P9-AFA-602

VOLUME 28 Venice to Wilmot, John

THE ENCYCLOPEDIA AMERICANA

INTERNATIONAL EDITION

COMPLETE IN THIRTY VOLUMES

FIRST PUBLISHED IN 1829

GROLIER INCORPORATED

International Headquarters: Danbury, Connecticut 06816

Library of Congress Cataloging in Publication Data
Main entry under title:

THE ENCYCLOPEDIA AMERICANA

Includes bibliographies and index.
1. Encyclopedias and dictionaries. I. Grolier Incorporated.
AE5.E333 1989 031 88-16397
ISBN 0-7172-0120-1 (v. 1)

PRINTED AND MANUFACTURED IN THE U.S.A.

FRITZ HENLE/PHOTO RESEARCHERS

Venice's Grand Canal sweeps by Santa Maria della Salute before entering the city to become its major waterway.

VENICE, ven'is. Sometimes called the Queen of the Adriatic, Venice has a physical site that few cities in the world can rival. The city proper is situated on more than 100 islands in a lagoon of the Adriatic Sea, 162 miles east of Milan. It is connected to the mainland by a 2.5-mile railroad bridge and a vehicular causeway of 228 arches built in 1932–1933. The central city is part of a unit of government called a commune that extends to the mainland and includes Porto Marghera and Mestre. The population of the commune is 360,293.

Plan of the City. Venice lies between the Alps on the northwest and the Adriatic on the southeast. Approximately in the center of a large lagoon, which comprises an area of about 180 square miles, are the muddy islands on which the first Venetians sank oak piles as foundations for their rude fisherman homes. On these small islands has arisen the almost magical city of Venice—its churches, palaces, and public buildings resting on piles buried beneath the lagoon's waters.

Along the borders of the islands are more than 100 canals. The Grand Canal, shaped roughly like a reversed letter S, over 2 miles long and varying in width from 33 to 77 yards, is the main artery, cutting the city into two unequal parts and connecting the railway station at the northwest with the open lagoon at the southeast. It is spanned by three bridges, of which the most notable is the Ponte di Rialto, a stone arch of the 16th century with small shops on each side, and connecting the central and oldest section of the city with the western quarter. From the Grand Canal extends an intricate network of smaller canals, averaging 4 to 5 yards in width, and measuring some 28 miles in total length. These lesser waterways are spanned by almost 400 bridges. On each of the tiny islands is a tortuous labyrinth of narrow, paved streets and lanes, some of which widen and join to form small, open squares. These narrow streets (*calli*) permit pedestrian travel, but much travel in Venice is by water, either in the *vaporetti* (little steamers) or *motoscafi* (motorboats) or by gondolas, which constitute one of the most distinctive features of Venetian life and which are so constructed as to permit passage through the narrowest canal. Barges propelled by men using long poles carry all the freight.

The largest square in Venice is the Piazza San Marco, one of the most beautiful squares in the world. Enclosed on three sides by the arcades of the Procuratie and on the fourth by the magnificent façade of St. Mark's Basilica, it is the center of the city's activities. At tables set outside the numerous cafés, citizens and visitors enjoy refreshments while listening to the lighthearted music of local bands. To the south of St. Mark's is a smaller square, the Piazzetta, with the Palazzo Ducale on the east and the Old Library on the west. The Piazzetta extends to the Canale di San Marco, and from this spot can be seen some of the outlying islands and, across the open lagoon, the Lido, one of the world's most famed bathing resorts. At the northeast corner of the Piazza di San Marco is a clock tower erected in 1496–1499, which serves as a portal to the Mercerie, a narrow, winding street of shops leading to the Rialto and the Grand Canal.

Proceeding along the Grand Canal, one passes Venice's most beautiful and most representative buildings. North and west of the Rialto, for instance, are the Fondaco dei Turchi, a 13th century example of Veneto-Byzantine architec-

SIPA PRESS, FROM BLACK STAR

The misty view of San Giorgio Maggiore beyond the gondolas recalls the paintings of Canaletto and Guardi.

The nearly 400 bridges in this city of water are high enough for barges and gondolas to pass under them.

SIPA PRESS, FROM BLACK STAR

ture, now largely restored; the 15th century Ca' d'Oro, a masterpiece of Venetian Gothic design; and the Palazzo Vendramin-Calergi, completed in 1509 and representative of the Lombardesque style of the early Renaissance (named for the Lombardo or Lombardi family). South and east of the Rialto are other palaces, representing every phase in the creative genius of Venetian architecture. Near St. Mark's the canal broadens into the lagoon surrounding Venice. The sections of this part of the city are bordered by a wide promenade and public gardens.

Of the islands not forming part of the main mass of the city the chief ones are (1) Giudecca, by far the largest, on the south, separated from Venice proper by the Canale della Giudecca; (2) San Giorgio Maggiore, immediately east of the former and separated from Venice by the broad Canale di San Marco, where the Teatro Verde, opened in 1954, is located; (3) San Pietro, east of the main island group; (4) San Michele, with the cemetery, to the north; (5) Murano, a group farther north, with an ancient glass industry; (6) Burano, to the northeast, famous for its laces; (7) Torcello, to the northeast, with an ancient Byzantine cathedral; and to the southeast, (8) San Servolo, with the province's insane asylum, and (9) San Lazzaro.

Historic Buildings and Other Points of Interest.—During the early period of Venetian art the city-state was closely associated with the Byzantine Empire. Thus techniques and forms of that culture were adapted by Venetian builders in their palaces, public buildings, and churches. By the 13th century, after Gothic design had begun to make itself felt, the Venetian palace was fully evolved. Venice, later than other cities in Italy, adopted by the 15th century some of the features of the early Renaissance, thus developing the Lombardesque Renaissance style.

Of many architecturally important structures in Venice the one most representative of the city's historic wealth and glory is St. Mark's

Basilica, a magnificent example of Byzantine influence, begun in 829 to enshrine the body of St. Mark, patron of the city. It was restored after a fire in 976, later demolished and rebuilt in the 11th century in the Byzantine style. The fine marbles date from the 13th to the 15th century. Formed in the shape of a Greek cross, the church is adorned with five Oriental domes and a two-tiered façade of predominantly pink marble, crowned with ogee arches and Gothic tabernacles. Four gilded bronze horses, brought from Constantinople in 1204, stand in the terrace of the upper story of the façade. Both exterior and interior are decorated with a wealth of mosaics, the ceiling of the church being completely faced with mosaics on a gold ground. Other examples of the profuse riches within the church include the Pala d'Oro, an altarpiece of precious jewels, enamel, and old gold; and the Baptistery, adorned with 14th century mosaics. At the southwest corner of the square stands the 323-foot-high Campanile (1912), an exact replica of the bell tower which, built and restored at various times between the 10th and 16th century, collapsed in 1902. At the base of the Campanile and facing the church is the graceful Loggetta di San Marco (1537–1540), one of Jacopo Sansovino's finest works.

Other churches of special significance include, in the eastern quarter, Santa Maria dei Miracoli, a masterpiece of the Lombardesque Renaissance style, built in 1481–1489; the Gothic church of Santi Giovanni e Paolo, containing the burial vaults of the doges; and the 15th century church of San Zaccaria, with one of Giovanni Bellini's finest madonnas. In the northern quarter are Santi Apostoli and San Giobbe, a Renaissance structure with a Gothic bell tower. In the western quarter is Santa Maria Gloriosa dei Frari, church of the Franciscans, begun in 1250 and rebuilt in Gothic style in the 14th–15th centuries; it contains some fine examples of Venetian painting. Here too is the Church of San Rocco, with its Scuola Grande containing a series of paintings by Tintoretto, executed between 1564 and 1587 and depicting scenes from the Old and New Testament; this grandiose cycle is considered by many the painter's masterpiece. The southwestern quarter contains the 14th century church of Santo Stefano, and the octagonal church of Santa Maria della Salute, begun in 1631 by the architect Baldassare Longhena. On the island of San Giorgio Maggiore stands the church of the same name, built by Andrea Palladio in the 16th century, and on the island of Giudecca is the church of Il Redentore, constructed from Palladio's plans and consecrated in 1592.

Second only to the churches in magnificence are the many palaces. Made for the most part of pink and white marble, with gracefully arched and decorated windows, balconies, loggias, and colonnades, they rise like dream castles from the lapping waters of the canals. The Palazzo Ducale, former residence of the doges and chief magistrates of the republic, is the most important of these unique structures. Erected between 1309 and 1549, this imposing and yet graceful building, resting on Gothic arcades, is one of the most beautiful palaces in Venice. The famous Bridge of Sighs, constructed about 1600, connects the palace with the prisons. Within the courtyard is the impressive Giants' Staircase. The palace contains some of the best examples of Renaissance painting, including works by Tintoretto and Paolo Veronese. Across the Piazzetta from the Palazzo Ducale stands the Old Library of St. Mark's, a building started by Jacopo Sansovino in 1536 and completed by his pupil Vincenzo Scamozzi in 1588 in the Renaissance style. It contains the Biblioteca Nazionale Marciana, with 500,000 books, 3,000 incunabula, and 13,000 manuscripts, and also the archaeological museum. Adjoining the library toward the Canale di San Marco is the Zecca (formerly the mint). Of special interest are the Procuratie Vecchie, former residences of the procurators of the republic, built by Bartolomeo Buon in 1514, and the Procuratie Nuove, begun in 1584 by Vincenzo Scamozzi.

The Accademia di Belle Arti (Venice Academy) is notable for the number of paintings by the great masters of the Venetian school. Other museums include the Correr, the Marciano (connected with St. Mark's), and the Galleria d'Arte Moderna and Museo d'Arte Orientale, both housed in the Palazzo Pesaro. Ca'Rezzonico, a palace on the Grand Canal, has a museum dedicated to the Venetian arts of the 18th century. Since 1895 an international exhibition of modern art has been held biennially in the pavilions of the Public Gardens.

The Piazza San Marco has been called Venice's living room. Tourists and Venetians crowd its café terraces.

FREELANCE PHOTOGRAPHER'S GUILD

Painting.—The critic Bernard Berenson has said that with "exquisite tact in their use of colour," the Venetians were able to express in painting the special values of the Renaissance—"delight in life with the consequent love of health, beauty, and joy. . . ." The great artists—the brothers Gentile (c. 1429–1507) and Giovanni (c. 1430–1516) Bellini, Giovanni Battista Cima (c. 1459–c. 1517), and Vittore Carpaccio (c. 1455–c. 1526) painted "magnificent processions" which satisfied "the Venetian's love of. . .splendor, beauty, and gaiety." Il Giorgione (c. 1477–c. 1510) quieted down the passions of the earlier painters, and Titian (c. 1477–1576) perfected the portrait, gaining the effect of great reality through new media. At the end of the period stands Tintoretto (1518–1594), expressing overwhelming power and mastering light and shadow in such a way as to infuse the human spirit of individualism even into his largest canvases. Other important painters of the late Renaissance include Paolo Veronese (1528–1588), with his paintings expressive of joyous worldliness, and Jacopo Bassano (1510–1592) and his sons, who so charmingly depicted country life. Just before its final decline, painting in Venice exerted its force once more in Giovanni Battista Tiepolo (1696–1770). See also PAINTING—*Modern Painting* (Venice).

Commerce and Industry.—Venice is no longer the important merchant city that it was from the 13th to the 16th centuries, and much of its present economic structure depends on the tourist trade. There are, however, some industries of economic importance. The Arsenale (or shipyards), which supplied all ships for the powerful Venetian fleet from the 12th century on, has long ago lost most of its importance. The glass and glass mosaic industry, whose origins may be traced back to the 10th century and which reached its greatest excellence in the 16th, is flourishing again on the island of Murano; Venetian wares, including glass beads, are widely exported. Beautiful laces are still made on the island of Burano and shipped abroad. Other traditional Venetian products are fine jewelry, leather goods, imitations of ancient art objects, and brocades and damasks. Porto Marghera, on the mainland, is the commercial and industrial port of Venice; it has become one of Italy's most important oil-refining centers and has also large chemical and metallurgical industries.

History.—Historians are in general agreement that before 452 A.D., when Attila invaded northern Italy, the islands of the Venetian lagoon had a small native population of simple, poor fishermen. Refugees from the mainland occasionally fled from the barbarian invasions to the safety of the islands, but, when the danger had passed, most of them returned to their mainland homes. Some of these newcomers remained, however, and by 568, when the Lombards were beginning their conquest of Italy, a considerable population had gathered on the islands and formed small townships. These townships, centered around the present Rialto, gradually consolidated to handle their common affairs, and in 697 the power passed to a single leader, called the doge. Pressed by the Byzantine Empire to the east and by the Lombards and Franks to the

Columns supporting a winged lion, the symbol of Saint Mark, and Saint Theodore frame San Giorgio Maggiore.

FREELANCE PHOTOGRAPHER'S GUILD

EUGENIO AIELLO/FPG

St. Mark's sumptuous Byzantine architecture recalls the past glory of Venice, when it linked east with west.

west, Venice struggled for, and achieved, independence as a republic. Her excellent position at the crossroads of East and West helped her to build up an empire in the Levant. She started her expansion in the 10th century by subduing pirates along the Dalmatian coast, thus gaining control of the Adriatic, then gradually secured trading and other privileges in a number of Mediterranean seaports. The city became one of the ports of embarkation for the Crusades. The growth of trade produced a merchant aristocracy which step by step gained ascendancy in state affairs. In 1172 the Grand Council of 480 members was established; the counselors to the doge formed the Council of the Invited (Pregadi), which became the forerunner of the Senate.

During the 13th and 14th centuries the possessions of Venice in the Levant continued to grow. In 1204 Doge Enrico Dandolo (q.v.) was a leader of the Fourth Crusade which conquered Constantinople, and the republic gained footholds in the Eastern Mediterranean, in the islands of the Ionian and Aegean seas, including Crete, and in seaports of Thessaly and other parts of the Greek mainland. Thus Venice had a long line of direct communication with Constantinople and the Levant. She ruled her colonies with skill, interfering little in local institutions and encouraging trade. Venetian merchants traveled to the Crimea, Asia Minor, and the Persian Gulf; Marco Polo brought glowing accounts from China and Persia. In her commercial expansion, however, Venice encountered the rivalry of another Italian maritime republic, Genoa, and a long struggle between the two powers was inevitable. The Genoese fleet, after reaching Chioggia in the Adriatic and endangering the existence of Venice itself, was utterly defeated there in 1380 leaving Venice the undisputed queen of the seas. In the meantime the oligarchy in Venice was gaining more and more power in the government of the republic. In 1297 membership of the Grand Council was restricted to members of certain families and names of those eligible were inscribed in a Golden Book. The only serious revolution, inspired by Baiamonte Tiepolo in 1310, failed, and in order to prevent further uprisings the Council of Ten (see TEN, COUNCIL OF) was instituted. Presided over by the doge himself, it was entrusted with the protection of public safety and with the vigilance against conspirators. In the second half of the 14th and during the 15th centuries, Venice began to acquire areas on the Italian mainland to protect her trade routes toward the north and west. By 1454 her possessions reached as far west as the Adda River, south to Ravenna, and north to the Alps. Such cities as Padova, Vicenza, Verona, Bergamo, Brescia, and Piacenza were in Venetian hands. The republic was an ally of Florence and the Duchy of Milan. This wide territory she held until the League of Cambrai, formed in 1508 by Pope Julius II, Emperor Maximilian I, and the kings of France and Aragon, stripped her of many of her possessions. However, most of the territory now comprised in the region Veneto returned soon after to Venice and remained under her administration until the dissolution of the republic in 1797.

After the conquest of Constantinople by the Turks in 1453, their power started to make itself felt throughout the Mediterranean. At first Venice succeeded in making commercial and financial agreements with the Ottoman Empire and to continue her oversea trade, but soon the Turks became able to press their expansion. In a long series of wars in the second half of the 15th and during the 16th century Venice lost more and more ground. Not even the victory of the Christian nations at Lepanto (1571) succeeded in checking the Ottoman advance. One by one the overseas possessions were lost. At the end of the 16th century the Venetian empire was shattered; gone were her military and commercial power, the first as a result of the long struggle with the Turks, the second also as a consequence of the new route to the Far East opened by the Portu-

GEORGES VIOLLON/PHOTO RESEARCHERS

The octagonal Santa Maria della Salute was built in the 17th century on the edge of the Grand Canal.

guese around the Cape of Good Hope. Also, with the discovery of the New World much world trade shifted toward the Atlantic. A last flash of Venetian strength came in 1683 when Morea was retaken from the Turks only to be lost some 30 years later. The republic, with its unchanged aristocratic government and its outdated institutions, continued its steady decline until the Napoleonic conquest of Italy. In May 1797 the Grand Council voted itself out of existence and soon after, by the Treaty of Campoformio, Venice was attached to the Austrian Empire; then, in 1805, she became part of the Kingdom of Italy under Napoleon's sponsorship. After the collapse of the Napoleonic empire in 1815, Venice was incorporated in the Lombardo-Venetian Kingdom under Austrian rule. In 1848, when revolutionary movements swept over Europe and the Risorgimento was in full swing in Italy, Venice rose against her Austrian rulers. The patriot Daniele Manin proclaimed a republic and, soon afterward, union with the Kingdom of Sardinia was voted. Even after the Piedmontese defeat at Novara in March 1849, Venice continued her resistance to the siege by Austrian forces, but in August she was forced into surrender, more by famine and cholera than by force of arms. Austrian domination was reestablished, and continued until 1866 when Venice was ceded by Austria to France. In the plebiscite that followed, the people of Venice voted overwhelmingly for union with the Kingdom of Italy, which took place the same year.

After the union, Venice suffered from the competition of the port of Trieste, which was the outlet of the Austro-Hungarian Empire until 1918. During World War I, Venice was subjected to aerial attack and damage to buildings and art work occurred. Although occupied by the Germans during World War II, the city escaped serious damage. A major flood in 1966 focused increased attention on a problem that had plagued Venice for centuries—it had been sinking into the sea at an alarming rate. Capping the city's artesian wells caused the underground water table to refill, and by the 1980's, Venice was even rising slightly. Air pollution was being brought under control, and efforts were under way to improve the sewage system. Studies were being conducted on ways to control the high tides.

Bibliography

Cole, Toby, ed., *Venice: A Portable Reader* (Lawrence Hill 1978).

Hale, John R., *Renaissance Venice* (Rowman & Littlefield 1973).

King, Margaret L., *Venetian Humanism in an Age of Patrician Dominance* (Princeton Univ. Press 1986).

Lovell, Margaretta M., *Venice: The American View 1860–1920* (Univ. of Wash. Press 1984).

McNeil, William H., *Venice—the Hinge of Europe: 1081–1797* (Univ. of Chicago Press 1974).

Martineau, Jane, and Hope, Charles, eds., *The Genius of Venice 1500–1600* (Abrams 1984).

Morris, Jan, *The World of Venice*, rev. ed. (Harcourt 1974).

Muir, Edward, *Civil Ritual in Renaissance Venice* (Princeton Univ. Press 1986).

Shaw-Kennedy, Ronald, *Venice Rediscovered* (A.S. Barnes 1978).

Zorzi, Alvise, *Venice* (Abbeville Press 1983).

VENING MEINESZ, ven′ing mī′nes, **Felix Andries** (1887–1966), Dutch geophysicist, who made major contributions to the study of the earth's gravity and suboceanic crust.

Vening Meinesz was born in Scheveningen, the Netherlands, on July 30, 1887. He received a degree in civil engineering from the Technical University of Delft in 1910 and then accepted a position with the Dutch government to work on a gravimetric study of the country. He developed a method using two pendulums from which it was possible to obtain accurate gravity readings free from disturbances such as the effects of shifting soil. By 1921 he succeeded in measuring gravity at stations throughout the Netherlands.

For over 15 years beginning in 1923, Vening Meinesz developed a complex system of measuring and recording devices that afforded accurate gravity measurements at sea. He found that certain areas along deep-sea trenches exhibited lower-than-expected gravitational attraction. These bands, later called the Vening Meinesz belts of negative anomalies, he believed were caused by convection currents under the earth's crust.

Vening Meinesz was professor of geodesy at the Technical University of Delft from 1938 to 1957. In 1963 a new institute for geophysics and geochemistry at Utrecht University was named for him. He died in Amersfoot, the Netherlands, on Aug. 12, 1966.

VENIRE, və-nī′rē, a judicial writ at common law directing a sheriff or other officer to select and summon jurors. In a few states of the United States, venire is still issued before the drawing of a jury list, but statutes limit the method of selection. In most states, however, the issuance of process comes after a list of qualified persons is prepared. Statutory substitutes for summoning juries are sometimes called "venire," but may be designated as "order," "precept," "summons," or "process." Venire may also mean the list of jurors drawn who are to be summoned.

VENIZELOS, vâ-nē-zâ'lôs, **Eleutherios** (1864–1936), Greek political leader, who was especially skillful in the administration of foreign policy. He was born in Crete on Aug. 23, 1864. After studying at Syros and the University of Athens, he practiced law in Crete. He played an active role in the anti-Turkish revolt of 1896, was elected to the Cretan assembly, and subsequently became minister of justice. When Prince George of Greece, as commissioner of Crete, sought to monopolize power, Venizelos countered by establishing a rival provisional government and proclaiming union of Crete with Greece. This daring feat, though unsuccessful, forced George's resignation in 1906 and brought Venizelos much new support. In 1909 he was called to Athens to advise the Military League shortly after its coup d'état and in 1910, Venizelos became prime minister of Greece.

Although a republican, Venizelos preferred constructive revisionist solutions to violent revolt against the crown. He reformed the army and navy, adjusted taxes, and stabilized the nation politically. Even more successful in foreign policy, he initiated a Greek-Bulgarian alliance that was instrumental in the defeat of Turkey in the First Balkan War (1912–1913). During World War I, he supported the Allied cause in direct opposition to the pro-German, though nominally neutral, Constantine I (reigned 1913–1917, 1920–1922). When Venizelos became convinced that the royalists were aiding the Germans, he set up a revolutionary provisional government in Salonika (Oct. 9, 1916). Constantine abdicated under Anglo-French pressure, and Venizelos took over the government of the whole country and brought Greece into the war on the Allied side on July 2, 1917.

Venizelos' diplomatic skill at Sèvres (1920) won much territory for Greece, including some of the Aegean Islands, East Thrace, and Smyrna. In spite of these triumphs, he was defeated at the polls by a war-weary electorate (November 1920) and went into exile. The exhausted nation then suffered defeat in Asia Minor at the hands of the aroused Turks, and Venizelos returned to represent his country at the Lausanne Conference (1922–1923).

He served again as premier in 1924 (for less than a month) and from 1928 to 1932. This time he failed to institute major internal reforms, but his foreign policy continued to be effective. He arrived at agreements with Italy (1928) and Yugoslavia (1929) and reopened full diplomatic relations with Bulgaria. His most notable triumph was an understanding with Turkey that paved the way for the Balkan pacts of the 1930's.

The misfortune of being in power when the world depression broke cost Venizelos his parliamentary majority and his office in September 1932. His reputation was gravely damaged the following March when certain republican officers, without his consent, sought to seize power by revolution. After barely escaping assassination in June 1933, Venizelos became implicated in another attempt to overthrow the government (March 1935). The failure of this coup led to his final exile and set the stage for the Ioannes Metaxas dictatorship (August 1936). Venizelos died in Paris, France, on March 18, 1936.

W. G. Vettes
University of Wisconsin–La Crosse

VENOM, ven'əm, a poisonous secretion of some animals, usually delivered by bite or sting. Venom generally is produced in special glands that often are associated with spines, teeth, or other piercing apparatus. Venom is most often used to subdue and kill prey or for defense, but in some animals it also functions as a digestive juice.

Most venoms are complex and act on the body in many ways. Most venoms that have been analyzed contain various mixtures of toxic enzymes and other proteins, including nerve poisons, tissue-destroying agents, heart poisons, and several enzymes that interfere with the body's complex biochemical machinery. One major group, the neurotoxic venoms, affects the brain and nervous system primarily, producing symptoms of nervous excitation or depression such as incoordination, tremors, convulsions, or paralysis. If poisoning is severe, death can result from respiratory paralysis. Another major group acts primarily by causing local tissue damage and disruption of blood cells. In severe cases death may result from circulatory collapse. Still other venoms produce a histaminelike response with manifestations of an allergic reaction. A severe allergic reaction in persons previously sensitized to such a venom can result in anaphylactic shock and even death. These and other venoms can also cause local skin irritation, redness, swelling, and itching.

The severity of a venom attack depends on several factors besides the nature of the venom. The age, size, and general health of the victim are important. Venom attacks in children are, for example, much more serious than in healthy adults. The site of the bite or sting is also significant, with those inflicted on the extremities generally less serious than those on the head or trunk.

Among marine animals, many sponges, sea anemones, and jellyfish produce venoms that cause skin irritations, sometimes severe; occasionally systemic symptoms; and rarely death. However, the Portuguese man-of-war and certain jellyfish and sea anemones produce highly toxic venoms that can cause severe illness and even death very quickly. The cone shell is also dangerous, producing a neurotoxic venom. Certain fishes—chiefly scorpionfishes (particularly the deadly stonefish), ratfishes, and some sharks—also secrete potentially lethal neurotoxins.

Many insects and arthropods inflict bites and stings that produce local effects and occasional systemic effects, but a few pose a more serious threat. In some persons bee and wasp stings may cause anaphylactic shock or even death. Ticks produce a neurotoxic venom that can occasionally cause paralysis and death. The bites of black widow and certain other spiders cause nervous-system excitation, muscle spasms, pain and hardening of the abdomen, and sometimes blood-system disturbances. Such bites can be but rarely are fatal. Similarly the neurotoxic venom of certain scorpions is dangerous. Local tingling or burning at the site of the bite is followed by malaise, restlessness, increasing agitation, and sometimes coma and death.

By far the best-known venomous animals are snakes. The venom of cobras, kraits, and coral snakes is primarily neurotoxic, with death—if it occurs—resulting from respiratory paralysis. The venom of rattlesnakes, moccasins, and copperheads causes local tissue damage, hemorrhage, and circulatory collapse.

VENTILATION, the process of supplying or removing air, by natural or mechanical means, to or from any space.

The ventilation of buildings was originally advocated for the purpose of removing from the air such impurities as the products of human respiration and perspiration and the gaseous products of combustion. Before 1920, the carbon dioxide (CO_2) content of air was considered as the most reliable index for determining its purity, and a maximum limit was set at ten parts of CO_2 per 10,000 parts of air on a volume basis. In fact, ventilation rates for public buildings were established in which the maximum permissible CO_2 content was limited to seven parts per 10,000. Normal free atmosphere has a CO_2 content of about four parts per 10,000, and in industrial atmospheres the content may be considerably greater. Subsequent studies have shown that CO_2 contents as great as 100 parts per 10,000 (or 1%) are not harmful, and that it is only when CO_2 contents reach 5% or 6% that breathing becomes difficult. The limit of ten parts per 10,000 can be considered as unrealistic.

A distinction must be clearly made between the ventilation requirements for carbon monoxide (CO) and those for CO_2. Carbon monoxide is deadly to animal life, and where continuous exposure to the gas is necessary, as in garages, vehicular tunnels, and mines, the concentration must not exceed one part in 10,000.

Under normal conditions, where noxious gases are not present, modern standards for ventilation have been based on the outdoor air required in order to avoid objectionable body odors. These ventilation rates were established in the mid-1930's by laboratory studies in which controlled quantities of ventilation air were supplied to various occupants of a sealed chamber. The studies indicated that people in small rooms required more ventilation air than people in large spaces, and that children required more than adults. Odors from tobacco smoke are as annoying as those from the body. Ventilation rates for the reduction of tobacco odors are considerably greater than those for reduction of body odors alone. In fact, in large assembly halls with unrestricted smoking, tremendously large ventilation rates must be provided if reasonably clear vision is to be maintained in the hall. Thus the danger of fire is not the only reason for the prohibition of tobacco smoking in many auditoriums.

Physiological Aspects of Ventilation. The effect of odors on the occupant is likely to be more psychological than physiological. It is true that appetites may be dulled and headaches may result from exposure to odors, but physical damage to the body will be difficult to prove. As far as most of the common odors are concerned, the purpose of ventilation is an aesthetic one. However, certain toxic chemical substances, which may or may not have detectable odors, pose a definite threat to health. This is especially true in industrial situations. See INDUSTRIAL HEALTH.

Ventilation for the purpose of reducing airborne bacteria is only partly effective, since it does not prevent accumulation of bacteria on surfaces. Treatment of room surfaces with disinfectants and removal of bacteria-bearing dust are more effective than ventilation in reducing airborne infection.

Accepted Standards for Ventilation. Recommended ventilation rates for most public and private enclosures are dependent mainly on the extent of smoking in the space. The following table lists outdoor-air (or "fresh-air") requirements according to usual practice.

OUTDOOR-AIR REQUIREMENTS

Application	Smoking	Recommended cfm.[1] per person
Apartment	Some	20
Barbershop	Considerable	15
Beauty parlor	Occasional	10
Broker's boardroom	Heavy	50
Department store	None	7½
Drugstore	Considerable	10
Factories	None	10
Hospitals, private rooms	None	30
Hospitals, wards	None	20
Hotel rooms	Heavy	30
Offices, general	Some	15
Offices, private	None to considerable	25-30
Restaurant, cafeteria	Considerable	12
Restaurant, dining room	Considerable	15
Schoolrooms	None	30
Theater	None	7½

[1] cfm.: cubic feet per minute.

The most common examples of ventilation, and the principal reasons for ventilation, are:

(1) Removal of excess heat, as in a foundry.

(2) Removal of body odors, as in locker rooms.

(3) Removal of moist air, as in laundries.

(4) Removal of gases and fumes, as from plating tanks, spray-paint booths, and steel mills.

(5) Removal of dust, as in grinding operations.

(6) Removal of animal odors, as in shelters.

(7) Removal of gas fumes or dust to prevent explosions, as in flour mills or hospital operating rooms. (Some anesthetics are explosive or combustible gases.)

In the United States, both national and state industrial codes specify the ventilation rates for commercial and industrial establishments.

Natural Ventilation. The simplest form of ventilation results from the action of wind, which builds a positive pressure on the windward side of a building and reduces the pressure on the leeward side. Wind action is variable, both in magnitude and direction, so that the resulting ventilation is not controllable.

A second cause of natural ventilation is referred to as "chimney action," because of the following analogy: A column of hot gas in a chimney is lighter than a corresponding column of cold air outside of the chimney. The result is that the column of heavier outdoor air displaces the column of lighter air inside the chimney, causing a flow of air to occur. A building is similar to a chimney, since cool air will flow in at openings near the lower level and out through openings near the roof. Ventilation by chimney action may be accomplished on calm days, but the effect again, is variable.

Mechanical Ventilation. Ventilation by wind or chimney action is not only capricious but frequently insufficient. For this reason, mechanical ventilation by means of a fan is often introduced.

Centrifugal and Propeller Fans. The two most common types of fans are the propeller type and the centrifugal type. Desk and window fans are common examples of propeller fans, which are capable of moving large airflow rates against relatively low resistance. The centrifugal fan can move air against a high resistance, such as that imposed by ductwork and filters. The ductwork may be connected to the inlet and discharge sides of the fan.

Exhaust fans are commonly of the propeller type, since air is discharged directly to the outdoors against small resistance. These fans are frequently combined with roof caps or provided with automatically operated shutters.

Supply and exhaust fans connected to a duct system are usually of the centrifugal type. In many applications, the noise of fan operation and air movement is of great concern, as in broadcasting studios and auditoriums. Noise can be minimized by careful engineering design and proper installation. In general, the higher the speed of a given fan, the higher the noise level of operation. Hence, large, low-speed fans are frequently selected over small, high-speed fans.

Air Distribution. Most ventilation systems require the use of an air distribution system, consisting of a central fan, a main duct, several branch ducts to the various rooms, and supply outlets to distribute the air to individual spaces.

The maximum velocity in a standard commercial duct system is about 2,200 feet per minute (fpm), but in high-velocity systems it may be as high as 8,000 fpm, with correspondingly smaller duct sizes for handling the same airflow rate.

Conveying a given airflow rate to a space is only part of the problem of proper air distribution. Air must be introduced into the space without the occupants being aware of the air distribution system. Furthermore, they should not be subjected to drafts, a draft being defined as air motion greater than 50 fpm. Air motion between 15 and 35 fpm is considered acceptable, and less than 15 fpm is considered to be stagnant. Location of supply outlets is also important. Favorably placed outlets include: (1) high sidewall vents so situated as to project air above the heads of the occupants; (2) ceiling outlets that spread the air at the ceiling level and mix it with room air; and (3) outlets at the floor or in window sills that discharge air vertically so that it spreads across the ceiling and mixes with the room air. Design procedures for air distribution systems are given in engineering books.

Exhaust Ventilation Systems. Industrial exhaust systems remove fumes, dusts, and vapors that may be harmful to the workers or would interfere with the manufacturing process. A complete exhaust system consists of an exhaust hood located at the source of contamination, branch ducts and main ducts to convey the air, and a fan. In the vicinity of the exhaust hood, the air velocities required to carry the air contaminants into the hood are: 50–100 fpm to remove vapors and gases from washing, degreasing, and welding operations; 100–200 fpm to remove paint from spray booths or dust from package filling; and 500–2,000 fpm to capture coarse material removed in grinding processes or abrasive cleaning.

In an exhaust system, air introduced into a ventilated space must be removed at the same rate. Make-up air may enter through windows or doors, but during cold weather these may be closed and interfere with proper operation. Inlet ducts provided with heating coils permit make-up air to be admitted to the space without causing discomfort to the occupants. Air introduced into a conditioned space can be regulated so that the air pressure within the space will be higher than that outside of the space. Under these conditions, a positive internal pressure will be created so that air, instead of leaking into the enclosure through window and door cracks, will filter out through these fissures. This will prevent the inflow of dust, pollen, and other pollutants present in the outside air.

Special Problems—Mines. Ventilation is required for safety and health in underground mines. In deep mines, ventilation air serves to remove dust, gases, and excessive humidity, and helps to regulate air temperatures. Not only does the presence of finely divided dust in the air present a potential explosion hazard, but rock dust is also a factor in the incidence of lung diseases. High humidity and temperatures affect not only the comfort of the men, but also the rate at which they can work without heat injury. The fan should be located outside the mine, where it will not be damaged in case of fire or explosion. The main shaft through which men are transported into the mine should not be used as a duct to convey exhaust air, since it may expose the men to smoke and fumes in the event of an explosion or fire. It may serve as a fresh-air intake except where freezing temperatures occur, in which case it is likely to accumulate ice. See also MINING—*Mine Safety*.

Garages. Garages should be ventilated to remove carbon monoxide gas and combustible vapors. An idling car produces carbon monoxide gas at an average rate of 0.59 cfm (cubic feet per minute). Outdoor air at the rate of 5,900 cfm per car would be required to maintain the carbon monoxide content at a safe level of one part in 10,000. This amount of outdoor air during the cold months would be prohibitively expensive to heat for the purpose of maintaining comfortable temperatures indoors. For this reason, exhaust systems with individual connections that fit over the automobile exhaust pipes are often used. These connections prevent the escape of exhaust gases into the working space, and the outdoor-air requirement is reduced from 5,900 cfm to only 100 cfm.

Tunnels. For a discussion of ventilation of major tunnels, see TUNNEL—*Ventilation*.

Pollen Removal. The problem of removing pollen grains and dust particles from outdoor air that is to be used for ventilation purposes is dealt with by the use of air-filtering devices, of which several effective types have been developed. See FILTER, MECHANICAL.

See also AIR CONDITIONING.

SEICHI KONZO
EDWARD JOSEPH BROWN
University of Illinois

Bibliography

Alden, John L., and Kane, John M., *Design of Industrial Ventilation Systems,* 5th ed. (Industrial Press 1982).

Brumbaugh, James, *Heating, Ventilating, and Air Conditioning Library,* 3 vols., 2d ed. (Macmillan 1983).

Clark, Deborah B., and Bradford, Debra, *Pressure Cycled Ventilators* (Prentice-Hall 1984).

Clifford, George, *Heating, Ventilating and Air Conditioning* (Reston 1984).

Croome, D. J., and Roberts, B. M., *Air Conditioning and Ventilation of Buildings,* 2d ed. (Pergamon 1981).

European Heating and Ventilating Association, eds., *The International Dictionary of Heating, Ventilating and Air Conditioning* (Methuen 1982).

Lindeke, Wolfgang, *Dictionary of Ventilation and Health* (State Mutual Bk. 1980).

Traister, John E., *Heating, Ventilating and Air Conditioning* (Prentice-Hall 1987).

VENTRILOQUISM, ven-tril'ə-kwizm, an ancient art of vocal and visual illusion, the production of speech and other sounds that appear to emanate from a source outside the speaker's person. Ventriloquial words are formed by retracting the tongue and moving only its tip, the voice being expelled from the slightly opened mouth. As the breath is released slowly through the glottis, narrowed by the retraction of the tongue, pressure is created, diffusing the sound. With the narrowed glottis muffling the tone, the illusion of distance increases in ratio to the degree of pressure built up when the mouth is nearly closed and the tongue retracted. These facts are contrary to the erroneous assumption that ventriloquial sounds originate in the abdominal region and are produced while the performer is inhaling, an assumption that may be partly due to the Latin roots of the word "ventriloquism" (*venter,* "belly" or "paunch," and *loqui,* "spoken"). The use of a ventriloquist's dummy, with moving lips operated by the ventriloquist and timed to coincide with the ventriloquist's speech, completes the speech and sight illusion. Pantomime is also used to create the auricular and optical illusion that sound is emanating from an area or object some distance from the ventriloquist, whose lips remain immobile.

The art of ventriloquism is presumed to have been handed down from person to person, although its precise origin is lost in antiquity. Archaeological studies trace ventriloquism to early Hebrew and Egyptian civilizations. It is also presumed that certain members of ancient priesthoods were practitioners of the art of voice diffusion. Tradition has it, for instance, that miraculous sounds of warning issuing from the stone of the River Pactolus in Lydia repelled thieves who were bent on stealing the golden sands of that stream. The speech of the Greek oracles and the speaking statues of the Egyptians give further credence to this theory of ventriloquial priestcraft. Among the ancient Greeks, Aurycles of Athens has been identified as a master of ventriloquism and leader of a group of practitioners referred to both as Eurycleides and Engastrimanteis ("belly-prophets"). India and China are areas in which ventriloquism is a familiar art. The Eskimo, Zulu, and Maori are among contemporary peoples of relatively primitive cultures among whom skilled practitioners of ventriloquism may be found.

Generally defined in the entertainment field as a form of conjury, ventriloquism continues to provoke mystery and call forth controversy. The point at issue is whether the ventriloquist throws his voice or whether this is an optical illusion that the artist creates by immobilizing his lips while speaking and effectively directing attention to the supposed source of the sound. At variance with the optical illusion theory is voice diffusion as practiced by birds and animals. The chickadee creates distinct ventriloquial effects by its note. A species of rabbit in Canada uses a high-pitched sound reputedly impossible to locate and capable of deceiving the rabbit's enemies as to its whereabouts. In further refutation of the optical illusion theory is the fact that dogs, in spite of their sensitivity to sound, seek the source of a ventriloquist's voice at the distant point from which it appears to emanate, and not in the person of the ventriloquist himself.

EDGAR BERGEN, *Ventriloquist*

VENTURA, ven-tŏŏr'ə, a city in California, on the Pacific Ocean, 70 miles (112 km) northwest of Los Angeles. It is the seat of Ventura county. Oil and agriculture (lima beans, citrus fruit, and English walnuts) are its chief sources of income. Ventura county ranks among the highest in oil production in California, and the city's oil-tool manufactures compete in national and world markets.

Chumash Indians, Spanish rancheros, and American settlers contributed to the city's history. San Buenaventura Mission, founded by Junípero Serra in 1782, is still in use (the city's official name is San Buenaventura). The Ventura County Historical Museum has collections on local history.

Ventura was incorporated as a town in 1866 and as a city in 1906. Government is by council and manager. Population: 83,475.

VENTURI TUBE, ven-tŏŏr'ē, a type of conduit and metering device, named after G. B. Venturi, the Italian physicist, who about 1791 first investigated the principles upon which it operates. Clemens Herschel, the American engineer who first used it in 1886 to measure the flow of water, is generally credited as the inventor. The venturi tube consists of a pipe or other closed conduit with a constricted throat, followed by a gradually diverging section, as shown in the illustration. The effect of the constriction at point 2 is to increase the velocity and thus reduce the pressure of the fluid flowing through it. In the following diverging section between points 2 and 3, the velocity gradually decreases and the pressure increases until, at point 3, velocity and pressure are the same as they were at point 1, except for a slight loss due to friction.

VENTURI TUBE

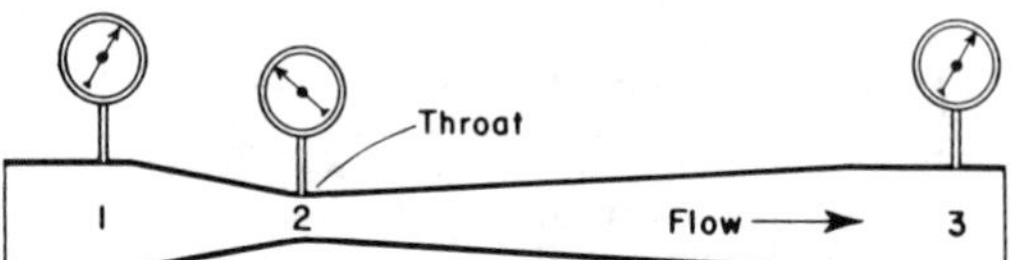

A major application of the venturi is in the measurement of the flow of fluids, both liquid and gaseous. It is also used in the common carburetor and in some pumps. In all cases its operation depends on the fact that there is a definite relationship between the rate of flow and the pressure differential between points 1 and 2. As a meter it is accurate within plus or minus 3% in measuring the flow of all types of fluid. By a suitable recording device, it can integrate the flow rate so as to give the total quantity of fluid that has gone through it in a certain period of time.

The venturi meter is the standard means of measuring water or steam flow in many industrial applications because it can be a permanent part of the system. In such cases, it is important that pressure loss be held to a minimum, and the diameter at the throat (point 2) will accordingly be made relatively large, with some sacrifice of gauge accuracy. There is no limit to the size of meter or the quantity of fluid that it can measure.

ELEANOR ALLEN, "*SAE Journal*"

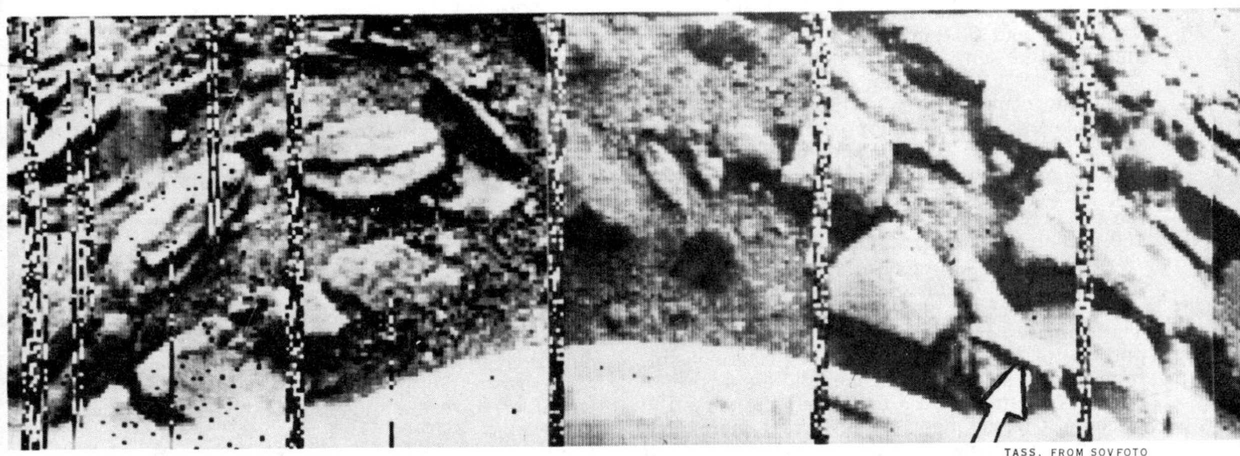

TASS, FROM SOVFOTO

First photograph of the surface of Venus was returned to earth by the Soviet spacecraft Venera 9 on Oct. 22, 1975. The rounded rocks may indicate some wind and sand erosion. The arrow (*bottom right*) points to a density meter.

VENUS, vē′nəs, the second planet in the solar system (after Mercury) in order of increasing distance from the sun. It revolves around the sun in a nearly circular orbit, which lies between the orbits of Mercury and the earth. Like the other planets, Venus shines by reflected sunlight. As seen from the earth at night it is brighter than any other planet or star, both because of its proximity to the earth and because it is covered by highly reflective clouds.

Scientists believe that Venus and the other planets in the solar system were formed about 4.5 billion years ago when they condensed out of a cloud of dust and gas. Of the planets, Venus is most similar to the earth in size and mass, but with a much more massive atmosphere and a surface pressure 90 times greater.

Venus is a solid spherical body having a diameter of about 7,520 miles (12,100 km), as compared with the earth's diameter of about 7,920 miles (12,240 km). Its mass is about 81% and its density about 90% that of the earth. On the surface of Venus the acceleration due to gravity is about 88% of that on earth. Thus an object weighing 100 pounds (45 kg) on earth would weigh about 88 pounds (40 kg) on the surface of Venus. Extremely sensitive measurements made in 1979 from the U. S. spacecraft Pioneer Venus 1 (the Orbiter) were unable to detect any planetary magnetic field, though fluctuating fields originating in the solar wind are always present.

The first successful flyby of Venus was made by the U. S. spacecraft Mariner 2 in 1962, and the first drop of an instrument-carrying capsule into the atmosphere of Venus was made from the Soviet spacecraft Venera 4 in 1967. Subsequent U. S. and Soviet space missions radioed back data that greatly increased knowledge of the planet and its cloud cover. But man did not have his first look at the surface until Oct. 22 and 25, 1975, when Venera 9 and 10 landed on the planet and returned photographs. Venera 9 functioned for 53 minutes, and its pictures revealed piles of angular rock strewn about the landing site and resembling a young mountainscape. Venera 10 functioned for 65 minutes and photographed older, more weathered rock formations, presumably showing the effects of erosion.

In December 1978, Pioneer Venus 2 sent four probes to the surface; the carrier "bus" burned up in the upper atmosphere after sending back its own series of measurements. Pioneer Venus 1 (the Orbiter) was placed in a highly elliptical orbit, penetrating the upper atmosphere once per revolution and taking pictures of the cloud tops when farther away. A radar mapper disclosed a strikingly rugged topography at midnorthern latitudes, in contrast to the rather flat equatorial landscapes obtained by radar from earth. The first results included observations of a huge canyon, comparable to the African rift valley, and plateaus as high as the Himalaya and twice the size of the Tibetan plateau. Also in December, the USSR's Venera 11 and 12 probes reached the surface. All probes sent back information on the clouds, the atmospheric gases, and the energy flows that maintain a hot surface.

Orbit. Venus travels around the sun in a nearly circular orbit at a mean distance of about 67.2 million miles (108 million km), compared with about 93 million miles (150 million km) for the earth and 36 million miles (58 million km) for Mercury. As viewed from above the solar system, Venus and the other planets move counterclockwise around the sun. The mean orbital velocity of Venus is about 22 miles (35 km) per second, compared with about 18.5 miles (30 km) per second for the earth. Venus takes about 225 earth days to go around the sun, compared with

KEY FACTS ABOUT VENUS

Mass	5.3×10^{21} tons (4.8×10^{21} metric tons)
Volume	3.3×10^{22} cubic feet (9.3×10^{20} cu meters)
Density	318 lbs/cu ft (5.1 grams/cu cm)
Diameter	7,520 miles (12,100 km)
Surface gravity	28.3 ft per sec/sec (8.6 meters per sec/sec)
Escape velocity	6.5 miles/sec (10.4 km/sec)
Orbital velocity	22 miles/sec (35 km/sec)
Eccentricity of orbit	0.007
Mean distance from sun	67.2 million miles (108 million km)
Greatest distance from earth	160 million miles (257 million km)
Least distance from earth	25 million miles (40 million km)
Rotation period	243 earth days
Sidereal revolution period	225 earth days
Albedo (reflectivity of light)	70%
Surface temperature	885° F (475° C)
Surface atmospheric pressure	1400 psi (90 bars)
Number of satellites	None

about 365 days for the earth. At its closest, Venus is about 66.8 million miles (107.5 million km) from the sun. At its farthest, it is about 67.7 million miles (108.9 million km) from the sun.

Venus comes closer to the earth than any other planet. Its closest approach to earth, when Venus is between the sun and the earth, is at a distance of about 25 million miles (40 million km). Its greatest distance from the earth, when the sun is between Venus and the earth, is about 160 million miles (257 million km).

When viewed through a telescope, Venus displays a complete cycle of phases—similar to those of the moon—as the planet travels around the sun. These phases are due to the fact that different portions of the sunlit area of Venus are visible from earth as Venus reaches different orbital positions relative to the earth and the sun. But in contrast to the moon, Venus varies enormously in apparent diameter, from 10 seconds of arc when full to 64 seconds as a thin crescent. Because of the total cloud cover, no permanent detail can be seen. In the near ultraviolet, however, markings of low contrast can be photographed. Their motion is used as a tracer of wind speeds.

Rotation. As Venus travels around the sun, it rotates slowly on its axis in a direction opposite to that in which it moves around the sun. This rotation, called retrograde rotation, is clockwise as seen from above the north pole of the planet. Venus makes one complete rotation once every 243 earth days. The combination of these two motions gives Venus a solar day of 117 earth days—58.5 days each of light and darkness. The equator is very nearly in the plane of the orbit.

By what seems to be a remarkable coincidence, the same face of Venus (after five Venus solar days) is presented to earth every time the two planets come closest to each other, the longitude drifting by only a fraction of a degree per period. Attempts have been made to explain this phenomenon as a tidal lock between the earth and a permanent bulge on Venus, but they are unconvincing. One consequence is that earth-based radar maps, which are best at the shortest ranges, are largely confined to the one side.

Atmosphere and Clouds. As seen from earth, Venus is completely enveloped in clouds and haze. Remote measurements, always difficult and subject to varying interpretations, are therefore even more ambiguous. Much of our best information comes from the direct probing by U. S. and Soviet spacecraft missions. It has been found that the polar clouds have significant holes (invisible from earth) that permit viewing to much greater depths than the 40 miles (65 km) typical of lower latitudes. The temperature at this level is −30° C (−22° F), and it increases steadily with depth to the surface temperature of 475° C (885° F). The temperatures of cloud top and surface are uniform to within a few degrees, day to night and equator to poles. The cloud base is near 30 miles (48 km), where the temperature is not far below the boiling point of water. Some haze extends down another 10 miles (16 km) or so. The clouds proper are divided into three regions (lower, middle, and upper) by the characteristics of the particles measured by several entry probes. The boundaries lie at 32 and 35 miles (51 and 57 km). Measurements from earth and from orbit indicate the presence of a thin haze extending well above the 40-mile (65-km) level of the visible cloud top. The lowest cloud layer is sometimes very dense and sometimes nearly absent, and it may be the source of the possible lightning discharges reported by the 1978–1979 missions. A major component of the clouds is concentrated sulfuric acid,

An artist's rendering of a huge canyon on Venus, mapped by radar carried on the spacecraft Pioneer Venus 1.

NASA

GODDARD INSTITUTE FOR SPACE STUDIES

Ultraviolet photographs of the changing cloud layer enveloping Venus. Right photo taken one day after left photo.

but chlorine, sulfur, and other compounds seem to be present as well.

The atmosphere is about 95% carbon dioxide (CO_2), most of the rest being nitrogen (N_2). Water vapor is scarce, reported values ranging from 0.1% to a hundredth as much. At low altitudes there are reports of various sulfur compounds (SO_2, H_2S, COS) that seem to be decomposition products of the cloud particles. Oxygen is also very rare. The high temperature and noxious environment are extremely hostile to life as we know it.

If all the CO_2 in the earth's crust is counted, the two planets have similar total amounts. On Venus, the high temperature and the scarcity of water keep the CO_2 in the atmosphere.

Venus' slow rotation exerts a marked control over the winds, which blow from the east, the same direction as the rotation itself. At the cloud tops, the speed can be measured by following the motion of the features found in ultraviolet photographs and from the Doppler shift of spectral lines. The result is about 220 miles (360 km) per hour. At lower altitudes, the motion of entry probes (particularly the four vehicles of Pioneer Venus) has been tracked by radio. The speeds are found to drop steadily with depth to a very small value at the surface. Surface winds have been measured by cup anemometers on Soviet landers. Though small, the winds are adequate in the dense atmosphere to produce some erosion. The winds undoubtedly help maintain the global uniformity of temperatures at each level.

The high surface temperature itself is maintained by the "greenhouse effect," in which solar radiation heats the atmosphere on the way down to the surface, where the last few percent is also converted to heat. Cooling by thermal (infrared) radiation is inhibited by the blanketing effect of clouds and atmosphere. A similar, but much smaller, greenhouse effect is important on earth. Venus is by far the most extreme example known.

Upper Atmosphere and Ionosphere. Even if Venus turns out to have a small magnetic field, it is certainly too weak to withstand the solar wind (a very fast stream of ionized hydrogen carrying a weak magnetic field of its own). Venus is by far the best-studied body whose upper atmosphere is subjected directly to solar-wind impact, and in this respect it offers an interesting analogy with comets. The atmosphere is itself partly ionized by solar radiation (the resulting medium is called the ionosphere). This electrically conducting medium has electric currents and magnetic fields generated in it by the solar wind, which is therefore deflected around the planet in much the same way that air flows around a solid obstacle. Part of the ionosphere is caught up in the flow and carried around to the night side. The neutral atmosphere at these heights does not share the remarkable uniformity of temperature found at lower altitudes: it is near 200° F (about 100° C) on the day side but as cold as −240° F (−150° C) on the night side.

Surface and Interior. One lander photograph of the surface shows what appear to be sharp-edged rocks. On the large scale of radar maps are features reminiscent of continents, ocean basins, and rifts. There are objects resembling large volcanoes, and perhaps large impact basins as well. Natural radioactivity, measured by the Soviet landers, suggests that the rocks are granitic (continental) at two sites and basaltic (oceanic) at one. It is an irresistible temptation to conclude that Venus is tectonically active, although we certainly cannot say that it exhibits seafloor spreading as does the earth.

Planetary magnetic fields are believed to be generated by dynamo action in a fluid core. The behavior of earth, Mercury, and Jupiter would lead one to expect a magnetic field on Venus that would easily have been detected, even in the face of the fluctuating fields from the solar wind. The absence of such a field is one hint that Venus is fundamentally different from earth in some unknown way.

DONALD M. HUNTEN, *University of Arizona*

Further Reading: Burgess, Eric, *Venus: An Errant Twin* (Columbia Univ. Press 1985). The following issues of the journal *Science* are largely given over to reports of the findings of the Venus Pioneer Venus 1 and 2 spacecraft: Vol. 203, no. 4382, 743–808 (1979) and Vol. 205, no. 4401, 41–121 (1979).

VENUS, vē′nəs, in Roman religion, goddess of love, beauty, grace, and fertility. Originally an Italian deity, she later was identified with the Greek goddess Aphrodite, whose nature and deeds were assimilated to the Roman Venus. Venus was one of the least important Roman divinities before her association with Aphrodite. Though there is some evidence that Venus was worshiped in Rome at an early date as a spirit that particularly prospered the fertility of vegetation, it was not until 217 B.C. that her cult, as equivalent to that of Aphrodite, was introduced into Rome from Sicily, where as Venus Erycina (or Erucina) she had been established on Mt. Eryx.

In the developed mythology, Venus was the daughter either of Jupiter and Dione or of Uranus, whose severed genitals mingled with the sea and produced her from the foam. As the most beautiful goddess, Venus married Vulcan, the ugliest god, but she bestowed her love on various gods, such as Mars and Mercury, and several mortals, including Anchises and Adonis. Among her children were Cupid (god of love), Hymen (god of marriage), Priapus (god of gardens), and Aeneas (the Trojan ancestor of the Romans). Plants sacred to her included the myrtle, rose, and poppy. Among animals her chief favorites were doves and sparrows. As Venus Genetrix (Venus the Ancestress), she received special honors from Gaius Julius Caesar, who professed his descent from her through Iulus, her grandson by Aeneas. From Caesar's devotion was derived the subsequent incorporation of Venus Genetrix into the imperial cult. In art, Venus appears sometimes clothed or partly draped, but usually nude. Among her celebrated statues are the *Venus de Milo* and the copies of Praxiteles' *Aphrodite of Cnidus.*

P. R. Coleman-Norton
Princeton University

VENUS AND ADONIS, vē′nəs, ə-don′is, an amatory poem in 199 six-line stanzas by William Shakespeare. It was first published in 1593 by Richard Field (like Shakespeare, a Stratford man) and was dedicated to the brilliant 20-year-old earl of Southampton, already a court favorite, whose patronage the poet sought. The poem, probably written the previous year after the theaters had been closed by the plague, was both Shakespeare's first published work and an immediate and continuing success. Sixteen editions appeared before 1640. The first edition was carefully printed and proofread and is the most authoritative one. For the narrative, Shakespeare combined two stories from Ovid's *Metamorphoses* and added other suggestions from the fashionable erotic poetry of Christopher Marlowe and Thomas Lodge.

Venus and Adonis, however, is less Ovidian than English and Renaissance. Deliberate artifice and aloofness are eschewed in favor of Warwickshire landscape and Elizabethan flora and fauna, sensuously presented. The story is not important. As Coleridge said later, we "seem to be told nothing but to see and hear everything." Nor should the poem be read as an erotic experience. It was Coleridge, too, who pointed out: "In this beautiful poem there is an endless activity of thought. . . ." The thoughts are embodied in discourses and argument about love and beauty, abstemiousness and excess, the nature of virtue. Beauty resides in the lover and is perpetuated by the union of lovers. What is not used is wasted, and all creation is essentially good. The poem is not about an attempted seduction but about the good and full life as the Renaissance conceived it, a life less of abnegation or licentiousness than of an approach to beauty. So read, Shakespeare's lovely verses have a meaning for all time.

Robert Hamilton Ball
Queens College, New York

VENUS DE MILO, vē′nəs də mē′lō, a Greek statue, probably the most celebrated that has survived from classical antiquity. Found on Melos, one of the Cyclades islands, in 1820, the statue, also called *Aphrodite of Melos,* was bought by the marquis de Rivière, the French ambassador to the Ottoman Empire, and presented to Louis XVIII, who in turn gave it to the Louvre in Paris. Once ascribed to the 5th or 4th century B.C., it probably dates from between 110 and 88 B.C.

The statue is draped from the hips down. This invention, borrowed from the 4th century B.C. sculptor Praxiteles, asserts the beauty of the torso and gives the work a satisfactory foundation. The arms are broken off, and the problem of their original position continues to fascinate scholars and aestheticians. Some have conjectured that she was holding a shield to look at her reflection; others, that she was spinning thread. The unknown sculptor, a supremely gifted eclectic, produced an extraordinarily subtle figure that has both dignity and simplicity.

Venus de Milo was found on the island of Melos in 1820.

THE MANSELL COLLECTION, LONDON

VENUS' FLYTRAP, vē′nəs, also called Venus-flytrap and Venus's flytrap, a perennial flowering plant known for its unusual habit of capturing and digesting insects and other small animals. The digestion of animal protein provides the plant with nitrogen-containing amino acids, and—as in the case of other carnivorous plants—is probably an adaptation to nitrogen-poor soils.

The Venus' flytrap (*Dionaea muscipula*) is a member of the sundew family Droseraceae. Although known throughout the world, it is native only to one small area in the United States, a strip of mostly swampy ground covering perhaps as little as 700 square miles (1,800 sq km) in the vicinity of Wilmington, N. C.

The plant bears white flowers in clusters on stalks up to 12 inches (30 cm) long. Spreading from the stalk base are leaves 3 to 6 inches (7.5–15 cm) long. Each leaf broadens into a pair of kidney-shaped lobes that normally lie like a partially opened book and are fringed with long stiff bristles.

The Venus' flytrap is the most dramatic of insectivorous plants. Unlike the sundew, for example, which traps its victims with a sticky secretion, the flytrap imprisons its prey by suddenly snapping the lobes of a leaf together. Secretions inside the margin of the leaf act as a lure for crawling insects. Each leaf has six slender hairs, spaced so as to form a triangle on each lobe. When a crawler touches two of these hairs (or one hair twice, since a double stimulus is necessary), the lobes of the leaf close. Wind and rain usually do not trigger the mechanism.

Venus' flytrap screens its prey by not immediately pressing too tightly. The marginal bristles, which fold over loosely like the interlaced fingers of two clasped hands, form prison bars for prey large enough to constitute a worthwhile meal, but tiny insects can escape through the spaces between the bristles. After a few minutes' time, the lobes of the leaf slowly press more and more tightly together, killing soft-bodied insects. Digestion is usually completed in five to ten days, whereupon the leaf opens wide again, ready for the next victim.

DR. WILLIAM E. HARLOW/PHOTO RESEARCHERS

A fly about to enter a Venus' flytrap. If the fly touches any two of the tiny trigger hairs on the inner surface, the bristled lobes of the trap will snap shut.

VERACRUZ, ver-ə-krōōz′, a state in Mexico, bordering the Gulf of Mexico from the Tamesí River in the northwestern part of the state to the Isthmus of Tehuantepec in the southeastern part. It extends no more than 100 miles (160 km) inland from a coastline more than 400 miles (644 km) long. It is bounded (north to south) by the states of Tamaulipas, San Luis Potosí, Hidalgo, Puebla, Oaxaca, Chiapas, and Tabasco. The area of Veracruz is 27,759 square miles (71,896 sq km).

Veracruz is predominantly mountainous. It has a narrow border of hot, humid coastland below the Sierra Madre Oriental, a range occupying the state's central and western portions. Pico de Orizaba (or Citlaltéptl), an extinct volcanic cone rising to 18,700 feet (5,700 meters) in central Veracruz, is the highest peak in Mexico and the third highest in North America. Cofre de Perote (14,048 feet, or 4,270 meters) is another major extinct volcano. In the north, the Tamiahua Lagoon, which extends 65 miles (105 km), has many large islands. Of the numerous rivers, the chief navigable one is Coatzacoalcos in the southeast. Rainfall is heavy, and the growth of tropical vegetation is exceedingly dense.

The state is an important agricultural and mining area. Important petroleum deposits underlying the coastal strip are being exploited. Leading agricultural products are cereal, corn, beans, fruits and vegetables, and sugarcane. Natural pasturage in the central highlands yields cattle and hides for export. The forests produce rubber, dyewoods, cabinet wood, chicle gum, and jalap. Manufactures include rum, textiles, tobacco products, paper, and chocolate.

The chief city is Veracruz. Other important cities include Orizaba, a resort and textile center; Pánuco and Coatzacoalcos, petroleum centers; the industrial towns Córdoba and Tuxpan; and Jalapa, the capital.

The region now occupied by the state of Veracruz was the center of an Indian civilization antedating that of the Aztecs, farther west. Interesting ruins exist, and archaeological finds have been many. Population: (1976 est.) 4,917,000.

VERACRUZ, ver-ə-krōōz′, a city in Mexico, the principal Mexican port of entry, located on the Gulf of Mexico, in the state of Veracruz about 200 miles (320 km) by air east of Mexico City. It has a harbor protected by breakwaters.

Veracruz (officially, Veracruz Llave) was the site of the first Spanish colonial post in Mexico, built in 1519 by Hernán Cortés, who used it as his base for the conquest of Mexico. He called it La Villa Rica de la Vera Cruz ("the rich town of the true cross"). The original settlement later was moved elsewhere, but it was reestablished in 1599 and subsequently served as a port for the Spanish fleet. Its lack of natural fortifications led to pillaging by pirates, especially in the years 1653 and 1712.

The city was captured by U. S. troops under Gen. Winfield Scott on March 29, 1847. Veracruz also fell to the French, first in 1838 and again in 1861. In 1914, U. S. forces occupied it for several months during a conflict with President Victoriano Huerta that led to his resignation.

Camera Press, Ltd.

Plaza and City Hall in the port of Veracruz. In the evening, following a Spanish tradition, chaperoned young ladies may stroll in the square and greet admirers.

The city of Veracruz is the terminal of several railroads and has air and passenger steamship services. Its manufactures include cigars, chocolate, liquors, tiles, and footwear. Its fine port facilities make it an export and import trade center. Important buildings include the colonial Fortress of Santiago, the Federal Custom House, and the City Hall. "Guarding" the harbor is the famous fort known as the Castillo De San Juan de Ulúa, built on Gallega Island, about a mile from the mainland. It was notorious as a prison before 1914. Not far from Ulúa is the Isla de los Sacrificios, a resort island important archaeologically for its ruins. There are excellent beaches south of the city.

Veracruz is an interesting mixture of the old and the new, with quaint old white-walled houses on narrow, cobbled streets contrasting with modern structures on broad thoroughfares. There are several spacious plazas, including the central Plaza Constitución, with its early 18th century parish church. The Alameda, or Plaza Zamora, has a bronze statue of Manuel Gutiérrez Zamora, a former governor of the state of Veracruz. There is also a monument to Benito Juárez, built to commemorate the Reform Laws, in the Parque Porfirio Díaz. Pop. (1950) 101,469.

VERACRUZ, Capture of. See MEXICAN WAR—*The Campaigns.*

VERAGUAS, bā-rä'gwäs, province, Panama, situated in central Panama, west of the canal, and extending across the peninsula from Mosquito Gulf of the Caribbean Sea, in the north, to the Pacific shore in the south, taking in the western part of the Azuero Peninsula and Coiba Island in the Pacific. The province covers an area of over 4,600 square miles. The land is amply forested, with stands of mahogany and other valuable hardwoods supporting a lumbering industry. Gold is mined in the Veraguas Mountains in the north, and there are deposits of magnesium, lead, mercury, zinc, and iron. Coffee, rice, sugarcane, and corn are grown in lower-lying regions. The province is bisected by the Inter-American Highway, which passes through Santiago, the provincial capital and principal town. Pop. (1950) 106,998.

VERATRUM, və-rā'trəm, genus of plants of the subfamily Melanthioideae, in the lily family (Liliaceae). The best known species are *V. viride,* the American false hellebore (also called green, or swamp hellebore and Indian poke), a native of the eastern United States and southeastern Canada; and *V. album,* the European hellebore (also called white hellebore). These species should not be confused with *Helleborus,* of the family Ranunculaceae. From fleshy, perennial rootstocks, the plants send up annual stalks three to eight feet tall, bearing panicled flowers and large, plaited leaves. Roots and rhizomes of *V. viride* and *V. album* contain many alkaloids, some of which are pharmacologically active. *V. album* is more toxic than the American species and no longer is used medicinally in the United States, although its powdered roots and rhizomes are employed as insecticides.

V. viride and extracts containing its hypotensive alkaloids are prescribed for primary (essential) hypertension. Only a small margin separates therapeutic and toxic doses. Major symptoms of veratrum poisoning, which may follow ingestion or inhalation of powdered rootstocks or ingestion of liquid preparations of the alkaloids, are vomiting, nausea, and retching, followed by prostration, muscular weakness, pallor, and shallow respiration. Death occurs from respiratory arrest. Antidotal treatment depends on the stage to which poisoning has progressed and may entail use of activated charcoal, morphine (if respiration is unaffected), carbon dioxide and oxygen inhalation, atropine, ephedrine, or caffeine.

ROBERTSON PRATT.

VERAVAL, vā-rä'vəl, town, India, a port of the Kathiawar Peninsula in Gujarat State. It is situated on the Arabian Sea, about 45 miles south of the town of Junagadh. The port once carried on a brisk trade with areas along the Persian Gulf, the Red Sea, and the East African coast, and was for a time the chief port of embarkation of Indian Muslim pilgrims to Mecca. Sea traffic is still brisk and varied and there is a variety of light manufacturing. Three miles to the southeast is the renowned Somnath Temple. Veraval was formerly included in the Muslim-ruled state of Junagarh (Junagadh) and retains a substantial Muslim minority. Pop. (1951) 40,378.

JOSEPH E. SCHWARTZBERG.

VERAZZANO, Giovanni da. See VERRAZANO.

VERB, vûrb, a term used by grammarians to designate a certain class of words, or part of speech, in a language. Formal, semantic, and functional criteria define the verb. To be recognizably distinct from other classes of words in a language, the verb must be different in form, the two most usual formal differentiators being inflection and a characteristic position in a sentence. In English, the word that can take the forms *cook, cooks, cooked* is a verb; the word that can take only the forms *cook* and *cooks* (including *cook's* and *cooks'*), but not *cooked,* is a noun. In the sentences *The cook cooks* and *The cooks cook,* the inflectional ambiguity of *cook* and *cooks* is resolved by word order; in the sentence *The cook cooked,* both word order and inflection distinguish the noun from the verb. In English, the inflectional possibilities are few and word order is correspondingly important; in a highly inflected language like Latin, inflection may be so rich that word order need not be used to make this distinction: *amant* is a verb in any position.

The semantic and functional characteristics of the verb cannot be used to distinguish it from another part of speech; we may speak of the meaning of the word *cook* only after we have identified it, through formal means, as noun or verb. At the same time, which of several formally differentiated classes is to be called verb is indicated by the semantic and functional characteristics of the words in the class.

Semantically, verbs are typically indicators of actions and processes (as are nouns, too, but verbs are very rarely indicators of objects and places). Functionally, variations in the inflection, or syntactic combination, of a verb usually indicate differences in the time or manner of an action. (Such differences in a noun are of spatial relationship or in the relation of person or thing to an action, as *performer, benefiter.*)

The extent to which functional variations are indicated by the verb varies greatly among languages. At one extreme is a language of the type of Vietnamese, in which inflection is negligible, so that the verb indicates only the action itself and separate words make other distinctions. At the other extreme is a language like Turkish, in which modifications of the form of the stem and endings can make such distinctions as: intensive, reciprocal, reflexive, impersonal, causative, negative, incapacity, necessity, infinitive, imperative, optative, time (present, past, and future), voice (active, passive, middle), aspect (perfective, imperfective), person (first, second, third), and number (singular and plural).

English, of course, stands between these two extremes, probably somewhat nearer to Vietnamese than to Turkish. The distinctions indicated by the Turkish verb are in English, shown partly by inflection, partly by auxiliary words, and partly by independent words (that is, not by the verb at all). English inflection consists of *-s,* which indicates third person singular (other person-number combinations are indicated nonverbally), and *-ed,* for past time. Some auxiliaries—such as *shall, will, must, may,* and *might*—occur only as adjuncts of the verb, never independently, and indicate temporal and modal distinctions that are typically indicated by inflection in some other languages. Auxiliaries such as *have* perform similar functions but also exist as independent words, homonyms of the auxiliaries. Still other functions are indicated by such words as *not, always,* and *would like to,* among others.

The concept of verb has almost universal application, but the details of its semantic and functional characteristics, like its formal markers, are unique for each individual language.

William Diver,
Department of Linguistics, Columbia University.

VERBANO, Lake. See Maggiore.

VERBASCUM. See Mullein.

VERBENA, vər-bē′nə, a complex genus of about 352 known specific and subspecific plant taxa and named natural and artificial hybrids. They are native to temperate and tropical America, with two species indigenous to the Mediterranean region and the Near East and introduced elsewhere in the Old World. Several American species have become naturalized in parts of Europe, Asia, Africa, and Australia. Approximately a hundred species, varieties, forms, and hybrids are cultivated of which *V. hybrida* is the most commonly seen and comprises no less than 125 horticultural races with showy spicate racemes of phloxlike flowers in various shades of red, blue, purple, yellow, and white.

The plants of this genus are usually referred to in English as "verbenas" when large-flowered, and as "vervains" when small-flowered. The latter term is a Middle English word (with "verveine" an Old French modification) derived from the celtic *fer,* to take away, and *faen,* stone, in allusion to the former use of the type species, *V. officinalis,* in the treatment of bladder stones. "Verbena" appears to be the Old Latin adaption of this term, used by Virgil and Pliny, and later adopted by Linnaeus. Numerous species have been employed medicinally in various localities.

The large-flowered species are sometimes segregated as the separate but closely related genus *Glandularia.* On the other hand, plants now referred to the genera *Bouchea, Ghinia, Junellia, Priva, Stachytarpheta,* and *Stylodon* were formerly included in *Verbena.* It is the type genus of the Verbenaceae, a plant family of worldwide distribution, comprising 76 genera and approximately 3,250 species and varieties, including the commercially very valuable wood, teak.

Harold N. Moldenke,
Director, Trailside Museum, Mountainside, N.J.

VERBENACEAE. See Verbena.

VERBOECKHOVEN, vĕr′bo͞ok-hō-vən, **Eugène Joseph,** Belgian painter: b. Warneton, West Flanders (now Belgium), June 9, 1798; d. Brussels, Jan. 19, 1881. His father, who was a sculptor, taught him to draw and model. Verboeckhoven became celebrated for his animal paintings, executed in a naturalistic, rather bland style. He produced an enormous number of canvases, including many landscapes with cattle, sheep, and horses. The outstanding features of his art are his careful drawing and the refinement and smoothness of his artistic execution.

VERCELLI, vār-chĕl′lē, province, Italy, in the Piedmont Region, extending from the peaks of the Pennine Alps, through the Alpine foothills, to the plain and the Po River. The area is 1,157 square miles, and the capital is Vercelli. The province is bounded north and east by the province of Novara, south by that of Alessandria, and west by the province of Turin and the Aosta Autonomous Region. The plain is highly irrigated and is watered by the Cavour Canal and by the

Sesia, Cervio, and Dora Baltea rivers. Rice is by far the chief agricultural product, followed by wheat, corn, and grapes. Industries are located at Vercelli, Biella (noted for its high-quality woolen fabrics), and Borgosesia. The province was formed in 1927 from part of Novara province. Population: (1981) 394,000.

VERCELLI, vâr-chĕl′lē, a city in northwestern Italy and the capital of Vercelli province, in the Piedmont region. It is situated on the Sesia River, some 35 miles (55 km) southwest of Milan, and is a rail and highway junction on the Milan-Turin routes. An important agricultural center, it is noted as one of Europe's most active markets for rice, which is cultivated on the surrounding irrigated plain. The city has rice and flour mills and factories producing textiles, shoes, and agricultural implements.

The city's most notable landmark is the imposing 13th century Basilica of Sant'Andrea, in the Lombard Romanesque manner; it has a Gothic interior and a striking octagonal cupola. In the library of the Cathedral of Sant'Eusebio are several valuable manuscripts, including the Anglo-Saxon *Codex Vercellensis* (or Vercelli Book), containing Old English sermons, religious poems, and a prose narrative, all dating from the early 11th century or before. Also worthy of note are the Church of San Cristoforo and two museums.

Probably founded by the Celts, the city became a Roman municipium, Vercellae. In the Raudian Fields nearby, the Roman general Gaius Marius defeated the Cimbri in 101 B. C. Vercelli became the see of a bishop in the 4th century. It was, in turn, a Lombard duchy and a Frankish county, developing into a free commune by the end of the 12th century and witnessing long factional struggles. In 1335 it came under the rule of the Visconti, dukes of Milan, but was ceded by them to the dukes of Savoy in 1427. Repeatedly sacked and conquered by French and Spaniards, it remained, with few interruptions, part of the domains of the dukes of Savoy (later kings of Sardinia) until its incorporation into the Kingdom of Italy in 1860. It became an archbishopric in 1817. The painter Giovanni Antonio de' Bazzi (1477–1549), called Il Sodoma, was a native of the city. Population: (1981) 51,975.

VERCHÈRES, ver-shâr′, **Marie Madeleine Jarret de** (1678–1747), French Canadian heroine. She was born in Verchères, Quebec, Canada, on March 3, 1678. The event that made her famous occurred at the farm of her father on the St. Lawrence River, about 20 miles (32 km) northeast of Quebec. On Oct. 22, 1692, when her parents were away, Iroquois Indians attacked the settlement. Most of the male settlers were ambushed and killed where they worked in the fields. The 14-year-old Madeleine escaped to the manorial fort, which was occupied by two soldiers, an old man, several women with infant children, and the girl's two younger brothers. She distributed guns to all who were capable of handling them, directed the defense of the fort, and stood off the Indians until relief arrived from Montreal a week later. For this act of heroism she was awarded a pension by the French crown. She married Pierre Thomas Tarieu de la Pérade in 1706 and is said to have saved his life in 1722 when he was assaulted by an Indian. Verchères died in Ste. Anne de la Pérade, Quebec, on Aug. 8, 1747.

VERCINGETORIX, vûr-sin-jet′ə-riks (died 52 B.C.), Gallic patriot. He interrupted Julius Caesar's conquest of Gaul in 52 B.C. by leading the Arverni and other Gauls in revolt. By guerrilla warfare, by raiding Roman lines of supply, by offering battle wherever possible on terrain unfavorable to the Romans, Vercingetorix won some successes. But his cause collapsed at Alesia (Alise-Sainte-Reine, France) when Caesar besieged that fortress and captured him. Caesar kept Vercingetorix in chains and exhibited him in his Gallic triumph in Rome, where after six years in captivity the defeated chieftain was put to death. In the seventh book of *De bello Gallico,* Caesar relates his version of the rebellion.

P. R. COLEMAN-NORTON, *Princeton University*

VERDAGUER, ver-thä-ger′, **Jacint** (1845–1902), Spanish poet. Born on May 17, 1845, of Catalan peasants, he entered the seminary at Vich at the age of 11 and was ordained a priest in 1870. While still a young man, he won various prizes in poetry contests. After traveling extensively as a chaplain for a steamship company, he became chaplain to the Comillas family.

His poetry runs the gamut from the secular to the mystical, the most famous single poem being the epic *L'Atlàntida* (1877). The first complete edition of his works appeared in 1905. With Joan Maragall, he was an important figure in the so-called *Renaixença,* a 19th century revival of Catalan literature. He died in Barcelona province on June 10, 1902.

GREGORY RABASSA
Queens College, New York

VERDE RIVER, vûr′dē, a river in west central Arizona. It rises in Yavapai county, flows generally in a southerly direction more than 100 miles (160 km), and empties into the Salt River, east of Phoenix. About 20 miles (32 km) north of its confluence with the Salt is the 287-foot (87-meter) Bartlett Dam. Further upstream are Horseshoe Dam and Reservoir. These works, with those on the Salt River, make possible the irrigation of a large part of semiarid central Arizona.

VERDEN, fâr′dən, a town in the West German state of Lower Saxony, on the Aller River, 21 miles (34 km) southeast of Bremen. It is an industrial center producing a widely diversified list of manufactures, including precision instruments, bookbinding machinery, chemicals, and furniture. Among places of local interest are a museum of equestrianism, one devoted to the history of the region, and a racetrack. Sachsenhain, a memorial park, commemorates Charlemagne's execution in 782 of 4,500 hostages to quell a Saxon rebellion. Verden has numerous religious structures: St. John's Church, erected in the 12th century and rebuilt three centuries later; the cathedral, with a Romanesque tower, built in the 13th to 15th centuries; and the Andreas Church, constructed early in the same period. The city hall dates from 1730.

Verden was established as a fishing settlement by the 8th century and assumed its position as a market center toward the end of the 10th century. It was incorporated as a town in 1192. The bishopric founded by Charlemagne passed to Sweden as a secularized duchy in 1648, but in 1719 it was ceded to Hannover. Population: (1980 est.) 24,200.

VERDI, vâr′dē, **Giuseppe** (1813–1901), Italian composer, who is best known for his operas, including *Rigoletto, Il Trovatore, La Traviata, Aïda,* and *Otello.* His principal nonoperatic work is the *Manzoni Requiem,* written in honor of Alessandro Manzoni, a poet and novelist whom Verdi revered. He also composed choral works, songs, and a string quartet.

To Italians he holds a special place as both an artistic and a patriotic hero. His face appears on the 1,000 lire note, a significance roughly equivalent to that of Washington on the American dollar bill. Although Verdi held no major political office, he came to be regarded as a hero during the struggle for the unification of Italy—the *Risorgimento*—when his music, particularly his choruses with patriotic overtones, were hailed as expressions of national aspiration. Standing above all parties and factions, Verdi continues today to enjoy undiminished popularity among his countrymen.

Early Life. Giuseppe Fortunio Francesco Verdi was born sometime between Oct. 9 and 11, 1813, in the village of Le Roncole, near Busseto, in the duchy of Parma. His birthdate is uncertain: although he always celebrated October 9 as his birthday, an ambiguous baptismal record is dated November 11. His parents kept the local tavern. Verdi liked to boast he came from peasant stock, but his remarks about himself and events in his life frequently turn out to be misleading, if not downright false. Research has shown that his forefathers had lived in the region since the 17th century and, for the most part, were engaged in trade.

By the age of three Verdi displayed sufficient musical ability to receive lessons from the local organist. When Verdi was nine his first teacher died, and the boy had made enough progress to assume some of his teacher's musical responsibilities. Later, in Busseto, he attended the local school and continued to study music with Ferdinando Provesi. The patronage of a local businessman, Antonio Barezzi, allowed Verdi to go to Milan in 1832 to complete his musical education.

Denied acceptance at the Milan Conservatory because he was beyond the age for admission, he studied privately with the composer Vincenzo Lavigna. Although Lavigna had had five operas produced at La Scala, he kept his young student working for three years at traditional counterpoint. In 1835, Verdi returned to Busseto to teach music and to conduct concerts, for which he composed occasional pieces. He married Barezzi's daughter Margherita, who died in June 1840. They had two children, a son and a daughter, neither of whom survived infancy.

Having given up his post in Busseto, Verdi moved to Milan in February 1839. Here his first completed opera, *Oberto,* was accepted and produced at La Scala in November. This work was sufficiently successful that Bartolomeo Merelli, director of La Scala, commissioned three additional operas from him. Verdi next wrote a comic opera in two acts, *Un giorno di regno,* which failed so decisively that it was withdrawn after a single performance. Depressed by this fiasco and by the loss of his family, Verdi considered abandoning his chosen career.

Merelli overcame Verdi's reluctance to write another opera by sending him the libretto to *Nabucco.* Verdi's eye was caught by the text for the Hebrew exiles, the chorus "Va, pensiero," and gradually brought himself to finish the score during the autumn of 1841. When *Nabucco* was presented at La Scala in March 1842, it made such an impression that it was presented again in the autumn for a run of 57 performances. In a short time *Nabucco* helped make Verdi's name known in all the leading opera centers.

THE BETTMANN ARCHIVE

Giuseppe Verdi was one of Italy's greatest opera composers and a hero to those seeking national unification.

In later years Verdi liked to refer to the decade following *Nabucco* as his "galley" years, when he regarded himself as a slave chained to his obligation to turn out several operas in most years. Of Verdi's 26 operas, 16 of them had been composed by 1851, while the remaining 10 were spaced out over the next 42 years. This marked change of pace indicates not only the improving status of composers in the second half of the 19th century, an improvement Verdi contributed to, but the greater study and reflection that went into his mature operas.

If the most widely popular of these early operas was *Ernani* (1844), the most significant of them in the light of Verdi's future was *Macbeth* (1847), his first work based on Shakespeare. In another sense 1847 was an important year for Verdi, for he left Italy for the first time, going to London, for *I masnadieri* with Jenny Lind, and to Paris for *Jérusalem,* a revision of his *I Lombardi* (1843) for the Opéra.

It was during this early phase of his career, but chiefly after 1846, that Verdi's music, particularly in such passages as the aria-like choruses in *Nabucco, I Lombardi,* and *Macbeth,* provided anthems for the *Risorgimento.* There is a clear stratum of nationalistic propaganda in *La battaglia di Legnano* (1849). But it was not until 1859 that crowds started shouting "Viva Verdi," making thereby an acronymic allusion to Vittorio Emmanuele Re D'Italia.

Middle Years. *Rigoletto* (1851), with its often free adaptation of the conventions of Italian opera up to that time, marks the division between Verdi's earlier "galley" years and the more leisurely pace he would generally adhere to in the future. Two influences contributed to Verdi's settling down after this decade of strenuous activity. One was his association with the retired soprano Giuseppina Strepponi, who had been a champion of his works at the onset of his career. After living together for more than a decade, they were married unobtrusively in 1859. The other was his purchase of land at Sant'Agata, just north of Busseto, the region his ancestors had come from. There he would gradually develop a model estate, which was to be his chief residence for the rest of his life. The library at Villa Sant'Agata, with its wealth of literary and historical works as well as books on science and agriculture, clearly indicates the breadth of Verdi's reading.

Il Trovatore (January 1853) and *La Traviata* (March 1853) were both successful—the former immediately; the latter, however, not until it was revived with a more appropriate cast in 1854. These two, along with *Rigoletto*, established his reputation as the most popular opera composer of the day, and they have held a permanent place in the core repertory ever since.

Verdi lived in Paris with Giuseppina almost continuously from October 1853 until January 1857. Here he was mainly involved in composing and staging *Les Vêpres siciliennes*, his first entirely new score for the Paris Opéra. While he was there, both *Il Trovatore* and *La Traviata* were produced at the Théâtre-Italien—the former with his active participation, the latter from a pirated version. He further helped solidify his reputation in Paris by making a French adaptation of *Il Trovatore*, with ballet and an expanded ending, for the Opéra.

Returning to Italy, Verdi settled in at Sant'Agata. But his first months were clouded by the disappointing receptions accorded *Simon Boccanegra* (March 1857) and *Aroldo* (June 1857), the latter being a reworking of his 1850 score *Stiffelio*. *Un ballo in maschera* was originally scheduled for Naples, but troubles with the censors there caused Verdi to withdraw his score, which was produced, further modified by Roman censors, in February 1859. Verdi became increasingly dissatisfied with slipshod performance practices in Italian opera houses and with the unpredictable censors, and for the next 10 years he accepted commissions for new works only outside Italy.

Verdi and his wife went to St. Petersburg for the launching of *La forza del destino* (March 1862). When that opera was first presented at La Scala in 1869, Verdi rewrote about a third of the score and personally prepared the performances. He was in Paris between November 1865 and March 1867, where he worked on *Don Carlos*, the most elaborate of his three works for the Opéra. To celebrate the opening of the Suez Canal and the new Cairo opera house, Verdi was commissioned to write a new opera. This was to be *Aïda*, with its Egyptian setting. Verdi did not attend the Cairo premiere (December 1871), but concentrated on its first Italian performance (La Scala, February 1872). Since 1869, Verdi's rapport with La Scala had undergone a marked improvement and its stage became his artistic home. The almost universal recognition of Verdi as the grand old man of Italian music dates from the time of *Aïda*.

Last Years. When Rossini died in 1868, Verdi had proposed a list of composers to contribute to a *Requiem*, for which he was to supply the concluding "Libera me." That project fell into abeyance, but after the death of Manzoni in 1873, Verdi was moved to complete the *Requiem* himself. Although he was active as a conductor of his works during the next several years, he seemed to have renounced composition, apparently content to divide his year between Sant'Agata and Genoa, where the winters were milder.

The reemergence of Verdi to compose his two final masterpieces was due to the efforts of his music publisher, Giulio Ricordi, who arranged for a collaboration with Arrigo Boito, who provided the librettos for *Otello* and *Falstaff*. Work on *Otello* proceeded hesitantly at first and in secret, since Verdi was unsure he was capable of finishing it at his advanced age. The premiere at La Scala (February 1887) provided him with the grandest success of his career.

Seemingly rejuvenated by it, Verdi expressed his desire to write a comic opera. The subject of *Falstaff* struck sparks of mercurial inventiveness and wit in Verdi. The composition of the opera advanced without the delays and hesitations that had marked the writing of *Otello*. Verdi was in his 80th year when *Falstaff* was first performed at La Scala (February 1893). That he was capable of producing such a lighthearted work at his age was generally regarded as little short of a miracle.

Although Boito tried to tempt him with composing a *King Lear*, Verdi knew such an effort was now beyond him. He spent most of his declining years at Sant'Agata. Here Giuseppina died in November 1897. Verdi was staying in a Milanese hotel when he suffered a stroke and died in his sleep on Jan. 27, 1901. He is buried beside Giuseppina at the Casa di Riposo, Milan, a home for retired musicians he endowed.

Personality. Verdi was a proud and private man who had no patience with flattery or idle curiosity. As a young man he was regarded as taciturn, but he seems to have mellowed somewhat with age, thanks to Giuseppina's influence. His sense of humor was wry, and with those he had confidence in he could be charming. With those who worked for him at Sant'Agata he was strict but scrupulously fair. His many surviving letters are sprinkled with irony and common sense, and are often moving, particularly when he expresses his lofty idealism for Italian music. He demanded of others what he demanded of himself—the best.

Works. The style of Verdi's early operas depends on the conventions for arias, duets, and finales established by Rossini and exploited in their several ways by Bellini and Donizetti, although Donizetti's influence can be observed in works that Verdi had composed as late as the 1850's. Yet his individuality, the presence of a potent musical personality, is clear from *Nabucco* onward. This is felt in his rhythmic vigor and his ability to develop melodies possessing a forward propulsiveness. The early works are relatively brief and often advance in a series of striking contrasts—at times crude, at their best irresistible.

Macbeth, customarily performed today in its revision (1865) for the Théâtre-Lyrique of Paris, stands out for its inventiveness in the distinctive color of such moments as the Act I duet for Macbeth and Lady Macbeth and the eerie Sleepwalking Scene. But it also points forward to Verdi's increasing sensitivity to dramatic characterization and his growing interest in plots of some psychological complexity. His exposure to the Paris Opéra that same year marks the beginnings of his effort to transmute the spectacle and more flexible structure of French grand opera into his own idiom.

The triad of *Rigoletto, Il Trovatore,* and *La Traviata,* each in its own way testifies to Verdi's developing mastery of his craft. The last act of *Rigoletto* approaches being a continuous musicodramatic unit, even though separate numbers, such as the astonishing Quartet, can still be discerned. *Il Trovatore,* outwardly the most faithful of the three to conventional forms, is notable for containing the earliest of his great roles for a dramatic mezzo-soprano in the old gypsy Azucena. In *La Traviata* he achieves new depth of intimate psychological portraiture in the figure of Violetta.

Although scarcely one of his best-known operas, *Les Vêpres siciliennes* indicates a change of course for Verdi that was to influence him through *Aïda. Les Vêpres* was his longest score up to this point, and within this larger framework there is much evidence of a new suppleness of technique, of richer harmonic inflection, and of a growing sophistication in the application of orchestral color. Although burdened with a somewhat rickety libretto by Eugène Scribe, *Les Vêpres siciliennes* stands among Verdi's major scores as the least generally appreciated.

Verdi's assimilation of the French grand opera style, particularly as he inherited it from Auber and Meyerbeer, can be observed progressively through *Un ballo in maschera, La forza del destino* and *Don Carlos,* attaining a new justness of proportion in *Aïda.* Much tauter than its two sprawling successors, *Un ballo in maschera* expertly fuses both public and private events, lightening the tragic mood with occasional touches of humor. It shows Verdi's greater freedom in adapting conventional forms, as when he substitutes for a cabaletta (the final section of a double-aria structure) a few highly charged phrases in Riccardo's Act III aria. Although the most episodic of Verdi's later works, *La forza del destino* is bound together by many pages of sincere eloquence beautifully wrought, such as Leonora's famous prayer, "Pace, pace, mio Dio." In its original form the longest of Verdi's operas, *Don Carlos* presents a complex drama, containing detailed portraits of six major characters. Long out of favor, it has ultimately taken its rightful position as one of Verdi's noblest, most thought-provoking works.

Aïda marks a new level of accomplishment for Verdi, with its finely attuned blend of exoticism, its pervasive sense of atmosphere, its integration of ballet into ongoing action (rather than being confined to a single *divertissement* in the French manner), and its equilibrium between public spectacle and private dilemma. The Nile Scene (Act III) of *Aïda* reveals his mastery of working aria and duet forms into a coherent act-long unit. The economy and dramatic symmetry of *Aïda* are an advance upon that achieved in *Un ballo in maschera* and clearly superior to the looser musicodramatic structure of either *La forza del destino* or *Don Carlos.*

Otello and *Falstaff,* coupled with the sections of *Simon Boccanegra* revised by Verdi in 1881, show him at the apex of his expressive powers. The ability to connect and articulate scenes of potent contrast with ease is everywhere apparent in *Otello*—for instance in the transition from the riot scene to the succeeding love duet that closes Act I. The old cabaletta function of expressing a new plateau of emotional perception is compressed into a single irrepressible outburst at the close of Desdemona's "Willow Song" (Act IV). In *Otello* the expression of moods ranging from hysteria to moments of inner resignation is achieved with startling vividness.

The extraordinary concentration of musical ideas in the comic *Falstaff* is responsible for its relative slowness to equal the popular appeal of *Otello,* but today it is more widely appreciated than it was a generation ago. Its quick wit and breathtaking pace, along with the frequent miniaturizing of structure, require a promptness of response opposed to the more leisurely gait of romantic *melodrama* or of grand opera.

For the sophisticated appropriateness of its orchestration, *Falstaff* occupies a unique place among Verdi's works. The telescoping of structure is observable in Falstaff's "Quand'ero paggio" (Act II, Scene 2) and in the love duets for Nanetta and Fenton. Verdi's mastery of ensemble writing is everywhere evident: in the nonet of Act I, Scene 2, and, most of all, in the splendid final fugue.

Reputation. Verdi's popularity has moved through at least three distinct phases. The earliest of these is his emergence in the later 1840's and 1850's as a symbol of Italian aspirations toward nationhood. Outside of Italy his fame was originally based upon his gifts as a melodist. Yet by the end of the 19th century, with the rise of the vogue for Wagner, Verdi's great popular successes of the 1850's were regarded with condescension by those shapers of taste who would admit virtues only in *Otello* and *Falstaff.*

The beginnings of the reappraisal of Verdi as a major composer occur in two places: the series of revivals of his lesser-known operas in new translations that began in Germany during the late 1920's, and in the productions prepared by Toscanini at La Scala in the same decade. Once started, the movement gained ground, until after World War II he came to be accepted, along with Mozart, as one of the greatest masters of opera.

The significance of Verdi as a link between the singer-oriented operas of Rossini, Bellini, and Donizetti and the dramatic volatility of the so-called veristic operas of Mascagni, Leoncavallo, and Puccini is now plain to see. Taking an approach different from Wagner's basically symphonic style, with its emphasis on the orchestra, Verdi evolved his musical syntax from vocal melody, using harmony to inflect and direct it and coming to employ orchestration as a means of characterizing it, thereby achieving a stylistic evolution in genuinely Italian terms.

William Ashbrook
Indiana State University

Bibliography

Budden, Julian, *The Operas of Verdi,* 3 vols. (Oxford 1984).

Godefroy, Vincent, *The Dramatic Genius of Verdi,* 2 vols. (St. Martin's 1975, 1978).

Kimbell, David R., *Verdi in the Age of Italian Romanticism* (Cambridge 1981).

Martin, George W., *Verdi: His Music, Life, and Times* (1963: reprint, Dodd 1983).

Walker, Frank, *The Man Verdi* (Univ. of Chicago Press 1982).

Weaver, William, and Chusid, Martin, eds., *The Verdi Companion* (Norton 1979).

VERDICT, vûr′dikt, in law, the determination of a jury on matters submitted in the course of a trial. Three types of verdict are utilized. The traditional form, a general verdict, fixes liability or the lack of it and involves both the finding of facts and the application of apposite legal principles presented in the instructions of the trial judge. A verdict is special when the jury passes on questions of fact only, with the court reserving the tasks of applying the law and rendering the final decision. Where a special verdict is available, its use may be either discretionary with the judge or mandatory upon the request of either party. A general verdict with special findings (interrogatories) combines the general verdict with answers to specific controlling questions of fact.

Although a verdict at common law had to represent the consent of all jurors, statutes in some jurisdictions provide that verdicts may be less than unanimous in civil cases. If the required vote for a verdict is not obtained, the jury is sent back for further deliberation or a new trial is ordered. In criminal cases, the verdict must be unanimous.

At common law a verdict was announced orally by the foreman of the jury in open court. In many states, the jury either writes out the verdict or signs a verdict form which is delivered to the clerk or judge. Special verdicts and special findings are usually rendered in written form. The verdict is confirmed when the jury is asked collectively if the decision as announced is their own. Generally, the parties have the right to have the jury individually "polled." If all jurors are agreed, the verdict is recorded and becomes final at that time. If the verdict has errors in form only, the judge may amend or correct. Some other defects can be cured by further deliberation of the jury, but if the verdict is contrary to the evidence or to law, or is otherwise fatally defective, it cannot stand and may be set aside. A verdict of acquittal of a criminal charge, however, is normally conclusive.

When a verdict may not be found until after adjournment of court for the day, the judge in a civil action and in certain criminal actions in some states may direct the jury to seal its verdict and to deliver it to an officer of the court to hold until court reconvenes.

ALAN A. MATHESON
Columbia University

VERDIGRIS, vûr′də-grēs, in popular usage, the greenish patina that forms on copper after long exposure to the atmosphere. It is a copper carbonate created on copper surfaces by the action of carbonic acid in the atmosphere. This type of verdigris produces the characteristic mottled green coloring of copper roofing and of bronze statues.

In chemistry, the term is applied to acetates of copper formed by reaction of copper with acetic acid. The acetates are powdery or minutely crystalline substances that are green or blue-green in color. Verdigris is used as a pigment in paints, as a mordant in dyeing, and as a fungicide and mildew preventive. It is poisonous if ingested.

VERDIN, vûr′din, a very small American songbird (*Auriparus flaviceps*) believed by some authorities to be related to the penduline titmouse (family Remizidae). The verdin is about 4 inches (10 cm) in length and has a very sharply attenuated bill. The male is gray above, grayish white below, has a yellow head, and is marked with chestnut on the forehead and wing. The female resembles the male but is duller. The nest is quite curious, consisting of a very large ball of twigs with an entrance at the side. The verdin is sedentary and ranges from southern California and southern Texas to the Lower Californian peninsula and southern Mexico.

CHARLES VAURIE, *Author of "The Birds of the Palearctic Fauna"*

VERDUN, vər-dun′; French ver-dûɴ′, a city in northeastern France, and the site of one of the greatest battles of World War I. Verdun (in full Verdun-sut-Meuse) is situated in the fertile valley of the Meuse and Meuse department. Its strategic position between the upland forests of the Argonne and Woëvre, commanding one of the principal routes between the Rhineland to the east and Champagne and Paris to the west, was recognized in early antiquity; indeed, its name derives from the Celtic *Verodunum*, meaning "great fortress." Already an urban center in the days of Roman Gaul, Verdun became an episcopal see in the 4th century. During the partitions of the Frankish empire after the death of Charlemagne, Verdun was included within the unstable central kingdom by the treaty made there in 843. By the late 10th century, German control was undisputed. Though the county of Verdun became a fief held by the bishop, the town itself developed as a fairly independent city of the Holy Roman Empire and grew prosperous during the Middle Ages by virtue of its active trade.

Its strategic significance led to its next major shift in political control, when Henry II, as "imperial vicar," took it under French administration in 1552. It passed formally to France by the Peace of Westphalia (1648). The Marquis de Vauban, Louis XIV's great military engineer, modernized its fortifications, taking particular advantage of the steep slopes of the Meuse. When France lost Alsace-Lorraine to the German Empire in 1871, Verdun, with Vauban's works brought up to date, became the key to the French eastern defenses. It sustained the assaults of the Germans during World War I but fell to them during World War II; it suffered major damage in both wars and has been largely rebuilt. Architectural features include an 11th century cathedral, a 14th century city gate, and a baroque city hall. Principal modern industries are candymaking, food processing, and leathercraft, and there is some hardware manufacturing. Population: (1975) 22,889.

See also VERDUN, BATTLE OF; VERDUN, TREATY OF.

HERBERT H. ROWEN, *Rutgers University*

VERDUN, vər-dun′; French, ver-dûɴ′, a city in the province of Quebec, Canada, on Montreal Island, directly south of and adjoining the city of Montreal. It was named after Saverdun, the birthplace of the first settler, who arrived in 1660. The settlement, at the foot of the Lachine Rapids, was the site of a fort built in 1662.

Verdun is primarily residential, although it supports some manufacturing. The population is almost equally divided between English-speaking and French-speaking residents, who are served by bilingual weekly newspapers and radio broadcasts. Verdun is noted for its hospitals, several parks, and a 3-mile (5-km) riverside boardwalk.

The community, then called Rivière St. Pierre, was incorporated as a village in 1875. As Verdun, it was incorporated as a town in 1907 and as a city in 1912. In 1959 it joined the Montreal Metropolitan Corporation. Population: 61,287.

FERNAND GRENIER, *University of Quebec*

VERDUN, Battle of, vər-dun′, one of the longest battles of World War I. It absorbed the major energies of Germany and France on the western front during most of 1916, caused casualties of about 1 million killed and wounded, and prepared the transition of the strategic initiative from the German to the Allied forces. Verdun, its earlier fortifications replaced by the most recent defensive works, including artillery turrets set in concrete forts almost at ground level, was the linchpin of the entire Allied system of field (trench) fortifications from the Swiss frontier to the North Sea. The German commander, Erich von Falkenhayn, decided to seek a breakthrough at this most difficult position in the hope of achieving final victory by one gigantic blow; at the least, he anticipated, he would force the French into expending irreplaceable forces in battle with his superior numbers and equipment.

The battle began with a sustained artillery bombardment on Feb. 21, 1916, followed by initial successes, including capture of the forts of Douamont and Hardaumont. Before the end of the month, Gen. Henri Philippe Pétain took command of French forces at Verdun, and resistance stiffened. However, the defenders' motto, *"Ils ne passeront pas!"* ("They shall not pass!"), exacted an immense toll of lives before it was made good. A combined French-British attack on the Somme in July compelled Falkenhayn to divert a portion of his forces, and during the remainder of the summer the French went over to the counteroffensive, regaining a major part of the lost ground by the end of the year. The French made additional gains during 1917 and in the final offensives of 1918. The tremendous French casualties triggered the French military mutinies of 1917. The Germans, however, were able to mount only the desperation Spring Offensive of 1918, their last important initiative on the western front. See also under WORLD WAR I—*Western Front: 1915–1917—Stalemate*.

HERBERT H. ROWEN, *Rutgers University*

VERDUN, Treaty of, vər-dun′, an agreement reached on Aug. 10, 843, at Verdun, France. From this treaty, made by the three sons of Louis I (the Pious), dates the first step in the emergence of the modern national states of France and Germany out of the empire of Charlemagne.

The death of Louis I in 840 was followed by civil war among the brothers: Charles the Bald (later emperor of the Carolingian empire as Charles II), Louis the German (later king of Germany as Louis II), and Lothair (Lothair I), heir to the imperial title. The victory of Charles and Louis at Fontenoy (June 25, 841) resulted in partition of the Frankish empire. Louis received territories inhabited principally by Germans to the east of the Rhine. Charles was awarded the area between the Escaut-Meuse-Saône-Rhône river line and the Pyrenees, inhabited largely by Gallo-Romans, with a ruling stratum of Franks. Lothair retained his imperial crown, but his territory was limited to a narrow strip of lands extending from Friesland on the North Sea to Italy. This "middle kingdom," with its ethnically disparate elements, did not survive and was itself parceled out between the German and French kingdoms. The text of the treaty has not survived, but its provisions are known from other sources.

HERBERT H. ROWEN, *Rutgers University*

VERDY, vâr-dē′, **Violette** (1933–   ), French ballerina and dance director. She was born Nelly Guillerm on Dec. 1, 1933, in Pont-l'Abbé, Brittany, France.

Verdy studied dance principally with Madame Rousanne and Victor Gsovsky in Paris. A child prodigy, she first appeared in *Les Forains* with Les Ballets des Champs-Elysées in 1945, remaining with the company until 1949. In 1950 and again in 1953–1954 she danced with the Ballets de Paris de Roland Petit. Her most famous role with the Ballets de Paris, and one created for her, was the bride in *Le Loup* (1953). She performed with the London Festival Ballet (1954–1955). As a leading dancer with the American Ballet Theatre (1957–1958) she appeared in the title role in *Miss Julie*. From 1958 until 1977 she was a principal dancer with the New York City Ballet.

Some of Verdy's important ballet roles were in *Romeo and Juliet* (1955), *Cinderella* (1955), *Episodes* (1959), *Jewels* (1967), *Dances at a Gathering* (1969), and *Pulcinella* (1972). She also appeared in the motion pictures *Ballerina* (1949) and *The Glass Slipper* (1954).

Verdy was director of the Paris Opera (1977–1980) and associate artistic director of the Boston Ballet (1980–1984). She became a teacher in the New York City Ballet in November 1984.

VEREENIGING, fə-rā′nə-ging, a town in the Republic of South Africa, on the Vaal River in southern Transvaal, 35 miles (55 km) south of Johannesburg. Coal, the principal local resource, has been mined since 1879 and largely accounts for the rise of Vereeniging as one of the nation's major industrial centers. The town has large power stations and manufactures iron and steel, steel tubing, electrical conduits, farm equipment, oxyacetylene, nuts and bolts, glass, and bricks and tiles.

Vereeniging was founded in 1882. Here British and Boer representatives met in 1902 to arrange terms for ending the South African War. Although the agreement was signed (May 31) in Pretoria, it is known as the Treaty of Vereeniging. In 1960 serious disturbances occurred in the nearby black township of Sharpeville. Vereeniging's civic center, completed in the 1970's, includes a museum and a library. Population: (1980) of the district, 149,410.

VERGA, vâr′gä, **Giovanni,** Italian novelist and short-story writer: b. Catania, Sicily, Sept. 2, 1840; d. there, Jan. 27, 1922. Born to wealth, he wrote his first novel at the age of 21. Such early works as *Eva* and *Tigre reale* (1873), published while he was living in Florence and Milan, were romantic and melodramatic. His literary manner changed after his return in 1880 to Sicily, where he wrote about peasants, fishermen, and impoverished noblemen. Outstanding among these later works are the collections of short stories *Vita dei campi* (1880) and *Novelle rusticane* (1883) and the novels *I Malavoglia* (1881) and *Mastro Don Gesualdo* (1880). *Cavalleria rusticana* (q.v.), one of the tales in *Vita dei campi,* inspired the well-known opera by Pietro Mascagni.

Verga's Sicilian stories and novels established him as the leader of the literary school of *verismo,* a native kind of naturalism aimed at an objective, documentary rendering of life, and he strongly influenced modern Italian fiction, particularly that of the neorealists. The translation of several of his works by D. H. Lawrence contributed to his international reputation. Verga's greatness lies not only in the perfection of his dramatic narrative, in the compactness and dryness of his art, and in his bold use of colloquial idiom and local dialect, but also in his combination of realism with subtle irony, and of stylistic sobriety with human compassion and warmth.

MARC SLONIM.

VERGENNES, věr-zhěn', **COMTE de (CHARLES GRAVIER),** French diplomat and statesman: b. Dijon, France, Dec. 20, 1717; d. Versailles, Feb. 13, 1787. Vergennes represents with unusual clarity the characteristics of French diplomacy during the Old Regime—its breadth of knowledge, its brilliance in conception and execution of plans, and its failure to encompass deep social and political transformations within its understanding. Born into a family of Burgundian magistrates, he early entered a diplomatic career as secretary to his uncle, who was ambassador to Portugal (1740) and Frankfurt (1741). His first independent appointment was as minister to Trier in 1750; his success in winning German support for French policy during a period of great diplomatic complexity led to his becoming ambassador to Constantinople (1754–1768). He obtained the sultan's alliance for France in 1756.

A successful embassy in Stockholm (1771–1774) was followed by his appointment as foreign minister for Louis XVI (1774–1786). He achieved his grand purpose—French revenge for the defeat by Great Britain in the Seven Years War (1756–1763)—by supporting the American rebellion against British sovereignty, first covertly and then in an open military alliance (1778). In 1776 he helped persuade the king to discard Turgot, the controller general, whose projected fiscal and social reforms stood in the way of the costly American campaign. After London acknowledged defeat in the Peace of Versailles (1783), Vergennes sought friendlier relations with England, to which he accorded favorable terms in the Eden Commercial Treaty of 1786. He continued to oppose any thoroughgoing reform of the French state and society until his death in 1787. His *Mémoire historique et politique sur la Louisiane* was published in Paris in 1802.

HERBERT H. ROWEN.

VERGIL, Roman poet. See VIRGIL.

VERGIL, vûr'jĭl, **Polydore,** Italian-English historian and ecclesiastic: b. Urbino, Italy, c. 1475; d. there, 1555. The first products of his humanist training in Italy were a collection of Latin proverbs, *Adagia* (1498), and his account of the "beginnings of things," *De rerum inventoribus* (1499). Both gained wide circulation and were expanded by him in later editions; the second of these works remains of importance for a contemporary view of progress and inventions. In 1502 he came to England as a deputy collector of papal taxes. With very few interruptions he remained there until 1553, writing various Latin essays and dialogues. He was encouraged by Henry VII (r. 1485–1509) to undertake a history of England and was rewarded with several church livings, of which the most important was the archdeaconry of Wells. An early draft of *Anglica Historia* was complete in 1513. This was revised for publication and in the first edition (Basel 1534) follows English history as far as 1509. It was not until the third edition (1555, the year of Vergil's death in Italy) that the story entered on the dangerous reign of Henry VIII (to 1537).

Vergil's *Anglica Historia* was several times printed on the Continent in Latin but it was more immediately influential because it was used by the English historians Edward Hall and Raphael Holinshed. In this way his picture of the 15th century came to form the basic pattern of Shakespeare's history plays from *Richard II* to *Richard III.* In the last decades of his life, Vergil was attacked by chauvinist English writers, not least because he was sceptical of the historical reality of Brutus and Arthur. In support of these unfashionable views he published the first edition of the chronicles of the 6th century historian Gildas (1525). Even Vergil's enemies plundered his work, however, and he was one of the most important figures in the emergence in England of the new type of Renaissance scholarship.

DENYS HAY,
Professor of History, University of Edinburgh.

VERGNIAUD, věr-nyō', **Pierre Victurnien,** French lawyer and parlementarian: b. Limoges, France, May 31, 1753; d. Paris, Oct. 31, 1793. Under the protection of Anne Robert Jacques Turgot and others he became a member of the Bordeaux parlement in 1781, later administrator of the Department of the Gironde, and in 1791 deputy to the National Legislative Assembly. He achieved his first fame there when he asked that the words "Sire" and "Majesty" be dropped. He abandoned all compromise with the king when the latter dismissed Roland de La Platière, Joseph Servan de Gerbey, and Étienne Clavière. But on June 20, 1791, he opposed the establishment of martial law and privately offered to support the king if the latter would return the Girondists to power. Louis XVI took no heed of his letter. It was Vergniaud who had to announce on August 10 the suspension of the king but he protested against the September massacres and tried to save the Swiss guard. Nevertheless, as a member of the National Convention he finally voted for the king's death. Soon he began to struggle against the Commune of Paris, Jean Paul Marat, Georges Jacques Danton, Robespierre, and others. He was arrested with the other Girondist leaders on June 2, 1793 after Charles François Dumouriez had committed treason and gone over to the Austrian side. He was condemned to death on October 30, and was guillotined the following day, along with 21 other Girondist leaders.

ROBERT E. TAYLOR,
New York University.

VERHAEREN, věr-hä'rən, **Émile,** Belgian poet and dramatist: b. St.-Amand, near Antwerp, Belgium, May 21, 1855; d. Rouen, France, Nov.

27, 1916. He studied in Ghent at the Jesuit College of Sainte-Barbe, with Maurice Maeterlinck and Charles Van Lerberghe. He obtained his law degree in Louvain and was admitted to the bar of Brussells in 1881, but was destined to abandon the law to become an outstanding poet of the symbolist school in Belgium. His first volume of verse, *Les flamandes,* was published in 1883.

Though he wrote in French, Verhaeren's style is Germanic in its vigor and its extravagance. He sang of his native Flanders in rhythms which struck French readers as savage and barbaric, but which were perfectly suited to such subject matter as the splendor and arrogance of medieval Burgundian dukes, the clash of arms, or the thunder of modern machines. His principal subject was to be contemporary man, uprooted, caught up by gigantic forces. Verhaeren has been compared to Walt Whitman as a poet of the humming dynamos and roaring steel furnaces. In *Les villes tentaculaires* (1895), he pictures the great city not so much as a cultural and civic center but as a giant octopus, sprawled over the land, grasping simple rustics and sucking them into the drabness of the steel and cotton mills. He was eloquent and brutal, sonorous and convincing as he expressed the surging energy and uneasy, often unpleasant, beauty of modern industrial society. In later collections, such as *Les forces tumultueuses* (1902) and *La multiple splendeur* (1906), a fresh faith in human potentialities is in evidence, giving his work a hopeful, at times even triumphant tone.

His more ambitious verse dramas include *Les aubes* (1898; Eng. tr., *The Dawn,* 1898), *Le cloître* (1900; *The Cloister,* 1915), and *Hélène de Sparte* (1912; *Helen of Sparta,* 1916), the last being almost classical in mood and inspiration. During the last 20 years of his life, he also wrote quiet verses of married bliss which have a warm intimacy of manner: *Les heures claires* (1896; *The Sunlit Hours,* 1916); *Les heures d'après-midi* (1905; *Afternoon,* 1917); *Les heures du soir* (1911; *The Evening Hours,* 1918). His fame, once universal, has somewhat faded, although it is solidly founded. See also DAWN, THE.

JAN-ALBERT GORIS,
Director, Belgian Government Information Center, New York.

VERISMO, vā-rēs'mō (It., "realism"), in music, a 19th century operatic manner emphasizing vigorous presentation of everyday life at the expense of conventional nobility and beauty. Responding to the naturalistic stage of literary realism (as in the novels of Émile Zola and some plays of Henrik Ibsen), it dispensed with opera's traditional legends, myths, heroics, and pseudohistory in favor of violent, shocking incidents from peasant, proletarian, and bourgeois life. *Verismo* characteristically makes use of continuous heightened recitative or arioso occasionally blossoming into arias, duets, and other pauses of lyric expansion. It had a prehistory in Georges Bizet's *Carmen* (1875) and operas that Alfred Bruneau (1857–1934) based on Zola.

The first overtly veristic operas were Pietro Mascagni's *Cavalleria rusticana* (1890) and Ruggiero Leoncavallo's *I Pagliacci* (1892), followed by *Louise* (1900), by Gustave Charpentier, and at least three of the operas of Giacomo Puccini: *Tosca* (1900), *La fanciulla del West* (1910), and *Il tabarro* (1918). Other composers who at times wrote veristic operas included Nicola Spinelli (1865–1909), Umberto Giordano (1867–1948), Ermanno Wolf-Ferrari (1876–1948), and Riccardo Zandonai (1883–1944). *Verismo* has persisted, but mostly in mixed, diluted forms.

HERBERT WEINSTOCK.

VERKAUFTE BRAUT, Die. See BARTERED BRIDE, THE.

VERLAINE, vĕr-lĕn, **Paul,** French poet: b. Metz, France, March 30, 1844; d. Paris, Jan. 8, 1896. His parents brought him to Paris as a child of seven. His first employment (1862) was in an insurance office, during which period Verlaine, who was eventually to rank among the foremost symbolist poets, began to experiment with verses in the Parnassian style. According to his own confession, his life was dominated by a number of indiscreet and wrongful acts, chiefly originating in his turbulent relationship with Arthur Rimbaud (q.v.). His liaison with the younger poet was punctuated by numerous violent quarrels and culminated in disgrace and imprisonment for Verlaine, who shot his companion in the arm in an apparent attempt to kill him in 1873. While in prison, Verlaine was converted to Catholicism. For many years after his release in 1875, he tried to restore his marriage, (he had married Mathilde Mauté de Fleurville in 1870) and recover social status. Poverty and dereliction blighted the last few years of his life, when he was again in the grip of forces beyond his control and fell victim to drink and debauchery.

If Verlaine's poetry appears today more immediately accessible than that of other French symbolists, his character is one of the most difficult to understand. He is usually described as weak and unstable. This judgment can be substantiated, but there is also evidence indicating tenacity and determination. He went further than most poets in practicing willed impassivity when he tried, early in life, to follow the Parnassian ideal in poetry. He was fervently *communard* at the time of the Paris Commune (1871). After his religious conversion, he denounced in vigorous terms those aspects of the modern spirit which he conceived to be erroneous.

During his last years, Verlaine was looked upon by many as the greatest living poet. He is still, in France, one of the few major poets who have reached the general public. However, his influence on the development of French poetry has been slight, despite the fact that he exploited brilliantly the resources of the language. In his first volume, *Poèmes saturniens* (1866), Verlaine revealed the influence of Charles Pierre Baudelaire and a new phase of the *mal du siècle,* a form of melancholia associated with the early Romantics. Among his best volumes are *Fêtes galantes* (1869), inspired by the paintings of Jean Antoine Watteau, and *Romances sans paroles* (1874); both works are notable for their evocative and musical qualities. His poem on the adventure with Rimbaud, *Crimen amoris,* echoing a "marriage of heaven and hell," is a deeply felt, essentially religious interpretation of the episode by a poet who, for the first time, understands the meaning of remorse and makes it a part of his nature.

Verlaine's *Art poétique,* written in 1874 and published a decade later in his *Jadis et naguère,* expresses his opposition to the Parnassian doctrine of objectivity and impassivity, and defines some of the basic theories of symbolism. Poetry should be primarily music, he states. It should stress nuance rather than color and should unite the vague with the precise. This music of poetry, which Verlaine advocated and created, is the most original feature of his art. In this kind of writing, language is vaporized as the poet tries to translate the evanescence of his dreams and to express the ineffable. Thus Verlaine might be more accurately described as an impressionist than as a symbolist. In the application of his principles, however, he did not go as far as he promised to go. From the standpoint of construction, although he often used an uneven number of syllables in his verse and succeeded in making the Alexandrine line more supple, his poetry exhibits a fairly conservative regularity.

WALLACE FOWLIE
Department of French, Bennington College

VERMEER, vər-mār′, **Jan** (sometimes called JAN VAN DER MEER VAN DELFT to distinguish him from painters of the same name who worked in Haarlem), Dutch painter: baptized Delft, Holland, Oct. 31, 1632; d. there, Dec. 15, 1675. Vermeer, today one of the rarest and most highly prized of painters, was virtually unknown during the 18th century and the first half of the 19th. His present fame began in 1866 when a French critic calling himself William Bürger (E. J. T. Thoré, 1807–1869), wrote three articles on him for the *Gazette des Beaux-Arts* which were published in book form, *Notice sur Van der Meer de Delft*, in the same year. Subsequent studies, as well as documents, tell a good deal about the short life of this extraordinarily gifted artist. He is said to have been a pupil of Carel Fabritius (1624?–1654), but this is not at all certain. In 1653, the year of his marriage, Vermeer was admitted to the painter's guild in Delft, and he was twice elected to the guild committee. His principal source of income was derived not from his painting but from his trade as an art dealer, a business he probably inherited from his father; nevertheless he was recurrently hard pressed for funds. There is no record that he sold any of his own pictures, which, at any rate, were not highly valued in his lifetime.

Jan Vermeer's *Girl Reading a Letter* is typical of his paintings featuring sunlit domestic interiors.

EDITORIAL PHOTOCOLOR ARCHIVES

Vermeer's especial gift of endowing ordinary objects with subtle significance by bathing them in light places him among the great painters of all time. His *Views of Delft* (1660), in the Mauritshuis at The Hague, immortalized his native town with luminosity and scintillant color. Among other masterpieces are *Maidservant Pouring Milk* (1660, Amsterdam Rijksmuseum), *A Painter in His Studio* (1666, Kunsthistorisches Museum, Vienna), *Girl with a Red Hat* (1667, National Gallery, Washington, D.C.), *Soldier and Laughing Girl* (1657, Frick Collection, New York City), and *Woman with a Water-Jug* (1663, one of four Vermeer paintings in the Metropolitan Museum of Art, New York City).

MARGARETTA SALINGER
The Metropolitan Museum of Art

VERMICULITE, vər-mĭk′yə-līt, a mineral of complex structure, a hydrous iron magnesium aluminum silicate, resembling certain clay minerals such as montmorillonite, produced in part through alteration of micaceous minerals by the addition of water in the molecular lattice. On heating, the contained water expands explosively to produce a porous light material having a volume as much as 20 times that of the original mineral. Vermiculite is used as a sound and temperature insulation, in filters for purifying oil, in incombustible packing, and as a medium for seed culture. It is mined in several states, including Montana (site of the largest vermiculite mine in North America, near Libby), North Carolina, South Carolina, and Wyoming.

MARSHALL KAY
Columbia University

VERMILION, village, Ohio, in Erie County, on Lake Erie, near the mouth of the Vermilion River, 40 miles due west of Cleveland, at an altitude of 605 feet. Three fisheries operate during the summer, and vacationists are attracted by the boating facilities. A fluorescent-light factory and olive-processing plant are among the industries, and there are many stone quarries in the vicinity. The name is believed to be derived from the red clay banks of the river. First settlement was in 1808; the village was incorporated in 1837. The village was once the home port of a fleet of lake vessels. Government is by mayor and council. Pop. 11,012.

VERMILION, a bright red pigment, or the color of this pigment, obtained from crystallized mercuric sulfide. See also CINNABAR.

VERMILION RANGE, mountain range, Minnesota, in St. Louis County, lying north of the Mesabi Range, the two forming part of the richest iron ore region in the Unites States. First discovered in 1865, Vermilion ore is now transported to Two Harbors on Lake Superior for shipment to the steel mills.

UNITED STATES DEPARTMENT OF AGRICULTURE

A dairy farm near Randolph. Vermont is the leading dairying state in the New England region.

VERMONT

State Seal of Vermont

TABLE OF CONTENTS

VERMONT, ver-mont′, a northern New England state of the United States. It is bounded on the north by the Canadian province of Quebec; on the east by the Connecticut River, which separates it from New Hampshire; on the south by Massachusetts; and on the west by New York state, the border for some 100 miles (160 km) passing through Lake Champlain.

The state gets its name from the French words *vert mont,* meaning "green mountain." Vermont is famous for its Green Mountains, which bisect the central part of the state from north to south and gives it its nickname, the "Green Mountain" state.

1. The Land

Having only two cities with populations exceeding 15,000 (Burlington and Rutland), Vermont is the least populous state east of the Mississippi River. Although the forests, farms, and villages give the state a rustic, agricultural appearance, industry represents its chief economic activity. Small industries are spread throughout the state, which is well known for its granite, marble, ski resorts, and maple syrup.

Physical Features. The variety of scenery in the small state of Vermont is obtained through a pleasant combination of mountains and river valleys connected by gaps known as gulfs and notches. Unlike the other New England states, Vermont does not have direct access to the sea, but it does have two north and south lines of easy ingress, the Lake Champlain–Hudson River valley on the west and the Connecticut Valley on the east. These valleys have had a significant influence on agriculture and transportation in New England. Between these two depressions lie Vermont's mountains. The Green Mountain range is the verdant backbone of the state and is unbroken except for the deep gaps through which flow the Winooski and Lamoille rivers. From this ridge, at the town of Granville, a branch range swings to the northeast and comes close to the Connecticut River. Just east of the Green Mountains in the Mansfield region lies the Worcester Range, set in parallel array. To the south are the northern end of the Hoosac Range, around Stamford and Readsboro, and the Taconic

VERMONT DEVELOPMENT DEPARTMENT

The Old First Church in Bennington overlooks a cemetery where American Revolutionary War dead are buried.

Range, running along the southwestern side of the state. This scenic range includes Mt. Equinox (3,816 feet, or 1,163 meters) and Green Peak (3,185 feet, or 971 meters). Beginning a few miles to the north of the Taconic are the Red Sandrock Hills, which extend north along Lake Champlain to St. Albans near the Canadian boundary; this low range rises no higher than Snake Mountain (1,271 feet, or 387 meters). The four highest peaks in the state are Mansfield (4,393 feet, or 1,339 meters), Killington (4,241 feet, or 1,293 meters), Ellen (4,135 feet, or 1,260 meters), and Camel's Hump (4,083 feet, or 1,245 meters). Interspersed among Vermont's mountains are pleasant valleys such as are found along the arms of the White River or at the ski center of Stowe, a resort town at the foot of Mt. Mansfield.

The state's geological formations have in part determined the environment of its citizens. During the course of long geologic ages, several bands of rock formations appeared on the north-south axis—schists, slates, granites, gneisses, and sandstones. Over this rough-hewn foundation spread the great icecap that three times altered the face of Vermont, wearing down the mountains, gouging river and lake valleys, and depositing traces of its mighty forces.

Rivers and Lakes. Because of the central Green Mountain watershed, most Vermont streams flow down the eastern slopes to the Connecticut River or westward to Lake Champlain, although the Lamoille, Winooski, and Missisquoi rivers move across the state from east to west before emptying into Lake Champlain, the latter first detouring into Quebec. The Connecticut River on the eastern boundary, although officially in New Hampshire, is the longest river in which Vermont has an interest. Its chief tributary is the White River, which enters the Connecticut at White River Junction. The longest stream entirely within the state is Otter Creek, which extends for about 90 miles (145 km) from Dorset to Lake Champlain. The latter, about 120 miles (193 km) in length, comprises nearly 100 miles (160 km) of the state's western border. The second-largest lake associated with Vermont, Lake Memphremagog, is on the Quebec border; about one fourth of its 60 square miles (155 sq km) is included in the state's area. The largest lake lying wholly within Vermont is Lake Bomoseen (8 square miles, or 20 sq km), at Castleton. Sterling Pond, at Stowe, with an elevation of 3,200 feet (975 meters), is the highest body of water of any importance.

Climate. Because Vermont is located halfway between the equator and the North Pole, the state is clearly in the north temperate zone, but temperatures are subject to considerable extremes. This variety is not only one of mountain and valley, but also of year-to-year and sectional changes. For instance, the Champlain Valley has a longer growing season (150 days) than the Connecticut Valley (120 days), but both seasons are longer than that found in the mountain intervales between. Rainfall likewise varies from 34 inches (864 mm) in the west and east central sections to 40 inches (1,016 mm) in the northern and central mountain regions. The mountain area also has the heaviest snowfall, a 10-foot (3,048-mm) average (thus supporting the ski industry). At Northfield, where there is a U. S. Weather Bureau Station, the highest temperature ever recorded was 98° F (37° C) and the lowest, −41° F (−41° C). The average range of annual temperature is from 38° to 46° F (3°–8° C).

More than 60% of Vermont's surface is covered with forests, both deciduous and conifer,

INFORMATION HIGHLIGHTS

Location: Vermont is a northeastern state, bordered on the north by the Canadian province of Quebec, on the east by the Connecticut River and New Hampshire, on the south by Massachusetts, and on the west by New York state.
Elevation: *Highest point*—Mt. Mansfield, 4,393 feet (1,339 meters); *lowest point*—Lake Champlain, 95 feet (29 meters); *approximate mean elevation*—1,000 feet (305 meters).
Area: 9,614 square miles (24,900 sq km); rank, 43d.
Population: 1980 census, 511,456; rank, 48th. Increase (1970–1980), 15.0%.
Climate: Long winters, warm summers.
Statehood: March 4, 1791; order of admission, 14th.
Origin of Name: French words *vert mont* ("green mountain") for the Green Mountains that bisect the state from north to south.
Capital: Montpelier.
Largest City: Burlington.
Number of Counties: 14.
Principal Products: *Manufactures*—machines and machine tools, scales and measuring devices, electrical and computer equipment, stone and marble products, processed foods; *farm products*—cheese and other milk products, sheep, poultry, apples, maple sugar and syrup; *minerals*—granite, marble, slate.
State Motto: "Freedom and Unity."
State Song (unofficial): *Hail, Vermont.*
State Nickname: Green Mountain State.
State Bird: Hermit thrush.
State Flower: Red clover.
State Tree: Sugar maple.
State Flag: The state arms and a view of rural Vermont centered on a deep blue ground. See also FLAG—*Flags of the States*.

which dominate the summits and ridges of the mountain area and reach down even to the typical wood lots on the farms at lower altitudes. The broken pattern persists as some pastures ascend the uplands. Leading examples of evergreens are pine, spruce, fir, and hemlock. Among the deciduous trees, the maple, elm, birch, beech, oak, ash, cherry, and butternut are the most prominent. The cool forest floor displays many varieties of ferns. No fewer than 1,482 species of flowers are represented.

When the first settlers arrived in Vermont they found a hunter's paradise. Wildlife abounded, some forms of which, such as the wolf and the cougar (catamount), now are rarely seen. Deer and bear were numerous enough to provide the Vermont pioneer with a living during the first winters. The white-tailed deer is still the most popular big game in Vermont. Vermont has the usual complement of smaller animals: foxes, rabbits, squirrels, woodchucks, hedgehogs, lynxes, bobcats, skunks, muskrats, and raccoons. Some, like the rabbit, furnish quarry for the hunter; others, like the raccoon, fall prey to the trapper.

Vermont has a variety of birdlife, beginning with the hermit thrush (the state bird) and including the robin, crow, bluebird, blue jay, phoebe, sparrow, hawk, woodpecker, and flicker. The most esteemed game bird is the partridge, or ruffed grouse.

The angler will find trout and landlocked salmon in some of the lakes. Those devoted to lake fishing also take bass, pickerel, and smelt, often in the winter when the lakes are dotted with little fishing shacks on the ice.

Mineral Resources. The extractive industries of Vermont fall into the category of quarrying rather than extensive mining. The quarrying and processing of granite and marble are important industries. The granite center is around Barre, and the marble belt is located in western Vermont, based at Rutland and its surrounding towns. In addition to this, Vermont is a major producer of asbestos. Slate and small amounts of copper, silver, and talc are also mined in Vermont.

Conservation. Vermont long ago turned its back on indiscriminate waste of natural resources, recognizing that its scenery is a prime recreational asset. Moreover, the state board of forests and parks maintains recreational areas, supervises state forests, and raises 4 million seedlings a year in response to demand for tree plantings. The water conservation board is attempting to eradicate stream pollution.

2. The People

From the time Vermont existed as an independent republic to the present, it has been a state noted for its independence of thought and action, giving rise to the expression, "Vermonters will do nothing that you tell them to; most anything that you ask them to." In addition to independence, industry and thrift usually are attributed to Vermonters.

Characteristics of the Population. The first settlers came to Vermont from Connecticut, Massachusetts, New Hampshire, and New York. Before the middle of the 19th century, Irish laborers were imported to build the railroads, and many of them remained. Next the Canadians, both French and non-French, made their appearance, coming mainly from the province of Quebec.

From Europe, Scottish and Italian artisans were introduced to make refinements in the granite and marble industries, while the Welsh were engaged in the slate industry. A small number of Poles settled in the state.

The early decades of the 19th century showed promise of a populous state, but this growth slackened thereafter. The lure of the West (especially after the passage of the Homestead Act

The town of Newport on the shores of Lake Memphremagog, whose waters straddle the Vermont-Quebec boundary.

VERMONT DEVELOPMENT DEPARTMENT

GROWTH OF POPULATION SINCE 1790

Year	Population	Year	Population
1790	85,425	1920	352,428
1820	235,981	1940	359,231
1840	291,948	1950	377,747
1860	315,098	1960	389,881
1880	332,286	1970	444,732
1900	343,641	1980	511,456

Gain, 1970–1980: 15.0% (U.S. gain, 11.4%). **Density,** 1980: 55.2 persons per sq mi (U.S. density, 62.6).

URBAN-RURAL DISTRIBUTION

Year	Percent urban	Percent rural
1920	31.2 (U.S., 51.2)	68.8
1930	33.0 (U.S., 56.2)	67.0
1940	34.3 (U.S., 56.6)	65.7
1950	36.4 (U.S., 64.0)	63.6
1960	38.5 (U.S., 69.9)	61.5
1970	32.2 (U.S., 73.5)	67.8
1980	33.8 (U.S., 73.7)	66.2

LARGEST CENTERS OF POPULATION

City or town	1980	1970	1960
Burlington	37,712	38,633	35,531
Rutland	18,436	19,293	18,325
Bennington	15,815	14,586	13,002
Essex	14,392	10,951	7,090
Brattleboro	11,886	12,239	11,734
South Burlington	10,679	10,032	6,903
Springfield	10,190	10,063	9,934

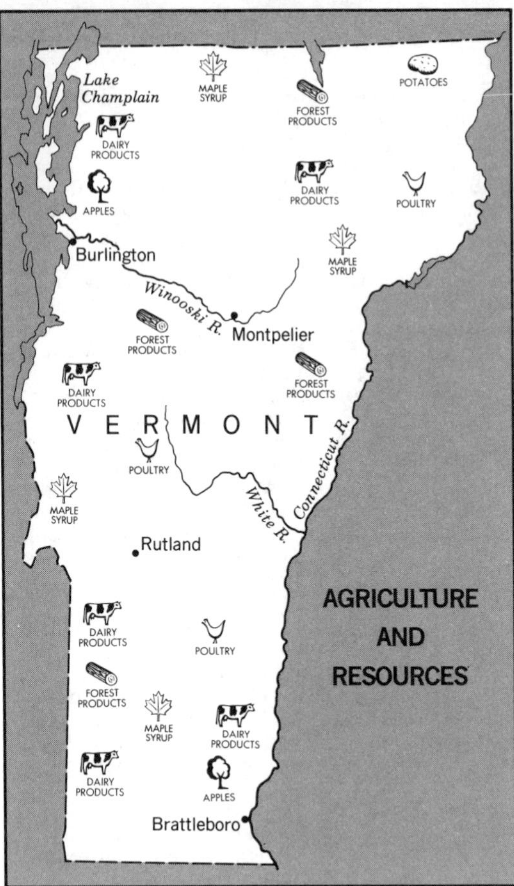

A skier negotiates a snowfield at Vermont's renowned Big Bromley ski area in the Green Mountains.

VERMONT DEVELOPMENT DEPARTMENT

of 1862), the Civil War, and gravitation to the cities all conspired to reduce the rate of population growth.

Almost 70% of the population lives in rural areas. The most rapidly growing areas are in the northern portion of the state and in the Champlain Valley. The state is predominantly Republican, and has voted for more Republican presidential candidates than any other state. The largest religious group in Vermont is Roman Catholic, followed by the United Church of Christ, Methodist, Baptist, and Episcopalian. Like other New Englanders, the people who live in Vermont are called Yankees.

Way of Life. Vermont has held steadfast to a traditional lifestyle. Conservation and ecology are an integral part of everyday living. Although a multilaned interstate highway spans the length of the state, no billboards or advertisements along the highway mar the natural beauty of the surrounding countryside. The rustic rest areas and information centers are state supported, and no commercial sale of goods is permitted on the premises. The state's leisurely lifestyle and simplicity are in sharp contrast to the congested, fast-paced East Coast areas that surround it.

Vermonters are hardy, outdoors people, particularly geared to winter sports such as skiing, skating, and hunting. Cottage industries, crafts, and antiques are in evidence at roadside stalls, where many of the skills of the past are kept alive. Square dancing and venison dinners are popular social events. The state also has attracted a number of well-educated corporate "drop-outs" who have chosen a simpler way of life closer to the land. Families seeking refuge in the more remote areas of the state have built their own log homes and established a self-sufficient lifestyle.

VERMONT

COUNTIES

Addison 29,406 .... A2
Bennington 33,345 .... A4
Caledonia 25,808 .... C1
Chittenden 115,534 .... A2
Essex 6,313 .... D1
Franklin 34,788 .... B1
Grand Isle 4,613 .... A1
Lamoille 16,767 .... B1
Orange 22,739 .... C3
Orleans 23,440 .... C1
Rutland 58,347 .... A3
Washington 52,393 .... B2
Windham 36,933 .... B5
Windsor 51,030 .... B4

CITIES and TOWNS

Addison○ 889 .... A2
Albany○ 705 .... C1
Albany 174 .... C1
Alburg○ 1,352 .... A1
Alburg 496 .... A1
Andover○ 350 .... B4
Arlington○ 2,184 .... A4
Arlington 1,309 .... A4
Ascutney 274 .... C4
Averill○ 15 .... D1
Bakersfield○ 852 .... B1
Barnard○ 790 .... B3
Barnet○ 1,338 .... C2
Barre○ 7,090 .... C2
Barre 9,824 .... C2
Barton○ 2,990 .... C1
Barton 1,062 .... C1
Beebe Plain 500 .... C1
Beecher Falls 950 .... E1
Bellows Falls 3,456 .... C4
Belvidere○ 218 .... B1
Bennington○ 15,815 .... A5
Bennington⊙ 9,349 .... A5
Benson○ 739 .... A3
Berkshire○ 1,116 .... B1
Bethel○ 1,715 .... B3
Bethel 1,016 .... B3
Bloomfield○ 188 .... D1
Bolton○ 715 .... B2
Bomoseen 700 .... A3
Bradford○ 2,191 .... C3
Bradford 831 .... C3
Braintree○ 1,065 .... B3
Brandon○ 4,194 .... A3
Brandon 1,925 .... A3
Brattleboro○ 11,886 .... B5
Brattleboro 8,596 .... B5
Bridgewater○ 867 .... B3
Bridport○ 997 .... A3
Bristol○ 3,293 .... A2
Bristol 1,793 .... A2
Brookfield○ 959 .... B2
Brookline○ 310 .... B4
Brownington○ 708 .... C1
Burke○ 1,385 .... D1
Burlington⊙ 37,712 .... A2
Burlington‡ 114,070 .... A2
Cabot○ 958 .... C2
Cabot 259 .... C2
Calais○ 1,207 .... B2
Cambridge○ 2,019 .... B1
Cambridge 217 .... B1
Canaan○ 1,196 .... D1
Castleton○ 3,637 .... A3
Cavendish○ 1,355 .... B4
Center Rutland 465 .... B3
Charlotte○ 2,561 .... A2
Chelsea○ 1,091 .... C3
Chester○ 2,791 .... B4
Chester-Chester Depot 1,267 .... B4
Chittenden○ 927 .... B3
Clarendon○ 2,372 .... A4
Colchester○ 12,629 .... A1
Concord○ 1,125 .... D2
Corinth○ 904 .... C2
Cornwall○ 993 .... A3
Coventry○ 674 .... C1
Craftsbury○ 844 .... C1
Craftsbury Common 55 .... C1
Cuttingsville 200 .... B4
Danby○ 992 .... A4
Danville○ 1,705 .... C2
Derby○ 4,222 .... C1
Derby (Derby Center) 598 .... C1
Derby Line 874 .... C1
Dorset○ 1,648 .... A4
Duxbury○ 877 .... B2
East Arlington 600 .... A4
East Barre-Graniteville 2,172 .... C2
East Berkshire 200 .... B1
East Burke 150 .... D1
East Dorset 550 .... A4
East Fairfield 150 .... B1
East Hardwick 200 .... C1
East Haven○ 280 .... D1
East Jamaica 200 .... B4
East Middlebury 550 .... A3
East Montpelier○ 2,205 ...... B2
East Poultney 450 .... A3
East Ryegate 210 .... C2
East Thetford 30 .... C3
East Wallingford 500 .... B4
Eden○ 612 .... B1
Eden Mills 200 .... C1
Enosburg Falls 1,207 .... B1
Essex○ 14,392 .... A1
Essex Junction 7,033 .... A2
Fairfax○ 1,805 .... B1
Fairfield○ 1,493 .... B1
Fair Haven○ 2,819 .... A3
Fair Haven 2,363 .... A3
Fairlee○ 770 .... C3
Ferrisburg○ 2,117 .... A2
Fletcher○ 626 .... B1
Florence 250 .... A3
Forest Dale 500 .... A3
Franklin○ 1,006 .... B1
Georgia○ 2,818 .... A1
Georgia Center A1
Gilman 600 .... D2
Glover○ 843 .... C1
Grafton○ 604 .... B4
Granby○ 70 .... D1
Grand Isle○ 1,238 .... A1
Graniteville-East Barre 2,172 .... C2
Granville○ 288 .... B3
Greensboro○ 677 .... C1
Groton○ 667 .... C2
Guildhall○ 202 .... D1
Guilford○ 1,532 .... B5
Halifax○ 488 .... B5
Hancock○ 334 .... B3
Hardwick○ 2,613 .... C1
Hardwick 1,476 .... C1
Hartford○ 7,963 .... C3
Hartland○ 2,396 .... C3
Highgate○ 2,493 .... B1
Highgate Center 350 .... B1
Highgate Falls A1
Highgate Springs 100 .... A1
Hinesburg○ 2,690 .... A2
Holland○ 473 .... D2
Hubbardton○ 490 .... A3
Huntington○ 1,161 .... A2
Hyde Park○ 2,021 .... B1
Hyde Park⊙ 475 .... B1
Hydeville 500 .... A3
Ira○ 354 .... A3
Irasburg○ 870 .... C1
Island Pond 1,216 .... D1
Isle La Motte○ 393 .... A1
Jacksonville 252 .... B5
Jamaica○ 681 .... B4
Jay○ 302 .... C1
Jeffersonville 491 .... B1
Jericho○ 3,575 .... B2
Jericho 1,340 .... A2
Johnson○ 2,581 .... B1
Johnson 1,393 .... B1
Jonesville 300 .... B2
Killington 700 .... B3
Leicester○ 803 .... A3
Lemington○ 108 .... D1
Lincoln○ 870 .... B2
Londonderry○ 1,510 .... B4
Lowell○ 573 .... C1
Ludlow○ 2,414 .... B4
Ludlow 1,352 .... B4
Lunenburg○ 1,138 .... D2
Lyndon○ 4,924 .... C1
Lyndonville 1,401 .... D1
Maidstone○ 100 .... D1
Manchester○ 3,261 .... A4
Manchester⊙ 563 .... A4
Manchester Center 1,719 .... A4
Manchester Depot B4
Marlboro○ 695 .... B5
Marshfield○ 1,267 .... C2
Marshfield 301 .... C2
Mendon○ 1,056 .... B3
Middlebury○ 7,574 .... A2
Middlebury⊙ 5,591 .... A2
Middlesex○ 1,235 .... B2
Middletown Springs○ 603 .... A4
Milton○ 6,829 .... A1
Milton 1,411 .... A1
Monkton○ 1,201 .... A2
Montgomery○ 681 .... B1
Montgomery Center 400 ..... B1
Montpelier (cap.)⊙ 8,241 .... B2
Moretown○ 1,221 .... B2
Morgan○ 460 .... D1
Morristown○ 4,448 .... B1
Morrisville 2,074 .... B1
Morses Line A1
Moscow 250 .... B2
Mount Holly○ 938 .... B4
Mount Tabor○ 211 .... B4
Newark○ 280 .... D1
Newbury○ 1,699 .... C2
Newbury 425 .... C2
Newfane○ 1,129 .... B4
Newfane⊙ 119 .... B4
New Haven○ 1,217 .... A2
Newport○ 1,319 .... C1
Newport⊙ 4,756 .... C1
Newport Center 250 .... C1
North Bennington 1,685 ...... A5
North Clarendon B3
North Ferrisburg 150 .... A2
Northfield○ 5,435 .... B2
Northfield 2,033 .... B2
Northfield Falls 600 .... B2
North Hartland 500 .... C3
North Hero○ 442 .... A1
North Hero⊙ 50 .... A1
North Hyde Park 450 .... B1
North Montpelier 188 .... C2
North Pomfret 400 .... B3
North Pownal 700 .... A5
North Springfield 1,200 ...... C4
North Troy 717 .... C1
North Westminster 310 .... B4
Norton○ 184 .... D1
Norwich○ 2,398 .... C3
Old Bennington 353 .... A5
Orange○ 752 .... C2
Orleans 983 .... C1
Orwell○ 901 .... A3
Panton○ 537 .... A2
Passumpsic 140 .... D2
Pawlet○ 1,244 .... A4
Peacham○ 531 .... C2
Perkinsville 187 .... B4
Peru○ 312 .... B4
Pittsfield○ 396 .... B3
Pittsford○ 2,590 .... A3

⊙County seat. ‡Population of metropolitan area. ○Population of town or township.

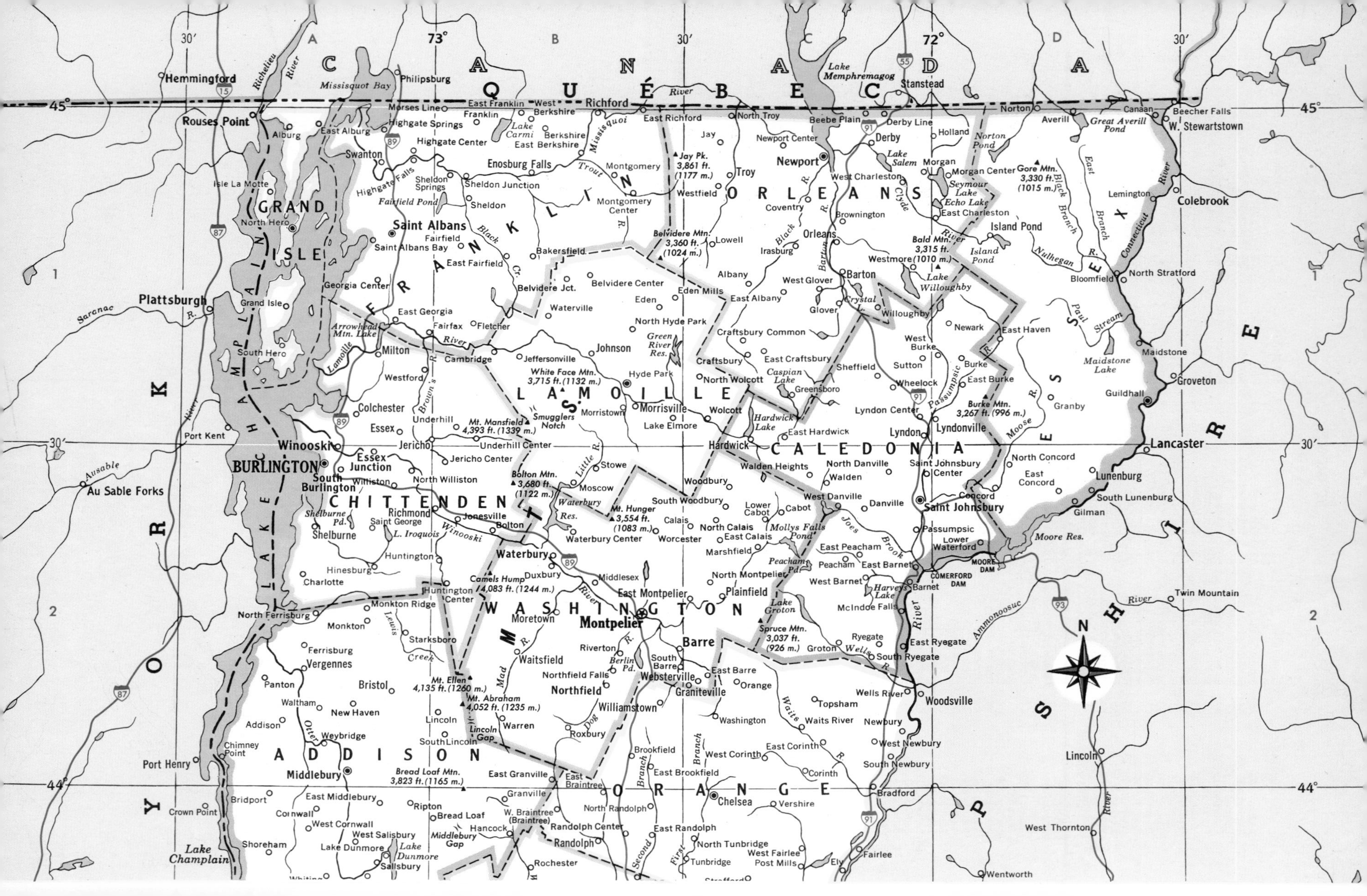

QUÉBEC
CANADA
NEW YORK
NEW HAMPSHIRE
GRAND ISLE
FRANKLIN
ORLEANS
ESSEX
LAMOILLE
CALEDONIA
CHITTENDEN
WASHINGTON
ADDISON
ORANGE
LAKE CHAMPLAIN
Lake Champlain
Missisquoi Bay
Lake Memphremagog
Richelieu River
Hemmingford
Rouses Point
Philipsburg
Stanstead
Beecher Falls
W. Stewartstown
Colebrook
Plattsburgh
Port Kent
Au Sable Forks
Port Henry
Crown Point
Saint Albans
Swanton
Highgate Springs
Highgate Center
Enosburg Falls
Richford
East Richford
North Troy
Jay
Troy
Newport
Derby
Derby Line
Beebe Plain
Norton
Averill
Canaan
Great Averill Pond
Island Pond
Orleans
Barton
Lake Willoughby
Jay Pk. 3,861 ft. (1177 m.)
Belvidere Mtn. 3,360 ft. (1024 m.)
Gore Mtn. 3,330 ft. (1015 m.)
Bald Mtn. 3,315 ft.
Burke Mtn. 3,267 ft. (996 m.)
White Face Mtn. 3,715 ft. (1132 m.)
Mt. Mansfield 4,393 ft. (1339 m.)
Smugglers Notch
Bolton Mtn. 3,680 ft. (1122 m.)
Mt. Hunger 3,554 ft. (1083 m.)
Camels Hump 4,083 ft. (1244 m.)
Mt. Ellen 4,135 ft. (1260 m.)
Mt. Abraham 4,052 ft. (1235 m.)
Lincoln Gap
Bread Loaf Mtn. 3,823 ft. (1165 m.)
Middlebury Gap
Spruce Mtn. 3,037 ft. (926 m.)
BURLINGTON
Winooski
Essex Junction
South Burlington
Shelburne
Colchester
Milton
Jericho
Underhill
Richmond
Waterbury
Stowe
Morrisville
Hyde Park
Johnson
Hardwick
Montpelier
Barre
Northfield
Waitsfield
Saint Johnsbury
Lyndonville
Lyndon
Lancaster
Groveton
Guildhall
Lunenburg
Woodsville
Bradford
Chelsea
Randolph
Middlebury
Vergennes
Bristol
North Ferrisburg
Moore Res.
MOORE DAM
COMERFORD DAM
Connecticut River
Winooski
Lamoille
Otter
Twin Mountain
Lincoln
West Thornton
Wentworth

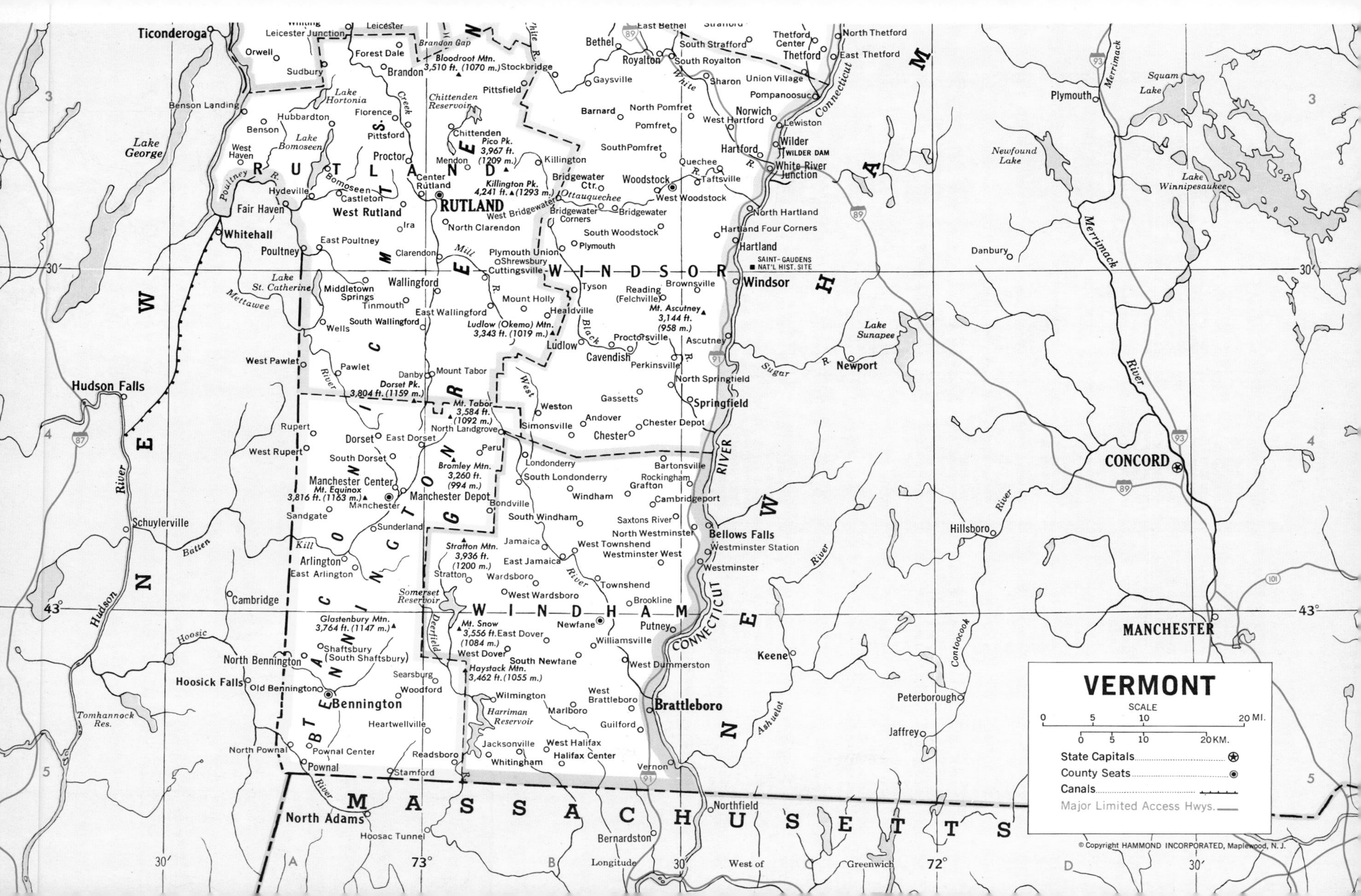
VERMONT
SCALE
0 5 10 20 MI.
0 5 10 20 KM.
State Capitals
County Seats
Canals
Major Limited Access Hwys.
© Copyright HAMMOND INCORPORATED, Maplewood, N. J.
RUTLAND
WINDSOR
BENNINGTON
WINDHAM
NEW HAMPSHIRE
NEW YORK
MASSACHUSETTS
Ticonderoga
Leicester Junction
Leicester
Orwell
Sudbury
Forest Dale
Brandon Gap
Bloodroot Mtn. 3,510 ft. (1070 m.)
Stockbridge
Brandon
Benson Landing
Lake Hortonia
Florence
Chittenden Reservoir
Pittsfield
Hubbardton
Benson
Lake Bomoseen
Pittsford
Chittenden
Pico Pk. 3,967 ft. (1209 m.)
Killington
Lake George
West Haven
Proctor
Mendon
Center Rutland
Killington Pk. 4,241 ft. (1293 m.)
Poultney R.
Hydeville
Bomoseen
Castleton
RUTLAND
West Rutland
West Bridgewater
Fair Haven
Whitehall
Ira
North Clarendon
East Poultney
Poultney
Clarendon
Mill R.
Plymouth Union
Shrewsbury
Cuttingsville
Lake St. Catherine
Mettawee
Middletown Springs
Wallingford
Tinmouth
East Wallingford
Mount Holly
Wells
South Wallingford
Ludlow (Okemo) Mtn. 3,343 ft. (1019 m.)
West Pawlet
Pawlet
Danby
Mount Tabor
Dorset Pk. 3,804 ft. (1159 m.)
Hudson Falls
Mt. Tabor 3,584 ft. (1092 m.)
Rupert
North Landgrove
West Rupert
Dorset
East Dorset
Peru
South Dorset
Bromley Mtn. 3,260 ft. (994 m.)
Manchester Center
Mt. Equinox 3,816 ft. (1163 m.)
Manchester
Manchester Depot
Sandgate
Schuylerville
Sunderland
Batten Kill
Arlington
East Arlington
Cambridge
Hudson River
Hoosic
Glastenbury Mtn. 3,764 ft. (1147 m.)
Shaftsbury (South Shaftsbury)
North Bennington
Hoosick Falls
Old Bennington
Bennington
Searsburg
Woodford
Tomhannock Res.
Heartwellville
North Pownal
Pownal Center
Pownal
Readsboro
Stamford
North Adams
Hoosac Tunnel
Bethel
East Bethel
Royalton
South Strafford
South Royalton
Gaysville
White R.
Sharon
Union Village
Thetford Center
Thetford
North Thetford
East Thetford
Pompanoosuc
Connecticut
Barnard
North Pomfret
Pomfret
West Hartford
Norwich
Lewiston
SouthPomfret
Hartford
Wilder
WILDER DAM
White River Junction
Quechee
Taftsville
Bridgewater Ctr.
Woodstock
Ottauquechee
West Woodstock
Bridgewater Corners
Bridgewater
North Hartland
Hartland Four Corners
South Woodstock
Plymouth
Hartland
SAINT-GAUDENS NAT'L HIST. SITE
Windsor
Tyson
Reading (Felchville)
Brownsville
Mt. Ascutney 3,144 ft. (958 m.)
Healdville
Black R.
Proctorsville
Ascutney
Ludlow
Cavendish
Perkinsville
North Springfield
Springfield
Gassetts
Weston
Andover
West R.
Simonsville
Chester
Chester Depot
Londonderry
South Londonderry
Bartonsville
Rockingham
Grafton
Windham
Cambridgeport
Bondville
South Windham
Saxtons River
North Westminster
Bellows Falls
Westminster Station
Jamaica
West Townshend
Westminster West
East Jamaica
Westminster
Stratton Mtn. 3,936 ft. (1200 m.)
Stratton
Wardsboro
Townshend
West Wardsboro
Somerset Reservoir
Brookline
Deerfield
Newfane
Putney
Mt. Snow 3,556 ft. (1084 m.)
East Dover
Williamsville
West Dover
South Newfane
West Dummerston
Haystack Mtn. 3,462 ft. (1055 m.)
Wilmington
West Brattleboro
Brattleboro
Harriman Reservoir
Marlboro
Guilford
Jacksonville
West Halifax
Whitingham
Halifax Center
Vernon
Northfield
Bernardston
CONNECTICUT RIVER
Plymouth
Merrimack
Squam Lake
Newfound Lake
Lake Winnipesaukee
Danbury
Merrimack River
Lake Sunapee
Sugar R.
Newport
CONCORD
Hillsboro
River
Contoocook
Keene
Ashuelot
Peterborough
Jaffrey
MANCHESTER
Greenwich
Longitude West of
30′
73°
72°
43°
A
B
C
D
3
4
5

VERMONT

Pittsford 666 ... A3
Plainfield○ 1,249 ... C2
Plainfield 599 ... C2
Plymouth○ 405 ... B3
Pomfret○ 856 ... B3
Post Mills 500 ... C3
Poultney○ 3,196 ... A3
Poultney 1,554 ... A3
Pownal○ 3,269 ... A5
Pownal Center ... A5
Proctor○ 1,998 ... A3
Proctorsville 481 ... B4
Putney○ 1,850 ... B5
Quechee 900 ... C3
Randolph○ 4,689 ... B3
Randolph 2,217 ... B3
Reading○ 647 ... B4
Readsboro○ 638 ... B5
Readsboro 402 ... B5
Richford○ 2,206 ... B1
Richford 1,471 ... B1
Richmond○ 3,159 ... A2
Richmond 865 ... A2
Ripton○ 327 ... A3
Riverton ... B2
Rochester○ 1,054 ... B3
Rockingham○ 5,538 ... C4
Roxbury○ 452 ... B2
Royalton○ 2,100 ... B3
Rupert○ 605 ... A4
Rutland○ 3,300 ... B3
Rutland⊙ 18,436 ... B3
Ryegate○ 1,000 ... C2
Saint Albans○ 3,555 ... A1
Saint Albans⊙ 7,308 ... A1
Saint Albans Bay 350 ... A1
Saint George○ 677 ... A1
Saint Johnsbury○ 7,938 ... D2
Saint Johnsbury⊙ 7,150 ... D2
Saint Johnsbury Center 400 ... D2
Salisbury○ 881 ... A3
Sandgate○ 234 ... A6
Saxtons River 593 ... B4
Searsburg○ 72 ... A6
Shaftsbury○ 3,001 ... A5
Sharon○ 828 ... C3
Sheffield○ 435 ... C1
Shelburne○ 5,000 ... A2
Sheldon○ 1,618 ... B1
Sheldon Springs 300 ... A1
Shrewsbury○ 866 ... B3
South Barre 1,301 ... B2
South Burlington 10,679 ... A2
South Dorset 200 ... A4
South Hero○ 1,188 ... A1
South Londonderry 500 ... B4
South Pomfret 250 ... B3
South Royalton 700 ... C3
South Ryegate 400 ... C2
South Shaftsbury ... A5
South Woodstock 360 ... B3
Springfield○ 10,190 ... C4
Springfield 5,603 ... C4
Stamford○ 773 ... A5
Starksboro○ 1,336 ... A2
Stockbridge○ 508 ... B3
Stowe○ 2,991 ... B2
Stowe 531 ... B2
Strafford○ 731 ... C3
Stratton○ 122 ... B4
Sudbury○ 380 ... A3
Sunderland○ 768 ... A4
Sunderland 500 ... A4
Sutton○ 667 ... C1
Swanton○ 5,141 ... A1
Swanton 2,520 ... A1
Taftsville 260 ... C3
Thetford○ 2,188 ... C3
Thetford Center 180 ... C3
Tinmouth○ 406 ... A4
Topsham○ 767 ... C2
Townshend○ 849 ... B4
Troy○ 1,498 ... C1
Tunbridge○ 925 ... C3
Underhill○ 2,172 ... B1
Underhill Center 575 ... B2
Union Village 161 ... C3
Vergennes 2,273 ... A2
Vernon○ 1,175 ... B5
Vershire○ 442 ... C3
Waitsfield○ 1,300 ... B2
Walden○ 575 ... C2
Wallingford○ 1,893 ... A4
Wallingford 1,141 ... A4
Waltham○ 394 ... A2
Wardsboro○ 505 ... B4
Warren○ 956 ... B2
Washington○ 855 ... C2
Waterbury○ 4,465 ... B2
Waterbury 1,892 ... B2
Waterbury Center ... B2
Waterville○ 470 ... B1
Websterville 700 ... B2
Wells○ 815 ... A4
Wells River 396 ... C2
West Barnet 175 ... C2
West Brattleboro 2,795 ... B5
West Burke 338 ... C1
West Charleston 170 ... C1
West Cornwall ... A3
West Dummerston 100 ... B5
West Fairlee○ 427 ... C3
Westfield○ 418 ... C1
Westford○ 1,413 ... A1
West Hartford 300 ... C3
West Haven○ 253 ... A3
West Haven 250 ... A3
Westminster○ 2,493 ... C4
Westminster 319 ... C4
Westminster Station 200 ... C4
Westminster West 400 ... B4
Westmore○ 257 ... C1
Weston○ 627 ... B4
West Pawlet 300 ... A4
West Rupert 300 ... A4
West Rutland○ 2,351 ... A3
West Rutland 2,169 ... A3
West Woodstock ... B3
Weybridge○ 667 ... A2
Wheelock○ 444 ... C1
White River Junction 2,582 ... C3
Whiting○ 379 ... A3
Whitingham○ 1,043 ... B5
Wilder 1,461 ... C3
Williamstown○ 2,284 ... B2
Williston○ 3,843 ... A2
Wilmington○ 1,808 ... B5
Windham○ 223 ... B4
Windsor○ 4,084 ... C4
Windsor 3,478 ... C4
Winooski 6,318 ... A2
Wolcott○ 986 ... C1
Woodbury○ 573 ... C2
Woodford○ 314 ... A5
Woodstock○ 3,214 ... B3
Woodstock⊙ 1,178 ... B3
Worcester○ 727 ... B2

OTHER FEATURES

Abraham (mt.) ... B2
Arrowhead Mountain (lake) ... A1
Ascutney (mt.) ... B4
Bald (mt.) ... D1
Barton (riv.) ... C1
Batten Kill (riv.) ... A4
Belvidere (mt.) ... B1
Black (creek) ... B1
Black (riv.) ... B4
Bloodroot (mt.) ... B3
Bolton (mt.) ... B2
Bomoseen (lake) ... A3
Brandon Gap (pass) ... B3
Bread Loaf (mt.) ... A2
Bromley (mt.) ... B4
Brown's (riv.) ... A1
Burke (mt.) ... D1
Camels Hump (mt.) ... B2
Carmi (lake) ... B1
Caspian (lake) ... C1
Champlain (lake) ... A1
Chittenden (res.) ... B3
Clyde (riv.) ... C1
Comerford (dam) ... D2
Connecticut (riv.) ... C5
Crystal (lake) ... C1
Dog (riv.) ... B2
Dorset (peak) ... A4
Dunmore (lake) ... A3
East Branch, Nulhegan (riv.) ... D1
Echo (lake) ... D1
Ellen (mt.) ... B2
Equinox (mt.) ... A4
Fairfield (pond) ... A1
Glastenbury (mt.) ... A5
Gore (mt.) ... D1
Green (mts.) ... B4
Green River (res.) ... B1
Groton (lake) ... C2
Hardwick (lake) ... C1
Harriman (res.) ... B6
Harveys (lake) ... C2
Haystack (mt.) ... B5
Hoosic (riv.) ... A5
Hortonia (lake) ... A3
Hunger (mt.) ... B2
Iroquois (lake) ... A2
Island (pond) ... D1
Jay (peak) ... B1
Joes (brook) ... C2
Killington (peak) ... B3
Lamoille (riv.) ... A1
Lewis (creek) ... A2
Lincoln Gap (pass) ... B2
Little (riv.) ... B2
Mad (riv.) ... B2
Maidstone (lake) ... D1
Mansfield (mt.) ... B1
Memphremagog (lake) ... C1
Mettawee (riv.) ... A4
Middlebury Gap (pass) ... B3
Mill (riv.) ... B3
Missisquoi (bay) ... A1
Missisquoi (riv.) ... B1
Mollys Falls (pond) ... C2
Moore (dam) ... D2
Moore (res.) ... D2
Moose (riv.) ... D1
Norton (pond) ... D1
Nulhegan (riv.) ... D1
Okemo (Ludlow) (mt.) ... B4
Ottauquechee (riv.) ... B3
Otter (creek) ... A2
Passumpsic (riv.) ... D1
Paul (stream) ... D1
Pico (peak) ... B3
Poultney (riv.) ... A3
Saint Catherine (lake) ... A4
Salem (lake) ... C1
Seymour (lake) ... D1
Shelburne (pond) ... A3
Smugglers Notch (pass) ... B1
Snow (mt.) ... B5
Somerset (res.) ... A4
Spruce (mt.) ... C2
Stratton (mt.) ... B4
Tabor (mt.) ... B4
Taconic (mts.) ... A5
Trout (riv.) ... B1
Waits (riv.) ... C2
Waterbury (res.) ... B2
Wells (riv.) ... C2
West (riv.) ... B4
White (riv.) ... C3
White Face (mt.) ... B1
Wilder (dam) ... C3
Willoughby (lake) ... D1
Winooski (riv.) ... B2

⊙County seat. ○Population of town or township.

Cities and Towns. Of the nine cities in Vermont, Burlington is the largest. Situated on Lake Champlain. Burlington is a distribution rather than a manufacturing center. Rutland, second in size, depends commercially on the marble industry and the manufacture of scales and electrical products. Winooski, across the Winooski River from Burlington, maintains several small manufacturing concerns. Montpelier, the state capital, about 10 miles (16 km) northwest of the geographical center of Vermont, is the home of a national insurance firm. A few miles to the southeast is Barre, the hub of the state's granite industry. The two largest communities in the southern part of the state are Brattleboro and Bennington.

3. The Economy

The driving economic forces in Vermont have been: (1) the need to wrest from the poor soil a specialized agriculture, which changed the character of farming from pioneer conditions to the 19th century boom in raising Merino sheep, followed by the shift to dairying after the Civil War; (2) the substitution of quarrying for mining by exploiting the great resources of marble and granite; (3) "Yankee inventiveness," which led to hundreds of inventions and fostered the small mills of the 19th century and the machine-tool industry of modern times; and (4) the preoccupation with the tourist trade, including the skiing industry.

Manufacturing. Vermont's leading industry is the manufacture of machines and machine tools, particularly in Springfield and Windsor. Other important manufacturing industries produce scales and other measuring devices, electrical equipment, computer equipment, stone and marble products, and processed foods.

Agriculture. Dairying is the dominant agricultural pursuit in Vermont, as evidenced by the fact that the state has two thirds as many cows as people. Among the many dairy products that are produced in Vermont is the distinctive cheddar cheese that comes from the rural areas of the state.

Vermont's farms have remained fairly constant in number (about 6,000) but have decreased in average size (276 acres, or 112 hectares).

Vermont contains two strips of relatively fertile soil: one in the Connecticut Valley and the other in the valley and islands of Lake Champlain. Grass and ensilage are the principal products because they are the ingredients for the important dairy industry and its concentration on fluid milk and cheese as products. Minor phases of farming include sheep raising, poultry production, and apple growing, the last especially in the Lake Champlain islands. More colorful is the maple sugar and syrup industry. Lumbering, whose products range from clothespins to plywood, is represented by the sawmills scattered through the mountain valleys.

Quarrying. The quarries around Barre produce excellent gray granite that is polished and

PERSONAL INCOME IN VERMONT

Source	1960	1970	1980
	(Millions of dollars)		
Farms	60	65	139
Mining	6	8	12
Construction	42	124	170
Manufacturing	168	339	907
Transportation, communications, and public utilities	42	76	182
Wholesale and retail trade	98	189	440
Finance, insurance, and real estate	26	55	128
Services	80	221	534
Other industries	2	4	15
Government	77	180	439
	(Dollars)		
Per capita personal income	1,879	3,302	7,827
Per capita income, U.S.	2,216	3,945	9,521

Source: U.S. Department of Commerce, *Survey of Current Business.*

VERMONT DEVELOPMENT AGENCY

VERMONT DEVELOPMENT AGENCY

A quiet village in the autumn foliage of central Vermont (*above*). Granite is quarried, cut, and polished in Barre (*left*), from a quarry in continuous operation for more than 100 years.

processed to make building stone and memorial markers. Pink granite is quarried east of Newport. The celebrated Vermont marble is quarried along the western flank of the Green Mountains and processed for tile and markers. Nonfading green, purple, and mottled slate is quarried in the Taconic Mountains.

Tourism. Tourism has become the state's second-largest source of income. Vermont has always been an ideal summer vacation spot and a major attraction when the autumn foliage bursts into color. Since World War II, winter sports and ski resorts have swelled the number of winter visitors as well.

Transportation. Vermont business tended to gravitate toward the Canadian markets until the railroads riveted the state to the rest of the nation and gave it access to Boston and New York markets. The competition for Western trade stimulated the building of the first railroad, the Vermont Central, which began operating in 1848. The railroads have declined; and some, like the Montpelier and Wells and the Rutland Railroad, have suspended operations. There is still some movement of bulk products such as oil from New York City via the New York State Barge Canal System to Lake Champlain. Vermont has air connections with Boston, New York, Albany, Hartford, and Canadian cities.

4. Government

Constitution. Vermont declared itself a free and independent republic on Jan. 15, 1777, and adopted its constitution on July 8 of the same year. A major revision was accomplished in 1786. Two years after Vermont was admitted to the Union, a new constitution was adopted on July 9, 1793. This is the basic document under which the state still operates. The amending process is as follows: every ten years amendments may be proposed with the support of a two-thirds vote in the Senate and a majority in the House. The proposals are then resubmitted to the next General Assembly; if approved by the assembly, they are submitted to popular vote and, if approved by the people, the proposals become part of the constitution.

Vermont citizens enjoy universal suffrage—universal manhood suffrage dates from the beginning of the state—but a voter must qualify by taking the Freeman's Oath to vote "without fear

GOVERNMENT HIGHLIGHTS

Electoral Vote—3. **Representation in Congress**—U. S. senators, 2; U. S. representatives, 1. **General Assembly**—Senate, 30 members, 2-year terms; House of Representatives, 150 members, 2-year terms. **Governor**—2-year term; may succeed self.

GOVERNORS OF VERMONT

Name	Party	Term
Thomas Chittenden		1778–1789
Moses Robinson		1789–1790
Thomas Chittenden		1790–1797
Paul Brigham, acting		1797
Isaac Tichenor	Federalist	1797–1807
Israel Smith	Democratic Republican	1807–1808
Isaac Tichenor	Federalist	1808–1809
Jonas Galusha	Democratic Republican	1809–1813
Martin Chittenden	Federalist	1813–1815
Jonas Galusha	Democratic Republican	1815–1820
Richard Skinner	"	1820–1823
Cornelius P. Van Ness	"	1823–1826
Ezra Butler	National Republican	1826–1828
Samuel C. Crafts	"	1828–1831
William A. Palmer	Anti-Masonic	1831–1835
Silas H. Jennison	Whig	1835–1841
Charles Paine	"	1841–1843
John Mattocks	"	1843–1844
William Slade	"	1844–1846
Horace Eaton	"	1846–1848
Carlos Coolidge	"	1848–1850
Charles K. Williams	"	1850–1852
Erastus Fairbanks	"	1852–1853
John S. Robinson	Democrat	1853–1854
Stephen Royce	Republican	1854–1856
Ryland Fletcher	"	1856–1858
Hiland Hall	"	1858–1860
Erastus Fairbanks	"	1860–1861
Frederick Holbrook	"	1861–1863
John Gregory Smith	"	1863–1865
Paul Dillingham	"	1865–1867
John B. Page	"	1867–1869
Peter T. Washburn	"	1869–1870
George W. Hendee, acting	"	1870
John W. Stewart	"	1870–1872
Julius Converse	"	1872–1874
Asahel Peck	"	1874–1876
Horace Fairbanks	"	1876–1878
Redfield Proctor	"	1878–1880
Roswell Farnham	"	1880–1882
John L. Barstow	"	1882–1884
Samuel E. Pingree	"	1884–1886
Ebenezer J. Ormsbee	"	1886–1888
William P. Dillingham	"	1888–1890
Carroll S. Page	"	1890–1892
Levi K. Fuller	"	1892–1894
Urban A. Woodbury	"	1894–1896
Josiah Grout	"	1896–1898
Edward C. Smith	"	1898–1900
William W. Stickney	"	1900–1902
John G. McCullough	"	1902–1904
Charles J. Bell	"	1904–1906
Fletcher D. Proctor	"	1906–1908
George H. Prouty	"	1908–1910
John A. Mead	"	1910–1912
Allen M. Fletcher	"	1912–1915
Charles W. Gates	"	1915–1917
Horace F. Graham	"	1917–1919
Percival W. Clement	"	1919–1921
James Hartness	"	1921–1923
Redfield Proctor	"	1923–1925
Franklin S. Billings	"	1925–1927
John E. Weeks	"	1927–1931
Stanley C. Wilson	"	1931–1935
Charles M. Smith	"	1935–1937
George D. Aiken	"	1937–1941
William H. Wills	"	1941–1945
Mortimer R. Proctor	"	1945–1947
Ernest W. Gibson	"	1947–1951
Lee E. Emerson	"	1951–1955
Joseph B. Johnson	"	1955–1959
Robert T. Stafford	"	1959–1961
F. Ray Keyser, Jr.	"	1961–1963
Philip H. Hoff	Democrat	1963–1969
Deane C. Davis	Republican	1969–1973
Thomas Salmon	Democrat	1973–1977
Richard A. Snelling	Republican	1977–1985
Madeleine Kunin	Democrat	1985–

or favor of any person." Vermont is represented in the U. S. Congress by two senators and one representative.

The Executive. The governor is elected for a two-year term. He heads the executive branch, which includes the lieutenant governor, secretary of state, auditor of accounts, treasurer, attorney general, and the commissioners of various departments. For nearly a century (1777–1870) the governor was elected on an annual basis. From 1870 to 1914 elections were held in odd-numbered years. After 1914 balloting has taken place in November of even-numbered years.

The Legislature. Vermont's first legislature was unicameral, and it was not until 1836 that the Senate was added. The full legislature is called the General Assembly. It consists of a 30-member Senate and a 150-member House of Representatives.

Under a reapportionment plan passed by the legislature in 1965 and accepted by a federal court, the number of senators was fixed at 30, chosen from 28 districts. The number of representatives was set at 150, elected from 71 districts. Populous districts have been subdivided so that no citizen may vote for more than two representatives. The legislature meets in odd-numbered years. The length of sessions is not limited, and special sessions may be called by the governor.

The Judiciary. Vermont's highest court is the supreme court, which has a chief justice and four associate justices elected to six-year terms by the legislature, as are judges of the superior court. It is customary for these judges to be reelected until retirement or death. Judges in the probate courts are elected for four-year terms, and district court judges are appointed by the governor for six-year terms, with legislative approval.

Taxation and Revenue. The basic taxes for local government are the poll tax and the property tax. For a long period Vermont levied a direct tax, but in 1931 this was abolished and a state income tax substituted. Although the state derives revenues also from licensing, corporate income taxes, excise taxes, and inheritance taxes, the individual income tax supplies about 42% of Vermont's total tax revenue.

5. Education and Culture

Elementary and Secondary Education. The educational background for Vermont is to be found in Massachusetts, where as early as 1647 legislation was enacted to provide a teacher for every town of 50 households and a school for every town with 100 households. Even during the period when the state was fighting for its existence, its founders found time (in framing the constitution of 1777) to provide for a school or schools in each town and a grammar school in each county. The establishment of school districts was ordered in Vermont's first school law, adopted in 1782, although the district was abandoned finally in 1892 and replaced by a compulsory town system. Before that, in 1780, the first secondary school in the state was opened at Bennington. A law of 1797 required town support of schools and established a minimum of weeks to be taught each year.

Early in the 19th century the goal of the secondary school was the academy—early examples were at Montpelier and Randolph—and by 1830, 20 academies had been established through-

VERMONT DEVELOPMENT DEPARTMENT

Vermont's State House in Montpelier, built in 1836, boasts a classic portico and a gold-covered dome.

out the state. The high-school movement began in Brattleboro in 1841 and spread rapidly.

Vermont's public-school system is administered by a state commissioner of education who is appointed for an indefinite term by members of the board of education, with the governor's approval. The members of the board of education are appointed to six-year terms by the governor with Senate approval. School attendance is compulsory for children between the ages of 7 and 16.

Higher Education. Vermont's colleges are few, but a number of them have received national acclaim. The University of Vermont, founded in 1791 at Burlington, benefited from the Morrill Act of 1862 (sponsored by a Vermont senator, Justin Smith Morrill) granting public land to states for the establishment of agricultural and technical colleges, and added a State Agricultural College in 1865. Middlebury College, located in the town of the same name, dates from 1800. It sponsors the famous summer conferences held annually at nearby Bread Loaf. Norwich University, for men, specializes in engineering and science. It was founded by Capt. Alden Partridge in Norwich in 1819 and moved to Northfield in 1866. The state-supported colleges in Castleton, Johnson, and Lyndon Center were originally founded as teacher-training schools. Bennington College for women places an emphasis on the "learn and earn" policy by having its students seek out related employment during the winter term. Roman Catholic institutions of collegiate level are St. Michael's College in Winooski Park and Trinity College in Burlington. Goddard College is a liberal arts institution in Plainfield. Junior colleges include Green Mountain College (Poultney), Vermont College (Montpelier), and Champlain College (Burlington).

Libraries and Museums. Vermont's first library was opened in 1791. Early libraries were called "social libraries," a kind of joint stock affair in which individuals combined to support libraries on a share basis. The Vermont Free Public Library, with headquarters in Montpelier, began the practice of sending out its first bookmobile in 1922, and by 1960 its mobile libraries covered the state.

The state library in Montpelier not only serves the general public, but it also acts as a law library to the supreme court. Other special libraries are the Vermont Historical Society Library in Montpelier, with its collection of Vermontiana; the library at the University of Vermont, which is the largest in the state; the Abernathy Library of American Literature, with collections of folk ballads and material relating to Henry David Thoreau; the Edward Clark Crossett Library at Bennington College; and the Jeremiah Durick Library at St. Michael's College.

The fine arts museums in the state include the Bennington Historical Museum and Art Gallery, featuring Bennington pottery, Grandma Moses' paintings, and the Grandma Moses Schoolhouse; the Thomas W. Wood Art Gallery in Montpelier, which displays Wood's work and American art of the 1920's; the Bundy Art Gallery, which features contemporary paintings and a sculpture garden; the Robert Hull Fleming Museum at the University of Vermont; and the Johnson Gallery of Middlebury College.

Among the museums that house historical memorabilia are the Shelburne Museum, consisting of 35 restored early American buildings on 100 acres (40 hectares); the State Historical Society Museum in Montpelier; and the Sheldon Museum in Middlebury, featuring displays of early Vermont life.

The Museum of American Fly Fishing, containing the fishing rods of such famous men as Presidents Herbert Hoover and Dwight Eisenhower, is in Manchester, as is the Southern

Vermont Art Center. The Morristown Historical Museum in Morrisville displays articles relating to early New England life.

Other museums of special interest include the Fairbanks Museum of Natural Science, the Maple Grove Museum, and St. Johnsbury Athenaeum Gallery, all in St. Johnsbury; and the Woodstock Historical Society in Woodstock, which features costumes, dolls, dollhouses, toys, farming equipment, and furnishings from the period 1800–1860.

Restorations. The John Strong D. A. R. Museum in Addison is a restored two-story brick home with authentic period furnishings. Other interesting restorations include the Victorian Park McCullough House in North Bennington; the Flemish-style Wilson Castle in Proctor, which contains museum pieces from around the world; the Old Rockingham Meeting House and Vermont Country Store in Rockingham; and the Farrar-Mansur House in Weston, a restored tavern dating from 1797.

Other Cultural Activities. The Vermont Symphony Orchestra is the first such group to be organized (1948) on a statewide level. The Bread Loaf Writers' Conference and the School of English, sponsored by Middlebury College each summer, are famous in their respective fields. The Southern Vermont Art Center (Manchester), the Mid-Vermont Artists (Rutland), and the Northern Vermont Artists (Burlington) sponsor notable exhibits of work produced by state artists.

Vermont is a popular setting for summer theaters. The Champlain Shakespeare Festival at the University of Vermont (Burlington) takes place each summer. The Marlboro Summer School of Music and Festival is internationally famous.

Vermont's natural beauty, its rustic tranquility, and the deep spiritual roots of its people have inspired writers since the colonial period. In the 20th century several prominent authors made their homes in Vermont, though born elsewhere. Foremost in this group was the poet Robert Frost, who was a founder of the Bread Loaf School of English.

Among artists, Thomas Waterman Wood, the outstanding Vermont painter of the 19th century, established the Wood Gallery of Art in Montpelier. Two Vermont sculptors, Hiram Powers and Herbert Adams, each became known for his portrait busts of famous Americans. Another sculptor, Larkin G. Mead, designed the Lincoln Tomb in Springfield, Ill., and created two statues of Ethan Allen, one for the state capital and another for the Capitol Building in Washington, D. C. His brother, William R. Mead, was a noted architect. Two other Vermont-born brothers who gained fame outside the state were William Morris Hunt, a painter whose works are represented in the Metropolitan Museum of Art in New York City, and Richard Morris Hunt, an architect who designed the main section of the Metropolitan Museum as well as the Fogg Museum at Harvard and the National Observatory in Washington, D. C. In modern times, a great many painters and sculptors have lived and worked in Vermont during at least part of their careers.

Communication. The first newspaper in Vermont was *The Vermont Gazette* published briefly in Westminster in 1780–1781. This was followed by the *Windsor Vermont Journal* in 1783. *The Rutland Herald,* begun as a weekly in 1794, is the state's oldest continuously published newspaper. The largest of the state's 11 dailies is the *Burlington Free Press.*

Vermont's first radio station, WSYB, began operation in 1930 in Rutland. Television was introduced by WCAX-TV in Burlington in 1954. Educational television was established in 1968. The state has about 40 radio stations and six television stations.

6. Recreation and Places of Interest

With 63 state parks and forests offering camping, hiking, and a variety of seasonal activities, Vermont is a favored vacation spot and tourist attraction. The state's main resort areas are in the Green Mountains, and its numerous lakes and streams are well stocked with several varieties of trout, black bass, perch, and pike.

Resort Areas. Ski areas abound, especially on Mt. Mansfield at Stowe, "Suicide Six" at Woodstock, Madonna Mountain in Jeffersonville, Pico Peak in Sherburne, Mt. Snow in Wilmington, and Jay Peak. Basin Harbor, near Vergennes, is a popular Lake Champlain summer resort. The Long Trail (261 miles, or 420 km), threading the summits of the Green Mountains for the length of the state, presents a challenge and a delight to hikers. The trail has shelters every few miles, and drinking water is always handy.

The rugged 266,000-acre (108,000-hectare) Green Mountain National Forest offers a vast recreational area. State parks include Camel's Hump State Park at Huntington Center, Bomoseen at

A town meeting in Corinth gives citizens the opportunity to participate individually in local government.

GRANT HEILMAN

H. ARMSTRONG ROBERTS

A memorial to the town's Civil War dead stands in a quiet churchyard in Chester, Vermont.

West Castleton, and Groton between Montpelier and St. Johnsbury.

Historic Sites and Monuments. "History by the wayside" in Vermont is displayed by 98 markers set up by the Vermont Historic Sites Board. In addition, the commission maintains the Bennington Battle Monument; the Jedediah Hyde log cabin (1783) on Grand Isle; a replica of President Chester A. Arthur's birthplace in Fairfield; the Hubbardton Battlefield; the Calvin Coolidge Homestead in Plymouth; the Constitution House in Windsor, where the Vermont Constitution (1777) was written; and the Eureka School House in Springfield.

Other Attractions. The Doric style state capitol in Montpelier is built of Barre granite. A statue of Ceres, the Roman earth goddess, is mounted atop the gilded dome. The state office building, directly across from the capitol, is a fine example of contemporary architecture, faced in Vermont marble.

Marble exhibits may be seen in Proctor and granite exhibits in Barre. Lake Champlain and its islands are picturesque in the summertime. Also of interest is the Mt. Mansfield Toll Road at Stowe, a winding, treacherous 4.5-mile (7.2-km) gravel road with a 50–70-mile (80–112-km) view from its summit.

Annual Events. The Vermont Maple Festival is held in St. Albans in April, followed by the Enosburg Falls Dairy Festival in June. The Marlboro Music Festival in July and August features world-famous musicians in concert, and the University of Vermont holds a Mozart Festival in the summer as well.

August and September are popular times for fairs, antique shows, and festivals, including the arts festival in Stratton Mountain. The fall foliage peaks between mid-September and mid-October. By mid-November, Alpine and Nordic events and races begin on the ski slopes. The most notable of the many winter carnivals is held in January at Stowe.

7. History

The first inhabitants of Vermont were the Algonkian Indians. Sometime during the 16th century they were routed from the land by the Iroquois. Vermont was the hunting ground of the Iroquois Confederacy when the first European, Samuel de Champlain, arrived in the territory in the 17th century.

Exploration. On July 4, 1609, Samuel de Champlain entered the lake that now bears his name. Half a century later (1666), the French erected Fort Ste. Anne on Isle La Motte, and the government of New France granted a number of seigniories along the Richelieu River in Quebec and on Lake Champlain. In 1690, Capt. Jacobus de Warm of Albany established a small fort at Chimney Point (in present-day Addison county). But the first permanent English settlement appeared in the Connecticut Valley when Massachusetts in 1724 sent Lt. Timothy Dwight to erect Fort Dummer, just below present-day Brattleboro. Further protection of river settlements was assured by the construction (1740) of Fort Number Four at Charlestown, N. H. The success of British arms in the French and Indian War (1754–1763) meant the removal of the French threat to Vermont.

Settlement and Early Years. With the fall of Montreal in 1760, settlers began swarming into southern Vermont. This movement was assisted materially by the Crown Point Military Road between Charlestown, N. H., and Crown Point, N. Y., and it was further expedited by the liberality with which Governor Benning Wentworth made grants west of the Connecticut in the area then called the New Hampshire Grants.

These grants did not go unnoticed by the governor of New York. He protested to King George III and obtained a decision (1764) in his favor to prevent further grants by New Hampshire. Not content, New York insisted upon regranting land the pioneers had already obtained under New Hampshire title. Naturally there was objection, and resistance became organized, particularly west of the mountains where Ethan Allen assembled the Green Mountain Boys. The "outlaws" not only were strong enough to defend their lands but bold enough to punish Yorkers with the "Beech Seal" (whipping), to defy sheriffs, and even to carry their operations across the New York border.

The Revolution. In 1775 when the news of Lexington came to Vermont, the Yankees ceased their hostile actions against the Yorkers and began to resist the British crown. In less than a month Ethan Allen, joined by Benedict Arnold, captured Fort Ticonderoga (May 10), and Seth Warner did the same at Crown Point. Vermont forces participated in the ill-fated Canadian expedition (1775), and Ethan Allen was captured outside Montreal (to be exchanged in 1778). The British grand strategy of 1777, to divide New England from New York, threatened to achieve a measure of success when a force under John Burgoyne appeared on the lake, recaptured Fort Ticonderoga and Crown Point, and began to press toward Albany. In the retreat that followed, the only battle of the Revolutionary War fought on Vermont soil occurred at Hubbardton on July 7, 1777 (the Battle of Bennington was waged just across the New York line). Although technically a defeat for the Green Mountain Boys, the Hubbardton clash was a successful rear-guard action that allowed the retreating Americans to regroup. The next month Burgoyne sent two detachments to capture military supplies at Bennington, only to meet with resounding defeat (August 16) at the hands of the Green Mountain Boys and Brig. Gen. John Stark's New Hampshire command, as well as elements of Massachusetts militia.

This campaign ended fighting in Vermont except for Tory and Indian raids (notably at Royalton, 1780). During the remainder of the war Vermont defended itself not so much by arms as by diplomacy. The much-disputed Haldimand negotiations, whether traitorous or only pretended on Vermont's part, did prevent invasions for the remainder of the war.

During the war Vermont found time to declare her independence under the name "New Connecticut" (at the Westminster convention, Jan. 15, 1777); to adopt the name "Vermont" (June 4, 1777); and to frame a constitution (at the Windsor convention, July 2–8, 1777) which forbade Negro slavery and granted universal manhood suffrage. Vermont also carried on (temporary) territorial aggrandizement against both New Hampshire and New York. At one time Vermont annexed 16 (later 35) New Hampshire border towns and a line of towns across the New York border. Eventually, Vermont returned to its present boundaries, and land claims were adjusted with New York by payment to the latter of a lump sum. Vermont continued its way as an independent republic until March 4, 1791, when it was admitted to the Union.

Although Vermont was "linked in friendly tether" to the United States, the trend of trade

FAMOUS VERMONTERS

Allen, Ethan (1738–1789), leader of the Green Mountain Boys.
Allen, Ira (1751–1814), Vermont statesman and brother of Ethan, who donated land for the establishment of the University of Vermont in 1789.
Arthur, Chester A. (1830–1886), 21st president of the United States.
Chittenden, Thomas (1730–1797), first governor of Vermont.
Coolidge, Calvin (1872–1933), 30th president of the United States.
Davenport, Thomas (1802–1851), inventor of the electric motor.
Dewey, George (1837–1917), naval commander and distinguished war hero in the Spanish-American War.
Dewey, John (1859–1952), philosopher.
Douglas, Stephen A. (1813–1861), senator and presidential candidate.
Fairbanks, Thaddeus (1796–1886), prominent manufacturer in the scale industry.
Hunt, Richard Morris (1827–1895), architect who designed the main section of the Metropolitan Museum in New York, the Fogg Museum at Harvard, and the National Observatory in Washington, D. C.
Hunt, William Morris (1824–1879), brother of Richard, painter whose works are in the Metropolitan Museum.
Marsh, James (1794–1842), transcendentalist, philosopher, and educator.
Mead, Larkin G. (1835–1910), sculptor who designed the Lincoln Tomb at Springfield, Ill., and created two statues of Ethan Allen, one for the state capital and another for the Capitol Building in Washington, D. C.
Mead, William R. (1846–1928), architect, brother of Larkin.
Morton, Levi P. (1824–1920), vice president of the United States.
Powers, Hiram (1805–1873), sculptor.
Smith, Joseph (1808–1844), leader of the Mormon Church.
Taft, Alphonso (1810–1891), secretary of war and attorney general.
Thompson, Daniel P. (1795–1868), author of *The Green Mountain Boys.*
Tyler, Royall (1757–1826), writer of the first American comedy, *The Contrast,* produced in New York in 1787.
Wood, Thomas Waterman (1823–1903), painter of the 19th century who established the Wood Gallery of Art in Montpelier.
Young, Brigham (1801–1877), founder of the Mormon Church.

A statue at Vermont's State House commemorates Ethan Allen's surprise seizure of Fort Ticonderoga in 1775.

VERMONT DEVELOPMENT DEPARTMENT

VERMONT DEVELOPMENT DEPARTMENT

Delegates at the Constitution House in Windsor adopted a charter for an independent Vermont in 1777.

for half of the state was with Canada. Montreal was the natural entrepôt for lumber, potash, grain, and provisions. Not even the embargo of the War of 1812 could end this trade, scandalous as it might be in wartime. It took the Champlain Canal (opened in 1823) and the coming of the railroads to turn Vermont southward economically. In the meantime, the northern townships continued to be occupied until the state had no more land to grant.

The War of 1812 brought with it the old British plan of thrusting a wedge between New England and New York through the Champlain Valley. The governor of Vermont considered the crisis sufficient to recall the Vermont militia from Plattsburgh. At Burlington, three British war vessels ineffectively bombarded a battery on the lake front. But more vigor was manifested by Lt. (later Commodore) Thomas MacDonough, who, in a remarkably short time, constructed near Vergennes a fleet that he led to victory against the British at Plattsburgh (Sept. 11, 1814), thus saving Vermont from immediate occupation by the British.

During the 1820's, Vermont embraced the Anti-Masonic movement to such a degree that Masons were excluded from town offices and juries, ministers were driven from their pulpits, and families were disrupted. An Anti-Masonic governor, William A. Palmer, was elected in 1831, and Vermont was the only state to cast its vote for William Wirt, the Anti-Masonic presidential candidate in 1832. (See also ANTI-MASONIC PARTY.) Vermonters began to show a growing interest in the antislavery movement and in temperance reform. By the same token, Vermont showed little enthusiasm for the Mexican War.

More enthusiasm was generated, however, for internal improvements. The Champlain Canal, completed in 1823, drew the Champlain Valley into the orbit of the Hudson River system, and canals on the Connecticut River aided the flatboat trade. Turnpikes were next to receive attention, leading eventually to a modern state highway system. But it was rather the coming of the railroads that evoked economic eagerness on the part of Vermonters. In June 1848 the first "train of cars" ran from White River Junction to Bethel on the Vermont Central line. Soon the state was covered with a railroad network, stimulating such industries as mining and lumbering.

When the Civil War came, Vermonters were at last united in its prosecution. The legislature made quick response to Abraham Lincoln's call for volunteers, Vermont ultimately furnishing 34,328 men to the Union cause. Its soldiers acquitted themselves well on the field of battle, and a token of the regard for their zeal may be found in Maj. Gen. John Sedgwick's order at Gettysburg: "Put the Vermonters ahead and keep the column well closed up." While no battle occurred on Vermont soil, St. Albans suffered a celebrated "raid" (actually a bank robbery) on Oct. 19, 1864, when Confederate soldiers, operating from Canada in civilian disguise, took more than $200,000 from town banks.

During the period that followed the Civil War, Chester A. Arthur in 1881 became the first vice president from Vermont. Later that year, on the death of James A. Garfield, he also became the first U. S. president from Vermont. Levi P. Morton was elected vice president in 1888. The naval side of the Spanish-American War found two Vermonters in hero's roles: Admiral George Dewey, victor at Manila Bay, was from Montpelier, and Admiral Charles E. Clark, who took the *Oregon* around South America in time for the Battle of Santiago, came from Bradford.

The Modern Era. The peaceful era that began for Vermont in the 19th century was shattered by World War I. Early in 1917, before the declaration of war, the Vermont legislature granted $1 million for war purposes. About 16,000 Vermonters served with the armed forces, and 642 of them lost their lives.

HISTORICAL HIGHLIGHTS

1609 Samuel de Champlain, probably the first white man to arrive in the area, claimed the region for France.
1724 English settlers established the first permanent settlement at Fort Dummer (Brattleboro).
1763 England took control of Vermont.
1764 New York gained jurisdiction over Vermont.
1770 New York courts ruled that Vermont landholders must have New York land grants or lose their land.
1775 The Green Mountain Boys, led by Ethan Allen, captured Fort Ticonderoga in the Revolutionary War.
1777 Vermont declared itself an independent republic and became the first state to include universal manhood suffrage in its constitution.
1791 Vermont joined the Union as its 14th state on March 4.
1823 The Champlain Canal was opened, creating a waterway from Vermont to New York City.
1850 Vermont legislature nullified the U. S. Fugitive Slave Law.
1864 In the northernmost action of the Civil War, Confederate soldiers robbed banks and raided St. Albans.
1881 Chester A. Arthur, born in Fairfield, became the first U. S. president from the state of Vermont.
1923 Calvin Coolidge, born in Plymouth Notch, became the second U. S. president from Vermont.
1927 Severe floods killed 60 persons and caused millions of dollars worth of damage.
1958 Vermont elected its first Democratic congressman in 106 years.
1964 Vermont's electoral votes went to the first Democratic presidential candidate since 1824, Lyndon B. Johnson.
1970 Environmental control law limiting major developments and protecting the environment were passed by the legislature.

Politically, Vermont showed devotion to the Republican party until the 1960's. In two presidential elections Vermont and one other state stood alone in that devotion: in 1912 (with Utah) for William Howard Taft, and in 1936 (with Maine) for Alfred M. Landon. In 1920, Vermont-born Calvin Coolidge was elected vice president on the Republican ticket; and when Warren G. Harding died in office, Coolidge was inaugurated president (Aug. 3, 1923) in his father's simple homestead at Plymouth. He won the election of 1924 in his own right.

In 1962, Philip H. Hoff became the first Democrat to be elected governor of Vermont in 109 years, thereby ending the Republicans' undisputed control of the governor's mansion.

Bibliography

Aiken, George D., and others, *Vermont for Every Season* (Vt. Life Mag. 1980).
Bassett, T. D., *Vermont: A Bibliography of Its History* (Univ. Press of New England 1984).
Beck, Jane C., *Always in Season: Folk Art and Traditional Culture in Vermont* (Univ. Press of New England 1982).
Bryan, Frank M., *Yankee Politics in Rural Vermont* (Univ. Press of New England 1974).
Danziger, Jeff, *The Vermont Mind* (New England Press 1986).
Denis, Michael J., *Vermont* (Danbury House Bks. 1983).
Duffy, John, *Vermont: An Illustrated History* (Windsor Pub. 1965).
Federal Writers' Project, *Vermont: A Guide to the Green Mountain State* (1937; reprint, Somerset, no date).
Goodman, Lee, *Vermont Saints and Sinners* (New England Press 1985).
Graffagnino, J. Kevin, *The Shaping of Vermont: From the Wilderness to the Centennial* (Vt. Heritage Press 1983).
Haviland, William, and Power, Marjory W., *The Original Vermonters: Native Inhabitants Past and Present* (Univ. Press of New England 1981).
Johnson, Charles W., *The Nature of Vermont: Introduction and Guide to a New England Environment* (Univ. Press of New England 1980).

VERMONT, University of, a coeducational, nondenominational university in Burlington, Vt., officially named the University of Vermont and State Agricultural College. Chartered in 1791, the university is the second oldest in the United States (after the University of North Carolina) to be established by a state legislature. The State Agricultural College was added to the corporate structure in 1865. The institution became a state university in 1955. The University of Vermont was the first New England university to admit women as regular students and the first in the country to establish a chemistry laboratory and a department of English language and literature. The university's Robert Hall Fleming Museum is the largest art museum in the state.

The university has colleges of arts and sciences, education and social services, engineering and mathematics, agriculture and life sciences, and medicine; schools of business administration, natural resources, and nursing and allied health sciences; and a graduate college. The programs lead to associate, bachelor's, master's, Ph.D., and M.D. degrees.

VERMOUTH, vər-mo͞oth′ (Fr. *vermout,* from Ger. *wermut* or *wermuth,* wormwood), a compound of white wines, mildly fortified with brandy and incorporating the flavors of numerous herbs and other aromatics, some of which have tonic properties. Forerunners of this bitter-noted appetizer ranged from spiced wines prepared by Hippocrates (460?–?377 B. C.) and Marcus Tullius Cicero (106–43 B. C.) to medieval mixtures that involved such exotics as myrrh and sandalwood. The vermouth industry had its beginnings toward the end of the 18th century in southern France and northern Italy, which regions are dominated today by large producers who keep secret their house formulas. Pale amber "French" is dry; dark reddish amber "Italian" is luscious-sweet. Both types are now produced in virtually all countries that grow wine grapes, notably the United States and Canada. Vermouth's chief bitter is wormwood.

VERNAL EQUINOX. See EQUINOX.

VERNALIZATION, vûr-nəl-ə-zā′shən, the exposure of plants to low temperature to induce or accelerate the development of the ability to form flowers. Many perennial and biennial plants, sown in spring, will not flower the same year, but will flower the following spring or summer. Such plants must experience winter in order subsequently to flower. Winter can, however, be replaced by exposure of the plants to temperatures between 1° and 10° C for a period of several weeks or months. Cold-requiring plants treated in this way flower soon after transfer from the treatment to warm temperatures and suitable photoperiod. The length of cold treatment required and the range of effective temperatures are genetically determined and differ from plant to plant.

The stem or bud meristem perceives the low temperature, and cold-requiring plants can be vernalized by cold treatment of the bud alone. Some plants, such as the winter cereals, are sensitive at a very early age. Thus five-day-old embryos of Petkus winter rye developing in the ear of the mother plant can be vernalized so that they have no subsequent cold requirement.

Other species are not sensitive until a leafy plant of a certain size or age has developed. This is true, for example, for carrots and many other vegetables. Cold treatment is effective only when the tissues are sufficiently active. When the amount of water, oxygen, or carbohydrate is inadequate, vernalization cannot take place. Dry seeds cannot be vernalized. However, seeds containing 50 percent water, and therefore barely active, can be vernalized.

Two to four days of moderate temperature following cold treatment permanently stabilizes the vernalized state. High temperature (30° C or higher) or lack of oxygen immediately after cold treatment destroys its effect. This is known as devernalization. Devernalized seeds can, however, be successfully vernalized again.

The nature of the events during and immediately after vernalization is unknown. It has been suggested that vernalization induces the production by the plant of a hormone, vernaline. This hypothetical substance has never been isolated. The suggestion of its existence is based on the discovery that in a few cases the vernalization effect can be transmitted through a graft union from a vernalized donor to an unvernalized receptor. In general, however, the vernalization effect is restricted to the treated part of the plant.

H. J. KETELLAPPER
California Institute of Technology

VERNATION, vûr-nā'shən, the arrangement of leaves within the bud. The development of leaves is continuous and essentially uninterrupted in plants grown from seed each year or in herbaceous annuals. But in woody dicotyledons, where growth continues from year to year, leaves are initiated and begin to develop in one season, enter the winter period of dormancy within buds, and complete their development and expansion the following spring. If the dormant bud is examined, it is immediately evident that the developing leaves are arranged within the bud in a pattern. This pattern is called *vernation.*

Vernation is specific for each plant and among the terms most commonly used to describe it are reclinate or inflexed, conduplicate, plicate, circinate, convolute, involute, and revolute. In the tulip tree, where the terminal portion of the leaf is bent downward over the basal part, the arrangement is *reclinate* or *inflexed.* In cherry and oak, the arrangement is *conduplicate,* with the leaf folded lengthwise along its midrib to bring the two halves of the leaf face to face. When the leaf blade is folded like a closed fan, as in maple and geranium, the arrangement is *plicate.* When the leaf is rolled from the tip toward the base, in pinwheel fashion, the descriptive term is *circinate.*

In many members of the rose family, leaves are rolled, much as a scroll, from one edge to the other, an arrangement called *convolute.* The terms *involute* and *revolute* describe an arrangement where both leaf margins are rolled, scroll-like, toward the midrib of the leaf. In the case of such plants as violet and water lily, the margins are rolled upward and the undersurface of the leaf lies outside. This is an *involute* arrangement. In azalea and dock, the margins are rolled similarly but downward and the upper surface of the leaf lies outside, an arrangement referred to as *revolute.*

ALVIN R. GROVE, JR.
The Pennsylvania State University

VERNE, vûrn, **Jules** (1828–1905), French novelist. He was born in Nantes, France, on Feb. 8, 1828, and attended the lycée there. Subsequently he studied law in Paris but later turned his attention primarily to literary and theatrical activities. His first successful play was produced under the patronage of Alexandre Dumas in 1850. In 1863 his novelette *Cinq Semaines en ballon* (Eng. tr., *Five Weeks in a Balloon*) brought him popular acclaim and set a pattern for a series of extravagant romances about science and invention that established Verne as the first novelist of modern science fiction. Some of his fiction has become fact: his submarine *Nautilus* predates the first successful power submarine by a quarter century, and his spaceship is remarkably prophetic of developments a century later.

For over 40 years he averaged more than a novel per year on a wide range of subjects. *Voyage au centre de la terre* (1864; Eng. tr., *Voyage to the Center of the Earth*) concerns subterranean fantasy; *De la Terre à la lune* (1865; Eng. tr., *From the Earth to the Moon*), space travel; *Les Aventures du capitaine Hatteras* (1866), polar exploration; *Vingt Mille Lieues sous les mers* (1869–1870; Eng. tr., *Twenty Thousand Leagues Under the Sea*), submarine travel; *L'Île mystérieuse* (1874; Eng. tr., *Mysterious Island*), industrial exploits of men stranded on an island; and *Michel Strogoff* (1876), Russians and Tatars. *Le Tour du monde en quatre-vingts jours* (1873; Eng. tr., *Around the World in Eighty Days*), Philéas Fogg's daring but realistic travel feat on a wager, remains one of Verne's best-loved and most popular novels. Verne died in Amiens, France, on March 24, 1905.

WILLIAM BRACY
Beaver College

VERNER, ver'nər, **Karl Adolph** (1846–1896), Danish philologist. He was born in Aarhus, Denmark, on March 7, 1846, and attended the University of Copenhagen, where he later (1883–1888) taught Slavonic languages. Meanwhile he was librarian at the University of Halle in 1876–1883. In 1875 he discovered an exception to Grimm's law, which he published two years later as "Eine Ausnahme der ersten Lautverschiebung" in the *Zeitschrift für vergleichende Sprachsforschung.* His discovery of this exception, which later became known as Verner's law, proved of far-reaching importance for Indo-European comparative grammar.

VERNER'S LAW, a philological formula propounded by the Danish philologist Karl Adolph Verner in 1875, containing certain modifications of Grimm's law concerning consonantal shift as between the Indo-European and Germanic languages. However, Verner's formula may be considered as an acceleration of the consonantal shift in Grimm's law rather than as an exception to it. According to Grimm's law, the Indo-European voiceless stop sounds (labial *p*, dental *t*, and palatal as well as velar *k*) develop into the corresponding voiceless spirant sounds in Germanic (labial *f*, dental *þ* = *th* in English *think*, and *χ* = *ch* in German *ich* or *Bach*). Thus the Indo-European voiceless labial stop *p* becomes the voiceless labial spirant *f* in Germanic, as Latin *pēs*, Greek πώς, Sanskrit *pâd* > Germanic *f* (Gothic *fōtus*). This *f* remains unchanged in English and German (*foot, Fuss*).

The Indo-European voiceless dental stop *t* becomes the voiceless dental spirant *þ* in Germanic, as Latin *tongēre* > German *þ* (Gothic *þagkjan*). This *þ* remains in English *th*, but becomes the voiced dental stop *d* in German (*think, denken*). Likewise the Indo-European voiceless palatal or velar stop *k* (Latin *c*) becomes the voiceless back spirant χ in Germanic (usually represented by *h*), as Latin *caput* > Germanic χ (Gothic *háubiþ*, German *Haupt*, and English *head*).

However, it was observed by Verner that the voiceless spirants *f*, *þ*, and χ, as well as the voiceless dental spirant *s* (from Indo-European *s*), sometimes develop still further in Germanic into the corresponding voiced spirants *đ* (as *v* in English *even*), *đ* (voiced as *th* in English *then*), *ǥ* (as *g* in North German pronunciation of *Wagen*), and *z*. This accelerated action of the consonant shift takes place when the Indo-European *p, t, k,* or *s* was not in initial position or when the original accent did not immediately precede the consonant in question. This same phenomenon is evident in the pronunciation of English *éxit* (with voiceless pronunciation *-ks-* when the accent precedes), but *exért* (with voiced *-gz-* when the accent follows). Thus Sanskrit *saptá* and Greek ‘επτά in contrast to Latin *séptem* indicate that the original accent followed the *p*. This word appears in Gothic not as *sifun* but as *sibun* (Gothic *b* is merely orthographic for *ƀ* in this intervocalic position). This *ƀ* normally remains in English *v*, but becomes the voiced labial stop *b* in German (*seven, sieben*). Likewise, whereas Indo-European *t* (Latin *trēs*, Greek τϱεις, Sanskrit *tráyas*) > *þ* in Germanic according to Grimm's law (Gothic *þreis*, English *three*, German *drei*), the second *t* of Indo-European *tritjó-* becomes *đ* in Germanic because of the suffixal accent. The *d* of Gothic *þridja* = *đ* in this position. This *đ* normally develops into English *d* and German *t* (*third, dritt-*).

Likewise, whereas Indo-European *k* (Latin *decem*, Greek δέκα) > χ in Germanic according to Grimm's law (Gothic *taíhun*, German *zehn*, and English *ten* with loss of intervocalic *h*), the *k* of Greek δέκα, with accent following > Germanic *tig* (Gothic *tigjus*, German *-zig* in *zwanzig*, and English *-ty* in *twenty* from the older form *-tig*). A similar interchange may be seen in English *lose* and *forlorn*. The *s* of the infinitive shows original Indo-European root accent and therefore no change of *s*, whereas the *r* of *forlorn* from Germanic *z* shows that the past participle originally had suffixal accent. The *s* therefore becomes *z* according to Verner's law and is then rhotacized (> *r*) in English and German. In German, to be sure, the *r* of the past participle is then leveled out to the infinitive *verlieren* (from Middle High German *verliesen*).

These consonantal changes may be indicated as follows, the first shift representing Grimm's law and the second shift Verner's law:

p	*t*
↓	↓
f (English and German *f*)	*p* (English *th*, German *d*)
↓	↓
ƀ (English *v*, German *b*)	*đ* (English *d*, German *t*)
k	*s*
↓	↓
χ (English and German *h*)	*s* (no change)
↓	↓
ǥ (English and German *g*)	*z* (English and German r)

CARL F. BAYERSCHMIDT,
Professor of Germanic Philology, Columbia University.

VERNET, vĕr-nĕʹ, name of a family of French painters:

(CLAUDE) JOSEPH VERNET: b. Avignon, France, Aug. 14, 1714; d. Paris, Dec. 3, 1789. Son of a decorative painter who taught him the rudiments of design, he found a patron who sent him to Rome. Vernet went by sea from Marseille to Civitavecchia and was so impressed by the sights that he determined to become a marine painter. He was soon saying, "Others may know better how the paint the sky, the earth, the ocean; no one knows better than I how to paint a picture." Despite conventionality of design, his paintings, whether landscapes or seascapes, have their human elements located with such attention to pervasive mood that Vernet is pre-eminent in this respect. His Italian pictures are more dramatic than the great series of the seaports of France commissioned by Madame de Pompadour and now in the Louvre. These, which in some instances dispose of many human figures, are serenely decorative in effect and mildly official in tone, as if the royal seal of approval had been passed gently over the surface.

(ANTOINE) CHARLES (HORACE) VERNET (known as **CARLE**), son of the preceding: b. Bordeaux, France, Aug. 14, 1758; d. Paris, Nov. 27, 1836. Precocious, he received instruction from his father and later from Michel Lépicié. His first interest was animal life. Otherwise, he imitated François Boucher and, after his return from Rome, Jacques Louis David. *The Triumph of Paulus Aemilius* (Metropolitan Museum of Art, New York), in the latter's style, was Vernet's first important picture. His success was assured, but the French Revolution, during which his sister died on the scaffold, made him despair. He rallied eventually and during the Directory named and satirized fashionable foibles as exemplified in the *Merveilleuses* and the *Incroyables*. Later he celebrated Napoleon I and his victories (*Battle of Marengo, Morning of Austerlitz*) but at the restoration of the Bourbons reverted to his love of animals and satirical comments on everyday life.

(EMILE JEAN) HORACE VERNET, son of the preceding: b. Paris, France, June 30, 1789; d. there, Jan. 17, 1863. Once the best known of the Vernets, he has dwindled to somewhat below his merits. His father was frenziedly active on his behalf, and as early as 1812 he was courted by the Bonapartists, to whom he remained substantially loyal for years. In 1814, when the Allies were closing in upon Paris, he fought in defense of the Barrière de Clichy and for his bravery received the Legion of Honor on the battlefield from the emperor himself. In 1822 he submitted *The Defense of the Barrière de Clichy* (Louvre) to the Salon, and when it was turned down for political reasons, he exhibited it in his own studio with overwhelming success. Charles X, in view of Vernet's popularity, showered him with honors: for instance, membership in the Institut de France (1826) and the directorship of the French Academy in Rome. In 1833, he rushed off to the Algerian campaign, just as in 1855 he went to the Crimean War. His battle scenes are absurdly large, but at the time they flattered French ambitions.

WALLACE BROCKWAY,
Consultant to the Bollingen Foundation.

VERNEUIL OVEN. See GEMS—*Synthetics and Imitations.*

VERNIER, vĕr-nyā′, **Pierre,** French mathematician: b. Ornans, France, 1580; d. there, Sept. 14, 1637. He was captain commanding the château d'Ornans, counselor of the king of Spain, and director general of the mint for the Franche-Comté. He devoted his leisure to mathematics, applying it to the study of elementary ballistics in his *Traité d'artillerie*. His only noteworthy contribution in the field of mathematics lay in his invention of the vernier, which was for a long time mistakenly attributed to the Portuguese mathematician, Pedro Nunes. The vernier is described in his work *Construction, usage et des propriétés du quadrant nouveau de mathématiques* (1631).

EUGENE A. AVALLONE

VERNIER, vûr′nē-ər, a mechanical device invented by Pierre Vernier (q.v.), used to read linear or angular scales to a higher degree of accuracy than possible with the usual scale. As usually constructed, the *direct* vernier consists of a short auxiliary scale (the vernier) having one more graduation in the same length than the larger (main) scale. Thus, each division on the vernier is proportionally smaller than the corresponding division on the main scale. In the accompanying illustration the vernier has 25 divisions, while the main scale has 24 divisions in the same length. Letting each main-scale division = 1/40 of an inch (0.025 inch), then each division on the vernier is 1/25 smaller than a main-scale division, or 1/25 × 0.025 = 0.001 inch, smaller than a main-scale division. The total reading shown is obtained by adding the main and vernier readings, that is, 1.625 inches (the point on the main scale before the zero of the vernier scale) + 16 × 0.001 inch = 1.641 inches.

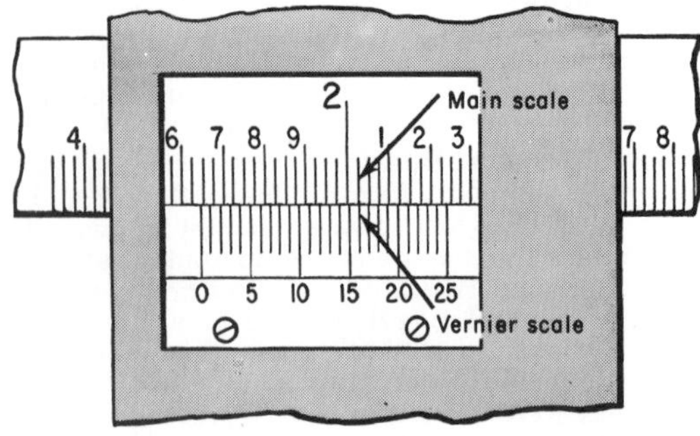

In the *direct* vernier, both main scale (*n* divisions) and vernier scale (*n* + 1 divisions) read in the same direction, whereas in the *retrograde* vernier, the main scale (*n* divisions) and vernier scale (*n*−1 divisions) read in the opposite direction. Of the two types, the direct vernier is the one that is almost universally employed.

Vernier scales can have any number of divisions (*n*) and are applied to measuring lengths and/or angles on such instruments as micrometers, protractors, sextants, and barometers.

EUGENE A. AVALLONE,
Associate Professor of Mechanical Engineering, City University of New York.

VERNIS MARTIN. See LACQUER; LACQUERWORK—*Europe*.

VERNON, vûr′nən, **Edward,** English admiral: b. Westminster, England, Nov. 12, 1684; d. Nacton, Suffolk, Oct. 30, 1757. He joined the navy in 1700, was elected to Parliament in 1722, and in November 1739, as vice admiral commanding an expedition against the Spanish West Indian colonies, captured Portobelo (Porto Bello). Subsequently he was naval commander in the unsuccessfull sea and land assaults on Cartagena (1741) and Santiago de Cuba (1741) and was dismissed from the navy (1746) in a dispute with the Admiralty.

Known as "Old Grog" because he wore gorgram clothing, Vernon originated the practice (adopted throughout the navy) of diluting the seamen's daily half-pint rum ration with four parts of water (a drink dubbed "grog") instead of issuing it neat, which had tended to cause drunkenness. Lawrence Washington, George Washington's half-brother, served under Vernon at Cartagena and in the admiral's honor gave the name Mount Vernon to his Virginia estate. After Lawrence's death, the estate became the property and home of George Washington and eventually a national shrine.

See also MOUNT VERNON.

VERNON, city, Province of British Columbia, Canada, near the north end of Okanagan Lake. It is served by the Canadian National Railways from Kamloops, by the Canadian Pacific Railway from Sicamous, and by bus services. There is also a municipally owned airport. The surrounding country, including approximately 12,000 acres (4,850 hectares) under irrigation, favors fruit and vegetable production and farming. The principal industries of the city include marketing, canning, and fruit-processing. It is also a fruitpacking center and a shipping center for poultry, eggs, dairy and beef products, and lumber. It was named in 1887 after Forbes George Vernon, a provincial official. Incorporated in 1892, the city has a radio station (CJIB) and a weekly newspaper *(Vernon News)*. The recreational facilities in and near the town for both winter and summer sports are many and varied. Population: 19,987.

ROBERT ENGLAND

VERNON, town, Connecticut, in Tolland County, approximately 12 miles (19 kilometers) by road northeast of Hartford, on the Wilbur Cross Highway. The town is served by a railroad. Covering about 18½ square miles (48 square kilometers) it lies partly in the central lowland of the state, consisting of gently rolling terrain below 300 feet (90 meters) altitude, and partly in the rugged eastern highland with altitudes to more than 500 feet (150 meters).

Vernon is situated in an agricultural area (major crop, potatoes). It contains the urban center of Rockville, and its manufacturing base includes fabric dyeing and finishing and production of envelopes, paper boxes, sound control and television equipment, plastic products, baseballs, fishline, and paint.

Settled from East Windsor in 1726 and North Boltin in 1760, it was incorporated in 1808 and attributes its name to George Washington's Virginia home, Mount Vernon. Rockville was named in 1836 and chartered in 1889. The town is governed by selectmen and town meeting. Pop. 27,974.

ROBERT C. SALE

VERNON, city, Texas, seat of Wilbarger County, situated near the right bank of the Pease River about 10 miles from its confluence with the Red River (forming the boundary with Oklahoma) and 50 miles by road west-northwest of Wichita Falls. Its altitude is 1,205 feet. It is a crossroads of four federal highways and is on the Forth Worth and Denver railroad. The city is a commercial center for a rich cotton- and wheat-growing, ranching, and oil-producing area, and has industries producing clothing, meat products, stock feed, athletic equipment, and metal goods. The W. T. Waggoner estate ranch, comprising over 500,000 acres in southern Wilbarger and neighboring counties, has its headquarters here. There is a radio broadcasting station, KVWC. Founded in 1880 on the cattle trail from Texas to Dodge City, Kans., it was incorporated in 1889 and adopted a commission form of government in 1916. Annual events include a picnic and pageant (May 1) commemorating the cattle crossings at Doan's Crossing on the Red River, and the Santa Rosa Rodeo and Quarter Horse Show (June) held on the Waggoner ranch. Pop. 12,695.

VERNONIA. See IRONWEED.

VERNY. See ALMA-ATA.

VERO BEACH, vēr'ō, city, Florida, Indian River County seat, on the Atlantic about midway down Florida's east coast, 15 miles north of Fort Pierce; altitude 14 feet. Primarily a residential and resort community, with 20 miles of beaches and two golf courses, it is also an important shipping center for the region's citrus farms. Cattle raising, light industry, and tourism are other economic factors. Transportation facilities include two airports and the Intracoastal Waterway (here the Indian River). Vero Beach is known to baseball devotees as the elaborate training base of the Los Angeles (formerly Brooklyn) Dodgers. Settled in 1880, the city was incorporated in 1919 under the name "Vero"; the present name was adopted in 1925. A council-manager plan of government became effective in 1951. Pop. 16,176.

KATHRYN M. OBENAUS.

VERONA, və-rō'nə, It. vā-rō'nä, province, Italy, in the north, in the Veneto Region. It borders on the provinces of Trento on the north, Vicenza and Padova on the east, Rovigo on the south, and Mantova on the southwest. The western boundary runs along the middle of the Lago di Garda, whose opposite shore is part of the Province of Brescia. The area is 1,196 square miles. The terrain is covered in the north by Alpine foothills—including the Monte Baldo and Monti Lessini chains—which slope southward to a fertile plain, part of the Po Valley. The province is well watered by the Adige River and its tributaries; some areas have been reclaimed and there are several hydroelectric power plants. The chief agricultural products are wheat, corn, sugar beets, rice, vegetables, and fruit (especially peaches); there is also stock and silkworm raising. Among the wines produced in Veronese vineyards Valpolicella and Bardolino (red table wines) and Soave (a white wine) are the best known. Red and white marble is quarried, and ocher is found in the hills. There is little manufacturing except in the city of Verona which is the provincial capital; Legnago, Bussolengo, and Villafranca di Verona are mainly agricultural trade centers. Pop. (1951) 645,536.

NELDA CASSUTO.

VERONA, city and commune, Italy, capital of Verona Province and the second most important center (after Venice) of the Veneto Region. It lies 90 miles east of Milan, on both banks of the Adige River, between the foothills of the Monti Lessini and the Po Valley plain. Rich in monuments and art treasures, Verona is also a thriving commercial and industrial center, the site of one of Europe's most important agricultural fairs, and a vital communications hub. Because of its position at the junction of the Milan-Venice and Rome-Brenner Pass railroad lines and highways, it was the target of destructive Allied air raids during World War II; further damage was caused by the retreating Germans, who blew up the nine bridges spanning the Adige. Many of Verona's monuments suffered, and 44 percent of its homes were destroyed, but reconstruction has since been completed. Food processing, printing, and the manufacture of agricultural and industrial machinery, leather products, pharmaceuticals, plastics, and paper are the city's chief activities.

Points of Interest.—There are four major Roman remains: the amphitheater, or Arena, the third largest extant of its kind, a great ellipse where 22,000 people can now be seated on the 44 tiers of steps and where an opera season is held each year; the Arco dei Gavi, dating from the age of Augustus; the Porta dei Borsari, a gate of the old Roman walls; and the theater on the left bank of the Adige, whose remains, buried until 1830, have been restored so that dramatic performances may now be presented there. The busiest and most picturesque square of the city is the Piazza delle Erbe, on the site of the Roman forum, where the daily vegetable and fruit market is held; it is surrounded by picturesque old houses and has a 14th century fountain. In contrast, Piazza dei Signori has a noble appearance; among the beautiful buildings that enclose it are the Loggia del Consiglio, a masterpiece of the Renaissance (late 15th century), attributed to Fra Giocondo; the town hall (1193) with the Lamberti tower; and the Palazzo del Governo, originally the residence of the della Scala family, where Dante and Giotto stayed during their sojourn in Verona. Nearby in a small square are the Arche Scaligere, the monumental Gothic tombs of several members of the della Scala family.

The most imposing building of the city is the Castelvecchio, a fortress built by Cangrande II della Scala in 1354–1357, and completed in 1375; the adjoining Ponte Scaligero has been rebuilt as it was before World War II. The most notable churches are the cathedral (12th–16th centuries), housing Titian's *Assumption;* San Zeno Maggiore, a beautiful Romanesque church of large proportions; the Gothic Sant'Anastasia; the Renaissance Church of San Giorgio; the Benedictine abbey of Santa Maria in Organo; and San Bernardino. The Bevilacqua, Pompei, and episcopal palaces are among the finest in the city. Verona's well-preserved walls, originally built by the della Scala family in the 14th century to supersede the Roman walls, were fortified by the Austrians.

SILBERSTEIN/MONKMEYER

The city of Verona, built on both banks of the Adige River in northern Italy, is among the country's richest in architectural monuments.

History. Nothing definite is known about the founding of Verona; it was inhabited by Rhaetians, Etruscans, and Gauls before its conquest by the Romans in 89 B.C. During the barbarian invasions it was a favorite residence of Theodoric, king of the Ostrogoths (d. 526 A.D.), and of the Lombard king Alboin (d. 573). In 774 it fell to Charlemagne and in the 10th century was given by Emperor Otto I to the dukes of Bavaria. The feudal landowners and rising merchant class cooperated in establishing a free commune in the early 12th century. With other towns of the Veneto, Verona formed (1164) the Veronese League, which developed (1167) into the Lombard League against the German emperors. The city was torn by rivalries among its noble families, an episode of which is depicted by Shakespeare in *Romeo and Juliet*. From 1226 Ezzelino III da Romano, a partisan of Emperor Frederick II, played a leading role in the struggle between Guelphs and Ghibellines and virtually ruled Verona from 1236 until his death in 1259. Then came the rule of the della Scala family, which lasted from 1260 to 1387 and marked the beginning of the most glorious period of the city's political and artistic history. Cangrande I della Scala (r. 1311–1329) was its most prominent and successful member, but his successors were weak, and the Visconti lords of Milan finally caused the family's downfall.

In 1405 Verona voluntarily accepted Venetian rule and enjoyed a long period of peace and prosperity until 1796. First occupied by the French, against whom an unsuccessful uprising took place (the *Pasque Veronesi*, Verona's Easter), it was ceded to Austria in 1797. Except for the years 1801–1814, it remained under Austrian rule until its incorporation into the Kingdom of Italy in 1866; Austria restored its fortifications and made it the main fortress of the Quadrilateral defense system, which played an important role in the wars of the *risorgimento*. The architects Fra' Giocondo (d. 1515) and Michele Sanmicheli (1484–1559) and the painters Pisanello (Antonio Pisano, c. 1395–c. 1455) and Paolo Veronese (Paolo Cagliari or Caliari, 1528–1588) were the most prominent native artists of Verona. Pop. (1971) 264,363.

NELDA CASSUTO

VERONA, borough, New Jersey, in Essex County. Bordered by Montclair, it is seven miles north-northwest of Newark, at an altitude of 255 feet. A residential community, within easy driving distance of New York City, it has modern shopping facilities and a substantial amount of light industry. The municipal center is renowned for its authentic colonial design. Incorporated in 1907, the borough is administered by a mayor and council. Pop. 14,166.

VERONESE, vā-rō-nā'zā, **Paolo** (real name PAOLO CAGLIARI or CALIARA), Venetian painter: b. Verona (whence his nickname), Italy, 1528; d. Venice, April 19, 1588. Through Antonio Badile, his first master, he became a recognizably Venetian painter before migrating to Venice in 1553. In his formative years he had obviously scrutinized the work of such diverse artists as Andrea Mantegna, Giulio Romano, and Il Moretto. Battista

Zelotti, another pupil of Badile, assisted Veronese in some of his early work, including decorations in the Palazzo Ducale (1553). By the late 1550's he had shed his predilection for mannerism and had arrived at a style of his own. About 1560 he produced sumptuous frescoes for the villa that Andrea Palladio had built for the famous Barbaro brothers, Marcantonio and Daniello, at Maser. Somewhat before 1560 he had begun, in the *Supper at Emmaus* (Louvre), that series of banquet pictures which, with an arrogant disregard for the unities of time, place, and action, seek only to vary, in detail and arrangement, one aspect in the life of a society whose luxury has never been surpassed. He introduced many contemporary notables into these highly secularized Biblical feasts: of the 120 figures in the *Marriage at Cana* (Louvre) a large number are recognizable portraits. Whether the *Marriage at Cana* or *Feast in the House of Levi* (Academy, Venice) is his masterpiece among banquet scenes is a question that needs no answer. The latter is certainly the more extravagant of the two, and his use in it of fools, dwarfs, and other curiosities led to his being called before a tribunal of the Inquisition. Accused of making mock of religion, Veronese replied that these motifs had stirred his interest and that, moreover, he had the right to use them decoratively.

In the late 1560's, Veronese began to show that he was at last willing to admit that Tintoretto, his elder by a decade, was a great force; but he was past imitating—he assimilated or borrowed with good-natured condescension. His inventiveness seems never to have flagged. *The Family of Darius Before Alexander* (National Gallery, London) is not good history but is a superb bit of pageantry, with its glowing portraits of the healthy, rich, and happy Pisani family. Religious scenes, mythological scenes, figure painting, and allegories poured from his brush, and as he was deluged with commissions, he employed many assistants in his workshop, including three of his sons and a brother. During his last years he worked on the vast decorative frescoes in the Palazzo Ducale, including *The Rape of Europe* (about 1580) and *The Triumph of Venice* (1578–1585), the latter one of the world's finest painted ceilings. It is, besides, an architectonic triumph, so skillfully managed that his way of solving the problem of a ceiling painting from the spectator's point of view remained a valid convention in Western painting for almost 200 years. *The Triumph of Venice* was Veronese's last gift to his adopted city, where his work quite exceeds Titian's in quantity and may be not less than Tintoretto's. He was a supreme master of decorative art, and his true successor was another Venetian, Giovanni Battista Tiepolo (1696–1770), born more than a century after Veronese's death. Veronese is best represented in the United States by *Mars and Venus United in Love* at the Metropolitan Museum of Art, New York, and by *Wisdom and Strength* and *The Choice of Hercules* in the Frick Collection, New York.

WALLACE BROCKWAY

VERONICA, və-rŏn'ĭ-kə, SAINT, a legendary Judaeo-Christian woman, who, when Jesus carried the Cross through Jerusalem to Calvary (c. 29 A.D.), wiped perspiration from his face with a cloth, which miraculously retained an imprint of

EDITORIAL PHOTOCOLOR ARCHIVES

The grandiose *Triumph of Venice* is a fresco by Veronese on the ceiling of the Palazzo Ducale in Venice.

his countenance. The scene is commemorated in the sixth of the 14 Stations of the Cross portrayed in Roman Catholic churches. Among the various veils purported to be the original cloth, the most celebrated is preserved in St. Peter's Basilica, Rome, Italy. Modern scholars suppose that the name Veronica was corrupted from the Latin phrase *vera icona* (true image), which originally was applied to the likeness itself.

P. R. COLEMAN-NORTON

VERONICA. See SPEEDWELL.

VERRAZANO, vār-rä-tsä'nō, or **VERRAZZANO,** vär-rät-tsä'nō, **Giovanni da,** Italian navigator: b. Greve, near Florence, Italy, ?1485; d. ?1528. In the service of Francis I of France, he led an expedition in 1524 which explored the North American coast from the vicinity of Cape Fear northward probably as far as Cape Breton; during the voyage he discovered New York and Narragansett bays. In 1528 he set out on another transatlantic voyage purportedly to Central America or Brazil and possibly in the hope of finding a passage to Asia; from this voyage he never returned and the circumstances of his death are unknown—although one story holds that he was killed and eaten by natives of an island of Darien (Panama). The Verrazano-Narrows Bridge across New York Bay, begun in 1959 and completed in 1964, was named in his honor.

VERRES, vĕr'ēz, **Gaius,** Roman politician: d. Marseille, France, 43 B.C. After he was quaestor in Rome (82) and proquaestor in Cilicia (79), where he acquired a taste for the fine arts, he became urban praetor in Rome (74). In this last-named magistracy Verres initiated the callous cupidity and the vicious venality which afterward characterized his Sicilian administration and made his name notorious as the most corrupt and the cruelest provincial governor in Roman history. As propraetor of Sicily (73–71), Verres almost ruined the island by maladministration of justice, peculation of provincial funds, extortionate exactions from provincials, mistreatment of both resident Romans and native Sicilians, and, above all, seizure of countless *objets d'art* of every description from public and private sources. The result was his trial on his return to Rome (70).

Though Verres was defended by Quintus Hortensius Hortalus, the leader of the Roman bar, his prosecutor, Marcus Tullius Cicero, destined to be Rome's greatest orator, presented so clear a case against him that after three days in court Verres departed into voluntary exile at Marseille. There he was able to live in luxury on what loot he had exported from Rome before his trial, until Mark Antony, the triumvir, who wanted Verres' wealth, caused his death.

Cicero's seven speeches against Verres give a detailed account of Verres' crimes. In addition, they present a clear picture of cruelty and rapacity that is perhaps unparalleled in classical antiquity.

P. R. Coleman-Norton

VERRI, vär'rē, **Pietro,** Italian political economist and philosopher; b. Milan, Italy, Dec. 12, 1728; d. there, June 28, 1797. Born of a noble family, he studied in Milan, in Rome, and at the College of Nobles in Parma. In 1759 he served as a captain in the Seven Years' War, after which he spent the rest of his life writing on economic and political matters and the reform of civic administration. Although he had a profound influence on the thought of his times, his proposals were generally thwarted by strongly entrenched groups.

From 1762 to 1764 Verri led a group of vocal and aggressive young intellectuals known as the "Accademia dei pugni" because of their lively meetings. In 1764 he founded *Il caffe* (The Coffeehouse), a periodical whose contents were supposedly transcriptions of actual discussions. The articles, many by Verri, dealt with a wide range of subjects, from natural history to medicine, philosophy, music, ethics, law, and literature, all expounding the same theme: the need for social, economic, and political reform. The magazine had considerable impact on contemporary Italian social consciousness.

In 1769 Verri published *Riflessioni sulle leggi vincolanti principalmente nel commercio de' grani* (Thoughts on the Laws Concerning Mainly the Trade in Grains), and two years later his anonymous *Meditazioni sull' economia politica* (Reflections on Political Economy), which was translated into French, German, and Dutch. In these and other writings, Verri supported liberalism and laissez faire, and maintained that the true wealth of a nation is increased by the growth of industry and trade. Disagreeing with the physiocratic principle of the net product, Verri held that taxes are paid by consumers through reduced consumption and not solely from the land. Verri here anticipated the modern concept of the shifting of taxes. In his theory of taxation, as well as in his definition of economic wants, his view of value or price as determined by both utility and scarcity, and in other concepts, Verri presented in germ many ideas which later became important in economic theory.

In *Storia di Milano* (1783), Verri traced Milan's history from the beginning of the Middle Ages to 1447, and in *Decadenza del papato* (Decline of the Papacy), written in 1783 and published in 1825, he argued that the church had fulfilled its historic function and should be deprived of its power, especially in the field of education. Verri was sympathetic toward the French Revolution and held municipal office during the occupation of Milan by the French. At first he showed indulgence toward their excesses, preferring "frenzy to lethargy," as he had done during the Reign of Terror in France; but in the end he appeared disillusioned.

Piero Pieri,
University of Turin.

VERRILL, vĕr'əl, **Addison Emery,** American zoologist: b. Greenwood, Me., Feb. 9, 1839; d. Santa Barbara, Calif., Dec. 10, 1926. Educated at Harvard College, where he graduated from the Lawrence Scientific School in 1862 and was assistant to Louis Agassiz, naturalist, at the Museum of Comparative Zoology from 1860 to 1864, he went to Yale University as professor of zoology in 1864 and held that position for 43 years—until his retirement in 1907. During this period he became an outstanding student, discoverer of new species, classifier, and authority in the field of marine invertebrates; he built up a large zoological collection at the Peabody Museum at Yale, of which he was curator for 43 years (1867–1910), and served for 16 years (1871–1887) as scientific chief of the United States Commission of Fish and Fisheries in southern New England. Verrill's work on marine invertebrates, including sponges, starfish, worms, mollusks, Crustacea, and coral and other coelenterates, extended during his lifetime from the waters of the New England coast and the Gulf Stream to those of the Bermudas, the West Indies, the Pacific coast of North and Central America, and Hawaii. He published important works on invertebrates of Vineyard Sound and adjacent waters (1873), starfishes of the North Pacific coast (1914) and of the West Indies, Florida, and Brazil (1915), and the coelenterates of the Canadian Arctic, as well as many other papers and a two-volume naturalist work, *Bermuda Islands* (1901–1907). For over 50 years (1869–1920) he was associate editor of the *American Journal of Science.*

VERRIO, vĕr'ē-ō, **Antonio,** Italian decorative painter: b. Lecce, Italy, about 1639; d. Hampton Court Palace, near London, England, June 15, 1707. Much of his early life is obscure, although he worked for a time in France. By 1671 he had arrived in England, probably at the invitation of Lord Arlington (Henry Bennet). From 1676 to the revolution of 1688 he was in the employ of Charles II and his successor, James II. The former paid him extremely well, and at Windsor Castle he painted large areas, mostly destroyed during the alterations of the 19th century. His ceilings must have been of great historical interest as reflecting the Stuart version of royal absolutism. Verrio worked at Chatsworth, seat of the duke of Devonshire in Derbyshire, and at Burghley House, that of the earl of Exeter near Stamford, before again becoming a royal painter, first for William III and then for Queen Anne. He painted chiefly at Hampton Court Palace, where much of his work survives. Verrio's success with the later Stuarts was based on the simple formula of being in the right place at the right time. He came forward in a barren period, when there were few painters to compete with him.

WALLACE BROCKWAY, *Former Consultant to the Bollingen Foundation*

VERROCCHIO, vār-rôk'kyō, **Andrea del** (real name ANDREA DI MICHELE DI FRANCESCO CIONE), Italian sculptor, painter, and goldsmith: b. Florence, Italy, 1435; d. Venice, Oct. 7, 1488. Best known as a sculptor, he may have been a pupil of Donatello and has acquired additional prestige from his influence on Leonardo da Vinci, who was his pupil. Verrocchio took his name from his teacher, the goldsmith Giuliano dei Verrocchi. Although his output was rather slight—Bernard Berenson lists 9 paintings, only 5 of which are entirely from his own hand, and 11 pieces of sculpture—his importance is altogether disproportionate to the number of his works.

Like Donatello, Verrocchio was a realist and therefore in the more important of the two currents of Florentine art. Except in detail here and there, he was little influenced by antiquity. The bronze *David* in the Bargello and the *Boy with a Dolphin* in the courtyard of the Palazzo Vecchio, both in Florence, reveal Verrocchio's characteristic style and are among his most popular works. The grandest and most universally praised is the equestrian statue of the military commander Bartolommeo Colleoni, on the Campo San Zanipolo in Venice. This was the last work of Verrocchio's life. He died before he had quite finished the model from which the casting was done, and the statue was completed by Alessandro Leopardi, who also designed the base. Many authorities consider the *Colleoni* the finest existing equestrian statue. Another notable bronze is a life-size group called *Christ and St. Thomas*, which fills one of the exterior niches of Or San Michele in Florence.

The most celebrated of Verrocchio's paintings is the *Baptism of Christ* in the Uffizi, Florence. The angel at the extreme left is in a different style, suggesting that perhaps it was painted by Leonardo. Other works include a sculptured *Angel* (Louvre, Paris); a terra-cotta *Madonna and Child* (Bargello, Florence); a silver relief, the *Beheading of John the Baptist* (Opera del Duomo, Florence); a marble relief of Alexander the Great (National Gallery of Art, Washington, D.C.); the bronze tomb of Cosimo de' Medici (San Lorenzo sacristy, Florence); and several paintings of the *Madonna and Child*, one of which is in the National Gallery of Art, Washington, D.C., and another in the Metropolitan Museum of Art, New York.

ARTHUR K. MCCOMB, *Editor of "Selected Letters of Verrocchio"*

VERS LIBRE, vĕr' lē'brə, a form of verse free from any fixed number of syllables or feet and from other traditional regularities of metrical verse, such as rhyme, hiatus, and caesura. Vers libre achieves internal unity and design by recurrent accents creating the rhythm. The French term has universal acceptance, although the term "free verse" is more commonly applied to this type of poetry in English.

Jean de La Fontaine's *Fables*, John Dryden's *Song for St. Cecilia's Day*, James Macpherson's Ossianic verse, and certain poems by Friedrich Gottlieb Klopstock have been called vers libre or free verse. But these terms are more significantly and characteristically applicable to the experiments of the French symbolists, the poetry of Walt Whitman, and that of some of the later poets of the 19th and 20th centuries.

The association of vers libre with modern poetry is not accidental. Vers libre is an extension of the intense re-elaboration of poetry by romanticism and a reformation which culminated in the poetry of the second half of the 19th century. It is one order of which the spoken language is capable. The modern poet, like anyone else, has had to find new order and has had to look for it first in his own speaking voice. Hence, vers libre is the least conventional of of all verse and the most individual in character.

Vers libre varies more widely than metrical verse in length and structure of grammatical units, and discloses less systematically the design of its movement and the collaboration of its rhythmical units. But it is not different in nature or source from metrical verse. Phonetic experiments, for example, have been conducted by the French linguists Robert de Souza and Georges Lote to prove that the syllable is not the essential constituent of French verse. Jean Baptiste Racine's Alexandrines in *Phèdre*, as read by Sarah Bernhardt, proved to have 13 and 14 syllables; Edmond Rostand, as read by Coquelin aîné, to have an Alexandrine once in every three lines only. George L. Trager and Henry L. Smith (*An Outline of English Structure*, 1951) have shown in effect that traditional English prosody rests on misleading elements of regularity and that pitch, intensity, and duration are as characteristic of regular as of vers libre. The Spanish scholar Tomás Navarro (*Métrica española*, 1956) shows that vers libre is as much governed by an accent of duration as is regular verse.

"No verse is free," T. S. Eliot has said, "for the man who cares to write poetry" ("Reflections on Vers Libre," *New Statesman*, March 3, 1917). Arno Holz in Germany, Vladimir Mayakovski in the USSR, Arthur Rimbaud, Jules Laforgue, and Guillaume Appolinaire in France, Giuseppe Ungaretti in Italy, Jorge L. Borges in Argentina, Vicente Huidobro in Chile, Federico García Lorca in Spain, and Carl Sandburg and others in the United States are among the modern poets who have found a new discipline of feeling and thought in vers libre.

EUGENIO C. VILLICANA, *Assistant Professor of Comparative Literature, Bard College.*

VERSAILLES, vĕr-sä'y; Eng. vər-sī', city, France, capital of Seine-et-Oise Department, place of residence and the court of the kings of France before the French Revolution, and, since the Concordat of 1801 with the Vatican, the seat of a bishopric. Situated on a plateau 12 miles west-southwest of Paris, it is also an important military and administrative center, and has metalworks and a national agricultural research station. The population in 1961 was 84,445.

The city of Versailles was deliberately designed in relation to its famous château, built by Louis XIV in the 17th century. The vast elongated palace of pink and cream stone, consisting of three wings extending from a central square, stands on an eminence facing west and east; its gardens and park lie to the west, where the terrain descends from a broad terrace, while the residential section of the city lies to the east, with its three main avenues converging symmetrically on the Place d'Armes, fronting the palace. The town derived its first century of livelihood from the activities of the court, and expanded with the addition of numerous government buildings and private residences; however, its newer districts are of relatively recent origin. Versailles, to this day, remains a quiet residential town, with several notable buildings, such as the Cathedral of St. Louis (1743–1754), besides the palace. It is one of the great tourist attractions of the Paris metropolitan area.

Camera Press Ltd.

View of the palace at Versailles, showing a part of the celebrated Hardouin-Mansart façade. The urn stands at the corner of a terrace which overlooks the gardens.

History of the Palace.—The first château at Versailles was built by Louis XIII (r. 1610–1643), an enthusiastic huntsman who erected in 1623 a small hunting lodge in the Val de Galie amid surrounding woodlands. His son, Louis XIV (r. 1643–1715), decided as early as 1660 to enlarge this estate and turn it into the most splendid residence in Europe. Accordingly, he gathered around him a brilliant team of artists who, from 1665 to 1683, completed the immense palace, large enough to hold the court and its officers. These artists were the architect Louis Le Vau (1612–1670), who was succeeded on his death by Jules Hardouin-Mansart (1646–1708); the landscape gardener André Le Nôtre (1613–1700), and the painter Charles Le Brun (1619–1690).

To these four men is owed most of the beauty that visitors can admire today. In designing the park, Le Nôtre created the most perfect type of formal French gardens. He also is responsible for the long straight avenues enclosing groves and fountains ornamented with marble, bronze, and gilded lead statues, and for the immense vistas for which Versailles is noted, particularly those of the Swiss Lake south of the palace and the mile-long Grand Canal extending beyond the gardens, where Louis XIV staged so many water festivities.

The 730-yard-long façade overlooking the gardens is chiefly the work of Hardouin-Mansart, and is considered a masterpiece of French classical style. Its main body contains the state apartments of the king and queen, connected by the famous Hall of Mirrors, which Le Brun and his team decorated with marble, paintings, gilded bronze sculpture, and 483 mirrors. On the east side, overlooking the entrance court, are the private apartments of the king and queen, whose present design stems mostly from the reigns of Louis XV (r. 1715–1774) and Louis XVI (r. 1774–1793). In the park, which today covers more than 20 acres, are the minor buildings erected by Louis XIV, Louis XV, and Louis XVI, including the Grand Trianon of white and pink marble, with Hardouin-Mansart's famous colonnade, and the Petit Trianon of Louis XV. Near the latter is Marie Antoinette's Hamlet, where she played at being a shepherdess, far from the strict etiquette of the French court.

The Versailles Museum.—At the outbreak of the revolution in 1789, the royal family was removed from Versailles by revolutionaries and taken to Paris. The furniture was sold as well as some of the paintings and works of art in the royal collections. However, in 1833 Louis Philippe (r. 1830–1848) ordered the establishment of a museum of French history in the palace. This is recalled by the inscription under the pediments: *A toutes les gloires de la France* (To all the glories of France). A part of the palace thus became a museum. Since then, with further enrichment of its collections—now numbering thousands of paintings, statues, pieces of furniture, tapestries, and other works of art—the palace has become one of the world's leading historical museums. At the same time, the untouched setting of the main part of the apartments enables the visitor to recall the prerevolutionary days of the *ancien régime.*

Notable Events at Versailles.—The declaration suspending hostilities between Great Britain and the United States in the American Revolution was signed at Versailles on Jan. 20, 1783 (the definitive peace treaty was signed in Paris on Sept. 3, 1783). During the Franco-Prussian War of 1870–1871, Versailles was the headquarters of German armies besieging Paris, and on Jan. 18, 1871, William I was crowned emperor of Germany in the Hall of Mirrors. During World War I Versailles was the seat of the Allied War Council, and the Treaty of Versailles was signed in the Hall of Mirrors on June 28, 1919. During World War II Allied General Headquarters were located at Versailles from September 1944 to May 1945. Today the palace is used for state receptions to distinguished guests. On such occasions splendid festivities take place, with illuminations, water displays in the park, and gala performances in the Salle de l'Opéra built for Louis XV by Jacques Ange Gabriel in 1768–1770.

GÉRALD VAN DER KEMP,
Conservateur en Chef du Musée de Versailles et des Trianons.

Further Reading: Arthaud, G., *The Fully Illustrated Guide to the Treasures of Versailles* (1935; reprint, Foundation for Classical Reprints 1984); Berger, R. W. *Versailles* (Penn. State Univ. Press 1985).

VERSAILLES, vər-sālz′, city, Kentucky, seat of Woodford County, located 13 miles west of Lexington at an altitude of 923 feet. It is on two federal highways and the Southern Railway (freight only). In the bluegrass agricultural region (tobacco, bluegrass seed, livestock, dairy products, poultry, hemp), it has manufactures of whisky, clothing, boats, and brooms, and has flour and feed mills. Margaret Hall School, an Episcopal school for girls, is here. Nearby are Pisgah Presbyterian Church (1812) and Buck Pond (1784), home of Thomas Marshall, father of John Marshall (1735–1855), United States chief justice. It is governed by a mayor and council. Pop. 6,427.

VERSAILLES, Treaty of, vər-sī′, the major treaty ending World War I, signed at Versailles, France, on June 28, 1919, and in force on Jan. 10, 1920, following ratification by Germany and four of the Principal Allied and Associated Powers, Great Britain, France, Italy, and Japan. It was not ratified by the United States which made a separate treaty of peace with Germany in 1921 incorporating much of the Treaty of Versailles by reference. The lesser Allied powers, except China, were also parties. Separate treaties of peace were made subsequently with Germany's allies, Austria, Hungary, Bulgaria, and Turkey.

The Treaty of Versailles was based on the pre-armistice agreement among the Allies of Nov. 5, 1918, and the armistice with Germany of Nov. 11, 1918, accepting President Woodrow Wilson's Fourteen Points as the basis for peace, with modification by the Allies of the points dealing with freedom of the seas, reparations, and the status of the Habsburg empire which had, in fact, broken up.

The treaty was negotiated in two stages. The Paris Conference of the Allies from December 1918 to May 1919, dominated by the Council of Four (President Wilson of the United States, Prime Minister David Lloyd George of the United Kingdom, Prime Minister Georges Clemenceau of France, and Prime Minister Vittorio Orlando of Italy) resulted in a practically complete draft. The negotiations, mostly by exchange of notes, by the Allies with Germany followed from May 7, 1919 to June 23, 1919. Germany protested that the treaty violated many of the Fourteen Points and imposed impossible economic burdens, but the Allies denied most of these contentions and made only minor changes in the draft which Germany reluctantly signed.

The League of Nations Covenant constituted the first section of the treaty. Apart from its general functions of maintaining peace, encouraging disarmament, and promoting international cooperation, important functions were delegated to the League in connection with certain territories renounced by Germany in other sections of the treaty.

Germany renounced territory in Europe to Poland (the larger part of Posen and West Prussia, including the Polish Corridor), to France (Alsace-Lorraine), and to Belgium (Eupen, Malmédy, and Moresnet), and ceded its leasehold in Shantung, China, to Japan (which restored it to China at the Washington Conference of 1922–1923). International arrangements for the Saar Valley, Danzig, and Memel were placed under the supervision of the League of Nations. Most of these territories as well as several others, including Upper Silesia, Schleswig, and the East Prussian districts of Allenstein and Marienwerder, were subject to plebiscites. Some of them, including northern Schleswig (which joined Denmark) and the areas assigned to Belgium, voted themselves out of Germany, while others (Allenstein, Marienwerder, southern Schleswig, part of Upper Silesia, and the Saar Valley) chose to remain in Germany. Alsace-Lorraine, however, which had been ceded by France to Germany in 1871, and the Polish Corridor area were not subjected to plebiscites. Germany also renounced all its overseas colonies in favor of the Principal Allied and Associated Powers who were obliged to place them under mandate of the League of Nations. The mandates were actually given to the Allied powers which had occupied the territories during the war. Most have subsequently become independent states.

Germany was required to pay reparations, over and beyond damages, as contemplated by the Fourteen Points, resulting from breaches of the law of war and of the guaranteed neutrality of Belgium. In accordance with the "war guilt clause," Germany accepted responsibility to compensate the Allies and their nationals for all the losses consequent upon the war imposed on them "by the aggression of Germany and her allies." This provision was qualified by consideration of Germany's capacity to pay, on which estimates by the Allies varied from $10 billion (Great Britain) to $100 billion (France). Final determination of this matter was left to the Reparations Commission on which it was intended that the United States should exert a moderating influence. The United States, however, withdrew from the treaty and the ultimate demand of the commission was for $33 billion, more than twice the original United States estimate.

The treaty imposed drastic limitations on German armaments and trade, internationalized several rivers and the Kiel Canal, and demilitarized a 30-mile-wide belt on the right bank of the Rhine, and provided sanctions in the form of Allied occupations of defined zones of German territory for a maximum period of 15 years.

France had accepted guarantees of the League of Nations Covenant and special alliances with Great Britain and the United States in lieu of extensive territorial cessions which it first demanded of Germany. When American withdrawal weakened these guarantees, France felt insecure and sought to continue occupation of German territory in the Ruhr Valley on the ground that Germany had defaulted in reparations obligations. This led to German economic resistance, galloping inflation of the German currency, and differences between Great Britain and France, the former favoring moderation of reparations and occupation policies, especially after the severe criticisms of the economic consequences of the peace by the British economist, John Maynard Keynes.

These differences and American withdrawal prevented strict enforcement of the treaty and encouraged Germany, after the collapse of its currency, to engage in a campaign for revision. Adolf Hitler, during his rise, constantly denounced the "*Dictat von Versailles*" and in the 1930's, after he had come to power and the general disarmament conference of 1932–1933 had failed, he repudiated the armament and reparations clauses of the treaty. The withdrawal of the United States, the differences among the Allies, the German economic collapse, the rise of communism in Russia and of fascism in Italy, and the propaganda of Hitler were more important than the actual terms of the Treaty of Versailles itself in bringing about its eventual failure and in the initiation of World War II 20 years after its signature.

The most significant features of the treaty were its initiation of the general system of international organization in the League of Nations and the World Court, continued as an outgrowth of World War II in the United Nations, and its development of the principle of self-determination, a phrase originated by the Soviet government but implied by President Wilson's Fourteen Points. This principle was the basis of the territorial dispositions of the treaty, the application of plebiscites, and the mandate system for liquidating empires, carried further by provisions of the United Nations Charter for self-determination, trusteeships, and nonself-governing territories.

See also DISARMAMENT; FOURTEEN POINTS; WORLD WAR I—15. *Diplomatic History of the War* (The Peace Conferences and Peace Treaties).

QUINCY WRIGHT,
Professor of Foreign Affairs, University of Virginia.

Bibliography

Dockrill, Michael, and Goold, Douglas J., *Peace Without Promise: Britain and the Peace Conferences, 1919–1923* (Shoe String 1981).

House, Edward M., *Intimate Papers of Colonel House*, ed. by Charles Seymour, 4 vols. (1928; reprint, Scholarly Press 1971).

Keynes, John M., *The Collected Writings*, vols. 2 and 3 (Cambridge 1971–1972).

Lentin, A., *Lloyd George, Woodrow Wilson, and the Guilt of Germany: An Essay in the Prehistory of Appeasement* (La. State Univ. Press 1985).

VERSE, vûrs. The term "verse" has been used with widely different meanings. Perhaps its most specific use has been for a single line of metrical composition and, less frequently, for a stanza. It has also been applied to metrical composition in general. While this is an extremely ancient usage, there has always competed with it a third and wider application of the term, to poetry as such. Thus, Plato (*Republic*, 601 B) suggests that the essence of poetry is "rhythm, meter and harmony," that whatever is versified is poetry. He is supported by later theorists like Julius Caesar Scaliger and Richard Whately. On the other hand, Aristotle (*Poetics*, 1447 b) objects that medicine or physical philosophy can be versified but will have nothing in common with Homer except a meter. Many theorists have seconded his objection; Sir Philip Sidney, for example, observes that the elements of verse are only an "ornament and no cause" of poetry. Given, especially, an extensive tradition of didactic and rhetorical work in verse—and now of modern advertising—it seems necessary to agree with these objections.

Thus, a twofold distinction is required. Whatever the basis for the distinction between *poetry* and *prose* (it would seem to involve a difference in the structuring of meaning as well as of sound and, ultimately, a different role for structure as such), the distinction between *verse* and *prose* can be made rather simply. Verse can be thought of as speech with a regular pattern or structure of sound; this may be of the *quantities* of sound, as in an iambic meter, or of the *qualities* of sound, as in rhyme or assonance, or of both these aspects of sound (see VERSIFICATION). Prose is speech without any sustained patterning of these elements. At the extreme of the verse quality, speech presents the effect of repetitiveness and of system. At the extreme of the prose quality, the sound of speech suggests a continuity of difference and a series. But between these extremes, of course, some of the patterns of verse do occasionally occur in prose, as in the consciously cultivated terminal rhythms of Greek and Latin orators. Similarly, between the extraordinary quality of poetry and the plainness of grammatical statement, there exists the middle ground of rhetoric and literary prose.

If verse is not to be identified completely with poetry, it is clear, nevertheless, that most of its history and development have been in connection with poetic effort. This is particularly true of the definition of basic rhythms and meters and the elaboration of stanzaic forms in the various modern literatures. The beginnings of verse, on the other hand, antedate the most ancient literatures. It is not necessary, however, to assume from the early appearance of verse that "warbling rose/Man's voice in verse before he spoke in prose." It may only be that by the time writing systems were invented, usually relatively late in the history of a language, verse was so highly esteemed that it was committed to written form before prose.

See also POETRY; RHYME.

BROTHER FIDELIAN BURKE, F.S.C.,
Academic Vice President and Professor of English, La Salle College.

VERSIFICATION, vûr-sə-fə-kā'shən, the act, art, or practice of making poetic lines or verses. In particular, versification is concerned with the patterns of sound which characterize verse. Such patterns are studied for the practical purpose of explaining some of the elementary conventions for writing verse and, as in the scansion taught in schools, for reading it properly. More detailed study may seek to understand how verse was written by one poet or by a group of poets in one or more historical periods. Descriptions of this type may further provide the basis for judgments about the aesthetic value of poems or for theorizing about the nature and function of sound patterns in verse and about poetry itself.

Patterns of sound in verse are of two general types—qualitative and quantitative. First are those patterns which involve the repetition and variation of the kinds or qualities of speech sounds. By this is meant those elements which differentiate one sound or letter from another, as *a* from *o* or *b* from *k* without reference to the intensity, duration, or musical pitch with which either sound is pronounced. These latter are the quantitative elements and are the basis for another large design of sound in verse. In the study of a poem's versification, both of these designs of sound, the qualitative and the quantitative, are considered in abstraction from the various patterns of meaning with which they occur simultaneously. But it is in the harmonious interplay of all such patterns that the poem exists and is enjoyed.

Design for Qualities of Sound.—Rhyme, alliteration, assonance, and other figures usually associated with the "melody" of verse are basically repetitions of the qualities of sounds, of their inherent characters. The most important of these figures are repetitions of whole syllables or of parts of syllables. Thus *rhyme* may repeat a whole syllable (supp*lied* . . . rep*lied*) or an essential part of a syllable (br*aid* . . . j*ade*)—normally, that is, the vowel and any consonant which may follow it. Complete repetition of syllables (*braid* . . . *braid*) has not been considered normal rhyme. As in other figurations and designs, a play of sameness and difference is expected. Hence, in normal rhyme, initial consonants contrast with syllabic elements otherwise repeated (r*aid* . . . m*ade*).

Two major varieties of rhyme are traditionally distinguished: *masculine,* which repeats the final stressed syllables of words (ar*cade* . . . bro*cade*) and *feminine,* which begins the repetition on a syllable other than the last (t*ending* . . . m*ending*). Repetition of more than one syllable in masculine rhyme is unusual (r*ecline* . . . d*ecline*), but is normal, of course, in feminine (th*undering* . . . s*undering*). Such richness of repetition may extend to lines and whole stanzas of refrain. However, in modern verse, especially, even full single rhymes are sometimes avoided for more subtle figurations called *imperfect* or *slant rhymes* (*blade* . . . *bled, cat* . . . *cad*) which only approximate one of the elements of repetition. Between the extremes of complete sameness (*braid* . . . *braid*) and complete difference (*braid* . . . *so*), slant rhyme moves beyond normal rhyme in the direction of difference.

Taking the same direction are some of the simpler traditional figures, such as alliteration, consonance, and assonance, and the less formal patterns of repeated sounds which occur in verse. While there is not complete agreement about terminology, *alliteration* is the name usually given to the repetition of a consonant or vowel at the beginning of words: "*D*oom is *d*ark and *d*eeper." *Consonance* repeats the same consonantal sound after different accented vowels, as in *pressed* . . . *past,* while *assonance* repeats the same vowel with different consonants following, as in *man* . . . *hat.* What also differentiates these simpler figures from the whole family of rhymes is the fact that the character of the syllable is not repeated. Even the repetition of *p* . . . *t* in a slant rhyme like *pit* . . . *pat* creates the effect that part of a syllable is being repeated. When only a single sound is repeated in contrasting syllabic contexts, as *p* in *tip* . . . *pool* or in *pit* . . . *pool,* the effect is quite different.

Beyond these figures, there are an indeterminate number of more random and casual phonetic echoes, as, for instance, the patterns of *r, s,* and *n* which support the alliteration of *rains* . . . *ruins* in Swinburne's line: "Fo*r* winte*r's* *rains* and *ruins* a*r*e over." While all these figurations are basically repetitions of qualitative or so-called "segmental" elements of sound, it is clear that "suprasegmental" features like stress affect the formalization and, in large measure, the conspicuousness of sound patterns. Thus, a stressed syllable is not ordinarily rhymed with an unstressed, and *end rhyme* (that is, rhyme at the end of metrical lines) is normally more conspicuous than *internal rhyme* (rhyme at the middle and end of the same line). Modern descriptive linguistics has provided the researcher with rather precise tools for weighing the effect of these factors.

In most cases, patterns of the qualities of sound present themselves as distinct but sporadic concentrations of similarity in a sequence of dissimilar syllables. The total design of sound qualities embraces, of course, the distinct patterns as well as their less organized background. Many of the finer effects of verse depend upon the poet's "ear" for the proper adjustment of pattern and background as much as on the conscious creation of the figures themselves.

Qualitative figures of sound play a role in the verse of all languages. End rhyme, for example, frequently contributes to the elaboration of larger metrical systems like stanzas. Rhyme was, however, practically unknown in classical Greek or Latin verse, though it became a familiar feature in medieval Latin and thence in the Romance languages. It is basic to Chinese verse, but generally avoided in Japanese. Arabic is peculiar in using a single rhyme throughout a poem. Assonance is also frequent in Romance verse of all periods, while alliteration is a prominent feature of early Germanic verse. The older forms of Celtic verse, especially Welsh, employ all the forms of qualitative figuration of sound in the greatest elaboration. The taste for richness in such figuration varies considerably; especially identified with this taste in English poetry since the early Renaissance are John Skelton, Edmund Spenser, William Shakespeare, John Milton, John Keats, Edgar Allan Poe, Algernon Swinburne, Gerard Manley Hopkins, and Dylan Thomas.

Design for Quantities of Sound.—The study of the sound patterns usually called rhythm and meter has generally been more systematic and detailed than the corresponding analysis of rhyme and other design of the qualities of sound. The term *prosody* is often applied to the former study, as is *metrics* and, less frequently, *rhythmics.* Prosodic study began quite early in the West. Aristotle, for example, already invokes a tradition of such study as he discusses in *The Poetics* (see POETICS OF ARISTOTLE, THE) the appropriateness of certain meters to satire, tragedy, and epic, and in the *Rhetoric,* the use of less obtrusive rhythms by the orator. The philosopher is important, too, for drawing a clear distinction (*Poetics,* 1447a, ll. 18ff.) between the art of poetry, with its own patterning of sound, and the arts of music and dance with which it had been and would continue to be closely associated. Aristotle's pupil Aristoxenus of Tarentum wrote a treatise on rhythm; part of the second book survives. The earliest complete treatise on metrics extant is by Hephaestion (130–169 A.D.). Like most of his predecessors, Hephaestion offers more information on types of metrical feet than on the precise basis of Greek meter.

From the beginning, however, there has been general agreement about the large object of prosodic study: it is the quantitative aspects of sound (length or duration, relative pitch, and intensity or force) and, in particular, the harmonious patterning of these elements in the flow of speech. For a poet creates a rhythm or meter by arranging the elements of conspicuousness or emphasis operating in his ordinary language. Rather than the haphazard prose arrangement of emphases, though, in a sentence like "The plowman is plodding his weary way homeward" (o ó o o ó o o ò o ó ó o), a poet like Thomas Gray may create a more formal and stylized pattern with "The plowman homeward plods his weary way" (o ó o ó o ó o ó o ó).

Types of Basic Rhythm.—The conventions which govern the creation of such patterns and, indeed, the particular quantifiable elements which may be patterned, vary from language to language and even, at times, from period to period of the same language. In Indo-European a basic type of meter seems to have utilized the lengths of speech sound and this mode developed into the "durational" or so-called "quantitative" meters of Sanskrit and Greek. A basic principle affecting these meters in Greek was the distinction between short and long syllables, the latter considered twice the length of the former. Various combinations of long and short syllables were possible; the resulting elementary units (*feet*) could then be repeated to form a longer rhythmic series. In Greek epic verse, for example, the dactylic foot (one long syllable followed by two shorts: ¯˘˘) was repeated with only occasional variations by other feet of equal duration, like the spondee (two long syllables: ¯¯). The regular patterned effect of alternating long and short durations was further formalized by the division of the whole metrical series into lines which, though they might vary from 12 to 17 syllables, had an equal durational value (namely, 24 short syllables). Other common feet besides the dactyl and spondee were the iamb (˘¯), anapaest (˘˘¯), trochee (¯˘), pyrrhic (˘˘), cretic (¯˘¯), paeon (¯˘˘˘), and choriamb (¯˘˘¯). More complicated than the regularly repeated dactylic verses of epic or the iambic lines of dramatic dialogue were the meters of Greek lyric. In these, different feet were combined in large rhythmic phrases (*cola*) and then arranged in stanzas.

Early Latin meters, in particular the Saturnian verse of Lucius Livius Andronicus and Gnaeus Naevius, appear to have been constructed on the basis of syllabic intensities rather than durations. But under the prevailing influence of Greek culture the "quantitative" system was adopted some time before the end of the 2d century B.C. Thereafter one finds Virgil imitating the dactylic verse of Homer, and Horace and other lyric poets the stanzas of Sappho and Alcaeus.

In the first centuries of Christianity, however, the linguistic distinction of long and short syllables fell into decay. At the same time, poets like St. Augustine and St. Ambrose introduced hymn meters in which lines had an equal number of syllables and concluded with simple rhymes. In addition, rhythmic figures similar to the end patterns of classical prose (*clausulae* or *cursus*) occurred in the middle and end of these lines. It was, perhaps, the extension of these patterns, based now on the intensities of regular word accents rather than on the duration of syllables, that led to a fully accentual meter. The transition, observable in hymns like the *Pange Lingua Gloriosi* and *Vexilla Regis Prodeunt* of Venantius Fortunatus (c. 530–c. 600), was completed by the 10th century; the earlier quantitative system, however, continued an artificial existence into the Renaissance. The versifications of the various Romance languages inherited from medieval Latin the principle of stable line length maintained by count of syllables. Their fundamental rhythmic effects, though, depend more on the manipulation of pauses and of stronger and weaker syllables in the phrases created by pauses, than on the regular recurrence of an accentual foot. In its long history, therefore, Latin verse utilized different aspects of sound as the basis of its verse rhythms. Originally this basis was intensity, in the classical period it became duration, and later it returned to intensity. (The other quantifiable element of sound, pitch, is never used as the basis of rhythm and meter; but in some languages, notably Chinese, it is used as an important adjunct to a rhythm the basis of which is count of syllables.)

Total Rhythmic Design.—The total design for the quantities of sound is, however, more complicated than the steady pulse of a meter or the looser harmony of a rhythm. Even in a very regular accentual meter, the simple alternation of light and heavy stresses has its variations. To begin with, there is some inequality in the stresses being patterned. For example, phrases like "and thus invoke" (o ó o ó), "another's hermitage" (o ó o ó o o), and "half-acre tombs" (ò ó o ó) all have iambic cadences, though various degrees of light and heavy stress occur. The iambic cadence requires simply that a less conspicuous sound precede a more conspicuous one. The measure of more or less is a relative one provided by the immediate context of syllables; it tolerates a certain range of difference. Another element of complexity is *metrical variation,* or the use of feet different from the one normally repeated. In English iambic meter, for instance, a trochee is frequently used to begin a line. This is the case in the first line of Shakespeare's Sonnet 30, which also has a pyrrhic and a spondee: "When to the sessions of sweet silent thought" (ó o o ó o o ó ó o ó).

More subtle variations are provided by the natural *groups* into which syllables fall as they cluster around strong stresses. Such groups are then separated by slight hesitations and pauses. For example, "tomorrow and tomorrow and tomorrow" (o ó o, ò o ó o, ò o ó o). Grouping occurs in all speech, but, with the greater deliberateness used to enunciate verse, groups in verse tend to be smaller and more frequent. The boundaries of groups may coincide with or overlap the boundaries of feet and thus provide a play between the conspicuousness of the two kinds of units. One can contrast, for example, the two textures in these passages of iambic meter from John Donne's "Canonization":

And if unfit for tombes and hearse
Our legend bee, it will be fit for verse

o ó, o ó, o ó, o ó,
o ó o, ó, o ó, o ó, o ó

As well a well wrought urne becomes
The greatest ashes, as halfe-acre tombs

o ó, o ò ó, ó, o ó,
o ó o, ó o, o ò ó o, ó

Given the basic rhythmic effect with its consistent or varying textures, the total design for the quantities of sound is further developed by larger systems and balances. For instance, in metrical verse like Alfred E. Housman's "To an Athlete Dying Young," the basic but varied pattern is iambic. This serial recurrence is sectioned into lines of four feet. (The lines in eight instances are varied by omission of a syllable and once by the suggestion of a *run-on line,* that is, a line in which a phrase is carried on to the next line.) The lines are then combined in *couplets* and the couplets repeated in seven four-line stanzas or *quatrains:*

The time you won your town the race
We chaired you through the market-place;
Man and boy stood cheering by,
And home we brought you shoulder-high.

Thus, a total rhythmic design is usually a complex hierarchy of line and stanza patterns developed from the basic rhythm of the poem and elaborated within individualized norms of repetition and variation.

Line and Stanza Patterns.—The names of metrical lines have traditionally indicated the basic foot and the number of times it is repeated or varied in the line: iambic dimeter, anapaestic trimeter, trochaic pentameter, and so forth. Stanzas combine lines of similar or different lengths and emphasize their unity by a pattern of end rhymes. The history of versification traces the rise and fluctuating popularity of a great variety of line and stanza patterns. In the verse of different languages, these patterns frequently become associated with special forms and genres of literature. The dactylic hexameter, for example, was associated chiefly with classical epic. It was combined with a dactylic pentameter in the *elegiac distich,* a couplet that was a staple of Latin love poetry. Among Romance poets, the troubadours of Provence were especially inventive in stanzaic patterns, sometimes with intricate rhyme schemes, like the *ballade, rondeau, triolet,* and *sestina.* Their followers in Italy produced the intertwining tercets called *terza rima* and the *sonnet,* a 14-line stanza with a slightly variable rhyme scheme. The latter was to have a distinguished history in most European literatures, and especially in English with Wyatt, Spenser, Sidney, Shakespeare, Donne, Milton, Wordsworth, Keats, and others. Comparable to the popularity of the sonnet in Western literature is the *hokku* in Japanese poetry; this is a short "stanza" of 17 syllables divided into 3 lines of 5, 7, and 5 syllables respectively. Among important lineal forms in the modern period have been the iambic pentameter in English (rhymed in couplets or "blank"), the 12–syllable iambic *Alexandrine* in French, and the hendecasyllabic in Italian. Major stanza forms utilizing the iambic pentameter in English are *rhyme royal* (rhyming a b a b b cc), the *Spenserian stanza* (a b a b b c b cc), which ends with an Alexandrine, and *ottava rima* (a b a b a b cc), borrowed from Italian narrative poetry, as, for instance, by Lord Byron for his *Don Juan.* These and numerous other types continue to flourish despite the 19th and 20th century experiments in *free verse,* which sought original effects outside the conventions of metrical, lineal, and stanzaic patterns.

The variety of contemporary English verse reflects a rich and complex history. Unfortunately the details of this history and even the fundamental nature of the rhythms involved are still matters of debate by prosodists. Existing differences of opinion can be surveyed in Thomas S. Omond's *English Metrists* (Oxford and New York 1921) and Pallister Barkas' *A Critique of Modern English Prosody* (Halle, Germany, 1934).

The nature of accentual meter is especially debated. Some maintain that its rhythm depends on recurring cadences of syllables more and less conspicuously stressed, others that it is a matter of recurring isochronous durations (that is, of feet or of intervals between stresses). It is generally agreed that in addition to *metrical verse,* there are at least two other varieties of English verse that demand a different kind of analysis. Old English *stress verse* or *alliterative verse,* practiced into the Renaissance and revived in the 19th century by S. T. Coleridge and G. M. Hopkins, had basically a loose rhythm of natural groups. In the repeated line unit, however, a sense of isochronous balance was created by the use of a determinate number of heavily stressed (often alliterated) syllables and by a strong medial pause. *Free verse* of the 19th and 20th centuries relies for its rhythmic effects on a simple combination of different but harmonious cadences of natural groups. In the poetry of Ezra Pound, T. S. Eliot, and their followers, it is influenced to some extent by the separate traditions of metrical verse and stress verse.

See also HEROIC VERSE; LITERATURE; ODE; POETRY; RHYME; SONNET; VERSE.

BROTHER FIDELIAN BURKÈ, F.S.C.,
Academic Vice President and Professor of English, La Salle College.

Bibliography

Bright, John W., and Miller, Raymond O., *The Elements of English Versification* (1910; reprint, Folcroft 1973).
Brooks, Cleanth, and Warren, Robert Penn, *Understanding Poetry,* 4th ed. (Holt 1976).
Carruth, William H., *Verse Writing* (1925; reprint, Norwood Eds. 1980).
Chatham, Seymour, *Theory of Meter* (Mouton Pub. 1964).
Crapsey, Adelaide, *A Study in English Metrics* (1918; reprint, Longwood 1977).
Cutler, A., and Ladd, D. R., eds., *Prosody: Models and Measurement* (Springer-Verlag 1983).
Fraser, G. S., *Metre, Rhyme, and Free Verse* (Methuen 1970).
Galyon, Aubrey E., *The Art of Versification: Matthew of Vendome* (Iowa State Univ. Press 1980).
Gross, Harvey, *The Structure of Verse,* rev. ed. (Ecco Press 1980).
Kaluza, Max, *A Short History of English Versification* (1911; reprint, Folcroft 1972).
Scott, Clive, *The French Verse-Art* (Cambridge 1980).
Woods, Susanne, *Natural Emphasis: English Versification from Chaucer to Dryden* (Huntington Lib. Pub. 1985).

VERST, vûrst, vĕrst (also VERSTA or VERSTE), a Russian measure of length equal to 0.6629 of a mile.

VERSUNKENE GLOCKE, Die. See HAUPTMANN, GERHART.

VERT, Cape. See CAPE VERDE.

VERTEBRA, a segment of the backbone. See ANATOMY, COMPARATIVE; BONE; MAMMALS.

VERTEBRATA, vûr-tə-brā'tə, all those animals that have a backbone or vertebral column as their axial supporting skeleton. The name is derived from the Latin *vertebratus,* meaning jointed. The group includes the primitive, jawless lamprey, all kinds of fish, the amphibians, the reptiles, the birds, and the mammals. The vertebrates themselves belong to a somewhat more inclusive animal group known as the Chordata which, in addition to the vertebrates, includes two marine types, the tunicates and *Amphioxus.* All of these have certain fundamental features in common that set them aside from the rest of the animal kingdom. These are (1) the notochord, which is the forerunner of the vertebral column both in evolution and in individual development; (2) a dorsal, tubular nerve cord; (3) gill slits on either side, opening from the throat to the exterior of the body; and (4) a heart on the ventral side of the body. In vertebrates only, a series of vertebrae develop around the notochord. In addition to the axial skeleton, and associated with it, is a series of muscular blocks or segments on each side of the body. This segmentation of the musculature is reflected in the segmental arrangement of the vertebrae, the spinal nerves and arteries, and to some extent in the excretory organs or kidneys.

Locomotion in aquatic vertebrates is effected by muscle contraction initiated in the muscle segments behind the head and transmitted as a wave passing down the length of the body to the tail. In the primitive cyclostomes, of which the lamprey is a common example, a longitudinal dorsal and ventral fin alone serves to stabilize the forward movement. In all fishes two sets of paired fins, the pectoral and pelvic fins respectively, each with an internal supporting skeletal girdle, serve as additional stabilizers and controls. Fish also have true jaws, whereas the more primitive cyclostomes have only a circular, jawless mouth.

The more fundamental features common to all vertebrates are well established in the aquatic forms. The vertebrate head is primarily a region of fused body segments with which are associated pairs of sense organs. The sense organs relate to perception of the environment and to analysis of food. Perception of the environment includes vision, represented by the eyes in their orbits; the nasal organs of smell, for the detection of chemicals brought from a distance; and the detection of water flow and pressures over the face and body surface.

Taste, associated with the mouth and throat, relates to food and water already entering the food canal. In addition to these senses, a labyrinth, consisting of a sac and three semicircular canals located in the three planes of space, serves for the analysis of body motion and is located on each side within the head immediately behind the eyes.

The primitive brain is essentially the enlarged anterior end of the spinal cord with local paired swellings associated with the various sense organs. This is encased in a protective structure, the skull, to which the jaws and the front end of the vertebral column are articulated.

Evolution of Vertebrates.—Primitive vertebrates are and seem always to have been the inhabitants of fresh water. Marine fish of all kinds appear to have arisen as migrants from the freshwater stock, from which terrestrial vertebrates are also derivations. The most primitive of these are the amphibians, mostly frogs and salamanders, which still lay small eggs in water. These eggs necessarily develop into aquatic larvae that subsequently must metamorphose into the terrestrial adult form preparatory to leaving the water. Reptiles, which retain a scaly skin, are better adapted to terrestrial existence and lay large eggs of the shelled, amniote type, which can be laid on land and develop directly into miniature adults. The stabilizing fins of the fish have become walking legs, and the tail is either lost or is retained mainly for balance. Other changes associated with terrestrial life are the development of the organ of hearing as an outgrowth of the labyrinth, the development of lungs to obtain oxygen from air instead of water, with a corresponding reduction of gill slits to stages seen only in the embryo, and an elaboration of the heart from the two-chambered type of the fish to the four-chambered kind typical of the higher vertebrates. Birds and mammals have arisen independently from a reptilian stock. Both have acquired a high, constant, body temperature that enables them to inhabit cold latitudes, with feathers forming insulating material in birds, and hair in mammals. Birds have become highly specialized, mainly as flying machines in which forelegs have become wings, but also in evolving a toothless beak in place of toothed jaws.

Mammals are not only warm blooded and hairy but have an efficient respiratory mechanism, the diaphragm, and a more generally developed and better brain. Mammals typically retain the developing egg within the body of the mother, nourishing the embryo and fetus before birth by means of the fetal placenta attached to the uterine wall, and after birth by means of the milk or mammary glands, from which the class derives its name.

The ancestry of vertebrates is obscure. The oldest vertebrate fossil remains are of freshwater animals equipped with a heavy external coat of armor, but with an internal structure already as complex and typically vertebrate as the modern lamprey, which is closely allied to them. In other words, vertebrates were already fully established as vertebrate types in the Ordovician period of 450 million years ago. Man himself is a vertebrate and a mammal, but of a particular kind that has come into existence only during the last million years.

Taken as a whole, vertebrates are animals that have had an extremely remote marine ancestry as primitive chordates, that became highly structured swimmers in fresh water, and that have in later times become progressively adapted to living out of water. They are outstanding in having become successively independent of the aquatic environment and also of change in the environmental temperature; the present human endeavor to travel through space and reach other worlds is a continuation of this fundamental vertebrate trend. From the first to the last, vertebrates have been the most adventurous creatures of this planet.

See also AMPHIBIA; ANATOMY, COMPARATIVE—*Skeleton;* BIRDS; CHORDATA; CYCLOSTOMATA; EYESIGHT IN THE LOWER ANIMALS—*Vertebrates;* MAMMALS; NERVOUS SYSTEM; REPTILES; SKELETON.

N. J. BERRILL,
Strathcona Professor of Zoology, McGill University.

VERTICAL CIRCLES, vûr′tĭ-kəl sûr′kəlz, in astronomy, imaginary great circles on the celestial sphere which pass through the zenith of a place (the point directly overhead) and intersect the celestial horizon at right angles. The vertical circle which passes through the north and south

THE SKELETON FROM FISH TO MAN. The skeleton of man, like that of all other vertebrate animals, is the passive part of the locomotor machinery, while the muscles and nerves are the active part. Comparative study of the skeletons of all known types of fossil and modern animals has made it possible to decipher the record of progress from fish to man. The series of forms here shown does not form a direct line of descent from fish to man but each stage shown is the nearest to the direct line so far discovered.

The earliest vertebrates lived exclusively in the water and swam by undulating the body. The fins were projections of the skin and body wall that served chiefly as rudders and balancers (Stage 1).

Gradually, in the swamp-living, air-breathing fishes, the pectoral and pelvic fins were transformed first into paddles (Stage 2) and then into limbs (Stage 3), as the animals crawled out of the swamps. After many ages the animals invaded the uplands (Stage 4) learning to crawl like turtles and lizards.

Next, they learned to raise the belly off the ground and run about (Stage 5). Then they climbed up into the trees and became very expert in running and leaping about among the branches (Stages 6, 7, 8).

At first these tree-living animals ran about mostly on top of the branches (Stage 7). Then some of their descendants adopted the suspension grasp as they began to swing from branch to branch. The gibbon (Stage 8), is rather overspecialized in this direction.

Avoiding extreme overspecialization for "brachiation" (swinging with arms), the ancestors of man came down from the trees, running perhaps occasionally on all fours but more and more often erect as do the gibbons when on the ground.

From his prehuman anthropoid ancestors, which were related to the chimpanzee and the gorilla (Stage 9), man has inherited his ability to hold the body erect or balanced on the hind legs (Stage 10). The forelimbs, being relieved from their former function as locomotor organs, were set free to serve the enlarging brain in defending the body and providing for its needs.

Based on an exhibit in The American Museum of Natural History points of the horizon (and hence also through the north and south celestial poles) is known as the celestial *meridian* (q.v.). The vertical circle which passes through the east and west points of the horizon is termed the *prime vertical.* Vertical circles are used in the horizon system of coordinates to measure the azimuths of stars. See also AZIMUTH; HORIZON—*Celestial Horizon.*

FERGUS J. WOOD.

VERTICAL TAKEOFF AND LANDING. See AERONAUTICS—2. *Aircraft Design and Structures* (The Vertical Takeoff and Landing [VTOL]).

VERTIGO, vûr'tə-gō, a state of being dizzy or lightheaded, caused by varying degrees of loss of equilibrium. True equilibrium is controlled by the labyrinthine and vestibular apparatus of the ear, the eyes, which transmit position information to the brain, the cortex of the brain, which coordinates position sense, the cerebellum (see BRAIN, ANATOMY OF), and finally the proprioceptive nerve fibers in tendons and muscles, which tell us the positions of our arms and legs without visual association.

Vertigo has always been a challenge to the clinician. The sufferer gives a varied history of attacks. He may have a mild dizzy or giddy feeling or he may have a more acute sense of objects rotating about him, associated with nausea and vomiting. This may cause him to stagger or even fall violently to the ground. The mechanism of this last type of vertigo centers in the labyrinths of the ear or the vestibular portion of the eighth nerve. (See MÉNIÈRE'S SYNDROME.) Ocular causes of vertigo include paralysis of extraocular muscles with double vision, or a temporary readjustment when the individual has acquired bifocal lenses. Direct brain involvement in the cortex or cerebellum is very rare and should be investigated by a trained neurologist when other more obvious causes have been ruled out.

There are a number of medical conditions which cause vertigo, most of which produce brain anoxia. Chronic pulmonary disease, such as emphysema, asthma, and pulmonary fibrosis, may cause repeated episodes of vertigo. Severe anemia, particularly pernicious anemia, is another cause. Patients with hypertension easily become dizzy or giddy, especially when there is a paroxysmal rise in blood pressure. Old, debilitated, or invalid patients are prone to become dizzy or black out when they change position from the reclining to the upright. This is called postural hypotension. Certain drugs produce vertigo by causing a chronic toxic labyrinthitis when used in large doses. These are quinine, salicylates, and streptomycin. Tension or hysterical states in which the individual hyperventilates and blows off his reserve supply of carbon dioxide can cause vertigo and fainting.

Of all the causes mentioned, labyrinthitis, or fluid and irritation in the middle and inner ear, is by far the most common reason for the vertigo sufferer to consult a doctor. Dehydration programs with ammonium chloride diuretics and salt restriction, heavy supplementary vitamin use of B_{12} and thiamine, control of nausea with Bonamine and Dramamine, and finally local ear attention generally relieve the symptoms.

REAUMUR S. DONNALLY, M.D.

VERTUE, vûr'tū, **George,** English engraver and antiquary: b. London, England, 1684; d. there, July 24, 1756. As an engraver he is known for his renderings of portraits and of illustrations for such works as Paul de Rapin's *History of England* (1736), the Society of Antiquaries' *Vetusta Monumenta* (1717–1756), and the *Oxford Almanac* (1732–1751), and for his series of fine historical prints. His antiquarian interests included the collection of a mass of material for a history of the fine arts in England; his notebooks (now in the British Museum) were used extensively by Horace Walpole, English writer, in his *Anecdotes of Painting in England* (1762–1771). He was buried in the cloisters of Westminster Abbey.

VERTUMNUS, vər-tŭm'nəs, or **VORTUMNUS,** vôr-tŭm'nəs, in Roman religion, a deity of uncertain functions. He seems to have been imported early from Etruria. Some support in ancient authors appears for the tradition of the Romans' worship of Vertumnus in connection with the change of seasons, the transformation of plants from blossoms to fruit, and tradesmen's activities, particularly in purchase and sale. His festival, the Vortumnalia, was celebrated on August 23 under the supervision of a special priest (*flamen Vortumnalis*).

P. R. COLEMAN-NORTON.

VERULAM, LORD. See BACON, FRANCIS.

VERULAMIUM. See SAINT ALBANS (England).

VERUS, vēr'əs, **Lucius Aurelius** (original name **LUCIUS CEIONIUS COMMODUS**), Roman emperor: b. Rome, Italy, Dec. 15, 130; d. Altino, January 169; r. 161–169. Adopted by Emperor Hadrian in 136 and then, with Marcus Annius Verus (later Marcus Aurelius Antoninus), by Emperor Antoninus Pius in 138, he and his adopted brother became imperial heirs. Verus was quaestor (153) and consul (154; 161). At Pius' death Verus and Marcus (r. 161–180) shared the sovereignty, but the latter, who was 10 years older, was considered the senior sovereign. Verus' character was inferior to that of Marcus, who employed him as commander of an expedition against Parthia (162–166) and campaigned with him against German invaders of Italy (168). Verus' death soon relieved Marcus of a partner who, if he had lived longer, probably would have been more of a hindrance than a help.

P. R. COLEMAN-NORTON.

VERVAIN. See VERBENA.

VERVIERS, vĕr-vyā', town, Belgium in Liège Province, situated at an altitude of 541 feet on the Vesdre River, 13 miles east of Liège. It lies on both banks of the river, here flowing through a picturesque narrow valley. Its chief industries, wool combing, weaving, and dyeing, owe their success partly to the exceptional purity—and hence suitability for wool processing—of the waters of the Vesdre and Gileppe rivers, including those of nearby Gileppe Lake (formed by Gileppe Dam), which are brought to the mills by aqueduct. There are also leather-tanning works and manufactures of shoes, earthenware, machine tools, felt and wool hats, and chocolate. The town has 18th and 19th century churches and a museum. Pop. (1956) 37,401.

VERWEY, vər-vī', **Albert,** Dutch poet, writer, and critic: b. Amsterdam, the Netherlands, May

15, 1865; d. Noordwijk aan Zee, March 8, 1937. He was one of a group of writers known as "the generation of 1880" (see NETHERLANDS, KINGDOM OF THE—*Cultural Life:* Literature) who helped revitalize Dutch literature of their period. Coeditor with Lodewijk van Deyssel (pseudonym of Karel J. L. A. Thijm, 1864–1952) of *Tweemaandelijksch tijdschrift* (1894–1902) and *De twintigste eeuw* (1902–1905), founder and editor of *De beweging* (1905–1919), and professor of Dutch literature at Leiden University (1925–1935), Verwey achieved a place of leadership as a critic and poet who believed in poetry as a social as well as aesthetic force. His life and work were influenced by a close friendship with Stefan George (1868–1933), German poet. His many publications include *Verzamelde gedichten* (3 vols., 1911–12) and *Proza* (10 vols., 1921–23).

VERWOERD, fâr-vōōrt′, **Hendrik Frensch,** South African prime minister: b. Amsterdam, Netherlands, Sept. 8, 1901; d. Cape Town, South Africa, Sept. 6, 1966. He was taken to South Africa when still an infant. After graduate work in Germany, he was professor of applied psychology and of sociology and social work at Stellenbosch University from 1927 to 1937.

In 1937, Verwoerd became editor of *Die Transvaler,* a pro-National party newspaper. He was appointed a senator by the new National government in 1948 and in 1950 became minister of native affairs, guiding much of the apartheid (q.v.) legislation through parliament. Verwoerd was elected prime minister in 1958. He led South Africa out of the Commonwealth of Nations in 1961 rather than soften his country's racial policies. He was stabbed to death on the floor of parliament.

L. GRAY COWAN
Columbia University

VERY, Jones, American poet and essayist: b. Salem, Mass., Aug. 28, 1813; d. there, May 8, 1880. He graduated from Harvard University in 1836, taught Greek there while studying at the divinity school, and in 1843 was licensed as a Unitarian preacher, but did little preaching. An associate of the transcendalists (see TRANSCENDENTAL PHILOSOPHY) and a religious ecstatic who believed that all his inspirations were of divine origin, he claimed that his religious sonnets were communicated to him during visions of the Holy Ghost. Often melodious and deep in sentiment, his poems won high praise from his friend, Ralph Waldo Emerson, and from William Cullen Bryant, and other contemporaries. On his sanity being questioned, he allowed himself to be committed to an insane asylum for a period in 1838. However Emerson, among others, affirmed his belief in Very's sanity and helped in the selection of his *Essays and Poems* (1839), Very's only work published during his lifetime. Posthumous works are *Poems* (1883) and *Poems and Essays* (1886).

VESALIUS, vĭ-sā′lē-əs, **Andreas,** Flemish anatomist and physician: b. Brussels, Flanders, Dec. 31, 1514; d. Oct. 15, 1564. Born into a family long associated with the medical care of the imperial dynasty, he studied at the universities of Louvain and Paris and took the degree of doctor of medicine in December 1537 at Padua, where he immediately joined the faculty to teach surgery and anatomy. Vesalius enjoyed great success as a teacher and was responsible for the great prestige of the chair of anatomy at Padua. During this period he composed his great work, *De humani corporis fabrica,* published by Johannes Oporinus in Basel on or about Aug. 1, 1543. The *Fabrica,* a book of epochal importance in the history of human anatomical studies, marked the overthrow of traditional Galenic anatomy based upon nonhuman material and the foundation of modern observational science. The most important portions of the work are those dealing with osteology myology, and cardiology. It was influential for two centuries, and because of its typographical excellence and also because of its beautiful and remarkable woodcut illustrations, the work of Titian's studio, it remains one of the finest examples of 16th century bookmaking.

With the publication of the *Fabrica,* Vesalius abandoned his academic career to become one of the imperial physicians serving Holy Roman Emperor Charles V and eventually acquired international fame as a consultant. During this period, and despite limited opportunity for research, he published a revised edition of the *Fabrica* in 1555.

Upon the abdication of the emperor, Vesalius removed to Spain in 1559 where he became physician to the Flemings at the court of Philip II. In 1564 he was permitted to leave Spain in order to make a pilgrimage to the Holy Land. Traveling by way of Venice, he sought and obtained his old chair at Padua, left vacant by the death of Gabriel Fallopius, but on the return voyage from the Holy Land he died suddenly and was buried on the island of Zante, Greece. Although he published other writings, the earlier ones are not of great significance and the later are merely addenda to the *Fabrica,* albeit with many alterations of content and style of presentation.

C. D. O'MALLEY
Professor of Medical History, School of Medicine, University of California, Los Angeles

VESICANTS, vĕs′ĭ-kənts, substances which, when applied to the skin, cause the formation of blisters. They cause first a dilation of the fine blood vessels of the skin (rubefaction) and subsequently an increased permeability of the capillaries. This results in the seeping of plasma from the capillaries into the extracellular spaces under the epidermis, and as the amount and pressure of the accumulating fluid increase, the skin bulges out and blisters are formed. When these are opened, the fluid escapes and the blister collapses. When not covered by a sterile dressing, the raw area exposed by the collapse of the blister may become infected and ulcerated.

Vesicants were formerly used extensively in a great number of inflammatory conditions to divert the blood flow from various areas in the body. However, their use has been replaced by other drugs which are more effective. Only two vesicants are still used, mostly by the laity, namely mustard and cantharides (Spanish or Russian flies). The former is used in the form of a mustard plaster and the latter as cantharides cerate (blistering cerate). It should, however, be pointed out that the prolonged contact of the latter, especially in exposed areas with raw skin, may eventually lead to injury of the kidneys (nephritis).

Blisters may be produced by prolonged contact with certain plant juices such as that of *Rhus toxicodendron* (poison ivy), *Chelidonium majus* (celandine), croton oil, from the seeds of *Croton tiglium* (croton), *Daphne mezereum* (wild pepper, spurge flax, or dwarf bag), or with certain chemicals and solvents, such as chloroform, hydrofluoric acid, iodine, methyl bromide (used in certain fire extinguishers), methyl chloride (used for refrigeration), mustard gas (dichlorodiethyl sulfide), nitrosomethylurethane, phenyldichloroarsine, and trichloroethylene.

W. F. VON OETTINGEN, M.D.

VESPASIAN, vĕs-pā'zhən (Lat. TITUS FLAVIUS SABINUS VESPASIANUS), Roman emperor: b. Reate (modern Rieti), Italy, Nov. 17, 9 A.D.; d. there, June 23, 79 A.D.; r. 69–79 A.D. His father was a tax collector, but a Roman senator was his maternal uncle. Vespasian served as military tribune in Thrace and as quaestor of Crete and Cyrene before he won his first important political office, the aedileship (38), which was followed by the praetorship (40). Vespasian married Flavia Domitilla, by whom he had two sons, Titus and Domitian, both of whom later served as emperor. Then turning to a military career, he was a legionary commander in Germany (42) and Britain (43). For his British campaign he received the triumphal decorations (44), since celebration of a triumph (q.v.) had become an imperial prerogative. For the next 20 years Vespasian lived in quasi retirement, which was interrupted twice: by his suffect consulship (51) and his proconsulship of Africa (?63). When the Jewish War began (66), Emperor Nero appointed him to lead the Roman forces against the rebellious Jews. Vespasian campaigned so successfully that he was about to end the war by besieging Jerusalem when the legions in Egypt and Judaea saluted him as emperor (July 69) and the Roman Senate formally conferred the sovereignty on him (December 69). Leaving his son (and successor) Titus to conclude the war, Vespasian returned to Rome to restore public order after the civil war which, following Nero's suicide (68) had brought three emperors (Servius Sulpicius Galba, Marcus Salvius Otho, and Aulus Vitellius) to the throne (68–69).

Vespasian began his reign by reforming the imperial revenues; he exacted strictly provincial tributes, regained public lands illegally occupied by individuals, instituted new taxes, and carefully supervised expenditures. The increased revenue financed many public works, such as the Colosseum (q.v.) in Rome and public buildings, bridges, and roads in the provinces, as well as subsidies (*alimenta*) for support and education of poor children. He reinvigorated the Senate, with which he closely cooperated, by enrolling in it distinguished Italians and provincials who enjoyed Roman citizenship. He decreased the number of freedmen (ex-slaves) in the civil service by substituting knights. He reorganized the provincial system, encouraged municipal life in the provinces by conferring Latin rights on many communities, and founded numerous colonies to advance the Romanization of the provinces. He reimposed discipline on the legions. He patronized artists and littérateurs, but expelled from Rome several Stoic and Cynic philosophers involved in conspiracies against the regime (71).

In foreign affairs Vespasian, through able generals, ended the Jewish War (70) and the Batavian revolt (70) and continued the conquest of Britain. He annexed the eastern client kingdoms of Lesser Armenia and Commagene (72). The German frontier was extended and strengthened by a series of fortresses and roads between the Danube and the Rhine rivers (73–74).

Vespasian was affable, blunt, courageous, honest, and parsimonious, detested ostentation, and toiled so indefatigably in the public interest that he restored prosperity to the empire that had been in disarray at his accession. The Senate deified him at his death.

P. R. COLEMAN-NORTON
Formerly, Princeton University

VESPER. See EVENING STAR, HESPERUS, or VESPER.

VESPER SPARROW, vĕs'pər spăr'ō, a widespread North American finch (*Pooecetes gramineus*) of the family Fringillidae, occurring in grasslands and pastures. About five inches in length, the bird has plumage of blended gray, brown, and white, with a patch of chestnut feathers on the shoulder from which it acquired its former name of bay-winged sparrow. Its colors blend with the field but as it takes wing the white outer tail feathers identify it. The song is sweet and, as the name implies, is often given toward evening. In the northeast, perhaps because so many old pastures and fields have gone back to woodland, the vesper sparrow is less often seen than some of the other members of the family. It migrates to the Southern states in the winter. The nest is a grass-lined cup, sometimes placed in a hoofprint of a cow. It would rarely be found were it not for the incubating bird's habit of flying only at the last minute when one is about to walk over the nest.

DEAN AMADON.

VESPERS, vĕs'pərz, a part of the official prayer of the Roman Catholic Church known as the Divine Office. It is essentially an evening prayer and is connected with the *sacrificium vespertinum*, the evening sacrifice, of the Old Law. Vespers became established in its present form in the 6th century. While the contents of vespers change with the day and season, the structure remains the same and can be illustrated by vespers for Sundays. Certain brief introductory prayers are followed by (1) five psalms, each concluded by the doxology, "Glory be to the Father . . ." and preceded and followed by appropriate antiphons; (2) a brief passage from Scripture called the little chapter; (3) a hymn with a versicle and response; (4) the *Magnificat* (q.v.) with its special antiphons; (5) the prayer proper to the particular Sunday, and in certain instances, where another feast coincides with the Sunday, commemoration of the feast day by an antiphon, versicle and response, and proper prayer.

Vespers are either first or second, according as they are said on the evening before the first day or on the day itself. Traditionally, first vespers ranked higher than second vespers. However, with new liturgical rules that became effective on Jan. 1, 1961, feasts with first vespers were greatly reduced in number and are now restricted to Sundays and the more important feast days throughout the year. Since the vesper service sanctified the end of the day and was thus more accessible in time to the faithful than the other parts of the Divine Office, it was long a popular devotion. Until recent times public chanting of vespers in parish churches was a not infrequent practice. At present, public recitation of vespers is carried out for the most part in seminaries, monasteries, and other religious houses, and in great cathedrals and churches such as the National Shrine of the Immaculate Conception in Washington, D.C.

JOHN K. RYAN,
Professor of Philosophy, The Catholic University of America.

VESPERS, Sicilian. See SICILIAN VESPERS.

VESPERTILIONIDAE. See BAT.

VESPUCCI, vās-pōōt'chē, **Amerigo,** Italian explorer: b. Florence, Italy, bap. March 18, 1454; d. Seville, Spain, Feb. 22, 1512. Of a noble Florentine family, he early developed a keen interest in geography and cosmography, and became business representative in Spain for one of the Medici. The erroneous claim by Christopher Columbus that he had opened a westward route to Asia excited Europeans, but failure to find the riches of India caused doubts to arise, and the Spanish and Portuguese rulers began to ask just what lands Columbus had found. With the world divided by the papal Line of Demarcation (1493), there was also a question as to which of those lands belonged to Spain and which to Portugal. Vespucci, as a man of "sagacious" (scientific) mind, was sent to find out. In letters to his Medici patron (1500–1502), he described two voyages he made along the coast of what is now known as South America, the first in 1499–1500 for Spain and the second in 1501–1502 for Portugal, exploring on the two voyages 6,000 miles of coastline on the north and east of a great land, "which we observed to be a continent."

In the "Letter to Soderini" (1504), purportedly written by Vespucci to a Florentine schoolmate, it is asserted that Vespucci made four voyages, the "first" in 1497, the "fourth" in 1503. In *Mundus novus* (1504), Vespucci said that the land he had followed to latitude 50° S. could not be part of Asia, because it extended too far to the south, and was therefore a hitherto unknown continent. This factual finding dampened the enthusiasms that Columbus had awakened in dreamers who sought to get rich quickly by taking a westward passage to India. Yet Columbus, neglected, sick, and in want, found Vespucci sympathetic and friendly, and in 1505 wrote of him: "He has at all times shown a desire to serve me, and is an honorable man." Columbus died the next year, and in 1507 Martin Waldseemüller (q.v.), a geographer in Lorraine, issued a map showing the new continent (the present South America), along with a pamphlet in which he proposed naming it "after its discoverer, Americus, and let it be named America, since both Europa and Asia bear names of feminine form."

The public instantly adopted the name, but controversy arose; it was charged that Vespucci was jealous, and since Columbus had made four voyages, Vespucci had claimed to have made as many. There was dispute over Vespucci's "first" voyage, which gave him a one-year priority over Columbus in sighting and landing on the coast of South America. Some believed the voyage to be spurious, and that Vespucci was a boaster, liar, and thief of another man's rightful honors. Some thought his friends in Florence might have invented that voyage to win credit for their city. Among modern investigators, Frederick J. Pohl, in *Amerigo Vespucci, Pilot Major* (New York 1944), assumed that Vespucci did not make the "first" voyage; Germán Arciniegas, in *Amerigo and the New World* (New York 1955), argued that he did. The dispute misses the essential point, however, for Waldseemüller was motivated in proposing the name "America" by the acceptance of Vespucci's proof of the existence of the new continent, much more than by his supposed priority in reaching it.

The Bettmann Archive

Amerigo Vespucci, for whom the Americas were named.

The southern continent was given the name "America," not on Waldseemüller's large map, but on a small inset map which presented two important geographical innovations for which Vespucci was solely responsible: the fact that there was a new continent and the concept of another ocean between that new continent and Asia. Vespucci was the first man to realize that, sailing westward from Europe, one must cross two oceans to reach Asia. He knew the approximate placement of the land and water masses of the earth because he had developed an original method of celestial navigation. By comparing the hour of the moon's conjunction with a planet observed in a Western land and the hour at which it was observed in Spain, he obtained longitude. He was surprisingly close to the correct figure in estimating the earth's circumference, being only 50 miles in error.

Until his death, Vespucci was astronomer to the king of Spain. One of his duties as pilot major was to prepare and revise a master chart of the Atlantic Ocean and the Western lands, and to provide copies for sea captains. As for the name America, people liked it so well that they applied it to the North American continent as well as to South America.

FREDERICK J. POHL.

Further Reading: Delpar, Helen, *The Discoverers: An Encyclopedia of Explorers and Exploration* (McGraw 1979); Pohl, Frederick J., *Amerigo Vespucci, Pilot Major* (Hippocrene Bks. 1966).

VESSELS, in anatomy. See ANATOMY, COMPARATIVE–*Circulatory System;* ARTERIES; BLOOD –*Circulation of the Blood;* CAPILLARIES; LYMPH.

VESSELS, vĕs′əls, in botany, part of the xylem (wood) of plants. They consist of series of vessel elements united end to end to form a somewhat pipelinelike conducting structure. Vessels conduct from the roots to all parts of the plant the water absorbed by the root hairs, together with various substances dissolved in it. (Elaborated food substances are conducted through sieve tubes in the phloem.) The unit cells of a mature vessel are elongate and empty, mere skeletons of cells. Typically, their walls are pitted, thick, and woody. Connection of the cell cavities is by perforation of the wall at or near each end. In form, the vessel elements range from slender and tapering to short and roughly cylindrical, even barrel shaped where highly specialized. Vessels that are composed of slender, elongated cells with ladderlike (scalariform) perforations at or near each end represent the primitive form; those in which the unit cells are short, of large diameter, and with solitary perforations at each end are highly specialized types.

Individual vessels may extend for long distances in the plant; they may fork and unite to form a meshwork of conducting lines. Vessels vary in type, abundance, and arrangement in different kinds of plants. Pits are present in their walls where they are in contact with other vessels and with living cells. The vessel system, in its distribution in the plant and in its conduction function, resembles the blood system of animals.

See also PLANTS AND PLANT SCIENCE–2. *Anatomy* (Tissues).

ARTHUR J. EAMES,
Professor Emeritus of Botany, Cornell University.

VESSELS, in shipping. See BOAT; FERRY; SAILING VESSELS; SHIP; SHIPBUILDING INDUSTRY AND CONSTRUCTION; STEAM VESSELS; TANKERS AND SUPERTANKERS; WARSHIPS.

VEST-AGDER, vĕst′äg-dər, county (Nor. *fylke*), Norway, bounded on the south by the Skagerrak and North Sea, on the west by Rogaland County, and on the north and east by Aust-Agder County. Its area is 2,817 square miles, and its capital is Kristiansand; other towns are Mandal, Flekkefjord, and Farsund. It is mostly wooded, with the Ruven Mountains in the north; several rivers (the Sira, Kvina, Lygna, Audna, Mandal, and Otra) flow southward into the North Sea or Skagerrak. Agriculture (in the lower river valley and coastal peninsulas), fishing, and lumbering are the chief occupations. There is also molybdenum mining. The county (then called *amt*) was known until 1918 as Lister and Mandal. Pop. (1950) 96,930.

VESTA, vĕs′tə, in Roman religion, virgin goddess of the hearth and its fire. Though she had an honorable place in the domestic devotions of Roman families, her state worship was more important. Vesta's cult apparently arose from the necessity of obtaining fire conveniently from a common center in primitive times; but, after such need had ceased, the custom of maintaining a perpetual fire persisted and received religious sanction. Ruins of the Temple of Vesta, a round edifice symbolical of the primitive Roman house, remain in the Forum in Rome, Italy. It contained no image of the deity, whose statue was in an adjacent shrine, but in it the Vestals (q.v.) tended a constantly burning fire. This fire was extinguished officially and annually on March 1 (the Roman New Year's Day) and then was rekindled ceremonially by friction of fagots. Its extinction at any other time, whether naturally or by negligence, foreboded calamity to the commonwealth. Vesta's festival (*Vestalia*) was on June 9, when barefooted women walked to worship in her temple, which was purified on June 15. The emperor Theodosius I (Theodosius the Great) in 394 abolished her cult in his policy of eradicating paganism in the Christianized Roman Empire.

P. R. COLEMAN-NORTON.

Further Reading: Guerber, H. A., *Myths of Greece and Rome* (1893; reprint, Arden Library 1985); Perowne, S., *Roman Mythology* (Bedrick Bks. 1984).

VESTA, in astronomy, the brightest of the asteroids (q.v.) and, with a mean opposition magnitude of 6.5, the only such object ever recurrently visible to the unaided eye. Discovered telescopically by Heinrich W. M. Olbers on March 29, 1807, as the fourth known asteroid, it has a diameter of about 240 miles and a period of revolution around the sun of 3.63 years.

FERGUS J. WOOD.

VESTALE, La, vās-tä′lā, an opera in three acts by Gaspare Spontini, with libretto by Victor Joseph Étienne de Jouy. It was first performed at the Opéra, Paris, on Dec. 16, 1807. The cast comprises: Giulia, a vestal virgin (soprano), the High Priestess of Vesta (contralto), Licinio, a Roman captain (tenor), a consul (tenor), Cinna (baritone), the Pontifex Maximus (bass). The action occurs in Rome. Giulia has become a vestal virgin while her betrothed, Licinio, has been campaigning in Gaul. Returning, he tries to abduct her from the Temple of Vesta. Responding to his ardor, she allows the sacred fire to die out, and is condemned to be buried alive. At the climax of her funeral procession, while Licinio is trying to rescue her, lightning rekindles the sacred fire, and the opera ends happily. In addition to the overture, the most renowned excerpts from *La Vestale* are Giulia's two second-act arias, *"Tu che invoco"* and *"O nume tutelar."*

HERBERT WEINSTOCK.

VESTALS, vĕs′təlz, or **VESTAL VIRGINS,** vĕs′təl vûr′jĭnz, maidens consecrated to the Roman goddess Vesta (q.v.) and to maintenance of the sacred fire constantly burning on her altar. Vestals, in number originally 2, then 4, and finally 6, served for 5 and finally 30 years, during which they were vowed to chastity. When their service expired, they might marry, but few wed, because marriage of an ex-vestal was considered unlucky. The pontifex maximus, as head of the state religion, filled vacancies from candidates, who were between 6 and 10 years old, without defects, and whose parents were freeborn, living citizens. Vestals wore the primitive sacral dress, which otherwise only brides used, had choice seats at public spectacles, were attended on promenades by lictors, and enjoyed other privileges, especially emancipation from paternal power, in exchange for which, however, they passed into the control of the pontifex maximus. Punishment for failure to keep the fire alive and for offenses other than unchastity was scourging by the pontifex maximus. Vestals who violated their vow of virginity were buried alive.

Vestals lived in the Atrium Vestae, an edifice whose ruins remain near the Forum in Rome, Italy. It contained a rectangular and colonnaded court adorned with gardens, fountains, and statues of the senior vestals; official rooms of the vestals; and domestic offices, the best-preserved portion of the palace.

P. R. Coleman-Norton.

VESTAVIA HILLS, vĕ-stā′vē-ə, city, Alabama, in Jefferson County, situated atop Shades Mountain (elevation 1,100 feet), 6 miles south of Birmingham, on a federal highway. A residential community, it derives its name from its outstanding landmark, Vestavia Temple, a home built in 1924 from plans based on the Roman Temple of Vesta. Its beauty is enhanced by widespread planting by residents of red maples and climbing roses. Founded in 1946 and incorporated in 1950 (with a population of 608), it has a mayor-and-council form of government. Pop. 15,733.

Oliver Roosevelt.

VESTED RIGHTS, vĕs′tĭd rīts, in law, a term denoting fixed, consummated interests in a particular person or persons. Rights are vested when they have settled so completely that they are not subject to being defeated without consent by the act of another private party. Interference with vested rights is duly compensable; such rights are carefully protected by the law and can be divested only for the public welfare under recognized procedures. An interest in property may vest even though possession or enjoyment is deferred until another interest has terminated, as, for example, in the case of a remainder after a life estate. Vested rights are distinguishable from contingent interests which are dependent upon the happening or performance of a certain event or condition which may not come before another event prevents their vesting.

Alan A. Matheson.

VESTERALEN (islands). See Lofoten.

VESTFOLD, vĕst′fôl, county (Nor. *fylke*), Norway, bounded on the east by the Oslo Fjord, on the south by the Skagerrak, on the southwest by Telemark County, and on the northwest and north by Buskerud County. Smallest but most densely populated of Norway's rural counties, its area is 903 square miles. Its capital is Tonsberg, port and Norway's oldest city (founded 871); other towns are Larvik, Horten, Sandefjord (an Antarctic whaling center), and Holmestrand. Hilly in the west and north, the terrain levels out into an eastern coastal plain. Agriculture, dairying, lumbering, and fishing are the chief activities. The country has excellent rail connections with Oslo. Offshore, on the east, are Notteroy and other islands popular among Oslo vacationers. The county (then called *amt*) was known until 1918 as Jarlsberg and Larvik. It is rich in Viking history. Pop. (1978) 184,355.

VESTMENTS, Ecclesiastical. See Costume, Religious.

VESTRIS, vĕs′trĭs, **Madame** (nee **Lucia Elizabeth Bartolozzi**), English actress: b. London, England, 1797; d. there, Aug. 8, 1856. Granddaughter of Francesco Bartolozzi, the engraver, in 1813 she married Auguste Armand Vestris, grandson of Gaetan Vestris, the great ballet dancer, but separated from him a few years later. She began her 40-year stage career as Proserpina in Peter von Winter's opera *Il ratto di Proserpina,* and might have had a great future in opera if she had troubled to train her contralto voice. As it was, her singing of such songs as *Cherry Ripe* and *I've Been Roaming* was incomparable. As an actress, she excelled in light rather than high comedy. She scored great successes in *The Haunted Tower,* as Phoebe in *Paul Pry,* and, in male costume, as Macheath in *The Beggar's Opera* and Cherubino in *The Marriage of Figaro.* Having become rich by 1830, Madame Vestris became lessee of the Olympic Theatre, London—possibly she was the first woman lessee in the history of the stage—and was involved in theatrical management there and at Covent Garden and the Lyceum for the rest of her life. She was a first-rate manageress, and improved scenery, costume, and methods of staging. In 1838 she married Charles James Mathews, the noted actor.

Wallace Brockway.

VESTRY, vĕs′trē, originally a room in which ecclesiastical vestments or apparel were kept (Latin *vestiarium;* consult II Kings 10:22). Such a room is now usually called a sacristy, as it also contains the sacred vessels and other liturgical utensils. In the Anglican churches, such as the Church of England and the Protestant Episcopal Church in the United States, the term is also used for the body of elected representatives of the parish, who are charged with the overseeing and administration of its "temporalities" (land, buildings, finance) and are legally responsible for its affairs. This use of the term is due to the fact that originally these elected bodies met in the vestry room or house. The presiding officer is the rector or vicar. Two members (usually senior) are chosen as wardens, whose special concern is the maintenance of the church fabric. Meetings are usually held monthly, and all parish business of a secular character may properly be considered.

In some of the older dioceses in the United States, the choice and duties of vestries are regulated by state law. (In England their duties have been considerably restricted since 1894, the parish councils now taking over many of their ancient responsibilities.) Subject to the bishop's approval, the vestry may call a clergyman when the office of rector is vacant. In some dioceses the bishop nominates three or more candidates, and the vestry (or parish meeting) chooses one.

Frederick C. Grant.

VESUNNA. See Perigueux.

VESUVIANITE, the former name for idocrase. See Idocrase.

FRITZ HENLE/PHOTO RESEARCHERS

Vesuvius is an active volcano on the eastern shore of the Bay of Naples. The city of Naples is in the foreground.

VESUVIUS, və-so͞o'vē-ŭs, a composite volcano, approximately 4,000 feet high, located on the eastern shore of the Bay of Naples, Italy, at 40° 49′ north latitude and 14° 26′ east longitude. Although its crater is one and one-half miles in diameter, Vesuvius is actually a small cone within the limits of a vast prehistoric cone and crater. This ancient crater, a remnant of which is represented by Monte Somma, on the north and east of Vesuvius, was probably nearly 10 miles in diameter. Its old eruptive focus lies about a quarter of a mile north of the present vent of Vesuvius.

Prior to 79 A. D., Vesuvius was not recognized as an active volcano, and it is believed to have been in repose for almost a thousand years. But in 79 A. D., the vegetation-covered volcano erupted and buried Herculaneum and Pompeii under many feet of ash and pumice. According to Pliny the Younger, at about 7 o'clock on the morning of Aug. 24, 79, a cloud appeared over the summit of the mountain. It took the shape of a pine tree with a tall trunk and widely distended branches, a form not uncommon in volcanic eruptions. There were also "flashes of fire as vivid as lightning and darkness more profound than night."

The records of subsequent eruptions are somewhat confused. It appears, however, that among the more violent were those of 203 and 472, during which fine ash was carried as far as Constantinople, as well as one in 512. There seems to be reasonable agreement that there were large outbreaks also in 685, 993, 1036, 1139, and 1500. Following this, there was an interval of relative quiescence during which time the mountain was again overgrown with vegetation. Then in 1631, there was a tremendous eruption. This ushered in the modern period of moderately continuous eruption, highlighted by unusually strong ones in 1794, 1872, and 1906.

The larger eruption of 1906 has been fully described in a special monograph by Frank A. Perret, American volcanologist. The morning of April 4, he relates, began with the emergence of a massive white cloud of gas and steam into which there were shot great quantities of dark ash probably derived from demolition of the upper part of the cone. Residents of Naples, seven miles away, carried umbrellas to protect themselves from the volcanic sand. By midnight lava was issuing rapidly from a new fissure on the south side of the cone at a low level. At 8 A. M. on April 6, a new vent opened on the southeastern side of the cone only 1,800 feet above sea level. From this came a tremendous flood of very fluid lava which fountained at the vent and flowed rapidly down into Boscotrecase. According to Perret, the volcano hummed and trembled like a gigantic boiler under an overload of steam pressure. There was a notable increase in earthquake activity and in the number of explosions in the crater. Electrical discharges were prominent in the ash clouds. The outstanding characteristics of this phase of the eruption were the explosive force and the quantity of highly fluid lava. Another phase began with the emission of steam blasts of compressed gases which rushed up for many hours carrying relatively small quantities of ash and forming a gigantic cauliflower cloud seven miles in height. This was a vast continuous emission of gas like a huge locomotive boiler blowing off. Beginning on April 8, the eruption passed into the "dark ash" phase. Throughout this, gas clouds were so charged with volcanic debris as to be solid black. At each outbreak Naples and the surrounding country were covered by a pall of darkness.

Vesuvius' eruptions have been cyclical. There have been long periods of repose during which energy was being accumulated to be catastrophically released during a short major eruption. After the 1906 eruption Vesuvius was quiet for seven years. In 1913, the conduit reopened and normal activity was resumed. It erupted with a tremendous explosion on June 3, 1929, hurling masses of material into the air. Its central cone split and collapsed. As the cone fell into the crater, lava welled out of the northeast section of the crater, ran down the sides toward the town of Terzigni, and ultimately halted 400 yards from the houses. In World War II, after the Allies had gained control of the area in 1944, Vesuvius erupted again. This eruption was preceded by several days of seismic activity. Then, at 4:30 on the afternoon of March 18, molten lava welled up through fissures in the floor of the crater. It poured over the rim and flowed down the side of the volcano. At 5:30 P.M. on the 20th the explosive phase began. The ruins of Pompeii were reburied under nearly a foot of ash. See also VOLCANO.

L. DON LEET, *Harvard University*

Further Reading: Jashemski, Wilhemina F., *The Gardens of Pompeii, Herculaneum and the Villas Destroyed by Vesuvius* (Caratzas 1986); Marx, Walter H., *Claimed by Vesuvius* (Ind. School Press 1975); Temple, F. J., *Vesuvius*, tr. by Gregory Barr (Capra Press 1977).

VETCH, the common name for about 150 species of annual or perennial plants of the genus *Vicia* in the pea family, Leguminosae. The annual types are of considerable economic importance; they are grown for pasture, hay, or silage, for soil improvement, as cover or green-manure crops, and for seed. Annual types generally thrive in warmer areas, while a few hardy species are grown successfully in areas where climatic conditions are more rigorous. Perennial types sometimes are used as a ground cover, but they are quite localized in native habitats and seldom are grown under cultivation. Most vetches are climbing, viny plants. Their compound leaves may have up to a dozen pairs of oval leaflets and end in tendrils. The small, pealike flowers are blue, violet, white, or yellow, and the fruits are small, flat pods.

Cow vetch (*Vicia cracca*), also called bird vetch or tufted vetch, is a climbing perennial with purple flowers.

JOHN J. SMITH

The most commonly grown vetches in the United States are hairy vetch (*V. villosa*), common vetch (*V. sativa*), and purple vetch (*V. benghalensis*). All are native to Europe. Hairy vetch is very adaptable to soil and climate conditions, while common vetch requires a milder climate, and purple vetch is the least winter hardy of the three. Other vetches include cow vetch (*V. cracca*), a climbing perennial with purple flowers; broad bean or horse bean (*V. faba*), a coarse, erect species with violet-veined white flowers and seeds that are edible; and woolly pod (*V. dasycarpa*), somewhat similar to hairy vetch (*V. villosa*).

Other members of the pea family called vetch are crown vetch (genus *Coronilla*), horseshoe vetch (*Hippocrepis*), and milk vetch (*Astragalus*).

VETERANS ADMINISTRATION (VA), an independent agency of the United States government established by executive order on July 21, 1930. The order consolidated into a single agency the Bureau of Pensions, the United States Veterans Bureau, and the National Home for Disabled Volunteer Soldiers.

The agency administers laws authorizing benefits for veterans and their dependents and for beneficiaries of deceased veterans. These benefits include medical care and treatment, compensation payments for disabilities or death related to military service, pensions based on financial need for certain veterans and survivors for disabilities or death not related to military service, education and rehabilitation, home-loan guaranty, life insurance, and burial.

To administer these benefits the agency has three main departments: (1) the Department of Medicine and Surgery; (2) the Department of Veterans Benefits; and (3) the Department of Memorial Affairs. The physical organization of the Veterans Administration includes a central office in Washington, D. C., regional offices, hospitals, outpatient clinics, nursing homes, domiciliaries, cemeteries, insurance centers, and data-processing centers.

The administrator of veterans affairs directs the agency. Assisting him are the three departments already listed and 13 staff offices: Administrative Services, Board of Veterans Appeals, Office of Construction, Controller, Data Management and Telecommunications, General Counsel, Human Goals, Information Services, Inspector General, Management Services, Manpower Programs, Personnel, and Planning and Program Evaluation.

See also VETERANS BENEFITS.

MAX CLELAND
Administrator of Veterans Affairs

VETERANS BENEFITS. There were 4,600,000 veterans in civilian life when the Veterans Administration was created in 1930. By the time the VA observed its 50th anniversary the estimated number of living veterans of the Spanish-American and subsequent wars, as well as peacetime service, had surpassed 30 million.

The largest centrally directed health-care system in the United States, the chain of VA medical centers and outpatient clinics provides medical care for ailing and disabled veterans. Its aim is to return patients to their homes as rehabilitated, independent, and self-supporting members of their communities.

Since the first of three GI bills became effective in 1944, approximately 18 million veterans have received education and training under a VA program. Through the vocational rehabilitation program, service-disabled veterans are provided counseling and special training to help them prepare for, obtain, and hold productive employment. Educational assistance is available to survivors of veterans who died from service-connected causes, and to dependents of veterans whose service-connected disabilities are rated total and permanent.

The VA also made possible more than $170 billion in VA-guaranteed home loans for nearly 10.5 million veterans over four decades. In addition, grants administered under the specially adapted housing program provide certain eligible veterans financial assistance in acquiring or remodeling "wheelchair" homes with special features suited to their individual needs.

The VA administers approximately $32 billion worth of government life insurance for about 4.2 million policyholders and supervises an additional $72 billion worth of life insurance for more than 3.5 million servicepersons, active and retired reservists, and veterans. The VA also supervises about $144 million in mortgage life insurance for severely disabled veterans with specially adapted housing grants.

The VA provides monthly compensation to veterans who are disabled by injury or disease incurred in or aggravated by active duty. Death benefits are available to dependents of a veteran who died of service-connected causes. Subject to specific income limitations, wartime veterans who are totally and permanently disabled for reasons not traceable to military service are entitled to disability pensions. Also subject to specific income limitations, death pensions are available to the surviving spouse and children of a war veteran who died of nonservice-connected causes.

The VA also provides certain burial benefits, including a flag to drape the casket of a deceased veteran and grave markers for all gravesites in national cemeteries and for the unmarked graves of veterans in private cemeteries. The VA's Department of Memorial Affairs oversees the system of 109 national cemeteries.

MAX CLELAND
Administrator of Veterans Affairs

VETERANS DAY, formerly Armistice Day, proclaimed annually by the president of the United States and by the governors of the various states in honor of former members of all branches of the United States armed services—to recall their sacrifices in war and contributions to peace.

November 11 was first proclaimed a holiday in 1919 as Armistice Day to commemorate the signing on Nov. 11, 1918, of the armistice that brought an end to World War I. It continued to be observed through 1953.

On June 1, 1954, President Dwight D. Eisenhower signed an act of Congress "to honor veterans on the eleventh day of November of each year . . . a day dedicated to world peace." Thus Veterans Day came into being with suitable observances held throughout the nation and in Arlington National Cemetery outside Washington, D. C. New legislation enacted in 1968 changed the date of the federal holiday to the fourth Monday in October, effective in 1971. Most states observe Veterans Day on this latter date.

VETERANS OF FOREIGN WARS OF THE UNITED STATES (VFW), an organization created by the merger in 1914 of three societies of United States overseas veterans that were founded after the Spanish-American War of 1898–1899. These societies were the American Veterans of Foreign Service, chartered by the State of Ohio on Oct. 11, 1899; the Colorado Society of the Army of the Philippines, organized at Denver, Colo., on Dec. 1, 1899; and another group, also known as American Veterans of Foreign Service, formed shortly thereafter at Altoona, Pa. The organization was chartered by Congress on May 28, 1936. With its membership vastly increased after World War I and World War II, the organization, popularly known as the VFW, became a major national veterans' society. It operates on a nonpartisan, nonsectarian, nonprofit basis. On the community level, it has over 10,000 local units. National headquarters are at Kansas City, Mo.

Membership of the VFW is restricted to males, specifically to any active or honorably discharged male officer or enlisted man who is a citizen of the United States and who has served in its military or naval service "in any foreign war, insurrection or expedition, which service shall be recognized by the authorization of the issuance of a campaign medal" by the military or naval service. The basic aims of the organization, dating back to its earliest roots, are expressed in a nationwide program of activities with a fourfold purpose: (1) to ensure the national security through maximum military strength; (2) to speed the rehabilitation of the nation's disabled and needy veterans; (3) to assist the widows and orphans of veterans, and the dependents of disabled and needy veterans; (4) to promote Americanism through education in patriotism and constructive service to communities.

The organization maintains a National Legislative Service office in Washington, D. C., which works for the benefit of all United States war veterans—and to implement policies endorsed at annual VFW national conventions. Also in Washington is the central office of the National Rehabilitation Service, which serves all disabled United States veterans of all wars, members and nonmembers alike, in such matters as government compensation and pension claims, hospitalization, and civil service employment preference.

At Eaton Rapids, Mich., the organization maintains the VFW National Home, founded in 1925 as a home for the children of deceased or totally disabled members of the organization. Functioning under the "family-unit" plan, the home includes on its 640-acre campus more than 30 family size dwellings, each housing a typical family group of children under the care of a trained housemother. The children receive education, food, clothing, constructive play, and physical welfare—all the essentials to well-rounded American youth—free of cost, plus financial assistance if they desire college or special vocational training.

Affiliated with the VFW, and also with headquarters at Kansas City, Mo., is the organization's Ladies Auxiliary, open to wives, sisters, daughters, mothers, and widows of overseas veterans and to women who served overseas in the armed forces.

BARNEY YANOFSKY
Editor, "V. F. W. Magazine"

VETERANS ORGANIZATIONS, a loose term for formal associations of people based upon their previous military service, usually in wartime. The term is inexact, since various "veterans organizations" have been formed for commercial or political purposes, or for private gain. These, however, are not true veterans organizations.

Veterans organizations exist in most modern nations, and in large countries there may be hundreds of them. Since World War II the number in the United States has been more than 700. There are numerous veterans organizations in most of the nations of continental Europe, Asia, Africa, Australia, and North and South America. The British Commonwealth Ex-Services League included more than 40 organizations, loosely federated, in 1961.

Largest veterans groups in the United States —all national in scope and chartered by Congress—are the American Legion, the Veterans of Foreign Wars, the Disabled American Veterans, and the American Veterans of World War II and Korea. Their chief interests, beyond fraternization, are the relief of distress in the families of their members and of other veterans; support of measures to promote the welfare and security of the nation; and reinforcement of the moral and social values which their members defended by their former military service. They maintain local posts and chapters, conduct civic projects, and give aid and various services to war veterans. They also have county and state divisions and national offices and staffs. They promote their aims through the accepted channels of civilian influence in public affairs.

The largest number of veterans organizations in the United States are small groups, such as veterans of specific military units, veterans with the same postwar problems (such as the blind or amputees), and veterans with the same unique military experiences (such as former POW's). More than 500 of these organizations hold annual reunions in the United States.

Modern veterans organizations stem from the service of vast numbers of civilians in the wars of the 19th and 20th centuries. The organizations are civilian in character, in aims, purposes, and methods of influence on society. By contrast, in earlier centuries of Western civilization, war veterans, as a class, were professional soldiers unemployed in their profession, and their impact on society was that of a potential military threat to the civilian establishment. Thus the significance of Julius Caesar's crossing the Rubicon was not his own return to Rome, but the return of his loyal legions, tacitly understood by all to be the force that would deliver political power to Caesar. By contrast, the constitution of the American Legion forbids the use of military titles and participation of the organization in partisan politics.

In Paris in 1950, the World Veterans Federation was formed as a congress of the veterans organizations of many nations. Within a few years it listed 157 affiliates in 46 nations. However, many veterans organizations did not join the federation, and many of its affiliates admit members without previous military service.

See also American Legion; AMVETS; British Legion; Disabled American Veterans; Veterans of Foreign Wars of the United States (VFW).

Robert B. Pitkin
"American Legion Magazine"

VETERINARY MEDICINE, the science dealing with the prevention and treatment of diseases of domestic animals. One who practices this science is a veterinarian, a name derived from the Latin *veterinarius,* meaning of or pertaining to beasts of burden and draft.

HISTORY

The origin of veterinary medicine is inseparable from that of human medical knowledge. The pathology of animal diseases was considered useful information by Hippocrates, the father of medicine. The histories of ancient Greece and Rome contain references to veterinary medicine. Horseshoers or farriers, in the ages when horses were essential in peace and war, often practiced veterinary skills, and farrier was a term formerly used for veterinarians. A more recent reference distinguishing between veterinarians and farriers, however, was recorded in 1646 by Sir Thomas Browne, English physician: "The second Assertion, that a horse has no gall, is very general, not only swallowed by the people, and common farriers, but also received by good veterinarians. . . ."

The earliest veterinary schools were founded in France, the first in 1761 in Lyon and the second in 1766 at Alfort. Approximately 10 veterinary schools were founded in European countries during the next 30 years. In the United States numerous private institutions were established for teaching veterinary medicine but the first unit associated with a college or university was the Division of Veterinary Medicine established in 1879 at Iowa State College of Agriculture and Mechanic Arts (now Iowa State University of Science and Technology).

Other U. S. institutions with schools of veterinary medicine that are accredited by the American Veterinary Medical Association include Auburn University, University of California at Davis, Colorado State University, University of Georgia, University of Illinois, Kansas State University, Louisiana State University at Baton Rouge, Michigan State University, University of Minnesota, University of Missouri, Ohio State University, Oklahoma State University, University of Pennsylvania, Purdue University, State University of New York Veterinary College (Cornell), Texas A&M, Tuskegee Institute, and Washington State University. In Canada there are schools of veterinary medicine at St. Hyacinthe, Quebec (1886) and at Guelph, Ontario (1862).

Originally, veterinary schools in the United States were privately owned; they depended on funds from tuition and other fees. Beginning with New York Veterinary College in 1894, they have become mostly state supported, only those at the University of Pennsylvania and at Tuskegee Institute remaining private.

The American Veterinary Medical Association, founded in 1863, with headquarters in Chicago, Ill., has done much to raise the standards of veterinary education as well as the level of ethics and practice of veterinary medicine.

Veterinary Medicine Throughout the World. Besides the United States and Canada, most of the well-developed countries of the world have had veterinary schools for many years, and the education given their veterinarians is of comparable quality in many instances. However, in Japan the majority of veterinarians have no more than a high school education in which veterinary science is emphasized, and only a small

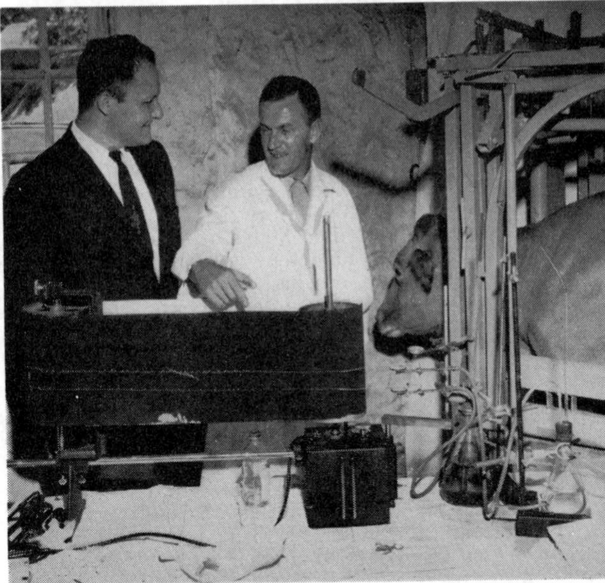

Jules Schick

Above: **A physician and a veterinarian in consultation. The methods and equipment used in their respective fields are often similar, as are many of the diseases studied.** ***Left:*** **Technicians in a modern veterinary laboratory.**

percentage can be considered veterinarians by United States standards.

Some variations in numbers of veterinarians compared with animal populations are interesting. Communist China, a leading livestock producer and the world's largest swine producer, has only two schools of veterinary medicine, with a disproportionately small number of veterinarians. India ranks 10th in number of veterinarians and leads the world in numbers of cattle, buffaloes, goats, and elephants. Japan reports the world's third largest number of veterinarians and is not among the world's 20 leading livestock producers.

In most English-speaking and some western European countries, the majority of veterinarians are engaged in private practice, while government service occupies a majority of veterinarians in other countries. The United States has the largest number of veterinarians dealing with health needs of pet animals.

EDUCATION

Entrance requirements for veterinary schools throughout the world have steadily risen. In the United States the advance is exemplified by comparing the early requirement by the New York legislature in 1895 that a high school diploma be earned before admission, to the modern minimum of two years of preveterinary college training required by all veterinary schools. Chemistry, physics, zoology, and certain liberal arts courses are prerequisite to admission to the modern school. The veterinary course in the United States comprises four years of a minimum of nine months each, as required by the American Veterinary Medical Association for admission of graduates to the association. Courses in anatomy, biochemistry, physiology, pathology, parasitology, microbiology, clinical diagnosis, medicine, and surgery are the backbone of veterinary medical education. In more advanced schools there is close correlation between courses given during the three phases of the curriculum. The phases generally recognized are: the basic sciences—physiology, chemistry, and anatomy; the veterinary sciences—pathology and bacteriology; the therapeutic sciences—medicine and surgery and their application. The organization of the different courses in one of these groups under a single chairman facilitates coordination of the material presented.

Veterinary education today incorporates the most advanced medical knowledge and techniques. The cooperation and exchange of information between veterinarians and physicians in research and teaching institutions work to the advantage of both fields. At the successful completion of the curriculum the student in the United States receives the degree of Doctor of Veterinary Medicine (D.V.M.). To qualify as a licensed veterinarian, the individual must pass an examination given by the state or states in which he wishes to practice. Efforts by the American Veterinary Medical Association to introduce a national board of examiners have met with partial success, but some states have retained their own state board examinations.

In Canada graduates from the veterinary schools also receive the Doctor of Veterinary Medicine degree. In Great Britain the doctor's degree is not granted but upon admission to membership of the Royal College of Veterinary Surgeons the graduate may append the letters M.R.C.V.S. to his name.

PUBLIC HEALTH ASPECTS

The protection of the health of the public is an integral part of all aspects of veterinary medicine. The inspection of meat food products, the recognition and eradication of communicable diseases, research in diseases causing great economic losses, and vaccination of individual animals are all services of veterinarians to safeguard the public health.

Treatment of Diseases Communicable to Man.—In the protection of public health from the menace of diseases of animals communicable to man, the practicing veterinarian occupies the first line of defense. His vaccination and immunization programs prevent uncounted cases of communicable disease. The diagnosis of the approximately 54 diseases which may spread from animals to man and the subsequent arrest of this spread depend on the veterinarian. The arrest of infectious diseases before they can assume epidemic proportions is usually done in cooperation with government veterinarians. Three of these serious communicable diseases are tuberculosis, brucellosis, and rabies.

Bovine Tuberculosis.—Of all the diseases of animals, none has been more important than bovine tuberculosis. The disease has appeared among cattle of all parts of the world wherever tubercle bacilli have been carried to them, but it was not until the tuberculosis test became available that the prevalence of tuberculosis in cattle could be determined. There was apparently no tuberculosis among the descendants of the Spanish Longhorn cattle in the southwestern part of the United States and Central and South America; the disease is thought to have been introduced into the Americas through the importation of fine beef and dairy cattle. By 1901, the incidence of tuberculosis among cattle in certain states of the United States varied from 4 to 50 per cent. In the 1920's the daily list of surgical operations in large American hospitals was made up of a considerable proportion of operations for the removal of tuberculous glands of the neck in children. This particular form of the disease was largely due to infection with the bovine type of tuberculosis contracted by drinking unpasteurized milk from tuberculous cows. There is scarcely a medical graduate of recent years who has seen an operation of this type; for the most audacious undertaking to control tuberculosis among animals and man in the entire history of the world began in the United States in 1917. Including a test and slaughter plan, it resulted in the only truly successful demonstration of controlling the disease. As of Jan. 1, 1941, every one of the 3,071 counties in the United States had been accredited as free of bovine tuberculosis.

Brucellosis.—The successful control of undulant fever in human beings probably will be achieved when the control of brucellosis in cattle and swine becomes fully implemented. The disease is transmitted to man by his handling cattle and swine infected with brucellosis and by drinking unpasteurized milk from infected cows. While the percentage of resultant deaths is not so high as from tuberculosis, undulant fever is the cause of much chronic ill health. The difficulty of diagnosis in the later stages and the lack of effective treatment make it a highly important public health problem today. Despite all the medical research on undulant fever, it remains the task of the veterinary profession to conquer this disease at its source.

Rabies.—Primarily an infection of the canine species, rabies may affect any of the warm-blooded animals such as the fox, skunk, and bat. Although the disease is usually transmitted by the bite of an infected dog, the farmer and the stockman are often exposed when handling cattle and horses which have contracted the disease. Ingestion of the rabies virus is not dangerous unless wounds are present in the throat or mouth, because the gastric juice quickly destroys the virus. While infection by means of the milk from cows suspected of having been exposed to rabies is exceedingly rare, it is nevertheless advised that all such milk be thoroughly boiled or pasteurized. Once rabies develops in man it is invariably fatal, as there is no cure for the disease. The public health significance of rabies is not confined to the fatal cases alone, for the cost of manufacturing and administering rabies vaccine to individuals who have been exposed to this disease is enormous. When the cost of valuable domestic animals which have to be destroyed because of rabies infection is reckoned, it can be seen that man pays a high price for the privilege of allowing rabies to remain uncontrolled.

Government Activities.—Government veterinary authorities in many countries are concerned with regulation of animal diseases which may sap the national health and economy, and with controlling animal products utilized for food by the general public. In the United States the eradication programs against bovine tuberculosis and brucellosis are under the direction of and largely carried out by veterinarians in the Agricultural Research Service of the Department of Agriculture. Aid in eradication or control of foot-and-mouth disease, vesicular exanthema, anthrax, and screwworm flies has also been carried out by this organization, which is also responsible, through its Livestock Regulatory Program, for the inspection of meat food products in packing houses. This inspection includes the ante- and postmortem examination of animals for evidence of disease as well as the maintenance of sanitary environment and processing. Research in animal disease by government veterinarians is carried out at modern laboratories located at Plum Island, N.Y.; Beltsville, Md.; and Ames, Iowa. Air pollution studies on animals to evaluate the disease-producing effects of smog have been undertaken at Philadelphia, Pa.

Veterinary services remain important in the military field despite the mechanization of the forces. Both the United States Army and Air Force maintain veterinary corps in their medical departments, composed of graduate veterinarians as officers and specially trained laymen as enlisted men. The mission of these corps is threefold: (1) to safeguard the health of the troops by inspection of all foods of animal origin procured for consumption by military personnel; (2) to provide professional veterinary medical service for animals owned by the military services; (3) to furnish adequate veterinary service in occupied countries.

The possibility of biological and radiological warfare has added new responsibilities to both military and civilian veterinarians. Contamination of food and animals and other hazards of these weapons have become matters of international concern, and have resulted in studies by military and other government agencies utilizing the special knowledge of the veterinarian.

The preservation of food by means of irradiation is another development under study by research teams which include veterinarians. In the United States, numerous military, industrial, and academic research groups have participated in such studies under the direction of the United States Army and the surgeon general. Feeding studies with chickens, rats, mice, dogs, and monkeys as test animals use specific food items preserved by irradiation and require the professional guidance and interpretation of the veterinarian.

PRACTICE

The practice of veterinary medicine varies according to locality, animal population, and special skills and interests of the veterinarian. For many years it was confined to the treatment of horses and cattle. As the use of the horse for transportation and work diminished, the emphasis in practice shifted to livestock and pets. Horses have assumed greater importance and value in racing, and in some countries are still important as livestock. The health of other livestock, namely, cattle, swine, sheep, goats, and poultry, is the concern of the rural practitioner frequently characterized as a large-animal practitioner. The small-animal practitioner deals with dogs, cats, and cage birds. Many veterinarians have mixed practices and divide their time between livestock and pets. Some practitioners treat only horses, usually race horses.

Vaccination Methods.—Prevention of disease constitutes a large and important portion of any veterinarian's efforts. Advice on nutrition, sanitation, breeding, and other husbandry practices is valuable, as is the vaccination of animals against many infectious diseases—for example, rabies, brucellosis, distemper, Newcastle disease, hog cholera, and feline panleukopenia.

Vaccination may be employed to produce two forms of immunity, active and passive. Active immunity results when the agent or some modification of the agent which causes the disease is introduced into the animal, stimulating it to produce antibodies. The antibodies produced against a modified or attenuated disease agent in the vaccine are also effective in protecting the animal against the virulent agent. An animal retains the ability to produce a specific antibody for varying periods of time. For some diseases it is a year; for others it is the balance of the animal's life. In passive immunity, antibodies produced in another animal's body are introduced and serve to protect the recipient against that disease. This form of immunity is of only about two weeks' duration.

Disease agents are used in several forms in the production of vaccine. The disease agent may be killed by substances such as formalin or ether; the agent may be attenuated by growing it on artificial media or in a different species of animal, or a variant of the agent which is less virulent may be used in the vaccine. Another method of vaccination introduces the virulent agent simultaneously with the antibodies produced by an immune animal, thus protecting as well as stimulating active immunity.

Large-Animal and Small-Animal Diseases.—The diseases the large-animal practitioner is called upon to diagnose, treat, and, if possible, prevent in other animals in the herd vary even within the breeds. For example, dairy cattle are subject to diseases of the udder and associated metabolic upsets such as ketosis and hypocalcemia. Beef cattle are subject to parasites, poisonous plants, and nutritional deficiencies. Many infectious diseases (anthrax, brucellosis, tuberculosis, shipping fever, and actinomycosis) are common to all breeds and types of cattle. Diseases such as blackleg, anaplasmosis, and coccidioidomycosis are prevalent in some localities but almost never occur in others. Common sheep diseases are parasitism, ketosis, listeriosis, anthrax, and clostridial diseases. Swine are subject to hog cholera, erysipelas, swine influenza, and certain nutritional diseases of baby pigs. Among the more common poultry diseases are chronic respiratory disease, leukosis, Newcastle disease, laryngotracheitis, blackhead, and erysipelas of turkeys.

The small-animal practitioner is frequently located in or near an urban population. The diseases of dogs commonly dealt with are distemper, infectious hepatitis, leptospirosis, and parasitism as well as many injuries. The small-animal practitioner is frequently requested to perform surgery and can often carry out many minor operations in his office. Perhaps one of the most valuable and common surgical procedures is the ovariohysterectomy or spay to sterilize a female dog or cat. The feline diseases commonly encountered are panleukopenia, cystic calculi, and respiratory diseases.

In addition to the contrast in size and function of their patients, the large- and small-animal practitioners differ from an economic standpoint. The common breeds of livestock are raised for purely commercial reasons. If the cost of treatment would eliminate the profit resulting from raising that animal, this treatment is usually not carried out. On the other hand, treatment may prolong the animal's life and allow financial gain to the owner, as for example in the case of a valuable stallion or bull used for breeding purposes. The value of a pet is not so frequently measured in purely monetary terms and treatment may consequently become more expensive and still be to the satisfaction of the animal's owner.

Zoological Problems.—Diseases of zoo animals are of interest to a small group of veterinarians. A few zoological gardens employ a veterinarian and others will call one as needed. Prevention of disease is an important factor in maintaining a healthy zoo collection. Advice on diet, sanitation, and environment will actually be of more value than treatment of individual animals. Immunization of the wild cats against feline panleukopenia and the wolf, jackal, coyote, and dingo against distemper and infectious hepatitis is of positive value.

The diagnosis of disease in wild animals is unsatisfactory; clinical study as in the domestic animal is impossible. The veterinarian must rely on such general precepts as similarity in anatomy and diseases between domestic and wild species. Deer, antelope, and buffalo are ruminants and are subject to the same diseases as domestic cattle. The wart hog, babirusa, and peccary are closely allied to swine, and the zebra is related to the domestic horse. A certain group of symptoms accompanies all diseases—dull, rough coat or feathers, refusal to eat, weakness in the hind quarters. By the time the disease has advanced to the point of becoming externally noticeable, it has usually gone beyond the reach of medical treatment. Occasionally animals are found dead in their cages without having shown any signs of illness whatsoever.

Treatment will sometimes be attempted if the condition appears to be one easily corrected. Sometimes it is possible to conceal medication in the food or drinking water without arousing the animal's suspicion. General anesthetics may be similarly administered to aid in carrying out tooth extractions, fracture reductions, or suturing major wounds. The principal danger here lies in the frantic and violent reactions exhibited by the animal as the effect of the drug wears off. Little is gained by removing an infected tooth only to have the animal break its neck dashing into the yard fence.

Quarantine of all newly acquired specimens is essential to prevent the introduction of infectious diseases. Veterinary supervision of quarantine allows such procedures as vaccination and worming to be carried out during this period. Gradual introduction of the zoo diet at the same time permits closer observation of an animal's reaction to this strange form of nutrition.

Specialization.—The advent of specialization in veterinary medicine has inevitably followed the trend in human medicine. The increasing volume of factual information and demands of special techniques require more complete individual attention in order that competent service may be offered. Some of the veterinary specialties now developed are surgery, obstetrics and gynecology, medicine, neurology, cardiology, dermatology, ophthalmology, pathology, and radiology.

Surgery.—Modern veterinary surgeons employ the methods of anesthesia and aseptic technique used in human surgery. Preanesthetic sedation and preparation are of particular importance in veterinary surgery to prevent the struggles of the animal patient, which may injure itself as well as the surgeon. The common inhalation and intravenous, as well as local, anesthetics are in general use. Sterile preparation of instruments, gloves, masks, caps, and gowns and the adequate preparation of the patient's operative site are procedures taught in all schools of veterinary medicine and widely employed by practitioners. The limitations imposed by farm conditions during surgery on livestock are obvious, but may be minimized by care.

Some of the common major surgical procedures carried out are rumenotomy, ovariohysterectomy, herniorrhaphy, intestinal anastomosis, caesarian delivery, fracture reduction, biopsy, and removal of tumors. The techniques of fluid

Above: On a Scottish farm, a shepherd girl inoculates an ailing young lamb with penicillin.

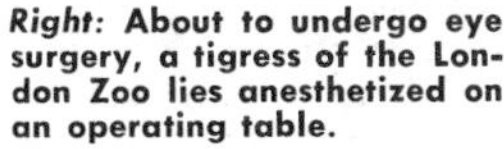

***Right:* About to undergo eye surgery, a tigress of the London Zoo lies anesthetized on an operating table.**

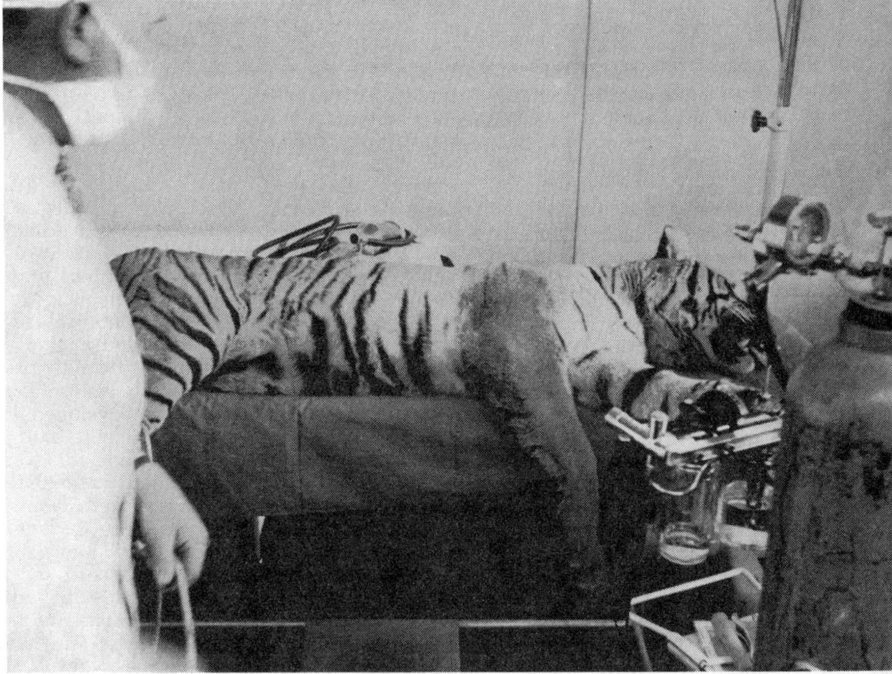

(Above) Thomas A. Wilkie; (right) Michael Ward

administration or blood transfusion are employed when needed. The problem of blood incompatibilities is not so severe in veterinary medicine as in human medicine, but pretransfusion matching is routinely carried out. In dogs, according to one authority, there are five distinct blood groups. There is only one type which is incompatible with all the others; the remaining four may be safely mixed. Incompatibility may arise in an individual dog after one transfusion of any of the four types as a result of acquired immunity. Thus a dog which is to be given a transfusion should always have its blood and the blood to be administered cross-matched. Postoperative care varies with each case—for example, in the exercise allowed to fracture cases or in the diets of animals recovering from intestinal surgery.

Medicine.—The beginning of any clinical examination is the case history. This includes such facts as the age of the animal, its diet, the general health as regards appetite, the vaccinations the animal has received, the diseases or accidents previously encountered, or prior treatment for the present complaint. Unless answers to these questions are accurate the veterinarian will be misled and the history will not coincide with the clinical findings. The diagnosis of animal diseases is facilitated by many laboratory techniques and mechanical aids, but it remains the task of the veterinarian to evaluate all the findings and make the decision.

The infectious diseases of animals which the veterinarian is expected to recognize and treat comprise a formidable list. Each species of livestock and pet is subject to its own special group, as are additional species ordinarily wild or confined to a zoo. One approach to this problem of classification and diagnosis is to consider diseases by organ systems. The respiratory diseases, the gastrointestinal diseases, and the urogenital diseases are groups taking in all conditions found in those systems. Another method of disease classification is by the type of agent responsible for causing the disease. There are bacterial, viral, mycotic, protozoan, and metazoan agents.

Another complicating factor in the diagnosis of animal disease is the accuracy of the findings. The fact arises that altered structure of organs and deviations of the chemical composition of the body fluids do not always disturb body functions to the extent that detectable signs appear. Abdominal enlargement due to pregnancy may resemble bloat, or the temporary elevation of temperature in a severely exercised animal or one confined to a hot stable may resemble that of fever.

The question of parasites is another problem to which there is no flat answer. When does the presence of parasites indicate a disease condition? One may think that the number of parasites present would be the guide; but this cannot be depended upon because a resistant host may harbor without ill effect a large number of parasites that would cause severe disease in a less resistant individual.

In spite of these reservations which any clinician who is honest in his approach to diagnosis must entertain, reliance must be placed on laboratory findings. The care with which a sample is taken and its handling until delivery to the laboratory influence the accuracy of the results. For example, a fecal sample for the identification of intestinal parasites must be fresh. Blood cell counts and determinations of specific substances in the blood such as protein, sugar, various cations, and nitrogenous substances are employed in veterinary medicine. Urine analysis, skin scrapings, fecal examinations, and bacteriological cultures are additional procedures of diagnostic value. Tests of blood serum for antibodies against disease agents are employed. Exposure to the agents of diseases such as brucellosis, leptospirosis, histoplasmosis, and pullorum may result in detectable blood changes. Another diagnostic tool is the skin test. This is best known for its application in the diagnosis of bovine tuberculosis and is also employed in some of the systemic fungus diseases. The specialities of neurology, ophthalmology, and cardiology are rapidly assuming greater proportions as diagnostic aids; yet the services of specialists are often not available to the individual veterinarian, who must employ ophthalmoscope, electrocardiograph, and roentgenograph himself to carry out a complete examination and arrive at an accurate diagnosis.

Following diagnosis, the treatment must be decided upon, and here again a wide variety of drugs, biological preparations, and procedures are available. The restless nature and fear on the part of the animal and the veterinarian's inability to communicate with it impose certain restrictions on technique in veterinary medicine, but the use of sedation, safe restraint, and cage confinement can frequently help accomplish difficult procedures. The latest pharmaceutical products are used in veterinary medicine, and some companies produce drugs exclusively for veterinary use. All the ethical drug firms produce veterinary adaptations of their products.

Pathology.—The postmortem examination of animals is called a necropsy in veterinary medicine as distinguished from the autopsy, or human postmortem examination. As an aid in the diagnosis of obscure causes of death the necropsy is of great value. It is also used to determine the extent of spread of a specific disease when large numbers of animals are dying in a region. Specific diseases cause characteristic postmortem appearances, and rapid recognition is possible by a trained veterinary pathologist. The necropsy is also of value to the future diagnosis and treatment of difficult cases. Veterinary pathologists examine tumor biopsy material to determine whether it is malignant. Comparing pathologic processes and lesions in the various species of animals as well as humans increases knowledge concerning basic principles of disease. The specialty of pathology requires highly technical support and the facilities of a laboratory. Pathologists are usually associated with a school or medical research organization. They are employed in the drug industry for evaluating the toxicity of new preparations.

The specialty of performing these examinations has developed to a high degree in veterinary medicine. In the United States, an examining board for veterinary pathologists was established in the District of Columbia in 1948, and the accepted applicants become members of the American College of Veterinary Pathologists. This group is at present the country's only examining board for a veterinary specialty. As a prerequisite to taking the examination, the applicant must have been a graduate veterinarian for five years and have had three years' experience in pathology.

Obstetrics and Gynecology.—In veterinary medicine, this specialty is of greatest importance in cattle practice. All animal species have occasional reproductive problems, but the specialist devotes a large portion of his time to cows. The services of veterinarians specializing in this field include breeding advice, treatment of sterility, artificial insemination, pregnancy diagnosis, assisting the animal in difficult delivery, and postnatal care.

The causes of sterility or difficult conception in animals are numerous. In animals of economic importance sterility reduces the value of the individual animal to the market value of its flesh for food. Sterility is not a complete lack of reproducing ability, but frequently only a temporary or partial failure, and in correcting the condition the veterinarian renders a valuable service. Diagnosis of the cause of sterility is highly technical and requires evaluation of the anatomy, hormone balance, sterility-producing disease agents, and general condition of the animal. Use of the appropriate techniques and drugs may often result in conception and successful completion of pregnancy. Infectious diseases, among them brucellosis, trichomoniasis, and viral equine abortion, are responsible for economic losses through interference with reproduction. Abortion or failure to conceive may result also from numerous diseases not primarily of the reproductive system, but which disturb the health of the animal seriously.

The techniques of artificial insemination have been greatly improved, allowing more general and successful use. They have now been used in the cow, horse, pig, sheep, dog, and various breeds of poultry. The implantation of the fertilized ova from purebred females into foster "scrub" females has been carried out successfully in cattle, sheep, and rabbits. However, this procedure of implantation remains in the experimental stage.

Difficult birth, or dystocia, through malposition, improper anatomy of the fetus or dam, improper function of one part of the reproductive tract, an abnormal number of fetuses, or debilitation of the dam may be relieved by the intervention of a veterinarian. The use of anesthetics, manipulation, traction, or surgery are techniques employed in the safe deliverance of the fetus and preservation of maternal life. This phase of veterinary medicine is one of the most satisfactory to client and veterinarian in terms of service and tangible results. Postnatal care of cows is often necessary; perhaps the two most common diseases following birth are retained placenta and hypocalcemia. Here again, relief may be swift and satisfactory.

Cardiology.—Heart disease of animals at present is best understood in dogs, although advances are being made in equine and bovine cardiology. The veterinary cardiologist employs instruments such as stethoscope, electrocardiograph, percussion hammer, blood pressure cuff, and radiograph. The examination of an animal for cardiac disease varies from a general examination only in that more precise instruments are used to concentrate on the cardiovascular system. The stethoscope may be used to give information about leaking heart valves, their location, and the degree of their incompetence. The percussion hammer may give an estimate of the size of the heart; the pressure cuff, together with the stethoscope, may be used to evaluate blood pressure. The radiograph will give information about the size, position, and shape of the heart as well as of the large vessels around the heart in the chest. Perhaps the most valuable tool in diagnosis of cardiac disease is the electrocardiograph. The instrument used by veterinary cardiologists is the same in all respects as electrocardiographs used in human cardiology. Contact with the animal's body is made by means of the standard plates or by alligator clips attached to the lead wires. The points of attachment are the four legs and various points over the animal's chest. The problem of hair interfering with good electrical contact arises occasionally, but use of a standard electrode paste and careful attention to application usually eliminate this problem. The electrocardiogram of animals varies with the species. Of great interest to human cardiologists is the similarity in the tracings of man, monkey, and dog. This similarity is of value in experimental cardiology and the interpretation of human electrocardiograms.

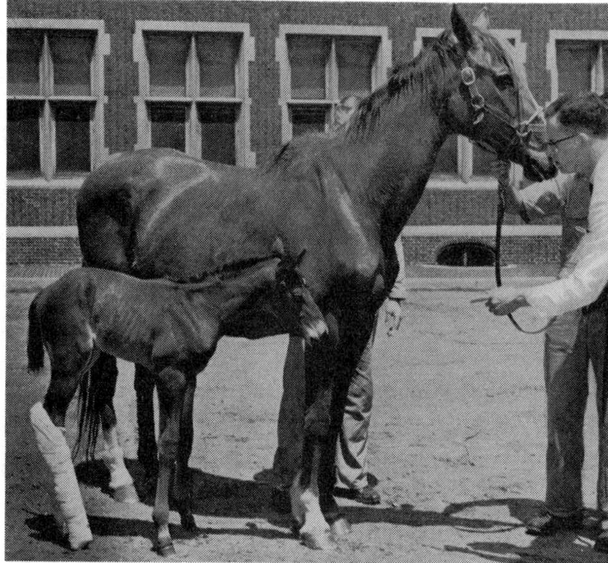

Leg fractures in foals are treated with splints, much as are broken bones in human beings.

Abnormal findings by means of the electrocardiogram in veterinary medicine are similar to human findings. Animals have arrhythmias such as left and right bundle branch block, extrasystoles, paroxysmal ventricular tachycardia, and auricular fibrillation. Other types of heart disease are present in animals. Congenital malformations are not uncommon. Such malformations as patent ductus arteriosus, patent foramen ovale, pulmonic stenosis, tetralogy of Fallot, and Eisenmenger's complex have been demonstrated in animals.

Cardiovascular diseases due to circulatory changes are not as common in animals as in man. Animals suffer from arteriosclerosis, but not from the type seen in man. In man, arteriosclerosis leads to clotting of the blood and death of the tissue supplied by the vessel. In the case of coronary arteries, the result is commonly called a heart attack or a coronary occlusion. This type of cardiovascular disease is much less common in animals than man, although certainly not unheard of. Another type of heart disease is valvular incompetence or insufficiency. This occurs most commonly in old dogs and particularly commonly in association with kidney disease. The results of valvular incompetence are many. The extra work of pumping blood resulting from the leaking valve causes the heart to enlarge. Eventually the heart will fail and fluid will accumulate in the lungs or elsewhere. This is known as congestive heart failure. The veterinary cardiologist may detect the murmur and hear sounds resulting from fluid accumulation in the lungs. If necessary, an electrocardiogram will be taken to evaluate the functioning of the heart's conduction system. A radiograph of the chest may then be taken to determine the degree of enlargement and congestion present. An animal with this condition may be treated with preparations used in similar cases of human heart failure.

Certain heart diseases are unique in animals. Dogs suffer from a parasite, *Dirofilaria immitis*, commonly called the heartworm, which enters the blood stream and eventually lodges in the right ventricle. If a large number gather here, the dog will experience difficulty in respiration and be of no value. The parasite is transmitted by means of a mosquito bite; consequently the disease is more common in areas in the United States and foreign countries where mosquitos are prevalent. Heartworms in dogs may be treated with chemicals injected into the blood stream or by surgical removal.

Another type of heart disease unique with animals is traumatic pericarditis, which is encountered in cattle. An animal will occasionally ingest a nail or piece of wire, which, upon entering the stomach, remains there because of its weight. The normal contraction of that portion of the ruminant stomach may cause this sharp object to pierce the stomach wall. If the object is moved in the direction of the animal's heart it may eventually come in contact with the sac around the heart and irritate it. The result of irritation and contamination by bacteria from the stomach is inflammation, or traumatic pericarditis. This condition is commonly called hardware disease. Uncorrected pericarditis will interfere with the function of the heart and death will result. If it is not too far advanced, surgical removal of the metal may relieve the condition. Some individuals, veterinarians as well as farmers, immobilize metallic objects or even remove them from bovine stomachs by means of a magnet. In a somewhat similar manner, a mine detector is occasionally utilized to diagnose hardware disease, although this method is not reliable.

Dermatology.—Diseases of the skin in animals present a wide and varied field. Viral, bacterial, mycotic, protozoan, endocrine, metabolic, nutritional, and neoplastic diseases of the cutaneous and subcutaneous tissues are frequently encountered in veterinary medicine. Diagnosis depends on special techniques such as culture and microscopic examination of scrapings as well as a broad and fundamental knowledge of normal physiology and the effects of imbalances in secretion, function, and interrelation between organs. Mange, eczema, and the various dermatides are becoming better understood and characterized with the development of this specialty in veterinary medicine.

Radiology.—This specialty is one of the most widely utilized special techniques by practitioners as well as radiologists. Radiology may be roughly divided into two categories, therapeutic and diagnostic. Therapeutic radiology is not as extensively employed in veterinary medicine as in human medicine. The outstanding example of the therapeutic use is in treatment of bovine actinomycosis. This is a disease which is characterized by enlargement of the lower jaw due to granulomatous inflammation. The disease organism is deeply buried in bone and scar tissue, and irradiation is one of the methods employed to halt the spread into surrounding tissue. The use of therapeutic radiology is generally limited to schools and large clinics.

Diagnostic radiology has a large place in veterinary medicine. The fact that only objective symptoms are available to guide him makes the radiograph even more valuable to the veterinarian than to the physician. The predilection of dogs and cats to swallow foreign bodies and the high incidence of fractures make every practitioner rely heavily on this technique. The method of restraint is of prime importance in veterinary radiology. Some animals may be restrained simply by holding or gentle tying. In other instances, general anesthesia must be employed to accomplish clear detail or to allow radiographs to be taken while the animal is in an uncomfortable or unusual position. The recommended kilovoltage for veterinary use is high since the exposure time may thus be reduced. The use of faster X-ray film also allows reduction of the time. Shorter time exposure improves radiographic detail by allowing less time for the animal to move. Interpretation of radiographs requires a complete knowledge of normal anatomy and a careful detailed examination of the radiograph by system, that is, skeletal, gastrointestinal, and so forth.

Special applications of radiology through use of radiopaque substances has increased the value of this technique, which is used in the diagnosis of gastrointestinal abnormalities, strictures, or malpositions. The radiopaque substance is swallowed by the animal and lines the wall of the organs as it passes through them. A radiograph taken at this time gives unusually clear detail and allows a more thorough visualization of the gastrointestinal system. The radiopaque medium is also used to diagnose congenital anomalies in the hearts of the animals. The visualization of the various chambers of the heart as the blood containing the radiopaque substance is pumped through it by its own contraction is a dramatic procedure indeed. The process is so rapid that occasionally moving pictures are utilized to capture the details. Injection of the ventricles of the brain with radiopaque medium or air is another development used in veterinary radiology. This serves to outline abnormal size or shape as well as unusual objects in the cavities of the brain. Other organs such as the kidney and uterus may also be visualized more clearly by means of radiopaque media.

Ophthalmology.—The demand for the specialist in diseases of the eye is somewhat limited in veterinary medicine. The average practitioner will carry out some routine ophthalmology, but only under rare circumstances will he refer a case to a specialist. The specialist in turn usually devotes only part of his time to ophthalmology. This situation does not result from a lack of

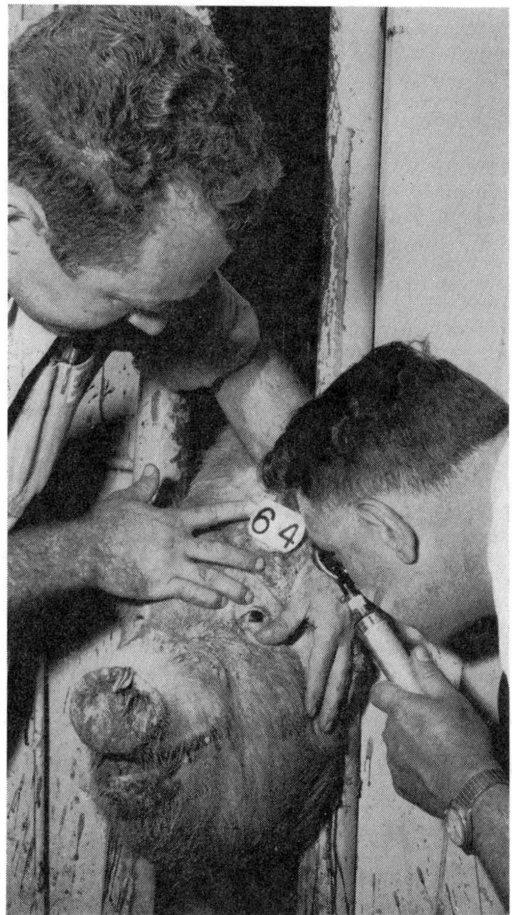

A veterinary ophthalmologist uses an ophthalmoscope to examine the eye of a hog.

knowledge or familiarity with ocular diseases in veterinary medicine, but rather from a slower development of specialists and specialties than has been evident in human medicine. Instruments employed by a veterinary ophthalmologist are binocular glasses that magnify 5 to 10 times, a small flashlight, and an ophthalmoscope. Among the more common eye diseases or conditions encountered in animals are entropion, or introversion of the margin of the eyelid; ectropion, or eversion of the same structure; conjunctivitis, which may be due to bacterial or viral agents; allergic conditions; foreign bodies; or chemical irritants. Conditions of the cornea, iris, and lens which interfere with vision are encountered in veterinary ophthalmology. Glaucoma and cataracts, known in human medicine, are not uncommon in animals. Infectious conditions of the eye are infectious keratitis of cattle, sheep, and goats, and periodic ophthalmia of horses and mules. The use of extremely fine and demanding surgical techniques is employed to correct some ocular conditions, and the employment of antibiotics and steroids has contributed to the success of medical handling of other eye diseases.

Neurology.—The veterinary neurologist, by means of neurologic symptoms and examination, attempts to localize diseases of the central nervous system. Occasionally certain symptoms strongly indicate that a specific area of the brain or spinal cord is affected. With a complete neurologic examination this localization may be confirmed, denied, or found to be merely a dominant sign of a more generalized condition. Identification of the site leads the veterinary neurologist to the next step, the nature of the lesion. Two broad classes of central nervous lesions are recognized: organic and functional. Certain diseases or conditions in other parts of the animal body will reflect themselves by altering the metabolism of the nervous system and produce functional neurologic symptoms.

The organic diseases of the central nervous system encountered in animals are of several types: congenital abnormalities such as hydrocephalus, absence or reduced size of the cerebellum, optic nerve hypoplasia, epilepsy, and myoclonia congenita. Circulatory disturbances in the brain and spinal cord of animals are of a different nature than knowledge of human disease might lead one to suspect. Arteriosclerosis and strokes, relatively common in man, are extremely infrequent in animals. The disturbances of circulation encountered in veterinary medicine are usually secondary to some infectious disease or injury. Diseases which attack the brain and cause inflammation or encephalitis are found in all species. This category includes rabies, canine distemper, equine encephalitis, and avian pneumoencephalitis or Newcastle disease of chickens.

Another type of central nervous disease which is of great interest to veterinary neurologists as well as to physicians specializing in this field is that of tumors. These are primary or may have spread from some other location in the body to produce symptoms which cause confusion to the veterinarian but which may be localized with a high degree of accuracy and identified by the neurologist.

See also ANIMALS, DISEASES OF; CATTLE—*4. Cattle Diseases;* DOG, DISEASES OF THE; HORSE, CARE AND DISEASES OF.

MARK W. ALLAM,
Dean, School of Veterinary Medicine, University of Pennsylvania.

Bibliography

Allan, Duncan, *Outlines of Animal Immunobiology* (Saunders 1980).
Clarke, Anna P., *Canine Clinic* (Macmillan 1984).
Grunsell, C., *Veterinary Annual* (PSG Pub. Co. annually).
Klos, Heinz-Georg, and Land, Ernst M., *Handbook of Zoo Medicine,* tr. by Gunter Speckmann (Van Nostrand Reinhold 1981).
Lane, D. R., ed., *Jones's Animal Nursing* (Pergamon 1985).
Schnurenberger, Paul R., and others, *Attacking Animal Disease* (Iowa State Univ. Press 1986).
Ward, Amy, *Small Animal Health Care* (Veterinary Medicine Pub. 1984).

VETIVER, vĕt′ə-vər, a robust, tufted, perennial grass, *Vetiveria zizanioides,* native to tropical Asia, especially the Indian region, and cultivated in both the Old and New Worlds for hedges and for its aromatic roots. The roots, since ancient times in India, have been made into mats, screens, and baskets that are very fragrant when wet. A volatile oil derived from the roots is used in perfumes, soaps, and cosmetics. The grass, also called *khus-khus,* has escaped from cultivation in the southern United States.

RICHARD M. STRAW.

VETO, vē′tō, a term derived from the Latin *veto,* "I forbid," and referring to the power of one member of an electoral or decision-making group, or of an outside agency, to prevent action by such a group. In the first of these two senses the veto implies that the group can act only if its members are unanimous, as in many clubs where a single "black ball" vetoes the election of a new member. Such a *liberum veto* (free veto) existed in the Polish constitution from the 17th century to 1791 based on the claim to absolute political equality of all Polish gentlemen represented in the Sejm or legislative body. This procedure made legislation extremely difficult and subject to the influence of foreign diplomats who could often bribe one member, thus weakening the state.

Diplomatic conferences have customarily required unanimity of the delegates for the passage of resolutions, and such unanimity was required for organs of the League of Nations in the absence of express exception (Covenant, Art. 5). A number of other international organizations have departed from the unanimity rule, as does the United Nations which permits resolutions by a two-thirds vote of the General Assembly, by a majority of the Economic and Social Council and the Trusteeship Council, and by 9 out of the 15 members of the Security Council. In the latter case, however, each of the five permanent members has a veto on substantive matters unless it is a party to a dispute before the council. It has been held in practice that failure of a permanent member to concur because of abstention or absence does not constitute a veto. In the course of the "cold war," the Soviet Union has frequently exercised a veto, and other permanent members have occasionally done so; for example, Great Britain and France vetoed the resolution calling upon Israel to withdraw its forces from Egyptian territory in 1956. The United States cast its first Security Council veto in 1970. Frequent use of the veto has seriously impaired the capacity of the Security Council to function in the way anticipated by the charter.

In confederations such as those of the United States from 1781 to 1789 and of Germany from 1815 to 1866, the member states usually have had a limited veto, especially on constitutional amendments. Even in federations such a veto has been claimed, as in the doctrine of "nullification," elaborated in the United States by John C. Calhoun—a doctrine that led to the American Civil War.

Veto by an outside agency is illustrated by the right of the Holy Roman emperor in the early Middle Ages to veto the election of a pope. In the 16th century the claim of certain Catholic states to veto consideration of a candidate for the papacy in a conclave of the College of Cardinals was accepted by custom, and frequently exercised by Austria. This right was abolished by Pope Pius X in 1804.

In two-chambered legislatures, each chamber usually has the power to veto action by the other, though in parliamentary governments the veto of the upper house has tended to be qualified. In the United States and some other countries, the courts can declare acts of legislative bodies unconstitutional, thus exercising what has been called a "judicial veto."

Veto Power of the Executive.—The most common instance of a veto right is that of the executive over the legislature. Such a veto by the sovereign of Great Britain is in theory absolute. In law, Parliament is merely advisory to the sovereign who has supreme legislative authority, and whose signature is therefore necessary for the effectiveness of any legislation. In practice, however, this royal veto has not been exercised since 1708. With the rise of responsible government, it has been recognized that the British sovereign must accept the advice of the prime minister on all political matters. This advice will normally require the sovereign to sign all bills approved by Parliament, but if the bill is opposed by the prime minister, the latter may advise the sovereign to dissolve Parliament and call an election, thus vetoing the bill, unless the election results in a majority in the House of Commons favoring a new prime minister who approves the bill. The same practice exists in other states with a parliamentary form of government, including most of the British dominions and most of the states of western Europe.

The power of the executive to dissolve the legislature is sometimes qualified, as it was in France during the Third and Fourth Republics, with the result that governments were immediately responsible to parliamentary majorities and consequently, in view of the multiparty system, were short lived. Under the Fifth Republic, established in 1958, the president, after consultation with the premier and presidents of the National Assembly and Senate, can dissolve Parliament or, in certain cases, he may submit bills to a national referendum. He thus has a qualified veto.

The executive veto is a characteristic feature of the presidential form of government which exists in most of the Latin American countries and in the United States. During the colonial period royal governors exercised a veto over acts of the colonial legislatures in America. Because of opposition to this practice, expressed in the Declaration of Independence, the state constitutions, with the exception of Massachusetts, at first gave no veto to the governor. Today, however, the governor has a veto in all the states except North Carolina, and his veto power extends to particular items in appropriation bills in 41 states, a power that is not enjoyed by the president of the United States.

Under the Articles of Confederation there was no veto because there was no executive, but the United States Constitution provides for a presidential veto of congressional acts which can, however, be overridden by a two-thirds vote of both houses of Congress. In such circumstances the act becomes law without the president's signature, as it does if the president does not sign the act and does not return it to Congress with his veto within 10 days, excluding Sundays. If, however, Congress adjourns during this 10-day period, failure of the president to act kills the bill by the so-called "pocket veto."

The early presidents exercised the veto sparingly, and only on the grounds of unconstitutionality. President Andrew Jackson first used it for political purposes, vetoing 12 bills, including that rechartering the Second United States Bank and that distributing to the states proceeds of the sales of public lands. The use of the veto has tended to increase. President Ulysses S. Grant vetoed 92 bills and President Grover Cleveland 584, mostly private pension bills. President Franklin D. Roosevelt vetoed 63 bills, and President Harry S. Truman, 250. President Dwight D. Eisenhower vetoed 181 bills, especially those authorizing public housing or other welfare legislation which he felt would endanger balancing of the budget.

A presidential veto was overridden for the first time in President John Tyler's administration in the case of a tariff bill. Such action has become more common as the use of the veto has increased. Four bills were passed over vetoes by President Grant, 15 over vetoes by President Andrew Johnson, 9 over vetoes by President Franklin D. Roosevelt, and 12 over vetoes by President Truman. Only 2 were passed over vetoes by President Eisenhower. President Ford, though in office less than three years, vetoed 65 bills and seldom was overridden.

The objective of the veto is to maintain a constitutional order by enabling each important organ to protect its own authority, thus preventing overcentralization, and constitutional violation. The veto, however, may be abused. Normally, however, it is a feature distinguishing constitutional government, in which all authority is limited by law, from dictatorship based on the principle of maximum centralization of authority.

Quincy Wright,
University of Virginia

VEUILLOT, vû-yō', **Louis François,** French author: b. Boynes, France, Oct. 11, 1813; d. Paris, April 7, 1883. Converted during a sojourn in Rome in 1838, he became one of the most vigorous, intransigent apologists of Roman Catholicism and of papacy. Collaborator of the Catholic newspaper *L'Univers religieux* (1838), then its editor in chief (1843–1860), he attacked principally through this newspaper what he considered the errors of the day: liberalism, materialism, Gallicanism, the programs of the French universities, and the laws affecting Catholic schools. He also wrote novels: *Pierre Saintive* (1840), *L'honnête femme* (1844); works of travel: *Rome et Lorette,* 2 vols. (1841), *Çà et là,* 3 vols. (1859), *Le parfum de Rome,* 2 vols. (1861); satires: *Les libres penseurs* (1848); *L'esclave vindex,* a pamphlet (1849), *Les odeurs de Paris* (1866); literary criticism: *Molière et Bourdaloue* (1877); and poems: *Oeuvres poétiques* (1878). See also his *Correspondance,* 9 vols. (1883–1913). He was a most gifted polemist and controversialist and a prolific, powerful prose writer.

Fernand Vial.

VEVEY, və-vā' (Ger. **Vivis**), commune, Switzerland, in Vaud Canton, situated on the northeast shore of Lake Geneva at the mouth of the Veveyse River gorge, 10 miles east-southeast of Lausanne, at an altitude of 1,276 feet. A resort noted for its beauty, it commands excellent views of the lake and the Pennine (Valais) Alps. It has good steamer and rail service, including connections to nearby mountain resorts. Vevey lies amid steeply rising vineyards and is the site of the picturesque Fête des Vignerons, celebrated every 15 to 20 years. Its manufactures include chocolate, evaporated milk, and cigars. An ancient and historic town (Rom. Viviscus), Vevey was ruled by the counts and dukes of Savoy from 1257 until its conquest by the Bernese in 1536; upon the overthrow of the Bernese by French revolutionary forces in 1798, it joined the Swiss Confederation as part of the former Léman canton. It has a 12th century church (St. Martin) and a museum. Population: (1970) 17,957.

VÉZELAY, vā-zə-lā', village, France, in Yonne Department, site of a celebrated monastery founded about 860. Commanding extensive views of the surrounding countryside, it stands at an altitude of approximately 1,000 feet on an isolated hill near the Cure River, 8 miles west-southwest of Avallon. The monastery's fame, dating from the 11th century, stems from the claim that the remains of St. Mary Magdalen had been removed there from a tomb at St. Maximin, Provence, for safeguarding from the Saracens; during the 12th century hosts of pilgrims visited the monastery. In 1146, St. Bernard preached at Vézelay before Louis VII of France to inspire the Second Crusade; in 1190, Richard I (Coeur de Lion) of England and Philip II (Philip Augustus) of France met there to arrange the Third Crusade. The massive Church of the Madeleine dates from the 11th century and was restored in the 19th century by Eugene Emanuel Viollet-de-Duc. Ancient fortifications, including a gate and circuit wall, are extant.

VIA APPIA. See Appian Way.

VIA DOLOROSA, vī'ə dŏl-ō-rō'sə, the route in Jerusalem which Jesus is believed to have followed in carrying his Cross to Mount Calvary. There are 14 stations marked by tablets. The name, Latin for "sorrowful way" was not used before the 16th century, although the route had been marked out from earliest times. The Way of the Cross, a form of devotion in the Roman Catholic Church, is in commemoration of that dolorous journey of the Saviour. It consists of prayer and meditation successively before each of the 14 stations of the Cross familiar in all Catholic churches, representing incidents beginning with Jesus' condemnation to death, continuing through his journey to Calvary and his Crucifixion, and ending with the laying of his body in the tomb.

VIADUCT, vī'ə-dukt, a long bridge constructed to carry a road or railroad over a river, another road or railroad, a congested urban area, or other obstacle. The term is applied particularly to bridges consisting of short concrete, masonry, or timber spans that rest on high supporting towers or piers. Viaducts usually were built of masonry until the 19th century, when timber was widely used for railroad viaducts. In modern practice steel-reinforced concrete has been widely used, and steel girders and towers are also popular.

In the United States a notable railroad viaduct is the Tunkhannock Viaduct, constructed in 1916 for the Erie-Lackawanna Railroad near Scranton, Pa. One of the world's largest concrete railroad bridges, it is 2,375 feet (724 meters) long and 240 feet (73 meters) high. A notable highway viaduct is the steel and concrete Pulaski Skyway, extending from Jersey City to Newark, N.J., and is a major traffic artery for the New York metropolitan region. It is 3.4 miles (5.5 km) long and 154 feet (47 meters) high.

VIANA DO CASTELO, vyä'nə do͞o kəsh-te'lo͞o, a town and fishing port in Portugal, and capital of the district of Viana do Castelo in Minho province. Situated on the north bank of the Rio Lima estuary and lying at the foot of Monte Santa Luzia, it is about 50 miles (80 km) by road north of Oporto. The castle to which its name refers is to the north of the city, on a rocky spur extending into the sea.

The population depends mostly on fishing, the city serving as the home port of a cod-fishing fleet operating on the Grand Banks off

Newfoundland. Its beaches attract considerable numbers of vacationers. The annual August festival of Our Lady of the Agony, which centers on the town's Baroque pilgrimage church, is noted for its displays of colorful costumes and dances of the region.

Viana (known in Roman times as Velobriga) has many old granite houses with iron railings and windows in the ornate Manueline style. There are several historic buildings of architectural interest. Population: (1970) 13,451.

VIANGCHAN, vyang'chan', the capital and chief city of Laos, with a port on the Mekong River. Except mainly for the university, schools, temples, government offices, and foreign embassies, the city's buildings are wooden. Small-scale industries produce such items as construction materials, textiles, and simple personal and household necessities.

Founded before 1300, Viangchan was the seat of one of several Lao principalities until they were united in 1353 as the kingdom of Lan Xang. King Setthathirath, who moved his court to Viangchan in 1563, beautified the city. He built the stupa That Luang to preserve Buddhist relics and the temple Wat Phra Keo to house the Emerald Buddha, a green jasper sculpture than was an important symbol of sovereignty. In 1828 the Thai sacked Viangchan, destroying Wat Phra Keo and carrying the Emerald Buddha off to Bangkok. Invading Chinese later despoiled That Luang, but it was restored under the French.

As Vientiane, the city was headquarters of the French administration in the kingdom of Laos from 1899 to 1953, when the country gained independence. Afterward the city remained co-capital, with Louangphrabang still the royal capital, until the abolition of the monarchy in 1975. Population: (1981 est.) 210,000.

VIARDOT-GARCÍA, vyär-dō'-gär-thē'ä, **Pauline** (1821–1910), French mezzo-soprano opera singer. Michelle Ferdinande Pauline García was born in Paris on July 18, 1821, a daughter of the renowned tenor Manuel García and a sister of the great contralto Maria Malibran. After singing in concert in Belgium, Germany, and France, she made her operatic debut as Desdemona in Rossini's *Otello* in London in 1839. In 1841 she married Louis Viardot, journalist and director of the Théâtre-Italien in Paris. The couple thereafter toured Europe together.

At the Paris Opéra, Pauline Viardot created the role of Fidès in Meyerbeer's *Le Prophète* (1849) and the title role in Gounod's *Sapho* (1851). In 1859 she appeared in a revival of Gluck's *Orphée et Eurydice*, prepared for the Paris Opéra by Berlioz. She sang the role of Orpheus more than 150 times.

Pauline Viardot had a wide vocal range, taking both soprano and contralto roles. She also was known as a great singing actress and a woman of intellectual distinction. After retiring from the stage in 1863, she took up composing and teaching. Her opera *Le Dernier Sorcier*, to a libretto by her close friend (and possible lover) Ivan Turgenev, was sung at Weimar in 1869.

She died in Paris on May 18, 1910. The autographed score of Mozart's *Don Giovanni*, which she owned, was willed to the library of the Paris Conservatory.

HERBERT WEINSTOCK
Coauthor of "Men of Music"

VIAREGGIO, vyä-rād'jō, a town on the west coast of Italy, on the Ligurian Sea, in the province of Lucca in Tuscany. It extends for 2 miles (3 km) between the shore and dense pine woods, with the Apuan Alps towering in the background. An avenue lined with hotels and villas runs along the coast, skirting the sandy beach that has made Viareggio one of Italy's most popular seaside resorts. In winter the festival of the carnival season attracts thousands every year.

Viareggio is a railway junction, port, and fishing center. Its manufactures include glass, pumps, and hosiery.

The English poet Percy Bysshe Shelley was cremated on the beach in 1822 after drowning on a boat trip near La Spezia. On nearby Lake Massaciuccoli is the home and tomb of the Italian composer Giacomo Puccini. Population: (1981) 58,136.

VIATICUM, vī-at'ə-kəm, in the Roman Catholic Church, the Holy Eucharist given to a person who is in danger of dying. In its original meaning in Latin, *viaticum* is a provision for a journey, such as money, clothing, or food. In the early church this meaning was extended metaphorically to apply to various spiritual aids for the passage from life to life-after-death, including prayers said at the time of death. Eventually the term was limited to Holy Communion for the dying or for those in immediate danger of death, such as soldiers going into battle.

The need for Viaticum is the reason traditionally given for the reservation of the Blessed Sacrament. It is customary for a priest to administer Viaticum. However, until the 10th century, members of the laity were permitted to take the Host to the dying. Requirements with regard to receiving the Eucharist do not apply in the case of Viaticum.

VIAU, vyō, **Théophile de** (1590–1626), French poet and playwright, who is generally referred to simply as Théophile. He was born in Clairac, near Agen, the son of a Protestant member of the minor nobility of Gascony. He went to Paris at an early age and led the Bohemian life of a freethinker, which earned him the title "prince of the libertines." Suspected of atheism, he was sentenced to death but was pardoned after spending two years in jail. He died in Paris on Sept. 25, 1626.

The author of odes, elegies, caprices, and satires, and of a tragicomedy, *Pyrame et Thisbé* (1617), Théophile defended spontaneity against the set of rules laid down by François de Malherbe, the great classical reformer. Théophile's feeling for nature and for solitude is unusual for the time. His verse is extremely musical, and the mood of his poetry is epicurean without being vulgar. He was renowned during his short life and immediately afterward, but his reputation suffered an eclipse after Nicolas Boileau-Despreaux, the classical poet and critic, ridiculed him for the preciosity of his images and attacked his "bad taste." The Romantics rehabilitated Théophile, and many modern poets have considered him a precursor for his intellectual audacity, rejection of imitation, and poetic freedom.

RENÉ GIRARD
Stanford University

VIAUD, Julien. See LOTI, PIERRE.

VIBO VALENTIA, vē′bō vä-len′tyä, is a town in Catanzaro province, Calabria region, southern Italy. Lying at an altitude of 1,824 feet (556 meters), it is near the Gulf of Sant'Eufemia, on the toe of Italy. Known as Monteleone di Calabria until 1928, the town is an agricultural trading center and manufactures tools.

It occupies the site of the Greek colony Hipponion, founded by Locrians before 600 B.C. There are remains of the Greek town's walls. The Romans in 192 B.C. transformed it into their colony of Vibo Valentia, which became an important port and naval station. It was ravaged by the Saracens in 893. The Holy Roman emperor Frederick II revived its civic life about 1235. A castle survives from this period. The town has been damaged by earthquakes, particularly in 1783 and 1905. Population: (1970) 28,649.

VIBORG, vē′bôr, is the capital city of Viborg *amt* (county) in Denmark. Located 37 miles (60 km) northwest of Aarhus, it has textile, brewing, tobacco, and machine-shop industries.

Viborg was probably a center of pagan worship in the pre-Christian era. It became Jutland's most important trading town during the Viking period and remained Jutland's largest population center until the 17th century. The cathedral (founded in 1130) was restored in the 19th century. Only the crypts remain of the original structure. Population: (1974) 37,771.

VIBRAPHONE, vī′brə-fōn, a percussion musical instrument, similar to the marimba, consisting of tuned metal bars, which, when struck by mallets, are amplified by resonator tubes suspended below each bar. The characteristic vibrato effect of the instrument is produced by electrically driven fans at the upper openings of the tubes. The instrumentalist can control the speed of the fans and is able to dampen the vibrato with a pedal.

The vibraphone, also called the vibraharp and commonly known as vibes, is used primarily for popular music. However, some serious composers, among them Alban Berg in his opera *Lulu,* have included the instrument in their orchestration.

Vibraphone, played by jazz musician Gary Burton.

LUDWIG DRUM COMPANY, LUDWIG INDUSTRIES

VIBRATION, in mechanics and acoustics, any sustained motion in which an object moves back and forth about an equilibrium or rest position. Familiar examples of vibrating motion include an oscillating spring, a swinging pendulum, a bowed violin string, and a struck tuning fork. Numerous other man-made objects also undergo vibration, including the rotating parts of machinery and even buildings and bridges. In nature, the ground vibrates during an earthquake. Also, animals with vocal cords vibrate them to make noises to communicate with other animals, and insects vibrate their wings or other body parts to make sounds. Perhaps the most important occurrence of vibration is in the production, transmission, and reception of speech. See also SOUND.

Characteristics. Vibratory motion is a back-and-forth motion of a body over a limited path. One vibration consists of one complete round trip of the vibrating body. The time taken to complete one vibration is called the *period.* The number of vibrations per second is called the *frequency.* The *amplitude* of the vibration is the distance from the equilibrium position of the body to the point of its maximum displacement.

The simplest type of vibratory motion is called *simple harmonic vibration,* or *simple harmonic motion.* In simple harmonic motion the acceleration of the body is proportional to its displacement from its original position and is opposite in direction to the displacement.

Other vibrations, such as that of a violin string, are more complex in that there is more than one mode of vibration and more than one frequency of vibration. Complex vibrations can be studied in simplified form by using mathematical techniques such as harmonic analysis. See also HARMONIC ANALYSIS; MECHANICS—*Simple Harmonic Motion.*

Vibration Control. Vibrations can be harmful to machines, impair measuring instruments, and create undesirable noises. Vibration control is achieved by damping and by isolation. As examples, viscous damping of impact vibrations in automobiles is accomplished by means of shock absorbers, and vibration isolation in automobiles is accomplished by mounting the engine on resilient material that reduces the transmission of vibrations from the engine to the chassis. See also DAMPING.

VIBURNUM, vī-bûr′nəm, a large genus of about 120 species of shrubs and small trees, many of which are cultivated for their showy and sometimes fragrant flowers. Viburnums are members of the honeysuckle family (Caprifoliaceae). Various species are native to regions ranging from the north temperate to the tropical. The species usually cultivated range in height from 4 to 15 feet (1.2–4.5 meters).

Most viburnums are deciduous, although some are evergreen. The leaves are opposite, simple, toothed or lobed, and turn bright colors in the fall. The flowers of most species are white. They are borne in flat, rounded, or pyramidal clusters. In many species the outer flowers of the clusters are showy and sterile, whereas the inner flowers

ROCHE

Viburnum carlesii has fragrant white flowers.

are inconspicuous and fertile. The flowers of most snowball viburnums are sterile.

The viburnums are popular landscaping shrubs because of their attractive flower clusters, fruits, and fall foliage. The snowball viburnums, which have showy, usually globular, flower clusters, are especially popular. They include the Chinese snowball (*V. macrocephalum*) and the Japanese snowball (*V. tomentosum sterile* or *V. t. plicatum*).

Most viburnums are easy to grow and maintain. They are usually propagated by cuttings or layering, but nonhybrid kinds can also be propagated by stratified seeds.

VICAR, vik′ər, an official who represents a superior official, especially in the Christian church. The term is derived from the Latin *vicarius,* an administrative deputy, substitute, or representative. Vicars originally were government officials in the late Roman Empire, bearing such titles as "vicar of Rome," "judge vicar," and "vicar of Italy." The title was used in various ways for clerics in the medieval church and continues in the Roman Catholic, Anglican, and some Lutheran churches.

In Roman Catholic usage, the pope has borne the title "vicar of Christ" since the 8th century, that title gradually replacing the ancient one, "vicar of St. Peter." A *vicar apostolic* is a titular bishop representing the pope in countries where a normal hierarchy is not established, as in England from the Reformation to 1850. A *vicar general* is a priest appointed by a bishop as his representative in matters ordinarily subject to his jurisdiction but not those of his sacred office, such as ordination. A *vicar* is a priest assisting or substituting for the rector of a parish.

In the Church of England the duties of a *vicar general* are usually assigned to the chancellor of the diocese, although archbishops have vicars general as special assistants. The priest of a parish whose revenues belong to someone else is called a *vicar.* This custom arose in the Middle Ages when some parish churches had their revenues "appropriated," or annexed, by monasteries. A member of the order or a secular priest was appointed to serve as rector and administer the parish. Such a secular priest was called a *vicar.* He had the spiritual status of a rector but usually received only a third of the revenues. After the dissolution of the monasteries by Henry VIII, laymen who were granted former monastic properties chose the vicars of parishes, subject to the bishop's approval. "Perpetual curates," permanently attached to one parish, are also sometimes known as vicars.

In the Episcopal Church in the United States, a vicar heads a mission or "chapel" within a parish as representative of either the bishop of the diocese or the rector by whom he was appointed. In some Lutheran churches a vicar may assist the pastor of a congregation.

FREDERICK C. GRANT
Formerly, Union Theological Seminary

VICAR OF WAKEFIELD, vik′ər, a novel by the English poet and author Oliver Goldsmith. According to evidence, *The Vicar of Wakefield* was written in 1761 and 1762, when it was sold to a publisher. It did not appear in print, however, until 1766, after Goldsmith, thanks to the success of his poem *The Traveller* (1764), had attained a literary reputation.

Goldsmith's only novel, *The Vicar of Wakefield* is a first-person narrative set in 18th century rural England. The narrator is Dr. Charles Primrose, the vicar, a kindly clergyman, who recounts the calamities that befall his family. Dr. Primrose is based to some extent on Goldsmith's father, and his son George on Goldsmith himself, especially in regard to George's travels and adventures on the Continent.

Characterization and Plot. In both its characterization and story complications *The Vicar of Wakefield* adheres to the style and conventions of 18th century English fiction. The vicar loses his independent wealth through his agent's deceitful business dealings, and his son, no longer the eligible young bachelor he once was, sets forth to recoup the family fortune. The vicar's wife, an ambitious woman, schemes to make suitable matches for her daughters Olivia and Sophia. As a result, Olivia is tricked into a bogus marriage ceremony by an unscrupulous rake, Squire Thornhill. Adversity mounts on adversity, and the Primroses seem destined for a life of poverty, dishonor, and despair. But all ends happily. The vicar recovers his fortune. George returns, to be reunited with the fiancée he had been forced to abandon. Olivia's marriage was, in fact, genuine, and Sophia weds Sir William Thornhill, the squire's generous and good-hearted uncle, who had been helping the Primroses under the assumed name of Mr. Burchell.

Critique. *The Vicar of Wakefield* was an immediate success. Goethe regarded it as one of the best novels ever written, and a similar opinion was held by later critics, including Henry James. Samuel Johnson, however, was less kind. He called the book "very faulty," saying that "there is nothing of real life in it, and very little of nature."

The modern reader is likely to agree more with Johnson than with Goethe. The novel, which Goldsmith said had a "hundred faults," is overly sentimentalized, presenting an idealized picture of English country life. The virtuous characters display a fortitude in the face of misfortune that is difficult to accept. The villains are of the blackest stripe, with few redeeming qualities. Nevertheless, *The Vicar of Wakefield* still retains considerable charm, written, as it is, with an artless simplicity—and sense of irony—that have enormous appeal.

VICE PRESIDENT OF THE UNITED STATES, the second-highest ranking official in the U. S. government. The president and vice president are the only nationally elected officials. If the president dies, resigns, or is removed from office, the vice president succeeds him. The vice president may also serve temporarily as acting president if the president, for whatever reason, is unable to discharge his duties. Like the president, the vice president must be at least 35 years old.

The Constitution of the United States prescribes only one duty for the vice president. He is the president, or presiding officer, of the U. S. Senate, and if a Senate vote ends in a tie the vice president may vote to break the tie. The vice president has been assigned other duties by statute, and the president may give him other responsibilities. All such responsibilities, including that of presiding over the Senate, are relatively insignificant, and the importance of the vice president derives almost entirely from the fact that at any moment he may succeed to the most powerful office in the world.

The Succession Problem. The office of vice president was created at the constitutional convention in 1787. The Constitution, in Article II, Section 1, provided: "In Case of the Removal of the President from Office, or of his Death, Resignation, or Inability to discharge the Powers and Duties of the said Office, the Same shall devolve on the Vice President. . . ."

This passage was ambiguous. Did "the Same" refer to the words "Powers and Duties" or to the word "Office"? In short, if a president died, would the vice president become only the acting president or would he be president in every sense of the word? In 1841, President William Henry Harrison died after a brief illness. Vice President John Tyler, the first man to confront the problem, contended that he had become president. He took the presidential oath. Some constitutional scholars disputed his claim, but his precedent became established. Between 1841 and 1963, eight presidents died in office. In each case his successor was recognized both officially and by the public as the president.

Long after Tyler had successfully asserted his claim to the presidency, research established that the "founding fathers" had intended that the vice president serve only as acting president should the president die, and that the committee on style, in writing the Constitution, had introduced the ambiguity unintentionally.

Tyler's precedent created another problem. Suppose that Harrison had remained alive but seriously ill and unable to discharge his duties. Suppose further that Tyler, using the same reasoning as before, had claimed the presidency on the basis of the same clause quoted above. Also, suppose that Harrison had recovered and sought to regain his office. If Tyler were in fact president, instead of acting as president, there would be no apparent means by which Harrison could resume his office.

Later, Presidents James Garfield and Woodrow Wilson were seriously disabled for months. In neither case did the vice president—Chester Alan Arthur and Thomas Marshall, respectively—seek to displace the president. Both vice presidents were concerned that the president might recover from his disability, reassert his claim to the office, and create constitutional chaos.

VICE PRESIDENTS OF THE UNITED STATES

Vice President	Term	President
1. John Adams	1789–1797	Washington
2. Thomas Jefferson	1797–1801	J. Adams
3. Aaron Burr	1801–1805	Jefferson
4. George Clinton	1805–1809	Jefferson
George Clinton[1]	1809–1812	Madison
5. Elbridge Gerry[1]	1813–1814	Madison
6. Daniel D. Tompkins	1817–1825	Monroe
7. John C. Calhoun	1825–1829	J. Q. Adams
John C. Calhoun[2]	1829–1832	Jackson
8. Martin Van Buren	1833–1837	Jackson
9. Richard M. Johnson	1837–1841	Van Buren
10. John Tyler[3]	1841	W. H. Harrison
11. George M. Dallas	1845–1849	Polk
12. Millard Fillmore[3]	1849–1850	Taylor
13. William R. D. King[1]	1853	Pierce
14. John C. Breckinridge	1857–1861	Buchanan
15. Hannibal Hamlin	1861–1865	Lincoln
16. Andrew Johnson[3]	1865	Lincoln
17. Schuyler Colfax	1869–1873	Grant
18. Henry Wilson[1]	1873–1875	Grant
19. William A. Wheeler	1877–1881	Hayes
20. Chester A. Arthur[3]	1881	Garfield
21. Thomas A. Hendricks[1]	1885	Cleveland
22. Levi P. Morton	1889–1893	B. Harrison
23. Adlai E. Stevenson	1893–1897	Cleveland
24. Garret A. Hobart[1]	1897–1899	McKinley
25. Theodore Roosevelt[3]	1901	McKinley
26. Charles W. Fairbanks	1905–1909	T. Roosevelt
27. James S. Sherman[1]	1909–1912	Taft
28. Thomas R. Marshall	1913–1921	Wilson
29. Calvin Coolidge[3]	1921–1923	Harding
30. Charles G. Dawes	1925–1929	Coolidge
31. Charles Curtis	1929–1933	Hoover
32. John N. Garner	1933–1941	F. D. Roosevelt
33. Henry A. Wallace	1941–1945	F. D. Roosevelt
34. Harry S. Truman[3]	1945	F. D. Roosevelt
35. Alben W. Barkley	1949–1953	Truman
36. Richard M. Nixon	1953–1961	Eisenhower
37. Lyndon B. Johnson[3]	1961–1963	Kennedy
38. Hubert H. Humphrey	1965–1969	L. B. Johnson
39. Spiro T. Agnew[2]	1969–1973	Nixon
40. Gerald R. Ford[4]	1973–1974	Nixon
41. Nelson Rockefeller	1974–1977	Ford
42. Walter Mondale	1977–1981	Carter
43. George H. W. Bush	1981–1989	Reagan
44. J. Danforth Quayle	1989–	Bush

[1] Died in office. [2] Resigned as vice president. [3] Succeeded to presidency on death of president. [4] Succeeded to presidency on resignation of president.

After the assassination of President John Kennedy in 1963, the 25th Amendment to the Constitution was approved by Congress and ratified in February 1967. It surmounts the ambiguity in Article II, Section 1, declaring that if the president dies, resigns, or is removed from office, "the Vice President shall become President."

But the 25th Amendment also establishes that if the president declares himself unable to discharge his duties, the vice president becomes only "Acting President." Under certain conditions, the vice president may declare the president disabled—if he will not or cannot do so himself and he then becomes acting president. For the text of the amendment, see CONSTITUTION OF THE UNITED STATES; for more on the succession issue, see PRESIDENTIAL SUCCESSION.

Another clause of the 25th Amendment became dramatically relevant in 1973 and 1974. Within a year both Vice President Spiro Agnew and President Richard Nixon resigned their offices. The 25th Amendment provides that when the vice presidency becomes vacant the president shall appoint a successor, subject to the approval by majority vote of both houses of Congress. (As a result of 15 deaths and three resignations of presidents and vice presidents the office has been vacant a total of about 37 years.) After Agnew pleaded no contest to a charge of income tax evasion and resigned, Nixon nominated Congressman Gerald Ford (R-Mich.) to succeed him. After a thorough and relatively nonpartisan investigation, Congress approved Ford. Eight months later, Nixon's public career collapsed under the weight of the Watergate scandal, and he resigned. Ford succeeded him and nominated Nelson Rockefeller to be vice president. After an inquiry that consumed four months, Congress approved Rockefeller.

The Vice President's Job. The vice president is elected with the president and is his potential successor. The vice president, however, is also the presiding officer of the U. S. Senate—in a government supposedly founded on the principle of the separation of powers.

In this anomalous position, vice presidents have often experienced frustration. They may not participate in Senate debate, and attempts to "lobby" on Capitol Hill in behalf of the administration's programs may only antagonize the senators. In practice, the vice president presides on ceremonial occasions and when Senate leaders expect a close vote. On most other occasions, senators take turns as presiding officer.

Since 1933, the vice presidents have attended meetings of the president's cabinet. By statute, the vice president is a member of the National Security Council. By executive order, he serves on the Domestic Council, which formulates policy recommendations for the president. From the 1940's the office "grew" as presidents began assigning other substantive tasks to their vice presidents. During World War II, Henry Wallace served for a time as chairman of the Board of Economic Warfare. President Eisenhower sent Vice President Nixon on a number of missions abroad that involved both ceremonial occasions and some significant diplomatic conversations. Nixon's successors have also traveled extensively. President Ford named Vice President Rockefeller to head a commission to investigate allegations against Central Intelligence Agency officials. Vice President Walter Mondale became one of President Jimmy Carter's most trusted advisers.

Under the Constitution "the executive power" rests solely with the president. Therefore, areas of responsibility cannot simply be shifted from the president to the vice president. For that reason the office of vice president remains a relatively empty one, which many energetic and able leaders have been reluctant to accept.

Nominations, Elections, and "Politics." The Constitution originally prescribed that the president and vice president be chosen by members of the Electoral College, each of whom would cast two votes. The person receiving the second greatest number of votes would become vice president. Each elector, in casting his two votes, had no way of indicating which person he preferred for president. Within a few years, political parties were putting up two-man teams for the two national offices. In 1804 the Antifederalists chose Thomas Jefferson and Aaron Burr for president and vice president, respectively. Electors favoring Jefferson and Burr voted for both men, creating a tie vote in the Electoral College. In the House of Representatives, where the tie was resolved, the Federalists supported Burr against their archfoe Jefferson, who barely won election.

The original electoral system was then scrapped and replaced with the 12th Amendment (1804), which provides that electors vote separately for president and vice president. Unfortunately, after 1804 the vice-presidential nomination quickly became a consolation prize often awarded to the faction of the party that had lost out in the contest for the presidential nomination. This desire of political parties to "balance" their tickets carried the likelihood that the person succeeding a president who died in office would not share his political philosophy. In 1850, for example, President Zachary Taylor, who opposed the Compromise of 1850, died and was succeeded by Millard Fillmore, who supported it. Since World War II, however, most vice-presidential nominees have held views close to those held by the presidential nominees.

Vice-presidential nominees often have been selected in haste in conferences between the just-chosen presidential nominee and his advisers. The choice may not be given sufficiently serious thought. But in 1944, Democratic party leaders feared, accurately, that President Franklin Roosevelt would die during his next term, and they succeeded in denying renomination to Vice President Henry Wallace, whom they regarded as not suited to be president.

Despite longstanding criticism of the nomination process, both major parties were embarrassed as recently as 1972. The Republicans renominated Spiro Agnew, and the Democrats chose Sen. Thomas Eagleton (Mo.), who resigned from the ticket within three weeks after acknowledging that he had received electroshock treatments for depression. On the recommendation of Sen. George McGovern (S. Dak.), the presidential nominee, the Democratic National Committee named Sargent Shriver, former director of the Peace Corps, to replace Eagleton.

Once the vice-presidential nominee is chosen, he delivers speeches echoing the presidential nominee's views on the issues of the campaign. Presidential nominees have encouraged their running mates to speak out sharply against the opposition party, even to the extent of making charges that the presidential nominee eschews in order to preserve his lofty, statesmanlike image. Unfortunately, this practice has carried over into some administrations, with vice presidents serving as spearheads for White House attacks on the opposition party. Vice President Humphrey exalted President Lyndon Johnson in his public statements and harshly criticized opponents of Johnson's conduct of the Vietnam War. The Nixon administration's hostility toward the press found a voice in Agnew, who delivered a series of abrasive speeches approved by the White House. Agnew characterized some elements of the press and partisan opponents of Nixon as effete, reckless, and elitist.

Salary and Perquisites. The vice president's salary of $79,125, plus $10,000 for expenses, is supplemented (since 1975) by annual cost-of-living increases, as determined by the president. The Secret Service guards the vice president and family. In 1974, Congress designated a Washington mansion formerly occupied by the chief of naval operations as the vice president's official residence. The vice president maintains offices in the Capitol and the Executive Office Building.

DONALD YOUNG
Author of "American Roulette: The History and Dilemma of the Vice Presidency"

Further Reading: Goldstein, Joel K., *The Modern American Vice Presidency: The Transformation of a Political Institution* (Princeton Univ. Press 1981); Light, Paul C., *Vice Presidential Power* (Johns Hopkins Univ. Press 1983); Young, Donald, *American Roulette: The History and Dilemma of the Vice Presidency* (1965; reprint, Viking 1974).

VICENTE, vē-sāɴn'tə, **Gil,** Portuguese playwright of the 16th century, who is regarded as the father of Portuguese drama.

Life. Gil Vicente was born about 1470 and probably grew up in a rural area (perhaps in Beira province or near Guimarães), since he reveals amazing acquaintanceship with country life. His early years are veiled in uncertainty. His known activities cover the period 1502 to 1536, the dates of his first and last dramatic pieces. Gil Vicente, the dramatist, and Gil Vicente, the goldsmith of the same epoch, were apparently the same man, but doubt has been cast on that identity, and as late as the mid-20th century a noted Portuguese critic argued that the dramatist displays a religious-scholarly training, not that of an artisan, and that his financial status was not that of a prosperous craftsman. If, as most believe, there was one Gil Vicente only, it is of interest that the goldsmith was in the service of the dowager Queen Lianor at the turn of the 15th century and used the first gold tribute from the East to fashion a famous Belém monstrance. He was appointed overseer of gold and silver artifacts for several monasteries in 1509, and in 1513 became master of the mint, a post he held for four and one-half years. In any event, Gil Vicente is remembered above all as the dramatist, actor, and director who throughout 30-odd years held the unique position of providing entertainment for the Portuguese court upon the occasions of church feasts, royal birthdays and marriages, and other important events. He died about 1536.

Works. Gil Vicente's first known connection with the theater was the night of June 7, 1502, when, dressed in rustic costume, he recited his *Monólogo do vaqueiro* (Herdsman's Monologue) in the royal palace in Lisbon to congratulate Queen Maria upon the birth of a son (later John III). On that occasion, Vicente used Spanish. In fact, 11 of his plays are in Spanish, 16 are in Portuguese, and the remaining 17 combine both languages. The use of a foreign tongue was due to the fact that Spanish was then very fashionable in the higher circles of Portugal, for the court was thronged with ladies and gentlemen in the retinue of the Spanish queens. King Emanuel (Manuel I, reigned 1495–1521) married, successively, two daughters of Ferdinand and Isabella of Spain, and later a sister of Emperor Charles V. His son John III (reigned 1521–1557) married another sister of Charles. Vicente developed the popular peninsular medieval tradition of liturgical drama and secular farce with such improvement that he has been called the founder of the Portuguese theater. It was Spain that had the greatest influence upon him, and the contemporary Spanish dramatist Juan del Encina provided his first inspiration.

Remarkable for its variety, Vicente's theater included religious-allegorical, pastoral, and chivalrous plays, as well as plays of contemporary customs, serious and farcical. One of his earliest works, for Epiphany in 1503, was the *Auto dos Reis Magos,* the old story of the adoration of the Magi. For Holy Week and for various religious festivals he often produced plays of an allegorical, moralizing nature, of which the *Auto da alma* (The Soul's Journey) is a good example. In the medieval tradition of anticlericalism, Vicente often satirized the clergy and took them to task for their lack of holiness. The famous *Barca do Inferno, Barca do Purgatório,* and *Barca da Glória,* for example, are vigorous criticism. Despite this attitude, Gil Vicente was a devout Roman Catholic. His quarrel was not with the church and its dogmas, but with its backsliding servants. The monarchs of the day were often politically at odds with the Holy See, and Vicente's position was not unusual. He had a sincere desire to bring about an improvement in clerical morals, and his attacks anticipate the Counter Reformation, not the Reformation. Vicente's satire was directed against other aspects of society also. In the *Auto dos físicos,* the physician was ridiculed; in the *Farsa dos almocreves* (The Carriers), the penniless nobleman living beyond his means. These and many others were the target of Vicente's pen. On the other hand, Vicente the patriot frequently offered praise and encouragement to his fellow countrymen as they continued their expansion in the East and their battles for the faith in North Africa. A case in point is *Exhortação da guerra* (Exhortation to War) written for a campaign against the Mohammedan town of Azamor.

The books of chivalry inspired Gil Vicente to write two entertaining plays in Spanish: *Dom Duardos* (on Edward of England, in love with Princess Flérida of Constantinople) and *Amadis de Gaula* (on the fictional hero of the same name). The *Tragicomédia pastoril da Serra da Estrêla,* written to celebrate a royal birth, represents the pastoral tradition, and reveals, as usual, Vicente's fine feeling for nature and his abilities as a lyric poet. His was a verse theater, and he made much use of songs, at times invented by him, at times drawn from the people. Music, sometimes composed by him, and dancing were integral complements. Costumes were appropriate and often colorful. Staging was sometimes simple, but often elaborate; for example, a miniature ship, fully rigged, might be brought on the stage. Gil Vicente's meter was a continuation of the medieval popular 8-syllable and 12-syllable lines, each with or without its hemistich. Fluidity and flexibility were Vicente's forte, and in his strophes many variations are to be found. In spite of the fact that a rival poet, Francisco de Sá de Miranda, returned from Italy in the mid-1520's with a new style, the hendecasyllabic line, Gil Vicente's constant preoccupation was with the native, the popular, and the traditional. Although he was justly accused of writing plays lacking in plot, unity, action, and character study, his primitive improvisations carried the day sufficiently to keep him in a preferred position until the end of his career in spite of the growing artificialities that surrounded him. Occasionally he did produce a work which merited the praise of the learned critic: the *Farsa de Inês Pereira,* for instance. The study of character is excellent, the plot is unified and well developed, and there is more action than usual. All this is combined with Gil Vicente at his best: sparkling dialogue, lyricism, spontaneity, contrast of the serious and comic; in a word, entertainment, with an underlying lesson.

Influence. Seven of Vicente's plays were on the first Portuguese Index of Prohibited Books (1551). However, his son Luis published a complete works in 1562, unaltered, likely due to the influence of Queen Regent Catherine. Because of censorship, the spirit of the Renaissance, and bad imitators, Gil Vicente's successors in Portugal are negligible. In Spain, however, the picture is quite different. The great drama of the Golden

Age came after his day, and many of its best characteristics are to be found in embryo in the works of the Portuguese playwright. The variety of Lope de Vega's "new comedy" owes much to him. He is also a precursor of the *auto sacramental* (dramatic religious allegory) which reached its height in the mid-17th century with Pedro Calderón de la Barca.

J. H. PARKER
University of Toronto
Author of "Gil Vicente"

Bibliography

Plays by Gil Vicente have been translated into English by Aubrey F. G. Bell, including *Four Plays of Gil Vicente* (Cambridge 1920). Bell also translated poetry taken from the plays as *Lyrics of Gil Vicente* (Oxford 1921). The complete works of Gil Vicente, in Portuguese, have been edited by Marques Braga, and a bibliography has been published by the Biblioteca Nacional, Lisbon.

Hart, Thomas R., *Gil Vicente* (Longwood 1981).

Parker, J. H., *Gil Vicente* (Twayne 1968).

Stathatos, Constantine C., *A Gil Vicente Bibliography 1940–1975* (Longwood 1980).

Vicente, Gil, *Farces and Festival Plays*, ed. by Thomas R. Hart (Univ. of Oreg. Bks. 1972).

Vicente, Gil, *Floresta de enganos*, a critical edition ed. by Constantine Christopher Stathatos (Univ. of N.C. Press 1972).

Vicente, Gil, *Tragicomedia de Amadis de Gaula*, ed. by T. P. Waldron (Manchester Univ. Press 1959).

VICENZA, vē-chen′tsä, is a city and capital of Vicenza province, in Venetia region, northeast Italy. It is 38 miles (61 km) west of Venice, located at the confluence of the Bacchiglione and Retrone rivers. A rail and road junction on the Venice-Milan line, it has iron- and steelworks, foundries, and factories producing agricultural and textile machinery, furniture, and glass. The city is irregular in shape, with winding streets and picturesque squares, and is rich in art treasures. Three architectural styles may be distinguished: the rich and delicate Venetian Gothic (14th–15th centuries), the elegant Lombard (15th–16th centuries), and the solemn classic Renaissance of Andrea Palladio (1518–1580), continued by his followers into the 19th century. Known as "Palladio's city," Vicenza contains many of the architect's most beautiful and striking buildings in his characteristic style blending Roman majesty and Venetian grace. Among them are the marble Basilica, with its classic colonnaded façade; the Loggia del Capitanio, left unfinished by Palladio but recently completed and now a World War II memorial; the Chiericati and Valmarana palaces; the Rotonda, a villa in the outskirts; and the Teatro Olimpico, a wood and stucco building started in 1580 and completed by Vincenzo Scamozzi (1552–1616). Inaugurated in 1585 with Sophocles' *Oedipus Rex*, the Teatro Olimpico is still in use.

The artistic, topographic, and business center of Vicenza is the Piazza dei Signori, enclosed by Palladio's Basilica and Loggia; the 250-foot-high Torre di Piazza, a slender brick bell tower; and the Monte di Pietà (pawnshop) with the adjoining baroque church of San Vincenzo. Elsewhere in or near the central area are the town hall, Scamozzi's masterpiece, dating to 1588 although it was not finished until 1662; the cathedral (14th–16th centuries), built on the foundation of an early Christian church; and the churches of Santa Corona and San Lorenzo, with fine works of art. Also worthy of note are the Gothic-Renaissance Palazzo Da Schio, reminiscent of Venice's Ca' d'Oro; the Gothic Longhi and Pigafetta residences; and the Thiene Palace. The Chiericati Palace houses the municipal museum, consisting of an archaeological collection and a fine art gallery.

History. Ancient Vicetia was a city of the Venetians, although little is known of its history before it was occupied by the Romans, who gave it the rank of a city in 49 B.C. It suffered from the barbarian invasions, but later became the seat of a Lombard duchy and a Frankish county. After being ruled by its bishops, Vicenza became a free commune in the 12th century. It was involved in wars against, and was ruled by, the lords of Padua, Verona, and Milan. In 1404 the city came under the sovereignty of the Venetian Republic, prospering under its wise rule and reaching its greatest heights in the 16th century. Although Palladio was then its greatest glory, Vicenza also produced in that period a line of notable painters starting with Bartolommeo Montagna, continuing through Francesco Maffei in the 17th century, and on into the 18th century. After the fall of the Republic of Venice in 1797, Vicenza was under Austrian domination until 1866, when it was united with the kingdom of Italy. During World War II Vicenza's art treasures suffered severely from air bombings, but the damage has since been largely repaired.

Vicenza Province. The northern part consists of Alpine foothills, the southern part of an irrigated plain, with the Berici and Lessini mountains to the west and south respectively. Population: (1971) of the city, 115,747; (1969) of the province, 667,300.

VICEROY, vīs′roi, a species of butterfly best known for its mimicking of the monarch butterfly. It is an example of protective coloration, since birds that eat the distasteful monarch learn to avoid both the monarch and its mimic. Human observers can easily distinguish the viceroy by the black band that curves across the veins of each hind wing.

The viceroy is distributed throughout southern Canada and the United States east of the Rockies, as well as in the southwestern states. The larvae feed on the leaves of willows, poplars, aspens, apples, plums, oaks, and cottonwoods. There are usually several generations a year. The larvae overwinter in a rolled leaf lined with silk. The leaf is prevented from falling in the winter by silk threads that anchor it to its twig. Both the viceroy (*Limenitis archippus*) and the monarch (*Danaus plexippus*) are classified in the family Nymphalidae. See also MIMICRY.

VICEROY, in political science, the governor of a country or province, usually part of an imperial domain, who rules in the name and by the authority of a king. The representative of the crown in British India had the honorary title of viceroy during the period of British rule from 1858 to 1947, although he exercised his powers as governor general. The term was similarly applied to the lord lieutenant of Ireland until the establishment of the Irish Free State in 1922. After the Italian annexation of Ethiopia in 1936, that country was ruled by a viceroy, representing the Italian king, until its liberation in 1941. Viceroy was also the official designation of the governors of Naples, Mexico, and Peru under the old Spanish colonial system.

QUINCY WRIGHT, *Author of "A Study of War"*

VICH, vēch (ancient **AUSA**; later **VICUS AUSONENSIS**), city, Spain, in Barcelona province and Catalonia, situated at an altitude of 1,575 feet, 38 miles north of Barcelona. It is a meat-processing center and has leather and sawmilling industries and manufactures of textiles, dyes, furniture, tiles, flour, and dairy products. The city contains the restored remains of the interior of a 3d century Roman temple. The neoclassic cathedral, founded in 1038 and rebuilt in 1780–1803, retains the original crypt and a medieval tower and Gothic cloister; it is decorated with murals by José Maria Sert (1876–1945), Spanish painter, representing the Mystery of the Redemption. The Episcopal Museum has early Catalan paintings and some sculpture. Population: (1970) 25,906.

VICHY, vĭsh'ē, Fr. vē-shē', town, France, in Allier Department, situated on the right bank of the Allier River at an altitude of 859 feet, 28 miles north-northeast of Clermont-Farrand. It is France's most famous spa. The Aquae Calidae ("warm springs") of the Romans, it has been known since ancient times for its hot mineral springs of strongly alkaline water considered particularly beneficial for digestive troubles. With its many luxurious hotels, its bathing establishments, and its entertainment places, the town lies alongside a belt of pleasant parks bordering the river. It has nine springs, of which six, including the largest—the Source des Célestins, with a flow of 45,100 gallons daily—are state property. Water available at *buvettes* (drinking places at the springs) is free. Bottled Vichy water is a major export. Almost forgotten during the Middle Ages, the springs came into prominence when the Marquise de Sévigné visited Vichy for a cure in 1676–1677 and were popularized in 1861 and later by the patronage of Napoleon III. During World War II, following the fall of France, Vichy was the seat of the government of Marshal Henri Philippe Pétain from July 1940 until 1944, when the government fled before the Allied advance to Sigmaringen, Germany. Population: (1968) 33,458.

VICHY WATER, vish'ē, is a naturally effervescent mineral water obtained from springs at Vichy, France. It contains sodium bicarbonate and other alkaline salts, reputedly has medicinal benefits, and is bottled for worldwide export.

VICHYSSOISE, vish-ē-swäz', originally known as *vichyssoise à la Ritz,* is a soup created in 1917 by the French cook Louis Diat while chef at the Ritz-Carlton Hotel in New York City. A puree of leeks, onions, potatoes, butter, and cream topped with chives, it is served cold.

VICKSBURG, vĭks'bûrg, city, Mississippi, capital of Warren County, situated on bluffs towering above the Mississippi and Yazoo rivers. It rises impressively on a series of natural terraces, interlaced with wooded ravines, and is noted for its precipitous streets, ascending in part from the business district paralleling the waterfront. The city's altitude is 206 feet above sea level, although the bluffs reach a height of 302 feet. In the valley below, a railroad and vehicular bridge spans the Mississippi to the Louisiana shore. Lying 40 miles west of Jackson, the state capital, the city is a crossroads of federal highways and is served by the Illinois Central Railroad and by a municipal airport. Rich in history, it is famous for the siege of Vicksburg in the Civil War (see VICKSBURG CAMPAIGN). On its landward side, it is bounded entirely, in crescent fashion, by Vicksburg National Military Park (q.v.).

Vicksburg is a notable industrial, trade, residential, and tourist center, and river port. An important 250-acre planned industrial district, served by a combined river-rail-highway terminal, was completed in 1961—the only facility of its kind on the 500-mile stretch of the Mississippi between Memphis, Tenn., and Baton Rouge, La. Oil refineries, foundries, lumber trade, and manufactures of chemicals, clothing, cottonseed oil, electrical goods, and cement are typical industries. The city is the center for a rich cotton, livestock, corn, hay, fruit, vegetable, and dairying region. Since 1930 it has been headquarters of the United States Mississippi River Commission. It is the home of a United States Water Experiment Station (the city's largest employer with 2,400 workers), and of All Saints Episcopal Junior College (founded 1908) for women, 12 garden clubs, the Vicksburg Little Theatre, 62 churches representing 16 denominations, and excellent medical facilities. March is Pilgrimage Month in historic Vicksburg, highlighted by many special events.

The city is on the site of a French fort of the early 18th century and of a Spanish outpost (Fort Nogales) built in 1791; the area came into United States possession in 1798. In 1814 the Reverend Newitt Vick, a Methodist minister for whom the city is named, established a mission nearby; five years later he began laying out the town, which was incorporated in 1825. The city has a commission form of government, adopted in 1912. Pop. 25,434.

EDWARD H. HOBBS,
Director, Bureau of Business Research, University of Mississippi.

VICKSBURG CAMPAIGN, the campaign in the American Civil War culminating in the surrender of Vicksburg, Miss., to Union forces under Gen. Ulysses S. Grant on July 4, 1863. The fortifications on the bluffs above the Mississippi River at Vicksburg were the key Confederate defenses of the river. Their capture by Union forces would give the Union control of the Mississippi throughout its length, and also would isolate the Confederate states west of the Mississippi from those to the east. During the period May–July, 1862, several attempts to seize Vicksburg were made by Adm. David G. Farragut's fleet and troops under Gen. Thomas Williams. These ventures failed, primarily because the guns of the ships could not be directed effectively against the Confederate batteries high on the bluffs, and because the Confederate troops far outnumbered the Union contingents sent against them.

Grant's Early Probings.—In November, 1862, General Grant began an overland movement from northern Mississippi and Tennessee against Vicksburg. In December, this maneuver was modified to include an expedition down the Mississippi under Gen. William T. Sherman. On the 29th, Sherman's force of 30,000, accompanied by Adm. David D. Porter's fleet, assaulted Chickasaw Bluffs, just north of Vicksburg (see Map A). The Confederates, outnumbered but in excellent defenses, repulsed the attack (see CHICKASAW BAYOU OR BLUFFS, BATTLE OF). On the 31st, Sherman's attempt to

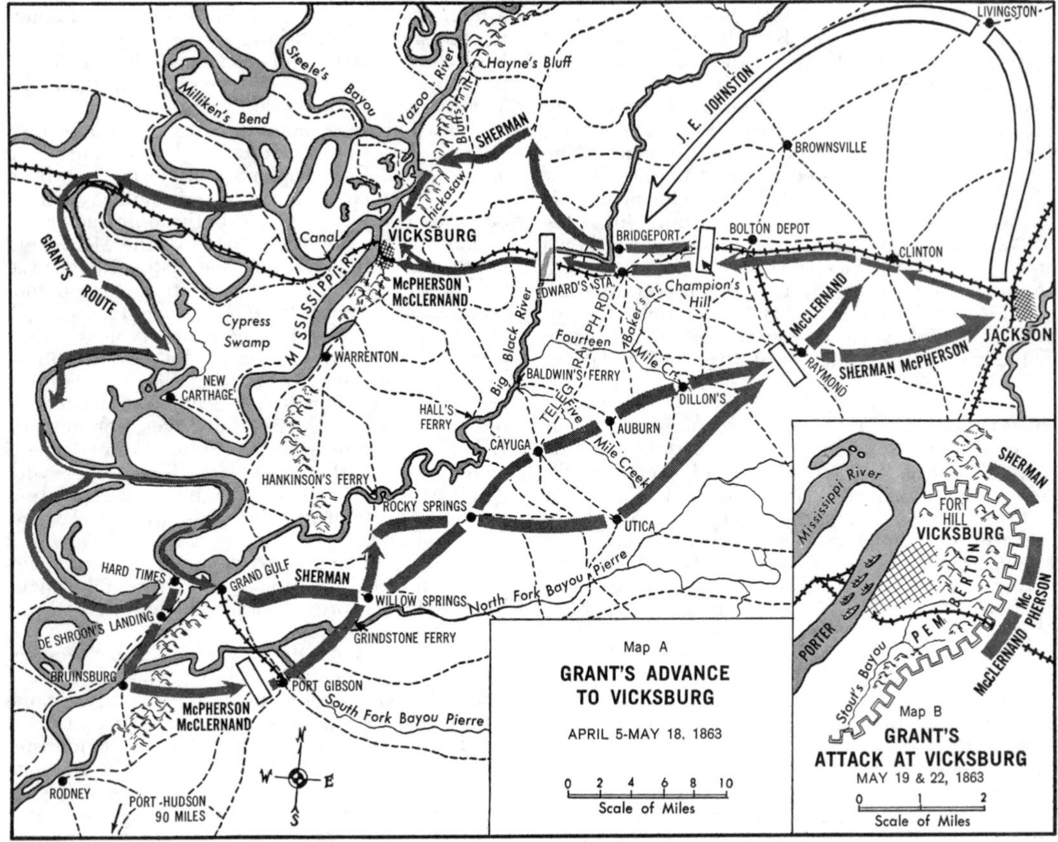

move up the Yazoo River and capture Hayne's Bluff also failed. He then retired westward to Milliken's Bend. Meanwhile, Confederate opposition to Grant's overland advance stiffened, while the cavalry of Gens. Nathan B. Forrest and Earl Van Dorn wrecked the Union line of communication and destroyed Grant's principal supply base at Holly Springs, in northern Mississippi.

These events, coupled with the receipt of orders to turn over command of the river expedition to Gen. John A. McClernand, whose fitness he doubted, caused Grant to abandon the overland advance and to reinforce the river expedition, over which he intended to assume personal command. Leaving Gen. Stephen A. Hurlbut's 16th Corps behind to protect the rear, he moved his remaining forces downstream to join Sherman.

General McClernand, meanwhile, had taken command of Sherman's forces and, seeking personal glory, embarked upon a diversionary expedition up the Arkansas River where he captured Fort Hindman (see Fort Hindman or Arkansas Post, Battle of). Grant sternly ordered him back to Milliken's Bend. On Jan. 29, 1863, Grant arrived at the bend and assumed personal command of the assembled forces. These comprised three corps—the 13th under McClernand; the 15th under Sherman; and the 17th under Gen. James B. McPherson.

An attempt was made to reach the high ground north of Vicksburg by way of Steele's Bayou and another along the Yazoo River. Both failed because of the swampy and difficult terrain and Confederate sniping and resistance along the narrow waterways. Efforts to build a canal across the peninsula opposite Vicksburg to bypass the city's batteries were defeated by rising waters. (Earlier, Williams had attempted to build such a canal at the same site, but rising waters forced him to abandon the project.) Similarly, an attempt to get below Vicksburg through Louisiana by way of Lake Providence, the bayous and streams leading therefrom into the Red River, and the Red River itself was frustrated by natural obstacles.

Grant Adopts A New Plan.—Grant finally evolved a plan which eventually proved successful. This was to reach the south of Vicksburg by means of the series of bayous just west of the Mississippi. Map A shows the route of advance. Much road and bridge construction through the swampy country was required initially, but later protracted clear weather dried some of the bayous and facilitated the movement. The corps of McPherson and McClernand reached Hard Times by April 29; here they were joined by Porter's fleet, which had forced its way south past the Vicksburg batteries. General John C. Pemberton, the Confederate commander in Mississippi, learned of these moves and anticipated an attack on Grand Gulf. However, instead of moving the bulk of his forces to the area, he increased the Grand Gulf garrison to 9,000—hardly sufficient to stave off Grant's force of some 40,000. Meanwhile, Gen. Benjamin H. Grierson's cavalry, on its famous raid throughout the length of the state of Mississippi, distracted Pemberton. Exaggerated reports of the damage being done by the Union cavalry led him to dispatch all of his cavalry and some infantry—forces he could better use around Vicksburg—to intercept the raiders. On April 29, the Union fleet attacked Grand Gulf without success.

Grant then moved farther south and, on April 30, crossed McPherson's and McClernand's corps at Bruinsburg, without Confederate opposition. That day, Sherman, who had been left before Vicksburg to conduct deceptive operations designed to draw attention from Grant's southward move, was ordered to proceed to Hard Times. Grant's plan provided that, once across the Mississippi, he would send a corps south to assist Gen. Nathaniel P. Banks advance from Baton Rouge to capture Port Hudson, which had been hastily fortified as a second Confederate stronghold on the Mississippi (see PORT HUDSON, SIEGE OF); then, with a shift of base of supply from Memphis to New Orleans, both armies would join in operations against Vicksburg. But Banks had set forth on a diversionary operation up the Red River and would not be ready to move against Port Hudson for more than a week. This news placed Grant in a quandary. Speed was essential to his success for, if he delayed, the Confederates might assemble forces superior to his own in the Vicksburg area. Also, his lengthy supply line to Memphis was exposed to Confederate raids. He decided to proceed without Banks.

Loading all available transportation with ammunition, he abandoned his long and vulnerable supply line and moved inland. His troops would have to feed off the country as they proceeded. On May 1, two Confederate brigades from Grand Gulf tried unsuccessfuly to stem the Union advance at Port Gibson (see PORT GIBSON, BATTLE OF). The next day, the Confederates abandoned Grand Gulf and withdrew toward Vicksburg. Sherman then crossed from Hard Times to Grand Gulf. The Confederates now were disposed with Pemberton's 32,000 men at Vicksburg and Gen. Joseph E. Johnston's 6,000 at Jackson; moving between them was Grant with 44,000. Johnston, overall Confederate commander in the West, ordered Pemberton delayed, contemplating instead a movement to cut off Grant's nonexistent supply line. After a skirmish at Raymond, Sherman's and McPherson's corps reached Jackson on May 14 and drove Johnston from the city; McClernand's corps occupied Raymond and Clinton to guard against Pemberton. That night, Grant received a copy of Johnston's order from a Union agent. Assuming that Pemberton would comply with the order, Grant started his forces to the west to meet him. Meanwhile, Pemberton, still bent on cutting Grant's supposed supply line, had advanced as far as Edward's Station. On May 16, the opposing forces finally clashed at Champion's Hill (see CHAMPION'S HILL, BATTLE OF), where the Confederates were driven back. A similar stand at the Big Black River failed and Pemberton withdrew his forces into the fortifications of Vicksburg, closely pursued by the Union forces.

Hoping to defeat the Confederates before they could get organized, Grant launched a hasty, and unsuccessful, attack on May 19 (see Map B). Fearing a long, dreary siege which would drain his force and allow Johnston to build up strength to his rear, Grant, on May 22, launched a better-prepared assault coordinated with a naval attack by Porter's fleet. Sherman's and McPherson's attacks made little headway and Grant was about to cancel the offensive when grossly exaggerated reports of success arrived from McClernand. Grant then ordered a renewal of the attack all along the line; its only result was to double the Union losses already sustained.

Siege and Surrender of Vicksburg.—A deliberate siege was now the only recourse, and Grant set about it methodically. As time passed, his besieging force increased until it outnumbered the Vicksburg garrison 71,000 to 20,000, and completely surrounded the defenses of the city. The siege continued, with daily losses on each side of from 10 to 100, until July 4 when the Confederates, on the verge of starvation, surrendered. In the meantime, Johnston had assembled a force of 31,000 and had moved to Grant's rear as far as the Big Black River. On July 4, learning of Pemberton's surrender, he withdrew toward Jackson, followed by 50,000 men under Sherman. He took position in Jackson awaiting Sherman's attack, but when the latter began to make preparations for a siege, Johnston, fearing Pemberton's fate, withdrew eastward on July 16.

The fall of Vicksburg on July 4 coupled with the Confederate defeat at Gettysburg on July 3 marked the turning point of the war and signaled the doom of the Confederacy.

VINCENT J. ESPOSITO,
Colonel, United States Army; Head, Department of Military Art and Engineering, United States Military Academy.

Bibliography

Catton, Bruce, *Grant Moves South* (Little 1960).
Catton, Bruce, *This Hallowed Ground* (Doubleday 1956).
Foster, William L., *Vicksburg: Southern City Under Siege* (Historic New Orleans Collection 1980).
Miers, Earl S., *The Web of Victory: Grant at Vicksburg* (1955; reprint, Greenwood Press 1978).
Milligan, John D., *Gunboats Down the Mississippi* (1965; reprint, Ayer 1980).
Sherman, William T., *Memoirs of Gen. W. T. Sherman* (Appleton 1891–1892).
U.S. War Department, *The War of the Rebellion: Official Records of the Union and Confederate Armies,* 70 vols. (USGPO 1882–1901).
Walker, Peter K., *Vicksburg: A People at War, 1860–1865* (Univ. of N.C. Press 1960).
Young, Harold, and others, *Vicksburg Battlefield Monuments: A Photographic Record* (Univ. Press of Miss. 1984).

VICKSBURG NATIONAL MILITARY PARK, a national park established on Feb. 21, 1899, commemorating the military activities in the American Civil War that led to the surrender of Vicksburg, Miss., to the Union forces on July 4, 1863, after a 47-day siege. Consisting of about 1,492 acres and including 27 miles of driveways, the park is in the shape of a crescent enclosing the city within a 9-mile-long arc which curves from the old bed of the Mississippi River north of the city to the riverbank on the south. Two main avenues, Union and Confederate, follow the respective siege lines. Remains of trenches, gun emplacements, and approaches are visible. The many monuments, memorials, and markers, numbering about 1,600, make Vicksburg one of the best marked of all the national military parks. In the administration building are a historical museum and a historical reference library. Within the park is Vicksburg National Cemetery, established on Feb. 22, 1867. Here are buried 17,077 Union soldiers, of whom only 4,305 are known. See also VICKSBURG; VICKSBURG CAMPAIGN.

VICO, vē'kō, **Giambattista,** Italian philosopher, legal theorist, and historical scholar: b. Naples, Italy, June 23, 1668; d. there, Jan. 22/23, 1744. The sixth among eight children of a semiliterate bookseller, he attended a Jesuit school, and was for a time enrolled in the law school of the University of Naples; in all essentials, however, he educated himself in the library of the Rocca family at Vatolla near Salerno, where he served as private tutor from 1686 to 1695. In 1699 he was elected professor of rhetoric at Naples; in the same year he married and, with a family that eventually included eight children, of whom three died in infancy, he subsisted for most of his life on the pittance afforded by his post, eked out by private teaching. In 1723 he competed for a chair in law, but was passed over in favor of a far less competent candidate. In 1735, when his health was already beginning to fail, Don Carlos of Bourbon (Charles III of Spain) made him royal historiographer of the new Kingdom of Naples, and in 1741 his son Gennaro was confirmed as professor of rhetoric in his place. The final version of his lifework, *Principi di scienza nuova d'intorno alla comune natura delle nazioni* (Principles of New Science Concerning the Common Nature of the Nations), was in press when he died.

Early Works.—Vico's lifelong preoccupation with the relation of theoretical ideals to social realities is already apparent in the inaugural orations which he delivered as part of his duties between 1699 and 1708. These orations show that the main influences in his early development were the Neo-Platonism of the Renaissance, and the mathematical rationalism of René Descartes, which was dominant at Naples in his time. The last of the series, however, *De nostri temporis studiorum ratione* (1709; On the Method of Studies of Our Time), was clearly influenced by Francis Bacon, whom Vico discovered about 1707. It contains the germ of the new theory of knowledge which he advanced—along with a very curious ontology of physical bodies as made up of "metaphysical points"—in his treatise *De antiquissima italorum sapientia ex latinae linguae originibus eruenda* (1710; On the Most Ancient Wisdom of the Italians Discoverable from the Origins of the Latin Language). As against the theory of "clear and distinct ideas," Vico claimed that "the rule and criterion of truth is to have made it," that "truth" and "fact" (or "deed") are convertible terms (*verum et factum convertuntur*). Thus we have mathematical knowledge because we construct the science ourselves, and such verisimilitude as we can achieve in the sciences of nature arises from our imitation of God's creative action in controlled experiments. By one of the oddest quirks of a mind whose extravagances have always been among the worst impediments to a just appreciation of its greatness, he affected to discover all this through a philological inquiry into the origins of the Latin language.

While writing his next published book, a life of Antonio Carafa (1716), Vico began to study Hugo Grotius, and this in turn led to his reading Thomas Hobbes, in whose work he found something like his own theory of knowledge applied to the science of society. Thus, the project of his "new science" was born. Its birth was announced in three large volumes, *Diritto universale* (1720–22; Universal Law), in which Vico sought to extract from the history of Roman law the eternal law or logic of the process by which fallen humanity advances from its primitive fear of authority to the reflective control of reason, and so turns its "certainty" into "truth." Like all of his previous works, this was written in Latin, but with the decisive defeat of his academic hopes in 1723 he turned to Italian for the successive versions of the *New Science* (1725, 1730, and 1744) and for his autobiography (1725, with continuations in 1728 and 1731).

The New Science.—The *New Science* in its final version contains five books: (1) Establishment of Principles, (2) Poetic Wisdom, (3) Discovery of the True Homer, (4) The Course (*corso*) of Nations, and (5) The Recurrence (*ricorso*) of Things in the Resurgence of the Nations. This design itself exhibits the complementary relation in which the mature Vico stood to the thinkers who had most influenced him. His new science is the science of the humane learning that Descartes despised, complete in book 1 with its own axioms and its own method; or the science of the "civil world, which, since men had made it, men could hope to know," with a theory of "the modifications of our human mind" to set against Bacon's experimental logic for investigating nature. The order of these modifications is the basis of the "ideal, eternal history" which is a pattern of development exemplified, like a Platonic "form" or "idea," in every culture; and thus the new science emerges in books 2 and 3 as the proper complement of Plato's theory of the ideal state. It restores poetry to honor and identifies Homer as "a heroic character of Grecian men insofar as they told their history in song." Vico's theories of poetry, myth, and language are probably the most important novelties of his new science.

The "ideal, eternal history" has three stages: the "age of the Gods," to which the earliest institutions, religion, the family, and burial, belong; the "age of the heroes," in which heads of families united against the class of serfs; and the "age of men," in which the plebs finally established their human rights and the legal principle of equity. But the assertion of private interests leads to a decay of public spirit and the consequent breakdown of institutions, until finally there is a return to the barbarism of the state of nature, and the cycle begins again on a higher level with the dawn of Christianity. The medieval period is the returned age of heroes, and the natural law theory of his own times marked for Vico the return of the age of men. The logic of this whole process clearly transcends the intentions of any historical agent, and Vico regarded this as a proof of the existence of divine providence, the power that preserves the human race in spite of its self-destructive tendencies. He was personally a devout Roman Catholic, and this complicated his view of the *corsi* and *ricorsi* of nations. Every nation goes through the cycles independently, and in different parts of the world the cycle will be at different stages; but the Judaeo Christian tradition is exceptional in that it exemplifies the direct action of providence revealing itself to men. Thus, either a Christian or a secular interpretation of Vico is possible, depending on one's attitude toward this exception.

Influence.—No summary can indicate the richness of the documentation or the fruitfulness of Vico's insights. The *New Science* was a work of epochal importance in historical method because it showed how the records of other ages (myths, legends, poetry) can be made to yield a rational history of the society that produced them. Vico's influence was probably greater and more widespread than is realized, because until about 1830 it was largely anonymous. Charles de Secondat, baron de Montesquieu, owned a copy of the book, and Jean-Jacques Rousseau was almost certainly influenced by it. Johann Wolfgang von Goethe recognized its greatness, and Johann von Herder knew of it; but Georg Wilhelm Friedrich Hegel, who restated so many of its principal theses, never alludes to it. Samuel Taylor Coleridge introduced Vico to England, but the *New Science* was not properly rescued from obscurity until the historian Jules Michelet published a partial French translation in 1827. Among the pioneers of sociology, both Auguste Comte and Karl Marx studied Vico, and he still enjoys a high reputation in Marxist circles as the first to understand the dialectic of the class struggle. But the founders of anthropology seem not to have known their greatest prophet, and he has had to wait until the present day to find in Pitirim Sorokin a genuine disciple in this area. The influence of his theories of poetry and language can be seen in James Joyce's *Finnegans Wake,* which is a reconstruction of the "heroic" thought processes contained in "poetic wisdom."

The revival of historical idealism in Italy by Benedetto Croce and Giovanni Gentile owes a great deal to Vico; their interpretations are often debatable, but their inspiration and scholarship have virtually created a new era in Vico studies.

H. S. HARRIS,
Associate Professor of Philosophy, University of Illinois.

Bibliography

The standard edition of Vico's works is edited by Fausto Nicolini, 8 vols. (G. Laterza 1911–1941). Thomas G. Bergin and Max H. Fisch have translated the *New Science* of 1744 (Doubleday 1961), with a discussion of Vico's reputation and influence in Fisch's introduction. The definitive commentary on the *New Science* is Nicolini's *Commento storico alla seconda Scienza nuova,* 2 vols. (Edizioni de Storia e Letteratura 1949–1950), and the definitive bibliography is *Bibliografia vichiana,* 2 vols. (R. Ricciardi 1947–1948).

Albano, Maeve, *Vico and Providence,* ed. by Donald P. Verene (Lang Pub. 1986).

Burke, Peter, *Vico* (Oxford 1985).

Mooney, Michael, *Vico in The Tradition of Rhetoric* (Princeton Univ. Press 1985).

Pompa, Leonard, tr., *Vico: Selected Writings* (Cambridge 1982).

Verene, Donald P., *Vico's Science of Imagination* (Cornell Univ. Press 1981).

VICTOR, vĭk'tər, name of three popes:

VICTOR I, SAINT: r. 189–199. Although the *Liber pontificalis* and the *Martyrologium Romanum* assert that he was martyred, this fact has been seriously questioned. His reign is remarkable chiefly because there was a notable development of the claim of the Roman See to exercise jurisdiction over all other churches. In this respect Victor's actions follow the line of conduct established by Clement I (r. 88–97) in his intervention in the affairs of the church of Corinth.

Victor was a vigorous opponent of the adoptionism which certain members of the Theodotian party attempted to propagate at Rome. According to their system of theological thought, called monarchianism (q.v.), Jesus was actually no more than an ordinary man whom God had adopted as His son and elevated to divine status. Eusebius of Caesarea, in the *Historia ecclesiastica* (book 5, sect. 28), referring to an anonymous treatise *Contra Artemonem* falsely attributed to St. Hippolytus, states that the original proponents of this heresy arose in Rome in Victor's time and claimed to represent authentic ecclesiastical tradition. The unknown author of the tract refutes the claims of this sect by pointing out that Victor had excommunicated Theodotus of Byzantium, the chief exponent of their ideas, and expelled him from Rome. Victor is also supposed to have condemned the modalism of Sabellius, but there is reason to believe that this error did not become troublesome until after his time. The *Liber pontificalis* attributes to Victor a decree pronouncing upon the validity of baptism when administered by any person whatsoever in a case of necessity, but Émile Amann (see *Bibliography*) regards this as "an anticipation."

The Roman martyrology and calendar mark July 28 as Victor's feast; more ancient martyrologies fix it as April 20. He was buried at the Vatican among his predecessors.

Bibliography.—Jaffé, Philippe, *Regesta pontificum Romanorum,* vol. 1, pp. 11–12 (Leipzig 1885); Duchesne, Louis, *Histoire ancienne de l'église,* vol. 1 (Paris 1923); Batiffol, Pierre, *L'église ancienne et le catholicisme,* pp. 267–276 (Paris 1938); Amann, Émile, "Victor Ier (Saint)," *Dictionnaire de théologie catholique,* ed. by A. Vacant and E. Mangenot, vol. 15, part 2, cols. 2862–2863 (Paris 1950).

VICTOR II (GEBHARD): d. Arezzo, Italy, July 28, 1057; r. 1055–1057. The successor of St. Leo IX, he attained the papal chair by the same means as Clement II, Damasus II, and St. Leo—as the nominee of Holy Roman Emperor Henry III, to whom he was related. As Gebhard, bishop of Eichstätt, he had become known as an excellent administrator. Henry nominated him in response to a suggestion made by a Roman delegation of which Hildebrand (the future Gregory VII) was a member. Although designated pope in September 1054, Victor did not consent to his election until the following March at Regensburg; he then went to Rome and was enthroned on either Holy Thursday (April 13) or Easter Day. At Pentecost (June 4), he joined the emperor at Florence, and a great council of 120 bishops was held under their joint presidency. At this council several bishops were deposed for simony and fornication, but political questions were given first place, and from the beginning of his reign Victor showed himself a strong supporter of the emperor's policy.

Victor was in Rome for the end of 1055 and the beginning of 1056, but in the autumn of the latter year he set out again for Germany to obtain imperial protection against the Normans, then regarded as the "new Saracens." He succeeded in reconciling the emperor and Godfrey, duke of Lorraine. On October 5, Henry died after a short illness, and Victor presided at the imperial obsequies at Speyer on October 28. On November 5 he caused Henry's young son to be recognized as emperor as Henry IV, and he established Henry III's widow Agnes as regent. Because of these and similar activities, he is sometimes said to have been chancellor of the Holy Roman Empire rather than head of the Roman Catholic Church.

Victor returned to Rome in time for Easter (March 30, 1057), and in April held a synod at the Lateran which was concerned with purely administrative affairs. He required the monks of Monte Cassino to accept Frederick, brother of the duke of Lorraine and later Pope Stephen X (IX), as their abbot in place of the man they had elected. He is supposed to have written to the empress at Constantinople to ask protection for pilgrims on their way to visit the tomb of Christ (consult *Patrologiae cursus completus . . . Series Latina,* ed. by J. P. Migne, vol. 149, col. 961, Paris 1853), although some authorities attribute this letter to Victor III. He was a patron of St. John Gualbert, who founded a new congregation of Benedictine monks at Vallombrosa.

After Victor's sudden death the people of Eichstätt wished to carry his body back to Germany. The Italians refused to allow this, however, and he was buried near the gates of Ravenna in the monument of King Theodoric, which had been transformed into a church and monastery.

Further Reading: Barraclough, Geoffrey, *The Medieval Papacy* (Norton 1979); Cheetham, Nicolas, *Keepers of the Key: A History of the Popes from St. Peter to John Paul II* (Scribner 1983); Ullmann, Walter, *A Short History of the Papacy in the Middle Ages* (Methuen 1974); Von Ranke, Leopold, *History of the Popes: Their Church and State,* 3 vols. (1901; reprint, Arden Library 1986); Walsh, M., *An Illustrated History of the Popes: St. Peter to John Paul* (St. Martin's Press 1980).

VICTOR III, BLESSED (DESIDERIUS): b. Benevento, Italy, c. 1027; d. Monte Cassino, Sept. 16, 1087; r. 1086–1087. Born of a noble family, he entered the monastery of Santa Sofia at Benevento. In 1055 he obtained authorization from Pope Victor II to transfer to Monte Cassino, and when Frederick, duke of Lorraine, abbot of that monastery, became pope as Stephen X (IX), Desiderius succeeded him as abbot on April 19, 1058. In 1059, Nicholas II made him cardinal of Santa Maria-in-Trastevere in Rome. Victor's chief personal interests lay in fostering the growth of his monastery, but elements in the church who had tired of the ceaseless activities of Gregory VII felt that the moderating spirit of the abbot of Monte Cassino would answer the needs of the church after Gregory's death (May 25, 1085). He was elected in May 1086 and consecrated on May 9, 1087.

The only point of interest in Victor's short reign lies in the complicated accounts of his election. The account by Peter of Monte Cassino is wholly favorable to him (consult *Patrologiae cursus completus . . . Series Latina,* ed. by J. P. Migne, vol. 173 (Paris 1854); the other is contained in a letter of a fanatical Gregorianist, Hugh of Lyon, inserted by Hugh of Flavigny in his *Chronicle* (consult *Patrologiae cursus completus,* vol. 154, cols. 339 ff., Paris 1853). Despite the openly avowed admiration of Peter for his subject, his account seems more trustworthy than that of Hugh, who appears to have been incapable of restraint or of sound judgment.

Those who hoped that the election of Desiderius would bring peace to the church were disappointed. Victor showed himself gentle and hesitant in character; his health was not good, and temperamentally he was as incapable of breaking with the policy of Gregory VII as of continuing it. His liturgical *cultus* was confirmed by Leo XIII on Sept. 23, 1887, and his feast is kept on September 16.

ALASTAIR GUINAN,
Hunter College of the City University of New York.

Further Reading: Cowdrey, H. E. J., *The Age of Abbot Desiderius: Montecassino, the Papacy, and the Normans in the Eleventh and Early Twelfth Centuries* (Clarendon Press 1983); Grisar, Hartmann, *History of Rome and the Popes in the Middle Ages,* 3 vols. (1912; reprint, AMS Press 1970); Korn, F., *From Peter to John Paul II* (Alba House 1980); Lancioni, Enrico, *A History of the Popes* (Woodhill Press 1979).

VICTOR AMADEUS, vĭk-tər am-ə-de′əs (It. VITTORIO AMEDEO), name of three rulers of the house of Savoy:

VICTOR AMADEUS I, duke of Savoy: b. Turin, Italy, May 8, 1587; d. Vercelli, Oct. 7, 1637. Son of Charles Emmanuel I, whom he succeeded as duke in 1630, he attempted unsuccessfully to maintain equilibrium between France and the Habsburgs and to enlarge his domain. After his marriage to the sister of Louis XIII of France (1619) and the outbreak of the Thirty Years' War, Savoy fell under French control, while attempts to annex Lombardy failed. With the cession of Pinerolo to France in 1631, Savoy's freedom was forfeited.

VICTOR AMADEUS II, duke of Savoy and later (as VICTOR AMADEUS I) king of Sicily and of Sardinia: b. Turin, Italy, May 14, 1666; d. Rivoli, Oct. 31, 1732. He was the son of Charles Emmanuel II, whom he succeeded as duke in 1675. His mother, Jeanne de Nemours, prolonged her regency and extended French influence over Savoy, but Victor Amadeus ousted her in 1684 and began to assert his authority. Married to the niece of Louis XIV, and with Pinerolo in French hands, he could not at first free himself from French tutelage. But after the League of Augsburg was formed against France in 1686, he joined it in 1690. French armies overran Savoy, while its attempts to invade France failed. Disgruntled at the Habsburg refusals to cede part of Lombardy, Victor Amadeus concluded a separate peace by which France restored Pinerolo. The War of the Spanish Succession (1701–1714) found Savoy allied at first with France, but, realizing that a French victory would lead to French encirclement of Savoy, Victor Amadeus joined the anti-French coalition in 1703. At the Peace of Utrecht in 1713, Savoy was elevated to a kingdom, obtained territorial concessions from France and Austrian Lombardy, and was given Sicily, which it was forced to exchange for Sardinia in 1720. Victor Amadeus abdicated in 1730 in favor of his son, Charles Emmanuel III.

VICTOR AMADEUS III, duke of Savoy and (as VICTOR AMADEUS II) king of Sardinia: b. Turin, Italy, June 26, 1726; d. Moncalieri, Oct. 16, 1796. Son of Charles Emmanuel III of Savoy (King Charles Emmanuel I of Sardinia), he succeeded his father in 1773. He reigned during a period of growing resentment by the middle class against its subordinate position, the conservative, militaristic government, and the king's absolute control. He gravitated in the French orbit until the French Revolution (1789) caused him to draw closer to Austria and Prussia. Revolutionary sentiment in his kingdom was aggravated by the French invasion of Savoy and occupation of Nice in 1792. Despite Austrian help, he was forced in 1796 to cede Savoy and Nice to France.

See also SAVOY, HOUSE OF; SARDINIA—*History*.

EMILIANA P. NOETHER,
Author of "Seeds of Italian Nationalism."

VICTOR EMMANUEL, vĭk′tər ĕ-măn′ūəl (It. VITTORIO EMANUELE), name of three Italian rulers:

VICTOR EMMANUEL I, king of Sardinia: b. Turin, Italy, July 24, 1759; d. Moncalieri, Jan. 10, 1824. Second son of Victor Amadeus III of Savoy (King Victor Amadeus II of Sardinia), he succeeded his brother Charles Emmanuel IV of Savoy (Charles Emmanuel II of Sardinia), who abdicated in 1802. Residing in Sardinia during the French control of Italy, Victor Emmanuel returned to Turin in 1814 and in 1815 obtained the Republic of Genoa at the Congress of Vienna, which, however, reaffirmed Austrian rule over Lombardy. Austria thus became the major threat to the house of Savoy's expansionist aspirations. Embittered by his exile and hostile to French-granted reforms, he alienated many of his people as the Carbonari and other secret societies pressed for liberalism, nationalism, and constitutionalism. Unwilling to accede to demands for a constitution and a campaign against Austria after the 1820 Neapolitan revolt, he abdicated in favor of his absent brother Charles Felix and entrusted the regency to Charles Albert.

VICTOR EMMANUEL II, last king of Sardinia and first king of Italy: b. Turin, Italy, March 14, 1820; d. Rome, Jan. 9, 1878. Succeeding his father Charles Albert, who abdicated in 1849 after his defeat by the Austrians at Novara, he resisted strong Austrian pressures to withdraw the constitution granted by his father in 1848. With the aid of his able prime minister, Camillo Benso di Cavour (q.v.), Victor Emmanuel strengthened his position at home and abroad. In Sardinia, many reforms were promulgated, and throughout Italy nationalists looked to him as the symbol of the *risorgimento*. Participation in the Crimean War against Russia and in the peace conference brought prestige to the little kingdom.

Secret negotiation between Cavour and Napoleon III assured French help in the war against Austria in 1859. As a result of this conflict, followed by revolts in the smaller states in central Italy and Giuseppe Garibaldi's expedition to southern Italy, most of the peninsula was united by 1861 and Victor Emmanuel was proclaimed king on March 17. Alliance with the victorious Prussians in the Prusso-Austrian war of 1866 resulted in the addition of Venetia. In 1870 the withdrawal of French troops from Rome and the fall of Napoleon III, who had been unwilling to see papal sovereignty limited, enabled Victor Emmanuel's troops to enter Rome, which was proclaimed the capital. Victor Emmanuel then faced the task of building a truly united country from its disparate parts. Not otherwise a great man, he rose to the demands of his time and displayed natural leadership in winning over the factions of the *risorgimento*.

VICTOR EMMANUEL III, king of Italy: b. Naples, Italy, Nov. 11, 1869; d. Alexandria, Egypt, Dec. 28, 1947. Carefully educated to be king and widely traveled as crown prince, he ascended the throne in 1900 on the assassination of his father Humbert I. During the first 22 years of Victor Emmanuel's reign, Italy made progress politically and economically and annexed *Italia irredenta,* the last Italian provinces still under Austrian control, at the end of World War I.

In 1922 he appointed Benito Mussolini, the leader of the Fascist Party, prime minister, hoping he would end postwar dissension and unrest. Mussolini established a personal dictatorship, using the king as a figurehead. But despite private differences with Mussolini over the whittling away of royal authority, Victor Emmanuel raised no objections to Mussolini's repressive domestic policies and aggression in Ethiopia, Spain, and Albania. Only when Italian defeat in World War II became inevitable did Victor Emmanuel try to dissociate the monarchy from fascism. Arresting Mussolini on July 25, 1943, he tried to take Italy out of the war with German consent. Failing in this, he opened negotiations with the Allies. When Germany began to move troops toward Rome to occupy the entire country against further Allied advances, he fled precipitately and found refuge in southern Italy under Allied protection. Anti-Fascist leaders, led by Benedetto Croce, demanded the abdication of the Fascist-tainted king and his son in favor of Victor Emmanuel's grandson. Victor Emmanuel refused and an impasse prevailed until Palmiro Togliatti announced that the Communists were willing to collaborate with the monarchy. The Allies pressed for a government representing all political parties. A compromise was finally reached whereby Victor Emmanuel would not abdicate, but would retire from public affairs and appoint his son lieutenant general of the realm when Rome was liberated from the Germans. This occurred on June 4, 1944.

In 1946, Victor Emmanuel formally abdicated in favor of his son, Humbert II, who reigned for one month until Italy was proclaimed a republic. Victor Emmanuel spent his exile in Egypt.

See also SARDINIA—*History;* SARDINIA, KINGDOM OF; ITALY—*3. History*.

EMILIANA P. NOETHER,
Author of "Seeds of Italian Nationalism."

VICTORIA, vĭk-tōr'ĭ-ə (in full ALEXANDRINA VICTORIA), queen of the United Kingdom of Great Britain and Ireland, and empress of India: b. Kensington, London, England, May 24, 1819; d. Osborne, Isle of Wight, Jan. 22, 1901. She reigned 63 years, 7 months, and 2 days, the longest reign known to English history. She was the only child of Edward Augustus (1767–1820), duke of Kent and the fourth son of George III, and Victoria Mary Louisa (1786–1861), daughter of the duke of Saxe-Saalfeld-Coburg and the widow of the prince of Leiningen-Dachsburg-Hardenburg. Her parents left their home in Franconia so that she might be born in England.

Early Years.—In infancy, the future queen was known as Drina. Her father, greatly encumbered by debts (which Victoria paid in 1839), died before she was a year old. The princess was brought up in seclusion and comparative poverty, though with infinite care, in Kensington Palace. She recalled that she had not been allowed to walk downstairs without someone holding her hand until she came to the throne. Her childhood was lonely and, as she later insisted, unhappy. Quarrels between her mother and the English royal family, especially William IV, greatly distressed the young princess. She became warmly attached to her governess, the Hannoverian baroness Louise Lehzen. Although quick and intelligent, the Princess was narrowly educated. When she was 13, she started to keep a journal, which she maintained to the end of her life, but her youngest daughter, who was her literary executor, burned all but some passages that seemed to her innocuous.

Accession.—Victoria came to the throne when William IV died on June 20, 1837, and she was

Photographic portrait taken in March 1861 shows Victoria with Prince Albert, who died in December of that year.

Gernsheim Collection

crowned in Westminster Abbey on June 28, 1838. She carried out her ceremonial duties with great poise and grace. Almost unknown by the official world, the young girl made an overwhelmingly favorable impression. For the first three years of her reign, she was in public affairs and in all the minutiae of her court under the influence of her prime minister, Lord Melbourne, for whom she developed a deep affection. A shrewd and amusing leader of the political aristocracy, he tutored her in politics and worldly wisdom, and she became a faithful partisan of the Whig party. Their conversations, recorded with artless skill by the queen, have been published in *The Girlhood of Queen Victoria, 1832–1840* (1912). Her desire to keep Melbourne in office was partly responsible for Sir Robert Peel's inability to form a Conservative government in 1839, when she refused Peel's request that she replace the ladies of her court appointed during the Whig administration (the "bedchamber crisis"). This, coupled with the unfounded imputations of immoral conduct to Lady Flora Hastings, supposedly instigated by Victoria's court ladies, cost the queen some of her popularity and made her family urge that she should marry.

Marriage and Family.—Her mother and her uncle, King Leopold of the Belgians, had long thought of Prince Albert (q.v.) of Saxe-Coburg-Gotha as a suitable consort. The handsome prince captured Victoria's heart, and she proposed to him at Windsor Castle on Oct. 15, 1839. They were married at the Chapel Royal, London, on Feb. 10, 1840. The life and character of the queen were profoundly changed by this happy marriage. She once told Albert, "It is you who have entirely formed me." Although some contemptuously referred to her as Queen Albertine, her position was strengthened by the marriage and the less partisan view of public affairs that resulted from Albert's conservative influence on her. They had nine children: Victoria, the princess royal, later Empress Frederick of Germany, 1840–1901; Albert Edward, the prince of Wales, later King Edward VII, 1841–1910; Alice, later grand duchess of Hesse-Darmstadt, 1843–1878; Alfred, duke of Edinburgh, later duke of Saxe-Coburg-Gotha, 1844–1900; Helena, later Princess Christian of Schleswig-Holstein, 1846–1923; Louise, later duchess of Argyll, 1848–1939; Arthur, duke of Connaught, 1850–1942; Leopold (who suffered from hemophilia), duke of Albany, 1853–1884; and Beatrice, later Princess Henry of Battenberg, 1857–1944.

The responsibilities of a large family allowed the queen less time for society. Under her husband's influence, she grew to dislike fashionable life and to enjoy country pursuits. In 1845 she acquired Osborne, a seaside estate on the Isle of Wight, and in 1848 she leased Balmoral in the Scottish highlands, which was purchased in 1852. She subsequently spent less time in the official residences, Buckingham Palace and

Four generations of royalty: Queen Victoria with her son (later Edward VII), grandson (George V), and great-grandson (who abdicated after a brief reign as Edward VIII).

The Bettmann Archive

Windsor Castle, both of which she disliked. On her accession, parliament allotted her £385,000 per year, which she received throughout her reign. She also enjoyed the revenues of the duchy of Lancaster, which rose to about £60,000 per year. In 1852, she was bequeathed £500,000 by a miserly eccentric, John Camden Neild.

Public Affairs.—During her married life, the queen paid several visits to the large industrial towns, a new departure in the history of the monarchy, but the highlights of her ceremonial work in these years were the opening of the Great Exhibition (1851) and the official visit to Napoleon III (1855). Guided by Prince Albert, she effectively intervened in politics, especially during the confusion of political parties that followed the repeal of the Corn Laws in 1846 and persisted through the 1850's. The resignation of Lord Melbourne in 1841 and the departure in 1842 of Baroness Lehzen (who exercised a baneful influence at court even after the queen's marriage) left Albert the supreme influence over her. Under Melbourne, she had accepted the plans of government without attempting to understand or criticize them; subsequently, this was not the case. Instead of finding her a willing rubber stamp, Victoria's ministers had to take account of the opinions and prejudices of the court. This first became known during the differences between the crown and Lord Palmerston, who was then foreign secretary (1846–1851). The queen was on terms of private friendship with the rulers of Belgium, Prussia, Portugal, and France and had a knowledge of foreign affairs that was in some ways better and more current than that of the government. Palmerston's attempt to build up the new democratic forces in Europe, especially at the expense of Austria, met with the queen's strong disapproval. She and the prince contemplated dismissing Palmerston, and in 1848 she told the prime minister, Lord John Russell, that she would have no "peace of mind as long as Palmerston was at the foreign office." Palmerston's unexpected departure from the cabinet in December 1851 was in part due to the prime minister's desire to please the queen. The formation of Lord Aberdeen's coalition government in 1852 was largely the work of the court and was described by the queen as "the realization of our most ardent wishes."

In 1853 the popularity of Victoria and her consort waned as their efforts to prevent the Crimean War were suspected of being counter to the country's interests. When war was declared in 1854, however, Victoria took an active part in organizing relief for the wounded, visited hospitals, distributed medals, and instituted the Victoria Cross.

Widowhood.—On Dec. 14, 1861, the prince consort (Albert was given this title in 1857) died from typhoid fever. The effect upon the queen was shattering. Indulging her grief as was characteristic of her generation, she donned the full regalia of widowhood and used writing paper with a mourning band for the rest of her days. For years, she lived in seclusion, appearing only to unveil memorials to the prince and in 1866 to open parliament, an event which she told the prime minister she could "only compare to an execution." She attempted to continue her former surveillance of public affairs, but, as events changed, the validity of what Albert had taught her diminished, and she found it increasingly difficult to make an effective contribution. Victoria had intense prejudices, which she never attempted to hide. Although she regarded herself as a liberal in politics, she loathed William Gladstone, the Liberal prime minister in 1868–1874, 1880–1885, 1886, and 1892–1894. She nearly exceeded her constitutional authority in trying to prevent his becoming prime minister in 1880, and she publicly blamed him for the death of Gen. Charles Gordon in 1885. Also open to constitutional objection was her excessive reliance on Benjamin Disraeli, 1st Earl of Beaconsfield (q.v.) and prime minister in 1868 and 1874–1880, who in 1876 introduced the bill conferring on her the title of empress of India. Fortunately, however, the prejudices of the queen were largely those of her most influential subjects. She was a strong imperialist. Her resolution and devotion to duty touched the public and helped to explain the almost frenzied acclaim of the jubilee of 1887, the diamond jubilee of 1897, her appearances during the Boer War from 1899, and her appearance in Dublin in 1900. She died after a brief illness and a rather longer failure of her powers.

Personal Characteristics.—Victoria is believed to have lamented on one occasion "we are rather short for a queen." She was very fair, with a clear, high-colored complexion. Even in old age she never lost her grace of movement, which gave the impression that she moved on wheels. She had a beautiful speaking voice, and, although she spoke German and French easily (and latterly a little Hindustani), she spoke English without a trace of a foreign accent. She never lost her shyness in public and was especially uncomfortable in the presence of those she thought cleverer than herself. It is not true that she lacked a sense of humor; her laughter was infectious and on occasions convulsive. She greatly enjoyed the theater, but never entered one after 1861, seeing only plays that were given privately. Victoria also showed deep interest in men and women of letters. Alfred Lord Tennyson, whose *In Memoriam* comforted her during her widowhood, was a great favorite. The queen's preoccupation with her journal and letter writing left her little time for reading, but she enjoyed the romantic novelists, especially Walter Scott and some of the early 19th century German writers, and there is evidence that she was fascinated by the novels of Anthony Trollope and George Eliot. She also greatly admired the historical writings of Thomas Babington Macaulay. Her taste in music was developed, with an inclination toward the German rather than the Italian composers, and she shared her consort's admiration for Felix Mendelssohn, who gave her some instruction. She played the piano and sang, and she danced beautifully. She formed a remarkable collection of early photographs, and she also collected dolls. Some extracts from her journal were published during her lifetime in *Leaves from the Journal of Our Life in the Highlands* (1868) and *More Leaves* (1883). Though hastily written and sometimes ungrammatical, her letters and journal are among the most vivid materials for a study of the 19th century.

See also GREAT BRITAIN AND NORTHERN IRELAND—*History*.

ROGER FULFORD
Author of "The Prince Consort," "Queen Victoria," and "Hanover to Windsor"

Bibliography

Bailey, John, *Some Political Ideas and Persons* (1921; reprint, Telegraph Bks. 1984).
Benson, E. F., *Queen Victoria* (1935; reprint, Darby Bks. 1985).
Duff, David, ed., *Queen Victoria's Highland Journals* (Holt 1983).
Fulford, Roger, *Hanover to Windsor* (Batsford 1960).
Hibbert, Christopher, *Queen Victoria in Her Letters* (Viking 1985).
Nevill, St. John B., ed., *Life at the Court of Queen Victoria* (Merrimack 1984).
Plowden, Alison, *The Young Victoria* (Stein & Day 1981).
Shearman, Dierdre, *Queen Victoria* (Chelsea House 1985).
Strachey, Lytton, *Queen Victoria* (1949; reprint, Harcourt 1966).
Weintraub, Stanley, *Victoria: An Intimate Biography* (Dutton 1987).
Woodham-Smith, Cecil, *Queen Victoria* (D. I. Fine 1986).

VICTORIA, vēk-tō'ryä, **Guadalupe** (real name MANUEL FÉLIX FERNÁNDEZ), Mexican general and president: b. Tamazula, Durango, Mexico, 1789; d. Perote, Veracruz, March 21, 1843. He joined the fight for Mexican independence in 1811 and was an officer in the army of José María Morelos y Pavón. When the Plan of Iguala was adopted in 1821, he retired from politics, but he joined the revolt of Antonio López de Santa Anna against Agustín de Iturbide's empire in 1822 (see MEXICO—26. *Mexico from 1810 to 1910*). After the proclamation of the republic, Victoria accepted a post in the provisional government and in 1824 was chosen as Mexico's first president. During his administration, the economy was organized, diplomatic relations with foreign nations were established, and slavery was abolished. He was succeeded as president in 1829 by Vincente Guerrero after a revolt, and he retired to private life.

VICTORIA, Tomás Luis de (Ital. TOMMASO LODOVICO DA VITTORIA), Spanish composer: b. Ávila, Spain, 1549?; d. Madrid, Aug. 27, 1611. In 1565, he began to study for the priesthood at the Collegium Germanicum in Rome, where he probably worked with Giovanni da Palestrina, whom he succeeded as master of music at the Roman Seminary in 1571. Ordained in 1575 Victoria served for the next 20 years in Roman churches. At the Church of San Girolamo della Carità he associated with St. Filippo de'Neri, who had founded there the Congregation of the Oratory, leading to the development of the oratorio. In 1592 Victoria is known to have been chaplain to the dowager Empress Maria, widow of Holy Roman Emperor Maximilian II; about two years later he became organist and choirmaster at the Convent of the Descalzas Reales in Madrid, where she lived in retirement. After her death in 1603, he stayed on as chaplain to her daughter, the Infanta Margarita, a nun. His crowning work, *Officio defunctorum*, a requiem mass for the empress, was published in 1605.

Victoria composed no secular music. His compositions, supported by ecclesiastical and royal patronage, were issued in splendid format from 1572 on. With those of Palestrina and Orlando di Lasso, his works mark the final summit of polyphony. His masses, psalms, motets, and magnificats assure his position among the great composers. They reveal fervid concentration, dramatic sweep, increasingly ecstatic and tragic tone, rhythmic inventiveness and audacity, and individuality that is at once intensely personal and unmistakably Spanish.

Consult Casimiri, Raffaele, *Il Vittoria* (Rome 1934), the first scholarly modern biography of Victoria.

HERBERT WEINSTOCK,
Author of "Music as an Art."

VICTORIA, vĭk-tōr'ĭ-ə, in Roman religion, goddess of victory, identified with the Greek goddess Nike (q.v.). Frequently conjoined with Jupiter and oftener with Mars, she was especially worshiped by soldiers. Her name supplied epithets (*Victrix* and *Victor*) for conquering legions and emperors. Though remains of her temple (built in 294 B.C.) are in Rome, her most celebrated memorial was the Altar of Victory in the Senate House (dedicated in 29 B.C.). In art Victoria wore a laurel wreath on her head, had wings on her shoulders, carried a palm branch, helmet, spear, or shield, and was clad in a flowing robe.

P. R. COLEMAN-NORTON.

VICTORIA, a state of the Commonwealth of Australia covering 87,884 square miles and occupying the southeastern portion of the island continent, between 34° and 39° south latitude and 141° and 150° east longitude. To the north, the River Murray divides the state from New South Wales; on the west it is bounded by South Australia, and to the south lies ocean, with Bass Strait dividing the mainland from Tasmania. The population was 2,952,883 according to the 1961 official estimate. The capital is Melbourne (pop., 1,907,000).

Physical Features.—In its eastern and western sections the coast is low and flat, with few inlets; in the central segment there are large bays and some high cliffs. Running east to west, the central highlands are a continuation of the continent's main mountain area: they form a wedge tapering from a broad and high mountain belt in the east until they disappear near the western boundary. The highest peak, in the Victorian Alps, is Mount Bogong (6,516 feet); there are six other peaks above 6,000 feet. In the west, the Grampians are a series of serrate ridges of sandstone rising to 3,829 feet in Mount William. North of the central highlands lie the Murray Basin plains, while the southern slopes fall away to the Gippsland plains (in the east) and the Western District plains (in the southwest), and between lies a drowned area represented by Port Phillip and Westernport bays. In the extreme south are two uplifted blocks, the South Gippsland Highlands and the Otway Ranges.

The climate is temperate and generally mild, with low humidity. The winter is cool to cold, with snow on the highland areas. The summer is usually hot. Average maximum daily temperatures in January (midsummer) in the north are between 80° and 90° F., and in the south between 75° and 80° F., with some upland areas under 70° F. The daily maximum in midwinter is in the 50's, and showery periods are common. Rainfall is lower in the northern parts (ranging from 12 inches to 25 inches), but the greater part is well watered with no marked seasonal concentration. High rainfalls (over 40 inches) are confined to the highlands.

Normal river flow totals about 17 million acre-feet a year. All streams have pronounced seasonal variation, though the greater rainfall and higher incidence of summer rains in the east give stronger and more regular flow. In very wet years the annual flow is three times the

Right: **Crews practicing on the Yarra at Melbourne, capital of the State of Victoria, Australia. In the background is St. Paul's Cathedral.**

Below: **Pall Mall, the main shopping street of Bendigo, Victoria, once a gold-mining town, now a tomato-canning and sheep-marketing center.**

Australian News & Information Bureau

average, whereas in severe drought years it falls to a quarter of the average. Water storages, totaling 6 million acre-feet, have been developed for irrigation. Winter flows are held in large reservoirs for use in the dry months; future development will involve very large storages to meet deficiencies in years of low rainfall. There is no prospect of water being available for irrigating all highly suitable land available. Approximately one fourth of the state's area is artificially supplied with water.

Hydroelectric undertakings are on a relatively small scale; there is one 135,000-kilowatt station and six smaller units operate. Power from the national Snowy Mountains hydroelectric project is fed into the state system.

In the highlands were some of the world's finest and most productive hardwood forests. Fires and settlement led to their reduction; since the early 1900's permanent forest areas have been set aside. In all, 16,790,000 acres are classed as forests, including 14 million acres of state forest; of this, half is primarily for lumber production and the balance is mainly protective forest. The best commercial forests are located where the rainfall exceeds 40 inches. The indigenous forests show a marked predominance of eucalypts. Plantations of introduced conifers (*Pinus radiata*) have developed to meet demands for softwoods and cover 35,000 acres.

Victorian soils are typical of Australian soils in their general poverty in phosphorus. In some areas, trace elements, including molybdenum, zinc, copper, and manganese, have also been shown to be lacking. Large areas of very sandy soils await development.

Population.—Average density of 33 people to the square mile compares with the national average of 3.5. Under the impact of immigration from abroad, recent population growth has been at the rate of about 3 per cent a year. The most striking feature of the distribution is the very high degree of urbanization, and efforts to decentralize industry have been defeated largely by the natural advantages of Melbourne. In 1961, 63 percent of the state's population lived in the Melbourne metropolitan area, as compared with 51 percent in 1921 and 55 percent in 1933. Other cities include Geelong (90,380 according to the 1960 official estimate), Ballarat (54,800), Bendigo (42,120), the Latrobe Valley settlements (aggregating about 40,000), and Mildura (12,620).

Religious affiliations follow the broad national pattern (see AUSTRALIA—*10. Cultural Affairs:* Religion) but Presbyterians are more numerous (13.3 percent).

Government.—Governmental activity is carried out through the legislative, executive, and judicial organs, and through semigovernment or statutory authorities and local government bodies (or municipalities). Executive authority is vested in a governor, appointed by the sovereign for a term of six years. He is assisted by an executive council, the members of which are ministers controlling the various administrative departments. The bicameral legislature comprises the Legislative Council, an upper house of 34 members elected for six years (one member for each of the 17 provinces retiring every three years), and the Legislative Assembly, a lower house of 66 members elected for the duration of Parliament (the maximum life of which is three years). Both houses are elected by universal adult suffrage, and voting is compulsory. A government can hold office only so long as it holds a majority in the Legislative Assembly.

The state raises funds from motor registration fees, probate duties, stamp duties, land tax, and entertainment tax. Income tax is collected by the federal government and reimbursement made on an adjustable formula. Annual revenue and appropriations are each about £A250 million.

Education, Health, and Welfare.—State education is secular and free, and school attendance is compulsory for children between the ages of 6 and 14. The registration of all schools and all teachers is required. There are three main groups of schools: state schools, Roman Catholic schools, and nongovernment schools, many of which are sponsored by Protestant churches but independently run. About 66 percent of pupils attend government schools; 20 percent, Roman Catholic; and 14 percent, other schools. The state also maintains a number of technical schools. There are two universities: the University of Melbourne (established 1853) and Monash University (opened 1961).

Melbourne's Public Library opened in 1856 as the first free public library in Australia. It houses about 700,000 volumes, including rare editions and manuscripts. The lending library has its own collection of 130,000 volumes.

Although the federal government is responsible for the broad social security program, important functions in social welfare are carried out by the state, including work in public health and education; child, youth, and family welfare; labor legislation; workers' compensation; and community services.

Economic Activities.—The net value of production shows the strong development of manufacturing. Of the total net value of £A880 million (1 pound = $2.23 U.S. currency) from all industries in 1958–1959, value of rural production was £A241 million and nonrural primary £A30 million compared with a net value in manufacturing of £A609 million.

Sheep number about 27 million. Fine wool comes from the Western District; fat lambs are more important in the north. Beef cattle, widely distributed, total about 1 million. Dairy cattle, mainly in the south and also in northern irrigation areas, total 1.65 million.

Year-round open-air dairying and livestock-and-grass farming are possible in southern districts and dry farming of grains is undertaken in the north, where there are also irrigated citrus and stone fruit orchards, truck gardens, and pastures. The climate does not favor small-scale farming because of poor rainfall distribution. Farms are on a commercial rather than a subsistence basis, and large estates persist.

Research has lifted yield per acre in cereal growing, pasture improvement has come with use of superphosphate, and there have been notable advances in sheep husbandry, dairying, hog raising, beef cattle fattening, and fruitgrowing. Irrigation areas have been extended and exceed 800,000 acres. Crops occupy about 6,978,201 acres. Wheat is by far the biggest crop, occupying 1,810,026 acres; the long fallow used in many districts accounts for another 2 million acres. Acreage sown to oats is about 970,688 and barley 383,000. Forages (700,000 acres), vineyards and orchards (111,547 acres), potatoes and vegetables (130,596 acres) and smaller crops, account for the remainder.

Manufacturing first became important during the 1860's when establishments concerned with rudimentary processing of raw materials began to extend their activities. The demands of World War II led to entry into many new fields. From the late 1940's there was large-scale United States and British investment, particularly in the automotive, textile, and chemical industries, in food processing, and in oil refining. By 1959 the number of factories exceeded 16,500, and more than 362,000 people were employed in them. Principal manufactures are motor vehicles, textiles and clothing, chemical fertilizers, agricultural implements, electrical goods, and petrochemicals, as well as butter, cheese, condensed milk, jam, and preserved fruit.

Principal imports from overseas are oil, vehicles, paper, lumber, textiles, iron, and steel. Imports from other states include iron and steel, sugar, and paper. Chief exports to overseas countries are wool, wheat, meat, fruit, flour, and dairy produce. Vehicles, machinery, refined petroleum products, beer, metals, and malt are shipped to other states.

Brown coal deposits in the Latrobe Valley are massive, with thicknesses up to 800 feet. Nearly 12 million tons a year are won by strip-mining methods for use in generating electricity (representing two thirds of the state's 1.5-million-kilowatt capacity), for compounding into briquette blocks for industrial and domestic use, and for town gas production. Clay is used for bricks, tiles, firebrick, and ceramic products; production exceeds 36 million cubic yards. Sands for use in building, glassmaking, and foundry work are available, together with limestone for cement-making. Salt and gypsum are won from shallow lakes. Other minerals include diatomite, limonite, magnesite, and fluorite, while gold continues to be the most important metal produced (annual production: 34,662 fine ounces).

Transportation and Communications.—Melbourne is the main port and focal point for the transport and communications system. The deep indentation of Port Phillip Bay allows sea transport to bring goods into the heart of the state. Geelong and Portland are other ports. Railroads had a total route mileage of 4,333 in 1959, all owned by the state. A line linking the narrower gauge New South Wales system with Melbourne was completed in 1961. There are over 100,000 miles of roads and streets, of which all but 4,000 miles of state highway are maintained by local authorities. Air services connect with other states and with New Zealand.

Places of Interest.—Extensive winter snowfields attract increasing numbers of visitors. Fishing is popular in inland streams and lakes and on the coast. The Grampians are notable for their wild flowers. Mildura, on the Murray, is a reminder of the work of the Chaffey brothers, who introduced irrigation. Of the many gold rush towns, only Ballarat and Bendigo have developed as commercial centers; others such as Walhalla and Clunes have fallen into disuse.

History.—The eastern tip of Victoria was sighted by Capt. James Cook in 1770, but it was left to George Bass, sailing in a whaleboat from Sydney in 1798, to indicate that a strait might divide this from Van Diemen's Land (Tasmania). An abortive settlement was made in 1803; permanent settlements came in 1834 at Portland and in 1835 at Melbourne, which was incorporated as a town in 1842. In 1851, the separate colony of Victoria was constituted with

A bronze statue of Queen Victoria stands in front of Parliament Building in the provincial capital of Victoria, British Columbia.

OFFICE OF TOURISM—CANADA

its own executive and legislature. Large deposits of gold uncovered in the same year brought a great influx of people, and the colony grew rapidly thereafter. Responsible government was introduced in 1856. In 1901 Victoria became one of the federated states of the Commonwealth of Australia.

R. M. YOUNGER

VICTORIA, city, British Columbia, Canada, capital of the province, situated at an altitude of 228 feet at the southeastern extremity of Vancouver Island. Victoria is a world port, with direct access to the Pacific through Juan de Fuca Strait. It is served by the Canadian National and Canadian Pacific Railways, Patricia Bay airport, extensive bus services, a provincially owned ferry to the mainland, and ferries to Seattle and Port Angeles, Washington. The city is governed by a mayor and council and forms a metropolitan region with the adjacent municipalities of Oak Bay, Saanich, Esquimalt, and others.

The city attracts a half million visitors annually. Its beautiful natural setting, flanked by the Malahat and Sooke Hills and overlooking the snow-clad Olympic Mountains across the strait, is enhanced by many parks and gardens, notably Beacon Hill Park and the Butchart Gardens. A mild, equable climate (the average annual precipitation is 26.19 inches and the frost-free period is 345 days), access to beaches, woods, and lakes, and facilities for yachting, golf, hunting, fishing, and other sports have attracted many retired persons, mostly of British origin. British pioneer influences are still evident in places.

Provincial and federal government services, including a naval and military establishment at Esquimalt and customs and immigration services, account for about 25 percent of the region's employment. Shipbuilding, shipping, machinery manufacturing, lumber processing, and fishing are major industries.

Victoria College, a coeducational institution originally a junior college, is now affiliated with the University of British Columbia and awarded its first degrees in 1961. Among the region's notable buildings are the provincial parliament buildings, Government House, the courthouse, the Empress Hotel, Craigdarroch Castle, Dominion Astrophysical Observatory, and Royal Roads Canadian Services College. Other institutions include museums and laboratories, an art gallery, a public library (149,000 volumes), the provincial library (400,000 volumes), the provincial archives, and the Pacific Naval Laboratory. There are also a number of theater groups.

History. Fort Camosun was established on the island site, by James Douglas, as western head-

J. Allan Cash

Buildings huddle along a narrow coastal strip and cling to steep hillsides in Victoria, the capital of crowded Hong Kong.

quarters of the Hudson's Bay Company in 1843 in anticipation of the partition of 1846, which placed the old headquarters within the United States.

Vancouver Island became a crown colony of the United Kingdom in 1850, and in 1856 a legislative assembly was summoned by Governor Douglas to the settlement, renamed Fort Victoria. After the Fraser River gold rush of 1858 brought sudden commercial growth to Victoria, it was incorporated as a city in 1862. When Vancouver Island was unified with the mainland of British Columbia in 1866, New Westminster was made the capital. In 1868 the capital was transferred to Victoria, which became the provincial capital when British Columbia entered the Dominion of Canada in 1871.

The 1976 population of Victoria was 62,551. In 1981 it had increased to 64,379.

ROBERT ENGLAND,
Economist; Author of "Contemporary Canada."

VICTORIA, city and capital of the British colony of Hong Kong. Victoria, at northern Hong Kong Island on the shore of one of the world's finest natural harbors, and Kowloon, across the harbor, form the colony's metropolitan area and together are usually known as Hong Kong. The population of Victoria was 633,138 according to the 1961 census.

Founded in 1843 on a strip of level land below a range of volcanic hills, the highest of which is Victoria Peak (1,823 feet), Victoria has developed its steep hillside and reclaimed land from the sea to provide room for expansion. By 1959 an area about 9 miles long and 600–1,200 feet wide had been reclaimed, but sections of the city, such as the Wanchai quarter, remained among the world's most densely populated places. Overcrowding, especially during periods of stress in China, has resulted in many disastrous fires and outbreaks of disease. Despite the continuing construction of reservoirs on Hong Kong Island and in the New Territories, water supply has not equaled demand, and rationing is sometimes necessary.

Victoria is the administrative and commercial center of the colony. Most of its businesses are associated with its function as a vital far eastern trading center. Dockyard and shipbuilding facilities have been modernized since World War II. Local industries, among them, textiles and machinery, burgeoned during the 1950s when trade with Communist China was curtailed. Its natural beauty, its colorful seaport atmosphere, its luxury hotels, and its low-priced merchandise from all parts of the world have made Victoria the center of Hong Kong's tourist trade, now one of the colony's major sources of income. Buses, an electric tramway, and 11 ferrying services provide public transportation. A funicular railroad to Victoria Peak has been in operation since 1888. The University of Hong Kong, founded in Victoria in 1912, had 1,268 students in 1959.

See also HONG KONG.

VICTORIA, city, Texas, seat of Victoria County, situated at an altitude of 187 feet on the

Guadalupe River, 30 miles from the Gulf of Mexico. It forms a geographical hub between Houston (124 miles by road), San Antonio (117 miles), and Corpus Christi (94 miles), and is served by two airlines, two bus lines, and the Missouri Pacific and Southern Pacific railroads. A barge canal was completed in the mid-1960's. Victoria's favorable climate, its abundance of water and natural resources, including gas and oil, and its location in prosperous ranch and farm country make it one of the fastest growing communities in the Southwest. There are oil refineries and a variety of industrial plants.

Don Martín de León established the city of Guadalupe Victoria in 1824 with a settlement of 41 families. In 1839 the town of Victoria was incorporated under the Republic of Texas. In 1957 a city manager system was adopted. Victoria college, a two-year institution established in 1926, is located on a 40-acre campus in the city. The second oldest newspaper in the state, the Victoria *Advocate*, established in 1846, is published daily. Pop. 50,695.

ORA LEE REYNOLDS.

VICTORIA, a genus of plants of the family *Nymphaeaceae,* resembling the common water lily, but most nearly allied to the genus *Euryale* of southeastern Asia, and distinguished from it particularly by the deciduous tips of the calyx, and the sterility of the innermost stamens. Three species of the genus have been found in South America. Best known of these is the *V. regia,* a magnificent water lily, of gigantic size, which is found especially in northern South America, frequently covering the surface for miles. *Victoria* was first observed by Thaddaeus Haenke in Bolivia in 1801. Rediscovered by Eduard Friedrich Poeppig about 1830 in the Amazon, it was named by him in 1832, *E. amazonum.* Plants of the genus *Victoria* were subsequently found in many rivers of the northeastern and eastern part of South America, as far south as Paraguay.

It was introduced with great difficulty to horticulture. Seeds were sent to England from Georgetown, British Guiana, in a bottle of water; they must be kept constantly wet to remain viable. The first flower that bloomed in England was presented to Queen Victoria, in honor of whom the genus was named. It is this northern species, therefore, which bears the name *V. regia.* The first flower was produced Nov. 9, 1849, at Chatsworth, England, the seat of the duke of Devonshire. By Nov. 9, 1850, this plant had produced 126 flowers throughout the year, and was still blooming.

The Indians of British Guiana called it the water platter, in reference to its remarkable floating leaves, which are six feet or more across, and are circular with an upturned rim four to six inches high. These gigantic leaves, which are of a purplish color on the under side, are orbicular-peltate; they have a sort of wickerwork of very prominent prickly veins underneath, and are borne on petioles longer than the depth of the water on which they float—an apparent provision against submersion by changes in the river level. The leaf tissues are full of air spaces and canals, which render the leaves so buoyant that they can support from 100 to 200 pounds of weight. The leaf is also punctured with minute holes, possibly for the escape of water from its fenced-in upper surface.

The water-lily-like flowers rise among the leaves upon prickly stalks; they are more than a foot across, nocturnal, and open on two successive evenings. The first time a *Victoria* opens, the inner petals over the stigma remain unexpanded and the flowers are creamy white, with a delicious fragrance. It closes the next forenoon, to open again at dark, this time expanding to its fullest extent, but has become rose-red in color and with a disagreeable odor. The flower is then closed forever, and is withdrawn beneath the surface of the water. The seeds are like peas, hidden in the cells of an inferior ovulary, or globular prickly capsule, about as large as a coconut; the starchy seeds are called *maíz del agua,* or water corn, in parts of South America, where they are used for food.

Victoria regia is found naturally in shallow inlets, lakes, and pools in bogs, and can be cultivated in greenhouses or in outdoor heated tanks. The other species, *V. amazonum* and *V. cruziana,* are more easily managed, especially the latter, which lives further from the equator (Paraguay). *Victoria* was introduced into India from seeds produced in Britain.

HENRY S. CONARD
Author of "How to Know the Mosses and Liverworts"

VICTORIA, Lake, a lake in Africa. In the center of the East African plateau, it lies mostly south of the equator, at a height of 3,720 feet (1,134 meters) above sea level and surrounded by Uganda, Kenya, and Tanzania. It was discovered by John Hanning Speke in 1858. In contrast to the other great lakes of eastern Africa, such as Tanganyika and Nyasa (Malawi), which are relatively narrow and deep with steep shores and smooth coastlines, Lake Victoria has a maximum depth of only 270 feet (82 meters), and its shores, except the western, are deeply indented. Its coastline exceeds 2,000 miles (3,220 km), although its greatest extent is only 250 miles (402 km) from north to south, and 160 miles (257 km) from east to west. Its area of 26,828 square miles (69,484 square km)—almost as large as the state of Maine—makes it the largest freshwater lake in the world after Lake Superior. It is the chief reservoir of the Nile basin, with a catchment area exceeding 100,000 square miles (259,000 square km). Headwaters of the Kagera River, which drain into the western side of Lake Victoria, are the most remote of all of the headwaters of the Nile.

The Victoria Nile emerges from Lake Victoria near Jinja, Uganda, where at Owens Falls a dam was constructed and a hydroelectric scheme inaugurated in 1954. The building of the dam resulted in the submergence of Ripon Falls and, after 1975, a rise in the lake level.

Among the numerous islands are the Sese Islands and the densely peopled Ukerewe Island. The largest gulfs are Winam (northeast), Speke (southeast), and Emin Pasha (southwest). Of the many ports the chief are Kisumu (Kenya), Mwanza and Bukoba (Tanzania), and Bukakata and Port Bell (Uganda). Regular steamer services are maintained along the chief ports, and rail systems connect the lake ports with ports on the Indian Ocean—Mwanza with Dar es Salaam (Tanzania) and Kisumu with Mombasa (Kenya).

The area surrounding Lake Victoria is well watered and there is considerable production of coffee and cotton, besides food crops such as

Fishing boats from Kisumu, Kenya, ply the waters of Lake Victoria, the largest freshwater lake in Africa and second largest in the world.

East African Railways & Harbours

sugar and maize. The density of population is in places high for East Africa, notably in Sukumaland (Tanzania), in Nyanza Province (Kenya), and in Buganda and Busoga (Uganda). More than 200 varieties of fish live in Lake Victoria, but the species *Tilapia* supplies most of the fishing industry.

ROBERT W. STEEL
Professor of Geography, University of Liverpool.

VICTORIA AND ALBERT MUSEUM, museum, London, in South Kensington. It houses one of the world's finest collections of post-ancient art, mostly decorative or applied art, in a building completed by Sir Aston Webb. Deriving originally from the Museum of Ornamental Art in Marlborough House, it was transferred to South Kensington in 1857 to become part of a collective museum of science and art. In 1899 the name was changed from the South Kensington Museum to the Victoria and Albert Museum, and in 1909 the name was limited to the art collections, the Science Museum being the name given to the scientific exhibits. The present museum comprises the departments of sculpture, ceramics, prints and drawings, paintings, metalwork, textiles, woodwork, circulation (for traveling exhibitions), and conservation and the Indian section, the National Art Library, and the museum extension services. The national collection of miniatures and watercolors are included in the museum. The V. & A., as it is widely known, attracts about 800,000 visitors annually, and has four outstations: the Bethnal Green Museum and the Wellington Museum in London; Ham House, near Richmond; and Osterley Park House in Middlesex.

C. H. GIBBS-SMITH

VICTORIA CROSS, a decoration instituted on Jan. 29, 1856, by Queen Victoria, is the most coveted of all British orders for conspicuous bravery. Originally granted only to British military and naval personnel, the right to receive the cross was extended to Indian soldiers in 1911, to members of the air force during World War I, and to the nursing services in 1920. Civilians may also receive the medal, but in only one case has it ever been awarded for a deed performed elsewhere than in the presence of the enemy. Since 1959 a tax-free annuity of £100 has been given to all recipients. Previously, recipients below commissioned rank were given an annuity of £10 and an additional annuity of £5 for each bar; in particular cases the £10 annuity was increased to the amount of £50.

The Victoria Cross consists of a Maltese cross of bronze and was made from Russian cannon captured at Sevastopol (September 1855); from March 1942, when the supply of Savastopol metal became exhausted, crosses were made of gunmetal supplied by the Royal Mint. The center contains a royal crown surmounted by the British heraldic lion. Below, on a scroll, is the inscription "For Valour." The reverse side of the bar bears the rank and name of the recipient. On the cross is inscribed the name and date of the action in which the honor was won. The clasp above, which is decorated with two horizontal branches of laurel, has a V appendage from which the cross is suspended. The cross, suspended by a crimson ribbon, is borne on the left breast. Until 1918, the ribbon for the Royal Navy was blue. Reward for any further act of exceptional bravery is presented in a bar attached to the ribbon.

See also DECORATIONS, MEDALS, AND ORDERS.

VICTORIA DAY, a holiday commemorating the anniversary of Queen Victoria's birthday, May 24, 1819. The movement to establish this date as Empire Day, in recognition of the unity of the British Empire, was initiated by Reginald Brabazon, Earl of Meath (1841–1929). Victoria Day or Empire Day, or both, are celebrated in various parts of the British Commonwealth of Nations, sometimes in conjunction with the observance of the anniversary of the reigning sovereign's birth. In Canada Victoria Day was established in 1952 as the first Monday preceding May 25, and Empire Day is observed in some provinces on the last school day before Victoria Day.

VICTORIA DE DURANGO, city, Mexico. See DURANGO.

VICTORIA DE JUNÍN, La, vēk-tō′ryä t͟hä ho͞o-nēn′, (The Victory of Junín), a poem by the Ecuadorian poet and politician José Joaquín Olmedo (1780–1847), one of Latin America's most important neoclassical poets. *La victoria de Junín,* written in 1825, was inspired by the victories of Simón Bolívar's troops over the Spanish at Junín (Aug. 6, 1824) and at Ayacucho (Dec. 9, 1824) in Peru. Although Bolívar had requested that Olmedo commemorate Junín in verse, he opposed the inclusion of what he regarded as unnecessary elements and criticized Olmedo's exaggerations and factual errors.

The poem is composed of 907 irregularly rhymed lines of 7 and 11 syllables. After a description of the battle at Junín, there occurs the supernatural appearance of Huayna Capac, last of the Inca rulers to reign over the entire empire, who speaks in praise of the struggle for independence, and predicts the battle at Ayacucho. His speech expresses the liberal outlook of the revolutionary leaders and their hopes for a Hispanic-American federation. The poem ends with a chorus of vestals and a description of the triumphal entry into Lima. *La victoria de Junín* suffers from grandiloquence and prosaic rhetoric, but at its best, particularly in descriptions of battle, it achieves considerable power. It continues to be one of the most widely read of Latin-American poems.

FRANK DAUSTER
Author of "Breve historia del teatro hispanoamericano"

VICTORIA FALLS, waterfall, Africa, on the Zambezi River at the border of Zambia and Zimbabwe, at a point 2,850 feet (869 meters) above sea level where the river is crossed by an outcrop of Tertiary basalt. The river falls abruptly, with a great roar and in a cloud of spray, over the edge of a chasm. The native Makololu name, *mosi-oa-tunya,* means "the smoke that thunders." The falls are 5,700 feet (1,737 meters) wide. Between Livingstone and Cataract islands are the Main Falls, 355 feet (108 meters) deep. The chasm varies in width from 80 to 200 feet (24–61 meters). The Zambezi then passes through a series of narrow zigzag gorges.

Over a mile wide, the Victoria Falls are among the most awesome of the African continent's many natural wonders.

Marilyn Silverstone from Nancy Palmer

David Livingstone discovered and named the falls on Nov. 16, 1855. Immediately below them, a 650-foot (198-meter) rail and road bridge was opened in 1904. The falls have become a tourist attraction, and a hydroelectric station, unobtrusively sited downstream, was opened in 1938.

ROBERT W. STEEL

VICTORIA HARBOUR, village, Ontario, Canada, in Simcoe County, on Hog Bay, an arm of Georgian Bay, about 25 miles northwest of Orilla, on the Canadian National Railway. The first building, a sawmill, was erected in 1869, and when the Midland Railroad arrived in 1871 the settlement was named in honor of Queen Victoria. The chief product is lumber. South of the village is the site of the Jesuit mission of St. Louis, where Jean de Brebeuf and Gabriel Lalement were captured by the Iroquois. Population: 1,125.

VICTORIA ISLAND, island, Northwest Territories, Canada, third largest island in the Arctic Archipelago north of the continental mainland. Although sighted by John Richardson of Sir John Franklin's second expedition, it was first explored by Peter Dease and Thomas Simpson in 1839 and named after the queen of England. Subsequent explorations were carried out by John Rae, Sir Robert McClure, Godfred Hansen, Vilhjalmur Stefansson, and others. The island has an area of 81,930 square miles and is characterized by a flat lowland topography covered by glacial drift. Flat lying Ordovician and Silurian dolomite predominate, but a minor occurrence of quartzite and granite at Hadley Bay and a belt of Coppermine Series rocks between the bay and Minto Inlet are of Pre-Cambrian age. The island contains three small settlements, the largest being Cambridge Bay, and a permanent population of about 500, mostly Eskimo. A sparse wildlife is its only known economic resource.

JOHN L. JENNESS.

VICTORIA LAND (formerly SOUTH VICTORIA LAND), region, Antarctica, between Ross Sea and Wilkes Land extending northward from latitude 78° to 70°30′S. at about 164°E. The eastern part is claimed by New Zealand as part of its Ross Dependency, and the western part by Australia.

Victoria Land was discovered in 1841 by Sir James Clark Ross. The Belgian expedition of Adrien de Gerlache (1897–1899), the British expedition of Carsten Egeberg Borchgrevink (1898–1900), and German, Swedish, and other British expeditions added to knowledge of this region. Robert Falcon Scott's British expedition of 1901–1904 established a base at Hut Point on McMurdo Sound at the western end of Ross Sea, from which two parties climbed the glaciers emanating from the polar ice cap and reached the Polar Plateau. Scott's 1910–1913 expedition contributed much additional scientific information. Exploration accelerated tremendously during the International Geophysical Year, 1957–1958, when Hallett Station was established by New Zealand and the United States on Cape

Adare, Scott Base by New Zealand, and Williams Air Facility Base by the United States on McMurdo Sound. From these bases scientists have gathered biological, geological, glaciological, geophysical, and meteorological information and traversed the surface of Victoria Land.

The interior is an ice-covered plateau, 9,000 feet above sea level, with ice 10,000–13,000 feet thick. On the eastern coast bordering McMurdo Sound is the largest ice-free area in Antarctica, about 100 square miles, comprising a number of valleys. The highest point in the region is Mount Lister (13,350 feet) in the Royal Society Range.

TROY L. PÉWÉ,
Head, Geology Department, University of Alaska.

VICTORIA NYANZA, lake in central Africa. See VICTORIA, LAKE.

VICTORIA REGIA. See VICTORIA (plant).

VICTORIA UNIVERSITY OF MANCHESTER, in Manchester, England, an outgrowth of Owens College, which was founded in 1851 as the result of a bequest of £96,000 by John Owens, a Manchester merchant. The Manchester School of Medicine was united with Owens College in 1872, and the Victoria University was created by charter in 1880 as a federal institution with constituent colleges, which later included University College, Liverpool (1884), and Yorkshire College, Leeds (1887). A new charter, issued on July 15, 1903, reconstituted the university as the Victoria University of Manchester and freed it from its association with all other colleges except Owens. The (Manchester) Institute of Science and Technology became associated with the university in 1905.

The university is governed, under the 1903 charter, by a chancellor, a vice chancellor, a court of governors, and a council. Academic matters are regulated by a senate consisting of the professors of the nine faculties: art, economic and social studies, education, law, medicine, music, science, technology, and theology. Most of the buildings, erected in the 20th century, are in the city; athletic grounds are at Fallowfield (30 acres) and Wythenshawe (50 acres) three miles away; and a health center is at Darbishire House, three quarters of a mile away.

Enrollment exceeds 16,000, including students attending the associated Institute of Science and Technology and the affiliated Manchester Business School.

RICHARD WEBB,
Director, Reference and Library Division, British Information Services, New York City.

VICTORIAN ORDER, The Royal. See DECORATIONS, MEDALS, AND ORDERS—*Great Britain.*

VICTORIAN STYLE, vĭk-tōr′ĭ-ən, the art, architecture, and decorative arts of English-speaking countries from about 1830 to 1900, roughly corresponding to the reign of Queen Victoria. The many Victorian styles generally display a decline of taste evidenced by eclectic use of past styles, overornamentation, sentimentality, and industrialized techniques, in an effort to appeal to a mass market. The term does not usually refer to such Victorian developments as the Arts and Crafts movement, art nouveau, or iron and glass construction. See also ARCHITECTURE; DRESS; ENGLISH ART AND ARCHITECTURE; FURNITURE; GLASS AND GLASSWARE; JEWELRY; PRE-RAPHAELITES; UNITED STATES—*Art and Architecture.*

VICTORIATE, vĭk-tō′rĭ-āt, or **VICTORIATUS,** vĭk-tō′rĭ-ā-təs, silver coin of the Roman Republic, struck after 235 B.C. It usually bore on the obverse the head of Jupiter and on the reverse the image of Victoria crowning a trophy and the word "Roma" beneath. It was used mostly for foreign trade.

P. R. COLEMAN-NORTON.

VICTORIAVILLE, vĭk-tōr′ĭ-ə-vĭl, town, Quebec Province, Canada, in Arthabaska County on the Nicolet River about 65 miles southwest of Quebec City. It is served by the Canadian National Railways. Situated in farming and dairying country, it includes among its manufactures furniture, clothing, shoes, and metal products. Originally called Demersville, it was incorporated as a village in 1860, renamed in 1861, and incorporated as a town in 1890. Population: 21,838.

VICTORINUS, vĭk-tō-rī′nəs, **Gaius Marius,** Roman grammarian, rhetorician, philosopher, and theologian: fl. 4th century A.D. An African by birth, he taught rhetoric at Rome. After his conversion to Christianity, which influenced St. Augustine toward his conversion, Victorinus retired in 362 when Emperor Julian the Apostate debarred Christians from teaching. Victorinus translated many Greek philosophical works into Latin, wrote extensively on philology, commented on several of St. Paul's epistles, and composed treatises against various heresies.

P. R. COLEMAN-NORTON.

VICTORY, vĭk′tə-rē, a novel, by Joseph Conrad, written in 1914 and published in 1915. It is a partially impressionistic tale based on Conrad's observations during his years at sea and told mostly from the point of view of an anonymous narrator who learns the details achronologically, bit by bit, over a long period of time. Axel Heyst, a nihilist philosopher and detached observer of life, chooses to remain a hermit on Samburan, an island in the East Indies, after the Tropical Belt Coal Company, of which he is local manager, goes bankrupt. On one of his rare excursions to civilization at Surabaja, Heyst rescues a young Cockney girl, Lena, a violinist of the touring Zangiacomo Ladies' Orchestra, from the cruelties of the conductor's wife and the insistent attentions of Schomberg, the hotelkeeper. The latter, in jealous rage, directs a trio of criminals —Jones, a sinister intellectual; Martin Ricardo, his sly agent; and Pedro, their monstrous, faithful half-wit—to Samburan with a false account of Heyst's tremendous wealth. As Heyst's relations with Lena gradually arouse in him "a greater sense of his own reality than he had ever known," and as her gratitude turns into a deep and devoted love, the nightmarish trio arrives to spend three tense days. Heyst, unarmed, finds himself morally paralyzed and unable to act, but Lena, deliberately luring the amorous Ricardo at the cost of suggesting to Heyst that she is faithless, sacrifices her life for him. By various devices all the criminals are killed, but Heyst, remorseful that he had never learned to love and trust in life, commits suicide by setting fire to his bungalow.

JOHN HAGOPIAN.

LEONARD LEE RUE III/PHOTO RESEARCHERS

A wild vicuña. The fine, soft, lustrous wool of vicuñas is used for luxurious natural-color garments.

VICUÑA, vi-kōōn′yə, a wild ruminant (*Vicugna vicugna*), related to the guanaco, llama, and alpaca. It lives in the Andes of southern Peru, Bolivia, and northern Chile and Argentina. Vicuñas inhabit open grassy or arid areas at elevations of 12,000 to 16,000 feet (3660–4880 meters). They have small heads and long necks and stand 27 to 35 inches (70–90 cm) high at the shoulder. The coat is buffy-brown (vicuña color) above, mainly of wool about 2 inches (50 mm) long, a protection against quick changes in temperature and strong sunlight. The breast has a bib of long white hair. The incisor teeth of the lower jaw have open roots and enamel on one side only, unlike those of other ruminants. As an adaptation to the reduced oxygen content of air at high elevations, red blood cells occur in great numbers (14 million per cubic millimeter).

Vicuñas live in herds of 15 to 20 or more, and can gallop as fast as 30 miles (48 km) an hour. In favorable areas they average one animal to 10 acres (4 hectares). Family bands have territories, which they often defend. They eat grass and some herbaceous plants. They spend about half of their time resting on the ground in dry open sites. Young, usually one per female, are born from mid-January to mid-April.

For centuries vicuñas have been exploited for their fine wool, excellent meat, or both. Under the Inca Empire, when vicuñas may have numbered between 1 million and 1.5 million, the animals were rounded up, sheared for their wool, and released. Many were killed for both meat and wool. Following the destruction of the empire by the Spanish, hunting increased and the number of vicuñas declined. In the 1950's a few hundred thousand remained, but increased hunting and competition for forage from domestic livestock resulted in a drastic reduction to about 10,000 in 1967. As a result of conservation measures, the number rose to 80,000.

TRACY I. STORER
University of California, Davis

VIDA BREVE, vē′dä brā′vā, an opera in two acts by the Spanish composer Manuel de Falla, with a libretto by Carlos Fernández Shaw. *La Vida Breve* (*The Brief Life*) was first performed in Nice, France, on April 1, 1913, eight years after it won first prize in a Madrid competition. It was staged at the Metropolitan Opera in New York City in 1926.

La Vida Breve is set in Grenada. Salud (soprano), a gypsy girl, is unaware that her lover, Paco (tenor), is about to marry Carmela (contralto), a girl from a higher social class than a gypsy's. Salud's grandmother (contralto) and her uncle, Sarvaor (bass), have spared her the truth. But she attends the wedding of Paco and Carmela, curses him, and turns against her family. Confronting Paco, she sings a song they have shared. He blanches at her sorrow, and she falls dead at his feet. Much of the music of the opera originated in Spanish folk music.

HERBERT WEINSTOCK
Coauthor of "Men of Music"

VIDAL, vi-däl′, **Gore** (1925–), American writer. Eugene Luther Vidal was born on Oct. 3, 1925, in West Point, N.Y., where his father was an aeronautics instructor at the U.S. Military Academy. Young Vidal was strongly influenced by his maternal grandfather, former U.S. Sen. Thomas Pryor Gore, and as a teenager he changed his first name to Gore.

Vidal's first novel, *Williwaw* (1946), drawn from his wartime experiences, was well received. The homosexual theme of his third novel, *The City and the Pillar* (1948), shocked many readers and hurt Vidal's critical reputation. His next five novels proved unpopular, and he turned to writing television plays. The most successful of these, *Visit to a Small Planet* (1955) and *The Best Man* (1960), were adapted for theater and film. In 1968 he published another controversial novel, *Myra Breckinridge*, which dealt humorously with transsexuality and lampooned contemporary American culture. He also wrote historical fiction, including *Washington, D.C.* (1967), *Burr* (1973), *1876* (1976), and *Lincoln* (1984).

Though disenchanted with the United States (which he called "the land of the dull and the home of the literal") and its political system, Vidal unsuccessfully sought U.S. Congressional seats in 1960 and 1982. His trenchant political essays are collected in *Rocking the Boat* (1962), *Reflections upon a Sinking Ship* (1969), and *The Second American Revolution* (1982).

VIDAL, vē-dȧl′, **Peire,** Provençal troubadour of the late 12th and early 13th centuries. Exact details of his life are uncertain, and he has been the subject of several legends, probably based on names or incidents in his poetry. Vidal is said to have been born in Toulouse and to have begun singing his songs in Marseille. He also is believed to have visited Spain, Italy, and Hungary.

Vidal embodied all the romantic qualities associated with the medieval troubadours. He had grace, courtliness, and a lyrical talent that won him the patronage of influential nobles. He was favored by Richard the Lion-Hearted and may have accompanied the king on the Third Crusade in 1189–1192. Vidal's lyrics, composed in the *langue d'oc* dialect of southern France, are intense and personal, expressing the sentiments of love in the best tradition of troubadour song.

© MARIO RUIZ

The typical home video game for use with a television set may satisfy interests ranging from ball games to basic math.

VIDEO. See TELEVISION.

VIDEO GAME, any of a variety of electronic games produced for a home television or computer display screen or for commercial consoles in amusement arcades. Most games are intended for entertainment and some for educational purposes. They may be played by one person or in competition with others.

Video games in arcades: to some, they are a harmless diversion; to others, an addictive and costly waste of time.

UPI/BETTMANN

Equipment for a typical home video game consists basically of a microprocessor module connected to a television set. A cartridge inserted into the module provides the program for the game's action and its accompanying sound. A keyboard, keypad, rotary knob, or "joystick" controls the action. A home computer system may also be used for playing video games.

Computers of the 1950's and 1960's, with transistors, resistors, and other components wired in intricate circuits, could be programmed for board games such as tick-tack-toe and checkers, and those of the early 1970's for such ball-and-paddle games as Odyssey and Pong. The development of integrated circuitry, capable of handling more complex functions, made possible such sports as soccer, hockey, baseball, and basketball. Additional refinements in microelectronics resulted in the microprocessor chip, which could accommodate programs for such games as Space Invaders, Pac-Man, Star Wars, The Empire Strikes Back, Asteroids, Kaboom, Wizard's Quest, and Donkey Kong. In the early 1980's the laser disk brought a three-dimensional sense to the player's participation.

The growing field of video games created several giants of software, including Atari, Coleco, Intellivision, Activision, and Parker Brothers. The volume of business in the home and commercial markets has been estimated to exceed $7 billion annually.

Video games, which became a virtual craze by the 1980's, have occasioned serious debate concerning their effect on children. Advocates claim that the games teach youngsters to become computer literate while also helping them to improve their concentration and motor (eye-and-hand) coordination. Opponents maintain that the games are addictive, involve excessive violence, take away too much time from reading and beneficial physical activities, and, when played in arcades, are too costly.

FRED FERRETTI, "*New York Times*"

VIDEO RECORDING, a technique for storing television programs or other pictorial and visual information as well as music, text, and numbers and other data. The two chief methods are optical recording on disks and magnetic recording on tapes. The two major types of optical disks are videodisks for use in home players and the more expensive professional optical disks. Both record television-type signals in frequency-modulated form. Since magnetic tapes for video recording are usually packaged in cassettes, they are called video cassettes and the machines that use them are called videocassette recorders (VCR's).

Optical Disks and VCR's Compared. Videodisks can be mass-produced like phonograph records and are therefore less expensive than videocassettes for prerecorded programs such as movies and music. In addition, they offer superior sound fidelity. Since there are no home recording systems for videodisks, they cannot be used for recording television programs at home or making home movies.

Professional recorders, both optical disk and magnetic tape, provide nearly instantaneous playback of what is being recorded. This makes it possible for the operator to monitor the recording continuously to verify that recording is taking place and that its quality is satisfactory.

Both home and professional disks can offer

random access to stored material. The disk pickup head can be directed almost instantly to a particular track on the disk to find and display a particular item—a specific picture or a specific encyclopedia article, for example. VCR's must search sequentially through tape until they find the desired item.

One of the main advantages of magnetic tape over optical disks is that it can be recorded, erased, and rerecorded an indefinite number of times with relatively inexpensive equipment. In addition, a single tape can hold up to eight hours of programming, compared to one hour on a two-sided videodisk. Because of these features, VCR's are popular for making home movies with a television camera, and even more popular for automatically recording television programs in order to replay them later at more convenient times. Because there is no inexpensive method for making many copies of a master tape, preprogrammed cassettes cost more than videodisks.

OPTICAL RECORDING

Principles. In the most successful types of optical systems the key recording instrument is a laser whose output is controlled by an electronic signal from a television camera or other source. Information is recorded on tracks consisting of a series of tiny pits. (See Fig. 1.) The pits are far too small to be seen with the naked eye.

In videodisks the series of pits is continuous, with variations in both the lengths of the pits and the widths of the ridges between them. These variations encode a frequency-modulated (FM) radio signal combining both video and audio TV signals.

A standard videodisk is 12 inches (30 cm) in diameter and carries recorded programs or pictures on a band about 4 inches (10 cm) wide.

Fig. 1. A videodisk with a greatly magnified section of two tracks. Program material is encoded by the lengths and spacing of the tiny pits.

PHOTO—COURTESY 3M

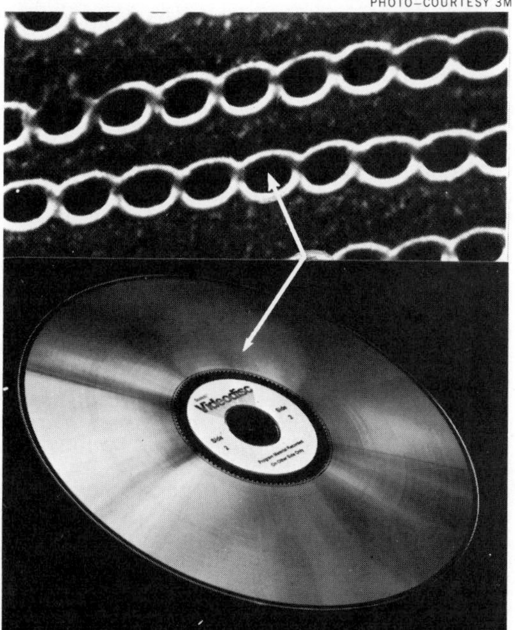

The information is recorded by a single spiral track consisting of 54,000 turns, with each turn carrying a single frame of a TV picture. On professional disks the tracks are concentric circles. Videodisks revolve 30 times per second (100,000 times per hour), providing a half hour of recording on each side. Professional disks generally revolve 60 times per second.

Videodisks—*Recording*. Production methods for videodisks are similar to those for audio disks. (See SOUND RECORDING AND REPRODUCTION.) A metal or glass disk is coated with a light-sensitive emulsion and exposed by a laser whose output is controlled by the signal being recorded. This process is called laser cutting. The unexposed area of the coating is dissolved away, and the disk is put in an etching solution that leaves "pimples" at spots protected by the exposed emulsion. The result is a master disk (a negative). The master disk is then electroplated. When the plating is separated from the master, it becomes the mother disk (positive), with pits where the master has pimples. The plating process is repeated to make one or more stamper disks (negatives).

The stamper disk is used to stamp out thousands of plastic disks (positives) for sale to consumers. Each pit in a plastic disk exactly matches the corresponding pimple in the master disk. The final steps are to vapor-deposit a very thin metal film that gives the disk a mirror finish and to apply a protective coating of transparent plastic. In some systems two disks are joined back to back to make double-sided disks.

***Playback*.** The finished disk is played back by focusing a laser beam on the track of pits as the disk rotates on a turntable. The variation in reflectance between pits and ridges creates an FM reflected beam that is a faithful copy of the original FM laser signal used to record the master disk. Dust particles, which would distort the signal, are kept out of focus by the disk's plastic coating. (See Fig. 2.) The reflected laser signal is then converted into electronic form for display on a television screen.

A phonograph record has at most 1,000 tracks with a track-to-track spacing of 2.8 mils (70 micrometers), while a videodisk has 54,000 tracks with a spacing of only 70 microinches (1.7 micrometers). Such extremely close spacing means that the recording and playback tracking systems must be highly accurate. The most successful system uses a three-spot tracking system on a grooveless disk. This system uses three spots of laser light—one for playback and two for the tracking system. See Fig. 3.

An equally precise electromechanical system focuses the laser on the recorded track. The focusing lens is mounted on a moving coil suspended above the disk. Its elevation above the disk depends on the coil current, which is controlled by the electrical capacitance between the lens mount and the metallized recording layer. This system can aim the focal point with a margin of error less than 40 microinches (1 micrometer).

Professional Disks—*Recording*. Unlike home videodisk systems, professional videodisk systems can record as well as play back. These disks are coated with a thin layer of sensitive material—usually tellurium—about 4 microinches (100 nanometers) thick. This layer is protected by a layer of transparent plastic. When the relatively high-power recording laser focuses

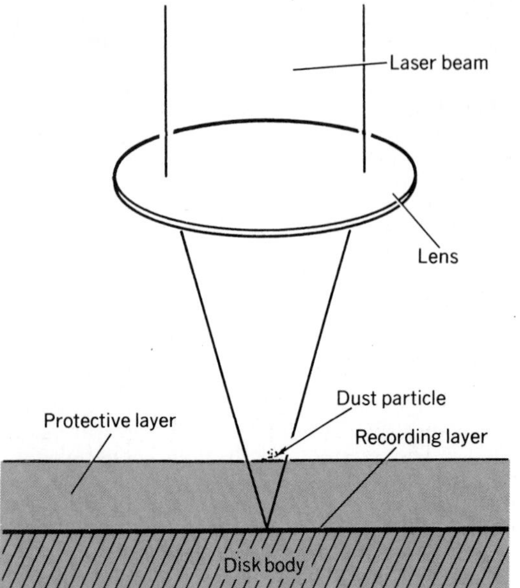

Fig. 2. Cross section of the upper layers of a videodisk. The transparent protective layer keeps dust particles away from the focal point of the playback beam.

on the tellurium, the heated spot melts and surface tension pulls it back. In this way, each burst of the laser forms a pit about 50 millionths of an inch (1.2 micrometers) in diameter.

Playback. Professional disk systems contain both recording and playback lasers. The playback systems are similar to those used for videodisks. However, the playback laser is focused on a spot only a few thousandths of an inch (about 0.1 mm) behind the recording spot, thus providing a check on what has just been recorded—a valuable tool in many professional applications. Such systems are called DRAW (Direct Read After Write) systems. DRAW systems are not suitable for home use because the recordable disks are too costly and there is no low-cost method of mass replication.

VIDEOCASSETTE RECORDERS (VCR's)

Two types of VCR are in widespread use: VHS and Betamax. Both use a helical recording format on 0.5-inch (13-mm) magnetic tape. (See TAPE RECORDING.) Two rotating heads record (or read) the helical video tracks. One stationary head records the audio track near one edge of the tape, and another head records a control track near the other edge. The control track carries a synchronizing signal that keeps the rotating heads on track during playback.

Although differences between the VHS and Betamax systems are minor, it is impossible to record a tape on one system and play it back on the other. A third system, designed to provide a single standard in any one country, was introduced in 1984. It uses 8-mm (0.3-inch) tape. However, differences in television systems continued to prevent compatibility between VCR's intended for use in different regions. For example, U.S. television stations transmit 30 pictures (frames) per second, while European stations transmit 25 per second.

Clock-driven switching circuits enable some VCR's to record automatically up to eight different television programs over a period of more than two weeks. Other common features include slow motion, freeze-frame, and remote operation.

Fig. 3. The videodisk playback tracking system uses three spots of light. The central spot reads the track. Any tendency to drift off center is corrected by signals generated by the outer spots.

HISTORY

The first successful video recorder was marketed by the Ampex Corporation in 1956. This recorder, which used reels of 2-inch (50-mm) tape, could only record monochrome pictures. Color video recorders were introduced by Ampex and RCA in 1959.

In 1969 the Sony Corporation of Japan introduced a system based on the U-matic format, using a 3/4-inch (20-mm) tape in a cassette. This cassette recorder was much smaller, cheaper, and more convenient than the earlier reel-to-reel recorders. Although it was originally intended for home use, the cost limited it mainly to such commercial uses as making training tapes. In 1975, following the introduction of the Betamax format by Sony and the VHS format by the Matsushita Corporation (also Japanese), prices of VCR's fell below $1,000, and the home market began a rapid expansion.

Optical recording on videodisks, using a mechanical stylus, was first demonstrated by the Telefunken Corporation in 1966, and an RCA system based on electrostatic capacitance was shown in 1969. However, the first commercially successful system was the VLP system, which was developed by the Philips Corporation of the Netherlands.

MICHAEL O. FELIX, *Ampex Corporation*

Further Reading: Cheshire, David, *The Video Manual* (Van Nostrand Reinhold 1982); Duton, Mark, and Owen, David, *The Complete Home Video Handbook* (Random House 1982); Isailovic, Jordan, *Videodisk and Optical Memory Technologies* (Prentice-Hall 1985); Sigel, Efrem, and others, *Video Disks: The Technology, the Applications and the Future* (Van Nostrand Reinhold 1981).

VIDOR, vē'dôr, **King** (1894–1982), American film director. In his 40-year career, he made more than 50 films, many of which were remarkable for their ground-breaking themes and technical innovations. King Wallis Vidor was born in Galveston, Tex., on Feb. 8, 1894. He developed a love for cinema as a boy, when he worked as a ticket taker and projectionist at the town's nickelodeon. He went to Hollywood in 1915 and began to write and direct silent films.

His first notable picture was *The Big Parade* (1925), a realistic, antiwar drama set during World War I. *The Crowd* (1928) masterfully depicts the impersonality of life in a big city. The film is memorable for its skillful camera techniques and location shooting in New York City. *Hallelujah* (1929), with an all-black cast, was Vidor's first sound picture. His other films include *The Champ* (1931), *Our Daily Bread* (1934), *The Citadel* (1938), *Northwest Passage* (1940), *Duel in the Sun* (1947), *The Fountainhead* (1949), and

The linear forms and shifting perspective of *Composition (Le Rêve)* are characteristic techniques of Maria Vieira da Silva.

COURTESY OF THE ARTIST

War and Peace (1956). Nominated five times for an Academy Award, Vidor received a special Oscar in 1979 for career achievement. His autobiography, *A Tree Is a Tree*, appeared in 1953. After retiring from filmmaking in 1959, Vidor taught film directing at the University of Southern California and other colleges. He died in Paso Robles, Calif., on Nov. 1, 1982.

VIE PARISIENNE, vē pȧ-rē-zyen′, an operetta in four acts by the French composer Jacques Offenbach, with a libretto by Henri Meilhac and Ludovic Halévy. *La Vie parisienne* (*Parisian Life*) was first performed at the Opéra Comique in Paris on Oct. 31, 1866.

La Vie parisienne, the first of Offenbach's internationally successful operettas to portray contemporary life, became synonymous with the dazzling, frivolous society of Second Empire Paris. The expertly designed libretto by the collaborators who later wrote the libretto for Bizet's *Carmen* furnished Offenbach with exactly the satiric, amorous, dance-inspiring material that he required for his best composition. Music from *La Vie parisienne*, like other Offenbach music, has been adapted for ballet.

HERBERT WEINSTOCK
Coauthor of "Men of Music"

VIEIRA, vyā′ē-rə, **Antonio** (1608–1697), Portuguese Jesuit missionary and diplomat. He was born in Lisbon on Feb. 6, 1608. At an early age he was taken by his parents to Bahia (now Salavador), Brazil, where he entered the Society of Jesus in 1623. Returning to Portugal in 1641, he became a friend of King John IV, who appointed him court preacher in 1644. Later he went on diplomatic missions for the king to Paris, The Hague, London, and Rome. He also performed other governmental services.

In 1652, Vieira returned to Brazil as a missionary to the Indians of the Maranhão region. However, by defending the Indians' rights, he incurred the wrath of the slave-owning aristocracy, who forced him to return to Portugal in 1661. Soon after, he lost his standing at court, and, as a result, his enemies succeeded in having him tried by the Inquisition. He was imprisoned in 1665.

Released two years later, Vieira lived in Rome from 1669 to 1675. There he labored for relief of the persecuted Portuguese Jews, a cause that he had long espoused. His efforts were only partly successful, but his oratorical brilliance impressed Pope Clement X and other church dignataries. In 1681 he returned to Bahia, becoming provincial of his order in 1688. He died there on July 18, 1697.

Vieira gained renown as a statesman, orator, writer, diplomat, and administrator. He was one of the great preachers of his era, and his pulpit was a powerful force for shaping public opinion on both sides of the Atlantic. His sermons, correspondence, and state papers provide a valuable repository regarding Portuguese-Brazilian relations in the 17th century. In his writing, Vieira's originality, lucidity, and emotional force place him among the great masters of Portuguese prose.

VIEIRA DA SILVA, vyā′ē-rə dä sil′və, **Maria Elena** (1908–), Portuguese-French abstract painter, whose works reflect the sense of dislocation experienced in the modern city. Vieira da Silva was born in Lisbon on June 13, 1908. She went to Paris in 1928 and studied sculpture with Charles Despiau and Antoine Bourdelle, followers of Auguste Rodin, whose work incorporated abstraction. She also studied printmaking at the Hayter atelier.

In painting, her teachers were the Fauve Expressionist Orthon Friesz and Fernand Léger. Léger's association with cubism and his celebration of technology are reflected in Vieira da Silva's works, which exemplify a controlled style of abstraction. A characteristic painting by her, such as *Composition (La Rêve)*, is made up of linear patterns, which convey a shifting between linear-perspective and nonperspective space. Reminiscent of synthetic cubism, the scene moves from an eye to an aerial view. Her colors are primarily earth tones with high-chroma accents.

Vieira da Silva became a French citizen in 1956. Her work is well represented in the Collection of the Museum of Modern Art in Paris.

WILLIAM ZIMMER
Art Critic, "New York Times"

© MICHEL HETIER

Vienna's Burgtheater faces the Ringstrasse. The Gothic spire of St. Stephen's Cathedral rises in the distance.

VIENNA, vē-en′ə, the federal capital and one of the nine provinces of Austria. Its name in German is Wien (vēn).

During the several centuries it served as the capital of the multinational Habsburg Empire and the economic hub of central eastern Europe it developed a sophisticated and rich culture. Home to a multitude of the world's greatest musicians in the past—Mozart, Beethoven, Schubert, Johann Strauss, Jr., and Brahms to name only a few—Vienna was for at least a century the capital of the Western world of music. It continues to thrive as a city of music, although its musical preeminence has passed to other cities. The city's architecture reflects some of the finest achievements of the ages that stretch from the Gothic through the Baroque to the modern period. Vienna's art museums are world renowned. Diplomatic congresses still gather in Vienna, and the city's gleaming Donaupark Center, completed in 1979, houses two major United Nations agencies: the International Atomic Energy Agency (IAEA) and the United Nations Industrial Development Organization (UNIDO).

Vienna emerged from the destruction of World War II a modern industrial and communications center. And in the years that followed, the *joie de vivre* of earlier decades returned to a considerable extent: the music, theater, coffeehouses, rich cuisine, and cosmopolitan outlook of Austria's imperial period are again in evidence.

Plan of the City. Vienna is located in the northeast corner of Austria, about 40 miles (65 km) from both Czechoslovakia and Hungary, which lie to the east. Its 160 square miles (415 sq km) are completely surrounded by the province of Lower Austria.

The city is a hub of major rail and auto routes. The Westbahn, which passes through Vienna, connects Istanbul in Turkey with Calais in France, following the route of the old Orient Express; and the Sudbahn carries traffic from Vienna to Trieste and Yugoslavia. The international airport in Schwechat is 12 miles (19 km) to the east of the city center, just beyond the city limits.

Of Vienna's 23 districts, 21 are located on the right bank of the Danube River. These extend westward to the hills of the Vienna Woods (Wienerwald). The first district forms the heart of the Old or Inner City (Innere Stadt). What used to be the main channel of the Danube skirts the first district on the northeast. Confined between earthworks, it is now called the Danube Canal (Donaukanal). The Danube itself flows in a broad and straight bed to the northeast of the canal on its course from the northwest to the southeast of the city. A still more northeasterly branch is separated from the main channel and has become a lake fed by springs and groundwater. This "Old Danube" ("Alte Donau") lies in a park that is popular for swimming and sailing.

In the west of the city the Vienna River divides the hills of the Vienna Woods to the north from those of the Lainzer Tiergarten to the south before joining the Danube Canal near the city center. The Kahlenberg, which rises to 1,585 feet (483 meters) in the Vienna Woods, is the last mild outcropping of the Austrian Alps, which reach their greatest heights far to the southwest.

The Vienna Woods offer paths for strolling and restaurants for relaxation. The Lainzer Tiergarten includes an enclosed park for exotic breeds of cattle, sheep, and deer.

The Ring Boulevard (Ringstrasse) has been a prominent feature of the city since 1857, when Emperor Francis Joseph ordered the old fortifications to be replaced by boulevards and buildings befitting the growing imperial city. In the shape of a horseshoe enclosing the Inner City and ending at the Danube Canal, it consists of several lanes of roadway, walkways, and four rows of trees, many of them flowering white chestnuts.

The subway, or U-bahn, has expanded along old City Express lines that originally connected the main railroad terminals. A newer High Speed Metropolitan Railway (Schnellbahn) speeds passengers from the south of the city and from across the Danube on the north.

The Viennese love to walk, whether in the crowded streets, the semiwildness of the Vienna Woods, or in the parks that dot the city. The Prater—the meadow and woodlands along the Danube once reserved for nobles—contains an amusement park with a famous giant Ferris wheel (the Riesenrad), a narrow-gauge railway leading to the Trade Fair Grounds, a planetarium, and major sports facilities.

Places of Interest. In the center of the Inner City stands the huge St. Stephen's Cathedral. The lofty south tower, completed in 1433, is one of the most beautiful of all Gothic spires.

The queen of shopping streets, the Kärntner Strasse, runs south from Stephansplatz in front of the cathedral to join the Ring at the Baroque State Opera House; en route, it passes the Hotel Sacher, famous for its Sachertorte, a typically Viennese confection of chocolate cake, marmalade, and chocolate icing.

Proceeding along the Ring in a clockwise manner, a pedestrian soon arrives at the Hofburg Gate and the magnificent Heldenplatz, built in the 1820's and now the site of Austria's monument to the unknown soldier.

Behind the Heldenplatz and enclosing it on two sides is the Hofburg. This imperial palace experienced continuous expansion from the 13th century to the close of the 19th. The complex of buildings that make up the Hofburg include magnificent state apartments where the Austrian president holds official receptions; the federal chancellery; the hall of the Spanish Riding School, where the world-famous white Lipizzaner stallions perform; the National Library, designed by Joseph Fischer von Erlach and constructed by his son Johann in the early 1700's; the Albertina, with a renowned collection of graphic arts; and the castle chapel where the Vienna Choirboys sing. The New Palace (Neue Hofburg), constructed in 1881–1913, houses the Ephesus Museum, with antiquities from Asia Minor, the Ethnological Museum, a huge museum of armor, and a museum for musical instruments.

Directly across the Ring from the Heldenplatz are two museums: one for natural history and one for fine arts. The latter, the Art History Museum, has important Egyptian-Oriental holdings and many works by Dürer, Titian, Bruegel, and Rubens.

The impressive mixture of parks, statues, and great buildings that line the Ring continues to the north with the Palace of Justice (seat of the

© MICHEL HETIER

Schönbrunn, the summer palace of the Habsburgs, is viewed at the end of a line of formally clipped hedges.

The Karlskirche, like Schönbrunn, is an excellent example of the Baroque architecture for which Vienna is famous.

© MICHEL HETIER

© LEO DEWYS INC.

Waltzing debutantes, wearing crowns, dance through the night at the Opera Ball, climax of the social season.

Supreme Court) and the Parliament, both completed in the 1880's in Greek Revival style. The Rathaus (City Hall), built in the same years, is an example of Neo-Gothic style. The mayor, who is also the governor of the province of Vienna, presides there. Across from the Rathaus is the Burgtheater (Imperial Theater), whose acting companies have held a leading place in German-language drama for two centuries. Farther to the north is the university, which was founded in 1364 and is the oldest university in German-speaking Europe.

South of the State Opera House, where the tour of the Ring began, is Vienna's most striking example of Baroque architecture—the Karlskirche, or Church of St. Charles Borromeo, which was built by the Fischer von Erlachs in the early 18th century. Its dome, like the spire of St. Stephen's, is a prominent feature of the skyline. Farther to the south is the Belvedere Palace of Prince Eugene of Savoy (1663–1736). Its secular Baroque culminates in the red marble halls of the Upper Belvedere.

White Lipizzaner stallions move through their complex paces to music in the hall of the Spanish Riding School.

© ANDY BERNHAUT/PHOTO RESEARCHERS

The culmination of Rococo style is found in the splendors of Schönbrunn Palace. Designed by the younger Fischer von Erlach and virtually completed by 1713, this summer residence of the imperial family is situated among the hills and what were then woods and meadows to the southwest of the city. About 45 of the 1,441 rooms are open to the public. Although the private rooms of Francis Joseph are spartan, others are lavish, such as the Room of Millions, a great Rococo display filled with Oriental miniatures. A splendid panorama of the city and the river can be enjoyed from the terraces and gardens of Schönbrunn and of the Belvedere.

Impressive as are the grand palaces and the museums, which range from museums of street cars to the home of Sigmund Freud, visitors are often most captivated by the calm pleasantness, or *gemütlichkeit,* of Viennese life. This may be experienced in the coffeehouses, where one may visit or read newspapers for hours over a single cup of coffee. Or it may be found at a Heurigen—a private vintner's tavern where the grower features "this year's wine." While tourists flock to the outlying district of Grinzing to sample the local wine, the Viennese are more likely to congregate for the same purpose in Sievering or Nussdorf.

Twice a year the Viennese indulge in special celebrations. Fasching, the carnival season between New Year's Eve and Lent, is a time of balls and parties, sponsored by numerous organizations and professions. And from late May through June the annual Vienna Festival provides a variety of theatrical and musical entertainment.

Population and Economy. As industrialization came to Austria in the last half of the 19th century, Vienna's population rose from 431,000 in 1851 to 2 million in 1905. Although the walls that choked urban expansion were torn down, the Inner City remained crowded. A World War I law banning rent increases or evictions while men were in military uniform perpetuated that condition. The law remains, with rents frozen for families where a member had once served in the armed forces, and apartments and business places are therefore kept in the family for generations. After the war large public-housing projects were undertaken in the suburbs to relieve the housing shortage.

The breakup of the Habsburg Empire and the arrival of hard times resulted in the departure of many Hungarians and Czechs. The depredations of the Nazis after the absorption of Austria by Germany in 1938 reduced the Jewish population—once a tenth of the city—to fewer than 10,000. The former ghetto was drastically depopulated.

Bombs destroyed 17% of all housing during World War II. Despite vigorous postwar reconstruction, modern units remain in high demand. Laws protect the city's Green Belt, and expansion therefore has had to take place in the eastern areas across the Danube.

Development of a major oil refinery in Schwechat, just to the east of Vienna, has helped to strengthen the city's economy. The refinery handles the crude oil produced north of Vienna as well as oil brought in by the Trieste-Vienna pipeline. Much of the Austrian petrochemical industry is situated at Vienna-Schwechat.

Vienna produces over half of the electrical products manufactured in Austria. Almost as important are the paper and woodworking industries, the metallurgical industries, and the clothing industry. The city is famous for its luxury goods, including petit point embroidery, fine leather products, and crystal.

The left bank region produces food for local consumption and wheat for export. Wine grapes are raised on the northwestern hills in a small, legally protected area of 1,917 acres (776 hectares).

A major economic contribution is made by the organizations located in the International (Donaupark) Center, which has extraterritorial status. Not only are the International Atomic Energy Agency and the UN Industrial Development Organization located there, but also the UN Relief and Works Agency for Palestine Refugees, the International Narcotics Control Board, and the center for Social Development and Humanitarian Affairs.

History. Where Vienna is now located, the Romans established a military encampment on the site of a Celtic settlement. The town that grew up about it, Vindobona, served as a garrison for the Romans until the decline of the Roman Empire. It was finally abandoned by the Romans in the early 5th century.

The first mention of the name "Wenia" is found in documents from the 880's. In the 10th century the German king Otto I seized the region from the Magyars, and it soon became the Holy Roman Empire's eastern province (Österreich). The Babenbergs of eastern Franconia were awarded the Austrian march (mark) in 976, and in 1156 the margravate of Austria was raised to a dukedom. The Babenberg dukes moved their court to Vienna in the 12th century.

The city grew as a trading center and staging area for crusades. The last Babenberg duke was killed in battle with the Hungarians in 1246. Ottokar II of Bohemia briefly held power there in the 13th century until he was ousted by Rudolf I of Habsburg, king of Germany. Thereafter until 1918, Vienna and the surrounding provinces served as the Habsburg heartland.

© ERIC CARLE/SHOSTAL

The sampling of the new wine at a wine tavern in the suburbs is a favorite pastime of the Viennese.

Minor insurrections by independently minded citizens of Vienna led the Habsburg Archduke Ferdinand I to abolish in 1526 the city's rights to self-government. Three years later the Turks surged westward from the Balkans to besiege the city, but Vienna refused to capitulate.

Threatened by a Swedish army in 1645 during the Thirty Years' War and devastated by the plague in 1679, Vienna was again besieged by the Turks in 1683. With the military assistance of John Sobieski, king of Poland, Vienna survived the Turkish threat. The Turks were driven back and were subsequently ousted from Hungary by the Treaty of Karlowitz (1699), after the great Habsburg field marshal Prince Eugene of Savoy had defeated the Turks at Zenta in 1697. Freed from external threats for the first time in over 100 years, Vienna celebrated by indulging in a Baroque building spree.

Under its 18th century Habsburg rulers Maria Theresa and her son Joseph II, Vienna prospered. Although it was twice occupied by Napoleon, once in 1805 and again in 1809, it triumphed over this humiliation by serving as host city for the congress that met in 1814–1815 to reconstruct Europe after Napoleon's final defeat.

The division of the empire into a dual Austro-Hungarian monarchy in 1867 did not adversely affect the city. During the second half of the 19th century the Ring was constructed and the city's suburbs were expanded to include outlying villages. But Vienna's prosperity did not reduce the increasing gap between rich and poor. Dismayed by the situation, Dr. Karl Lueger helped to found the Christian Social Party. On becoming Vienna's mayor (burgomaster) in 1897, Lueger undertook to improve living conditions in the city. Municipal housing and gas and electric works were built; hospitals, asylums, and city cemeteries were created; city bank and insurance companies were formed; tramways were constructed; and the Green Belt was begun.

© HARRY REDL/BLACK STAR

The Donaupark Center on the north bank of the Danube was opened in 1979. It houses various UN agencies.

As the twilight of imperial Austria set in, Vienna enjoyed a remarkable artistic and intellectual resurgence. Among Vienna's composers of the second half of the 19th century and the first half of the 20th were Anton Bruckner and Gustav Mahler, Franz Schmidt, Richard Strauss, and Hugo Wolf, Arnold Schoenberg, Alban Berg, and Anton Webern. The list of Vienna's world-famous painters during this golden age includes Gustav Klimt, Egon Schiele, and Oscar Kokoschka. Among Vienna's designers and architects of the day were Josef Hoffmann, Kolo Moser, Otto Wagner, and Adolf Loos. The Wiener Werkstätte, founded by the Vienna Secessionists, was rich in innovative design. Arthur Schnitzler and Hugo von Hofmannsthal are only two of a substantial group of outstanding writers of the period. Vienna's great medical tradition was carried on by Sigmund Freud. An Austrian school of economics arose in Vienna, and in the field of philosophy a group of scholars known as the Vienna Circle formulated the doctrine of logical positivism (later called logical empiricism).

The Vienna Woods, immortalized in the music of Johann Strauss, Jr., provide the setting for country outings.

© ANDY BERNHAUT/PHOTO RESEARCHERS

This remarkable flowering occurred just as the society from which it sprang was about to suffer a cataclysmic change. Losses in World War I and the breakup of the empire into several successor states spelled near disaster for Vienna. Deprived of traditional sources of food and raw materials, the city was in the position of being an industrial and financial center with no ready market for its goods or funds. The collapse of the Vienna Creditanstalt bank in 1931 further worsened the republic's economic situation.

An expansion of the franchise in 1919 brought about the election of Social Democrats to key positions in city government. The more conservative Christian Socialists, however, held the rest of the country. Conflicts between the two groups resulted in the bombardment of Vienna's pride—the new housing projects—in 1934 and the crippling of the Social Democrats, who might otherwise have later helped to oppose Hitler and prevent Germany's annexation of Austria in the Anschluss of 1938.

In the last days of World War II the city suffered severe damage before being occupied by the Soviet army in April 1945. For 10 years after the end of the war the city was divided into four occupation sectors (American, British, French, Soviet), with the Inner City changing hands each month. But even during Vienna's occupation by the four powers, its administration, unlike Berlin's, was unified. In May 1955 the Austrian State Treaty provided for the withdrawal of all foreign troops. Austria proclaimed military nonalignment, and in time Vienna once again became a center for international diplomacy.

JONATHAN E. HELMREICH
Allegheny College

Further Reading: Crankshaw, Edward, *Vienna* (Macmillan 1976); Johnston, William M., *Vienna, Vienna: The Golden Age, 1815–1914* (Crown 1981); Lehne, Inge, and Johnson, Lonnie, *Vienna—The Past in the Present* (Heinman 1985); Schorske, Carl E., *Fin-De-Siècle Vienna: Politics and Culture* (Knopf 1980).

GIRAUDON/ART RESOURCE

The Congress of Vienna's plenipotentiaries are shown in a wash drawing by Jean Baptiste Isabey.

VIENNA, Congress of, an assembly of powers that met at Vienna in 1814–1815 to reorganize Europe after Napoleon's downfall.

Representatives of the four major allies—Austria, Prussia, Russia, and Britain—as well as those of smaller allied countries—Spain, Portugal, and Sweden—began to arrive in Vienna in September–October 1814. It was the most brilliant gathering of diplomats and great personalities that Europe had ever seen. Three of Europe's most important rulers, Emperor Francis I of Austria, Emperor Alexander I of Russia, and King Frederick William III of Prussia, were active in the complex diplomatic negotiations. Britain was represented by its foreign minister, Castlereagh, and for a short period by Wellington. Austria was represented by Metternich, its foreign minister; Prussia by Hardenberg, its leading minister; Russia by the diplomat Nesselrode; and the France of Louis XVIII by Talleyrand.

The four major allies, bound together in an alliance by the Treaty of Chaumont (concluded in March 1814), actually did not expect the small countries to have a say in the reorganization of the continent; they were there merely to ratify their decisions. However, Talleyrand, taking advantage of the discontent of the small nations, moved to have at least some of the problems discussed by larger numbers of participants. A committee of eight was constituted, which included the four major allies, France, and the other signatories of the First Treaty of Paris of May 30, 1814—Portugal, Sweden, and a later signatory, Spain.

In the meantime, major frictions had developed within the Chaumont alliance. The Russian emperor had originally promised to divide the Grand Duchy of Warsaw, a creation of Napoleon's, between Russia, Austria, and Prussia. He now claimed all of Poland for Russia. He proposed that Austria should receive large slices of Italy, while Prussia should annex all of Saxony. Russia's enigmatic ruler not only hoped to expand his country to the shores of the Oder River, but he also wanted to unite all Poles under his scepter and to grant them self-government and a liberal constitution.

As the other powers were fearful of Russia's territorial ambitions, France, Austria, and Britain concluded a secret defense alliance on Jan. 3, 1815. By its terms the signatories promised to resist Russia's demands, if necessary by force. France probably profited most from this quarrel between the allies. Talleyrand wrote to his master in Paris: "The coalition is dissolved, France is no longer isolated in Europe."

Eventually a compromise was arranged: Prussia received two fifths of Saxony and other territorial compensation in Westphalia and the Rhineland, while Poland was again divided among Russia, Austria, and Prussia. Russia got most of the Grand Duchy of Warsaw as a separate kingdom under Russian sovereignty.

The sudden return to France of Napoleon in March 1815 and his victorious march to Paris contributed greatly to the restoration of unity among the allies. Napoleon was defeated at Waterloo in June 1815, and in the same month (on June 9) the final instrument of the Vienna Congress was signed by the powers with the exception of Spain, which was dissatisfied with the peace settlement for Italy.

The decisions of the Congress of Vienna brought about a complete reorganization of the European continent that in its essential features lasted for nearly a century. By acquiring Poland, Russia penetrated deeper into the European continent. Prussia was restored as a major power and received large slices of German territory. It was Castlereagh who insisted that Prussia be given the territories in western Germany so that it could guard the Rhine against future French aggression. Austria became the master of northern Italy by acquiring Lombardy and Venetia, while Tuscany and Modena were transferred to collateral branches of the Austrian imperial house. Parma was given to Marie Louise, Napoleon's former wife, who retained her title of empress; however, their son, the king of Rome, was excluded from the succession. The king of Sardinia regained his lands of Sardinia, Savoy, Piedmont, and Nice and added Genoa, thereby becoming once again one of the most important rulers in Italy.

The United Provinces and Belgium were joined as the United Netherlands under the rule of William I. Denmark gave up Norway to Sweden but received the German duchy of Lauenburg in exchange. Sweden was obliged to relinquish Swedish Pomerania to Prussia. The pope got back his territories in Italy, but his claims to Avignon were rejected. The German Confederation was established, with a federal diet that was to meet in Frankfurt am Main. The confederation's constitution, which provided for only loose ties between the German states, was a defeat for the friends of German unity, especially for Baron Stein who, in the service of Russia, had won over Emperor Alexander to his idea of the unification of the German states. Metternich, however, opposed this project, which would have strengthened Prussia's position in Germany. Switzerland also received a new confederate constitution.

The final treaty that emerged from the congress was the most important diplomatic document of the 19th century. Its main provisions remained unaltered for a period of 40 years. The peace settlement achieved at Vienna preserved Europe from any general conflagration for almost a century. Until the outbreak of World War I, the concert of the Great Powers continued to exist and the balance of power on the continent of Europe was a force for peace.

The treaty, however, contained some major flaws. It tried to settle 19th century problems with the methods of 18th century diplomacy. The rising nationalist movements in Europe were all but ignored by the European statesmen. Territories were shifted without consideration for the wishes of their populations. These shortcomings eventually brought about the collapse of the work of Vienna.

Further Reading: Alsop, Susan M., *The Congress Dances* (Washington Sq. Press 1985); Kissinger, Henry, *A World Restored: Metternich, Castlereagh and the Problems of Peace, 1812–1822* (Houghton 1957); Nicolson, Harold, *The Congress of Vienna* (1946; Harcourt 1970); Pallain, Georges M., *The Correspondence of Prince Tallyrand and King Louis XVIII during the Congress of Vienna* (1881; reprint, Da Capo 1973).

VIENNA, vē-en′ə, **University of,** a coeducational institution in Vienna, Austria, and one of Europe's most venerable academic centers, noted especially for its medical school. It was founded as an autonomous body in 1365 under a charter granted by Duke Rudolf IV and a papal bull issued by Pope Urban V. The original faculties were of law, medicine, and the arts; a faculty of divinity was established in 1384 by Pope Urban VI.

After becoming a state institution in 1554, the university was reformed completely in 1749–1760 under Empress Maria Theresa, who modernized the faculty of medicine, enabling it later to become one of the most advanced schools of its kind in the world. During the 19th century, under the aegis of Emperor Francis Joseph I, the modern organization of the university was effected, with emphasis on academic freedom and scientific research.

At present the university is a self-administrative governmental institute. It has faculties of humanities, law and political science, medicine, natural sciences, philosophy, social sciences and economics, Catholic theology, and Protestant theology. The library, restored in 1777, contains some 2 million volumes. The university archives, founded in 1708, preserve records back to the 14th century. The annual enrollment exceeds 40,000 students.

VIENNA BOYS CHOIR, vē-en′ə, a group of boy choristers, aged from about 10 to 14, who are trained and sing in Vienna, Austria, and enjoy a worldwide reputation through international tours. The choir, or Wiener Sängerknaben (also rendered in English as the Vienna Choir Boys), was established by Maximilian I in 1498 to perform in the chapel of the Hofburg, where they continue to sing on Sunday mornings.

The choir comprises four units of 22 voices each, which permits performance rotation and allows for home visits. The boys reside in the elegant Augarten Palace, but they must pay for their board and schooling out of performing and recording fees.

VIENNA CIRCLE, vē-en′ə, a group of scientists, mathematicians, and philosophers who initiated the movement of logical positivism (later called logical empiricism). Moritz Schlick, professor of philosophy at the University of Vienna, together with a number of colleagues and advanced students, formed a discussion group in 1924, which came to be known as *Der Wiener Kreis*, or the Vienna Circle. Prominent among the members were Rudolf Carnap, Otto Neurath, Hans Hahn, Felix Kaufmann, Victor Kraft, Kurt Gödel, Friedrich Waismann, Kurt Reidemeister, and Herbert Feigl. Among the more important visitors and collaborators were Philipp Frank, Richard von Mises, Hans Reichenbach, C. G. Hempel, Alfred J. Ayer, Eino Kaila, Ernest Nagel, Charles Morris, and Alfred Tarski.

A common interest in the logical foundations of mathematics and the clarifications of the concepts and assumptions of the empirical sciences led the group to formulate a viewpoint that was published in the form of a manifesto entitled *Wissenschaftliche Weltauffassung* (Scientific World View) in 1929. By that time the ideas of Ludwig Wittgenstein had made their full impression on the circle. Wittgenstein never participated in its sessions but was in contact with several of its members. By 1930 the periodical *Erkenntnis* (*Knowledge*, later called the *Journal of Unified Science*) began to propagate the group's views, as well as those of its Berlin counterpart, comprising the group of scientific empiricists led by Hans Reichenbach.

The Vienna Circle grew smaller with the departure of Carnap to Prague in 1931 (and to Chicago in 1936), with Feigl's removal to the United States in 1930, and with the departure of other members; but it continued its activities until Schlick's death in 1936. The circle dispersed in 1938 with Germany's annexation of Austria and was disbanded in 1939, but its influence in Britain and the United States continued to remain strong. The movements of analytic philosophy (or of linguistic analysis) in Britain, and of logical empiricism represented in many centers of higher learning in the United States—together with the ever-growing concern with the

H. VEILLER/EXPLORER, FROM CARL E. ÖSTMAN

The Vienna State Opera, nearly demolished by bombs in World War II, has been restored to its former grandeur.

philosophy of science—still bear in many ways the imprint of the Vienna ideas.

In its formative years the Vienna group was influenced most strongly by the works of Gottlob Frege, Ernst Mach, Bertrand Russell, David Hilbert, and Albert Einstein. The points of view that successively emerged from the minds of the group were phenomenalistic positivism, empirical realism, physicalism, and an emotivist ethical theory.

Though the doctrines of the Vienna Circle have been modified considerably since the 1930's, the basic outlook of scientific empiricism, with its exact analyses of the logical foundations of the sciences and its repudiation of speculative metaphysics, continues its authoritative position as a most influential factor in present day philosophy.

See also EMPIRICISM; LINGUISTIC ANALYSIS; SCHLICK, MORITZ.

HERBERT FEIGL, *Author of "Readings in the Philosophy of Science"*

VIENNA PHILHARMONIC ORCHESTRA, vē-en′ə, one of the two principal orchestras of Vienna, Austria, the other being the Vienna Symphony Orchestra. The Vienna Philharmonic Orchestra (Wiener Philharmoniker) is composed of members of the State Opera orchestra. The idea of forming such a group goes back to the 1830's, but it was not until 1860 that a regular concert series began. The Philharmonic is associated with many of the major figures of 19th and 20th century music, including Brahms, Liszt, Mahler, Wagner, Bruckner, Dvořák, Richard Strauss, and Schoenberg. Because of its obligation to the Opera, the orchestra's nine subscription concerts are given on Saturday afternoons and Sunday mornings. Performances are held in the Grosser Saal of the Musikverein, a concert hall noted for its acoustics.

The Vienna Symphony Orchestra (Wiener Symphoniker) is Vienna's regular concert orchestra. It was founded in 1900 and is not self-governing, as is the Philharmonic, but is controlled by the Gesellschaft der Musikfreunde, the Austrian Broadcasting Company, and the Konzerthausgesellschaft. During financial difficulties in the 1930's, the city assumed financial responsibility for the orchestra. It, too, performs in the acoustically superb Grosser Saal of the Musikverein.

VIENNA STATE OPERA, vē-en′ə, the major opera company of Austria and one of the foremost opera organizations in the world. The Vienna State Opera (Staatsoper) is located on the Ringstrasse, near the Hofburg, a former royal palace. The opera house, which was known as the Hofoper (court opera) until the end of the monarchy in 1918, opened on May 25, 1869, with a performance of Mozart's *Don Giovanni,* sung in German. In March 1945 the structure was almost completely destroyed during Allied bombing. However, it was restored to its former glory (the facade had remained intact) and was reopened on Nov. 5, 1955, with a performance of Beethoven's *Fidelio.*

Early History. Opera in Vienna dates from the first half of the 17th century. However, it was during the reign of Emperor Leopold I, from 1658 to 1705, that opera grew in popularity. For his marriage, Leopold commissioned Antonio Cesti to write an opera for the occasion—*Il pomo d'oro* (1666 or 1667). The opera required complicated staging, and an elaborate theater was built in the Hofburg.

In 1748 the Hofburg theater was succeeded by the Theater bei der Hofburg, or Burgtheater, where several of Mozart's operas, including *The Marriage of Figaro,* had their premieres. (The present Burgtheater, built in the late 19th century and restored after damage in World War II, presents only spoken drama.) Earlier, in 1708, the Theater am Kärntnerthor was built as an opera house for the public. This building, which gradually supplanted the Burgtheater as the court opera, was in continuous use until 1869, when it was replaced by the Hofoper, built in a grandiose neo-Baroque style.

Throughout the 18th century, opera in Vienna was dominated by Italians. For example, the celebrated Roman librettist Pietro Metastasio was court poet in Vienna from 1730 until his death in 1782 and wrote about 35 opera texts. Even works by native Germanic composers, such as Gluck and Mozart, were sung in Italian at the court theaters. However, in the early 19th century, as opera attracted audiences from a wider public, there was an increasing demand for singing in German, until by the time the Hofoper was built, that language predominated.

Later History. With the opening of the Hofoper the quality of performances increased. In the 19th century a series of able directors—Johann Herbeck, Franz Jauner, and Wilhelm Jahn—introduced important contemporary works to Vienna, with special emphasis on Wagner and the later Verdi. In 1875, Bizet's *Carmen* was a great success in Vienna after the cool reception at its premiere in Paris a few months earlier. Also significant was the popularity of works by the Hungarian-born Karl Goldmark and the Czech Bedřich Smetana.

The Hofoper's most celebrated epoch was during the directorship of Gustav Mahler in 1897–1907. He aimed to recreate authentic performances. He assembled an outstanding company of singers and placed greater emphasis on the visual aspects of opera. He broadened the repertory with important new works by Puccini, Richard Strauss, Tchaikovsky, and others.

After the establishment of the Staatsoper in 1918, Richard Strauss and Franz Schalk became codirectors. When Strauss resigned in 1924, Schalk continued until 1929 as sole director. His successors included Clemens Krauss, Felix Weingartner, and Bruno Walter. After the Anschluss in 1938, the Staatsoper was Nazified, and many of its members fled from Vienna. Following World War II the Staatsoper again attracted notable directors, including Karl Böhm and Herbert von Karajan. In addition, the singing of works in the original language replaced the former nearly exclusive German tradition.

Other opera theaters of importance in Vienna are the Volksoper, built in 1898, and the Theater an der Wien, built in 1801. Between 1945 and 1955 these houses were used by the Staatsoper while its own building was being reconstructed. Both the Volksoper and the Theater an der Wien specialize in operettas, for which Vienna is so justly famous.

WILLIAM ASHBROOK, *Indiana State University*

VIENNE, vyen, a department of France, occupying the eastern part of the former province of Poitou. The department is traversed from the southeast to the north by the Vienne River, a tributary of the Loire. The Clain River joins the Vienne south of Châtellerault, after flowing past Poitiers, the department capital. The department forms a corridor between two massifs, the Armorican massif on the northwest and the Massif Central on the southeast. Offering unimpeded access to the Paris Basin from Spain and the southwest of France, this Poitou gap has been prominent in the military history of France.

Vienne is chiefly agricultural, suited in some areas to the raising of livestock and in others to the cultivation of grains and fodder crops and to truck gardening. Heaths and forests stretch over other areas. Industry is less important to the economy. Population: (1980) 365,200.

VIENNE, vyen, a city in the department of Isère in France, on the Rhône River, about 20 miles (32 km) south of Lyon. It lies in a small basin of low-lying land, surrounded by ridges of hard rock that rise toward the Alps. The small Gère River joins the Rhône at Vienne.

A Gallic stronghold of the Allobroges before Gaul was conquered by the Romans, it became one of the most important cities in Roman Gaul. A Christian community had become established there by the 2d century, and in time Vienne became the seat of an archbishopric. It retained its importance through the Middle Ages, first as one of the chief cities of the kingdom of Burgundy and then as the capital of Dauphiné.

The city gradually declined in importance as Lyon overtook it commercially. It was also overshadowed by the growth of St. Étienne, an iron- and steel-working center 25 miles (40 km) to the west. Today the city's manufactures include textiles, pharmaceuticals, and metallurgical products.

The most impressive of its Roman remains is the Temple of Augustus and Livia, built during the reign of Augustus. The city's large Roman theater, which backs up against Mont Pipet, has been excavated. The most notable edifice of the Christian period is the former cathedral of St. Maurice, built between the 12th and 16th centuries. (The archiepiscopal see was suppressed during the French Revolution.) The former Church of St. Pierre, which is now a museum, dates partly from the 6th century. Population: (1975) 27,830.

NORMAN J. G. POUNDS*, *Indiana University*

VIENTIANE. See VIANGCHAN.

VIETCONG. See under VIETNAM—*History*.

VIETE, vyet, **François** (1540–1603), French mathematician, who invented symbolic algebra. Viète devoted his mathematical career to recovering in algebraic form the core of analytic methods by which Greek mathematicians such as Euclid, Apollonius, Archimedes, and Diophantus had reached their theorems. He proposed, in his *Introduction to the Analytic Art* (1590), a new alphabetic notation that made clear the relation between unknowns and their powers, differentiated between several different unknowns, and expressed general coefficients or parameters. In contrast to the algebra then current, which dealt with the solution of specific numerical problems, Viète's new "arithmetic of quantitative forms" focused on the structure and transformation of equations, and the treatises that make up his *Art of Analysis* constitute the first formal theory of equations.

Viète's program for the application of algebra to both geometry and arithmetic was the basis for the later development of analytic geometry and for the first steps toward the calculus by Pierre de Fermat and René Descartes. It was Descartes who reformed Viète's symbolism into the notation now commonly used.

Although famous as a mathematician, Viète was a lawyer by profession. He served as adviser to several noble Huguenot families and as a royal privy councillor during the French Wars of Religion.

MICHAEL S. MAHONEY, *Princeton University*

VIETMINH. See under VIETNAM—*History*.

BOCCON-GIBOD/SIPA SPECIAL FEATURES

The mausoleum of Ho Chi Minh, in Hanoi, contains the embalmed body of Vietnam's revolutionary leader.

VIETNAM

CONTENTS

VIETNAM, vē-et-näm′, a country on the east coast of the Indochinese Peninsula, embodying the oldest continuous civilization in Southeast Asia. Today it is best known as the principal arena of the Vietnam War (1957–1975), one of the most bitter and lengthy conflicts of the 20th century.

First appearing as a rice-growing society in the Red River Delta just prior to the Christian era, Vietnam was conquered by the Han dynasty of China in 111 B.C. and exposed to a thousand years of Chinese rule. The Vietnamese retained their separate identity, however, and in 939 A.D. regained their independence. During the next several centuries, Vietnam emerged as one of the most dynamic states in Southeast Asia. Ruled by a centralized monarchical system patterned after that of China, it gradually expanded from its confines in the Red River valley, conquering the neighboring state of Champa along the central coast and then seizing the Mekong Delta from Kampuchea.

In the 19th century, Vietnam was conquered by France and placed under colonial rule. Under the French, the economy began to develop a modern commercial and industrial sector, but living conditions did not markedly improve and political freedoms were limited. By the 1920's anticolonial sentiment was on the rise. In 1945 a coalition of nationalist forces called the Vietminh, led by the Communist party, took advantage of Japanese military occupation to seize power in the north. Subsequent negotiations between the Vietminh and the returning French broke down, and in December 1946 war broke out. After eight years of bitter conflict, the Geneva Agreements brought the war to an end. Vietnam was temporarily divided into two military regroupment zones at approximately the 17th parallel.

Nationwide elections to create a unified government were to be held in 1956 but did not take place. Thus the division of Vietnam lasted for 22 years. In the north, the Communist-dominated Democratic Republic of Vietnam began the march to socialism. In the south, non-Communist nationalists led by Ngo Dinh

INFORMATION HIGHLIGHTS

Official Name: Socialist Republic of Vietnam (Cong Hoa Xa Hoi Chu Nghia Viet Nam).
Name of Nationals: Vietnamese.
Head of State: Council of State (functioning as collective presidency).
Head of Governent: Chairman, Council of Ministers (premier).
Legislature: National Assembly (Quoc Hoi).
Area: 127,242 square miles (329,556 sq km).
Boundaries: *North,* China; *east,* Gulf of Tonkin and South China Sea; *south,* South China Sea and Gulf of Thailand; *west,* Kampuchea and Laos.
Elevations: *Highest*—Fan Si Pan (10,308 feet, or 3,142 meters); *lowest*—sea level.
Population: (1979 census) 52,741,766; (1983 est.) 57,036,000.
Capital: Hanoi.
Largest City: Ho Chi Minh City (formerly Saigon).
Major Languages: Vietnamese (official), Thai and Mon-Khmer languages, Chinese.
Major Religious Groups: Mahayana Buddhists, Roman Catholics, Cao Dai and Hoa Hao adherents, Theravada Buddhists, animists.
Monetary Unit: Dong (= 100 xu).
Flag: A large, five-pointed yellow star centered on a red field. See also FLAG.

© GEORGE COHEN/LIAISON

Steep cliffs shelter Ha Long Bay, an inlet of the Gulf of Tonkin near the port of Haiphong in northern Vietnam.

Diem set up a government in Saigon based on the Western democratic model. But Diem's autocratic methods alienated many South Vietnamese, and by 1960 popular discontent fanned and organized by the Communists was on the rise. In 1963, Diem was overthrown by a military coup, but the situation continued to deteriorate. In 1965, fearing a total collapse of the Saigon regime, the United States introduced American combat forces to stem Communist-led guerrillas. North Vietnam retaliated by infiltrating its own army units into the south. In 1973 the bloody conflict was brought to a temporary halt through a peace agreement signed in Paris, calling for withdrawal of the U.S. military and a negotiated political settlement between competing forces in Vietnam. The negotiating process soon broke down, however, and in 1975 the North Vietnamese army launched a major offensive. Saigon fell in late April. One year later, south and north were merged into the new Socialist Republic of Vietnam with its capital at Hanoi.

The Communist regime is attempting to bring all of Vietnam to socialism. It faces intimidating challenges in the forms of a stagnant economy and a southern population largely resistant to the doctrines of Marx and Lenin. In foreign affairs, Vietnamese efforts to create a close strategic alliance with the Communist governments in neighboring Laos and Kampuchea encountered opposition from Kampuchea. In December 1978, Vietnam invaded and set up a pro-Vietnamese government in Phnom Penh. This action was denounced by China, which launched a brief punitive invasion of Vietnam in 1979. Many other nations refused to recognize the legitimacy of a Kampuchean government kept in power by Vietnamese occupation forces.

1. The Land

Vietnam has a land area of 127,242 square miles (329,556 sq km). Shaped like a giant letter "S," it extends along the eastern edge of the Southeast Asian mainland from the Chinese border to the southern tip of the Ca Mau Peninsula, a straight-line distance of about 1,000 miles (1,600 km). Near the center of its double curve the country narrows to a width of less than 30 miles (50 km).

Relief. Vietnam is largely mountainous but contains three major lowlands. In the north lies the Red River (Song Hong) Delta. The Red River originates on the Yünnan Plateau of southwestern China and flows southeast to the Gulf of Tonkin. The delta is bounded by rugged mountains that extend to the Chinese border in the north and to the frontier with Laos in the west. Far to the south is the much larger delta of the Mekong, Southeast Asia's longest river. From its source on the Tibetan Plateau it flows south for some 2,600 miles (4,160 km) to the South China Sea. As it nears the sea it divides into several distributaries flowing through flat, marshy land that has been built up over the centuries by soils deposited by the river. This delta extends from the vicinity of Ho Chi Minh City (formerly Saigon) to the mangrove swamps of the Ca Mau Peninsula. Linking the two deltas is a lengthy, narrow lowland along the South China Sea. In the north, this coastal area consists of a relatively flat, sandy plain, with several small rivers flowing into the sea from the mountains to the west. South of the Hai Van Pass, near Da Nang, mountains often jut directly into the sea.

In northern Vietnam the mountains bordering the Red River Delta reach elevations of more than 10,000 feet (3,000 meters). From the southern side of the delta, the Annam Cordillera (Truong Son) stretches along the western frontier with Laos and Kampuchea, close to the coast. Southward it widens into a plateau of 20,000 square miles (50,000 sq km) called the Central Highlands.

Climate. Vietnam lies wholly within the tropics, but the north experiences some variation in temperature. From April to November, the temperature there is warm, averaging about 86°F (30°C). During the winter months the average drops to about 68°F (20°C) and can reach as low as 41°F (5°C). The south has more uniform temperatures, averaging about 81°F (27°C) throughout the year.

In Vietnam the seasons are most clearly marked by changes in precipitation. From April to the end of October, the summer monsoon sweeps across the southern half of the peninsula, bringing heavy rains, normally about 80 inches (2,000 mm) per year. In the north, rainfall averages 60 inches (1,500 mm) yearly.

Natural Resources. Although the Mekong and Red River deltas comprise only 23% of the total land area of the country, they contain about 60% of the population. These areas, with their warm climate and rich alluvial soils, are appropriate for the cultivation of wet rice, and some areas support two rice crops per year. However, in the north, cold and drought often cause severe damage to the rice crop and bring the threat of starvation to thousands of peasants. Vicious typhoons spawned in the South China Sea frequently sweep across the central coast and batter the rice lands with high winds and floods.

Only about 16% of the land is under cultivation. Much of the remainder is forested, and for the most part sparsely populated. The Northern and Central highlands are inhabited mainly by tribal minorities who traditionally use slash-and-burn techniques to cultivate dry crops. Vietnam's mountains are rich in hardwoods, game, and minerals such as iron, tin, and zinc.

Some plateau and hilly areas are planted with cash crops such as tea, coffee, and spices. In the rich basaltic red soil along the Kampuchean border, the French established rubber plantations that eventually became, after rice, Vietnam's primary source of export earnings. During the Vietnam War, some forest and plantation areas, notably along the frontier with Kampuchea, were defoliated by U.S. herbicides. There was concern that such areas might suffer permanent damage, but most appear to be recovering.

Several governments, such as the Saigon regime of Ngo Dinh Diem and the current Communist government, have attempted to resettle Vietnamese peasants from the densely populated lowlands into the highlands. In 1976 the current government announced plans to move 10 million Vietnamese by the end of the 20th century as part of a vast program of decentralization. By 1980, about 1.5 million were actually resettled.

2. The People

With more than 450 people per square mile (175 per sq km), Vietnam is the most densely populated country in Southeast Asia except for Singapore. In much of the Red River Delta, the rural population density exceeds 1,800 persons per square mile (700 per sq km).

As in most Southeast Asian countries, the population is divided into disparate ethnic groups. Relatively speaking, however, Vietnam is more homogeneous than are most of its neighbors, for 85% of its people are ethnic Vietnamese. Yet even here lies diversity, because the Vietnamese themselves are split according to religious preference and geographical location.

The Vietnamese. Like many of the peoples of Southeast Asia, the Vietnamese are of obscure origins. In prehistoric times they lived in the Red River Delta, where apparently they were one of the first peoples in Asia to cultivate wet rice. Ethnically, they are probably related to the Yüeh (Viet) peoples who lived throughout southeastern China, but by the time they first appear in history, they had already evolved into a distinctive society and called themselves the Lac peoples.

The language is hardly a better tool for tracing the people's origins. Like Chinese and Thai, Vietnamese is a tonal language but is considered to be a member of the Austroasiatic language family and has syntactical similarities to the nontonal Mon-Khmer languages of this group. A thousand years of Chinese rule resulted in the introduction of many Chinese words and phrases into the vocabulary, and the script in use until modern times was based on the Chinese ideograph system. Early in the 20th century, Vietnamese scholars successfully promoted the use of *quoc ngu*—a system of writing Vietnamese in the Latin alphabet. Originally invented by Catholic missionaries, it is the official script today.

Originally the Vietnamese were restricted to the area around the Red River Delta. After independence was restored in the 10th century, many Vietnamese peasants migrated southward in the wake of the Vietnamese conquest of Champa and the subsequent seizure of the Mekong Delta. This expansion more than doubled the size of the Vietnamese state and relieved population pressure in the densely inhabited areas of the Red

Fishing boats crowd the harbor of Vung Tau, a port near Ho Chi Minh City in southern Vietnam.

© DAVID AUSTEN/STOCK BOSTON

Flat farmland soon gives way to mountains in Vietnam, except in the deltas of the Red and Mekong rivers.

River valley, but it also introduced a new problem to a heretofore geographically compact society.

In the "frontier" atmosphere of the Mekong Delta a new type of Vietnamese began to emerge, less influenced by the hierarchical and familial traditions of the north. These differences were accentuated by a civil war that divided north and south in the 17th and 18th centuries and later by the French colonial regime. The French split the Vietnamese Empire into three parts: the protectorates of Tonkin (Tongking) in the north and Annam in the center, and the colony of Cochin China in the south. These correspond to the Vietnamese regional distinctions of Bac ky (the north), Trung ky (the center), and Nam ky (the south). Northerners, hardworking and traditional in their cultural orientation, were relatively little exposed to European influence, which in Tonkin was centered in the commercial cities of Hanoi and Haiphong. In Annam, too, the French presence was limited, and the local population as a whole remained under the influence of the conservative orientation of the court at Hue. Cochin China, however, was exposed to the full force of colonial economic exploitation, and Saigon became the vibrant center of Western influence and activity. The Western presence undoubtedly accentuated the already informal and easy-going but volatile characteristics of the local population. Today, these differences pose a serious challenge to the Communist party's attempt to create a unified socialist society.

Tribal Minorities. The most numerous of all ethnic minority groups in Vietnam are the tribal peoples. Numbering somewhat more than 3 million people, they live primarily in the mountains surrounding the Red River Delta and in the Central Highlands. They have a variety of ethnic and linguistic backgrounds. Some, like the Tho (Tay), the Thai (divided into Black, White, and Red Thai), and the Nung, speak languages of the Thai (Tai) group and may have migrated into northern Vietnam from southern China centuries ago. The Tho, who have a close cultural relationship with the Vietnamese, are the most populous tribal group, numbering more than 500,000. They live north of the Red River, and most are rice farmers. The roughly 500,000 Thai inhabit the upland areas in the far northwest and have been less influenced by the lowland Vietnamese. Other groups in the north are the Muong, the Meo, and the Yao.

In the Central Highlands, most tribal groups are ethnically unrelated to the majority Vietnamese, speak Mon-Khmer or Malay languages, and practice slash-and-burn agriculture. Some, like the Rhade and the Jarai, are apparently related to the lowland Cham.

Traditionally, most tribal peoples had only limited contacts with the lowland population. Recently, however, Vietnamese governments have made efforts to assimilate them. The present Communist regime has made cautious attempts to integrate the tribal peoples into Vietnamese society and persuade them to abandon their traditional ways of life. The results have been mixed. Several hundred thousand have apparently adopted a settled way of life, according to official statistics. Others may have resisted, however, for persisent rumors tell of dissident activity by tribal groups in the Central Highlands and along the Chinese border.

The Chinese. After the tribal peoples, the Chinese are the largest ethnic minority in Vietnam, totaling about 2 million at the end of the war in 1975. Most are the descendants of immigrants who entered Vietnam over a period of several generations prior to the colonial period. The majority settled in large cities like Saigon, Hanoi, and Haiphong, where they became active in commerce and manufacturing.

Like the tribal minorities, the Chinese have traditionally sought to avoid integration into Vietnamese society, and both the imperial government and the French permitted them to retain a degree of cultural and administrative autonomy. Before 1975 the Communist regime in the

© BRUCE GORDON/PHOTO RESEARCHERS

Something of a Parisian atmosphere persists in Ho Chi Minh City, the former Saigon.

north followed a similar practice and allowed the approximately 200,000 Chinese in its area to operate their own schools and maintain Chinese nationality. They dominated the small private sector in Hanoi and Haiphong. In 1978, however, the regime nationalized industry and commerce throughout the country. Many ethnic Chinese, fearing that the move was racially inspired, fled the country, some across the border into China, others by ship to other countries in Southeast Asia. According to some estimates, as many as half a million may have departed between 1978 and 1982. At first, government authorities denied any intention to eliminate Chinese distinctiveness. Later, however, Hanoi appeared to concede that many Chinese in Vietnam cannot be successfully integrated into socialist society and encouraged or at least tolerated their departure. The future of those who remain is uncertain.

The Cham and Khmer. The Cham are remnants of the dominant people of the old Champa kingdom, which the Vietnamese conquered during their "march to the south." Numbering, 50,000, they are of Malay extraction and make their living as fishermen or farmers along the central coast. The Khmer, about 300,000 strong, are descendants of settlers who were absorbed by the Vietnamese as they expanded into the Mekong Delta in the 17th century. Most are Theravada Buddhists and live in villages in the lower delta separate from the surrounding Vietnamese population. In neighboring Kampuchea, the Khmer are the majority ethnic group.

Religious Groups. Religious life in Vietnam is characterized by a variety of faiths, the absence of clear lines of division between different beliefs, mutual tolerance, and a willingness to adopt new creeds without giving up the old ones. The majority of the Vietnamese adhere to a diluted form of Mahayana Buddhism, which has always coexisted with Chinese ancestor worship, with the ethical concepts of Confucianism, and with popular forms of Taoism. The worship of national heroes and the appeasing of guardian spirits of the house and village are still widespread. Animist beliefs persist among tribal peoples. The chief religious minorities are the Roman Catholics and the followers of 20th century sects.

The Catholics. At the close of the Vietnam War, there were about 2 million Catholics in Vietnam. While most are ethnic Vietnamese, they have long been considered a separate group within the population because of their distinctive beliefs and practices. The Catholic community originated in the 17th century, when more than 500,000 were reported converted by French mis-

As of old, a rice vendor awaits customers in her shaded stall. A free market still exists on the family level.

© EDDIE ADAMS/GAMMA LIAISON

© JAMES PICKERELL/BLACK STAR

Members of the Cao Dai faith worship at their temple in Tay Ninh. The sect claims over a million followers.

sionaries. Despite official persecution, the community survived, and under French rule its numbers increased rapidly. Many Catholics became prominent in education, commerce, and the professions. Originally about half lived in the north, but after the Geneva Conference of 1954 nearly 700,000 migrated southward to flee Communist rule. In South Vietnam, they settled mainly in the vicinity of Saigon, where they formed the nucleus of the Westernized middle class and became a crucial source of support for the regime of Ngo Dinh Diem.

After 1975 the Communist regime attempted to conciliate southern Catholics because of their potential contribution to the nation-building effort. Freedom of religious worship was guaranteed, and the local church hierarchy was permitted to retain official ties with the Vatican. But Hanoi remains suspicious of the Western orientation of many Catholics and restricts the activities of church organizations. As a result, relations between the government and the Catholic community have often been strained, and several priests have been accused of treasonous behavior.

The Sects. The Cao Dai and Hoa Hao sects were founded in southern Vietnam between the two world wars. Each claims the support of more than 1 million followers today. Cao Dai ("High Tower"), a syncretistic belief incorporating elements of several major world religions, was founded shortly after World War I in Saigon. Later it took root in rural areas along the Kampuchean border and moved its headquarters to Tay Ninh province, where it remains. Hoa Hao (from the name of the village where it was founded) is a Buddhist reform sect. Founded by the Buddhist mystic Huynh Phu So in 1939, it spread rapidly among peasants in the lower Mekong Delta.

Both groups resented French efforts to limit their influence and cooperated with the Japanese during World War II. After the Japanese surrender they cooperated briefly with the local Vietminh, but relations soon became strained. After 1954, both organizations cooperated reluctantly with the Saigon regime against the Communists. Since 1975 the Hanoi regime has handled the sects with care and apparently has delayed collectivization in their areas. There have been reports, however, of resistance to the government by sect members.

3. Education and Cultural Life

Historically, Vietnam has served as a cultural bridge between China and Southeast Asia. Only after the end of the 19th century did Western influences begin to replace Chinese inspiration in national life. In today's Vietnam the primary goal of education and the arts is to inculcate in all citizens the virtues of the socialist system.

Education. During the precolonial period, Vietnamese education was patterned after the system used in China. Its chief goal was to train potential candidates for the bureaucracy. Promising young males were exposed to the Confucian classics at village schools in preparation for the civil service examinations and entry into officialdom.

During the colonial period, the Confucian educational system was abolished and replaced by the French model. Course content changed from Confucian ethics and philosophy to the social and natural sciences. The concept of education as a stepping-stone to an official career was discarded and emphasis placed on practical training and exposure to Western culture. Only a minority of school-age children, however, actually attended school.

After 1954 the Saigon government retained and expanded the French system. In the north the Communists turned to the Soviet model. Under today's socialist republic, emphasis is placed on Marxist doctrine, revolutionary ethics, and the value of combining book learning with manual labor.

Culture. During the centuries of Chinese rule, Vietnamese society was introduced to a variety of influences from the north. Chinese styles transformed Vietnamese literature, music, and visual arts and mixed with indigenous themes.

This tendency was particularly pronounced in literature. Under Chinese rule, literary Chinese was the official language of Vietnam and the primary mode of expression in philosophy, poetry, and historiography. But the vernacular survived, and when a native form of the Chinese writing system—*chu nom,* or "southern characters"—was developed sometime after the 8th century, the Vietnamese language came into increased use as a literary vehicle. During the Le dynasty (1428–1804) a new form of novel based on the vernacular began to flourish. Its distinguishing characteristics—such as its frequent use of irony and social criticism—set it apart from its contemporary Chinese equivalent.

Under French rule, Chinese cultural influence rapidly declined. Literary Chinese was abandoned, and many educated Vietnamese turned to the French language as a modern alternative. At first, some felt that Vietnamese was inadequate as a sophisticated means of written expression, but after Chinese ideographs were

© GEORGE COHEN/LIAISON

For new construction, economically pinched Vietnam relies heavily on old-fashioned muscle power.

replaced by *quoc ngu*, Vietnamese gradually became accepted as the national language of the country. Western music, painting, and architecture replaced traditional Chinese forms. Literature, poetry, fiction, drama, and essay writing were all transformed by French influence. In the 1920's and 1930's a new generation of Vietnamese novelists began to depict the habits and aspirations of the new Westernized middle class. At first some were simple imitations of popular romantic novels in the West. In the 1930's, however, a school of young writers influenced by the trend toward critical realism in the West began to use the novel as a vehicle for serious critique of colonial society.

After 1954 the popularity of Western culture continued and even intensified in the south. In some areas, such as popular music and literature, the dominant role of French tradition was replaced by that of the United States. In painting and the visual arts, French influence held its own. With the introduction of several hundred thousand U.S. troops after 1965, American rock music, popular literature, and individualistic lifestyles became increasingly prevalent, particularly among the young and in urban areas.

In the north, culture was viewed by the regime as a means of creating the New Man. During the Vietnam War, art, music, and literature all reflected themes of patriotism and sacrifice for the sacred cause of national reunification. Today, in unified Vietnam, culture continues to serve politics. Literature, music, and the visual arts are all used as a means of indoctrinating the mass of the population in the virtues of physical labor, revolutionary ethics, and the socialist system. But the effort to eliminate capitalist cultural influence in the south has not been particularly successful. Pornographic and escapist literature, rock music, and hedonistic attitudes continue to be popular, notably among the young. Concerned that such "noxious weeds of capitalism" could threaten the struggle to build a socialist society, the regime is waging a vigorous campaign to eradicate such foreign influences.

4. Government

Before the French conquest in the latter half of the 19th century, the Vietnamese political system was based on the Chinese model. Postcolonial governments have been based on Western models of parliamentary democracy in the south and Soviet-style "centralized democracy" in the north and since 1976 for a united Vietnam.

Imperial Government. Under the Chinese-derived Cult of Heaven, the emperor was presumed to rule by divine mandate. His authority was buttressed by Confucian doctrine, which emphasized the social virtues of obedience and hierarchy.

The emperor's power was not limitless. Imperial decisions were implemented by a bureaucracy whose members were selected through a complex series of examinations based on the mastery of the classical Chinese texts. The relatively permanent character of the bureaucracy and the emphasis on correct procedures and Confucian precedent served on occasion to restrict the authority of the monarch and prevent his arbitrary use of power. The stress on merit provided a ladder of upward mobility for talented youth and limited the arrogance of the landed aristocracy. At the same time, the bureaucracy was often cumbersome, ritualistic, and dominated by special interests.

Colonial Rule. The traditional system was abandoned under French rule. The emperor at Hue retained titular authority in the protectorates of Tonkin and Annam. Real power, however, resided in the colonial administration, headed by a Paris-appointed governor-general for all of French Indochina (Vietnam, Laos, and Kampuchea). In the colony of Cochin China, the French ruled directly. In the protectorates, colonial influence was channeled through a system of French advisers operating at the regional and provincial levels. The imperial bureaucracy was retained, but in emasculated form, and it lost its last shreds of legitimacy when the civil service examinations were abolished.

VIETNAM
0 50 100 150 MI.
0 50 100 150 KM.
International Boundaries
Capitals of Countries
Tropic of Cancer
Longitude East 104° of Greenwich
100°
104°
108°
112°
20°
16°
12°
8°
B
C
D
2
3
4
5
C H I N A
C H I N A
BURMA
L A O S
THAILAND
CAMBODIA
V I E T N A M
H A I N A N
GULF OF TONKIN
SOUTH CHINA SEA
GULF OF THAILAND
Paracel Islands (China)
Hanoi
Haiphong
HO CHI MINH CITY
(Saigon)
Vientiane
(Viangchan)
BANGKOK
(Krung Thep)
Phnom Penh
Gejiu
Mengzi
Wenshan
Simao
Manhao
Yen Minh
Bao Lac
Trung Khanh Phu
Nanning
Guiping
Xi Jiang
Heng Xian
Luoding
Yulin
Ha Giang
Muong Khuong
Cao Bang
Chongzuo
Fan Si Pan
10,308 ft.(3142 m.)
Lao Cai
Chapa
Bao Ha
Lai Chau
Luc An Chau
Bac Can
That Khe
Pingxiang
Muang Ou Tai
Jinghong
Phôngsali
Nghia Lo
Tuyen Quang
Yen Bai
Thai Nguyen
Lang Son
Phu Tho
Vinh Yen
Bac Giang
Tien Yen
Mong Cai
Beihai
Hepu
Maoming
Zhanjiang
Leizhou
Haikang
Leizhou Wan
Bandao
Anpu Gang
Weizhow Dao
Muang Sing
Son La
Dien Bien Phu
Muang Khoua
Van Yen
Son Tay
Bac Ninh
Hon Gai
Van Hoa
Ke Bao
Quang Yen
Dao Cat Ba
Hoa Binh
Phu Ly
Nam Dinh
Thai Binh
Ban Houayxay
Muang Xon
San Nua
Hoi Xuan
Ninh Binh
Muang Paktha
Dao Bach Long Vi
(Nightingale I.)
Qiongzhou Haixia
Haikou
Lingao
Louangphrabang
Bai Thuong
Thanh Hoa
Nong Het
Cua Rao
Con Cuong
Phu Qui
Xiangkhoang
Phou Bia
9,252 ft.(2820 m.)
Baisha
Qionghai
Dongfang
Wanning
Muang Xaignabouri
Nan
Phu Dien
Vinh
Vu Liet
Phuc Loi
Borikhan
Rao Co
7,500 ft.
(2286 m.)
Napè
Ha Tinh
Huong Khe
Mui Ron
Muang Pak-Lay
Chai Buri
Khamkeut
Phrae
Uttaradit
Nong Khai
Ba Don
Ron
Phou Cô Pi
6,358 ft. (1938 m.)
N
Dan Sai
Udon Thani
Nakhon Phanom
Muang Khammouan
Dong Hoi
Co Lieu
Hon Gio
Mui Lay
Kumphawapi
Nong Lahan
Phitsanulok
Savannakhét
Khe Sanh
Quang Tri
Hue
Vung Chon May
Phichit
Phetchabun
Mukdahan
Muang Xépôn
Ban Lahanam
Mui Da Nang
Da Nang
Maha Sarakham
Khemmarat
Quang Nam
Hoi An
Nakhon Sawan
Chaiyaphum
Suwannaphum
Saravan
Tam Ky
Mui Nam Tram
Plateau des Bolovens
Chu Lai
Binh Son
Mui Ba Lang An
Quang Ngai
Ubon
Pakxé
Sisaket
Attapu
Son Ha
Mo Duc
Nakhon Ratchasima
Mae Nam Mun
Lop Buri
Sara Buri
Surin
Ngoc Linh
8,524 ft.
(2598 m.)
Tam Quan
Kontum
Hoai Nhon
Phra Nakhon Si Ayutthaya
Dangrek (Dong Rak) Chain
Muang Không
Phu My
Pleiku
Plateau du Kontum
An Tuc
An Nhon
Prachin Buri
Phumi Samraong
Virochey
Qui Nhon
Ban Aranyaprathet
Chachoengsao
Samut Prakan
Sisophon
ANGKOR WAT
Stoeng Treng
Song Cau
Hau Bon
Chon Buri
Batdambang
Siemreab
Tonle Sap
Stoeng Sen
Cao Nguyen Dac Lac
Tuy Hoa
Ban Me Thuot
Van Ninh
Mui Varella
Chu Yang Sin
7,890 ft.(2405 m.)
Ben Goi
Sattahip
Chanthaburi
Pouthisat
Kampong Thum
Kracheh
Nha Trang
Kampong Chhnang
Kampong Cham
Bo Duc
Nui Lang Bian
Cam Ranh
Khanh Hoa
Vinh Cam Ranh
Loc Ninh
Da Lat
Phan Rang
Prey Veng
Nui Ba Den
3,235 ft.
(986 m.)
Phu Rieng
Binh Long (An Loc)
Di Linh
Kampong Spoe
Tay Ninh
Svay Rieng
Phu Cuong
Hoa Da
Mui Dinh
Ap Vinh Hao
Ap Long Ha
Xuan Loc
Bien Hoa
Gia Dinh
Phan Thiet
Takev
Plaine des Joncs
Moc Hoa
Tan An
Kampot
Kampong Saom
Chau Phu
Cao Lanh
My Tho
Hon Cu Lao
Long Xuyen
Sa Dec
Vung Tau
Duong Dong
Ha Tien
Dao Phu Quoc
Hon Chong
Rach Gia
Vinh Long
Can Tho
Truc Giang
Go Cong
Mouths of the Mekong
Phu Vinh
Quan Dao Nam Du
Kien Hung
Hon Tho Chau
(Hon Panjang)
Thanh Tri
Khanh Hung
Quan Long
Bac Lieu
Con Son
Dam Doi
Mui Bai Bung
(Pte. de Ca Mau)
Hon Khoai
Les Deux Frères
Mekong
Nam Tha
Nam Ou
Mae Nam Nan
Mae Nam Pa Sak
Se Khong
Se San
Srepok
Ia Drang
Song Ba
Song Cai
Song Ca
Black R. (Song Da)
Red R. (Song Hong)
Sip Song Chau Thai

The ostensible reason for the destruction of the traditional Confucian system was to introduce the Western political model. Yet the French were slow to promote democratic institutions in colonial Indochina. Legislative assemblies were established early in the 20th century but had a narrow franchise and only advisory powers. Only in 1949, under the pressure of civil war, did the French grant substantial autonomy to a Vietnamese government under ex-emperor Bao Dai.

Divided Vietnam. After 1954 the non-Communist government in South Vietnam, with U.S. advice, adopted a new political system based on a synthesis of the presidential and parliamentary models. But President Ngo Dinh Diem's political style was Confucian and autocratic. He was intolerant of opposition, and the unicameral National Assembly eventually did little but provide rubber-stamp endorsements of his decisions. After Diem's overthrow, a new constitution went into effect in 1967.

In the north the Communist regime adopted the institutions that had originally been established for the Democratic Republic of Vietnam (DRV), founded in Hanoi in September 1945. In 1946 a constitution was adopted, creating a government with sovereign power vested in a unicameral National Assembly. The Communist party was the dominant force in the government, but members of several other political parties, including some who were rivals of the Communists, were brought into the cabinet to broaden popular support for the struggle against the French. After the war began in December 1946, the party concentrated power in its own hands, while maintaining links with the population through the mass associations of the Vietminh Front.

In 1954 the DRV government returned to Hanoi. During the next few years, the regime gradually created an administrative structure based on the formation of elected bodies at provincial, district, and village levels. A new constitution ratified in 1960 contained many of the features of its predecessor but strengthened the office of the presidency in deference to the unique qualities of Ho Chi Minh. As before, the superficial resemblance to the Western democratic model masked the reality that real power was vested in the party, now renamed the Vietnam Workers' party. The party itself, whose members comprised about 3% of the total population, operated according to the Leninist principle of democratic centralism, providing for centralized leadership from the Politburo and the Central Committee. Popular participation in the political process was achieved by the regime and through the Fatherland Front. This was an omnibus organization consisting of several mass associations representing key social groups in the population: farmers, workers, students, women, and the various ethnic and religious minority groups. These associations served as a vehicle for the expression of popular aspirations and as a conduit for mobilizing popular support for the programs of the regime.

The SRV. After victory in the south in 1975, the Hanoi regime moved rapidly to complete administrative reunification of the two zones. Elections for a unified National Assembly (with representation split evenly between north and

VIETNAM

CITIES and TOWNS

Place	Key
An Loc (Binh Long) 15,276	C 5
An Nhon	D 4
An Tuc	D 4
Ap Long Ha	D 5
Ap Vinh Hoa	D 5
Bac Can	C 2
Bac Giang	C 2
Bac Lieu 53,841	C 5
Bac Ninh 22,560	C 2
Ba Don	C 3
Bai Thuong	C 3
Ban Me Thuot 68,771	C 4
Bao Ha	B 2
Bao Lac	C 2
Bien Hoa 87,135	C 5
Binh Long 15,276	C 5
Binh Son	D 4
Bo Duc	C 4
Cam Ranh 118,111	D 4
Can Tho 182,424	C 5
Cao Bang	C 2
Cao Lanh 16,482	C 5
Chapa	C 2
Chau Phu 37,175	C 5
Chu Lai	D 4
Co Lieu	C 3
Con Cuong	C 3
Cua Rao	C 3
Da Lat 105,072	D 5
Dam Doi	D 5
Da Nang 492,194	C 3
Dien Bien Phu	B 2
Di Linh 4,500	D 5
Dong Hoi	C 3
Gia Dinh	C 5
Go Cong 33,191	C 5
Ha Giang	C 2
Haiphong * 1,279,067	C 2
Hanoi (cap.) * 2,570,905	C 2
Ha Tien	C 5
Ha Tinh	C 3
Hau Bon	D 4
Hoa Binh	C 2
Hoa Da	D 5
Hoai Nhon	D 4
Ho Chi Minh City * 3,419,678	C 5
Hoi An 45,059	D 4
Hoi Xuan	C 2
Hon Chong	C 5
Hon Gai 100,000	C 2
Hue 209,043	C 3
Huong Khe	C 3
Ke Bao	C 2
Khanh Hoa	D 4
Khanh Hung 59,015	C 5
Khe Sanh	C 3
Kien Hung	C 5
Kontum 33,554	C 4
Lai Chau	B 2
Lang Son 15,071	C 2
Lao Cai	C 2
Loc Ninh	C 5
Long Xuyen 72,658	C 5
Luc An Chau	C 2
Moc Hoa 3,191	C 5
Mo Duc	C 4
Mong Cai	C 2
Muong Khuong	C 2
My Lai	D 4
My Tho 119,892	C 5
Nam Dinh 125,000	C 2
Nghia Lo	B 2
Nha Trang 216,227	D 4
Ninh Binh	C 2
Phan Rang 33,377	D 5
Phan Thiet 80,122	D 5
Phuc Loi	C 3
Phu Cuong 28,267	C 5
Phu Dien	C 3
Phu Ly	C 2
Phu My	D 4
Phu Qui	C 3
Phu Rieng	C 5
Phu Tho 10,888	C 2
Phu Vinh 48,485	C 5
Pleiku 23,720	C 4
Quang Nam	C 4
Quang Ngai 14,119	D 4
Quang Tri 15,874	C 3
Quang Yen	C 2
Quan Long 59,331	C 5
Qui Nhon 213,757	D 4
Rach Gia 104,161	C 5
Ron	C 3
Sa Dec 51,867	C 5
Saigon (Ho Chi Minh City) * 3,419,678	C 5
Song Cau	D 4
Son Ha	D 4
Son La	B 2
Son Tay 19,213	C 2
Tam Ky 38,532	D 4
Tam Quan	D 4
Tan An 38,082	C 5
Tay Ninh 22,957	C 5
Thai Binh 14,739	C 2
Thai Nguyen 110,000	C 2
Thanh Hoa 31,211	C 3
Thanh Tri	C 5
That Khe	C 2
Tien Yen	C 2
Truc Giang 68,629	C 5
Trung Khan Phu	C 2
Tuyen Quang	C 2
Tuy Hoa 63,552	D 4
Van Hoa	C 2
Van Ninh	D 4
Van Yen	C 2
Vinh 43,954	C 3
Vinh Long 30,667	C 5
Vinh Yen	C 2
Vu Liet	C 3
Vung Tau 108,436	C 5
Xuan Loc	C 5
Yen Bai	C 2
Yen Minh	C 2

OTHER FEATURES

Feature	Key
Bach Long Vi, Dao (isl.)	D 2
Ba Den, Nui (mt.)	C 5
Ba Lang An, Mui (cape)	D 4
Black (riv.)	B 2
Ca Mau (Mui Bai Bung) (pt.)	C 5
Cam Ranh, Vinh (bay)	D 5
Cat Ba, Dao (isl.)	C 2
Cháu, Hon Tho (isl.)	B 5
Chon May, Vung (bay)	C 3
Dac Lac, Cao Nguyen (plat.)	C 4
Da Nang, Mui (cape)	D 3
Deux Frères, Les (isls.)	C 5
Dinh, Mui (cape)	D 5
Fan Si Pan (mt.)	B 2
Gio, Hon (isl.)	C 3
Goi, Ben (bay)	D 4
Hon Panjang (Hon Tho Chau) (isl.)	B 5
Joncs (plain)	C 5
Khoai, Hon (isl.)	C 5
Kontum (plat.)	C 4
Lang Bian, Nui (mts.)	D 4
Lay, Mui (cape)	C 3
Mekong, Mouths of the (delta)	C 5
Nam Tram, Mui (cape)	D 4
Ngoc Linh (mt.)	C 4
Nightingale (Bach Long Vi) (isl.)	D 2
Phu Quoc, Dao (isl.)	B 5
Quan Dao Nam Du (isls.)	B 5
Rao Co (mt.)	C 3
Red (riv.)	C 2
Ron, Mui (cape)	C 3
Se San (riv.)	C 4
Sip Song Chau Thai (mts.)	B 2
Son, Con (isls.)	C 5
Song Ba (riv.)	D 4
Song Ca (riv.)	C 3
Song Cai (riv.)	C 4
Song Da (Black) (riv.)	C 2
Song Hong (Red) (riv.)	C 2
Tonkin (gulf)	C 3
Yang Sin, Chu (mt.)	D 4
Varella, Mui (cape)	D 4

south) were held in April 1976. In July a unified Socialist Republic of Vietnam (SRV) was created with its capital in Hanoi. The southern-based National Liberation Front was merged into the Fatherland Front of the north. To placate regional sensitivities, several southerners were given responsible posts in the national administration.

On the surface, unification took place without incident. To reduce the likelihood of resistance, thousands of individuals suspected of counterrevolutionary tendencies were sent to reeducation camps. Still, the regime ran into difficulties in imposing its will on the south. Experienced southern cadres were lacking, and personnel sent from the north often lacked the experience to shift from revolution to administration, or were easily corrupted by the affluence of the south. Southerners began to complain of official arrogance and high living. To cleanse the party of impure elements, the Politburo launched a rectification campaign that dismissed a reported 80,000 members. At the same time, more than 300,000 new members were added, many of them young people and veterans, resulting in a total membership of 1.7 million by 1981. Whether such measures can alleviate the malaise in the south, where much of the population resents northern domination and "social transformation," remains to be seen.

In December 1980 the National Assembly ratified a new constitution. Its main innovation was the creation of a Council of State to replace the office of the presidency. Other provisions strengthened the role of the assembly as the "supreme organ of the people's power" and reorganized the Council of Ministers and local administration. But the leading role of the party, expressed through the function of the dictatorship of the proletariat, was strongly reaffirmed.

One of the most crucial problems faced by the party was that of succession. Throughout the war, the party had been led by a few veterans of the revolutionary struggle: Ho Chi Minh (who died in 1969), Le Duan, Pham Van Dong, and Truong Chinh. By the mid-1980's, all were in their seventies but held the key positions of authority: Le Duan as party secretary-general, Pham Van Dong as chairman of the Council of Ministers (premier), and Truong Chinh as chairman of the Council of State. The delay in arranging succession to a new generation of leaders may be ascribed in part to disagreement over fundamental questions about the future course of the revolution. So long as this debate continued, the generation that had waged the struggle for unification was reluctant to step down. The three leaders finally did in 1987.

5. The Economy

Vietnam is a country with abundant natural resources and an intelligent, industrious citizenry. Yet today it is one of the poorest countries in Asia. Its standard of living is barely at the level of subsistence, and it is heavily dependent on outside financial aid. That paradox is rooted in history.

The Economic Background. In the precolonial era, Vietnam had a predominantly agrarian economy with a small commercial and manufacturing sector and some foreign trade. The population was essentially dependent for its survival on the cultivation of wet rice. The advent of colonial rule brought significant changes to the economy. Vietnam had little to offer France in the way of accessible mineral resources and spices. In order to facilitate the commercial exploitation of their new possession, the French developed export crops, such as rubber, tea, and rice. Beyond promoting exports, French economic interests in Vietnam were limited to creating a market for French manufactured goods. In consequence, colonial Vietnam did not enter into a period of rapid industrial growth, and development in the manufacturing sector was limited to small consumer-goods industries producing such items as textiles, paper, foodstuffs, and cement.

Vietnam entered the period of independence, then, with a modernized but basically unrestructured version of its precolonial economy. In the south, where mineral resources are scarce, the regime concentrated on the development of light industry and export crops. But war soon interrupted such efforts. By the mid-1960's the south—a rice exporter in the colonial era—was forced to import food and became increasingly dependent on U.S. economic assistance.

In the meantime, the north embarked on its road to socialism. The ultimate goal of the ruling party was to transform Vietnam into an advanced industrial society based on the socialist model. Because of the primitive state of the economy, however, the regime was forced to move slowly, initially nationalizing basic industries and utilities and carrying out an extensive program of land reform. The first stages of collectivization began in 1958, and by 1960 the vast majority of farm families in the north had been enrolled in low-level cooperatives. At its Third Congress held in September 1960, the party announced an ambitious five-year plan to begin socialist industrialization.

Within less than three years, however, the demands of the war in the south began to interfere with economic construction, and the regime was forced to shift its priorities. During the next decade, economic growth in the north was minimal, as material and human resources were mobilized for the cause of national reunification. Bombing by the United States severely damaged the industrial and transportation base of the north, and the Hanoi government became heavily dependent on the USSR, China, and other socialist countries for economic assistance and food shipments.

Economic Integration and Development. The end of the war in 1975 permitted the Hanoi regime to turn once again to economic development. The addition of the south represented real benefits. The south was the traditional "rice bowl" of the country, with the potential to feed the excess population in the north; it also possessed a relatively modern consumer-goods industry that could help provide for the needs of Vietnam's war-weary population.

At the same time, the situation presented the party with a severe challenge. How could the productive capacity of the capitalist south be most effectively mobilized in preparation for its integration into the socialist economy of the north? When should socialist transformation begin, and under what conditions?

At first, the regime simply announced that for the time being the capitalist sector would be relatively untouched. Only a few major enterprises were nationalized, and businessmen and farmers were assured that their property and their profits would not be confiscated. In the fall of 1975, however, the regime suddenly announced that after a short period of transition to encourage economic recovery, the south would be led gradually to socialism. In 1976 the schedule became clearer with the promulgation of a new five-year plan for 1976–1980. The primary objectives of the plan would be: (1) to begin the process of converting the Vietnamese economy from small-scale to large-scale production, a goal that the regime conceded would require at least a generation to attain; and (2) to undertake the socialist transformation of industry and agriculture in the south, an objective that should be "basically achieved" by 1980.

The plan's primary emphasis would be on the development of heavy industry, transportation, and communication; on the production of iron, coal, and hydroelectric power; and on the exploitation of offshore oil and gas resources. The plan also called for substantial increases in food production through improved irrigation, increased use of fertilizer, and the cultivation of subsidiary crops. To put more cropland under the plow, the regime planned to resettle substantial numbers of people from the densely settled Red River Delta to less-developed regions of the country, notably the Central Highland and along the Kampuchean frontier. In such areas, "agroindustrial centers" were to be set up at district level to become the foci of diversified economic development throughout the country. The ultimate goal was to move 10 million people over two decades. As a first stage, the regime planned to resettle several million people who had taken refuge in the cities of the south. They would be sent to "New Economic Areas" prepared in advance by government cadres in sparsely populated areas in Vietnam.

From the outset, these optimistic plans ran into difficulty. Foreign aid did not attain anticipated levels. Bad weather hampered efforts to increase food production. Mismanagement and corruption hindered efforts to make rational use of resources. Finally, the regime's attempt to regulate the private economy in the south foundered. Merchants hoarded goods to drive up prices. Farmers refused to sell rice at low official prices to state purchasing agencies. The resettlement program faltered as many settlers complained of poor conditions on the farms and returned to the cities.

By 1978 the economy was in a crisis, and the regime decided to accelerate the pace of socialization in order to strengthen its control over the southern economy. In March, Hanoi abruptly announced that all remaining private firms above the family level would be nationalized. Peasants were induced to enter low-level cooperative organizations, in line with the goal of ending private farming in the early 1980's. The results were disastrous. The announcement of nationalization provoked the flight of thousands of people from Vietnam, the majority of them resident Chinese. In the Mekong Delta, private farmers resisted efforts to herd them into collectives.

In the fall of 1979, with the economy in a shambles, Hanoi reversed course. The private urban economy was restored, and the pace of socialization in the countryside was slowed. To promote increased grain production, peasants in the north were permitted to lease land from their collective organizations in return for a mutually agreed-on grain quota. Excess production could be consumed privately or sold on the free market. Incentives were offered to encourage the cultivation of virgin lands and subsidiary crops.

The new pragmatic strategy had beneficial effect on production, and the economy gradually began to recover. In April 1982, government policy was reaffirmed at the party's Fifth National Congress, which also announced a new five-year plan (1981–1985) calling for emphasis on agriculture and consumer-goods production. Socialization of the south remained a top priority but would be delayed until later in the decade.

State of the Economy. The Vietnamese economy is gradually emerging from the collapse of the late 1970's. Grain production has increased significantly, and the country is now near self-sufficiency in food production, although at a low level of per capita consumption. Industrial production is growing, but progress is spotty. Certain key areas such as coal and hydroelectric power remain in serious difficulty, and hopes that substantial oil reserves would be found have yet to be realized. Foreign economic assistance remains inadequate, making the regime increasingly dependent on aid from the Soviet Union and its allies. In 1978, Vietnam joined the Soviet-dominated Council for Mutual Economic Assistance (CEMA).

Party hardliners are reported to be unhappy at the continued existence of capitalism in the south. Such elements are on the offensive and threaten to overturn the delicate balance between ideology and pragmatism within the party leadership.

6. History

According to Vietnamese legend, the ancestor of the Vietnamese people was Lac Long Quan (Lac Dragon Lord), a godlike figure who emerged from the sea to found the state of Vietnam and impart to it the benefits of civilization. Before returning to the sea, Lac Long Quan married Au Co, daughter of an invading conqueror from the north, and they parented the first in a series of kings who for more than 2,000 years ruled over Van Lang, in the Red River Delta. How much of this account reflects actual events is open to conjecture. However, the era of this semihistorical dynasty overlaps the rise of the Bronze Age Dong Son culture, which emerged in the Red River Delta as early as the 7th century B.C. The so-called Lac peoples of the region were rice farmers, and their rulers were a class of feudal lords. Their racial origins are obscure, but it is generally believed that they are ethnically related to Austroasiatic peoples who lived along the coast of southeastern China.

In the mid-3d century B.C. the kingdom of Van Lang was conquered by the armies of An Duong, an adventurer from southern China. An Duong then united the Lac peoples with inhabitants of the neighboring mountains into a kingdom called Au Lac. The new kingdom did not survive long, for its emergence had coincided with the expansion of the Chinese state of Ch'in, which in 221 B.C. completed the unification of China and founded the first centralized Chinese Empire. When the Ch'in Empire began to disintegrate after the death of its founder in 210 B.C., the southern provinces lapsed into anarchy. There a Ch'in general, Chao T'o (in Vietnamese, Trieu Da), established under his rule at Canton the independent kingdom of Nan Yüeh, meaning "southern Yüeh," in reference to the peoples who then inhabited coastal China south of the

DEANE DICKASON, FROM EWING GALLOWAY

The Purple Gate leads into the former Imperial Palace grounds in Hue, on the coast of central Vietnam.

Yangtze River. Chao T'o then conquered Au Lac and incorporated it into his kingdom, from whose Vietnamese name, Nam Viet, comes the name of modern Vietnam.

Chinese Rule. After the death of Chao T'o, Nam Viet rapidly declined, and in 111 B.C. the entire kingdom was conquered by the Han dynasty of China, successor of the Ch'in. So began a thousand years of Chinese rule over the Vietnamese people.

At first the Han ruled indirectly through the local landed aristocracy, who provided them with tribute. Eventually, however, Chinese governors strengthened their control over the area in order to increase tax revenues. The local lords, with their prestige and source of wealth threatened, began to resist. In 39 A.D., led by Trung Trac, widow of a local lord, and her sister Trung Nhi, they rose against Chinese rule and briefly restored Vietnamese independence. But the Han returned to the attack, and when the Trung sisters were abandoned by the local aristocracy, Chinese rule was restored.

After the Trung sisters' revolt, Chinese domination became more direct. Chinese officials were sent to fill top posts in the local administration and gradually merged with local aristocrats to form a new Sino-Vietnamese ruling class. During the next centuries, the Vietnamese were exposed to the full force of cultural Sinicization. Chinese political institutions were introduced, literary Chinese became the official language of administration, and the ruling class was educated in Confucian principles. Chinese social practices also were introduced, including the patriarchal family system, which served to reduce the traditionally prominent role of women in Vietnamese society.

The Han conquest of the Lac peoples in the Red River Delta was only one aspect of the process by which Chinese civilization had expanded southward from its origins in the Hwang Ho (Yellow River) valley over many centuries. In most of China south of the Yangtze River, the process of assimilation was successful, but in parts of southwestern China and especially in Vietnam, the local peoples successfully retained their cultural identity.

Owing either to the vitality of their culture or to their great distance from the center of the Chinese Empire, the Vietnamese persistently asserted local autonomy and launched periodic revolts against Chinese rule. Finally, in 939, Vietnamese rebels led by Ngo Quyen, son of a local magistrate, took advantage of the disintegration of the T'ang dynasty to set up an independent state. Its capital was Co Loa (just north of Hanoi), the site of the capital of Au Lac more than a thousand years earlier.

Dai Viet and the Southward Expansion. Ngo Quyen died in 944, and his kingdom soon collapsed. A period of instability ensued, lasting until the establishment of the first great Vietnamese dynasty, the Ly, in 1009. The new state, which was called Dai Viet (Greater Viet), with its capital at Hanoi, consolidated its position in the Red River Delta and secured its northern border by paying tribute to the new Sung dynasty of China.

In 1225 the Tran dynasty succeeded the Ly in Hanoi. A new threat from the north was presented by the Mongols, who completed their conquest of China in 1279. In 1285 and 1287 they attacked Dai Viet and occupied the capital. But Vietnamese forces, led by Tran Hung Dao, put up such vigorous resistance that the Mongols had to withdraw.

The expulsion of the Mongols from China in 1368 and their replacement by the native Ming dynasty did not end Dai Viet's northern security problem. In 1407 the Ming invaded on pretext of supporting the Tran ruler against a usurper. In its weakened condition, Dai Viet succumbed to Chinese rule. Once again, however, resistance rose rapidly, and at last in 1427 the rebel Le Loi expelled the Chinese. In 1428 he formed the new Le dynasty.

The Le presided over the southward expansion of the Vietnamese state and people. Since the restoration of independence in the 10th century, Vietnam had periodically clashed with the state of Champa along the coast to the south. On occasion Cham armies even sacked the Vietnamese capital.

Under the Le dynasty the Vietnamese assumed the offensive and in 1471 shattered the Cham state. After annexing most of Champa, they continued to advance southward, gradually absorbing the petty principalities that had been formed out of the remainder of Cham territory. The Vietnamese completed their expansion by the mid-18th century, having wrested the lower Mekong Delta from Kampuchea.

The Traditional Vietnamese State. The Ly dynasty, although breaking away from Chinese rule, had retained many of the institutions introduced by the Chinese. But the influence of Confucian advisers at court was diluted by the presence of Buddhist and Taoist monks and of members of the great feudal families who dominated the bureaucracy and restricted the power of the monarch.

Under the Tran and then the Le, the importance of Confucian institutions and practices increased. The influence of Buddhist and Taoist advisers declined at court. Commoners were permitted for the first time to take the civil-service examinations, thus limiting the power of the aristocracy. Large landed estates were confiscated and distributed to a new class of free landholding farmers loyal to the monarchy. The Le also attempted to rationalize the legal system through the creation of the Hong Duc Code during the reign (1460–1497) of Le Thanh Tong, the greatest of the dynasty's rulers. The new legal system served to bring Vietnamese social institutions closer in some respects to the Chinese model. But indigenous traditions were not entirely neglected, and the historically prominent role of Vietnamese women in the family was given legal expression in the new regulations.

Division and Reunification. Under the Le, then, a vigorous assertion of the power of the centralized state took place. But power and sophistication also led to decay. Confucian ideals often were not carried out in practice and degenerated into ritualism, pedantry, and arrogance. Weak rulers were unable to prevent the resurgence of noble families to power.

In 1527, Gen. Mac Dang Dung deposed the Le ruler and set up his own dynasty, touching off a long civil war to restore the legitimate ruling line. After 1592, when the country was reunited, the Trinh family served as viceroys in the north for effete Le rulers, while the Nguyen family exercised control south of the Red River Delta, though at first paying nominal allegiance to the throne. About 1620 the Nguyen refused obedience to Hanoi, and fighting broke out with the Trinh. This second civil war was inconclusive, ending in a truce reached in 1673.

The defacto division of Vietnam between the Trinh and Nguyen families lasted another century. In the 1770's the three Tay Son brothers (so called for their home district) led a popular revolt against both houses. In 1777 they deposed the Nguyen, and in 1786 they conquered the Trinh. Two years later the eldest brother proclaimed himself emperor over both north and south, but he died after a short reign. A surviving Nguyen prince continued the war until his final victory and the establishment of a new dynasty over the entire country in 1802.

Western Penetration and the French Conquest. Vietnam's period of weakness and division coincided with the appearance of a powerful new force in Southeast Asia. In 1511 a Portuguese fleet landed at Malacca (Melaka) on the west coast of the Malay Peninsula. In 1535 the Portuguese established a trading post (also called a factory) at Fai Fo, near the present Da Nang. They were followed in the 17th century by Dutch, English, and finally French traders.

The first stable mission in Vietnam was founded by Portuguese and Italian Jesuits in 1615 at Fai Fo. But the "apostle of Vietnam" was a French Jesuit, Alexandre de Rhodes, who arrived in 1624 and within three years had baptized more than 6,500 adults. The work of Catholic missionaries, especially those of the Paris Society of Foreign Missions, founded in 1659, was so successful that the Vietnamese authorities became alarmed. Persecutions began, and in 1750 nearly all the missionaries were expelled. By that time most Western factories were long closed, for Vietnam had relatively little to offer foreign traders.

Christian interests in France continued to seek official support for their activities from their government. The Tay Son rebellion offered an opportunity. When Nguyen Anh, a scion of the Nguyen house in the south, fled in the wake of the Tay Son conquest, he made the acquaintance of Pierre Pigneau de Behaine, a French bishop stationed on Ha Tien island in the Gulf of Thailand. Hoping to use his friendship with the young prince to restore French Catholic influence in Vietnam, Pigneau sought financial support from the court at Versailles for a military mission to restore the Nguyen to power. A treaty was signed in 1787 calling for French aid in return for trade and missionary privileges. Although the plan aborted, Pigneau on his own initiative helped form a fleet that assisted Nguyen Anh in overthrowing the Tay Son. In 1802, Nguyen Anh set up the Nguyen dynasty at Hue with himself as Emperor Gia Long.

Pigneau's hope that his efforts would lead to a restoration of French influence in Vietnam was misplaced. Though grateful to his benefactor, who had died in 1799, Gia Long was not particularly receptive to Western influence and limited the French to a small presence in his realm. His successors were even more suspicious of foreign influence and sought to eliminate it by driving all French advisers and European missionaries out of the country. In 1857, provoked by pressure from Catholic and commercial interests in France, the government of Emperor Napoleon III decided to use force in order to restore French influence in Vietnam. After an unsuccessful naval assault at Da Nang, a French fleet attacked in the south and defeated the imperial forces. In 1862 the court ceded three provinces in the Mekong Delta to the French. In 1867 the French seized the remainder of the delta.

In the early 1880's the French resumed their advance, attacking the Red River delta in 1882 and Hue the following year. In 1883 the intimidated court assigned France a protectorate over the north and central parts of the country.

Policies and Impact of the French. By the end of the century, the French had brought some order to their "balcony on the Pacific." Vietnam had been divided into the protectorates of Tonkin (in the north) and Annam (in the center) and the colony of Cochin China (in the south). In 1887 these were combined with a protectorate established in 1863 over Kampuchea to form the Indochinese Union, run by a governor-general appointed from Paris. In 1893 the French established a protectorate over Laos and added that country to the union.

In Cochin China, French rule was direct. Elsewhere, French administrators technically served as advisers to the local bureaucracies and royal courts. In actuality, their authority was virtually supreme, and the Vietnamese emperor became a mere figurehead.

With the colonial administration in place, the French began to exploit the area's natural resources. The swampy lands of the Mekong Delta were drained, and an irrigation system was constructed to permit an expansion of rice production in the south. Rubber seedlings imported from Brazil were planted in the rich *terre-rouge* (red-earth) lands along the Kampuchea border. Tea and other cash crops were grown in the sparsely populated Central Highlands, and coal mines were opened in Tonkin.

Apologists for the colonial regime argued that the French presence was beneficial to the local populace. Roads and bridges were built, and rail lines were gradually extended throughout the country. A small modern manufacturing and commercial sector began to appear in the big cities. Rice production increased with the opening of the new lands in the south. But the impact of such developments on the mass of the population was uneven. The modern sector was dominated by colonial interests or the resident Chinese, while manufacturing was hindered by French policies discouraging the development of local products that might compete with imports from France. The increase in grain production had little effect on the rural standard of living, for much of the land was held by absentee landowners who earmarked the rice for export. Peasants were forced into tenancy, or into coal mines or rubber plantations where the pay was low and working conditions miserable.

The colonial impact on political institutions was equally ambivalent. Publicists for the colonial regime sometimes maintained that France had a "civilizing mission" to transform Vietnam into an "advanced" society on the Western model. In practice, the colonial administration was slow to introduce Western political institutions. In Cochin China a colonial council was established, but it was dominated by colonial interests. In the first quarter of the 20th century, legislative assemblies were set up in Annam and Tonkin, but the franchise was limited and the assemblies had solely advisory functions.

This ambiguity was fully reflected in the official attitude toward culture and education. At first, ambitious officials attempted to abolish traditional educational institutions, at least in Cochin China. In the north and the center, the civil-service examinations were abandoned, and the use of the Chinese written language was discouraged. Eventually, however, the regime saw the political benefits of promoting traditional values, and dropped its efforts to Westernize the mass of the population.

The Rise of Nationalism. Vietnam has a well-deserved historical reputation for fiercely protecting its independence. Yet the initial resistance to the French conquest was ineffective, for the emperor was weak and his court was divided over how to respond to French power. Local officials and military commanders in the countryside offered some resistance, but it lacked centralized direction and collapsed after the death of the most renowned leader, Phan Dinh Phung, in 1895.

The first signs of a modern nationalist movement appeared during the first decade of the 20th century, when members of the traditional scholar-gentry, led by Phan Boi Chau, set up the Association for the Modernization of Vietnam to overthrow French rule and establish a modern state based on a constitutional monarchy. The society had its headquarters in Japan, where dedicated young patriots were trained and then sent back to Vietnam to provoke a mass uprising.

While Chau was building up his movement in Japan, others preferred reformist methods. They tried to persuade France to live up to its self-proclaimed civilizing mission and reform Vietnamese society from within. In 1906 progressive elements set up a new institution called the Hanoi Free School to promote Western learning. It was soon closed by the authorities, who feared its members were inciting rebellion.

Chau's group had little more success. When his initial efforts to overthrow the colonial regime by force made short headway, he turned to China, where Sun Yat-sen's revolutionary movement had overturned the Manchu dynasty in 1911. To win Sun's approval, Chau reorganized his own movement along republican lines. But several revolts failed, and after Chau's arrest in China in 1914, his movement declined.

Following World War I, a new generation of nationalists began to appear among the emerging middle class in Saigon, where small political factions dedicated to the realization of national independence were formed in the early 1920's. This radical agitation subsided after 1926 when several of its leaders were arrested. But discontent was on the rise throughout the country, and in 1927 the Vietnamese Nationalist party (popularly known as the VNQDD) was organized in the north. Across the border in China, the first avowedly Marxist revolutionary organization was created among Vietnamese exiles by Ho Chi Minh, a Vietnamese patriot and convert to Leninism, who had been sent by the Comintern to create a Communist organization in Vietnam.

The coming of the Great Depression added to the unrest. Labor strikes, fueled by rising unemployment, increased. High taxes, mandarin corruption, and the collapse of the price of rice led to rising peasant unrest. An attempt by the VNQDD to incite a revolt among soldiers at army garrisons in Tonkin was put down in February 1930, and most of the party's leaders were executed. But agitation continued, and during the summer and fall a major revolt broke out among peasants and factory workers in the central provinces of Nghe An and Ha Tinh. Although the revolt was based on genuine grievances, it was incited in part by local agitators from the Indochinese Communist party (ICP), which had been formed in February. The revolt was suppressed with brutal efficiency, and the Communist apparatus was virtually wiped out.

For the next several years, nationalist activity was minimal, as anticolonial groups were reduced to a struggle for sheer survival. Only after 1935 did it begin to revive, stimulated in part by the ascendancy of the Left in France under the Popular Front (1936–1938). Colonial policy became more conciliatory, and nationalist organizations, including the ICP, were tacitly permitted to engage in peaceful activities. The Communists took advantage of the tolerant atmosphere and attempted to strengthen their popular base among the urban working and middle classes and among the peasantry. By the end of the decade, the ICP had become the most active force in the Vietnamese anticolonial movement.

World War II and the War of Independence. After the collapse of the Popular Front, the colonial regime in Indochina cracked down on the nationalist groups. In September 1940, France, at the nadir of its fortunes in World War II and now under heavy pressure from Japan, granted Tokyo extensive military and economic concessions in Indochina. In return, the French colonial regime was allowed to maintain the semblance of its authority.

In the hope that the road to independence ran through Tokyo, some nationalist groups began to cooperate with the Japanese. Others retreated to China, which was at war with Japan, and sought Chinese assistance. In May 1941 the ICP attempted to unite all anti-Japanese groups in the area behind its own leadership in a broad united front called the Vietminh, or League for the Independence of Vietnam. For the next four years, party activists developed the political base of the front. Meanwhile, Japan had entered World War II, and Vietminh guerrilla forces had carved out a liberation zone in the mountains north of Hanoi. There they prepared for an uprising to be launched against Japanese and French forces at the end of the war. The ICP's task was made easier in March 1945, when Japanese authorities deposed the French administration and took power behind a puppet Vietnamese administration under Emperor Bao Dai.

The Vietminh insurrection was launched in August 1945 shortly after Japan's surrender and the end of World War II. Japanese resistance to the Vietminh was light, and most of Tonkin and Annam were occupied in a few days. On September 2, the Democratic Republic of Vietnam (DRV) was established in Hanoi with Ho Chi Minh as president. The Vietminh were less successful in the south, where the ICP encountered stiffer competition from other nationalist groups and the new religious sects and were forced to share power in a Committee of the South. In October, French military forces drove the Vietminh and their allies out of Saigon into the countryside, where they organized a guerrilla resistance.

During the fall of 1945 the DRV in Hanoi attempted to win popular support by adopting a moderate but progressive program and including rival parties such as the VNQDD in the cabinet. In March 1946, delicate negotiations with a French representative resulted in a preliminary agreement calling for the creation of a Vietnamese "free state" within the French Union. A plebiscite would be held in Cochin China to allow the population there to determine its own future. But formal negotiations held near Paris in July collapsed. Ho Chi Minh signed a *modus vivendi,* calling for renewed peace talks early in 1947, but tension increased during the autumn as clashes took place between Vietminh forces and French units newly arrived in the north. On Dec. 19, 1946, the Vietminh launched a surprise attack on French installations in the Hanoi area but afterward withdrew to prepared positions in the mountains.

For the next several years, both sides exercised the military option. At first the French resisted compromise and sought a military victory. That goal was elusive, however, and in 1949, faced with a deteriorating military situation in Vietnam and rising public opposition to the war at home, France created the autonomous Associated State of Vietnam under Bao Dai to fight alongside France. In 1950, despite evidence that many nationalists viewed the new government as a French puppet, the United States reluctantly agreed to provide it with military and economic assistance in the struggle against the Vietminh.

Ho Chi Minh gained Vietnamese independence from France, but died before national reunification in 1976.

For their part, ICP leaders hoped that aid from the newly victorious Communist government in China would enable them to achieve victory on the battlefield, but a Vietminh offensive in the Red River Delta failed to achieve its objectives. After 1951, ICP strategy concentrated on harassing French forces in Indochina while encouraging antiwar sentiment in France. In late 1953 this strategy paid off when the French agreed to attend peace talks in Geneva with the other Great Powers and the Indochinese governments concerned.

Public support for the war in France, already low, was further undermined by the fall of the military outpost of Dien Bien Phu in early May, on the very eve of the conference. In July the French and Vietminh military commands signed an agreement calling for an armistice and the temporary division of Vietnam near the 17th parallel, with Vietminh forces to be regrouped north of the line and French Union forces south of it. An unsigned protocol specified that general elections were to be held in 1956, for the understood though not directly stated purpose of creating a unified national government.

The Two Vietnams. The elections were not destined to take place. After the Geneva agreements, the U.S.-supported government of the Associated State of Vietnam administered the south from Saigon under the patriot Ngo Dinh Diem,

UPI PHOTO BY KYOICHI SAWADA

Faces reflecting war's misery: a mother and her children struggle across a river to escape the fighting in 1969.

who had been appointed premier by head of state Bao Dai before the end of the conference. Diem, a Catholic and rigid anti-Communist, refused to consult with the DRV, which had been reestablished in Hanoi.

The DRV protested Diem's thwarting of national elections, which it expected the Communists to win, but took no immediate action. During its first years in power the ICP—renamed the Vietnam Workers' party (VWP)—concentrated on consolidating its rule in the north and promoting economic reconstruction. To broaden its popular base, the regime adopted moderate social and economic policies, including a land-reform program that destroyed the landlord class and distributed holdings to poor and landless peasants. Major industries were nationalized, but a small private sector was tolerated. In 1958 the party began the transformation to socialism, urging the peasants into small cooperative organizations and announcing plans to initiate socialist industrialization.

In the meantime, Ngo Dinh Diem attempted to strengthen his position in the south. In 1955, in accordance with the outcome of a popular referendum, he proclaimed a republic with himself as the president. The following year a constitution was promulgated for the Republic of Vietnam. Diem considered the Communists the primary threat to his regime and energetically sought to suppress the small Vietminh apparatus that they had left to protect their interests in the south. But Diem's autocratic style, his alleged favoritism toward his fellow Catholics, and his failure to attack the sources of rural poverty alienated broad sections of southern society. By 1959, internal dissent was growing, and the party leadership in Hanoi adopted a new policy of revolutionary struggle to overthrow Diem. The symbolic leadership of the movement was a broad coalition entitled the National Front for the Liberation of South Vietnam (NLF), created in 1960. To provide maximum appeal to the diverse groups opposed to the Saigon regime, Hanoi's involvement in the front was disguised and the organization adopted a moderate program. Behind the scenes, however, the front was under the firm control of the VWP.

Aided by Diem's mistakes, NLF insurgency grew rapidly in the early 1960's, and the revolutionary armed forces—popularly known as the Vietcong—built up base areas in several provinces. As Diem became increasingly isolated from his people, military leaders in the south, with U.S. approval, overthrew his regime in 1963. But the new military government was weak and faction-ridden, and by late 1964, South Vietnam was in virtual chaos. The Johnson administration, fearing a total collapse of the Saigon regime, began to deploy U.S. combat forces in the south. Behind the shield of an increasing U.S. military presence, a new military leadership under Generals Nguyen Cao Ky and Nguyen Van Thieu seized power in June 1965. In 1967, under pressure from Washington, their government promulgated a new constitution and held elections that placed Thieu in the presidency. Social and economic reforms, including an extensive land-reform program, were carried out to rally support behind the government.

The Johnson administration had hoped that a display of U.S. might would demonstrate American resolve and persuade the Communists that a continuation of the insurgency in the south was fruitless. But Hanoi, with growing assistance from the Soviet Union, China, and other socialist countries, put the DRV on a war footing and began to infiltrate units of the North Vietnamese army into the south, where they played an increasing role in the fighting.

In early 1968 the Communists launched the Tet Offensive, a major series of attacks throughout South Vietnam, in an effort to destabilize the Saigon regime and provoke opposition to the war in the United States. Communist casualties were high, prompting some observers to declare the offensive a failure. But Hanoi had achieved at least one of its objectives, for the offensive increased antiwar sentiment in the United States and persuaded President Johnson to halt further escalation of U.S. troop levels in South Vietnam and seek a negotiated settlement of the war.

The opening of peace talks in Paris in May 1968 did not lead to an immediate end of the war, for neither side was yet willing to make major concessions. But the level of fighting on the battlefield declined as the Nixon administration, beginning in 1969, gradually withdrew U.S. troops, while simultaneously attempting to strengthen the capacity of South Vietnamese forces to defend themselves. In January 1973 the Paris Agreement brought the war temporarily to an end. The United States withdrew its remaining military forces. In return, Hanoi accepted the continued existence of the Theiu regime in Saigon. The agreement made no reference to the North Vietnamese troops, then numbering over 150,000, who remained in Communist-held areas of the south.

The Paris Agreement called for the creation of a tripartite National Council for Reconciliation and Concord, including supporters of the NLF, supporters of the Saigon regime, and neutralists. The council would confer on the formation of a government of national union in the south. But negotiations rapidly broke down, and clashes between government and revolutionary forces took place with increasing frequency in rural areas. In early 1975, Hanoi returned to the military option, launching a major offensive in the Central Highlands. Caught by surprise, the Thieu regime reacted slowly, and when it became clear that U.S. aid would be minimal, resistance rapidly collapsed. North Vietnamese military units entered Saigon on the last day of April. The long war was finally over.

The Socialist Republic of Vietnam. The party leadership in Hanoi had little time to savor the fruits of victory, for intimidating challenges lay ahead. The war-torn economy had to be revived and millions of refugees resettled from cities into rural areas. The capitalist economy in the south had to be abolished and the two Vietnams integrated into a single socialist state.

On the political scene, Hanoi moved with dispatch. Elections for a National Assembly representing both zones took place in April 1976. In July a unified Socialist Republic of Vietnam, representing a nation of 50 million people, was formally inaugurated with its capital at Hanoi.

In the economic sphere the regime was more cautious. Recognizing that the immediate need was to increase the productive capacity of the economy, Hanoi adopted a moderate policy in the south. The capitalist sector was left essentially intact, and few major industries and business firms were nationalized. In late 1976, however, the regime announced that the south would begin the transition to socialism at the end of the decade. Meanwhile, an ambitious five-year plan would inaugurate rapid industrial development.

The regime's plans quickly encountered difficulty. Faulty management hindered the recovery of the urban economy. Agricultural productivity suffered from bad weather and the refusal of farmers to sell grain at low official prices. Foreign aid did not reach anticipated levels. In 1978 the regime nationalized all industry and commerce above the family level in an effort to strengthen its control over the urban economy. The policy backfired, however, provoking the flight of thousands of refugees to China or to other countries in Southeast Asia. In 1979 the regime changed course, relaxing restrictions on private commercial activity and offering incentives to increase production.

The economic crisis coincided wih rising tensions in foreign affairs. The new Communist government in Kampuchea, which had come to power with Hanoi's assistance, suspected that Vietnam intended to dominate all of Indochina. Border clashes took place along their mutual frontier. In December 1978, after negotiations had failed, Vietnam launched an invasion that overthrew the Pol Pot regime and established a pro-Hanoi government in Phnom Penh.

China had assisted the DRV in its struggle for national reunification but was increasingly concerned at rising Vietnamese power in Southeast Asia, as well as Hanoi's growing intimacy with the Soviet Union. In mid-1978, China cut off its aid projects in the SRV. Hanoi retaliated by joining the Soviet-dominated Council for Mutual Economic Assistance and signing a treaty of alliance with Moscow. The following February, China launched a brief offensive across the Vietnamese border, contending that Hanoi had to be punished for its aggression in Kampuchea. Chinese forces were soon withdrawn, but Peking continued to assist Pol Pot's guerrillas, forcing

UPI PHOTO

A Woman's Day parade honors Trung Trac and Trung Nhi, sisters who led a revolt against Chinese rule in 39 A.D.

Vietnam to maintain over 150,000 troops in Kampuchea. Non-Communist Kampuchean forces fighting the pro-Hanoi government were supported by other Southeast Asian countries and the United States. Vietnam thus became isolated from many of its neighbors and more dependent on the Soviet Union.

Signs of economic revival, stimulated by the pragmatic policies adopted in 1979, were short-lived. In the south, widespread hostility to government policies persisted. Vietnam sought foreign investment to revitalize its economy but was unable to reverse deterioration of its business climate or overcome U.S. opposition to investment. Nguyen Van Linh, appointed head of Vietnam's Communist party in late 1986, made clear his intention to deal with Vietnam's overwhelming economic problems by using some capitalist economic strategies and by ending the drain on Vietnam's resources imposed by occupation of Kampuchea.

WILLIAM J. DUIKER*
Author of "Vietnam: Nation in Revolution"

Bibliography

Buttinger, Joseph, *The Smaller Dragon: A Political History of Vietnam*, 2d ed. (Westview Press 1986).
Duiker, William J., *Vietnam: Nation in Revolution* (Westview Press 1983).
Duiker, William, *Vietnam Since the Fall of Saigon*, 2d ed. (Ohio Univ. Press 1985).
Harrison, James Pinckney, *The Endless War: Fifty Years of Struggle in Vietnam* (Free Press 1982).
Hodgkin, Thomas, *Vietnam: The Revolutionary Path* (St. Martin's Press 1981).
Karnow, Stanley, *Vietnam: A History* (Viking 1983).
Sully, François, ed., *We the Vietnamese* (Praeger 1971).
Taylor, Keith Weller, *The Birth of Vietnam* (Univ. of Calif. Press 1983).
Thrift, Nigel, and Forbes, Dean, *The Price of War: Urbanization in Vietnam 1954–1985* (Allen & Unwin 1986).

UPI

U.S. Marines came under heavy fire in Hue during the Tet offensive launched by Communist forces in 1968.

VIETNAM WAR, vē-et-näm′. The Vietnam War—also called the Indochina War or Second Indochina War—may be said to have started in 1957 when Communist-led rebels began mounting terrorist attacks against the government of the Republic of Vietnam (South Vietnam). The rebel forces, commonly called the Vietcong, were later aided by troops of the Democratic Republic of Vietnam (North Vietnam). American combat personnel were formally committed to the defense of the South in 1965.

An agreement calling for a ceasefire was signed in January 1973, and by March the few remaining U.S. military personnel in Vietnam were withdrawn. However, the war between the two Vietnamese sides persisted inconclusively for two additional years before South Vietnamese resistance suddenly and unexpectedly collapsed. Saigon, the capital of South Vietnam, fell to the Communists on April 30, 1975.

1. Political Aspects of the War

The causes of the conflict can be traced back to the Indochina War of 1946–1954. After Japan's defeat in World War II, the French had returned to Indochina as colonial administrators but were challenged by the Vietminh, Communist-led Vietnamese nationalists who had proclaimed an independent government in 1945. France, in an attempt to seem to give Indochina independence while retaining control there, granted nominal sovereignty to Vietnam, Cambodia, and Laos as "associated states" of the French Union in 1949. The following year the United States recognized the three "associated states" and began supplying them with economic and military aid, although it was channeled through France. By 1954, the United States was furnishing 78% of the cost of the French war effort. In the spring of 1954, when the French were besieged at Dien Bien Phu, the administration of President Dwight D. Eisenhower gave serious consideration to providing them with air and even ground support.

Washington expected little of Ngo Dinh Diem, who assumed leadership in French-controlled Vietnam during the 1954 armistice negotiations that ended the war. After the Geneva Agreement of that year had temporarily divided Vietnam into northern and southern parts, Diem headed the government of South Vietnam in Saigon, while Ho Chi Minh presided over the Communist-dominated government of the North at Hanoi. The Geneva Agreement had provided for elections to be held in 1956 to reunify Vietnam, and the Communists had anticipated that they would win because of their elaborate political organization. For this reason Diem, a determined anti-Communist, blocked the elections—with the backing of the U.S. government. The Communists, unable to unify and dominate Vietnam through elections, then returned to military means of doing so.

First Years of the War. The terrorist incidents that began in 1957 intensified over the next two years. Initially the rebels were Communists left behind in the South after 1954, but they were soon reinforced by others who had moved to the North in accord with the Geneva Agreement. By 1964 the Vietcong rebels had been joined by regular North Vietnamese army units.

The objective of the Vietnamese Communists remained constant throughout the war: the overthrow of the non-Communist Saigon government and its replacement with a regime that would agree to ultimate unification with the Hanoi government. The tactics of North Vietnam, however, varied in response to the reaction its activities provoked on the part of the South and, more important, the United States. The U. S. buildup of South Vietnam's armed forces and American combat involvement from 1965 forced the Communists to fight a much larger, more conventional, and longer war than they had expected in the late 1950's.

The United States came to play a major role in the Vietnamese power struggle after Geneva because it feared that the rest of Southeast Asia would fall to communism if Ho Chi Minh prevailed in South Vietnam. In the late 1950's, and even into the 1960's, Washington tended to see Communist nations as constituting a politico-military monolith. Thus American support of the Diem government after 1954 was consistent with the U. S. strategy of containing communism throughout the world.

President Eisenhower had pledged in 1954 to assist the Diem government in "developing and maintaining a strong, viable state capable of resisting attempted subversion or aggression through military means." He sent several hundred military advisers to South Vietnam. The mounting Communist assault against the Diem government and Saigon's inability to deal satisfactorily with this threat prompted President John F. Kennedy to increase U. S. military advisory personnel to 16,000 by the time of his assassination in November 1963. Some of these men saw limited combat service.

Earlier in November 1963, Diem was overthrown and killed. The U. S. government had clearly despaired of him, and was aware of the plot to remove him. His overthrow increased the likelihood of direct U. S. intervention in the war, however, for a series of incompetent administrations rapidly followed one another in Saigon, and the military effort against the Communists suffered from the political preoccupation of South Vietnam's leaders.

The Tonkin Gulf Resolution, passed by the U. S. Congress in August 1964 after two naval incidents involving U. S. and North Vietnamese craft, authorized President Lyndon B. Johnson to "repel any armed attack against the forces of the United States and to prevent further aggression." The question was later raised in Congress and elsewhere as to whether the administration had misrepresented aspects of the Tonkin Gulf incidents, and subsequently it was established that the resolution had been drafted in advance of the crisis. After serving as the main legal basis for major U. S. escalation of the undeclared war, the Tonkin Gulf Resolution was repealed in 1970.

Failure of Escalation. Even as late as 1965, when the United States began to step up its participation in the war, Vietnam itself was not the primary consideration in Washington's Southeast Asian policy. What moved the Johnson administration to act was its desire to reinforce the credibility of the United States as an ally.

During the Johnson years the number of U. S. forces in Vietnam increased from 16,000 to more than half a million, although at the end of 1964 there were still only 23,000. The war also escalated in other ways: sustained U. S. bombing of North Vietnam began in early 1965; the annual cost of the war increased from $5.8 billion to $28.8 billion between 1966 and 1969; and

GILLES CARON—PIX

HELICOPTERS, widely used in the Vietnam War, carry troops on combat missions of all types.

adjacent Laos, through which ran the system of Communist supply routes known as the Ho Chi Minh Trail, was drawn into the Vietnam War as an increasingly important theater of conflict.

Realizing the value of international support for the U. S. war effort, President Johnson after 1965 sought to increase the participation of other nations in the fighting. As a result, South Koreans, Thais, Australians, Filipinos, and New Zealanders took part in the conflict.

President Johnson had ordered the bombing of North Vietnam in order to force the Communists to negotiate a settlement of the war. At various times he temporarily halted these attacks in hope of achieving the same result, but the Vietnamese Communists repeatedly expressed their unwillingness to negotiate before the withdrawal of U. S. and other foreign forces. Although the parties involved probably preferred a negotiated settlement to a prolongation of the war, none of them was willing to make sufficient concessions

The failure of President Johnson's policies to induce the Communists to negotiate, plus mounting domestic opposition to the war, prompted him on March 31, 1968, to order a partial halt of the bombing of North Vietnam. Direct talks between the United States and North Vietnam began in May in Paris. Following the complete cessation of the bombing of North Vietnam, announced by President Johnson on Oct. 31, 1968, the Paris talks were enlarged to include South Vietnam and the Communists' political orga-

CHAU VAN NAM, UPI

SOUTH VIETNAMESE troops in armored personnel carriers patrol flooded rice paddies in Chaudoc province near Saigon.

nization in the South, the National Liberation Front (NFL).

"Vietnamization." In the first years of the 1970's, although the Paris negotiations had made no apparent progress toward a political settlement of the war, the conflict seemed to be drawing to a close—at least with respect to U. S. ground participation. From a peak of 543,400 U. S. servicemen in Vietnam in April 1969, President Richard M. Nixon, who had taken office in January, reduced the U. S. military presence in Vietnam to 184,000 by December 1971. By mid-1971 the United States had almost completely ended its ground combat role in South Vietnam, major responsibility for ground defense having been taken over by the South Vietnamese themselves. This "Vietnamization" of the war had been preceded by a massive buildup of South Vietnam's armed forces, which numbered more than 1 million in 1971.

"Ceasefire." The Paris peace talks were broken off in March 1972 by the United States, which apparently believed that the Communists were not negotiating sincerely. In response to the major Communist offensive that followed, President Nixon ordered the mining of Haiphong and six other North Vietnamese harbors. Negotiations in Paris resumed in July, but after Secretary of State Henry Kissinger announced in mid-December that the talks had not been successful, the United States resumed air attacks against North Vietnam. The raids lasted 11 days and may have hastened the agreement that was finally signed on Jan. 27, 1973.

There were four main points to the pact: withdrawal of all U. S. forces from South Vietnam; release of all prisoners of war; an international 1,160-man peacekeeping force; and recognition of the right of the South Vietnamese people to determine their own future. North Vietnam was not required to withdraw its troops from the South, but was not to make replacements. The last American forces departed in March.

Despite the ceasefire and U. S. troop withdrawal, the fighting did not stop. More than 50,000 Vietnamese were killed in battle in the first year after the truce agreement. The taking of Phuoc Long province near the Cambodian border in January 1975 set the stage for the final Communist offensive, which began in March with an attack on Ban Me Thuot in the Central Highlands. South Vietnamese President Nguyen Van Thieu ordered the evacuation of the Highlands, and Saigon's military forces fell apart. The Communists subsequently moved with comparative ease to the outskirts of Saigon, capturing the city on April 30 without a major battle. Most of the top anti-Communist leaders had left with the last departing American civilians. The Vietnam War was over.

Costs of the War. By the time of their complete withdrawal in 1973, U. S. forces had participated in the Vietnam conflict longer than in any other war. A total of 57,605 Americans lost their lives in combat, compared with 33,629 in the Korean War (1950–1953). An additional 303,700 U.S. military personnel were wounded in battle. The United States spent an officially acknowledged $165 billion on the Vietnam War, as against $18 billion for the Korean conflict. Only in World War II were direct U.S. military expenditures higher.

Vietnamese losses were much greater than those suffered by the United States. The dead and wounded of the South Vietnamese military numbered respectively 220,357 and 499,000. North Vietnamese and Vietcong battlefield fatalities are difficult to estimate but were given by the United States as 444,000. The number of wounded Communist combatants was unknown. Hundreds of thousands of civilians were killed in Vietnam during the war, many by the American bombing of the North. About half of the South's population had become refugees by the war's end in April 1975.

The war shattered the economies of both parts of Vietnam. Agricultural production declined, and dependence on imports rose dramatically. One fifth of South Vietnam's extensive forest cover was sprayed with herbicides, and a substantial portion of the sprayed area was ruined. Chemical herbicides probably destroyed enough food for 600,000 persons for a year in South Vietnam and enough timber to meet the country's needs for 30 years. South Vietnam's $696 million trade deficit in 1974 indicated in part why prices had risen some 800% since 1963.

On the plus side, both halves of Vietnam were significantly modernized as a direct result of the war. New skills were introduced, and old ways of thinking and behaving were probably abandoned forever. Many people showed unaccustomed initiative when thrust into new roles on the battlefield and in the economic, administrative, and political spheres.

Wider Effects of the War. The period after the combat commitment of U. S. forces in Vietnam in 1965 saw the increasing involvement of two adjacent countries, Laos and Cambodia. From the mid-1960's, the Vietnamese Communists made major use of the territory of these neutrals, both for supply routes and for troop sanctuaries.

Prior to the overthrow of Prince Norodom Sihanouk in Cambodia in March 1970, that land had not been a major battleground. The U. S.–South Vietnamese military intervention of April–June 1970 had the unintended effect of exposing larger portions of the country to a Vietnamese Communist military presence. The Hanoi-directed forces apparently had no immediate designs on Cambodia, but they were quickly supplanted as the major antigovernment military force there by the Khmer Rouge—insurgent Cambodian Communists. The United States stepped up its aid to the weak Lon Nol regime, but to no lasting avail. After five years of increasingly intense fighting, the Cambodian capital, Phnom Penh, fell to the Khmer Rouge on April 17, 1975, just 13 days before the Communist takeover of Saigon.

The United States increased its air attacks against the Communist supply routes in Laos in 1968 and gave more aid to the anti-Communist Souvanna Phouma government. But it also used its influence to support a Laotian political settlement, which was reached in February 1973, a month after the Paris Vietnam agreement. Fighting did not resume on a significant scale, but the Communist Pathet Lao effectively took control of the government by peaceful means in May 1975 after the end of the Vietnam War. This change reflected the demoralization of the anti-Communists in Laos because of events in both Vietnam and Cambodia.

During the years of the Vietnam War, other important developments took place in Southeast Asia. Malaysia withstood guerrilla attacks launched from Indonesia, and subsequently Indonesian anti-Communists reversed their country's drift toward communism, meanwhile restoring much of its economic vitality. The economies of Singapore, Malaysia, and Thailand prospered, and inaugural moves were made on behalf of regional cooperation. Defenders of U. S. policies claimed that American participation in the Vietnam War had bought time for such developments. Critics, however, pointed to the deteriorating situations in Laos and Cambodia and a heightened threat to neighboring Thailand.

The "Nixon Doctrine," unveiled in July 1969, was a direct outgrowth of American intervention in the Vietnam War. It significantly revised U. S. policy, calling on Asian countries to be more "self-reliant" and disavowing a future American willingness to become involved in a combat capacity in a ground war between rival factions in a country. The new policy represented a change in the strategy, if not the values, that had prompted large-scale U. S. combat participation in the war.

The balance of power that existed in Southeast Asia following the fall of South Vietnam reflected both the ascendancy of the Nixon Doctrine—which survived Nixon's resignation—and widespread doubts about the credibility of the United States as an ally. The Americans, not the South Vietnamese, had held off the Communists for a decade. But when the Americans left, the South Vietnamese faltered—and the Communists won the war. Thailand, a longtime U. S. ally, quickly sought reconciliation with Hanoi, despite the recent use of Thai bases for American bombing attacks against North Vietnam. Another ally, the Philippines, displayed uneasiness about U. S. bases on its soil, while South Korea indicated its fear that the Americans would not come to its aid in the event of renewed Communist aggression.

After the fall of Vietnam, although the United States had suffered 46,000 combat deaths and had spent $139 billion, the Americans were perceived in most of the rest of Asia as an insufficiently reliable military and political partner. Ironically, the U. S. image as a credible ally might have been brighter in 1975, when the war ended, if Washington had never made the major effort it did in defense of South Vietnam.

RICHARD BUTWELL, *Author of "Southeast Asia: A Political Introduction"*

2. Military Aspects of the War

At the time of the Geneva Agreement in mid-1954, the United States had 342 military personnel in Indochina, mainly in Saigon, constituting the Military Assistance Advisory Group (MAAG), Indochina. From mid-1950, MAAG had furnished arms to the French Expeditionary Corps. Following the Geneva accords, MAAG coordinated U. S. assistance in evacuating those North Vietnamese who elected to move to South Vietnam.

At the request of the new South Vietnamese government, the United States in the fall of 1954 began providing arms, equipment, and advisers to Saigon's armed forces. The French continued to provide advisers for the Army of the Republic of Vietnam (ARVN—pronounced är′vin) until withdrawal of the French Expeditionary Corps in the spring of 1956. MAAG then became the exclusive advisory agency for ARVN, and the next year for the South Vietnamese Air Force and Navy. Meanwhile, in October 1955 "MAAG, Indochina" became "MAAG, Vietnam."

Because French transfer of U. S. arms to the Vietnamese caused logistic chaos, 350 more U. S.

U. S. SOLDIER signals his patrol to stay low while another checks the bushes for enemy soldiers.

WIDE WORLD

CAMERA PRESS—PIX

NORTH VIETNAMESE transport unit uses bicycles to carry ammunition boxes through the jungle trails.

soldiers were brought in to form the Temporary Equipment Recovery Mission early in 1956. The goal of MAAG was to create a South Vietnamese army of 150,000 to resist invasion long enough for an international force to intervene. MAAG functioned only through suggestion and training.

In withdrawing from South Vietnam under terms of the Geneva Agreement, the Communists took many of their rank-and-file to North Vietnam for insurgency training, leaving behind cadres and arms caches. So confident was North Vietnam of absorbing the south after elections prescribed by the Agreement that it took no military action. This left the South Vietnamese government of Ngo Dinh Diem free to fight the armies of two small but powerful religious sects, the Cao Dai and the Hoa Hao, and a band of Saigon gangsters, the Binh Xuyen. These were either defeated or joined government forces.

Formation of the Vietcong. Having crushed a popular revolt at home and conducted a reign of terror to bring farms under state control, the North Vietnamese government began in 1958 to infiltrate political cadres and guerrillas into the south, where they joined those left behind in 1954 to create an insurgent force, the Vietcong (VC), meaning "Vietnamese Communists." Hard-core Communist strength was estimated in 1959 to be 3,000. The first U. S. deaths from hostile action were two soldiers killed in a VC attack at Bien Hoa in July 1959.

By propaganda, coercion, and terror—assassinations, kidnappings, ambushes, attacks on consolidated villages—and by continued infiltration from the north, Vietcong numbers gradually increased. By mid-1961, after North Vietnam had sponsored a National Front for the Liberation of South Vietnam (NLF), the Vietcong had become a serious threat to the Diem regime.

U. S. Reaction. President Kennedy in the fall of 1961 decided to increase U. S. strength, but not for combat. During 1962 the U. S. military increased to more than 11,000, and early in the year a new headquarters was established—the Military Assistance Command, Vietnam (MACV) —which absorbed MAAG. MACV was a joint (Army, Navy, Air Force) command under the Commander in Chief, Pacific (CINCPAC). MACV's commander was also subordinate to the U. S. ambassador. Patrolling the coast, the U. S. Seventh Fleet was directly under CINCPAC.

Most U. S. effort in 1962 was to improve ARVN's mobility, communications, intelligence, and logistics. U. S. Army Special Forces (Green Berets) trained Vietnamese counterparts and civilian irregular defense groups. A U. S. helicopter company was assigned to each of four ARVN corps and subsequently increased to one company per division. The helicopter became the symbol of a new kind of war, a checkerboard campaign in which units might be picked up and set down swiftly almost anywhere.

The U. S. Air Force provided South Vietnam with 30 aircraft: B-26 bombers and armed T-28 trainers. Whenever a U. S. pilot flew, a Vietnamese student pilot was with him. Vietnamese air force strength increased to 219 planes, including troop and cargo carriers; 117 planes, including jet fighters, stayed under U. S. control as a defensive reserve. The U. S. Air Force headquarters in Vietnam was at first the 2nd Air Division, later the Seventh Air Force.

With increased U. S. effort and growth of South Vietnamese armed and paramilitary forces to over 400,000 men, hope of defeating the insurgents grew. But turbulent South Vietnamese politics culminated in the coup upsetting Diem in November 1963, and there was a succession of unstable governments.

The insurgents flourished, reaching a strength in 1964 of 35,000 in organized military units and 100,000 overall, including political cadres—the "infrastructure." A government program to relocate the rural population in supposedly secure "strategic hamlets" collapsed. U. S. troops, totaling 23,000, incurred increasing casualties: 42 killed in 1963, 118 in 1964. Two incidents in August 1964, involving U. S. destroyers and North Vietnamese patrol boats in the Gulf of Tonkin, resulted in strikes by U. S. Navy planes against North Vietnam and almost unanimous passage by Congress of the Tonkin Gulf Resolution.

Communist Moves. Late in 1964 intelligence indicated that three North Vietnamese Army regiments were moving toward or had entered South Vietnam, and Vietcong attacks in regimental and divisional strength were destroying ARVN units on an average of a battalion a week. ARVN leadership often failed. Desertions were high. The Communists seized and temporarily held some district and provincial capitals and entire provinces. U. S. installations, including the embassy in Saigon, were for the first time targets of VC attack.

Bombing North Vietnam. When in February 1965 the Vietcong shelled a U. S. compound in the Central Highlands at Pleiku, killing 8 soldiers, and attacked a barracks at Qui Nhon, President Johnson ordered air attacks on military targets that were situated in North Vietnam. He removed U. S. dependents, deployed a Hawk air-defense battalion to an air base at Da Nang, and authorized U. S. Air Force jets to assist ARVN units in emergencies. In March, U. S. Air Force and Navy planes began a bombing campaign against North Vietnam that ended only in November 1968. To guard U. S. installations, President Johnson ordered the first ground troops to Vietnam, two Marine Corps battalions that arrived at Da Nang in March 1965, followed by an Army military police battalion at Saigon. In early April he ordered two more Marine battalions and an air squadron to Da Nang and authorized the Marines to expand their operations beyond their defensive perimeters. This started a short-lived "enclave strategy," under which U. S. troops were to secure selected areas, free ARVN troops for other operations, and demonstrate U. S. resolve.

In May a U. S. Army airborne brigade arrived to protect an air base at Bien Hoa, and the next month U. S. B-52 strategic bombers, based on Guam and later in Thailand, began continuous raids against entrenched Communist bases in remote regions of the south. Under new authority granted by President Johnson to use ground troops when necessary to strengthen ARVN, the airborne brigade late in June conducted the first U. S. ground offensive, a brief incursion with ARVN units into War Zone D, a Communist sanctuary close to the Bien Hoa air base.

U. S. Buildup. Advised by the MACV commander, Gen. William C. Westmoreland, who had assumed command in June 1964, that South Vietnam could not long survive without U. S. combat troops, President Johnson decided in mid-July 1965 to send them. By the end of the year there were some 180,000 U. S. troops in Vietnam.

The first troops built a logistic base. New ports were made or vastly expanded at six sites. Over 4 million square yards (3.3 million sq meters) were paved for airfields. Vast storage facilities, several thousand miles of roads, and hundreds of bridges were constructed.

U. S. Operations. General Westmoreland used some incoming troops as a fire brigade to squelch major threats and keep the Communists off balance. Three North Vietnamese regiments in the Central Highlands apparently intended driving to the sea to cut the country in two. Against them Westmoreland committed the Army's first airmobile unit, the 1st Cavalry Division. In the battle of the Ia Drang Valley, the cavalrymen killed 1,300 Communists and chased the rest into Cambodia.

The pattern of U. S. commitment was soon set: U. S. Marines in the northern provinces (I Corps) and the U. S. Army in the central region (II Corps) and around Saigon (III Corps). For a time ARVN troops alone fought in the Mekong Delta (IV Corps).

Despite continued infiltration raising Communist strength by the end of 1965 to more than 220,000, the fire-brigade phase by mid-1966 had passed. ARVN and some U. S. units then concentrated on protecting villages and hamlets, thereby providing support for "pacification," a program supported by South Vietnamese and U. S. civilian agencies and aimed at eliminating local guerrillas and the infrastructure and providing government services. Other U. S. units tried to bring the Communist main forces, or regulars, to battle, driving them away from the population. This was called "search and destroy."

An additional objective was to eliminate Communist sanctuaries or logistic bases, such as War Zone C along the Cambodian border and War Zone D north of Saigon. Lacking sufficient resources to occupy the bases permanently, they destroyed bunkers and tunnels with explosives and eliminated forest cover by chemical defoliation or by razing with heavy bulldozers called "Rome Plows." Repeated forays into the sanctuaries were required.

It was a war without front lines. Communist troops could be anywhere, not always uniformed and often not distinguishable from the population. Without the usual standards for measuring progress, the military turned to imprecise statistics: number of dead, of villages "pacified," of miles of highway opened. MACV exercised no command over ARVN or forces of other countries. In an effort to keep the war localized, pursuit of Communists into Cambodia or Laos or beyond the Demilitarized Zone (DMZ) between South and North Vietnam was forbidden, though the Communists maintained bases in all three places and brought supplies through the Cambodian port of Sihanoukville (Kompong Som) and over the "Ho Chi Minh Trail." In hope of promoting negotiations, the United States sometimes halted bombing of North Vietnam, and there were truces for Vietnamese holidays.

All U. S. units operated from fortified base camps into neighboring districts on security and pacification missions. At times they shifted far afield, building a temporary base camp and forward fire-support bases from which helicopter-transported artillery could reinforce search-and-destroy operations. Long-distance patrols were common and ambush and counter-ambush familiar tactics. The U. S. and South Vietnamese navies sealed the long coastline and patrolled the extensive waterways of the Mekong Delta. In 1966 the U. S. Riverine Force was established in the Delta. It had an infantry brigade supported by barracks ships, armored troop-carrier and escort boats, and floating artillery platforms.

Civilians sometimes were evacuated to separate them from the Vietcong, and these cleared areas would be declared "free-fire zones." War conducted among a population sometimes sympathetic to the Communists led on occasion to excesses, as at the village of My Lai in 1968 when U. S. troops killed several hundred civilians.

Arms and Equipment. The radio and the helicopter (including rocket-firing gunships) were essential. Other sophisticated items included big troop- and cargo-carrying aircraft, armored personnel carriers, electronic sensors, beehive artillery projectiles, and electrically activated mines. Yet barbed wire and sandbags were used as ex-

HOMELESS after burning of their village, a Vietnamese mother and her child face an uncertain future.

DANA STONE—UPI

tensively as in World War I. The Communists also had excellent weapons, such as the automatic AK-47 rifle, although they had artillery only along the DMZ. They were masters of the booby trap, including sharpened bamboo spikes called "punji stakes." In the antiaircraft defense of North Vietnam, they used Soviet-supplied surface-to-air missiles. The Communist soldier displayed patience, stamina, courage, and a marked ability to avoid battle and escape entrapment.

Top U. S. Strength. Eventually, U. S. strength increased to almost 550,000, including 3 corps headquarters, 7 divisions, and 5 separate specialized brigades, plus 2 Marine divisions and a separate regiment. ARVN grew to 500,000 regulars and 500,000 paramilitary. The Republic of Korea furnished 48,000 men; Thailand, a division; Australia, a brigade; and the Philippines and New Zealand, smaller units. More than 30 nations gave nonmilitary aid. The Vietcong and North Vietnamese built their strength to over 250,000.

Tet Offensive. Toward the end of 1967, Westmoreland responded to a buildup in the northern part of South Vietnam by moving some U. S. Army units to I Corps. A Communist offensive began in the northern and central provinces before daybreak on Jan. 30, 1968, and in the Saigon and Delta regions that night. Some 84,000 men attacked 36 of 43 provincial capitals, 5 of 6 autonomous cities, 34 of 242 district capitals, and 50 hamlets, penetrating deep into 10 cities, including Saigon and Hue. ARVN cleared 4 cities quickly and 4 others in up to 3 days, but in Saigon and Hue fighting was protracted. Controlling Hue for almost a month, the Communists executed about 3,000 civilians.

The Communists apparently believed their offensive would engender a public uprising, but nowhere did substantial support develop. Neither did morale of ARVN units falter. In the first two weeks the Communists lost 32,000 killed, while U. S. and South Vietnamese losses were 1,000 and 2,000 respectively. Three times in the next six months the Communists tried to regain their momentum, but the attacks degenerated into sporadic mortar and rocket attacks. For 11 weeks at Khe Sanh 4 U. S. Marine battalions and an ARVN battalion were besieged. U. S. firepower, including 175mm artillery and B-52's bombing in close support, inflicted heavy losses and the North Vietnamese withdrew. Khe Sanh was abandoned in favor of mobile operations.

Damage to pacification proved to be temporary. The Communists had incurred heavy losses and their political infrastructure became more vulnerable. In late fall of 1968 the South Vietnamese government with expanded U. S. assistance launched an accelerated pacification program. On the U. S. side this was managed by Civil Operations and Revolutionary Development Support (CORDS), a component of MACV created in mid-1967 to fuse the pacification efforts of various U. S. civilian agencies and the military. The extent of damage to the Communists in the Tet offensive became more apparent in 1969 as the pacification program progressed and large military confrontations decreased.

Vietnamization. A new MACV commander, Gen. Creighton W. Abrams, who succeeded Westmoreland on July 1, 1968, was able to afford greater resources for pacification and for "Vietnamization"—the program to strengthen South Vietnamese forces for eventually taking over all military responsibilities. Beginning on June 8, 1969, with President Nixon's announcement of major U. S. troop withdrawals, this involved transferring U. S. bases and quantities of equipment.

With the overthrow of Prince Sihanouk in Cambodia and President Nixon's relaxation of restrictions against cross-border operations, ARVN troops on April 29 and U. S. troops on May 2, 1970, attacked to eliminate the long-sacrosanct Communist bases in Cambodia, while the Cambodians denied Sihanoukville as a port for Communist supplies.

By order of President Nixon, U. S. units advanced no deeper than 21 miles (34 km) inside the country. Some 43,000 South Vietnamese and 31,000 U. S. troops participated. In operations lasting until June 29, when the last U. S. troops withdrew, approximately 11,000 Communists were killed and 9,300 tons of supplies destroyed. More important were neutralization of the Communist sanctuaries and denial of Sihanoukville.

The only route for supplies and reinforcements left to the North Vietnamese was the Ho Chi Minh Trail, already subject to attacks by B-52 bombers. On Feb. 8, 1971, the vanguard of 21,000 ARVN troops entered Laos to raid the trail complex as far as 25 miles (40 km) inside the country at the road junction of Tchepone, taken on March 6. Temporarily reactivating the abandoned base at Khe Sanh, U. S. forces furnished air, artillery, and logistic support.

Contrary to earlier practice in Cambodia, the North Vietnamese fought savagely, inflicting sharp losses on 4 of 12 ARVN battalions. The heaviest concentration of antiaircraft fire yet encountered destroyed 89 U. S. helicopters. Near the end of March, the South Vietnamese withdrew. The Cambodian and Laotian operations showed improved performance of ARVN in fierce fighting.

On March 30, 1972, after most U. S. ground combat troops had departed, North Vietnam launched a conventional invasion across the DMZ and subsidiary thrusts from Laos and Cambodia. Achieving surprise with heavy tanks and artillery, the North Vietnamese captured Loc Ninh near the Cambodian border and all the northernmost province of Quang Tri before ARVN defense, with American air and naval support, stiffened. President Nixon ordered renewed bombing of North Vietnam, including first use of B-52's against the North, and mining of North Vietnamese harbors, including Haiphong. In mid-May the South Vietnamese began to counterattack, and on September 15 recaptured Quang Tri city. Yet the rest of the northern province and much of the Central Highlands remained under North Vietnamese control.

Despite the ceasefire agreement effective Jan. 28, 1973, by which time all American combat forces had departed, fighting continued sporadically while the North Vietnamese improved supply routes and sharply increased their strength in the South. Early in 1975 they captured Phuoc Long province along the Cambodian border, and on March 5 they began a major offensive in the Highlands and the northern provinces. Congress had forbidden further U. S. military involvement in Indochina as of Aug. 15, 1973, so that no American military reaction was possible. With all roads in the Highlands blocked and North Vietnamese forces far superior, the South Vietnamese began a withdrawal that under enemy pressure became a rout. A similar decision to abandon Quang Tri city and Hue led to panic.

One after another the coastal cities, including Da Nang, the country's second largest, were abandoned amid tragic scenes of refugees trying to escape. Having lost the equivalent of six divisions and three fourths of the country, threatened by 20 North Vietnamese divisions, and denied additional American military aid, the Saigon government surrendered on April 30.

CHARLES B. MACDONALD
Author of "The Mighty Endeavor"

3. Effects of the War on U. S. Society

The war had profound effects on American society, as well as on the U. S. role abroad. The unpopularity of the war with large portions of the American public was a major reason for President Johnson's refusal to run for the Democratic nomination to a second term in 1968. The strong showing of Sen. Eugene McCarthy in Democratic primary balloting was interpreted by the president as a repudiation of his leadership. Vice President Hubert H. Humphrey was not able to dissociate himself sufficiently from the Johnson war policies, and the result was the election of Republican Richard M. Nixon as president in 1968.

Other Political Effects. One of the war's early political effects on the domestic scene was its impact on the already developing radicalization and polarization of the country's youth. Young persons were in the forefront of the 1968 presidential drives of Senators McCarthy and Robert F. Kennedy. The young led demonstrations at the Democratic convention in Chicago and dominated antiwar demonstrations.

The intensity of youth's reaction against the war was shown in the spring of 1970. Almost all college campuses were disrupted, and some of the schools were forced to close, as students expressed their opposition to the U. S.–South Vietnamese intervention in Cambodia. Student leaders accused President Nixon of expanding the conflict, and the fatal shooting of four students by Ohio National Guardsmen during a demonstration at Kent State University in May intensified the reaction against the government.

The opposition of youth to the war drew the greatest attention, partly because of the dramatic ways in which it expressed itself. But many clergymen, educators, and businessmen had expressed their disapproval of the government's Vietnam policies as early as the mid-1960's, and their numbers grew in subsequent years. As late as 1968, however, a majority of the public apparently did not favor disengagement from Vietnam. Initially, the public believed that the United States should not have become involved in the conflict, but that since it was involved it should see the war through to the end. By mid-1971 a majority of the public seemed to believe that the United States should get out of the war. A Harris poll in May had shown that 60% of the persons polled favored continued U. S. withdrawal even if the government of South Vietnam should collapse.

Escalation of a war that was never formally declared led to a strain on the constitutional system of checks and balances. Although congressional and senatorial criticism of the war mounted after 1965, it was clear that public distrust of government was increasing. This attitude seemed to be dramatically justified when in 1971 several U. S. newspapers exposed high-level deception of the American public over Vietnam by publishing excerpts from the "Pentagon Papers," a classified government study. The subsequent illegal entry into the office of Dr. Daniel Ellsberg's psychiatrist—Ellsberg was chiefly responsible for the disclosure of the Pentagon Papers—underscored continued government irregularities. The Vietnam War thus contributed to a strong national reaction to the cover-up of the June 1972 Watergate break-in, which led to the attempt to impeach President Nixon, his historic resignation in 1974, and the succession of Gerald R. Ford to the presidency. The irony was that President Nixon was largely responsible for American disengagement from the Vietnam War.

The Congress elected in 1974 included an unusually large number of new faces. It was younger and more liberal than any Congress had been for years. The radicalization of some aspects of American politics, a feature of the late 1960's and early 1970's, had given way to a more measured liberal presence. But American polit-

DANA STONE—UPI

EXHAUSTED GI's rest in the rubble of shattered buildings after taking a small village near Hue, in Thua Thien province.

THE NEW YORK TIMES

PROTESTING AGAINST THE WAR, demonstrators stage a peaceful mass rally in Washington in 1969.

ical complacency had been shaken, a new responsiveness had been introduced into the political process, and the Vietnam War had played a significant role in the change.

There was also a domestic response to the overextension of American power abroad and to the excessive assumption of responsibility for other nations' affairs. Termed "neoisolationist," this sentiment was clearly a reaction to the length, cost, and outcome of the war.

Effects on U. S. Economy. The reaction against an activist foreign policy was not exclusively induced by the Vietnam War. Increasingly, Americans showed growing concern over neglected areas of domestic policy—the deteriorating state of many cities, environmental pollution, and expanding welfare rolls. But it was the general state of the economy as much as anything else that caused increasing public concern in the first half of the 1970's.

The economic cost of U. S. involvement in Vietnam was probably the least appreciated aspect of the decisions of those who first involved the United States in the war and then dramatically escalated the conflict in the mid-1960's. By the war's end in 1975, its total cost to the United States, including higher prices for other government activities not directly related to the conflict, was probably well over $200 billion. Because this level of expenditure had not been foreseen, government controls of the sort that had been introduced in previous major wars were not immediately established.

The inflation that gripped the nation in the first half of the 1970's, although not wholly induced by the Vietnam War, was much influenced by its cost. As early as the mid-1960's such areas as the construction industry were hard hit as war spending drove up mortgage interest rates. By the early 1970's, the inflation was the worst the nation had experienced since the years just after World War II. Overall economic activity slowed down considerably after nearly a decade of fairly rapid growth, and subsequent compensatory moves, combined with the decline of U. S. participation in the war, increased unemployment.

By 1974 the country was clearly in a recession, and the difficulties of the American economy were having worldwide effects. A largely uncontrolled war economy appeared to have driven up the costs of many American nonwar goods, to have forced capital and related activity out of the country, and to have laid the basis for overlapping inflation and recession.

The consequences of the Vietnam War for the United States were not limited to its domestic economy. The high priority accorded Vietnam had adverse effects for the United States internationally as well. While the United States was devoting billions of dollars a year to military expenditures for the Vietnam War alone, the Japanese economy, with a relatively small military investment, developed at an unprecedented pace. Japan began invading U. S. domestic markets and undercutting U. S. sales abroad. Eventually, as foreign confidence in the dollar sagged, the U. S. currency was allowed to float on the international market. In effect, it was devalued. Meanwhile the Soviet Union was expanding its missile and naval capacities, its economy unburdened by the adverse effects of a costly foreign war.

See also GENEVA AGREEMENT OF 1954; INDOCHINA; PENTAGON PAPERS; TONKIN GULF RESOLUTION; VIETNAM.

RICHARD BUTWELL, *Author of "Southeast Asia: A Political Introduction"*

Bibliography

Arnett, Peter, and Maclear, Michael, *The Ten Thousand Day War: Vietnam, 1945–1975* (St. Martin's Press 1981).

Bowman, John S., ed., *The World Almanac of the Vietnam War* (World Almanac 1986).

Buttinger, Joseph, *A Dragon Defiant: A Short History of Vietnam* (Praeger 1972).

Ellsberg, Daniel, *Papers on the War* (Simon & Schuster 1972).

Fitzgerald, Frances, *Fire in the Lake: The Vietnamese and the Americans in Vietnam* (Random House 1972).

Goodman, Alan E., *Politics in War: The Bases of Political Community in South Vietnam* (Harvard Univ. Press 1973).

Herring, George C., *America's Longest War: The United States and Vietnam* 2d ed. (Temple Univ. Press 1986).

Isaacs, Arnold R., *Without Honor: Defeat in Vietnam and Cambodia* (Johns Hopkins Univ. Press 1983).

Langer, Paul F., and Zasloff, Joseph, *North Vietnam and the Pathet Lao: Partners in the Struggle for Laos* (Harvard Univ. Press 1970).

McAlister, John T., Jr., and Mus, Paul, *The Vietnamese and Their Revolution* (Harper 1970).

Poole, Peter A., *Expansion of the Vietnam War into Cambodia* (Ohio University Center for International Studies 1970).

Poole, Peter A., *The United States and Indochina: From FDR to Nixon* (Dryden Press 1973).

Race, Jeffrey, *War Comes to Long An: Revolutionary Conflict in a Vietnamese Province* (Univ. of Calif. Press 1972).

Shaplen, Robert, *The Road from War: Vietnam 1965–1971*, rev. ed. (Harper 1971).

Zasloff, Joseph J., and Goodman, Allan E., *Indochina in Conflict: A Political Assessment* (Heath 1972).

VIEUX CARRÉ. See NEW ORLEANS—*Places of Interest*.

VIGÉE-LEBRUN, vē-zhā'lə-brûɴ', **Marie Anne Elisabeth,** French portrait painter: b. Paris, France, April 16, 1755; d. there, March 30, 1842. She was trained in painting by her father, Louis Vigée, and encouraged in art by Gabriel François Doyen (1726–1806) and Joseph Vernet (1714–1789). She married the painter Jean Baptiste Pierre Lebrun, and they had a daughter before they separated.

In 1779, Mme. Vigée-Lebrun painted Queen Marie Antoinette for the first time. This marked the beginning of her career as a painter of royalty that she pursued until her death. Her popularity was aided by a contemporary enthusiasm for the concept of equality of the sexes. She was elected to membership in the French Royal Academy in 1783.

At the outbreak of the French Revolution in 1789 she fled to Rome with her daughter. The next year she went to Naples, where she painted the queen of Naples, the queen's children, and Lady Emma Hamilton. Mme. Vigée-Lebrun then traveled through Austria and Russia, receiving patronage of Catherine the Great and painting members of the royal families. She went back to France in 1801, and in the following year she went to England, where she painted the Prince of Wales (later King George IV). She returned to Paris from her long exile in 1805 and painted Napoleon's sister, Mme. Marie Murat. Toward the end of her life, Mme. Vigée-Lebrun spent much of her time at her country house in Louveciennes.

Most of the large number of portraits that Mme. Vigée-Lebrun painted were of women, and her paintings expressed the prettiness expected by the sitters, with a fine, feminine interest in their costumes. She wrote her *Mémoires* in 1835 (Eng. tr. by Lytton Strachey, 1903). Her paintings are on display in the Louvre, Paris; the National Gallery and the Wallace Collection, London; and The Metropolitan Museum, New York City. Portraits of Marie Antoinette and her children are in the Versailles Museum, and a self-portrait is in the Galleria degli Uffizi, Florence.

H. D. Hale
Art Critic

VIGELAND, vē'gə-län, **Adolf Gustav,** Norwegian sculptor: b. Mandal, Norway, April 11, 1869; d. Oslo, March 12, 1943. His sculpture at first resembled Auguste Rodin's and Aristide Maillol's in style, but ultimately smoothed to an essentially realistic technique.

By far the greatest part of Vigeland's life work is found in the Frogner Park in Oslo. The park consists of a central axis with gates of decorative ironwork, a bridge with 58 small and 4 large figure groups, the fountain surrounded by 15 tree groups and 50 reliefs, a large mosaic labyrinth, and a hillock covered with circular stairs. The circular group is a doughnut-shaped composition of 7 figures. The circular stairs bear 36 large granite groups in 12 rows radiating from a column more than 55 feet tall, containing 121 figures in gray granite. Behind the column are a rectangular work of 21 figures and a large circular group.

In addition to the work that Vigeland did for Frogner Park, he left a number of early busts and reliefs, which are housed in the Oslo Museum.

H. D. Hale
Art Critic

VIGIL, vĭj'əl, in Roman Catholic liturgy, a day preceding a feast and in preparation for it. Since the holy day is a day of rejoicing and festivity, preparation for it traditionally, although not invariably, includes fasting. Pope John XXIII made liturgical changes which, beginning in 1961, set the number of vigils at seven: two of the first class, the vigils of Christmas and Pentecost; four of the second class, those of Ascension Thursday, the Assumption of Mary into Heaven, the Nativity of St. John the Baptist, and St. Peter and St. Paul; and one of the third class, that of St. Lawrence. The Easter Vigil is not a liturgical day, but is celebrated as a night watch.

John K. Ryan

VIGILANTES, vĭj-ə-lăn'tēz, the name given to self-appointed law-enforcement groups who appeared from time to time on the American frontier and occasionally in older communities where established authorities seemed unable to cope with lawlessness and disorder.

A precursor to frontier vigilante movements was found in the "claims associations," groups of settlers on public land who banded together to make certain that speculators would not outbid them when the land which they occupied was placed on sale at public auction. These were organized in the mid-19th century in Iowa and other parts of the Middle West.

Vigilantism also occurred in the gold rush towns of California, although, since formal municipal government was nonexistent, the term "popular tribunals" is probably a more accurate term. When outlawry disturbed peaceful citizens, they organized into democratic courts, appointed judges and juries, and dealt summarily with offenders. Dry Diggings was renamed Hangtown as a result of one of these episodes. Democratic legal procedure in gold rush towns was in most cases orderly and reasonably just; only occasionally did it degenerate into lynch law and mob rule.

Two of the most famous episodes of vigilante activity occurred in San Francisco. The first, in 1851, resulted from the inability of the new city administration to cope with gangs of outlaws, known as the "Hounds" or "Regulators," who preyed chiefly on minority groups and were suspected of complicity in the great fires that repeatedly destroyed portions of the city. Under the leadership of Sam Brannan, a group of vigilantes seized and executed a notorious criminal, John Jenkins, then sentenced various other suspects to death, deportation, whipping, or legal trial. Five years later, when a newspaper editor named James King was slain by James P. Casey, a county supervisor, the vigilantes reorganized, seized Casey and a criminal named Charles Cora, and tried and executed them. Under the leadership of William T. Coleman, the vigilantes barricaded the streets in an area known as "Fort Gunnybags," and worked their way through a long list of undesirable characters. Its work done, the committee formally disbanded. It was opposed by a group known as the "Law and Order" faction, including many city officials and attorneys.

Another dramatic episode of vigilante effectiveness in a frontier mining area occurred in Montana in 1864. A criminal named Henry Plummer managed to have himself elected as sheriff of the Bannack and the Virginia City area.

Because of Plummer's official position, news of gold shipments was easy to obtain. He organized a gang of 100 desperadoes who specialized in stage robberies. A vigilante group was organized, hunted the gang, and finally executed Plummer in 1864.

The city of New Orleans experienced two major incidents where self-appointed agencies attempted to cope with current problems. In 1858 when municipal politics seemed hopelessly entangled among several political groups and election procedures were suspect, a vigilance committee was organized, barricaded streets in the French Quarter, and tried to guarantee an honest election. City officials vacillated, and finally the vigilantes disbanded when a change in municipal administration occurred. In 1890 the Mafia, a secret society composed largely of Sicilian immigrants, engaged in extortion, racketeering, and murder, and finally assassinated the chief of police, David Hennessey. When the suspects, despite strong evidence as to their guilt, were acquitted, indignant citizens held a mass meeting, seized the jail, and shot down those whose complicity in the crime seemed clear, largely destroying the Mafia's influence.

Although vigilantism was often justified by circumstances and was in many cases carried out by citizens who were moderate and orderly in their application of force, it carried with it many dangers, the chief of which was that it sometimes degenerated into mob rule. This is well illustrated by a grave marker in Boot Hill Cemetery, Tombstone, Ariz., which bears the epitaph "Lynched by Mistake."

GLENN S. DUMKE,
President, San Francisco State College.

Bibliography

Beidler, John X., *X. Beidler: Vigilante*, ed. by Helen F. Sanders and William H. Bertsche, Jr. (1957; reprint, Univ. of Okla. Press 1969).
Brown, Richard M., *Strain of Violence: Historical Studies of American Violence and Vigilantism* (Oxford 1975).
Burrows, William E., *Vigilante* (Harcourt 1976).
Dimsdale, Thomas J., *Vigilantes of Montana* (Univ. of Okla. Press 1985).
Gard, Wayne, *Frontier Justice* (1949; reprint, Univ. of Okla. Press 1968).
Langford, Nathaniel P., *Vigilante Days and Ways*, 2 vols. (1890; reprint, AMS Press 1976).
Lindstrom, Joyce, *Idaho's Vigilantes* (Univ. of Idaho Press 1984).
Peltier, Jerome, ed., *Banditti of the Rockies* (Ross Bks. 1964).
Rosenbaum, H. Jon, and Sederberg, Peter C., eds., *Vigilante Politics* (Univ. of Pa. Press 1976).
Stevens, Herbert, *Vigilantes Ride in 1882* (Ye Galleon Press 1979).

VIGILIUS, vĭ-jĭl'ĭ-əs, pope: d. Syracuse, Sicily, June 7, 555; r. 537–555. Of Roman origin, he was the son of the consul Johannes and brother of a Roman senator. He was ordained to the diaconate probably during the pontificate of Boniface II (530–532), who designated him as his eventual successor. This designation was later revoked; but largely through the influence of Belisarius and Theodora, his star continued to rise, and he succeeded Silverius on the papal chair in March 537. Vigilius had engaged to annul the decrees of the Council of Chalcedon (451) relating to the pro-Nestorian "Three Chapters," which Emperor Justinian I wanted condemned to facilitate the return of the Monophysites to the church. When Vigilius failed to act, he was summoned by the emperor to Constantinople, where he issued his *Judicatum* (548), in which he condemned the chapters but disclaimed any disparagement of Chalcedon. His subsequent efforts to amend an impossible situation by his *Constitutum ad imperatorem* resulted in his condemnation by the Council of Constantinople of 553. Later, he agreed to ratify the decrees of that council and was permitted to return to Rome, after an absence of seven years, but died en route. Most church historians hold that it would be difficult to justify the character and actions of Vigilius.

ALASTAIR GUINAN.

VIGNA. See COWPEA.

VIGNETTE, vĭn-yĕt', a form of ornamentation employed in the graphic arts and architecture. The style originated in the representation of vines, leaves, and tendrils in classical Greek architecture; hence the term "vignette" (derived from the French *vigne*, vine). Further developed by the Romans, who introduced it into Europe, the vine pattern was preserved during the Middle Ages as a favorite form of manuscript illumination, and later it found a high expression in the embellishment of Gothic art and architecture. The vignette continues in wide use in printing, appearing as a small design or illustration immediately preceding the title page of a book or before and after individual chapters—often in conjunction with an initial letter. The term applies generally today to any small engraving or photograph—especially a portrait—of indefinite boundary, the marginal areas shading off into the surrounding page. By extension, the word is used in literature to refer to a brief portrayal of a scene or character. A short narrative piece sometimes is called a vignette.

VIGNOLA, vē-nyô'lä, **Giacomo da** (real name GIACOMO BAROCCHIO, BAROZIO, or BAROZZI), Italian architect, painter, and sculptor: b. Vignola, Italy, 1507; d. Rome, July 7, 1573. His influence spread the Baroque style of architecture throughout the Roman Catholic world. Vignola studied under Francesco Guicciardini, and in 1535 went to Rome to make measured drawings of monuments for the Academy of Architecture. He worked under Francesco Primaticcio at Fontainebleau, casting sculptures for the gardens there. From 1543 to 1548 he worked in Bologna, designing bridges, canals, and villas. Pope Julius III, to whom he had been introduced by Giorgio Vasari, called him to Rome in 1550, and for the next five years he collaborated with Michelangelo on the Farnese Palace in Rome; he became papal architect and worked for Julius III on the Villa di Papa Giulio in Rome. His pentagonal Villa Farnese at Caprarola, built for Alessandro Cardinal Farnese, contains one of the finest circular staircases of the Renaissance, as well as statues and frescoes, which Vignola executed; he also worked on a number of other splendid villas for the Roman aristocracy. After he succeeded Michelangelo as director of works for the basilica of St. Peter, in 1564, he built the cupolas at each side of the central dome. In 1568 he designed his most influential work, Il Gesù, mother church of the Jesuit order. Imitation of this church initiated the Baroque style, as did Vignola's *Regola delli cinque ordini d'architettura* (1562, Rules of the Five Orders of Architecture). In 1583, his *Due regole della prospettiva pratica* (Two Rules of Practical Perspective) was published. Vignola's work showed an increasingly sumptuous use of classical motifs, which reached a critical point in Il Gesù and influenced architecture for 200 years.

H. D. HALE
Art Critic

VIGNY, vē-nyē′, COMTE **Alfred Victor de,** French man of letters: b. Loches, Indre-et-Loire, France, March 27, 1797; d. Paris, Sept. 17, 1863. He was the only son of 60-year-old Léon Pierre de Vigny, former officer in the king's army, and of his 40-year-old wife, who belonged to the lower nobility, and had been ruined by the French Revolution; but pride ran high in their impoverished home. Young Vigny was austerely brought up in anticipation of the time when Napoleon would topple from power and the returning monarchy would call forth its loyal subjects. A mere adolescent in 1814, he entered military service, only to find himself lost between echoes of glamorous wars that were no more and dreams of new battles that never materialized. He resigned his commission in 1827, his heart set on a life of writing; but frustration continued to stalk him: in his marriage to Lydia Bunbury, whose fresh English beauty soon withered in torpid invalidism; in his stormy liaison with the actress. Marie Dorval; in the uneasy progress of his very career. The French Academy rejected his candidacy five times, finally admitting him in 1845. Yet, literature per se, with or without its worldly rewards, became ever more the refuge of this lonely man, or in Charles Augustin Sainte-Beuve's famous phrase, his "ivory tower."

Vigny's comparatively small output was a seminal one, more so than that of Alphonse de Lamartine and Victor Hugo. Maturity of thought distinguished his *Poèmes* of 1822, although they did not include the most mature of them all, *Moïse*, also composed that year. When it appeared in the enlarged edition of 1826 (*Poèmes antiques et modernes*), this dazzling prelude to romantic claims of divine mission and prophetic gift created a stir. Already in 1824 the short epic, *Éloa, ou la Soeur des anges,* had introduced a type of philosophical poetry that Lamartine, Hugo, and others were to emulate years later. Vigny's historical novel, *Cinq-Mars* (q.v., 1826) and his translation of *Othello* (produced at the Comédie-Française in 1829) likewise rank among the earliest and most significant episodes of the romantic campaign. After the revolution of 1830, it became apparent that his unique brand of metaphysical pessimism, far from being supine and misanthropic, made him peculiarly sensitive to the redeeming features of man's condition. *Stello,* a triptych of novelettes (1832), and *Chatterton,* possibly the high point of French romantic drama (1835), while exposing the vices of a materialistic society, held out hope for the ultimate triumph of the spirit. Meanwhile, *Servitude et grandeur militaires,* a collection of short stories (1835), preached abnegation, the soldier's obscure virtue, to all who toil in the service of mankind. Indeed, as if to confirm those premises, Vigny's greatest fame accrued to him from posthumous works. His poetical testament *Les destinées* (1864), contains unsurpassed examples of an art which, ever since *Moïse* and *Éloa,* strove to convey ideas by means of pregnant symbols (for example, *La maison du berger*). The unfinished novel, *Daphné,* with Julian the Apostate as its central figure, was first published in 1912 and actually bears a striking resemblance to religious disquisitions of the post-Renan period. Finally, Vigny's *Journal d'un poète* (to be consulted in *Oeuvres,* Pléiade edition, vol. 2, 1948) has taken its place among the great intellectual diaries of modern times, there being, in fact, no better witness to the depth and urgency of his thought.

JEAN-ALBERT BÉDÉ
Columbia University

Bibliography

Buss, Robin, *Vigny: Chatterton* (Longwood 1984).
Carter, Marion E., *Role of the Symbol in French Romantic Poetry* (1946; reprint, AMS Press 1977).
Dobay Rifelj, Carol De, *Word and Figure* (Ohio State Univ. Press 1986).
Higonnet, Patrice, *Class, Ideology and the Rights of Nobles During the French Revolution* (Oxford 1981).
Hunt, H. J., *The Epic in 19th Century France* (Gordon Press 1976).
Vigny, Alfred de, *Les Poemes,* ed. by Jean Chuzeville (French & European Pub. 1953).
Whitridge, A., *Alfred De Vigny* (1933; reprint, Telegraph Bks. 1982).

VIGO, vē′gō, **Joseph Maria Francesco** (known as FRANCIS VIGO), Italian-born trader and pioneer in the American northwest: b. Mondovì, Piedmont (now part of Italy), Dec. 3, 1747; d. Vincennes, Ind., March 22, 1836. He served with a Spanish regiment at New Orleans and after his discharge became active in the fur trade. In 1772 he established himself at St. Louis, where for a time he was secret agent for the Spanish governor. Vigo's chief claim to fame rests upon the invaluable aid which he rendered to George Rogers Clark (q.v.), especially in the campaign initiated at Kaskaskia which terminated British influence in the northwest country. Committing his fortune to the American cause, he supplied the hard-pressed Clark with the funds and equipment that made possible the latter's successful expedition against Vincennes in 1779, and he deserves much credit in the eventual awarding of the Northwest Territory to the United States. From about 1783 he resided in Vincennes, becoming a naturalized citizen soon after. His later claims for reimbursement for the aid furnished to Clark were ignored by the federal government, and he died impoverished. In 1876 the Supreme Court awarded about $50,000 to his heirs.

VIGO, city, Spain, in Pontevedra Province, Galicia, on Vigo Bay, an inlet of the Atlantic Ocean, 80 miles south-southwest of La Coruña near the Portuguese border. Built on a hill overlooking the bay, Vigo consists of two parts: the old town, on the slope of the hill, consisting of the harbor, steep winding streets, and ancient palaces; and the new town, at the top of the hill, with modern streets and a business center. The city dates from Roman days, when it was called Vicus Spacorum. A fleet of galleons carrying gold from the New World was partly captured and partly sunk in 1702 by a British-Dutch fleet. Part of the treasure is still believed to be at the bottom of the bay, but attempts to raise it have been unsuccessful. Vigo's economy to a large extent depends on the sea. A fishing industry is important, as are fish processing, boatbuilding, and a busy harbor that serves as a port of call on transatlantic steamship lines. There are also granite quarrying, chemical works, and manufacturing. The city is the chief center of modern Galicia. Pop. (1981) 258,724.

JEAN SERMET

VIHUELA, vē-wā′lä, name of at least two Spanish musical instruments, the *vihuela de arco,* a viola-like member of the violin family, and the more important *vihuela de mano,* a guitarlike lute. The lute proper never became acclimated in Spain, where the leading folk instrument was the guitar; the vihuela de mano evolved as a compromise instrument for aristocratic use. Shaped like a lute-sized guitar, it was equipped with double strings, most often tuned G-c-f-a-d′-g′ or G-c-f-g-c′-f′-g′. A large repertoire of compositions for it survives from the 16th century, most notably in the *Libro de música de vihuela de mano, intitulado El Maestro* (1535–1536), by Luis Milan (1500?–?1561), a teaching manual with numerous examples.

HERBERT WEINSTOCK.

VIIPURI. See VYBORG.

VIJAYANAGAR, vĭj′ə-yə-nŭg′ər or **BIJANAGAR,** bĭj ə-nŭg′ər (Indian, "City of Victory"), India, ruins of the capital of the ancient South Indian empire of the same name. The ruins, covering nine square miles, are near the modern village of Hampi on the south bank of the Tungabhadra River in the Bellary District of Mysore State. Founded in 1336 as the fortress of a petty chief, the city grew rapidly in importance, and by the 16th century, at the height of its glory, was the capital of an empire embracing all of India south of the Krishna (Kistna) River. In 1565, at the Battle of Talikota, the empire was decisively defeated by its traditional enemies, the combined Muslim sultanates of the Deccan, and the abandoned city was systematically destroyed. The most splendid part of the city was the palace enclosure, famous for its Temple of Razara Ramaswami (the Thousand Ramas), its baths, and its elephant stables. Some distance away, Vitalaswami Temple is noteworthy for its magnificent sculpture and massive construction.

JOSEPH E. SCHWARTZBERG.

VIJAYAVADA, vÿ′ə-yä-vä-dŭ (formerly **BEZWADA**), city, India, in the Kistna (Krishna) District of Andhra Pradesh State. Incorporated in 1888, it has since grown rapidly because of its importance as a transportation and commercial center in coastal Andhra Pradesh, and, in particular, in the fertile, populous agricultural tract including the large Krishna River delta. A dam 3,715 feet long and 20 feet high crosses the Krishna River at Vijayavada, and from the dam irrigation canals take water to 900,000 acres on both sides of the river. The city has rice milling, tobacco curing, and sugar refining, and industries such as cement and light engineering establishments. Nearby are the noteworthy Dravidian rock cave shrines at Undavalle. Pop. (1981) 544,958.

JOSEPH E. SCHWARTZBERG

VIKING, vī′kĭng, a designation of the adventurous people of the North, a collective name for the Norwegians, Swedes, and Danes in the 8th to 10th centuries. The term is derived from the Icelandic *vik,* bay or inlet, with the ending *-ing.* While it was perhaps primarily applied to one who lived in a bay area, the name was used by the Northmen themselves in the sense of "one who fares by the sea to his adventures of commerce and of war"; for among them a man could not hope for greater praise than to be called by his compatriots *vikingr mikill,* a great seafarer, while to go *i viking* was the usual way of speaking of their favorite enterprise of trading and plundering across the waters. Being a viking in that sense was considered highly honorable; this is attested by the fact that numerous runic inscriptions in the Scandinavian countries commemorate such exploits.

At the earliest stage of the Viking society the land was the property of the clan or group, and the individual could claim his share only by living on the land and taking part in its cultivation. At the time usually called the Viking age, individual holdings had become the rule, however, and landowning jarls were numerous. Their land and their retainers were inherited only by their sons. The aggressive freemen and the younger members of the clan began to yearn for the freedom of the open sea and for adventures beyond the fjords of their homeland.

Being excellent shipbuilders and expert seamen, the Scandinavian Vikings were able to navigate the open sea by the aid of the sun, moon, and stars. Bands of freemen and venturesome youth would go forth on expeditions of trading or on excursions simply for the sake of satisfying their lust for daring adventures. These seafaring projects soon developed into piratical incursions and savage plundering forays. Inspired by heroic tales of old, and fired by religious devotion to their courage-imparting war gods, Odin and Thor, they became the scourge of Europe for several generations. Year after year great hordes of bloodthirsty warriors were seized each season with an irresistible desire to leave their homes to go out to conquer, to burn, to pillage, and to kill; and in an almost insane rage they devastated cities and coastal towns. Monasteries and cathedrals with their rich stores of gold and silver and sacred objects were the favorite scenes of bawdy raids by the Northern marauders.

But the Vikings were not only thieves and destroyers of life and property. Even from the earliest times they were intent also upon securing dominions for themselves and establishing homes in other lands. Thus during the Viking age there was an important colonizing movement: westward to the Faeroes, Iceland, Greenland, the Orkneys, Shetlands, and Hebrides, to England and Ireland; southward to France, Normandy, and the Frisian coast; and eastward to the Baltic lands and the Dnieper Basin, where they founded the Russian state.

See also NORMANS; VINLAND.

E. GUSTAV JOHNSON,
Professor Emeritus of Swedish,
North Park College.

Bibliography

Jones, Gwyn, *A History of the Vikings,* rev. ed. (Oxford 1984).
Logan, F. D., *The Vikings in History* (B & N Imports 1983).
Magnusson, Magnus, *Viking:* (Merrimack 1985).
Mawer, Allen, *The Vikings* (1913; reprint, Arden Lib. 1978).
Redmond, Jeffrey R., *Tales of the Vikings: Saga Translations and Their Histories* (Exposition Press 1982).
Simpson, J., *The Viking World* (St. Martin's Press 1980).
Viking Society for Northern Research, *Saga Book,* 19 vols. (1892–1977; reprint, AMS Press 1980).
Wahlgren, Erik, *The Vikings and America* (Thames & Hudson 1986).

VIKRAMADITYA, vĭk-rə-mä′dĭt-yə, a title ("equal in valor to the sun") or name used by several kings of ancient India. A king of legend called Vikramaditya founded an era in 57 B.C., Vikrama Samvat, which is still current in India. Vikramaditya was the hero of numerous legends—miraculous, supernatural, romantic, and historical.

The Jaina Chronicles relate that the Sakas (Śaka) invaded Malwa in central India, drove away its king, and occupied his capital, Ujjain. But four years later, Vikramaditya, the son of the expelled king, defeated the Sakas and regained the kingdom. The date was 57 B.C., and to commemorate the event he inaugurated the Vikrama Samvat. There is nothing improbable in this account, and it fits in well with all that we know of the history of the period. But the literary sources, from which alone we derive the information, belong to a considerably later period, and the existence of a historical person named Vikramaditya in the 1st century B.C. is not authenticated by any record which may be regarded as contemporary or nearly so.

The Vikramaditya tradition must have been firmly established during the age of the Guptas (4th to 6th century A.D.). Two emperors of this dynasty assumed the title, and two others adopted its abbreviated form, Vikrama. Chandragupta II was a great emperor who defeated the Sakas. There is good reason to believe that his court was graced by the greatest Indian poet, Kalidasa, one of the "Nine Gems" (learned men) who adorned the court of the legendary king Vikramaditya. These three points of agreement have led modern scholars to look upon Chandragupta II as the historical king around whom the legend of Vikramaditya gradually grew. Many rulers of India in later times assumed the title, including eight kings of the Chalukya dynasty, one of whom even established an era in imitation of the legendary Vikramaditya, while some rulers of the powerful Rashtrakuta, Chola, and Pandya dynasties used the shorter form, Vikrama.

R. C. MAJUMDAR.

VILAS, vī′ləs, **William Freeman,** American lawyer and politician: b. Chelsea, Vt., July 9, 1840; d. Madison, Wis., Aug. 27, 1908. Moving to Madison as a boy, he was educated at the University of Wisconsin and took a law degree (1860) at the University of Albany. He interrupted his legal practice to serve in the Union Army, rising to the rank of lieutenant colonel; subsequently he was professor of law at the University of Wisconsin from 1868 to 1892, except for his four-year service in the cabinet of Grover Cleveland. An active Democrat, Vilas was permanent chairman of the 1884 convention which nominated Cleveland, under whom he served as postmaster general (1885–1888) and secretary of the interior (1888–1889). He proved himself to be an able administrator, and became one of the president's closest friends. Later he served one term (beginning in 1891) as United States senator from Wisconsin. Vilas was a leader of the Gold Democrats (q.v.) in 1896.

VILKITSKI or **VILKITSKY,** vĭl-kĭts′kē, Russ. vyĭl-kēts′kĭ, **Boris Andreyevich,** Russian explorer and scientist: b. Russia, 1885; d. Brussels, Belgium, March 6, 1961. He was graduated from the naval academy at St. Petersburg in 1903 and eventually rose to the rank of rear admiral. He is credited with being the first to navigate the Northeast Passage in an east-westerly direction (the course had been sailed previously, from west to east, by Nils A. E. Nordenskjöld in 1878–1880). Vilkitski used the two icebreakers, *Taimyr* and *Vaigach,* in searching for the passage north of Siberia in 1913, but at that time he was unable to sail through because of heavy ice floes near Nicholas II Land (now Severnaya Zemlya), an archipelago which he discovered on that journey. Upon his return he was commissioned to continue his exploration, and in the summer of 1915 he was successful in making the first passage from Vladivostok to Archangel.

Vilkitski's expeditions obtained valuable data in many fields, particularly in hydrography, which later contributed significantly to further exploration of the Arctic regions north of Siberia. Although a refugee from the Russian Revolution, he worked for the Soviet government for a short period in World War II as supervisor of convoys across the Kara Sea.

FINN RONNE.

VILLA, vē′yä, **Francisco** (known as **PANCHO VILLA**), Mexican bandit and general: b. Río Grande, Durango, Mexico, June 5, 1878; d. near Parral, Chihuahua, July 20, 1923. His parents, Augustín Arango and Micaela Arámbula, christened him Doroteo Arango. He borrowed the name "Francisco Villa" from that of an earlier outlaw after he had killed a man for betraying his sister. In 1903 federal troops captured him, but permitted him to avoid imprisonment by volunteering for the 14th Cavalry Regiment. He spent most of his youth in the mountains, where he lived as a bandit. From robbing trains, looting banks, and raiding mines, he learned to live off the land and to avoid pursuers. These experiences helped him to develop into an elusive guerrilla fighter.

The outbreak of the 1910 Revolution against the Díaz regime inspired Villa to support Francisco I. Madero, who had declared himself provisional president of Mexico. At the first Juárez battle in 1911, Villa fought courageously and shortly won fame for his valor. During the revolution he captured Juárez on three occasions (1911, 1913, and 1919), and he conquered Chihuahua, Parral, and Torreón numerous times. Though retaining the favor of Madero, he had difficulties with both Pascual Orozco and Victoriano Huerta, and the latter imprisoned him in Mexico City in 1912. Always elusive, Villa managed to escape four months later, and went to live in El Paso, Texas, where he soon began to reorganize his followers. Returning to Mexico in 1913, for the next two years he delivered crushing blows on the battlefield to his competitors for the presidency, winning the interested concern of the United States when President Woodrow Wilson dispatched to Villa his personal representative, George C. Carothers.

For a period Villa appeared to be the leader most likely to solve the vexing problems of the increasingly bloody revolution. He experienced a setback from which he never fully recovered, however, when he lost the crucial Battle of Celaya to Gen. Álvaro Obregón in 1915. Mexicans now shifted their allegiance to Obregón's superior, Venustiano Carranza. The United States, noting this enthusiasm, turned from Villa, and the Villistas felt themselves betrayed. The Santa Isabel massacre in Mexico in January 1916, when Villistas slaughtered 15 Americans, was an act of reprisal. After Carranza received permission to use United States rails to transport his troops, Villa vengefully raided Columbus, N. Mex., on March 9, 1916, killing 17 Americans.

Thereafter began Gen. John J. Pershing's epic chase of Villa during the 1916 punitive expedition into Mexico. The troopers killed a number of Villistas and dispersed the rest, Villa having with him at the last only three faithful men. But the United States contingent failed to catch him; instead, the unfortunate expedition made him a household hero. The Mexican government retired him as a general with full pay in 1920. In 1923 a group of his enemies, enlisting the aid of a pumpkin-seed vendor to alert them of his approach, ambushed him and assassinated him in his automobile at Parral, Chihuahua. In 1926 fiends desecrated his tomb and stole his skull. The perpetrators of these crimes were never identified with certainty.

Few men in modern history have maintained a stronger hold on the masses than has Villa. Although a vicious killer, he sometimes showed a merciful side: pity for children, sympathy for peons, and charity for widows. It was the irony of his life that he should have been betrayed by a street vendor, one of the peasant class from whom he sprang and for whose cause he had always expressed devotion and among whom he became a folk hero.

See also MEXICO—8. *History* (Modern Mexico).

HALDEEN BRADDY,
Professor of English, Texas Western College.

VILLA, vĭl'ə, possibly a diminutive form of *vicus,* a hamlet or village, a term applied to suburban summer residences in the days of the Roman republic and empire from about the 3d century before Christ and thereafter. Villas were of two types: one, the *villa rustica,* a farm in individual ownership or one operated for profit under absentee direction; the other, the *villa urbana,* a country seat belonging to the well-to-do. Although something is known of the construction and appearance of villas from excavations, our knowledge of them is derived primarily from descriptions by such writers as Pliny the Younger—who described two of his several villas at Tusculum and Laurentium in his letters—and by Seneca, Varro, and Vitruvius. In one form or another, the villa was always associated with the practice of agriculture.

The dawn of the Iron Age and the development of the iron plow and other implements greatly stimulated agricultural production and encouraged the development of new methods, the study of plant and soil differentiation, the practice of irrigation and crop rotation, and the import of new types of produce from other parts of the civilized world. Fresh impetus was given to this trend by the distribution to Roman citizens in the early 2d century B.C. of the *ager publicus,* the public domain composed of lands confiscated in war, expropriated from political opponents, or reverting to the state by escheat. Since the *villa rustica,* conducted by the slave *familia,* was more familiar with improved agricultural methods and because its owners alone possessed the resources needed to introduce new crops and breeds, great numbers of the newly landed peasants lost their properties to the villa owners, composed in part of the growing, rich, powerful, and corrupt senatorial class. This evolution coincided with the unification of the entire Italian Peninsula by conquest under Rome, which became the commercial and administrative center of the Mediterranean and created a new class of merchants, financiers, and contractors. These factors, coupled with a great demand for new varieties of food by the well-to-do consumer and the import of slave labor from Roman military victories, led to the evolution of the villa on the *latifundia* (q.v.), vast farms, one or two of which comprised perhaps 40,000 acres, although most were smaller. In the villa, the main room was the kitchen, with bakery and stables beyond, and special rooms for wine and oil presses. These estates, some near Rome and some in the provinces, were intensively cultivated to produce revenue for their owners from new types of animals, fruits, fowl, and fish introduced from abroad. Corn, flax, vegetables, olives, and grapes were cultivated. Pigeons, peacocks, and ducks were raised in aviaries, while fish and snails were cultivated in artificial ponds. The *latifundia* were treated as technically and economically self-sufficient units. Irrigation, manuring, and crop rotation were practiced; agricultural implements and specialized buildings were developed; and the holdings were run on a strict accounting basis.

These large estates survived as long as prisoners of war could be obtained cheaply as slaves but, with the passing of the slave economy toward the end of the republic, the *villa rustica* and its associated farm experienced profound changes. The slave *familia* gave way to the *colonus,* who rented the land or worked it on shares in small tracts. The *latifundium,* thus broken up into small units but still in individual ownership, developed partly as a produce farm and partly as a stock-breeding operation with thousands of head of cows, horses, sheep, and goats. Parallel to and succeeding this metamorphosis, the late Roman type of estate, the *villa urbana,* developed.

These elaborate country villas, at first built on terraced hills near Rome in the rich Campania and in parts of Etruria, were considered indispensable to maintain the position of the ruling classes. Even a man of such moderate means as Cicero owned six suburban and country houses. Greek architects were called on to design splendid mansions, on the construction of which sums as high as today's equivalent of a million dollars were lavished. These villas comprised great halls, loggias, baths, libraries, and formal gardens and were furnished at even greater expense with costly paintings, statuary, and exotic furniture, much of which was pillaged from the vanquished peoples of the East. The whole scheme of life of the villa was centered on dining in the vast banquet halls. High prices were paid for slaves trained in culinary practice, and cellars were stocked with vast quantities—sometimes as much as 8,000 gallons—of imported wines.

In the transition from the last days of the republic to the early period of the empire, expenditures for villas, already extreme in Cicero's day, grew even vaster, and estates were built at even greater distances from Rome—many overlooking the Bay of Naples and at similar spots of scenic beauty, and many in outlying provinces even as distant as Britain. Gardens and lakes were constructed on an ever more lavish scale; the halls of the villas were decorated with gilded beams and their walls constructed of multicolored imported marbles. The baths were built as luxurious separate structures, and outbuildings covered great stretches of the coast. Furniture, inlaid with tortoiseshell and ivory, grew even more elaborate; great candelabra were used for illumination; and gold and silver plate of incredible weight made its appearance.

Even the influence of the more austere emperors such as Trajan and Hadrian in the 2d century A.D. failed to deter the excesses of the moneyed proprietors, who continued to luxuriate in elaborate country villas and extended their building operations to the present areas of France, Switzerland, and Germany. Architecture achieved even greater freedom, and mosaic floors and glass windows were introduced. The final achievement was the installation of flues to conduct heat from a central fire to the various rooms.

Architecture and landscape design complemented each other to create even more luxurious villas, which evolved into unsymmetrical, rambling buildings designed to take advantage of the breeze and the view and embraced towers and colonnades on several levels. The outbuildings, dedicated to pleasure and ornament, were gradually separated from the main villa. Hadrian's own villa at Tibur (Tivoli) covered 180 acres; its gardens extended for many miles; and its numerous structures reproduced all the famous buildings the emperor had seen on his travels.

With the increasing incursions of the barbarian hordes, the decrease in Roman territory and the consequent loss of wealth, the decline of the monarchy, and the evolution of Rome from a pagan to a Christian center, the Roman villa fell into ruins and disappeared, to await its rebirth in the luxurious 15th century.

The Greeks had no passion for country life, preferring to build their residences in the city and confining their suburban slave estates and those in Sicily before the Roman conquest and on the coast of the Black Sea to scientific agricultural production for profit. The Egyptians in the time of the Ptolemies followed a similar system, but completely under government control. The ubiquitous Roman type of villa left its impress on the life of subsequent centuries. Many British country estates of totally different construction were, following the Roman tradition, styled villas. In Renaissance Italy, however, the true Roman villa enjoyed a revival, and several were built on the sites of famous Roman predecessors. The Villa d'Este near Tivoli, the Villa Pia in the Vatican gardens, and the Villa Barberini at Castel Gandolfo are a few of the many Renaissance villas that closely resemble Roman prototypes both in architecture and in their garden setting and terraces.

OTTO V. ST. WHITELOCK,
Consulting Editor of "The Encyclopedia Americana."

VILLA-LOBOS, vē'lə-lōm'bo͝osh, **Heitor,** Brazilian composer: b. Rio de Janeiro, Brazil, March 5, 1887; d. there, Nov. 17, 1959. He was an influential proponent of Brazilian nationalism in music as well as the creator of more than 1,300 compositions of almost every conceivable type. Villa-Lobos' father taught him to play the viola in the manner of a cello while the boy was still too small to hold it under his chin, and he picked up a variety of other instruments well enough to perform in cafés and theaters. Before he was 20, he traveled through many parts of Brazil collecting folk tunes and writing original compositions.

Villa-Lobos' 14 *chôros,* written between 1920 and 1929, probably contain his most characteristic and important work. Scoring them for a variety of instruments from single guitar to full orchestra with chorus, the composer regarded them as stylized syntheses of elements in Brazilian music, and as original additions to the development beginning with the suite and ending with the symphonic poem. Many critics do not find the structure so important, but generally admire their brilliance of color and timbre, their fecundity in theme, and their vigorous dance rhythms. In form the *chôros* resembles a rhapsody.

Influences upon Villa-Lobos have been much debated because of the composer's incredible musical memory, and because scholars sometimes disagree with his extensive program notes. Through friendship with Darius Milhaud and Artur Rubinstein, and through a Brazilian government fellowship for four years' study in France, he became acquainted with the new currents in European music, but he frequently disavowed alleged influences by voicing his hatred of "cults" and "systems." His suites, *Bachianas Brasileiras* show a debt to Johann Sebastian Bach that is perhaps not especially apparent to most listeners. The obvious influences on his work are folk songs, popular songs, and African and Indian music.

Villa-Lobos' interest in a great national musical movement in Brazil led him to become in 1932 director of music in education in Brazil; to found the Brazilian Academy of Music in Rio de Janeiro, an institution that has trained a very large percentage of the country's music teachers, as well as some performers and composers; and to edit a songbook for school and popular use. He originated a custom of celebrating Brazilian National Day with massed choruses and orchestras, conducting as many as 40,000 voices and 1,000 instruments. Speaking of this nationalism in his own works, Villa-Lobos once said: "I study the history, the country, the speech, the customs, the background of the people. I have always done this, and it is from these sources, spiritual as well as practical, that I have drawn my art."

His huge body of work includes several operas, ballets, oratorios, at least 12 symphonies, and 15 or more string quartets.

VILLA MARIA COLLEGE, vĭl'ə mə-rē'ə an accredited Roman Catholic college for women, in Erie, Pa., operated by the Sisters of St. Joseph. The institution was first chartered as a seminary in 1882, later offered instruction on the primary and secondary levels, and established itself as a college in 1925. A school of nursing was founded in 1953. Degrees offered include the bachelor of arts and the bachelor of science in liberal arts, and the bachelor of science in nursing, medical technology, home economics, and commercial education. Buildings and grounds total 45 acres. The annual enrollment approximates 600 students. The faculty includes both religious and lay teachers.

VILLA PARK, village, Illinois, in Du Page County, 17 miles east of St. Charles and 11 miles west of the Chicago city limits. Primarily a residential community, it is a rail-commuting suburb of Chicago. The surrounding area is devoted to the cultivation of a large variety of farm produce, and there are beverage and fertilizer plants in the village. Incorporated in 1914 it adopted the council-manager form of government in 1957. Pop. 23,185.

VILLA RICA, vĭl′ə rĭk′ə, town, Georgia, in Carroll and Douglas counties, 31 miles west of Atlanta, altitude 1,155 feet. The principal manufactures are clothing and fibers, fertilizer, and cottonseed oil; lumbering is another occupation. There is an airport. The town was incorporated in 1830, four years after the discovery of gold brought an influx of settlers. Pop. 3,420.

VILLACH, fĭl′äᴋ (Slovenian Bᴇʟᴊᴀᴋ), city, Austria, in the Province of Carinthia, on the Drau River at the western end of the Klagenfurt Basin. The city is the trade and commercial center of the province, with manufacturing of lead wares supplied by lead from the rich mines of nearby Bleiburg. There is also timber trading. Already important as a city in Roman times, Villach was part of the bishopric of Bamberg between the 10th and 18th centuries. St. Jacob's Church, in Gothic style with a detached 315-foot-high tower, was built in the 15th century. Near the city is Warmbad Villach, known for its mineral baths.

Gᴇᴏʀɢᴇ W. Hᴏғғᴍᴀɴ.

VILLAGE, vĭl′ĭj, a type of community, generally small but without exact or commonly accepted size limits. Generally, in the United States, the village is thought to be intermediate between the hamlet (a settlement with several families and some form of commerce but no more than 50 people) and the town (generally over 1,000 people). In New England and New York, and occasionally in other parts of the United States, the village is a recognized unit of local government and may be incorporated, with governing, policing, and taxing powers. Often in these areas, however, the village is simply the trading and social center of a "town" (that is, a township, which may include unsettled areas or single-family farmsteads). This pattern was so general in the northeastern United States that the business and social center of a community of 20,000 or 30,000 people may still be called "the village." The term "village" has little popular use in the United States outside of New England and New York, however. Even very small communities elsewhere are likely to be known to their residents as towns.

Origin and Evolution.—The village is the typical form of rural settlement in most of the world—in Europe (except for Great Britain), in Asia, in Africa, and in much of South America. The isolated farmstead or "open-country neighborhood," typical of much of the United States, Canada, Australia, New Zealand, and scattered regions elsewhere, appears to be fairly recent in world history. It often seems to be the result of the settlement of lands that previously were only thinly occupied by indigenous populations, but probably also derives from the emergence of clear-cut private proprietorship of land. In much of Europe and in many other areas of the world, communal land ownership prevailed in the past, and this property arrangement was one basis for the village form of rural settlement, the community being set amid the tillage and grazing lands.

The end of communal ownership or partly communal land use by peasants or serfs on feudal estates generally did not cause the end of villages or, except in England, any substantial increase of separate farmsteads. Generations of equal divisions of land among heirs, provided by the Napoleonic Code and persisting in most of western Europe since Napoleonic times, resulted in widespread fragmentation and scattering of hereditary plots. Thus the village commonly continued to lie near the center of a farming area, with residents often successively tending plots in several directions from their homes. In eastern Europe, under Communist regimes, consolidation of holdings, if not outright collectivization, has been the rule since World War II, but the village pattern remains. The scattered plots are still very common in rural France and Italy and not unknown in Germany and the Low Countries.

Growing awareness of the nearly universal appearance of the agricultural village prompted many social theorists in the 19th century to suggest that such communities represented a universal stage in human evolution. Such simplifying theories lost support as evidence of the great diversity of human cultures and their paths of change was accumulated. The interpretation of the village pattern is now more nearly a functional one. With settled agriculture, village orientation provides mutual protection, sociability, a measure of economic specialization (such as handicrafts), and at least the rudiments of local government.

Characteristics.—Since size limits will not precisely distinguish villages from other types of communities, the question arises as to whether the term has a precise meaning. All communities or settlements called villages in popular language or technical studies cannot be brought within a common definition. Sometimes the term is simply anachronistic or fanciful, as in "Greenwich Village" in New York City. Generally, however, a village is a residential and trading center for a predominantly agricultural economy. Its social controls are predominantly traditional and informal; more formal administration and government are typical of cities and towns. Its self-sufficiency may be nearly complete, as in some parts of the Far East and Latin America, or seriously impaired by modern transportation, communication, and agencies of central government. The population of the village, unlike that of most cities and many towns, is self-recruited rather than immigrant. This, and the traditional informality of social standards and controls, lends a distinct quality of homogeneity that the more cosmopolitan center does not have.

The collapse of the theory that the village is the basic community of all civilizations did not end the idealization of the village. Yet even the informal and traditional social controls of the village can be extremely restrictive, certainly more so than the formal tolerance of difference that the cultural heterogeneity of the city encourages or requires. And it cannot be assumed that villages are democratic. European villages are often dominated by one or a few families, some of which may claim descent from feudal rulers. The village in India is often ruled by a council (panchayat) of the leading caste or by a few principal landlords. Even in the United States, with its short history and absence of an officially recognized aristocracy, leading families are more likely to receive deference in villages than in larger and more impersonal communities. The integration of village life, or lack of social problems and tensions, has also been exaggerated. Conflicts may smolder or burn brightly, all the more because the parties know each other and personalize the antipathy.

In Europe and Asia, the village has exhibited a remarkable power of survival amidst currents of rapid social change. Rural America has been much more profoundly affected by the encroachments of an urban-industrial civilization. Many small towns, technically villages, have virtually disappeared as their economic and other social functions have been absorbed by nearby cities. Village life may endure a while longer in the United States, but the sense of continuity and communal integrity are difficult to maintain with high rates of residential mobility and in the face of steady inroads of an essentially urban civilization.

See also VILLAGE COMMUNITIES.

WILBERT E. MOORE,
Professor of Sociology, Princeton University.

VILLAGE COMMUNITIES. The village community may be defined as a group of people who live in permanent dwellings in a defined territory which includes arable land, sometimes held in common. If cattle is kept, as is often the case, it is pastured on noncultivated meadowland over which the community claims right. Further characteristics include a predominance of agricultural occupations, a close relationship to the natural environment, strong internal cohesion, and a relative absence of internal stratification and of occupational, territorial, and vertical social mobility. As such, the village is a specific type of rural settlement, but not the only one.

The definition given implies that village communities did not exist before the Neolithic period, which saw the invention of agriculture and domestication of animals. The pre-Neolithic mode of life, hunting of animals and collecting of wild plants and seeds, necessitated nomadism or seminomadism rather than sedentary settlement. The earliest known village sites were found by archaeologists in the same area in which agriculture seems to have originated, namely, in present day Iraq, Iran, Egypt, and Palestine (consult Robert J. Braidwood, *The Near East and the Foundations for Civilization,* Eugene, Oreg., 1952). Some of these sites are 7,000 to 8,000 years old. Of their socioeconomic structure, little is known.

Theory.—The scientific study of the village community did not start until the middle of the 19th century. Scholars such as Konrad von Maurer, Frederic Maitland, Frederic Seebohm, Baden Henry Baden-Powell, Sir Paul Vinogradoff, Max Weber, and many others directed their attention to the village community as a significant unit of study. Sir Henry Maine (1822–1888), one of the first English writers on this topic, held the theory that the village community was originally founded by a group of kin-related people who settled independently in a specified spot. In time, the original households branched out into many separate ones, clearing more land as the need arose. Occasionally they included strangers, who were sometimes adopted but more often relegated to second-class membership, tolerated rather than accepted. If one family became extinct, its share of land was returned to the common stock. Only in later times, under pressure of more highly developed political structures, did the village community become feudalistic. The land was then owned by a ruler, who received tribute in kind and promised protection in return. Often the responsibilities of supervision and collection were transferred to other members of the aristocracy. Maine based his case for this presumed development upon analysis of Roman law (*Ancient Law,* 1861) and upon practices in Russia, southeastern European countries, and specifically India, where he had carried out extensive field research (*Village Communities in the East and West,* 1871).

Several other scholars criticized Maine's theoretical reconstructions. Baden-Powell, who also had visited India, Sir Frederick Pollock and Frederic Maitland, Jan Lewiński, and Gorham Sanderson demonstrated that the manor and its surrounding village communities in the area of the Roman Empire did not develop out of individual villages but were historically associated with the latifundia established during the time of the empire.

Modern anthropologists and sociologists take the position that both developments took place. They recognize that the evolution and structure of human settlements in general, and of village communities in particular, are closely connected with specific historical developments and ecological, sociopolitical, economic, and religious circumstances which are different from place to place. With this recognition, questions of absolute origins have generally been replaced by an increased interest in the structure and function of village communities, in an attempt to gain a basic understanding of the essential nature of living arrangements therein.

Existing Village Communities.—Authentic communal-tenure village communities are not as common as they were in the past. The 19th century authors already noted their virtual absence from Europe at the time they were writing, although Maine still encountered some during his research in India. On Java, where communal tenure was the rule rather than the exception, only one third of all communities possessed such a system in 1927. In 1910, 90 percent of the villages in the central plateau of Mexico had no communal land of any kind. In other areas where villages with common tenure once existed (China, Africa, South America, and elsewhere), the system has also lapsed. Yet the village community, with or without communal tenure, remains a characteristic unit.

Peasant Villages.—Max Weber (1864–1920) made a very important distinction between peasant and farmer communities. Peasant life is closest to that of the village community: for peasants, agriculture is both a livelihood and a way of life. Farmers, on the other hand, carry out agriculture for the market, as a business to gain profit, looking on the land as commodity and capital. Peasant villages in this sense are still found over many parts of the world, although some are doubtless in transition to becoming farmer communities or industrialized towns.

As their characteristic features, peasant villages show strong internal cohesion and tendencies to restrict membership to those born within the community. Rules of local endogamy sometimes reinforce this trend. Membership in the community is demonstrated by participation in religious rituals, which frequently stress the power of the community to deal with the supernatural rather than reliance upon individual piety. Economically, a peasant produces mainly for his own household's consumption, although he also uses part of his product to exchange in a market for other goods and services. These markets are often local and differ in structure from those in the cities. Although some city-produced goods reach the peasant level, there is a tendency to limit the flow of city goods into the community.

Politically, peasant villages are now usually parts of national states and theoretically possess the rights and duties involved in such membership. But the village community has frequently retained mechanisms of internal control, whether through government-approved local leaders or through informal leadership and community sanctions. Emotional attachments face inward. The individual's first loyalty is to his family, then to his community, and only then to whatever is beyond. The various elements of this characterization may be developed more strongly in some villages than in others, but as a type they are recognizable and clearly distinct from tribal groups, farming settlements, and city formations.

See also VILLAGE.

ANNEMARIE DE WAAL MALEFIJT,
Lecturer in Anthropology, Hunter College, New York.

Bibliography

Maine, H. S., *Village-Communities in the East and West*, ed. by R. Mersky and J. Jacobstein, 2d ed. (1879; reprint, W. S. Hein 1972).
Samuel, R., ed., *Village Life and Labour* (Methuen 1983).
Seebohm, Frederic, *English Village Community* (1883; reprint, Associated Faculty Press 1971).
Slater, Gilbert, *English Peasantry and the Enclosure of Common Fields* (1907; reprint, Kelley 1968).

VILLAGE GOVERNMENT. See URBAN GOVERNMENT.

VILLAIN or **VILLEIN.** See VILLEINS.

VILLANELLE, vĭl-ə-nĕl′, originally a French pastoral roundelay, evolved in the Renaissance from an Italian three-part folk song. Jacques Grévin, Joachim du Bellay, and Honoré d'Urfé wrote amatory and light villanelles, and Jean Passerat gave the poem what is its nearest standard form. The villanelle consists of an indefinite number of tercets, usually five, followed by a final quatrain. Like the rondeau, it is a form with frequent repetitions. The first and third lines of the first tercet are alternately repeated as the third line of succeeding tercets, and together as the last refrain of the quatrain:

$$a^1\,b\,a^2\;a\,b\,a^1\;a\,b\,a^2\;.\,.\,.\;a\,b\,a^1\,a^2.$$

Andrew Lang and Ernest Henley, among 19th century English poets, rediscovered the modest lightness and charm of the form. Edwin Arlington Robinson, in *The House on the Hill*, also used the form, with his characteristic weight and consequence.

EUGENIO VILLICAÑA.

VILLANI, vĕl-lä′nē, **Giovanni,** Florentine chronicler: b. Florence, Italy 1275?; d. there, 1348. A member of the Florentine mercantile class which played a major role in Europe's international economy in the 14th century, he traveled extensively on business in Italy, France, and the Low Countries as a youth. Active in politics, he three times entered the Signoria, Florence's highest executive office. Toward the end of his life his fortunes declined, and he was imprisoned for debt in 1342, after the Bonaccorsi company, in which he was a partner, went bankrupt. He died in 1348, a victim of the Black Death.

While on a visit to Rome during the jubilee of 1300, Villani was inspired to write a history of Florence. He was convinced that the city, "the daughter and creature of Rome, was in the ascendancy and destined for great things." The history—*Cronica Universale*—traces human history from its origins. He based his early books upon the literary sources available to him. The last half of his work (books 7–12), treats of events during the author's lifetime, and is the most important. While describing Florentine history in great detail, he also wrote informative chapters on events elsewhere in Italy, France, England, and the Low Countries. A historical source of primary importance, the chronicle also reflects the outlook of the writer and his social class. Villani's mentality was bourgeois; his world was that of the countinghouse, the city hall, and the public square. While still accepting the medieval ideals which he had inherited, he reveals in his chronicle the extent to which these ideals had disintegrated in Florence's urban environment. His brother Matteo extended the chronicle to 1363, and after his death his son Filippo wrote a few additional chapters carrying the story through 1364. There is no modern critical edition of the *Cronica;* the best available is the Florence Magheri edition (8 vols.) of 1823.

GENE A. BRUCKER,
Professor of History, University of California.

VILLANOVA UNIVERSITY, vĭl-ə-nō′və, an institution of higher learning, at Villanova, Pa., 14 miles northwest of Philadelphia. Controlled by the Augustinian Fathers of the Roman Catholic Church, the school dates back to 1843, when classes were opened on a 200-acre tract of land (Belle Air) which the order had purchased the previous year. On March 10, 1848, the "Augustinian College of Villanova in the State of Pennsylvania" received its charter by an act of the legislature. Becoming a university in 1954, Villanova offers courses in arts and sciences, commerce and finance, engineering (civil, electrical, chemical, and mechanical), and nursing. About 4,200 students are regularly enrolled in full-time courses. Summer, part-time, and most full-time courses are co-educational.

EUGENE J. RUANE.

VILLANOVANS. See ITALY—7. *History* (Northern Influences).

VILLARD, vĭ-lär′, vĭ-lärd′, **Henry,** American journalist and financier: b. Speyer, Bavaria, April 10, 1835; d. Dobbs Ferry, N.Y., Nov. 12, 1900. He changed his name from Ferdinand Heinrich Gustav Hilgard when he went to the United States in 1853. Villard, who long desired to be a writer, started on German-American publications, later doing correspondent work for the Cincinnati *Commercial*, Chicago *Tribune*, New York *Tribune*, New York *Herald*, and others. In 1858 he reported the Lincoln-Douglas debates, starting a lifelong friendship with Abraham Lincoln. In 1859–1860, Villard, along with Horace Greeley, reported on the discovery of gold in Colorado. Villard's book, *The Past and Present of the Pike's Peak Gold Regions* (1860), was reprinted in 1932.

Villard gained fame reporting the Civil War, covering Bull Run, the Wilderness campaign, Missionary Ridge, Petersburg, Richmond, and other engagements. Out of this conflict he became a "convinced pacifist," a feeling that he passed on to his son, Oswald Garrison Villard (q.v.).

From 1868 to 1871 the family lived in Boston, Mass., where Villard was secretary of the American Social Science Association. His work with German bondholders in financial transactions with Pacific coast railways eventually placed him in the ranks of the top railroad promoters. He once lost his fortune but regained it with the aid of German capital. In 1890 he acquired control of the Edison Lamp Company at Newark, N.J., and later the Edison Machine Works at Schenectady, N.Y. For two years he headed the Edison General Electric Company, which he organized in 1889. His interest returned to journalism in 1881, when he purchased the New York *Evening Post* and the weekly *Nation,* and combined them, the latter becoming in large part the *Post's* weekly supplement. They were independent publications, with low circulations but much influence.

In 1866, Villard married Helen Frances "Fanny" Garrison, only daughter of William Lloyd Garrison, the famed abolitionist editor. Villard's life story is told in *Memoirs of Henry Villard* (2 vols., 1904).

William H. Taft,
School of Journalism, University of Missouri.

VILLARD, Oswald Garrison, American journalist: b. Wiesbaden, Germany, March 13, 1872; d. New York, N.Y., Oct. 1, 1949. Called an "aristocrat of liberalism," he, unlike his father, Henry Villard (q.v.), devoted his lifetime to journalism. At Harvard, where he was educated (B.A., 1893), Villard was an assistant in the history department until leaving in 1896 to begin his newspaper work with a six-month "course" on the old Philadelphia *Press.* He then moved to New York City, where his father recently had acquired the New York *Evening Post* and *The Nation.* As publisher and editor of the *Evening Post* from 1897 to 1918—when it was sold after having lost money and circulation during the war years—Villard fought for many a lost cause, becoming a recognized pacifist for his stand against the Spanish-American War and United States entry into World War I. He owned and edited *The Nation* from 1918 to 1932; in 1907 he founded *Yachting* magazine. He was one of the founders of the National Association for the Advancement of Colored People. Both father and son were suffragists.

His books include: *John Brown—A Biography Fifty Years After* (1910); *Germany Embattled* (1915); *Newspapers and Newspaper Men* (1923); *Prophets—True and False* (1928); *The German Phoenix* (1933); *Our Military Chaos* (1939); *Within Germany* (1940); and *The Disappearing Daily* (1944). Highlights of Villard's career are told in the autobiographical *Fighting Years; Memoirs of a Liberal Editor* (1939).

William H. Taft.

VILLARI, vēl'lä-rē, **Pasquale,** Italian historian and statesman: b. Naples, Italy, Oct. 3, 1826; d. Florence, Dec. 17, 1917. An ardent nationalist from his youth, Villari participated in the uprising against the Bourbons in Naples (1848); forced into exile after the revolt's failure, he went to Florence and began his historical studies. His reputation was established with the publication of his biography of Girolamo Savonarola, *Storia di Girolamo Savonarola e de' suoi tempi,* 2 vols. (1859–61), which was followed by a study of Niccolò Machiavelli, *Niccolò Machiavelli e i suoi tempi* (1877–82), and by other major works on Italian medieval history. He held university posts in Pisa and Florence, where he trained a generation of students in medieval and Renaissance history. Actively engaged in politics, he sat in both the Chamber of Deputies and the Senate, and served a brief term as minister of public instruction (1891).

Villari was closely identified with the movement that sought to build a firm foundation for the new Italian state by glorifying Italy's past. A passionate believer in individual liberty, his historical ideal was Savonarola, whom he admired more than Machiavelli. He was an articulate exponent of the liberal ideals of his age, and his books, translated into English by his wife, were widely read and admired in England. He also wrote several important political tracts, in which he exposed the evils of Italian society and criticized the government's failure to solve or alleviate these problems.

Gene A. Brucker.

VILLARRICA, bē-yä-rē'kä, city, Paraguay, capital of Guairá Department, and connected by railroad and highway with Asunción, 110 miles west-northwest. From the surrounding agricultural region comes a wide variety of goods for processing and marketing here, including cotton, yerba maté, tobacco, citrus fruits, and sugarcane. There are also textile, lumber, and flour mills, and trade is conducted in cattle and hides. Wine is manufactured by settlers of German origin. Founded on the Paraná in 1576 (and reestablished on the present site in 1682), the town is pleasantly situated on a hill dotted with orange groves, and retains its colonial flavor. There is a beautiful cathedral, and a religious shrine attracts large numbers of pilgrims each year. Pop. (1950) 27,795.

VILLARS, vē-lår', Duc **Claude Louis Hector de,** French soldier: b. Moulins, France, May 8, 1653; d. Turin, Italy, June 17, 1734. He distinguished himself under vicomte de Turenne (Henri de La Tour d'Auvergne) and Louis II, prince de Condé, in the famous crossing of the Rhine in the war with Holland, 1672. He campaigned in Flanders under the duc de Luxembourg, in Alsace under François de Bonne Créqui. During the War of the League of Augsburg (1689–1697) he became a major general in 1690 and lieutenant general in 1693. After the peace, he was appointed ambassador to Vienna, a post he held until 1701, having formerly served brilliantly there in 1683. In the War of the Spanish Succession (1701–1714) he crushed Prince Louis of Baden at Friedlingen, Oct. 14, 1702, and was acclaimed marshal of France by his troops on the field of battle, a title ratified by Louis XIV, who also appointed him commander in chief replacing Marshal Nicolas de Catinat. Although victorious at Höchstädt in 1703, he asked to be recalled in consequence of a disagreement with the elector of Bavaria, his ally in operations against the Austrians. In 1704 he led the royal army against the Camisards (q.v.); when he persuaded their leader, Jean Cavalier, to abandon the struggle and the rebellion collapsed, he was made a duke. Very successful in the eastern campaigns, 1705–1707, he became commander of the army of the Alps in 1708, and the next year commander of the army of the North. Pitted against Marlborough and Prince Eugene in the sanguinary Battle of Malplaquet (1709), he was severely wounded. After recovering at Versailles he was made a peer of France and governor of Metz in 1710. Again leading the French Army in 1712 he defeated Prince Eugene at Denain, which hastened the signing of the Treaty of Utrecht. A grateful sovereign made him governor of Provence. When Austria refused to accept the Treaty of Utrecht he again defeated Prince Eugene and imposed the Peace of Rastatt on Austria (March 1714). Elected to the French Academy, Villars served as minister of state in 1723, and was made a grandee of Spain. At the beginning of the War of the Polish Succession (1733–1735) he was created grand marshal of France and given command of the army in Italy where he won a series of battles despite his 81 years. A rough and bold commander he was more admired by his soldiers than by the nobles at court, who accused him of being avaricious and a braggart. However, he was the best French general of his day, and a worthy opponent of Marlborough and Prince Eugene.

Of Villars' *Mémoires* (3 vols., 1784) only the first volume is authentic, the other two being a worthless compilation by Guillaume Plantavit de la Pause.

ROBERT E. TAYLOR,
New York University.

VILLE PLATTE, vēl-plăt', city, Louisiana, seat of Evangeline Parish, 45 miles southwest of Alexandria, at an altitude of 72 feet. The city is in an agricultural area that produces rice, cotton, sweet potatoes, corn, and cattle. There is petroleum in the area, and a carbon plant is in the city. Settled by the French, the city was incorporated in 1858. Chicot State Park is to the north of the city. The government is administered by mayor and council. Pop. 9,201.

ALOYSIUS LAUNEY.

VILLEFRANCHE-SUR-SAÔNE, vēl-fränsh'sür-sōn', town, France, in the Department of Rhône, near the Saône River, 17 miles north-northwest of Lyon. An industrial center, it produces clothing and textiles (silk, satin, flannels), farm and viticulture implements, and food products, and it is a marketing center for the region's famous Beaujolais wines. Founded early in the 13th century, Villefranche has several Renaissance houses —one of which, the town hall, dates from 1660— and a Romanesque-Gothic church. Pop. (1982) 28,858.

VILLEHARDOUIN, vē-lär-dwăN', **Geoffroi de,** French chronicler: b. Villehardouin, near Troyes, France, about 1150; d. about 1218. He was marshal of Champagne (next to the highest military rank in that county) from about 1185, but most of what is known of him is revealed in his chronicle from 1199 on. During the Fourth Crusade he made important arrangements with the Venetians in early 1201 to transport the crusaders to the Holy Land. He played a key role with the poet Conon de Béthune in the negotiations with Alexius (later Alexius IV Angelus) of Byzantium which resulted in the Crusade being deflected from the Holy Land to the conquest of Byzantium. After the fall of Constantinople, April 25, 1204, he helped to reconcile Baldwin of Flanders, newly elected emperor, and his friend Boniface, marquess of Montferrat. He was granted as his share of the spoils a fief in Thrace in 1205 and the title of marshal of Rumania. He seems to have returned to France sometime after 1212. His *Conquête de Constantinople,* the first great history in French, probably written around the year 1212, covers the period 1199 to 1207, ending the year of Boniface's death, killed in an ambush by Bulgars. In form, the history is autobiographical, but the scrupulousness of the observation and the documentation makes it an excellent historical document.

The first printed edition of the *Conquête* was that of Blaise de Vigenère in 1585. The best available edition today is the one that was edited by Edmond Faral.

ROBERT E. TAYLOR,
New York University.

VILLEINS, vĭl'ənz. From the late Roman Imperial period in the 4th century down into the 13th century when western Europe was dominated by the seignorial (manorial) system, agrarian service was provided by humble rustics known as peasants. The word peasant is but a collective name for a variety of agrarian classes, among which was the villein (derived from the Latin *villanus,* meaning inhabitant of a village).

In a legal, social, and economic sense the villein is difficult to define. On the Continent a villein was generally a free peasant with less burdensome agrarian obligations than the unfree serf. In England, however, a villein was ordinarily unfree and endured the legal, social, and economic condition of the continental serf. Although the medieval lawyer felt that a distinction between free and unfree peasant could be made on the basis of the more onerous and less clearly defined services born by the latter, such legal distinction is unrealistic. Whatever may have been the legal status of the villein, his whole life was controlled essentially by economic conditions which kept him immobile and made him and his descendants responsible for working the same plot of land under the same seignorial obligations for centuries. Essentially, therefore, the condition of the villein was no different from that of other peasant classes whether defined as free or unfree by the lawyer.

A member of an agrarian community (seigniory or manor), which was basically self-sufficient, the villein possessed land enough to support him and his family. In return for his land he cooperated with other villeins in cultivating and harvesting the land of the lord of the manor as well as his own land. In addition, the villein rendered to the lord specified payments in kind and in money. The villein was under the legal jurisdiction of the lord and received justice in the local seignorial court. For approximately 900 years the villein, who comprised the great mass of western Europe's population, lived under the private political, economic, and legal control of the feudal aristocracy, which did the governing and the fighting. Only with the emancipation of the villein in the late Middle Ages did the feudal aristocracy lose this direct and complete control of the agrarian masses. As this control was lost, the villein then became a free farmer subject to the laws of the state and entitled to basic legal, social, and economic rights.

See also SEIGNORIALISM.

BRYCE LYON
University of California at Berkeley

VILLENAGE. See VILLEINS.

VILLENEUVE, vēl-nûv', **Jean Marie Rodrigue,** Canadian cardinal and archbishop of Quebec: b. Montreal, Canada, Nov. 2, 1883; d. Alhambra, Calif., Jan. 17, 1947. He was educated in Montreal at Sacré Coeur School and Mont St. Louis College, before joining the Oblates of Mary Immaculate as a novice in 1902. He received his philosophical and theological training at the Oblate scholasticate in Ottawa, and was ordained a priest on May 27, 1907. He taught philosophy and theology at the University of Ottawa from 1907 to 1920, when he was appointed superior of St. Joseph's Scholasticate. Earning the degrees of doctor of philosophy in 1919, doctor of theology in 1922, and doctor of canon law in 1930, he became dean of philosophy at the University of Ottawa in 1923 and founded the Academy St. Thomas, a society devoted to the study of Thomism. He also launched the closed-retreat movement. He was named first bishop of Gravelbourg, a French-Canadian center in Saskatchewan, in June 1930, and in 1932 was made the 20th bishop of Quebec. The following year he was made the 10th archbishop of Quebec, and he became the fourth Canadian cardinal in 1933. As leader of the Quebec Roman Catholics he led the province's Roman Catholic Church through the Depression and World War II years.

In his younger days Cardinal Villeneuve had nationalist inclinations, and took an active part in the struggle for French separate schools in Ontario. He was a friend of Abbé Lionel Groulx, the French-Canadian nationalist leader of the 1920's and 1930's, defending his controversial novel *L'Appel de la race* (1922) and supporting him in 1937 as "one of the masters of the hour . . . one of those to whom our race owes much." Cardinal Villeneuve favored corporatism as a remedy for the social injustice of the depression-ridden 1930's, and worked to promote the Catholic Action movement in Canada.

After Canada's entry into World War II the cardinal developed a broader Canadian nationalism, vigorously supporting the war effort and opposing the antiwar *Bloc Populaire* movement. In a speech at Toronto in April 1941, he observed: "Patriotism should extend to the whole of Canada. Divine Providence seems to have destined the English- and French-speaking Canadians to cooperate in building a nation based on Anglo-Saxon and French civilization." His continuing interest in social reform was manifested in the important joint pastoral letter of October 1943, which declared that the socialist Co-operative Commonwealth Federation (CCF) was a theologically neutral party for which Catholics were free to vote, while condemning Communism. In the fall of 1944 and early in 1945 he issued vigorous warnings against the worldwide menace of Communism, after a visit to Britain and the European battlefronts. He strongly supported agricultural colonization as the answer to postwar resettlement problems in a notable joint pastoral letter of the Quebec bishops, "La Colonisation: Notre salut" (1946).

Cardinal Villeneuve was the author of *L'Un des vôtres* (1927), a series of theological treatises on the sacraments (1936–42), and of numerous articles on religion, philosophy, and sociology in scholarly reviews and journals.

MASON WADE,
University of Rochester.

VILLENEUVE, Pierre Charles Jean Baptiste Sylvestre de, French naval officer: b. Valensole, Provence, France, Dec. 31, 1763; d. Rennes, April 22, 1806. Born of a noble family, he entered the French navy and won rapid promotions —to post captain in 1793 and to rear admiral in 1796. In his first major command, he led a section of the Napoleonic fleet during the Mediterranean campaign of 1798. In the action at Abukir Bay in August, Villeneuve's flagship, the *Guillaume Tell,* was one of but two French ships of the line to escape after the crushing defeat suffered at the hands of Horatio Nelson.

The British plan of forestalling Napoleon's threatened cross-Channel assault by blockading his sail in various continental ports found Nelson off Toulon in December 1804 when Villeneuve, in command there, received orders to make for the West Indies. More than a mere diversion, the French strategy involved a rendezvous of French warships at Martinique, attacks on several of the islands and on British commercial shipping, and then a secret return to Europe for the invasion of England. Nelson, thinking that Villeneuve's design lay in the Mediterranean, permitted his adversary to slip the blockade, then pursued him across the Atlantic, reaching Barbados in early June 1805. The fact of Nelson's presence in the islands spurred the departure of Villeneuve for Europe.

On July 22, 1805, Villeneuve's returning fleet encountered an English squadron under Sir Robert Calder. Following a confused and indecisive engagement, the French admiral put in at El Ferrol, where he next was ordered by Napoleon to unite with the squadrons at Brest or Rochefort. Such a merger might have given the French a total of 50 sail to dominate the Channel. But Villeneuve, putting to sea on August 13, mistook some frigates of a French supporting squadron for British ships, and, in a characteristic display of timidity, fled for Cádiz followed by the British fleet under Horatio Nelson. This failure effectively ended the emperor's hopes for a venture against England.

In Cádiz, on September 14, Villeneuve, lacking supplies and facilities, received instructions to sail the Franco-Spanish fleet into the Mediterranean for an attack on Naples. While making preparations, Villeneuve learned that he was to be replaced in command, and he impetuously decided to embark at once. On October 19 he stood out from port with 33 ships of the line to face the waiting Nelson who had 27 ships; and the result was the French disaster off Cape Trafalgar in which 18 French ships were lost and Nelson was killed (see TRAFALGAR, BATTLE OF).

Taken to England as a prisoner, Villeneuve was soon released and he returned to France. Fearful of a court martial, he tarried at Rennes to ascertain the emperor's disposition toward him. For several days he heard no word. On April 22, he was found dead of knife wounds, and is generally supposed to have taken his own life. There is no conclusive evidence that he committed suicide, however, and one interesting theory holds that the luckless officer was murdered by agents of Napoleon.

VILLEROI, vēl-rwä', DUC DE (FRANÇOIS DE NEUFVILLE), French marshal: b. Lyon, France, April 7, 1644; d. Paris, July 18, 1730. Brought up with Louis XIV he never lost his courtly charm and manners. A colonel in 1664 he fought in the war with the Turks and was wounded at the Battle of Saint Gothard (Szentgotthárd) in Hungary. He rose in rank rapidly during the Dutch War (1672–1678), becoming lieutenant general in 1677. At his father's death in 1685 he became governor of Lyonnais, Forez, and Beaujolais. He fought courageously in the Battle of Steenkerke (1692) and was made a marshal of France in 1693. Commanding the army in 1695, he proved incompetent in failing to prevent William of Orange from recapturing Namur. At the start of the War of the Spanish Succession he took command of the Army of Italy, was beaten at Chiari (1701), and made prisoner at Cremona in 1702. Sent to the Low Countries in 1703, three years later he suffered disastrous defeat at Ramillies. This ended his military career, but not the king's favor, for Louis XIV willed that he become tutor to the future Louis XV, a post he held until 1722, when the duc d'Orléans exiled him to Lyon. He was able to return to court two years later, but never to favor.

ROBERT E. TAYLOR.

VILLIERS, vĭl′ərz, a distinguished English family which owed its fortunes to its charms, in both sexes, for three generations of Stuart kings.

GEORGE VILLIERS, 1ST DUKE OF BUCKINGHAM: b. England, Aug. 28, 1592; d. Portsmouth, Aug. 23, 1628. He was the son of a Leicestershire squire, and his handsome looks and exquisite manners caught the fancy of the susceptible James I. Promoted to the post of gentleman of the king's bedchamber by a cabal headed by Archbishop Abbott, young Villiers was the candidate of the anti-Spanish party and hopes were entertained of his following a popular course. In 1619 he was made lord admiral, in which office he displayed administrative energy and a strong desire to recover the navy from the wretched state into which it had fallen. But it was not until James' declining years that Buckingham—he had been rapidly advanced in the peerage, monopolies and grants loaded upon him and his family—dominated foreign policy. He achieved a personal domination over Prince Charles, heir to the throne, greater than that he had ever exercised over the old, tired king. In pursuit of the scheme of a marriage with the Infanta, with the mirage of political and financial advantages, Charles and Buckingham rushed off on a harebrained journey to Madrid. Inevitably rebuffed, Buckingham made himself the leader of the war party against Spain, enjoying temporary popularity with Parliament, and forced war upon the unwilling James to aid the Protestant cause in Germany engaged in the Thirty Years' War. The expedition sent in 1625 accomplished nothing, and was the favorite's first total failure.

In 1625 Charles I came to the throne, and for the next three years Buckingham ruled England. His idea now was a French alliance, in pursuit of which the favorite crossed over to France. Disappointed here too, he revenged himself by paying his addresses to the French queen in public, and returned to advocate a war with France. The incoherence, extravagance, and incapacity of such a course lost Buckingham his former friends and aroused the Commons to impeach him. To protect him Charles dissolved Parliament and supported his minister more blindly than ever. Though Buckingham had energy and some administrative drive, he was totally incapable of statesmanship. By 1627 he had involved the country in war with France as well as with Spain. An expedition to Cadiz, which accomplished nothing, was followed by an expedition to La Rochelle to aid the Huguenots and raise Richelieu's siege. In spite of Buckingham's personal bravery the effort was another failure. To gain sufficient supplies for a renewed attempt, Charles accepted the Commons' Petition of Right, setting forth their grievances against his government. The nation's indignation concentrated against the favorite, but Charles would not drop him. On Aug. 23, 1628, at Portsmouth, where Buckingham was desperately making preparations for another expedition to relieve La Rochelle, he was assassinated by a discharged naval officer, in the house of Capt. John Mason, founder of New Hampshire.

GEORGE VILLIERS, 2D DUKE OF BUCKINGHAM: b. Westminster, England, Jan. 30, 1628; d. Kirkly Moorside, Yorkshire, April 16, 1687. He inherited the indescribable charm and grace, the mercurial wit, and something of the talent that was in this family, but was without his father's willpower and determination. On the father's assassination, the children were brought up along with the king's, so that the young duke was from infancy a companion of Charles II. Though only a boy, Buckingham fought for the king in the Civil War and took part in the royalist plots against Commonwealth and Protectorate for the restoration of the monarchy. In exile he opposed Clarendon's strict Anglican policy and favored toleration, and this was the only subject on which he followed a consistent course. After the Restoration he allied himself with the opposition in the Commons to Clarendon, upon whose fall he became the leading member of the cabal that took over the government. His public liaison with the Countess of Shrewsbury, whose husband he killed in a duel, hardly improved his credit with his Presbyterian allies. Far too volatile, he could not stay the course and was gradually pushed aside by Arlington, who kept him out of the secret of the Treaty of Dover, by which Charles II promised to bring the country over to Catholicism. On learning of it Buckingham went into opposition and cooperated with the Whig Party. Having run through an immense fortune, he retired during his last years to Yorkshire, most of his estates having been sold or mortgaged.

Buckingham wrote one successful satirical play, *The Rehearsal*, a number of tracts, and occasional verses; but he lives in English literature through Dryden's famous description of him in *Absalom and Achitophel*.

BARBARA VILLIERS, DUCHESS OF CLEVELAND, better known to history as LADY CASTLEMAINE: b. Westminster, England, autumn 1641; d. Chiswick, Oct. 9, 1709. Her grandfather was half-brother of the 1st duke of Buckingham; her father was killed in the Civil War. Extremely beautiful, with all the Villiers vivacity and temperament, she became Charles II's mistress at the age of 19 on his restoration and the mother of a number of his children. It is chiefly through these activities that the Villiers blood has suffused itself through the English peerage. (Consult the essay, "The Great Villiers Connection" by J. M. Keynes.) Lady Castlemaine was insatiably importunate, and equally extravagant, so that her pensions, grants from public funds, and gifts became a drain upon the state. Granted Henry VIII's famous palace of Nonsuch, she pulled it down and sold the materials. She also sold the mansion and gardens of Berkshire House, St. James's, which Charles had given her. Cleveland Court and Cleveland Row, on the site of the gardens, remain as monuments to this side of her activities. Politically she had less importance than has been thought, though she played a part in Clarendon's fall from power.

By 1673 Charles II had tired of her tantrums, and her place was taken by the French duchess of Portsmouth. Barbara took up with other lovers, among them her cousin, young John Churchill; her last child is usually considered his. Many portraits remain to attest her beauty.

ELIZABETH VILLIERS, COUNTESS OF ORKNEY, Mistress of William III: b. England, 1657; d. London, April 19, 1733. Though without the Villiers looks, she was a woman of great sense, wit, and tact. Swift said she was the wisest woman he ever knew, and William III valued her advice on English politics. She used her influence tactfully to aid the Dutch king's difficult personal relations with the English nobles.

GEORGE WILLIAM FREDERICK VILLIERS, 4TH EARL OF CLARENDON, b. London, England, Jan. 12, 1800; d. there, June 27, 1870. He early entered the diplomatic service, and won confidence by his handling of the problems created by the Carlist civil war in Spain. In 1847 appointed lord lieutenant of Ireland, he had to carry the country through the terrible crisis of the potato famine, and did all he could to alleviate suffering and improve methods of Irish agriculture. Foreign secretary in 1853, he failed to prevent the outbreak of the Crimean War; though at the conclusion the peace he negotiated was considered the best settlement obtainable. He renounced the right of seizure of neutral goods at sea in time of war, and attached a declaration of belligerent rights to the Treaty of Paris, 1856. After the American Civil War, in which the *Alabama* incident, with its damage to American shipping, had endangered Anglo-American relations, Lord Clarendon concluded a convention with the United States to settle the *Alabama* claims.

A. L. ROWSE,
Fellow of All Souls College, University of Oxford.

VILLIERS, vĭl'yərz, **Alan John,** Australian sailor and author: b. Melbourne, Australia, Sept. 23, 1903. Since first putting to sea at the age of 15, he devoted his life to sailing and to writing on maritime adventure and history. In 1923 he joined a Norwegian whaling expedition to the Ross Sea (Antarctica), describing his experiences in *Whaling in the Frozen South* (rev. ed. 1931) and *Vanished Fleets* (1931). The last of the Australian grain vessels was the subject of *Grain Race* (1933), written after he had twice sailed the four-masted *Parma* to victory in the Australia-to-England race—the second time (1933) in 83 days. *Cruise of the Conrad* (1937) tells of his 60,000-mile voyage around the world (1934–1936) with a crew of cadets aboard the *Joseph Conrad*.

Villiers wrote *Sons of Sinbad* (1940) after studying Arabian dhows and ancient navigation techniques in the Red Sea and Persian Gulf. *The Quest of the Schooner Argus* (1951), a history of early deep-sea fishing, resulted from a period of dory fishing in the Grand Banks and off Greenland. In 1957 he skippered the *Mayflower II*, an exact replica of the original, in a commemorative voyage from Plymouth, England, to Plymouth, Mass., in 54 days. *Give Me a Ship to Sail* (1959) is an account of the event. His autobiography, *The Set of the Sails,* appeared in 1949. Among his many other books on sea lore are *The Making of a Sailor* (1938), *Monsoon Seas* (1952), and *Wild Ocean* (1957).

VILLIERS DE L'ISLE-ADAM, vē-lyä' də lēl-à-dän', COMTE **Philippe Auguste Mathias de,** French writer: b. St. Brieuc, Britanny, France, Nov. 7, 1838; d. Paris, Aug. 18, 1889. He was one of the loftiest figures of French symbolism, a belated and unhappy embodiment of European romanticism, whose works are crossed with fitful flashes of genius. The scion of an ancient noble family from Brittany, he was raised by a mother who adored him and by an impecunious father who nurtured his disdain for the modern world and his dreams of legendary grandeur.

Villiers read much idealistic German philosophy in his youth, and was profoundly impressed by Charles Baudelaire, who introduced him to Richard Wagner and to the works of Edgar Allan Poe. To the latter, Villiers may have owed a longing for death as the only worthy culmination of pure and ardent loves; but his imagination is less morbid than Poe's and his tales are more subtle. Wagner helped him dream his impossible dreams of a return to medieval heroism.

After an early volume of verse, Villiers realized that he was most gifted as a sumptuous poet in prose. His early symbolic novel, *Isis* (1862), full of occult idealism, and his sarcastic satire of the democratic and prosaic bourgeois, *Tribulat Bonhomet* (1887), proclaimed in fictional form the haughty count's contempt for the modern world and his longing for the "land of heart's desire." His play, *La révolte* (1870), would not have been unworthy of Henrik Ibsen and appeared long before Ibsen became known in western Europe. Villiers' *Contes cruels* (1883; Eng. tr., *Sardonic Tales,* 1927) ranks among the most original body of short stories of the 19th century. The tales are far less brutal and pessimistic than the contemporary stories of Émile Zola and Guy de Maupassant, and are instinct with Catholic faith and with pity for the wretched inhabitants of the modern world.

Villiers' masterpieces are the strange novel of anticipation, *L'Eve future* (1886), in which science, represented by Thomas A. Edison, creates a woman embodying the lover's impossible ideal—but the spirit alone could endow her with life; and *Axël* (1890), a poetic drama replete with glittering descriptions and visionary dreams of medieval Germany, in which the author relates the pursuit of treasure by two lovers whose passion is not for earthly riches: they reject life, like Tristan and Isolde, preferring the fulfillment of death. William Butler Yeats was fascinated by the book, and Edmund Wilson gave the title of *Axel's Castle* (1931) to his study of the imaginative literature of 1870–1930.

HENRI PEYRE,
Sterling Professor of French, Department Head, Yale University.

VILLON, vē-yôn', **François,** French poet: b. Paris, France, 1431; d. after 1463. The greatest French medieval poet, he is one of the most widely admired in English-speaking countries. His life, one of the most irregular lives that poet ever lived, has been told, more or less faithfully, in many novels and films; but much in it remains shrouded in mystery. His poetry, which is contained in one slim volume, is, after that of Dante and Geoffrey Chaucer, the first in Europe which has a tone of intense sincerity. It strikes the modern reader as if the passing of centuries had worked no effect upon its freshness.

Nothing is known about the poet's origins and family. His real name was François de Montcorbier, probably taken from a small place in Burgundy whence his humble ancestors must have come. But he was a Parisian to the bone and a peculiarly urban poet, who left the capital only unwillingly and when banished for his misdeeds or hunted by the police. *"Il n'est bon bec que de Paris,"* alluding to the biting wit of which Parisians like to boast, and also to their taste for humorous satire, is one of Villon's famous octosyllabic lines. He took the name "Villon," as was then customary, from that of Maître Guillaume de Villon, a priest who was the chaplain in the collegiate church of Saint-Benoît-le-Bestourné and a professor of canon law, and who adopted him and took care of his education.

The year of Villon's birth was also that in which Joan of Arc, after reviving French national feeling, was burned at Rouen. Five years later, in 1436, Paris, occupied by the English since 1419, was recaptured by Charles VII of France. When Villon was 20, Sandro Botticelli and Ghirlandajo had just been born in Italy (Girolamo Savonarola and Leonardo da Vinci were to come into the world in 1452); the great portrait painter Jean Fouquet was completing his *Book of Hours;* and a grave and profound master was doing the *Pietà* of Avignon.

François grew up in a milieu of clerics and law students, close to the Sorbonne. He studied avidly, and received his degrees of bachelor, then of licentiate and of master of arts, between 1449 and 1452. Allusions to ancient learning recur in his poems. But Villon also spent, or wasted, much time among scoundrels, adventurers, and thieves.

In June 1455 he was involved in a quarrel concerning a woman and he killed the young priest who had attacked him. He fled to Angers, where he appears to have taken part in some burglaries. He was pardoned by the king early in 1456, but again became involved in burglary (this time a theft of 500 gold coins from the Collège de Navarre in Paris), and, after composing his *Lais* or *Petit testament,* he took refuge away from Paris, perhaps at the court of the prince and poet Charles d'Orléans, at Blois. In 1460, Villon was again in jail, at Orléans, and the following year at Meung-sur-Loire, where he was released, along with the other prisoners, when King Louis XI went through that city. Villon was inspired by his misdeeds and misfortunes to write more poetry, and in 1461 he produced his masterpiece, the *Testament* or *Grand testament,* a long poem of 173 stanzas in which he included some ballades and rondeaux composed earlier.

Caught by the police after another brawl in 1462, Villon composed his celebrated *Ballade des pendus* ("Ballad of Hanged Men") after being sentenced to be "hanged and strangled." A decree from the Paris court of justice on Jan. 5, 1463, changed the death penalty to banishment for 10 years. No trace is found of Villon after that fate. The first dated edition of his poetry appeared in 1489.

The themes of Villon's verse are regret for the time misspent away from study and even keener regret for the great and lovely women of olden days ("But where are the snows of yesteryear?"); passionate yearning for the companionship of women of low estate (*Ballade de la belle heaulmière*) of whom he sang instead of the noble ladies that courtly poets had idealized before him; and naive faith in the Virgin Mary and in his own native country torn by wars. His most unforgettable accents are those in which he conjures up the physical horrors of death and imagines his own body hanging from the gallows, pecked by birds, washed by hail and rain, an object of pity and perhaps a lesson of morality for those who would avoid a similar fate. Nowhere had the medieval theme of man's equality before the triumph of death—which inspired many a painting in Italy and France and several contemporaries of William Shakespeare—been treated with less sentimentality, more sensual directness, and a starker realism. For the first time in western Europe, the "I" of a weak and unfortunate sinner appears through every stanza of his direct and intense poetry. Villon deserved a better fate than was meted out to him, but his will was unequal to the temptations to which he yielded.

The octosyllabic line and the concrete, fast stanza of eight lines in which Villon enclosed his racy language, as well as his graphic images, were admirably adapted to the direct effect he wanted to produce. He was still a man of the Middle Ages, but one who had left behind conventionality in feelings, allegories, pseudomysteries, and clever virtuosity. He is the most sincere of French poets, and Charles Beaudelaire, Paul Verlaine, and Guillaume Apollinaire, four centuries later, were proud of being the successors of that earliest of all *"poètes maudits."* Villon's poetry was translated into English by Dante Gabriel Rossetti, Algernon Swinburne, and Ezra Pound.

HENRI PEYRE,
Sterling Professor of French, Department Head, Yale University.

VILLUPURAM, vĭl-ə-pŏŏr'əm, town, India, in the South Arcot District of Madras State, about midway between Madras City and Tiruchirapalli. It is connected by a rail spur line to the port of Pondicherry, 33 miles east, which was a French enclave until its cession to India in 1954. The region around Villupuram supports an economically depressed, overwhelmingly agricultural population. In addition to its commercial functions, the town has some sugar milling. Pop. (1981) 77,052.

JOSEPH E. SCHWARTZBERG.

VILNA. See VILNYUS.

VILNYUS, vĭl'nĭ-əs (Russ. **VILNA** or **VILNO,** Pol. **WILNO,** Ger. **WILNA**), city, USSR, capital of the Lithuanian SSR, located in southeast Lithuania where the Vilnya (Vileika) River joins the Neris (Viliya) River, a tributary of the Neman flowing into the southern Baltic Sea. The city is built on river terraces, with the outskirts on wooded plateaus. The chief industries are machine building, food processing, woodworking, textile mills, and tanneries. Vilnyus is a major railway junction, with lines radiating to Latvia, Belorussia, Poland, and Leningrad.

Vilnyus is the largest cultural and educational center of the Lithuanian SSR. The state university, founded in 1579, is one of the oldest universities in all Europe. In addition there is an academy of science, a teachers' college, a music conservatory, an art college, and a law school.

History.–Vilnyus is one of the oldest cities in the USSR Baltic area, being founded in the 10th century. In 1322–1323 it became the capital of the Lithuanian principality. Because of its strategic location between east central Europe and Russia, it became a battleground for many wars in the succeeding centuries. The Teutonic Knights captured and destroyed the city in 1377. In 1569 it became part of the joint Polish-Lithuanian kingdom. During the Great Northern War between Sweden and Russia, Swedish troops occupied the city in 1702 and 1706. Russian armies seized Vilnyus from 1655 to 1660, again in 1788, and finally annexed the city to the Russian Empire in 1795. The city participated in the unsuccessful Polish revolutions of 1831 and 1863 against Russian rule.

During World War I, Vilnyus fell under German occupation from 1915 to 1918. At the war's end, the city became the capital of the re-created country of free Lithuania. In 1920, however, Poland annexed the city by force, an annexation which Lithuania was too weak to oppose. In September 1939 the USSR conquered eastern Poland, and on Oct. 10, 1939, returned Vilnyus to free Lithuania. This proved to be an empty gesture, because in June 1940 the USSR forcibly annexed all Lithuania, including Vilnyus. During World War II, the city fell again under German rule from 1941 to 1944, when it was reconquered and reannexed by the Soviet Union. Forty percent of the city buildings were destroyed in this war as a result of battle damage and the scorched-earth policies of first the retreating Russians and later the retreating Germans. This war damage has now been repaired. Both the Germans and Russians conducted vast wartime purges of the city's population. Lithuanians, Poles, Russians, Belorussians, and Jews constitute the majority of the city's inhabitants. Pop. (1959) 235,000.

ELLSWORTH RAYMOND,
Associate Professor of Soviet Government and Economics, New York University.

VIMINAL, vĭm′ə-nəl, hill, Rome, Italy. Smallest of the city's traditional seven hills, it is 183 feet in altitude, almost 766 yards long, and about 60 acres in area; it extends northeastward from the city's center, and lies between the Quirinal and Esquiline hills, whence it is separated, respectively, by the Via Nazionale and the Via Cavour. In antiquity the Viminal was an unimportant district, inhabited by lower-class citizens, and traffic passed it on either side; but on it was the Altar of Jupiter Viminalis. The massive Palazzo del Viminale (1902), its most important modern building, contains the ministry of the Interior.

P. R. COLEMAN-NORTON.

VIMY RIDGE, vĭm′ē, Fr. vē-mē′, ridge, France, in the Department of Pas-de-Calais, about 10 miles north of Arras, and scene of an engagement (as part of the Battle of Arras) in World War I. The 475-foot prominence presented a formidable obstacle to the Allied offensive against the northern pivot of the German line in the spring of

Society for Cultural Relations with the USSR

A pavilion at the collective farm market in Vilnyus.

1917. Strongly fortified by the Germans, the ridge was subjected to shattering fire from Allied artillery for four days before a direct assault was launched by the Canadian Corps on April 9. The four Canadian divisions under Sir Julian Byng courageously stormed and took the position in two days of bitter combat, but the rest of the general operation, through April 14, cost the corps more than 11,000 casualties. In 1936 a memorial was dedicated on the ridge in honor of Canadians who gave their lives in World War I.

VIÑA DEL MAR, bē′nyä thēl mär′, city, Chile, in Valparaiso Province, on the Pacific coast, four miles northeast of Valparaiso. One of the leading

The beach and waterfront hotels at Viña del Mar, Chile.

Pan American

seaside resorts and playgrounds of South America, Viña del Mar is a city of spacious boulevards, lovely parks and gardens, luxury hotels, and handsome villas. Wealthy visitors from Santiago, as well as from Argentina and other foreign countries, are attracted in large numbers by such features as the municipal gaming casino, racetrack, golf course, theaters, and clubs. The social season reaches its peak in the summer (December–February), although the region is blessed with an equable climate the year round. The city is situated on a sheltered bay, along which extend several fine beaches.

In addition to its high standing as a resort, Viña del Mar is a manufacturing center, with a large sugar refinery and installations producing chemicals, alcohol, petroleum products, vegetable oils, and soaps. Wines, fruits, and vegetables are marketed for the surrounding farm districts. Pop. (1959) 100,000.

VINCA. See PERIWINKLE.

VINCENNES, vĭn-sĕnz′, Fr. văN-sĕn′, **SIEUR de (FRANÇOIS MARIE BISSOT),** French-Canadian soldier and explorer: b. Montreal, Canada, June 17, 1700; d. near the headwaters of the Tombigbee River, Mississippi, March 25, 1736. He was the son of Jean Baptiste Bissot, Sieur de Vincennes (q.v.), and the similarity of their work, together with the fact that the younger Vincennes often used the name of his godfather, François Margane, Sieur de la Valterie, led to a confusion of their identities by early historians. From boyhood François was his father's companion on frontier duty, and upon his death the 19-year-old youth took over his post at Ke-ki-onga, the Miami Indian village then occupying the site of Fort Wayne, Ind. In 1722 young Vincennes was commissioned ensign in the French colonial army, and later he built a fort near Lafayette, Ind., commanding it for four years.

The general drift of the Indians being south along the Wabash River into Louisiana, Vincennes eventually allied himself with that territory, and in 1731 or 1732 he erected a fort at the site of Vincennes, Ind., a city which was named in his honor. He was in command there when in 1736 new fighting broke out between Louisiana and the Chickasaw Indians. At the call of Louisiana's governor, Jean Baptiste le Moyne, Sieur de Bienville, Vincennes joined forces with other French officers who were stationed along the Wabash and Illinois rivers, and reached the appointed rendezvous near present-day Memphis, Tenn., in advance of the Louisiana troops. There, urged by the restive and overconfident Indians under their command, Vincennes and his brother officer, Pierre D'Artaguiette, attacked the enemy and were badly defeated. Nearly a score of young Frenchmen, including Vincennes and a chaplain, were carried off by the Chickasaw, tortured, and burned at the stake.

VINCENNES, SIEUR de (JEAN BAPTISTE BISSOT), French-Canadian soldier and explorer: b. near Quebec, Canada, Jan. 19, 1668; d. near the site of Fort Wayne, Ind., 1719. His father, François Bissot, was a Norman emigrant to New France who established a tannery and mill across the St. Lawrence River from Quebec, and who was granted a seigniory there in 1672. Jean Baptiste was a younger brother-in-law and ward of Louis Jolliet (q.v.), the explorer, who entered him in the seminary at Quebec, and a godchild of Jean Baptiste Talon (q.v.), through whom he was appointed ensign in the French marine, the branch of the army in America.

From his youth Vincennes was familiar with Indian affairs, and he was already held in high esteem by the Miami when appointed their commander in 1696 by the governor of New France, the Comte de Frontenac. He made his headquarters with the Indians successively on the St. Joseph River and at the great Miami village of Ke-ki-onga, on the Maumee River. There, on the site of Fort Wayne, Ind., Vincennes established in 1704 a fort and trading post. Living and trading with the Miami for the rest of his life, he served as a bulwark of French influence in the West. He went to the rescue of the post at Detroit during the Fox Indian uprising of 1712; and as late as 30 years after his death his name held sufficient prestige among the Miami to induce them to return to their French allegiance. He was succeeded in the command of Ke-ki-onga by his son, François Marie Bissot, Sieur de Vincennes (q.v.).

VINCENNES, city, France, in the southeastern suburbs of Paris, between the Marne and Seine rivers, four miles from the Cathedral of Notre Dame, in the Department of the Seine. The city is close to the outermost walls of Paris, and grew around a medieval castle that was converted into a prison in the 17th century, a factory in the 18th century, and was extensively modified in the 19th century. The donjon, or keep, and the late medieval Gothic chapel, have survived. The castle was one of the residences of French kings. It lies on the northern edge of the Bois de Vincennes, a wooded park with several lakes and the remains of some of the former outer defenses of Paris. Vincennes has a museum devoted to the history of the French colonies, and a museum of military history. Pop. (1962) 50,425.

NORMAN J. G. POUNDS.

VINCENNES, city, Indiana, Knox County seat, on the Wabash River (here the Illinois boundary), 55 miles south of Terre Haute, at an altitude of 430 feet. An attractive residential community with a rich historical background, it is also a busy retail and industrial center. Its factories manufacture principally glass, batteries, shoes, structural steel, and paper products. Oil, bituminous coal, natural gas, and sand and gravel deposits are found in the vicinity. Vincennes is an important rail-shipping hub. The surrounding fertile farm country has large nursery interests and dairy, stock, and poultry farms, and raises such crops as corn, soybeans, wheat, peaches, and apples.

Vincennes abounds in points of interest related to its storied past. Vincennes University, now a junior college, was incorporated in 1806, becoming the first institution of higher learning in Indiana. The handsome George Rogers Clark Memorial, a national monument erected (1931–1933) on the site of old Fort Sackville, commemorates the winning of the Northwest and the intrepid deeds of Clark and his followers during the War for Independence. The memorial contains a heroic bronze statue of Clark by Hermon A. MacNeil. Adjoining the monument is the Lincoln Memorial Bridge, spanning the

Wabash. Also nearby is the Church of St. Francis Xavier, begun in 1825; known as the Old Cathedral, it is the first Catholic house of worship west of the Alleghenies. The Old Cathedral Library (completed in 1843) houses a valuable collection of rare manuscripts and historical objects dating from the region's early days. Other points of interest are the old territorial Legislative Hall (dating from about 1800); Grouseland, the one-time residence of William Henry Harrison, first territorial governor and later president of the United States; and the Judge Abner T. Ellis Mansion, where Abraham Lincoln was a frequent visitor. (The Indiana "Lincoln country" is within short driving distance.) In the region of Vincennes are some of the most notable Indian mounds in the state.

History.—The oldest town in Indiana, Vincennes was founded in 1731 or 1732 by the ill-fated sieur de Vincennes on the site of an Indian village (see VINCENNES, SIEUR DE, FRANÇOIS MARIE BISSOT). Earlier, in 1702, it had been a French mission. The name "Vincennes" was adopted shortly before the territory was occupied in 1763 by the British. They, however, paid little attention to the settlement until the outbreak of the American Revolution, when (in 1777) the British dispatched a military contingent to take possession of the fort and rename it Sackville. The strategic importance of the Northwest Territory induced George Rogers Clark (q.v.) to undertake his daring expedition, and his Virginia-supported force captured Vincennes in 1778. Although the British regained possession of the place later that year, Clark, alerted by the Italian-born patriot Francis Vigo (q.v.), attacked and won the fort in the following February. Vincennes was held by Virginia until 1784, when it was ceded to the United States. The first court was held here in 1787, and for 13 years, beginning in 1800, Vincennes was the capital of the new Indiana Territory. It was incorporated as a borough in 1815 and as a city in 1856. Present government is administered by a mayor and council. Pop. 20,857.

VINCENT, vĭn'sĕnt, SIR **(Charles Edward) Howard,** English public official: b. Slinfold, Sussex, England, May 31, 1849; d. Menton, France, April 7, 1908. Educated at Sandhurst, he was commissioned in the army in 1868 but resigned after five years to study law and was admitted to the bar in 1876. He had already traveled widely in Europe, part of the time (1871, 1876) as military correspondent for the *Daily Telegraph,* and was an accomplished linguist. In 1877 he went to Paris to study methods of police work, and after further observations in Belgium, Germany, and Austria, was named the first director of criminal investigation at Scotland Yard (1878). In this post Vincent reorganized the operations of the London detective force completely and did pioneer work in the rehabilitation of criminals; his book, *A Police Code and Manual of Criminal Law* (1882), became a standard text and went through many editions. Resigning from Scotland Yard in 1884, he was elected to Parliament as a Conservative the following year and retained the seat until his death. He was a leading advocate of the protective tariff and the imperial preference system. He was knighted in 1896.

VINCENT, văɴ-säɴ', **(Jean) Hyacinthe,** French epidemiologist: b. Bordeaux, France, Dec. 22, 1862; d. Paris, Nov. 23, 1950. Educated at the School of Military Medicine, he was professor of bacteriology and epidemiology (1897–1912) at Val-de-Grâce, the military hospital and medical school in Paris, and founded the Antityphoid Vaccination Laboratory there. From 1925 until his death he was director of the Laboratory of Epidemiology and Infectious Diseases at the Collège de France. Vincent discovered the fusiform organism (Vincent's bacillus) and spirochete (Vincent's spirillum) which cause the disease known as trench mouth (Vincent's angina or Vincent's infection), common among soldiers in World War I. He also discovered the value of the application of chlorine to infected wounds; a vaccine for typhoid and paratyphoid; and a serum against gas gangrene.

VINCENT, vĭn'sĕnt, **John Heyl,** American Methodist bishop: b. Tuscaloosa, Ala., Feb. 23, 1832; d. Chicago, Ill., May 9, 1920. Licensed as a Methodist preacher in Pennsylvania at the age of 18, he moved to Illinois in 1857 and seven years later became pastor of Trinity Church in Chicago, where he began his important work of reforming Sunday school instruction. Through the monthly *Sunday School Teacher,* which he founded in 1865, a standard Sunday school curriculum was established and soon was adopted widely by other Protestant denominations. Vincent was transferred to the staff of the Methodist Sunday School Union in New York City and from 1868 to 1888 was its corresponding secretary and editor of publications.

In 1874, with Lewis Miller, he organized a summer training institute for Sunday school teachers at Lake Chautauqua in New York State; and in 1878, under Vincent's direction, this was broadened into the Chautauqua Literary and Scientific Circle, which presented lectures by prominent persons on public affairs, literature, and science as well as on religion. Other centers were soon developed throughout the United States, and the so-called Chautauqua movement (q.v.) became a major pioneering project in adult liberal education. Vincent was made a bishop of the Methodist Episcopal Church in 1888, and in 1900 he was sent to Switzerland to take charge of the church's work in Europe. He retired in 1904. Among his books are *The Chautauqua Movement* (1886) and *The Modern Sunday School* (1887).

GEORGE EDGAR VINCENT (1864–1941), his son, was professor of sociology at the University of Chicago from 1904 until resigning in 1911 to become president of the University of Minnesota. As president of the Rockefeller Foundation (1917–1929), he played a leading role in medical relief work during and after World War I, and under his direction the foundation's worldwide efforts in the health field were greatly enlarged. He also was active in the Chautauqua movement that had been founded by his father. He published *An Introduction to the Study of Society* (with Albion W. Small; 1895) and *Social Mind and Education* (1896).

VINCENT DE PAUL, văɴ-säɴ' də pôl', SAINT, French Roman Catholic ecclesiastic: b. Pouy, Gascony, France, April 24, c. 1580; d. Paris, Sept. 27, 1660. He was the third of six children of Jean de Paul and Bertrande de Moras, who raised their family on a very small farm at Pouy near Dax in southwest France. Vincent received his basic education at Dax, finished his studies at the University of Toulouse, and in 1600 was ordained priest. After four years of additional study at Toulouse, he took the degree of bachelor of theology. Captured by Barbary pirates on a voyage from Marseille to Narbonne, he was sold as a slave in Tunis and spent two years there under various masters before escaping to Rome. Vincent spent a year in Rome before returning to France in 1607.

St. Vincent de Paul

The Bettmann Archive

At Paris, Vincent became acquainted with Father Pierre de Berulle, afterward cardinal, and soon held a place of confidence among important court people. He was appointed chaplain to Queen Margaret of Valois and became tutor to the eldest son of Philippe Emmanuel de Gondi, general of the royal galley. In 1617, Vincent preached a mission to the country people of Picardy in the church at Folleville and was appalled by the spiritual needs of the peasantry of France. For a short time he was pastor of Châtillon-les-Dombes and then went to Paris, where he worked untiringly for convicts and galley slaves, with the result that he was made royal chaplain of the galleys in 1619. He later had a hospital built at Marseille for the convicts.

Aided by an endowment from Mme. de Gondi, Vincent founded (1625) a company of zealous missionaries to preach to the tenants on the Gondi estates and to the people of the countryside in general. This company of priests, known as the Congregation of the Mission (see Congregation of the Mission), first was centered at the Collège des Bons Enfants but in 1632 was given the priory of St. Lazare in Paris, from which the members are sometimes called Lazarists. Its members renounced ecclesiastical preferment, took four simple vows of poverty, chastity, obedience, and stability, and dedicated themselves to the salvation of the country folk and to the direction of diocesan seminaries. The congregation, which also became known as the Vincentians, was officially approved by Pope Urban VIII in 1633, and Vincent lived to see 25 houses founded in France, Poland, and other countries, including Madagascar.

In addition to his work for the spiritual alleviation of the needy, Vincent established confraternities of charity to attend poor sick persons in each parish. From this program the Daughters of Charity came into being, with the help of St. Louise de Marillac. These sisters were not to be religious but rather seculars, whose "convent is the sickroom, their chapel the parish church, their cloister the streets of the city." Their work was widespread—in hospitals and schools, in homes for foundlings and the aged. To finance these various charitable organizations, Vincent invoked the assistance of wealthy women of Paris and brought them together as the Ladies of Charity to collect funds and to assist in works of mercy. The Daughters of Charity was founded in 1633 by Vincent and Saint Louise de Marillac, and approved by Rome in 1668, eight years after Vincent's death.

Vincent showed great organizational ability in all these foundations. His charity extended to every emergency that arose in his time, from ransoming Christian slaves in North Africa to collecting alms for the war-devastated areas of Lorraine. He was the confidant of the queen regent, Anne of Austria. Against the Jansenists he effectively asserted his belief in the mercy of God. Vincent remained always simple and humble, ascribing the success of his works to the grace of God. He was canonized by Pope Clement XII in 1737, and was declared by Pope Leo XIII, in 1885, the Universal Patron of Works of Charity. He also inspired the famous lay organization of the St. Vincent de Paul Society. His feast day is Sept. 27.

Alvin Burroughs, C. M.
St. Mary's Seminary, Houston, Texas

VINCENT FERRER, vĭn′sĕnt fĕr-rĕr′, Saint (Span. Vicente Ferrer), Spanish Dominican preacher: b. Valencia, Spain, ?1350; d. Vannes, Brittany, France, April 5, 1419. He entered the Dominican Order in 1367, studied at its schools in Barcelona and Toulouse, and joined the entourage of Pedro Cardinal de Luna in 1379, when the latter was legate of the Avignon antipope to the court of Aragon. After de Luna was chosen antipope at Avignon as Benedict XIII (1394), Vincent was summoned by him to his court, where he became his confessor and theologian and remained one of his most loyal supporters until the eve of his deposition by the Council of Constance in 1417.

Meanwhile, in 1399, Vincent embarked on a great evangelical mission that lasted until his death. He wandered through southern France, Switzerland, and northern Italy, preaching repentance and a renewal of faith to hundreds of thousands in vast outdoor meetings. From 1408 to 1416 he concentrated his efforts in Spain, where he was credited with the conversion of many Jews and Muslims. His last mission was to Brittany. In May 1418 he acceded to the request of King Henry V of England to preach before the regent at Caen. He was canonized by Pope Callistus III in 1455. His feast day is celebrated on April 5.

VINCENT OF BEAUVAIS, vĭn′sĕnt, bō-vĕ′, French encyclopedist: b. about 1190; d. ?1264. Of his personal history little is known except that he joined the Dominican Order about 1220 and enjoyed the favor of King Louis IX. Vincent undertook the stupendous task of compiling a comprehensive encyclopedia of all branches of human knowledge in his time, under the general title of *Speculum majus.* The first part, *Speculum naturale,* in 32 books, and 3,718 chapters, treats of cosmography, physiology, psychology, physics, theology, botany, zoology, mineralogy, and agriculture. The second part, *Speculum doctrinale,* in 17 books and 2,374 chapters, deals with logic, poetry, rhetoric, astronomy, geometry, education, industrial and mechanical arts, anatomy, surgery, medicine, jurisprudence, and other subjects. The third division, *Speculum historiale,* in 31 books and 3,793 chapters, brings the history of the world down to 1250 A. D. A fourth part, *Speculum morale,* was included in early editions, but its authenticity has been disproved. The entire *Speculum majus,* with its 80 books and 9,885 chapters, would equal some 60 modern octavo volumes. The standard edition is the one that was published by the Benedictines at Douai, France (1624).

VINCENT OF LÉRINS, vĭn'sĕnt lā-răNs', SAINT, Gallic theologian: d. after 434. What little is known of his life is provided by Gennadius' *De viris illustribus* (late 5th century). Vincent became a monk at Lérins, was ordained a priest, and under the pseudonym "Peregrinus" composed two *Commonitoria,* the second of which was quickly lost and is known only from a résumé given by Vincent. Apparently inspired by Tertullian's *De praescriptione* (c. 200), the surviving *Commonitorium* (434) displays no originality, but the author expresses the borrowed ideas in clear and striking formulas.

Vincent's aim is to establish a definite criterion of orthodoxy, which he finds in the rule: "what has been believed everywhere, always, and by all." More important is his discussion of the "progress" of revealed faith, by which he understands, not an alteration, but an organic development that consists in disengaging and placing in their own proper light truths implicit in the deposit of faith. Vincent's doctrine shows an affinity to that of his contemporaries Johannes Cassianus and Faustus of Riez, and like them he seems to regard Augustine's teaching on grace as an innovation. It is probable that the *Objectiones Vincentianae,* refuted by Prosper of Aquitaine, is also his work and that he at least inspired the *Objectiones Gallorum.*

ANSELM G. BIGGS, O. S. B.
Professor of History, Belmont Abbey College Belmont, N. C.

VINCENT OF SARAGOSSA, vĭn'sĕnt, săr-ə-gōs'ə, SAINT, Christian martyr: d. Valencia, Spain, about 304. He was instructed by St. Valerius, bishop of Saragossa in Spain, ordained a deacon, and appointed to preach and to teach the people. He and Valerius were arrested by Dacian, the Roman governor, in pursuance of the Diocletian persecution of Christianity, and were taken to Valencia, where Valerius was condemned to exile, but Vincent was subjected to cruel tortures that led to his death. Accounts of his sufferings, or "Acts," were soon written, and were quoted by St. Augustine; later versions were greatly elaborated. St. Vincent became a figure of widespread veneration in Spain, France, and Italy, and his name won great popularity in Roman Catholic countries. In Burgundy he is the patron of vinedressers. Among his symbols in art is the raven, since, according to legend, his dead body was protected by a raven from being devoured by beasts and birds of prey.

JOHN K. RYAN

VINCENTIANS. See CONGREGATION OF THE MISSION.

VINCETOXICUM, vĭn-sē-tŏk'sĭ-kəm, a genus of plants in the milkweed family (Asclepiadaceae), comprising some 80 species of erect or twining perennial herbs and subshrubs mostly native to Old World temperate and warm regions, with a few in the tropics. Their leaves are usually opposite. The flowers are white or greenish yellow to purplish or black, with five-parted calyxes, corollas, and coronas. The name has been variously used and has included species of *Cynanchum,* also of the Old World, which should be distinguished from *Vincetoxicum.* In the New World the name *Vincetoxicum* has been given to many species that are now assigned mostly to the genus *Gonolobus.*

RICHARD STRAW

VINCI, Leonardo da. See LEONARDO DA VINCI.

VINDHYA PRADESH, vĭnd'hyə prə-dāsh' former Indian state, created in 1948 by union of the 34 native states of the Bundelkhand and Baghelkhand agencies, plus one state of the Gwalior Residency; absorbed by Madhya Pradesh State (q.v., former Central Provinces) in the states' reorganization of Nov. 1, 1956. The region, which is mainly dependent on agriculture, is a community of some economic backwardness. It has an area of about 24,600 square miles. The eight component districts of the former state—Datia, Tikamgarh, Chhatarpur, Panna, Satna, Rewa, Sidhi, and Sahdol—continue as districts within Madhya Pradesh. Population: (1961 est.) 4,453,876.

JOSEPH E. SCHWARTZBERG

VINDHYA RANGE MOUNTAINS, a low mountain or hill range in India which forms the divide between the drainage basins of the Ganges and Narbada rivers. With its western end in the State of Gujarat, the Vindhyas and their extension, the Kaimur Range, stretch east-northeastward nearly 700 miles to southwest Bihar State. The designation of "mountains" is a misnomer, since the Vindhyas actually form the steep, fault-controlled, southern escarpment of a plateau rising to elevations normally ranging between 1,500 and 2,000 feet, and seldom exceeding 3,000 feet. The aspect from the north is in no way impressive. The Vindhyas consist mainly of high-quality sandstone with a cap of Deccan traprock in the west. They are part of the Pre-Cambrian rocks of India.

JOSEPH E. SCHWARTZBERG

VINE. See GRAPE.

VINE IN ART AND SYMBOLISM, vīn. The vine was used in Greek antiquity as the symbol of Dionysus (Bacchus), the god of plant life and the spirit who caused all vegetation to grow. In the Old Testament, the vine is frequently mentioned as symbolic of the fruitfulness of the Promised Land, and as such appears on ancient coins. From the Christian point of view, the vine is used as a metaphor to express the relationship between God and His people, and the vineyard as the protected place where the children of God flourish under His care. "For the vineyard of the Lord of hosts is the house of Israel, and the men of Judah his pleasant plant . . ." (Isaiah 5:7).

For the New Testament, the vine became the symbol of Christ and the Church of God, life eternal, and the Eucharist itself, based largely on the parable: "I am the true vine, and my

Father is the husbandman . . . ye are the branches: He that abideth in me, and I in him, the same bringeth forth much fruit. . . . Herein is my Father glorified . . ." (John 15:1, 5, 8).

The vine with grapes being harvested by *putti* (cupids) is a Dionysian motif which appears in the Pompeian frescoes and the mosaic pavements of Rome and persists as pagan symbolism in the mosaics decorating the ring vault of the ambulatory of the early Christian Church of Santa Costanza in Rome. Its Christian symbolism appears clearly established in the mosaics and decorations of early Christian and Byzantine sarcophagi in Rome and particularly in Ravenna, where Hellenistic, Coptic, and Syrian decorative influences are crystallized into a new and vigorous style. The most famous example is probably the carved ivory throne of Archbishop Maximianus (d. 556) in the archiepiscopal palace of Ravenna, with its vigorous vine pattern with grapes being eaten by doves and peacocks, symbolic of the eternity of the soul through Christ. This symbolism becomes the established meaning when the vine is used as a decorative motif in Christian churches throughout succeeding styles in Europe.

LAURENCE SCHMECKEBIER
Director, The School of Art, College of Fine Arts, Syracuse University

VINEGAR, vĭn'ə-gər, derived from the French *vinaigre,* meaning sour wine, is the acidic liquid resulting from oxidative bacterial conversion of dilute alcoholic solutions from a wide variety of materials, but generally derived from fruits, to acetic acid.

In vinegar manufacture, the sugary materials or those produced by hydrolysis of starches are first converted to alcohol by yeasts of the genus *Saccharomyces.* Then the vinegar or acetic acid bacteria are used to transform the alcohol to acetic acid. Air is essential as these bacteria do not grow in the absence of oxygen. If the right nutritive conditions are maintained, the bacteria produce enzymes which cause the oxidation of the alcohol. These nutrients include simple sugars (glucose), amino acids and other nitrogenous compounds, vitamins particularly of the B complex, and inorganic compounds, especially phosphates. The chemical reaction is most simply represented as:

$$CH_3CH_2OH + O_2 + \text{bacterial enzymes} \rightarrow CH_3COOH + H_2O$$

Three methods are used to produce vinegar. The *slow* process, commonly known as the French method, the oldest commercial procedure, is almost obsolete. To start this process, the ends of barrels first are fitted with air vents, drilled about three inches in from the side but parallel to the side bung. Then the barrel is placed on a rack with the side bung up and filled one fourth to one third with sound vinegar containing active bacteria. This mass of bacteria is called "mother of vinegar." Vinegar stock is then added until the barrel is one half to two thirds full. The mixture of vinegar and alcohol is allowed to remain in the barrel until its maximum acid content develops (up to three months). Then two thirds to three fourths of the vinegar is withdrawn and replaced with fresh vinegar stock and the process repeated.

The *generator* process, first introduced into Germany, has been used almost universally for over 100 years for the production of commercial vinegars. A typical generator is a cylindrical wooden tank equipped with cooling coils, air vents, and a grating two or more feet above the bottom to support packing material, preferably beechwood shavings, and a sparger for dispersal of vinegar stock evenly over the surface of the packing. The liquid trickles over the packing covered with vinegar bacteria and meets a rising current of air admitted through the bottom. Circulation of the mash through the generator is continued a number of times until acetification is practically complete.

The *submerged* process for making vinegar is an outgrowth of the spectacular technological advances made in antibiotic manufacture during World War II. The submerged method employs a cylindrical stainless steel or wood tank suitably equipped with devices for ensuring an adequate, continuous air supply and cooling coils to control temperature fluctuations. To start acetification, the unit is filled with a mixture of vinegar containing bacteria and the alcohol to be oxidized, supplemented with nutrients and aerated. The temperature is maintained at about 86° F. After acetification about half of the vinegar is withdrawn and the remainder is left in the tank as seed for the next batch. This method, in one form or another, developed in West Germany and the United States, is rapidly replacing the older processes throughout the world.

Apple cider vinegar is the most common table vinegar used in the United States. Wine vinegar is used extensively in the grape-growing regions of the world. Malt vinegar is very popular in England. Distilled vinegar, also known as grain, spirit, or white vinegar, made from industrial alcohol, is commonly used in the food industries as an acidulant and as a preservative. In some countries a synthetic vinegar is made by diluting concentrated (glacial) acetic acid with water. Rice vinegar, which has a piquant quality, is often used in Oriental countries for marinades and salad dressings.

Table vinegar (as it is used for salad dressing and cooking) contains between 4 and 5 percent acetic acid (grams per 100 milliliters). Distilled vinegar as used in the food industries generally is 10 to 12.5 percent acid.

REESE H. VAUGHN
Professor of Food Science and Technology, University of California, Davis, Calif.

VINEGAR BIBLE, the popular name for a Bible printed at Oxford, England, in 1716–1717, and so named because of a misprint in the page heading of Luke 20 which reads "The Parable of the Vinegar," instead of "The Parable of the Vineyard." The fine folio edition in two volumes was the work of John Baskett, king's printer.

VINEGAR EEL. See EELWORM.

VINELAND, vīn'lənd, city, New Jersey, in the southern part of the state, 7 miles north of Millville and 35 miles south of Camden, at an altitude of 95 feet. Situated in the heart of a truck-farming and poultry-raising region, it is the business and marketing center of southern New Jersey. Industry also is important in the economy; principal manufactures include glassware, clothing, cement blocks, paper boxes, fireworks, chemicals, machinery, and foundry products; and fruits, vegetables, and other foods are processed. The city is the home of several state institutions, including a school for retarded children which is acclaimed for its high standards, a school for feebleminded women, and a veterans' home.

Vineland was planned and developed in 1861 by Charles K. Landis, who successfully united agriculture and industry in the area. It was incorporated as a borough in 1880. In 1952 the borough annexed Landis Township to form the city of Vineland, greatly expanding its area and population. Government is administered by mayor and council. Pop. 53,753.

VINES, vīnz, **H(enry) Ellsworth, Jr.,** American tennis player: b. Los Angeles, Calif., Sept. 28, 1911. He rose to sudden prominence in 1931 by winning the national singles tennis championship at Forest Hills, N.Y. The following year, at the age of 21, he emerged as a likely successor to the great William T. Tilden, Jr. (q.v.), with a series of brilliant performances, including a repeat triumph in the nationals and a victory at Wimbledon. Twice in 1932 he defeated the French star Henri Cochet, who had dominated amateur tennis for years. In 1934, Vines joined Tilden's professional troupe, helped to popularize the pro game, and won the championship in 1939. In later years he took up competitive golf with some success.

VINET, vē-nĕ', **Alexandre Rudolphe,** Swiss Protestant theologian: b. Ouchy, near Lausanne, Switzerland, June 17, 1797; d. Clarens, May 4, 1847. He studied for the Protestant ministry in which he was ordained in 1819, having previously been appointed, when only 20, professor of French language and literature at the gymnasium at Basel. A stanch advocate of religious liberties and of the separation of church and state, he ably defended these principles in his forceful sermons and writings, including *Mémoire sur les libertés des cultes* (1826), *Essai sur la conscience* (1829), *Essai sur la manifestation des convictions religieuses* (1842), and *Du socialisme considéré dans son principe* (1846). Having accepted the chair of practical theology at Lausanne in 1837, he abandoned it 10 years later when the curtailment of Protestant freedoms led to his withdrawal from the national chuch as part of the Free Church movement in Vaud Canton. Vinet's highly personal approach to Christian theology and his pragmatic attitudes toward dogma left a considerable mark on Protestantism not only in his own country, but in France, England, and elsewhere in Europe. His sermons were collected as *Discours sur quelques sujets religieux* (1831, 1841). He is remembered also for his valuable surveys of French philology and literature, including *Chrestomathie française,* 3 vols. (1829–30), *Études sur la littérature française au XIXme siècle* (3 vols., 1849–51), and *Histoire de la littérature française au XVIIIme siècle* (2 vols., 1853). Also published posthumously was his excellent *Études sur Blaise Pascal* (1848). His *Oeuvres* were published in Lausanne and Paris, beginning in 1910.

VINEYARD. See GRAPE.

VINEYARD SOUND, vĭn'yərd, a body of water off the southeastern coast of Massachusetts, separating Martha's Vineyard from the Elizabeth Islands. About 20 miles in length and from 3 to 7 miles in width, it joins Nantucket Sound on the northeast and the Atlantic Ocean on the southwest, and it is a passage for coastal ships.

VINGT-ET-UN, văɴ-tā-ûɴ', a card game played with a whole pack and with any number of players. The cards count according to the number of pips (or spots), the face cards counting 10 and the ace 1 or 11 as the holder chooses. The object of the game is to obtain a hand the total value of which equals 21 (hence the name). Two cards are dealt to each player, and if no one has a hand equal to 21, on the first deal, the players have the right of drawing cards in turn; if the cards drawn bring the total to more than 21 the player is out of the game. The player first obtaining a hand of 21 takes the pool or any other winning determined upon.

VINITA, vĭ-nē'tə, city, Oklahoma, seat of Craig County, located 60 miles northeast of Tulsa, at an altitude of 702 feet. Vinita lies in a stock-raising and agricultural area. The city was named by Col. Elias C. Boudinot, a Cherokee Indian and one of the promoters of the townsite, in honor of Vinnie Ream (1850–1914). Miss Ream, a sculptress, received a congressional commission to model the life-size statue of Abraham Lincoln which stands in the capitol at Washington, D.C. Manufactures include metal products, machinery, dairy products, beverages, and packaged meats. There is some coal mining. Foremost in interest for thousands of Oklahoma citizens are rodeo performances. The Will Rogers Memorial Rodeo is held at Vinita annually each fall. The city is governed by a mayor and council.

Although there was a small settlement, known as Downingville, here in 1870, Vinita was not founded until 1871 when two railroads were extended into the region. Will Rogers (1879–1935), American humorist, attended a secondary school here, and in his writing facetiously referred to Vinita as his "college town." Pop. 6,740.

VINJE, vĭn'yə, **Aasmund Olafsson,** Norwegian poet and essayist: b. Telemark, Norway, April 6, 1818; d. Gran, Opland, July 30, 1870. Born the son of a poor cotter, he retained throughout his life the peasant's earthy view of culture and society. Although he studied law at the University of Oslo, he never practiced, but eked out an existence by government clerical work, teaching, and writing. In 1851 he began working as Oslo correspondent for a provincial newspaper, but in 1858 he began publication of his own journal, *Dølen* (The Dalesman), in which he could express his ideas on any subject. It was written in the newly constructed rural language of Ivar Andreas Aasen, called Landsmaal or New Norse, which set him apart from such friends and contemporaries as Henrik Ibsen and Bjørnstjerne Bjørnson, and limited his reading public. But it permitted him to give full expression to his native Telemark dialect, particularly in the lyrics, which he began publishing after 1858. Like Heinrich Heine, whom he admired, Vinje was a psychologically torn personality, at once caustic and romantic, with a critical outlook on contemporary life and a deeply felt enthusiasm for the beauties of nature. Vinje's lyrics are classics in Norwegian literature, and many of his essays are still highly readable for their wit and common sense. He embedded many of them in his best-known work, *Ferdaminni fraa Sumaren 1860* (1861; Eng. tr., *Travelogue from the Summer of 1860,* 1861), an account of a walking tour in the mountains between Oslo and Trondheim. After visiting England, he wrote a caustic commentary on English life, *A Norseman's View of Britain and the British* (1862).

EINAR HAUGEN,
University of Wisconsin

VINLAND, vin'lənd, the name of the southernmost of the North American lands discovered in about 1000 A. D. by the Norseman Leif Ericson (q.v.). The earliest mention of Vinland (or Wineland) appears in the ecclesiastical history written about 1075 by Adam von Bremen. The most detailed information about Vinland and the Vinland voyages appears in the *Saga of the Greenlanders,* found in the *Flateyarbók* codex written in the last part of the 14th century, and in the *Saga of Eric the Red,* found in the *Hauksbók* codex written somewhat before 1334 and in the 15th-century *Skálholtsbók.*

The *Saga of the Greenlanders* tells of Bjarne Herjulfsson, who, sailing from Iceland to Greenland in 986, was driven off course by storms; he sighted strange coasts but did not go ashore. Then Leif Ericson, the son of Eric the Red (q.v.), set out from Greenland on a voyage of exploration. Sailing southward he discovered a barren country he called Helluland (Flat-stone Land), next, Markland (Wood Land), and then a pleasant country he called Vinland, where he built large houses and stayed a year. The Vinland expeditions of Thorwald, Thorfinn Karlsefni (q.v.), and Freydis followed.

Eric the Red's saga presents a somewhat different version. It relates that Leif Ericson discovered Vinland during a voyage from Norway to Greenland and describes Thorfinn Karlsefni's Vinland expedition with three ships, 160 people —including women—and cattle. Thorfinn stayed three years in Vinland but had to leave because of dangerous native inhabitants, whom he called the Skraelings.

The two sagas contain controversial and legendary material but also material so authentic that the Norse discovery of some parts of North America can hardly be disputed.

Vinland's Location. Ascertaining the location of Vinland has been a puzzle. Most experts, referring to the name Vinland and to the fact that the sagas mention grapes and wine, concluded that Vinland must be situated south of the northern limit of wild grapes. New England, New York, and other areas have been proposed. The explorer Fridtjof Nansen, however, held that the mention of grapes and wine was legendary. The philologist Sven Søderberg claimed that "Vin" in Vinland referred not to wine but was the old Norse syllable meaning "pasture," used in place names.

Accepting and supplementing this, the writer theorized that Vinland probably was in northern Newfoundland, as earlier suggested by W. A. Munn and V. Tanner. In 1960, I extensively searched the coasts and discovered at the northern tip of Newfoundland, in an area called L'Anse aux Meadows, some overgrown sites. During subsequent archaeological expeditions eight house sites were excavated and finds of Norse type were made. Archaeological assessment and carbon-14 dating procedures confirmed that the sites are Norse and pre-Columbian, dating from about the year 1000, but the exact site of the Vinland settlement remains in doubt.

The "Vinland Map." In 1965, Yale University published the so-called "Vinland Map," a world map showing Vinland and supposedly drawn in Switzerland and dating from around 1440—well before Columbus' voyage in 1492. But in January 1974, Yale announced that tests of the ink had shown the New World portions of the map to be a forgery. See also AMERICA—*Pre-Columbian Voyages.*

HELGE INGSTAD
Author of "Land under the Pole Star"

VINNITSA, vĭn'ĭt-sə, Russ. vyĕn'nyĭ-tsə, oblast, USSR, in the Ukrainian SSR, located in the west central Ukraine in the basin of the Southern Bug River. The area (10,300 square miles) is a rolling plain with black soil and some forests. The climate is moderate, with warm humid summers and mild winters. More sugar beets are grown here than in any other oblast of the USSR. Other major crops are wheat, rye, beans, fruit, vegetables, and tobacco. One fifth of all USSR sugar is refined in the oblast. There also are factories producing flour, canned fruit, vodka, beer, dairy products, shoes, clothing, bricks, tiles, chemical fertilizer, and farm machinery. Granite, kaolin, and limestone are mined. The oblast formed on Feb. 27, 1932, has seven cities: Vinnitsa (q.v.), the capital, Mogilev-Podolski, Zhmerinka, Tulchin, Kazatin, Gaisin, and Bar. The population (mainly Ukrainians, Russians, and Jews) is 83 percent rural. Population: (1983) 1,997,000.

ELLSWORTH RAYMOND

VINNITSA, city, USSR, in the Ukrainian SSR, located in the western Ukraine about 124 miles southwest of the Ukrainian capital of Kiev. Vinnitsa is built on steep banks along both sides of the Southern Bug River. It has many gardens and parks, and is so picturesque that it is nicknamed "Little Kiev." It is the capital and largest city of Vinnitsa Oblast (q.v.). The main city industry is sugar refining; other factories produce candy, packaged meat, textiles, chemical fertilizer, tools, and spare parts for agricultural machines. Educational institutions include two teachers' institutes, a medical college, and a Communist Party college. The city was founded in the 14th century, and lived under Polish rule from 1569 until 1793, when it was annexed by Russia. In 1941–1944, during World War II, it was occupied by invading Germans, whose war damage was quite extensive. Most of the inhabitants are Ukrainians and Jews. Population: (1983) 350,000.

ELLSWORTH RAYMOND

VINOGRADOFF, vyə-nŭ-grä'dôf, SIR **Paul Gavrilovich,** Anglo-Russian scholar: b. Kostroma, Russia, Dec. 1, 1854; d. Paris, France, Dec. 19, 1925. Educated at the University of Moscow, he had a great ability for languages, and traveled widely in his youth. He went to Italy in 1878, and wrote his master's thesis, which in 1881 became his first published work, *The Origin of Feudal Relations in Lombard Italy.* He went to England in 1883, and while working in archives found an important collection of legal cases compiled for a judge during the reign of Henry III.

After marrying Louise Stang, of a well-known Norwegian family in 1887, he published the work for which he is most widely known, *Villainage in England* (1892). In this work he advanced the theory that the manor in England derived not from serfdom but from the free village community. He became one of England's first and most renowned medievalists, despite his Russian background. He returned to Russia and became interested in the Zemstvo (q.v.) movement (local self-government) and in the reform of Russian education. After his plan for a professorial committee to air the grievances of the students at the University of Moscow was turned down in 1901, he resigned his post at the university. He returned to England, where he received an honorary degree from Oxford University. In 1902 the same university appointed him Corpus Christi professor of jurisprudence, a post he held until his death. He was the first director of the Selden Society (1907–1918) and in 1917, one year before he became an English citizen, was knighted.

Vinogradoff's other works include *The Growth of the Manor* (1905); *English Society in the Eleventh Century* (1908); *Roman Law in Mediaeval Europe* (1909); *Self-Government in Russia* (1915); and *Outlines of Historical Jurisprudence* (1920–22), for which he was especially cited when he was awarded a doctor's degree *honoris causa* by the University of Paris in 1925. He also contributed to the *Cambridge Medieval History*.

SHEPARD B. CLOUGH,
Professor of History, Columbia University.

VINOGRADSKI, vyə-nŭ-gräd′skē, or **WINOGRADSKY,** wĭ-nŭ-gräd′skē, **Sergei Nikolayevich**, Russian phytochemist and biochemist: b. Kiev, Russia, Sept. 1, 1856; d. Paris, France, Aug. 31, 1946. After first attending Kiev University, he was graduated from St. Petersburg University in 1881. He next studied in central Europe, and then returned to Russia, where he was chief of microbiology and later director (1902–1905) of the Institute of Experimental Medicine at St. Petersburg. After the Bolshevik Revolution of 1917, Vinogradski emigrated to France, where he joined the Pasteur Institute in 1922 as head of its division of agricultural microbiology. He retired in 1940.

In 1887 Vinogradski discovered chemosynthesis, a process through which certain microbes can oxidize nonorganic substances; this was one of the most important discoveries in plant physiology up to that time. In 1889 he applied "selective" fertilization to soil, thus increasing types of soil microbes that he wished to multiply; and in 1893, without using nitric fertilizer, he successfully grew plants which obtained nitrogen from the atmosphere. His new methods in soil microbiology in general proved that earth contains many more microorganisms than had been believed up to that time.

Although most of his research was in plant and soil microbiology, Vinogradski also contributed to medicine and industry through his discoveries. Despite his anti-Soviet views and the fact that he was a refugee from the USSR, Soviet history books honor him as the greatest Russian microbiologist of the 19th century. A collection of his many writings was published posthumously in 1949.

ELLSWORTH RAYMOND.

VINSON, vĭn′sən, **Frederick M(oore),** American legislator, government official, and 12th chief justice of the United States: b. Louisa, Ky., Jan. 22, 1890; d. Washington, D.C., Sept. 8, 1953. His service in the national legislature and executive was probably of greater importance than his short—seven-year—tenure on the high court. For it may be said of Vinson, as Associate Justice Oliver Wendell Holmes said of Chief Justice Edward Douglass White: he was "built rather for a politician than a judge."

Vinson was born, strange as it may seem, in a jail at Louisa, Ky., where his father was the jailer. He was a thorough product of Kentucky, taking his A.B. (1909) and LL.B. (1911) at Centre College, each time at the head of his class. An athlete of some ability, he eschewed professional baseball in favor of the law and immediately entered politics. Admitted to practice in 1911, he became city attorney of Louisa in 1913, served as commonwealth attorney (1921–1924), and was elected as a Democrat to the United States House of Representatives in 1922, serving for 13 years (1923–1929; 1931–1938). He failed of re-election in 1928, when he managed the Al Smith presidential election in Kentucky, but surged rapidly to leadership after being returned in 1930. As an influential member of the Ways and Means Committee, he performed yeoman service for President Franklin D. Roosevelt's New Deal, becoming a specialist in tax and fiscal matters. He secured passage of the Revenue Bill in May 1938 just before resigning to take an appointment as justice of the U.S. Court of Appeals for the District of Columbia, where he served from 1938 to 1943, and in 1942 he was appointed chief judge of the U.S. Emergency Court of Appeals, charged with reviewing the legality of price control orders under the Emergency Price Control Act.

Anxious to make a more direct and active contribution to the war effort, he was appointed director of the Office of Economic Stabilization in May 1943 and in April 1945 was made director of the Office of War Mobilization and Reconversion, the "economic czar" of the country. In July of that year he was appointed secretary of the treasury by President Harry S. Truman and held that post until June 1946, when he was appointed chief justice of the United States in succession to the late Harlan Fiske Stone.

Vinson was not constitutionally suited to be a high court justice for he was a "team worker" rather than the solo performer that the post demands. Although intelligent, he lacked breadth of intellect, and was very much dependent on his law clerks for the written product demanded of a justice. He also lacked understanding of the court as an institution. Politics remained too much a part of him, and his opinions, such as those in the "steel seizure" case, *Youngstown Sheet & Tube Co.* v. *Sawyer*, 343 U.S. 579 (1952), and *United States* v. *United Mine Workers*, 330 U.S. 258 (1947), reveal an insurmountable loyalty to the executive branch of government. Probably his most important civil liberties opinions were *Dennis* v. *United States*, 341 U.S. 494 (1952), *American Communications Assoc.* v. *Douds*, 339 U.S. 382 (1950), *Shelley* v. *Kraemer*, 334 U.S. 1 (1948), and the early school segregation cases, *Sweatt* v. *Painter*, 339 U.S. 629 (1950), and *McLaurin* v. *Oklahoma State Regents*, 339 U.S. 637 (1950). In the *Dennis* case, he upheld the constitutionality of the Smith (Alien Registration) Act of 1940 as applied to the leaders of the Communist Party; *Douds* sustained the requirement of the non-Communist oath by labor union leaders; *Shelley* held that states could not enforce restrictive racial covenants in land deeds; and *Sweatt* and *McLaurin* invalidated the "separate but equal" test as applied to professional and graduate schools of state universities.

In his evaluation of Vinson, Francis Alfred Allen, American educator who served as legal secretary to the chief justice in 1946–1948, appropriately wrote: "We may be too disposed . . . to underestimate the man of action, the master of political techniques, the architect of compromise .... Such a man is not likely to found a school of thought or leave behind him a coterie of intellectual disciples. But the chief justice found other important ways to serve his nation."

While there are many who do not regard Vinson's contributions to American jurisprudence with admiration, there are almost none who do not credit him with great executive and political abilities, as well as a deep capacity for warmth and friendship.

PHILIP B. KURLAND
Professor of Law, University of Chicago

VINTON, vĭn'tən, city, Iowa, seat of Benton County, on the Cedar River, 32 miles northwest of Cedar Rapids; altitude 805 feet. Principal manufactures in this agricultural trading center are screw machines and farm implements. A large vegetable cannery (corn and peas) operates here, and there is poultry packing. Vinton is the site of a state school for the blind, whose graduates may matriculate at any college in Iowa. Settled in 1839 as Northport, and later called Fremont, the city received its present name in 1846, and was incorporated in 1869. Pop. 5,040.

VINTON, town, Virginia, in Roanoke County, situated at an altitude of 910 feet. It is chiefly a residential community, whose western limits coincide with the limits of the city of Roanoke. Vinton's economic activities are integrated in the diversified industries of the Roanoke Valley. The town is known as the "Dogwood Capital of Virginia," and a special celebration, highlighted by a band festival, is held each spring at the peak of the blossoms. The Smith Mountain Dam area is nearby. Settled in 1837, Vinton was known originally as Gish's Mills. Incorporation came in 1884, and town manager government was introduced in 1904. Pop. 8,027.

HERBERT L. KEATON

VINYL COMPOUNDS. See PLASTICS.

VIOL, vī'əl, a family of stringed instruments. The viols, descended from earlier European fiddles, had their peak of popularity in the 16th and 17th centuries. Scholars divide the viol family into *viole da braccio* (arm viols) and *viole da gamba* (leg viols); the former largely became obsolete as the latter paralleled the violins of later periods. A classic viol differs from a violin chiefly thus: its shoulders slope down from its body rather than projecting at right angles; the body has a flat rather than a bulging back; its strings number six or seven rather than four; it has gut frets around the fingerboard; its sound holes are *c*-shaped rather than *f*-shaped; its bridge is comparatively flat, permitting the bowing of full chords on its comparatively thin strings; it is held downward, on or between the knees, rather than pressed against the left shoulder, and is played with a bow whose stick curves outward and is held palm upward. The characteristic sound of the viol is comparatively faint, soft, and lacking in brilliance. By the 17th century, viols classically came in three sizes: treble, tenor, and bass; a "chest of viols" was made up of two instruments of each size. English composers who wrote for the viol include William Byrd, John Coperario, Orlando Gibbons, and John Jenkins.

See also VIOLA; VIOLA DA GAMBA; VIOLA D'AMORE; VIOLIN; VIOLONCELLO.

HERBERT WEINSTOCK

VIOLA, vē-ō'lə, Italian for viol (q.v.), but in modern usage the second, or alto, member of the violin family. Tuned a fifth lower than the violin (c g d' a') and an octave higher than the violoncello, it is only slightly larger than the former, but much smaller than the latter; this noticeable difference in the relationship between pitch and size gives the instrument its unique, somewhat nasal, timbre among the strings. Its two lower strings are covered with copper wire. Music for the modern viola is commonly written on the alto clef, although the highest notes appear on the treble clef. The German term for viola is *Bratsche,* and the French term *alto.* Although the viola has been scored for chiefly as an ensemble instrument in chamber and orchestral music, it has also been composed for as a solo instrument, notably by Hector Berlioz (*Harold en Italie*) and, more recently, by Paul Hindemith (solo sonatas; *Der Schwanendreher,* for viola and orchestra).

HERBERT WEINSTOCK

VIOLA DA GAMBA, vē-ō'lä dä-gäm'bä (It. for "leg viol"), originally the name of a class of viol (q.v.), larger than the *viola da braccio* (arm viol), but in later usage specifically applied only to the bass member of the viol family. Even after the viols generally had been displaced by the more brilliant violins, the *viola da gamba* long persisted. Johann Sebastian Bach (1685–1750) wrote notable sonatas for it, and Karl Friedrich Abel (1723–1787) was a famous performer on the instrument.

HERBERT WEINSTOCK

VIOLA D'AMORE, vē-ō'lä dä-mō'rā (viol of love, probably from the blindfolded head of Amor often used on the instrument instead of a terminal scroll), a viol the size of a treble viol, but having sympathetic wire strings stretched below the bowed strings, and therefore having a timbre with an aura of silvery echo. Until the middle of the 18th century, the name was applied to a violin with metal strings; by 1740, however, the instrument sometimes heard today had usurped the name.

Notable parts for this later *viola d'amore* occur in music by Antonio Vivaldi (1680?–1743) and Johann Sebastian Bach (1685–1750), and, later, in many operas, including *Les Huguenots* by Giacomo Meyerbeer, *Le jongleur de Notre-Dame* by Jules Massenet, and *Madama Butterfly* by Giacomo Puccini. Paul Hindemith (1895–) has written both a sonata and a concerto for the *viola d'amore.*

HERBERT WEINSTOCK

VIOLACEAE, vī-ō-lā′sē-ē, a fairly well-defined family containing herbs, shrubs, and trees. The majority of genera are woody and tropical, but *Viola* itself is an important exception, consisting mainly of low north-temperate herbs. The leaves have stipules at their base, are arranged alternately, and are generally undivided. The inflorescences are spicate, racemose or cymose, or the flowers are solitary; and each flower stalk bears a pair of bracteoles. The flowers are either regular or zygomorphic with parts free and in fives. The sepals persist, the anthers open inward, and the superior ovary is single celled with three parietal placentae and a single style and stigma. The fruit is either a capsule or a berry, and the seeds have abundant fleshy endosperm.

The family is placed by Adolf Engler in the order Parietales. There are 16 genera and about 800 species, the main center of distribution being in the Southern Hemisphere, particularly South America. The largest genera are *Rinorea* (tropical trees or shrubs with regular flowers) and *Viola* (mainly nontropical herbs with zygomorphic flowers). There are no important uses, but some species of *Viola* are cultivated in gardens.

See also VIOLET.

DAVID H. VALENTINE,
M. J. HARVEY.

VIOLET, vī′ə-lĭt. The violets comprise the genus *Viola,* the largest genus of the Violaceae, with some 400 species. They are predominantly perennial herbs, but a few are annuals, and a few are small shrubs.

Viola is characterized by its bilaterally symmetrical, spurred flower and by its fruit, a capsule that splits to give three valves containing the seeds. In most species the valves contract on drying, squeezing the hard smooth seeds and shooting them several feet.

The flowers are highly adapted to cross-pollination by insects. The lowest petal forms a landing platform with guide markings radiating from the throat of the spur, which varies in length from 2 to 30 millimeters according to the species. The stamens surround the ovary and open inward; the pollen which collects is liberated when the stamens are disturbed. The two lowermost stamens bear appendages which secrete nectar into the spur. The stigma of the violet is very variable in shape.

The conspicuous open flowers described are formed at the beginning of the growing season. Later many species produce petalless flowers which never open and are invariably self-pollinated. The same plant may thus produce seed from both cross- and self-fertilization in a single season.

Wilhelm Becker has divided the genus into 14 sections, 7 confined to the Southern Hemisphere. Most of the Eurasian and North American violets fall into three sections. The blue violets (section *Nomimium*) form a large north-temperate group. Familiar subsections are: (1) *Rostratae* (dog violets), circumpolar, with flowers on overground stems; (2) *Uncinatae,* Eurasian, with flowers on a short rootstock (remarkable in having nonexplosive capsules and ant-dispersed seeds; includes the sweet violet, *V. odorata,* native to Europe); (3) *Stolonosae,* circumpolar, generally marsh violets with creeping stems; and (4) *Boreali-Americanae,* the North American "stemless blue" violets with fleshy rhizomes.

The section *Chamaemelanium,* predominantly yellow flowered, is common in North America and parts of Asia. The petals are arranged like those of pansies, but the spur is shorter, and the style is straight at the base; both in this and the section *Nomimium,* regular polyploid series are found.

The pansies (section *Melanium*) have leafy stipules, and the lateral petals are directed more or less upward; the capitate style is bent at the base. Some are large-flowered perennials, some small-flowered weedy annuals. All are Eurasian except for one species native to North America. Garden pansies probably arose from hybrids between the European species *V. tricolor* and *V. lutea* and the Asiatic *V. altaica.* Wild hybrids are frequent in the genus, and in some groups this has led to the blurring of species boundaries and to introgressive hybridization.

Roche

Canada violet (*Viola canadensis*), in blossom.

Violet flowers can be candied or used to make jelly. The leaves are sometimes added to salads.

DAVID H. VALENTINE,
M. J. HARVEY,
Department of Botany, Science Laboratories, The Durham Colleges, University of Durham, England.

VIOLET, the first color of the rainbow, a pure hue in its own right. Historically it is the hue of royalty. Colorants having a pure violet hue occur mostly in single chemical entities, sometimes referred to as red-violet, magenta, or purple, which are shade variations. Certain shades of violet may be produced by mixing bluish reds with reddish blues, but the single-body violet chemical compounds available are purer in hue and more brilliant and generous in variety. In the visible spectrum, violet excites energy at wavelengths

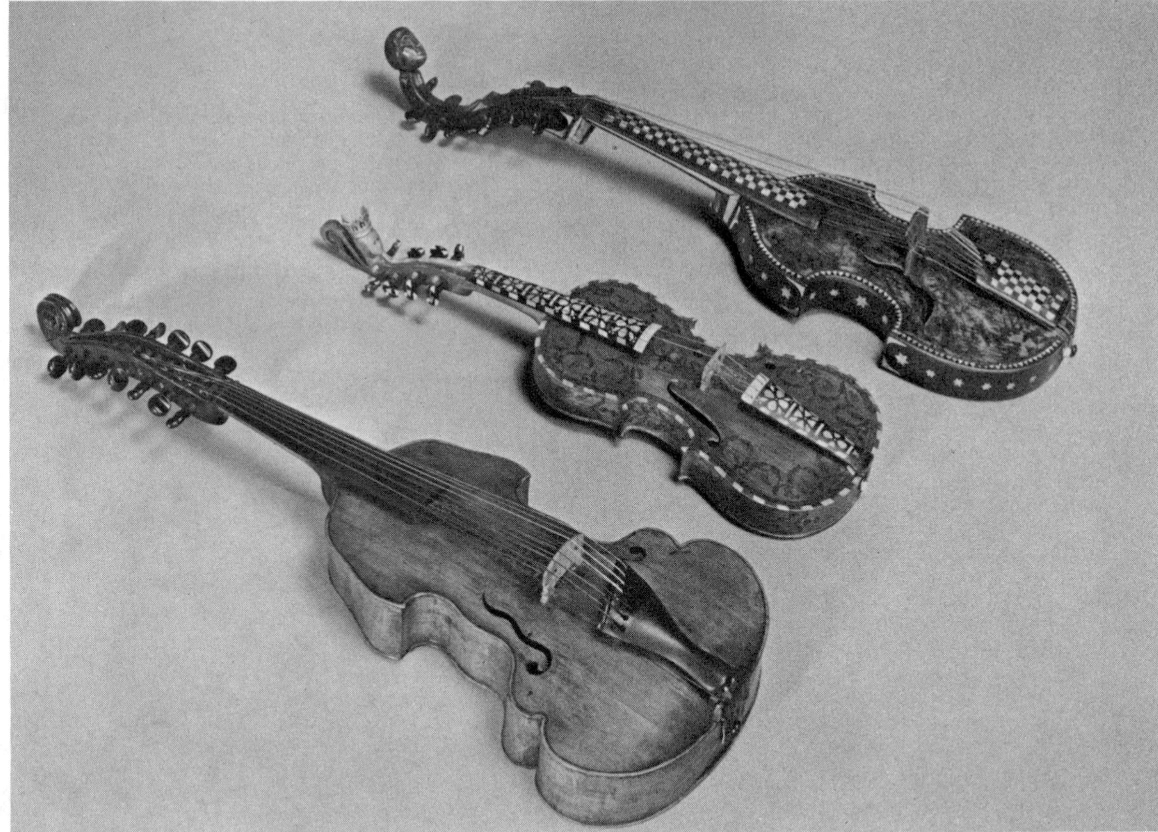

THE METROPOLITAN MUSEUM OF ART

A French example of the 18th century *viola d'amore* (top). A Bohemian example of the 18th century *viola d'amore* (middle). A related 19th century Norwegian instrument known as a Hardanger viol (bottom).

of 400 to 450μ; a second but important peak is observed in the pure red portion at a wavelength of around 700μ.

Violet pigments are utilized in many ways. As deep tones they depict hues of richness and beauty unmatched in the visible spectrum. Also, they may be used with opaque whites to produce half tones and such delicate and individual pastels as iris. Violets may also be employed in mixtures with red and light oranges to deepen them without losing richness. Perhaps the most important use of violet pigments is that of "bluing" whites. Advantage is taken of the fact that yellow is the complementary color of violet by using violet pigments in trace amounts to neutralize the yellow cast characteristic of most so-called white compounds.

Among the inorganic violet pigments are two well-known examples: cobalt violet and mineral violet, sometimes called Nürnberg violet. Both are weak tinctorially, but possess clean violet hues. Organic violet pigments are widely used for colorants and comprise several chemical groups that produce pigments used in the manufacture of carbon paper, printing inks, plastics, industrial and automotive finishes, and a variety of other products. Among the chemical groups that produce violet pigments are the thioindigos, the quinacridones, the alizarines, and the carbazole dioxazines.

VINCENT C. VESCE,
National Aniline Division, Allied Chemical Corporation.

VIOLET-GREEN SWALLOW. See SWALLOWS.

VIOLIN, vī-ō-lĭn′, the most important family of modern stringed instruments; specifically, the soprano member of that family, with strings tuned g, d′, a′, e″. Developed during the second half of the 16th century from such earlier European instruments as the rebec, gigue, lyra, kit, and vielle, the violins gradually displaced the members of the earlier viol family. Violins are distinguished from viols by much greater brilliance, flexibility, and audibility. True violins differ from viols in having shoulders that project from their bodies at right angles instead of sloping downward; by bodies with outward-bulging rather than flat backs; by having shallower ribs between back and table; by having four rather than six or seven strings; by having no keyboard frets; by having sound holes shaped like the letter *f* rather than like the letter *c;* by having an arched bridge that makes the bowing of full chords impossible under ordinary circumstances (though two strings can be bowed simultaneously); by being played (except for the double bass, not a true violin) with a bow having a straight or slightly inward-curving stick held palm downward; and, in the violins and violas, by being played pressed against the performer's left shoulder rather than held downward on or between the knees.

The members of the violin family are the violin proper, the viola, the violoncello, and the double bass (this last, often called contrabass viol, may be viewed as a development of the deepest size of viol rather than as a true violin). The violins make up the string section of a modern symphony orchestra; except for the double bass, they also are the most important instruments in chamber music: a typical string quartet consists of two violins, a viola, and a violoncello.

Renowned early makers of violins, all Italians, included Gasparo Bertolotti "da Salò" (1540–1609), Giovanni Paolo Maggini (1580–1632), the brothers Antonio and Girolamo Amati (respectively 1550–1638 and 1556–1630), Antonio Stradivari (1644?–1737), and, in the 17th and 18th centuries, members of the Guarneri, Ruggieri, Rogeri, and Testore families. Notably excellent violins were made in Austria (Jacob Stainer or Steiner, 1621?–1683); Germany (Klotz or Kloz family, 17th and 18th centuries); England (Thomas Urquhart, 17th century; Barak Norman and Benjamin Banks, 18th century); and France (Lupot family, 18th and 19th centuries).

A very early passage for solo violins occurs in the aria *Possente spirto* in Claudio Monteverdi's opera *La favola d'Orfeo* (1607). The earliest recognized extensive composer for the violin was Giovanni Battista Fontana (d. 1630); like several early violin makers, he lived in Brescia, Italy. Italian composers for the violin and (late 17th century) their German contemporaries and successors quickly evolved virtuoso techniques of performance. It was again Italians who capitalized on the more specifically expressive, melody-carrying capacities of the violin, notably in the compositions (including trio sonatas) of Giovanni Legrenzi (1626–1690), Arcangelo Corelli (1653–1713), and such members of the Bologna School as Giovanni Battista Vitali (1644?–1692), Domenico Gabrielli (1659–1690), Giuseppe Torelli (1658–1709), Tommaso Antonio Vitali (1665?–?1747), and Giuseppe Aldrovandini (1673–?1707). More virtuosic, as characterized by increasing demand for accuracy in rapid passagework, were the high baroque violin sonatas and concertos of Antonio Vivaldi (1669?–1741), Francesco Maria Veracini (1690–?1750), Giuseppe Tartini (1692–1770), and Pietro Locatelli (1695–1764).

In the German states, baroque violin music was developed by Georg Philipp Telemann (1681–1767), Johann Georg Pisendel (1687–1755), and Johann Sebastian Bach (1685–1750). The vitality and dynamism of the German manner fused with more specifically Italianate styles in the compositions of George Frideric Handel (1685–1759), Francesco Geminiani (1687–1762), Antonio Lolli (1730?–1802), Gaetano Pugnani (1731–1798), and Giovanni Battista Viotti (1755–1824). Meanwhile, violinist-composers of the Mannheim School, notably Johann Schobert (1720–1767), tended clearly toward the high Viennese rococo-classical manner of both solo and ensemble violin music to be found in the sonatas, concertos, and quartets of Franz Joseph Haydn (1732–1809), Luigi Boccherini (1743–1805), Wolfgang Amadeus Mozart (1756–1791), and Ludwig van Beethoven (1770–1827). Since the compositions of Beethoven's middle and late periods, developments both in violin playing and in composing for the instrument generally have paralleled the evolution of musical idioms and styles rather than having separable, meaningful histories of their own. Familiar styles of violin playing were developed during the 19th century in Hungary, Russia, Germany, and France. After World War II, an enduring renaissance of violin playing took place in Italy.

HERBERT WEINSTOCK
Author of "Music as an Art"

See Bibliography next page.

Right: Back and face views of a violin made by the best known member of the Guarneri family, Giuseppe (del Gesù) (1698–1744). *Below:* Three views of the Hellier Stradivarius, produced by Antonio Stradivari in 1679.

(Left and right) THE BETTMANN ARCHIVE

Bibliography: Violin

Abele, Hyacinth, and Niederheitman, Friedrich, *The Violin: Its History and Construction,* tr. by John Broadhouse (1952; reprint, Longwood 1977).
Auer, Leopold, *Violin Masterworks and Their Interpretation* (1925; reprint, Hyperion Press 1979).
Bachmann, Alberto, *An Encyclopedia of the Violin,* ed. by Albert E. Wier, tr. by Frederick H. Martens (1925; reprint, Da Capo 1975).
Clarke, A. Mason, *The Violin and Old Violin Makers* (Scholarly Press 1976).
Courvoisier, Karl, *Technics of Violin Playing* (1899; reprint, Longwood 1978).
Cremer, Lothar, *The Physics of the Violin,* tr. by John S. Allen (MIT Press 1984).
Delbanco, Nicholas, *The Beaux Arts Trio* (Morrow 1985).
DuBourg, G., *The Violin* (1852; reprint, Longwood 1977).
Gill, Dominic, ed., *The Book of the Violin* (Rizzoli Int. Pub. 1984).
Heron-Allen, Edward, *Violin-Making As It Was and Is* (Sterling 1984).
Menuhin, Yehudi, *The Compleat Violinist* (Summit Bks. 1986).
Roth, Henry, *Master Violinists in Performance* (Paganiniana Pub. 1982).
Schwarz, Boris, *Great Masters of the Violin* (Simon & Schuster 1983).
Staliner, Cecie, *Dictionary of Violin Makers* (1896; reprint, Longwood 1977).
Wenberg, Thomas J., *The Violin Makers of the United States* (Mt. Hood Pub. 1986).

VIOLLE, vyôl, **Jules,** French physicist: b. Langres, France, 1841; d. Fixin, near Dijon, 1923. A graduate of the Ecole Normale Supérieure of Paris, he received the doctor of science degree in 1870. He taught at the University of Lyon from 1883 and from 1890 at the Ecole Normale Supérieure; in 1891 he was also appointed professor at the Conservatoire des Arts et Métiers. Violle made important studies in the radiation of bodies at high temperatures; in solar radiation and the measurement of high temperatures; in the origin of hail and ways of combating it. He determined the solar constant, atmospheric absorption, the point of fusion of gold, platinum, and paladium; but he is best known for having created in 1881 the unit of luminous intensity that bears his name, the Violle, or Violle's standard, defined as the light emitted by a square centimeter of platinum at the temperature of solidification, about equal to 18.5 British standard candles. The Academy of Sciences admitted him to membership in 1897. Among his works are *Théorie mécanique de la chaleur* (1869–72); *Sur la radiation solaire* (1879); *Eclairage électrique* (1883); *Polarisation par emission* (1892); *Rayonnement des corps incandescents* (1893); *De l'avenir de nos industries physiques après la guerre* (1915).

VIOLLET-LE-DUC, vyô-lĕ'lə-dük', **Eugène Emmanuel,** French architect and writer: b. Paris, France, Jan. 21, 1814; d. Lausanne, Switzerland, Sept. 17, 1879. He studied architecture in Paris and began his career by restoring minor medieval buildings in the south of France. In the 1840's, with Jean Baptiste Lassus he restored the Sainte Chapelle in Paris, and from 1845 to 1855 they restored the Cathedral of Notre Dame, building a new spire over the crossing and a new pulpit. Among his other restorations, Viollet-le-Duc worked on the cathedrals at Laon and Amiens, the town walls of Carcassonne, and the Château de Pierrefonds. As a writer, he is best known for his immense *Dictionnaire raisonné de l'architecture française du XIe siècle* (1854–1869), in 10 volumes, and his *Dictionnaire raisonné du mobilier français jusqu'à la Renaissance* (1853) in 6 volumes, both with innumerable plans, sections, and illustrations by his hand, covering every aspect of medieval building and furniture. He also wrote a monograph on Notre Dame and an essay on medieval military architecture. He was a confirmed academic Gothicist, and said that a youthful visit to Versailles offended him so that he could never have any sympathy for the unfunctional arts of the Renaissance. He has been accused of over-restoration, with some justice, but his service to Gothic architecture as publicist and codifier outweighs his damage to the few structures he saved from ruin.

H. D. HALE,
Art Critic.

VIOLONCELLO, vī-ə-lən-chĕl'ō (commonly abbreviated as 'cello or cello), the bass member of the violin family. Tuned an octave and a fifth below the violin (C, G, d, a), an octave below the viola, it is more than twice as wide and long, and exactly four times as thick, as the violin. Music for the cello is commonly written on the bass clef, but the highest notes may appear on the tenor (or even treble) clef. Among the oldest surviving cellos are two believed to have been made by Andrea Amati (1530?–?1611) at Cremona, Italy, about 1565.

After being employed almost exclusively in thorough-bass accompaniment, the cello began to emerge as a solo instrument in the late 17th century. *Ricercari per violoncello solo* by Domenico Gabrieli (1659–1690) prefigured the famous sonatas for unaccompanied cello by Johann Sebastian Bach (1685–1750). Other noted early composers for the cello included Giuseppe Jacchini (17th–18th centuries) of Bologna, Antonio Vivaldi (1669?–1741), Evaristo Felice dall'Abaco (1675–1742), Leonardo Leo (1694–1747), Giacomo Bassevi, called Cervetto (1682?–1783), and his son Giacomo (1747–1837). One of the most outstanding and prolific composers for the instrument was Luigi Boccherini (1743–1805). Since Boccherini's sonatas, concertos, and quintets (with two cellos), developments in both cello playing and in composing for the instrument have paralleled the evolution of musical idioms and styles rather than having separable, meaningful histories of their own. The Catalan cellist Pablo (Pau) Casals (1876–) became one of the most famous performing musicians of the 20th century.

HERBERT WEINSTOCK.

VIOTTI, vyôt'tē, **Giovanni Battista,** Italian composer and violinist: b. Fontanetto da Po, Italy, May 12, 1755 (not May 23, 1753, as often stated); d. London, England, March 3, 1824. Child of a blacksmith, he early attracted wealthy patrons, studied with Gaetano Pugnani, and made international tours as a virtuoso violinist, often playing his own compositions. After being a court musician and opera impresario in Paris, he went to London in 1792 as a conductor, also playing in the famous concerts organized by Johann Peter Salomon. His fortunes declined after 1798, though he directed the Théâtre-Italien in Paris in 1819–1822, and he died in obscurity. His importance in the evolution of modern violin playing was decisive, and in his nearly 30 violin concertos he worked out the full pattern of a sonata-based form exploiting the richest resources of both orchestra and solo instrument. His very numerous compositions also include

Upper right: **Russel's viper has been known to bear over 60 young in a single litter.** ***Lower right:*** **the horned head of a rhinoceros viper.** ***Below:*** **The enormous Gaboon viper develops fangs nearly two inches long.**

R. Van Nostrand from National Audubon Society

chamber pieces and both piano sonatas and piano concertos.

HERBERT WEINSTOCK
Author of "Music as an Art"

VIPERS, vī'pərz, limbless reptiles of the family Viperidae, which includes many dangerously venomous snakes inhabiting Europe, Asia, and Africa. Vipers have tubular fangs that are tilted back against the roof of the mouth when not in use. The venom apparatus is essentially the same as that of the rattlesnake and other pit vipers, which are not true vipers (see RATTLESNAKE; SNAKE—*Classification of Snakes*.

The fangs of both vipers and pit vipers are proportionately longer than those of cobras and their allies in the family Elapidae, in which the fangs are permanently erect at the front of the jaw. While such primitive vipers as the African night adders (*Causus*) have relatively short fangs, those of the big vipers are comparatively enormous. The Gaboon viper (*Bitis gabonica*), at its maximum length of approximately six feet, has the largest fangs known, nearly two inches in length if measured along the curve. The venom apparatus serves primarily as a means of killing or subduing the prey, and secondarily as a means of defense.

In older classifications snakes equipped with the fang-tilting mechanism characteristic of vipers and pit vipers were placed in the suborder Solenoglypha as a subdivision of the order that includes all snakes. At present the vipers and pit vipers are placed in separate families, or sometimes in subfamilies (Viperinae and Crotalinae, respectively) of the family Viperidae. The presence on each side of the head of a pit located behind and below the nostril distinguishes the crotalids or pit vipers from the viperids, or true vipers, which lack the heat receptors contained in the pair of pits.

Form and Coloration.—With few exceptions vipers are rather heavy bodied. The head is commonly broad, and sharply set off from the body in most species, but the night adders and especially the burrowing vipers (*Atractaspis*) are relatively slender, with narrow heads. Along with the rare Fea's viper (*Azemiops feae*) of Upper Burma and the adjacent parts of China and Tibet, they retain enlarged plates instead of having small scales on the top of the head, as is characteristic of most vipers.

Vipers vary from the uniform black or lead color of burrowing forms, through the pale gray or buff typical of the desert dwellers, to the complex symmetrical patterns of yellowish brown, purple, and reddish colors seen in such forest-dwelling forms as the Gaboon viper. Most arboreal vipers (*Atheris*) are green, rarely yellow, often with ill-defined darker markings.

Distribution.—The true vipers are represented in Europe by one genus containing 8 species, and in Asia by 5 genera that include 14 species. In Africa, the center of their abundance, there are approximately 40 species belonging to 7 genera.

Habitats.—The principle of adaptive radiation is exemplified by the vipers in Africa, where those in one genus (*Atheris*) have prehensile tails and are largely arboreal, living either in trees or shrubs. A second group, comprising species of the genera *Bitis, Causus, Echis, Aspis*, and *Vipera*, are primarily terrestrial, though the Sahara horned viper (*Aspis cerastes*) buries itself in the sand. There are no truly aquatic species, but the rhinoceros viper (*Bitis nasicornis*) frequents swamps or moist forest habitats. Burrowing vipers, (*Atractaspis*), found only in Africa and the adjacent portions of Asia Minor, are the only vipers that move beneath the soil; they rarely appear on the surface except after rains.

Terrestrial vipers are widely distributed in Europe and Asia. The adder (*Vipera berus* and its subspecies) inhabits an extensive range, from the British Isles (except Ireland) eastward across Europe and Asia to Sakhalin Island on the Pacific coast, including areas within the Arctic Circle, north of the Baltic Sea. In Africa, vipers occur as far south as the Cape of Good Hope.

Breeding.—All vipers give birth to living young, with the exception of the night adders (*Causus*) and the burrowing forms (*Atractaspis*), which lay their eggs in the ground, or in decaying vegetation. Some large vipers are extremely prolific. The widely distributed puff adder (*Bitis arietans*) of Africa and the Arabian Peninsula may produce 70 young at a time, and 63 are reported in a single litter produced by Russell's viper (also known as the "daboia" and "tic-polonga") in Asia. In contrast, the smaller night adder (*Causus rhombeatus*) seldom lays more than 20 eggs, and the secretive burrowing viper may lay only one egg at a time.

Vipers use their sense of smell in finding mates. Rival males indulge in a spectacular performance called the "dance of the adders." With the head and the fore part of the body held erect, competing males face each other as each endeavors to push his opponent to the ground. This "dance" sometimes continues for hours, accompanied by elaborate swaying movements, until one male or the other is momentarily forced over on his back. There is no biting in such contests, which may be interpreted as a manifestation of territoriality, or in some instances as males competing for mating rights. Similar behavior in American pit vipers was mistakenly interpreted as a "courtship dance."

Vipers commonly produce a brood every year, but in northern Europe, and at higher elevations in the Alps, gestation in the adder (*Vipera berus*) requires two growing seasons. Thus under such extreme conditions a brood is produced only on alternate years by these vipers.

Size.—Vipers range in size from slender burrowers scarcely a foot long to the maximum length encountered in Russell's viper, which may exceed six feet. Other vipers attain dimensions between these extremes, ranging in size from two to three feet. Arboreal vipers, and those dwelling in regions with short growing seasons or in sandy deserts, tend to be smaller. Males often attain larger dimensions than females.

Feeding Habits.—Most vipers prey on the smaller mammals, principally rodents, but night adders feed upon toads, and burrowing vipers occasionally devour blind snakes (*Typhlops*). The common adder eats field mice, voles, shrews, the eggs and nestlings of birds, as well as lizards, frogs, and salamanders. Juvenile vipers select such small prey as insects, slugs, and worms.

Enemies.—The principal enemy of vipers is undoubtedly man. In addition to destroying or disturbing natural habitats, human beings, because of their fear of being bitten, kill great numbers of vipers. Predatory birds, hedgehogs, foxes, badgers, other snakes, and even fishes devour vipers. They are subject to infestations of mites and ticks, and commonly harbor internal parasites.

Viper Bite.—There are few reliable statistics concerning the incidence of snakebite. Some 20,000 to 25,000 deaths from venomous snakes are said to occur annually in India. In Europe, where vipers are the only dangerous snakes, fewer than 20 deaths from snakebite are reported annually. In Africa, bites of the burrowing vipers, the saw-scaled vipers (*Echis*), and the puff adder (*Bitis arietans*) and its allies, are probably responsible for more human fatalities than bites from mambas, cobras, and other venomous snakes.

The venoms of vipers differ from species to species. Many venoms contain a powerful depressant that may cause death from cardiac failure when sufficiently large amounts reach the bloodstream of the victim. Other elements in the venom affect the central nervous system. Vipers normally kill small animals within minutes or even seconds, but large animals seldom succumb unless the viper manages to inject a large amount of venom when biting the victim.

Symptoms of viper bite in human beings are usually extreme pain and swelling, with discoloration at the site of the penetration. Neurotoxic elements in the venom may cause vomiting, diarrhea, or prostration, sometimes with the loss of consciousness. In fatal cases the pulse and respiration weaken gradually until death ensues, usually five or six hours after a bite, though in rare instances it may be delayed until the third day. Victims surviving for longer periods usually recover.

CHARLES M. BOGERT
The American Museum of Natural History

Further Reading: Leetz, Thomas, *T.F.H. Book of Snakes* (TFH Pub. 1983); Marais, Johan, *Snake Versus Man* (Intl. Specialized Bk. Ser. 1985); Mattison, Christopher, *Snakes of the World* (Facts on File 1986); Seigel, Richard A., *Snakes: Ecology and Biology* (Macmillan 1987); Visser, John, and Chapman, David, *Snakes and Snakebite* (State Mutual Bk. 1980).

VIPER'S BUGLOSS. See BUGLOSS.

VIPSANIUS. See AGRIPPA, MARCUS VIPSANIUS.

VIRACOCHA, the highest in rank of the gods of the Inca. The Inca believed that he lived in the sky, where he ruled over lesser deities. See under INCA.

VIRAMGAM, vĭr'ŭm-gäm, town, India, in the Ahmadabad District of Gujarat State, 35 miles west-northwest of the city of Ahmadabad. The ancient, walled town is an important rail junction and a regional market for cotton ginning and milling, and for oilseed milling. Cotton weaving is conducted both as a handloom and as a factory industry. Population: (1961) 38,955.

JOSEPH E. SCHWARTZBERG.

VIRCHOW, fĭr′кнō, **Rudolf,** German pathologist, anthropologist, and political leader: b. Schivelbein, Pomerania (now Swidwin, Poland), Oct. 13, 1821; d. Berlin, Germany, Sept. 5, 1902. After receiving a medical degree at Berlin in 1843, he was appointed prosector at Charité Hospital and in 1847 became assistant professor (*Privatdozent*) at Berlin. Leaving in 1849 to accept the chair of pathological anatomy at Würzburg, he returned to a similar position at Berlin seven years later.

Virchow started his medical career with experimental and chemical work after 1843. His many discoveries included embolism and leukemia, and the substances amyloid, hematoidin, and myelin. His microscopic studies added tremendously to medical knowledge of connective tissue, inflammation, and tumors (he discovered myxoma, myoma, glioma, psammoma, and he redefined sarcoma and melanoma). He cleared up the life cycle of the trichinae. More important even than the detail work was his establishment (with John Goodsir and Robert Remak) of the basic biological rule: "Every cell descends from another cell"; and his giving a common denominator to all pathology: all pathology is eventually "cellular pathology"—the foundations of which he laid in his epochal *Die Cellular-pathologie in ihrer Begründung auf physiologische und pathologische Gewebelehre* (1858). This localist pathology was an important stimulus for surgery, as well as for Paul Ehrlich's specific drug therapy. He was at the same time an important pioneer of public health, and he successfully fought for better sewerage, hospitals, schools, and meat inspection.

As an anthropologist, Virchow was a leader in the movement toward greater emphasis on laboratory research which marked anthropological study in the 1860's. His unique survey of 7,000,000 German schoolchildren showed only 30 percent to be blond and blue eyed. He dug out German pile dwellings and walled mounds, and helped Heinrich Schliemann at Troy. Virchow's opposition to bacteriology and Darwinism has been exaggerated. He founded societies, and was editor of the *Zeitschrift für Ethnologie* from 1869 until his death.

Virchow's political career culminated in his opposition (as leader of the Progressive Party) to Bismarck during the constitutional conflict of 1862–1866. After Bismarck's victory in 1870, Virchow devoted himself mostly to anthropological and archaeological work. He was a member of the Berlin City Council from 1859, of the Prussian Diet from 1861 to 1902, and of the Reichstag from 1880 to 1893.

During the last third of the 19th century, Virchow probably was the best-known medical man in the world. He trained many students, Germans and foreigners—among the latter, William Osler; and his influence still is widely felt. Most of his research was published in his *Archiv für pathologische Anatomie und Physiologie und für klinische Medizin,* founded in 1847 and still appearing today.

See also MEDICINE, HISTORY OF—9. *Medicine in the Nineteenth Century;* PATHOLOGY—*History.*

ERWIN H. ACKERKNECHT,
Institute of Medical History, University of Zurich, Switzerland.

VIRDEN, vûr′dən, city, Illinois, in Macoupin County, 20 miles south of Springfield at an altitude of 674 feet. It is an important market center for the agricultural products of the area, chief of which are corn, wheat, soybeans, cattle, and hogs. Industries include lumbering, small boat making, dress manufacture, and food processing. Coal deposits in the area were exhausted in 1952.

Settled in 1847, Virden was incorporated as a village in 1861 and chartered as a city in 1873. It has a mayor and council government. Pop. 3,899.

VIRDEN, town, Province of Manitoba, Canada, 193 miles west of Winnipeg. It is the center of an agricultural community. When oil was discovered in the area in 1951, the resultant boom doubled the population. The first producing well within the town was brought in in 1955 and drilling still continues (1961). Formerly known as Gopher Creek, the name was changed to Manchester in 1882, and the town was incorporated as Virden in 1901. Population: 2,940.

VIREOS, vĭr′ē-ōz, a family (Vireonidae) of about 35 exclusively American songbirds, prevailingly greenish and inconspicuous in color, from which the name "greenlets" came. Vireos live mostly in broad-leaved woodlands. The red-eyed vireo, *Vireo olivaceus,* is one of the most common birds of eastern and northern North America, migrating to Central America and northern South America in winter, there to join other closely related forms. The bird is about five inches long, with a gray crown and a greenish-brown back; the underparts and a line above the eyes are dull white. As with other vireos, the song is rather unmusical, but is uttered very persistently, even when the bird is seeking insects. The nest is a cup suspended between horizontally forked twigs. The four or five eggs are white, sparingly spotted with reddish brown. Eggs of the parasitic cowbirds are often found in a vireo's nest. The yellow-throated vireo, *V. flavifrons,* is one of the few brightly colored species of the group, with a buzzy alto quality to its song. The white-eyed vireo, *V. griseus,* is a bird of bushy areas, found in Bermuda and the West Indies as well as in North America. The Philadelphia vireo, *V. philadelphicus,* rather uncommon, is an obscurely marked species that often eludes bird watchers.

DEAN AMADON.

VIRGIL or **VERGIL,** vûr′jəl, **(Publius Vergilius Maro),** Roman poet: b. near Mantua in Cisalpine Gaul, Oct. 15, 70 B.C.; d. Brundisium, Italy, Sept. 21, 19 B.C. (For a discussion of the spelling of his name, see section on *Fame.*)

Early Years.—Much concerning the poet's life is unknown or uncertain, and even the best of the ancient biographies of Virgil, the *Life* by Aelius Donatus in the 4th century, contains many inferences wrongly made from Virgil's poetry, although it does accurately give the main details of his life. Andes, the place of his birth, is identified by many with modern Pietole, 3 miles south of Mantua, but by others with Carpenedolo, 30 miles northwest of Mantua. His father, said to have been a potter or a farmer, was sufficiently wealthy to provide his son with excellent educational opportunities. After attending school at Cremona and Milan, Virgil went to Rome, where he studied medicine, mathematics, and rhetoric, and later to Naples to study philosophy under the Epicurean Siro. He was apparently still at Naples when his or his father's property in Cisalpine Gaul was confiscated for veterans after the Battle of Philippi in 42 B.C. Whether the estate was restored to him is uncertain, but there is no evidence that he ever again lived in northern Italy. Most of his life was spent in Campania and Sicily, but he had a house at Rome, on the Esquiline Hill. A member of the literary circle of the statesman and patron Gaius Cilnius Maecenas, he was well acquainted with Octavian (later the emperor Augustus), and numbered among his closest friends Plotius Tucca, Varius Rufus, Gaius Cornelius Gallus, and Horace, the famous lyric poet and satirist, who in his *Odes* (book 1, ode 3) referred to Virgil as "half of my soul" (*animae dimidium meae*).

The two major influences upon Virgil during his formative years were philosophy—especially the recently published *De rerum natura* of Lucretius—and the poetry of Gaius Valerius Catullus and his contemporaries; these, known as "new poets," had introduced into Latin literature various forms of Alexandrian poetry such as epigram, elegy, and the short epic. If Virgil had written poetry in his youth or early manhood it would in all probability have been of this type. Curiously enough, in addition to the three works of Virgil which are undoubtedly genuine, there have come down under his name a number of such short poems: *Culex, Ciris, Moretum, Aetna, Dirae, Copa,* and a collection called *Catalepton* (In Light Vein). The ancient *Lives* attribute poems with these titles to Virgil, and the poets Lucan, Publius Papinius Statius, and Martial mention a *Culex* of Virgil.

About these poems, known as *Appendix Vergiliana,* there is little unanimity of opinion. Scholars in 1900 agreed that the poems were spurious, but by 1930 many looked upon them as authentic works of Virgil's youthful days and valuable as such for providing additional biographical details and enlarging our understanding of the development of his poetic art. By 1960 the majority of scholars again rejected the poems, viewing them largely as post-Virgilian imitations or forgeries. Two or more of the *Catalepton* are usually accepted as genuine.

Productive Period.—Between 42 and 37 B.C. Virgil composed the 10 pastoral poems known as *Bucolics* or *Eclogues;* he spent the next seven years on the *Georgics,* a didactic work on farming, and devoted the remainder of his life, from 30 to 19 B.C., to the composition of the *Aeneid,* the national epic of Rome. Virgil wrote his poetry to be heard; this is indicated by the fact that he and Maecenas took turns reading to Augustus the completed *Georgics* and that he read books 2, 4, and 6 of the *Aeneid* to Augustus and his sister Octavia; it is said that Octavia fainted when Virgil read the tribute in book 6 to young Marcellus, her son who had recently died.

In 19 B.C., Virgil began an extended trip to Greece and Asia Minor, planning to spend three years on the final revision of the *Aeneid* and to devote the remainder of his life to the study of philosophy. At Athens he met Augustus and, being ill, returned with him to Italy. He died shortly after landing at Brundisium and was buried near Naples. The so-called Tomb of Virgil in the area is probably not authentic.

Bucolics.—The *Bucolics,* or *Eclogues* (Selections), the earliest of Virgil's undoubtedly genuine work, are modeled upon the *Idyls* of Theocritus, greatest of the Alexandrian poets, and consist of dialogues and monologues by shepherds who discuss in polished hexameters their lives and love affairs, compete in amoebean, or responsive, singing matches, and lament the death of the shepherd youth Daphnis. The poems are arranged in an order which is artistic rather than chronological, with *Eclogues* 1 and 9 on country life and confiscations of land, *Eclogues* 2 and 8 on love themes, *Eclogues* 3 and 7 as song contests, and *Eclogues* 4 and 6 on the world of the future and the world of the past, enclosing and emphasizing *Eclogue* 5, the death and deification of Daphnis. The final poem, *Eclogue* 10, the love lament of the poet Cornelius Gallus as a shepherd, is also the latest and combines both the realism and the fantasy of the previous pastorals.

The earliest *Eclogues,* 2, 3, and 5, are the most Theocritean, the later poems being far less imitative. Virgil's originality takes several forms:

(1) He blends with the Sicilian scenery of Theocritus that of northern Italy and makes an important innovation—the introduction of the Greek Arcadia, from which was derived the Arcadia of later pastoral poetry, an idealized and happy realm of shepherds and shepherdesses.

(2) He adds pastoral allegory by referring to real persons in the guise of shepherds. This procedure makes the interpretation of the poems all the more fascinating, and all the more difficult. Is the dead and deified Daphnis in the fifth eclogue merely an ideal shepherd or is he, as seems more probable, Julius Caesar? Many commentators find allegory where the poet perhaps never intended it, and it seems especially unwise to view the collection as Virgil's poems about his literary friends and then to identify each of the shepherds with a specific person.

(3) Virgil differs from Theocritus also in praising by name real persons and in reflecting the historical events and political ideas of his day—the confiscations of land in northern Italy and the sufferings of the dispossessed, and the yearning for a new era of peace and happiness.

Eclogue 4, the most famous and most discussed poem in the collection, and hardly a pastoral, anticipates the poet's later treatment of loftier themes; it describes the birth of a child who will usher in a new Golden Age of peace and goodwill. The religious and philosophical ideas in the poem have been related to earlier Greek poetry, to Egyptian and Oriental thought, to Sibylline oracles, to Hebraic prophecy. The child has been considered a god, or has been identified with the expected son of the consul Asinius Pollio, to whom the poem is dedicated, or of Mark Antony, or (perhaps most likely) of Octavian. From the time of Constantine to that of Alexander Pope the poem was viewed as a prophecy of the coming of Christ, and hence is sometimes termed the "Messianic Eclogue."

Georgics.—Virgil's next work, the *Georgics,* also described the country life with which he was so familiar and which he loved so well. The poem was composed slowly over a seven-year period, from 36 to 30 B.C., an average of less than one verse a day. Virgil was indebted for technical information to many earlier works, both Greek and Roman. His sources include prose works by

Aristotle and Theophrastus, Hellenistic poems by Aratus of Soli and Nicander, and Roman treatises on farming by Marcus Porcius Cato and Marcus Terentius Varro, whose *Res Rusticae* was published in 37 B.C. The chief literary models were two, Hesiod's *Works and Days* and Lucretius' *De rerum natura.* Virgil claims to sing the song of Ascra (birthplace of Hesiod) throughout Roman towns; actually his indebtedness to Hesiod is limited largely to book 1 of the *Georgics,* which likewise deals with "Works" and "Days."

The four books of the *Georgics* are devoted to the management of fields, the care of trees and vines, the rearing of horses and cattle, and beekeeping. The material is arranged in units of two books each: 1–2 on inanimate nature (fields, trees, and vines), and 3–4 on living creatures (herds, flocks, and bees). The work is a masterpiece of artistic construction, with many similarities and contrasts between books 1 and 3 and between books 2 and 4.

Virgil skillfully avoids the dryness of a didactic work by introducing passages of especial interest or of a more universal nature—praise of Octavian, praise of Italy, the blessings of country life. These passages, sometimes called "digressions"—but not really so as they develop naturally from the context—lift the poem to themes of social and national interest, to the higher realms of religion and philosophy. Topics such as the evils of war, the Golden Age, and the praise of Octavian had appeared in the *Eclogues* and will reappear in the *Aeneid.* The emphasis in the *Georgics* upon *labor* and *pietas,* however, is something new, and these will become basic themes in Virgil's final work.

In the development of the poet's art, the *Georgics* stand between his more youthful pastorals and the severe style of national epic, but in content and significance much nearer the latter. The poem is itself an epic dealing with all aspects of life, and its universal nature is seen most clearly in the endings of the four books on the themes of War, Peace, Death, and Rebirth. The *Georgics* is considered by general agreement the most perfect Roman poem in existence.

Aeneid.—Virgil had originally planned to compose a historical epic about Rome and the achievements of Augustus, apparently somewhat in the style of the earlier Roman poets Gnaeus Naevius and Quintus Ennius. Instead, he chose as the central character of his epic Aeneas, one of the great heroes of Trojan legend, and recounted his wanderings and adventures from the fall of Troy to the establishment of his destined rule in Latium. The poet thus described the formation of the Roman people, and by means of prophecies and prophetic statements was able to relate famous events in later Roman history culminating with the victories and triumphs of Augustus.

Virgil was the Roman Homer, and many themes and episodes recalled or re-echoed passages in both the *Iliad* and the *Odyssey.* He was influenced also by Greek tragedy, the *Argonautica* of Apollonius of Rhodes, and the Latin poetry of Ennius, Lucretius, and Catullus. He had the ability which all great writers possess, an almost magical power of integration which enabled him to take material from many different sources and make it his own. The *Aeneid* is not only the national poem of Rome, but, because of the power and beauty of Virgil's verse and poetic imagery, the subtlety of his character delineation, and his sympathy for human suffering, it is one of the great epics of world literature. See also AENEID.

Fame.—Virgil's fame among his countrymen was immediate and permanent. The poet Sextus Propertius hailed the *Aeneid,* even before its completion, as "something greater than the *Iliad*" and later poets such as Tiberius Catius Silius Italicus and Statius endeavored to imitate Virgil's poetic style. The *Aeneid* was used as a textbook in Roman schools and made the subject of grammatical commentaries. In the late Roman period Virgilian cantos were composed by arranging lines and half lines from his works in such a way as to give a sense entirely different from the original. As Virgil acquired more and more a reputation for vast learning, the custom arose of consulting the *sortes Virgilianae,* by opening the *Aeneid* at random and foretelling the future from the passage first read.

Various legends about Virgil arose in the Naples area, and in the Middle Ages he was portrayed as a magician with marvelous inventions and disreputable adventures ascribed to him. The association of his name with *virga,* magician's wand, may have contributed to the spelling "Virgilius"—instead of the correct Latin "Vergilius"—and hence "Virgil." The name is spelled with an *i* in France and Italy, "Vergil" is the more usual form in Germany, and in England and America both forms are used. Other factors in the change of spelling may have been the *virga,* or poplar branch, which was said to have grown rapidly to a tree when he was born, thus foretelling his destiny, and *virgo,* or maiden, a name assigned to him for his shy and retiring nature.

In the Renaissance, Virgil was again revered as a poet, and from then to the present his influence on European poetry has been great. Dante, Geoffrey Chaucer, Edmund Spenser, John Milton, John Dryden, and Alfred, Lord Tennyson, as well as many others, bear testimony to their knowledge of and devotion to his works. The bimillenium of his birth in 1930 was celebrated with enthusiasm in both Europe and America, and was attended by the publication of many editions, commentaries, and interpretations of his poems. In 1945, T. S. Eliot called Virgil "the classic of all Europe."

GEORGE E. DUCKWORTH,
Giger Professor of Latin, Princeton University.

Bibliography

Bernard, John D., and Alessi, Paul T., eds., *Vergil at 2000: Commemorative Essays on the Poet and His Influence* (AMS Press 1986).

Garrison, D. H., *The Language of Vergil* (P. Lang, 1986).

Gransden, K. W., *Virgil's Iliad: An Essay on Epic Narrative* (Cambridge 1985).

Hardie, Philip, *Virgil's Aeneid* (Oxford 1986).

Johnson, W. R., *Darkness Visible: A Study of Vergil's Aeneid* (Univ. of Calif. Press 1976).

Leach, Eleanor W., *Vergil's "Eclogues", Landscapes of Experience* (Cornell Univ. Press 1974).

Miles, Gary B., *Virgil's Georgics: A New Interpretation* (Univ. of Calif. Press 1980).

Warwick, Henrietta H., *A Vergil Concordance* (Univ. of Minn. Press 1975).

Williams, Gordon, *Techniques and Ideas in the Aeneid* (Yale Univ. Press 1985).

Williams, R. D., and Pattie, T. S., *Virgil: His Poetry Through the Ages* (Longwood 1982).

English Translations

The Aeneid, tr. by Robert Fitzgerald (Random House 1983).

The Aeneid of Virgil: A Verse Translation, tr. by Allen Mandelbaum (Univ. of Calif. Press 1981).

The Eclogues, tr. by Guy Lee (Penguin 1984).

Eclogues and Georgics, ed. by R. D. Williams (St. Martin's Press 1983).

VIRGIL, Polydore. See VERGIL, POLYDORE.

FRITZ HENLE, FROM MONKMEYER

Virgin Islands National Park covers two thirds of the island of St. John and extensive offshore areas.

VIRGIN ISLANDS, a group of some 100 small islands lying between the Caribbean Sea and the Atlantic Ocean east of Puerto Rico. They are divided into the Virgin Islands of the United States (the former Danish West Indies) and the British Virgin Islands.

Christopher Columbus, noting the great number of islands when he discovered them in 1493, named them after Saint Ursula and the 11,000 virgins who shared her legendary voyage. During the next century the Spaniards killed or drove out the native Arawak and Carib Indians. The first permanent European colonies were founded by the Danes and the English in the 17th century. At that time Africans were brought in to work on the European plantations, and today the overwhelming majority of Virgin Islanders are of African descent.

VIRGIN ISLANDS OF THE UNITED STATES

The western Virgin Islands are an unincorporated territory of the United States. They were purchased from Denmark in 1917 for $25 million. The territory comprises 68 islands covering 132 square miles (342 sq km). Of the three main islands, St. Thomas is closest to Puerto Rico, which lies 40 miles (65 km) to the west. St. John is 3 miles (5 km) east of St. Thomas, and St. Croix is 40 miles to the south.

The territory had a population of 96,569 in the 1980 census. This figure represented a gain of 54.6% over the 1970 census total. The capital is Charlotte Amalie (1980 population, 11,842), on St. Thomas. The only other major towns are Christiansted (2,914) and Frederiksted (1,046), both on St. Croix.

Physical Features. The land consists of a dramatic procession of craggy mountaintops rising from an underwater shelf. On St. Thomas the mountains reach 1,556 feet (474 meters); on St. John, 1,277 feet (389 meters); and on St. Croix, 1,165 feet (355 meters).

The climate is one of the islands' chief assets, with a temperature that averages about 78°F (26°C). Humidity and pollen count are low. Annual rainfall averages about 40 inches (1,000 mm), but it may vary considerably, and most of it runs off. The first half of the year is slightly drier than the last.

The lack of rivers and streams and the mountainous terrain make extensive cultivation difficult, but some 1,220 plants have been catalogued on St. Thomas alone. Large wildlife is scarce, except for a few deer and wild boar. The mongoose was successfully introduced to kill off the snakes. Lizards, iguanas, and land crabs abound. There are more than 220 species of birds, including wild parakeets, doves, egrets, pelicans, tropical species, and boobies, whose eggs are a great delicacy. The surrounding seas contain some of the most beautiful underwater scenery in the world, with many varieties of coral, sponge, and brightly colored fish. Some 650 varieties of shells are found.

Virgin Islands National Park, dedicated in 1956, encompasses about two thirds of St. John and extensive offshore areas. The park conserves the island's natural beauty and wildlife, under-

ISLAND AREAS AND POPULATIONS

Island[1]	Land Area sq mi	Land Area sq km	Population (1980)
St. Croix	80	207	49,725
St. John	20	52	2,472
St. Thomas	32	83	44,372

[1] Including adjacent smaller islands and cays.

water marine gardens, and historical objects including stone writings of the aboriginal inhabitants and the ruins of old forts and sugar plantations. The island's facilities for tourists range from a luxury resort to guest houses and national park camping accommodations. St. John lies about 3 miles (4.8 km) east of St. Thomas and is nearest to the British Virgin islands.

St. Thomas, like St. John, is mountainous with a narrow coastline and steep, terraced hills leading up to the central ridge. The city of Charlotte Amalie has an excellent natural harbor and contains a number of tourist facilities. On the east side of the island, Magens Bay has one of the finest beaches in the Caribbean.

St. Croix is the flattest of the islands, but has mountains in the east and north. The north shore is bordered by coral reefs and numerous bays. Buck Island, which has been taken over as a national park site, is noted for its reefs, tropical fish, and underwater trail for snorkeling. The island has a variety of tourist accommodations.

The People. The 1980 census listed 60.9% of the people as rural and 39.1% as urban. Nearly three fourths of the people are classified as black and less than one fifth as white.

Between 1960 and 1980 the population nearly tripled, owing both to a high rate of natural increase and to immigration, especially from other Caribbean islands. The territory has one of the highest standards of living in the Caribbean. Many immigrants are attracted to the islands by better job opportunities and living conditions than are available in their respective countries.

The islanders speak English, most of them with a "Calypso" accent. The Roman Catholic and Jewish faiths and various Protestant denominations are represented among the territory's population.

A system of private and public schools at all levels serves the territory. The College of the Virgin Islands, with campuses on St. Thomas and St. Croix, enrolls about 2,000 students.

The Economy. The Virgin Islands possess few natural resources other than their attractive climate, scenery, and beaches. Opportunities for farming are limited, and the chief mineral resource is stone. Tourism therefore has become the territory's main industry.

During World War II, airfields were built on St. Thomas and St. Croix. Later converted to civilian use, they opened the territory to large-scale tourist traffic. In addition, many cruise ships stop at Virgin Islands ports. In 1950 about 15,000 tourists visited the islands. Currently more than 1 million visitors are spending over $100 million in the territory each year. The development of hotels, stores, restaurants, and recreational facilities to meet this tourist demand created thousands of new jobs in trade, services, and the construction industry. The territorial government is also a major employer.

Liberal tax exemptions have been granted to new industries in an effort to diversify the economy and enable the islanders to acquire higher skills. There are now oil refineries and an aluminum plant, as well as various light industries producing articles such as jewelry and lotions. Because of a scarcity of water, desalinization plants have been built to make seawater fresh. These installations also produce electric power for the islands.

St. Croix is the center of the territory's agricultural activities, mainly vegetable growing and cattle raising. Sugar production, which was once the mainstay of the islands' economy, all but ended as land became too valuable for large-scale farming. Commercial fishing also has been limited in scope.

Location map of the Virgin Islands

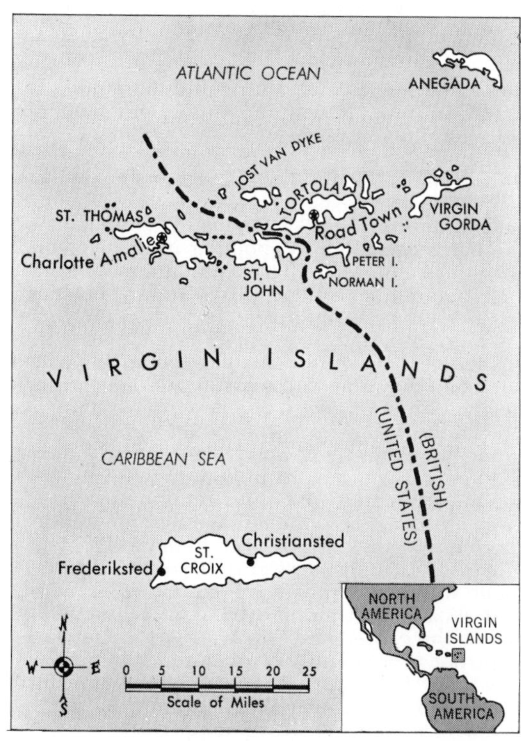

Government. The unincorporated territory is governed under provisions of an act of the U. S. Congress passed in 1954 and subsequently amended. The governor is elected by the people for a term of four years, and the legislature, elected by the people every two years, consists of 15 senators. The judiciary is headed by a federal district judge appointed by the president of the United States. Although Virgin Islanders are U.S. citizens with a nonvoting representative in the U.S. Congress, they do not vote in U.S. presidential elections. On July 10, 1981, President Reagan signed legislation authorizing a referendum on Nov. 3, 1981, on a proposed constitution for the territory.

Government operations are financed jointly from revenues collected locally and from federal taxes on certain articles produced in the Virgin Islands and transported to the United States. Separate federal grants are made for emergency purposes and essential public projects.

History. Columbus is believed to have landed at Salt River Bay, St. Croix, in 1493. During the 17th century the Dutch, English, French, and Spaniards established themselves in parts of the present territory, but without lasting success. The first permanent European settlement was made by the Danes in 1672, on St. Thomas. Slaves were first imported the following year, and eventually Africans of some 20 ethnic groups were working on the islands' highly profitable sugar plantations.

In 1717 the Danes began to settle St. John. The new colony prospered, but its economy suffered a temporary setback in 1733 when the slaves rebelled and held the island for six months, driving out the planters. The revolt caused the Danes to purchase St. Croix that year from the French. Before Denmark prohibited the slave trade in 1803, the Danish West Indies were known as the largest slave market in the world. Emancipation came in 1848, the year of another serious rebellion.

With the decline of the sugar industry, due largely to competition from other producing areas, the islands' economy stagnated. Between 1835 and 1930, the population fell steadily from 43,000 to 22,000. Although the United States expressed interest in acquiring the Danish West Indies as early as the 1860's, it did not buy the islands until the opening of the Panama Canal and the outbreak of World War I (both in 1914) had made their strategic value too evident to ignore.

The development of a tourist and industrial economy after 1945 restored prosperity to the islands but introduced social problems. The importation of foreign workers to meet a labor shortage created tensions between native residents and immigrants, who received lower wages. The concentration of economic power and its benefits in the hands of white residents and non-residents produced racial antagonisms. A wave of violent crimes that took the lives of more than a dozen persons during a two-year period abated in 1974.

The political aspirations of the black community were recognized in 1968 when the first native black governor was appointed and the governorship was made elective, starting in 1970. Since 1972 the Virgin Islands have been represented in the U. S. House of Representatives by an elected delegate who has a voice, though no vote, in congressional deliberations.

BRITISH VIRGIN ISLANDS

The eastern Virgin Islands, settled by English planters in 1666, are a British colony of 36 islands with a total area of 59 square miles (153 sq km). At the nearest point they are less than 1 mile (1.6 km) from the Virgin Islands of the United States, to which they are closely related geographically and economically. To preserve its economic ties with the U.S. territory, the colony did not join the 1958–1962 West Indies federation of British islands.

Under the constitution of 1967, which was amended in 1977, the British Virgin Islands are administered by an appointed governor, an executive council, and a partly elected legislative council. The governor consults with the executive council, which includes ministers chosen from the elected membership of the legislative council.

Physical Features. The British Virgin Islands are the easternmost extension of the Greater Antilles chain. They are separated from the Lesser Antilles by the Anegada Passage, one of the chief entrances into the Caribbean Sea. In climate, terrain, and natural resources, they are similar to the Virgin Islands of the United States, except that the British group has a main island which is low-lying and flat.

The largest islands are Tortola, with an area of 21 square miles (54 sq km); Anegada, 15 square miles (39 sq km); and Virgin Gorda, 8 square miles (21 sq km). Their names are Spanish. Tortola ("turtle dove") rises to 1,780 feet (543 meters) on Mt. Sage, the highest point in all the Virgin Islands. The xerophytic, or drought-adapted, vegetation on this island is of great scientific interest. Anegada (the "drowned" island) is nowhere more than a few feet above sea level. From the sea it sometimes appears to be covered by the surf that pounds its dangerous reefs. Virgin Gorda (the "fat" virgin) reaches an elevation of 1,359 feet (414 meters). Its "baths," a series of beautiful caves washed by the sea and roofed with huge boulders, are a popular tourist attraction.

The People and the Economy. The British Virgin Islands had a 1980 population of 11,006, more than 80% of which lived on Tortola. Almost all of the people are of African descent and English speaking. Various Protestant faiths predominate. The capital of the British Virgin Islands, Road Town, is on Tortola.

In the early 1980's more than 3,000 pupils were enrolled for primary and secondary education. Higher education was available at the University of the West Indies, with campuses on other Caribbean islands.

The rapidly growing tourist industry is believed to offer the best opportunity for economic development. There is some agriculture and stock raising, but little manufacturing. A large part of the labor force is employed in the Virgin Islands of the United States. Most of the export trade is with the U. S. territory and the currency in local use is the U. S. dollar.

Bibliography

Creque, Darwin D., *The U. S. Virgins and the Eastern Caribbean* (Whitmore 1968).

Eggleston, George T., *Virgin Islands* (1959; reprint, Krieger 1973).

Moore, James E., *Everybody's Virgin Islands* (Lippincott 1979).

Tansill, Charles C., *The Purchase of the Danish West Indies* (1932; reprint, Greenwood Press 1968).

Zabriskie, L. K., and Bush, George F., *The U. S. Virgin Islands*, Part I, ed. by Helen Nash (Mainespring Press 1985).

VIRGIN ISLANDS NATIONAL PARK. See VIRGIN ISLANDS—*Virgin Islands of the United States* (Physical Features).

VIRGIN MARY. See MARY, SAINT.

VIRGINAL, vûr′jə-nəl, a keyboard instrument of the harpsichord family, popular in the 16th and early 17th centuries. The virginal has one set of jacks and one set of strings, plucked by plectra of quill or leather. Virginals are without legs and are held in the player's lap. Their cases are box shaped, and they are made of decorative woods, such as rosewood, often with painted or inlay designs.

Confusion has arisen over the origin of the term "virginal." It was once believed that the virginal was named in honor of Elizabeth I, the Virgin Queen, but the instrument's use in the early 16th century precludes that possibility. More likely, the term derived from the Latin *virginalis* (relating to a virgin) because the instrument was played by young girls. This word, with its apparent plural ending, may have given rise to the expression "a pair of virginals" when referring to a single instrument. Also, the virginal was incorrectly called a spinet, probably because of the Italian (*spinetta*) and French (*épinette*) words for the instrument.

GRANT HEILMAN

The long, fertile Shenandoah Valley of Virginia is cradled by the Blue Ridge and Allegheny mountains.

VIRGINIA

CONTENTS

VIRGINIA, one of the South Atlantic states, has played a prominent role in the history of the United States. The Commonwealth of Virginia is sometimes spoken of as the "Mother of Presidents" because eight presidents of the United States were born there. More commonly, it is referred to as the *Old Dominion.* Charles II honored it by naming it a dominion when the colony recognized him as king after the execution of his father, Charles I, in the English Civil War.

Virginians formed the first representative assembly in America. They also were deeply involved in the Revolutionary movement and in shaping the Constitution and its Bill of Rights on which the United States government is based. It was Virginia's tragedy that it became the chief battleground during the Civil War, but in time it recovered from the devastating dislocations caused by that catastrophe.

Always on guard against federal encroachments on its rights as a state, Virginia has nevertheless been economically nourished since the Great Depression by federal government establishments located in the northeastern and southeastern sections. Government employment has contributed to the diversification of the economic base of this state that was once dependent almost exclusively on a single crop, tobacco.

State seal of Virginia.

Increasing urbanization and an influx of citizens from other states in the 1960's and 1970's have somewhat weakened Virginia's historical allegiance to Southern viewpoints. Nevertheless, its traditions, closely linked to those of the rest of the South, are so enduring that Virginia remains not only geographically but culturally a Southern state.

HARRY N. TAYLOR, PHOTO RESEARCHERS

The New River flows through gorges in the Alleghenies in the anthracite region of southwestern Virginia.

1. The Land

Virginia encompasses a wide range of landforms, river systems, soils, natural resources, and climate. This great variety has had a marked effect on the state's economy, society, and political history. It has also led to such local differentiation that Virginians are likely to identify themselves by the regions in which they live.

Major Physical Divisions. There are three major topographic regions in Virginia: the Tidewater, or Coastal Plain; the Piedmont; and the Mountain and Valley Province. The last has three subdivisions—the Blue Ridge, the Valley and Ridge, and the Appalachian Plateau.

Tidewater. The Tidewater, or Coastal Plain, including the Eastern Shore of Chesapeake Bay, is a low-lying area. The land rises gently from the bay to about 300 feet (90 meters) at the fall line, where the principal rivers drop from the Piedmont to the Tidewater. The fall line cuts across the Potomac at the Great Falls, the Rappahannock at Fredericksburg, the James at Richmond, and the Appomattox at Petersburg.

Narrow in the north, the Tidewater widens in the south to a maximum width of 100 miles (160 km) at the North Carolina border. The soils are clays, sands, shell marl, and gravel over beds of sedimentary rocks. The greater the distance from the coast, the greater the clay content.

Much of the Tidewater is cut by rivers descending slowly into broad estuarial, tidal basins near Chesapeake Bay. Between these rivers are three flat peninsulas, interlaced with creeks and tidal swamps: the Northern Neck between the Potomac and the Rappahannock; the Middle Peninsula between the Rappahannock and the York; and the Peninsula between the York and the James. Navigation by deep-draft vessels is now restricted by the lack of harbors and by river siltation. The Hampton Roads basin at the junction of the James with Chesapeake Bay, however, is an excellent deep-draft harbor.

The Eastern Shore, forming the lower tip of the Delmarva peninsula, is separated from the western mainland by Chesapeake Bay. It is as flat as the rest of the Coastal Plain. Isolated islands lie off its Atlantic coast, and tidal inlets indent the Chesapeake side.

The southern plain below the James is marshy. Its soils are thin, and it is coursed by sluggish, nonnavigable streams and rivers that drain into North Carolina rivers and sounds. The Dismal Swamp covers much of the southeastern area.

Piedmont. The Piedmont is a plateau ascending toward the west until it reaches about 1,000 feet (330 meters) at the beginning of the Blue Ridge. The rolling land is pierced here and there with sharply defined hills and crystalline rock outcroppings. It is crossed by rivers and streams. The soils, which increase in fertility toward the west, are red clays, limestone, and sand over sedimentary and igneous rocks. This ancient plateau varies in width from 40 miles (65 km) at the Potomac to 160 miles (260 km) at the North Carolina border.

Mountain and Valley Province. The Blue Ridge rises along the western edge of the Piedmont, running in a northeast-southwesterly direction. North of the Roanoke River the ridge is narrow and at one point reaches a height of over 4,000 feet (1,200 meters). South of the river the

INFORMATION HIGHLIGHTS

Location: A South Atlantic coast state bordered north and northeast by Maryland, east by the Atlantic Ocean, south by North Carolina and Tennessee, west by Kentucky, and northwest by West Virginia.
Elevation: *Highest point*—Mt. Rogers, 5,729 feet (1,747 meters); *lowest point*—sea level along the Atlantic coast; *approximate mean elevation*, 950 feet (290 meters).
Area: 40,767 square miles (105,587 sq km); rank, 36th.
Population: 1980 census, 5,346,818; rank, 14th. Increase (1970–1980), 14.9%.
Climate: Moderate, with mild winters and humid summers; abundant rainfall.
Statehood: June 25, 1788.
Origin of Name: For the "Virgin Queen" (Elizabeth I of England).
Capital: Richmond.
Largest City: Norfolk.
Number of Counties: 95.
Principal Products: *Manufactures*—Chemicals, tobacco manufactures, food products, electrical equipment and supplies, transportation equipment, textiles; *farm products*—cattle, milk, tobacco, broilers; *minerals*—coal, stone.
State Motto: *Sic semper tyrannis* ("Thus always to tyrants").
State Song: *Carry Me Back to Old Virginia.*
State Nickname: The Old Dominion.
State Bird: Cardinal.
State Flower and Tree: Dogwood.
State Flag: A deep blue field with a circular white center containing the state coat of arms; white silk fringes the outer edge. See under FLAG.

Ridge broadens into a broad plateau that rises to a height of over 5,000 feet (1,525 meters). The highest peaks in Virginia, Mt. Rogers and Whitetop, are found in this southern section.

In the Valley and Ridge division, the Great Valley, or the Valley of Virginia, lies between the Blue Ridge and the Appalachian Ridge on the West Virginia border. The Great Valley extends about 360 miles (580 km) from the Potomac, where it is about 35 miles (55 km) wide, to the Tennessee boundary, where it is about 100 miles (160 km) wide.

The Great Valley is actually a series of valleys separated by transverse ridges, plateaus, and gaps. The largest and northernmost is the Shenandoah, a rich and fertile region. The valley floors range from 300 feet (90 meters) in the north to 2,400 feet (730 meters) in the south. The Great Valley is drained to the north by the Shenandoah River, to the east through the Blue Ridge by the James and the Roanoke, and to the southwest into the Mississippi watershed by the New, Holston, and Clinch rivers.

The third division of the Mountain and Valley Province is the Appalachian Plateau, located in the southwestern corner of the state. The plateau, which extends into the state from Kentucky, is crossed by streams that have cut deep ravines. The Cumberland Gap in the Cumberland Mountains is at the extreme southwestern tip of Virginia. In this rugged Appalachian Plateau region and in the valleys just to the east of it, Virginia's major coal deposits are found.

Climate. Summer temperatures range from an average of 70°F (21°C) in the southwest to 80°F (27°C) in the east, with the mean being 77°F (25°C). Summer in eastern Virginia is usually accompanied by high humidity. The winter mean is about 39°F (4°C), although near-zero weather often occurs in the mountains.

The frost-free growing season ranges from 150 days in the west to 245 days in the east, averaging about 200 days. Annual precipitation averages 40 inches (1,015 mm), varying from 30 inches (760 mm) in the northwest to 50 inches (1,270 mm) in the southwest and 55 inches (1,400 mm) along the southeastern coast. Snow is on the ground about 10 days a year in the eastern regions, 20 days on the Piedmont, and up to 60 days in the western mountains.

Plant Life. Forest covers more than two thirds of the state, with pines predominating in the Tidewater and intermingling with hardwoods on the Piedmont. Hardwoods are predominant in the western mountains and valleys. Dogwood is common throughout the state. Rhododendrons, mountain laurel, wild azaleas, and redbud grow in the more mountainous regions.

Animal Life. In the mountains there are still some black bear, an increasing stock of deer, and much small game. The Piedmont and Tidewater have small game with a few deer. Game birds include quail, dove, grouse, woodcock, and the migratory waterfowl of the Atlantic flyway. The state has a large variety of songbirds.

Conservation. Virginia recognized earlier than most states the importance of protecting the environment. The development in the 1920's and 1930's of the large Jefferson National Forest in southwestern Virginia and the George Washington National Forest in the northwest, the protection and stimulation of the shellfish industry in the James River and Chesapeake Bay basins, and the control of rivers and streams through the fish and game commissions are examples.

Since the 1960's stringent water-pollution laws, administered by the state water-control board, have been applied to all rivers and streams. The present constitution contains a strong conservation section. Regional planning

A village center in Reston, Va., a residential-industrial complex near Washington, D. C., built in the 1960's.

ROBERT PERRON, PHOTO RESEARCHERS

The Chesapeake Bay Bridge–Tunnel, opened to traffic in 1964, connects Norfolk with the Delmarva peninsula. Tunnels do not obstruct the bay's shipping channels.

commissions coordinate the environmental control efforts of adjacent counties and cities. The absence of extensive heavy industry in the state is due in part to an unwritten policy not to encourage industries that might pollute the environment.

2. The People

In the four decades after 1940, Virginia experienced a population growth rate of about 100% or more than that of the nation. Increased urbanization accompanied this growth. Almost two thirds of the population is classified as urban, and many persons living in rural communities work in urban areas. Over half of all Virginians live in an urban corridor running from Washington, D.C., south to Richmond and east to the Hampton Roads—Norfolk area.

According to the official count in the 1980 decennial census, Virginia's population was 79.1% white, 18.8% black, and 2.1% other racial groups. In 1950 the population was 22.1% black.

Historical Components of the Population. Of the Indian tribes encountered by the first settlers in the 17th century, only a few descendants survive. The original European settlers were almost entirely rural Englishmen. In the 18th century, large numbers of Scots-Irish, Irish, and Germans migrated into the Valley of Virginia, many from Pennsylvania, Maryland, and New Jersey.

Black slaves, at first imported in small numbers, were brought in by the thousands after 1680 and composed almost half of the 550,000 colonists at the time of the Revolution.

Colonial Virginia's population doubled every 25 years after 1680, and in the early years of the republic, Virginia was the most populous of the states. However, in the 19th century its growth lagged behind that of the nation. Not only had Virginia lost the lands that were formed into the state of Kentucky in 1792, but West Virginia was shaped out of some of Virginia's counties in 1863 and 1866. Growth was also checked by the stagnation of the economy and by the bloodletting of the Civil War. From the 1870's to the 1930's, the growth rate remained low as Virginians migrated from the state. Thereafter the rate increased.

Religion. During the colonial era the Church of England (the Anglican Church) was the established church and as such was supported by public taxes. Nevertheless, dissenting groups were encouraged to settle in the Great Valley in the 18th century. The Scots-Irish brought with them their Presbyterian allegiance. In the same period German Lutherans settled in the Valley, as did many German Pietists (Mennonites, River Brethren, and Amish). The influx of these non-Anglicans led the colony in time to extend religious toleration to dissenters. Thomas Jefferson's famous Statute for Religious Freedom was passed by Virginia's House of Delegates in 1785 and accepted by its Senate in 1786. The reconstituted Protestant Episcopal Church was disestablished.

The Methodists and Baptists have outnumbered the other denominations in Virginia since the 19th century. After 1950 the Roman Catholic and Pentecostal churches grew substantially.

LARGEST CENTERS OF POPULATION

(Incorporated places and metropolitan areas[1])

City or metropolitan area	1980	1970	1960
Norfolk	266,979	307,951	304,869
Metropolitan area[2]	806,951	732,600	578,507
Virginia Beach	262,199	172,106	8,091
Richmond	219,214	249,332	219,958
Metropolitan area	632,015	547,542	408,494
Newport News	144,903	138,177	113,662
Metropolitan area[3]	364,449	333,140	224,503
Hampton	122,617	120,779	89,258
Chesapeake	114,486	89,580	...
Portsmouth	104,577	110,963	114,773
Alexandria	103,217	110,927	91,023
Roanoke	100,220	92,115	97,110
Lynchburg	66,743	54,083	54,790
Suffolk	47,621	9,858	12,609
Danville	45,642	46,391	46,577
Petersburg	41,055	36,103	36,750

[1]Standard metropolitan statistical areas. [2]Norfolk-Virginia Beach-Portsmouth. [3]Newport News-Hampton.

URBAN-RURAL DISTRIBUTION

Year	Percent urban	Percent rural
1920	29.2 (U.S., 51.2)	70.8
1930	32.4 (U.S., 56.2)	67.6
1940	35.3 (U.S., 56.6)	64.7
1950	47.0 (U.S., 64.0)	53.0
1960	55.8 (U.S., 69.9)	44.2
1970	63.1 (U.S., 73.5)	36.9
1980	66.0 (U.S., 73.7)	34.0

GROWTH OF POPULATION SINCE 1790

Year	Population	Year	Population
1790	691,737	1920	2,309,187
1820	938,261	1940	2,677,773
1840	1,025,227	1950	3,318,680
1860	1,219,630	1960	3,966,949
1880	1,512,565	1970	4,651,448
1900	1,854,184	1980	5,346,818

Gain, 1970–1980: 14.9% (U.S. gain, 11.4%). **Density,** 1980: 134.7 persons per sq mi (U.S. density, 62.6).

VIRGINIA

COUNTIES

Accomack 31,268 N5
Albemarle 55,783 G5
Alleghany 14,333 D5
Amelia 8,405 H6
Amherst 29,122 F5
Appomattox 11,971 G6
Arlington 152,599 K3
Augusta 53,732 F4
Bath 5,860 E4
Bedford 34,927 E6
Bland 6,349 B6
Botetourt 23,270 E5
Brunswick 15,632 J7
Buchanan 37,989 D1
Buckingham 11,751 G5
Campbell 45,424 F6
Caroline 17,904 K4
Carroll 27,270 C7
Charles City 6,692 K6
Charlotte 12,266 G6
Chesterfield 141,372 J6
Clarke 9,965 H2
Craig 3,948 D6
Culpeper 22,620 H3
Cumberland 7,881 H6
Dickenson 19,806 D2
Dinwiddie 22,602 J6
Essex 8,864 L5
Fairfax 596,901 K3
Fauquier 35,889 J3
Floyd 11,563 D7
Fluvanna 10,244 H5
Franklin 35,740 E6
Frederick 34,150 H2
Giles 17,810 C6
Gloucester 20,107 L6
Goochland 11,761 J5
Grayson 16,579 B7
Greene 7,625 H4
Greensville 10,903 J7
Halifax 30,599 G7
Hanover 50,398 J5
Henrico 180,735 K6
Henry 57,654 E7
Highland 2,937 E4
Isle of Wight 21,603 L7
James City 22,763 L6
King and Queen 5,968 L5
King George 10,543 K4
King William 9,334 K5
Lancaster 10,129 M5
Lee 25,956 B2
Loudoun 57,427 J2
Louisa 17,825 J5
Lunenburg 12,124 H7
Madison 10,232 H4
Mathews 7,995 M6
Mecklenburg 29,444 H7
Middlesex 7,719 M5
Montgomery 63,516 D6
Nelson 12,204 G5
New Kent 8,781 L5
Northampton 14,625 N6
Northumberland 9,828 M5
Nottoway 14,666 H6
Orange 18,063 H4
Page 19,401 H3
Patrick 17,647 D7
Pittsylvania 66,147 F7
Powhatan 13,062 J5
Prince Edward 16,456 H6
Prince George 25,733 K6
Prince William 144,703 K3
Pulaski 35,229 C6
Rappahannock 6,093 H3
Richmond 6,952 L5
Roanoke 72,945 D6
Rockbridge 17,911 F5
Rockingham 57,038 G4
Russell 31,761 E2
Scott 25,068 D2
Shenandoah 27,559 G3
Smyth 33,366 A7
Southampton 18,731 K7
Spotsylvania 34,435 J4
Stafford 40,470 K4
Surry 6,046 L6
Sussex 10,874 K7
Tazewell 50,511 B6
Warren 21,200 H3
Washington 46,487 E2
Westmoreland 14,041 L4
Wise 43,863 C2
Wythe 25,522 B7
York 35,463 L6

CITIES and TOWNS

Abingdon⊙ 4,318 E2
Accomac⊙ 522 N5
Achilles 525 M6
Afton 350 G4
Alberene 200 G5
Alberta 394 J7
Alexandria (I.C.) 103,217 N3
Allisonia 325 C7
Altavista 3,849 F6
Alton 500 F7
Amelia Court House⊙ 500 J6
Amherst⊙ 1,135 F5
Amissville 150 H3
Amonate 350 F1
Andover 180 C2
Annandale 49,524 N3
Appalachia 2,418 C2
Appomattox⊙ 1,345 G6
Ararat 500 C7
Arlington⊙ 152,599 O3
Arrington 500 G5
Arvonia 500 H5
Ashburn 345 K2
Ashland 4,640 J5
Atkins 1,352 B7
Augusta Springs 600 F4
Austinville 750 B7
Axton 540 E7
Aylett 100 K5
Baileys Crossroads 12,564 N3
Ballsville 150 H6
Bandy 200 F1
Banner 3,271 D2
Barboursville 600 H4
Barren Springs 125 C7
Bassett 2,034 E7
Bastian 600 B6
Basye 22,810 G3
Batesville 575 G5
Bealeton 200 J3
Beaverdam 500 J5
Beaverlett 200 M6
Bedford (I.C.)⊙ 5,991 E6
Belle Haven 589 N5
Ben Hur 400 B2
Bent Mountain 140 D6
Bentonville 500 H3
Bergton 150 G3
Berryville⊙ 1,752 H2
Big Island 500 F5
Big Rock 900 D1
Big Stone Gap 4,748 C2
Birchleaf 650 D1
Birdsnest 736 N6
Bishop 600 A6
Blackridge 32 H7
Blacksburg 30,638 D6
Blackstone 3,624 H6
Blackwater 130 C3
Blairs 500 F7
Bland⊙ 950 B6
Bloxom 407 N5
Bluefield 5,946 B6
Blue Grass 200 E3
Bluemont 200 J2
Blue Ridge 2,347 E6
Boissevain 975 B6
Bolar 135 E4
Bon Air 16,224 J5
Boones Mill 344 E6
Boston 400 H3
Bowling Green⊙ 665 K4
Boyce 401 H2
Boydton⊙ 486 H7
Boykins 791 K7
Bracey 106 H7
Branchville 174 K7
Brandy Station 400 J4
Breaks 550 D1
Bremo Bluff 200 H5
Bridgewater 3,289 F4
Brightwood 100 H4
Bristol (I.C.) 19,042 D3
Broadford 500 F2
Broadway 1,234 G3
Brodnax 492 J7
Brooke 245 K4
Brookneal 1,454 G6
Brownsburg 300 F5
Browntown 300 H3
Brucetown 250 H2
Buchanan 1,205 E5
Buckingham⊙ 200 G5
Buena Vista (I.C.) 6,717 F5
Buffalo Junction 300 G7
Bumpass 110 J5
Burgess 200 M5
Burke 33,835 M3
Burkes Garden 267 B6
Burkeville 606 H6
Burnsville 140 E4
Callao 500 L5
Callaway 225 D7
Calverton 500 J3
Cana 168 C7
Cape Charles 1,512 M6
Capeville 325 M6
Capron 238 K7
Cardwell 200 J5
Carrsville 300 L7
Carson 500 K6
Cartersville 100 H5
Casanova 370 J3
Cascade 835 E7
Castlewood 2,420 D2
Catawba 350 D6
Catlett 500 J3
Cedar Bluff 1,550 E2
Cedar Springs 200 B7
Cedarville 200 H3
Center Cross 360 L5
Ceres 200 B6
Champlain 160 K4
Chancellorsville 40 J4
Chantilly 12,259 K3
Charles City⊙ 5 K6
Charlotte Court House⊙ 568 G6
Charlottesville (I.C.)⊙ 39,916 G4
Charlottesville‡ 113,568 G4
Chase City 2,749 H7
Chatham⊙ 1,390 F7
Check 75 D6
Cheriton 695 M6
Chesapeake (I.C.) 114,486 M7
Chester 11,728 K6
Chesterfield⊙ 950 J6
Chester Gap 400 H3
Chilhowie 1,269 F2
Chincoteague 1,607 O5
Christiansburg⊙ 10,345 D6
Chula 150 J6
Church View 200 L5
Churchville 250 F4
Cismont 25 H4
Claremont 380 L6
Clarksville 1,468 G7
Claudville 180 D7
Clay Bank 200 L6
Clear Brook 300 H2
Cleveland 360 E2
Clifford 150 F5
Clifton Forge (I.C.) 5,046 E5
Clinchburg 250 E2
Clinchco 900 D1
Clinchport 89 C2
Clintwood⊙ 1,369 D2
Clover 215 G7
Cloverdale 850 E6
Cluster Springs 350 G7
Cobbs Creek 700 M6
Coeburn 2,625 D2
Coleman Falls 250 F6
Coles Point 100 L4
Collierstown 300 E5
Collinsville 7,517 E7
Colonial Beach 2,474 L4
Colonial Heights (I.C.) 16,509 K6
Columbia 111 H5
Concord 500 F6
Copper Valley 425 C7
Courtland⊙ 976 K7
Covesville 475 G5
Covington (I.C.)⊙ 9,063 D5
Craigsville 845 E4
Crandon 250 C6
Crewe 2,325 H6
Crimora 450 G4
Cripple Creek 200 B7
Critz 125 D7
Crockett 200 B7
Cross Junction 125 H2
Crozet 2,553 G4
Crozier 300 J5
Crystal Hill 475 G7
Cullen 725 G6
Culpeper⊙ 6,621 H4
Cumberland⊙ 300 H6
Dahlgren 950 K4
Dale City 33,127 K3
Daleville 450 E6
Damascus 1,330 E2
Dante 1,083 D2
Danville (I.C.) 45,642 E7
Danville‡ 111,789 E7
Davenport 230 D2
Dayton 1,017 G4
Deerfield 500 F4
Delaplane 100 J3
Deltaville 1,082 M5
Dendron 307 L6
Dewitt 140 J6
Dillwyn 637 H5
Dinwiddie⊙ 500 J6
Disputanta 800 K6
Doswell 50 J5
Drakes Branch 617 G7
Drewryville 200 K7
Drill 192 E2
Dryden 400 C2
Dry Fork 200 F7
Dublin 2,368 C6
Duffield 148 C2
Dumfries 3,214 K3
Dundas 200 H7
Dungannon 339 D2
Dunn Loring 6,077 N2
Dunnsville 800 L5
Eagle Rock 750 E5
Earlysville 210 H4
East Stone Gap 240 C2
Eastville⊙ 238 M6
Ebony 400 J7
Edgehill 100 K4
Edinburg 752 H3
Eggleston 350 C6
Elberon 25 L6
Elkton 1,520 G4
Elliston 1,172 D6
Emory 2,292 E2
Emporia (I.C.)⊙ 4,840 J7
Esmont 950 G5
Esserville 750 C2
Ettrick 4,890 K6
Evergreen 300 G6
Evington 175 F6
Ewing 800 B3
Exmore 1,300 N5
Faber 125 G5
Fairfax (I.C.)⊙ 19,390 M3
Fairfield 465 F5
Fairlawn 1,794 C6
Fairport 175 M5
Falls Church (I.C.) 9,515 N2
Falls Mills 800 B6
Falmouth 3,271 K4
Farmville⊙ 6,067 H6
Farnham 150 L5
Ferrum 200 D7
Fieldale 1,190 D7
Fincastle⊙ 282 E6
Fishersville 975 F4
Flint Hill 750 H3
Floyd⊙ 411 D7
Forest 497 F6
Fork Union 350 H5
Fort Blackmore 150 C2
Fort Mitchell 125 H7
Foxwells 400 M5
Franconia 22,310 N3
Franklin (I.C.) 7,308 L7
Franktown 500 N6
Fredericksburg (I.C.) 15,322 J4
Free Union 121 G4
Fries 758 B7
Front Royal⊙ 11,126 H3
Fulks Run 130 G3
Gainesville 600 J3
Galax (I.C.) 6,524 C7
Garrisonville 200 J4
Gasburg 150 J7
Gate City⊙ 2,494 C3
Georges Fork 200 C2
Gibson Station 150 B3
Gladehill 150 E7
Glade Spring 1,722 E2
Gladys 500 F6
Glasgow 1,259 F5
Glen Allen 6,202 J5
Glen Lyn 235 C6
Glen Wilton 190 E5
Glenwood 2,276 F7
Gloucester⊙ 1,545 L6
Gloucester Point 5,841 M6
Goldbond 250 C6
Goldvein 500 J4
Goochland⊙ 800 J5
Goode 200 F6
Gordonsville 1,421 H4
Gore 500 H2
Goshen 134 F5
Grafton 500 L6
Greenbackville 300 O5
Green Bay 500 H6
Greenbush 200 N5
Greenville 400 F5
Greenwood 800 G4
Gretna 1,255 F7
Grottoes 1,369 G4
Groveton 18,860 O3
Grundy⊙ 1,699 E1
Gum Spring 125 J5
Gwynn 205 M5
Hacksneck 111 N5
Hague 425 L4
Halifax⊙ 772 G7
Hallwood 243 N5
Hamilton 598 J2
Hampden-Sydney 1,011 G6
Hampton (I.C.) 122,617 M6
Hanover⊙ 500 K5
Harborton 200 N5
Hardy 325 E6
Harman-Maxie 650 D1
Harrisonburg (I.C.)⊙ 19,671 F4
Hartfield 700 M5
Haymarket 230 J3
Haynesville 500 L5
Haysi 371 D1
Head Waters 35 F4
Healing Springs 175 E5
Heathsville⊙ 300 L5
Henry 300 E7
Herndon 11,449 K3
Highland Springs 12,146 K5
Hillsboro 115 J2
Hillsville⊙ 2,123 C7
Hiltons 300 D3
Hiwassee 250 C7
Hoadly 400 K3
Hollins College 12,295 D6
Honaker 1,475 E2
Hopewell (I.C.) 23,397 K6
Hopkins 100 N5
Horntown 400 O5
Hot Springs 300 E4
Huddleston 200 F6
Hume 350 J3
Huntington 5,813 N3
Hurley 850 E1
Hurt 1,481 F6
Independence⊙ 1,112 B7
Indian Valley 300 C7
Iron Gate 620 E5
Irvington 567 M5
Isle of Wight⊙ 185 L7
Ivanhoe 900 C7
Ivor 403 L7
Ivy 900 G4
Jamestown 12 L6
Jamesville 500 N5
Jarratt 614 K7
Java 100 F7
Jeffersonton 300 J3
Jetersville 110 H6
Jewell Ridge 600 E1
Jonesville⊙ 874 B2
Keeling 680 F7
Keezletown 975 G4
Keller 236 N5
Kenbridge 1,352 H7
Kents Store 130 H5
Keokee 300 C2
Keswick 300 H4
Keysville 704 H6
Kilmarnock 945 M5
Kimballton 50 C6
King and Queen Court House⊙ 500 L5
King George⊙ 575 K4
King William⊙ 100 K5
Kinsale 250 L4
Lacey Spring 140 G3
La Crosse 734 H7
Ladysmith 360 J4
Lafayette 1,172 D6
Lake Barcroft 8,725 N3
Lakeside 12,289 J5
Lambsburg 800 C7
Lancaster⊙ 110 M5
Laurel Fork 300 C7
Lawrenceville⊙ 1,484 J7
Lebanon⊙ 3,206 E2
Lebanon Church 300 G2
Leesburg⊙ 8,357 J2
Lewisetta 125 M4
Lexington (I.C.)⊙ 7,292 E5
Lightfoot 120 L6
Lincolnia 10,350 N3
Linden 320 H3
Linville 500 G3
Lithia 105 E6
Little Plymouth 195 L5
Littleton 15 K7
Lively 400 L5
Loretto 150 K4
Lorton 5,813 K3
Louisa⊙ 932 H4
Lovettsville 613 J2
Lovingston⊙ 600 G5
Lowesville 500 F5
Lowmoor 700 E5
Lucketts 500 J2
Lunenburg⊙ 13 H7
Luray⊙ 3,584 H3
Lynchburg (I.C.) 66,743 F6

I.C. Independent City. ⊙County seat. ‡Population of metropolitan area.

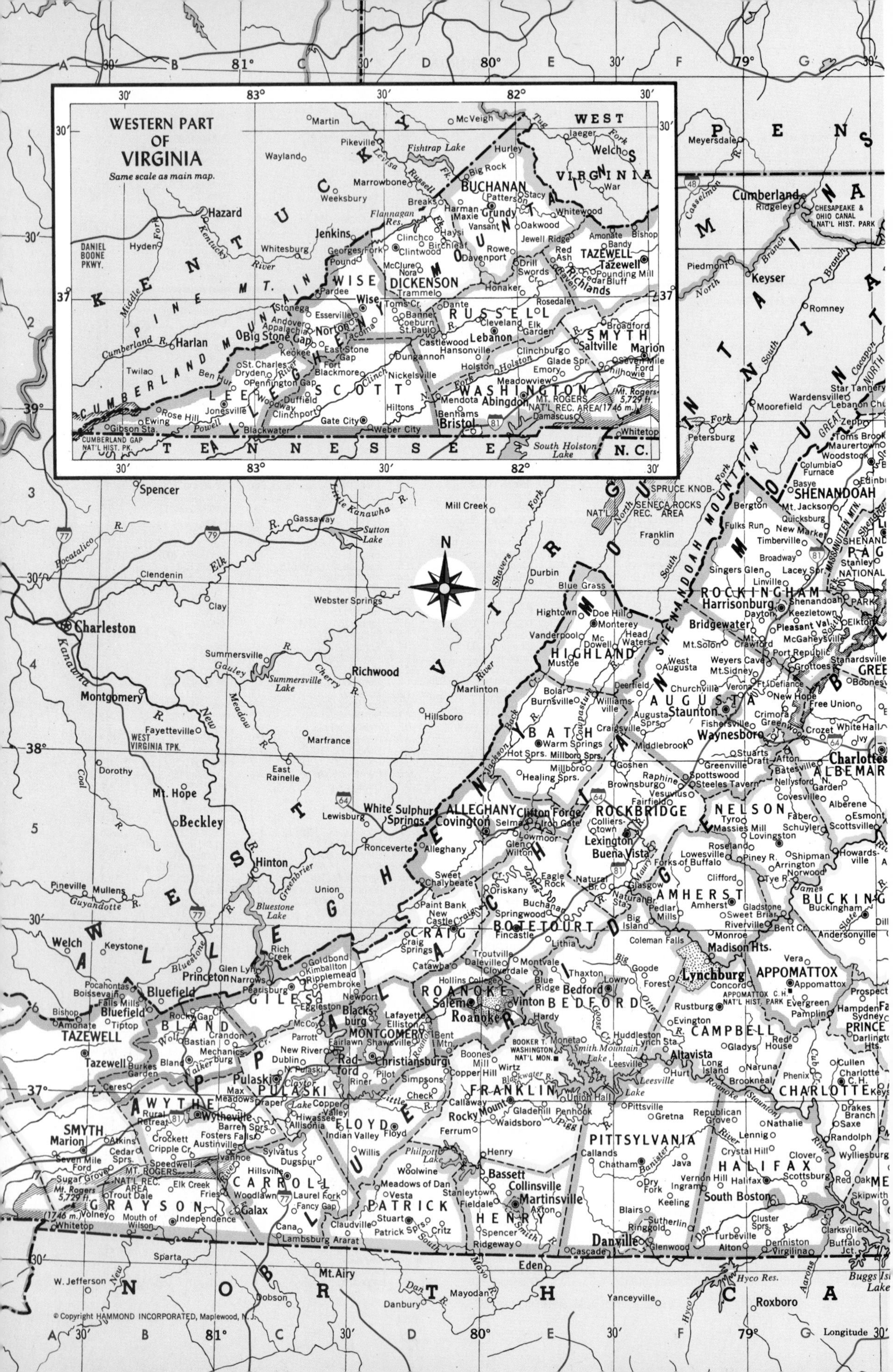

WESTERN PART OF VIRGINIA
Same scale as main map.
KENTUCKY
WEST VIRGINIA
TENNESSEE
N.C.
CUMBERLAND MOUNTAIN
PINE MT.
ALLEGHENY MOUNTAINS
BUCHANAN
DICKENSON
WISE
RUSSELL
SCOTT
LEE
WASHINGTON
SMYTH
TAZEWELL
Hazard
Hyden
Jenkins
Whitesburg
Harlan
Big Stone Gap
Norton
Wise
Grundy
Lebanon
Abingdon
Bristol
Marion
Saltville
Tazewell
Richlands
Pikeville
Welch
Fishtrap Lake
Flannagan Res.
South Holston Lake
DANIEL BOONE PKWY.
CUMBERLAND GAP NAT'L HIST. PK.
MT. ROGERS NAT'L REC. AREA (1746 m.)
Mt. Rogers 5,729 ft.
PENNSYLVANIA
MARYLAND
WEST VIRGINIA
NORTH CAROLINA
ALLEGHENY MOUNTAINS
SHENANDOAH MOUNTAIN
BLUE RIDGE
APPALACHIAN
GREAT NORTH MOUNTAIN
Cumberland
Keyser
Romney
Petersburg
Moorefield
Charleston
Clendenin
Spencer
Clay
Montgomery
Fayetteville
Summersville
Richwood
Webster Springs
Marlinton
Hillsboro
Lewisburg
White Sulphur Springs
Ronceverte
Union
Mt. Hope
Beckley
Hinton
Princeton
Bluefield
Welch
Pineville
Mullens
Sutton Lake
Summersville Lake
Bluestone Lake
SPRUCE KNOB-SENECA ROCKS NAT'L REC. AREA
CHESAPEAKE & OHIO CANAL NAT'L HIST. PARK
WEST VIRGINIA TPK.
HIGHLAND
BATH
ALLEGHENY
AUGUSTA
ROCKINGHAM
SHENANDOAH
ALBEMARLE
NELSON
ROCKBRIDGE
AMHERST
BOTETOURT
CRAIG
GILES
BLAND
TAZEWELL
ROANOKE
MONTGOMERY
PULASKI
WYTHE
SMYTH
GRAYSON
CARROLL
FLOYD
PATRICK
FRANKLIN
HENRY
PITTSYLVANIA
BEDFORD
CAMPBELL
APPOMATTOX
CHARLOTTE
HALIFAX
BUCKINGHAM
PRINCE EDWARD
Harrisonburg
Staunton
Waynesboro
Charlottesville
Monterey
Warm Springs
Hot Sprs.
Covington
Clifton Forge
Lexington
Buena Vista
Lynchburg
Roanoke
Salem
Vinton
Bedford
Blacksburg
Christiansburg
Radford
Pulaski
Wytheville
Galax
Independence
Marion
Floyd
Stuart
Rocky Mount
Martinsville
Danville
Chatham
South Boston
Halifax
Altavista
Appomattox
Fincastle
Pearisburg
Tazewell
Mt. Airy
Eden
Yanceyville
Roxboro
Smith Mountain Lake
Leesville Lake
Philpott Lake
Hyco Res.
BOOKER T. WASHINGTON NAT'L MON.
APPOMATTOX C. H. NAT'L HIST. PARK
MT. ROGERS NAT'L REC. AREA
Mt. Rogers 5,729 ft. (1746 m.)
Longitude
© Copyright HAMMOND INCORPORATED, Maplewood, N.J.

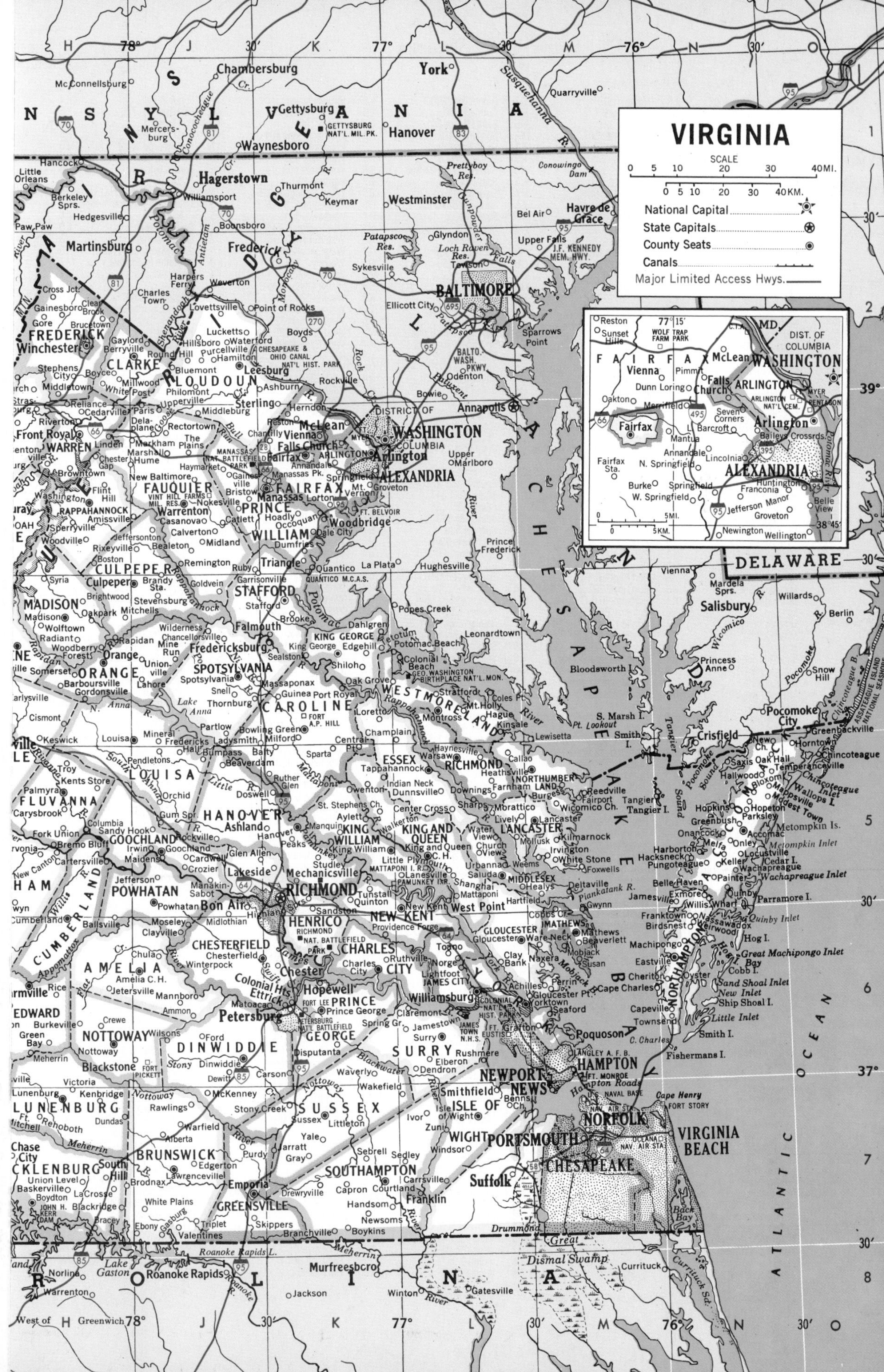
VIRGINIA
SCALE
0 5 10 20 30 40 MI.
0 5 10 20 30 40 KM.
National Capital
State Capitals
County Seats
Canals
Major Limited Access Hwys.
DIST. OF COLUMBIA
WASHINGTON
ARLINGTON
ALEXANDRIA
FAIRFAX
DELAWARE
BALTIMORE
RICHMOND
NORFOLK
VIRGINIA BEACH
CHESAPEAKE
PORTSMOUTH
NEWPORT NEWS
HAMPTON
Petersburg
Fredericksburg
Williamsburg
Suffolk
Annapolis
Frederick
Hagerstown
Winchester
CHESAPEAKE BAY
ATLANTIC OCEAN
West of Greenwich 78° 77° 76°
39° 37°

VIRGINIA

Lynchburg‡ 153,260 .... F6
Lynch Station 500 .... F6
Machipongo 400 .... N6
Madison⊙ 267 .... H4
Madison Heights 14,146 ..... F6
Manakin-Sabot 200 .... J5
Manassas (I.C.)⊙ 15,438 ... K3
Manassas Park
(I.C.) 6,524 .... K3
Mannboro 175 .... J6
Manquin 576 .... K5
Mantua 6,523 .... N3
Mappsville 700 .... O5
Marion⊙ 7,029 .... F2
Markham 300 .... J3
Marshall 800 .... J3
Martinsville
(I.C.)⊙ 18,149 .... E7
Massies Mill 225 .... F5
Mathews⊙ 500 .... M6
Matoaca 1,967 .... J6
Mattaponi 300 .... L5
Maurertown 158 .... G3
Max Meadows 782 .... C6
McClure 300 .... D2
McCoy 600 .... C6
McDowell 110 .... E4
McGaheysville 600 .... G4
McKenney 473 .... J7
McLean 35,664 .... N2
Meadows of Dan 150 .... D7
Meadowview 2,292 .... E2
Mechanicsburg 350 .... C6
Mechanicsville 9,269 .... K5
Meherrin 400 .... H6
Melfa 391 .... N5
Mendota 375 .... D2
Merrifield 7,525 .... N3
Middlebrook 125 .... F4
Middleburg 619 .... J3
Middletown 841 .... H2
Midland 600 .... J3
Midlothian 950 .... J6
Milford 650 .... K4
Millboro 400 .... E5
Millboro Springs 200 .... E4
Millwood 400 .... J2
Mineral 399 .... J4
Mine Run 450 .... J4
Mitchells 88 .... J4
Mobjack 210 .... M6
Modest Town 225 .... O5
Mollusk 800 .... L5
Moneta 300 .... E6
Monroe 500 .... F6
Monterey⊙ 247 .... E4
Montross⊙ 456 .... L4
Montvale 900 .... E6
Morattico 225 .... L5
Moseley 210 .... J6
Mount Crawford 315 .... G4
Mount Holly 200 .... L4
Mount Jackson 1,419 .... G3
Mount Sidney 500 .... F4
Mount Solon 124 .... F4
Mount Vernon 24,058 .... K3
Mouth of Wilson 400 .... B7
Mustoe 150 .... E4
Narrows 2,516 .... C6
Naruna 175 .... G6
Nassawadox 630 .... N6
Nathalie 200 .... G7
Natural Bridge 200 .... E5
Natural Bridge
Station 450 .... F5
Naxera 300 .... M6
Nellysford 290 .... G5
New Baltimore 125 .... J3
New Canton 96 .... H5
New Castle⊙ 213 .... D5
New Church 427 .... N5
New Hope 200 .... G4
Newington 8,313 .... N3
New Kent⊙ 25 .... L5
New Market 1,118 .... G3
Newport 600 .... D6
Newport News
(I.C.) 144,903 .... L6
Newport News-
Hampton‡ 364,449 .... L6
New River 500 .... C6
Newsoms 368 .... K7
Nickelsville 464 .... D2
Nokesville 520 .... J3
Nora 550 .... D2
Norfolk (I.C.) 266,979 .... M7
Norfolk-Virginia Beach-
Portsmouth‡ 806,691 .... M7
Norge 750 .... L6
North Garden 200 .... G5
North Pulaski 1,405 .... C6
North Springfield 9,538 ...... N3

Norton (I.C.) 4,757 .... C2
Nottoway⊙ 170 .... H6
Oak Hall 221 .... N5
Oakton 19,150 .... M3
Oakwood 715 .... E1
Occoquan 241 .... K3
Onancock 1,461 .... N5
Onley 526 .... N5
Orange⊙ 2,631 .... H4
Oriskany 116 .... E5
Owenton 400 .... K5
Oyster 200 .... N6
Painter 321 .... N5
Palmyra⊙ 250 .... H5
Pamplin 273 .... G6
Pardee 190 .... C2
Paris 90 .... J3
Parksley 979 .... N5
Parrott 750 .... C6
Patrick Springs 800 .... D7
Patterson 500 .... E1
Peaks 500 .... K5
Pearisburg⊙ 2,128 .... C6
Pedlar Mills 50 .... F5
Pembroke 1,302 .... C6
Pendletons 100 .... J5
Penhook 500 .... E7
Pennington Gap 1,716 .... C2
Perrin 250 .... M6
Petersburg (I.C.) 41,055 ..... J6
Petersburg-Colonial Heights-
Hopewell‡ 129,296 .... J6
Phenix 250 .... G6
Philomont 265 .... J2
Pilot 360 .... D6
Pimmit 6,658 .... N2
Piney River 778 .... G5
Pittsville 600 .... F7
Pleasant Valley 150 .... G4
Pocahontas 708 .... B6
Poquoson (I.C.) 8,726 ...... M6
Port Republic 75 .... G4
Port Royal 291 .... K4
Portsmouth (I.C.) 104,577 . M7
Potomac Beach 200 .... L4
Pound 1,086 .... C2
Pounding Mill 399 .... E2
Powhatan⊙ 600 .... J5
Prince George⊙ 150 .... K6
Prospect 275 .... G6
Providence Forge 500 .... L6
Pulaski⊙ 10,106 .... C6
Pungoteague 500 .... N5
Purcellville 1,567 .... J2
Purdy 350 .... J7
Quantico 621 .... K3
Quicksburg 160 .... G3
Quinby 350 .... N5
Quinton 121 .... K5
Radford (I.C.) 13,225 .... C6
Radiant 250 .... H4
Randolph 150 .... G7
Raphine 500 .... F5
Rapidan 176 .... H4
Raven 4,000 .... E2
Rawlings 200 .... J7
Rectortown 225 .... J3
Red Ash 300 .... E2
Red House 150 .... G6
Red Oak 250 .... G7
Reedville 400 .... M5
Rehoboth 100 .... H7
Reliance 150 .... H2
Remington 425 .... J3
Republican Grove 125 .... F7
Reston 36,407 .... M2
Rice 194 .... H6
Rich Creek 746 .... C6
Richlands 5,796 .... E2
Richmond (I.C.) (cap.)⊙
219,214 .... K5
Richmond‡ 632,015 .... K5
Ridgeway 858 .... E7
Riner 360 .... D6
Ringgold 150 .... F7
Ripplemead 600 .... C6
Riverton 500 .... H3
Rixeyville 150 .... H3
Roanoke (I.C.) 100,220 ...... D6
Roanoke‡ 224,341 .... D6
Rockville 290 .... J5
Rocky Gap 200 .... B6
Rocky Mount⊙ 4,198 .... E7
Rosedale 760 .... E2
Rose Hill 700 .... B3
Roseland 300 .... F5
Round Hill 510 .... J2
Rowe 150 .... E2
Ruby 188 .... J3
Rural Retreat 1,083 .... B7
Rushmere 1,070 .... L6
Rustburg⊙ 650 .... F6

Ruther Glen 200 .... K5
Ruthville 300 .... L6
Saint Charles 241 .... C2
Saint Paul 973 .... D2
Saint Stephens
Church 500 .... K5
Salem (I.C.)⊙ 23,958 .... D6
Saltville 2,376 .... E2
Saluda⊙ 150 .... L5
Sandy Hook 700 .... H5
Saxe 110 .... G7
Saxis 415 .... N5
Schuyler 250 .... G5
Scottsburg 335 .... G7
Scottsville 250 .... G5
Seaford M6
Sealston 200 .... K4
Sebrell 160 .... K7
Sedley 523 .... L7
Selma 500 .... E5
Seven Corners 6,058 .... N3
Seven Mile Ford 425 .... A7
Shanghai 150 .... L5
Shawsville 950 .... D6
Shenandoah 1,861 .... G4
Shiloh 150 .... K4
Shipman 350 .... G5
Simpsons 150 .... D6
Singers Glen 155 .... F3
Skippers 150 .... K7
Smithfield 3,718 .... L7
Snell 300 .... J4
Somerset 200 .... H4
South Boston (I.C.) 7,093 ... G7
South Hill 4,347 .... H7
Sparta 485 .... K4
Speedwell 650 .... B7
Spencer 500 .... E7
Sperryville 500 .... H3
Spotsylvania⊙ 350 .... J4
Springfield 21,435 .... N3
Springwood 120 .... E5
Stafford⊙ 750 .... K4
Stanardsville⊙ 284 .... G4
Stanley 1,204 .... G3
Stanleytown 1,761 .... D7
Star Tannery 500 .... G2
Staunton (I.C.)⊙ 21,857 .... F4
Steeles Tavern 200 .... F5
Stephens City 1,179 .... H2
Sterling 16,080 .... J2
Stonega 275 .... C2
Stony Creek 329 .... J7
Strasburg 2,311 .... H3
Stuart⊙ 1,131 .... D7
Stuarts Draft 1,776 .... G4
Studley 500 .... K5
Suffolk (I.C.)⊙ 47,621 .... L7
Sugar Grove 1,027 .... B7
Surry⊙ 237 .... L6
Susan 500 .... M6
Sussex⊙ 75 .... K7
Sutherlin 180 .... F7
Sweet Briar 900 .... F5
Swords Creek 315 .... E2
Sylvatus 200 .... C7
Syria 75 .... H4
Tacoma 150 .... C2
Tangier 771 .... M5
Tappahannock⊙ 1,821 ...... K5
Tazewell⊙ 4,468 .... E2
Temperanceville 400 .... O5
Thaxton 450 .... E6
The Plains 382 .... J3
Thornburg 135 .... J4
Timberville 1,510 .... G3
Tiptop 175 .... B6
Toano 950 .... L6
Toms Brook 226 .... G3
Townsend 525 .... M6
Trammel 450 .... D2
Triangle 4,470 .... K3
Triplet 300 .... J7
Trout Dale 248 .... B7
Troutville 496 .... E6
Tye River 80 .... G5
Tyro 125 .... F5
Union Level 100 .... H7
Unionville 500 .... J4
Upperville 250 .... J2
Urbanna 518 .... L5
Valentines 400 .... J7
Vansant 2,708 .... D6
Vera 150 .... G6
Vernon Hill 250 .... F7
Verona 2,782 .... F4
Vesta 350 .... D7
Vesuvius 500 .... F5
Victoria 2,004 .... H6
Vienna 15,469 .... M2
Vinton 8,027 .... E6
Virgilina 212 .... G7

Virginia Beach
(I.C.) 262,199 .... N7
Volney 105 .... B7
Wachapreague 404 .... N5
Wakefield 1,355 .... K7
Walkerton 985 .... K5
Ware Neck 100 .... M6
Warfield 100 .... J7
Warm Springs⊙ 325 .... E4
Warrenton⊙ 3,907 .... J3
Warsaw⊙ 771 .... L5
Washington⊙ 247 .... H3
Waterford 350 .... J2
Water View 265 .... L5
Waverly 2,284 .... K6
Waynesboro (I.C.) 15,329 ... F4
Weber City 1,543 .... D3
Weems 500 .... L5
Weirwood 300 .... N6
West Augusta 325 .... F4
West Point 2,726 .... L5
West Springfield 25,012 ..... N3
Weyers Cave 300 .... F4
White Hall 250 .... G4
White Stone 409 .... M5
Whitetop 860 .... A7
Whitewood 350 .... E1
Wicomico Church 500 .... M5
Wilderness 200 .... J4
Williamsburg
(I.C.)⊙ 9,870 .... L6
Williamsville 145 .... E4
Willis 170 .... D7
Willis Wharf 360 .... N5
Winchester
(I.C.)⊙ 20,217 .... H2
Windsor 985 .... L7
Winterpock 100 .... J6
Wirtz 500 .... E6
Wise⊙ 3,894 .... C2
Wolftown 350 .... H4
Woodberry Forest 450 .... H4
Woodbridge 24,004 .... K3
Woodlawn 1,689 .... C7
Woodstock⊙ 2,627 .... G3
Woodville 200 .... H3
Woodway 400 .... C2
Woolwine 150 .... D7
Wylliesburg 213 .... G7
Wytheville⊙ 7,135 .... C7
Yale 115 .... K7
Yorktown⊙ 550 .... M6
Zuni 300 .... L7

OTHER FEATURES

Aarons (creek) G7
Allegheny (mts.) D5
Appalachian (mts.) E5
Appomattox (riv.) H6
Appomattox C.H. Nat'l Hist.
Park F6
Arlington Nat'l
Cemetery O3
Assateague Island Nat'l
Seashore O4
Back (bay) N7
Banister (riv.) F7
Big Otter (riv.) F6
Blackwater (riv.) E6
Blackwater (riv.) K6
Blue Ridge (mts.) E6
Bluestone (lake) C5
Booker T. Washington Nat'l
Monument E6
Buggs Island (lake) H7
Bull Run (creek) J3
Cedar (isl.) N5
Charles (cape) M6
Chesapeake (bay) M5
Chesapeake and Ohio Canal
Nat'l Monument K2
Chincoteaque (bay) O4
Chincoteague (inlet) O5
C.I.A. N2
Claytor (lake) C6
Clinch (riv.) D2
Cobb (isl.) N6
Colonial Nat'l Hist.
Park L6
Cowpasture (riv.) E4
Craig (creek) D5
Cub (creek) G6
Cumberland (mt.) B2
Cumberland Gap Nat'l Hist.
Park A3
Dan (riv.) F7
Dismal (swamp) M8
Drummond (lake) L7
Fishermans (isl.) N6
Flanagan (res.) D1
Flat (creek) H6

Fort A.P. Hill K4
Fort Belvoir 7,726 .... K3
Fort Eustis L6
Fort Lee 9,784 .... K6
Fort Monroe M6
Fort Myer O2
Fort Pickett J6
Fort Story N7
Gaston (lake) H8
George Washington Birthplace
Nat'l Mon. L4
Goose (creek) E6
Goose (creek) J3
Great Machipongo (inlet) N6
Hampton Roads (est.) M7
Henry (cape) M7
Hog (isl.) N6
Hog Island (bay) N6
Holston, North Fork
(riv.) D2
Hyco (riv.) F8
Jackson (riv.) E4
James (riv.) K6
Jamestown Nat'l Hist.
Site L6
John H. Kerr (dam) H7
Langley A.F.B. M6
Levisa Fork (riv.) D1
Little (inlet) N6
Little (riv.) J5
Little (riv.) D7
Manassas Nat'l Battlefield
Park J3
Massanutten (mt.) G3
Mattaponi (riv.) K5
Mattaponi Ind. Res. K5
Maury (riv.) F5
Meherrin (riv.) H7
Metompkin (inlet) N5
Metompkin (isl.) N5
Mobjack (bay) M6
Mount Rogers Nat'l Rec.
Area E2
New (inlet) N6
New (riv.) B8
Ni (riv.) J4
North Anna (riv.) H4
Nottoway (riv.) K7
Oceana Naval Air Sta. N7
Pamunkey (riv.) K5
Pamunkey Indian
Reservation L5
Parramore (isl.) N5
Pentagon O3
Petersburg Nat'l
Battlefield K6
Philpott (lake) D7
Piankatank (riv.) M5
Pigg (riv.) E7
Po (riv.) J4
Pocomoke (sound) N5
Potomac (riv.) K4
Powell (riv.) B3
Quantico Marine Corps Air
Station 7,121 .... K4
Quinby (inlet) N6
Rapidan (riv.) H4
Rappahannock (riv.) L4
Richmond Nat'l Battlefield
Park K6
Rivanna (riv.) H5
Roanoke (riv.) J8
Rogers (mt.) E2
Russell Fork (riv.) D1
Sand Shoal (inlet) N6
Shenandoah (mt.) F3
Shenandoah (riv.) J2
Shenandoah Nat'l Park G3
Ship Shoal (isl.) N6
Slate (riv.) G5
Smith (isl.) N6
Smith (riv.) E7
South Anna (riv.) J5
South Holston (lake) E3
South Mayo (riv.) D7
Staunton (Roanoke)
(riv.) F6
Stony (creek) J6
Swift (creek) K6
Tangier (isl.) M5
Tangier (sound) N5
Tug Fork (riv.) E1
U.S. Naval Base M7
Vint Hill Farms Military
Reservation J3
Wachapreaque (inlet) N5
Walker (creek) B6
Wallops (isl.) O5
Willis (riv.) H5
Wolf (creek) B6
Wolf Trap Farm Park N2
York (riv.) L6

I.C. Independent City. ⊙County seat. ‡Population of metropolitan area.

NEWPORT NEWS SHIPBUILDING PHOTO

Newport News, at the head of Hampton Roads, is a large shipbuilding center and a major coal and tobacco port.

3. The Economy

By the latter half of the 20th century, Virginia had developed a stable, diversified, and balanced economy that enjoyed a faster economic growth rate than that of the nation. It is perhaps ironic that politically conservative Virginia, traditionally opposed to extensive federal expenditures, has been economically sustained to a large degree by the rapid mid-20th century growth of federal and military agencies within the state. Manufacturing is the second most important generator of personal income. Industry has been attracted to Virginia from both Eastern and Midwestern states by its favorable tax and labor laws, its excellent transportation system, its adequate labor supply, and its natural environment.

Transformation of the Economy. Virginia had a flourishing tobacco-based economy during the colonial period. In the early national period it shifted gradually to more diversified farming as a result of the depletion of the Tidewater lands and the loss of important English markets for tobacco. The financial panics of 1819 and 1837 introduced further changes in the state's economy. Beginning in 1840, manufacturing centers sprang up in the areas of Richmond-Petersburg and Wheeling (now in West Virginia), and farming flourished in the Valley of Virginia and the Southside region (the area south of the James from the Blue Ridge to Suffolk). From 1830 to the Civil War, work advanced slowly on the canals and railroads that would link the eastern and western parts of the state. One sixth of the nation's pre-Civil War railroad trackage was in Virginia.

PERSONAL INCOME IN VIRGINIA

Source	1960	1970	1980
	(Millions of dollars)		
Farms	249	242	279
Mining	84	177	662
Construction	359	867	2,195
Manufacturing	1,243	2,641	7,057
Transportation, communications, and public utilities	475	906	2,577
Wholesale and retail trade	938	1,925	5,333
Finance, insurance, and real estate	252	558	1,775
Services	736	1,795	6,089
Other industries	20	41	120
Government	1,574	4,090	9,796
	(Dollars)		
Per capita personal income	1,889	3,712	9,392
Per capita income, U.S.	2,216	3,945	9,521

Source: U.S. Department of Commerce, *Survey of Current Business.*

The physical devastation caused by the Civil War was tremendous. However, full recovery was achieved by the end of the 19th century, thanks to the expansion of the railroad system, the discovery of a bright-leaf tobacco strain that could grow in Southside soil, the development of the tobacco-processing industry in Richmond, and the construction of deepwater facilities in Hampton Roads.

In the early 20th century the use of chemical fertilizers made farmers less dependent on tobacco. During World War II the expansion of manufacturing, military activities, and the growth of the federal establishment accelerated the trends toward both industrialization and urbanization.

Government Services. The growth in federal and state government services after 1933 brought about the rapid development of the urban areas around Washington, Richmond, and Hampton Roads. In the 1970's more than 34% of the state's work force was engaged in government services. Since the 1930's federal and, to a lesser extent, state agencies have generated the greatest amount of personal income in the state. The rate of growth of personal income from this source has been second only to that from the contract construction industry. The government has stimulated this industry by a multitude of building projects. It has also benefited private research companies by placing them under contract to do specialized work for its various agencies.

Manufacturing. Light industry accounts for most of Virginia's manufactures. They are highly diversified, producing chemicals, tobacco products, processed foods, transportation equipment, textiles, electrical equipment, paper and pulp, furniture, lumber, and processed stone and masonry. The major heavy industry is shipbuilding in Newport News and Portsmouth.

Tobacco processing is centered in Richmond. Textiles are manufactured in Roanoke, Danville, and Lynchburg. Chemical plants are situated along the Appomattox River and in Norfolk and Portsmouth.

Mining. Coal mining in western and southwestern Virginia developed rapidly after the Civil War. It reached its peak in the 1920's, then went into decline after World War II as oil and natural gas steadily replaced coal in the fuel market. But by the mid-1970's the coal industry began to revive as oil became less plentiful and more costly. Most of Virginia's coal is bituminous and is found in southwestern fields, of which the best known is the Pocahontas Field in Buchanan and Tazewell counties.

Tobacco, here being examined after curing, has been a mainstay of Virginia's economy since colonial times.

ROD HEINRICHS/GRANT HEILMAN

Various stones such as granite, limestone, marble, and shale are quarried. Clays and sand and gravel come from the Tidewater. Virginia is a leading source of kyanite, and ranks among the top ten states in the production of pyrites, titanium, and limestone.

Power. Electric power production in the mid-20th century kept pace with the rapidly expanding demands for electricity, which were nearly six times greater in 1975 than in 1945. Less than 5% of the power is hydroelectric. One nuclear power facility is in operation at Surry on the James River. But meeting future power needs may depend, as it has in the past, on the continued expansion of coal-fueled generating capacity at existing plants in the state and in adjacent West Virginia counties.

Agriculture. After 1945, farms in Virginia decreased in number, increased in size, and produced about the same total income annually as they had before. Because of the overall growth of total income within the state, the relative importance of farm income has therefore declined.

Farm income is evenly divided between field and orchard crops and livestock and livestock products. Southside Virginia produces tobacco, grain, apples and other fruits, and poultry (particularly broilers and turkeys) are raised in the Valley. Livestock and dairy farming predominate in the northern Piedmont. Truck farming is mainly on the Eastern Shore and in the Tidewater. Peanuts are grown in the southeastern counties. The famous Smithfield hams also come from the southeast.

Fishing. The Chesapeake Bay and offshore fisheries provide an important source of income. Shellfish, particularly oysters and crabs, represent one third of the total catch and three fifths of its total cash value. Menhaden (used for fertilizer and for oil), alewives, and white fish are leading fish catches.

Labor Force. An indicator of Virginia's expanding economy has been the growth rate of its labor force, which after 1950 increased faster than the state's population as a whole. Government, trade and sales, light manufacturing, and service industries employ the majority of workers. The decrease in the number of farms has been accompanied by a continuing drop in the number of farm workers.

The percentage of workers in labor unions is low. This is partly due to the nature of the state's business activities, which primarly employ service workers. It is also due to the dispersion of manufacturing concerns to suburbs and small towns, and to a right-to-work law.

Tourism. The many historic sites of the colonial, Revolutionary, and Civil War periods, the national parks, monuments, and forests, the scenic parkways of the western mountain regions, the ocean beaches of the Eastern Shore and Virginia Beach, and the many rivers and bays along the Chesapeake are all within easy reach of the densely populated eastern United States. Extensive promotion of these attractions by state and local agencies has helped to make tourism an important segment of the state's economy.

Transportation. Virginia retains a large part of its railroad trackage because it is an essential link in the Eastern Seaboard traffic and in the freight-traffic system of the Deep South. Coal continues to move by rail eastward to the Hampton Roads ports. Many cities still have passenger train services.

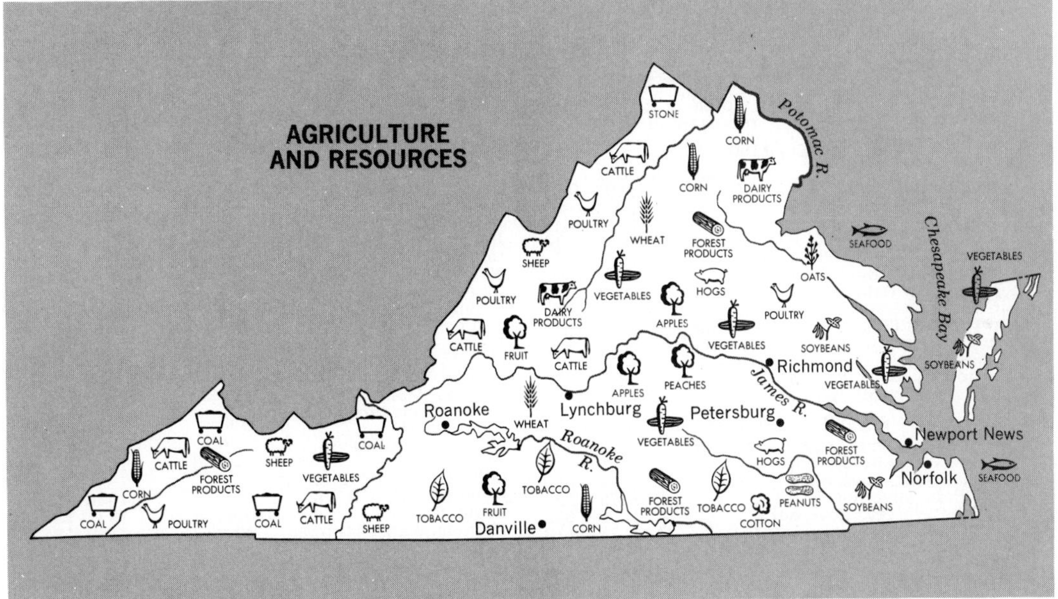

Virginia has completed most of its interstate and arterial highways. These have helped to stimulate economic diversification in many small towns and formerly isolated rural areas. The Chesapeake Bay Bridge-Tunnel links the Eastern Shore with the Tidewater mainland.

The deepwater shipping facilities in the Hampton Roads area are almost unrivaled along the Atlantic coast. Newport News–Norfolk is the world's largest coal-shipping port. Norfolk is home base for both the U. S. Atlantic Fleet and that of the North Atlantic Treaty Organization (NATO). There is also a deepwater terminal at Richmond.

Dulles International Airport, west of Washington, D. C., and the airports of Richmond and Norfolk offer worldwide flight service. All other major cities are served by domestic airlines.

4. Government and Politics

In the two centuries since the Commonwealth of Virginia adopted its first constitution in 1776, the voting franchise has gradually been broadened, the counties have lost much of their autonomy, and the executive branch has been strengthened.

Virginia's Constitutions. Under the first constitution, the General Assembly dominated the executive and judiciary branches, and within the assembly the House of Delegates was given more power than the Senate, the upper house. The executive and the judiciary were chosen by the General Assembly. The governor was further restrained by a privy council, the Council of State. County government was semiautonomous. Not only was the franchise restricted to property owners, but representation in the General Assembly was heavily weighted in favor of the eastern part of the state.

The next constitution, that of 1830, broadened the franchise slightly, increased the governor's powers, and reapportioned the legislature, although the trans-Allegheny region remained underrepresented. The reform constitution of 1851 again increased the power of the governor, made most state officers elective rather than appointive, instituted a poll tax, and provided for universal white manhood suffrage. It corrected many of the apportionment inequities, but not enough to prevent the western counties from seizing the opportunity provided by the Civil War to break away and form the state of West Virginia in 1863.

The Underwood Constitution, ratified in 1869 during the Reconstruction period, provided for secret ballots, enfranchised Negroes, revamped county government, shifted the tax base to landed property, and established a free public school system throughout the state.

The constitution of 1902 limited suffrage by renewing the poll tax and by imposing an "understanding clause" that required an applicant-voter to interpret constitutional provisions to an examiner's satisfaction. It created the State Corporation Commission to regulate corporations, such as railroads. It also eliminated the county-court system dating from 1634.

In 1970 the electorate approved a complete revision of the constitution, which went into effect in 1971. The revisions streamlined the document, especially those articles dealing with the judiciary. They committed the state to a quality public education system, enlarged the state borrowing capacity, and removed the possibilities for abuse and arbitrary restriction of the franchise. The revised constitution also included a broad conservation clause.

Executive. The Virginia governorship has evolved into one of the strongest in the nation. With the reorganization of the executive branch in 1928 and 1948, control of the state agencies was consolidated, and the governor was empowered to appoint most state officials. Thereafter elections were limited to the offices of governor, lieutenant governor, and attorney general.

The governor has the power of veto over General Assembly bills, including an item veto on appropriation bills. He may also veto a bill

GOVERNMENT HIGHLIGHTS

Electoral Vote—12. **Representation in Congress**—U. S. Senators, 2; U. S. representatives, 10. **General Assembly** (legislature)—Senate, 40 members, 4-year terms; House of Delegates, 100 members, 2-year terms. **Governor**—4-year term; cannot serve successive terms.

EXECUTIVES OF VIRGINIA

(During the colonial period some of the governors never left England. These titular governors were represented in the colony by deputy governors.)

Company Era (1607–1624)

Edward M. Wingfield, council president	1607
John Ratcliffe, council president	1607–1608
John Smith, council president	1608–1609
Lord De La Warr, governor	1609–1618
George Percy, council president	1609–1610
Sir Thomas Gates, lt. governor	1610
George Percy, deputy governor	1611
Sir Thomas Dale, deputy governor	1611
Sir Thomas Gates, lt. governor	1611–1614
Sir Thomas Dale, deputy governor	1614–1616
George Yeardley, deputy governor	1616–1617
Samuel Argall, deputy governor	1617–1619
Sir George Yeardley, governor	1619–1621
Sir Francis Wyatt, governor	1621–1624

Royal Era (1624–1652)

Sir Francis Wyatt, governor	1624–1626
Sir George Yeardley, governor	1626–1627
Francis West, governor	1627–1629
John Pott, governor	1629–1630
Sir John Harvey, governor	1630–1635
John West, governor	1635–1637
Sir John Harvey, governor	1637–1639
Sir Francis Wyatt, governor	1639–1642
Sir William Berkeley, governor	1642–1652

Commonwealth Period (1652–1660)

Richard Bennett, governor	1652–1655
Edward Digges, governor	1655–1656
Samuel Mathews, governor	1656–1660

Royal Era (1660–1776)

Sir William Berkeley	1660–1677
Herbert Jeffreys, lt. governor	1677–1678
Thomas, Lord Culpeper	1678–1683
Sir Henry Chicheley, deputy governor	1678–1680
Francis, Lord Howard of Effingham	1684–1692
Francis Nicholson, lt. governor	1690–1692
Sir Edmund Andros	1692–1698
Francis Nicholson	1698–1705
Edward Nott	1705–1706
Edmund Jennings, council president	1706–1710
Alexander Spotswood, lt. governor	1710–1722
Hugh Drysdale, lt. governor	1722–1726
Robert Carter, council president	1726–1727
William Gooch, lt. governor	1727–1749
Thomas Lee, council president	1749–1750
Lewis Burwell, council president	1750–1751
Robert Dinwiddie, lt. governor	1751–1758
John Blair, council president	1758
Francis Fauquier, lt. governor	1758–1768
John Blair, council president	1768
Lord Botetourt	1768–1770
William Nelson, council president	1770–1771
Earl of Dunmore	1771–1776

Governors of the Commonwealth

Name	Party	Years
Patrick Henry		1776–1779
Thomas Jefferson		1779–1781
Thomas Nelson, Jr.		1781
Benjamin Harrison		1781–1784
Patrick Henry		1784–1786
Edmund Randolph		1786–1788
Beverley Randolph		1788–1791
Henry Lee		1791–1794
Robert Brooke		1794–1796
James Wood, Jr.	Demo.-Rep.	1796–1799
James Monroe	"	1799–1802
John Page	"	1802–1805
William H. Cabell	"	1805–1808
John Tyler, Sr.	"	1808–1811
James Monroe	"	1811
George William Smith	"	1811
James Barbour	"	1812–1814
Wilson Cary Nicholas	"	1814–1816
James P. Preston	"	1816–1819
Thomas Mann Randolph	"	1819–1822
James Pleasants, Jr.	"	1822–1825
John Tyler	"	1825–1827
William B. Giles	"	1827–1830
John Floyd	Democrat	1830–1834
Littleton W. Tazewell	"	1834–1836
Wyndham Robertson	"	1836–1837
David Campbell	Democrat	1837–1840
Thomas Walker Gilmer	Whig	1840–1841
John Rutherford (acting)	Whig	1841–1842
John M. Gregory (acting)	"	1842–1843
James McDowell	"	1843–1846
William Smith	Democrat	1846–1849
John B. Floyd	"	1849–1852
Joseph Johnson	"	1852–1856
Henry A. Wise	"	1856–1860
John Letcher	"	1860–1864
William Smith	"	1864–1865
Francis H. Pierpont	Republican	1865–1868
Henry H. Wells	"	1868–1869
Gilbert G. Walker	"	1869–1874
James L. Kemper	Democrat	1874–1878
Frederick Holliday	Conservative	1878–1882
William E. Cameron	Readjuster	1882–1886
Fitzhugh Lee	Democrat	1886–1890
Philip W. McKinney	"	1890–1894
Charles T. O'Ferrall	"	1894–1898
J. Hoge Tyler	"	1898–1902
Andrew J. Montague	"	1902–1906
Claude A. Swanson	"	1906–1910
William H. Mann	"	1910–1914
Henry C. Stuart	"	1914–1918
Westmoreland Davis	"	1918–1922
E. Lee Trinkle	"	1922–1926
Harry Flood Byrd, Sr.	"	1926–1930
John Garland Pollard	Democrat	1930–1934
George C. Peery	"	1934–1938
James H. Price	"	1938–1942
Colgate W. Darden, Jr.	"	1942–1946
William M. Tuck		1946–1950
John S. Battle	"	1950–1954
Thomas B. Stanley	"	1954–1958
J. Lindsay Almond, Jr.	"	1958–1962
Albertis S. Harrison, Jr.	"	1962–1966
Mills E. Godwin, Jr.	"	1966–1970
Linwood Holton	Republican	1970–1974
Mills E. Godwin, Jr.	"	1974–1978
John Dalton	"	1978–1982
Charles S. Robb	Democrat	1982–1986
Gerald L. Baliles	"	1986–

Persons serving only a short time as council president or acting governor have been omitted from this list.

and return it as altered by executive agreement, with recommendations for repassage. The governor is responsible for the administration of numerous state agencies, which after 1972 reported to the governor through five secretaries—administration and finance, education, human affairs, commerce and resources, and transportation and public safety.

Legislature. Members of the Senate and the House of Delegates, jointly called the General Assembly, are elected in odd-numbered years and meet annually in January for 60-day sessions in even-numbered years and for 30-day sessions in odd-numbered years. Both the 60-day and the 30-day sessions can be extended by a two-thirds vote of both houses. The governor may call special sessions.

Judiciary. The principal courts are the supreme court of appeals, circuit courts for counties and towns, and local courts not of record. The General Assembly elects the justices of the supreme court for 12-year terms and judges of the circuit courts for eight years.

Political Subdivisions. The state has two separate political divisions, and the independent cities and the counties. The independent cities, of which there were 39 in 1975, must at one time have had at least 5,000 residents. There are also more than 200 incorporated towns, with populations between 1,000 and 5,000 which provide some local services and management but are otherwise integral parts of the counties.

Public Finance. The division of motor vehicles collects gasoline and vehicle taxes. The State

The state capitol in Richmond, with its Ionic portico, was built in the late 18th century. The wings were added in 1904–1905. Thomas Jefferson provided the design, which was based on a late Roman temple in Nîmes, France.

VIRGINIA CHAMBER OF COMMERCE, PHOTO BY FLOURNOY

Corporation Commission handles taxes paid by insurance companies and public-service corporations. The department of taxation, in conjunction with county and city officials, handles all other taxes, including corporation, sales, inheritance, real and personal property, and graduated income taxes. In addition, the state derives considerable income from the taxing and selling of liquor through the Alcoholic Beverage Control Board.

Sales and gross receipt taxes produce the greatest amount of the state's revenue, followed by individual income taxes, license taxes, and corporation net income taxes.

Social Services. The state has long provided an extensive program for deaf, blind, handicapped, and occupationally displaced persons. However, until the establishment of 22 state planning districts in the 1970's, many counties and localities lacked adequate public-health and social-service facilities, often rejecting federal assistance in favor of local autonomy. The planning districts have led to a rapid improvement in social-service programs. Long-planned revision of prison and mental-health programs are under way.

Political Parties. Until 1952, when Dwight D. Eisenhower carried the state, Virginians had voted Republican in a national election only once—in 1928. Though Eisenhower won the state again in 1956, and Richard Nixon in 1960 and 1968, the voters continued to elect Democrats to state offices and to Congress until 1969. In that year the Republicans captured the governorship with Linwood Holton and again in 1973 with Mills Godwin, a former Democrat who ran as a Republican. Simultaneously, the Republicans captured a majority of the congressional seats. Thus Virginia returned to a statewide two-party system, which it had abandoned in the 1880's. Both parties tend to operate independently of the national parties.

5. Education and Culture

Throughout the colonial period and the 19th century, most education was provided by private schools. Agitation from western elements in the 1840's and 1850's secured some state funds for public schools, but there was no constitutional provision for them until 1869. Public school funds then became involved in politics, and it was not until the constitution of 1902 that adequate provision was made for public schools.

Elementary and Secondary Schools. The school system is locally administered. General policy and management of state-aid funds are vested in the state superintendent of public instruction and a nine-member board of education.

Although Virginia's expenditures per pupil have lagged behind the national average, they rose markedly in the mid-1960's. Virginia now ranks about 25th among the states in such expenditures for education.

Integration of the races was limited in the decade after the 1954 U.S. Supreme Court decision barring racial segregation (*Brown* v. *Board of Education*). This separation of black and white students continued until the mid-1960's, when all school districts were integrated.

Higher Education. The state supports 14 colleges and universities: Clinch Valley College of the University of Virginia (Wise), George Mason College (Fairfax), Longwood College (Farmville), Madison College (Harrisonburg), Mary Washington College (Fredericksburg), Norfolk State College (Norfolk), Old Dominion University (Norfolk), Radford College (Radford), University of Virginia (Charlottesville), Virginia Commonwealth University (Richmond), Virginia Military Institute (Lexington), Virginia Polytechic Institute and State University (Blacksburg), Virginia State College (Petersburg), and the College of William and Mary (Williamsburg). In 1966 the state established a system of two-year community colleges. Completed in the 1970's, the system includes 27 colleges operating under a state department of community colleges.

There are 18 accredited, privately controlled four-year colleges and universities, among which the best known are Hampden-Sydney (Hampden-Sydney), Hampton Institute (Hampton), Hollins College (Hollins College), Mary Baldwin (Staunton), Randolph-Macon (Ashland), Randolph-Macon's Woman's College (Lynchburg), the University of Richmond (Richmond), Sweet Briar (Sweet Briar), Virginia Union University (Richmond), Virginia Wesleyan College (Norfolk), and Washington and Lee University (Lexington). There are also four private, accredited junior colleges.

The University of Virginia is the chief center for graduate and graduate-professional education, and Virginia Polytechnic Institute is the center for agricultural and engineering training.

Libraries and Museums. The principal research libraries are the Virginia Historical Society, the

UNIVERSITY OF VIRGINIA, DEPARTMENT OF GRAPHICS

The Rotunda of the University of Virginia is one of several campus buildings designed by Jefferson.

Valentine Museum Library, and the Virginia State Library (all in Richmond); the Alderman Library of the University of Virginia (Charlottesville); the Mariner's Museum (Newport News); and the Swem Library of the College of William and Mary (Williamsburg). As a result of the regional planning commissions formed in 1971, all cities and counties have access to public library programs.

The museums with which two of the research libraries are associated have displays relating to Virginia's past. Exhibits on the history of Richmond and of the state are offered in the Valentine Museum, and on the history of shipping in the Mariner's Museum. The Douglas MacArthur Museum in Norfolk contains memorabilia from World War I to the Korean War. Mementos of the Civil War, including the provisional constitution of the Confederacy, are exhibited in the Confederate Museum (once the White House of the Confederacy) in Richmond. The Edgar Allan Poe Museum is also in Richmond.

There are major art galleries at the Virginia Museum of Fine Arts (Richmond) and the Walter Chrysler Museum (Norfolk). The Virginia Museum displays art on tour throughout the state by means of an ingenious artmobile.

The Performing Arts. The Barter Theater (Abingdon), established in 1932, was the first state-supported theater in the nation. The Virginia Museum of Fine Arts Theatre performs in Richmond and on tour throughout the state. A major center for outdoor theater and concerts is Wolf Trap Farm near Washington, D.C. Summer stock and little theater groups abound in the state.

Historical Societies. The Virginia Historical Society (Richmond), established in 1931, publishes the *Virginia Magazine of History and Biography* and historical monographs and manuscripts. The Virginia State Library (Richmond) houses the state archives and publishes state documents, historical guides, and the quarterly *Virginia Cavalcade*. The Institute of Early American History and Culture (Williamsburg) publishes the *William and Mary Quarterly* and books about early America. County historical societies and patriotic and ancestral organizations publish historical records and preserve historical shrines.

Research. Research programs are carried on by the National Aeronautics and Space Administration (NASA) at its Langley Field headquarters in Hampton. The former NASA rocket launch site at Wallop's Island on the Eastern Shore is a major civilian center for conducting atmospheric and satellite tests. Nuclear reactors are maintained at the University of Virginia and Virginia Polytechnic Institute. The state supports a marine biology research program at Gloucester Point. Major medical and health research is carried out at the University of Virginia and the Medical College of Virginia in Richmond.

Communications. Virginia has more than 100 weekly newspapers and more than 30 daily papers, the principal ones being the Norfolk *Virginian-Pilot,* the Richmond *Times Dispatch,* and the Roanoke *Times*. There are nearly 200 radio stations, more than a dozen commercial television stations, and a state-supported educational television station.

6. Historical and Recreational Sites

Much of Virginia's history and important phases of America's history are encapsulated in the state's beautifully preserved historic buildings and battlefields. In addition to its abundant reminders of the past, Virginia also offers a great variety of parks, forests, and beaches to the nature lover and those who seek relaxation.

Historical Sites. Perhaps the best-known historic area in Virginia is the triangle formed by Jamestown, Williamsburg, and Yorktown. The Jamestown Festival Park includes a reproduction of James Fort, with wattle and daub houses, an Indian lodge, a glass factory, and full-scale models of the three ships that brought the first settlers to Jamestown. The scene of the culminating battle of the American Revolution can be seen at Yorktown. Williamsburg, the second capital of colonial Virginia, has been restored as an 18th century town. The reconstructed Capitol, governor's palace, Raleigh Tavern, Bruton parish church, and the Christopher Wren building of the College of William and Mary are among its most outstanding monuments to the past. See also WILLIAMSBURG, COLONIAL.

Beautiful plantations border the James River, including Carter's Grove, Berkeley (the birthplace of President William Henry Harrison), Westover, and Shirley. Richmond, the state capital, lies farther west on the James River. Thomas Jefferson designed the Capitol, modeling it on the Maison Carée, a Roman temple in Nîmes, France. The John Marshall House in Richmond was planned by the chief justice himself. Patrick Henry called for liberty or death in a memorable speech in Richmond's St. John's Church.

Westmoreland county, which lies between the Potomac and the Rappahannock rivers on the Northern Neck, is the site of Stratford Hall, near Montross, where Robert E. Lee was born. It is also the site of the George Washington Birthplace National Monument, which includes the Washington family plantation of Wakefield. The house where George Washington was born burned down in 1799. A reconstructed colonial plantation house has replaced it.

Several houses of historical interest are in Fredericksburg, including Kenmore, a Georgian manor house that belonged to George Washington's sister, and the James Monroe Law Office and Museum.

Gunston Hall, the home of George Mason, is southwest of Alexandria. South of the city is Mount Vernon (see MOUNT VERNON), George Washington's home on the Potomac. Woodlawn, which belonged to Washington's step-granddaughter Nelly Custis Lewis, was built on what was once part of the Mount Vernon estate. Both Washington and Lee worshiped in Christ Church in Alexandria. North of Alexandria, in Arlington, is Arlington House (the Custis-Lee Mansion), built by Martha Washington's grandson George Washington Parke Custis. It became the home of Robert E. Lee after his marriage to Custis' daughter. The Arlington National Cemetery surrounds the mansion.

Woodrow Wilson's birthplace is in Staunton, in the Valley west of the Blue Ridge. Just east of the Blue Ridge is the town of Charlottesville, which has two fine examples of Thomas Jefferson's architectural inventiveness: the original buildings of the University of Virginia and, outside of Charlottesville, his home of Monticello (see MONTICELLO). Nearby is Ash Lawn, the home of James Monroe. To the southwest, near Roanoke, is the Booker T. Washington National

NATIONAL PARK SERVICE, PHOTO BY JACK E. BOUCHER

Horseback riders follow a bridle path along the Blue Ridge in Virginia's Shenandoah National Park.

FAMOUS VIRGINIANS

Byrd, Harry Flood, Sr. (1887–1966), Virginia's foremost spokesman in national affairs as U. S. senator (1933–1965).

Byrd, Richard Evelyn (1888–1957), polar explorer, first man to fly over the North and South poles.

Cabell, James Branch (1879–1958), writer, best known for his novel *Jurgen* (1919).

Cather, Willa (1873–1947), writer, best known for *Death Comes for the Archbishop*.

Clark, George Rogers (1752–1818), military leader, won important victories over the British and their Indian allies during the Revolution.

Clark, William (1770–1838), American explorer; he and Meriwether Lewis led an expedition to the Pacific.

Freeman, Douglas Southall (1886–1953), journalist and historian, wrote biographies of Robert E. Lee and George Washington.

Glasgow, Ellen (1874–1945), writer, noted for her novels dealing with Virginia's social history.

Glass, Carter (1858–1946), U. S. representative and senator, chief author of Federal Reserve Act.

Harrison, William Henry (1773–1841), 9th president of the United States.

Henry, Patrick (1736–1799), Revolutionary leader and orator; 1st governor of the Commonwealth of Virginia.

Jackson, Thomas J. ("Stonewall"; 1824–1863), Confederate general and one of the outstanding tacticians in military history.

Jefferson, Thomas (1743–1826), 3d president of the United States.

Johnston, Joseph Eggleston (1807–1891), Confederate general, instrumental in winning the first Battle of Bull Run (Manassas).

Lee, Francis Lightfoot (1734–1797), signer of the Declaration of Independence; instrumental in winning Virginia's approval of the Constitution.

Lee, Henry ("Light-Horse Harry"; 1756–1818), skillful cavalry officer during the Revolution, signer of the Declaration of Independence, governor of Virginia, U. S. congressman.

Lee, Richard Henry (1732–1794), political leader and orator, introduced a resolution in the Continental Congress on which the Declaration of Independence was based.

Lee, Robert E. (1807–1870), general of the Confederate armies in the Civil War.

Lewis, Meriwether (1774–1809), American explorer; he and William Clark led the first official U. S. expedition to the Pacific.

McCormick, Cyrus Hall (1809–1884), inventor of the mechanical reaper.

Madison, James (1751–1836), 4th president of the United States.

Marshall, John (1755–1835), 4th chief justice of the U. S. Supreme Court whose decisions profoundly affected the country's constitutional growth.

Mason, George (1725–1792), author of Virginia's bill of rights, on which the federal bill of rights is modeled.

Maury, Matthew Fontaine (1806–1873), hydrographer, wrote first textbook on modern oceanography (1855).

Monroe, James (1758–1831), 5th president of the United States.

Page, Thomas Nelson (1853–1922), writer and diplomat, author of romantic, sentimental novels.

Pickett, George Edward (1825–1875), Confederate general, led famous charge at Gettysburg.

Poe, Edgar Allan (1809–1849), poet, critic, and pioneering short-story writer.

Randolph (family), influential in the history of the colony and of the early years of the republic.

Reed, Walter (1851–1902), bacteriologist, proved that yellow fever was carried by a certain variety of mosquito.

Scott, Winfield (1786–1866), general in chief of the U. S. Army (1841–1861), won significant victories in the Mexican War; Whig candidate for president in 1852.

Stuart, James Ewell Brown ("Jeb"; 1833–1864), Confederate cavalry leader, successfully scouted the enemy in several important battles.

Taylor, Zachary (1784–1850), 12th president of the United States.

Tyler, John (1790–1862), 10th president of the United States.

Washington, Booker T. (1856–1915), Negro social reformer and educator, established Tuskegee Institute; spokesman for cooperation between the races.

Washington, George (1732–1799), 1st president of the United States.

Wilson, Woodrow (1856–1924), 28th president of the United States.

PHOTO RESEARCHERS

Natural Bridge, once purchased by Jefferson from King George III, is all that remains of a collapsed cavern.

Monument, which marks the birthplace of the Negro educator and social reformer.

Civil War Monuments. The major Civil War battlefields and military cemeteries have been preserved, mainly as part of the National Park system. The Manassas National Battlefield Park covers the site of two major battles, called First Manassas (1861) and Second Manassas (1862), or the battles of Bull Run. Four Civil War battles—Fredericksburg, Chancellorsville, Wilderness, and Spotsylvania Court House—were fought on the grounds now included in the Fredericksburg and Spotsylvania National Military Park. Richmond National Battlefield Park commemorates the various battles fought in defense of the Confederate capital. To the south of Richmond is the Petersburg National Battlefield. After a nine-month siege of the city by the forces of Gen. Ulysses S. Grant, Lee was forced to abandon both Petersburg and Richmond. The war ended with the surrender of the Confederate Army at Appomattox, east of Lynchburg. McLean House, where the terms of surrender were agreed on, is preserved in the Appomattox Court House National Historical Park.

Parks and Forests. The most extensive parks and forests of Virginia are west of the Piedmont. The Shenandoah National Park extends along the Blue Ridge from Front Royal in the north to the vicinity of Waynesboro. The Skyline Drive runs along its crest. The park has extensive camping, recreational, and hiking facilities. The Blue Ridge Parkway links the Shenandoah National Park with the Great Smoky Mountains National Park in North Carolina and Tennessee.

The Valley of Virginia, lying west of the Blue Ridge, contains some remarkable natural formations. Among the many caverns are the Grand Caverns, the Luray Caverns, and the Endless Caverns. But the most famous natural phenomenon is the Natural Bridge, south of Lexington. Near Mt. Solon are the Natural Chimneys, seven limestone pillars that resemble a ruined fortress. Bath county in the west is noted for its mineral springs. The historic mountain pass on Daniel Boone's Wilderness Road is in the Cumberland Gap National Historical Park in the southwestern corner of the state.

Two large national forests extend along Virginia's western border: the Jefferson National Forest in the southwest, and the George Washington National Forest in the northwest. The latter includes the Alleghenies on the west, part of the Blue Ridge on the east, and part of Massanutten Mountain, which rises from the floor of the Shenandoah Valley.

The major resort areas in eastern Virginia are Seashore State Park in Virginia Beach and Westmoreland State Park on the Potomac. Two undeveloped wilderness seashore parks are located at Back Bay, Virginia Beach, and Assateague Island, a long, narrow island off the Eastern Shore of Virginia and Maryland.

Annual Events. The Shenandoah Apple Blossom Festival in Winchester and the International Azalea Festival in Norfolk are both held in the spring. During Virginia Garden Week in April, private homes and gardens are opened to the public. On Pony Penning Day held in July on Chincoteague Island, wild ponies from neighboring Assateague Island are sold at auction.

7. History

In 1606 the Virginia Company of London (also known as the London Company), a stock company controlled by a council in London, sent a fleet of three ships—the *Sarah Constant,* the *Goodspeed,* and the *Discovery*—with more than 100 settlers to establish a permanent settlement in the New World. On May 13 (May 23, New Style), 1607, the three ships were moored to trees on a peninsula on the James River. The next day the men disembarked. James Fort, named after King James I of England, was soon built.

The early years of Jamestown were marked by poor leadership and planning, an inadequate food supply, Indian raids, and an inability to find a marketable product. Only Capt. John Smith, one of the colony's councillors, showed real capacity for leadership. Gravely injured in an accident in 1609, he returned to England for good. In the winter of 1609–1610, the colonists were reduced by starvation to near savagery. The survivors were about to abandon the colony in June when the colony's first full governor, Lord De La Warr, arrived with a relief ship.

Conditions improved somewhat between 1610 and 1616 under the able and sometimes stern administration of De La Warr and his deputies. And the colony gained a valuable crop for export with the planting of West Indian tobacco seed by John Rolfe in 1612. With the marriage in 1614 of Rolfe to Pocahontas, daughter of the Indian chieftain Powhatan, peace was achieved with the Indians for eight years. America's first representative assembly met in 1619, when elected burgesses convened in a General Assembly, composed of the House of Burgesses, as well as the governor, and the council.

LIBRARY OF CONGRESS

Westover is one of the grandest of the James River plantations. William Byrd built the mansion in the 1730's.

Settlers began to arrive in greater numbers, and the colony took on a permanent character, despite the Indian massacre of 1622 and epidemics. In 1624 it became a royal colony when King James dissolved the London Company.

Royal Colony. By 1635 the colonial population had grown to almost 5,000. In 1644, during the governorship of Sir William Berkeley, another Indian massacre devastated the colony, but this caused only temporary setbacks.

When Civil War broke out in England, Virginia remained loyal to the crown. It recognized Charles II as king in 1649 when his father Charles I, was executed, and welcomed hundreds of new colonists, some of whom became the founders of Virginia's gentry society. However, the colony submitted to the Commonwealth in England in 1652. The Commonwealth period lasted until the Restoration in 1660, when the House of Burgesses reelected the popular Sir William Berkeley as governor.

Less flexible than before, Berkeley kept one General Assembly in session from 1661 to 1676, refusing to call new elections, and tended to favor the new gentry over the old settlers. He also lacked vigor in combating the restless Indians. A severe tobacco depression and social unrest in the counties compounded problems and led to rebellion in 1676. Led by young Nathaniel Bacon, a councillor, Bacon's Rebellion lasted

Monticello, the home Jefferson designed and built on a hill commanding a view of the Blue Ridge and Piedmont.

GEORGE LAYCOCK, PHOTO RESEARCHERS

GRANT HEILMAN

James Fort has been reconstructed at Jamestown, the Virginia colony's first capital.

only a few months and achieved little. Berkeley was recalled by the king in 1677.

After Britain's Glorious Revolution of 1688, more compatible career governors were sent to Virginia. The College of William and Mary was established in 1693, and the capital was moved from Jamestown to Williamsburg in 1699.

Negro chattel slavery, an incidental source of labor before 1680, became the basis for the great plantations of the Tidewater and lower Piedmont. The smaller Tidewater planters left to join a new wave of English and Scottish immigrants in settling the Piedmont up to the Blue Ridge. In the 1730's and 1740's, Scotch-Irish and Germans from Pennsylvania began to move into the Valley of Virginia. Despite differences in religious and social views, the Virginians welcomed them as a buffer against the French and Indians.

The planter society developed in this period permanently affected Virginia's character. The aristocratic society was a frank imitation of English country-gentry society. Its hierarchy of about 350 families perpetuated itself by intermarriage and a virtual monopoly of political offices. The aristocrats lived in comfortable splendor and multiplied their wealth by speculating in land and slave trading. The aristocracy defended self-government, viewed political service as a duty, and, most important, produced in one generation the great leaders of the Revolutionary and early national periods.

In 1753, conflicting claims by the French and British to the upper Ohio Valley led Virginia's Gov. Robert Dinwiddie to send the 21-year-old George Washington to warn the French away from the area. This diplomatic mission and a military expedition led by Washington the next year were failures. When a British force under Gen. Edward Braddock was defeated in 1755 by the French near Fort Duquesne (the site of Pittsburgh), the whole western frontier, including the Valley, lay open to Indian raids. Not until 1758, when the French evacuated Fort Duquesne during the French and Indian War (1754–1763) was the Valley again secure.

During the Pistole Fee Dispute (1752–1755) over taxation privileges, Virginians had served notice that they would zealously defend their supposed rights. The Parson's Cause (1758–1763), a highly unpopular attempt by the established clergy to collect regular salaries during an economic depression, undermined the church, brought Patrick Henry to prominence, and strained relations between crown and colony. The closing of western lands by the Proclamation of 1763 angered large land speculators and small frontiersmen, even though the law was not enforceable. Later Indian treaties gave Virginians full access to the Kentucky country, but Governor Dunmore violated orders in attacking the Ohio Indians in Dunmore's War (1774).

Revolution. The Proclamation line of 1763 proved to be only a minor irritant, since it could be ignored with impunity. But the various taxes imposed on the colonies by Parliament in the 1760's and 1770's provoked widespread colonial resistance, since those who were taxed had no representation in Parliament. Parliament's imposition of a stamp tax in 1765 drew from Patrick Henry and other members of the House of Burgesses from the western and northern counties the famous Stamp Act Resolves, which stated that only the General Assembly had the right to tax Virginians. Repeal of the Stamp Act in 1766 was followed by the equally disputed Townshend Acts of 1767, which imposed customs duties on certain imported products. Repeal of the Townshend Acts in 1770 on all imports but tea momentarily eased the tension.

However, when Britain passed the so-called "Coercive and Intolerable Acts" in retaliation for the "Boston Tea Party" in 1773, the House of Burgesses stood fast by the Boston patriots. When Governor Dunmore dissolved the General Assembly, the burgesses, meeting at Raleigh Tavern in Williamsburg, proposed that representatives from all the colonies meet in convention. This proposal led to the first Continental Congress of 1774. A Virginia Convention held in Williamsburg selected a distinguished delega-

HISTORICAL HIGHLIGHTS

1607 Jamestown settled.
1619 America's first representative assembly, the House of Burgesses, met at Jamestown; first blacks arrived in Virginia.
1622 About 350 settlers killed in Indian massacre.
1624 London Company's charter revoked; Virginia became a royal colony.
1676 Bacon's rebellion against Governor Berkeley.
1693 College of William and Mary founded.
1699 Capital moved from Jamestown to Williamsburg.
1765 Patrick Henry's Stamp Act speech and passage of Stamp Act Resolves by General Assembly.
1774 Virginia Convention formed, called for first Continental Congress.
1776 Virginia Convention declared Virginia independent and adopted bill of rights and state constitution.
1779 Richmond designated new capital.
1781 Cornwallis surrendered at Yorktown.
1788 Virginia ratified constitution.
1819 University of Virginia founded.
1831 Nat Turner's insurrection.
1859 John Brown's raid on Harpers Ferry.
1861 Virginia seceded, joined Confederate States; Richmond became confederate capital.
1865 Lee surrendered to Grant at Appomattox.
1870 Virginia readmitted to the Union.
1902 New state constitution restricted voting by poll tax and literacy requirements.
1954 U. S. Supreme Court ending segregation in public schools was met with massive resistance; but by 1967 most schools were integrated.
1969 For the first time in the 20th century, Virginia elected a Republican as governor.
1971 Revised state constitution went into effect.

tion to the first Continental Congress, over which House of Burgesses Speaker Peyton Randolph presided. The convention system after April 1775 virtually took over operation of government from Dunmore.

Randolph called for a convention to be held at St. John's Church in Richmond in March 1775 to approve the decisions made at the first Continental Congress. Patrick Henry then urged that a militia be called up. Seconded by Richard Henry Lee, and supported by Thomas Jefferson, the motion was passed.

Alarmed by these events, Dunmore seized the available powder supplies and then in May fled to a British man-of-war anchored in the York River. In the following months Dunmore attacked the coast several times, after which he sailed for England in 1776.

At the second Continental Congress, George Washington was elected commander in chief of the Continental Army on June 15, 1775. Nevertheless, most Virginians hoped for reconciliation and refused to heed the radical calls of Thomas Jefferson, Patrick Henry, and Richard Henry Lee for independence. The radical voice finally triumphed in May 1776, when the Virginia Convention met in Williamsburg. On May 15, both radicals and conservatives in that convention voted that Virginia's delegates in Philadelphia should call for independence from Britain. At the request of the convention, George Mason drew up a bill of rights for Virginia (on which the federal bill of rights was later modeled). He also helped draft Virginia's first constitution, adopted by the convention on June 29.

At the Continental Congress, Richard Henry Lee proposed on June 7 that the colonies declare themselves independent. The Virginia Resolution was approved on July 2, and Thomas Jefferson's Declaration of Independence was adopted on July 4. Jefferson then returned to Virginia, seeking liberalization of the state constitution, a more proportional representation in the legislature, and greater protection for the dignity of the individual. The reactions to this program set the tone of political debate in the state for several generations. A new judicial and penal system, abolition of primogeniture and entail, and the establishment of religious freedom were achieved by 1786, but universal white manhood suffrage was delayed until 1851 and public education until 1869.

Virginia until 1780 had little direct contact with the war beyond raising and supplying troops. George Rogers Clark, with a poorly equipped army of Virginia frontiersmen, wrested the Northwest from the British in 1778–1779. By 1780, Virginia had so stripped itself of troops for the Continental Army that it was easy prey when Benedict Arnold, on a raiding expedition for the British, laid waste to the new capital of Richmond in January 1781. By May, British Gen. Lord Charles Cornwallis had reached Virginia from the Carolinas. He was unable to destroy Lafayette's army. On Oct. 19, 1781, the British surrendered at Yorktown.

The First Decades of the Republic and the Virginia Dynasty. Virginia's cession of its claims to the Northwest Territory, which were based on the charter of 1609 and on Clark's conquest of the area in 1778–1779, was accepted by the United States in 1783, and the deed was signed in 1784. Virginia stipulated that new states formed from the territory be equal in rights and privileges to the older states. This condition was translated into the Ordinance of 1787, the basic statement for the admission of new states.

Many Virginians were concerned with the weaknesses of the national government. Partly at the instigation of James Madison, a convention was convened in Philadelphia in 1787 to consider revision of the Articles of Confederation. Madison, Edmund Randolph, and George Mason all played prominent roles in the debates at the Philadelphia Constitutional Convention. But though Virginians took a leading part in drafting the Constitution, such distinguished Virginians as Patrick Henry and George Mason feared a strong national government. Only after the Constitution's proponents promised to seek the addition of a bill of rights did the Virginia Convention of 1788 vote to ratify.

For the first 40 years of the national period, Virginia statesmen dominated national politics. George Washington's terms as president were from 1789 to 1797. Between 1801 and 1825, Jefferson, Madison, and Monroe served consecutively as presidents. The chief justice of the U.S. Supreme Court between 1801 and 1835 was the distinguished Virginian John Marshall. But as the Virginia dynasty became more nationalistic and Marshall's decisions strengthened federal power, Virginians turned away from the national leadership. The Jeffersonian Republicans split, and the states'-rights agrarians, including John Randolph, John Taylor, Judge Spencer Roane, and John Tyler, won out over the reformers in the 1820's.

The Capitol, in colonial Williamsburg, was the meeting-place of the Burgesses, General Court, and Council.

COLONIAL WILLIAMSBURG

Sectionalism, Secession, and Civil War. Virginia failed to keep pace with national growth after the War of 1812. Virginians blamed the tariff, but equally important was the exhaustion of the soil by the cultivation of tobacco and by the resistance of eastern Virginians to an east-west canal system. Nominally a Democratic state, Virginia moved in and out of the Whig and Democratic parties, seeking the best guarantor of states' rights and agrarian principles.

Internal sectionalism dominated state politics. The vital, growing western counties demanded that the suffrage be given to all taxpayers, and not limited to freeholders, and that the legislature be reapportioned to give the western counties greater representation. They also demanded manumission of slaves. The easterners gradually yielded to certain of their demands in the constitutions of 1830 and 1851. But all hope for manumission ended in 1831 when about 60 slaves, led by the slave Nat Turner, massacred whites in Southampton county. After a plan for gradual emancipation of slaves failed in the General Assembly in 1832, opposition to slavery in the state faded away.

Virginians tried to maintain a moderate but pro-Southern position. They deplored the extremism of Southern "fire-eaters," but were even more hostile to Northern abolitionists. Virginia refused to support South Carolina's Ordinance of Nullification (1832), which declared the federal tariff acts of 1828 and 1832 null and void because they infringed on the state's constitutional rights. But Virginia upheld the right of a state to secede from the union under certain extreme circumstances.

The chances of avoiding a clash between North and South were jeopardized by John Brown's raid on Harpers Ferry on Oct. 16, 1859. Brown and several followers, including five blacks, seized the U.S. arsenal at Harpers Ferry (now in West Virginia) in an attempt to persuade slaves to rise against their owners. He was taken prisoner and hanged. The raid and Brown's execution drove the proslavery and antislavery groups even further apart, with the moderate position greatly weakened.

Virginia refused to join South Carolina and some other Southern states in seceding after the election of Abraham Lincoln. Its state convention voted against secession as late as April 4, 1861. But when Lincoln called for volunteers from all the states to put down the "insurrection," it voted on April 17 in favor of secession.

Virginia was the center of military and political operations throughout the Civil War. Richmond became the capital of the Confederacy. Serious fighting opened with the battles of Bull Run and Ball's Bluff in 1861. In the spring of 1862, Union troops under George McClellan pushed up the peninsula to within sight of Richmond, only to be repulsed by the brilliant defensive tactics of Robert E. Lee and T. J. (Stonewall) Jackson. Lee then broke John Pope's offensive at the second Battle of Bull Run, and took the offensive himself, but was checked by McClellan at Antietam (Maryland) in September. Lee won defensive victories in December 1862 at Fredericksburg and in May 1863 at Chancellorsville. Emboldened by these victories to seek a decisive climax to the war, Lee moved north into Pennsylvania, where he was beaten at Gettysburg in July. Badly battered and inadequately supplied, Lee's Army of Northern Virginia resisted for nearly a year before yielding Richmond, retreating to the west and surrendering at Appomattox Court House on April 9, 1865.

Reconstruction and Recovery. Peace found Virginia prostrate. The transmontane counties had become the state of West Virginia in 1863 with the support of the provisional Union government in Virginia. Provisional Gov. Francis H. Pierpont took office in Virginia at the war's end, steering a moderate course until military reconstruction was instituted in 1867. Even then, an attempt to write a radical reconstructionist constitution disfranchising Confederate leaders failed in 1869 through the intervention of Gen. John M. Schofield, the military governor, and President Ulysses S. Grant. Virginia was readmitted to the Union in 1870.

An alliance of Conservatives (former Democrats and Whigs) and moderate Republicans ended radical Republican control in 1870. Serious differences over the readjustment of the state debt, the subversion of school funds to political ends, and an indifference to the needs of small farmers brought to power in 1881 a coalition of western Virginians, the Readjusters (a party calling for a scaling down of the state's debt), small farmers, Negroes, and Republicans, led by railroad magnate Gen. William Mahone. Once the debt had been readjusted downward, the coalition fell apart. Mahone's faction moved toward the Republican party. The Readjusters returned to the Conservative ranks and helped rejuvenate the Democratic party. The Democrats recaptured control of the governor's office and the

In St. John's Church in Richmond, the Virginia Convention heard Patrick Henry's eloquent call for freedom.

VIRGINIA CHAMBER OF COMMERCE, PHOTO BY FLOURNOY

VIRGINIA DEPARTMENT OF CONSERVATION AND ECONOMIC DEVELOPMENT

Stratford Hall, built in the 1720's, was the birthplace of Robert E. Lee, Confederate general in the Civil War.

General Assembly in 1885. The Democrats dominated state politics thereafter until 1969.

The economy gathered momentum in the late 19th century following railroad expansion, agricultural diversification, a revitalization of the tobacco industry, and the opening of southwestern coalfields. Nevertheless, Virginia lagged behind the nation in per capita income until World War I stimulated the economy. Prosperity continued until the Depression of the 1930's.

Depression and Wartime Virginia. During the 1920's political leadership passed to a Democratic party faction headed by Harry F. Byrd, Sr., who served as governor from 1926 to 1930. Governor Byrd reorganized the decentralized executive branch, inaugurated a program of highway expansion, and continued the social-welfare measures of Westmoreland Davis, governor from 1918 to 1922. Becoming a member of the U.S. Senate in 1933, Byrd continued to act as the state's political leader. Although Virginians generally disapproved of the New Deal, the expansion of federal agencies made government service the state's leading source of income after 1932. World War II stimulated the growth of Virginia even more than World War I had done.

Virginia Today. Massive resistance to the U.S. Supreme Court's desegregation decision of 1954 dominated state politics for a decade. Devised by Senator Byrd and pushed through the General Assembly by the Byrd organization, a powerful political coalition that controlled Virginia government for 30 years, a policy of "massive resistance" closed schools in several communities in 1958. Gov. Lindsay Almond and the assembly finally bowed to the federal courts and business pressure in 1959 and accepted limited integration. But it was not until late in the administration of Albertis Harrison (1962–1966) that Virginia politicians could address themselves to the needs of a rapidly growing state.

Electoral changes in the 1960's increased the representation and influence of the cities and broadened the electorate. In 1964 the poll tax in federal elections was eliminated by the 24th Amendment. In the same year the state legislature was reapportioned. The Civil Rights Voting Act of 1965 permitted federal examiners to register blacks under certain circumstances. And in 1966 the U.S. Supreme Court struck down Virginia's poll tax in state elections.

The Byrd organization itself underwent changes in 1966. In that year Byrd died and was succeeded by his less influential son, Harry F. Byrd, Jr. At the same time two major organization stalwarts, U.S. Sen. A. Willis Robertson and Rep. Howard W. Smith, were defeated by more liberal Democrats in the Democratic primaries. In this more progressive climate Democrat Mills E. Godwin, Jr., was elected governor. During his tenure (1966–1970), he guided the assembly toward a program of financial and educational reforms and improved social services.

The "Solid South" of the Democrats showed serious cracks in several Southern states, including Virginia, in the 1970's. In the case of Virginia, three successive gubernatorial elections were won by Republicans, and only in 1981 did the Democrats win back the governor's mansion. It seemed by that time that Virginia had been established as a two-party state.

D. ALAN WILLIAMS*
University of Virginia

Bibliography

Ashe, Dora J., ed., *Four Hundred Years of Virginia, 1584–1984: An Anthology* (Univ. Press of America 1985).
Beeman, Richard R., *The Old Dominion and the New Nation, 1788–1801* (Univ. Press of Ky. 1972).
Beverley, Robert, *History and Present State of Virginia* (Univ. Press of Va. 1969).
Dabney, Virginius, *Virginia: The New Dominion* (1971; reprint, Univ. Press of Va. 1983).
Federal Writers' Project, *Virginia: A Guide to the Old Dominion* (1940; reprint, Somerset 1980).
Gottman, Jean, *Virginia in Our Century* (Univ. Press of Va. 1969).
Heinemann, Ronald L., *Depression and New Deal in Virginia: The Enduring Dominion* (Univ. Press of Va. 1983).
Jefferson, Thomas, *Notes on the State of Virginia*, ed. by William Peden (Norton 1972).
Morgan, Edmund S., *American Slavery—American Freedom: The Ordeal of Colonial Virginia* (Norton 1975).
Morger, Allen, *Virginia Bourbonism to Byrd, 1870–1925* (Univ. Press of Va. 1968).
Morris, Shirley, *The Pelican Guide to Virginia* (Pelican 1981).
Randolph, Edmund, *History of Virginia*, ed. by Arthur H. Shaffer (Univ. Press of Va. 1970).
Rouse, Parke, Jr., *Virginia: The English Heritage in America* (Hastings 1976).
Tate, Thad W., and others, *Colonial Virginia: A History* (Kraus International Pubs. 1985).
Ward, Harry M., *Richmond: An Illustrated History* (Windsor Pub. 1985).

VIRGINIA is a city in northeastern Minnesota, in St. Louis county, 60 miles (97 km) north of Duluth. It primarily is a residential community, mainly supported by nearby iron-ore mining and processing operations in the Mesabi Range. Clothing and foundry products are made in Virginia. Virginia was founded as a village in 1892 and became a city in 1895. It has a mayor and council form of government. Population: 11,056.

VIRGINIA, University of, a state-controlled, coeducational institution of higher learning, located in Charlottesville, Va. It was chartered under the sponsorship of Thomas Jefferson in 1819 and opened to students in 1825. The university is governed by a rector and a 16-member board, known as the Visitors of The University of Virginia. Until 1904 it was administered by a faculty chairman. Since then it has been headed by a president. Enrollment in the university exceeds 20,000.

The university still bears the impress of Jefferson, its first rector. He planned the initial curriculum, laid out the campus, and designed the original buildings, including the Rotunda, an adaptation of the Pantheon in Rome, which has been declared a registered national historic landmark. Two other presidents of the United States played important roles in the university's early years. James Madison was the second rector, and James Monroe was a member of the first governing body.

Curriculums. The University of Virginia grants undergraduate and graduate degrees. Its components are the College of Arts and Sciences, the McIntire School of Architecture, the McIntire School of Commerce, the Curry Memorial School of Education, the School of Engineering and Applied Science, the School of Nursing, the School of Law, the School of Medicine, the Graduate School of Arts and Sciences, and the Graduate School of Business Administration.

Clinch Valley College, in Wise, Va., is a coeducational liberal arts college that is a branch campus of the university. It grants baccalaureate degrees in biology, business and public administration, education and psychology, English, history and sociology, humanities, mathematics, modern foreign languages, and the physical sciences. In addition, the university operates a school of general studies that provides undergraduate and graduate credit and noncredit extension courses at various locations throughout the state: Abingdon, Arlington, Charlottesville, Lynchburg, Madison, Norfolk, Richmond, and Roanoke. (Mary Washington College, founded in 1908, a state-aided, coeducational liberal arts college in Fredericksburg, was a part of the university system from 1944 until 1972, when it resumed independent status.)

Special Activities and Publications. The University of Virginia conducts a variety of special academic programs. In astronomy it operates the Leander McCormick Observatory, the Fan Mountain Observing Station, and the National Radio Astronomy Observatory. Related to the biological sciences are the Mountain Lake Biological Station, Seward Forest, and the Blandy Experimental Farm. The Thomas Jefferson Center for Studies in Political Economy sponsors visiting scholars and conducts lectures, seminars, and research in problems dealing with social policy. The Institute of Government conducts research with regard to Virginia state, county, and municipal governments. The Center of the Study of Science, Technology, and Public Policy, which functions through a grant by the National Science Foundation, conducts programs related to public policy on contemporary social problems. Journals published by the university include the *Virginia Quarterly Review, Military Law Review, Virginia Journal of International Law,* and *New Literary History.*

VIRGINIA AND KENTUCKY RESOLUTIONS, three resolutions protesting the adoption of the Alien and Sedition Acts during the administration of President John Adams. One resolution, passed by the Virginia legislature in 1798, was drawn up by James Madison. The others, passed by the Kentucky legislature in 1798 and 1799, were written by Vice President Thomas Jefferson, but his authorship was not known at the time.

The Jeffersonians viewed the Alien and Sedition Acts, which had been supported by the Federalists, as a threat to the freedom of speech guaranteed by the Constitution. The resolutions advocated repeal of the acts, but the issues were more far reaching. Madison and Jefferson held that the national government possessed only limited and delegated powers. Jefferson contended that the national government could not be the final judge of whether it had exceeded its authorized powers in particular cases and that the states, or perhaps even one of them, should judge. Madison was less precise, but in 1828 he argued that his resolution could not be considered a basis for John Calhoun's theories of state sovereignty and nullification.

All states were sent copies of the resolutions for comments, and some replied that the decision on the constitutionality of federal laws rested with the judiciary. Eventually, the Supreme Court assumed the responsibility.

VIRGINIA BEACH is an independent city in southeastern Virginia, on the Atlantic Ocean and Chesapeake Bay, centered about 15 miles (24 km) east of Norfolk. Primarily a tourist and resort center, it was incorporated as a town in 1906 and as a city in 1952. In 1963 all of Princess Anne county was merged with the city, giving it an area of 310 square miles (803 sq km), with 38 miles (61 km) of shoreline.

Within the city limits, a granite cross at Cape Henry marks the spot where the English colonists who founded Jamestown made their first landing in 1607. The first settlement within the city limits was made on Lynnhaven Bay in 1621. Virginia Beach has a manager and council form of government. Population: 262,199.

VIRGINIA CITY, a town in southeastern Montana, is near the site of a major gold discovery. It was the territorial capital from 1864 to 1876 and is now the seat of Madison county. The town, 90 miles (145 km) south of Helena, has been restored, as has nearby Nevada City.

Six prospectors discovered a rich vein of gold in Alder Gulch in 1863, and Virginia City soon had a population of 10,000. An outlaw gang, led by the sheriff, robbed and killed scores of miners. Nearly $300 million in gold was mined in the area during the boom. Many buildings have been restored or reconstructed. Points of interest include St. Paul's Episcopal Church, the Opera House, and Boot Hill. Population: 192.

VIRGINIA CITY, an unincorporated area in western Nevada, the seat of Storey county, is 22 miles (35 km) southeast of Reno. It was first settled as a mining camp on the eastern slope of Mt. Davidson in 1859, when the Comstock Lode was discovered. The resulting silver and gold rush was spectacular, and fantastic fortunes were made. Reckless speculation in San Francisco brought fortunes to men in no way connected with the actual mining. Virginia City enjoyed balls, grand opera, Broadway hits, and private entertainments in the mansions of "Millionaire's Row." Evening dress, formal servants, champagne, and splendid carriages flourished in the Nevada desert. The Virginia & Truckee Railroad, connecting with the Central Pacific at Reno, carried sleepers to and from San Francisco and was the richest short line on record. Mark Twain made his name as a reporter on the staff of *The Territorial Enterprise* when it was published in Virginia City in the 1860's.

When the price of silver fell, Virginia City's population rapidly dwindled from its all-time high of about 25,000 in 1876. Fires wiped out larges areas, and many frame buildings were transported to Los Angeles and Oakland. Virginia City, now advertised as the world's liveliest ghost town, has as many as 40,000 weekly visitors in a summer. There is no industry except tourism, which supports atmospheric saloons and a handful of Victorian lodging houses.

Virginia City was incorporated in 1865. It has a combined county and city form of government. Population: (Virginia Township) 1,459.

See also COMSTOCK LODE.

LUCIUS BEEBE
Author of "The Big Spenders"

VIRGINIA COMPANIES. See LONDON COMPANY; PLYMOUTH COMPANY.

VIRGINIA CONVENTIONS, five extralegal conventions that met at Williamsburg and Richmond between 1774 and 1776. Four of the conventions called for self-government and freedom for the American colonies as part of the British Empire, and the last called for independence.

First Convention. On May 26, 1774, the royal governor, Lord Dunmore, dissolved the Virginia Assembly at Williamsburg because the House of Burgesses had called for fasting and prayer out of sympathy for Boston, whose port had been closed after the Boston Tea Party. The next day, most of the burgesses met in Raleigh Tavern, where they denounced Parliament's action and called for a congress of all the colonies to meet annually to consider the united interests of America. Later, about 25 burgesses called for a convention to meet in Williamsburg on August 1.

Delegates were chosen from four boroughs and 56 of the 61 counties, at least 31 of which had adopted strong resolutions concerning Boston and British repression. The convention was much like the House of Burgesses, whose speaker, Peyton Randolph, was chosen president. The delegates repeated the call for a general congress and elected seven representatives. The convention also agreed not to import goods from England or to import or purchase slaves after Nov. 1, 1774, and to stop all exports to England by Aug. 10, 1775, unless American grievances were redressed. Thomas Jefferson's *A Summary View of the Rights of British America* was made known to the convention and, although not acted upon, had much influence later. The convention remained in session for six days.

Second Convention. On March 20–27, 1775, the second convention met in St. John's Church in Richmond, where it was free from the influence of the governor. Patrick Henry, who had led the fight for an aggressive program against the mother country, introduced resolutions designed to put the colony in a state of defense. Public sentiment was strongly favorable, and Henry's famous "liberty or death" speech crystallized it into approval of the resolutions. A committee was appointed to draw up a defense plan.

Third Convention. Meeting in Richmond on July 17, 1775, the third convention stated its reasons for coming together: the governor's arbitrary dissolutions of the assembly; his secret removal of powder from the magazine at Williamsburg and his escape to a British man-of-war at Yorktown; his threats to burn Norfolk; and his gathering of troops and ships against Virginia.

The convention began to act as the government of the colony, replacing the royal government and passing ordinances as laws rather than resolutions or recommèndations. For the third time, Randolph was made president. The 115 delegates created a committee of safety and elected Patrick Henry commander in chief of Virginia forces. The committee of safety, headed by Edmund Pendleton, was to execute ordinances of the convention, direct military forces, and remain in authority until the next convention. Revenue was provided and new representatives were elected to the Continental Congress. The convention adjourned on Aug. 26, 1775.

Fourth Convention. Organized at Richmond on Dec. 1, 1775, the convention moved to Williamsburg. Edmund Pendleton was chosen president. The convention increased the work and responsibility of the committee of safety so that it remained the real executive authority of Virginia until July 1776. Virginia was considered part of the "united colonies," and its troops were to serve under an officer commissioned by Congress. The convention adjourned on Jan. 20, 1776.

Fifth Convention. The last, and most important, convention met at Williamsburg on May 6, 1776, and was attended by 131 delegates, many of whom had been instructed to cast off the British yoke. James Madison and Edmund J. Randolph were prominent new members, and Pendleton was reelected president.

On May 15, 1776, the convention instructed its representatives in Congress to move "to declare the United Colonies free and independent states." Virginia was the first state to instruct its representatives to move for independence. On June 12 the convention adopted the Virginia Bill of Rights, prepared by George Mason, which influenced similar declarations in the other states, the Bill of Rights added to the U.S. Constitution in 1791, and the French Declaration of the Rights of Man in 1789. It has been retained in every Virginia constitution adopted since that time. On June 29 the convention unanimously approved Virginia's first constitution as a commonwealth, making Virginia the first state to adopt a new constitution. Under the new constitution, the convention chose Patrick Henry as the first governor. The convention adjourned on July 5, 1776, and reconvened in October as the first House of Delegates.

ALLEN MOGER
Washington and Lee University

GRANT HEILMAN
Virginia creeper, also called American ivy.

VIRGINIA CREEPER, a strong, high-climbing, woody vine, also called woodbine or American ivy. The Virginia creeper, *Parthenocissus quinquefolia,* is a native North American member of the grape family (Vitaceae). Its leaves are usually compound, commonly with five coarsely toothed leaflets, 2 to 5 inches (5–12 cm) long on stalks.

The plant climbs by means of tendrils, each of which has five to eight tiny branches ending in adhesive disks. The disks attach the plant firmly to stone walls, masonry, trees, and other objects. Many small, greenish white flowers appear in July. In the fall, small inedible bluish black berries appear, and the leaves turn a deep crimson and scarlet.

Also called Virginia creeper is *P. inserta,* whose tendrils do not have adhesive disks but attach the plant by twining about a support. Like *P. inserta* and *P. tricuspidata* (Boston ivy or Japanese ivy), Virginia creeper is widely used, because of its attractive foliage and its climbing habit, to cover unsightly external walls and other objects.

VIRGINIA MILITARY INSTITUTE, a state-supported institution of higher learning in Lexington, Va. Commonly known as V.M.I., it admits only men for the regular session (August to May), although women may attend during the summer. Chartered in 1839, it is the oldest state military college in the United States. It is governed by a board of visitors, including the state adjutant general, and is administered by a superintendent of military rank. Army or Air Force officer training is required of all regular students, most of whom receive military commissions upon graduation. The institute offers B. A. and B. S. degrees.

During the Civil War, nearly all of the students and alumni served with the Confederate forces. At the beginning of the war, the students, called cadets, were transferred to Richmond to instruct Confederate enlistees. However, the institute was reopened in 1862, and in 1864 the cadet corps fought as a unit at the Battle of New Market. The institute was burned that year by federal troops, but it resumed instruction in 1865.

VIRGINIA POLYTECHNIC INSTITUTE, a state-controlled, coeducational institution of higher learning in Blacksburg, Va. A land-grant college, it was founded as the Virginia Agricultural and Mechanical College in 1872. In 1885 its name was changed to the Virginia Agricultural and Mechanical College and Polytechnic Institute, and, in 1944, to the Virginia Polytechnic Institute. Its present official name, the Virginia Polytechnic Institute and State University, was adopted in 1970.

Popularly known as V.P.I., it is governed by a 14-member board of visitors and administered by a president. Enrollment totals approximately 19,000.

The institute is made up of seven colleges: arts and sciences, agriculture, architecture, business, engineering, home economics, and education, all of which offer undergraduate degrees. Through the Graduate School, a separate unit, each of the divisions also grant master's and doctor's degrees. Special programs and facilities include the Reynolds Homestead Research Center for agriculture, the Reston Program in Urban Studies, and the Experimental Inner College for human environmental problems. A quarterly, *Coptext,* is published at V.P.I.

VIRGINIA REEL. See REEL.

VIRGINIA RESOLUTIONS OF 1847, the state of Virginia's official rejection of the Wilmot Proviso. The Wilmot Proviso was an amendment to a presidential bill, moved in the U. S. House of Representatives on Aug. 8, 1846, to appropriate money for the acquisition of territory from Mexico, with which the United States was at war. The Wilmot Proviso stipulated that "as an express and fundamental condition to the acquisition of any territory . . . neither slavery nor involuntary servitude shall ever exist in any part of said territory. . . ." Eventually, in 1847, a bill shorn of the controversial amendment was passed, but the bitter debates in the House and the Senate had roused controversy in all sections of the country. Virginia's General Assembly was the first of the state legislatures to make a pronouncement against the proviso, and its resolutions served as models that were followed by other Southern states.

VIRGINIAN, The, a novel by the American writer Owen Wister, published in 1902. *The Virginian,* a tale of "a horseman of the plains," is a romance of the old American West, in the cattle country of Wyoming between 1874 and 1890. It was the time when a newcomer to the area was a "tenderfoot," when steers by the thousands pastured on the open range, when cattle thieves were hanged on the nearest cottonwood without benefit of a trial. Wister, an Easterner, was familiar with both the locale and the period, since he spent his summers in the West. From his experiences and observations he fashioned a number of stories and novels, of which *The Virginian* is the best known.

The plot revolves around the Virginian (as he is known throughout the book), a tall, handsome, rough-hewn cowboy who has settled on Judge Henry's Sunk Creek ranch, and Molly Wood, who has come from Vermont to teach at the new schoolhouse. At first the contrast between the backgrounds and breeding of the New England schoolmarm and the poker-playing, hard-drinking cowpuncher seems an insurmountable barrier between them, but soon she has him reading and enjoying Scott, Browning, Dickens, and even Shakespeare. The dramatic climax is reached in a pistol duel at sunset, in which the Virginian kills the cattle rustler Trampas, his sworn enemy. Molly and the Virginian are married, and he rises from foreman to partner in the Sunk Creek ranch.

Wister handled his material realistically, and created believable characters. *The Virginian* was immensely successful as a book, play, and motion picture. Popular with every generation since publication, the novel became the prototype of countless "Westerns." In the Virginian, Wister created the model cowboy-hero—the defender of law and order, who will not compromise his ideals, and the stalwart leader of men, who does not flinch in the face of danger and whose best friends are his horse and pistol.

VIRGINIANS, The, a novel by the English writer William Makepeace Thackeray, first published serially between 1857 and 1859. In a sense, *The Virginians: A Tale of the Last Century* might be considered a sequel to Thackeray's *Henry Esmond* (1852), since its major characters, the brothers George Esmond Warrington and Harry Esmond Warrington, are descendants of the hero of the earlier novel. But the later novel lacks cohesion with the earlier, and, by comparison, it fails to succeed in regard to structure.

The Virginians is set in colonial Virginia, where the aristocratic Esmond had emigrated, and in London, between the French and Indian War and the American Revolution. The plot, after a brilliant beginning, is diffused by amorous and familial complications that ultimately weaken its effectiveness. According to Gordon N. Ray, author of a major Thakeray biography, *The Virginians* is a rich book, if a chaotic one.

VIRGINIUS AFFAIR, vər-jin′ē-əs, a violent incident in the harbor of Santiago de Cuba in 1873 that almost caused a war between the United States and Spain. The *Virginius*, a ship registered in the New York customhouse as the property of an American citizen, was captured on the high seas near Jamaica by the Spanish man-of-war *Tornado* on Oct. 31, 1873. The Spanish charged, accurately enough, that the ship was about to land men and arms in Cuba, which was then engaged in the Ten Years' War against Spain. At the time of capture the *Virginius* was flying the American flag. The ship was taken to Santiago. President Ulysses S. Grant remonstrated with the Spanish government, and through the U. S. minister to Spain, Gen. Daniel E. Sickles, demanded the release of the *Virginius* and its crew.

While Spain, which was at that time a republic under President Emilio Castelar y Ripoll, asked for time to obtain information, the authorities in Cuba took matters into their own hands. On Nov. 7–8, 1873, the captain of the *Virginius*, Joseph Fry, and 52 crewmen and passengers were shot. President Grant ordered the Navy to be mobilized for war. President Castelar maintained that his orders had been received too late to prevent the execution.

It seemed that hostilities could not be prevented. On November 28, however, a protocol was signed between Secretary of State Hamilton Fish and the Spanish minister at Washington by which Spain agreed to surrender the survivors and the ship and to salute the flag of the United States. However, Secretary Fish later announced that he was satisfied that the ship had no right to fly the U. S. flag, and the salute was dispensed with. Spain paid indemnities to the United States as well as to Britain for the British subjects who were among the victims. But the Spanish officers responsible for the massacre were not punished.

VIRGIN'S BOWER. See CLEMATIS.

VIRGO, vûr′gō, is a large constellation between the constellations Leo and Libra. In the Northern Hemisphere, it reaches its highest position above the horizon late in May and is visible throughout the summer.

Spica, its brightest star, is a first-magnitude binary star about 220 light-years distant from earth. Next in brightness are three third-magnitude stars, including Gamma Virginis, a binary star about 32 light-years from earth. These four stars and others give Virgo a total of about 160

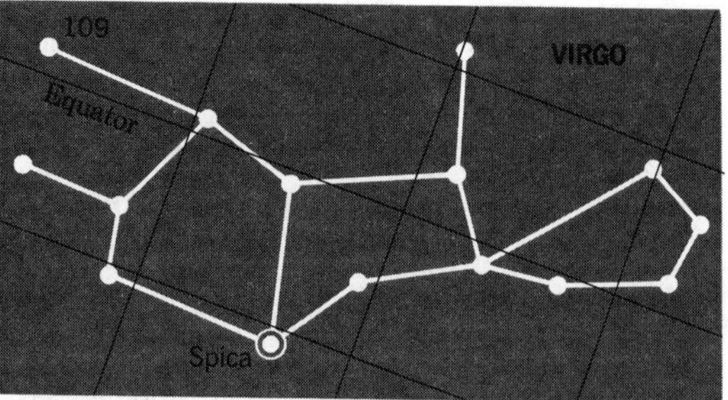

stars visible to the naked eye. Virgo also contains thousands of galaxies and clusters of galaxies.

Virgo's line pattern represents the figure of a virgin holding an ear of wheat. The constellation was known to ancient peoples and was listed in the *Almagest* of Ptolemy. In astrology, Virgo is the sixth sign of the zodiac. See also SPICA; ZODIAC.

VIRTANEN, vir′tä-nen, **Artturi Ilmari** (1895–1973), Finnish biochemist, who received the 1945 Nobel Prize in chemistry for his development of improved silage-making techniques. From the beginning of his career, Virtanen was interested in finding the practical applications of science.

After 1920 his attention was directed to the problem of fodder storage. Northern countries such as Finland had always been faced with the difficulty of providing food for cattle during winter. Virtanen showed that if fodder were kept sufficiently acid (pH 4) no serious spoilage occurred. The result was that the quality of dairy products could be sustained at summer levels using winter silage, and human nutrition was thereby improved.

Virtanen was born in Helsinki, Finland, on Jan. 15, 1895. He studied biochemistry at the University of Helsinki as well as at other European universities. He died in Helsinki on Nov. 11, 1973.

VIRTUAL IMAGE. See LENS.

VIRTUES, Cardinal. See CARDINAL VIRTUES.

VIRUS, vī'rəs, a very simple, noncellular parasite that can reproduce only inside living cells. The simple structure of viruses is their most distinctive characteristic. Most of them consist only of a genetic material—either DNA (deoxyribonucleic acid) or RNA (ribonucleic acid)—and a protein coat. Some also have membranous envelopes. But all lack the structures normally found in cells that are necessary for metabolism, growth, and reproduction.

Viruses are "alive" in that they can reproduce themselves—although only by taking over a cell's synthetic machinery—but they have none of the other characteristics of living organisms. While scientists once thought that viruses might be an evolutionary link between nonliving chemicals and living cells, they now think that viruses probably evolved from cells. This could happen if a small piece of cellular DNA were excised from a chromosome. If the excised DNA could replicate, it could then evolve independently of the parental chromosome. Such independently replicating pieces of DNA frequently occur in bacteria, where they are called plasmids. Those pieces of replicating DNA that evolved a mechanism for infecting additional cells would have an obvious survival advantage.

Viruses cause a large variety of significant diseases of plants and animals, including humans. In addition, they have provided a simple tool with which scientists can study DNA replication and protein synthesis, and thus have contributed to the solution of some of the most fundamental problems of genetics and molecular biology.

Size and Structure. Viruses are small—much smaller than the cells they infect. Roughly speaking, they range in size from 20 to 400 nanometers (nm) in diameter. (One nanometer is one billionth of a meter. About 25 million nanometers make up an inch.) For comparison, a small bacterium such as *Escherichia coli* has an average diameter of about 1,500 nm, and a typical plant

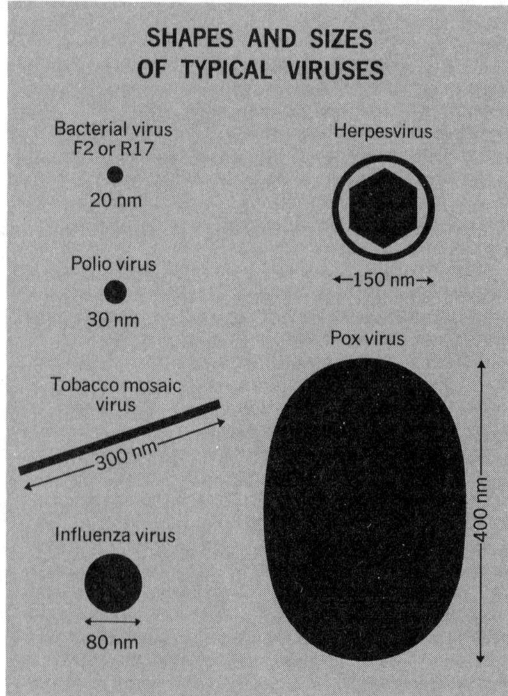

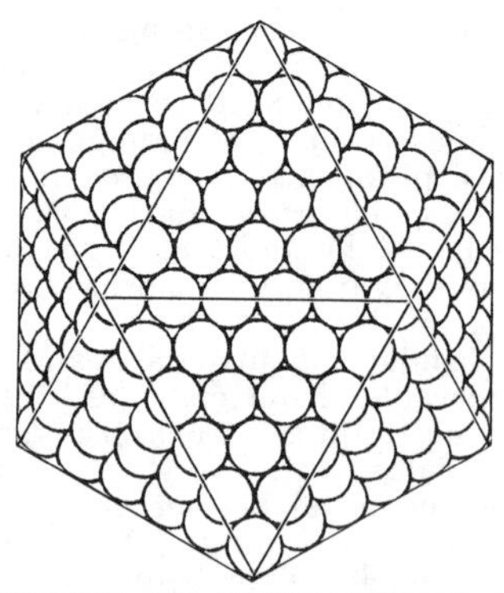

STRUCTURE OF ICOSAHEDRAL VIRUS

or animal cell has a diameter of about 10,000 nm. With a few exceptions, viruses are too small to be seen under the light microscope. Scientists knew they existed because extracts of infected tissues, which had been filtered to remove bacteria and cell debris, could infect other susceptible hosts. Viruses could not be seen, however, until after the invention in 1933 of the electron microscope, with its great magnifying power.

The two most common shapes of viruses are the icosahedron and the rod. An icosahedron is a regular polyhedron having 20 triangular faces, 12 corners, and 30 edges. In icosahedral viruses, the nucleic acid with its associated proteins forms an inner core. Surrounding the core is the capsid, or coat, which is composed of protein subunits called capsomeres. Together the core plus the capsid form the nucleocapsid. The nucleocapsid is the entire virus, except in the case of viruses that have envelopes. Icosahedral viruses appear to be roughly spherical in electron micrographs. The diameters of the capsids range from about 20 to 100 nm. Adenoviruses are typical icosahedral viruses.

The coat-protein subunits of the rod-shaped viruses are arranged in a helical pattern around the axis of the rod, with the nucleic acid sandwiched between them in adjacent turns of the helix. The capsomeres completely cover the nucleic acid. Tobacco mosaic virus is an example of a helical virus. The rod is 300 nm long and has a diameter of 18 nm.

Both icosahedral and helical viruses may have envelopes. The envelope contains lipids and polysaccharides in addition to proteins. It has a structure similar to that of the outer membrane of cells. In order to be enveloped, helical nucleocapsids must be flexible enough to fold into an irregular core within the envelope. Herpesviruses are enveloped icosahedral viruses, and myxoviruses are enveloped helical viruses.

Certain bacteriophages (viruses that infect bacteria) have a relatively complex structure. These are the "T-even" phages. They consist of a polyhedral head containing the DNA and of a tubular tail. A thin disk called the collar is located between the head and the tail. The tail has a hexagonal plate at its base, and a fiber is attached to each corner of the plate. The T-even phages are about 210 nm from head to tail.

Classification. Viruses are classified according to the type of organism that they infect: animals, plants, or bacteria.

Bacterial viruses, or phages, may contain either DNA or RNA. They were discovered, probably independently, by British bacteriologist F. W. Twort in 1915 and by the French microbiologist Félix d'Hérellel in 1917. Because multiplication of phage within a bacterium results in the *lysis,* or rupture, of the host cell, d'Hérelle thought that phages could be used to control bacterial diseases. He was wrong, but investigations of phages have contributed much of the fundamental knowledge of gene function and protein synthesis.

Virtually all plant viruses contain RNA as their genetic material. They have either helical or icosahedral structures. In 1899 the Dutch botanist M. W. Beijerinck proposed that the agent causing tobacco mosaic disease was a self-reproducing, subcellular form of life. In 1935 the American biochemist Wendell Stanley proved the unusual nature of the tobacco mosaic virus (TMV) when he crystallized it. At that time, crystallization was thought to be a property of inorganic molecules. Now it is known that organic substances, too, including purified virus, will crystallize if their molecules or particles can form orderly structural arrays.

No generalizations can be made about the structure of animal viruses. They may have either DNA or RNA for their genetic material. Some have envelopes, while others exist as naked nucleocapsids. They may be as simple in structure as is the polyoma virus, the DNA of which weighs about a billionth of a billionth of a gram and contains fewer than 10 genes, or they may be as complex as the poxviruses, which have almost 50 times as much DNA as the polyoma virus. Poxviruses are big enough to be seen with the light microscope.

REPRODUCTION

In order to reproduce, a virus must first enter a susceptible host cell. Once inside, the virus takes over the synthetic machinery that normally makes all cellular components and uses it to synthesize viral constituents and reproduce the virus in large numbers. Synthesis of cell constituents stops as a result of viral infection. Reproduction of many kinds of viruses results in the dissolution and death of the host cell. Such virus-caused dissolution is called *lysis,* and the virus is said to *lyse* the host cell.

The exact mechanism by which a virus reproduces depends on the type of nucleic acid it contains. All four possible types, double- or single-stranded DNA and double- or single-stranded RNA, have been found. The life cycles of phages have been most thoroughly studied and are the best understood. In general, the reproduction of animal and plant viruses parallels that of phages with the same type of nucleic acid.

Phages with DNA. The first step in the multiplication of any virus is adsorption—that is, attachment to the susceptible cell. Viruses usually attach to a specific, limited range of cell types. The specificity of attachment depends both on the viral coat (or envelope) and on the presence of receptors on the cell surface. The T-even phages attach to the bacterium *Escherichia coli* by means of the tail fibers. The virus then injects its double-stranded DNA through the tail into the bacterial cell. (See photograph on page 175.) The period following injection is the *eclipse,* during which infectious viruses cannot be recovered from disrupted bacteria. The virus coat remains outside the cell, and naked viral nucleic acid is only infectious under special circumstances.

Synthesis of viral components and enzymes completely replaces that of bacterial constituents in infected cells. The viral DNA replicates in the normal manner according to the principles of base-pairing suggested by James Watson and Francis Crick. Viral genes direct the synthesis of messenger RNA's and, ultimately, of viral coat proteins. For descriptions of the replication of DNA and RNA and of the synthesis of cell proteins, see GENE.

During maturation, the various components assemble spontaneously to form complete infectious virus particles. A hundred or more may form in each cell. The final step is the release of the newly synthesized viruses. This is accomplished by means of a viral enzyme, called lysozyme, that breaks down the bacterial cell wall. The viruses then escape from the bacterium into the surrounding medium, where they can infect additional cells, and the lysed bacterium dies.

A few simple phages, such as ΦX174, have a single-stranded DNA molecule for their genetic material. When ΦX174 infects a bacterium, the first step, once the DNA is inside the cell, is the synthesis of a DNA strand (the minus strand) complementary to the original parental (or plus) strand. The resultant double-stranded DNA replicates to form additional double-stranded progeny. Later in the ΦX174 life cycle, only plus strands are formed. These associate with capsid proteins to form virus particles.

A virus does not "grow" in the usual sense. Instead, the virus is "fully grown" as soon as its component parts have assembled themselves into the structure that is characteristic of that particular virus.

Phages with RNA. The RNA phages, including phages f_2 and $Q\beta$, have only enough RNA to code for three proteins. These are the coat protein, an attachment protein needed for adsorption of the virus to the host bacteria, and an enzyme called RNA synthetase or replicase. A replicase, which transcribes viral RNA to form RNA strands complementary to it, is necessary for replication of all RNA viruses. The viral RNA serves both as a messenger for the synthesis of viral proteins and as a template on which the replicase synthesizes a complementary minus strand. The minus strand in turn serves as a template for the synthesis of additional plus RNA strands. These plus strands have three options: they can serve as templates for the synthesis of minus strands; they can act as messengers for the synthesis of more viral proteins; or they can be incorporated into intact virus particles. As many as 10,000 RNA virus particles may form in a single cell.

Animal Viruses. Although the reproduction of animal viruses resembles that of the corresponding types of bacteriophages, some differences exist. The complete naked virus—not just the nucleic acid—usually enters the host cell. In the case of enveloped viruses, the envelope first fuses with the cell membrane, after which the nucleocapsid is released into the cell. Uncoating of the viral nucleic acid inside the cell is carried out by cellular enzymes that digest the capsid proteins.

The DNA of most DNA viruses replicates in the nucleus of the infected cell. (Replication of animal viruses differs in this respect from replication of phages in bacteria, because bacteria do not have nuclei.) The messenger RNA of these viruses is also synthesized in the nucleus but it then migrates to the cytoplasm where protein synthesis occurs. The proteins must be transported back into the nucleus since assembly of the nucleocapsids takes place there. The assembly of the nucleocapsids of animal viruses is spontaneous and resembles that of the phages. The DNA-containing poxviruses reproduce entirely in the cytoplasm, as do viruses with RNA.

Naked viruses may be released by lysis of the cell or by the formation and subsequent rupture of virus-containing vacuoles at the cell surface. The release of enveloped viruses is more complicated. After viral proteins are incorporated into the cell membrane, the nucleocapsid adheres to its inner surface and causes the membrane to bud outward. Eventually the membrane completely surrounds the nucleocapsid and the completed enveloped virus pinches off from the cell. The lipids and polysaccharides of the envelope are derived from the host-cell membrane.

Plant Viruses. Much less is known about the reproduction of plant viruses than about that of animal and bacterial viruses. This is due mainly to the previous lack of plant cell cultures in which the virus could be grown in a synchronized manner—that is, with all the particles in the same phase of the reproductive cycle. Such synchronization is required for studying the details of virus reproduction. Suitable cultures have recently become available, however.

It appears that plant viruses reproduce in a manner similar to that of other RNA viruses. One difference is that some, probably including TMV, may replicate their RNA in the nucleus. The cellulose cell walls of plants constitute something of a barrier to viral infection, which requires wounding of the plant cell. This is most often done by insect carriers of viruses, but man and his machinery may also spread viral infections. Transmission between cells of a plant is through plasmodesmata, links of cytoplasm that extend through the cell wall and connect cells.

LYSOGENY

Viruses that always lyse cells are called *virulent* viruses. *Temperate* viruses, however, do not always kill their host cells. Infection of a susceptible bacterial strain by a temperate phage produces either of two results. In some cases the virus multiplies and causes lysis of the cell. In other cases, involving only DNA viruses, the phage establishes a *lysogenic* relationship with the cell. In 1950 the French microbiologist André Lwoff showed that in lysogeny the virus is maintained in the bacterial cell in a stable, heritable, but noninfectious form called the *prophage,* which does not reproduce in the lysogenized cell.

One of the best-studied lysogenic relationships is that between phage lambda and strain K12 of the bacterium *E. coli.* The structure of phage lambda somewhat resembles that of the T-even phages, but it has much less DNA for its genetic material. Once this phage establishes a lysogenic relationship with a bacterial cell, that bacterium cannot be infected by additional viruses of the same type. The cell is said to be "immune" to infection. (This "immunity" has no relation to the immune system of higher animals.) Both immunity and the lack of reproduction by the phage are caused by the presence of a repressor protein that prevents transcription of the viral genes needed for reproduction. The repressor is specified by a lambda phage gene. The French molecular biologist François Jacob concluded that when a temperate phage enters a suitable bacterial cell, a race occurs between the synthesis of the gene products needed for reproduction and the synthesis of the immunity repressor. The outcome of the race determines whether the cell will be lysed (destroyed) or will be lysogenized and survive.

When lysogenization occurs, the viral prophage is inserted into the bacterial chromosome, usually at a fixed site. Its replication is controlled by bacterial genes so that it replicates only when the bacterial chromosome does. Occasionally the integrated prophage is spontaneously excised, and the virus then reproduces normally and lyses the cell. A number of treatments, including irradiation with ultraviolet light, certain chemicals, and carcinogens, can greatly increase the frequency of excision.

TRANSDUCTION

Viruses sometimes carry bacterial DNA from a donor bacterium to a recipient. The American geneticists Joshua Lederberg and Norton Zinder, who discovered this phenomenon in 1951, called it *transduction. Restricted,* or *specialized, transduction* is the transfer of a limited number of specific genes by a lysogenic phage. Specialized transduction requires excision of the virus from the chromosome of the donor bacterium. During excision, neighboring bacterial genes are removed together with viral DNA. Thus only those bacterial genes near the site of the prophage in the donor's chromosome are transferred to the recipient bacterium.

In *general transduction,* any portion of the bacterial chromosome may be transferred to a recipient. It is caused by encapsulation of bacterial DNA into the phage coat. The transducing phage preparation can be obtained either from lysogenic bacteria or from a lysing viral infection. Many such transductants carry no phage genes. They are still infectious, because infectivity is a property of the coat. Only a small fraction of the bacterial chromosome can be transferred, however, because the bacterial chromosome is much larger than the normal viral chromosome. Thus only genes close together on the donor bacterial chromosome can be transduced to a recipient bacterium.

This property of general transduction gave investigators a tool for constructing detailed maps of bacterial chromosomes. For example, the American microbiologists Charles Yanofsky and E. Lennox used general transduction to map the region of the *E. coli* chromosome containing the genes required for synthesis of the amino acid tryptophan. Yanofsky later prepared an even more detailed map of one of these genes. This map served as the basis for Yanofsky's proof in 1966 of a tenet of molecular biology that had long been assumed—namely, that the amino acids that make up a protein molecule are joined together in exactly the same sequence as are the corresponding codons (a codon is a sequence of three nucleotides that specifies or codes for a particular amino acid).

CULTIVATION

Because viruses are obligate intracellular parasites, they must be grown in living cells. Virus preparations are needed in large quantities for the manufacture of vaccines against viral diseases and in smaller quantities for scientific in-

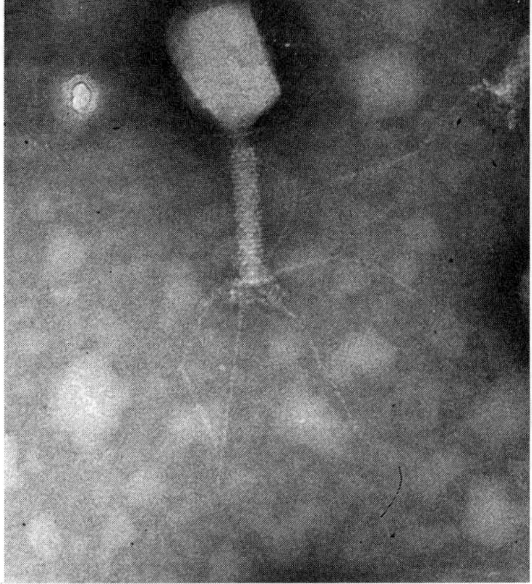

DR. THOMAS F. ANDERSON, THE INSTITUTE FOR CANCER RESEARCH

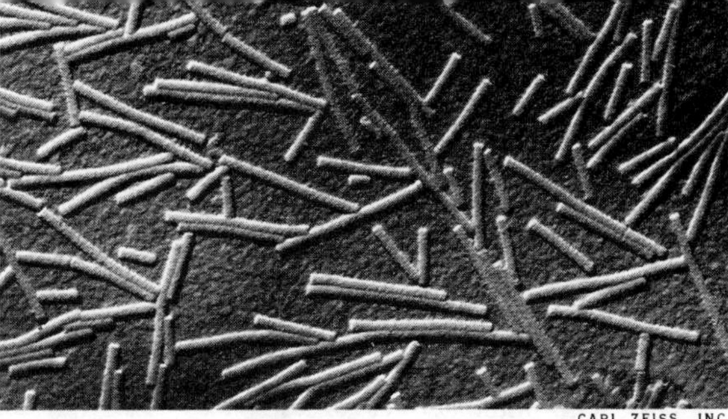

CARL ZEISS, INC.

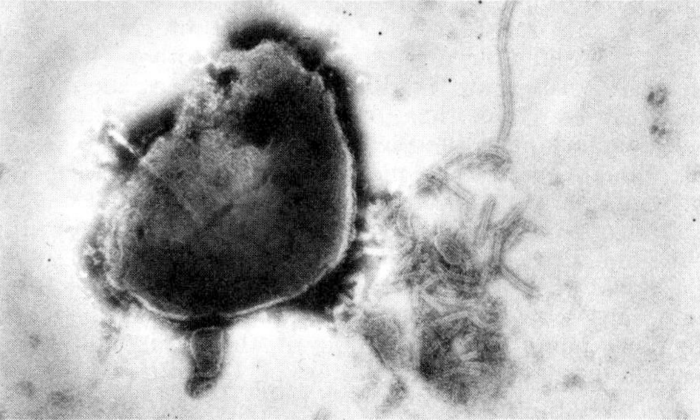

DR. F. A. MURPHY, CENTER FOR DISEASE CONTROL, ATLANTA, GA.

Three types of viruses: (*Top right*) Rod-shaped viruses cause the tobacco mosaic plant disease. (*Bottom right*) Filaments of viral particles emerge from a mumps virus. (*Above*) Bacteriophage T4 has a "head" containing DNA, a tail, and tail fibrils for attaching itself to a bacterium.

vestigations. Finding suitable cells for growing a virus is sometimes a major problem. For example, research on polio was greatly hindered until 1939 when the American microbiologists John Enders, Thomas Weller, and Frederick Robbins discovered that poliovirus could reproduce in cultures of certain human or monkey tissues.

Cells that tend to become cancerous are considered unsuitable for growing viruses for vaccines that will be injected into humans. Cultures of normal cells may be used for this purpose. Another alternative is the use of fertile chicken or duck eggs. The rabies virus, for example, is now grown in duck eggs. Until recently, this virus had to be cultivated in nerve tissue—the normal site of viral multiplication—and the vaccines contained some of the nerve tissue, which often caused dangerous allergic reactions. With the newer vaccines, immunization against rabies has become less hazardous.

VIRUSES AND HUMAN DISEASES

Viruses cause a number of infectious diseases in humans, ranging in seriousness from the merely uncomfortable common cold to severe, often fatal, diseases such as smallpox, yellow fever, and rabies. Rubella (German measles) virus is a major cause of fetal death and birth defects. In addition to these acute, infectious diseases known to be caused by viruses, there is growing evidence that viruses may be involved wholly, or at least partially, in several chronic degenerative conditions. Among them are cancer, diabetes, multiple sclerosis, rheumatoid arthritis, systemic lupus erythematosus, and certain degenerative diseases of the central nervous system.

Most pathological symptoms of viral disease are the result of cell death or damage due to reproduction of the viruses in the cell. Viral diseases may be localized, disseminated, or inapparent. In *localized* infections such as the common cold, the virus multiplies in, and damages cells near, the site of entry. In *disseminated* viral diseases, an initial round of reproduction occurs near the site of entry, but the virus then spreads through the blood to additional organs, where further damage occurs. *Inapparent* infections may cause no noticeable symptoms but are important means of spreading virus diseases.

Adenoviruses. Adenoviruses are naked icosahedral viruses containing double-stranded DNA. They multiply in the nuclei of susceptible cells. Adenoviruses cause respiratory infections similar to flu, and some eye inflammations. They are not the major viral cause of respiratory infections, however. That distinction belongs to the influenza viruses and rhinoviruses.

Herpesviruses. Herpesviruses are large enveloped viruses that have double-stranded DNA as their genetic material. They replicate in the nucleus and kill the cells that they infect. The herpesviruses are widely disseminated in the human population.

The herpes simplex viruses, HSV I and HSV II, cause lesions around the mouth (cold sores) and eyes, and around the genital area. Among adults, HSV infections are uncomfortable rather than life threatening. Among newborn infants, however, HSV infections may be fatal in up to 70% of those infected. A woman with a genital herpes infection may transmit the virus to her child at birth. One of the most striking characteristics of HSV I and II is their capacity to persist in a latent, asymptomatic state and then flare up to cause recurrent lesions, especially during physical or emotional stress.

Another herpesvirus that shares this characteristic is the varicella, or herpes zoster, virus. In individuals—usually children—who have not been previously exposed to the virus, it causes chicken pox. Shingles is a recurrent form of the disease afflicting adults who have previously had chicken pox. The disease involves an inflammation of the ganglia (clusters of nerve-cell bodies), where the virus is apparently maintained in a latent state between outbreaks.

The Epstein-Barr virus (EBV), another herpesvirus, is the probable cause of infectious mononucleosis, sometimes called the "kissing disease." When infection with EBV occurs early in life, it causes no characteristic symptoms. If the first infection occurs in adolescence or later, mononucleosis apparently results. The symptoms of mononucleosis resemble those of leukemia, a cancer of the lymphoid system, although mononucleosis is a relatively mild, nonfatal disease. EBV has been associated with Burkitt's lymphoma, a lymphoid cancer that afflicts children in certain areas of Africa.

Poxviruses. Poxviruses are the largest and most complicated of the animal viruses. They consist of a central nucleoid that contains the DNA. The nucleoid is surrounded by two membranous envelopes. The outer surface of the virus is covered by tubular or threadlike structures. Poxviruses are resistant to common disinfectants, heat, cold, and drying, although most other enveloped viruses are readily inactivated by such treatments. The variola, or smallpox, virus is the most important of the poxviruses.

Picornaviruses. The picornaviruses are a class of small, nonenveloped viruses that contain single-stranded RNA. They include the poliovirus and the rhinoviruses.

Poliovirus, a widespread virus, only occasionally causes severe disease in humans. Most infections begin with ingestion of the virus and its multiplication in the lining of the digestive tract. From there it is carried by the blood to the lymph nodes. In most individuals the disease proceeds no further. In about 1% to 2% of all cases, however, the virus builds up a persistent population in the blood and spreads to the central nervous system. Damage here can produce permanent paralysis or death. Vaccines have virtually eliminated the paralytic form of the disease.

Rhinoviruses cause many of the upper respiratory infections known collectively as the common cold. At least 89 distinct, but related, rhinoviruses have been identified. They have no group-specific antigen (one found in all members of a group). This practically rules out development of a vaccine to prevent what may be mankind's most common affliction, since the vaccine would have to contain all of the cold-causing viruses.

Myxoviruses. The influenza viruses are myxoviruses. These are enveloped viruses containing single-stranded RNA that is in five or six pieces. The influenza viruses are an additional major cause of upper respiratory infections. Although influenza itself rarely causes death, bacterial pneumonia may follow the viral infection and prove fatal. The old, the young, and the chronically ill are the most frequent victims of this secondary pneumonia.

The influenza viruses are classified into three distinct types—A, B, and C—depending on the kind of antigen they have. Types A and B cause the periodic influenza epidemics that may sweep the globe. Each major type may be further divided into subtypes. These subtypes may be sufficiently different so that immunity to one does not confer protection against others. Moreover, new subtypes arise occasionally as a result of antigenic shifts. The major antigenic shifts are thought to result from an interchange of genetic material between two different subtypes that have infected the same cell. This interchange is made possible by the fact that the RNA of influenza viruses is in several pieces.

Vaccines of moderate effectiveness can be prepared from killed influenza viruses, but control of the disease is complicated by the antigenic shifts. Vaccines against the parent subtypes are usually ineffective against the newly formed subtype.

Paramyxoviruses. Once classified with the myxoviruses, the paramyxoviruses are now recognized as different enough to warrant a category of their own. The paramyxoviruses are enveloped viruses with single-stranded RNA, but their RNA is in one piece. This group of viruses includes the parainfluenza viruses, which also cause upper respiratory infections, and the mumps and measles viruses. Measles virus has also been identified as a possible cause of subacute sclerosing panencephalitis, one of the slow virus diseases. Measles vaccines have been prepared from both attenuated live virus and inactivated virus.

Rhabdoviruses. These large, bullet-shaped viruses have a single-stranded RNA and an envelope. A rhabdovirus causes rabies, one of the most feared diseases of humans. Rabies, which can infect all mammals, is usually transmitted to humans by the bite of an infected animal.

The virus spreads from the point of entry by migrating along the nerves to the brain, where it multiplies and causes encephalitis. Because rabies has a long incubation period—up to a year—immunization following exposure is effective.

Togaviruses. Togaviruses are enveloped viruses with single-stranded RNA. They are carried and transmitted to humans by arthropod vectors, usually insects. A togavirus is the cause of yellow fever, a serious disease affecting the internal organs, especially the liver and kidneys. Walter Reed demonstrated in 1900 that yellow fever is transmitted by mosquitoes.

The togaviruses cause several kinds of encephalitis. Among these are three forms of equine encephalitis—western, Venezuelan, and eastern—all of which can be transmitted to humans. The first two diseases are relatively mild in man, but eastern equine encephalitis is often fatal and may result in severe neurological damage.

Rubella or German measles—not to be confused with rubeola, or measles—is probably caused by a togavirus. The course of German measles resembles that of measles, but rubella is usually milder and may be inapparent. Rubella is dangerous because of the damage it causes in fetuses during the first three months of gestation. Thus prevention of infection of pregnant women is of great importance. This can be accomplished by vaccination with attenuated virus of susceptible persons, especially young children, who are the principal carriers of rubella.

Viruses and Cancer. It has been established that viruses cause certain animal cancers. In the case of human cancers the evidence is less conclusive, but the involvement of both DNA and RNA viruses is suspected. The evidence for involvement of DNA viruses is largely indirect, and includes data drawn from several different kinds of studies. Epidemiological studies are done to determine whether people who have been infected with a virus are more or less likely than those not infected to develop a particular cancer. They are often done in conjunction with immunological studies that determine whether a suspect virus has left traces of its presence in the form of antibodies against it in the patient's blood. Examination of tumor cells may detect the presence of viral DNA or RNA or of virus-associated antigens. The pathological changes associated with a human cancer are compared with those of an animal cancer caused by a virus in a search for similarities that might suggest similar causation. And study of the cancer-causing potential of a virus in both cultured cells and in living animals—especially nonhuman primates—may tend to incriminate the virus as a cause of human cancer.

Thus far the evidence suggests—but does not prove—that three herpesviruses contribute to the development of certain cancers. The Epstein-Barr virus has been associated with Burkitt's lymphoma. Herpes simplex viruses I and II have been associated with carcinomas of the head and neck and of the urogenital regions, respectively.

Two groups of investigators in the United States have isolated RNA viruses from human cancer patients. One group, led by the virologist Marvin Rich, has isolated one from a line of cultured cells derived from a breast carcinoma. The other group, led by the cell biologist Robert Gallo, has isolated a different type of virus from a leukemia patient.

Malignant transformation of a cell is permanent and inheritable. That is, when the transformed cell divides, the daughter cells are also cancerous. This implies that the information specifying the cancerous transformation is somehow incorporated into the cell's genetic material. This is easy to explain for DNA viruses. Lysogeny provides a model for such incorporation of viral DNA into cellular DNA. It was more difficult to explain for RNA viruses, several of which are known to cause tumors in animals, until the American virologists Howard Temin and David Baltimore independently, in 1970, discovered an enzyme called reverse transcriptase or RNA-dependent DNA polymerase in certain animal tumor viruses. This enzyme transcribes RNA into DNA, which might then be incorporated into cellular DNA. The enzyme is also found in the RNA viruses discovered by Rich and Gallo.

Three points must be made about the evidence implicating viruses as causes of human cancer. First, a virus found in cancer cells does not necessarily prove that it caused a cancerous transformation. Second, there is little or no evidence that cancer is contagious. And third, it is possible that a virus by itself does not cause cancer but that additional factors, such as chemical carcinogens or radiation, must also participate in the process.

The Slow Virus Diseases. The slow virus diseases are a group of degenerative diseases characterized by a long incubation period. They usually follow a protracted course that ends in death. Many affect the brain.

Some slow viral infections appear to be caused by conventional viruses. These include two neurological diseases, subacute sclerosing panencephalitis (SSPE) and progressive multifocal leukoencephalopathy (PML). Measles virus has been associated with SSPE. This disease occasionally develops in children and adolescents several years after they have had a typical measles infection. Measles virus has been isolated from the brains and lymph nodes of such patients. Individuals with defective immune systems may develop PML, another rare neurological disease. A DNA virus of the papovavirus type has been isolated from the brains of PML patients. Although SSPE and PML are quite rare, there is some evidence that two common diseases—multiple sclerosis and diabetes—are caused by slow viruses.

Other slow virus diseases are caused by unconventional agents that have properties unlike those of typical viruses. The unconventional agents have never been observed with the electron microscope and do not elicit an immune response, as do true viruses. It is even doubtful whether they contain nucleic acids. It is possible, however, to transmit the unconventional slow viral diseases to experimental animals with cell- and bacteria-free extracts of infected brains. Two similar neurological diseases of the human, Kuru and Jacob-Creutzfeld disease, are caused by unconventional agents. The discovery that these rare degenerative diseases are caused by transmissible agents raises the possibility that other chronic degenerative diseases of the nervous system are similarly caused.

DEFENSES AGAINST VIRAL DISEASE

Viruses are antigenic. They are able to elicit a response from the immune system of an infected host. This ability is the basis for vaccination, in which a killed or an attenuated live virus is used to evoke an immune response without producing severe disease symptoms. Since the immune system has a "memory," the immunized host will be able to fight off subsequent natural infections.

Both the humoral and cellular branches of the immune system are involved in providing protection against, and recovery from, viral infections. Humoral immunity depends on the production of antibodies. When viruses invade the body, they stimulate the production of antibodies that are specific for each kind of virus. However, if the viruses are closely related and have common antigens (vaccinia and variola viruses, for example), antibodies to one may also work against the other. After the antibodies are formed, they complex (unite) with the virus and prevent it from infecting cells. The complexed virus can still adsorb to the cells. The block against infection appears to be in the uncoating step following penetration.

Although antibodies provide the main immune protection against viral infection, cellular immunity plays a role, especially in recovery from the disease. Cellular immunity is provided by direct attacks of "killer" cells on viruses and virus-infected cells. During the reproduction of many viruses, viral components are incorporated into the cell membrane. These components are recognized as foreign by the immune system, and the cells carrying them are destroyed by the killer cells. This cell destruction limits the reproduction and spread of viruses, but it also produces inflammation and other pathological symptoms.

In fact, the immune system may be a major contributor to the destructive effect of viral diseases. A classic example is lymphocytic choriomeningitis (LCM) in mice. The LCM virus forms complexes with the antibodies against it. When the complexes become trapped in small blood vessels of the kidney, they cause a kidney inflammation called glomerulonephritis that usually results in death. When killer immune cells attack virus-infected brain cells, the neurological symptoms of LCM result. Many investigators think that such reactions between viruses and the immune system may be involved in the human autoimmune diseases, including rheumatoid arthritis and systemic lupus erythematosus.

Interferon. The production of interferon is another defense against viral infection. Interferon is a protein produced by a virus-infected cell that inhibits virus reproduction. Interferon is species-specific but not virus-specific—that is, human interferon is effective against many kinds of viruses.

Although interferon production is induced by viruses, its synthesis and action depend on the expression of three cellular genes. One specifies the interferon itself and is turned on to begin production of interferon by the presence of the virus. The interferon then turns on the other two genes in the cell where it was formed and in other cells to which it may diffuse. One gene directs the synthesis of a protein that prevents viral multiplication. The other, however, produces a repressor of interferon production. This means, therefore, that interferon synthesis is self-limiting.

Much interest has developed in the clinical use of interferon to combat viral infections. But this has been on a limited experimental scale because isolation of interferon for therapeutic use is impractical. Cells produce only minute quantities of the protein. Certain synthetic double-stranded RNA's can induce interferon production in animal cells, but the toxicity of these materials limits their use for inhibiting infection in humans.

Chemotherapeutic Agents. A number of chemical agents inhibit viral reproduction. They include adamantanamine, carboxypeptides, isatin-β-thiosemicarbazone, halogenated derivatives of deoxyuridine, arabinosyl cytosine, and the antibiotic rifamycin. But their use in humans is limited by their toxicity. Since viruses must take over cellular machinery in order to multiply, drugs that inhibit viral reproduction frequently do it by inhibiting reactions necessary for cellular functions. Another phenomenon that may limit the application of these therapeutic agents is their capacity to cause the development of virus strains that are resistant to the effects of the drugs. However, some drugs are used for combating external, local viral infections.

JEAN L. MARX
Research News Staff of "Science"

Bibliography

Andrewes, Sir Christopher, *Natural History of Viruses* (Norton 1967).
Brooks, Stewart M., *World of the Viruses* (Barnes, A. S. 1970).
Davis, Bernard D., *Microbiology,* 3d ed. (Lippincott 1980).
Stent, Gunther S., and Calendar, Richard, *Molecular Genetics: An Introductory Narrative,* 2d ed. (W. H. Freeman 1978).
Watson, J. D., and others, *Molecular Biology of the Gene,* ed by J. Roberts and others (Benjamin/Cummings 1986).

VIRUS PNEUMONIA. See PNEUMONIA.

VISA, vē′zə, or **VISÉ,** vē-zā′, an official indorsement, usually of a passport, indicating examination and authenticity. Customarily, consular offices issue visas. A visa is affixed in the country issuing the passport by an official of the country to be visited; it grants permission for entry, although it does not necessarily guarantee admission. The type secured depends upon the regulations of the country and the length of the expected visit. Visas of short term are called transit, tourist, or passport visas; those of longer duration are visitors' visas. Persons intending permanent residence must obtain an immigration visa after proving eligibility. Visas are not needed to enter many countries, especially by tourists. See also PASSPORT.

ALAN MATHESON

VISAKHAPATNAM, vi-sä-kə-put′nəm, is a city in India, on the Bay of Bengal, roughly midway between Calcutta and Madras. It is the chief port between those cities. The inner harbor was opened to ocean vessels in 1933, and since India became independent in 1947 the port has been developed as the country's major shipbuilding center. Special loading quays have been built to handle manganese ore, which is the principal export.

The suburb of Waltair, a seaside resort, lies 2 miles (3 km) to the north. Waltair is the site of Andhra University.

Visakhapatnam (also Vishakhapatnam, and formerly Vizagapatam) is the capital of the district of the same name in Andhra Pradesh. Population: (1981) 594,259.

VISALIA, və-sāl′yə, a city in central California, is the seat of Tulare county. Located in the San Joaquin Valley on the fertile delta of the Kaweah River, it is 42 miles (67 km) southeast of Fresno. Economically, the community is both agricultural and industrial. The chief agricultural products are citrus fruits, grapes, and cotton. The College of the Sequoias, a public junior college, is here. Nearby Mooney Grove, a county park, contains a historical museum.

Visalia was incorporated in 1874 and since 1923 has been governed by a manager and council. Population: 49,729.

VISAYAN ISLANDS, vē-sä′yən, or **BISAYAS,** bē-sä′yəz, the central and largest group of the Philippine Archipelago, lying south of Luzon and north of Mindanao between latitude 9°5′ and 13° N., and between longitude 121°49′ and 125°51′E. Their land area is 23,535 square miles distributed over a total area of 77,840 square miles. The group, which encompasses the Visayan Sea, comprises 490 islands, including Bohol, Cebu, Leyte, Masbate, Negros, Panay, Romblon, and Samar and their dependent islands. The most important of the dependent islands are: Lapinin, Grande, and Panglao, belonging to Bohol; Mactan, belonging to Cebu; Biliran and Panain, belonging to Leyte; and Guimaras, belonging to Panay. The islands are inhabited primarily by Visayans, a Malay people speaking the Visayan language and forming the largest ethnological group in the Philippines.

VISBY, viz′bi, town, Sweden, capital of the County of Gotland, located on the island of Gotland in the Baltic Sea, about 120 miles southeast of Stockholm. Accessible by rail, ship, and the Scandinavian Airlines System, Visby (or Wisby) is a tourist center, resort, and seaport, ice-free the year round. Its industries include sugar refining and lumber milling.

Of ancient origin, Visby retains much of its appearance of the medieval period, during which it enjoyed great prosperity, coined its own money, and formulated a widely used code of sea laws. In the 12th century, it was the headquarters of the Hanseatic League. The town hall, which has 42 massive towers, and the Cathedral of St. Mary, which is still in use, are from the 13th century. The town declined at the end of the 13th century and did not recover until the end of the 19th century. The Gotland Museum houses an excellent collection of medieval art. Population: (1984) 20,442.

See also GOTLAND.

VISCHER, fish′er, **Friedrich Theodor** (1807–1887), German writer. He was born in Ludwigsburg, Germany, on June 30, 1807. After becoming a vicar, he returned to the University of Tübingen, where he earned his doctorate (1832) and became a lecturer (1836) and professor (1837). He was suspended from 1844 to 1846 for his liberal views and in 1848 was a member of the Frankfurt Parliament. In 1855, he received a professorship at Zürich, but in 1866 he accepted the position at Tübingen again and at Stuttgart, lecturing only at the latter from 1869. He died in Gmunden, Austria, on Sept. 14, 1887.

In his *Ästhetik, oder Wissenschaft des Schönen* (3 vols., 1846–1857), Vischer applied Georg W. F. Hegel's system to aesthetics. Later rejecting Hegel, he unsuccessfully tried to revise it. *Auch Einer* (2 vols., 1879), a novel, was his most popular work, humorously describing an idealist's struggle with life. *Faust, Der Tragödie dritter Teil* (1862), a comedy in the manner of Aristophanes published under the pseudonym Deutebold Symbolizetti Allegorowitsch Mystifizinski, assails philologists and idolizers of Johann von Goethe. Vischer's other works include *Über das Erhabene und Komische* (1837; On the Sublime and the Comic); and *Kritische Gänge* (2 vols., 1846; new series, 6 vols., 1860–1873).

F. E. Coenen
Formerly, University of North Carolina

VISCHER, fish′ər, **Peter** (c.1460–1529), the most distinguished member of a family of German sculptors and bronzesmiths whose works mark the transition from the Gothic to the Renaissance styles in Germany.

Peter Vischer the Elder, as he is known, was born in Nuremberg, the son of Hermann Vischer the Elder (died 1488), who established the family foundry. Peter's most celebrated work is the reliquary shrine of Saint Sebald in St. Sebald's Church, Nuremberg. He first submitted a model (now in Vienna) for the shrine in 1488, but it was never executed. Between 1507 and 1519 he and his sons worked on a new design of this masterpiece, a Gothic canopy carried by six pillars on a base supporting the 14th century sarcophagus of the saint. Though the conception is Gothic, many of the details are Renaissance. The shrine has statues of the 12 apostles, 12 prophets, and 72 lesser figures, including a portrait of Vischer in his workman's apron.

Vischer's other notable works include the monument to Count Otto IV of Henneberg (Römhild), the monument to Bishop Georg II (Bamberg Cathedral), the tomb of Archbishop Ernst of Saxony (1495; Magdeburg Cathedral), and the tomb of Bishop John IV (1496; Breslau Cathedral). The monuments to Count Eitel Friedrich II of Hohenzollern (parish church, Hechingen) and Count Hermann III of Henneburg (Römhild) are after designs by Albrecht Dürer. Peter the Elder died in Nuremberg on Jan. 7, 1529.

Four of Vischer's sons worked in the family foundry: Peter the Younger (1487–1528), Hans (1489–1550), Hermann the Younger (1486?–1517), and Paul or Paulus (died 1531). Peter the Younger traveled to northern Italy and is credited by some critics with introducing Renaissance elements into the family's works. In 1513 he worked with his father on the figures of King Arthur and Theodoric for the tomb of Emperor Maximilian at Innsbruck.

VISCONTI, vēs-kōn′tē, ruling family of Milan, a fief of the Holy Roman Empire, from 1277 to 1447. At the end of the 10th century, members of the family became vassals of Archbishop Landolfo of Milan. By the early 11th century, the family had probably obtained the office of *visconte* (viscount) and its emblem, the bronze serpent of St. Ambrose.

The first known member of the principal line was Uberto (d. 1248), whose son Ottone (1207–Aug. 8, 1295) was made archbishop of Milan in 1262. Defeating his enemy, Napoleone della Torre, ruler of Milan, Ottone took possession of his see in 1277 and founded the Visconti *signoria* (lordship) over Milan. His grandnephew Matteo I (Aug. 15, 1250–June 24, 1322) was legitimated as Ottone's successor when Emperor Adolf of Nassau appointed him imperial vicar of Lombardy in 1294. Expelled from Milan in 1302 by the della Torre family, Matteo returned in 1310, aided by Emperor Henry VII, and extended his rule over Alessandria, Tortona, Vercelli, Novara, Pavia, Lodi, Cremona, Piacenza, Bergamo, and Como. Caught in the papal-imperial feud, Matteo was excommunicated in 1320. His eldest son, Galeazzo I (1277?–Aug. 6, 1328) succeeded him and, aided by Emperor Louis IV and the imperial faction (the Ghibellines), defeated the papal faction (the Guelphs). Subsequently, he lost Louis' favor and was exiled.

His only son, Azzo (1302–Aug. 16, 1339), bought the title of imperial vicar of Milan from the emperor. Mild and prudent, Azzo defended his domain from Louis and King John of Bohemia and captured Brescia from the della Scala family. He ruled over a semiautonomous confederation of cities that included Bergamo, Brescia, Crema, Lecco, Lodi, Cremona, Piacenza, Parma, Bobbio, Vercelli, Asti, Alessandria, and Tortona. With Azzo, the Visconti became the most powerful family in Northern Italy.

Azzo was succeeded by two uncles, ruling jointly. Luchino (1292–Jan. 24, 1349), holding the real power, exiled his three nephews, Matteo, Galeazzo, and Bernabò, as possible rivals, and extended his rule in the Ticino Valley, Piedmont, and Tuscany. His military victories excited the admiration of Petrarch. At Luchino's death, Giovanni (1290–Oct. 5, 1354), the archbishop of Milan, remained sole ruler. He recalled his nephews and had them recognized as his successors. While promoting peace with his neighbors, he annexed Bologna in 1350 and Genoa in 1353. An able ruler, he reorganized the statutes of Milan, reformed the clergy, and supported the arts.

The Visconti domain was divided among the three nephews, but Matteo II died in 1355. Ruling from Milan, Bernabò (1323–Dec. 19, 1385), aggressive, cruel, bizarre, able, father of 37 children and owner of 5,000 hunting dogs, kept Italy in turmoil for 30 years. Papal-led coalitions regained Bologna from him. Mild in comparison, Galeazzo II (1320–Aug. 4, 1378), ruled from Pavia and attracted artists and scholars to his court. He founded the university (1361) and built the castle at Pavia.

His only son, Gian Galeazzo (Oct. 16, 1351–Sept. 3, 1402), succeeded him and became sole ruler when he imprisoned, and probably poisoned, Bernabò. Gian Galeazzo hired the best mercenaries and was hailed by the humanists of his court as the new king of Italy. His occupation of Verona and Vicenza in 1387 and Padua in 1388 aroused the opposition of the republics, led by Florence. He bought the titles of duke of Milan (1395) and of Lombardy (1396) from Emperor Wenceslaus, captured Pisa, Siena, Perugia, Assisi, Spoleto, and Bologna, and threatened Florence itself. The Visconti domain attained its greatest size, and its system of centralized administration was borrowed by later rulers. Gian Galeazzo founded the Certosa and fostered the growth of the university and library at Pavia, and promoted the construction of the cathedral at Milan. Gian Galeazzo's daughter, VALENTINA (1366–Dec. 14, 1408), was the grandmother of Louis XII of France, whose claim to Milan derived from her.

Gian Galeazzo's sons were GIANMARIA (1389–May 16,1412), duke of Milan, and FILIPPO MARIA (Sept. 3, 1392–Aug. 13, 1447), count of Pavia. Gianmaria was assassinated, leaving no male heirs and a disintegrating state. Filippo Maria, trying to reconstruct his father's domain, provoked coalitions led by Florence and Venice. He occupied Genoa in 1421, but lost Brescia and Bergamo to Venice. A cruel and suspicious ruler, he died without a male heir, ending the direct line.

The Milanese in 1447 proclaimed the Ambrosian Republic, which was overthrown by Francesco Sforza, husband of Filippo Maria's daughter, BIANCA MARIA (1423–Oct. 23, 1468). Sforza was proclaimed duke of Milan (1450) thus beginning the Sforza dynasty. A branch of Visconti descending from Uberto, brother of Matteo I, survives in Milan.

VINCENT ILARDI
University of Massachusetts

VISCOSITY, vis-kos′ə-tē, is a property of a matter that inhibits flow. The successful use of fuels, lubricants and paints, among many other things, depends upon the correct choice of their viscosities. Even solids will flow if high enough stresses are employed. Metal wires, if stretched beyond their ordinary elasticity, will elongate continuously under constant stress. Other substances like pitch, if left long enough, will flow even under their own weight. The concept of viscosity is therefore not confined to simple liquids and gases. Much of rheology, the science of flow, is concerned with materials whose viscosities show complicated anomalies and that are sometimes difficult to classify as either solid or liquid.

Viscosity, essentially, is a resistance to a shearing force. Imagine two parallel rigid plates separated by a gap that is filled with a fluid. If the upper plate is moved while the lower plate remains stationary, the intervening fluid will be sheared—that is, the upper layers will be dragged by the moving sheet and in turn will drag the lower layers. Each layer is moved by the faster layers above and retarded by the slower-moving ones below. Because of the friction between layers, a definite force is required to keep the upper sheet moving at any particular speed. The greater this force, the higher the viscosity of the fluid.

VISCOUNT, vī′kount, a British title of nobility, ranking next below earl and above baron. It was first conferred by letters patent on John, Lord Beaumont, by Henry VI, in 1440. The title is frequently attached to an earldom as a second title and is held by the eldest son during the lifetime of the father. The title came to Britain from France, where the vicomte was originally the deputy of the comte or count, whose official powers they were delegated to exercise. As the title of count eventually became hereditary, so did the title of viscount. Created in 1550, the viscountcy of Hereford is the oldest surviving viscountcy in Britain.

VISHNU, vĭsh′nōō (Sanskrit VIṢṆU), the second member of the supreme Hindu divine trinity, the others being Siva, or Shiva, and Brahma. Brahma, an intellectual creation personifying conceptions found in Vedic literature, receives little worship. Vishnu and Siva, however, are syncretic deities, composed of elements drawn from many sources and very real to their followers. Between them, they embrace almost all of sectarian Hinduism, as expressed in cults centered on themselves, their wives and sons, or figures associated with them. To his sectaries, each god is supreme, fulfilling all the functions of creation, maintenance, dissolution, and, in due time, re-creation of the universe, and the other god is his inferior.

Like most Indian gods, Vishnu has many names. The *Puranas* give him a thousand. The commonest are Hari, Vikramaditya, and the names of his various incarnations. Vishnu appears in the *Rig Veda* as a solar deity who takes three gigantic strides; with one he rises from the region below and encompasses the earth, with a second he encompasses the atmosphere, and with the third he ascends to the highest point of heaven. He is thus a type of conquering hero. Associated or identified with him in later times are other Vedic solar deities, such as Surya, god of the sun.

The Vaishnavas (q.v.), the followers of Vishnu, regard him as the primal being, Narayana, who lies upon the cosmic waters supported in the folds of the endless serpent Ananta, or Shesha, and canopied by its thousand heads, while a lotus sprouts from his navel bearing the god Brahma. Vishnu has a heaven, Vaikuntha; usually two wives, Lakshmi or Shri, goddess of wealth, and Bhu, the earth; and, in some texts, a son, Kama, the god of love. He has a lucky curl (*śrīvatsa*) on his breast, carries a mace, conch, discus, and lotus in his four hands, and has slain innumerable demons. In color he is dark.

He is worshipped directly as Vishnu or, more commonly, in his avatars (see AVATAR), among them Rama, Krishna, and Buddha (qq.v.). In addition to the 10 principal avatars mentioned in the *Puranas*, many lesser incarnations are honored. Many bhakti cults (cults of ecstatic devotion to a deity) are associated with Vishnu, especially in his form as Krishna, in whose worship erotic practices may appear.

See also HINDUISM.

W. NORMAN BROWN,
Professor of Sanskrit and Chairman, South Asia Regional Studies, University of Pennsylvania

VISIGOTH. See GOTHS.

VISION. See EYE; OPHTHALMOLOGY; SENSES AND SENSATION; and Index entry *Vision.*

VISION OF PIERS PLOWMAN, The. See PIERS PLOWMAN.

VISITING CARD, a card inscribed with a person's name, and sometimes an address or title, used to send in as an announcement when calling, and for other social purposes governed by the customs of the time and place. The use of visiting cards is thought to have originated in the 16th century, when German students, at Padua, before returning to their homeland, called on their professors and left symbols of friendship in the form of a miniature drawing in color of a coat of arms, below which the visitor wrote his name and the date. Several such tokens survive, the earliest dated 1560, but there is no record of other use of visiting cards until the 18th century. The earliest such card known is a handwritten one dated 1731 from Florence, Italy. Engraved cards began to appear between 1750 and 1760, and by 1770 were in common use in Milan and Rome.

Early cards were decorated with a garland of flowers surrounding the name; later ornamental bands and symbols appeared, and finally whole scenes—landscapes, architectural monuments, or human figures—covered the card so fully as to leave little space for the name. In France visiting cards sometimes imitated playing cards, with the name written across or between rows of hearts or other suit symbols. When Louis XVI (r. 1774–1792) ascended the throne, card styles in France became more sober, and in the late 18th century Russian and German visitors to France and Italy had simple cards ornamented with a border of conventional motif. In early 19th century France embossed white cards were fashionable for a time, and engraved cards in which the name followed the curves of a monogram. Later in the century lithographed designs appeared both on the Continent and in England. Such lithographed cards continued in use into the 20th century in some places, but by 1900 plain white cards bearing the name engraved in typographic characters had come into fashion. During the 20th century there was little change in the appearance of visiting cards except for a trend toward greater simplicity in the typographic style of the engraved lettering.

VISSER 'T HOOFT, vis′ərt hōft, **Willem Adolf** (1900–1985), Dutch Protestant leader. He was born in Haarlem, the Netherlands, on Sept. 20, 1900. He studied at the University of Leiden, where he took a doctor's degree in theology in 1928, and was ordained in the Reformed Church of Geneva (Switzerland) eight years later.

Meanwhile, in 1924, Visser 't Hooft had become secretary of the World Alliance of Young Men's Christian Associations. He was named general secretary of the World's Student Christian Federation in 1931. When a provisional committee was formed (1938) to establish the World Council of Churches, he was invited to become general secretary of the organization and served in that capacity from its formal inception in 1948. He also founded and edited its quarterly publication, the *Ecumenical Review*.

Among his books are *The Church and Its Function in Society*, with Joseph H. Oldham (1937); *The Kingship of Christ* (1948); *The Renewal of the Church* (1956); and *Has the Ecumenical Movement a Future?* (1977). Visser 't Hooft died in Geneva on July 4, 1985.

VISTA, acronym for Volunters in Service to America. See Peace Corps.

VISTULA RIVER, vis′tū-lə, the longest river in Poland. Rising on the north slopes of the western Beskids, a range of the Carpathian Mountains, the Vistula (Polish, Wisła) flows generally east, then north, west, and north again for about 680 miles (1,095 km) until it reaches the Baltic Sea. Near the end of its course its eastern arm, known as the Nogat River, flows into the Vistula Lagoon, which is separated from the Baltic by a sandspit. The main western arm flows north through a region of drained marshland to the Gulf of Danzig (Gdańsk). A channel parallel to the sea links the main Vistula arm with Nowy Port, the seaport of Danzig. Other major cities along its course are Warsaw, Cracow, and Toruń.

The Vistula is linked with the Pripet and Dnieper rivers of the Soviet Union via its main eastern tributary, the Bug, and with the Oder River on the East German border by the Brda River, the Bydgoszcz Canal, and the Noteć River.

The Vistula has been of less economic utility to Poland than the well-developed waterway of the Oder River system. Most of the Vistula cannot be used by larger vessels, which can navigate only in the lower course. During the winter the river is frozen for 50 to 60 days.

VITAL STATISTICS are records of life events such as births, marriages, divorces, migration, sickness, and death, and the numerical analysis of these recorded events in the form of rates and trends. The records may pertain to the smallest village or to a whole state or nation.

Basically, there are two sources of information about a population. One is *vital statistics*—the continuous registration of life changes as they occur. The other is *census enumeration*—the counting of people and their characteristics as of one moment in time. *Demography*, the statistical and mathematical analysis of population, is based on both these sources and has the task of reconciling them. It checks the accuracy and furthers the understanding of vital statistics by viewing them in the light of census results, and vice versa. Thus vital statistics are both a branch of demography and dependent on it.

History. Although the idea for keeping records of vital events is an old one, it proved more difficult than the taking of censuses. In medieval Europe ceremonies such as baptisms, burials, and weddings were ordinarily paid for, and the recording of these payments in the parish church produced a rudimentary register. However, what was recorded was the ceremony rather than the event itself, and the entries were confined to parishioners. Furthermore, the entries gave the date of the ceremony rather than the date of the event, and information considered necessary today was not included. The forms were not standard from parish to parish, and the collection and compilation of data for whole regions were not attempted.

In the 16th century, efforts were made to improve the church records. These efforts were generally more successful in Protestant countries. By 1608 the first systematic parish register system was established in Sweden, by 1610 in Quebec, by 1628 in Finland, and by 1646 in Denmark. The purpose and control were still religious, and the recording was confined to ceremonies. Consolidation for whole countries was not attempted until the 18th century in France and the early 19th century in England.

Massachusetts Bay and New Plymouth colonies became the first governments in Christendom to require (1) that the actual events rather than the ceremonies be recorded and (2) that this registration be performed by civil authorities rather than the clergy. This important step of secularizing the recording of vital statistics was continued once the United States became independent. In France the Napoleonic Code (1804) made the state responsible for recording births, deaths, and marriages, and set forth who should record each kind of event and what the record should include.

Despite the progress made, there were few attempts to consolidate the data for whole countries. This had been tried in France in the 18th century, and in England in 1801. England sought not only to collect data for 1801 but also to get the returns for 1700–1780 as well, though some of the records had perished. In America the process of settling the continent hindered the establishment of a complete registration. The federal government did not begin collecting death statistics until the "Death Registration Area," comprising ten states, the District of Columbia, and a few cities, was constituted in 1900. The area was gradually expanded until in 1933 it embraced the entire United States. A "Birth Registration Area" with ten states was set up in 1915 and had been extended to the whole nation by 1932.

Purposes. The main purpose of vital records is to serve as legal documents. The individual must often prove his identity, age, citizenship, or marital status. An authorized record of vital events, kept in an official repository and available upon proper demand, is necessary both for him and for the state. Such records, however, can be kept without statistics. The reason for the compilation and analysis of registration data is to inform the government and the public of basic trends in the population and thus to guide policy, particularly regarding public health. The need for future population estimates has led to an increased interest in birth statistics. Statistics on marriages, divorces, annulments, separations, adoptions, and legitimate and illegitimate births are valuable for legislative and administrative purposes in the welfare field and for analysis in the social fields.

See also CENSUS; POPULATION.

VITALE, vē-tä'lā, **Ferruccio,** Italian-American landscape architect: b. Florence, Italy, Feb. 5, 1875; d. New York, N.Y., Feb. 26, 1933. He studied at the Classical School of Florence and graduated from the Royal Military Academy of Modena, he was commissioned in the Italian Army, serving as military attaché in Washington, D.C. (1898–1899), and as military observer with the United States Army in the Philippines. Resigning from the army, he studied landscape architecture in Italy, where his father was a leading architect. Vitale returned to the United States in 1904 and opened an office in New York City for the practice of landscape architecture. He designed the gardens for a number of great estates in the vicinity of New York City, Cleveland, Ohio, and Chicago, Ill., and was a consultant in the planning of the Rockefeller estate at Pocantico Hills, N.Y. In addition, he drew up the town plans of Scarsdale and Pleasantville, N.Y., and designed Meridian Hill Park in Washington. In 1920 he was awarded the gold medal of the Architectural League of New York. He became an American citizen in 1921.

As a trustee of the American Academy of Rome, Vitale was instrumental in establishing a department of landscape architecture there, and a series of fellowships. He also was one of the founders of the Foundation for Architecture and Landscape Architecture at Lake Forest, Ill. Appointed a member of the National Commission of Fine Arts in 1927 by President Calvin Coolidge, he served until 1931. Vitale was also involved in the architectural planning for the Century of Progress exposition held in Chicago in 1933.

VITALIAN, vĭ-tăl'yən, SAINT, pope: b. Segni, Italy; d. Jan. 27, 672. Nothing is known of his life before his consecration as pope on July 30, 657.

In the controversy then raging over the Monothelite formula (see MONOTHELETISM), Vitalian tried to restore the Eastern Church to Roman authority by placating the Byzantine emperor Constans II, but the emperor requited the hospitality shown him in Rome in 663 by carrying off a quantity of bronze works of art. Vitalian was more successful in Britain; Theodore of Tarsus, whom he sent there as archbishop of Canterbury in 668, was the first to be accepted by the entire English church.

VITALISM, vī'tə-lĭz-əm, the philosophical view that a special life principle, a particular quality or essence, distinguishes living from nonliving objects. A dualistic philosophy, it maintains that something nonmaterial regulates the material components of living organisms, as opposed to the monistic philosophy of mechanism, which believes that animate beings differ from inanimate matter only by virtue of the greater complexity of organization of the molecular systems of which they are constructed.

The supposed life principle has been given many different names throughout biological and philosophical history. Aristotle called it *psyche*, and it was also called *pneuma, anima,* and *entelechia* by the ancients. Georg Ernst Stahl (1660–1734), whose writings brought about the development of modern vitalistic concepts, called it *anima sensitiva,* or sensitive soul. Caspar Friedrich Wolff (1733–1794) named it *vis essentialis,* and Johann Friedrich Blumenbach (1752–1840), *nisus formativus.* Other important proponents of vitalistic doctrines have included Albrecht von Haller (1708–1777), Marie François Xavier Bichat (1771–1802), Augustin Pyrame de Candolle (1778–1841), François Magendie (1783–1855), Johannes Müller (1801–1858), Jacob Johann vom Uexküll (1864–1944), and Hans Adolf Eduard Driesch (1867–1941).

Henri Bergson (1859–1941) considered organisms to differ from inorganic objects by the possession of a creative force, the *élan vital,* which he thought to be an important factor in evolution. Bergson, like a number of other vitalists, considered life to be a psychological manifestation comparable to mind. Many vitalists regard living processes as purposive, hence the arguments of teleology are often adduced as support for vitalistic tenets. Mechanistic and vitalistic views are philosophical rather than scientific, and are subjects of belief rather than of scientific proof.

See also MECHANISM; TELEOLOGY.

JANE OPPENHEIMER
Professor of Biology, Bryn Mawr College

VITAMIN, an organic compound required in tiny amounts in the diet of all organisms for proper biological functioning and maintenance of health. The term "vitamin" has no chemical significance, since most of the vitamins are chemically unrelated. Vitamins were originally called *vitamines,* a term coined to suggest that they were nitrogen-containing amine compounds vital for life. The final "e" was dropped from *vitamine* after it was discovered that some of these essential compounds are not amines.

Although vitamins are essential to the metabolism of all species of animals, they need not be part of the diet of every species. Those animals that do not need a dietary source of a vitamin can synthesize the compound within their bodies or obtain it from their intestinal tracts, where microorganisms synthesize it for them. In cattle and other ruminants, for example, the B vitamins are supplied by colonies of microorganisms that live in the rumen. In this case, therefore, compounds that are vitamins for man are not vitamins for a cow, since they need not be part of the cow's normal diet.

Vitamins are commonly classified into two groups, the fat-soluble and the water-soluble. This is not an absolute division, but one of degree, for some of the fat-soluble vitamins have been made in water-soluble form, and some water-soluble vitamins are soluble to some extent in fat solvents. Vitamins A, D, E, and K are fat-soluble. Vitamin C and members of the vitamin B complex are water-soluble.

Vitamin requirements vary greatly from one form of life to another. The higher plants can apparently synthesize all the vitamin compounds they need. Although the compounds are not vitamins for plants, the fact that plants synthesize them is evidence that the compounds are essential in plant metabolism. While relatively little is known about insect vitamin requirements, some insects are known to require vitamin C and several of the B vitamins. All vertebrates need vitamins A, B_1, B_2, B_6, pantothenic acid, and vitamin D. In the case of man, however, the vitamin status of vitamin D has been called into question on the ground that the body can synthesize the vitamin if given adequate exposure to sunlight. Most animals synthesize the vitamin C they need, but a few primates—including man—require vitamin C in their diet.

WEIGHT EQUIVALENTS OF INTERNATIONAL UNITS

Vitamin	Chemical form	Weight of 1 IU in micrograms
A	all-trans retinol	0.300
	all-trans retinyl acetate	0.344
	beta-carotene	0.600
D	pure crystalline D_3	0.025
E	natural *dl*-alpha-tocopherol acetate	735
	dl-alpha-tocopherol	910
	synthetic *dl*-alpha-tocopherol acetate	1,000

The ability to synthesize a vitamin confers a clear advantage on an organism, since it makes the organism independent of its environment for a supply of the compound. On the other hand, a vitamin-synthesizing capability exacts a price. In order to synthesize the vitamin, the body's cells must construct the cellular machinery needed for synthesis and expend energy in carrying out the synthesis. While the price in materials and energy may be low, animals that do not need to pay the price may have a significant evolutionary advantage over other animals. Man's recent ancestors, for example, probably lived on a diet rich in vitamin C, in which case the ability to synthesize the vitamin would have been superfluous. Thus, mutations that took away the vitamin C-synthesizing capability of some of these early ancestors may have spread because of the fact that they conferred an appreciable evolutionary advantage on the individuals that carried them.

In general, the vitamins play catalytic and regulatory roles in the body's metabolism. Among the water-soluble vitamins, the B vitamins apparently function as coenzymes (nonprotein parts of enzymes). Vitamin C's coenzyme role, if any, has not been established. At least part of the importance of vitamin C to the body may result from its strong antioxidant action. The functions of the fat-soluble vitamins are less well understood. Some of them, too, may contribute to enzyme activity, and some of them are essential to the functioning of cellular membranes. Unlike the so-called macronutrients (proteins, carbo-

Vitamins and vitamin-like substances	Outstanding sources	Effects of deficiency	Areas primarily affected
A and its precursors	Fish-liver oils, green plants, yellow vegetables	Night blindness, xerophthalmia	Eyes, skin, mouth, respiratory tract, urogenital tract
B complex			
Thiamine (B_1)	Yeast, pork, liver, whole grains	Beriberi	Brain, nerves, heart
Riboflavin (B_2)	Yeast, milk, egg white, liver, leafy vegetables		Skin, mouth, eyes, liver, nerves
Niacin	Yeast, wheat germ, meats	Pellagra	Gastrointestinal tract, skin, brain
B_6	Whole grains, yeast, egg yolk, liver		Skin, red blood cells, brain, kidneys, adrenals
Pantothenic acid	Liver, kidney, green vegetables, egg yolk		Adrenals, kidneys, skin, brain, spinal cord
Biotin	Liver, kidney, yeast		Skin, muscles
Folic acid	Liver, deep green leafy vegetables	Macrocytic anemias	Red blood cells
B_{12}	Liver, meats	Pernicious anemia	Red blood cells
C (ascorbic acid)	Citrus fruits, fresh vegetables, potatoes	Scurvy	Bones, joints, mouth, capillaries
D	Fish oils	Rickets, osteomalacia	Bones, teeth
E	Grains and vegetable oils		Reproductive tract, muscles red blood cells, liver, brain
K	Green vegetables		Blood prothrombin
Inositol	Whole grains, liver		
Para-aminobenzoic acid	Yeast		
Choline	Egg yolk, brain, grains		Liver, kidneys, pancreas

hydrates, and fats), none of the vitamins provides energy to the body.

Many vitamins must be converted into other forms before they can be active in the body. All of the B vitamins are biologically inactive until they are converted into their coenzyme forms by various structural modifications of their molecules. The B_1, B_2, and B_6 molecules, for example, are activated by the addition of phosphate groups.

For most of the vitamins, the body's quantitative requirements are not known precisely. Recommended Dietary Allowances (RDA's) have been specified by the National Research Council for ten vitamins—A, C, D, E, and the B vitamins thiamine (B_1), riboflavin (B_2), B_6, B_{12}, folic acid, and niacin. Even for these ten, the body's requirements may vary considerably from person to person. See also NUTRITION.

Only three vitamins are considered to be toxic to man if taken in excessive doses. They are vitamin A, vitamin D, and—to a lesser extent—niacin.

Intestinal Synthesis. The differences in the vitamin requirements of various species may be explained partly on the basis of intestinal (or rumen) synthesis. The ruminant has no need for dietary B vitamins, since the microflora of the rumen synthesize these vitamins, and they are absorbed as they reach the small intestine. The importance of intestinal synthesis in the nonruminant animal was not realized until experimental animals had been placed on raised screens to prevent the large-scale ingestion of feces. As a result, need for increased amounts of certain vitamins became evident. The niacin in the feces of rats, for example, may be 100 times as large as the dietary intake. Remarkable responses were produced by feeding the feces of normal animals to rats that had been on a deficient diet.

There is considerable evidence that the bacteria present in the intestinal tracts of animals and man synthesize many of the B vitamins and vitamin K, but the evidence for the availability of these vitamins to the host through absorption is still debatable. Animals that practice coprophagy (consumption of feces), on the other hand, benefit from the intestinal synthesis. The reason is that the major sites of intestinal synthesis are the cecum and large intestine, and these are not actively absorbing surfaces for the vitamins. Even if some absorption from the lower gut occurs, only those vitamins that have been released from the bacterial cells will be available. Niacin, riboflavin, and thiamine are held within the cells and hence are available only after the feces are ingested and digestion of the bacterial cells liberates the vitamins. Pantothenic acid, folic acid, vitamin B_6, and biotin, on the other hand, diffuse from the cells to the medium and are ready for absorption. Vitamin K is also available for absorption.

Diet plays an important role in intestinal synthesis of vitamins. Different carbohydrates have been shown to influence the growth of the symbiotic organisms in the intestinal tract in different ways. For example, more vitamin synthesis occurs on a diet of dextrin or of starch than on a cane sugar diet. It is therefore important to feed not only the host, but also the microorganisms.

In man, under optimum conditions, intestinal microorganisms can synthesize large amounts of the B vitamins. Biotin, folic acid, and vitamin K synthesized by intestinal organisms may be absorbed to a small extent in man, but there is considerable doubt as to the importance of intestinal synthesis of vitamins for animals that do not practice coprophagy.

THE VITAMINS

The following survey discusses the vitamins in alphabetical order. All vitamins of the B group, including those that do not have alphabetical designations, are discussed under the B heading.

Vitamin A. All vertebrates require an outside source of vitamin A or of its carotenoid precursors. One of the first symptoms of a vitamin A deficiency in animals is a decreased ability to see in dim light. This has been shown to be caused by a decrease in a photosensitive pigment in the retina of the eye, which contains vitamin A aldehyde as a part of its structure. A deficiency of this vitamin results in changes in the epithelial tissues throughout the body, causing xerophthalmia in the eyes when the deficiency state is far advanced, and pathological changes in the digestive tract, bones, reproductive organs, skin, and respiratory tract. Secondary infections are quite common. Thus the main functions of vitamin A are to maintain normal epithelial tissue and to form the retinal pigment, rhodopsin.

The most important source of vitamin A is fish-liver oil, since the liver has the ability to store large amounts of the vitamin. Vitamin A is found in good quantities in egg yolk, whole milk, and cream. Also, many plants contain compounds, known as *provitamins,* that are converted into vitamin A after they are eaten. These are the carotenoids, mainly beta-carotene and other carotenoid pigments that show varied vitamin A activity in the animal. Because these pigments are yellow, the provitamin A activity of a plant product is roughly proportional to the yellow or green color present. Chlorophyll, the green pigment, parallels the carotenoid concentration. Green leafy vegetables, yellow vegetables (pumpkin, squash, sweet potatoes), and apricots are rich sources. Carotenoids are the parent source of all vitamin A, since animals make the vitamin from these precursors.

Vitamin A and carotene are rapidly destroyed by oxidation and ultraviolet light. Rancidity produced in oils containing vitamin A hastens its destruction. The cooking of food has little effect on the vitamin or provitamin present. However, since the partial hydrogenation of fats decreases the amount of vitamin contained in them, many such products on the market have vitamin A restored to them.

The conversion of carotene to the colorless vitamin A takes place mainly in the intestinal wall. Certain animals such as sheep, goats, pigs, rats, guinea pigs, and rabbits have white body

VITAMIN A CONTENTS OF FISH-LIVER OILS

Fish	Vitamin A[1]
Black sea bass	300,000
Swordfish	250,000
Lingcod	175,000
Soupfin shark (male)	120,000
Sablefish	90,000
Halibut	87,000
Bonito	35,000
Albacore tuna	25,000
Cod	2,000

[1] Average content in International Units per gram of oil

fat and possess very little carotene in their tissues. These animals rapidly convert most of the ingested carotenoids into vitamin A during absorption. On the other hand, human beings, cattle, horses, and chickens are less efficient converters of carotene to vitamin A, and these species have a considerable quantity of yellow pigment in the body fat.

Vitamin A or carotene is stored to a large extent in the liver of animals, and this reserve supply makes it possible for an animal to exist for some time without a dietary source of the vitamin. The polar bear is reported to store such large quantities that individuals eating polar bear livers have become severely ill. Extremely high levels of vitamin A are definitely toxic. Ingestion of excessive amounts of vitamin A over a prolonged period of time, especially by children, will result in hypervitaminosis A, characterized by anorexia, loss of weight, cracking and bleeding of lips, thickening of skin, edema, pruritis, and seborrheic eruptions. The hair becomes coarse and may fall out, the bones may show tender swelling, and the child may be unable to walk. In adults, headache, nausea and vomiting, nervous manifestations, and peeling of the skin may occur.

Vitamin B Complex. The first vitamins named were fat-soluble A and water-soluble B. As time passed, it was found that vitamin B was a composite of several vitamins, so that the terms B_1 and B_2 came into being. As more vitamins were discovered, they were classified as B vitamins if they were soluble in water and present in yeast. This classification has been seriously questioned—and rightly so. It is to be hoped that, when the functions of all vitamins are known, a more rational grouping can be made. Meanwhile, nutritionists have begun to abandon the B designation in favor of a more descriptive name based on the chemical nature of the compound.

Thiamine (Vitamin B_1). Thiamine functions as a coenzyme for a number of important reactions in metabolism. It is essential in the metabolism of carbohydrates in every cell of the body. It is also involved in fat and protein metabolism to some extent. Since more thiamine is required in the utilization of carbohydrates than fats, diets high in fat decrease the thiamine requirement. All animals require a dietary source of thiamine except cattle and other ruminants, whose rumens contain microorganisms that synthesize the vitamin. The young calf needs thiamine until the rumen becomes functional.

THIAMINE CONTENTS OF SOME COMMON FOODS

Food	Thiamine[1]
Yeast, dried brewers'	10,000
Wheat germ	3,000
Yeast, fresh	3,000
Ham	1,200
Peas (dry)	800
Oats, rolled	800
Beans (dry)	500
Soybean flour	500
Wheat flour (whole wheat)	500
Bread, white (enriched)	400
Cornmeal, yellow	400
Peanuts	400
Rice, brown	300
Veal chop	290
Beef liver	250
Beefsteak	200
Eggs	170
Potato	150
Beans, green	90
Bread, white (unenriched)	80
Orange juice	60
Rice, white	50
Beets	40
Cheese, American	40
Milk, cow's	40

[1] Approximate, in micrograms of thiamine per 100 grams of food

Thiamine is widespread in nature, though in relatively small concentrations. Whole grains, legumes, pork, liver, nuts, egg yolk, and yeast are good sources. Fruits and milk are poor sources. In the milling of wheat as much as 80% of the thiamine may be removed. A fair amount is leached out of vegetables during cooking. Since thiamine is not stored to any appreciable extent in the body, a daily intake is necessary. Thiamine is stable to cooking temperatures in neutral or acid solution for short periods of time, although it is destroyed by heat in basic solution.

Thiamine deficiency has been shown to exist in most animals with the exception of ruminants. It was discovered first in birds (pigeons, chickens) that are unable to stand, exhibit opisthotonos (head retraction), and die with a condition called polyneuritis. In all species a decreased growth rate is observed. Rats on a thiamine-deficient diet have slower heartbeats, enlarged hearts, convulsions, paralysis, and polyneuritis. In man the severe deficiency state is called beriberi. Three general types of symptoms are observed: heart changes, nervous symptoms, and edema. A less severe state of thiamine deficiency is more often encountered in the Americas. The symptoms involved are loss of appetite, headache, gastrointestinal disorders, inability to sleep, fatigue, dizziness, and possible palpitation of the heart. Infant beriberi occurs in children nursed by mothers with beriberi. Thiamine deficiency in the form of polyneuritis is observed also in chronic alcoholics. Many alcoholics eat ill-balanced, inadequate diets that are deficient in many vitamins, including thiamine.

Thiaminase disease has been reported in foxes, chickens, and man as the result of the destruction of the vitamin in the digestive tract. Thiaminase is an enzyme that destroys thiamine. It occurs in uncooked freshwater fish and mollusks, in some saltwater forms, and in some microorganisms and plants. If animals consume these substances or the microorganisms inhabit their intestinal tracts, a thiamine deficiency is induced, even though the diet contains adequate thiamine.

Riboflavin (Vitamin B_2). Riboflavin functions as a part of several enzyme systems concerned with the oxidation of amino acids and cellular respiration. Riboflavin is important in the production of energy from foodstuffs in all cells. Its importance in so many enzyme systems makes it easy to understand why so many different deficiency symptoms occur in various species.

Milk, cheese, muscle meat and organs, fish, yeast, eggs, and green leafy vegetables are good sources of riboflavin. Cereals, fruits, and nonleafy vegetables are rather poor sources. Little riboflavin is stored in the body, although some retention occurs in certain tissues. Large intakes result in excretion of excess amounts.

Riboflavin is very sensitive to light. Exposure of milk in bottles to sunlight for as little as several hours results in as much as a 70% loss in riboflavin. In slightly basic solutions riboflavin is much more sensitive to light. Cooking losses are slight, except for what is lost in the cooking water.

APPROXIMATE RIBOFLAVIN CONTENTS OF SOME COMMON FOODS

Food	Riboflavin[1]
Yeast, dried brewers'	3,000
Beef liver	2,000
Yeast, fresh	1,500
Wheat germ	600
Cheese, American	500
Peanuts	400
Soybean flour	400
Beans (dry)	300
Beefsteak	300
Bread, white (enriched)	300
Eggs	300
Ham	300
Peas (dry)	300
Veal chop	220
Cornmeal, yellow	200
Milk, cow	150
Oats, rolled	150
Beans, green	120
Bread, white (unenriched)	100
Wheat flour (whole wheat)	100
Beets	70
Orange juice	55
Rice, brown	50
Potato, white	40
Celery	30
Rice, white	20

[1] Approximate, in micrograms of riboflavin per 100 grams of food

While it is possible for a pure riboflavin deficiency to occur in man, a deficiency of this vitamin is found most frequently in conjunction with deficiencies of several other B vitamins. The most common symptoms of uncomplicated riboflavin deficiency are lesions of the eyes, mouth, and skin. Cracks at the corners of the mouth (cheilosis), inflamed lips and purple-red tongue, glossitis, inflammation of the cornea of the eye, itching and light-sensitive eyes, and seborrheic lesions of the skin are the symptoms observed, depending upon the severity of the deficiency.

Niacin (Nicotinic Acid). The significance of niacin in metabolism was understood before its importance in nutrition was known. Niacin is closely associated with riboflavin and is a part of many enzymes responsible for the oxidation of foodstuffs in the body.

Liver, meat, yeast, and fish are excellent sources of niacin. Good sources are whole grains (except corn), peanuts, and eggs. Fruits and vegetables are fair sources, but milk and milk products are low in niacin. Milk and milk products, however, are among the best pellagra-preventing foods because of their high tryptophan content. Little niacin is stored. As with the other B vitamins, niacin in the tissues decreases as the deficiency progresses. When excess levels of niacin are taken by man, a flushing occurs accompanied by itching and burning sensations due to vasodilation of the subcutaneous vessels of the face, neck, and arms. Still higher levels may impair the functioning of the liver. Very high levels when fed to rats produce toxic symptoms and at times paralysis of the respiratory center.

Niacin is one of the most stable vitamins. Some is lost during cooking if the cooking water is discarded.

A deficiency of niacin results in a serious disease known as pellagra. This disease is often complicated by deficiencies of riboflavin and thiamine, as well as of other members of the vitamin B complex. It usually occurs in warm climates of the world and is still a rather widespread disease.

This disease can be counteracted, if it is purely a niacin deficiency, by the addition of niacin or the amino acid tryptophan. Tryptophan is converted into niacin in the walls of the intestinal tract and within the tissues themselves. From experiments with man it has been shown that it takes 60 milligrams of tryptophan to yield one milligram of niacin. Pellagra has been associated with corn-eating populations. However, certain diets, composed largely of rice, are lower in niacin than the corn diets, yet no pellagra occurs. The reason for this is that corn is deficient not only in niacin but also tryptophan, whereas the rice diets contain larger quantities of the amino acid.

Vitamin B_6. The name vitamin B_6 was originally applied to one compound, pyridoxine. Since the discovery of this vitamin, two closely related substances, pyridoxal and pyridoxamine, have been shown to occur naturally and to possess vitamin B_6 activity. Vitamin B_6 is now used as a class name to include all compounds with vitamin B_6 activity.

Vitamin B_6 plays an important role in protein metabolism and in the synthesis of hemoglobin, serotonin, and γ-aminobutyric acid. The latter two compounds may be important chemicals in the metabolism of the brain.

Vitamin B_6 is widely distributed in both animal and plant products. In plants and seeds the usual form of the vitamin is pyridoxine, whereas in animal products it usually occurs as pyridoxal and pyridoxamine. The richest sources are whole-grain cereals, fish, milk, eggs, vegetables, and yeast. It is not stored to any significant extent. Extremely large doses are required before any signs of toxicity are evident in animals.

Pyridoxine is stable to heat, but pyridoxal and pyridoxamine are partially destroyed by autoclaving (pressure cooking). All forms of the vitamin are sensitive to light and vigorous oxidation.

The rat was the first species in which vitamin B_6 was shown to be required. One of the most characteristic symptoms of deficiency in the rat is a dermititis of the extremities (mouth, paws, ears, nose, tail) with accompanying swelling. There is also decreased growth and hyperirritability, followed by convulsions.

The most convincing evidence that man requires a dietary source of vitamin B_6 was the rather widespread occurrence of convulsive seizures in young infants receiving a canned liquid milk formula. The simulated milk was heat-treated, and as a result the level of vitamin B_6 was below that required by the infant. A change of formula or treatment with pyridoxine dramatically cured the condition. Attempts to produce a dietary deficiency in adult men have failed. However, the inclusion of deoxypyridoxine, an inhibitory analogue of the vitamin, in a deficient diet results in a syndrome characterized by dermatitis, cheilosis, glossitis, and mental depression.

The early use of excessive levels of isoniazid in the treatment of tuberculosis caused peripheral neuritis that could be prevented by simultaneous administration of pyridoxine. Isoniazid induces a vitamin B_6 deficiency by combining with the active form of the vitamin, pyridoxal phosphate, and causing its elimination in the urine.

Evidently the need for vitamin B_6 is increased in pregnancy, and many women with marginal intakes are thrown into a vitamin B_6 deficiency state. This is detected by an abnormal tryptophan load test among women with severe nausea during the first trimester, since vitamin B_6 is concerned with normal tryptophan metabolism and, with inadequate vitamin, xanthurenic acid (an abnormal product of tryptophan metabolism) occurs in the urine.

Pantothenic Acid. Pantothenic acid has been shown to function as a part of enzymes involved in fat, carbohydrate, and energy metabolism. It is essential for the synthesis of steroids, including cholesterol, the adrenal cortical hormones, and sex hormones.

Pantothenic acid is abundantly distributed in nature. Yeast, cereals, liver, kidney, and eggs are very good sources. Milk and vegetables contain a moderate amount. Fruits and muscle meat are rather poor sources. There is little storage of pantothenic acid in the body, although levels of the vitamin in the liver and kidneys decrease markedly as the deficiency disease develops. Pantothenic acid is stable to heat in neutral solution, but is destroyed by heat in acid and basic solution.

The primary lesions in experimental animals attributed to a pantothenic acid deficiency involve the nervous system, skin, and adrenal cortex. A pantothenic acid deficiency was induced in adult men by feeding a pantothenic acid-deficient diet plus omega-methylpantothenate, an inhibitor of the vitamin. There were subjective neurological symptoms, such as numbness and tingling of the feet, burning feet, and an impaired sense of balance. It seems probable that pantothenic acid is a dietary essential for man, but the wide distribution of it in foods makes a dietary deficiency seem unlikely.

Biotin. All the functions of biotin have not been determined. However, it is known to function in the synthesis of fatty acids and in several other processes involving carbon dioxide fixation. Indirect evidence implicates its function in carbohydrate and protein metabolism as well.

Liver, yeast, kidney, and egg yolk are excellent sources of biotin. Fresh vegetables, grains, fish, and dairy products contain considerable amounts. A small amount of biotin is transferred into human milk. Biotin is not affected by heat, acid, or basic solution. It is inactivated by oxidation.

Biotin deficiency is not likely to be a naturally occurring disease, because of biotin's widespread occurrence and its great biological potency. In the chick a dietary deficiency can be produced with a characteristic symptom of dermatitis that is severe around the mouth, eyelids, and feet. Perosis also occurs. Experimental biotin deficiency has been induced in many species, including man, by the inclusion of high levels of raw or cold-dried egg white. Raw egg white contains a protein, avidin, that combines with biotin in the digestive tract and makes it unavailable to the animal. Heating egg white destroys the avidin's ability to join with biotin. Similar symptoms are produced on an experimental diet lacking in biotin with sulfonamide added to decrease the intestinal synthesis of the vitamin. Human volunteers on a diet of raw egg white developed a dry, scaly skin with extremely gray pallor, slight anemia, muscle pains, weakness, mental symptoms (depression), and loss of appetite.

Folic Acid (Folacin, Pteroylglutamic Acid). Folic acid functions in the synthesis of methionine (an amino acid), and in the formation of thymine and purines (components of nucleic acids), which are essential elements of all cells. The maturation of the red and white blood cells is evidently very sensitive to a deficiency of folic acid.

Folic acid occurs in several forms in nature, and these may be free or conjugated with other substances. Yeast, liver, green leafy vegetables, and grass are excellent sources of folic acid compounds. Cereals, milk, and meat contain somewhat less. Folic acid is stored to a slight extent in tissues, especially liver, in the conjugated form. A folic acid-deficient diet, therefore, markedly decreases the level of this vitamin in the liver.

Folic acid is heat-stable in neutral and basic solution, though very unstable to heat in acid solution. It is inactivated by light. There is a considerable loss of folic acid during storage, processing, and cooking of foods.

Blood disorders are the main symptoms of a folic acid deficiency in most animals. In man the anemias associated with pernicious anemia, sprue, nutritional macrocytic anemia, and macrocytic anemia of pregnancy are relieved by administering folic acid. Since the discovery of vitamin B_{12} as the antipernicious anemia factor, the use of folic acid in the disease has been largely discontinued, since it tended to aggravate the nervous symptoms of the disease.

The use of antifolic acid compounds in the treatment of leukemia and other neoplastic disease has resulted in toxic manifestations reflecting a tissue depletion of folic acid. These symptoms are oral lesions (glossitis, inflamed mucous membranes) and gastrointestinal disorders (nausea and diarrhea). These may be prevented by administering N^5-formyltetrahydrofolic acid, a metabolic derivative of the vitamin.

Vitamin B_{12}. Vitamin B_{12} is the most recent of the B vitamins to be discovered. Its isolation from liver was announced simultaneously by scientists in England and the United States in 1948. It is classed as a B vitamin despite the fact that it does not occur in yeast, as do the other members of this group. Its discovery was a direct result of an intensive search for the anti-pernicious anemia factor. Vitamin B_{12} has also been shown to be responsible for the greater part of the activity of the "animal protein factor" required for the growth of chicks and turkeys on all-vegetable diets.

The exact functions of vitamin B_{12} are unknown, although there is some evidence that it is concerned with nucleic acid synthesis and methionine formation in close conjunction with folic acid. Vitamin B_{12} is needed in such minute amounts that it must be involved in some very fundamental biochemical reactions.

It seems likely that the occurrence of vitamin B_{12} in nature is the result of microbial synthesis. There is no convincing evidence that the vitamin is produced in the tissues of higher plants or animals. A great many bacteria and actinomyces synthesize it. It is distributed widely in foods of animal origin, such as meat, milk, eggs, fish, oysters, and clams. Its presence in these tissues occurs as a result of the ingestion of vitamin B_{12} in the food or from rumen synthesis. The best sources are fermentation residues, kidney, and liver. Plant products are practically devoid of the vitamin. None is present in yeast. Vitamin B_{12} is heat-stable in neutral solution, but is destroyed in basic solution.

Vitamin B_{12} alleviates all symptoms of pernicious anemia in man, including macrocytic anemia, neurological symptoms, and tongue lesions. It is also effective to some extent in the other macrocytic anemias, but folic acid has been more effective in some cases of sprue, nutritional anemias, and macrocytic anemia of pregnancy.

To be absorbed from the intestinal tract, vitamin B_{12} requires the presence of a substance called the *intrinsic factor,* produced by the gastric mucosa. It is this factor that is missing in pernicious anemia patients. Total gastrectomy (removal of the stomach) results in the production of an artificial pernicious anemia several years after the operation unless vitamin B_{12} is injected or fed along with the intrinsic factor. The delay in the onset of the symptoms is caused by the unusual ability of the liver to store the vitamin.

In areas of the world where raw fish is eaten, a fish-tapeworm anemia may occur as the worm deprives the host of the dietary vitamin B_{12}. The best treatment is to get rid of the worm, but injected vitamin B_{12} is effective.

Vitamin B_{12} deficiencies sometimes occur in vegetarians who eat no animal products at all—the so-called "vegans." After some years on an all-vegetarian diet, some vegans experience the neurological symptoms of pernicious anemia. The symptoms can be corrected by orally administered vitamin B_{12}. The anemia itself is not present because of the large amount of folic acid contained in the vegetable diet.

Vitamin C (Ascorbic Acid). Vitamin C is needed to maintain the integrity of the capillary blood vessels and to aid in the formation of normal teeth and bones. Specifically, vitamin C regulates the formation of intercellular substances having collagen or related substances as the basic constituents. In the absence of vitamin C the intercellular cementing substances fail to be deposited in the normal way. Collagen is not deposited by the fibroblasts of the connective tissue, osteoid is not deposited by osteoblasts of the bone, and dentine is not deposited by the odontoblasts of the teeth. Because of this the supporting tissues are particularly affected, especially those in which the intercellular substance is calcified. Little is yet known of the biochemical role of vitamin C, but in view of the ease with which it undergoes reversible oxidation and reduction, it may serve as an antioxidant in living organisms. Vitamin C also appears to play some role in preventing or reducing the severity of colds.

VITAMIN C CONTENTS OF SOME COMMON FOODS

Food	Vitamin C[1]
English walnuts (green, unripe)	500–2,000
Turnip greens	100–150
Strawberries	40–80
Orange juice (fresh)	40–70
Cabbage (fresh)	40–70
Lemon juice	40–60
Tomato (fresh)	20–30
Potato, white	20–30
Pineapple (fresh)	20–30
Cabbage (cooked)	15–20
Tomato juice	10–20
Sauerkraut	10–20
Potato (winter-stored)	5–10
Lettuce, head	5–10
Watermelon	5–8
Apple	3–10
Pineapple (canned)	2–10
Beans, green (canned)	2–5

[1] In milligrams of vitamin C per 100 grams of food

Citrus fruits and tomatoes are excellent sources of vitamin C, as are strawberries, cabbage, spinach, and other green leafy vegetables. The potato is not a concentrated source, but because of the large quantities commonly consumed, it represents an important source. Cow's milk is a fair source until pasteurized, when some of this vitamin is destroyed. Human milk contains several times as much ascorbic acid as fresh cow's milk. It is common practice to fortify an infant's diet with synthetic vitamin C.

Since little ascorbic acid is stored in the tissues, a daily intake is required. One of the few clinical tests of some importance is the white blood cell and platelet vitamin C content, which reflects rather well the vitamin C status of the body.

Ascorbic acid is highly susceptible to oxidation, especially in the presence of copper or in a basic solution such as sodium bicarbonate. It is most stable in acid solution. The oxidation product of ascorbic acid, dehydroascorbic acid, is biologically active. Dehydroascorbic acid, however, readily undergoes an irreversible change with the formation of a biologically inactive compound. Certain vegetables contain an enzyme that destroys the vitamin. In the cooking of fruits and vegetables as much as 80% of the ascorbic acid can be lost by oxidation or leaching into the cooking water. There is less loss by oxidation in acid foods. Vitamin C is used as an antioxidant in the processing of fruits in order to prevent the peeled fruit from turning brown.

Man, monkeys, the guinea pig, and a Persian songbird (the bulbul) are species of animals that require a dietary source of this vitamin and develop scurvy when they lack it. Scurvy is characterized by subcutaneous hemorrhages, swollen and bleeding gums, loosened teeth, weakened bones, and at times an anemia. Scurvy in advanced stages is now seldom seen in man, but the less acute symptoms are known to occur occasionally.

Vitamin D. Vitamin D is concerned with absorption and metabolism of calcium and phosphorus. The amounts of these minerals, as well as the ratio between them, are important considerations in the prevention of rickets and osteomalacia. In man and other animals the need for the vitamin is more critical. If the level of either mineral is very low in the diet, no amount of vitamin D will correct the deficiency. When calcium and phosphorus are present in proper amounts and ratio, the need for vitamin D will be at a minimum. The amount of vitamin D required varies with the amounts of these two minerals in the diet, and with the species. The major role of vitamin D is to promote the absorption of calcium from the intestinal tract, and to maintain the concentrations of calcium and phosphate in the blood at the proper levels. Indirect evidence implicates this vitamin in carbohydrate metabolism.

The need for vitamin D is especially great in the growing child and in the pregnant and lactating woman. This is true because, during growth and pregnancy, bone development progresses rapidly, and during lactation the mineral metabolism of the mother is under continued stress. The vitamin D status of the unborn young and the nursing infant is influenced by the nutritional status of the mother, since vitamin D is stored to some extent in the liver of the fetus and is passed in fair amounts into the milk.

VITAMIN D CONTENTS OF SEVERAL FISH-LIVER OILS

Fish	Vitamin D[1]
Albacore tuna	25,000–250,000
Bonito	50,000
Swordfish	2,000–25,000
Black sea bass	5,000
Lingcod	1,000–6,000
Halibut	1,000–5,000
Sablefish	600–1,000
Cod	85–500
Soupfin shark (male)	5–25

[1] Range of vitamin D contents or average content in International Units per gram of oil.

The amount of vitamin D in nature is very limited. There are two forms of vitamin D of importance: vitamin D_2 is found in plants and yeasts after irradiation with ultraviolet light, and vitamin D_3 is found in fish-liver oils and in animals and animal products after irradiation. Egg yolk and butter are good sources. Fish-liver oils are extremely rich sources, and it is usually in this form that animals and infants receive dietary supplements of vitamin D. Fortunately, there are some 11 provitamins D in certain animal and plant materials that, when eaten by animals, are converted into vitamin D by the action of sunlight on the skin. The adult animal eats enough of these provitamins for the body to make sufficient vitamin D to meet its needs, given adequate exposure to sunlight. The discovery by Alfred F. Hess and Harry Steenbock that ultraviolet light increases the vitamin D potency of foods resulted in the practice of irradiating certain foods, especially milk. However, pure vitamin D is now added to milk in an oil emulsion.

Massive doses of vitamin D have been shown to be toxic, causing deposition of calcium in arteries and soft tissues throughout the body. In children large doses cause anorexia, nausea, vomiting, abdominal pain, colic, sometimes diarrhea, more frequently constipation, loss of weight, and dehydration. The child becomes sleepy, apathetic, and pale. He may suffer from headache and possibly fever, muscle cramps, and occasionally from convulsions. In severe cases visual disturbances may develop, the heart action may be affected, and there may be bone changes. The clinical picture may resemble that of tuberculosis, meningitis, or encephalitis. The therapeutic dose used for the prevention or cure of rickets, however, is well below this toxic level. The amount of vitamin D used to treat premature or very young infants may at times approach a toxic level.

Vitamin D can be stored in the liver, although the amounts are not comparable with the quantity of vitamin A stored there. It is stable at ordinary cooking temperatures and in the presence of most chemicals.

Vitamin E. The biochemical function of vitamin E is not yet known. It probably acts as an antioxidant, protecting unsaturated fatty acids in various tissues from oxidation, which would result in the formation of products detrimental to the structural integrity of cells in general.

Vitamin E seems to play a role in the structural integrity of muscle and in the reproductive, nervous, and vascular systems. However, there is no evidence that the vitamin can cure impotence or sterility in the human male, nor that even massive doses can relieve angina pectoris or prevent heart attacks. In fact, there is little or no evidence to support any of the many specific claims made for vitamin E in the popular medical literature.

Vitamin E is synthesized solely in plants, so that it is found mainly in plant products, concentrated in the seeds. There are several recognized forms of the vitamin, but one, alpha-tocopherol, is the most active compound. The richest sources of this vitamin are the vegetable oils, such as wheat-germ oil, cottonseed oil, peanut oil, and soybean oil. Many green leafy vegetables, such as lettuce, are good sources. Most animal products are poor sources. Since vitamin E is so widespread in occurrence, it is unlikely that any animal or human diet will be lacking in this factor, although there is evidence that an increased consumption of unsaturated fatty acids (vegetable oils) increases the amount of vitamin E required in the diet.

Vitamin E is stored in various tissues of the animal, although not to so great an extent as vitamins A and D. Placental transfer is limited, so that the newborn animal has a low reserve. The vitamin can be increased in the milk by feeding the mother larger amounts, so that the diet of the female is of great importance in the early vitamin E status of the young animal.

Vitamin E is readily destroyed by oxidation, a reaction that occurs very fast in the presence of rancid fats. Because of this ease of oxidation, vitamin E protects vitamin A from oxidation by being preferentially oxidized. Vitamin E is termed an antioxidant in this case, but by acting in this capacity, it loses its vitamin activity. Vitamin E is stable to heat in the absence of air, although an increase in temperature in the presence of air increases its rate of oxidation.

The pathological lesions of a deficiency state of vitamin E are many and varied, depending upon the species involved. Changes occur in completely unrelated tissues, and although vitamin E therapy corrects the biochemical lesions, there is usually a lack of restoration of structure. A vitamin E deficiency was first discovered in the rat, with different results in the male and female, although the reproductive performance is disturbed in both. In the female there is usually a resorption of the fetus, which can be prevented by feeding vitamin E during pregnancy.

Muscular dystrophy is a common manifestation of a vitamin E deficiency in rabbits and herbivores. However, muscular dystrophy in man does not respond to vitamin E therapy.

Vitamin E is related in the animal to two other dietary components, unsaturated fatty acids (present in vegetable oils in large amounts) and selenium. Unsaturated fatty acids accentuate the symptoms of vitamin E deficiency in most instances, and selenium will prevent or correct some of them.

Vitamin K. One of the functions of vitamin K is to promote the formation of prothrombin (a blood-clotting factor) and several other plasma proteins made in the liver, which are needed in the blood-clotting process. The mechanism of its action is not known. The fact that vitamin K functions also in plants and some microorganisms indicates that blood clotting is not its only, or even most important, function. Evidence points to a participation of vitamin K in photosynthesis in plants and in the process in all living organisms whereby the chemical energy of carbohydrates, fats, and proteins is converted into useful energy in the form of adenosine triphosphate, the so-called "energy currency" of living things.

There are two naturally occurring forms of vitamin K, K_1 made by green plants and K_2 synthesized by microorganisms. A synthetic compound called menadione (K_3) is as potent as the natural vitamins for some functions in certain species. Several water-soluble substances with vitamin K activity have been produced. Green leafy plants are rich sources of the vitamin. Cereals and fruits are poor sources. Liver and eggs are animal sources containing significant quantities of vitamin K. Other animal materials are low in the vitamin.

There is no evidence that the natural vitamins K in massive doses cause toxic effects. However, menadione has produced toxic symptoms in dogs, rabbits, and man when administered in excessive doses, and some of the water-soluble forms have produced toxic symptoms in newborn infants.

Vitamin K is not stored in any appreciable amount in the body. It is rapidly metabolized in some as yet unknown manner. Small quantities are transferred across the placenta and deposited in the fetal liver. The small amounts excreted into the milk cannot be increased appreciably by feeding more vitamin K to the mother. Vitamin K is heat-stable, but is destroyed by exposure to light and basic solutions.

Vitamin K deficiency was first observed in chicks reared on purified diets. Hemorrhages occurred in the intestines, under the skin, and in the muscles. If prolonged feeding of these diets continued, the disease was fatal. Prothrombin levels in the blood were decreased, resulting in an increase in the time required for coagulation of blood. Vitamin K deficiency has not been observed to any great extent in other species because of its intestinal synthesis and the practice of coprophagy (consumption of feces). Possibly the relatively short intestinal tract of the chick limits vitamin K synthesis.

Man shows a need for vitamin K under certain circumstances associated with poor absorption of the vitamin due to diarrhea, ulcerative colitis, sprue, or bile-duct obstruction, since bile salts are needed in the absorption process. In obstructive jaundice and sprue, administration of vitamin K by injection or by feeding water-soluble forms of the vitamin has proved beneficial. In the newborn infant a hemorrhagic condition often develops, accompanied by low levels of blood prothrombin. To prevent this, it was formerly common practice to give vitamin K to the pregnant woman before parturition or to the child at birth. However, the use of water-soluble forms at excessive levels proved potentially dangerous, and in some cases resulted in a hemolytic anemia.

Hemorrhage from the injudicious use of dicumarol (an anticoagulant and inhibitor of vitamin K used to reduce occurrence of blood clots) is probably the most common cause of vitamin K deficiency in man. Vitamin K_1 and K_2 are effective in controlling the desired prothrombin level during dicumarol therapy.

VITAMIN-LIKE COMPOUNDS

Inositol. The functions of inositol are mostly unknown. It may be involved in fat transport, and it is a constituent of compounds (phospholipids) found in the heart and the brain. The requirement for inositol of those species needing it in the diet is many times greater than that for most vitamins. This may be attributed to the fact that inositol is a part of a structural unit in the body and does not serve as a coenzyme, as do the B vitamins.

Cereal grains, fruits, vegetables, liver, and milk are good sources of inositol. Meat is a rather poor source. Inositol occurs in most plant materials as phytin, a substance composed of phosphorus, inositol, magnesium, and calcium.

Inositol deficiency was first observed in mice, with loss of hair, retarded growth, and dermatitis as symptoms. Similar symptoms, as well as "spectacle eye" and fatty livers, were seen in rats on a diet deficient in inositol. It is difficult to explain these observations in view of the fact that glucose, which is present in all cells, is converted to inositol in the rat. It may be that under certain conditions insufficient inositol is synthesized. Inositol has been reported to be a growth factor for chicks, pigs, hamsters, guinea pigs, and turkey poults.

Para-Aminobenzoic Acid. Para-aminobenzoic acid (PABA) was discovered when it was shown to counteract the effect of sulfanilamide on bacteria in 1940. The next year it was reported to be required for the growth of chicks and by the rat to prevent graying of hair.

Probably the most important function of PABA is as a nutrient for the microorganisms that inhabit the intestinal tracts of animals and man. It increases intestinal synthesis of various B vitamins, including folic acid, of which it is a part. In bacteria, PABA functions as a precursor of folic acid, and thus indirectly in the synthesis of purines and certain amino acids (methionine and serine). It is widely distributed in both the plant and the animal world. Yeast is an especially rich source.

Choline. Choline is a dietary essential used as a structural component of tissue. No catalytic role has been discovered for it. In this respect it differs from the vitamins of the B complex.

Choline is a structural part of some phospholipids. It may be in this form that choline functions in the transport and metabolism of fat. It also functions in transmethylation, a process of fundamental importance. Methionine, along with choline, contains methyl groups that are passed intact to other compounds that are methyl acceptors. Although it has been demonstrated that methyl groups can be synthesized in the body, such insufficient amounts are produced that dietary sources are necessary. This function of choline can be replaced by methionine. However, methionine cannot replace choline in the metabolism of fat or in the prevention of perosis. These are essential functions of choline per se. In addition, choline is the precursor of acetylcholine, which is present in nerve tissue and functions in transporting nerve impulses. The requirement for choline is in the same order of magnitude as that of amino acids, due to its structural function in the animal body.

A choline deficiency results in marked symptoms in all species: rats show slow growth, hemorrhagic kidneys, fatty livers, paralysis of the hind legs, and impaired reproduction and lactation; dogs develop extremely fatty and cirrhotic livers; in the chick, besides poor growth, perosis is a characteristic symptom.

Choline is so widespread in nature that there is little chance of a dietary deficiency occurring in man or animals when natural diets are consumed. Meat, fish, cereals, and legumes are rich sources, but fruits are devoid of it.

ANTIVITAMINS

The concept of antivitamins developed as the result of the discovery that para-aminobenzoic acid reversed sulfanilamide action. It was evident, when the chemical structures were compared, that these two substances were very similar. This discovery led organic chemists to synthesize many compounds chemically related to other vitamins. Many of these compounds, when fed to animals, caused a vitamin deficiency state, which usually could be corrected by feeding the vitamin concerned.

Since 1940 several antivitamins have proved of importance in chemotherapy. The sulfonamides (anti-PABA) have been used successfully in the treatment of certain bacterial infections. Dicumarol (antivitamin K) has been found useful in preventing the formation of potentially fatal blood clots. Folic acid analogues have proved of some use in the treatment of leukemia and several other types of neoplastic disease.

Antivitamins were responsible for the demonstration of man's need of pyridoxine, pantothenic acid, and biotin. In addition, antivitamins have provided an excellent tool for the study of biochemical functions of several vitamins. The natural occurrence of antivitamins may be a consideration in future studies of nutrition. Examples of these are not numerous, although several deserve mention. Raw fish and clams possess an antithiamine, actually an enzyme, that destroys the thiamine in the diet. An antithiamine in ferns has produced thiamine deficiency symptoms in horses. Spoiled sweet-clover hay contains dicumarol, which produces a vitamin K deficiency in animals that consume it.

History and Research. The history of the recognition of the importance of vitamins to man is interesting. Evidence of scurvy and rickets existing in prehistoric man has been discovered in examining skeletal remains. Night blindness (vitamin A deficiency) and its treatment with goat's liver were known to physicians in biblical times. Various navies in the world were using citrus fruits to prevent scurvy as early as the 18th and 19th centuries. Beriberi (thiamine deficiency) was also known in the Orient in early times, and the Japanese Navy attempted to prevent this condition by making dietary changes as early as 1887.

Up to this time, with few exceptions, scientists believed that an animal could be maintained in normal health on a diet containing carbohydrates, fats, proteins, minerals, and water. Diseases which were cured by dietary means had been attributed to some toxic material present in foodstuffs. The concept of a deficiency of a specific substance in food as the cause of a disease originated as a result of the studies on beriberi conducted by Christiaan Eijkman (a Nobel Prize winner in 1929) in the Netherlands East Indies in 1893–1897. He produced a polyneuritic condition (closely resembling beriberi) in fowls by feeding them a diet of polished rice, and found that he could prevent or cure the condition by feeding the rice polishings with the milled rice. Several years later Gerrit Grijns, an associate of Eijkman, announced that beriberi was cured by a substance that was lacking in the diet. With this impetus the next two decades were notable for the discovery of other vitamins.

In 1907, Axel Holst and Theodor Frölich in Norway produced experimental scurvy in guinea pigs and showed that it could be cured by small quantities of cabbage. In England, from 1906 to 1912, Sir Frederick Gowland Hopkins (who shared the 1929 Nobel Prize with Eijkman) made extensive studies of the effects on animals of purified diets of carbohydrate, fat, protein, minerals, and water. He found that rats did not grow well on these diets, but responded to small amounts of milk. Hopkins concentrated the growth-producing substances in milk by chemical means. As a result of this work he asserted that there existed certain "accessory food factors"—other than the energy-containing foods, proteins, and minerals—that animals require for life.

In 1912, Casimir Funk made a survey of all knowledge then existing of vitamin deficiency diseases. In attempting to classify all known dietary essentials he coined the word *vitamine* to designate the substances which Hopkins had called "accessory food factors." This word was changed to *vitamin* at the suggestion of Jack C. Drummond in 1920. In 1913, Elmer V. McCollum and Marguerite Davis at the University of Wisconsin and Thomas B. Osborne and Lafayette B. Mendel at Yale, working independently, discovered the existence of a fat-soluble factor required for the growth of animals, vitamin A.

After this time rapid progress was made in the concentration, isolation, chemical identification, and synthesis of many new vitamins. This progress was facilitated by the use of experimental animals on special diets. After 1940 microorganisms were used extensively in the discovery and isolation of the newer vitamins.

Research in the field of vitamins after 1948 centered on the study of the biochemical functions of each vitamin and of vitamin interrelationships with other vitamins, amino acids, hormones, and minerals. Most of the vitamins whose functions have been determined have been shown to function as parts of enzyme systems concerned with the metabolism of carbohydrates, fats, and proteins.

In retrospect there seem to be three distinct periods in the history of vitamin research. First was the period characterized by recognition of the existence of nutrients different from those needed for energy and the building of tissues. This period began centuries ago and lasted until early in the 1900's. The second period (1925–1955) was devoted to the isolation, determination of structure, and synthesis of the vitamins. The third period was concerned with the attempt to understand the physiology and biochemistry of the vitamins. This began about the same time as the second period and is continuing.

LOUISE J. DANIEL*
Formerly, Cornell University

Bibliography

Beaton, G. H., and McKenry, E. W., eds., *Vitamins, Nutrient Requirements and Food Selection*, vol. 2 of *Nutrition, A Comprehensive Treatise* (Academic 1964).

Davidson, Stanley, and Passmore, R., *Human Nutrition and Dietetics*, 5th ed. (Longmans 1972).

De Luca, H. F., and Suttie, J. W., eds., *Fat-Soluble Vitamins* (Univ. of Wis. Press 1970).

Kutsky, Roman J., *Handbook of Vitamins and Hormones* (Van Nostrand-Reinhold 1973).

Marks, John, *The Vitamins: A Practical Manual* (Kluwer 1985).

Mervyn, Leonard, *The Dictionary of Vitamins: The Complete Guide to Vitamins and Vitamin Therapy* (Thorsons Pub. 1984).

Wagner, Arthur, and Folkers, Karl, *Vitamins and Coenzymes* (1964; reprint, Krieger 1975).

VITEBSK, vē-tepsk′, a city in the Belorussian republic of the Soviet Union, is the capital of Vitebsk oblast. Located at the junction of the Western Dvina and the Luchesa rivers in northeastern Belorussia, it is a river port and a major junction for several railroad lines linking Moscow, Leningrad, the Ukraine, and the Soviet Baltic republics.

Vitebsk is the largest center in Belorussia for the manufacture of linen textiles. Its factories also produce machine tools, furniture, shoes, glass, ceramic goods, and construction materials, and they process foods. There are teacher training, polytechnical, veterinary, and medical institutes in Vitebsk.

Vitebsk first appeared as a fortified area in the 11th century. For a time it was the center of its own small principality. It came under the control of the Lithuanian state in the 14th century and subsequently passed to the crown of Poland in the 16th century. Czarist Russia conquered and annexed the city in 1772. Some medieval churches are still intact, although the city has been almost destroyed several times, most recently by the Germans during their advance into the Soviet Union in World War II.

Vietbsk oblast lies in the basins of the western Dvina and the Dnieper rivers. Its cities include Vitebsk, Orsha, Polotsk, and Lepel. The uplands are farmed, principally for flax and rye. Population: (1983 est.) of the city, 324,000; of the oblast, 1,392,000.

VITELLIUS, vi-tel′ē-əs, **Aulus,** Roman emperor: b. Sept. 24, 15 A. D.; d. Rome, Dec. 20, 69. A favorite of emperors Tiberius, Caligula, Claudius, and Nero, he was incompetent, indolent, profligate, cruel, and gluttonous. He served as consul (48) and as proconsul of Africa (60). Emperor Galba appointed him to command the army in Lower Germany (68), where he so pampered the soldiers that they saluted him emperor on Jan. 2, 69. His legates invaded Italy and overcame Emperor Otho, who committed suicide in April.

Vitellius proceeded to Rome, where the Senate accepted him in June, but he made no preparation to withstand the general Vespasian, whom the eastern legions proclaimed emperor in July. Deserted eventually by most of his troops, Vitellius was restrained by the Roman populace from abdicating. Vespasian's advance forces discovered him hiding in the palace, dragged him through the Forum, and threw him into the Tiber River.

P. R. COLEMAN-NORTON
Formerly, Princeton University

VITERBO, vē-ter′bō, city and commune, Italy, capital of Viterbo Province, in Latium (Lazio). Situated at an altitude of about 1,000 feet (300 meters), it lies 38 miles (60 km) northwest of Rome on a rolling plain at the foot of the Cimini Mountains. It is the manufacturing and commercial center of the province; food processing and the production of tools, textiles, leather, and paper are the chief local industries. Viterbo preserves many 12th and 13th century buildings, and was little affected by the Renaissance and baroque styles. The medieval quarter, in the southern part of the city, looks much today as it did 700 years ago. The encircling pinnacled medieval walls with their towers and seven gates are also well preserved. The city's most important landmark is the 13th century papal palace and adjoining Gothic loggia, built for the popes when they took refuge here in times of strife in Rome. In the same square is the Romanesque 12th century cathedral with a tall campanile. Other landmarks are the Farnese Palace; the Fontana Grande, the finest fountain in the city; the Poscia residence; and the churches of San Giovanni in Zoccoli, San Francesco, and Santa Maria della Quercia.

Originally settled as an Etruscan town and later a Roman colony, Viterbo was included in the territories donated to the popes by the Franks in the 8th century, and was a pawn between the Holy Roman emperor and pope for centuries. Eugene III (r. 1145–1153) was the first pope to take refuge there. By the 15th century, however, Viterbo had been completely eclipsed by Rome as the seat of papal power. Population: (1983 est.) 58,009.

VITORIA, bē-tō′ryä, a city in northern Spain, is the capital of the Basque province of Álava. The old town is situated on a hillside and centers on the old Cathedral of Santa María. Founded in the 12th century, most of it dates from the 14th century. The modern city, where the unfinished new cathedral (begun in 1906) is located, lies on a level plain. Vitoria is an agricultural market center. Its factories process food and manufacture agricultural machines.

During the Peninsular War, British forces under the duke of Wellington decisively defeated the French here on June 21, 1813. Population: (1981) 192,773.

VITRUVIUS, vi-tro͞o′vē-əs, Roman architect and engineer of the 1st century B. C., whose treatise *De architectura* inspired the revival of classical architecture that began in the Renaissance and continued into the 20th century. Marcus Vitruvius Pollio was probably a military engineer under Julius Caesar. He superintended the construction of military engines for Emperor Augustus, was engineer of the water supply of Rome, and built a basilica at Fanum (Fano, Italy).

De architectura, written after 27 B. C. and dedicated to Augustus, is based on Vitruvius' own experience and on the works (now lost) of earlier Greek architects. Its ten books preserve the aesthetic principles and proportions of classical Greek architecture, which Vitruvius favored, rather than the technically impressive domed and vaulted Roman style then developing.

Book 1 deals with the training of architects, who should be cultivated in arts and sciences as well as technically skilled, and the principles of architecture and urban planning. Book 2 discusses building materials. Books 3 and 4 cover temples and the Greek orders. Other public buildings and private houses are the subjects of Books 5 and 6. Book 7 deals with interior design, including wall painting. The last three books are concerned with engineering: Book 8 on water supply, Book 9 on measuring time, and Book 10 on mechanical engineering.

De architectura was known in the Middle Ages, but its importance as the only written source for the classical style was first recognized by the Renaissance architect Leone Battista Alberti. Michelangelo, Bramante, and Vignola were influenced by its precepts. First printed about 1486, it appeared with illustrations by Palladio in 1556.

VITTORINO DA FELTRE, vēt-tō-rē'nō dä fāl'trā (originally VITTORINO RAMBOLDINI or DE' RAMBOLDINI), Italian humanist and educator: b. Feltre, Italy, 1378; d. Mantua, Feb. 2, 1446. Born in poverty, he worked his way through the University of Padua by teaching, and afterward kept a school in Venice while learning Greek. Called to Mantua in 1423 by Giovanni (Gian) Francesco I Gonzaga to tutor his children, Vittorino established there "the first great school of the Renaissance."

In addition to the Gonzaga children and other noble boys and girls, his 60 or 70 students always included many penniless scholars. His "Joyous House" set a pattern for Renaissance and later schools by combining strict moral training, the new humanist emphasis on classical literature, and the classical belief in development of the body by athletics. In each respect Vittorino himself set a high example for his students, among them such later ruler-scholars as Ludovico Gonzaga and Duke Federigo da Montefeltro of Urbino.

LINTON S. THORN
Hofstra College

VITTORIO VENETO, vēt-tô'ryō vâ'nā-tō, town and commune, Italy, in Treviso Province in the region of Venetia, 22 miles (35 km) north of Treviso at the edge of the Venetian plain near the foothills of the Alps. Agricultural machinery, textiles, paper, and furniture are some of its products. The town is a summer resort noted for its mineral springs. There are several Gothic and Renaissance buildings, the Castle of San Martino, and an 18th century cathedral.

Vittorio Veneto gave its name to a series of battles fought nearby in October–November 1918, toward the close of World War I. The defeat of the Austrian armies by the Italians, supported by British, French, and American troops, led to the armistice that was signed between the Allies and Austria on Nov. 3, 1918. Population: (1981 census) 30,028.

VITUS, vī'təs, SAINT, Christian martyr: d. Lucania, Italy, between 286 and 305. According to legend, when he was either 7 or 12 years old, he and his tutor, St. Modestus, and his nurse, St. Crescentia, were tortured for fidelity to Christianity. As a saint of succor, Vitus is invoked for protection against various diseases, especially the nervous disorder known technically as chorea and popularly as St. Vitus's dance (see CHOREA). The feast of the three saints is celebrated on June 15.

P. R. COLEMAN-NORTON
Formerly, Princeton University

VIVALDI, vē-väl'dē, **Antonio** (1678–1741), Italian composer and violinist, who, before Bach, carried the concerto form to its most advanced stage of technical development and artistic expression. Vivaldi's life is imperfectly documented. Many statements about him prove unfounded upon close examination, and it is impossible to date his compositions with any degree of certainty.

Vivaldi was born in Venice on March 4, 1678. He studied music with his father, a violinist, and entered the priesthood sometime before 1703, the year he began teaching music at and composing for the Ospedale della Pietà, a school for orphaned girls in Venice.

Because of asthma or a similar respiratory affliction, he never celebrated mass after his first year as a priest—though throughout his life he was known as the "red priest," presumably because of the color of his hair. He continued to teach at the Pietà until 1709, and again between 1711 and 1716.

Vivaldi travelled widely throughout Italy. He served as chapelmaster to Prince Philip of Hesse-Darmstadt, governor of Mantua, from 1718 to 1722. Toward the end of his life he went to Vienna, hoping to find employment and preferment at the court of Emperor Charles VI. He was disappointed, however, and died destitute in Vienna, where he was buried in a pauper's grave on July 28, 1741.

Works and Influence. Vivaldi, a phenomenally prolific composer, wrote approximately 40 or 50 operas and some 500 concertos, in addition to church music of all kinds. His operas, for the most part, have been forgotten, as has most of his church music except the Gloria Mass and the oratorio *Juditha Triumphans*. Vivaldi's present-day eminence rests on his superb instrumental music, especially his concerti grossi and solo concertos.

His first volume of concertos was published about 1712 and contains four solo concertos and eight concerti grossi. From this volume the best known of the solo concertos is the Violin Concerto in A Minor, and the most enduring of the concerti grossi is the D Minor. It is in the volume *The Trial of Harmony and Invention*, Opus 8, that Vivaldi's most frequently played concertos are found. These are the four concertos collectively called *The Four Seasons*, and each example is intended as a musical description of a different season of the year, beginning with spring.

Vivaldi greatly influenced Johann Sebastian Bach, who as a boy copied Vivaldi's music and memorized it. As an adult, Bach transcribed nine of Vivaldi's concertos as concertos for other instruments. It is probable that Vivaldi's solo concertos for violin served as the models for Bach's own solo concertos for that instrument and that Bach owed the excellence of his celebrated Brandenburg Concertos to Vivaldi's precedent.

Although much admired during his lifetime, Vivaldi was all but forgotten by the end of the 18th century, and his ultimate recognition as a major composer of the baroque period was delayed until the 20th century. In the 1920's a large collection of Vivaldi's scores was discovered, and in 1947 a complete edition of his instrumental works appeared.

VIVARINI, vē-vä-rē'nē, the name of a family of Italian painters important in the history of Renaissance painting.

ANTONIO VIVARINI (known also as ANTONIO DA MURANO): b. Murano, Italy, c. 1415; d. Venice, c. 1476/1484. Early in his career he collaborated with Giovanni d'Allemagna (probably from Cologne), his brother-in-law. He went to Venice after 1450. Stylistically he was a follower of Gentile da Fabriano, and he is remarkable as the first Venetian painter to break away from Byzantine influences, although traces of these are still to be seen in his work. Characteristic of his painting is the anxious expression on the faces of his figures and the closely spaced uprights of his architectural backgrounds. His best-known works are the *Madonna Enthroned*, in the Venice Academy; three altarpieces in the church of San Zaccaria, Venice; and a polyptych in the Vatican Gallery, Rome. In the United States his work may be seen in the Metropolitan Museum, New York City, and the National Gallery, Washington, D. C.

BARTOLOMEO (or BARTOLOMMEO) VIVARINI: b. Murano, c. 1432; d. Venice, c. 1491. He was the brother of Antonio. Bartolomeo's painting shows the influence of the Paduan school. A distinct, linear quality, garlands of fruits, and earnest construction characterize his work. He collaborated with Antonio on several altarpieces; his first known independent work was *St. John of Capistrano* (1454, now in the Louvre, Paris). Paintings of his are to be found in Santa Maria Formosa and the Academy in Venice, and in the United States in public collections at the National Gallery, Washington, D.C. (*Crowning of the Virgin* and *Madonna and child*); the Metropolitan Museum, New York City (*Mother and Child*); the Fogg Art Museum, Cambridge, Mass.; the De Young Memorial Museum, San Francisco, Calif.; and the Yale University Art Gallery, New Haven, Conn.

ALVISE VIVARINI: b. about 1446/1447; d. Venice, c. 1503/1505. Son of Antonio, he also shows traces of Byzantine influence in his painting, but to a lesser degree than his father. His work is characterized by the bell-shaped, almost closed eyelids of his Madonnas, the pupils of the eyes intersected by the lower lids, and by a peculiar linear treatment of the nostrils. His first dated work was in 1475. In 1488 he asked and obtained permission to work for the doge and the Signoria in the Great Council Hall of the Doge's Palace in Venice; he died during the course of this work, which was destroyed by fire. The *Madonna Enthroned with Six Saints* and *Santa Clara* in the Venice Academy, *Madonna with a Sleeping Child* in the Church of the Redeemer in Venice, and *Madonna Enthroned* in Berlin are his best-known works. A *Virgin and Child with Four Saints* in the Hermitage, Leningrad, which had been ascribed to Bellini, has recently been attributed to Alvise Vivarini. His paintings in public collections in the United States include *St. Sebastian*, at the Brooklyn Museum, New York City; *Virgin and Child*, at the Walters Art Gallery, Baltimore Md.; and a head at the Philadelphia Museum.

H. D. HALE,
Art Critic

VIVEKANANDA, vē-və-kä′nən-də, **SWAMI** (real name, **NARENDRANATH DUTTA** or **DATTA**), Hindu religious leader: b. Calcutta, India, 1863; d. Belur, 1902. A disciple of Ramakrishna (q.v.) he was inspired by his teacher to serve men as visible manifestations of God.

Desiring to further India's material advancement, he visited the United States in 1893 and made a deep impression at the Parliament of Religions which was held in Chicago. During a three-year stay in America and Europe that followed, he founded the Vedanta movement and adopted the name Vivekananda.

The Ramakrishna Mission, which became a worldwide organization embodying a cultural synthesis of East and West, was established by him in 1897. Although he was an ardent patriot, he dreamed of One World through the integration of science and Vedanta.

VIVES, vē′vās, **Juan Luis** (1492–1540), Spanish scholar, who was one of the most important humanists of the 16th century. He was born in Valencia on March 6, 1492, into a noble family. He studied in Valencia and at the University of Paris, which, because of its Scholastic orientation, he left in 1514 to go to Bruges, Flanders, the center of Renaissance humanism. There he met Erasmus, the leading humanist, and Guillaume Budé, the great scholar of ancient Greek.

Vives' edition of Saint Augustine's *City of God* brought him to the attention of Henry VIII of England, who invited him to serve as tutor to Princess Mary. While in England, Vives became a friend of Sir Thomas More and taught at Oxford. In 1528, Vives left England because he opposed the king's divorce suit against Catherine of Aragon and returned to Bruges, where he died on May 6, 1540.

Vives made important contributions to educational methodology. He advocated the use of the vernacular in teaching, with grammar reduced to a minimum; the establishment of public schools to prepare students for the academy; the introduction of recreation as a part of the curriculum; and the education of women. Vives also evolved an inductive method in the fields of education, philosophy, and psychology that later became associated with Francis Bacon. As a psychologist he was concerned with problems related to the nature of memory and the apprehension and association of ideas. A practical scholar, he held that knowledge was of value only if it could be put to use to bring about what he called the *Summum Bonum* (the greatest good), which he found in God. Vives' most important works were written in Latin, including *De institutione feminae Christianae* (1523); *De tradendis disciplinis* (1531); *De anima et vita* (1538), probably one of the first works on psychology; *Linguae Latinae exercitatio* (1538); and *De veritate fidei Christianae* (1543).

VIVIANI, vē-vyȧ-nē′, **René** (1863–1925), premier of France at the outbreak of World War I. He was born in Sidi-bel-Abbès, Algeria, on Nov. 8, 1863. Trained as a lawyer, he proved to be a fiery orator and gifted debater. When he entered politics in the late 1880's, his commitment to advanced social reforms led him to join the Socialist movement. Elected to the Chamber of Deputies from Paris in 1893 (reelected 1898), he soon became a leader of the moderate wing of the Socialist group.

Viviani believed that collaboration between Socialists and liberal elements of the middle class was indispensable for the realization of social reforms. After the unified Socialist party was founded (April 1905) and such collaboration was prohibited, he joined other moderate Socialists in creating what became the Republican Socialist party.

He served as minister of labor from 1906 to 1910. In December 1913 he became minister of public instruction, then formed his own ministry in June 1914. To prove his country's peaceful intentions, he ordered the withdrawal of French troops several miles behind the frontier. When war came, he rallied the nation with his appeal for a political truce and a "sacred union" of all Frenchmen. In October 1915 he resigned the premiership, but continued to serve in the cabinet of Aristide Briand until 1917. He died in Le Plessis-Robinson, France, on Sept. 7, 1925.

VIVIPAROUS ANIMALS, vī-vip′ə-rəs, include all those animals that produce living young developed in the female, in contrast to *oviparous animals,* which lay eggs. In mammals the entire development from egg to fetus occurs in the uterus or womb. The growing young is attached there by a special structure, the placenta, in which blood vessels of mother and young are interlaced; food and oxygen from the parental blood diffuse into the embryo circulation, and wastes follow the opposite path. Viviparous development also occurs in some sharks, insects, starfishes, and other animals. In *ovoviviparous animals* the egg develops within the parent oviduct, using its own large yolk supply as food, and live young are born. This type occurs in rattlesnakes, garter snakes, some lizards, a few salamanders, various fishes, and a miscellany of invertebrates. Plants in which seed develops while attached to the parent plant are also called viviparous. See also ANATOMY, COMPARATIVE—*Reproductive Organs.*

TRACY I. STORER

VIVISECTION, viv-ə-sek′shən, literally, is the dissection of a living animal. The term is now used to apply to all types of experiments on living animals, whether or not cutting is done. Since the earliest days of biological science, information obtained from experiments on invertebrates, fishes, amphibians, and rodents has contributed enormously to our understanding of the life processes. An outstanding example of this kind of research was that of the English court physician William Harvey in the first quarter of the 17th century. His experiments on a large variety of invertebrate and vertebrate organisms clearly demonstrated the relationship between the heartbeat and the circulation of blood. Experiments on larger mammals, especially the dog and cat, had sometimes been performed even in ancient times by so-called physicians and surgeons; but it was not until the development of the newer biomedical sciences of physiology, pharmacology, and experimental pathology in the 19th century that the use of these mammals in the research laboratory became general on the European continent. A complete understanding of the normal and abnormal functioning of man has always been an important goal of biological research. The intimate connection between animal experimentation and rational therapeutics, however, did not gain widespread acceptance from scientists and physicians until the 19th century, after prolonged and bitter controversy. The performance of live animal experiments to educate and train biologists and physicians and to develop new surgical techniques was also firmly established at this time.

Many early animal experiments, particularly on the larger mammals, undoubtedly caused the subjects to experience much discomfort and pain, just as therapeutic and surgical procedure was responsible for much human suffering until relatively recent times. However, significant advances in anesthetic technique and in neurophysiology —chiefly the result of animal experiments— have enabled the scientist to develop laboratory animal methods as humane as those used in modern medical practice. Humane treatment of the animals is now considered a chief prerequisite for efficient and successful research in the biomedical sciences. Such treatment involves adequate housing, feeding, and general care in addition to the careful handling of animals during experiments. In the years since the end of World War II, both aspects of laboratory animal treatment have been complicated by the phenomenal increase in the number of experimental animals used for many different purposes: research in the biological, medical, and veterinary sciences; education and training of scientists, physicians, surgeons, and veterinarians; the manufacture of vaccines, toxoids, and antitoxins; diagnosis of disease; drug testing and standardization; and space research.

Many organizations now exist to determine the most humane procedures for treating animals under all types of laboratory conditions and to publicize these procedures to appropriate individuals and institutions. The United Nations Educational, Scientific and Cultural Organization is involved in this activity. Other organizations, such as the American Association for Laboratory Animal Science (formerly the Animal Care Panel) and the American Association for Accreditation of Laboratory Animal Care in the United States, are private professional societies made up of scientists, veterinarians, animal breeders, caretakers, and research institutions. Still others are governmental bureaus such as the Institute of Laboratory Animal Resources of the National Research Council in the United States and the Laboratory Animal Bureau in Great Britain. In many countries there are also "humane societies" that are genuinely interested in the adoption of standardized humane methods for treating experimental animals. The advice offered by these groups may not always be useful or constructive, but they continually challenge the scientist to defend and improve his position concerning the treatment of the animals. Such societies frequently contend that only through governmental regulation can proper treatment of laboratory animals be assured. The British Cruelty to Animals Act of 1876 (amended in 1906) exemplifies this approach, but it is still debatable whether the treatment of laboratory animals is more humane in Great Britain than in countries having no comparable law. Under the British system, animal experiments can be made only in a registered laboratory open to government inspection; individuals require licenses in order to perform such experiments, and each type of animal experiment must be approved.

Organized antivivisectionists have sought to influence lawmakers and the lay population in virtually all countries where animal experiments are performed. Almost yearly since 1897, antivivisectionist-sponsored bills have been offered in the United States Congress, but none has yet passed. On a local level, however, the antivivisectionists have frequently succeeded in such matters as preventing the acquisition of dogs and cats by research laboratories and professional schools. As a countermeasure, the National Society for Medical Research was founded in 1946 under the sponsorship of the Association of American Medical Colleges. This society has the support of professional schools and research and philanthropic institutions. State chapters comprise individual scientists and responsible public figures. Largely because of the activities of these groups, many states now have specific laws that permit approved institutions to obtain unwanted stray animals for research purposes.

ALBERT S. KUPERMAN
Field Staff Member, Rockefeller Foundation

VIZCAÍNO, vēth-kä-ē′nō, **Sebastián,** 16th–17th century Spanish navigator, who made the first detailed exploration of the coast of California. He was probably born in Corcho, Spain. About 1585 he went to Mexico to seek his fortune, and by the end of the decade he had made at least one trip to Manila. In 1596 he led an unsuccessful expedition up the Gulf of California in search of pearls. Six years later he set out with three ships to explore the coast of California for good harbors and the end of a possible sea passage from the Atlantic.

Leaving Acapulco in May 1602, the ships reached San Diego Bay in November and Monterey Bay in December. From there Vizcaíno sent one ship back with disabled crewmen. He led the other ships as far north as Cape Mendocino, where they had to turn back because of the miserable condition of the crews. They missed the bay of San Francisco.

Arriving in Mexico in February 1603, Vizcaíno recommended the use of Monterey as a Spanish naval port and as a refitting station for the Manila galleons. His advice was not taken. In 1611–1614 he led an expedition from Mexico to Japan and back. He died sometime after 1615.

Vizcaíno was not the first to explore California. But the detailed information he gathered remained definitive until the Portolá-Serra expedition of 1769.

VIZSLA, vizh′lô, a hunting dog developed in the great central plain of Hungary, an agricultural region noted for its abundant small game. The vizsla is about the size of a dalmatian. It stands about 23 inches (60 cm) at the shoulder and weighs about 60 pounds (28 kg). In Hungary, vizslas having two types of coats—short-haired and wire-haired—are raised. The short-haired vizsla, recognized by the American Kennel Club in 1960, has a smooth coat with colors of rusty gold to dark sandy yellow preferred.

EVELYN SHAFER

Vizsla (short-haired), also called a Hungarian pointer.

The vizsla was bred as a general-purpose hunting dog. It has an excellent nose and can track rabbits, point and retrieve game birds on land, and retrieve geese and ducks in water.

V-J DAY refers to the date (Sept. 2, 1945) of Japan's formal surrender in World War II.

VLAARDINGEN, vlär′ding-ən, a city in the Netherlands, is in South Holland province, just west of Rotterdam. Situated on the north bank of the Nieuwe Waterweg (New Waterway), it is the Netherlands' third-largest port. Vlaardingen is the base of a large fishing fleet, and herring and cod are cured here. Dairy goods are also processed. The manufacture of chemical fertilizers is a leading industry. Population: (1972) 81,579.

VLACHS, vläks, a European people who today make up a large part of the population of Rumania and the Moldavian republic of the USSR. The name is derived from Volokh, a name given to them by the Slavs. They prefer to call themselves Romani or a variant of that name.

Their origins are traced to the Roman province of Dacia, an area corresponding to modern Rumania. The native inhabitants of Dacia intermarried with the Roman colonists and soldiers, adopting their culture and language. In the Middle Ages they spread over much of the Balkans. Those in Bulgaria joined the Bulgarians to form the Empire of Vlachs and Bulgarians in 1184. Others settled in what was to become Wallachia and Moldavia. These principalities joined in the 19th century to form Rumania.

VLADIMIR, vlad′ə-mir (c. 956–1015), grand prince of Kiev. Vladimir the Great (also Saint Vladimir) was the son of Svyatoslav, grand prince of Kiev, who shortly before his death divided his state among Vladimir and his two other sons, Yaropolk and Oleg. They soon quarreled with each other; Oleg was killed, and Vladimir fled to Scandinavia. Returning with a band of Varangian mercenaries, Vladimir treacherously slew his brother Yaropolk and became grand prince of Kiev about 978.

Vladimir's victory signified the temporary triumph of paganism over Christianity in Kiev. According to a chronicle of a later period, missionaries from neighboring states tried to convert Vladimir to their respective faiths. Before accepting any of them, Vladimir sent envoys abroad to see how the people lived under the different religions. He and his supporters, according to this chronicle, decided in favor of Eastern Orthodoxy when the envoys reported that they "no longer knew whether we were in heaven or on earth" when they witnessed the religious ceremony of the Greeks.

Vladimir's preference for the Eastern Orthodox rite was strengthened by his desire for the hand of Princess Anna, sister of the Byzantine emperor Basil II. A condition of the marriage, which was celebrated at Kherson in the Crimea, was Vladimir's submission to baptism (about 989). Vladimir was the last of the great European princes to accept Christianity.

Upon his return to Kiev, Vladimir embarked immediately upon the Christianization of his people. He devoted the remainder of his life to building churches, furthering education, and dispensing charity. He also greatly expanded his territories. Yet he maintained unity within the state by appointing his sons as governors of different areas and by requiring them to pay tribute to him. Vladimir died in Berestovoye, Russia, on July 15, 1015. His death was the signal for fratricidal warfare among his sons.

CHARLES MORLEY
The Ohio State University

VLADIMIR, vlad′ə-mir, is the name of a city and an oblast in the Russian republic of the USSR. It is located on a hill rising above the Klyazma River, a tributary of the Oka. Vladimir is an important textile center but also manufactures machine tools, tractors, chemicals, and automobile parts.

History. Vladimir II Monomakh, grand prince of Kiev, founded the city, which was named after him, in the early 12th century. Andrew Bogolyubsky, grandson of Vladimir and son of Yuri Dolgoruky,, prince of Rostov-Suzdal, made this his capital when he became ruler of the principality of Rostov-Suzdal on his father's death in 1157. His brother Vsevolod III continued to rule there after Andrew's death in 1174. These rulers of what is sometimes known as the principality of Vladimir, and their successors, were generally recognized as the senior princes of Kievan Russia until Vladimir was pillaged and burned by the Tatars in 1238. Thereafter the princes of Vladimir gradually lost their influence in northeastern Russia. In the 15th century, Vladimir came under Moscow's rule.

Historical Monuments. The Golden Gates on the west, made of panels of gilded copper, were built in 1164. They are the only examples of 12th century Russian military architecture that survive in Russia. The Silver Gates on the east no longer exist. Andrew Bogolyubsky had the Cathedral of the Dormition (Uspensky Sobor) built in 1158. In 1189, Vsevolod III had it rebuilt and enlarged after a fire. Vsevolod also had the Dimitri (Demetrius) Cathedral built in 1194–1197. These churches, which have been preserved, are masterpieces of Russian architecture. Most of the remaining historic buildings in Vladimir date from the 16th to the 19th centuries. Population: (1972) of the city, 248,000; (1970) of the oblast, 1,511,000.

VLADIMIR II MONOMAKH, vlad′ə-mir mu-nu-mäkh′ (1053–1125), grand prince of Kiev. He was born in Kiev, the eldest son of Vsevolod I and grandson of Yaroslav I, both of whom were grand princes of Kiev. His mother, Irina, was the daughter of the Byzantine emperor Constantine Monomachus.

When Vsevolod died, the townspeople of Kiev asked Vladimir Monomakh to be their prince, but he stood aside in favor of his cousin Svyatopolk II, whose claims to the position were superior to his own. He led the princes of his family on three successful expeditions against the heathen Polovtsy (Kipchak Turks, also called Cumans). When Svyatopolk died in 1113, the democratic *veche* (town assembly) passed over those in direct line of succession and appealed to Vladimir again to accept the principality. This time Vladimir agreed.

During his reign, Kiev prospered and reached the zenith of its political power. Vladimir repeatedly campaigned against the Polovtsy. He also founded the city of Vladimir on the Klyazma River, which was to become the center of Kievan Russia before the end of the century.

Vladimir was a skillful and humane leader. His humanity is clearly evidenced in his famous *Book of Instruction*, written for his children about 1117. A typical passage that conveys the tenor of the book is: "Give to the orphan, protect the widow, and permit the mighty to destroy no man." Vladimir Monomakh died near Kiev on May 19, 1125.

VLADIVOSTOK, vla-di-vos-tok′, is a city in the Russian republic, USSR, and capital of the Primorski krai (Maritime Territory). The Soviet Union's largest port on the Pacific Ocean, it is located in the extreme southeastern part of Siberia near the Korean and Manchurian (Chinese) frontier. The city is built like an amphitheater on hills around Golden Horn Harbor, which is an inlet of Peter the Great Bay. It is at the southern end of the Muraviev-Amurski peninsula, which separates the Gulf of Amur on the west from the Ussuri Bay on the east.

Because of an intermixture of summer monsoons and Siberian winters, the climate is unusual, with damp springs, hot wet summers, long dry autumns, and frigid winters. The harbor freezes for several months each winter, but it is kept open by icebreakers.

Vladivostok is the economic and cultural center of the entire Soviet Far East. It is the eastern terminus of the Trans-Siberian Railway and the main supply base for other Soviet ports on the Pacific and east Arctic coasts. Vladivostok is also the home port for the Soviet Pacific naval and fishing fleets. The city and surrounding region are heavily fortified.

The city has more than 200 industries, chief among which are ship building and repair, fish canning, metalworking, and construction. Oil, coal, grain, and lumber are major exports. There are engineering, education, fishing, and merchant marine colleges.

The site of the city was first fortified in 1860. The town grew slowly at first, but as the hinterland was explored and developed, it began to grow more rapidly. By 1890 it had become the administrative center of the region. It was bombarded by the Japanese Navy in 1904. For several years after World War I, it was occupied by United States, British, French, and Japanese troops. Late in World War II, it was a major port receiving United States lend-lease supplies for the USSR. Population: (1972) 472,000.

ELLSWORTH RAYMOND
New York University

VLAMINCK, vlà-maɴk′, **Maurice de** (1876–1958), French painter, whose bold use of color and exuberant personality typified the Fauvist movement with which he was associated. However, the spontaneous style of this period soon gave way to paintings in the more ordered manner of Paul Cézanne, and during the remainder of his long life he devoted himself increasingly to realism.

Vlaminck was born in Paris on April 4, 1876. At age 19 he took some drawing lessons but received no academic training. His interest in art was stimulated by his friendship with André Derain, whom he met about 1900, when both were in rebellion against the academic tradition as well as the neo-impressionists. A 1901 exhibit of Vincent Van Gogh reaffirmed Vlaminck's conviction in the unrestrained use of color.

Vlaminck was one of the original exponents of Fauvism, an artistic revolt launched by an exhibit at the Salon d'Automne in 1905. With his remarkable physical energy and vitality—reflected in his robust style of painting that featured heavy brushstrokes—Vlaminck proved to be the embodiment of a Fauve (literally, "wild beast"). But by 1908, claiming that he had explored the limits of intense colors drawn straight from the tube, he began to produce relatively subdued and well-structured composi-

MUSEUM OF MODERN ART, NEW YORK, GIFT OF MR. AND MRS. WALTER HOCHSCHILD

Vlaminck's *Winter Landscape* (1916–1917) has the dark colors, strong, spontaneous brush strokes, and clearly defined forms that followed his early Fauvist exuberance.

tions, rendered in darker tones. This trend became more pronounced after World War I, and from then on his work showed the influence of the Dutch naturalists, with clearly defined forms and tonal colors of gray, green, and blue dominating his canvases.

Works dating from Vlaminck's Fauvist years include *Picnic in the Country* and *Bridge at Châtou* (both painted in 1905 and now in private collections) and *Street at Marly-le-Roi* (1905–1906) and *Red Trees* (1906), both at the Musée National d'Art Moderne, Paris. From his later period are *Self-Portrait* (1910; private collection) and the somber *Hamlet in the Snow* (1943).

Vlaminck was also an illustrator, decorator, printmaker, and author (including novels, such as *Grains au vent,* his first). He died in Rueil-la-Gadeliére, near Paris, on Oct. 11, 1958. See also FAUVISM.

VLORË, vlôr′ə, is the second most important port city in Albania. Vlorë (also Vlonë, Vlora, or Valona) lies on the Bay of Vlorë and is sheltered by Karaburun, a peninsula to the west of the bay, and by Sazan Island at its mouth. The city's industries include fishing and canning, cement making, rice husking, and the refining of olive oil. It exports bituminous coal mined in nearby fields.

Called Aulon by the Greeks, it was one of the three ancient Greek colonies on the Illyrian coast. Possession of it was contested by the major powers in the area in the centuries that followed the fall of Rome. In 1464 it became part of the Ottoman Empire. At Vlorë on Nov. 28, 1912, Ismail Kemal (a native of the city) and other nationalist leaders proclaimed Albanian independence. At the end of World War II, Albania's Communist regime gave the naval base to the Soviet Union, but because it lacked breakwaters the USSR gradually reduced its personnel, and Soviet submarines abandoned the base. Population: (1981 est.) 61,500.

VLTAVA RIVER, vul′tə-və, Czechoslovakia, the most important river of Bohemia, flowing a distance of 267 miles (430 km) before emptying into the Elbe. It rises in the eastern Bohemian Forest, flows southeast to a point near the Austrian border, and then curves north, continuing past Cesky Krumlov, Budweis, and Prague until reaching the Elbe, near Melnik, about 20 miles (32 km) north of the capital. The Vltava (Moldau, in German) is open to large steamboats for about 50 miles (80 km) in its lower course, beginning below Stechovice.

VOCAL CORDS are the parts of the larynx, or voice box, that vibrate to produce sound. They are known in anatomy as *plicae vocales,* or *vocal folds,* because they are two folds of pearly white mucous membrane attached to the sides of the larynx. Every air-breathing vertebrate has a larynx, but only mammals (including man) and a few lower forms have vocal cords.

The vocal folds or cords project into the cavity of the larynx, slanting together to form a V with the apex in front. Each fold contains a strong band of yellow elastic tissue known as the *vocal ligament.* Between the folds is an elongated space called the *rima glottidis.* The vocal cords with their ligaments and the rima glottidis together constitute the *glottis,* the sound-producing apparatus of the larynx.

Vocalization (making sounds with the voice) is part of the breathing mechanism. The sound is produced when air enters the larynx from the lungs during exhalation and thus causes the vocal cords to vibrate. Because breathing is to a large extent voluntary, the force of the air in the glottis can be controlled. This is how the voice is modulated.

Vibration of the vocal cords makes vocalization possible, but other factors are involved in speaking or making articulate sounds. Movements of the tongue, lips, jaws, and cheeks mold the column of air in the glottis so that the tautness and rate of vibration of the vocal cords are regulated. In this way, sounds of different pitch and intensity may be produced.

During ordinary breathing, the vocal cords are draped apart in the V shape. In speech or singing, they are drawn together. When a very high note is uttered, the space between the cords is reduced to a narrow slit.

See also LARYNX; VOICE.

FPG

In an adult education class, students acquire the background necessary for understanding information processing.

VOCATIONAL EDUCATION. The aim of vocational education is to prepare young people and adults for useful occupations, particularly for skilled trades and semiprofessional careers. It also may serve to increase the knowledge and skills of those already employed in occupations of this kind. Vocational education is most often given at the high school or junior college level and does not normally include training for professions such as law and medicine.

Vocational education often stresses instruction in skills that the learner must use on a specific job. It also provides technical background that increases the student's understanding of a field of work. For example, a course in the physical properties of metals is a vocational course when given to young men preparing to be machinists. Programs to combine practical and theoretical instruction include work-study, on-the-job training, and cooperative training.

A work-study program is one in which a student works on a job during part of his regular school hours. Sometimes the school assists the student in obtaining his job. However, there may be no close coordination of practical experiences with classroom instruction.

On-the-job training provides a planned program of vocational instruction for persons on actual jobs. A supervisor or an experienced employee teaches the student the skills of a specific occupation. Some time is spent in classroom study, which may or may not be closely coordinated with training given on the job.

A cooperative training program stresses coordination of education in school and at work. Teachers and employers plan classroom and job training so that the student sees the relationship of theory and practice. The cooperative program usually gives the student a broader background of vocational knowledge than he could get from a work-study or on-the-job program.

Changes and innovations in business, industry, homemaking, marketing, and agriculture have increased the need for vocational education. Millions of jobs are changing, and new jobs are emerging. Displaced workers must learn new skills and must often relocate.

The most rapidly expanding occupations require the most training. Predictions of U.S. manpower distribution indicate that the greatest proportional growth will be in professional, sales, office, service, and technical occupations. Employment opportunities for highly skilled craftsmen and technicians are increasing even faster than those for scientists and engineers. A major task of vocational educators is to prepare people for these skilled and technical fields.

VOCATIONAL EDUCATION PROGRAMS

The federal government, schools, and industry group vocational training programs into seven categories. These are: (1) trade and industrial, (2) office or business, (3) distributive, (4) agricultural, (5) home economics, (6) health occupations, and (7) technical.

Trade and Industrial Education prepares people for skilled occupations, particularly in the manufacturing, building, and maintenance industries. It trains such craftsmen as machinists, pattern-makers, carpenters, plumbers, auto mechanics, and air conditioning repairmen. Other trades, such as those of the printer and the baker, also fall in the skilled category.

A young person who wants to learn a skilled trade or craft can choose one of several programs. He can enroll in a vocational high school and take a combination of academic and practical courses. In this program he would spend half his school week in general education courses such as English, history, science, and mathematics, and the other half in shop or laboratory courses that teach the skills of a specific trade.

SYBIL SHELTON/PETER ARNOLD

Students gain practical experience in a class training high-school students as dental technicians.

A second option is to take a cooperative program in a vocational high school. The student would divide his time equally between classes in school and practical experience in a factory or shop. Classroom study and practical work are coordinated. If, for example, a boy is studying TV repair, his shop work on wiring might be backed up by a course in basics of electricity.

A third kind of trade and industrial program is apprenticeship. Some trades are customarily learned through a period of work under the direction of experienced craftsmen. The period of apprenticeship varies—three years for bricklayers, five years for plumbers, and four to six years for men in the printing trades. In most programs, work experience is supplemented by classroom study in the evenings or during part of the working week.

In addition to these various programs to train young people to start work in skilled jobs, there are programs for workers in a field. Part-time courses help craftsmen learn to use new machines and new techniques. Other programs train unemployed workers to start new trades. For example, some factory workers displaced by automation have been retrained to service TV sets.

Office Education programs range from typing and filing to business management and computer programming. Most high schools offer basic business courses in shorthand, typing, and bookkeeping. Many large high schools also provide courses in clerical procedures, office machine operation, and data processing. Some programs take place entirely in the school. Others are cooperative, with part of the school week spent in a business office for on-the-job training.

Young people who aim for more responsible positions in business may take post-high school training. An example of a program at this level is a two-year curriculum to train legal secretaries. Courses include general education (English and history), basic business (typing and word processing), and special studies (legal terminology and business law). Other two-year programs train men and women in accounting, in the operation of electronic computers, and in the principles of office supervision or store management.

Distributive Education prepares students for careers providing goods and services to consumers. The term "distributive occupations" covers a wide range. It includes the jobs of retailing and wholesaling workers such as salesmen, managers, buyers, demonstrators, and deliverymen. It also includes personal service workers such as desk clerks in hotels and motels.

A young man or woman who wants to prepare for a distributive occupation can take a cooperative program in high school. Many high schools offer a two-year program in 11th and 12th grades, or a one-year program in 12th grade. School periods are divided between general education courses and special courses in merchandising and marketing, including such topics as business costs and consumer preferences. For practical experience the student spends at least 15 hours a week on an actual job. His work is supervised both by a distributive education coordinator, who is a member of the school staff, and by a representative of the management of the company that is helping to train the student.

In addition to high school programs there are programs for advanced students and for adults. Post-high school courses train men for careers in such fields as retail store management, wholesale company management, and hotel and motel management. Adult classes help people in sales and management to improve their techniques.

Agricultural Education covers a complex range of activities. The modern farm owner or manager is often called an agricultural businessman. In addition to being an expert on plants and animals, he must understand such matters as erosion control, machinery operation, and the processing of his products by freezing or other methods. Agricultural education is not restricted to farming but also takes in related businesses. These include selling fertilizer, feed, tools, and machinery; transporting produce; and providing such services as soil testing and well drilling.

To prepare foı careers in agriculture, students can take four-year programs in high school. As in other kinds of vocational education, students mix classroom study and practical experience. Young farmers who have left high school can enroll in part-time courses.

For more advanced training, high school graduates can take two-year programs. One example is the agriculture technology program, which includes study of agronomy, farm tractors, farm surveying, welding, technical mathematics, and applied psychology.

Adult farmers who want special training can enroll in part-time programs. Courses teach farm management methods and crop production.

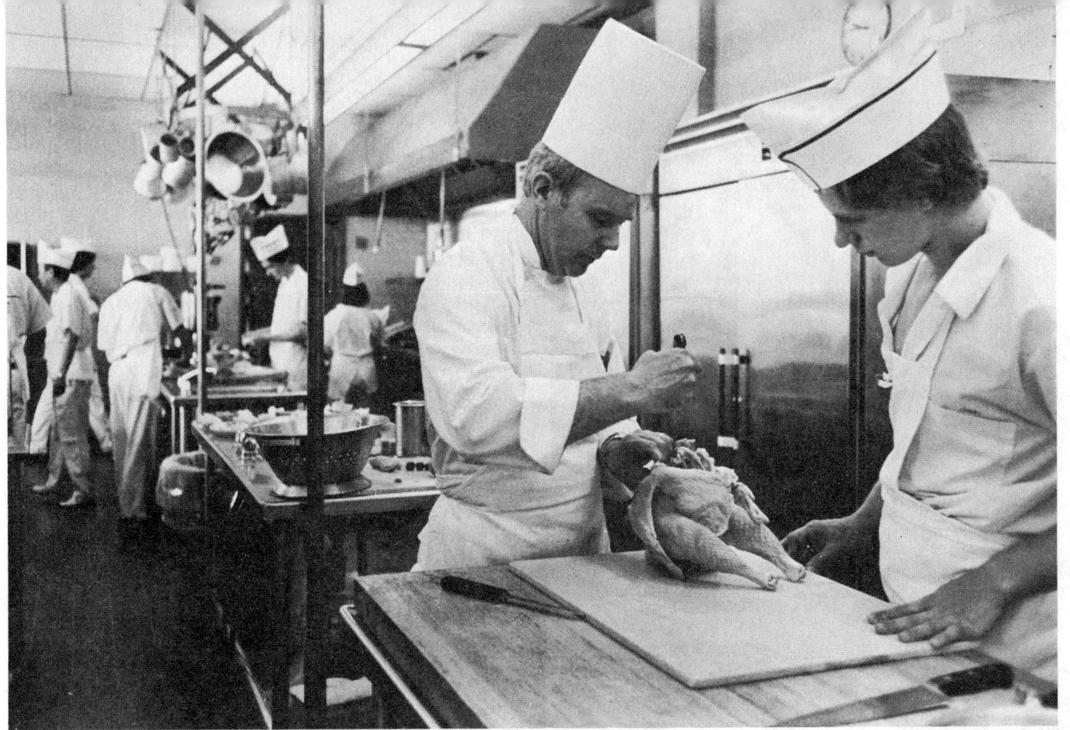

SYBIL SHELTON/PETER ARNOLD

In this well-equipped high school, a student is given individual attention in a restaurant-management class.

Home Economics Education, as part of vocational education, focuses chiefly on preparation for family life rather than on training for a paid job. The objective of homemaking programs is to help girls (and some boys) learn how to handle the routines and problems of family living.

High school homemaking programs may last two, three, or four years. The basic courses usually include foods and nutrition; clothing and textiles; child care and development; housing and interior decoration; family management and finance; care of the sick and aged; and personal, family, and community relations. To teach these courses, home project or home experience activities are integrated with classroom study. Teachers visit students and their parents to plan home projects that will put classroom learning to work in practical situations.

Part-time homemaking programs are offered to young people who are not in school, and to adults. Some courses, like those in high school, aim to help students in their homes. Other courses train men and women for jobs as cooks, tailors, dressmakers, assistants in care for the aged, and assistants to dietitians.

Health Occupations Education trains men and women to assist doctors, dentists, registered nurses, and other professional people in the field of health. The largest enrollments are in programs to train practical nurses. These programs usually last one year, combining classroom study and supervised work in hospitals. In all states of the U.S. training is available for high school graduates and for adults who want to qualify as practical nurses. In some states high school seniors can enroll in these programs.

Other programs in the health occupations field vary greatly in length and content. Training for nurse's aids may be completed in 4 to 10 weeks. On the other hand, training for dental technicians, medical laboratory assistants, and other semiprofessional men and women may require two or more years of study.

Technical Education prepares men and women to work as expert assistants to professionals in many fields. The work of technicians multiplies the effectiveness of professional and managerial experts. Professional mechanical engineers, for example, need the assistance of semiprofessional engineering aides and precision measurements technicians. Electrical and electronic engineers delegate some of their work to technicians. In business, data-processing technicians speed the work of executives by handling masses of facts and figures in banks and insurance companies. In agriculture, soil technicians assist soil scientists. In the health field, technical workers include X-ray technicians and dental hygienists.

These semiprofessional jobs are called "middle-level" occupations because they require more training than skilled crafts but require less education than professional positions do. Nearly all technicians must take training beyond high school, usually a two-year program. Typical programs give the student a core of knowledge that is basic to his field of interest. A mechanical technology student, for example, studies analytical geometry, calculus, chemistry, physics, and metallurgy. He also takes more specific courses such as welding, machine shop practice, industrial electricity, and machine design. A person who has completed this program has a broader base of knowledge than a skilled worker such as a machinist. A trained technologist is able to work alongside a mechanical or industrial engineer on a variety of projects.

VOCATIONAL EDUCATION AGENCIES

Many kinds of agencies provide programs of vocational education: public high schools, public and private junior colleges and technical institutes, extension services, correspondence schools, labor unions and industrial firms, and the armed forces. Some of these agencies offer dozens of programs, while others specialize in training for one type of occupation.

HUGH ROGERS/MONKMEYER

(*Above*) An instructor discusses TV transmission problems at a state university. (*Below*) At a private institution, students learn aircraft-engine maintenance.

CARY WOLINSKY/STOCK, BOSTON

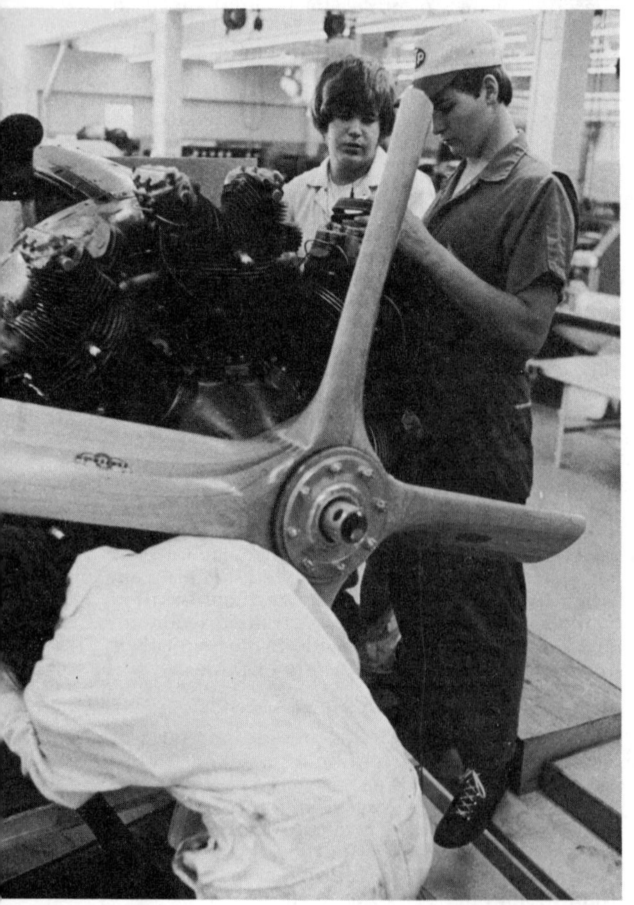

Public Schools lead the vocational education field in terms of number of people trained and variety of programs offered. Public high schools train millions of boys and girls and thousands of adults each year in skills ranging from carpentry and auto repair to dressmaking and commercial art. High schools prepare skilled workers in six of the seven varieties of programs discussed earlier: trade and industry, business, distributive occupations, agriculture, home economics, and health. They do not usually provide training for semi-professional and technical occupations.

Two main plans are used for organizing high school vocational training. One is to give job training in addition to general education courses in a high school. The second plan is to organize separate vocational high schools.

A high school that provides both vocational and general education has certain advantages. Vocational students have access to a large number of general courses such as science, social studies, and languages. They can use the library and other facilities of the high school and share in sports and social activities. Only a large community, however, can support a school that offers both a general program and dozens of vocational courses requiring specialized teachers and expensive shops and workrooms. Small high schools may have to limit their vocational programs to business and home economics.

Large city school systems are able to maintain specialized vocational high schools. New York City, for example, has a High School of Art and Design, a High School of Fashion Industries, and a Machine and Metal Trades High School. In rural districts, a number of towns can pool their tax resources to build and run a well equipped regional vocational school that will serve them all. Pre-job programs are designed to meet the needs of business, industry, and agriculture in the area. General education courses are given, but not on the same scale as in a comprehensive high school.

Junior Colleges are leading agencies for training men and women to enter semiprofessional and technical occupations. Junior colleges give two-year programs keyed to the growing number of jobs that require training beyond high school. A sample of occupations of this type includes missile technicians, office supervisors, insurance salesmen, agricultural research technicians, and medical record technicians. Some junior colleges offer training in crafts such as automobile repair and office machine repair. In addition to pre-job training, junior colleges offer courses for adults who want more training for their present work or retraining for new careers.

Both public and private junior colleges offer vocational education. Many private two-year colleges specialize in business courses, although some give other programs such as engineering technology. See JUNIOR COLLEGE.

Technical Institutes specialize in training engineering technicians. These institutes resemble junior colleges in that they give two-year programs above the high school level but below the level of the four-year college or university. To prepare men to work as assistants to professional engineers, technical institutes emphasize both "thinking" and "doing" courses. Programs are planned to fit the requirements of industry and are changed as new industrial techniques come into use. Private technical institutes are noted for developing new training methods.

SYBIL SHELTON/PETER ARNOLD

A vocational-high-school masonry course prepares students for entry into professional apprenticeship programs.

Extension Education is a service that provides vocational training for young people and adults who cannot enroll in full-time classes. Particularly important is the Agricultural Extension Service, a joint project of the U.S. Department of Agriculture and the state colleges and universities. Agents for this program advise and instruct farm families. See AGRICULTURAL EDUCATION.

Correspondence Schools offer vocational education programs for home study. Dozens of courses are available in subjects ranging from drawing to cooking. Studying any subject through the mail has obvious disadvantages. The learner cannot talk directly to his teacher, and he does not have the laboratories, shops, and libraries provided by vocational schools. The advantage of correspondence study is that it can be fitted into after-work hours and can be carried on by people who cannot get to a school or college. Some employers encourage men and women to take correspondence courses so that they can increase their knowledge and skills without losing valuable time from work.

Correspondence courses are offered by many well-established colleges and universities. Courses are also sold by firms that specialize in teaching by mail. While many of these firms are reputable, some make misleading promises of easy study leading to high-paying jobs. Reputable schools are listed by the Accrediting Commission of the National Home Study Council, an association of U.S. correspondence schools. See also CORRESPONDENCE SCHOOLS AND COURSES.

Labor Unions and Industrial Firms provide vocational education in several ways. Apprenticeship programs are among the oldest kinds of job training to prepare craftsmen for trade and industry. Apprentice programs are planned and run by joint action of union officials and employers. Public high schools, and sometimes public junior colleges, are involved to the extent that they provide classroom study to supplement on-the-job learning of manual skills. A division of the U.S. Department of Labor, the Bureau of Apprenticeship and Training, promotes training of craftsmen and advises unions and management on the conduct of programs.

Unions and industry also sponsor training programs for employees who are not enrolled as apprentices. Some industries give training on the job, but a number of large firms have set up elaborate training centers. In equipment and operation these centers resemble vocational high schools or even technical institutes. However, industrial training centers concentrate on one kind of education. They prepare craftsmen to produce or service a specific product.

Armed Forces. The U.S. Army, Air Force, and Navy train large numbers of skilled technicians. Many former servicemen and women use their military training in civilian jobs after they complete their enlistments. About half of all enlisted personnel in the armed forces are classified as skilled craftsmen or technicians, such as metal-workers, aircraft mechanics, automotive repairmen, electricians, radio operators, photographers, and medical laboratory technicians. The armed services provide training in special schools and on the job. Trade and technical training can be supplemented by correspondence courses available through the U.S. Armed Forces Institute (USAFI) and the Military Extension Correspondence Course Program.

There are advantages and disadvantages to learning a trade in the armed forces. On the one hand, hundreds of thousands of men and women who have learned and used skills in the service have moved into related civilian jobs. For example, a technician who has spent four or more years learning to install and operate radar sets for the Navy or Air Force can often get a position with a commercial airline. Nevertheless, educa-

W.VA. STATE DEPT. OF EDUCATION

Mechanical drawing is taught in many vocational programs as a prerequisite to various technical courses.

tors and guidance counselors caution youths against considering the services as free trade or technical schools. The armed forces cannot guarantee training in the chosen field. The needs of the service determine who goes to which training school. Thus a would-be rocket technician may end up in a school for clerks—or in the infantry.

Associations. Each area of vocational education is represented by at least one professional association in the United States. The organization with the largest membership and broadest scope is the American Vocational Association. Founded in 1906, the association now has member groups in all 50 states. Publications include the *American Vocational Journal,* issued nine times a year. Headquarters are at 1510 H Street, N.W., Washington, D.C. 20005.

In addition to the professional associations, there are student organizations in several fields of vocational education. For example, the Distributive Education Clubs of America (DECA) is a national association designed to supplement the high school programs in distributive education. Many students in vocational agriculture programs are members of Future Farmers of America (FFA) or of 4-H Clubs. The Future Homemakers of America (FHA) is the national organization of high school students who are enrolled in home economics courses.

U.S. VOCATIONAL EDUCATION LEGISLATION

The federal government has been active for more than a hundred years in stimulating vocational education in the United States. The first federal legislation in this area was the Morrill Act of 1862, providing funds for the agricultural and mechanical colleges later known as *land-grant colleges.* Thus, vocational education was identified with colleges. This was unique because in Europe vocational education had been separated from academic studies.

The establishment in 1906 of the National Society for the Promotion of Industrial Education was another milestone in the history of vocational education. This group urged that the federal government help train young men and women for jobs in industry. In 1913 the Commission on National Aid to Vocational Education was created to provide federal aid to the states in this field. The Smith-Lever Act, passed by Congress in 1914, provided federal grants to the states on a matching basis to be used for instruction in agriculture and home economics.

Federal aid to vocational education was broadened in 1917 with the passage of the Smith-Hughes Act. This legislation gave the states about $7.2 million a year for vocational programs in high schools, including agricultural, trade and industrial, and home economics education. The Smith-Hughes Act also established a Federal Board of Vocational Education to administer the program. The responsibilities of this board were transferred in 1933 to the office of the U.S. Commissioner of Education.

The George-Deen Act of 1936 authorized on a continuing basis an appropriation of $13 million a year for vocational education in agriculture, trade and industry, home economics, and, for the first time, distributive occupations.

In 1940, Congress appropriated money for defense training, later called War Production Workers. The 11 million people given vocational training from 1940 to 1945 helped make America the arsenal of democracy.

The George-Barden Act was passed by Congress in 1946. It authorized an increase in federal aid to vocational education from $14 million to $29 million.

In the next decade Congress approved several bills increasing the scope of aid to vocational education. The 1958 National Defense Education Act (NDEA), also called Public Law 864, authorized increased funds for certain designated subject areas, including technical education. Title VIII of the act provided funds to states for allocation to local districts to encourage vocational education programs for highly technical occupations. Other legislation provided federal funds for training in the fishing trades and in practical nursing.

Following the report of a Panel of Consultants on Vocational Education appointed by President John F. Kennedy, Congress passed the Vocational Education Act of 1963. This was more comprehensive than any previous vocational education act. The law authorized a new program of permanent federal assistance for vocational education. These funds were in addition to those annually appropriated under previously existing laws and to appropriations for residential schools and work-study programs. The funds under the new act were allocated among the states on the basis of population and per capita income. Each state was required to match federal funds on a 50–50 basis, and to provide assurance that the federal government's money would not replace local and state expenditures.

State boards for vocational education became the sole agencies for administering the federal funds allocated to the states. The new funds were not earmarked for specific occupational fields. They could be expended for vocational education programs that prepare people for employment in any occupation not requiring a college degree. Programs could be conducted in

SYBIL SHELTON/PETER ARNOLD

Cosmetology programs in many vocational high schools prepare their students directly for employment.

comprehensive or specialized high schools, area vocational schools, junior and community colleges, or universities that offer terminal vocational programs. Federal funds could be used to assure quality in vocational programs such as teacher training, supervision and administration, and research and program evaluation. Ten percent of each year's appropriation was required to be reserved for grants by the U.S. Commissioner of Education, for research and demonstration projects in vocational education.

The Vocational Education Act of 1963 permitted more flexibility in the use of funds for agricultural education and distributive education. It restricted the use of some of the home economics funds to job-oriented instruction. The area technical education program, authorized under NDEA in 1958, was made permanent. In addition, states were permitted to spend funds on a 50-50 matching basis for the construction of area vocational school facilities. The act also provided $5 million yearly to support vocational education programs that train practical nurses.

VOCATIONAL EDUCATION AROUND THE WORLD

In Canada, the development of vocational education has been similar to that in the United States. In 1913 the Dominion accepted a measure of financial responsibility for the development of provincial schools to meet the demands of agriculture, commerce, and industry. The Agricultural Instruction Act of 1913 made provision for a contribution of $1,000,000 annually for 10 years. The Technical Education Act of 1919 approved an additional $1,000,000 a year for 10 years on a matching fund basis with the provinces. However, Ontario was the only province to meet the condition within 10 years.

The Technical Vocational Training Assistance Act of 1942, passed while Canada was engaged in World War II, was not implemented. Instead, vocational training was conducted as on-the-job training to meet the needs of the time.

Technological changes in the 1950's and 1960's renewed interest in vocational education. The Training Assistance Act of 1962 united Canada in an all-out effort for vocational education. Three types of institutions now offer vocational education in Canada—trade schools, vocational high schools, and institutes of technology.

Courses at the trade school level do not require high school graduation. The aim is to prepare a student for a specific occupation. Courses are provided for the building trades, the mechanical and metalworking trades, the electrical trades, automotive trades, and a few others.

Vocational high school students receive a broader training, combining vocational subjects with cultural academic subjects. The vocational student is not committed to any particular occupation. After the completion of four years of high school, he receives a diploma. Business subjects such as typing, bookkeeping, and business law are prominent in the curriculums of most vocational high schools; but other subjects are also offered, such as agriculture, home economics, automobile mechanics, and drafting.

Institutes of technology prepare students to bridge the gap between skilled tradesmen and professional engineers. These schools accept only high school graduates.

In Britain, apprenticeship disappeared earlier than on the European continent. A series of acts in 1851, 1860, 1872, and 1889 made possible day and evening schools for the working class. In 1902 the program of vocational instruction was broadened. During the same period employers were providing classes of instruction for workers.

Great Britain has higher elementary schools, evening schools, and day trade schools to meet the needs of vocational education. Vocational learners may be full- or part-time students. Many enter soon after leaving secondary school at the age of 15. Vocational education prepares students for all types of jobs in industry and commerce. Technical colleges offer a wide range of vocational studies, including merchant marine, agriculture, illustrating and drafting, nursing, and many others.

In Russia. An important contribution to the development of vocational education was made in Russia in 1888 with the beginning of shop classes. Better-trained engineers were needed quickly. The apprenticeship system was too slow. Victor della Vos, the director of the Imperial Technical Railway School at Moscow, established shop classes in which a problem was developed and specially prepared drawings were made. The teacher, an expert mechanic, gave a demonstration lesson. Then, each member of the class performed the same exercise at his own bench. This procedure was quickly adopted in other countries. The idea of breaking a skill or trade down into its various steps as a basis for teaching became widely accepted in educational circles.

Under the communist government of the Soviet Union, the ministry of labor reserves has the task of training skilled workers for the different branches of the country's economy. It does this through a variety of vocational schools. The commonest types are: (1) trades and railway schools, where a two-year course is given in skilled mechanical trades; and (2) factory schools for less complex skills, where the course lasts only a year. Students live at the schools, and train on the job in factories.

Many Russian workers receive training through the apprenticeship system, learning on the job and attending evening classes. The classes are provided by a specialized secondary school called a *technicum.* A technicum is devoted to a single field and is designed to produce middle-level specialists for industry, transport, agriculture, medicine, and education. The medical schools, for example, train midwives, nurses, and doctors' assistants. The teacher training schools produce primary school teachers. While technicums may be set up and maintained by any government department or public enterprise, the ministry of education exercises educational supervision. Courses last for four years and combine practical training with general education. Upon completing the course, students take a state examination. The brightest may then go on directly to higher education, while the others are required to work for at least three years before doing so.

In France, vocational education dates back to 1794 when the Conservatory of Arts and Crafts was founded. The decrees of 1888 established agricultural education. Each French department provided instruction in crafts, such as weaving, metal- and woodwork, and furniture making. Nevertheless, vocational education in France has developed mainly since 1940. Each French department now has a vocational guidance center. French industry makes a major contribution in this field, with most of the larger corporations providing vocational training shops and classes.

Vocational education is also conducted by the national government as a joint enterprise between the public schools and the commerce or agriculture ministries. Other vocational education is conducted in separate schools that have high admission standards.

In West Germany, all boys must continue their education beyond the elementary grades in one of three types of schools: (1) general, (2) industrial, or (3) commercial. The curriculums are broad, providing many general education subjects. Control of the schools is widely dispersed among the ministries of commerce, labor, and interior. Vocational schools differ widely in the north and south of Germany. In the north the schools stress theoretical instruction, while in the south they favor practical teaching.

The Munich System, organized by School Superintendent G. Kerschensteiner, has attracted worldwide attention. His program of studies endeavors to bridge the gap between the elementary school and employment. The chief emphasis is on skill training. Groups of employers provide materials, equipment, and professional advice for each school.

In Switzerland, vocational training is a respected part of the educational system. The country is noted for the number and excellence of its technical and trade schools. The government grants subsidies for vocational training in many important industries as well as in trade, agriculture, and housework.

In Latin America, Africa, and Asia. In the underdeveloped areas of the world, vocational training was nonexistent for a long time. Even when special educational institutions were founded, they tended to grow slowly until recently. As a result, commerce and industry have for many years had to rely upon a foreign labor supply for skilled technicians. Countries that have been independent for many years have established vocational training schools, but these have been few in number.

See also ADULT EDUCATION; AGRICULTURAL EDUCATION; BUSINESS EDUCATION; EXTENSION EDUCATION; INDUSTRIAL EDUCATION; JUNIOR COLLEGE; TECHNICAL EDUCATION; VOCATIONAL GUIDANCE; VOCATIONAL REHABILITATION.

WILLIAM B. LOGAN
Director of Distributive Education Institutes
The Ohio State University

Bibliography

American Vocational Association. *Facts YOU Should Know About Agricultural Education in the Public Schools; Facts YOU Should Know About Distributive Education; Facts YOU Should Know, Home Economics Education; Facts YOU Should Know, New Developments and Their Impacts on Trade and Industrial Education; Facts YOU Should Know, Vocational Education, Gateway to Opportunity; Facts YOU Should Know, Relation of Vocational and Practical Arts Education to Economic Well-Being* (Washington, D.C.; American Vocational Association).

Bailey, Larry J., *Career Education for Teachers and Counselors: A Practical Approach* (Carroll Press 1985).

Bauer, Betsy, *Getting Work Experience: The Student's Directory of Professional Internship Programs* (Dell 1987).

Campbell, Richard, and Thompson, Mary, *Working: Today and Tomorrow* (EMC 1986).

Eggleston, John, ed., *Work Experience in Secondary Schools* (Methuen 1983).

Finch, Curtis R. and McGough, Robert C., *Administering and Supervising Vocational Education* (Prentice-Hall 1982).

Miller, Melvin D., *Principles and a Philosophy for Vocational Education* (National Center of Research for Vocational Education 1985).

Roberts, Roy W., *Vocational and Practical Arts Education* (Harper 1971).

Swanson, Steve, *When You Graduate* (Augsburg 1985).

UNESCO, *World Survey of Education, Secondary Education* (United Nations 1979).

Venn, Grant, *Man, Education, and Work* (American Council on Education 1964).

PETER VANDERMARK/STOCK, BOSTON

A school guidance counselor reviews a student's academic program as it applies to career choices.

VOCATIONAL GUIDANCE, one of many guidance activities included within the broad classification of guidance services. The National Vocational Guidance Association has defined vocational guidance as "the process of assisting the individual to choose an occupation, preparing for it, entering it, and progressing in it." Vocational guidance expanded beyond the achieving of occupational goals is directly related to educational guidance. As a matter of fact, they both become a part of the total guidance process directed toward aiding the individual to make satisfactory adjustment to his environment in all of its aspects. Making a career choice is just one of the many common problems facing students.

Development. A recognized historian of vocational guidance, Professor John M. Brewer, formerly of Harvard University, gave six reasons for the rise of the vocational guidance movement in the United States. They are:
(1) The removal of work from the home, which meant that most young people could not acquire the necessary skills from their parents or receive information from them about the world of work which they would enter.
(2) The increasing complexity of the world of work, which multiplied the possible occupational areas that a young person might enter.
(3) The failure of many who had undertaken vocational training for occupations to which they were not suited.
(4) The difficulty of finding appropriate employment in a world of increasing specialization.
(5) The transformation of secondary schools from specialized institutions serving the minority of students preparing for college to schools serving all youth.
(6) Finally, the importance in a democratic society for each individual to have freedom of choice in preparing himself for an occupation in which he might receive the maximum satisfaction from his efforts and make the maximum contribution to society.

Frank Parsons is credited with initiating the vocational guidance movement in the United States. In 1908, in a Boston social settlement house, he established and directed the "Breadwinner's Institute" or Vocation Bureau of Boston. The bureau was a pioneer effort in the field of vocational guidance. In addition to counseling, Parsons tried to spread the idea of vocational guidance, urging that the work be taken over by the schools. He explained his methods in *Choosing a Career,* published posthumously in 1909. Parsons observed that "society is very shortsighted as yet in its attitudes toward the development of its human resources. It trains its horses better, as a rule, than its men. It spends unlimited money to perfect the inanimate machinery of production, but pays very little attention to the business of perfecting human machinery, though it is by far the most important in production." Counselor training courses were set up at Boston and Harvard universities by Meyer Bloomfield, Parsons' successor. The vocation bureau was moved to Harvard in 1917 and became the Bureau of Vocational Guidance of the Graduate School of Education.

Following Parsons, Eli M. Weaver, a teacher in the public schools of New York City, pioneered in vocational guidance by developing a program designed "to find the right vocations for young people by the time they had completed secondary education."

As indicated above, vocational guidance is comparatively new in the educational process, both within the school systems and in other agencies of society. Full realization of its potential as a means for greater national strength and better utilization of human resources did not ap-

ELLIS HERWIG/STOCK, BOSTON

At the college level, a guidance counselor is generally a highly trained and experienced educator.

pear until the era of World War II and immediately thereafter. It is now a recognized principle that the manpower needs of the United States call for the full utilization of the talents of all individuals. Such can be achieved only when men and women through good vocational guidance are provided with a program of assistance in selecting an occupation, preparing for it, finding a job in it, and progressing in it.

Phases. There are four major steps involved in the vocational guidance process: (1) testing and appraisal, (2) information services, (3) counseling, and (4) placement. Actually, these steps may need to be repeated many times during the occupational life of any one individual.

Testing and Appraisal. Original research of such noted psychologists as Alfred Binet (1857–1911) and Edward Lee Thorndike (1874–1949) led to the development of testing and measurement instruments to determine certain mental characteristics. The four major areas where such instruments have been developed are mental ability, individual interests, aptitudes, and personality characteristics. Measured mental ability identifies native intelligence and suggests a range of occupational choice within which work potential is most appropriate. Appraisal of interest identifies those types of activity that tend to stimulate and hold the attention of an individual. Appraisal of aptitudes identifies those inherent abilities which each of us possesses in specialized fields such as mathematics, mechanics, art, clerical activities, and music. Appraisal of personality characteristics identifies the personality traits of an individual and serves as a guide to his behavior in particular situations.

Such measurements can only provide clues in these four areas and must not be used as final determining factors. Final choices and decisions are influenced by an accumulation of all the information about an individual. Such accumulation of information is generally recorded in what is referred to as a student's cumulative file. This file is used by both counselor and student. The information commonly found in such a file, in addition to the test information, refers to health, scholastic achievement, family history, social background, economic status, hobbies, extracurricular activities, employment experience, and observations by teachers, parents, and others who have had contact with the student.

This cumulative file becomes the basic document used in making educational plans and establishing occupational goals. The cumulative file is most useful when it follows the student from grade to grade and school to school, giving a current picture and summarizing past details. See INTERESTS AND THEIR MEASUREMENT.

Information Services. Many factors in the dynamic economy found in the United States present a confusing and constantly changing pattern to those seeking to determine the best avenues of employment to pursue. Hence, the collecting and organizing of information about occupations is an important phase of the guidance process. The volume of information necessary today has increased many times over that required in the past. To illustrate, the directory of occupational titles of the United States Department of Labor now includes in excess of 25,000 job classifications.

Occupational information available to students generally includes at least four areas: (1) the nature of occupations, salary, working conditions, advancement potential, and so on; (2) the minimum requirements to be met in order to enter the occupation—educational background, specific training, health, age, personality characteristics, and so on; (3) the educational programs available that will prepare for entry into employment—where they are offered, the length of training, the cost, the entrance requirements, and so on; and (4) the opportunities for employment in the occupation—locally, adjacent areas, nationwide, permanent or temporary.

Sources of Information. There can be found in the public libraries many books, pamphlets, brochures, government publications, and other types of material giving information about occupations. Furthermore, the public library is one of the best sources for bibliographies and indexes on all types of publications relating to the world of work. Most secondary schools, universities, and colleges, both public and private, maintain special occupational information libraries containing the same types of information as found in public libraries. These, however, are somewhat more specialized and localized in terms of the curriculum in the particular school and the special needs of its students. In addition, school occupational libraries normally will contain brochures describing local community jobs and job requirements, economic surveys, employment trends, and new industrial and commercial developments on the drawing boards.

At a community workshop for learning the techniques for getting a job, unemployed people can view themselves on videotape as they take part in a mock interview.

SYBIL SHELTON/PETER ARNOLD

The United States Employment Service and affiliated state employment services form a nationwide organization which constitutes probably the richest source of occupational information for counseling and guidance purposes. There are several thousand local offices located in cities and towns throughout the nation. In addition to providing occupational and labor market information, they offer testing, counseling, and placement services, both to in-school youth and to experienced workers who wish or need to change their field of work. State employment offices offer special services to job seekers who have vocational handicaps, to veterans, to middle-aged and older workers who are finding it difficult to obtain employment, and to job applicants of minority groups.

Trade unions, employers' associations, and professional societies are other good sources of guidance information. Such organizations may be local, state, or national. Often there will be found local branches of state or national organizations where information relating to occupations, job opportunities, economic trends, and requirements are readily available.

Many state and federal government agencies are involved in some aspect of vocational guidance and provide occupational information. Probably the best single document providing occupational information is the *Occupational Outlook Handbook*, published by the United States Department of Labor, Bureau of Labor Statistics. This handbook deals with and interprets trends in occupations, and provides fundamental information about job situations and future outlook which users—students, counselors, workers—can apply to advantage in making decisions on career choices.

A new source by which occupational information is disseminated is through modern media such as radio, television, and motion pictures. Many films are published by private industrial and commercial concerns and professional organizations and are made available to schools. Public service time on television and radio often is devoted to giving occupational information to the public. Employers seeking employees frequently use these media as a means of contacting potential new workers.

Counseling. Counseling refers to the process which takes place between the counselor (an adviser) and the counselee (the individual who is seeking assistance in making decisions on occupational choices). Its purpose is to assist the individual in assessing his potentialities and in making wise decisions on the basis of the information available from the appraisal process and other sources of information referred to above.

The counseling process most often takes place between a counselor and an individual student. However, during recent years there has been a trend toward the group counseling process in which, under the leadership of a counselor, a small group of students work together in studying occupations, appraising potentials, exchanging information about one another, and testing tentative decisions. The advantage of the individual conference approach is that it focuses attention on the individual and his special needs. The advantage of the group counseling approach is that it enables the individual to recognize that others have questions and problems not unlike his and to profit from their experience and knowledge.

It must be recognized, however, that in any school much counseling takes place above and beyond that which is done by personnel identified as counselors. For example, the classroom teacher-student relationship is a constant counseling process, as are the many contacts which a student has in the community and the home. Particularly helpful to students in selecting an occupation are the vocational teachers in the secondary schools, and the professional staffs in the professional schools of the universities and colleges. Furthermore, within most school systems

SYBIL SHELTON/PETER ARNOLD

In a city-sponsored program, a guidance counselor teaches local youths the skills of preparing job applications.

there are many professional personnel who provide special counseling services; for example, the school psychologist and psychiatrist, the school doctor and the school nurse, and the child welfare and attendance officers.

More recently, many community agencies are becoming involved in the counseling process. These include counseling services of industry and business, service clubs, religious organizations, the military services, the Veterans Administration, veterans' organizations, and the Young Men's Christian Association and Young Women's Christian Association. Many communities throughout the nation have organized community councils for the purpose of coordinating their counseling and guidance efforts.

Placement. The final step in the vocational guidance process is that of helping students (once they have made their decision and have prepared themselves for work) to find suitable employment—matching the job and the worker. Most schools have a placement officer, who is responsible for maintaining current files on job opportunities and on students seeking employment, and then selecting the best candidates available. In the school and college program, he has the further responsibility of cooperating especially with the vocational teachers and professional school staff members who are in daily contact with the needs and opportunities in particular fields. Finally, he is responsible for gathering and recording follow-up information about students after they are on the job.

Preparation of Staff. Tremendous strides have been made in recent years in the professionalization of guidance personnel, both in and out of school service. Higher standards have been set and improved programs of preparation have been developed in order to improve the quality of guidance services. Most states require teaching experience in addition to special course work before certification is granted. Included among the special courses in any certification requirement are tests and measurements, basic principles and practices of guidance, counseling techniques, occupational and educational information, group guidance, child growth and development, mental hygiene, and supervised practice in guidance.

Professional Guidance Organizations. The original professional guidance organization was the National Vocational Guidance Association, founded in 1913. This was amalgamated in 1952 with several related associations into the American Personnel and Guidance Association. There are now six divisions of this latter organization, each representing special interests in guidance and the personnel profession. They are the American College Personnel Association, Association for Counselor Education and Supervision, National Vocational Guidance Association, Student Personnel Association for Teacher Education, American School Counselor Association, and Division of Rehabilitation Counseling. Together they span personnel and guidance work in elementary and secondary schools, in higher education, and in community agencies and organizations, and encompass many personnel interests in government and business.

Significant Changes and Trends. Generally, those services identified as guidance services have not been found in the elementary school programs. More recently, however, school people throughout the nation are giving consideration to the strengthening of guidance services in the elementary grades. It is at this level, many claim, that those responsible for education can get to know students more intimately, can influence them more readily, and can direct their learning experiences more effectively in accordance with their potential.

In the past, educational programs have been designed primarily for the average student. Now, throughout the nation are found special programs and special financing for the gifted and the less able, for the hard of hearing, for the mentally retarded, for the aged, and for other types of special students. Such special programs require extended and strengthened guidance services. See VOCATIONAL REHABILITATION.

The advent of data processing is enabling counseling personnel to gather information, record it, and make it more readily available at lower cost.

There is greater recognition today that counseling must be a continuous process in the schools from the elementary school through college, on to the first job. From this point, the individual is in continuous need of counseling services of one kind or another, either for assistance with personal problems or for retraining for new job placement.

It is now recognized that a direct relationship exists between guidance and curriculum development and instruction. As a matter of fact, there are those who refer to guidance as the heart of the educational program. It is through effective guidance services that identification of basic pupil characteristics is made and the educational needs of and opportunities within the service area of any institution are determined. Information about students and the community to be served are the two essentials to curriculum building and the total instructional process.

See also VOCATIONAL EDUCATION.

J. GRAHAM SULLIVAN
Chief, Bureau of National Defense Education Act Administration, California State Department of Education

VOCATIONAL REHABILITATION, a term that refers specifically to those services that are necessary to render a disabled individual fit to engage in remunerative employment.

History and Legislation. Historically, vocational rehabilitation services grew out of the interest of organized labor prior to World War I in securing certain retraining services for workmen who were injured in industry. The first federal legislation which was introduced actually bore the title "An Act to Provide Vocational Rehabilitation Services for Those Injured in Industry," but before adopted by Congress the measure was broadened to include other than industrially injured. The first federal program became effective in 1921.

The 1921 Vocational Rehabilitation Act was very limited and simply provided grants to the states for the purpose of retraining persons barred from employment due to a physical disability. The act was drastically amended with the passage of the Barden-La Follette Act of 1943 (Public Law 113) which added to the program the mentally ill and mentally retarded as well as the physically handicapped. In addition, the 1943 amendments greatly expanded the range of services to be provided by the various state agencies, particularly including physical restoration services. The act was further amended in 1954 with the passage of Public Law 565, which changed the financing formula and added many new features, such as special research and demonstration projects and funds for training personnel.

Federal-State Program. Currently the program is operated as follows. Federal funds are appropriated by Congress to the United States Office of Vocational Rehabilitation, an agency of the Department of Health, Education, and Welfare. On the basis of the per capita income in the various states, a formula is established for allocation of funds which must be matched by state funds in accordance with the financing formula. The state programs are almost without exception

DAN BRINZAC/PETER ARNOLD

Vocational rehabilitation qualifies disabled workers for useful employment. (*Above*) A blind man sorts merchandise. (*Below*) A handicapped worker in an electronics plant.

MIMI FORSYTH/MONKMEYER

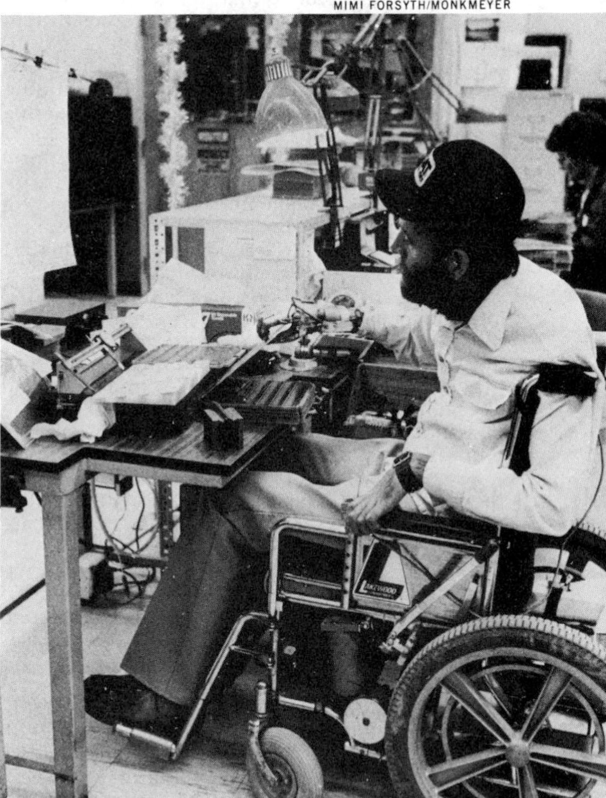

Sheltered workshops operated by nonprofit institutions for the mentally retarded provide simple, productive work such as packaging and assembling.

SYBIL SHELTON/MONKMEYER

operated as a unit of the state department of education, although the federal law does permit operation of the program as an independent agency within the state.

Eligibility for vocational rehabilitation is based upon the following federal requirements: (1) the presence of a physical or mental disability and the resulting functional limitations or limitations in activities; (2) the existence of a substantial handicap to employment caused by the limitations resulting from such disabilities; and (3) a reasonable expectation that vocational rehabilitation may render the individual fit to engage in a remunerative occupation.

Even with the substantial increase in appropriations since 1954, no state vocational rehabilitation agency has been able to meet the needs of all handicapped persons seeking such assistance. A president's task force report indicated in 1951 that there were over 2 million handicapped persons in the United States who could be assisted to remunerative employment through vocational rehabilitation services, and estimated that this figure was being increased by a quarter of a million persons yearly. Thus each state is required to establish a system of priorities for determining which of many applicants it will be able to serve with existing staff and funds.

States vary widely in the manner in which they select applicants, and there is little uniformity in the manner in which priorities are applied. In the less wealthy states of the South much greater emphasis is placed upon the provision of direct medical services because of limited public health facilities for persons with remediable handicaps. In other states greater emphasis is placed upon counseling and training.

Procedures and Facilities. The process of vocational rehabilitation begins with case finding, in which cooperative arrangements are made with various potential referral agencies, such as doctors, hospitals, clinics, public employment agencies, industrial accident commissions, schools, and various public and private health and welfare agencies. An initial evaluation is made to determine whether the individual meets the requirements of legal eligibility, following which a counselor is assigned to work with the disabled applicant, usually throughout the entire program of services. Medical information concerning the nature and extent of the disability is mandatory, and wherever it is found that the disability may be removed or ameliorated through any type of medical service, such aid is usually provided by the agency.

The object of all vocational rehabilitation services is restoration to employment. Through counseling, which usually involves the use of standard psychological tests, a job objective is mutually decided upon between the counselor and the client, and steps are taken to carry out the rehabilitation plan. If this involves training in a new occupation, the agency may pay the cost of such training in a public or private trade school, business college, and college or university, or through correspondence schools, tutorial instruction, and on-the-job training—or through any combination of these. If a person is in financial need, he may be provided (while undergoing service) maintenance assistance, transportation, payment for books and supplies, training supplies, or customary occupational tools.

Following completion of services it is the agency's responsibility to ensure that the disabled client is satisfactorily placed in a remunerative job. The public employment service is utilized to the greatest possible extent in the placement process, but often in the case of a severely disabled applicant it is necessary to provide this placement service directly through utilization of vocational rehabilitation counselors.

Among the facilities which have been developed to expedite the vocational rehabilitation services are comprehensive rehabilitation centers and workshops for the disabled. Such a center is most often a medically oriented facility which provides a variety of services under one roof—usually to the severely disabled—and generally including social, psychological, vocational, and medical evaluation and treatment where indicated. In recent years workshops for the disabled have greatly broadened the scope of the traditional "sheltered workshop" program, and now offer work evaluation, work adjustment, job tryout, and actual vocational training in certain occupations.

Social and Economic Merits.—The social importance of restoring disabled persons to usefulness is of course widely accepted, and the economic value which this represents has come to be recognized as having great significance for society. It has been estimated that a disabled person who has been provided with vocational rehabilitation services, and has been placed in employment, will pay back in taxes in the course of his working life 10 times the amount of money spent for his rehabilitation. In recent years attention has been focused upon the problem of disability in relation to dependency, and large numbers of persons receiving public assistance because of a disabling condition now are being restored to employment.

Number and Types of Cases.—Case load trends throughout the United States are reported periodically to the Federal Office of Vocational Rehabilitation, and a record of successful cases is reported in detail. Since federal standards are quite general in nature, there are widespread differences between the states in their definitions of a "rehabilitated" case. Consequently, statistics have to be viewed with a certain amount of caution, since it is difficult, if not impossible, to compare states on the basis of their quantitative results. In the fiscal year 1960 over 90,000 cases were reported nationally as having received vocational rehabilitation services and having been placed successfully in employment.

The types of disabilities served by vocational rehabilitation agencies run the gamut of almost every known disabling condition. The two largest groups of disabled persons currently receiving vocational rehabilitation services are those with orthopedic impairments resulting from congenital causes, illness, or trauma, and the chronically ill who suffer from such diseases as tuberculosis, heart disease, and diabetes. Service to the mentally ill and mentally retarded has been slow in developing in the federal-state vocational rehabilitation program, largely due to the lack of staff trained in the particular problems of these disability groups. In late years considerably greater emphasis has been placed upon serving this very large segment of the disabled population, and it is anticipated that this group will continue to grow as a significant factor in the case loads.

Recent Advances.—Following the passage in 1954 of Public Law 565 a tremendous variety of special research and demonstration projects have been financed with vocational rehabilitation funds. These have ranged from the establishment of special facilities, such as rehabilitation centers and workshops, to intensive research into restorative treatment of the cerebral palsied, the chronically ill, the mentally retarded, and so on.

Training funds authorized under Public Law 565 have resulted in the establishment of graduate programs in rehabilitation counseling in major colleges and universities in practically every part of the United States. In addition, financial assistance has been provided to schools of social work, of occupational therapy, of physical therapy, of medicine, of nursing, and so on, to increase the rehabilitation content in these programs as an aid in meeting the severe personnel shortage in the entire rehabilitation field.

See also BLIND—*The United States* (Rehabilitation of the Adult Blind); EDUCATION OF THE PHYSICALLY HANDICAPPED; MENTAL RETARDATION—*The Retarded Pupil in School;* VOCATIONAL GUIDANCE.

Further Reading: Smith, Christopher, *Training and Technology for the Handicapped* (Material Dev. Ctr. 1986).

ANDREW MARRIN,
Chief, Vocational Rehabilitation Service, California State Department of Education.

VOCATIVE CASE. See CASE (grammar); DECLENSION.

VODKA, vŏd′kə (the "little water"—as its name means—of Russia), a colorless liquor made from any starchy material such as grain (rye, barley, corn), potatoes, or sugar beets. It is distilled at so high a proof that virtually none of the flavors in the mash comes through, resulting in a spirit which is neutral and, even after the proof has been reduced for palatability, ardent. By Slavic custom, vodka is served in small glasses, not sipped but gulped, as an accompaniment to appetizers or snacks. The use of vodka as a base for mixed drinks is largely an American innovation, which has given rise to a vodka industry using grain only and rectifying with charcoal.

LAWTON MACKALL.

VOGEL, fō′gəl, **Hermann Wilhelm,** German photochemist: b. Doberlug, Lower Lusatia, Germany, March 26, 1834; d. Berlin, Dec. 17, 1898. In 1863 he conducted his first researches on the reaction of silver halides toward exposure to light, a work for which he received his doctorate at the University of Berlin. He served as professor of photochemistry, spectrum analysis, and photography at the Royal Technical College, Berlin, from 1879 until his death.

Vogel's most important contribution to photography was his discovery in 1873 of optical or dye sensitizing, the method by which the sensitiveness of the silver halides employed in photography is extended from the blue to include the green, orange, red, and infrared. His discovery was a necessary step to color photography, to the photography of the spectrum beyond the blue, and to the representation of colors in the proper tones of gray in ordinary black and white photography. One of the early workers in spectral photography, he also contributed importantly to the technique of star classification according to their spectra. Vogel was the author of *Handbuch der Photographie* (3 parts in 1 vol., 1867–70), and he edited *Photographische Mitteilungen* from 1864.

See also PHOTOGRAPHY—2. *Black-and-White Still Photography.*

C. B. NEBLETTE.

VOGELWEIDE, Walther von der. See WALTHER VON DER VOGELWEIDE.

VOGLER, fō′glər, **Georg Joseph** (usually called **ABT** or **ABBÉ VOGLER**), German musical pedagogue, inventor, and composer: b. Würzburg, Germany, June 15, 1749; d. Darmstadt, May 6,

1814. He studied music in northern Italy and took holy orders at Rome in 1773, receiving high pontifical preferment and thereafter styling himself Abbé ("Abt") Vogler. Returning to Germany, he founded (1775) a music school at Mannheim in order to spread his theories about the teaching of composition. From 1781, he wandered about Europe, teaching, conducting, and composing; during these years he acquired, not altogether unjustly, a reputation as a learned dilettante and charlatan. Settling in Darmstadt in 1807, he founded another school there, attracting such notable pupils in composition as Giacomo Meyerbeer, Carl Maria von Weber, and Peter von Winter.

Vogler's very numerous operas and compositions in many forms have not remained in the active repertoire, and his mechanical instruments and devices for the organ and other instruments have largely disappeared. But he is guaranteed a niche in the archives of music because of the accomplishments of his pupils, his writings on acoustics and pedagogy, and the fact that Robert Browning used him as the point of departure for the well-known poem *Abt Vogler*.

HERBERT WEINSTOCK.

VOGÜE, vô-gü-ā′, VICOMTE DE (EUGÈNE MELCHIOR), French writer and diplomat: b. Nice, France, Feb. 25, 1848; d. Paris, March 24, 1910. After serving in the Franco-Prussian War, he entered the government foreign service in 1871 and was assigned to embassies and missions in Constantinople, Egypt, and St. Petersburg. Leaving his diplomatic career in 1882 to devote himself to writing, he produced a series of essays and novels which exerted a considerable influence on younger French writers, and he helped to foster the trend away from naturalism and toward idealism and mysticism in French fiction. Of major importance in this respect was his *Le roman russe* (1886), a collection of essays on such Russian authors as Fyodor Dostoyevsky, Leo Tolstoy, and Ivan Turgenief (Turgenev) which aroused wide interest in Russian fiction and thereby affected the course of the French novel. His own novels include *Jean d'Agrève* (1897), *Les morts qui parlent* (1899), and *Le maître de la mer* (1903).

VOICE, vois, in grammar, a term indicating certain formal and functional characteristics of a verb. In classical grammar three voices are distinguished: active, passive, and middle. Active is opposed to passive on the one hand and to middle on the other, but passive and middle actually have nothing in common.

The opposition of active to passive occurs with transitive verbs (verbs that take an object). In the active construction the performer of the action (or "actor," hence the term "active") is the subject of the sentence, as is indicated by its inflection (in Latin, the nominative case) or by word order (in English, before the verb). In the passive the receiver of the action (or "patient," hence "passive") is the subject, and is so indicated, while the performer of the action is either indicated by some other grammatical device or is not mentioned at all. The grammatical form of the verb indicates whether the construction is active or passive; that is, whether the subject is agent or patient. Thus, in English: *Brutus killed Caesar/Caesar was killed (by Brutus)*; in Latin: *Brutus Caesarem interfecit/Caesar (a Bruto) interfectus est.*

The opposition of active to middle occurs in transitive and intransitive verbs alike; transitivity is irrelevant. The middle voice indicates that the actor is involved to some degree in the result of the action (the range is very great, from direct involvement to the merest hint of what is in the speaker's mind, and translation into a language without a middle voice is correspondingly difficult). A typical example would be: Greek active, φυλάττειν (phuláttein), "stand guard"; middle, φυλάττεσθαι (phuláttesthai), "be on one's guard."

WILLIAM DIVER,
Department of Linguistics, Columbia University.

VOICE, the sound uttered by living beings. In singing, the voice functions like a musical instrument, depending for its quality and volume upon the same acoustical principles that control the production of tone in reed instruments.

Mechanics of Singing.—The three elements necessary to produce a singing tone are an air supply (the lungs), a reed (the vocal cords), and a space in which the fundamental tone can be strengthened (the throat, mouth, and head cavities).

The outflow of air from the lungs provides the motive power in singing. Inhalation takes place with the expansion of the lower ribs and the lowering of the diaphragm, a large muscle that separates the upper chest from the abdomen. Exhalation, in turn, is controlled by the muscles of the lower ribs and abdomen. In singing, the proper use of diaphragmatic and lower rib breathing is essential; other kinds of breathing, such as clavicular or pancostal, are generally thought unsatisfactory.

The reed is the next element in the production of vocal tone. It is found in the larynx, whose framework consists of nine cartilages. The largest is the thyroid, whose point makes the lump in the throat called the Adam's apple. This is joined to other cartilages to which the vocal cords are attached in front and back. The vocal cords themselves are the elastic inner edges of the vocal ligaments. They are protected during swallowing by the epiglottis, a cartilage at the root of the tongue. During ordinary breathing the vocal folds are draped apart, but in speech or singing they draw together to initiate sound. Thus they oppose the air in the windpipe, and the pressure built up makes their edges vibrate up and down. The speed of their vibration is varied by certain unconscious muscles of the larynx controlled by the ear; the faster the cords vibrate, the higher is the pitch of the fundamental tone they produce. The vocal cords also are able to reduce their normal thickness, if necessary, so that they can vibrate with greater ease at high frequencies. (See also LARYNX.)

Once the tone has been initiated, it must be strengthened. This is the function of the resonators, whose importance cannot be overestimated. The motion of the air caused by the vibration of the vocal cords and the puffs of air escaping through them stirs the air in the throat cavity into vibration. Then the air in the mouth and windpipe vibrates, as do the hard palate and bony structures of the head. All of this vibrating air, contained in a cavity that is itself vibrating, reinforces the fundamental tone made by the vocal cords. This complex acoustical phenomenon is further enhanced by the fact that the mouth and throat can be varied in size and shape to make vowel sounds, each of which has a formant that lies just under those that characterize voice quality. At times the adjustment of mouth and throat that must be made to produce a certain vowel sound and that which must be made to reach a certain pitch are in conflict, and in singing the purity of the vowel sound gives way to musical demands.

Early History.—Man's interest in the voice reaches far back into his history. By the Hippocratic age the Greeks knew that air motivated the voice. Aristotle (384–322 B.C.), in his *De audibilibus,* speculated on phonation and the variance of voice quality. Galen (129/130–199/200 A.D.), the father of laryngology, described the principal cartilages and muscles of the larynx and called the vocal cords the glottis. The Romans, with their concern for oratory, were interested in the care of the voice, and Quintilian (35/40–after 90 A.D.), in his *Institutio oratoria,* gives many suggestions for its preservation. Even in the early Middle Ages, when music was securely under the thumb of philosophy, singing was a prime concern of the Western church, which, through its singing schools, and particularly the Schola Cantorum in Rome (probably founded 4th century A.D.) kept alive whatever vocal technique survived this tumultuous period.

The later Middle Ages saw a revival of interest in vocal problems. St. Bernard of Clairvaux (1090–1153) mentioned the falsetto, a thin, reedy sound used for singing high notes and produced by a partial vibration of the edges of the vocal cords. The first mention of registers, that series of tones of similar quality produced by a delicate adjustment of the vocal cords, occurred in the work of John of Garland (Johannes de Garlandia, fl. early 13th century) and soon after that in the writings of Jerome of Moravia (fl. mid-13th century). Derived from the sensation a singer feels as he sings in them, the terms "chest," "throat," and "head" which these early theorists gave to the registers still are in use. Marchettus of Padua (fl. early 14th century) and Theodoricus de Campo (fl. 1450) named the natural instruments of the body that formed the voice. Adam de Fulda (c. 1445–1505) attempted to describe how the voice is formed and gave a rudimentary description of the functioning of the lungs.

The 16th century saw many advances. About 1500, Berengarius of Pavia discovered that there were two arytenoid cartilages instead of one. Andreas Vesalius (1514–1564) made laryngeal dissections, while Gabriel Fallopius (1523–1562) described the muscles of the larynx. The musical treatises of the time, such as those of Sylvestro di Ganassi (fl. early 16th century) and Giovanni Battista Bovicelli (fl. about 1600), mentioned practical vocal problems such as breathing and deportment. Lodovico Zacconi (1555–1627), whose *Prattica di Musica . . .* has been called the best source for the vocal practices of his time, gave, in addition, exercises for flexibility to be practiced on all vowels.

The Castrato.—Most important to the subsequent history of voice, however, was the introduction into the Western church, as music grew complex and choirboys scarce, of the castrato (q.v.). By 1557 castrati were used in religious celebrations in Spain, and in 1562, Padre Soto, a castrato from Spain, entered the Sistine Chapel. These singers were able to perform amazing vocal feats as the result of an operation that, by removing their sexual organs in boyhood, kept their voices from changing at puberty. Training improved the native flexibility of this kind of voice, while abnormally large chest dimensions and an unusually small larynx, that allowed the voice to be produced with very little air, contributed to their superb breath control. With such superior vocal equipment, they were able to, and soon did, take over the art of singing as their own.

The 17th Century.—Secular vocal music, and the techniques for singing it, flowered in the 17th century. Studies on the larynx continued. At Oxford, Thomas Willis (1621–1675) gave the first accurate description of the superior laryngeal nerve, while a theoretician, Marin Mersenne (1588–1648), indicated in his *Harmonie universelle* (2 vols., 1636–37) that the study of musical reeds might furnish a clue to the cause of pitch in the human voice. Books on singing multiplied, beginning with Giulio Caccini's (1550–?1618) observations in the preface to his *Le nuove musiche* (1601) and continuing with the work of many other musicians later in the century who gave advice on solfeggi (q.v.), ornamentation, the use of registers, the control of breath, and the acquiring of agility.

The 18th Century.—Further refinements were brought in the 18th century to an art that was already flourishing. Antoine Ferrein (1693–1769) showed in 1741 that phonation occurred when the lips of the glottis came together and vibrated. Zaccaria Tevo (b. 1651) was the first musical authority to include a plate of the larynx in a musical text. In voice teaching, both composers and castrati were prominent. The composer Nicola Porpora (1686–1768) was a most famous teacher; two of his pupils were the castrati Carlo Farinelli (1705–1782) and Gaetano Majorano (known as Caffarelli, 1703–1783). Pietro Francesco Tosi (1647?–1732), a castrato, wrote an enormously influential treatise on singing (*Opinioni de' cantori . . .*, 1723) that was translated into German and English. In Germany, his translator Johann Friedrich Agricola followed his ideas exactly, venturing to disagree with him only on his conception of the falsetto. France, too, followed suit, save for Jean Blanchet (1724–1778), with his curious theory that pitch could be controlled by conscious manipulation of the larynx without reference to the ear. Another castrato, Francesco Pistocchi (1659–1726), founded a famous singing school in Bologna. His ideas, transmitted through his pupil Antonio Bernacchi (1685–1756) found expression in the work of Giambattista Mancini (1716–1800), author of perhaps the finest book on singing of the 18th century (*Pensieri e riflessioni pratiche sopra il canto figurato,* 1774). With his empirical approach to vocal problems, his insistence on the value of demonstration, and his concern for every detail of the singer's art, he is still read and appreciated.

The 19th Century.—Continued scientific research, a decline in standards of singing, the rise of national schools of singing, and the diffusion of the Italian method were significant features of the 19th century. Manuel García, Jr. (1805–1906), invented the laryngoscope (q.v.), an instrument for examining the interior of the larynx. Experimental work revealed many of the acoustical properties of musical sound and culminated, in 1863, in Hermann L. F. von Helmholtz' definitive book on the laws of tone color in sound (*Lehre von den Tonempfindungen als physiologische Grundlage für die Theorie der Musik*, 1863; Eng. tr., *On the Sensations of Tone as a Physiological Basis for the Theory of Music*, new and rev. ed., 1948). The decline in singing has been attributed to the growth of the declamatory style, the rise in pitch, and the dissappearance of the castrati. By the turn of the century, the operation that created the castrato was looked upon with moral indignation, and although a few survived, among them the famous Giovanni Battista Velluti (1781–1861), their day was over. They continued to sing in churches, but even there they were replaced, as the century progressed, by boys and falsettists. The last of their number, Alessandro Moreschi, whose voice was recorded, died in 1922.

The rise of national schools of singing was another development of the 19th century. The transfer of Italian opera to Paris shifted the center of vocal instruction to France, where at first Italian methods were followed. Bernardo Mengozzi's *Méthode de chant du Conservatoire de Musique* (1803) borrowed from Mancini. By 1825, however, Alexis de Garaudé (1779–1852), in his revised *Méthode complète de chant*, was forced to attempt a reconciliation of the old method with the new bravura style. His attempt was only partly successful, however, and new techniques mushroomed. Giovanni Battista Rubini (1794–1854) was the first modern singer, according to many sources, to use vibrato; while Louis-Gilbert Duprez (1806–1896) introduced the use of the high voice without falsetto to France in 1836 or 1837.

Meanwhile, in Germany, the rise of national opera gave impetus to a school that achieved individuality with Peter von Winter's *Vollständige Singschule* (1824). Friedrich Schmitt's *Grosse Gesangschule* (1824) paved the way for a highly articulate movement that found its chief exponent in his pupil Julius Hey (1832–1909), whose four-volume *Deutscher Gesangsunterricht* (1886) embodied Wagnerian concepts of voice and voice production.

It must be emphasized, however, that during this entire period the Italian tradition had many representatives even in countries with active national schools of their own, and while it did not dominate vocal teaching as it once had, it gave to the 20th century the bulk of its methodology intact. Its leaders were Francesco Lamperti (1811–1892) and his son, Giovanni Battista Lamperti (1839–1910), in Milan and Manuel García, Jr., in Paris and London. García—with his sister Pauline Viardot-García (1821–1910), and his pupils, Jenny Lind (1820–1887) and Mathilde Marchesi (1821–1913), who herself taught Mme. Nellie Melba (1861–1931), Emma Calvé (1858–1942), and Emma Eames (1865–1952), among others—was certainly the most prominent teacher of his day, and it is unlikely that even those who did not agree with him escaped his influence. Certainly he colored the thinking of two generations of voice teachers who followed him, and many of his conceptions, such as the *coup de glotte* (a particular method of attacking a note), are still debated today.

The Modern Era.—The 20th century has seen continued research in acoustics and phonetics, the continued exploration of ways of training the voice, and the revival of the countertenor voice and florid singing. The instruments of modern physics, such as the spectroscope and planigraph, have been used in the study of voice production. The phonograph and magnetic tape recorder have been employed not only for self-instruction, as by Amelita Galli-Curci (1882–1963), but also to preserve the work of great artists and as a teaching aid in the voice studio.

University study projects have resulted in a number of important doctoral dissertations on the voice and, in the case of Dr. Carl E. Seashore's (1866–1949) work on vibrato at the University of Iowa, some definitive results were obtained.

Approximate ranges of the various human singing voices. The voice of the professional may extend from a third to a fourth or more above and below these averages.

Other research has led to some conflicting theories. For example, Raoul Husson's assertion that the recurrent laryngeal nerve starts vibration of the vocal cords was challenged by Janwillem van den Berg's belief that they are actuated by subglottic pressure.

Vocal teaching has concerned itself largely with the psychological basis of singing and an attempt to give some kind of uniform meaning to the singer's vocabulary. Some new theories of vocal production have sprung up. Ernest George White developed a method built around the conception that tone originated in the sinuses. In England, Alfred Wolfsohn worked out a method of voice production that produced pupils

SUBDIVISIONS OF VOCAL RANGES

Voice	Quality
Soprano	
Coloratura	High, flexible
Lyric	Medium size, cantabile singing
Lyric spinto	Full, bright
Dramatic	Largest soprano voice
Tenor	
Leggiero	Similar to lyric soprano
Robusto	Full, vigorous
Heldentenor	Largest tenor voice, used in Wagnerian operas
Bass	
Cantante	Like lyric soprano
Profondo	Deep, dark
Buffo	Comic

with seven- to nine-octave ranges. Renewed interest in the countertenor, the highest of the male voices and one often produced by the use of falsetto, brought attention to the problems of technique that face this delicate instrument. Out of fashion since the 17th century, except in English church choirs and Negro minstrel shows, the modern revival of this voice resulted in Benjamin Britten's making use of it for the role of Oberon in *A Midsummer Night's Dream* (premiere 1960).

Most significant, however, has been the recent flowering of coloratura singing. Long ignored because singers with large voices trained in the dramatic school could not negotiate their *fioriture,* the operas of Gioacchino Rossini, Vincenzo Bellini, and Gaetano Donizetti have received increased attention in recent years. This rebirth of florid singing, actuated by Maria Callas, has found its finest expression to date in the singing of Joan Sutherland, whose artistry promises to sustain continued interest in an area of vocal technique largely ignored by contemporary singers.

See also separate articles on MUSIC; OPERA.

JEAN BOWEN
Music Division, The New York Public Library

Further Reading: Barbereaux-Parry, M., *Vocal Resonance: Its Source and Command* (1941; reprint, Christopher Pub. Hse. 1979); Butenschon, S., and Borchgrevink, H., *Voice and Song* (Cambridge 1982); Christy, V. A., *Foundations in Singing,* 4th ed. (W. C. Brown 1979); Longo T., *Fundamentals of Singing and Speaking* (S. F. Vanni 1945).

VOICE OF AMERICA (VOA), a radio broadcasting function of the U.S. government, forming a semi-autonomous unit of the U.S. International Communication Agency. It broadcasts news, music, and other programs in 38 languages throughout the world. VOA's principal purpose is to promote understanding of the United States and its policies in foreign countries. Formerly part of the U.S. Information Agency, VOA was transferred to the International Communication Agency in 1978.

VOILE, voil, a fine, sheer textile used in women's clothing and in curtains. It may be produced of wool, cotton, silk, or rayon, and is fashioned in a plain weave of warp and weft yarns which are tightly twisted. Voile is soft and light in appearance, and its draping qualities make it a desirable fabric for blouses and dresses.

VOIT, foit, **Karl von** (1831–1908), German physiologist, known for his research on human metabolism. He was born in Amberg, Bavaria, Germany, on Oct. 31, 1831. He attended Munich, Würzburg, and Göttingen universities and began his research at Munich, studying with the chemist Justus von Liebig. While only 26, Voit published a major paper on the process known as "nitrogen equilibrium," and thereafter devoted himself entirely to basic research in nutrition and metabolism, often in concert with Max von Pettenkofer, whose ingenious apparatus facilitated their work. With one device, large enough to house a man, they were able to observe how food is assimilated by the body, during both the active and restful states; they also measured the amounts of oxygen consumed and heat produced.

From 1863 until his death Voit served as professor of physiology at Munich. He wrote voluminously on his specialty, including a series of standard texts on metabolism in humans and animals. In particular, his work on metabolism during the presence of illnesses, such as diabetes and leukemia, established his reputation as the father of modern nutritional science. With Pettenkofer and Ludwig von Buhl he founded the periodical *Zeitschrift für Biologie* in 1865. He died in Munich on Jan. 31, 1908.

VOITURE, vwä-tür', **Vincent** (1597–1648), French poet and writer of letters. He was born in Amiens, France, on Feb. 24, 1597. He studied law, but from 1625 he found his true place as a wit at the salon of the marquise de Rambouillet. He took the side of Gaston, duke d'Orléans, against the king but made his peace with Richelieu when he composed a letter on the recapture of Corbie. For that letter the king rewarded him in 1638 with the post of chamberlain. Voiture's letters made him the rival of Guez, seigneur de Balzac, and his verse made him the center of heated literary disputes. Although highly polished, his poems are more akin to those of Clément Marot and the Renaissance than to those of François de Malherbe. Voiture died in Paris on May 26, 1648.

ROBERT TAYLOR, *University of Massachusetts*

Further Reading: Voiture's works were first published in Paris in 1650. The best editions are those of A. Ubicini, 2 vols. (Paris 1855) and Octave Uzanne (Paris 1879). See also Magne, Émile, *Voiture et les origines de l'Hôtel de Rambouillet* (Paris 1911) and *Voiture et l'Hôtel de Rambouillet,* 2 vols. (Paris 1929–1930).

VOJVODINA, voi'vô-dē-nä, an autonomous province in northern Serbia, Yugoslavia, bordering Hungary on the north and Rumania on the east. Vojvodina (also spelled Voivodina or Voyvodina) comprises about 8,360 square miles (21,650 sq km) and has 8.5% of the country's area and about 10% of its population. The region is a fertile plain, with about 83% of its area devoted to agriculture. Corn, wheat, rye, barley, oats, sugar beets, and tobacco are the chief crops. Oil has been found near Velika Greda. Industry consists principally of food processing, beer brewing, sugar refining, and textile manufacturing. The capital is Novi Sad (German, Neusatz).

History. Long a part of Hungary, the territory came under Turkish domination in the 16th century, but was restored to the Habsburgs by the treaties of Karlowitz (1699) and Passarowitz (1718). Leopold I (1640–1705) began an active colonization program, settling peoples of many nationalities here, although Serbians continued to predominate. By a charter of 1690 the emperor granted special privileges: the inhabitants were to elect their own Voivode (literally, "leader of an army"; hence the name "Voivodina") and their own patriarch. Although true autonomy never materialized, the patriarchate served to maintain the rights and status of the Serbs of the area.

In recognition of their aid in suppressing the Hungarian Revolution of 1848, Francis Joseph I established an Independent Crownland of the Voivodina (1849–1860), which included the Banat. Subsequently these territories were placed again under direct Hungarian control, but at the end of World War I those portions of the Baranya, Backa, and the Western Banat that were ceded by Hungary to Yugoslavia were organized into one of the seven governmental districts of the new state, known as the Vojvodina. The organization of the territory underwent several changes during the next decades. The Vojvodina of today comprises territory north of the Sava (Save) and Danube rivers, and is made up of the historic geographic areas of Srem (Syrmia), Backa, and the Western Banat. Most of the Germans either left or were deported after World War II, but a large minority of Magyars (25% of the population) remains. Population: (1976) 1,984,000.

E. C. HELMREICH, *Bowdoin College*

VOLANS, vō'lanz, the constellation of the Flying Fish, one of 12 Southern Hemisphere asterisms added by Johann Bayer in his *Uranometria*

(1603) from star observations made by the Dutch navigators Petrus Theodori and Frederik Houtman. It is a faint constellation, consisting mainly of five stars of the 4th magnitude. The configuration is centered in right ascension 8^h0^m, declination −69°, and reaches the meridian at 9 P.M. about March 1.

FERGUS J. WOOD.

VOLAPÜK, vō-lə-pük', the first man-made universal language (q.v.) to attain a measure of success, when it was demonstrated that it actually could be spoken, written, printed, and read. Its author was Johann Martin Schleyer (1831–1912), a German Roman Catholic priest and linguist, of Constance.

Preoccupied with the idea of furthering world trade and universal brotherhood, Schleyer started by inventing a "universal alphabet" which professedly covered the sound range of all languages and could therefore be used for any one of them. Then he worked out a basic vocabulary and grammar, making them operate as a new constructed language, *Volapük,* which in the new tongue meant "world speech." Launched in 1880, Volapük soon achieved a spectacular success, making converts among amateurs and arousing the curiosity of professional linguists in Germany, France, and the United States. By 1889 the Volapük movement claimed 200,000 adherents, 24 publications, and the support of 300 societies. Three International Volapük conferences were held: in Friedrichshafen, Germany (1884), Munich (1887), and Paris (1889). At the first two conferences most discussions and meetings were conducted in German. At the third conference it was decided that Volapük was to be used exclusively in the proceedings. Thus put to the test, Volapük failed to operate smoothly, causing a great deal of confusion. It became apparent that the language was too difficult for nonlinguists. In spite of this Schleyer was emphatic in refusing to consider any suggested simplifications. From then on Volapük began to lose supporters, first to Esperanto (q.v.), and in later years to Idiom Neutral (a modification of Volapük) and other rival languages.

Construction of the Language.—The vowels of the Volapük alphabet, *a, e, i, o, u, ä, ö, ü,* are taken, together with their pronunciation, from the German. The consonants are, with a few exceptions, pronounced as in English. The system of word formation demands that the root words, mostly nouns, should be monosyllables with a consonant at the beginning and a nonsibilant consonant at the end to accomodate the plural ending *-s.* Derived mostly from English, German, and Latin, the root words are in some cases easily recognizable, in other cases their meaning is hard to guess; for example, *man* (man), *tim* (time), *gud* (the good), *dom* (house, Latin *domus*), *vol* (world), *pük* (speech), *löf* (love), *nol* (knowledge), *plim* (compliment).

From these roots, by the addition of *-ik* and a further *-o,* adjectives and adverbs are formed; for example, *gudik* (good), *gudiko* (well). To the nouns are added the case endings: *-a* (genitive), *-e* (dative), *-i* (accusative), and an additional *-s* for the plural. In verbs a prefix denotes the tense; the personal pronouns (I, thou, he, she, we, and so on—*ob, al, om, of, obs,* and so on) are added as suffixes; for example, *löfob* (I love), *älöfob* (I loved), *elöfom* (he has loved), *ilöfof* (she had loved), *olöfobs* (we shall love), *ulöfob* (I shall have loved).

Having appeared at a time when the need for a world language was strongly felt, Volapük enjoyed a brief success. At present it is remembered only as the pioneer among the constructed international auxiliary languages.

NICOLAI RABENECK,
Writer on European Nations and Cultures.

VOLATILE OILS. See ESSENTIAL OILS.

VOLCANISM, vŏl'kən-ĭz-əm, or **VULCANISM,** vŭl'-kən-ĭz-ə̄m, volcanic power or activity. The term ordinarily includes all natural processes resulting in the formation of volcanoes, volcanic rocks, lava flows, and the like. See also GEOLOGY—*Internal (Endogenous) Processes;* ROCKS—*Igneous Rocks* (Extrusions and Intrusions); VOLCANO.

VOLCANO, vŏl-kā'nō, a place on the earth's surface from which gases, molten rock, and fragmentary materials have been extruded. The term "volcano" is derived from Vulcano, one of the Lipari Islands north of Sicily, which in classical

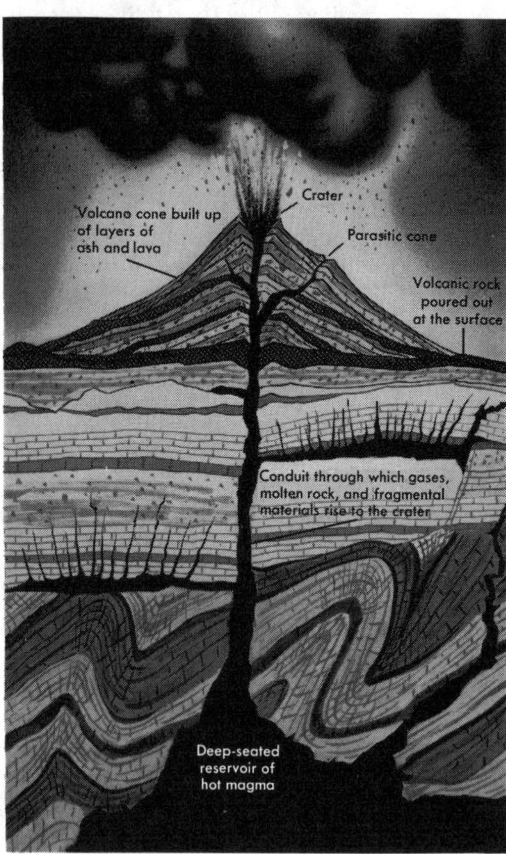

Schematic drawing showing the subterranean and surface structure of a volcano.

times was thought to be the entrance to the netherworld, the domain of Vulcan, the blacksmith god.

Volcanoes differ in the materials which they extrude and the form in which they develop. A universal feature of volcanoes is that they are motivated by molten rock which has invaded the

VOLCANO

ERUPTION OF A VOLCANO

The photographs on this page were taken during a protracted eruption of Kilauea Iki on the Island of Hawaii. The eruption began in November 1959, when molten lava briefly filled the crater of the volcano and then subsided. Earthquakes repeatedly shook the area, and in January 1960 a fissure opened on Kilauea Iki's flank. Lava erupted in a spectacular string of fire fountains along the line of the crack. The lava bubbled and spurted for 36 days. Flows as deep as 50 feet engulfed most of the nearby village of Kapoho and added more than 500 acres to Hawaii's coast. This type of eruption is characteristic of Kilauea: there is a heavy flow of fluid basaltic magma, but no explosion. Thus, although this eruption was one of the most destructive in recent Hawaiian history, it was less violent than eruptions usually are in other parts of the world.

Lava fills the crater of Kilauea Iki in first phase of eruption.

All photographs by Alpha Photo Associates

Flames and poisonous gases threaten Kapoho during the fissure eruption of Kilauea Iki. Although partially destroyed by a lava flow, the village was evacuated without loss of life.

PLATE 1

Lava pouring from Kilauea Iki's flank invades a papaya grove at a speed of several inches a minute.

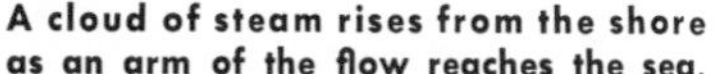

A cloud of steam rises from the shore as an arm of the flow reaches the sea.

VOLCANOES AROUND THE WORLD

Birnback

A new volcanic island, Surtsey, emerges from the sea near Iceland, the northern anchor of the Atlantic chain of volcanoes.

As shown on the map below, most volcanoes lie in the two principal zones of recent mountain building, the Alpine-Himalayan zone and the zone bordering the Pacific.

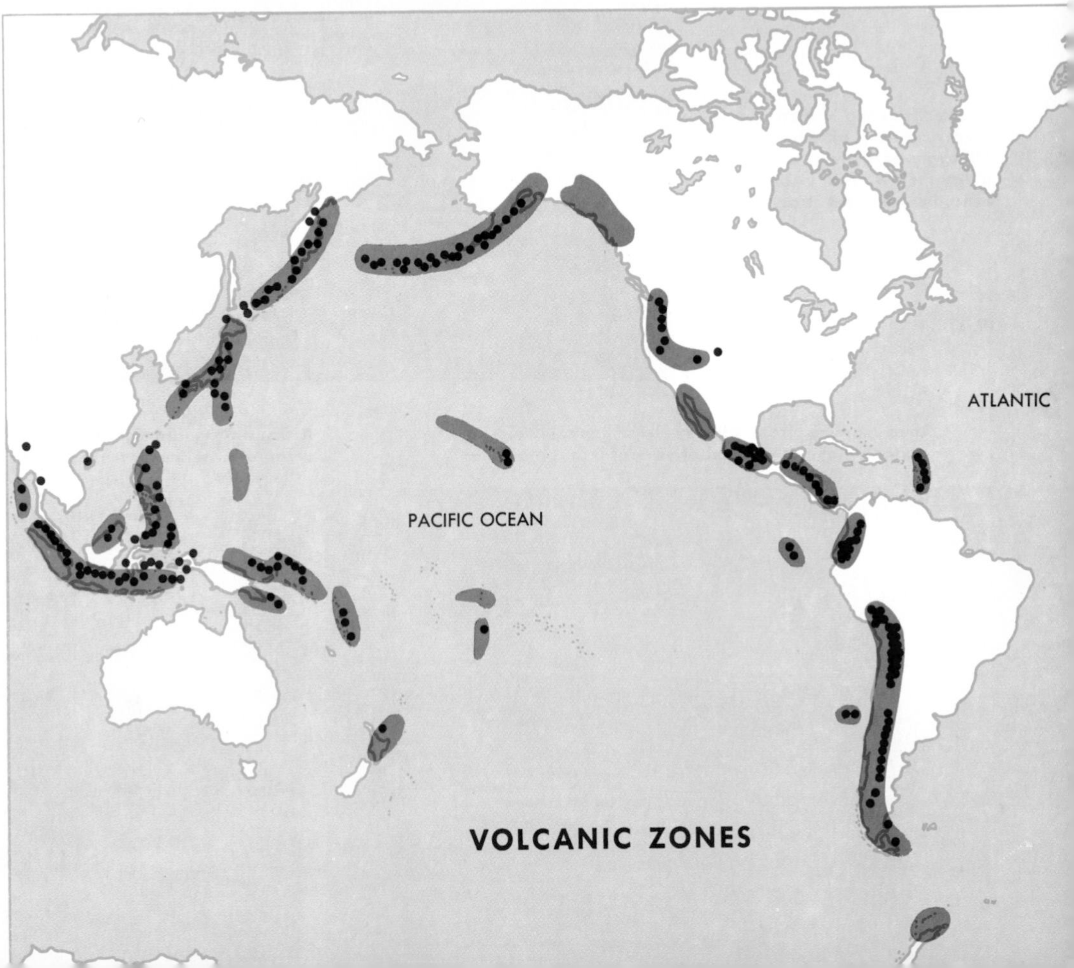

ATLANTIC

PACIFIC OCEAN

VOLCANIC ZONES

Freelance Photographers Guild

Steaming Mount Etna looms over Taormina, Sicily, near the west end of a volcanic zone reaching eastward to Asia.

Shostal

Known as "the lighthouse of Central America" because of its nearly constant activity, Izalco first erupted in the eighteenth century in the highlands of El Salvador.

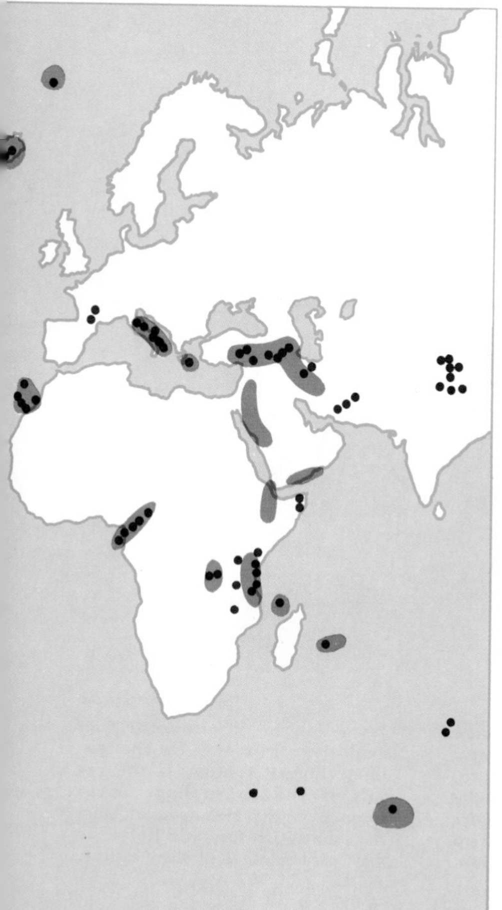

Photo Researchers

Rising about 12,390 feet, Mount Fuji is the highest peak in Japan. The celebrated volcano last erupted in 1707.

CONES

Shostal

Shostal

Each of the mountains shown on this page represents a principal type of volcanic cone. The *cinder cone*, made of lightweight exploded materials, generally has the high rounded profile of Cinder Cone Mountain (above) in Lassen National Park, California. The *shield volcano* (below), built up by repeated flows of liquid lava, is characterized by gently sloping sides. The *composite volcano*, containing layers of both exploded cinders and lava flows, is steeper than the shield volcano but less steep than the cinder cone. Mount Mayón (left) in the Philippines is typical.

Freelance Photographers Guild

Hawaii's gently rising Mauna Loa is the crest of an enormous shield volcano rising nearly 30,000 feet from the floor of the Pacific. Flow is seen in foreground.

LAVAS

Lavas assume various characters depending on their temperature at eruption, rate of cooling, mineral content, and other factors. Fine-grained *basalt* (above) occurs when cooling is slow enough to permit minerals to begin crystallization.

The glassy character of *obsidian* (above) is produced by extremely rapid cooling of a viscous lava. Unlike basalt, which occasionally forms underground, obsidian always forms at the earth's surface where cool air prevents crystallization.

Fundamental Photographs

***Scoria* (above) is associated with explosive eruptions. Its sponge-like, cindery texture is the result of sudden cooling. Gases trapped in the molten lava leave thousands of tiny air holes as they accumulate and then escape.**

(*Top*) Mt. Saint Helens, Washington, erupted violently on May 18, 1980, after remaining dormant for over 100 years. (*Bottom*) Kilauea, on the island of Hawaii, one of the world's most active volcanoes, sends a river of molten lava toward the sea during its November 1959 eruption.

(TOP) ROGER WERTH, 1980 LONGVIEW DAILY NEWS/WOODFIN CAMP; (BOTTOM) UPI

outer crust of the earth as what is called *magma*. Sometimes this merely supplies the heat which produces a steam or gas explosion with the resultant fragmentation of nearby materials. On other occasions it wells out at the surface, where it is called *lava*.

The manner in which lava and fragmental materials combine to determine the form of a volcano has been used as a basis for classification. Thus the majority of the world's volcanoes may be divided into two main types, lava domes or shield volcanoes, and composite volcanoes.

In the *shield* volcano, the mountain is a gently sloping dome composed of a series of lava flows. An individual flow rarely exceeds 25 feet in thickness. Fragmental materials thrown out by explosions are present but in very small quantities and have virtually no effect on the form of the mountain. As such a volcano grows, eruptions of lava often take place from fissures in the flanks as well as from the central vent. Eventually, the column of lava is no longer able to rise to the summit of the mountain and all the eruptions come from lateral fissures. From then on the volcano increases in diameter but not in height. Closely spaced lava domes may unite as they grow in size and form a compound lava volcano. The island of Hawaii, for example, has been formed by the union above sea level of five huge lava domes. The mid-ocean archipelagoes such as Hawaii, Samoa, the Society group, the Tuamotus (Paumotus), and many others are lava dome ranges or groups of great volcanoes built along major rifts in the suboceanic crust.

The *composite* volcano develops a form which is dominated by rock fragments exploded from the throat, interspersed with lava flows from this vent or from fissures in the side of the mountain. A volcano of this type is normally steeply sloping and symmetrical, with a small crater in the top. The crater is a funnel-shaped depression which rarely exceeds a mile or so in diameter. Many composite volcanoes rise 10,000 feet or more above their base. Mayon Volcano in the Philippine Islands, Vesuvius in Italy, and Fuji in Japan are good examples of composite volcanoes.

The great majority of high places on the globe which are called mountains are composed of folded sedimentary rocks. Volcanoes are distinguished from these in part by their characteristic shape and in part by the nature of their materials.

Ashes and lava in the vicinity of a volcano mark an active vent. Many which have not erupted within historical times may still be classed as probably just dormant if their symmetry has not been badly disturbed by erosion and their lava and ash deposits are fairly well preserved. As far back as records in the rock take us into the earth's history, volcanoes are found to have been present. The ancient, truly dead ones have been worn away so that today we can view remnants of their throats and the pools of once-molten rock upon which they drew, as in the White Mountains of New Hampshire.

Distribution.—There are approximately 430 volcanoes in the world which have erupted within historical times. Of these, 275 are located in the Northern Hemisphere and 155 in the Southern Hemisphere. There are records of about 2,500 eruptions, of which more than 2,000 took place in and around the Pacific Ocean, where there are 336 of the active volcanoes. Many volcanoes are dormant or dead; these have not been counted, but probably would number in the thousands.

A general feature of the distribution of volcanoes is that they occur within or near the two great zones of recent mountain building. One of these, the Alpine-Himalayan zone, extends through the Mediterranean area across the Caspian Sea through the Himalaya and down the Malay Peninsula. The other borders the Pacific Ocean. In addition to these, there is volcanic activity within the three great oceanic regions of the Pacific, Atlantic, and Indian oceans.

Notably active groups occur in the Aleutian Islands of the North Pacific; along the Kamchatka Peninsula and Kuril Islands; throughout the Japanese Islands, the Philippine Islands (with 98 eruptive centers), Indonesia, and the South Pacific groups of islands. The west coast of South America has its share, while Central America is particularly active. The west coast of North America is relatively inactive, though Mt. Lassen erupted in 1914 (see LASSEN PEAK) and Mt. St. Helens erupted in 1980 (see SAINT HELENS, MOUNT). Such peaks as Baker and Rainier in Washington, Crater Lake and Hood in Oregon, and Shasta in California are volcanoes with historical or geologic evidence of youth.

The Atlantic Ocean region contains some very important volcanic centers. In the northern part lies Iceland, the greatest lava field of modern times. There are believed to be between 20 and 30 active vents. The uncertainty is introduced by the fact that some are probably hidden beneath ice sheets. In the lower latitudes close to the African coast are the Canary Islands with several active volcanic centers and the Cape Verde Islands with one active cone. The Azores, farther to the west, are volcanic islands near which four submarine eruptions have occurred. In the Indian Ocean, Kerguelen is a large island apparently built of flood or shield lavas and may be regarded as the counterpart of Iceland.

One of the most striking features of the distribution of volcanoes is their arrangement along lines or narrow elongated zones. This feature is particularly well illustrated in the Pacific and circum-Pacific regions. The alignment can best be explained by assuming that the original molten material has ascended along deep-seated fractures, although it is usually emitted at the surface only at certain favored points. These points are sometimes at the intersections of fractures running in different directions. A spectacular example of alignment is to be found in the islands of the Hawaiian chain. They are all the protruding peaks of volcanic mountains. The related islands are strung on a line 1,500 miles long trending north of west nearly parallel to the trends of the Marquesas, Society, Tuamotu, Tubuai, Samoa, and other volcanic chains of the Pacific, each group presumably fed by a great abyssal crack in the earth's crust. At the northwest end of the Hawaiian chain are the low Ocean and Midway Islands. At the southeast is Hawaii, highest deep-sea island in the world, with Mauna Loa towering more than five miles above the ocean floor nearby and still growing. The history of this chain appears to have been one of activity beginning in the northwest and moving progressively southeastward. Most of the earlier vents are now extinct and modern activity is concentrated in the southeastern end.

Materials Erupted.—Lava, the molten rock which is poured out on the surface during an eruption, comes from a parent magma which is a silicate melt with varying amounts of iron, calcium, aluminum, magnesium, potassium, and sodium, with minor quantities of other elements. These magmas are divided into two groups on the basis of their silica percentage, the acid and the basic magmas. The so-called acid lavas, such as rhyolite, contain 70–75 percent silica while the basic rocks such as basalt contain as little as 40–48 percent silica. Ferromagnesian minerals are more common in basic rocks. The lime content also increases on going from the acid to the basic end of the series. Of the most common effusive igneous rocks, rhyolite is at the acid end of the series, basalt at the basic end, and intermediate lavas ranging from acid toward basic are dacite, trachyte, and andesite. The two most common lavas in the world are basalt and andesite. The difference between the two is essentially the difference in the proportion of the magnesium-iron minerals.

Chemical composition is of interest mainly because it affects the viscosity of the molten lava. By so doing it influences the rate and distance of flow, degree of crystallization, the shape of cones, and the surface forms and structures of the solidified rock. Acid lavas are usually of high viscosity whereas basic lavas are extremely fluid. As lava rises and flows out on the earth's surface, diminished pressure permits the escape of the bulk of its gases. The escaping gas produces bubbles which leave empty vesicles when the lava consolidates. Extreme distention of the lava in this way produces the kind of molten froth which solidifies as the material known as pumice.

In terms of physical appearance, there are literally scores of lava types, but two are best known: aa (ah-ah) and pahoehoe. The surface of aa lava is covered with a mass of rough, jagged, angular blocks of all sizes and shapes. Pahoehoe lava, on the other hand, is characterized by wrinkled, ropy forms. In general it is believed that aa lavas are erupted at lower temperatures and with higher gas content than pahoehoe. The pahoehoe flows with relative smoothness and the gas escapes rapidly and quietly. Aa is so highly charged with gas that, although it is erupted at comparatively low temperature, it is still somewhat fluid. The gas escapes explosively, breaking the surface into masses which immediately congeal into rough blocks which move with the advancing flow like a river of clinkers.

Eruptions.—An eruption is a difficult thing to define. Volcanologists at observatories at Kilauea and Vesuvius have concluded that the most distinctive feature of a volcanic cycle is a short period of repose at its end. This is often preceded by an explosion which constitutes the phase popularly known as an eruption. At volcanoes like Kilauea and Vesuvius, the lava column is visible most of the time and serves as a gauge of activity. Repose is followed by an increase in the internal pressure which may or may not manifest itself by the appearance of lava and building up of the cone as at Vesuvius.

Right: **Vesuvius, on the Bay of Naples, Italy, is famed for eruptions since ancient times. Here it is seen in wartime upheaval (March 1944) after the Allies captured the area.**

(Right) Ewing Galloway; (below) United States Navy

Below: **On the Alaska Peninsula and on some of the Aleutian Islands are volcanoes which constantly emit smoke or steam and occasionally erupt violently. This one in Alaska was photographed from a high-flying Navy plane.**

The volcano literally swells like a toad. At Hawaii, instruments record the tilt of the ground which results from this swelling. As the climax of pressure approaches, lava may break through the flanks or overflow the top. This is followed by collapse. At this stage some volcanoes explode violently. Others simply send out lava floods. Kilauea usually does the latter, but in 1924 it closed a 132-year supercycle with a spectacular steam-blast eruption which tossed eight-ton boulders nearly a mile from the vent and released tremendous cauliflower clouds of smoke. Steam blasts are believed to differ from normal explosive eruptions in that the energy comes from superheating of ground waters as contrasted with the rise of gas and lava from depth. Scientists at the Hawaiian Volcano Observatory have concluded that the internal pressure under a volcanic cone may be thought of as accumulating at a nearly steady rate throughout the ages. The volcanic vents are safety valves and the entire island by its weight acts like the spring control of the valve, opening only when the pressure inside has passed a certain amount. Such a mechanism might naturally be expected to give rise to a sort of periodicity of eruptions. Hawaiian eruptions have shown a tendency to follow a rough pattern. The apparent connection may be a coincidence, but this pattern seems to be related rather closely to sunspot cycles. The details of the relationship are not simple.

The normal type of Hawaiian eruption which is dominated by the welling out of large quantities of lava is characteristic of thinly fluid basaltic magma of very high temperature (1200°–1300° C.). The activity which accompanies such an eruption sometimes includes the rapid emission of gases from the surface of a lava lake which may throw particles of molten lava into the air to be caught by the wind and blown out into long glassy threads. These are called Pele's hair after the Polynesian goddess of volcanoes.

When the lava is more acidic or at a lower temperature (1100°–1200° C.), its viscosity is greater than that of the Hawaiian lava, and escaping gas is from time to time unable to maintain open passages to the air. The lava then solidifies, and gas accumulates below the plug until its pressure is sufficient to bring about release by explosion. In this type of eruption there is a rhythmic blowing out of clots of lava, bombs, and scoria at relatively closely spaced intervals. A classic example of activity along this pattern is Stromboli in the Mediterranean Sea, north of Sicily. Its habitual luminosity at night led it to be called the lighthouse of the Mediterranean.

Still more acidic lavas possess greater viscosity at temperatures of 1100° C. or less. These solidify quickly upon exposure to the atmosphere and cap an erupting vent so that complete quiescence ensues between eruptions. In the intervals of quiet, magmatic gases gather energy. They finally explode, disrupting the plug with tremendous violence and shooting out clouds black with particles of solid lava. Such eruptions are called Vulcanian because of their typical occurrence in Vulcan, another Mediterranean volcano. Bread-crust bombs are characteristic of this mode of eruption.

An extreme case of a long interval of quiet followed by a particularly violent explosion occurred at Vesuvius (q.v.) in the eruption of 79 A.D. The eruption consisted first of comminuted plug rock, then light froth which had accumulated in the pipe, then scoria, and finally heavy lava was extruded. The temperature of the lava in such an eruption is about 1000° C.

Another special form of explosive eruption is typified by that of Pelée in Martinique in 1902 (see PELÉE, MONT). Here again there was a viscous acidic magma capping pent-up gases under great pressure. The unique feature of this eruption was the intermittent ejection of white-hot clouds composed of an emulsion of glowing gas and solid particles. These instead of rising into the air were projected downward and spread devastation and death over the surrounding country. Closely connected with the emission of these death-dealing clouds was the slow upheaval of a dome of recently solidified lava. Such a mode of eruption is called Peléean. In it the temperature appears to be about 1100° C. at the point of ejection.

An example of the extreme in low temperature eruptions was furnished by Bandai-san in Japan, July 15, 1888. In this type the lava loses heat before it is able to reach the surface. As a result, the materials which appear are shattered old rock, masses of water and steam, and gas.

Cause.—In thinking about the ultimate cause of volcanism, it is natural at first to consider the possibility of the earth as consisting of a solid skin resting on a molten interior. Historically, speculation on the cause of volcanism followed just that reasoning. But today it is known from the study of earthquake waves that the earth is solid down to a depth of 1,800 miles. Below that, it is possible that the material is molten; this, however, cannot be looked upon as a source for the materials ejected from volcanoes, since it is not possible for this molten material to travel 1,800 miles to the surface. There are many facts of observation regarding the behavior of volcanoes which lead to the conclusion that the immediate source reservoirs are relatively small in dimension and located near the surface. Studies of the volcanoes on the island of Hawaii show that they may be supplied from a primary magma chamber located at an approximate depth of 20 miles below the crust. The main problem is to explain how molten rock has accumulated in these reservoirs.

Since the ejected materials of the world's volcanoes are overwhelmingly dominated by basalt or close relatives of that rock type, there has been speculation on the existence of a worldwide layer of basalt at considerable depth. The earth's heat at a point 20 miles below the surface would be sufficient to melt this rock if the overlying pressure were reduced locally. Such a reduction of pressure is believed to occur in areas of the world where mountains still are being formed. The wrinkling of the crust which accompanies mountain building could initiate an abyssal fracture. At a depth of 20 miles basalt would liquefy locally and start working its way upward. The melting process would be accelerated by the fluxing action of gases which would come out of solution as the liquid worked toward regions of lower pressure. When such a mass neared the surface, it would send off tongues through some of the many fractures available to it in the outermost rocks. These could supply a series of small reservoirs from which volcanoes could be fed.

Obviously, these thoughts on the ultimate cause of volcanoes wander far into the realm of speculation. No single theory has yet embraced all the myriad details of volcanic behavior and distribution. This fact alone suggests the possibility of more than one explanation for the phenomenon. At any rate, throughout geological time—as far back as it is recorded in the rocks now open for inspection (3 billion years)—volcanoes have lived and died. There were more in some periods than others, but, by and large, it seems highly probable that their general characteristics were not greatly different from those of modern ones.

Related Phenomena.—Some volcanoes in the process of their growth under water have not yet reached the surface, while others have extended only a portion of their cones above water. In the case of the former, the addition of some new material by bringing it above water level gives birth to a new island. The violent explosion of a partially submerged cone, on the other hand, may remove all visible evidence and cause the disappearance of an island. Again, by the normal operation of wave action a dome, which is in intermittent eruption, may be worn away between eruptions. Bogoslof in the Aleutian chain at about 56° north latitude, 168° west longitude is one of that type. Falcon Island (or Fonuafoo) at 20°23′ south latitude, 175°25′ west longitude, blew its head off one day in 1913 and disappeared. On Oct. 4, 1927, to the accompaniment of a series of explosions, it just as suddenly reappeared—only to vanish again in 1949.

In one of the most famous eruptions in history, a major engulfment of one of the peaks of Krakatau (Krakatoa) in the straits between Java and Sumatra reduced it to a height below sea level and caused a tidal wave 120 feet high which drowned more than 36,000 people. This followed a terrific explosion on Aug. 27, 1883. (See also KRAKATAU.)

Most volcanoes have a habit of issuing warnings before they erupt. These take various forms. In Hawaii, as has been mentioned, scientific measurement of the tilt of the ground and of small local earthquakes supply some of the evidence. At Krakatau the series of events which culminated in the greatest explosion began on May 20, 1883, and continued in the form of intermittent explosions throughout the summer of that year. At Sakura-jima, Japan, in the latter part of 1913, smoke began to issue from the mountain, local earthquakes increased greatly in number, and springs on the mountain accelerated their flow. Heeding these warnings, the authorities evacuated the entire population of 23,500. At 10 A.M., Jan. 12, 1914, an explosion opened the west wall of the mountain. Ten minutes later the east side blew out, sending clouds of dust to 20,000 feet. One half the entire volume of the mountain was blown to bits but not a life was lost because of the recognition of the warning signs.

Proposals have often been made for the utilization of volcanic heat. This does not mean the harnessing of eruptions of volcanoes but rather making use of fumaroles, boiling springs, and heat found in volcanic districts. For many years the steam of fumaroles has been used in Iceland and Japan for heating schools and public buildings. Most of this is the steam of groundwater brought to the boiling point through the agency of underground magma or of volcanic gases combining with oxygen in the air. In Iceland, North America, the tropics, and New Zealand, hot springs have been used as laundries. They have also been exploited as baths for the treatment of physical ailments. Near Lardarello in Tuscany, boric acid has been produced from scalding natural steam for more than a century. In order to obtain higher temperatures and pressures, holes have been drilled into the ground in a number of places. At the Geysers in the St. Helena Range in California, a region overlying volcanic magma, a great store of hot steam was discovered by drilling. Temperatures from 200°–350° F. and pressures from 60–175 pounds per square inch were found. Wells varied in depth from 150 to 600 feet.

Except for the relatively small areas immediately adjacent to vents which have erupted recently, volcanism, especially in tropic regions, has produced exceptionally fertile countryside. This is accomplished in part by frequent renewal of potash and phosphates through eruptions.

Volcanic eruptions at Skaptar Jokull and Asama in 1783; Babuyan in 1831; Krakatau in 1883; Santa Maria and Pelée in 1902; and Katmai in 1912 are known to have hurled great quantities of dust into the stratosphere (above 50,000 feet). There, free from marked convection or washing by rain, it was returned to lower levels only by the action of gravity. From the evidence of high haze and colored sunsets throughout the world, it required from two to three years to make the trip in some cases. In the case of Krakatau, it was estimated that the dust reached an altitude of not less than 130,000 feet. It has been computed that such volcanic dust particles are of the order of 1½ to 2 microns in diameter (1 micron = 0.001 millimeter).

In June 1912, an observer of the United States Geological Survey was in Algeria making measurements of the quantity of heat coming to the earth from the sun. At Bassau, Algeria, during the observations of June 19, 1912, streaks of dust were noted lying along the horizon. These were joined by others and in a few days the sky appeared "mackereled" although no clouds were present. Finally the phenomenon became so marked that observations were discontinued. On June 29, the whole sky was filled with haze which continually became worse until the expedition departed, September 10. It was later learned that this was part of a worldwide condition produced by the eruption of Mt. Katmai, Alaska, on June 6, 1912. Calculations revealed that the dust from this eruption had traveled at 25 miles per hour. The haziness of the atmosphere during the summer of 1912 produced a decrease in direct solar radiation which amounted to nearly 20 percent of the total heat at high sun. The dust of Katmai diminished the heat available to warm the earth by an amount sufficient to produce a fall of nearly 13° F. in the temperature of the earth as a whole. If it were effective for a long enough period of time such a fall would bring a large section of the present temperate zones within a region of year-round ice. This is the basis for the theory attributing glacial periods to increases in volcanic activity.

Indonesian Information Office

Volcanic cones of Tengger Range, East Java, Indonesia. Range contains the Bromo and other active volcanoes.

See also LAVA AND LAVA FLOWS; ROCKS—*Igneous Rocks*. For a listing of some of history's great volcanic eruptions, see DISASTERS—*Earthquakes and Volcanoes*.

L. DON LEET.

VOLCANO ISLANDS (Jap. KAZAN-RETTO), island group in the western Pacific Ocean, northeast of the Marianas, and southeast of the Bonin Islands, annexed by Japan in 1891. Largest of the three islands of the group is Iwo Jima (q.v.), 760 miles south of Tokyo; it is 5 miles long and has an area of 8 square miles. Kita-Iwo-Jima lies to the north of Iwo Jima, and Minami-Iwo-Jima to the south. There is a population in the islands of about 1,200, of whom 1,000 inhabit Iwo Jima. Suribachi, an extinct volcano, rises to 546 feet on the southern edge of Iwo Jima.

In 1945, Iwo Jima was invaded by the American 5th Amphibious Corps. Although encountering strong opposition ashore, marines stormed Mount Suribachi on February 23, planting the American flag on the crater's rim (and providing one of the famous photographs of the war). Under the Japanese peace treaty of 1951, it was agreed that the United States might propose that the Volcano Islands be assigned as a trusteeship, and that meanwhile the United States would administer the islands. In 1968 the United States returned the islands to Japanese control.

VOLCANUS. See VULCAN.

VOLE, vōl, field mouse, a small rodent belonging to the subfamily Microtinae (family Cricetidae or Muridae of some authors) distinguished from other mice by dental and cranial characters, and by its comparatively stout body, short, rounded ears, short tail, and tuberculated feet. The name, of European origin, means "field mouse" and has been applied to several genera of rodents in North America, including *Microtus* (meadow voles), *Clethrionomys* (red-backed voles), *Phenacomys* (heather voles), *Lagurus* (sagebrush vole), and *Pitymys* (pine vole). Voles can also be found in Central America and in northern parts of Eurasia.

Various species of meadow voles may become especially numerous and cause great loss to grain crops, or to orchards by girdling the trunks of the trees. They eat almost their own weight in vegetable matter each day, consuming seeds, bark, roots, and leaves. Their reproductive potential is legend. They can give birth to their first litter at five weeks of age and, under proper conditions, produce offspring almost every three weeks. Under ideal conditions, if all the progeny of a pair of meadow voles lived, and bred when sexually mature, at the end of one year there would be over one million mice. Their population is kept within reasonable limits by the vole's many enemies. As prey, they constitute a major food item to many important furbearing animals, and may, at times, limit the numbers of the latter by their own abundance.

R. L. PETERSON
Curator, Department of Mammals, Royal Ontario Museum, Toronto

VOLENDAM, vō'lən-däm, village, the Netherlands, on the Ijsselmeer 11 miles northeast of Amsterdam in North Holland Province. It is traditionally a fishing village, and duck breeding has become important in the economy. The community attracts many tourists and artists because of the picturesque costumes and setting. Volendam had its origin in the building of the great sea dam for the new waterway to Edam in the mid-14th century. There is a ferry from Volendam to nearby Marken Island, another tourist center. Population: (1984 est.) 24,019.

VOLGA RIVER, vŏl'gə, Russ. vôl'gə, river, USSR, in the Great Russian Plain, the principal waterway of the Soviet Union, 2,290 miles in length, and the longest river in Europe. It rises in the Valdai Hills at an elevation of 748 feet and falls into the Caspian Sea, forming a large delta at Astrakhan. Its basin has an area of 530,000 square miles. It flows at first 90 miles southeast past Rzhev, then northeast past Kalinin, Ivankovo, and Uglich to the Rybinsk Reservoir. It then turns east past Rybinsk, Yaroslavl, Kostroma, and Kineshma, and southeast and east past Gorki and Cheboksary to Kazan. Here it turns south, flowing circuitously past Ulyanovsk and forming a hairpin bend around the Zhibuli Mountains at Kuibyshev. The Volga then proceeds southwest past Syzran, Balakovo, Volsk, Saratov, and Kamyshin to Volgograd (former Stalingrad), where it changes course southeastward before reaching the Caspian. Below Volgograd, the Volga sends off a parallel branch, the Akhtuba. The two main branches and a multitude of cross channels form a braided flood plain which, like the Caspian Sea, is situated below sea level. The principal tributaries of the Volga River are (on the right) the Oka and Sura rivers, and (on the left) the Unzha, Vetluga, and Kama rivers.

Hydroelectric Projects.—The construction of dams, reservoirs, and hydroelectric installations has greatly changed the appearance of the Volga River course under the Soviet regime. The first hydroelectric project was completed in 1937 at Ivankovo. It dammed the Volga River, forming the Volga Reservoir, from which a canal was built to Moscow. This was followed in 1941, just before the Soviet Union's entry into World War II, by the completion of the hydroelectric projects of Uglich and Rybinsk (called Shcherbakov from 1946 to 1957). The Rybinsk dam formed the Rybinsk Reservoir, with an area of 1,760 square miles. Its hydroelectric plant, generating 330,000 kilowatts, was the first large waterpower installation on the Volga. The next dam was completed in 1955 at Gorodets, above Gorki; its hydroelectric station has a generating capacity of 400,000 kilowatts.

The two largest hydroelectric projects on the Volga River are near Kuibyshev and Volgograd. The Kuibyshev dam, completed in 1955 at Zhigulevsk, has a hydroelectric station with a generating capacity of 2,300,000 kilowatts. The Volgograd dam, completed just north of the city in 1958, was designed to attain a full capacity of 2,575,000 kilowatts by 1961. Additional dams and hydroelectric stations were planned for Balakovo (1,000,000 kilowatts), between Saratov and Kuibyshev, and for Cheboksary (800,000 kilowatts), between Gorki and Kazan.

Navigation and Canals.—The construction of dams and reservoirs has improved navigation along the Volga River by regulating the water level. Navigation was formerly impeded by shallows and sandbanks during the normal low-water stage in late summer, which followed a flood stage in May and June. During the winter season, ice closes the Volga River for a period ranging from about four months in the lower course to five months in the upper reaches. In order to maintain transportation in the Volga Valley even during the winter season, a railroad was built parallel to the right bank of the river in World War II and completed in 1944. In spite of the relatively short navigation season, the Volga River is by far the most important inland waterway of the Soviet Union. In 1955, the Volga system, including the Kama River, handled 55 percent of all goods carried on Soviet rivers and canals.

The importance of the Volga River is enhanced by canals that link it with other river systems. These canals are the Moscow Canal, linking the Volga at Ivankovo with the Soviet capital; the Volga-Don Canal (opened in 1952), which connects the Volga at Volgograd with the Don River; and the Mariinsk waterway, a series of lakes, rivers, and canals linking the Volga with the Baltic at Leningrad. The Mariinsk waterway, to be known as the Volga-Baltic waterway, was being expanded and modernized under the Seven-Year Plan (1959–1965).

History.—The Volga River area was settled in the early Middle Ages by Slavic and Finnic tribes, which used it as a trade route to the Caspian lands and central Asia. The Mongol invasions found the Russians entrenched in the upper reaches of the Volga and the Oka, extending their control as far as Nizhni Novgorod (the present Gorki, founded in 1221). The entire Volga Valley did not pass to Russian control until the 16th century, when the Tatar khanates of Kazan (1552) and Astrakhan (1556) were conquered by Ivan the Terrible. After the building of east-west railroads in the late 19th century, the Volga became an important north-south transportation link (made famous by the Volga boatmen). Nowadays these have been replaced by motorized barges and modern river steamers, traveling the 1,900-mile course between Moscow and Astrakhan in nine days.

THEODORE SHABAD,
Author of "Geography of the USSR."

VOLGOGRAD, vŏl′gō-grăd, Russ. vôl-gə-grät′ formerly STALINGRAD), oblast, USSR, in the southeast European part of the Russian SFSR, 36,300 square miles in area. The capital is Volgograd (q.v.). The oblast is a dry steppe and semidesert area with a population consisting mostly of Russians and Ukrainians. Annual rainfall is about 14 inches; average July temperature, 75° F.; average January temperature, 10° F. Salt is mined in the east, and unmined deposits of iron ore exist in the northwest. Agriculture is the chief occupation in the north, and grazing in the south, the main farm products being wheat, sunflower seed, dairy produce, meat, and wool. Cattle, hides, wool, and salt are oblast surplus products. The area became part of the newly formed Stalingrad Krai in 1934 and was organized separately as Stalingrad Oblast in 1936. The name was changed to Volgograd in 1961. Pop. (1959) 1,849,000.

ELLSWORTH RAYMOND.

VOLGOGRAD (formerly STALINGRAD; originally TSARITSYN), city, USSR, capital of Volgograd Oblast in the southeast European part of the Russian SFSR. Stretching in a narrow belt for 30 miles along the west bank of the Volga River where it most nearly approaches the Don, the city is an important river port and transshipment point, with railways to the Caucasus, the Donets Basin, Moscow (580 miles northwest), and up the west bank of the Volga. A rail line terminating on the east bank of the Volga across from Volgograd runs to the Urals. Caucasian oil coming up the Volga by river tanker is transshipped to railway tank cars for delivery to Moscow, while timber floated downriver from northern European Russia to Volgograd is transferred to the railroad and sent to the Donets coal basin. Donets coal is also transshipped from railway to riverboat and sent upriver to other Volga cities.

Because of this easy access to Donets coal, Caucasian oil, and north Russian timber, Volgograd in Soviet times has developed into a great industrial center. Its tractor factory, one of the largest tractor and tank plants in the world, is supplied with alloy steel by the Red October steelworks, which operates on scrap iron collected throughout the Volga area. There also are machine-building, chemical, leather, and food-processing factories, as well as sawmills, shipping yards for building and repairing riverboats, and an oil refinery. Airlines radiate to the Caucasus, Rostov, Moscow, and the Urals. The importance of Volgograd as a transportation center was increased when the 60-mile canal between the Don and Volga rivers was opened in 1952. In 1958 one of the largest hydroelectric power dams in the world was completed on the Volga just north of the city.

History.—During the 13th century the region surrounding the site of Volgograd was occupied by Tatars of the Golden Horde. Following the conquest of Kazan and Astrakhan from the Tatars, in the early 1550's the Russians built a fortified town called Tsaritsyn on an island opposite the junction of the Volga and the small river Tsaritsa. Remote from Moscow and surrounded by nomadic tribes, the town was of considerable strategic importance, and in 1556–1558 a fortress was built there. In the 19th century Tsaritsyn lost its military importance but became an important commercial center, particularly for transshipping naphtha and kerosine overland from the river.

The town fell into Communist hands immediately after the Bolshevik Revolution of 1917 but was attacked twice during the ensuing Civil War by White armies. In 1918 Piotr N. Krasnov's White forces reached the outskirts but were driven back. In the summer of 1919 Gen. Anton I. Denikin's White Army seized the city for three months but was driven out by Red Army units under the command of Joseph Stalin. As this seems to have been the only occasion when Stalin actually commanded troops during the Civil War, the battle won a prominent place in Soviet history books, and the city was renamed Stalingrad in 1925. Its growth was great under the Soviet regime, as shown by its population increase from 55,000 in 1897 to almost 446,000 in 1939.

In 1942, a year after the German invasion of the USSR in World War II began, the German Army struck at Stalingrad from the Ukraine in an attempt to cut off the supply of Caucasian oil to central European Russia and the Red Army on the front (85 percent of Soviet oil came from the Caucasian fields at the time). By late autumn the German troops had reached and occupied most of the city, Soviet troops holding only a narrow strip of land along the river. The city was temporarily destroyed, as fighting took place from house to house. After the river froze, however, large reserves of the Red Army crossed from the east bank, completely encircling the city and the German forces within it. Some 22 German divisions were trapped and captured. This battle was later recognized as the turning point of the entire European phase of World War II.

In November 1961, after Nikita S. Khrushchev, at the 22d Party Congress, made further revelations about the crimes of Stalin, the name of the city was changed again, to Volgograd. Pop. (1959) 591,000.

ELLSWORTH RAYMOND,
Associate Professor of Soviet Government and Economics, New York University.

VOLHYNIA, vŏl-hĭn′ĭ-ə, a historic region of Russia, in what is now the Ukrainian SSR of the Soviet Union. It is situated in the upper reaches of the Bug River, a tributary of the Vistula, and of the Pripet River, a tributary of the Dnieper. The region derives its name from the Volhynians, an early Slavic tribe, which had its political center in what is now the city of Vladimir-Volynski (the Volhynian Vladimir, to be distinguished from the Vladimir east of Moscow). Volhynia was an early Russian principality in the 11th and 12th centuries. It was raided by the Mongols in 1240, then passed to Lithuania in the 14th century. It remained in Lithuania and, after 1569, in the merged Polish-Lithuanian state, until it passed to Russia in the second (1793) and third (1795) partitions of Poland. In Czarist Russia, Volhynia was a guberniya (administrative division) with its capital at Zhitomir. Between World Wars I and II, Volhynia was divided between Poland and the Soviet Union. Under Soviet rule, the regional name Volhynia (Russian Volyn) was revived in the name of the Volyn (q.v.) Oblast of the Ukrainian SSR.

THEODORE SHABAD.

VOLITION, the act or power of willing or choosing. See FREE WILL AND DETERMINISM.

VOLK, vōlk, **Leonard Wells,** American sculptor: b. Wellston (now Wells), N.Y., Nov. 7, 1828; d. Osceola, Wis., Aug. 19, 1895. The son of a stonecutter, he learned the craft in his father's shop. In 1848 he went to St. Louis, Mo., where he taught himself drawing and modeling, and married a cousin of Stephen A. Douglas, who supplied funds for study in Rome (1855–1857). On his return Volk set up a studio in Chicago and organized the first art exhibition held there; he was one of the founders of the Chicago Academy of Design (1867).

Volk studied both Abraham Lincoln and Douglas closely during the Lincoln-Douglas debates, and is probably the only sculptor to have modeled Lincoln from life. In 1860 he made a life mask of Lincoln and casts of his hands; these are not only of great value to sculptors, but invaluable historic momentos. Volk's marble bust of Lincoln was destroyed in the great Chicago fire of 1871, but the original model was preserved. His colossal statue of Douglas survives in Chicago, as do his statues of Lincoln and Douglas in the Illinois state capitol at Springfield, and one of Lincoln in the city of Rochester, N.Y.

(STEPHEN ARNOLD) DOUGLAS VOLK (1856–1935), his son, became a portrait and figure painter. He organized and directed the Minneapolis (Minn.) School of Fine Arts (1886–1893), and later taught at the National Academy of Design, Cooper Union, and the Art Students League of New York City. His portrait of Felix Adler is in the Metropolitan Museum in New York City, while those of Gen. John Joseph Pershing and Albert, king of the Belgians, are in the National Gallery of Art, Washington, D.C.

VÖLKLINGEN, fûlk'lĭng-ən, city, Germany, in the State of Saarland, near the French border, on the Saar River, at the mouth of the Rossel River, 7 miles west of Saarbrücken, at an altitude of 700 feet. It is an important element in the Saar's industrial complex, with the largest steel plant in the area, and serves as an important rail junction and coal-mining center. Völklingen also manufactures coke, heavy machinery, electrical equipment, building materials, and cement. Three large electric plants, one in the suburb of Wehrden, produce power for the region's industry. In keeping with the character of the district, Völklingen maintains a trade school, while Schiller Park and a surrounding municipal forest serve to ameliorate the industrial environment. Under the name of Fulcolingas, the city was first mentioned at the beginning of the 9th century, when it was under the domination of the Frankish kings; its present name came into use in 1518. Industry was first established toward the end of the 16th century, following the discovery of coal and iron deposits. Napoleon I founded a school of mines in the southern suburb of Geislautern in 1807. Pop. (1959 official est.) 42,600.

VOLKMANN, fōlk'män, **Richard von** (pen name RICHARD LEANDER), German surgeon and writer: b. Leipzig, Germany, Aug. 17, 1830; d. Jena, Nov. 28, 1889. Educated at Halle, Giessen, and Berlin, he served as privat-docent (1857–1867) and professor of surgery at Halle, and director of the surgical clinic there. He was the first to describe cancer resulting from irritation of the skin by coal tar and paraffin oils (1873), and to excise the rectum for cancer (1878). He described ischemic contracture of the muscles due to pressure or injury accompanied often by muscle degeneration; this is called Volkmann's contracture, and the resulting paralysis is known as Volkmann's paralysis. Volkmann founded the *Sammlung klinischer Vorträge* (Collection of Clinical Lectures 1870), and was the foremost German advocate of Listerian antisepsis. Under the pen name of Richard Leander, he published several collections of folk tales.

ALFRED WILHELM VOLKMANN (1801–1877), his father, was a physiologist who specialized in the physiology of blood movement, the nervous system, vision, and muscle irritability. He contributed important work on the histology of the central nervous system and described the small canals, known as Volkmann's canals, which transmit blood vessels in the compact bone of the long bones. His publications include *The Independence of the Sympathetic Nervous System* (1842) and *Elasticity of Muscles* (1856).

VOLLARD, vô-lär', **Ambroise,** French art dealer and publisher: b. Réunion, Indian Ocean, 1865; d. Versailles, France, July 21, 1939. Going to Paris from his native isle, he was able to set up as a dealer as early as 1893. He specialized in the routine portraitist Ferdinand Roybet (1840–1920), but he was carefully watching developments in modern art. In 1895, he defied the general public with the first Cézanne show, which, however, immediately attracted some influential connoisseurs.

From then until his death, Vollard showed most of the significant avant-garde artists, and often helped them out by buying their (at the time) unwanted works at unabashedly bargain rates. For instance, he organized the first Picasso show in 1901, and in 1905 bought 30 Picasso canvases for 2,000 francs. He sat for many of his artists (the Cézanne portrait required 115 sittings). He induced many artists to become illustrators and thus became a famed publisher of superbly illustrated books. His autobiography, *Recollections of a Picture Dealer,* appeared in 1936, a year before the publication of the French edition.

WALLACE BROCKWAY

VOLLEYBALL, vŏl'ē-bôl, a team game in which a large inflated ball is hit with the hands back and forth across a net. Six players constitute an official team, and, in the modern game, the ball need not be immediately returned across the net, although this is permissible. A player may relay the ball to a teammate who in turn may relay it to another teammate or back to the original one—or may elect to return it across the net. Thus, the ball may be hit one, two, or three times, but no more, on one side of the net. It may not be hit twice in a row by the same player. Points are made basically as in lawn tennis—by striking the ball into the opponents' court or when the opponents fail to make a good return. Points are scored only by the serving side, and a game is for 15 points except that after the score reaches 14—all one side must gain a 2-point advantage—16-14, 17-15, and so on.

A full-sized court is 60 feet long and 30 feet wide, divided laterally by a net 8 feet high for men players, 7½ feet high for women players,

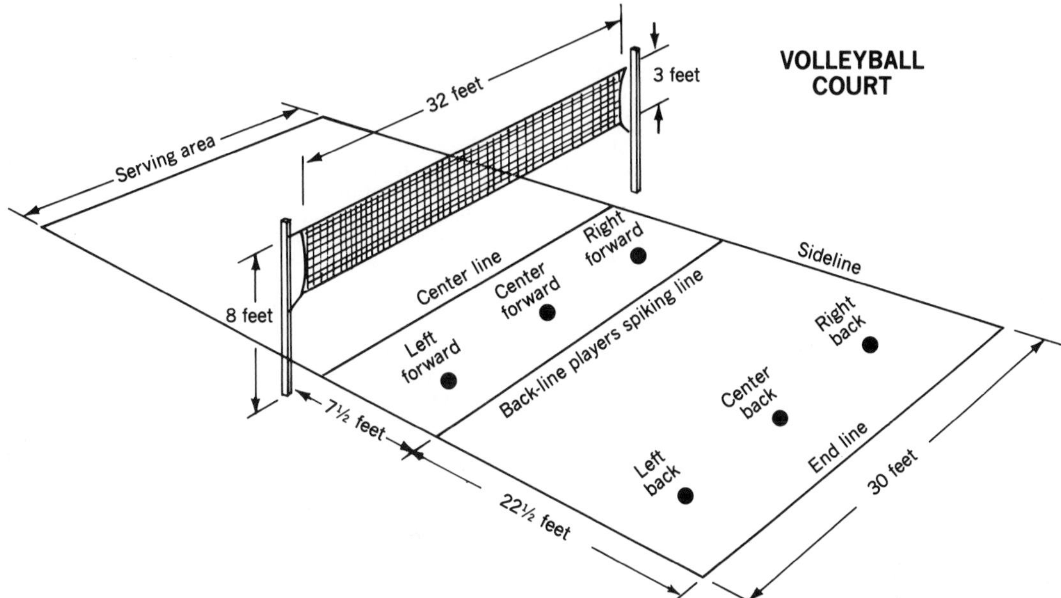

and sometimes as low as 7 or 6½ feet for young or inferior ones. The six players of a team occupy equal sections of the court—each one of them 15 by 10 feet—and are divided into three forwards (those nearest the net) and three backs. Team designations are accordingly right forward, center forward, left forward; right back, center back, left back. However, players rotate one position clockwise every time the serve changes hands.

The ball, leather-covered, is between 26 and 27 inches in circumference, weighs between 7 and 10 ounces, and is inflated to between 7 and 8 pounds pressure. It is served from the back of the court, usually deep to the opponents court. The usual custom is to attempt to relay it toward the net to a forward who "sets it up" by hitting it directly up into the air. Another forward then attempts to "spike" the ball by reaching up and hitting it down crisply into the opponents' court, as in badminton, where smashes are more effective when made close to the net.

William G. Morgan, physical director of the Holyoke, Mass., Young Men's Christian Association, was credited with the invention of the game in 1895. It has been modified since, and remains a popular YMCA game. It is also played outdoors, and is included in the Olympic Games.

PARKE CUMMINGS
Author of "The Dictionary of Sports"

VOLNEY, Comte de, vôl-nā' (CONSTANTIN FRANÇOIS DE CHASSEBOEUF; original family name BOISGIRAIS), French scholar and political philosopher: b. Craon, Anjou, France, Feb. 3, 1757; d. Paris, April 25, 1820. After studying law and medicine, Volney spent eight months in a Coptic monastery in the Lebanon studying Arabic, then traveled extensively through Egypt and Syria. An account of this trip, *Voyage en Egypte et en Syrie*, was published in 1787. In 1789 he was a member of the States-General, and in 1790 secretary of the Constituent Assembly. Imprisoned during the Terror, he escaped the guillotine, and in 1794 became the first professor of history at the newly founded École Normale. He served in the Senate under Napoleon, and in the Chamber of Peers under Louis XVIII.

Volney's *Les ruines ou méditations sur les révolutions des empires* (1791), a mixture of description and philosophy, sets forth his theories on the equality of man and on the need for tolerance and agnosticism where truth is not verifiable. In 1792 he bought an estate in Corsica, where he attempted to put his politico-economic theories into practice. In 1795 he went to the United States, where he traveled widely until forced to leave in 1798 because of American suspicions that he was a spy. His observations on this trip are incorporated in *Tableau du climat et du sol des États-Unis* (1803).

VOLOGDA, city, USSR, capital of Vologda Oblast in the Russian SFSR, 250 miles north-northeast of Moscow. The city is located on the small Vologda River, which joins the Sukhona 20 miles below the city and is navigable for Sukhona river boats. Vologda is a transportation center situated at the crossing of the Leningrad-Kirov and Moscow-Archangel railroads. Its industries include locomotive and car repair shops, machine shops, a furniture factory, a linen mill, and a plant producing lumbering equipment. The city is the center of a dairying district, and its name is believed to be derived from an old word *vologa*, meaning "dairy products." Founded in 1147, the city was first ruled by Novgorod, then became an independent principality (1397–1481) before falling to Moscow. Historic buildings include St. Sophia cathedral (built about 1570) and an 18th century bishop's palace (now a museum), which are located on the site of a former kremlin. Pop. (1959) 138,000.

THEODORE SHABAD

VOLOGESUS, vŏl-ō-jē'səs, or **VOLOGASES,** vŏl-ō-gā'sēz, name of five Parthian kings, whose chronology is controversial and whose history is confused.

VOLOGESUS I (r. 51?–?77 A.D.) warred with Rome (54–62) over the buffer state of Armenia and finally succeeded in confirming Tiridates, his brother, as its king, but on Roman terms. He fostered the spread of Zoroastrianism.

VOLOGESUS II (r. 130?–147) bribed invading

Alans to retire (133) and maintained peaceful relations with the Romans.

VOLOGESUS III (r. 148–191) continued at peace with Rome until he invaded (162) Armenia and Syria, whence he was expelled. The Romans then advanced into Mesopotamia, Assyria, and Armenia. The war ended favorably (166) for Rome, which received part of Mesopotamia in the peace settlement.

VOLOGESUS IV (r. 191?–?209) aided Gaius Pescennius Niger Justus against Lucius Septimius Severus in their contest for the Roman sovereignty (193). The Parthian capture of Nisibis, Mesopotamia, brought (197) Severus eastward for two years of successful campaigning, which ended in his annexation of all Mesopotamia (199).

VOLOGESUS V (r. 209?–?222) won his crown by defeating his brothers, endured a Roman invasion (216), made favorable terms with the Romans (217), but lost so many troops that the Persians asserted their independence of Parthia, which soon succumbed (226) to the Persian dynasty of the Sassanids.

P. R. COLEMAN-NORTON,
Princeton University.

VOLOS, vô'lôs, city, Greece (coextensive with the municipality of PAGASAE), capital of Magnesia nome (prefecture). Situated 100 miles north-northwest of Athens, near the foothills of Mount Pelion and at the end of a fine harbor (the Gulf of Volos), it is the chief port of Thessaly, the fertile, undulating plain of central Greece. Greater Athens, with a population of about 2,000,000, absorbs most of the products of the Volos area (fresh fruits, vegetables, olives, olive oil, hides and skins, and tobacco).

Mythology associates Volos with Iolcus, from where the mythical Jason led the Argonautic expedition in quest of the Golden Fleece. Volos itself is a relatively new city, built in the 1860's. Together with the rest of Thessaly, it was annexed by Greece in 1881 by virtue of the Berlin Treaty (1878). At that time the city's population was less than 4,000. In the 1880's, Volos was connected with Larisa and the other cities of the region by the Thessalian Railways. Port facilities were developed in the years preceding the Balkan Wars (1912–1913). After World War II the building of good roads and the relatively cheap transportation available by overland truck resulted in the decline of the port.

Volos was threatened with extinction on April 19–21, 1955, when, after a series of seismic warnings, a devastating earthquake leveled more than one third of its buildings and damaged most of those remaining, leaving about 40,000 persons homeless. With government support the city now has been fully reconstructed and has returned to a condition of moderate prosperity. Pop. (1951) 51,144; (1960 est.) 55,000.

G. G. ARNAKIS,
Professor of History, The University of Texas.

VOLPONE OR THE FOX, vŏl-pō'nē, a comedy by Ben Jonson, written in early 1606 (Old Style 1605) and performed at the Globe Theatre by the King's Men. The entire play, according to the prologue, was written in five weeks. It was published two years later with a dedicatory epistle addressed to the universities at Oxford and Cambridge and was popular on the English stage until the late 18th century. It was the first of Jonson's four great masterpieces of realistic comedy and takes a place of distinction beside *Epicoene, or The Silent Woman* (1609), a tour de force of delightful and ingenious farce; *The Alchemist* (1610), his greatest achievement in dramatic structure; and *Bartholomew Fair* (1614), a realistic panorama of low life.

Volpone, unlike these companion pieces, does not have a contemporary London setting and contains less topical allusion and purely ephemeral subject matter. The basic situation is taken from the practice of legacy hunting in ancient Rome. The setting has been transferred to a more contemporary Italy and the characters universalized by the clever beast epic device of animal names. Volpone (meaning fox) is a crafty grandee of Venice who makes a game of gulling a group of legacy hunters whose names suggest birds of prey—the lawyer Voltore or vulture, the old miser Corbaccio or carrion crow, and the merchant Corvino or raven. They compete with one another in bestowing favors in order to be designated heir to the avaricious and wily old fox who dissembles the role of invalid. Mosca or the gadfly is Volpone's clever and agile servant or parasite who manipulates the Plautine-like intrigue.

Jonson had been practicing his craft as a stage satirist for at least nine years and had experimented with a type of play known as "humour" comedy ("humour" referring to popular concepts of anatomy and psychology) in which amusing or objectionable eccentricities of character and stock comedy types such as fops or braggarts were exhibited in carefully contrived situations for the purpose of ridicule and correction. In *Volpone* Jonson sports less with human folly (his avowed purpose in "humour" comedy) than with crime. The spirit of comedy becomes sinister and grotesque. A farcical subplot is developed around a tedious English knight named Sir Politic Would-Be and his Lady Would-Be, a satire on English travelers. But the main plot is well sustained. The denouement, meting out justice to the malefactors, verges on tragedy. Throughout the play the texture of the poetry is richly ornate with eloquent satirical digressions and lyric passages of great beauty. Jonson the classicist and satirist is at the height of his creative powers.

There have been some notable 20th century revivals, and a popular adaptation by Stefan Zweig and Jules Romains in the spirit of *commedia dell'arte,* performed in Paris in 1928, was translated into English by Ruth Langner (1928).

WILLIAM BRACY,
Humanities Editor of "The Encyclopedia Americana."

VOLSCI, vŏl'sī, an ancient Italian tribe dwelling in Latium, central Italy, in the middle Liris (Liri) River valley and southeast of the Alban Hills. Allies of the Aequi, they were a threat to Rome during the 5th and 4th centuries B.C., but by 304 B.C. they had become subject to Rome. They were quickly absorbed into Roman society. A brief inscription dating from the early 3d century B.C. suggests linguistic affinities with Umbrian.

VOLSK, vŏlsk, city, USSR, in Saratov Oblast in the Russian SFSR, on the right bank of the Volga River, 75 miles northeast of Saratov. Volsk is one of the leading cement-manufacturing centers of the Soviet Union. The city is surrounded on three sides by the steep clifflike slopes of the Volga uplands, containing vast reserves of cement clays, writing chalk, and sand. These materials provided the basis for the establishment of four large cement mills at Volsk in the 1870's. The mills, expanded and modernized in the Soviet period, supply cement for large dam projects on the Volga River, as well as for construction in central European Russia, the Urals, and Kazakhstan. Besides cement, Volsk also manufactures roofing slate, lime, chalk, bricks, tanning materials, leather goods, and equipment for the construction materials industry. Volsk is an important transportation center, at the junction of a railroad and the Volga River. More than 90 percent of the city's shipments by river barges consist of building materials. Pop. (1959) 62,000.

THEODORE SHABAD.

VOLSTEAD, vŏl'stĕd, **Andrew J.,** American lawyer and legislator: b. Goodhue County, Minnesota, 1860; d. Granite Falls, Jan. 20, 1947. He was admitted to the bar in 1884, and, after serving in several local political offices, was elected in 1902 to the United States House of Representatives. Normally an obscure backbencher, he rose to national prominence when in January 1919 he was selected to draw up the act, known as the Volstead Act, to enforce prohibition of the manufacture, sale, and transportation of intoxicating beverages under the 18th Amendment. After his defeat for reelection in 1922 he resumed his law practice in Granite Falls and became legal adviser to the chief of the Northwest prohibition enforcement district. See also LIQUOR LAWS—*United States;* PROHIBITION.

VOLSTEAD ACT. See VOLSTEAD, ANDREW J.

VOLSUNGS, vŏl'so͝ongz, a lineage of Teutonic legend descended from the culture hero Volsung, a great-grandson of Odin. Volsung, who was born to King Rerir and his wife after she had eaten a miraculous apple of fruitfulness, became a powerful and wealthy king and begat nine sons and one daughter. He thrust a sword through the oak which grew in his great hall, declaring that the sword would belong to the hero who could pull it out. His youngest son, Sigmund, was able to do so but, according to one version of the legend, Siggeir, king of the Goths, who had married Volsung's daughter Signy or Sieglinde, coveted the sword, and by treachery killed Volsung and all the brothers except Sigmund. Sigmund had a son Sigurd or Siegfried, last of the Volsungs, by his sister. According to another version, Sigmund married Hiordis, daughter of the King of the Islands, whose rejected suitor slew all the Volsungs, including Sigmund, before the birth of Sigurd. The legend is found in the Icelandic *Edda,* the Scandinavian *Volsunga Saga,* and the German *Nibelungenlied,* and Richard Wagner used it in his operatic cycle *Der Ring des Nibelungen.*

VOLT. See ELECTRICAL AND MAGNETIC UNITS.

VOLTA, vôl'tä, COUNT **Alessandro,** Italian physicist, chemist, and discoverer of constant-current electricity: b. Como, Italy, Feb. 18, 1745; d. there, March 5, 1827. His first electrical publications, in which he described improved electrometers, appeared in 1769 and 1771. He became professor of physics at Como in 1774 and five years later professor of natural philosophy at Pavia, where he remained for 25 years. Volta made improvements in the electrophorus (q.v.) in 1777 and in the electroscope (q.v.). After analyzing marsh gas he published his most popular treatise, *Lettere sull aria infiammabile delle paludi* (1776); and another paper on an improved electroscope appeared in 1782. A series of inventions followed, including an eudiometer, an electric pistol, and a lamp that burned inflammable air.

Prompted by Luigi Galvani's treatise on animal electricity (1791), Volta commenced a new series of experiments that resulted in his announcement on March 20, 1800, of his discovery of the "voltaic pile," the first source of constant-current electricity. He communicated the results of his work to the Royal Society of London, which published the experiments in its *Philosophical Transactions* in 1800. With this he and other scientists decomposed water by electrolysis, electroplated precious metals, formed the electromagnet, and thereby opened the electrical age.

At the invitation of Napoleon I, Volta went to Paris in 1801 and performed experiments before the Institut de France. To honor the occasion a gold medal was struck, a sum of 6,000 francs was awarded to him, and a commission was created to repeat his experiments. He also was granted the title of count and made a senator of the kingdom of Lombardy; later he received the Cross of the Legion of Honor.

Volta's publications appeared in the *Giornale Fisico-Medico* and the *Scelta d'Opuscoli,* as well as the aforementioned *Transactions* of the Royal Society of London, which elected him a fellow in 1791 and presented him the Copley medal in 1794. His published works were collected in five volumes in 1816 and in seven volumes in 1918–1929. The volt, the unit of electromotive force, was named in his honor in 1881.

See also BATTERY, ELECTRIC—*Primary Battery* (Development); ELECTROCHEMISTRY—*Early History.*

BERN DIBNER,
Chairman of the Board, Burndy Corporation, Norwalk, Conn.

VOLTA, vŏl'tə, a West African river system and basin of 150,000 square miles which lies south of the great bend of the Niger River. The basin is funnel shaped, being more than 500 miles across in its northern source area but tapering to about 25 miles near the Gulf of Guinea. The several sections of the Volta system display sharply angled courses resulting from the capture of previously established segments by headward eroding streams.

The Black Volta, the chief tributary, rises in the northwestern corner of the drainage basin and flows northeastward along a course inherited from the time it was a tributary of the Niger River. Where it turns southeast it is joined by the Sourou from the northeast. In high flood the Sourou distributes water from the upper Black Volta, because it was the original course of the latter. In its southward valley the Black Volta in part forms the boundary between the Ivory Coast Republic and Ghana. It bends sharply east to enter Ghana and join the White Volta.

The White Volta rises in the northeast corner of the drainage basin and follows a southerly course characterized by angular bends. Its principal tributary, the Red Volta in the north central basin, joins it in Ghana after leaving Upper Volta Republic. The junction of the White and Black Voltas forms the Volta proper which has a principal left bank tributary, the Oti, entering Ghana from Togo. The Volta ends in a marshy delta which it is building into the Bight of Benin.

The Volta River is not a major navigable system because of its many rapids. Heavy cargo canoes operate on sections of the Black and White Voltas and launches use the Volta proper, but most navigation is on Lake Volta.

The Akosombo Dam at Ajena, constructed in 1961–1965, created Lake Volta, one of the world's largest man-made lakes. The lake extends about 200 miles (320 km) into northern Ghana and covers an area of 3,275 square miles (8,482 sq km). Energy produced at the dam—over 500,000 kw annually—is used to smelt alumina and to power mines, factories, and cities, and eventually may be increased for export.

HIBBERD V. B. KLINE, JR.,
Department of Geography, University of Pittsburgh.

VOLTA REDONDA, vôl′tə rə-thônn′də, town, Brazil, in Rio de Janeiro State just south of the Minas Gerais border, on the Paraíba River, 60 miles northwest of the city of Rio de Janeiro. Brazil's leading steel-milling center, it is served by the Rio-São Paulo railroad. The government-operated National Steel Mills, which produced its first steel in 1947, processes high-grade iron ore and alloys which it receives by electrified railway from Itabira in Minas Gerais. The plant uses coal from Santa Catarina (Paraná State) mixed with imported coking coal, as well as hydroelectric power generated at the Ribeirão das Lages plant 20 miles to the southeast on the Paraíba River. Volta Redonda is one of the most ambitious industrial projects in South America. Clustered around the buildings of the main plant are a number of privately owned plants which manufacture materials for the government-owned mills or process byproducts. On the side of the valley overlooking the mills is a model town housing the workers. Pop. (1950) 33,110; (1970) 120,645.

VOLTAGE. See ELECTRICITY; ELECTROMETER; GENERATOR, ELECTRIC; MOTOR, ELECTRIC; POWER, ELECTRIC; TRANSFORMER.

VOLTAIC BATTERIES. See BATTERY, ELECTRIC.

VOLTAIC CELL. See BATTERY, ELECTRIC.

VOLTAIC REPUBLIC. See UPPER VOLTA, REPUBLIC OF.

VOLTAIRE, vŏl-târ′ (pseudonym of **FRANÇOIS MARIE AROUET**), French author, philosopher, and apostle of free thought: b. Paris, Nov. 21, 1694; d. there, May 30, 1778. He came from a cultured middle-class family, was educated by the Jesuits at the Collège Louis-le-Grand, steeped in the classics, and attracted early by a literary career, for which he gave up the study of law. His health was poor and he was thus by necessity and by inclination a temperate man at a time when pleasure was openly worshipped, during the years of gay relaxation which followed the death of Louis XIV (1715). He was twice confined to the Bastille, most unjustly, in 1717 and in 1726. That experience strengthened his passion for justice and he decided to uphold the rights of men of letters against the arbitrary power of the king and of the nobles.

Upon Voltaire's liberation in 1726, he went over to England where he spent three important years. He discovered William Shakespeare and much of English literature, he admired Isaac Newton, and he envied the freedom of thought and the commercial prosperity of England. He praised England in contrast with France in vivid prose in his *Lettres philosophiques* (known also as *Lettres sur les Anglais*, 1734; English version, 1733). The book was forbidden in Paris and Voltaire had to exile himself for a while. He chose to live until 1749 at Cirey in Lorraine, close to the border and thus able to escape if his writings were judged subversive.

In 1749 he lost his intimate friend, the Marchioness of Châtelet, and accepted the often repeated invitation of Frederick the Great of Prussia to live at his court at Potsdam. Voltaire was then a very skillful poet, both serious and playful, the author of some good tragedies—which were considered in his day worthy of Jean Baptiste Racine (*Brutus*, 1730; *Zaïre*, 1732; *Mahomet*, 1742; *Mérope*, 1743) but are no longer performed today—a moralist, a historian,

Voltaire

New York Public Library

and a polemist. He was curious of everything, vivacious, nervous, and at times egotistic. His friendship with Frederick II soon deteriorated into unpleasantness, and the king failed to behave philosophically or even courteously. Voltaire left in 1753, took to a wandering life for some years, then lived in Switzerland near Geneva and in 1758 established his residence at Ferney (now in France, on the Swiss border outside Geneva) with his niece, Madame Denis. Ferney was not under the jurisdiction of the French king and Voltaire enjoyed security there. His writings then became more outspoken, and their author enjoyed universal fame: kings, noblemen, foreign visitors, all flocked to Ferney to pay homage to the sovereign of literature. A great number of persons corresponded with Voltaire, who stands supreme among the letter writers of all ages.

He first produced works of history: *Le Siècle de Louis XIV* (1751), *Essai sur les moeurs* (1753, 1756). They constitute the first modern historical treatises composed according to a critical method and with a gift for analytical clarity. Voltaire does not bring the past back to life with the imaginative power which later historians will possess; but the shrewdly discriminates among the causes and the consequences of events. He moreover lays the stress upon civilization and upon the manners, beliefs, and daily lives of the people, forsaking the earlier exclusive emphasis on kings and on wars. His history of mankind (*Essai sur les moeurs*) is not impartial: Voltaire decreases the role traditionally granted to the Jewish people and underlines that of Asiatic nations. History to him is, or should be, the progressive victory of enlightenment and of fraternity over ignorance, fanaticism, and evil.

At the same time, Voltaire composed philosophical poetry: *Poème sur la loi naturelle* (1756), inspired in part by Alexander Pope's *Essay on Man*, and *Poème sur le désastre de Lisbonne* (1756) which treats of the problem of evil in nature as posed in 1755 by the catastrophic Lisbon earthquake. Voltaire scathingly ridiculed the systematic optimism which sees every event as willed by God and as the condition for a greater good. He prefers to believe that all is not well today, but may be better some day if we take up arms vigorously against natural and human evils.

But Voltaire is incomparably greater as a prose writer than as a poet: he lacked the gift of imagery and the sense for half shades and mysterious suggestiveness which we require today from poetry. His masterpieces are, along with his witty, vivacious letters, his novels. *Zadig* (1747) is an allegorical Oriental tale; *Micromégas* (1752) is a delightful Swiftian philosophical fantasy; *Candide* (1759) is Voltaire's highest achievement. It is a satire on the previous adventure novels of the age, an attack upon the claims of unlimited optimism, an entertaining and at times very free story of a candid and gullible young man gradually shedding all his illusions and concluding in the end that the best is to "cultivate one's garden" without excessive idealism and without the dubious assistance of nebulous metaphysics or of a God who helps best those who help themselves.

Voltaire's activity was tireless: he was an eager contributor to the great *Encyclopédie* started by his friends Jean Le Rond d'Alembert and Denis Diderot. He published in 1763 an important treatise on tolerance and in 1764 the famous and influential *Dictionnaire philosophique*. He poured out a considerable number of other treatises, pamphlets, tales, and ironical works in which he expressed his views on the abuses which he condemned and on how to put an end to injustice, arbitrary power, and the greed of the privileged ones which reduces the underprivileged to misery.

Voltaire's philosophy is not original or profound: some historians of thought even refuse to call him a philosopher, for he did not formulate a coherent system claiming to explain the whole universe. But Voltaire repudiated such systems as logical but ineffective structures which closed the eyes of many to the actual state of things. Voltaire's thought is pragmatic and practical. He believes in God and calls himself a theist: the world is a complex clock which cannot be explained without a clockmaker. But Voltaire's God does not intervene in the course of events. There is no Providence, no miracle, no divine revelation. Christ is left out of Voltaire's philosophical outlook; the Scriptures are far from revered by the Frenchman's irony; immortality counts but little or is scorned as a selfish illusion of man's pride. Voltaire's creed is natural religion, that is, religion viewed as equivalent to morality and reduced to the self-evident truths of justice, goodness, and truth. God's only advice to man could be: "Be just." Our service is to humanity as a whole. Fanaticism is the most dangerous of all evils, and religious intolerance and the wars which it fosters must be eradicated. Hence Voltaire's war cry: "*Ecraser l'infâme.*" The infamous foe to be crushed is Roman Catholic fanaticism, from which Voltaire and his friends, the "philosophes" of the 18th century, had to suffer most. For Voltaire lived in an age when the press did not exist, thought was not free, and men were not equals before civil law.

Voltaire was not content with writing intelligent and witty works. Several times he intervened courageously to save freethinkers or Protestants martyred or persecuted—to rehabilitate Frenchmen whom a partial justice had gravely wronged. He took an active interest in political economy, in social reform, in improving the lot of the common man through better agriculture and expanding industry. Much maligned by his enemies, sometimes too quick tempered and addicted to ferocious polemics, forced to wear masks and to resort to duplicity by the backward laws of his age, Voltaire has often been misjudged by posterity. He was a fighter, and has not been easily forgiven for the skill with which he attacked the excesses of religion. Yet he did more good with his pen than perhaps any other writer. He taught the virtue of doubt which should precede, examine, and strengthen positive faith. He promoted civilization and humanism, and helped weaken man's inhumanity to man. When he died in 1778, he was mourned by the whole of Europe. During the Revolution, his ashes were laid to rest in the Paris Pantheon.

HENRI PEYRE,
Sterling Professor of French, Yale University.

Further Reading: Ayer, A. J., *Voltaire* (Random House 1986); Morley, John, *Voltaire* (1913; reprint, Century Bookbindery 1982); Noyes, A. *Voltaire* (1936; reprint, Darby Bks. 1983); Torrey, Norman L., *Spirit of Voltaire* (1938; reprint, Russell & Russell 1968); Voltaire, *Candide: Bilingual Edition*, ed. by Peter Gay (St. Martin's Press 1969); id., *Philosophical Letters*, tr. by Ernest N. Dilworth (Bobbs 1961); id., *The Portable Voltaire*, ed. by B. R. Redman (Penguin 1977).

VOLTAMETER. See COULOMETER.

VOLTERRA, vōl-tĕr'rä, **Daniele da** (real name DANIELE RICCIARELLI), Italian painter and sculptor: b. Volterra, Italy, 1509; d. Rome, April 4, 1566. He was known also as "Il Braghettone" (breeches maker) after he was commissioned in 1558 by Pope Paul IV to clothe the nudes in Michelangelo's *The Last Judgment* in the Sistine Chapel. Volterra's best-known paintings are in the style of Michelangelo, whose follower and friend he was, and include *Descent from the Cross* (1541) at the church of the Trinità dei Monti in Rome, a crowded *Massacre of the Innocents* in the Uffizi, Florence, and *David Killing Goliath* in the Louvre. From 1547 to 1550 he was in charge of paintings at the Vatican. He had the reputation of being an incredibly slow worker: commissioned by Catherine de'Medici to design an equestrian statue of Henry II of France, he finished only the horse. A statue of Louis XIII later was mounted on Volterra's horse, but both pieces were destroyed in the French Revolution.

H. D. HALE.

VOLTERRA, Vito, Italian mathematician: b. Ancona, Italy, May 3, 1860; d. Rome, Oct. 11, 1940. After studying at Florence, Pisa, and Padua, he served as professor at Padua (1883–1892) and Turin before going in 1900 to the University of Rome. In 1931 he resigned to avoid taking an oath of allegiance to the Fascist regime. Volterra isolated the concept of permutable functions and began the systematic elaboration of integral and integro-differential equations. Constantly guided by scientific problems, he was able to test his theories, and derived from these problems the new ideas which caused him to be ranked as "one of the most imaginative inventors in the history of analysis." His publications include *The Theory of Permutable Functions* (1915) and *Theory of Functionals and of Integral and Integro-differential Equations* (1930).

VOLTERRA, town and commune, Italy, in Pisa Province, Tuscany, 31 miles southeast of Pisa and about 20 miles from the Tyrrhenian Sea. It is the terminus of a railroad from Cecina on the Tyrrhenian coast. The town stands on a hill at an altitude of about 1,600 feet, in a ridge separating the Era and Cecina valleys. Almost completely enclosed by its medieval walls, Volterra has preserved the flavor of the Middle Ages and produces a lasting impression on the visitor. The Etruscan town covered a much wider area, as testified by the perimeter of the Etruscan walls, parts of which, in gigantic stones, are still standing. The typical local industry is alabaster work, the stone being quarried nearby. In the vicinity are important salt mines, worked since the 9th century.

In Piazza dei Priori, one of Italy's finest medieval squares, stand the 13th century Palazzo dei Priori or town hall, housing an art gallery; the Palazzo Pretorio, with its imposing tower; and the episcopal palace. The Romanesque cathedral and the adjoining 13th century baptistery, with its black and white marble stripes, are in the Pisan architectural style. In the narrow winding streets are numerous medieval houses and towers which lend the city an austere and somber aspect. San Michele, San Francesco, and the Badia are fine medieval churches. The imposing fortress at the southeast edge of the hill dates from the 14th and 15th centuries. Of outstanding interest is the Etruscan Museum, containing over 600 cinerary urns, bas reliefs, and a wealth of objects unearthed in nearby necropolises. The hills around Volterra have been subject to landslides due to erosion, as may be observed in the Balze, a deep precipice into which Etruscan cemeteries, churches, and other buildings have fallen.

Velathri, as Volterra was known in ancient times, was one of the most powerful administrative divisions of the Etruscans. The Roman general Lucius Cornelius Scipio defeated the Etruscans near here in 298 B.C. and soon after the town was conquered by the Romans, who called it Volaterrae. Volterra became an episcopal see in the 5th century and was ruled by its bishops in the Middle Ages. A free commune arose in the 12th century but, weakened by internecine conflicts and wars with its neighbors, it succumbed to Florence, which sacked and conquered it in 1472. Thereafter Volterra followed the fortunes of the Florentine state. Pop. (1961) commune 17,938.

NELDA CASSUTO.

VOLTMETER. See ELECTRICAL MEASUREMENTS—*D-C Measurements* (Voltage).

VOLTURNO RIVER, vōl'tōōr'nō, chief river of southern Italy, for most of its 109-mile course in Campania. It rises in Molise in the La Meta mountain group of the Apennines and flows first south and southeast through the mountains, then, after a wide swing where it receives the waters of its chief tributary, the Calore, it takes a westward course past Capua across the Campanian plain and empties into the Tyrrhenian Sea near Castel Volturno, 22 miles northwest of Naples. In 1860, Giuseppe Garibaldi won on the Volturno a decisive victory over Francis II, last Bourbon king of Naples, who was then forced to retreat to Gaeta. During World War II the Germans established a strong defense line along the river and only after heavy fighting were American troops able to cross it in October 1943 on their northward march toward Rome.

NELDA CASSUTO.

VOLUME, vŏl'yōōm, the three-dimensional measurement of the total space occupied by any object or substance. The volume of a solid possessing three sides mutually at right angles to each other may be obtained by multiplying together the lengths of the respective sides. The product is the volume. The volume of a sphere is given by the formula $\frac{4}{3}\pi R^3$, and that of a cylinder is equal to πR^2h, where R is the radius of the sphere or cylinder and h is the height of the cylinder.

The volume of any irregularly shaped object may be obtained most accurately (if it is feasible to do so) by completely immersing it in water in a container just filled to the brim or to the height of a small orifice, and catching the exact amount of overflow water which the immersed object displaces. This quantity of water is then weighed, and since 0.998 gram of water occupies 1 cubic centimeter at 20° C. (68° F.) the volume of the object may be obtained directly from the weight of water displaced. The volumes of liquids and gases, being fluids, may be measured from the volumes of the containers which they occupy.

See also CALCULUS—7. *Applications of the Definite Integral* (Volumes of Solids); HEAT—*Thermal Expansion;* MENSURATION—*Volumes and Surface Areas.*

FERGUS J. WOOD.

VOLUMETRIC ANALYSIS. See CHEMICAL ANALYSIS—*Quantitative Inorganic Analysis.*

VOLUNTARY CONVEYANCE, vŏl'ən-tĕr-ē kŏn-vā'-əns, in law, a transfer of property without a valuable consideration. A typical example is a deed from a husband to his wife or from a parent to his child for an expressed consideration of love and affection. The significance of "voluntariness," in this rather technical legal sense, is that creditors or others having legal or equitable rights to the property thus transferred can have the transaction nullified.

Under modern bankruptcy law, a voluntary conveyance is included within the general term "voidable transfer." The federal Bankruptcy Act provides, in part, that a trustee in bankruptcy may set aside any transfer made or obligation incurred by a debtor, within one year of filing a petition for bankruptcy, "without fair consideration" if the debtor "is or will be thereby rendered insolvent, without regard to his actual intent." Furthermore, the statute provides that a transfer "without fair consideration" is voidable if made by a debtor who is engaged or about to engage in a business or transaction for which the property remaining in his hands after such transfer is "an unreasonably small capital," without regard to his actual intent.

Where the consideration paid is very small in comparison to the value of the property conveyed, the conveyance will probably be held to be "voluntary" even though it is not literally "without any valuable consideration." In the absence of insolvency or precarious financial condition, the law allows a person to transfer his property without any consideration or with only nominal consideration regardless of whether he has debts.

RICHARD L. HIRSHBERG.

VOLUNTEERS OF AMERICA, a national religious-social welfare organization founded in 1896 in New York City by Ballington and Maud Booth. With national headquarters in New York City, it operates about 470 service programs in more than 100 cities and towns throughout the nation. The organization is quasi-military; officers are uniformed and hold rank.

The organization's basic aim is to give spiritual and material aid to the needy without regard to race or creed. Spiritual aid in the form of nondenominational Protestant worship services, Sunday schools, Bible study classes, and personal religious counseling is offered in mission churches usually located in areas not served by denominational churches. Material aid is offered through maternity homes, summer camps, homes for the aged, salvage and rehabilitation programs, girls' residences, services to prisoners and prisoners' families, community centers, day nurseries and family day care programs, emergency homes, school clothing programs, and other services. More than 2 million persons are aided each year.

DAVID R. BALCH.

VOLVOX, vŏl′vŏks, a genus of minute (just visible to the unaided eye), freshwater, motile, colonial, spherical organisms, the cells of which contain chlorophyll. The spheres are filled with watery colloids, and the individual cells are embedded near the surface of the colony. Each of these bears two rapidly beating flagella and a stigma, one or more pyrenoids, a single nucleus, and two or more contractile vacuoles. In most species, a given cell is connected to all the cells which surround it by protoplasmic threads which pass through the cell wall.

Only certain cells have the capacity for forming daughter colonies, and these are located in the posterior hemisphere of the colony. By cell division, these form daughter colonies which turn inside out during development and which are finally shed from the parent colonies. *Volvox* also reproduces by sexual reproduction in which minute sperms fertilize large pear-shaped eggs. The product of this fusion is a thick-walled

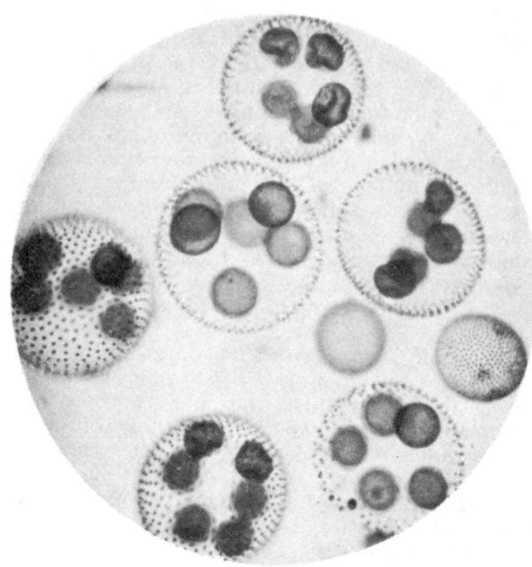

***Volvox*, a colonial green alga. Note daughter colonies within parent colonies. Magnified about 100 times.**

zygote, which, after a period of dormancy, germinates to form a single motile cell; this cell, by further division, gives rise to the typical *Volvox* colony. This organism is classified by some as a plant (see ALGAE) and by others as an animal (see PROTOZOA).

HAROLD C. BOLD.

VOLYN, vŭ-lĭn′yə, oblast, USSR, in the Ukrainian SSR, in the Pripet Marshes. Its capital is Lutsk. Volyn Oblast was established in 1939 when the Polish section of historic Volhynia (q.v.) was returned to Soviet control. The oblast borders on Poland along the Bug River, has some agriculture (grains and tobacco) in the south, and lumbering industries in the north along the Pripet River and its tributaries. In the 1950's a large brown-coal industry developed around the mines of Novovolynsk, in the southwestern part of the oblast near the Bug River. Industry is concentrated at Lutsk (1956 est. pop., 53,000), which produces processed foods and farm implements; at Kovel (1956 est. pop., 23,000), a railroad center; and at Vladimir-Volynski, near the brown-coal basin. Pop. (1959) 890,000.

THEODORE SHABAD.

VOMER, vō′mər, the posterior portion of the nasal septum in the skull. See SKULL.

VOMITING, vŏm′ĭt-ĭng, the spontaneous evacuation of the stomach contents by reverse peristalsis through the esophagus and the oral cavity. This action is assisted by the diaphragm and the muscles of the abdominal wall. The cardia of the stomach and the muscle walls of the esophagus are relaxed while the glottis is closed and respiration is inhibited to prevent aspiration of stomach contents into the lungs. Vomiting is controlled by the vomiting center at the base of the brain in the medulla. Vomiting is almost always a sufficient cause for immediate medical consultation. It may mean a severe electrolyte disturbance such as seen in diabetes mellitus, uremia, or vomiting of the newborn. It is a cardinal symptom in intestinal obstruction and acute appendicitis. Increased intracranial pressure from brain tumor and other space-occupying lesions within the skull can trigger projectile vomiting. The vomiting center may be stimulated centrally by such drugs as apomorphine, emetine, picrotoxin, morphine, and a host of others; or by adrenaline, histamine, and choline, which are also produced by the body itself. Finally, mental stress, fatigue, pregnancy, and hysteria can be responsible for severe vomiting. Continual loss of electrolytes from the stomach, notably chlorides, may prove fatal unless promptly restored by proper intravenous therapy.

REAUMUR S. DONNALLY, M. D.

VON, fôn, a German word meaning "of," is used as a prefix to surnames. First used indiscriminately, the *von* gradually became a mark of distinction and its use confined to those of noble birth. Rulers exercised the right of ennobling others, and this took the form of allowing them to use the prefix *von.* The same usage prevails in Austria and the successor states of the Austro-Hungarian empire, but not in Switzerland, where *von* often is found in nonaristocratic names. In the *Americana,* German names are usually alphabetized under the proper name—for example, August von Mackensen is found under the style MACKENSEN, AUGUST VON. In some cases, however, particularly in American usage, *von* has become a part of the proper name. Thus Wernher von Braun is listed as VON BRAUN, WERNHER.

VON BÉKÉSY, George. See BÉKÉSY.

VON BRAUN, fôn broun, **Wernher** (1912–1977), German-American engineer, who pioneered in the development of rockets for warfare and space exploration. He was born in Wirsitz, Germany, on March 23, 1912. As a youth he became interested in space flight and interplanetary travel. His education along these lines was gained at technical institutes in Zürich, Switzerland, and Berlin, and at the University of Berlin (Ph.D., 1934).

In 1930 he began experimental work with rockets under the sponsorship of the German Rocket Society, of which he was a founding member, and in 1932 the German Army employed him as liquid-fuel rocket expert for its rocket experiment station at Kummersdorf. When the proving ground was moved in 1937 to Peenemünde on the Baltic Sea, von Braun was appointed technical director. Here, in 1938, he and his associates launched a rocket with a range of 11 miles (17.7 km)—the direct forerunner of the V-2 that was first turned against Britain on Sept. 7, 1944.

In March 1945, when Russian armies were approaching Peenemünde, von Braun and many of his staff went to Bavaria, where they surrendered to American troops. He signed a contract with the U. S. Army and was assigned to White Sands Proving Grounds, N. Mex., as technical adviser, and to Fort Bliss, Texas, as technical director of its missile project. In 1950, when the project was moved to Redstone Arsenal near Huntsville, Ala., von Braun was appointed chief of the guided-missile development division.

In 1956 he became director of the development-operations division of the Army Ballistic Missile Agency at Huntsville. Von Braun and associated Redstone scientists were responsible for the development of the 200-mile (320-km) range Redstone missile and its successor, the intermediate-range Jupiter; the Jupiter-C rocket assemblies; the Juno II rocket; and the huge Saturn rockets used to launch Apollo spacecraft.

Von Braun became director of the Marshall Space Flight Center of the National Aeronautics and Space Administration (NASA) at Huntsville in 1960. He left NASA in 1972 to become vice president of Fairchild Industries, Inc. He died in Alexandria, Va., on June 16, 1977.

Von Braun became an American citizen in 1955. He is the author or coauthor of several books, including *Conquest of the Moon* (1953), *The Exploration of Mars* (1956), *History of Rocketry and Space Travel* (rev. ed., 1969), and *Space Frontier* (rev. ed., 1971).

VON KARMAN, Theodor. See KÁRMÁN.

VON NEUMANN, fôn noi′män, **John** (1903–1957), Hungarian-American mathematician. Johann (later changed to John) von Neumann was born in Budapest, Hungary, on Dec. 28, 1903. He studied at the University of Berlin, the Technical Institute in Zürich, and the University of Budapest (Ph.D. in mathematics, 1926). After a year at the University of Göttingen as a Rockefeller Fellow (1926–1927) he taught mathematics at the universities of Berlin (1927–1929) and Hamburg (1929–1930). In 1930 he went to the United States as visiting professor at Princeton University, where he was appointed professor of mathematical physics in 1931. Two years later he became associated with the Institute for Advanced Study, Princeton, N. J., and in 1937 he became an American citizen.

In 1945, von Neumann became director of the institute's Electronic Computer Project, which developed a number of major electronic computers. These included MANIAC (mathematical analyzer, numerical integrator and computer), NORC (naval ordnance research computer), and ORDVAC (ordnance variable automatic computer). MANIAC's computing speed enabled the United States to complete the calculations necessary for building and testing its hydrogen weapon in a vastly shorter time than might otherwise have been possible. During World War II, von Neumann acted as adviser on research essential to national defense for a number of federal agencies, including the Los Alamos (N. Mex.) Laboratory.

Von Neumann's contributions to the quantum theory (in 1932 he had published in German his *Mathematical Foundations of Quantum Mechanics;* Eng. tr., 1955) and his knowledge of the practical application of nuclear energy were of major importance in developing the first atomic bomb. In collaboration with Oskar Morgenstern he published a pioneering study, *Theory of Games and Economic Behavior* (1944; 3d ed. 1953), a new approach to the study of economic behavior that was applied to problems of military strategy by the U. S. armed forces.

From 1955 until his death, in Washington, D. C., on Feb. 8, 1957, von Neumann served on the U. S. Atomic Energy Commission. which he had served as a member of the General Advisory Committee from 1952.

See also COMPUTERS—*History.*

VONDEL, vôn′dəl, **Joost van den,** Dutch poet, dramatist, and prose writer: b. Cologne, Germany, Nov. 17, 1587; d. Amsterdam, the Netherlands, Feb. 5, 1679. From 1582 to 1596 his parents, exiles from Antwerp as members of the persecuted Anabaptist sect, were compelled to flee intermittently from the inquisitorial terror instituted in the Lowlands by the Spanish duke of Alva. Thus it was that the senior Joost acquired, a year after his arrival in Amsterdam, the powerfully protective Amsterdam citizenship (the date was March 27, 1597). Few cities in Europe at the turn of the century had so fascinating a commercial and cultural life as did the "Venice of the North." The young Vondel reacted strongly. He soon became a member of *Het wit Lavendel* (White Lavender), a chapter of the popular "Chambers of Rhetoric"—societies of enthusiastic poets and poetasters. The contacts made here with leading intellectual and artistic figures inspired the beginnings of the poet's long career as lyricist and dramatist.

From the performance (1610) of the Biblical drama *Het Pascha* (The Passover; printed 1612), for over a half century he composed an abundance of lyrics, translations (Lucius Annaeus Seneca, Virgil, Sophocles, Euripides), and original dramas. His fame rests especially on such plays as *Maria Stuart* (1646), *Lucifer* (1654), and *Jephtha* (1659). But even long before these successes Vondel had attracted admiration and hostility with the drama *Palamedes* (1625), in which he plunged passionately into the storm aroused in Holland, and all of Europe, by the execution in 1619 of Holland's lord advocate, Johan van Oldenbarnevelt. Preeminent in dramatic force and loftiness of language and conception is the drama *Lucifer,* dealing as does John Milton's *Paradise Lost* with a theme popular in Renaissance and 17th century baroque literature, the mysterious rebellion of heaven's angels against God.

Although evidently happily married for 25 years to Maria (Mayken) de Wolff (1586–1635), Vondel was saddened by the irresponsible behavior of his son Joost (d. 1660). This, much more than any feeling aroused in Calvinistic Holland by Vondel's return to Catholicism (about 1640), clouded the poet's later years. Even so his fame was universally recognized at his death; and he constitutes along with Rembrandt and Hugo Grotius the most brilliant constellation of Holland's Golden Age. His burial place is in De Nieuwe Kerk in Amsterdam, the city of his adoption.

CLARENCE K. POTT,
Professor of German, The University of Michigan.

VONNEGUT, von′ə-gət, **Kurt, Jr.** (1922–), American author, whose novels and stories focus on the dehumanizing effects of powerful institutions and entrenched beliefs. Vonnegut's blend of iconoclasm, fantasy, tragicomic situations, sardonic humor, and colloquial style using coined words made his works widely popular.

In *Player Piano* (1952), his first novel, engineers and executives take over America and attempt complete computerization and automation. In *Cat's Cradle* (1963), a physicist invents a catalyst ("ice-nine") that turns all liquids into solid ice, and a religious prophet preaches comfortable untruths ("foma") to members of corporations, clubs, and other "granfalloons." *Slaughterhouse-Five* (1969), about an American soldier in a German prison camp who witnesses the destruction of Dresden by Allied firebombs, is considered Vonnegut's most powerful novel. His other works include the story collection *Welcome to the Monkey House* (1968); a play, *Happy Birthday, Wanda June* (1970); and *Wampeters, Foma & Granfalloons* (1974), miscellaneous essays; as well as *Breakfast of Champions* (1973); *Slapstick* (1976); and *Galápagos* (1985).

Vonnegut was born in Indianapolis, Ind., on Nov. 11, 1922. He attended Cornell University, studied anthropology at the University of Chicago (M. A., 1971), and has taught creative writing. His internment in Germany during World War II is the basis of *Slaughterhouse-Five.*

VOODOO, vo͞o′do͞o, the folk religion of Haiti, consisting of African, Roman Catholic, and local elements. The term is derived from the Dahomean (West African) *vodun,* meaning "spirit." The Creole French word *vaudou* stems from *vodu,* of the African Ewe language. Many of the Africans brought to Haiti during the period of slavery came from Dahomey, but others such as the Yoruba (Nago) and Ibo also have contributed to the cult. Syncretic religions of this type exist also in other areas to which many Africans were brought —for example, *santería* in Cuba, *Shango* in Trinidad, *Condomblé, Xangó,* and *macumba* in Brazil. In the United States, the term "voodoo" (or hoodoo) often is used to mean any type of magic. More specifically, it refers to the magical and curative activities of "voodoo doctors," particularly among Negroes in the South. However, there is no evidence at present of a cult of the type found in Haiti, although such a cult does appear to have existed in New Orleans during the 19th century.

Eve Arnold from Magnum

"Burning of the pots"—a Haitian *vodu* ceremony. The cult includes spirit possession, in which participants take on the characteristics of *loa*, or lesser divinities.

The Haitian *vodu* cult involves belief in a Supreme Deity (*Bon Dieu*), as well as in *loa,* the dead, and the twins. The *loa* are a large group of lesser deities, known variously by the names of

Catholic saints and those of African gods. *Vodu* worship centers in family groups and cult groups, headed by a priest (*hungan*) or priestess (*mambo*), and there are various grades of initiates. They perform ceremonies on an annual cycle (such as Christmas, harvest) and for special occasions (initiations, memorial services). Families of believers have obligations for the worship of their *loa* and their ancestors, and the twins among them; and cult groups are called in to provide the expert help with the necessary ceremonies, which consist principally of Roman Catholic prayers, drumming and dancing, and the preparation of feasts.

The *loa* are invited to participate in these rites and they do so through spirit possession; that is, certain participants take on the characteristics of individual *loa*. This means not only certain items of clothing (such as a red kerchief for "Ogun-St. James"), but also the behavior, gestures, facial expression, and so on, of the *loa*. Such trance states are introduced by specific drum rhythms associated with each *loa*. The deity may sing, dance, greet people, give advice, perform cures, eat, drink, and so on. "Possession" may last from a few minutes to several hours, and the individual is supposed not to have any memory of the event. A possessed person is referred to as the *loa's* "horse" (*cheval*). Possession is central to the life of the cults since it presents tangible evidence of the gods and brings their reassuring presence to the believers.

Each group of worshipers is an independent unit, and there is no central organization, hierarchy, or dogma. There is much variation between groups in the specific *loa* worshipped—the choice of which depends on family tradition—and there is variation also in specific ceremonies and details of belief. However, there is contact between groups and there exists some general consensus.

Haitian peasants fear black magic, and the cults provide protection against it and other evils. There is much poverty, disease, and a high rate of infant mortality, with little empirical defense against these ills. Efforts by the church to destroy the cults often have led to an increased fear of magic. Under these conditions, the cults fulfill an important function.

ERIKA BOURGUIGNON
Associate Professor of Anthropology
The Ohio State University

VOORTREKKERS. See SOUTH AFRICA, REPUBLIC OF—*History*.

VORARLBERG, fōr'ärl-berkh, is the second-smallest province in Austria and its most westerly. It is connected to the rest of the country by the Arlberg Pass. The Silvretta and Rhätikon ranges of the Rhaetian Alps form its southern boundary with Switzerland. Liechtenstein is on the southwest. The Rhine River forms its western frontier with Switzerland. The Bregenzer Forest borders West Germany on the north.

The people of Vorarlberg speak a German dialect that closely resembles Swiss German. Most of the inhabitants are Roman Catholics. Over one third of the population lives in the five main towns: Bregenz, the capital; Feldkirch; Dornbirn; Lustenau; and Bludenz.

Only a little more than 1% of Vorarlberg's area of 1,004 square miles (2,600 sq km) is arable. Forest occupies about 25%, and most of the rest consists of meadows and pastures. The best agricultural areas are in the Rhine Valley, where fruits are grown, and the Ill Valley.

Vorarlberg is Austria's most industrialized province after Vienna. Abundant water from its mountains is the main power source for the many small- and medium-sized industries. The province is best known for its textiles, especially cotton goods and lace.

Most of Vorarlberg had been acquired by the Habsburgs by 1523. It was briefly attached to Bavaria during the Napoleonic Wars. Between 1815 and 1918, Vorarlberg and Tyrol (Tirol) were combined administratively as part of the Austrian Empire. Although a referendum held in 1919 overwhelmingly indicated Vorarlberg's desire to unite with Switzerland, it became a province of Austria because of Switzerland's lack of interest. During World War II the province again was united with Tyrol, but its independent status was reestablished at the end of the war. Population: (1961) 226,323.

GEORGE W. HOFFMAN, *University of Texas*

VORONEZH, vu-rô'nyəsh, is a city in the USSR, in the Russian SFSR. It is the capital of Voronezh oblast, and the largest city in the fertile agricultural black-earth belt. It is situated 290 miles (467 km) southeast of Moscow, on the Voronezh River, a tributary of the Don.

The city's manufacturing industries have received a major impetus during the Soviet period. Voronezh produces forge and press equipment, agricultural machines, bridge assemblies, and radio and television sets. A large synthetic rubber plant supplies a local tire factory. The city has expanded to the new industrial districts on the left bank of the Voronezh River.

Voronezh was founded in 1586 as a Russian outpost against the nomads of the southern steppes. It flourished under Peter I the Great, who built a navy at Voronezh for his campaigns against the Turks. In the 18th and early 19th centuries, when livestock was raised on the nearby steppe, Voronezh developed a large trade in livestock, hides, and wool. With the agricultural settlement of the area in the late 19th century, crop raising gradually displaced animal husbandry.

During World War II, Voronezh became a frontline city. The Germans occupied the older, right-bank section in July 1942 in their drive on Stalingrad. The Voronezh battle, which lasted 200 days, resulted in the virtual razing of the old city, including the arsenal of Peter the Great and the prominent bell tower of the former Mitrofan monastery. When the Germans were expelled in January 1943, the city's population was only a fraction of the 327,000 it had had in 1939. The war damage, exceeded in the Soviet Union only by that of Stalingrad and Sevastopol, was largely repaired after the war. Population: (1970) 660,000.

THEODORE SHABAD
Editor of "Soviet Geography"

VORONOFF, vô-rô-nŏf', **Serge,** French surgeon and physiologist: b. Voronezh, Russia, July 10, 1866; d. Lausanne, Switzerland, Sept. 1, 1951. He studied medicine in Paris and became a French citizen in 1897. As surgeon in chief of the Russian hospital in Paris in World War I, he performed remarkable bone-graft operations. After the war he was appointed director of the experimental surgery laboratory at the Collège de France, Paris, and while there completed the research that led to his highly publicized claim to have effected rejuvenation in elderly men by the transplant of sexual glands from young animals. In the lower animals, those of an animal of the same species were used; in man, those of one of the higher apes (hence the name "monkey glands"). Later, Voronoff proposed that retarded children could be developed both physically and mentally through the grafting of monkey thyroid glands. Among his publications (Eng. tr.) are *Rejuvenation by Grafting* (1925), *Love and Thought in Animals and Men* (1937), *From Cretin to Genius* (1941), and *The Sources of Life* (1943).

VOROSHILOV, vu-ru-shi′lôf, **Kliment Yefremovich,** Russian general and politician; b. Verkhneye, Yekaterinoslav Province, Ukraine, Russia, Feb. 4, 1881. The son of a railway watchman, he worked in his youth as a miner, farmhand, and factory machinist, and joined the Russian Social Democratic Party in 1903. After the Bolshevik Revolution of 1917 he helped organize the Soviet secret police. During the Russian Civil War (1918–1920) he was a Red Army commander and police chief in south Russia and the Ukraine. He later commanded military districts, and from 1925 to 1940 was war commissar (minister) of the USSR. In 1940 he was dismissed from the war ministry and made a vice premier.

During the Soviet-German War (1941–1945), Voroshilov briefly commanded the Baltic front, suffered many defeats, and spent much of the rest of the war training troops. From 1945 to 1947 he headed the Soviet Control Commission in Hungary. In 1953, after Joseph Stalin's death, Voroshilov was removed from his vice premiership and made chairman of the Supreme Soviet Presidium (president of the USSR). In 1960 he resigned from the USSR presidency and from the Communist Party Presidium (which he had joined in 1926), being succeeded as head of state by Leonid I. Brezhnev. At the 22d Party Congress (1961) he was publicly attacked as a member of the 1957 "anti-party" group. He died in Moscow on Dec. 2, 1969.

VOROSHILOVGRAD, vu-ru-shi-lôf-grát′, a city in the USSR, is the capital of Voroshilovgrad oblast in the Ukrainian SSR. It is on the Lugan River, about 100 miles (160 km) northeast of the Sea of Azov. Originally known as *Lugansk*, the city was renamed in 1935 for Kliment Yefremovich Voroshilov (see above). It reverted to "Lugansk" in 1958, and again became "Voroshilovgrad" on Voroshilov's death in 1970.

The city has been one of the Donets Basin's leading manufacturing centers since a naval armaments plant was established there in 1796 to supply the Russian fleet on the Black Sea. A steam locomotive factory founded in 1896 was expanded under the Soviet regime and converted to diesel production. Other manufactures are machine tools, cast-iron pipe, and coal-mining equipment.

Voroshilovgrad oblast covers part of the industrial Donets Basin and a farming region to the north. It has an area of 10,300 square miles (26,700 sq km). Population: of the city (1981), 474,000; of the oblast (1979), 2,788,000.

THEODORE SHABAD
Editor of "Soviet Geography"

VÖRÖSMARTY, vû′rûsh-mŏrt-yə, **Mihály,** Hungarian poet and playwright: b. Nyek, Hungary, Dec. 1, 1800; d. Pest, Nov. 19, 1855. A practicing attorney, he became a judge in 1849, but already he had established a great reputation as a poet. Much of his writing was inspired by nationalist sentiment, to which he added a classical flavor. His patriotic lyric *Szózat* (The Call), composed in 1836, became a national anthem. Contributing to his rank as one of his country's foremost poets are the epics *Zalán futása* (1824), *Cserhalom* (1825), and *Két szomséd vár* (1831). The finest of his many plays is *Vérnász* (1833). In 1837, Vörösmarty founded the outstanding literary periodicals *Athenaeum* and *Figyelmezö*. Pál Gyulai edited his collected works (2d ed., 1884) and published his biography in 1866.

VORSTER, fôr′stər, **Balthazar Johannes** (1915–1983), South African public official. He succeeded Hendrik Verwoerd after Verwoerd's assassination in 1966, and served until 1979.

Vorster was born in Jamestown, Cape province, on Dec. 13, 1915. He studied law at Stellenbosch University, where he was a Nationalist party student leader. During World War II he was a member of the Ossewa Brandwag (Ox-Wagon Guard), which opposed South Africa's participation in the war. Arrested in 1942, he was interned for a year and a half.

After his election to parliament as a Nationalist in 1953, he became deputy minister of education, arts, and sciences, and of social welfare and pensions. In 1961 he was appointed minister of justice, police, and prisons, with the responsibility of administering South Africa's controversial security laws. Elected prime minister in September 1966, he resigned in 1978 and was elected president. He resigned the presidency on June 4, 1979, accused of testifying falsely in an investigation into government expenditures for propaganda projects. Later he worked behind the scenes to promote apartheid. He died in Cape Town on Sept. 10, 1983.

VORTEX, vôr′tĕks, a form of fluid motion in which the fluid particles travel in a closed (generally circular) path around an axis or a curved line. Forced vortices have a motion essentially the same as if the fluid were rotating as a solid around the axis; that is, the speed of each particle is proportional to the distance from the axis of rotation. This type of motion tends to be developed within the impeller of a turbomachine, such as a pump. If a cylinder containing liquid is rotated around its axis, the action of viscosity will eventually cause it to be set into motion as if it were solid.

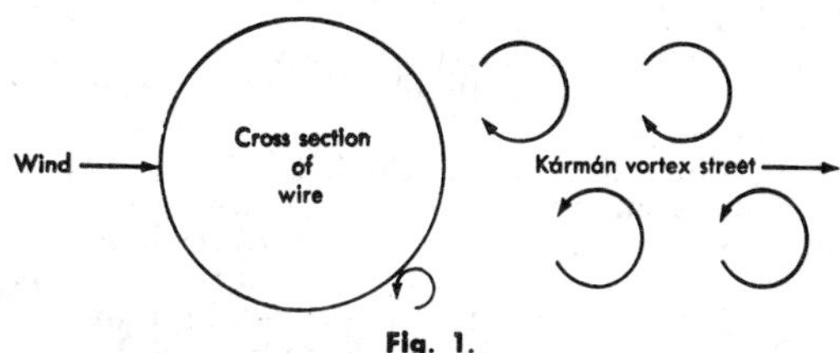

Fig. 1.

In forced vortex motion every particle has the same angular velocity. Free vortices follow a different law, where the speed of a particle is inversely proportional to its distance from the axis. In this motion the individual particles do not rotate (irrotational flow) although the particle describes a circular path. If one imagines the fluid composed of small spheres with a dot of red in the northern direction, then, as these spheres move in a circular path around a central axis, the dots would always stay on the north side of the sphere. This type of motion occurs frequently in nature in a whirlpool, cyclone, hurricane, and waterspout, except that the center or "eye" is more likely to follow the forced vortex law. This combination is called the Rankine combined vortex (named after William J. M. Rankine).

Vortices form behind blunt objects that have liquids or gases flowing over them. An example would be a boulder in a riverbed, or the wind blowing around a house. One interesting case is that of wind blowing across a stretched wire, as a telephone wire. A small eddy or vortex forms behind the wire, and, after growing to a certain size and strength, separates from the wire and moves along with the airstream. Another eddy starts to grow as the earlier one is shed, from the opposite side of the wire, as indicated in Fig. 1. As each vortex is shed it exerts a force on the wire. These form and shed at a rate that causes the wire to vibrate at an audible frequency–the common "singing" or humming of wires. The alternate vortices, rotating in opposite directions, are known as the Kármán vortex street (after Theodore von Kármán, who was the first to identify and demonstrate the effect).

Under certain conditions wind speed, wire length, and wire tension are such that the oscillations become very large causing the wires to break. A similar effect occurs when other shapes with insufficient bracing are subjected to the wind. When the Tacoma Narrows Bridge collapsed during a gale in 1940, it was because of the large oscillations produced by shedding vortices from the bridge's structural members.

See also AERODYNAMICS—*3. Induced Drag Resulting from Lift;* HYDRODYNAMICS.

VICTOR L. STREETER
Professor of Hydraulics, Department of Civil Engineering, The University of Michigan

VORTEX MOTION. See VORTEX.

VORTEX THEORY. See DUST CLOUD THEORY OF PLANETARY EVOLUTION—*Von Weizsäcker's Theory.*

VORTICELLA, vôr-tə-sĕl'ə, probably the commonest genus of ciliate protozoa within the order Peritrichida. A wreath of cilia at the anterior end makes a whirlpool which sweeps food into the gullet. The body, which has a shape that resembles an inverted bell, usually rests on a contractile stalk which is usually attached to a solid surface. When disturbed, vorticellae may become free swimming. They are ubiquitous in freshwater aquariums and ponds, where they attach to the walls, vegetation, and even the backs of water-dwelling animals, such as crayfish and turtles. Vorticellae, along with related colonial (arboroid) forms, teem in activated-sludge sewage disposal plants, where their preference for well-oxygenated waters rich in bacteria is exploited in converting noxious bacterial bodies to a much smaller—and harmless—bulk of protozoan bodies.

Vorticellae are becoming objects of research because (1) their springlike stalk offers a parallel to muscle; and (2) species with sexually differentiated mating types parallel sexuality in higher animals. Several laboratories are trying to obtain them in pure culture so that they can be "domesticated," so to speak, into research objects amenable to experimental studies. See also PROTOZOA.

SEYMOUR H. HUTNER
Haskins Laboratories
New York, N.Y.

VORTICISM, vôr'tĭ-sĭz'əm, an artistic movement, closely allied in its literary aspects to imagism (q.v.). Its leaders were the American poet Ezra Pound (1885–1972), the French sculptor Henri Gaudier-Brzeska (1891–1915), and the English poet and painter Percy Wyndham Lewis (1884–1957). The last was the editor of the vorticist review, *Blast: Review of the Great English Vortex,* which was issued twice, in June 1914 and July 1915. The principles of vorticism were never clearly defined; however, its primary concern was with the form, rather than with the content, of art. It was loosely related, therefore, to other avant-garde artistic movements, such as cubism. According to Pound, the vorticist uses "only the primary media of his art"—in painting, color and line; in sculpture, the arrangement of planes; and in poetry, the image. The movement was short lived—confined to about the period of World War I—and its importance lies in its historic role as one of the many innovations and experiments in art during the early decades of the 20th century.

VORTICITY. See HYDRODYNAMICS.

VORTIGERN, vôr'tĭ-gûrn, British tribal king: fl. 450. As chief of Britons in southern England and Wales, he invited a band of Jutes, led by the brothers Hengist (Hengest) and Horsa, to assist him in repelling his enemies, the Picts and Scots. The traditional account is based on the writings of Gildas (shortly before 547) and Bede, the latter mentioning Vortigern by name. Bede adds that the Jutes arrived in England in 449, and that a subsequent falling out between the allies, which precipitated a battle in 455, the consequences of which included Vortigern's overthrow and the establishment by the Jutes of the kingdom of Kent. However, this version of the Jute invasion continues to raise serious doubts among historians.

VOS, vŏs, **Cornelis de,** Flemish painter: b. Hulst (now in the Netherlands), 1585; d. Antwerp (now in Belgium), May 9, 1651. He began painting in Antwerp in 1608, and became an art dealer about eight years later. In 1627 he represented the Seville dealer Chrysostom van Immerseel, who imported Dutch and Flemish paintings for sale in Spain, Portugal, and the New World. A friend of Peter Paul Rubens, de Vos was said to have had portrait commissions–to be done in the Rubens manner–passed on to him by the overworked master.

De Vos' most popular works are multiple portraits which he painted in a drier, more detailed style than Rubens, but with the same feeling of mastery and confidence in his goal that characterized Rubens' oils. The adults in his portraits are embued with a convincing sincerity, and the children glow with a candor and innocence that ensure his popularity to this day.

His mythological paintings in the Prado (Madrid) and his religious paintings lack the sincerity of his portraits, which are exhibited in the United States by the Boston Museum, the Detroit Institute, the Metropolitan Museum, New York, the Philadelphia Museum, and the Portland (Oreg.) Art Association.

H. D. HALE,
Art Critic.

VOS, Martin de, Flemish painter: b. Antwerp (now in Belgium), c. 1532; d. there, Dec. 4, 1603. He was a pupil and assistant of Frans Floris (1516?–1570), and went to Rome, Florence, and Venice, where he was Tintoretto's assistant from 1552 to 1558. By this time de Vos was a master in the Antwerp guild and in demand for his religious paintings and portraits. Between about 1579 and 1592 he was a court painter.

De Vos' portrait *Gilles Hoffman and His Wife* (1570, Rijksmuseum, Amsterdam) is a stiff, formal work. *Antoine Anselmo and His Family* (1577, Brussels) lightens the formality of the parents' pose with the appealing awkwardness of their two children. His religious paintings in the Flemish Mannerist style include *Tribute Money* (1601, Antwerp), *St. Paul at Ephesus* (1568, Brussels), and the masterful *Panhuys Family Moses with the Tablets* (The Hague), in which he surrounds Moses and Aaron with a crowd of portraits of the Panhuys family, with servants bearing his characteristic ewers and jugs, and with his self-portrait in the background.

H. D. HALE.

VOSGES, vōzh, department, France, in the eastern part of the country, lying on the western flank of the Vosges Mountains and drained mainly by the Moselle and Meuse and their tributaries. The southwest, however, is drained southward to the Saône. Vosges, with an area of 2,279 square miles, is a rather hilly region, characterized in the west by part of the limestone Plateau of Langres, in the center by a dissected region built up mainly of sandstone and known as the Monts Faucilles, and in the east by the steeper ascent to the summit of the Vosges Mountains. The latter rise in the department to 4,100 feet in the Ballon d'Alsace, which constitutes the southeastern corner of the department (see also VOSGES, mountain range).

The higher ground, especially in the Vosges Mountains, is mainly forested, but much of the remainder is under cultivation. Soils, however, vary greatly in quality, and that developed on the Triassic sands of the central region is generally rather poor and acid. Cereal, fodder crops, and sugar beets are grown.

The Department of Vosges long has been noted for its light manufactures and textile industries, which use the water power provided by the rivers as they issue from the Vosges Mountains. An early textile industry was reinforced by textile workers who abandoned Alsace when it passed into German hands in 1871. Épinal (1954 pop., 26,288) is the capital of the department and its chief industrial city, with paper, lace, and glass manufactures; and it is the focus of a number of smaller industrial communities in the surrounding hills. St.-Dié and Remiremont also have textile industries. Vosges is crossed by the main railroad from Basel and Belfort to northern France and also by the canal linking the Moselle with the Saône. Pop. (1962) 380,676.

NORMAN J. G. POUNDS,
Professor of Geography, Indiana University.

VOSGES, mountain range, eastern France, extending north and south for about 120 miles, parallel with the river Rhine. The range consists of a core of crystalline rocks, including granite, but these come to the surface only in the High Vosges of the south; elsewhere they are covered by Permian and Triassic deposits. The Vosges rise abruptly from the plain of the Rhine along a line marked by a system of faults, and in their main features they are closely paralleled by the Black Forest, which rises to the east of the river.

The range is divisible into the southern or High Vosges and the northern or Low Vosges, separated from one another by the Saverne (Zabern) Gap. The fairly regular crest of the High Vosges lies at over 2,000 feet, and rises toward the south to culminate in the Ballon de Guebwiller (4,672 feet). To the south the Belfort Gap separates the Vosges from the Jura Mountains. The western slope of the Vosges is more gentle than the eastern, and is trenched by the deep valleys of the Moselle and its tributaries, all of which rise within the Vosges themselves. The Low Vosges, an undulating plateau built of infertile Triassic sandstone, is a sparsely settled area which has always presented a greater barrier to movement than its low altitude would suggest.

The Vosges Mountains are mostly forested, though the rounded upper surfaces of the High Vosges are covered with a coarse pasture. Valley bottoms generally are cultivated, and extensive vineyards are situated along the eastern flanks. The Vosges never have been important for mining, but water power was a factor in attracting the textile, paper, and other industries to a number of small cities along the western margin. The Saverne Gap is used by an important road and railroad, as well as by the Rhine-Marne Canal.

NORMAN J. G. POUNDS,
Professor of Geography, Indiana University.

VOTE, VOTERS, VOTING. See ELECTIONS; VOTING BEHAVIOR.

VOTING BEHAVIOR, vōt′ĭng bē-hāv′yər. Despite the drama and excitement of election campaigns in the United States, the major influences on the vote in the presidential elections lie only partly in the personalities of the candidates or the impact of the immediate issues. Deep-lying predispositions that have their origins far back in the country's history provide a substratum of partisanship on which all contemporary political movements depend.

Two-Party Rivalry.—For over 100 years virtually all political activity in the United States has been organized around the two major parties. The Democratic Party first came clearly into being with the election of Andrew Jackson in 1828. Although not organized specifically as a working class party, it had a certain "common man" flavor reflecting in part the character of Jackson himself. The Democrats were subsequently opposed by the Whigs and other lesser parties. The Republican Party came into being in an explosive reaction throughout the Midwest and East to the passage of the Kansas-Nebraska Bill (q.v.) in 1854. The election of the first Republican president, Abraham Lincoln, in 1860, led to the secession of the Southern states and the subsequent American Civil War. In the ensuing 100 years numerous minor parties have appeared as protest or special interest movements, but they have faded quickly as the nation has become increasingly committed to its two major parties.

During this 100-year period, ascendancy in national politics has moved in a slow cycle from one party to the other. The dominant position of the Democrats prior to 1860 was broken by the division within the party over the issue of slavery and the loss of a considerable part of its normal vote to the newly created Republican Party. Following the substantial victories of Lincoln in 1864 and Ulysses S. Grant in the two subsequent elections, the strength of the two parties at the polls swung back toward an even division, the Democrats finally winning again with Grover Cleveland in 1884.

Cleveland's victory did not resolve the uncertain balance of party strength, but in 1896 the election of William McKinley demonstrated a clear shift of the electorate to the Republican Party, which therewith acquired an ascendant position which it held with only a single interruption until 1932. The election of Woodrow Wilson in 1912 was made possible only by the division of the Republican vote between William Howard Taft and Theodore Roosevelt, and Wilson's reelection undoubtedly was influenced by the sense of crisis associated with World War I. During the 1920's Republican dominance was reasserted, and Republican presidents were elected with heavy majorities.

Political Realignment.—In the 1930's the political pendulum swung again as the great depression created extensive political realignment, similar to the 1850's. Millions of citizens who had previously voted Republican or had not voted at all turned to Franklin D. Roosevelt and the New Deal. The Democratic Party, which had been the minority party at least since 1896, now became the majority party. It not only won five successive presidential elections, but also captured state and local offices in areas that had been solidly Republican for generations.

The Democratic ascendancy was interrupted in 1952 by the election of General Dwight D. Eisenhower as the Republican candidate for president. His election and his re-election in 1956 introduced a uniquely personal, almost nonpartisan quality into presidential politics. Eisenhower's great popularity did not greatly alter the underlying partisanship of the electorate, however—a fact convincingly demonstrated by the failure of the Republican Party to control the two houses of Congress during the greater part of his terms of office. In 1960, Democratic control of both the executive and legislative branches of the federal government was reinstated, and there was substantial evidence that the country was still in a phase of Democratic ascendancy.

Special Interests.—In most European democracies the party system is more or less closely organized around basic social divisions within the electorate. These divisions are primarily economic, religious, and regional. The parties tend to focus their appeal on a particular social stratum: working-class people, farmers, Roman Catholics, business and professional persons, people of particular sectional interests, and the like. All of these dimensions also have been present in United States politics for many years. The sharpest cleavage is the regional division inherited from the Civil War period, which created the "solid South" for the Democrats and established the Republicans as the dominant party in many parts of the North.

Religion has played a role in United States politics ever since the heavy immigration from Roman Catholic countries, particularly Ireland, began in the middle of the last century. The Democratic Party in the large cities succeeded in capturing these new citizens, and it has held a diminishing claim on their loyalty ever since. In contrast to farmers in many other countries, American farmers have not closely identified themselves with any party, but have been distinguished by their violent swings from one party to the other as their economic circumstances fluctuated.

Underlying all of these and other aspects of political loyalty has been the dimension of social-class status. Although social class has never had the significance in the United States that it has had in many European societies, the Democratic Party has had a long-standing attraction for people of working-class status. Middle-class people have tended to identify themselves with the Republican Party, which is generally seen by the public as the party of conservatism and respectability.

Although these group components may be found in the national vote in every presidential election, it is important to realize that neither party has an exclusive claim on any of these groups. Both parties attempt to make their appeals sufficiently broad to attract them all. In this sense they are "parties of integration"; they both seek to represent all strata of American society rather than to speak for one particular stratum, as the parties in the European multiparty systems attempt to do.

Crossing Party Lines.—It is also clear that, from one election to the next, these various social attributes of the vote may become more or less important, as immediate circumstances polarize political opinion along one dimension rather than another. The economic disasters of the 1930's, for example, greatly heightened the political significance of social class, and support of the two parties tended to separate along class lines during this period. During World War II the importance of class position as a determiner of the vote diminished, and it receded still further during the Eisenhower period of the 1950's.

Similarly, the religious dimension, which is relatively latent in most national elections, came into prominence in 1928 and 1960, when the Democratic presidential nominees were Roman Catholics. The vote tended to align itself along religious lines, with Catholics voting much more heavily Democratic than would ordinarily have been the case, and many Protestants crossing their usual party line to vote against a Catholic nominee. From time to time other issues have activated other social groups—Negroes, labor union members, Southerners, for example—introducing new forms of social orientation into the vote.

In every national election in the United States the vote represents an interaction of long-standing partisan loyalties, commonly handed down from one generation to the next, and the impact of contemporary personalities and events. In most elections the party holding the majority of the committed partisans in the electorate will elect its candidates. On occasion, the force of immediate circumstances may place the majority party at such a disadvantage that it will lose an election, but it usually returns to office after a short interval. On rare occasions in United States history a period of massive realignment of political loyalties has taken place in response to national crises, and the two parties have exchanged their majority and minority relationships. Under ordinary circumstances, however, partisan commitments are highly resistant to change; it is these loyalties, distributed unevenly through the major strata of American society, that provide the principal element of stability in the United States electoral system.

See also ELECTIONS—*United States.*

ANGUS CAMPBELL,
Director, Survey Research Center, The University of Michigan.

Further Reading: Campbell, A., and others, *The American Voter* (1960; reprint, Univ. of Chicago 1980); Dummett, Michael, *Voting Procedures* (Oxford 1985).

VOTING MACHINE. The intricate mechanism which casts and counts the votes of millions of citizens in the United States today is in marked contrast to the simple devices which served as the first voting machines. Near the close of the 19th century machines which combined voting and counting were used. The first official use of voting machines in the United States occurred in Lockport, N.Y., in 1892. Four years later they were employed on a large scale in Rochester, N.Y., and within a short time came into wide use throughout the state. The movement for the use of the voting machine, especially in states with numerous presidential electors, has paralleled that for the adoption of the presidential short ballot (the form which omits the names of the electors, showing only names of candidates for president and vice president).

The voting machine, a mechanical Australian ballot, grew out of the need to correct the abuses which developed with the paper ballot (in spite of its uniform and official character and of its being marked in secrecy at the official polling place), and the need to provide a prompt and accurate count. Its use eliminates, as much as possible, fraud, error, and carelessness on the part of both the voter and the election officials, and, at the same time, greatly facilitates the totaling of election results.

Operation.—The counters of the machine must be inspected and set at 000 before the polls open; then the machine adds the votes as they are cast. When the last voter opens the curtain to leave the machine, the total votes for each candidate and for each proposition appear on the counters. The election judge or the inspector locks the machine against further voting and opens the counting compartment in the presence of all persons who are lawfully in the polling place. A certificate of the number of votes cast for each candidate and for each proposition on the machine and on the "irregular ballots" (those cast on paper for persons whose names do not appear on the ballot label of the machine) is then made and signed as required by law for election returns. When the canvass is completed the machine must remain locked for a stated period, usually 30 days. If a recanvass is demanded, the court may order the machines to be opened and examined—a procedure more accurate and less expensive than a recount of paper ballots.

Economy.—The voting machine also cuts down election costs. Precincts may be consolidated since the voter can cast his vote in a shorter time on the machine than on a paper ballot. This reduction in the number of precincts cuts cost of personnel, supplies, and rent. Since the machine is equipped with a curtain which conceals the voter the expense of constructing booths is eliminated. There is a saving in printing costs since the ballot label fits into the frame of the machine. Some paper ballots must still be printed for educational purposes and for absent voters. Although there are admitted economies in the use of the voting machine over the paper ballot, there are expenses in connection with the machine in addition to the initial cost: storage, insurance, upkeep, replacement, and the education of election officials and voters.

Constitutionality.—The constitutionality of voting machine legislation was challenged in many of the states. Some adopted elastic constitutional provisions delegating power to the legislature to prescribe the method of voting provided that secrecy be preserved (for example, Arizona constitution, 1912, Art. 8, sect. 1). The Supreme Courts of several states invalidated the first voting machine laws on the ground of unconstitutionality. In Kentucky (*Jefferson Co. ex rel. Grauman* v. *Jefferson Co. Fiscal Court,* 273 Ky. 674 [1938]) the state Supreme Court ruled: "Unquestionably the framers of the Constitution meant that a paper ballot with the names of the candidates upon it should be furnished." On the other hand the Supreme Courts of certain other states interpreted more liberally—for example in Iowa (*U.S. Standard Voting Machine Co.* v. *Hobson,* 109 N.W. 458 [1900]) the court said: "Voting by means of a voting machine is voting by ballot. The constitutional provision that elections shall be by ballot was intended to require and protect the secrecy of the ballot, with the general purpose of guarding against intimidation, securing freedom in the exercise of the elective franchise and reducing to a minimum the incentive to bribery."

Requirements for Use.—The states that have adopted voting machine laws have prohibited the approval by commissioners of any machine which does not meet certain requirements. The machine must allow each elector to vote in secrecy either a straight party ticket (when the law so provides) or a split ticket; prevent any elector voting for more candidates for a given office than he is entitled to; enable each elector to vote by irregular ballot for a person whose name does not appear on the machine; be of such character that each elector may readily and intelligently vote for all candidates of his choice; allow a voter to change his choice before he completes his vote; and possess one or more locks which would forestall any fraudulent manipulation. In polling places using the machines, provision is made for the voter whose right to vote is challenged—by supplying him an official paper ballot or an absent voting ballot marked "Challenged Ballot" on the back, or by allowing him to vote on the keyboard of the machine or in the space provided for voting an "irregular ballot" and marking "challenged" beside his name on the poll list.

Much of the early dissatisfaction with the machines was caused by lack of understanding on the part of officials and voters. Now all states using machines provide training for election officials. In Florida no one may serve as a member of any board of election where machines are used without being certified by the custodian of machines as qualified to perform the duties in connection with the machine. Sample or specimen ballot labels on a reduced scale are distributed for educational purposes before the election and are on display at the polling places. Some states (New York, for example) place a machine on public exhibition in charge of a competent instructor at least three days before an election. Many states require that a miniature functioning model be in the polling place for the voter to operate before going in to cast his vote.

Machines are manufactured today to meet the requirements of the party-column ballot and of the office-group ballot, with or without facilities for voting a straight ticket. A machine can be found to meet the needs of any election district for the primary as well as for the general election. The largest machines will record the votes of nine parties of 70 candidates each and provide space for 35 questions.

SPENCER D. ALBRIGHT
Professor of History and Political Science, University of Richmond

VOTING TRUST, an arrangement in the operation of corporations whereby some or all of the stockholders transfer their shares to one or more trustees, who are authorized to vote the stock during the life of the agreement. In exchange, stockholders receive trust certificates, which may be bought and sold just as other securities. Certificate holders receive the dividends on the deposited shares; the voting rights of the shares, however, rest with the trustees. Such arrangements are legal throughout most of the United States. However, abuse of the trust device in organizing and operating businesses during the late 19th century stimulated many restrictions through the so-called antitrust laws.

Voting trusts centralize and expedite control of the corporation in the hands of a relatively few persons. Going concerns may use the device as a form of permanent proxy. The voting trust occurs most frequently, however, in reorganization, providing concentrated and positive control to guide the corporation out of its difficulties. Such trusts usually are limited to a fixed period of years, at the end of which the voting rights revert to the stockholders.

Finally, a voting trust may be established when a court rules that a large institutional stockholder—such as a foundation or a labor union—may not vote its shares.

WILLIAM N. KINNARD, JR.
The University of Connecticut

VOTIVE OFFERINGS. See OFFERINGS.

VOUET, vwĕ, **Simon,** French decorative and portrait painter: b. Paris, France, Jan. 9, 1590; d. there, June 30, 1649. In 1604 he was already painting portraits in London. In 1612 he went to Italy where he studied the works of Paolo Veronese in Venice. Vouet spent the next years in Rome, where he was elected president of the Académie de Saint-Luc. In 1627 he was called to Paris as court painter to Louis XIII. He painted a portrait of the king (Louvre), murals for the Louvre and Luxembourg palaces, and decorations for Cardinal Richelieu. Vouet was the teacher of Pierre Mignard, Eustache Lesueur and Charles Le Brun, and through Le Brun he influenced French decorative painting up to the end of the century.

Other paintings by Vouet include *Apollo and the Muses* and *Venus* at the Budapest Museum of Fine Arts, the *Investiture* and *Martyrdom of St. Francis* in the Church of San Lorenzo in Lucina, Rome, and a *Madonna and Child with Saints* in the Prado, Madrid. His style indirectly derives from the realism of Michelangelo da Caravaggio, but Vouet discarded the Italian's exaggeration and developed a calm, monumental style which was ideally suited to French taste.

H. D. HALE
"Art News" Magazine

VOUGHT, vôt, **Chance Milton,** American aeronautical engineer and designer: b. New York, N.Y., Feb. 26, 1890; d. Southampton, Long Island, July 25, 1930. After learning to fly at the age of 20 under the tutelage of the Wright brothers, he achieved his first success as a designer four years later with an advanced trainer used by the British in World War I. This was followed (1916) by the famous Vought-Wright Model V military biplane. In 1917, with the financial backing of Birdseye B. Lewis, he formed the Lewis & Vought Corporation (later the Chance Vought Corporation), which, utilizing Vought's streamlined designs, produced such outstanding aircraft as the Vought VE-7 trainer (1919); the Vought UO-1 convertible observation plane (1922–1925), which could be catapulted from the deck of a ship; and the FU-1 high-altitude fighter (1925). His well-known O2U Corsair convertible seaplane established world speed and altitude records. In 1929 the firm was merged into the United Aircraft & Transport Company; later it again became an independent concern, known (from 1961) as the Chance Vought Corporation.

VOUSSOIR, vōō-swär′, any of the wedge-shaped stones making up an arch or a vault. The bottom stones on either side are called *springers,* and the top center stone is the *keystone.*

VOWEL, vou′əl, a simple articulated sound, which is produced merely by breathing, accompanied by a constriction in the larynx, a greater or less elevation or depression, expansion and contraction of the tongue, and contraction or expansion of the lips. The vowel sounds of the English alphabet are imperfectly represented by five letters: *a, e, i, o, u* (and sometimes *w* and *y*); the deficiency of our alphabet, therefore, is apparent when it is recalled that there are at least 13 distinct shades of vowel quality in the spoken language, as heard in the following words: *ale, an, ask, ah, all, ell, err, eel, ill, old, ore, pull, ooze.* The long sound of *i,* as in *ire,* and of *y,* as in *by,* although represented by one letter, are really compound vowel sounds or diphthongs. The French simple vowel sounds *u* and *eu,* and the German *ö* and *ü,* are not heard in the English language.

See also ACOUSTICS—*Sound Sources: The Human Voice;* PHONETICS; and the individual articles on the several vowel letters.

VOYVODINA. See VOJVODINA.

Painter Édouard Vuillard is best remembered for the brooding portraits of his sister and mother at home in their wallpapered rooms.

MUSEUM OF MODERN ART

VOZNESENSKY, voz-nye-syen'skē, **Andrei Andreyevich,** Russian poet: b. Moscow, USSR, May 12, 1933. He cut short his architectural studies (1951–1957) to turn to poetry, becoming a protégé of Boris Pasternak. His poems, reflecting the influences of Pasternak and Vladimir Mayakovsky, were first published in 1958. Voznesensky's long poem *The Masters* (1959) won him recognition, and two volumes published in 1960, *Parabola* and *Mosaics,* attracted attention for their wit, subtlety, and experimentation with meter and rhythm. *Thirty Digressions from the Poem "The Triangular Pear,"* inspired by a visit to the United States in 1961, caused wide discussion in the USSR. Despite his commitment to Communist principles, Voznesensky became known, with Yevgeni Yevtushenko, as a leader of the revolt against Soviet literary censorship. Another volume of poems, *Antiworlds* (1964), was followed in 1966 by his collected poems, published as *An Achilles Heart. Stikhi* (1967) and *Ten zvuka* (1970) followed. Selected English translations appear in *Nostalgia for the Present* (1978).

VRIESLAND. See FRIESLAND.

VUILLARD, vü-ē-yár', **Jean Édouard,** French painter: b. Cuiseaux, Saône-et-Loire, France, Nov. 11, 1868; d. La Baule, Loire-Atlantique, June 21, 1940. In 1884, at the Lycée Condorcet, he met Ker-Xavier Roussel and Maurice Denis, future fellow members of the Nabis group, and Alexandre Lugné-Poë, who, as an actor-manager, would later commission programs and scenery from him. In 1886 Vuillard began to study art at the École des Beaux-Arts, and two years later left it with Roussel to study at the Académie Julian. Denis, Pierre Bonnard, Paul Sérusier, and Félix Vallotton were also at the Académie Julian, and in 1889 they founded the Nabis (Hebrew word meaning "prophets"), a group under the influence of Paul Gauguin.

Vuillard designed his first program for Lugné-Poë's Théâtre Libre in 1890, and a year later he exhibited with the Nabis at Le Barc de Boutteville's and had his first one-man show. In the same year he met Stéphane Mallarmé, at whose house he encountered the leading figures of the Parisian intellectual world. From 1892 he made programs and scenery for Lugné-Poë and began a series of decorative panels. In 1899, Ambroise Vollard published Vuillard's lithographs *Paysages et Intérieurs.*

Vuillard wryly called himself an "Intimist." He stayed close to home, painting by preference his mother and sister and their wallpapered rooms. His entire work is recognizable from the play of patterns in wallpaper, upholstery, and dress materials. From 1903 he exhibited at his dealer's and at the salons, but the popularity he had enjoyed in the 1890's dwindled until a revival of his first one-man show, in 1936. In 1938 he was elected to the Institut, and held a retrospective in the Musée des Arts Décoratifs. His popularity now is at a peak, and his paintings set auction records yearly. H. D. HALE

VULCAN, vŭl'kăn (Lat. VULCANIS or VOLCANUS), in Roman religion, god of fire, originally of volcanic fire, and patron of arts and crafts (particularly metallurgy) associated with fire. His cult came early to the Romans from Asia Minor, by way of Etruria, and later was assimilated to that of Hephaestus, the Greek fire god. Vulcan's parents were Jupiter and Juno, one of whom hurled him from heaven and thereby lamed him. Early myth made him husband of Maia, goddess of growing vegetation, but later legend married him to Venus, goddess of love, and thus allegorized the union of artistic craft with grace and beauty. Volcanoes were the natural chimneys of his subterranean smithies, of which the most famous was beneath Mount Etna, Sicily, where the Cyclopes aided Vulcan in manufacture of mechanical marvels, objects of art, arms and armor for gods and heroes, and thunderbolts for Jupiter.

Vulcan's festival (*Volcanalia*) was celebrated on August 23 with rites to avert destructive fire. Such propitiation rites probably caused erection of his earliest temples outside a city's walls. In Ostia, the port of Rome, Vulcan's worship surpassed that of any other Italian deity. In art Vulcan appears as bearded, wearing a conical cap and a sleeveless tunic, holding hammer and tongs, exhibiting powerful muscles in arms and legs, and having one leg shortened to show his lameness.

P. R. COLEMAN-NORTON,
Princeton University.

VULCANIZATION, vŭl-kən-ə-zā'shən, a method of treating crude rubber with sulphur or a sulphur compound so as to make it strong, elastic, and resistant to the actions of solvents and abrasives, as well as to heat and cold. See also RUBBER—*Discovery of Vulcanization; Making Rubber Products.*

VULCANO, vōōl-kä'nō (anc. HIERA and VULCANIA), island, Italy, the southernmost of the Lipari Islands (q.v.), situated in the Tyrrhenian Sea, 16 miles (26 km.) north-northwest of Milazzo on the northern coast of Sicily; area 8 square miles (21 sq km.).

There are several volcanoes on the island, including those of Monte Aria (1,637 feet, 499 meters) and Vulcanello (403 feet, 123 meters). The Gran Cratere volcano (1,266 feet, 386 meters) has had active eruptions throughout recorded history. Pop. 413.

VULGATE, The, vŭl'gāt, the name that has been given since the 16th century to the standard Latin version of the Bible used in Western Christendom from the early Middle Ages to the present. The word (Medieval Latin *vulgata* [*editio*], common or well-known [version]) came to be used as a proper name with this meaning only after the Council of Trent (1545–1563). Before that time, *vulgata* was simply a descriptive adjective, and when patristic or medieval Latin writers applied it to a Bible, they referred usually to the Septuagint Greek translation or to the Old Latin version made from it.

First Latin Bibles.—The sacred books of the Jews were written in Hebrew (some parts in Aramaic) and translated successively into Greek between the 3d and 1st centuries B.C. This work of translation was done for the benefit of Jews living outside Palestine, in Egypt especially, who no longer understood Hebrew. The Greek collection thus formed (generally known as the Septuagint), including some works which later were not recognized as sacred by the Palestinian rabbis, was taken over by the Christian community from its beginnings, and treasured as the Word of God which prophesied the salvation worked through Jesus of Nazareth. As Greek was the common language of all the peoples in the lands bordering on the eastern Mediterranean, the first and second generations of apostles and missionaries found this version of the collection adequate both for their preaching and for liturgical use in the assemblies, whether they were located in Syria, Asia Minor, Greece, Egypt, or southern Italy.

By the 2d century A.D., however, the Christian faith was spreading to such areas as northern Italy, North Africa, Spain, and Gaul, where not Greek but Latin was the language in general use. The Scriptures, both those taken over from the Jews (the Old Testament, translated into Greek) and the new collection formed by the apostolic writings (the New Testament, written in Greek), therefore had to be Latinized for use in these communities. Presumably the first translations were oral, following the practice in Jewish synagogues, where the sacred text was read in Hebrew and translated sentence by sentence into the vernacular. Thus in the Christian reunions the texts may at one time have been read in Greek and then translated at sight into Latin. We know at least that before the end of the 2d century there existed written Latin translations of both Old and New Testaments, and in the Western provinces of the Roman Empire the Greek texts gradually ceased to be used except by a decreasing number of bilingual scholars. These Latin translations are known collectively as the Old Latin version of the Bible.

It is still disputed whether a single such version was composed and prescribed by authority for all Latin-speaking churches, or whether, as St. Augustine seems to have believed, different translations originated in different localities and influenced each other without ever constituting a fixed and official text. In any case, it is very likely that the first complete Latin translation appeared in North Africa, where Greek was least known, and that the European Latin version was in its origin independent of the former. It has even been suggested that a pre-Christian Latin translation of the Old Testament had been produced in North Africa by Jews and was then taken over by Christians, but there is no direct evidence for this. By the early 3d century the Christian community in Rome also had changed the language of its liturgy and Scripture reading from Greek to Latin.

The haphazard origin and growth of these Old Latin texts meant endless variety and disagreement in the manuscripts and consequently in the texts as read in different churches. Further, the most frequently used passages, those of the New Testament especially, had suffered much from harmonizing (inserting phrases from one Gospel in another) and glosses and additions of all kinds. By the mid-4th century some standardizing of the Gospel text was urgently required; to be effective, it had to be patronized by some central authority. The scholarly Pope St. Damasus I, bishop of Rome from 366 to 384, decided to have it undertaken, and he called on the man who seemed best qualified for this delicate task: his secretary, Eusebius Hieronymus, better known to us as St. Jerome (q.v.).

St. Jerome's Early Life.—Jerome was born about 347 A.D., a native of the town of Stridon, near the northwestern frontier of what is now Yugoslavia. His parents were Christians, but according to a custom frequent in those days his baptism was deferred until after boyhood. Sent to Rome for his secondary education, he received a thorough grounding in the literary and oratorical training of the time; and there, at about the age of 18 or 20, he was received into the church by baptism.

Jerome was peculiarly gifted for his future work. Small and frail in appearance, he nevertheless had a remarkably tough constitution. He had great intellectual curiosity, an immense capacity for work, and a gift for languages and literary studies. With these, he was a fervent Christian, intensely loyal to the church and to orthodox doctrine, and always proud of having received his baptism in Rome itself. His defects of temperament—impatience, touchiness, hasty

Council of Trent. Its approval of St. Jerome's *"vulgata"* (well-known) Latin translation of the Bible in 1546 led to adoption of the tradional name for the work: Vulgate.

The Mansell Collection, London

temper, a passionate partisanship which made him unfair to his opponents—were the defects of his qualities. Ardently devoted to the intellectual apostolate, he first interested himself in church history. But when circumstances and his devotion to study led him into the Biblical field, he had the insight to grasp both the need that existed and his own unique qualifications for satisfying it. By his lifetime of labor devoted to the Scriptures, he had an influence on future generations and left a legacy to the church comparable only to those of his great contemporary, Augustine.

His education completed, Jerome traveled in Gaul, and there he came in contact with groups of ascetics, religious men and women practicing the primitive form of monasticism which had lately spread to the West from the communities of Egypt. Feeling an ardent attraction to this most heroic form of Christian life, he journeyed to the Middle East and joined a community of hermits living in the Syrian Desert outside Chalcis, near Antioch. Here, among the rigors and severe penances of 4th century monasticism, he maintained his scholarly interests: he improved his knowledge of Greek, acquired some Syriac, and began the study of Hebrew under the tuition of a Jewish convert to Christianity. At first he fully intended to spend the rest of his life in this retreat, but after four years a theological controversy raised such a commotion even among the hermits that Jerome, then about 30 years of age, left the desert in disgust. He pursued his Scripture studies first in Antioch and later in Constantinople; in 382 he accompanied two bishops who had been summoned to Rome to attend a church council. There Pope Damasus, impressed by the young ascetic's command of languages and Biblical learning, kept him as his secretary for Greek affairs, encouraged him to write works of exegesis, and finally commissioned him to revise the current Latin text of the Gospels.

Gospel Revision.—The pope's commission is known to us only by Jerome's letter of dedication, and this refers only to the Gospels, which were issued in 383 or 384. Jerome's account of his work is fairly detailed and is borne out by comparisons that can still be made with surviving manuscripts of the Old Latin. As his standard he chose the oldest Greek manuscripts available as being the least corrupt, and he chose well, for they evidently belonged in the main to the Alexandrian text tradition (*Codex Vaticanus* and others), regarded as the purest by modern textual critics. To avoid a too radical change, he left the colloquial diction and syntax of the Old Latin pretty much as he found them, but wherever the meaning was at variance with the Greek he corrected it, and he removed the additions and expansions that had been inserted. He also rearranged the Gospels in the Greek order—our familiar Matthew, Mark, Luke, John; the Old Latin had arranged them by length—Matthew, John, Luke, Mark. As for the rest of the New Testament, Acts, Epistles, and Revelation, though Jerome speaks in one place as though he had revised the whole of it, we cannot be sure that this was so. The existing text differs little from one form of the Old Latin, so the revision, if it was made, must have been slight and superficial.

The Psalter.—Having been officially commissioned and long desired, the revised Gospel text was generally welcomed in the Latin-speaking church. But another section of the Scriptures, liturgically just as important and familiar as the Gospels, was in even more urgent need of revision: namely, the Psalter. On this, Jerome labored repeatedly. While still in Rome (before 385), he revised the Old Latin Psalms according to the Greek, working on the same principles as he had with the Gospels. A few years later, in Palestine, using the famous *Hexapla* of Origen (185?–?254) available in the library at Caesarea, he produced a more thorough emendation, partly corrected according to the Hebrew text. Finally, about 392, as part of his complete new version, he translated the Psalms anew from the Hebrew. But whereas the rest of his translation eventually found general acceptance, this Psalter "according to the Hebrews" was too radical a departure from the familiar liturgical text and never found acceptance in the use of any church. Rather it was the second revision from the Greek, the Gallican Psalter (so called, apparently, because it was first popularized about the 8th century in Gaul), that gradually became and remained the standard Psalm book of the Latin church and the Psalm text of the Vulgate. Only in modern times (1945) has a new official Latin translation been made, from a critically established Hebrew text, and recommended for liturgical use; but this is not part of the Vulgate.

Translation from the Hebrew.—After Damasus' death, Jerome, finding himself out of favor with the clergy of Rome, migrated to Palestine in 385. He settled in Bethlehem, where henceforward he devoted himself to the monastic life, to his Hebrew studies, and to the production of Scriptural translations and commentaries. He had conceived the ambitious project of a complete new version of the Old Testament Scriptures, directly from the original texts, so that Latin-speaking Christians should have available a Bible more faithful to the original than the Old Latin version made from the Septuagint. With the moral and financial support of friends, particularly among the laity of Rome, he completed this great undertaking in 15 years—years occupied also with duties of administration (he was head of a monastery), with much controversial writing and correspondence, and, latterly, with increasingly bad health. He died in his Bethlehem monastery at about the age of 72, in 419 or 420.

The work was launched in 390 with the books of Samuel and Kings, introduced by the famous helmeted prologue in which Jerome set forth his aims and principles. There followed, at fairly regular intervals, the Psalter, the Prophets, Job, Ezra, Chronicles, and the wisdom books. The five books of the Pentateuch were issued between 398 and 404, followed by Joshua, Judges and Ruth, and Esther. At the special request of friends, Jerome also did a Latin translation of two of the rejected books (those not regarded as canonical by the Jews): Tobit and Judith.

Old Testament Canon.—Something must be said of Jerome's attitude to the canon of the Old Testament as it affected the composition of the Vulgate. The early church had taken over the Old Testament Scriptures in their Greek form, and in this collection several books were included which the rabbis of Palestine, toward the end of the 1st century A.D., had decided were not to be reckoned as canonical. Two at least, the Wisdom of Solomon and II Maccabees, had never existed in Hebrew, being original Greek compositions. But the Christian Church, which claimed to follow apostolic tradition rather than the rules of the synagogue, had never considered itself bound by these Jewish exclusions, and at first raised no question about the sanctity of any of the books found in the Greek collection believed to have been used by the apostles.

In this connection it is important to remember that the Bible, for Christians as for Jews, was still a collection of physically separate books. A single large volume containing all, and only, the books considered to be divinely inspired, was unknown in Latin before the time of Flavius Magnus Aurelius Cassiodorus (6th century), and indeed it could not well exist as long as there was uncertainty as to how far the canon extended. No universally acknowledged list existed, though the African churches, for example, in the 4th century expressly recognized a canon identical with that later found in the Vulgate (therefore including the Apocrypha), and this was approved by the bishop of Rome to whom they submitted it. The question was gradually settled by a consensus of usage and an appeal to tradition. The books which had been publicly read in the majority of churches "from time immemorial" became established as canonical, and the rank and file bishops and faithful, in the East as in the West, remained unmoved by the preference of Jerome and other 3d and 4th century scholars for the more restricted canon of the Jews.

Although Jerome was not one to accept any man's authority blindly, still he had learned from his Jewish teachers a great deal besides the bare knowledge of Hebrew. Along with much valuable erudition, he had acquired their exaggerated idea of the infallibility of the 4th century Hebrew text and its superiority to the Septuagint. He was also disposed to accept their authority when they told him which books were canonical and which were not, especially since their list had been clearly fixed for three centuries, while the extent of the Christian canon was still somewhat indefinite. Hence he omitted from his program of translation most of the extra books of the Septuagint (that is, the Apocrypha of the Authorized Version)—Wisdom of Solomon, Ecclesiasticus, Baruch, I and II Maccabees—and only reluctantly translated Tobit, Judith, and the Greek additions to the books of Daniel and Esther. Yet Jerome too witnesses, in a way, to the larger Christian canon, for in his letters and other writings he frequently cites the Apocrypha as passages of Scripture and the Word of God. See also APOCRYPHA.

Reception of Jerome's Translation.—Thus Jerome had set circulating in the Roman world a series of Latin translations of Old Testament books differing in varying degrees, and sometimes very considerably, from the familiar Old Latin. Save for an occasional convert from Judaism, no one in that world was capable of checking his work or of verifying the claims he made for its faithfulness. Nor could he allege, since the death of Damasus, any official sanction for the enterprise. His versions had to be accepted, if at all, on faith in his reputation as a churchman and a scholar and on their intrinsic merits of greater clarity and better Latin style. Against this acceptance two factors weighed heavily. The first was personal animosity: Jerome's quickness to take offense was matched only by his readiness to give it, and the saddest part of his story is the list of personal quarrels which he managed to set going and only seldom allowed to subside. There were many clerics in the West who believed that no good at that time could come out of Bethlehem. The second factor, more general, was simply the novelty of the work. For generations the Latin-speaking faithful had been used to the Old Latin; the readings and chants of the liturgy, the rites of baptism and the Eucharist, were largely constituted of its texts, which thus had entered deeply into each Christian's religious life. Further, it was known to be (in the Old Testament) a close and literal reproduction of the Septuagint, the Bible hallowed by apostolic use, and many felt a deep repugnance at Jerome's preference for the Bible of the Jews and his apparent abandonment of the Christians' heritage. (On this point, Jerome himself was sensitive. He repeatedly insisted that by translating the Hebrew he intended no disrespect to the Greek and justifiably pointed to the large amount of work he had already done on the latter version.) Even Augustine, himself a keen student of the Bible and alive to textual problems, sought to dissuade Jerome from issuing these translations; from the point of view of a bishop, concerned for the Christian life of his flock, he preferred simply a revision of the existing Latin texts.

On the other hand, the immense superiority of Jerome's work in intelligibility and clarity could not fail to be obvious to every student. Slowly but surely, as his texts were more and mode widely copied and studied, they gained in popularity, first in Gaul and then in other parts of the empire. A few years after the translator's death, Augustine was quoting his version of the Minor Prophets, and other books are cited or even made the basis of commentaries by several writers before the end of the 5th century. About the middle of the 6th century, Cassiodorus, the organizer of the great Biblical scriptorium at Vivarium in southern Italy, was the first to compose an entire Bible containing all Jerome's translations, the other books being supplied from the Old Latin. By 800, Jerome's text had become practically universal.

Composition of the Vulgate.—Thus the Vulgate, to the best of our knowledge, was actually put together by Cassiodorus. It is a composite work, and its part may be distinguished according to their origins, as follows:

(1) The books of the Hebrew Bible (except the Psalter) as translated by Jerome.

(2) The Psalms according to Jerome's second revision (Gallican Psalter) of the Old Latin.

(3) Tobit and Judith, translated by Jerome from the Aramaic.

(4) The additions to Daniel and Esther, translated by Jerome from the Greek of Theodotion and the Septuagint, respectively.

(5) The other five books of the Apocrypha (called by Roman Catholics Deuterocanonica) from the Old Latin, unrevised.

(6) The Gospels, according to Jerome's revision of the Old Latin.

(7) Acts, Epistles, and Revelation, according to the Old Latin, but whether revised, and by whom, is uncertain.

The order in which the books were arranged varied considerably from one manuscript to another, especially in the Old Testament. The Apocrypha were usually mingled with the rest.

Transmission of the Vulgate.—Before the invention of printing, a literary work, to be published, had to be copied repeatedly by hand, and the more often it was copied the more the text became corrupted by scribal errors. The process was cumulative: each copyist reproduced the mistakes of his predecessors and inevitably added some of his own. A careless or incompetent scribe might fall into errors on every page. Only the most rigorous control and minute supervision of every copy made—and ruthless destruction of those that fell below standard—could check this tendency. Such a control was achieved by the medieval rabbis in their supervision of Hebrew manuscripts, but for the Vulgate it was not even attempted, and in any case the number and distribution of copies were far too great. Medieval Vulgate manuscripts still existing are numbered in the thousands, and they are only a fraction of what once existed. In addition to copyists' mistakes, the long-surviving tradition of the Old Latin text had its effect on the Vulgate wording; many manuscripts contained books from both versions, and their readings were sometimes confused by scribes. Finally, just as with the Old Latin, glosses and harmonizations gradually expanded the Vulgate text.

Medieval scholars of course were well aware of this process, and successive attempts were made to counteract it. Alcuin (735–804), Theodulf (d. 821), Lanfranc (1005?–1089), and Abbot St. Stephen Harding (1048?–?1134) are some of those associated with attempted restoration of a purer text, but none had more than a temporary effect. The techniques of the time were simply not adequate to achieve the end sought; a corrected edition could never overtake, much less supersede, the existing corrupt ones. In the 13th century the great demand for Bibles

British Museum

Part of a rendering of the Vulgate by Alcuin (735-804), English theologian. Alcuin was among several medieval scholars who tried to restore the purity of St. Jerome's text after much hand copying had led to corruptions.

for student use at the University of Paris occasioned the formation of a standard text, which unfortunately was full of glosses and interpolations. A partial remedy was provided by the *correctoria* composed by Dominican and Franciscan professors, which were lists of false readings and their emendations.

Printed Editions.—The invention of printing about 1450, which theoretically made possible the multiplication of copies without error, threatened at first to make things worse. In the first half-century about 100 editions of the Vulgate were printed, and almost without exception they contained the badly corrupted Paris text. In the next 50 years appeared the first critical editions—that is, those that took their text from older and more accurate manuscripts and omitted some at least of the interpolations. Such were the Complutensian or Spanish Polyglot (issued

1522), the Hittorpian (1530), and the various editions of Robert I Estienne (1528 ff.).

By reason of the revival of Hebrew learning among the Christians other possibilities now occurred. The laborious task of reconstituting Jerome's original text might be avoided by the short cut of simply emending the text according to the Hebrew; this was attempted by the Reformer Andreas Osiander and by the Roman Catholic Isidoro Clario. More ambitiously, others undertook to duplicate Jerome's work by making new Latin translations from the originals, with or without added commentaries. Between 1512 and 1579, 10 different new translations were published, half by Roman Catholics and half by Reformers. At the same time, translations into the different vernaculars were being multiplied, some from the Vulgate, others from the Hebrew and Greek.

Council of Trent.—Faced with this confusion of claims and counterclaims on behalf of various texts and editions, the Council of Trent set out to clarify and fix the Roman Church's traditional position. After determining the canon of the Scriptures (in which the apocryphal or deuterocanonical books were at last definitely included), it decreed in 1546 that "of all the Latin versions now in circulation . . . this particular ancient and well-known version, approved by so many centuries of use in the Church," should be considered "authentic" for public use, and no one should venture to repudiate it. The word here translated "well-known" is in the text of the decree *vulgata*, and it is from its use in this document that the name comes. *Authentic* means "authorized" or "official," much as the King James Bible is also called the Authorized Version. The decree gave the Vulgate an official status over all the new Latin versions but decided nothing about its standing relative to the Hebrew and Greek originals nor about vernacular translations, which the council, after discussion, deliberately refrained from mentioning. All of this is quite clear since the modern publication of the minutes of the council's debates. Unfortunately, in the controversies of the time, the term "authentic" was sometimes misinterpreted. Protestant controversialists accused the council of ranking the corrupt Vulgate above the "pure" original texts, while some Roman Catholic theologians in the 17th century held that the Vulgate was the normative Bible, and the originals might be neglected or "corrected" into conformity with it. This view lingered in some quarters among Roman Catholics even into modern times, though expressly reprobated by the Holy See.

Modern Editions.—The council had also ordered that the Scriptures (the Vulgate especially but also the older texts) be printed as accurately as possible. The first fulfillment of this directive was the excellent Sixtine edition of the Septuagint, published in 1587. The Vulgate correction, curiously, ran into greater difficulties. An improved though still rather corrupt edition was published at Louvain by the Dominican Johannes Henten (1547 ff.) and for a while served as a standard text. After several abortive projects an expert commission appointed in 1586 by Pope Sixtus V (r. 1585–1590) prepared in two years an excellent text, based on the best surviving Vulgate manuscript, the *Codex Amiatinus,* which represents the text tradition stemming from Cassiodorus. Unfortunately, Sixtus, disturbed at the quantity of matter thus omitted from the text then familiar in the church, insisted on editing the work himself and largely nullified the commission's labors by restoring many of the old interpolations and corrupt readings. His edition, thus modified, was published in May 1590, but its distribution was not far advanced when the pope died three months later. There was so much dissatisfaction among the experts with this Sixtine edition that 10 days after the pope's death the cardinals ordered it withdrawn from circulation, and later all the copies that could be recovered were destroyed. After some intervening brief pontificates a new commission prepared a compromise text, a partial correction of the Sixtine, and this, now known as the Sixto-Clementine or Clementine, was published under Pope Clement VIII (r. 1592–1605) in 1592. It has remained the official Vulgate ever since.

In 1889 two Anglican scholars, John Wordsworth and Henry Julian White, began the publication of a critical edition of the Vulgate New Testament, which was completed by H. F. D. Sparks in 1954. Meanwhile, a group of Benedictine scholars was commissioned to prepare a new official and critical edition of the whole Vulgate, to be issued in about 26 volumes. Publication began in 1926 with Genesis, and by 1957 more than one half of the Old Testament had been completed with the publication of volume 11, through the Canticle of Canticles (Song of Solomon).

Value of the Vulgate.—As a translation, the Vulgate is the best of the ancient versions. Jerome's work is eclectic to this extent, that he drew not only on the learning of the rabbis, but also on the writings of Origen and other Christian scholars, and made constant use of the Septuagint and the 2d century translations of Aquila of Pontus, Theodotion, and Symmachus. His vast erudition ensured that no traditions available at the time escaped him, and on the whole his work is an impressive monument of literary skill and linguistic learning. He deliberately broke with the older tradition of ultraliteral translation, preferring, as he said, to translate the meaning rather than just the words. Further, he was a gifted writer, and his Old Testament is perhaps the greatest monument of early church Latin. This is not the Latin of the pagan classics, yet it preserves much of their concision and majestic gravity and is remarkably apt at reproducing the terseness and emphasis of the Hebrew. The Latin liturgy of the Western Church continually echoes the rhythms and language of this Bible, and its style governed the Latin of the Middle Ages.

More generally, the influence of the Vulgate in the history of Western European culture is incalculable. All languages and literatures of the Western World are indebted to it in greater or less degree. For 1,000 years it was *the* Book (Bible, from the Latin *biblia,* book), familiar to all who learned to read, the standard of language and writing, the text most studied and commented, which supplied the foundations of law, political organization, and the plastic arts, as well as of the Christian religion.

English Translations.—Aside from the incomplete Anglo-Saxon versions of the 8th to 11th centuries, the first Bible in English was a translation of the Vulgate: the version begun by John Wycliffe (1320?–1384) and completed after his death. In the 16th century, Roman Catholic exiles on the Continent again translated the Vulgate, the New Testament appearing in Reims in 1582, the Old at Douai in 1609–1610 (see DOUAY BIBLE). A modern translation, approved for liturgical use, was published by Ronald Knox in 1944–1949.

See also BIBLE—*3. Manuscripts and Versions of the Old Testament;* and *12. The Text of the New Testament: Textual Criticism, Manuscripts, and Versions.*

R. A. F. MACKENZIE, S. J.,
Professor of Old Testament, Jesuit Seminary, Toronto.

Bibliography

Ackroyd, P. R., and Evans, C. F., eds., *Cambridge History of the Bible*, vol. 1, *From the Beginnings to Jerome* (Cambridge 1979).

Berschin, Walter, *Greek Letters and the Latin Middle Ages: From Jerome to Nicholas of Cusa*, tr. by Jerold Frakes (Catholic Univ. of Am. Press 1987).

Hornblower, Jane, *Hieronymus of Cardia* (Oxford 1981).

Jerome, Saint, *Letters of Saint Jerome*, vol. 1 (Paulist Press 1963).

Metzger, Bruce, *The Early Versions of the New Testament* (Oxford 1977).

Schroeder, H. J., tr., *Canons and Decrees of the Council of Trent* (TAN Bks. Pub. 1978).

VULPECULA, vŭl-pĕk′yə-lə, the Northern Hemisphere constellation of the Little Fox, delineated by Johannes Hevelius in the late 17th century. It contains no stars brighter than the 5th magnitude. An important constituent is the Dumbbell Nebula (Messier 27), so called because of its shape when seen in larger telescopes. Lying in right ascension $20^h\ 0^m$, declination 25°, the constellation crosses the meridian at 9 P.M. about September 8.

FERGUS J. WOOD.

VULPIUS, vo͝ol′pē-o͝os, **Christian August,** German novelist and playwright; b. Weimar, Germany, Jan. 23, 1762; d. there, June 25, 1827. He was educated at Jena and Erlangen, and in 1790 returned to Weimar, where he became friendly with Johann Wolfgang von Goethe, through whose influence he became secretary of the court theater, librarian, and curator of coins. In 1797 he published the first of a series of novels about robbers, *Rinaldo Rinaldini, der Räuberhauptmann;* although these were lurid picaresque stories without literary merit, they were widely popular, and were translated into many languages and imitated by a number of other writers.

His sister CHRISTIANE VULPIUS (1765–1816) formed a romantic attachment with Goethe in 1788 and bore him several children before marrying him legally in 1806.

VULTURE, vŭl′chər, the name of various birds of prey of the order Falcones or Accipitres that habitually feed on carrion. This order, comprising the eagles, hawks, and their relatives, is divided into several families, to two of which belong the vultures of the Old World on the one hand, and those of the New World on the other.

The vultures of the New World form a separate family (Cathartidae), which is believed to have developed independently from all other birds of prey. They consist of six species, similar in their feeding habits to their namesakes of the Old World but differing from them and the other birds of the order through a number of skeletal and other variations. Among these may be cited a difference in the nostrils, which are not separated by a bony septum; a differently shaped sternum; a much longer middle finger; and weaker feet. The better-known species are the turkey vulture or turkey buzzard (*Cathartes aura*), the black vulture (*Coragyps atratus*), the South American condor (*Vultur gryphus*), the California condor (*Gymnogyps californianus*), and the king vulture (*Sarcorhamphus papa*). The first two are black with a naked head, which is red in the turkey vulture—hence its name. The turkey vulture is more buoyant in the air than the black vulture, with a longer tail and a somewhat longer wing spread (almost 6 feet as against about 4.5 feet), and ranges from the tip of South America to southern Canada. The black vulture does not extend so far north, reaching Maryland and the central states, and is commoner in the more southerly parts of the United States. The condors are huge species which live in the Andes and the Sierras of California. Their wing spread of nearly 10 feet places them among the largest of all the flying birds, exceeded only slightly by some of the largest albatrosses. The South American species is common, but the numbers of the California condor have been reduced so drastically that less than 50 individuals remain in existence. The king vulture of tropical America is the most colorful. The body is white, the wings and tail are black, and the bare head is gaudily tinted with red, yellow, blue, and violet and ornamented by wattles.

Pat Kirkpatrick, from National Audubon Society

King vulture

The Old World vultures are related to the eagles and hawks and belong to the same family (Accipitridae); they range from southern Europe and parts of Africa to India, central Asia, and China. They include, among others, such well-known species as the celebrated lammergeier or bearded vulture (*Gypaëtus barbatus*), the griffon (*Gyps fulvus*), the sinister-looking white-headed vulture (*Trigonoceps*) of Africa, and the Egyptian vulture (*Neophron percnopterus*). The last named is all white with black wings. It is relatively small, with a wing spread of about 3.5 feet, but some of the other species are fully as large as the condors, and the magnificent lammergeier stands nearly 4 feet high.

Vultures feed on carrion, which they usually detect from aloft, and normally inhabit open regions, but some feed on any sort of garbage, and in the eastern countries of the Old World and in parts of tropical America many frequent towns and villages, where they are tolerated as scavengers. These birds show no fear of man, perching or walking sedately about in even the most crowded bazaars or markets. In Tibet and India they dispose of human dead exposed in certain sites or structures when religious custom forbids burial or cremation. Vultures are repulsive in many ways but beautiful when aloft. Gliding on almost motionless wings and soring in wide circles often to immense heights, the larger ones are among the most majestic of all birds.

See also CATHARTIDAE; CONDOR; EGYPTIAN VULTURE; LAMMERGEIER; TURKEY BUZZARD.

CHARLES VAURIE,
Assistant Curator, The American Museum of Natural History.

VYATKA. See KIROV.

VYBORG, vē'bôrg (**VIBORG, VIIPURI**), city, USSR, in the Russian SFSR, in northwest Leningrad Oblast about 70 miles northwest of Leningrad, on the Karelian Isthmus where the Saimaa Canal enters the Gulf of Finland. The city is near the Finnish frontier and is a junction of railways between Finland, Leningrad, and the Karelian Autonomous SSR. The civic center is on the mainland, with suburbs on peninsulas and islands. Cool summers and mild winters have made Vyborg a beach resort, and there are many tuberculosis sanatoriums. Its industries specialize in wood products, flour, perfume, and farm machinery. There are many historic buildings, including an ancient castle.

Vyborg was founded in the 12th century, and in 1293 fell under Swedish rule. Russia conquered it in 1710 and annexed it in 1721. It was incorporated in free Finland in 1920, when the latter gained independence from Soviet Russia. As a result of the Soviet-Finnish War of 1939–1940, the city was annexed by the USSR on March 12, 1940. During the Soviet-German War, Vyborg was reoccupied by Finland from 1941 to 1944 and suffered great damage, which has since been repaired. The city is the capital of Vyborg district. The inhabitants are mainly Russians. Pop. (1959) 51,000.

ELLSWORTH RAYMOND.

VYCHEGDA RIVER, vĭ'chəg-də, river, USSR, in the Russian SFSR, mostly in the Komi Autonomous SSR. Rising in the southern Timan Ridge, it flows generally south and west for 700 miles, emptying into the Northern Dvina River near Kotlas. From May to November it is navigable for some 600 miles. The river is also important for floating timber cut from the forests along its banks.

VYE, vī, **Eustacia,** heroine of *The Return of the Native* (1878) by Thomas Hardy. Described as "the raw material of a divinity," she is Hardy's most ambitious attempt to portray a *femme fatale*. In her craving for pleasure she is kin to Gustave Flaubert's Emma Bovary. She marries Clym Yeobright, and wrecks his life. On the verge of eloping with Damon Wildeve, a former suitor, she drowns herself; Wildeve, trying to rescue her, shares her fate. See also RETURN OF THE NATIVE, THE.

DELANCEY FERGUSON.

VYERNY. See ALMA-ATA.

VYRNWY RIVER, vûr'nōō-ĭ, river, Wales rising in northwestern Montgomeryshire and flowing southeast, northeast, and north for 35 miles into the Severn River on the Shropshire border. Lake Vyrnwy, near its source, was created in 1890, when a dam 1,170 feet wide and 160 feet high was constructed across the valley to form a reservoir to supply water to Liverpool. At an altitude of 825 feet, the lake is 5 miles long and averages a mile in width.

VYSHINSKY or **VISHINSKY,** vĭ-shĭn'skē, **Andrei Yanuaryevich,** Russian public official: b. Odessa, Russia, Feb. 10, 1883; d. New York, N.Y., Nov. 22, 1954. Joining the Social Democratic Party in 1902, he was active in the revolution of 1905 and imprisoned briefly thereafter. In 1913 he took his law degree at the University of Kiev. At the outbreak of the revolution of 1917 Vyshinsky sided with the Mensheviks, but after his party's collapse, he joined the Bolsheviks in 1920. He then began to teach at the University of Moscow, where he was professor of criminal law procedure (1923–1925) and rector (1925–1928). He also served as prosecutor in the Division of Criminal Cases of the Supreme Court of the USSR (1923–1925) and prosecutor of the Russian SFSR (1931–1933). In 1933 he was appointed deputy public prosecutor of the USSR and in 1935 public prosecutor, an office he filled until 1939. In this capacity he attracted international attention as the relentless prosecutor in the purge trials of 1936–1938. Vyshinsky became first deputy commissar for foreign affairs in 1940, and in 1943 was named Soviet representative on the Allied Mediterranean Commission. In 1944–1945 he was active in the Balkans, particularly in Rumania, which he brought under Communist control. From 1946, as chief Russian delegate to the United Nations, he made use of his great legalistic skill and ability as an orator to launch virulent attacks on Western "warmongers." Appointed foreign minister in 1949, he held this post until 1953, when he was replaced by Vyacheslav M. Molotov and became first deputy foreign minister again and permanent delegate to the United Nations. There he continued his sharp denunciations of Western policy, although he modified his violence somewhat after Stalin's death. He edited *The Law of the Soviet State* (Eng. tr., 1948); other translated works include *Lenin and Stalin* (1948) and *The U.S.S.R. and World Peace* (1949).

VYSHNI VOLOCHEK, vish'nyĭ vŭ-lô'chək, city, USSR, in west central Kalinin Oblast, Russian SFSR, 70 miles northwest of Kalinin and 175 miles northwest of Moscow. Although it has lost some of the importance that it had as a port on the Vyshni-Volotsk Canal connecting the Baltic with the Volga (constructed by Peter the Great in the early 18th century), it is still an important road and railroad junction. Its chief industries are cotton milling, lumber milling, and the manufacture of glass. It was chartered in 1770. Pop. (1959) 66,000.

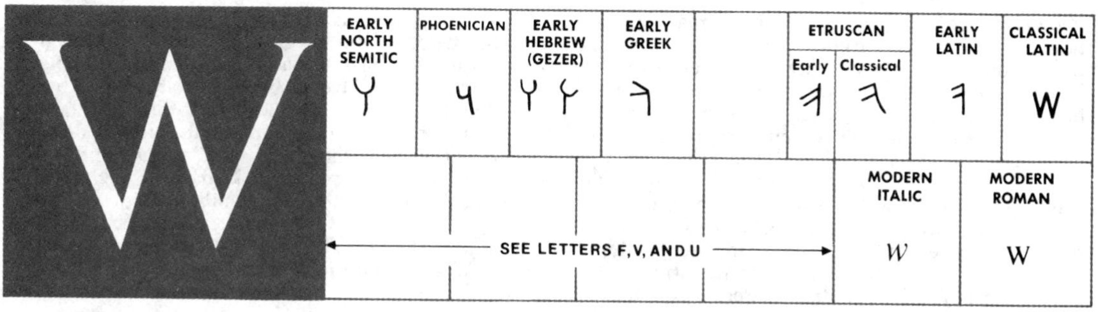

W

EARLY NORTH SEMITIC	PHOENICIAN	EARLY HEBREW (GEZER)	EARLY GREEK		ETRUSCAN Early	ETRUSCAN Classical	EARLY LATIN	CLASSICAL LATIN
								W

← SEE LETTERS F, V, AND U →	MODERN ITALIC	MODERN ROMAN
	w	w

A. C. SYLVESTER, CAMBRIDGE, ENGLAND

The development of the letter W is illustrated in the chart above, beginning with the early North Semitic letter. The evolution of the majuscule (capital) W is shown at top; that of the minuscule (lowercase) at bottom.

W, the 23d letter of the English alphabet. Its name, double u, well describes its shape and origin. The French *double vé* is essentially the same name; *u* and *v* are variants of Latin V or *u,* which was used in ancient Roman times for the sounds of both *w* and *u.* Both the shape of the letter and its uses are far older than the first mention of the name. In the Latin of the Roman republic a vowel was written twice to indicate its length; and the *uu* (with the value of English *w*) is found in early writings of the empire (after 27 B.C.). The second *u,* which might or might not appear in the spelling, was originally used as a glide between *u* and a different vowel, as in *Danuius* and *Danuuius,* later *Danubius* (Danube). This practice had been common in the Italic dialects, as in the Oscan *eítiuvam* and Umbrian *kastruvuf,* both similar to Latin *noctua* in formation. Conversely, Latin might omit the glide *u,* even where usually written, as in *iuenta* for *iuuenta.* The same use of *uu* appeared at Praeneste in 385 A.D. and in the provinces, especially in native names to indicate the sound *w* that Latin had lost, as in *Seuuo* (about 150 A.D.), *Seuuonianus* (102 A.D.), *Piauuonius* (266 A.D.) and *Vuitildes* (597 A.D.).

Since the *w* sound had gone from Latin itself the letter is usually not found in the Romance languages except in borrowed words. There is no *w* in the Italian alphabet. In French it is pronounced *v* in *wagon* and *w* in *tramway,* but *ou* is written for *w* in *oui,* and the dipthong *wa* is written *oi* in *poids.* In Gothic, *w* was written as Y (Greek *υ*), and Old English used the rune ƿ (wen). The emperor Claudius I (r. 41–54 A.D.) attempted unsuccessfully to introduce into Latin an inverted digamma (Ⅎ) for *w.*

Confusion is inevitable, since the sound is a semivowel, sometimes pronounced *w* and sometimes *u.* Phonetically, *w* is a bilabial voiced fricative, produced by an expulsion of voice through slightly pursed lips, but there is some closure at the back of the mouth, and Germanic words may appear in Romance languages with complete closure. Thus, Old high German *werra* is in French *guerre* (war). A voiceless variety of *w* is heard in North America, as in *what,* written hw in Old English (hwæt). In Gothic the Greek θ was diverted to this use. Gaelic changed *w* into *f,* and *fat* and *fot* may be heard in Aberdeenshire for *what.* English has lost *w* before *l,* as in *lisp* (Anglo-Saxon *wlisp*). Variants such as *enow* and *enough* are due to inflectional differences stabilized in standard usage from different dialects. *Whore,* from Old English *hore,* cognate with Latin *carus* (dear) may be a dialect form, like Lancashire *wham* for "home." The *w* survives in spelling but not in pronunciation, in *answer* and *Greenwich.* In *assuage* French influence is obvious.

JOSHUA WHATMOUGH
Chairman, Department of Linguistics, Harvard University

WAAGEN, vä′gən, **Gustav Friedrich,** German art historian and museum director: b. Hamburg, Germany, Feb. 11, 1794; d. Copenhagen, Denmark, July 15, 1868. A nephew of the poet and aesthetician Ludwig Tieck, he was destined for an art-historical career. A searching pamphlet on the brothers Hubert and Jan van Eyck brought him, as director, to Berlin (later Kaiser Friedrich) Museum, which had just been founded. In Great Britain his reputation was based on *The Treasures of Art in Great Britain,* 3 vols. (1854, 1857), an amplified version of a work published in Germany almost 20 years before. A painstaking catalogue of art treasures in private hands, it stimulated further collecting.

WALLACE BROCKWAY

WAAL River, väl, river, the Netherlands, the southern and larger arm of the Rhine. The Rhine enters the Netherlands near Millingen and forks into the Lower Rhine and the Waal, which flows through the Province of Gelderland to its border and there unites with the Maas, or Meuse, to form the Merwede.

WAALS, väls, **Johannes Diderik van der,** Dutch physicist: b. Leiden, Netherlands, Nov. 23, 1837; d. Amsterdam, March 9, 1923. At the age of 25 he entered the University of Leiden from which he was graduated in 1865. After graduation he taught physics, first at Deventer and then at The Hague, returning to Leiden to work for the doctorate which he received in 1873.

One of the exciting new areas in physics when van der Waals was a young student was thermodynamics. The concept of heat as a fluid (caloric) had been shattered in the 1850's when it became clear that heat could be converted into mechanical work and could not, therefore, be a substance. Instead heat was defined as the kinetic energy of the constituent molecules of a body. In 1857, the German physicist Rudolf Clausius applied this idea to gases. He showed how the ordinary gas laws could be deduced mathematically from the assumptions that gas molecules had no appreciable volume, were in constant motion, and did not act upon one another. The law derived from these postulates is known as the ideal gas law for no real gas behaves exactly in accordance with it. The deviations from the ideal gas law intrigued van der Waals. He subjected Clausius' work to a searching criticism and was soon able to detect the source of error. If one assumes that gas molecules do have a volume and that they do act upon one another by weak but not negligible forces (known today as van der Waals forces), then the equation of state for individual gases may be written so that it is in much closer agreement with experimental determinations.

Van der Waals' equation states: $(P + a/V^2)(V - b) = RT$.

P = pressure; V = volume; R = the gas constant; T = absolute temperature; a = the mutual attractions between gas molecules, differing for different gases; b = the volume of gas molecules, also differing for each gas. (See also KINETIC THEORY OF GASES.)

In 1910, van der Waals was awarded the Nobel Prize in physics for his work on gases. From 1877 until his retirement in 1907, he was professor of physics at the University of Amsterdam.

L. PEARCE WILLIAMS,
Professor of History, Cornell University.

WABANA, wô-bă'nə, is a town in Newfoundland, Canada. Situated on Bell Island, in Conception Bay, about 15 miles northwest of St. John's, Wabana's economy is based entirely on its iron mines which form one of the largest deposits of red hematite ore in the world. Since the start of mining operations in 1895 more than 50 million tons of ore have been produced, and the known reserves are many times that amount. The mines are owned and operated by the Dominion Steel and Coal Corporation; much of the ore is transported to the company's steel mills in Sydney, Nova Scotia, but there are also substantial shipments to western Europe. Wabana is connected with the Newfoundland mainland by ferry to Portugal Cove, eight miles by paved highway from the provincial capital. Population: 4,254.

ALLAN M. FRASER.

WABASH, wô'băsh, city, Indiana, seat of Wabash County, situated on the Wabash River, 45 miles west of Fort Wayne, at an altitude of 745 feet. Located in the heart of a wheat- and corn-producing region, it is an industrial and commercial center in which rubber goods, woodworking machinery, paperboard, rock wool insulation, electronic equipment, and magnetic coils are manufactured. It has an airport.

A Carnegie Library, the Memorial Hall which houses the county historical society's museum, and the Honeywell Memorial Community Center are features of the city's cultural and civic life. The Salamonie and Frances Slocum state forests nearby offer camping and picnic areas.

Settled in 1835, Wabash received its city charter in 1866. The river on which it stands and from which it takes its name was one of the early trade routes from Lake Erie to the Ohio Valley, and the word Wabash is the English derivation of the Indian word Ouaboukigou meaning "shining white." Later the Wabash and Erie Canal paralleled this same route, and traces of the old canal and locks may still be seen. Wabash was the girlhood home of Gene Stratton Porter, whose birthplace is only a few miles east of the city, and was the scene of several of her novels. One of the original arc lamps used in 1880 when Wabash became the first city in the world to light its streets by electricity is on display in the courthouse, and another item of historical interest is the monument commemorating the site where the Treaty of Paradise Springs was signed with the Miami Indians in 1826. A massive, bronze statue of Abraham Lincoln by the noted sculptor, Charles Keck, stands on the courthouse lawn. The city is governed by a mayor and city council. Pop. 12,985.

NANCY A. COWGILL,
Wabash Carnegie Public Library.

WABASH COLLEGE, a small liberal arts college for men located in the town of Crawfordsville, Ind., 45 miles northwest of Indianapolis. Since its founding in 1832 the college has remained independent of both church and state support, conservative in curriculum, and vigorous in its pursuit of both academic excellence and athletic competition. The guiding philosophy of the institution insists that students be given a wide degree of freedom and responsibility in their personal concerns, and a single rule, that a man shall behave as a gentleman, governs relations between administration and student body. The bachelor of arts degree program is the only one which the college feels itself competent to offer, and each student is required to complete courses in the natural sciences, humanities, and social sciences before being admitted to upper-class standing.

Academic, administrative, and residence halls are situated on 50 acres of wooded land. On the edge of the campus national fraternities maintain chapter houses which feed and house about 60 percent of the students. The independent men are housed and fed in college facilities. Students are drawn primarily from the Midwest but an increasing number enter from eastern and far western states.

The school color is red, and the nickname "Little Giants" reflects an era when a small college engaged in athletic competition with major universities. The average enrollment is 750.

STEPHEN G. KURTZ,
Associate Professor of History, Wabash College.

WABASH RIVER, river, Ohio, Indiana, and Illinois. It rises in Grand Lake, Mercer County, in the western part of Ohio, and flows northwest into Indiana, where it takes a generally western course to Logansport. It then flows southwest to Covington in Fountain County and then nearly south past Terre Haute to the Ohio River. For about 200 miles of its sinuous lower course it forms the boundary between Indiana and Illinois. About 475 miles in length, it is the largest tributary of the Ohio entering it from the north.

WAC, an acronym for the Women's Army Corps of the U. S. Army, established by Congress in 1943. It replaced the earlier WAAC, an auxiliary corps. See WOMEN'S ARMY CORPS.

WAC CORPORAL. See ROCKETS.

WACE, wäs, Norman-French cleric and poet: b. Island of Jersey, about 1100; d. about 1175. He spent most of his life in Caen and Bayeux, where he became a canon about 1169, but he visited southern England sometime before 1155. He dedicated his two verse chronicles, the *Roman de Brut*, to Eleanor of Aquitaine, queen of England, and about 1160, under the patronage of Henry II, he began a chronicle of the dukes of Normandy.

His best-known work is the *Roman de Brut* (1155), a translation into verse of Geoffrey of Monmouth's *Historia regum Britanniae* (History of the Kings of Britain). Wace adapted freely from Geoffrey's legendary chronicle, showing poetic skill in vivid depiction and a concern for verisimilitude. He also drew upon contemporary oral traditions about King Arthur and provides the earliest extant allusions to the Round Table. The poem furnished an important source for Chrétien de Troyes and Layamon, two other important poets in the development of the Arthurian legend.

VERNON HARWARD.

WACKENRODER, väk'ən-rō-dər, **Wilhelm Heinrich,** German writer: b. Berlin, Germany, July 13, 1773; d. there, Feb. 13, 1798. Though he followed a legal career, he became known as a writer of the romantic school. Early in life Wackenroder formed a lasting friendship with a fellow student, Ludwig Tieck (q.v.), who subsequently became one of the leaders of the romantic movement.

While studying law at Halle, Erlangen, and Gottingen, Wackenroder devoted considerable time to broadening his knowledge of art. He went to Berlin with his friend Tieck in 1794, and later the two visited the rich picture galleries of Dresden, Cassel, Salzdahlum and Pommersfelden, and became well acquainted with Bamberg and Nürnberg. These ancient cities imbued Wackenroder with the spirit of their long and unbroken development in which art had played an intrinsic role. Among those who shaped Wackenroder's taste should be mentioned Karl Philipp Moritz, writer and art educator, Johann Dominik Fiorillo, painter and art historian, and, in matters of music, the composer Johann Friedrich Reichardt.

Wackenroder's fame is based on a slim volume of essays published anonymously in 1797 under the title *Herzensergiessungen eines kunstliebenden Klosterbruders* (Heart Outpourings of an Art-Loving Friar). These were papers supposedly written by a monk on the subject of paintings and music by old masters. This included papers presumably written by Raphael and Bramante, recounting the origins of masterpieces of art. The book also contained four essays generally believed to have been written by Tieck. The main thesis of the book contends that great art cannot be taught or learned merely by following theories; instead, great works of art emanate from the intuition of a master, prepared by intense studies. This results, however, only if the artist is rooted within a system of culture, devoted to great ideals such, for example, as those offered by the Roman Catholic Church. One of Tieck's essays went so far as to describe a painter who, overwhelmed by the inspiration he received from the Catholic Church, accepts conversion convinced that only thus might he attain mastery in art. The general tone of the book was such as to persuade Goethe, in keeping with his negative attitude toward the upcoming romantic school, to reject it. To this school, however, as represented by the so-called Nazarene group of German artists living in Rome, the book appeared as a manifesto of their intention to follow the ideals of the early Gothic painters. It is not at all certain that Wackenroder would have agreed with his self-appointed followers, for they apparently overlooked the fact that he did not extoll the medieval world or any of the early masters. Instead he glorified the masters of fulfillment, Raphael, Dürer, Leonardo, and Michelangelo, and even exalted the trends leading into the later period we now call baroque. This tendency is even more evident in Wackenroder's essays on music. Here he praises contemporary and near-contemporary music, such as the great choral works of his century. After Wackenroder's death, Tieck published some essays by Wackenroder under the title: *Phantasien über die Kunst für Freunde der Kunst* (1799, Fantasies on Art for Friends of Art), a volume which expounds some fine traits involved in Wackenroder's understanding of music.

HANS HUTH
Curator of Decorative Arts, The Art Institute of Chicago

WACO, wā'kō, city, Texas, seat of McLennan County, situated on the Brazos River, just below its confluence with the Bosque River, 90 miles south of Fort Worth and 98 miles southwest of Dallas by road. Its altitude is 427 feet. It is a focal point of state and federal highways and of four railroads—the Missouri Pacific, St. Louis Southwestern, and Southern Pacific (freight only), and the Missouri-Kansas-Texas (passengers and freight). Air service is provided by Braniff Airways and Continental Air Lines. James Connally Air Force Base is nearby. The city is the hub of a rich agricultural blackland region producing chiefly cotton and grain (also hay and dairy products), and is an important cotton market. Tires, glass, furniture, cement, clothing, sporting goods, caskets, dry-cleaning equipment, textiles, phonograph records, and cottonseed oil are leading products of its more than 250 manufacturers. Waco is also the home of several life insurance companies.

Higher education is provided by Baylor University (q.v.) and Paul Quinn College. The latter, for Negroes, founded in 1881 by the African Methodist Church, is a four-year coeducational college accredited by the state Department of Education. The city has excellent public schools, also a public library, Baylor University library, and (on the Baylor campus) the Armstrong-Browning library dedicated to Robert Browning, English poet. There are several hospitals including a large veterans' hospital; also state and Methodist orphanages. Fronting the Brazos River is 650-acre Cameron Park. The city is also served by Lions Park, 17 other neighborhood parks, and the recreational facilities of nearby Lake Waco (an artificial lake created by erecting a dam on the Bosque River). The Fort House and Mann House are two of Waco's historic restored homes.

Formerly inhabited by Waco (Hueco) Indians (hence the name), the area was first surveyed by Neil McLennan and Capt. George B. Erath about 1840. The town was laid out in 1849 on the site of a Waco village burned by Cherokees in 1830, and was incorporated in 1856. A Methodist female college was established in 1859, and Waco University (absorbed by Baylor University in 1886) was founded in

1861). The city expanded rapidly following the arrival of the railroads (1881). In 1870, the 475-foot suspension bridge across the Brazos—at that time the country's largest single-span suspension bridge—was opened. The city has a council-manager form of government. Pop. 101,261.

DAVID M. HENINGTON,
City Librarian, Waco.

WACO INDIANS. See WICHITA INDIANS.

WAD MEDANI, wăd mĕ'dă-nĭ, city, Sudan, headquarters of the Blue Nile Province, in the Gezira, 110 miles southeast of Khartoum, on the left bank of the Blue Nile, south of the influx of the Rahad River. It is a major center for the production of long staple cotton, its chief agricultural product. Barley, corn, wheat, durra, and fruits are also grown. Site of an agricultural research station, virtually the whole working population is engaged in agricultural or pastoral production. The people are of mixed Arab, Nubian, and Black descent. Pop. (1977 est.) 184,501.

JOHN RALPH WILLIS, JR.

WADAI, wä-dī' (Fr. **OUADAÏ** or **OUADDAÏ**), a principal region in the Republic of Chad, and a former Muslim sultanate occupying this region. The adjective Wadaian is sometimes used to describe the Negro *mesakin,* or peasantry of the region. Wadai forms a part of the eastern boundary with the Republic of Sudan in the vicinity of 14° north latitude. To the north lies the Sahara, including the Ennedi Plateau. To the south is the forested region of Dar Runga. On the west are the scrub and grass plains of the Baguirmi and Kanem regions. Wadai lies mostly above the 1,500-foot contour and has a general slope westward. It is part of the vast interior basins of Lake Chad and Bodele depression. The western portion of Wadai is an almost flat clay plain with patches of sandy soil and of black-cotton soil. The Ba Tha is the major stream which, after rains, flows westward across the plain. Its course of more than 300 miles ends short of Lake Chad. The plain is mostly bush covered, but in places there are tall grasses after the rains, and elsewhere scattered trees occur among the grasses. The eastern portion of Wadai is broken hill country of scrub-covered granite rocks rising nearly to 5,000 feet and interspersed with forested valleys. There are no permanent streams in Wadai.

Wadai is a major transitional area between Negro and Arab peoples and cultures. The region was so remote that it was known to Europeans only through the accounts of the Arab geographers until it was traversed by the German explorer Gustav Nachtigal (1834–1885) in 1873. About 1635–1640 the Tunjur, the ruling Arab dynasty of Wadai, was overthrown by a Black Maba chieftain known as Abd-el-Kerim. Thereafter, Blacks of Arab culture ruled the sultanate. Wadai sometimes dominated the neighboring sultanates of Darfur (in the Sudan), Kanem, and Baguirmi.

The French advanced from the Congo and Lake Chad in the 1890's to find the powerful Senussi sect ruling Wadai. An Anglo-French treaty of 1899 recognized Wadai as in the French sphere, but the sultanate resisted effective occupation. A *jihād* or holy war was declared in 1908. There was much fighting between 1909 when the French captured the major city of Abéché (Abeshr) and 1912, when Sultan Doumourah surrendered and the sultanate was abolished.

The population of Wadai was estimated at more than 2,000,000 by Nachtigal. Colonel Jean Tilho set it at 300,000 in 1917. Nachtigal claimed 30,000 inhabitants for Abéché, whereas in 1922 it was stated to be 5,000. French figures for 1950 gave a total of about 800,000 people in Wadai on an area of almost 95,000 square miles. Insofar as these differences are real, they reflect the changing economy of the region. Whereas Wadai was once a great caravan center and known for its tremendous traffic in slaves, it is now an isolated region subsisting largely on maize and millet with a limited traffic in cotton, peanuts, cattle, and horses. Wadai and its capital Abéché lie on the famous overland pilgrim route between Central and West Africa and Mecca and the city has an airport. During World War II, this route furnished a difficult supply line to the Middle East.

HIBBERD V. B. KLINE, JR.,
Chairman, Department of Geography, University of Pittsburgh.

WADDELL, wŏ-dĕl', **Helen (Jane),** British scholar and translator: b. Tokyo, Japan, May 31, 1889; d. March 5, 1965. After working in Belfast, she studied at Somerville College, Oxford (1920–1922). She was the recipient of the Susette Taylor fellowship from Lady Margaret Hall, Oxford, an honor decisive in her career, for it entailed residence in Paris for several years (1923–1925). She imbibed the French scholarly indulgence for the *ouvrage de vulgarisation,* and indeed her finest book is precisely that. This is *The Wandering Scholars* (1927), a work that manages to be a delight without sacrificing any measure of authority. Not less engaging are *Beasts and Saints* (1934) and *The Desert Fathers* (1936), in which the complex apparatus of impeccable scholarship never rises to the surface. *Mediaeval Latin Lyrics* (1929) shows her as a singularly sensitive translator. Her single novel, *Peter Abelard* (1933), is a fiercely passionate recountal that brings the 12th century clearly into view and keeps it there without a single creaking wheel.

WALLACE BROCKWAY.

WADDELL, James Iredell, American naval officer: b. Pittsboro, N.C., July 13, 1824; d. Annapolis, Md., March 15, 1886. He was appointed midshipman in the United States Navy in 1841, became lieutenant in 1855, and resigned his commission to join the Confederate Navy in 1862. After serving as a battery officer at several engagements within the Confederacy, he was sent to Europe in 1863, and in October 1864 at Madeira he took command of the *Shenandoah* (q.v.), with which he raided the United States whaling fleets in the Pacific. Waddell carried the Confederate flag around the world and captured 39 vessels by August 1865 when he heard of the end of the war. He then sailed 17,000 miles to Liverpool, England, and surrendered his ship to the British. After amnesty was declared he returned to the United States and became a captain for a private steamship company in 1875. In 1877 his ship, the *San Francisco,* struck a reef and sank, but all passengers were saved. At the time of his death he commanded the Maryland state flotilla for policing oyster beds.

WADE, wād, **Benjamin Franklin,** American lawyer and legislator: b. Feeding Hills, near Springfield, Mass., Oct. 27, 1800; d. Jefferson, Ohio, March 2, 1878. One of the 11 children of poor parents, Wade had little formal education. Admitted to the Ohio bar in 1827, he began law practice at Jefferson, thenceforth his home. After two years as prosecuting attorney he was elected (1837) to the Ohio Senate on the Whig ticket, and in 1841–1843 served another term; there he led a successful fight to strengthen laws against divorce and worked to make the state's fugitive slave law ineffective. Appointed circuit judge (1847), he kept out of the antislavery fight until the popular verdict was unmistakable, then took a leading part while campaigning for the United States Senate in 1851. Elected, Wade, with his colleague Senator Salmon P. Chase, fought the Southern senators' efforts to extend slavery. He began the first of two terms as a Republican senator in 1857.

During the Civil War (1861–65) Wade was one of the Republican "Radicals" or "Jacobins" who opposed Lincoln. He was a founder and chairman of the Committee on the Conduct of the War that aspired to take its direction out of the president's hands. Angered at Lincoln's humane plans for Southern reconstruction and unable to induce the Republican Party to choose another nominee in 1864, he joined Henry Winter Davis of Maryland in a violent attack on Lincoln published in the Aug. 5, 1864 issue of the New York *Tribune.* The two Jacobins demanded immediate emancipation, arming of the Negroes, confiscation of rebel property, and execution of prominent Southerners.

To Wade's disgust, President Andrew Johnson chose to be guided by Lincoln's reconstruction policy. In March 1867 Wade became president pro tem of the Senate, and had Johnson been convicted of the impeachment, he would have succeeded him. But Wade had made many enemies; Johnson may have been spared because to some of his, Senate judges he seemed the lesser of two evils. Failing to obtain the nomination as vice president in 1868, Wade returned next year to his Ohio law practice.

Of average height and strongly built, his white mane, piercing black eyes and aggressive manner in the war years impressed the public, while his colleagues respected his talent for invective, fearlessness, and skill at intimidating opponents. He was called "Bluff Ben."

William Frank Zornow,
Department of History, Kent State University.

WADENA, wŏ-dē'nə, village, Minnesota, seat of Wadena County, located at an altitude of 1,372 feet about 45 miles west of Brainerd. Located in an agricultural area, Wadena is primarily a trading center for dairy and poultry products, livestock, and grain. It was settled in 1871 and incorporated in 1881. The name is derived from an Indian word meaning "little round hill." Population: 4,699.

WADESBORO, wādz'bûr-rō, town, North Carolina, seat of Anson County, located at an altitude of 433 feet about 45 miles southeast of Charlotte, near the South Carolina border. Lumber, underwear, hosiery, flour, feed, cotton yarn, and cottonseed products are among the manufactures of Wadesboro, which is surrounded by cotton and tobacco plantations. The site was given by Capt. Patrick Boggan and the town was named after Col. Thomas Wade, both Revolutionary War soldiers. It was first settled about 1785. Pop. 4,119.

WADHAM COLLEGE. See Oxford University.

WADI or **WADY,** wä'dĭ, an Arabic term meaning valley, ravine, river, or riverbed. The word was borrowed by Turkish, Persian, and other Near Eastern languages and is now extensively used throughout western Asia and North Africa. In Spanish it appears as *guadi* in such names as Guadalquivir (al-Wādi al Kabīr, the great river) in Córdoba. As a geological term it is generally used for a channel or bed of a watercourse which is dry except in rainy seasons.

Philip K. Hitti.

WADI HALFA, wä'dĭ hăl'fə, town and district, Republic of the Sudan, in the Northern Province situated on the right bank of the Nile just south of the Egyptian border. The people are of Nubian and Arab origin. The town came into existence in the 19th century as the terminus of a steamboat service from Upper Egypt. From 1885 to 1898 it was an advance base for Anglo-Egyptian military operations against the Mahdists and became the northern terminus of the railway to Khartoum. The town lost some importance when a railroad was built between Khartoum and Port Sudan in 1908–1910. From 1940 to 1942 Wadi Halfa was an important staging post on the Allied line of communication with Egypt via Central Africa. Parts of the town were to become inundated by the reservoir of the Aswan High Dam begun in 1960. Pop. (1956) 11,007.

Kenneth D. D. Henderson.

WADSWORTH, wŏdz'wûrth, **James,** American educator: b. Durham, Conn., April 20, 1768; d. Geneseo, N.Y., June 7, 1844. He graduated from Yale in 1787. In 1790 he moved to the Genesee Valley, western New York, where success as a land promoter for his uncle, Jeremiah Wadsworth (q.v.), and especially as an investor in lands of his own made him one of the state's richest landowners. As landlord of many tenants, he took special interest in scientific agriculture and public education. In 1811, he urged the state to establish normal schools and in 1838 procured the creation of a state system of district-school libraries. He himself spent over $90,000 to subsidize lectures, articles, and textbooks on education and to found a library and an academy at Geneseo. He believed that a man educated in science was a "double man."

Edward K. Spann.

WADSWORTH, James Jeremiah, American diplomat and administrator: b. Groveland, N.Y., June 12, 1905; d. Rochester, N.Y., March 13, 1984. After graduating from Yale in 1927, he served in the New York State Assembly (1931–1941). During World War II he was active in business. In 1948 he was named assistant to the head of the Economic Cooperation Administration and in 1950 director of the civil defense program. Appointed in 1953 deputy representative to the United Nations, he became chief representative in August 1960 for the rest of the year. He was instrumental in the creation of the International Atomic Energy Agency in 1957 to implement the "Atoms for Peace" plan of President Eisenhower. From 1958 to 1961, he served as Chief American negotiator at the three power Geneva conference, working for an effective ban on nuclear weapons tests. Following his service with the United Nations he was named president of the National Research Institute in Washington, D.C.

EDWARD K. SPANN.

WADSWORTH, James Samuel, American soldier and politician: b. Geneseo, N.Y., Oct. 30, 1807; d. near Fredericksburg, Va., May 8, 1864. Although educated for the law, he preferred to be a landed gentleman on the model of his father, James Wadsworth (q.v.). But his hatred of slavery made him a founder in 1848 of the Free Soil Party. In 1856, he led the antislavery Democrats of New York into the Republican Party and in 1860 backed the nomination and election of Abraham Lincoln. In 1861, he volunteered both time and money to aid the union cause. Commissioned a brigadier general in August, he was appointed military governor of the District of Columbia in March 1862. In November he ran for governor of New York in defense of Lincoln's emancipation and war policies but lost to Horatio Seymour (q.v.). He commanded a field division at Fredericksburg and then at Gettysburg where his men bore the brunt of the attack. Mortally wounded at the Battle of the Wilderness, he died in an enemy field hospital.

EDWARD K. SPANN.

WADSWORTH, James Wolcott, Jr., American legislator: b. Geneseo, N.Y., Aug. 12, 1877; d. Washington, D.C., June 21, 1952. He graduated from Yale in 1898. His observations in 1898–1899, both as a private and a civilian, of American army operations in Puerto Rico and in the Philippines made him a lifelong advocate of military training and preparedness. He was a member of the New York State Assembly (1905–1910) and speaker of that house (1906–1910). He served in the United States Senate from 1915 until defeated in 1926 by Robert F. Wagner. A conservative, he opposed the popular election of senators, woman's suffrage, and national prohibition and backed the Henry Cabot Lodge "reservationists" in killing Woodrow Wilson's plan for the League of Nations. From 1933 to 1951, he sat in Congress. In the 1930's he was a critic both of the New Deal and of isolationism, and in the 1940's he was an ardent advocate of strong national defense. He sponsored the Selective Training and Service Act of 1940 and in 1941 procured its extension just five months before the Japanese attack on Pearl Harbor.

EDWARD K. SPANN.

WADSWORTH, Jeremiah, American businessman and Revolutionary officer: b. Hartford, Conn., July 12, 1743; d. there, April 30, 1804. After 10 years as a sailor and sea captain, he served in the American Revolution as commissary first for Connecticut regiments and then, from 1777, for the Continental Army, being made commissary general in 1778. In 1780, he agreed to procure supplies for the French Army sent to aid America. As a merchant and speculator, he wanted strong government and in 1788 supported ratification of the federal Constitution in Connecticut. In 1789, following his election as a member of the House of Representatives, he fought unsuccessfully for national military training. One of the richest men in his state, Wadsworth was a founder of the Bank of North America and the Hartford Bank, a director of the United States Bank, and a promoter of the Hartford Manufacturing Company, a pioneer in the use of power-driven textile machines. He invested heavily in the Phelps-Gorham land purchase in western New York.

EDWARD K. SPANN.

WADSWORTH, Peleg, American soldier: b. Duxbury, Mass., May 6, 1748; d. Hiram, Me., Nov. 12, 1829. He became a schoolmaster after graduating from Harvard and a captain of a company of minute men in 1774. In 1775 he laid out the defenses of Roxbury and Dorchester Heights, Mass. After serving as aide-de-camp to Artemas Ward in 1776 he fought under Washington at the Battle of Long Island. In 1778 he was made adjutant general and in 1779 brigadier general of the Massachusetts militia. Wadsworth was second in command in the unsuccessful expedition against the British at Penobscot Bay, Maine. After receiving command of the eastern department he was captured by a British raiding party in February 1781, but he escaped in June. He was elected as representative in Congress from 1793 to 1807. In 1806 he returned to Maine where he settled on an estate in Oxford County. Henry Wadsworth Longfellow was his grandson, named after Peleg's son Henry, who was killed in the Tripolitan War.

WADSWORTH, city, Ohio, in Medina County, located 11 miles west of Akron and 33 miles south of Cleveland, at an altitude of 1,173 feet. It is served by the Cleveland Hopkins airport. The city is industrial and residential, with half the population employed in nearby cities. The chief manufactured products are matches, valves, cardboard containers, salt, shoe soles, and rubber products. There is a public library and a municipal hospital. Government is by mayor and council.

The community, which was first settled in 1814 by Vermonters, was named for Elijah Wadsworth, a Revolutionary War general. It was a trade and farming area until the Civil War, after which the major interest was coal mining. Pop. 15,166.

KENNETH F. EMERICK.

WAESCHE, wā-shē, **Russell Randolph,** American coast guard officer: b. Thurmont, Md., Jan. 6, 1886, d. Bethesda, Md., Oct. 17, 1946. Appointed cadet in the Revenue Cutter Service in 1904, he was commissioned in 1906 and served in cutters in the Atlantic, Great Lakes, and Alaskan waters. At headquarters during World War I, he later commanded destroyers during the prohibition period and in 1928 was again assigned to Washington where he served for the remainder of his career. He was appointed commandant in 1936, being promoted from commander to rear admiral, was reappointed in 1940 and again in 1944. In April 1945, Waesche became the first Coast Guard admiral. Under his guidance the

Coast Guard became the primary maritime agency of the government. It expanded to over 200,000 during World War II and manned ships in every theater. Dynamic and dedicated, Admiral Waesche ranks as the outstanding officer in his service.

JOHN D. HAYES
Rear Admiral, U.S. Navy (Ret.)

WAF. See WOMEN IN THE AIR FORCE.

WAGENAAR, vä'gə-när, **Bernard,** American composer and teacher: b. Arnhem, Holland, July 18, 1894; d. York, Me., May 19, 1971. He was the son of the composer Johan Wagenaar. He began musical studies at an early age with his father and studied the violin with Gerard Veerman in Utrecht. He settled in the United States in 1920, and was a violinist in the New York Philharmonic from 1921 to 1923. Later he returned to this orchestra to conduct first performances of some of his own compositions. From 1927 to 1971 he was associated with the Juilliard School of Music, primarily as teacher of composition.

Aside from several groups of songs and a chamber opera (*Pieces of Eight*, 1943), Wagenaar concerned himself primarily with abstract music including four symphonies (ranging from 1925 to 1949), the *Triple Concerto* (flute, harp, cello, and orchestra, 1934), a violin concerto (1940), and chamber music including four quartets. While reflecting many of the innovations of the earlier part of the 20th century, Wagenaar emerged as a composer with a strong neoclassical bent, writing chromatically in expressive lyricism within a diatonic framework. He is regarded as a conservative tonal composer who nevertheless reveals an urbane sophistication and admirable craftsmanship in his treatment of form and structure.

SAUL NOVACK
Queens College

WAGENAAR, Jan, vä'gə-när, Dutch historian: b. Amsterdam, the Netherlands, Oct. 28, 1709; d. there, March 1, 1773. Holland's most eminent historian in the 18th century, Wagenaar brought a new emphasis to voluminous presentation of unpublished documentary sources, many of which survive only in his works. Although passionately involved in the political controversies of his own day, his position as a moderate republican enabled him to achieve unusual balance and fairness in his historical writings.

HERBERT H. ROWEN*, *Rutgers University*

WAGENAAR, vä'gə-när, **Johan,** Dutch organist and composer, father of Bernard Wagenaar: b. Utrecht, Holland, Nov. 1, 1862; d. The Hague, June 17, 1941. After working as a church organist, he became director of the Utrecht Music School in 1904 and from 1919 to 1937 was director of the Royal Conservatory in The Hague.

He wrote the operas *The Venetian Doge* (1904) and *The Cid* (1916); the symphonic poems *Saul and David* (1906) and *Elverhöt* (1940); the overtures *King John* (1889) and *Cyrano de Bergerac* (1905); and choral works, songs, and organ pieces.

WAGER, a bet or gambling bargain. The essence of a wager is that it is performable only on the happening of a condition, a fortuitous event such as a sporting contest, horse race, or election, or upon the ascertainment of a disputed fact. Wagers are generally illegal, unrecognized by law as contrary to public policy since enforcement would compel payment, without commensurate value in return, to one who had suffered no detriment. If a wager is paid, statutes in some states permit recovery by the loser in all or in specified kinds of gambling transactions. While the wager is still executory, money deposited with a stakeholder may be recoverable. Ordinary contracts of suretyship or insurance, where assumption of risk for compensation is an established business, are not invalid as wagers.

ALAN MATHESON
Arizona State University

WAGES, the price of, or the payment for, labor services. Wages can be interpreted narrowly as consisting of cash payments or, broadly, to include a wide variety of noncash payments as well. In order to discuss wages in meaningful economic terms, it is desirable to define wages as all payments to employees, in cash or in kind, that impose costs upon employers.

Methods of Wage Payments. In the wages system that initially developed in the manufacturing and construction sectors of the economy, wages are paid on a weekly basis. The income base is determined by the basic hourly rate for the job multiplied by the number of hours worked per week. Beyond weekly wages, employees receive income, broadly construed, in three other forms of compensation: premium pay, pay for time not worked, and employee benefits.

Premium pay consists of payments for overtime (hours in excess of a standard determined by the union contract or by legislation) and for working on second or third shifts, Sundays, and holidays. *Pay for time not worked* occurs when payment is made and no work is performed. Examples are paid holidays, vacations, and sick leave, portal-to-portal pay (for time spent getting ready for or leaving work), and "dead time" in transportation.

Employee benefits, called "fringe benefits" when they were a small fraction of total remuneration, are the fastest-growing component of the wages package. Originally granted during World War II when unions received pensions as an alternative to cash, they now account for approximately one third of payrolls. Employees in government service, in the manufacture of chemicals, petroleum, and transportation equipment, and in public utilities receive the largest benefits; employees in agriculture and construction receive the smallest. The largest category of benefit expenditures is employer contributions to retirement, life, and health insurance.

Salaries also are payments for labor services. Wages and salaries may be classified according to the time period of payment. "Blue-collar" or production workers usually are paid on an hourly basis; "white-collar" or managerial employees usually are paid salaries on a weekly, monthly, or annual basis. As the composition of employment has changed from agricultural and mining to manufacturing and, then, to services, so has the method of payment changed from wages to salaries.

In addition to wages paid on the basis of time, part of an employee's pay may be based on the number of units of production. This is called the *piece-rate* system. Management traditionally has preferred the piece-rate approach because labor costs tend to be stabilized. Such systems are generally opposed by employees and unions because of the difficulty of establishing a "fair" rate. Also the worker who produces too much may be ostracized as a "rate buster."

Incentive systems of payment have been acceptable when negotiated or when the union is able to appeal management decisions. The use of incentive systems varies among industries. They are more likely to be adopted if they have been in existence for a long time and when the proportion of labor costs to total costs is high.

Wage Theory. Like all prices, the price of labor—wages—is determined by the interaction of the forces of demand and supply. The demand for labor originates with employers who hire labor, capital, and other factors of production based on the relationship between productivity and cost. The supply of labor originates with the individual worker. Whether the worker supplies labor to one employer or another, whether he chooses to buy leisure (not to work) or to work many hours, depends primarily on the wage rate offered for his services. Although wages are a crucial determinant of labor supply, the worker also considers such items as working conditions and opportunities for advancement. The demand for and the supply of a particular kind of labor will determine the wages in a given labor market. The demand for and supply of all labor determine the general wage level.

Wage determination, however, is a dynamic process. For example, higher money wages will, in the short run, usually result from increases in the demand for products and corresponding increases in the demand for the labor that produces those products. Higher money wages, however, also affect the supply side as new workers are attracted into the labor market. The supply response of labor to higher wages will have a dampening effect on the forces that caused the initial wage increases.

Wage Structure. The hierarchy of wage rates among different groups of employees is called the *wage structure*. The most important of these wage relationships are those based on regional location and type of industry and occupation. The *geographical wage structure* describes wage rates for different regions of the country in the same industry and occupation. Historically, occupations of similar skill have commanded lower wages in the South than elsewhere. However, the migration of less-skilled employees from the South and the increased industrialization of the South have narrowed this differential and, in some occupations, have eliminated it.

The *industry wage structure* is determined largely by the amount of capital investment per worker and the skill mix of the employees. High-wage industries are firms that use a large amount of machinery per worker.

The location of a job in the *occupational wage structure* depends largely on the investment in education and training of the employees involved. In manufacturing and construction, such craft occupations as carpenter and electrician have been at the top of the wage structure. In the middle are jobs that require the ability to operate machinery, and at the bottom are the unskilled labor and service classifications. Increased education and training, the elimination of restrictions on entry into skilled occupations, and encouragement of minorities and women have succeeded in promoting upward occupational mobility. This process has resulted in a considerable narrowing of wage differentials between the most- and least-skilled jobs.

Wage Trends, Prices, and Productivity. Over the past century, the trend of *money* wages and *real* wages (money wages deflated by the price level) has been strongly upward in the Western world. Since the end of World War II, this growth has been shared also by Japan and other industrialized countries. Since the Great Depression, there has not been a year in which money wages have not risen in the United States. However, increases in money wages have not always been commensurate with—or even moved in the same direction as—real wages. In fact, the largest increase in real wages over a ten-year period occurred between the depression years of 1930 and 1940. It is real wages that determine the worker's purchasing power and standard of living.

The trends in money and real wages in the United States since 1900 are analyzed here for two periods, 1900 to 1960 and 1960 to 1980, in order to account for the increasing importance since 1960 of employee benefits in the wages package. Between 1900 and 1960, money wages increased tenfold, from $418 per year to $5,130 per year. Over the same period, the consumer price index increased threefold; thus the American worker received a very substantial advance in real wages, amounting to slightly under 2% per year. From 1960 to 1980, the trend in real wages was flatter as measured only by cash wages. In those 20 years, the earnings of manufacturing workers increased from $2.26 to $7.27 per hour, or at the rate of 6% per year, while prices advanced by 5% per year over the same period. The average gain in money wages, then, was about 1% larger than the rise in prices. If, however, employee benefits are counted as part of wages, then the average gain in real compensation per worker between 1960 and 1980 reverts to 2% per year.

One need look no further than at the affluence of the American worker to see the favorable impact of rising real wages. But it is important to note that workers have taken part of their benefits in the form of leisure time. Hours per week have decreased from 60 in 1900 to less than 40, and further, significant increases in the number of paid holidays and weeks of vacation have been received by workers.

While real wages have increased steadily, there is increasing evidence that inflation and other factors, notably falling productivity, are eroding the living standard of the American worker. Since 1950, each passing decade resulted in a smaller increase in real wages. The American economy has experienced three spurts of inflation: (1) the rising prices of the early 1950's associated with the Korean War; (2) the cost-push inflation between 1956 and 1958; and (3) the lengthy inflation of the late 1960's and 1970's, largely attributed to the Vietnam War, oil price increases, lagging productivity, and Federal Reserve policy. Inflation since 1965, accompanied by increasing unemployment, has been popularly known as stagflation.

Wage Regulation. As the livelihood of workers and their families became increasingly dependent on the factory system of production, the government stepped in to protect wage earners by regulating wages, hours, and other conditions of employment. Workers in firms in interstate commerce are covered by the laws of the federal government; otherwise, state laws prevail. The major legislation in this area is the Fair Labor Standards Act, passed in 1938. At that time, the minimum wage was 25 cents per hour; with inflation, it has been periodically adjusted upward to provide a wage that is about half of the actual average hourly earnings in manufacturing. Some 38 states have established minimum wages, most of them below the federal level.

Maximum wage rates also have been set by government, usually in conjunction with price controls, as part of economic stabilization policies. Rigid wage-price controls have been instituted only during war periods. Since the 1960's, more flexible *income policies* have been adopted, which have been formulated as "guideposts" in order to limit wage increases to the increase in output per man hour or to some level considered noninflationary.

Unions and Wages. Do unions have the power to raise wages above what they would be in the absence of unions? Do unions cause inflation or increase labor's share of the national income? The public tends to answer affirmatively, but the economic power of unions is greatly exaggerated. This power varies among unions, but on the average the union effect is only 10%. Because unions resist wage decreases strongly, union effect is relatively larger during downturns in economic activity and weaker in inflationary periods when unionized workers are trying to catch up. Unions are strongest in industries where they can control entry, where the firm has monopoly power, and where it is difficult for the employer to substitute capital for union labor.

Union power over wages weakens with time as employers and consumers make substitutions in favor of lower-priced factors and products. Inflation results in most cases from expansionary policies rather than from cost or union pressure. Indeed, organized labor's share of the national income has changed little.

MELVIN LURIE
University of Wisconsin—Milwaukee

Bibliography

Douty, H. M., *The Wage Bargain and the Labor Market* (Johns Hopkins Univ. Press 1980).
Harrop, David, *World Paychecks: Who Makes What and Why* (Facts on File 1982).
Henderson, Richard I., *Compensation Management: Rewarding Performance,* 4th ed. (Reston 1985).
Remick, Helen, ed., *Comparable Worth and Wage Discrimination* (Temple Univ. Press 1984).
Rima, Ingrid, *Labor Markets, Wages, and Employment* (Norton 1980).
Wallace, Marc J., Jr., and Fay, Charles A., *Compensation Theory and Practice* (Kent Pubs. 1983).

WAGNER, Cosima. See WAGNER, RICHARD.

WAGNER, wag′nər, **Honus** (1874–1955), American baseball player, who is generally regarded as the finest shortstop in major league history. Barrel-chested and bowlegged (at 5′11″ and 200 pounds), he did not fit the image of the sleek shortstop, but he was deceptively fast as a fielder and baserunner. The "Flying Dutchman" led the National League in stolen bases five times and amassed 720 in his career.

Wagner achieved his greatest success, however, as a hitter, with eight batting titles (surpassed only by Ty Cobb with 12), and a career average of .329. He also set NL career records for games played (2,785), hits (3,430), singles (2,426), doubles (651), and triples (252), all of which stood at the time of his death, and he averaged over .300 in batting 17 consecutive times.

NATIONAL BASEBALL LIBRARY, COOPERSTOWN, N.Y.
Honus Wagner has been hailed as the all-time best player.

John Peter Wagner, nicknamed Honus and Hans, was born in Mansfield (later Carnegie), Pa., on Feb. 24, 1874. He worked in coal mines as a youth and signed his first professional contract in 1895. After a year with Paterson (N.J.) he played three seasons with Louisville and in 1900 signed with the Pittsburgh Pirates. He retired in 1917 after 18 seasons. A genial player, noted for his sportsmanship in a rough-and-tumble era, Wagner was acclaimed by many as the greatest all-around performer in baseball annals. He was one of the first five elected to the Baseball Hall of Fame in 1936. He died in Carnegie on Dec. 6, 1955.

MARTIN APPEL, *Coauthor of "Baseball's Best: The Hall of Fame Gallery"*

WAGNER, väg′nər, **Otto** (1841–1918), Austrian architect. He was born in Vienna, Austria, on July 13, 1841. He studied at the Technical High School in Vienna; at the Bauakademie, Berlin; and from 1861 to 1863 at the Imperial and Royal Academy in Vienna, where he was a professor from 1894 to 1913. From 1899 to 1905 he was a member of the Vienna Secession, a group interested in *art nouveau.*

Wagner's best-known publication was *Moderne Architektur* (1896), in which he broke with academic practice and recommended the use of new materials, new principles of construction, and new forms that should express 19th century changes in culture. Until 1894 he had a successful career building apartments and villas in Florentine and High Renaissance style, but with the publication of his book he began a series of public transportation stations outside Vienna in the *art nouveau* style. His mature work culminated in the Postal Savings Bank, Vienna (1904–1906). He died in Vienna on April 12, 1918.

H. D. HALE, *"Art News" Magazine*

THE GRANGER COLLECTION

Richard Wagner in about 1867, photographed at his villa near Lucerne, where he wrote much of *Die Meistersinger*.

WAGNER, väg′nər, **Richard** (1813–1883), the most important German composer of opera in the second half of the 19th century. He was often compared with his equally important Italian contemporary, Giuseppe Verdi. Each created a musical language that seemed to contemporaries a manifestation of deep national instincts, and each placed his new idiom in the service of dramas with a political mission.

Wagner's works assumed a particular character in that the texts he set to music, unlike Verdi's, were completely his own creation and, moreover, often embodied a pernicious jingoism and racism. Wagner looked upon his operas as projections into art of what he wished to accomplish as a social reformer; he strove for recognition, above all, as a political philosopher poetically expounding Germany's destiny. If the obscurity of his literary style and of his mind has made nonsense of this claim, posterity has nonetheless celebrated the extraordinary beauty of the music with which he enveloped his words. His place is not, as he wished, in the pantheon of great thinkers but, rather, among the great composers.

Early Years. Wilhelm Richard Wagner was born in Leipzig in the kingdom of Saxony, on May 22, 1813. His mother, Johanna, was the wife of Carl (Karl) Friedrich Wagner, a Leipzig police official. There has been some dispute about Wagner's paternity, and it has been claimed that Wagner was the natural son of Ludwig Geyer, an itinerant actor who, from time to time, lodged in the Wagner home. Carl Friedrich died half a year after the birth of the child, and Geyer and Johanna soon married and set up a household in Dresden, the Saxon capital.

Although Richard had been baptized as Carl Friedrich's son, his parents enrolled him in the Dresden Kreuz School as Richard Geyer (1822). His academic interests were literary for the most part, and he tried his hand at poetic drama. In 1827 he returned to Leipzig. Geyer had died, and it seemed politic for the boy to reclaim his legal name and connections with the Wagner family. In 1828 he entered Leipzig's St. Nicholas School but neglected his studies to attend plays, operas, and concerts. A performance of Goethe's drama *Egmont* with Beethoven's incidental music determined his future: he decided to write poetic texts and clothe them with his own music. At 16 years of age and with no background in music beyond fingering favorite pieces at the keyboard, he determined to learn to compose. No other major composer made so late a start.

He threw aside attempts at traditional education and sought help from private music tutors. His studies with the contrapuntalist Christian Theodor Weinlig proved especially profitable. Yet, like Verdi, Wagner learned most by reading scores and listening to performances. His student work included piano sonatas, a piano fantasia, concert overtures, incidental vocal music to Goethe's *Faust*, and an ambitious symphony. These works freely mixed elements from Bach, Mozart, Beethoven, Pleyel, Bellini, and Rossini.

A more familiar Wagner appeared in his first attempt at opera, *Die Hochzeit* ("The Wedding," 1832). Inspired by his first disappointment in love, the text already treated the classic Wagnerian situation of a guilty relationship in conflict with the social order. Despite original touches, the surviving fragment of the score reveals a young composer in search of a style. He arrived at one in his first completed opera, *Die Feen* ("The Fairies," 1834), by again creating a composite. He artfully adapted bits and pieces from the leading German Romantic composers: Mendelssohn, Weber, and Marschner. The text of *Die Feen*, based upon a tale by Gozzi, is also an inventive, if bizarre, pastiche: it parades a variety of literary motives that would reemerge in later Wagnerian operas, the most significant being a weak male's redemption through the devotion of a strong woman.

Die Feen came into being in Bavaria, where Wagner had fled in 1833 to escape service in the Saxon army. He became chorus director and coach at the Würzburg theater and began to build what would become a formidable baton technique. When *Die Feen* failed to achieve production, the practical young composer turned his back on its German style to follow the banner of the more popular Italian opera. Bellini was his inspiration as he wrote *Das Liebesverbot* ("The Ban on Love," 1835). Its libretto, derived from Shakespeare's *Measure for Measure*, is technically accomplished; the boisterous superficial score, however, is a hodgepodge of materials not adapted but shamelessly purloined from a variety of composers. The opera died on the stage of the Magdeburg theater, whose music director Wagner had become in 1834. Consolation came from Minna Planer, the leading lady of the theater's acting company and by now his mistress.

He continued to gain experience as conductor in provincial theaters: in Königsberg, where he married Minna in November 1836, and then in Riga. Here he again opportunistically changed artistic direction. Finished with his Italian flirtation, he embraced grand opera. A sumptuously staged historical pageant accompanied by music, this pompous genre had recently been brought into being by Spontini and Meyerbeer. With them as models, Wagner began composition of his mammoth *Rienzi,* with Paris, the center of grand opera, clearly in his mind.

His creditors in pursuit and his passport forfeit, Wagner found himself forced to flee Riga after two seasons. By stealth he and Minna made their way to the Prussian coast, and set sail for England. In September 1839 they were in Paris. The city cruelly frustrated Wagner's hopes. The French showed little interest in him, even when, in desperation, he turned his hand to the salon song and vaudeville chorus. No theater was willing to discuss *Rienzi,* which he completed (November 1840) during a confinement of several weeks in a Parisian debtors' prison.

His misery made him increasingly prize things German: now German history, literature, and myth commanded his time. It was in France that Wagner first studied the legends of Tannhäuser and Lohengrin and began to occupy himself with both a symphonic work inspired by Goethe's *Faust* (later called the *Faust Overture*) and a new opera, *Der fliegende Holländer* ("The Flying Dutchman," 1841), which unfolded amid the mists and wild cliffs of the Teutonic north. Thoroughly disenchanted with Meyerbeer's grand opera aesthetic, he came to despise this enormously successful Jew. An obsessive—and soon to be pathological—anti-Semitism had begun to play its destructive role in the development of Wagner's character.

Irony doubly mocked the fitness of things when, thanks to Meyerbeer's generous recommendation, the Dresden opera house accepted *Rienzi* for production, Wagner's Parisian-style grand opera serving as his passport back to Germany. Within months of *Rienzi*'s enormously successful premiere (October 1842), Wagner became the theater's presiding conductor. The Dresden public, however, received his *Holländer* (1843) without enthusiasm. He was irked that Germans relished the Gallic glamor of *Rienzi* and had little patience with the German gravity of *Holländer.* Though he had gained recognition in Dresden as a conductor, he resented what he held to be his superficial success as an operatic composer.

His *Tannhäuser,* which had premiered in 1845, further underscored the dilemma. Audiences applauded those elements of grand opera the work preserved—brilliant vocal ensembles and refulgent pageantry. But they remained indifferent to its more serious sections—those darker and dramatically rich passages touched with German mysticism, in which the singers expressed complex emotions not in the traditional aria but in a new kind of impassioned, often overwrought musical recitation. *Lohengrin,* completed in Dresden during 1848, continued to explore these tendencies, exploiting them more consistently. Wagner saw his immediate artistic direction clearly: his new musical style, purified of any residue of grand opera, was to expound German myth and saga. Before the end of the year he had put to paper a scenario called *The Nibelung Myth as Scheme for a Drama.*

With debts again engulfing him, he once more fled a city, creditors and police in pursuit (May 1849). This time, if apprehended, he faced a possible death sentence for treason, for during several days of civil war in Dresden he had been at the center of revolutionary activity. It was providential that he was able to escape to Zürich.

Middle Years. His Swiss exile brought forth four ambitious essays: *Art and Revolution, The Art Work of the Future* (both of 1849), *Jewry in Music* (1850), and *Opera and Drama* (1851). The first two celebrated the socialist revolution as the political setting that would nourish the coming Wagnerian drama. It would bring together the arts of poetry, music, drama, and design (the so-called *Gesamtkunstwerk,* or all-embracing work of art) as they once had been brought together in Athens. The third essay excoriated the Jews as a materialistic element alien to the German Folk and to its need for the Wagnerian national drama. The fourth described the techniques this drama could call into play to achieve a new and closer union between word and tone. The orchestra was to assume an expanded role, the instruments commenting on the action. Moreover, a system of reiterated musical phrases associated with particular situations, characters, or emotions would both explicate the poem and unify the whole, a device that would become associated with the term *Leitmotif* (leading motif).

In Switzerland, Wagner's Nibelung drama grew to gigantic proportions. By the close of 1852 he had finished assembling his material from Teutonic saga and legend into four poetic dramas. He called the cycle *Der Ring des Nibelungen* ("The Ring of the Nibelung"), the individual units eventually taking the titles of *Das Rheingold* ("The Rhinegold"), *Die Walküre* ("The Valkyrie"), *Siegfried,* and *Götterdämmerung* ("The Twilight of the Gods"). The last title suggests the change that had overtaken his perception of a work conceived in Dresden as an allegory of triumphant revolution. Reading Schopenhauer had reinforced a growing pessimism and resignation, and, despite adjustments and revisions in his text, he was at a loss to find a coherent and satisfactory ending for it.

In 1853 the musical drought that had afflicted him since the completion of *Lohengrin* ended, and he proceeded to compose the *Ring* up to the point (the final act of *Siegfried*) at which the ebullient hero breaks through the magic fire and claims his bride. Here Wagner put down his pen. Too much had changed. Not only had the socialist revolution foundered, but so had his marriage. He turned from the deeds of joyous Siegfried to take up the tale of rueful Tristan and produced an uncompromisingly serious work, *Tristan and Isolde,* whose iridescent music exudes an extraordinary melancholy passion.

Not even with the completion of Tristan (1859) was he ready to return to the *Ring.* His socialist fever had completely subsided, and he now wished to exalt not blazing revolution but, rather, the staid values of Germany's past. He no longer identified himself with either Siegfried seeking victory or Tristan seeking death, but instead with the poet-musician Hans Sachs, a wise and settled man seeking accommodation. This figure, taken from the chronicles of Renaissance Germany, became the pivot of a new opera that Wagner had begun to plan—*Die Meistersinger von Nürnberg* ("The Master Singers of Nuremberg"). Its text came into being in France.

Soon after writing the final notes of *Tristan,* Wagner had taken up residence in Paris to prepare a revised and expanded version of *Tann-*

häuser for the Opéra. Despite the production's failure (1861), he came under the spell of the great theater, and it is both ironic and fitting that the eminently Germanic libretto of *Meistersinger* (1862) took the form of a grand opera in the tradition of the Opéra and Meyerbeer. Wagner had executed not only a political but, once again, an aesthetic turnabout. The music, which he began to put to paper even before the libretto was finished, shunned the sinuous chromatic idiom of *Tristan* and anchored *Meistersinger* in a sober, diatonic tonal vocabulary. He would complete the opera years later under extraordinary patronage.

Late Years. Amnestied and thus able to reenter Germany, he accepted the summons of young King Louis (Ludwig) II of Bavaria (1864) to settle in Munich, there to complete the *Ring* under royal patronage. But how to finish this product of the revolutionary spirit increasingly perplexed the strict authoritarian and monarchist that Wagner had become. For the most part, the unfinished *Ring* remained locked in his desk, and he filled his days in Munich by writing political articles and preparing model productions of his works, among them the premiere of *Tristan* (1865). However, he went too far in his political meddling and before the end of the year found himself expelled from Munich and again in exile in Switzerland.

King Louis continued to support Wagner, who settled in Triebschen (near Lucerne) and resumed the composition of *Meistersinger*. In Munich, hostility toward him soon cooled, and he returned for visits, which were climaxed by the triumphant premiere of *Meistersinger* (1868). At this time he openly took as his mistress Cosima von Bülow, wife of his chief disciple, the conductor Hans von Bülow, and daughter of Franz Liszt. The resulting scandal again closed Munich's gates to Wagner. Ever pragmatic, he loosened his ties with Louis of Bavaria and sought patronage from the Prussian royal house of Hohenzollern in Berlin. Wagner now wanted to complete and mount the *Ring* as a celebration of Prussia's political ascendancy. With confidence that Berlin would provide subsidies for such a festival, he started to build his ideal theater in the Franconian town of Bayreuth. When Berlin proved uninterested, he turned again to King Louis, whose treasury paid the costs of the Bayreuth theater (Festspielhaus) and Wagner's palatial home (Haus Wahnfried).

In 1869, Wagner again took up composition of the *Ring*, the exuberant closing duet of *Siegfried* reflecting his joy with Cosima. Minna had died in 1866. Cosima finally succeeded in dissolving her marriage in 1870, and the lovers legalized their union that same year. Work on the score of *The Twilight of the Gods* (the conclusion to which Wagner tinkered to the end) and the preparations for the first Bayreuth Festival occupied their household. The last note of the *Ring* was written in 1874, and the festival took place two years later. It consisted of the *Ring*'s first three complete performances, *Rhinegold* and *Valkyrie* having already received their premieres in Munich at King Louis' command in 1869 and 1870, respectively.

Wagner was less than satisfied with the festival and wished to approach the *Ring* differently the next time. But for him there was to be no next time, for he devoted the second—and for him the last—Bayreuth Festival (1882) to the unveiling of *Parsifal*. He had completed its text in 1877, thereafter laboring at its score in Bayreuth and on travels that took him as far as Palermo, where he finished the work early in 1882. If a series of violently anti-Semitic tracts written during these closing years of his life reveal the accelerating poisoning of his mind, the subtle music of *Parsifal* with its superb tone-painting betrays nothing of decline. After its premiere performance he returned to Italy in search of a cure for his failing health. In Venice on Feb. 13, 1883, he succumbed to a stroke. He is buried in Bayreuth.

Wagner's Achievement. In addition to the scores of Weber, Marschner, Mendelssohn, and Spontini, those of Liszt and Berlioz contributed to Wagner's musical vocabulary. He bent this magpie heritage to his will, his musical language quickly developing its own personality. However, his unique contribution was not in the area of melody, harmony, or tone color, his brilliance in these areas notwithstanding, but rather in his dissolution of the independence of traditional opera "numbers"—aria and ensemble—by blurring their contours and thus making entire acts of his mature works into single spans of uninterrupted music. He enhanced the role of the orchestra to a commanding position so that it might provide the medium that could bind these large units together musically and, at the same time, give them dramatic coherence.

Converting the venerable reminiscence theme into his flexible leitmotif, he formed his orchestral tissue in the tradition of classical variation technique by joining, interweaving, superimposing, and transforming these motifs. Their literary associations, moreover, formed a subtext explicating the speech-song of the singers on stage. Thus the orchestra, in the spirit of the chorus of ancient Greek drama, comments on the action, following and revealing the state of the characters' minds and souls.

Wagner's attempt to create a new species of musicodramatic art by following the formulas codified in his Swiss essays proved abortive. Only *Rhinegold, Valkyrie,* and the first two acts of *Siegfried* reflect these precepts consistently. But, though he returned to the aesthetic of grand opera—an apostasy he refused to admit—he used its monumental plan and stagecraft to epoch-making effect. At its best the Wagnerian music drama (he did not want the term opera applied to his works) achieved a fusion of text and music no less complete than in the finest operatic pages of Gluck, Mozart, Beethoven, Berlioz, and Verdi.

ROBERT W. GUTMAN, *Author of "Richard Wagner: The Man, His Mind, and His Music"*

Bibliography

Donington, Robert, *Wagner's Ring and Its Symbols* (1963; reprint, Faber 1969).

Gutman, Robert W., *Richard Wagner: The Man, His Mind, and His Music* (Harcourt 1968).

Mann, Thomas, *Thomas Mann Pro and Contra Wagner,* tr. by Allan Blunden (Univ. of Chicago Press 1986).

Millington, Barry, *Wagner* (Biblio. Dist. 1984).

Newman, Ernest, *The Life of Richard Wagner,* 4 vols. (1933–1946; reprint, Cambridge 1976).

Newman, E., *The Wagner Operas,* 2 vols. (Harper 1983).

Shaw, George Bernard, *The Perfect Wagnerite* (1911; reprint, Dover 1966).

Stein, Jack M., *Richard Wagner and the Synthesis of the Arts* (1960; reprint, Greenwood 1973).

Wagner, Richard, *Richard Wagner's Prose Works,* tr. by William Ellis and William Ashton (1892–1899; reprint, Scholarly Books 1972).

Watson, D., *Richard Wagner: A Biography* (McGraw 1983).

THE BETTMANN ARCHIVE

Robert F. Wagner served in the U.S. Senate.

WAGNER, wag′nər, **Robert Ferdinand** (1877–1953), American politician, who was the sponsor of key social legislation during the Franklin Roosevelt administration. Sometimes called the "legislative pilot of the New Deal," Wagner could claim as his greatest achievement the National Labor Relations Act (the "Wagner Act").

Wagner was born in Nastätten, Germany, on June 8, 1877, and moved with his family to New York when he was eight years old. He grew up in a slum area in upper Manhattan. He worked his way through City College in New York, graduating in 1898. Two years later he received a law degree from New York Law School.

Wagner began his long career in politics in 1904, when he was elected to the New York State Assembly. He served in the state legislature from 1905 to 1918, and was a justice of the New York supreme court from 1919 to 1926.

In 1926 he was elected to the U.S. Senate, where he served for more than two decades. In the late 1920's, Wagner worked tirelessly but in vain to obtain passage of legislation to control unemployment. Then, in 1932, when the Great Depression was at its worst, Congress passed the Relief and Construction Act, the first legislation that gave the federal government the responsibility for preserving a desirable level of national employment.

Wagner helped draft and pass through the Senate several other important bills that committed the federal government to aid the national economy. One of the most important of these was the National Industrial Recovery Act (1933), designed to improve labor standards and to prevent unfair competitive practices. Others included the National Labor Relations Act (1935) and the bills that set up the Civilian Conservation Corps and the farm-mortgage refinancing plan. Wagner also sponsored housing legislation and an unemployment insurance bill that later became a cornerstone of the Social Security Act (1936). He was chairman of the Senate banking and currency committee. Wagner resigned from the Senate in 1949. He died in New York City on May 4, 1953.

WAGNER, wag′nər, **Robert Ferdinand, Jr.** (1910–), American politician, who served as mayor of New York City from 1954 to 1965. He was born in that city on April 20, 1910. As a boy, he traveled with his father, U.S. Sen. Robert F. Wagner, on campaign tours. After graduating from Yale College and Yale Law School, he served in the New York State Assembly from 1937 to 1941. He resigned to volunteer for service with the Army Air Force in World War II, advancing to lieutenant colonel.

After 1945, Wagner held appointive posts in the New York City government, including those of commissioner of housing and buildings and chairman of the city planning commission. He was elected borough president of Manhattan in 1949. He was defeated for the Democratic nomination for U.S. senator in 1952, but won election as mayor of New York the following year.

In his 12 years as mayor, Wagner initiated significant reforms in education and housing, and gained a reputation as an able mediator of labor disputes. He established the office of city administrator, and in 1962 prevailed on a Republican-controlled state legislature to approve a new city charter giving unprecedented powers to the mayor. Deciding not to seek reelection in 1965, Wagner went into private law practice. He was U.S. ambassador to Spain in 1968–1969 and envoy to the Vatican in 1978–1980.

WAGNER ACT. See NATIONAL LABOR RELATIONS ACT.

WAGON TRAINS, caravans of covered wagons that served as the principal means for the settlement and supply of the far-western United States before the coming of the railroads. The vast Great Plains area, with its level treeless prairies and its lack of navigable streams, was well suited to the covered wagons.

Although they had been used to haul freight between the Eastern seaboard and the Ohio Valley after the War of 1812, wagon trains were first used extensively in the 1820's on the Santa Fe trail. Long trains of covered wagons drawn by oxen or mules carried manufactured goods from Missouri to be exchanged for fur, gold, and silver in Santa Fe. The independent traders who pooled their resources to form these trains usually elected a captain and four lieutenants, who commanded the parallel columns in which the wagons moved in hostile Indian country. These officers enforced the rules, selected the route, and designated stopping places for "nooning" and night. One or more caravans made the journey each year from 1824 until the outbreak of the Mexican War in 1846.

William Lewis Sublette, a fur trader, used wagons to carry goods to the annual traders' rendezvous in 1830, when he successfully crossed the Rocky Mountains via South Pass. In 1841 a party of 69 persons under John Bidwell and John Bartleson opened the trails to California and the Oregon country, although they were forced to abandon their wagons on the way. Each year thereafter long trains of wagons pulled out of Independence, Mo., bound for the Sacramento Valley in California or the Willamette Valley in Oregon. This migration reached its peak in 1849 and 1850 during the California gold rush. See FORTY-NINERS, THE; OREGON TRAIL.

At first, isolated settlements were supplied with Eastern goods by small merchants, operating

Wagon trains played an important role in the settlement of the American West. Pulled by oxen, mule, or horse teams, the wagon caravans carried settlers and essential goods westward over the Santa Fe, Oregon, and other trails. They declined in importance in the late 19th century with the coming of the railroads.

THE BETTMANN ARCHIVE

one or more trains, but by 1859 the firm of Russell, Majors & Waddell dominated the business. With dozens of trains, each containing 26 wagons pulled by 12 oxen and commanded by a wagon master and assistant wagon master, the company virtually monopolized western freighting until the Civil War. Smaller concerns continued to use wagon trains after Russell, Majors & Waddell became a victim of overexpansion. Even after the coming of the railroads in the 1870's, wagon trains were employed to reach isolated camps and settlements.

RAY ALLEN BILLINGTON
Northwestern University

Bibliography

Billington, Ray Allen, *Westward to the Pacific: An Overview of America's Westward Expansion* (Univ. of Wash. Press 1979).

Connor, Seymour V., and Skaggs, Jimmy M., *Broadcloth and Britches: The Santa Fe Trade* (Texas A & M Univ. Press 1977).

Federal Writers Project, *Oregon Trail: The Missouri River to the Pacific Coast* (1939; reprint, Somerset Pub. 1971).

Schlissel, Lillian, *Women's Diaries of the Westward Movement* (Schocken 1982).

Sunder, John E., *Bill Sublette, Mountain Man* (1959; reprint, Univ. of Okla. Press 1982).

WAGTAIL, any of the 10 species of the genus *Motacilla,* the type genus of the Motacillidae family of songbirds, which also includes the pipits. Wagtails are natives of Europe, Asia, and Africa. The more northern species migrate in winter to such tropical areas as the Philippines, where they are common at that season. One species, the yellow wagtail, *M. flava,* reaches North America, but only as a local summer resident in Alaska. Like other wagtails, it is a slender, long-tailed bird, about 8 inches (20 cm) in length. It runs about on the ground in open muddy or rocky areas, often on the shore. Wagtails incessantly wag the tail up and down, hence their name. They feed on insects, some being partial to butterflies that have congregated on mud. They snip the wings from these insects before eating them. The pied or white wagtail, *M. alba,* and other species are conspicuous in Britain and elsewhere in Europe.

DEAN AMADON
The American Museum of Natural History

WAHHABISM, wä-hä'bizm, a puritan Muslim reform movement, founded about 1744 by Muhammad Ibn Abd al-Wahhab (1703–1792), a native of Nejd, who traveled to Hejaz and elsewhere for religious study. Convinced that innovations and immorality had corrupted Islam, he dedicated himself to restoring its purity. His movement, which became known as Wahhabism, emphasized the transcendental in Islam and opposed saint worship and veneration of tombs. After returning to Nejd, Muhammad allied himself with a local ruler, Muhammad Ibn Saud. Wahhabism thus sparked Saudi political expansion—resulting eventually in the creation of modern Saudi Arabia. See also under SAUDI ARABIA—*History and Government.*

R. BAYLY WINDER, *New York University*

WAHOO, wä-hōō', a name of American Indian origin most commonly applied to a shrub (*Euonymus atropurpureus*), also known as burning bush. See BURNING BUSH.

WAHOO, wä-hōō', a large and highly prized game fish (*Acanthocybium solandri*) closely related to the Spanish mackerel. Wahoos are widely distributed in warm waters of the Atlantic, Pacific, and Indian oceans. Off North American shores they range as far north as Maryland and Lower California. They are found in open water near the surface or around reefs, traveling alone or in small groups. They eat other fish.

The wahoo is dark greenish above and silvery below, often showing lighter bands on the body—particularly when fighting an angler's hook. It has a long body with a long snout and large teeth. The fins are dark. Each fin is followed by small finlets, as in tunas, and the lateral line curves downward abruptly a little beyond the tip of the pectoral fin. Wahoos over 120 pounds (55 kg) in weight and nearly 5 feet (1.5 meters) in length have been caught, but the average size is 25–65 pounds (11–30 kg).

The wahoo is a member of the tuna group in the mackerel family (Scombridae). Its distinctive features include a caudal keel.

CHRISTOPHER W. COATES
*New York Zoological Society**

WAHPETON, wô'pə-tən, is a city, in North Dakota, and the seat of Richland County, located at an altitude of 969 feet on the Red River of the North, 46 miles south of Fargo. Cattle, grain, and dairy and poultry products from the surrounding area are marketed and processed in Wahpeton. Its industries include printing and binding and the manufacture of pottery, culverts, and sheet iron. There is an airport.

The city was settled in the 1860's and incorporated in 1883. Its name was changed from Chahinkapa to Wahpeton in 1893. The North Dakota State School of Science, which has a junior college, a business school, and a trade school, is located there. There is also a U.S. Indian school, serving both Dakotas and Minnesota. The city has a conservatory of music and a municipal band. Chahinkapa Park provides recreational facilities. Government is by mayor and council. Population: 9,064.

WAIANAE, wī-ä-nī', village, Hawaii, in Honolulu County, near the western end of the island of Oahu, about 31 miles from the business center of the city of Honolulu. Originally and for many years, Waianae was a plantation village —the center of the now abandoned Waianae Sugar Company. It is located on the seashore at Pokai Bay and is in an area of low rainfall resulting in a hot and dry climate. Much of the land formerly cultivated in irrigated sugarcane is now occupied by small farms producing fruits and vegetables. There are also a number of dairymen, poultrymen, and several small cattle ranches in the surrounding area. The world-famous Makaha beach for surfing is nearby and Pokai Bay includes protected anchorage for small boats of all kinds. Population: 7,941.

H. H. WARNER.

WAIKATO RIVER, wī'kä-tō, river, New Zealand, in the northwest part of North Island, flowing first into Lake Taupo and then out of it north to the Tasman Sea 25 miles south of Manukau Harbor on the west coast. The longest river in New Zealand, it has a total course of 220 miles, of which only 80 miles are navigable. There are hydroelectric installations at Arapuni and Horahora.

WAIKIKI, wī-kĭ-kē', or **WAIKIKI BEACH,** resort, Hawaii, a part of the metropolitan district of the city and county of Honolulu. It is about 4 miles from the downtown business center of the city in the opposite direction from Pearl Harbor. Extending some 2½ miles along the oceanfront, its inland boundary is the Ala Wai Canal about ½ mile back from the beach. Waikiki is the tourist center of the state with many hotels and apartment houses for the accommodation of visitors. The beach is protected by a submerged coral reef about one half mile offshore where the waves break for the famous sport of surfing on boards and in outrigger canoes. Kapiolani Park (155 acres) affords other types of recreation and includes a covered stage for outdoor concerts, a driving range, zoo, and tennis courts. The tourist industry centering in Waikiki is the fastest growing segment of the state's economy.

H. H. WARNER.

WAILING WALL, wāl'ĭng wôl, a section of the 59-foot-high west wall of the present-day Muslim el-Haram-esh-Sharif (the "Noble Sanctuary" containing the Dome of the Rock, q.v., built in 691 A.D.), on the east side of Jerusalem. It is believed to be a part of the original wall surrounding the Temple of Solomon, but it was probably rebuilt by Herod. Since the Middle Ages, Jews have been accustomed to gather below this wall, especially on Fridays, and bewail the fall of the city and the destruction of the temple (in 597–586 B.C. and in 70 and 135 A.D.), and to pray for their restoration. As a symbol of Judaism, both the choice of site and also the custom are subject to criticism, and many modern Jews, especially in the West, would prefer a more positive expression of their faith in Israel's survival and its prospects for social and religious power and security. Access to the Wailing Wall was barred to Jews by the Jordanians beginning in 1948, when Jerusalem was divided into the Old City, held by Jordan, and the New City, held by Israel.

FREDERICK C. GRANT.

WAILUKU, wī-lōō'kōō, village, Hawaii, on the island of Maui. It is the county seat of Maui County which includes the two smaller islands of Molokai and Lanai. In addition to these government offices, Wailuku is the headquarters of the Wailuku Sugar Company which employs many of its residents. It is also the site of one of the earliest primitive sugar mills built in 1825. Located about three miles inland from the seaport town of Kahalui, it has a newspaper and a radio-television station. It is an unincorporated community which is governed by the chairman of the county board of supervisors. Population: 10,260.

H. H. WARNER.

WAIMANALO, wī'mə-nä'lō, village, Hawaii, in Honolulu County, 14 miles from the business center of Honolulu. It is situated on the windward side of the island of Oahu and is considered a residential suburb reached by a cross-island highway tunnel through the mountains. It is also served by the 21-mile sea level highway around the east end of the island. Waimanalo was originally a typical plantation village for the Waimanalo Sugar Company, which ceased operating several years ago. Residents now include fruit and vegetable farmers, poultrymen, dairymen, a considerable number of Hawaiian homesteaders, as well as others who work in Honolulu. The area includes an attractive beach adjacent to Bellows Field, which was an Air Force installation during World War II. Pop. 3,562.

H. H. WARNER.

WAINEWRIGHT, wān'rīt, **Thomas Griffiths,** English art critic and criminal: b. Chiswick, England, October 1794; d. Hobart Town, Tasmania, 1852. He wrote art criticism for the *London Magazine* under the pseudonyms Egomet Bonmot and Janus Weathercock, and exhibited his pictures at the Royal Academy. A wit, dandy, and man of elegant tastes, he included among his friends Thomas De Quincey, William Hazlitt, and Charles Lamb. Although his uncle, mother-in-law, and sister-in-law and a friend in Boulogne all had died to his convenience or profit under circumstances suggesting poisoning, Wainewright was apprehended in 1837 for forging an order on the Bank of England 11 years before. He was banished for life to Van Diemen's Land (Tasmania), where he died of apoplexy. His life and his crimes provided the inspiration for a number of authors, and he is represented in Edward Bulwer-Lytton's novel *Lucretia,* Charles Dickens novelette *Hunted Down,* and Oscar Wilde's essay *Pen, Pencil, and Poison.*

WAINWRIGHT, wān′wrīt, **Jonathan Mayhew,** American army officer: b. Walla, Walla, Wash., Aug. 23, 1883; d. San Antonio, Texas, Sept. 2, 1953. He graduated from the United States Military Academy in 1906 and served in an expedition against the Moros in the Philippines in 1909–1910. During World War I he was with the 82d National Army Division in France and afterward with the Third Army in Germany. He returned to the United States and remained there, attending the Command and General Staff School (1928–1931) and the Army War College (1933–1934), until he was ordered to the Philippines in October 1940. In March 1942 he succeeded General Douglas MacArthur as Philippine commander. After a heroic resistance he was forced to surrender Corregidor and the survivors of the Philippine campaign to the Japanese on May 6, 1942. (See WORLD WAR II —9. *War in the Southern and Southwestern Pacific.*) General Wainwright was released from a Manchurian prison camp in August 1945 and participated in the Japanese surrender ceremonies in September which took place aboard the U.S. battleship *Missouri.* When he returned to the United States in the same month he was recognized with the prestigious Congressional Medal of Honor, promoted to the rank of general, and appointed to head the Eastern Defense Command. He was commander of the Fourth Army from 1946 until his retirement in 1947, after which he was engaged in business.

WAINWRIGHT, Richard, American naval officer: b. Washington, D.C., Dec. 17, 1849; d. there, March 6, 1926. A graduate of the United States Naval Academy (1868), he was executive officer of the battleship *Maine* when she was destroyed in Havana Harbor in 1898. During the Spanish-American War he commanded the *Gloucester,* a poorly armed vessel that had been J. P. Morgan's yacht, and vanquished the Spanish destroyers *Furor* and *Pluton* at Santiago de Cuba on July 3, 1898. For this action he was cited by Congress. Wainwright was superintendent of the Naval Academy from 1900 to 1902, commander of the *Newark* from 1902 to 1904, and commander of the *Louisiana* from 1907 to 1908. From 1908 to 1910 he was in command of divisions of the Atlantic fleet. He retired with the rank of rear admiral in 1911. He edited with Robert M. Thompson *The Confidential Correspondence of Gustavus Vasa Fox* (1918–19), Civil War assistant navy secretary.

WAINWRIGHT, town, Alberta, Canada, about 125 miles southeast of Edmonton on the Canadian National Railway. Wheat growing and cattle raising are the important agricultural activities in the surrounding district. There is an oil refinery just west of the town which produces gasoline, various fuel oils, and asphalt. There are over 200 producing wells as well as a number of gas wells in the area. Adjacent to the town is a military camp administered by the federal Department of National Defense. Population: 4,266.

ERIC V. HANSON.

WAIPAHU, wī-pä′hōō, village, Hawaii, in Honolulu County, located on the island of Oahu, about 14 miles west of the center of the city of Honolulu. It is situated on the leeward side of the island and is adjacent to one arm of Pearl Harbor. It is an unincorporated community and a part of the city and county of Honolulu which includes the whole island of Oahu. Waipahu was originally a plantation village centering about the Oahu Sugar Company mill but in recent years has grown rapidly as a suburban residential area for workers at Pearl Harbor and nearby industrial plants. Subdivisions have been developed on surrounding land which was formerly planted to sugarcane and it is now a bustling community of diverse interests. The Hawaiian name Wai-Pahu meaning "gushing water" refers to the many large springs in that area which in earlier days were developed as artesian wells. Pop. 29,139.

H. H. WARNER.

WAITE, wāt, **Morrison Remick,** American lawyer and chief justice of the United States: b. Lyme, Conn., Nov. 29, 1816; d. Washington, D.C., March 23, 1888. He was a son of Henry Matson Waite, a chief justice of Connecticut. After graduating from Yale College in 1837, he moved to Maumee (City), Ohio, in 1838, and was admitted to the Ohio bar the next year. Settling in Toledo in 1850, he had great success as a lawyer specializing in corporate finance and real property—matters of particular importance to his railroad clients. His professional attainments, though, were not patently matched by his success in politics, for he was twice defeated for Congress (1846 and 1862), although he did serve a single term in the Ohio legislature (elected 1849). Nevertheless, his poor showing at the polls did not prevent him from playing a prominent behind-the-scenes political role, especially as a leader of the Union cause in Ohio. His efforts in this regard were of sufficient importance to secure for him in 1863 the tender of an appointment to the Ohio Supreme Court—an offer which he rejected, preferring to serve as unofficial counselor to the governor.

In 1871, President Grant named Waite as an American counsel, along with his Yale classmate, William M. Evarts, and Caleb Cushing (qq.v.), in the *Alabama* claims (q.v.) proceedings at Geneva. On his return to the United States, Waite served as president of the Ohio constitutional convention in 1873–1874. In the latter year, after President Grant was unable to secure Senate approval of either George H. Williams (q.v.), his attorney general, or Caleb Cushing to succeed Salmon P. Chase as chief justice of the United States, he nominated Waite (January 19), who was accepted by the Senate without enthusiasm, but without objection.

Waite's major contribution as chief justice was the preservation of legislative power, as against judicial power. He wrote the court's opinion in *Munn* v. *Illinois,* 94 U.S. 113 (1877), which sustained the power of a state to fix rates charged by businesses that are "clothed with a public interest." Major restraints on state power deriving from the Constitution's contract clause (Art. I, Sec. 10, par. 1) were eliminated by him in such cases as *Spring Valley Water Works* v. *Schottler,* 110 U.S. 347 (1884), and *Stone* v. *Mississippi,* 101 U.S. 814 (1880). He also wrote opinions rigorously effecting the 11th Amendment's protection of states against suit without their consent (*Louisiana* v. *Jumel,* 107 U.S. 711 [1882], and *Antoni* v. *Greenhow,* 107 U.S. 769 [1883]), and he contributed to the expansion of congressional power over interstate commerce (*Pensacola Telegraph Co.* v. *Western Union Telegraph Co.,* 96 U.S. 1 [1878]). Where state and federal interests conflicted, he reluctantly protected the latter, extending the negative implications of the Constitution's commerce clause (Art. I, Sec. 8, par. 3), in *Hall* v. *De Cuir,* 95 U.S. 485 (1878). His most important opinion in the area of civil liberties sustained the power of the United States to make bigamy a crime, even in reference to Mormons, who asserted a right against such inhibition on the grounds of religious freedom (*Reynolds* v. *United States,* 98 U.S. 145 [1879]).

Unlike his predecessor, Waite refused to use the dignity and prestige of his office for political purposes, specifically, making himself unavailable for the Republican presidential nomination in 1876. Although he possessed great legal talent, Waite was probably the most colorless figure ever to occupy the position of chief justice, and his important contributions to constitutional jurisprudence are overshadowed by the drabness of his opinions and personality.

See also SUPREME COURT OF THE UNITED STATES—*Political History of the Court* (From the Civil War to the New Deal).

PHILIP B. KURLAND,
Professor of Law, University of Chicago.

WAITOMO CAVES, wī-tō′mō, a series of limestone caves on North Island, New Zealand, near Te Kuiti, comprising the Waitomo, Ruakuri, and Aranaui caves. They were first explored in 1887 and subsequently developed as a major tourist attraction. Floodlighting at strategic points has enhanced the natural beauty of the formations, which have been given names like "the organ-loft" and "the cathedral." Underground limestone formations occur elsewhere. What makes the Waitomo Caves unique is the remarkable Glowworm Grotto. A high vaulted dome over an underground river is lit only by pinpoints of insect light. The visitor's boat is pulled silently along an unseen wire and the most hardened traveler is moved by the beauty of the underworld scene. The "glowworms" are not the fireflies or glowworms of other areas, but the larvae of the *Boletophela luminosa,* which spin a sticky web from the roof and attract by their light the midges abounding in the underground stream.

IAN A. GORDON.

WAITS, wātz′, the king's minstrels, who in England and other countries used formerly to guard the streets at night and proclaim the hour. The name was afterward applied to the town's musicians, who, however, did not perform the duties of watchmen, and to private bands, when employed as serenaders.

In modern times the waits are musicians who play during the night hours on the approach of the Christmas or New Year seasons. Traditionally, they call at the houses of the inhabitants for donations.

WAITZ, vīts, **Georg,** German historian: b. Flensburg, Germany, Oct. 9, 1813; d. Berlin, May 24, 1886. This foremost German medieval historian of the 19th century intended to study law, but at the University of Berlin he came under the influence of Leopold von Ranke and transferred to history. While Ranke was concerned mainly with the modern period and diplomatic history, Waitz' interests focused on the institutional developments of the Middle Ages. Waitz' first work, a constitutional history of Germany, is comparable in its significance to William Stubbs' studies in English history. In 1842 Waitz became professor at Kiel, where he worked on the history of the Hanseatic League. At Kiel he took an active part in local political struggles, fighting to prevent the incorporation of Schleswig-Holstein with Denmark; in 1848, representing Holstein in the Frankfurt Parliament, he played a leading role in drafting the abortive liberal German constitution of this assembly. Forced out of Kiel because of his politics, Waitz became professor at Göttingen, which he made a center for German medieval studies. In 1875 Waitz became director of the Monumenta Germaniae Historica in Berlin. For many years he had collaborated in this great enterprise of collecting medieval documents, and he devoted the remainder of his life to its reorganization and modernization. Waitz' development, from wide intellectual interests and active political commitments to concentration on highly specialized and technical scholarly problems, is typical of the careers of many 19th century German scholars.

FELIX GILBERT,
Professor of History, Bryn Mawr College.

WAITZ, Theodor, German philosopher and anthropologist: b. Gotha, Germany, March 17, 1821; d. Marburg, May 21, 1864. After studying at Leipzig and Jena, he became lecturer in 1844 and professor of philosophy in 1848 at Marburg. His philosophical works largely derive from those of Johann Friedrich Herbart.

Waitz is best known as one of the first to envision the scope of the science of anthropology. In his *Anthropologie der Naturvölker* he analyzed anthropology as the study of the relation between man's physical and mental composition and his social development or history. He critically examined the existing descriptive material about the peoples of the world and was an early proponent of the view that the differences in degree of civilization of various races are due to differences of opportunity rather than native capacity.

WAIVER, wā′vər, in law, the surrender of a known right or an excuse for nonperformance. The term "waiver" is used with different meanings and must therefore be related to particular situations. An agreement for consideration made in substitution for a previous obligation or a choice of one right which causes the loss of others is sometimes called a waiver. More often waiver refers to a promise or permission excusing some condition of a duty to render performance or an obligation due presently or in the future or relinquishing a legal defense. Action in reliance often supports the promise. Generally, a waiver must be intentional or voluntary, and a knowledge of the facts necessary to effectuate a waiver is required. Conduct evidencing an intention to waive may be sufficient to work a relinquishment of a right or advantage.

ALAN MATHESON.

WAKASHAN INDIANS, wä-kăsh′ən (from *waukash,* the Nootka word "good," which Capt. James

Cook mistook for the tribal name), a linguistic stock of North American Indians inhabiting an area centering in Vancouver Island, the neighboring mainland of British Columbia, and a small area on Cape Flattery, Washington. The stock is composed of two major divisions: the Kwakiutl Indians, which include the Bella Bella; and the Nootka Indians, which include the Makah.

FREDERICK J. DOCKSTADER

WAKATIPU LAKE, wä-kä-tē′pōō, lake, New Zealand, on the South Island, 54 miles in length and 112 square miles in area. It is picturesquely situated in Otago Province, in the midst of magnificent mountain scenery. Queenstown and Glenorchy, on the borders of the lake, are favorite tourist resorts.

WAKAYAMA, wä-kä-yä-mä, city, Japan, situated on the island of Honshu. The city is the capital of Wakayama Prefecture and is located at the head of Kino Valley in the central part of the west coast of Kii Peninsula where the Naruto Channel leads into the eastern end of the Inland Sea, 35 miles southwest of Osaka. Its small port is restricted largely to domestic trade. The principal industries are the manufacture of textiles (spinning, weaving, dyeing, and bleaching of cotton), lumber, and chemicals. Although regarded as an outlier of the Osaka industrial belt, the city functions principally as political, economic, cultural, and educational center for the prefecture. Historically, Wakayama was an important castle town and the headquarters of one of "The Three Houses" (*Go-sanke*) established by the first Tokugawa ruler, Ieyasu. "The Three Houses" were Kii, Mito, and Owari and were heads of the powerful and wealthy fiefs of those names, conferred by Ieyasu on his three youngest sons, from whose families the heir to the Shogunate was to be selected in case of failure of the direct line. The House of Kii was established in 1619 at Wakayama. Ieyasu's direct line came to an end with Ietsugu, the seventh Tokugawa shogun, and the next seven shoguns (1716 to 1867), from Yoshimune downward, were all members of the House of Kii. The present castle was rebuilt in 1959, as its predecessor had been destroyed during World War II. The former castle was one of the best-preserved feudal castles in Japan. Notable buildings in the city include the princely Kishu Palace and the beautiful Temple of Kimiidera, the latter believed to have been founded in 770 A.D. Wakayama became a city on April 1, 1881. Pop. (1960) 285,155.

WAKAYAMA PREFECTURE was formed principally from the former Kii Province and occupies the southwestern portion of Kii Peninsula in central Japan. The area is composed mainly of mountainous land; three quarters of the area is covered by forests. Consequently, one of the more important industries of the prefecture is lumbering, and many of the cities located at the mouths of rivers are centers of lumber markets and industry. Most of the agricultural areas are concentrated in the river valleys and along the narrow coastal plains. The main staple crops are rice, rye, wheat, and barley. Mandarin oranges are an important cash crop, especially in the Arita River district. Both high-sea and coastal fisheries are important industries, the ports for the former being concentrated along the southern Kii coast. Although manufacturing is not significant, after World War II a large petroleum refinery was built at Shimotsu in the central part of the west coast facing the Kii Channel. The prefecture has many resort centers; the Shirahama hot springs serve as a weekend resort center for the Osaka area. Pop. (1960) 1,002,191.

GEORGE H. KAKIUCHI
Assistant Professor of Geography, University of Washington

WAKE, wāk (Old English *wacu*, in *nihtwaco*, night watch), a vigil or watch, usually by night, kept primarily as a religious rite. Ethnologically, wakes are widely practiced and are to be found in tribal cultures throughout the world. Among the Pueblo Indians of the American Southwest, vigils are observed by the Hopi and Zuñi. The Hopi bride and her female attendants stay up all night making wafer bread the night before the marriage. At Zuñi, during Shalako night, everyone present in the dance house is expected to stay awake to help with a prayerful state of mind. Abstinence from sleep is encouraged by the belief that magical penalties will befall sleepers, such as loss of their properties to those who stay awake. A person sleeping during a Hopi ceremony is said to retard the growth of the crops. Some such idea of sympathetic magic probably runs through other Pueblo rules about staying awake on ritual occasions. Similarly, in Japanese villages, a night watch is kept by designated individuals at the end of the lunar year and prior to opening of the fishing season.

Wakes are frequently observed prior to the disposal of the dead and are motivated by respect for the dead and the fear of evil spirits. Sometimes a wake is kept prior to burial; in other cultures the body is buried temporarily, and a watch is kept prior to cremation. Christian custom up to the time of the Reformation in Europe encouraged wakes at the side of a corpse prior to burial, but the custom became obsolete thereafter in Protestant countries. It survived in Ireland, where it was often associated with drinking parties, which doubtless cheered the mourners. In contemporary times, the honor guard set to keep watch over a body lying in state is a secular version of the wake tradition.

Vigils (Lat. *vigiliae*) or devotional watches were observed in the medieval Christian church on the eves of feast days. Pentecost, Assumption, All Saints', and Christmas provided special occasions for vigils. The *vigiliae* were originall· the services celebrated during the night preceding the feast, but the abuses connected with these nocturnal vigils led to their discontinuation, and the vigil services were transferred to the day preceding the feast. The Roman Catholic midnight mass at Christmas and the Church of England services at Easter Eve are survivals of the earlier custom. New Year's Eve parties are secular vigils reminiscent of ancient rites.

DAVID BIDNEY
Department of Anthropology, Indiana University

WAKE FOREST UNIVERSITY, a coeducational institution in Winston-Salem, N.C., affiliated with the Baptist State Convention of North Carolina. It was chartered in 1833 as the Wake Forest Manual Labor Institute, opened to students in 1834, and rechartered as Wake Forest College in 1838. Its present name dates from 1967.

The greater part of its endowment was lost during the Civil War, but the college continued work and regained its financial prosperity. In

THE BETTMANN ARCHIVE

United States Navy airplanes attack Japanese-held Wake Island in February 1942.

1956 it was relocated on a new $20 million campus at Winston-Salem. The university offers undergraduate degrees through Wake Forest College and the Charles H. Babcock School of Business Administration. Professional degrees are offered in the School of Law and the Bowman Gray School of Medicine. M.A., M.S., and Ph.D. degrees in several fields are offered in the graduate school, the faculty of which comes from Wake Forest College and the Bowman Gray School of Medicine. The university's average enrollment exceeds 4,500, of whom about 3,000 are undergraduates.

WAKE ISLAND, a North Pacific possession of the United States, located at latitude 19°17′ N. and longitude 166°35′ E. and situated some 2,300 miles west of Honolulu and 1,989 miles southeast of Tokyo. Wake and its companion islands Peale and Wilkes, to the east and west of it, respectively, lie on the route from the United States and Hawaii to China and the Philippines. They enclose a lagoon about 4½ miles long, 2¼ miles wide, and 9 feet deep. The islets, of coral formation, have a land area of about 3 square miles.

Wake was first visited by Capt. William Wake in 1796 and was charted by Lieut. Charles Wilkes in 1841, during his South Seas exploration, when one islet was named for him and the other for Titian Ramsay Peale, the expedition's naturalist. Wake was formally claimed by the United States in 1900. For years it was chiefly a cable station. In 1934 it was made a United States naval reservation. Pan American Airways, using it for their China Clipper service, built a hotel and seaplane base there in 1935.

Wake was proclaimed a naval defense area on May 15, 1941. More than 1,000 civilian workers were completing an air and submarine base when a Japanese air squadron attacked a few hours after the bombing of Pearl Harbor on Dec. 7, 1941. On Dec. 11, Maj. James P. S. Devereux commanding 400 marines repulsed a Japanese naval task force, sinking a cruiser. A few obsolete planes defended the island against air attack until Dec. 23, when 1,100 Japanese troops were put ashore and the garrison surrendered. On Feb. 14, 1942, a flotilla commanded by Adm. William F. Halsey raided Wake Island, but no effort was made to recapture it until the Japanese surrendered on Sept. 4, 1945. After the war the United States Navy built an air facility on Wake Island and it was also used as a fueling stop for commercial airlines. During the Korean War President Harry S. Truman went to the island on Oct. 15, 1950, to confer with Gen. Douglas MacArthur.

WAKE-ROBIN, the first of John Burroughs' collections of essays, published in 1871. In its charm and character it may well stand as an example of all. It is mostly about birds and their ways, but it has also essays and passages that show his wider knowledge and love of nature and the outdoor life in general. Burroughs was a great naturalist; one would not exactly say a great scientist, for he rarely put into scientific form the observations and generalizations that science seems to demand. Yet he was a great naturalist, for his life was passed in observing nature and learning her secrets. *Wake-Robin* (the popular name of the nodding white trillium) is an invitation to do likewise. It was written mostly in Washington, where in the 1860's, Burroughs was a clerk in the Treasury Department, but it is made out of recollections of earlier days in the Catskill country where Burroughs was born. It has more in it of birds than of other things, but it is full of the flavor of outdoor life. "Look about you," he says, "and see the beautiful and wonderful things all around." In *Wake-Robin* we have an invitation to the fields and the woods, to the daily pleasures of bird and flower or fish and deer, of the naturalist or the camper. John Burroughs and Henry David Thoreau are the two chief masters in a form of literature in which the United States is preeminent, the literature of nature; and if one will read *Wake-Robin* (as well as *Walden*) one will known why. The book has not only the keen observation that detects every fact, but the humanity that enables one to state the fact so as to be interesting to those of lesser powers.

EDWARD EVERETT HALE.

WAKEFIELD, wāk'fēld, **Edward Gibbon,** English colonial statesman: b. London, England, March 20, 1796; d. Wellington, New Zealand, May 16, 1862. He was a member of the legation staff at Turin, Italy, from 1814 until the death of his wife in 1820, after which he lived in Paris. In 1826 a scandal resulted when he returned to England, deceitfully abducted a young heiress from school and married her. The unconsummated marriage was annulled by special act of Parliament, and Wakefield was sentenced to three years' imprisonment. In prison he studied criminal law, and his *Facts Relating to the Punishment of Death in the Metropolis* (1831) had a great influence in its reform. His primary interest, however, was colonial affairs. His views were first presented in *A Letter from Sydney* (1829) and were expanded in *England and America* (2 vols., 1833) and in *A View of the Art of Colonization* (1849). He advocated the control of emigration to meet the demands of the colonies and to maintain the numerical equality of the sexes; the abolition of free grants of all agricultural land except pastureland to alleviate the labor shortage; and the sale of new land at prices that would allow a laborer to purchase a holding in four or five years.

In 1830 the National Colonization Society was founded to carry out his ideas, and the government adopted his plan the next year for New South Wales. The South Australian Association was formed in 1834, and under its auspices the colony of South Australia was founded two years later on Wakefield's principles. In 1838 he accompanied the earl of Durham to Canada as the governor general's unofficial adviser, and he assisted in the drawing up of Durham's *Report on the Affairs of British North America.* (1839).

In 1837 Wakefield had helped to organize the New Zealand Association, which was amalgamated with the New Zealand Land Company in 1839 and sent a shipload of colonists in the *Tory* to New Zealand. The British government was thereby forced to assume sovereignty over the colony in 1840, and its annexation by France was forestalled. Wakefield was also a prime mover in the founding of an Anglican colony at Canterbury in 1849. In 1852 he went to New Zealand and became an adviser to Col. Robert H. Wynward, the acting governor. In 1854 his health broke down, and he lived in retirement in Wellington until his death.

His brother WILLIAM HAYWARD WAKEFIELD (1803–1848) was also a colonist. He served as an agent of the New Zealand Land Company and founded Wellington in 1840.

A second brother, ARTHUR WAKEFIELD (1799–1843), was also an agent of the New Zealand Land Company. He founded Nelson in 1841, but was killed in the Wairau Massacre.

A third brother, FELIX WAKEFIELD (1807–1875), was an engineer. He was one of the founders of Canterbury.

A son, EDWARD JERNINGHAM WAKEFIELD (1820–1879), lived in New Zealand from 1839 to 1844 and from 1852 until his death. He was the author of *Adventures in New Zealand* (2 vols., 1845).

WAKEFIELD, city and county borough, England, situated in Yorkshire, in the West Riding (of which it is the county town) on the Calder River, nine miles south of Leeds. A woolen-manufacturing town since the 13th century, it now has a wide range of industries and is a market town for the surrounding agricultural and coal-producing area. In addition to good rail and road communications, it has access to the Humber River ports by way of the Calder.

The cathedral (the former parish church) is a 15th century building with a spire 247 feet high. Abutting on a 14th century bridge across the Calder is the chapel of St. Mary, founded in 1357. It is one of the few remaining medieval bridge chapels in England, but was drastically restored in 1847. In 1460 Wakefield was the scene of the battle in which Richard Plantagenet, 3d duke of York, was seized and beheaded. The Towneley or Wakefield miracle plays of the 15th and 16th centuries probably originated in the district.

Wakefield became a town as early as 1231. It was incorporated in 1848, became a city and the seat of a bishopric in 1888, and became a county borough in 1915. It forms part of the Wakefield parliamentary borough. Pop. (1959 est.) 59,860.

GORDON STOKES.

WAKEFIELD, town, Massachusetts, in Middlesex County, 10 miles north of Boston, at an altitude of 88 feet. The villages of Greenwood and Montrose lie within its borders, along with Crystal and Quannapowitt lakes. Settled as part of Reading in 1639, it became South Reading in 1812, adopting its present name in 1868 in honor of Cyrus Wakefield, a leading citizen, who established the first rattan factory in the world at Wakefield. Wakefield now produces leather products, electronics components, electrical machinery, chemicals, and a variety of minor manufactures. Cultural organizations include an art association and a historical association. The Lucius Beebe Memorial Library, and the ancient Hartshorne House, a restored colonial dwelling dating from 1663 with period furnishings, are attractions in the community. Wakefield has retained the town-meeting system of government. Population: 24,895.

WAKEFIELD, city, Michigan, in Gogebic County, at an altitude of 1,555 feet on the Northern Peninsula, 18 miles south of Lake Superior. Wakefield is in an iron-mining and agricultural area and has three sawmills. A summer resort, it also serves as a center for winter sports. It was first settled in 1866. Government is by council and manager. Population: 2,591.

WAKEFIELD, unincorporated village, Rhode Island, situated in Washington County, in the town of South Kingstown at an altitude of 40 feet, 27 miles south of Providence. The surrounding area has dairy, fruit, and poultry farms, and the village has cotton and woolen mills. Situated at the head of Point Judith Pond, an Atlantic Ocean inlet, Wakefield is a popular summer resort. Population, with adjacent Peacedale: 6,474.

WAKEFIELD, George Washington's birthplace, situated in Westmoreland County, Virginia, on the south bank of the Potomac River, about 30 miles east-southeast of Fredericksburg. The estate of Wakefield was purchased by Augustine Washington in 1718. The house in which George Washington was born was destroyed by fire in 1780. In 1923, the estate was acquired by the Wakefield National Memorial Association which conveyed the property to the United States in 1930 as the George Washington Birthplace National Monument. The monument covers 394 acres and includes the burial ground of the Washington family and a memorial building erected in 1931.

WAKKANAI, wäk-kä-nī, city, Japan, situated on Soya Bay at the northern tip of Hokkaido Island, 247 miles by rail north of Sapporo, the capital of Hokkaido. Wakkanai is separated from Sakhalin (USSR) by the Soya Straits. It is the northernmost city in Japan and the northern terminus of the Hokkaido rail system. The settlement was established at the end of the 18th century as a fishing village. Prior to the end of World War II, it flourished as the chief port connecting Hokkaido with Karafuto (South Sakhalin), which was then Japanese territory. It was also an important fishing port both for high-sea (mainly in the North Pacific area) as well as coastal fishing. It has lost its functions as a base for high-sea fisheries and ferry port and has reverted to a small fishing base for coastal fisheries. Within the administrative boundary of Wakkanai are found the Tempoku oilfield and a part of the Tempoku (or Soya) coalfield. Wakkanai became a city on April 1, 1949. Population: (1980) 54,493.

George H. Kakiuchi.

WAKSMAN, wăks′măn, **Selman Abraham,** American microbiologist: b. Priluki, Russia, July 22, 1888; d. Hyannis, Mass., Aug. 16, 1973. He went to the United States in 1910, attended Rutgers University (B. S., 1915; M. S., 1916), became an American citizen in 1916, and was granted a doctorate by the University of California in 1918. He returned to Rutgers as lecturer on soil microbiology, advancing to full professor in 1930, and after 1921 also served as microbiologist at the New Jersey Agricultural Experiment Station. During this period he directed his research toward soil conservation, elucidating the formation of humus, developing methods for studying biochemical processes in soil, and explaining the decomposition of plant materials in compost. From 1930 to 1942 he was also marine microbiologist at the Woods Hole Oceanographic Institute.

Waksman undertook the search for antibiotics in soil in 1939. Observing that *Streptomyces,* a genus of saprophytic soil bacteria, survived where other species perished, Waksman and his staff sought a strain that would exert a toxic effect on disease microorganisms without poisoning the patient or injuring animal tissue. In 1943 they derived from S. *griseus* a fine mycelium that met all requirements, and in January 1944 Waksman and his assistants, Albert Schatz and Elizabeth Bugie, announced the discovery of streptomycin (q.v.). It quickly proved its therapeutic value and led to the development of actinomycin, Terramycin, Aureomycin, and other forms for which Waksman coined the term antibiotics (q.v.).

During World War II Waksman served as a member of the National Defense Research Council. In 1949 he established the Rutgers Institute of Microbiology, which is supported by royalties from streptomycin, and served as its director until his retirement in 1958. In 1952 Waksman was awarded the Nobel Prize in physiology and medicine. His written works include *Principles of Soil Microbiology* (1931), *Humus* (1938), *Actinomycetes* (1950), and *My Life with the Microbes* (1954), an autobiography.

WALACHIA or **WALLACHIA,** wŏ-lā′kĭ-ə, a historic division of the old Kingdom of Rumania. It was originally two provinces: Oltenia (9,305 square miles), or Lesser Walachia, to the west; and Muntenia (20,270 square miles), or Greater Walachia, to the east. Oltenia, bounded on the north and west by the Carpathian Mountains and on the east by the Olt River, is marked by densely populated valleys, rich forests, grazing grounds, and a fertile lowland bordering the Danube. Muntenia, lying east of the Olt, is more advanced economically, having very fertile soil in which maize, wheat, and fodder are raised. The valuable oilfields of Ploesti and Campina are in Muntenia, and Bucharest, the Rumanian capital, is its largest city.

The redistricting of Rumania's historic provinces eliminated Walachia as an integral unit of the state. According to the 1956 census Muntenia contained 31.4 percent and Oltenia 13.8 percent of the total population of Rumania (17,-489,450). More than 90 percent of the inhabitants are Rumanians, with very small enclaves of Magyars, Jews, Serbs, and Bulgarians.

See also Romania—*History*.

Sherman D. Spector.

WALAFRID STRABO, văl′ə-frĭd strā′bō (Walafrid the Squinter), German theological writer and Latin poet: b. Swabia, c. 809; d. Aug. 18, 849. His early days were spent as a monk and student at the abbey of Reichenau where he began his career as a writer. Later he removed to Fulda where he studied under Rabanus Maurus. During the period 829 to 838 he became a confidant of the court of Louis the Pious and tutor of the young Charles the Bald. From 838 until his death, he was (except for a brief interval) abbot of Reichenau.

A friend of most of the notables of his time, Walafrid was a poet, composer of saints' lives, and a compiler of encyclopedic materials for school use. His poetry is significant for its fine descriptions of nature and warm expressions of passion. His *Visio Wettini* is one of the earliest dream accounts of the other world. His prose pamphlet on the sources and development of certain liturgical practices exercised considerable influence. It is worthy of note that the author did not engage in mystical speculation, but tried to present his subject in terms of historical evolution. The great *Glossa ordinaria,* a widely read commentary on the Scriptures, may owe something to his scholarship, but some of its substance is earlier and most of it is of a later period than Walafrid.

His most famous poem is the *Hortulus*. It is an account of a little garden that he used to tend with his own hands and is largely made up of descriptions of the various herbs he grew there and their uses, both medicinal and for other purposes.

ALLEN CABANISS,
Professor of History, University of Mississippi.

WALAM OLUM, wä'läm ō'lŭm, the tribal chronicle of the Delaware or Leni-Lenape Indians. In the Lenape language, *walam* means "painted," and *olum*, "tally." The title is usually translated into English as *Red Score*. The chronicle was first published in 1836 by Constantine Rafinesque in *The American Nations*. Rafinesque claimed that the work was a translation of a manuscript interpreting a pictographic record. Although scholars at first doubted the authenticity of the record, Daniel G. Brinton, in *The Lenape and Their Legends* (1885), concluded that it was a genuine chronicle of the Delaware migrations.

The *Walam Olum* tells of the wanderings of the Delaware from the Labrador region southward and westward, and again eastward to the Middle Atlantic area. According to Brinton, the "narrator was probably one of the native chiefs or priests, who had spent his life in the Ohio and Indiana towns of the Lenape."

WALBRZYCH, väl'bzhĭκ (Ger. WALDENBURG), city, Poland, formerly a part of Prussia, on the Polsnitz River, 42 miles southwest of Breslau and before 1945 known as Waldenburg. It lies in the Lower Silesia district of Poland which is the important hard coal district of the Waldenburger Gebirge, a branch of the Sudetic chain. Walbrzych is also noted for its manufacture of porcelain, glass, soap, brick, wire, machinery, linen, flax, hemp, and pharmaceuticals. The city contains a noted school of mining. Pop. (1982 est.) 134,300.

WALBURGA, väl-bŏŏr'gä, SAINT (also WALPURGA or WALPURGIS), English missionary to the Germans: b. England, c. 710; d. Heidenheim, Germany, Feb. 25, 779. She was the sister of St. Willibald, first bishop of Eichstätt, Germany, and of St. Winnebald (Winebald), first abbot of Heidenheim, and the niece of St. Boniface, the apostle of Germany. About 750 she followed her brothers to Germany and became the abbess of a convent at Heidenheim. She is said to have been a learned woman and may have been the author of an account of St. Willibald's travels in Palestine, written in Latin. After her death she received the honors of a saint and was believed to have worked many miracles, especially through the medicinal oil found in her burial place. Her festivals are held on May 1 and February 25. The legend of Walpurgis (Walburga's) Night, when witches are said to congregate with the devil, originated from the coincidence of one of her feast days, May 1, with a festival commemorating Waldborg, a pagan fertility goddess. See also WALPURGIS NIGHT.

WALCHEREN, wäl'κə-rən, island, the Netherlands, in the Province of Zeeland, at the mouth of the Scheldt, 10 miles long and 11 miles wide. A bridge connects with Zuid-Beveland and a railway to the mainland. It is well wooded and fertile and fruit is abundant. Though not the largest island of the Netherlands, it is the most densely populated. The largest town is Flushing (Vlissingen) whence are steamer connections with England; other towns include Middelburg (capital of Zeeland Province), Westkapelle, and Veere. The chief products are vegetables, cereals, sugar beets, and fruit. In 1809, during the Napoleonic campaigns, a British expedition under the 2d earl of Chatham captured the island of Walcheren but failed to seize Antwerp, the ultimate objective; when Austria collapsed the expedition was withdrawn after suffering heavy losses. British forces were landed once more on Walcheren Island in September 1944, during World War II; after incurring casualties exceeding 40,000, they drove out the Germans and went on to capture Antwerp, which became the main Allied base. The island is popular with tourists who enjoy the old town of Middelburg. Pop. (1956 est.) 77,839.

WALCOTT, wôl'kət, **Charles Doolittle,** American geologist, paleontologist, and administrator: b. New York Mills, N.Y., March 31, 1850; d. Washington, D.C., Feb. 9, 1927. His formal education ended in 1868 when he was forced to work, but he continued his study of geology and in 1876 found employment with the state geologist of New York. In 1879 he joined the staff of the United States Geological Survey and became its director in 1894. From 1907 until his death he was secretary of the Smithsonian Institution. He was instrumental in founding and organizing the Carnegie Institution of Washington, The Freer Gallery of Art, the National Research Council, and the National Advisory Council for Aeronautics, and he held executive positions with the Carnegie Institution and the National Academy of Sciences.

Despite his heavy administrative responsibilities he continued his geological and paleontological research, specializing in Cambrian trilobites and stratigraphy. His numerous writings include *The Trilobite* (1881), *The Cambrian Faunas of North America* (2 vols., 1884–85), *The Fauna of the Lower Cambrian or Olenellus Zone* (1890), and *Cambrian Brachiopoda* (2 vols., 1912).

WALD, wôld, **Lillian D.,** American social worker: b. Cincinnati, Ohio, March 10, 1867; d. Westport, Conn., Sept. 1, 1940. She is best known as the founder of the Henry Street Settlement in New York City and as the organizer of the first nonsectarian public health nursing system in the world. At the age of 22 she decided to become a nurse after meeting one who had been sent to care for her sister during childbirth. She studied medicine at the New York Hospital Training School for Nurses and the Woman's Medical College in New York. In 1893 she and another nurse, Mary Brewster, enlisted the financial support of several wealthy friends and established a small settlement on Rivington Street, New York City, before moving to the famous settlement at 265 Henry Street, which was Miss Wald's home for nearly 40 years. At first known as the Nurses' Settlement, the institution provided visiting nurse service as well as settlement services. In 1902 she initiated in New York City the first city school nurse service in the world. Other services originated by her were the plan for town and country nursing adopted by the American Red Cross, and the Federal Children's Bureau, established by Congress in 1908. She was a bitter opponent of slums and child labor and an advocate of more parks and play areas.

In 1915 she became the first president of the American Union against Militarism, but after the United States entered World War I she became a subcommittee member of the Council of National Defense, and after the war she represented the Children's Bureau at international conferences in Europe. She also served on numerous state and city commissions in the interest of public health and became first president of the National Organization for Public Health Nursing. In 1933 she resigned as president of the settlement's board of directors. In addition to a number of popular magazine articles and pamphlets, she also wrote two books: *The House on Henry Street* (1915); and *Windows on Henry Street* (1934).

WALDECK-ROUSSEAU, våld-dĕk'rōō-sō', **Pierre Marie René,** French statesman: b. Nantes, France, Dec. 2, 1846; d. Paris, Aug. 10, 1904. He studied law in Paris and began to practice at St.-Nazaire and from 1873 at Rennes. Advocating a strong republic to secure individual liberties and promote moderate social reforms, he was elected deputy for Rennes in 1879. He was minister of the interior from 1881 to 1885, in the ministries of Léon Gambetta and Jules Ferry, and was largely responsible for securing legal recognition of trade unions (*syndicats*) in 1884. In 1886 he was admitted to the Paris bar and withdrew from politics in 1889 to practice law. He defended Ferdinand Marie De Lesseps in 1893.

In 1894 he became senator from Loire, and in the following year he unsuccessfully bid for the presidency of the republic. In 1889, during the political and social agitation surrounding the Dreyfus affair, President Émile Loubet called upon Waldeck-Rousseau to form a government. His ministry included Republicans of all nuances as well as Alexandre Millerand, the first socialist minister of the Third Republic. In it was born the "Left Bloc," a coalition of Republicans and Socialists that dominated the political scene until 1905. Waldeck-Rousseau retained for himself the ministry of the interior and acted to liquidate the Dreyfus affair. He prosecuted extreme nationalists and restored respect for the law. In 1899 Alfred Dreyfus was pardoned, and an amnesty law, which ended prosecutions arising out of the affair, was passed in 1900. The following year, the Associations Act was passed, subjecting religious establishments to the regulations governing other forms of association. The Left Bloc scored a striking success in the general elections of 1902, and Waldeck-Rousseau, weakened by ill-health and considering his task completed, resigned on June 3, 1902, ending the longest ministry since 1875.

AARON NOLAND,
Associate Professor of History, City College of New York.

WALDEMAR, wôl'də-mär (Danish **VALDEMAR,** val'də-mär), the name of four kings of Denmark, notably:

WALDEMAR I (called THE GREAT); b. Jan. 14, 1131; d. Dec. 5, 1182. The son of Canute (Knud) Lavard, he was born eight days after his father's murder. He was named for his mother's grandfather, Russian Grand Prince Vladimir. When King Eric III died in 1147, Waldemar claimed the throne and took control of Jutland. By 1157 he was undisputed king of Denmark. His first task was to protect the coasts against raiding Wends. He built effective armed forces and, in 1169, backed by leaders of north Germany, conquered Rügen and forced the Wends to accept Christianity.

For a decade, he was in conflict with Archbishop Eskil of Lund, but was supported by most of the bishops, led by Absalon of Roskilde. At Ringsted, on June 25, 1170, the reconciliation of church and crown was symbolized by the proclamation of Canute Lavard as saint, and Waldemar's first legitimate son, Canute was crowned in a temporarily successful effort to change the kingship from elective to hereditary. From 1170 to Waldemar's death in 1182, Denmark experienced a relatively peaceful and prosperous period.

WALDEMAR II (called THE VICTORIOUS), son of Waldemar I: b. 1170; d. March 28, 1241. He succeeded his childless brother, Canute VI, in 1202. For a time he played a role in European politics. In alliance with Philip Augustus of France, he supported Pope Innocent III's candidate for emperor, Frederick II of Hohenstaufen. He succeeded in extending the Danish frontier from the Eider River to the Elbe and meddled in the internal politics of Norway and Sweden. In 1219, he was able to take control of Estonia.

In the first 20 years of Waldemar II's reign, Denmark continued the prosperity begun under his father and brother, but Waldemar could not maintain his conquests. In 1223 he was treacherously captured by Henry of Schwerin and forced to pay ransom and to relinquish the lands south of the Eider. His attempt to upset the agreements led to a crushing defeat at Bornhøved in 1227, which ended all hope of recovering the lost lands.

Despite his failures, he lived in popular memory as the Victorious, but an earlier and better designation is that of "Lawgiver." Waldemar II's Jutland Code is a landmark in Danish law. It was promulgated by the king and accepted by the people at an assembly in March 1241, a few days before his death.

WALDEMAR IV ATTERDAG (another day), son of Christopher II: b. about 1320; d. Oct. 24, 1375. After the murder of Count Gerhard of Holstein by Niels Ebbeson in 1340, Waldemar returned from his refuge in Bavaria and by 1349 was in possession of Jutland and the Danish islands. Although he ceded Skåne to Sweden and sold Estonia to the Teutonic Knights, he recovered Skåne with its valuable herring markets in 1361.

By this time he was the dominant political factor in his realm, generally able to maintain law and order. In restoring the royal power, he profited from the widespread longing for order and peace after years of misrule by German nobles. As a material foundation for his authority, he increased the royal domain. He also enforced royal rights to demand military service from nobles and peasants and ships and crews from the market towns. He created royal courts of appeal.

Walden Pond, near Concord, Mass. In these placid surroundings, Henry David Thoreau, living in solitude, penned thoughts that influenced men's minds in many lands.

His capture in 1361 of the richest market of Baltic trade, Visby in Gotland, led to war with Sweden and the Hanseatic League. On the eve of hostilities, Waldemar went to Germany to seek allies and left his council to face defeat by foreign and domestic enemies. The peace of Stralsund (1370), granted fishing and market rights to the Hanseatic League. After a successful campaign in South Jutland, Waldemar died in 1375 without male heirs.

LAWRENCE D. STEEFEL
Emeritus Professor of History,
University of Minnesota

WALDEN, väl'dən, **Paul,** Russian organic chemist: b. Tsesis (Ger. Wenden), Latvia, July 26, 1863; d. Gammertingen, near Sigmaringen, Germany, Jan. 24, 1957. After studying at Riga, Leipzig, and Munich, he joined the faculty of the physics department of Riga Polytechnic, where he subsequently became director. He went to the St. Petersburg Academy of Science as head of the chemistry department in 1910, and from 1919 to 1934 was professor and director of the Chemical Institute at the University of Rostock.

In 1895 Walden discovered a type of optical inversion (Walden inversion) which constituted a change in configuration which occurs in many metathetical reactions involving atoms or radicals attached to asymmetric atoms. The concept of rearward attack mechanism gives experimental evidence that in most metathetical reactions the entering group attaches itself to the back face of the atom from that occupied by the displaced group, although the process is not readily detectable except in optically active substances. Walden is also noted for his investigations into the electrical conductivity of aqueous solutions of organic acids and the dielectric constants of solutions.

WALDEN, OR LIFE IN THE WOODS, a book of philosophical observations by Henry David Thoreau related to his experiences between 1845 and 1847, when he built a cabin with his own hands and lived alone at Walden Pond, near Concord, Mass. Both his words and his manner of living were a protest against commercialism and conformity in American society. The book is a testament of personal dedication to transcend the sterility and meanness of days "frittered away by detail"—"to front only the essential facts of life."

The first and longest chapter, "Economy," explains how he obtained the economic freedom thus to "live deliberately" and find out what life "had to teach." In so doing, he turned conventional values topsy-turvy. Instead of living to make money, like many citizens of Concord, he made money only to live. While at Walden, he supported himself by working as a day laborer and surveyor, and he grew his own vegetables. Materials for his cabin cost $28.12½. He itemized his almost inconsequential expenses to show that it was "not necessary that a man should earn his living by the sweat of his brow, unless he sweats easier than I do."

Thoreau never defined in simple generalizations the kind of life that this economy should make possible. Like other transcendentalists, he believed that "every man is tasked to make his life, even in its details, worthy of the contemplation of his most elevated and critical hour." But he did not advocate that other men should build cabins and live isolated. For himself, he found this way of life a convenient road to the philosophers' old search for truth. All the other chapters in *Walden* reveal aspects of this quest.

He brought special vision to what he felt his contemporaries had not clearly seen in both society and nature. It was characteristic of his relationships with people that awareness of individuality became more sharp as blinders imposed by conventional values were removed. Thus, he felt the wholesomeness of solitude in contrast with the cheapness of too much sociability; yet he relished certain visitors and neighbors, particularly a Canadian woodchopper—"a Homeric man"; and he helped "to forward" a runaway slave "toward the north star." Attacking the dead weight of customs and institutions, he urged reading as "noble intellectual exercise" rather than as a "paltry convenience"; he called society "a desperate party" running amok to collect his poll tax. Regarded by some as primarily a naturalist, he also observed nature with passionate originality and great acumen, reporting such phenomena as a battle of ants; the nesting, calls, and flights of birds; the habits of field mice and rabbits; and the myriad evidences of changing seasons. He concluded: "We are asleep nearly half our time. . . . Only that day dawns to which we are awake. . . . The sun is but a morning star."

On its publication in 1854, *Walden* was acclaimed by some literary intellectuals but had little financial success. However, the book has never been out of print since that date and has affected men's ideas in many parts of the world. Mohandas Gandhi, Leo Tolstoy, many early leaders of the British Labour Party, William Butler Yeats, and Marcel Proust have been among those influenced.

JOHN ASHWORTH.

WALDENBURG. See WALBRZYCH.

WALDENSES, wŏl-dĕn'sēz. The origin of the Waldenses is mainly to be attributed to Peter Waldo (q.v.), though a much earlier existence was formerly claimed for the movement. It was represented as the pure remnant of the primitive church maintained after the secularizing acts of Constantine. A specific connection was alleged with the teachings of Claudius, bishop of Turin (817–839), whose diocese extended over the valleys in which Waldensianism was later to maintain itself. These historical errors have been abandoned. But anticipations of Waldo's teaching were widespread in the 12th century and were characteristic of such sects as the Petrobrusians, Henricians, Arnaldists, and Humiliati. It is likely that the Waldenses drew many recruits from these groups. Catharism was also widely prevalent, and in some locations Albigenses and Waldenses were street neighbors and shared the same persecution. But the Manichaean dualism and peculiar usages of the Cathari (q.v.) were alien to the Waldenses. Inquisitors usually distinguished clearly between the two and represented the Waldenses as disciples of Waldo. Thus Walter Map, reporting events of 1179, speaks of those called *Valdesii* from the name of their founder Valdes, and in Latin texts of about 1200 they are called *Valdenses* or *Waldenses* for the same reason. From *Valdenses* lexicographers derive *Vaudois*, the name by which they are commonly known in French.

Doctrines and Practices.—The Waldenses based their teachings strictly on the Scriptures. Following Waldo's example, they continued to circulate the vernacular Bible, using fresh translations from the Vulgate. At some points the scriptural principle caused revisions of doctrine similar to those of the 16th century Reformation, but notably the doctrine of justification by faith was not adopted. Ernesto Comba indeed ascribes to the Waldenses "a singular reluctance to innovate in the dogmatic field." However, they rejected the doctrine of purgatory, masses for the dead, indulgences, the invocation of saints, and the use of images, and they venerated but declined to adore the Virgin Mary. They observed two sacraments only, and some of them rejected infant baptism. The Waldenses were conscientiously industrious and favored artisan callings, generally avoiding merchandising as morally perilous. They stressed family virtues and abhorred lying. On principle they rejected military action but were led to break this rule in instances of extreme peril to their families and religion.

Writings Before the Reformation.—No authoritative canon of extant medieval Waldensian writings has been made. Versions of the New Testament in Italian and French dialects are preserved, and at least one of the pre-Reformation German Bibles appears to be Waldensian. Some of their most impressive writings are in verse, the outstanding being *La Nobla Leyczon* (the Noble Lection), a work of poetic quality in a Provençal dialect. Misrepresented as earlier than Waldo, it was probably written in the 15th century. It presents a devout affirmation of Waldensian positions. The Bible history is extensively surveyed, with emphasis on the superiority of the perfect law of Christ to that of Moses. Auricular confession, sacramental absolution, the Mass, and papal authority are repudiated. Among other documents of the same period is a catechism containing expositions of the Lord's Prayer, the Commandments, the Sacraments, and discussions of love, hope, and the gifts of the spirit. Under the Second Commandment there is a sharp attack on St. Gregory's statement that images are the books of the laity.

Ministry and Polity.—The Waldensian ministry consisted of bishops, presbyters, and deacons, vowed to poverty, chastity and obedience. The term *barba* (Fr. *barbe*), which meant "maternal uncle," was applied to these ministers in affection and reverence, replacing the traditional "father" because in the New Testament this word is associated with God. Bishops were elected by vote of all three classes of ministers. We read of a superior bishop for southern France elected in a synod and designated *maioralis omnium*. The presbyters were those chiefly engaged in missionary preaching. Deacons could be made presbyters only after intensive Bible study. Annual general conventions or synods were held whenever possible. At these meetings, missioners were assigned to fields near and far, often for two years. They preached and talked their message in streets and buildings, or in homes to which they gained admission sometimes in the guise of peddlers. A feature of the organization was the erection of hospices for the use of the preachers on journey.

Persecutions.—Attempts of popes and rulers to suppress heresy by armed crusades and the Inquisition subjected the Waldenses to severe, if intermittent, persecution which at times imperiled their very survival. From historians we have vivid accounts of the atrocities and martyrdoms of this long struggle. By the time of the Reformation the principal settlements left to them were in the high valleys of Piedmont and the adjacent French Dauphiné and Provence. They were, however, ofttimes pursued into their mountains and suffered untold losses and miseries. Their survival as a church and community is an outstanding historical example of the tenacity generated by religious conviction. In Bohemia their groups mingled somewhat uncomfortably with the Hussites, and from their episcopate the *Unitas Fratrum* obtained episcopal orders. Early colonies in Apulia and Calabria survived until 1560, when they were extinguished by the sword.

The Waldenses and the Reformation. The beginnings of the Reformation in Germany and Switzerland aroused great interest in the valleys. In 1530 two *barbes,* George Morel and Peter Masson, bringing letters from their brethren, visited the Reformers of Basel, Strasbourg, and Bern. They asked searching questions and revealed their own scruples over concessions they had been making to escape persecution, such as bringing their children to priests for baptism. They held fruitful conferences with Johannes Oecolampadius of Basel and made the acquaintance of Guillaume Farel in Neuchâtel.

Discussions followed in the Vaudois villages, and a synod was called, which met at Chanforan on the Angrogne, Sept. 12–18, 1532. Here the Waldenses adopted a confession of faith reflecting the impact of Reformed teachings. The articles on predestination and providence (articles 2–5), and on the marriage and local settlement of ministers (12–16), are startlingly new among Waldensian statements, and may have been suggested by Farel and Antoine Saunier (both natives of the Dauphiné) who attended the synod as fraternal delegates from a conference of Swiss pastors. It was also resolved that there should be no equivocation in relations with Roman Catholicism. Provision was made for a new version of the Bible, and Pierre Robert Olivétan, a cousin of John Calvin and a Paris-trained scholar, was commissioned to prepare it. This celebrated work, composed not in one of the old dialects but in literary French, and translated not from the Vulgate but from the Bible languages with help from the earlier French version of Jacques Lefèvre d'Étaples, was published in Neuchâtel in 1535. Two of the *barbes* voiced dissatisfaction with the actions of the synod, went to Bohemia to consult with sympathetic Hussites, and failing to raise serious resistance finally left the Waldensian church.

The interest taken by Calvin in the Waldenses, and the work of pastors from Geneva and Lausanne helped further to identify the Waldenses with Reformed Protestantism. However, their new circle of foreign friends could not shelter them from persecution. In 1545, Francis I was induced on false information to send an expedition which massacred the inhabitants of 22 villages. At this and other crises of persecution, Geneva and other Protestant communities uttered protests and aided survivors, without being able to prevent later measures of repression. In 1655, Charles Emmanuel II of Savoy, prompted by the Congregation *De Propaganda fide,* authorized an attack which at Easter devastated the Piedmont valleys with savage fury. Oliver Cromwell's protests to Louis XIV induced Louis to permit belated entry of some of the refugees from this massacre into France, and Sir Samuel Morland, Cromwell's ambassador extraordinary to Savoy, obtained at least a hearing for English resentment. Morland also brought back valuable Waldensian manuscripts, which were deposited in Cambridge. Meanwhile a troop under Josué Janavel in surprising victories began a recovery of the Vaudois which resulted in the "Glorious Return" of a remnant under Henry Arnaud in 1689. Many vicissitudes followed before Charles Albert of Sardinia on Feb. 17, 1848, issued the Edict of Emancipation, by which the Waldenses were given civil rights.

Revival and Expansion. The Waldensian church was then taking on new vitality through help received especially from England. Canon William S. Gilly (1789–1855), by his visits and writings, obtained funds for a college (1831). Major General John C. Beckwith (1789–1862), a maimed veteran of Waterloo, gave nearly 40 years of service in the communities, imparting new vision and establishing many schools. Another agent of their revival was the able Italian convert, Luigi Desanctis (1808–1869), leader of the new center at Turin. Italian replaced French as the language of the church, and Italy was taken as its mission field. In the past century Waldensian churches to the number of about 200 have arisen in many parts of the peninsula and Sicily. Though mainly self-supporting, the denomination has been aided, especially in building, by American, British, and other Protestants. It has thus been able to establish numerous educational centers and hospitals, and to maintain the Alpine retreat "Agape," frequented by foreign Protestant youth. Its theological seminary, opened at Torre Pellice in 1855, was removed to Florence and later (1892) to Rome. The work of the church is under the general supervision of the *Tavola* or administrative board. Migration to the Americas has led to the formation of various colonies of which the most populous are at Valdese, N.C. (1893) and Colonia Valdense (1858) and neighboring settlements in Uruguay.

JOHN T. MCNEILL
Auburn Professor Emeritus of Church History
Union Theological Seminary

Bibliography

American Waldensian Aid Society, *Annotated Reading List on the Waldenses* (1939).
Cameron, Evan, *The Reformation of the Heretics: The Waldenses of the Alps, 1480–1580* (Oxford 1984).
Comba, Emilia, *History of the Waldenses of Italy* (1889; reprint, AMS Press).
Jones, William, *The History of the Waldenses,* 2 vols., 2d ed. (1816; reprint, AMS Press).
Tourn, Giorgio, *The Waldensians: The First 800 Years,* rev. ed. (Friendship Press 1980).

WALDERSEE, väl′dər-zā, COUNT **Alfred von** (1832–1905), German soldier. He was born in Potsdam, Germany, on April 8, 1832, and died in Hannover on March 5, 1905. He entered the Prussian Army in 1850, and in the Franco-Prussian War (1870–1871) was aide-de-camp to the king. In 1882, as quartermaster general, he was made virtually chief of the general staff under Count Helmuth von Moltke, whom he succeeded in 1888. He strengthened the political independence of the general staff from the civil government and began through his friendship with Prince William, heir to the throne, to meddle in politics. He openly favored the Christian anti-Semitic movement led by the court chaplain Adolf Stoecker, which brought him into opposition to Bismarck. In the European diplomatic crisis of 1887–1889 he got into even sharper conflict with the chancellor by advocating a preventive war against Russia. Waldersee bore a large responsibility for the dismissal of Bismarck by William II. But William's friendship cooled off quickly. In 1891, Waldersee was made corps commander in Schleswig-Holstein. In 1900–1901 as a field marshal he commanded the European forces assembled in China after the Boxer Rebellion. Three volumes of his memoirs, *Denkwürdigkeiten,* were published in 1922–1925.

HAJO HOLBORN
Author of "A History of Modern Germany"

WALDHEIM, vält′hīm, **Kurt** (1918–), Austrian president, who was formerly a career diplomat and secretary-general of the United Nations. He was born in St. Andrae-Wörden, near Vienna, on Dec. 21, 1918. He attended the Consular Academy of Vienna, served with the German Army during World War II, and earned a doctorate in law from the University of Vienna in 1944.

Entering the foreign service, Waldheim was assigned to Paris in 1945, then returned to Vienna to head the personnel division in 1951. Among other posts, he was director of political affairs (1960–1964) and minister of foreign affairs (1968–1970). He was also minister and ambassador to Canada (1956–1960).

Waldheim's association with the United Nations began in 1955 with his appointment as Austria's observer. With Austria's admission in 1958, he headed its first permanent delegation to the General Assembly and was its permanent UN representative (1964–1968, 1970–1971). He succeeded U Thant as secretary-general of the UN on Jan. 1, 1972, and was reelected in 1976. He won praise for his quiet diplomacy in settling disputes among members, but was criticized for failing to act decisively. He organized relief programs for Bangladesh, Cambodia, and other countries, but was unable to secure the withdrawal of Vietnamese troops from Cambodia, Israeli forces from occupied areas, South Africans from Namibia, and Soviet forces from Afghanistan, as well as the release of American hostages in Iran. His bid for a third term was opposed by China, and he was succeeded by Javier Pérez de Cuéllar in 1982.

In April 1971, Waldheim failed in his bid for the presidency of Austria. Fifteen years later he mounted a successful campaign and on July 8, 1986, was inaugurated for a six-year term. His candidacy had been strenuously opposed by Jewish and other groups, contending that Waldheim had misrepresented his military service under the Nazi occupation of Yugoslavia and Greece and had been involved in, or at least privy to, liquidations and deportations of partisans and civilians.

WALDO, wôl′dō, or **VALDO,** văl′dō, **Peter** (c. 1140–c. 1218), French religious reformer. Waldo first comes to notice as a wealthy merchant of Lyons experiencing a religious crisis.

One tradition is that he obtained his wealth by "usury," a term then used for any interest on money. According to an anonymous inquisitor he was religiously startled in 1173 by witnessing the sudden death of a prominent citizen. Another source tells how he heard a minstrel sing the legend of Alexis, a 4th century saint of poverty, and resolved to follow the pattern of apostolic poverty. Knowing little Latin, he employed two clerics to translate extensive portions of Scripture into the local dialect of French. Some selections from the "saints," possibly the Church Fathers, were also translated for him. Waldo deeded his house to his wife, settled his daughters in a nunnery, gave his remaining wealth to the poor, and began preaching.

He gathered disciples, instructing them in the Scripture. He became the directing leader of a society of propertyless, celibate, biblical lay evangelists who were known as the Poor Men of Lyon. Traveling in pairs, they preached informally, featuring the recital of memorized passages of Scripture in the vernacular. When Archbishop Guichard of Lyon forbade this activity, Waldo continued it, saying that he would obey God rather than men; but he also sought church approval. At the Third Lateran Council (1179) two of the Poor Men brought an appeal against the archbishop's ruling. They exhibited a book "in the dialect of Gaul" containing the Psalms and other excerpts from the Bible. Walter Map, who questioned them before a commission of the council, says they were unlettered men who went about two by two, garbed in wool and barefooted, "naked following the naked Christ." They encountered the amused disdain of their examiners in theology. They were forbidden to preach without permission of the local clergy. They persisted, and Waldo became more antagonistic to the papacy and hierarchy. He rejected nonscriptural elements in worship and belief, such as purgatory, the adoration of saints, the use of images, and the formula "I absolve thee" in absolution. He also opposed oath taking, war service, and capital punishment. In 1182, Guichard's successor, John of the Fair Hands, expelled the Poor Men from the diocese, and in 1183 the Council of Verona pronounced them heretics.

Waldo's later life is not reliably recorded. Flight from persecution and zeal to make converts may have taken him to Metz, to Lombardy, and finally to Bohemia. His death was probably recent when in 1218, at a synod in Bergamo, Waldenses of Lombardy disagreed with those of France who held that at death he had been received immediately to Paradise for his holiness. He takes his place in history as a pre-Franciscan exemplar of disciplined Christian poverty, and as the first to make widely effective use of the vernacular Bible in preaching.

JOHN T. MCNEILL
Auburn Professor Emeritus of Church History
Union Theological Seminary

WALDSEEMÜLLER, vält′zā-mül-ər, or **WALTZEMÜLLER,** väl′tsā-mül-ər, **Martin** (Lat. HYLACOMYLUS or ILACOMILUS) (c. 1470–c. 1518), German cartographer. He was born in Radolfzell or Freiburg, Baden, Germany, and died in St. Dié, Alsace (now in Vosges Department, France). He was regarded as an able young geographer by a group of learned men of his time. His *Cosmographiae introductio* and his map of the world (the latter prepared as a globe also), both published at St. Dié in 1507, attracted much attention, and originated the name "America" (from Amerigo Vespucci). The name conferred upon the transatlantic lands, in the little Latin treatise and on the huge wall map and globe, was so promptly and generally popular that its originator himself was powerless to recall it.

When he issued his *Carta marina* in 1516, he had changed his opinion as to the relative value of the achievements of Columbus and Vespucci, for the word America does not appear on the map of 1516. But it was too late to impose a name less significant and less appropriate.

Of the Waldseemüller map of 1507, 1,000 copies were printed, yet all but one were destroyed or lost, and the same fate overtook the *Carta itineraria Europae* of 1511 and the *Carta marina* of 1516. The *Carta itineraria* was the first to be recovered; the more interesting maps of 1507 and 1516 did not come to light until 1901, when their discovery created a sensation. The geographical world was suddenly startled

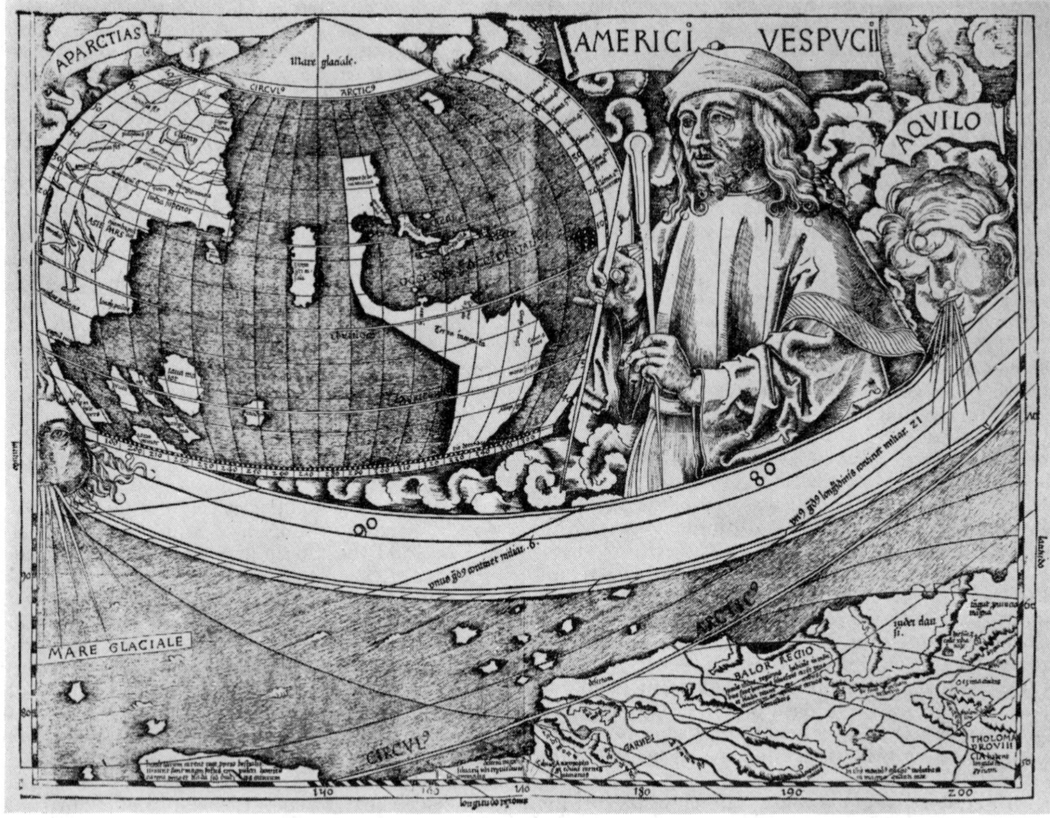

New York Public Library

Part of Waldseemüller's map of 1507. His works of that year originated the name America, from Amerigo Vespucci.

by a brief announcement that Waldseemüller's long-lost map of 1507, together with another of his of 1516, had been found by Professor P. Joseph Fischer of Feldkirch, in the library of Prince Waldburg at Wolfegg Castle. The assertion, that Waldseemüller intended to bestow the name America upon the southern continent only, appears at first sight to find support in the map of 1507, but is disproved by a comparison of the map with the explanatory passage in the *Introductio*. The Greek form of his own name on the map of 1516 is Ilacomilus, showing plainly his preference for that spelling toward the end of his life. His name does not appear in any form upon the map of 1507. The only copy of the first edition of the *Introductio* is in the New York Public Library. Waldseemüller was canon of St. Dié at his death.

WALDSTEIN. See WALLENSTEIN, ALBRECHT WENZEL EUSEBIUS VON.

WALDTEUFEL, vál-tû-fəl′, **Emil,** Alsatian composer: b. Strasbourg, France, Dec. 9, 1837; d. Paris, Feb. 16, 1915. After studies at the Strasbourg Conservatoire, he settled permanently in Paris, continuing his education at the Paris Conservatoire. When waltzes printed at his own expense proved popular, he narrowed his interests to the composition of dance music. He soon became internationally famous, making gaudily heralded tours as conductor of his own dances. In 1865 he was appointed court musician to the Empress Eugénie, for whom he conducted lavish court balls. Composer of approximately 250 orchestral dances, he long shared the domain of light music with Daniel Auber, Jacques Offenbach, and Johann Strauss, Jr. The best-remembered of his works are waltzes: *Dolores, España* (on themes by Emmanuel Chabrier), *Estudiantina, Mon rêve, Les patineurs* (*The Skaters*), *Les sirènes, Toujours ou jamais, Très jolie,* and *Les violettes.*

HERBERT WEINSTOCK.

WALDWICK, wôld′wĭk, borough, New Jersey, in Bergen County, situated west of Saddle River in the foothills of the Ramapo Mountains at an elevation of 335 feet. First known as New Prospect, its name was changed to Waldeck, later to Waldwick. Located 7 miles north of Paterson and 25 miles from New York City, Waldwick is a residential community. It has excellent shopping centers, schools, a library, and two churches, one of which, the Methodist Episcopal, has records going back to 1791. The borough covers about four square miles, containing a park and picnic space. A swimming pool and lake add to its attractions, as does Ho-Ho-Kus Brook which eventually joins the Saddle River. During the American Revolution, Washington's army camped here. Indian graves and artifacts are still found, relics from Chief Gray Wolf's occupancy. Incorporated as a borough in 1919, it is governed by a mayor and council. Pop. 10,802.

WALES, wālz, **PRINCE OF,** title customarily conferred, by investiture, upon the eldest son of the sovereign of Great Britain. Of all the native rulers of Wales, it was held only by the last, Llewelyn ap Gruffydd, and was acknowledged by the English crown in 1267. Fifteen years later, Llewelyn was killed during the conquest of Wales by Edward I. Edward's son (later Edward II) was born in Caernarvon in 1284, and was invested with the title in 1301. The title is not hereditary, for while the king's son is born earl of Cornwall he has to be invested as Prince of Wales. When the blind King John of Bohemia was killed at the Battle of Crecy (1346), the prince of Wales (Edward, the Black Prince), who was in command of the English army, appropriated his standard, a plume of three ostrich feathers, with its motto *Ich Dien* (I serve), and these have ever since been held by each succeeding prince of Wales.

DAVID WILLIAMS
Author of "A History of Modern Wales"

WALES (formerly **WALES AND MONMOUTHSHIRE;** Welsh **CYMRU**), a historical, ecclesiastical, and administrative unit also termed the principality of Wales, occupies the central western peninsula of Great Britain. Its area is 8,016 square miles (20,761 sq km), and its population (1981 census) is 2,749,640. Cardiff is the capital.

The position of Monmouthshire has, since the union of England and Wales in the 16th century (see section 3. *History and Government*), been ambiguous. It is sometimes regarded as an English shire, but, in legislation, it has almost invariably been linked with Wales.

For the convenience of the reader this article is divided into the following sections:

1. The Land and the Economy

The Welsh peninsula is bounded on the north and west by the Irish Sea, on the south by the Bristol Channel, and on the east by the English counties of Cheshire, Salop, Hereford and Worcester, and Gloucestershire. Its north-to-south length is 136 miles, and its breadth, 112 miles. At the northwest extremity of the peninsula is the former island county of Anglesey, separated from the mainland by the Menai Strait. The greater part of Wales lies at an elevation of more than 600 feet above sea level. Snowdon, the highest peak in the British Isles (3,560 feet), gives its name to the Snowdonia National Park, an area of some 837 square miles. Other heights are Carnedd Llywelyn (3,484 feet), Carnedd Dafydd (3,426 feet), Cader Idris (2,927 feet), and Plynlimon (2,468 feet). Wales has several rivers, the most notable of which—the Severn (210 miles) and the Wye (130 miles)—both rise on the slopes of Plynlimon and flow into the Bristol Channel. The largest natural lake is Bala in Merioneth; Lake Vyrnwy is an artificial reservoir which forms the water supply of Liverpool, while Birmingham gets its water from reservoirs in the Elan and Claerwen valleys in the moorlands of central Wales. Like other highland areas of the British Isles, Wales is a region of heavy rainfall; areas above 1,000 feet in elevation have more than 60 inches of rain each year. Wales lies, however, on the warmer, western side of Britain, and the valleys of the west coast are sheltered from the cold east winds so that they enjoy an extremely mild climate.

Under the so-called Local Government Bill of October 1972, Wales' 13 counties ceased to exist and in their place eight new counties were created, effective in April 1974. The original 13 counties were as follows: Anglesey, Breconshire, Caernarvonshire, Cardiganshire, Carmarthenshire, Denbighshire, Flintshire, Glamorganshire, Merionethshire, Monmouthshire, Montgomeryshire, Pembrokeshire, and Radnorshire.

The eight counties, with populations (1981 census) are as follows:

THE COUNTIES OF WALES

County	Population (1981 census)	County	Population (1981 census)
Clwyd	385,581	Mid Glamorgan	533,770
Dyfed	323,040	Powys	108,121
Gwent	436,500	South Glamorgan	376,718
Gwynedd	222,291	West Glamorgan	363,619
Total Wales			2,749,640

Wales is a region of great scenic beauty. Its wide expanse of coastline varies from rugged-rock scenery to stretches of golden sand. This has made the seaside resorts of the north Wales coast into playgrounds for the industrial population of Lancashire, and those of south Wales for the people of the English Midlands. Towns have therefore grown up which cater to the popular tourist trade, notably Rhyl and Llandudno in the north and Porthcawl and Barry in the south. Others, such as Beaumaris in Anglesey and Tenby in Pembrokeshire, are still unspoiled, with houses of Georgian architecture that give them the air of watering places of a bygone age. The island of Anglesey (ancient Mona) is joined to the mainland by a suspension bridge (1,000 feet long), which was built by the Scottish engineer Thomas Telford in 1825 and is itself an object of beauty. At the far end of the Lleyn Peninsula, the long arm of Caernarvonshire that stretches out into the Irish Sea, is Bardsey, the "island of the saints," reputed to be the burial place of a thousand Celtic saints. Across Cardigan Bay is the southern Welsh promontory, the rocky headland of St. David's, situated on the Pembrokeshire coastline, which has been designated a national park. Here, in a little hollow near the coast, lies the cathedral church of St. David's, undoubtedly the most picturesque cathedral in the British Isles; its history goes back to the days when this headland, as well as Bardsey, were landfalls on the ancient sea routes from northern Spain, Brittany, and Cornwall to Ireland and the Isle of Man. Here it was that the Briton, St. Patrick, took ship for the "Emerald Isle" on the journey that led to the Christianization of Ireland.

The mountains of Snowdonia are famous for their beauty. Equally remarkable are the wide open moorlands of the interior, of Hiraethog and the Plynlimon Range, of the Radnor Forest and the Brecon Beacons. Nor are the more fertile areas without their beauty; despite its proximity to the great south Wales coalfield the Vale of Glamorgan has been aptly called "the garden of Wales."

Adding greatly to the attractiveness of the country are its numerous ruined castles, not merely the great structures erected by Edward I in the late 13th century to keep the Welsh in subjection—at Beaumaris, Conway, Caernarvon, and Harlech—but scores of others of Norman and of Welsh origin which make Wales into a veritable land of castles.

Agriculture.—The traditional occupation of rural Wales was the breeding of cattle. These were often driven hundreds of miles along country roads and over moorlands, swimming across the Menai Strait and fording the rivers, to the cattle markets of the English Midlands and of London, to supply meat for the growing industrial towns. The drovers remained important members of the Welsh community until their occupation was taken away from them by the railway. Sheep were introduced by the Cistercian monks and in time became more important than cattle in the rural economy. Welsh mountain lamb still remains a delicacy, but originally sheep were reared more for their wool, and the wool trade of Wales became important. Small woolen mills were set up in many country towns, but they declined when the market became flooded with woolen goods from the Yorkshire factories. Because of its elevation, rainfall, and the nature of the soil, Wales has been unsuitable for arable farming. Areas in which wheat will grow are limited generally to the coastal fringes and the broad valley floors, but oats will tolerate more extreme conditions and are extensively used in fattening livestock. Most of the arable farming is found in the coastal lowlands of south Wales, where the Vale of Glamorgan stands out as a particularly rich area.

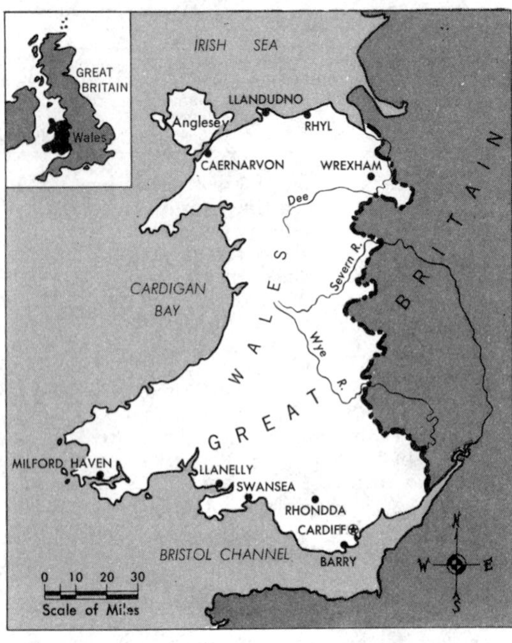

Wales

Conditions in rural Wales in the early 19th century closely resembled those in Ireland. The population grew rapidly, as it did in Ireland before the great famine of 1846. This led to economic distress, which brought grievances to the surface. Rack-renting by absentee landlords was as common in Wales as in Ireland, and the country people suffered from the rigors of the poor law, the tithes, and the tolls on the turnpike roads. The "hungry forties" saw the outbreak of the so-called Rebecca Riots, when men assembled at night, dressed in women's clothes and with their faces blackened, and destroyed the turnpike gates. Conditions were eased with a return of prosperity, especially as the railway was introduced into Wales in the 1850's and syphoned off the surplus population. There now began a stream of migration to the industrial areas, and also of emigration, particularly to the United States. The United States census of 1890 listed over 100,000 natives of Wales in its population, mainly from the rural areas. On the other hand, each succeeding British census from 1851 to 1961 (except 1911) showed a continuous decrease in the number of people engaged in agriculture. In particular, the population withdrew from the marginal lands in the uplands of Wales. There were acute economic crises in 1876 and in the years after World War I; throughout the last hundred years, problems of depopulation have remained unsolved. Efforts have been made to introduce social amenities into the countryside, such as better roads and greater electrification, as well as to encourage afforestation and to foster light industries in the country towns, but the census of 1961 showed that the drift from the land had continued.

Industry.—Wales has extensive coal deposits. There are two coalfields. That of north Wales is situated in the northeast around Wrexham, in the shires of Denbigh and Flint. Here coal mining was first developed as a subsidiary to the iron industry, and the process by which coal could be used to smelt iron was introduced, soon after its discovery, at the Bersham ironworks near Wrexham. The local iron ore quickly became exhausted. The industry continued with imported ores, and after World War II great developments were made at the Shotton steelworks in Flintshire. The local coal is of inferior quality, but is particularly suitable for gas producing. There are several brickworks in the area, an important chemical industry at Ruabon, and rayon factories on the Dee estuary.

The south Wales coalfield, an elongated area of about 1,000 square miles covering much of Monmouthshire, Glamorgan, and south Carmarthenshire, is of vastly greater importance. It is the largest continuous coalfield in Great Britain, with deposits ranging from bituminous and steam coal to anthracite. Here also the coal industry was, for several decades, a subsidiary to iron smelting. In the early stages of the Industrial Revolution a number of ironworks came into existence along the northeastern rim of the coalfield, from Hirwaun to Blaenavon, where coal outcrops could be easily worked and there were adequate supplies of timber and water, as well as of limestone, which was used in smelting. The center of this development was at Merthyr Tydfil, where the Cyfarthfa and Dowlais works were, for a time, the most extensive in Europe. The first steam-driven locomotive in the world drew a load of 10 tons, 70 persons, and 5 wagons for 9.5 miles out of Merthyr Tydfil on Feb. 21, 1804, and the first iron rails also were made in Merthyr. An important discovery in the western part of the coalfield was the process by which anthracite coal could be used in smelting iron. The credit for this goes primarily to David Thomas, who successfully applied the process at the Ynyscedwyn works in the Swansea Valley in February 1837. Two years later he was in-

(Above) Ewing Galloway; (right and below) Black Star

***Above:* End of a hard day's work below ground—coal miners of South Wales leaving a pit head. *Right:* Slate quarrying. Once a major factor in the Welsh economy, the industry was hit hard by a change in roofing tastes in favor of tiles. *Below:* A hot-strip steel mill in Ebbw Vale, Gwent county. Wales also produces tinplate.**

vited by the Lehigh Coal Company of Pennsylvania to emigrate, and he became one of the most successful ironmasters in the United States.

The local supplies of iron soon became exhausted, and several iron companies turned to the production of coal. Because of the proximity of the coalfield to the coast, as well as the downhill gradient from the pit heads to the ports, a great export trade grew up, both with foreign countries (especially those of South America) and with the bunkering ports of the world. The Powell-Duffryn Company, centered in the Aberdare Valley, became celebrated. This trade was revolutionized by the opening up of the valleys of the two Rhondda rivers in the 1860's. These were in the center of the coalfield, where the coal seams were at the greatest depth from the surface, and this had delayed their development, but the steam coal which they produced was unrivaled. On the eve of World War I, Cardiff had become the largest coal-exporting port in the world.

The iron industry was also revolutionized at the same time. Bessemer's process for manufacturing steel on a large scale (1856) was immediately adopted at Dowlais, and the rival Siemens (open-hearth) process (1868) was first successfully applied at Landore near Swansea. Equally important was the discovery (1879) by two Welsh cousins, Percy Gilchrist and Sidney Gilchrist Thomas, of a method by which phosphoric iron ore could be used in the Bessemer and Siemens processes, a discovery which, among other things, enabled Prussia to use the coal of Alsace and the phosphoric iron ore of Lorraine to build up its economic wealth and its political power. The local iron ore of south Wales proved to be entirely inadequate for these new developments, and ore had to be imported from Spain. As it was cheaper to bring coal to the coast than to transport ore inland, the industry tended to migrate from the northeastern rim of the coalfield to the seacoast, and a great steelworks was opened at Cardiff (completed 1936).

Much of the steel was used for the manufacture of tinplate, which at one time was almost a Welsh monopoly. (In 1875, out of 77 tinplate works in Great Britain, 57 were in south Wales.) This industry was badly affected by the McKinley tariff on tinplate imposed by the United States government in 1890, and a great many skilled Welsh workers emigrated to the

United States. The industry recovered when it obtained other markets in Argentina, Russia, and the Far East. Between World Wars I and II, Welsh industry suffered an intense depression. To counteract it the government assisted in the opening, in 1935, of an enormous tinplate works at Ebbw Vale, in northern Monmouthshire, a location which reversed the trend to the coast. World War II brought a new demand for coal and steel, and the postwar years saw further development. Four leading companies pooled their resources to form the gigantic Steel Company of Wales, which opened a vast new steelworks at Margam near Swansea in 1951. In the following year a great tinplate works was opened at Trostre, near Llanelly, and in 1956 another at Velindre near Swansea. These involved an outlay of over £100 million, and made south Wales the leading steel and tinplate producing area in Great Britain.

One other heavy industry played a great part in the life of the Welsh community. This was the slate industry, located mainly (but not exclusively) in Caernarvonshire in northwest Wales. Disastrous strikes in the early years of the 20th century crippled the industry, and a great many slate quarrymen emigrated to the slate-producing areas of Pennsylvania and upper New York. A change of taste to tile as a roofing material brought the industry almost to a standstill.

After 1934 some new manufacturing industries were introduced in Wales to ensure diversity of employment and to provide capital and consumer goods on a more extensive scale. These new industries include plastics, chemicals, textiles, electrical and radio equipment, and aircraft. An oil refinery has been built at Llandarcy, and Swansea and Milford Haven are now counted among the great oil ports of Europe.

The industrialization of Wales led to a network of roads, canals (which soon became obsolete), and railways. Most means of transport tended to link Wales with England, rather than to integrate the Welsh countryside. A notable event was the opening of the Severn Tunnel (reducing the journey from south Wales to London by an hour), which, as was appropriate, was used for the first time by a coal train in Jan. 9, 1886.

Living and Working Conditions.—Industrialization also led to the concentration of the population in the coalfield areas and to the growth of towns. Of these the most notable are the towns of Cardiff and Swansea (pop. 166,740). Rhondda received borough status in 1955. Both Cardiff and Swansea are major seaports; other ports include Newport, Barry, Port Talbot, and Llanelly.

The coalfield of south Wales was, before its

Right: **The City Hall, Cardiff.** ***Below:*** **Harlech Castle, founded by Edward I in 1283. Standing on a height near the Gwynedd county coast and still well preserved, it commands magnificent views of the surrounding area.**

(Right) Pix Inc.; (below) Josef Muench

development, a barren moorland, interspersed with deep parallel valleys running from north to south. It was, therefore, sparsely populated, and the industrial population had to be brought in from the outside. Apart from skilled workers, drawn from England, this population was recruited mainly from the Welsh hinterland, but there was also a considerable Irish element, especially after the famine of 1846; later, Spanish workers migrated to south Wales because of the trade in iron ore with northern Spain. Because of the topography of the area, the mining towns took the form of long narrow strips along the valley beds, with houses built in terraces on the hillsides. Drainage and sanitation were difficult in these circumstances, and living conditions were poor. Many settlements were the property of the mineowners, who also had company (or "truck") shops where their workmen were forced to buy their provisions. Working conditions were difficult, and there were numerous accidents, the most disastrous being that at Senghenydd in 1913, when 439 lives were lost. In consequence of these living and working conditions, there was much industrial discontent. Early in the 19th century, the working-class movement took the form of Chartism (q.v.), and on Nov. 4, 1839, a body of 5,000 Monmouthshire ironworkers and miners marched on Newport. The absence of an industrial tradition, the isolation of the mining valleys, the heterogeneous nature of the population, all made it difficult for a working-class movement to develop. There were frequent strikes, most of them ineffective until the formation of the South Wales Miners' Federation in 1898. South Wales therefore obtained a reputation for industrial unrest. This unrest, however, was largely confined to the mining industry; the other great industries, such as steel, had a remarkable record of industrial peace. A great many industrial workers emigrated to the United States (among them a large number of converts to Mormonism) and took an active part in labor movements in the country of their adoption. Both James J. Davis (United States secretary of labor in the Coolidge administration) and John Llewellyn Lewis (president of the United Mine Workers of America) were, like Aneurin Bevan, natives of Monmouthshire.

2. The People and Their Cultural Heritage

Ethnic Composition and Language.—The population of Wales is mixed in origin. Short, dark people, who predominate on the moorlands of central Wales, are supposed to represent the early inhabitants. At the dawn of history, however, the land was occupied by taller, fair people who spoke a Celtic language. The Celtic-speaking invaders were divided into two groups, the Goidelic and the Brythonic. It was formerly thought that the Goidels came from the Continent across the North Sea, displacing the original inhabitants, and were themselves displaced and driven to the west and to Ireland by the Brythons; but recent scholars consider it more likely that the Goidels came by a western sea route from Spain and crossed from Ireland into Britain. The linguistic division is easily appreciated by considering the Celtic word for "son," embedded in so many personal names. An original *qu* gave a *k* sound in Goidelic, found, for example, in MacDonald (the son of Donald) or MacDowell (the son of the dark man). In Brythonic this became *map* or *mab*, found in Pugh (the son of Hugh) or Prichard (the son of Richard), and before a vowel, in Bevan (the son of Evan) or Bowen (the son of Owen). In modern times the Goidelic branch is represented by Erse, Scottish Gaelic, and Manx, and the Brythonic branch is represented by Welsh, Breton, and Cornish (the last of which is now extinct). The language was greatly influenced by the four centuries of Roman occupation, and modern Welsh has in it a strong Latin element.

The 20th century has seen the decline of the Welsh language. While each succeeding census until 1921 showed a relative decrease in the number of Welsh speakers in the population (owing to the increase of monoglot English speakers), there was still an absolute increase of Welsh speakers, because of the natural growth in the population. The census of 1931 showed both a relative and absolute decrease. The proportion of those able to speak Welsh then stood at 36.8 percent. By the time of the census of 1951, this figure had fallen to 28.4 percent. Numerous reasons account for the decline in the language. A premium had been placed on English by its exclusive use in the law courts and in administration; the gentry had, in the course of the centuries, become Anglicized through contact with the same class in England; industrialization brought an influx of English workers, and at the same time rural Wales, which was predominantly Welsh in speech, suffered from depopulation. Also, until recent years, official policy discouraged the use of Welsh in schools, and the people themselves were indifferent. Great efforts have been made in recent years to reverse this trend, but without apparent success.

See also CELTIC LANGUAGES—*Celtic Language Groups* (British or Brythonic).

Literature and the Arts.—The Welsh language evolved in the 6th century, and Welsh is possibly unique in having a continuous literary tradition from that time. The great Welsh epic, the *Gododdin* (*Gododin*) of the poet Aneirin, dates, in fact, from the 6th century, and was written, not in the area now called Wales, but in the Edinburgh district. It describes an unsuccessful attempt by the Welsh of that territory to regain the old Roman fort of Cataractonium (modern Catterick) in Yorkshire from the Saxons. The petty Welsh princes of the Middle Ages all had their court poets, who wrote in the "strict meters," an elaborate form of alliterative verse. The greatest of all Welsh poets, Dafydd ap Gwilym (who flourished in the mid-14th century and was a contemporary of Petrarch), introduced simpler forms and new themes, singing, in particular, of nature and of love. Medieval Welsh prose finds its highest expression in the tales of the *Mabinogion* (q.v.) and in numerous romances.

As Wales remained throughout many centuries a sparsely populated region with few large centers of population, it was poor in those arts which are dependent upon town life, such as architecture and orchestral music, but the Welsh creative genius continued to find expression in poetry, and particularly in lyric poetry. An outstanding poet of the 18th century was Goronwy Owen (1723–1769), who ended his troubled life in Virginia. The romantic movement had profound influence on Wales. It led to the revival, in 1789, of the Eisteddfod (q.v.; literally, seance or session), a medieval poetical and musical contest, which has since been held

A farmer sets out with his sheep dogs in rugged northern Wales. Sheep farming is an important factor in Welsh agriculture.

British Travel and Holidays Association

annually and has grown to great proportions. With it is associated the gorsedd, a coterie of bards and musicians with an elaborate ritual that purports to go back to the time of the druids but was, in reality, an invention of Edward Williams (1747–1826; better known by his bardic title of Iolo Morganwg), a litterateur of the romantic period. The Eisteddfod (which meets annually in the first week of August, alternately in north and south Wales, and is attended by thousands of people) has had immense influence, for it has canalized the recreation of the Welsh people into musical and literary competitions. Welsh choirs have thereby become celebrated. An entirely independent institution is the international folk dancing and musical festival held every year in Llangollen, in the valley of the Dee.

The 20th century has witnessed a remarkable efflorescence of Welsh literature, both in prose and in poetry. Notable poets were T. Gwynn Jones, W. J. Gruffydd, and R. Williams Parry. Welshmen writing in English have developed into an Anglo-Welsh school. They have included several novelists and prose writers, and at least one poet of genius, Dylan Thomas.

Other arts are represented by the painters Richard Wilson, Augustus Edwin John, and David Jones, and the architect Sir Percy Thomas.

See also BARD; CELTIC LITERATURES—*Welsh Literature*.

Religion.—Christianity was introduced into Britain toward the end of the Roman period, but the Christianization of Wales was due to a number of Celtic saints, who established churches in Brittany, Cornwall, and Wales. Of them, the most notable was St. David (q.v.; d. about 601), who still remains the patron saint of Wales. For some centuries, Celtic Christianity differed from that of Rome, particularly in respect of the date of Easter, but the Roman form was finally accepted in 768. Medieval Wales owed much to the Cistercian monks, who planted their houses in desolate places and kept in close touch with the native population. In their monasteries, the great chronicle of Wales, *Brut y Tywysogion*, was compiled. The Reformation, when these monasteries were dissolved, was introduced into Wales from England. It was in no sense a spiritual awakening in Wales; it was accepted with much indifference but with no opposition. It produced, however, a magnificent translation of the Bible (1588, by William Morgan, later bishop of St. Asaph), which adapted the language to modern purposes and saved it from the fate of the other Celtic tongues. Puritanism, also, despite its later importance, was introduced from England into Wales, and had meager success until the mid-18th century.

The religious revivals of the 18th century gave Wales its present-day religious complexion. The Methodist movement in Wales was, in origin, unconnected with the Wesleys. A Welsh clergyman, Griffith Jones (1683–1761), brought literacy to a large number of people by a unique system of circulating schools, and native Methodist leaders, notably Howell Harris (1714–1773), Daniel Rowland (1713–1790), and William Williams (1717–1791), built on the foundations laid by him. The emotionalism of Methodism permeated the older dissenting denominations, the Baptists and the Independents, and led to a great increase in their numbers. When the census of religious worship was taken in 1851 (the only religious census in British history), it was found that well over three quarters of the people of Wales were dissenters from the Established Church. Religious, political, and economic motives then led to a movement to disestablish the Church of England in Wales, and the struggle culminated in an act of Parliament which was implemented in 1920 during the premiership of the Welshman David Lloyd George. The Anglican Church, however, still remains the denomination with the largest number of adherents.

Education.—Like the Scots, the Welsh people have shown a passion for education. This led to

(Above) L. Bruce Mayne; (right) Pix Inc.

Above: St. David's Cathedral, Dyfed county, one of the most picturesque churches in the British Isles. The building dates back to 1180. *Right:* Talyllyn Lake, at the foot of Cader Idris, in southwest Gwynedd county.

the foundation of university colleges at Aberystwyth (1872), Cardiff (1883), and Bangor (1884), which were incorporated in the University of Wales in 1893, and to which a fourth college at Swansea was added in 1920. An act of 1889 provided Wales with a system of state-aided secondary schools, a dozen years before a similar measure was passed for England. Primary education, which is the concern of local government authorities, was placed under the control of a separate Welsh Department of the Ministry of Education in 1907, the year which saw, also, the establishment of a National Library at Aberystwyth and a National Museum in Cardiff. In recent years, a number of primary schools have been set up in which instruction is entirely through the medium of the Welsh language.

3. History and Government

Wales became separated politically from the rest of Britain when Germanic tribes invaded the island from across the North Sea. In the wars that ensued, the shadowy but historical figure of Arthur emerges (6th century). In later centuries, through the writings of Geoffrey of Monmouth, he became the central figure in cycles of romance, and the Arthurian legend is possibly Wales' greatest contribution to European civilization. The last ruler of a united Britain was Cadwaladr (Cædwalla, d. 664), whose standard, a red dragon on a green background, remains the standard of Wales. In the following century, Offa, king of Mercia (d. 796), delimited the frontier between the English and the Welsh by building Offa's Dyke (q.v.). Even today England is spoken of in Wales as being "beyond Offa's Dyke."

During the succeeding centuries Wales was divided into a number of small units, constantly at war among themselves. In the 9th century the land was unified under Rhodri the Great (d. about 877), who defended Wales against the Norsemen and again in the next century, under Howel the Good (Hywel Dda, d. 950). Welsh society was tribal; with Howel's name is associated a remarkable body of law (the Law of Hywel Dda), which pictures this society in great detail. After 1066, the Normans quickly overran most of south Wales, individual Norman lords conquering the small states one by one and taking over the semiregal powers of the Welsh rulers whom they displaced. Thereby the lordships of the March (borderland) of Wales came into existence. In the lowlands of these lordships the Normans introduced a manorial system. In north Wales, on the other hand, a strong line of princes withstood the Anglo-Norman kings.

Llywelyn ab Iorwerth (d. 1240) played an active part in English politics in the struggle for Magna Carta, and his grandson, Llywelyn ap Gruffydd (d. 1282), allied himself with the revolt of Simon de Montfort. In 1267 Llywelyn assumed the title of prince of Wales, and this was acknowledged by the English crown. However, his death in war against Edward I of England in 1282 brought the dynasty to an end, and the conquest of Wales was completed. The land was organized by the Statute of Rhuddlan (1284), and Llywelyn's territory became a separate principality bestowed on the English king's son as prince of Wales.

Revolts against English domination occurred from time to time, the most notable being in the first decade of the 15th century when Owen Glendower (Owain Glyndŵr, 1354–?1416) proclaimed himself prince of Wales. In the Wars of the Roses which followed, Wales played a significant part, for both York and Lancaster derived much of their support from the Welsh March. The Lancastrian claim devolved on Henry Tudor, the representative of a Welsh house. He unfurled the red dragon of Cadwaladr at the Battle of Bosworth Field (1485), which his supporters hailed as a Welsh victory. Richard III was killed, and Tudor ascended the throne of England as Henry VII.

By the Act of Union of England and Wales (1536), passed in the reign of Henry VIII, both the principality and the March were assimilated to the realm of England. Wales was divided into 13 shires, which were given parliamentary representation, and Welshmen obtained complete equality with Englishmen before the law, except that official business had to be transacted in English. For the next three and a half centuries (until the Local Government Act of 1888) Wales was governed by its own gentry, who represented it in Parliament and administered justice and local government as magistrates in quarter sessions. In time this class became Anglicized in speech and alienated from their tenantry, especially after the religious revival of the 18th century, for the gentry remained Anglican in religion, whereas the people of Wales became predominantly Nonconformist. The later 19th century witnessed a struggle between them, which came to a head in the movement to disestablish the Church of England in Wales. This also acted as a catalyst in party politics, for the Liberal Party supported disestablishment whereas the Tory Party was opposed to it. Hence Wales became solidly ranged on the side of the Liberal Party. In the election of 1906, which ushered in the greatest of Liberal administrations, not a single Tory candidate was returned for a Welsh constituency. The leadership of the Liberals passed to the Welshman David Lloyd George (1863–1945), the World War I leader and architect of the Versailles settlement.

With its success in securing disestablishment (1920), the Liberal Party in Wales seemed to have run its course. The year 1925 saw the foundation of the Welsh Nationalist Party (Plaid Cymru), which advocated dominion status for Wales, while remaining loyal to the crown. It contested several parliamentary elections without success; nevertheless, it forced on the major parties an awareness of Welsh problems. The intense depression in industry in the interwar period, when the unemployment figure for Wales stood at about 250,000 out of a total population of 2,500,000, led to the rapid growth of the Labour Party. As early as the election of 1929, Wales returned 25 Labour members out of its total of 35, and this proportion, with slight variations, remained constant in subsequent elections despite the varied fortunes of the Labour Party in England. Among the party's outstanding Welsh leaders have been Aneurin Bevan and James Griffiths. In 1942 the provision that the law courts must be conducted in English was at last repealed. The Labour government established an Advisory Council for Wales in 1949 to advise it on Welsh affairs, and the Conservative government in 1954 entrusted the oversight of Welsh administration to a minister for Welsh affairs (who combined this with another office) and in 1957, in addition, appointed a minister of state for Welsh affairs. Cardiff was officially made the capital in 1955. In April 1974, Wales' 13 counties (shires) were discontinued, and eight new counties were created in their place.

DAVID WILLIAMS
University College of Wales, Aberystwyth

Further Reading: Carr-Saunders, A. M., and Caradog-Jones, D., *A Survey of the Social Structure of England and Wales* (Garland 1985); Jones, Gareth E., *Modern Wales: A Concise History, 1485–1975* (Cambridge 1985); Morris, Jan, *The Matter of Wales: Epic Views of a Small Country* (Oxford 1985); Williams, David, *A History of Modern Wales* (Musson 1950); Williams, Gwyn A., *The Welsh in Their History* (Longwood 1982).

Lech Wałesa, Polish leader who founded the Solidarity union, was awarded the Nobel Peace Prize in 1983.

WALES, University of (Welsh, Prifysgol Cymru), a British institution established by charter in 1893 and formed by the union or association of three existing colleges: the University College of Wales, Aberystwyth (founded in 1872); the University College of South Wales and Monmouthshire, Cardiff (1883); and the University College of North Wales, Bangor (1884).

The Welsh National School of Medicine, at Cardiff, was founded in 1893 as a department and school of the University College of South Wales and Monmouthshire. It was made a separate college of the university in 1931, and since that time preclinical courses have been provided at the university. Three other colleges are now affiliated with the University of Wales: the Institute of Science and Technology, at Cardiff; the University College of Swansea; and St. David's University College, at Lampeter.

WAŁĘSA, va-wenz'ə, **Lech** (1943–), Polish labor leader who was awarded the Nobel Peace Prize for 1983. He was born in Popowo, a small village near Włocławek, Poland, on Sept. 29, 1943, during the Nazi occupation in World War II. After attending a state vocational school in Lipno, he began work as an electrician at the Lenin Shipyard in Gdansk, where he participated in the bloody "bread riots" over increased food prices in 1970. In 1976, as a delegate to the government-sponsored trade union, he was fired for having drawn up a list of workers' grievances at the shipyard.

In 1978, as strikes and protest demonstrations against the Communist regime's food policies increased throughout Poland, Wałęsa, then working at a machine repair shop, founded the Baltic Free Trade Unions Movement, a predecessor of Solidarity. In August 1980 workers took over the Lenin Shipyard and demanded the reinstatement of Wałęsa. On August 31 the government reached an agreement with a strike committee headed by Wałęsa to allow the workers to form independent trade unions. Despite official obstructions, the union called Solidarity, with Wałęsa as its chairman, was sanctioned by the country's supreme court on Nov. 10, 1980.

In the ensuing months, as the threat of Soviet intervention hung over a troubled Poland, Wałęsa followed a careful, diplomatic course between the Communist government and the country's 13 million workers. In February 1981, Wojciech Jaruzelski became premier, and it soon became apparent that Moscow had ordered the Polish government to toughen its labor policies. Nationwide strikes followed, and in mid-December the government declared martial law and arrested Wałęsa and other Solidarity leaders. On Oct. 8, 1982, Solidarity was dissolved by Parliament. Wałęsa was released from prison in November, only to be subjected to almost continuous harassment by the government. On Oct. 5, 1983, he was awarded the Nobel Peace Prize for his struggle in behalf of workers' rights.

WALKER, Alice (1944–), American novelist, poet, and social activist. Underlying much of her fiction and poetry is the struggle of black women for self-fulfillment and public recognition. She was born in Eatonton, Ga., on Feb. 9, 1944, the youngest of eight children in a family of sharecroppers. At Spelman College in Atlanta, she took part in civil rights demonstrations. A gifted student, she won a scholarship to Sarah Lawrence College, from which she graduated in 1965. Her marriage (1967) to Melvyn Rosenman Leventhal, a white civil rights attorney, ended in divorce (1976).

Walker's first volume of poems, *Once* (1968), occasioned by her summer tour of Africa in 1964, was praised for its insightful views of black Africans, civil rights, love, and despair. Subsequent collections, generally well received for their lyrical grace and originality of theme, include *Revolutionary Petunias and Other Poems* (1973), *Goodnight, Willie, I'll See You in the Morning* (1979), and *Horses Make a Landscape More Beautiful* (1984).

In her first novel, *The Third Life of Grange Copeland* (1970), Walker analyzed the plight of black men who fail in their family relationships, partly because of environmental constraints but also because of their inability to treat women as equals. Another novel, *Meridian* (1976), examines the civil rights movement from the point of view of a black woman who tries to preserve idealistic commitments from convenient slogans. For *The Color Purple* (1982), about a resolute black woman who weathers the physical and psychological abuses of domineering men and succeeds, Walker won the Pulitzer Prize and the American Book Award. The film version was well received.

Walker's short stories are exemplified in *Love and Trouble: Stories of Black Women* (1973) and *You Can't Keep a Good Woman Down* (1981). Her essays are represented in *In Search of Our Mothers' Gardens: Womanist Prose* (1983).

WALKER, David (1785–1830), American black abolitionist, who called for slaves to rebel and secure their freedom. He was born in Wilmington, N. C., on Sept. 28, 1785, of a slave father and a free mother, and was himself considered free. He traveled widely through the South observing the condition of slaves. Settling in Boston, he taught himself to read and write, and in 1827 went into the clothing business. He joined the abolitionist movement and became a correspondent for *Freedom's Journal*, a weekly devoted to the antislavery cause.

In 1829, Walker published a pamphlet, *Appeal . . . to the Colored Citizens of the World . . . but in particular to those of the United States of America*, urging slaves to rise and declare themselves free, using force if necessary.

The *Appeal*, a rousing though closely reasoned document, went through three editions and alarmed many slaveholders. Several Southern states enacted legislation prohibiting the circulation of abolitionist literature. Georgia declared it a crime to teach slaves to read and write. Virginia barred black ministers from preaching to blacks for fear that they would read from Walker's pamphlet.

A reward for Walker's capture or death was offered by a group of Georgians, and friends urged him to seek safety in Canada, but he refused. In the summer of 1830, under unexplained circumstances, Walker was found dead outside his clothing shop in Boston, possibly from poisoning.

Walker's marriage in 1828 produced a son, Edward G. Walker, who in 1866 became the first black elected to the Massachusetts legislature.

WALKER, Sir Emery (1851–1933), English typographer. He was born in Padington, London, England, on April 2, 1851. His formal schooling ended when he was 13. In 1873 he joined a firm of process engravers and in 1886 founded his own firm.

Walker's friendship with William Morris was fruitful in its influence on the improvement of typography, since out of their association came the Kelmscott Press, in 1891. Although Walker had no financial interest in this famous press, for which Morris designed the type and ornaments, he was nevertheless a virtual partner. Following the death of Morris in 1896, Walker and Thomas James Cobden-Sanderson founded the Doves Press, from which Walker withdrew in 1909. He was knighted in 1930 and died in Hammersmith, London, on July 22, 1933.

WALKER, Francis Amasa (1840–1897), American economist and educator. He was born in Boston, Mass., on July 2, 1840. The son of the political economist Amasa Walker (1799–1875), he graduated from Amherst in 1860 and began the study of law, which he gave up to enlist in the Union Army. His rank during the greater part of the Civil War was lieutenant colonel, but in 1865 he was brevetted brigadier general. After serving as chief of the U.S. Bureau of Statistics from 1869 to 1871 and superintending the 9th census (1870), he was commissioner of Indian affairs from 1871 to 1872. From 1873 to 1881 he was professor at the Sheffield Scientific School of Yale, and in 1878 he was the representative of the United States at the International Monetary Conference in Paris. In 1879 he was appointed the superintendent of the 10th census. He accepted the presidency of the Massachusetts Institute of Technology in 1881 and held it until his death in Boston on Jan. 5, 1897. He was president of the American Statistical Association from 1882 to 1897 and of the American Economic Association from 1885 to 1892.

Walker was an earnest advocate of international bimetallism and was deeply interested in the economics of wages and profits. His writings include *The Wages Question* (1876), *Money* (1878), *Political Economy* (1883), *Land and Its Rent* (1883), and *International Bimetallism* (1896). His *Discussions in Economics and Statistics* (2 vols., 1899) was edited by D. R. Dewey, and his *Discussions in Education* (1899) by J. P. Munroe.

WALKER, Horatio (1858–1938), Canadian painter. He was born in Listowel, Ontario, Canada, on May 12, 1858. He began his studies under J. A. Fraser, a miniature painter, in Toronto; visited Europe in 1882; and in the following year settled permanently on the Île d'Orléans in the St. Lawrence River.

He visited New York City in 1885, and in 1891 he was elected to the National Academy of Design. He was the recipient of awards at expositions in Paris, Chicago, Buffalo, St. Louis, and San Francisco.

Walker specialized in paintings of French Canadian peasant life and scenes, particularly studies of farm animals, and his work shows the influence of the Barbizon school, particularly of Jean François Millet. Among his best-known works are *The Harrower* (Metropolitan Museum, New York City); *Oxen Drinking* (National Gallery, Ottawa, Canada); *Ave Maria* (Corcoran Gallery, Washington, D.C.); *Sheep Yard by Moonlight* (National Gallery, Washington, D.C.); and *Sheepshearing* (Albright Art Gallery, Buffalo). He died on the Île d'Orléans, Quebec, on Sept. 27, 1938.

WALKER, Jimmy (1881–1946), American politician. James John Walker was born in New York City on June 19, 1881. After attending St. Francis Xavier School and LaSalle Academy, he entered St. Francis Xavier College. He left after a year to enroll at the New York Law School and was admitted to the bar in 1912. Three years earlier he had been elected to the New York State Assembly, and in 1915 he progressed to the state Senate, becoming minority leader of that body in 1921. With the combined support of Tammany Hall and Gov. Alfred E. Smith, he defeated the Republican-Fusion candidate, Frank Waterman, and was elected New York City's 97th mayor in 1925.

Jimmy Walker came to typify the sophisticated New York of the "Fabulous Twenties," the era of speakeasies, limitless speculation, and a free-and-easy political philosophy. Soon after his reelection in 1929, however, rumors of civic corruption prompted the state legislature to order an investigation of the city's affairs. The Hofstadter investigation committee named Samuel Seabury as its counsel, and widespread graft and maladministration were revealed. On the witness stand, when questioned by Seabury, Mayor Walker had difficulty making plausible the explanation of some of his transactions, which were alleged to have yielded him large sums of money.

In 1932, Gov. Franklin D. Roosevelt called him to Albany to discuss his finances, and on Sept. 1, 1932, Walker resigned as mayor. He then moved to Europe until 1935 and there married the film actress Betty Compton (he had divorced his first wife, Janet Allen). In 1940 he became impartial chairman of the National Cloak and Suit Industry. He died in New York City on Nov. 18, 1946.

WALKER, Mary Edwards (1832–1919), American physician and advocate of women's rights. She was born in Oswego, N.Y., on Nov. 26, 1832. Notably ahead of her time in her views on women's rights, she studied medicine and in 1855 received a physician's certificate from the Syracuse Medical College. After practicing briefly in Columbus, Ohio, she moved to Rome, N.Y. During the Civil War she served as a nurse in the Union Army until 1864, when she was commissioned and made an assistant surgeon.

As a girl she had begun to wear trousers, partly concealed by a skirt, and in the Army she wore a uniform like that of the other officers. After leaving the Army in 1865 she worked briefly as a journalist in New York City and then took up medical practice in Washington, D.C. There she wore men's clothes in the daytime, but full evening dress when she was lecturing on social reforms.

In 1865 she became the first woman to receive the Congressional Medal of Honor, awarded for her medical work in the Civil War. The medal was withdrawn by the Board of Medal Awards in 1917 but restored by the Army in 1977.

WALKER, Robert J(ohn), American legislator: b. Northumberland, Pa., July 19, 1801; d. Washington, D.C., Nov. 11, 1869. For "a mere whiffet of a man, stooping and diminutive, with a wheezy voice and expressionless face," Walker in the course of his career sustained a multitude of activities that would have taxed the strength of a more outsize individual.

His father was the jurist and Jeffersonian Jonathan Hoge Walker. Financial problems, which troubled Walker intermittently because of his speculations, began early and he had to borrow money to pay tuition at the University of Pennsylvania. Graduating in 1819 at the top of his class, Walker was admitted to the bar in Pittsburgh two years later. By 1824, Walker was a leader of the Democratic Party in Pennsylvania and a force in rallying its strength behind the presidential ambitions of Andrew Jackson.

Greener fields beckoned in Mississippi where he joined his brother Duncan in a lucrative law practice and was drawn into the vortex of the speculative boom in cotton, plantations, and slaves. Although his speculations were astronomical, Walker retained enough of the common touch to enable him to defeat George Poindexter in the senatorial campaign of 1835. Walker's victory was aided by the reputation for eccentricity that Poindexter had acquired and by the latter's expressed preference for Jeffersonian to Jacksonian democracy, whereas Walker eagerly claimed Gen. Andrew Jackson's support.

In the Senate, Walker was typical of many statesmen of the middle period of American history in his avowed advocacy of sectional interests. He favored the award of public lands to new states, supported the cause of preemption, endorsed a low tariff, and opposed the distribution of the federal surplus lest the result provide an excuse for increasing tariff rates. A good Jacksonian Democrat, he supported the independent treasury scheme and opposed the Bank of the United States. An ardent expansionist, he enthusiastically supported the annexation of Texas, and his *Letter of Mr. Walker of Mississippi, Relative to the Annexation of Texas* (1844) was widely publicized by the proannexationists.

President John Tyler's treaty of annexation was defeated in the Senate despite Walker's ardent defense and it was not until the election of James K. Polk, whose candidacy Walker had favored, that a compromise resolution of the annexation of Texas was passed. Polk further rewarded Walker by making him secretary of the treasury in 1845. Four years in this office provided additional evidence of Walker's position as a supporter of the independent treasury system and of a tariff for revenue. His negotiation of a public loan for support of the Mexican War was, on the whole, a commendable operation; the warehousing system that he established for handling imports had a lasting influence that extended beyond his years in the cabinet; and he sponsored a bill for the creation of the Department of the Interior.

After leaving the Treasury, Walker continued to live in Washington, using his political connections to advance business interests that concerned him or those who retained him. He was engrossed in land speculation, projects for a Pacific railroad, mining, and the marketing of corporate securities, but he found it impossible to resist an offer to be governor of the strife-torn Kansas Territory in 1857. There a breach developed between Walker and the Southern extremists and he was compelled to resign after a relatively brief tenure.

Walker became a Unionist and supported Stephen A. Douglas for the presidency in 1860. During the Civil War his financial talents were exploited in the sale of federal bonds in England, an operation which was notably successful. After the war he was again active as a lobbyist. Walker supported the annexation of Alaska with the same enthusiasm that he had once urged the acquisition of Texas. On his deathbed he was hopeful that the United States would yet acquire Nova Scotia.

EDWARD N. SAVETH,
Graduate Faculty, New School for Social Research.

WALKER, Sears Cook, American mathematician and astronomer: b. Wilmington, Mass., March 23, 1805; d. Cincinnati, Ohio, Jan. 30, 1853. After graduating from Harvard College in 1825 he taught school for a time, then worked as an insurance actuary, devoting his leisure time to the study of astronomy. In 1837 he was asked to set up an astronomy observatory for the Philadelphia High School, one of the first in the United States. In 1845 he joined the staff of the newly established United States Naval Observatory in Washington, D.C. From 1847 until his death he was responsible for computing longitudes for the United States Coast Survey. His most famous contribution to astronomy was the conclusion, based on a large number of observations, that the electric telegraph furnished the best means of determining the difference of longitude from place to place. He initiated the telegraphing of transits of stars, and what came to be known as the American method of applying the graphic registration of time results to the registry of time observations.

WALKER, Thomas, American physician, trader, and explorer: b. King and Queen County, Va., Jan. 25, 1715; d. Albemarle County, Nov. 9, 1794. After studying medicine with his sister's husband he set up practice in Fredericksburg, Va., and became noted as a surgeon. He also ran a general store and engaged in an import-export trade. By marriage he acquired the 11,000-acre estate known as Castle Hill, from which he carried on trading operations. In 1748 he joined a group of land speculators who explored lands to the west and staked out claims for themselves; in 1749 he became chief agent of the Loyal Land Company which had received a grant of 800,000 acres from the Council of Virginia, and in the following year he led an expedition to explore the lands of this grant. He kept a journal of the trip, which is the first record of a white man in what was to become Kentucky.

In 1755, during the French and Indian Wars, he became commissary to the Virginia troops under George Washington, and was later charged with fraud in his accounts, but acquitted. He served in the Virginia House of Burgesses for a number of years and represented Virginia in negotiations with the Indians in 1768 and 1775. Active in the revolutionary movement, he was a member of the executive council when Virginia became a state. At Castle Hill, where he built a homestead in 1765, Walker was a neighbor of the Jefferson family, and for a time he was guardian of the young Thomas Jefferson.

WALKER, William, American adventurer: b. Nashville, Tenn., May 8, 1824; d. Trujillo, Honduras, Sept. 12, 1860. Walker's short stature, slight frame, and habit of reticence were hardly suggestive of his role as "gray-eyed man of destiny" and intrepid filibuster. His various careers and his capacity for audacity involved him in the practice of three professions and motivated a life of derring-do, culminating in death before a firing squad.

Walker graduated from the University of Nashville in 1838, and five years later received a medical degree from the University of Pennsylvania. There was a year of postgraduate medical study in Paris followed by a *wanderjahr* on the European continent—a rather unusual educational background for a man born at that time in the Southwest. But the medical profession palled upon him as did his next profession, the law, which he practiced in New Orleans and gave up to become editor and proprietor of the *Daily Crescent.* His career as journalist lasted for about two years, after which, in 1850, Walker was on his way to California.

In booming San Francisco and later in Marysville, Walker devoted himself to law and journalism. But in an atmosphere of national expansion, other horizons beckoned. In 1853, Walker commanded an expedition which landed at La Paz, Lower California, which Walker proclaimed an independent state and with himself as president. But with the Mexicans hostile and the American authorities refusing to allow his supplies to follow him, Walker could only retreat to the border, surrender to the American force stationed there, and stand trial in San Francisco for violating the neutrality laws. He was acquitted by a sympathetic jury.

With appetite whetted, soaring personal ambition, and the fever of manifest destiny in his blood, Walker turned his attention to Nicaragua. At the head of a small band and aided by the Accessory Transit Company, an American company operating as a transportation factor across the isthmus, Walker had little trouble in seizing Nicaragua and proclaiming himself president in 1856.

Walker's activities in Nicaragua had the support of an important segment of Southern opinion in favor of both slavery and expansion. This included Joseph Brown, Alexander H. Stephens, Thomas L. Clingman, Robert Toombs, and others equally prominent. While the federal authorities frowned upon his filibustering activities, Walker received considerable regional support. He repealed an earlier Nicaraguan decree for the abolition of slavery, an action "calculated to bind the Southern States to Nicaragua, as if she were one of themselves."

Walker dreamed magnificent dreams of a military empire constituted of Central American states; an interoceanic canal that would attract the shipping of the world; and the use of slave labor in the development of the economy of Central America. But the fantasies exploded before the reality of British and French interests in the area and Walker's error in supporting, in the councils of the Accessory Transit Company, a faction opposed to the redoubtable Cornelius Vanderbilt. There was soon another revolution in Nicaragua and Walker was deposed.

Back in the United States, Walker tried to return to Central America and reestablish his authority. In August 1860 he landed in Honduras, whence he tried to reach Nicaragua by land. The British apprehended him, however, and turned him over to the Honduran authorities, who executed him by firing squad.

EDWARD N. SAVETH,
Graduate Faculty, New School for Social Research

WALKERTON, wôk'ər-tən, town, Ontario, Canada, seat of Bruce County, on the Saugeen River, about 30 miles southeast of its entry into Lake Huron at Southampton. Served by the Canadian National and Canadian Pacific railways, it is the trading and service center for an extensive general farming area. Its industries, formerly based on local water power but now served by the Ontario hydroelectric system, include furniture and woodworking, flour milling, metalworking, and dairying. Population: 4,682.

D. F. PUTNAM.

WALKIE-TALKIE, wôk'ē-tôk'ē, a portable two-way radio set developed by the United States Army Signal Corps in 1933 and employed extensively during World War II by the infantry for communication between platoon and company commanders. It weighed about 30 pounds, had a telescoping antenna and French-type telephone, and was worn strapped to the back of a soldier who remained at the side of his unit commander. Both the transmitter and receiver operated on one preset frequency, thus eliminating tuning, and were automatically switched on when the antenna was extended to its full length.

Wide World Photos

When snow disrupted telephone service in Washington, D.C., White House police resorted to walkie-talkies.

Following the war, the size was greatly reduced by the development, first, of small batteries and tiny vacuum tubes and, later, of transistors and other miniaturized parts. Combination transmitters and receivers, now called transceivers, have since found many police, fire, railroad, trucking, and other civilian applications in addition to their military use.

FRANK DORR.

WALKING, wôk'ĭng, a term generally applied to progressing on foot, never having both feet off the ground at the same time. This provision, rather than the speed attained, differentiates walking from running, since a person may walk faster than he runs.

As a recreational activity walking may be divided into two main branches. The first is walking over terrain for the exercise and pleasure derived thereby. This branch is more commonly called *hiking*.

WALKING RACES

The second branch is *competitive walking*, that is, racing. The rules, in essence, state that contact with the ground must always be maintained with some portion of one foot. The heel must touch the ground first, and the toe be the last portion to leave it. The heel of the foremost foot must touch the ground before the toe of the other foot breaks off contact. For these reasons walking is often called the "heel-and-toe" sport.

Currently, competitive walking is far less popular than competitive running in the United States, although events for sectional and national championships are held under the auspices of the Amateur Athletic Union. There is no interscholastic or intercollegiate competition. Distances vary from 1 to 25 miles where United States records are considered, and there are recognized world records for various distances between 2 and 30 miles and 3,000 and 50,000 meters, as well as for distances covered in one and two hours.

In the Olympic Games walking races have been a fixture since 1908, although the distances have varied. Currently the distances are 20,000 and 50,000 meters. In modern times Americans have fared indifferently in the sport. They hold no world records and have won no Olympic titles since 1906. The USSR, Sweden, Australia, and Czechoslovakia have dominated the sport, Soviet athletes in particular having established many world records.

As an example of contrasts in speed between walking and running, the record for the mile walk is slightly under 6.5 minutes as against slightly under 4 minutes for the mile run. At longer distances the disparity is less, but not markedly so.

PARKE CUMMINGS,
Author of "The Dictionary of Sports."

Wide World Photos

Competitors in the 1960 Olympics pass Castel Sant' Angelo in Rome during the 50-kilometer (31-mile) walk.

WALKING FISH. See SERPENT HEAD.

WALKING LEAF. See LEAF INSECT.

WALKING PURCHASE, The, a measure of land purchase common among certain North American Indian tribes—the distance a man could walk in a specified time. In 1682 the Delaware Indians sold to William Penn a tract of land at the junction of the Delaware and Lehigh rivers, extending in depth as far as a man could walk in a day and a half. Penn and a group of Indians walked 40 miles and the deed to that much land was given him.

In 1737, when the Delaware agreed to sell another tract of land, Thomas Penn engaged expert walkers who, in the allotted time and over a prepared trail, advanced 66½ miles and the resultant claim embraced about 12,000 square miles. When the Delaware complained that their venerable custom had been abused, Penn invited the Iroquois to expel them, whereupon the Delaware allied themselves with the French. The result of Thomas Penn's departure from his father's policy of fair dealing with the Indians were the savageries of Indian warfare. In 1758, Penn gave over the northern part of the purchase to the Iroquois and four years later the colony compensated the Delaware for the southern portion by a payment of £400.

EDWARD N. SAVETH.

WALKING STICK, an elongated insect of the family Phasmidae, order Orthoptera, which simulates twigs, grass stems, and leaves. These insects remain absolutely motionless when alarmed, so that it is almost impossible to see them. There are about 700 species, confined mainly to the tropical regions of the world. Some of the larger species attain a length of 9 to 13 inches and are the longest of all living insects. Over a half of this great length is formed by the overdeveloped second and third thoracic segments of the body. The mouth parts are of the biting type, the eyes are small, the antennae are fairly long, and the legs are long and slender. These insects have the unusual ability of at least partially regenerating lost limbs. The female drops her eggs singly on the ground and at short intervals, letting them fall where they may.

WILLIAM D. FIELD.

WALKÜRE, Die, dē väl-kü'rə (THE VALKYRIE), the second music drama of Richard Wagner's *Der Ring des Nibelungen* (text by the composer), first performed at the Court and National Theater, Munich, June 26, 1870. (See NIBELUNGEN, THE RING OF THE.) Between the close of *Das Rheingold,* the first music drama in the cycle, and the opening of *Die Walküre,* Wotan (baritone) has realized that the evil resulting from the theft of the Rhine gold can be ended only if the Ring is returned to the Rhine. Needing an innocent hero who will shoulder the gods' guilt, retake the Ring, and restore it to the Rhine maidens, Wotan, disguised as Wälse, a hero, has fathered the twins Siegmund (tenor) and Sieglinde (soprano) by a mortal woman.

Act I.—Into the forest home of the Neiding warrior Hunding (bass)—a huge room built around the trunk of an ash tree—Siegmund staggers in exhaustion. Hunding's wife Sieglinde (soprano) tenderly takes care of Siegmund. Hunding, who has recognized the intruder as an enemy, nevertheless respects the duty of giving him refuge for one night. Sieglinde, attracted by Siegmund, and half aware that he is her brother, puts Hunding into a drugged sleep and shows Siegmund the sword embedded in the ash tree by a one-eyed wanderer (Wotan) at her wedding feast. It is to belong to him who can extract it from the tree trunk. When the infatuated Siegmund easily withdraws the sword, Sieglinde recognizes him as her hero brother. Leaving Hunding asleep, the two acknowledge their love and disappear into the surrounding forest.

Act II.—In a wild forest place Wotan tells Brünnhilde (soprano)—his favorite among the Valkyrie daughters he has had by Erda—to protect Siegmund in the coming fight between him and Hunding. Fricka (mezzo-soprano), Wotan's wife and the protectress of marriage, demands that Siegmund be punished for having stolen Hunding's wife, his own twin sister. Reluctantly, Wotan orders Brünnhilde to drain the strength from Siegmund's sword. The Valkyrie informs Siegmund of his coming death, but disobeys Wotan during the actual fight, attempting to save

HOUSE & GARDEN

WEYERHAEUSER

Above: Hardwood veneer mounted on lightweight plywood makes easily installed paneling and provides the natural beauty of hickory to this modern living room.

Left: Entrance hall of a restored 18th century American home. The painted murals so popular in that period have returned to favor, sometimes in the form of wallpaper.

Siegmund. Wotan places his spear between Hunding and Siegmund, and Siegmund's sword shatters against it; Hunding kills him. In a mixture of rage, remorse, and disappointment, Wotan in turn kills Hunding. But Brünnhilde succeeds in saving Sieglinde, who will bear Siegmund's child.

Act III. Brünnhilde brings Sieglinde to her eight Valkyrie sisters, who have assembled on their rock with the bodies of heroes which they are carrying to Walhalla. She begs them to protect her from Wotan's wrath over her disobedience. Knowing that Wotan cannot be appeased, Brünnhilde gives Sieglinde the pieces of Siegmund's sword and sends her down into the forest to bear her child there. She then faces Wotan, who, rejecting her pleas and those of her sisters, deprives her of her godly attributes. He rules that Brünnhilde must be put into a magic sleep on the summit of the rock; he promises only that whatever hero shall reach her and awaken her will be allowed to lead her into a new life. He then calls upon Loge, god of fire, to surround the Valkyries' rock with a ring of flame that can be penetrated only by a hero who has never discovered fear. Wotan knows, as Brünnhilde half knew before falling asleep, that this hero will be Siegfried, the son of Siegmund and Sieglinde.

HERBERT WEINSTOCK
Author of "Music as an Art"

WALKYRIE. See VALKYRIE.

WALL COVERINGS, wôl kŭv'ər-ĭngs, decorative materials used to cover walls whether for decoration or for concealing or correcting architectural defects. They are not part of the actual wall construction as is tile or plaster. Since they are applied directly to the wall, they are subject to the same style influence as the rooms of which they are a part, so that in traditionally styled rooms the system of proportioning the walls into separate spaces, such as dado or frieze, which commenced with the Renaissance, has been followed ever since.

Wall coverings follow closely contemporary fashions, and many effects formerly unattainable because of the expense have become possible with materials simulating marble, embossed leather, cabinet woods, textiles (including satins and brocades) and metal surfaces. This decorative flexibility is supplemented by many interesting artistic effects, including those of painted mirrors, deeply incised and sculptured linoleum, photomurals, paintings on canvas, and hand-painted wallpaper in narrow strips. Indeed the adaptability of wall coverings to a decorative scheme is limited only by the relative versatility of the interior decorator.

One of the most usual decorative wall coverings is *paint*, brushed, rolled, or sprayed on; it not only introduces color into a room but also serves as a protective covering. Most painted walls are of plaster—rough or smooth—which is the most widely used wall material. No wall should be painted unless the surface is smooth and dry. At least three coats are needed for a new painted surface or for covering a dark color. Paint is available in almost any color desired. In fresco decoration the painting is done directly on the wet plaster.

Murals in any medium—oil, watercolor, or pastels—are usually painted on canvas, paper, or other material which is then mounted on the wall. Finally a glaze or a coating of clear lacquer is applied so that the mural may be cleaned without spoiling it. Photomurals are enlargements of photographs on paper or cloth which are mounted on walls in sections or as a single unit for decoration.

Fabrics are frequently applied to walls, and they may or may not be the same pattern as the

Grass cloth was a common type of wall covering earlier in the century and its soft texture recommends it for use today. Here, an elegant blue grass cloth is used on the walls of a bedroom decorated in an unusual and very personal way.

draperies in the room, depending upon the decorative effect desired. Fabric is applied to the wall with a binder in the same way as wallpaper, and, if desired, a narrow braid or gimp is pasted at the edges for a neat finish; if the fabric is used in panels a narrow molding, painted the color of the woodwork, is used instead of the braid. A highly decorative, but rather formal, treatment can be achieved with fabric dipped in plaster, draped on the wall, and allowed to dry into stiff folds. Another effective method of decorating walls with plaster is to enclose mirrors, paintings, or *objets d'art,* set into the wall, with molded plaster frames.

The transience from apartment to apartment or from house to house, year after year, precludes solid wood paneling as a decorative treatment, but the owner can have an economical effect of paneling by employing flexible *wood veneers* that are obtainable mounted on strong plywood backing wallboard, heavy cloth, or on paper which can be applied directly to the wall. The expense is but a fraction of what wood planks and buttresses would cost, is easily hung, and requires only an occasional rewaxing for a beautiful finish. Many varieties of cabinet woods are available in this form, including satinwood, walnut, and bleached oak.

Insulating boards, made of fiber treated to be moisture- and verminproof, are to be had in various sizes and with beveled edges and grooves cut in the surface to give the effect of beveled planks. (See WALLBOARD.) Other types are either enameled in a plain surface or marked off in squares to simulate tile.

Even *glass* is not to be overlooked as a wall covering. Manufacturers of glass offer tinted, clear, and antiqued mirrors for walls, as well as heat-resisting glass for mantelpieces and structural glass for partitions. Opaque colored glass is useful as a wall covering in kitchens and bathrooms.

Lustrous washable and fadeless wall coverings can be obtained in innumerable colors and variety of designs, and highly artistic schemes can be evolved from the new wall coverings of *spun glass* or *metal.* The spun glass is made by cementing tiny threads of glass to a paper backing which enables it to be applied easily to the wall. The result is a washable and durable wall covering eminently suitable as a background for either contemporary decoration or the delicate 18th century styles. The metal wall coverings have a thin coating of metal bonded to a paper backing by means of an electrochemical process while being manufactured.

Handwoven *grass cloth,* made of thin strips of wild honeysuckle bark in natural and other colors, with a metallic or a brilliantly colored paper backing, give a richly textural surface that constitutes an artistic and durable wall covering.

Linoleum resembling fine paneling or marble, and also available in many plain and textural effects, is an important and comparatively new wall covering. Natural *cork* is also a useful medium, and highly decorative effects are being achieved with tiles in natural, dark, and mottled colors applied at random or to form a pattern.

Leather, popular since the Renaissance as a wall covering, has continued in popularity, and ideas abound in the ways in which it can be applied: either nailed, quilted, stretched tightly over boards of almost any shape applied to the wall, or used as a background for a mural.

The numerous types of *laminated synthetic materials* and the range of decorative possibilities make them worthy of serious consideration. They are strong and light, flexible enough for application to rounded surfaces, and unaffected by water, grease, or grime. These fabricated materials, resembling leather, find favor because of increasing style range and the broadening of their application.

WALLPAPER

Of the many types of wall coverings, perhaps the most familiar is wallpaper, printed, painted, embossed, or grained, and available in patterns and various degrees of texture—from smooth glossy surfaces to those resembling rough plaster —and in finishes to suit every taste and budget. Wallpapers constitute an extensive range which—excepting the papers customarily applied on sidewalls—may be divided into five categories: ceiling papers, borders, scenics and panels, imitative papers simulating various materials, and three-dimensional papers with a relief surface. Many of these are guaranteed sunfast and washable, and special coatings of some make them also resistant to stains and grease—even those in delicate colors. Of the various types, there are papers covered in silk, as well as those manufactured to resemble chintz and other printed fabrics. Velvety flock papers—made by printing the design on paper of various colors with glue, instead of a color, and then blowing fine colored wool or silk shavings over the wet glue design—simulate the rich texture and sheen of expensive Genoese velvets. The solid-colored wallpaper in a wide range of hues, either plain or with self-colored motifs, is best as a background for furniture and fabrics, but the most difficult to hang. Patterned wallpapers include various types: isolated motifs and classic designs for formal rooms; small overall patterns for bedrooms and rooms in Early American or Provincial styles; stripes, geometric patterns, and small repeat designs for small rooms or where broken wall areas need to be brought into line; and, for contemporary rooms, there are stylized patterns and abstract motifs well designed and beautifully colored. Wallpapers and fabrics, printed from the same rollers, make a pleasing combination when no other pattern appears in the room. Wallpapers with specially durable surfaces are obtainable for kitchens, bathrooms, and children's rooms. The very young child will appreciate a storytelling paper, while an older child will be interested in a paper showing various sports, or perhaps a map of the world, or one depicting historical events or the development of the railroad and steamship.

Except for scenic papers, sold by the panel, wallpaper is sold in double rolls, 16 yards long, 20, 22, or 30 inches wide, untrimmed; European wallpapers are 19 to 22 inches trimmed. The more expensive custom-made papers are screen printed or stenciled, and the cheaper papers are roller printed; a few fine papers are still printed by hand from wood blocks, a separate set of blocks being used for each color.

The first wallpapers were hand painted in China and as early as the middle of the 16th century examples had begun to arrive in Europe, brought by Dutch and Portuguese traders. They were a luxury, however, and competitive cheaper imitations soon began to appear. These were crudely printed in black on 15-inch squares of colored paper in allover geometric designs from wood blocks, the first appearing in France at Rouen in 1620–1630, made by one Le François. They were pasted up in haphazard fashion, with no attempt at matching repeats, as a substitute for expensive tapestry hangings used on walls as protection against drafts. Similar papers were printed in England as early as the reign of Henry VIII (1509–1547), although the first patent was not issued until 1692, in the reign of William and Mary. The art was perfected in the middle years of the 18th century by Reveillon in Paris, who popularized paper panels designed by Pillement as a substitute for expensive painted decoration. Papers of an even later period were still printed from wood blocks, with finishing touches added by hand. By 1760 the French were pasting the small sheets together in strips before printing, in a fixed length of 24 sheets 20 inches wide called endless paper. Jean Papillon was the first to produce wallpaper in a continuous repeating design.

In the United States the first wallpaper factory was established in 1790 by John B. Howell at Albany, N.Y. In 1803 Zuber began publishing his series of superb scenic papers, rivaled only by Joseph Dufour, which reached a zenith in popularity about 1830. Within 10 years papers were being printed by machine, and by 1867 expensive hand-blocked papers had come to an end, although they occasionally enjoyed subsequent revivals in popularity.

A considerable part of the wallpaper market is concerned with reproductions of old papers, of which many authentic antique examples are still available. These include papers from old original wallpaper documents, and paper removed from trunk linings, hatboxes, and the like. Some Chinese hand-painted examples are 200 years old. Modern adaptations of documentary wallpapers are especially useful in giving an authentic atmosphere to interiors decorated in the traditional styles, particularly those expressing the English and French periods. For these, small floral prints, toile patterns, fruit motifs, swags, and plumes are suitable. For formal rooms of the Regency, Directoire, Empire, and American Federal periods the scenic wallpapers are appropriate; for more informal rooms of the same

Far left: **Plastic is now available in proper weights for wall covering, as shown here. It is particularly recommended for service areas such as kitchens and bathrooms. The braided rug is also of plastic.**

Left: **A simply striped wallpaper decorates one wall of this room, providing an excellent background for the large bed. Another wall, in whitewashed wood paneling, furnishes an interesting contrast.**

periods, there are stripes, wreaths, medallions, shocks of wheat, Napoleonic bees, pilasters, and contrasting borders. For rooms in the Louis XV and XVI styles, there are papers imitating the rare silks and damasks of the period, particularly appropriate for use in small rooms. These papers reproduce motifs including toile vignettes, bowknots, stripes, ribbons, wreaths of flowers, festoons, and swags.

In decoration wallpapers are esteemed for their magical qualities of illusion; scenic designs will make small rooms appear larger; they can supply architectural details and furnishings in a room with printed designs of furniture, windows, and shelves of books; they can widen a room with their designs arranged horizontally, or lift a low ceiling with stripes printed vertically; they can give a remodeled look with the various textures available; architectural irregularities can be accented or minimized as desired with such designs as grilles, windows, and louver shutters; or they can contribute dramatic interest as decorative panels.

See also INTERIOR DESIGN.

LEE CANNON,
Managing Editor, "Interior Design."

Bibliography

Little, Nina F., *American Decorative Wall Painting, 1700–1850* (Dutton 1980).

Lynn, Catherine, *Wallpaper in America: From the 17th Century to World War I* (Norton 1980).

Schoeser, Mary, and Cooke, Fred, *Twentieth Century Design: Fabrics and Wallpapers* (Dutton 1986).

Yeager, Robert C., *Painting and Wallpapering*, ed. by Sally W. Smith (Ortho Bks. 1986).

WALL CREEPER, a beautiful and interesting songbird (*Tichodroma muraria*) of Eurasia. The wall creeper inhabits mountainous regions, and frequents steep rock faces and occasionally the walls of ruins or stone buildings while searching their crevices for food. The nest is built also in rocks and walls, deep in a narrow crevice or hole. The bird is about 5 inches in size, not counting its long decurved bill which may reach a length of 1½ inches. The body plumage is soft gray and the bird is inconspicuous when at rest but becomes a burst of color when it flies, for its large wings are beautifully patterned with carmine, red, black, and white. It creeps on rocks and because of this and the long curved bill, was classified until very recently among the true creepers (family Certhiidae). However, it is related to the titmice (family Paridae), which it resembles in its anatomy and physiology, rather than to the true creepers.

CHARLES VAURIE.

WALL PAINTINGS. See MURAL PAINTING; WALL COVERINGS.

WALL STREET, a street in New York City, extending from Broadway to the East River, which takes its name from the fact that it follows the line of the old wall erected across lower Manhattan Island by the Dutch colonists as a protection against their enemies. At the southwest corner of Wall and Broad streets is the New York Stock Exchange; at the southeast corner, the building of J. P. Morgan & Co.; and at the northeast corner, the old U.S. Sub-Treasury Building (now a museum), standing on the site where George Washington made his first inaugural address. Abutting on Wall Street are many of the greatest financial institutions in America. Because of this concentration the term "Wall Street" came into popular use as referring to the financial center of the United States. See also NEW YORK—*10. Places and Activities of Interest.*

WALLA WALLA wŏl'ə wŏl'ə, city, Washington, seat of Walla Walla County, situated on the Walla Walla River 6 miles north of the Oregon border and 161 miles southwest of Spokane by road. The city lies at an altitude of 900 to 1,000 feet in a broad valley at the edge of the Blue Mountains to the south. Its name comes from a Nez Percé Indian word meaning "little river." It is served by a federal highway and for freight only by the Union Pacific, Northern Pacific, and Walla Walla Valley railways; passenger services are provided by Greyhound Bus Lines and West Coast Airlines. The city is primarily a residential, trade, office, and processing center for a large and prosperous farming region, with chief products of wheat, peas, sugar beets, alfalfa seed, cattle, sheep, poultry, asparagus, strawberries, carrots, onions, and spinach. It has food-processing plants, a container factory, and lumber mills, and does a large business in insecticides, chemical fertilizers, and farm machinery. There are a veterans' and two general hospitals. The state penitentiary is within the city.

The city is the seat of Whitman College (q.v.), containing the Whitman Museum of historical and other exhibits, St. Paul's School (Episcopal) for girls, and the usual public and parochial schools. Walla Walla College (Seventh-Day Adventist), founded in 1892, is at nearby College Place. A Little Theatre, the Symphony Society and Orchestra (founded in 1907), and public and college libraries contribute to cultural and educational activities, while the many recreations include mountain hunting and skiing. The Southeastern Washington Fair, held every September, features a rodeo.

The area is rich in history. Six miles west of the city is the Whitman National Monument, commemorating the work of Marcus Whitman (q.v.), American missionary and pioneer who was massacred by Indians with his group in 1847. In 1856 United States cavalry forces established a post (Fort Walla Walla) at the present city site, and the village that grew there, at first called Steptoeville but named Walla Walla in 1859, served as a supply point for Washington and Idaho miners. The city was incorporated in 1893. It adopted a commission form of government in 1911 but changed to the council-manager system in 1960. Population: 25,618.

SARAH CORCORAN,
Librarian, Walla Walla Public Library.

WALLA WALLA INDIANS (meaning "little river"), a North American Indian tribe of the Shahaptian language stock, most closely related to the Nez Percé and Cayuse tribes. They once inhabited the lower Walla Walla River region and the junction of the Columbia and Snake rivers of Oregon and Washington, but they have been removed to the Umatilla Reservation in Oregon, where some 623 Walla Walla resided in 1960. Through intermarriage and a long period of intermixture, their culture has been so thoroughly enmeshed with that of the Nez Percé, Cayuse, and Umatilla peoples that differentiation is almost impossible.

FREDERICK J. DOCKSTADER.

WALLABY, wŏl′ə-bē, the small kangaroo (q.v.) of Australia, New Guinea, and adjacent islands. Compared with the kangaroo, the tail is more hairy, the feet larger, and the third incisor tooth has a central notch. Wallabies live in shrub, brushwood, or open country. One of the largest, the red-necked wallaby (*Macropus ruficollis*), measures 40 inches in head and body, and has a tail 30 inches long. Rock wallabies (*Petrogale*) inhabit rocky areas, shelter by day in caves, and can ascend trees. The hare wallabies (*Lagorchestes*), found in grassy places, have the size, habits, and speed of hares.

Arthur W. Ambler from National Audubon Society

A pair of wallabies, diminutive cousins of the kangaroo.

TRACY I. STORER.

WALLACE, wŏl′əs, **Alfred Russel,** British naturalist: b. Usk, Monmouthshire, England, Jan. 8, 1823; d. Broadstone, Dorset, Nov. 7, 1913. Wallace ended his formal education at the age of 14 and for several years worked variously as apprentice watchmaker, surveyor, and schoolteacher. While employed as a surveyor he became interested in geology and botany and the problems of botanical classification, and began systematically to write down his ideas. While teaching at the collegiate school in Leicester, he took up hypnotism, engaging in experiments in what he called phrenomesmerism, which were actually concerned with suggestion and telepathy. More important he met Henry Walter Bates, the naturalist, who introduced him to the science of entomology. At this time also he read *An Essay on the Principle of Population* (1798) by Thomas Robert Malthus, which greatly influenced Wallace's thinking on selection as a factor in evolution.

In 1846 Wallace persuaded Bates to accompany him on a collecting trip up the Amazon, defraying expenses by the sale of specimens. They sailed in 1848. In 1850 they separated to follow different routes and Wallace traveled up the Rio Negro and mapped unexplored portions of the Uaupés River. A fire at sea on the return voyage in 1854 destroyed everything he had with him, but from notes and collections sent home earlier he published *Palm Trees of the Amazon and their Uses* (1853) and *A Narrative of Travels on the Amazon and Rio Negro* (1853).

While working on his collections in London, Wallace came to the conclusion that the Malay Archipelago offered the richest field for a collector. In 1854, therefore, he set out for the East Indies, where he traveled until 1862. The following years were spent in studying his collections—he obtained 125,660 specimens altogether—and in publishing the results. Wallace supported himself entirely by the sale of collections and by lectures, books, and articles on many subjects until 1881, when, through the influence of Charles Robert Darwin and Thomas Henry Huxley, he was granted a Civil List pension of £200 a year. In his later years he espoused a number of unorthodox theories and causes, both scientific and social, which tended to obscure his genuine contributions to the natural sciences. His writings encompass the full range of his eclectic interests.

One of Wallace's most famous achievements was his independent discovery of the means of evolutionary change. In a paper published in 1855, *Essay on the Law which has regulated the Introduction of New Species,* he stated that the geographical distribution of species and genera required some sort of evolutionary explanation. In 1858, while lying ill with fever at Ternate in the Molucca Islands, he realized that natural selection was the method by which evolution operated. He wrote out his ideas and mailed his essay to Charles Darwin, who, unknown to him, had been developing the same theory for 20 years. Darwin resolved his dilemma by having read, at a meeting of the Linnaean Society on July 1, 1858, Wallace's essay together with a sketch of his own written in 1844 and a letter written in 1857. The three documents were published in the *Journal* of the Linnaean Society in 1858. Wallace's section was entitled "On the Tendency of Varieties to Depart Indefinitely From the Original Type." As presented in these papers, there is no significant difference between the theories of Darwin and Wallace. Both men stress variation and heredity, acted upon by natural selection, as sufficient to explain evolutionary change.

Wallace's greatest contributions were in the field of zoogeography. In three important works, *The Malay Archipelago* (1869), *The Geographical Distribution of Animals* (1876), and *Island Life* (1880), he mapped out a series of zoogeographic regions and discussed the patterns of continuity and discontinuity in the distribution of animal types. He reasoned that the present continents and oceans were essentially permanent in position, and made a distinction between isolated oceanic islands and continental islands, which rise through shallow seas from shelves which link them to the continental land mass. Finally, on the basis of his vast collections, he demonstrated that the boundary between the Asiatic and Australian zoogeographic regions passed between the islands of Bali and Lombok in the East Indies, a theoretical dividing line which is known as Wallace's Line.

Wallace was married in 1866 to a daughter of botanist William Mitten. He received the Order of Merit in 1910.

See also ZOOGEOGRAPHY—*Historical Factors* and *Zoogeographical Regions.*

GERALD M. HENDERSON,
Department of Sociology and Anthropology, Brooklyn College

WALLACE, DeWitt, American publisher: b. St. Paul. Minn., Nov. 12, 1889; d. Mount Kisco, N.Y., March 30, 1981. William Roy DeWitt Wallace attended Macalester College in St. Paul and the University of California at Berkeley. After working as a salesman for St. Paul publishers, he enlisted in the Army in World War I. While selling books he had conceived the idea of a magazine consisting of condensations of articles appearing elsewhere, and while convalescing in an Army hospital in France he practiced making digests of the articles he read. On returning to St. Paul he studied magazines in the public library to discover what subjects were of enduring interest, and by January 1920 had prepared a sample copy of the *Reader's Digest*. Unable to find a publisher, he went to New York, determined to publish the periodical himself. The first issue appeared in February 1922, and in 1938 the first British edition was published in London. By the 1980's the *Reader's Digest* had a circulation of approximately 30 million—the largest of any American magazine—and was printed in 17 languages for international distribution.

Lila Bell Acheson Wallace (1889–1984), his wife and the cofounder, coeditor, and coowner of the *Reader's Digest*, was the daughter of a Presbyterian minister. After graduating from the University of Oregon in 1917, she engaged in social service work until her marriage to Wallace on Oct. 15, 1921, four months before the first issue of the *Reader's Digest* was published. Lila Wallace became known for her philanthropic activities, including the restoration of Boscobel, a mansion near Garrison, N.Y., and gifts to the Metropolitan Museum of Art in New York City.

WALLACE, (Richard Horatio) Edgar, English novelist, playwright, and journalist: b. Greenwich, England, April 1, 1875; d. Hollywood, Calif., Feb. 10, 1932. Brought up in the family of a poor but respectable London fish porter, he left school at the age of 12, and engaged in a number of occupations before enlisting at 18 in the army. Sent to South Africa in 1896, he began to contribute to various journals there, and on his discharge in 1899 became a correspondent for Reuters and the London *Daily Mail*. In 1902 he served as first editor of the *Rand Daily Mail* in Johannesburg. In 1905 his first novel, *The Four Just Men*, was published, and with the appearance of *Sanders of the River* (1911) his reputation as an author was established. The very quantity of his output is worthy of record; in 28 years he produced over 170 books, in addition to numerous music-hall songs, plays, magazine and newspaper articles, and, in his last years, motion-picture stories. One of his most successful plays, *On the Spot* (1931), was written in four days. His novels and plays, mostly thrillers concerned with crime detection, were notable for the freshness and originality with which he worked out basic plots. As many as 5 million copies of his books were sold in a single year.

WALLACE, George Corley, American political leader: b. Clio, Ala., Aug. 25, 1919. His election to the governorship of Alabama in 1962, 1970, 1974, and 1982 helped make him an important figure on the national political scene.

Wallace grew up in rural Alabama, where his father owned and managed several small tenant farms. In high school he won and successfully defended the state bantamweight boxing championship. He also boxed professionally to help meet expenses at the University of Alabama law school. After graduating from law school in 1942, he served three years in the Air Force.

After several years in private law practice and two terms in the state legislature, Wallace was elected a state district court judge in 1952. His defiance of a federal court order to produce voting records in 1956 brought him his first statewide support. He lost a race for governor in 1958, but was elected in 1962. His administration adopted extensive programs for the poor. A segregationist, he sought to bar the path of black students seeking to enroll at the University of Alabama, but both the university and the public schools were integrated. He received some support for the 1964 Democratic presidential nomination. Ineligible by state law to succeed himself, Wallace successfully backed his wife, Lurleen, for governor in 1966, with the understanding that he would continue to set policies for the state. Lurleen became the nation's third woman governor, but she died in office in 1968.

In 1968, Wallace ran for president on the American Independent party ticket. He supported "law and order" and condemned urban riots and protest demonstrations, and won 13% of the popular vote. The state constitutional bar against gubernatorial succession was repealed in 1969. Wallace was elected again in 1970 and became a moderate on racial issues, winning increasing black support. On May 15, 1972, while campaigning for the Democratic presidential nomination, he was shot in Laurel, Md., by Arthur Bremer. Though partially paralyzed and unable to walk, Wallace was reelected in 1974. He failed again in his bid for the Democratic presidential nomination in 1976. Elected for the fourth time in 1982, he served out his term in progressively poor health, then retired in 1987.

WALLACE, Henry Agard, Vice President of the United States: b. Adair County, Iowa, Oct. 7, 1888; d. Danbury, Conn., Nov. 18, 1965. After graduating from Iowa State College with a bachelor of science degree in agriculture in 1910, he became associate editor of *Wallaces' Farmer*, succeeding his father as editor in 1924. When this journal was merged with the *Iowa Homestead* in 1929, Wallace remained editor until 1933. Meanwhile, he had developed several high-yielding strains of hybrid corn, selling the seed with great success through his own company.

Originally a Republican, Wallace supported the Democratic presidential candidate Alfred E. Smith in 1928, and in 1932 he helped to swing Iowa for Franklin Delano Roosevelt. As secretary of agriculture during the first two Roosevelt administrations, he was an ardent supporter of New Deal policies, and set up within the Department of Agriculture the Agricultural Adjustment Administration (*q.v.*) to administer the farm price support program.

In 1940 Wallace was elected vice president and served in this capacity during Roosevelt's third term in office. He was sent on goodwill tours to Latin America and the Far East, and from 1942 to 1943 was head of the short-lived Board of Economic Warfare. In 1944, after the nomination of Harry S Truman as vice president, Wallace was appointed secretary of commerce, being confirmed by the Senate on March 1, 1945, shortly before Truman succeeded to the presidency. A speech made by Wallace on Sept. 12,

1946, attacking the administration's firm policy toward the Soviet Union, led to his resignation by presidential request. He then became editor of the liberal weekly, the *New Republic*, whose circulation more than doubled before he left it in 1947.

In 1948 Wallace became presidential candidate of the Progressive Party, a newly organized third party with a pro-Soviet platform attacking the Marshall Plan and calling for disarmament Although polling a popular vote of over a million, Wallace and the vice-presidential candidate, Senator Glen H. Taylor of Idaho, failed to carry any state. In 1950 Wallace left the party after it had repudiated his endorsement of the United States-United Nations police action in Korea. He subsequently published a statement, "Why I Was Wrong" (*This Week*, Sept. 7, 1952), explaining his shift from sympathy for the aims of the Soviet Union to a deep distrust of these aims. Wallace withdrew from politics and resumed his activity with the Pioneer Hi-Bred Corn Company, from his farm in New York State. Wallace was a prolific writer. His publications include *Corn and Corn-Growing* (with Earl N. Bressman, 1923; 5th ed., 1949); *America Must Choose* (1934); and *Sixty Million Jobs* (1945).

HENRY CANTWELL WALLACE (1866–1924) was the father of Henry Agard. After graduating from Iowa State Agricultural College (1892) and teaching there for a time, in 1895 he joined his father (Henry Wallace, 1836–1916) and brother in acquiring the periodical *Farm and Dairy*, which they renamed *Wallaces' Farm and Dairy* and later *Wallaces' Farmer*. Under the editorship of Henry Wallace (until his death in 1916) and Henry Cantwell Wallace (1916–1924) this became one of the leading farm journals in the United States. Through editorial policy and his activities in several farm organizations, Henry Cantwell Wallace became a leader in promoting farm interests, working particularly for the equalization of railroad rates for farm products. While secretary of agriculture from 1921 until his death in 1924 he reorganized the agriculture department. During his term in office he also championed conservation and improved marketing methods. He wrote *Our Debt and Duty to the Farmer* (1925).

WALLACE, Lew(is), American lawyer, soldier, author, and diplomat: b. Brookville, Ind., April 10, 1827; d. Crawfordsville, Feb. 15, 1905. After studying law in his father's office, he served in the Mexican War as a 2d lieutenant. Admitted to the bar in 1849, he practiced in Indianapolis, Covington, and Crawfordsville, and was elected to the state Senate in 1856. During the Civil War he rose from colonel to major general in the Union Army, distinguishing himself in battles at Romney, W.Va., Fort Donelson, Tenn., and the second day (April 7, 1862) of the Battle of Shiloh, Tenn. At the Battle of the Monocacy (July 9, 1864), he held off Lieut. Gen. Jubal A. Early's Confederate Army with a smaller, unseasoned force, suffering defeat but preventing Early's capture of Washington. Wallace served on the court-martial which tried the assassins of Abraham Lincoln, and presided over the military court which convicted the superintendent of Andersonville Prison (q.v.) of cruelty in allowing the death of Union prisoners.

Returning to Crawfordsville in 1865, Wallace practiced law and ran unsuccessfully for Congress in 1870. He was appointed governor of New Mexico Territory in 1878 by President Hayes and settled the then-raging Lincoln County cattle war. He stayed in New Mexico until 1881 and then served ably as minister to Turkey from 1881 to 1885.

In 1873 Wallace published *The Fair God*, a historical romance inspired by Prescott's *Conquest of Mexico*, and in 1880 came *Ben Hur; A Tale of the Christ*, one of the best sellers of all time, translated into many languages and successfully dramatized on stage and screen. His later works such as *The Boyhood of Christ* (1888) and *The Prince of India* (1893), did not have the enduring appeal of this classic.

WALLACE, SIR Richard, English connoisseur and collector of art: b. London, England, July 26, 1818; d. Paris, France, July 20, 1890. Wallace was reputed to be the illegitimate son of either the 4th marquess of Hertford or of that nobleman's mother. Known in youth as Richard Jackson, he spent much of his life in Paris, where he was well known in society and art circles. After 1857 he assisted the 4th marquess in building up the finest private art collection in the world, and in 1870 he inherited this together with Hertford House in London and other properties. In 1871 he was created a baronet in recognition of his relief services during the siege of Paris in the Franco-Prussian War. He bequeathed the Hertford-Wallace collection to his French wife, the former Julie Amélie Charlotte Castelnau, who on her death in 1897 left it to the English nation.

WALLACE, Robert Charles, Canadian geologist and educator: b. Orkney, Scotland, June 15, 1881; d. Kingston, Ontario, Canada, Jan. 29, 1955. Educated at the University of Edinburgh (M.A. 1901; B.Sc. 1906; D.Sc. 1912) and at Göttingen University (Ph.D. 1909), he specialized in the physical chemistry of rock magmas, petrology, and crystallography. Coming to Canada in 1910, he became lecturer (1910–1912) and professor (1912–1928) of geology and mineralogy at the University of Manitoba, also serving from 1926 to 1928 as commissioner of mines and natural resources for Manitoba. From 1928 to 1936 he was president of the University of Alberta, which acquired a school of nursing and expanded university extension work under his leadership. Wallace became principal and vice chancellor of Queen's University in Kingston in 1936. During his 15 years as principal, schools of nursing, fine arts, and physical and health education were established, as well as departments of industrial relations and biological research. In 1951 he became executive director of the Arctic Institute of North America. In 1945 he participated in the London conference which formed the United Nations Educational, Scientific, and Cultural Organization (UNESCO). He served as Canadian advisory editor for THE ENCYCLOPEDIA AMERICANA from 1940. Among his publications are *Liberal Education in a Modern World* (1932) and *Religion, Science, and the Modern World* (1952).

WALLACE, William, American manufacturer: b. Manchester, England, March 16, 1825; d. Washington, D.C., May 20, 1904. In 1832 his family migrated to the United States, and in 1848 he joined his father and brothers in founding, first at Derby, Conn., and in 1850 at Ansonia, Conn., the firm of Wallace & Sons, which soon became one of the leading manufacturers of copper and brass in the United States. In cooperation with Moses Gerrish Farmer, Wallace began to make dynamos employing armatures of various types, one of which, the Farmer-Wallace dynamo, was used to illuminate the buildings and grounds of the Centennial Exhibition at Philadelphia in 1876, the first general electric lighting in the United States. In 1877 he patented a plate-carbon arc lamp for use with this dynamo, by means of which a number of arc lights could be placed in series on the circuit, thus originating the series method of arc lighting.

WALLACE, SIR **William,** Scottish patriot: b. probably at Elderslie, family estate near Paisley, Scotland, about 1272; d. London, England, Aug. 23, 1305. Such little as is known of Wallace's early life is derived from a metrical biography written nearly 200 years after Wallace's death by Henry the Minstrel, who based his work on a manuscript of John Blair, personal friend and chaplain of Wallace, but also adorned it with later legends. Wallace appears to have been the second son of a landed family of Cymric (Welsh) ancestry with holdings in Renfrewshire, west of Glasgow. He emerged as a leader of Scottish independence in 1297, at a time when Edward I (q.v.) of England, taking advantage of virtual civil war in Scotland between the parties supporting two contenders for the throne of Scotland, had imprisoned one, John de Baliol (1249–1315; see BALIOL), won over the rival Bruce family, carried the Scottish coronation stone from Scone to Westminster, and made himself king of Scotland. When Edward was called to France by war with Philip IV, Wallace rallied his countrymen to fight for Scottish freedom.

In May 1297 Wallace led a band of 30 men in burning Lanark and killing its sheriff (an appointee of Edward), and he soon formed a disciplined army from the Scotsmen, mostly commoners or small gentry, who flocked to his standard. In September Wallace's forces met an English army near Stirling Castle, and gained a signal victory by cutting down the enemy as they crossed a narrow bridge over the Forth River. Soon much of Scotland was under his control and he crossed the border to ravage northern England. By 1298 he was ruling Scotland as guardian of the kingdom for Baliol. According to tradition he was knighted at about this time, perhaps by a Scottish nobleman.

Edward I, on his return from the French war, inflicted on July 22, 1298 at Falkirk a crushing defeat on Wallace, who had been deserted by many of the Scottish nobles and was thus deficient in cavalry. Wallace then gave up the guardianship of Scotland and in 1299 went to France to beg aid from Philip IV. The Anglo-Scottish war continued, but what part Wallace took is not certain. In 1304 the Scottish barons submitted to Edward, who outlawed Wallace and put a price on his head. On Aug. 5, 1305 the patriot was captured by a fellow countryman, Sir John de Menteith, and taken to London. There Wallace was tried and executed for treason although, as he maintained, he could not be guilty of treason because he had never sworn allegiance to Edward. Wallace had never had the support of the entire Scottish nation—the nobles were particularly undependable—but after his execution Wallace's name became a symbol of the Scottish struggle for independence, and he continues to be one of the great national heroes of Scotland.

WALLACE, William Stewart, Canadian historian: b. Georgetown, Ontario, June 23, 1884; d. Toronto, Ontario, March 11, 1970. Educated at the University of Toronto (B. A. 1906) and Balliol College, Oxford (B. A. 1909; M. A. 1912), he was professor of history at McMaster University (1909–1920) and special lecturer on that subject at the University of Toronto (1910–1922). At the latter institution he joined the university library in 1920, and held the position of librarian from 1923 until his retirement in 1954. During World War I he served in the Canadian Expeditionary Force (1915–1918).

Wallace was editor of the *Canadian Historical Review* (1920–1930), the *Encyclopedia of Canada* (6 vols., 1937), and two volumes for the Champlain Society. In addition he was author of a number of books chiefly on Canadian history, including *The United Empire Loyalists* (1914); *The Family Compact* (1915); *By Star and Compass* (1922; rev. ed. 1953); *Dictionary of Canadian Biography* (1926; rev. ed. 1945); *Murders and Mysteries* (1931); and *The Pedlars from Quebec* (1954).

WALLACE, William Vincent, Irish composer and concert artist: b. Waterford, Ireland (Eire), March 11, 1812; d. in the Pyrenees, France, Oct. 12, 1865. The son of a bandmaster, Wallace became a professional violinist at the age of 15 and began composing about 1831. In 1835 he set out on a series of concert tours and adventures which took him to Australia, North and South America, Germany, Holland, and England, where he made his London debut in 1845. His first opera, *Maritana,* was produced at Drury Lane in 1845. Wallace also wrote *Matilda of Hungary* (1847), *The Amber Witch* (1861), *Love's Triumph* (1862), and *The Desert Flower* (1863), but *Lurline* (1860) was the only other successful opera. He composed a vast number of light piano pieces such as *La Gondola* and *Tarantelle.*

WALLACE, city, Idaho, Shoshone County seat, situated at an altitude of 2,729 feet; 75 miles east of Spokane, Wash. The trading center of the Coeur d'Alene mining and lumbering district, it has smelting and woodworking industries. The city was founded in 1884 under the name of Placer Center and incorporated as Wallace in 1888. Pop. 1,736.

WALLACEBURG, wôl'əs-bûrg, town, Ontario, Canada, a port on the Sydenham River, in Kent County, about 16 miles northwest of Chatham. The port admits lake steamers up to 19-foot draft. Wallaceburg is also an industrial center, producing glass and glass containers, brass and brass tubing, pressure cookers, iron castings, builders' hardware, and dried cereal grass. It was settled early as a river crossing and local service center on the Chatham-Sarnia road and incorporated in 1896. Population: 11,506.

D. F. PUTNAM.

WALLACE'S LINE. See WALLACE, ALFRED RUSSEL.

WALLACH, väl'äĸ, **Otto,** German chemist: b. Königsberg, Prussia, March 27, 1847; d. Göttingen, Germany, Feb. 26, 1931. After receiving his doctorate at Göttingen in 1869 he went to Bonn as assistant to Friedrich August Kekulé von Stradonitz (q.v.). Made professor at Bonn in 1876 and director of instruction in pharmacy in 1879, he became interested in the chemical structure of ethereal oils such as camphene, citrene, and related terpenes. He continued this research as director of the Chemical Institute at Göttingen (1889–1915), and for his masterly analysis and identification of the complex terpenes or alicyclic compounds, which laid the foundation of the modern perfume industry, Wallach was awarded a Nobel Prize in 1910.

WALLACK, wŏl'ək, a family of actors of English origin who played an important part in the development of the New York theater:

JAMES WILLIAM WALLACK: b. London, England, about 1795; d. New York, N.Y., Dec. 25, 1864. The son of actors, he made his first stage appearance in a pantomime at the age of 4 and became a member of the Drury Lane company at 12. He received great acclaim in his New York City debut in 1818, and until 1851 divided his time between England and the United States. From 1852 he made his permanent home in America. In 1837 he took over the management of the National Theatre in New York, where his older brother, Henry John Wallack, became stage manager and his nephew, James William Wallack, the juvenile lead. In 1852 he acquired Brougham's Lyceum at Broadway and Broome streets and renamed it Wallack's, under the stage management of his son, Lester Wallack. In 1861 father and son opened a new Wallack's Theatre at Broadway and 13th Street. Wallack was regarded as a remarkably versatile actor, equally successful in melodrama and light comedy, and an unusually competant stage manager.

LESTER WALLACK (christened JOHN JONHSTONE WALLACK): b. New York, N.Y., Jan. 1, 1820; d. Stamford, Conn., Sept. 6, 1888. The son of James William Wallack, he was educated in England, and did not make a professional stage appearance until he was nearly 20. He returned to the United States only in 1847. Unwilling to take advantage of his father's famous name, he acted under such names as Allan Field and John Wallack Lester, and it was not until 1861, when he had achieved a reputation of his own as an actor, and had become the real manager of his father's theater, that he appeared as Lester Wallack. In addition to acting in such popular plays of the period as Dion Boucicault's *Used Up*, he played in a number of his own works, including *First Impressions* (1856), *Rosedale* (1863), and *A Scrap of Paper* (1879).

The Wallack's Theatre company attracted some of the most famous players of the period, and although Lester Wallack retired in 1887, the theater continued under the name of Wallack's until 1915, when it was demolished after a final season under Harley Granville-Barker (q.v.). Lester Wallack's memoirs, *Memories of Fifty Years*, were published in 1889.

WALLAROO. See KANGAROO.

WALLAS, wŏl'əs, **Graham,** English political thinker: b. Sunderland, Durham, England, May 31, 1858; d. Portloe, Cornwall, Aug. 9, 1932. Educated at Oxford University (1877–1881), he was a schoolmaster (1881–1890) before becoming a university extension lecturer. He joined the Fabian Society in 1886 and contributed to *Fabian Essays on Socialism* (1889). Wallas helped to plan the London School of Economics where he lectured (1895–1923), becoming professor of political science in 1914. His political experience was gained in local government, for he sat on the London School Board (1894–1904) and on the London County Council (1904–1907). He was a member of the Royal Commission on the Civil Service (1912–1915) and lecturer at the Lowell Institute at Boston (1914).

His influence, which was widespread, was exerted mainly through his brilliant lecturing and teaching, and through his few but seminal writings. According to George Bernard Shaw his lectures on Chartism and his *Life of Francis Place* (1898) did much to persuade the Fabians of the need for scholarly study of earlier radical movements, and paved the way for the researches of Beatrice and Sidney Webb on trade unionism and other 19th century working-class movements. But his chief importance lies in his pioneer work in social psychology. He criticized the intellectualist assumptions of current political thought and emphasized the place of irrational forces in politics and in the making of public opinion. His studies of *Human Nature in Politics* (1908) and *The Great Society* (1914) did much to widen and deepen English political thought in the 20th century. In witty, persuasive style he showed the dangers to democracy of failure to realize how much political decisions rest on subconscious processes of habit, suggestion, and imitation. His reputation has grown as his independence, originality, and perceptiveness have become more fully appreciated.

DAVID THOMSON,
Sidney Sussex College, Cambridge University, England.

WALLASEY, wŏl'ə-sĭ, county borough, England, on an upland of the Wirral Peninsula in Cheshire, facing Liverpool across the estuary of the Mersey River. The town of Wallasey is largely residential, housing white-collar workers who commute to Liverpool by ferry. The borough also includes the seaside resort of New Brighton, famous for its seven-mile promenade along the waterfront. Industry is limited to the southern part of the borough, where its dock system is linked with that of Birkenhead on Wallasey Pool. Pop. (1961) 103,213.

WALLBOARD, wôl'bōrd, a general term used to designate a number of materials employed on walls and ceilings in place of or over plaster. Common types include pulpboard of relatively soft or intermediate consistency, gypsum (sheetrock), plywood and other wood products, plastic laminates, and various kinds of hardboard. They range in thickness from ⅛ to 1 inch. Most are available as planks 8 and 16 inches wide and as building boards or panels in 32- and 48-inch widths. Lengths are commonly 8 and 10 feet, sometimes 12 feet and, especially in the case of composition products, 16 feet. They are applied by cementing to the wall surface or nailing to studs or furring strips. Edges may be plain for butting or they may be tongue-and-grooved or lapped to conceal nails or clips.

Pulpboard, or paperboard, is made directly from pulp. Gypsum is a mineral, hydrous calcium sulphate, used in making plaster. Gypsum wallboard consists of a gypsum core encased in thick tough manila paper. For greater resistance to fire, some gypsum boards have vermiculite, glass fibers, and other noncombustible mineral products embodied in the gypsum core. Plywood is built up of a number of bonded thin veneers. Another manufactured wood product consists of a core of bonded wood chips faced with bonded wood flakes. Plastic laminates are made of synthetic resins reinforced with glass fibers. Hardboard is reconstituted natural wood fabricated by reducing the wood to fibers and then pressing the fibers together into panels. It may be standard or tempered, the tempered hardboard being denser, harder, and having higher moisture resistance than standard board. The surface of any wallboard may be natural or treated. One popular treated finish is with vinyl, which provides a hard, mar-resistant face in wood-grain, striated woven, or figured patterns.

FRANK DORR
Associate Editor of "Popular Science Monthly"

WALLENBERG, väl'ən-berg, **Raoul** (1912–), Swedish diplomat, who is credited with saving at least 100,000 Hungarian Jews from deportation to concentration camps by German occupation authorities during World War II.

Wallenberg was born in Stockholm on Aug. 4, 1912, of a family of prominent bankers, industrialists, and diplomats. He traveled widely as a youth and became proficient in several languages. At the University of Michigan he studied architecture and city planning, and after graduating in 1935 worked for a business firm in South Africa and for a Dutch bank in Haifa, Palestine, where he met Jewish refugees from Germany. He later managed an export-import business in Stockholm.

In July 1944, Wallenberg was appointed an attaché to the Swedish mission in Budapest, Hungary. Amply funded by the U.S. War Refugee Board and the American Jewish Joint Distribution Committee, he distributed fabricated passports and identification papers to thousands of Jews assigned for deportation to Nazi death camps and placed other Jews in buildings under Swedish government custody.

On Jan. 17, 1945, he left Budapest by car in the company of a driver and two Russian officers, ostensibly for a meeting with Soviet officials in Debrecen, Hungary. Neither he nor his driver returned. Wallenberg was believed to have been arrested by Soviet authorities, presumably on espionage charges.

The Soviet government disclaimed any knowledge of Wallenberg but in 1957 reported that he had died in prison of a heart attack ten years before. Some former Soviet prisoners testified that they had seen Wallenberg as late as 1976, and an international committee concluded in January 1971 that he was still alive.

On Oct. 5, 1981, President Ronald Reagan approved a special act of the U.S. Congress making Wallenberg an honorary American citizen, a distinction awarded to only one other person—Sir Winston Churchill. This action empowered the State Department to take the case to the Soviet authorities.

Further Reading: Bierman, John, *Righteous Gentile: The Story of Raoul Wallenberg, Missing Hero of the Holocaust* (Viking 1981); Lester, Elenore, *Wallenberg: The Man in the Iron Web* (Prentice-Hall 1982); Rosenfeld, Harvey, *Raoul Wallenberg: Angel of Rescue* (Prometheus 1982); Werbell, Frederick E., and Clarke, Thurston, *Lost Hero: The Mystery of Raoul Wallenberg* (McGraw 1982).

WALLENSTEIN, väl'ən-shtīn, **Albrecht Wenzel Eusebius von** (1583–1634), Austrian general in the Thirty Years' War. He was born in Hermanič, Bohemia (now Czechoslovakia), on Sept. 24, 1583, of a noble family named Waldstein. His family was neither wealthy nor influential. Driven by a passion for power, he resolved to make his own way. Although he converted from Lutheranism to Catholicism, he had no strong religious convictions. His faith was in astrology, and he strongly believed in the horoscope cast for him by the astronomer Johannes Kepler.

At age 22 he received his first army commission in an expedition against the Turks in the Balkans. In 1609 he married a wealthy Moravian widow, Lucretia von Wičkov, and on her death five years later inherited her extensive estates. Wallenstein's bravery in the relief of Gradisca, besieged by the Venetians, won the attention of Ferdinand of Styria (later Emperor Ferdinand II). Wallenstein supported the Habsburgs in the Bohemian revolt of 1618.

His military exploits in the Bohemian war were, however, less notable than his shrewd business sense and his administrative ability. He borrowed money from bankers which he used to recruit soldiers and to purchase landed properties, some of them the confiscated estates of the Bohemian nobility. In turn, he made large loans to the emperor, and Ferdinand II repaid him in land and dignities. By 1623, Wallenstein possessed 2,000 square miles in northeast Bohemia and was the wealthiest man in the country. The emperor appointed him governor of the kingdom, quartermaster general of the army, and bestowed on him the title of prince of Friedland. He married a daughter of Count von Harrach, one of the emperor's closest advisers.

When Christian IV of Denmark threatened the Habsburg cause in 1625, Wallenstein offered to raise an army of 20,000 men. Ferdinand II accepted and appointed him commander in chief and created him duke of Friedland. Wallenstein then proved his military ability by routing Count von Mansfeld at Dessau Bridge on April 25, 1626, and contributing to the final defeat of Christian IV. As General of the North and Baltic Seas, Wallenstein sought control of the Baltic but was checked at the Siege of Stralsund in 1628.

Jealous of Wallenstein's wealth and his new rank of duke of Mecklenburg, and in fear of the emperor's great power which depended on the duke's army, the German princes forced Ferdinand to dismiss Wallenstein on Aug. 13, 1630. He was recalled in December 1631 to stem the successes of Gustavus Adolphus of Sweden. His strategy against Gustavus Adolphus and his repulse of the king at Nuremberg on Sept. 3, 1632, earned him a high rank among military commanders. At the Battle of Lützen on Nov. 16, 1632, the Swedes defeated Wallenstein at the expense of their great king's death.

Wallenstein's complex personality and spectacular career have been treated in numerous scholarly and literary works. He has been portrayed as a loyal servant of the emperor and a traitor, a soldier who also sought peace, a Bohemian patriot as well as a good German. After his dismissal in 1630, he offered his services to Gustavus Adolphus and intrigued with exiled Bohemian rebels, perhaps to secure the Bohemian throne. When he was reinstated as commander in chief, he carried on negotiations with Saxony in the furtherance of a general peace. There can be no doubt that after Lützen, Wallenstein degenerated in mind and body. The Saxon and Bohemian intrigues were renewed, and he approached Cardinal Richelieu. But he followed no line of action with consistency. Ferdinand II was finally convinced that his general plotted treason, and on Jan. 24, 1634, he ordered Wallenstein's seizure dead or alive.

Wallenstein was murdered at Eger in Bohemia on Feb. 25, 1634, by Walter Devereux, an English captain. His officers also were murdered by soldiers who were part of the forces of Walter Butler, an Irish general, and Walter Leslie and John Gordon, Scottish colonels. The German poet Johann Christoph Friedrich von Schiller immortalized Wallenstein in a dramatic trilogy.

E. A. BELLER
Princeton University

WALLENSTEIN, wol′ən-stīn, **Alfred Franz** (1898–1983), American conductor, who introduced classical music on radio. He was born in Chicago, Ill., on Oct. 7, 1898, the son of an Austrian father and a German mother. After his family moved to Los Angeles, Calif., Wallenstein began to study the cello at the age of eight. A year later he made his first public appearance. Soon he was playing in theater orchestras and on the vaudeville circuit. In 1916 he played with the San Francisco Symphony Orchestra, and in 1917 was engaged by the ballerina Anna Pavlova for an extensive tour of Central and South America. After two years of study in Europe, he became first cellist of the Chicago Symphony Orchestra in 1922, and remained there until 1929, when Arturo Toscanini invited him to join the New York Philharmonic Orchestra. He resigned in 1936, when Toscanini retired.

Meanwhile Wallenstein became director in 1931 of a radio orchestra which broadcast the first all-classical program in the United States with commercial sponsorship; in 1933 he began to direct his Sinfonietta for radio station WOR (New York City) of the Mutual Broadcasting System, presenting classical music several times a week in choice evening time, and demonstrating that classical music could find favor with the public. As music director of WOR from 1935 to 1945, he developed a balanced program of music broadcasts, ranging from Bach to modern composers and from opera to folk music. For this service to American music he received the George Peabody Award of the University of Georgia (1941) and the Alice M. Ditson Award of Columbia University (1947).

As music director of the Los Angeles Philharmonic Orchestra from 1943 to 1956, Wallenstein developed programs for young people, including the concert series Symphonies for Youth. He was music director of the Hollywood Bowl from 1952 to 1956 and conductor of the Symphony of the Air from 1961 to 1963. Wallenstein appeared as guest conductor with a number of leading orchestras and in 1966 became visiting conductor at the Juilliard School of Music. He was awarded the French Legion of Honor in 1955. He died in New York City on Feb. 8, 1983.

WALLENSTEIN, a dramatic poem by Johann Christian Friedrich von Schiller consisting of *Wallensteins Lager* (Wallenstein's Camp), a prologue in one act; *Piccolomini,* a drama in five acts; and *Wallensteins Tod* (Wallenstein's Death), a tragedy in five acts. The three parts were first performed at Weimar, Germany, in 1798 and 1799. The idea of a dramatic treatment of the towering figure of Wallenstein had come to Schiller as early as 1791 during his intensive study of the Thirty Years' War.

According to Johann Wolfgang von Goethe, Schiller's *Wallenstein* is "so great that nothing else of its kind exists a second time." The best in Schiller's manner of thinking and in his writing technique seems to be most happily combined: the inspiring buoyancy of his language, the structure of the plot which rises dynamically to its climax, the wealth of male figures and male conflicts, and—the unique accomplishment of a genius—his success in bringing to life with the most economical means the world-historical background of an important period in the history of the Occident. Nowhere is the drama burdened by the ballast of Schiller's massive source studies. Everything is real and lifelike to the spectator or reader.

The central figure is the ambitious general, driven by impulses, who, far beyond his historical model, has become a unique character in world literature. To be sure, his actions are determined by his desire for power and by his ambition. But it is difficult to understand him in view of his indecision, his tactics of never committing himself in writing, his mania of bringing his worldly actions in harmony with cosmic events by means of astrology, his blind trust on the one hand, and his hesitant distrust on the other. He cannot, in any event, be brought down to a common denominator. Just for that reason he is again and again the most fascinating—now the most pleasing, now the most repulsive—central character of the entire trilogy.

Wallenstein's opponent, Octavio Piccolomini, a general, is also individually delineated. He, too, is not a common traitor against Wallenstein, but an important personage representing the crown. He may seem a "fox" and a "snake" to his brother-in-law, Count Terzky. But his loyalty to the emperor is not lacking in justification. Also his actions are tragic, as his victory over Wallenstein is linked with the death of his son (a character invented by Schiller). Countess Terzky, who thinks like a man and proudly chooses death in preference to disgrace, and the charming Thekla (Wallenstein's daughter), who is equal to Max Piccolomini (son of Octavio) in her unconditional idealism, belong to Schiller's best woman characters.

FREDERIC E. COENEN
University of North Carolina

WALLER, wol′ər, **Edmund,** English poet and politician: b. Coleshill, Buckinghamshire, England, March 3, 1606; d. Beaconsfield, Oct. 21, 1687. Educated at Eton and King's College, Cambridge, he began his parliamentary career at the age of 16, as member for Amersham, and became noted for his considerable rhetorical powers. Though a royalist, he showed sympathy to the parliamentary cause and in 1643, after the Battle of Edgehill, was trusted as a parliamentary commissioner to treat with the king. Shortly afterward, an unwise and probably superficial connection with a violent royalist plot earned him a court-martial sentence of death, which he evaded by bribery and a servile denunciation of various friends and associates. These methods secured the commutation of his sentence to a fine and exile, which poverty and a family connection with Oliver Cromwell enabled him to terminate in 1652. His Cromwellian connections found expression in his best-known serious poem, *A Panegyric to My Lord Protector* (compare the analogous *Horatian Ode on Cromwell's Return from Ireland* by Andrew Marvell). Nevertheless, he managed to ingratiate himself by his charm and wit at the court of Charles II after the Restoration, characteristically excusing his inferior poem *Upon His Majesty's Happy Return* by observing, "Poets, Sir, succeed better in fiction than in truth." He also returned to Parliament in 1661 and maintained his reputation for eloquence.

Waller's love affairs, after the death of his first wife (Anne Bankes) in 1634, called forth many of his better-known poems. He vainly courted first "Sacharissa" (the 18-year-old Lady Dorothy Sidney) and then "Amoret" (Lady Sophia Murray?), but he finally married Mary Bracey in 1644.

Waller's first book of poems appeared in 1645 and was very popular, running through several editions in the 17th century. His poetry has a conversational ease and urban wit, usually devoted either to love themes (as in *To a Lady in Retirement, Of Sylvia,* and *An Apology*) or to occasional topics (*Instructions to a Painter*). His best meditative poem is *Of the Last Verses in the Book.* His contemporaries admired most his technical polish and considered him the first to write "correctly." Marvell, John Cleveland, and John Dryden are all indebted to him—Dryden particularly observing, "unless he had written, none of us could write." He is thus traditionally considered the first Augustan poet, but apart from his best songs (*Go, Lovely Rose,* and *On a Girdle*) his verse has been decried since the 18th century, partly for its suave tone and slight themes.

H. M. Richmond,
Assistant Professor of English, University of California.

WALLER, Sir **William,** English general and member of Parliament: b. about 1597; d. London, England, Sept. 19, 1668. He first served in the Venetian Army and then took part in the English defense of the Palatinate at the beginning of the Thirty Years' War. Waller was elected to the Long Parliament in 1640, and when the Civil War began, he was made a colonel in the Parliamentary Army; it was later said that he was probably unequaled on either side as a master of defensive tactics. Early successes won him promotion to general and the nickname "William the Conqueror," but in July 1643 he suffered defeat near Devizes. Undaunted, he raised a new army with the help of Parliament and prevented Royalist forces from penetrating Sussex and Kent. In June 1644 he was defeated by Royalist forces at Cropredy Bridge near Banbury, and his undisciplined, unpaid troops were unable to keep King Charles from marching into Cornwall. About this time he is credited with having suggested the idea of the New Model Army to Oliver Cromwell, leader of the king's opponents who had previously served as a general under Waller.

In 1645, under the Self-denying Ordinance, which debarred members of Parliament from military command, Waller resigned his commission and returned to Parliament as one of the leaders of the Presbyterian party. In 1647 he was one of the 11 Presbyterian members impeached as having encouraged the Scottish invasion and intrigued with the Royalists; the next year he was arrested in Pride's Purge of the Commons and imprisoned for three years without trial. During the Protectorate he was twice again arrested and charged with complicity in Royalist plots. With the accession of Charles II to the throne in 1660, Waller was elected to the Convention Parliament, but retired from political life soon afterward.

WALLEYED PILE. See Pikeperch.

WALLFLOWER, wôl′flou-ər, the colloquial name of plants in the genus *Cheiranthus,* especially *C. cheiri,* in the mustard family, Cruciferae. *C. cheiri* is a perennial, native to southern Europe, about two feet high, with gray-green, hairy stems, narrow, entire leaves, and fragrant, yellow to red-brown or purplish, four-petaled flowers, these are about an inch across, in conspicuous racemes. Double-flowered forms occur. It is a common garden plant, especially in Europe, often grown on walls. Although it is spring blooming, it may flower at Christmas in favored places in England. The western or Siberian wallflower, *Erysimum asperum,* of North America, which has orange blossoms, is similar and closely related to the European form.

Edwin B. Matzke.

WALLIN, väl-lēn′, **Johan Olof,** Swedish poet and ecclesiastic: b. Dalecarlia (Dalarna), Sweden, Oct. 15, 1779; d. Uppsala, June 30, 1839. He was educated at Uppsala University and ordained in 1806. Subsequently he was pastor at the Royal Military Academy at Karlberg, and after a distinguished career in the church (including pastorates at Solna, Västerås, and Stockholm), he was made archbishop of Sweden in 1837. He was an outstanding church administrator and had few equals as a pulpit orator. He is known especially as a prolific writer of hymns and as an adapter and translator of older and foreign psalms. In the Swedish Psalm Book of 1819, compiled under his direction and often referred to as "Wallin's Psalm Book," there are some 130 hymns by him. His great achievement lies in his skill in combining the awe-inspiring Biblical tradition with the sincere simplicity of folk religion, and it is indicative of his high repute that his famous contemporary Esaias Tegnér called him "David's Harp of the North." Apart from his hymns, Wallin's finest poem is *Dödens ängel* (1834; The Angel of Death), devoted to the theme of death and judgment. His secular poems cannot compare with his religious songs. To his early production belong didactic poems in the spirit of the Enlightenment; two of these, *Uppfostraren* (The Educator) and *Sång öfver Gustaf III* (Song to Gustavus III), earned prizes from the Swedish Academy. During the same period he also wrote idyllic and humorous verse. Toward the end of his life he composed a number of poems on themes from his native province, Dalecarlia, among them *Höbergningen* (The Hay Harvest) and *Smeden* (The Smith). Of interest to Americans is his dithyrambic song *George Washington.* His collected works have appeared in many editions, the first in 1847–1848.

Gösta Franzen,
Professor of Scandinavian, The University of Chicago.

WALLING, wŏl′ĭng, **William English,** American labor reformer and socialist: b. Louisville, Ky., March 14, 1877; d. Amsterdam, Holland, Sept. 12, 1936. He graduated from The University of Chicago in 1897 and then took graduate work in economics and sociology there. Endowed with independent means, he devoted himself to the labor movement. In 1903, with Jane Addams and others, Walling founded the National Women's Trade Union League, and through immigrant friends in New York City he became interested in the Russian revolutionary movement. In Russia in 1905 he met Vladimir Ilich Lenin, Maksim Gorki, and other leaders, and while still in Europe met and married Anna Strunsky, a socialist writer who had collaborated with Jack London on *The Kempton-Wace Letters.* Inspired by a race riot that he and his wife witnessed in Illinois in 1908, he became one of the founders of the National Association for the Advancement of Colored People in 1909. He joined the Socialist Party in 1910, but resigned in 1917 because of its antiwar policy. After World War I he worked actively with the American Federation of Labor, and in 1935 he became executive director of the Labor Chest, which was organized to help workers in Fascist countries. His publications include *Russia's Message* (1908), *The Larger Aspects of Socialism* (1913), and, with Samuel Gompers, the anti-Soviet *Out of Their Own Mouths* (1921).

WALLINGFORD, wŏl′ĭng-fərd, town, Connecticut, in New Haven County, on the Quinnipiac River, 13 miles north of New Haven.

The altitude varies from 20 feet along the river to 750 feet in the highlands of the Fowler and Beseck Mountains on the eastern border. Agriculture, particularly the raising of vegetables, is important in the area. Chief industries are the manufacture of silverware, instruments, electrical equipment, specialty steels, plastics, resins, and apparel. Two notable preparatory schools, Choate and Putnam, are located here. The Wharton Brook State Park provides recreational facilities, and there is a large area of state leased land for hunting. The Wallingford Historical Society maintains a collection of antiques and documents in the Samuel Parsons House, an early dwelling.

Named for a town in Berkshire, England, Wallingford was settled in 1667 by former residents of New Haven on land purchased from the Indians in 1638. It was incorporated as a town in 1670. In 1853 a separate borough of Wallingford was incorporated, but in 1958 the borough and town were reconsolidated. In the period from 1850 to 1880 a branch of the Oneida Community flourished here. Government is by mayor and council. Population: 37,274.

ROBERT C. SALE.

WALLINGTON, wŏl′ĭng-tən, borough, New Jersey, in Bergen County, near the Passaic River just southeast of Passaic and nine miles north of Newark. It has diversified industries, including the manufacture of steel tubing, electrical equipment, plastics, paint, and paper boxes. Government is administered by mayor and council. Population: 10,741.

WALLIS, wŏl′ĭs, **John,** English mathematician: b. Ashford, Kent, England, Nov. 23, 1616; d. Oxford, Oct. 28, 1703. Educated at Emmanuel College, Cambridge, he was ordained in the Church of England, and in 1641 became chaplain to a Yorkshire baronet. Skilled in the art of cryptography, Wallis assisted the Parliamentarians by deciphering captured Royalist documents when the Civil War began, and in 1643 he was rewarded by being made rector of a church in London. Notwithstanding his opposition to the execution of Charles I, he was appointed Savilian professor of geometry at Oxford in 1649, and he continued to occupy the chair until his death more than half a century later; when Charles II was restored to the throne in 1660, Wallis was made one of the royal chaplains. He was one of the divines appointed in 1661 to revise the Book of Common Prayer; and when the Royal Society was founded in 1663, he was one of the earliest members.

Modern algebra owes much of its completeness to Wallis' elucidation of its principles. In his most important work, *Arithmetica infinitorum* (1655), he reduced the idea of limit to arithmetic form and extended the application of the law of continuity formulated by Johannes Kepler. He also anticipated the differential and integral calculus, and introduced the symbol for infinity. Other mathematical studies included *Mathesis universalis* (1657) and *De algebra tractatus* (1685); he also published less important works on cryptography, grammar, logic, and theology.

WALLIS AND FUTUNA, two island groups of volcanic origin in the Southwest Pacific, constituting an overseas territory of France. They are located about 250 miles (400 km) west of Samoa. The Wallis Islands include Wallis Island (Uvéa) and 22 small islets, and the Futuna (Hooru) Islands include Futuna and Alofi. Their combined area is 106 square miles (274 sq km). The capital is Mata Utu, on Wallis (Uvéa). The inhabitants are Polynesian, most of them Roman Catholics.

The islands' principal agricultural products, grown in a hot and humid climate, are taro, yams, copra, and tropical fruits. Other leading products include lumber and fish.

The Wallis Islands were named for Samuel Wallis, the English circumnavigator who discovered them in 1767 along with Tahiti and other Pacific islands. In 1837, French missionaries arrived there, and in 1842 the two groups were claimed by France as dependencies, attached administratively first to Tahiti and later to New Caledonia. They became a protectorate of France in 1887 and were given colonial status in 1917. In December 1959 the islanders voted overwhelmingly to become a French overseas territory, and on July 29, 1961, the Territory of the Wallis and Futuna Islands came into being. The territory is governed by a French administrator, assisted by a 20-member Territorial Assembly. Population: (1976) Wallis (Uvéa), 6,109; Futuna, 31,173; Alofi, uninhabited.

WALLON, wȧ-lôɴ′, **Henri Alexandre,** French historian and statesman: b. Valenciennes, France, Dec. 23, 1812; d. Paris, Nov. 13, 1904. Educated at the Normal School in Paris, he was appointed to the chair of modern history and geography at the Sorbonne in 1846, served in the Legislative Assembly in 1849–1850, and was elected to the National Assembly in 1871. His constitutional amendment of 1875, providing for the method of electing the president, was largely responsible for the final establishment of the republic. He was minister of public instruction (1875–1876) and a life member of the Senate from the latter year. He had become permanent secretary of the Academy of Inscriptions in 1873. Among his numerous writings are *La terreur* (1873) and *Les représentants du peuple en mission*... (5 vols., 1888–90).

WALLOONS, wŏ-lo͞onz, the people who live in the French-speaking parts of Belgium, or more precisely in the provinces of Liège, Luxembourg, Namur, and Hainaut, and in the district of Nivelles in the Province of Brabant. The name "Walloon" was probably derived from that of a Celtic tribe, the Volcae, but according to the famous Belgian historian Henri Pirenne (1862–1935), Germanic tribes in ancient times knew the people of the Walloon region as Wala. At all events, the inhabitants of this area were conquered by Julius Caesar and incorporated into the Roman Empire; thus they were subjected to the Latin language. When the Franks invaded the empire, the Walloons were not driven from their lands, for the settlements of the Germanic newcomers were stopped by a dense forest (the Carbonaria Silva), on the east by the rugged Ardennes, and by Roman defenses on a road which ran approximately along what is now the linguistic frontier between the Netherlandish- and French-speaking peoples, that is, from Dunkerque in France, south of Brussels and north of Liège.

The Walloons adopted Roman Catholicism after the conversion of Clovis (496) and became divided into feudal principalities after the breakup of Charlemagne's empire in the last part of the 9th century. The Walloon region was subsequently brought together with the Netherlandish provinces by the dukes of Burgundy, whose holdings fell (1482) to the Spanish Habsburgs through marriages and inheritances upon the death of Mary of Burgundy.

Protestantism made some headway in Wallonia in the 16th century, but the Spaniards were able to prevent the Belgian provinces from attaining their independence as did the northern provinces, and were also successful in stamping out Protestantism by employing ruthless measures, including the Inquisition. Because of Spanish religious oppression, some Walloon Protestants fled to the neighborhood of Leiden in the northern Netherlands; here they developed plans for emigrating to the New World and may have had contacts with the Pilgrims. In 1624 a goodly company of them left the Netherlands to settle in New Amsterdam (now New York).

By the Treaty of Utrecht (1713) the Belgian provinces went to the Austrian Habsburgs, and during the French Revolution and the Napoleonic period they were annexed to France. At the Congress of Vienna (1815) they were joined with the northern Netherlands to form the Kingdom of the United Netherlands. This new state was short lived, however, for the religious and linguistic policies of King William I antagonized many of the southerners, who rose in revolt in 1830 and established the separate kingdom of Belgium. Walloons played an especially important role in the affairs of the new state, for their language (French) was at first the only official language, and their wealth, resulting from early industrialization, was greater than that of the Flemings. Since World War I the Walloons have lost their predominant position in the state, and much of their area has become economically depressed because of the exhaustion of mines, as in the Borinage.

Literature and Language.—Once spoken in all of the Walloon region of what is now Belgium, the Walloon language has generally disappeared in current parlance except near Liège. Its literature dates back to the 12th and 13th centuries. Although traces of the language are found in *Aucassin and Nicolette* (q.v.), probably written in Hainaut, it was for a long time used exclusively for pious writings, such as *Li ver del Juïse* and *Li dialoge Gregoire lo pape,* and for 14th and 15th century chronicles such as *Chronique de Floreffe.* In the 17th century it enjoyed a modest revival with the appearance of the first drama in the language, *Moralité* (1623), and in the 18th century it was employed for songs, comments on current happenings, and popular comedies. In the 19th century the language was supported, as were so many others of tertiary importance, by romanticists organized for the purpose; the Societé Liègeoise de Littérature Wallonne was founded for this reason in 1856. Today, however, Walloon literature is largely of a folklore nature.

Only in recent times have the Walloons attained some degree of united action in the linguistic struggles in Belgium, although the country is divided fairly equally between those who speak Flemish, which is essentially the same as Netherlandish (Dutch), and those who speak French. French was adopted as the official language of the government when Belgium became an independent state after the revolution of 1830, since it was the language of the revolutionary leaders. Subsequently the Flemish strove to raise their language to an equal footing with French, and put pressure on political parties to favor their programs. In the course of time they achieved their goals, which included simultaneous use of Flemish and French in all state business, ranging from parliamentary debates to inscriptions on coins; the use of Flemish in courses at the University of Ghent; the creation of Flemish-speaking regiments in the armies; bilinguality in all judicial cases; and the use of the "child's mother tongue" in elementary and secondary school instruction. In 1932 a new law was passed requiring schools to adopt the language most used in the district which they served; the Walloons became particularly incensed at this reform, which meant that in certain areas, especially on the linguistic border, children of Walloon parents would sometimes be required to study in Flemish. Moveover, the general success of the Flemish movement in the matter of linguistic laws and the population growth in the Flemish provinces, which was such that Flemish-speaking people became more numerous than those who spoke French, made the Walloons fear for the future. They organized for their defense a Walloon movement, proposing a kind of federal state in which the two linguistic areas would be equal and which would pledge to defend Walloon linguistic interests. In fact, competing Flemish and Walloon interests are visible in many public issues, such as state-church relationships (Catholicism being stronger in Flemish-speaking than in French-speaking sections); the formation of cabinets; and in areas of economic development where the Flemish-speaking provinces tend to be more devoted to agriculture, shipping, and textiles, while the French-speaking sections lean toward heavy industry and mining.

See also BELGIUM—*1. The People* and *7. Culture* (Literature); FLEMISH LANGUAGE; FRANCE—*38. Language.*

SHEPARD B. CLOUGH,
Professor of History, Columbia University.

WALLPAPER. See WALL COVERINGS—*Wallpaper.*

WALNUT, wôl'nŭt, the common name for trees of the genus *Juglans* in the walnut family, Juglandaceae, important for their valuable wood and nuts. Most of the 20 species are found in the Northern Hemisphere, mainly in temperate regions. These deciduous hardwoods have rough furrowed bark; alternate pinnately compound leaves with a distinctive odor when bruised; and greenish flowers, the male in drooping catkins. The large edible nuts have a husk that does not split open, and usually a hard shell. The trees sometimes exceed 100 feet in height with trunks 3 feet in diameter; they are used for roadside planting, shade, ornament, and shelter belts.

Black walnut (*Juglans nigra*). Clockwise from the upper right, the details include a nut in its husk, a winter silhouette, nut shell, bark, leaves, and male flowers.

Six species are native in the United States: black walnut (*J. nigra*) and butternut or "white walnut" (*J. cinerea*), both widely distributed in the Eastern states and extending to adjacent Canada; little walnut (*J. microcarpa*) and Arizona walnut (*J. major*) in Southwestern states and northern Mexico; and California walnut (*J. californica*) and Hinds walnut (*J hindsii*) in California. About 11 other species with the Spanish name "nogal" occur southward in the high mountains of Mexico, Central America, and the Antilles, and in the Andes from Venezuela to Argentina. Native to the Old World are Persian ("English") walnut (*J. regia*), Siebold walnut (*J. ailantifolia*) and its variety heartnut in Japan, and three other species in China.

Black walnut is one of the best-known, largest, and most valuable native hardwoods. Though not plentiful, the trees grow rapidly in mixed forests on rich, moist, well-drained soil such as is found in valleys. They are planted on farms as a valuable timber crop, and efforts are being made to select superior nut trees. The supply of black walnut sawtimber in the United States is estimated at more than 1.5 billion board feet with an average annual cut of roughly 55 million board feet. Indiana, Ohio, Missouri, and the neighboring states are the leading producers.

The wood of black walnut is often beautifully figured, as with stripes or sometimes with wavy or curly grain, especially in certain stumps prized for veneer. Heartwood varies from light to chocolate brown, and sapwood is whitish. Principal uses are in furniture for home and office, cabinets (as for television and radio), gunstocks, pianos, caskets, and interior woodwork and paneling. Limited quantities go into railway ties, fence posts, and fuel wood. The nuts are a popular food, especially in ice cream, candy, and cakes.

Persian walnut ranks among the important nut trees in the temperate zone and provides a fine cabinet wood. It has been cultivated so long that its original home is uncertain, perhaps from southeastern Europe east to the Himalayas, or in China, unless the tree was introduced there at an early date. The name English walnut is misleading, for production in England is relatively small. The lumber is usually designated according to its origin as Circassian, Turkish, Italian, or French walnut.

The United States leads in the production of Persian walnuts, with more than 90 percent coming from California and nearly all the rest from Oregon. The harvest usually exceeds 75,000 short tons annually. Other important producers are Italy, France, Turkey, China, and India. In the walnut orchards, grafted trees from selected varieties are intensively cultivated. The harvested nuts are promptly hulled and dried, then graded and bleached, and marketed mostly unshelled. The Persian walnut has not thrived in the eastern and southern United States, and planting orchards there is not recommended.

ELBERT L. LITTLE, JR.,
United States Forest Service.

Bibliography

Flint, Mary L., ed., *Integrated Pest Management for Walnuts* (Agric. & Natural Res., Univ. of Calif. 1986).
Ramos, David E., *Walnut Orchard Management* (Agric. & Natural Res., Univ. of Calif. 1985).
Thompson, Bruce, *Black Walnuts for Profit*, rev. 4th ed. (Walnut Press, AZ 1983).
Vavasour, B. T., *Growing Walnuts* (AG Access Pub. 1984).

WALNUT CANYON NATIONAL MONUMENT, a United States national monument in Arizona, 11 miles east of downtown Flagstaff. The canyon contains the remains of over 400 dwellings built by the Sinagua Indians about 1100 A.D.; the overhanging ledges of the canyon walls formed the roofs for their homes. Walnut Creek furnished an abundant supply of water for household use. The Sinagua successfully cultivated corn, beans, and pumpkins, but because of severe drought were compelled to abandon the area in the 13th century. The canyon flora varies from the cactus of the Arizona deserts to the fir of the high Rockies. The cliff dwellers utilized many of the plants for food, medicine, and fiber. In addition to its scenic attractions the monument is an area of great geological and biological interest. It is open to visitors all year round.

MEREDITH M. GUILLET.

WALNUT CREEK, city, California, in Contra Costa County, at an elevation of 142 feet, 13 miles east of Oakland. The name is derived from the drainage creek which serves the surrounding watershed of 65 square miles, a region of steep hills and deep valleys dominated by Mount Diablo (3,849 feet). The city is a trading center for an area with a population of over 200,000, most of the residents living outside the limits of the three incorporated cities of Walnut Creek, Concord, and Martinez (the county seat). Walnut Creek has a walnut-processing plant, a canning factory, and an electronics plant. It dates from 1849, achieving minor importance in gold-rush days as "The Corners" because the mission road from San Jose to Martinez here crossed the east-west overland route to the goldfields. Incorporated in 1914, it adopted a council-manager form of government in 1956. Pop. 53,643.

JOHN R. HOLLIS.

WALNUT RIDGE, city, Arkansas, seat of Lawrence County, 21 miles northwest of Jonesboro, at an elevation of 275 feet. The city lies on a gently rolling ridge and was named for the walnut trees growing in the region. Cotton, rice, and soybeans are produced in the vicinity, and manufactures include mobile houses, girls' dresses, fertilizer, and shoe lasts. The city has a county library and a junior college. Incorporated in 1873, it is governed by a mayor and council. Pop. 4,152.

NADEAN LEE.

WALPI, wôl'pē (from Hopi *wala ovi,* meaning "place of the gap," referring to a gap in the mesa), the best-known and most picturesque of the Hopi Indian villages, situated on the tip of First Mesa, in northeast Arizona, about 65 miles north-northeast of Winslow. The first site of Walpi was on a lower terrace, where a village was built about 1300 A.D. Following the Pueblo Revolt of 1680 (see PUEBLO INDIANS—*History*), the Indians moved to the top of the mesa, fearing retaliation by the Spaniards, and built the present village. The famous Snake Dance is held here in odd-numbered years, demonstrating the ceremony in its most dramatic form. Long exposed to white and alien Indian contacts, Walpi residents reflect a combination of many outside influences in their life and customs. The population is approximately 100.

FREDERICK J. DOCKSTADER.

WALPOLE, wŏl'pōl, **Horace** (baptized **HORATIO**), **4TH EARL OF ORFORD,** English letter writer, historian, connoisseur, and amateur architect: b. London, England, Sept. 24, 1717 (Old Style); d. there, March 2, 1797. The youngest and third surviving son of the statesman Sir Robert Walpole (q.v.; later 1st earl of Orford), he went to school at Eton (1727–1734) and at King's College, Cambridge (1735–1738), and made the "grand tour" of France and Italy (1739–1741) with the poet Thomas Gray. In 1741 he entered the House of Commons, representing family boroughs there until 1768. He seldom spoke in Parliament, but was a keen observer of politics, and sometimes was a participant behind the scenes. After his retirement from Parliament, his activities centered mostly about Strawberry Hill (near Twickenham), the country house which he had taken in 1747, and in his constructions, gardens, and collections there.

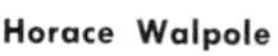

Horace Walpole

National Portrait Gallery, London

Walpole was a pioneer in reviving Gothic architecture, and Strawberry Hill was remodeled by him into a miniature Gothic castle. Antiquarian pursuits, correspondence, and social activity also filled much of his time. He never married. At Strawberry Hill he established a private printing press, from which he issued works by his friends (including two of Gray's odes), books on antiquarian subjects (some of them by himself), and small occasional pieces. On his nephew's death in 1791, he became earl of Orford, with possession of the embarrassed Norfolk estates of his family, but through his own prudence he was already well-to-do. He never sat in the House of Lords. His collections at Strawberry Hill were sold ultimately in 1842, but many of them have been reassembled by Wilmarth S. Lewis at Farmington, Conn., and Strawberry Hill itself is now occupied by St. Mary's College.

Publications and Letters.—Walpole initiated the so-called Gothic romances when he published *The Castle of Otranto* in 1764. His *Anecdotes of Painting in England* (4 vols., 1762–71), based partly on George Vertue's notes, was the first art history of England. He also wrote an art catalogue, *Aedes Walpolianae* (1747), listing and discussing his father's collection of paintings; *The Mysterious Mother* (1768), a tragedy in verse, privately printed and never acted; historical memoirs of the last 10 years of George II's reign and the first 11 of George III's, with continuations in rougher form (all published after his death, in 1822, 1845, and 1859 respectively); *A Catalogue of the Royal and Noble Authors of England* (1758); *Historic Doubts on the Life and Reign of King Richard the Third* (1768, a defense of Richard); *Essay on Modern Gardening* (1785); and various poems, political articles, and small catalogues of art collections.

Though the *Anecdotes of Painting* is still useful to art historians, and the *Castle of Otranto* is a minor landmark in literary history, Walpole's fame now rests on his letters, of which over 3,000 survive. Historically, they are 18th century England's truest record, portraying social life, public affairs, and contemporary arts and letters with wit, vividness, and accuracy, and from a liberal point of view. They are far more brilliant than his memoirs, which are more studied in style and too often marred by personal animosity. Walpole had many of his letters returned to him, and he annotated them himself. In each interchange he stressed the topics most interesting to his correspondent; he wrote about social events to George Montagu and Lady Ossory, about antiquities to William Cole, about literature to William Mason, and about politics to Sir Horace Mann, his distant cousin, who, as English representative in Tuscany, corresponded with him for 45 years after Walpole's departure from Florence. Walpole's closest friend was his cousin, Gen. Henry Seymour Conway, though there was a rift between them in 1765 when Walpole felt slighted by Conway's political neglect of him. Some of his liveliest letters are to feminine correspondents. The warmth of personal feeling gives to his best letters the brilliance and spontaneity which make them so dazzling and, even today, so fresh in their appeal.

Character.—Thomas Babington Macaulay and other critics, particularly in the 19th century, accused Walpole of superficiality and frivolity. His attitude of detached amusement exposes him to this charge, but his abhorrence of slavery, his sympathy with the oppressed, his generosity to many individuals, and his condemnations of many fashionable vices have gone largely unnoticed. A more valid charge is that of spitefulness: his portraits of his father's political opponents are usually biased and bitter. Walpole was a nervous and sensitive man, too temperamental for political success and too amateurish to be a thorough scholar. As a friend, he was untiring in his attentions, but too sensitive to slights. His gift for friendship, however, is one reason why he is now remembered, since, combined with his supreme verbal artistry, it makes him one of the greatest letter writers.

See also CASTLE OF OTRANTO, THE.

WARREN H. SMITH,
Yale University Library.

Bibliography

Walpole's works appeared in 9 vols. (R. Phillips 1798–1825) and his letters in 19 vols. (Oxford 1903–1905; 1918–1925) and in 48 vols. (Yale Univ. Press 1937–1983).
Greenwood, Alice D., *Horace Walpole's World* (1913; reprint, Arden Library 1985).
Ketton-Cremer, Robert W., *Horace Walpole* (1959; reprint, Arden Library 1979).
Lewis, Wilmarth S., *Horace Walpole* (Pantheon 1961).
Sabor, Peter, *Horace Walpole* (G. K. Hall 1984).

WALPOLE, SIR Hugh (Seymour), English novelist: b. Auckland, New Zealand, March 13, 1884; d. near Keswick, England, June 1, 1941. His father, an Anglican priest, held various posts in England, New Zealand, and the United States before becoming bishop of Edinburgh in 1910. Hugh was educated at Emmanuel College, Cambridge, and tried lay mission work and teaching before deciding to become a writer in 1909. He wrote novels energetically, lived a full social life in London, and collected friends enthusiastically, notably "Elizabeth" (Elizabeth Mary Beauchamp, later countess von Arnim and Countess Russell), Henry James, and Arnold Bennett. During World War I he served as a medical orderly with the Russian Army, and saw the revolution of 1917 in Petrograd (Leningrad) while acting as chief of Anglo-Russian propaganda. After the war he conducted (1919) the first of many successful lecture tours in the United States and later traveled widely. From 1934 to 1936, in Hollywood, he worked on scenarios of *David Copperfield, Little Lord Fauntleroy,* and *Kim.* Walpole collected books, manuscripts, and pictures insatiably, gave generous help to individuals, and devoted much time to the Book Society and the Society of Bookmen. He was knighted in 1937.

Walpole achieved a vast popular reputation in his lifetime. He wrote 42 novels, as well as essays, autobiographies, and criticism, with facility. Critics have often been less than just to his work. Suspense and tension, for instance, make *Mr. Perrin and Mr. Traill* (1911), his realistic story of schoolteachers, still eminently readable. Underestimated novels like *The Dark Forest* (1916) and *The Secret City* (1919) show what he could achieve artistically in responding to new scenes and temperaments. *The Cathedral* (1922) has strength of narrative purpose and symbolism in its study of an ecclesiastic, showing the influence of Anthony Trollope. Walpole's desire to write in the grand manner, combined with his exuberant sense of romance and love of Cumberland's scenery, produced *Rogue Herries* (1930), a highly colored 18th century novel, continued in *Judith Paris* (1931), *The Fortress* (1932), and *Vanessa* (1933).

A good introduction to Walpole as a raconteur is provided by his autobiographical writings, of which *Roman Fountain* (1940) is the liveliest. These are intelligently literary and reveal something of the personal tensions that underlay his superb talent for storytelling.

Consult Hart-Davis, Rupert, *Hugh Walpole* (New York 1952), an excellent biography with a useful bibliography.

A. NORMAN JEFFARES,
Professor of English Literature, The University of Leeds.

WALPOLE, SIR Robert, 1ST EARL OF ORFORD, English statesman: b. Houghton, Norfolk, England, Aug. 26, 1676; d. London, March 18, 1745. The son of a Norfolk squire, he was educated at Eton and King's College, Cambridge, and began his 40-year parliamentary career in 1701 as a member first from Castle Rising and then from King's Lynn. In 1705 he was appointed to the council that advised Prince George, Queen Anne's husband, in his duties as lord high admiral. In 1708, as secretary at war, he became an active member of the Whig administration. Walpole was made treasurer of the navy two years later and was one of the managers of the trial of Dr. Henry Sacheverell (q.v.). After the ministry of the 1st earl of Godolphin was dismissed, he resigned his offices and became a recognized leader of the Opposition in the Commons. He defended the late ministry and attacked the new government so strongly that in 1711–1712, as a means of removing him from the scene, he was charged with peculation while secretary at war, expelled from Parliament, and committed to the Tower of London for six months. Reelected by the voters of King's Lynn in 1713, he continued his opposition to the Tory ministry of Robert Harley (1st earl of Oxford) and Henry St. John (1st Viscount Bolingbroke) until the death of Queen Anne in August 1714.

Townshend Ministry and After.—With the accession of George I the Whigs came into their own. Walpole was made paymaster general of the forces and served as chairman of the committee which impeached the Tory leaders for treason in 1715. The same year, with his brother-in-law Charles Townshend (2d Viscount Townshend) as chief minister, he became first lord of the treasury and chancellor of the exchequer. But the intrigues of the court and differences with other members of the Whig majority over foreign policy led to Townshend's dismissal, and Walpole followed him out of office early in 1717. For three years he sat on the benches of the Opposition during the government of Charles Spencer (3d earl of Sunderland) and James Stanhope (1st Earl Stanhope), speaking against the Mutiny and Peerage bills and repeal of the Schism Act (1718), and objecting strenuously to the formation of the Quadruple Alliance against Spain. Reconciliation within the party came in 1720, and he rejoined the ministry as paymaster of the forces. Not of the inner cabinet, however, he escaped the odium with which the ministry was connected in the South Sea affair (see SOUTH SEA COMPANY, THE); and after the so-called bubble burst, he was called upon to lead the nation back to financial stability. Named first lord of the treasury and chancellor of the exchequer in April 1721, he soon took over the full leadership of the ministry.

Walpole's Ministry.—For the next 21 years Walpole's history is the history of England. The South Sea troubles were overcome, the Atterbury plot was crushed (see ATTERBURY, FRANCIS), and disturbances in Scotland and Ireland were resolved. The alliance of Austria and Spain was checked by the Treaty of Hannover (1725) between England, France, and Prussia; and peace was later furthered by the treaties of Seville (1729) and Vienna (1731). On the death of George I in 1727, Walpole found himself faced with the possibility of being superseded, but he soon proved his ability to get things done and continued to serve George II as loyally as he had George's father. His friendship with Queen Caroline was a decided asset.

As Walpole gave loyalty, so he expected it, and soon there grew up an opposition of dissident Whigs, led by William Pulteney (later 1st earl of Bath), John Carteret (later 1st Earl Granville), and Philip Dormer Stanhope (4th earl of Chesterfield), and backed by the jealous old Tory Bolingbroke. This opposition was strong, but Walpole retained the royal favor and continued to hold the majority in Parliament. In 1733 he suffered his only defeat when the Opposition successfully aroused public feeling and forced him to abandon his excise scheme. In 1734 he was much blamed for keeping aloof from the War of the Polish Succession, and in the same year the Opposition joined without success to attack the Septennial Act. In 1737, Queen Caroline's death deprived him of a staunch and faithful friend. The Opposition, now reinforced by William Pitt (later 1st earl of Chatham) and joined by the London merchants, continued to attack his pacific policy. Nevertheless, Walpole concluded a convention with Spain, and not until October 1739 did he, reluctantly, declare war, the so-called War of Jenkins' Ear.

The duties of office weighed increasingly on Walpole, and his health declined. Taking his defeat on an election petition as a test, he resigned in February 1742. He was created 1st earl of Orford, gave up his career in the House of Commons, and retired to the House of Lords, but he retained his influence with the king to the end.

Walpole's Achievement.—Throughout his ministry Walpole showed his intense loyalty to the king, the Hanoverian family, and the Whig Party. He was a sound administrator, a skillful financier, powerful in debate, a shrewd judge of men, and wise in the way of politics. Even better than his contemporaries he knew the sources of power in the 18th century and used them advantageously. His major aims included the firm establishment of the Hanoverian line, the maintenance of peace, friendship with France, and the prosperity of England through commerce and trade (although he remained ever mindful of the landed interests). In all of these he was successful. Reductions were made in the national debt, land tax, and customs duties; commerce and industry were stimulated; and colonial prosperity was promoted, a foundation being laid for the worldwide development of the British Empire that was to follow. Above all, a strong and steady government was maintained; more than any other leader he made the cabinet system a reality, establishing the principle of unanimity and the collective responsibility of the prime minister and cabinet members to Parliament. By leadership and example, Walpole was truly Britain's "first prime minister."

ALFRED J. HENDERSON,
Professor of History, MacMurray College, Jacksonville, Ill.

Sir Robert Walpole, 1st earl of Orford.

National Portrait Gallery, London

Bibliography

Coke, William, *Memoirs of the Life and Administration of Sir Robert Walpole,* 3 vols. (W. Davies 1798).
Goldgar, Bertrand A., *Walpole and the Wits* (Univ. of Neb. Press 1976).
Morley, John M., *Walpole* (1889; reprint, Greenwood Press 1981).
Plumb, John Harold, *Sir Robert Walpole,* 3 vols. (Crescent Press 1956–1960).
Taylor, George Robert Sterling, *Robert Walpole and His Age* (J. Cape 1931).

(Above) American Museum of Natural History; (right) Annan Photo Features

***Above:* The Pacific walrus; old males like this one often weigh over 2,000 pounds. *Right:* Walrus young in a zoo; the tusks which characterize the adult are undeveloped.**

WALPOLE, town, Massachusetts, in Norfolk County, at an elevation of 200 feet, on the Neponset River, 19 miles south of Boston and 26 miles north of Providence, R.I. It is a manufacturing as well as a residential town; products include floor coverings, papers, machinery, chemicals, artificial leathers, surgical dressings, and cedar woodwork. Norfolk County Agricultural School and the Massachusetts Correctional Institution are located here.

South Walpole was purchased from King Philip, the Indian chief, for £20, and the town was settled in 1659. Originally within the boundaries of Dedham, it was incorporated separately in 1724 and named in honor of Sir Robert Walpole, the prime minister of England. The charter outlining the authority of the town and its bylaws was adopted in 1926. The town is governed by a general town meeting. Pop. 18,859.

DORIS M. QUINN.

WALPURGA or **WALPURGIS, SAINT.** See WALBURGA.

WALPURGIS NIGHT, väl-po͞or'gĭs nīt (Ger. WALPURGISNACHT), in central Europe, the night before May 1. According to popular belief, the power of witches was at its height at this time, and on the night of April 30 they would assemble at some meeting place such as a crossroads or mountaintop, arriving on broomsticks or with demons to perform their evil rites, indulge in wild dances and orgies, affirm their allegiance to their master the devil (who would be there in person or in the form of a goat or some other animal), initiate new members, and receive their assignments for the coming year. While some authorities hold that the legends about these festivals originated in the meetings of some heretical sects, it is more likely that the ceremonies and rituals were a survival of a pagan fertility cult. The first of May marked the advent of the growing season, and it was an important day for the German cultivator; many contracts were made, and the labors of the field assumed new activity. It was not surprising,- therefore, that at so important a time the witches and powers of evil should be especially active and that steps must be taken to circumvent them. Fires were lighted to burn out the witches or drive them away, in some places on Walpurgis Night and in others on May Day. The same custom prevailed in Celtic regions, where similar fires were lighted on Beltane (May Day). There were other times of the year when witches were especially active, and in many ways the beliefs about Halloween (q.v.) in England paralleled those about Walpurgis Night. Witches and evil spirits were again abroad, and had to be dealt with by lighting fires and by other methods.

The association with St. Walburga (Walpurga) came about because one of her feasts was held on May Day, and her influence as a protector against magic could be invoked to banish the powers of evil. The place most conspicuously associated with Walpurgis Night orgies was the Brocken or Blocksberg, the highest peak in the Harz Mountains in central Germany, which had been the site of ancient pagan sacrifices. In Part I of *Faust,* Johann Wolfgang von Goethe presents a vivid picture of the witches' sabbath held here.

WALRAS, vȧl-rȧ', **(Marie Esprit) Léon,** French economist: b. Évreux, France, Dec. 16, 1834; d. Clarens, Switzerland, Jan. 25, 1910. Becoming interested in social reform, he abandoned the profession of mining engineering to study economic theory. Walras became professor of political economy at the University of Lausanne in 1870, holding the post until 1892. He applied the so-called mathematical method to economics —the reduction of economic laws to mathematical formulas and the use of simultaneous equations to determine unknown quantities. The method is expounded in his *Élements d'économie politique pure* (1874–77). Other works include *Théorie mathématique de la richesse sociale* (1883) and *Études d'économie politique appliquée* (1898). His work in connection with marginal utility and general equilibrium was especially notable. His influence on economic theory, although slow to take effect, has been considerable.

WALRUS, wôl'rəs, an Arctic marine pinniped mammal, *Odobenus rosmarus,* of which there are two subspecies: the Atlantic (*O. rosmarus rosmarus*) and the Pacific (*O. rosmarus divergens*). It is distinguished from the related hair seals (see SEALS AND SEALING) by the two upper canine teeth that project downward as stout tusks (walrus ivory). They grow from persistent pulp to a length of 15 inches or more, and are slightly curved. All the other teeth are small and simple. The head is small, with a squarish muzzle bearing short coarse "whiskers" (vibrissae), small eyes, and ear openings, but no external ears. The body is short, massive in the neck region, and the hide is a thick armor, wrinkled on the shoulder and warty on the hind feet. The sparse short grayish-brown hair mostly disappears on old males. Bulls are 10 to 12 feet long and 5 feet high, and weigh 2,000 pounds or more; cows are one third smaller with more slender and curved tusks. The species rarely comes ashore, living mainly in water and on ice floes around margins of the Arctic Ocean south to Hudson Bay and Bristol Bay, with some seasonal movements. It lives in groups of a few to over 100, notable for their noisy bellowing. To feed, a walrus descends as much as 300 feet, head down, and uses its tusks to grub mollusks and other marine animals from the ocean floor. Pads on the muzzle move food into the mouth, discarding the shells. Occasionally a seal is eaten.

Adult walruses mature at about 5 years. Gestation lasts 11 months, and a single four-foot pup is born in April, May, or June. The animals are inoffensive except when mating or guarding their young, or if they are attacked. In earlier centuries they occurred south to Massachusetts and the Gulf of St. Lawrence, but persistent hunting, mainly for walrus ivory and oil from blubber, has reduced their numbers and range. In 1957 the total population was thought to be only from 40,000 to 50,000. Eskimos and other Arctic peoples depend much on walrus, using every part of the body—for food, fuel, clothing, or equipment. The uniform and hard structure of the big canine teeth has been much used as an alternative for the ivory of elephant tusks in carving small decorative objects; this craft has been learned with much skill by the Eskimos since white explorers and traders penetrated the Arctic.

TRACY I. STORER,
Professor of Zoology, Emeritus, University of California at Davis.

WALSALL, wôl′sôl, county borough, England, in Staffordshire, eight miles north of Birmingham. It is a large and progressive industrial town on the edge of the coalfield and since very early times has been noted for its tanneries and leather manufactures, to which ancillary items such as buckles, harness, and harness furniture were added. Modern industries include printing and the manufacture of electrical switchgear, machine tools, tubes, chains, and clothing. There are 300 acres of parks and open spaces, including a notable arboretum. The 15th century Church of St. Matthew crowns the hill on which the old town was founded. Walsall is of ancient foundation, having been a royal borough in the 11th century, in the time of Edward the Confessor; it had a mayor as early as 1377 and a merchant guild in 1390. Charters were granted by Henry II (1159) and later kings. It became a county borough in 1888. Pop. (1961) 117,836.

H. GORDON STOKES.

WALSENBURG, wôl′sən-bûrg, city, Colorado, seat of Huerfano County, on the Cucharas River, at an altitude of 6,200 feet, 48 miles south of Pueblo. It is a residential city, with coal mining and ranching in the vicinity. Walsenburg is located near the famous Spanish Peaks (Huajatolla, or "Breast of the World") and is the gateway to San Isabel National Forest. There are summer and winter resorts nearby, with excellent hunting and fishing. Annual festivals include a rodeo and the Spanish El Fandango. Formerly a small village called La Plaza de los Leones, Walsenburg was incorporated in 1873 and named for Fred Walsen, an early settler. The government is by mayor and council. Pop. 3,945.

CORA MOCKMORE.

WALSH, wôlsh, **Ed(ward Augustin),** American baseball player: b. Plains, Pa., May 14, 1881; d. Pompano Beach, Fla., May 26, 1959. A 6-foot 1-inch 196-pound right-handed pitcher known as Big Ed, he broke into the majors with the Chicago White Sox of the American League in 1904 and played with them through 1916. His best pitch was the "spitball," since outlawed. Walsh achieved his greatest year in 1908, when he gained 40 victories (1 less than the modern record) while appearing in 66 games and pitching 464 innings for a major league mark that remained at his death. Twice he pitched and won doubleheaders. His career record was 195 victories and 128 losses. He was elected to the Baseball Hall of Fame in 1946.

GEORGE MCNICKLE.

WALSH, Edmund A(loysius), American educator and expert on international politics: b. Boston, Mass., Oct. 10, 1885; d. Washington, D.C., Oct. 31, 1956. Educated at Boston College and in Europe, he joined the Society of Jesus in 1902 and was ordained a priest in 1916. After teaching literature at Georgetown University for five years, he became dean of arts and sciences there in 1918; he was then called almost immediately by the United States War Department to administer the Students' Army Training Corps. In 1919 he organized the School of Foreign Service at Georgetown University, the first organization of its kind in the country, serving as its regent and becoming vice president of the university in 1924. He soon became an outstanding authority on international politics; he made a study of the schools of political science and commerce in Europe (1921–1922); served as representative for Roman Catholic interests in Russia and dispensed relief for various Roman Catholic organizations there (1922–1923); helped negotiate the differences between Mexico and the Roman Catholic Church (1929); assisted in founding Baghdad College in Iraq; and was consultant to the chief of counsel for the United States at the trial of German war criminals at Nürnberg in 1945. Among his books are *The Fall of the Russian Empire* (1928); *Total Power* (1948); and *Total Empire* (1951).

WALSH, Thomas James, American lawyer and legislator: b. Two Rivers, Wis., June 12, 1859; d. near Rocky Mount, N.C., March 2, 1933. He took a law degree at the University of Wisconsin in 1884 and practiced at Redfield, S.Dak., until 1890, when he removed to Helena, Mont. There he became a leader of the Montana bar and an authority on constitutional law. A Democrat in politics, he served as United States senator from 1913 until his death. Walsh was an able proponent of the war policies of President Woodrow Wilson and a strong advocate of the woman suffrage and child labor amendments; he also upheld the rights of farm and labor organizations under the Clayton Act. During 1922–1923 he was in charge of the investigation of the leasing of naval oil reserves in Wyoming and California, as a result of which he became widely known for uncovering the Teapot Dome and Elk Hills oil scandals. He was appointed attorney general by President Franklin D. Roosevelt in 1933, but died on his way to Washington to take office.

WALSINGHAM, wôl′sĭng-əm, **Sir Francis,** English statesman: b. either at Chrislehurst, Kent, or London, England, c. 1530; d. London, April 6, 1590. He attended King's College, Cambridge, and, because of his Protestant convictions, chose to live abroad during the reign of Mary I. With the accession of Elizabeth I, he returned to England and sat in Parliament from 1558 to 1567, supporting William Cecil (later 1st Baron Burghley). Walsingham was English ambassador in Paris from 1570 to 1573, and thereafter, until his death, he served as secretary of state, sometimes jointly with others. He was knighted in 1577. As secretary of state he favored English colonization in America and induced Elizabeth to throw her support to the Dutch in the struggle with Spain.

He maintained numerous private agents and spies at foreign courts, and many stories are told of his diplomatic skill and profundity. He had chief direction of the measures for the discovery of the conspiracy of Anthony Babington (q.v.) against Elizabeth, as a result of which he was instrumental in bringing about the trial and execution of Mary, Queen of Scots. However, Elizabeth rejected his advice on many important matters, notably in regard to the preparations to be made against the Spanish Armada.

In his private character he is said to have been ascetically strict in his morals and puritanical in his religious zeal. After the death of his son-in-law Sir Philip Sidney in 1586, Walsingham was at the mercy of Sidney's creditors and died deeply in debt.

WALTARI, väl-tä′rĭ, **Mika Toimi,** Finnish novelist: b. Helsinki, Finland, Sept. 19, 1908; d. there, Aug. 26, 1979. His first published novel, *Suuri illusioni* (1928), was written in Paris. He then completed a master's degree in philosophy at Helsinki University (1929) and worked for a few years as an editor. After his successful novel *Vieras mies tuli taloon* (1937; Eng. tr., *A Stranger Came to the Farm,* 1952), he was able to give full time to research and writing except during World War II.

Waltari's masterpiece is *Sinuhe, egyptiläinen* (1945; Eng. tr., *The Egyptian,* 1949). Other novels in English translation include *The Adventurer* (1950), *The Wanderer* (1951), *The Dark Angel* (1953), *The Etruscan* (1956), and *The Tongue of Fire* (1959).

In *The Egyptian,* Waltari deals with religious, political, and domestic affairs of people who lived about 3,000 years ago, but makes these events in many ways suggestive of conditions of his own day. Critics acclaim the accuracy of his handling of historical details as well as his skill in creative imagination.

William Bracy

WALTER, wôl′tər, a family of English publishers, founders and managers of *The Times* of London.

John Walter (known as John Walter I): b. 1736 or 1739; d. Teddington, Middlesex, England, Nov. 16, 1812. He was in the coal export trade and the associated marine insurance business until shipping losses brought him to insolvency in 1781. Friends assisted him to start afresh in a new business as a printer, and in 1783 he was installed in Printing House Square, the site of the old King's Printing House, where he was equipped with a new invention, the logographic press, the type of which was cast in syllables instead of separate letters. As an example of what the press could do, he started, on Jan. 1, 1785, a small news sheet called the *Daily Universal Register,* which was renamed *The Times* three years later. As a polemical journalist, John Walter I came in conflict with the brothers of George III who secured his imprisonment for criminal libel. *The Times* seemed moribund when he retired in 1795 and handed its conduct over to his eldest son, William Walter, who transferred sole management to his younger brother, John Walter II, in 1803.

John Walter (known as John Walter II): b. London, England, Feb. 23, 1776; d. there, July 28, 1847. From the age of 19 to 20 he was at Trinity College, Oxford. On coming of age he was brought into the office as his father's partner in the printing business and to assist in the management of *The Times.* Upon assuming control, his first concern was to cut adrift from the 18th century tradition of journalistic subservience to politicians. The break was accomplished by 1806, but the consequence was a long and severe struggle to vindicate the paper's new liberty against counterattack in the form of withdrawal of government printing contracts and advertising, and the denial of government sources of foreign news to *The Times,* while they were open to its competitors. During this struggle, Walter was mainly responsible for founding a foreign news service in Europe; initiating the profession of war correspondent; and, above all, for proving that a newspaper could be financially supported by commercial advertisers who, unlike political patrons, would not seek to dictate the policy of the paper. By 1814 the paper was solvent. Walter was ready to withdraw from daily supervision of the content of *The Times* and allow the editor, a previously obscure employee, to emerge as the responsible figure that the title suggests today. Walter retained commercial control of the paper and became a member of Parliament for Berkshire (1832–1837) and Nottingham (1841–1842).

John Walter (known as John Walter III): b. London, England, Oct. 8, 1818; d. Bear Wood, near Reading, Nov. 3, 1894. Educated at Exeter College, Oxford, he was called to the bar in 1847 and in the same year became manager of *The Times.* He introduced the Walter press, which was the forerunner of modern newspaper printing presses. A member of Parliament from 1847 to 1865, and from 1868 to 1885, he was strongly interested in politics and left much of the management of the paper to Mowbray Morris. His eldest son, who was to have succeeded him as John Walter IV, died at the age of 26 in

1870 after coming to the aid of some skaters who had fallen through the ice. His brother, Arthur Fraser Walter, was the next successor to control.

ARTHUR FRASER WALTER: b. London, England, Sept. 12, 1846; d. Bear Wood, near Reading, Feb. 22, 1910. He was educated at Christ Church, Oxford. After the death of his father, he became chief proprietor of the paper until 1908 when, owing to financial difficulties, *The Times* was converted into a limited company and a majority interest was bought by Sir Alfred Harmsworth (later Baron and Viscount Northcliffe). Arthur Walter remained as chairman of the company.

JOHN WALTER (known as JOHN WALTER V): b. 1873; d. Hove, Sussex, Eng., Aug. 11, 1968. He succeeded his father as the chairman of the company. In 1922 the paper was bought by John Jacob Astor (later Lord Astor of Hever) in Walter's name. Astor became chairman of the company, but Walter retained one tenth of the shares and continued to be known as "co-chief proprietor."

DERMOT MORRAH,
Formerly of "The Times," London.

WALTER, väl'tər, **Bruno** (real surname SCHLESINGER), German conductor: b. Berlin, Germany, Sept. 15, 1876; d. Beverly Hills, Calif., Feb. 17, 1962. In 1894 he was appointed assistant to Gustav Mahler as conductor at Hamburg, rejoining him at the Vienna Opera in 1901; he later became a persuasive propagandist for Mahler's compositions. In 1914 he was appointed music director at Munich, where he became famous for his performances of Mozart operas. From 1922 on, he conducted at the annual Salzburg festivals. Walter made his American debut in New York City in 1923; headed the Berlin State Opera from 1925 to 1929; and then succeeded Wilhelm Furtwängler as conductor of the Leipzig Gewandhaus Concerts. When the Nazi regime stopped his activities in Germany, he made guest appearances elsewhere. He became music director of the Vienna Opera in 1936, but again was driven out by the Nazis. During World War II he became an American citizen and subsequently conducted many American orchestras as well as at the Metropolitan Opera House in New York City. He was most appreciated for his performances and recordings of the Viennese classic repertoire. An accomplished pianist, he also composed, and wrote several books, including *Von den moralischen Kräften der Musik* (1935), *Gustav Mahler* (1936; rev. Eng. tr., 1958), and the autobiographical *Theme and Variations* (1946).

HERBERT WEINSTOCK.

WALTER, wôl'tər (incorrectly WALTERS or WATERS), **Lucy,** English beauty, mistress of Charles II: b. near Haverfordwest, Pembrokeshire, Wales, ?1630; d. Paris, France, 1658. She met the future Charles II while he was an exile in The Hague in 1648, and was his mistress until 1651. In 1649 she bore him a son, James Scott, who was made duke of Monmouth in 1663 and received the support of the Whigs in their attempt to exclude James II from the throne. (See MONMOUTH, DUKE OF.) Although Charles admitted paternity, he denied ever having married Lucy, and she led a life of considerable promiscuity both before and after her association with him. In 1656 she was briefly imprisoned in the Tower of London under suspicion of being a spy, but was released and deported to the Continent. She also used the alias of Mrs. Barlow or Barlo.

WALTER, Thomas Ustick, American architect: b. Philadelphia, Pa., Sept. 4, 1804; d. there, Oct. 30, 1887. He studied at the Franklin Institute and in the office of William Strickland. In 1830 he opened his own office, and the following year designed the Philadelphia City Prison. Walter's design for Girard College was accepted in 1833, and for six years he worked on plans for this building, which became known as a model of classic purity. In 1851 he succeeded Robert Mills as architect of the Capitol in Washington, D.C. He held this position until 1865 and was responsible for adding the wings and the dome. He also completed the Treasury Building and added wings to the Patent Office. A founder of the American Institute of Architects (1857), he was its president from 1876.

WALTER REED ARMY MEDICAL CENTER, an army medical center in and near Washington, D.C., created in 1923, 14 years after its first component, Walter Reed General Hospital, opened its doors on May 1, 1909. Named for Maj. Walter Reed (q.v.), the famed conqueror of yellow fever, the center also houses the Walter Reed Army Institute of Research, Armed Forces Institute of Pathology, Central Dental Laboratory, Army Prosthetics Research Laboratory, Army Audiology and Speech Center, and the Historical Unit, United States Army Medical Service.

Outgrowing its original 113 acres in northwest Washington during World War II, the center acquired the 188-acre site of a boarding school for young women at Forest Glen, Montgomery County, Md., 5 miles to the north. The Army has maintained the school's unique architecture and relaxed environment for the beneficial effect such surroundings have on convalescing hospital patients. A spacious community of homes for noncommissioned officers and their families is also located on a 22-acre tract at Glenhaven, Md., a few miles north of the Forest Glen section.

Major William Cline Borden, then commander of the hospital at Washington Barracks (now Fort McNair), was the first to envision a complete army medical center capable of carrying on research, teaching, and care of the sick and wounded. His dream was realized in 1905 when Congress authorized construction of the hospital.

Walter Reed General Hospital, with a capacity of 1,500 beds, carries on an intensive intern and resident training program. It is accredited in 21 of 24 specialties approved by the American Medical Association. The research institute, an element of the Army Medical Service Research and Development Command, also maintains a medical unit at Fort Detrick, Md., and a medical research unit in Malaya.

WALTERBORO, wôl'tər-bûr-ō, town, South Carolina, seat of Colleton County, at an altitude of 91 feet, 45 miles west of Charleston. It has an airport. Walterboro is the trading center of a lumbering and agricultural region which raises cotton, truck crops, livestock, and dairy cattle. Industrial establishments include sawmills; plants for manufacturing baskets, laminated plywood boxes, and asbestos drier felts; a dress factory; and a meat-packing plant. The town is also a winter resort and tourist center, with excellent hunting and fishing in the vicinity. It was settled by a family of rice planters named Walter in the early 18th century. It has a mayor-council form of government. Pop. 6,036.

MARGUERITE G. THOMPSON.

WALTERS, wôl'tərz, **William Thompson,** American businessman and art collector: b. Liverpool, Pa., May 23, 1820; d. Baltimore, Md., Nov. 22, 1894. He trained as a civil and mining engineer in Philadelphia, entered the iron industry, and in 1841 went into the produce commission business in Baltimore. From 1847 to 1883 he was in partnership with Charles Harvey in the liquor trade. Because of his Confederate sympathies, Walters spent the Civil War years in Paris with his son Henry, and here his active interest in the arts began. After the Civil War he began to buy up small, disorganized Southern railroads, and in 1889 he consolidated his holdings in the Atlantic Improvement & Construction Company, which in 1893 became the Atlantic Coast Line Company. Walters was a patron of the sculptor William Henry Rinehart and a trustee of the Corcoran Gallery of Art in Washington, D.C. He formed the nucleus of what is now the Walters Art Gallery in Baltimore by purchasing the works of such contemporary painters as Camille Corot, François Millet, Eugène Delacroix, Léon Gérôme, and Sir Lawrence Alma-Tadema. He also imported the first Percheron horse to America.

HENRY WALTERS (1848–1931), his son, was also a railroad executive and art collector. Educated at Georgetown University, the Lawrence Scientific School at Harvard University, and in Paris, where he met the art dealer Paul Durand-Ruel, he was able to devote more time than his father to collecting. He added prints, ceramics, sculpture, jewelry, textiles, manuscripts, and a large art library to his father's collection, and in 1907 built the Walters Art Gallery in Baltimore, which he left, with a quarter of his estate, to the city of Baltimore.

HERBERT D. HALE,
Art Critic.

WALTHAM, wôl'thəm, city, Massachusetts, in Middlesex County, on the Charles River, 9 miles west of Boston, at an altitude of 67 feet. Once famous as a watchmaking center, it is now the home of some 250 diversified industries, mostly in the electronics and precision-instrument fields. The city's "showcase" is a four-mile stretch known as the "Golden Circle," where widely spaced factories have been built in attractively landscaped settings. Waltham is also a center for agricultural information and research, with headquarters of the county farm bureau and an agricultural field station of the University of Massachusetts. Brandeis University is located here. The city's library houses a rare collection of Waltham watches. Two historic homes are of special interest: Gore Place (1805), home of Gov. Christopher Gore, famous for its English bricks and imported shrubs; and the Lyman House (1793), with fine gardens and old trees.

Organized as a precinct of Watertown in 1630, Waltham was incorporated as a separate town in 1738 and became a city in 1884. In 1813 Francis Cabot Lowell introduced cotton manufacturing, a major factor in the city's economy until 1930; he installed the first power loom in the United States, and for the first time combined all operations in cotton cloth production in one plant. In 1854 the Waltham Watch Company was established and remained the city's most famous enterprise until it closed in 1950. Waltham is governed by a mayor and 15-member council. Pop. 58,200.

BERNICE K. COWAN.

WALTHAMSTOW, wôl'thəm-stō, municipal borough, England, in southwest Essex, on the Lea River, nine miles northeast of London and included in Greater London. Adjacent to Epping Forest, it was formerly a rural suburb with many large estates, but has developed rapidly as an industrial and residential suburb of London, with fine public buildings, parks, and housing developments on a large scale. South Essex Technical College is located here. Almshouses, several manors, and St. Mary's Church all date from the 16th century. William Morris (1834–1896) was born in Walthamstow. Pop. (1961) 108,788.

WALTHARII POESIS, wäl-tä'rĭ-ē pō-ā'sĭs or **WALTHARIUS MANU FORTIS,** wal-tä'rĭ-o͞os mä'-no͞o fôr'tĭs, a poem of 1,456 Latin hexameter lines, the only complete extant work about Walter of Aquitaine. Fragments survive of an Old English *Waldere* and of a Middle High German *Walther und Hildegund.* Slavic versions also exist. Waltharius is a youth brought up with his fiancée Hildegund as a hostage at the court of Attila the Hun. Although kindly treated, he flees with Hildegund and a great treasure. He eludes his pursuers, but his arrival in the territories of the Burgundian king, Gunther, is reported by a ferryman. The king takes his best warriors to seize the treasure, but Waltharius kills them in a series of brilliantly described single combats. The feeble Gunther finally persuades his greatest warrior, Hagen, a close friend of Waltharius, to join him in an attack. All three receive grave wounds, but Hagen and Waltharius feast together before Waltharius goes on to his home in Aquitaine—with the treasure.

Some critics date the poem in the 9th century, but the prevailing view is that it was written by Ekkehard I, abbot at St. Gall in Switzerland, about 940 and revised about a century later by Ekkehard IV. The attitudes and morality are Germanic—notions of honor, scorn of pain and death—but the language is classical and therefore some critics have denied the existence of a Germanic original and regard the *Waltharius* as a mere imitation of classical epic with German names. This is unlikely. The poem is vigorous and well organized and is probably the best Latin epic of the Middle Ages.

W. T. H. JACKSON,
Professor of German, Columbia University.

WALTHER, väl'tər, **Carl Ferdinand Wilhelm,** German-American Lutheran leader: b. Langenchursdorf, Saxony, Germany, Oct. 25, 1811; d. St. Louis, Mo., May 7, 1887. After completing theological studies at the University of Leipzig, he encountered opposition to his strongly conservative Lutheran position and emigrated to the United States in 1839 with 750 Lutherans headed by Martin Stephan, Lutheran pastor at Dresden. Succeeding Stephan as leader of the

Lutheran colony in Perry County, Mo., Walther also succeeded his brother as pastor of Trinity Congregation in St. Louis (1841). That same year he married Christine Emilie Bünger, who bore him six children. A log-cabin school he had helped to found in Altenburg in 1839 was moved in 1850 to St. Louis, where it became known as Concordia Theological Seminary. He was its first elected professor (1849). He was also president (1847–1850, 1864–1878) of a new church body that was organized in 1847 largely under his direction, the German Evangelical Lutheran Synod of Missouri, Ohio and Other States. This is now the Lutheran Church-Missouri Synod, with a membership comprising one third of all Lutherans in North and South America.

Walther hoped to achieve one "united Evangelical Lutheran Church of North America" through a federation, The Lutheran Synodical Conference of North America, which was organized in 1872 with Walther as its first president. His hopes, however, were frustrated by theological controversy, namely that of the nature of predestination.

A prolific writer, Walther edited the influential periodical *Der Lutheraner* from 1844 and the professional journal *Lehre und Wehre* from 1855 (now the *Concordia Theological Monthly*). He was also the author of a number of definitive theological works, written in German, many of which have been translated into English. His works include *Amerikanisch-Lutherische Evangelien-Postille* (1871) and *Americanisch-Lutherische Pastoraltheologie* (1872). Proceeds from the sale of his works were always given to the church's treasury.

Walther's other talents lay in music. His skill as an organist and as a baritone singer caused him to consider music as a career before he took up the study of theology.

Possessed of a powerful, magnetic personality, Walther has been called "the most commanding figure in the Lutheran Church of America during the 19th century." He is buried in Concordia Cemetery in St. Louis.

OSWALD C.J. HOFMANN
The Lutheran Church, Missouri Synod

WALTHER VON DER VOGELWEIDE, väl'tər fôn dûr fō'gəl-vī-də, German poet, b. probably in Austria, c. 1160; d. about 1230. He learned his art in Austria from Reinmar von Hagenau. Although noble birth is generally assumed, he could have owed his title of "Sir" (*hêr*) to his position as court singer, for in moral outlook he seems closer to the clergy and the later bourgeoisie than to the nobility. After mastering the art of the *minnesang* (courtly love lyric), Walther rejected the restrictive conventions of *hôhe minne* (languishing love for inaccessible ladies) and devoted his talents to *nidere minne* (natural love for women regardless of rank). Declaring *wîp* (woman) a more honorable term than *frouwe* (lady), he glorified womanhood by praising women's ennobling influence upon men even more than their physical beauty.

Walther was the first minnesinger to cultivate the *Spruch,* a type of gnomic verse derived from scriptural, classical, and popular wisdom. Previously shunned by noble minnesingers, the *Spruch* achieved literary status when perfected by Walther, who mastered most lyric genres of his day including courtly and noncourtly love songs, complaints, salutations, disputes, dance songs, summer songs, nature songs, *botenlieder* (songs to be sung by a messenger), allegories, Crusade songs, hymns, panegyrics, philippics, parodies, elegies, fables, riddles, and nursery rhymes. His most original contribution was his political songs, in which he championed the German Empire in its struggle against the papacy. Never questioning Christian dogma, he castigated clerical greed and the secular ambitions of the church and composed scathing invectives against Innocent III and Gregory IX for prolonging civil strife by playing one imperial claimant against the other.

Although long famous, Walther is mentioned in only one historical document, a travel account of Bishop Wolfger of Passau, who in 1203 gave five *solidi* to "Walthero cantori de Vogelweide" to purchase a fur coat. Approximate dates can be deduced from historical allusions in Walther's political songs, but it is impossible to reconstruct his life from the limited evidence in his surviving works. Nevertheless, much is revealed by his subjective songs, which, unlike most contemporary works, seem based on personal experience. Even when put into traditional literary forms, his verses suggest genuine feeling, especially in his reflections on abstract problems such as man's proper relation to God and to other men. Sincere patriotism pervades his praise of the German lands through which he wandered as a mendicant singer until he finally received a small fief from Emperor Frederick II.

Apparently ingenuous, Walther's songs conceal his subtle artistry in metrical patterns and rhyme schemes, and despite their varied forms and subject matter, they all bear the imprint of a strong personality. Sometimes merry and sometimes serious, they are all affirmative except for his political diatribes. Even the elegiac plaints of his old age are affirmative; when finally disillusioned with the blandishments of the world, he still has unshaken faith in a better life to come. This universality of interest and deep and abiding faith make Walther a fitting spokesman for his age, certainly Germany's greatest medieval poet, and often acclaimed Europe's greatest lyric genius of the High Middle Ages.

GEORGE FENWICK JONES,
Associate Professor of German, Goucher College.

WALTON, wôl'tən, **Ernest Thomas Sinton,** Irish physicist: b. Dungarvan, County Waterford, Ireland, Oct. 6, 1903. The son of a Methodist minister, he was admitted at the age of 12 to Methodist College in Belfast, where his interest in science was first aroused. He later attended Trinity College, Dublin, graduating with first class honors in mathematics and experimental physics in 1926. In 1927 he was awarded a research scholarship at the Cavendish Laboratory of Cambridge University and there was introduced by Sir Ernest (later 1st Baron) Rutherford to the exciting new field of nuclear transformations. He also met John Douglas Cockcroft and with him began work on a method of producing fast subatomic particles by means of high voltages. By 1932 Cockcroft and Walton were able to create constant high potentials which permitted them to bombard the nuclei of lithium with hydrogen ions (protons) and observe the effects. They interpreted the production of helium nuclei as the result of the splitting of the lithium nuclei by the high-energy protons. Modern particle accelerators and artificial nuclear fission date from these experiments, for which Walton and Cockroft received the Nobel Prize in physics in 1951. In 1946, Walton returned to Trinity College as Erasmus Smith's professor of natural and experimental philosophy.

L. PEARCE WILLIAMS
Cornell University

WALTON, George (1741–1804), American political leader. He was born near Farmville, Va., in 1741. After serving as a carpenter's apprentice, he went to Savannah, Ga., in 1769, where he studied law and was admitted to the bar in 1774. With three others, he organized a meeting at Savannah on July 27, 1774, to discuss measures of resistance against Great Britain. Walton became a member of the resulting Committee of Correspondence and later was president of the Council of Safety in Georgia. In 1776 he was sent as a delegate to the Continental Congress and was one of the signers of the Declaration of Independence and the Articles of Confederation. He continued to serve in Congress until 1781. In 1778 he was appointed colonel of the 1st Regiment, Georgia Militia. Wounded and taken prisoner when the British captured Savannah, he was exchanged in September 1779 and two months later became governor of Georgia, serving until January 1780. He also served as chief justice of the state from 1783 to 1789 and as judge of the Superior Court from 1790, with interruptions, until his death. He was governor again in 1789–1790 and United States senator in 1795–1796. He died in Augusta on Feb. 2, 1804.

WALTON, Izaak (1593–1683), English author. He was born in Stafford on Aug. 9, 1593. His father died when Izaak was an infant. Izaak must have had some schooling in Stafford, but his first appearance in public records is in 1614 as proprietor of an ironmonger's shop in London, and in

Izaak Walton

NATIONAL PORTRAIT GALLERY, LONDON

1618 he became a freeman of the Ironmongers' Company. In 1626, at Canterbury, he married Rachel Floud or Floyd (d. 1640), a collateral descendant of Archbishop Thomas Cranmer; his second wife, Anne Ken (d. 1662), was a stepsister of Thomas Ken, later bishop of Bath and Wells.

In London, Walton was a friend and parishioner of John Donne, whose life he wrote as a preface to a volume of Donne's sermons (1640); this biography was enlarged and published separately in 1658. Other friends and acquaintances included Sir Henry Wotton, poet and diplomat; George Herbert, poet and divine; and Robert Sanderson, bishop of Lincoln, whose lives he published in 1651, 1670, and 1678, respectively. The only one of his biographical subjects with whom he had no personal contact was the theologian Richard Hooker (1554–1600), whose life he published in 1665.

Walton seems to have retired from business about 1644. As an Anglican and Royalist, he was unhappy under the Cromwellian dictatorship, and perhaps to take his mind off the evil times he wrote, or compiled, the book that is his chief claim to literary immortality, *The Compleat Angler* (see COMPLEAT ANGLER). This was first published in 1653 and revised and enlarged in 1655; a 5th edition in 1676 was still further enlarged, and a section of "instructions how to angle for a trout or grayling in a clear stream" by Charles Cotton was added.

After the Restoration (1660) and the death of his second wife, Walton lived much of the time at Farnham Castle as permanent guest of George Morley, bishop of Winchester. He died on Dec. 15, 1683, in the home of his daughter Anne, wife of William Hawkins, prebendary of Winchester. He was buried in Winchester Cathedral.

DELANCEY FERGUSON
Brooklyn College

WALTON, Sir William Turner, (1902–1983), English composer. He was born in Oldham, Lancashire, on March 29, 1902. He attended Christ Church, University of Oxford, and was a tutorial student of Ernest Ansermet, Ferruccio Busoni, and Edward Joseph Dent. He then won fame overnight with the performance (June 12, 1923) of *Façade*, a sardonic, flippant setting of poems by Edith Sitwell for declaiming voice, flute, clarinet, saxophone, trumpet, cello, and percussion. In a more serious vein, the oratorio *Belshazzar's Feast* (1931) solidified his reputation, and he continued to produce both serious and light music with meticulous craftsmanship. He was knighted in 1951. His first opera, *Troilus and Cressida* (Covent Garden, London, 1954), won considerable applause. Other works include two symphonies, ballets, overtures (notably *Portsmouth Point*, 1926, and *Scapino*, 1940), concertos (for cello, viola, violin), marches, suites, chamber music, film scores, and ceremonial pieces, such as coronation marches for George VI and Elizabeth II and a *Te Deum* for Elizabeth's coronation. With Ralph Vaughan Williams and Benjamin Britten, Walton was regarded as one of the leading 20th century English composers. He died on the island of Ischia, Italy, on March 8, 1983.

HERBERT WEINSTOCK,
Coauthor of "Men of Music"

WALTON, village, New York, in Delaware County, 20 miles southwest of the county seat, Delhi. It lies at an altitude of 1,235 feet on the Delaware River, in a picturesque valley in the foothills of the Catskill Mountains.

Formerly a lumbering center, it is in a thriving dairy-farming area and supports several large dairies and smaller industries. Excellent fishing and hunting and two scenic reservoirs nearby attract tourists and sportsmen. Delhi Agricultural and Technical Institute, Hartwick College, and Oneonta State University College of Education are all within 25 miles. Incorporated in 1851, Walton is governed by a mayor and board of trustees. Pop. 3,329.

WALTZ, a term now mainly associated with a round dance to music in triple measure. Its origin reaches back to the 16th and 17th centuries, when it was best known as the *Weller*, an Austrian and Bavarian peasant dance with wild wide steps in rapid turning movement. Its sliding, gliding steps caught the fancy of the people, and when higher society joined the peasants in the *Weller*, the "mad" movements became more moderate.

Another forerunner of the waltz was the *Ländler*, a turning dance from Styria, a mountain region of Austria, which included separate figures, such as hand clapping or spinning the girls on the upraised hands of their stamping partners. The name *Walzer* does not appear before the middle of the 18th century. At first, the dance held all of Germany and Austria in its spell, and emerging bourgeois society welcomed it as the expression of a new era. In 1790 it invaded France, but it was not accepted in England until 1812. Despite the resistance of courts and dancing masters, the waltz quickly conquered the world.

The French created their own version, the skipping waltz, while the Germans had such variations as the schottische and the two-step. The classical waltz, however, had its cradle in Vienna; Vicente Martín y Soler's opera *Una cosa rara* (produced there in 1786) featured what is usually considered the original Viennese waltz. Ever since then the waltz has remained the expression of youthful exuberance and longing passion; even its successors, such as the slow boston, or the hesitation waltz introduced by Vernon and Irene Castle in the decade following 1910, have retained some of its sensual, ecstatic feeling. It is not surprising that this dance superseded the famous minuet of the 18th century and outlived the quadrille and the cancan, once the favorites of their era.

In spite of the vehement movements of the original *Ländler* and *Weller*, the music of these dances was marked by an evenness of the three beats or an accentuation of the second beat of the measure. The Viennese waltz increased the tempo to about 200 quarter notes to the minute. Emphasis of the first beat and underemphasis of the second beat developed, while the extreme movements turned into floating lightness. Smooth progression in music and dance became the hallmark of the classical waltz, and the 8-measure period of the *Ländler* became 16 measures. Carl Maria von Weber, for example, used 16 measures in his *Invitation to the Dance* (1819). Franz Schubert composed several *Ländler* and waltzes, and the influence of the early waltz melodies can be detected in the music of Joseph Haydn and Wolfgang Amadeus Mozart (notably in the ballroom scene in *Don Giovanni*). Richard Strauss' *Der Rosenkavalier* is waltz inspired, and waltzes are found in many operas, among them *La Bohème, Eugene Onegin, Faust, Mefistofele*, and *Hänsel and Gretel*.

Johannes Brahms and Frédéric Chopin, Peter Ilich Tchaikovsky and Maurice Ravel were also among those who wrote waltzes, but this musical form reached its greatest popularity with the Viennese composers Johann Strauss the Younger (the *Blue Danube* and *Tales from the Vienna Woods* waltzes), Eduard Strauss, Franz Lehár, and Oscar Straus.

WALTER SORELL
Columbia University

WALTZEMÜLLER, Martin. See WALDSEEMÜLLER, MARTIN.

WALVIS BAY, wôl′vĭs, a port and surrounding territory (434 square miles, or 1,124 sq km) on the Atlantic coast of Namibia (South West Africa). It is administered as part of the Republic of South Africa's Cape of Good Hope province but is also claimed by Namibia. The harbor, open to the north, is sheltered by Pelican Point peninsula. Annual rainfall amounts to less than 1 inch (25 mm), making the region the driest in Africa south of the equator. Water is obtained from Rooibank, 28 miles (45 km) inland.

Between 1916 and 1930, Walvis Bay served as a whaling station and subsequently was a repair depot for whaling ships operating in the Antarctic. A channel was dredged to a long wharf equipped with electric cranes. Several of the oil companies use Walvis Bay as a petroleum storage depot; the port serves mining and stock-raising regions; and a chilled meat export trade has been developed.

Other leading industries are the processing of fish and the collection of guano. There is a small airfield and a radio station, and the town is linked by rail with South Africa through Swakopmund.

The first recorded visit to Walvis Bay by a European was made in 1487 by the Portuguese navigator Bartholomeu Dias. Later known as Woolwich Bay, it was frequently used in the late 18th and in the 19th century as a rendezvous for whaling ships (many of them American) operating in the South Atlantic. A German mission station was established nearby in 1845. The territory was annexed by Great Britain in 1878 and added to Cape Colony in 1884; it remained under British control after Germany annexed South West Africa in the latter year. After South Africa conquered South West Africa in 1915, Walvis Bay was developed as the region's principal port. It was administered as part of South West Africa (now Namibia) from 1922 to 1977 and since then as part of Cape of Good Hope province. Population: (1978) 25,000.

NEWELL M. STULTZ,
African Studies Program, Boston University.

WAMPANOAG INDIANS, wŏm-pə-nō′ăg ("Eastern people"), a tribe of the Algonkian linguistic stock, closely related to the Massachusetts Indians. They were sometimes call Pokanoket, from their principal village, or Massasoit, from their noted chief. The Wampanoag occupied what are now Bristol County, R.I., and Bristol County, Mass., but claimed the territory between Narragansett Bay, the Pawtucket River, and the Atlantic Ocean, including Martha's Vineyard and Nantucket Island. They were visited by the English navigator Bartholomew Gosnold as early as 1602, at which time they numbered some 5,000 individuals; an epidemic in 1617 seriously decreased the population. When the Pilgrims established themselves at Plymouth Colony in 1620, the Wampanoag inhabited about 30 villages, and their chief, Massasoit, negotiated a treaty with the whites which was faithfully observed until his death. He was succeeded by two sons, the younger of whom, Metacom, was called "King Philip" by the colonists. Brutal treatment of the Indians by the white settlers so incensed Metacom that he tried to organize all of the Algonkian tribes of the region to resist them. In 1675 most of

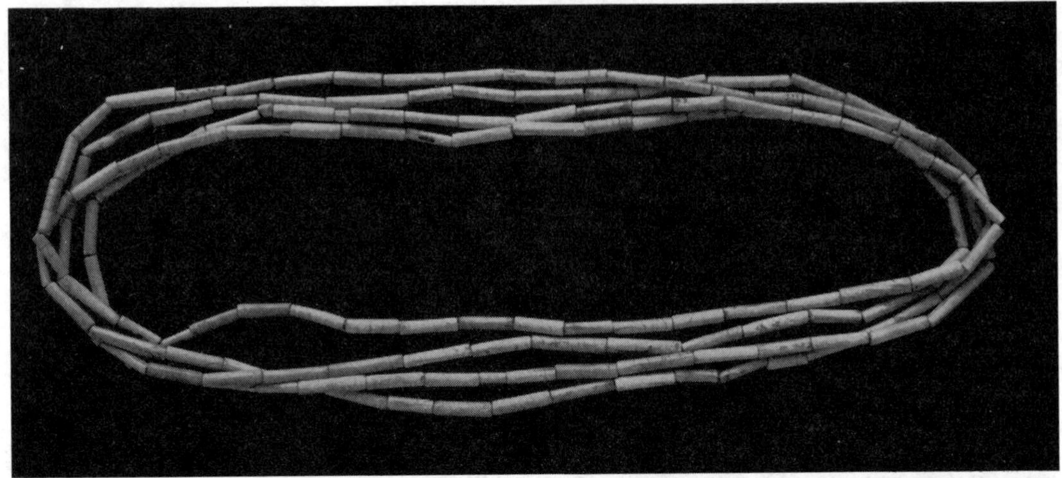

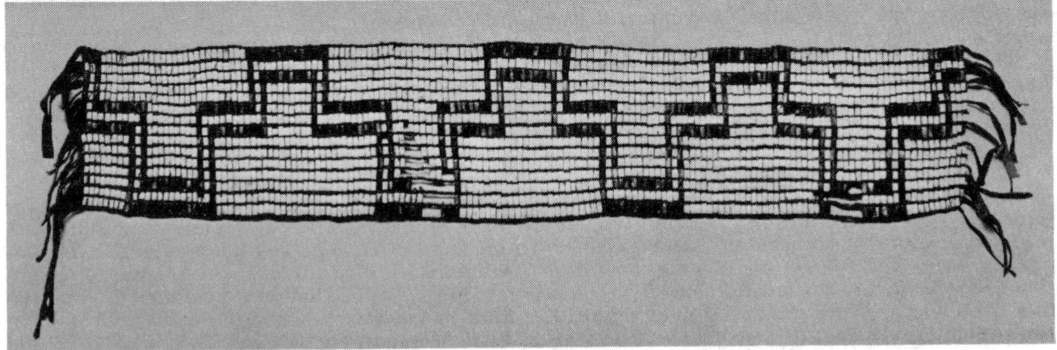

Museum of the American Indian, Heye Foundation

Top: Shawnee wampum beads from Oklahoma. **Bottom:** Wampum belt given by Lenni-Lenape (Delaware) Indians to William Penn.

these tribes united to begin King Philip's War (q.v.), during which most of the Wampanoag and Narragansett peoples were exterminated. Their survivors settled with other remnant groups, and some descendants are to be found today among the groups on Martha's Vineyard and Nantucket. These people are a greatly mixed-blood population, who have infused several tribal and racial strains; there are perhaps 500 individuals today with some degree of Wampanoag blood.

FREDERICK J. DOCKSTADER.

WAMPUM, wŏm′pəm (from Algonquian *wampumpeak,* a string of white shell beads; also called *sewan, peak,* or *peag*), specifically, a cylindrical shell bead, drilled longitudinally, measuring about ⅛ inch in diameter, and from ¼ to 7/16 inch in length. These beads were commonly made from the shell of the quahog clam, *Venus mercenaria,* and were used by Indian tribes throughout the Northeast as a medium of exchange and standard of value. When used as ornaments, the beads became symbols of wealth or position; in the hands of the appointed "keeper of the wampum," they were historical records or documents. The religious aura which was attached to wampum added an air of solemnity to meetings in which it was included. Beads made from the purple section of the shell, usually called "black beads," were twice as valuable as the more common white beads which came from the larger part of the shell.

In the making of wampum, small pieces of the shell were broken up, roughly shaped, polished smooth on rough stones, and then drilled. We have no records of the aboriginal technique of wampum manufacture; as soon as the white man came, his iron tools greatly simplified and tremendously accelerated the process. The great center of the wampum industry was Long Island; hence the aboriginal name Sewanhacky for the island. The manufactured beads were carried across Manhattan into the territory of the Wappinger, who controlled the distribution of wampum up into the Iroquois and neighboring regions.

Lack of sufficient currency for commercial needs forced the New England colonists to use wampum as a medium of exchange, not only with the Indians, but among themselves as well, during times of coin shortage. Rhode Island recognized wampum officially until as late as 1670, and in New York it was used into the 1700's—as for example in payment of ferriage between New York and Brooklyn. Values varied greatly; in some areas, 3 dark or 6 white beads were equivalent to an English penny. But wampum was usually sold by the fathom, and the price varied between 5 and 10 shillings per fathom. In many interior regions, the beads continued in use well down into the late 19th century.

Naturally, counterfeit wampum was a serious problem; many early English and Dutch documents stress the problem caused by the manufacture of huge quantities of spurious shell beads. The Dutch seem to have been the most active in this industry, but in 1746 John W. Campbell set up a factory at Pascack, N.J., for the specific purpose of making wampum and other shell items. Out of this grew a business which did not die out until the death of his great grandson, Alexander Campbell, in 1899; during this time, Campbell wampum played an important role in the establishment of John Jacob Astor's fur business, was distributed throughout the northern and western part of the United States, and had no small effect upon the economic relationships of the Indian tribes concerned.

Wampum beads were strung in varying combinations for many purposes. Messengers usually carried them as tokens of safe conduct when traveling between tribes; "condolence strings" announced the death of an important chief, and strings were used as invitations to council meetings. When a new Iroquois chief was installed, he was given his wampum "horns of office" by the matron as evidence of his new position.

The colors enabled the Indians to make ornaments out of wampum in a variety of pleasing designs. When woven into great belts, averaging 6 inches wide and 30 inches long, these designs frequently became mnemonic devices, recording a particular event. Thus the famous wampum belts given to William Penn at the Treaty of Shackamaxon in 1682 not only transferred the Pennsylvania territory to him, but recorded the event pictorially. It was traditional to exchange these belts at such occasions, to make the agreement binding upon all parties; the act had much the same impact as affixing an official seal to a document.

True wampum was distributed from the Atlantic coast to the Mississippi River, and from the general Great Lakes region to the lower Ohio Valley. In the western parts of the country, other types of shell beads are often popularly known as "wampum," but the term is properly applied only to the beads previously discussed. Along the Pacific coast, the dentalium shell was used both as a standard of value and as an ornament; the flat, drilled disc-shell bead common throughout the West and Southwest is often also miscalled wampum. None of these Western varieties had the same many-sided use and importance to the individual tribes as did the wampum of the Algonquian and Iroquian peoples.

The two great collections of wampum and belts still extant are housed in the Museum of the American Indian, New York City, and in the New York State Museum in Albany. That these and two or three smaller collections are essentially all that survives of the great quantities of wampum once in existence is mute testimony to the erosion that time has levied upon much of Indian culture.

FREDERICK J. DOCKSTADER,
Director, Museum of the American Indian, Heye Foundation.

Bibliography

Lyford, Carrie A., *Quill and Beadwork of the Western Sioux* (Johnson Bks. 1979).
Orchard, William C., *Beads and Beadwork of the American Indian,* 2d ed. (Mus. of the Am. Indian 1975).
Quimby, G., *Indian Culture and European Trade Goods: Archaeology of the Historic Period in the Western Great Lakes Region* (1966; reprint, Greenwood Press 1978).
Saletore, R. N., *Encyclopedia of Indian Culture,* 4 vols. (Humanities Press 1981–1984).
Speck, Frank G., *Functions of Wampum among the Eastern Algonkian* (1919; reprint, Kraus 1976).
Stites, Sara H., *Economics of the Iroquois* (1905; reprint, AMS Press 1976).
Weeden, William B., *Indian Money as a Factor in New England Civilization* (1884; reprint, AMS Press 1978).
Wildschut, William, and Ewars, John, *Crow Indian Beadwork,* ed. by M. Smith, rev. ed. (Eagles View 1985).

WANAMAKER, wŏn'ə-mā-kər, **John,** American merchant: b. Philadelphia, Pa., July 11, 1838; d. there, Dec. 12, 1922. Starting in 1857 as a paid secretary (first in the United States) of the Philadelphia Young Men's Christian Association, he went into the men's clothing business (1861) with his brother-in-law, Nathan Brown, and in 1869 established John Wanamaker & Company, a more fashionable men's store on

John Wanamaker

Culver Service

Chestnut Street. In 1876 he founded the Grand Depot, which he soon developed into a complete department store. Having risen to the top of the mercantile field in Philadelphia, Wanamaker took over (1896) the business of A. T. Stewart and Company in New York City, which under his direction became one of the leading department stores there but finally closed in 1954. He was a pioneer in merchandising methods, notably the use of newspaper advertising, and also in the application of employee welfare and training systems.

Wanamaker was active in the public life of Philadelphia and took part in many reform movements. As a stanch Republican he helped to finance the presidential campaign of 1888 and was made postmaster general (1889–1893) by President Benjamin Harrison. Wanamaker instituted a number of improvements in the Post Office Department but was criticized for continuing to apply the "spoils system." Active all his life in religious work, he organized (1858) the Bethany Sunday School (Presbyterian), which became one of the largest in the United States, and was president (1870–1883) of the Philadelphia Young Men's Christian Association.

(LEWIS) RODMAN WANAMAKER (1863–1928), his son, became his father's right hand in the business after the death (1908) of an elder brother Thomas, and was sole owner after his father's death. In addition to his business activities, he was a noted collector of French art and rare musical instruments. He also supported studies of the North American Indians and pioneered in financing transatlantic aviation, including the first such flight by Richard Byrd in

1927. He donated the war-dead memorial in Madison Square, New York City.

WANAPAM INDIANS, wä'nä-pəm ("river people"), a Shahaptian-speaking tribe of North American Indians, who were referred to as the Sokulk by Meriwether Lewis and William Clark. They range along both banks of the Columbia River in the State of Washington, from above Crab Creek to the mouth of the Snake River. The Wanapam are not officially recognized as a tribe by the United States government. Their fame is chiefly due to the "Dreamer Society," which is a religious revivalist group started by Smohalla (q.v.), the prophet, in the latter half of the 19th century. His preaching strongly influenced Indians of the whole Northwest area, particularly Chief Joseph and the Nez Percé Indians.

FREDERICK J. DOCKSTADER

WANAQUE, wŏn'ə-kē, borough, New Jersey, in Passaic County, on the Passaic River, at an elevation of 255 feet in the Ramapo Mountains, 10 miles northwest of Paterson. It includes the villages of Haskell and Midvale, which produce metal powder, knitted goods, and calendars. Nearby is Wanaque Reservoir, which is the largest one in New Jersey. It encompasses an area six miles long and one mile wide. The borough of Wanaque was incorporated in 1918. Pop. 10,025.

WANCHÜAN. See CHANGKIAKOW.

WANDERER, The, wŏn'dər-ər, one of the finest examples extant of the alliterative lyric poetry of the Old English period. It was preserved in the Exeter Book (q.v.) and may be described as a 115-line lament. After a general statement about the hardships of life, the poet gives the wanderer's song of sorrow. The dominant theme is mutability or the fleeting nature of life and worldly things. The wanderer is alone, without family and friends, having been cut off from all security and happiness by the death of his master and protector. He recalls his former joys and his dreams of better days but in sadness he comes to accept and resigns himself to his ultimately harsh fate.

WILLIAM BRACY

WANDERING JEW, wŏn'dər-ĭng jōō, a name applied to several common greenhouse plants. All are trailing or creeping, have ornamental foliage, and grow easily. The name is commonly used for *Zebrina pendula* (lance-ovate leaves, commonly red-purple beneath and purplish above with silver stripes) and *Tradescantia fluminensis* (spiderwort; ovate-acute green leaves, red-purple beneath in brighter light). Sometimes *Commelina nudiflora* (day flower; lance-ovate leaves) is also called wandering Jew. These three are closely related and difficult to tell apart, especially when variegated (leaves striped, yellow or white); they are distinguished by the color of the flowers (respectively rose-red, white, and blue) and by leaf sheath characters. In England, *Saxifraga sarmentosa* (strawberry geranium; orbicular leaves toothed, reddish below and white-veined above) and *Linaria cymbalaria* (*Cymbalaria muralis,* Kenilworth ivy; leaves three- to nine-lobed) are known locally as wandering Jew. *Commelina nudiflora* and *Linaria cymbalaria* grow outdoors in the United States as far north as New York and New Jersey.

GEORGE E. WHEELER

WANDERING JEW, The, a legendary figure in many countries. As early as 1228, according to the English chronicler Roger of Wendover, there were reports from the Orient of "Joseph, a man of whom there was much talk in the world who, when our Lord suffered, was present and spoke to him, and who is still alive in evidence of the Christian faith." Though in this version he is identified with Joseph of Arimathea, and elsewhere with Judas, Pilate, the Man in the Moon, or the Wild Rider of German storm legends, the title of the Wandering Jew was first given to Cartaphilus, a porter in Pilate's court, who struck Jesus and told him not to loiter; Jesus answered, "I am going, and you will wait until I return." When he reaches the age of 100, Cartaphilus turns 30 again, his age at the time of his sin; and though he has been baptized, he lives on, humble, ascetic, and a friend to bishops and holy men, and will continue to live so until the Last Judgment. In 16th century Germany the legend was given new force with "eyewitness" accounts of how Ahasuerus, a shoemaker, urged Jesus to hasten on the road to Golgotha and was told, "I shall stand and rest, but you shall know no rest."

Appearances of the Wandering Jew were many times reported: in Saxony (1564), in Holland (1575) and in the West Indies shortly thereafter, in France (1604), in Belgium (1774) under the name of Isaac Laquedem, and even among the Mormons in Utah (1868). German lore had him wearing a flowing red mantle and a broad-brimmed or cocked hat; and charity dictated that two harrows be fitted together in the fields so that he might have an interval of rest. When hurricanes came to Brittany and Picardy, the peasants crossed themselves and said, "It is the Wandering Jew who passes by!" Speaking all languages, he appears in French and English balladry and chapbook literature, in Lithuanian and German saga, a figure who has well atoned for his impiety and who, with our modern humanitarian sympathy, loses his anti-Semitic coloring. Hence in the sensational novel of Eugène Sue (q.v.), *Le juif errant* (1844–45), Ahasuerus became a symbol of the poor and of their helper, occasionally intervening in the action, but serving mainly as a scaffolding for a story about the intolerable lot of women and the working classes, the machinations of a Jesuit villain, and Fourierist socialism. Like the Flying Dutchman, the Wandering Jew has paid bitterly for a moment of careless error, but he has been rewarded by becoming a figure of dignity and resignation, which has attracted the literary interest not only of Goethe and Shelley, but of recent writers who have seen in him an allegory of the painful exile and persecution of the Jewish people.

FRANCIS LEE UTLEY
Chairman, Department of English, The Ohio State University

WANDEROO, wŏn-də-rōō', the lion-tailed monkey, *Macaca silenus,* of the Malabar coast in southern India. The head and body are 18 to 21 inches long, and the tail, tufted at the tip, 10 to 13 inches long. The body hair is black, and the face is encircled by a gray to white ruff or beard. This monkey lives in herds of 12 to 20 in dense forests, using both plant and animal material for food.

The name is also applied to the bear monkey, *Presbytis senex,* a species of langur found in the mountains in southern Ceylon. The head and body are 21 to 22 inches long, and the tail 26 inches. The body fur, 4 to 5 inches long on the sides, is uniform dusky brown, that on the cheeks and chin being grayish to white. The animal's cry is a loud *how-how,* often repeated.

TRACY I. STORER.

WANDSWORTH, wŏnz'wərth, metropolitan borough of London, England, the largest of the city's boroughs (over 14 square miles in area), on the south bank of the Thames, at the mouth of the small Wandle River. It includes the districts of Wandsworth proper, Putney, Earlsfield, Upper and Lower Tooting, Balham, Streatham, and part of Clapham. It is a highly industrialized as well as a residential district, with dyeing and textile printing, oil processing, paper milling, brewing, and the manufacture of hats. Wandsworth Prison and a technical college are located here. Many Huguenots took refuge in Wandsworth after the revocation of the Edict of Nantes in 1685. Population: (1983 est.) 258,400.

WANER, wa'nər, **Paul Glee,** American baseball player: b. Harrah, Okla., April 16, 1903; d. Sarasota, Fla., Aug. 29, 1965. One of the greatest hitters and fielders in the game's history, he played as an outfielder with the Pittsburgh Pirates (1926–1940), Brooklyn Dodgers (1941, 1943–1944), Boston Red Sox (1941–1942), and New York Yankees (1944–1945). A left-handed batter, he won the most valuable player award in 1927 and the National League batting championship in 1927, 1934, and 1936. Waner's lifetime batting average was .333. Known as "Big Poison," he and his brother Lloyd ("Little Poison") formed a famous brother combination with the Pirates. Paul was elected to the Baseball Hall of Fame in 1952.

WANG CHING-WEI, wäng' jĭng'wā', Chinese political leader: b. Canton, China, ?1884; d. Japan, Nov. 10, 1944. After studying law in Tokyo, he joined the Chinese revolutionary movement and in 1910 was imprisoned for plotting the death of the Chinese prince regent. Freed in 1912 after the success of the revolution, he became one of Sun Yat-sen's chief supporters and most favored aids, his influence rivaling that of Chiang Kai-shek. After Sun's death in 1925, Wang Ching-wei headed the left wing of the Kuomintang and was premier of China from 1932 to 1935. His vacillations, however, made him unpopular with both left and right, and an attempt was made on his life in 1935. In 1938 he deserted the Nationalist government and two years later became head of the puppet government that Japan set up in Nanking. His reputation as a revolutionary hero in 1911 was forgotten, and the Kuomintang sought his assassination. He held his post as premier and obeyed Japan's dictates until his death.

WANG WEI, wäng' wā (courtesy name MO-CHIEH or MO-CH'I; official title YU CH'ÊNG), Chinese landscape painter, poet, and calligrapher: b. 699; d. 759. He is traditionally the founder of the southern school of Chinese landscape painting, his reputation being based on copies of a winter landscape scroll of his home, *Wang Ch'uan,* and on the *Portrait of the Scholar Fu Shêng* in a Japanese private collection, which may possibly come from the artist's own hand. The essay on landscape attributed to him, *The Spirit of the Brush* (tr. by Shio Sakanishi, 1939) is almost certainly of a later date. Wang Wei is credited with the invention of painting in light washes with "broken ink" brushstrokes for depth. The truth of this claim cannot be determined, but since his *Wang Ch'uan* was a winter landscape, it can be assumed that he did paint in this manner, which would best suit such a scene. *The Spirit of the Brush* contains mostly Wang Wei's commentary on the nature of what is painted (mist, clouds, leaves, water, and the like) and only a little theory: "In landscape, the idea must come first; the carrying out of the idea follows. . . . Ink painting perfects nature and completes the Creator's work." The essay ends with the Zen Buddhist statement: "Profound truths cannot be explained in words."

HERBERT D. HALE.

WANG YANG-MING, wäng' yäng'mĭng' (also called WANG SHOU-JÊN), Chinese philosopher: b. 1472; d. 1529. He served in many governmental posts from magistrate to governor. In 1506, when he protested the imprisonment of a good official, he was beaten with 40 strokes and banished for about 3 years to the frontier. Here he developed his famous doctrine that principles are inherent in the mind and that therefore to investigate things is to investigate the mind. He also pronounced the doctrine that knowledge is the beginning of action and action is the completion of knowledge–that they are one. No one had taught such a doctrine in China before. This new and dynamic philosophy was a direct challenge to Chu Hsi (1130–1200), who taught the objective investigation of things on the ground that principles are in things. Since Chu's philosophy was the established and dominant one, Wang's severe attack on it as a static and decadent doctrine—stereotyped, formalistic, narrow, and lacking originality or vigor—aroused strong antagonism.

In 1517–1519, by imperial order, Wang suppressed several rebellions. He was not rewarded but was ignored by the court, since his frank criticism of the corrupt government and his opposition to Chu Hsi had created many enemies. In 1521 he arrived at the doctrine of the extension of innate knowledge–that the knowledge of the good is inborn in man and one can naturally extend it into action if one's mind is pure and follows its own natural principle. For six years thereafter he lived in retirement, lecturing on sincerity, purposefulness, and alertness, and attracting followers from all parts of China. He suppressed another rebellion in 1527–1528 but died a year later on his way home.

Wang's vigorous and vital philosophy exercised tremendous influence in China for 150 years. It also became an outstanding school in Japan, producing a number of brilliant leaders of modern Japanese reform movements. Its influence was subsequently felt in the early 20th century, in the convictions of Sun Yat-sen and Chinese idealists.

WING-TSIT CHAN,
Professor of Chinese Culture and Philosophy, Dartmouth College.

WANKEL ENGINE, wang′kəl, a rotary internal-combustion engine invented by the German engineer Felix Wankel in the mid-1950's and first tested successfully in endurance trials in 1959. Since then the engine has been intensively developed for use as an automobile engine, notably by NSU and Mercedes-Benz in Germany, Toyo Kogyo in Japan, Citroën in France, and the Curtiss-Wright Corporation in the United States. Toyo Kogyo's Mazda RX-2 and RX-3 automobiles, powered by two-rotor Wankel engines, were successfully introduced in the United States in the early 1970's.

For equivalent horsepower, the Wankel engine has about half the size and half the weight of a conventional piston-cylinder reciprocating engine. It also has less than half as many moving parts and is smoother running and quieter than a piston engine. Perhaps more important, the Wankel engine has greater potential for reducing air pollution caused by automobile emissions. Although the gasoline-burning Wankel is not inherently pollution-free, it works better with thermal-reactor or catalytic-reactor pollution control equipment than does the piston engine.

Wankel engines have many possible applications, including the powering of trucks, boats, electric generators, lawn mowers, snowmobiles, and golf carts. High horsepowers are obtained by using two or more rotors on a common main shaft.

Engine Components. A Wankel engine consists basically of a housing, a rotatable triangular rotor whose sealed apexes are always in contact with the housing, three chambers formed between the rotor faces and the inner surface of the housing, a ring gear on the inner part of the rotor, a stationary nonrotating gear fixed rigidly to the housing and concentric with the main shaft, a rotatable main shaft that transmits the rotations of the rotor, an eccentric on the main shaft placed so that the eccentric is in sliding contact with the inner bore of the rotor, an intake port that admits the fuel-air mixture, one or two sparkplugs for igniting the mixture, and an exhaust port for spent gases.

The inner surface of the housing, comparable to a cylinder wall in a piston engine, has a shape that resembles a fat-waisted figure 8. This shape is called a two-lobe epitrochoid. The rotor is the analog of the pistons in a piston engine. The three chambers opposite the rotor faces are the analog of cylinders in a piston engine, but each chamber changes continuously in volume, shape, and position as the rotor turns. The volume changes provide the pumping action for a fuel-air intake, compression, combustion, and exhaust cycle. Also, the rotor faces open and close the inlet and exhaust ports at appropriate times in a cycle, eliminating the need for valves.

The rotor ring gear meshes with the stationary gear to maintain the rotor in proper orientation with the inner surface of the housing. In the case of a two-lobe inner housing configuration and a three-faced rotor, the number of rotor-ring gear teeth and the number of stationary gear teeth must be in the ratio of three to two. These gears do not transmit the engine's torque.

Operation. Like a piston engine, the Wankel engine requires a battery, starter motor, and distributor to put the engine in operation, and a cooling system and lubrication system to keep the engine running properly. After the engine is started, the rotor is constantly turned by the gas pressure on the face of the rotor opposite the chamber then in the combustion (or power) stage. This is the third stage of a four-stage cycle—namely, intake, compression, power, and exhaust. In one revolution of the rotor, each of the three chambers undergoes a complete four-stage cycle. A complete cycle for one chamber is shown in the accompanying diagram. The other two chambers undergo the same cycle in their turn. Thus there are three power impulses in one revolution of the rotor.

Main Shaft Drive. All motion in the Wankel engine is rotary, and therefore there is no need to convert reciprocating (up-down) motion to rotary motion as in a conventional piston engine. In the Wankel, part of the center bore of the rotor is machined smooth and mounted on the eccentric on the main shaft. When the rotor turns, its center bore pushes directly on the eccentric at a point away from the center line of the main shaft and thereby exerts leverage on the main shaft, causing it to turn. At the same time, there is a hula hoop-like interaction of the rotor ring gear and the stationary gear. As a result, when the rotor makes a one-third turn about its center, the main shaft makes one full turn. This one full turn of the rotor results in three turns of the main shaft, with one power impulse per turn of the shaft.

Further Reading: Ansdale, Richard R., *The Wankel RC Engine* (A. S. Barnes 1969); Faith, Nicholas, *Wankel: The Curious Story Behind the Revolutionary Rotary Engine* (Stein & Day 1975); Norbye, Jan P., *The Wankel Engine* (Chilton Bks. 1971).

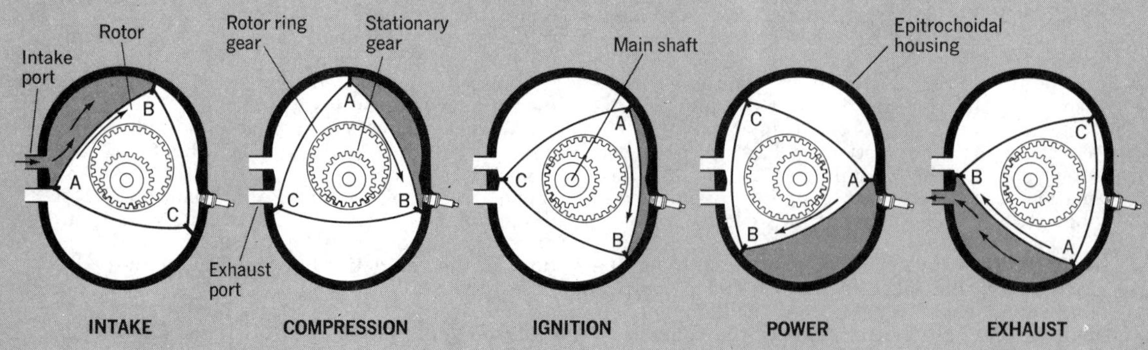

WANKIE, wong'kē, is a city in western Zimbabwe. It is connected by rail with Bulawayo to the southeast and Livingstone, Zambia, to the northwest. Wankie is economically important for its coal, of which there are proved reserves of 500 million tons. Other industries include the manufacture of coal by-products, bricks, and coke. In the area surrounding Wankie are dairy, citrus, and vegetable farms and cattle ranches. Wankie National Park, one of the finest game reserves in Africa, lies to the south.

Wankie is named for a former Bantu chief. The enormous coal deposits were located in 1895. Population: 33,000.

WANNE-EICKEL, vän'ē-ī'kəl, is a city in the Ruhr in the state of North Rhine-Westphalia, West Germany. It was formed in 1926 by the merger of the cities of Wanne and Eickel. Wanne-Eickel is primarily a coal-mining center. It is also a port city on the Rhine-Herne canal and an important rail junction. The city manufactures chemicals, electrical goods, refrigeration apparatus, and machinery. There are also breweries. Population: (1975 est.) 92,500.

WANTAGH, won'tô, is an unincorporated community on the south shore of western Long Island, N.Y., in Nassau county, about 25 miles (40 km) east of New York City. Wantagh is chiefly a residential community in the township of Hempstead. On the shore of East Bay is a large park, which is connected to a series of bridges and causeways to Jones Beach State Park. Population: 19,817.

WAPITI. See Elk.

WAPPINGER INDIANS, wop'in-jər, an important confederacy of Algonkian Indians who formerly occupied the territory along the east bank of the Hudson River from Manhattan to Poughkeepsie and eastward to the lower Connecticut River valley. The Wappinger ("Easterners") were closely related to the Mahican and are regarded as having been part of the tribe. The confederacy included many minor groups, the most important of which were the Wappinger proper, who were dominant, and the Wecquaesgeek, Siwanoy, Tunxis, Kitchawank, Nochpeem, Quinnipiac, Mattabesec, and Tankiteke.

In the face of expanding white settlement of Connecticut, the eastern tribes of the confederacy gradually sold their lands and dwindled away, the survivors joining other remnant groups at Scaticook near present Kent, Conn., and Stockbridge, Mass. A few went to Canada. The Hudson River tribes became involved in war with the Dutch (1640–1645), in which some 1,600 Indians were killed, most of them Wappinger. The survivors retained their identity and some of their lands in Westchester county until 1756, when these, too, abandoned their homelands and joined in with the Nanticoke, then living near present Binghamton, N.Y., and the Delaware. Some joined the Moravian and Stockbridge Indians, while a few still lived in Dutchess county, N.Y., until about 1775.

The confederacy, which numbered about 5,000 at its height, was the major provider of *sewan*, or wampum, to the rest of the Eastern Woodlands tribes.

Frederick J. Dockstader
Director, Museum of the American Indian

WAQIDI, al-, al-wä'ki-dē (747–823), Arab historian. Abu Abdullah Muhammad Ibn Umar al-Waqidi was born in Medina, Arabia. He flourished in Baghdad under the patronage of the powerful vizier Jaafar al-Barmaki. (See Barmecid.) Young al-Waqidi had served the vizier and the caliph as a guide when they were on a holy pilgrimage. In Baghdad he was appointed a judge and contributed a score of books centering on the Prophet Mohammed and the Islamic conquests. Of these only one, *Kitab al-Maghazi* (The Book of Campaigns), has survived as an independent work. It was published in part by Alfred von Kremer in 1856. A synopsis of this was translated into German by Julius Wellhausen in 1882.

Al-Waqidi used the annalistic method in presenting historical events, in which he was followed by leading Arab historians, many of whom included in their material extensive quotations from his work.

Philip K. Hitti

WAR is a violent conflict between states. Though the word is used to describe other types of conflict—civil war, class war, or even the war between the sexes—war is an aspect of politics. The state outlaws many formerly acceptable types of group violence, but uses those types, such as war or even controlled rioting in some cases, that its leaders find useful.

War and the Individual. The social psychologist William McDougall (1871–1938) traced war to an "instinct of pugnacity," an instinct not triggered by specific stimuli but by the blocking of other instincts. William James (1842–1910) hoped that peaceful competition would gradually replace conflict and that states would find a "moral equivalent" for war by drafting young men for socially useful projects. Violent emotions may be sublimated by work, sports, or by reading or watching movies or television programs dealing with war and violence. The work of Ivan Pavlov (1849–1936) on conditioned reflexes raised the problem, on the other hand, of deliberate state education for violence. Societies have always regarded some forms of violence as good and others as bad, and have trained some men as soldiers or police. These pioneer psychologists and psychiatrists were merely applying scientific analysis to well-known social phenomena.

The modern soldier may be more likely to develop combat neuroses or psychoses than the soldier of the past, but he also may be less likely to desert or mutiny. Modern combat may produce more neuroses or psychoses because modern states can keep men in combat for longer periods, because modern weapons are more destructive, and because the open formations of modern armies make it more necessary for the individual to force himself to activities that all soldiers know are potentially self-destructive. Because psychologists and psychiatrists are more successful in treating individuals than groups, they can answer the practical military question of which men will fight effectively under certain conditions more confidently than they can resolve social questions about the causes of war, the processes by which states choose their leaders and by which these leaders make decisions, and the question of whether these decisions reflect the desires and delusions of the led or whether the leaders infect the led with their own delusions. For the present, a student of war must use also the voluminous writings of soldiers, statesmen, philosophers, novelists, and other observers of group behavior.

The Literature of War. Groups of men used their hunting weapons against other men long before the dawn of history. Much of man's oral and written record—perhaps as much of it as is devoted to any other human problem—deals with war. The soldier developed a professional literature long before other men began to write of alleviating war's hardships or of doing away with war entirely.

Though the historian John Richard Green (1837–1883) saw war as a story of senseless butchery, its stakes—the individual's survival or his sacrifice for society—are so high that it has provided many examples of individual and collective heroism or individual and collective cowardice and self-seeking and major themes for imaginative literature. Many of the epics whose collective heroes and narratives synthesize the experience of whole civilizations deal with war. For centuries man regarded war as an inevitable part of his fate, like his struggles with the weather, disease, or the mysterious ocean. By the early 19th century, however, pioneer social scientists claimed to have discovered some of the laws of human society. One of the greatest of modern novelists, Leo Tolstoy (1828–1910), wrote *War and Peace* (*Voina i mir*, 1865–1869)—around the epic destruction of Napoleon's army in Russia in 1812—to exemplify the individual's fate in the elemental "swarm, in which a man must inevitably follow the laws laid down for him." Had the greatest of the great captains changed history? Or was the little man with the "yellow, puffy, heavy face, dim eyes, a red nose, and a husky voice" only "submissively performing the cruel, gloomy, irksome, and inhuman role assigned" to him by destiny? (See also WAR AND PEACE.)

Scientists cannot answer Tolstoy's question. But they can observe the collective consequences of collective action. As one of the most highly organized types of social activity, war has stimulated social, economic, and political changes at increasing tempos as all social organizations have become more complex. The literacy level achieved by state education has enabled states to turn farmers into sailors or housewives into welders with surprising speed. Whether modern states and armies are better able to resist the sudden shocks of war, however, is an unanswered question.

Social scientists can apply two criteria to the vast criteria of war: (1) a work dealing with war in general must deal with society; and (2) since war is a form of social activity, there can be no simple answers to its questions. Many military or pacifist works merely reflect man's quest for certainty, for simple rules to govern his personal or social activities, or for slogans which seem politically popular.

War and the Modern State. Since wars are waged by states, and since preparation for war is the most expensive activity of those sovereign entities which began to emerge in Europe at the end of the 15th century, most military problems should be approached from the political standpoint. This includes the factors once grouped under the term "political economy": the aims of the opposing states in any particular conflict, and the resources—social, economic, and diplomatic, since the division of the world into such units is a major trend in modern history—which each has at its disposal. One other trend is equally important: while some states (the Great Powers) have grown more powerful than others, all states have increased their power over the human and economic resources of their respective societies.

The greatest of military philosophers, Karl von Clausewitz (1780–1831), based his work *On War* (*Vom Kriege*, 1833) on the idea that war is "nothing but a continuation of political intercourse with an admixture of other means." The essence of war is violence. "War is thus an act of force to compel our adversary to do our will." Force, "that is to say physical force, [is the] *means;* to impose our will upon the enemy is the *object.*" To attain this object the enemy must be disarmed, and this "disarming is by definition the proper aim of military action."

Disarming the enemy may be more difficult now than it was in Clausewitz' day. Some of the weapons developed since the Industrial Revolution have changed the character of war. The principles of war do not change, but this technological factor influences specific wars. The development of aircraft, aircraft carriers, and landing craft between the two World Wars, for example, made it possible for the United States and Japan to wage war across the Pacific much more effectively in the 1940's than would have been possible in the 1920's.

Weapons competition is not new, but only recently has technological change been rapid and continuous enough to make the scientist as important in war as the soldier or the statesman. Even the introduction of gunpowder was so gradual that the development of fire weapons was discontinuous. The 19th century invented "the method of invention." For the first time scientists and engineers turned their attention to a "disciplined attack on one difficulty after another." World War I (1914–1918) was the first general conflict in which the belligerents constantly used all the resources of modern industry and the sciences. Thirty-one years after Germany invaded Belgium (Aug. 3, 1914), a nuclear weapon destroyed the Japanese city of Hiroshima (Aug. 6, 1945) and opened the possibility of the military destruction of civilization. This revolution in military technology occurred in a time span only one year longer than that between Columbus' discovery of the New World and the first voyage around the world (1492–1522).

Military systems reflect political and technological developments and create organizational patterns of their own which form the third factor in war. The ways in which men are recruited, trained, commanded, supplied, and fight are discussed elsewhere, but soldiers' ideas about war are very important. The Prussian general staff's ideas were a decisive factor in Germany's becoming the greatest military power in Europe in the third quarter of the 19th century, but none of the general staffs foresaw the deadlock of World War I. Had they done so, they might have told their governments that the game was not worth the candle. If an enemy cannot be disarmed by nuclear warfare without disarming oneself and perhaps all the neutrals as well, psychological warfare or subversion might be better ways to compel him "to do our will."

Clausewitz thought, on the whole correctly, that wars would become more total with "the participation of the people in this great affair of

UPI

World War I involved the total industrial, scientific, and moral resources of the world's greatest powers.

state." Unlike some of his followers, however, he always recognized the possibility of limited war. A state's efforts should be proportioned to the enemy's "powers of resistance," the product of "two inseparable factors: the extent of the means at his disposal and the strength of his will."

States have increased their power over individuals and their ability to persuade other individuals that resistance is futile. Though the men who handle absolute weapons are psychologically steeled and physically protected, Clausewitz knew that the commander is less fearful for himself than for the men and society in his charge. The "searching, cool, comprehensive" mind of a man who is both general and statesman might be overwhelmed by the responsibility for all civilization. But Tolstoy was aware of an "unwavering, irrefutable consciousness of freedom," though he later regarded violence to others as the greatest of possible evils. The key question is political. Will the use of specific forces in specific ways in specific cases advance the ends of the state? Since the state is neither a suicide pact nor one for mutual enslavement, complete nonresistance or unrestricted violence are extremes which allow no freedom of choice and are equally immoral.

War in Graeco-Roman Civilization. The transformation of the ancient city-states into a universal state dominated by the ruler of Rome fascinated early historians, but they did not speculate on war itself or on the importance of technology in its history. The iron weapons which had enabled the Greek cities to defeat the Persian Empire (499–479 B.C.) were used by these cities against each other in the Peloponnesian War (431–404 B.C.), analyzed by Thucydides (460/455–c. 400 B.C.), the defeated and exiled Athenian admiral who became the first great critical historian. Where the chroniclers of the Persian Wars had used the traditional explanation of divine intervention, Thucydides traced human events to human causes, perhaps because it was easier to explain defeat in these terms.

Centuries later Niccolò Machiavelli (1469–1527) founded political science with a treatise on *Il Principe* (see PRINCE, THE), written in 1513, based in part on his study of Livy's (Titus Livius, 59 B.C.–17 A.D.) Roman history. Though Machiavelli lived in an age of technological change, the future victory of gunpowder weapons was not clear in his day. The rise of the universal Graeco-Roman state could be adequately explained by political skill, different combinations of the same weapons (spear, sword, javelin, and ballista), or the genius of such great captains as Alexander the Great or Julius Caesar.

These conquerors plundered the civilizations of the East and enslaved the Western barbarians. Unable to compete with the slaveholders during these long wars, the small Italian farmers became professional soldiers. Their leaders dominated Roman politics and ruined the state with their civil wars when no outside worlds remained to plunder. But they also established universal law, a transportation network, and a unified economy, and fortified the frontiers against the remaining barbarians. The Roman military system included these walls, the roads and waterways which gave their armies mobility, an economic system which supplied them, and a traditional tactical doctrine. This system held back the barbarians while Christianity triumphed over the other universal religions within the empire. The Byzantine or Eastern Roman Empire survived into the medieval period of the civilization which arose in western Europe after the barbarians had destroyed the Western Roman Empire.

War in Western Civilization. Medieval warfare depended on local fortifications—a great charge on a less productive agriculture than that of the Romans. Roman roads and waterways had not been repaired or were blocked to movement by artificial obstacles. Armies could supply themselves for only a few weeks, and many of the Roman principles of command and logistics had been forgotten. Armored cavalry, with stirrups and iron horseshoes to increase the impetus of horse and lancer, had appeared in the later Roman Empire. Within the localized framework of medieval society, such cavalry could move faster and hit harder than any existing infantry. Castles, armor, horses, and training were the capital of the feudal nobility, who were not anxious to arm or train their peasants in the fighting skills. When religious fanaticism submerged local jeal-

THE BETTMANN ARCHIVE

The bomb dropped on Hiroshima on Aug. 6, 1945, introduced the potential for the destruction of all civilization.

ousies during the Crusades, medieval armies carried on extensive campaigns. But the West expanded against the Moors or the primitive Scots or Balts by means of chains of castles garrisoned by military monks or other professional soldiers. The church enlisted the nobility in these common enterprises, limited warfare in certain seasons, fostered knightly conduct, and protected students, traders, and pilgrims.

The first modern armies were raised by the new monarchs, who came to command greater moral and economic resources (the church and the middle classes welcoming their efforts to establish order) than the feudal barons or the trading cities. Bowmen and disciplined pikemen broke the absolute supremacy of the armored knight, and gunpowder battered down castles and gave the infantry better missiles. War retarded economic development in some areas, but stimulated mining, manufacturing, and transportation in others. Businessmen developed military management and, along with impoverished noblemen, entered the service of successful monarchs.

Gunpowder weapons had become standardized by the 18th century. The horrible religious wars of previous centuries had resulted in new rules of warfare—an example which in the 20th century has raised hopes for limits on nuclear warfare. Military technology was again comparatively static, and monarchs could not raise larger forces without increasing the power of the middle and lower classes and decreasing that of the now loyal nobility.

The French monarchy collapsed in 1789 as a result, in part, of mismanagement and unsuccessful and expensive wars. The revolutionaries broke the nobility's near-monopoly of higher commands, supplied their conscript armies with the stockpiled weapons of the Old Regime, manufactured new weapons, and adopted tactics which spent lives in battle in order to save lives—by winning decisive victories over armies which had become too rigid to survive. The monarchs eventually defeated the revolutionaries by adopting their methods, by calling on their own peoples, and by reforms which gave their people something to fight for.

The development of the railway, steamship, and telegraph made it possible to supply and command even larger armies. An era of comparative peace (1815–1848) was followed by one of revolution and war (1848–1871). The American Civil War (1861–1865) foreshadowed modern total war, but Prussia's quick victories over Austria (1866) and France (1870–1871) called attention to her general staff and system of peacetime conscription. Germany and France were then equal in industrial power and German weapons were not markedly superior.

Prussia's speedy victories and Germany's postwar industrial prosperity had major psychological results. War was glorified as a test of national fitness. By 1914 every power but Great Britain and the United States had adopted peacetime conscription, and every power had a general staff and higher military schools based more or less on the German pattern. Most soldiers thought that the next war would be decided quickly. Industrial mobilization was neglected. The new rapid-firing weapons (repeating rifles, machine guns, and artillery) could be overcome by resolute attackers. Germany planned to defeat France quickly by driving through neutral Belgium to the flank and rear of the French armies along the Franco-German border. Deployed infantry with horsed artillery and transport could not easily change fronts. Railroads piled armies onto the frontiers, but fighting armies could move no faster than those of the Romans and their great size made them much less flexible.

The unknown factor was the effect of the new weapons. His study of military literature convinced the Polish banker, Ivan S. Bloch (1836–1902) that these weapons would strengthen the defenders. His six-volume *Budushchaya Voina* (1898; last volume translated as *The Future of War in Its Technical, Economic, and Political Relations*, 1898) predicted battles lasting for days, and observed: "At the end it is very doubtful whether any decisive victory can be gained." Like the inventor of dynamite, Alfred Nobel (1833–1896), Bloch thought that such a war would entail "even upon the victorious Power, the destruction of its resources and the breakup of society." The Hague peace conferences of 1899 and 1907 expanded and codified the laws of war and provided a court for certain disputes, but failed to deal with the basic political problems arising from unrestricted national sovereignty.

The Age of Violence. The western European era of Western Civilization was ended by World War I. When the Germans were stopped at the Marne River, the war in the West became a siege involving the total industrial, scientific, and moral resources of the world's greatest industrial states. Russia's defeat by the Central Powers precipitated the Russian Revolution of 1917. All of the major belligerents encouraged nationalist revolutions in enemy countries. All of them experimented with economic controls. The victors set up a League of Nations, took greater shares of a restive colonial world, and recognized the new states of eastern Europe. But they neither placated nor dismembered a disarmed Germany and failed to overthrow the Communist regime in Russia. Wartime nationalist passions and war weariness made a stable postwar settlement nearly impossible. The human and material costs of this war of attrition led to a widespread belief that war accomplishes nothing.

DIETER LUDWIG/GAMMA LIAISON

Modern wars, especially ones involving guerrilla action, tend to directly threaten civilian populations.

Western civilization's recuperative powers proved to be almost as great as its powers of destruction. Even Communist Russia recovered industrially in a comparatively short time, though all of the western European states lost markets to the United States and Japan, who had not been as deeply involved in the war. The great depression of the 1930's was partly due to wartime overexpansion and to peacetime trade barriers aimed at promoting wartime self-sufficiency. Germany became a totalitarian dictatorship, one rooted, like those established earlier in the Soviet Union and Italy, in wartime discontents. All of these states mobilized their peoples morally and economically. Germany and Italy glorified war and conquest as solutions for their economic problems. The Communists held that war was inherent in capitalistic competition for markets and raw materials and a useful revolutionary tool in a world disrupted by conflict. The League of Nations failed to deal with the underlying causes of war and to prevent German rearmament and Japanese, Italian, and German aggression. Germany planned for sudden victory over her divided enemies with the weapons which had broken the deadlock in the last years of World War I, particularly the tank and the airplane. Air power's extreme partisans hoped to win wars by directly attacking war industries and destroying the morale of enemy civilian populations.

Germany, Italy, and Japan failed to defeat the United States, Great Britain, China, and the Soviet Union in World War II (1939–1945). The belligerents again threw all of their resources into the conflict. Postwar economic recovery again was surprisingly rapid. Communism was spread by conquest in eastern Europe, but was defeated in western Europe by nationalist resistance, United States economic aid, and the threat of war against further Russian expansion. In the war, Japan's bid for empire in China and East Asia was defeated, but China became Communist during the turmoil accompanying Japan's collapse.

Nationalist revolutions, aided by western Europe's unwillingness and inability to retain political control, spread from East Asia to Africa. Again war speeded up industrialization, increased the power of the state and, concurrently, its welfare activities. It was a forcing house for western European unity, but it did not shake the belief in the state sufficiently to prevent the new United Nations from being organized on the old principle of national sovereignty. The chief political result of this war has been mentioned. It produced weapons so powerful that those scientists, politicians, and military men who are most familiar with them have declared almost unanimously that total war no longer will solve political problems.

See also BELLIGERENCY; INTERNATIONAL LAW; WAR, LAWS OF; WAR CRIMES. For the military aspects of war, see such articles as AMPHIBIOUS WARFARE; MILITARY SCIENCE; STRATEGY, MILITARY; TACTICS. Articles on individual wars will be found under their own headings.

THEODORE ROPP
Professor of History, Duke University

Bibliography

Aron, Raymond, *On War,* tr. by Terence Kilmartin (1968; reprint, Univ. Press of Am. 1985).
Boulding, Kenneth E., ed., *Peace and the War Industry,* 2d ed. (Transaction Bks. 1973).
Bush, Vannevar, *Modern Arms and Free Men* (1949; reprint, Greenwood Press 1985).
Clausewitz, Karl von, *On War,* ed. by Anatol Rapoport (Penguin 1968).
Delbruck, Hans, *History of the Art of War Within the Framework of Political History,* tr. by Walter J. Renfroe, Jr. (1975; reprint, Greenwood Press 1985).
Earle, Edward M., ed., *Makers of Modern Strategy* (Princeton Univ. Press 1943).
Eibl-Eibesfeldt, Irenaus, *The Biology of Peace and War* (Viking 1979).
Friedman, Leon, *The Law of War,* 2 vols. (Random House 1972).
Howard, Michael, *War in European History* (Oxford 1976).
Larteguy, Jean, *The Face of War: Reflections on Men and Combat* (Bobbs 1979).
Montross, Lynn, *War Through the Ages* (Westview Press 1985).
Stoessinger, John G., *Why Nations Go to War* (St. Martin's Press 1985).
Taylor, A. J., *How Wars Begin* (Atheneum Pub. 1979).
Wright, Quincy, *Study of War,* 2d ed. (Univ. of Chicago Press 1965).

WAR, AMERICAN CIVIL. See CIVIL WAR; also articles on individual campaigns and engagements.

WAR, Articles of. See ARTICLES OF WAR.

WAR, Department of, a former executive department of the United States government with supervision over the military establishment. Until the organization of the federal government in 1789, military affairs were managed by a War Office (created in 1781). The act of Aug. 7, 1789, which in effect continued the activities of the War Office unchanged, established a Department of War headed by a civilian secretary of cabinet ranking. Originally, the department's jurisdiction included the navy, but in 1798 that function was taken over by the new Department of the Navy. Numerous changes in organization and responsibilities occurred during the War Department's 158 years of existence, notably during the periods of World Wars I and II.

The move toward unification of the armed services was climaxed by the National Security Act of 1947 (as amended in 1949), which combined the nation's defense organizations into the National Military Establishment, later redesignated the Department of Defense. The War Department thus became the Department of the Army (within the Defense Department), headed by a civilian secretary who is subordinate to the secretary of defense and who does not hold cabinet rank. The reorganization also transferred certain of the War Department's functions and property, including the Army Air Forces, to the new Department of the Air Force. See also DEFENSE, DEPARTMENT OF.

WAR, Laws of. Operations of war by civilized countries are governed by rules known as the laws of war. Some of these, like the British or American common law, are unwritten, although generally recognized. Others are set forth in treaties and conventions to which many nations are parties. This article deals with the principal subjects of both written and unwritten laws of war. Many of the important written laws are contained in the Geneva conventions of 1929 relating to the treatment of prisoners of war, and to the care of the wounded and sick, and the Hague conventions of 1899 and 1907. The latter deal specifically with such questions as the opening of hostilities, the laws and customs of war on land, the duties and rights of neutrals, submarine mines, bombardment by naval forces, and projectiles from balloons. Earlier conventions, while still effective, are largely superseded by these conventions. The written rules are in general a formal application of principles of the unwritten laws of war.

The bases of the laws of war are military necessity, humanity, and chivalry. It has been said that the unwritten rules are binding on all civilized nations, and it is recognized that signatories to the conventions are bound by their terms, possibly subject to certain exceptions, even when the enemy is not a signatory.

In early days, the customs of armies depended on might, rather than right. There were no laws of war as we know them today. Prisoners of war were slain or made slaves. Captured towns were sacked and ravished. The conqueror's will was supreme. However, over the centuries the influences of civilization, and especially Christianity, brought ameliorating changes. The proper and decent treatment of prisoners of war, the sick and wounded, and the civil population became increasingly recognized, sometimes by special agreement or conventions between belligerents or local commanders, sometimes because of a more civilized influence on the victor.

While certain rules have been the subject of different interpretations by signatory nations, and although some of them have been violated by some belligerents recently, the laws of war generally have been followed, more especially on land. They are well known to trained officers and have been set forth in a number of military and naval manuals of the defense forces of civilized countries.

Armed Forces.—The laws of war, and their rights and duties, apply to regular armies, navies, and air forces. They also apply to militia and volunteer corps which are properly commanded, have distinctive emblems, and carry arms openly. Even a *levée en masse* (mass uprising) in unoccupied territory, if carrying arms openly but without time to organize, may resist invasion, and are recognized as having the rights of belligerents if they respect the laws and customs of war. However, those who rise against an occupying army are not entitled to the protection of the laws of war.

Hostilities.—The Hague conventions call for previous and explicit warning, either in the form of a reasoned declaration of war or of an ultimatum before the commencement of hostilities. This provision was complied with by Great Britain in the famous ultimatum to Germany of Aug. 4, 1914, and again at the start of her hostilities with Germany in September 1939. The provision was disregarded by Japan when her carrier planes attacked Pearl Harbor in December 1941. In view of the invention of atomic bombs and guided missiles, there may well be a need for more specific provisions, but conventions unfortunately do not always prevent nations from violations.

While military necessity is held to justify the destruction of life or limb of armed enemies and enemy property, it never justifies cruelty. Neither torture, wounding (except in combat), nor the imposition of unnecessary suffering are permitted.

For this reason the Hague convention prohibits the use of poison or poisoned weapons, the killing or wounding of an enemy who has laid down his arms and surrendered, the refusal

According to an early visitor, Indians in Florida declared war by planting arrows to which hair had been attached.

The Bettmann Archive

of quarter, or the use of arms or material likely to cause unnecessary injury. The Geneva Protocol of 1925 prohibiting the use of gas or bacteriological methods of warfare is also in force and effective among a substantial number of signatories. Even Adolf Hitler observed this prohibition and did not use poison gas or bacterial weapons in combat, so far as is known.

Among the other subjects dealt with in the conventions are the permissibility of stratagems and ruses of war, the forbidding of the misuse of flags, insignia, and military uniforms of the enemy, the requirement to spare religious works, works of art, and hospitals, so far as possible, and the prohibition against the attack or bombardment of undefended towns or buildings. Pillage is forbidden, even when a town is taken by assault. There is, however, no general restraint against bombing from the air of defense forces or of defended places. It is doubtful whether the convention prohibits the bombing from the air of lines of communication such as railroads or roads used or useful in supplying enemy forces. The bombing of railroads in France by the Allies before the Normandy landings in World War II was considered to be an essential means of preventing reinforcements of the German troops defending the coastline, and hence a permissible act of war.

A number of rules govern the laying of contact mines, among which are prohibitions against laying of automatic contact mines off an enemy coast or port in order to intercept commercial shipping, and against any use of such mines unanchored unless they become harmless within an hour after the loss of control. Neutral powers must observe similar rules, and belligerents are to remove all mines laid by them at the end of the war. Also forbidden is the use of torpedoes which do not become harmless after missing their target. The prohibition against laying of contact mines was violated by Germany in World War II, and apparently all belligerent navies in that war used torpedoes that did not become harmless after missing their targets.

The status of enemy merchant ships at the outbreak of war, and the rules as to their conversion into warships, are dealt with in the 1907 Hague conventions. Provision is made for the free departure of merchant ships, and the prohibition of confiscation of them or of those found on the high seas in ignorance of the outbreak of war. Either merchant ships or warships may be detained or requisitioned on paying compensation, and the latter may be destroyed on payment of compensation and provision made for the safety of those on board. These rules are not, however, agreed to by all the principal nations.

Neutrality.—Rules regarding neutrality and the duties and rights of neutrals are dealt with in the Hague conventions. Neutrality on the part of a nonbelligerent consists of abstaining from participation in the war and in impartially governing various acts on its part, on the part of its people, or on the part of belligerents. The territory of neutrals is declared to be inviolable. Thus, belligerents are not to move forces or matériel across neutral territory, nor form corps of combatants, nor open recruiting agencies in a neutral country. It is not a hostile act for a neutral to resist violations of its neutrality. While a neutral state may not furnish supplies or munitions of war or make loans to a belligerent, commercial transactions between belligerents and citizens or residents of neutral countries are not prohibited, and the latter can sell supplies or munitions to the former, if they can be exported without involving the neutral nation. Belligerents, however, cannot build wireless stations on neutral territory to communicate with belligerent forces on land or sea, nor use an installation of the kind established by them before the war on neutral territory for purely military purposes, if it is not open for the service of public messages. A question remains as to whether there is a violation of neutrality involved in flights over neutral territory by planes engaged in a raid or other act of war against the area of a hostile belligerent where no harm is done to the neutral.

A neutral state is not required to prevent belligerent forces from entering its territory, but it is bound to intern them, as far as possible at a distance from the theater of war, and may allow officers their liberty, upon their parole not to leave neutral territory without permission. The neutral state is to supply the interned with food, clothing, and relief at the ultimate expense of the belligerents concerned. There are special provisions for the care of the sick and wounded, with respect to medical personnel, and regarding railway material. See also NEUTRALITY.

Prisoners of War.—Perhaps the greatest humanitarian advance in the laws of war over the centuries has to do with the treatment to be accorded to prisoners of war. This reached a culmination in the conventions of the 19th and 20th centuries, and especially in the Geneva convention of 1929. The rules there set forth govern most of the civilized nations of the world. They are extremely detailed and specific, giving full consideration to the prisoner, and broadly speaking in this century they have been followed by belligerents, although there have been notable and tragic exceptions.

The underlying principles are those of humanity and reciprocity. The convention states that prisoners of war, a term including both combatants and noncombatants, as well as followers such as correspondents and contractors (provided they have military credentials), are to be treated with humanity and protected against violence and insult. Women are to be treated with all the regard due their sex. That the convention is a noble effort to assure humane treatment is shown by the meticulous and numerous provisions laid down to this end. They include: prohibitions against bad treatment, the retention of personal effects (except arms, military papers, and equipment), accounts of their moneys, evacuation out of the combat zone, prohibition against needless exposure to danger while awaiting evacuation, notification to the enemy of the capture, and information as to the official addresses to which letters from families to prisoners of war may be sent. The rules further govern the details of internment, care of health, safeguards as to hygiene, the provision of clothing, the heating and lighting of quarters, and precautions against fire. The food ration is to be equal in quantity and quality to that of troops at base camps, and prisoners are to receive facilities for preparing additional food. Sufficient water must be furnished and the use of tobacco permitted.

Imperial War Museum, London

The British bring in captured Germans in 1916. The rights of prisoners are strictly defined under the laws of war.

Infirmaries, medical care and inspection, recreation and religious freedom, officers' camps, and pay are all provided for in detail.

Prisoners of war, except officers and *assimilés,* that is, those of like rank, may be required to work, according to their rank and aptitude, if not physically unfit. Fair working hours and conditions must govern, and the work must have no direct relation with war operations. Unhealthful or dangerous work is prohibited. Various other provisions are made for correspondence of and to prisoners, who are to be allowed also to receive parcels by mail containing food, clothing, and books, subject to censorship.

Other clauses include rules relating to wills, complaints, requests, agents, intermediaries, application of local and military laws, punishment, attempted escapes (which must not be unduly punished), repatriation under certain conditions, prohibition against transfer to penitentiaries, summary punishment, judicial prosecution, and the right to counsel and of appeal. Seriously sick and wounded prisoners are to be returned to their own country when brought to a condition permitting transport. The dead must be buried, their graves marked, and their relatives notified. In case of an armistice convention, repatriation of prisoners is to be agreed on by the belligerents as soon as possible, and in any case with the least delay after the conclusion of peace.

Remaining rules of the convention include provisions as to facilities for relief societies, a neutral central agency, the posting of the convention in prisoner of war camps, and the right of the representatives of the protecting powers to visit prisoners.

The International Red Cross has helped to enforce the rules for the amelioration of the conditions of prisoners of war. See also PRISONERS OF WAR.

Sick, Wounded, and Dead.—The rules of war also prescribe that the wounded and sick of the armed forces must be treated with humanity and cared for by belligerents, without distinction of nationality. After battle, the belligerent in possession of the field is responsible for the search for the wounded and dead and for their protection from robbery and abuse. Cessation of fire or local armistice to permit removal of wounded is encouraged. Special provisions of the Geneva (Red Cross) convention of 1929 apply. The dead are to be identified, their deaths verified, and reports furnished. They are to be honorably buried, with each belligerent providing a graves service.

While mobile sanitary formations and their establishments are to be respected and protected by the belligerents, the protection may be lost if they are used against the enemy. They may, however, use arms in self-defense or in defense of their wounded and sick.

Other provisions of the Geneva convention relate to the protection of sanitary personnel, certain relief societies, such as the American Red Cross, sanitary transportation, and the use of the Red Cross or other distinctive emblem. Special rules govern aircraft and vessels used as a means of sanitary transportation. It should be noted that aircraft engaged in this service, even when properly painted and marked, are to avoid flights over the firing line and generally over areas in control of the enemy.

Belligerents are required, so far as military conditions permit, to render the distinctive emblems, such as that of the Red Cross, visible to the land, air, and sea forces of the enemy, in order to prevent aggressive action. Unfortunately, they do not always prevent such action. A plane at a distance, a vessel at night in bad weather, an ambulance against a dark background, are none of them easy to identify as engaged in sanitary operations, even when properly marked.

Espionage.—Spying and treason have always been treated summarily in time of war. The conventions purport to define spies and specify the necessity of clandestine action. Thus soldiers who, not wearing a disguise, make their way into the enemy lines to obtain information, are not spies. In the United States both espionage and treason are defined by statute as set forth in the Articles of War.

Intercourse.—By the customs and laws of war, nonintercourse between belligerents is the rule. There are certain well-recognized exceptions relating to safe-conducts for ambassadors and diplomatic agents of neutrals, *parlementaires* (commanders' agents), flags of truce, passports, and cartels. The Hague conventions lay down the rule that an authorized *parlementaire* may enter into communication with the enemy, advancing with a white flag. He, as well as the bugler, flag bearer, and interpreter who accompany him, have a right to inviolability. The commander to whom he is sent is not bound to receive him, and may take steps, including detention, to prevent his taking advantage of his mission.

Civil Population.—The rights and duties of civilians in occupied territory and of the occupying forces are dealt with in the laws of war. Generally, so long as the civil population refrains from active aid to their own forces, they are to be allowed to pursue their peaceful occupations, without interference from the occupying forces, so far as military necessities permit. They cannot be compelled, lawfully, to assist the latter, however, in actions, including espionage, against their own forces. They must not be allowed to starve, and it is customary for the military government set up by the occupying power to maintain law and order, to enforce sanitary regulations, to prevent epidemics, to assure the water supply, to restore communications, to provide for a wholesome economy, and to prevent interference by the civil population with military operations and the supply of food, ammunition, and other needs of the military forces of the occupying power.

Military government is the organization through which a belligerent exercises authority over occupied enemy territory. The Hague convention annex (1907) establishes its duty to restore law and order and ensure public order and safety. The same convention forbids the abolition by declaration of the rights and rights of action of enemy nationals; however, the occupying commander may regulate commerce, establish censorship, and seize and utilize all means of transportation. The occupant may levy taxes, and is accordingly bound to pay the expenses of administration of the occupied territory to the same extent as the legitimate government.

It is forbidden to compel the inhabitants of occupied territory to swear allegiance to the hostile power. Family honor and rights, the lives of persons, and religious convictions and practices must be respected. It is the duty of the inhabitants in return to behave peacefully, to refrain from hostilities, and to obey the military government officials of the occupying power. For the purposes of administration, the services of the inhabitants may be requisitioned in order that public works, trades, professions, public utilities, sanitation, railroads, and communications may be resumed.

A belligerent may destroy or seize all property, public or private, hostile or neutral, unless specifically protected, if and only if the destruction or seizure is imperatively demanded by the necessities of war. The Hague annex regards an occupying power as administrator of public real estate and buildings belonging to the enemy state, and it is required that these be safeguarded. Buildings of direct military use, doubtless, may be destroyed or damaged if necessary in military operations. Property dedicated to religion, charity, or education is to be treated as private property. Movable property belonging to the occupied state, especially if useful for military purposes, may be seized by the forces of the occupying power.

Private property is to be respected according to the Hague annex, yet articles useful in war may be seized, even if privately owned, although the owner has a right to compensation upon the declaration of peace.

Pillage and private gain by members of the armed forces are prohibited. The Hague annex also forbids the seizure or destruction of submarine cables connecting occupied territory with neutral territory, unless it is unavoidable, in which case they must be restored and compensation fixed when peace is made. While jamming may interfere with wireless communication, the wide use of radio probably has reduced the importance of this prohibition.

Requisitions have long been recognized by civilized nations, provided that they were needed by the army of occupation or invasion, were demanded by order of the commander, and payment made or receipts given and the articles paid for in due course. The Hague annex is probably only declaratory of the unwritten laws of war in its similar provisions.

The matter of collective punishments, such as general penalties for the acts of individuals for which the population as a whole is not responsible, has given rise to debatable incidents. Such collective punishments are condemned by the Hague annex, and perhaps by the unwritten laws of war. However, reprisals for violations of the laws of war or of the regulations of the occupying power by members of the enemy's civil population are not forbidden. In practice it has at times been difficult to distinguish between collective penalties and retaliations, particularly in cases of general disorder or of widespread resistance, whether passive or otherwise. See also MILITARY LAW.

Robert Capa from Magnum

Medical personnel, at work in war-torn Paris in 1944, are protected only by the rules of the 1929 Geneva Convention.

Blockades and Contraband.—Blockades are recognized if successfully maintained, but not otherwise. This does not mean that the blockading forces must assure the prevention or capture of every vessel attempting to run the blockade. It does mean that the attempt must be made extremely hazardous. Ships of neutral nations caught violating the blockade may be captured and made subject to condemnation by a prize court.

How far the old rules are affected by air power and the modern use of the air service in war is difficult to say. Obviously a certain number of planes can always penetrate an air blockade and drop supplies on belligerent territory. There would seem to be a real need for new and up-to-date rules on this subject.

Among the questions that have plagued governments in time of war are those relating to contraband and to the shipment from one neutral to another of articles, products, or materials where a belligerent had reason to believe that the ultimate destination was an enemy country. It is most unlikely that any country having control of the seas, roads and railroads, or of the air would permit the free passage of supplies needed for carrying on the war. Many articles, especially arms and munitions of war, are clearly contraband, but there is lack of agreement as to many others, and the tendency is toward recognition of a greatly increased number and variety of goods as constituting contraband in time of war. Since in modern warfare there are few things that are not useful in one way or another in the war effort of the enemy, it is obvious that nothing useful will be allowed to reach the enemy if it can be prevented. The major deterrent is the fear of bringing neutrals into the war on the side of the enemy. This may be a controlling factor if the neutral is strong militarily or economically. See also BLOCKADE; CONTRABAND.

Maritime War.—Privateering was abolished by the Declaration of Paris (q.v.) in 1856. The United States, however, did not adhere.

The Hague conventions contain provisions, beyond those already mentioned, relating to naval bombardments, adaptation of the Geneva convention, restrictions as to the right of capture, and the rights and duties of neutrals.

The bombardment by naval forces of undefended ports, towns, or buildings, not including military works and factories, is prohibited. Bombardment may be commenced, however, if local enemy authorities refuse requisitions for provisions or supplies necessary for the immediate use of the naval force.

The conventions also contain special provisions for the protection of hospital ships, the shipwrecked, and those who are sick and wounded.

Belligerent warships may revictual in neutral ports only to bring their supplies up to peacetime standards, and may ship only sufficient fuel to reach the nearest port of their own country, with their time to do so limited.

Many provisions of the Hague conventions are stated to apply only to the contracting powers and only if all belligerents are parties to the convention. Insofar as the conventions are declaratory of the unwritten laws of war, however, they would appear to be binding on all civilized states.

Owing to differences of interpretation by nations and prize courts, the reservations made by several of the great powers and the effect of submarine and air weapons, the rules of maritime warfare are dependent today, to a great extent, more on conscience than on written laws.

Enforcement.—The remedies of the injured belligerent for violations of the laws of war by the enemy include punishment of individual offenders and reprisals. For many military offenses, individual members of the enemy forces are protected if acting by order of their government or commanders. The commanders are subject to punishment if captured. Nonbelligerents who commit hostile acts are considered war criminals, if captured. Those who rise in arms in occupied territory are subject to the death penalty. There are rules regarding other crimes, such as acts of marauders and armed prowlers, and acts specifically forbidden by the occupying power or by a belligerent. Punishment of war crimes should be only after trial and conviction by a military or other competent court. All war crimes may be punished by death, or a lesser penalty.

Reprisals are recognized by the laws of war, where necessary in an endeavor to force the enemy to desist or refrain from violations of these laws. They are peculiarly distasteful, however, to the modern conscience, and should be resorted to only in extreme cases, and after careful inquiry by the responsible commanders. There may be rare cases where the safety of the troops requires immediate action. Reprisals may take the form of punishment of hostages, of enemy forces, or even of the civil population. Collective punishment may be necessary, despite the general rule against this form of penalty. The Geneva convention of 1929 expressly forbids reprisals against prisoners of war. Hostages are said to be entitled to treatment as prisoners of war when duly accepted as hostages. In cases where they have been taken to assure that the enemy will not commit unlawful acts, and the enemy does commit such acts, they may be punished.

End of Hostilities.—The cessation or termination of hostilities is usually accomplished by a truce, a surrender or capitulation, or an armistice. A truce is usually a temporary and often local cessation of hostilities to permit removal of the dead or wounded from the battlefield, or for other temporary purposes such as the arranging of a surrender. It is brought about by agreement between the opposing commanders of the forces concerned. A longer cessation of hostilities, usually for a definite period, and suspending military operations between belligerents, may be provided by agreement in a formal written armistice. The armistice of Nov. 11, 1918, between the Allies and Germany—and its several extensions—is a good example. The Hague annex provides that if the duration is not fixed, military operations may be resumed at any time, if the enemy is warned within the time agreed upon according to the armistice terms. The annex further provides that an armistice may be general or local, that notice thereof must be given in good time to the troops and to competent authorities, and that hostilities are suspended at once after such notice or at the time fixed by the agreement. It is also provided that any serious violation of the armistice by a party gives the other party the right to denounce it, and, if the matter is urgent, of renewing hostilities without delay. These provisions are declaratory of the unwritten laws of war. The difficulty with a general armistice agreement, from the viewpoint of the conqueror, is that the terms may be differently interpreted by the belligerents and lead to unsatisfactory results. This occurred after World War I. Hostilities in World War II did not result in a true armistice, but in enforced unconditional surrender of the principal defeated nations.

This did not mean, however, that the victors would or could impose inhuman provisions or conduct themselves like barbarians toward the defeated enemy.

Future Changes.—As special committees and commissions of the United Nations have been studying international law, disarmament, and definition of aggression, it is possible that the results of these studies, when and if adopted by the United Nations, will change or affect existing rules or laws of war.

See also BELLIGERENCY; HAGUE COURT; INTERNATIONAL LAW; WAR CRIMES.

CORNELIUS W. WICKERSHAM,
Lieutenant General, New York Guard (Retired); Former Regent of the University of the State of New York.

Bibliography

Bailey, Sydney D., *How Wars End: The United Nations and the Termination of Armed Conflict 1946–1964*, 2 vols. (Oxford 1982).
Green, L. C., *Essays on the Modern Law of War* (Transnational Pub. 1985).
Roberts, Adam, and Guelff, Richard, eds., *Documents on the Laws of War* (Oxford 1982).
Trooboff, Peter D., ed., *Law and Responsibility in Warfare: The Vietnam Experience* (Univ. of N.C. Press 1975).
Wells, Donald A., *War Crimes and Laws of War* (Univ. Press of Am. 1984).

WAR, Prisoners of. See PRISONERS OF WAR.

WAR, Prize of. See CONTRABAND; PRIZE; PRIZE COURTS AND PRIZE JURISDICTION.

WAR AND PEACE (*Voina i mir,* 1865–69), the masterpiece of Leo Tolstoy (q.v.), and one of the two or three greatest novels of world literature. This vast work was carefully planned and slowly written over the course of some six years. Tolstoy was about 40 when he finished *War and Peace,* which is essentially a historical novel concerned with family life and war in Russia between the years 1805 and 1814. The work concentrates on five major families—the Bezukhovs, the Rostovs, the Bolkonskys, the Kuragins, and the Drubetskois—but scores of other characters appear. Besides peasants and aristocrats, there are privates and officers of the army and many historical figures connected with the French invasion of Russia in 1812, such as Napoleon I, Alexander I, Mikhail Ilarionovich Kutuzov, and celebrated generals of the two armies. The narrative moves with ease from St. Petersburg to Moscow, then to country estates, revels in restaurants, merrymaking in the fields, and to the realistically perfect pictures of war. No other novel has ever conveyed such a complete picture of human life, of everything in which people find their happiness and greatness, their grief and humiliation.

Tolstoy's art of characterization achieves unsurpassed perfection in *War and Peace.* Even the dogs and horses, as one critic remarked, are individualized. The Rostovs are simplehearted country squires modeled on Tolstoy's own family: Nikolai Rostov and his father were suggested by the author's father and grandfather. The unforgettable heroine Natasha was inspired by Tolstoy's sister-in-law. And the intellectual pride of Prince Andrei Bolkonsky recalls a pronounced trait in Tolstoy's own nature, as do certain of the characteristics of the easygoing Pierre Bezukhov. In some respects, the moral conflict between Prince Andrei and Pierre represents the dualism of Tolstoy's nature—that is, living for the sake of doing good for himself as opposed to living for the sake of serving humanity.

When the reader leaves this region of peace, of family life, for the field of war, then he encounters the only serious difficulty in appreciating this great masterpiece. Although the scenes of war are magnificent, Tolstoy's laboring of his theories on history, on what causes war, and on the significance of the so-called leaders of war strikes many readers as excessive. Long after the publication of the novel, Tolstoy admitted that he had committed an artistic mistake in obtruding his theories upon the essential unity of his story. Yet, out of his insistence that victory in battle depended upon the collective will of the people to win emerged the image of one of the finest characters of the novel, Platon Karatayev, the small, cheerful, soft-spoken peasant who stands as a symbolic personification of the simplicity and truth living in the great gray masses of Russia.

In general, however, Tolstoy avoided preaching in his purely creative works; at least, he did so before his spiritual revelation which came some years after *War and Peace.* And his great masterpiece, apart from the one exception mentioned, is remarkably free from didacticism. In truth, no novel he ever wrote is quite so full of the stuff of life as *War and Peace,* and nowhere else has he made so much of life live so vividly and realistically in his fiction.

Bibliography.—Noyes, George, *Tolstoy* (New York 1918); Mirsky, Dimitri S., *History of Russian Literature,* ed. by Francis J. Whitfield (New York 1958); Steiner, George, *Tolstoy or Dostoevsky* (New York 1959); Simmons, Ernest J., *Tolstoy,* 2 vols. (New York 1960).

ERNEST J. SIMMONS,
Formerly Professor of Russian Literature, Columbia University.

WAR BETWEEN THE STATES. See CIVIL WAR IN AMERICA; also articles on individual campaigns and engagements.

WAR CENSORSHIP. See CENSORSHIP—*Wartime Censorship.*

WAR COLLEGE, a term generally applied to the highest level of military educational institutions in the major countries of the world. The present war colleges developed from the various military schools which were established during the latter part of the 18th and the early part of the 19th centuries for the development of professional military officers. This need was felt when the "general staff" organizations of the major armies of Europe took on a directing role in the management of their armed forces.

Originally the war colleges were intended to teach the principles of warfare, primarily land warfare. Thus they were, in a sense, technical schools occupied solely with the military aspects of national policy. In the late 18th century, however, the Kriegsakademie of Prussia began to include in its curriculum the study of philosophy, particularly that of the nationalist philosophers. Similar trends are to be noted at a slightly later date in the École de Guerre of France and the advanced military schools of Russia.

Today the curricula of the war colleges have been extended to consider economic, social, political, and psychological aspects which influence or affect national policy decisions. The teaching of the purely military arts has become the responsibility of lower level "staff colleges."

The student bodies have been expanded to

permit representation from civilian governmental agencies and departments. In one instance, that of the Escola Superior de Guerra of Brazil, leaders of the national civilian communities with no direct connection with the government are enrolled as students.

In the United States, the war college system follows a dual course. Each service has at the pinnacle of its educational system a war college; that is, the Army War College at Carlisle, Pa., the Naval War College at Newport, R.I., and the War College, Air University, at Maxwell Air Force Base, Ala. Each of these colleges concerns itself with the overall principles of warfare as they apply to its particular service, set against a study of national policy and strategy, including the political, psychological, economic, and social considerations.

In addition to these service war colleges, there are two which come under the direct supervision of the Joint Chiefs of Staff: the National War College, which emphasizes the political aspects of national policy, and the Industrial College of the Armed Forces, which concentrates on the study of economic considerations. Both colleges are located in Washington, D.C.

Other major war colleges located in the Western nations include the École de Guerre of France, the Imperial Defence College of the United Kingdom, and the National Defence College of Canada. Relatively little is known of the program of study of the senior service (that is, war colleges) of the Soviet Union.

B. D. LOCKER,
Major, Information Officer, Institute of Technology, Wright-Patterson Air Force Base, Ohio.

WAR CORRESPONDENCE, a term applied to accounts by newspaper reporters from battle areas. Such reports became important in the middle of the 19th century. There were several correspondents present to report the Mexican War (1846–1848), and in the Crimean War (1854–1856) reporters dominated the news. In the conflicts of the 1860's and 1870's, most important of which were the American Civil War and the Franco-Prussian War, scores of "war correpondents" covered most of the important battles and other developments.

There had always been, of course, ways of circulating war news. With the expansion of printing in the 16th century, war news became a salable commodity. In the 17th century there arose a flourishing business in England and in western Europe in pamphlets, broadsides, and newsbooks that dealt with the wars of the period. All of these continued into the 18th century when regular (ultimately daily) newspapers took over the news. Also, the habit was formed of publishing dispatches of field commanders, usually in official gazettes at first; Napoleon Bonaparte's famous bulletins were the most successful war news of this kind, both for his time and later.

Probably John Bell (1745–1831), who reported the duke of York's expedition to the Netherlands in 1794 for the London *Oracle and Public Advertiser,* has the strongest claim as the first war correspondent, but Sir William Howard Russell (1820–1907) of the London *Times* earned the title "Father of War Correspondents" for his reporting in the Crimean War. Russell's vivid style had wide appeal, and his influence was felt for more than half a century. He also introduced the issue of battlefield censorship. By his time the press, in particular the London *Times,* was strong enough to support reporters against the objections of the authorities.

The period between the end of the Crimean War in 1856 and the beginning of World War I in 1914 was the great era of war correspondents who counted themselves members of a separate, glamorous profession. The professionals, nearly all of whom were British or American, monopolized the reporting of the numerous small imperialistic wars. Archibald Forbes (1838–1900) and George W. Steevens (1869–1900) were leading British war correspondents, while Januarius A. MacGahan (1844–1878), who reported mostly for London papers, and Richard Harding Davis (1864–1916) were outstanding American reporters. The larger wars of the time usually were covered by scores, sometimes hundreds, of correspondents who were of numerous nationalities and who represented a wide range of ability and integrity. Their news was a mixture of serious and anecdotal accounts, of truth and fabrication, of important and trivial information.

Censorship was applied in varying degrees in most of the pre-World War I conflicts. It often delayed and sometimes distorted the news, but the field representatives of an increasingly powerful press managed to keep the public reasonably well informed. A combination of genuine allegiance to press freedom and a conviction that the practical advantages of military publicity outweighed the arguments for silence justified a seemingly insatiable public demand for news.

At the same time the increasing speed of communications enhanced the dangers of divulging military information. Soon after World War I began, rigid restrictions were initiated by all of the belligerent powers, both in the fighting areas and at home, although in countries of traditional press freedom voluntary censorship was more usual. Once again basic war news became official through a carefully systemized scheme of communiqués and other releases. The system proved hopelessly inadequate in an age of publicity and in warfare waged almost equally on psychological and material levels.

As a consequence, there occurred in 1917–1918 another revolution in war news, and by the end of the war the supply of news had reached unprecedented quantities. News quality had improved, too, but it was a product of rigid controls, enormously expanded official news machinery, reporting inspired by patriotism, and the integration of independent and official news. Three of the most outstanding correspondents of the war were Sven Anders Hedin (1865–1952) of Sweden, Sir Philip Gibbs (1877–1962) of England, and Frederick Palmer (1873–1958) of the United States.

Following World War I there was a period of disillusionment and bitter denunciation of the "propaganda" news that had resulted from the new system. But there was little possibility of turning from the directions that had been taken. World War II was the heir not only of the factors that had made psychological warfare inevitable in 1917–1918 but also of developments that pushed the news further in the same directions. Technical inventions and improvements in communications—radio and photographic advances especially—offered almost limitless means for influencing opinion.

Early in World War II the estimated number of people engaged in reporting the war was 10,000. They included photographers, broadcasters, columnists, artists, and desk writers as well as field reporters; all armies had their public information officers, and all reporters with the armies were in uniform. In total warfare, *war news* tends to merge with *news in wartime*. Although war correspondence had lost much of its traditional meaning, it still was possible for reporters to achieve great eminence. The American Ernie Pyle (1900–1945) did so by concentrating on the individual soldier and the human aspects of warfare. Leland Stowe (1899–), another American, did outstanding work in reporting the peripheral wars in Finland and Norway. Alan Moorehead (1910–), a British reporter in the Mediterranean area, managed somehow to stick fairly close to the traditional type of reporting. Ilya Ehrenberg (1891–1967), an outstanding Russian reporter, possessed great writing skill. Both during and after World War II it was the general belief that the war had been more fully and accurately reported than its predecessor.

JOSEPH J. MATHEWS,
Professor of History, Emory University.

Bibliography

Bolling, Landrem R., *Reporters under Fire: U.S. Media Coverage of Conflicts in Lebanon and Central America* (Westview Press 1985).
Clardy, Andrea, ed., *Gordon Gammack: Columns from Three Wars* (Iowa State Univ. Press 1979).
Desmond, Robert W., *Tides of War: World News Reporting 1931–1945* (Univ. of Iowa Press 1984).
Harris, J. D., *War Reporter* (Woodhill Press 1979).
Knight, Oliver, *Following the Indian Wars* (Univ. of Okla. Press 1960).
Knightley, Phillip, *The First Casualty: From the Crimea to Vietnam: The War Correspondent as Hero, Propagandist, and Myth Maker* (Harcourt 1976).
McNamara, John, *Extra: U.S. War Correspondents in Action* (1945; reprint, Ayer 1973).
Mankekar, D. R., *Leaves from a War Reporter's Diary* (Intl. Bk. Dist. 1977).
Mathews, Joseph J., *Reporting the Wars* (1957; reprint, Greenwood Press 1972).

WAR CRIMES. War crimes are violations of the rules of war. These rules, which limit the type and extent of violence permissible in war, are partly laid down in written treaties (laws) and partly consist of unwritten customs.

There are at least four compelling reasons for the existence of rules of war. First, every belligerent has a selfish interest not to provoke reprisals from the enemy, and not to provoke neutrals to join the enemy. Second, wars, however bitter, are to usher in a new era of peace. Hence, reconciliation should not be made too difficult: yesterday's enemy may be needed as a friend tomorrow. Third, nations do not wish their armed forces to "get out of hand"; for, as history has also shown, they may otherwise easily turn against their own government and conationals. Last, but not least, war has always been decried, for humanitarian and many other reasons; if wars cannot be prevented their cruelty and destructiveness must at least be limited, for the purpose of sheer self-preservation. For all of these reasons, the law of war is the oldest and one of the most important parts of international law. Especially since the Middle Ages, the rules of war—as well as the conditions under which it is lawful to start a war—have greatly occupied the attention of governments, jurists, and, indeed, military men.

Rules of War.—The rules of war fall into several categories:

(1) Rules concerning the status of combatants. These determine whether or not a person has the right to engage in combat and other military activities. For example, professional and conscripted soldiers may kill enemy soldiers in battle, but neither an individual civilian nor a soldier disguised as a civilian may do so.

(2) Rules concerning the conduct of hostilities. These circumscribe the type and extent of damage and suffering that may be inflicted upon the people and territory of the enemy, the treatment of prisoners of war, and the like.

(3) Rules dealing with the behavior of the occupying power in occupied enemy territory. The longer a wartime occupation lasts (for example, in the war which ended in 1945, Japan occupied large parts of China for over a decade), the more important are these rules.

(4) Rules pertaining to such important matters as the rights and duties of the belligerents and their citizens toward neutral nations and their citizens, and to the behavior of the parties under a truce and during an armistice.

Offenses against any of these rules, whether established by treaties or by international custom, constitute *war crimes*.

Historical Developments.—At different periods of history, the laws and customs of war varied greatly; and for long stretches of time, and in many regions of the world, practices were considered acceptable which at other times were regarded as utterly repugnant and not permissible. Nor did this evolution constitute a continuous process of amelioration. For some periods of time, or in some parts of the world, usages would improve, only to relapse again into barbarity. For example, the periods of the Crusades and, again, of the Thirty Years' War (1618–1648) were marked by a cruelty of military customs which had been overcome in previous periods and elsewhere.

Surveying the history of warfare, we find that often it was considered permissible to plunder or even physically to destroy a conquered city, and to slay the inhabitants, irrespective of sex and age. At other times, at least certain places—such as places of worship—had to be spared, and/or persons who had found rescue there, and/or women and children. For example, the Old Testament (Deuteronomy 20:19, 20) forbids the destruction of fruit-bearing trees in enemy territory. The Greeks of the heroic age had very cruel usages of war; thus, indignities were inflicted even on the corpse of a fallen enemy leader—as shown in the description, by Homer, of the treatment of Hector's body by Achilles. On the other hand, quarter was given during the Trojan wars even during battle, if ransom was offered. And the ancient code of Manu, the legendary legislator of India, ordered long before the Trojan wars that an enemy must not be harmed if he is asleep, or naked, or turning to flight, or defenseless, or folding his hands to ask for mercy. But at diverse periods of history, captured enemy soldiers were slain, or at least it was permitted to slay them.

A relative improvement in the law of war was the gradually developed custom not to slay prisoners but to make them into slaves (agricultural workers, household servants, and the like) or to exchange them for one's own soldiers who had fallen into captivity of the other side. Yet, for example, Hemocratus, a general in the service of Syracuse (on the island of Sicily), was condemned to exile by his government for having ordered his troops to treat the invading Athenian armies with moderation; while Julius Caesar was not reprimanded for having sold, rather than killed, 33,000 Belgian prisoners during his second campaign in Gaul.

Under the law permitting the enslavement of conquered people, the Hebrews were taken in servitude to Egypt. The custom of selling enemy prisoners at slave auction developed into the custom of allowing the payment of ransom for their liberty. There are examples of freeing captives without ransom; while, on the other hand, in the 16th and 17th centuries it was again considered permissible to make slaves of prisoners.

Religious views greatly influenced the rules of war. When the outcome of war was regarded to be the judgment of heaven, or the vanquished were regarded as being abandoned by the gods, such doctrines were used as justification for the cruel treatment of the defeated. On the other hand, the Stoics (for example, Marcus Tullius Cicero, 106–43 B.C.) taught that the vanquished must be spared; and according to the law as it existed at certain times in antiquity, generals who had received the surrender of towns or even nations actually became their patrons.

At some periods, more lenient rules applied in wars between "equals" (for example, conflicts between Christian princes or between Muslims) than in wars against "outsiders" or "infidels" (for example, between Christians and Muslims). Thus, in 1179, Pope Alexander III requested that enslaving be limited to non-Christians.

Very important to the development of international law was the fact that, however brutal the rules of war may have been, the violations of such limitations as did exist were considered as grievous wrongs; and in times of deep religious convictions punishments of a religious nature were threatened as the most powerful deterrent available. Thus, during the 11th century, church councils proclaimed the so-called "Truce of God" (q.v.), forbidding warfare on certain days and the harming during hostilities of certain categories of persons, especially priests, women, pilgrims, and merchants (and also sometimes of beasts of burden), under penalty of excommunication. Similarly, in wars between peoples of different religions, "treachery"—the violation of a treaty-created or customarily sacrosanct rule, such as the molestation of heralds of truce, or the breach of a promise of free conduct—would be "punished" by severest reprisals.

The first war crimes trial in history in the technical sense of the term (that is, punishment of transgression of the law of war through judicial procedure) appears to have been the trial by an English court in 1305 of the celebrated Sir William Wallace (q.v.), for waging a war of extermination against the English population, "sparing neither age nor sex, monk nor nun." Since the latter part of the Middle Ages, customs and practices have evolved which eventually led to the modern law of war; and, in the words of a leading British jurist, Lord Wright of Durley (Robert Alderson Wright), chairman of the United Nations War Crimes Commission, "there have been hundreds of cases in which national military tribunals have tried and convicted enemy nationals of breaches of the laws of war." To illustrate, during the Franco-Prussian War of 1870–1871, the Germans executed numerous French *francs-tireurs* (irregular combatants) for violations of the laws of war.

The teachings of jurists and philosophers of the 17th and 18th centuries did much to humanize the conduct of belligerents. For example, Montesquieu (1689–1755) held that to murder prisoners of war is contrary to all law, and Jean Jacques Rousseau (1712–1778) added that they must not be held in dungeons or prisons, or put in iron, but should be placed in healthy conditions and liberated after the end of the war. Rules to such effect were agreed upon in the Treaty of Commerce and Friendship between the United States and Prussia, signed by Benjamin Franklin and King Frederick the Great.

Geneva and The Hague.—Decisive progress in the evolution of the laws of war was made after the 1860's partly under the impact of the horrors of the Crimean War and the American Civil War, through international treaties concluded between states. The Geneva Conventions of 1864 and 1906, for example, were to ameliorate the conditions of wounded soldiers in the field (see GENEVA CONVENTION). The most important among the treaties adopted prior to World War I were the various conventions and regulations approved at international conferences held at The Hague in 1899 and 1907, and especially the "Convention respecting the Laws and Customs of War on Land" and the "Regulations" of the same name, annexed to the convention of 1907. (See also HAGUE COURT.) The rules and principles laid down therein constitute the most ambitious effort so far to "define with greater precision" the rules and customs of war on land.

Although subsequently further refined by various international conventions—for example, the Geneva Prisoner of War Convention of 1929 and the Geneva conventions of 1949—the Hague Regulations of 1907 (as they are called for short) have continued to form the core of the law of war of the 20th century. They have been so generally accepted by the community of nations that, as numerous tribunals have stated, they are binding upon all states and all individuals, which means that their violation constitutes war crimes.

Some of the provisions of the 1907 regulations, cited here at random, may indicate their range and significance: "Volunteer corps" (now often known as organized partisans or guerrillas), if fulfilling specific conditions laid down in the regulations, have the same rights and duties as have armies. Prisoners of war must be humanely treated. For example, their board, lodging, and clothing must be "on the same footing" as furnished to the troops who captured them. "It is especially forbidden to employ poison or poisoned weapons" or "to kill or wound an enemy who . . . has surrendered" or "to declare that no quarter will be given." "The attack or bombardment, by whatever means, of towns, villages, dwellings, or buildings which are undefended is prohibited." "Escaped prisoners who are retaken before being able to rejoin their own army . . . are liable [only] to disciplinary punishment. Prisoners who, after succeeding in escaping, are again taken prisoner, are not liable to any punishment on account of the previous flight." In belligerently occupied territory, "family honor and rights, the lives of persons, and private property, as well as religious convictions and practices, must be respected. Private property cannot be confiscated. Pillage is formally forbidden. No general penalty, pecuniary or otherwise, shall be inflicted upon the population on account of the acts of individuals for which they cannot be regarded as jointly and severally responsible." "The property of municipalities, that of institutions dedicated to religion, charity and education, the arts and sciences, even when State property, shall be treated as private property"—that is, must be "respected" and cannot be confiscated by the occupant.

Basic Principles Regarding War Crimes.—(1) Since the rules of war are part of international law, no nation can one-sidedly change them. No legislature or government or general can decree that something which is a war crime is permitted to their own forces. In 1842, Daniel Webster, United States secretary of state, declared: "The law of war forbids the wounding, killing, impressing into the troops of the country, or enslaving or otherwise maltreating the prisoners of war unless they have been guilty of some grave crime, and from the obligations of this law no civilized state can discharge itself."

(2) War crimes can be punished, not only by the organs of the country of which the offender is a citizen—for example, a guard who tortures, or a camp commander who orders the torturing of, prisoners of war will in a civilized country be court-martialed by his own authorities—but also by the enemy. The right of the enemy to try a war crime suspect has been uncontested throughout the centuries.

(3) In fact, since the rules of war are *international* law, such enemy suspects may be tried, and, if found guilty, punished even by a nation which has *not* passed any legislation for such procedures. Hence, Gen. George Washington acted correctly when in 1780, during the American Revolutionary War, he had Maj. John André (q.v.) tried by a Board of General Officers, and André was correctly convicted by them as a spy "under the laws of war" (that is, under the then existing *international* rules of war) even though no *American* legislature had by 1780 stipulated the criminality of André's behavior. The matter was lucidly stated by United States Attorney General James Speed in 1865 in connection with the trial of President Abraham Lincoln's assassins: "The laws of war . . . exist and are of binding force upon the departments and citizens of the government though not defined by any law of Congress . . . . When war comes, the laws and customs of war come also, and . . . during the war are part of the law of the land." Similarly, the United States Supreme Court stated shortly after the Civil War (in *Dew* v. *Johnson*): "What is the law which governs an army invading an enemy's country? It is not the civil law of the invaded country; it is not the civil law of the conquering country; it is the law of war."

(4) War crimes are very serious offenses. In the words of the United States basic field manual: "All war crimes are subject to the death penalty, although a lesser penalty may be imposed."

(5) Not only military personnel are bound by the law of war. Hence, any civilian may become guilty of a war crime—for example, a physician who subjects an enemy citizen to inhuman "medical experiments," or a businessman participating in the plunder of enemy property.

(6) Even in the heat of war, persons suspected of war crimes may not be punished without their guilt being properly established. To shoot them out of hand constitutes itself a war crime. International law does not lay down the procedure to be followed. Summary procedure may suffice, if it affords the accused the minimum guarantees of a fair trial according to the general principles of law as recognized by civilized nations.

(7) In a wider sense, the term "war crimes" covers two other types of behavior violating international law, namely "crimes against peace" and "crimes against humanity."

Crimes Against Peace.—These consist in planning, preparing, initiating, or waging of war of aggression. After World War II, the International Military Tribunal at Nürnberg (composed of one each American, British, French, and Russian judge) tried top leaders of Adolf Hitler's Germany, and the International Military Tribunal for the Far East, at Tokyo (composed of one judge each from Australia, Canada, [pre-Communist] China, France, Great Britain, India, the Netherlands, New Zealand, the Philippines, the USSR, and the United States), tried top leaders of Japan. Both tribunals stated in their judgments that to unleash a war of aggression "is not only an international crime; it is the supreme international crime." But both tribunals emphasized that only persons actually formulating or influencing governmental policy can be charged with "crimes against peace." For example, the Tokyo judgment declared that "the duty of an army is to be loyal." Hence, neither privates nor generals of an aggressor nation can be blamed if they "merely performed their military duty of fighting a war waged by their government," as long as they did not personally participate in the making of the policy of aggression.

The concept that aggression is a crime is intimately connected with the distinction between "just" and "unjust" war. "Unjust war" means, in essence, aggressive war, and includes especially aggression made in violation of a solemn pledge (treaty) *not* to attack. The distinction between just and unjust war goes back for more than 2,000 years. It has been insisted upon, for example, by Roman statesmen and jurists in antiquity; by the two most influential "doctors" of the Catholic Church, St. Augustine in the 5th century and St. Thomas Aquinas in the 13th century; by the father of the modern law of nations, Hugo Grotius (1583–1645), and other famous Dutch jurists; and by Spanish scholastics and French and German thinkers of the age of enlightenment. Approximate precedents for the proposition that "crimes against peace" are punishable also exist. Thus, the Senate of Rome requested the extradition for trial of Hannibal for inciting nations to make war upon Rome, and of Brutulus Papius of Samnium for attacking Rome in breach of treaty. (Both committed suicide.) In 1474, Sir Peter of Hagenbach, governor of Breisach, was tried by a court composed of Austrian and Swiss judges and executed for having waged a terroristic war.

During the period of absolutism in Europe, the distinction between just and unjust war fell into oblivion. But when in 1815, Napoleon Bonaparte, violating his pledge, escaped from Elba to France and rekindled the war, the Great Powers of Europe declared him an outlaw "as an enemy and disturber of the tranquility of the world [who] has incurred public vengeance." Thereafter, Britain, with the consent of the other Great Powers, punished him by banishing him to the grim island of St. Helena.

Under the Versailles Treaty (1919), the German emperor William II was to be tried by an international tribunal "for a supreme offence against international morality and the sanctity of treaties" (especially including the violation of the German-guaranteed neutrality of Belgium and Luxembourg). But the Netherlands, where William had fled, refused to extradite him, and the trial never took place.

During the interwar period, several international pronouncements condemned wars of aggression as illegal and criminal. Thus, in February 1928, the sixth Pan American Conference of 21 American republics resolved that "war of aggression constitutes an international crime against the human species . . . all aggression is illicit." The Nürnberg and Tokyo international tribunals attached special importance to the "General Treaty for the Renunciation of War" (Kellogg-Briand Pact, q.v.) of Aug. 27, 1928, because it was ratified before World War II by virtually all countries of the world. The pact does not specify that aggression is criminal, but the Nürnberg international tribunal declared: "The solemn renunciation of war as an instrument of national policy [pledged in the Kellogg-Briand Pact] involves the proposition that such a war is illegal in international law; and that those who plan and wage such a war, with its inevitable and terrible consequences, are committing a crime in so doing." This, as well as all other principles enunciated by the Nürnberg international tribunal, received added weight by the fact that the General Assembly of the United Nations, by a unanimous resolution of Dec. 11, 1946, identified itself with these principles, as did subsequently the 11-nation Tokyo tribunal.

It should be noted, however, that after World War II only 36 leaders (12 German and 24 Japanese), out of the many thousands of war crime suspects tried, were convicted for "crimes against peace."

Crimes Against Humanity.—These are outrages (murder, extermination, deportation, torture, and other mass atrocities) and persecutions of entire racial, religious, and political groups. If the victims are enemy citizens, such deeds constitute "war crimes" in the narrow sense of the term. But if the victims were, for example, German nationals, such deeds were considered punishable under international law (that is, also by non-German courts), *provided* they were committed in connection with "crimes against peace," or "war crimes." The Nürnberg international tribunal interpreted these crimes cautiously. Its judgment states that "revolting and horrible" as was "the policy of persecution, repression and murder of civilians in Germany before the war of 1939," the tribunal was not competent to deal with them. It did, however, find certain defendants guilty of atrocities, irrespective of the nationality of the victims, because they were committed "in execution of or in connection with the aggressive war." In other words, when, for example, mentally or physically deficient persons were systematically exterminated as "useless eaters" in occupied territories as well as in Germany, or when German Jews and gypsies were transported to concentration and extermination camps just as were foreign Jews and gypsies pursuant to the Nazi master race theory, all this was part and parcel of a criminal war policy. Other war crimes tribunals which had to deal with indictments for "crimes against humanity" followed the interpretation of the Nürnberg international tribunal.

It will be noted, therefore, that the post-World War II war crimes trials left open the question as to whether mass atrocities committed by or with the complicity of a government *in peacetime* against entire groups of its *own* population constitute international crimes; that is, whether the culprits can be brought to justice before an outside court.

War Crimes Trials After World War I.—The practices of "terror," in violation of the laws of war, which Germany used in World War I led to an insistent demand to punish the individuals responsible for them. The Versailles Treaty provided that Germany should hand over to the Allies the persons wanted for trial. But when in February 1920 the first such list of some 900 names—including the former imperial crown prince, Field Marshal Paul von Hindenburg, and Gen. Erich F. W. Ludendorff—was presented, German indignation was so strong that the Allies agreed to a compromise, namely, that investigations and trials would be handled by the German Supreme Court. The outcome was a farce. Of the 901 persons grievously incriminated by evidence furnished by the Allies (mainly Great Britain, France, and Belgium), 888 were either acquitted or not indicted. The whole procedure gave rise to fanatical chauvinistic demonstrations, and greatly helped the early spread of nazism. The 13 who were found guilty received insignificant prison sentences but were celebrated inside and outside the court as national heroes.

War Crimes Trials in Connection with World War II. *Wartime Trials.*—The most famous trial held during the war was that staged by the Germans at Riom (France) of French statesmen for "crimes against peace." The intention was to prove that the accused, and especially Léon Blum, the former French prime minister who was of Jewish ancestry, had been involved in a Jewish plot to start a world war against Germany. But the evidence immediately pointed in the opposite direction. The trial was quickly abandoned, and the defendants put in concentration camps. The first trial of an officer of the notorious Nazi Elite Guard extermination troops was held in Kharkov, USSR, in 1943.

Postwar Trials.—In view of the unparalleled mass atrocities systematically carried out by Germany from the inception of the war, numerous formal warnings were issued by the Allies during World War II that the culprits would be brought to justice. Resolve was also strong to punish Japanese atrocities committed in the far-flung Asian and Pacific theaters of war. In 1943, a "United Nations Commission for the Investigation of War Crimes," composed of representatives of 17 nations, was established with its seat in London as a clearinghouse of information and evidence. In May 1944, at the request of China, the commission established a Far Eastern subcommission.

The trial before the International Military Tribunal (Nov. 20, 1945, to Oct. 1, 1946) of Hermann Goering and 20-odd other leading personalities of the Third Reich was held at Nürnberg for symbolic reasons, Nürnberg having been the citadel of national socialism where Hitler had held his huge annual rallies. The trial was presided over by the British member of the tribunal, Lord Justice Geoffrey Lawrence. The tribunal was established and functioned pursuant to an agreement signed in London in August

Wide World Photos

Nazi leaders are sentenced during the final session of the War Crimes Trial in Nürnberg's Palace of Justice (1946).

1945 by representatives of the United States, Britain, France, and the USSR, and formally adhered to also by 19 other nations.

Of the 24 former leading Nazis indicted, 22 were tried, including Martin Bormann *in absentia;* one of the defendants committed suicide before judgment and the other was not tried for medical reasons. Death sentences were imposed on 12 defendants, 3 were given life imprisonment and 4 lesser prison sentences, and 3 were acquitted.

Thereafter, 185 other leading German personalities—cabinet ministers, field marshals and admirals, industrialists, ambassadors, jurists, physicians, and so on—were indicted before 12 tribunals, composed exclusively of United States judges, at Nürnberg between December 1946 and March 1949 under a law issued by the Allied Control Council for Germany. Four defendants committed suicide; four were severed from the proceedings for health reasons. Of the remaining 177, these United States tribunals sentenced 25 to death, 20 to life imprisonment, 97 to lesser prison terms, and acquitted 35.

The Tokyo international tribunal was established on Jan. 19, 1946, by General of the Army Douglas MacArthur, as Supreme Commander of the Allied Powers (SCAP). The substantive and procedural law applied by it was very similar to that applied by the Nürnberg international tribunal. However, there were four chief prosecutors (one each from the four powers represented on the bench) at Nürnberg, and only one chief prosecutor (an American, Joseph B. Keenan, former assistant to the United States attorney general) at Tokyo. The trial lasted (including a seven-month recess to prepare the 1,200-page judgment) from May 3, 1946, to Nov. 4, 1948. The Australian member, Chief Justice of the Supreme Court of Queensland William Flood Webb, presided. Probably the best known of the defendants was Gen. Hideki Tojo, Japan's prime minister in 1941–1944, who was hanged as a war criminal in 1948. Of the 25 defendants brought to trial, 7 were given the death sentence, 16 were sentenced to life imprisonment, and 2 to other prison terms.

Furthermore, many trials were conducted from 1945 by American, British, French, Australian, Belgian, Dutch, Polish, Norwegian, Soviet, Czechoslovak, and other courts in many parts of Europe and the Far East. The defendants were mainly citizens of former enemy countries, but numerous nationals of the respective countries also were tried as collaborators in the war crimes of the enemy. The most famous of the latter trials were probably those of Marshal Henri Philippe Pétain and Pierre Laval—respectively head of state and prime minister of France's wartime Vichy regime—and the Norwegian Vidkun Quisling, whose name had become synonymous for fifth columnist during World War II. One reason why many trials could be held was the unique fact that huge masses of official, top-secret documents of the former Axis powers had become available.

As the decade of the 1960's opened, the war crimes trials connected with World War II were not entirely over. This was particularly true of the Federal Republic of Germany, where since the 1950's many gravely incriminated persons who had lived under assumed names were brought to trial. German authorities estimated that these trials—long since held exclusively by German courts under German law—involving several additional thousands of suspects, were to come to an end by 1963. As far as these "late" trials were concerned, world attention focused on the trial in 1961, before the High

Werner Braun from Camera Press, London

Charged with complicity in the murder of six million Jews, Adolf Eichmann stands trial before an Israeli court (1961).

Court of Israel, of Adolf Eichmann (who had lived incognito in Latin America, whence he was abducted to Israel in 1960), for having been a top figure in, and largely master mind of, the extermination of millions of Jews and others considered "inferior" by the Hitler regime.

See also INTERNATIONAL LAW; WAR, LAWS OF.

JOHN H. E. FRIED,
Adjunct Professor of Political Economy, New York University; Formerly Special Legal Consultant to the United States War Crimes Tribunals in Nürnberg.

WAR DANCES. To the European, encountering for the first time hostile Africans or American Indians, dance rituals seemed to be primarily warlike in intent. The donning of "war paint" and feathers, the brandishing of weapons, and the monotonous thudding of the feet of Plains Indians could only be construed by the foreigner as being designed to put valor into the hearts of warriors; and this frightening picture has become a common one in Western tales and narratives which mirror the clash of the aboriginal and the civilized. Hence, the war dance has been overemphasized: it is merely one form of those many processional and dancing rites which all over the world—in Oceania, Africa, India, and both of the Americas—are used to achieve "spirit power" or "medicine" for the participants and to weld them together into a cohesive social group.

From such religious and psychological sources, dance rites may proceed to many functions: worship, the increase of human and agricultural fertility, the passage of the adolescent into manhood, the encouragement of success in hunting, the cure of disease, or ecstasy and mere entertainment. Among these functions may be success in war or celebration of victory. The Arunta of central Australia, *after* a battle, paint their bodies, thrust twigs through their nostrils, and, forming a square, approach the main camp waving their shields. Old women with clubs strike the shields, and the mimicry of warfare is impressive. But the presence of women in the rite and the time of the action make it clear that the purpose is anything but the incitement of martial spirit.

Even the American Indian "scalp dances" had a purpose far from that of war—they marked virility and often were used to seek rainfall. The morisco or morris dance, common in Spain and naturalized in England, probably had little to do with Christian warfare against the Moors; the name and the blackened faces have caused students to misinterpret what was in essence a vegetation rite. Children in their games still wage sham battles, and the hostility of these and of savage miming, both group and dual, may serve as well to suppress aggression as to incite it.

FRANCIS LEE UTLEY,
Professor of English, The Ohio State University.

WAR DEPARTMENT. See WAR, DEPARTMENT OF.

WAR HAWKS. See UNITED STATES—*16. The Founding of the Nation, 1763–1815* (War Hawks).

WAR INDEMNITY. See REPARATIONS.

WAR INFORMATION, Office of. See OFFICE OF WAR INFORMATION.

WAR LABOR BOARDS. World War I.—As the United States speeded up its industries for the prosecution of World War I, the need for a stable and efficient labor corps soon became apparent. In January 1918, a conference between the Department of Labor and the Council of National Defense formulated a program of labor administration designed to achieve this end. The program, which was approved that month by President Woodrow Wilson, called for the creation of agencies to establish federal labor exchanges, to deal with questions arising from hours and wages, to secure proper working conditions and adequate housing, to collect and digest labor information, and to disseminate such information to the public. Secretary of Labor William B. Wilson, whom the president appointed war labor administrator, formed an advisory council to make specific recommendations, and its suggestions resulted in the establishment of the War Labor Policies Board and the National War Labor Board. The latter, set up in March 1918, was empowered to settle through mediation and conciliation all labor disputes occurring in industries deemed essential to the war effort. Specialized agencies, such as the United States Employment Service and the Women in Industry Service, were organized shortly after.

World War II.—Within two weeks after the United States entered World War II, a joint labor-management conference proposed the establishment of a new National War Labor Board (NWLB) to effect the peaceful settlement of labor disputes. The board, created by executive order of Jan. 12, 1942, comprised four representatives each from labor, industry, and the general public. A second major function of the board, that of stabilizing wage levels as an anti-inflation measure, was initiated on Oct. 3, 1942.

Superseding the National Defense Mediation Board, the NWLB was granted the power of final arbitration in labor disputes; and from the time of its inception until the surrender of Japan the board dealt with nearly 18,000 such cases (affecting 12,300,000 workers). The effectiveness of the program is reflected in the fact that, during the whole period of the war, production time lost because of strikes and lockouts declined by nearly two thirds of the peacetime level (from 27/100 of 1 percent of total working hours in 1935–1939 to 11/100 of 1 percent in World War II). Correspondingly, the average duration of strikes was reduced from 23 days in 1939 to 5 days in 1944. Compliance by labor and management was voluntary in most instances, although the board invoked its powers of compulsion when necessary. The NWLB, terminated by executive order on Dec. 31, 1945, was succeeded (with respect to its wage stabilization program) by the National Wage Stabilization Board.

WAR OF 1812, a conflict between the United States and Great Britain, beginning with a declaration of war by the American Congress, June 18, 1812, and closing officially with the signing of the Treaty of Ghent, Dec. 24, 1814. The war was begun by the United States in retaliation for British interference with American trade and shipping on the high seas and, to a lesser degree, for alleged British complicity in Indian hostilities on the frontier.

Background and Causes.—On the high seas the United States suffered violation of its rights as a neutral (as it conceived them) by both Great Britain and France, antagonists in the wars of the French Revolution and Napoleon. These powers were at war from 1793 to 1801 (formally terminated by the Peace of Amiens, 1802) and again from 1803 to Napoleon's defeat and first surrender in 1814. The war, in its early years, was profitable to American shipowners and merchants. American shipping employed in the foreign trade grew from a tonnage of 363,100 in 1791 to 848,300 in 1807. American ships could trade with both belligerents. With French and Spanish ships driven from the seas by the British Navy, American shippers found it especially profitable to carry merchandise between France and Spain on the one hand and French and Spanish Caribbean colonies on the other. To permit such trade was contrary to British policy (under the so-called "Rule of the War of 1756"),[1] but for some years British authorities winked at it when the voyage between mother country and colony was "broken" at an American port. United States ports were thronged with ships which brought tropical cargoes from the Caribbean, went through the motions of importing them, and then, with new papers, carried the same cargoes to Europe as exports from the United States. This lucrative practice was halted by a British court decision in the case of the *Essex* (1805), holding that such a voyage was not legalized by the device of breaking it at an American port.

The Bettmann Archive

Francis Scott Key composed *The Star-Spangled Banner* after witnessing the British bombardment of Fort McHenry in 1814.

To American protests at the *Essex* decision and threats of retaliation through an act excluding certain British products from the United States, the British responded by substituting for enforcement of the *Essex* policy a blockade of part, and only part, of the English Channel and North Sea coast of France and her European dependencies (Charles James Fox's blockade, declared May 16, 1806). Elsewhere American ships might enter, even though carrying

[1] This was a rule, enforced by British prize courts, upholding the notification of Great Britain to Holland that she would not permit neutrals to engage in trade with nations with whom Great Britain was at war if the trade had not existed in peacetime.

colonial produce. Intended as a concession to the United States, Fox's blockade really opened the fierce Anglo-French competition in blockades and other restrictions on neutral commerce, which eventually involved the United States in war. Napoleon, whose hopes of invading England had perished when Horatio Nelson destroyed the French and Spanish fleets at Trafalgar (Oct. 21, 1805), seized upon this British measure as an excuse for launching a new attack upon England through her commerce. Destruction of British trade, he believed, would defeat proud Britannia as effectually as armed invasion. By his Berlin Decree (Nov. 21, 1806), therefore, he declared the British Isles under blockade and ordered that any vessel coming from England or her colonies should be seized as if it were British property. It was now Britain's turn to retaliate. In two orders in council (Jan. 7 and Nov. 11, 1807) the British government announced a blockade of the ports of France, her possessions, and her allies, and ordered the seizure of neutral ships attempting to trade with such ports unless—an important proviso—they had first put in at a British port and paid duty on their cargoes. It is evident that the British aim was not to shut off trade with the Continent, but rather to levy tribute upon neutral trade with His Majesty's enemies. To those orders in council Napoleon responded with his Milan Decree (Dec. 17, 1807). Any neutral ship, he warned, that had visited a British port, paid British taxes, or submitted to search by a British naval vessel, would be regarded as in effect British and hence as liable to seizure and confiscation if it should fall into French hands. Subsequent decrees (Bayonne, April 17, 1808; Rambouillet, March 23, 1810) ordered the confiscation of American ships in French ports which were held to have violated the previous French decrees or the restrictions placed on them by their own government.

Napoleon, without a navy, obviously could not enforce a blockade of the British Isles; nor could Britain, with the greatest navy in the world, effectively police all the sea lanes leading to French-controlled ports. The United States contended that as a principle of international law, "blockades to be binding must be effective." In American eyes, therefore, both British and French blockades were mere "paper blockades" and hence illegal.

Also illegal and injurious from the American standpoint was the British practice of impressment when carried out against neutral ships. The impressment of sailors was a crude form of "selective service" by which the British Navy had, for generations, recruited its personnel in times of stress. Trouble arose when British naval vessels stopped American ships on the high seas and removed sailors who were alleged to be (and often were) British subjects. In justification the British pointed to the unquestioned facts that numerous sailors deserted the British Navy and entered the easier and more agreeable service of the American merchant marine, and that such deserters often equipped themselves with fraudulent papers purporting to prove their American citizenship. British authorities, therefore, claimed that they were within their rights in stopping American ships on the high seas and removing seamen who, in the opinion of the officer conducting the search, looked and talked like Englishmen. The British principle of indelible allegiance, colliding with the liberal naturalization policy of the United States, created further complications.

The United States, for its part, denied that the British had any right to remove personnel from American ships on the high seas and pointed out truly that many of those seized were bona fide American citizens. American protests contrasted the arbitrary character of such removals, carried out under the direction of a naval officer who was an interested party, with the treatment of alleged contraband property, which could be taken only upon decision by a prize court.

The impressment controversy reached a tragic climax in the *Chesapeake-Leopard* affair of June 22, 1807. Ordinarily United States naval vessels were spared the humiliation of the practice, but on this occasion the frigate *Chesapeake*, suspected of harboring British deserters, was fired upon when she failed to stop at the order of the *Leopard's* commander, and four sailors were removed, of whom only one proved to be a British subject. American tempers flared at this flagrant insult to the American flag. President Thomas Jefferson tried in vain to extract from Britain's acknowledgment of error in this instance a settlement of the entire impressment controversy. Though the British made tardy reparation for the attack on the *Chesapeake*, they continued to remove sailors from American merchant ships.

Unwilling to submit tamely to violation of American rights, and yet reluctant to resort to war in their defense, President Jefferson had recourse to measures of "peaceable coercion" aimed at both belligerents. After the *Chesapeake-Leopard* incident, he excluded British naval vessels from American ports. At his request, Congress passed the Embargo Act (Dec. 22, 1807), closing the ports of the United States to all commerce other than the coastwise trade, on the theory that denial of the American trade and the services of the American merchant marine would wring concessions from both belligerents. The results were disappointing. Though the embargo and subsequent restrictive measures injured British merchants and manufacturers, and finally led—too late—to the repeal of the orders in council, the opening of Spanish and Spanish colonial markets partly made up the loss. Napoleon complimented the Americans on standing up for their rights and "assisted" them by confiscating American ships that entered French ports in violation of the American law. The embargo was more injurious to the people of the United States than to the foreign nations which they sought to punish. Seaport towns stagnated, and southern agriculture, largely dependent on export markets, languished; only smugglers profited. Domestic opposition to Jefferson's policy became intense, particularly among the commercial classes of the Northeast, for whose protection the embargo was in theory designed. To them the remedy appeared worse than the disease. After 14 months Congress repealed the embargo, substituting a milder Non-Intercourse Act (March 1, 1809), which reopened trade except with France and England and empowered the president to reopen it with either or both of them upon their agreeing to rescind their illegal blockades. A friendly but inept British envoy, David M. Erskine, promised revocation of the Orders in Council of 1807 in return for trifling concessions from the United States. James Madison (inaugurated president March 4, 1809) thereupon suspended nonintercourse with Great Britain, only to be informed that Erskine had acted without authority. Nonintercourse was reapplied. Erskine's successor, Francis James Jackson, adopted such an overbearing attitude that Madison refused to deal with him.

Meanwhile, nonintercourse was proving as ineffectual a weapon as the embargo. Congress replaced it with "Macon's Bill Number Two" (May 1, 1810), which reopened trade with all the world, but with the proviso that if one of the belligerents should cease its interference with American trade, and the other failed to do likewise, nonintercourse would be reimposed against the delinquent. This last proviso enabled Napoleon to trick Madison. By pretending that the French decrees had been withdrawn insofar as they affected American ships, the French foreign minister induced Madison to reimpose against Great Britain the nonimportation features of the former nonintercourse law. Negotiations in the summer and fall of 1811 (between James Monroe, the new secretary of state, and Augustus John Foster, the new British minister) were fruitless. The British still refused to revoke their orders in council. An impasse had been reached over commercial restrictions. An impasse had long existed over impressments. Madison called Congress to meet a month early, in November 1811, and recounted the history of disputes with both France and Great Britain. British practices, he complained, had "the character as well as the effect of war on our lawful commerce." To resist Britain's "hostile inflexibility," the president asked Congress to put the United States "into an armor and an attitude demanded by the crisis."

The 12th congress, elected in 1810, was led by the War Hawks, a group of youngish men, several of them from frontier states, who demanded more drastic measures than embargo and nonintercourse to avenge the nation's wrongs. They elected Henry Clay, one of their number, speaker of the House of Representatives. John C. Calhoun of South Carolina, John A. Harper of New Hampshire, and Peter B. Porter of western New York became leaders of the war party. These men were animated in part by a new set of grievances against Great Britain. Since 1807 a Shawnee Indian named Tecumseh had been constructing an Indian confederation in the West for the purpose of checking cessions of Indian land to the United States. In this enterprise he had the sympathy of British agents in Canada, who wished the American Northwest kept as a preserve for Indians and fur-bearing animals. Sporadic Indian attacks on frontier settlers, symptoms of rising Indian hostility, grew in number, and Westerners blamed the British for inciting them. In the fall of 1811, Gen. William Henry Harrison led an army of regulars and militia into the Indian country in an effort to overawe the red men. Shortly before dawn on November 7 his encampment on the banks of Tippecanoe Creek in Indiana was surprised by an Indian attack. The assailants were beaten off, but not till they had inflicted heavy losses on Harrison's command. The West cried for vengeance and, since British arms were found on the fallen foe, demanded that the British be driven from Canada. Canada in British possession, said one Kentucky paper, would be "a never failing source of Indian hostility."

Western opinion, calling for the conquest of Canada in self-defense, was not unmindful of the positive advantages of such an acquisition—among them the full control of the waterways and the fur trade. War with England also promised benefits to the South, which eyed greedily Spain's possessions in East and West Florida. A portion of the latter, to which the United States laid dubious claim as included in Louisiana, had already been occupied without Spain's consent. In the spring of 1812 an agent of the United States stirred up a revolt against Spanish authority in East Florida and led United States troops into the province at the invitation of the insurgents. His too transparent operations were disavowed in Washington, but Southerners expected that a declaration of war against Great Britain, with which Spain was now allied, would be the signal for the seizure of the remainder of the Floridas. Thus to the Northwest and the South war offered the lure of territorial expansion.

The Bettmann Archive

The burning of Washington by British military and naval forces (August 1814), in a fanciful early engraving.

It is significant that, while the seaboard communities showed strong opposition to the war, the most ardent War Hawks came from the frontier states—from the crescent of lands facing British and Spanish territory and the Indian frontier between. To their sections successful war would mean not only the punishing of injuries and perhaps the liberation of closed European markets for their goods but also the acquisition of valuable territory.

On June 1, 1812, Madison sent to Congress a special message advising a declaration of war against Great Britain. He listed as grievances: first, impressments; second, interference with legitimate trade; third, intrigues with the western Indians. Congress responded, June 18, with a declaration of war, passed with disturbingly large negative votes—62 out of 160 members of both houses. Two days before, the British foreign minister had announced that the orders in council would be revoked; and the revocation order was issued June 23—the slowly ripened fruit of peaceable coercion. Moves to halt hostilities in recognition of this major concession were blocked; the war went on over the issues of impressments and Western grievances and ambitions.

Campaigns.—The United States was ill prepared for conflict. Congress, while it had moved steadily toward war during the winter and spring of 1811–1812, had made no adequate provision for carrying it on. It had provided, on paper, for a regular army of 36,700 men, but fewer than 10,000 had been raised, and these were ill trained and scattered about the country in small garrisons. The state militias were poorly disciplined and unreliable. Many were ready to take advantage of their supposed exemption from duty on foreign soil; some state governors, in fact, refused to permit their militiamen to leave their states. Though preparing to fight Great Britain in defense of maritime rights, Congress had rejected all proposals for building up the navy. That the prowar West was most emphatic in this rejection supports the theory that Western eyes were fixed elsewhere than on the sea. When war began, the United States possessed 16 frigates and sloops of war (the heavy and light cruisers of that day) against over 600 vessels of the British Navy. Even on the lakes, command of which was essential for a successful invasion of Canada, and where both sides must "start from scratch," nothing had been done to ensure naval control. Fearing the odium of war taxes, Congress had proposed to finance the war by loans; but since most of the country's ready capital was in New England and New England sentiment was largely antiwar and pro-British, the loans were never fully raised.

The Bettmann Archive

Andrew Jackson directs the American defense of New Orleans.

Plans for territorial conquest, North and South, quickly went awry. The desire of the South and the administration to seize the Floridas was frustrated by Northern opposition in Congress. Early attempts to invade Canada failed because of poor planning and poor generalship. The initial American plan, instead of concentrating on one point, such as Montreal, where communications to the west might have been cut, called for three simultaneous invasions—one directed at Montreal from Lake Champlain, one across the Niagara River at or near Buffalo, and a third across the Detroit River from Detroit. The third of these campaigns was the first to get under way and the first to collapse. Brig. Gen. William Hull, with a force of some 2,000 men, reached Detroit soon after the declaration of war. Thence he advanced into Canada and threatened the British post at Malden. Soon, however, he found that the British control of Lake Erie cut him off from his base in Ohio, while his rear was menaced by British and Indians who had taken Michilimackinac and came pouring south. Hull retreated to Detroit, where on Aug. 16, 1812, he surrendered the post and its garrison to the energetic British commander, Maj. Gen. Isaac Brock. On the preceding day Fort Dearborn (Chicago) had been surrendered and its garrison treacherously massacred by Indians in the process of evacuation. The entire Northwest was in British hands.

In October Maj. Gen. Stephen Van Rensselaer, commanding the New York militia and a small number of regulars on the Niagara, sent a part of his force across the river to attack Queenston, only to see it cut to pieces and the survivors captured by the enemy, while the remainder of the militia refused to go to the rescue. General Brock, victor over Hull, also commanded in this action, but paid for the victory with his life. In the following month, Maj. Gen. Henry Dearborn, senior officer in the United States Army, led a force of regulars and militia from Plattsburgh on Lake Champlain to the Canadian border. Farther than that the militia refused to advance, and the Army returned to winter quarters at Plattsburgh.

In 1813 Brig. Gen. William Henry Harrison avenged Hull's failure and recovered control of the Detroit area. This success was made possible by the naval victory of Master Commandant Oliver Hazard Perry, who had superintended the building of a small fleet at Erie, Pa., over the British squadron on Lake Erie (Sept. 10, 1813), giving the United States command of the lake. Harrison's army, ferried across the lake, overtook the retreating British on the Thames River (Oct. 5, 1813) and inflicted a severe defeat, in which the chief casualty was the famous Indian leader, Tecumseh. Elsewhere the second year of the war brought no important successes. A two-pronged campaign against Montreal, down the St. Lawrence and down the Richelieu, was brought to an inglorious end by minor defeats and the coming of winter. During a temporary naval supremacy on Lake Ontario American forces had taken York (Toronto) and inexcusably set fire to the Parliament building of Upper Canada. For this and for other needless acts of devastation by the Americans, the British took revenge in December. Crossing the Niagara River, they surprised and captured Fort Niagara, which they held until the end of the war, burned the villages of Black Rock and Buffalo, and laid waste the Niagara frontier from Lake Ontario to Lake Erie.

The year 1814 brought a new situation. Napoleon's defeat in Europe released thousands of veteran British troops for service in America. The problem for the United States became not the conquest of Canada but the defense of its own territory. Fortunately, capable officers had replaced the incompetents who had commanded the American armies of 1812 and 1813. In July a small army commanded by Maj. Gen. Jacob Brown and Brig. Gen. Winfield Scott crossed the Niagara River, defeated a British force at Chippawa or Chippewa (July 5, 1814), and fought a reinforced British Army to a standstill at Lundy's Lane (July 25, 1814), but got no farther. Early in September, 11,000 British troops commanded by Gen. Sir George Prevost invaded New York at the foot of Lake Champlain and advanced to Plattsburgh. Here on Sept. 11, 1814, the naval squadron covering Prevost's flank was annihilated by an American fleet skillfully commanded by Master-Commandant Thomas Macdonough. With his communications thus exposed, Prevost found it expedient to retreat to Canada.

Meanwhile, a British fleet and army ravaged the shores of Chesapeake Bay, scattered the militia defending Washington, D.C. (Battle of Bladensburg, Aug. 24, 1814), and burned the public buildings in the capital in retaliation for the American behavior at York. A subsequent attack on Baltimore was repulsed. The British fleet then convoyed an army to the mouth of the Mississippi for an attack on New Orleans. There, on Jan. 8, 1815 (two weeks after the signing of a peace treaty at Ghent), Maj. Gen. Andrew Jackson, with an army of regulars, volunteers, and Western militia, inflicted on the British under Maj. Gen. Sir Edward M. Pakenham, who lost his life in the battle, the severest military defeat of the war. While the British were thus foiled in their attempt to seize the mouth of the Mississippi, their agents in the Northwest had taken possession of the upper course of the river and were in full control of present-day Wisconsin and the northern part of Illinois.

While the war on land had, until its closing months, gone generally against the United States, American privateers had scoured the seas, taking hundreds of British prizes, and the American Navy had won honors in a series of notable single-ship actions on the Atlantic. The most famous of these were the victories of the *Constitution* over the *Guerrière* (Aug. 19, 1812), the *Constitution* over the *Java* (Dec. 29, 1812), and the *United States* over the *Macedonian* (Oct. 25, 1812). These were frigate actions. In the encounters of the smaller sloops of war, also, the advantage lay with the Americans. But there were victories on the British side, too (for example, the defeat and capture of the frigate *Chesapeake* by the *Shannon,* June 1, 1813), and in reality the American successes, while glorious in themselves and a tonic to a depressed morale, were but pinpricks to the dominant British Navy. British sea power, in fact, closed in upon the American ports and coasts with a progressively tighter blockade. Before the end of the war, nearly all the ships of the American Navy were either captured or bottled up in port, and American seaborne trade had disappeared from the oceans.

The Bettmann Archive

The *Constitution* (right) defeats the *Guerrière*, one of many events which make the War of 1812 famous in American naval annals.

End of the War.—A Russian offer of mediation, though rejected by Great Britain, led indirectly to the meeting of British and American commissioners in Ghent, Belgium, in August 1814. The British, who had thus far had the ad-

Brown Brothers

With the signing of the Treaty of Ghent in December 1814, the War of 1812 was officially ended.

vantage in the war, asked adjustments of the boundary line in their favor and the setting aside of a large area in the American Northwest for the permanent and exclusive use of the Indians. The Americans (John Quincy Adams, James A. Bayard, Henry Clay, Albert Gallatin, and Jonathan Russell), while rejecting British demands, asked neither territory nor concessions with regard to maritime rights; they asked merely a return to the status quo *ante bellum.* American victories during the fall, the reluctance of the British public to bear further war burdens, and the advice of the duke of Wellington persuaded the British government to drop its demands and accept the American proposal. A treaty on this basis, restoring territory occupied by either side, was signed Dec. 24, 1814, and unanimously approved by the United States Senate, Feb. 16, 1815.

Federalist New England, strongly pro-British in sentiment, had opposed the war as well as the commercial restrictions that preceded it. In the final months of the war this opposition came to a head in the Hartford Convention (q.v.), which brought together delegates from three New England states and from towns or counties in two others. The convention held potentialities of nullification or even disunion, but more conservative counsels prevailed, and the body went no further than to propose certain amendments to the federal Constitution designed to safeguard sectional interests. These proposals were forgotten in the general satisfaction that attended the termination of the war.

If judged by the Treaty of Ghent, the War of 1812 attained none of the objectives for which the United States had fought—neither territorial acquisitions nor acceptance of its theory of maritime rights. But not all the results appeared in the treaty. The war did break the power of the Indians in the Northwest and also (through Andrew Jackson's campaign of 1813–1814 against the Creeks) of those in the South. Thus it removed the grievance that had led to the demand for the acquisition of Canada, and paved the way for the purchase of the Floridas from Spain (1819). That there were no further disputes over blockades and impressments was the consequence, not of American valor, but of the end of the European war and the long peace that followed. The ending of these troubles, for whatever cause, and the American victories in the last six months of the war, overshadowed in popular consciousness the earlier defeats and humiliations. A feeling that the young nation had successfully defended its rights produced a new spirit of national unity, self-satisfaction, and patriotism.

See also separate articles on principal battles of the War of 1812, and biographies of leading military and naval commanders.

Bibliography

Brannan, John, ed., *Official Letters of the Military and Naval Officers of the United States, During the War with Great Britain in the Years 1812–1815* (1823; reprint, Ayer 1971).

Carr, Albert H. A., *The Coming of War: An Account of the Remarkable Events Leading to the War of 1812* (Viking 1960).

Dudley, William S., and Crawford, Michael J., eds., *The Naval War of 1812: A Documentary History*, Vol. 1 (USGPO 1985).

Everest, Allan S., *The War of 1812 in the Champlain Valley* (Syracuse Univ. Press 1981).

Garitee, J. R., *The Republic's Private Navy: The American Privateering Business as Practiced by Baltimore during the War of 1812* (Mystic Seaport Mus. Pub. 1977).

Pratt, Julius W., *Expansionists of 1812* (P. Smith 1925).

Pratt, Julius W., *"Fur Trade Strategy and the American Left Flank in the War of 1812" (American Historical Review* (January 1935).

Smith, Dwight L., *The War of 1812* (Garland 1984).

Sugden, John, *Tecumseh's Last Stand* (Univ. of Okla. Press 1985).

Taylor, George R., ed., *The War of 1812: Past Justifications and Present Interpretations* (1963; reprint, Greenwood Press 1980).

JULIUS W. PRATT,
Professor of American History, Emeritus, University of Buffalo.

WAR OF 1870. See FRANCO-PRUSSIAN WAR.

WAR OF INDEPENDENCE, American. See AMERICAN REVOLUTION, THE.

WAR OF THE PACIFIC (also known as the **CHILE-PERUVIAN WAR**), a conflict waged by Chile against an alliance of Bolivia and Peru, and ending in complete victory for the Chileans. Hostilities began in 1879 and ended in 1881, although guerrilla activity continued for two more years and peace was not finally concluded until 1884. The war grew out of a dispute between Chile and Bolivia over nitrate deposits in the latter's Atacama Province, where an export tax was imposed on Chilean exploiters in 1878. When a Chilean company operating at Antofagasta refused to pay the tariff, the Bolivian government ordered confiscation of the property in February 1879. Chile responded by dispatching a warship with troops to seize the port of Antofagasta, which it accomplished on February 14. Bolivia declared war on March 1. Peru, which had a secret alliance (of 1873) with Bolivia, now threatened, and on April 5 Chile declared war upon the allies.

The Bolivian and Peruvian presidents, commanding their respective troops, enjoyed some initial successes, but by the end of 1879 the Chilean fleet had overcome the Peruvian, thereby gaining control of the sea. On land the Chilean forces were increasingly successful, and their decisive victory over allied troops at Tacna, Peru (May 26, 1880), knocked Bolivia out of the conflict. Finally, on Jan. 17, 1881, a Chilean army under Gen. Manuel Baquedano captured Lima and forced Peru to sue for peace.

As the fruits of her victory Chile took from

Bolivia her access to the Pacific Ocean and from Peru the coast north of the Bolivian possessions to and including the districts of Arica and Tacna (the latter reverted to Peru in 1929). Peru obtained the evacuation of Lima and made peace by the Treaty of Ancón in 1883, and Bolivia by the Treaty of Valparaiso in the following year, although its terms were not made final until 1904.

See also CHILE–*History* (Liberal Era).

WAR OF THE ROSES. See ROSES, WARS OF THE.

WAR RELIEF. See DISPLACED PERSONS; LEND-LEASE; RED CROSS.

WAR REPARATIONS. See REPARATIONS.

WARANGAL, wŭ′rəng-gəl, district, city, and former Hindu kingdom, India, of the Telangana region of the State of Andhra Pradesh. As a district of the now-defunct State of Hyderabad, Warangal comprised 8,139 square miles; but as a part of Andhra, to which it was ceded in 1956, its area has undergone a net reduction to 4,984 square miles, due to the separation of Khamman District in the east while a part of Nalgonda District was added in the west. The area is a rather open plain, with numerous isolated rocky hills, and fertility is generally not high. Tank irrigation is widespread, supplementing the moderate rainfall (averaging about 40 inches annually). Rice and jowar are the chief grains, and peanuts are the main cash crop.

Warangal city, the district headquarters, is near the site of the Hindu kingdom of the same name which lasted from the mid-12th through the early 14th century. Its present importance, however, is due to rather recent growth. The only true city in eastern Telangana, it is primarily a commercial center which also manufactures excellent carpets and has handloom- and mill-cotton and leather industries. Pop. (1961 provisional) city 156,163; district 1,545,750.

JOSEPH E. SCHWARTZBERG.

WARBECK, wôr′bĕk, **Perkin,** Walloon impostor, pretender to the English throne in the reign of Henry VII: b. Tournai (Tournay), Flanders, about 1474; d. London, England, Nov. 23, 1499. The son of Jehan de Warbecque, a local official, he was taken to Portugal by the wife of Sir Edward Brampton, a Yorkist partisan. Later he sailed to Ireland in the service of a Breton merchant, landing at Cork—clad in his master's costly silks—in 1491. The excited townspeople concluded that here must be the son of Edward IV's brother George, Duke of Clarence. Warbeck at first denied the identity, and also that he was a son of Richard III, as some had supposed; but he finally was prevailed upon by the dukes of Desmond and Kildare to dissemble the role of Richard, duke of York and younger brother of the murdered boy king, Edward V.

In March 1492, Warbeck set forth his claim in a letter to James IV of Scotland. The pretender was recognized by Charles VIII of France, who, however, had to dismiss him from his realm after the peace of Étapes (November 1492), and by Emperor Maximilian I, who provided him with money and soldiers for attempted invasions of Kent, England, and Waterford, Ireland (1495). He also was received in Flanders by Margaret, dowager duchess of Burgundy and sister of Edward IV, as her nephew.

Warbeck next went to Scotland, where James credited his claims, and gave him his cousin, Catherine Gordon, in marriage. At length, Warbeck landed with a force in Cornwall in 1497, but, after gaining some support and advancing to Exeter, was taken prisoner by noblemen loyal to Henry. Confessing in full his imposture before the king, he was dealt with lightly at first; however, after an abortive escape from the Tower of London, and his implication in intrigue with Edward, earl of Warwick, he was hanged on the gallows at Tyburn in 1499.

WARBLE FLY. See OX-BOT.

WARBLER, wôr′blər, a small, insectivorous songbird. The name "warbler" often is loosely applied to birds of quite distinct families, but in ornithology the term is restricted to two families: the Old World warblers (Sylviidae), and the New World or wood warblers (Parulidae). The two groups are not related and are far removed in bird classifications. Some authorities consider the Old World warblers to be closely related to the Old World flycatchers and the wood warblers to be near relatives of the tanagers.

Old World Warblers.—The Old World warblers are the more numerous of the two groups with well over 300 species, compared with about 110 for the wood warblers. Some authorities include some American species (mentioned below) among the Old World warblers, but only one typical species, the arctic warbler (*Phylloscopus borealis*), has extended its range to the New World. It is widespread throughout northern Eurasia but has invaded western Alaska, returning after the breeding season, however, to the ancestral winter quarters of the species in southeastern Asia.

The American birds which sometimes are included among the Old World warblers are the kinglets and gnatcatchers and their allies. The kinglets (genus *Regulus*) are not strictly American, as their four species are divided between the New and Old Worlds—two in North America and the others in Eurasia and north Africa. The kinglets seem to be closely related to the Old World warblers, but the affinities of the gnat-

The ovenbird (*Seiurus aurocapillus*) seldom takes wing.

Allan D. Cruickshank from National Audubon Society

catchers and their allies are more uncertain. They are restricted to the Americas, and most authorities believe that they constitute a distinct subfamily, the Polioptilinae, with about 10 species. The best known is the blue-gray gnat-catcher (*Polioptila caerulea*) of the open woodlands. It is a tiny and lively sprite, barely over four inches in size with a long tail which it continually waves about, the tail being longer than the body.

The Old World warblers, in the strict sense, are divided into many genera, but, despite their diversity, almost all the species are small birds, varying from about 3½ to 6 inches in length, with a thin and relatively long bill and a very plain plumage. The pigments are never bright, the prevailing coloration being grayish, greenish, buffy, or brown, with the back having blackish streaks in the species of the grasslands.

The species which inhabit temperate regions are the most homogenous and belong to a relatively few genera which are abundant in species; nearly 100 species belong to only about six or seven genera. The most numerous of these, as well as one of the most typical of all genera, is *Cisticola*, with 40 species. All but 2 of these species are restricted to Africa, where they inhabit grasslands. Of the other 2 species, one ranges from China and India to Australia, and the other, the common fantail warbler (*Cisticola juncidis*), is one of the most widespread of all birds. It breeds throughout most of Africa and from southern Europe eastward to Arabia, India, China, Japan, and northern Australia. The willow or leaf warblers (genus *Phylloscopus*) consist of 30 species which inhabit the wooded regions of temperate and northern Eurasia.

In the larger genera, such as *Cisticola* and *Phylloscopus*, the species tend to resemble each other so very closely in appearance that they are difficult to identify in the field by sight. Even specimens in collections are often misidentified. In life, however, species which inhabit the same regions have very different call notes and songs. In Europe, for instance, the contrast between the songs of the willow warbler (*Phylloscopus trochilus*) and the chiffchaff (*P. collybita*) are so great that the two birds seem to belong to different families, though they are virtually indistinguishable in appearance. The song of the willow warbler is a very beautiful regular musical phrase, while the chiffchaff repeats endlessly and irregularly the two notes which gave it its name.

American redstart (*Setophaga ruticilla*) feeding its young.

Allan D. Cruickshank from National Audubon Society

The genus *Sylvia*, with about 20 species, is another well-known genus, best represented in Europe where its species inhabit gardens and open woodlands. Some of these warblers are considered by many to be the most accomplished singers of all birds—the song consisting of a remarkably rich and varied musical warble without discordant notes. Other genera, such as *Acrocephalus*, inhabit only reedbeds.

A famous member of the family, the well-named tailorbird (*Orthotomus sutorius*) of India and China, builds a most remarkable nest. The bird selects large and tough leaves and actually sews two or more together by piercing their edges with its long and very sharp beak. A strand of some cotton fiber, tough cobweb, or silk obtained from a cocoon is drawn through the holes and knotted on the outside. The bird then builds the actual nest in the aerial cradle which it has so cleverly fashioned. It is said that some leaves are so well and regularly stitched that it is hard to believe that the work was not done by a human.

New World Warblers (Wood Warblers).— The wood warblers inhabit woodlands, as the name indicates, but only in a very broad sense: their habitat varies from canebrakes or scattered bushes in abandoned fields to the dense, unbroken coniferous forests of the north. Some inhabit swamps, others the banks of streams; some seldom leave the forest floor, while others frequent only the treetops. Habitat, behavior, and coloration vary so much that to describe the wood warblers adequately would require a good-sized book.

The three well-known and interesting species selected here differ widely in their habitat and behavior. The American redstart (*Setophaga ruticilla*) is typically arboreal and one of the most handsome of all warblers. It is about 5½ inches in size. The male is black and white with large orange-red areas on the sides of the breast and on the wing and tail; the female is gray, green, and white with bright yellow areas where the male is red. It is an active bird, constantly diving and whirling in the air in pursuit of an insect, or, when not feeding, coquettishly pirouetting about on a branch, gracefully spreading its tail and wings to display the bright markings. The American redstart breeds from Alaska and Canada south to Alabama, Louisiana, Utah, and Oregon, and winters in the West Indies and from Mexico to northern Brazil. Other arboreal and handsome species will come to mind, especially in the large genus *Dendroica*.

The ovenbird (*Seiurus aurocapillus*) is the favorite warbler of many bird watchers. Six inches in length, it is more heavybodied than the other wood warblers and, together with the water thrushes, has longer legs. It inhabits the forest floor, from which it very seldom flies up, and where it builds a domed nest of leaves and fibers. Most of its time is spent daintily walking about, stepping over dead leaves and twigs in search of food. The sexes are alike, olive green above with an orange crown, and white below, streaked with black. The ovenbird breeds from Canada south to Colorado and some southern states, and winters in the southeastern United States, West Indies, and from Mexico to northern South America.

Allan D. Cruickshank from National Audubon Society

Louisiana water thrush (*Seiurus motacilla*) over its nest.

The Louisiana water thrush (*Seiurus motacilla*) is related to the ovenbird, which it resembles in size and coloration with the exception of the orange crown; but it is more slender, less deliberate, and occupies a very different habitat. It frequents only the banks of streams, preferably small and running, to glean its food from the edge of the water. It continually teeters as it walks, and resembles a miniature wagtail more than it does a wood warbler; the ovenbird resembling more a tiny thrush. The Louisiana water thrush breeds from southern Ontario and the north central and northeastern United States to parts of Texas, Louisiana, Alabama, and Georgia, and winters in the West Indies and from Mexico to northern South America.

CHARLES VAURIE,
Assistant Curator
The American Museum of Natural History

Bibliography

Bent, Arthur C., *Life Histories of North American Wood Warblers,* 2 vols. (Dover 1963).
Carlson, Carl W., and others, *Sutton's Warbler: A Critical Review and Summation of Present Data* (Audubon Naturalists Soc. 1981).
Harrison, Hal H., *Wood Warbler's World* (Simon & Schuster 1986).
Walkinshaw, Lawrence H., Kirtland's Warbler (Cranbrook Inst. of Science 1983).

WARBURG, Ger. vär'bo͝ork, Eng. wôr'bûrg, **Otto Heinrich,** German biochemist: b. Freiburg, Baden, Germany, Oct. 8, 1883; d. West Berlin, Aug. 1, 1970.

Warburg took his degree in chemistry under Emil Fischer in 1906 and was graduated doctor of medicine in 1911. From 1931 he served as director of the newly constructed Kaiser Wilhelm Institute for Cell Physiology (since 1953, the Max Planck Institute for Cell Physiology), in Berlin-Dahlem. Under his guidance this institute achieved world leadership in technological competence and biochemical achievement.

Warburg's scientific interests centered around three fundamental biological phenomena: cellular respiration, photosynthesis, and cancer. The impact of his contributions in all of these areas is difficult to overestimate. In 1931 he received the Nobel Prize in physiology and medicine for his identification of the oxygen-activating respiratory enzyme as an iron porphyrin derivative. Subsequently he discovered and characterized the pyridine nucleotide dehydrogenases and flavoproteins as members of the respiratory chain, and worked out the mechanism whereby the energy released in the oxidation of foodstuffs may be conserved and transferred for use in synthesis and growth. The mechanism of cellular respiration provided the first explanation of the chemical mechanism of enzyme action.

In photosynthesis, Warburg's main effort was directed toward an understanding of the mechanism of the process. He commenced these studies in 1920 with his father, Emil Warburg (1846–1931), a distinguished physicist and a pioneer in the measurement of energy yields of photochemical reactions. The details of the energetics of photosynthesis can now be understood as a result of Otto Warburg's work in collaboration with Dean Burk; and the unraveling of the chemical mechanism was able to get under way, greatly facilitated by the solution of the energetics problem.

Warburg's investigation of the metabolism of cancer cells led him to the view, which was subsequently confirmed, that cancer cells exist in the body as facultative anaerobes, capable of growth without oxygen, whereas the normal body cells are obligate aerobes, incapable of anaerobic growth. This discovery was expected to have far-reaching results in aiding the understanding of—and ability to control—neoplastic growth.

In the face of the prevalent academic tendency to berate "mere technicians," Warburg described himself as a technician, thus revealing the great importance he attached to proper and adequate experimental procedures. Research laboratories everywhere have adopted his manometric and optical techniques—a tribute to their quality and usefulness. Warburg contributed to biochemistry, however, not only as a master technician, but also as a highly original thinker. His theories, daring in scope and far in advance of contemporary thought, have repeatedly turned out to be correct. He was in the forefront of scientific controversy throughout most of his life, a fearless—and peppery—champion of truth.

BIRGIT VENNESLAND,
Department of Biochemistry, The University of Chicago.

WARBURTON, wôr'bər-tən, **William,** English prelate: b. Newark, Nottinghamshire, England, Dec. 24, 1698; d. Gloucester, June 7, 1779. Following a grammar school education, he abandoned the legal profession and took holy orders in the Church of England (1727). A prolific and polemical writer, he became involved in innumerable theological and literary controversies. He gained the favor of the court by his *The Alliance Between Church and State* (1736), in which he strove to justify the degree of religious toleration granted by the established church in 1689, and by his *The Divine Legation of Moses* (2 vols., 1737–41), in which he upheld the divine origin of the Mosaic law.

Ecclesiastical preferment for Warburton followed rapidly. He became chaplain to the prince of Wales (1738), preacher to Lincoln's Inn (1746), prebendary of Gloucester (1753), a royal chaplain (1754), prebendary of Durham (1755), dean of Bristol (1757), and bishop of Gloucester (1760). Meanwhile, his defense (1739) against Jean Pierre de Crousaz' criticism of the *Essay on Man* earned him the friendship of Alexander Pope, who made Warburton his literary executor (1744). In 1747, Warburton published an annotated edition of William Shakespeare's works that was severely criticized for its arrogance and its lack of scholarship. His attack on Methodism in *The Doctrine of Grace* (2 vols., 1762) evoked an effective reply from John Wesley.

ALLAN M. FRASER.

WARD, wôrd, **Aaron Montgomery,** American businessman: b. Chatham, N. J., Feb. 17, 1843; d. Highland Park, Ill., Dec. 7, 1913. As a child he moved with his family to Niles, Mich., where he attended public school until the age of 14. After working at a number of jobs, he became a traveling salesman for a dry goods firm in St. Louis. Selling to the rural market acquainted him with the problems of farmers, whose income from produce sold at wholesale prices was often inadequate to pay for consumer goods and farm equipment at retail prices. While working in Chicago for another dry goods house, he conceived the idea of a mail order business to serve the rural trade, buying in large quantities for cash and selling for cash at low markups. In 1872 with a capital of $2,400, of which $800 was furnished by his partner, George R. Thorne, he founded Montgomery Ward and Company.

The company's first catalog was a single-sheet price list of a small selection of hardware items. Ward's judgment in choosing merchandise and his offer of a money-back guarantee were important factors in the firm's early success. In 1874, after the National Grange had begun to stock its retail cooperatives through Montgomery Ward, the line of merchandise was greatly expanded, and by 1876 the catalog had grown to a 150-page illustrated book. By 1891 the company was grossing more than $1 million annually, and at the time of Ward's death annual sales totaled about $40 million. Ward retired as active head of the firm in 1901.

WARD, Artemas, American Revolutionary general: b. Shrewsbury, Mass., Nov. 26, 1727; d. there, Oct. 28, 1800. After graduating from Harvard (1748), he held several public offices in Shrewsbury and represented his town in the Massachusetts General Court, where he regularly opposed British authority. During the French and Indian War he served in the provincial militia, rising to the rank of colonel.

In 1774, Ward was appointed brigadier general by the provincial congress and in May 1775 was made commander in chief of the Massachusetts troops. As a major general in the Continental Army he directed the siege of Boston until George Washington took command in July 1775.

Ward resigned from the army in March 1776 on account of poor health. He returned to political life and served as president of the Massachusetts executive council, as a delegate to the Continental Congress, and as a Federalist congressman.

WARD, Artemus (real name CHARLES FARRAR BROWNE), American humorist: b. near Waterford, Me., April 26, 1834; d. Southampton, England, March 6, 1867. He left school at the age of 13, when his father died, and worked 10 years as a printer's apprentice and typesetter in New England and the Middle West. In 1857 he joined the staff of the Cleveland *Plain Dealer* and began writing the sketches that established him as one of the most popular humorists of the mid-19th century. Under the signature of Artemus Ward, the supposed manager of a traveling carnival show, he wrote of current events and contemporary institutions, poking fun at insincerity and sentimentality. The sketches, written in a kind of New England dialect with comic misspellings, bad grammar, and intentionally atrocious puns, caught the public fancy and made Artemus Ward's name a household staple throughout the United States.

In 1859, Ward joined the staff of *Vanity Fair,* a humorous journal in New York created as a rival to the British *Punch.* His continued success induced him to take to the lecture circuit. Ward's fame as a lecturer was immediate and far exceeded that of his writings. A tall, lean figure on the lecture platform, he delivered his material in a bemused, self-deprecating style characterized by understatement and folksy common sense. He was a master of the long pause, during which he seemed to grope painfully for the right word and be delighted when he found it. Among the most popular of his lecture-sketches were *Babes in the Wood, Among the Mormons,* and *The Shakers.*

Ward went to England in 1866, became a regular contributor to *Punch,* and enjoyed great success as a lecturer. He died of tuberculosis at the height of his career.

His chief works in book form include *Artemus Ward: His Book* (1862); *Artemus Ward: His Travels* (1865); and *Artemus Ward in London* (1867).

WARD, Barbara, English economist and journalist: b. York, England, May 23, 1914; d. Lodsworth, England, May 31, 1981. She was educated at Somerville College, Oxford, where she took an honors degree in 1935 and was an extension lecturer from 1936 to 1939. In 1939 she joined the staff of the *Economist,* Britain's leading financial weekly, becoming its foreign editor in 1940. In the period after World War II she earned recognition throughout Europe and in the United States, where she often lectured, as one of the most influential writers and commentators on economic and political subjects.

Her publications include *The International Share-Out* (1938), a study of the colonial system; *The West at Bay* (1948); *Faith and Freedom* (1954); *Five Ideas That Change the World* (1959); *India and the West* (1961); and *The Rich Nations and the Poor Nations* (1962). She was an early advocate of European economic union and urged the establishment of a broad Western policy to counter that of the Communist bloc in dealing with emergent nationalism in underdeveloped areas. Accordingly, she stressed the importance of basing that policy on the same principles of social justice that had tended to mitigate extremes of wealth and poverty in the industrial democracies of the West.

In 1950 she married Commander (later Sir) Robert Jackson, an Australian. She was created a Dame of the British Empire in 1974 and, as Baroness Jackson of Lodworth, a life peeress in 1976.

WARD, Frederick Townsend, American military leader in China: b. Salem, Mass., Nov. 29, 1831; d. Ningpo, China, Sept. 21, 1862. From 1848 he led the life of a military and commercial adventurer, engaging in various wars and trading schemes. He served under William Walker in one of the latter's filibustering expeditions to Central America and with the French Army during the Crimean War. In 1860 he was in China, where the Taiping Rebellion was in progress. There he gathered a band of adventurers of several nationalities and approached the local Chinese authorities in Shanghai with an offer to capture the nearby town of Sungkiang in return for a large sum of money. The town was held by about 10,000 rebels, but, after an initial failure, Ward cleared the rebels from the Shanghai areas and thus made good his promise and received his prize.

He then set about clearing the country around Shanghai of rebels, earning a monetary reward for each victory. By early 1862, he had organized and drilled three regiments of native troops and, in August of that year, used them to drive a much larger force of Taipings from the town of Tsingpu, the last rebel stronghold within a 30-mile radius of Shanghai. He was made a mandarin of the highest rank and was appointed admiral general by the emperor. Several weeks later, however, at a time when he was making arrangements to return to the United States to take part in the Civil War, he was mortally wounded in a skirmish near Ningpo. The Chinese accorded him a gigantic state funeral and erected a memorial temple in his honor at Sungkiang. His admirably trained and disciplined military force afterward became the nucleus of Charles George ("Chinese") Gordon's famous "Ever Victorious Army."

WARD, MRS. Humphry. See WARD, MARY AUGUSTA.

WARD, James, English psychologist and philosopher: b. Hull, England, Jan. 27, 1843; d. Cambridge, March 4, 1925. He studied theology in England and continued his education in Berlin and Göttingen. At the latter university he studied under the philosopher Rudolf Hermann Lotze, whose influence on him was lasting. After preaching for a year at a Congregationalist church in Cambridge, Ward turned from formal religion, entered Trinity College, and delved further into psychology. After 1894 the emphasis of his work was in philosophy, which he treated in *Naturalism and Agnosticism* (1899) and *The Realm of Ends, or Pluralism and Theism* (1911), based on his Gifford lectures. His views are also summarized in *Psychological Principles* (1913) and *Essays in Philosophy* (1927). In addition to Lotze, the ideas of Gottfried Wilhelm Leibniz and Charles Darwin's views on evolution helped to shape Ward's views. From 1897 until his death he occupied the chair of mental philosophy and logic at Cambridge University.

WARD, John Quincy Adams, American sculptor: b. Urbana, Ohio, June 29, 1830; d. New York, N.Y., May 1, 1910. At the age of 19 he entered the Brooklyn studio of Henry Kirke Brown, the sculptor, almost as much as helper as student. Here he remained seven years, among other things working on, and in, Brown's noted equestrian statue of George Washington. Ward said, "I spent more time inside that horse than Jonah did inside the whale." His ultimate reward was to people various towns of the eastern seaboard with statues, statuettes, and busts. His *Indian Hunter* (1868) in Central Park, his masterly *Washington* (1883) on the steps of the Subtreasury, and the pediment (1903) of the New York Stock Exchange are among his many works in New York City. His *Henry Ward Beecher* (1891) is in front of Borough Hall, Brooklyn, and his fine equestrian statue of Maj. Gen. Winfield Scott Hancock (which was finished by Paul Bartlett) stands in Fairmount Park, Philadelphia.

WALLACE BROCKWAY
Bollingen Foundation

WARD, Lester Frank, American sociologist: b. Joliet, Ill., June 18, 1841; d. Washington, D.C., April 18, 1913. Educated at Columbian University (now George Washington University), where he took a law degree in 1871, he became a geologist and later a paleontologist in the United States Geological Survey. His contributions to the natural sciences were significant, but it was as a pioneer in the development of modern American sociology that he is remembered. A staunch advocate of the theory of evolution, he also saw social development as deriving from society's deliberate striving for the improvement of the human condition, and he urged the importance of universal education in both the physical and social sciences for achieving an era of progress and enlightment. Ward made a great impact on sociology with his *Dynamic Sociology* (1883). Other of his publications in this field are *The Psychic Factors of Civilization* (1893), *Outlines of Sociology* (1898), *Pure Sociology* (1903), *Applied Sociology* (1904), which explains Ward's ideas of "social telesis," a sociocracy and social planning, and the six-volume *Glimpses of the Cosmos* (1913–18), which is an autobiographical presentation of his beliefs. From 1906 he was professor of sociology at Brown.

WARD, Lynd Kendall, American illustrator: b. Chicago, Ill., June 26, 1905. He grew up in Boston and was educated at Teachers College, Columbia University. At Leipzig, Germany, he spent a year at the National Academy for Graphic Arts studying etching under Alois Kolb, lithography under George Mathéy, and wood engraving under Hans Mueller. In 1929, Ward published *God's Man,* a novel consisting entirely of woodcuts, and followed this with *Madman's Drum* (1930), *Wild Pilgrimage* (1932), *Prelude to a Million Years* (1933), *Song Without Words* (1936), and *Vertigo* (1937)—all published in New York City. At the same time he made numerous illustrations in lithography, wood engraving, watercolor, oils, and crayon for children's books and trade books, as well as lecturing on his work.

H. D. HALE
"Art News" Magazine

WARD, Mary Augusta (nee ARNOLD; better known as MRS. HUMPHRY WARD), English novelist and social worker: b. Hobart, Tasmania, Australia, June 11, 1851; d. London, England, March 24, 1920. The granddaughter of Dr. Thomas Arnold of Rugby, and a niece of Matthew Arnold, she was married in 1872 to Thomas Humphry Ward (1845–1926), an editor. Her father, Thomas (1823–1900), a colonial school administrator, returned to England in 1856 after becoming a Roman Catholic (he later served as professor of English literature at a new Catholic university in Dublin), and Mary was raised and educated in England. From 1865 until removing to London in 1880, she lived at Oxford, and her long residence there undoubtedly inclined her toward the ethical concerns which permeated her writing.

Mrs. Ward published a children's story, *Millie and Olly,* in 1881, but her first important literary work was a worthy translation (1884) of Henri Frederic Amiel's *Journal Intime.* In 1888 appeared the book which brought her immediate and worldwide fame. The novel *Robert Elsmere,* which enjoyed an immense sale and was translated into several languages, expressed her strongly held conviction that Christianity could best be served by minimizing its mystical qualities and striving toward fulfillment of the gospel's social ideas. Among her many novels which skillfully delineated social personalities were: *The History of David Grieve* (1892), *Marcella* (1894), *Sir George Tressaday* (1896), *Helbeck of Bannisdale* (1898), *Eleanor* (1900), *Lady Rose's Daughter* (1903), *The Marriage of William Ashe* (1905), *Fenwick's Career* (1906), *The Testing of Diana Mallory* (1908), *Daphne* (1909), *Canadian Born* (1910), *The Case of Richard Meynell* (1911), *Delia Blanchflower* (1915), and *The War and Elizabeth* (1918).

Mrs. Ward is well remembered also for her outstanding achievements as a social worker. In 1890 she founded a settlement house in a poor district of London, and from this effort grew the famous Passmore Edwards Settlement. Here Mrs. Ward expended great amounts of energy and thought; among her significant contributions was the introduction of "children's play hours," a movement which became an integral part of London recreational center programs. *A Writer's Recollections* (1918) contains autobiographical material; and her daughter, Janet Penrose Trevelyan, published *The Life of Mrs. Humphry Ward* in 1923.

WARD, Nathaniel, Anglo-American divine and pamphleteer: b. Haverhill, Suffolk, England, c. 1578; d. Shenfield, Essex, October 1652. The son of a Puritan minister, he was educated at Emmanuel College, Cambridge, graduating in 1599. For at least a decade he practiced law; but about 1618 he took holy orders, serving until 1624 as a British chaplain in Prussia, later as a curate in London (1626–1628), and finally as rector of Stondon Massey, Essex (1628–1633), until removed by Archbishop William Laud for his ardent Puritanism.

Ward sought haven in Massachusetts, and in 1634 became co-pastor at Agawam (Ipswich). Retiring after two years, he was called upon to help draft the first Massachusetts code of laws, known as the *Body of Liberties* (q.v., adopted 1641), for whose influential system of civil safeguards and procedures he is said to have been primarily responsible. He was also active in formulating the 1648 code. By 1647, Ward himself was again in England, and from 1648 until the time of his death he held a parish at Shenfield.

Several Puritan pamphlets by Ward appeared after his return, but none has the fame of the manuscript he carried back for publication. The title was seriously racy: *The Simple Cobler of Aggawam in America. Willing to help 'mend his Native Country, lamentably tattered, both in the upper-Leather and sole, with all the honest stitches he can take* (London 1647). In it Ward threaded verbal inventions against both the frippery of "nugiperous Gentledames" and the "gay-nothings" of the new "Phrantasticks" who thought they had "discovered the Nor-west passage to Heaven." No man for Roger Williams' tolerance, Ward gave dissenters "free Liberty to keep away from us." Five editions and a parody appeared within the year. Ward remains one of the most readable early colonial writers.

NORMAN HOLMES PEARSON
Associate Professor of English
Yale University

WARD, Wilfrid Philip, English Roman Catholic author and apologist: b. Ware, Hertfordshire, England, Jan. 2, 1856; d. London, April 9, 1916. The son of the Roman Catholic theologian William George Ward (q.v.), he was educated at Ushaw College, Durham, and the Gregorian University in Rome, and became a lecturer at the former in 1890.

In contrast to the religious extremism of his father, Wilfrid's position in church matters was a more liberal one, and he exerted a stabilizing influence on fellow Catholics engaged in the great debate over Modernism (q.v.). As a writer his manifest ability lay in the field of biography. He produced the *Life and Times of Cardinal Wiseman* (1897) and a superb *Life of Cardinal Newman* (1912). Considered to be equally valuable is a two-volume work which traced his father's role as a leader in the ideological upheaval that had taken place at Oxford earlier in the century: *William George Ward and the Oxford Movement* (1889) and *William George Ward and the Catholic Revival* (1893).

WARD, William George, English Roman Catholic theologian: b. London, England, March 21, 1812; d. there, July 6, 1882. He entered Christ Church, Oxford, and was elected fellow at Balliol in 1834. After taking holy orders, he lectured in mathematics and soon became a strong influence in Oxford life. Joining the Oxford Movement in 1838, he became one of its most forceful spokesmen, and stoutly defended in two pamphlets John Henry Newman's momentous *Tract XC* (1841), in which Newman argued in behalf of Roman Catholic doctrine.

Ward's most famous work, *The Ideal of a Christian Church* (1884), carried his attack on Anglican attitudes to its furthest point, and resulted in a motion of censure by Oxford authorities which failed only because of a technicality. He was degraded from his university degrees, however, resigned his post, and in 1845 was received into the Roman Catholic Church, along with Newman and other Tractarians. Ward lectured in moral philosophy at St. Edmund's College, Ware, in 1851–1858, and edited the *Dublin Review* (1863–1878), in which he contended vigorously on behalf of ultramontane principles. These articles were collected as *Essays on the Philosophy of Theism* (1884). A two-volume study of Ward and the Oxford Movement was written by his son, the author Wilfrid Philip Ward (q.v.).

See also OXFORD MOVEMENT.

WARD, in law, a minor or incompetent person placed legally under the care of a guardian or court. A minor may become a ward simply by reason of infancy or because of delinquency, dependency, or neglect. Court-appointed guardians may be necessary as well for other persons considered unable to care for themselves or manage their own property, such as those mentally incapacitated or insane, habitual drunkards, spendthrifts, and, in a few jurisdictions, physically disabled persons. Generally, a friend or relative petitions the court on behalf of an incompetent, but voluntary application for wardship also is recognized. The court may appoint a guardian of the person to supervise control, care, and education of the ward; a guardian of the property charged with protecting the ward's estate; or both. A special guardian to represent the ward in litigation also may be chosen. Wardship of a child terminates at majority, or in some instances at the time of marriage.

See also GUARDIAN.

ALAN MATHESON.

WARDEN, wôr'dən, a title applied to certain executive or supervisory officials entrusted with duties which imply wardship or guardianship. In the United States, it is applied to such public officers as game wardens, who enforce the game laws; port wardens, who are harbor officers; and prison wardens, the chief administrative officers in penitentiaries. In Connecticut, it is also the title of the chief executive officer of a borough.

In the Protestant Episcopal Church, the churchwardens are two parochial officers, chosen annually at Easter vestries, one by the minister and one by the parishioners. Their duties are to protect the church building and its appurtenances, to superintend the ceremonies of divine worship, and generally to act as the legal representatives of the parish.

In England the heads of several colleges at Oxford are known as wardens. Certain officers of the crown or of the royal household are also known by that title.

WARDEN, The, a short novel published in 1855, which quietly announced the arrival of Anthony Trollope (q.v.) as a major new writer in a decade dominated by a galaxy that included William Thackeray, Charles Dickens, George Eliot, and Gustave Flaubert. Followed in 1857 by *Barchester Towers*, it inaugurated a series of six novels (generally called "The Chronicles of Barsetshire") dealing with clerical life in an English cathedral town. Trollope said that the idea for *The Warden* came to him as he stood on the bridge at Salisbury looking at the cathedral. *The Warden* and *Barchester Towers* are so closely linked in characters, story, and setting that they form a continuous novel in two parts; yet each is capable of an individual existence.

Nathaniel Hawthorne correctly praised the novels for their human nature. English readers were intrigued with their clerical setting and characters, and delighted to find in the bishop's palace and in a cathedral town a group of human, flesh-and-blood men and women possessing all the worldly frailties and concerns of ordinary mortals. It is this preoccupation with recognizable people that gives such freshness to the novels in their historic setting.

In a spirit of kindly but urbane comedy, with occasional flashes of irony, Trollope tells the story of the Rev. Septimus Harding, the kindly and gentle warden of an ancient charitable hospital who is accused by the reformers of exploitation of the legacy. The novel unfolds a cast of characters, whom we meet in later books, as the warden wrestles with and finally resolves his difficult problems. The central situation is based on an actual case widely discussed in the newspapers of the day.

HARLAN HATCHER,
President, The University of Michigan.

WARDHA, wŭrd'hä, district, town, and river, India, in Maharashtra State. The district, split off from Nagpur in 1862, comprises 2,429 square miles. It occupies an undulating tract along the northeast flank of the Wardha River in the eastern rimland of the Deccan lavas. The river flows southeast to join the Penganga. The fertile soil and the 40-inch annual precipitation are well suited to the growing of cotton. Jowar, a sorghum, is the chief staple crop. According to the 1951 census, agriculture supported 65 percent of the population. The Marathi-speaking district was ceded in 1956 by Hindi-speaking Madhya Pradesh to a then bilingual Bombay State and became, in turn, a part of the newly constituted unilingual State of Maharashtra in 1960.

The town of Wardha is the headquarters and chief commercial center for the district. A fairly important rail junction, it has a major cotton mart and is a center for cotton handloom and other handicraft industries. Mahatma Gandhi made his headquarters here for a time, and Sevagram Ashram (four miles east-southeast), which he founded in 1936, continues to function as a Gandhian training center for village workers. Pop. (1951) city 39,827; district (1961 provisional) 631,367.

JOSEPH E. SCHWARTZBERG.

WARD'S ISLAND, wôrdz, island, New York. Owned by New York City, it lies in the East River, northeast of the borough of Manhattan, between Randall's Island, to the north, and Welfare Island to the south, marking the western boundary of Hell Gate. It is crossed by the Triborough Bridge. The island, which has an area of over 250 acres, served as a British military post during the Revolutionary War. After 1847, the state's immigration service used it as a refuge for sick and destitute aliens. For nearly 50 years it was the site of a mental hospital (known from 1896 as the Manhattan State Hospital for the Insane); the institutional buildings were abandoned in the early 1940's and the grounds given over to recreational facilities. A municipal sewage disposal plant, at the time one of the three largest in the world, was constructed on the northeast end of the island in 1937. Since 1951, Ward's Island has been connected to Manhattan by a pedestrian drawbridge.

WARE, wâr, town, Massachusetts, in Hampshire County, on the Ware River, 22 miles west of Worcester, at an altitude of 490 feet. An industrial community, it manufactures woolens, knitted wear, sporting goods, converted papers, and other products. A new high school was under construction in 1961. Quabbin Reservoir, a short distance to the northwest, is a major scenic attraction and recreation area. The town's name is derived from the Nenameseck (meaning "fishing weir"), an Indian tribe which took salmon from the falls here. Settled about 1717, Ware was incorporated in 1761. After the Revolution, many townspeople supported the insurrection led by Daniel Shays (q.v.), and one local home was used as a supply depot. Present-day government is by the town meeting. Pop. 8,953.

MARY L. SMITH.

WAREHAM, wâr'hăm, town, Massachusetts, in Plymouth County, at the head of Buzzards Bay, 16 miles northeast of New Bedford, at an altitude of 20 feet. Part of a famous summer resort area, it has many fine beaches and other facilities which attract thousands of visitors annually. Its chief industries are the manufacture of nails and the culture and canning of cranberries. Settled in 1678, the town was incorporated in 1739. It contains the villages of Onset, Wareham, East Wareham, West Wareham, and South Wareham. The town meeting form of government is used. Pop. 18,457.

MAE C. REED.

WAREHOUSE, wâr'hous, a building for the storage of wares, or goods, until such time as they are required for consumption, sale, or other use. A warehouse may be privately operated for the sole use of its owner, or it may be a public enterprise charging a fee for storage space and other services. Public warehousing, or the business of conducting a warehouse, is licensed and regulated by law. It has become a vital factor in the expansion of trade. A census of business taken by the United States Bureau of the Census in 1954 showed that in that year there were 7,565 public warehouses operating in the continental United States, Alaska, and Hawaii, doing an annual business of $757,000,000 and employing 94,444 workers with an annual payroll of $304,000,000.

Warehousing is an ancient business, probably dating as far back as when the Phoenicians ruled the trade lanes and found it necessary to build storage vaults for their cargoes until the goods could be disposed of to merchants. There are records of public warehousing transactions in the Middle Ages in Venice and Genoa, to which ports ships brought valuable cargoes from all over the then known world.

Warehousing began in the United States in early colonial times, buildings for storage being erected in the principal ports to receive shipments from Europe and to hold them in safekeeping until they could be sold to local merchants. The advent of railroading required the opening of similar storage buildings in important inland cities as well as those on the seacoast, and at first these warehouses were operated at terminals by the railroads themselves. Under the Hepburn Act of June 29, 1906, however, the Interstate Commerce Commission, which had been given authority over the railroads, separated this service from transportation. The United States Warehouse Act of Aug. 11, 1916, provided for licensing by the secretary of agriculture of warehouses in which farm commodities were stored for interstate shipment. A Uniform Warehouse Receipts Act is the law in 48 states and Puerto Rico, and its provisions are embodied in the commercial codes of Pennsylvania and Massachusetts. It defines a warehouseman as one lawfully engaged in the business of storing goods and limits to him the privilege of issuing warehouse receipts, which are certificates containing a list of goods stored by him. They may or may not be negotiable as circumstances warrant.

There are various kinds of public warehouses: those storing general merchandise; those for household goods; refrigerated warehouses primarily for perishable foods; warehouses for farm products, such as cotton, wool, tobacco, grain (called elevators), and potatoes; and special warehouses for storing such commodities as furs, bulk petroleum, vegetable oils, sirups, and other bulk liquids. There are two types of United States bonded warehouses: one for holding imports until the customs duty is paid, and the other for holding goods produced in the United States and subject to the internal revenue tax. Both afford valuable facilities to business.

FRANK DORR,
Associate Editor of
"Popular Science Monthly."

WARFARE. See AMPHIBIOUS WARFARE; ARMY; ARTILLERY; CHEMICAL WARFARE; GUERRILLA WARFARE; GUIDED MISSILES; GUN; MILITARY AERONAUTICS; MILITARY COMMUNICATIONS; MILITARY ENGINEERING; MILITARY INTELLIGENCE; NAVAL AVIATION; NAVAL INTELLIGENCE; NAVAL STRATEGY AND TACTICS; NUCLEAR WEAPONS; ROCKETS; SIEGE; STRATEGY; SUBMARINE; TACTICS; WAR; WARSHIPS; and the Index entry *War*.

WARFIELD, wôr'fēld, **David,** American actor: b. San Francisco, Calif., Nov. 28, 1866; d. New York, N.Y., June 27, 1951. He played his first speaking role on stage in a San Francisco production of *The Ticket-of-Leave Man* in 1888, and from 1890 was seen in New York at the Casino and at Weber and Fields' Music Hall, where, in a burlesque setting, he perfected his talent for mimicking Italian, Scottish, German, Jewish, and other accents. His popular impersonation of a Russian Jewish immigrant attracted the attention of the producer David Belasco, for whom Warfield was to star in a series of phenomenal successes, beginning in 1900 with *The Auctioneer,* a play written especially for him. During a quarter century of stardom, Warfield, often hailed as America's leading actor, appeared only in a half a dozen roles, in all of which he portrayed unusual old gentlemen, pathetic and amusing, but always appealing.

The Auctioneer, in which he created one of his greatest characters, Simon Levi, had a run of well over 1,000 performances in 1900–1903. It was followed (1903–1907) by the equally successful *The Music Master*. He played in *The Grand Army Man* for the first time in 1907; in *The Return of Peter Grimm* in 1911; and in *Van Der Decken* in 1916. In 1916–1918 Warfield was again acting in *The Auctioneer* and *The Music Man,* and in 1924, shortly before he retired, he played Shylock in Shakespeare's *The Merchant of Venice*. He was one of the few millionaire actors of the legitimate stage and in the early 1920's refused a million-dollar offer to appear in films. During the penny arcade era, he was associated with Marcus Loew in the venture which was to become the giant motion-picture distribution and production enterprise, Loew's Incorporated.

WARFIELD, village, British Columbia, Canada, two miles southwest of Trail on the Canadian Pacific Railway line and the highway to Rossland. It was originally known as Annable. Its modern development began in 1935, when it was opened as a residential subdivision for employees of the Consolidated Mining and Smelting Company at Trail, seven miles north of the State of Washington. There is a fertilizer plant. The village shares in the utilities of Trail, which is able to make use of the Columbia River. Population: 1,969.

WARHAM, wôr'əm, **William,** English prelate: b. Hampshire, England, c. 1450; d. Hackington, near Canterbury, Aug. 22, 1532. He was educated at Winchester and New College, Oxford (fellow, 1475). After taking his doctor's degree in law, he went up to London (1488) and practiced as an advocate in the Court of Arches, the consistory court of the Province of Canterbury, from which there was at that time no appeal save to the pope. He was also moderator of the Civil Law School at Oxford (c. 1490), master of the rolls (1494), and archdeacon of Huntingdon (1496). In 1502 he became bishop of London, and in 1503 he was nominated by Pope Julius II to be archbishop of Canterbury. He received the pallium in the following year, when he was also made lord chancellor by Henry VII. The chancellorship of Oxford University was added to his honors in 1506, and in 1509 he married and crowned Henry VIII and Catherine of Aragon.

Although Warham conferred the cardinal's hat in 1515 upon Thomas Wolsey, who succeeded him the next month as lord chancellor, friction arose between the two men in 1518 when Wolsey became papal legate. In 1527, however, Warham assisted Wolsey in the secret inquiry into the validity of the king's marriage, and in 1530 he signed the petition to Pope Clement VII asking for the king's divorce, in spite of the fact that he was chief counselor for the queen. This act of submission to royal tyranny was scarcely wholehearted, for a year later when Henry ordered the English clergy to acknowledge him as "supreme head of the Church," the archbishop added the significant clause, "so far as the Law of Christ allows." In 1532 Warham protested against all acts of the Parliament of 1529 that were inimical to the interests of the church or the pope, appealing to the principles of Magna Carta (*Ecclesia Anglicana libera sit*), but to no avail. He was a patron of the New Learning and a benefactor of scholars (including Erasmus), but he had no sympathy with Protestantism.

FREDERICK C. GRANT
Author of "Basic Christian Beliefs"

WARHOL, wôr'hôl, **Andy,** American artist and filmmaker: b. Pennsylvania (place unknown) on Aug. 6, 1928 (most commonly accepted date); d. New York, N.Y., on Feb. 22, 1987. He was a leader in the avant-garde pop art movement of the early 1960's and a pioneer in commercial silk-screen reproduction. Using photographs of his subjects, he had silk screens made from them in mass quantity in his studio, which he named "the factory." Among the subjects he depicted, often in series or duplications with minor variations in color and tone, were soup cans, soap-pad boxes, and soft-drink bottles; public figures, including Marilyn Monroe; and news events.

Warhol graduated from the Carnegie Institute of Technology with a degree in pictorial design in 1949. He became a successful fashion illustrator in New York and in the late 1950's began to show his controversial pop art. He soon became a leader of the pop art school. Turning to filmmaking in the 1960's, he made a series of experimental pictures with such titles as *Eat, Sleep, Kiss, Chelsea Girls, Blue Movie, Bike Boy, Flesh,* and *Trash.* He also produced recordings of the Velvet Underground rock music group and wrote such books as *The Philosophy of Andy Warhol: From A to B and Back Again* (1975) and *Andy Warhol's Exposures* (1979).

WARLOCK, Peter. See HESELTINE, PHILIP.

WARM-BLOODED ANIMALS, mammals and birds which have a regulated body temperature usually above that of the environment. By contrast, reptiles, amphibians, fishes, and invertebrates are "cold-blooded," generally at the temperature of their surroundings. See also ANIMAL HEAT.

WARM FRONT. See FRONT.

WARMING, vär'mĕng, **Johannes Eugenius Bülow,** Danish botanist: b. Manø, North Frisian Islands, Denmark, Nov. 3, 1841; d. Copenhagen, April 1, 1924. He developed an early interest in botany and in 1863–1866 made a long voyage of exploration to Brazil, returning to complete his doctorate in 1871 at Copenhagen, where he began to teach in 1873. In 1882 he was appointed professor of botany at the Royal Institute of Technology in Stockholm, and in 1884 he traveled to Greenland; his classic studies of Brazilian flora and Arctic vegetation were the result of this and his earlier expeditions. In 1886 he was named director of the botanical garden and professor of botany at Copenhagen, where he spent the remainder of his life, except for periodic voyages of exploration.

Warming worked on problems of plant morphology and created a system of classification. He also carried out important studies on the nature of ovules (immature seeds). His greatest contribution, however, was as a pioneer in the field of ecology, and he may be said to have laid the foundations of this science through his studies of the relationships of plants to such factors of the environment as temperature, light, precipitation, and soil conditions. He showed that plants, trees, and shrubs adapt themselves to changes in their surroundings through spontaneous modifications of structure and function. His ingenious demonstrations that environmental conditions control the internal processes that initiate, restrain, and regulate the growth of roots, leaves, stems, and other tissues and organs are the basis of all modern work in the field.

Warming's *Plantesamfund* (1895), a pioneer work in ecology, was rewritten and enlarged for its English-language edition, *Oecology of Plants,* published in 1909.

WARNER, wôr'nər, **Charles Dudley,** American editor and author: b. Plainfield, Mass., Sept. 12, 1829; d. Hartford, Conn., Oct. 20, 1900. He graduated from Hamilton College in 1851 and from the law school of the University of Pennsylvania in 1858. After practicing law in Chicago, he joined the Hartford (Conn.) *Evening Press* in 1860. His association with this paper, merged with the *Courant* in 1867, lasted until his death. He served as assistant editor, editor, part owner, and literary contributor. He was also contributing editor to *Harper's New Monthly Magazine* from 1884 to 1898.

Although he wrote travel books, novels, and biographies, Warner contributed most to American letters as an essayist. *My Summer in a Garden* (1871) placed him high on the list of humorists. Later volumes of essays include *Backlog Studies* (1873), *Being a Boy* (1878), *On Horseback* (1888), and *Fashions in Literature* (1902). Warner is probably known most widely for his collaboration with Mark Twain in *The Gilded Age* (1873). While his essays are marked by warm humor, his novels are sternly moralistic. *A Little Journey in the World* (1889), *The Golden House* (1894), and *That Fortune* (1899) deal with the social responsibility of great wealth. His travel sketches include *Saunterings* (1872), *My Winter on the Nile* (1876), *A Roundabout Journey* (1883), and *Our Italy* (1891). He also edited the *American Men of Letters Series* and was co-editor of *A Library of the World's Best Literature* (30 vols., 1896–97). *The Complete Writings of Charles Dudley Warner* (1904), edited by Thomas R. Lounsbury, has a biographical sketch by the editor.

WARNER, Glenn Scobey (known as POP WARNER), American football coach: b. Springville, N.Y., April 5, 1871; d. Palo Alto, Calif., Sept. 7, 1954. Graduated from Cornell University with a law degree in 1894, he began his coaching career at the University of Georgia in 1895. Warner won national fame at Carlisle (Pa.) Indian School (from 1899) as the coach of Jim Thorpe and other all-American players. In 1915 he went to the University of Pittsburgh, where he remained for nine years and led three undefeated teams. In 1924 he joined the staff of Stanford University, coaching three Rose Bowl teams in nine years. His 46 years of continuous coaching, a record exceeded only by Amos Alonzo Stagg, included service at such other schools as Cornell and Temple universities and San Jose (Calif.) State College. Warner pioneered the crouch start, the single and double wing formations, and the clipping block.

WARNER, Seth, American Revolutionary officer: b. Roxbury, Conn., May 17, 1743; d. there, Dec. 26, 1784. Settling in Bennington, Vt., in 1763 under a grant from New Hampshire's Gov. Benning Wentworth, he joined with Ethan Allen and others in resisting New York's territorial claims in the area. On Nov. 27, 1771, the governor of New York offered £20 for his arrest, and in 1774 the General Assembly of New York declared him an outlaw. When the American Revolution began, Warner, with Allen and Benedict Arnold, captured Ticonderoga (May 10, 1775), and on the next day he took Crown Point. He was elected lieutenant colonel commandant of the Green Mountain Boys on July 26, later serving on the Canadian border under Gen. Richard Montgomery. While Montgomery besieged St. John, New Brunswick, Warner defeated Sir Guy Carleton's relieving force at Longueuil, on October 31. During the retreat from Canada in 1776, he commanded the rear guard. When Ticonderoga was abandoned in 1777 to Gen. John Burgoyne, Warner commanded the rear guard of Arthur St. Clair's army and was defeated by Gen. Simon Frazer at Hubbardton on July 7. Retreating to Vermont, his regiment helped to defeat the British at Bennington on August 16. The Vermont Assembly appointed him brigadier general in 1778, but he saw little more active service because of failing health.

DRAKE DE KAY.

WARNER, Susan Bogert (pseudonym ELIZABETH WETHERELL), American novelist: b. New York, N.Y., July 11, 1819; d. Highland Falls, March 17, 1885. She began her writing career with the publication of *The Wide, Wide World* (1850), which concerns the religious development of a 13-year-old orphan. Her second and almost as successful novel, *Queechy* (1852), also illustrates the spiritual growth of a young girl. Although she wrote many other novels, she is remembered for the unusual popularity of these first books, which appealed to the age's sentimental piety.

WARNER, Sylvia Townsend, English novelist: b. Harrow-on-the-Hill, Middlesex, England, December, 1893; d. Maiden Newton, Dorset, England, May 1, 1978. Educated privately, she wrote a book of poems, *The Espalier* (1925), followed by her first novel, *Lolly Willowes* (1926), which had the distinction of being the first Book-of-the-Month Club selection. Subsequent novels, such as *The Corner That Held Them* (1948), set in a medieval convent, and *The Flint Anchor* (1954), about a 19th century English family, as well as her short stories and poems, confirmed her critical reputation as a subtle and imaginative writer. She has a polished, delicate style, which reveals a sometimes whimsical wit intermingled with the prevailing realism.

WARNER ROBINS, city, Georgia, in Houston County, 16 miles south of Macon, at an altitude of 356 feet. Known as Wellston, with about 50 inhabitants, before World War II, it was incorporated as Warner Robins in March 1943, following the establishment of a nearby Air Force base. The city and the extensive Warner Robins Air Materiel Area here were named after Brig. Gen. Augustine Warner Robins (1882–1940). The city expanded rapidly as the base became one of the largest Air Force installations in the South. It is governed by a mayor and council. Pop. 39,893.

SALLY WELLING.

WARNING COLORATION. See MIMICRY; PROTECTIVE COLORATION.

WARP. See WEAVING; TEXTILE.

WARPATH, wôr′păth, among the American Indians, the route or path taken on going to war; a warlike expedition or excursion. "On the warpath" means on a hostile or warlike expedition; hence also, figuratively, a person or persons in a hostile frame of mind, or about to take a hostile course of action.

WARR ACRES, wôr′ ā-kərz, town, Oklahoma, in Oklahoma County, a residential suburb, five miles northwest of Oklahoma City. Pop. 9,940.

WARRAGAMBA RIVER, wŏr-ə-găm′bə, river, Australia, in east New South Wales. Part of the Hawkesbury River system, the Warragamba flows 14 miles northeast from the junction of the Cox and Wollondilly rivers into the Nepean River near Wallacia. Located on the river is the Warragamba Dam, 379 feet high, one of the largest in Australia, used to supply water to Sydney and for hydroelectric power and flood control.

WARRANT, wŏr′ənt, a legal process issued by competent authority directing an officer of the law or other party to perform a specific act. Warrants are issued by magistrates, justices of the peace, or others designated by statute. A *warrant of arrest* commands an officer to arrest and bring the party named before a magistrate or court to answer or be examined concerning an offense with which he has been charged. The basis of issuance is probable cause shown, normally upon a formal charge by one appearing and alleging the commission of an offense. Usually the charge must be supported by oath or affirmation of the complaining party. To be valid, an arrest warrant must identify the accused by name or other sufficient description; it must state facts constituting an offense and essential to establish the jurisdiction of the issuing official. In order to secure personal protection for his actions, the person executing the warrant must make a return showing compliance with its command. Unless otherwise provided by statute, the territorial validity of a warrant is limited to the jurisdiction of the court or magistrate issuing it.

A *search warrant* is a written order authorizing an official to examine specified premises usually for the presence of stolen property or other unlawful goods, and to secure their production before the issuing body. Issued only on a showing of reasonable grounds for suspicion affirmed or sworn to by a complainant, the warrant must contain a particular description of the place to be searched and the goods to be seized.

Other types of warrants include *warrants of commitment*, by which a court directs the confinement of a person in prison either before or after trial; *land warrants*, issued by land offices to purchasers of public lands; *landlords' warrants*, issued to compel the sale of personal chattels at public sale to meet the requirements of a lease; *bench warrants*, issued by a court to compel the appearance of a witness or for the arrest of a person in contempt proceedings; *death warrants*, issued usually by a governor to carry out a sentence of death imposed by a court on a convicted criminal; and *distress warrants*, which authorize the levy of a distraint upon chattels, usually for the nonpayment of rent. Warrants are also used in financial, governmental, and commercial dealings. These include dividend warrants, treasury warrants, mercantile warrants, municipal warrants, school warrants, reclamation warrants, and stock warrants.

ALAN A. MATHESON,
School of Law, Columbia University.

WARRANT OFFICER, an officer of the armed forces ranking between commissioned and noncommissioned officers. The grade has existed in European armies and navies since the 17th century, signifying an officer whose authority stems from a warrant rather than from the sovereign's commission. In the United States Army and Marine Corps warrant officers fill an increasing number of important specialist positions, including helicopter pilots and missile technicians; the Navy and Air Force, however, are replacing warrant officers with limited-duty commissioned officers. The British Army's two grades (WO I and WO II) include the position of sergeant-major and several specialist appointments. In the French Army and Air Force the NCO grades of *adjudant-chef* (created 1912) and *adjudant* (created 1776) correspond to warrant officers in the United States and British services.

A. P. WADE.

WARRANTY, wŏr'ən-tē, a guarantee, assurance, or covenant, or an undertaking to indemnify against loss. The term "warranty" is used with varying meanings in different kinds of contracts. There are two general classes: *express warranties*, created by explicit statement of the seller or person to be bound; and *implied warranties*, which are derived by inference from the acts of the parties or the circumstances of the transaction. In a contract of insurance, a warranty is a stipulation or statement of facts on the part of the insured in the nature of a condition upon which the duty of the insurer's preformance may depend. When real property is conveyed by warranty deed, the grantor covenants that he has title and binds himself and his heirs to defend the title in the grantee. A warranty in the sale of personal property is a statement made by the seller at the time of and as part of the contract of sale that the quality or character of the article sold is or shall be as represented. Warranties of title, of fair merchantability, and in certain cases of quality may be imputed by law in a sales transaction. Breach of warranty may subject the warrantor to liability in damages and in some cases excuse the other party from performing.

ALAN A. MATHESON,
School of Law, Columbia University.

WARRAU INDIANS, wä-rä'o͞o, or **GUARAUNO INDIANS,** gwä-rou nō, a numerous South American Indian tribe and linguistic family living in the Orinoco Delta (Venezuela), British Guiana, and Surinam. They were possibly the original inhabitants of Trinidad. Fishing is the chief food activity of the Warrau, whose settlements are composed of six or eight small dwellings each; no contemporary population figure is known. Basketry, weaving, and some pottery are known, but their major craft is the manufacture of excellent dugout canoes, which are in great demand among neighboring tribes. Their religion is primarily shamanism, but the Warrau also worship a supreme being called Grandfather. Their name means "boat people".

FREDERICK J. DOCKSTADER.

WARREGO RIVER, wŏr'ĭ-gō, river, Australia, flowing south-southwest from Queensland into New South Wales. Rising in the Carnarvon Range, a section of the Great Dividing Range, it receives several tributaries from the Warrego Range to the west and runs for 495 miles, reaching the Darling River northeast of Louth. It was first explored in 1846 by Sir Thomas Livingstone Mitchell (q.v.), who retained the native name for the river.

WARREN, wŏr'ən, **Charles,** American lawyer and legal historian: b. Boston, Mass., March 9, 1868; d. Washington, D.C., Aug. 15, 1954. Educated at Harvard College and Harvard Law School, he was admitted to the bar in 1892. From 1905 to 1911 he was chairman of the Massachusetts Civil Service Commission. Although most of his career was spent in private law practice, he was United States assistant attorney general from 1914 to 1918, and in that capacity was in charge of the prosecution of German espionage agents. He also was responsible to a large degree for the drafting of the Espionage Act (1917), the Trading with the Enemy Act (1917), and the Sabotage Act (1918). His memorandum on neutrality to the State Department in 1934 served as the basis for the neutrality acts passed by Congress in 1935, 1936, and 1937. Warren's major contribution as a legal historian was *The Supreme Court in United States History* (3 vols.,

1922), which won the Pulitzer Prize in 1923. Other important works include *A History of the American Bar, Colonial and Federal, to 1860* (1911) and *The Making of the Constitution* (1928).

WARREN, Earl, 14th chief justice of the United States (from 1953 to 1969): b. Los Angeles, Calif., March 19, 1891; d. Washington, D. C., July 9, 1974. He served on the court during a period of unparalleled developments in civil rights. The term "Warren Court" came to be used to describe the bold, liberal outlook of the Supreme Court in those years. Before his appointment to the court, Warren was governor of California.

Early Career. Warren grew up in Bakersfield, Calif. He received his higher education at the University of California at Berkeley, earning a bachelor of laws degree in 1912 and a doctorate of jurisprudence in 1914. After brief law practice and Army service during World War I, he held

Earl Warren

Hartley Alley—Pix

the offices of deputy city attorney for Oakland (1919–1920), deputy district attorney (1920–1925) and district attorney (1925–1939) for Alameda county, and attorney general of California (1939–1943). He also assisted in establishing legal aid associations and organizing a public defender system in the state.

Governor. A liberal Republican, Warren was three times elected governor of California with unprecedented bipartisan support (1942, 1946, and 1950). Coping effectively with diverse, powerful interests, he managed to reduce taxes while expanding state services. In 1948 he was the unsuccessful vice presidential candidate on the Republican ticket headed by Thomas E. Dewey. Warren resigned the governorship in 1953 to accept President Dwight D. Eisenhower's recess appointment as chief justice.

Chief Justice. During Warren's tenure [he resigned in 1968, effective in 1969], the court faced a variety of critical issues, but most important decisions involved civil rights questions. As Warren explained, "The very atmosphere in which we live is charged with the subject." Despite his early reputation as a "hard prosecutor" and his support of wartime internment of Japanese-Americans, he stood consistently for a broad interpretation of the constitutional protections of the individual. Through all of Warren's judicial performance ran a preoccupation with "fairness." His opinions, reflecting political judgment and a sense of justice more than precise legal scholarship, brought him both praise and condemnation.

In May 1954, only two months after Senate confirmation of his permanent appointment, Warren, for a unanimous court, wrote the landmark opinion in *Brown* v. *Board of Education* holding that racial segregation in public elementary schools denied equal protection of the laws. "Separate educational facilities," he contended, "are inherently unequal." This ruling, which precipitated the first of a series of attacks on the members of the Warren Court, later was extended sweepingly to transportation, recreation, and other activities.

Across a wide spectrum the Chief Justice guarded individual liberties—defense of citizenship as a basic right (*Perez* v. *Brownell* and *Trop* v. *Dulles*, 1958), refusal to permit criminal sanctions for Communist party members who accept positions of union leadership (*United States* v. *Brown*, 1965), curbing of racial discrimination in voting (*South Carolina* v. *Katzenbach*, 1966), invalidation of state miscegenation laws (*Loving* v. *Virginia*, 1967), and limitation of the use of libel laws to inhibit freedom of the press (*Curtis Publishing Company* v. *Butts*, 1967). He endorsed broadening the interpretation of the 14th Amendment to apply more and more to the state governments the restrictions placed on the federal government by the Bill of Rights. Maintaining that almost all election districts that were not apportioned on a population basis were unconstitutional, he spoke for the court in *Reynolds* v. *Sims* (1964) and subsequent cases, holding the view that malapportionment in either house of a state legislature denied equal protection of the laws.

With Warren's support, the court expanded the rights of the accused in many areas, including search and seizure, self-incrimination, and the right to counsel. One of the Chief Justice's most notable opinions, *Miranda* v. *Arizona* (1966) enlarged both the right to counsel and the right of suspects to be informed that they need not answer questions. Warren's opinion in *Watkins* v. *United States* (1957) also limited legislative investigatory power.

Warren insisted that the military be kept subordinate to civil government. First as a dissenter and then with the majority, he took the position that military trial of civilians was always unconstitutional (*Reid* v. *Covert*, 1957; *Kinsella* v. *United States, et al.*, 1960).

As Chief Justice, Warren vigorously performed the special duties of his office, such as presiding over the Judicial Conference, but largely abstained from participating in extrajudicial activities. Only reluctantly did he yield to President Lyndon Johnson's plea that he head the official investigation into the assassination of President John F. Kennedy (see WARREN COMMISSION REPORT).

CARL BRENT SWISHER*, *Author, "Growth of Constitutional Power in the United States"*

WARREN, Howard Crosby, American psychologist: b. Montclair, N.J., June 12, 1867; d. Princeton, Jan. 4, 1934. He graduated from Princeton in 1889 and, after further study in Germany, began to teach psychology at Princeton in 1893. Warren worked to establish the independence of psychology from philosophy, and in 1920 became the first chairman of the Department of Psychology at Princeton. In 1921 he published his great book, *History of the Association Psychology*, upon which he had worked for 20 years. It is generally regarded as a major contribution to psychological literature. Warren upheld the double-aspect theory of the body-mind relationship and taught that the method of introspection is indispensable in scientific psychology. Though he was in sympathy with the behaviorism of John B. Watson, he did not believe that observations of overt behavior alone were adequate methods. Under his leadership the *Psychological Review,* of which he was senior editor from 1910, became a forum for debates on basic issues in psychology and for discussions of the methods advocated by Edward B. Titchener and the proponents of behaviorism. In 1925 he dedicated Eno Hall at Princeton, the first college building in America solely devoted to psychology.

PHILIP L. HARRIMAN

WARREN, John Collins, American surgeon: b. Boston, Mass., Aug. 1, 1778; d. there, May 4, 1856. His father, JOHN WARREN (1753–1815), younger brother of Joseph Warren (q.v.), was one of the founders of the Harvard Medical School (1782) and first professor of anatomy and surgery there. John Collins Warren graduated from Harvard College in 1797, studied medicine under his father, and entered medical practice in Boston. He joined the faculty of Harvard Medical School in 1809 and was professor of anatomy and surgery there from 1815 to 1847. With James Jackson he founded the *New England Journal of Medicine and Surgery* (1812) and the Massachusetts General Hospital (1821), where he was surgeon until 1853.

Assisted by William T. G. Morton, Warren performed the first surgical operation in which ether was used as an anesthetic (1846). He also performed the first strangulated hernia operation in the United States and introduced John Hunter's operation for aneurysm. Warren was interested in paleontology and geology and became the owner of the most complete mastodon skeleton (now in the American Museum of Natural History, New York City) known in his day. His collections formed the nucleus of the Warren Museum at Harvard. His most important book was *Surgical Observations on Tumours with Cases and Operations* (1837). His *Physical Education and the Preservation of Health* (1845) and *The Preservation of Health . . .* (1854) went through many editions.

JOHN COLLINS WARREN (1842–1927), his grandson, was also a distinguished Boston surgeon and member of the faculty at the Harvard Medical School (1871–1907). He played a major role in securing funds for the new medical center at Harvard (1906) and also for the Collis P. Huntington Memorial Hospital for Cancer Research in Boston. Among his publications were *The Anatomy and Development of Rodent Ulcer* (1872), for which he received the Boylston Medical Prize, and *Surgical Pathology and Therapeutics* (1895).

WARREN, Joseph, American physician and Revolutionary army officer: b. Roxbury, Mass., June 11, 1741; d. Charlestown, June 17, 1775. Graduated from Harvard College in 1759, he studied medicine with a physician in Boston and entered practice there in 1764. When the Stamp Act was passed (1765), he plunged into politics and soon became one of the leaders of the militant patriot group in Boston, with Samuel Adams and John Hancock. Warren was a member of the original Boston committee of correspondence (November 1772) and one of the three authors of *A State of the Rights of the Colonists* (1772), detailing their grievances. In September 1774 he presented to the Suffolk County convention at Milton, Mass., the historic Suffolk Resolves, which were later carried to Philadelphia by Paul Revere and endorsed by the Continental Congress, protesting and refusing obedience to the British Intolerable Acts. In October he became a member of the newly formed Massachusetts Committee of Safety, assigned to organize the provincial militia.

Warren was the man who sent Paul Revere and William Dawes on their famous ride (April 18, 1775). He was killed fighting in the ranks at the Battle of Bunker Hill, three days after being made a major general by the Massachusetts Provincial Assembly.

WARREN, Leonard (originally WARRENOFF) American baritone: b. New York, N.Y., April 21, 1911; d. there, March 4, 1960. After singing in the Radio City Music Hall Chorus, he won (March 26, 1938) the Metropolitan (Opera) Auditions of the Air. He then studied briefly in Italy and made his operatic debut at the Metropolitan Opera as Paolo Albiani in Verdi's *Simon Boccanegra* on Jan. 13, 1939. During the next 21 years, Warren's powerful, dark voice and dedicated, growing artistry triumphed over his short, puffed figure and his rudimentary histrionic sense to establish him among the star operatic performers of his time. Besides 406 Metropolitan performances in New York City and 230 on tour, he gave many recitals, made guest appearances in North and South America and Europe, and sang for phonograph recordings.

He was noted as a Verdi baritone (*Aïda, La Traviata, Il Trovatore, Rigoletto, Falstaff, Otello, Ernani, Macbeth*), and also sang in *La Gioconda, Pagliacci, Tosca,* and other operas. While singing the role of Don Carlo in *La forza del destino* at the Metropolitan, he collapsed, dying a few minutes later.

HERBERT WEINSTOCK

WARREN, Mercy Otis, American author: b. Barnstable, Mass., Sept. 25, 1728; d. Plymouth, Oct. 19, 1814. Sister of the revolutionary leader James Otis, she married another Massachusetts patriot leader, James Warren, in 1754 and was acquainted in the years that followed with many of the chief figures of the American Revolution, notably the members of the Adams family and Thomas Jefferson.

Mrs. Warren wrote poems and plays in support of the patriot cause, including the dramatic satires *The Adulateur* (1773) and *The Group* (1775). Her *Poems Dramatic and Miscellaneous* was published in 1790. Her chief work was the *History of the Rise, Progress, and Termination of the American Revolution* (3 vols., 1805), which is important for its firsthand account of the events and personalities of the period.

WARREN, Robert Penn (1905–), the first American poet laureate, much of whose verse constitutes a poetic mix of memory and meditation on the mystery of humanity's kinship with all life. As a New Critic he sought the same integration in literature; as a novelist he offered this web of being in *All the King's Men* (1946) and other works; as a social commentator he ar-

ROLLIN A. RIGGS, NYT PICTURES

Robert Penn Warren, one of America's most versatile writers, became poet laureate of the United States in 1986.

gued the similarity of seeming inseparables in *Segregation* (1956) and *Who Speaks for the Negro?* (1965). For himself he required the same completeness, managing also to be playwright, biographer, professor, and author of short stories and children's books.

Born in Guthrie, Ky., on April 24, 1905, he acquired his impulse for reconciliation from being heir to the South's sense of community and from closeness to his maternal grandfather, who remembered the divisiveness of the Civil War. At Vanderbilt University in the early 1920's, Warren became a member of the Fugitive-Agrarian group (named for their magazine, *Fugitive*), which explored the middle ground between exploitive capitalism and radical communism. His Rhodes scholarship (1928–1930) was only the first of honors that later included Pulitzer prizes for both fiction and poetry, the Bollingen Prize, and the National Medal for Literature. He was named poet laureate of the United States in 1986.

No contemporary American matched the historical relevance of Warren's long narrative poems: *Brother to Dragons* (1953)—how the brutal murder of a slave by Jefferson's nephew shook the author of the Bill of Rights; *Audubon* (1969)—the inseparability of beauty and even such radical changes as death; *Chief Joseph of the Nez Percé* (1983)—Indian courage in the face of genocide. But the intimately personal lyric became his favorite, after his marriage in 1952 to the writer Eleanor Clark and the birth of their two children, memorialized in *Promises* (1957). In lectures published as *Democracy and Poetry* (1975) he spoke of poetry as "love knowledge," a moral centering of the self balanced with society achieved through the dramatic tension created between their shared moments of elegy and ecstasy.

All Warren's novels use the South to image universal concerns. His poems, however, provide a wider range of reflectors; those on the earliest explorations of the Kentucky-Tennessee wilderness, the tight metaphysical verses reminiscent of Andrew Marvell, the exuberant and elegant Italianate stanzas exclaiming over his children, and the later works with broken rhythms and colloquialisms, written in his converted-barn workshop in Connecticut. Ever the spiritual "yearner," Warren was driven to discover whether what he sensed of the immanent-transcendent in all global life was a sign of God's dual nature as well.

LEONARD CASPER
Author of "Robert Penn Warren: The Dark and Bloody Ground"

WARREN, Whitney (1864–1943), American architect. He was born in New York City on Jan. 29, 1864, and studied at the École des Beaux-Arts in Paris. He began to practice as an architect in New York in 1894.

Together with Charles D. Wetmore, Warren designed many hotels and railroad stations, including Grand Central Terminal in New York City, Grand Trunk Station in Winnipeg, and the Ritz-Carlton, Ambassador, Biltmore, and Commodore hotels in New York. He also designed the New York Yacht Club Building, the John Paul Jones Crypt at the United States Naval Academy, the bronze gates of the Cathedral of St. John the Divine in New York, and the rebuilt Louvain Library in Belgium. He died in New York City on Jan. 24, 1943.

WARREN, a city in Arkansas, 90 miles (145 km) by road south of Little Rock. It is the seat of Bradley county. The city is a farming center, with truck and row crops, poultry, and livestock providing the major income. Warren was incorporated in 1851 and has a mayor-council form of government. Population: 7,646.

WARREN, a city in Michigan, in Macomb county, north of and adjacent to Detroit and 8 miles (13 km) west of Lake St. Clair. It is a major automotive manufacturing center as well as a producer of steel, electrical equipment, tools and dies, and plastic molding. The General Motors Technical Center and the Detroit Tank Arsenal are located in the city.

Organized as Hickory township in 1837, the community changed its name to Aba the following year and to Warren shortly thereafter. It was incorporated as a village in 1893 and as a city in 1955. Warren is governed by a mayor and council. Population: 161,134.

WARREN, a city in Ohio, on the Mahoning River, 20 miles (32 km) by road northwest of Youngstown. It is the seat of Trumbull county. Its principal industries are steel production and fabrication and automotive and appliance wiring.

Settled in 1797 by Ephraim Quinby and named after Moses Warren, a surveyor for the Connecticut Land Company, Warren was the first and only capital of the Western Reserve. (See also WESTERN RESERVE.) The community was incorporated as a village in 1834 and became a city in 1869. The Dana Musical Institute, founded by William H. Dana in 1869, gained prominence in the area and operated until the early 1940's, when it was merged with the School of Music at Youngstown University.

Warren has a mayor and council. Noted citizens were James Ward Packard and his brother William Doud Packard, and Earl Derr Biggers.

Near the city is Phalanx Mill, a relic of a Fourierist colony of the 1840's. Pop. 56,629.

MARJORIE COCHRAN.

WARREN, borough, Pennsylvania, Warren County seat, 40 miles by road from Bradford, at the junction of Conewango Creek and the Allegheny River, at an altitude of 1,193 feet. It was laid out in 1795 and incorporated in 1832. Located in a fertile agricultural and timber area, it was formerly a lumbering center. With the discovery of oil in Pennsylvania in 1859, oil refining became an important industry in the borough. It manufactures metal products, oilfield equipment, furniture, electrical equipment, and plastics. It is the principal gateway to the Allegheny National Forest. Northeast of the borough is the Cornplanter Indian Reservation. Warren is governed by a burgess and council. Pop. 12,146.

WARREN, town, Rhode Island, in Bristol County, 9 miles east of Providence, at an altitude of 30 feet, on the Kickemuit and Warren rivers, at the mouth of Narragansett Bay. Originally known as Sowamsett, it was the home of Massasoit, the Wampanoag Indian chief. In 1632 an English trading post was established here, and in 1747 it was incorporated as a town, named after the English admiral Sir Peter Warren. During the Revolutionary War it was the headquarters for a time of the marquis de Lafayette. Today it is an industrial and resort town. In addition to seafood canneries, Warren has automotive-equipment, slide-fastener, clothing, rubber-flooring, plastic, and luggage factories. It is governed by a town council. Pop. 10,640.

JANICE E. MUMMA.

WARREN COMMISSION REPORT, the published findings of the investigation of the U. S. President's Commission on the Assassination of President John F. Kennedy. The Warren Commission was established by order of President Lyndon B. Johnson on Nov. 29, 1963, one week after the murder of his predecessor in Dallas, Texas, on Nov. 22, 1963. It was directed to evaluate all circumstances surrounding the assassination as well as the killing of the alleged assassin, Lee Harvey Oswald (q.v.), by a Dallas nightclub owner, Jack Ruby. After a 10-month investigation the commission determined that Oswald was the assassin, that he acted alone, and that he had not known Ruby.

Headed by U. S. Chief Justice Earl Warren, the 7-member commission included two senators, Richard B. Russell and John Sherman Cooper; two representatives, Hale Boggs and Gerald B. Ford; and two attorneys long active in public service, Allen W. Dulles and John J. McCloy. James Lee Rankin was appointed chief counsel. The commission evaluated reports made by the Federal Bureau of Investigation, the Secret Service, the Dallas police department, government departments and agencies, and congressional committees. In addition it took the sworn testimony of 552 witnesses.

The report, released on Sept. 27, 1964, concluded that Oswald fired three shots from the Texas School Book Depository building; that those shots killed President Kennedy and wounded Texas Gov. John B. Connally; and that he later killed policeman J. D. Tippitt, who tried to apprehend him. Without ascribing a motive, it pointed out relevant character traits of Oswald, such as deep-seated hostility and resentment of authority. Despite Oswald's past defection to the Soviet Union and his activities on behalf of Cuba, the commission found no evidence implicating either country and discounted reports of any conspiracy. Neither could it relate the killing of Oswald to the other murders. The commission criticized the conduct of the Secret Service and the FBI before the assassination and made proposals for improved protection of the president.

The Warren Report at first received almost universal acclaim. But as Oswald could never be brought to trial, doubts of his guilt and speculations of conspiracy gave rise to a rush of books and articles challenging the commission's findings. Perhaps most influential were *Rush to Judgment* by Mark Lane and *Inquest* by Edward Jay Epstein, both published in 1966. These books sought to show that the commission had conducted a superficial investigation, and Lane proclaimed Oswald's innocence. All the commission's detractors were attacked for their unproved premises, and none offered an acceptable alternative explanation, but they served to tarnish the Warren Report in the public mind. William Manchester, commissioned by the Kennedy family to write an account of the assassination, conducted an investigation of his own, and his book, *The Death of a President* (1967), basically corroborated the official report. But because many people could not accept the verdict of a murder without meaning, lingering doubts continued to manifest themselves as attacks on the report.

WARRENSBURG, wŏr'ənz-bûrg, city, Missouri, seat of Johnson County, 65 miles southeast of Kansas City, at an altitude of 881 feet. Named for Martin Warren, veteran of the American Revolution, who settled here in 1833, it was incorporated as a city in 1856. During the Civil War loyalty was divided between the Union and the Confederacy, and troops of both sides occupied the city. In 1870, at the Old Courthouse, Senator George Graham Vest delivered his classic oration, "Tribute to the Dog," during a suit for damages over the killing of a dog by a farmer. The center of a grain- and livestock-producing area, Warrensburg manufactures uniforms, cotton goods, shoes, and lawn mowers. It is the home of Central Missouri State College, founded in 1871. A manager form of city government was adopted in 1957. Pop. 13,807.

W. A. STANTON.

WARRENSVILLE HEIGHTS, wŏr-ənz-vĭl, village, Ohio, in Cuyahoga County, adjacent on the southeast to Cleveland, of which it is a residential suburb. It was incorporated in 1927. Pop. 16,565.

WARRENTON, wŏr'ən-tən, town, Virginia, seat of Fauquier County, in the northeast part of the state, 43 miles southwest of Washington, D.C. Situated at the foot of the Blue Ridge Mountains, it is a center for the breeding of Thoroughbred horses and dairy and beef cattle, and is noted for its fox-hunting events. The town also has a steel plant and lumber industries. The area was settled at the beginning of the 18th century, and in 1718 a large tract of land here was granted to Thomas Lee, father of the American Revolutionary statesman Richard Henry Lee. Leeton Forest nearby was the home built by Charles Lee, son-

©PORTEFIELD—CHICKERING/PHOTO RESEARCHERS

View of Warsaw, Poland, looking northwest from the Palace of Culture across a complex of new apartment houses.

in-law of Richard Henry Lee and attorney general of the United States in 1795–1801. The town was incorporated in 1810 and named for Gen. Joseph Warren of Bunker Hill fame. It adopted the council-manager form of government in 1920. Pop. 3,907.

WARRINGTON, wŏr'ĭng-tən, county borough, England, in Cheshire, on the Mersey River and the Manchester Ship Canal, 16 miles (26 km) east of Liverpool. Although its suburbs were located in Cheshire, Warrington was not transferred from Lancashire to Cheshire until 1974. Warrington grew up at the lowest convenient crossing of the Mersey, and there is evidence that such a crossing has existed here since Roman times. A bridge was first mentioned in 1305. Modern Warrington is a busy industrial borough, with wire manufactures, leather tanning, soapmaking, chemicals, engineering, and the manufacture of iron, steel, and aluminum goods and electrical products. One of its three breweries has for over 200 years been based on exceptionally pure water from wells in the Bunter sandstone.

Notable buildings include the municipal headquarters, housed in a beautiful 18th century mansion; the Georgian building of Warrington Academy, associated with Joseph Priestley, the discoverer of oxygen, and other notable men of the time; the parish church, dedicated to St. Elfin, with a spire 280 feet high; and Bewsey Hall, dating from 1600. There is a good museum and art gallery. Pop. (1981) 168,846.

H. Gordon Stokes
Author of "English Place-Names"

WARRINGTON, village, Florida, in Escambia County, on Pensacola Bay, adjacent on the southwest to the city of Pensacola and on the north to the U.S. Naval Air Station. Pop. 15,792.

WARS OF SUCCESSION. See Succession Wars.

WARS OF THE ROSES. See Roses, Wars of the.

WARSAW, wôr'sô, city, Indiana, Kosciusko County seat, on the Tippecanoe River, 40 miles west-northwest of Fort Wayne, at an altitude of 825 feet. It has a municipal airport. Located in an agricultural area, it is an industrial, trade, and resort center. Its manufactures include orthopedic and surgical equipment, metal products and machinery, furniture and other wood products, toys, and breakfast foods. Nearby Winona Lake, the home of Grace College and Seminary, is a religious and cultural center. Warsaw, named for the capital of Poland, was settled in 1836, incorporated as a town in 1854, and as a city in 1875. It is governed by a mayor and city council. Pop. 10,647.

A. James Sloan

WARSAW (Pol. Warszawa), city and capital, Poland, on both sides of the Vistula River, at an altitude of 240 feet. Its winters are cold and summers are warm, with an average temperature of 25.7° F. in January and 65.4 °F. in July. The average annual rainfall is 22.2 inches.

Warsaw is a major industrial center producing automobiles, steel, pharmaceuticals, cement, radio and television sets, electrical equipment, and clothing. The city is also the transportation hub of the country; seven railroad trunk lines connect it with the major cities of Poland, as well as with Berlin, Kiev, Leningrad, Moscow, Prague, and Vienna. The airport and Okęcie connects Warsaw with 14 European capitals. Zerań serves as the port of the city.

Located in Warsaw are the government ministries, the economic planning agencies, the Parliament, the National Bank of Poland, and the Polish Chamber of National Trade, the central export and import agency. It is the seat of the primate of Poland (Roman Catholic) and the metropolitan of Poland (Orthodox) as well as the heads of the other religious bodies. The three national political parties maintain their principal headquarters in Warsaw.

As the intellectual center of the country, Warsaw houses the Polish Academy of Sciences, the chief scientific institution, with more than 74 affiliated research institutes throughout Poland. Major libraries of the city include the National Library, the Library of the University of Warsaw, the Public Library of Warsaw, the Central Medical Library, and the Library of Parliament.

Fourteen institutions of higher learning are in the city including the University of Warsaw, the Central School of Agriculture, the Warsaw Polytechnic, the Foreign Service College, the Central School for Planning and Statistics, and the Catholic Theological Academy. Of the 15 museums, the National Museum is outstanding, with a fine collection of ancient, medieval, and modern art.

Many of the major newspapers and magazines of Poland are published in Warsaw. Its chief newspapers are *Trybuna Ludu*, *Głos Pracy*, *Express Wieczorny*, *Zycie Warszawy*, and *Slowo Powszechne*. Among the major periodicals are found *Świat*, *Polityka*, and *Nowa Kultura*. The city has three radio stations and one television channel. The major theaters are the Teatr Polski, well known for its renditions of Polish and foreign classics, and the National Theater, which has a more contemporary repertoire. The National Philharmonic Hall in Warsaw is the home of the outstanding symphony orchestra of Poland.

The city contains many world-famous palaces and churches. Łazienki Palace, home of Stanislas II Augustus, the last king of Poland, is an outstanding example of Polish classicism. Other historic buildings are Namiestnikowski Palace, now the seat of the government; Staszic Palace, which houses part of the Academy of Sciences; and the Palace of John III Sobieski in Wilańow. The 14th century Gothic Cathedral of St. John, the Church of the Visitation Nuns, and the baroque-style Holy Cross Church are outstanding examples of Warsaw's ecclesiastical architecture. Noted postwar buildings include the 40-story Palace of Culture and Science and the Ten-Year Stadium, which seats more than 80,000 people. Most of Warsaw was destroyed during World War II, but the old town, Stare Miasto, with its famous Sigismund III Column, has been

EDITORIAL PHOTOCOLOR ARCHIVES

The 40-story Palace of Culture, a gift to Warsaw from the USSR, is built in Soviet architectural style.

The late Renaissance and baroque buildings of the Old City were rebuilt after total destruction in World War II.

EASTFOTO

Malo Darrat from Black Star

A monument in the former Warsaw Ghetto honors Jewish heroes of the 1943 revolt against the German forces.

fully restored to its original state, and the area appears today as it did centuries ago.

History.—Warsaw first appears in the 12th century as a village adjoining Ujazdów, a castle of the princes of Masovia. It became the capital of Masovia in 1413. In the 16th century it was the seat of the joint Polish-Lithuanian Sejm, and the kings of Poland were elected at Wola, a nearby suburb. In 1596 Sigismund III moved his court from Kraków to Warsaw, and from that time Warsaw assumed a central position in the life and history of Poland. In the 17th and 18th centuries it was occupied at various times by the Swedes and the Russians; and when Poland was finally partitioned in 1795, the city was given to Prussia. Captured by Napoleon I in 1806, it became the center of the short-lived Grand Duchy of Warsaw under Napoleon's protection, but in 1813 it was taken again by the Russians, to whom it was awarded by the Congress of Vienna in 1815.

During the 19th century, under Russian rule, Warsaw grew into a large industrial center. Its population increased from 127,000 in 1832 to 383,000 in 1882 and 884,000 in 1914. Despite bloody insurrections in 1830–1831 and 1863 and serious rioting in 1905, Russia held the city until it was lost to Germany in August 1915.

In November 1918 Warsaw became the capital of newly independent Poland, and by 1939 the city's population had grown to 1,289,000. Attacked at the outbreak of World War II, it capitulated to Germany on Sept. 27, 1939. During the next five years, more than 85 percent of the city was destroyed, and more than 600,000 inhabitants of Warsaw lost their lives. On April 19, 1943, the Jews in the ghetto rose against the Germans, and after a few weeks of fighting the entire area was razed and its people annihilated. The city revolted against the Germans on Aug. 1, 1944, but after 62 days of bitter fighting the revolt ended in defeat. Nevertheless, the Soviet and 1st Polish armies liberated Praga on Sept. 14, 1944, and the entire city was retaken by Jan. 17, 1945. Population: (1978 est.) 1,552,300.

WARSAW, University of, a Polish institution of higher education founded in Warsaw in 1816 and opened in 1818. Closed by the Russians after the failure of the Polish revolt of 1830–1831, it was not reopened until 1869. From 1884 to 1916 it was completely Russianized. The university made substantial progress during the interwar years. With other Polish educational institutions, it was closed by the Germans after they captured Warsaw in 1939 and was not reopened until 1945. During this period, however, some instruction was given in secret. Russian influence, dominant in the decade after the war, lessened to some extent after 1956.

The university has faculties of biology and geography, chemistry, journalism, political economy, philosophy, philology, geology, mathematics and physics, history, law, and pedagogy.

WARSAW PACT, a military alliance between the Soviet Union and its European satellites. The pact was conceived as an answer to the North Atlantic Treaty Organization (NATO), and it was concluded soon after West Germany's rearmament and admission to NATO.

More formally known as the Warsaw Treaty of Friendship, Cooperation, and Mutual Assistance, the treaty was signed in Warsaw, Poland, on May 14, 1955. Its signatories were Albania, Bulgaria, Czechoslovakia, East Germany, Hungary, Poland, Romania, and the Soviet Union. Besides representatives of the signatory nations, an "observer" from Communist China attended the Warsaw conference that led to the treaty and announced that his government would come to the aid of its European partners in the event of a war with the West. The defense treaty was automatically renewed in 1975 when its 20-year term expired.

The joint command of the armed forces, with its headquarters in Moscow, was placed under Marshall Ivan Konev, a Soviet military hero of World War II. Soviet troops stationed in Hungary under the Warsaw Pact crushed the 1956 revolution in that country. All the Warsaw signatories with the exception of Albania and Romania participated in the invasion of Czechoslovakia in 1968 to end the liberalization policies of Alexander Dubček. Albania had supported China in its split with the USSR and in 1961 boycotted Warsaw Pact activities. In 1968 it formally withdrew from the pact. Romania condemned the invasion of Czechoslovakia and later, as an expression of its fundamental disagreement with the Soviet Union on matters of policy, withheld its troops from maneuvers of Warsaw Pact forces.

ROBERT D. WARTH*, *University of Kentucky*

WARSHIPS, wôr'shĭps. Down through the ages warships have tended to fall into three major categories. *Capital ships,* representing maximum strength, have ordinarily operated together in large fleets or in smaller squadrons. *Cruisers,* including frigates and similar earlier types, have generally emphasized speed rather than strength; they have often acted singly in scouting, raiding or protecting commerce, or in carrying messages. Finally, there have often been various lesser types of *auxiliaries and specialized craft;* a large group of small vessels is called a flotilla. A nation's total force of all categories of warships comprises its navy. While warships have generally differed from cargo-carrying merchantmen, in the days of sail merchant vessels were often licensed by a government to operate as privateers against enemy shipping.

There has been a constant interplay between warships and tactics. The nature of the ships has influenced fighting methods and in turn has been influenced by them. There has been a gradual trend from close-range shock action toward long-range missile action. For centuries naval actions were really infantry fights on floating platforms; then came gunnery at gradually increasing distances, and finally very long-range attack by airplanes and guided missiles. Formerly almost all fighting was by surface vessels, but the 20th century has seen increasing activity in the air and by submarines beneath the surface of the sea.

THE AGE OF OARS

Mediterranean Galleys.—For more than 2,000 years the principal warships of the world were the slender Mediterranean galleys, propelled by oars, at least when they went into action. They dominated naval battles from Salamis in 480 B.C., and even earlier, down to Lepanto in 1571 A.D. Naturally they underwent various changes in size and structure during those centuries, but as distinct from later warships, the galleys of different periods had much in common.

First and foremost, they were built for speed and maneuverability rather than for sturdy seagoing qualities; compared with most sailing vessels, they were narrow in proportion to their length. They might raise their big, square sail to take advantage of a following wind while cruising, but for effectiveness in battle they generally relied on their numerous oars, which gave them a control of direction and speed not possible in vessels dependent on wind alone. Such a tactical advantage was achieved only at the sacrifice of important strategic qualities. Since the low sides of the galleys gave scant protection against high seas, the vessels usually hugged the coast, moving from one headland to the next; virtually all the great naval battles of the galley era were fought within sight of land. The slender craft had no room for crews to sleep aboard or for food, water, or other stores sufficient for more than a few days at a time. It was customary to go ashore every night, and in earlier days the boats were often pulled onto the beach. To avoid the boisterous winter seas the galleys were usually laid up between October and April. For these reasons, protracted campaigns and long blockades of enemy ports were seldom feasible. Throughout the long galley period cargoes in the Mediterranean were generally carried in tubby "round" ships, propelled by sails rather than by oars, and slower than the galleys but much more seaworthy.

Long before the galley proper had been developed by the Greeks, there were scattered recorded examples of Mediterranean fighting vessels having some of its general qualities. Around 1400 B.C., pirate raiders in fast, slender vessels threatened Egypt's commercial communications with Phoenicia and other parts of the eastern Mediterranean. Some two centuries later the Greeks captured Troy with a major expedition. Homer, the Greek poet, gave a detailed description of the Greek galleys in his *Iliad* (c. 850 B.C.), but he was writing long after the event. He described the Greek warships as swift and graceful craft, largely undecked; the larger ones were about 90 feet long with 50 oars, and the smaller ones approximately half that size. Throughout antiquity the rowers were freemen rather than galley slaves, who did not become common until medieval times. Those Homeric galleys apparently used their big, square sail when the wind was favorable, and oars only when it blew from the wrong direction or for battle action. The sea fighting was largely missile action between infantrymen armed with spears and bows.

Eventually a new concept of naval tactics led to galleys designed for effective shock action. The galley itself became the principal weapon. Propelled at top speed (ultimately 7 knots) by its rowers, it sought to sink or cripple an enemy craft by crashing into it with the strong, pointed ram at its bow. The evolution of galley design reflected efforts to increase man power at the oars without unduly increasing the size of the vessel.

The first such ram-equipped galleys began to appear before 800 B.C. The capital ship was the 50-oared penteconter, with 24 rowers on each side and 2 men with steering oars at the stern. A fighting platform, from which the marines could operate, ran fore and aft over the center of the galley. While the large number of oarsmen gave good power for ramming, the galleys were so long and narrow that they were often unseaworthy and difficult to maneuver. Around 700 B.C., the Phoenicians and Greeks began to meet that problem with the two-banked penteconter. Instead of 24 rowers seated one behind the other on each side, there were now 12 on the gunwale and 12 below them, operating their oars through ports in the hull. This resulted in a vessel with all the ramming power of its predecessor, yet at least a third shorter, with a stronger and more seaworthy hull, presenting a smaller target to the enemy.

The three-banked trireme, the most famous of all galley types, suddenly replaced the two-banked penteconter between 550 and 500 B.C., just in time for the great battles between the Greeks and the Persians. Additional oar power was secured without a serious increase in size by placing a third bank of rowers on an outrigger built above the gunwale and projecting beyond it. The largest triremes were apparently about 120 feet long and nearly 20 feet in beam. Like most galleys, they had low freeboard, with the gunwales only about 8 feet above the waterline. The trireme drew only about 3 feet, so that it could easily be beached at night. Its oars were about 14 feet long. In addition to its 170 rowers and 2 steersmen, it carried 5 officers, approximately 15 petty officers and specialists, and a number of spearsmen and archers.

The ancient fleets contained far more numerous capital ships than those of later days. Whereas there were only 27 British and 33 French and Spanish ships of the line at Trafalgar in 1805, and similar small numbers in the later great battles of Jutland (1916) and Leyte Gulf (1944), there seem to have been at least 1,000 triremes, and possibly 1,800, in the decisive Battle of Salamis in 480 B.C. At Aegospotami, in 405 B.C., the Spartans captured 171 of the 180 Athenian triremes, whose crews had gone ashore to forage for food.

By that time the first of the supergalleys were beginning to appear. In the new quadriremes (fours) and quinquiremes (fives) several men pulled at a single oar, instead of only one man, as in a trireme. (The exact rowing arrangements in the larger galleys have caused much speculation without satisfactory conclusions.) Competition in galley size reached its peak shortly after 300 B.C. in the fleets of Alexander the Great's successors in Greece and Egypt. They not only had many sevens, nines, and elevens, but went on past thirteens, with 1,800 rowers each, to include tremendous thirties and even larger ships. Some of the galleys carried catapults and movable wooden turrets. Those oversized galleys gradually disappeared; later fleets might have a few big tens, but fives were much more common. When the Romans suddenly took to the sea in force against the Carthaginians in 260 B.C., they invented the corvus, a sort of gangplank with a heavy spike. Dropped on the enemy decks, it gave the Roman legionaries a chance to fight an infantry action at sea.

Along with these heavy capital ships, some navies included lighter, faster vessels to serve the purposes of later frigates or cruisers, particularly in running down pirates and other raiders. Such were the *hemiolia* and *triemiolia,* which could use both sail and oars during a chase and then have some of the rowers leave their oars to stow away the mast and sail as action approached. In later days the Romans developed the *liburna* (Liburnian galley) for the same purpose.

Naval activity died out in the late Roman Empire, and no important innovations appeared until the Arabs attacked the Byzantine forces in the 7th century A.D. The Byzantine use of Greek fire (q.v.) and the Arab use of huge grappling hoops made the old ramming tactics impracticable, and the new Byzantine galleys, called dromons, emphasized speed and maneuverability. In the 10th century the Byzantines built larger galleys and even some specialized landing craft, while the Arabs countered with their own large galleys, some of them 250 or 300 feet long, using Greek fire and huge catapults.

By the 13th century, Venice, Genoa, and other Italian cities were bringing galleys to a final high peak of development, particularly to convoy the precious cargoes of silks and spices from Constantinople, Syria, and Egypt. The standard Venetian galley, in vogue from about 1290 to the late 1500's, had much in common with the old Greek triremes. It was 125 feet long, 15 to 18 feet in beam, and 4.5 feet in draft. Each of its 150 rowers operated a separate oar about 30 feet long, with 3 men sitting side by side on a slanting bench on either side of a central gangway. A fighting platform or forecastle was built in the bow, and a larger, higher castle in the stern. There, and sometimes along the gangway, the bowmen marines were stationed for action. There was usually one mast with a big lateen sail. The other Christian navies as well as that of the Turks used similar galleys. The Venetian rowers were generally freemen who often took part in the fighting, but chained galley slaves propelled most of the other fleets. By the 16th century the advent of gunpowder had led to the use of the primitive harquebus, while one or more cannon were placed in the bow.

Such galleys, little changed from the wars of 2,000 years earlier, made up most of the rival naval forces at Lepanto, where in 1571 the Christians defeated the Turks in the last great sea fight of the age of oars. The Christian fleet, about half Venetian, consisted of 208 galleys, 6 big three-masted galleases with cannon, 24 sailing vessels with supplies, and about 50 light rowing craft. The fleet was manned by 44,000 rowers and other mariners in addition to 30,000 soldiers. The Turkish force was similar. Each force went into battle in three divisions in line abreast; the fighting was at close range. While some navies, particularly the French, maintained galley forces two centuries longer, their role in action was negligible.

See also GALLEY; TRIREME.

Other Early Warships.—There was no such clear-cut continuity in warship development outside the Mediterranean. In northern Europe naval activity was usually a part-time affair, carried on in vessels that customarily served other purposes. Moreover, the warships were ordinarily simply transports carrying invaders to the scene of activity ashore; regular fights at sea were rare. The records of this northern naval activity are so scanty that, even after ingenious scholarly conjecture, ship types remain vague for most of the ancient and medieval period.

One important exception is the type of vessel in which the Scandinavian Vikings performed wonders in the century following 800 A.D. The well-preserved remains of such a ship, discovered in 1880 at Gokstad, south of Oslo, give a clear idea of its distinctive features. Like the galley, it combined a single big, square sail, for cruising with a following wind, with oars. Since the latter were carried chiefly for operating against a contrary wind rather than for shock action in battle, however, the rowers were less numerous—the Gokstad ship had 16 pairs of oars. It had elevated, planked deck sections fore and aft and could carry 60 or 70 persons. The ship differed from the galley most significantly in the sturdy seagoing qualities that enabled it to encounter the gales and long swells of the high seas, which would have swamped a galley with its low freeboard. In such vessels the Vikings ranged from Russia out to Iceland and later to Greenland, and southward to the British Isles and France. These were not full-time warships, however; they were used for trading and colonizing as well, and even when there was fighting, it usually occurred in raids ashore.

Around the end of the 9th century the English king Alfred the Great (r. 871–901) introduced two new features: a fairly full-time naval force and a larger type of warship. Both features were carried further by Canute and other Scandinavian rulers, some of whose dragon ships had 60 pairs of oars and carried 400 or 500 men.

Those big dragon ships, revived for a while around 1200, finally died out. During the later Middle Ages most naval activity became a part-time affair, with cargo-carrying "round" ships taken over temporarily for war service. That usually meant the construction of temporary castles fore and aft from which the fighting men could more easily attack the enemy. Dependent on sail alone, these tubby vessels were not capable of effective ramming or other tactical maneuvering; they simply provided floating platforms for infantry encounters at sea. Even when gunpowder was first employed, it was in the form of little "murthering pieces"—225 in one case—for use against the enemy's men rather than his ships. Those guns gradually transformed the temporary castles into permanent parts of the ship's structure.

Naval warfare was usually a part-time affair also in the Indian Ocean and in the Far East, where Arab dhows or Chinese junks were pressed into service for temporary action. The Koreans, however, in the years 1592–1598, produced one highly specialized type of vessel which was far ahead of its time. This was the strongly armored, tortoise-shaped ship with which they helped to drive Japanese invaders from their country.

THE AGE OF SAIL

Only 17 years after the last great galley fight at Lepanto, the defeat of the Spanish Armada by the English in 1588 marked a major turning point in naval history. In place of shock action at close range, the conventional naval battle for the next 250 years would be fought by sailing vessels firing cannon at each other, usually at a distance of a few hundred yards. This meant a radical change in the tactical and strategic capacity of the warship. The galley could more or less disregard wind and tide when the time came to attack in battle; its rowers could work up to a speed of 7 knots for short spurts. The sailing vessels, on the other hand, had far less tactical freedom of action; wind from the wrong direction or the absence of wind meant constant difficult adjustments and put a high premium on ship handling. Strategically, exactly the reverse was true. The slender galley was not capable of long cruises away from land, nor could it maintain a long blockade. The sailing vessel, however, could keep to the seas for months on end; her stout, seaworthy hull could withstand stormy seas and could carry sufficient food, water, and munitions to free her from constant dependence on a shore base. The nature of naval warfare naturally underwent a significant change.

One of the men who did most to bring about this change was John (later Sir John) Hawkins, an outstanding Elizabethan sea dog who had been a pioneer in penetration of the Spanish Main. In 1573 he became treasurer and comptroller of the navy, with responsibility for naval construction. In this capacity he was influential in evolving a type of warship that was sufficiently weatherly to get to windward of the enemy and pound him with long guns instead of engaging him in the traditional infantry fight at sea. Early in the Tudor period the English had taken the lead in shifting the ordnance emphasis from little man-killers in lofty castles to heavier ship killers placed down inside the hull, with gun ports cut through the side. The big galleons, however, kept their lofty superstructures until Hawkins cut them down to improve the sailing qualities. When the great Spanish fleet appeared off the south coast of England, Hawkins and the others were successful in keeping to windward of the Spanish ships and pounding them, while their thousands of infantrymen had no chance to get into action. Some of those Spaniards, incidentally, had participated in the successful hand-to-hand action at Lepanto.

See also ARMADA.

Ships of the Line.—All through the 17th century there was a gradual evolution of new types designed for long-range action. The larger ones were capital ships which fought in fleets or squadrons; the lesser ones were frigates and smaller cruisers, more apt to serve singly. In all cases, the principal weapon was the long gun, similar to the artillery used by armies ashore, but mounted on solid wooden carriages with little wheels instead of the big wheels of the army gun. These guns were muzzle loading, unlike the later breechloaders, and smoothbore instead of rifled; normally they fired solid round shot. For a long time, they were designated by the weight of that shot: a 32-pounder, for instance, fired a

Science Museum, London

The stern of an 18th century British warship.

ball approximately 6.5 inches in diameter, with an effective range of about 1,200 yards. Other guns in common naval use ranged from 12- to 64-pounders. Later, around the time of the American Revolution, carronades, which could fire large projectiles for short distances, were also often used.

The new tactics required a naval commander to become a ship handler as well as a fighting man. Formerly it had usually sufficed to tell the sailing master to lay alongside the enemy for hand-to-hand fighting. Now one's whole ship had to be maneuvered in order to aim one's broadside guns. The old galleys had charged into action side by side in long lines. Now, with one's guns arranged in broadsides, it became standard procedure for capital ships to go into action in a line-ahead (column) formation, since that gave the greatest freedom of maneuver and was least apt to interfere with the fire from the other ships. That is why the capital ships became known as ships of the line or line-of-battle ships. For years this formation was rigidly required by the British *Fighting Instructions* (1673); the standard naval action saw the rival fleets or squadrons fighting in parallel lines, each ship picking out an enemy opponent and blasting at her until something gave way. Late in the 18th century, however, a few bold admirals achieved success by breaking the line. In individual ship actions each captain sought to get to windward of his opponent and, if possible, to rake with his whole broadside, while the enemy could use few guns in reply.

A few notable ships were produced early in the 17th century, especially Britain's very successful capital ship, the *Sovereign of the Seas,* which was designed by Phineas Pett and launched in 1637. Rapid advances were made during the three stubbornly fought Anglo-Dutch Wars (1652–1674). By the end of that time warships were taking on uniform characteristics that would change little for more than a century. There was general similarity among the fleets of all maritime nations: captured vessels were constantly being absorbed by their captors. By and large, the whole 18th century was a static period with little change in ships or fighting methods. The average active life of warships and merchantmen, wooden ships or modern steel ones, has been about 20 years, but there were occasions where durable warships far older went into action. Lord Nelson's *Victory* was 40 years old at Trafalgar[1], and the *Royal William* was 63 when she fought in 1782, yet they differed little from the latest vessels of their type.

By the 18th century warships were designated by the number of guns they normally carried and also by the number of complete, covered gun decks. Largest of all were the clumsy, towering first-rate ships of the line, with 100 guns or more on their three decks. Like the slightly smaller second-rates, also three-deckers, with 90 guns or so, a few of them served in major fleets, usually as flagships. Their towering height gave them a certain advantage in action, but they were seldom as seaworthy as the two-decked third-rates, which made up the bulk of the battle lines. Some of these, especially in the French and Spanish navies, carried 80 guns. Others, with only 64, were barely strong enough for the line of battle but could be useful for convoy duty and on distant stations. Most popular of all the ships of the line was the third-rate 74, which could be relied on to sail well and fight well under most conditions. Of the 60 ships of the line in the rival fleets at Trafalgar in 1805, 7 were first-rate and 4 were second-rate three-deckers, 7 were 80's, and 4 were 64's; all the rest, a total of 38, were the popular 74's.

A typical 74 was the British *Ajax,* built on the Thames in 1798. Her tough hull extended 182 feet on her gun deck, between the captain's cabin at the stern and the broad, apple-cheeked bows that butted through the waves. Her beam was nearly 50 feet between her bulging yellow sides. She drew about 13 feet forward and 18 feet aft, and she measured 1,953 tons, as compared with about 2,300 tons for the first-rates. Through the ports on her gun deck poked the snouts of thirty 32-pounders, with thirty 24-pounders on the upper deck, and six more 24-pounders on her open quarterdeck and forecastle, along with 16 carronades, not all of which were counted in her nominal 74-gun rating. In those relatively cramped quarters, 600 officers and men often lived for weeks and even months without setting foot on shore.

It took 2,000 oak trees, many of them a century old, to build such a ship. The British were sentimental about those "hearts of oak" in their "wooden walls," but after 1800 their woodlands could scarcely keep up with the demand, and Britain had to search the world for Indian teak and other tough, exotic woods to fill the gap. Neither Britain, France, the Netherlands, or Spain had native firs or pines suitable as masts or yards for those square-rigged vessels. All were full-rigged ships, with square sails on the foremast, mainmast, and mizzenmast. It was necessary to send to the Baltic or North America for those masts and yards: the mainmast of a first-rate, for example, measured 40 inches in diameter and 40 yards in length.

Frigates and Lesser Warships.—Frigates, smaller and usually speedier, came next below the ships of the line. The British had a few two-decked fourth-rates of 50 guns or so; this was a rather unsatisfactory intermediate type, like the later armored cruisers, not strong enough for the battle line. The most numerous and important frigates were the fifth-rates, ranging usually from 32 to 38 guns; also numerous and useful were the sixth-rates, with 24 or 28 guns. They all had only one gun deck, but they carried some guns on the forecastle or poop. The same classes were general in the various continental European navies.

Like the later cruisers, the frigates had several functions. They were useful for commerce protection, which often involved the escort of groups of merchantmen in convoy; and in commerce raiding, normally welcome to officers and crews because of the chance for prize money. Frigates also served with the fleet for the rapid transmission of dispatches and for scouting—Nelson called them the "eyes of the fleet." Often they were employed to show the flag in foreign ports, especially on distant stations. With its far-flung commerce and colonial empire, Britain needed large numbers of such frigates.

In 1812 the British Navy had 112 frigates in active commission along with 124 ships of the line and nearly 400 lesser vessels. The United States, when it declared war that summer, had only 6 frigates and a few smaller vessels. Three of the frigates, however, were supercruisers of a type that would give the Royal Navy grave concern. Back in 1794 the Americans had decided that since they could not afford many ships, the few they had should be the best possible. That decision led to the 44-gun *Constitution, United States,* and *President;* fast and well gunned, they could run away from any individual ships they could not easily defeat. When the *United States* defeated the *Macedonian,* a conventional 38-gun frigate, in 1812, she had the advantage of displacing 1,576 tons, as compared with 1,325 tons for the British vessel. She measured 175 feet in length to the *Macedonian's* 158 feet, and had 478 men in officers and crew to the British 301. Of particular significance was the weight of her broadside: 846 pounds in contrast to 561 pounds for the *Macedonian.* The British finally captured the *President* by attacking her with four ships simultaneously in an encounter very similar to the action of three of their cruisers against the German supercruiser or pocket battleship *Admiral Graf Spee,* which presented a similar problem in 1939.

Below the frigates were lesser cruisers, headed by the sloops of war, not to be confused with the little, single-masted sloops of the merchant marine. Some earlier naval sloops had been two-masted brigs, but by 1800 most of them were full-

[1] Her keel was laid down in 1759, and she was launched in 1765.

Above: **Galleys in close action, first half of the 16th century.**

Right: **An English man-of-war of the period 1580 to 1600.**

Above: **A historic tug-of-war between two British naval sloops, April 3, 1845, when the propeller overcame the paddle wheel.**

WARSHIPS

Right: **Deck of the frigate U.S.S. *Constellation*, launched in 1797, now preserved as a public memorial at Fort McHenry, Baltimore, Md.**

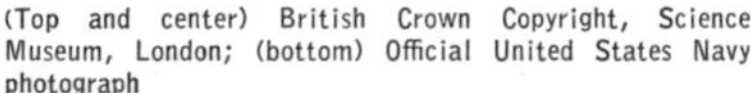

rigged ship sloops. One of these, the U.S.S. *Wasp*, captured the very similar H.M.S. *Frolic* in 1812; each was rated at 18 guns; their broadsides weighed 268 and 292 pounds, respectively, and their crews numbered 138 and 110. At the next lower level, in an 1813 fight between two 14-gun brigs, the American *Enterprise*, with a 135-pound broadside, defeated the *Boxer* with 126 pounds; their respective crews numbered 102 and 72. Beyond those cruisers proper, the navies contained numerous bomb ketches, cutters, storeships, and lesser craft; the United States built large numbers of rather worthless little gunboats just before 1812.

The years of almost continuous Anglo-French naval warfare between 1793 and 1815, into which the War of 1812 blended, saw the last major action, with a few exceptions, in the sailing ship era proper. In the case of the smaller classes of cruisers, moreover, this was the last time when merchantmen could be utilized on a large scale for warlike purposes. From time to time various nations converted merchant vessels to naval purposes, but merchantmen which received letters of marque and reprisal to serve as privateers in raiding enemy commerce were far more numerous.

See also FRIGATE; SAILING VESSELS.

THE PERIOD OF TRANSITION

By the time the ships of the line, frigates, and lesser craft had completed their combat duty in 1815, the long static naval era was about to give way to a period of continued and drastic change. By the end of the 19th century the world's navies would be transformed completely. Gradually sails gave way to steam for propulsion, while iron and then steel hulls, heavily armored in the case of capital ships, replaced the time-honored hearts of oak. The two movements were fairly distinct, merging only eventually to produce the final new types. The first steam warship was completed in 1815, but steam did not become general until the middle of the century, and even in the 1880's many cruisers on distant stations used sail much of the time in order to conserve coal. The shift to iron hulls and armor did not get under way until the 1850's, but once started it became general in the next two decades.

From Sail to Steam.—The shift from sail to steam produced far-reaching effects, of which the most important was freedom from dependence on winds and tides. In tactics it restored the freedom of action enjoyed by the oar-driven galleys; commanders could now choose a battle formation without having to wonder what the winds might do to it. In the field of strategy ships could now take a direct course instead of having to conform to trade winds, westerlies, or monsoons. Times of arrival, moreover, could be predicted with relative accuracy. But there were also strategic limitations. Whereas sailing ships could keep the seas for months on end without putting into port, steam warships were tied down to shore bases to replenish their bunkers—a situation that would not be finally relieved until the United States by World War II had evolved the art of fueling at sea and later had developed atomic power.

The first steam warship was the brainchild of Robert Fulton, who sought to break the strangling British blockade of New York in the War of 1812. His *Demologos* or *Fulton the First*, as she was later called, was designed for that specific local purpose with a tough, catamaranlike double hull. The paddle wheel was thoroughly protected in the middle of the ship. Her sides were 5 feet thick, and she carried thirty 32-pounder guns, measured 2,475 tons, and could make 5.5 knots. Unfortunately a shortage of government funds delayed her completion until the spring of 1815, after the war had ended and Fulton had died. After her trial runs she lay idle at Brooklyn Navy Yard until she exploded and burned in 1829.

The United States also provided the first naval action under steam. For operations by Commodore David Porter against West Indian pirates in 1823–1825, a little river steamer was commissioned as the galliot *Sea Gull*. She actually fired the first shots under steam at a time when the other vessels were becalmed.

In the next two decades the British and French added a few paddle-wheel vessels to their navies. These were useful for carrying dispatches and for towing becalmed sailing ships, but as fighting vessels they encountered two valid objections. Their paddle wheels were highly vulnerable to enemy fire, and, to a lesser degree, so was their machinery, which was located above the waterline. Moreover, their paddle wheels broke up the traditional broadside batteries, which were still regarded as the essential main armament.

Those objections were overcome by the introduction of the screw propeller (q.v.) in the early 1840's. The credit for its invention goes primarily to John Ericsson, a Swedish engineer, and to an Englishman, Francis Pettit (later Sir Francis) Smith, both of whom patented the idea in 1836. Skepticism and conservatism delayed its adoption for a few years. The first regular screw warship was the very satisfactory 954-ton *Princeton*, built by the United States in 1843, just ahead of the British *Rattler*, which failed to convince the Admiralty of the propeller's merits until, in 1845, she towed the paddle-wheeler *Alecto* backward at 2.5 knots.

The obvious advantages of the screw led to its speedy adoption in frigates and smaller craft. It was extended quickly to ships of the line after the French in 1850 launched the 92-gun *Napoléon*, whose 960-horsepower engines gave her almost 14-knot speed. The Crimean War (1853–1856) showed clearly the relative helplessness of the big sailing vessels, as did the American Civil War (1861–1865). No new purely sailing warships were built, although not until 1869 was the first capital ship laid down without masts or sails. Out on distant stations, where coal was scarce, ships still used sail for some time. Speed gradually increased: in 1886, British cruiser types averaged 12.6 knots; in 1914, 23.3 knots; and in 1939, 30.8 knots. United States Navy averages at those dates were 8.0, 20.4, and 32.9 knots, respectively.

From Oak to Iron and Steel.—Two separate developments, often confused, were the substitution of iron for wood as the material for hulls and the placing of heavy iron armor on the sides of major warships (by the 1890's steel had generally supplanted iron). There were, for a while, some armored ships with wooden hulls, and most of the smaller, faster iron or steel ships had no armor.

Two French engineers, graduates of the École Polytechnique, Henri Joseph Paixhans and Stanislas C. H. L. Dupuy de Lôme, played the principal roles in this transition. In 1822, Paixhans, who had been an engineer officer under Napoleon, produced his *Nouvelle force maritime,* which advocated the use of horizontal shellfire in place of the usual solid shot. He had been impressed with the fact that naval actions were usually far less deadly than land battles, and proposed to alter that situation by shells which would make a shambles of wooden ships. Using guns bored to larger calibers, he demonstrated in 1824 what shells could do to a ship of the line. Shell guns were gradually adopted in several navies, and then a clamor arose to "keep out the shells!" Paixhans thereupon wrote a pamphlet, *Expériences faites par la marine française, sur une arme nouvelle* (1825), advocating the use of heavy armor as the only protection against his shells. Before long the proving grounds in France, Britain, and elsewhere were firing heavy guns at slabs of iron to find out what was needed.

In 1843 the United States Congress made a heavy appropriation to start construction of a seagoing armored vessel proposed by the brothers Edwin A. and Robert L. Stevens of Hoboken, versatile inventors in several fields. After several shifts of policy and plans, a promising 4,683-ton twin-screw ship with powerful engines and armor 6.75 inches thick was left partly completed in 1856. Despite constant pressure in Washington, this first armored ship was allowed to rust unfinished at Hoboken.

Two events in the Crimean War accelerated the adoption of armor. At Sinop on the Black Sea, 11 wooden Turkish warships were quickly destroyed by the shell guns of a Russian squadron on Nov. 30, 1853. Later, when the allies found that their big wooden ships were unsuited to the close bombardment of the Russian fortifications, the French and British each built five shallow-draft floating batteries. On Oct. 15, 1855, the French *Tonnant, Lave,* and *Dévastation* bombarded the Kinburn forts successfully with relative impunity; the British vessels arrived just too late for that initial action.

Under the initiative of Dupuy de Lôme, the French next proceeded to apply armor to a seagoing vessel. He had already applied steam to the ship of the line *Napoléon* in 1850, and he was an ardent advocate of iron hulls. Now, in 1857, Napoleon III appointed him naval director of matériel. In March 1858, in a bold bid for command of the seas, France ordered four armored frigates. The first of these, the *Gloire,* was completed in 1859. Dupuy de Lôme believed in iron hulls, but, in order to get the ships to sea quickly, she and two others were built with wooden hulls, with iron used only in the *Couronne,* launched in March 1861.

See also Armor Plate; Floating Battery.

THE DEVELOPMENT OF MODERN WARSHIPS

Ironclads and Battleships.—The term "ironclad" was generally applied to armored vessels until steel supplanted iron in the 1890's, when the term "battleship" came into use. The original ironclads, though classed as frigates because of the number of their guns, quickly ousted the traditional wooden ships of the line from their long-lived role as capital ships exercising maximum power.

The ambitious French ironclad program stirred Great Britain into immediate action. It was standard policy for the British not to undertake any major innovation that might render obsolescent the commanding position of their existing fleet, but to be ready to meet quickly any foreign threats of such a nature. On May 25, 1859, shortly before the *Gloire* was ready for sea, the British answered the challenge by laying the keel of the *Warrior,* which was followed in October by the identical *Black Prince.* These ships were designed to "overtake and overwhelm any other warship in existence." They measured 9,210 tons to the *Gloire*'s 5,617 tons and had 30 or more heavy guns arranged in the conventional broadside manner; they could make 14 knots, as compared with the French ship's 13 knots. All three ships had 4.5-inch armor, which for the moment could give protection against the strongest smoothbore or rifled guns. Whereas the *Gloire*'s armor belt covered the whole length of her hull, however, the British armor covered only the vulnerable 213-foot midships section, the rest of the hull being protected by internal compartments.

The most significant difference in these pioneer ironclads was that the British ships had iron instead of wooden hulls. Great Britain and France had each built several unarmored iron warships between the early 1840's and mid-1850's, but they had then shifted back to wood. Although each was now once more fairly convinced of the value of iron, with the command of the seas possibly at stake both countries put armor plate on wooden hulls as a temporary expedient. The French announced a very ambitious ironclad program in 1860, but superior industrial facilities soon enabled the British to recover their old lead. Meanwhile, several other navies soon built or ordered armored ships. By the spring of 1862, when news of the dramatic *Monitor-Merrimac* (*Merrimack*) encounter in Hampton Roads crossed the Atlantic, 40 seagoing armored vessels and 30 armored coast defense vessels were built, building, or authorized in Europe.

When the Civil War began, the Americans had no armored ironclad except the rusting, unfinished Stevens battery, but both sides quickly improvised such ships. The South, despite its lack of industry, built several; in particular, it erected an iron structure over the hull of the frigate *Merrimac,* burned and sunk at Norfolk. The North tried three different types. One, the *Galena,* was worthless; and the second, the *New Ironsides,* was a seagoing armored frigate along the lines of the British and French ironclads. The third, designed by Ericsson, was the *Monitor.* It had a revolving turret with 8-inch armor, equipped with two 11-inch smoothbore guns and mounted on an armored hull with a very low freeboard.

On March 8, 1862, the *Merrimac* terrorized the wooden Union ships at Hampton Roads, ramming and sinking the *Cumberland* and setting the *Congress* afire with her shells. The *Monitor* arrived from New York that night, just in time to prevent further destruction on the next day. The two ironclads then fought an indecisive action with neither able to damage the other seriously. Unfortunately, the *Monitor* type, which was unsuited to general use on the high seas, became unduly popular in the United States for years to come. Had the *New Ironsides* been completed in time to win such popular acclaim against the *Merrimac,* the United States Navy might have secured more vessels of a useful type.

As it was, the Navy laid up or sold all of its ironclads after the war and reverted to obsolete wooden cruisers until the 1880's.

During those years the British and other European navies experimented constantly with many different types of ironclads. Not until 30 years after the appearance of the *Gloire* and the *Warrior* did a fairly standard type of predreadnought appear, and even then changes kept coming. The constant race between the offensive and defensive caused that situation, the steadily increasing power of the guns necessitating stronger and stronger armor. The 4.5-inch plate of the first ironclads, strong enough to withstand the 8-inch projectiles of the 68-pounders, quickly became inadequate.

The substitution of a turret with a few much heavier guns for the old broadside was the first major change. The *Devastation,* laid down in 1869, carried four 12-inch rifled guns with 706-pound projectiles, or more than 10 times the weight of those of the *Warrior.* In keeping with the general principle that a battleship's armor should withstand the sort of blows her guns delivered, the *Devastation's* side armor was 12 inches thick instead of 4.5 inches. Finally, to give a wider range of fire for her turret guns, she was the first capital ship without lofty masts and rigging. In 1872, even before she was completed, Italy was planning even bigger guns and thicker armor for her *Duilio* and *Dandolo,* which finally had 17.7-inch guns and 17-inch armor. The British *Inflexible,* designed to match them, had 16-inch guns and armor that reached an all-time thickness of 24 inches. The dimensions in inches thereafter declined somewhat, but a series of important technological developments led to even harder-hitting guns and tougher armor. Between the mid-1880's and mid-1890's smokeless powder, high-explosive shells, and steel armor plate created new conditions.

Until then, traditional black powder had served both to propel the projectile and to explode the shells. Now science moved in two directions. The new propellants, based on guncotton, gave a long, slow push instead of going off with a sudden bang. To take advantage of this development, gun barrels were made longer; the smokeless feature was an incidental by-product. The 12-inch gun of 1895 was 35.4 feet long, as compared with the 13.6-foot length of the 1870 gun. It was a steel breechloader rather than an iron muzzle-loader; with its muzzle energy increased from 9,400 tons to 33,000 tons, it 850-pound projectile could pierce 33 inches of wrought iron instead of 13 inches. At the same time, new devices were developed for more rapid loading and firing, and black powder gave way in the shells to picric acid and other nitro derivatives producing much more violent high-explosive results.

In the meantime, with the substitution of steel for wrought iron, armor became steadily better able to resist such increased blows. Compound armor, with hard-faced steel plate to resist penetration cemented to wrought iron backing to prevent cracking, appeared in the 1880's. After further experiments by the American Hayward Augustus Harvey and the Frenchman Joseph Eugène Schneider, the Krupp Works of Germany produced a plate, soon adopted by most navies, that combined great toughness with reduced weight. Krupp plate 5.75 inches thick gave as much protection as 12 inches of compound steel or 15 inches of the old wrought iron. For the same overall weight, therefore, a battleship could protect more of its hull or increase its guns or speed.

Midway in those developments, Britain provided a naval landmark with the *Royal Sovereign,* laid down in 1889 and completed in 1892. After three decades of constant change, she and her six sister ships embodied the features of the predreadnought type general in most navies until the *Dreadnought* herself appeared in 1906. The triple-expansion engines of this 14,150-ton battleship could drive her at 15.5 knots (16.5 knots under forced draft). Almost a third of her weight came from her compound steel armor, which measured 18 inches at its thickest. She carried four 13.5-inch guns in two turrets, fore and aft, with a secondary battery of ten 6-inch quick-firing guns, plus 24 much smaller ones. The combination of four big guns and several medium-sized ones was the distinguishing feature of the predreadnoughts, as compared with the all-big-gun dreadnoughts. With her 1,000 tons of coal, the *Royal Sovereign* had a cruising radius of 2,780 miles at 14 knots or 4,720 miles at 10 knots.

British Crown Copyright, Science Museum, London

Midship section of British ironclad H.M.S. *Devastation*.

The battleship now entered its heyday, which extended from the appearance of Capt. Alfred Thayer Mahan's *Influence of Sea Power upon History, 1660–1783* in 1890 to the Washington Conference of 1921–1922. As against the cruiser and commerce destruction, Mahan stressed the essential position of the capital ship in the command of the seas. His teachings spurred on three major newcomers: the United States, Germany, and Japan. When the Americans emerged from their naval dark ages in the early 1880's, they maintained at first their traditional predilection for cruisers, but in 1890 they too shifted to battleships. The first three American battleships proper, the *Indiana, Massachusetts,* and *Oregon,* each displacing about 10,300 tons, were somewhat smaller than those of the British; they carried four 13-inch and eight 8-inch guns. In 1907–1909 the Great White Fleet of 16 American battleships made a spectacular cruise around the world. The chief concern of the British, however, came from the Germans, who in 1900 announced a building program aimed at Britain. Meanwhile, the Japanese had turned to Britain for most of their new battleships, which soundly beat the Russians in 1904–1905. By 1904 there were nearly 100 first-class battleships built or building in the major fleets, Britain leading with 48, followed by the United States, with 24; Germany, with 22; Russia, with 19; and France, with 17.

Gunnery at long ranges was not very effective until after 1900, when the British and Americans, goaded by Percy Moreton (later Sir Percy) Scott and William S. Sims, began to develop fire-control devices that greatly improved accuracy at long distances. Spotting of ranges was confused by the mixture of splashes from the big and secondary guns. Moreover, if the secondary guns were omitted and the big guns increased, an all-big-gun ship might smother a conventional ship with its salvos before the latter's secondary guns could come into range. The Americans took a step in the new direction in 1905, planning to install eight 12-inch guns and no medium-sized ones in their *Michigan* and *South Carolina*. In the same year the Admiralty made a radical exception to its usual policy of "follow and overtake rather than initiate." Primarily concerned with German naval competition and realizing that in any case the new idea was in the air, the British decided that a quick and secret shift would give them a long head start with the new type, even though it would render their huge existing battle fleet obsolescent. The new *Dreadnought* was rushed through in a year instead of the usual three or four years. Laid down on Oct. 2, 1905, she took her trials on Oct. 3, 1906. She had ten 12-inch guns and no secondary battery, measured 17,900 tons, and could make 21 knots. Her effect was so revolutionary that her predecessors became known as predreadnoughts and her successors as dreadnoughts (later, superdreadnoughts). The gamble was successful, for the *Nassau*, the first German dreadnought, laid down in 1906, was not completed until 1909. When World War I broke out in 1914, Britain had been able to maintain her three-to-two lead over the Germans.

The importance of the battleship was at its peak in that conflict. Most of the scores of capital ships built during the previous half century had never fired a gun at an enemy; the only major fleet action had been the crushing victory of the Japanese battleships over the Russians at Tsushima on May 27–28, 1905. Now Britain's command of the seas depended primarily on the few additional dreadnoughts of her Grand Fleet, charged with the task of confining Germany's High Seas Fleet to the North Sea. The greatest sea fight in history (until Leyte Gulf) was an indecisive encounter between those two fleets on May 31–June 1, 1916, in the Battle of Jutland, which showed that battleships could absorb punishment that battle cruisers, with their lighter armor, could not.

The battleship situation was strongly affected when the Washington Conference of 1921–1922 accepted the American suggestion of a naval holiday in the building of capital ships, with a ratio of five-five-three for the United States, Britain,

Science Museum, London

The British battleship H.M.S. *Dreadnought*.

and Japan. Several partly completed American superdreadnoughts were then scrapped. Battleship construction was resumed after 1936, when Japan withdrew from the limitation agreements and Germany began to rearm; by 1941 powerful new ships appeared in several navies. Japan's huge 69,100-ton *Yamato* and *Mushashi*, with 18-inch guns, were the largest battleships ever built; they missed their chance for surface action and were sunk by American bombers. Germany built the 52,600-ton *Bismarck* and *Tirpitz*, which caused grave alarm before being sunk. The British and Americans, adhering to the 35,000-ton treaty limit, each built several of that size. Since the 28-knot American *North Carolina* and the rest were not fast enough to keep up with the new carrier task forces, four new ships capable of 33 knots, the *Iowa, Missouri, New Jersey*, and *Wisconsin*, were built during the war. Having about the same guns and armor as the 35,000-ton ships, they needed 10,000 additional tons for the extra speed. The four ships were 887 feet long with a 108-foot beam, and they each carried 2,700 men at war strength. Their 16-inch guns, 66 feet long, could throw a 2,700-pound armor-piercing projectile 23 miles and were quite accurate at 19 miles. To withstand that type of projectile they had armor belts 16 to 19 inches thick. The very fact that those latest models were designed to keep pace with carriers indicated the passing of the old primacy of the battleship. The battleship era finally came to an end on March 8, 1958, when the *Wisconsin*, the last one in commission, was laid up in reserve; the British had laid up their last battleship, the *Vanguard*, in 1956.

The cost of capital ships mounted at a rate much faster than that of prices in general. The *Warrior* (1861) had cost only $1.8 million; the *Royal Sovereign* (1892), $4.5 million; and the *Dreadnought* (1906), $8.9 million. The 45,000-ton *Missouri*, on which the Japanese surrendered in Tokyo Bay in 1945, cost $100 million, the same as the whole 16-ship Great White Fleet, and 10 times as much as the 27 British ships of the line that won Trafalgar. By 1959 a single submarine would be in the same $100 million class.

Cruisers.—Corresponding in function to the frigates, sloops, and gun brigs of the age of sail, modern cruisers of various types have stood midway between capital ships and the little vessels of the flotilla. Responding to many of the same innovations as the capital ships, they have undergone a complex evolution since the coming of steam and iron. In 1886, when Baron (later 1st Earl) Brassey began his *Naval Annual,* the lists of cruising ships showed most of them to be unprotected and almost half of them to be partly or wholly of wood. By the eve of World War I nearly all of them were protected or armored, their speed had almost doubled, and some rivaled battleships in size. When World War II began, the larger cruisers were almost gone, leaving two similar types of moderate size. The figures given in Table 1 do not include the little gunboats, as distinct from gun vessels, which Admiral Sir John (later 1st Baron) Fisher eventually eliminated from the Royal Navy, remarking that they could "neither fight nor run away" but were "absorbing valuable officers and men."

The cruiser type that survived longest comprised the moderate-sized, moderately armed, and relatively speedy vessels, particularly useful in time of war for guarding one's own commerce or for raiding the enemy's; in peacetime many of them showed the flag on distant stations. By 1886 all of them were equipped with steam, but to conserve coal many still did much of their cruising under sail. This was especially true of the American ships, whose propellers had even been reduced to improve their sailing qualities. Most of the active United States fleet still consisted of old wooden vessels, some of them built before 1861. Except for the very latest ones, they were armed largely with old smoothbore guns, whereas virtually every other navy had nothing but rifled guns, many of them breechloading. Half of the British cruisers were of composite construction, with wooden planking over iron frames; a few were all wooden, and a few all iron; and an increasing number had steel hulls. The protected ships, a category which grew steadily, had an internal iron deck about 2 inches thick, which sloped down to the waterline at each side, with coal piled on top. The American *Atlanta* and *Boston,* completed in 1886, each had a 1.5-inch belt over her machinery. The British preferred this type to the armored cruiser until the end of the century and built a considerable number of various sizes.

Other nations, however, began to turn to armored cruisers by 1890. With their side armor, they often approached battleships in size, gunpower, and appearance and usually exceeded them in speed. In the eternal compromise between armor, armament, and speed, a few extra knots were often secured at the expense of a few inches of armor protection. Such ships presented a real threat to Britain, with its widespread empire and trade. British strategy traditionally called for confining enemy capital ships in port. The most serious threat lay in potential enemy supercruisers fast enough to evade any ship they could not defeat. Such had been the American 44-gun frigates in 1812 and the American *Wampanoag,* which made 17.75 knots in 1868, almost a decade before any other ship traveled that fast. The Americans accomplished the same thing with their 21-knot armored cruiser *New York* in 1891, but the real British concern was for the French armored cruiser *Dupuy de Lôme* of 1890, the forerunner of an avowed program of threatening British commerce. When the new light, tough Krupp armor plate made it possible to gain protection against 6-inch shells, the British began to turn out 12,000-ton and even 14,000-ton armored cruisers to offset those French threats. Then they moved on, in an unhappy moment, to the big battle cruisers, conceived at the same time as the *Dreadnought.* The *Invincible, Inflexible,* and *Indomitable* were almost identical with the *Dreadnought* in tonnage and in cost; each had eight 12-inch guns to her ten. But they had only 6 or 7 inches of armor in place of her 11 inches; that was the price for their extra 4 knots or more of speed. The three ships were only a start; by 1914 the British had nine, and the Germans four. Once the term "battle cruiser" had been applied to the type, both countries began to count them with dreadnoughts for the battle service for which their sides were too thin.

Compared with battleships and ordinary cruisers, armored cruisers and battle cruisers suffered very heavy losses in World War I. Three British armored cruisers were sunk by a submarine on Sept. 22, 1914. A few weeks later, on November 1, two more were sunk off Coronel, Chile, by two German armored cruisers, which in turn succumbed on December 8 to two British battle cruisers off the Falkland Islands. The Battle of Jutland, the classic dreadnought encounter, discredited those big, lightly armored ships; three British battle cruisers and two armored cruisers were sunk, while the similar German cruisers were badly mauled. Altogether, the British lost 11 of their 34 armored cruisers in the war, and the Germans 7 of their 9. Nevertheless, the British built a few more battle cruisers, culminating in 1920 in the 42,000-ton *Hood,* with 8-inch armor and a speed of 32 knots. For many years the *Hood* was the largest warship afloat, but on May 24, 1941, she blew up after being hit by the *Bismarck.* The United States converted two projected battle cruisers to aircraft carriers after the Washington Conference.

Another variation of the armored cruiser pattern consisted of the German pocket battleships, built to meet the prohibition of the Treaty of Versailles against German possession of new warships of more than 10,000 tons. With aluminum, welding, and other weightsaving means, the three ships, each of which actually displaced 12,000 tons, carried six 11-inch guns and many smaller ones, and could make 26 to 28 knots with 3- or 4-inch side armor and a protected deck. The British met the threat in World War II by sending out ordinary cruisers in groups; three of them ended the *Admiral Graf Spee's* career off the Río de la Plata in December 1939.

Between the wars cruiser categories were generally narrowed down to heavy cruisers with 8-inch guns and light cruisers with 6-inch guns. Some had side armor, seldom more than 3 inches thick; some had thin protective decks; and most of them could make 30 knots or more. The Washington Conference limited cruisers to 10,000 tons, but the five-five-three ratio was not extended to them until the London Conference (1930), following a bitter dispute between the British "6-inch admirals," who wanted many smaller cruisers, and the American "8-inch admirals," who wanted fewer but larger ones. With the additional weight demands of antiaircraft and radar equipment, American designers felt cramped by the 10,000-ton limit. Once it had been removed, they built two 14,700-ton cruisers of the *Worcester* class, with twelve 6-inch guns, and three 17,000-ton heavy cruisers of the *Des Moines* class, which had quick-firing 8-inch guns.

A bow-on view of the nuclear-powered aircraft carrier USS *Dwight D. Eisenhower*.

U.S. NAVY

H. ARMSTRONG ROBERTS

Early sea trials of a nuclear-powered attack submarine in waters of Long Island Sound.

U.S. NAVY

The nuclear-propelled guided missile cruiser USS *Virginia* underway in the Atlantic.

Cruisers of these relatively moderate sizes continued into later new developments, but the very large types, such as the battle cruisers and big armored cruisers, were abandoned, as were the little gun vessels and gunboats at lower levels. Scattered around the world, they had long exercised gunboat diplomacy but, "too slow to run and too weak to fight," they gave way to the versatile destroyers.

See also CRUISERS; NAVAL CONFERENCES.

Destroyers and Escort Craft.—Naval development was strongly affected by Robert Whitehead's invention of the automobile torpedo between 1864 and 1875. The earlier spar torpedoes had to be carried directly into contact with their target, but the Whitehead torpedoes could be discharged from a distance, which increased steadily. When swift, little cigar-shaped torpedo boats were built to approach the enemy stealthily, the doom of the capital ship was predicted prematurely. One of the first, if not the first, of such craft was Britain's 27-ton *Lightning*, completed in 1877; 84 feet long and only 10.9 feet in beam, it carried 15 officers and men and could make 19 knots. France adopted boats of this type as a means of cutting down Britain's long lead in battleships, building them by the score and setting up many nests of them just across the English Channel. Britain was naturally alarmed; battleships at anchor protected themselves with nets, while quick-firing guns and searchlights were developed. By 1886 the British had 10 torpedo cruisers to combat the menace, but at 17 knots they were too slow. In 1892, Alfred (later Sir Alfred) Yarrow proposed to Admiral Fisher a new class of larger, stronger, and faster vessels to meet the menace. "We'll call them 'Destroyers,'" said Fisher, "as they're meant to destroy the French boats." No time was lost; the first two, the 240-ton *Havock* and *Hornet*, were completed in 1893. With the 10-to-1 ratio of length to beam (180 feet to 18 feet) that would become general, they could make 27 knots. As anticipated by Yarrow, they gradually eliminated torpedo boats by taking over their offensive function as well as providing defense against sneak attacks. Soon they developed into one of the most versatile and useful types of warships, able to take over some of the old gunboat functions in addition to their work in torpedo defense and attack. By 1914, Britain had 218 destroyers; Germany, 142; Russia, 105; France, 83; and the United States, 52. France alone had a sizable torpedo flotilla.

The destroyer came into its own in World War I as an antidote to the submarine. Fast, maneuverable, and equipped with depth charges and other antisubmarine devices, it was in demand for convoy duty besides service with the fleet. Between 1917 and 1922 the United States turned out 272 four-stacker destroyers (DD-75–DD-347) of 1,090 to 1,190 tons with a 35-knot speed, Many served in World War II as light minelayers (DM), high-speed minesweepers (DMS), and high-speed transports (APDO); 50 were transferred to Britain in 1940 in exchange for bases in British possessions. With so many destroyers on hand, no new ones appeared until the 1,350-ton *Farragut* class in 1934. During World War II large numbers of vessels of the 2,050-ton *Fletcher* and 2,485-ton *Gearing* classes were built. By 1958 the new *Hull* class, largest of the regular destroyers, reached 2,850 tons, with three 5-inch and four 3-inch guns and a 33-knot speed. One of this class, the *Turner Joy*, was DD-951, indicating the cumulative number of the United States Navy's regular destroyers since the original 420-ton *Bainbridge* of 1901.

In a much shorter time the smaller, slower destroyer escorts (DE) had reached a total of 1,036. With the very heavy demand for convoy escort work during World War II, the need was felt for more substantial vessels than the 110-foot submarine chasers (PC, SC) and other patrol craft, but the 33-knot speed of the regular destroyers, requiring scarce machinery, was not needed for slow convoys. The answer was a vessel ranging from 1,140 to 1,400 tons and about 300 feet long, usually armed with three 3-inch or two 5-inch guns capable of 22 to 24 knots. A few with a 25-knot speed were built in the mid-1950's. The British counterparts of such lesser patrol vessels, originally designated by such names as sloops and corvettes, were finally included in the flexible category of frigates, indicating vessels usually older, smaller, or slower than the newer destroyers. In the United States Navy, on the other hand, the term "frigate" was applied to certain vessels larger than the regular destroyers, such as the 3,500-ton destroyer leaders (DL) of the *Mitscher* class and certain guided missile vessels (DLG).

In the meantime, while the original little torpedo boat of 1877 had gradually evolved into a veritable cruiser, the cycle began again with the very fast little motor torpedo boats to restore the original purpose of approaching stealthily to deliver a torpedo attack. The possibilities of this type were revealed in World War I, when Italian boats sank two Austrian dreadnoughts. Various navies adopted the type; in World War II the United States patrol-torpedo (PT) boats had 27-ton wooden hulls and speeds of 40 knots or more.

See also MOTORBOATS—*Naval Motorboats;* TORPEDO.

Submarines.—The submarine was developed to deliver torpedo attacks more safely than by means of small surface vessels. Early experiments with submersibles had been made by David Bushnell, Robert Fulton, the Confederates, and others, but the appearance of the modern submarine proper had to await the invention of the electric battery for submerged operation, coupled with the internal combustion engine for surface cruising. The French Navy commissioned the little *Gymnote* as early as 1888 and took a long lead in building primitive submarines, and there were experiments in other European countries in the 1890's. The distinctive features of the modern submarine, however, were first embodied in the *Holland* (actually, *Holland No. 9*), named for its inventor, John P. Holland, an Irish-born resident of Paterson, N.J. This 54-foot, 75-ton boat, which could make 7 knots surfaced and 6 knots submerged and dive in 8 seconds, was purchased and commissioned by the United States Navy in 1900. Holland's designs and those of another American, Simon Lake, were soon used in building submarines for several navies. By 1914 the British had 97 submarines built or building; France had 86; the United States, 49; and Germany, 45. The adoption of the gyrocompass in 1908 and the diesel engine in 1909 greatly increased submarine effectiveness.

By that time most of the standard submarine

features had been developed. The new vessel was a long, narrow cigar-shaped tube of steel, filled with elaborate machinery. Ballast tanks placed between the outer and inner shells of the hull could be suddenly filled with water to submerge her and then emptied to bring her to the surface again. Diesel engines for propulsion on the surface were far more satisfactory than the original gasoline engines, but they required fresh air to operate and were useless when submerged. Storage batteries were employed to run beneath the surface, but the speed was much slower, and the batteries could operate only briefly; then the vessel had to rise to the surface to recharge them. While torpedoes, discharged through tubes placed either forward or aft, were the principal weapon, there was often a 3- or 4-inch gun, and some submarines carried mines to lay instead.

Early in World War I some submarines carried out their originally planned function of approaching by stealth and sinking enemy warships. The real importance of the submarine, however, dates from the German attacks on merchant shipping in February, 1915, which, when renewed in an unrestricted manner in February 1917, almost forced Great Britain into submission before the convoy system and other antisubmarine devices had been perfected. Because of their compact size and vulnerability, the U-boats (*Unterseeboote*) could not follow the traditional surface practice of search and seizure. At the Washington Conference of 1921–1922 the British sought the abolition of the submarine, but France and other nations objected, and they remained a part of all major navies.

In World War II the United States had the dual role of combating German submarine attacks in the Atlantic while very effectively sinking Japanese shipping in the Pacific. American submarines of the *Gato* class, built in large numbers during the war, measured 311 feet in length and 27 feet in beam, displaced 1,525 tons on the surface and 2,425 tons submerged, had a complement of 85 officers and men, and could make 21 knots on the surface and 10 knots submerged. They had six tubes for 21-inch torpedoes in the bow and four in the stern and carried a 3-inch or 5-inch gun and a small antiaircraft gun. One of the chief difficulties in submarine operation was the need to surface frequently in order to recharge batteries. Toward the end of the war the Germans began to use the snorkel, which, projected above the surface, obviated the need to expose oneself. This naturally made detection much more difficult.

See also SUBMARINE.

Aircraft Carriers.—During World War II the aircraft carrier supplanted the battleship as the principal warship. Its prime value has lain in its ability to deliver heavy blows at far greater distances than the 20 or more miles which a 16-inch shell can reach. On the other hand, the carrier has lacked the armor that has enabled the battleship to absorb heavy blows, and so has depended on escorting cruisers, destroyers, and even battleships to ward off enemy attacks. The carrier task force has replaced the old battle line as the major tactical formation. The most conspicuous feature of the carrier, accounting for its nickname "flattop," is the huge flight deck from which planes can take off and on which they can land again, checked by arresting gear. The planes are brought up by elevators from their hangars below decks, and launching is assisted by catapults. To leave the flight deck as nearly clear as possible, the funnel and bridge are generally crowded at one side. The necessity of carrying large quantities of aviation gasoline has constituted a serious fire hazard.

The airplane was even more of a naval novelty than the submarine in World War I. At first emphasis was placed on the seaplane, which was used primarily for scouting. In 1913 the British had equipped the cruiser *Hermes* for carrying a few seaplanes, which were hoisted in and out by a crane, Later the converted passenger liner *Engadine,* similarly equipped, was present, with scant effect, at Jutland. Then came the more difficult task of launching and receiving wheeled land planes. This led during the war to the first of several conversions of the abnormal 19,000-ton, 30-knot cruiser *Furious* into what became the first carrier. The British had acquired several more carriers before the Americans, in 1922, completed the conversion of the 11,000-ton collier *Jupiter* into their first carrier, the *Langley* (CV1). By 1927 two projected American battle cruisers had been converted into the 33,000-ton *Lexington* and *Saratoga.* By that time, Japan had built the 7,500-ton *Hosho* and had converted the *Kaga* and *Akagi* from battleship and battle cruiser hulls, respectively. Carrier design, like naval aviation techniques in general, proceeded slowly, with constant experimentation, between the wars. Gradually bombing attacks overshadowed the early emphasis on scouting; carriers had to carry protective light fighters in addition to bombers. By 1939 the British had 12 carriers built or building, while the United States and Japan each had 7. The marginal value of a single vulnerable carrier was consequently very high.

A landmark in the history of naval warfare was the Battle of the Coral Sea on May 7–8, 1942, when the ships of the rival American and Japanese carrier forces did not come within sight of each other. The Japanese attack on Pearl Harbor and the American raids on Tokyo showed the possibilities of carrier warfare. The major American carriers during World War II were those of the 30,800-ton *Essex* class. With flight decks usually measuring 876 by 113 feet, they could carry about 100 planes and 2,800 officers and men. Their armament consisted simply of a few 5-inch guns. Like the cruisers and destroyers, they could make at least 33 knots. In later days they were classed as support carriers (CVS), while the smaller *Saipan* and *Cowpens* classes, wartime conversions from cruiser hulls, were called light carriers (CVL).

The escort carrier (CVE) was a wartime innovation designed to give convoy protection in mid-ocean beyond the range of land-based planes. As in the case of the destroyer escorts, high speed was not necessary. Large numbers of these so-called jeep carriers were produced, some of the early ones being converted from merchant marine hulls. The 9,800-ton *Bogue* (CVE-1), completed in 1942, had a flight deck measuring 492 by 112 feet, could accommodate 30 planes, and made 18 knots. In conjunction with destroyers or destroyer escorts, they made possible very effective hunter-killer antisubmarine tactics.

By the end of the war the first of the still larger attack carriers (CVA) began to appear, with the 51,000-ton *Midway* and *Franklin D. Roosevelt,* which were followed in 1947 by the *Coral Sea.* The three ships alternated as the nucleus of the Sixth Fleet in the Mediterranean. Then, to accommodate the huge new jet bombers, the 56,000-ton *Forrestal* class carriers (CVA-59–CVA-64) began to appear by 1955. Their very strong flight decks, measuring about 1,040 by 252 feet, were capable of accommodating about 100 of the largest planes. The United States Navy also undertook extensive modernization of many older carriers to adapt them to the new demands. Some important innovations were borrowed from the British. In particular, in place of the former axial or fore-and-aft flight deck, the after portion was angled or canted so that landing planes, if not properly arrested, would not endanger planes on the forward deck. This arrangement also permitted planes to be launched and landed at the same time. In addition, the hydraulic catapults formerly used for launching began to give way to more powerful steam catapults that could thrust a 35-ton plane, with its engines going at full speed, from a standing start to a speed of 115 knots in 15 seconds. Armored decks also were introduced in the newer carriers.

Other Ships.—Besides the principal warships described separately, navies maintain numerous auxiliary ships, including submarine tenders (AS), destroyer tenders (AD), oilers (AO), hospital ships (AH), attack transports (APA), attack cargo ships (AKA), and ammunition ships (AE). Many specialized types of these vessels and various landing craft were developed in connection with amphibious warfare operations in World War II. More than 100 different types of landing craft grew out of that conflict, among them infantry landing ships (LSI), tank landing ships (LST), and landing craft—personnel (LCP).

See also AMPHIBIOUS WARFARE.

CHANGES OF THE POSTWAR PERIOD

The 1950's saw warships undergo more profound changes than in any other decade except the years around 1860. Nuclear power was introduced for both submarines and surface ships, and guided missile launchers began to replace gun turrets. With its substantial resources and worldwide responsibilities, the United States took the lead in these developments.

The new trend was particularly apparent in the steadily increasing variety of specialized ship types designed to meet particular needs and techniques. Previously scores or even hundreds of fairly uniform vessels had been designated by the same symbols—destroyers (DD), submarines (SS), carriers (CV), and cruisers (CA and CL). Now dozens of new symbols were added to designate specialties. The most significant of the postwar changes were denoted by adding an N for nuclear propulsion and a G or a B for guided or ballistic missiles. Sometimes the nuclear and missile features were combined in the same vessel, such as the *Long Beach* (CGN-9), the first nuclear guided missile cruiser, launched in 1959, and the *George Washington* (SSBN-598), a nuclear submarine designed to fire the intermediate-range ballistic missile Polaris.

Development of Atomic Propulsion and Guided Missiles.—Scientists were quick to realize that in addition to its potentialities for explosive purposes, atomic fission could develop useful power. In the naval field this meant a form of propulsion combining better strategic and tactical characteristics than oars, sails, coal, or oil had possessed. With a nuclear core scarcely the size of a basketball and capable of propelling a small vessel more than 100,000 miles without the necessity of replenishing its fuel supply, atomic power could be very useful in surface vessels. Moreover, its use would open up entirely new possibilities in the strategic employment of submarines, which would be able to cruise almost indefinitely, even under polar ice, without having to approach the surface to charge their batteries, as conventional submarines, even those equipped with snorkels, must do.

It was the problem of adapting atomic power to submarines that first received attention from the United States Navy. The Navy had been interested in nuclear fission since 1939, but the direct development of atomic propulsion dated from 1946, when Capt. (later Vice Admiral) Hyman G. Rickover, a naval engineer, went with some young officers to study the problem at the United States Atomic Energy Commission's laboratories in Oak Ridge, Tenn. In 1948 work on the development of a reactor for naval use began at the Argonne National Laboratory in Chicago. The reactor finally developed was able to generate steam for running the engines by heating water that would not be radioactive. (An alternative method using sodium proved less satisfactory in use and was discarded in favor of the water coolant.) A heavy lead sheath was needed for protection against radiation. Before installing the new machinery in the first submarines, it was tested in a submarine hull at Arco, Idaho.

While Rickover's group was developing the atomic reactor, another naval-scientific force, based at Johns Hopkins University, worked on guided missiles. The damage suffered by the United States Fleet from Kamikaze attacks as it approached Japanese waters in World War II had emphasized the need for weapons more effective than ships' antiaircraft fire or fighter planes. The V-1 and V-2 missiles used by the Germans against Great Britain in 1944–1945 directed attention to missile possibilities. In January 1945, the Navy Bureau of Ordnance and the Johns Hopkins Applied Physics Laboratory, with the cooperation of other universities and laboratories, began work on the Bumblebee project in missile research and development.

Of the wide variety of surface-to-surface, surface-to-air, air-to-surface, and air-to-air missiles developed by this and other projects, warships were most directly affected by the series of surface-to-air missiles with the popular names Terrier, Tartar, and Talos. These missiles were designed primarily for protection against fast, powerful high-altitude bombers. With their use, carriers, which had devoted much of their plane capacity to protective interceptor fighters, could accommodate greater numbers of offensive bombers.

The Terrier, Tartar, and Talos are graceful, slender missiles, with sharp points and small fins or wings. In addition to the missile proper, each has a large rocket booster which drops off quickly after launching. They use a solid rather than a liquid propellant, which might create a serious fire hazard. All three are guided in flight by shipboard radar, at least until within homing distance of their targets.

The first Bumblebee missile in operation was the Terrier, in 1953. With a diameter of about 45 inches and a length of 15 feet (exclusive of its 10-foot booster), it has a range of about 20 miles (32 km). Its heavy twin launcher can fire two missiles simultaneously. The missiles can be fired automatically at the rate of eight per minute once the radar has been fixed on the target. The Tartar, a lighter version of the Terrier, is similar in size and range but has lighter equipment for use aboard destroyers or in place of a larger ship's secondary batteries. The Talos, first used in 1958, is a much more potent weapon, with a range of about 70 miles (115 km) and the ability to attain an altitude of 75,000 feet (22,-860 meters). It weighs 3,000 pounds (2,160 kg), measures 20 feet (6 meters) in length, and has a 30-inch (76-cm) diameter. In addition to fulfilling its antiaircraft function, it can be used against ships, shore targets, or submarines.

Use of Atomic Propulsion and Guided Missiles. On Aug. 20, 1951, with the Rickover and Bumblebee projects showing results, the Navy ordered its first nuclear submarine. On December 4 of that year, it ordered the conversion of the first cruiser for guided missiles. By the late 1950's new developments crowded one after the other. The most important was the world's first application of atomic power to ship propulsion in the submarine *Nautilus*. Beginning with her first trials late in 1954, her performance was highly satisfactory. In August 1958 she made the first passage under the Arctic ice, proceeding from the Pacific to the Atlantic via the North Pole. See also NAUTILUS, THE U. S. S.

Meanwhile, the Navy had been experimenting with submarine hull design. The earlier submarines had been essentially submersibles, spending much of their time on the surface. Nuclear propulsion called for designs that would give the best results while the vessel was submerged. The teardrop or whale-shaped hull, broad at the bow and tapering aft, was tested in 1953 in the *Albacore,* which achieved a record underwater speed. This type of hull and the new nuclear power were combined in 1959 in the *Skipjack,* which was able to make 25 knots while submerged and proved highly maneuverable. Unlike the conventionally powered submarines, the nuclear submarines were designed to be faster submerged than surfaced. The two major features of nuclear propulsion and missiles were combined in the *Halibut* (1960) and the *Permit* (1962), both of which were designed to carry Regulus missiles capable of shore bombardment.

In the 1950's, guided missiles steadily replaced the conventional rifled guns on surface vessels. The pioneer ship in this development was the heavy cruiser *Boston,* whose after 8-inch (20-cm) gun turrets were replaced by two Terrier twin mounts in 1955. In the same way the destroyer *Gyatt* was transformed from DD-712 to DDG-1 with a single Terrier launcher. In 1956 it became the first missile-armed destroyer. The next step, when the heavier Talos missiles became available in 1958, was to use them on some of the cruisers, starting with the *Galveston* (CLG-3). Since Terrier installations were too heavy for destroyers, the lighter Tartar missiles were installed on eight large destroyers of the *Charles Francis Adams* class, but the ten still larger *Farragut*-class frigates were equipped with single twin Terrier launchers. All of these vessels were known as single-end ships because they retained the traditional rifled guns in turrets forward in addition to the missiles aft. Finally, the Navy decided to substitute missile launchers for the forward guns as well. The first of these double-end ships was the converted heavy cruiser *Albany,* equipped in 1961 with two twin Terriers forward and two twin Talos mounts aft. Without requiring major transformations, Regulus ship-to-shore missiles with a range of about 500 miles (800 km) were installed on most of the largest carriers and on some of the heavy cruisers.

The first two nuclear-powered surface warships were commissioned in 1961. They were the guided-missile-armed cruiser *Long Beach* and the aircraft carrier *Enterprise*. The *Long Beach,* with Terriers forward, Talos aft, and Regulus missiles amidships, is estimated to have a cruising radius of 140,000 miles (225,000 km) without having to replenish fuel or stores and to have a top speed of 45 knots. The *Enterprise,* an 85,000-ton attack carrier, became the largest warship afloat, a distinction previously held by the conventionally powered carriers of the *Forrestal* class. Although the *Enterprise* with her eight nuclear reactors can remain longer in active front areas and carry more fuel for her planes and escorts, the tactical advantages of nuclear power in aircraft carriers are not so striking as in submarines, where there is a difference in kind and not simply in degree. Nuclear power would be more useful in the little destroyers, which have to refuel every two or three days when operating at top speed, but the weight of the reactor-protection lead shield and other equipment presents a problem in slender hulls crowded with intricate gear.

More fundamentally significant than the huge 1,100-foot (335-meter)-long *Enterprise* was the development of the 1,500-mile (2,400-km) Polaris ballistic missile and the large nuclear submarines to carry and launch it. This enabled the Navy to create a strategic deterrent of prime importance in the weapons competition of the cold war. In addition to short- and medium-range guided missiles, that competition produced intercontinental ballistic missiles (ICBM's), designed to cover the entire distance between the competing nations, and intermediate-range ballistic missiles (IRBM's), capable of reaching part of the way. While the ground-launching sites of ICBM's and IRBM's could be destroyed in an initial enemy attack to prevent a counterstroke, missile-bearing nuclear submarines would still be capable of destroying the enemy's cities, thus providing a substantial deterrent effect.

The next step was to devise a missile that could be carried aboard a submarine and fired while submerged. Rear Adm. William F. Raborn, Jr., was largely responsible for that development. Ballistic missiles of the U. S. Army and Air Force were too large and their liquid fuel too dangerous for use on a submarine. The use of solid fuel, as in guided missiles, solved the problem of devising a missile suitable for carrying on submarines. A powerful missile that could be fired from a submerged submarine became possible after the Atomic Energy Commission found that the weight of a thermonuclear warhead could be radically reduced. The result was the Polaris, which the Navy terms a fleet ballistic missile (FBM), measuring 27 feet (8.2 meters) in length and 8 feet (2.4 meters) in diameter and weighing about 14 tons.

As vehicles for such weapons, the Navy in 1958 began construction of five specially designed nuclear submarines (SSBN's, denoting ballistic-missile-armed, nuclear-powered submarines). The first of these, the *George Washington,* was completed in 1959. Each of these vessels was designed to carry 16 Polaris missiles. Elaborate navigation devices had to be perfected to enable a submerged missile-carrying submarine to ascertain its location in relation to potential targets.

LATER DEVELOPMENTS

In the United States in the 1960's and 1970's the nuclear-powered ballistic-missile submarine (SSBN) became and remained the most important type of warship because of its role in the U. S. strategic offensive forces. In this role, the SSBN provides underwater speed, endurance, and concealment combined with a capability of firing nuclear-warhead missiles over distances that have been stepped up from 1,400 miles (2,250 km) to more than 2,500 miles (4,000 km).

SSBN Program. The first five SSBN's, including the *George Washington,* joined the fleet in 1959–1961. While submerged in July 1960, the *George Washington* successfully test-fired the Polaris A-1 missile, the first underwater launching of a ballistic missile. This original version of the Polaris had a range of about 1,400 miles (2,250 km).

The next five SSBN's, including the *Ethan Allen,* joined the fleet in 1961–1963. Each sub is equipped with tubes for launching 16 Polaris A-2 missiles. The Polaris A-2, first launched from the *Ethan Allen* in 1962, has a range of about 1,700 miles (2,735 km).

The next 31 SSBN's, *Lafayette*-class submarines, joined the fleet in 1963–1967. Each of them originally was equipped to carry 16 Polaris A-2 or 16 Polaris A-3 missiles. One *Lafayette*-class sub, the *Andrew Jackson,* launched the first Polaris A-3 missile in 1963. This missile is about 30 feet (9 meters) long, weighs 15 tons, and has a range of about 2,900 miles (4,670 km).

By the end of 1967 the United States had 41 SSBN's. Each sub carried 16 Polaris missiles with thermonuclear warheads, totaling 656 missiles, most of which were originally fitted or retrofitted Polaris A-3 missiles.

By the mid-1970's most of the 31 *Lafayette*-class SSBN's had been refitted with Poseidon missiles, and the rest were to follow suit. This missile has about the same range as the Polaris A-3, but each Poseidon can be fitted with ten independently targetable warheads (MIRV's). When this program is completed the United States will have 496 (31 × 16) Poseidon missiles installed in submarines. The Poseidon missile was first test-fired from the *James Madison* in 1970.

Trident Project. Development of a nuclear-powered Trident submarine was under way in the mid-1970's. This submarine will be larger and quieter than the *Lafayette*-class submarines and will have tubes for launching 24 Trident missiles. The Trident missile, which will be fitted with MIRV's, will have a range of at least 4,000 miles (6,500 km).

Aircraft Carriers. During the 1960's the United States strengthened its naval forces by the addition of four conventionally powered aircraft carriers. They were the *Kitty Hawk,* commissioned in 1961; the *Constellation* (1961); the *America* (1965); and the *John F. Kennedy* (1968). Each of these ships has a capacity to carry about 90 aircraft.

In the mid-1970's two nuclear-powered aircraft carriers were scheduled to join the fleet. They were the *Nimitz,* which was commissioned in May 1975 and superseded the *Enterprise* as the world's largest warship, and the *Dwight D. Eisenhower.* A third, the *Carl Vinson,* was scheduled for service in 1980. Each ship carries about 100 aircraft.

Battleships. The United States has four battleships—the *Iowa, Missouri, New Jersey,* and *Wisconsin*—laid up in reserve. In perhaps the last appearance of the battleship in warfare, the *New Jersey* was in service in 1968–1969 during the Vietnam War to provide heavy gunfire support for land operations in coastal areas.

Nuclear-Powered Frigates. The Navy's first nuclear-powered guided-missile frigate (DLGN), the 8,600-ton *Bainbridge,* was commissioned in 1962, and the second, the *Truxton,* joined the fleet in 1967. Several other DLGN's, including the *California* and the *South Carolina,* were added to the fleet during the 1970's.

Amphibious Assault Ships. The *Iwo Jima,* commissioned in 1961, was the first ship in the world to be specifically designed and built to carry helicopters. Five other amphibious assault ships (LPH's) joined the fleet during 1962–1970 to strengthen the use of helicopters for attack landings by Marines.

A new type of amphibious assault ship (LHA) having a full-length flight deck and a landing-craft docking well was being added to U. S. naval forces in the mid-1970's.

Soviet Warships. At the end of World War II the Soviet Union had very few warships, but it soon embarked on a massive construction program featuring submarines, cruisers, and destroyers. By the mid-1970's the Soviet Navy and the U. S. Navy were the world's largest and most powerful.

By the mid-1970's the Soviet Union had the world's largest submarine force, including about 40 nuclear-powered ballistic-missile submarines and about 250 submarines of other types.

In terms of surface vessels the Soviet Navy was second only to the United States. In the mid-1970's its surface-vessel forces consisted of approximately 225 ships, including 2 *Kiev*-class aircraft carriers, 2 guided-missile-armed helicopter cruisers, 17 missile-armed cruisers, 14 gun-armed cruisers, 42 missile-armed destroyers, 36 gun-armed destroyers, and 110 escort ships.

Other Countries. By the mid-1970's, Britain had four nuclear-powered ballistic-missile submarines, each carrying 16 Polaris A-3 missiles. France had an approximately similar force of SSBN's. It was estimated that Communist China had about 50 submarines, with none being an SSBN.

See also GUIDED MISSILES; GUN; NAVAL ARCHITECTURE; NAVAL AVIATION; NUCLEAR WEAPONS.

ROBERT G. ALBION, *Harvard University*

Bibliography

Burt, R. A., *British Battleships of World War I* (Naval Inst. Press 1986).
Couhat, Labayle, and Baker, A. D., III, eds., *Combat Fleets of the World 1986–1987* (Naval Inst. Press 1986).
Harland, John, *Seamanship in the Age of Sail* (Naval Inst. Press 1985).
Institute of Strategic Studies, *The Military Balance* (The Institute for Strategic Studies, London, annually).
Lenton, Henry T., ed., *Navies of the Second World War: American Battleships, Carriers, and Cruisers* (Doubleday 1968).
Lyon, Hugh, *An Illustrated Guide to Modern Warships* (Arco 1986).
Moore, John E., ed., *Jane's Fighting Ships* (Jane's Pub., Inc. annually).
Morrison, John, and Coates, John, *The Athenian Trireme* (Cambridge 1986).
Thornton, J. M., *Warships, 1860–1970* (Arco 1973).

WART, a small noncancerous tumor that grows in the skin. Warts are caused by a virus. They are small hard growths, usually 2 to 10 millimeters (0.04–0.4 inch) across. They may come and go, lasting for months or years at a time and then disappearing—sometimes only to reappear at the same site at a later time.

Warts occur most commonly on the fingers, elbows, knees, face, and scalp. When they occur at a spot where they are subjected to pressure, especially on the soles of the feet (plantar warts), they may be flattened and covered with a callus. Plantar warts are often painful and may be very hard to eradicate. Occasionally warts occur in unusual shapes, resembling a thread or even a tiny cauliflower. Such warts are most often seen on the head and neck, especially on the scalp and in bearded areas. *Moist,* or *venereal,* warts are transmitted by sexual or other physical contact. They occur around the rectum or, in women, around the vagina. Venereal warts are often multiple and sometimes coalesce to form large plaques.

Treatment. A variety of local treatments are used to remove warts. These treatments, which should be used only under a physician's supervision, include podophyllin (for venereal warts), caustic chemicals such as phenol or silver nitrate, freezing with dry ice, burning with an electric needle, X rays, or even surgical removal. Unfortunately, warts of all kinds tend to recur after removal.

LOUIS J. VORHAUS, M. D.
Cornell University Medical College

WARTA RIVER, vär'tä (Ger. **WARTHE**), river, Poland, rising 35 miles northwest of Kraków and flowing 474 miles northwest and west to the Oder River, which it joins at Kostrzyn (Küstrin). It is the third longest river in Poland; main tributaries are the Ner, Noteć, Obra, and Prosna rivers. Navigable for 250 miles, it is connected with the Vistula River by the Noteć River and the Bydgoszcz Canal. Poznań is the largest city on its banks.

WARTBURG, värt'bo͝orKH, a castle, in East Germany, in Thuringia, overlooks Eisenach, on a hill (1,276 feet) in the Thuringian Forest. Built about 1075 to 1080 by Louis the Leaper, landgrave of Thuringia, during the Saxon risings against Emperor Henry IV, it was the seat of the landgraves of Thuringia until the middle of the 15th century. In the 13th century it was the scene of poetical contests of bards and minnesingers, celebrated in song and story, including Richard Wagner's opera *Tannhäuser.* Elizabeth (St. Elizabeth), wife of Landgrave Louis IV, lived at Wartburg from 1221 to 1227. Historically the castle is most famous as the place where Martin Luther translated the New Testament into German, after having been brought to Wartburg under the protection of Frederick III, elector of Saxony. In October 1817 at the Wartburg Festival commemorating the 300th anniversary of the Reformation, the first joint assembly of *Burschenschaften,* nationalist student organizations, was held. The castle has been restored several times.

WARTHOG, a wild pig of the genus *Phacochoerus* in the Suidae family of the order Artiodactyla. It is found only in Africa south of the Sahara Desert and north of Cape Province. The species *P. africanus* inhabits the northern portions of this area, and *P. aethiopicus* the south. Except for the forests of Ethiopia, thinly forested areas with open spaces are the preferred habitats. Warthogs are seldom found above an altitude of 8,000 feet.

SATOUR
An adult warthog (with tusks) and youngsters.

A rather hideous animal, the warthog has thin legs and a massive barrel-shaped body, standing about 28 inches high at the shoulder. Its neck and back are covered with long, bristly hair, but the remainder of its body is naked. The tail, which is long and tufted at the end, ordinarily hangs limply, but is carried upright with the tufted tip hanging over when the animal is running. The head is large with a flat, wide muzzle. The eyes are set far back, and the ears are small and sharply pointed. Both sexes have two sets of huge, upward-curving tusks; unlike those of the true pigs, the tusks of the upper jaw are longer than the set below. Large warts protrude between the tusks and the eyes. Warthogs have poor eyesight, but scent and hearing are keenly developed.

An omnivorous animal, the warthog lives principally on roots, berries, and grasses. Though diurnal, it has been observed feeding in the moonlight. It lives in large holes in the ground, usually excavating deserted ant-bear or porcupine holes. Its principal enemies are leopards.

WARD J. RUDERSDORF, *Michigan State University*

WARTON, wôr'tən, **Thomas** (1728–1790), English literary historian and poet, who was named poet laureate in 1785. He was born in Basingstoke, Hampshire, on Jan. 9, 1728. He spent most of his life at Trinity College, Oxford, where he received his B. A. degree in 1747. From 1757 to 1767 he was professor of poetry at Oxford, and in 1785 was elected Camden professor of history. Warton wrote verse, essays, biographies, and a book on architecture, but his chief work is *The History of English Poetry . . .* (3 vols., 1774–1781). He died in Oxford on May 21, 1790.

Once compared by Samuel Johnson to a turkey cock, grown fat and lazy from too much collegiate comfort, Warton was an odd mixture: an antiquarian who enjoyed ale, practical jokes, and the conversation of workmen as much as he did old manuscripts and books. One of his poems was entitled *The Pleasures of Melancholy* (1747), but the humorous pieces he collected in *The Oxford Sausage* (1764) are more representative of his natural bent. There is no question of his importance as a scholar. His *Observations on the Faerie Queene of Spenser* (1754) and his critical edition of John Milton's early poems (1785) are still valuable. As Johnson remarked, Warton showed later students the way to success in interpreting the older poets "by directing them to the perusal of the books those authors read." In his *History*, too, critic René Wellek wrote, Warton, "showed the way." Though often inaccurate, the book was one of the first to study systematically the great Oxford and Cambridge collections of Middle English manuscripts.

JOSEPH WARTON (1722–1800), Thomas' brother, was also a critic, poet, and educator. He served as headmaster of Winchester College from 1766 to 1793. Essentially, however, he was a man of letters. His first poem was published at the age of 17, and his first volume of poetry, *Ode on Reading West's Pindar*, appeared four years later, in 1744, followed by *Odes on Various Subjects* (1746). His most important achievement as a critic was *An Essay on the Genius and Writing of Pope* (2 vols., 1756; 1782).

HOYT TROWBRIDGE, *University of New Mexico**

WARWICK, EARLS OF, famous title of English nobility, originating in 1088 when William II created the earldom for Henry de Newburgh. The title has been held by the following families: Newburgh or Beaumont (1088–1242), Beauchamp (1268–1449), Neville (1449–1471), Plantagenet (1471–1478, 1483–1499), Dudley 1547–1554, 1561–1590), Rich (1618–1759), and Greville (1759 to present). The most important bearers of the title were the following:

THOMAS DE BEAUCHAMP: b. about 1345; d. July 8, 1401. He was one of the lords appellant in opposition to Richard II in 1387. Upon the defeat of this opposition by Richard in 1389, Warwick retired to his estate, but was accused of an obscure conspiracy in 1397 and confined in the Tower of London, a part of which is still named Beauchamp Tower after him. Warwick was tried by Parliament for high treason, pleaded guilty, and was sentenced to life imprisonment, but was freed by Henry IV in 1399.

RICHARD DE BEAUCHAMP: b. Salwarp, Worcestershire, England, Jan. 28, 1382; d. Rouen, France, May 31, 1439. Son of the preceding, he was a pattern of medieval chivalry. In 1403 he put Owen Glendower, leader of the Welsh national uprising, to flight and helped to defeat the Percy family at Shrewsbury. In 1408 he left on a pilgrimage to the Holy Land, returning in 1410 by way of Russia, Poland, and Germany. Warwick was then made deputy of Calais and represented England at the Council of Constance in 1414–1415. Henry V subsequently gave him one of the three commands in Normandy and in his will entrusted Warwick with the education of his infant son Henry VI. In 1437 the earl returned to France in an effort to save the English possessions there. He died while governing Normandy and lies buried in St. Mary's Church at Warwick. His tomb is one of the finest of such medieval works of art.

RICHARD NEVILLE, called the KINGMAKER: b. Nov. 22, 1428; d. Barnet, Hertfordshire, April 14, 1471. He obtained the earldom by marrying Anne, daughter of the preceding. The owner of vast estates and a man of great energy and ambition, he was the last great leader of baronial opposition to the crown. Throwing in his lot with the Yorkists against the feeble Lancastrian king Henry VI, Warwick won the victory at the first Battle of St. Albans (May 22, 1455), which opened the Wars of the Roses. In consequence, he was made captain of Calais, which he used as a base against pirates and foreign shipping in the English Channel, winning great popularity for his exploits. Warwick and his family, the Nevilles, were mainly responsible for the triumph of the Yorkists and for making Edward IV king in 1461. For the next three years he was in fact ruler of England, but Edward's secret marriage to Elizabeth Woodville shattered Neville's plans for a French marriage for the king, to strengthen the new dynasty; it also indicated Edward's desire to be independent of his overmighty subject. Warwick moved into opposition, allying himself with Louis XI of France in support of the Lancastrians, and succeeded in restoring Henry VI to the throne in 1470. When the exiled Edward IV, supported by Charles the Bold of Burgundy, returned to England in 1471, Warwick found that he had lost the support of the country. Engaging in battle at Barnet, he was routed and slain. His younger daughter Anne married Richard, duke of Gloucester, who became King Richard III, in 1472 and in 1483 his vast estates were merged in the crown.

JOHN DUDLEY: b. ?1502; d. London, England, Aug. 22, 1553. The son of Edmund Dudley (1462?–1510), Henry VII's privy councilor, he was a man of marked military ability. In 1542, during Henry VIII's last war, he was appointed admiral, leading the attack against the Scottish coast (1543) in which Edinburgh was burned, and capturing Boulogne, France (1544). Dudley was created earl of Warwick in 1547 (the title having become vacant at the end of the preceding century), and on September 10 defeated the Scots at Pinkie. In 1549 he suppressed the Kett (Ket) peasant rebellion in Norfolk. On his return to London in October 1549, he overthrew the protectorship of Edward Seymour, duke of Somerset, and for the next four years he was the real ruler of England. Created duke of Northumberland in 1551, on the ground of his descent from Richard de Beauchamp, earl of Warwick, he tried to bring his daughter-in-law, Lady Jane Grey, to the throne on Edward VI's death in 1553, but the attempt failed, and he was subsequently executed by Mary I.

ROBERT RICH: b. 1587; d. April 19, 1658. His father had been created earl of Warwick by James I in 1618, the title having lapsed again in 1590. Inheriting the earldom in 1619, Warwick became a leading figure in the colonial enterprises in America and took part in the struggle for power within the Virginia Company from 1620. Coming from a Puritan family, he was instrumental in securing patents for the Plymouth and Massachusetts Bay colonies and opposed Sir Ferdinando Gorges' projects for New England. When the break between Charles I and Parliament reached its climax, Warwick was made lord high admiral by Parliament and contributed considerably to the king's defeat in the Civil War. He also was appointed to head the commission that was created by Parliament to administer the New World colonies and used his influence there to further religious freedom. Although his commission as admiral was repealed in 1649, he supported Oliver Cromwell, whose daughter married his grandson and heir.

A. L. ROWSE
All Souls College, Oxford University

WARWICK, GUY of. See Guy of Warwick.

WARWICK, municipal borough, England, county town of Warwickshire, on the Avon River, 19 miles southeast of Birmingham. The modern town manufactures film and carpets and assembles automobiles. It is famous as the site of Warwick Castle, hereditary home of the earls of Warwick, which dates mainly from the 14th century, though many alterations have been made, notably by Fulke Greville in the 17th century. Warwick traces its history back to the building of a stronghold by Ethelfleda, daughter of Alfred the Great, in 915; its municipal history goes back to the time of Edward the Confessor. Rebuilding after the fire of 1694 produced many houses which contribute to its present charm. St. Mary's Church contains the Beauchamp Chapel dating from 1443, an outstanding example of florid Perpendicular architecture, with the elaborate tombs of the Warwick family. Over the east gate of the town is the 15th century Chapel of St. Peter; over the west gate, built in the 12th century, is St. James's Chapel, now part of Lord Leycester's Hospital, founded by Robert Dudley, earl of Leicester, in 1571. Population: (1971) 18,289.

H. Gordon Stokes
Author of "English Place-Names"

WARWICK, city, Rhode Island, in Kent County, 10 miles south of Providence, on the Pawtuxet River and East Greenwich and Narragansett bays, at an altitude of 25 feet. Warwick is principally a residential community with widely spread individual centers. A few small industrial plants are located in the city, but the large cotton mills that were its chief industry have been closed. Theodore Francis Green State Airport and Goddard Recreational Park are located nearby. Rocky Point is one of New England's oldest shore resorts, and the long shoreline, with its navigable inlets, attracts many small boat owners.

Warwick was established in 1642 by Samuel Gorton (q.v.), who obtained a charter through the influence of Robert Rich, earl of Warwick, for whom the city is named. Originally called Shawomet, after the Indian tribe from whom the land was purchased, it was incorporated as a town in 1644 and chartered as a city in 1931. Government is administered by mayor and council. Pop. 87,123.

WARWICKSHIRE, wôr'ik-shər, is a county in the Midlands, England. Warwick is the county seat. Until the local-government reorganization of 1974, the county included the important industrial cities of Birmingham and Coventry. In 1974 these boroughs and others contiguous to them were formed into the metropolitan county of West Midlands. Today, Warwickshire is bounded by Staffordshire on the north, Leicestershire and Northamptonshire on the east, Oxfordshire and Gloucestershire on the south, the county of Hereford and Worcester on the west, and West Midlands on the northwest.

Drained by the westward-flowing Avon and its tributaries Warwickshire is well wooded in parts. The county is highly cultivated, with wheat and oats the main crops, supplemented by barley, fruit, garden produce, and dairying. Scattered remains of the Forest of Arden are found in the west. Little remains of industrial importance except for the electrical and machinery works of Rugby.

One Roman road remaining from the past is Watling Street. The Avon Valley was the first part of the county to be settled in the early Middle Ages. In the later Middle Ages Warwick and Kenilworth were fortified. Both towns have castles, which, however, date from a later period than the original Norman fortifications. There are interesting 14th century manors such as Maxstoke Castle. Near Maxstoke are the ruins of Maxstoke Priory. Stoneleigh Abbey, just east of Kenilworth, is a large 18th century edifice, with some remains of the original Cistercian monastery. Leamington, near Warwick, known for its spa, is a residential and holiday resort. There is an outstanding Tudor mansion at Compton Wynyates. The best-known building, however, is William Shakespeare's birthplace at Stratford-on-Avon, a town that is also famous for its annual Shakespeare festival.

WASATCH RANGE, wô'sach, mountain range, western United States, part of the Rocky Mountains, extending from Bannock County in southeast Idaho to Sanpete County in central Utah. Dividing Utah into approximately two equal sections, it is the source of the Ogden, Provo, Spanish Fork, and Weber rivers. The major cities of Utah are on its western slopes. Its highest peak is Mount Timpanogos, 12,008 feet. The range includes part of Wasatch National Forest and contains the Timpanogos Cave National Monument. Found in the Wasatch Range are fossilized corals, snails, clams, and mussels, as well as gold, copper, silver, and lead.

WASCO, wos'kō, city, California, in Kern County, 28 miles northwest of Bakersfield, at an altitude of 273 feet. Located in a fertile cotton and potato area, it manufactures oil-well casings, irrigation pipes, agricultural chemicals, farm machinery, vitamins, and antibiotics. It was incorporated in 1946 and is governed by a mayor and city council. Originally called Dewey, after Adm. George Dewey, it was renamed Wasco in 1900. Pop. 9,613.

WASCO INDIANS, wos'kō, a tribe of the Chinook linguistic family. They are also known as the Dalles Indians and occasionally as Wascopums. The name is derived from *wask'o*, meaning a horn cup or bowl, which referred to the bowl of a large rock near the main village.

The tribe once inhabited the region around The Dalles, on the south bank of the Columbia River in Oregon. The Wasco were the major Upper Chinook tribe, having gradually absorbed the other smaller groups. With the Wishram, they formed the easternmost extension of the Chinook family. They were a sedentary tribe, living primarily on salmon and other fish. After signing a treaty in 1855, they were removed to the Warm Springs Reservation in Oregon, where some 700 lived in 1975.

Frederick J. Dockstader
Director, Museum of the American Indian

WASECA, wo-sē'kə, city, Minnesota, Waseca County seat, on Clear Lake, 27 miles east of Mankato, at an altitude of 1,115 feet. It was built in 1867 as a shipping point for the fertile wheat region in which it is located. Its principal industry is canning. The University of Minnesota maintains an agriculture school here. Pop. 8,219.

WASH, The, a shallow bay of the North Sea on the east coast of England between Lincolnshire and Norfolk counties. The bay is about 20 miles (32 km) long and 15 miles (24 km) wide. It receives the Nene, Ouse, Welland, and Witham rivers, which drain the Fens. The ports of King's Lynn and Boston are located on The Wash. Boston was a major port for exporting wool during the 14th century. The Wash, once a larger body of water before centuries of silting, now is a fishing center. It has low marshy shores and sandbanks that make navigation hazardous.

WASHAKIE, wosh'ə-kē (1804?–1900), was a Shoshoni Indian chief. Originally called Pinaquana, he left the Umatilla tribe of his father and went to the Shoshoni tribe of his mother, where he was given the name Washakie, which means "shoots the running buffalo," or according to some sources, "a gambler's gourd."

At an early age, by sheer ability and military prowess, he became chief of the Eastern Shoshoni of Wyoming, often called Washakie's Band. He was always friendly with the whites, and his efforts to aid and protect emigrants to California were attested to by a document signed by more than 9,000 settlers. He was an autocrat who exerted firm control over his people but was an effective force for progress. Washakie often scouted for the United States Army during its campaigns against the Sioux, Cheyenne, and other tribes. He died at Fort Washakie, Wyo., on Feb. 20, 1900, and was buried there.

FREDERICK J. DOCKSTADER
Director, Museum of the American Indian

WASHBURN, Israel (1813–1883), American public official. He was born in Livermore, Me., on June 6, 1813. He practiced law, held several local offices, and served in the U. S. House of Representatives (1851–1861), where he opposed slavery and helped found the Republican party.

As governor of Maine (1861–1863), Washburn supported the Union cause, raising ten regiments of volunteers. He was collector of customs at Portland, Me., from 1863 to 1877. He died in Philadelphia on May 12, 1883. Elihu Washburne was his brother.

WASHBURNE, Elihu Benjamin (1816–1887), American political leader and diplomat. He was born in Livermore, Me., on Sept. 23, 1816. After attending law school he practiced law in Galena, Ill., and invested successfully in Western lands.

Entering politics, he served in the U. S. House of Representatives (1853–1869) as a Whig and Republican. Known as the "Watchdog of the Treasury," he opposed lobbyists and waste of the public lands. His friendship with Abraham Lincoln and his support for Ulysses S. Grant, also from Galena, enhanced Washburne's reputation. During Reconstruction, Washburne, a Radical Republican, was an outspoken foe of President Andrew Johnson.

Under President Grant, Washburne was secretary of state in 1869 and minister to France from 1869 to 1877. He was the only official foreign representative to stay in Paris during the German siege and the Paris Commune. His bid for the Republican nomination for president in 1880 led to a break with Grant, who wanted the nomination. Washburne died in Chicago on October 22, 1887.

WASHING MACHINE, a machine for washing clothes or fabrics. The modern electrically powered washing machine eliminates the drudgery of doing laundry by hand or by a manually operated machine.

Automatic Washer. The automatic washer is by far the most popular and versatile type. After the user opens the top lid, loads articles to be laundered into the wash basket, and sets the controls, the washer fills with water at a selected temperature, washes, rinses, extracts water from the articles by spinning them rapidly, and stops without further attention.

The washing action is accomplished by a finned agitator driven by an electric motor. The agitator creates strong water currents in the wash basket and forces the water through the laundry. Generally, the agitator provides two washing actions—regular and gentle. Regular action is used for cotton, linen, and permanent-press articles, and gentle action is used for delicate fabrics, knitted garments, and washable woolens.

After the wash water is drained, a spray rinse introduces clean water into the wash basket while it is spinning. The rinse water is then extracted by the spinning of the wash basket, which has perforations over its entire surface that serve to pass the water driven outward by the spinning action.

Other features of automatic washers include automatic dispensing of bleach, fabric softener, and detergent; a water-level control; a mixing valve to combine hot and cold water for the proper warm-water temperature; and safety features, such as automatic shutoff if the top lid is opened while the machine is running.

Most automatic washers have controls enabling the user to choose one of three cycles: "regular," for ordinary laundry; "permanent-press," to minimize wrinkle formation in permanent-press fabrics; and "delicate," for fabrics of low strength.

History. One of the first mechanical washing machines was patented by Hamilton E. Smith of Pittsburgh, Pa., about 1858. His home washer was operated by turning a crank that rotated paddles on a vertical shaft inside a tub filled with water and clothes. However, his machine and other early ones had little success because they were hard on clothes and required tiresome hand operation. For some years before and after the end of the 19th century a family's home washing commonly was done manually by using a water-filled wooden tub, a corrugated washboard, and a rubber-roller wringer to extract most of the water from the clean clothes.

The first electrically powered washing machine was invented in 1910 by Alva J. Fisher and manufactured in Chicago. Several electric washers were available by World War I, but they did not gain a sizable market until the 1920's. In 1922 the agitator-type washer was invented by Howard Snyder. Made in Newton, Iowa, it gained immediate widespread favor.

The first automatic washer, introduced in 1937, was a front-loading model that took up to 9 pounds (4 kg) of wash in a drum. The drum rotated on a horizontal shaft, washing the articles by tumbling them from the top to the bottom of the water-filled drum. In the late 1940's the first of the modern top-loading, agitator-type automatic washers was introduced. Present-day washing machines are more highly automated and versatile versions of this type.

WASHINGTON, Booker Taliaferro (1856–1915), American black educator and social reformer, who believed that blacks should work for advances in education and employment instead of trying to win social equality with whites. He was born on April 5, 1856, on the James Burroughs plantation, 13 miles (21 km) southeast of Roanoke, Va. His mother, Jane Furguson, was a cook on the plantation. After the Civil War, Washington moved to Malden, W. Va., where he attended school while working in salt furnaces and coal mines. From 1872 to 1875 he studied at Hampton (Va.) Institute and Industrial School. He returned to Malden to teach school for two years, briefly attended Wayland Seminary in Washington, D. C., and in 1879 joined Gen. Samuel C. Armstrong's staff at Hampton Institute. In 1881, Armstrong chose Washington to head a normal school at Tuskegee. Under his leadership Tuskegee Normal and Industrial Institute grew from one teacher and fewer than 50 students in an old church and shanty to one of the world's leading centers of black education.

After speaking briefly at the Cotton States and International Exposition at Atlanta, Ga., on Sept. 18, 1895, Washington was regarded by many as Frederick Douglass' successor as the chief spokesman for his race. In this speech, and in other speeches and writings, Washington advocated cooperation between the races and urged blacks to stay in the South, accept social segregation, and temporarily abandon efforts to win political and civil rights. Convinced that the South was not yet willing to share political power with the blacks, and that the masses of freedmen were illiterate and impoverished, Washington emphasized the need for gaining more wealth and culture as necessary prerequisites for equality of citizenship. Instead of focusing on the limitations that his race faced, he habitually stressed areas open for positive action. In 1900 he founded the National Negro Business League, which reflected his emphasis on skill, thrift, and enterprise.

Booker T. Washington, American leader in education

LIBRARY OF CONGRESS

Washington's program and pronouncements were well attuned to the economic and social views that were dominant in the United States for several decades after Reconstruction ended in 1877. This retreat from the emphasis on equality caused William E. B. Du Bois and others to lead a vigorous opposition to his leadership. Prodded by the virtual disfranchisement of blacks in the South, the ineffectiveness of industrial training for handicrafts that were rapidly being displaced by machines, and the institution of a rigid color caste system, Washington began, in his last years, to come closer to agreement with the leaders of the protest against inequality. Washington died at Tuskegee on Nov. 14, 1915.

In 1945, he was elected to the Hall of Fame for Great Americans. His birthplace is now the Booker T. Washington National Monument.

EARLIE THORPE
North Carolina Central University

Bibliography

Drinker, Frederick E., *Booker T. Washington: The Master Mind of a Child of Slavery* (1915; reprint, Greenwood Press 1977).

Harlan, Louis R., *Booker T. Washington: The Making of a Black Leader* (Oxford 1972).

Harlan, Louis R., *Booker T. Washington: The Wizard of Tuskegee, 1901–1915* (Oxford 1983).

Harland, Louis R., and others, eds., *The Booker T. Washington Papers, 13 vols.* (Univ. of Ill. Press 1972–1984).

Spencer, Samuel R., *Booker T. Washington and the Negro's Place in American Life* (1955; reprint, Little 1965).

WASHINGTON, Bushrod (1762–1829), American Supreme Court justice. He was born in Westmoreland county, Va., on June 5, 1762. A scion of two of Virginia's first families, he was a nephew of George Washington. After graduating from the College of William and Mary in 1778 and serving a short time in the Continental Army, he studied law under James Wilson, whom he would later succeed on the U. S. Supreme Court. In 1787 he was elected to the Virginia House of Delegates, and in 1788 he was a delegate to the Virginia state convention, where he supported the ratification of the federal Constitution. In the following years he built a flourishing law practice.

When John Marshall rejected an appointment to the Supreme Court, John Adams appointed Washington, who was confirmed on Dec. 20, 1798. The court soon developed into a vital organ of government with the addition of Marshall in 1801 and William Johnson in 1804. Under Marshall's leadership few important opinions were written by associate justices, and it is difficult to evaluate the role played by Washington in the development of constitutional theory.

But Washington's duties on the Supreme Court included "riding circuit" to U. S. district courts, and his work as a trial judge can more easily be measured. His decisions reveal a man of great courage but narrow of intellect, painstaking and methodical rather than imaginative or brilliant. His most important opinions on circuit were *Corfield* v. *Coryell* (1823), where he narrowly construed the privileges-and-immunities clause of Article IV of the Constitution, and *Golden* v. *Prince* (1814), where he anticipated some of the commerce-clause problems that were to reach the court. Washington did his work well without staking out any great claim on history.

Washington lived at Mount Vernon after the death of George and Martha Washington. He served on the court for 31 years until his death in Philadelphia on Nov. 26, 1829.

PHILIP B. KURLAND, *University of Chicago*

NATIONAL GALLERY OF ART

GEORGE WASHINGTON

1st PRESIDENT OF THE UNITED STATES
IN OFFICE FROM 1789 TO 1797

BORN	Feb. 22, 1732, in Westmoreland county, Va.
HIGHER EDUCATION	None.
RELIGION	Anglican.
OCCUPATION	Statesman, soldier.
MARRIAGE	Jan. 6, 1759, to Martha Dandridge Custis.
CHILDREN	None.
MILITARY SERVICE	Officer of Virginia troops in the colonial period and commander in chief of the American Army during the Revolution.
KNOWN AS	Father of his country.
POLITICAL PARTY	Federalist.
LEGAL RESIDENCE WHEN ELECTED	Virginia.
DIED	Dec. 14, 1799, at Mount Vernon, Va.
BURIAL PLACE	Mount Vernon, Va.

WASHINGTON, George (1732–1799), 1st president of the United States. When Washington retired from public life in 1797, his homeland was vastly different from what it had been when he entered public service in 1749. To each of the principal changes he had made an outstanding contribution. Largely because of his leadership the Thirteen Colonies had become the United States, a sovereign, independent nation.

As commander in chief during the American Revolution, he built a large army, held it together, kept it in a maneuverable condition, and prevented it from being destroyed by a crushing defeat. By keeping the army close to the main force of the British, he prevented them from sending raiding parties into the interior. The British did not risk such forays because of their belief that their remaining forces might be overwhelmed. The British evacuation of Boston in 1776, under Washington's siege, gave security to nearly all New England.

Drawing from his knowledge of the American people and of the way they lived and fought, Washington took advantage of British methods of fighting that were not suited to a semiprimitive environment. He alternated between daring surprise attacks and the patient performance of routine duties. Washington's operations on land alone could not have overcome the British, for their superior navy enabled them to move troops almost at will. A timely use of the French fleet contributed to his crowning victory at Yorktown in 1781.

After the war Washington took a leading part in the making of the Constitution and the campaign for its ratification. Its success was assured by 1797, at the end of the second term of his presidency. In 1799 the country included nearly all its present-day territory between the Atlantic coast and the Mississippi River.

President Washington acted with Congress to establish the first great executive departments and to lay the foundations of the modern federal judiciary. He directed the creation of a diplomatic service. Three presidential and five congressional elections carried the new government, under the Constitution, through its initial trials.

A national army and navy came into being, and Washington acted with vigor to provide land titles, security, and trade outlets for pioneers of the trans-Allegheny West. His policy procured adequate revenue for the national government and supplied the country with a sound currency, a well-supported public credit, and an efficient network of national banks. Manufacturing and shipping received aid for continuing growth.

In the conduct of public affairs, Washington originated many practices that have survived. He withheld confidential diplomatic documents from the House of Representatives, and made treaties without discussing them in the Senate chamber. Above all, he conferred on the presidency a prestige so great that political leaders afterward esteemed it the highest distinction to occupy the chair he had honored.

Most of the work that engaged Washington had to be achieved through people. He found that success depended on their cooperation and that they would do best if they had faith in causes and leaders. To gain and hold their approval were among his foremost objectives. He thought of people, in the main, as right-minded and dependable, and he believed that a leader should make the best of their good qualities.

As a Virginian, Washington belonged to, attended, and served as warden of the established (Anglican) church. But he did not participate in communion, nor did he adhere to a sectarian creed. He frequently expressed a faith in Divine Providence and a belief that religion is needed to sustain morality in society. As a national leader he upheld the right of every sect to freedom of worship and equality before the law, condemning all forms of bigotry, intolerance, discrimination, and persecution.

Throughout his public life, Washington contended with obstacles and difficulties. His courage and resolution steadied him in danger, and defeat steeled his will. His devotion to his country and his faith in its cause sustained him. Averse to harsh measures, he was generous in victory. "His integrity," wrote Thomas Jefferson, "was the most pure, his justice the most inflexible I have ever known. He was, indeed, in every sense of the word, a wise, a good, and a great man."

EARLY CAREER

George Washington was born in Westmoreland county, Va., on a farm, later known as Wakefield, on Feb. 11, 1731, Old Style (Feb. 22, 1732, New Style). His first American ancestor, John Washington, came to Virginia from England in 1657. This immigrant's descendants remained in the colony and gained a respected place in society. Farming, land buying, trading, milling, and the iron industry were means by which the family rose in the world. George's father, Augustine, had four children by his first wife and six by his second wife, Mary Ball, George's mother. From 1727 to 1735, Augustine lived at Wakefield, on the Potomac River between Popes Creek and Bridges Creek, about 50 miles (80 km) inland and close to the frontier.

Of George's early life little is known. His formal education was slight. He soon revealed a skill in mathematics and surveying so marked as to suggest a gift for practical affairs akin to youthful genius in the arts. Men, plantation life, and the haunts of river, field, and forest were his principal teachers. From 1735 to 1738, Augustine lived at "Little Hunting Creek" (later Mount Vernon). In 1738 he moved to Ferry Farm opposite Fredericksburg on the Rappahannock River. Augustine died when George was 11, leaving several farms. Lawrence, George's half brother, inherited Mount Vernon, where he built the central part of the now famous mansion. Another half brother, Augustine, received Wakefield. Ferry Farm went to George's mother, and it would pass to George after her death.

These farms bounded the world George knew as a boy. He lived and visited at each. Ambitious to gain wealth and eminence, mainly by acquiring land, he was obliged to depend chiefly on his own efforts. His mother once thought of a career for him in the British Navy but was evidently deterred by a report from her brother in England that an obscure colonial youth could not expect more at Britain's hands than a job as a common sailor. George's youthful model was Lawrence, a cultivated gentleman, whom he accompanied on a trip to Barbados, West Indies, in 1751. Here George was stricken with smallpox, which left lasting marks on his face.

When but 15, George was competent as a field surveyor. In 1748 he went as an assistant on a surveying party sent to the Shenandoah Valley by Thomas, 6th Baron Fairfax, a neighbor of Lawrence and owner of vast tracts of land in northern Virginia. A year later George secured a commission as surveyor of Culpeper county. In 1752 he became the manager of a sizable estate when he inherited Mount Vernon on the death of Lawrence.

George's early experiences had taught him the ways of living in the wilderness, had deepened his appreciation of the natural beauty of Virginia, had fostered his interest in the Great West, and had afforded opportunities for acquiring land. The days of his youth had revealed a striving nature. Strength and vigor heightened his enjoyment of activities out of doors. Quick to profit by mistakes, he was otherwise deliberate in thought. Not a fluent talker, he aspired to gain practical knowledge, to acquire agreeable manners, and to excel in his undertakings.

French and Indian War. In the early 1750's, Britain and France both strove to occupy the upper Ohio Valley. The French erected Fort Le Boeuf, at Waterford, Pa., and seized a British post, Venango, on the Allegheny River. Alarmed by these acts, Virginia's governor, Robert Dinwiddie, sent Washington late in 1753 on a mission to assert Britain's claim. He led a small party to Fort Le Boeuf, where its commander stated France's determination to possess the disputed area. Returning to Williamsburg, Washington delivered the defiant reply. He also wrote a report which told a vivid winter's tale of wilderness adventure that enhanced his reputation for resourcefulness and daring.

Dinwiddie then put Washington in command of an expedition to guard an intended British fort at the forks of the Ohio, at the present site of Pittsburgh. En route, he learned that the French had expelled the Virginia fort builders and were completing the works, which they named Fort Duquesne. He advanced to Great Meadows, Pa., about 50 miles (80 km) southeast

Martha Dandridge Custis was a wealthy widow with two small children when she married Washington in 1759.

LAWRENCE D. THORNTON

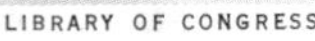

LIBRARY OF CONGRESS

LAWRENCE D. THORNTON

As a young man, George Washington spent several years as a land surveyor. Some of the instruments he used are at right.

of the fort, where he erected Fort Necessity. On May 28, 1754, occurred one of the most disputed incidents of his career. He ambushed a small French detachment, the commander of which, Joseph Coulon de Villiers, sieur de Jumonville, was killed along with nine of his men. The others were captured. This incident started the French and Indian War. The French claimed that their detachment was on a peaceful mission; Washington thought that it was engaged in spying. He returned to Fort Necessity, which a large French force attacked on July 3. It fell after a day's fighting. In making the surrender, Washington signed a paper that imputed to him the blame for "*l'assassinat*" (murder) of Jumonville. Not versed in French, Washington later explained that he had not understood the meaning of the incriminating word.

By the terms of the surrender, he and his men were permitted to return, disarmed, to the Virginia settlements. The news of his defeat moved Britain to send to Virginia an expedition under Gen. Edward Braddock, whom Washington joined as a voluntary aide-de-camp, without command of troops. Braddock's main force reached a point on the Monongahela River about 7 miles (11 km) southeast of Fort Duquesne where, on July 9, 1755, he suffered a surprise attack and a defeat that ended in disordered flight. Washington's part was that of inspiriting the men. His bravery under fire spread his fame to nearby colonies and abroad. Dinwiddie rewarded him by appointing him, in August, to the command of Virginia's troops, with the rank of colonel.

His new duties excluded him from leadership in the major campaigns of the war, the operations of which were directed by British officials who assigned to Virginia the humdrum task of defending its inland frontiers. No important battles were fought there. Washington drilled his rough and often unsoldierly recruits, stationed them at frontier posts, settled disputes, struggled to maintain order and discipline, labored to procure supplies and to get them transported, strove to have his men paid promptly and provided with shelter and medical care, sought support from the Virginia government, and kept it informed. His command trained him in the management of self-willed men, familiarized him with the leaders of Virginia, and schooled him in the rugged politics of a vigorous society.

The French and Indian War also estranged him from the British. Thereafter, he never expressed a feeling of affection for them. He criticized Braddock for blaming the Virginians as a whole for the shortcomings of a few local contractors. He also thought that Braddock was too slow in his marches. As commander in Virginia, he resented his subordination to a British captain, John Dagworthy, and made a trip to Boston early in 1756 in order to get confirmation of his authority from the British commander in America. He objected that one of his major plans was upset by ill-considered orders from Britain, and in 1758 he disputed with British officers about the best route for an advance to Fort Duquesne. The war ended in such a way as to withhold from him a suitable recognition for his arduous services of nearly six years and to leave him, if not embittered, a somewhat disappointed man.

Life at Mount Vernon. Resigning his commission late in 1758, he retired to Mount Vernon. On Jan. 6, 1759, he married Martha Dandridge, widow of Daniel Parke Custis, whose estate included 15,000 acres (6,000 hectares) and 150 slaves. Washington became devoted to Martha's two children by her first marriage, John Parke Custis and Martha Custis.

As a planter, Washington concentrated at first on tobacco raising, keeping exact accounts of costs and profits. He soon learned that it did not pay. British laws required that his exports should be sent to Britain, sold for him by British merchants, and carried in British ships. Also, he had to buy in Britain such foreign finished goods as he needed. On various occasions he complained that his tobacco was damaged on shipboard or sold in England at unduly low prices. He thought that he was often overcharged for freight and insurance, and he objected that British goods sent to him were overpriced, poor in quality, injured in transit, or not the right type or size. Unable to control buying and selling in England, he decided to free himself from bondage to British traders. Hence he reduced his production of tobacco and had his slaves make goods of the type he had imported, especially cloth. He developed a fishery on the Potomac, increased his production of wheat, and operated a mill. He sent fish, wheat, and flour to the West Indies where he obtained foreign products or money with which to buy them.

From the start he was a progressive farmer who promoted reforms to eliminate soil-exhausting practices that prevailed in his day. He strove to improve the quality of his livestock, and to increase the yield of his fields, experimenting with crop rotation, new implements, and fertilizers. His frequent absences on public business hindered his experiments, for they often required his personal direction.

He also dealt in Western lands. Virginia's greatest estates, he wrote, were made "by taking up . . . at very low prices the rich back lands" which "are now the most valuable lands we possess." His Western urge had largely inspired his labors during the French and Indian War. At that time, Britain encouraged settlement in the Ohio Valley as a means of gaining it from the French. In July 1754, Governor Dinwiddie offered 200,000 acres (80,000 hectares) in the West to colonial volunteers. Washington became entitled to one of these grants. After the war he bought claims of other veterans, served as agent of the claimants in locating and surveying tracts, and obtained for himself (by July 1773) 10,000 acres (4,000 hectares) along the Ohio between the Little Kanawha and Great Kanawha rivers, and 10,000 acres on the Great Kanawha. In 1775 he sought to settle his Kanawha land with servants.

Washington lived among neighbors who acquiesced in slavery and, if opposed to it, saw no feasible means of doing away with it. In 1775 he endorsed a strong indictment of the slave trade, but in 1776 he opposed the royal governor of Virginia who had urged slaves of patriot masters to gain freedom by running away and joining the British army to fight for the king. When Washington was famous as a world figure he dissociated himself, publicly, from slavery, although he continued to own many slaves. He favored emancipation if decreed by law. In his will he ordered that his slaves be freed after the death of Mrs. Washington.

Early Political Activity. After expelling France from North America, Britain decided to reserve most of the Ohio Valley as a fur-producing area.

INDEPENDENCE NATIONAL HISTORICAL PARK

This portrait of Washington as commander of the Army was painted by James Peale sometime in 1787–1790.

By the Quebec Act (1774), Britain detached from Virginia the land it claimed north of the Ohio River and added it to the royal Province of Quebec. This act struck at Washington's plans because it aimed to leave the Indians in possession of the north bank of the Ohio, where they could menace any settlers on his lands across the river. In April 1775 the governor of Virginia, John Murray, 4th earl of Dunmore, canceled Washington's Kanawha claims on the pretext that his surveyor had not been legally qualified to make surveys. At this time, also, Britain directed Dunmore to stop granting land in the West. Thus Washington stood to lose the fruits of his efforts during the French and Indian War.

As a member of the Virginia House of Burgesses from 1759 to 1774, Washington opposed the Stamp Act, which imposed crushing taxes on the colonies for the support of a large British army in America. Virginia, he said, was already paying enough to Britain: its control of Virginia's trade enabled it to acquire "our whole substance." When the Townshend Revenue Act (1767) levied taxes on tea, paper, lead, glass, and painter's colors, Washington pledged not to buy such articles ("paper only excepted"). By mid-1774 he believed that British laws, such as the Boston Port Act and the Massachusetts Government Act, showed that Britain intended to do away with self-government in the colonies and to subject them to a tyrannical rule. In May he joined other Virginia burgesses in proposing that a continental congress should be held, and that a "provincial congress" be created to take the place of the Virginia assembly, which Dunmore had disbanded.

Washington was chairman of a meeting at Alexandria in July that adopted the Fairfax Resolves, and he was elected one of the delegates to the 1st Continental Congress, which met in

Philadelphia in September. There the Fairfax Resolves provided the basis for the principal agreement signed by its members—the Continental Association. This forbade the importing into the colonies of all goods from Britain and all goods subject to British taxes. Moreover, it authorized all towns and counties to set up committees empowered to enforce its provisions. The Continental Congress thus enacted law and created a new government dedicated to resisting British rule. Washington spent the winter of 1774–1775 in Virginia, organizing independent military companies which were to aid the local committees in enforcing the Continental Association and, if need be, to fight against British troops.

THE AMERICAN REVOLUTION

When the 2d Continental Congress met on May 10, 1775, the fighting near Boston (Lexington-Concord) had occurred. The British Army was cooped up in Boston, surrounded by nearly 14,000 New England militiamen. On Feb. 2, 1775, the British House of Commons had declared Massachusetts to be in a state of rebellion. This imputed to the people of that colony the crime of treason. Washington, by appearing at the 2d Congress in uniform (the only member thus attired), expressed his support of Massachusetts and his readiness to fight against Britain. In June, Congress created the Continental Army and incorporated into it the armed New Englanders around Boston, undertaking to supply and pay them and to provide them with generals. On June 15, Washington was unanimously elected general and commander in chief.

The tribute of a unanimous election reflected his influence in Congress, which endured throughout the American Revolution despite disagreements among the members. In 1775 they divided into three groups. The militants, led by Samuel Adams, Benjamin Franklin, and Richard Henry Lee, favored vigorous military action against Britain. Most of them foresaw the need of effective aid from France, which the colonies could obtain only by offering their commerce. Before that could be done they must become independent states. Another group, the moderates, represented by Benjamin Harrison and Robert Morris, hoped that a vigorous prosecution of the war would force Britain to make a pro-American settlement. Only as a last resort would the moderates turn to independence. The third group, the conciliationists, led by John Dickinson, favored defensive measures and looked to "friends of America" in England to work out a peace that would safeguard American rights of self-taxation, thereby keeping the colonies in the British Empire. Washington agreed with the militants and the moderates as to the need for offensive action. The conciliationists and the moderates, as men of fortune, trusted him not to use the army to effect an internal revolution that would strip them of their property and political influence.

Early in the war, Washington and the army had to act as if they were agents of a full-grown nation. Yet Congress, still in an embryonic state, could not provide suddenly a body of law covering all the issues that figure in a major war. Many actions had to be left to Washington's discretion. His commission (June 17, 1775) stated: "You

The Capture of the Hessians at Trenton, painted by John Trumbull, shows Hessian commander, Colonel Rall, surrendering to Washington.

YALE UNIVERSITY ART GALLERY

VIRGINIA MUSEUM OF FINE ARTS, GIFT OF COL. AND MRS. EDGAR W. GARBISCH

Washington (*standing, right*) addresses the delegates to the Constitutional Convention in Philadelphia in 1787. The painting is by Junius Brutus Stearns.

are hereby vested with full power and authority to act as you shall think for the good and welfare of the service." There was a danger that a strong general might use the army to set up a military dictatorship. It was therefore urgent that the army would be under a civil authority. Washington agreed with the other leaders that Congress must be the superior power. Yet the army needed a good measure of freedom of action. A working arrangement gave such freedom, while preserving the authority of Congress. If there was no need for haste, Washington advised that certain steps should be taken, and Congress usually approved. In emergencies, he acted on his own authority and at once reported what he had done. If Congress disapproved, he was so informed, and the action was not repeated. If Congress did nothing, its silence signified assent. So attentive was Washington to Congress, and so careful was he when acting on his own initiative, that no serious conflict clouded his relations with the civil authority.

Washington Takes Command. When he took command of the army at Cambridge on July 3, 1775, the majority of Congress was reluctant to adopt measures that denoted independence, although favoring an energetic conduct of the war. The government of Lord North decided to send an overpowering army to America, and to that end tried to recruit 20,000 mercenaries in Russia. On August 23, George III issued the Royal Proclamation of Rebellion, which branded Washington as guilty of treason and threatend him with "condign punishment." Early in October, Washington concluded that in order to win the war the colonies must become independent.

In August 1775, Washington insisted to Gen. Thomas Gage, the British commander at Boston, that American officers captured by the British should be treated as prisoners of war—not as criminals (that is, rebels). In this, Washington asserted that the conflict was a war between two separate powers and that the Union was on a par with Britain. He defended the rank of American officers as being drawn from "the uncorrupted choice of a brave and free people, the purest source and original fountain of all power." In August–September he initiated an expedition for the conquest of Canada and invited the king's subjects there to join the 13 colonies in an "indissoluble union." About the same time he created a navy of six vessels, which he sent out to capture British ships bringing supplies to Boston. Congress had not favored authorizing a navy, then deemed to be an arm of an independent state. Early in November, Washington inaugurated a campaign for arresting, disarming, and detaining the Tories. Because their leaders were agents of the British crown, his policy struck at the highest symbol of Britain's authority. He urged the opening of American ports to French ships and used his prestige and the strength of the army to encourage leaders of the provincial governments to adopt measures that committed their colonies to independence. His influence was evident in the campaigns for independence in Connecticut, New Hampshire, Rhode Island, Massachusetts, Virginia, Pennsylvania, and New York. He contributed as much to the decision for independence as any man. The Declaration of Independence was formally adopted on July 4, 1776.

The Military Campaigns. Washington's military record during the revolution is highly creditable. His first success came on March 17, 1776, when the British evacuated Boston. He had kept them surrounded and immobilized during a siege of more than eight months. He had organized a first American army and had recruited and trained a second. His little fleet had distressed the British by intercepting their supplies. Lack of powder and cannon long kept him from attacking. Once they had been procured, he occupied, on March 4–5, 1776, a strong position on Dorchester Heights, Mass., where he could threaten to bombard the British camp. The evacuation made him a hero by proving that the Americans could overcome the British in a major

HISTORICAL PICTURES SERVICE

CONTINENTAL INSURANCE COMPANIES

(*Above*) Washington is inaugurated the first president of the United States in New York City in 1789. (*Left*) In E. P. Ottendorf's painting of Washington and his first Cabinet, Washington stands at the right, and the Cabinet members are (*left to right*) Edmund Randolph, Henry Knox, Thomas Jefferson, and Alexander Hamilton.

contest. For five months thereafter the American cause was brightened by the glow of this outstanding victory—a perilous time when confidence was needed to sustain morale.

Washington's next major achievement was made in the second half of 1776, when he avoided a serious defeat and held the army together in the face of overwhelming odds. In July and August the British invaded southern New York with 34,000 well-equipped troops. In April, Washington's force had consisted of only 7,500 effective men. Early in June, Congress had called 19,800 militia for service in Canada and New York. In a few weeks Washington had to weld a motley throng into a unified force. Even then his men were outnumbered three to two by the British. Although he suffered a series of minor defeats (Brooklyn Heights, August 26–29; Kip's Bay, September 15; Harlem Heights, September 16; White Plains, October 28; Fort Washington, November 16), the wonder is that he escaped a catastrophe.

After the setbacks in New York, he retreated through New Jersey, crossing the Delaware River in December. The American cause now sank to its lowest ebb. Washington's main army, reduced to 3,000 men, seemed about to disintegrate. It appeared that the British could march easily to Philadelphia. Congress moved to Baltimore. In these dire straits Washington made a dramatic move that ended an agonizing campaign in a blaze of glory. On the stormy night of December 25–26 he recrossed the Delaware, surprised Britain's Hessian mercenaries at Trenton, and captured 1,000 prisoners. This move gave him a striking position in central New Jersey, whereupon the British ceased offensive operations and pulled back to the vicinity of New York.

On Oct. 17, 1777, Gen. John Burgoyne surrendered at Saratoga, N. Y., his army of 5,000 men—all that were left of the 9,500 who had invaded New York from Canada. To this great victory Washington made two contributions. First, in September 1775, he sent an expedition to conquer Canada. Although that aim was not attained, the project put the Americans in control of the approaches to northern New York, particularly Lake Champlain. Burgoyne encountered so many obstacles there that his advance was seriously delayed. That in turn gave time for the militia of New England to turn out in force and to contribute decisively to his defeat. Second, in 1777, Washington conducted a campaign near Philadelphia that prevented Gen. William Howe from using his large army for the relief of Burgoyne. Washington's success at Trenton had placed him where he could both defend Philadelphia and strike at British-held New York. Howe had thereupon undertaken a campaign with the hope of occupying Philadelphia and of crushing Washington's army. Although Washington suffered minor defeats—at Brandywine Creek on September 11 and at Germantown on October 4—he again saved his army and, by engaging Howe in Pennsylvania, made possible the isolation and eventual defeat of Burgoyne.

Unable to overcome Washington in New Jersey and Pennsylvania, the British shifted their main war effort to the South. In 1781 their invasion of Virginia enabled Washington to strike a blow that virtually ended the war. France had joined the United States as a full-fledged ally in February 1778, thereby putting French troops at Washington's disposal and, more important, giving him the support of a strong navy which he deemed essential to victory. His plan of 1781 called for an advance from New York to Virginia of a large American-French army which would act in concert with the French fleet, to which was assigned the task of controlling Chesapeake Bay, thereby preventing an escape by sea of the British forces under Lord Cornwallis. Washington's army trapped Cornwallis at Yorktown, Va., on the York River, and the French admiral, count de Grasse, gained command of the bay. Outnumbered, surrounded on land, and cut off by sea, Cornwallis surrendered his 7,000 troops on October 19. Although Britain still had large forces in America, the Yorktown blow, along with war weariness induced by six years of failure, moved the war party in England to resign in March 1782 in favor of a ministry willing to make peace on the basis of the independence of the United States.

Political Leadership During the War. Washington's political leadership during the Revolution suggests that of an active president of later times. He labored constantly to keep people of all classes at work for the cause. He held a central position between two extremes. He strove to retain the support of the common people, who made up the army and—as farmers and workers—produced the supplies. Composing the left wing, they cherished democratic ideas that they hoped to realize by popular rule in the state governments. Washington appealed to them by his faith in popular sovereignty, his sponsorship of a republic and the rights of man, and his unceasing efforts to assure that his soldiers were well paid and adequately supplied with food, clothing, arms, medical care, and shelter. His personal bravery, industry, and attention to duty also endeared him to the rank and file, as did his sharing of dangers and hardships, as symbolized by his endurance at Valley Forge during the bleak winter of 1777–1778. The right wing consisted of conservatives whose leaders were men of wealth. Washington retained their confidence by refusing to use the army to their detriment and by insisting on order, discipline, and respect for leadership. It was his aim that the two wings should move in harmony. In this he succeeded so fully that the American Revolution is rare among political upheavals for its absence of purges, reigns of terror, seizures of power, and liquidation of opponents.

Before 1778, Washington was closely affiliated with the left wing. Afterward, he depended increasingly on the conservatives. In the winter of 1777–1778 there was some talk of replacing him with Gen. Horatio Gates, the popular hero of Saratoga. This estranged Washington from some of the democratic leaders who sponsored Gates. The French alliance, coming after the American people had made heavy sacrifices, tended to relax their efforts now that France would carry much of the burden. These developments lessened the importance of the popular leaders in Washington's counsels and increased the standing of the conservatives. Washington sought maximum aid from France, but also strove to keep the American war effort at a high pitch lest France should become the dominant partner—a result he wished to avoid. His character and tact won the confidence and respect of the French, as typified by the friendship of the Marquis de Lafayette.

In 1782 some of the army officers, irked by the failure of Congress to fulfill a promise concerning their pay, threatened to march to Philadelphia and to use force to obtain satisfaction. In an address on March 15, 1783, Washington persuaded the officers to respect Congress and pledged to seek a peaceful settlement. Congress responded to his appeals by granting the officers five years' full pay, and the crisis ended. It evoked from Washington a striking statement condemning government by mere force. "If men," he wrote, "are to be precluded from offering their sentiments on a matter which may involve the most serious . . . consequences, . . . reason is of no use to us, the freedom of speech may be taken away, and dumb and silent we may be led, like sheep, to the slaughter."

Throughout the war, Washington retained a commanding position in the army. Generals Philip Schuyler, Henry Knox, Nathanael Green, and Henry Lee were especially attached to him. His relations with Horatio Gates became strained but not ruptured. A rebuke to Charles Lee so angered that eccentric general as to cause him eventually to retire and to denounce Washington as a demigod. General Benedict Arnold suffered a somewhat milder, though merited, rebuke shortly before he agreed to sell information to Britain about the defenses at West Point.

(In 1976 an act of Congress promoted Washington to six-star General of the Armies so that he would rank above all other American generals.)

THE CONFEDERATION YEARS

After the war, several states were beset with troubles that alarmed Washington and conservative leaders who were close to him. British merchants flooded the United States with British goods. Inadequate markets abroad for American products obliged American merchants to export coin or to buy imports on credit. Britain excluded American ships from the trade of the British West Indies, to the distress of New England. A shortage of money depressed the prices of American products and enhanced the difficulty of paying debts—not only those owed to British merchants but also those that had been contracted by Congress or the states to finance the war. As the debt burdens grew, debtors demanded that the states issue large quantities of paper money. About half the states did so. Such paper depreciated, to the loss of creditors. The strife between debtor and creditor in Massachusetts exploded in an uprising, Shays' Rebellion, that threatened to overthrow the state government.

Apprehensive men turned to Washington for leadership. It seemed to them, and to him, that the troubles of the times flowed from the weaknesses of the central government under the Articles of Confederation. The Union could not provide a single, stable, adequate currency because the main powers over money were vested in the states. Because Congress could not tax, it could not maintain an army and navy. Nor could it pay either the principal or the interest on the national debt. Washington believed that the central government should be strengthened so that it could safeguard property, protect creditors against hostile state laws, afford the Union a uniform, nondepreciating currency, and collect taxes in order both to pay the national debt and to obtain revenues sufficient for current needs. He also thought that Congress should be empowered to foster domestic manufacturing industries as a means of lessening the importation of foreign goods. Washington's anxieties over events in the 1780's were deepened by his memories of bitter experiences during the Revolution, when the weakness of Congress and the power of the states had handicapped the army in countless ways.

The Constitutional Convention met at Philadelphia in May 1787. Washington, a delegate of Virginia, served as its president. His closest associate then was James Madison. The Constitution, as adopted, embodied Washington's essential ideas. It provided for a "mixed" or "balanced" government of three branches, so devised that all three could not easily fall under the sway of any faction, thus assuring that every important group would have some means of exerting influence and of protecting its interests in a lawful manner. The federal government, as remodeled, was vested with powers adequate for managing the common affairs of the Union, while leaving to the states control over state-confined property and business, schools, family relations, and nonfederal crimes and lesser offenses. Washington helped to persuade the Virginia legislature to ratify the Constitution, making use of *The Federalist* papers written in its defense by James Madison, Alexander Hamilton, and John Jay.

THE PRESIDENCY

Unanimously elected the first president, Washington was inaugurated in New York City on April 30, 1789. Acting with a cooperative Congress, he and his aides constructed the foundations on which the political institutions of the country have rested since that time.

His qualifications for his task could hardly have been better. For 15 years he had contended with most of the problems that faced the infant government. By direct contact he had come to know the leaders who were to play important parts during his presidency. Having traveled widely over the country, he had become well acquainted with its economic conditions and practices. Experience had schooled him in the arts of diplomacy. He had listened closely to the debates on the Constitution and had gained a full knowledge both of its provisions and of the ideas and interests of representative leaders. He had worked out a successful method for dealing with other men and with Congress and the states. Thanks to his innumerable contacts with the soldiers of the Revolutionary army, he understood the character of the American people and knew their ways. For eight years after 1775 he had been a de facto president. The success of his work in founding a new government was a by-product of the qualifications he had acquired in the hard school of public service.

The Executive Departments. The Constitution designated the president as the only official charged with the duty of enforcing all the federal laws. In consequence, Washington's first concern was to establish and develop the executive departments. In a sense such agencies were arms of the president—the instruments by which he could perform his primary duty of executing the laws. At the outset, Washington and his co-workers established two rules that became enduring precedents: the president has the power to select and nominate executive officers and the power to remove them if they are unworthy.

Congress did its first important work in 1789, when it made provision for five executive departments. The men heading these departments formed the president's cabinet. One act established the war department, which Washington entrusted to Gen. Henry Knox. Then came the creation of the treasury department, its beginnings celebrated by the brilliant achievements of its first secretary, Alexander Hamilton. The department of state was provided for, and Thomas Jefferson took office as its first secretary in March 1790. The office of postmaster general came into being next, and the appointment went to Samuel Osgood. Washington's first attorney general, Edmund Randolph, was selected after his office had been created.

In forming his cabinet Washington chose two liberals—Jefferson and Randolph—and two conservatives—Hamilton and Knox. The liberals looked to the South and West, the conservatives to the Northeast. On subjects in dispute, Washington could secure advice from each side and so make informed decisions.

In constructing the new government, Washington and his advisers acted with exceptional energy. The challenge of a large work for the future inspired creative efforts of the highest order. Washington was well equipped for the work of building an administrative structure. His success arose largely from his ability to blend planning and action for the attainment of a desired result. First, he acquired the necessary facts, which he weighed carefully. Once he had reached a decision, he carried it out with vigor and tenacity. Always averse to indolence and procrastination, he acted promptly and decisively. In everything he was thorough, systematic, accurate, and attentive to detail. From subordinates he expected standards like his own. In financial matters he insisted on exactitude and integrity.

The Federalist Program. From 1790 to 1792 the elements of Washington's financial policies were expounded by Hamilton in five historic reports. Hamilton was a highly useful assistant who devised plans, worked out details, and furnished cogent arguments. The Federalist program consisted of seven laws. Together they provided for the payment, in specie, of debts incurred during the Revolution; created a sound, uniform currency based on coin; and aimed to foster home industries in order to lessen the country's dependence on European goods.

The Tariff Act (1789), the Tonnage Act (1789), and the Excise Act (1791) levied taxes, payable in coin, that gave the government ample revenues. The Funding Act (1790) made provision for paying, dollar for dollar, the old debts of both the Union and the states. The Bank Act (1791) set up a nationwide banking structure owned mainly by private citizens, which was authorized to issue paper currency that could be used for tax payments as long as it was redeemed in coin on demand. A Coinage Act (1792) directed the government to mint both gold and silver coins, and a Patent Law (1791) gave inventors exclusive rights to their inventions for 14 years.

The Funding Act, the Excise Act, and the Bank Act aroused an accelerating hostility so bit-

LIBRARY OF CONGRESS

Mount Vernon, Washington's Virginia estate, was his home for most of his life. This aquatint depicts the president's mansion in 1800, the year after he died.

Washington had no children of his own, but he was devoted to the son and daughter of his wife, Martha, by her first marriage.

NATIONAL GALLERY OF ART, WASHINGTON, D. C., ANDREW MELLON COLLECTION 1940

ter as to bring into being an opposition group. These opponents, the Republicans, precursors of the later Democratic party, were led by Jefferson and Madison. The Funding Act enabled many holders of government certificates of debt, which had been bought at a discount, to profit as the Treasury redeemed them, in effect, at their face values in coin. Washington undoubtedly deplored this form of private gain, but he regarded it as unavoidable if the Union was to have a stable currency and a sound public credit. The Bank Act gave private citizens the sole privilege of issuing federal paper currency, which they could lend at a profit. The Excise Act, levying duties on whiskey distilled in the country, taxed a commodity that was commonly produced by farmers, especially on the frontier. The act provoked armed resistance—the Whiskey Rebellion—in western Pennsylvania, which Washington suppressed with troops, but without bloodshed or reprisals, in 1794.

The Republicans charged that the Federalist acts tended to create an all-powerful central government that would devour the states. A protective tariff that raised the prices of imported goods, a centralized banking system operated by moneyed men of the cities, national taxes that benefited the public creditors, a restricted currency, and federal securities (as good as gold) that could be used to buy foreign machines and tools needed by manufacturers—all these features of Washington's program, so necessary to industrial progress, repelled debtors, the poorer farmers, and the most zealous defenders of the states.

The Judiciary System. Under Washington's guidance a federal court system was established by the Judiciary Act of Sept. 24, 1789. The Constitution provided for its basic features. Because the president is the chief enforcer of federal laws, it is his duty to prosecute cases before the federal courts. In this work his agent is the attorney general. To guard against domination of judges, even by the president, the Constitution endowed them with tenure during good behavior.

The Judiciary Act of 1789 was so well designed that its most essential features have survived. It provided for 13 judicial districts, each with a district court of federal judges. The districts were grouped into three circuits in which circuit courts were to hear appeals from district courts. The act also created a supreme court consisting of a chief justice and five associate justices to serve as the final arbiter in judicial matters, excepting cases of impeachment. Washington's selection of John Jay as the first chief justice was probably the best choice possible for the work of establishing the federal judiciary on a sound and enduring basis.

Foreign Affairs. In foreign affairs, Washington aimed to keep the country at peace, lest involvement in a great European war should shatter the new government before it could acquire strength. He also sought to gain concessions from Britain and Spain that would promote the growth of pioneer settlements in the Ohio Valley. In addition, he desired to keep up the import trade of the Union, which yielded revenue from tariff duties that enabled the government to sustain the public credit and to meet its current expenses.

The British and French. The foreign policy of Washington took shape under the pressure of a war between Britain and revolutionary France. At the war's inception Washington had to decide whether two treaties of the French-American alliance of 1778 were still in force. Hamilton held that they were not, because they had been made with the now-defunct government of Louis XVI. Washington, however, accepted Jefferson's opinion that they were still valid because they had been made by an enduring nation—a principle that has since prevailed in American diplomacy.

Fearing that involvement in the European war would blight the infant government, Washington issued a proclamation of neutrality on April 22, 1793. This proclamation urged American citizens to be impartial and warned them against aiding or sending war materials to either belligerent.

Because Britain was the dominant sea power, France championed the doctrine of neutral rights that was asserted in the French-American alliance. The doctrine held that neutrals—the United States in this case—might lawfully trade with belligerents in articles not contraband of war. Britain acted on a contrary theory respecting wartime trade and seized American ships, thereby violating rights generally claimed by neutrals. Such seizures goaded the Republican followers of Jefferson to urge measures that might have led to a British-American war. Washington then sent John Jay on a treaty-making mission to London.

Jay's Treaty of Nov. 19, 1794, outraged France because it did not uphold the French-American alliance and because it conferred benefits on Britain. Although Washington disliked some of its features, he signed it (the Senate had ratified it by a two-thirds vote). One reason was that keeping open the import trade from Britain continued to provide the Treasury with urgently needed revenues from tariff duties.

Unable to match Britain on the sea, the French indulged in a campaign to replace Washington with their presumed partisans, in order to vitiate the treaty. They also waged war on the shipping of the United States, and relations between the two countries went from bad to worse.

The Western Frontier. Washington's diplomacy also had to deal with events in the West that involved Britain and Spain. Pioneers in Tennessee, Kentucky, and the Ohio country, who were producers of grain, lumber, and meats, sought good titles to farmlands, protection against Indians, and outlets for their products via the Ohio and Mississippi rivers and New Orleans.

In the northern area, Britain held, within the United States, seven trading posts of which the most important were Niagara, Detroit, and Mackinac. The determination of the Indians to preserve their hunting lands against the inroads of pioneers seeking farms encouraged the British in Canada in their efforts to maintain their hold on the fur trade and their influence on the Indians of the area north of the Ohio River.

The focus of the strife was the land south of present-day Toledo. The most active Indian tribes engaged were the Ottawa, the Pottawatomi, the Chippewa, and the Shawnee. Two American commanders suffered defeats that moved Washington to wrath. British officials in Canada then backed the Indians in their efforts to expel the Americans from the country north of the Ohio River. A third U. S. force, under Gen. Anthony Wayne, defeated the Indians so decisively in 1794 in the Battle of Fallen Timbers, at the site of present-day Toledo, that they lost heart and the English withdrew their support. Wayne then imposed a victor's peace. By the Treaty of Greenville (1795) the tribes gave up nearly all their lands in Ohio, thereby clearing the way for pioneers to move in and form a new state.

In 1796 the British evacuated the seven posts that they had held within the United States. Because Jay's Treaty had called for the withdrawal, it registered another victory for Washington's diplomacy.

The Spanish Frontier. On the southwestern frontier the United States faced Spain, then the possessor of the land south of the 31st parallel, from the Atlantic coast to the Mississippi River. Intent upon checking the growth of settlement south of the Ohio River, the Spaniards used their control of the mouth of the Mississippi at New Orleans to obstruct the export of American products to foreign markets. The two countries each claimed a large area, known as the Yazoo Strip, north of the 31st parallel.

In dealing with Spain, Washington sought both to gain for the western settlers the right to export their products, duty free, by way of New Orleans, and to make good the claim of the United States to the territory in dispute. The land held by Spain domiciled some 25,000 people of European stocks, who were generally preferred by the resident Indians (Cherokee, Creek, Choctaw, and Chickasaw, with 14,000 warriors), to the 150,000 frontiersmen who had pushed into Kentucky, Tennessee, and western Georgia.

The selection of Jefferson as the first secretary of state reflected the purpose of Washington to aid the West. But before 1795 he failed to attain that goal. His task was complicated by a tangle of frontier plots, grandiose land-speculation schemes, Indian wars, and preparations for war that involved Spanish officials, European fur traders, and the Indian tribes, along with settlers, adventurers, military chieftains, and speculators from the United States.

Conditions in Europe forced Washington to neglect the Southwest until 1795, when a series of misfortunes moved Spain to yield and agree to the Treaty of San Lorenzo. The treaty recognized the 31st parallel as the southern boundary of the United States and granted to Americans the right to navigate the whole of the Mississippi, as well as a three-year privilege of landing goods at New Orleans for shipment abroad.

When Washington left office the objectives of his foreign policy had been attained. By avoiding war he had enabled the new government to take root, he had prepared the way for the growth of the West, and by maintaining the import trade he had safeguarded the national revenues and the public credit.

Washington Steps Down. By the end of 1795, Washington's creative work had been done. Thereafter he and his collaborators devoted their efforts largely to defending what they had accomplished. A conservative spirit became dominant and an era of "High Federalism" dawned. As his health declined, Washington became saddened by attacks made by his Republican opponents, who alleged that Hamilton had seized control of the administration, that a once-faithful ally, France, had been cast aside, that the Federalists were plotting to create a monarchy on the British model, and that they had corrupted Congress in order to effect their program. The attack reached its high (or low) point when Washington's foes reprinted forged letters that had been published to impugn his loyalty during the Revolution. He made no reply to his detractors.

Washington had been reelected unanimously in 1792. His decision not to seek a third term established a tradition that has been broken only once and is now embedded in the 22d Amendment of the Constitution. In his Farewell Address of Sept. 17, 1796, he summarized the results of his varied experience, offering a guide both for that time and for the future. He urged his countrymen to cherish the Union, to support the public credit, to be alert to "the insidious wiles of foreign influence," to respect the Constitution and the nation's laws, to abide by the results of elections, and to eschew political parties of a sectional cast. Asserting that America and Europe had different interests, he declared that it "is our true policy to steer clear of permanent alliances with any portion of the foreign world," trusting to temporary alliances for emergencies. He also warned against indulging in either habitual favoritism or habitual hostility toward particular nations, lest such attitudes should provoke or involve the country in needless wars.

LAST YEARS

Washington's retirement at Mount Vernon was interrupted in 1798 when he assumed nominal command of a projected army intended to fight against France in an anticipated war. Early in 1799 he became convinced that France desired peace and that Americans were unwilling to enlist in the proposed army. He successfully encouraged President John Adams to break with the war party, headed by Hamilton, and to end the quarrel.

Washington's last public efforts were devoted to opposing the Virginia and Kentucky Resolutions of 1798, which challenged his conviction that the Constitution decreed that federal acts should be the supreme law of the land. Continuing to work at his plantation, he contracted a cold and died on Dec. 14, 1799, after an illness of two days.

Among Americans, Washington is unusual in that he combined in one career many outstanding achievements in business, warfare, and government. He took the leading part in three great historic events that extended over a period of 20 years. After 1775 he was animated by the purpose of creating a new nation dedicated to the rights of man. His success in fulfilling that purpose places him in the first rank among the figures of world history.

CURTIS P. NETTELS, *Cornell University*

Bibliography

Alden, John R., *George Washington: A Biography* (La. State Univ. Press 1984).
Fitzgerald, John C., *George Washington Himself* (1933; reprint, Greenwood Press 1975).
Flexner, James T., *George Washington: A Biography*, 4 vols. (Little 1965–1972).
Flexner, James T., *Washington: The Indispensable Man* (1974; reprint, New Am. Lib. 1979).
Ford, Paul L., *The True George Washington* (1986; reprint, Arden Library 1981).
Freeman, Douglas S., *George Washington*, completed by John A. Carroll and Mary W. Ashworth, 7 vols. (Scribner 1948–1957).
Hansen, William P., and Haney, John, eds., *Washington* (Chelsea House 1987).
Higginbotham, Don, *George Washington and the American Military Tradition* (Univ. of Ga. Press 1985).
Irving, Washington, *Life of George Washington*, 5 vols. (1883; reprint, Darby Bks. 1983).
Jackson, Donald, and Twohig, Dorothy, eds., *The Diaries of George Washington*, 6 vols. (Univ. Press of Va. 1976–1980).
Ketchum, Richard M., *The World of George Washington* (Crown 1984).
Morgan, Edmund S., *The Genius of George Washington* (1980; reprint, Univ. Press of Am. 1985).
Nettels, Curtis P., *George Washington and American Independence* (1951; reprint, Greenwood Press 1977).
Wills, Garry, *Cincinnatus: George Washington and the Enlightenment* (Doubleday 1984)).

WASHINGTON, Martha (1731–1802), wife of George Washington. Martha Dandridge was born in New Kent county, Va., on June 2 (May 22, Old Style), 1731. Her parents, John and Frances Jones Dandridge, belonged to respected but not aristocratic families. An attractive, capable girl, Martha in 1749 married Daniel Parke Custis, son of John Custis, a wealthy planter. The couple lived in the "White House" on a plantation on the Pamunkey River. Two of their four children died in infancy. On the death of her husband on July 8, 1757, Martha inherited a sizable fortune.

This fortune gave her a wide choice of suitors, so that her choice of George Washington denoted a strong preference. They were married on Jan. 6, 1759, and in the following spring settled in Mount Vernon. They started to rebuild the estate, which had been neglected during Washington's service in the French and Indian War. Destined not to have any children of their own, they gave attentive care to her son "Jackie" and daughter "Patsy."

Martha was a cheerful companion, of good nature and abundant common sense. Her principal weakness was an excessive fear concerning her children when they were sick or absent. Her portrait suggested to Ralph Waldo Emerson a line in Proverbs, "She looketh well to the ways of her household and eateth not the bread of idleness." During the Revolution she spent her winters with General Washington and supervised Mount Vernon during the remainder of the year. The death of Patsy in 1773 and of Jackie in 1781 were grievous blows to Martha and George, who helped raise Jackie's children—Elizabeth, Eleanor, George Washington, and Martha.

After the war she often entertained distinguished visitors. As the wife of the first president she performed her social duties with generous hospitality, dignity, and reserve. She gave a clue to her life when she wrote that she had been taught by the "great example" before her never to oppose her private wishes to the public will.

After Washington died in 1799, Martha lived in seclusion at Mount Vernon. She died there on May 22, 1802.

CURTIS P. NETTELS, *Cornell University*

T. M. GREEN/WEST STOCK

Mount Rainier, Washington's highest mountain, towers over Cascade Range and Mount Rainier National Park.

WASHINGTON

TABLE OF CONTENTS

State seal of Washington

WASHINGTON, a northwestern state of the United States, bordered on the north by the Canadian province of British Columbia and the Strait of Juan de Fuca, on the east by Idaho, on the south by Oregon and the Columbia River, and on the west by the Pacific Ocean. It extends 360 miles (580 km) east to west and 240 miles (385 km) north to south. It was named for George Washington, whose portrait is on the state seal.

The rugged natural setting of the state with its great mountains, forests, and Pacific seacoast is a reminder of the primitive wilderness that still existed here less than a century ago. Washington has kept much of the pioneering spirit of the men and women who opened this Northwest country, one of the last frontiers in the United States. In the period up to World War I, the state had a notable record in the enactment of progressive social legislation. Later, the energy potential of Washington's mighty rivers led to the construction of great dams for power generation and desert reclamation. The creation of abundant power helped attract the aluminum industry to the state during and after World War II. Washington's aircraft industry produced the Boeing Flying Fortress and the first American commercial jet, and the state assumed a major role in American atomic-energy research and production of fissionable materials through the Hanford Atomic Works in the central area. Along with these industries of the space and atomic age, Washington cares for its natural heritage through the conservation and improvement of its basic agricultural, forest, and fishing resources.

The state flag, adopted in 1923, consists of the state seal centered in a field of dark green.

INFORMATION HIGHLIGHTS

Location: Washington is a northwestern state, bordered on the north by the Canadian province of British Columbia and the Strait of Juan de Fuca, on the east by Idaho, on the south by Oregon and the Columbia River, and on the west by the Pacific Ocean.
Elevation: *Highest point*—Mt. Rainier, 14,410 feet (4,392 meters); *lowest point*—sea level; *approximate mean elevation*—1,700 feet (519 meters).
Area: 68,139 square miles (176,480 sq km); rank, 20th.
Population: 1980 census, 4,132,180; rank, 20th. Increase (1970–1980), 21.1%.
Climate: Mild winters and summers, especially in western Washington, which also has more rainfall than the eastern part of the state.
Statehood: Nov. 11, 1889; order of admission, 42d.
Origin of Name: Named for George Washington.
Capital: Olympia.
Largest City: Seattle.
Number of Counties: 39.
Principal Products: *Manufactures*—aircraft and aerospace systems and wood products; *farm products*—wheat, dairy products, cattle, chickens, fruits and vegetables, and barley and other grains; *mining*—coal, portland cement, lime, clay products, sand and gravel, stone, and magnesite.
State Motto: "Alki" (Chinook dialect, "By and By").
State Song "Washington My Home."
State Nicknames: Evergreen State; Chinook State.
State Bird: Willow goldfinch.
State Flower: Rhododendron (Western variety).
State Tree: Western hemlock.
State Flag: Green, with the state seal centered and bearing the year of Washington's admission to the Union. See also FLAG—*Flags of the States*.

1. The Land

The topography of the state of Washington is highly varied. The coastal climate in the west is separated from the interior continental climate in the east by the Cascade Range. To the west are deep canyons and towering mountains with rushing streams, dense forests, and numerous bays. To the east lie rolling farmlands and wheat fields.

Washington has 175 miles (280 km) of coastline on the Pacific Ocean, but a tidal shoreline of 3,026 miles (4,869 km) that includes the Strait of Juan de Fuca and the islands in Puget Sound. Its seaports long have been the gateway to Alaska and the Far East.

A chain of volcanic peaks dominate the Cascades, all of which have been dormant for many years, with one exception. This is Mt. St. Helens, which began spewing ash and steam on the afternoon of March 27, 1980, the first of many small eruptions that culminated with a major blast on May 18, 1980. The volcano had been dormant since 1857, and its activity in 1980 was the first volcanic eruption in the United States since 1917. The gas and ash killed everything within a 154-square-mile (400-sq-km) area, and about 60 persons lost their lives.

The land supports the economy. The lumbering industry and waterpower production are by-products of the forests and the falls formed by the rivers as they cascade down the mountains. The state's rugged beauty, preserved by its conservation program, holds great appeal for those who appreciate the wonders of nature.

Major Physical Divisions. A relief map of Washington reveals a wide range of variation in altitude from sea level to the top of Mt. Rainier. Several geographic regions may be noted.

Starting with the Olympic Peninsula in the northwest, the topography rises from sea level on the west (Pacific Ocean), north (Strait of Juan de Fuca), and east (Puget Sound), to the highlands of the Olympic Mountains. The coastal plain is narrow (20 to 30 miles, or 32 to 48 km) on this peninsula and is dominated by the rugged terrain of the Olympics, rising to a maximum height of 7,954 feet, or 2,324 meters (Mt. Olympus). Unique among American mountains, the Olympics comprise a broad mass of snow-clad peaks surrounded by virgin evergreen rain forests. At many points almost inaccessible, these mountains are very irregular, being cut by intricate, deep valleys and bulwarked with high ridges and glacier-carrying peaks. The mountains have many snowfields, alpine meadows, lakes, cascades, and streams. This wilderness area, approximately 50 miles wide by 35 miles deep (80 by 56 km), is one of the few remaining regions in the United States containing virgin forests. It has been preserved as a national park since 1938.

The Puget Sound region is dominated by a long arm of the Pacific Ocean that reaches deep into the heart of the western part of the state. Beginning with the Strait of Juan de Fuca, Puget Sound extends approximately 60 miles (96 km) eastward from the Pacific, and from Whatcom county on the Canadian border south to Thurston county, a total sweep of about 125 miles (200 km). Varying in width up to 40 miles (64 km), Puget Sound has an irregular shoreline and is dotted with some 300 islands. Many of these are small, but there are also several big ones, including Whidbey Island. Puget Sound provides numerous deepwater bays and harbors. The region, as defined by the Puget Sound Regional

Wilderness Beach on Washington's Olympic Peninsula is an unspoiled recreation area of rugged vistas.

KEITH GUNNAR/WEST STOCK

H. NOSEWORTHY/FREELANCE PHOTOGRAPHERS GUILD

The arch on the Canadian border in Blaine commemorates more than a century of U. S.–Canadian amity.

Planning Conference, includes the 12 counties bordering on the sound. The area is characterized as a wide valley extending south from the British Columbia line to Lewis county, and lying between the Olympic Mountains on the west and the Cascade Range on the east. The valley is cut by numerous streams flowing into Puget Sound from the mountains on each side. The land itself is rolling, with occasional level tracts, some of which are quite extensive. The soil is largely glacial, with alluvial overlay along the lower levels.

Southwestern Washington includes the six counties lying south of the Olympic Peninsula and the Puget Sound area and extends from the Pacific Ocean to the Cascade Range and south to the Columbia River. From the coastal plain eastward this area is characterized by ranges of hills or low mountains that gradually rise to the foothills of the Cascades. Here are found numerous rivers and streams, fertile valleys, a limited amount of prairie land, and heavily forested areas. Small lakes abound.

The backbone of the state is the Cascade Range, which extends from the Canadian border to the Columbia River. Rising some 8,000 feet (2,438 meters) above sea level, the higher ranges are snow clad much of the year and soar into half a dozen great peaks. These, from north to south, are: Mt. Baker (10,750 feet, or 3,276 meters); Mt. Shuksan (9,038 feet, or 2,755 meters); Glacier Peak (10,436 feet, or 3,181 meters); Mt. Rainier (14,410 feet, or 4,392 meters); Mt. Adams (12,307 feet, or 3,751 meters); and Mt. St. Helens (9,671 feet, or 2,948 meters). A natural barrier to east-west traffic, the Cascades are cut by several passes, five of which—Stevens, White, Cayuse, Blewitt, and Snoqualmie—are kept open the year around. Forests cover a great proportion of the Cascades, much of the area being in national forests. Lakes and streams provide recreational opportunities.

The Okanogan Highlands comprise the northeastern portion of Washington, running from the Cascades on the west to Idaho on the east and from the Canadian border south to the Columbia and Spokane rivers. They cover the four counties of Okanogan, Ferry, Stevens, and Pend Oreille. The region consists of a series of mountain ridges with valleys and rolling land between them. Unlike the Olympics and Cascades, these ridges do not rise much above 5,000 feet (1,524 meters), and taper off to the south. The slopes are long, gentle, and forest clad. Construction of the great dam across the Columbia River at Grand Coulee created the large artificial Franklin D. Roosevelt Lake, which extends 151 miles (243 km) north and east through this region.

South of the Okanogan Highlands and east of the Cascades the major part of the remainder of the state is known as the Columbia Plateau. Rising gently east and west from the Columbia River at an elevation of 500 to 600 feet (152–183 meters) above sea level, the plain reaches maximum heights of 2,000 feet (610 meters) with occasional ridges and hills reaching 1,000 (305 meters) and 2,000 feet higher. Much of it is flat, arid desert, but portions of the plain are rolling. In general it may best be described as an elevated plateau cut by occasional coulees and marked with ridges extending down the Cascades on the west and the Blue Mountains on the southeast. The hills of the fertile Palouse country characterize the southeastern part of the region.

The Blue Mountains reach northward from Oregon into the southeastern corner of Washington, with altitudes as high as 7,000 feet (2,134 meters) above sea level, or 5,000 feet above the Columbia plain.

Rivers, Lakes, and Harbors. The principal river of Washington is the Columbia, which enters the state from British Columbia, at approximately 117° 30′ west longitude. Its principal tributaries in the eastern section are the Pend Oreille (or Clark Fork), the outlet of Lake Pend Oreille in northern Idaho; the Spokane, which is the outlet of Coeur d'Alene Lake, also in Idaho; the Okanogan, flowing from the north through Lake

Okanogan in British Columbia; the Methow; Lake Chelan and its outlet; the Wenatchee and the Yakima, flowing down from the Cascade Range; and the Snake River, its most important tributary, which rises in the western part of Wyoming and flows through southern Idaho. In western Washington the Lewis and Cowlitz rivers are also tributaries of the Columbia. The Columbia is navigable for oceangoing vessels to Vancouver and for steamboats over the greater part of its course. The Snake is navigable for more than 150 miles (241 km). The Okanogan, Lewis, Cowlitz, Nooksack, Skagit, Snohomish, Duwamish, Puyallup, and Chehalis rivers are also navigable for considerable distances.

There are 948 named freshwater lakes in the state, the largest natural one being Lake Chelan, lying between the eastern ridges of the Cascade Range. It is 55 miles (89 km) long, from 1 to 3 miles (1.6–4.8 km) wide, and more than 1,500 feet (457 meters) deep in many places, extending from a point near the Columbia River into the very heart of the mountains. This part of the state is noted for its grand scenery. Lake Washington, lying in the western part of King county and bounding Seattle on the east, is a beautiful body of water 26 miles (42 km) long and from 2 to 4 miles (3.2–6.5 km) wide. Its surface is about 20 feet (6 meters) higher than the mean high tide in Puget Sound; a government canal and locks have been constructed at Seattle to connect Lake Washington with the sound through Lake Union. Lakes Crescent, Cushman, Quinault, and Ozette are the largest lakes in the Olympic Mountains; Lakes Wenatchee, Kachess, Keechelus, and Cle Elum are the largest in the Cascades. Moses and Soap lakes are among the larger lakes in the Columbia Basin area.

Willapa Bay and Grays Harbor are the only good ports on the Pacific coast of Washington, but Neah Bay, Clallam Bay, Port Angeles, and Dungeness are all excellent ports on the Strait of Juan de Fuca. Puget Sound includes all the waters of the great inland sea and is from 60 to 1,000 feet (18–305 meters) in depth. The rise and fall of the tide ranges from 9 to 18 feet (2.7–5.5 meters) and there are no sunken reefs or other dangerous obstructions to navigation. Vessels can land at almost any point along the whole 1,600-mile (2,575-km) coastline. The principal harbors are Bellingham Bay, Everett Harbor, Port Townsend, Seattle Harbor or Elliott Bay, Commencement Bay or Tacoma Harbor, and Port Orchard.

Climate. Conditioned by location and topography, the climate of Washington varies considerably from west to east. West of the Cascades the influence of Pacific Ocean breezes, tempered by the North Pacific Drift, an extension of the warm Japan Current, ensures a mild, healthful climate the year around. Rainfall averages 36 inches (914 mm) over this section. A wide variation prevails, however, on the southwestern slopes of the Olympic Mountains, whose rainfall ranges from 142 inches, or 3,607 mm (the heaviest in North America) to an average of 17 inches (432 mm) on the northeastern edge of the Olympic Peninsula, where the same mountains cast their "rain shadow." Apart from the restricted heavy rainfall area on the coast, rainfall in western Washington is spread lightly over a fairly long period, with heaviest precipitation occurring usually in December. The summer months, especially July and August, are relatively free from rainfall, though every month may have a few rainy days. Every month usually has clear and sunny days even in winter. In contrast to the rainfall, snowfall is limited to the higher altitudes, the average being only 5 inches (127 mm) or so on the coast and 10 inches

Great Dry Falls in central Washington, created by ice and water, is a geological wonder of the world.

FPG

BOB AND IRA SPRING

The giant Grand Coulee Dam harnesses the Columbia River and provides power and irrigation to a vast region.

(254 mm) throughout the Puget Sound basin. The protection given by the Cascade Range against cold air flowing from the interior explains this phenomenon. In the foothills and mountains, snowfall is much heavier, being 400 inches (10,160 mm) at Snoqualmie Pass, where the elevation is 3,000 feet (915 meters), and even more at higher altitudes in the Cascades and Olympics.

In winter (January) the average temperature of western Washington is 35° to 40° F (2°–4° C); the summer (July) average is 60° to 70° F (16°–21° C). The winter daily average minimum is 35° F, and the summer daily average maximum is 74° F (23° C). Thus both winters and summers are mild. A relatively long frost-free crop season results, with an average growing season ranging from 180 to 260 days in the Puget Sound lowlands and diminishing to a range of 80 to 120 days in the Cascade uplands. The frost-free season normally extends from March to November. Eastern Washington between the Cascades (which cast a "dry shadow" over parts of the Columbia Basin) and the Rockies (which shield the area somewhat from severe storms originating in the interior) has a more arid climate than that prevailing on the coast. It also has greater extremes of temperature. The wide gate cut through the Cascades by the Columbia River on its rush to the sea opens an avenue for mild Pacific Ocean breezes to enter the area, and extend to it some of the tempering effects of the coastal climate. Rainfall is low, total precipitation ranging from 10 to 20 inches (254–508 mm) over the Columbia Basin and Okanogan Highlands. From 10 to 60 inches (254–1,524 mm) of snow falls on this area, depending on the elevation. Mean temperatures range from 25° to 35° F (−4–2° C) in January and from 63° to 77° F (17°–25° C) in July. The growing season averages from 80 to 200 days. The Puget Sound region has but 40% to 45% sunshine; the Columbia Basin enjoys from 40% to 60%.

Plant and Animal Life. The flora of the state is conditioned by the varied geography and climate. Starting in the west with the sea, many marine plants abound, including various forms of algae, lichens, eelgrass, and related species. The sand dunes on the coast produce abroma, beach pea, lupine, saltbush, and similar plant life. Farther east, in the rain forests of the Olympic Peninsula and the forested foothills of the Cascades, are lush growths of Douglas fir, western red cedar, Sitka spruce, and other conifers. Interspersed are such deciduous types as alder, vine maple, dogwood, cottonwood, oak, rhododendron, salmonberries, ferns of many varieties, and a profusion of vines, flowering shrubs, and mosses, which thrive in the damp forests.

The character of the flora changes markedly on the eastern slopes of the Cascades. Pines predominate in the forests. In the arid lowlands the native plant life includes such types as sagebrush, rabbit brush, hopsage, and greasewood. Grasses and flowering plants abound where the rainfall is heavier. The high mountain meadows are filled with colorful Indian paintbrush, lupines, phlox, and many other grasses and flowers.

Forests cover over half the area of the state; many of them are in national or state forest reserves. Virgin growth has largely disappeared except in Olympic National Park and the higher reaches of the Cascades. The chief commercial species in the west are Douglas fir, western red cedar, and hemlock. In the eastern forests of Washington various species of pine predominate.

Outstanding land animals are the mountain elk, deer, bear, and numerous fur-bearing animals, such as raccoon, skunk, badger, marten, and mink. Forest and shore birds abound.

Salmon, in abundance, are found in the Columbia River, and many varieties of trout are among the migratory fish of the state. The squawfish, white sturgeon, and spinyrayed fish are important freshwater fish, and halibut, albacore tuna, herring, pilchard, flounder, eel, and devilfish (octopus) are among many of the saltwater varieties. Other marine life includes sponges, mussels, sea urchins, clams, oysters, scallops, crabs, shrimp, opalescent squid, and porpoise.

Mineral Resources. Extensive coalfields are found in the western part of the state, the only large deposits on the Pacific Coast. The Okanogan Range of the Rocky Mountains, which cuts across the northeastern corner of the state, holds deposits of clay, copper, gold, lead, limestone, magnesite, silver, and zinc. Other ores found in the state are barite, copper, gypsum, iron, peat, tungsten, and uranium.

Conservation. The people of Washington are becoming more and more conscious of the need to conserve all their natural resources. Conservation of water for irrigating arid but otherwise fertile land was one of the earliest steps taken toward husbanding resources.

Many storage and diversion dams have been built in the state. The largest and most ambitious project stems from the construction of the Grand Coulee Dam, known as the Columbia Basin Irrigation Project. Although this project was delayed somewhat by World War II, rapid progress was made in the construction of pumping stations, canals, and storage reservoirs after the war. No irrigation work had more careful detailed planning of every phase, from size of

WASHINGTON

COUNTIES

Adams 13,267 .... G3
Asotin 16,823 .... H4
Benton 109,444 .... F4
Chelan 45,061 .... E3
Clallam 51,648 .... B2
Clark 192,227 .... C5
Columbia 4,057 .... H4
Cowlitz 79,548 .... C4
Douglas 22,144 .... F3
Ferry 5,811 .... G2
Franklin 35,025 .... G4
Garfield 2,468 .... H4
Grant 48,522 .... F3
Grays Harbor 66,314 .... B3
Island 44,048 .... C2
Jefferson 15,965 .... B3
King 1,269,749 .... D3
Kitsap 147,152 .... C3
Kittitas 24,877 .... E3
Klickitat 15,822 .... E5
Lewis 56,028 .... C4
Lincoln 9,604 .... G3
Mason 31,184 .... B3
Okanogan 30,639 .... F2
Pacific 17,237 .... B4
Pend Oreille 8,580 .... H2
Pierce 485,667 .... C3
San Juan 7,838 .... C2
Skagit 64,138 .... D2
Skamania 7,919 .... D5
Snohomish 337,720 .... D2
Spokane 341,835 .... H3
Stevens 28,979 .... H2
Thurston 124,264 .... C4
Wahkiakum 3,832 .... B4
Walla Walla 47,435 .... G4
Whatcom 106,701 .... D2
Whitman 40,103 .... H4
Yakima 172,508 .... E4

CITIES and TOWNS

Aberdeen 18,739 .... B3
Acme 500 .... C2
Addy 180 .... H2
Adna 55 .... B4
Aeneas 5 .... F2
Airway Heights 1,730 .... H3
Albion 631 .... H4
Alder 300 .... C4
Algona 1,467 .... C3
Allyn 850 .... C3
Almira 330 .... G3
Aloha 140 .... A3
Altoona 15 .... B4
Amanda Park 495 .... A3
Amber 32 .... H3
Amboy 480 .... C5
Anacortes 9,013 .... C2
Anatone 88 .... H4
Appleton 120 .... D5
Arden 30 .... H2
Ardenvoir 150 .... E3
Ariel 386 .... C5
Arlington 3,282 .... C2
Ashford 300 .... C4
Asotin⊙ 943 .... H4
Auburn 26,417 .... C3
Ayer 20 .... G4
Azwell 152 .... F3
Bainbridge Island-Winslow (Winslow) 2,196 .... A2
Baring 200 .... D3
Battle Ground 2,774 .... C5
Bay Center 187 .... A4
Bay City 187 .... B4
Beaux Arts Village 328 .... B2
Beaver 450 .... A2
Belfair 500 .... C3
Bellevue 73,903 .... B2
Bellingham⊙ 45,794 .... C2
Bellingham‡ 106,701 .... C2
Belmont 30 .... H3
Benge 50 .... G4
Benton City 1,980 .... F4
Beverly 200 .... F4
Bickleton 90 .... E5
Biglake 105 .... C2
Bingen 644 .... D5
Black Diamond 1,170 .... D3
Blaine 2,363 .... C2
Blanchard 125 .... C2
Bluecreek 40 .... H2
Blyn 100 .... B3
Boistfort 75 .... B4
Bonney Lake 5,328 .... C3
Bossburg 66 .... H2
Bothell 7,943 .... B1
Bow 200 .... C2
Boyds 125 .... G2
Bremerton 36,208 .... A2
Bremerton‡ 146,609 .... A2
Brewster 1,337 .... F2
Bridgeport 1,174 .... F3
Brier 2,915 .... C3
Brinnon 500 .... B3
Brooklyn 50 .... B4
Brownstown 200 .... E4
Brownsville 50 .... A2
Brush Prairie 200 .... C5
Bryn Mawr-Skyway 11,754 .... B2
Buckley 3,143 .... C3
Bucoda 519 .... C4
Buena 590 .... E4
Burbank 211 .... G4
Burien 23,189 .... A2
Burley 300 .... C3
Burlington 3,894 .... C2
Burton 650 .... C3
Camas 5,681 .... C5
Carbonado 456 .... D3
Carlsborg 500 .... B2
Carlton 410 .... F2
Carnation 913 .... D3
Carrolls 50 .... C4
Carson 500 .... D5
Cashmere 2,240 .... E3
Castle Rock 2,162 .... B4
Cathlamet⊙ 635 .... B4
Cedar Falls 200 .... D3
Centerville 100 .... D5
Centralia 11,555 .... C4
Central Park 2,709 .... B3
Chattaroy 250 .... H3
Chehalis⊙ 6,100 .... C4
Chelan 2,802 .... E3
Chelan Falls 250 .... E3
Cheney 7,630 .... H3
Chesaw 15 .... G2
Chewelah 1,888 .... H2
Chimacum 275 .... C3
Chinook 928 .... B4
Cinebar 200 .... C4
Clallam Bay 600 .... A2
Clarkston 6,903 .... H4
Clayton 175 .... H3
Clearlake 750 .... C2
Clearwater 194 .... A3
Cle Elum 1,773 .... E3
Cliffdell 50 .... E4
Clinton 900 .... C3
Clipper 25 .... C2
Cloverland 80 .... H4
Clyde Hill 3,229 .... B2
Coalfield 500 .... B2
Colbert 225 .... H3
Colby 150 .... A2
Colfax⊙ 2,780 .... H4
College Place 5,771 .... G4
Colton 307 .... H4
Columbia Heights 2,515 .... C4
Colville⊙ 4,510 .... H2
Conconully 157 .... F2
Concrete 592 .... D2
Connell 1,981 .... G4
Conway 150 .... C2
Cook 80 .... D5
Copalis Beach 600 .... A3
Copalis Crossing 500 .... B3
Cosmopolis 1,575 .... B4
Cougar 96 .... C4
Coulee City 510 .... F3
Coulee Dam 1,412 .... G3
Coupeville⊙ 1,006 .... C2
Cowiche 150 .... E4
Creston 309 .... G3
Cumberland 250 .... D3
Cunningham 50 .... G4
Curlew 168 .... G2
Curtis 60 .... B4
Cusick 246 .... H2
Custer 300 .... C2
Daisy 15 .... G2
Dallesport 600 .... D5
Danville 215 .... G2
Darrington 1,064 .... D2
Davenport⊙ 1,559 .... G3
Dayton⊙ 2,565 .... H4
Deepcreek 73 .... H3
Deep River 50 .... B4
Deer Harbor 400 .... B2
Deer Park 2,140 .... H3
Deming 200 .... C2
Denison 100 .... H3
Des Moines 7,378 .... B2
Diablo 55 .... D2
Diamond 26 .... H4
Dishman 10,169 .... H3
Dixie 210 .... G4
Doe Bay 150 .... C2
Donald 100 .... E4
Doty 245 .... B4
Douglas 27 .... F3
Dryad 125 .... B4
Dryden 500 .... E3
Dungeness 675 .... B2
Du Pont 559 .... C3
Dusty 25 .... H4
Duvall 729 .... D3
East Olympia 300 .... B4
Easton 250 .... D3
Eastsound 800 .... B2
East Wenatchee 1,640 .... E3
Eatonville 998 .... C4
Edison 250 .... C2
Edmonds 27,679 .... C3
Edwall 150 .... H3
Elbe 150 .... C4
Elberton 35 .... H4
Eldon 60 .... B3
Electric City 927 .... F3
Electron 74 .... C4
Elk 100 .... H2
Ellensburg⊙ 11,752 .... E3
Elma 2,720 .... B4
Elmer City 312 .... G2
Eltopia 200 .... G4
Endicott 290 .... H4
Enetai 2,638 .... A2
Entiat 445 .... E3
Enumclaw 5,427 .... D3
Ephrata⊙ 5,359 .... F3
Erlands Point 1,254 .... A2
Espanola 75 .... H3
Ethel 180 .... C4
Eureka 100 .... G4
Evans 100 .... H2
Everett⊙ 54,413 .... C3
Everson 898 .... C2
Ewan 37 .... H3
Fairfax 75 .... C4
Fairfield 582 .... H3
Fairview-Sumach 2,788 .... E4
Fall City 1,528 .... D3
Farmington 176 .... H3
Ferndale 3,855 .... C2
Fife 1,823 .... C3
Finley 70 .... F4
Fircrest 5,477 .... C3
Fords Prairie 2,582 .... B4
Forks 3,060 .... A3
Four Lakes 500 .... H3
Frances 144 .... B4
Freeland 50 .... C2
Freeman 150 .... H3
Friday Harbor⊙ 1,200 .... B2
Fruitland 150 .... G2
Fruitvale 3,967 .... E4
Galvin 250 .... B4
Gardiner 80 .... B2
Garfield 599 .... H3
Garrett 1,134 .... G4
Gate 75 .... B4
Geiger Heights H3
George 261 .... F3
Gig Harbor 2,429 .... C3
Glacier 150 .... D2
Glenoma 500 .... C4
Glenwood 626 .... D4
Gold Bar 794 .... D3
Goldendale⊙ 3,575 .... E5
Goodnoe Hills 40 .... E5
Gorst 750 .... C3
Grand Coulee 1,180 .... G3
Grand Mound 100 .... C4
Grandview 5,615 .... F4
Granger 1,812 .... E4
Granite Falls 911 .... D2
Grapeview 250 .... C3
Grayland 750 .... A4
Grays River 350 .... B4
Greenacres J3
Greenbank 600 .... C2
Grotto 60 .... D3
Hadlock-Irondale 1,752 .... C2
Hamilton 268 .... D2
Hansville 250 .... C3
Harper 300 .... A2
Harrah 343 .... E4
Harrington 507 .... G3
Hartline 165 .... F3
Hatton 81 .... G4
Havillah 20 .... F2
Hay 55 .... H4
Heisson 200 .... C5
Hobart 500 .... D3
Home Valley 75 .... D5
Hoodsport 500 .... B3
Hooper 75 .... G4
Hoquiam 9,719 .... A3
Humptulips 275 .... A3
Hunters 200 .... G2
Hunts Point 480 .... B2
Huntsville 100 .... G4
Husum 200 .... D5
Hyak 50 .... D3
Ilwaco 604 .... A4
Impach 44 .... G2
Inchelium 206 .... G2
Index 147 .... D3
Indianola 800 .... A1
Ione 594 .... H2
Irby 30 .... G3
Issaquah 5,536 .... C3
Joyce 375 .... B2
Juanita 17,232 .... B1
Kahlotus 203 .... G4
Kalaloch 30 .... A3
Kalama 1,216 .... C4
Kapowsin 500 .... C4
Keller 195 .... G2
Kelso⊙ 11,129 .... C4
Kendall 100 .... C2
Kenmore 7,281 .... B1
Kennewick 34,397 .... F4
Kent 23,152 .... C3
Kettle Falls 1,087 .... H2
Kewa 63 .... G2
Keyport 900 .... A2
Kingston 950 .... C3
Kiona 230 .... F4
Kirkland 18,779 .... B2
Kittitas 782 .... E4
Klickitat 750 .... D5
Krupp (Marlin) 83 .... F3
La Center 439 .... C5
Lacey 13,940 .... C3
La Conner 633 .... C2
Lacrosse 373 .... H4
La Grande 100 .... C4
Lake Forest Park 2,485 .... B1
Lake Stevens 1,660 .... D3
Lakewood 250 .... C2
Lamont 101 .... H3
Langley 650 .... C2
La Push 500 .... A3
Latah 155 .... H3
Laurel 9 .... D5
Laurier 50 .... G2
Leadpoint 20 .... H2
Leavenworth 1,522 .... E3
Lebam 275 .... B4
Lester 26 .... D3
Liberty 25 .... E3
Liberty Lake 1,599 .... J3
Lilliwaup 75 .... B3
Lincoln 60 .... G3
Lind 567 .... G4
Littlerock 850 .... B4
Long Beach 1,199 .... A4
Longbranch 640 .... C3
Longmire 30 .... D4
Longview 31,052 .... B4
Loomis 150 .... F2
Loon Lake 500 .... H2
Lopez 100 .... C2
Lummi Island 675 .... C2
Lyle 580 .... D5
Lyman 285 .... D2
Lynden 4,022 .... C2
Lynnwood 22,641 .... C3
Mabton 1,248 .... E4
Malaga 125 .... E3
Malden 200 .... H3
Malo 240 .... G2
Malone 175 .... B4
Malott 350 .... F2
Manchester 400 .... A2
Mansfield 315 .... F3
Manson 220 .... E3
Maple Falls 300 .... D2
Maple Valley 900 .... C3
Marblemount 300 .... D2
Marcus 174 .... H2
Marietta-Alderwood 2,324 .... C2
Markham 117 .... B4
Marlin 83 .... F3
Maryhill 90 .... E5
Marysville 5,080 .... C2
Matlock 255 .... B3
Mattawa 299 .... F4
McCleary 1,419 .... B3
McKenna 300 .... C4
McMurray 62 .... C2
Mead H3
Medical Lake 3,600 .... H3
Medina 3,220 .... B2
Melbourne 100 .... B4
Menlo 237 .... B4
Mercer Island (city) 21,522 .... B2
Merritt 10 .... E3
Mesa 278 .... G4
Metaline 190 .... H2
Metaline Falls 296 .... H2
Methow 60 .... E2
Mica 105 .... H3
Milan 150 .... H3
Millwood 1,717 .... H3
Milton 3,162 .... C3
Mineral 550 .... C4
Moclips 500 .... A3
Monitor 650 .... E3
Monroe 2,869 .... D3
Monse 29 .... F2
Montesano⊙ 3,247 .... B4
Morton 1,264 .... C4
Moses Lake 10,629 .... F3
Mossyrock 463 .... C4
Mountlake Terrace 16,534 .... B1
Mount Vernon⊙ 13,009 .... C2
Moxee City 687 .... E4
Mukilteo 1,426 .... C3
Naches 644 .... E4
Nahcotta 200 .... A4
Napavine 611 .... C4
Naselle 500 .... B4
Navy Yard City 2,594 .... A2
Neah Bay 800 .... A2
Neilton 250 .... B3
Nespelem 284 .... G2
Newhalem 350 .... D2
Newman Lake 102 .... J3
Newport⊙ 1,665 .... H2
Nine Mile Falls 150 .... H3
Nisqually 500 .... C3
Nooksack 429 .... C2
Nordland 706 .... C2
Normandy Park 4,268 .... A2
North Bend 1,701 .... D3
North Bonneville 394 .... C5
North Cove 50 .... A4
Northport 368 .... H2
Oakesdale 444 .... H3
Oak Harbor 12,271 .... C2
Oakville 537 .... B4
Ocean City 350 .... A3
Ocean Park 918 .... A4
Ocean Shores 1,692 .... A3
Ocosta 369 .... B4
Odessa 1,009 .... G3
Okanogan⊙ 2,302 .... F2
Olalla 500 .... A2
Olga 100 .... C2
Olympia (cap.)⊙ 27,447 .... C3
Olympia‡ 124,264 .... C3
Omak 4,007 .... F2
Onalaska 600 .... C4
Opportunity 21,241 .... H3
Orchards 8,828 .... C5
Orient 50 .... G2
Orondo 130 .... E3
Oroville 1,483 .... F2
Orting 1,787 .... C3
Oso 150 .... D2
Othello 4,454 .... F4
Otis Orchards-East Farms 4,597 .... H3
Outlook 300 .... E4
Oysterville 150 .... A4
Ozette 50 .... A2
Pacific 2,261 .... C3
Pacific Beach 900 .... A3
Packwood 800 .... D4
Palisades 150 .... E3
Palmer 200 .... D3
Palouse 1,005 .... H4
Paradise Inn 10 .... D4
Parker 500 .... E4
Parkland 23,355 .... C3
Pasco⊙ 18,425 .... F4
Pataha 91 .... H4
Pateros 555 .... E2
Paterson 250 .... F5
Pe Ell 617 .... B4
Peshastin 500 .... E3
Pine City 48 .... H3
Plain 50 .... E3
Plaza 20 .... H3
Plymouth 220 .... F5
Point Roberts 500 .... B2
Pomeroy⊙ 1,716 .... H4
Port Angeles⊙ 17,311 .... B2
Port Blakely 600 .... A2
Porter 200 .... B4
Port Gamble 122 .... C3
Port Ludlow 200 .... C3
Port Orchard⊙ 4,787 .... A2
Port Townsend⊙ 6,067 .... C2
Potlatch 100 .... B3
Poulsbo 3,453 .... A1
Prescott 341 .... G4
Preston 500 .... D3
Prevost 60 .... B2
Prosser⊙ 3,896 .... F4
Pullman 23,579 .... H4
Puyallup 18,251 .... C3
Queets 180 .... A3

⊙County seat. ‡Population of metropolitan area.

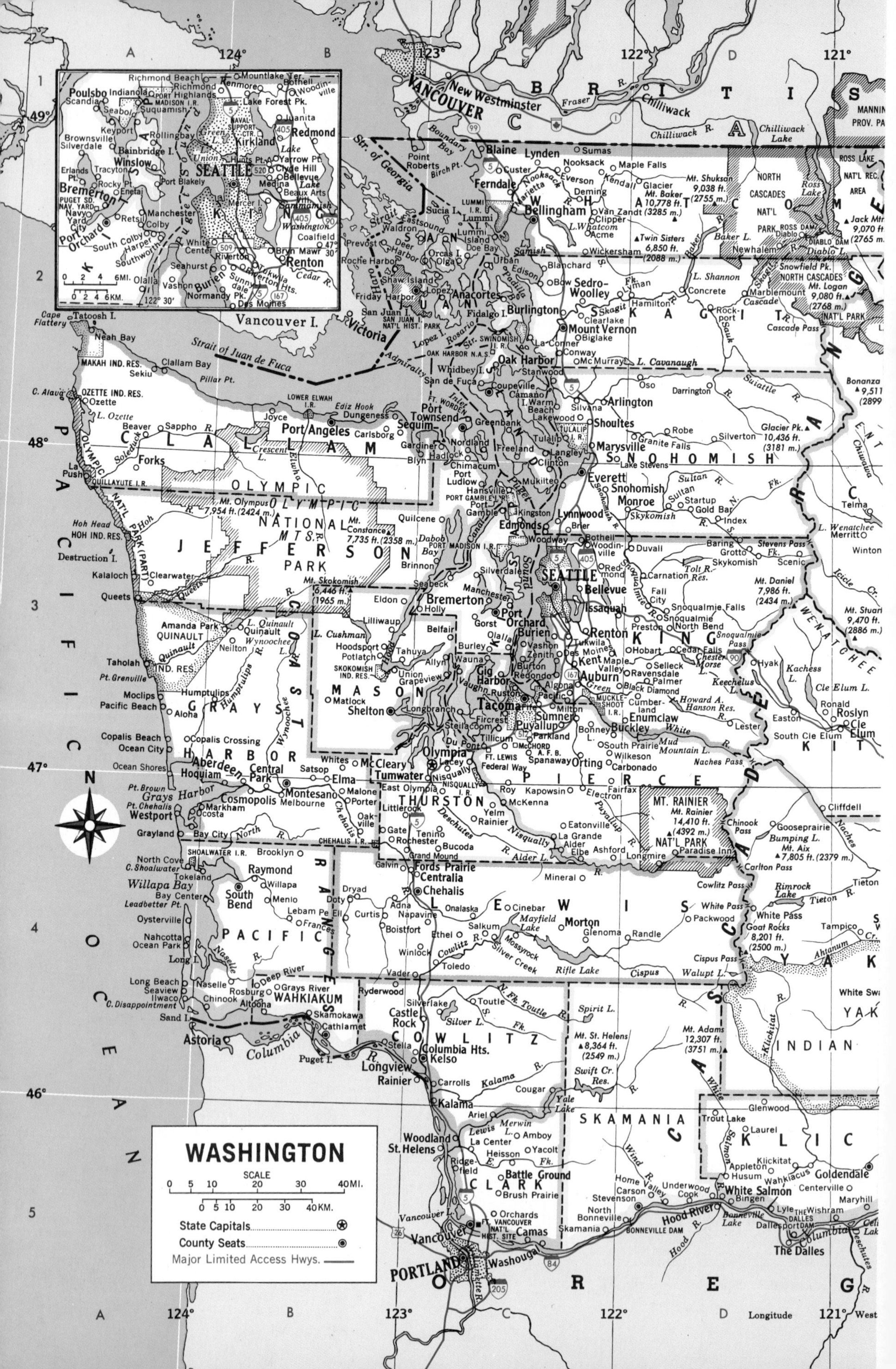

WASHINGTON
SCALE
0 5 10 20 30 40 MI.
0 5 10 20 30 40 KM.
State Capitals
County Seats
Major Limited Access Hwys.
A
B
C
D
124°
123°
122°
121°
49°
48°
47°
46°
1
2
3
4
5
Longitude
West
N
BRITISH COLUMBIA
VANCOUVER
New Westminster
Fraser R.
Chilliwack
Chilliwack R.
Chilliwack Lake
MANNING PROV. PARK
Vancouver I.
Victoria
Str. of Georgia
Strait of Juan de Fuca
Boundary Bay
Point Roberts
Birch Pt.
Blaine
Lynden
Sumas
Nooksack
Maple Falls
Custer
Ferndale
Everson
Kendall
Glacier
Mt. Shuksan 9,038 ft. (2755 m.)
Mt. Baker 10,778 ft. (3285 m.)
Deming
Van Zandt
Clipper
Acme
L. Whatcom
Twin Sisters 6,850 ft. (2088 m.)
Bellingham
WHATCOM
LUMMI I.R.
Lummi I.
Sucia I.
Waldron
Eastsound
Prevost
Deer Harbor
Orcas I.
Olga
Doe Bay
Roche Harbor
Shaw Island
Lopez
Friday Harbor
San Juan I.
SAN JUAN I. NAT'L HIST. PARK
SAN JUAN
Anacortes
Fidalgo I.
Burlington
Mount Vernon
Sedro-Woolley
Lopez I.
Rosario Str.
SWINOMISH I.R.
La Conner
Conway
Biglake
Clearlake
Hamilton
Lyman
Concrete
Rockport
Marblemount
Newhalem
Diablo
ROSS DAM
DIABLO DAM
Ross Lake
ROSS LAKE NAT'L REC. AREA
NORTH CASCADES NAT'L PARK
Jack Mtn. 9,070 ft. (2765 m.)
Snowfield Pk.
Mt. Logan 9,080 ft. (2768 m.)
Cascade Pass
L. Shannon
Baker L.
Blanchard
Bow
Edison
Samish
Wickersham
Urban
SKAGIT
OKANOGAN
Oak Harbor
OAK HARBOR N.A.S.
Whidbey I.
Admiralty Inlet
San de Fuca
Coupeville
Camano
Stanwood
Mc Murray
L. Cavanaugh
Oso
Darrington
Arlington
Suiattle R.
Bonanza 9,511 (2899
Silvana
Warm Beach
Lakewood
TULALIP I.R.
Tulalip
Shoultes
Robe
Silverton
Marysville
Granite Falls
Glacier Pk. 10,436 ft. (3181 m.)
Langley
Clinton
Lake Stevens
SNOHOMISH
Everett
Mukilteo
Snohomish
Sultan
Startup
Gold Bar
Index
Monroe
Skykomish R.
Lynnwood
Edmonds
Brier
Woodway
Bothell
Woodinville
Duvall
Baring
Grotto
Stevens Pass
Skykomish
Scenic
Telma
L. Wenatchee
Merritt
Winton
Tolt R.
Carnation
Redmond
SEATTLE
Bellevue
Issaquah
Fall City
Snoqualmie
Snoqualmie Falls
North Bend
Preston
Mt. Daniel 7,986 ft. (2434 m.)
Mt. Stuart 9,470 ft. (2886 m.)
Snoqualmie Pass
WENATCHEE
Renton
KING
Tukwila
Des Moines
Kent
Hobart
Cedar Falls
Chester Morse L.
Maple Valley
Selleck
Ravensdale
Hyak
Kachess L.
Keechelus L.
Cle Elum L.
Auburn
Black Diamond
Palmer
Howard A. Hanson Res.
Ronald
Roslyn
Cle Elum
South Cle Elum
Easton
Lester
MUCKLESHOOT I.R.
Cumberland
Enumclaw
Buckley
Bonney L.
White R.
Mud Mountain L.
South Prairie
Wilkeson
Carbonado
Naches Pass
Orting
Spanaway
PIERCE
Fairfax
Electron
Kapowsin
Puyallup R.
MT. RAINIER NAT'L PARK
Mt. Rainier 14,410 ft. (4392 m.)
Paradise Inn
Longmire
Ashford
Elbe
Alder
La Grande
Eatonville
Alder L.
Chinook Pass
Goosepraire
Bumping L.
Mt. Aix 7,805 ft. (2379 m.)
Cliffdell
Naches
Carlton Pass
Cowlitz Pass
White Pass
Packwood
Rimrock Lake
Tieton
Goat Rocks 8,201 ft. (2500 m.)
Tampico
Ahtanum
YAKIMA
Cispus Pass
Walupt L.
CASCADE RANGE
Olympia
Tumwater
Lacey
McCleary
East Olympia
Nisqually
NISQUALLY I.R.
FT. LEWIS
McCHORD A.F.B.
Federal Way
Roy
McKenna
Yelm
Rainier
Nisqually R.
Deschutes R.
THURSTON
Littlerock
Tenino
Gate
Rochester
Bucoda
Grand Mound
CHEHALIS I.R.
Tacoma
Puyallup
Sumner
Fircrest
Steilacoom
Tillicum
Parkland
Du Pont
Ruston
Milton
Algona
Pacific
Gig Harbor
Vaughn
Longbranch
Burton
Redondo
Vashon
Zenith
Burien
Port Orchard
Bremerton
Manchester
Silverdale
Gorst
Olalla
Holly
Seabeck
Belfair
Burley
Wauna
Allyn
Tahuya
Union
Grapeview
MASON
Shelton
Matlock
Hoodsport
Potlatch
SKOKOMISH IND. RES.
Lilliwaup
L. Cushman
Eldon
Hood Canal
Brinnon
Dabob Bay
PORT MADISON I.R.
Kingston
Port Gamble
PORT GAMBLE I.R.
Hansville
Port Ludlow
Chimacum
Hadlock
Nordland
Port Townsend
FT. WORDEN
Greenbank
Freeland
Quilcene
Mt. Constance 7,735 ft. (2358 m.)
Mt. Skokomish 6,446 ft. (1965 m.)
Puget Sound
Sequim
Gardiner
Blyn
Dungeness
Carlsborg
Port Angeles
Ediz Hook
LOWER ELWHA I.R.
Joyce
Elwha R.
CLALLAM
Crescent L.
Sappho
Beaver
Forks
Soleduck R.
La Push
QUILLAYUTE I.R.
L. Ozette
Ozette
OZETTE IND. RES.
C. Alava
Sekiu
Clallam Bay
Pillar Pt.
MAKAH IND. RES.
Neah Bay
Cape Flattery
Tatoosh I.
OLYMPIC NAT'L PARK
OLYMPIC MTS.
Mt. Olympus 7,954 ft. (2424 m.)
OLYMPIC NATIONAL PARK
JEFFERSON
Hoh R.
Hoh Head
HOH IND. RES.
Destruction I.
Kalaloch
Clearwater
Queets R.
Queets
Amanda Park
QUINAULT
L. Quinault
Quinault
Neilton
Wynoochee L.
Taholah
IND. RES.
Pt. Grenville
Moclips
Pacific Beach
Humptulips
Aloha
GRAYS HARBOR
Copalis Beach
Copalis Crossing
Ocean City
Ocean Shores
Aberdeen
Hoquiam
Central Park
Montesano
Satsop
Elma
Malone
Porter
Oakville
Whites
Cosmopolis
Melbourne
Pt. Brown
Grays Harbor
Pt. Chehalis
Markham
Westport
Ocosta
Grayland
Bay City
North R.
Chehalis R.
SHOALWATER I.R.
Brooklyn
North Cove
C. Shoalwater
Tokeland
Willapa Bay
Raymond
Willapa
Bay Center
South Bend
Menlo
Leadbetter Pt.
Oysterville
Lebam
Pe Ell
Frances
Nahcotta
Ocean Park
PACIFIC
Naselle R.
Long I.
Long Beach
Seaview
Ilwaco
C. Disappointment
Naselle
Chinook
Rosburg
Deep River
Grays River
WAHKIAKUM
Altoona
Skamokawa
Cathlamet
Sand I.
Astoria
Columbia R.
Puget I.
COAST RANGES
PACIFIC OCEAN
Galvin
Fords Prairie
Centralia
Chehalis
Dryad
Doty
Adna
Curtis
Napavine
Boistfort
Onalaska
LEWIS
Cinebar
Mayfield Lake
Morton
Mineral
Salkum
Glenoma
Randle
Ethel
Winlock
Cowlitz R.
Mossyrock
Silver Creek
Toledo
Rifle Lake
Cispus R.
Vader
Ryderwood
Silverlake
Silver L.
Toutle
N. Fk. Toutle R.
Spirit L.
Castle Rock
COWLITZ
Stella
Columbia Hts.
Kelso
Longview
Rainier
Carrolls
Kalama R.
Cougar
Kalama
Ariel
Yale Lake
Merwin L.
Lewis R.
Amboy
La Center
Yacolt
Heisson
E. Fk.
Woodland
St. Helens
Ridgefield
Battle Ground
CLARK
Brush Prairie
Orchards
Vancouver L.
Vancouver
FT. VANCOUVER NAT'L HIST. SITE
Camas
Washougal
PORTLAND
Willamette R.
OREGON
Mt. St. Helens 8,364 ft. (2549 m.)
Swift Cr. Res.
Mt. Adams 12,307 ft. (3751 m.)
SKAMANIA
Wind R.
Home Valley
Carson
Stevenson
North Bonneville
Skamania
BONNEVILLE DAM
Underwood
Cook
Hood R.
Hood River
White Salmon
Bingen
Bonneville Lake
Trout Lake
Glenwood
Laurel
Salmon R.
KLICKITAT
Klickitat
Klickitat R.
Appleton
Husum
Wahkiacus
Goldendale
Centerville
Lyle
Wishram
THE DALLES DAM
Dallesport
The Dalles
Maryhill
Deschutes R.
White Sw
YAKIMA INDIAN
KITTITAS
CHELAN
Chiwawa R.
Icicle Cr.
Poulsbo
Indianola
Scandia
PORT MADISON I.R.
Suquamish
Seabold
Keyport
Brownsville
Silverdale
Rollingbay
Bainbridge I.
Winslow
Erlands Pt.
Tracyton
Bremerton
Rocky Pt.
Enetai
PUGET SD. NAV. YARD
Navy Yard City
Port Blakely
Retsil
Manchester
Colby
Port Orchard
South Colby
Harper
Southworth
Olalla
Vashon
Richmond Beach
Richmond Highlands
Mountlake Ter.
Kenmore
Bothell
Woodinville
Lake Forest Pk.
NAVAL SUPPORT CTR.
Juanita
Kirkland
Redmond
Green L.
Union L.
Hunts Pt.
Yarrow Pt.
Clyde Hill
Bellevue
Medina
Beaux Arts Vill.
Lake Washington
Lake Sammamish
Mercer I.
White Center
Riverton
Coalfield
Bryn Mawr
Renton
Cedar R.
Seahurst
Burien
Tukwila
Riverton Hts.
Sunnydale
Normandy Pk.
Des Moines
KITSAP
KING
0 2 4 6 MI.
0 2 4 6 KM.
122° 30′
47° 30′

E
F
G
H
J
120°
119°
118°
117°
49°
48°
47°
46°
2
3
4
5
B R I T I S H
C O L U M B I A
R O C K Y
Similkameen R.
Oliver
Osoyoos L.
Kettle R.
Midway
Grand Forks
Christina L.
Rossland
Trail
Fruitvale
BOUNDARY DAM
Mt. Abercrombie 7,308 ft. (2227 m.)
Boundary
Metaline Falls
Metaline
BOX CANYON DAM
Sullivan L.
Ione
Tiger
Pend Oreille R.
Lost Creek
Ruby
PEND OREILLE
KALISPEL IND. RES.
Cusick
Usk
Dalkena
Priest L.
Priest R.
ALBENI FALLS DAM
Newport
Priest River
Sacheen L.
Diamond L.
Deer L.
Loon Lake
Loon L.
Elk
Deer Park
Milan
Mt. Spokane 5,878 ft. (1792 m.)
Clayton
Tumtum
Long Lake
Denison
Chattaroy
Colbert
Newman L.
Mead
Otis Orchards
Newman Lake
Coeur d'Alene
Greenacres
Liberty Lake
Coeur d'Alene L.
Millwood
Spokane
Town & Country
Opportunity
Veradale
Dishman
Nine Mile Falls
Reardan
Deepcreek
FAIRCHILD A.F.B. Hts.
Airway
Espanola
Medical Lake
Four Lakes
Geiger Hts.
Latah Cr.
Valleyford
Mica
Freeman
Rockford
Waukon
Edwall
Cheney
Tyler
Amber
Spangle
Fairfield
Plummer
Plaza
Waverly
Latah
S P O K A N E
Pasayten R.
Remmel Mtn. 8,690 ft. (2649 m.)
Nighthawk
Oroville
Molson
Chesaw
Palmer L.
Loomis
Havillah
Mt. Bonaparte 7,267 ft. (2215 m.)
Wauconda
Tonasket
Bonaparte Cr.
Harts Pass
Methow R.
Mazama
Chewack R.
Tiffany Mtn. 8,275 ft. (2522 m.)
Conconully
Okanogan R.
Gardner Mtn. 8,760 ft. (2670 m.)
O K A N O G A N
Twisp Pass
Winthrop
Riverside
Aeneas
W. Fk.
CHELAN NAT'L REC. AREA
Twisp R.
Twisp
Omak
Okanogan
Stehekin
SAWTOOTH RIDGE
Malott
Carlton
Omak L.
Lucerne
Lake Chelan
Methow
Brewster
Monse
Pateros
Lake Pateros
CHELAN RANGE
Entiat R.
Bridgeport
WELLS DAM
CHIEF JOSEPH DAM
Azwell
C H E L A N
Manson
Chelan
L. CHELAN DAM
Chelan Falls
Mansfield
Plain
Ardenvoir
D O U G L A S
Withrow
Entiat
Waterville
Lake Entiat
Leavenworth
Peshastin
Wenatchee R.
Dryden
Orondo
Douglas
ROCKY REACH DAM
Cashmere
Monitor
MOSES COULEE
GRAND COULEE
Palisades
East Wenatchee
W. Wenatchee
Wenatchee
Rock Island
Malaga
ROCK ISLAND DAM
Liberty
Curlew
Curlew Lake
Malo
Danville
Laurier
Republic
KETTLE RIVER RANGE
Snow Pk. 7,109 ft. (2167 m.)
F E R R Y
Sanpoil R.
Franklin D. Roosevelt Lake
Inchelium
Impach
Twin Lakes
Kewa
COLVILLE INDIAN RESERVATION
Nespelem
Keller
COULEE DAM NAT'L REC. AREA
Rufus Woods Lake
Elmer City
GRAND COULEE DAM
Coulee Dam
Electric City
Grand Coulee
Orient
Northport
Leadpoint
Columbia R.
Bossburg
Evans
Boyds
Marcus
Kettle Falls
Colville
Colville R.
Orin
Park Rapids
Arden
Rice
S T E V E N S
Addy
Daisy
Bluecreek
Gifford
Chewelah
Valley
Cedonia
Hunters
Springdale
Fruitland
SPOKANE IND. RES.
Wellpinit
Ford
Spokane R.
Little Spokane R.
Banks Lake
Hartline
DRY FALLS DAM
Coulee City
Almira
Wilbur
Lincoln
Creston
Davenport
L I N C O L N
Billy Clapp L.
Blue L.
Lenore L.
Wilson Cr.
Stratford
Wilson Creek
Crab Cr.
Harrington
Lake Cr.
Mohler
Soap L.
Soap Lake
Marlin (Krupp)
Tule L.
Coal Cr.
Lamona
Sylvan L.
Irby
Odessa
Sprague
Ephrata
Winchester
Quincy
G R A N T
Trinidad
Moses L.
Ruff
Wheeler
Ritzville
Sprague L.
Rock L.
Lamont
Pine City
Malden
Rosalia
Pine Cr.
Tekoa
Oakesdale
Rock Cr.
Ewan
Thornton
Belmont
Farmington
Saint John
Steptoe
Garfield
Elberton
Cow Cr.
Marengo
George
Moses Lake
A D A M S
Lind
Ralston
Winona
Endicott
Diamond
Colfax
Palouse
Wanapum Lake
Potholes Reservoir
Warden
O'SULLIVAN DAM
Benge
W H I T M A N
Palouse R.
Albion
Moscow
Lacrosse
Dusty
Pullman
Othello
Cunningham
Hatton
Washtucna
Hooper
Almota
LOWER GRANITE DAM
Lower Granite L.
L. Bryan
Hay
T I T A S
Thorp
Ellensburg
Kittitas
Vantage
Columbia R.
WANAPUM DAM
Royal City
Beverly
Lower Crab Cr.
Smyrna
Schawana
SADDLE MTS.
Priest Rapids L.
Mattawa
PRIEST RAPIDS DAM
Yakima R.
Wenas Cr.
Naches
Cowiche
Selah
Yakima
Terrace Hts.
Fruitvale
Broadway
Fairview
Moxee City
Union Gap
YAKIMA RIDGE
Parker
Donald
Wapato
Buena
Brownstown
Zillah
Harrah
Granger
Toppenish
Outlook
Toppenish Cr.
Sunnyside
Grandview
IMA
RESERVATION
Satus Cr.
Mabton
Prosser
HANFORD RESERVATION
U.S. DEPT. OF ENERGY
Connell
Kahlotus
Lower Monumental Lake
LOWER MONUMENTAL DAM
LITTLE GOOSE DAM
Riparia
Mesa
Ayer
Starbuck
Tucannon R.
Deadman Cr.
G A R F I E L D
Pomeroy
Pataha
Pataha Cr.
Colton
Uniontown
F R A N K L I N
Eltopia
Snake Lake
Clyde
Snake River
Sacajawea
Turner
Clarkston
Lewiston
C O L U M B I A
Asotin
ASOTIN DAM (SITE)
Eureka
Prescott
Huntsville
Dayton
W. Richland
Richland
ICE HARBOR DAM
Pasco
Benton City
Kiona
Burbank
Waitsburg
A S O T I N
Cloverland
Kennewick
B E N T O N
WALLA WALLA
Touchet R.
Dixie
BLUE MTS.
Anatone
Finley
Garrett
Walla Walla
WHITMAN MISSION NAT'L HIST. SITE
Wallula
Lake Wallula
Touchet
Walla Walla R.
College Place
CHINA GARDENS DAM (SITE)
Bickleton
Milton-Freewater
Grande Ronde R.
HELLS CANYON NAT'L REC. AREA
K I T A T
Paterson
Plymouth
Blalock I.
Umatilla
MCNARY DAM
Joseph Cr.
Umatilla Lake
River
Boardman
Goodnoe Hills
Roosevelt
Willows
Arlington
JOHN DAY DAM
John Day R.
Willow Cr.
Umatilla R.
Pendleton
Wallowa
Elgin
Moro
Birch Cr.
Pilot Rock
Enterprise
O
N
I D A H O
of
Greenwich
© Copyright HAMMOND INCORPORATED, Maplewood, N. J.

WASHINGTON

Quinault 450 B3
Quincy 3,525 F3
Rainier 891 C4
Ralston 35 G4
Randle 950 D4
Ravensdale 400 D3
Raymond 2,991 B4
Reardan 498 H3
Redmond 23,318 B1
Redondo 950 C3
Renton 30,612 B2
Republic⊙ 1,018 G2
Retsil 1,524 A2
Richland 33,578 F4
Richland-Kennewick‡ 144,469 F4
Richmond Beach-Innis Arden 6,700 A1
Richmond Highlands 24,463 A1
Ridgefield 1,062 C5
Ritzville⊙ 1,800 G3
Riverside 243 F2
Riverton 14,182 B2
Riverton Heights B2
Robe 36 D2
Roche Harbor 200 B2
Rochester 325 C4
Rockford 442 H3
Rock Island 491 E3
Rockport 200 D2
Rocky Point 1,495 A2
Rollingbay 950 A2
Ronald 200 E3
Roosevelt 60 E5
Rosalia 572 H3
Rosburg 419 B4
Roslyn 938 E3
Roy 417 C4
Royal City 676 F4
Ruff 25 F3
Ruston 612 C3
Ryderwood 367 B4
Saint John 529 H3
Salkum 390 C4
San de Fuca 150 C2
Sappho 100 A2
Satsop 300 B3
Scandia 75 A1
Schawana 150 F4
Seabeck 200 C3
Seabold 250 A1
Seahurst A2
Seattle⊙ 493,846 A2
Seattle-Everett‡ 1,606,765 A2
Seaview 500 A4
Sedro-Woolley 6,110 C2
Sekiu 328 A2
Selah 4,500 E4
Selleck 150 D3
Sequim 3,013 B2
Shaw Island 125 B2
Shelton⊙ 7,629 B3
Shoultes C2
Silvana 92 C2
Silver Creek 175 C4
Silverdale 950 A2
Silverlake 42 C4
Silverton 65 D2
Skamania 200 C5
Skamokawa 450 B4
Skykomish 209 D3
Smyrna 36 F4
Snohomish 5,294 D3
Snoqualmie 1,370 D3
Snoqualmie Falls 250 D3
Soap Lake 1,196 F3
South Bend⊙ 1,686 B4
South Broadway 3,500 E4
South Cle Elum 449 D3
South Colby 500 A2
South Prairie 202 D3
Southworth 175 A2
Spanaway 8,868 C3
Spangle 276 H3
Spokane⊙ 171,300 H3
Spokane‡ 341,835 H3
Sprague 473 G3
Springdale 281 H2
Stanwood 1,646 C2
Starbuck 198 G4
Startup 350 D3
Stehekin 98 E2
Steilacoom 4,886 C3
Steptoe 215 H3
Stevenson⊙ 1,172 C5
Stratford 70 F3
Sultan 1,578 D3
Sumas 712 C2
Sumner 4,936 C3
Sunnydale B2
Sunnyside 9,225 F4
Suquamish 1,498 A1
Tacoma⊙ 158,501 C3
Tacoma‡ 485,643 C3
Taholah 550 A3
Tahuya 150 B3
Tekoa 854 H3
Telma 50 E3
Tenino 1,280 C4
Terrace Heights 3,199 E4
Thornton 90 H3
Thorp 500 E3
Tieton 528 E4
Tiger 69 H2
Tillicum C3
Tokeland 500 A4
Toledo 637 C4
Tonasket 985 F2
Toppenish 6,517 E4
Touchet 450 G4
Toutle 825 C4
Town and Country 5,578 H3
Tracyton 2,304 A2
Trinidad 30 F3
Trout Lake 900 D5
Tukwila 3,578 B2
Tulalip 250 C2
Tumtum 250 H3
Tumwater 6,705 B3
Turner 14 H4
Twisp 911 E2
Tyler 69 H3
Underwood 640 D5
Union 380 B3
Union Gap 3,184 E4
Uniontown 286 H4
Usk 180 H2
Vader 406 B4
Valley 156 H2
Valleyford 175 H3
Vancouver⊙ 42,834 C5
Vantage 300 E4
Van Zandt 25 C2
Vashon 350 A2
Vaughn 600 C3
Veradale 7,256 H3
Wahkiacus 30 D5
Waitsburg 1,035 G4
Waldron 90 B2
Walla Walla⊙ 25,618 G4
Wallula 148 G4
Wapato 3,307 E4
Warden 1,479 F4
Warm Beach 75 C2
Washougal 3,834 C5
Washtucna 266 G4
Waterville⊙ 908 E3
Waukon 15 H3
Wauna 300 C3
Waverly 99 H3
Wellpinit 250 G3
Wenatchee⊙ 17,257 E3
Westport 1,954 A4
West Richland 2,938 F4
West Wenatchee 2,187 E3
Wheeler 75 F3
White Center-Shorewood 19,362 A2
Whites 70 B3
White Salmon 1,853 D5
White Swan 270 E4
Wickersham 200 C2
Wilbur 1,122 G3
Wiley City 250 E4
Wilkeson 321 D3
Willapa 300 B4
Wilson Creek 222 F3
Winchester 70 F3
Winlock 1,052 C4
Winona 42 H4
Winslow (Bainbridge Island-Winslow) 2,196 A2
Winthrop 413 E2
Winton 25 E3
Wishram 575 D5
Withrow 32 F3
Woodinville B1
Woodland 2,341 C5
Woodway 832 C3
Yacolt 544 C5
Yakima⊙ 49,826 E4
Yakima‡ 172,508 E4
Yarrow Point 1,064 B2
Yelm 1,294 C4
Zenith-Saltwater 8,982 C3
Zillah 1,599 E4

OTHER FEATURES

Abercrombie (mt.) H2
Adams (mt.) D4
Admiralty (inlet) B2
Ahtanum (creek) D4
Aix (mt.) D4
Alava (cape) A2
Alder (lake) C4
Asotin (creek) H4
Asotin (dam) J4
Bainbridge (isl.) A2
Baker (lake) D2
Baker (mt.) D2
Baker (riv.) D2
Banks (lake) F3
Birch (pt.) C2
Blalock (isl.) F5
Blue (lake) F3
Blue (mts.) H4
Bonanza (peak) E2
Bonaparte (creek) F2
Bonaparte (mt.) F2
Bonneville (dam) D5
Bonneville (lake) D5
Boundary (bay) C1
Boundary (dam) H2
Boundary (lake) H2
Box Canyon (dam) H2
Brown (pt.) A4
Bumping (lake) D4
Camano (isl.) C2
Carlton (pass) D4
Cascade (pass) D2
Cascade (range) D4
Cascade (riv.) D2
Cavanaugh (lake) D2
Cedar (riv.) B2
Celilo (lake) E5
Chehalis (pt.) A4
Chehalis (riv.) B4
Chehalis Ind. Res. B4
Chelan (lake) E2
Chelan (range) E2
Chester Morse (lake) D3
Chewack (riv.) E2
Chief Joseph (dam) F3
China Gardens (dam) J4
Chinook (pass) D4
Chiwawa (riv.) E2
Cispus (pass) D4
Cispus (riv.) D4
Cle Elum (lake) E3
Coal (creek) G3
Coast (ranges) B3
Columbia (riv.) B4
Colville (riv.) H2
Colville Ind. Res. G2
Constance (mt.) B3
Coulee Dam Nat'l Rec. Area G2
Cow (creek) G3
Cowlitz (pass) D4
Cowlitz (riv.) C4
Crab (creek) F3
Crescent (lake) B2
Curlew (lake) G2
Cushman (lake) B3
Dabob (bay) C3
Dalles, The (dam) D5
Daniel (mt.) D3
Deadman (creek) H4
Deer (lake) H2
Deschutes (riv.) C4
Destruction (isl.) A3
Diablo (lake) D2
Diamond (lake) H2
Disappointment (cape) A4
Dry Falls (dam) F3
Ediz Hook (pen.) B2
Elwha (riv.) B3
Entiat (lake) E3
Entiat (mts.) E2
Entiat (riv.) E3
Fairchild A.F.B. 5,353 H3
Fidalgo (isl.) C2
Flattery (cape) A2
Fort Lewis 23,761 C3
Fort Vancouver Nat'l Hist. Site C5
Fort Worden C2
Franklin D. Roosevelt (lake) G2
Gardner (mt.) E2
Georgia (str.) B2
Glacier (peak) D2
Goat Rocks (mt.) D4
Grand Coulee (canyon) F3
Grand Coulee (dam) F3
Grande Ronde (riv.) H5
Grays (harb.) A4
Green (lake) A2
Green (riv.) C3
Grenville (pt.) A3
Hanford Reservation-U.S. Dept. of Energy F4
Haro (str.) B2
Harts (pass) E2
Hells Canyon Nat'l Rec. Area H5
Hoh (head) A3
Hoh (riv.) A3
Hoh Ind. Res. A3
Hood (canal) B3
Howard A. Hanson (res.) D3
Humptulips (riv.) B3
Ice Harbor (dam) G4
Icicle (creek) E3
Jack (mt.) E2
John Day (dam) E5
Juan de Fuca (str.) A2
Kachess (lake) D3
Kalama (riv.) C4
Kalispel Ind. Res. H2
Keechelus (lake) D3
Kettle (riv.) G2
Kettle River (range) G2
Klickitat (riv.) D4
Lake (creek) G3
Lake Chelan Nat'l Rec. Area E2
Latah (creek) H3
Leadbetter (pt.) A4
Lenore (lake) F3
Lewis (riv.) C5
Little Goose (dam) G4
Little Spokane (riv.) H3
Logan (mt.) E2
Long (isl.) A4
Long (lake) H3
Loon (lake) H2
Lopez (isl.) C2
Lower Crab (creek) F4
Lower Elwah Ind. Res. B2
Lower Granite (lake) H4
Lower Monumental (lake) G4
Lummi (isl.) C2
Lummi Ind. Res. C2
Makah Ind. Res. A2
Mayfield (lake) C4
McChord A.F.B. 5,746 C3
McNary (dam) F5
Merwin (lake) C5
Methow (riv.) E2
Moses (lake) F3
Moses Coulee (canyon) F3
Mount Rainier Nat'l Park D4
Muckleshoot Ind. Res. C3
Mud Mountain (lake) D3
Naches (pass) D3
Naches (riv.) E4
Naselle (riv.) B4
Naval Support Ctr. B1
Newman (lake) H3
Nisqually (riv.) C4
Nisqually Ind. Res. C4
Nooksack (riv.) C2
North (riv.) B4
North Cascades Nat'l Park D2
Oak Harbor Naval Air Station C2
Okanogan (riv.) F2
Olympic (mts.) B3
Olympic Nat'l Park B3
Olympus (mt.) B3
Omak (lake) F2
Orcas (isl.) C2
Osoyoos (lake) F1
O'Sullivan (dam) F4
Ozette (lake) A2
Ozette Ind. Res. A2
Padilla (bay) C2
Palmer (lake) F2
Palouse (riv.) G4
Pasayten (riv.) E2
Pataha (creek) H4
Pateros (lake) F2
Pend Oreille (riv.) H2
Pillar (pt.) A2
Pine (creek) H3
Port Angeles Ind. Res. B2
Port Gamble Ind. Res. C3
Port Madison Ind. Res. A1
Potholes (res.) F3
Priest Rapids (lake) E4
Puget (isl.) B4
Puget (sound) C3
Puget Sound Navy Yard A2
Puyallup (riv.) C4
Queets (riv.) A3
Quillayute Ind. Res. A3
Quinault (lake) B3
Quinault (riv.) A3
Quinault Ind. Res. A3
Rainier (mt.) D4
Remmel (mt.) E2
Rifle (lake) C4
Rimrock (lake) D4
Rock (creek) H3
Rock (lake) H3
Rock Island (dam) E3
Rocky (mts.) H2
Rocky Reach (dam) E3
Rosario (str.) C2
Ross (dam) D2
Ross (lake) D2
Ross Lake Nat'l Rec. Area E2
Rufus Woods (lake) F2
Sacajawea (lake) G4
Sacheen (lake) H2
Saddle (mts.) E4
Saint Helens (mt.) C4
Samish (lake) C2
Sammamish (lake) B2
Sand (isl.) A4
San Juan (isl.) B2
San Juan Island Nat'l Hist. Park B2
Sanpoil (riv.) G2
Satus (creek) E4
Sauk (riv.) D2
Sawtooth (ridge) E2
Shannon (lake) D2
Shoalwater (cape) A4
Shoalwater Ind. Res. B4
Shuksan (mt.) D2
Silver (lake) C4
Similkameen (riv.) F1
Skagit (riv.) C2
Skokomish (mt.) B3
Skokomish Ind. Res. B3
Skykomish (riv.) D3
Snake (riv.) G4
Snohomish (riv.) C3
Snoqualmie (pass) D3
Snoqualmie (riv.) D3
Snow (peak) G2
Snowfield (peak) D2
Soap (lake) F3
Soleduck (riv.) A3
Spirit (lake) C4
Spokane (mt.) H3
Spokane (riv.) H3
Spokane Ind. Res. G3
Sprague (lake) G3
Stevens (pass) D3
Stuart (mt.) E3
Sucia (isl.) C2
Suiattle (riv.) D2
Sullivan (lake) H2
Sultan (riv.) D3
Swift Creek (res.) C4
Swinomish Ind. Res. C2
Sylvan (lake) G3
Tatoosh (isl.) A2
The Dalles (dam) D5
Tieton (riv.) D4
Tiffany (mt.) F2
Tolt River (res.) D3
Toppenish (creek) E4
Touchet (riv.) G4
Toutle, North Fork (riv.) C4
Toutle, South Fork (riv.) C4
Tucannon (riv.) G4
Tulalip Ind. Res. C2
Tule (lake) G3
Twin (lakes) G2
Twin Sisters (mt.) D2
Twisp (pass) E2
Twisp (riv.) E2
Umatilla (lake) E5
Union (lake) B2
Vancouver (lake) C5
Walla Walla (riv.) G4
Wallula (lake) F4
Walupt (lake) D4
Wanapum (lake) E3
Washington (lake) B2
Wells (dam) F3
Wenas (creek) E4
Wenatchee (lake) E3
Wenatchee (mts.) E3
Wenatchee (riv.) E3
Whatcom (lake) C2
Whidbey (isl.) C2
White (pass) D4
White (riv.) D3
White Salmon (riv.) D4
Whitman Mission Nat'l Hist. Site G4
Willapa (bay) A4
Wilson (creek) F3
Wind (riv.) D5
Wynoochee (lake) B3
Wynoochee (riv.) B3
Yakima (ridge) E4
Yakima (riv.) F4

⊙County seat. ‡Population of metropolitan area.

farm, analysis of soil, and the projection of probable crops to the solution of community problems.

The rapid depletion of virgin forests with little regard for the future finally yielded to a policy of conservation. The planting and protection of tree farms is a recognized and rapidly growing practice. Programs of fire prevention and selective logging also have been put into effect. Where selective logging is not possible, the practice is to leave enough trees for natural reseeding. The state government, the National Forest Service, and private industry cooperate in this vital work of reforestation.

Conservation also is practiced by the fisheries, where a conflict of basic interests exists. Dams such as the Grand Coulee, however beneficial for irrigation and electric energy, completely block the salmon from reaching their spawning grounds. After the completion of Grand Coulee, efforts were made to provide means, such as fish ladders, for the salmon to surmount the obstacles. Research indicates that much more needs to be done. While fish ladders may get a large share of the mature fish upstream, this is but half the battle. Still to be solved is how to return the fingerlings safely downstream—far too many of them are swept over the dams or destroyed as they seek a way down through the great power turbines.

The extensive conservation programs in the state covering soil conservation, fish and wildlife management, forest management, flood control, and land reclamation are administered by state and federal agencies. The latter include the Forest Service, the National Park Service, the Fish and Wildlife Service, the Bureau of Land Management, the U. S. Army Corps of Engineers, and the Bureau of Reclamation.

2. The People

The population of Washington, according to the 1980 census, comprised about 3.8 million whites, 106,000 blacks, and 248,000 members of other races, chiefly American Indians and Orientals. Of the foreign-born whites, Canadians formed the largest group. Scandinavians (particularly Norwegians and Swedes), Britons, and Germans also contributed substantially to the foreign-born population. Of the more than 60,000 Indians in the state, more than half live on reservations or other government-granted areas.

Roman Catholics form the largest religious grouping, followed by Lutherans and Methodists.

Characteristics of the Population. In spite of steady population growth, Washington remains one of the more sparsely populated states. Washington pioneers were largely farmers or farm dwellers. Not until 1880 did the census reports show evidence of urban growth. The attraction of war industries during World War II caused an accelerated shift of population from farms to cities. A continuation of this trend is expected, even when allowance is made for the countermovement from city centers to suburban developments. About three fourths of the state's population live in urban areas.

More than half the population lives in or near the state's three largest cities—Seattle, Spokane, and Tacoma. Seattle and Tacoma are important shipping and manufacturing centers. Spokane, in the eastern, agricultural half of the state, is a manufacturing and grain center. Most of the cities and towns in this less populated part of the

KEITH GUNNAR/WEST STOCK

Goat Lake in Foggy Park offers a quiet refuge away from the populated centers of coastal Washington.

River rafters plunge through the glacier-fed turbulent waters of the Sauk River, northeast of Seattle.

KEITH GUNNAR/WEST STOCK

LARGEST CENTERS OF POPULATION
(Incorporated places and metropolitan areas[1])

City or metropolitan area	1980	1970	1960
Seattle	493,846	530,831	557,087
Metropolitan area[2]	1,607,469	1,424,605	1,107,213
Spokane	171,300	170,516	181,608
Metropolitan area	341,835	287,487	278,333
Tacoma	158,501	154,407	147,979
Metropolitan area	485,643	412,344	322,950
Bellevue	73,903	61,196	12,809
Everett	54,413	53,622	40,304
Yakima	49,826	45,588	43,284
Bellingham	45,794	39,375	34,688
Vancouver	42,834	41,859	32,464
Bremerton	36,208	35,307	28,922
Kennewick	34,397	15,212	14,244
Richland	33,578	26,290	23,548
Longview	31,052	28,373	23,349
Renton	30,612	25,878	18,453

[1]Standard metropolitan statistical areas. [2]Seattle-Everett.

URBAN-RURAL DISTRIBUTION

Year	Percent urban	Percent rural
1920	54.8 (U.S., 51.2)	45.2
1930	56.6 (U.S., 56.2)	43.4
1940	53.1 (U.S., 56.6)	46.9
1950	63.2 (U.S., 64.0)	36.8
1960	68.1 (U.S., 69.9)	31.9
1970	72.6 (U.S., 73.4)	26.6
1980	73.5 (U.S., 73.7)	26.5

GROWTH OF POPULATION SINCE 1870

Year	Population	Year	Population
1870	23,955	1940	1,736,191
1880	75,116	1960	2,853,214
1900	518,103	1970	3,413,244
1920	1,356,621	1980	4,132,180

Gain, 1970–1980: 21.1% (U.S. gain 11.4%). **Density,** 1980: 62.1 persons per sq mi (U.S. density, 62.6).

state developed as lumber or mining towns or agricultural and trade centers.

The rural portion of the population is engaged in agriculture or lumbering. The small rural towns serve as trade and recreational centers and provide employment in the mills, grain elevators, and food-processing plants.

Main Centers of Population. In the Puget Sound region is located Washington's chief trading center and largest city, Seattle, whose economic influence extends throughout the Pacific Northwest and overseas to Alaska and the Orient. Also in the Puget Sound region is Tacoma, the third-largest city in Washington and a prominent industrial and trading center. Secondary trading centers in this region are Bremerton, seat of the Puget Sound Navy Yard; Bellingham; Everett; and Olympia, the state capital.

Southwestern Washington has no major trading center but is in the radius of Portland, Oreg. Secondary trading centers are Vancouver, the Longview-Kelso, Aberdeen-Hoquiam, and Centralia-Chehalis districts. Central Washington contains no large cities, Yakima and Wenatchee being the chief secondary trading centers of apple and other orchard areas.

Northeastern Washington is dominated by Spokane, the second-largest city in the state and center of the "Inland Empire" region that extends from the Cascade Range in Washington, eastward into western Montana, and from British Columbia on the north into northeastern Oregon and Idaho on the south. Southeastern Washington, which also comes under the economic influence of Spokane, has but one secondary trading center, Walla Walla, seat of Whitman College and center of a flourishing agricultural region. Richland, with its two rapidly growing satellites Pasco and Kennewick (known as the Tricity area), is rapidly becoming a trade center rivaling

Seattle is the largest city in the Pacific Northwest and the thriving gateway port to Alaska and Asia.

JAY LURIE/FPG

Loggers in Washington's rich forests use mechanical equipment to cut, load, and haul Douglas fir to sawmills.

Walla Walla in this region. The great Hanford Atomic Works, managed for the Energy Research and Development Administration by Battelle-Northwest, provides a strong economic base for this new trading center.

3. The Economy

With few exceptions the economic development of Washington rests on and parallels the exploitation of the state's natural resources. In the lush virgin forests that grew down to the edge of the sea, lumbering began late in the 18th century. One of the earliest sawmills started in 1825. Rich fisheries were exploited also in the early days.

Today the economy is built basically on the tripod of forests, agriculture, and hydroelectric energy. Although virgin forests largely have been depleted, much forest wealth remains and is now being utilized on a sustained-yield basis. A substantial payroll stems from lumber and plywood mills, pulp and paper processing, and subsidiary forest-products industries. Agriculture is diversified, producing wheat and other field crops; horticultural products, including the famous Washington apples; livestock, dairy products, and poultry; and bulbs and seeds. With the development of hydroelectric energy, electrochemical and electrometallurgical industries were attracted to the state, notably a very substantial aluminum smelting and refining business that now accounts for a third of the nation's output.

Two notable exceptions to the general pattern are the Boeing airplane plant in Seattle and the atomic-energy plant in Hanford near Richland in eastern Washington. The aerospace industry employs about 80,000 persons. The atomic-energy project was located in Washington largely because of the need for secrecy—a need satisfied by the availability of a large tract of desert land remote from population centers. Both the Hanford project and Boeing continue to make major contributions to national defense.

Manufacturing. Measured in value of products, contribution to income, and employment, manufacturing is Washington's leading industry. Its chief manufactured products are transportation equipment, particularly aircraft and aerospace systems; wood products, including lumber, plywood, and shingles; and processed food. Washington is also a major shipbuilding center. The Boeing Company, the nation's largest producer of commercial airliners, employs more people than any other manufacturer in the state. Other important manufactures are paper products, including paperboard, and metal products.

Industrial activity is concentrated around Puget Sound, but it is widely distributed throughout the state. This is made possible by the availability of large quantities of hydroelectric power and the electricity rates that were set to inhibit industrial clustering at dam sites.

Agriculture and Lumbering. Almost half of the total land area in Washington is covered with farmland, about half of which is devoted to crops and the other half to pastureland and woodland. The state's farms have grown slightly in number (about 34,000) but have decreased slightly in average size (about 481 acres, or 195 hectares).

PERSONAL INCOME IN WASHINGTON

Source	1960	1970	1980
	(Millions of dollars)		
Farms	268	356	803
Mining	13	17	84
Construction	372	685	2,421
Manufacturing	1,384	2,495	7,468
Transportation, communications, and public utilities	390	768	2,288
Wholesale and retail trade	1,045	1,849	5,394
Finance, insurance, and real estate	671	549	1,810
Services	631	1,493	5,289
Other industries	30	67	325
Government	1,016	2,447	5,903
	(Dollars)		
Per capita personal income	2,372	4,046	10,309
Per capita income, U.S.	2,216	3,945	9,521

Source: U.S. Department of Commerce, *Survey of Current Business.*

HAROLD LANEY/FPG

The fertile volcanic soil of Washington's Wenatchee Valley produces central Washington's renowned apples.

Rough weather is an everyday occurrence for those who gather the succulent crab along Washington's coasts.

SAMUEL CROOT COMPANY, INC.

Wheat is the number one crop. The state is also a major producer of dairy products, cattle, hay, eggs, potatoes, sugar beets, hops, chickens, dry beans, asparagus, green peas, barley and other grains, and a wide assortment of fruits including apples, pears, berries, plums, apricots, and cherries.

Washington is the nation's leading producer of apples and is well known for its Red Delicious and Golden Delicious varieties. Most of its orchards are located in the irrigated valleys in the central part of the state.

Cattle, horses, and sheep are raised on large ranches in eastern part of the state, but most of the dairy farms are in the western section.

Flower bulbs are another important Washington crop. The state is a leading producer of iris, tulip, and daffodil bulbs and also produces greenhouse plants such as azaleas, Easter lilies, and poinsettias.

Approximately 53% of the state is timberland. The timberlands are divided by the Cascades, with ponderosa pines to the east and Douglas firs to the west. Washington has about one fifth of all the Douglas fir in the nation.

Fishing. More than 200 species of edible fish and shellfish make fisheries an important industry in the state. Salmon is the most prized catch, and halibut is second. Other fish and seafoods include Pacific cod, ocean perch, sole, flounder, oysters, clams, crabs, rockfish, herring, and tuna.

Mining. Coal is one of the most important mineral resources of the state. The major fields are on the western slopes of the Cascade Mountains, chiefly in King county. An important exception is the low-grade bituminous variety, which is located in Pierce county and is the only source of coking coal in the Pacific Coast states.

Washington's mineral resources have been exploited in varying degrees since 1853. Minerals are divided into two broad groups, metallics and nonmetallics. Nonmetallic minerals have always had a greater value of total production than metallic minerals. Coal, portland cement, lime, clay products, sand and gravel, stone, magnesite, and less important nonmetallic minerals and aggregates have generally accounted for about 90% of the state's total mineral output. The ores of gold, silver, copper, lead, zinc, and other metallic elements such as tungsten, manganese, iron, magnesium, and nickel have accounted for the other 10%. The chief metallic mining operations are carried on in Stevens, Pend Oreille, Ferry, Chelan, and Okanogan counties.

Electric Power. Washington has more potential waterpower than any other state in the country. The state's energy sources include hydroelectric power, native coal, petroleum refineries, and natural gas. The greatest source of hydroelectric power is the Columbia River, which is spanned by huge dams. The greatest of these is the Grand Coulee Dam, built by the federal government during the Depression of the 1930's. Other large dams on the Columbia River are Bonneville, Chief Joseph, John Day, McNary, Priest Rapids, Rock Island, Rocky Reach, The Dalles, and Wanapum. Washington state shares power produced by the Columbia with other Northwest states.

As the more economical sites are utilized, hydroelectric power projects become more expensive to construct. At the same time progress in the technology of harnessing nuclear energy is rapidly cutting the cost of atomic sources of electric energy. The result may be that much of the hydroelectric potential of Washington's rivers will never be harnessed. Contributing to this end is the growing opposition by fishery interests to high dams that jeopardize important salmon spawning grounds. Attention also is being given to the possibilities of utilizing Washington's coal for thermoelectric plants.

A further addition to the energy base of the state has been the construction of petroleum refineries. These are supplied with crude oil either by pipelines from Canada or Montana or by sea. Natural gas is piped to Washington from the rich sources of the Peace River area in Canada as well as from the more remote San Juan Basin in New Mexico.

Transportation. The location of Washington makes transportation and communications facilities of vital importance. Remote from the great centers of population of the United States, the people of this state have welcomed the air age. Washington has long enjoyed the enviable position of being the point in the United States closest to Alaska and the Orient by the great-circle route for waterborne traffic. The progress of air traffic has publicized the state's strategic situation.

Nearly every community is within range of one of the state's 300 airports or airfields. In addition to the 12 domestic airlines serving the state, there is an international airport in Seattle.

A network of roads covers the state, and transcontinental systems have links in Washington's highway system. Washington is also well served by local and transcontinental bus and railroad lines. Two floating concrete pontoon bridges cross Lake Washington in Seattle, and the state has one of the most extensive automobile passenger ferry systems in the world.

4. Government

The constitution of the state of Washington was adopted in 1889 following an earlier draft at the Walla Walla Convention in 1878, which the people of the territory adopted but the U. S. Congress rejected, possibly because it included a provision for woman suffrage. Amendments are proposed by a two-thirds vote of the legislature and ratified by a majority of the voters voting on the amendment, or by a constitutional convention. No changes have been made in the basic organization of the state government, which provides for executive, legislative, and judicial bodies.

Suffrage is extended to citizens of the United States, 18 years of age or over, who have resided in the state one year. Each voter must register in order to be eligible to exercise his franchise. A division of permanent registration is maintained in the election division of the office of the secretary of state. Provision is made for the initiation of laws by the voters and for the referral of proposed laws by the legislature to the voters—the initiative and referendum. Petitions for initiative or referendum measures must be signed by 50,000 or more legal voters. Recall petitions against state officials also are filed with the secretary of state. Voting machines are used in the larger cities.

Structure of Government. The people of Washington elect their governor and lieutenant governor for four-year terms, the election coinciding with those for president of the United States. A governor may succeed himself in office. The state has eight United States congressmen, one elected from each of eight congressional districts.

Legislative. The state constitution provides for a bicameral legislature with apportionment to both

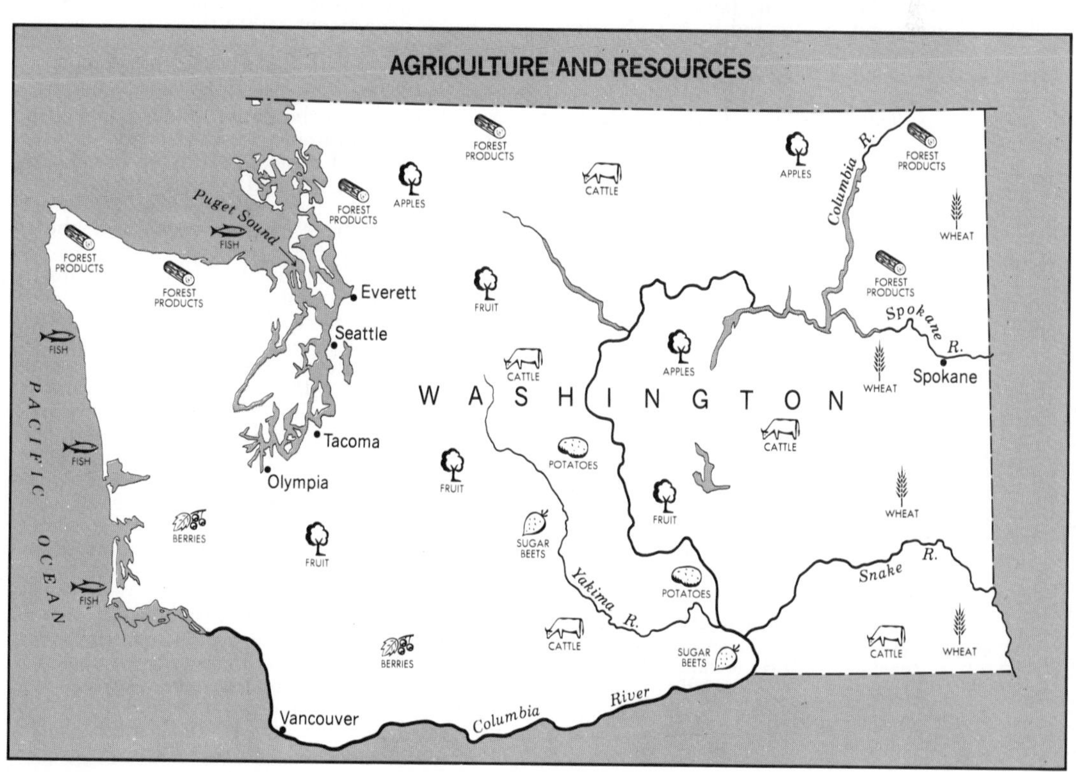

WASHINGTON STATE DEPARTMENT OF COMMERCE AND ECONOMIC DEVELOPMENT

Washington's imposing State Capitol in Olympia enjoys a striking setting at the southern end of Puget Sound.

the House and Senate on a population basis, limiting the total to 99 in the House and 49 in the Senate. Currently, however, one senator and two representatives are elected from each of the 49 districts.

State senators are elected for four-year terms, about half of them being chosen at each of the biennial elections held in even-numbered years concurrently with the national general elections. All representatives are elected for two-year terms. The regular sessions of the legislature convene on the second Monday in January in odd-numbered years and are limited by the constitution to not more than 60 days. Special or extraordinary sessions may be called by the governor. The legislature may determine the matters to be dealt with by its members during the session.

Judiciary. The highest court in Washington is the state supreme court. Nine supreme court judges are elected on a nonpartisan basis, three every two years for six-year terms. The position of chief justice of this court goes to the judge with the shortest remaining term. If two or more judges have equal terms remaining, the chief justice is selected by the other judges.

A court of appeals was established in 1969 with 12 judges also elected for six-year terms on a nonpartisan ballot. Other state courts include district superior courts and justice-of-the-peace courts.

Public Finance. A state income tax has been rejected by the people on several occasions, and the state relies for revenue largely on a retail sales tax. For the most part, property taxes are levied by counties, cities, and other special districts. Excise taxes on beverages, motor fuels, and tobacco, taxes on public utilities, and motor-vehicle licensing are additional sources of income for the state.

GOVERNMENT HIGHLIGHTS

Electoral Vote—10. **Representation in Congress**—U.S. senators, 2; U.S. representatives, 8. **State Legislature**—Senate, 49 members, 4-year terms; House of Representatives, 98 members, 2-year terms. **Governor**—4-year term; may serve successive terms.

Social Services. Public health service was provided for by the state constitution, which established the state board of health. This governing and supervisory body of five members, appointed by the governor with the consent of the Senate, is charged with responsibility for all matters relating to the preservation of the life and health of the people of the state. Since 1921 the state has had a department of health led by a director and assistant director.

Washington is among the leading states in social legislation. The workmen's compensation act of 1911 set up the nation's first monopolistic state industrial insurance fund. In 1917 a medical act established a medical-aid fund, including hospital care for injured workmen, to which contributions are made by employers and workers. These acts have been amended and liberalized from time to time.

In 1921 the department of labor and industry was created to coordinate and centralize state activities in the field of labor and labor conditions. This department is under the charge of a director appointed by the governor with Senate confirmation. Disabled workers or those incurring designated occupational diseases are paid compensation based on the number of their dependents during their incapacity. Pensions are provided for total disability and for dependents of those killed by or dying as a result of industrial accidents. Safety standards are enforced throughout the various industrial establishments in the state. Periodic inspection is maintained for all extraordinarily hazardous industries.

Public assistance began with the Washington Emergency Relief Administration created by law in January 1933. In 1935 the work was placed in a state department of public welfare, which was succeeded in 1937 by the state department of social security. The law of 1937 established a public-assistance code, abolished the poor laws,

GOVERNORS OF WASHINGTON

Territorial		
Isaac Ingals Stevens	Democrat	1853–1857
J. Patton Anderson[1]	"	1857
Fayette McMullin	"	1857–1859
Richard D. Gholson	"	1859–1861
William H. Wallace[1]	Republican	1861
William Pickering	"	1862–1867
George E. Cole[2]	Democrat	1867
Marshall F. Moore	Republican	1867–1869
Alvan Flanders	"	1869–1870
Edward S. Saloman	"	1870–1872
James F. Legate[1]	"	1872
Elisha P. Ferry	"	1872–1880
William A. Newell	"	1880–1884
Watson C. Squire	"	1884–1887
Eugene Semple	Democrat	1887–1889
Miles Conway Moore	Republican	1889
State		
Elisha P. Ferry	Republican	1889–1893
John Harte McGraw	"	1893–1897
John Rankin Rogers	Democrat-Populist	1897–1901
Henry McBride	Republican, acting	1901–1905
Albert Edward Mead	Republican	1905–1909
Samuel G. Cosgrove	"	1909
Marion E. Hay	Republican, acting	1909–1913
Ernest Lister	Democrat	1913–1919
Louis Folwell Hart[3]	Republican, acting	1919
Louis Folwell Hart	Republican	1919–1925
Roland H. Hartley	Republican	1925–1933
Clarence D. Martin	Democrat	1933–1941
Arthur B. Langlie	Republican	1941–1945
Monrad C. Wallgren	Democrat	1945–1949
Arthur B. Langlie	Republican	1949–1957
Albert D. Rosellini	Democrat	1957–1965
Daniel J. Evans	Republican	1965–1977
Dixie Lee Ray	Democrat	1977–1981
John Spellman	Republican	1981–1985
Booth Gardner	Democrat	1985–

[1] Failed to qualify. [2] Appointment not confirmed by Senate. [3] Acting from February, when Lister retired, to June 14, when Lister died; sworn as governor on June 15, 1919; elected for another term beginning in 1921.

and coordinated federal, state, and county activities, designating boards of county commissioners as local administrative units. In 1930 unemployment compensation and employment service were reorganized into a separate state department. Provisions have been liberalized by subsequent initiative and legislative action.

State institutions charged with responsibility for health and welfare include two custodial schools for the care and training of retarded young people, one at Medical Lake and the other at Buckley; mental hospitals at Fort Steilacoom, Medical Lake, and Sedro-Wooley; hospitals, including the Washington Infirmary at Grand Mound and McKay Memorial Research Hospital at Soap Lake; a training school for boys under 18 at Chehalis and one for girls under 18 at Grand Mound; a school for the deaf and one for the blind, both in Vancouver; and soldiers' homes, including Washington Veterans' Home in Retsil and State Soldiers' Home and Colony in Orting.

5. Education and Culture

The first schools in the state of Washington were established in the early 1830's. One was for the Hudson's Bay Company employees at Fort Vancouver, and the other was established by missionaries in Spokane to teach the Indians. The first territorial legislature provided for the establishment of common schools in 1854. The state constitution provides that "it is the paramount duty of the state to make ample provision for the education of all children residing within its borders, without distinction or preference because of race, color, caste, or sex."

Elementary and Secondary Education. Washington's public schools are under an elected state superintendent of public instruction and a state board of education. The superintendent supervises all public elementary, junior, and senior high schools, all state junior colleges, and Indian education.

Free education is provided through high school for all individuals between the ages of 6 and 21, and education is compulsory between the ages of 8 and 15. Children between the ages of 15 and 16 must attend school unless they have regular jobs.

Higher Education. Six colleges and universities are supported by the state. These are the University of Washington, in Seattle; Washington State University, in Pullman (until 1959 the State College of Washington); Western Washington University in Bellingham; Central Washington University in Ellensburg; Eastern Washington University in Cheney; and Evergreen State College, near Olympia.

Private schools and colleges include Whitman College, in Walla Walla; the University of Puget Sound, in Tacoma; Whitworth College and Gonzaga University, in Spokane; and Seattle Pacific University and Seattle University, in Seattle. The University of Washington has the largest enrollment.

Libraries and Museums. Washington's oldest library is the State Library in Olympia, founded in 1853 as the Territorial Library. The state is

Mount Rainier dominates the horizon from the imposing campus of the University of Washington in Seattle.

MONKMEYER PRESS PHOTO

well supplied with library facilities. Practically every community has some library service. The University of Washington has a large and growing collection and houses the Bibliographic Center for the Pacific Northwest. Washington State University and the four state colleges, as well as the private colleges and universities, also have ample library facilities. The Seattle Public Library has an unusually fine collection of books and offers excellent library service through its many branches. The *Seattle Times,* a daily newspaper, maintains a reference library and a library service free to the public.

The Seattle Art Museum has a celebrated collection of Oriental art and jades. Also in Seattle are the Henry Art Gallery, the Frye Museum, and the Thomas Burke Memorial Washington State Museum. Other museums of interest are the Eastern Washington State Historical Society and Museum in Spokane, containing a fine collection of Indian arts and handicrafts; the Tacoma Art Museum and the Washington State Historical Society Museum, in Tacoma; the Bellevue Art Museum, in Bellevue; the Whatcom Museum of History and Art, in Bellingham; the Pioneer Village and Willis Carey Historical Museum, in Cashmere; Cowlitz County Museum, featuring pioneer and Indian artifacts, a log cabin, a country store, a post office, a barbershop, a livery stable, and a kitchen and parlor of a stagecoach inn; the Maryhill Museum of Art, a massive building containing a large collection of Rodin originals; and the Adam East Museum in Moses Lake, which contains artifacts of early man and prehistoric animals.

Other Cultural Activities. The cultural pattern of the people of Washington is definitely Western. Life is freer and more relaxed than in the eastern United States. Informality and hospitality are characteristic of the state. The pioneer tradition still is strong and is reflected in the living pattern.

However, interest in art, literature, music, and other cultural activities is great. Seattle supports an excellent symphony orchestra. The School of Drama of the University of Washington is nationally acclaimed and has contributed many stars to the American stage and screen. Great interest is attached to the cultural patterns of the original Indians, and museums contain excellent collections on the Northwest and Alaska.

Communication. The earliest newspaper in Washington was the weekly *Columbian,* first published in Olympia in 1852. Eleven years later the *Gazette* began at Seattle; it was the direct ancestor of the *Post-Intelligencer.* All the larger cities in the state have one or two dailies, and many of the smaller communities are served by weekly or semiweekly journals. The *Seattle Times* and *Post-Intelligencer* have the largest circulations in the state.

National and local radio and television services blanket the state. The first regularly scheduled broadcasting in the state began in Seattle in 1921. Television was introduced in Seattle in 1948, and in 1954 one of the first educational TV stations in the nation began transmitting from the University of Washington.

6. Recreation and Places of Interest

The state of Washington appeals to the sportsman and those interested in recreation. Mount Rainier National Park and Olympic National Park offer the spectator unrivaled scenery and at the same time lure mountain climbers as well as devotees of skiing. The site of the first state legislative hall is preserved in the state capital in Olympia, and the old capitol building, con-

The "Citizen's" crosscountry ski race at Gold Creek Valley attracts skiers from all over Pacific Northwest.

KEITH GUNNAR/WEST STOCK

JAY LURIE/FPG

The sheltered waters of Seattle's Lake Washington offer ideal conditions for the weekend sailor.

structed in 1893, is famous for its Romanesque architecture. Seattle, the largest city in the Pacific Northwest, is important as a center of import and export trade. Here also are located the University of Washington, the largest university of the Pacific Northwest, and the Boeing Company plant, one of the West's pioneer establishments in the aeronautical field. The Covington House, the oldest house in the state, is preserved in Leverich Park, Vancouver. The numerous dams, notably Bonneville and Grand Coulee, always attract many tourists.

National Areas. The state of Washington has three national parks: Mt. Rainier National Park, consisting of 378 square miles (979 sq km) centered on the largest single-peak glacial system in the United States, and one of the most awesome sights in the Northwest; North Cascades National Park, 505,000 acres (204,366 hectares) in the north central part of the state, which is characterized by jagged peaks, canyons, and rivers and lakes and is populated by mountain goat, deer, and black bear; and Olympic National Park, a scenic wilderness of 901,216 acres (364,091 hectares) where Mt. Olympus (7,965 feet or 2,427 meters) is located.

The state also has hundreds of acres of national recreation areas. One of the most appealing to tourists is the Coulee Dam National Recreation Area. It contains one of the largest concrete dams in the world, Grand Coulee Dam, on the Columbia River. The area is further enhanced by the Franklin D. Roosevelt Lake, which covers 81,000 acres (32,780 hectares). The other two national recreation areas are Lake Chelan and Ross Lake.

In addition to these, there are six national forests in the state, one of which is Okanogan with 1,520,456 acres (614,264 hectares) of woodland threaded by trails along its precipitous terrain. The other national forests are Mt. Baker–Snoqualmie, Colville, Gifford Pinchot, Wenatchee, and Olympic. The national recreation areas, parks, and forests offer a broad range of outdoor activities, including camping, picnicking, mountain climbing, hiking, boating, fishing, and winter sports.

State Parks. Washington has set aside approximately 83,380 acres (33,685 hectares) that are devoted to a great number of state parks for scenic, historic, and recreational value. The state parks are administered by the state parks committee. Camping facilities are provided in many of these areas. Of outstanding interest among the developed parks are Lake Chelan, Dry Falls, Deception Pass, Gingko Petrified Forest, Moran on Orcas Island, and Mt. Spokane.

Indian Reservations. Indian reservations are administered from four headquarters: the Taholah Indian Agency of Hoquiam, with jurisdiction over the Chehalis, Makah or Neah Bay, Nisqually, Ozette, Quinaielt, Skokomish, and Squaxin Island reservations; the Tulalip Agency in Tulalip, in charge of the Lummi, Muckleshoot, Port Madison, Puyallup, Swinomish, and Tulalip reservations; the Colville Agency, administering the Spokane and Colville reservations; and the Yakima Agency, administering the Yakima Reservation.

Other Points of Interest. In Seattle the University of Washington Arboretum with its Japanese Tea Garden is a noteworthy attraction, as are the two floating bridges spanning Lake Washington. The USS *Missouri*, on which the U. S. treaty with Japan was signed at the end of World War II, is anchored near the naval shipyard in Bremerton. The town of Leavenworth, modeled after a Bavarian village, is a year-round resort area, with its Alpine architecture, scenery and sporting events. At Maryhill on a cliff overlooking the Columbia River the visitor will find a replica of the 4,000 year-old Stonehenge in England. The Dungeness State Salmon Hatchery and Olympic Game Farm, both in Sequim, are open to the public. The state also has important restorations, wildlife preserves, city parks and zoos, monuments, and museums.

Annual Events. Washington's most outstanding annual events center on rodeos, sea fairs, and pow wows. Rodeos include Spokane's Diamond Spur Rodeo in April, the Omak Stampede and Suicide Race in August, and the Ellenburg Rodeo, one of the major rodeos in the state, held on Labor Day weekend.

Seattle's ten-day Seafair held in late July and early August features hydroplane races on Lake Washington. The Tri-Cities Water Follies and Columbia Cup Hydroplane Races are held in Kennewick in late July. Indian pow wows are held throughout the summer in White Swan, Colville, Toppenish, and Spokane.

The wonders of nature are feted in the spring with the Washington State Apple Blossom Festival in Wenatchee, the Lilac Festival in Spokane, Port Townsend's Rhodedendron Festival and

FAMOUS WASHINGTONIANS

Auslander, Mrs. Joseph (1911–1960), poet and winner of the 1935 Pulitzer Prize for poetry, known as Audrey May Wurdemann.
Boeing, William Edward (1881–1956), aircraft manufacturer who founded Boeing Airplane Company.
Crosby, Bing (Harry Lillis, 1904–1977), popular singer and film actor.
Denny, Arthur Armstrong (1822–1889), pioneer and author who founded the settlement that was to become Seattle, and wrote *Pioneer Days on Puget Sound.*
Douglas, William Orville (1898–1980), Associate Justice of the U. S. Supreme Court.
Garry, Spokane (1811–1892), an American Indian missionary who was a leader among the tribes of the Columbia Basin for nearly 60 years.
Gould, Carl F. (1873–1937), one of the leading architects of the Northwest.
Jackson, Henry Martin (1912–1983), lawyer and politician, serving as U. S. Congressman 1941–1953 and U. S. Senator after 1953; chairman of the Democratic National Committee 1960–1961; sought Democratic presidential nomination in 1972 and 1976.
Johnston, Eric A. (1896–1963), Spokane businessman who became president of the United States Chamber of Commerce from 1942 to 1946 and holder of government posts under Presidents Franklin D. Roosevelt, Harry Truman, and Dwight D. Eisenhower.
Jones, Wesley Livsey (1863–1932), U. S. Congressman 1899–1909, U. S. Senator 1909–1932, author of Jones Act of 1929 providing for strict enforcement of Prohibition.
Leschi (?–1858), a Nisqualli chief who was hanged for murders committed by his tribe in the uprising at Seattle in 1856.
McClintic, Guthrie (1893–1961), theatrical producer and director of many Broadway plays, husband of Katharine Cornell.
Munsel, Patrice (1925–), singer who made her operatic debut at the Metropolitan Opera in New York City in 1943.
Parrington, Vernon Louis (1871–1929), author and professor of English who won the Pulitzer Prize for history in 1928 with the first two volumes of his *Main Currents in American Thought.*
Seattle (c. 1786–1866), an Indian chief of the Dwanish, Suquamish, and other tribes, who befriended the white settlers of that region.
Smohalla (c. 1815–1907), Indian prophet and chief of a small tribe who was founder of the Dream religion.
Wainwright, Jonathan Mahew (1883–1953), U. S. Army general in World War II.
Whittaker, James W. (1931–), mountain climber, member of the U. S. Mount Everest Expedition in 1963, and first American to reach its peak.

Victorian Homes Tour, and the Washington State Autumn Leaf Festival in Leavenworth.

Other interesting annual events are Port Angeles' Salmon Derby and Derby Days celebration on Labor Day weekend; Snake River Days in Clarkston in August; and the Pacific Northwest Wagner Festival held in Bellevue in July.

7. History

The region that is now Washington had a substantial Indian population when it was first discovered by white explorers. The Cayuse, Colville, Nez Percé, Okanogan, Spokane, and Yakima tribes inhabited the plains and valleys east of the Cascades. The coastal tribes were the Chinook, Clallam, Clatsop, Nisqually, Nooksack, and Puyallup.

Exploration. The earliest history of Washington is contained in the records of expeditions and discoveries by Spanish, British, and American explorers. The territorial claims made by these men on behalf of their countries laid the groundwork for the later disputes about which nation had paramount rights to the Pacific Northwest. The claim of Juan de Fuca (Apostolos Valerianos) to have discovered in 1592 the strait that bears his name is not generally accepted by historians. In 1775 the Spanish navigator Bruno Heceta (Hezeta) sailed up the Pacific coast from California and discovered the mouth of the Columbia River. He did not attempt to enter the river, but went ashore farther up the coast and formally laid claim to the entire area for his country.

Settlement. Sixteen years after this event a small band of Spanish colonists established on Neah Bay the first white settlement in what later became Washington, but at the end of five months the post was abandoned. For further discussion of territorial claims, see OREGON QUESTION.

The next white people to make settlements in Washington were fur traders. In 1810 the North West Company's Spokane House was established by Canadian agents a few miles northwest of the present city of Spokane. The following year John Jacob Astor's Pacific Fur Company set up a post at Fort Okanogan, which was the first American settlement in the area, and another at Astoria, now in Oregon. In 1812, Astor's Fort Spokane began operations as a rival of Spokane House in eastern Washington.

After the fur traders, during the earliest years of settlement, came the missionaries and their wives. A settlement was established by Marcus Whitman in 1836 near the site of the present city of Walla Walla. In 1843, Whitman, returning from a visit to the East, helped guide a large party of American settlers, and that same year a provisional Oregon Country government was formed at Champoeg, now in Oregon.

The earliest American settlement in the area north of the Columbia River was made at Tumwater on Puget Sound in 1845. A year later the disputed ownership of the Oregon Country was settled by the Oregon Treaty, under the terms of

HISTORICAL HIGHLIGHTS

- **1775** Spanish explorers Bruno Heceta and Juan Francisco de la Bodega y Quadra landed on Washington soil.
- **1792** Captain Robert Gray discovered the Columbia River; Captain George Vancouver surveyed Puget Sound.
- **1805** Lewis and Clark reached the mouth of the Columbia River at the Pacific Ocean.
- **1810** The North West Company, a British-Canadian fur-trading company, established a post near Spokane.
- **1818** The United States and Great Britain entered into joint occupation of the Oregon region, which included Washington.
- **1825** The Hudson's Bay Company established Fort Vancouver.
- **1846** The U. S.-Canadian boundary was established at the 49th parallel.
- **1853** Congress created the Washington Territory.
- **1881** The Northern Pacific Railroad reached Spokane.
- **1889** Washington was admitted to the Union on November 11 as the 42d state.
- **1909** The Alaska-Yukon-Pacific Exposition was held in Seattle.
- **1917** The Lake Washington Ship Canal opened.
- **1928** The Capitol at Olympia was completed.
- **1937** The Bonneville Power Administration began operations.
- **1942** Grand Coulee Dam was opened.
- **1962** The Century 21 World's Fair was held at Seattle.
- **1964** The Columbia River Treaty of 1961 received final approval from the United States and Canadian governments.
- **1974** The Spokane World's Fair, Expo '74, took place.

which Britain took all the territory north of the 49th parallel and the United States all territory to the south, except the south end of Vancouver Island. The American part was organized as Oregon Territory on Aug. 14, 1848. The same year, settlement began at the site of Olympia, in 1851 at Seattle, and at Bellingham and Tacoma the next year. A rapid growth in population led to division of the territory, and on March 2, 1853, the portion north of the Columbia River and the 46th parallel was separately organized as Washington Territory.

Gold was discovered in northeastern Washington in 1855 and along the Fraser River in Canada in 1858. The rush of prospectors through the country and the ensuing growth of new settlements contributed much to the increase of Indian anxiety over the fate of their hunting grounds. The years from 1855 to 1859 were marked by intermittent war between settlers and Indians. Oregon became a state in 1859, and Washington Territory was enlarged to include all of the former Oregon Territory not in the new state. The Idaho gold strikes of 1860–1863 brought boom times to Walla Walla, the chief supply point for gold prospectors, and it became the largest city in the territory. Partly as a result of the rapid growth of eastern Washington, sections of it were broken off in 1863 and incorporated in the new Territory of Idaho. Thus the permanent boundaries of the future state of Washington were fixed except for the adjustment in the area of the San Juan Islands in 1872. See San Juan Boundary Dispute.

During the Civil War, sentiment in favor of statehood grew strong in the territory. In 1867 the territorial legislature sent a resolution to Congress urging admission. However, 11 years passed before a territorial convention drew up a constitution for the proposed new state, and it was not until Feb. 22, 1889, that Congress passed an enabling act providing for the admission of the state of Washington into the Union. The state constitution was adopted and ratified by the people in an election held on Oct. 1, 1889. On Nov. 11, 1889, in accordance with the provisions of the enabling act, statehood was proclaimed by the president of the United States.

Because of its remoteness and the difficulty of reaching it from the eastern states, Washington had slow population growth until the advent of the first railroad in 1883. Since that time the development of the state has been rapid. Steamship service from Puget Sound to Alaska began in 1886 and to the Orient in 1891. The discovery of gold in Alaska and the Yukon Territory in 1896 found Seattle in the position that Walla Walla had been in a generation before, and its population tripled in a decade. During this time eastern Washington developed its agriculture and horticulture.

The Modern Era. World War I caused a sudden expansion of the state's industrial activities, especially in shipbuilding. World War II also greatly affected Washington's growth, with the creation of large shipbuilding and military aircraft industries and the development of the atomic-energy plant at Camp Hanford. The rates of population and economic growth slowed in the 1950's, but during the 1960's easily exceeded national rates, largely through the impact of the aerospace industry.

Thus Washington has based its growth successively on being a supply depot for gold strikes, on fishing and forestry, agriculture, and finally the manufacture of transportation equipment and shipbuilding. Although part of the last significant geographic frontier of continental United States, Washington is shedding its lusty frontier past and emerging into a period of balanced social and economic development.

LARRY IKENBERRY/WEST STOCK

An awesome mushroom-shaped ash cloud rose miles in the air following the 1980 eruption of Mt. St. Helens.

To stabilize its economy, Washington is trying to attract new industries that will make it less dependent on federal aerospace and government contracts. The major challenge facing the state is to encourage this industrial growth without destroying the environment. A compromise between the conservationists who want to protect the natural resources and recreational areas and the progressive industrialists who see the need to build the state's economy seems to be Washington's main concern in the 1980's.

N. H. Engle* and Warren W. Etcheson*
University of Washington

Bibliography

Avery, Mary W., *Washington: A History of the Evergreen State* (Univ. of Wash. Press 1965).
Cameron, Mary A., ed., *Snow Tours in Washington*, rev. ed. (Signpost Bk. Pub. 1979).
Carpenter, Cecelia S., *They Walked Before: The Indians of Washington State* (Wash. State Hist. Soc. 1977).
Clark, Norman H., *Washington* (Norton 1976).
Kirk, Ruth, *Washington State: National Parks, Historic Sites, Recreation Areas, and Natural Landmarks* (Univ. of Wash. Press 1974).
Kirk, Ruth, and Daugherty, Richard D., *Exploring Washington Archaeology* (Univ. of Wash. Press 1978).
Lewis, Paul M., *Beautiful Washington*, 2 vols., rev. ed. (Beautiful Am. 1985).
Majors, Harry M., *Exploring Washington* (Van Winkle Pub. 1975).
Ogden, Daniel M., and Bone, Hugh A., Jr., *Washington Politics* (1960; reprint, Greenwood Press 1981).
Roberts, Philip, *A Date with Washington History* (Skyline West Press 1986).
Spring, Bob, and Spring, Ira, *Wildlife Areas of Washington* (Superior Pub. 1976).
Sunset Editors, *Travel Guide to Washington*, 4th ed. (Lane 1978).
Swan, James G., *Almost Out of the World, Scenes from Washington Territory* (Wash. State Hist. Soc. 1971).
Williams, Burton J., *Washington: Readings in the History of the Evergreen State* (Coronado 1977).

WASHINGTON, D. C., is the capital of the United States. It is one of the few national capitals founded solely as a seat of government. The original plan of the city anticipated its future growth. As the new republic increased in size and wealth, Washington grew to become one of the most important and beautiful cities in the world. It is the site of impressive government buildings, magnificent monuments, important historical landmarks, fine museums, and broad, tree-shaded avenues and malls. Every year Washington is visited by millions of tourists from all parts of the United States and from many other countries of the world. But the city is also home to a large number of people—the place where they live, work, and raise families. As such, it is confronted by the same problems facing most large cities.

Washington, District of Columbia, was named for George Washington and Christopher Columbus. The present-day city of Washington is coextensive with the District of Columbia, and the names are synonymous. It is the only city in the United States that is not part of a state.

Washington lies on the Potomac River between Maryland and Virginia. The city's site was selected by President Washington in 1791. Maj. Pierre Charles L'Enfant, a French engineer and architect, was commissioned to plan the future capital. In 1800 the still unfinished city replaced Philadelphia as the nation's capital.

THE FACE OF THE CITY

Physical Setting and Climate. Washington is situated on the northeastern bank of the Potomac River where it joins the Anacostia River. It initially occupied lands ceded by Maryland and Virginia and extended across the Potomac. But in 1846 the portion given by Virginia was returned to that state, and the city has since comprised only former Maryland territory, an area of 67 square miles (174 sq km).

As the federal government grew in size and complexity, it became impossible to contain all necessary facilities within the district, and many large federal agencies established headquarters outside the city. As a result, metropolitan Washington today stretches over 1,500 square miles (3,885 sq km) and includes parts of Virginia as well as Maryland.

Much of the land surface of the city is flat, with gently rolling areas in the northwest corner broken by the narrow gorge of Rock Creek. Washington's weather is generally cold and damp in winter and hot and humid in summer.

L'Enfant's Plan. L'Enfant's plan for Washington is considered the country's principal achievement in municipal planning. For a new republic of just 3 million people, he conceived a magnificent plan, envisioning the growth of the city along with the nation. In its grandeur and baroque emphasis the plan was reminiscent of Versailles and Paris. L'Enfant placed the "Federal House" (Capitol) and the "President's House" (White House) on high ground that commanded views down to the Potomac River. The site of the Capitol was selected as the focal point of the city, with streets and avenues radiating out from it. L'Enfant's basic design for the city still prevails, in spite of many revisions and much unregulated construction.

Sections of the City. Washington is divided into four unequal quadrants with the Capitol at the center. North Capitol Street, East Capitol Street, South Capitol Street, and the Mall form the lines of division of the city's four sections—Northwest (NW), Northeast (NE), Southwest (SW), and Southeast (SE). Over this arrangement has been placed a grid of streets, with those running north-south designated by number and those running east-west by letter. Broad avenues named for states slash diagonally across the city. Street systems in the four sections are identically labeled, and the quadrant initials are therefore an integral part of every Washington address.

At strategic spots L'Enfant's plan placed decorative circles, each consisting of a landscaped plot with streets and avenues radiating from it like the spokes of a wheel. Later additions to the circles were statues of military heroes, often Civil War figures. As the motor age burgeoned, the circles, with vehicles pouring into them from the grid system, proved to be major traffic bottlenecks. Some relief was achieved by building tunnels under several circles to speed the traffic of heavily traveled thoroughfares. The circles are confusing to motorists new to Washington.

Neighborhoods. The northwestern section is the heart of Washington, the site of the most important government buildings, monuments, museums, and other tourist attractions. The city's principal shopping district is there, in the area north of Pennsylvania Avenue between the White House and the Capitol.

Within this area too are several of the city's loveliest neighborhoods. Embassy Row, extending along the portion of Massachusetts Avenue running northwest from Dupont Circle, is a section of handsome consulates and embassies. Georgetown, the city's oldest section, lies west of Rock Creek Park. It is a carefully preserved neighborhood, and many of its lovingly restored townhouses, 100 to 200 years old, are beautiful examples of early American architecture. It is also noted for its smart boutiques.

The Watergate apartment and office building complex along the Potomac has some of Washington's most luxurious housing. After the break-in at the Democratic National Committee headquarters in the complex in June 1972, Watergate became the name of the scandal that led to President Richard Nixon's resignation in August 1974.

SITES OF THE U. S. CAPITAL

The capital of the United States was situated in many cities before it was finally established in Washington, D. C., in 1800. The federal government met temporarily in Philadelphia, Pa. (1775–1776, 1778–1783, 1790–1800); Baltimore, Md. (1776); Lancaster, Pa. (1777); York, Pa. (1777–1778); Princeton, N. J. (1783); Annapolis, Md. (1783–1784); Trenton, N. J. (1784), and New York City (1785–1790).

PLACES OF INTEREST

Tourism, virtually a year-round activity, reaches its peak in early spring, when visitors arrive to view the Japanese cherry trees in bloom around the Tidal Basin. That is when the city is most beautiful, and its many trees and large and small parks brighten the stones and brick. There is too much to see in Washington for just a short stay, and many return again and again to revisit favorite places and discover new ones.

CARL SCHOLFIELD, RAPHO/PHOTO RESEARCHERS

The Capitol, Washington, D. C., houses both the U. S. Senate and U. S. House of Representatives.

Official Washington. Because of its great size, central location, and elevated position on Capitol Hill, the Capitol dominates the Washington skyline. The U. S. Congress meets in this building. Visitors may attend congressional sessions to watch the legislators in action.

The Capitol is one of Washington's most magnificent buildings. It is constructed of white sandstone and marble and crowned by an immense dome. On top of the dome stands a bronze 19.5-foot (6-meter) high statue of Freedom. Public rooms include the Rotunda, decorated with paintings and statues of events and people in American history, and Statuary Hall, which contains statues of distinguished citizens from every state.

The Capitol is set in a small park around which are a number of impressive government buildings. To the east is the Supreme Court Building, constructed of white marble and modeled after a Greek temple. Nearby stands the Library of Congress, one of the two largest libraries in the world—only the Lenin State Library in Moscow may be larger. Among the many priceless items of historical interest on display are Abraham Lincoln's first and second drafts of his Gettysburg Address. In addition to books the library houses photographs, musical scores, maps, microfilmed newspapers, and movies—in all, some 75 million items. Nearby is the Folger Shakespeare Library, with unmatched resources for Shakespearean study.

The White House, known also as the Executive Mansion, stands northwest of the Capitol at 1600 Pennsylvania Avenue. Every four years the parade for the newly inaugurated president travels the historic route along Pennsylvania Avenue from the Capitol to the White House. The White House, whose foundation was laid in 1792, has been the home of every president with the exception of George Washington.

The 132-room White House, which has been renovated and enlarged several times, is a white sandstone building in neoclassical style. It consists of a main building, flanked by east and west wings. The main building has two columned porticoes—the square north portico, which is the main entrance, and the curved south portico.

Tourists may visit portions of the ground floor and first floor, including the Blue Room, the State Dining Room, and the East Room, which is used for many of the president's public receptions. The White House grounds are open to the public only once a year—for the annual Egg Roll held on Easter Monday.

The White House stands in a landscaped area that is bounded on the north by Lafayette Square and on the south by the Ellipse, a circular park. These parks and the White House grounds are often referred to as the President's Square. In the center of Lafayette Square is an equestrian statue of President Andrew Jackson. On each corner of the square is a statue of a European who aided the American Revolution—the French Marquis de Lafayette and Count de Rochambeau, the Polish Thaddeus Kosciusko, and the German Baron von Steuben. At the northern edge of the Ellipse is the Zero Milestone, from which all distances from the capital are measured.

Several historic buildings border Lafayette Square, including Decatur House, built in 1819, and Blair House, the official guest residence for high-ranking foreign visitors. President Harry Truman and his family lived in Blair House from

1948 to 1952 while the interior of the White House was being renovated.

Between the White House and the Capitol on Pennsylvania Avenue are a group of federal buildings occupying an area known, because of its shape, as the Federal Triangle. One of the best-known buildings in the triangle is the National Archives, the depository of important federal documents. Three of the nation's most precious documents—the Declaration of Independence, the Constitution, and the Bill of Rights—are on permanent display. To ensure their preservation they are exhibited in helium-filled cases under tinted laminated glass.

Monuments. Monuments to three presidents—George Washington, Thomas Jefferson, and Abraham Lincoln—are among the most popular sights in the city. They stand in a vast green triangular area, within full sight of one another.

The Washington Monument is a white marble obelisk about 555 feet (169 meters) high. Its interior is hollow, and visitors may climb the stairs or ride the elevator to the top for a panoramic view of the city and its surrounding area.

The Washington Monument stands at the edge of the Mall, a long, narrow park extending from the Capitol. Continuing in a straight line from the monument is West Potomac Park with its Reflecting Pool. Beyond it is the Lincoln Memorial, a monumental structure resembling a classic Greek temple. Its exterior is a white marble colonnade consisting of 36 Doric columns representing the states in the Union at the time of Lincoln's death in 1865. Dominating the interior is an impressive seated statue of Lincoln, the work of the American sculptor Daniel Chester French. The texts of Lincoln's Gettysburg Address and Second Inaugural Address are inscribed on the walls.

Near the Lincoln Memorial, at the west end of Constitution Gardens, is the Vietnam Veterans Memorial, dedicated in 1982. Its walls, made of black granite, are inscribed with the names of over 58,000 servicemen who died or remain missing. The design was by Maya Ying Ling, a student at Yale University. A lifesize sculpture in bronze depicting three servicemen armed and in combat gear, created by Frederick Hart of Washington, D.C., was installed on the grounds in 1984.

South of both the Washington Monument and the Lincoln Memorial is the Jefferson Memorial, standing amid the famed cherry trees on the shore of the Tidal Basin. The Jefferson Memorial is a circular, colonnaded marble structure topped by a beautiful dome. Inside stands a heroic statue of Jefferson. Selections from his writings are inscribed in bronze on panels on the walls.

Museums and Galleries. Washington's museums and art galleries are among the finest in the world. The Smithsonian Institution, a scientific and cultural organization sponsored by the U.S. government, consists of museums or similar units in the areas of science, technology, history, and art. Several of its museums are on the Mall.

The Smithsonian's best-known scientific bodies include the National Museum of Natural History and the National Air and Space Museum. The Museum of History and Technology has one of the city's most popular exhibits—the collection of First Ladies' gowns. The National Gallery of Art, Washington's principal art gallery, houses a superb collection of American and European art. The Hirshhorn Museum and Sculpture Gar-

INDEX TO PLACES OF INTEREST IN WASHINGTON D.C. AND VICINITY

1. Agriculture, Department of ... C-4
2. American Red Cross Headquarters ... B-3
3. Arts and Industries Building ... C-5
4. Blair House ... B-4
5. Bureau of Engraving and Printing ... C-4
6. Capitol ... C-6
7. Chesapeake and Ohio Canal ... A-2
8. Commerce, Department of ... B-4
9. Constitution Hall ... B-4
10. Corcoran Gallery of Art ... B-4
11. Custis-Lee Mansion ... D-1
12. Ellipse ... B-4
13. Executive Office Building ... B-3
14. Federal Bureau of Investigation (J. Edgar Hoover Building) ... B-5
15. Federal Reserve Board ... B-3
16. Federal Trade Commission ... B-5
17. Folger Shakespeare Library ... C-6
18. Ford's Theater ... B-5
19. Fort Lesley J. McNair ... E-5
20. Fort Meyer ... D-1
21. Freer Gallery of Art ... C-4
22. George Washington University ... B-3
23. Georgetown University ... A-1
24. Government Printing Office ... B-6
25. Health, Education, and Welfare, Department of ... C-5
26. Hirshhorn Museum and Sculpture Garden ... C-5
27. House Office Buildings ... C-6
28. Housing and Urban Development, Department of ... C-5
29. Interior, Department of the ... B-3
30. Internal Revenue Building ... B-4
31. Jefferson Memorial ... D-4
32. John F. Kennedy Center for the Performing Arts ... B-2
33. John F. Kennedy Eternal Flame ... D-1
34. Judiciary Square ... B-5
35. Justice, Department of ... B-5
36. Labor, Department of ... B-5
37. Lafayette Square ... B-4
38. L'Enfant Plaza ... C-5
39. Library of Congress ... C-6
40. Lincoln Memorial ... C-3
41. Marine Corps War Memorial ... C-1
42. Martin Luther King Memorial Library ... B-5
43. Museum of African Art ... C-6
44. Museum of History and Technology, National ... C-4
45. National Academy of Sciences ... B-3
46. National Aeronautics and Space Administration ... C-5
47. National Air and Space Museum ... C-5
48. National Archives ... B-5
49. National Gallery of Art ... C-5
50. National Historical Wax Museum ... A-5
51. National Museum of Natural History ... C-4
52. National Portrait Gallery ... B-5
53. Octagon House ... B-3
54. Pan American Union Building ... B-4
55. Pentagon (Department of Defense) ... E-2
56. Petersen House ... B-4
57. Postal Service ... B-4
58. Reflecting Pool ... C-3
59. Robert A. Taft Memorial ... B-6
60. Senate Office Buildings ... B-6
61. Smithsonian Institution Building ... C-4
62. State, Department of ... B-3
63. Supreme Court ... C-6
64. Theodore Roosevelt Memorial ... B-2
65. Tomb of the Unknowns ... D-1
66. Transportation, Department of ... C-5
67. Treasury Building ... B-4
68. Union Station ... B-6
69. United States Botanic Garden ... C-6
70. United States Information Agency ... B-3
71. United States Weather Bureau ... A-3
72. Vietnam Veterans Memorial ... C-3
73. Washington Monument ... C-4
74. Washington Navy Yard ... D-7
75. Watergate Complex ... B-2
76. White House ... B-4
77. World Bank ... B-3

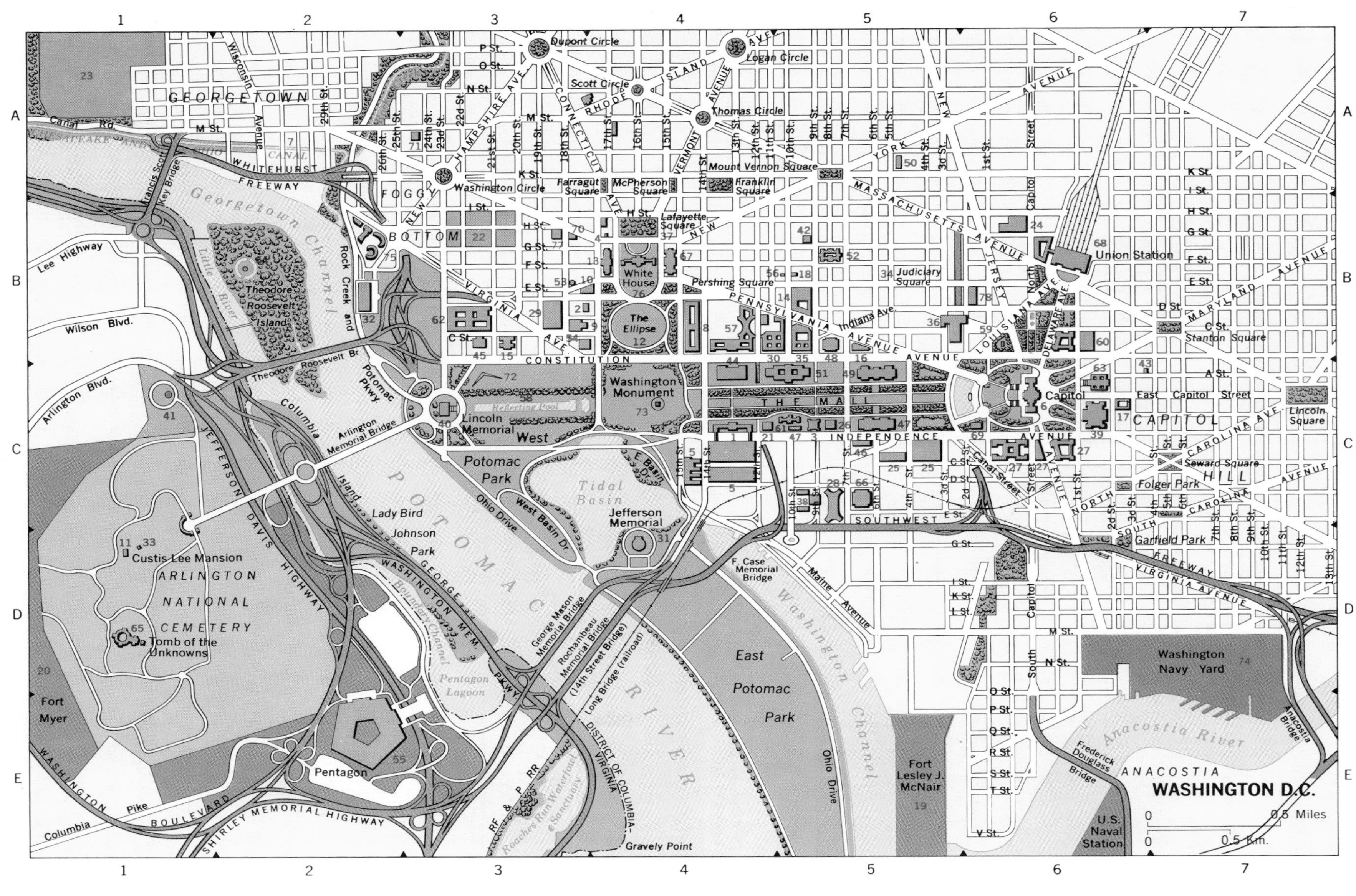
WASHINGTON D.C.
0 0.5 Miles
0 0.5 Km.
GEORGETOWN
FOGGY BOTTOM
Dupont Circle
Logan Circle
Scott Circle
Thomas Circle
Washington Circle
Mount Vernon Square
Farragut Square
McPherson Square
Franklin Square
Lafayette Square
Pershing Square
Judiciary Square
Stanton Square
Lincoln Square
Seward Square
Folger Park
Garfield Park
Union Station
White House
The Ellipse
Washington Monument
Lincoln Memorial
Reflecting Pool
Jefferson Memorial
Tidal Basin
Capitol
CAPITOL HILL
THE MALL
West Potomac Park
East Potomac Park
Washington Channel
Washington Navy Yard
Fort Lesley J. McNair
U.S. Naval Station
Anacostia River
ANACOSTIA
Frederick Douglass Bridge
Anacostia Bridge
POTOMAC RIVER
Georgetown Channel
Theodore Roosevelt Island
Little River
Columbia Island
Lady Bird Johnson Park
Boundary Channel
Pentagon Lagoon
Pentagon
ARLINGTON NATIONAL CEMETERY
Custis-Lee Mansion
Tomb of the Unknowns
Fort Myer
Gravely Point
Roaches Run Waterfowl Sanctuary
DISTRICT OF COLUMBIA
VIRGINIA
Francis Scott Key Bridge
Theodore Roosevelt Br.
Arlington Memorial Bridge
George Mason Memorial Bridge
Rochambeau Memorial Bridge
(14th Street Bridge)
Long Bridge (railroad)
F. Case Memorial Bridge
CHESAPEAKE AND OHIO CANAL
Canal Rd.
Wisconsin Avenue
WHITEHURST FREEWAY
Rock Creek and Potomac Pkwy.
Lee Highway
Wilson Blvd.
Arlington Blvd.
JEFFERSON DAVIS HIGHWAY
GEORGE WASHINGTON MEM. PKWY
SHIRLEY MEMORIAL HIGHWAY
WASHINGTON BOULEVARD
Columbia Pike
RF & P RR
Ohio Drive
West Basin Dr.
E. Basin Dr.
Maine Avenue
CONSTITUTION AVENUE
PENNSYLVANIA AVENUE
INDEPENDENCE AVENUE
VIRGINIA AVE
NEW HAMPSHIRE AVE
CONNECTICUT AVE
RHODE ISLAND AVENUE
VERMONT AVENUE
NEW YORK AVENUE
MASSACHUSETTS AVENUE
NEW JERSEY AVENUE
LOUISIANA AVE.
DELAWARE AVE.
MARYLAND AVENUE
NORTH CAROLINA AVE.
SOUTH CAROLINA AVENUE
Indiana Ave.
East Capitol Street
North Capitol Street
South Capitol Street
Canal Street
SOUTHWEST FREEWAY
VIRGINIA AVENUE
M St.
N St.
O St.
P St.
K St.
I St.
H St.
G St.
F St.
E St.
D St.
C St.
A St.
L St.
Q St.
R St.
S St.
T St.
V St.
29th St.
26th St.
25th St.
24th St.
23d St.
22d St.
21st St.
20th St.
19th St.
18th St.
17th St.
16th St.
15th St.
14th St.
13th St.
12th St.
11th St.
10th St.
9th St.
8th St.
7th St.
6th St.
5th St.
4th St.
3d St.
2d St.
1st St.

CARL SCHOLFIELD, RAPHO/PHOTO RESEARCHERS

A heroic statue of Thomas Jefferson stands in the central rotunda of the Jefferson Memorial.

The Lincoln Memorial is dominated by a huge, white marble statue of America's Civil War president.

VAN BUCHER, PHOTO RESEARCHERS

den is a cylindrical structure with a sunken outdoor sculpture garden. Its collection includes 20th century American paintings and works of sculpture dating from ancient times to the present. Other Smithsonian art galleries include the National Collection of Fine Arts, devoted to American art; the Freer Gallery of Art, with an outstanding collection of Oriental and Islamic art; and the National Portrait Gallery.

Washington also has many smaller museums that are privately administered. Among the most popular are the Phillips Collection, devoted to 19th and 20th century European and American painting, and the Corcoran Gallery of Art, specializing in American art. Dumbarton Oaks has a fine collection of pre-Columbian and Byzantine art. It is part of the estate in Georgetown where the Dumbarton Oaks Conference was held in 1944 to draft the basic plan for the organization of the United Nations. The Museum of African Art and the Douglass Institute of Negro Arts and History are housed in the first Washington home of Frederick Douglass, 19th century black abolitionist. When it opened in 1964 the museum was the first in the United States devoted exclusively to African art.

Cultural Life and Recreation. The John F. Kennedy Center for the Performing Arts, which opened in 1971, provided Washington with a much-needed theater, concert hall, and opera house. It is the home of the National Symphony Orchestra and the American Ballet Theatre. The center is a popular sightseeing attraction. Stage productions are also presented regularly at the National Theater, the Arena Stage, and historic Ford's Theater, where President Lincoln was assassinated in 1865.

Parks are scattered throughout Washington. The largest is Rock Creek Park, which follows the course of Rock Creek through the northwestern part of the city. It contains natural wood-

G. MARTIN, PHOTO RESEARCHERS

The south facade of the White House, which has been the home of every U. S. president from John Adams on.

lands and picnic, hiking, and sports facilities. It is also the site of the National Zoological Park, a unit of the Smithsonian Institution.

Sailing is popular on the Potomac River, and the Reflecting Pool is used for races of model sailboats in the spring and summer and for ice skating in the winter. The Chesapeake and Ohio Canal, now a national monument, is traveled for a part of its length by sightseers in mule-drawn barges. Robert F. Kennedy Stadium is the home of the Washington Redskins of the National Football League. Capital Centre, in Landover, Md., is the home of the Washington Bullets of the National Basketball Association and the Washington Capitals of the National Hockey League.

Suburban Washington. There are many interesting and popular sites in the areas outside the city. Overlooking the Potomac River in Virginia is Mount Vernon, which was George Washington's estate. His home and many of the other estate buildings have been preserved, and the mansion and museum contain much of the original furniture.

Arlington National Cemetery, directly across the Potomac from Washington, is the largest national cemetery in the United States. It is the burial place of President John F. Kennedy, whose grave is marked by an eternal flame. Nearby is the grave of his brother Sen. Robert F. Kennedy. In the Tomb of the Unknown Soldier (also known as the Tomb of the Unknowns) are buried three unidentified American servicemen, one each from World War I, World War II, and the Korean War. The Custis-Lee Mansion, overlooking the cemetery, is a national memorial.

North of the cemetery is the Marine Corps War Memorial, a bronze sculpture of the raising of the American flag on Iwo Jima during World War II. Also in Arlington is the Pentagon, the world's largest office building, headquarters of the Department of Defense.

The Washington Monument is an austere, white marble shaft at the edge of the Reflecting Pool.

CECIL W. STOUGHTON, NATIONAL PARK SERVICE

FRED E. MANG, JR., NATIONAL PARK SERVICE

The Supreme Court Building, modeled after a Greek temple, was erected on Capitol Hill in 1935.

THE LIFE OF THE CITY

Population. Washington had a population of 638,432 in 1980, a decline of 15.6% from the 1970 census of 756,668. The population of the metropolitan area increased by 5.2%, from 2,910,111 in 1970 to 3,060,922 in 1980. The Washington metropolitan area includes Arlington, Fairfax, Loudoun, and Prince William counties in Virginia; the Virginia cities of Alexandria and Falls Church; and Montgomery and Prince Georges counties in Maryland.

Washington had long been one of the fastest-growing metropolitan areas in the country. But by the 1970's its population growth rate had fallen to its lowest level in the 20th century. In the 1960's the metropolitan area had grown by 37.8% whereas the growth rate in the 1970's dropped to only 5.2%.

About 66% of the residents of Washington are blacks, compared with slightly more than one third in 1950. The city's suburban areas, however, have remained largely white. Washington's population is drawn from all 50 states and from many foreign nations. Numerous residents live in the area only temporarily, moving there to work for the government for several years and leaving when a new administration takes office. Others are drawn to the city to staff the foreign diplomatic, military, and trade missions.

Education and Libraries. Washington's public school system is run by an elected board of education. About 95% of the pupils are black. The city also has a large number of private schools.

Washington is the site of several well-known colleges and universities. The oldest is Georgetown University, founded in 1789, the first Roman Catholic college in the United States. Howard University is the largest predominantly black university in the country. Other schools in the city include George Washington University, American University, Gallaudet College for the deaf, and Catholic University of America.

In addition to the famed Library of Congress, Washington has a large public library system. The main library is the Martin Luther King Memorial Library. There are numerous local branch libraries.

Churches. Washington has a number of imposing religious buildings. The largest church in the city is the Episcopal Cathedral Church of St. Peter and St. Paul, usually known as the Washington Cathedral. Begun in 1907, it is built in Gothic style. Its Gloria in Excelsis Central Tower is the highest point in Washington. The National Shrine of the Immaculate Conception is the largest Roman Catholic church in the United States. A blend of Byzantine and Romanesque architecture, it adjoins Catholic University. St. John's Episcopal Church, located near the White House, is known as the "Church of the Presidents" because many of the country's presidents have worshipped there. The Islamic Center is an institution of Muslim worship, education, and culture. Its mosque is decorated with brilliant mosaics.

Economy. Government is by far Washington's biggest industry, and the federal government dominates both the economic and social life of the city. The largest number of federal workers are those in the lower ranks who are responsible for the day-to-day operations of government at home and abroad. Washington is also the headquarters of many labor unions, and of business and professional organizations and nonprofit agencies that work for the government or try to influence its decisions.

Tourism ranks second in importance in the economy, and every year millions of tourists visit the capital. Washington has also become increasingly important as a convention center. The construction industry is a source of many jobs, as residential and government office buildings continue to rise in all parts of the city. Manufacturing is less important in Washington than in most major cities. Printing plants employ the largest number of manufacturing workers.

Transportation and Communication. Automobiles are the principal means of transportation within the city and its main link with the suburbs. The movement of commuters to and from work has given the capital traffic problems with few equals anywhere. In 1969 the Washington Metropolitan Transit Authority began construction of a 98-mile (158-km) transit rail system (Metro), including subway and surface lines, which would extend into the suburbs. By 1978, three sections of the subway were operating.

Washington's railroad terminal is Union Station, located north of the Capitol. The city is served by three airports. Washington National Airport, just across the Potomac River in Virginia, is one of the country's busiest airports. Dulles International Airport is about 25 miles (40 km) west of the city in Virginia, and Baltimore-Washington International Airport is in Maryland, 30 miles (48 km) northeast.

Washington is one of the world's major communication centers. The large press corps consists of representatives of most of the major newspapers, magazines, and radio and television stations. They gather and report news of Washington for American and international audiences. Washington itself is served by one daily newspaper, the morning *Post*.

GOVERNMENT

Congress granted Washington a self-governing charter in 1974, for the first time in 100 years. Until then residents had no voice in their own government. The district is governed by a mayor and 13-member city council, all elected for four-year terms. The local government has the authority to raise money through taxation, but Congress has retained control of the city's budget and the right to overrule most local decisions.

Washington residents had long been denied the vote in national elections, causing them to call their city the "last colony." Since the adoption of the 23d Amendment in 1961, they have had the right to vote in presidential elections. In 1970 the district was granted the right to elect a nonvoting delegate to the House of Representatives.

HISTORY

Site Selection and Planning. During the American Revolution and the early years of the new republic, Congress sat in several different cities. The need for a permanent capital was apparent, but conflict developed over its location. Northerners wanted the new capital to be situated in the North, and Southerners wanted it in the South. Finally, a compromise was worked out by Alexander Hamilton and Thomas Jefferson in 1790. The North agreed to a Southern location for the capital in exchange for the South's agreement to support federal assumption of debts incurred by all states during the Revolution.

On July 16, 1790, Congress authorized the selection of a site "not exceeding 10 miles square" (260 sq km) somewhere in the Potomac region. President Washington was empowered to choose the exact location and appoint the building commissioners. In January 1791 he chose the land in Maryland that now comprises the district

ESTHER HENDERSON, RAPHO/PHOTO RESEARCHERS

Georgetown, a residential section near downtown Washington, preserves its 18th century architecture.

The Hirshhorn Museum and Sculpture Garden, a component of the Smithsonian Institution, contains one of the most comprehensive collections of 20th century art.

SMITHSONIAN INSTITUTION

THE METROPOLITAN MUSEUM OF ART, PURCHASE 1942, JOSEPH PULITZER BEQUEST

A wooden dome sheathed with copper covered the rotunda connecting the wings of the unfinished Capitol in 1824.

and a small area in Virginia, including the town of Alexandria.

President Washington appointed Maj. Pierre Charles L'Enfant, a French engineer and architect who had fought in the American Revolution, to design the new city. Maj. Andrew Ellicott was commissioned to survey the federal territory. For his assistant, Ellicott chose Benjamin Banneker, a black mathematician and astronomer.

L'Enfant quickly encountered problems, and he was dismissed in 1792 for forging ahead regardless of his orders, the budget, or landowners with prior claims. Ellicott was asked to complete the work, and his map of the projected city, based on L'Enfant's plan, became the first official map of Washington.

Early Years. The White House, the oldest public building in Washington, was begun in 1792. In the following year President Washington laid the cornerstone of the Capitol. Washington officially became the U. S. capital in 1800, when the federal government moved there from Philadelphia. The transfer was not very difficult since the entire clerical staff numbered just 137. President John Adams and his wife, Abigail, were the first occupants of the still incomplete Executive Mansion. At the time the district became the U. S. capital, it had a population of about 8,000. Although the area was still primarily covered with swamps and pastureland, construction had been started on a number of homes, shops, and taverns.

During the War of 1812, Washington was burned by the British in August 1814, causing President James Madison and his wife to flee the city. Before leaving, Dolley Madison rescued a famous Gilbert Stuart portrait of George Washington from the White House. Reconstruction began almost immediately.

Growth of the City. Washington's growth rate was very slow for many years. In 1846, Congress agreed to return to Virginia the land that the state had previously ceded to the federal government, thus reducing the district's area to its present size.

A period of rapid growth began during the Civil War, when Washington's population increased greatly. The city was a military arsenal, and thousands of Union troops were stationed there to protect it in case of Confederate attacks. In addition, freed slaves from the South streamed into the city.

At the end of the war, with a serious housing shortage and its public facilities totally inadequate for the growing population, Washington began a major rebuilding program. Civil improvements during the 1870's included paved streets and sidewalks, parks, sewer lines, and hundreds of trees that still shade the capital. The city of Georgetown, originally included in the district, became part of Washington in 1871—making the city and the district coterminous.

Political Developments. During most of its early years, Washington was governed by an elected mayor and council. But in the 1870's the district's residents lost the right to elect their own local government. In 1871, Congress made the city a federal territory. It was administered by a governor appointed by the president and a bicameral legislature—an 11-member council appointed by the president and a 22-member house of delegates elected by the people. In 1874, Congress established a new municipal government consisting of three commissioners appointed by the president. The commissioners' acts were subject to approval by the District of Columbia committees of the Senate and the House of Representatives. Washington was the only city in the

United States denied the right of self-government. Not until 100 years later was home rule restored.

The 20th Century. The period of most rapid growth in Washington began during the Depression of the 1930's. Thousands of New Dealers arrived in the capital to help plan and implement new federal programs designed to ease the economic crisis, and the federal government assumed increasing importance in domestic affairs. The rate of growth accelerated during World War II. Between 1930 and 1950 the population nearly doubled, increasing from 486,869 to 802,178. In the years after the United States entered World War II, Washington became the political capital of the Western world.

In the 1960's and 1970's, Washington was at the center of many of the conflicts facing the nation, especially the civil rights struggle. The assassination of civil rights leader Martin Luther King, Jr., in Memphis, Tenn., on April 4, 1968, touched off six days of rioting in the capital. Large areas in the city's black sections were looted and burned before calm was finally restored.

Washington has paid a price for its rapid rate of growth in the 20th century. The city confronts many problems common to most U. S. metropolises—crime, slums, water and air pollution, traffic congestion, and rapid population changes. There have been many encroachments on the idealized plan for a federal city put before the founders in the early days of the republic. Despite such changes, however, there remain the long, tree-lined vistas, the parks, the majestic buildings and monuments, and, above all, a sense of history and of history-in-the-making.

STUART E. JONES
Formerly, National Geographic Magazine

Bibliography

Cox, Warren J., and others, eds., *A Guide to the Architecture of Washington, D.C.* (McGraw 1974).
Furer, H. B., *Washington, D.C., A Chronological and Documentary History* (Oceana 1974).
Green, Constance M., *Washington: A History of the Capital* (Princeton Univ. Press 1976).
Gutheim, Frederick, *Worthy of the Nation* (Smithsonian Inst. Press 1977).
Lee, Richard M., *Mr. Lincoln's City: An Illustrated Guide to the Civil War Sites of Washington* (EPM Pub. 1981).
Leech, Margaret, *Reveille in Washington, 1860–1865* (Carroll & Graf 1986).
Reps, John W., *Monumental Washington: The Planning and Development of the Capital Center* (Princeton Univ. Press 1967).
Smith, Sam, *Captive Capital: Colonial Life in Modern Washington* (Ind. Univ. Press 1974).

WASHINGTON, a city in southwestern Pennsylvania, is the seat of Washington county, 28 miles (45 km) southwest of Pittsburgh. An industrial center, the city supplies glass food containers, clay products for glass furnaces, stainless steel, ferroalloys, truck bodies, and other durable goods. Washington and Jefferson College, situated in the city, was chartered in 1787. Bradford House, restored in the 1960's, was the home of David Bradford, leader of the Whiskey Rebellion in 1794. The LeMoyne crematorium, built by Francis J. LeMoyne in 1876, was the first one built in the United States.

Washington county, the first county so named in the United States, was established in 1781. Catfish Camp, the place chosen for holding the first election, was renamed Washington in 1781 and incorporated as a borough in 1810 and as a city in 1924. Washington has a city council form of government. Population: 18,363.

WASHINGTON, Mount, a mountain in north central New Hampshire, in Coos county, about 15 miles (25 km) southwest of Berlin. It is the highest peak in the northeastern United States, rising 6,288 feet (1,916 meters) above sea level. Mount Washington is in the White Mountains of the Presidential Range, which also includes Mt. Madison, Mt. Adams, Mt. Jefferson, and Mt. Monroe. In 1642, Darby Field was the first white man to climb to the summit of Mt. Washington, which was named after George Washington by Manasseh Cutler in 1784. Mount Washington has been a major tourist attraction and a popular summer and winter vacation area for many years.

The summit of Mt. Washington may be reached by hiking along marked trails maintained by the U. S. Forest Service and the Appalachian Mountain Club. The summit may also be reached by a 3-mile (4.8-km) cog railway that ascends 3,625 feet (1,105 meters) from a base station near Crawford Notch. This cog railway, completed in 1869, was the first of its kind in North America. There is also a highway to the summit from Pinkham Notch. Buildings at the summit include the Tip Top House, the Summit House, and the Mt. Washington Observatory.

Mount Washington is formed chiefly of granite that once was scoured by glaciers, as evidenced by Tuckerman Ravine on its southeastern slope. Its snowcap melts during the summer and forms again in the winter. Its summit is rocky and has little vegetation, but its lower slopes are covered by coniferous trees.

WASHINGTON, Treaty of, a treaty between Britain and the United States, signed on May 8, 1871, that settled a series of controversies between Washington and London. During the American Civil War the British government had permitted a British company to build and sell the cruiser *Alabama* and several other ships to the Confederate government. The United States insisted that the British must pay for the damages inflicted by these vessels on Northern shipping, but the British refused to pay these so-called *Alabama* claims.

Other disputes had arisen about the ill-defined water boundaries between the United States and Vancouver Island, the Canadian claims for compensation for the raids by the pro-Irish Fenians in the United States, Canadian-American trade problems, and the Canadian insistence that American fishermen stay outside Canadian territorial waters.

In the late 1860's relations between Britain and the United States grew steadily worse. Several attempts to settle the disputes by diplomatic negotiation collapsed, and bellicose statements were made on both sides of the Atlantic. Sen. Charles Sumner (R-Mass.), chairman of the Committee on Foreign Affairs, demanded the annexation of Canada. Britain, fearing war with Russia, was anxious to end its quarrel with the United States in order to ensure U. S. neutrality.

Early in 1871 a series of informal Anglo-American conversations opened the way for the appointment of a Joint High Commission with ten members, five from each country. It was hoped that this commission would be able to settle the major disputes between the two parties. Secretary of State Hamilton Fish headed the American delegation, and the British representatives included Sir John A. Macdonald, the Canadian prime minister.

The text of the Treaty of Washington was completed in May 1871. By its terms the *Alabama* claims were to be submitted by the United States to an international tribunal of arbitration at Geneva, Switzerland, which later awarded the United States $15,500,000 as compensation for the damages inflicted by the *Alabama* and the other Confederate vessels. William I, emperor of Germany, selected by the commission to decide whether Haro Strait or Rosario Strait was the boundary between Vancouver Island and the state of Washington, accepted the American claim—Haro Strait—and awarded the San Juan Islands to the United States. A fisheries commission appointed under the terms of the agreement decided that the United States should pay Canada $5,500,000 in return for special fishing privileges. The Joint High Commission also concluded that the United States should not be required to pay Canada any compensation for life and property damage suffered by the Canadians in the Fenian raids.

The Treaty of Washington showed the value of good sense, moderation, and compromise, and ended a period of confusion, hostility, and danger of war between Britain and the United States. The negotiations at Washington also stimulated the development of self-government in Canada.

See also ALABAMA CLAIMS; ARBITRATION, INTERNATIONAL; FISHERIES QUESTION.

GOLDWIN SMITH
Wayne State University
Author of "The Treaty of Washington, 1871"

WASHINGTON, University of, a state-controlled, coeducational institution of higher learning, located in Seattle, Wash. It has both undergraduate and graduate curriculums. The university is governed by an 11-member Board of Regents, of which seven members are appointed by the governor, with the approval of the state Senate. Administration is under a presiden'

Opened to students in 1861, 28 years before Washington was admitted to the Union, the University of Washington is the oldest state-supported university on the Pacific Coast. It enrolls more than 30,000 students.

Curriculums and Programs. The University of Washington is composed of 17 schools and colleges. Those granting both undergraduate and graduate degrees are the College of Arts and Sciences, the College of Architecture and Urban Planning, the School and Graduate School of Business Administration, the College of Education, the College of Engineering, the College of Fisheries, the College of Forest Resources, the School of Nursing, the College of Pharmacy, the School of Public Health and Community Medicine, the School of Dentistry, and the School of Medicine. Those granting only graduate degrees are the School of Law, the Graduate School, the School of Librarianship, the Graduate School of Public Affairs, and the School of Social Work.

Among the university's special facilities are the Institute for Governmental Research, the Center for Asian Arts, the Center for Studies in Demography and Ecology, the Center for Education in Politics, the Developmental Psychology Laboratory, the Fisheries Research Institute, the Institute for Marine Studies, the Institute of Forest Products, the Laboratory of Radiation Ecology, the Child Development and Mental Retardation Center, the Computer Science Laboratory, and the Regional Primate Research Center.

WASHINGTON AND JEFFERSON COLLEGE is a private, coeducational liberal arts college in Washington, Pa. Until 1970 its enrollment was limited to men. Washington and Jefferson has about 1,600 students.

The college has its origins in two academies: one, chartered in 1787, in Washington; the other, in 1794, in nearby Canonsburg. The Canonsburg academy became Jefferson College in 1802, and the Washington academy became Washington College in 1806. In 1865 the two colleges joined and took the present name.

WASHINGTON AND LEE UNIVERSITY is a private, liberal arts institution of higher learning in Lexington, Va. It is primarily an undergraduate school, granting bachelor's degrees in the arts and science. Postgraduate training is offered by the School of Law. On the undergraduate level, enrollment is limited to men. The School of Law began admitting women in 1972.

Washington and Lee has a distinguished history, closely associated with the two men after whom it is named. It was founded in 1749 as Augusta Academy, in Augusta county, north of Lexington. The academy became Liberty Hall in 1776 and was moved to Lexington in 1780. In 1782 it was incorporated as Liberty Hall Academy by the Virginia state legislature. In 1796, George Washington gave the academy shares of stock in a canal company that were valued at $50,000. This was, up to then, the largest gift to education in the history of the United States. In gratitude the academy was renamed after the nation's first president in 1798, and in 1813 it became Washington College.

Following the Civil War, Gen. Robert E. Lee accepted the presidency of the college. Under his leadership the resources of the institution grew, and enrollment increased significantly. The law school was established, and courses in engineering and applied science were introduced. During his tenure plans were also made for introducing instruction in commerce and business and in journalism. In 1868, while he was president, Lee built the chapel that bears his name. He maintained his office in the building, now a national historic landmark, and was buried there after his death in 1870. In his honor the institution was renamed Washington and Lee University in 1871.

WASHINGTON COLLEGE is a coeducational nonsectarian college in Chestertown, Md. It originated as the Kent County School in 1723 and was chartered as Washington College in 1782. George Washington consented to the use of his name, contributed to its endowment, and served on the governing board. The college maintains a full curriculum of courses in the arts and sciences leading to the bachelor of arts or the bachelor of science degree.

WASHINGTON CONFERENCE. See NAVAL CONFERENCES—*Washington Conference (1921–1922)*.

WASHINGTON ELM, a tree in Cambridge, Mass., at the edge of the Common. It was the first of a line of six magnificent elms planted on Garden Street shortly after the year 1700. According to local tradition, George Washington took command of the colonial troops on July 3, 1775, under the tree and gave an inspiring address, but some historians doubt the complete authenticity of the tradition. The elm stood until 1923, when it finally collapsed. Pieces were sent to public officials, museums, and collectors all over the United States, and a part of the trunk is at Mount Vernon, Va. The city has built a small park with appropriate memorials on the site.

GEORGE D. BLACKWOOD
Formerly, Boston University

WASHINGTON MONUMENT, a national memorial in Washington, D. C., erected in honor of George Washington. An unadorned, white marble shaft, floodlit at night, it is rivaled only by the Capitol dome for first place on the Washington skyline. Though somewhat austere, it is beautiful in its simplicity and, from an engineering point of view, is one of the world's most remarkable masonry structures. From a square base of 55 feet (17 meters) on a side, the tapering, wind-resistant, hollow shaft towers 555 feet (169 meters), in exactly the same proportions of ancient Egyptian obelisks. An interior stairway and elevator lead to the top, which affords an excellent view of the city.

The monument was constructed at a cost of $1,187,000. The first $300,000 was contributed privately through the initiative of the Washington National Monument Society, formed in 1833. The design, by the architect Robert Mills, called for a shaft surrounded by a colonnaded statuary hall, to be used as a national pantheon; this was finally omitted. The cornerstone was laid on July 4, 1848. Construction rose to a height of some 150 feet (46 meters) but was then virtually abandoned for lack of funds. In 1876, in a flourish of enthusiasm for the centennial of American independence, Congress appropriated $200,000 for resumption of work. The U. S. government took title, and construction was completed in 1884. The monument was dedicated on Feb. 21, 1885, and opened to the public on Oct. 9, 1888.

HOMER T. ROSENBERGER
Columbia Historical Society

WASHINGTON STATE UNIVERSITY is a state-controlled coeducational institution of higher learning, located in Pullman, Wash. The university was chartered as a land-grant college in 1890, under the name Washington State Agricultural College and School of Science. It became the Agricultural College, Experiment Station, and School of Science of the State of Washington in 1891 and the State College of Washington in 1905. Its present name was adopted in 1959. Washington State is governed by a seven-member board of regents, appointed by the governor and confirmed by the state senate, and administered by a president. In addition to the campus at Pullman, the university operates extension and research centers at Lind, Mount Vernon, Prosser, Puyallup, Vancouver, and Wenatchee.

The university comprises eight colleges, all of which offer undergraduate degrees and graduate programs through doctorates—sciences and arts, agriculture, economics and business, education, engineering, home economics, pharmacy, and veterinary medicine. Special academic programs include Asian, black, and Chicano studies; environmental and resource studies; and cooperative work with various industries. The university operates a water-research center and hydraulics laboratory for dam construction, nuclear reactor facilities, and computer installations. Enrollment is about 15,000.

WASHINGTON UNIVERSITY is a private, coeducational institution of higher learning, located in St. Louis, Mo. It was founded in 1853 as Eliot Seminary. Its present official name, The Washington University, was adopted in 1857, when instruction was first offered. It is governed by a self-perpetuating 38-member board of trustees and is administered by a chancellor.

Undergraduate degrees are granted by the College of Arts and Sciences, the School of Architecture, the School of Business and Public Administration, the School of Engineering and Applied Sciences, and the School of Fine Arts. All of these offer advanced degrees except the College of Arts and Sciences and the School of Engineering and Applied Sciences. Advanced degrees are also offered by the School of Dentistry, the School of Law, the School of Medicine, the Graduate School of Arts and Sciences, the Henry Edwin Sever Institute of Technology, and the School of Social Work.

Special academic programs include the Urban Research and Design Center, the Consortium of Graduate Study in Management, and the off-campus Tyson Research Center for sculpture, painting, and printing. The library has special collections on musicology, Missouriana, St. Louisiana, and Western Americana. Publications include the *Urban Law Annual*, the *Industrialization Forum*, and the *Philosophy of Science*. Enrollment is about 10,000.

WASHINGTON'S FAREWELL ADDRESS, the valedictory of George Washington on leaving public life. It was never delivered orally, but presented to the public through the press on Sept. 17, 1796. It soon acquired an almost legendary quality as a major state paper, and has influenced American thinking about foreign policy ever since. The address was political in its inspiration, designed to assist the Federalists in the election of 1796. Revised and largely rewritten by Alexander Hamilton, who had left the administration, it represents a blend of Washington's strong sentiments and Hamilton's facile intellect. It removed speculation about a third term for Washington and seriously handicapped Thomas Jefferson in his campaign for the presidency in 1796.

Its original political orientation has now been largely forgotten, but for generations the address has been cited in favor of isolation and as a warning against "entangling alliances"—a phrase that was invented by Jefferson and does not appear in the Farewell Address. A close reading of the text, however, reveals that Washington was not preaching withdrawal for its own sake. Instead he was arguing a much more realistic policy line. What Washington urged on the American people was no more than the single-minded pursuit of the national interest, as soberly and objectively derived from the controlling circumstances. He rejected the idea of "habitual hatred" or "habitual fondness" toward particular nations; he called instead for dedication to purely American goals. Whether Hamiltonian or Washingtonian, these are no more than standard precepts of classical *Realpolitik*.

Even the realism and appropriateness of the sentiments do not explain the hold that the Farewell Address has had on Americans. It has struck so deep because of its eloquent evocation of American uniqueness: the United States is fortunate in having "so peculiar a situation" that it need not engage in the "ordinary vicissitudes" and "ordinary combinations and collisions" of international politics. Contact with the system of international politics may be made in "extraordinary emergencies," but America's regular path lies elsewhere. No argument more suited to the traditional predispositions of Americans can be imagined, but few thoughtful citizens would maintain its relevance as a basis of policy for the present era.

CHARLES O. LERCHE, JR., *Author "Foreign Policy of the American People"*

EXCERPTS FROM THE FAREWELL ADDRESS

Friends and fellow citizens: The period for a new election of a citizen to administer the executive government of the United States being not far distant, and the time actually arrived when your thoughts must be employed in designating the person who is to be clothed with that important trust, it appears to me proper, especially as it may conduce to a more distinct expression of the public voice, that I should now apprise you of the resolution I have formed to decline being considered among the number of those out of whom a choice is to be made.

I beg you, at the same time, to do me the justice to be assured, that this resolution has not been taken without a strict regard to all the considerations appertaining to the relation which binds a dutiful citizen to his country; and that, in withdrawing the tender of service which silence in my situation might imply, I am influenced by no diminution of zeal for your future interest; no deficiency of grateful respect for your past kindness; but am supported by a full conviction that the step is compatible with both . . . .

Of all the dispositions and habits which lead to political prosperity, religion and morality are indispensable supports. . . . And let us with caution indulge the supposition that morality can be maintained without religion. Whatever may be conceded to the influence of refined education on minds of peculiar structure, reason and experience both forbid us to expect that national morality can prevail in exclusion of religious principle.

It is substantially true that virtue or morality is a necessary spring of popular government. The rule indeed extends with more or less force to every species of free government. Who that is a sincere friend to it can look with indifference upon attempts to shake the foundation of the fabric? . . .

Observe good faith and justice toward all nations. Cultivate peace and harmony with all. . . .

In the execution of such a plan nothing is more essential than that permanent, inveterate antipathies against particular nations and passionate attachments for others should be excluded, and that in place of them just and amicable feelings toward all should be cultivated. The nation which indulges toward another an habitual hatred or an habitual fondness is in some degree a slave. It is a slave to its animosity or to its affection, either of which is sufficient to lead it astray from its duty and its interest. Antipathy in one nation against another disposes each more readily to offer insult and injury, to lay hold of slight causes of umbrage, and to be haughty and intractable when accidental or trifling occasions of dispute occur.

So, likewise, a passionate attachment of one nation for another produces a variety of evils. Sympathy for the favorite nation, facilitating the illusion of an imaginary common interest in cases where no real common interest exists, and infusing into one the enmities of the other, betrays the former into a participation in the quarrels and wars of the latter without adequate inducement or justification. . . .

Against the insidious wiles of foreign influence (I conjure you to believe me, fellow citizens) the jealousy of a free people ought to be *constantly* awake, since history and experience prove that foreign influence is one of the most baneful foes of republican government. . . .

The great rule of conduct for us in regard to foreign nations is, in extending our commercial relations, to have with them as little *political* connection as possible. So far as we have already formed engagements let them be fulfilled with perfect good faith. Here let us stop.

Europe has a set of primary interests which to us have none or a very remote relation. Hence she must be engaged in frequent controversies, the causes of which are essentially foreign to our concerns. Hence, therefore, it must be unwise in us to implicate ourselves by artificial ties in the ordinary vicissitudes of her politics or the ordinary combinations and collisions of her friendships or enmities.

Our detached and distant situation invites and enables us to pursue a different course. If we remain one people, under an efficient government, the period is not far off when we may defy material injury from external annoyance; when we may take such an attitude as will cause the neutrality we may at any time resolve upon to be scrupulously respected; when belligerent nations, under the impossibility of making acquisitions upon us, will not lightly hazard the giving us provocation; when we may choose peace or war, as our interest, guided by justice, shall counsel. . . .

The inducements of interest for observing that conduct will best be referred to your own reflections and experience. With me, a predominant motive has been to endeavor to gain time to our country to settle and mature its yet recent institutions, and to progress without interruption to that degree of strength and consistency, which is necessary to give it, humanly speaking, the command of its own fortunes. . . .

Further Reading: Binney, Horace, *Inquiry into the Formation of Washington's Farewell Address* (1859; reprint, Da Capo 1969); Washington, George, *Diaries of George Washington: January 1770 to December 1799*, vol. 6, ed. by Donald Jackson (Univ. Press of Va. 1980).

WASHITA, Battle of the, wosh′ə-tô, a military engagement in which a U. S. Army unit destroyed a Cheyenne Indian camp on the Washita River in present-day Oklahoma. The Cheyenne had resisted the construction of a railroad, and in 1868 the 7th U. S. Cavalry, led by Lt. Col. George Custer, moved against them.

Custer picked up the Indian trail at the Canadian River near the Texas border and followed it to a camp on the Washita River. On the bitterly cold dawn of November 27, Custer attacked. Chief Black Kettle, who had been negotiating for peace, was killed as the Cheyenne, caught by surprise, were defeated after desperate resistance. Women and children joined the defense, and many were killed. Some Cheyenne escaped. Custer later reported killing 103 warriors, an unverified number. On orders of Gen. Philip Sheridan, he destroyed the village and hundreds of ponies. Six soldiers died at the village, and Maj. Joel Elliott and 14 men were surrounded and wiped out by other Indians they had pursued nearby.

Many persons called the attack a massacre. Custer was also criticized for failing to reconnoiter and discover other Indian camps nearby and for failing to aid Elliott.

Black Kettle Museum, in Cheyenne, Okla., honors Indians killed on the Washita.

WASHO INDIANS, wosh′ō, a small North American tribe inhabiting areas along the Truckee and Carson rivers and the borders of Lake Tahoe in Nevada and several small valleys in neighboring California. The language of the Washo once was thought to be an independent one, but it is now regarded as a distant part of the great Hokan linguistic family.

The Washo were losers in a contest with the Northern Paiute over land that is now Carson City, Nev. As a result they were dispossessed and permanently prohibited from owning horses. However, from this relatively destitute tribe comes some of the finest Indian basketry. The work of Datsolali (1831–1926) is one of the few instances in American Indian art in which the name of the craftsman has been recorded. Her work is highly prized both by private collectors and by museums.

Probably there never were more than 1,000 members of the Washo tribe at any one time. Today, about 800 are reported living on reservations in California and Nevada.

WASP is the common name for insects of the order Hymenoptera, other than ants and bees, generally characterized by slender bodies with abdomens attached by narrow stalks ("wasp waists") and more or less painful stings.

In its broadest sense, the name wasp includes certain plant-feeding kinds such as gall and seed wasps and leaf and wood wasps, which in North America are commonly called sawflies. (See SAWFLY.) The vast majority of wasps, however, attack other insects or spiders. Many of these deposit their eggs in or on another insect, and their larvae consume the body fluids of the host, finally killing it shortly before they are ready to pupate. These are the so-called "parasitic Hymenoptera." (See CHALCID FLY; ICHNEUMON FLY.) True wasps belong to another group, the Aculeata, in which the ovipositor (egg-laying tube) is modified to form a sting, the egg being discharged from the tip of the abdomen proper.

True Wasps. True wasps vary in length from 2 mm (about 0.1 inch) to as large as 5 cm (2 inches). They belong to three major groups—the solitary wasps, the social wasps, and the nest parasites.

Solitary wasps prey upon insects or spiders, which they paralyze by stinging and then carry to a somewhat isolated nest as food for their larvae. Social wasps live in large, communal nests with a caste system and a division of labor. These wasps macerate their prey and feed it directly to the larvae. The sting serves mainly in defense of the colony. Social wasps that are banded with black and yellow, as many are, are often called yellow jackets, while the larger kinds are called hornets. The third group consists of wasps that have become nest parasites of other wasps or of bees. This includes two large families—the Mutillidae or "velvet ants" and the Chrysididae or "cuckoo wasps"—as well as a number of smaller families.

There are about 3,800 kinds of true wasps in America north of Mexico, and an estimated 25,000 kinds in the world as a whole. The vast majority of these are solitary wasps, there being only about 30 species of social wasps in America north of Mexico and about 800 species of wasps that are nest parasites of other Hymenoptera. In the tropics, however, social wasps are much more abundant, and their large, aerial nests are often a conspicuous feature of forests and farmland.

GENERAL CHARACTERISTICS

The structural features of wasps resemble those of ants and bees in every major respect. The resemblance is so close, in fact, that ants and bees are believed to have evolved from wasplike ancestors.

Wings. Most wasps are strong fliers, having two pairs of membranous wings that are held together by small hooklets as in other Hymenoptera. However, winglessness is fairly common among females of some groups, and in one entire family, the Mutillidae or "velvet ants," the females always lack wings.

Waist and Antenna. One of the more striking features of wasps is the "wasp waist." In many wasps this "waist" is no different from that in many other Hymenoptera, but the base of the last body section is so long and thin in some wasps that they are often referred to as "thread-waisted" wasps. The slender "waist" permits movement of the abdomen in various directions in such activities as stinging, egglaying, and nest construction. Another striking feature of wasps is the fixed number of antennal segments, females nearly always having 12 and males 13.

W. T. DAVIDSON, FROM NATIONAL AUDUBON SOCIETY

(*Above*) The yellow jacket (*Vespula*), a social wasp, has a distinctive yellow-and-black banded abdomen. (*Below*) A cicada killer (*Sphecius speciosus*), a large solitary wasp, pounces on a cicada that will provide food for the wasp's larva.

LYNWOOD M. CHACE, FROM NATIONAL AUDUBON SOCIETY

Sting. The most characteristic feature of wasps is the sting, which is a modified ovipositor (egg-laying structure) and thus present only in the females. Poison glands are associated with the sting and discharge their contents into the puncture. The venom of solitary wasps serves either to kill the prey or—more commonly—to place it in deep paralysis so that the wasp's larva can have a living food supply. Solitary wasps do not often use the sting in defense of the nest, and the sting has no serious effects on man, though it may be painful for a few moments. The venom of social wasps is quite different chemically and often causes swelling and systemic effects on man. Perhaps 15 to 20 persons die each year in the United States from anaphylactic shock following stings by wasps and bees.

Feeding. Since adult wasps commonly feed on nectar, their mouthparts are variously modified and tonguelike for probing the blossoms of flowers. Although velvet ants and some of the winged solitary wasps have rather hairy bodies, they lack the branched hairs and specialized pollen-collecting devices of bees. One exceptional family of wasps, the Masaridae, does in fact feed its larvae with pollen and nectar in the manner of bees, but in this case the food is carried in the crop and regurgitated in the nest.

Life Cycle. The eggs of wasps are delicate, thin-walled, and somewhat sausage-shaped. Solitary wasps typically lay the egg on the paralyzed prey, but a few solitary wasps and most social wasps place it in the empty cell before prey is brought in. The larvae are legless and grublike but have a distinct head capsule with strong mandibles, short sensory organs known as palpi, and a spinneret in the form of a transverse slit or a pair of slender projections. Development of the larva is rapid, not more than 5–7 days of feeding being required for many solitary wasp larvae and 12–20 days for social wasp larvae. In most species, the mature larva spins a silken cocoon. The cocoon may be flimsy or absent in some of the twig-nesters, and social wasps spin only a silken cap over the cell. Following spinning, the larva enters a resting or "prepupal" stage. Most solitary wasps overwinter in the prepupal stage, transforming to pupae in the spring and emerging as adults a few weeks later. Social wasp larvae typically pupate soon after spinning and give rise to adults—males, worker females, and potential queens—about two weeks later. The fertilized adult females, or queens, overwinter and found colonies the following spring. The fertilizing sperm is stored in an abdominal receptacle—the spermatheca—for use as needed. These females may have a total life span of about a year as adults, although adult solitary wasps rarely live more than 1–2 months. The males of both social and solitary wasps are more short-lived, and play at most a very minor role in the nesting process.

Types of Nests. The vast majority of solitary wasps nest in the ground, usually in soil that is at least slightly sandy. The mandibles and front legs form efficient digging organs, and the oblique or vertical burrow may reach a depth of anywhere from 5 cm (2 inches) to more than a meter (40 inches) depending upon the species. Some wasps prepare a single terminal cell, and when it is fully provisioned fill up the burrow with soil and make a new nest, while others make several successive cells in a single burrow. A few wasps maintain a single nest for their whole lifespan, making numerous cells from branches of one burrow. Ground-nesters often leave a pile of soil at the entrance, but some species scrape away this pile, rendering the nest very difficult for a human observer to find unless the wasp is seen entering or leaving. A few species prepare an elaborate earthen "chimney" at the nest entrance.

Many solitary wasps nest aboveground. Best known are the various kinds of mud daubers and mason wasps, which make cells of mud and attach them to rocks, bridges, buildings, and other objects. Other kinds of solitary wasps nest in hollow twigs or in borings in wood made by beetles. These prepare a series of cells separated by partitions of mud, pitch, grass, or detritus. These wasps will often accept artificial "trap nests," consisting of pieces of wood with a hole bored through one end.

Social wasps most commonly build their nests of paper. Old wood scraped from logs and fence posts and mixed with saliva is spread out in thin layers to form the cells, pedicel (supporting stalk), and covering of the nest. Some tropical wasps produce a very tough carton, and some even have thin places or "windows" in the nest covering. Temperate-zone species have nests of two major types. Paper wasps, mainly of the genus *Polistes,* construct single naked combs suspended by a pedicel. Hornets and yellow jackets, mainly of the genus *Vespula,* construct tiers of combs surrounded by an envelope. In each case the combs are hexagonal in cross section and are directed downward.

The nests of paper wasps rarely contain more than 100 individuals and usually contain many fewer. Nests of some of the hornets and yellow jackets may house much larger populations. Both types of nests are built annually. They are abandoned in the fall and not used again.

CLASSIFICATION OF WASPS

All wasps are members of the insect order Hymenoptera. The true wasps, together with bees and ants, are classified in the Aculeata, a division of the suborder Apocrita. (See also HYMENOPTERA.) The true wasps are classified in the following five superfamilies:

Bethyloidea includes the Bethylidae, tiny wasps that attack the larvae of beetles and moths; the Chrysididae (cuckoo wasps); and several small families.

Scolioidea includes the Scoliidae and Tiphiidae, which prey on beetle larvae but do not make a true nest, and Mutillidae ("velvet ants"), which parasitize the nests of other wasps and bees.

Pompilioidea are the spider wasps, all of which attack spiders and use a single large spider per nest cell; the "tarantula hawks" belong to this group.

Sphecoidea are a large group of solitary wasps—including the sand wasps, mud daubers, and thread-waisted wasps—that prey on a great variety of insects and spiders and commonly use several per nest-cell.

Vespoidea includes the Masaridae, which use pollen and nectar as larval food, and Eumenidae, the mason and potter wasps, nearly all of which use mud in their nests. The group of most interest is the Vespidae, the social wasps. Vespidae and Eumenidae fold their wings longitudinally when at rest and are often called "plaited-winged" wasps.

SOCIAL WASPS

The social wasps have a caste system, consisting of a queen, short-lived drones, and a number of sterile females called workers. In temperate regions the colony is founded in the spring by a fertilized female that has hibernated successfully. She builds the initial small nest, lays several eggs, and feeds the larvae with chewed-up insects. These larvae produce sterile females that, in hornets and yellow jackets, are notably smaller than the queen. These workers then take over the tasks of enlarging the nest and feeding the larvae.

After several weeks the workers build cells of somewhat greater diameter. These cells are supplied with a greater amount of food and ultimately produce females of larger size, potential queens of the next generation. About this time the queen begins to lay male-producing eggs. As in all Hymenoptera, the female can control the sex of her offspring by means of a sphincter muscle on the spermatheca. Males are produced from unfertilized eggs. Mating occurs in late summer, and the mated females enter hibernation, while the drones and workers are soon killed by cold temperatures.

This is the usual pattern of colonies of hornets and yellow jackets, although some details vary with the species involved. Some, such as the bald-faced hornet, make aerial nests in trees and bushes, while others occupy cavities in the ground, which they may enlarge in the course of the summer. The temperature in these nests re-

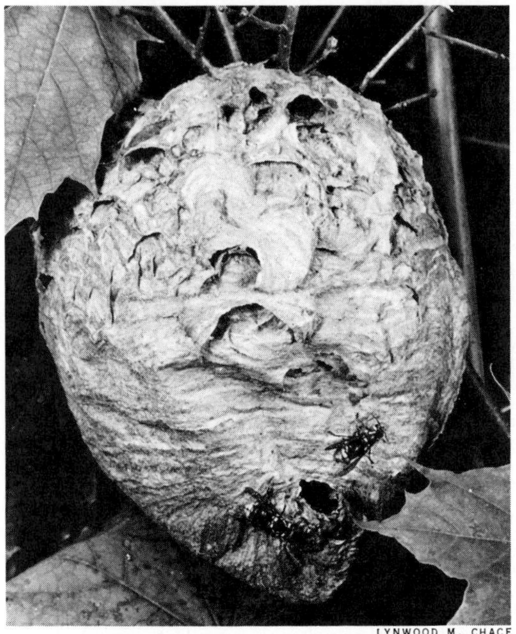

LYNWOOD M. CHACE

GRANT HEILMAN

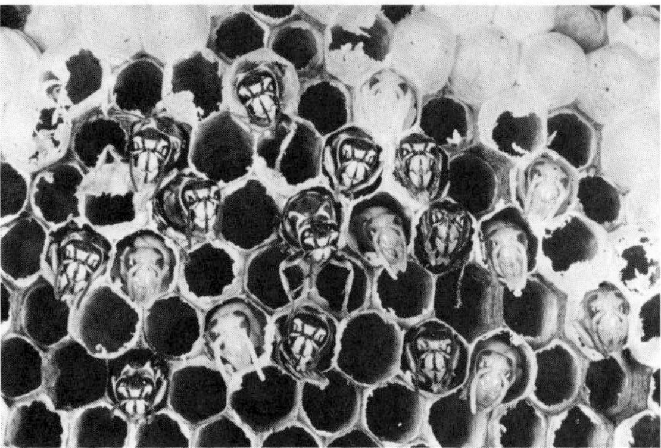

LYNWOOD M. CHACE, FROM NATIONAL AUDUBON SOCIETY

(*Above*) The envelope-enclosed nest of the bald-faced hornet (*Vespula maculata*). (*Top right*) Unenclosed nest of the paper wasp (*Polistes*), showing cells with eggs, capped cells, and larvae. (*Right*) Young yellow jackets emerge from cells.

mains relatively constant despite wide fluctuations in the outside temperature. In cold weather the nest is kept warm by heat produced by the wasps' activities and by closing the entrances. In hot weather the wasps ventilate the nest by fanning with their wings.

Nest founding by paper wasps of the genus *Polistes* differs considerably from that of the hornets and yellow jackets. Although a single female starts the nest in the spring, she is often joined by others, occasionally, as many as four or five. A dominance hierarchy, or "pecking order," is soon formed, the dominant female doing most or all of the egg-laying and the others acting as workers. If the dominant female dies or is injured, another will assume the role of queen. When the new generation emerge, they are similar in size and appearance to the foundress females, although they are in fact sterile workers. Later in the summer, males are produced, as well as females that are destined to mate, enter hibernation (often in country houses), and provide the foundresses of next year's nests.

Polistes' many tropical relatives are diverse almost beyond description. Some make naked combs, while others make enveloped nests not unlike those of yellow jackets, although the building materials vary and may include plant gums or mud. Because there are many predators in tropical forests, the nests are protected in various ways—some by camouflage, some by being suspended from the tips of high branches or in a tree inhabited by ants that are aggressive toward mammals but not toward the wasps. Certain inhabitants of naked combs build a long pedicel to which they apply a substance secreted by abdominal glands that repels ants. Occupants of covered nests may vibrate the envelope to produce a drumming sound, while others display their bright-colored, sting-tipped abdomens on the outside of the nest. As a last resort the wasps may attack the intruder as a group. Some tropical species have barbed stings, which—like honeybee stings—remain in the wound.

SOLITARY WASPS

Solitary wasps are abundant and highly beneficial, since many prey upon noxious insects such as cutworms, aphids, and weevils. While most social wasps are unselective regarding prey, solitary wasps are quite specific. For example, one species was brought from Japan to the United States to control larvae of the Japanese beetle, to which its attacks are confined. Another was imported to Puerto Rico to control mole crickets in sugarcane fields, and it has proved effective.

Solitary wasps show little tendency to protect their nests aggressively, but the nests are usually so inconspicuous as to attract little attention. Ground-nesting species often have elaborate behavior designed to conceal the entrances to their nests. Such wasps have remarkable powers of orientation and are able to find their nests readily even when scattered among many other nests and quite invisible to man. They remember landmarks at varying distances from the entrance, and usually find the entrance even when some of the landmarks are destroyed.

HOWARD E. EVANS, *Colorado State University*

Further Reading: Evans, Howard E., *Wasp Farm* (Comstock Pub. 1985); Evans, Howard E., and Eberhard, Mary Jane, *The Wasps* (Univ. of Mich. Press 1970); Krombein, Karl V., *Trap-nesting Wasps and Bees* (Smithsonian Inst. Press 1967); Spoczynska, Joy D., *The World of the Wasp* (Crane, Russak 1975); Spradbery, J. P., *Wasps: An Account of the Biology and Natural History of Solitary and Social Wasps* (Univ. of Wash. Press 1973).

WASPS, The, wosps, a comedy by the Greek playwright Aristophanes, dating from 422 B. C. Like earlier plays by Aristophanes, *The Wasps* satirizes the political life of contemporary Athens, led by the radical demagogue Cleon—in this instance, the city's judicial system and the Athenians' fondness for litigation.

The Wasps has many farcical scenes, particularly the mock trial of a dog accused of stealing cheese. The main characters are Philocleon (Cleon lover) and his son Bdelycleon (Cleon hater). Philocleon is a paid juror, one of the many wasps (the chorus of irresponsible jurors). Bdelycleon persuades his father and the wasps that they are merely lackeys for unprincipled politicians. But Philocleon, personifying the people of Athens, remains unregenerated, becoming drunk and riotous and indulging his sexual appetite with a common flute girl.

WASSAIL, wos′əl, is a toast and a liquor. The term, in its Old English and Old Norse forms, was simply a salutation meaning "be in good health." In early medieval England, however, it came to be associated with drinking the health of a person, and by the 12th century the formula was well established in which the response to "wassail" was "drink-hail." Such toasts were probably used chiefly at holiday times, for in the 16th century and later the term also applied to the liquor with which the toast was drunk, particularly the spiced ale served on Twelfth Night, Christmas Eve, and New Year's Eve. The vessel from which this holiday ale was drunk was called a wassail bowl. Wassailing was often practiced outdoors by villagers, who carried a wassail bowl from door to door and drank the health of those who received them kindly.

"Wassail-drink-hail" also became a formula for drinking parties, with a bowl drained at each "wassail." In the 12th century, Frenchmen observing this practice among English travelers in French taverns regarded the English as a nation of drunkards, and by the time of Shakespeare the term "wassail" was used in England as a synonym for drinking bout.

ELIZABETH E. BACON
Formerly, Michigan State University

WASSERMANN, väs′ər-män, **August von** (1866–1925), German bacteriologist, who worked with the German physicians Albert Neisser and Carl Bruck in developing a test for the diagnosis of syphilis in 1906. This test, known as the Wassermann test, was a great advance in the diagnosis of syphilis. Wassermann's other contributions to medicine included an antitoxin treatment for diphtheria; inoculations against typhoid, cholera, and tetanus; and a serum for diagnosing a predisposition to tuberculosis.

Wassermann was born in Bamberg on Feb. 21, 1866. He received an M. D. degree from the University of Strassburg (Strasbourg) in 1889, joined the staff of the Robert Koch Institute for Infectious Diseases at Berlin in 1890, and became a director of experimental therapy and biochemistry there in 1906. In 1913 he became director of experimental therapy at the Kaiser Wilhelm Institute in Berlin. Wassermann died in Berlin on March 16, 1925.

WASSERMANN, väs′ər-män, **Jakob** (1873–1934), German novelist, whose works, psychologically oriented, treat the interrelationships among people. He was born in Fürth, Bavaria, on March 10, 1873. He grew up in poverty and, at 17, went to work in a factory. He gradually turned to writing, and his first stories and poems were published in the journal *Simplicissimus.*

Die Juden von Zirndorf (1897; Eng. tr. *The Dark Pilgrimage,* 1933) was the first of the novels that were to make Wassermann famous. The theme concerns the longing of the Jews for a messiah to deliver them from a world of oppression, and the need for justice and kindness in human relations. *Caspar Hauser* (1908; Eng. tr., 1928) restated the latter theme and established Wassermann as a mature writer. It was based on a true incident of a youth, who could not walk or speak, who suddenly appeared on the streets of Nuremberg in 1928.

Critics regard Wassermann's most distinguished book to be *Christian Wahnschaffe* (1918; Eng. tr., *The World's Illusion,* 1920). International in scope and theme, it portrays a man who gives up wealth and ease to succor the suffering people of the world.

Wassermann was not a member of the naturalist school, although there are many naturalistic elements in his books. He made frequent use of symbolism and introduced eccentric characters to present his view of human nature. He also had a tendency to manipulate characters and situations to fit his philosophical ends. Other major works include an autobiography, *Mein Weg als Deutscher und Jude* (1921; Eng. tr., *My Life as German and Jew,* 1933); *Der Aufruhr um den Junker Ernst* (1926; Eng. tr., *The Triumph of Youth,* 1927); and *Der Fall Maurizius* (1928; Eng. tr., *The Maurizius Case,* 1929). Wassermann died in Altaussee, Austria, on Jan. 1, 1934.

WASSERMANN TEST, wä′sər-mən, named for August von Wassermann, a test developed in 1906 for diagnosing syphilis but now no longer used. When the blood or spinal fluid of a patient was tested, a positive Wassermann reaction generally indicated the presence of antibodies formed as a result of a syphilis infection, although false positive reactions are possible.

WASTE, Industrial, solid, liquid, or gaseous waste products discharged into the environment by an industrial enterprise. They are important causes of pollution. Industrial gases, smoke, and dust particles are major contributors to air pollution, while chemicals and heat are among the major pollutants of water.

Factories and electric power plants are among the major industrial sources of air pollution. They contaminate the air with millions of tons of carbon monoxide, sulfur dioxide, hydrocarbons, and particulate matter each year. Although nuclear power plants do not cause air pollution, they discharge heated water into rivers and streams, causing thermal pollution. Industrial water pollution is also caused by the dumping of toxic chemicals, plant nutrients, metal particles, mining wastes, and radioactive materials into bodies of water. Oil seepage from underwater drilling sites and oil leakage from tankers are other forms of water pollution.

See also AIR POLLUTION; ENVIRONMENT; NUCLEAR ENERGY—*Environmental and Health Hazards;* PETROLEUM—*Environmental Problems;* THERMAL POLLUTION; WASTE DISPOSAL; WATER POLLUTION.

UNITED PRESS INTERNATIONAL

Waste disposal by abandonment: junked cars surround antilitter sign outside Denton, Texas.

WASTE DISPOSAL, the collection, storage, and processing of waste materials. In nature, wastes are for the most part returned to the environment through chemical action, bacterial activity, and weathering. Some man-made wastes are also processed, or degraded, by these natural processes. However, many of the wastes of an industrial society are not readily degraded and absorbed into the environment and must undergo special processing. This article deals primarily with the disposal of the solid portion of man-made wastes, from kitchen garbage to old cars. Liquid wastes are discussed in the article WASTEWATER, and gaseous wastes are covered in the article AIR POLLUTION.

For centuries man's nondegradable waste materials have generally been hauled, along with the degradable wastes, for disposal in open gulleys or abandoned pits. This type of disposal has led to a deterioration of the local environment around the dumping sites because the wastes attract insects and vermin, produce unpleasant odors, and sometimes catch fire. The dumping sites also often mar the natural beauty of the landscape.

Such centers of local environmental deterioration were multiplying and concentrating rapidly in both developed and developing countries, partly because of growing population densities and partly because of the great increase in the use of waste-generating goods and services by those concentrated populations. However, because of increasing public concern about the deterioration of the environment, old waste-disposal practices are no longer acceptable in most countries. As a result, some of the old methods are being refined and new ones sought. Since 1968, when a survey revealed that 94% of the land-disposal sites in the United States were inadequate, many states and municipalities have made major strides toward use of sanitary landfill or other improved processing and disposal practices.

About 80% of all community waste in the United States is disposed of by sanitary landfill. About 10% is deposited in open dumps, and about 10% is incinerated. Other disposal methods, such as composting, salvage, and reclamation, treat only a small portion of the total.

Practically every material used by man appears at some time as waste. Even tiny amounts of gold and silver are found in municipal refuse. The following table shows the composition of solid wastes produced by a typical community in the United States.

TYPES OF SOLID WASTES*

(Estimated U. S. Annual Average)

Component	Percentage
Paper	50.6
Food wastes	19.6
Metal	9.9
Glass	10.1
Wood	3.5
Textiles	3.0
Leather and rubber	1.7
Plastics	1.4
Miscellaneous	0.2

* Excluding grass, leaves, and other yard wastes.

There are also large quantities of community and other types of wastes that, because of their large size or origin, are usually segregated for separate handling. These items include automobiles, household appliances, furniture, industrial metal scrap, demolition wastes, manure from cattle feedlots, radioactive materials, and power-plant fly ash.

In the United States the per capita production of solid wastes has increased steadily to a daily rate of over 10 pounds (4.5 kg) per person, including both industrial and residential wastes. This is equivalent to a national total of about 360 million tons per year. This total includes 55 billion cans, 26 billion glass bottles, 30 million tons of paper, 7 million automobiles, and 100 million tires. In addition, 2,000 million tons of waste are produced by agriculture, and over 1,100 million tons are mining and mineral wastes.

These enormous quantities of wastes are not "burying" us, as has been frequently claimed. We have neglected their proper handling—and much more must be done—but our wastes will not bury us.

The various methods of waste disposal used in the United States cost an estimated total of $4.5 billion a year, or more than $10 per ton. About half the cost is for the collection and transportation of the wastes to the processing or disposal site. The other half is incurred in the processing and ultimate disposal of the residue at some permanent storage site.

STORAGE AND COLLECTION METHODS

At one time garbage, such as kitchen waste, was kept separate from dry rubbish and trash. Each type of waste was stored in a separate, covered container usually made of steel. Sometimes the garbage was used for hog feeding. However, it was found that raw garbage could spread disease, and it was required that garbage for feeding hogs be cooked to sterilize it. Because of the high cost of garbage sterilization and other economic and environmental factors, the use of garbage for hog feeding has been discontinued. Most cities have not continued to separate their dry trash and garbage, but collect the two types of waste together as combined waste.

The storage containers for solid household wastes also have changed. Often, the storage containers are lined with or replaced by plastic bags. The use of plastic liners helps to keep the containers clean. Another aid to clean and odor-free waste handling—where it is permitted legally—is the household garbage grinder (garbage disposal unit), which discharges finely ground food wastes directly into the sewer systems. This disposal method reduces the load on the solid-waste disposal system at the cost of an increased load on the liquid-waste disposal system.

An interesting result of the growing use of paper and plastics in packaging and in the manufacture of many items has been a reduction in the water and ash content of community wastes. With this change in the composition of wastes has come a noticeable increase in the calorific value of these wastes when they are burned as fuel. In the United States, the heat value of a pound (0.45 kg) of average community refuse is about half that of a pound of bituminous coal (5500 Btu per pound).

Waste collection systems for apartment houses, stores, office buildings, and industrial plants use large standardized steel containers that are emptied regularly by special trucks that are equipped to lift and empty the containers into compaction compartments. In industrial plants a large container may be equipped with its own compaction mechanism for compressing the waste as it is received. Depending on the compaction method and forces used, the refuse is usually compacted from a loose density of about 350 pounds per cubic yard (210 kg per cubic meter) to at least 600 pounds per cubic yard (355 kg per cubic meter).

Another method of reducing the volume of refuse for collection is on-site incineration. This method reduces the waste to a small fraction of its original volume. When properly maintained and operated, on-site incinerators equipped with fuel-fired afterburners and fly-ash control systems are very effective and contribute very little to air pollution. If neglected and allowed to deteriorate, however, they may become sources of objectionable odors, gases, smoke, and dust.

During the 1960's two alternative collection methods were devised. One method, used to a limited extent in apartment houses in Sweden, uses a system of vacuum-sealed air-suction pipes in the building to convey the solid refuse in a stream of air to a central collection point. A similar system that has been devised in the United States shreds the waste and mixes it with water. The resulting slurry is then conveyed from the building to a collection point through large pipes. Both systems eliminate the dust and odors of handling the refuse at the building, but have had only limited use because of the high costs of operation in comparison with conventional systems.

Sanitary Landfill. The formerly widespread practice of unsightly open dumping has been re-

MOUNTAIN OF TRASH in Blackwell Forest Preserve near Chicago will serve as an area of ski slopes and toboggan runs. The mountain, a honeycomb of cells made of garbage and clay, helps solve waste disposal problem.

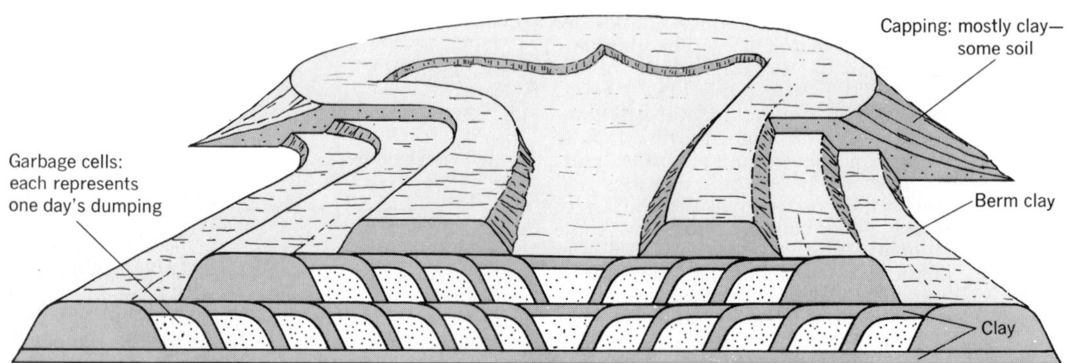

TOM CARDAMONE ASSOCIATES, INC. FOR FORTUNE MAGAZINE.

WIDE WORLD PHOTOS

TWO METHODS of disposing of automobiles: (*above*) a car is hoisted onto a conveyor belt, sent up to a shredder, and chewed into small bits; and (*right*) cars are put through a crusher that molds them into blocks.

placed in most areas by sanitary landfills. Frequently, landfill sites are later used for purposes that may not have been feasible before landfilling. Among common landfill sites are abandoned quarries, gravel pits, or strip mines, and canyons and swamps.

The landfill process involves daily spreading and compacting of the waste into a layer of uniform thickness. At the close of each day, the layer is covered by a thick layer of compacted soil to seal the waste from rodents and insects and to prevent the release of unpleasant odors from decaying organic material.

Long experience has established the requirements of this method and has demonstrated its potentialities under many different circumstances. Groundwater conditions in the vicinity of the landfill site are of critical importance, because leaching of soluble portions of the waste may cause excessive water contamination in unusual cases.

Slow decomposition of the organic and cellulosic portions of the waste occurs, resulting in a very gradual settling of the filled surface. However, such areas are frequently satisfactory for recreation and park use. After ten or more years of natural settling, the site may be suitable for industrial, commercial, or residential building. Many marshy areas in large metropolises have been reclaimed for building purposes through landfilling. However, in some areas marshes are needed for the preservation of wildlife, and in those regions landfilling should be limited to only the particular areas that are deemed important both for waste disposal and for ultimate use as dry land.

The decomposition of cellulose in a landfill is accompanied by a very slow formation of methane gas, which seeps out into the atmosphere. When methane gas forms by natural decay in swamps it is called swamp, or marsh, gas. Normally, much more methane is released into the air by the natural decay of trees and other vegetation than by the decay of waste in landfills. In a rare misapplication of landfilling too close to a building, the methane may accumulate inside the building and cause an explosion.

WIDE WORLD PHOTOS

A disadvantage of landfilling in metropolitan areas is that as the need for waste disposal grows, the number of suitable sites diminishes. This problem is enormously complicated when the city is completely surrounded by residential suburbs that are hostile to all forms of waste processing in their areas, especially the processing of waste from a neighboring community. The well-founded hostility to the formerly widespread practice of open dumping has, however, prejudiced many taxpayers against any form of landfilling regardless of the demonstrated success of the sanitary landfill method.

To solve the problem of suitable sites, some experiments have been conducted using "trash-trains" to haul compacted or baled refuse from transfer stations in metropolitan areas to landfill sites in unused quarries, gravel pits, or strip mines. Because the economic prospects of such a system are not encouraging, no city has yet invested in trash-trains as a major solution to its waste-disposal problem. A similar system, long used in the Netherlands, has been abandoned in favor of incineration.

Another variation of the landfill concept greatly increases the disposal capacity of certain sites and provides recreational slopes in otherwise flat terrain. In this variation, wastes are compacted in layers to create a landscaped hill 100 feet (30 meters) or more in height. Such hills, sometimes nicknamed Mount Trashmore, have been built in DuPage county and Evanston, Illinois; Virginia Beach, Virginia; Frankfurt, West Germany; and Stockholm, Sweden. Not all potential landfill sites are suitable for conversion into hills, but many are. In regions where natural hills are scarce, a carefully built, covered, and landscaped hill of waste can solve a waste-disposal problem and at the same time actually enhance the environment.

Another site sometimes used for waste disposal, and under consideration for more extensive use is the ocean floor. A major deterrent to wider use of the ocean floor is the long-term threat of contamination of the deep-sea environment by materials that injure marine life.

Incineration. Incineration reduces community refuse approximately 90% by volume and 75% by weight. The "missing" material is discharged innocuously into the atmosphere in the form of carbon dioxide and water vapor. The remaining incombustible solid residue may be processed to remove the useful metals, but more commonly it is deposited in a landfill.

On-site incineration is useful in reducing the amount of residue to be hauled away if the incinerator is operated under properly controlled conditions. One major problem with incineration is that many incinerator units contribute to air pollution by spewing carbon monoxide, hydrocarbons, and particulate matter into the air. Afterburners can burn most of the polluting gases, and special dust collectors can be used where needed to clean the exhaust gases, but the smaller the incinerator, the more difficult it becomes to reduce air pollution. Accordingly, there is a trend to using large municipally operated incinerators that are controlled by trained operators and equipped with highly effective air-pollution-control devices.

Another significant trend well under way in Europe and beginning in the United States is to use city incinerators to generate electric power or steam for heating. A major advantage of such incinerators is that the extraction of heat from the combustion process results in a reduced temperature of the exhaust gases, to a point where the use of high-efficiency air-pollution-control equipment is feasible. Another advantage of this type of system is that the sale of electric power or steam can partially offset the cost of operating the incinerator. The heat value available in the solid waste from a community in the United States is usually enough to generate about 10% of the total electric power used by the community. Thus even though a saving can be made through the use of solid waste as a fuel for power generation, about 90% of the usual power requirement of the community must still be obtained from other energy sources.

Although the power- or steam-generating incinerators with efficient air-pollution-control equipment are inherently clean, such units have rarely been built in the United States because of their high cost. A further deterrent has been the reluctance of private power-generating companies to burn heterogeneous municipal waste instead of a uniform fossil fuel. Also, some products of waste combustion are corrosive and have attacked boiler tubes in some of the units used in Europe. Nevertheless, the value of such systems for energy conservation, coupled with their clean operation, will encourage their wider use in the future.

Another type of incineration system operates at such high temperatures that the residue is melted, forming a slag that may have many uses as construction material. However, the variability of the wastes fed into the incinerators results in nonuniform products, and the potential for air pollution by constituents volatilized by the high temperatures is a serious problem.

The secondary-materials industry is primarily concerned with reclaiming scrap, principally metals. Unfortunately, fluctuating economic and metal-supply conditions have often discouraged metal recovery. A significant development has been the use of large and costly grinders and associated equipment to reduce old automobiles to small clean steel pieces suitable for recycling into some steelmaking processes. The large investment required to build these plants means that they must be kept busy by locating them near major collection points for old cars. The cost of transportation prohibits moving abandoned cars from thinly populated areas to metropolitan sites, with the result that junked cars will undoubtedly continue to accumulate throughout the countryside. One possible way of solving the problem is to add a disposal fee to the purchase price of every car.

Many attempts are being made to salvage useful raw materials from wastes, and a few have been successful. For example, some plants are de-inking clean waste newspaper so that it can be reprocessed into paper. Also, pulping machinery from the pulp and paper industry has been demonstrated to be capable of reclaiming cellulose fibers. Two full-scale plants of this type were constructed in the United States in 1978.

Another experimental process is pyrolysis, in which useful liquids and gases are distilled from the waste, leaving a charred residue that may be used as fuel or in industrial processes. Finding markets for such by-products has often been an insurmountable obstacle in similar pyrolysis schemes developed in the past.

Over 100 million tons of fine fly ash are collected annually by air-pollution-control equipment on coal-fired power plants. Despite considerable research, uses for this extremely fine dust consume only about 10% of the total, mostly in asphalt paving and as an additive in making concrete. Most of it is pumped in a water slurry to large storage ponds.

Composting. The production of useful soil-conditioning material from the cellulosic and organic portions of community wastes remains an attractive concept, but most large-scale attempts have failed because of marketing problems and costs. Research in composting is continuing, and under special supply and marketing conditions, composting will eventually find some limited applications. In the large industrial city of São Paulo, Brazil, a Danish compost system has been successful because nearby small vegetable farms, operated largely by Japanese immigrants, have found the compost useful for improving the compacted soil of the area.

AGRICULTURAL WASTE

Modern farming produces enormous quantities of stalks, vines, stems, and other plant waste materials, but the biggest problem is animal wastes—1.5 billion tons a year in the United States, for example. The traditional solution of manure spreading to improve the soil is highly beneficial. Research to find better methods of utilizing animal wastes is under way.

RICHARD B. ENGDAHL
Battelle Memorial Institute

HAZARDOUS WASTE LANDFILL

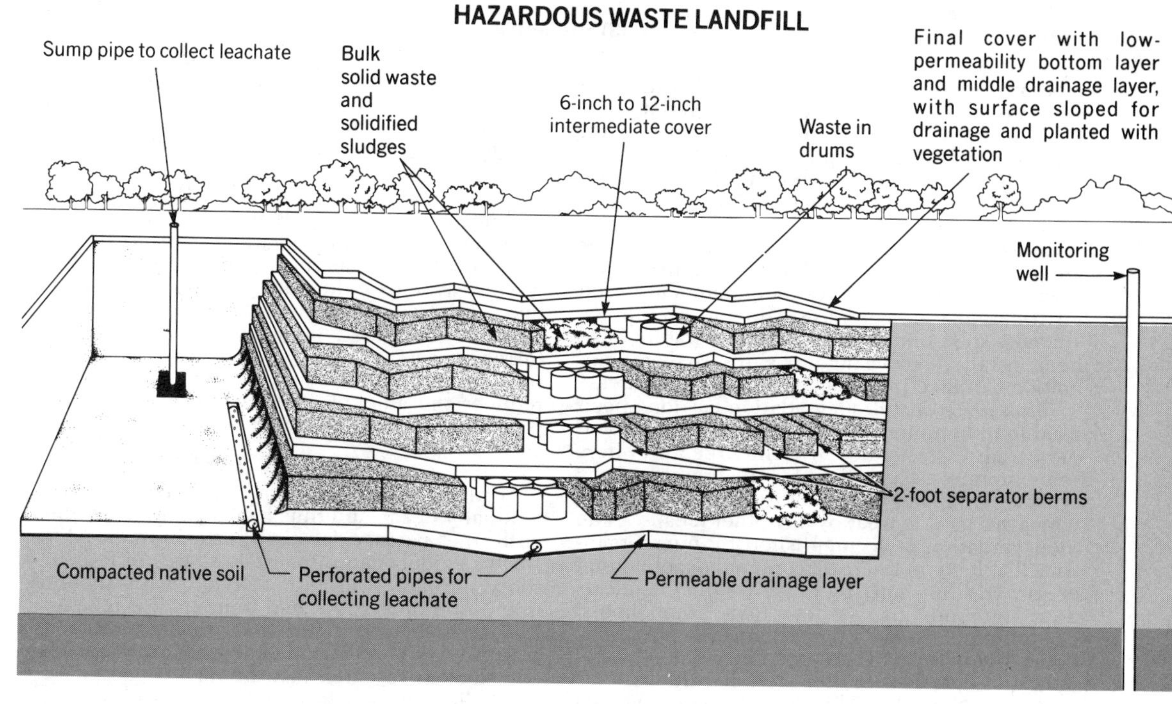

An example of a landfill designed to contain hazardous wastes. Even this design, which meets U.S. federal standards, may yield a toxic leachate that requires disposal by some other means.

HAZARDOUS WASTES

Hazardous wastes include a wide variety of waste materials that may be a threat to human health or to the environment. They are produced by many industries, including chemical, nonferrous metal, and electronic industries. The magnitude of the problem is hard to appraise. Most estimates of the amounts produced in the United States alone fall between 40 million and 275 million tons each year. Estimates of worldwide hazardous-waste production are not available.

Hazardous wastes became a national issue in the United States in the mid-to-late 1970's, when it was widely recognized that toxic industrial wastes in landfills and open dumps had begun to contaminate water-supply systems. In response, the federal government passed the Resource Conservation and Recovery Act (RCRA) in 1976 and the Comprehensive Environmental Response Compensation and Liability Act (CERCLA) in 1980.

RCRA. This act established a program for identifying and tracking hazardous wastes. It also set standards and required permits for treatment, storage, and disposal systems. The act classified wastes as hazardous if they posed a substantial actual or potential hazard to human health or the environment when improperly treated, stored, transported, or disposed of.

Under this classification, any waste material that is ignitable, corrosive, chemically reactive, or toxic is hazardous. Examples include metal sludges from the manufacture of paint and nonferrous metals, sludge from toxaphene production, chlorinated hydrocarbon wastes, and distillation residues from the production of acetaldehyde, nitrobenzene, and acrylonitrile.

Wastes that are not classified as hazardous under RCRA—and therefore not regulated—include those associated with the production of coal, oil, and other fossil fuels; those from mining and processing other minerals; cement-kiln dust; domestic sewage sludge; and household wastes.

CERCLA. Popularly known as Superfund, this act was designed to respond to emergencies created by chemical spills and leakage from hazardous waste sites. It is financed by a tax on crude oil, imported petroleum, and the manufacture of certain chemicals. However, the liability for cleanup costs rests with the parties whose actions are found to have caused the emergencies. The cost of cleaning up a single site can be hundreds of millions of dollars.

Superfund deals with a much broader range of hazardous substances than does RCRA. It empowers the government to act in two kinds of situations. For emergencies, such as a dangerous chemical spill, it authorizes immediate action to preserve human health or the environment. For ongoing threats, such as leakage from a waste site into water supplies, it authorizes long-term action to find a permanent remedy.

Disposal Methods—*Landfill*. The most commonly used method of disposal is to bury the waste in a landfill similar to the sanitary landfill used for nonhazardous wastes. This is not a permanent solution, since the buried waste generally remains hazardous indefinitely—it is only out of sight. Over a long period of time it may be impossible to prevent the release of toxic leachates or gases. Liquid wastes are especially difficult to contain. To prevent liquids from leaking, landfills designed for hazardous wastes are often lined with a sheet of plastic or a layer of clay.

Nearly 6,000 hazardous waste landfills exist in the United States. Many of them are "in house" landfills, maintained by companies that generate large amounts of hazardous wastes. Others are commercial landfills, operated by companies whose main business is waste disposal and which receive waste materials from many manufacturers. In the event of a leak from either type of landfill, the operator may be required to clean up the site and recompense injured parties. If an operator goes out of business, however, subsequent problems with the landfill may have to be dealt with by government agencies. Superfund was created to finance cleanups at such sites.

Incinerators. Incinerators for hazardous wastes are similar to those used for municipal solid wastes. Different types of incinerators are used for different types of wastes, including liquids, sludges, and solid materials. Incinerators have been installed on oceangoing ships, so that incineration can take place far from populated areas.

Biodegradation. Biodegradation has long been used to treat municipal sewage sludge and some industrial wastes. (See WASTEWATER.) It offers some promise as a method for treating very toxic organic compounds in dilute waste streams, which are hard to treat by any other means. The biodegradation is accomplished by microorganisms that feed on the toxic compounds, obtaining energy and nutrients by breaking the chemicals down into nontoxic or less toxic components. For example, some microorganisms can break down highly toxic PCB's (polychlorinated biphenyls) and thus render them less hazardous.

Ocean Disposal. This highly controversial method has long been used for disposing of municipal sewage and other liquid wastes, including industrial acids. Proponents argue that the ocean is large enough to assimilate toxic materials without appreciable harm. Opponents contend both that the local effects of ocean dumping may be significant and that long-continued dumping may be harmful on a wider scale.

Chemical Detoxification. Some hazardous wastes can be detoxified by the addition of another chemical. For example, acids can be neutralized with bases, and ions of toxic metals in liquid wastes can be chemically converted into metallic salts that can be precipitated and removed from the liquid. Detoxification is useful for liquid wastes that contain only a single hazardous compound, provided that the compound is reactive and that the product of the detoxification reaction either is recoverable or is nonhazardous and nonreactive.

Injection. Liquid hazardous wastes have been disposed of by injecting them into porous rock formations deep underground. Most wells used for this purpose were originally drilled for oil or gas. Injection has been used to dispose of waste hydrocarbon compounds, acids, and dilute solvents. Disposal of such wastes by injection has the same drawbacks as landfill disposal—only more so, because the wells were originally drilled to obtain oil and gas and not to create leakproof storage sites.

Effectiveness of Disposal Methods. No method of disposal can totally destroy the hazardous components of wastes. Each method leaves a residue of some kind. Burial or dispersal only contains the hazardous material waste for a time, as in landfill disposal, or dilutes its concentration, as in ocean disposal. Incineration creates both gaseous emissions and ash, which may contain metals or other hazardous compounds. Chemical detoxification often results in a sludge that may contain toxic metallic salts and must be disposed of in turn by some other method.

Overall, the various methods of disposal do not solve the problem of hazardous wastes. At best they make disposal more manageable by making the waste less hazardous, by reducing its quantity, or by concentrating it in a location where it can be monitored easily.

Alternatives to Waste Disposal. The best way to deal with hazardous waste is not to produce the waste at all—or at least to minimize the amount produced. Four methods are useful for this purpose: (1) Manage the hazardous waste carefully to prevent contamination of nonhazardous wastes, which would magnify the disposal problem. (2) Use alternative materials that do not generate the same type of waste in the manufacturing process. (3) Recycle the wastes for futher processing. (4) Use a manufacturing process that reduces the amount of the waste or changes or produces a less hazardous waste.

RADIOACTIVE WASTE

Unlike chemical wastes, radioactive wastes gradually decay and thus become less dangerous with the passage of time. Some radioactive wastes contain more than one source of radioactivity. Sources of radioactive wastes include uranium mines, spent fuel from nuclear reactors, fuel reprocessing operations, nuclear weapons plants, hospitals with nuclear medicine facilities, and nuclear research institutions.

Radioactive wastes are classified as low level or high level, depending on the intensity of their radioactivity. Both types of radioactive wastes can be treated to reduce the volume and/or the hazard of the waste, just as can be done with hazardous chemical wastes. The bulk of nuclear waste is low level. The safe disposal of such waste is relatively simple, both because of its low radioactivity and because it usually has a relatively short half-life—the time needed for a material to lose half its radioactivity. Low-level wastes are sometimes handled by direct contact and are disposed of by shallow burial underground.

High-level wastes present a much more serious disposal problem than do low-level wastes. However, the quantity of material to be disposed of is much smaller than the quantity of low-level wastes. Also, high-level waste with a short half-life can be held until it becomes low-level waste and then disposed of in the same way as other low-level wastes.

High-level wastes occur in both liquid and solid forms. In general, safe containment is most feasible for solid forms. However, both liquid and slurry wastes can be solidified by several different processes, such as vitrification (or glassification) and incorporation into concretes or clays. Sites under consideration for permanent containment of high-level wastes include reservoirs in deep salt or rock formations, reservoirs under the ocean floor, the polar ice caps, and outer space.

LINDA M. CURRAN
Battelle

Bibliography

Committee for Energy Awareness, *The Management of Radioactive Wastes: An Annotated Bibliography* (1982).

Muller, K. R., and others, eds., *Chemical Waste* (Springer-Verlag 1986).

Murray, R. B., *Understanding Radioactive Waste,* 2d ed. (Battelle Press 1983).

National Research Council, *Management of Hazardous Industrial Wastes: Research and Development Needs* (National Academy Press 1983).

Office of Technology Assessment, Congress of the United States, *Technologies and Management Strategies for Hazardous Waste Control* (USGPO 1983).

Weinberg, D. B., and others, *Hazardous Waste Regulation Handbook* (Wald, Hackrader, & Ross 1982).

WASTEWATER consists of the liquid and water-carried wastes from residences, commercial buildings, industrial plants, and institutions, together with any groundwater, surface water, and storm water that may be present. The terms "wastewater" and "sewage" are sometimes used interchangeably.

In United States communities, an average of 150 gallons (567 liters) of water per person is used every day for all purposes. About 70% of this water—100 gallons (378 liters)—becomes wastewater. However, there are large variations among communities. The domestic wastewater from a city of one million persons averages about 100 million gallons (378 million liters)—more than 400 thousand tons (360 thousand metric tons)—a day, not including storm water runoff.

The rate at which wastewater is produced by households, commercial establishments, and industries varies considerably from hour to hour so that collection systems must be designed to handle the peak flows. Such peaks may vary from two to four times the average output, amounting to 200 to 400 gallons (750–1,500 liters) per person per day.

COMPOSITION AND CHARACTERISTICS

The composition of wastewaters depends on their origin and the volume of water in which the wastes are carried. Wastewaters that originate entirely from residential communities are made up of excreta, bathing and washing water, and kitchen wastes. These urban wastewaters do not vary widely among different communities. In rural communities and communities in the developing countries, the characteristics of the wastewaters may be quite different. Also, wide variations in composition and concentration occur where large industrial or commercial establishments add their wastes to the system.

There are several basic characteristics used to evaluate wastewater quality. They include the biochemical oxygen demand, the concentration of suspended particles, the acidity or alkalinity of the water, and the quantity and type of microorganisms present.

Biochemical Oxygen Demand. The biochemical oxygen demand (BOD) is the oxygen required for the biochemical decomposition of the organic matter in wastewater. It is determined by measuring the amount of oxygen used by decay microorganisms in a sample of the wastewater over a specific period of time, usually five days, at a specific temperature, generally 68° F (20° C). The BOD is indicative of the impact that the wastewater can be expected to make on the oxygen content of the stream receiving the waste. The per capita contribution of BOD in the United States is about one sixth of a pound (0.075 kg) per day. In 100 gallons (378 liters) of wastewater per capita per day, the BOD amounts to a concentration of about 200 milligrams per liter (11.5 grains per gallon), nearly equal to 200 parts per million.

Suspended Solids. On the average, about one fifth of a pound (0.09 kg) of suspended solids is added to wastewaters per capita per day in the United States. This results in a concentration of about 240 milligrams per liter (14 grains per gallon). The suspended solids are a burden in the receiving streams because of the BOD that the organic particles exert, because of the turbidity the particles impart to the receiving water, and because of the sludge deposits that may build up in the stream. The handling and disposal of the solids removed in treatment constitute a major function of wastewater treatment plants.

Suspended solids in wastewater are classified as either fixed or volatile. The fixed solids are essentially inert and the volatile solids make up the organic fraction that is suitable for biological degradation or incineration. Suspended solids may also be classified as either settleable or nonsettleable. The settleable solids can be readily removed by a period of quiescence in a sedimentation tank (primary treatment). The nonsettleable solids can be removed by other means (secondary treatment).

Acidity and Alkalinity. With respect to acidity or alkalinity, domestic wastewaters are generally neutral. Industrial wastes, however, may make the water too acidic or too basic. When this happens special pretreatment is needed before the waters undergo biological treatment, because extremes of acidity or alkalinity are toxic to the microorganisms responsible for biological treatment.

Microorganisms. Many viruses and other microorganisms, particularly the enteric organisms that live in the intestines of man and other warm-blooded animals, are found in large numbers in wastewaters. Some of these organisms are pathogenic, causing such diseases as typhoid, cholera, and dysentery. The numbers of these organisms are usually small and their identification and enumeration are difficult. For routine purposes, therefore, the presence of certain so-called enteric indicator organisms, such as the coliform group (which includes the common intestinal bacterium *Escherichia coli*), is used to provide evidence that pathogens may be present. Because human feces discharged each day contains about one million coliform organisms per capita, all wastewaters are heavily loaded with coliforms and their numbers are indicative of the overall degree of water contamination.

The drinking water standards of the U. S. Public Health Service require that drinking water contain an average of no more than one coliform organism per 100 milliliters of water, about 10 per quart. This low concentration suggests that pathogenic organisms are not likely to be present. Ordinary wastewaters may have hundreds of thousands of coliform organisms per milliliter, and because conventional wastewater treatment can remove only from 99.0% to 99.9% of them, chemical disinfection is required for complete safety if the water is to be reused.

Chlorine Demand. The chlorine demand of wastewaters is important where the water is to be disinfected, because chlorine is the most commonly used disinfectant. The higher the degree of wastewater treatment, the less the chlorine demand of the treated effluent is likely to be. Chlorine requirements may range from 20 to 200 pounds (9–90 kg) per million gallons (3.78 million liters) of wastewater to be treated.

Nutrients. Nutrients, particularly nitrogen and phosphorus compounds, are present in significant concentrations in all domestic wastewaters, chiefly from human excreta and detergents. The nutrients in domestic wastewaters as well as those from fertilizers used on cultivated fields encourage the growth of large populations of algae and other aquatic organisms in the receiving waters. This enrichment, called eutrophication, may interfere with the normal ecological balance of the receiving waters. Many bodies of water, such as Lake Constance in central Europe and parts of Lake Erie in North America, have been ruined by excessive eutrophication. See EUTROPHICATION.

Heavy Metals and Synthetic Organic Chemicals. Heavy metals and synthetic organic chemicals pose special problems in wastewaters. High concentrations of them may interfere with the treatment processes.

The heavy metals, particularly lead and mercury, are toxic to man and other animals. Mercury pollution in the Great Lakes and other lakes and streams has seriously endangered many fish as well as the people who eat the fish. Some synthetic organic compounds, such as the chlorinated hydrocarbons (DDT, lindane, and similar broad spectrum insecticides), may also be toxic if they get into water supplies or into the food chain. The identification and determination of the concentration of these chemicals are difficult, but where industrial wastes and agricultural runoffs containing heavy metals and synthetic organic compounds are known to find their way into the wastewater collection system, their detection is important.

WASTEWATER COLLECTION SYSTEMS

The first sewers for the collection of wastewater were storm sewers that were installed to collect rainwater in the commercial centers of large cities. In modern times London was the first major city to use sewers. London's example was then followed by Paris, New York, and Boston. Household wastes were collected and hauled in wagons for disposal outside the city. As indoor water supplies became common, the storm sewers were used to carry off domestic wastes as well as storm water. These combined sewer systems succeeded in removing wastes from the immediate vicinity of the households, but by discharging them into the nearest watercourse, created serious problems of water pollution, particularly during dry periods when the water level in the streams was low.

When wastewater treatment was introduced in the middle of the 19th century, separate sanitary sewer systems for domestic wastewaters were installed. A sanitary system collects the wastewaters from household, commercial, industrial, and institutional establishments and conducts them through a sanitary sewerage, or wastewater, collection system to a treatment site. The storm sewers required for handling surface runoff empty into the nearest watercourse.

Collection systems for domestic and industrial wastewaters involve part of all of the following elements: plumbing systems, connections from plumbing systems into the collection system, sewers, manholes, and pumping stations. Because the materials in domestic and industrial wastewaters may be corrosive, the sewers are usually made out of vitrified clay tile, cement-asbestos mixtures, centrifugally cast concrete, or rigid plastic materials. Sanitary sewers usually range in size from a minimum of 8 inches (200 mm) to 6 to 8 feet (1.8–2.4 meters) in diameter.

Storm water collection systems collect surface runoff through inlets in gutters in city streets, through inlets in large paved areas, or through collectors from building roofs. Storm sewers range in size from 15 inches (380 mm) in diameter to conduits 10 feet (3 meters) or more across. Small storm sewers may be made of precast concrete or corrugated steel, and large sewers are often of concrete constructed in place. When a city, like New Orleans, La., is below the level of the waters surrounding it, all the rain that falls on the city is collected in storm sewers and is pumped out of the city.

Usually water is moved through sewers by gravity, and the sewers must have enough slope to prevent the sedimentation of wastewater solids. Slopes may vary from 6 inches to 15 feet (150 mm–4.5 meters) per mile (1.6 km). To avoid the excessive excavation that would result from maintaining adequate sewer grades in cities built on flat terrain, pumping stations may be installed at points throughout the system.

Where combined sanitary and storm sewers are used, it is not feasible to conduct the large volumes of mixed wastewaters to a treatment plant so that special storm overflows leading directly into the receiving water are necessary. These overflows discharge substantial amounts of raw wastewater to the receiving waters during rainstorms, causing considerable pollution of the water. For this reason, combined storm and sanitary systems are no longer being built and attempts are being made to separate combined systems where they do exist.

DEVELOPMENT OF WASTEWATER TREATMENT

Human body wastes are naturally decomposed and stabilized by microorganisms, either in the ground or in the topsoil or receiving waters. In the middle of the 19th century, when rivers flowing past the major urban industrial centers in Europe and the United States became heavily polluted, the first wastewater treatment on a community-wide scale was initiated. This treatment, which utilized natural decomposition, consisted of using the wastewater on agricultural lands, and it is still practiced in some parts of the world. The acreage necessary for such disposal is great, usually from 20 to 200 acres (8–80 hectares) of land per thousand population. With the growth of densely populated urban areas, however, the space required for natural decomposition became scarce and special processes for treatment were developed.

Modern wastewater treatment is generally divided into three phases: primary, secondary, and tertiary. Each of these steps produces sludge, which can be disposed of or used for various purposes.

Primary Treatment. Primary treatment, or plain sedimentation, developed in the early 1900's, removes only the settleable solids from wastewaters. This process is considered to be the absolute minimum of treatment that every community must afford. By 1970, about 9% of the sewered population in the United States was still without any treatment at all while about 33% of the sewered population was provided with only primary treatment.

A modern system for primary treatment entails collecting the wastewaters, conveying them to a central point for treatment, using screens to remove large objects and grit chambers to remove grit, and using primary sedimentation tanks to remove the suspended settleable solids. This type of system produces about one third of a gallon (1.3 liters) of wet sludge per person per day, and facilities for handling and disposing the sludge are also needed. Primary treatment reduces the concentration of suspended solids by about 60% and reduces the BOD by about 35%,

WIDE WORLD

Actress and singer Ethel Waters delighted audiences with the warmth of her stage and screen performances.

biography (written with Charles Samuels), *His Eye Is on the Sparrow,* which critics hailed for its candor and sensitivity. Beginning in the late 1950's she participated as a gospel singer in the crusades of evangelist Billy Graham. She died in Chatsworth, Calif., on Sept. 1, 1977.

In both her acting and singing, Ethel Waters showed a freshness, exuberance, and warmth that captivated audiences. Popular songs with which she is identified include *Dinah, Having a Heat Wave,* and *Stormy Weather.*

WATERS, Muddy (1915–1983), American blues singer and guitarist. McKinley Morganfield was born on April 14, 1915, in Rolling Fork, Miss. At 13 he began to play the harmonica at local gatherings. He later learned to play the guitar, emulating the "bottleneck" style of blues musicians Robert Johnson and Eddie "Son" House. His reputation grew, and in 1941 a recording of his music was made for the Library of Congress folk-music archives. Encouraged by this recognition, Waters moved to Chicago in 1943 to pursue a career in music. With his band, he began to transform the country-blues style, adopting electric guitar and adding amplification to produce the more urbanized sound of rhythm and blues. He was a popular rhythm-and-blues recording artist throughout the 1950's.

Beginning in 1958, when he toured England, Waters became more widely known. His electric blues style inspired a generation of young British musicians who later became innovators in rock music. He also was venerated by jazz and folk musicians and performed frequently at the Monterey and Newport festivals. He played at Carnegie Hall and the White House and in the 1970's won six Grammy Awards. He died near Chicago on April 30, 1983.

WATERS, Territorial. See TERRITORIAL WATERS.

WATERSHED, as defined in the United States, all the land that drains into an individual stream or lake. Thus a watershed may be only a few acres in area or may consist of a drainage basin tens of thousands of square miles in size. In British usage, the term designates the divide between two different drainage basins.

The word watershed has become a very common subject of conversation. This is true because more and more people have come to the realization that a large part of their well-being relates to a watershed in some manner or other; that the water they use comes from a watershed; and that terribly destructive floods also come from a watershed. Concurrent with this realization has come an increasing knowledge concerning the effect that man may have upon various characteristics of a watershed.

Management of the land and natural resources of a watershed in such a manner as to bring about or maintain certain desired characteristics of water yield is known as watershed management. Any program for management of a watershed may include one or more of the following broad objectives: (1) rehabilitation (2) protection, and (3) increasing water yields.

Rehabilitation Watershed lands may include urban, rural, forest, or rangelands. Urban areas constitute a condition most drastically altered from the natural state. These areas are covered largely with impermeable surfaces (such as paved streets and buildings), and natural channels have been greatly encroached upon by man's structures. The total area involved is not very great; all that can be done in water control is to get storm water away with the minimum of damage by the use of engineering works, such as storm sewers and lined channels. Urban areas generally comprise lands that are permanently lost to productive watershed uses.

Rural areas include the farmlands of the country. Watershed management on lands in this category may include one or both of the two broad objectives, rehabilitation and protection. Rehabilitation may include such measures as planting gullied areas, installing minor structures to supplement such planting, and changing land use from crops to pasture or forest. Rehabilitation is usually needed where nonconservation farming practices have been used over a period of time and excessive erosion has resulted in serious deterioration of the land. Protection involves those practices that would prevent excessive erosion while production of various crops is carried on. Such measures as contour plowing, terracing, and stripcropping may be used, depending upon the steepness of slope and the soil type. Although some of these measures may moderately increase the rate at which water can enter the soil, the primary objective is to get storm waters off the land with a minimum of soil erosion. On agricultural lands there is little opportunity to accomplish much in the way of increasing total water yields.

Forests, ranges, and other wildlands are the areas where the maximum opportunity for watershed management occurs. The headwaters of most streams are usually forested, and also mark the zones where the most precipitation occurs. As these areas are the principal water sources of most drainage basins, it is here that the major effects upon water yield may be produced by land management practices. Here watershed management may be aimed at one or more of the three broad objectives—rehabilitation, protection, and increasing water yields.

The degeneration of a watershed area is usually started by destructive logging, overgrazing, fire, or other practices that tend to remove the protective vegetative cover and compact the soil. The degenerative process becomes apparent when excessive volumes of surface runoff, together with increasing soil erosion, occur during intense storm periods. Unless remedial measures are taken, the degenerative process occurs at an accelerated rate until a degree of stability is reached under a condition of low infiltration and storage capacity for the watershed, high rates of surface runoff and flood discharge from the streams, and large movement of sediment down the channels to the valleys below. If steps are taken early enough in the degeneration process, rehabilitation may be accomplished with comparative ease through artificial revegetation and minor structural works. With increasing degeneration, the restoration process becomes progressively more difficult and expensive. In all cases, the first and most important step toward rehabilitation is to discontinue or modify the practice or use that produced the destructive process. In the case of range watersheds, this may consist of discontinuing grazing of livestock for a period of time until the vegetative cover is adequately restored; or it may consist of grazing management so as to prevent the concentration of livestock in seriously eroding areas. In forest lands logging operations would be modified so as to ensure perpetuation of a good tree cover. Wildfire should in all cases be prevented. In some areas where the degeneration process has not progressed too far, it is possible to rehabilitate the area in a few years and very effectively reduce surface runoff and erosion; but other areas, where the destructive processes have continued for many years, often require a longer time before rehabilitation can become fully effective.

Protection. With the more intensive use of forest and rangeland, the need for protection of water values becomes more and more important. This is probably the most challenging phase of watershed management at the present time. As the need for increased wood products and forage continues, the possibilities of doing damage to the water resource also increases. In order to ensure that the water resource is fully protected, land managers must critically examine all practices to ensure that watershed values are fully recognized and protected. As a general theory, one might say that each forest land area has a characteristic critical level which determines the comparative safety or danger of any manipulation of the forest environment. Some environmental changes are induced whenever the forest cover is manipulated in a silvicultural operation. These operations are safe as long as the forest complex tends to regenerate good conditions over a reasonable period of time. If the operation strikes too severe a blow at the forest community, however, an accelerated cycle of degenerative change is likely to occur. The same reasoning applies equally to rangeland. Therefore, the objective in managing these types of lands is to control the processes so that the critical level is not passed. This may mean, in the case of forest land, a modification of cutting operations so as to ensure perpetuation of a good vegetative covering; or, in the case of rangelands, it may mean management practices that provide a good distribution of livestock and utilization of not over a certain percentage of the forage. The specifications needed will vary, depending upon the soil, vegetation, climate, topography, and similar elements. In general, the essence of this phase of watershed management is maintenance of a status quo through careful use of the various resources of the land.

Increase of Yields. Increasing water yields from a watershed in general represents a challenge for the future. Of the total amount of water arriving on a watershed in the form of rain or snow, a large percentage is returned to the atmosphere by evaporation and transpiration. Research carried on at several locations in the United States indicates that it may be feasible to manipulate the vegetative cover in such a manner as to reduce evaporation and transpiration water losses and thereby increase water available to streamflow. The effectiveness of such practices will vary depending upon the type of vegetative cover, soil depths, air temperatures, type and time of occurrence of precipitation, and similar factors. For example, studies in the Rocky Mountains of Colorado indicate that partial cuttings in dense coniferous forest stands may increase water available for streamflow as much as 15 to 20%. Studies in Utah, California, and South Carolina indicate that if deep-rooted species are replaced by shallow-rooted species, transpiration losses are decreased where soil depths are greater than four feet. In North Carolina, watershed studies showed that water yields might be increased by various methods of timber cutting. In all cases cutting must be tempered by due regard for maintaining a protective covering for the soil to prevent erosion and deterioration of the site.

In all phases of watershed management the chief consideration is the integration of all uses of the watershed lands so as to best maintain the productive capacity for all the renewable resources. Primary consideration should be given to maintaining maximum sustained yields of good quality water. See also WATER SUPPLY—*Sources and Collections; Conservation.*

HERBERT C. STOREY
United States Forest Service

WATERSKIING. See WATER SKIING.

WATERSPOUT, a whirling, funnel-shaped, cloud-filled wind that occurs over water and is similar in appearance to a tornado, which occurs over land. The typical waterspout extends downward from the base of a towering cumulus or cumulonimbus cloud to the water surface. Spray is kicked up on the water surface before the waterspout touches down. The funnel may have an overall length of 300–600 meters (about 1,000–2,000 feet). It is made visible by the condensation of water vapor as air rushes inward and upward. The inrushing air spins cyclonically—counterclockwise in the Northern Hemisphere and clockwise in the Southern. In a few waterspouts the rotation is anticyclonic.

Waterspouts differ from tornadoes in several respects. First, they are not as violent as tornadoes. The air may rotate around a waterspout at a speed of 20–40 meters per second (mps), or 45–90 miles per hour (mph), far less than the 100 mps (225 mph) wind speeds that may occur in tornadoes. Second, waterspouts tend to move more slowly and not last as long as tornadoes. A typical waterspout may drift along at 5 mps (about 10 mph) and last for 10 minutes. Third, a waterspout may range from 10 to 100 meters (about 35–350 feet) across, whereas a tornado may be ten times as wide. Fourth, waterspouts tend to occur under fair weather conditions.

Waterspouts pose a hazard to small boats, and on rare occasions they may cross over land and cause personal injuries and property damage.

Waterspouts generally occur when there is a large temperature difference between the base of the cloud and the water surface. This condition occurs often over the tropical oceans and over portions of the Gulf of Mexico and western Atlantic Ocean in the summer. It also occurs when cold air crosses much warmer water, for example, over the Great Lakes and North Atlantic Ocean in winter.

In the United States waterspouts are most common near the Florida Keys in summer and over the Great Lakes and North Atlantic coastal margins in the cooler part of the year.

LANCE F. BOSART
State University of New York at Albany

NOAA

A large temperature difference between the base of a cloud and the water surface can produce a waterspout.

WATERTON-GLACIER INTERNATIONAL PEACE PARK, an international park, established on June 18, 1932, by acts of the Canadian Parliament and the United States Congress. It comprises two separately administered parks—Waterton Lakes National Park in southwestern Alberta and Glacier National Park in northwestern Montana. An area of 1,560 square miles (4,039 sq km) athwart the Rocky Mountains, Glacier Park is linked with Waterton Lakes Park (203 square miles, or 526 sq km) by the Chief Mountain International Highway and the Continental Divide. Together the two parks boast some 300 lakes, 60 glaciers, and 1,200 miles (1,932 km) of hiking trails; a large variety of animal life, including more than 200 species of birds; and more than 1,000 varieties of wildflowers.

Geologists trace the history of the region to the Proterozoic era, at least 600 million years ago. In late Cretaceous time (70 million years ago) an upheaval called the Lewis Overthrust propelled the rock crust into jagged crags and peaks, after which (about 1 million years ago in the Pleistocene epoch) the peaks and valleys were hewn to their present state by gigantic ice masses. Glacier's highest point is Mt. Cleveland at 10,448 feet (3,185 meters); Waterton's highest is Mt. Blakiston, 9,600 feet (2,930 meters). Logan Pass on the Continental Divide, which is crossed by Glacier Park's scenic Going-to-the-Sun Road, has an elevation of 6,664 feet (2,030 meters).

Called the "Land of the Shining Mountains," Waterton-Glacier is considered to have panoramic beauty rivaling the Swiss Alps. Campgrounds and lodging are available from mid-June to mid-September. See also GLACIER NATIONAL PARK.

Glacier National Park, in northwestern Montana, is part of the Waterton-Glacier International Peace Park, which straddles the U.S.–Canadian border. Swiftcurrent Lake and the adjacent Lewis Range are notable tourist attractions.

WATERTON LAKES NATIONAL PARK, a wilderness area in southwestern Alberta, Canada, on the eastern slopes of the Rocky Mountains, set aside as a national park in 1895. Within its area of 203 square miles (526 sq km) are sharp peaks, noted for their extraordinary coloring, valleys carved by glaciers, and numerous lakes. Its highest point is Mt. Blakiston, at 9,600 feet (2,930 meters). The park has a rich variety of plantlife and an abundance of animals, including bighorn sheep, moose, and elk.

Waterton Park and Glacier National Park in Montana make up the Waterton-Glacier International Peace Park, which was established in 1932. See also WATERTON-GLACIER INTERNATIONAL PEACE PARK.

WATERTOWN, a town in west central Connecticut, in Litchfield county. It is situated on the west bank of the Naugatuck River, just northwest of Waterbury. Watertown has a number of industries, principally the manufacture of plastics, synthetic fabrics, brass and wire goods, and hardware. In the center of town, along the green, are several houses dating from the late 18th century. Nearby is the Taft School, a leading private, coeducational preparatory school. Portions of the Black Rock State Park and the Mattatuck State Forest are located in Watertown.

The first permanent settlement of the area occurred about 1720, and in 1738 an ecclesiastical society called Westbury was formed. In 1780 the societies of Westbury and Northbury were separated from Waterbury and incorporated into the present community of Watertown. The town has a council-manager form of government. Population: 19,489.

WATERTOWN, a town in eastern Massachusetts, in Middlesex county, on the Charles River. It is a residential and industrial suburb of Boston, about 8 miles (13 km) to the east. Watertown's principal manufactures include fabricated metal products, electrical and other machinery, precision instruments, rubber products, electronic equipment, and chemical products. The town has two junior colleges; the Perkins School for the Blind, founded in Boston in 1633, moved to Watertown in 1912.

One of the four earliest Massachusetts Bay settlements, Watertown has retained many of its early houses. Among them is the Abraham Browne House, whose original section dates from 1633. Also of interest is the U.S. arsenal (1816), a section of which is used by the U.S. government as an engineering and research center for information on weapons manufacture.

In 1630 a group of Englishmen led by Sir Richard Saltonstall settled Watertown. From its inception the community was devoted to democracy. The first New England town to elect a board of selectmen (1634), Watertown became known as "the Cradle of the Town Meeting." During the Revolution it was a hotbed of anti-British sentiment, and many Whigs fled here from Tory Boston.

Watertown was the home of many artists, writers, and other intellectuals who were attracted by the cultural climate. In the 19th century it was a gathering place for such transcendentalists as Ralph Waldo Emerson and Margaret Fuller.

The town is governed by a council and manager. Population: 34,384.

WATERTOWN, a city in northern New York, the seat of Jefferson county, about 65 miles (105 km) north of Syracuse. Bisected by the Black River, the city has a 112-foot (34-meter) waterfall, which supplies power for industry. Papermaking, begun in 1809, and the manufacture of paper machinery and paper products are major economic activities. The city also produces air brakes, hydraulic equipment, snowplows, electric motors, thermometers, clothing, and ski lifts. Watertown is the commercial center of a large dairy-farming and agricultural region. As the gateway to the Thousand Islands and Adirondack resort areas, it also benefits from tourism.

Notable public buildings include the Flower Memorial Library and the Jefferson County Historical Society home, both containing relics from Indian times and the period of French settlement. A Woolworth building on the Public Square marks the site where Frank W. Woolworth in 1878 introduced the five-and-ten-cent store.

Settled in 1800, Watertown was incorporated as a city in 1869. It is governed by a council and manager. Population: 27,861.

WATERVILLE, a city in southern Maine, in Kennebec county, 18 miles (29 km) north of Augusta. Situated on the west bank of the Kennebec River at the Ticonic Falls, Waterville is a distributing and wholesale marketing center. It also manufactures paper and wood products, shirts, and woolen goods. The city is the seat of Colby College (1813) and Thomas College (1894).

Long before the English colonization of the area, the Indians had maintained a village at the confluence of the Kennebec and Sebasticook rivers, across from what is now Waterville. The first English trading post here dated from 1653. On the site of the Indian village, the English in 1754 constructed Fort Halifax, which commanded a strategic Indian route during the French and Indian War. By 1800 two settlements had grown up on opposite sides of the Kennebec River, and administration of the area became difficult. As a result, in 1802, Waterville was incorporated as a separate town. Chartered as a city in 1888, Waterville has a mayor-council government. Population: 17,779.

WATERVLIET, wô′tər-vlēt, a city in eastern New York, in Albany county, on the west bank of the Hudson River opposite the city of Troy. An industrial city, Watervliet produces steel products, textiles, abrasives, and bricks. Its U.S. arsenal, established in 1813, has produced arms for wars since the War of 1812.

Watervliet was settled about the time of the Dutch colonization of Albany in 1624. Part of a tract of land bought from the Mohawk Indians, it was given the name Watervliet (meaning "flowing stream") about 1630. In 1836 it was incorporated as the village of West Troy, and in 1896 it was chartered as a city under its present name.

Overlooking the Hudson is the Schuyler Homestead (1666), where Philip Schuyler and his wife hosted many notables. In 1776 the first informal community of Shakers in America was founded in Watervliet by Ann Lee.

Watervliet has a council-manager form of government. Population: 11,354.

WATERWAY, Inland. See ATLANTIC INTRACOASTAL WATERWAY.

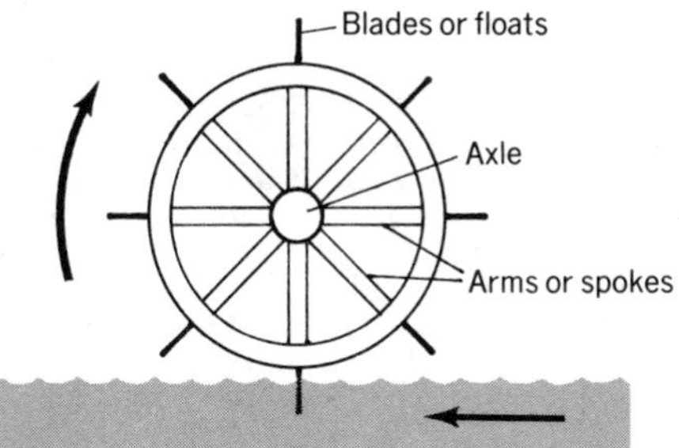

Traditional undershot

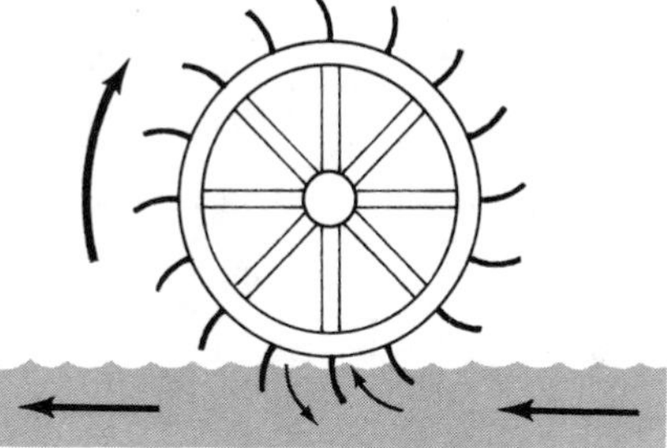
Poncelet undershot

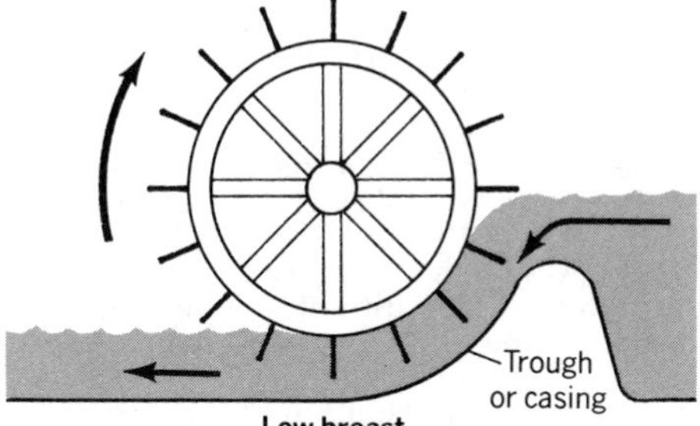

Low breast

High breast (pitchback)

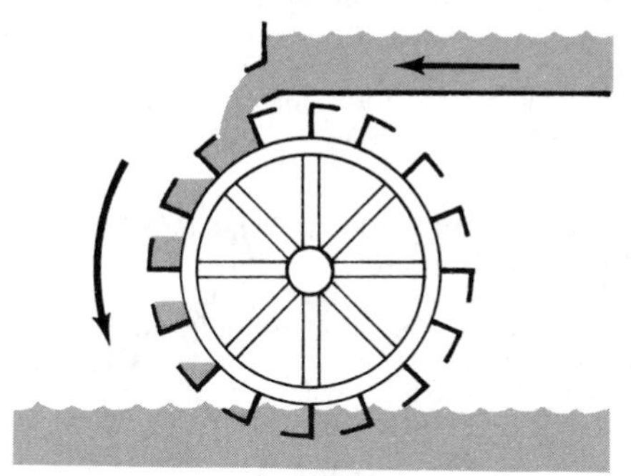
Overshot

WATERWHEEL TYPE	HEAD REQUIRED (feet)	TYPICAL WATER VOLUME (cu. ft./sec.)	TYPICAL EFFICIENCY
Undershot			
Traditional	less than 4	10-175	0.20-0.30
Poncelet	less than 6	7-175	0.60-0.65
Breast			
Low	4-10	5-150	0.45-0.60
High	10-40	2-40	0.60-0.80
Overshot	10-50	2-30	0.60-0.80

WATERWHEEL, one of the basic devices used to convert the flow or fall of water into mechanical work. The term is usually applied to wheels with vertical planes of rotation and horizontal axles. For wheels with horizontal planes of rotation and vertical axles, see TURBINE.

Kinds of Waterwheels. Vertical waterwheels are generally divided into three main groups: overshot, undershot, and breast.

The overshot waterwheel has containers, commonly called buckets, distributed around its rim. Water passed over the wheel enters these buckets and turns the wheel by its weight.

The undershot waterwheel usually has radial blades, or paddles. Water is passed beneath the wheel, where it strikes these blades and turns the wheel by impulse. One form, the Poncelet wheel, has curved rather than flat blades and operates by reaction or pressure, like a turbine, instead of by impulse.

The breast wheel receives its water at some point between the summit and the bottom of the wheel and is usually equipped with a close-fitting trough or casing on its lower quadrant to prevent water from leaving the wheel prematurely. Breast wheels are subdivided into low and high types. The low breast wheel usually has blades and receives water at or below axle level. The close-fitting casing causes water to act on its blades largely by weight. The high breast (or pitchback) wheel normally has buckets like an overshot wheel and receives its water above axle level. Although breast wheels operate by both weight and impulse, the contribution of weight should be maximized for efficient operation.

History. For more than a thousand years vertical waterwheels were the most reliable source of energy for industry. The first firm evidence of their use dates from the 1st century B.C., when several Greek writers mention watermilling. By the 1st century A.D. undershot waterwheels occasionally were used to grind grain or raise water in the Mediterranean area. During the same century some type of water-activated device was used in China to provide air blasts for smelting iron. However, several factors, such as abundant human labor, long inhibited the wide use of waterwheels.

Medieval Europeans were the first to extensively use the waterwheel for a variety of industrial purposes, beginning about the 6th century. By the 10th century, European millwrights had begun to expand the applications of waterpower. By 1600, waterwheels were used for dozens of industrial processes, including sawing wood, boring pipes, drawing wire, pumping water, producing paper, smelting and shaping metals, grinding flour, preparing hemp for rope, crushing olives for oil, and fulling wool. England alone had more than 5,600 watermills by the late 11th century and probably 20,000 by 1800. France had an estimated 80,000 by 1700.

As the use of waterpower grew, European engineers improved the natural flow of streams with dams and canals. By the 14th century, for example, the use of dams to increase the fall of water and make water flow more dependable for waterwheels had created serious problems for navigation in England, leading to attempts by Parliament to regulate such dams. Hydropower canals, which led water from streams to more convenient locations, or to sites where a higher fall could be developed, were also used with greater frequency. By 1800, German mining engineers had constructed in the Harz Mountains near Clausthal a hydropower system consisting of 60 dams and 120 miles (193 km) of canals. These provided water to 225 waterwheels driving mining and metallurgical equipment.

The increased demand for industrial waterpower, especially in Britain, provided the stimulus for several improvements in waterwheels. Beginning about 1760, British engineers such as John Smeaton and, later Thomas Hewes, began replacing wood with iron. By 1830, British industrial waterwheels were built largely of iron, with power taken from the wheels by means of iron gear teeth mounted on their rims instead of wooden gear wheels mounted on their axles. Rim gearing reduced the strain on the spokes or arms of the waterwheel, permitting the construction of lighter wheels, and reduced the amount of step-up gearing needed for high-speed machinery. Iron industrial wheels often were built on the suspension principle; the thick wooden arms that linked the axles and rims of the old wooden waterwheels were replaced by thin wrought-iron spokes held in tension like the spokes of a bicycle wheel.

Additional improvement in waterwheel utilization came from experimental investigations, especially those of John Smeaton (1759). His experiments on 2-foot (60-cm)-diameter model wheels revealed that water acting by weight produced twice the power of water acting by impulse under the same conditions of fall and volume. This led Smeaton to advocate the replacement of impulse-driven undershot wheels with weight-driven overshot or breast wheels. By 1800, wherever the efficient use of water was important, overshot and low breast wheels had displaced the undershot. Early in the 19th century, high breast wheels superseded overshot wheels in heavy industry, since they were better able to deal with variable water levels.

By the 1830's, British and American iron and iron-wood industrial breast wheels wee able to operate at efficiencies as high as 0.70 to 0.80. Some of the largest examples developed 200 to 300 horsepower.

As British engineers pioneered the development of the iron breast wheel, French engineers were applying scientific theory to analyze the performance of waterwheels. This work culiminated with Jean Charles Borda (1767) and Lazare Carnot (1782), who demonstrated that for maximum efficiency water should enter waterwheels with minimal impact and leave them with minimal velocity. Ultimately, this led to Jean Victor Poncelet's design of an improved undershot wheel with curved blades, which reduced impact and water exit velocity, and to Benoit Fourneyron's development of an efficient water turbine.

The importance of vertical waterwheels as industrial prime movers declined sharply in the mid-19th century as a result of the emergence of the water turbine—a more compact, cheaper, faster, more versatile, and more efficient device—and of the spread of the steam engine—a prime mover without the locational restrictions of the waterwheel. By the early 20th century the vertical waterwheel had become a rarity.

TERRY S. REYNOLDS
Author of "Stronger Than a Hundred Men: A History of the Vertical Waterwheel"

WATFORD, wot'fərd, a municipal borough in southeastern England and the largest town in Hertfordshire. A residential suburb of London, 15 miles (24 km) to the southeast, it is situated in the Colne Valley, between the rivers Colne and Gade. Its early growth as a market town stems from the fact that the Colne is easily forded at this point. Although still a marketing center for the surrounding agricultural region, the town also has printing, brewing, and paper industries.

Watford has two old churches: St. Mary's, noted for its memorial monuments, and St. James', largely restored in the 19th century. Mrs. Elizabeth Fuller's Free School (1704) and the Bedford Almshouses (1580) are also of interest. Watford was incorporated in 1922. Population: (1981) 74,356.

WATIE, wä'tē, **Stand** (1806–1871), Cherokee Indian, who was a Confederate officer in the Civil War. He was born in Rome, Ga., on Dec. 12, 1806, educated at a mission school and in Cornwall, Conn., and afterward edited a Cherokee newspaper. In 1835 he was one of four Cherokees to sign the Treaty of New Echota, by which the Cherokees relinquished their lands east of the Mississippi and moved to Oklahoma. All four signers were sentenced to death by their tribesmen. Watie alone escaped and became a planter in Oklahoma.

After the Cherokees allied with the Confederacy in the Civil War, Watie volunteered for military service. He led a Cherokee regiment in many battles in the Indian Territory. He was made a brigadier general in 1864 and was one of the last Confederate soldiers to surrender. After the war, he returned to planting. Watie died in Honey Creek Indian Territory (now Delaware County, Okla.) on Sept. 9, 1871.

WATKINS GLEN, wot'kinz, a resort village in western New York and the seat of Schuyler county. It is situated at the southern end of Seneca Lake in the Finger Lakes region, about 60 miles (97 km) southwest of Syracuse. Watkins Glen State Park contains a spectacular gorge and many waterfalls. The Watkins Glen Grand Prix, an international sports-car race, is held annually.

Settled in 1791, the village was incorporated as Jefferson in 1842 and became known as Watkins Glen in 1926. Population: 2,440.

WATLING STREET, wot'ling, an 11th century name for one of four Roman roads included in the list of four Royal Roads recorded or invented by Norman lawyers after the Norman Conquest. The others are Icknield Street, Ermine (or Erning) Street, and Fosse (or Foss) Way.

Watling Street extended in a northwesterly direction from London (the Roman Londinium) to Wroxeter (Viroconium), passing through St. Albans (Verulamium), and intersecting Fosse Way at a point southwest of Leicester. The same name has been used to designate many Roman roads or roads that are reputed to be Roman roads that exist in other parts of Britain, such as the road from Dover to London via Canterbury. Watling Street has retained its importance since the Middle Ages, and today forms part of the Great North Road connecting London with Scotland.

The derivation of the name of Watling Street is unknown, but some authorities feel that it may be related to an English personal name. Early charters mention the road originally as Waecling (or Waetlinga) Straet, which may mean "the way of the Waetlingas (an ancient tribe)," or the "sons of Waetla."

WATROUS, wô'trəs, **Harry Willson,** American artist: b. San Francisco, Calif., Sept. 17, 1857; d. New York, N.Y., May 9, 1940. After schooling in New York City, he studied at the Atelier Bonnat and Académie Jullian in Paris. Upon his return, he devoted himself to genre and still-life paintings of a meticulously detailed nature, as well as specializing in faithfully detailed renditions of ecclesiastical statuettes and lustrous ceramics. He was the recipient of many awards and prizes such as the Clark Prize (1894); the $1,000 Altman Prize (1929); the National Arts Club Medal (1931); and the Lippincott Prize (1935). Watrous was secretary of the National Academy of Design from 1898 to 1920, and president in 1933. His works include *Passing of Summer* (Metropolitan Museum, New York City), *A Study in Black,* and *My Mother.*

WATSEKA, wôt-sē'kə, city, Illinois, and Iroquois County seat, on the Iroquois River and Sugar Creek, at an altitude of 634 feet. The city, about 78 miles south of Chicago, is in an agricultural and stock-raising region. Industry consists of plants which manufacture condensers, transformers, electric parts, and business forms. The town was platted as South Middleport in 1860 on the site of a trading post. In 1865 it was renamed for Watch-e-kee (pretty lady), the Potawatomi wife of Gurdon Hubbard, the first white settler of the region. Henry Bacon, the architect, was born in Watseka in 1866. The town was incorporated in 1867, and the form of government is by mayor and council. Pop. 5,543.

GLADYS GORDON

WATSON, Homer Ransford, Canadian painter: b. Doon, Ontario, Canada, 1855; d. there, May 30, 1936. He studied landscape painting in the United States (under George Inness) in 1876 and later in England. For his subjects he chose the pioneer life of Ontario and the rural scenes around his native Doon, where he lived most of his life. He was president of the Royal Canadian Academy from 1918 to 1922. Two of his paintings hang in Windsor Castle, England, and six are in the National Gallery in Ottawa. *The Flood Gate* (1900) is considered his best work. Other paintings include *The Pioneer Mill* (1878); *The Truants* (1900); and *Storm Clouds, Grand River* (1924).

WATSON, James Dewey, American biochemist: b. Chicago, Ill., April 6, 1928. He shared the 1962 Nobel Prize in physiology or medicine with Francis H. C. Crick and Maurice H. F. Wilkins for their discovery of the molecular structure of DNA (deoxyribonucleic acid).

Watson received his Ph.D. in zoology from Indiana University in 1950. In 1951 while doing postgraduate work in Europe, he saw Wilkin's X-ray diffraction studies of DNA and became interested in the molecular structure of DNA. Shortly thereafter he began work on the problem with Francis Crick at Cambridge University.

Biochemical analysis had previously revealed that DNA was composed of alternating phosphate and sugar groups along with nitrogenous bases joined to the sugars. Watson and Crick studied both Wilkin's X-ray diffraction evidence and the stereochemical configurations possible for such a molecule and were finally able in 1953 to construct a molecular model of DNA. This model, now known as the Watson-Crick model of DNA, showed DNA to be a double helix with the bases forming the core and the sugar and phosphate groups on the outside. Watson told the story of his collaboration with Crick in the best-seller *The Double Helix,* published in 1968.

In 1956 Watson joined the staff of Harvard University and in 1968 became director of the Cold Spring Harbor Laboratory of Quantitative Biology in New York.

WATSON, John (pseudonym IAN MACLAREN), Scottish-English clergyman and author: b. Manningtree, Essex, England, Nov. 3, 1850; d. Mount Pleasant, Iowa, May 6, 1907. After graduating from Edinburgh University in 1870 with an M.A., he studied for the ministry at New College, Edinburgh, and, briefly, at Tübingen University, Germany. After serving in various ministerial posts, he was appointed to the Presbyterian Church in the Sefton Park district of Liverpool, England, in 1880. He remained there for 25 years, during which time he won fame as a preacher, built a church, and was one of the founders of Liverpool University.

Watson's second career, that of an author of fiction under the name "Ian Maclaren," began in 1894 when he published a collection of stories and sketches of the Scottish peasantry, entitled *Beside the Bonnie Brier Bush.* The book was a success throughout Great Britain and the United States. It was followed the next year by a similar collection, *The Days of Auld Lang Syne* (1895, new ed., 1929), and by other fiction such as *Kate Carnegie and Those Ministers* (1897), *Afterwards, and Other Stories* (1898), and *Young Barbarians* (1901), a book for boys. Watson also produced a number of theological works under his own name such as *The Mind of the Master* (1896). His fame as an author led to three lecture tours in the United States, during the first of which, in 1896, he delivered the Lyman Beecher lectures at Yale University, published as *The Cure of Souls* in the same year. His appearances were well received, and he returned in 1899. In the course of his third tour in 1907 he became ill and died.

Watson's secular writings have been severely criticized on the grounds of sentimentality, but his works are redeemed by his wit and his lack of pretensions to realism.

See also KAILYARD SCHOOL.

WATSON, John Broadus, American psychologist: b. Greenville, S.C., Jan. 9, 1878; d. New York, N.Y., Sept. 25, 1958. Educated at Furman University (M.A. 1900) and the University of Chicago (Ph.D. 1903), he taught at the latter from 1903 to 1908. During 1908–1920 he was professor of experimental and comparative psychology and director of the psychological laboratory at Johns Hopkins University. In 1920 he entered the advertising field, becoming a vice president of the J. Walter Thompson Company, New York City, in 1924. He was vice president of William Esty & Company from 1936 until 1946.

The school of objective psychology, called behaviorism, was originated by Watson at Johns Hopkins with the publication of his paper "Psychology as the Behaviorist Views It" (1913). In it, he argued against the old school of introspection and mentalist concepts and proposed an objective, functional, and experimental method of psychology which would study the relationships between environmental events (stimuli) and behavior (response). Watson rejected the significance of motive and concentrated on conditioned responses. The leading psychologists of the day regarded Watson's thesis as a rejection of classical principles, and there was much controversy in psychological circles as a result.

Watson next published a comparative psychology, *Behavior* (1914). His activities were then interrupted by World War I, during which he served as a major in the aviation section of the Signal Corps. Afterward he wrote *Psychology from the Standpoint of a Behaviorist* (1919), which served to present his definition of psychology and his method. At this time he was also conducting experiments in conditioning on animals and infants. After Watson turned to the advertising field, he maintained his interest and writing in psychology.

Behaviorism, as Watson conceived it, was dominant in the psychology of the United States in the 1920's. By the late 1940's its influence had declined, but it left a decided impact on psychological principles as a whole. Watson's other books include *Animal Education* (1903); *Behaviorism* (1925; rev. eds., 1930, 1958); *Ways of Behaviorism* (1928); and *Psychological Care of the Infant and Child*, with Rosalie A. Watson, his second wife (1928).

See also Behavior and Behaviorism.

WATSON, John Christian, Australian political leader: b. Valparaiso, Chile, April 9, 1867; d. Sydney, Australia, Nov. 18, 1941. Educated in New Zealand, Watson was apprenticed to a printer and in 1880 made his way to Sydney, where he worked as a compositor. In 1893 he was elected president of Sydney's Trades and Labour Council, and in 1894 he became head of the Australian Labour Federation and presided at a conference of union representatives from New South Wales which approved the principle that Labour Party candidates for Parliament must pledge themselves not to vote against majority decisions taken in caucus. He also entered the state's Legislative Assembly in 1894 and remained until elected to the House of Representatives in the first Federal Parliament in 1901, when he was chosen as party leader. At an election late in 1903, Labour gained several seats in Parliament, and in April 1904 Watson formed the first federal Labour cabinet. After four months his administration fell, but until he resigned leadership of his party in 1907, Watson continued to influence the government of Alfred Deakin (q.v.), while his sincerity, courtesy, and moderate views strengthened public support for the Labour Party.

R. M. Younger.

WATSON, Richard, English clergyman and chemist: b. Heversham, Westmorland, England, August 1737; d. Calgarth Park, Westmorland, July 4, 1816. Educated at Trinity College, Cambridge, he was elected professor of chemistry in 1764. His experiments with salt solutions won him election to the Royal Society in 1769, and in 1772 he discovered the principle of the black-bulb thermometer. His second, and greater, interest—theology—began in 1771 when he obtained the regius chair of divinity at Cambridge, although he continued to write on chemistry for many years. He became archdeacon of Ely in 1779 and was consecrated bishop of Llandaff in 1782. Of his many theological writings, two are noteworthy: a defense of Christianity against Edward Gibbon (1776), and a defense of the Bible against Thomas Paine (1796), both of which gained wide circulation and endorsement, the latter in the United States as well.

WATSON, Sereno, American botanist: b. East Windsor Hill, Conn., Dec. 1, 1826; d. Cambridge, Mass., March 9, 1892. After completing his education at Yale University in 1847, he tried his hand in various fields with indifferent results. In 1867 he went to California and later that year, after an arduous journey, joined the exploration party of Clarence King (q.v.), then beginning a government geological survey of the Cordilleran ranges of Colorado. When the party's botanist left, Watson was assigned to collect plant data. His thoroughly catalogued collections involved many group revisions and served to establish his reputation in the field. His work was published as *Botany* (also called "Botany of the King Expedition"), in 1871, and was the fifth volume in the survey's famous *Report of the Geological Exploration of the Fortieth Parallel* (7 vols., 1870–80).

In 1873, Watson became assistant in the Gray Herbarium at Harvard. The next year he was named curator, a post he held until his death. Here he undertook his major work, *Botany of California* (2 vols., 1876–80), which listed the first flora of that region, and was used as the basis for subsequent classifications. Asa Gray and William Henry Brewer aided in the first volume. Watson's other work includes the *Bibliographical Index to North American Botany* (1878), and the 1889 revision, with John Merle Coulter, of Gray's *Manual of Botany*.

WATSON, Thomas, English poet and literary scholar: b. ?London, England, c. 1557; d. there, Sept. 26, 1592. He presumedly attended Oxford University for a time and later studied law in London, but his main interests were literary. His first published work was a Latin translation of Sophocles' *Antigone* (1581), and in 1585 he wrote a paraphrased version of Tasso's pastoral *Aminta*. *Meliboeus* (1590), a Latin elegy on the death of his patron, Sir Francis Walsingham, which he also translated into English, and *Amintae Gaudia* (published posthumously in 1592), an original Latin pastoral, are two other out-but removes very little of the other constituents of the wastewater.

Secondary Treatment. Secondary treatment involves the addition of a biological treatment phase following plain sedimentation. In the United States, about 58% of the sewered population is served by some form of secondary wastewater treatment. At best, this treatment removes about 85% to 95% of the organic matter in wastewater. It has little effect on dissolved materials or on the nutrients that stimulate the growth of algae in the receiving waters. Thus, efficient secondary treatment for a community of one million persons still permits the discharge of untreated wastewater equivalent to that of a community of 100,000 persons. It also discharges all the community's nutrients and dissolved solids, as well as any contaminants that may be added to the water by industrial plants that are located in the community.

There are two basic methods used in modern secondary treatment: the trickling filter and the activated-sludge process. In small communities, secondary treatment is usually accomplished by the trickling-filter method, which evolved from two earlier methods: the sand filter and the contact bed. In larger communities it is generally accomplished by the activated-sludge process.

Sand Filter. Early sand filters were beds of fine sand, usually 3 feet (1 meter) deep, through which the wastewater slowly seeped. As it seeped through the sand, the organic matter was decomposed and stabilized by the microorganisms in the wastewater. Sand filters required about 4 acres (1.6 hectares) of sand beds for each thousand people. Because of this large space requirements, sand beds are seldom used.

Contact Bed. The contact bed, consisting of many layers of stone, slate, or other inert material, provided a relatively large surface area for the growth of microorganisms. It operated on a fill-and-draw basis, and the organic matter delivered during the fill period was decomposed by the microorganisms on the bed. The oxygen required by the microorganisms was provided during the resting period, when the bed was exposed to the air.

Trickling Filter. The trickling filter came into use in the early 1900's. In the modern version of this system, the wastewater is applied to the filter through rotary distributors and it is allowed to trickle down over large stone or plastic beds that are covered with microorganisms. The beds are not submerged, thus air can reach the organisms at all times. The area requirements for trickling filters are about 5 to 50 acres (2–20 hectares) per million people.

Activated-Sludge Process. In the second decade of the 20th century a more efficient method of biological treatment was developed, the activated-sludge process. In this process, heavy concentrations of aerobic microorganisms, called biological floc or activated sludge, are suspended in the liquid by agitation that is provided by air bubbled into the tank or by mechanical aerators. Final sedimentation tanks are needed to separate the floc material from the flowing liquid. Most of the biologically active sludge is then returned to the aeration tank to treat the incoming water. The high concentration of active microorganisms that can be maintained in the aeration tank permits the size of the treatment plant to be relatively small, about 1 to 5 acres (0.4–2 hectares) per million population.

Tertiary Treatment. Tertiary treatment is designed for use in areas where the degree of treatment must be more than 85% to 95% or where the wastewater, after treatment, is reused. It is primarily intended to further clean, or polish, secondary treatment plant effluents by removing additional suspended material and lowering the BOD, generally by filtration. This polishing, however, has little impact on the dissolved solids, including the nutrients, synthetic organic chemicals, and heavy metals. To eliminate these constituents of wastewater, other methods of treatment have been devised. These processes include coagulation and sedimentation, precipitation, adsorption on activated carbon or other adsorbants, foam separation, electrodialysis, reverse osmosis, ion exchange, and distillation.

Handling Sludge. The accumulated solid materials, or sludge, from wastewater treatment processes amount to 50 to 70 pounds (22–31 kg) per person per year in the dry state or about one ton (0.9 metric ton) per year in the wet state. A city of one million produces about 35,000 tons (31,500 metric tons) of dry sludge per year.

Sludge is highly capable of becoming putrid and can itself be a major pollutant if it is not biologically stabilized and disposed of in a suitable manner. Biological stabilization may be accomplished by aerobic or anaerobic digestion. In aerobic digestion, the solids are decomposed over long periods of time in the presence of aerobic microorganisms. In anaerobic digestion, which is much more common, the solids are placed in an airless tank containing anaerobic organisms. Methane, carbon dioxide, and water are produced as a result of anaerobic digestion. The methane is often recovered for fuel to heat the tank (and thus increase the rate of anaerobic digestion) or to produce power. Where the gas is used to drive engines for power, the cooling water of the engine is used for heating the tank, increasing the efficiency of the process. Digestion of sludge, whether anaerobic or aerobic, reduces the volume of sludge and renders it nonputrescible.

Digested sludge, whether in its wet form or after being dried on open beds, is a useful soil builder but has little value as a fertilizer. Wet digested sludge is often used for the reclamation of arid and barren soils in parks, along highways, and similar public places. However, caution must be exercised when these sludges are used for edible crops because disease-causing organisms may survive the processing. Only heat-drying at high temperatures assures that the sludges are free of these organisms.

In modern wastewater treatment plants, mechanical dewatering of sludge by vacuum filters, centrifuges, or other devices is becoming widespread. The dewatered sludge may then be heat-dried if it is to be reclaimed or it may be incinerated. In large communities where large amounts of sludge are produced, mechanical dewatering and incineration are commonly practiced.

The reclamation of sludges for their organic value was actively pursued at one time. A treatment plant built in Milwaukee, Wis., in the 1920's markets heat-dried sludge, sold under the name Milorganite, as fertilizer. With the development of inexpensive, easily applied chemical fertilizers, the market for sludge dwindled, and no new treatment plant can expect to sell all of its sludge.

WASTEWATER RECLAMATION

The unintentional reuse of wastewaters occurs often because wastewaters are generally discharged into streams and lakes that are used as sources of water supply. In the United States, about 40% of the population is served by waters containing municipal or industrial discharges. Sometimes wastewaters are intentionally used for replenishing groundwaters, for industrial processes or cooling, for the creation of recreational lakes and other facilities, or for irrigation. Direct reuse of wastewaters for drinking purposes is not practiced. In areas where the water supply for drinking purposes is limited, wastewaters may be reclaimed for secondary uses, such as lawn and park irrigation, industrial processes, toilet flushing, clothes washing, and fire fighting.

By far the greatest potential for wastewater reclamation is for irrigation, particularly in arid regions. For irrigation, quality requirements are minimal, and wastewaters may be used after primary or secondary treatment, though not to irrigate crops that are to be eaten raw. Irrigation with wastewaters is thus appropriate for such crops as cereals, hay, trees, and cotton. Well treated wastewater effluents from a community of about 1,000 persons can irrigate 10 to 25 acres (4–10 hectares) of land.

Wastewater treatment plant effluents are extremely useful for industry, particularly as cooling water. The required quality of the wastewater depends on the industry and the use. Industrial plants often install their own treatment facilities to improve and regulate the quality and quantity of the wastewater they use.

Recreational usage of wastewater effluents is common in arid regions. Wastewater effluents have been used for many man-made lakes, including those in Golden Gate Park in San Francisco, Calif., and the lakes for swimming, boating, and fishing in Santee, Calif. Where the lakes and ponds are to be used for bathing or water sports, the wastewater has to be disinfected.

The use of wastewater treatment plant effluents for groundwater recharge is increasingly popular as an ultimate method of disposal and for the conservation of water resources. However, the quality requirements for recharge are exceedingly high, and some form of tertiary treatment may be required. The recharge of groundwaters may be accomplished by spreading the wastewaters in large basins where they may percolate into the ground. In areas where the aquifer (the water-bearing bed) is well below the surface of the ground, the wastewaters may be injected into deep wells. In places where recharge is important in protecting or developing groundwater resources, the capture of storm water for recharge is becoming increasingly popular.

DANIEL A. OKUN
University of North Carolina, Chapel Hill

Bibliography

Curds, C. R., and Hawkes, H. A., eds., *Ecological Aspects of Used Water Treatment* (Academic Press 1975).
Escritt, L. B., *Sewage and Sewage Treatment: International Practice* (Wiley 1984).
Hammer, Mark J., *Water and Waste-Water Technology,* 2d ed. (Wiley 1986).
Korbitz, W. E., *Modern Management of Wastewater Utilities* (Garland 1981).
National Association of Home Builders, *Alternatives to Public Sewers* (1978).
Okun, D. A., and Ponghis, G., *Community Wastewater Collection and Disposal* (World Health Org. 1975).

WATCH, a portable timepiece, usually a cased mechanism small enough to be worn or carried.

The watch developed into its modern form by slow stages from the late medieval tower clock after the invention of the mainspring, which replaced weights as a source of power. Peter Henlein of Nuremberg was long credited with being the first to apply this critical invention to a portable timepiece, but his priority was never clear and is disputed. At any rate, it is known that spring-drive movements were in use by the early 15th century, and that clock-watches containing a mainspring began to appear shortly after 1500 all over Europe. These first portable timepieces were drum-shaped, about 6 inches (15 cm) high, made entirely of iron, and often suspended from the neck or waist by a hoop soldered to the case. They had only one hand and were highly inaccurate. Through the centuries further refinements resulted in smaller and smaller timepieces capable of ever-greater accuracy. A true pocket watch appeared by the mid-17th century, and in England watches were customarily worn in a pocket after 1675, when Charles II made the long waistcoat fashionable. Wristwatches are products of the 20th century.

Components. The components of a mechanical watch include (1) a source of power; (2) a train of wheels (the power train) to transmit the power to an escapement, which intermittently releases the power; (3) a balance mechanism to regulate the flow of power from the escapement; and (4) another train of wheels (the dial train), which turns the dial hands to indicate the passage of time. Electric watches, an innovation of the 1950's, differ from this scheme only in that the balance wheel provides the motive force for the gear train. Integrated circuitry has resulted in the production of watches containing no moving parts.

MECHANICAL WATCHES

In the mechanical watch, power is transmitted from the mainspring through the escape pinion by a wheel train consisting of four pairs of gears. The step-up ratio, approximately 4,000:1, produces 18,000 half cycles of vibration per hour in the balance (5 per second). In more expensive chronographs the balance vibrates more rapidly to permit the recording of tenths or hundredths of a second.

The rate of going (timekeeping) of the mechanism is controlled by a hairspring, attached to the balance wheel. The balance serves the same function in a watch as a pendulum in a clock. The spring acts in the place of gravity to provide the restoring torque that keeps the rate of going regulated. A hairspring was first devised by Robert Hooke about 1660, and an improved spiral balance spring was introduced by Christiaan Huygens in 1675.

The escapement was originally the same verge or vertical type as that in use for clocks. Such an escapement limited the portability of watches and made them so inaccurate that many early ones had a small sundial built in for convenience in making the necessary daily correction. By the end of the 17th century better types of escapement began to appear for use in clocks, and watchmakers experimented with all of them. The lever escapement was developed into its modern form by the French watchmaker Abraham Louis Breguet by the beginning of the 19th century, and finally became universally adopted

(*Left*) A 16th century German watch that can be used for either 12-hour or 24-hour time.

THE METROPOLITAN MUSEUM OF ART, GIFT OF PIERPONT MORGAN, 1917.

A 17th century quarter-hour-repeating watch by the British maker Thomas Tompion. The gold-cased timepiece was carried in a gold and leather outer case.

PHOTOGRAPH BY STEPHEN PITKIN, THE TIME MUSEUM, ROCKFORD, ILL.

An 18th century chronometer by the British maker John Harrison.

NATIONAL MARITIME MUSEUM, GREENWICH, ENGLAND

about 1915 when automatic machinery made it easier to construct.

A major problem with early portable timepieces was the variation in output of the mainspring: the watch ran faster when fully wound and more slowly as it wound down. The first attempt to remedy this was with the stackfreed, a crude auxiliary spring that acted against the pull of the mainspring when fully wound, and exerted relatively less restraint as the mainspring wound down. The stackfreed was superseded by the fusee in the mid-16th century. Jacob Zech, who invented the fusee in 1525, utilized a conical, grooved cylinder as a reel for a length of catgut attached to the mainspring barrel. The catgut, which in versions after 1600 began to be replaced by a chain, gave the timepiece increasing leverage by unwinding toward the larger end of the spindle as the watch ran down. Modern watches avoid the problem by housing the mainspring inside the going barrel. This makes it possible to reduce torque variations to a minimum by carefully proportioning the barrel arbor and barrel diameter to mainspring thickness. In some watches stopwork is used to eliminate the serious variation in torque that occurs when the spring is fully wound.

By the mid-16th century timepieces had become considerably smaller, and men and women of fashion began a fad of wearing pendant watches. To meet the growing demand, watchmakers responded with small watches of all shapes with intricate cases, often of gold or rock crystal, decorated lavishly with precious stones. From about 1590 to 1630, the oval shape predominated, in part because that shape made it easier to house the fusee. In the next century the principal innovations involved techniques for making the watch flatter while also increasing its accuracy. From about 1575, brass began to be used more than iron in the mechanism. By 1625, steel was being used for more delicate pieces.

Toward the end of the 17th century the epicycloidal curve began to be applied to cutting gears to replace the trial-and-error hand filing that had been common earlier, and Huygens' improved spiral balance spring was in common use. With increasing accuracy and the adaptation of smaller trains of gear wheels to watches, it became practical to add a minute hand. By 1700 the best watches had a daily error of five to ten minutes, and most watches employed both an hour and a minute hand. The use of pierced jewels, for which an English patent was issued in 1704, made it possible to increase the accuracy still further by decreasing the friction on the pivots.

Early Manufacturing. Primarily because of the existing clockmaking and toolmaking capacity, Nuremberg became the first center of watchmaking and Germany remained in the lead throughout the 16th century. England, France, and, by the late 16th century, Switzerland, accounted for most of the other watchmaking activity. A

PHOTOGRAPHS BY STEPHEN PITKIN, THE TIME MUSEUM, ROCKFORD, ILL.

(*Above*) Front and back dials of a watch by Patek Phillipe & Co. (Swiss, 1932). (*Right*) A self-winding, minute-repeating watch by A. L. Breguet (French, about 1812). It sounds the hour and minute at the press of a button. Dial sectors show the state of winding and the temperature.

watchmakers' guild, founded in Geneva in 1589, helped to make that city an important center. The guild established a formal apprenticeship program, rigidly limited entry into the trade, and established standards of quality that became the model throughout Europe. The Geneva monopoly was so effective that no other Swiss city became an important watchmaking center until nearly a century later, when a Neuchâtel locksmith, Daniel Jean Richard, independently designed a machine for milling watch wheels and organized a guild in his district to compete with Geneva.

Developments in 18th century watchmaking were aimed at further refinements in accuracy, primarily to serve navigational needs. Thus it was only natural that leadership should move during this period to the principal sea power, Britain. A reward of 20,000 pounds (equivalent to about $2 million in today's money) announced by the British government in 1714 for any method of determining a ship's longitude to a certain degree of accuracy was finally claimed by John Harrison in 1765. His timekeeper was accurate to three seconds a day over the required six-week period, making it possible to compute longitude within 34 miles (55 km). The invention of the spring detent escapement 10 years later by John Arnold and Thomas Earnshaw, Englishmen working independently of each other, allowed the marine chronometer to achieve the greatest accuracy possible under handcrafting methods. British superiority was sustained during the 18th century by a number of technical innovations including its monopoly on pierced jewels. This was maintained until the 1770's, when Swiss and French watchmakers learned the secret of making them.

By 1840, Switzerland had surpassed Britain, primarily by virtue of superior organization, the early adoption of mechanization and assembly-line production, and generally innovative manufacturing practices. The Swiss were the first to profit from the economies that could be realized from even an imperfect application of the principle of interchangeable parts. By the late 18th century, factories were turning out rough movements, or *ébauches*, consisting of plates, bridges, wheels, and barrels, and these were being supplied in huge quantities to finishers who applied the jewels, mainspring, escapement, hands, and dial.

The availability of uniform ébauches at very small cost permitted savings at all later stages of manufacture, and it led to the greatest quantity of production achievable in the absence of automatic machinery. Because the same ébauche could be used to make watches of greatly varying quality, the Swiss became known as the makers of both the best and the worst of watches. Mass production of ébauches actually was begun across the French border by Frédéric Japy of Beaucourt, using Swiss equipment in 1776. Within a few years power-operated machinery was in use, and similar factories were opened in Switzerland to meet the seemingly inexhaustible demand.

Manufacturing in the United States. The first watch factory in the United States was established in 1809 in Shrewsbury, Mass., by Luther Goddard. Over the next few years, Goddard produced about 500 watches by manufacturing the wheels, plates, and other brass parts, while importing the other parts from England. Like other industries of the time, Goddard's apparently fell victim first to the Jefferson embargo, which prevented the import of needed parts, and then to the flood of cheaper British imports at the end of the War of 1812.

The second American watch factory, established in 1838 in Hartford, Conn., by James and Henry Pitkin, became the first to attempt to manufacture by machine. Even though the Pitkin brothers invented and made their own watchmaking equipment, they were still not able to compete with the cheaper imports produced by the British and the Swiss systems, and were forced out of business within four years.

Full machine manufacture on the principle of interchangeable parts was not achieved until 1850, when the American Horologe Company (later to become the Waltham Watch Company) went into operation. The problem with earlier efforts had been that machine-tool makers had not been able to meet the extremely close tolerances required for watchmaking and in every case had ended by depending too much on hand labor. Thus, European manufacturers, with both cheaper labor and superior organization, had the edge. The Waltham factory was finally able to overcome this edge by using such steam-powered equipment as a stamping machine that formed the entire watch plate in one action and a set of dies and punches with which all the holes could be made simultaneously.

Although American factories produced some very fine watches, including the highly accurate railroad models, the American forte, in watches

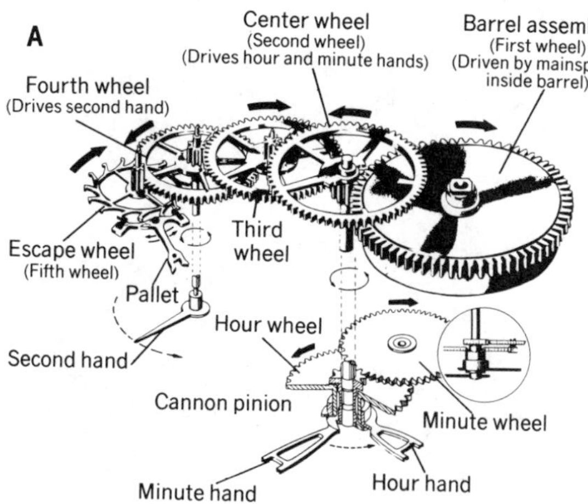

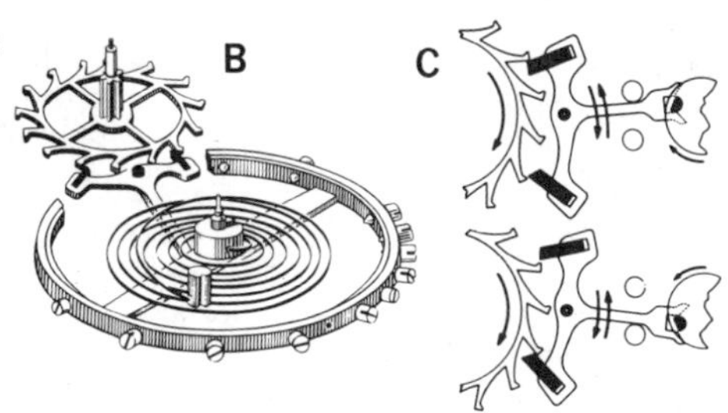

STEM-WIND WATCH

The mechanism of a stem-wind watch includes a mainspring to drive a train of geared wheels; an escapement to arrest and release the power flow; and a balance assembly to control the rate of power flow. In the Hamilton watch wheel train (A) shown here, rotation rates of the wheels increase from once in 8 hours for the barrel assembly to once in 6 seconds for the escape wheel. Control is supplied by the balance wheel and hairspring (B, foreground), operating on the principle of isochronism. The balance wheel, swinging back and forth 300 times a minute, controls the rotation of the escape wheel — and hence that of all the other wheels in the train — by means of the rocking escape lever and its pallet jewels (C), which permit only 1 of the 15 teeth on the escape wheel to move by at a time. As a tooth moves by one pallet jewel, the other pallet jewel locks another tooth, halting the wheel. When the balance wheel swings back, it releases the escape lever to permit another tooth to move by. Meanwhile, movement of the escape wheel transmits enough energy to the balance wheel to keep it in motion.

as in most other manufactured goods, was in using the automatic machinery in quantity production for the masses. The Waterbury Watch Company pioneered with the cheap watch in 1878, at first selling for four dollars and dropping to three very soon. In 1892 a mail-order merchant, Robert H. Ingersoll, contracted with the Waterbury company to supply him these watches, which he sold under his own name as the famous Ingersoll "Dollar Watch." In 1908 the Ingersoll company began manufacture of these watches on its own and kept the price at one dollar until it went out of business in the 1920's. Following in the same tradition, U.S. Time, beginning in 1949, produced its Timex watch by pushing mass production and machine manufacturing techniques to the limit. In 1960 this company was producing annually 8 million watches for shipment all over the world.

ELECTRIC AND ELECTRONIC WATCHES

Electricity was first used as the motive force in clocks as early as 1840, and by 1929 the quartz crystal was being used to produce a clock accurate to a hundredth of a second a day. Application of both electricity and quartz vibrations to watches became possible with the development of miniature high-energy batteries. Experiments were made by a number of companies in the 1950's, and the first marketable electric watch was produced in 1957 by the Hamilton Watch Company (U.S.).

In the electronic watch the balance wheel is replaced by a tuning fork, which vibrates several hundred times a second and is a great deal more accurate than the balance spring. Vibrations are maintained by a battery-driven transistorized oscillating circuit interacting with two permanent magnets attached to the ends of the tuning fork. Called the Accutron, the tuning fork wristwatch was invented by Max Hetzel and was first marketed by the Bulova Company. From the beginning it was guaranteed to maintain accuracy to within two seconds a day throughout its life.

The next step in the long search for a better oscillator was the quartz-crystal, which relies on integrated circuitry to electronically count the vibrations of the crystal resonators. Integrated circuitry also makes it possible to combine many functions in the same watch with little increase in cost, and to provide digital read-outs from luminous elements controlled by electrical signals. Digital models contain no moving parts and can be accurate to less than one minute per year.

The first marketable quartz-crystal watches were introduced in 1969 by Seiko in Japan and Hamilton in the United States. Seiko, which already had become the world's largest manufacturer of high-precision jeweled watches in the mid-1960's, quickly moved into leadership in the use of integrated circuits. The Swiss continued to concentrate on mechanical watches utilizing a tuning-fork balance or analog models (with hands) employing the quartz-crystal. Heavy investment in equipment that turns out mechanical components made the Swiss firms and the one surviving U.S. manufacturer, Timex, slow to adopt the movement-free digital designs, and the result was that leadership passed permanently to Japan and Hong Kong. Switzerland went from 80% of the world's production in the late 1940's to 22% in 1980, the year that Japan moved into production leadership. See also CLOCK.

GEORGE H. DANIELS
University of South Alabama

Further Reading: Clutton, C., and Daniels, G., *Watches* (Sotheby Pub. 1979); Kahlert, H., and others, *Wristwatches* (Schiffer 1986); Landes, D. S., *Revolution in Time* (Harvard Univ. Press 1983).

WATCHUNG MOUNTAINS, wä′chung, a range of hills in New Jersey, beginning at a point southwest of Paterson and curving to the southwest for about 40 miles (64 km) before terminating in the area north of Somerville. The hills consist of two ridges at an elevation of 400 to 500 feet (122–152 meters), lying largely in Somerset and Essex counties. The ridges are referred to as the First Watchung and the Second Watchung Mountains. Of volcanic origin, the hills are composed of traprock (once a lava flow) covered by shale and sandstone, except where erosion has revealed the original igneous rock.

WATER, the most abundant of all chemical compounds. Water is both an essential ingredient of all living organisms and a major component of the environment in which they live. It occurs naturally in three states: solid (ice or snow), liquid (water), and gas (water vapor or steam). Water and ice cover about 75% of the earth's surface, and water vapor is an important constituent of the atmosphere.

1. Physical and Chemical Properties

Water is an excellent solvent, a catalyst for many chemical reactions, a good storehouse for both heat and cold, and a poor electrical conductor when pure. The unique properties of water are based on its unusual structure in the liquid and solid states and on the polarity of its molecule.

Structure of Water—*The Water Molecule.* The water molecule consists of two hydrogen atoms and one oxygen atom (H_2O). Its angular structure is shown in Fig. 1. The hydrogen atoms are about 1 angstrom unit (1 Å = 10^{-8} cm) away from the oxygen atom, bound to it by covalent bonds.

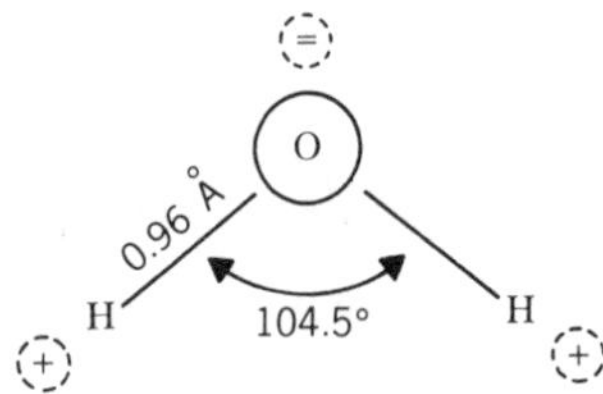

Fig. 1. Structure of the water molecule.

Each covalent bond is due to the mutual sharing of a pair of electrons between each hydrogen and the oxygen. However, the sharing is unequal, because an oxygen atom is considerably more electronegative than a hydrogen atom. Thus the oxygen atom is able to pull both electron pairs much closer to it. As a result, the oxygen has a partial double negative charge, indicated in the figure by (=), and each hydrogen has a partial positive charge, (+).

Although the water molecule as a whole is electrically neutral, it is highly polar: that is, it has a negatively charged pole (at the oxygen atom) and a positively charged pole (centered between the hydrogens). The polarity results from the bent shape of the molecule and the distribution of electrical charges within it.

Solid State: The Structure of Ice. There are eight known forms of solid water, or ice, each with a distinctive crystal structure. These forms are identified by the Roman numerals I through VIII. The oxygen atoms in ordinary ice are arranged in a tetrahedral pattern (see Fig. 2). As the diagram shows, each oxygen atom is attached by hydrogen bonds to four surrounding oxygen atoms from four other molecules. All of the oxygen atoms are about 2.8 Å apart. See also ICE.

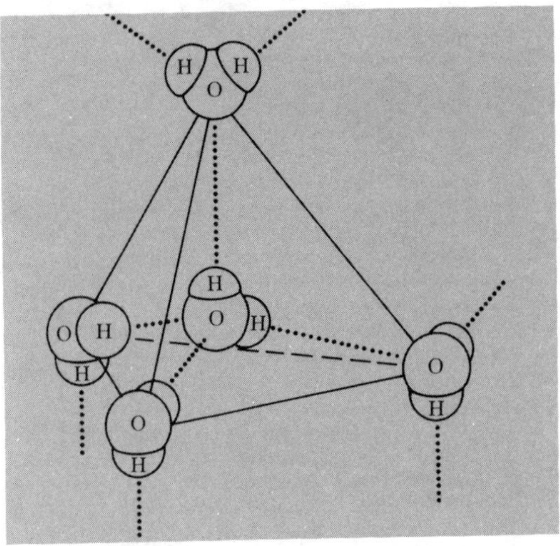

Fig. 2. Tetrahedral arrangement of oxygen atoms in ice I.

Gas State. The water molecules in the gas state—water vapor or steam—are so far apart that very little association occurs between them. Hence, gaseous water consists mostly of monomers—single independent H_2O molecules. A few of the molecules are dimers, $(H_2O)_2$—two H_2O molecules joined together—and even fewer are trimers, $(H_2O)_3$.

Liquid State. Over short distances, liquid water has an order that is similar to the overall order in the lattice of ice. Over greater distances, however, the ordering disappears, as in the gas phase. Liquid water consists of clusters or aggregates of H_2O molecules—$(H_2O)_n$, where n represents the number of associated water molecules—perhaps about 40.

Phase Diagram. The phase diagram of water represents the various pressure and temperature conditions in which all the phases of water can exist (see Fig. 3). From the phase diagram it can be seen that ice I, the ordinary form of ice, exists at low temperatures and moderate pressures. Water vapor exists at low pressures and high temperatures. Liquid water occurs at pressures and temperatures intermediate between those for ice I and gaseous water. The other forms of ice, ice II and higher, can exist only at pressures in excess of 2000 atmospheres (atm).

Point B is the normal boiling point of water, which is measured at a temperature of 100°C at 1 atm of pressure. Point M is the normal melting point (or freezing point) of ice I and occurs at 0.000°C at 1 atm.

Fig. 3. Phase diagram for water.

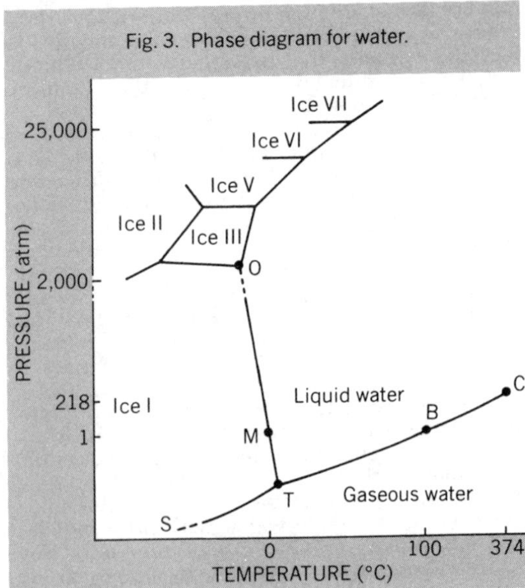

The critical point of water, Point C—the highest temperature at which gaseous water may be liquefied no matter how high the applied pressure—is 374.1°C at 218.2 atm. Above this temperature, water vapor cannot be liquefied under any pressure.

Point T is the triple point at which three phases—ice I, liquid, and gas—are all present in equilibrium with each other, at an assigned temperature of 0.01°C occurring at a pressure of about 0.006 atm. Other triple points also exist on this phase diagram. For example, at point 0, ice I, ice III, and liquid water all coexist in equilibrium at −22.0°C and 2045 atm.

Curve TC, the boiling point curve, shows that as the external pressure decreases, the boiling point also decreases. For example, when the atmospheric pressure is 0.5 atm, water boils at 81.7°C (179°F).

The melting point of ordinary ice lies along the curve TO. The negative slope of this curve—enlarged for clarity—shows that the melting point of ordinary ice decreases with increasing pressure. This is very unusual behavior for a solid. However, the melting point of ordinary ice is not very sensitive to pressure changes. An increase in pressure of about 100 atm will decrease the melting point of ice I by only 1°C.

The sublimation curve, TS, represents the temperature and pressure conditions under which ordinary ice can change directly to water vapor (sublimation) and the vapor can change directly to ice, bypassing the liquid state.

Physical Properties. Many anomalous physical properties of ordinary ice and liquid water can be explained by the high degree of hydrogen bonding in water. Properties associated with separation of the water molecules, such as viscosity, surface tension, boiling point, melting point, and heats of boiling and melting, have anomalously high values.

The density of ordinary ice is less than that of liquid water—an extremely unusual property. This anomaly is due to the open structure of ordinary ice brought about by the hydrogen-bonding network. As ice melts, about 15% of the hydrogen bonds break, causing the water molecules to become more closely packed and thus increasing the density. The density increases to a maximum value (0.999975 g/cm^3) at 3.98°C. Above that point the density decreases as the temperature increases—the usual behavior. The lower density of ordinary ice explains why it floats on water. The other forms of ice—ice II through ice VIII—are all denser than the liquid.

Thermal Properties. The modern definition of the calorie (cal) is based on the Joule (J), a unit of energy: accordingly, 1 cal = 4.184 J (exactly). This value agrees closely with the previous definition of the calorie as the quantity of heat required to raise one gram of water from 14.5° to 15.5°C at one atm. Hence, the specific heat capacity of water is 1.0 cal/g°C.

When water undergoes a phase change, such as from ice to liquid or liquid to ice, heat is either absorbed or given off. The heat of fusion (or melting) of water at 0°C is 80 cal/g. Thus, 80 cal of heat is needed to melt 1 gram of ice. Conversely, when 1 gram of liquid water freezes at 0°C, 80 cal are released. The heat of vaporization (or condensation) of water at 100°C is 540 cal/g. Hence, 540 cal are needed to convert 1 gram of liquid water to steam, and 540 cal are released when 1 gram of steam condenses at 100°C. The heat of condensation is put to use in domestic and industrial steam heating systems.

Water as a Solvent. Water is an excellent electrolytic solvent: it can easily dissolve many substances whose molecules contain ionic bonds. This property is due to the high dielectric constant of water, 78.3 (at 25°C) relative to 1 for a vacuum. Because of its high dielectric constant, water can reduce the attractive forces between the cations and the anions of salt that is dissolved in it by a factor of about 80.

Electrical Properties. Pure water is a very poor conductor of electricity, because the concentration of the ions resulting from the autoionization of water—hydronium and hydroxide—is extremely small. However, water molecules can take into solution and dissociate into ions ionic (or electrolytic) and other solutes. This can greatly increase the concentration of ions, with a corresponding increase in the conductivity of the solution.

Heavy Water. Heavy water, or deuterium oxide (D_2O), is water whose molecules contain deuterium, a heavier isotope of hydrogen, instead of hydrogen.

Chemical Properties—*Dissociation.* Water may dissociate to hydrogen and oxygen gases by the reaction

$$2H_2O \rightleftarrows 2H_2 + O_2.$$

However, water is thermally stable; it is only about 2% dissociated at 2000°C.

Autoionization. Water can ionize itself to a very small extent by the reaction

$$2H_2O \rightleftarrows H_3O^+ + OH^-.$$

In pure water the amounts of hydronium ions (H_3O^+)—a hydrated hydrogen ion (H^+) or proton—and hydroxide ions (OH^-) are equal. Hence, pure water is neither acidic (having an excess of H_3O^+) nor basic (an excess of OH^-). At 25°C, there are only one H_3O^+ ion and one OH^- ion for every 140 million H_2O molecules.

Acid-Base Reactions. Water is an amphoteric species, in that it can act as either an acid, a proton donor, or as a base, a proton acceptor. When hydrogen chloride gas is dissolved in water, water acts as a base:

$$HCl(g) + \underset{\text{(base)}}{H_2O(l)} \rightarrow H_3O^+ + Cl^-.$$

When ammonia gas is dissolved in water, it acts as an acid:

$$NH_3(g) + \underset{\text{(acid)}}{H_2O(l)} \rightleftarrows OH^- + NH_4^+.$$

Oxidation-Reduction Reactions. Water can act either as an oxidizing agent or as a reducing agent. For example, water can oxidize carbon to carbon monoxide, liberating hydrogen gas:

$$C + \underset{\text{(oxidant)}}{H_2O} \rightarrow CO + H_2.$$

It may also reduce chlorine gas to hydrogen chloride, releasing oxygen gas:

$$2Cl_2 + \underset{\text{(reductant)}}{2H_2O} \rightarrow 4HCl + O_2.$$

ZVI C. KORNBLUM, *The Cooper Union*

Further Reading: Deming, H. G., *Water: The Fountain of Opportunity* (Oxford 1975); Hawkins, David T., *Physical and Chemical Properties of Water* (Plenum Pub. 1976); Leopold, Luna B., *Water: A Primer* (W. H. Freeman 1974); Petrucci, R. H., *General Chemistry*, 4th ed. (Macmillan 1985).

2. Water Resources of the World

The total volume of the world's water resources, including both fresh water and salt water, is tremendous: more than 350 quintillion (350×10^{18}) gallons. (See Table 1.) This is about 330 million cubic miles, or 1.4 billion cubic kilometers (cu km). (See Table 1.) About 97% of this total is the salt water of the oceans and seas. Of the remaining 3% that is fresh, nearly 70% is in relatively inaccessible ice caps, glaciers, and permanent snow cover, mostly in Antarctica. The next-largest store of fresh water is groundwater, estimated at 2.8 quintillion gallons (2,526 cubic miles, or 10.5 million cu km). The fresh water in rivers and streams at any time is comparatively small: 560 trillion (560×10^{12}) gallons (500 cubic miles, or 2,100 cu km). Yet rivers and streams are the most common sources of large freshwater supplies for people, agriculture, and industry.

Global Circulation. Much of the world's water is in constant circulation. Its general pattern of movement is known as the hydrologic cycle, or water cycle. A simplified form of this cycle for a typical year is shown in Fig. 1. The figure shows, for example, that each year about 118 quadrillion (118×10^{15}) gallons (107,000 cubic miles, or 445,000 cu km) enters the atmosphere by evaporation from the world's oceans and seas. More than 90% of this water returns to the oceans and seas in the form of rain, hail, and snow. See also HYDROLOGIC CYCLE.

Most of the water precipitated onto land originally entered the atmosphere from the oceans. A large proportion of the water that reaches the land returns to the atmosphere either by direct evaporation or by transpiration from plants.

The length of time that water remains in one environment, called its residence time, varies greatly from one environment to another. For example, water that enters the atmosphere may remain there about 10 days before leaving in the form of precipitation, while most of the water in the oceans remains there for several thousands of years. The residence time of water in rivers and streams is generally a period of days or weeks, depending on the water's point of entry. On the other hand, the residence time of groundwater varies from days to hundreds of thousands of years, depending on the depth of the water below the surface and the characteristics of the aquifer in which it occurs.

Fig. 1. Annual circulation of the world's water, expressed in thousands of cubic miles.

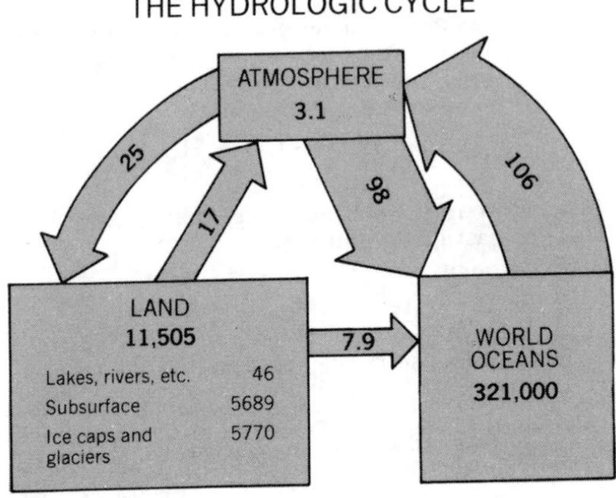

Table 1—WATERS OF THE WORLD: AREAS AND VOLUMES

Fresh and slightly mineralized waters	Area covered 1,000 square miles*	Volume of water 1,000 cubic miles	Volume of water 1,000 billion gallons
Atmospheric water	197,000	3.1	3,410
Biological water (plants, animals)	—	0.26	296
Freshwater lakes	477	22	24,000
Rivers	—	0.50	560
Marsh waters	1,036	2.76	3,030
Glaciers and permanent snow cover	6,265	5.772	6,358,000
Soil moisture	32,000	3.96	4,360
Ground ice in zones of permafrost strata	8,100	70	80,000
Groundwater (freshwater zone)	52,050	2,526	2,782,000
Total fresh water	—	8,400	9,255,000
Salty and brackish waters			
Saltwater lakes	317	20.5	22,600
Oceans and seas	139,500	321,000	353,500,000
Groundwater (saline-water zone)	52,050	3,088	3,400,000
Total salt water	—	324,100	356,900,000
Grand total	—	332,500	366,200,000

*Conversion factors: square miles to square kilometers, 2.59; cubic miles to cubic kilometers, 4.17; gallons to liters, 3.79.

Adapted from: United Nations Educational, Scientific, and Cultural Organization, *World Water Balance and Water Resources of the Earth:* Paris, Unesco, 1978, page 43.

Supplies of Fresh Water—*Streams.* The accompanying map (Fig. 2) shows the drainage basins of the world's major rivers (outlined areas) and the location of deserts and other arid regions (shaded areas). A rough indicator of the water supply potentially available in each basin is provided by the average annual discharge at the mouth of the river (see Table 2).

Another indicator of the maximum potential water supply in a particular area is the average flow of all the streams in the area. Such data for each continent are given in Table 3. These estimates are based on the assumption that high flows caused by heavy rains and melting of ice and snow could be stored in reservoirs and subsequently released downstream during periods of little or no rainfall.

Groundwater. Groundwater is by far the most widespread source of fresh water. It is available in nearly every part of the globe, often at depths easily reached by wells. The aquifers that provide the largest rates of yield to wells are in extensive layers of sand, gravel, porous limestone, or porous basalt. Wells that tap such aquifers may yield hundreds of gallons of water per minute.

The water supply of most water-bearing rock formations, or aquifers, is replenished to some extent each year by precipitation that seeps down below the soil to the water table—the upper surface of an aquifer that is not confined above by an impervious rock layer.

standing examples of Watson's facility with different kinds of Latin verse. He was considered the foremost Latinist of his day, but it was as a sonneteer that he left his stamp on English literature. Watson's *The Hecatompathia, or Passionate Centurie of Love* (1582), a collection of 18-line "sonnets" in English, revitalized an interest in the sonnet form. He was the first writer of sonnets after Sir Thomas Wyatt and Henry Howard, earl of Surrey, and his work preceded Sir Philip Sidney's *Astrophel and Stella.* Another collection of poems, this time in the true sonnet form, *The Tears of Fancie, or Love Disdained* (published posthumously in 1593), is considered Watson's best work. His poetry lacks feeling, but his technical skill and choice of topics influenced the later sonnets of the 16th century. His work was closely studied by William Shakespeare and others, and Watson, at the time of his death, was praised by fellow poets and scholars as the equal of Edmund Spenser and Sidney.

WATSON, Thomas Augustus, American electrical engineer and shipbuilder: b. Salem, Mass., Jan. 18, 1854; d. Passagrille Key, Fla., Dec. 13, 1934. After leaving public school at a young age, he went to work in 1872 at an electrical shop in Boston which constructed models for a number of inventors, including Alexander Graham Bell. Watson began his association with Bell in 1874, and served as his assistant during the experiments which led to the invention of the telephone. Their efforts were crowned on March 10, 1876, when Bell spoke the first sentence transmitted by telephone: "Mr. Watson, come here; I want you." When the Bell Telephone Company was formed in 1877, Watson was given an interest in the business. He resigned in 1881, and, three years later, in partnership with Frank O. Wellington, began building ships and engines. The business flourished, and government contracts for large war vessels necessitated expansion of the shipyard, so the Fore River Ship & Engine Company was organized in 1901. Watson retired in 1904 and spent the remainder of his life exploring other interests, taking courses in geology and literature, studying music and painting, and even acting (he had speaking roles in the Shakespeare Festival at Stratford-on-Avon, England, in 1911). His autobiography, *Exploring Life,* was published in 1926.

WATSON, Thomas Edward, American political leader and author: b. Columbia County, Ga., Sept. 5, 1856; d. Washington, D.C., Sept. 26, 1922. Born into a wealthy slaveholding family made destitute by the Civil War, he early developed the instincts of rebellion and reform which were to characterize his political career. He attended Mercer University for two years and later studied law privately; after being admitted to the bar in 1875 he opened a practice in Thomson, Ga., winning a statewide reputation as a criminal lawyer. Armed with a fiery, combative nature and a hatred for the Northern industrialists who controlled the new South, he entered politics as an agrarian reformer, fighting the Democratic machine to win a term in the state legislature in 1882. He was elected to Congress in 1890 as a Farmers' Alliance Democrat but soon joined the new People's (Populist) party (see POPULIST PARTY) and served as the voice of the agrarian revolt in the House, as well as introducing reform bills and the first resolution for free rural delivery of mail. Watson was defeated by the Democrats in the next two turbulent elections, marked by gerrymandering and fraud, but he pressed his fight for reform and campaigned against capitalist finance. In 1896 the Populists named him their vice presidential candidate, which, because it involved harmony with the Democrats, he accepted reluctantly.

Discouraged by his defeats, Watson left the political scene in 1896 and devoted his time to writing history and biography. In 1904 he was back again, this time as the presidential candidate of the Populists; he was a nominal candidate again in 1908. Now, disillusioned, he shifted his attention to new issues, forsook the old agrarian-industrial struggle and, to the dismay of his Populist supporters, directed his energies against the Catholics, Negroes, Jews, and Socialists. He became the champion of the Ku Klux Klan. He actively fought United States entry into World War I and the conscription of troops. Elected to the Senate in 1920, he was an outspoken foe of Woodrow Wilson and the League of Nations. He died in office two years later.

Watson's writings include *The Story of France* (1899); *Napoleon: a Sketch of His Life* (1902); *The Life and Times of Thomas Jefferson* (1903); and *The Life and Times of Andrew Jackson* (1912). For his vitriolic attack on Catholicism in *The Roman Catholic Hierarchy* (1910), he was prosecuted but acquitted. He founded *Tom Watson's Magazine* in New York in 1905, and later published the *Weekly Jeffersonian* and *Watson's Jeffersonian Magazine* (1906).

WATSON, Thomas John, American industrialist: b. Campbell, N.Y., Feb. 17, 1874; d. New York, June 19, 1956. He attended Addison (N.Y.) Academy and the Elmira (N.Y.) School of Commerce, and began his business career at 17 as a store clerk in Painted Post, N.Y. In 1898 he joined the National Cash Register Company, rising to the position of general sales manager during his 15-year service. In 1914 he became president of the Computing-Tabulating-Recording Company (formed as a holding company in 1911), which changed its name in 1924 to International Business Machines Corporation (IBM). Watson embarked on a program of expansion, instituted an elaborate system of sales and technical training, and in 1949 created a subsidiary, the IBM World Trade Corporation, to direct the company's vast overseas operations. He retired as president in 1949 to become chairman of the board.

The phenomenal growth of IBM under Watson's personal management is part of the history of American business. Through the years he widened the firm's original scope from the manufacture of business machines of all types to encompass the fantastically complex electronic calculators and giant computers which are widely used in business today.

Given to moralism and maxim (he created IBM's famous watchword, "THINK"), Watson personally supported extensive philanthropies; was a noted art patron and collector; and materially aided medical research, religious groups, young people's organizations, educational enterprises, welfare societies, and numerous other charitable activities.

See also COMPUTERS—*History.*

WATSON, Thomas John, Jr. (1914–), American businessman and ambassador, who succeeded his father as head of the International Business Machines Corporation (IBM). The elder of the two sons of Thomas J. Watson, he was born in Dayton, Ohio, on Jan. 8, 1914. He received his B. A. degree from Brown University in 1937, and that same year joined the IBM company as a junior salesman. He served (1940–1946) with the Air Force in World War II, flew combat missions, won his senior pilot's wings, and advanced in rank to lieutenant colonel. During this period he spent six months in the USSR under the lend-lease airlift program.

Returning to the company in 1946, he served as its president in 1952–1961, chairman of the board in 1961–1971, and chairman of the executive committee in 1971–1979. Under his direction IBM achieved leadership in the field of automation. He also devoted much of his time to other companies, to educational institutions, and to the federal government as he became director of several corporations, trustee of a number of universities, and member of several presidential advisory boards. He also presided over the General Advisory Committee of the Arms Control and Disarmament Agency. Appointed by President Carter, Watson was ambassador to the Soviet Union from 1979 to 1981. His many honors include the Presidential Medal of Freedom.

WATSON, Tom (1949–), American golfer, who in 1980 became the first in the sport to win more than $500,000 in a single season. Thomas Sturges Watson was born in Kansas City, Mo., on Sept. 4, 1949. He began playing as a boy and in his teens won the Missouri amateur championship four times. A graduate of Stanford University (1971), he turned professional in his senior year. He failed to win a single tournament, although his earnings jumped from about $2,000 in 1971 to $75,000 in 1973.

As his game improved, he overcame the stigma of "choking" in the late rounds of close matches. He broke into prominence by capturing the British Open in 1975, repeating in 1977, 1980, 1982, and 1983. He also won the World Series of Golf in 1977 and 1980 and the Masters title in 1977 and 1981, and was voted Player of the Year in 1977 and 1978. He was awarded the Vardon Trophy (for lowest scoring average) in 1978. After several failures, Watson triumphed in the U.S. Open in 1982.

With consistent victories or high-place finishes on the Professional Golfers Association tours, Watson was the leading money winner from 1977 to 1980. His total earnings by 1983 passed $3 million, second to Jack Nicklaus on the all-time list of prizewinners.

WATSON-WATT, wŏt'sən-wôt, SIR **Robert (Alexander)** (1892–1973), Scottish physicist, who pioneered in the development of radar. He was born in Brechin, Scotland, on April 13, 1892, and attended University College, University of St. Andrews, where he taught natural philosophy in 1912–1921. In 1919, while a government meteorologist, he took out his first patent for a radiolocation (radar) instrument to be used in atmospheric study. While serving (1921–1936) in the Department of Scientific and Industrial Research and the National Physics Laboratory, he continued to improve his radiolocation equipment in accuracy and sensitivity, and in 1935, after lengthy experiments, he patented a new type of radiolocator which formed the basis of British wartime radar. By the time of the Battle of Britain radiolocation had become a powerful defense against German air raids, and this device has been credited with swinging the balance of that critical phase of the war in Britain's favor. In 1941, Watson-Watt visited the United States to confer with American scientists who had developed a similar device, and from that time on radar became a joint project of Britain and the United States. As a result of his achievements, Watson-Watt was knighted in 1942 and received the United States Medal of Merit in 1946. His works include *Through the Weather House* (1935) and *Pulse of Radar* (1959), an autobiography. He died in Inverness, Scotland, on Dec. 5, 1973.

WATT, James (1736–1819), Scottish engineer whose inventions led to an improved steam engine. He was born in Greenock, Renfrew, Scotland, on Jan. 19, 1736, and at age 18 he went to London where he studied mathematical instrument making. Later, when he tried to open a shop in Glasgow, he was deterred by a craft guild. Glasgow University friends came to his aid, and he was appointed mathematical instrument maker to the university. While here he made his great invention, in 1765, of a separate condensing vessel for the steam engine. The idea first occurred to him the year before when he was given the university's model of the Newcomen engine to repair. This apparatus, invented in 1705 by Thomas Newcomen and John Calley (or Cawley), used the steam cylinder itself as a condenser, by introducing a jet of cold water into the cylinder to condense the steam. Watt found that this method

James Watt, Scottish engineer, whose invention of a condensing vessel in 1765 led to an improved steam engine.
NATIONAL PORTRAIT GALLERY

so reduced the temperature of the cylinder that three times as much steam was required as was necessary. He set to work to condense the steam in a separate receptacle, insulate the cylinder against heat loss, and pump out noncondensable gas, and he patented the processes in 1769, nearly four years after the inventions covered by the patent had been made. Although he did not invent the steam engine, his improvements were of such importance that he is popularly credited with this distinction.

In 1775, Watt entered into partnership with Matthew Boulton, the owner of the Soho Engineering Works, near Birmingham, and the plant began producing engines on a large scale. Watt left the business in 1800, when his patent, renewed in 1775 for 25 years, expired. Besides the separate condenser, the inventor made a number of other improvements in the steam engine. He devised the sun-and-planet gear wheel, in order to convert reciprocating motion to rotary motion; made use of the expansion principle to design the double-acting engine; applied a speed governor to steam engines; and invented the throttle valve. He also built the first indicator for drawing a diagram of steam pressure, patented an improved-combustion furnace, invented a special ink for coyping letters, and discovered independently the chemical composition of water. His memory was retentive and the range of his reading wide, and he had knowledge of language, music, and chemistry. The significance of his work places him among the foremost of inventors.

Watt was a fellow of the royal societies of both London and Edinburgh. He originated the term "horsepower," and the units of power called "watt" and "kilowatt" were named in his honor. He died in Heathfield Hall, near Birmingham, England, where he had retired to devote his time to mechanical pursuits and inventions, on Aug. 25, 1819.

See also STEAM; STEAM ENGINE.

WATT (symbol W), a unit of power, or amount of energy expended per unit time. Named for Scottish engineer James Watt, it is equal to one joule per second. One watt-hour is a unit of energy equal to 3,600 joules or 3.413 BTUs. One kilowatt hour is equal to 1,000 times that amount. A watt-hour meter measures the amount of electric energy consumed.

WATTEAU, wo-tō′; Fr. vȧ-tō′, **Jean Antoine** (1684–1721), French painter known as the founder of the French school. He was born of Flemish parents in Valenciennes on Oct. 10, 1684. He went to Paris in 1702, where, after a period of impoverishment, he entered the studio of Claude Gillot, an able painter of arabesques and other ornamentation. While there (1704–1708), young Watteau developed the propensity for theater design which was to identify his future work. He next came under another master, Claude Audran, and this association seems to have been of primary significance to the young artist's career. Through Audran's position as keeper at the Luxembourg Palace, Watteau gained entrance to the gallery, where he could study the great Marie de Médicis cycle of Peter Paul Rubens. From these 21 huge compositions Watteau was able to assimilate the baroque master's dynamics of form and coloration, which he then adapted to his own rococo art.

THE METROPOLITAN MUSEUM OF ART, MUNSEY FUND, 1934

Watteau's *Mezzetin* is a portrait study of a costumed actor playing a stock character in Italian comedy.

Distressed by his failure to achieve the Prix de Rome in 1709 (he took second place), Watteau left Audran and returned briefly to Valenciennes, where some of his military scenes probably originated. Upon his return to Paris, he gained the friendship of the financier Pierre Crozat, whose great art collection centered on the Flemish and Venetian masters whom Watteau admired. The artist stayed with Crozat for a time, both in Paris and at his Montmorency villa, whose formal gardens appear in many subsequent paintings. In 1712 he became an associate of the Académie Royale de Peinture et Sculpture, and a full member five years later. His health now failing, he went to live in Paris with his friend Edmond Gersaint, an art dealer, for whose shop he painted the famous *enseigne* (signboard), now in the Berlin Museum. Continuing to work diligently despite his illness, he finally moved to a country home in Nogent-sur-Marne, where he died on July 18, 1721.

Watteau's Art. One of the true luminaries of French painting, Watteau dominated the art of that country in the early 18th century to the extent that he may be regarded as the founder of the French school. Although he began painting during the declining days of Louis XIV, his work showed a complete independence of the bigoted court of Versailles and anticipated the way of life (among the leisured) that would inevitably burst forth when France passed into the hands of the Régent Orléans. On Watteau's small, intimate canvases Watteau created a world of unconstrained elegance, finding his favorite subjects among the fine ladies and gentlemen of the regent's court, and portraying them in attitudes of dalliance in parks and glades. Pervading these *fêtes champêtres*, however, is an air of wistfulness tinged with melancholy, as though the artist were impressed by the transitory nature of romantic love. In this half-real realm of shadow and illusion, Watteau's delicate color harmonies and sensitive brushstrokes seem to pass a layer of scrim over the precise details of costume and scenic milieu.

Above all, Watteau's art is of the theater, and his paintings, whether of court life or rural genre, rely on the stock characters of Italian comedy so popular during the Regency. His many canvases on the theme of love are summarized in the classic *Embarquement pour Cythère* (Louvre)—painted in 1717 as his diploma piece for the Académie—in which he grouped his amorous figures into a *fête galante* of compelling charm. This work is clearly indebted to Rubens' *Jardin d'amour*, but the influence is transformed by Watteau's own subtleties. Through such scenes he helped to free French painting from its inhibitions and opened the way to the coloristic and ornamentive vitality of the rococo.

Although Watteau's ideas were widely imitated in the 18th century—by his pupils Jean Baptiste Pater and Nicolas Lancret, and notably by François Boucher and Jean Honoré Fragonard—he alone remains above the vulgarism that vitiated much of the aristocratic art of tha era. His paintings are sensuous, but not licentious; rather they are infused by a spiritual purity that far transcends the sentimentality of his emulators.

The structure of Watteau's art rests firmly on his superb draftsmanship; and his drawings, of which perhaps 300 survive, have been acclaimed as his "surpreme achievement" (K. T. Parker). The splendid collections in the British Museum and the Louvre reveal the full range of his technique, and include, in addition to the notes for the familiar theatrical pieces, lesser-known landscapes, designs, portraits, nudes, animals, and especially fine studies of hands. Conceived realistically from life, the drawings for the most part represent finished products, rather than preparatory sketches. Red chalk predominates, although this often is fused with white to produce remarkably warm and lifelike flesh tones. Many of the drawings are executed in red, white, and black, a technique (*à trois crayons*) in which Watteau was unrivaled.

Watteau's paintings appear in museums and galleries throughout Europe and, to a lesser extent, the United States. Much of his work is concentrated in Germany, largely because of the admiration of Frederick II the Great, who avidly collected his finest pieces for the palaces at Potsdam. In Berlin are *La comédie française* and *Le déjeuner en plein air*. The Louvre paintings, in addition to the *Embarquement pour Cythère*, include *Gilles*, *L'indifférent*, *La finette*, and *L'assemblée dans un parc;* in the Wallace Collection (London) are *La leçon de musique*, *Le concert de famille*, and *Les amusements champêtres*. Among his works in the United States are *Mezzetin*, a portrait study, in the Metropolitan, and *La gamme d'amour* in the National Gallery. Interest in Watteau revived with the publication in 1875 of Edmond de Goncourt's *Catalogue raisonné de l'oeuvre peint, dessiné et gravé d'Antoine Watteau*, and his paintings subsequently soared in value.

See also PAINTING—*The 18th Century*.

WATTENSCHEID, vät'ĕn-shīt, city, Germany, in the State of North Rhine-Westphalia, located in the heart of the Ruhr basin at an altitude of 200 feet, 6 miles northeast of Essen. It is primarily an industrial city, engaged in the mining of anthracite coal and the manufacture of electrical products and metal and textile goods. As in many of the Ruhr's industrial centers, a trade school is prominent in the educational system. Wattenscheid was chartered as a city in 1425. Its most notable historical landmark is the Probstei Church, completed about 1400 and incorporating a baptismal font of the 10th century. After World War II, the city was included in the Federal Republic of Germany (West Germany). Pop. (1959 official est.) 77,800.

WATTERSON, wŏt'ər-sən, **Henry** (known as MARSE HENRY), American journalist and politician: b. Washington, D.C., Feb. 16, 1840; d. Jacksonville, Fla., Dec. 22, 1921. Son of a newspaper editor, he received an informal but thorough schooling. In spite of his regard for Abraham Lincoln, he served with the Confederate Army in the Civil War out of loyalty to the South. Before the war was over, he began to work as a newspaper editor in Tennessee. In 1868 he became editor of the Louisville, Ky., *Daily Journal*, which he immediately merged with Walter N. Haldeman's *Courier*, Haldeman remaining as publisher. As editor of the *Courier-Journal* until 1919, Watterson exerted nationwide influence, expressing his strongly held convictions in fiery prose. He fought both for the restoration of home rule in the South and for the rights of the blacks; promoted Samuel J. Tilden's candidacy for the presidency; and as a member of the House of Representatives (1876–1877), worked in vain to have Tilden certified as victor. In later years he conducted a vitriolic editorial campaign against President Theodore Roosevelt, whom he accused of dictatorial tendencies. From 1914 Watterson urged the United States to declare war on Germany in World War I, and his editorials on the subject won him a Pulitzer Prize in 1917. He broke with President Woodrow Wilson on the League of Nations issue, however. Watterson's books include *The Compromises of Life and Other Lectures and Addresses* (1903), and *"Marse Henry": an Autobiography* (2 vols., 1919).

WATTLEBIRD, wŏt'əl-bûrd, or **WATTLED CROW,** a New Zealand bird, *Callaeas cinerea*, discovered by Capt. James Cook's party and so called by them because of two blue and orange unfeathered wattles at the corners of its mouth. About a foot in length, it is plain gray, with black on the sides of the head. A closely allied race occurs on the North Island of New Zealand. A fruit-eating forest bird of weak flight, it is now greatly reduced in numbers. With the saddleback and the huia, two other New Zealand species, it forms a family, the Callaeidae, allied, presumably, to the birds of paradise and Australian bell magpies.

WATTLES, wŏt'əlz, name given in Australia to trees and shrubs of genus *Acacia*. See ACACIA.

WATTMETER, wŏt-mēt-ər, in electricity, a device which measures electrical power in terms of watts. See WATT.

WATTS, wŏtz, **George Frederic,** English painter and sculptor: b. London, England, Feb. 23, 1817; d. there, July 1, 1904. He studied at the Royal Academy and in the studio of sculptor William Behnes. After winning the Westminster Palace design competition in 1852 with *Caractacus Led in Triumph Through the Streets of Rome,* he studied in Italy. From 1843 to 1847 he lived mainly in Florence, painting many portraits as well as treating Italian literary themes such as *Paolo and Francesca* (Dante), and *Anastasio degl'Onesti* (Boccaccio). In 1847 another Westminster competition called Watts to England, and he won the prize with *Alfred Inciting his Subjects to Prevent the Landing of the Danes,* now hanging in a committee room in the House of Commons. About this time Watts painted a long series of outstanding Victorian portraits of such notables as Matthew Arnold, Thomas Carlyle, Alfred, Lord Tennyson, John Stuart Mill, Robert Browning, William Gladstone, and Giuseppe Garibaldi.

Watts led a very uneventful life, except for an allegedly stormy 13-year marriage to the young actress, Ellen Terry. Artistically, his aim was to make English art the equal of English literature, and he believed that art must not only represent beauty but point a moral. He carried his ethical beliefs into his commissions, but he was rarely able to realize his conceptions. In style he was one of the few British painters who worked in the grand manner with something of the quality of Titian's effects. He painted many allegorical works, most of which were successful. After 1867, he devoted much of his time to experimenting in sculpture, and afterward his paintings became more solid and less complicated. His most successful sculpture was the massive bronze *Physical Energy* in Kensington Gardens, cast as a memorial to Cecil Rhodes. Watts was elected to the Royal Academy in 1867, twice refused a baronetcy, but finally accepted the Order of Merit in 1902. He is represented in the Tate Gallery, to which Watts presented over 50 of his works, the National Gallery, and the National Portrait Gallery, all in London, as well as in other museums and galleries in the United States. A biography and compilation of his writings were published by his second wife in 1912.

JEAN ANNE VINCENT.

WATTS, Isaac, English theologian and hymnist: b. Southampton, England, July 17, 1674; d. London, Nov. 25, 1748. He was educated for the ministry at the nonconformist academy at Stoke Newington, London, from 1690 to 1694. In 1696 he became a tutor in the family of Sir John Hartopp, and in 1699 he was chosen assistant minister of the Independent Congregation in Mark Lane, London, becoming its pastor in 1702. Never robust in health, from 1712 he lived in semiretirement at the home of Sir Thomas Abney, devoting most of his time to writing as well as to a voluminous correspondence. He died at the Abney home in Stoke Newington and was buried in Bunhill Fields. There is a monument to his memory in Westminster Abbey.

Watts was the creator of the modern hymn, as opposed to the medieval office hymn and the Reformation metrical paraphrase of the Psalms. He wrote about 600 hymns, many of which are still found in various Protestant hymnals. He created the new genre with rapidity, and many of his best hymns were written between the ages of 20 and 22, before he began his ministerial career. None was published until his *Horae Lyricae* came out in 1706. The following year his *Hymns and Spiritual Songs* (2d ed., 1709) appeared, and his *Divine Songs* (1715), later called *Divine and Moral Songs* (1729), was a pioneer hymnal for children. *The Psalms of David* was published in 1719. Watts's psalms are free paraphrases, rather than metrical versions. Some of them have become the most famous hymns in the English language, including "O God, our help in ages past."

In addition to his poetic gifts, Watts had the mind of a teacher and clear thinker. His *Logick* (1725), *Knowledge of the Heavens and Earth* (1726), *Philosophical Essays* (1733), and *The Improvement of the Mind* (1741) were used as basic textbooks at Cambridge, Oxford, Harvard, and Yale universities until the beginning of the 19th century. Edinburgh University honored him with the doctor of divinity degree in 1728. Among his theological treatises are *Doctrine of the Trinity* (1722), *Essay on the Freedom of the Will* (1732), and *Useful and Important Questions Concerning Jesus, the Son of God* (1746). In addition, Watts wrote treatises on various other subjects.

He was a forceful preacher, and a man wholly absorbed in the mystery of God. Never a political nonconformist, he was rather a spiritual dissenter whose entire theology was expressed in the following lines from his hymn, "When I survey the wondrous cross:"

Were the whole realm of nature mine,
  That were an offering far too small;
Love so amazing, so divine,
  Demands my soul, my life, my all.

His was a mind which at one moment could be combating the empiricism of John Locke and in the next could be writing for children:

Were I so tall to reach the pole,
  And grasp the ocean in my span,
I must be measured by my soul:
  The mind's the standard of the man.

LEONARD ELLINWOOD
Author of "The History of American Church Music"

WATTS-DUNTON, wŏts'dŭn'tən, **(Walter) Theodore,** English critic, novelist, and versifier: b. St. Ives, Huntingdonshire, England, Oct. 12, 1832; d. Putney, London, June 6, 1914. After a private education at Cambridge, Watts became a solicitor and practiced briefly in London. His talents, somewhat limited, showed best in his intimacies with those of greater fame, such as Dante Gabriel Rossetti and Algernon Charles Swinburne in particular. His acquaintance with such men was facilitated by his positions, first as literary and art critic for the *Examiner* (1874–1876), and then as critic for and contributor of verse to the *Athenaeum* for a quarter of a century. He had a curious therapeutic effect on a Rossetti debilitated by whiskey and chloral, but even more positively showed himself an amazingly resourceful and patient male nurse for Swinburne. From 1879 to the time of Swinburne's death in 1909, Watts-Dunton devotedly controlled the life of the once-tempestuous poet, adding no doubt to the life-span and, perhaps necessarily at the same time, quenching the early Swinburne glow.

An admirer of George Borrow and his gypsies, Watts-Dunton wrote verses about these cultish wanderers and published them in the *Athenaeum*. In 1897 he collected his gypsy poems under the title, *The Coming of Love, and Other Poems*. The poems are somewhat cluttered and lack the singing quality the subject matter suggests as appropriate. A year later he had his most pronounced literary success with the publication, long delayed, of *Aylwin*, a romantic novel notable for a good plot, some memorable scenes, and a sketch of Rossetti as one of the characters.

Next to his two chief claims to fame—caretaker of Swinburne and a novel—Watts-Dunton could be remembered for coining the phrase "the renascence of wonder" as the romantic essence, and for his article on "Poetry" (*Encyclopaedia Britannica*, 9th ed., 1885). For a look at how he remembered his friends, one may consult the leisurely *Old Familiar Faces*, published posthumously (1916).

KENNETH L. KNICKERBOCKER, *University of Tennessee.*

WAUCONDA, wô kŏn′də, village, Illinois, in Lake County, on Bangs Lake, 16 miles west-southwest of Waukegan. At an altitude of 800 feet, it lies in a dairy and farm area. The main basis of the economy is the farm trade although added trade is gained from summer colonists. The village had its beginnings in 1836 when Justus Bangs built his house on the shore of the lake now named after him. The name of Wauconda was adopted in 1839 at the suggestion of a schoolteacher who took a fancy to the name of an Indian character in a legend. Pop. 5,688.

WAUGH, wô, **Alec** (in full ALEXANDER RABAN WAUGH), English author: b. London, July 8, 1898; d. Tampa, Fla., Sept. 3, 1981. A brother of Evelyn Waugh, he won success as a novelist and travel writer. His books include *The Loom of Youth* (1917); *No Truce with Time* (1941); *Guy Renton* (1952); *The Sugar Islands* (1958); *Fuel for the Flame* (1960), and *A Family of Islands* (1964). His *Island in the Sun* (1956) was adapted as a motion picture.

WAUGH, Evelyn Arthur St. John, English novelist: b. London, Oct. 28, 1903; d. Taunton, Somerset, April 10, 1966. He was a son of Arthur Waugh (1866–1943), critic, publisher, author, and editor of many books. Educated at Lancing and Oxford University, he was received into the Roman Catholic Church in 1930. Between 1939 and 1945 he served as a commando officer in West Africa and Crete, and as a British liaison officer in Yugoslavia. At heart a romantic, but endowed with incisive qualities of mind and an impeccable English style, he is an outstanding satirical novelist of our time, expressing the shocked horror of the moralist when observing the social, religious, and political infirmities of modern society. The abiding theme of his plots is that of the innocent who ventures into a world of chaos and unreason, where he perishes, or from which he withdraws.

The basic tone may be serious (*A Handful of Dust*, 1934; *Work Suspended*, 1942; *Helena*, 1950), or more commonly farcical and burlesque (*Decline and Fall*, 1928; *Vile Bodies*, 1930; *Black Mischief*, 1932; *Scoop*, 1938; *Put Out More Flags*, 1942; *Scott-King's Modern Europe*, 1947; *The Loved One*, 1948; *Love Among the Ruins*, 1953), but it is always mordant. His greatest public success, *Brideshead Revisited* (1945), has definite artistic faults, which he attempted to correct in a revised edition (1960). His own favorite novel is *Helena*, the fictional life of the mother of Constantine, who discovered the fragments of the True Cross. The trilogy of novels, *Men at Arms* (1952), *Officers and Gentlemen* (1955), and *Unconditional Surrender* (1961), depict his attitude to World War II, and to army life. *The Ordeal of Gilbert Pinfold* (1957) reveals much of his own attitude to his work and personality. *Edmund Campion, Jesuit and Martyr* (1935), was an act of thanksgiving for his conversion. *The Life of Ronald Knox* (1959) is a memorial to a great writer and priest. Waugh traveled constantly and recorded his impressions of the impact of Western civilization of indigenous social patterns, both in his novels (*Black Mischief, Scoop*) and in travel books (*Labels*, 1930; *Remote People*, 1932; *Ninety-two Days*, 1934; *A Tourist in Africa*, 1960). The first volume of *A Little Learning*, a projected three-volume autobiography, appeared in 1964.

Waugh is a moralist by conviction; a traditionalist by temperament. But the voice which expresses distaste for all manifestations of modernity, for politics, psychology, plastics, and Picasso, is also that of the artist, stimulated to production by what he derides. This double identity is confusing to those critics who would praise his writing while condemning his views. The tendency, with affluence and age, to restrict immediate contact with the surrounding irritants led, after the war, to the cultivation of a more allusive, symbolical mode of narration, which further disconcerts many who prefer the brilliant parodies written in Waugh's youth.

FREDERIC J. STOPP, *Cambridge University.*

WAUGH, Sidney, American sculptor: b. Amherst, Mass., Jan. 17, 1904; d. New York, N.Y., June 30, 1963. He studied at Massachusetts Institute of Technology (1920–1923), but later concentrated on art at the Scuola delle Belle Arte, Rome (1924), and under sculptor Henri Bouchard, Paris (1925–1928). The Prix de Rome, won in 1929, exerted a great influence on his style. His success as an architectural sculptor may be traced in part to Waugh's academic intellectualism which stems from the classical rather than from the modern world. By 1930, he had become acquainted with etched glass at the Swedish Exposition in Stockholm. A visit to the factory so stimulated him that he soon established a designer relationship with the Steuben Division of the Corning Glass Works. Today he is in the forefront of glass designers and holds a unique position among sculptors. Outstanding works in this unusual medium include *The Merry-Go-Round Bowl*, designed as a wedding gift to Princess Elizabeth of England from President and Mrs. Harry Truman, and a three-foot, glass-cast *Atlantica* for the New York World's Fair (1939), which was the largest single piece of clear polished crystal glass ever made.

In 1936 he was the first contemporary American glass designer to see his work enter the collection of The Metropolitan Museum, New York City. In the same year, he was elected to the

National Academy of Design which made him a full member two years later. He distinguished himself in World War II and later, serving as teacher as well as sculptor, headed the Rinehart School of Sculpture of the Maryland Institute, which is in Baltimore.

Waugh's monumental works adorn many buildings in Washington, but interest in his work has not been confined to public edifices, as commissions from the Bethlehem Steel Company and the Bank of Manhattan attest. He is represented in many public and private collections in Europe and America.

DOROTHY GRAFLY,
Editor and Publisher "Art in Focus."

WAUKEGAN, wô-kē′gən, city, Illinois, Lake County seat, on Lake Michigan, 40 miles north of Chicago, at an altitude of 595 feet. The name is derived from the Potawatomi, meaning "little fort."

Waukegan is an industrial city with port facilities for lake and ocean vessels. Major products include outboard motors, wire and steel, gypsum, asbestos, building materials, leather, and pharmaceuticals. The Great Lakes Naval Training Station is just south of the city limits, and the Illinois Beach State Park is north of the city. The Waukegan Memorial Airport was dedicated in 1961.

The city was originally populated by the Potawatomi Indians. Permanent settlers arrived in 1835 and the town of Little Fort was incorporated in 1841. The name was changed to the Indian synonym in 1849 and Waukegan became a city on Jan. 4, 1859. Government is by mayor and city council. Pop. 67,653.

RUTH W. GREGORY.

WAUKESHA, wô′kĕ-shô, city, Wisconsin, seat of Waukesha County, on the Fox River, 15 miles west of Milwaukee, at an altitude of 821 feet. An industrial city in an agricultural area, the city has a symphony orchestra, and is the seat of Carroll College. There is an airport. The chief industries make internal combustion motors, castings, and foundry products. The lands of the Potawatomi Indians, who had a village here, were ceded to the federal government in 1833. Three prehistoric Indian mounds of the 55 known to have been here are preserved in Cutler Park. The first white settlement was in 1834 and was known as Prairieville until 1845. The present name is Indian for "little fox." The health-giving fame of the water from the many springs made Waukesha well known, and the city was a noted watering place from about 1870 to the early 1900's. The form of government is mayor and council. Pop. 50,365.

EDWARD W. LYNCH.

WAUKON, wô-kŏn′, city, Iowa, seat of Allamakee County, 19 miles east of Decorah, at an altitude of 1,216 feet. The region is agricultural and supports a big dairy industry and a flourishing business district. There is an airstrip. Traditionally a trading center, Waukon was founded in 1849 and incorporated in 1883. The city was named for a Winnebago chief, known to the settlers as John Wawkon. In Winnebago, Wawkon means "thunder." A county fair is held in August of each year. Effigy Mounds National Monument is 18 miles from the city. The monument is a park centered around burial mounds in the shape of various animals and birds. Government is by mayor and council. Pop. 3,983.

LAVERNE HULL.

WAUPACA, wô-păk′ə, city, Wisconsin, seat of Waupaca County, 47 miles northwest of Oshkosh, at an altitude of 868 feet, in an agricultural and stock-raising region. The surrounding area was formerly engaged principally in lumbering, but Waupaca became one of the state's first centers for potato production and marketing, and still stands high in this activity. Within a few miles of the city there are more than a score of small picturesque lakes, which have brought Waupaca into favor as a summer resort. The streams and lakes afford excellent sport. The name is derived from an Indian word for "white sand bottom." Pop. 4,472.

WAUPUN, wô-pŭn′, city, Wisconsin, in Dodge and Fond du Lac counties, 70 miles northwest of Milwaukee, at an altitude of 903 feet. It lies in a fertile agricultural area producing grain and food for the local canneries. Two state institutions, the Wisconsin State Prison and the Central State Hospital for the criminal insane, are located here. The beauty and fertility of the Rock River valley brought the first settlers here in 1838. The community was incorporated in 1878 under the name of Waupun, which is a variation in spelling of the Indian name Waubun, meaning "dawn of day." Government is by mayor and council. Pop. 8,132.

MABEL W. JONES.

WAUSAU, wô′sô, city, Wisconsin, seat of Marathon County, 85 miles west northwest of Green Bay on the Wisconsin River, at an altitude of 1,200 feet. Set in the heart of Wisconsin's rich and prosperous dairy country, it serves as a trade center for a radius of some 50 miles. Its industry includes paper, paper pulp, industrial machinery, woodworking, and insurance. Wausau Technical Institute trains students in residential design, electronics, and business, and there is a two-year branch of the University of Wisconsin Extension Division located here. Founded in 1839 by George Stevens, who walked from St. Louis, Mo., in search of pineries and a good millsite, the place was originally called Big Bull Falls. The name was changed to Wausau, a Chippewa Indian word meaning "far, far away," in 1872 when the city charter was granted. Rib Mountain State Park, four miles southwest of the city, is widely known as a winter sports area and is frequented by summer tourists as well. Fifteen miles to the east, the Dells of the Eau Claire River are a favorite recreation spot. Government is by mayor and aldermen. Pop. 32,426.

DOROTHEA M. KRAUSE.

WAUSEON, wô′sē-ŏn, village, Ohio, seat of Fulton County, 32 miles west of Toledo, at an altitude of 775 feet. The village is a residential center of three square miles surrounded by rich farmlands. Agriculture is a chief industry with poultry, cattle, and dairy products leading. Several manufacturing companies produce and assemble automotive products for nearby Detroit. Named for a chief of the Ottawa of the Maumee Valley, Wa-se-on, which signifies "far off," the village was settled in 1835 and incorporated in 1852. Pop. 6,173.

DOROTHY SQUIRE.

WAUTERS, wou'tərs, **Émile Charles Marie,** Belgian painter: b. Brussels, Belgium, Nov. 29, 1846; d. Paris, France, Dec. 11, 1933. He studied in Brussels under Charles Albert and Jean François Portaels, and in Paris under Jean Léon Gérôme. His first painting to attract wide notice was a typically academic subject, anecdotal yet historical, *Fair Edith Finding the Body of Harold on the Field of Hastings.* As a result of this public attention, the artist was sent by his government to attend the opening of the Suez Canal. Like Eugène Delacroix and others before him, Wauters was inspired by the exoticism of the oriental scenes, and made many notes and sketches which were later faithfully put on canvas with exact archaeological detail, as in his panorama called *Cairo and the Banks of the Nile.* However, Wauters went beyond the careful drawing and rather dry painting technique that characterized the painting of many of his contemporaries in the academic tradition, as may be seen in his "*The Madness of Hugo Van der Goes* (1875). He demonstrated that he was not unaffected by the lighter colors and loose handling of the brush of the Impressionists. He specialized in chiaroscuro effects, which was probably the result of his study of Italian paintings. Besides historical subjects, Wauters also painted more than 200 portraits, mainly royalty and public figures. He is represented in important public galleries in Antwerp, Brussels, Dresden, Philadelphia, Vienna, and Zurich.

JEAN ANNE VINCENT.

WAUWATOSA, wô-wə-tō'sə, city, Wisconsin, in Milwaukee County, five miles west of Milwaukee, on the Menomonee River, at an altitude of 634 feet. Although the city is predominately residential, an area along the Menomonee Valley is classed as a light manufacturing district with such industries as a chemical plant, concrete products manufactory, millwork factory, foundry, lumber yards, and a motor-manufacturing plant. A memorial center built in 1957 includes the city hall, an auditorium, and a public library. The name of the city comes from "Wau-wau-tae-sie," an Indian chief of the Potawatomi tribe. In the Indian language it means "firefly," and was adopted because of the many fireflies seen in the dense thickets that bordered on the Menomonee River. The city, settled in 1834, has a mayor and a common council form of government adopted in 1897 when it was incorporated as a city of the fourth class. Pop. 51,308.

ESTHER REGLI.

WAVE, The, wāv, a novel of the Civil War, by Evelyn Scott, first published in 1929. It is a notable example of the experimental school of fiction so popular between the two world wars.

The book takes its title and its method from the physical definition of a wave. A wave travels always in a definite direction, though the particles which compose it at any given instant do not advance with it but are merely whirled in circular movement. As Miss Scott applies the symbol in her narrative, the wave is the Civil War—the social and ideological forces which made the conflict; the particles are the human beings whom the war disturbs or destroys, but does not alter. The book has no plot in the ordinary sense; no one character, or group of characters, is carried through the war as Stephen Benet, in *John Brown's Body,* carries Jack Ellyat and Clay Wingate. Instead, we have a long series of vignettes of men and women, North and South, each coming to some individual crisis. Some of the people are real—Davis and Lincoln, Grant and Lee; many are fictitious representatives of classes and types. The leaders may recur in more than one episode; most of the others appear only once. The story touches most of the military high spots, from Bull Run to Appomattox, but each is told as it is seen by individual participants, who may be generals, or may be privates, deserters, or civilian bystanders. The life at home, behind the lines, receives as much attention as the battles, and here again the range is as wide as the nation, from the bankers who helped finance the Union cause to the runaway Negroes who trailed in the wake of Sherman's army. Bread riots in Richmond; draft riots in New York; preachers, statesmen, editors, lunatics, thieves; all the human gamut of America is represented, and all are merely particles stirred by the wave of war.

DELANCEY FERGUSON.

WAVE GUIDE, Electric, a term for any assemblage of conductors and insulators used to transmit electrical energy from one place to another. In normal usage the term "wave guide" refers to metallic pipes or solid tubes of insulating material which are used to direct very high frequency electrical energy along desired paths.

Methods of Transmission.—A pair of copper wires serves as an economical and efficient electrical transmission line up to frequencies of hundreds of megacycles. At frequencies above 50 to 100 megacycles the efficiency and usefulness of a two-wire line begins to drop off rapidly because of heating of the line itself, and because the line acts as an antenna and radiates some of its electrical energy into space rather than conducting it to the desired place. Unwanted radiation may be avoided by use of a coaxial line which is built with a central copper wire surrounded by an insulating material, and with a braided copper sleeve and insulating jacket on the outside. The electrical energy is contained between the inner and outer conductors and unwanted radiation is no longer a serious problem. Heating of the copper conductors as well as heating of the insulating materials limit the usefulness of coaxial lines in most applications to frequencies below about 5,000 megacycles.

Rectangular Wave Guides.—At frequencies above 1,500 to 3,000 megacycles hollow metallic wave guides become practical. They are not useful at lower frequencies because of the large size required. Wave guides are ordinarily made of copper or brass, and may be silver or gold plated to improve their electrical performance. If electrical energy is to be transmitted in a wave guide, one inside dimension, such as a in Fig. 1(A), must be at least one half wavelength at the operating frequency. Electrical energy whose frequency is lower than this critical frequency will not be transmitted down the guide. The dimension b determines the allowable voltage which can exist between the top and bottom walls of the guide and fixes the maximum power which can be transmitted.

The electric field intensity (similar to voltage) across the guide is maximum at the center and tapers off to zero at the sides as shown in Fig. 1(B). In contrast, the magnetic field intensity (similar to current), along a horizontal section such as c-c'-c''-c''' in Fig. 1(C), is a

RIVER BASINS AND ARID REGIONS OF THE WORLD

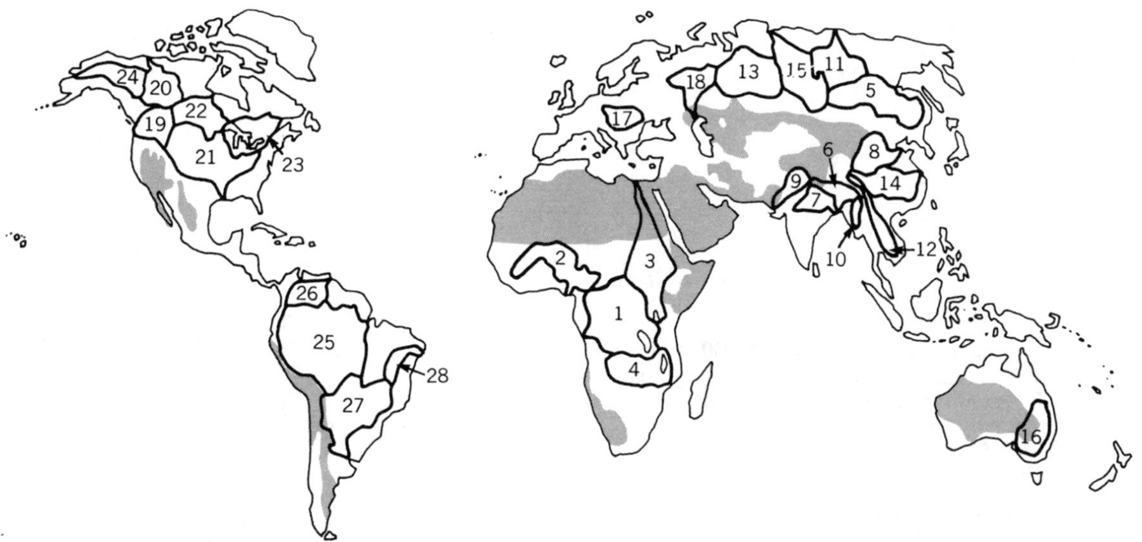

Fig. 2. River drainage basins of the world's major rivers are shown in outline, and arid regions are shaded. The numbered basins are identified in Table 2.

Groundwater is an important source for streams. Wherever a streambed cuts below the water table, groundwater seeps through the banks and bed of the stream. This seepage, called base flow, generally supplies 20% to 50% of the water in most streams. During an extended drought, base flow becomes the main supply.

Water Usage. Of the water withdrawn from streams, lakes, or wells for human use, nearly two thirds is used for irrigating crops, and most of this is used in southern Asia. Irrigation also consumes more water than any other use. In the United States, for example, an average of 55% of the water used for irrigating crops evaporates or transpires to the atmosphere in the form of water vapor. This 55% is classified as consumed, because it is not returned directly to streams or groundwater aquifers and thus is not available for immediate reuse. In the case of water withdrawn for personal and industrial uses, nearly all of it may be available for reuse either directly or after suitable treatment.

Personal survival requires only a few quarts of water a day. But the development of industry, irrigated agriculture, and urban life-styles bring great increases in water use. In the United States, for example, daily water use averages about 1,600 gallons per capita. This figure includes 50–100 gallons for domestic uses, 650 gallons for irrigation, and 820 gallons for industry.

Water Shortages. Although the quantity of the world's freshwater resources is more than adequate to meet present and projected human needs, the uneven distribution from place to place and from time to time results in severe shortages. In Africa, for example, a population of over 500 million has an average water supply of nearly 2.5 trillion gallons (9.5 trillion liters)

Table 2—AREA AND ANNUAL RUNOFF OF MAJOR RIVER BASINS

No. on map	CONTINENT River (Nation at mouth)	Basin drainage area (1,000 sq. miles)	Average annual runoff (inches per year)
	AFRICA		
1	Congo (Zaire)	1,440	13.2
2	Niger (Nigeria)	850	3.4
3	Nile (Egypt)	1,170	0.4
4	Zambezi (Mozambique)	548	6.2
	ASIA		
5	Amur (USSR)	730	8.2
6	Brahmaputra (Bangladesh)	220	43.2
7	Ganges (Bangladesh)	382	23.5
8	Yellow River (China)	290	2.5
9	Indus (Pakistan)	378	9.6
10	Irrawaddy (Burma)	153	42.5
11	Lena (USSR)	961	8.2
12	Mekong (Vietnam)	303	23.8
13	Ob (USSR)	1,160	5.2
14	Yangtze (China)	698	20.1
15	Yenisei (USSR)	977	9.6
	AUSTRALIA		
16	Murray (Australia)	410	0.8
	EUROPE		
17	Danube (Romania, USSR)	315	9.2
18	Volga (USSR)	533	7.1
	NORTH AMERICA		
19	Columbia (U.S.)	236	15.1
20	Mackenzie (Canada)	697	6.7
21	Mississippi (U.S.)	1,250	7.0
22	Nelson (Canada)	414	3.1
23	St. Lawrence (Canada)	396	12.0
24	Yukon (U.S.)	324	9.2
	SOUTH AMERICA		
25	Amazon (Brazil)	2,370	40.7
26	Orinoco (Venezuela)	382	43.5
27	Paraná (Argentina)	890	8.0
28	São Francisco (Brazil)	247	6.1

Conversion factors: square miles to square kilometers, 2.59; inches to millimeters, 25.4

Table 3—WATER SUPPLY AND WATER USAGE BY CONTINENT[1]

	SUPPLY				USAGE					
Continent	Area (square miles)	Annual runoff (inches)	Total supply	Per capita supply	Irrigation	Thermo-electric power	Other industry	Domestic	Total usage	Per capita usage
Africa	11500	4.5	2460	4633	44	8	3	9	64	121
Asia	17030	10.9	8830	3098	1014	49	22	71	1156	406
Australia-Oceania	3440	10.6	1740	108750	9	6	4	1	20	1250
Europe	3860	11.0	2030	2915	84	127	133	29	373	536
North America	9310	9.6	4270	10810	148	168	55	28	399	1010
South America	6910	24.4	8030	30417	25	5	3	8	41	155
Antarctica	5440	5.6	1450							
World	57490	10.5	28800	6048	1324	363	221	146	2054	431

[1]Per capita supply and usage figures in gallons per day; all others in billions of gallons per day.
Conversion factors: inches to millimeters, 25.4; square miles to square kilometers, 2.59; gallons to liters, 3.79.
Sources: A. Baumgartner and E. Reichel, *The World Water Balance;* The Global 2000 Report to the President.

per day, nearly 5,000 gallons (19,000 liters) per person per day—more than enough for all personal, agricultural, and industrial uses if it were distributed uniformly in place and time. Nevertheless extensive regions are perennially dry and experience severe droughts when rainfall is even lower than normal.

Comparable droughts have occurred in many other parts of the world, including the southwestern and central parts of the United States during the dust-bowl years of the 1930's. Some areas with relatively generous water supplies, such as the northeastern United States, draw on those supplies so heavily that a period of lower-than-normal precipitation may result in widespread shortages. See also CONSERVATION.

Conservation. Many water shortages could be eliminated or substantially alleviated by conservation measures. Personal water usage, for example, could be greatly reduced by installation of water-efficient showers, toilets, dishwashers, and other water-consuming appliances. In industry, water can be saved by recycling and other conservation measures. In irrigated agriculture, a substantial reduction in water usage usually follows a change from conventional surface flooding to sprinklers or drip irrigation techniques. The use of such measures can be encouraged by metering water usage and pricing it at its true cost.

JOHN C. KAMMERER, *Hydrologist*

Bibliography

Baumgartner, A., and Reichel, E., *The World Water Balance* (Elsevier Pub. Co. 1975).

Davies, Delwyn, *Fresh Water* (Aldus Books 1967).

Frater, Alexander, ed., *Great Rivers of the World* (Little 1984).

International Hydrological Programme, *Ground Water in Hard Rocks* (Unipub 1985).

L'Vovich, M. I., *World Water Resources, Present and Future* (Am. Geophysical Union 1979).

Meyer, G., "Water—Sources and Utilization," *Encyclopedia of Chemical Technology* (Wiley 1984).

Nace, R. L., *Are We Running Out of Water?* (USGPO 1967).

U.S. Council on Environmental Quality and the Dept. of State, *The Global 2000 Report to the President, The Technical Report* (USGPO 1980).

Van der Leeden, F., *Water Resources of the World, Selected Statistics* (Water Information Center 1975).

White, G. F., and others, "Resources and Needs—Assessment of the World's Water Situation," in *U.N. Water Conference, Summary and Main Documents* (Oxford 1978).

WATER, Heavy. See HEAVY WATER.

WATER BABIES, The, subtitled *A Fairy Tale for a Land-Baby,* a story for children by Charles Kingsley, published in 1863, with a dedication "To my youngest son, Grenville Arthur, and to all other good little boys." It is a fairy story heavily charged with didacticism.

Tom, an apprentice chimney sweep, blunders into a wrong room at Harthover Place. The whole household chases him, thinking him a thief. He finally escapes across the moors, plunges into a river, and is changed by the fairies into a water baby. The rest of the story is devoted to his aquatic adventures, first in the river and then in the ocean.

Kingsley works into the narrative a great deal of his wide knowledge of natural history, but adds still more in the way of moral preaching. The training of the water babies is handled by two fairy godmothers whose functions are sufficiently defined by their names: Mrs. Bedonebyasyoudid and Mrs. Doasyouwouldbedoneby. The underwater world is conceived of as a kind of purgatory in which imperfect spirits are gradually purified by punishments and rewards. Tom's own purification is completed when he makes a toilsome pilgrimage to the Other-end-of-Nowhere to release the soul of his old, cruel master, Mr. Grimes, the chimney sweep.

Kingsley hated cruelty, selfishness, and stupidity, and made his dislike abundantly plain to his child readers. Only their parents, however, are likely to get the full significance of his ironic comments on materialistic scientists, or of his theological overtones. To the modern adult reader (children can probably still take it in their stride) the relentless underscoring of moral preachments is the greatest defect of the book. It is worth noting that *Alice in Wonderland* by Lewis Carroll was published just two years after *The Water Babies.* Lewis Carroll may have got from Kingsley some hints for the character of the Duchess.

DELANCEY FERGUSON
Brooklyn College

WATER BALLET. See SWIMMING—*Synchronized Swimming.*

WATER BEAR. See TARDIGRADE.

WATER BEETLE, any of numerous water-living beetles that swim by using their legs as oars. The largest family, the Dytiscidae, contains more than 2,000 species, grouped in 120 genera. All of the dytiscids are aquatic, although they pupate in soil near the edges of lakes, ponds, and streams.

Dytiscids range in length from 0.04 to about 1.5 inches (1–35 mm). They have convex backs and undersides and a smooth body covering (exo-

© B. J. COATES/BRUCE COLEMAN, INC.

Water buffalo plow rice fields in Thailand. They are a major source of agricultural power in the tropics.

skeleton). The legs, flattened and fringed with long hairs on the edges, are adapted for swimming. The beetles can hang from the surface film of water by means of long hairs on the last two body segments; the hairs also serve as a breathing tube. Adults can trap air under their wing shields (elytra) as a supply for diving.

Both adults and larvae are voracious, attacking other insects, mollusks, worms, salamanders, tadpoles, and small fish. Adults leave the water at night and may travel long distances in search of suitable breeding places. They are frequently attracted to light. Large adults of some species are eaten in parts of eastern Asia.

Another large family of water beetles is the Hydrophilidae, the water scavengers. These are about the same size as dytiscids but have club-shaped instead of filamentous antennae. Both adults and larvae are vegetable scavengers. See Beetle for illustration.

Charles Howard Curran*
The American Museum of Natural History

WATER BOATMAN, a worldwide group of small to medium-sized water bugs that swim by rowing with their very long hind legs. The rowing legs are flattened like oars and fringed with swimming hairs. Water boatmen swim with a short, jerky motion. They can remain underwater for long periods, drawing on a supply of air carried mostly under the wings.

The wide, flat body of the water boatman has a smooth, dark-brown outer covering (exoskeleton). The head is blunt and convex, and the antennae are concealed in a recess between the head and the thorax.

Water boatmen feed mostly on algae and decaying vegetation but also eat some tiny animals found on pond and stream bottoms. They attach their eggs to pond vegetation in variously sized groups. They fly at night, and most species are attracted to light.

The bugs often are found in large numbers. In Mexico, two species of *Arctocorixa* occur in such quantities that the eggs are collected and used for food, and the adults are dried for use as food for fish, poultry, and pet birds.

The eight genera and 300 species of waterbugs make up the family Corixidae, order Hemiptera.

Charles Howard Curran*
The American Museum of Natural History

WATER BUFFALO, buf′ə-lō, a domestic cud-chewing, plant-eating mammal distantly related to domestic cattle. The water buffalo (*Bubalus bubalis*) may have been domesticated more than 4,000 years ago in Iraq and the Indus Valley. Domesticated populations certainly existed in southern China more than 3,000 years ago. Until recently, wild populations survived near most of the domesticated animals. As a result, interbreeding was common and relatively little difference exists between the wild and domesticated forms.

Adult wild males reach head-and-body lengths of 7.9–9.2 feet (2.4–2.8 meters) and are about 6 feet (1.8 meters) high at the shoulders. Weights are generally about 2,200 pounds (1,000 kg). Females are usually smaller than males, and most domestic varieties are smaller than wild specimens. The distinctive horns are more or less triangular in cross section, flat above and

A water boatman swims by using its legs as oars.

© EDWARD S. ROSS

strongly ribbed below. The length and curvature of the horns varies from individual to individual, and among domesticated animals they vary from breed to breed.

Two major groups of domestic breeds are generally recognized: the larger swamp buffalo, which are the work buffalo of the rice-growing regions of Asia, and the smaller river buffalo, which have been selected as dairy animals, especially in India and Pakistan. Water buffalo milk has much more fat, more nonfat solids, and less water than cow milk.

The world population of domestic water buffalo is about 140 million, including 60 million swamp buffalo and 80 million river buffalo. Most of the swamp buffalo are in China (30 million), and most of the river buffalo are in India (60 million) and Pakistan (10 million). Domestic water buffalo have been introduced into the lower Nile Valley in Egypt, southeastern Europe, Brazil, and parts of Australia.

E. LENDELL COCKRUM, *University of Arizona*

WATER BUG, any of several kinds of swimming bugs, but especially the giant water bugs, which are also known as electric-light bugs, toe biters, or fish killers. They are nearly worldwide in distribution, although most species are tropical.

The giant water bugs are very large—up to 4 inches (100 mm) long in the United States and even longer in the tropics. The front legs are adapted for grasping prey, and the hind legs are flattened like oars for swimming. The long, strong beak rests under the head and front of the thorax.

The adults and nymphs live in ponds and small lakes where they feed on insects, snails, tadpoles, small frogs and toads, salamanders, fish, and any other animals they can overcome. They are voracious and sometimes bite the feet of bathers. If held in the hand they sometimes inflict painful wounds. The adults fly at night and are sometimes attracted to light in such enormous numbers as to be serious pests. Females of some genera deposit their eggs on the backs of males, temporarily preventing flight. In parts of tropical America and the East Indies, the adults are used as food.

The giant water bugs make up the family Belostomatidae in the order Hemiptera. The family includes about 100 species grouped in eight genera. See also WATER BOATMAN; WATER SCORPION; WATER STRIDER.

CHARLES HOWARD CURRAN*
The American Museum of Natural History

WATER CHESTNUT, a small family of Old World water plants that yield an edible fruit, also called water chestnut. The name is applied especially to *Trapa natans,* also called the water caltrop, caltrops, trapa nut, and saligot. Water chestnuts have long been cultivated as ornamental pond plants and for their fruits. In eastern North America they have escaped from cultivation and are established in ponds and streams.

The water chestnut has two kinds of leaves, submerged and floating. The submerged leaves are finely divided feathery structures that grow from nodes in the underwater stem. The floating leaves are fan-shaped and often variegated or mottled. The flowers are small and white. The hard, nutlike fruits are about 1 to 2 inches (25–50 mm) across with two pairs of spines or horn-shaped protrusions that develop from flower sepals. The fruit somewhat resembles the caltrop, an ancient weapon with two pairs of opposed spines. It is usually boiled or roasted for eating.

Another member of the family, ling (*T. bicornis*), is cultivated for its fruit in China, Japan, and Korea. As its specific name indicates, its fruit has only two horns. Singhara nut (*T. bispinosa*), which is native to tropical Asia, is also grown for its fruit, which may have one or two horns.

The Chinese water chestnut sold in Oriental food shops in the United States is the corm of a sedge, *Eleocharis dulcis.*

WATER CLOCK. See CLEPSYDRA.

WATER COLOR. See WATERCOLOR.

WATER CONSERVATION. See CONSERVATION—*Water Conservation.*

WATER CRESS. See WATERCRESS.

WATER CYCLE. See HYDROLOGIC CYCLE.

WATER DESALINIZATION. See DESALTING.

WATER DOG. See MUD PUPPY.

WATER FLEA. See DAPHNIA.

WATER GAS, a clean, low-energy fuel gas usually made by passing air and steam through a bed of incandescent coal or coke. It is used in industry as a fuel for furnaces and gas turbines. See GAS, FUEL—*Manufactured Gas* (Low-Btu Gas).

WATER HEN, a common name for a group of chickenlike marsh birds. See COOT; GALLINULE; RAIL.

WATER HYACINTH, a common name for *Eichhornia crassipes,* a floating perennial herb of the pickerelweed family (Pontederiaceae) native to tropical America. Widely cultivated as an ornamental, it has escaped as a weed in warm

Water hyacinth (*Eichhornia crassipes*)
GRANT HEILMAN

temperature and tropical waterways. The floating leaves are clustered at the nodes and have ovate to round fleshy or leathery blades one to three inches broad, constricted at their bases above bulbous inflated petioles. These petioles, whose internal tissues have large intercellular air spaces, support the plant in the water; submerged leaves, if present, are long and narrow. The flowering stalk, from a few inches to two or more feet tall, rises erect from the leaf cluster and bears a loose terminal spike of conspicuous, funnel-shaped, somewhat two-lipped lavender flowers, the uppermost of whose six petals has a blue patch surrounding a bright yellow central spot. The attractive flowers bring it also the name water orchid. Long pendant roots may hang freely in the water or, in shallow water, penetrate the soil beneath. The plants propagate themselves profusely by thick horizontal rhizomes, and in areas where they become established, as in the rivers and bayous of the southeastern United States, constitute a menace to navigation by obstructing channels with impenetrable masses of tightly bound plants. In Florida the water hyacinth is called the "million-dollar plant," because of the extent to which it has hindered navigation on the St. Johns River.

RICHARD M. STRAW

© JACK DERMID/NATIONAL AUDUBON SOCIETY/PR

Water lily *(Nymphaea odorata)*

WATER LILY, a plant of the aquatic family Nymphaeaceae, and of the genus *Nymphaea*. These are found in fresh, still waters throughout the warm and temperate regions, and are often cultivated. Some can be raised easily from seed, and those which are hardy in the North will stand a very low temperature without damage, even to be encased in ice. They may be grown in tanks, or even in half-barrels, as well as in ponds. The tropical species must be raised nearly to blooming size in a greenhouse before being planted outside. The water lilies are handsome plants, having more or less orbicular leaves, either floating, or more rarely immersed, and solitary flowers, of similar varying habit. The blossoms have four sepals and many petals, stamens, and carpels, the latter united and immersed in a thickened receptacle; in color they may be white, pink, yellow or blue, and are sometimes very fragrant. The flowers of some species open by day and close at night; others open at night and close by day. The duration of one flower is usually three days. If pollinated the flower is drawn to the bottom of the pond or tank by a bending or spiral coiling of the stalk.

The fruit is indehiscent, somewhat fleshy, and like a large berry filled with seeds. The seeds have small embryos and abundant starchy perisperm, and are enclosed in pulpy arils. When the seeds are ripe the pod breaks open irregularly. The seeds are borne to the surface of the water by the buoyant arils, where they repel each other and float far and wide by changes in surface tension and by currents of water and wind. After one or two hours the aril contracts, breaks loose, and lets the seed drop to the bottom of the pond. Nearly all of the known 40 species have been brought into cultivation, and countless hybrids have been produced, both in the hardy and tropical groups. One of the finest is the Australian water lily (*N. gigantea*). Its flowers are sometimes a foot across, with hundreds of stamens, and the color is blue, pink, or white. It does not close so completely at night as do other water lilies. The Egyptian lotus (*N. caerulea*) that was a favorite plant of the ancient Egyptians is often confounded with the Indian lotus (*Nelumbo*), but is really a blue-flowered water lily, with flowers borne on stiff stalks a foot above the water. It was a valuable plant to the decorators of Egypt, who copied it, and conventionalized its form in many of their architectural ornaments, and also introduced it constantly into their painted pictures of life and customs. Its rootstock and seeds served as food. The European water lily (*N. alba*) has white flowers that usually float upon the surface of the water. The flowers are not fragrant, as are those of the American water lily (*N. odorata*). The latter lovely water lily rides upon the water, with snow-white petals radiating in circles, the inner gradually narrowing, and passing by various stages into golden stamens in the center. They open in sunshine about 6 A.M., and close in the early afternoon. The fruit is ovate and baccate and ripens underwater. The leaves, or lily pads, a favorite food of deer, are ovate-orbicular, with a deep sinus, and have very long cylindrical stems of unvarying thickness, great flexibility, and toughness. The thick, fleshy creeping rootstock furnished a brown dye for the early settlers, and was also used as a styptic and tonic. A variety of this water lily is smaller and has rose-colored flowers. There are four other species of *Nymphaea* in the United States, including the golden-flowered water lily (*N. mexicana*) of Florida and Mexico.

See also LOTUS; NYMPHAEACEAE; VICTORIA.

HENRY S. CONARD
Grinnell College

WATER LINE. See WATERLINE.

WATER METER, a device installed in a pipe under pressure for measuring and registering the quantity of water passing through it.

Sextus Julius Frontinus (c. 30–104), a *curator aquarum* in charge of the many aqueducts delivering upland water to Rome, had bronze apertures installed where the quantities of water diverted to large consumers could be observed and estimated; for smaller users, orifices were installed. The original United States patent for measuring the flow of water under pressure was granted in 1850 to William Sewell, and in 1852, Joseph Maudsley took out a British patent on a similar principle. In 1875, a patent providing legible dials above water greatly facilitated meter reading. General interest in meters increased during the next decade; 39 patents were issued in 1886. The Venturi meter, based on principles laid down by Giovanni Battista Venturi (1746–1822), was given practical reality by Clemens Herschel in 1887. (For further history, see William L. Herron, *Water Works Engineering*, 1930, p. 1897.) Standard specifications for cold-water meters have been issued by the American Water Works Association, and designated C-700 (displacement type); C-701 (current type); C-702 (compound type); C-703 (fire-service type); and C-704 (current type, propeller driven).

There are in use six principal types of meters for pressure pipes: disk (or displacement), velocity, compound, fire-service, orifice, and Venturi. Domestic meters generally are of the disk, velocity, compound, or fire-service types; for larger quantity measurements the orifice and Venturi meters are used.

The *disk* (or *displacement*) meter is provided with a measuring chamber of a known size. As this chamber fills and empties, the mechanism of the meter records the quantity of water displaced each time the water leaves the chamber. The mechanism is operated by various means, including nutating disk, oscillating piston, and rotating gear. The disk type is costlier than the velocity type; it is made in ⅝-inch to 6-inch sizes. While relatively accurate at low flows, the disk meter has a limited capacity range for a given size and high friction loss at high flow. If improperly installed, it tends to be noisy. For high capacities, a battery of disk meters, a velocity meter, or a compound meter will prove more practical.

A *velocity* meter (also termed *current, turbine,* or *torrent*) is provided with a piston or impeller, the speed of the mechanism being calibrated to the quantity of water passing through it. This type is low in initial cost, inexpensive in repairs, and measures relatively large quantities with little friction loss. It comes in sizes 1½ to 16 inches. Inasmuch as there is no obstruction to the free flow of water through this meter, it meets the requirements of the National Board of Fire Underwriters for use on fire-service lines. However, it is difficult to maintain at a high degree of accuracy, and to repair.

A *compound* meter comprises a combined disk and velocity meter. The low flow is measured through the disk mechanism, after the flow reaches a predetermined rate, measurement is picked up by the velocity mechanism. It is available in 1½- to 10-inch sizes. Compound meters have a wide capacity range, measuring both large and small flows accurately; at the "change point" from displacement to velocity mechanisms, there is usually a sharp drop in accuracy. Because of its size, it ordinarily must be tested in place, a hindrance to effective repair. A battery of two or more small disk meters is frequently used in place of a compound.

In the *fire-service* meter, a certain proportion of the total flow passing through the meter is bypassed through a measuring device which is usually of the disk type, although sometimes of the velocity type.

Where there is little or no frost or snow, it is advantageous to set the meter in a box in the sidewalk area, affording easy access for reading or changing the meter. In climates where the winters are severe, however, it is practically a necessity to install a domestic meter in the basement to prevent damage from freezing.

The working parts of domestic meters are made light and durable. Hard rubber generally is used for disks, and also for the rotary pistons of some meters. Where the liquids are hot, or consist of chemical solutions, brass generally is employed. Possible damage due to clogging by the entry of fish or gravel is prevented by various forms of strainers and sieves, while the effect of frost is abated by frost cases.

Orifice meters have no moving parts in the pipe, merely an orifice in a thin plate. Their merits are low initial cost, short length, ease of installation, adaptability to large capacity, and their freedom from clogging which promotes continuous accuracy; however, the head loss is high.

The *Venturi* meter is based upon the hydraulic principle that when water flows at an increased velocity, there will be a corresponding reduction in head, or pressure. The meter usually consists of an upstream reducer whereby the area is diminished to approximately one fourth to one ninth of the pipe area. Downstream from the reducer is a short throat piece and a relatively long section to increase from the throat diameter back to the normal pipe diameter. The upstream pressure is measured just above the point at which the pipe begins to taper down to the throat; pressure is also measured in the throat, where the high velocity occurs. The relatively long downstream section permits a gradual change, with little loss of head, from the high velocity to the normal pipe velocity; this loss is estimated generally to be about one tenth of the velocity head in the throat.

Venturi meters are relatively inexpensive. For large flows they have a high degree of accuracy over a broad range, with a very small friction loss; but they do not measure accurately at low flows. They require a substantial space for installation, and once installed cannot readily be removed to a new position. With reasonable care they may be operated for years without adjustment; the clear waterway through the meter prevents clogging.

Registering mechanism consists of a series of gear wheels and dials. The flow of the water actuates the gear wheels and the number of revolutions are recorded on the dials. The arrangement of the mechanism converts the number of revolutions into any desired unit of volume, such as cubic feet, United States gallons, imperial gallons, or liters. Mercury wells are also employed.

For the effects of metering, see WATER SUPPLY—*Uses and Consumption.*

CLINTON L. BOGERT
Coauthor of "Waterworks Handbook."

Further Reading: DeCarlo, Joseph P., *Fundamentals or Flow Measurement: An Independent Learning Module of the Instrument Society of America* (Instr Soc 1984); Scott, R. W., ed., *Developments in Flow Measurement*, vol. 1 (Elsevier 1982); American Water Works Association, *Water Meters: Selection, Installation, Testing, and Maintenance* (1973).

WATER MILFOIL, any plant in the genus *Myriophyllum,* in the water milfoil family, Haloragidaceae. There are some 40 species of *Myriophyllum,* widely distributed in both warm and cold regions, many native to Australia. These aquatic plants grow in still water or rooted in the mud. The leaves, often ½ to several inches in length, are whorled or alternate; the submerged ones are usually once-pinnately divided into fine, threadlike segments, hence the name *Myriophyllum* (from the Greek *myrios*, numberless, and *phyllon*, leaf). Leaves above the water may be similar, but frequently are less deeply cut or entire. The small flowers are either in the axils of the submerged leaves, or in aerial spikes, the upper often staminate, the lower pistillate, the central ones perfect. They are characteristically four-parted, usually with four sepals, four petals (or none), eight (or four) stamens, and an inferior, four-celled ovary which splits at maturity into four single-seeded segments. The flowers are often purplish, reddish, or yellow. The species of *Myriophyllum* are difficult to separate. *M. brasiliense,* also called parrot's feather because of its feathery leaves, is native to South America; it is grown in aquariums and has escaped from cultivation. *M. exalbescens* and *A. verticillatum* are common species of extensive occurrence in North America, Europe, and Asia.

EDWIN B. MATZKE

WATER MOCCASIN. See COTTONMOUTH.

WATER MOTOR. See HYDRAULIC ENGINE; HYDRAULIC MACHINE; TURBINE; WATERWHEEL.

WATER OUZEL, or **DIPPER,** a songbird of the family Cinclidae, with two species each in the Old and New World. Water ouzels are very plump brown birds with or without a white breast and abdomen, and with short wings and tail. They resemble the wrens, to which they may be distantly related, but are aquatic and much larger, varying from about seven to nine inches in size. The plumage is very dense and provided with an undercoat of down. They frequent the banks of shallow clear lakes and especially swift and turbulent streams in hilly or mountainous country. Their food consists chiefly of the larvae of aquatic insects which they secure by wading or submerging, walking deliberately on the bottom when underwater. The name "dipper" is derived from their habit of constantly jerking up and down, as though hinged at the knee, while walking out of water. The single species in North America (*Cinclus mexicanus*) inhabits the mountains of the West from Alaska south to Panama.

CHARLES VAURIE

Water plantain (*Alisma triviale*)

WALTER SCHLEGEL

WATER PARSNIP, a small group of plants commonly found in wet meadows and swamps. Water parsnips make up the genus *Sium* of the parsley family (Umbelliferae). They are native to southern Africa and many regions of the northern temperate zone.

A familiar North American species is *S. suave,* which grows from Newfoundland and British Columbia south to Florida, Louisiana, Utah, and California. It may reach a height of 6 feet (1.8 meters) and bears flat-topped clusters of small white flowers. Its narrowly segmented leaves have toothed edges. A somewhat similar plant, *Berula pusilla,* is also called water parsnip.

The skirret (*S. sisarum*), an Asian species, is sometimes cultivated for its thick tuberous root, which is eaten as a vegetable.

JOHN J. SMITH

Water pennywort (*Hydrocotyle umbellata*)

WATER PENNYWORT, a group of small plants that grow in mud or shallow water and bear small round, scalloped leaves sometimes called "pennies." Water pennyworts, also called "marsh pennyworts," make up the genus *Hydrocotyle* of the parsley family (Umbelliferae). They are widespread throughout North America. Their tiny white or greenish flowers are borne in clusters either on stems or at the bases of the leaf stalks.

The name "water pennywort" is also applied to *Centella erecta,* a small North American plant that resembles members of the genus *Hydrocotyle.*

WATER PLANTAIN, a small group of plants of the genus *Alisma* (arrowhead family, Alismataceae) that live in mud or shallow water. Water plantains have clumps of grasslike or ovate leaves borne on stalks that may be 1 foot (30 cm) or longer. A central stem bears a loose cluster of tiny flowers, each of which has three green sepals and three white or pinkish petals.

North American species include *Alisma subcordatum,* found from New England to Minnesota and Nebraska, and *A. triviale,* from Nova Scotia, Quebec, and British Columbia to Florida, Texas, Mexico, and California. The bulblike bases of these plants were once used as food by Indians.

WATER PLANTS. See AQUATIC PLANTS.

D. P. A.—PICTORIAL PARADE

SEVERE WATER POLLUTION, believed caused by pesticides, in the Rhine River in Germany, caused the death of millions of fish and made the water unusable either for drinking or for swimming.

WATER POLLUTION. Water, one of man's most precious resources, is generally taken for granted until its use is threatened by reduced availability or quality. Water pollution is produced primarily by the activities of man, specifically his mismanagement of water resources. The pollutants are any chemical, physical, or biological substances that affect the natural condition of water or its intended use. Because water pollution threatens the availability, quality, and usefulness of water, it is of worldwide critical concern.

In the late 1960's and early 1970's the seriousness of the water pollution problem was brought to public attention by several events. These included the spill in 1967 of 30 million gallons of oil into the ocean off the southern coast of England from the tanker *Torrey Canyon* and the spill of 8 million gallons of oil from offshore drilling on the California coast near Santa Barbara, the death of millions of fish in the polluted Rhine River in Germany, and drastic changes in the ecological balance of such lakes as Lake Erie in the northeastern United States, Lake Tahoe in California, Lake Constance on the border of Switzerland, Austria, and Germany, and Lake Zurich in Switzerland.

Nature of Water Pollution. The increase in the number and variety of uses for water throughout the world has produced a wide range of standards of water quality that must be satisfied. These demands include (1) preservation of rivers in their natural state; (2) potability of the water supply; (3) preservation and enhancement of fish and wildlife; (4) safety for agricultural use; (5) safety for recreational use, including swimming; (6) accommodation to a great variety of industrial purposes; (7) freedom from nuisance; (8) generation of power for public utilities; (9) dilution and transport of wastes. Besides the specific chemical, biological, and physical requirements for the multitude of uses noted above, there are constraints reflecting public health requirements, aesthetics, economics, and short- and long-term ecological impacts. Consequently, there is no rigid or specific definition of water pollution, since the intended use or uses of the water must be taken into consideration in any definition of what constitutes polluted water.

One method of classifying the gaseous, liquid, and solid constituents of water that constitute pollution depends on the intended use of the water. The pollutants are then grouped as not permissible, as undesirable and objectionable, as permissible but not necessarily desirable, or as desirable. For example, if water is to be used immediately for animal consumption, toxic compounds are not desirable, whereas a certain amount of oxygen is not objectionable. On the other hand, if the water is to be used in a power plant for steam generation, toxic materials might be allowable or even perhaps desirable, whereas oxygen that could possibly corrode equipment would be objectionable.

Another method of classifying pollutants that enter water as a result of man's domestic, industrial, or other activities is to distinguish between conservative and nonconservative pollutants. *Conservative pollutants* are those that are not altered by the biological processes occurring in natural waters. These pollutants are for the most part inorganic chemicals, which are diluted in receiving water but are not appreciably changed in total quantity. Industrial wastes contain numerous such pollutants, including metallic salts and other toxic, corrosive, colored, and taste-producing materials. Domestic pollution and return flow from irrigation may contain numerous such pollutants, including chlorides and nitrates.

Nonconservative pollutants, on the other hand, are changed in form or reduced in quantity by chemical and physical processes involved in biological phenomena occurring in water. The most common source of nonconservative pollutants is domestic sewage—highly putrescible organic waste that can be converted into inorganic materials such as bicarbonates, sulfates, and phosphates by the bacteria and other microorganisms in the water.

If the water is not too heavily laden with wastes, it will undergo "self-purification." This process involves the action of aerobic bacteria—that is, bacteria that require free oxygen—to break down wastes, and it produces no offensive odors.

If, however, the water is laden with wastes beyond a certain amount, the process of biological degradation becomes anaerobic—that is, it proceeds by the action of bacteria that do not require free oxygen. In this process, noxious hydrogen sulfite gas, methane, and other gases are produced. The aerobic and anaerobic processes that occur naturally in streams are used in sewage treatment plants and are, in fact, major elements in sewage treatment.

SCOPE OF THE PROBLEM

The problem of water pollution has been and is almost worldwide.

History. By the 20th century, people had become concerned about water pollution, largely because of the prevalence of waterborne diseases such as typhoid fever. The coliform test, still the major indicator of the biological safety of water, was developed to detect the presence or absence in water of bacterial organisms from the human intestinal tract. Measures were aimed also at controlling water temperature. Other measures were developed to attack organisms, to make use of the natural assimilation capacity of flowing streams in purifying wastes, and to pass water through treatment plants to provide safe drinking water. Later, pollution control was directed toward problems caused by processing wastes from industry. Control was aimed primarily at protecting downstream public water supplies or at stopping or preventing public nuisances.

Factors Affecting Water Pollution in the Mid-20th Century. The growth and changes in the United States and in many parts of the world, particularly in the more developed nations, in the mid-20th century have contributed substantially to water pollution. Population growth, the rate of industrial progress and technological developments, changing land practices, and other factors have accelerated water pollution—largely through the need for waste disposal.

Rapidly growing urban areas have created demand for disposal of domestic wastes through already overburdened waterborne collection and disposal systems. The increased production of goods has greatly increased the amount of common industrial wastes. New processes in manufacturing produce new and complex wastes that are not removed by existing treatment and control technology. Increased use of commercial fertilizers and the development of new pesticides applied to agricultural and urban areas have created a host of new pollution problems. Expansion in the nuclear energy field and the use of radioactive materials have presented new and complex water pollution problems. Leapfrogging urban developments have made it difficult to construct and extend well-designed sewer systems and to develop treatment plants of adequate size. The intrusion of seawater in response to excessive pumping of groundwater supplies has created new problems of groundwater degradation.

Present Conditions. Pollution is a problem in almost all waterways—rivers, lakes, estuaries, and even oceans, once erroneously thought to be able to assimilate almost everything.

The seriousness of the water pollution problem can be illustrated by a few examples in the United States. In the mid 1960's the Arkansas River was found routinely to have large amounts of sodium in the water, making it unuseable for drinking. A 1964 outbreak of encephalitis in New Jersey was attributed in part to water pollution since polluted streams provided extensive breeding grounds for the mosquito carriers of the disease. As late as 1965 a midwestern city was dumping 300,000 pounds of paunch manure (partly digested material in the stomachs of slaughtered cattle) into the Missouri River each day. This material contributed to the unsightliness of the river, led to its condemnation for recreation and sports, and of course, presented public health hazards.

Some of the Great Lakes provide prime examples of serious lake pollution. Lake Erie, for example, receives waste discharge of over ten million people, of which 45% receives primary and secondary sewage treatment, 50% only primary treatment, and 5% no treatment at all. Pollutants from these discharges and others have lead to a reduction in the commercial and sport fishery in the area. For example, in 1925 about 25,000 pounds (11,350 kg) of cisco were harvested each year, while in the mid 1960's only about 1,000 pounds (454 kg) were harvested, the cisco population largely replaced by undesirable species such as carp and catfish. Parts of Lake Michigan are also used as a "dumping ground" for many wastes. A steel plant has discharged into the lake over 230 million gallons of wastes per day; this includes 13,750 pounds of nitrogen that enhances algae growth and 54,000 pounds of oil that is damaging to the aquatic life and waterfowl.

Estuaries serve as the breeding grounds for many animals, and pollution of these areas often has very serious effects on the well-being and reproductive success of many species. The metropolitan area of New York City has been pouring over ½ billion gallons of inadequately treated sewage into its rivers and harbors each year with the result that now only 35 of the city's 575 miles of estuary coastline is considered safe for swimming.

Although the ocean serves as a biological wasteland, one-half of the world's fish comes from only 0.001% of the ocean, and these coastal waters are where pollution is the greatest. The New York City area is one of the largest polluters of sea water. It annually dumps 17 million cubic yards of refuse (sewage, sludge, excavation dirt, acids, chemical wastes, and other wastes) into coastal waters, killing much of the shellfish and other marine life of the areas. Recent oil spills in harbors and in offshore drilling operations have also contributed to substantial losses in marine life, waterfowl, and the use of beaches for recreation.

Prognosis. If widespread water pollution continues unabated, it will result in a lack of potable water for domestic purposes at a time when demand is increasing; a reduction in crop production and consequent higher food costs; the elimination of certain fishes used for food and sport and the destruction of other aquatic life; and higher costs for products whose manufacture depends on high water quality.

MAJOR WATER POLLUTANTS

Water may be considered polluted because of an excess or burden of any gaseous, liquid, or solid constituent. The list of substances that may pollute water is almost endless, but the major pollutants are discussed here briefly.

Organic Wastes. Organic wastes are contributed by domestic sewage from both rural and urban areas and by industrial wastes of animal and plant origin. Although domestic sewage is the most widespread source of degradable organic wastes, industry contributes about an equal amount of such wastes. The greatest industrial generators of organic wastes are the food and pulp-and-paper industries, which have numerous plants, many of which discharge massive loads of organic wastes into waters. One sugar beet processing plant during its brief seasonal operation may produce organic wastes equivalent to the sewage flow of a city of half a million people.

The breakdown of organic wastes by bacteria removes oxygen from the water, producing a serious problem. Since fish and aquatic life depend on dissolved oxygen, oxygen-demanding organic wastes damage the aquatic environment. When such wastes consume oxygen excessively, conditions of gross septic pollution result. Rivers grossly polluted by organic wastes include the Detroit River, the Merrimac River in Massachusetts, and sections of the Mississippi River and its tributaries.

Living Agents. Living agents that can pollute water include bacteria, viruses, and other microorganisms that can cause disease. These organisms may enter water through domestic sewage or through certain kinds of industrial wastes, especially those associated with the tanning industry or animal slaughter. Although the bacteria causing typhoid and cholera are effectively controlled in most developed countries of the world, they still present a danger in many underdeveloped areas. Harder-to-destroy viruses that may cause intestinal or other infections pose a continuing water pollution problem.

Plant Nutrients. Plant nutrients—substances that stimulate the growth of plants—are also major polluters of water. The two principal water polluting elements in plant nutrients are nitrogen and phosphorus, but trace amounts of other elements are also present. These elements are usually present in small amounts in natural waters, but much larger amounts are contributed by sewage, certain industrial wastes, and drainage from fertilized lands and underground materials high in nitrates. Biological waste treatment processes do not remove plant nutrients from water. In fact, such treatment makes them more usable by plant life.

When plant nutrients spill over in large amounts into water, they act as fertilizers, stimulating the intensive and extensive growth of water plants, such as algae and water weeds. Such growth often causes unsightly conditions, interferes with water treatment processes, and creates unpleasant and disagreeable tastes and odors. When these plant growths die and decay, they not only produce a foul taste and odor but also cause secondary oxygen consumption, thus lowering the level of dissolved oxygen in the water. Such excessive development of plant life from surplus nutrients in surface streams, lakes, and ponds is known as *eutrophication*. It has occurred, for example, in Lake Erie in the northeastern United States, in Lake Washington in the northwestern United States, Lake Constance in Switzerland, Austria, and Germany, and in Lake Baikal in Siberia. See also EUTROPHICATION.

Synthetic Organic Chemicals. The steady output of new chemical compounds for a variety of purposes has produced new pollutants of increasing concern. New products are developed and old ones abandoned before their pollution significance can be determined. In many chemical industries, for example, a majority of sales are of products unknown only two or three years earlier. Included in this group are detergents and many other household cleaning products, new synthetic pesticides, synthetic industrial chemicals, of a wide variety, and wastes from the manufacture of these products. In particular, pesticides, such as DDT, dieldrin, and chlordane, used to control insect pests in agricultural situations but eventually found in water, are of growing concern. The synthetic organic chemicals or their residues are often toxic to fish and other aquatic life as well as detrimental to man. Their stability and persistence in the water environment produce new and complex problems in conventional water and waste treatment.

Inorganic Chemical and Mineral Substances. Inorganic chemicals and minerals may also pollute water—interfering with stream purification, destroying fish and aquatic life, causing excessive hardness of water supply, having corrosive effects on machinery, and, in general, adding to the cost of water treatment. Included in this group are a vast array of metals, metal salts, acids, solid particulate matter, and many other synthetic chemical compounds and their by-products and wastes.

Mercury pollution has just recently been recognized as a very serious and widespread danger in many waterways. Abnormal amounts of mercury have been found in water and in fish and game birds in more than half of the states. Mercury, even in very small amounts, can cause very serious physiological effects and in some cases death. It, like the pesticides, travels along the food chain—that is, is passed from organism to organism, such as from minute aquatic microorganisms to fish to game birds or to man. Waterways known to be polluted with mercury include Lake Erie, the Connecticut River, the Savannah River, Lake St. Clair, the Rio Grande River, Lake Onondaga in New York, the Wisconsin River, and many others.

Inorganic chemical pollutants are contributed to water through the wastes from mining and manufacturing processes, oil-field operations, agricultural practices, and natural sources. Irrigation, particularly in the western United States, leaches large amounts of mineral salts from the soil, adding substantially to the salt load of downstream water supplies. Natural salt and gypsum deposits in the southwestern United States are particularly serious sources of pollution in that area, damaging or making unusable large quantities of ground, stream, and impounded water. Oil-field brines compound the salt problem in that region. Acids of a wide variety are discharged as waste by industry, particularly from abandoned workings and tailings of acid mine operations. Acid mine drainage is a major problem in the Ohio, Delaware, and Susquehanna rivers and in certain tributaries of the Mississippi River.

Sediment. In some areas, land erosion, slippages, and particles washed from hard-surfaced areas, such as streets, buildings, and airports contribute significantly to water pollution. Such sediments are not as insidious in their pollutional characteristics as other pollutants, but they can be a major problem because of the sheer magnitude of the sediment load. It has been estimated that the suspended solids from sediments are at least 700 times greater than those contributed by sewage. Sediments fill streams, channels, and harbors, necessitating excessive dredging. They also fill reservoirs, reducing their capacity and usefulness, and erode power turbines and pumping equipment. Sediments increase the treatment costs for municipal and industrial water supply as well as for sewage. Sediment also reduces the sun's penetration of water, and this in turn reduces the production of oxygen—which is necessary to normal stream balance—by aquatic plants.

Silt and suspended sediment in a river or lake

OFFICIAL RATINGS ON SOME MAJOR U.S. WATERWAYS[1]

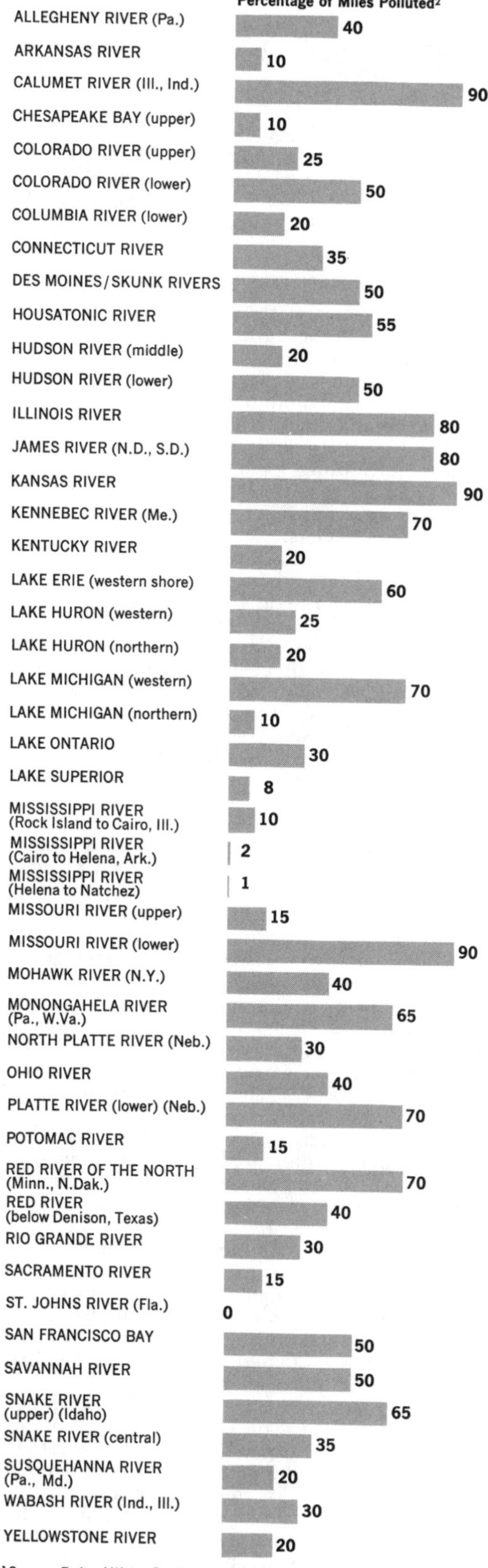

[1] Source: Federal Water Quality Administration.

[2] Waters are considered polluted when they contain more man-made wastes than minimum government standards specify. Figures given indicate the mileage that fails to meet government standards; it does not indicate the degree of pollution, which may vary considerably, often being greater near large cities.

EXTENT OF WATER POLLUTION IN THE UNITED STATES
(Percent of stream miles polluted)

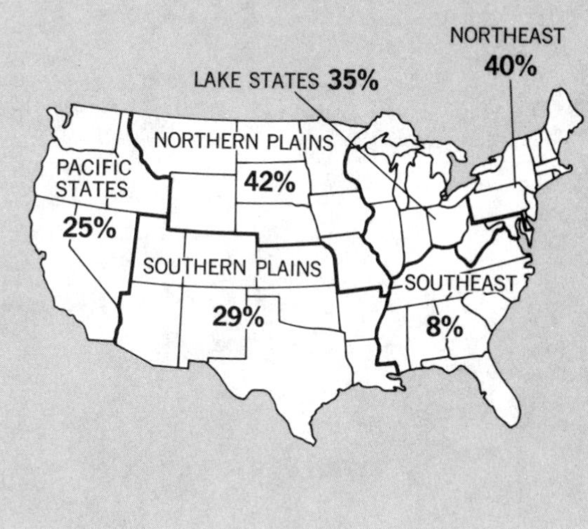

can harm aquatic life in a number of ways: (1) by direct action on the aquatic organisms swimming in the water; (2) by killing, slowing the growth, decreasing the disease resistance, or in other ways preventing the successful development of the eggs and larvae of aquatic organisms; (3) by modifying the natural movements and migrations of organisms; and (4) by reducing the abundance of food available to the aquatic organisms.

Radioactive Materials. The atomic power industry has led to pollution of waters by radioactive wastes. A radioactive waste is a solid, liquid, or gaseous waste produced during the manufacture or use of radioactive substances. Such wastes may result from mining and processing of radioactive ores, from the use of refining radioactive materials and power reactors, from industrial, medical, and research uses of radioactive materials, and from fallout resulting from the testing of nuclear weapons. The two most common radioactive materials found in water are strontium–90 and radium–226.

The problems posed by radioactive materials introduced into natural bodies of water must be considered in terms of their possible effects on aquatic organisms and on man. People may be exposed to radioactivity by using contaminated waters as a source of domestic water supply, by swimming in such waters, or by using them for other recreational purposes. Such water may also be used to irrigate crops and may contaminate freshwater and saltwater fish. Industrial use of contaminated water and work in sewage treatment plants might also expose workers to radioactivity. Since radiation is cumulative in human beings, total exposure to radiation from all environmental sources must be carefully considered.

Hot Water. The increased use of natural bodies of water for cooling operations in industry presents another water pollution problem—the addition of damaging amounts of heat to streams. Tremendous volumes of water are used for cooling in electric power plants, steel mills, petroleum refineries, petrochemical plants, and other industries. Most of this water, with the added heat, is returned to the lakes, streams, and coastal waters from which it was originally withdrawn. When returned, it raises the water temperature.

Heat is considered a water pollutant for several reasons. First, it reduces the solubility of

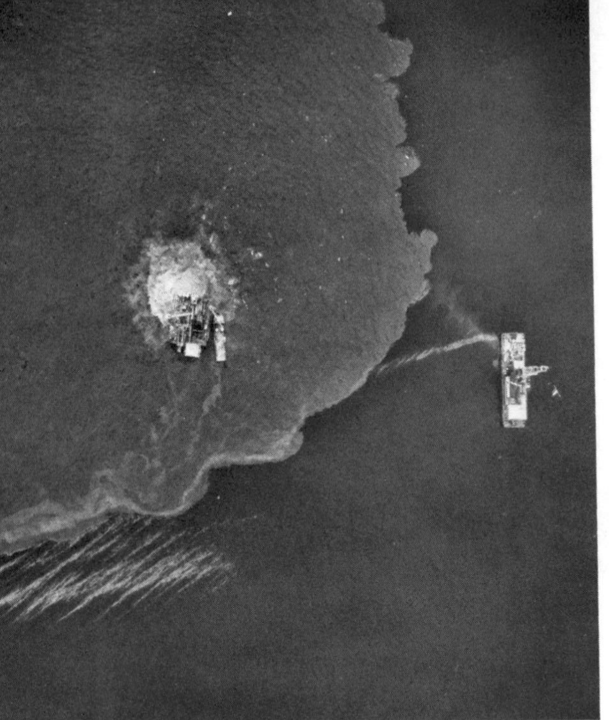

MARK HURD AERIAL SURVEYS

OIL SLICKS, such as one near Santa Barbara, Calif., present a particularly serious water pollution problem.

oxygen in water, thereby reducing the ability of receiving water to assimilate oxygen-consuming pollutants and support fish and aquatic life. Second, the higher water temperature may have a direct detrimental effect on fish and aquatic life by changing their physical environment. Since some fish can tolerate only a few degrees of temperature increase, a substantial increase can virtually eliminate normal aquatic life. Eggs from chinook salmon, for example, incubated in water at temperatures above 60° F (51° C) suffer excessive mortality. Third, heated water can also harm water stored in reservoirs. Summer temperatures heat up the surface layer in lakes and impoundments, causing the water to stratify, with the cooler water settling to the deeper layers. Decomposing vegetative matter from natural and man-made pollutants depletes the oxygen from these cooler layers with detrimental effects on aquatic life. When these oxygen-deficient waters are discharged from the lower gates of a dam, they may have serious effects on downstream aquatic life and the ability of the stream to assimilate downstream pollution.

Cold Water. Cold water can also be a water pollutant, harming the production of some agricultural crops. Cold water released from the deep layers of storage reservoirs into surface streams of irrigation canals can, for example, have undesirable physiological effects on crops, retarding germination and reducing yields. This has happened in rice-growing areas in the Sacramento Valley of California. Cold water is also undesirable from the standpoint of recreational use.

Oil. Water is polluted by oil discharge from barges and ships or from the accidental or careless handling of crude oil in transport, development, and drilling operations. It is estimated that 1.5 million tons of oil are spilled into the ocean each year. Oil-polluted water results in great damage to aquatic life and other wildlife. Waterfowl alighting on oil sump areas or oil-covered waters usually become so oil soaked that they are unable to fly. Oil destroys much of the aquatic life of oceans, including the food of fishes and shellfish. There is little information on the toxicological effects of oil on man or other warmblooded animals. Experience along the Santa Barbara coast of California indicates that severe oil spills also result in substantial immediate economic losses to the nearby communities.

SOURCES OF POLLUTANTS

Pollutants enter water from industrial wastes, from urban areas and agricultural areas, and from transport vehicles.

Industry. Industrial wastes provide the widest range of complex pollutants, including various kinds of organic and inorganic chemicals and heat. Steel mills, for example, have been identified as contributing phenolic compounds, dissolved iron, increased fluoride and manganese concentrations, elevations in water temperature, and undesirable odors.

A particularly complex dimension of water pollution has emerged in recent years with the growth of the synthetic chemical industry. Industrial wastewaters that tend to increase or decrease the hydrogen ion concentration of the water—that is, that affect the acidity of the water —can be particularly harmful to aquatic life. Coal mine stripping, for example, can produce acids that cause widespread damage to vegetation and aquatic animal life. Other toxic elements commonly found in industrial wastes include arsenic, bromine, chlorine, sodium chlorate, and sodium fluoride.

Large power plants also constitute a hazard because they often give off heat. A plant planned for the St. Croix River at Oak Park Heights in Minnesota with a heat rejection rate of 2,520,000,000 Btu per hour would raise water temperatures considerably, causing serious damage to aquatic life.

Urban Areas. Pollutants that enter water from urban areas are largely wastes from sewage treatment plants and septic tanks, dust, dirt, and other contaminants carried in storm sewer systems and materials leached or transported from land fills or dumps.

Agriculture. Agriculture, including the processing of agricultural products, is the source of a number of water pollutants, such as sediment from the erosion of croplands, animal wastes, pesticides used to destroy crop pests, and fertilizers that contain phosphorus and nitrogen. A steadily growing agricultural problem is the runoff from areas contaminated by livestock and poultry wastes, particularly from feedlots. Overall waste production by farm animals in the United States is estimated at about 20 times that of human production.

Although animal wastes are normally disposed of by physical means on land, the sheer volume makes this material a potential source of contamination of public water supplies. On the basis of the oxygen needed by microorganisms for the biological degradation of organic material, wastes from a feedlot with 10,000 animals are equivalent to those of a city of about 45,000 people. The overall problem of agricultural waste and runoff from agricultural lands is compounded by the expansion of urban areas into regions of agricultural production.

Transport Vehicles. Many of the common forms of transport contribute directly to water pollution. A major source of pollution of the world's waterways is the discharge of raw sewage and other wastes from commercial passenger and transport ships into bays, estuaries, and harbors. The increasing use of private boats that discharge waste into waters also contributes to the problem. Over 8 million watercraft navigate in U. S. waters, discharging a variety of pollutants that include sanitary wastes, oil, litter, and bilgewater. There is also the danger of accidents, such as the *Torrey Canyon* disaster, leading to increased pollution. The problem is especially difficult since no specific international regulations deal with pollution of oceans or other international waterways.

Passenger trains also contribute to water pollution by discharging sewage and garbage directly onto railroad right-of-ways where it can move into surface or underground water supplies.

MEASURING AND DETECTING WATER POLLUTION

To define and attempt to solve the problem of water pollution, accurate measurements of the level of water pollution are absolutely essential. The volume and concentration of waste plus its overall polluting effect must all be measured.

Volume and Concentration of Solids. The volume of waste is measured in terms of total flow in gallons per day or of per capita flow in gallons per day. The normal per capita flow of domestic sewage, for example, varies from 50 gallons (190 liters) per capita per day in small towns to about 200 gallons (755 liters) in large cities.

The concentration of the waste is expressed both by the type and amount of solids it contains and by the biological activity that these solids will support. The solids in a stream will normally consist of suspended and dissolved solids and both organic and inorganic materials. For example, the solids in normal domestic waste are approximately 60% organic and 40% inorganic. Organic materials—those representing living or dead plant and animal matter—serve as food for microorganisms and constitute the major pollution-producing solids. Examples of organic materials include fecal matter, paper, bacteria, and alkyl benzene sulfonate (ABS) detergents. Such organic solids can be burned off readily, leaving the inorganic solids, such as sand and ash.

Solids in wastes are expressed either in terms of concentration, such as pounds of solids per million pounds (ppm) of waste or in total weight, such as pounds per day. Some of the organic constituents of pesticides and herbicides present complex measuring problems since their polluting effect may be significant at concentrations of less than one part per billion (ppb). A test of solids gives a measure of the total amount of solids in a waste material and their relative division into suspended and dissolved fractions and into organic and inorganic fractions. It does not, however, give specific information on the waste's susceptibility to treatment or its pollutional effect. This information is provided by chemical tests.

Chemical Tests. Chemical tests such as the chemical oxygen demand (COD) test and the biochemical oxygen demand (BOD) test determine the amount of oxygen required to stabilize waste. The COD test determines the amount of chemical oxidizing agent, such as potassium dichromate, required to oxidize completely the organic material present in a sample of water. The BOD test measures the amount of oxygen needed for the biological decomposition of organic solids under aerobic conditions during a standardized temperature (normally 43° F, or 20° C). The BOD test is the principal test for determining the polluting power of a waste, because it measures the total amount and rate of oxygen that is needed to prevent odor, nuisance, and oxygen depletion of streams.

The rate at which a given quantity and type of organic waste exerts oxygen demand depends on a variety of factors, including the temperature and the chemical characteristics of the receiving water. For example, toxins may appreciably slow BOD by inhibiting bacterial action. In extreme instances of toxic pollution, a body of water may become bacteriologically "dead." High temperatures, on the other hand, accelerate bacterial action, so that wastes are degraded more rapidly and dissolved oxygen in the water is drawn upon heavily.

The COD and BOD tests do not provide information on the many wastes contributing to water pollution, such as ABS herbicides, insecticides, weed killers, acid wastes, residual dissolved organic chemicals, and electroplating wastes. For some wastes, standardized tests are available. For others, the tests are not very accurate, and for still others, there are no tests at all. In some cases, it is better to use bioassay tests, using insects or fish to determine pollutant concentrations, than to develop specific quantitative chemical tests.

Measuring Radioactivity. The level of radioactivity in water must also be measured, and the length of exposure considered. A dose-response relationship for the biological effects of ionizing radiation has not yet been determined. See also Radiation.

EFFECTS OF WATER POLLUTION

Water pollution biologically affects all living organisms and also produces economic, industrial, and aesthetic effects.

Plants. As mentioned earlier, the addition of plant nutrients (nitrates and phosphates) to water stimulates the growth of undesirable aquatic weeds and algae—eutrophication. In addition, certain chemicals, such as chlorides, can, when present in water in large amounts, reduce the yields and adversely affect the quality of some crops.

Animals. Fish and other aquatic animals such as lobsters, shrimp, and mussels, live in a precise physiological adjustment with the various factors in their aquatic environment—temperature, oxygen content of the water, salinity, bottom sediments and suspended material, and light. Various pollutants in water may affect any or all of these factors.

Fish and aquatic invertebrates are poikilothermic—that is, their body temperature varies with that of their external environment. Some fishes are sensitive to temperature changes of only 1.6° F (about 1° C). Rapid temperature changes produced by water pollution can be harmful and even lethal to some organisms in a very short period of time.

The concentration of oxygen in the water is another very important environmental variable to which fish and aquatic invertebrates must adapt. Generally, oxygen concentrations of about 9 parts per million, are most acceptable, whereas concentrations lower than 5 parts per million cause asphyxia in some species.

Changes in water salinity also impose a stress on aquatic organisms. For example, an organic organism may lose water and shrink or gain water and swell if subjected to a change in salinity. The presence of silt may result in a physical smothering and interference with light penetration. Light penetration is necessary for growth of green plants and if impaired may lower biological productivity of aquatic organisms.

Nonaquatic animals can also be affected by water pollution. Land animals and birds, for example, are affected by water pollution through feeding on fish and aquatic animals taken from polluted or contaminated waters.

Man. Water pollution affects man's health, aesthetic appreciation and recreational use of water, and industrial use of water.

The transmission of waterborne disease is of great concern. In highly developed countries in particular, emphasis has shifted from concern over bacterial disease to concern over waterborne viral disease. Viral hepatitis, for example, has been found to occur more frequently in cities whose water supplies have comparatively high levels of water turbidity. Toxic chemicals found in streams that are ultimately used for water supplies also pose an important public health problem.

It is clear that toxic chemicals, such as arsenic and cyanides, must be excluded from the water, but the increasing number of chemicals from new pesticides, fertilizers, and other new products found in water is of increasing concern since the public health significance of these chemicals is not yet fully known. Nitrates, fluorides, and phosphates are also finding their way into water supplies from groundwater pollution.

Man's views on water pollution are also based on aesthetic values. The smells associated with anaerobic processes in sewers, stagnant ponds, septic tanks, and other places are repulsive. Floating materials, such as sewage solids and other suspended sediment, including dyes found in industrial waste, are also repulsive. Dense algae growth resulting from large amounts of sewage residue and plant nutrients dumped into water also makes the water unattractive and malodorous.

As man's desire for water-based recreation increases, greater demands are placed on the quality of water. The water must not only be aesthetically attractive but must also meet certain other conditions. If, for example, the level of dissolved oxygen in the water is reduced by the load of organic waste, or toxic chemicals affect fish, sport fishing may be seriously affected. Sports such as swimming that involve direct contact with water raise the water standards even higher.

Water pollution also has other indirect economic effects on man. When water becomes so polluted that industrial growth and development are curtailed, the incomes and health standards of workers are lowered. Continued pollution can actually reduce the number of jobs.

The range of water quality necessary or desirable for industrial processes varies greatly with the intended use of the water. The water used in steel mills, for example, must have a lower chloride level than that accepted for drinking water, and commercial fisheries demand water qualities similar to those required for sport fishing and for swimming. On the other hand, cooling water can often be of comparatively low sanitary quality, although the presence of heat and corrosive and scale-forming materials is undesirable. Some industrial processes require unusually soft water, whereas others need comparatively hard water. A large part of the water used in the paper-and-pulp industry can be of relatively low quality in some respects, but must, however, contain little iron, magnesia, and carbon dioxide.

Overall Environmental Equilibrium. Approximately 70% of the total surface area of the earth is water. Since this water is a dynamic system, any changes in its normal constituents and processes affect local, regional, and eventually the worldwide environment.

COMBATING WATER POLLUTION

Effective pollution control systems depend on policies that combine technical, economic, social, and aesthetic considerations. The decisions involved require answers to many complex questions. How can we provide water of what quality, when, how much, to what people, and for what purposes? Who is to be restrained from putting how much of what kinds of wastes into what parts of the water system? Who is to be permitted to use waters for waste disposal and under what terms and conditions? Who will pay the high cost of protecting surface and groundwaters?

The extreme view of demanding absolutely clean or pure water is as unacceptable as uncontrolled water pollution, since technical and financial feasibility must be included in all practical considerations of the problem.

There are several ways in which water pollution can be combated. First, through treatment of wastewater to make water reusable and of high quality. Second, by the enactment and enforcement of governmental regulations prohibiting and limiting pollution of waters. Third, by development of practices and techniques that will prevent or limit the natural runoff of pollutants—for example, from agricultural areas—into water.

Water Treatment. The traditional method of controlling water pollution in the United States has been to collect waste in a system of sewers and transport it to a waste treatment plant where the wastewater is treated for discharge into streams and for reuse.

There are two kinds of sewer systems—combined and separate. Combined sewers carry both water polluted by human use and storm water polluted as it drains off homes, streets, or land. In separate systems, sanitary sewers carry only sewage, while storm sewers carry the large volumes of storm runoff water. During dry weather when combined sewers are handling only the normal amount of wastewater, all of it is carried to the waste treatment plant. But, during a storm, when combined sewers have to carry a much larger amount of water, part of the water, including varying amounts of raw sewage, often bypass the treatment plant and flow directly into receiving streams. In these cases, the process of dilution is depended on to minimize the pollution, but this is a highly undesirable situation.

Wastewater is usually treated by two processes, called primary and secondary treatments. In *primary* treatment, solids are allowed to settle out from the water, and the effluent from the tank is then treated by chlorination to kill disease-causing bacteria and reduce odors. Although

30% of the municipalities in the United States give sewage only primary treatment, this process is inadequate for most water needs. In *secondary* treatment, up to 90% of organic material in sewage is removed simply by making use of the bacteria in the organic material. In this process the effluent leaving sedimentation tanks is acted on by bacteria that consume a substantial amount of the organic material in the sewage. Secondary treatment is completed by the addition of chlorine, which kills more than 90% of harmful bacteria in the effluent. In a very few areas, notably near Lake Tahoe, water is subjected to advanced tertiary treatment involving many new processes that further purify the water.

In areas lacking a sewer system or treatment plant, lagoons or septic tanks are used. A septic tank receives wastewater from a home and holds it while bacteria in the sewage break down the organic material so that clearer water flows out into a leaching field. Lagoons that provide for proper depth and detention while sunlight, algae, and oxygen interact can also restore water to a quality equal to that provided by the standard secondary treatment. See also WASTEWATER.

Government Activity. In the United States, water pollution control has evolved in the 20th century largely as a federal activity, with the states only in later years taking an active part in developing laws and procedures for water pollution control. From the first federal legislation concerning water pollution—the 1899 Rivers and Harbor Act—through the 1965 Water Quality Act, the 1966 Clean Water Restoration Act, and the 1987 Clean Water Act, the federal government has gradually established criteria for all interstate and coastal waters, granted assistance for research and treatment facilities, and provided for enforcement of laws against pollution.

The 1987 Clean Water Act allocated $20 billion to help provide states with federal funds for water pollution control as well as laws and programs to help protect the environment from toxic chemicals. The major provisions of this act were: $9.6 billion in federal grants to pay 55% of costs to help communities build sewage treatment facilities; $8.4 billion in federal grants for state revolving-loan funds to finance municipal sewage treatment facilities; $2 billion for additional programs to clean up the nation's water supplies; and the establishment of stricter laws governing the use of toxic chemicals and the development of programs to monitor and control water pollution in the Great Lakes and Chesapeake Bay.

The Federal Water Quality Administration administers the government's water pollution laws. Its activities include research and development, technical assistance, comprehensive water pollution control programs, and regulatory and enforcement actions. The work of a number of other government agencies, such as the Soil Conservation Service, Forest Service, Corps of Engineers, Public Health Service, Bureau of Reclamation, Bureau of Land Management, Bureau of Mines, Bureau of Outdoor Recreation, Fish and Wildlife Service, Bureau of Sport Fisheries and Wildlife, National Park Service, and the Coast Guard also includes efforts to prevent pollution.

Many states have also established agencies with specific responsibilities for water quality and pollution control, and a number of interstate groups have been organized to meet the problem of pollution in rivers and river basins that cross state lines. Considerable progress has been made by the Ohio Valley Water Sanitation Commission and the Interstate Sanitation Commission covering New York metropolitan areas.

Research and Development. Water pollution research is under way on a number of different fronts, including the search for a more efficient way to remove oxygen-demanding contaminants and organic contaminants now untreated, complete disinfection of wastes, control of agricultural runoff, prevention of seawater intrusion, retarding or reversal of eutrophication, reuse of wastes and others.

POLLUTION CONTROL ALTERNATIVES

It is technically possible to treat most municipal and industrial wastewaters so as to restore the quality they had before use, but the cost may be too high. Fortunately, various technical procedures other than wastewater treatment may help protect and enhance the quality of water. Among these are dilution, reaeration, temporary storage and programmed release of waste, changing industrial production processes or products, and recovery of waste, sometimes for profitable reuse or sale in by-products. One alternative to these procedures is the use of sewage effluents in irrigation procedures. In most cases, the problem is to select the best combination of measures to achieve specified water quality at least cost. The technical alternatives present problems from the standpoint of political and institutional jurisdiction and decision-making, and the decisions involve consideration of benefits and overall costs, economic and other.

There are at least three basic procedures for implementing governmental decisions for maintaining or improving water quality: (1) direct regulation through setting up water quality standards; (2) grants or payments for treatment or other improvement techniques; and (3) charges levied for treatment of waste or for disposal of effluents into public waters. The first two are already in use to varying degrees in the United States. The third, that of making effluent charges a major element in an efficient and equitable system of pollution control, has been given little attention except in the Rhur Valley in West Germany where organized regional districts have imposed effluent charges.

VERNE H. SCOTT*
University of California, Davis

Bibliography

Angeletti, G., and Bjorseth, A., eds., *Analysis of Organic Micropollutants in Water* (Kluwer 1984).
Banik, Allan E., and Wade, Carlson, *Your Water and Your Health* (Keats 1974).
Bitton, Gabriel, and Gerba, Charles. eds., *Groundwater Pollution Microbiology* (Wiley 1984).
Canter, Larry W., and Knox, R. C., *Ground Water Pollution Control* (Lewis 1985).
Dugan, Patrick, *Biochemical Ecology of Water Pollution* (Plenum Pub., 1975).
Grava, Sigurd, *Urban Planning Aspects of Water Pollution Control* (Columbia Univ. Press 1969).
Keith, Lawrence H., *Advances in the Identification and Analysis of Organic Pollutants in Water,* 2 vols. (Butterworth's 1982).
Kneese, Allen V., *Water Pollution: Economic Aspects and Research Needs* (Johns Hopkins Univ. Press 1962).
Pye, Veronica I., and others, *Groundwater Contamination in the United States* (Univ. of Pa. Press 1983).
Richardson, Genevra, and others, *Policing Pollution: A Study of Regulation and Enforcement* (Oxford 1982).
Stiff, M. J., ed., *River Pollution Control* (Halsted Press 1980).
Suess, M. J., ed., *Examination of Water for Pollution Control,* 3 vols. (Pergamon 1985).
Thomas, Bill, *American Rivers: A Natural History* (Norton 1978).

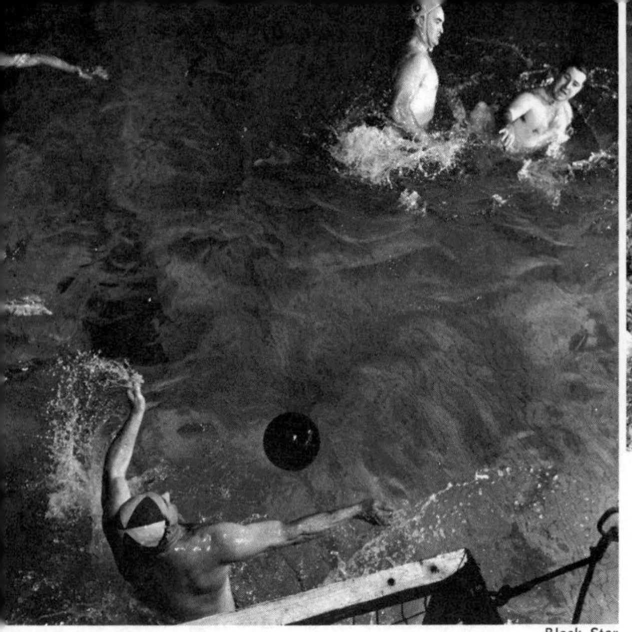

Black Star

Black Star

Above: Tackling a player in water polo. Ball may be held in one hand only, and only the player with the ball may be tackled. After contact is made, the player must keep the ball above the water.

Left: Goalkeeper saves a backhand shot. A goal may be scored by hand, head, or foot. Netted goals are 10 feet wide. Each goal scored counts one point.

WATER POLO, an aquatic team game played by swimmers in indoor and outdoor pools with an inflated ball. As in other goal games, such as soccer and lacrosse, the objective is to place the ball through the opponents' goal, thereby scoring one point. Usually this is accomplished not by individual effort but by relaying the ball to teammates.

The game saw its start in England in the 1870's and has grown in popularity during the 20th century. Two types evolved: one, especially popular in the United States, was a "softball" variety (the ball not fully inflated) and was extremely rough—a player was often tackled and held underwater until he released the ball; in Europe, however, a "hardball" variety was adopted, and the sport was first played in the Olympic games in 1900. Because of Olympic games prestige, this hardball game may now be considered the "official" international game, although the softball type continued to enjoy some popularity in the United States until the end of the 1930's.

International game rules call for a fully inflated, leather-covered ball between 27 and 28 inches in circumference, weighing between 14 and 16 ounces. The pool is not less than 20 nor more than 30 yards long; the width may not exceed 20 yards and must be uniform. No part of the pool may be shallower than 3 feet. Netted 10-foot-wide goals are placed at least 1 foot in front of the center of each pool end; the crossbar is 3 feet above the water, provided the pool is at least 5 feet deep, otherwise it is 8 feet above the bottom of the pool. (In major play, such as the Olympic games, a "shallow-end" pool would not be used.)

A team consists of 7 players—the goalkeeper; left, center, and right forwards (essentially offensive players); and left, center, and right backs (essentially defensive). Limited substitutions are permitted. The 20-minute game is divided into four 5-minute periods, with 1-minute rests between the first and second and between the third and fourth periods. There is a 5-minute rest between halves in which the teams change ends. In case of a tie, a 3-minute overtime is played. A goal may be scored by hand, head, or foot. At the start of a game the ball is thrown by the referee into the middle of the pool, and the two teams—lined up at the far ends—vie for possession. After an interruption the referee returns the ball to the goaltender, who must put it into play within 5 seconds. The ball may be held—balanced—in one hand only. Many rules penalize unnecessary roughness; only the player with the ball may be tackled, and he must not hold it underwater after contact is made. For a complete understanding of the game, the official rules should be studied.

The United States scored its sole Olympic victory to date in 1904. Great Britain, France, Germany, Italy, and Hungary have been other victors, with Hungary—a perennial "power"—winning in 1932, 1936, 1952, and 1956. However, the United States has produced a number of fine players from American national championship teams, such as the Illinois Athletic Club, the Chicago Athletic Club, the New York Athletic Club, and the Los Angeles Athletic Club.

PARKE CUMMINGS,
Author of "The Dictionary of Sports."

WATER POWER, the utilization of water as a natural liquid to produce energy, or power, in controlled amounts.

The power of water in the natural processes of nature is enormous and often awesome. Great waterfalls and storm-tossed waters sending tremendous waves crashing on the beaches are visible evidence of the mighty power of water. Although the potential for water power is great, practical limitations relating to the gathering and control of the power of water permit only an infinitesimal percentage to be developed. For example, the power of water resulting from the action of the ocean waves throughout the world represents an enormous amount of energy; however, no practical method of utilizing this potential has yet been devised. The most common form of using the power of water is in the exploitation of the difference in head, or the drop of water through a height, by developments on rivers.

Water power thus produced is renewable by natural processes. Evaporation takes place from the oceans and other water surfaces, adding to the water vapor content in the air. The air and water vapor is moved, both horizontally and vertically, over the earth's surface. Under appropriate conditions the water vapor becomes separated from the air in the form of rain, snow, or ice and, under the action of gravity, falls to earth. When this takes place in uplands or in the mountains, water collects at elevated locations and proceeds to flow back to the ocean through a network of rivers, using up its potential energy in soil erosion and the production of heat through turbulence and viscous action. By construction of a water power plant or hydroelectric plant, a portion of this potential energy may be made available in controlled form.

Power Production. A water power plant consists of many elements. The prime mover for converting the energy in the water to mechanical energy is a waterwheel or a hydraulic turbine. In hydroelectric plants, the prime mover shaft is connected (usually directly) to the shaft of an electric generator which changes the mechanical energy into electrical energy. Auxiliary control equipment such as speed governors, wicket gates, and control valves are provided. Since river flow is variable, as well as the load demands on the plant, water storage may be provided by construction of a dam with waterways to convey the water to the prime mover.

Mechanical work may be accomplished by water when the pressure, elevation of the free surface, or a change in the average velocity takes place in a suitable flow system. W pounds of a liquid possess potential energy in the amount WXh foot-pounds when the center of gravity is at an elevation h feet above the base from which the potential energy is measured. When water passes through a conduit from a high to a low elevation, the potential energy is changed to kinetic energy and friction losses. Mechanical work may be obtained when the water flows through a suitable water motor or turbine, the amount of work being a maximum when the water is discharged from the turbine with minimum pressure and velocity. Neglecting losses, the theoretical power available from a steady stream of water dropping from a surface elevation h feet above a lower elevation may be determined by the expression

$$62.4\ \frac{XQXh}{550} = \text{horsepower (theoretical)}$$

where Q is the rate of flow in cubic feet per second. The overall efficiency of a water power plant is the power output (mechanical or electrical) divided by the theoretical power available. Efficiencies of greater than 80 percent are achieved in modern large installations.

When the load on a hydraulic turbine changes, the water flow control valve setting must be altered correspondingly or the turbine rotative speed will change. Since load changes may occur very rapidly (for example, a short circuit in the transmission will trip the generator overload protection device and the whole load on the hydraulic turbine generator unit may be removed in a matter of microseconds) it may be necessary to operate the control valve rapidly. If the penstock is of appreciable length, the valve cannot be closed in a time less than about $10\frac{L}{C}$ (L = length of penstock, feet; C = velocity of sound in water in the penstock, feet per second) without producing pressure surges. In the event the closure time is less than $2\frac{L}{C}$, the full water-hammer pressure surge is developed with a magnitude of rise about equal to 60 ΔV pounds per square inch, where ΔV is the change in average velocity in feet per second in the penstock produced by the valve action. Surge chambers are installed to protect the penstock from failure. Since the water-hammer waves may be reflected as negative pressure waves, protection is provided for the penstock against collapse due to internal high vacuum conditions.

Selection of Sites. For the determination of locations for water power plants and the selection of proper size of equipment, studies are made of the available records of water flow at the proposed sites over long periods of time. When records of length sufficient to produce statistically significant data are not available, use has been made of partial rainfall records, crop records, thickness of tree rings, and similar indirect methods to estimate water flow magnitudes. Records from adjacent drainage areas are sometimes used as a basis for water flow estimates, but due to geographical and meteorological phenomena, the comparison is seldom valid without large and frequently not well-known correction factors. A knowledge and application of modern meteorology is important. Increasing attention is being given to control of weather; cloud seeding, or the introduction into the upper atmosphere under suitable cloud conditions of silver iodide or other substances, has been used to augment precipitation and thus to increase the amount of water flowing in a stream. Water flow rates vary greatly throughout the year as well as from year to year. In addition to the variable of precipitation and snowfall, the runoff is influenced by evaporation and transpiration losses, ground storage, and percolation. Water flow studies are made to determine expected magnitudes of minimum, maximum, and average daily flows, and the expected frequency of each. The minimum flow is used as the basis to determine available primary power; the maximum flow to indicate flood conditions; and the daily average to provide information fundamental to the design of a storage reservoir and to estimate the amount of secondary power available. Hydrograph and flow-duration curves are useful ways in which to study flow data. The hydrograph is a time history of flow rates plotted with discharge rates as ordinates and the time of occurrence in sequence as abscissas. The flow-duration curves are plotted with (daily, weekly, or monthly) flow rates or any proportional factor like power (when the head available is fixed) as ordinates, and the percentage of time for a year during which the flow rate equals or exceeds the given quantity as abscissas. Figure 1 presents a dimensionless flow-duration curve where the ordinates are expressed as a percentage of the minimum flow rate, which in turn establishes the amount of firm power to be expected from the unregulated flow. The area *oabc* on this curve represents the total amount of power available during a year. The area *odbc* is proportional to the annual primary or firm power. For a proposed water power plant having an installed capacity three times (300 percent) the firm power capacity, the area *defb* is proportional to the annual secondary or surplus power. The power of area *eaf* is wasted. By construction of a storage reservoir it is possible to store some water during flood periods and release it during periods of low flow, thus increasing the primary power to the area *ojhc* and changing the flow-duration curve at the power site to the curve in the figure marked *with storage*. The economics of proposed power instal-

OMIKRON/PHOTO RESEARCHERS

A powerhouse is located at the base of Fontana Dam on the Little Tennessee River in western North Carolina.

lations can be investigated with the aid of this curve to ascertain the significance of changes in selected power capacity and reservoir capacity.

By construction of a dam, water is impounded in a reservoir and the elevation of the water surface increased. By such means the potential power of water as it flows naturally down a river is seized by concentrating the more gradual drop of water over a reach of the river into one single fall and backing the water behind the dam to form a pool or reservoir. Many factors are given attention: the dam must be safe against overturning, sliding, excessive stresses, floods, surface water waves, possible ice action, effects of earthquakes, and other contingencies; in the reservoir area, land, real estate, water rights, railroads, highways, and similar items are usually involved

Fig. 1.

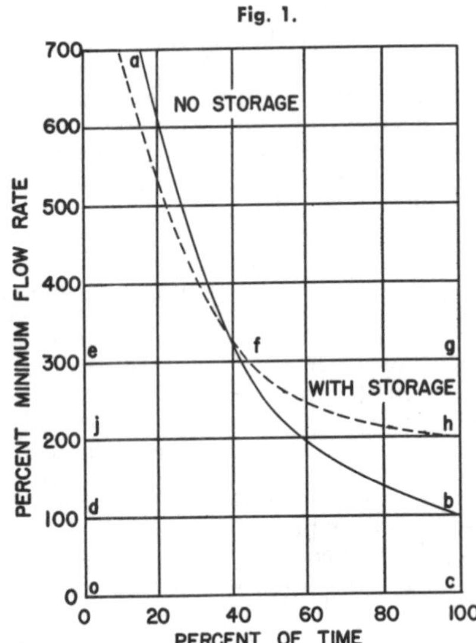

in varying degree; and facilities for passing anadromous fish are frequently required. Recreation has been given increasing attention.

In many projects the powerhouse is located at a distance from the dam, usually to gain additional head. In such cases, a waterway is provided to carry the water to the powerhouse. The waterway may be an open channel or canal, a closed conduit, or combinations of both. Canals are constructed along surface contours. Flumes, or open channels, are constructed of wood, metal, or concrete and are carried on supports to cross narrow valleys or ravines. Tunnels become practical when carrying water from one watershed to another, or in mountainous country where rock conditions are suitable and to avoid ice, snow, and landslide hazards. Penstocks are pipes conveying water from the waterway to the turbines, and may be constructed of wood or reinforced concrete, although they are more commonly made of steel.

When producing electrical energy for commercial use, the speed of rotation of the hydraulic turbine driving the generator must be controlled automatically within small limits to produce electric current of a constant voltage and frequency. Hence, a speed governor is used.

For centuries waterwheels have been in existence, making use of the velocity of the water flowing in a river (much the same as a windmill obtains energy due to the velocity of the wind), or an elevation drop in the water surface about equal to the diameter of the wheel. The power thus generated was adequate only for small mechanical works to be utilized on or very near the location of the waterwheel. Examples include power for gristmills or for operation of mechanical equipment in a manufacturing plant by transmission through gears or belting.

Hydraulic Turbines. The prime mover for modern water power developments is the hydraulic turbine, developed during the late 19th century in Europe and America. Hydraulic turbines are classified broadly in two main divisions: impulse turbines and reaction turbines. Impulse turbines are represented in modern practice by a single type called the Pelton waterwheel or turbine (inventor Allen Pelton, 1829–1908). Reaction turbines are divided in two types: the Francis turbine (James B. Francis, 1815–1892) and propeller turbine. The latter type is subdivided into the fixed-blade type and the Kaplan type (Victor Kaplan, 1876–1934) with movable blades. The range of specific speeds for maximum efficiency are: Pelton (single nozzle), 3.5 to 5.5; Francis, 15 to 100; and Kaplan, 90 to 190. Specific speed is defined as the ratio of the product of the speed of shaft rotation (revolutions per minute) and the square root of the horsepower output to the hydraulic head (feet of water) raised to the five fourths power. Efficiencies up to 94 percent have been obtained and are expected to be usually over 90 percent in modern installations. Pelton turbines have been used for heads of up to more than one mile (Chandoline plant, Switzerland—three Pelton turbines of 50,000 horsepower each under 5,740 feet head); Francis turbines up to more than 1000 feet (Piottino plant, Switzerland—two Francis turbines of 28,000 horsepower each under 1,060 feet head); and Kaplan turbines up to a little over 100 feet (Marne plant, northeast of Milan, Italy—Kaplan turbine, 7,320 horsepower under 105 feet).

The powerhouse provides protection for the important mechanical and electrical equipment. The turbine-generator unit is usually housed for protection against the weather and to increase ease of maintenance. In temperate climates, these units may be installed out of doors. Automatic control equipment, operator's control panel, instruments, low tension switching equipment, maintenance shops, office, and storage supplies are typical items included within the powerhouse. Space and hoisting equipment are provided for installation, repair, and maintenance of the hydraulic turbine and electrical generator units. Normally one or more operators are on duty at the powerhouse, but some fully automatic hydroelectric plants only require a maintenance visit and check at intervals of a week or longer.

Figures 2 and 3 illustrate typical hydroelectric station arrangements. Figure 2 shows a single nozzle Pelton turbine. Turbines of this type are used for heads of 1,000 feet and greater and

Fig. 2

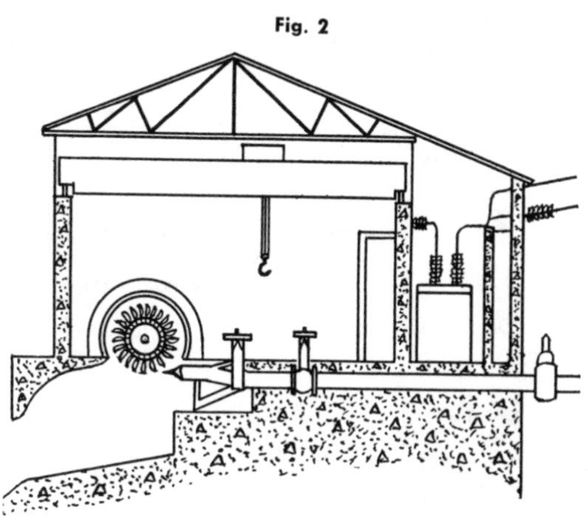

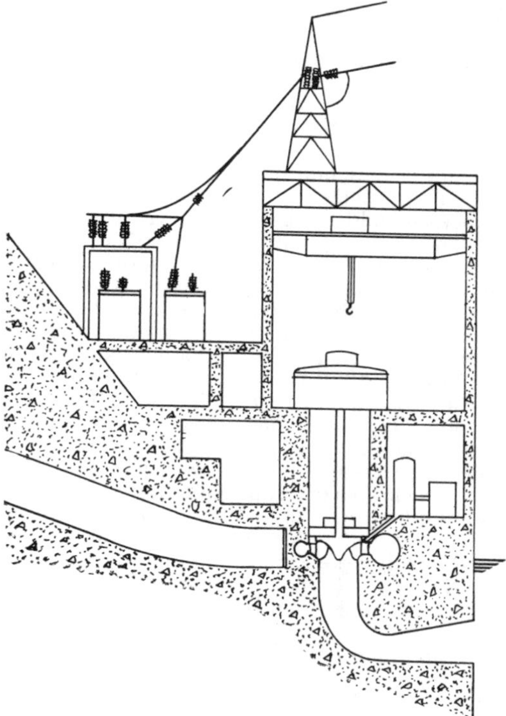

Fig. 3

in sizes up to about 70,000 horsepower. Most installations use one or two nozzles per wheel, but recent developments include efficient operation with four and six nozzles. The penstock terminates in a needle nozzle which is automatically adjusted by the governor to maintain constant rotative speed of the wheel. The nozzle guides the high velocity water into the buckets mounted on the wheel where the water is deflected so that the forward component of velocity approaches zero. The water then falls from the housing and passes into the tail pit.

Figure 3 shows a vertical shaft Francis turbine mounted in a semioutdoor type of powerhouse located at the base of the dam. Water flows from the conduit through the dam into the spiral case, through the wicket gates, the runner, and the draft tube. The wicket gates are adjusted by governor action to maintain constant speed of rotation. These turbines have been constructed for use with heads from 3 to over 1,000 feet, but modern designs are seldom used for heads of less than 50 feet. One of the larger American units is rated at 115,000 horsepower at 475 foot head and 180 revolutions per second.

See also DAM; HYDRAULIC ENGINEERING; TURBINE—*Hydraulic Turbine.*

R. G. FOLSOM
Professor of Mechanical Engineering and Director of the Engineering Research Institute, University of Michigan
Revised by E. ROBERT DE LUCCIA
Vice President and Chief Engineer, Pacific Power and Light Co., Portland, Oreg.

WATER PRESSURE. See HYDRAULICS.

WATER PURIFICATION. See WATER SUPPLY—*Treatment and Conditioning.*

WATER SCORPION, the common name of a small family of aquatic bugs of the family Nepidae of the order Hemiptera. The species of *Nepa* are elongate-oval in form, of *Ranatra* long and subcylindrical; other genera are intermediate in form. The front legs are raptorial, thickened, and directed forward. The middle and hind legs are long and slender and are used in crawling. The single segment of the front tarsi is sickle shaped and folds back into a groove in the tibiae. The end of the abdomen bears a pair of short or long respiratory filaments which form a breathing tube which is projected through the surface film to obtain air. The adults crawl laboriously about on submerged portions of plants in search of prey, but usually they remain in ambush to await their prey. In swimming the front legs are moved up and down while the other four legs perform a kicking motion. Flight takes place at night. The eggs are laid on water plants and in cracks and crevices of debris. The adults of some species make a squeaking noise by jerking back the front legs so that the coxae rub against the coxal cavities. Many feign death when captured. Only seven species occur in temperate America, the commonest being *R. americana*. The length ranges from about one to two inches.

CHARLES HOWARD CURRAN
The American Museum of Natural History

WATER SHIELD, a perennial aquatic herb, *Brasenia schreberi*, with floating, elliptic entire or shallowly crenate leaves 4 to 12 centimeters long and 2 to 6 centimeters wide, purple beneath. The petiole is attached to the center of the leaf (peltate or shield-shaped) and covered, as is the stem and underside of leaf, with 2 or 3 millimeters of clear, firm jelly. Flowers are dull purple, just above the surface of the water; petals 3 or 4, narrow, 12 to 16 millimeters long, persistent. There are 12 to 18 stamens, of two lengths; 4 to 8 carpels separate, becoming indehiscent, 1- to 3-seeded follicles. The herb is native to North and South America, Asia, Africa, Australia, and New Zealand. *Brasenia* has only the one species. It is closely related, in structure of flower and fruit, to Cabomba, a popular aquarium plant. It is placed in the water-lily family (Nymphaeaceae) because, like *Nymphaea*, the seed contains both endosperm and perisperm and has a hard shell which opens at germination by shedding a circular lid bearing the hilum and micropyle; also the first leaf is awl shaped. The separate carpels, becoming follicles, relate *Brasenia* to the marsh marigolds (Ranunculaceae). *Brasenia* has the reduced vascular system and large air cavities common to water plants. The tissues lack the internal stellate hairs of the water lily tribe. The stems and petioles are as elastic as india rubber, a condition which is useful for floating leaves in flowing water. *Brasenia* is usually found in 2 meters of water, but can get along in 2 centimeters.

HENRY S. CONARD
Grinnell College

WATER SKIING, the sport of riding on skis while being towed by a motorboat. Introduced in the 1920's, water skiing has grown dramatically in popularity since World War II. Riding behind a boat is the most basic type of water skiing. More experienced skiers advance to slalom skiing, jumping, and trick riding.

Conventional water skis are about 5 feet 8 inches (1.75 meters) long and 6½ inches (17 cm) wide. There is a rubber foot binding on each ski. A keel on the bottom provides stability. The skier grasps a wooden handle that is connected to a 75-foot (23-meter) tow line. The line has one end attached to the motorboat, either inboard or outboard, that pulls the skier. Flotation vests are usually worn for safety.

The traditional method of skiing is to begin in the water, sitting on the back ends of the skis, which slant upward. As the boat accelerates, the skier rises on his legs, keeping his arms straight. While skiing, the body is almost erect, and the knees are slightly bent. Experienced skiers may start from a beach, dock, or float.

Competition skiing has slalom, jumping, and trick riding events. World championships have been held since 1949. In slalom, skiers twist

CALLAWAY GARDENS

Water skier sends up a gigantic sheet of water as he leans into a turn during a slalom competition.

through a course marked by buoys. Slalom skiers usually ride a single ski that has two foot binders and has an extradeep keel. Slalom skiing is especially eyecatching as the skiers turn up huge sheets of spray as they maneuver through a course. Jumpers use longer, heavier skis and skim up a ramp that is 6 feet (1.8 meters) above the water at the take-off point. The variations of trick riding are limited only by the skier's ingenuity. Trick skis are shorter and lighter and have no keels, so skiers can turn around. Other types of water skiing include barefoot skiing and skiing with a kite attachment, which lifts the skier into the air.

Whether water skiing was invented in Europe or the United States remains a matter of controversy. Count Maximilian Pulaski claimed to have introduced it on the French Riviera in 1929, but Fred Waller appears to have skied on Long Island Sound as early as 1924. Water skiing was a novelty until the boom in motorboating brought skiing within reach of all water-sports enthusiasts.

WATER SNAKE, in eastern North America, any one of about 18 members of the worldwide genus *Natrix*, but principally any one of the half dozen forms of *N. sipedon* or northern water snake. These common semiaquatic reptiles are to be found in marshes, swamps, and ponds, or beside streams and rivers, into whose waters they dive and swim with ease when disturbed. If cornered or captured most water snakes depress their bodies and discharge the foul contents of their cloacal glands. Their aggressive behavior often results in these nonpoisonous snakes being mistaken for, and locally called, moccasins, which are unrelated and very venomous reptiles. Water snakes prey chiefly on fish, frogs, newts, and tadpoles. The adults average 30 inches in length, and are covered with crossbands and blotches in dull colors.

ARTHUR LOVERIDGE

WATER SOFTENING. See WATER SUPPLY—*Treatment and Conditioning* (Softening).

WATER SPANIEL. See AMERICAN WATER SPANIEL.

WATER STARWORT. The water starworts are soft, slender plants of the genus *Callitriche*, usually growing in crowded patches, either on moist ground, or in shallow water and with floating leaves, or wholly submerged. Leaves are opposite, narrow in submerged parts, nearly round when floating, and then 3 to 5 millimeters in diameter and practically sessile, forming rosettes, in patches 2 to 10 decimeters across. Flowers are axillary, sessile, with 2 tiny bractlets. The staminate flower consists of 1 stamen only, which bears its yellow anther 1 or 2 millimeters above the rosette of leaves. The pistillate flower consists of a 2-lobed ovulary, bearing 2 divergent, filiform styles, stigmatic along the distal part. The fruit is 2 lobed; each lobe is divided by a false partition, making a total of four compartments, each containing a seed. At maturity the four parts separate as drupelets. These peculiar characteristics have no parallel in other plants. The genus *Callitriche* has a family of its own: Callitrichaceae. Henry A. Gleason attributed 40 species to this genus, inhabiting all of the continents, as well as Greenland and New Zealand. The distinguishing characters of the species can be seen only with mature fruits, and with a magnification of 10 times or more. Six species of water starworts occur in northeastern North America.

HENRY S. CONARD

AUSTRALIAN NEWS & INFORMATION SERVICE
In calm water and brilliant sunshine, four Australian skiers fan out behind a powerful inboard motor boat.

WATER STRIDER, any member of the family Gerridae of the order Hemiptera. They are also known as water skippers and pond skaters. They have a chunky thorax and the abdomen is long and narrow in the freshwater species, short and narrowed apically in the marine forms. All are somber colored. They get their name from the fact that both adults and nymphs swim about the surface of water with a very efficient but jerky motion. The middle legs are elongated, their tarsi provided with a bristle bearing long plumes which provide propulsion and buoyancy. Water striders move rather clumsily when crawling over emergent plants or damp soil, upon which they rest. Most of the adults are winged, and fly at night; the number of apterous ones is relatively small. They are more or less gregarious, the numbers in a group varying from 6 to more than 30. On slow-flowing streams they drift downstream a few inches, then stride swiftly forward, which enables them to maintain the same relative position with objects on the bank. The most curious species, one in the Atlantic and one in the Pacific, belong to the genus *Halobates*. These apterous creatures have been observed in enormous numbers hundreds of miles out to sea.

CHARLES HOWARD CURRAN

© GEORG GERSTER/PHOTO RESEARCHERS

The 80-mile-long All-American Canal takes irrigation water from the Colorado River to California's Imperial Valley.

WATER SUPPLY. This article deals with the methods and equipment required to collect, conserve, and deliver to consumers a potable, conditioned product, acceptable to both domestic and industrial users as to quantity, quality, and pressures. It is organized into discussions of (1) history, (2) use and consumption, (3) sources and collection, (4) distribution, (5) treatment and conditioning, and (6) conservation. For additional material on various other aspects of the subject, see also AQUEDUCT; DAM; DRAINAGE; HYDRAULICS; HYDROLOGY; IRRIGATION; PUMPS; RIVER; TUNNEL; WATER POWER.

HISTORY

Community Waterworks of the Ancients. Waterworks—wells, canals, aqueducts, reservoirs, and distribution pipes—built as community efforts to provide central supplies from which man could carry water in gourds, skins, jars, waterpots, or other vessels to their abodes, appear to have had their beginnings in earliest historical times. All early waterways were of the gravity-flow type, since they antedated by centuries the use of power pumps and high pressure pipes. In Egypt, however, the shadoof, or water sweep, was probably used in ancient times to raise water a few feet from the Nile and the canals.

The Bible contains three references to public water supplies. Genesis 26 records that the herdsmen of Isaac, the son of Abraham, strove with the natives of the valley of Gerar for wells in the valley, one of which was dug by Abraham sometime before 1700 B.C. In the 8th century B.C., King Hezekiah of Judah ". . . made a pool, and a conduit, and brought water into the city . . ." of Jerusalem (II Kings 20:20; II Chronicles 32:4, 30); the pool has been identified as Siloam, which received water from Gihon spring through a tunnel or conduit 1,777 feet long. In later years, several other conduits were built from the spring at Gihon. The woman of Samaria had a waterpot at a public well, known as Jacob's Well (John 4:6), donated centuries before by Jacob.

Centuries before Christ, community waterworks were built by the Egyptians, Babylonians, Mesopotamians, Persians, and Phoenicians. It may be surmised that reservoirs and canals were built in the flat lands of countries flooded seasonally by great rivers, to conserve the water for the dry season. In Egypt, remains indicate that an extensive system of canals was built under Rameses II (r. 1292–1225 B.C.). It is possible that an extensive series of canals was utilizable for water supply in the age of the Pyramids, generally considered to have extended from 3000 to 2000 B.C.

In Mesopotamia, fed by the Tigris and Euphrates rivers, both wood and stone were scarce materials. Under the necessity of conserving materials, it is not unlikely that the true arch and similar fundamental structural forms were developed in this region. It has been held that the true arch was used as early as 3000 B.C. in Asia Minor; both the Egyptians and later the Greeks knew of the arch, but with them it never became the important feature of aqueduct bridges that it did in the times of Roman activity. (See also ARCH—*History of Arch Construction.*)

In Assyria, watered by the Tigris, King Sennacherib (about 704 B.C.) built the aqueduct of Jerwan to serve Nineveh, in place of an earlier system of canals. It was about 30 miles long, and delivered "pure mountain water" from Mount Tas. It crossed a valley 30 feet deep and 920 feet wide on an aqueduct bridge of cut stone, consisting of very heavy piers on 50-foot centers and gable-shaped "arches" of 8-foot-span, formed by corbeling the squared stone from layers of horizontal masonry in the piers. This waterway far exceeded the Roman aqueducts in dimension: 52½ feet wide and about 5½ feet deep.

The works of the Phoenicians (at their peak of power from 1000 to 900 B.C.) are among the most important of the preclassical waterworks structures, even when gaged by the monumental structures of the Romans in later times. The wells of Ras el 'Ain may be cited as an example. Here four adjoining deep artesian wells are surmounted by hexagonal towers of masonry, rising 18 to 20 feet above the plain. From these tower reservoirs, water was piped to the seashore for shipping in skins to nearby islands.

The early water supply for Greek cities came from nearby large springs, such as the Pirene at Corinth and the Callirrhoe at Athens. Among the earliest water-carrying structures are the tunnels driven to drain Lake Copais in Boeotia. Vertical construction shafts were sunk at intervals to facilitate tunneling; the deepest shaft was 216 feet. Remains of 16 shafts are still discernible, spaced from 210 to 666 feet apart. Polybius records a tunnel with intermediate shafts built near Hecatompylus about 500 B.C. Similar remains of Greek waterworks are to be found in Asia minor, Syria, Phoenicia, and Palmyra. On the Aegean island of Samos, a tunnel described by Herodotus was constructed late in the 6th century B.C. by Eupalinus of Megara, to conduct water through a solid limestone mountain for a town supply. The construction tunnel was 8 by 8 feet and about 1,100 feet long; in its bottom was dug a trench from 7 to 27 feet deep in which was laid a 7½-inch clay pipe to carry the water supply. Rock excavation was done laboriously with hand tools, perhaps aided by fire setting (the shattering of heated rock by sudden cooling with water). No intermediate shafts were used which might guide the diggers, and the result was that the headings failed to meet. (It must be recognized that the ancients lacked surveying techniques.) The gangs in the two headings heard each other, however, and dug a crosscut about 20 feet long to complete the passage. Dean Emeritus J. K. Finch of Columbia University explains the large tunnel and small pipe at Samos as follows: "The tremendous amount . . . of excavation . . . for such a small pipe is however exceptional; in other Greek water supplies, the pipes vary in diameter from 4 to 6 inches, and the tunnels are so small that we wonder how the diggers could ever have wriggled in and out of the 'rabbit burrows,' as the Romans called them."

When the city of Athens grew, the spring supply no longer sufficed. About 510 B.C., a supplementary supply was obtained from the neighboring hills by drilling a tunnel through rock; from Hymettus two tunnels were driven through rock under the Illisus. The course of another tunnel originating in the Pentelikon (Pendelikon), is still traceable from the ruins of air shafts rising 5 feet above the ground at about 150-foot intervals. An underground conduit from the Pentelikon, started by Emperor Hadrian (76–138 A.D.), was still in use in the 20th century.

The Greeks also advanced the science of hydraulics. Hero (Heron) of Alexandria (3d century A.D. or earlier) proposed a method of ascertaining the rate of flow of water from springs by digging a pit of measurable dimensions at a lower level than the spring and examining, by means of a sundial, the time taken to fill the pit to a measured height.

BLACK STAR

This Roman aqueduct at Segovia, Spain, is 2,683 feet long and contains 119 mortarless granite arches.

Roman Waterworks. The more than 200 aqueducts built by the Romans between 312 B.C. and 455 A.D. throughout the then known world, and observable now chiefly at the many ruins of aqueduct bridges, are justifiably the best known of ancient waterworks structures. Ruins stand to be admired in Rome and throughout Italy, in Africa, Spain, Portugal, France, Germany, Asia Minor, and many other regions. The waterworks of the Romans differ from similar modern systems in that the theory of impounding reservoirs had not yet been developed. In almost every system—Metz in France was an exception—an aqueduct diverted water from a spring or stream; no impounding reservoir was provided to conserve flood flows for utilization in dry weather. History fails to record how these Roman water supply systems fared in dry seasons.

Thanks to the writings of Sextus Julius Frontinus (c. 30–104 A.D.), more is known about the 11 aqueducts that were built to supply Rome during a 530-year period under the republic and the empire than is known about the waterworks of the provinces. Frontinus, water commissioner of Rome, notes that the populace utilized local wells, springs, or the Tiber River for about 440 years (assuming that the city was founded in 753 B.C.). Most of the aqueducts extended from distant spring-fed areas or the river Anio (Aniene) across the Campagna di Roma, a low-lying plain completely surrounding the Seven Hills of Rome. Underground, the aqueducts were in tunnel or in cut-and-cover construction, crossing depressions on aqueduct bridges. Where an aqueduct crossed a wide valley, it was generally supported on a series of piers and true arches. In a deep valley an upper series of arches would be placed on the first tier, and in the case of a very deep valley a third tier of arches would be employed to secure the desired elevation.

The aqueducts terminated in various distribution reservoirs built on the Seven Hills of Rome, from which water was piped to smaller reservoirs, public baths or fountains, and to a few privileged consumers. Surreptitious consumers, according to Frontinus, also contrived private taps to the public supply. The people as a rule, just as they do today in many South American and Asiatic localities lacking a distribution system, carried water in containers from the fountains to their homes or shops. Herschel estimates the combined capacity of the 11 aqueducts at 80 m.g.d. (million gallons per day); some later authorities give 40 m.g.d. Four of the aqueducts, restored, are still in use.

Eleven Aqueducts of Rome. The 11 aqueducts of ancient Rome, in chronological order, were:

(1) Aqua Appia, built by Appius Claudius (Caecus) about 312 B.C., started at springs near Tivoli, northeast of Rome. It was 10.3 miles long and had a waterway about 2½ feet wide and 5 feet high. For tactical reasons, all but 300 feet was built underground, some in tunnel.

(2) Anio Vetus was constructed about 40 years later, in 272 B.C. It started at springs in the upper Anio valley in the Apennines, and was more than 43 miles long. It was largely underground, except for an aqueduct bridge 1,100 feet long. It delivered water into the city 90 feet higher than did Aqua Appia.

(3) Aqua Marcia, "the pride of Ancient Rome," was built under Quintus Marcius Rex, praetor of the Republic, about 144 B.C. It started from the river Anio, high in the hills near Tivoli, and was about 58 miles long, of which over 6 miles was supported on an aqueduct bridge across the Campagna di Roma. It had the largest waterway of the 11 aqueducts: 4½ to 5½ feet wide and 8 to 9 feet high. Water was delivered high enough (195 feet above Tiber level) to supply the Capitoline, Caelian, and Aventine hills. This aqueduct was reconstructed in part in 1869–1870.

(4) Aqua Tepula was constructed in 127 B.C. from a source in Tusculum. It was 11 miles long. Crossing the Campagna di Roma for about 6 miles, it was built on top of the first tier of arches of Aqua Marcia. The water is recorded as being "warm and not of the best quality."

(5) Aqua Julia was built by Marcus Vipsanius Agrippa about 33 B.C. It tapped a source not far from that of Tepula, and for 4 miles utilized the waterway of the Tepula. It was 15½ miles long and was carried across the Campagna di Roma as the third tier of arches on the Aqua Marcia. Both Tepula and Julia were of cheaper construction (brick and concrete) than the Marcia, in which only stones were used.

(6) Aqua Virgo was completed by Agrippa in 20 B.C., under the Empire. From copious springs on the estate of Lucius Licinius Lucullus, it extended almost entirely underground to the Campus Martius. It was 14 miles long, and the water was termed "excellent."

(7) Aqua Alsietina (or Augusta) was built under Emperor Augustus about 2 A.D. to supply water to his private pond where sham naval battles were staged. Built underground to Trastevere, it was 22 miles long, a short distance on arches. No remains have been found.

(8) Aqua Claudia and (9) Anio Novus were begun under Emperor Caligula about 38 A.D. and finished by Emperor Claudius I about 52 A.D. They are on the same aqueduct bridge across the Campagna di Roma, Novus superimposed on Claudia, which shows a reversion to the use of massive cut stones in place of the cheap masonry of the two preceding structures; the ruins still stand. They delivered water to the highest hills, including the Palatine. Claudia was 43 miles long, of which 9¼ miles was on aqueduct bridges across the lower Campagna di Roma. About 65 A.D., Claudia was shortened by constructing a tunnel 3 miles long. Novus started at an intake in the Anio. It was 62 miles long, including 9¼ miles on the same arches as Claudia.

(10) Aqua Trajana, built by Emperor Trajan about 109 A.D., started at the springs of Lagodi, and was about 36½ miles long.

(11) Aqua Alexandrina, the last of the great aqueducts, was built about 226 A.D. by Marcus Aurelius Alexander Severus. It was about 14 miles long, largely supported on arches.

Roman Provinces. The Roman provinces contain many ruins of aqueduct bridges, splendid examples of the engineering skills of the Roman builders. In Algeria, for instance, famed ruins may be observed at valley crossings of the Constantine aqueduct. In Spain, there is an aqueduct at Segovia (815 yards long, 92 feet high) which was built about 100 A.D. and is still in use; at Mérida (where the valley crossing is 2,500 feet), the bridge consists of 100 arches of fine masonry in two tiers; and near Tarragona is an aqueduct about 22 miles long which is in use today after restoration in the 19th century.

Pont du Gard, near Nîmes, France, was built by Agrippa in 19 B.C.; it is 900 feet long, 160 feet high, and the span of the largest arch is 74 feet. All masonry, except for the water channel on top, was laid "dry." Four aqueducts built for Lyon in France by the Romans utilized siphons, made up of groups of lead pipes, to cross depressions, there being 14 on the Gier River. Vandals have long since removed the valuable metal pipes. Similar siphons are reported as being used in Italy on the Alatri aqueduct about 134 B.C.

Accessories. Pipes for conveying water from reservoirs and local sources of supply closer to the consumer evidently were utilized to some extent by the ancient engineers. In Rome, water was piped from the terminal reservoirs of the 11 aqueducts to subreservoirs. Ruins have been found that indicate that some form of sedimentation basin was erected near the reservoirs, possibly to clarify the muddy water before delivery to public baths and fountains. The Romans are reputed to have used lead pipes to some extent. Ruins of conduits of drilled stones have been uncovered at Jerusalem and elsewhere. Wooden pipes joined by iron collars were evidently used by the Romans in Germany, Britain, and other places. Ruins of distribution chambers have been found at Nîmes, Minturnae, and Thuburbo Majus. At Lincoln in England was found the single example of a primitive type of pump to raise water. The Greeks used clay pipe at Samos, and later developed standard-dimension bell-and-spigot pipe in sizes corresponding to about 4 and 6 inches in diameter for water flow not under pressure.

Early Waterworks in the United States. From 1652 to 1800, 16 waterworks systems were built in the American colonies or states: Boston, Mass. (1652); Bethlehem, Pa. (1754); Providence, R.I. (1772); Geneva, N.Y. (1787); Plymouth, Mass. (1796); Salem, Mass. (1795); Hartford, Conn. (1797); Portsmouth, N.H. (1798); Worcester, Mass. (1798); Albany, N.Y. (1798); Peabody, Mass. (1799); New York, N.Y. (1799); Morristown, N.J. (1799); Lynchburg, Va. (1799); Winchester, Va. (1799); and Newark, N.J. (1800).

When the distance to remote sources made construction too expensive for a single community to finance, regional water-supply systems were set up. The earliest in the United States was in 1895—the Metropolitan Water District of Massachusetts, serving Boston and suburban communities within 10 miles of the city. It originally served 18 communities with a population below 900,000 and now serves 30 communities with a population of 1,600,000.

Beginnings of Water Treatment. Of remote antiquity is the appreciation of the relation of the drinking water supply to disease. In the 4th century before Christ, Hippocrates, known as the "Father of Medicine," advocated the boiling and filtering of polluted water before drinking. Pliny the Elder (23–79 A.D.), in his *Historia Naturalis*, discusses the characteristics of potable water. From olden times, the Chinese were accustomed to putting alum in tubs of water to clarify it; the same thing was done in Egypt. Elisha (9th century B.C.) is recorded in II Kings 2:19–22 as treating a worthless spring ("the water is naught") with salt so that it became usable "unto this day."

The treatment of water to remove pathogenic organisms had its beginning about 1892, after Dr. Robert Koch had traced the cholera epidemic in Hamburg, Germany, to its unfiltered raw water supply. This he did by observing that Altona, on the opposite bank of the Elbe, which used the same river water, but filtered it, had no disease. Previously, since 1855, London had been required by parliamentary statute to filter its water supply through slow sand filters, but the efficacy of the process was clearly demonstrated by Dr. Koch. Filters were not introduced into the United States until about 1870 and were made of the slow type; the first important modern rapid-sand filtration plant was built in 1902 at Little Falls, N.J., and is still used by the Passaic Valley Water Commission.

In 1909, liquid chlorine was developed for the disinfection of water supplies, and the subsequent development of modern equipment for its automatic application has made this procedure standard practice for combating pathogenic bacteria, with less and less reliance placed on other chemicals. (See section on *Disinfection and Chlorination.*)

USES AND CONSUMPTION

This section deals only with water diverted into waterworks structures. The uses of water from waterworks are (1) primary, for such strictly domestic purposes as drinking, preparation of foods and beverages, bathing, cleansing, and watering of lawns and gardens; and (2) secondary, comprising industrial processes, commercial products, disposal of wastes in sewers, fire fighting, street sprinkling, swimming pools, and public fountains. For a composite United States community, the reasonable requirements in gallons per capita of resident population per day are: residential, 50; commercial, 20; industrial, 50; public, 10; unaccounted for losses, 10, for a total of 140.

Domestic water use was reported by the American Water Works Association (AWWA) as 50 gallons per capita per day east of the 100th meridian (near the center of North Dakota), and 100 gallons per day west of that longitude. The AWWA also reported the tendency of meter sales to rise with family income. The maximum daily

AMERICAN WATER WORKS ASSOCIATION

Water intake on Skinner Reservoir, which supplies the San Diego Aqueduct in southern California.

demand, including all types of municipal use, has been placed at 200 percent of the yearly average, and the hourly peak rate at 200 to 300 percent. Summer consumption runs about 140 percent of the yearly average, and winter, 90 percent. A survey of five large cities showed special summer loads caused peak days of 100 percent above corresponding days when the special demands of hot weather were absent.

Waste and Control. Unaccounted-for water, which passes through the master meters at the sources of supply but not through the consumers' meters, constitutes 20 to 50 percent of the master meter reading. It comprises water lost in leakage in pipes and services, and water used for street sprinkling, snow removal, sewer flushing, and fire fighting. Undue waste of water proves a serious consideration when it requires the purveyor to seek additional sources or to install larger pumps and pipes; it can be curbed, however, by public appeal and ordinances prohibiting lawn sprinkling and other purposes in an emergency, by waste surveys, and by installation of meters. The water requirements of air conditioners have become so heavy—a 10-horsepower compressor, for instance, requires about 1,000 gallons per 8-hour day—that many municipalities have strict ordinances which require the recirculation of such water.

The effect of pressure on consumption is direct; high pressures induce leakage and freer domestic use. When the pressure at Oak Park, Ill., was reduced from 45 to 25 pounds, the consumption rate fell from 65 to 45 gallons per capita per day.

Meters. The installation of house meters confronts owners with a personal responsibility for the amount of water used and soon produces a marked reduction in consumption; but as the novelty of responsibility fades, the rate starts to rise. Many large cities require meters only of industries, commercial establishments, and large apartment houses. Disadvantages of residential meters are the cost and the nuisance to the householder of meter reading and replacement, and the expense of installation. There is also considerable loss of pressure through the meter. See also WATER METER.

© GEORG GERSTER/PHOTO RESEARCHERS

An array of center-pivot irrigators in an Oregon field distributes water from the Snake River.

SOURCES AND COLLECTIONS

Hydrological conditions as to rainfall, runoff, and percolation must be understood in developing and collecting a water supply. Rainfall infiltrates into the soil, runs off over the surface, or is transpired by vegetation; evaporation follows; then condensation into cloud formation, and return to earth as rain or snow. Although precipitation is the source of all water supply, only a small part is divertible to man and his uses, since less than half of it appears promptly as streamflow, the remainder undergoing either percolation into the porous substrata, transpiration from vegetation, or evaporation. See also HYDROLOGY; WATERSHED.

Sources of Supply. Underground waters are more feasible as sources in small communities, while large cities, with some exceptions, either go great distances for upland surface supplies or utilize the large lakes or rivers nearby. Groundwater resources are near at hand and such systems are cheap to install; surface supplies entail expensive reservoirs and aqueducts, or large offshore intakes and tunnels to the pumping station.

The method of development of sources to produce a dependable yield varies with the type of source. In the case of streams, it involves a large impounding reservoir, intake works, and a transmission conduit between the reservoir and the distribution system. With groundwater, development involves wells, infiltration galleries or springs, distribution reservoirs, pumps, and, in many regions, recharging facilities (see below) for sustaining groundwater levels.

Surface Waters. ***Impounding Reservoirs.*** Where the supply is dependent on large reservoirs on upland streams of variable flow (as in Boston, New York, and San Francisco), consideration must be given to the amount of runoff which can be caught in the reservoirs and held for use in dry years. Such a reservoir is formed by constructing a dam across a narrow valley just downstream from a region where the valley has a wide floor, in order to provide large storage and minimum cost of dam. The capacity to be developed requires statistical, economic, hydraulic, and hydrological studies; statistics of past records help in predicting future rates of demand; economic studies entail the correlative costs of dams and storage capacity secured, and the costs of real estate at various prospective sites; hydraulic studies fix the flowline of the depleted reservoir high enough so that the distribution system can be fed largely by gravity.

Not all storage capacity is available for use; the lowest outlet port in the headworks is located several feet above the bottom to avoid discharging silt into the conduit. (In 1916, the designers of Elephant Butte Reservoir, New Mexico, estimated that the 45-mile-long, 3-mile-wide lake would silt up in about 233 years.) Evaporation must also be considered in reckoning available storage. New monomolecular film techniques may cut evaporation losses in the United States more than 20 billion gallons of water daily.

Intake Works. Intake works are essential to divert the water of reservoirs, lakes, or large rivers into transmission conduits or suction wells of the waterworks system. On large bodies of water, studies are required to determine the least polluted area for locating the intake. If the source of supply is a large river, as in the case in St. Louis, Philadelphia, and Kansas City, Mo., or the Great Lakes, as in Chicago, Buffalo, and Cleveland, intake structures are designed only to obtain water of the highest quality, with little concern for lack of water in dry years. Since the quality in large bodies of water varies according to depth and season of the year, gated inlet ports must be stationed at several levels. Intakes of the tower type are used at Chicago and Cincinnati, the latter providing for a 70-foot variation in the stage of the Ohio River. Generally, intakes are equipped with inlet and outlet gates; coarse screens to exclude cumbersome floating debris; and, in cold climates, heating devices to prevent ice cakes from plugging the waterways.

Groundwaters. Works for the collection of underground water may comprise springs, infiltration galleries, or wells of several types: large open, driven, drilled, and gravel packed. For years Roanoke, Va., got most of its water from a spring in rock formations; Havana, Cuba, gets most of its supply from the Vento Spring, in limestone formation. Brooklyn was supplied for many decades by two infiltration galleries on Long Island; since Catskill water became available they have been held in reserve.

Wells. Wells in unconsolidated formations constitute the most common method of utilizing shallow or deep aquifers; at comparatively low cost a well can be put down to tap water resources at any reasonable depth. In calculating the spacing of wells tapping the same aquifers, consideration must be given to the drawdown curve of each well, caused by the rapid withdrawal of water by the pump. Wells too closely spaced fail to yield the anticipated quantities; this circle of influence may extend for several thousand feet in porous formations, and less in tighter soils. Water supplies for single farms or homes can usually be obtained from a shallow dug or driven well at little expense, but the purity must be properly safeguarded by sealing the top against pollution from the surface.

Where water is to be obtained from a fine-sand layer, as on Long Island, the gravel-packed or gravel-wall well assures uninterrupted flow; an ordinary well in this material would clog readily. This type of well is double cased, the ground surrounding the proposed screen location is under-reamed, and the space filled with pea gravel and sealed off with mortar at the groundline.

Rock wells are the chief source of underground water in the North Central states from Ohio to North Dakota. Madison, Wis., is an outstanding example of a population supplied entirely from rock wells. Drilled in water-bearing rock known as Potsdam sandstone, its wells are widely spaced over an area of 27 square miles and yield an average of 37 million gallons a day.

Problems. Groundwater supplies, in comparison with surface waters, require constant vigilance for their conservation as to quality, quantity, pumping level, freedom from saltwater intrusion and pollution, and conditions of the screens and casings. Wear on screens and pumps by sand often shortens the lives and reduces the yields of wells. Close spacing may decrease the quantity per well, and overpumping may cause the static level to drop. Geophysical methods, both seismic and electrical, for locating the water table fast and cheaply, are in use by many state water control departments.

Encroachment of homes and industries may bring pollution problems. In Nassau County, Long Island, a dump containing old auto bodies raised the iron content of a shallow well several hundred feet away to such an extent that the well had to be deepened to a formation where the pollution had not penetrated.

Artificial Recharge. When water is pumped out at a greater rate than the supply is replenished by nature, static groundwater levels will fall, and costs of pumping will be increased. If the well is near the ocean, the lowered level may create hydraulic conditions which induce the inflow of seawater, ruining the well. One remedy for this condition is to force more water than the normal percolation into the ground, a process known as "artificial recharging." This is accomplished by water spreading on the surface from an adjacent stream at floodtime (a majority of projects are of this type), or by injecting water, usually from a public water supply system, into the wells. Water spreading is done on permeable flat lands adjoining the stream, either by plowing to provide ditches and furrows, or by excavating a series of basins from 1 to 10 acres in area. Replenishment of underground reservoirs from surface supplies has been practiced in the United States since 1889.

Where the surface is not permeable or where impervious lenses intervene, surface spreading is ineffective and recharge wells must be used. A survey has shown that this method has been only moderately successful, however; wells may be more successful in resisting saltwater intrusion. Sewage reclamation for groundwater recharge appears to be thoroughly feasible if the heavy development costs are spread over a long period and if careful control is maintained to prevent pollution by poorly treated influents. A well system is more complicated and expensive than surface recharge, but in some regions it is the only practicable method, as in the rice fields of Arkansas, where an annual rainfall of 50 inches cannot percolate through the impermeable clay and silt on the surface.

DISTRIBUTION

Conduits. The conveyance of water supply from an impounding reservoir, or an intake, to the distribution system entails the construction of conduits of some form: canals or open channels, large masonry aqueducts or pressure tunnels, or metal or reinforced concrete pipes. The ancients had no materials available to withstand high pressures, so they had to content themselves with masonry aqueducts following the hydraulic grade line, with aqueduct bridges across valleys. But in modern waterworks, with a wide choice of materials, equipment, and skills, the engineer places less dependence on topographical conditions, and is free to utilize canals, pipelines of wood, metal, reinforced concrete and asbestos cement, grade and pressure tunnels, and siphons.

Reinforced-concrete conduits may be monolithic, precast, or prestressed. Precast pipe is made in sizes up to 180 inches. Steel cylinder pipe is recommended where the head exceeds 100 feet. Prestressed concrete steel cylinder pipe is available in sizes 24 to 144 inches; it requires a better grade of steel, but only 70 to 80 percent of the amount needed in non-prestressed pipe; concrete is of better quality, and wall thickness can be reduced. The hydraulic carrying capacity of concrete, asbestos cement, or cement-lined metal pipes does not deteriorate as rapidly as in tar-coated metal pipe; however, slimes will build up in such pipes and reduce the carrying capacity.

For high heads, and where water hammer is a dominant factor, plate steel with modern welded shop joints and Dresser couplings for field joints, and steel cylinder prestressed pipe produce satisfactory conduits. Metal conduits should be safeguarded against tuberculation by cement-mortar lining, bituminous coating, or cathodic protection.

Cast-iron pipes are used for conduits in sizes up to about 24 inches. The modern tendency is to use centrifugally cast pipe, which is lighter in

© PETER MENZEL/STOCK, BOSTON

This automatic pumping station lifts reservoir water over hilly terrain to a municipal storage system.

weight than pit cast, and comes in 20-foot lengths. Mechanical joints are fast replacing the ball-and-spigot joint.

Appurtenances essential to the successful operation of transmission conduits include: high level overflows on flow-line aqueducts; sectionalizing valves or stop planks at convenient intervals so that sections may be taken out of service without too much water loss; blowoffs for emptying sections for repairs and inspection; air valves on summits of all pressure lines; drainage shafts and blowoffs on pressure tunnels; and air-and-vacuum valves on all steel lines.

The size of conduits from distant reservoirs can be reduced, and continuity of service better ensured, if distribution reservoirs (see below) are installed; these provide for hourly and daily peak rates of demand, or for several days' storage in case of a break in the conduit. See also AQUEDUCT.

Pumping Systems. Deep wells are generally equipped with motor-driven turbine pumps. Closely spaced groups of shallow wells, if the pumping depth is less than 20 feet, can sometimes be connected to a common suction header and served by a pumping station at ground level. Two stations, comprising about a dozen wells each, were operated successfully for years by a Jamaica, Long Island, water company. Although wells can be pumped directly into the system, this often leads to overpumping of the stratum during high demand periods; a more conservative practice is to pump at a low, constant rate into a tank at ground level, whence water is boosted by other pumps to meet fluctuating rates of demand. The choice of steam or electricity for power depends on many factors. Electricity is essential for automatic or semiautomatic operation. Freedom from interruption of service on many large systems is assured by having power lines from two separate stations; on small systems engine-driven standby units are more economical, and distribution reservoirs can serve as standbys for a short time. Philadelphia completed electrification of its system in 1954, ending 155 years of steam-driven pumping.

Three types of pumping systems are in use in the United States: direct, indirect, and direct-indirect. In direct pumping there is no open reservoir on the distribution system and the pressure at the pumps depends on the number of taps open; water hammer is a constant menace, and fire demands can be met only by speeding up the pumps. In indirect pumping an open storage reservoir receives the water; from there it flows by gravity into the system. In direct-indirect pumping an open storage reservoir is located on the far side of the distribution system, allowing the pumps to operate against fairly constant pressure. This system best meets fire demands, permits smaller pumps and reduced power charges, and eliminates water hammer on pumps and plumbing fixtures. For a description of the various kinds of water pumps, see PUMPS.

Distribution Reservoirs. Impounding reservoirs, discussed above, are situated only at the source of surface supplies, whereas distribution reservoirs (also termed "equalizing" or "storage" reservoirs) are utilized with both surface and groundwater supplies. They are located at or near that side of the distribution system opposite to the source of supply. Numerous useful purposes are served: (1) in indirect or direct-indirect pumping a cushion is provided against which the pumps react; they are operated more evenly; (2) storage is provided where wells are the sole source of supply; (3) an emergency reserve is provided to lessen the damages or discomfort consequent on a breakdown elsewhere in the system; (4) water pressure is improved; (5) reserve storage permits the design of systems for the average rather than the peak demand, at marked economies; (6) on small systems the distribution reservoir can be filled during an 8-hour day, or during periods of low-priced power, thereby saving two labor shifts, and considerable power; (7) where the supply is filtered, distribution reservoirs allow operation of filters at normal rather than peak demand, saving wash water, power, and depreciation; (8) peak rates of fire flow are provided for more economically.

The volumes of available storage vary slightly in gravity and pumping systems. Gravity systems involve a long transmission conduit from the upland impounding reservoir; the size of this conduit can be reduced if storage for a week or two can be provided in a distribution reservoir. On a direct-indirect pumping system, storage of a few days should suffice. Distribution reservoirs should be located centrally, as close as possible to the district to be served, and, if practicable, should be on the side of the distribution system opposite the source of supply. They should also be at sufficient elevation to afford adequate pressures even when emptied to the one-quarter stage. They may be built by excavating to form earth embankments; they may be reinforced-concrete-covered, groined-arch structures; standpipes of reinforced concrete or steel, or steel tanks on towers.

Distribution Systems. The network of interconnecting pipes extending from the pumping station, wells, or the end of the transmission conduit to the consumers' premises and to hydrants is termed the distribution system. Its function is to deliver to the consumer water in required quantities and at satisfactory pressures, under all conditions and despite a break in any pipe in the system. While various materials were formerly used for pipes—wood, wrought iron, cement-lined stovepipe, wrought steel, steel plate, reinforced concrete, galvanized steel, and cast iron—the present trend is to use cast-iron pipe (cement lined in regions where the water is aggressive) or asbestos-cement pipe. The sizes of pipe where hydrants are to be served should never be less than 8 inches, except in small, limited systems. Street mains larger than 48 inches are uneconomical, although 72-inch pipes are sometimes used, as in Jersey City and in Brooklyn. Large cast-iron pipes are subject to shrinkage and other stresses, which make them less reliable than steel or reinforced concrete in cases of heavy pressure or traffic loads. Plastic pipe, in sizes ½ to 2 inches, has been used since 1950, chiefly for house services. The merits of plastic pipe include resistance to rust, corrosion, and chemical and electrolytic attack; ease and economy of installation; and pliability and minimal use of fittings. Its disadvantages are reported as the tendency to fail from ruptures, brittleness, and shrinkage; sensitivity to truck impact loads, necessitating deeper laying; and destruction by rodents.

The primary function of hydrants is to afford hose connections for fire fighting, and they should be spaced close enough so that no more than 300 feet of hose is needed. Gate valves are essential for segregating a section of pipe in event of a break; they should be placed on all pipes in an intersection, and not more than 1,000 feet apart between intersections. Check valves at pumps are required to prevent backflow. Pressure-regulating valves are installed in low parts of the system to maintain pressure within proper limits. Altitude-controlling valves are spring operated to close at a prescribed pressure and prevent overflow of distribution reservoirs and tanks. Cone valves, a new development, may be operated manually, automatically, or electrically to maintain a constant level in a distribution reservoir, to prevent water hammer, or to reduce pressures.

TREATMENT AND CONDITIONING

A large part of this section is taken from *Water Quality and Treatment*, American Water Works Association (1950).

Quality. Waters subjected to treatment have qualities broadly characteristic of their sources—modified by pollutional, chemical, and physical agencies to which they have been exposed between the point where the sky water reaches the earth and the treatment plant. Natural pollution results from material absorbed by the fresh sky water in its travels over or through forest covers of leaves, fertilized croplands, and pasture lands strewn with manure and other organic debris. Pollution by humans, comprising industrial wastes and untreated sewage, is more injurious. Chemical agents comprise primarily the soluble minerals with which the water has been in contact, air dust, and chemical wastes discharged into streams; such agents increase the hardness and alkalinity, and add carbonic acid, color, and odor. In addition, streams in flood pick up floating debris and silt; and water in storage is subject to algae, microorganisms, worms, and fish. The advent of nuclear power has added new contaminating agents.

EAST BAY MUNICIPAL UTILITY DISTRICT

Huge automatic water pumps are visible in the interior of this municipal pumping station.

UPI

A chemist checks the mineral content of a water sample in the laboratory of a city water-treatment plant.

The net effect of these various contaminating influences is to add algae, alkalinity, bacteria, color, floating debris, hardness, microorganisms, odors, tastes, toxicity, and turbidity in varying intensities to the water delivered for treatment. Counteragents in streams, such as sedimentation, oxidation, sunlight, and biological agents, contribute to self-purification; but time, temperature, and character of the pollution are important factors. Streams of the United States have divergent characteristics; those of the West are likely to be hard, turbid, and low in color; those of New England, soft, clear, and colored.

Groundwaters are generally clear, cold, colorless, and harder than the surface waters of the same region; bacterially, they are usually cleaner than surface waters. Water from limestone formations is apt to be hard and may be polluted through fissures from the surface; it forms deposits in pipes and is relatively noncorrosive. In granite formations, groundwaters are soft, low in dissolved minerals, relatively high in carbon dioxide, and actively corrosive. Groundwater temperature remains fairly stable during the year; at 10 to 50 feet below the surface it is usually the same as the mean atmospheric temperature of the locality; below 50 feet it rises about 1 degree for each 60 feet of depth.

The contaminational load on groundwaters from synthetic detergents (termed also "syndets") is presenting a major problem. In 1948, syndets represented only 16 percent of the total soap and detergent sales, but by 1957 they had risen to 67 percent. Syndets in water produce an unpleasant taste and frothing, which can be detected when the concentration is 1.5 ppm. (parts per million) or higher.

Types of Treatment. Since the characteristics of raw water vary widely, as do its uses, the habits of consumers, and the kinds of appurtenances in the waterworks systems, different types of treatment have been developed. These include longtime storage in reservoirs, screening, plain sedimentation, sedimentation following coagulation with chemicals, filtration, disinfection, softening and aeration, and the use of chemicals.

Longtime storage, it has been found, will reduce color and nitrates, increase albuminoid ammonia, reduce bacteria of all sorts, and remove some suspended matter. Many large cities in the United States use this as the chief water treatment, supplemented by chlorination. New York City applies chlorine after the water leaves the distribution reservoirs at Kensico, Hillview, and Silver Lake; and promotes sedimentation in Kensico Reservoir by applying alum to the Catskill and Delaware aqueducts before their waters enter the reservoir.

Coarse screens are generally placed in intakes to divert large, floating objects, including ice from the conduits. Fine screens are placed inside the coarse screen to intercept leaves, larva, aquatic vegetation, and fish. Microstrainers with openings of 0.001 inch on a revolving drum, have been used since about 1945.

Plain sedimentation (not induced by the use of coagulants) takes place whenever the velocity of water is reduced suddenly. In a water treatment plant, water is held in a quiescent stage in basins for a sufficient time to permit the gravitational deposit of the large suspended particles, which settle at a rate dependent on their size, weight and shape, and the viscosity of the water. Modern practice favors upward flow rather than horizontal flow basins, with skimming troughs closely spaced to pick up the cleanest water at the top. Mechanisms are installed to remove sludge before it mingles with the incoming water; this ensures greater silting depth and removes the sediment without periodically taking the basin out of service to hose out the mud.

The addition of a coagulant chemical to the water brings about an agglomeration of colloidal and fine suspended matter into larger masses which will settle more readily. This process involves violent mechanical stirring of the water, called flocculation, to disperse the chemicals uniformly throughout. Filtration is then necessary to remove the agglomerated chemicals and impurities. Coagulation is recommended when the turbidity of the raw water exceeds 30 to 50 ppm. Sulphate of aluminum, commonly called alum, is the most widely used coagulant; ferric salts have also been used extensively; and, in late years, activated silica and polyelectrolytes (including starch and its derivatives) have been used as supplements. Coagulation periods vary from 3 to 90 minutes; the current trend is to periods of 30 to 60 minutes. Velocities of 1.0 to 1.3 feet per second are now extensively used for basin design.

Filters. In general, two types of filters are in successful use in treatment plants: the rapid-sand, or mechanical (see Fig. 1), and the slow-sand, or "sand" or "English" (see Fig. 2). The latter is now used chiefly where there are large areas of land available, and where turbidity and color removal are not prime considerations. Slow-sand filters differ from rapid in many other respects: they are available only for gravity flow; they are operated at slow filter rates of 3 to 8

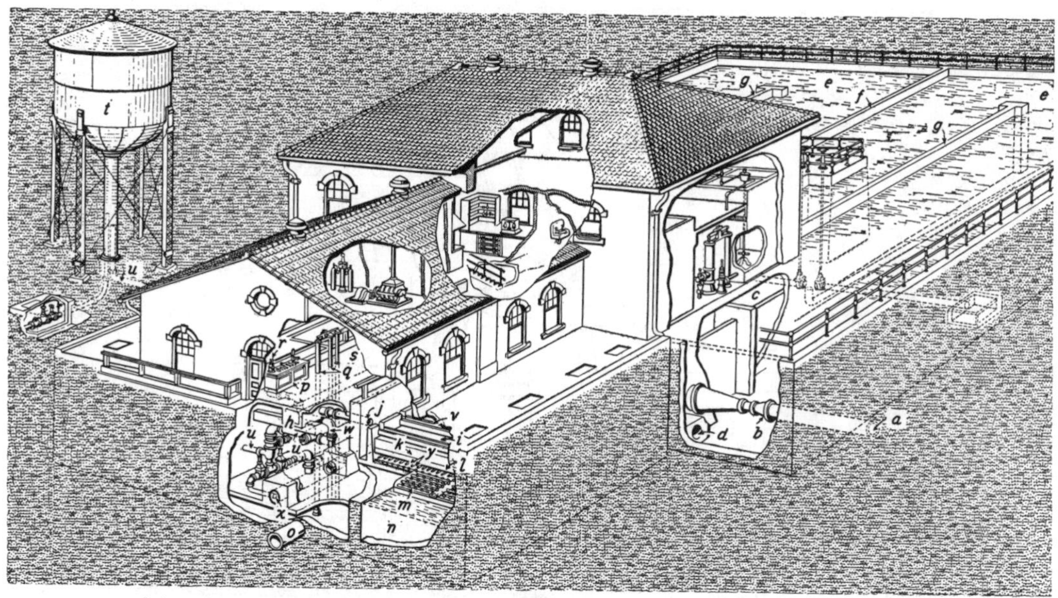

Redrawn by permission from "Water Supply and Purification" by William A. Hardenbergh; International Textbook Company, 1945

Fig. 1. Typical arrangement of rapid, or mechanical, filter plant.

The water enters through pipe, *a* (lower right-hand corner), and through the Venturi meter, *b*, into mixing chamber, *c*, where the coagulant is applied. (The flocculator is not shown.) The coagulated water then passes to sedimentation basins, *e*, through conduit, *d*; here, part of the floc settles out. The two basins are separated by wall, *f*, so that they may be operated separately, one being used while the other is being cleaned or held in reserve. (In some plants, sludge-removing equipment would be installed here.) Wall, *g*, provides a baffle to guide the water in even flow and prevent crosscurrents and short circuiting. (Valves in the bottom of the basins, for cleanout of sediment, are not shown.) The flume, *h*, leads the water from the sedimentation basin to the various filter boxes, *i*, through the influent pipe, *j*. The water percolates down through the sand, *k*, which is supported on the strainer filter bottom, *m*. This collects the filtered water and delivers it into the clear-water reservoir, *n*, beneath the filters. From here water is pumped through the pipe, *o*, to tank, *t*, or to the distribution system. The filtering and washing operations are controlled from the operating table, *p*, the rate regulator, *q*, and the loss-of-head gage, *r*, which are located on the operating floor, *s*, over the operating gallery. Filtered water for backwashing the filters is stored in the elevated wash-water tank, *t*, from which it is fed through pipes, *u*, into the filter bottom, *m*, and flows upward at high velocity through the gravel and the sand, causing the sand to float to a limited extent so that it is more easily freed of dirt. The wash water and dirt are carried into the gutters, *v*, and thence into the drains, *w* and *x*. Air for agitating sand during cleaning is supplied through the piping, *y*.

m.g.d. (million gallons per day) per acre; they do not require the pretreatment of water by coagulation and sedimentation; and they require longer periods of cleaning and servicing. Rapid filters, on the other hand, can be built for either gravity or pressure flow; can be operated at rates of 125 to 200 m.g.d. per acre; and can be cleaned quickly by backwashing. Either type can be relied upon to produce an agreeable water under practically all circumstances.

A filter consists of a bed of sand or prepared crushed anthracite (about 24 to 30 inches thick in rapid filters and up to 40 inches in slow), supported on a bed of gravel or some coarse porous material, and contained in a basin with various operating accessories. Layouts of rapid-sand filter plants vary, but in general follow the scheme shown in Fig. 1. The filter boxes range in capacity from 0.3 to 2.0 m.g.d. and are arranged symmetrically about either side of the operating gallery, the enclosure under the operating floor. In northern climates the entire filter is enclosed, but in the deep South only the operating floor is roofed over. The filtered water basin, or clear water reservoir, is situated beneath the filter boxes. A layout of a typical slow-sand filter, such as that in Springfield, Mass., is shown in Fig. 2.

Diatomite Filter. The diatomite, or diatomaceous, earth filter, developed for military use during World War II, is a pressure vessel utilizing diatomaceous earth as the filtering medium. The earth is deposited as a coating one-eighth inch thick before the filter is put into operation, and rests on a fine screen of metal. A slurry of diatomaceous earth is added to the influent water to build up the thickness of the filter. Filtration rates vary from 1 to 5 gallons per minute per square foot.

Disinfection and Chlorination. Disinfection is the process of killing a large amount of microorganisms by means of chemicals, heat, ozone, ultraviolet rays, etc. Liquid chlorine was first employed in 1909 and was commonly added just prior to filtration; now it is applied both before and after filtration. Chlorination materially improves the coagulation of some waters. Prechlorination may also control the growth of algae, reduce biological accumulation in filters, and contribute to improved filter efficiency. Postchlorination appreciably reduces the number of bacteria of all types entering the distribution system. When ammonia is combined with chlorine, a slower acting disinfectant results which has been found beneficial in retarding growths in long conduits, and for suppressing the development of iron-fixing or slime-forming types of bacterial growths. Chlorination, however, is not a substitute for more general treatment; preliminary coagulation and sedimentation plus filtration are generally required also.

Chlorine is a greenish yellow gas which under pressure is converted to a liquid. It is available commercially in steel cylinders ranging

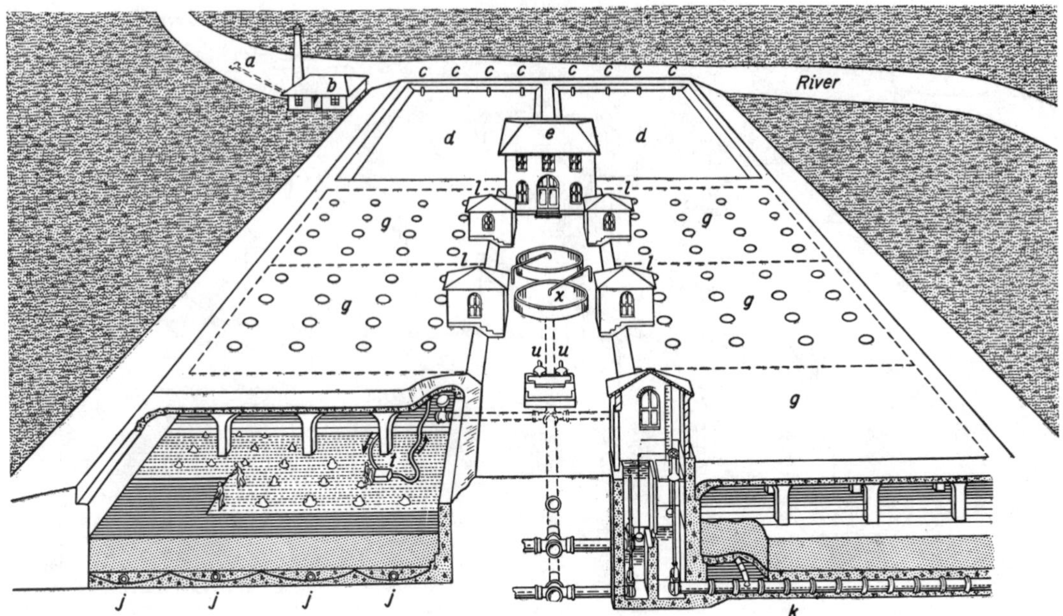

Fig. 2. General view of slow filter plant.

This consists of such sections as the duplicate sedimentation basins, *d*, the filter units, *g*, and the laboratory, *e*. Low lift pumps, *b*, take water from intake, *a*, and deliver through aerating risers, *c*, to sedimentation basins, *d*. Water is uniformly distributed to filters, *g*, by a float valve. Collector pipes, *j*, collect the filtered water and lead to the main collector, *k*, which leads to the regulator house, *l*, whence it flows through regulating orifices to the clear water well (not shown). A portable sand ejector, *t*, is employed when the sand requires washing. Sand washers, *u*, discharge the clean sand to sand storage bins, *x*, for eventual placing again in the filters.

Based on "Water Purification Plants and Their Operation," by Milton F. Stein; John Wiley & Sons, Inc.

to 2,000 pounds or larger. At 70° F., the pressure required to maintain the liquid form is about 85 pounds per square inch, but the pressure increases as the temperature rises. When the liquid is drawn from the cylinder, the release of pressure causes it to change back into a gas. Liquid chlorine is fed from the pressure cylinders to the water through a machine called a chlorinator, which automatically proportions the gas to the rate of water flow.

The mechanism of the action of chlorine in destroying bacteria and microorganisms has been the subject of much conjecture. The general belief today is that there is a physicochemical reaction between chlorine and the proteins and amino groups in the cell wall and contents, causing disintegration of the cell. Another theory suggests that the action is based on the inhibition of a key enzymatic process which oxidizes the glucose of the cell; when chlorine destroys this power of oxidation, the bacterial cells die.

A late development in the use of chlorine has been the breakpoint method, whereby more effective bactericidal action can be obtained, and tastes and odors removed, with a minimum quantity of chlorine.

Chlorine dioxide, first introduced in water treatment about 1940, produces a more rapid oxidation of some organic compounds, and removes taste-producing substances (such as chlorophenol) which frequently result from chlorination. See also CHLORINE.

Ozonization. This method of treating water involves the application of ozone, a faintly blue gas of pungent odor which readily breaks down into nascent oxygen, a powerful oxidizing agent. It is applied to water by discharging into a scrubber or an injector, or by spraying the water into ozonized air. At Ashton, England, ozonization was reported to disinfect and to reduce color, tastes, and odors; similar reports came from Germany, but costs of operation were found to be higher than with chlorine. Ozonization was discontinued at the Belmont filters in Philadelphia in 1959 due to the degradation of raw water; improvements were to provide large basins for the long detention time needed for free residual chlorination before other chemical treatment. See also OZONE.

Fluoridation. The addition of fluorides to the water delivered into the distribution system has been a moot political and religious problem since 1945, when fluorides were first introduced into public water supplies. In 1958, the World Health Organization's Expert Committee on Water Fluoridation issued its first conclusions: (1) drinking water containing about 1 ppm. fluoride has a marked preventive action on dental caries; (2) there is no evidence that water containing this concentration of fluoride impairs general health; (3) controlled fluoridation of drinking water is a practicable and effective public health measure. On Dec. 5, 1957, the American Medical Association reaffirmed safety, as to general health of consumers, of fluoridation up to 1 ppm. in drinking water. Fluoridation at public demand, and when approved by local medical and dental societies, was endorsed repeatedly by the American Water Works Association.

In 1975, about half of the U.S. population used water that contained natural or added fluorides. A number of states have water with a high content of natural fluorides, Texas and North Dakota leading. Controlled fluoridation programs are also in operation in communities throughout the world.

Softening. Sky water becomes "hard" by the addition of minerals which are dissolved as the water runs over the surface or percolates underground. Hardness can become a source of considerable expense to the consumer unless it it reduced by softening.

Water-softening processes for municipal plants are either the cold lime-soda process, the cation-exchange process (formerly called the zeolite process) or a combination of the two. In the cold lime-soda process, the steps are usually: addition of chemicals (generally lime and soda ash), mixing, sedimentation in basins for the reaction to take place, rapid sand filtration, and recarbonation to prevent the formation of incrustants and scale. If the water were not recarbonated (by diffusing carbon dioxide gas through it, to restore the carbon dioxide removed by the reaction with lime) the water would be unstable as to the solubility of carbonates and the corrosion of metals. The lime-soda process involves the handling of dusty lime, the disposal of great quantities of sludge, and expert supervision of recarbonation; if the recarbonation is not properly done, the sand, gravel, filters, and pipes will accumulate coatings of carbonates.

The cation-exchange softener is the most widely used type in municipalities, industries, and homes. In industries and homes, a water of zero hardness is produced, while in municipalities, completely softened water is mixed with hard water, to produce a water of tolerable hardness. The softener occupies comparatively little space, and is simple to operate. A cation-exchange water softener consists essentially of a container (gravity or pressure type) for the bed of exchange material, and piping and appurtenances for passing water through that material in one direction for softening the water, and in the reverse direction for the regeneration of the bed. In the reverse flow, the water carries brine. There is also required a storage bin for the salt, and a tank for saturated salt brine. The principle of this process lies in the ability of certain sodium compounds, which are insoluble, to exchange cations with other substances in the water; when a hard water is passed through a sodium cation exchanger, the calcium and magnesium in the hard water are replaced by sodium from the exchanger. Since the action is reversible, the "exhausted" cation exchanger can be "regenerated," with a solution of common salt, once all the readily replaceable sodium has been exchanged for calcium and magnesium from the hard water. In the regeneration, the calcium and magnesium of the exhausted cation exchangers are replaced with a fresh supply of sodium from the regenerating brine unit. Then, after washing with water to free it of brine, the exchange material in the filter is in condition to soften a fresh supply of hard water.

Corrosion may be an incidental result of cation-exchange softening, unless provision is made to guard against it. Water softened by this process is not in itself corrosive, but the absence of magnesium and calcium compounds prevents the formation of a coating based on alkaline hard water which protects the metal from attack by oxygen, the real corrosive agent. To protect pipelines in distribution systems, it is therefore advisable to mix the softened water with the raw, or make such adjustments to the *p*H and alkalinity as will produce substantial saturation with calcium carbonate.

DETROIT WATER AND SEWERAGE DEPT.

Sand filters at a Detroit water plant are used to remove fine impurities before the water is chlorinated.

Aeration. Aeration is the process of bringing about the intimate contact of air and water by any of the following methods: spraying the water in the air, bubbling air through the water, or by agitation of the water by cascades, etc. Aeration removes hydrogen sulphide, simple chlorine odors, and odors caused by decomposing organic matter; it can also greatly reduce odors caused by microorganisms, and can remove some iron and manganese. The method employed depends on the efficiency desired. Jet aerators are most effective, but cause a loss of 10 to 20 pounds pressure. Cascades, much used in industry, comprise 3 or 4 open metal steps down which the water tumbles. A series of slag-filled trays built vertically over each other, with screened or slatted bottoms, are termed tray aerators or trickling beds. Compressed air can be blown into the water mechanically through porous plates so set as to induce spiral flow.

Tastes and Odors. These conditions are caused by (1) dissolved gases, such as hydrogen sulphide; (2) organic matter, either living or in process of decay; (3) industrial wastes, of which phenol is the most troublesome; and (4) chlorine. In surface waters, the predominant problem is odor rather than taste. Most tastes, except those caused by chlorine alone, can be removed by an oxidizing agent; one such agent used in the United States is activated carbon. Chlorine itself is most valuable for taste and odor control.

Corrosion Control. By the addition of lime or soda to water containing free CO_2 (carbon dioxide) in such quantities that unprotected metal pipes would be corroded and tuberculated, water can be maintained in such chemical balance that the pipe coating is not dissolved. In recent years sodium hexametaphosphate (sold under the trade names of Calgon and Nalco-18) has come into increasing use to prevent "red water" caused by iron pickup in the distribution system or to minimize the growth of tubercules.

CONSERVATION

Although cities and other areas plagued by water shortages grow in number each year, there is ample water if it is properly conserved and developed under responsible government agencies. It has been estimated that the runoff from annual rainfall, spread evenly over the United States, would yield 8.7 inches, far greater than the 1 to 1.5 inches needed to meet national demand for domestic, industrial, and agricultural purposes. Water can be conserved in many ways, including universal metering of all services, holding back floodwaters in oversize reservoirs, desalting seawater and guarding against the intrusion of seawater into groundwater, reducing evaporation in reservoirs, using large groundwater reservoirs more extensively, recharging ground storage where geological conditions are favorable, and, in emergencies, discharging treated sewage into groundwater reservoirs under rigid controls. See also WATERSHED.

Intrusion of Seawater. The conservation of groundwater resources is particularly important near the seacoast because heavy pumping lowers the water table to such an extent that seawater will flow landward and force abandonment of the well. This has happened to New York City wells on Long Island, to deep wells at Atlantic City, N.J., and to wells in the Los Angeles district, at Savannah and Brunswick, Ga., and in the Panhandle region of Texas. Since 1940, long-continued draft on the coastal groundwaters of California, a period of protracted drought, and increasing municipal and agricultural demands have lowered the static groundwater level to a point below sea level. Several ways have been suggested to combat seawater intrusion, such as reduction of pumping, or use of stage pumping; recharge of overdrawn aquifers to raise groundwater level; maintenance of a freshwater barrier above sea level along the coast; construction of artificial subsurface barriers; and the sinking of closely spaced wells along the coast to pump seawater back to sea. All evidence to date is that degraded aquifers can be reclaimed by pressure recharge through wells.

Desalting Seawater. Supplementing deficient supplies of freshwater by using desalted seawater has received increasing study and research. Its use has been considered by such seaside metropolises as New York and Los Angeles, in view of the successful desalting to supply thousands of persons on South Pacific islands in World War II.

The federal government has set up a special agency to work on the problem. The Office of Water Research and Technology in the Interior Department is charged with developing economically feasible processes for converting saltwater to freshwater. Processes being tested include vapor-compression distillation, solar distillation, electrodialysis, and those utilizing freezing, critical pressures, and osmosis. The goal is to bring down the cost of desalinization. Desalting plants are now in full operation for public supplies in Aruba, Curaçao, the Virgin Islands, Bermuda, and in Kuwait and the Bahrein Islands on the Persian Gulf.

Sewage Plant Effluent. Consideration is being given seriously to the use of sewage treatment plant effluent for public use to tide over periods of water shortage, provided it is restricted to the most severe emergency conditions. (Its use in industry is growing increasingly.) This method was practiced successfully in the city of Chanute, Kans. during a drought period. Secondarily treated and chlorinated sewage from its new treatment plant was diverted into a pond—providing 17 days detention—formed by a dam on the Neosho River, on which the city also had a waterworks intake one mile upstream. There was no measurable flow from the Neosho from August to February, and use of treated sewage began in October and recycling was practiced until March. There were no known cases of waterborne disease resulting from the emergency measure. Studies in California supported the practicability of reclamation, and it is now used in the Southwest and the Far West for recharge or for irrigation.

CLINTON L. BOGERT
Consulting Engineer, Coauthor of "Waterworks Handbook"

Bibliography

American Water Works Association, *Water Quality and Treatment: A Handbook for Public Water Supplies,* 3d ed. (McGraw 1971).

Frederick, Kenneth D., *Scarce Water and Institutional Change* (Resources for the Future 1986).

Geraghty, Miller, *Water Atlas of the U.S.,* 3d ed. (Water Info. 1973).

Hofkes, E. H., *Small Community Water Supplies: Technology of Small Water Supply Systems in Developing Countries* (Wiley 1984).

Holtz, David, and Sebastian, Scott, eds., *Municipal Water Systems: The Challenge for Urban Resource Management* (Indiana Univ. Press 1978).

Kasperson, Roger E., and Kasperson, Jeanne X., eds., *Water Re-Use and the Cities* (Univ. Press of New England 1977).

Robinson, Michael C., *Water for the West: The Bureau of Reclamation, 1902–1977* (American Public Works 1979).

Rosenkrantz, Barbara G., ed., *Clean Water and the Health of the Cities: An Original Anthology* (Arno 1977).

Skinner, Brian J., *Earth Resources,* 3d ed. (Prentice-Hall 1986).

Steel, E. W., and McGhee, Terence, *Water Supply and Sewerage,* 5th ed. (McGraw 1979).

White, Gilbert F., *Strategies of American Water Management,* rev. ed. (Univ. of Michigan Press 1971).

WATER TABLE, *in architecture,* a horizontal band or other projection to throw off water, especially the table at the juncture of the foundation of a building and the upper wall.

In hydraulic engineering, the topmost level of that part of the ground which is saturated with water. Known also as a *waterline,* it determines the depth at which a well or spring must penetrate to reach water. When the water table recedes below that point, the well dries up. See also CONSERVATION—*Water Conservation.*

In road engineering, the gutter beside the road which carries off water is called a water table.

WATER TRANSPORT. See TRANSPORTATION.

WATER TURBINE. See TURBINE—*Hydraulic Turbine;* WATERWHEEL.

WATER VAPOR. See BOILING; STEAM.

WATER WILLOW, common name for several swamp or water herbs; especially in the United States and eastern Canada, the species of *Justicia* (family Acanthaceae), such as *J. americana,* a two- to three-foot-tall perennial with lanceolate leaves and dense spikes of pale violet to white, tubular, two-lipped flowers; and *Decodon verticillatus* (family Lythraceae), or swamp loosestrife, a six-foot-tall perennial with lanceolate leaves and axillary magenta flowers.

WATERBURY, a city in Connecticut, in New Haven county, 90 miles (145 km) northeast of New York City. Situated in the Naugatuck River valley, Waterbury is Connecticut's fourth-largest city in population—after Bridgeport, Hartford, and New Haven. With hills of granite to the east and west, the city parallels the north-south course of the Naugatuck River. The Mad River flows through the eastern part of the city and then curves to the west, where it joins the Naugatuck.

Industry and Commerce. The city's earliest industry began about 1750. Some 50 years later the first brass mill began operation. Soon Waterbury gained a worldwide reputation as a brass center. The foundries produced brass and bronze for further fabrication into sheets, rods, and tubing. The mills also processed aluminum, steel, and numerous alloys. By the 1970's the brass industry had declined as technological innovations, federal regulations, and the use of plastics increased. Cheap watches also formerly were manufactured in great numbers, and the well-known Waterbury and "dollar" watches originated here.

Goods other than brass include electrical equipment, computer components, machine tools, precision instruments, chemicals, rubber, and plastics.

Educational and Cultural Life. Educational institutions include public and parochial elementary and secondary schools. A well-known private school is St. Margaret McTernan School. Higher education facilities include Post College (1890), Waterbury State Technical College (1964), Mattatuck Community College (1967), and a branch of the University of Connecticut.

Opportunity for informal education is provided by the Silas Bronson Public Library. The Mattatuck Historical Society, organized in 1877, maintains colonial collections, a museum, and a genealogical library.

Waterbury's architecture is enhanced by several buildings by Cass Gilbert, a noted 20th century architect whose work features a combination of white marble and red brick. Another red brick structure, the railroad station designed by the architects McKim, Mead, and White, and completed in 1906, is particularly elegant.

Holy Land, a 13-acre (5-hectare) hilltop site dominated by a 20-foot (6-meter) cross, has attracted thousands of tourists, with its statues of the saints, representations of biblical events, and model buildings that are meant to depict Jerusalem.

History and Government. Known to the Indians as "Matetacoke" (land without trees), later contracted to Mattatuck, the site of the Waterbury settlement was first deeded by the Indians to white men in 1657. The area in this deed later became a part of the Mattatuck grant, which was subsequently incorporated as a town in 1686 upon being separated from the town of Farmington. The first settlement in 1674 was on a plateau at the top of a steep rise to the west of the Naugatuck River and was known as the Town Plot. This settlement was abandoned in King Philip's War, and soon thereafter a new settlement was made, on the east side of the river, which became the present city of Waterbury.

For more than a century the town's growth was slow. In addition to the natural disadvantages of its location for a community dependent upon agriculture, it underwent such calamities as the "great flood" of 1691 and the "great sickness" of 1712. In 1902 a disastrous fire practically wiped out the city's business section, and in 1955 a devastating flood caused severe property damage.

The government consists of a mayor and a board of aldermen. Incorporation as a city took place in 1853. From 1895 until 1960, when county government in Connecticut was abolished, Waterbury was one of two county seats of New Haven county. Population: 103,266.

ROBERT C. SALE*
State Librarian of Connecticut

WATERBUCK, the name applied to various African antelopes that inhabit swampy areas or hide in tangles of high reeds, sometimes coming into the more open country to feed in early morning and late evening. The defassa waterbuck (*Kobus defassa harnieri*) is a large and handsome species, tan in color, with slightly curved horns that measure up to 3 feet (1 meter) in length. It generally is found in small herds and ranges some distance from water onto the dry plains in thornbush country of the Sudan. The lechwe waterbuck (*Onotragus leche*) is a smaller species, confined to swampy areas along the Zambezi River. Both these species have been bred in captivity and are commonly shown in zoological gardens.

Despite their name, the waterbucks are not the most aquatic of African antelopes. This distinction belongs to the sitatunga (*Limnotragus*) and other forms having expanded and flattened hoofs especially adapted for travel on soft, wet ground. Waterbuck hoofs are normally shaped, and, except for their more sculptured horns, the adult waterbucks resemble superficially the adult deer (*Odocoileus*) found in much of North America.

EDWARD S. HODGSON
Tufts University

A male defassa waterbuck. Waterbucks are found near rivers and swamps in most of the sub-Saharan Africa.

WATERCOLOR. The term watercolor may be defined in three ways. It can refer to any type of painting that uses water-bound pigments; or to the pigments themselves; or it may be used to designate an art form, that is, watercolor painting as distinguished from oil painting.

Technique and Materials. The earliest method of painting in a water-bound medium is *a fresco*. Applied directly to damp, fresh (*fresco*) plaster, the color is totally absorbed, becoming an integral part of the plaster itself. This dries to a rock-hard amalgam, the result of a chemical action between the lime (calcium hydroxide) in the plaster and the carbon dioxide in the atmosphere. In a later method, pigmented color was bound with egg, and the resulting emulsion, known as tempera, could then be diluted with water. Gouache, an opaque form of watercolor used with great effect by Chinese artists, is achieved by mixing white with pigmented color.

As an art form, "true" or "pure" watercolor painting consists of glazing transparent colors, applied in delicate washes, one upon the other, allowing the paper to act as an illuminating agent. Considerable luminosity and brilliance is created by the contrast between the reflective luster of the raised surfaces of a granular paper and the depth and richness of the heavily loaded color in the hollows. But although watercolor is transparent, successive washes cause the interaction of absorption and reflection to become more complex, resulting in a loss of luminosity and freshness and giving rise to a "muddy" quality. The maxim "Never lose your paper" thus remains as true today as when it was first coined.

A careful selection of paper has always been considered of paramount importance, and watercolorists each have their favorite one. Some prefer a heavy, thick paper; others, a light, thin variety. These range in weight from 72 pounds (32.4 kg) per ream, to 400 pounds (180 kg) for pasteless boards. Watercolor paper is available with three types of surface: smooth, or "hot-pressed"; with a medium grain, or "not" surface; and a "rough" surface, which, as its name implies, carries a heavy grain. The best quality watercolor papers are handmade from white linen rags. Although expensive, they withstand rough treatment, and color on them retains a fresh and lively character. Many of today's good quality mold-made papers are much cheaper, and although made by machine, offer an acceptable substitute for handmade papers. Not all watercolor papers are white. The 19th century English watercolorists David Cox and Peter de Wint favored tinted, coarse-grained wrapping papers with a mottled surface, modern versions of which are still manufactured.

Brushes also play a major role in watercolor painting, and great attention is given to their preparation. The best and most costly brushes are made from pure red sable, taken from the tail hairs of the Siberian kolinsky, a type of mink. Although expensive, these soft yet springy brushes will last for many years if treated with care. Other brushes are made from the hair of camel, ox, badger, and squirrel and from nylon and other man-made fibers. The ideal brush should be of reasonable length—never short and stubby. It should be thick at the ferrule and should taper to a fine point. Yet some great watercolorists have seen fit to break this rule. Although both the broadest wash and the finest detail can be achieved with a single large sable, most watercolor artists use three or more different-sized brushes.

In the manufacture of watercolor paint, the finely ground pigment—fine enough to pass through a screen of 325 meshes to the square inch—is not simply mixed with water. A binding agent must be added to ensure that the paint adheres to the paper and remains stable, not flaking off when dry. In the past, when artists ground their own colors and prepared their own paints, all manner of binding agents were mixed with the pigments to provide a vehicle: flour, animal size, rice paste, casein of cheese, and other ingredients secret to a particular artist. The most successful, however, were found to be a variety of gums: gum arabic, tragacanth, and fish glue, among others. Today, artists' colormen bind their pigments with gum arabic, counteracting brittleness by adding honey and sugar and keeping the paint moist with glycerin. Adding glycerin is doubly important in preparing the moist color packaged in tubes, the most efficient and economical way for the artist to use watercolor. Gum arabic is preferred as a binder, for although it readily dissolves in water, enough remains in the paint to act as a thin varnish, which gives the color additional luminosity. A quaint conceit of English watercolorists was to add alcohol, usually brandy or whiskey, to their paint water to accelerate drying.

The four or five simple colors at the disposal of the ancients has grown steadily over the centuries into a rich range of colors, and today the watercolor artist can choose from over 100 different ones, obtained from vegetable, mineral, and synthetic sources. This in itself can be a snare, for although only an approximate hue can be obtained by mixing pigmented primary colors (red, yellow, and blue), it is nevertheless advisable to restrict a palette to less rather than more colors.

History. Very early examples of watercolor painting appear in subterranean caves in south central France and northern Spain. There, by the feeble light of guttering animal-fat lamps, early artists depicted a variety of animals with magnificent spirit and vitality, using primitive brushes and sometimes spraying on the unbound color through hollow bone blowpipes. These masterpieces have been preserved for posterity by the fortuitous chemical action of the limestone surface on which they were painted. Later, artists of ancient Egypt consciously used *a fresco* technique in their tomb paintings, produced to be gazed upon by the souls of the dead, not publicly admired. They were also the first to use watercolor on a paperlike material (papyrus). It remained for the Mediterranean cultures of Crete, Greece, Etruria, and Rome to compose wall paintings intended to delight living viewers.

During the Middle Ages, artist-clerics used watercolor, both transparent and opaque, with great skill to produce illuminated manuscripts. These works, painted on vellum, were the forerunners of the 16th and 17th century miniatures painted on paper, wood, and ivory. Wall painting, both *a fresco* and *a secco* (painting on dry plaster) reached its peak during the Renaissance, with artists such as Giotto, Piero della Francesca, and Michelangelo. In the 16th century, artist-explorers such as John White and Jacques de Morgues Le Moyne found watercolor a conve-

THE METROPOLITAN MUSEUM OF ART, AMELIA B. LAZARUS FUND, 1910

Winslow Homer's luminous, freely painted watercolors, such as *Hurricane, Bahamas,* redefined the medium in America.

nient medium for immediate record, and Albrecht Dürer drew a number of breathtakingly realistic watercolor studies. Otherwise watercolor was neglected in Europe until the 18th century.

The Far East. In China, and later in Japan, pure watercolor was developed as the exclusive means of visual expression. Chinese artists painted for an elite audience of intellectuals, and often for themselves alone. They sought to capture the quintessence of nature in their work, regarding man very much as an afterthought. Painting was considered an extension of poetry and calligraphy. Great importance was placed on the control and handling of the brush—the "strength of brushstroke" (Japanese, *fude no chikara*). The artist strove for absolute coordination between mind and hand. As the point of the brush touched the surface of the paper, he attempted to communicate an inner feeling, which flowed through his hand to the tip of the brush and thence to the content of the painting. Once the brush made contact with the paper, the artist worked quickly—"As the buzzard swoops when the hare jumps out."

Painting implements were sticks of black ink, which when diluted with water produced an infinite range of soft grays, and color pigments stiffened with gum, whose strength was controlled by mixing the color with a white pigment ground from seashells. With these materials, the scholar-artists of China and Japan created delicate watercolors of great beauty. At first derivative of Chinese painting, Japanese watercolor gradually took on a softer quality, while still retaining perfect precision of brushstroke. The flower paintings of Tani Buncho epitomize Japanese watercolor at its best.

THE BRITISH MUSEUM, LONDON

Hibiscus, by Tani Buncho, exemplifies the Japanese emphasis on simplicity and perfect control of the brush.

VICTORIA AND ALBERT MUSEUM, LONDON

With landscapes like *An Ancient Beech Tree,* Paul Sandby helped raise the status of watercolor painting in England.

English Watercolor. It may be said that Albrecht Dürer was the father of Western watercolor, but more than 200 years elapsed before the English watercolorists raised it to an art in its own right.

The flowering of watercolor began in England during the early part of the 18th century. Until then it had been used only to tint pen-and-pencil drawings with washes of blue and sepia. Yet the monochrome sketches of Claude Lorrain and Rembrandt van Rijn not only suggest a sense of immense space but, in a miraculous way, a feeling of color.

The 16th century German artist Albrecht Dürer drew meticulously detailed watercolor studies, such as *Young Hare*.

ALBERTINA, VIENNA, AUSTRIA

Influenced on the one hand by Italian classicism and on the other by Dutch realism, the early watercolor artists turned to landscape for inspiration, a theme that was to reach unparalleled heights during the early part of the 19th century. As they began to use color, three distinct styles emerged: (1) Washes of transparent color were added to enrich pen drawings made in sepia or black on white paper; (2) Gouache, or opaque body color, was used alone, usually on tinted paper; and (3) Transparent washes were strengthened by the judicious use of gouache in the light passages.

Paul Sandby was by far the most significant figure in the first period of the English watercolor movement (roughly 1720–1780), doing more than anyone to raise its status. Timidly at first, he gradually began to add stronger color to monochromatic washes flooded over a fine "etcher's" pen outline, achieving the chiaroscuro (interplay of light and shade) so much admired by his contemporaries.

It was during the second phase of the movement (1780–1850) that watercolors of great power and unsurpassed beauty were produced. Building on the foundation laid by earlier artists, the painters of the heyday of English watercolor tended to divide into three schools: topographical, romantic, and mystical. On occasion the work of an individual painter overlapped all three areas.

In three words, the poet Thomas Gray captured the essence of the topographical school: "Scenes, situations, antiquities." An increasing number of art patrons were traveling abroad, and they called for paintings of the buildings and

Venice: The Grand Canal with the Salute, by J. M. W. Turner, illustrates the English artist's mastery of light and atmosphere and his ability to capture the glassy surface of placid water.

THE ASHMOLEAN MUSEUM, OXFORD, ENGLAND

places seen on their travels. In addition, demand was growing for scenes of the British countryside, while the advent of sea bathing and the seaside resort began to popularize the seascape.

Such artists as John Robert Cozens, while satisfying these popular demands, also took the development of watercolor a stage further. Abandoning restrictive pen line and monochromatic underpainting, Cozens built up his sensitive pictures in a series of delicate low-toned washes, putting dark color over light. This approach had a marked influence on the great romantics, Thomas Girtin and J. M. W. Turner, who as young men copied Cozens' work by candlelight. Other topographical watercolorists of the time were John "Warwick" Smith, Edward Dayes, Michael Angelo Rooker, and Francis Towne.

Thomas Girtin, although he died tragically young, led the way to a highly romantic, imaginative approach to watercolor, forging a tradition that was perpetuated by Turner, John Constable, and others. As one critic wrote of him, "No one characteristic watercolor of the early 19th century could be imagined without presupposing Girtin." Whereas Girtin was content to create beauty from observable reality, Joseph Mallard William Turner invented, imposing his own ideas on the subjects he painted. Obsessed by color and "flittering light," he created watercolors that sparkle and scintillate in a manner that no one since has achieved. The vortexing waves and feel for water in his seascapes belie the English critic John Ruskin's words, "The sea has never been, and I fancy, will never be or can be painted."

John Constable, whose watercolors went unappreciated until 50 years after his death, and who came as close as anyone to matching Turner's sense of space, was a master of skies. Unlike Turner, who allowed his romantic vision to dictate the view before him, Constable was the first to prove that a landscape could be a great work of art and yet remain a faithful likeness of nature.

John Sell Cotman, David Cox, and Peter de Wint, though contemporaries, developed completely different styles. Cotman, who with John Crome was a leader of the Norwich school of painting, ordered the elements of nature within his watercolors into a preconceived pattern, laying one limpid, carefully conceived wash upon another. Cox threw himself vigorously into his work, especially in later life when freed from financial constraints, and excelled at capturing a fleeting windswept moment in time. ("How fond you are of painting wind, Mr. Cox," an admirer once exclaimed.) De Wint's painting, in contrast, has a calm serenity. He used rich, balanced color derived from a limited palette to depict calm reflections on water and the mellow stone of old buildings. Among other leading watercolorists of this period were John Varley, Cornelius Varley, A. V. Copley Fielding, and John White Abbott.

William Blake was supreme among the visionaries, mystical painters who saw and painted with the inner eye. One of the most imaginative artists of all time, Blake once said of himself, "Men think they can copy nature as correctly as I copy imagination." The other English great visionary was Samuel Palmer, who brought to watercolor an unbelievable richness of color. Artists influenced by Blake and Palmer were Edward Calvert, John Linnell, and Henry Fuseli.

From 1850 onward, as the number of exhibitions and watercolor societies increased, more and more artists took to the medium of watercolor, which was by now accepted as an independent art form. However, the work itself degenerated into a vehicle for technical virtuosity and cloying prettiness, in which overbright color was used to ape oil painting. In an attempt to revitalize British painting, a group of young artists formed the Pre-Raphaelite Brotherhood, taking for their theme "truth to nature." Among the more famous of these who worked in watercolor were Dante Gabriel Rossetti, Ford Madox Brown, and Sir Edward Burne-Jones.

The beginning of the 20th century saw British watercolor take on a fresh impetus, as the influ-

GIRAUDON/ART RESOURCE

The French artist Paul Cézanne used watercolor to create studies such as *Table de cuisine: pots et bouteilles.*

THE BROOKLYN MUSEUM, PURCHASED BY SPECIAL SUBSCRIPTION

Economical, rapid brushstrokes produce portraiture of remarkable sensitivity in *Bedouins,* by the American artist John Singer Sargent.

ence of the Postimpressionists, Fauves, Expressionists, Cubists, and Futurists began to be felt. The New English Art Club, founded to shake the Royal Academy out of its lethargy, encouraged such painters as Philip Wilson Steer, Walter Richard Sickert, Christopher Nevinson, Paul Nash, David Jones, Graham Sutherland, and John Piper.

France. In France watercolor has never enjoyed the popularity as a medium that it has in Britain and the United States, yet a number of great French artists have turned to it on occasion. It was introduced into France during the early part of the 19th century, by French artists working in England who had come under the influence of the English Romantics. Eugène Delacroix, encouraged by a highly talented young English watercolorist living in France, Richard Parkes Bonington, discovered that watercolor could be an extremely expressive medium, as did Théodore Géricault.

Although the Impressionists used what was essentially a watercolor technique, allowing the ground of their paintings to come through as a reflective surface, they never fully exploited the medium. Some of them who used watercolor, either as studies or to explore the play of light, were Édouard Manet, Edgar Degas, Auguste Renoir, Camille Pissarro, Claude Monet, and Alfred Sisley.

Paul Cézanne, who turned from the instant image of the Impressionists to, as he said, "something more solid and endurable," used watercolor as a means of relaxation from oil painting. These studies, never intended for the public eye, nonetheless follow his goal of producing "constructions after nature." Paul Gauguin also created powerful watercolors, rich in color and strong in pattern. Later, Henri Matisse, Georges Braque, Pablo Picasso, and Georges Rouault carried on the tradition.

United States. Watercolor painting, regarded in its early stages as a poor relation of oil painting by American artists, rapidly grew in importance. Today, much of the exciting exploration of the medium is being carried out in the United States. In the early part of the 19th century, watercolor painting in America, following closely the lead of the English school, showed little promise of the tremendous impetus that it was to gain 50 years later.

From 1850 onward a revolution among American watercolorists resulted in a move from drawing in watercolor to painting with the medium. More than anyone, Winslow Homer was responsible for this revolution. His watercolors, far in advance of his oil paintings, were at first influenced by the Impressionists Monet and Degas. By the end of the century they had grown in stature to completely personal works of art that had a considerable influence on his contemporaries. He simplified the masses in his work, and his cleaner color, chosen with discretion, became almost synonymous with light.

John Singer Sargent, though best known for his oil paintings, believed that his watercolors held greater artistic significance. In these impressionistic works, he manipulated light and color with technical brilliance to create a personal romanticism. Even more in advance of his time, Maurice Brazil Prendergast met with little contemporary acclaim, but his works, with their woven patterns of positive color, had a marked influence on succeeding generations of American watercolor artists.

Another artist of distinction who turned to watercolor at this time was James McNeill Whistler. His watercolors, which along with the rest of his works are influenced by Japanese art, have a remarkable spontaneity, their clear, restrained color being used to capture an instant in time. The paintings of Thomas Eakins also halt time and motion to freeze a passing impression, but in an entirely contrary manner. His carefully analyzed work is almost mathematical in its photographic concept.

John Marin, more than any other artist, was responsible for the explosive growth of American watercolor. His work, at first conservative, under the influence of the Futurists developed a swift, subjective style. Representational imagery was replaced by intense inner perception. He himself said, "Painting is founded on the heart controlled by the head." The beginning of the 20th century saw more and more American artists turning to watercolor as a medium—Childe Hassam, Arthur Davies, Gifford Beal, Rockwell Kent, and a host of others.

Subsequent generations of American watercolor artists, motivated by the work of Raoul Dufy, Rouault, Paul Klee, and the Expressionists as well as Marin, believing watercolor to be the most flexible mode of expression, have turned it into an exciting experimental medium. Exploiting color and texture to the full, spattering, dribbling, grasping at the happy accident and controlling it, they achieve a shattering, controlled vibrancy. A far cry from the sedate 18th century topographical studies, watercolor has become, particularly in the United States, the medium of adventurous artistic expression in the hands of such modern masters as Jackson Pollock, Mark Tobey, Morris Graves, Sam Francis, Andrew Wyeth, Lyonel Feininger, Robert Rauschenberg, Hilda Levy, Ben Shahn, Jack Kling, Edward Reep, and many others.

BERNARD BRETT
Author of "A History of Watercolor"

Bibliography

Brett, Bernard, *A History of Watercolor* (Simon & Schuster 1984).
Hoopes, Donelson, *American Watercolor Painting* (Watson-Guptill 1977).
Reep, Edward, *The Content of Watercolor* (Van Nostrand 1969).
Reynolds, Graham, *A Concise History of Watercolors* (Oxford 1971).
Wilton, Andrew, *British Watercolors, 1750 to 1850* (State Mutual Book 1977).

WATERCRESS, any of six species of perennial aquatic herbs of the mustard family. Watercress leaves are widely used as salad greens and garnishes. Native to Europe, watercress (*Nasturtium*) has been naturalized throughout much of temperate North America. The plants have smooth succulent stems and pinnate compound leaves with up to 11 roundish leaflets.

The common green watercress (*Nasturtium officinale*) is cultivated nearly worldwide. This species, which remains green in the fall, is subject to frost damage. Brown, or winter, watercress, which turns purplish brown in the fall, is more resistant to frost. It is a hybrid between *N. officinale* and the wild species *N. microphyllum*.

Watercress beds can be established by inserting stems discarded from salad plants in the bed of a shallow stream with a gentle but continual flow of water. The stems creep along the streambed, taking root as they grow. Watercress is harvested anytime except during the summer flowering period. Frequent harvesting stimulates prolific branching.

A bed of common green watercress in a shallow stream.

© DEREK FELL

Victoria Falls viewed from Zambezi Gorge. Over a mile wide, the falls are partly hidden by the gorge walls.

WATERFALL, a stream of water that descends freely over a precipice. It is formed when a stream flows from a resistant rock to one that is more readily eroded by the stream, or when a stream drops from a resistant rock to a depression formed by other natural agencies.

Waterfalls are among the most impressive spectacles of nature. Some falls are distinctive because of their beauty, especially those that drop from a great height. Others are notable because of the great volume of water that flows over the precipice. A few of the greatest waterfalls are impressive for both reasons.

Because waterfalls impede navigation, they became the sites of portages, canals, rail and road heads, or ports at the head of navigation. Mills were built to use the power of the falls, and industrial settlements grew up around them. Many communities are situated at falls, and some towns and cities have names referring to this position. The largest in the United States are Niagara Falls, N. Y., Wichita Falls, Texas, and Sioux Falls, S. Dak.

Among the great falls of the world, the most spectacular in North America is Niagara Falls. Goat Island divides it into Horseshoe (Canadian) Falls, between New York state and the Canadian province of Ontario, and American Falls, in New York. Horseshoe Falls receives nine tenths of the Niagara River's flow. It is about 2,500 feet (762 meters) wide and 160 feet (49 meters) high. American Falls is about 1,000 feet (305 meters) wide and 167 feet (51 meters) high. At Niagara Falls, the river flows over resistant Lockport limestone of Silurian age. The limestone lies above less resistant shales in the face of the falls. As the waters undercut the lip of the falls, portions of the face break away, causing the falls to retreat gradually upriver. This retreat has been observed in modern times, and is marked by great rock-falls. Niagara Falls has receded several miles in the 10,000 years since glacial ice melted from the region.

Other falls over horizontal limestone are St. Anthony Falls on the Mississippi River in Minneapolis, Minn., and Chaudière Falls on the Ottawa River in Ottawa, Ontario. Each of these waterfalls is about 50 feet (15 meters) high.

Angel Fall, in southeastern Venezuela, is the highest known waterfall of consequence. A tributary of the Caroni River drops 3,212 feet (979 meters) over a face of flat-lying quartzite. The descent is made in two falls, the upper one measuring 2,648 feet (807 meters).

Victoria Falls, on the Zambezi River in southern Africa, plunges 355 feet (108 meters) and more through flat lava layers. The falls are more than a mile wide but drop into a narrow chasm that may have been eroded along a fracture zone.

At Multnomah Falls, in Oregon, a tributary of the Columbia River descends about 850 feet (260 meters) over lavas. In ancient times, the Columbia also dropped over lavas as it flowed through the Grand Coulee, its prehistoric course in the northeastern part of Washington. The falls were 3 miles (4.8 km) wide and as high as 400 feet (125 meters). The falls of the Passaic River at Paterson, N. J., drop 75 feet (23 meters) over ancient lava. Yellowstone Falls in Yellowstone National Park, Wyo., has an upper fall of 109 feet (33 meters) and a lower fall of 308 feet (94 meters). Vertical dikes of lava, intruded into less resistant volcanic sediments, prevent Yellowstone Falls from retreating with erosion.

Montmorency Falls, near Quebec, Canada, is 275 feet (84 meters) high. It occurs along a fault that brought the falls' resistant granitic rocks into a position opposite easily eroded shales.

Some of the highest waterfalls issue from hanging tributary valleys above main valleys deepened by glaciers. Yosemite National Park in California has several spectacular falls of this sort. Before glaciation, the deep stream valley had rapidly descending tributaries along its sides. Ice eroded and broadened the valley floor. When the ice melted, the upper courses of the tributaries entered the steep-walled main valley far above its floor. Ribbon Falls drops 1,612 feet (491 meters); Yosemite Falls has an upper fall of 1,430 feet (435 meters) and a lower

SELECTED MAJOR WATERFALLS OF THE WORLD

Name of Falls	Height (feet)	Height (meters)	Stream	Location
North America				
Bridalveil	620	189	Merced River tributary	Yosemite National Park, California
Churchill	245	75	Churchill River	Labrador, Newfoundland, Canada
Comet	320	98	Van Trump Creek	Mt. Rainier National Park, Washington
Fairy	700	210	Stevens Creek	Mt. Rainier National Park, Washington
Feather	640	195	Fall River	California
Grand	150	45	Mississagi River	Ontario, Canada
Illilouette	370	113	Illilouette Creek	Yosemite National Park, California
Latourelle	224	68	Merced River tributary	Oregon
Montmorency	275	84	Montmorency River	Quebec, Canada
Multnomah	850	260[1]	Columbia River tributary	Oregon
Highest fall	680	207		
Nevada	594	181	Merced River	Yosemite National Park, California
Niagara			Niagara River	New York–Ontario, Canada
American	167	51		
Horseshoe (Canadian)	160	49		
Ribbon	1,612	491	Ribbon Creek	Yosemite National Park, California
Shawinigan	150	46	St. Maurice River	Quebec, Canada
Shoshone	210	64	Snake River	Idaho
Silver Strand	1,170	357	Silver Strand Creek	Yosemite National Park, California
Takakkaw	1,248[1]	380[1]	Glacier source; flows into Yoho River	British Columbia, Canada
Highest fall	1,000	305		
Virginia	315	96	South Nahanni River	Northwest Territories, Canada
Yellowstone			Yellowstone River	Yellowstone National Park, Wyoming-Montana-Idaho
Upper	109	33		
Lower (Grand)	308	94		
Yosemite	2,425[1]	740[1]	Yosemite Creek	Yosemite National Park, California
Upper	1,430	435		
Lower	320	98		
South America				
Angel	3,212[1]	979[1]	Caroní River tributary	Venezuela
Highest fall	2,648	807		
Cuquenán	2,000	610	Cuquenán River	Venezuela
Iguassú	210	64	Iguassú River	Brazil-Argentina
Kaieteur	741	226	Potaro River	Guyana
King Edward VIII	840	256	Mazaruni River tributary	Guyana
King George VI	1,600	488	Mazaruni River tributary	Guyana
Paulo Afonso	270[1]	82[1]	São Francisco River	Brazil
Tequendama	482	147	Bogotá River	Colombia
Europe				
Gastein			Gasteiner Ache	Austria
Upper	207	63		
Lower	279	85		
Gavarnie	1,385	422	Gave de Pau	France
Giessbach	1,150[1]	350[1]	Giessbach	Switzerland
Glomach	370	113	Elchaig River tributary	Scotland
Kile	1,840[1]	560[1]	Kile River	Norway
Highest fall	490	149		
Krimml	1,246[1]	380[1]	Krimml River	Austria
Marmore	525[1]	160[1]	Velino River	Italy
Reichenbach	300[2]	91[2]	Reichenbach	Switzerland
Rheinfall (Schauffhausen)	100[1]	30[1]	Rhine River	Switzerland
Rjukan	983	300	Mana River	Norway
Skykje	650	198	Hardanger Fjord tributary	Norway
Staubbach	980	299	Staubbach	Switzerland
Trümmelbach	950[1]	290[1]	Trümmelbach	Switzerland
Vettis	850	259	Mörkedola River	Norway
Africa				
Aughrabies	450	137	Orange River	South Africa
Baratieri	460	140	Ganale Dorya	Ethiopia
Boyama (Stanley)	200[1]	61	Lualaba River	Zaire
Kabalega (Murchison)	400[1]	122[1]	Victoria Nile	Uganda
Kalambo	704	215	Kalambo River	Tanzania-Zambia
Maletsunyane	630	192	Orange River tributary	Lesotho
Ruacaná	406	124	Cunene River	Angola
Tugela	2,800[1]	854	Tugela River	South Africa
Victoria	355	108	Zambezi River	Zambia-Zimbabwe
Asia				
Gersoppa	830	253	Sharavati River	India
Khone (8-mile, or 13-km, wide series of falls)	70	21	Mekong River	Laos-Kampuchea
Nachi	430	131	Nachi River	Japan
Oceania				
Bowen	540[1]	165[1]	Glacier source	New Zealand
Highest fall	470	143		
Sutherland	1,904[1]	580[1]	Arthur River	New Zealand
Highest fall	815	248		
Tully	800[1]	244[1]	Tully River	Australia
Wentworth	614[1]	187[1]	Murray River	Australia
Highest fall	360	110		
Wollomombi	1,580	482	Wollomombi River	Australia
Highest fall	1,100	335		

[1]Total height of a series of falls. [2]Highest fall in a series.

one of 320 feet (98 meters); Bridalveil Falls is 620 feet (189 meters) high.

Many other falls are noted for their height. Gavarnie Falls in the French Pyrenees drops 1,385 feet (422 meters) into a glacial amphitheater. The highest fall of Takakkaw Falls, in Yoho National Park, British Columbia, is about 1,000 feet (305 meters). Sutherland Falls near Milford Sound, South Island, New Zealand, has three falls with a total drop of 1,904 feet (580 meters), the highest being 815 feet (248 meters).

Among falls of great volume, Niagara Falls and Victoria Falls have been named. Churchill Falls on the Churchill River in Labrador, northeastern Canada, has a flow that cascades 245 feet (75 meters) over resistant granitic rocks into a narrow canyon, with rapids descending nearly as far. Great Falls on the Missouri River in Montana, 75 feet (23 meters) high, and Shawinigan Falls on the St. Maurice River about Three Rivers (Trois Rivières), Quebec, 150 feet (46 meters) high, are important sources of waterpower. The Iguassú River on the border of Argentina and Brazil falls about 210 feet (64 meters) with large volume. The greatest in terms of volume of discharge is the Khone cataract on the Mekong River in southeastern Laos. Although the total drop of the river is only 70 feet (21 meters), an average of 400,000 cubic feet (11,325 cu meters) is discharged per second. The previous world record was held by the Guaíra Falls on the Paraná River in South America, but these rapids were submerged following the completion of the Itaipú dam in 1982.

Angel Falls in southern Venezuela. The upper one, shown here, is the world's highest major waterfall.

WATERFORD, a town in southeastern Connecticut, in New London county. It is on Long Island Sound just west of the city of New London, which adjoins it. Waterford includes the communities of Morningside Park, Quaker Hill, and Pleasure Beach. The town is chiefly residential, but it has some resort attractions and a few industries. The Millstone granite quarry, opened in 1830, is one of the largest active quarries in the state. A nuclear power plant that generates electrical energy is located in the town. The Harkness Memorial State Park has extensive grounds with flower gardens and greenhouses and a 42-room mansion with exhibitions of bird paintings by the 20th century ornithologist Rex Brasher. The Eugene O'Neill Theater Center, which includes works by new playwrights, is located in Waterford.

The area of Waterford was settled in 1653 and was long part of New London. It was incorporated as a separate town in 1801. Waterford is governed by a town meeting, selectmen, and a board of finance. Population: 17,843.

WATERFORD, county borough and seat of County Waterford, and the leading port in the southeast of Ireland. Its Gaelic name is Port Láirge. It is 85 miles (135 km) south-southwest of Dublin. From its excellent location on the south bank of the River Suir, it exports livestock, dairy products, and containerized products. In addition to ship repairs, local industries process meats and cattle feed and produce farm equipment, footwear, furniture, paper, and electrical goods. Since 1950 there has been a revival of the industry—renowned in the 18th century—that produced the cut Waterford glass highly prized by collectors.

Danish Vikings, who settled here about 850, selected the name Waterford (Vadrefjord). One of their leaders, Reginald, son of Sigtryg, is supposed to have built Holy Trinity Church about 1050. Richard Strongbow led a Norman force that occupied Waterford in 1171. King John granted the city a charter in 1206. Waterford remained for centuries one of the principal centers of English occupation in Ireland. In 1649 it resisted a memorable siege by Oliver Cromwell, but it fell to his son-in-law Henry Ireton the next year.

Of the old Danish fortifications, Reginald's Tower, a fort dating probably from 1003, remains. Vestiges of the Norman wall and fortifications also survive. Other historic buildings include Blackfriars' Priory, a Dominican house founded in 1226; the ruins of a Franciscan friary, founded in 1240; and Christ Church cathedral (Protestant) on the site of Sigtryg's church, begun in 1773.

County Waterford has an area of 710 square miles (1,840 sq km). It is drained principally by the rivers Suir and Blackwater. The area is one of contrasting scenic beauty, with the Knockmealdown and Comeragh mountains in the northern and central portions, and the cliffs and bays of the coast. Sloping hills and valleys—where farming, dairying, and livestock raising are carried on—are characteristic of the rest of the county. Economic activity, in addition to that of the city of Waterford, includes fishing, leather tanning, and marketing of farm produce. Slate, limestone, quartz, and marble are quarried. Population: (1981) of the city, 31,344; of the county, 81,462.

WATERGATE AFFAIR, the worst political scandal in U. S. history. It led to the resignation of a president, Richard M. Nixon, after he became implicated in an attempt to cover up the scandal. Narrowly, "Watergate affair" referred to the break-in and electronic bugging in 1972 of the Democratic National Committee (DNC) headquarters in the Watergate apartment and office building complex in Washington, D. C. Broadly, the term was also applied to several related scandals. More than 30 Nixon administration officials, campaign officials, and financial contributors pleaded guilty or were found guilty of breaking the law. Nixon, facing possible indictment after his resignation, received from his successor, Gerald Ford, a full pardon "for all offenses . . . which he . . . has committed or may have committed. . . ."

Americans were deeply troubled by the scandal. Attempts by Republican officials to discredit Democratic leaders and disrupt their campaign threatened the political process. Electronic surveillance presented a threat to civil liberties. Abuse of "national security" and "executive privilege" to thwart the investigation suggested that those concepts needed more precise definitions. The misuse of large campaign donations suggested the need for further reform legislation. The willingness of Nixon and his aides to use the Federal Bureau of Investigation (FBI), the Internal Revenue Service (IRS), and the Central Intelligence Agency (CIA) in unlawful or unethical ways against their "enemies" was a reckless exploitation of the bureaucracy.

"National Security." The antecedents of Watergate were steps taken by Nixon from 1969 to 1971 allegedly in the cause of national security. To uncover the sources of leaked news about such matters as the bombing of Cambodia, Nixon authorized, without court approval, the wiretapping of the phones of government officials and newspapermen. But some of the men whose phones were wiretapped had no involvement with security matters, and taps on two men continued after they had joined the staff of Sen. Edmund Muskie (D–Me.), who was seeking the Democratic presidential nomination.

In 1971, Nixon approved an intelligence operation that contemplated burglaries and the opening of mail to detect security leaks. The author of the plan, Tom Huston, acknowledged that part of his plan was "clearly illegal." Nixon revoked the operation after a protest by FBI Director J. Edgar Hoover.

Also in 1971, Nixon created the Special Investigations Unit—known as the "plumbers"—to plug news leaks. In September, agents of the unit broke into the office of Dr. Lewis Fielding, the psychiatrist of Dr. Daniel Ellsberg, who had given copies of the Pentagon Papers, a secret account of U. S. involvement in Indochina, to newspapers. (See PENTAGON PAPERS.) After Nixon learned of the break-in, he and his top aides agreed to say that the break-in had been carried out for national-security reasons. But in 1974, Charles Colson, a former special counsel to the president, who had pleaded guilty to obstructing justice, admitted that the agents wanted to find derogatory information about Ellsberg before Ellsberg's espionage trial. Colson said that "on numerous occasions" Nixon had urged him to disseminate such information. Egil Krogh, Jr., head of the plumbers unit, pleaded guilty to violating Dr. Fielding's civil rights, saying that he could not in conscience assert national security as a defense. Colson and Krogh were imprisoned. Two other persons, including John Ehrlichman, former chief domestic adviser to Nixon, were convicted of conspiring to deprive Dr. Fielding of his civil rights. Ehrlichman, who had approved a "covert entry" into Dr. Fielding's office, also was imprisoned.

The Watergate Break-in. In 1971, H. R. Haldeman, Nixon's chief of staff, was notified by an assistant, Gordon Strachan, that U. S. Attorney General John Mitchell and John Dean, counsel to the president, had discussed the need to develop a "political intelligence capability" at the Committee for the Re-election of the President (CRP). Some of the personnel and tactics identified with the activities described above became associated with efforts aimed at the Democrats. Early in 1972, Mitchell—both before and after he assumed his new position as director of CRP—discussed political espionage plans with Dean; Jeb Magruder, deputy director of CRP; and G. Gordon Liddy, counsel to the Finance Committee to Re-elect the President.

Magruder later testified that on March 30, 1972, Mitchell approved a proposal by Liddy that included the Watergate break-in. Mitchell vehemently denied this. Long after the scandal was revealed, investigators could not determine (1) who gave the ultimate order to break into Watergate, or (2) what the conspirators hoped to find there.

In any event, at 2:30 A. M. on June 17, 1972, police arrested five men at the DNC headquarters. The men were adjusting electronic equipment that they had installed in May. One of those arrested was James McCord, security coordinator for CRP.

Cover-up. Magruder later admitted that he and others began immediately to cover up White House and CRP involvement in the break-in. He and others destroyed incriminating documents and testified falsely to official investigators. L. Patrick Gray later resigned as acting director of the FBI after admitting that he had destroyed documents given him by Ehrlichman and Dean.

On June 23, 1972, Nixon learned from Haldeman of Mitchell's possible link with the operation. Nixon instructed Haldeman to stop an FBI inquiry into the source of money used by the wiretappers, using the excuse that the investigation would endanger CIA operations. Dean and others subsequently sought to induce CIA officials to cooperate with this plan. On July 1, Mitchell left CRP, citing personal reasons.

Nixon declared publicly on August 29 that no one in the administration, then employed, was involved in Watergate. Although money found in the possession of the wiretappers was traced to CRP, such evidence was insufficient to implicate high officials. On September 15, only the five men first arrested, plus Liddy and E. Howard Hunt, one of the plumbers, were indicted. Nixon congratulated Dean for "putting your fingers in the dikes every time that leaks have sprung here and sprung there."

Collapse of the Cover-up. In January 1973, two months after Nixon's reelection, the seven indicted men were tried before Judge John Sirica in the U. S. district court in Washington, D. C. Five pleaded guilty, and McCord and Liddy were convicted of conspiracy, burglary, and illegal wiretapping. Meanwhile, suspicions grew that the break-in was part of a broad program of political espionage. The U. S. Senate voted to conduct an investigation. The grand jury continued to hear witnesses.

During hearings on his nomination to be permanent director of the FBI, Gray revealed that he had given FBI Watergate files to Dean. His testimony suggested that other top White House aides were involved in clandestine activities.

In March and April, Nixon met often with his top aides to plan responses to the Gray revelations and to prepare for the investigations. On March 21, Dean warned Nixon of a cancer growing on the presidency. He said that Hunt had issued a thinly veiled threat to tell about the plumbers' activities unless he received hush money. Although Nixon later denied ordering such payments, he told Dean to "get it." That night, $75,000 was passed to Hunt. Nixon later stated publicly that he had begun a new investigation of Watergate on March 21. On March 22 he told Mitchell, "I want you all to stonewall it, let them plead the Fifth Amendment, cover-up or anything else, if it'll save it—save the plan." At other times he urged aides to tell the truth.

On March 23, Judge Sirica read a letter from McCord charging that witnesses had committed perjury at the trial and that the defendants had been pressured to plead guilty and remain silent. McCord, hoping to avoid a severe sentence, cooperated with investigators and implicated Dean and Magruder in the break-in. Dean and Magruder then abandoned the cover-up and implicated other White House and CRP officials. Investigators were told that Mitchell had approved the break-in, that transcripts of conversations taped at the DNC were given to Strachan for delivery to Haldeman, and that Ehrlichman had ordered the destruction of documents. On April 30, Nixon announced the resignation of Haldeman, Ehrlichman, and Dean. Attorney General Richard Kleindienst resigned rather than prosecute men he knew. Nixon and Elliot Richardson, the new attorney general, approved the creation of a special prosecutor's office, headed by Archibald Cox of the Harvard Law School.

The Senate's Select Committee on Presidential Campaign Activities, under the chairmanship of Sen. Sam Ervin (D–N. C.), opened public hearings in May. Dean's testimony linked Nixon to the cover-up. Haldeman, Ehrlichman, and Mitchell denied wrongdoing and defended the president. The testimony revealed the president and his aides as isolated and as hostile toward and fearful of scores of "enemies."

"Dirty Tricks." Donald Segretti, a young lawyer, admitted trying to disrupt the campaigns of Democratic presidential aspirants. After pleading guilty, he served a short prison term. Segretti testified that he had 28 agents working for him in 12 states. He said that he had been hired by Strachan and Dwight Chapin, Nixon's appointments secretary, and paid by Herbert Kalmbach, Nixon's personal attorney. The "tricks" included planting stink bombs and writing a fake letter in which a U. S. senator accused two colleagues of sexual misconduct. Chapin was convicted of lying to a grand jury concerning his relationship with Segretti. He was imprisoned.

In another "dirty trick," Hunt faked State Department cables in an effort to implicate President John Kennedy in the assassination in 1963 of South Vietnamese President Diem, a Catholic. Hunt tried to get the cables published in *Life* magazine in order to anger Catholic voters.

Campaign Contributions. By the fall of 1974, 18 corporations and 21 corporate executives had admitted making illegal contributions to Republicans and Democrats for the 1972 campaign. Kalmbach acknowledged raising and disbursing large sums of money that were subsequently used for illegal purposes. In 1974 he pleaded guilty to two counts, including one that he promised an ambassador a better assignment in return for a $100,000 contribution. Kalmbach was imprisoned.

Investigators could not establish that the settlement of an antitrust suit against the International Telephone and Telegraph Corporation (ITT) was in return for ITT's pledge of money for the 1972 Republican convention. But former Attorney General Kleindienst pleaded guilty to a misdemeanor count of failing to testify fully before the Senate. He had denied, falsely, that he had been pressured by Nixon to drop the antitrust suit. California Lt. Gov. Ed Reinecke was convicted of testifying falsely that he had not discussed the ITT money pledge with Attorney General Mitchell until after the antitrust suit was settled. His conviction was reversed; a Senate quorum had not been present during his testimony.

In 1975 ex-Treasury Secretary John Connally was acquitted of charges that he had accepted a bribe from a dairy organization eager to have the Nixon administration increase price supports.

Mitchell and Maurice Stans, chairman of the Finance Committee to Re-elect the President, were acquitted of charges that they had attempted to impede the investigation of a wealthy contributor. Stans later pleaded guilty to charges relating to illegal handling of campaign funds, as did former Montana Gov. Tim Babcock and former Nixon counsel Harry Dent.

Dispute over the Tapes. Alexander Butterfield, a former White House official, testified in July 1973 that Nixon had taped conversations in his office. Prosecutor Cox subpoenaed tapes relevant to the investigation. Nixon refused to release them. Judge Sirica directed Nixon to let him hear the tapes. Nixon appealed the order, arguing that a president was immune from judicial orders enforcing subpoenas and that under the concept of executive privilege only he could decide which communications could be disclosed.

The U. S. court of appeals upheld Sirica, but Nixon then proposed that Sen. John Stennis (D–Miss.) listen to the tapes and verify an edited version that Nixon would submit to the grand jury and to the Senate committee. Cox rejected this proposal and Nixon's order that he make no further attempts to obtain tapes. Attorney General Richardson, having assured Congress that the prosecutor would be free to pursue the investigation, resigned rather than obey Nixon's order to fire Cox. On October 20, Nixon dismissed both Deputy Attorney General William Ruckelshaus and Cox. This "Saturday night massacre" ignited a "fire storm" of criticism, and triggered serious moves to impeach Nixon. Nixon then agreed to give the tapes to Sirica, and he appointed Leon Jaworski, a Texas attorney, to succeed Cox. Nixon guaranteed that Jaworski would be free of White House control.

One shocking disclosure followed another. The White House said that two subpoenaed conversations had never been taped. One tape contained an 18-minute gap. White House officials and Nixon's secretary, Rose Mary Woods, gave confusing testimony on how the gap might have occurred. Six court-appointed electronics experts said that at least five separate erasures had caused the gap. Many persons concluded that someone had deliberately destroyed evidence.

On March 1, 1974, seven former aides of the president—Haldeman, Ehrlichman, Mitchell, Colson, Strachan, Robert Mardian, and Kenneth Parkinson—were indicted for conspiring to hinder the Watergate investigation. (The grand jury had named Nixon an unindicted co-conspirator, and Dean, Magruder, and lesser figures in the scandal had already pleaded guilty.) Colson later pleaded guilty to charges concerning the Ellsberg case and was relieved of the cover-up charges. Charges against Strachan were dropped. The remaining five went on trial in October 1974, and on Jan. 1, 1975, all but Parkinson were found guilty. In 1976, the U. S. court of appeals ordered a new trial for Mardian, and subsequently all charges against him were dropped. Haldeman, Ehrlichman, and Mitchell exhausted their appeals in 1977. Ehrlichman voluntarily entered prison in 1976 and the other two entered prison in 1977.

Evidence against Nixon, given to Judge Sirica by the grand jury, was turned over by the judge to the House Judiciary Committee, which had begun its impeachment investigation. When the committee subpoenaed 42 more tapes in April 1974, Nixon agreed to release publicly and to the committee the edited transcripts—but not the actual recordings—of 46 conversations. Legal experts disagreed on whether the transcripts established that Nixon was a part of the conspiracy. But most persons found the tone of the conversations to be distasteful, with the participants mostly concerned with how Nixon and his top aides could avoid being implicated.

Meanwhile, Jaworski asked Sirica to subpoena 64 tapes and documents. Nixon refused to honor the subpoena, and Jaworski took the issue to the U. S. Supreme Court. In a historic 8–0 decision on July 24, the court rejected Nixon's claim that he had absolute authority to withhold material from the prosecutor, and ordered him to obey the subpoena. Nixon did so.

The Culmination. In late July the House committee approved three articles of impeachment. (See IMPEACHMENT.) Shortly thereafter James St. Clair, the president's lawyer, learned that one of the 64 tapes that Nixon had been compelled to surrender was the June 23, 1972, conversation with Haldeman in which Nixon sought to thwart the FBI investigation. He insisted that Nixon publish the tape. Nixon did so, and his support in Congress virtually disappeared. Facing certain impeachment and removal from office, Nixon resigned, effective at noon August 9.

Further Reading: Bernstein, Carl, and Woodward, Bob, *All the President's Men* (Simon & Schuster 1974); Dean, John, *Blind Ambition: The White House Years* (Simon & Schuster 1976); Drew, Elizabeth, *Washington Journal: The Events of 1973–1974* (Macmillan 1984); White, Theodore H., *Breach of Faith: The Fall of Richard Nixon* (Atheneum and Reader's Digest 1975).

WATERHOUSE, Benjamin (1754–1846), American physician, who introduced in the United States the practice of vaccination with cowpox vaccine to prevent smallpox. In 1800 he published *A Prospect of Exterminating the Small Pox*, giving the results of tests on his five-year-old son and others with cowpox vaccine, developed by Edward Jenner in England. Its publication inspired others to practice vaccination, including laymen who often used impure vaccines. The result was a serious epidemic of smallpox, for which Waterhouse was at first blamed, though he was soon vindicated. In part two of *A Prospect* (1802), he offered conclusive evidence that proper inoculation with pure cowpox vaccine provided complete security against smallpox.

Waterhouse was born in Newport, R. I., on March 4, 1754. He studied in London, Edinburgh, and Leiden, and in 1783 was appointed professor of the theory and practice of physic at the newly established medical department of Harvard College, where he taught for the next 29 years. Waterhouse died in Cambridge, Mass., on Oct. 2, 1846.

WATERLOO, a city in northeastern Iowa, the seat of Black Hawk county, situated on both banks of the Cedar River, 110 miles (177 km) northeast of Des Moines. The city's most important industries are meat-packing and the manufacture of tractors.

Waterloo has an extensive system of parks. Its Museum of History and Science includes a planetarium. The Waterloo Recreation and Art Center–Municipal Galleries contains art exhibits and a theater. The Foursquare Gospel Church occupies the building of the Old Stone Schoolhouse, built in 1858. The National Dairy Cattle Congress is held in Waterloo every October.

The area was settled in 1845 and called Prairie Rapids Crossing. The community was given its present name in 1851 and incorporated in 1868. Waterloo is governed by a mayor and council. Population: 75,985.

WATERLOO, a regional municipality of Ontario, Canada, in Waterloo county, 63 miles (101 km) southwest of Toronto and adjacent to Kitchener. Its chief industries are furniture and farm implements. The site of one of Canada's largest liquor distilleries, it also manufactures bicycles, cotton goods, paper boxes and bags, and metal products. Because the head offices of five national insurance companies are located here, the city is frequently described as the "Hartford of Canada" (a reference to Hartford, Conn.).

Waterloo has always been a center of music and the arts. Bands were organized about 1860, and the Waterloo Band held its first music festival in 1932. The twin cities of Waterloo and Kitchener support a symphony orchestra, a choir, an art society, and a community theater. Waterloo College, a coeducational institution that became a four-year college of arts in 1924, is affiliated with the University of Western Ontario. It was made a university in 1959.

History. The region was settled by large bands of Mennonites who came from the United States at the beginning of the 19th century. Abraham Erb, who settled here in 1806, is recognized as the founder. The original settlers, known as Pennsylvania Dutch, were hardworking, thrifty people, and the area has always been a hive of industry. The old log schoolhouse erected in 1820, still stands in Waterloo Park. Bertha Mabel Dunham (1881–1957), of Pennsylvania Dutch ancestry, has written about the early settlers.

Incorporated as a village in 1857, Waterloo became a town in 1876, a city in 1948, and "the Regional Municipality of Waterloo" by parliamentary act of 1972. Part of the city was merged with other nearby communities to form the new city of Cambridge as of Jan. 1, 1973. Population: 49,428.

WATERLOO, Battle of. This battle, fought on June 18, 1815, brought to an end the "Great War" in Europe between Revolutionary France and its neighbors, which had started in 1792 and persisted, with brief intervals, for nearly a quarter of a century. It took place 12 miles (19 km) south of Brussels and about 2 miles (3 km) south of the village of Waterloo, in Belgium. The one-day battle was the final act of a four-day campaign—by far the shortest and yet the most decisive of all the Napoleonic campaigns.

The end of the long struggle had appeared to come in April 1814 with Napoleon I's abdication and enforced retirement to the isle of Elba. But while the peace settlement was still being worked out at the Congress of Vienna (see VIENNA, CONGRESS OF), news came that Napoleon had left Elba and had landed in southern France on March 1, 1815. Twenty days later he reentered Paris in triumph.

The disbanded soldiers of France, forgetting all the sacrifices that his ambition had caused, rallied to Napoleon once again, and the recently restored Bourbon king, Louis XVIII, fled to Belgium. By following him there, ejecting him, together with the British, and regaining the Low Countries, Napoleon hoped to gain a spectacular opening success that would paralyze the opposing coalition. Within two months he reconstituted an army of a quarter of a million men, a total that was increasing weekly, and was able to assemble a picked striking force of about 125,000 for the invasion of Belgium.

The British Army had been reduced or dispersed so quickly in 1814 that little more than 30,000 men could be found for the use of the 1st duke of Wellington (Arthur Wellesley), and four fifths of them were raw troops. The Allied troops placed under his command amounted to a further 70,000 men—Belgians, Dutch, and various German contingents—but the Belgian and Dutch forces included many who had been in Napoleon's service, while only a fraction of the Germans were fully trained. In later years Wellington used to say that if he had had his old Peninsular Army he would have swept Napoleon "off the face of the earth in two hours." See PENINSULAR WAR, THE.

The Prussian Army under Gebhard Lebrecht von Blücher amounted to nearly 120,000 men, with more than half consisting of recruits or militia, and its equipment was poor. Still larger Austrian and Russian armies were on their way to join in the general invasion of France, which was intended to open early in July.

Meanwhile the armies of Wellington and Blücher were widely distributed to protect the frontier of Belgium, the former covering the western half and its own line of supply from Ostend and Antwerp, and the latter covering the eastern half and its line of supply from the Rhine. The whole front stretched nearly 90 miles (145 km), and the depth of the Allies' dispositions was 30 to 40 miles (48–64 km). They reckoned on having sufficient warning of any move by Napoleon to concentrate forward and meet him with their combined forces—a concentration that would take about three days.

Napoleon saw clearly that he must strike before the Austrian and Russian armies appeared, and aimed to strike at the joint between Wellington's and Blücher's armies, so as to drive a wedge between them and then crush them separately. He hoped to profit by the way their lines of supply ran divergently westward and eastward, so that if they were surprised and split by his stroke their natural tendency would be to fall back in different directions.

They had foreseen this possibility, and to meet it Wellington had gone so far as to agree that, in the event of a retreat being necessary, he would abandon his own communications and withdraw along with Blücher toward the Rhine. But, with an Englishman's sense of the sea, he instinctively felt that Napoleon would try to cut him off from his own seaports. He had never fought Napoleon, and perhaps had not realized that Napoleon had an instinctive preference for operating on "interior lines," and piercing joints—especially when faced with numerically superior forces. Under the influence of that instinctively preconceived idea, Wellington kept his British divisions far out on his right flank, while his Netherlander divisions were posted near the joint with Blücher's army—and he continued to keep a large detachment out on his right during the Battle of Waterloo.

Napoleon Crosses the Sambre. Napoleon had assembled his whole striking force in the angle between the Sambre and the Meuse rivers, and had achieved its concentration close to the frontier with remarkable secrecy and speed. In the early hours of June 15 he advanced over the frontier, forced the crossings of the Sambre near Charleroi a few miles farther on, and that evening the bulk of his force was massed beyond the river on a narrow front. On the next morning it advanced in a Y formation, of two wings and a central reserve, which was ready to be swung in support of either wing as circumstances indicated. The right wing pushed up the Liège road toward Ligny, and the left wing up the Brussels road toward Quatre Bras. That expanding advance promised to widen the breach that had already been made in the Allies' front.

Blücher had been quick to recognize the danger and to concentrate his own army—but slow to make it clear to his ally. It was midafternoon before Wellington received the bare and belated news that French troops were attacking the line of the Sambre. Still believing that Napoleon would come round his outer flank, he issued orders whereby the bulk of his forces assembled west of the road from Mons to Brussels, though part of the left corps made a short sidestep toward the Charleroi-Brussels road.

Fortunately, the chief of staff of that corps, Jean Victor Constant de Rebecque, took the initiative of continuing the sidestep to that road by sending Prince Bernard of Saxe-Weimar's brigade to occupy the key road junction of Quatre Bras. Fortunately also, Prince Bernard handled his small force so skillfully as to bluff the enemy as to its size. It was to the credit of these two men that the French cavalry were prevented from having a clear ride to Brussels. At 10 P.M. of June 15 Wellington ordered his whole force to start moving eastward. But he was still so unconcerned as to go to the Duchess of Richmond's ball instead of forward to get closer knowledge of the situation, as was his usual practice. It was at the ball, at about 1 A.M. of the 16th, that he received news the French had captured Charleroi and were close to Quatre Bras. Although he now accelerated the eastward move of his army, it was too far distant to give any direct help to Blücher the next day, though the fraction of it at Quatre Bras had an important indirect effect.

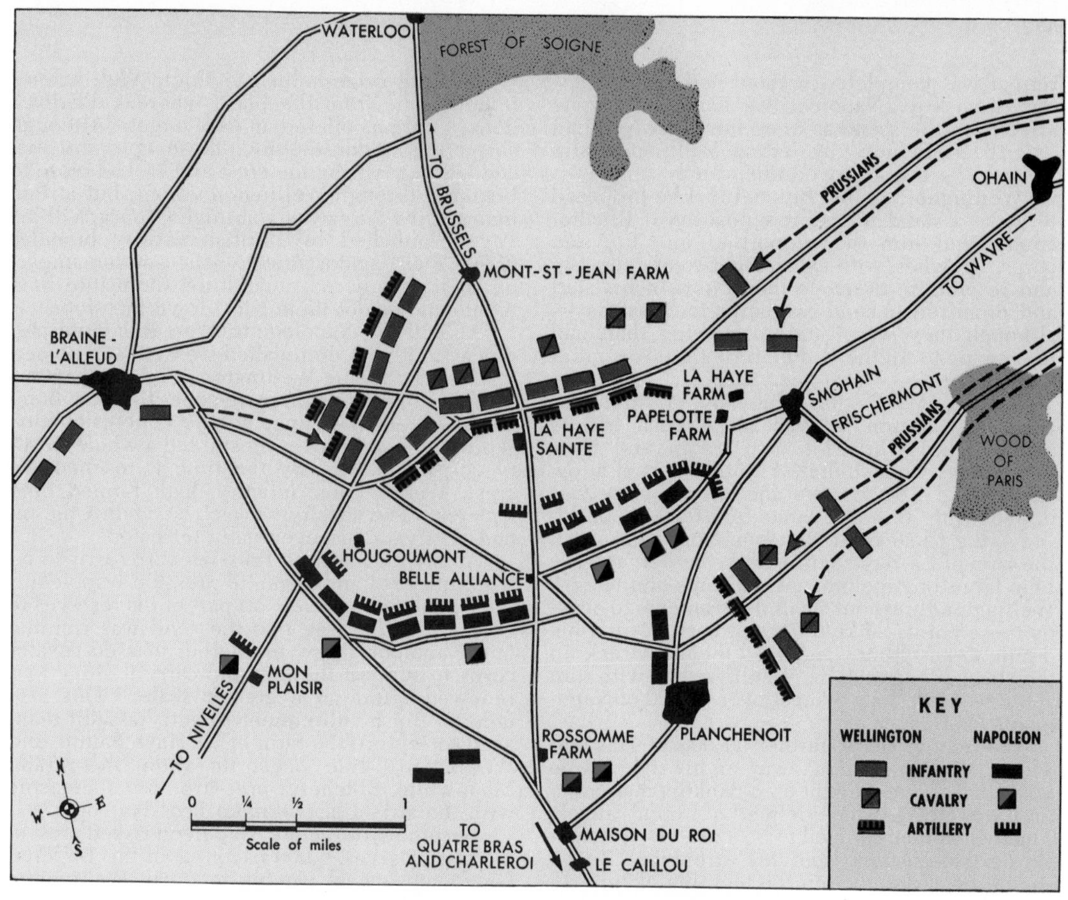

Field of the Battle of Waterloo, June 18, 1815.

At 6 A.M. Wellington rode out to Quatre Bras and approved the dispositions of the two brigades there. The French had not yet shown themselves in great strength, so Wellington, still thinking that a French flanking move might come through Mons, kept his reserve back instead of bringing it up at once. About noon he rode over to see Blücher near Ligny, where three of the four Prussian corps had arrived.

He was shocked to find that they were drawn up on the forward slope of a hill, exposed to the enemy's artillery fire. Such a disposition, contrary to his own Peninsular practice, seemed to him an invitation to trouble. He said to Blücher: "Everyone knows his own army best, but if I were to fight with mine here, I should expect to be beat." Blücher retorted: "My men like to see their enemy." Wellington said no more at the moment but remarked to one of his own officers that the Prussians would be "damnably mauled."

Soon after he had left—to return to Quatre Bras—the Prussians were attacked by the French right wing under Emmanuel de Grouchy. For five hours the battle swayed to and fro and the issue looked uncertain, though the Prussian infantry were suffering excessive loss as Wellington had predicted. Then late in the evening Napoleon intervened with his reserve, and the battered Prussian center broke—a collapse that led to a general retreat under cover of darkness.

Blücher's defeat might have become an irretrievable disaster if Napoleon had been able to fulfill his afternoon intention of swinging his left wing under Marshal Ney round against Blücher's flank and rear. But that part of the plan had miscarried owing to confusion of orders.

Quatre Bras. Ney had been slow to advance in the morning when he could have overwhelmed the slender force at Quatre Bras and captured the crossroads with ease prior to an eastward turn. Perhaps he remembered too well the traps that Wellington had set in the Peninsular War. When Ney ordered his leading corps (under Honoré Charles Michel Joseph Reille) to the attack about 2 P.M.—after lengthy reconnaissance and preparation—it quickly routed the Netherlander division there. But at this crisis Wellington's reserve was beginning to arrive and by throwing the first two battalions into a counterattack through the woods, Wellington bluffed the French to a standstill long enough for the rest of the reserve to occupy the position. Ney's renewed assault was repelled by a much-stiffened defense.

Meanwhile Ney's other corps (Jean Baptiste Drouet d'Erlon) had been diverted toward Ligny without Ney's knowledge. Furious at this step and failing to grasp Napoleon's intentions, Ney sent d'Erlon orders to return at once. So d'Erlon turned round when he had almost reached the Ligny battlefield and then arrived back at Quatre Bras too late to redeem the check that Ney had suffered there.

On the next morning Wellington, receiving belated news of Blücher's defeat, withdrew from Quatre Bras to a position at Mont-St.-Jean, south of Waterloo and about midway to Brussels. So skillfully did he screen his movements that his retreat was completed without serious interference from Ney. Napoleon was so angry when he arrived on the scene as to exclaim that Ney had "sacrificed France" by letting Wellington slip away. The event proved this exactly so.

Wellington notified Blücher that he proposed to make a stand in the new position if Blücher could send him the support of one Prussian corps. Blücher, with characteristic comradeship and resolution, overrode the doubts of his staff and promised to send two corps the next day—although they were later in arriving than had been hoped. In the end he brought three out of the four.

June 18. Wellington's defensive position was admirably chosen, so that the French had to attack uphill while his own troops and their movements were sheltered by the crest of a low ridge. The open glacis of the forward slope was dotted with three separate clusters of buildings—the Château of Hougoumont on the west, the farm of La Haye Sainte in the center, and the twin farms of Papelotte and La Haye on the east. Wellington threw out small detachments to occupy these points—like prongs projecting from his 3-mile (5-km) front—and used them to break up the attacker's formation. In all, he had with him about 64,000 troops to meet over 70,000 of Napoleon's veterans.

Wellington left a further 17,000 at Hal and Tubize, 8 miles (13 km) away on his right, as he felt that Napoleon might try a flanking maneuver that way rather than deliver a frontal attack. That detachment proved to be a useless and dangerous subtraction from his strength. Yet it should be added that on the morning of June 18 several of the French generals—those who had met Wellington in the Peninsular War—warned Napoleon against attempting a frontal attack against Wellington's army in a defensive position. But Napoleon would not listen. A move round Wellington's flank might only drive him back toward Blücher. Napoleon was confident in the power of attack when directed by himself and retorted, "Because you have been beaten by Wellington you consider him a good general. But I tell you that Wellington is a bad general and the English are bad troops. This whole affair will not be more serious than swallowing one's breakfast."

He was equally contemptuous of the possibility that the Prussians might intervene. For when it was reported that a waiter who had served Wellington at breakfast the previous day had overheard an aide-de-camp refer to Blücher's coming, Napoleon scornfully said: "After such a battle as Fleurus [Ligny], the Allies couldn't join forces for at least two days—besides the Prussians are pressed by Grouchy's forces who are at their heels."

The battle opened about 11:30 A.M. on the morning of June 18, Napoleon having postponed the start several hours in order to allow the ground to dry. To clear his path he began with attacks to break the right and left "prongs," but both attacks were repulsed. Indeed, Hougoumont with its small garrison of 500 guardsmen, eventually reinforced to 2,000, absorbed the whole effort of Reille's corps of 13,000 throughout the battle.

About 1 P.M. Napoleon, growing impatient, launched d'Erlon's corps of 16,000 men in an assault on the center of the main position following a massed artillery bombardment. But the crest of the ridge helped to shield Wellington's infantry line from the blast, whereas d'Erlon's dense columns offered an easy target. Although shriveling under the fire, these columns succeeded in reaching the crest and looked close to breaking through Wellington's front, but at that moment the 2d earl of Uxbridge (Henry William Paget) launched two British cavalry brigades (2,000 men) against them. The sudden impact on their disordered ranks burst them into fragments and swept them back down the slope.

At 3:30 P.M. Napoleon tried another battering-ram assault with diminished strength and no better result. Seeing Wellington's line withdraw a little—actually to gain more cover from the bombardment—Ney jumped to the conclusion that Wellington was retreating and led a whole cavalry corps forward. By the time it reached the crest Wellington's infantry had formed into squares. The cavalry waves beat against the infantry in vain and eventually retreated.

At last, the leading Prussian corps arrived on the battlefield and began to press on Napoleon's right flank, which drew off part of his reserves to check it. Realizing that the sand was running out, Napoleon threw in another massed cavalry corps to support the first and carry it along in a renewed effort on a greater scale. This also failed. But a subsequent infantry assault managed to capture the farm of La Haye Sainte, and Wellington's line began to show the strain. Meanwhile Blücher's pressure was increasing with the arrival of two more Prussian corps.

Becoming desperate, Napoleon risked most of his last reserves, 6,000 bayonets of the Imperial Guard, on a final gamble to break Wellington. After another intense bombardment the assault came in three waves about 8 P.M. across ground that was now a quagmire after so much trampling. Each wave was repulsed. Then Wellington rode forward to the crest and raised his cocked hat as a signal for the whole line to advance in a general counterstroke. His army poured down the slope sweeping Napoleon's shattered army before it, while the Prussians surged in from the flank. As the sun set the darkness swallowed an army and an empire.

The Hundred Days of Napoleon's second reign had been terminated in one day of battle. The costs were heavy on both sides. Estimated losses in dead and wounded on that day were 12,000 for Wellington's army, 7,000 for Blücher's, and 25,000 for Napoleon's; an additional 8,000 of the French were captured.

Escaping from the field, Napoleon reached Paris safely on June 21, but he was forced to see the hopelessness of further resistance and on the next day signed his second abdication. It proved final. There was no escape from the remote island of St. Helena to which he was banished.

B. H. LIDDELL HART
Author of "The British Way in Warfare"

Bibliography

Becke, Archibald F., *Napoleon and Waterloo* (1914; reprint, Books for Libs. 1972).
Chalfont, Lord, ed., *Waterloo: Battle of Three Armies* (Knopf 1980).
Chandler, David, *Waterloo: The Hundred Days* (Macmillan 1981).
Howarth, David, *Waterloo: Day of Battle* (Atheneum 1969).
Keegan, John, *The Face of Battle* (Penguin 1983).
Longford, Elizabeth, *Wellington: The Years of the Sword* (Academy Chicago 1982).
Pericoli, Ugo, *Eighteen-Fifteen: The Armies at Waterloo* (Scribner 1973).
Weller, Jac, *Wellington at Waterloo* (Crowell 1967).

WATERMARK, a design or distinguishing mark, used in paper manufacture to identify the maker and to guard against counterfeiting in paper used for stamps, bonds, and some currencies. It is produced by a raised or depressed pattern on the mold that forms the surface of the wet paper.

The Italian papermakers of the late 13th century were the first to use watermarks; their designs were simple twists of wire sewn in the screen of the mold. In England, Sir William Congreve invented watermarking in color in 1818, and in 1845 light-and-shade watermarks were devised by William Henry Smith. The design is now applied on the dandy roll, a cylinder covered with wire cloth and riding on the wet web of paper in a fourdrinier machine.

WATERMELON, an annual trailing vine grown for its sweet, crisp-textured, watery fruit. Watermelons range in size and shape from small round "icebox" varieties about the size of a large muskmelon to large oblong varieties more than 2 feet (0.6 meter) in length. The fruit has a hard rind and is dark or light green in color and sometimes striped. Red-fleshed varieties are most common.

Watermelons (*Citrullus lanatus* or *C. vulgaris*) are members of the gourd family, Cucurbitaceae. They have been cultivated for many centuries. Native to Africa, they early spread to India and other tropical and subtropical regions. In North America cultivation is known to have been attempted in Massachusetts in 1629, and the fruit was grown by Florida Indians before 1664.

Most large varieties of watermelon mature best in warm southern climates, although some small short-season varieties such as Sugar Baby and Yellow Baby can be grown successfully in cooler climates. The season can be artificially lengthened by starting the plants indoors or by protecting plants outdoors with hot caps or cloches. A black plastic mulch stops weed growth and warms the soil enough to speed maturation by about a week. The watermelon tolerates higher humidities than the muskmelon, although it is more susceptible to leaf blights in high humidity. Successful culture requires well-drained soils, preferably sandy loam, with a good content of organic matter. Light soils are particularly necessary in areas with a short growing season. Crop rotation helps to prevent disease from carrying over from year to year.

The most serious insect pest of watermelons, as of many other cucurbits, is the cucumber beetle—both because of feeding by larvae and adults and because the beetle is a carrier of cucurbit mosaic, a plant virus.

It is hard to know when a watermelon is ripe. Helpful signs include size of fruit, a slight bumpiness of the rind, and a hollow sound when the melon is thumped with the knuckles. The most reliable test of ripeness seems to be a change in the color of the rind in contact with the ground from white to pale yellow.

GRANT HEILMAN

The watermelon plant has distinctive, deeply lobed leaves. Most varieties require a warm climate.

WATERPROOF FABRIC, broadly, any fabric treated to resist water penetration. Strictly, a waterproof fabric is one that can be exposed to water over a prolonged period without being penetrated by the water, while a water-repellent fabric can shed water for a shorter period but eventually will allow some water to pass through.

Most waterproof fabrics are coated with a vinyl or rubber finish that closes all the pores or openings in the fabric. A fabric so treated is virtually impenetrable by water. Waterproof fabrics of this type are used mainly to make tarpaulins to protect goods from rain and snow when shipped or stored outdoors. They are used to some extent to make rain garments for use by sailors and others who are exposed to foul weather for long periods. But since waterproof fabrics do not "breathe," they are uncomfortable to wear and thus are little used for rainwear.

Chemical Water Repellents. Fabrics have traditionally been made water-repellent by application of some kind of chemical finish. The finish is usually a waxy material, a silicone, or a material containing fluorine—such as Zepel or Scotchgard. The cost of the finish and the durability are directly related. The wax finishes are the least expensive but also the least durable. The Scotchgard or Zepel type of finishes are the most durable and the most expensive. The silicone finishes are intermediate in both cost and durability. They have a stiff feel because of the high concentration of chemical that must be applied.

All three kinds of water-repellent finishes are normally applied during the finishing stages of fabric production. The fluorine-containing finishes are also packaged and sold for application at home. The results of home application are generally good, but the factory-applied finish is more durable because of the high temperatures used in the industrial process. Fluorine-based water repellents can be reapplied several times during the life of the fabric with reasonably good results.

Water-Excluding Fabric Structures. Beginning in the 1980's, new fabrics appeared that keep out water by the structure of the fabric rather than by a chemical finish. These fabrics have microscopic openings that resist penetration by water but permit air to pass freely. Since the fabrics can breathe—like chemically finished fabrics—they make comfortable garments. The waterproof Gore-tex fabric consists of a Teflon film with microscopic pores glued to a conventional synthetic fabric. Versatech fabric is tightly woven of superfine yarn. With larger fabric openings than Gore-tex, Versatech breathes more freely but is classed as water-repellent rather than waterpoof.

CLIFF L. SEASTRUNK
North Carolina State University

WATERPROOFING BASEMENTS. Basement walls of poured concrete or concrete block construction tend to leak when water accumulates in the soil beside the wall instead of draining quickly away. The pressure of the accumulated water then forces it through any existing cracks or joints. The water also makes the adjoining soil more fluid, creating pressure that widens the cracks further. This problem can be avoided in new construction by the following measures:

1. Start with a structurally sound basement.
2. Coat the basement wall with a good waterproofing material.
3. Provide proper drainage and backfill.
4. Slope walks, driveways, and lawns downward from the basement wall.
5. Provide regular annual maintenance.

Basement Walls. Basement walls should be constructed on a footing adequate for the local terrain and climate. Typically, poured-concrete walls should be cured for seven days, and the surfaces should be dry and relatively smooth before applying waterproofing. Concrete-block walls are usually given a ⅜-inch (1-cm) coat of plaster before waterproofing is applied.

Waterproofing and Dampproofing Materials. The term waterproofing materials is here reserved for long-lasting materials that protect a concrete wall against penetration by water under pressure. These coatings have three characteristics: (1) They remain elastic at low temperatures, so that they can stretch without cracking even in subzero weather. (2) They can bridge cracks in the basement wall of up to ⅛ inch (0.3 cm) without failing. (3) They have a long life and do not become brittle or dissolve in water.

The six main types of waterproofing materials for poured-concrete or concrete-masonry walls are membranes of polymer modified asphalt, urethane elastomers, bentonite clay materials, rubberized asphalt sheets, vulcanized rubber sheets, or cementitious materials.

Dampproofing materials are less durable materials that retard penetration if the water is not under pressure. These materials, which are usually unmodified asphalt or coal-tar residues, have three disadvantages: (1) They slowly dissolve in the presence of water. (2) They become brittle with time. (3) They have little low-temperature elasticity. Dampproofing materials provide much less protection than waterproofing materials but may be adequate if the backfill around the basement is well drained or drainage boards are used. They are usually recommended only for above-grade walls or building exteriors.

Grade-line flashings should extend at least 3 inches (7.5 cm) above the soil backfill. Never allow the waterproofing membranes to terminate below grade. An unsightly membrane can be concealed (and protected) by special skirts of coated metal or fiberglass. Foundation insulation board, now required in most northern communities, can serve the same purpose. Flashing must be placed over the board to protect it from ultraviolet radiation and mechanical damage.

Drainage and Backfill. The backfill around basement walls must be a free-draining granular material such as a soil with a high percentage of sand and gravel. A drainage board should be placed on the wall to enhance water percolation if sand-and-gravel backfill material is not available.

A perimeter drain tile is essential. It should be adjacent to the footing and 4 inches (10 cm) below the basement floor slab. It should be covered with a filter fabric and connected to a sump or other drainage sink of adequate capacity. A drain tile cleanout also is recommended. If roof gutters are used, the downspouts should direct roof water to a well-drained area no less than 8 feet (2.5 meters) from the basement wall.

Sloping. Sidewalks, driveways, and lawns should slope away from the basement wall at least ½ inch per foot (4 cm/meter). Avoid trapping runoff next to the basement wall.

Maintenance. Maintenance usually consists of filling in low spots with soil if settling is detected in the lawn, caulking grade-line flashing and downspouts, caulking or cleaning joints in concrete walks adjoining basement walls, and cleaning roof gutters and downspouts to keep them clear of leaves and twigs.

STOPPING LEAKS IN EXISTING BASEMENTS

The major sources of water that leaks into basements are surface runoff, high ground-water tables, cracked sewer or water lines, and damaged drain tile systems.

Leaks are best repaired by digging to expose the exterior of the basement wall and then treating the surface as recommended for new construction. If this is too costly, satisfactory repairs sometimes can be made from inside the basement by injecting grouts of urethane or epoxy plastics or cementitious materials. If repair from inside is effective, water pressure may build up behind the wall. The resulting stress may cause additional cracks, which in turn may lead to the creation of new leaks.

BRENT ANDERSON ASSOCIATES, INC.

WATERS, Ethel (1900–1977), American actress and singer, who won acclaim for her performances on radio, television, stage, and screen. She was born in Chester, Pa., on Oct. 31, 1900, and spent her childhood in conditions of extreme poverty in black slums in and around Philadelphia. After working for a time as a hotel domestic, she began her career as a vocalist in a theater in Baltimore, Md., and first appeared in New York City in 1925 at the Plantation Club in Harlem. After making her bow on Broadway in 1927 in a Negro revue, *Africana,* she combined nightclub work with the theater. She appeared in the Irving Berlin success *As Thousands Cheer* (1933); costarred with Beatrice Lillie in *At Home Abroad* (1935); and in 1938 gave a concert recital at Carnegie Hall.

Waters' first straight dramatic role was in *Mamba's Daughters* (1939), which attracted attention to her acting ability. She both acted and sang in the 1940–1941 hit *Cabin in the Sky* and in the film version produced in 1942. Her greatest artistic success was as the wise and patient cook in Carson McCullers' *The Member of the Wedding* (1950), which received the New York Drama Critics' Circle Award. She repeated this role in the film version of 1953. She also appeared extensively on radio and television.

In 1951, Ethel Waters brought out her auto-

Actress and singer Ethel Waters delighted audiences with the warmth of her stage and screen performances.

biography (written with Charles Samuels), *His Eye Is on the Sparrow,* which critics hailed for its candor and sensitivity. Beginning in the late 1950's she participated as a gospel singer in the crusades of evangelist Billy Graham. She died in Chatsworth, Calif., on Sept. 1, 1977.

In both her acting and singing, Ethel Waters showed a freshness, exuberance, and warmth that captivated audiences. Popular songs with which she is identified include *Dinah, Having a Heat Wave,* and *Stormy Weather.*

WATERS, Muddy (1915–1983), American blues singer and guitarist. McKinley Morganfield was born on April 14, 1915, in Rolling Fork, Miss. At 13 he began to play the harmonica at local gatherings. He later learned to play the guitar, emulating the "bottleneck" style of blues musicians Robert Johnson and Eddie "Son" House. His reputation grew, and in 1941 a recording of his music was made for the Library of Congress folk-music archives. Encouraged by this recognition, Waters moved to Chicago in 1943 to pursue a career in music. With his band, he began to transform the country-blues style, adopting electric guitar and adding amplification to produce the more urbanized sound of rhythm and blues. He was a popular rhythm-and-blues recording artist throughout the 1950's.

Beginning in 1958, when he toured England, Waters became more widely known. His electric blues style inspired a generation of young British musicians who later became innovators in rock music. He also was venerated by jazz and folk musicians and performed frequently at the Monterey and Newport festivals. He played at Carnegie Hall and the White House and in the 1970's won six Grammy Awards. He died near Chicago on April 30, 1983.

WATERS, Territorial. See TERRITORIAL WATERS.

WATERSHED, as defined in the United States, all the land that drains into an individual stream or lake. Thus a watershed may be only a few acres in area or may consist of a drainage basin tens of thousands of square miles in size. In British usage, the term designates the divide between two different drainage basins.

The word watershed has become a very common subject of conversation. This is true because more and more people have come to the realization that a large part of their well-being relates to a watershed in some manner or other; that the water they use comes from a watershed; and that terribly destructive floods also come from a watershed. Concurrent with this realization has come an increasing knowledge concerning the effect that man may have upon various characteristics of a watershed.

Management of the land and natural resources of a watershed in such a manner as to bring about or maintain certain desired characteristics of water yield is known as watershed management. Any program for management of a watershed may include one or more of the following broad objectives: (1) rehabilitation (2) protection, and (3) increasing water yields.

Rehabilitation Watershed lands may include urban, rural, forest, or rangelands. Urban areas constitute a condition most drastically altered from the natural state. These areas are covered largely with impermeable surfaces (such as paved streets and buildings), and natural channels have been greatly encroached upon by man's structures. The total area involved is not very great; all that can be done in water control is to get storm water away with the minimum of damage by the use of engineering works, such as storm sewers and lined channels. Urban areas generally comprise lands that are permanently lost to productive watershed uses.

Rural areas include the farmlands of the country. Watershed management on lands in this category may include one or both of the two broad objectives, rehabilitation and protection. Rehabilitation may include such measures as planting gullied areas, installing minor structures to supplement such planting, and changing land use from crops to pasture or forest. Rehabilitation is usually needed where nonconservation farming practices have been used over a period of time and excessive erosion has resulted in serious deterioration of the land. Protection involves those practices that would prevent excessive erosion while production of various crops is carried on. Such measures as contour plowing, terracing, and stripcropping may be used, depending upon the steepness of slope and the soil type. Although some of these measures may moderately increase the rate at which water can enter the soil, the primary objective is to get storm waters off the land with a minimum of soil erosion. On agricultural lands there is little opportunity to accomplish much in the way of increasing total water yields.

Forests, ranges, and other wildlands are the areas where the maximum opportunity for watershed management occurs. The headwaters of most streams are usually forested, and also mark the zones where the most precipitation occurs. As these areas are the principal water sources of most drainage basins, it is here that the major effects upon water yield may be produced by land management practices. Here watershed management may be aimed at one or more of the three broad objectives—rehabilitation, protection, and increasing water yields.

The degeneration of a watershed area is usually started by destructive logging, overgrazing, fire, or other practices that tend to remove the protective vegetative cover and compact the soil. The degenerative process becomes apparent when excessive volumes of surface runoff, together with increasing soil erosion, occur during intense storm periods. Unless remedial measures are taken, the degenerative process occurs at an accelerated rate until a degree of stability is reached under a condition of low infiltration and storage capacity for the watershed, high rates of surface runoff and flood discharge from the streams, and large movement of sediment down the channels to the valleys below. If steps are taken early enough in the degeneration process, rehabilitation may be accomplished with comparative ease through artificial revegetation and minor structural works. With increasing degeneration, the restoration process becomes progressively more difficult and expensive. In all cases, the first and most important step toward rehabilitation is to discontinue or modify the practice or use that produced the destructive process. In the case of range watersheds, this may consist of discontinuing grazing of livestock for a period of time until the vegetative cover is adequately restored; or it may consist of grazing management so as to prevent the concentration of livestock in seriously eroding areas. In forest lands logging operations would be modified so as to ensure perpetuation of a good tree cover. Wildfire should in all cases be prevented. In some areas where the degeneration process has not progressed too far, it is possible to rehabilitate the area in a few years and very effectively reduce surface runoff and erosion; but other areas, where the destructive processes have continued for many years, often require a longer time before rehabilitation can become fully effective.

Protection. With the more intensive use of forest and rangeland, the need for protection of water values becomes more and more important. This is probably the most challenging phase of watershed management at the present time. As the need for increased wood products and forage continues, the possibilities of doing damage to the water resource also increases. In order to ensure that the water resource is fully protected, land managers must critically examine all practices to ensure that watershed values are fully recognized and protected. As a general theory, one might say that each forest land area has a characteristic critical level which determines the comparative safety or danger of any manipulation of the forest environment. Some environmental changes are induced whenever the forest cover is manipulated in a silvicultural operation. These operations are safe as long as the forest complex tends to regenerate good conditions over a reasonable period of time. If the operation strikes too severe a blow at the forest community, however, an accelerated cycle of degenerative change is likely to occur. The same reasoning applies equally to rangeland. Therefore, the objective in managing these types of lands is to control the processes so that the critical level is not passed. This may mean, in the case of forest land, a modification of cutting operations so as to ensure perpetuation of a good vegetative covering; or, in the case of rangelands, it may mean management practices that provide a good distribution of livestock and utilization of not over a certain percentage of the forage. The specifications needed will vary, depending upon the soil, vegetation, climate, topography, and similar elements. In general, the essence of this phase of watershed management is maintenance of a status quo through careful use of the various resources of the land.

Increase of Yields. Increasing water yields from a watershed in general represents a challenge for the future. Of the total amount of water arriving on a watershed in the form of rain or snow, a large percentage is returned to the atmosphere by evaporation and transpiration. Research carried on at several locations in the United States indicates that it may be feasible to manipulate the vegetative cover in such a manner as to reduce evaporation and transpiration water losses and thereby increase water available to streamflow. The effectiveness of such practices will vary depending upon the type of vegetative cover, soil depths, air temperatures, type and time of occurrence of precipitation, and similar factors. For example, studies in the Rocky Mountains of Colorado indicate that partial cuttings in dense coniferous forest stands may increase water available for streamflow as much as 15 to 20%. Studies in Utah, California, and South Carolina indicate that if deep-rooted species are replaced by shallow-rooted species, transpiration losses are decreased where soil depths are greater than four feet. In North Carolina, watershed studies showed that water yields might be increased by various methods of timber cutting. In all cases cutting must be tempered by due regard for maintaining a protective covering for the soil to prevent erosion and deterioration of the site.

In all phases of watershed management the chief consideration is the integration of all uses of the watershed lands so as to best maintain the productive capacity for all the renewable resources. Primary consideration should be given to maintaining maximum sustained yields of good quality water. See also WATER SUPPLY—*Sources and Collections; Conservation*.

HERBERT C. STOREY
United States Forest Service

WATERSKIING. See WATER SKIING.

WATERSPOUT, a whirling, funnel-shaped, cloud-filled wind that occurs over water and is similar in appearance to a tornado, which occurs over land. The typical waterspout extends downward from the base of a towering cumulus or cumulonimbus cloud to the water surface. Spray is kicked up on the water surface before the waterspout touches down. The funnel may have an overall length of 300–600 meters (about 1,000–2,000 feet). It is made visible by the condensation of water vapor as air rushes inward and upward. The inrushing air spins cyclonically—counterclockwise in the Northern Hemisphere and clockwise in the Southern. In a few waterspouts the rotation is anticyclonic.

Waterspouts differ from tornadoes in several respects. First, they are not as violent as tornadoes. The air may rotate around a waterspout at a speed of 20–40 meters per second (mps), or 45–90 miles per hour (mph), far less than the 100 mps (225 mph) wind speeds that may occur in tornadoes. Second, waterspouts tend to move more slowly and not last as long as tornadoes. A typical waterspout may drift along at 5 mps (about 10 mph) and last for 10 minutes. Third, a waterspout may range from 10 to 100 meters (about 35–350 feet) across, whereas a tornado may be ten times as wide. Fourth, waterspouts tend to occur under fair weather conditions.

Waterspouts pose a hazard to small boats, and on rare occasions they may cross over land and cause personal injuries and property damage.

Waterspouts generally occur when there is a large temperature difference between the base of the cloud and the water surface. This condition occurs often over the tropical oceans and over portions of the Gulf of Mexico and western Atlantic Ocean in the summer. It also occurs when cold air crosses much warmer water, for example, over the Great Lakes and North Atlantic Ocean in winter.

In the United States waterspouts are most common near the Florida Keys in summer and over the Great Lakes and North Atlantic coastal margins in the cooler part of the year.

LANCE F. BOSART
State University of New York at Albany

NOAA

A large temperature difference between the base of a cloud and the water surface can produce a waterspout.

WATERTON-GLACIER INTERNATIONAL PEACE PARK, an international park, established on June 18, 1932, by acts of the Canadian Parliament and the United States Congress. It comprises two separately administered parks—Waterton Lakes National Park in southwestern Alberta and Glacier National Park in northwestern Montana. An area of 1,560 square miles (4,039 sq km) athwart the Rocky Mountains, Glacier Park is linked with Waterton Lakes Park (203 square miles, or 526 sq km) by the Chief Mountain International Highway and the Continental Divide. Together the two parks boast some 300 lakes, 60 glaciers, and 1,200 miles (1,932 km) of hiking trails; a large variety of animal life, including more than 200 species of birds; and more than 1,000 varieties of wildflowers.

Geologists trace the history of the region to the Proterozoic era, at least 600 million years ago. In late Cretaceous time (70 million years ago) an upheaval called the Lewis Overthrust propelled the rock crust into jagged crags and peaks, after which (about 1 million years ago in the Pleistocene epoch) the peaks and valleys were hewn to their present state by gigantic ice masses. Glacier's highest point is Mt. Cleveland at 10,448 feet (3,185 meters); Waterton's highest is Mt. Blakiston, 9,600 feet (2,930 meters). Logan Pass on the Continental Divide, which is crossed by Glacier Park's scenic Going-to-the-Sun Road, has an elevation of 6,664 feet (2,030 meters).

Called the "Land of the Shining Mountains," Waterton-Glacier is considered to have panoramic beauty rivaling the Swiss Alps. Campgrounds and lodging are available from mid-June to mid-September. See also GLACIER NATIONAL PARK.

© GARY WUNDERWALD/MONTANA TRAVEL PROMOTION UNIT

Glacier National Park, in northwestern Montana, is part of the Waterton-Glacier International Peace Park, which straddles the U.S.–Canadian border. Swiftcurrent Lake and the adjacent Lewis Range are notable tourist attractions.

WATERTON LAKES NATIONAL PARK, a wilderness area in southwestern Alberta, Canada, on the eastern slopes of the Rocky Mountains, set aside as a national park in 1895. Within its area of 203 square miles (526 sq km) are sharp peaks, noted for their extraordinary coloring, valleys carved by glaciers, and numerous lakes. Its highest point is Mt. Blakiston, at 9,600 feet (2,930 meters). The park has a rich variety of plantlife and an abundance of animals, including bighorn sheep, moose, and elk.

Waterton Park and Glacier National Park in Montana make up the Waterton-Glacier International Peace Park, which was established in 1932. See also WATERTON-GLACIER INTERNATIONAL PEACE PARK.

WATERTOWN, a town in west central Connecticut, in Litchfield county. It is situated on the west bank of the Naugatuck River, just northwest of Waterbury. Watertown has a number of industries, principally the manufacture of plastics, synthetic fabrics, brass and wire goods, and hardware. In the center of town, along the green, are several houses dating from the late 18th century. Nearby is the Taft School, a leading private, coeducational preparatory school. Portions of the Black Rock State Park and the Mattatuck State Forest are located in Watertown.

The first permanent settlement of the area occurred about 1720, and in 1738 an ecclesiastical society called Westbury was formed. In 1780 the societies of Westbury and Northbury were separated from Waterbury and incorporated into the present community of Watertown. The town has a council-manager form of government. Population: 19,489.

WATERTOWN, a town in eastern Massachusetts, in Middlesex county, on the Charles River. It is a residential and industrial suburb of Boston, about 8 miles (13 km) to the east. Watertown's principal manufactures include fabricated metal products, electrical and other machinery, precision instruments, rubber products, electronic equipment, and chemical products. The town has two junior colleges; the Perkins School for the Blind, founded in Boston in 1633, moved to Watertown in 1912.

One of the four earliest Massachusetts Bay settlements, Watertown has retained many of its early houses. Among them is the Abraham Browne House, whose original section dates from 1633. Also of interest is the U.S. arsenal (1816), a section of which is used by the U.S. government as an engineering and research center for information on weapons manufacture.

In 1630 a group of Englishmen led by Sir Richard Saltonstall settled Watertown. From its inception the community was devoted to democracy. The first New England town to elect a board of selectmen (1634), Watertown became known as "the Cradle of the Town Meeting." During the Revolution it was a hotbed of anti-British sentiment, and many Whigs fled here from Tory Boston.

Watertown was the home of many artists, writers, and other intellectuals who were attracted by the cultural climate. In the 19th century it was a gathering place for such transcendentalists as Ralph Waldo Emerson and Margaret Fuller.

The town is governed by a council and manager. Population: 34,384.

WATERTOWN, a city in northern New York, the seat of Jefferson county, about 65 miles (105 km) north of Syracuse. Bisected by the Black River, the city has a 112-foot (34-meter) waterfall, which supplies power for industry. Papermaking, begun in 1809, and the manufacture of paper machinery and paper products are major economic activities. The city also produces air brakes, hydraulic equipment, snowplows, electric motors, thermometers, clothing, and ski lifts. Watertown is the commercial center of a large dairy-farming and agricultural region. As the gateway to the Thousand Islands and Adirondack resort areas, it also benefits from tourism.

Notable public buildings include the Flower Memorial Library and the Jefferson County Historical Society home, both containing relics from Indian times and the period of French settlement. A Woolworth building on the Public Square marks the site where Frank W. Woolworth in 1878 introduced the five-and-ten-cent store.

Settled in 1800, Watertown was incorporated as a city in 1869. It is governed by a council and manager. Population: 27,861.

WATERVILLE, a city in southern Maine, in Kennebec county, 18 miles (29 km) north of Augusta. Situated on the west bank of the Kennebec River at the Ticonic Falls, Waterville is a distributing and wholesale marketing center. It also manufactures paper and wood products, shirts, and woolen goods. The city is the seat of Colby College (1813) and Thomas College (1894).

Long before the English colonization of the area, the Indians had maintained a village at the confluence of the Kennebec and Sebasticook rivers, across from what is now Waterville. The first English trading post here dated from 1653. On the site of the Indian village, the English in 1754 constructed Fort Halifax, which commanded a strategic Indian route during the French and Indian War. By 1800 two settlements had grown up on opposite sides of the Kennebec River, and administration of the area became difficult. As a result, in 1802, Waterville was incorporated as a separate town. Chartered as a city in 1888, Waterville has a mayor-council government. Population: 17,779.

WATERVLIET, wô'tər-vlēt, a city in eastern New York, in Albany county, on the west bank of the Hudson River opposite the city of Troy. An industrial city, Watervliet produces steel products, textiles, abrasives, and bricks. Its U.S. arsenal, established in 1813, has produced arms for wars since the War of 1812.

Watervliet was settled about the time of the Dutch colonization of Albany in 1624. Part of a tract of land bought from the Mohawk Indians, it was given the name Watervliet (meaning "flowing stream") about 1630. In 1836 it was incorporated as the village of West Troy, and in 1896 it was chartered as a city under its present name.

Overlooking the Hudson is the Schuyler Homestead (1666), where Philip Schuyler and his wife hosted many notables. In 1776 the first informal community of Shakers in America was founded in Watervliet by Ann Lee.

Watervliet has a council-manager form of government. Population: 11,354.

WATERWAY, Inland. See ATLANTIC INTRACOASTAL WATERWAY.

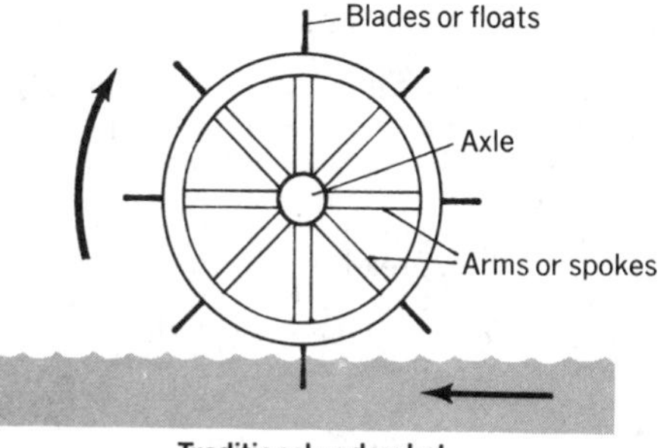

Traditional undershot

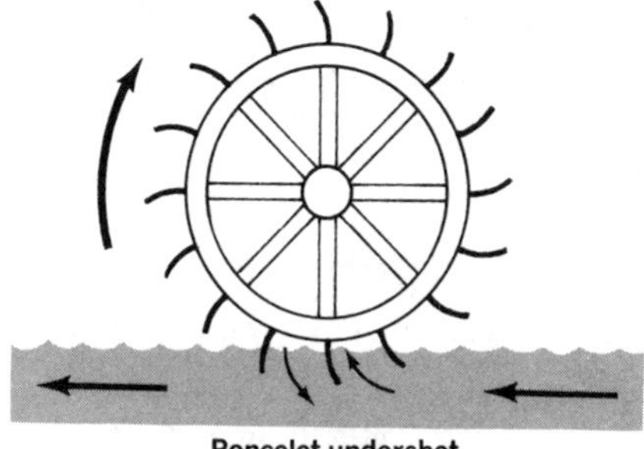
Poncelet undershot

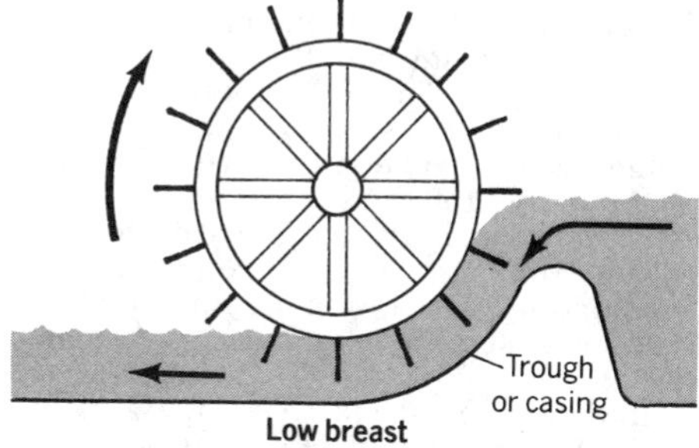

Low breast

High breast (pitchback)

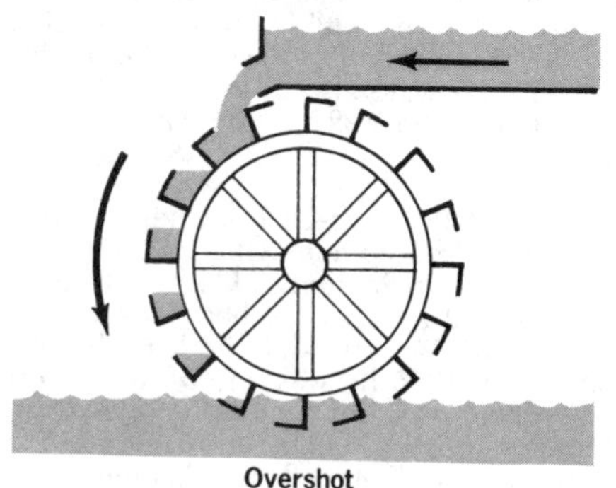
Overshot

WATERWHEEL TYPE	HEAD REQUIRED (feet)	TYPICAL WATER VOLUME (cu. ft./sec.)	TYPICAL EFFICIENCY
Undershot			
Traditional	less than 4	10-175	0.20-0.30
Poncelet	less than 6	7-175	0.60-0.65
Breast			
Low	4-10	5-150	0.45-0.60
High	10-40	2-40	0.60-0.80
Overshot	10-50	2-30	0.60-0.80

WATERWHEEL, one of the basic devices used to convert the flow or fall of water into mechanical work. The term is usually applied to wheels with vertical planes of rotation and horizontal axles. For wheels with horizontal planes of rotation and vertical axles, see TURBINE.

Kinds of Waterwheels. Vertical waterwheels are generally divided into three main groups: overshot, undershot, and breast.

The overshot waterwheel has containers, commonly called buckets, distributed around its rim. Water passed over the wheel enters these buckets and turns the wheel by its weight.

The undershot waterwheel usually has radial blades, or paddles. Water is passed beneath the wheel, where it strikes these blades and turns the wheel by impulse. One form, the Poncelet wheel, has curved rather than flat blades and operates by reaction or pressure, like a turbine, instead of by impulse.

The breast wheel receives its water at some point between the summit and the bottom of the wheel and is usually equipped with a close-fitting trough or casing on its lower quadrant to prevent water from leaving the wheel prematurely. Breast wheels are subdivided into low and high types. The low breast wheel usually has blades and receives water at or below axle level. The close-fitting casing causes water to act on its blades largely by weight. The high breast (or pitchback) wheel normally has buckets like an overshot wheel and receives its water above axle level. Although breast wheels operate by both weight and impulse, the contribution of weight should be maximized for efficient operation.

History. For more than a thousand years vertical waterwheels were the most reliable source of energy for industry. The first firm evidence of their use dates from the 1st century B.C., when several Greek writers mention watermilling. By the 1st century A.D. undershot waterwheels occasionally were used to grind grain or raise water in the Mediterranean area. During the same century some type of water-activated device was used in China to provide air blasts for smelting iron. However, several factors, such as abundant human labor, long inhibited the wide use of waterwheels.

Medieval Europeans were the first to extensively use the waterwheel for a variety of industrial purposes, beginning about the 6th century. By the 10th century, European millwrights had begun to expand the applications of waterpower. By 1600, waterwheels were used for dozens of industrial processes, including sawing wood, boring pipes, drawing wire, pumping water, producing paper, smelting and shaping metals, grinding flour, preparing hemp for rope, crushing olives for oil, and fulling wool. England alone had more than 5,600 watermills by the late 11th century and probably 20,000 by 1800. France had an estimated 80,000 by 1700.

As the use of waterpower grew, European engineers improved the natural flow of streams with dams and canals. By the 14th century, for example, the use of dams to increase the fall of water and make water flow more dependable for waterwheels had created serious problems for navigation in England, leading to attempts by Parliament to regulate such dams. Hydropower canals, which led water from streams to more convenient locations, or to sites where a higher fall could be developed, were also used with greater frequency. By 1800, German mining engineers had constructed in the Harz Mountains near Clausthal a hydropower system consisting of 60 dams and 120 miles (193 km) of canals. These provided water to 225 waterwheels driving mining and metallurgical equipment.

The increased demand for industrial waterpower, especially in Britain, provided the stimulus for several improvements in waterwheels. Beginning about 1760, British engineers such as John Smeaton and, later Thomas Hewes, began replacing wood with iron. By 1830, British industrial waterwheels were built largely of iron, with power taken from the wheels by means of iron gear teeth mounted on their rims instead of wooden gear wheels mounted on their axles. Rim gearing reduced the strain on the spokes or arms of the waterwheel, permitting the construction of lighter wheels, and reduced the amount of step-up gearing needed for high-speed machinery. Iron industrial wheels often were built on the suspension principle; the thick wooden arms that linked the axles and rims of the old wooden waterwheels were replaced by thin wrought-iron spokes held in tension like the spokes of a bicycle wheel.

Additional improvement in waterwheel utilization came from experimental investigations, especially those of John Smeaton (1759). His experiments on 2-foot (60-cm)-diameter model wheels revealed that water acting by weight produced twice the power of water acting by impulse under the same conditions of fall and volume. This led Smeaton to advocate the replacement of impulse-driven undershot wheels with weight-driven overshot or breast wheels. By 1800, wherever the efficient use of water was important, overshot and low breast wheels had displaced the undershot. Early in the 19th century, high breast wheels superseded overshot wheels in heavy industry, since they were better able to deal with variable water levels.

By the 1830's, British and American iron and iron-wood industrial breast wheels wee able to operate at efficiencies as high as 0.70 to 0.80. Some of the largest examples developed 200 to 300 horsepower.

As British engineers pioneered the development of the iron breast wheel, French engineers were applying scientific theory to analyze the performance of waterwheels. This work culiminated with Jean Charles Borda (1767) and Lazare Carnot (1782), who demonstrated that for maximum efficiency water should enter waterwheels with minimal impact and leave them with minimal velocity. Ultimately, this led to Jean Victor Poncelet's design of an improved undershot wheel with curved blades, which reduced impact and water exit velocity, and to Benoit Fourneyron's development of an efficient water turbine.

The importance of vertical waterwheels as industrial prime movers declined sharply in the mid-19th century as a result of the emergence of the water turbine—a more compact, cheaper, faster, more versatile, and more efficient device—and of the spread of the steam engine—a prime mover without the locational restrictions of the waterwheel. By the early 20th century the vertical waterwheel had become a rarity.

TERRY S. REYNOLDS
Author of "Stronger Than a Hundred Men: A History of the Vertical Waterwheel"

WATFORD, wot'fərd, a municipal borough in southeastern England and the largest town in Hertfordshire. A residential suburb of London, 15 miles (24 km) to the southeast, it is situated in the Colne Valley, between the rivers Colne and Gade. Its early growth as a market town stems from the fact that the Colne is easily forded at this point. Although still a marketing center for the surrounding agricultural region, the town also has printing, brewing, and paper industries.

Watford has two old churches: St. Mary's, noted for its memorial monuments, and St. James', largely restored in the 19th century. Mrs. Elizabeth Fuller's Free School (1704) and the Bedford Almshouses (1580) are also of interest. Watford was incorporated in 1922. Population: (1981) 74,356.

WATIE, wä'tē, **Stand** (1806–1871), Cherokee Indian, who was a Confederate officer in the Civil War. He was born in Rome, Ga., on Dec. 12, 1806, educated at a mission school and in Cornwall, Conn., and afterward edited a Cherokee newspaper. In 1835 he was one of four Cherokees to sign the Treaty of New Echota, by which the Cherokees relinquished their lands east of the Mississippi and moved to Oklahoma. All four signers were sentenced to death by their tribesmen. Watie alone escaped and became a planter in Oklahoma.

After the Cherokees allied with the Confederacy in the Civil War, Watie volunteered for military service. He led a Cherokee regiment in many battles in the Indian Territory. He was made a brigadier general in 1864 and was one of the last Confederate soldiers to surrender. After the war, he returned to planting. Watie died in Honey Creek Indian Territory (now Delaware County, Okla.) on Sept. 9, 1871.

WATKINS GLEN, wot'kinz, a resort village in western New York and the seat of Schuyler county. It is situated at the southern end of Seneca Lake in the Finger Lakes region, about 60 miles (97 km) southwest of Syracuse. Watkins Glen State Park contains a spectacular gorge and many waterfalls. The Watkins Glen Grand Prix, an international sports-car race, is held annually.

Settled in 1791, the village was incorporated as Jefferson in 1842 and became known as Watkins Glen in 1926. Population: 2,440.

WATLING STREET, wot'ling, an 11th century name for one of four Roman roads included in the list of four Royal Roads recorded or invented by Norman lawyers after the Norman Conquest. The others are Icknield Street, Ermine (or Erning) Street, and Fosse (or Foss) Way.

Watling Street extended in a northwesterly direction from London (the Roman Londinium) to Wroxeter (Viroconium), passing through St. Albans (Verulamium), and intersecting Fosse Way at a point southwest of Leicester. The same name has been used to designate many Roman roads or roads that are reputed to be Roman roads that exist in other parts of Britain, such as the road from Dover to London via Canterbury. Watling Street has retained its importance since the Middle Ages, and today forms part of the Great North Road connecting London with Scotland.

The derivation of the name of Watling Street is unknown, but some authorities feel that it may be related to an English personal name. Early charters mention the road originally as Waecling (or Waetlinga) Straet, which may mean "the way of the Waetlingas (an ancient tribe)," or the "sons of Waetla."

WATROUS, wô'trəs, **Harry Willson,** American artist: b. San Francisco, Calif., Sept. 17, 1857; d. New York, N.Y., May 9, 1940. After schooling in New York City, he studied at the Atelier Bonnat and Académie Jullian in Paris. Upon his return, he devoted himself to genre and still-life paintings of a meticulously detailed nature, as well as specializing in faithfully detailed renditions of ecclesiastical statuettes and lustrous ceramics. He was the recipient of many awards and prizes such as the Clark Prize (1894); the $1,000 Altman Prize (1929); the National Arts Club Medal (1931); and the Lippincott Prize (1935). Watrous was secretary of the National Academy of Design from 1898 to 1920, and president in 1933. His works include *Passing of Summer* (Metropolitan Museum, New York City), *A Study in Black,* and *My Mother.*

WATSEKA, wôt-sē'kə, city, Illinois, and Iroquois County seat, on the Iroquois River and Sugar Creek, at an altitude of 634 feet. The city, about 78 miles south of Chicago, is in an agricultural and stock-raising region. Industry consists of plants which manufacture condensers, transformers, electric parts, and business forms. The town was platted as South Middleport in 1860 on the site of a trading post. In 1865 it was renamed for Watch-e-kee (pretty lady), the Potawatomi wife of Gurdon Hubbard, the first white settler of the region. Henry Bacon, the architect, was born in Watseka in 1866. The town was incorporated in 1867, and the form of government is by mayor and council. Pop. 5,543.

GLADYS GORDON

WATSON, Homer Ransford, Canadian painter: b. Doon, Ontario, Canada, 1855; d. there, May 30, 1936. He studied landscape painting in the United States (under George Inness) in 1876 and later in England. For his subjects he chose the pioneer life of Ontario and the rural scenes around his native Doon, where he lived most of his life. He was president of the Royal Canadian Academy from 1918 to 1922. Two of his paintings hang in Windsor Castle, England, and six are in the National Gallery in Ottawa. *The Flood Gate* (1900) is considered his best work. Other paintings include *The Pioneer Mill* (1878); *The Truants* (1900); and *Storm Clouds, Grand River* (1924).

WATSON, James Dewey, American biochemist: b. Chicago, Ill., April 6, 1928. He shared the 1962 Nobel Prize in physiology or medicine with Francis H. C. Crick and Maurice H. F. Wilkins for their discovery of the molecular structure of DNA (deoxyribonucleic acid).

Watson received his Ph.D. in zoology from Indiana University in 1950. In 1951 while doing postgraduate work in Europe, he saw Wilkin's X-ray diffraction studies of DNA and became interested in the molecular structure of DNA. Shortly thereafter he began work on the problem with Francis Crick at Cambridge University.

Biochemical analysis had previously revealed that DNA was composed of alternating phosphate and sugar groups along with nitrogenous bases joined to the sugars. Watson and Crick studied both Wilkin's X-ray diffraction evidence and the stereochemical configurations possible for such a molecule and were finally able in 1953 to construct a molecular model of DNA. This model, now known as the Watson-Crick model of DNA, showed DNA to be a double helix with the bases forming the core and the sugar and phosphate groups on the outside. Watson told the story of his collaboration with Crick in the best-seller *The Double Helix,* published in 1968.

In 1956 Watson joined the staff of Harvard University and in 1968 became director of the Cold Spring Harbor Laboratory of Quantitative Biology in New York.

WATSON, John (pseudonym IAN MACLAREN), Scottish-English clergyman and author: b. Manningtree, Essex, England, Nov. 3, 1850; d. Mount Pleasant, Iowa, May 6, 1907. After graduating from Edinburgh University in 1870 with an M.A., he studied for the ministry at New College, Edinburgh, and, briefly, at Tübingen University, Germany. After serving in various ministerial posts, he was appointed to the Presbyterian Church in the Sefton Park district of Liverpool, England, in 1880. He remained there for 25 years, during which time he won fame as a preacher, built a church, and was one of the founders of Liverpool University.

Watson's second career, that of an author of fiction under the name "Ian Maclaren," began in 1894 when he published a collection of stories and sketches of the Scottish peasantry, entitled *Beside the Bonnie Brier Bush.* The book was a success throughout Great Britain and the United States. It was followed the next year by a similar collection, *The Days of Auld Lang Syne* (1895, new ed., 1929), and by other fiction such as *Kate Carnegie and Those Ministers* (1897), *Afterwards, and Other Stories* (1898), and *Young Barbarians* (1901), a book for boys. Watson also produced a number of theological works under his own name such as *The Mind of the Master* (1896). His fame as an author led to three lecture tours in the United States, during the first of which, in 1896, he delivered the Lyman Beecher lectures at Yale University, published as *The Cure of Souls* in the same year. His appearances were well received, and he returned in 1899. In the course of his third tour in 1907 he became ill and died.

Watson's secular writings have been severely criticized on the grounds of sentimentality, but his works are redeemed by his wit and his lack of pretensions to realism.

See also KAILYARD SCHOOL.

WATSON, John Broadus, American psychologist: b. Greenville, S.C., Jan. 9, 1878; d. New York, N.Y., Sept. 25, 1958. Educated at Furman University (M.A. 1900) and the University of Chicago (Ph.D. 1903), he taught at the latter from 1903 to 1908. During 1908–1920 he was professor of experimental and comparative psychology and director of the psychological laboratory at Johns Hopkins University. In 1920 he entered the advertising field, becoming a vice president of the J. Walter Thompson Company, New York City, in 1924. He was vice president of William Esty & Company from 1936 until 1946.

The school of objective psychology, called behaviorism, was originated by Watson at Johns Hopkins with the publication of his paper "Psychology as the Behaviorist Views It" (1913). In it, he argued against the old school of introspection and mentalist concepts and proposed an objective, functional, and experimental method of psychology which would study the relationships between environmental events (stimuli) and behavior (response). Watson rejected the significance of motive and concentrated on conditioned responses. The leading psychologists of the day regarded Watson's thesis as a rejection of classical principles, and there was much controversy in psychological circles as a result.

Watson next published a comparative psychology, *Behavior* (1914). His activities were then interrupted by World War I, during which he served as a major in the aviation section of the Signal Corps. Afterward he wrote *Psychology from the Standpoint of a Behaviorist* (1919), which served to present his definition of psychology and his method. At this time he was also conducting experiments in conditioning on animals and infants. After Watson turned to the advertising field, he maintained his interest and writing in psychology.

Behaviorism, as Watson conceived it, was dominant in the psychology of the United States in the 1920's. By the late 1940's its influence had declined, but it left a decided impact on psychological principles as a whole. Watson's other books include *Animal Education* (1903); *Behaviorism* (1925; rev. eds., 1930, 1958); *Ways of Behaviorism* (1928); and *Psychological Care of the Infant and Child,* with Rosalie A. Watson, his second wife (1928).

See also BEHAVIOR AND BEHAVIORISM.

WATSON, John Christian, Australian political leader: b. Valparaiso, Chile, April 9, 1867; d. Sydney, Australia, Nov. 18, 1941. Educated in New Zealand, Watson was apprenticed to a printer and in 1880 made his way to Sydney, where he worked as a compositor. In 1893 he was elected president of Sydney's Trades and Labour Council, and in 1894 he became head of the Australian Labour Federation and presided at a conference of union representatives from New South Wales which approved the principle that Labour Party candidates for Parliament must pledge themselves not to vote against majority decisions taken in caucus. He also entered the state's Legislative Assembly in 1894 and remained until elected to the House of Representatives in the first Federal Parliament in 1901, when he was chosen as party leader. At an election late in 1903, Labour gained several seats in Parliament, and in April 1904 Watson formed the first federal Labour cabinet. After four months his administration fell, but until he resigned leadership of his party in 1907, Watson continued to influence the government of Alfred Deakin (q.v.), while his sincerity, courtesy, and moderate views strengthened public support for the Labour Party.

R. M. YOUNGER.

WATSON, Richard, English clergyman and chemist: b. Heversham, Westmorland, England, August 1737; d. Calgarth Park, Westmorland, July 4, 1816. Educated at Trinity College, Cambridge, he was elected professor of chemistry in 1764. His experiments with salt solutions won him election to the Royal Society in 1769, and in 1772 he discovered the principle of the black-bulb thermometer. His second, and greater, interest—theology—began in 1771 when he obtained the regius chair of divinity at Cambridge, although he continued to write on chemistry for many years. He became archdeacon of Ely in 1779 and was consecrated bishop of Llandaff in 1782. Of his many theological writings, two are noteworthy: a defense of Christianity against Edward Gibbon (1776), and a defense of the Bible against Thomas Paine (1796), both of which gained wide circulation and endorsement, the latter in the United States as well.

WATSON, Sereno, American botanist: b. East Windsor Hill, Conn., Dec. 1, 1826; d. Cambridge, Mass., March 9, 1892. After completing his education at Yale University in 1847, he tried his hand in various fields with indifferent results. In 1867 he went to California and later that year, after an arduous journey, joined the exploration party of Clarence King (q.v.), then beginning a government geological survey of the Cordilleran ranges of Colorado. When the party's botanist left, Watson was assigned to collect plant data. His thoroughly catalogued collections involved many group revisions and served to establish his reputation in the field. His work was published as *Botany* (also called "Botany of the King Expedition"), in 1871, and was the fifth volume in the survey's famous *Report of the Geological Exploration of the Fortieth Parallel* (7 vols., 1870–80).

In 1873, Watson became assistant in the Gray Herbarium at Harvard. The next year he was named curator, a post he held until his death. Here he undertook his major work, *Botany of California* (2 vols., 1876–80), which listed the first flora of that region, and was used as the basis for subsequent classifications. Asa Gray and William Henry Brewer aided in the first volume. Watson's other work includes the *Bibliographical Index to North American Botany* (1878), and the 1889 revision, with John Merle Coulter, of Gray's *Manual of Botany.*

WATSON, Thomas, English poet and literary scholar: b. ?London, England, c. 1557; d. there, Sept. 26, 1592. He presumedly attended Oxford University for a time and later studied law in London, but his main interests were literary. His first published work was a Latin translation of Sophocles' *Antigone* (1581), and in 1585 he wrote a paraphrased version of Tasso's pastoral *Aminta. Meliboeus* (1590), a Latin elegy on the death of his patron, Sir Francis Walsingham, which he also translated into English, and *Amintae Gaudia* (published posthumously in 1592), an original Latin pastoral, are two other outstanding examples of Watson's facility with different kinds of Latin verse. He was considered the foremost Latinist of his day, but it was as a sonneteer that he left his stamp on English literature. Watson's *The Hecatompathia, or Passionate Centurie of Love* (1582), a collection of 18-line "sonnets" in English, revitalized an interest in the sonnet form. He was the first writer of sonnets after Sir Thomas Wyatt and Henry Howard, earl of Surrey, and his work preceded Sir Philip Sidney's *Astrophel and Stella*. Another collection of poems, this time in the true sonnet form, *The Tears of Fancie, or Love Disdained* (published posthumously in 1593), is considered Watson's best work. His poetry lacks feeling, but his technical skill and choice of topics influenced the later sonnets of the 16th century. His work was closely studied by William Shakespeare and others, and Watson, at the time of his death, was praised by fellow poets and scholars as the equal of Edmund Spenser and Sidney.

WATSON, Thomas Augustus, American electrical engineer and shipbuilder: b. Salem, Mass., Jan. 18, 1854; d. Passagrille Key, Fla., Dec. 13, 1934. After leaving public school at a young age, he went to work in 1872 at an electrical shop in Boston which constructed models for a number of inventors, including Alexander Graham Bell. Watson began his association with Bell in 1874, and served as his assistant during the experiments which led to the invention of the telephone. Their efforts were crowned on March 10, 1876, when Bell spoke the first sentence transmitted by telephone: "Mr. Watson, come here; I want you." When the Bell Telephone Company was formed in 1877, Watson was given an interest in the business. He resigned in 1881, and, three years later, in partnership with Frank O. Wellington, began building ships and engines. The business flourished, and government contracts for large war vessels necessitated expansion of the shipyard, so the Fore River Ship & Engine Company was organized in 1901. Watson retired in 1904 and spent the remainder of his life exploring other interests, taking courses in geology and literature, studying music and painting, and even acting (he had speaking roles in the Shakespeare Festival at Stratford-on-Avon, England, in 1911). His autobiography, *Exploring Life,* was published in 1926.

WATSON, Thomas Edward, American political leader and author: b. Columbia County, Ga., Sept. 5, 1856; d. Washington, D.C., Sept. 26, 1922. Born into a wealthy slaveholding family made destitute by the Civil War, he early developed the instincts of rebellion and reform which were to characterize his political career. He attended Mercer University for two years and later studied law privately; after being admitted to the bar in 1875 he opened a practice in Thomson, Ga., winning a statewide reputation as a criminal lawyer. Armed with a fiery, combative nature and a hatred for the Northern industrialists who controlled the new South, he entered politics as an agrarian reformer, fighting the Democratic machine to win a term in the state legislature in 1882. He was elected to Congress in 1890 as a Farmers' Alliance Democrat but soon joined the new People's (Populist) party (see POPULIST PARTY) and served as the voice of the agrarian revolt in the House, as well as introducing reform bills and the first resolution for free rural delivery of mail. Watson was defeated by the Democrats in the next two turbulent elections, marked by gerrymandering and fraud, but he pressed his fight for reform and campaigned against capitalist finance. In 1896 the Populists named him their vice presidential candidate, which, because it involved harmony with the Democrats, he accepted reluctantly.

Discouraged by his defeats, Watson left the political scene in 1896 and devoted his time to writing history and biography. In 1904 he was back again, this time as the presidential candidate of the Populists; he was a nominal candidate again in 1908. Now, disillusioned, he shifted his attention to new issues, forsook the old agrarian-industrial struggle and, to the dismay of his Populist supporters, directed his energies against the Catholics, Negroes, Jews, and Socialists. He became the champion of the Ku Klux Klan. He actively fought United States entry into World War I and the conscription of troops. Elected to the Senate in 1920, he was an outspoken foe of Woodrow Wilson and the League of Nations. He died in office two years later.

Watson's writings include *The Story of France* (1899); *Napoleon: a Sketch of His Life* (1902); *The Life and Times of Thomas Jefferson* (1903); and *The Life and Times of Andrew Jackson* (1912). For his vitriolic attack on Catholicism in *The Roman Catholic Hierarchy* (1910), he was prosecuted but acquitted. He founded *Tom Watson's Magazine* in New York in 1905, and later published the *Weekly Jeffersonian* and *Watson's Jeffersonian Magazine* (1906).

WATSON, Thomas John, American industrialist: b. Campbell, N.Y., Feb. 17, 1874; d. New York, June 19, 1956. He attended Addison (N.Y.) Academy and the Elmira (N.Y.) School of Commerce, and began his business career at 17 as a store clerk in Painted Post, N.Y. In 1898 he joined the National Cash Register Company, rising to the position of general sales manager during his 15-year service. In 1914 he became president of the Computing-Tabulating-Recording Company (formed as a holding company in 1911), which changed its name in 1924 to International Business Machines Corporation (IBM). Watson embarked on a program of expansion, instituted an elaborate system of sales and technical training, and in 1949 created a subsidiary, the IBM World Trade Corporation, to direct the company's vast overseas operations. He retired as president in 1949 to become chairman of the board.

The phenomenal growth of IBM under Watson's personal management is part of the history of American business. Through the years he widened the firm's original scope from the manufacture of business machines of all types to encompass the fantastically complex electronic calculators and giant computers which are widely used in business today.

Given to moralism and maxim (he created IBM's famous watchword, "THINK"), Watson personally supported extensive philanthropies; was a noted art patron and collector; and materially aided medical research, religious groups, young people's organizations, educational enterprises, welfare societies, and numerous other charitable activities.

See also COMPUTERS—*History*.

WATSON, Thomas John, Jr. (1914–), American businessman and ambassador, who succeeded his father as head of the International Business Machines Corporation (IBM). The elder of the two sons of Thomas J. Watson, he was born in Dayton, Ohio, on Jan. 8, 1914. He received his B. A. degree from Brown University in 1937, and that same year joined the IBM company as a junior salesman. He served (1940–1946) with the Air Force in World War II, flew combat missions, won his senior pilot's wings, and advanced in rank to lieutenant colonel. During this period he spent six months in the USSR under the lend-lease airlift program.

Returning to the company in 1946, he served as its president in 1952–1961, chairman of the board in 1961–1971, and chairman of the executive committee in 1971–1979. Under his direction IBM achieved leadership in the field of automation. He also devoted much of his time to other companies, to educational institutions, and to the federal government as he became director of several corporations, trustee of a number of universities, and member of several presidential advisory boards. He also presided over the General Advisory Committee of the Arms Control and Disarmament Agency. Appointed by President Carter, Watson was ambassador to the Soviet Union from 1979 to 1981. His many honors include the Presidential Medal of Freedom.

WATSON, Tom (1949–), American golfer, who in 1980 became the first in the sport to win more than $500,000 in a single season. Thomas Sturges Watson was born in Kansas City, Mo., on Sept. 4, 1949. He began playing as a boy and in his teens won the Missouri amateur championship four times. A graduate of Stanford University (1971), he turned professional in his senior year. He failed to win a single tournament, although his earnings jumped from about $2,000 in 1971 to $75,000 in 1973.

As his game improved, he overcame the stigma of "choking" in the late rounds of close matches. He broke into prominence by capturing the British Open in 1975, repeating in 1977, 1980, 1982, and 1983. He also won the World Series of Golf in 1977 and 1980 and the Masters title in 1977 and 1981, and was voted Player of the Year in 1977 and 1978. He was awarded the Vardon Trophy (for lowest scoring average) in 1978. After several failures, Watson triumphed in the U.S. Open in 1982.

With consistent victories or high-place finishes on the Professional Golfers Association tours, Watson was the leading money winner from 1977 to 1980. His total earnings by 1983 passed $3 million, second to Jack Nicklaus on the all-time list of prizewinners.

WATSON-WATT, wŏt'sən-wôt, SIR **Robert (Alexander)** (1892–1973), Scottish physicist, who pioneered in the development of radar. He was born in Brechin, Scotland, on April 13, 1892, and attended University College, University of St. Andrews, where he taught natural philosophy in 1912–1921. In 1919, while a government meteorologist, he took out his first patent for a radiolocation (radar) instrument to be used in atmospheric study. While serving (1921–1936) in the Department of Scientific and Industrial Research and the National Physics Laboratory, he continued to improve his radiolocation equipment in accuracy and sensitivity, and in 1935, after lengthy experiments, he patented a new type of radiolocator which formed the basis of British wartime radar. By the time of the Battle of Britain radiolocation had become a powerful defense against German air raids, and this device has been credited with swinging the balance of that critical phase of the war in Britain's favor. In 1941, Watson-Watt visited the United States to confer with American scientists who had developed a similar device, and from that time on radar became a joint project of Britain and the United States. As a result of his achievements, Watson-Watt was knighted in 1942 and received the United States Medal of Merit in 1946. His works include *Through the Weather House* (1935) and *Pulse of Radar* (1959), an autobiography. He died in Inverness, Scotland, on Dec. 5, 1973.

WATT, James (1736–1819), Scottish engineer whose inventions led to an improved steam engine. He was born in Greenock, Renfrew, Scotland, on Jan. 19, 1736, and at age 18 he went to London where he studied mathematical instrument making. Later, when he tried to open a shop in Glasgow, he was deterred by a craft guild. Glasgow University friends came to his aid, and he was appointed mathematical instrument maker to the university. While here he made his great invention, in 1765, of a separate condensing vessel for the steam engine. The idea first occurred to him the year before when he was given the university's model of the Newcomen engine to repair. This apparatus, invented in 1705 by Thomas Newcomen and John Calley (or Cawley), used the steam cylinder itself as a condenser, by introducing a jet of cold water into the cylinder to condense the steam. Watt found that this method

James Watt, Scottish engineer, whose invention of a condensing vessel in 1765 led to an improved steam engine.

NATIONAL PORTRAIT GALLERY

so reduced the temperature of the cylinder that three times as much steam was required as was necessary. He set to work to condense the steam in a separate receptacle, insulate the cylinder against heat loss, and pump out noncondensable gas, and he patented the processes in 1769, nearly four years after the inventions covered by the patent had been made. Although he did not invent the steam engine, his improvements were of such importance that he is popularly credited with this distinction.

In 1775, Watt entered into partnership with Matthew Boulton, the owner of the Soho Engineering Works, near Birmingham, and the plant began producing engines on a large scale. Watt left the business in 1800, when his patent, renewed in 1775 for 25 years, expired. Besides the separate condenser, the inventor made a number of other improvements in the steam engine. He devised the sun-and-planet gear wheel, in order to convert reciprocating motion to rotary motion; made use of the expansion principle to design the double-acting engine; applied a speed governor to steam engines; and invented the throttle valve. He also built the first indicator for drawing a diagram of steam pressure, patented an improved-combustion furnace, invented a special ink for coyping letters, and discovered independently the chemical composition of water. His memory was retentive and the range of his reading wide, and he had knowledge of language, music, and chemistry. The significance of his work places him among the foremost of inventors.

Watt was a fellow of the royal societies of both London and Edinburgh. He originated the term "horsepower," and the units of power called "watt" and "kilowatt" were named in his honor. He died in Heathfield Hall, near Birmingham, England, where he had retired to devote his time to mechanical pursuits and inventions, on Aug. 25, 1819.

See also STEAM; STEAM ENGINE.

WATT (symbol W), a unit of power, or amount of energy expended per unit time. Named for Scottish engineer James Watt, it is equal to one joule per second. One watt-hour is a unit of energy equal to 3,600 joules or 3.413 BTUs. One kilowatt hour is equal to 1,000 times that amount. A watt-hour meter measures the amount of electric energy consumed.

WATTEAU, wo-tō'; Fr. vȧ-tō', **Jean Antoine** (1684–1721), French painter known as the founder of the French school. He was born of Flemish parents in Valenciennes on Oct. 10, 1684. He went to Paris in 1702, where, after a period of impoverishment, he entered the studio of Claude Gillot, an able painter of arabesques and other ornamentation. While there (1704–1708), young Watteau developed the propensity for theater design which was to identify his future work. He next came under another master, Claude Audran, and this association seems to have been of primary significance to the young artist's career. Through Audran's position as keeper at the Luxembourg Palace, Watteau gained entrance to the gallery, where he could study the great Marie de Médicis cycle of Peter Paul Rubens. From these 21 huge compositions Watteau was able to assimilate the baroque master's dynamics of form and coloration, which he then adapted to his own rococo art.

THE METROPOLITAN MUSEUM OF ART, MUNSEY FUND, 1934

Watteau's *Mezzetin* is a portrait study of a costumed actor playing a stock character in Italian comedy.

Distressed by his failure to achieve the Prix de Rome in 1709 (he took second place), Watteau left Audran and returned briefly to Valenciennes, where some of his military scenes probably originated. Upon his return to Paris, he gained the friendship of the financier Pierre Crozat, whose great art collection centered on the Flemish and Venetian masters whom Watteau admired. The artist stayed with Crozat for a time, both in Paris and at his Montmorency villa, whose formal gardens appear in many subsequent paintings. In 1712 he became an associate of the Académie Royale de Peinture et Sculpture, and a full member five years later. His health now failing, he went to live in Paris with his friend Edmond Gersaint, an art dealer, for whose shop he painted the famous *enseigne* (signboard), now in the Berlin Museum. Continuing to work diligently despite his illness, he finally moved to a country home in Nogent-sur-Marne, where he died on July 18, 1721.

Watteau's Art. One of the true luminaries of French painting, Watteau dominated the art of that country in the early 18th century to the extent that he may be regarded as the founder of the French school. Although he began painting during the declining days of Louis XIV, his work showed a complete independence of the bigoted court of Versailles and anticipated the way of life (among the leisured) that would inevitably burst forth when France passed into the hands of the Régent Orléans. On Watteau's small, intimate canvases Watteau created a world of unconstrained elegance, finding his favorite subjects among the fine ladies and gentlemen of the regent's court, and portraying them in attitudes of dalliance in parks and glades. Pervading these *fétes champêtres,* however, is an air of wistfulness tinged with melancholy, as though the artist were impressed by the transitory nature of romantic love. In this half-real realm of shadow and illusion, Watteau's delicate color harmonies and sensitive brushstrokes seem to pass a layer of scrim over the precise details of costume and scenic milieu.

Above all, Watteau's art is of the theater, and his paintings, whether of court life or rural genre, rely on the stock characters of Italian comedy so popular during the Regency. His many canvases on the theme of love are summarized in the classic *Embarquement pour Cythère* (Louvre)—painted in 1717 as his diploma piece for the Académie—in which he grouped his amorous figures into a *fête galante* of compelling charm. This work is clearly indebted to Rubens' *Jardin d'amour,* but the influence is transformed by Watteau's own subtleties. Through such scenes he helped to free French painting from its inhibitions and opened the way to the coloristic and ornamentive vitality of the rococo.

Although Watteau's ideas were widely imitated in the 18th century—by his pupils Jean Baptiste Pater and Nicolas Lancret, and notably by François Boucher and Jean Honoré Fragonard—he alone remains above the vulgarism that vitiated much of the aristocratic art of tha era. His paintings are sensuous, but not licentious; rather they are infused by a spiritual purity that far transcends the sentimentality of his emulators.

The structure of Watteau's art rests firmly on his superb draftsmanship; and his drawings, of which perhaps 300 survive, have been acclaimed as his "surpreme achievement" (K. T. Parker). The splendid collections in the British Museum and the Louvre reveal the full range of his technique, and include, in addition to the notes for the familiar theatrical pieces, lesser-known landscapes, designs, portraits, nudes, animals, and especially fine studies of hands. Conceived realistically from life, the drawings for the most part represent finished products, rather than preparatory sketches. Red chalk predominates, although this often is fused with white to produce remarkably warm and lifelike flesh tones. Many of the drawings are executed in red, white, and black, a technique (*à trois crayons*) in which Watteau was unrivaled.

Watteau's paintings appear in museums and galleries throughout Europe and, to a lesser extent, the United States. Much of his work is concentrated in Germany, largely because of the admiration of Frederick II the Great, who avidly collected his finest pieces for the palaces at Potsdam. In Berlin are *La comédie française* and *Le déjeuner en plein air.* The Louvre paintings, in addition to the *Embarquement pour Cythère,* include *Gilles, L'indifférent, La finette,* and *L'assemblée dans un parc;* in the Wallace Collection (London) are *La leçon de musique, Le concert de famille,* and *Les amusements champêtres.* Among his works in the United States are *Mezzetin,* a portrait study, in the Metropolitan, and *La gamme d'amour* in the National Gallery. Interest in Watteau revived with the publication in 1875 of Edmond de Goncourt's *Catalogue raisonné de l'oeuvre peint, dessiné et gravé d'Antoine Watteau,* and his paintings subsequently soared in value.

See also PAINTING—*The 18th Century.*

WATTENSCHEID, vät'ĕn-shīt, city, Germany, in the State of North Rhine-Westphalia, located in the heart of the Ruhr basin at an altitude of 200 feet, 6 miles northeast of Essen. It is primarily an industrial city, engaged in the mining of anthracite coal and the manufacture of electrical products and metal and textile goods. As in many of the Ruhr's industrial centers, a trade school is prominent in the educational system. Wattenscheid was chartered as a city in 1425. Its most notable historical landmark is the Probstei Church, completed about 1400 and incorporating a baptismal font of the 10th century. After World War II, the city was included in the Federal Republic of Germany (West Germany). Pop. (1959 official est.) 77,800.

WATTERSON, wŏt'ər-sən, **Henry** (known as MARSE HENRY), American journalist and politician: b. Washington, D.C., Feb. 16, 1840; d. Jacksonville, Fla., Dec. 22, 1921. Son of a newspaper editor, he received an informal but thorough schooling. In spite of his regard for Abraham Lincoln, he served with the Confederate Army in the Civil War out of loyalty to the South. Before the war was over, he began to work as a newspaper editor in Tennessee. In 1868 he became editor of the Louisville, Ky., *Daily Journal,* which he immediately merged with Walter N. Haldeman's *Courier,* Haldeman remaining as publisher. As editor of the *Courier-Journal* until 1919, Watterson exerted nationwide influence, expressing his strongly held convictions in fiery prose. He fought both for the restoration of home rule in the South and for the rights of the blacks; promoted Samuel J. Tilden's candidacy for the presidency; and as a member of the House of Representatives (1876–1877), worked in vain to have Tilden certified as victor. In later years he conducted a vitriolic editorial campaign against President Theodore Roosevelt, whom he accused of dictatorial tendencies. From 1914 Watterson urged the United States to declare war on Germany in World War I, and his editorials on the subject won him a Pulitzer Prize in 1917. He broke with President Woodrow Wilson on the League of Nations issue, however. Watterson's books include *The Compromises of Life and Other Lectures and Addresses* (1903), and *"Marse Henry": an Autobiography* (2 vols., 1919).

WATTLEBIRD, wŏt'əl-bûrd, or **WATTLED CROW,** a New Zealand bird, *Callaeas cinerea,* discovered by Capt. James Cook's party and so called by them because of two blue and orange unfeathered wattles at the corners of its mouth. About a foot in length, it is plain gray, with black on the sides of the head. A closely allied race occurs on the North Island of New Zealand. A fruit-eating forest bird of weak flight, it is now greatly reduced in numbers. With the saddleback and the huia, two other New Zealand species, it forms a family, the Callaeidae, allied, presumably, to the birds of paradise and Australian bell magpies.

WATTLES, wŏt'əlz, name given in Australia to trees and shrubs of genus *Acacia.* See ACACIA.

WATTMETER, wŏt-mēt-ər, in electricity, a device which measures electrical power in terms of watts. See WATT.

WATTS, wŏtz, **George Frederic,** English painter and sculptor: b. London, England, Feb. 23, 1817; d. there, July 1, 1904. He studied at the Royal Academy and in the studio of sculptor William Behnes. After winning the Westminster Palace design competition in 1852 with *Caractacus Led in Triumph Through the Streets of Rome,* he studied in Italy. From 1843 to 1847 he lived mainly in Florence, painting many portraits as well as treating Italian literary themes such as *Paolo and Francesca* (Dante), and *Anastasio degl'Onesti* (Boccaccio). In 1847 another Westminster competition called Watts to England, and he won the prize with *Alfred Inciting his Subjects to Prevent the Landing of the Danes,* now hanging in a committee room in the House of Commons. About this time Watts painted a long series of outstanding Victorian portraits of such notables as Matthew Arnold, Thomas Carlyle, Alfred, Lord Tennyson, John Stuart Mill, Robert Browning, William Gladstone, and Giuseppe Garibaldi.

Watts led a very uneventful life, except for an allegedly stormy 13-year marriage to the young actress, Ellen Terry. Artistically, his aim was to make English art the equal of English literature, and he believed that art must not only represent beauty but point a moral. He carried his ethical beliefs into his commissions, but he was rarely able to realize his conceptions. In style he was one of the few British painters who worked in the grand manner with something of the quality of Titian's effects. He painted many allegorical works, most of which were successful. After 1867, he devoted much of his time to experimenting in sculpture, and afterward his paintings became more solid and less complicated. His most successful sculpture was the massive bronze *Physical Energy* in Kensington Gardens, cast as a memorial to Cecil Rhodes. Watts was elected to the Royal Academy in 1867, twice refused a baronetcy, but finally accepted the Order of Merit in 1902. He is represented in the Tate Gallery, to which Watts presented over 50 of his works, the National Gallery, and the National Portrait Gallery, all in London, as well as in other museums and galleries in the United States. A biography and compilation of his writings were published by his second wife in 1912.

JEAN ANNE VINCENT.

WATTS, Isaac, English theologian and hymnist: b. Southampton, England, July 17, 1674; d. London, Nov. 25, 1748. He was educated for the ministry at the nonconformist academy at Stoke Newington, London, from 1690 to 1694. In 1696 he became a tutor in the family of Sir John Hartopp, and in 1699 he was chosen assistant minister of the Independent Congregation in Mark Lane, London, becoming its pastor in 1702. Never robust in health, from 1712 he lived in semiretirement at the home of Sir Thomas Abney, devoting most of his time to writing as well as to a voluminous correspondence. He died at the Abney home in Stoke Newington and was buried in Bunhill Fields. There is a monument to his memory in Westminster Abbey.

Watts was the creator of the modern hymn, as opposed to the medieval office hymn and the Reformation metrical paraphrase of the Psalms. He wrote about 600 hymns, many of which are still found in various Protestant hymnals. He created the new genre with rapidity, and many of his best hymns were written between the ages of 20 and 22, before he began his ministerial career. None was published until his *Horae Lyricae* came out in 1706. The following year his *Hymns and Spiritual Songs* (2d ed., 1709) appeared, and his *Divine Songs* (1715), later called *Divine and Moral Songs* (1729), was a pioneer hymnal for children. *The Psalms of David* was published in 1719. Watts's psalms are free paraphrases, rather than metrical versions. Some of them have become the most famous hymns in the English language, including "O God, our help in ages past."

In addition to his poetic gifts, Watts had the mind of a teacher and clear thinker. His *Logick* (1725), *Knowledge of the Heavens and Earth* (1726), *Philosophical Essays* (1733), and *The Improvement of the Mind* (1741) were used as basic textbooks at Cambridge, Oxford, Harvard, and Yale universities until the beginning of the 19th century. Edinburgh University honored him with the doctor of divinity degree in 1728. Among his theological treatises are *Doctrine of the Trinity* (1722), *Essay on the Freedom of the Will* (1732), and *Useful and Important Questions Concerning Jesus, the Son of God* (1746). In addition, Watts wrote treatises on various other subjects.

He was a forceful preacher, and a man wholly absorbed in the mystery of God. Never a political nonconformist, he was rather a spiritual dissenter whose entire theology was expressed in the following lines from his hymn, "When I survey the wondrous cross:"

> Were the whole realm of nature mine,
>   That were an offering far too small;
> Love so amazing, so divine,
>   Demands my soul, my life, my all.

His was a mind which at one moment could be combating the empiricism of John Locke and in the next could be writing for children:

> Were I so tall to reach the pole,
>   And grasp the ocean in my span,
> I must be measured by my soul:
>   The mind's the standard of the man.

LEONARD ELLINWOOD
Author of "The History of American Church Music"

WATTS-DUNTON, wŏts'dŭn'tən, **(Walter) Theodore,** English critic, novelist, and versifier: b. St. Ives, Huntingdonshire, England, Oct. 12, 1832; d. Putney, London, June 6, 1914. After a private education at Cambridge, Watts became a solicitor and practiced briefly in London. His talents, somewhat limited, showed best in his intimacies with those of greater fame, such as Dante Gabriel Rossetti and Algernon Charles Swinburne in particular. His acquaintance with such men was facilitated by his positions, first as literary and art critic for the *Examiner* (1874–1876), and then as critic for and contributor of verse to the *Athenaeum* for a quarter of a century. He had a curious therapeutic effect on a Rossetti debilitated by whiskey and chloral, but even more positively showed himself an amazingly resourceful and patient male nurse for Swinburne. From 1879 to the time of Swinburne's death in 1909, Watts-Dunton devotedly controlled the life of the once-tempestuous poet, adding no doubt to the life-span and, perhaps necessarily at the same time, quenching the early Swinburne glow.

An admirer of George Borrow and his gypsies, Watts-Dunton wrote verses about these cultish wanderers and published them in the *Athenaeum.* In 1897 he collected his gypsy poems under the title, *The Coming of Love, and Other Poems.* The poems are somewhat cluttered and lack the singing quality the subject matter suggests as appropriate. A year later he had his most pronounced literary success with the publication, long delayed, of *Aylwin,* a romantic novel notable for a good plot, some memorable scenes, and a sketch of Rossetti as one of the characters.

Next to his two chief claims to fame—caretaker of Swinburne and a novel—Watts-Dunton could be remembered for coining the phrase "the renascence of wonder" as the romantic essence, and for his article on "Poetry" (*Encyclopaedia Britannica,* 9th ed., 1885). For a look at how he remembered his friends, one may consult the leisurely *Old Familiar Faces,* published posthumously (1916).

KENNETH L. KNICKERBOCKER,
University of Tennessee.

WAUCONDA, wô kŏn′də, village, Illinois, in Lake County, on Bangs Lake, 16 miles west-southwest of Waukegan. At an altitude of 800 feet, it lies in a dairy and farm area. The main basis of the economy is the farm trade although added trade is gained from summer colonists. The village had its beginnings in 1836 when Justus Bangs built his house on the shore of the lake now named after him. The name of Wauconda was adopted in 1839 at the suggestion of a schoolteacher who took a fancy to the name of an Indian character in a legend. Pop. 5,688.

WAUGH, wô, **Alec** (in full **ALEXANDER RABAN** WAUGH), English author: b. London, July 8, 1898; d. Tampa, Fla., Sept. 3, 1981. A brother of Evelyn Waugh, he won success as a novelist and travel writer. His books include *The Loom of Youth* (1917); *No Truce with Time* (1941); *Guy Renton* (1952); *The Sugar Islands* (1958); *Fuel for the Flame* (1960), and *A Family of Islands* (1964). His *Island in the Sun* (1956) was adapted as a motion picture.

WAUGH, Evelyn Arthur St. John, English novelist: b. London, Oct. 28, 1903; d. Taunton, Somerset, April 10, 1966. He was a son of Arthur Waugh (1866–1943), critic, publisher, author, and editor of many books. Educated at Lancing and Oxford University, he was received into the Roman Catholic Church in 1930. Between 1939 and 1945 he served as a commando officer in West Africa and Crete, and as a British liaison officer in Yugoslavia. At heart a romantic, but endowed with incisive qualities of mind and an impeccable English style, he is an outstanding satirical novelist of our time, expressing the shocked horror of the moralist when observing the social, religious, and political infirmities of modern society. The abiding theme of his plots is that of the innocent who ventures into a world of chaos and unreason, where he perishes, or from which he withdraws.

The basic tone may be serious (*A Handful of Dust,* 1934; *Work Suspended,* 1942; *Helena,* 1950), or more commonly farcical and burlesque (*Decline and Fall,* 1928; *Vile Bodies,* 1930; *Black Mischief,* 1932; *Scoop,* 1938; *Put Out More Flags,* 1942; *Scott-King's Modern Europe,* 1947; *The Loved One,* 1948; *Love Among the Ruins,* 1953), but it is always mordant. His greatest public success, *Brideshead Revisited* (1945), has definite artistic faults, which he attempted to correct in a revised edition (1960). His own favorite novel is *Helena,* the fictional life of the mother of Constantine, who discovered the fragments of the True Cross. The trilogy of novels, *Men at Arms* (1952), *Officers and Gentlemen* (1955), and *Unconditional Surrender* (1961), depict his attitude to World War II, and to army life. *The Ordeal of Gilbert Pinfold* (1957) reveals much of his own attitude to his work and personality. *Edmund Campion, Jesuit and Martyr* (1935), was an act of thanksgiving for his conversion. *The Life of Ronald Knox* (1959) is a memorial to a great writer and priest. Waugh traveled constantly and recorded his impressions of the impact of Western civilization of indigenous social patterns, both in his novels (*Black Mischief, Scoop*) and in travel books (*Labels,* 1930; *Remote People,* 1932; *Ninety-two Days,* 1934; *A Tourist in Africa,* 1960). The first volume of *A Little Learning,* a projected three-volume autobiography, appeared in 1964.

Waugh is a moralist by conviction; a traditionalist by temperament. But the voice which expresses distaste for all manifestations of modernity, for politics, psychology, plastics, and Picasso, is also that of the artist, stimulated to production by what he derides. This double identity is confusing to those critics who would praise his writing while condemning his views. The tendency, with affluence and age, to restrict immediate contact with the surrounding irritants led, after the war, to the cultivation of a more allusive, symbolical mode of narration, which further disconcerts many who prefer the brilliant parodies written in Waugh's youth.

FREDERIC J. STOPP, *Cambridge University.*

WAUGH, Sidney, American sculptor: b. Amherst, Mass., Jan. 17, 1904; d. New York, N.Y., June 30, 1963. He studied at Massachusetts Institute of Technology (1920–1923), but later concentrated on art at the Scuola delle Belle Arte, Rome (1924), and under sculptor Henri Bouchard, Paris (1925–1928). The Prix de Rome, won in 1929, exerted a great influence on his style. His success as an architectural sculptor may be traced in part to Waugh's academic intellectualism which stems from the classical rather than from the modern world. By 1930, he had become acquainted with etched glass at the Swedish Exposition in Stockholm. A visit to the factory so stimulated him that he soon established a designer relationship with the Steuben Division of the Corning Glass Works. Today he is in the forefront of glass designers and holds a unique position among sculptors. Outstanding works in this unusual medium include *The Merry-Go-Round Bowl,* designed as a wedding gift to Princess Elizabeth of England from President and Mrs. Harry Truman, and a three-foot, glass-cast *Atlantica* for the New York World's Fair (1939), which was the largest single piece of clear polished crystal glass ever made.

In 1936 he was the first contemporary American glass designer to see his work enter the collection of The Metropolitan Museum, New York City. In the same year, he was elected to the

National Academy of Design which made him a full member two years later. He distinguished himself in World War II and later, serving as teacher as well as sculptor, headed the Rinehart School of Sculpture of the Maryland Institute, which is in Baltimore.

Waugh's monumental works adorn many buildings in Washington, but interest in his work has not been confined to public edifices, as commissions from the Bethlehem Steel Company and the Bank of Manhattan attest. He is represented in many public and private collections in Europe and America.

DOROTHY GRAFLY,
Editor and Publisher "Art in Focus."

WAUKEGAN, wô-kē'gən, city, Illinois, Lake County seat, on Lake Michigan, 40 miles north of Chicago, at an altitude of 595 feet. The name is derived from the Potawatomi, meaning "little fort."

Waukegan is an industrial city with port facilities for lake and ocean vessels. Major products include outboard motors, wire and steel, gypsum, asbestos, building materials, leather, and pharmaceuticals. The Great Lakes Naval Training Station is just south of the city limits, and the Illinois Beach State Park is north of the city. The Waukegan Memorial Airport was dedicated in 1961.

The city was originally populated by the Potawatomi Indians. Permanent settlers arrived in 1835 and the town of Little Fort was incorporated in 1841. The name was changed to the Indian synonym in 1849 and Waukegan became a city on Jan. 4, 1859. Government is by mayor and city council. Pop. 67,653.

RUTH W. GREGORY.

WAUKESHA, wô'kĕ-shô, city, Wisconsin, seat of Waukesha County, on the Fox River, 15 miles west of Milwaukee, at an altitude of 821 feet. An industrial city in an agricultural area, the city has a symphony orchestra, and is the seat of Carroll College. There is an airport. The chief industries make internal combustion motors, castings, and foundry products. The lands of the Potawatomi Indians, who had a village here, were ceded to the federal government in 1833. Three prehistoric Indian mounds of the 55 known to have been here are preserved in Cutler Park. The first white settlement was in 1834 and was known as Prairieville until 1845. The present name is Indian for "little fox." The health-giving fame of the water from the many springs made Waukesha well known, and the city was a noted watering place from about 1870 to the early 1900's. The form of government is mayor and council. Pop. 50,365.

EDWARD W. LYNCH.

WAUKON, wô-kŏn', city, Iowa, seat of Allamakee County, 19 miles east of Decorah, at an altitude of 1,216 feet. The region is agricultural and supports a big dairy industry and a flourishing business district. There is an airstrip. Traditionally a trading center, Waukon was founded in 1849 and incorporated in 1883. The city was named for a Winnebago chief, known to the settlers as John Wawkon. In Winnebago, Wawkon means "thunder." A county fair is held in August of each year. Effigy Mounds National Monument is 18 miles from the city. The monument is a park centered around burial mounds in the shape of various animals and birds. Government is by mayor and council. Pop. 3,983.

LAVERNE HULL.

WAUPACA, wô-păk'ə, city, Wisconsin, seat of Waupaca County, 47 miles northwest of Oshkosh, at an altitude of 868 feet, in an agricultural and stock-raising region. The surrounding area was formerly engaged principally in lumbering, but Waupaca became one of the state's first centers for potato production and marketing, and still stands high in this activity. Within a few miles of the city there are more than a score of small picturesque lakes, which have brought Waupaca into favor as a summer resort. The streams and lakes afford excellent sport. The name is derived from an Indian word for "white sand bottom." Pop. 4,472.

WAUPUN, wô-pŭn', city, Wisconsin, in Dodge and Fond du Lac counties, 70 miles northwest of Milwaukee, at an altitude of 903 feet. It lies in a fertile agricultural area producing grain and food for the local canneries. Two state institutions, the Wisconsin State Prison and the Central State Hospital for the criminal insane, are located here. The beauty and fertility of the Rock River valley brought the first settlers here in 1838. The community was incorporated in 1878 under the name of Waupun, which is a variation in spelling of the Indian name Waubun, meaning "dawn of day." Government is by mayor and council. Pop. 8,132.

MABEL W. JONES.

WAUSAU, wô'sô, city, Wisconsin, seat of Marathon County, 85 miles west northwest of Green Bay on the Wisconsin River, at an altitude of 1,200 feet. Set in the heart of Wisconsin's rich and prosperous dairy country, it serves as a trade center for a radius of some 50 miles. Its industry includes paper, paper pulp, industrial machinery, woodworking, and insurance. Wausau Technical Institute trains students in residential design, electronics, and business, and there is a two-year branch of the University of Wisconsin Extension Division located here. Founded in 1839 by George Stevens, who walked from St. Louis, Mo., in search of pineries and a good millsite, the place was originally called Big Bull Falls. The name was changed to Wausau, a Chippewa Indian word meaning "far, far away," in 1872 when the city charter was granted. Rib Mountain State Park, four miles southwest of the city, is widely known as a winter sports area and is frequented by summer tourists as well. Fifteen miles to the east, the Dells of the Eau Claire River are a favorite recreation spot. Government is by mayor and aldermen. Pop. 32,426.

DOROTHEA M. KRAUSE.

WAUSEON, wô'sē-ŏn, village, Ohio, seat of Fulton County, 32 miles west of Toledo, at an altitude of 775 feet. The village is a residential center of three square miles surrounded by rich farmlands. Agriculture is a chief industry with poultry, cattle, and dairy products leading. Several manufacturing companies produce and assemble automotive products for nearby Detroit. Named for a chief of the Ottawa of the Maumee Valley, Wa-se-on, which signifies "far off," the village was settled in 1835 and incorporated in 1852. Pop. 6,173.

DOROTHY SQUIRE.

WAUTERS, wou'tərs, **Émile Charles Marie,** Belgian painter: b. Brussels, Belgium, Nov. 29, 1846; d. Paris, France, Dec. 11, 1933. He studied in Brussels under Charles Albert and Jean François Portaels, and in Paris under Jean Léon Gérôme. His first painting to attract wide notice was a typically academic subject, anecdotal yet historical, *Fair Edith Finding the Body of Harold on the Field of Hastings.* As a result of this public attention, the artist was sent by his government to attend the opening of the Suez Canal. Like Eugène Delacroix and others before him, Wauters was inspired by the exoticism of the oriental scenes, and made many notes and sketches which were later faithfully put on canvas with exact archaeological detail, as in his panorama called *Cairo and the Banks of the Nile.* However, Wauters went beyond the careful drawing and rather dry painting technique that characterized the painting of many of his contemporaries in the academic tradition, as may be seen in his *The Madness of Hugo Van der Goes* (1875). He demonstrated that he was not unaffected by the lighter colors and loose handling of the brush of the Impressionists. He specialized in chiaroscuro effects, which was probably the result of his study of Italian paintings. Besides historical subjects, Wauters also painted more than 200 portraits, mainly royalty and public figures. He is represented in important public galleries in Antwerp, Brussels, Dresden, Philadelphia, Vienna, and Zurich.

JEAN ANNE VINCENT.

WAUWATOSA, wô-wə-tō'sə, city, Wisconsin, in Milwaukee County, five miles west of Milwaukee, on the Menomonee River, at an altitude of 634 feet. Although the city is predominately residential, an area along the Menomonee Valley is classed as a light manufacturing district with such industries as a chemical plant, concrete products manufactory, millwork factory, foundry, lumber yards, and a motor-manufacturing plant. A memorial center built in 1957 includes the city hall, an auditorium, and a public library. The name of the city comes from "Wau-wau-tae-sie," an Indian chief of the Potawatomi tribe. In the Indian language it means "firefly," and was adopted because of the many fireflies seen in the dense thickets that bordered on the Menomonee River. The city, settled in 1834, has a mayor and a common council form of government adopted in 1897 when it was incorporated as a city of the fourth class. Pop. 51,308.

ESTHER REGLI.

WAVE, The, wāv, a novel of the Civil War, by Evelyn Scott, first published in 1929. It is a notable example of the experimental school of fiction so popular between the two world wars.

The book takes its title and its method from the physical definition of a wave. A wave travels always in a definite direction, though the particles which compose it at any given instant do not advance with it but are merely whirled in circular movement. As Miss Scott applies the symbol in her narrative, the wave is the Civil War—the social and ideological forces which made the conflict; the particles are the human beings whom the war disturbs or destroys, but does not alter. The book has no plot in the ordinary sense; no one character, or group of characters, is carried through the war as Stephen Benet, in *John Brown's Body,* carries Jack Ellyat and Clay Wingate. Instead, we have a long series of vignettes of men and women, North and South, each coming to some individual crisis. Some of the people are real—Davis and Lincoln, Grant and Lee; many are fictitious representatives of classes and types. The leaders may recur in more than one episode; most of the others appear only once. The story touches most of the military high spots, from Bull Run to Appomattox, but each is told as it is seen by individual participants, who may be generals, or may be privates, deserters, or civilian bystanders. The life at home, behind the lines, receives as much attention as the battles, and here again the range is as wide as the nation, from the bankers who helped finance the Union cause to the runaway Negroes who trailed in the wake of Sherman's army. Bread riots in Richmond; draft riots in New York; preachers, statesmen, editors, lunatics, thieves; all the human gamut of America is represented, and all are merely particles stirred by the wave of war.

DELANCEY FERGUSON.

WAVE GUIDE, Electric, a term for any assemblage of conductors and insulators used to transmit electrical energy from one place to another. In normal usage the term "wave guide" refers to metallic pipes or solid tubes of insulating material which are used to direct very high frequency electrical energy along desired paths.

Methods of Transmission.—A pair of copper wires serves as an economical and efficient electrical transmission line up to frequencies of hundreds of megacycles. At frequencies above 50 to 100 megacycles the efficiency and usefulness of a two-wire line begins to drop off rapidly because of heating of the line itself, and because the line acts as an antenna and radiates some of its electrical energy into space rather than conducting it to the desired place. Unwanted radiation may be avoided by use of a coaxial line which is built with a central copper wire surrounded by an insulating material, and with a braided copper sleeve and insulating jacket on the outside. The electrical energy is contained between the inner and outer conductors and unwanted radiation is no longer a serious problem. Heating of the copper conductors as well as heating of the insulating materials limit the usefulness of coaxial lines in most applications to frequencies below about 5,000 megacycles.

Rectangular Wave Guides.—At frequencies above 1,500 to 3,000 megacycles hollow metallic wave guides become practical. They are not useful at lower frequencies because of the large size required. Wave guides are ordinarily made of copper or brass, and may be silver or gold plated to improve their electrical performance. If electrical energy is to be transmitted in a wave guide, one inside dimension, such as a in Fig. 1(A), must be at least one half wavelength at the operating frequency. Electrical energy whose frequency is lower than this critical frequency will not be transmitted down the guide. The dimension b determines the allowable voltage which can exist between the top and bottom walls of the guide and fixes the maximum power which can be transmitted.

The electric field intensity (similar to voltage) across the guide is maximum at the center and tapers off to zero at the sides as shown in Fig. 1(B). In contrast, the magnetic field intensity (similar to current), along a horizontal section such as c-c'-c''-c''' in Fig. 1(C), is a series of closed, approximately concentric, curves. Many more complicated modes of transmission than the one illustrated in the diagram below are possible.

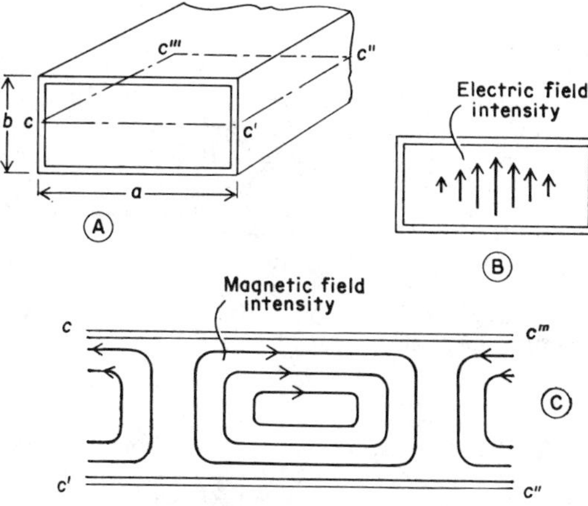

Fig. 1. Rectangular wave guide.

Other Wave Guide Shapes.—Wave guides of circular cross section are used in some applications. Wave guides may also be made of solid insulating material such as polyethylene. A dielectric guide operates in the same fashion as does a "light tube" for the transmission of visible light. Electrical energy is contained within the dielectric tube because of the different electrical properties of the tube and the surrounding atmosphere. Another kind of wave guide is called a "strip line" and consists of thin, narrow strips of an insulating material, and of a metal on a metallic base.

Wave guides have their widest usage in the radar field where they are used as a connection between various parts of radar transmitters, receivers, and antennas. Here the frequency ranges from 1,500 to above 10,000 megacycles. The corresponding half wavelengths, which dictate (approximately) the largest dimension of the guide, are 7.9 inches to 0.12 inches. In recent years wave guides have gained widespread usage in telephone and television systems, especially in transcontinental telephone and television microwave relay links. They are also used as critical elements of radar equipment, microwave ovens, and mass spectrometers.

See also RADAR—*How Radar Works;* TELEPHONE—*4. Transmission Methods;* TELEVISION—*Principles of Television.*

GLEN A. RICHARDSON,
Department of Electrical Engineering, Worcester Polytechnic Institute.

WAVE LENGTH. See WAVELENGTH.

WAVE MECHANICS. See ATOM—*The Bohr Atom;* QUANTUM THEORY—*Modern Theory.*

WAVELENGTH, wāv'lĕngth, the shortest distance at any instant of time from one crest (or trough) of a wave to an adjacent crest (or trough). This definition is strictly true only if the wave is vibrating at a uniform rate, that is, if its vibration is sinusoidal. The concept of wavelength may be applied to any wave phenomenon whether it be a sound wave, light wave, electromagnetic wave, water wave, or some other type of wave. The wavelength λ (lambda) in Fig. 1 is measured between points A and A' or between B and B'.

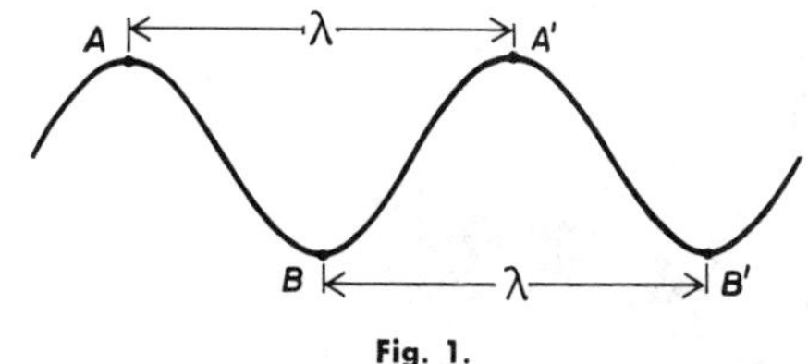

Fig. 1.

The quantity which is measured at the two points varies with the nature of the wave phenomena. With sound waves, sound pressure would ordinarily be measured; with light waves, light intensity would be measured; with electromagnetic waves, electric or magnetic field intensity would be measured; and with water waves, displacement of the water from a level surface would be measured.

The wave motion travels through a medium at a velocity which depends on the frequency, and perhaps on viscosity, temperature, humidity, and other factors peculiar to particular wave phenomena. The wavelength depends upon the velocity v and the frequency f of the wave. Wavelength is the quotient of velocity of propagation and frequency ($\lambda = v/f$). Thus, if any two of the quantities in the equation are known, the third quantity may be calculated. The velocity is approximately constant in many cases, and the wavelength and the frequency are then related by a simple constant. This is the case for radio or light waves transmitted in the atmosphere, and the constant velocity is 300 million meters per second.

See also ATOM—*The Present View of the Atom;* DOPPLER EFFECT; RADAR—*Principles;* RADIO—*8. Principles of Radio;* SOUND—*Diffraction and Reflection;* SPACE EXPLORATION; WAVE GUIDE; WIEN, WILLIAM—*Wien's Laws.*

GLEN A. RICHARDSON,
Department of Electrical Engineering, Worcester Polytechnic Institute.

WAVELL, wā'vəl, **Archibald Percival,** 1ST EARL WAVELL, British field marshal who was a leading commander in World War II. b. Colchester, England, May 5, 1883; d. London, May 24, 1950. Wavell came of a military family and was always destined for service in the army. He received his secondary school education at Winchester College and subsequently attended the Royal Military Academy, Sandhurst, but, having been appointed to his father's regiment, the Black Watch, left hurriedly for the tail end of the South African War in 1901. A highly versatile man, Wavell became a specialist in Russian, first visiting the country in 1911 after graduating at the Staff College in 1910. Subsequent visits enriched his knowledge of the Russian language and his familiarity with the Russian army and military system and, with Gen. Sir Giffard Le Quesne Martel, he was the first British officer to witness the parachute maneuvers that were held in the Soviet Caucasus in 1936.

At the outbreak of World War I Major Wavell was posted to the staff of general headquarters in France, where he was wounded and lost an eye. In 1917 he became liaison officer between the War Office and the Egyptian Expeditionary Force, and after a spell at the Supreme War Council in 1918 became chief staff officer of the 20th Corps. The war over, he served on Gen. Sir Edmund Allenby's staff in Egypt, a difficult assignment owing to the contrast between his chief's enlightened views on Egyptian independence, and those of the Foreign Office.

Earl Wavell

Wide World

A spell on the Rhine with his regiment and another at the War Office followed. In 1930 he assumed command of the 6th Brigade at home, and as a major general in 1935, was given the command of the 2d Division. His skill and originality in setting maneuver schemes made a deep impression. After a brief tenure of the Southern Command he became commander in chief of the Middle East in 1939.

The brilliance of his crushing victories over the Italians in Egypt, against vast odds, has become immortal. Many of his troops were withdrawn to Greece, however, owing to British intervention there. While the British were being defeated in Greece, the Germans recaptured the territory recently won by Wavell. He had no further success except against the "Vichy" French in Syria. Two offensives at Sollum, on the frontier, having aborted in May and June 1941, Wavell changed places with Gen. Sir Claude Auchinleck, commander in chief in India. After unavoidable heavy defeats at the hands of the Japanese he became viceroy. He was admirable in this position, but the appointment ended sadly. He advised the government that partition and the end of the British Raj should be preceded by some 15 years of firm rule. This was rejected; he was recalled; and the hand-over was made in haste amidst civil strife costing hundreds of thousands of lives. It is inadvisable to pontificate on the validity of his plan, but that which actually followed was calamitous.

Wavell became a field marshal in 1942 and was created Viscount Wavell of Cyrenaica and Winchester in 1943. In 1947 he became an earl. Immensely strong physically and mentally, intellectually lambent, taciturn, brave, and kindly, Wavell was the outstanding military figure of his time. Whether he was the greatest British commander remains unproved. Wavell's writings include *The Palestine Campaigns* (1928); *Allenby, A Study in Greatness* (1940); *Generals and Generalship* (1941); *Allenby in Egypt* (1943); *Other Men's Flowers: An Anthology of Poetry* (1944); *Speaking Generally* (1946); *The Good Soldier* (1947); and *Soldiers and Soldiering* (published posthumously, 1954). The two books on Allenby were reprinted in one volume in 1946.

CYRIL BENTHAM FALLS,
Chichele Professor of the History of War, Emeritus, Oxford University.

WAVELLITE, wā′və-līt, a hydrous basic aluminum phosphate mineral, $Al_3(OH)_3(PO_4)_2 \cdot 5H_2O$. It may contain fluorine substituting for OH. Characteristically, it occurs in globular aggregates with a radial fibrous structure. It is gray, yellow, green, or black, is translucent, and has a vitreous luster. The hardness is 3.5 to 4 and the specific gravity is 2.3 to 2.5. Wavellite is a rare secondary mineral formed in cavities in aluminum-rich rocks and minerals, such as low-grade aluminous metamorphic rocks, and in phosphorite and limonite deposits. Wavellite may be found in Pennsylvania and Arkansas.

ELIZABETH KAY BERNER.

WAVEMETER, wāv′mē-tər, an instrument which measures the wavelength of an electromagnetic wave. Devices which measure frequency rather than wavelength are also called wavemeters. A device for frequencies above 100 megacycles (wavelengths shorter than one meter), utilizes a traveling detector which is a short antennalike probe which is moved along a transmission line (Fig. 1), or along a slot in a coaxial line or wave guide. The probe connects to a crystal rectifier and a direct-current microammeter. The points at which minima occur are noted on the scale. The difference between two adjacent minima is one half wavelength.

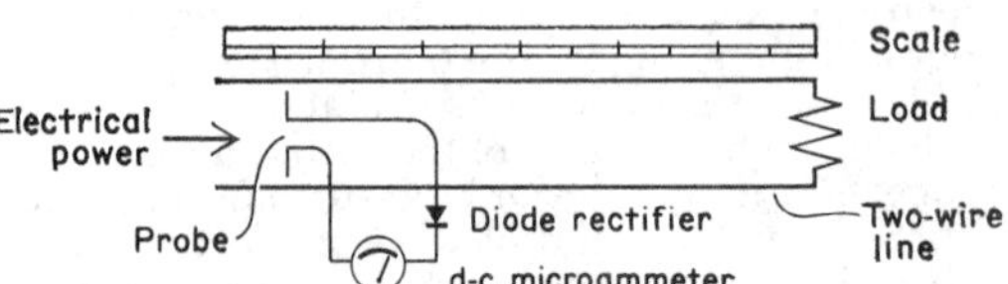

Fig. 1. Traveling detector wavemeter for measuring wavelength on a two-wire line.

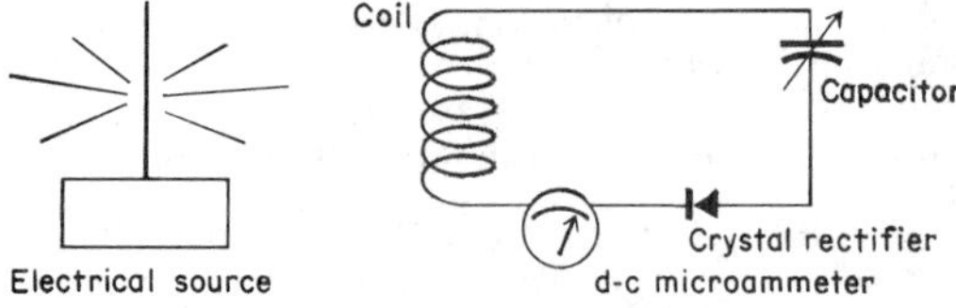

Fig. 2. Circuit of a frequency meter.

The wavelength of light may be measured by an interferometer in which a beam of light is split into two parts which follow almost identical paths to a viewing telescope. The length of one of the paths is adjustable. If the path lengths are identical, the two parts reinforce one another and the viewer sees a bright light. If the path lengths are different by one quarter of a wavelength, the two parts cancel and the viewer sees a minimum of brightness.

Nearly all types of frequency meters utilize the resonance property of a coil-capacitor combination which is designed to absorb electrical energy most readily at one frequency. The coil and capacitor are connected in series with a crystal rectifier and d-c meter (Fig. 2). The frequency meter is brought close to the electrical source, and the coil or capacitor is varied (tuned) until a maximum reading is obtained. The frequency is read from a calibrated dial. Other frequency meters are tuned-cavity, grid-dip, and heterodyne meters.

See also WAVE GUIDE; WAVELENGTH.

GLEN A. RICHARDSON,
Department of Electrical Engineering, Worcester Polytechnic Institute.

WAVERLEY, wā'vər-lē, municipality, Australia, in New South Wales, in the Sydney metropolitan area, southeast of Sydney, on Bondi Bay. Brass, shoes, and furniture are produced. Bondi Beach is a popular resort. Pop. (1966) 63,607.

WAVERLEY NOVELS, The, prose fiction of Sir Walter Scott, published from 1814 to 1831. The first, *Waverley* (1814), supplied the collective name; Scott remained anonymous until 1827, and the separate novels were ascribed to the "Author of Waverley." The term "novels" may be disputed. Scott's "Essay on Romance" (1823) distinguished his genre from the novel's "ordinary" events and "modern" milieu. But the distinction means little; Scott, said William Hazlitt, found "there is no romance like the romance of real life." And Aleksandr Pushkin defined Scott's contribution to fiction as a form which translated the historically remote and exotic into contemporary reality.

The Waverley Novels are "historical" in that they interweave domestic relations and events with public issues and political forces constituting specific epochs. Hence, they may be grouped by historical setting. The smallest group (for example, *Guy Mannering*, 1815; *St. Ronan's Well*, 1824) is set in Scott's own era. *Waverley*, *The Heart of Midlothian* (1818), and *Rob Roy* (1818) head the "Scotch" group (perhaps most effective), dramatizing cultural and ideological conflicts of recent Scottish history, from 17th century Cavalier-against-Puritan (*Old Mortality*, 1816; *Woodstock*, 1826) to the "end of an auld sang" with picturesque, pathetic Jacobitism a century later (*Redgauntlet*, 1824). Finally, *Quentin Durward* (1823) and *Kenilworth* (1821) typify the less colloquial, more "literary" romances of an older British and European past, from early 17th century London (*Fortunes of Nigel*, 1822) back to 12th century *Ivanhoe* (1820).

Whatever the epoch, the most typical Waverley pattern depicts a young person, his ancestral tradition deeply split in political or cultural loyalties, who is passive or "romantic" enough to become involved with heroic partisans of extreme causes. His love affairs are lifelessly artificial; his domestic and political relations with quasi-parental figures are central and vital. Through his experience, opposing cultural forces are portrayed; while he, committed to peace and moderation, encounters the mystery of fated involvement and the problems of conscience in the face of divided loyalties. He learns, with Scott's tragicomic view of history, that fanatic or rigid heroism verges on cruel folly; that men divided by ideal commitments (or prejudices) are men unable to find a language of the heart by which to transcend the barriers, however picturesque, of their traditional fidelities. The ending is usually "comic" in the Shakespearian sense. Good heart and balanced judgment triumph; community is restored; life, though unheroically, goes on.

The novels enjoyed a worldwide popularity, inspiring European novelists such as Honoré de Balzac, Victor Hugo; and Pushkin, and making Scott Europe's first literary figure of the age. In Britain they drew upon a deepening historical sense to serve history's first mass-reading public, and fostered the antienlightenment revival in religion and culture and the Tory socialism in politics which gave the Victorian age its character. Yet for most "moderns," they are unread. Walter Allen finds the "current view" of Scott in E. M. Forster's words: "a trivial mind and a heavy style. He cannot construct." The view is debatable, and the admirable recent Waverly criticism of Allen, Daiches, and Pritchett. (see *Bibliography*) suggests anew that The Waverly Novels are the work of a major artist.

See also SCOTT, SIR WALTER.

FRANCIS RUSSELL HART,
Assistant Professor of English, University of Virginia.

Bibliography

Allen, Walter, *Six Great Novelists* (1955; reprint, Arden Library 1978).
Canning, Albert S., *Philosophy of the Waverley Novels* (1879; reprint, R. West 1973).
Daiches, D., *Literary Essays* (Univ. of Chicago Press 1968).
Dickson, Nicholas, *Bible in Waverley* (1884; reprint, Arden Library 1980).
Lamont, C., *The Poetry of the Early Waverley Novels* (Longwood 1975).
MacKerchar, E., *Wit and Wisdom from the Waverley Novels* (Folcroft 1973).
Pritchett, V. S., *The Living Novel* (1946; reprint, Norwood Eds. 1985).
Rogers, May, *Waverley Dictionary*, 2d ed. (1967; reprint, Gale Res. 1985).
The Waverley Manual, or Hand-Book of the Chief Characters, Incidents and Descriptions (1871; reprint, Folcroft 1978).

WAVERLY, wā'vər-lē, city, Iowa, Bremer County seat, 17 miles north-northwest of Waterloo on the Cedar River, at an altitude of 940 feet. Waverly is primarily an agricultural community located in the farm belt of the Midwest. Its industries include condensed milk factories, a food-processing plant, and an excavating-equipment plant. In the heart of the city is Wartburg College, a four-year coeducational liberal arts school, owned and operated by the American Lutheran Church since 1868. The Bremer Historical Society Museum, founded in 1959, is also here. Incorporated in 1859, Waverly operates under a mayor and council form of government. Pop. 8,444.

MARJORIE HUMBY.

WAVERLY, village, New York, in Tioga County, 16 miles east-southeast of Elmira on the Chemung River, near the Pennsylvania border. Set in a general farming region, Waverly is mainly a residential center. The village was first known as Factoryville. In 1796, John Shepard, one of the earliest and most prominent settlers, bought 1,000 acres covering the land on which Waverly now stands. Another active early settler was Joseph E. Hallett who came to the village in 1833 and is credited with suggesting the present name. The village was incorporated in 1853. Pop. 4,738.

GEORGIA M. LUNN.

WAVERLY, village, Ohio, capital of Pike County, situated at an altitude of 570 feet on the Scioto River, 14 miles south of Chillicothe. It is an agricultural marketing center and has lumber, wood products, and concrete products industries. Nearby is Lake White State Park. Founded in 1829 as Uniontown and renamed Waverly the following year, the town benefited when the Ohio and Erie Canal was routed through it. It became the county seat, replacing Piketon, in 1861. Pop. 4,603.

WAVES (United States Naval Reserve). See WOMEN IN THE NAVAL SERVICE.

WAVES, Electromagnetic. See ELECTROMAGNETIC RADIATION; LIGHT—*Interaction of Light with Matter;* RADIO—*Radio Theory and Technology;* WAVES AND WAVE MOTION.

WAVES, Sea and Ocean, wāvz. A simple or idealized train of waves can be described in terms of their period, wavelength, and height. The height, which is twice the amplitude, is the vertical distance from crest to trough, and the period is the time required for a single complete wave to pass a fixed point. Although the waves travel over the surface, there is virtually no transport of the water itself. An object floating on the surface moves forward with the crest, but reverses its motion in the trough, traveling in the direction opposite that of the wave. Actually, such a floating object follows a circular vertical orbit, the diameter of which corresponds to the height of the wave. One orbit is completed with the passage of each wave in the interval corresponding to the period of the wave. This particle motion of the medium is characteristic of surface waves; the orbits are greatest at the surface, decrease with distance beneath the surface, and are essentially zero at a depth equal to one half the wavelength.

The speed of travel of surface waves depends on their wavelength or period. Wave speeds $= 1.34\sqrt{L}$ or $3.03\ T$, where the wave speed is in knots, the wavelength (L) in feet, and the period (T) in seconds. The speed of waves is independent of their height.

Wind and Waves.—Most of the surface waves observed in nature are the result of wind action. When the wind begins to blow across undisturbed water, the first waves produced are ripples. These small wavelets have the properties of capillary waves and are controlled in part by the surface tension of the water. The ripples are short lived. If the wind continues to blow at speeds greater than a few miles per hour, the size of the waves increases and the surface of the water assumes an irregular character in which it is difficult to recognize individual waves. This is due to the development of a spectrum of waves having different periods, wavelengths, and heights. The irregular and rough appearance of the water surface is most obvious when the winds are increasing in strength and while the waves are still growing in size. The drag of the wind on the water surface transfers kinetic energy from the atmosphere to the water. A part of this energy is transformed into wave energy, a part is dissipated in turbulent mixing, and a part is liberated by the molecular viscosity of the water. Relatively large amounts of energy are dissipated by the breaking of waves when they become too steep and unstable. In open water this is indicated by the presence of whitecaps and by patches of bubbles and foam.

The relationship between wind and waves depends on three major factors: the wind speed, the duration of the wind, and the fetch, the distance over which the wind has acted on the water. In general, as these three factors are increased, the height, period, and wavelength of the surface waves increase until they reach certain maximum values that correspond to those of the fully developed wind waves. Typical values are given in Table 1.

Table 1—MINIMUM TIME AND MINIMUM FETCH FOR THE FULL DEVELOPMENT OF WAVES FOR CERTAIN WIND SPEEDS[1]

Wind speed (knots)	10	20	30	40	50
Fetch (nautical miles)	10	75	280	710	1,420
Duration (hours)	2.4	10	23	42	69

For example, for a wind of 30 knots it requires a fetch of at least 280 nautical miles and the wind must blow for at least 23 hours in order to exert maximum wave development. If either the fetch or the duration of the wind is less, the size of the waves will be smaller.

[1] All tables in this article are adapted from *Practical Methods for Observing and Forecasting Ocean Waves,* by Willard J. Pierson, Gerhard Neumann, and Richard W. James.

The waves which break on beaches result from swells generated by the prolonged drag of the wind over many surface miles of ocean.

Ray Atkeson from A. Devaney

Table 2—CHARACTERISTICS OF FULLY DEVELOPED WAVES PRODUCED BY WINDS OF CERTAIN SPEEDS

Wind speed (knots)	10	20	30	40	50
Average period (seconds)	2.9	5.7	8.6	11.4	14.3
Average wavelength (feet)	28	111	251	446	696
Average height (feet)	0.9	4.9	13.6	27.9	48.7
Approximate wave speed (knots)	9	17	26	35	43

Table 2 gives the average period, wavelength, height, and approximate wave speed of the fully developed wind waves produced by winds of various speeds. For a 30-knot wind, for example, if it has blown for 23 hours over a fetch of 280 nautical miles, the average period is 8.6 seconds, the average wavelength is 251 feet, and the average height is 13.6 feet. It should be noted that these waves travel at a speed slightly less than that of the wind.

The figures given above apply to average waves. In practically all cases, the larger waves present are more important; consequently, it is often necessary to deal with the "significant" waves, that is, the waves that comprise one third of the highest waves. It is also possible to identify the properties of the largest one tenth of the waves. From Table 3 it can be seen that the larger waves present are approximately twice as high as the average waves.

Table 3—CHARACTERISTICS OF THE LARGER WAVES PRODUCED BY WINDS OF CERTAIN SPEEDS

Wind speed (knots)	10	20	30	40	50
Height of significant waves (feet)	1.4	8	22	44	78
Height of 1/10 highest (feet)	1.8	10	28	57	99

Swell.—When the wind speed decreases or when the waves have traveled out of the generating area, they are gradually transformed into swell, which is the term applied to surface waves that have more uniform profiles, longer crests, and longer periods and wavelengths. Swell can travel for thousands of miles; it comprises the waves that are transformed into the breakers and surf that occur along exposed ocean coasts. As the swell moves into shallow water, the wave profile is modified when the depths to the bottom are less than about one half the wavelength of the swell. The speed of the waves is reduced, the length is shortened, and the steepness of the waves is increased until the wave becomes unstable and the crest plunges forward as a breaker.

Wind waves and swell can be refracted when they enter an area where the depth of water is less than one half the wavelength of the waves. This can be clearly seen when the wave crests of a swell approach an ocean coast at an angle. The parts of the wave first entering shallow water will be retarded so that the breakers tend to approach the coast parallel to the beach. The energy of the waves and swell that is dissipated on the beach is an important process in shaping coastlines and in producing the sands, silts, and muds that make up the beaches and shallow-water sediments. Exposed coasts may be eroded by wave action and the sediments may be transported for long distances along a coast by the longshore littoral drift resulting from the combined effects of the breakers and the currents. During violent storms and periods of larger waves beaches are generally cut away, and the sediment is temporarily deposited outside the breaker zone. During calmer periods this sediment is transferred back to the upper portions of the beach.

Protected harbors and anchorages occur where there is a limited fetch to minimize the effects of local winds and where, because of natural topography or such man-made structures as breakwaters, the area is sheltered from the waves or swell present in the adjacent open water. Some wave energy will enter a harbor, and this may create seiches, to be discussed below, that are dangerous to moored and anchored vessels.

Because of their importance in military operations, in geological processes, and in many engineering problems, the characteristics of surface waves have been studied intensively since the beginning of World War II, and techniques have been developed for the prediction of wind waves, swell, and surf.

Long Waves.—When the wavelength of a wave is large compared to the depth of the water, the waves are known as long waves. In such long waves, the particle motions, instead of conforming to vertical circular orbits, are limited to reciprocating horizontal movements that are uniform from the surface to the bottom. The maximum speed of the particle motion is in the direction of the wave movement beneath the crest of the wave, and the maximum speed in the opposite direction is beneath the trough.

In a progressive long wave, the speed of the advance of the wave is dependent only upon the depth of water. If the depth of water (d) is in feet, the speed of wave travel in knots is equal to $3.36\sqrt{d}$. In the deep ocean basins the tides and tsunamis travel at about 400 knots.

In closed basins, such as lakes, or even in portions of the ocean it is possible to have standing long waves. In a standing wave the surface rises and falls with a definite period, but the maximum changes in elevation occur along the same lines, called antinodes, and midway between the antinodes the elevation remains constant along lines called the nodes. Depending upon the horizontal and vertical dimensions of a basin, there are a number of natural periods that correspond generally to the natural period and harmonics of an organ pipe. If some impulsive mechanism has a period that corresponds to one of the natural periods of a basin, standing waves will be generated. Seiches in lakes, harbors, and bays are standing waves. The very large tide in the Bay of Fundy is a standing wave generated in the embayment by the tides in the adjacent ocean because the natural period of the bay is the same as that of the semidiurnal tide.

Storm surges are another type of long wave associated with violent storms such as hurricanes and typhoons. Great damage can result from the high sea levels that flood low-lying coastal areas.

Tsunamis (sometimes called tidal waves) are long waves that are caused by violent displacements of parts of the sea bottom that also create certain earthquakes. The tsunamis may travel across oceans and even around the world. Flooding when the crests of the waves strike land can cause tremendous damage and loss of life.

See also WAVES AND WAVE MOTION.

RICHARD H. FLEMING,
Professor of Oceanography, University of Washington.

Further Reading: Bascom, Willard, *Waves and Beaches: The Dynamics of the Ocean Surface*, rev. ed. (Doubleday 1980); LeBond, P. H., and Mysak, L. A., *Waves in the Ocean* (Elsevier Pub. Co. 1981); Mei, Chiang C., *The Applied Dynamics of Ocean Surface Waves* (Wiley 1982); Sarpkaya, Turgut, and Isaacson, Michael, *Mechanics of Wave Forces on Offshore Structures* (Van Nostrand Reinhold 1981).

WAVES, Sound. See ACOUSTICS; WAVES AND WAVE MOTION.

WAVES AND WAVE MOTION. All things on the earth, the living and the inanimate, are continuously exposed to a shower of waves. Some of these stimulate our senses, others do not. We cannot escape from waves of some kind, wherever we may go. On a lake in the woods, far from the city noise, the call of a loon or the hum of a mosquito disturbs the quiet air. The astronaut in space outside the atmosphere receives no sound waves from earth, but he is constantly bombarded by electromagnetic waves from the stars or by cosmic rays coming from the outer parts of our galaxy, or possibly even from other galaxies.

Today the science and concept of waves permeate all of physics. Growing knowledge of waves and wave motion has contributed enormously to man's understanding of the physical universe. In this article only a general summary of waves and wave phenomena as they appear about us and are found to be associated with the physical universe will be attempted. The reader will, however, find many cross references to other articles dealing with particular aspects of the subject.

Wave motion is one of the modes of transferring energy. A motorboat starts a series of waves that eventually break on the shore. Much of the energy of the engine driving the boat is expended in producing waves. The two common ways of transferring energy are through the action of waves on or through a medium or by direct contact with some source of energy. The boat may strike a dock as well as produce waves. Action at a distance without an intervening medium has been difficult for man to visualize although he has always observed the effects of gravity without action or aid of a tangible medium. Bodies are pulled to the earth without the action of observable waves and without contact with the earth. Today, without assuming there is a medium, we speak of waves, for example light waves, or other phenomena with wave characteristics.

Characteristics of Waves.—The characteristics of waves are illustrated by waves on water. The distance from crest to crest is called the wavelength. The number of waves that passes a given point per second is called the frequency. The velocity of the wave form is then given by velocity = wavelength × frequency. This relation is appropriate for all types of waves.

In wave motion there is no transport of matter. Waves on a lake may seem to transport water up onto the shore, but there is no resultant flow of water as in a river. As the waves move into shallow water or strike the shore, the regular wave motion is modified, but flow of water from a distant point to the shore does not take place. (See WAVES, SEA AND OCEAN.) We have seen waves running across a field of grain in a summer breeze. Obviously there is no transport of the stalks of wheat from one point to another. They merely oscillate about a given position. In any wave, only a disturbance or wave form moves through or over (as in the case of waves on water) a medium.

If the particles of the medium through which the wave travels oscillate perpendicularly to the direction of wave travel, as indicated in Fig. 1, the wave is called a *transverse* wave. Transverse waves may be produced in a long stretched cord by vibrating the end in a direction perpendicular to the cord. The velocity of the wave will be determined by the tension in the cord and its mass per unit length. The relation is

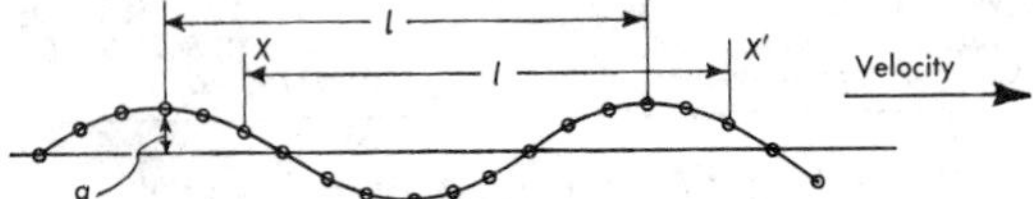

Fig. 1. Displacement of particles in a transverse wave. The distance *l* between two crests or between two points *X* and *X'* in the same phase is one wavelength.

$$\text{velocity} = \sqrt{\frac{\text{tension}}{\text{mass per unit length}}}$$

Another common type of wave is illustrated by sound waves in air. (See ACOUSTICS.) In this kind of wave the particles of air oscillate along a line parallel to the direction of travel of the wave. This is called a *longitudinal* or *compressional* wave.

In Fig 2, showing the displacement of particles in a longitudinal wave, we have represented particles of the medium by small circles along the line. Normally these are equally spaced, but when a longitudinal wave travels from left to right, the particles oscillate about their undisturbed positions. This results in a crowding at one point, a condensation, *C*, and a dispersion or region, *R*, with less than normal density or number of particles per unit volume. These regions of less than normal density are called rarefactions. The regions of normal density in the figure are designated *N*.

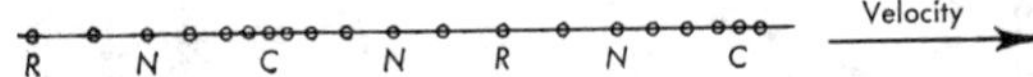

Fig. 2. Displacement of particles in a longitudinal wave.

In sound waves in air we should not assume that each of these particles is a simple molecule. Rather we can consider each particle to be an aggregate or cloud of molecules similar to a swarm of gnats. The center of mass of the swarm may oscillate with a small amplitude while each molecule (or gnat) darts about in a random fashion, often with an average mean free path between collisions or reversals of path greater than the amplitude of motion of the swarm itself. Longitudinal waves can be demonstrated by use of the toy called "Slinky," a closely wound weak spring which can slowly "walk" downstairs, somersault fashion, if placed on an upper step and set in motion by giving the upper rings a forward push. By hanging such a spring horizontally from long strings, as shown in Fig. 3, one has an ideal medium for the production of visible compressional waves. If one end of the spring is compressed, a region of condensation is seen to move along the spring. In Fig. 3, lower part, the regions of condensation in a compressional wave moving from left to right are at *J*, *K*, *L*, *M*, and *N*. Compressional waves can be transmitted through a liquid or gas which resists change of volume, but not change of shape. Transverse and longitudinal waves may be established in a solid which resists changes of both shape and volume. Transverse and longitudinal waves are not the only types of wave that can be produced, but are more easily described than others. Often a wave may be a combination of these two types, as for example, waves on a free water surface.

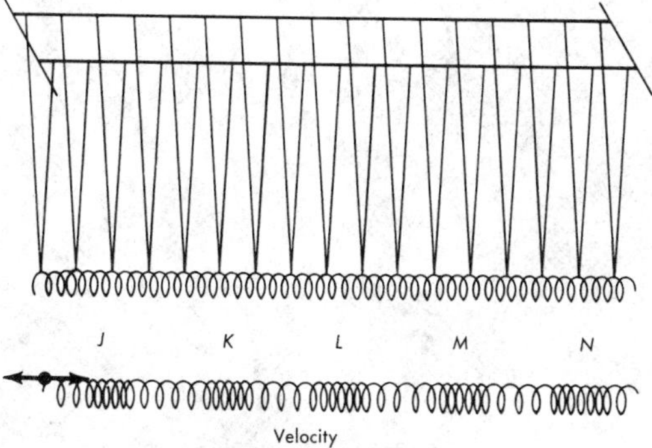

Fig. 3. Model to demonstrate longitudinal waves. The coiled spring is suspended from long strings. In the lower drawing, the positions of maximum density (the condensations) are shown at *JKLMN* for a given instant as the wave moves along the length of the spring.

To return to Fig. 1, this shows the wavelength, *l*, and also the amplitude, *a*, of a wave. The wave form shown is simple harmonic; that is, it may be obtained by attaching a pen to a vibrating tuning fork and moving it across a piece of paper. The displacement of the end of the tuning fork may be represented by the equation $y = a \sin \omega t$. This motion is called a simple harmonic motion. At a time t the displacement is y. The maximum displacement is a, the amplitude of the motion. The frequency of motion is proportional to ω. Not all waves are simple harmonic. The sound wave produced by a tuning fork is simple harmonic, but a note from a violin or one sung by the voice is more complex. However complex any wave found in nature may be, it can be represented by or produced by the addition of simple harmonic waves. These have frequencies that are integral multiples of the fundamental or lowest frequency. In music these harmonics are called overtones. The analysis into simple harmonic waves of any wave or periodic phenomenon, for example, the tides, was demonstrated in 1822 by Baron Jean Baptiste Joseph Fourier in his book, *The Analytical Theory of Heat*. We call the resolution of a periodic motion into simple harmonic motion a Fourier analysis.

Superposition of Waves.—Light waves, sound waves, and waves on the surface of water from different sources are often observed to pass through a given position without destruction. Light waves or rays (the paths along which the waves travel) from one source cross those from another, and each is observed as if the other were not present. However, if the region of crossing is observed, as it can be for waves on water, a very complex pattern may be seen. For many kinds of waves, the resultant motion when two or more waves cross can be described by application of the principle of superposition. This principle states that to find the resultant displacement (or value of magnetic or electric fields in electromagnetic waves) one may simpy add the displacement or field strength produced separately by each wave. The principle is valid as long as the forces acting are proportional to the displacement. This is usually true for waves whose amplitude is small compared to the wavelength.

By use of the principle of superposition one can conclude that if two waves, traveling in the same direction, or approximately the same direction, and having the same amplitude and wavelength, pass through a given point such that the crest of one coincides with the trough of another, the resultant displacement at that point will always be zero. The waves are said to interfere at the point in question (see INTERFERENCE). When two waves having the same amplitude and wavelength travel in opposite directions, the resultant motion is called a standing wave. At any instant there is a wave form, but it does not advance.

In Fig. 4 two transverse waves, represented by the solid line and the fine dotted line, are

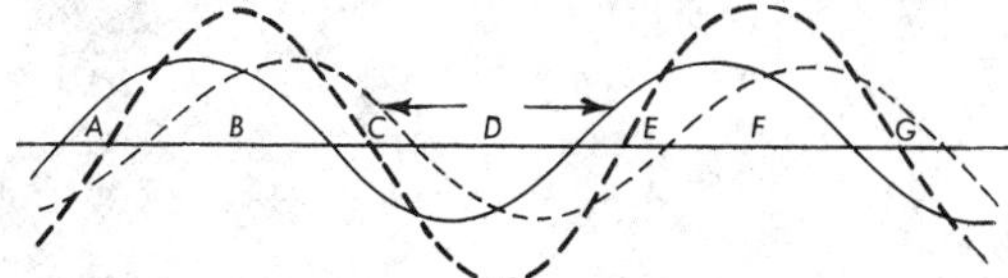

Fig. 4. Two waves traveling in opposite directions. The resulting displacement at a given instant is shown by the heavy dotted line. This is a standing wave with nodes at *A*, *C*, *E*, and *G* and loops or positions of maximum displacement at points *B*, *D*, and *F*, midway between the nodes.

shown at a given instant. One is moving toward the right (solid line), the other (dotted line) is traveling toward the left. By employing the principle of superposition and adding positive displacements above the reference line to negative displacements below the reference line, we obtain the heavy dashed line. We note that the displacement at the points *A*, *C*, *E*, and *G* is zero. These points are one half wavelength apart. If the positions of the waves are sketched at a slightly later time, one finds the displacement at *A*, *C*, *E*, and *G* is still zero; in fact, it will remain zero at all times under the conditions stipulated. These points are called nodes. At points midway between the nodes, the displacement varies with the position of the two traveling waves and changes from zero to a maximum value equal to twice the amplitude of the individual traveling waves. The standing wave is shown at one instant by the heavy dashed line.

A time-exposure photograph of standing waves on a rubber tube is shown in Fig. 5. Here the frequency of vibration (and hence the wavelength of the running waves) is such that an integral number of half wavelengths fits in between the ends of the tube. By vibrating one end of the tube, a wave is sent along its length. This is reflected at the other end, and thus two waves traveling in opposite directions are obtained. If standing waves are to be maintained on a string fixed at two ends, these must be at nodes. The vibrations of a piano or violin string can be considered as standing waves. The violinist touches the string at the proper point to produce standing waves of the desired wavelength and hence frequency and pitch. The bridge of the violin and the point of contact of the finger determine the ends of the vibrating string.

The superposition of waves is utilized in

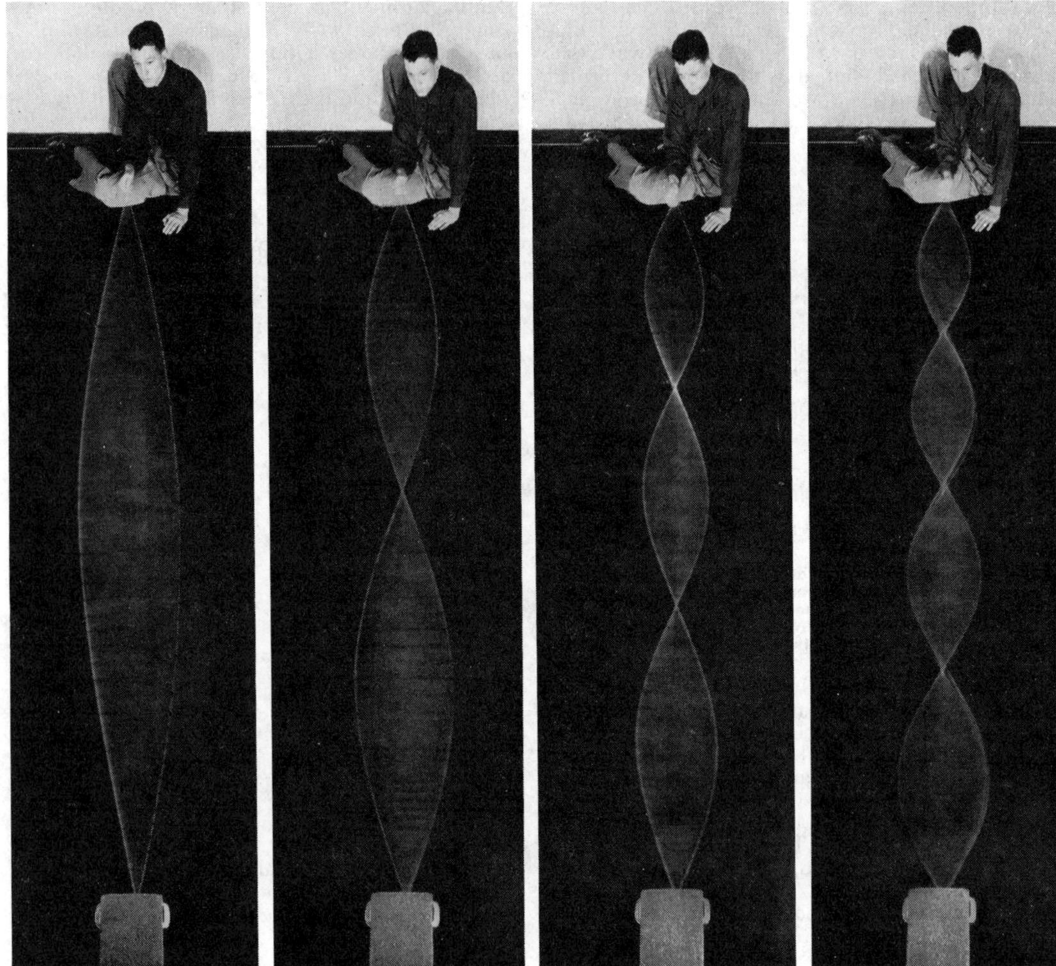

Physical Science Study Committee, "Physics," D.C. Heath & Company, Boston

Fig. 5. Standing waves. As one end of the rubber tube is moved from side to side with increasing frequency, patterns with more and more loops are formed. Note, however, that only certain definite frequencies produce fixed patterns.

synthesizing a complex wave out of a number of simple harmonic waves in accordance with Fourier's method.

Light as a Wave Motion.—The nature of light has long intrigued the scientist (see LIGHT). Can it be described as a wave motion in some medium? Or is it made up of small particles or corpuscles emitted from the source or reflected from the object observed? There is evidence for both hypotheses. But today we no longer say that a medium is required for its transmission. All attempts to detect the presence of a medium have failed. Probably the most decisive of these attempts was the so-called Michelson-Morley experiment launched in the 1880's (see MICHELSON, ALBERT ABRAHAM), which paved the way for the development of the theory of relativity (see RELATIVITY—*Absolute Motion*).

Nature appears to be such that the location and propagation of light can be best described by the wave hypothesis. The production of standing waves, the phenomenon of interference, and the bending of rays about an obstacle (diffraction) are described or "explained" in terms of waves. Indeed, we ascribe definite wavelength to light of different colors. Visible light is a small fraction of the total of the electromagnetic spectrum. However, the absorption and emission of light, in fact its reaction with matter in general, require us to consider it to be composed of particles or quanta, each quantum having energy proportional to the frequency of the light or equal to hf where h is Planck's constant and f is the frequency. This hypothesis is supported by observation of the photoelectric effect, the Compton effect, and the emission of light from electrically excited atoms. In the Compton effect, for example, the corpuscles or quanta of light bounce off electrons after collision just as a billiard ball recoils after colliding with other balls. The change in velocity and energy and the direction of the velocity of the quantum after collision are determined in the same manner as for billiard balls.

Thus, light or electromagnetic radiation appears to be such that neither the wave picture nor the corpuscular theory alone is sufficient to describe its characteristics. The human intellect tends to assume that one description or the other should suffice, but nature is not so limited. Light is not in every respect similar to waves on water, nor does it behave as small material bodies

(Newtonian mass particles). It behaves in accordance with its own laws.

It should be mentioned that the particle nature is more easily observed for light of very short wavelength, but there is no reason to suggest that the nature of radiation of long wavelength is essentially different.

The Wave Nature of Particles.—The physicist of 1920 could well have said that the totality of his science was represented by matter and radiation, and that these exhibited entirely different characteristics; at least electrons and protons, the basic units of matter, always behaved as particles and not as waves. But during the following decade this concept was changed. Louis Victor de Broglie of France proposed in 1924 that, because of the symmetry often found in nature, particles such as electrons may exhibit wave characteristics. For electromagnetic radiation the relation between frequency f and energy E is $f = E/h$, and the wavelength λ and the momentum p ascribed to photons are related such that $\lambda = h/p$, where h in each case is Planck's constant. For a particle the momentum would be written as mv (mass $\times$ velocity). Hence, for an electron having a velocity v and mass m, the associated wavelength is $\lambda = h/mv$. For an electron having a velocity it may acquire in any ordinary radio tube, the associated wavelength is about 1 angstrom unit, that is 10^{-8} centimeter.

In 1927, Clinton J. Davisson and Lester Halbert Germer, American scientists, while studying the scattering of electrons that had bombarded a nickel crystal, discovered that the electrons were reflected from the crystal in much the same manner as X-rays. Intense beams of electrons appeared at the same angles one would expect of X-rays (waves) whose wavelength was equal to the de Broglie prediction of the wavelength for electrons, that is $\lambda = h/mv$. Numerous experiments have verified de Broglie's hypothesis. It is interesting to note that Joseph John Thomson of England was awarded the Nobel Prize in 1906 in part for his experiments showing the definite ratio of charge to mass of electrons and for related experiments that demonstrated the particle properties of electrons. His son, George Paget Thomson, shared the prize in 1937 with Davisson for experiments that demonstrated the wave properties of electrons. The younger Thomson showed that the diffraction of electrons in passing through thin metallic foils was the same as that of X-rays, if one ascribed the de Broglie wavelength to the electrons.

The Schrödinger Wave Equation.—An extension of the concept of waves in the description of atomic particles led to Erwin Schrödinger's wave equation (1926). This is a differential equation that for a single particle takes the form

$$\frac{\rightarrow h^2}{8\pi^2 m}\frac{d^2\psi}{dx^2} + (E - V)\psi = 0$$

Here h is Planck's constant, m is the mass of the particle, E is its total energy, V is its potential energy, and ψ is the eigenfunction whose value determines the probability of finding the particle at the position x. For the simplest case of a free particle in a box, this equation has as a solution $\psi(x) = A \sin \omega x$. When the boundary conditions imposed by the box are employed to find the appropriate values of ω, the solution represents standing waves with nodes at the walls of the box. Thus there may be 1, 2, 3, or any integral number of half waves fitted into the box as they are between the fixed ends of the vibrating rubber tube in Fig. 5. These integral numbers are the quantum numbers of quantum mechanics (see QUANTUM THEORY—*Modern Theory*).

For a particle subject to an inverse-square force, the solutions yield the quantum numbers and energy states of the hydrogen atom that had previously been given by the Bohr theory (see BOHR, NIELS HENRIK DAVID) with very different postulates. The quantum numbers now are introduced "naturally." They are required to satisfy mathematically the boundary conditions of the system. The Bohr theory was successful only for a single particle in the electrical field of a "point" nucleus. The Schrödinger wave equation is found applicable to more complex atomic and molecular systems. It is the basis of the new quantum or wave mechanics. Physicists believe the equation is valid for larger systems, but with the larger mass the solutions become asymptotic with the classic mechanics for macroscopic systems.

See also ATOM; PHYSICS—*Modern Physics;* RADIO—*1. Nature of Radio Communications;* SOUND; WAVELENGTH; WAVES, SEA AND OCEAN; X-RAYS—*1. Physics of X-Rays.*

J. W. BUCHTA,
Professor of Physics, University of Minnesota.

WAX, wăks. Beeswax was probably the wax first known to man. Later, other materials having properties similar to those of beeswax were discovered and also called waxes. Waxes generally are slippery or tacky, opaque, water repellent, and soluble in hot turpentine or naphtha, and become glossy when rubbed. Different types of wax vary in these characteristics, as well as in such qualities as hardness, ductility, and melting point.

Natural Waxes.—Natural waxes are classified in accordance with their origin as mineral, insect or animal, and vegetable. Their purity depends on the place of origin, care in handling, and the method of extraction.

Mineral Waxes.—*Montan wax* is extracted from brown coal or lignite found in California, Czechoslovakia, Germany, and Russia. The coal is crushed, dried and processed with a solvent to extract a crude wax This is further refined by another solvent extraction and by oxidation with chromic acid. Montan wax contains varying amounts of resin, which contributes to its hardness and luster. When rubbed or heated, it releases a bituminous odor.

Peat wax is obtained from peat found in England, Scotland, and other countries. It resembles montan wax in composition, but is more brittle.

Ozokerite is obtained from wax shales found in Austria, Poland, and Russia. It is separated from earthy matter by boiling with water and then drawing off the layer of melted wax that forms at the top. This is refined by treatment with sulphuric acid and decolorizing earth. Since the mid-1950's, this wax has not been available in the United States. Ozokerite is an amorphous hydrocarbon mixture. Its most important property is its high absorbing power for oil, grease, and solvents. It is also resistant to acids and alkalies; in this respect it is superior to vegetable and animal waxes. *Ceresin* originally was a purified ozokerite. Today it consists of ozokerite with 50 to 80 percent paraffin wax.

Paraffin wax is the type most widely used. It is obtained from the high-boiling residues of petroleum-refining processes by solvent extraction, chilling, and filtering. Paraffin wax is white, soft, translucent, slippery, tasteless, and odorless. It is made in a number of grades with different melting points and containing various small amounts of mineral oil. *Microcrystalline wax* is also obtained by solvent extraction from the high-boiling residues remaining after the distillation or refining of petroleum. It differs from paraffin wax in having a much higher molecular weight, and its crystals are smaller and irregular. It is tougher, more ductile, and more coherent than paraffin wax.

Insect and Animal Waxes.—Commercially, *beeswax* is the most important of the insect types. It is produced as a digestive secretion by honeybees and then placed in a cell of the honeycomb in the hive. It is gathered in many agricultural countries and exported in crude form to more industrialized countries for refining. The crude wax is obtained by melting the honeycomb or boiling it in water. The melted wax is filtered and strained to remove foreign matter and cast into blocks. It is then refined by solvent extraction and bleached by chemical treatment or exposure to sunlight. Beeswax is noted for its plasticity, ductility, and its ability to form stable emulsions.

Chinese insect wax is deposited on the branches of certain trees by *Coccus ceriferus,* an insect native to China. The wax is scraped off, and refined by melting in hot water and filtering. It is fairly hard, shiny, and crystalline. *Shellac wax,* found in a resin produced by an insect native to India, is recovered when the shellac is refined. It is hard, tough, and lustrous, but usually contains some shellac and other impurities.

Spermaceti is present in sperm oil obtained from the head and blubber of the sperm whale. The oil is chilled, and the crude spermaceti is filtered off. It is refined by boiling with dilute caustic soda, separating, and washing with water until neutral; it is then dried, melted, and run into molds. Refined spermaceti is white, shiny, crystalline, brittle, and greasy. *Wool wax* or *wool grease* is extracted from sheep wool. The crude product is dark, sticky, and malodorous. It is refined chemically and by solvent extraction to yield lanolin and fatty waxes.

Vegetable or Plant Waxes.—The important commercial vegetable waxes are found as coatings on leaves, on stems of various shrubs and trees, and on certain berries and grasses, all usually found in tropical regions The wax functions to prevent loss of moisture by the plant.

Carnauba wax occurs as a fine, light powder on certain palms; it is gathered and refined mostly in Brazil. The leaves are stripped from the palms, dried, and shredded, and the waxy powder is then scraped off, melted, and run into molds. When cooled, it is either shipped as crude wax or melted in boiling water, skimmed off, and cast into slabs to be shipped as semirefined wax. A refined grade is obtained by extraction with a solvent, filtering, and then boiling off the solvent. Carnauba wax is the hardest type known; it is amorphous, tough, and lustrous, and has a pleasing aromatic odor. *Ouricury wax* is similar to the carnauba type and is obtained from a palm native to Brazil. It is recovered and refined by methods similar to those used for carnauba wax, but contains more resin and foreign matter than the latter.

Candelilla wax is found as a coating on a wild perennial rush native to northern Mexico and southern Texas. The rushes are submerged in vats of boiling water, and the melted wax is drawn off into a second tank to remove traces of water and to settle out impurities. This semirefined wax may then be treated chemically and with decolorizing earths to purify it further. Candelilla wax is second only to carnauba in hardness; it is brittle, lustrous, and has an aromatic odor. Under pressure it becomes sticky because of its resin content.

Sugarcane wax is found as a thin white deposit on sugarcane. In the sugar-refining process, the wax is concentrated with other impurities that are filtered off; this mass is dried and a semirefined wax is extracted by using a solvent. Repeated melting and extraction yield a refined product. Sugarcane wax is not as hard as carnauba wax, is more complex chemically, and contains a resin. *Esparto wax* is derived from a coating on certain reeds and grasses found in North Africa and Spain. The method of refining is similar to that used for sugarcane wax. Esparto wax is similar to candelilla wax, but is harder and less brittle.

Japan wax is obtained from the berries of sumaclike trees native to China and Japan. The berries are first dried and crushed, the husks are removed, and the pulp is squeezed in heated presses to produce an oil that solidifies to a soft wax upon cooling. This is refined by melting in hot water, skimming, and bleaching in the sun. Japan wax is soft and malleable, but sticky; it has a tallowlike odor and becomes rancid and discolored on aging.

Numerous other natural waxes, such as palm, bayberry, bark, rice-oil, flax, kapok, and raffia wax, are produced in relatively small amounts. Because their properties are not sufficiently important or because their costs of production are too high, they are of very little commercial interest.

Synthetic Waxes.—Certain chemical compounds have waxy properties and are known as synthetic waxes. In this group are the fatty alcohols, acids, and ketones; stearic acid esters of glycerin, glycols, and sorbitol; hydrogenated animal, fish, and vegetable oils; chlorinated paraffin wax and naphthalene; amides and diamides of stearic acid; fatty amines and nitriles; low molecular-weight polyethylene and polyvinylstearate; terphenyl hydrocarbons; and ethylene oxide polymers.

Properties and Cost.—Waxes are differentiated from one another by variations in the following essential properties: color; luster; odor; density; hardness; ductility; toughness; plasticity; flexibility; viscosity, stringiness, and expansion, when melted; penetration; contraction when cooled; tackiness; adhesiveness; water impermeability; moisture transmission; stability to light, air, acids, alkalies, solvents, and attack by microbes; solubility and gelling in solvents; emulsifiability; compatibility with other waxes, resins, and asphalt; melting or softening point; transparency or opacity; toxicity; presence of impurities; electrical resistance; structure; edibility; flammability; surface tension; and specific gravity. The accompanying table details the chemical and physical properties of a number of commercially utilized natural waxes.

CHEMICAL AND PHYSICAL PROPERTIES OF COMMERCIAL NATURAL WAXES

Wax	Melting range, °C.	Saponification number[1]	Acid number[2]	Iodine number[3]	Specific gravity[4]	Acetyl number[5]	Main constituents
Beeswax	62–70	86–96	17–21	8–11	0.955–0.975	15	Myricyl palmitate, cerotic acid, hydrocarbons
Candelilla	65–69	46–65	15–16	14–37	0.969–0.993	—	Hydrocarbons, melissic acid, myricyl alcohol, resins
Carnauba	83–91	73–86	1–8	8–13	0.990–0.999	55	Esters of alcohols, acids, hydrocarbons
Ceresin	64–77	0	0	0	0.88–0.92	—	Aliphatic hydrocarbons
Chinese insect	65–80	78–93	0.2–13	1.4–2	0.926–0.970	—	Ceryl cerotate
Japan	50–56	207–237	20	4–15	0.975–0.990	27–31	Glycerides of mono- and dibasic acids
Montan							
Crude	76–92	58	25	16		—	Esters of wax acids, free wax acids, free wax alcohols, resins
Distilled	72–77	75–89	73–85	10–15	1.0		
Refined	77–84	70–80	15–20				
Ouricury	79–84	62–85	3–24	7–15	0.99–1.06	—	Myricyl cerotate, hentriacontane free wax acids, resins
Ozokerite	58–100	0	0	0	0.85–0.95	0	Aliphatic hydrocarbons
Shellac	74–78	100–126	12.5–16.0	1.2	0.97–0.98	—	Esters of wax acids, free wax alcohols
Spermaceti	41–49	121–135	0.5	2.6–3.8	0.905–0.960	2.6	Cetyl palmitate
Sugarcane (refined)	76–79	65–77	23–28	5–10	0.997	30–40	Alkyl and steryl esters of fatty acids
Wool wax	31–42	82–140	0.2–40	15–47	0.924–0.960	—	Esters of cholesterol and lanosterol

[1] Milligrams of potassium hydroxide necessary to saponify completely one gram of wax. [2] Indication of the amount of free acid present. [3] Indication of the amount of iodine absorbed under specified conditions, a measure of stability toward oxidation. [4] Ratio of weight of a specific volume of wax to the same volume of water at 4°C. [5] A measure of the number of hydroxyl groups in each molecule.

Because of the very specific properties that any given wax possesses, it is usually necessary to blend various waxes with resins or other products to obtain the exact combination of characteristics necessary for a specific use. Thus carnauba wax, which is valued for its hardness and luster, is compounded with paraffin and with beeswax or oils, or both, to make it more flexible and adhesive when used for polishes. A dental carving wax may contain paraffin, ozokerite, montan, and carnauba waxes. This combination produces a finished product with the desired characteristics by utilizing specific features of each component wax. For economic reasons, low-priced waxes are added to those of higher cost when their addition does not significantly reduce the desirable properties of the latter.

The cost of waxes varies according to the amounts available, the demand for specific types, and the cost of production, which, in turn, tends to fall as demand increases. Thus, the widely used paraffin and microcrystalline waxes may sell for from 6 to 11 cents per pound; beeswax, candelilla, and shellac waxes, from 50 to 70 cents; and the highly prized carnauba type, from 60 to 90 cents.

Commercial Uses.—Waxes have become important industrial materials, annual consumption in the United States alone being over 1.7 billion pounds (1961). Paraffin and microcrystalline waxes account for over 93 percent of this total.

The greatest quantity of wax is used in paper products such as milk containers, bread wrappers, and containers for thousands of other food and consumer products. Paraffin is the main wax employed for this purpose, blended with various additives to improve its performance. Most candles are also made of paraffin, although beeswax is still employed for church candles and others of high quality. Protective coatings on fruit, cheese, wood, metal, and rubber usually contain paraffin wax. The electrical industry is one of the largest users of chlorinated naphthalene and paraffin wax for insulation and for encapsulating, sealing, and moisture proofing, although other synthetic waxes may be used where higher melting points are needed.

The drug industry uses waxes in such items as balms, ointments, suppositories, and tablet coatings; the cosmetic industry uses them in creams, lipsticks, eyebrow pencils, mascara, hair preparations, and other specialties. Dental products include carving, modeling, and impression waxes.

Wax is included in special lubricants to enable them to withstand high temperatures, to effect the release of rubber and plastic products from molds, and to prevent stickiness in such articles. Wax is also employed to soften textile fibers, to dull the gloss of varnishes, in the casting of molds by the lost-wax process, for protection against corona effect and ultraviolet rays, and as a component of crayons, acid and corrosion proofings, adhesives, matches, paint and varnish removers, and fireworks. The textile and leather industries use large quantities of wax for waterproofing. The polish industry is the largest user of carnauba wax, blended with other waxes and materials to produce the highest gloss and greatest durability. Carbon paper is manufactured by coating one side of a suitable paper with waxes, color, and oil; the wax dissolves and absorbs the color and prevents it from soaking through the sheet.

HARRY BENNETT,
President, Bennett-Rosendahl Co., Inc.

Further Reading: Kolattukudy, P. E., ed., *Chemistry and Biochemistry of Natural Waxes* (Elsevier Pub. Co. 1976).

WAX MODELING, the production of art or other objects in wax or through the use of wax. The medium used is chiefly beeswax because of its special properties.

The use of beeswax as an art medium predates recorded history. We can assume, however, that some primitive ancestor of man, while examining this material, discovered that the warmth of his hand made it plastic but that when the heat was removed, it retained the form he had given it. By the time man had emerged from the Stone Age, many of the present-day uses and techniques had been developed. The chief ones are direct modeling, casting, and the lost wax method.

Direct Modeling.—In this method, a lump of wax is shaped into the desired form by carving and tooling it. Usually the wax is first heated and applied over a rough form or manikin that follows the general shape of the object. One type of manikin is made of plaster of Paris which is reinforced by wire rods to give strength and support. Another type is made by wrapping absorbent cotton around wire and then brushing melted wax over it, to build it up to the desired thickness.

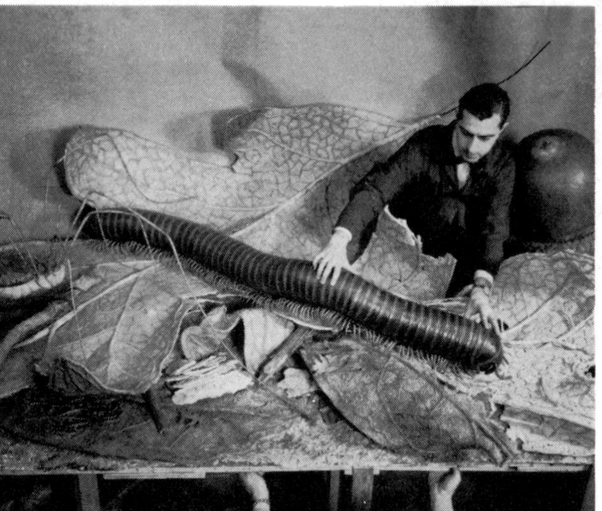

The American Museum of Natural History, New York

The author of this article prepares an exhibit, depicting life on the forest floor, by means of giant wax models.

Casting.—As man's knowledge increased, it was soon discovered that when wax was melted and poured into a cavity or mold, the wax, upon cooling, would conform to the shape of the mold. The first molds were hollowed-out depressions in blocks of stone. These were used to cast simple objects which were flat on one side. Such molds for casting flat celts or axheads have been found in Europe dating to the Bronze Age (about 2000–1800 B.C.).

By early Greek and Roman times, it was found that when calcium sulphate, which occurs in nature as alabaster and as gypsum, is heated, it becomes the powdery substance we now call plaster of Paris. When a little water is added to this material, it recrystallizes and becomes solid. Plaster of Paris as a mold material was first mentioned by Pliny the Elder (23–79 A.D.) who dated its use back to 300 B.C.

A simple object can be reproduced in wax by first coating the upper surface with liquid plaster and then allowing it to set or harden. The resultant plaster mold is then separated from the object and immersed in warm soapy water until it is completely saturated. It is then removed from the water and melted wax is poured into the mold cavity. The wax is allowed to cool and solidify. The soapy water acts as a separator and allows the wax cast to be removed from the plaster without sticking.

In more complicated objects the molds are made in several interlocking sections known as piece molds. This is necessary to allow the removal of the wax cast. Hollow wax casts are made in piece molds by partially filling the mold with melted wax and then rotating the mold until the wax has entirely coated the inner surface and has solidified.

Because of its fleshlike translucency when color pigment is added, wax has long been used in reproducing human portraits. Ancient Roman nobility were honored by such wax portraits which were placed in the vestibules of their homes. Lysistratus (fl. c. 300 B.C.) worked in this way. The Florentine artist, Andrea del Verrocchio (1435–1488), was one of the first to do life-size wax figures, complete with costume, glass eyes, and wig. A 14th century manuscript by Cennino Cennini of Padua, *Il Libro Del'Arte* (tr. by Daniel V. Thompson, Jr., 1933) gives a detailed description of the method of taking a plaster mold from a live model. This is probably the same method used since the early Roman times to produce molds in which the wax is cast. The wax figures in Madame Tussaud's famous exhibition in London incorporate these same techniques.

Lost Wax Process.—In this method, a model of the desired object is completed in wax, utilizing either the direct-modeling or the casting technique. It is then dipped in a bath of clay of creamy consistency, so that it is completely coated with a thin film. When this has dried, it is enveloped in a thicker clay covering to strengthen it. This is allowed to dry thoroughly and then is heated so that the wax is melted and runs out through an aperture left for this purpose. Molten metal is now poured through this opening and into the void vacated by the wax. When the metal has cooled, the clay is broken open to extract the cast. Each mold can thus serve for only one cast. Because of the loss of both the wax model and the clay mold in this process (hence, the term lost wax) archaeological evidence of its use in prehistoric times is mainly inferential. However, a few fragments from a later Bronze Age smith have been unearthed at Saint-Chély-du-Tarn (Lozère Department) in France. Among the remains was found a large lump of beeswax and some clay mold fragments.

RAYMOND H. DE LUCIA,
Exhibition Department, The American Museum of Natural History, New York.

WAX MYRTLE, wăks mûr'təl, a stiff shrub or small slender tree, *Cerothamnus ceriferus* (or *Myrica cerifera*), to 40 feet tall, but usually low and spreading, forming dense thickets, belonging to the bayberry family (Myricaceae). The bark is brownish-gray and smooth; the leaves narrow, oblong or oblanceolate, 1 to 4 inches long, much reduced toward the tips of the branches, mostly acute at the apex and wedge shaped at the base, often sparingly toothed, dark green and shiny above, paler and sometimes hairy beneath, golden resinous, often yellowish, fragrant when crushed, and usually persistent through the winter. The flowers appear in early spring before or with the new leaves, the staminate ones in short scaly cylindric catkins about ⅜ inch long and the pistillate ones in more or less globular or oblong clusters. The fruits, borne against the stems, are less than 1/10 inch in diameter, but are covered, when mature, with a pale blue, lavender, or grayish white, aromatic wax in microscopic rounded particles used in making candles which burn with a pleasing fragrance. The plants are popular ornamentals because the attractive fruit masses persist all winter. The wax is usually procured by boiling a quantity of the berries and skimming off the floating melted wax. The wax myrtle is native in sandy swamps, marshes, wet woodlands, and hammocks protected from fire on the coastal plain from southern New Jersey to Florida and the West Indies, west to Arkansas and Texas. It blooms in March and April. The related northern bayberry (*C. pensylvanicus*) is commonly sold as "wax myrtle" by nurserymen. The wax myrtle is also known popularly as candleberry, candleberry myrtle, sweet oak, tallow bayberry, tallow shrub, and waxberry.

H. N. MOLDENKE,
Director, Trailside Museum, Mountainside, N.J.

WAXAHACHIE, wôk-sə-hăch'ē, city, Texas, seat of Ellis County, situated 28 miles south of Dallas and 42 miles southeast of Fort Worth, at an elevation of 585 feet. It is a marketing center for a rich blackland region producing grain, cotton, and cattle, and has industries including clothing, furniture, boats, oil well equipment, cottonseed oil, poultry processing, sales books, commercial refrigerators, soft drinks, and a honey plant. Southwestern Bible Institute, a junior college founded in 1927, is located here. An annual livestock show and rodeo is held in September. Founded in 1847 and incorporated in 1871, the city gets its name from a stream called by the Indians Waxahachie, meaning "cow or buffalo creek." The Confederate government established a powder mill here but it was blown up in 1863. The city has a council-manager form of government, adopted in 1946. Pop. 14,624.

WAXBILL, wăks-bĭl', an African weaverbird (q.v.), one of the section of the family called blood finches because of the prevalence of red in the plumage. It has long been a favorite among cage birds and is sold by dealers all over the world. It is nearly five inches long. The beak is bright red and somewhat swollen. A bright red stripe passes between the eyes and the middle of the breast, and the belly is a beautiful reddish brown. The upper surface of the body is brownish gray, the lower surfaces lighter, everywhere traversed by very fine blackish wavy lines; wings and tail are brown.

WAXFLOWER or **MADAGASCAR JASMINE.** See STEPHANOTIS.

WAXWING, wăks'wĭng, a name applied to the three species of songbirds of the family Bombycillidae because the secondary flight feathers often have little bright red waxy projections at their tips. The common, sociable cedar waxwing (q.v.; *Bombycilla cedrorun*) of North America is about six inches long. The head is crested; the plumage, soft and silky, is brown becoming yellow on the abdomen and the tip of the tail. The voice is feeble and lisping. The bird nests in midsummer, laying four or five heavily marked eggs in a cuplike nest. The food is fruit. The Bohemian waxwing *(B. garrula)* is more northern in distribution and occurs in the United States (other than Alaska) only as a rare winter visitor. It is found in Europe and Asia as well as North America. The third species of the family, the Japanese waxwing *(B. japonica)*, is found only in northeastern Asia.

DEAN AMADON.

WAXWORKS, collections of wax figures, usually representations of real persons. See TUSSAUD, MARIE GRESHOLTZ; WAX MODELING.

WAY, Right of. See RIGHT OF WAY.

WAY OF ALL FLESH, The, a novel by the English author Samuel Butler (q.v.; 1835–1902), published posthumously, one year after his death. A severely critical study of Victorian life in general and domestic life in particular, it traces the history of four generations of the Pontifex family from that of John Pontifex, a rural carpenter of considerable amateur attainments in the arts, to that of his great-grandson, Ernest, who emerges as the hero of the tale and who is searchingly tested by circumstance before he is allowed to find his way to a secure plateau of worldly wisdom, literary accomplishment, inherited wealth, and permanent bachelorhood in London. Butler's well-known iconoclasm is directed with particular relentlessness upon Ernest's father, Theobald, a Church of England clergyman, who rears his son from infancy with equal parts of stupidity and impatience, plus liberal doses of cruelty and bullying, all the while convinced that he never departs from the loftiest possible conception of Christian duty. Lesser persons of thematic importance include Ernest's mother, a woman of limited intelligence but unlimited powers of self-dramatization; the pretty, dipsomaniac Ellen, onetime servant in Theobald's household with whom Ernest forms a temporary union after his release from prison; and Ernest's godfather, Overton. It is Overton who ostensibly tells the whole story from the point of view of an interested family friend. As spokesman for the author, he may be considered a self-portrait of Samuel Butler in later life.

Subsequent generations of readers are prone to find *The Way of All Flesh* somewhat too didactic and even at times improbable, more especially at moments when the lives of its characters are manipulated to illustrate one or another of the novelist's preconceptions concerning the role of heredity and environment in human affairs. At the same time, however, the book has been judged by time to contain its full share of gifted and compelling story, the illusion of life being very nearly absolute for long and brilliantly sustained passages. There is likewise the consideration that it has proved to be a rich mine of material for later writers with similar interests, however little the source may be recognized or admitted. Among those who openly acknowledged their indebtedness was George Bernard Shaw, who wrote of Butler's autobiographical masterpiece as follows in the preface to *Major Barbara:* "It drives one almost to despair of English literature when one sees so extraordinary a study of English life . . . making so little impression that when, some years later, I produce plays in which Butler's extraordinarily fresh, free and future-piercing suggestions have an obvious share, I am met with nothing but vague cacklings about Ibsen and Nietzsche. . . . Really, the English do not deserve to have great men."

MARKHAM HARRIS,
Department of English, University of Washington.

WAY OF THE CROSS, The. See VIA DOLOROSA.

WAY OF THE WORLD, The, a play by William Congreve (q.v.), his last and one of the finest English comedies of manners. First acted in London early in March 1700, it had a brilliant cast, including Thomas Betterton, Anne Bracegirdle, and Elizabeth Barry. It did not, however, have the immediate success of *The Old Batchelor* (1693) and *Love for Love* (1695), perhaps because, as Congreve implied in the preface, his last comedy did not conform to the more sentimental taste of the moment.

The plot, essentially original with Congreve, centers in the wooing of Millamant, a charming girl whose fortune is unfortunately under the control of Lady Wishfort, her aunt, by Mirabell, an equally charming sophisticate who has incurred the enmity of Millamant's aunt. With the aid of his former mistresses, Mrs. Marwood and Mrs. Fainall, Mirabell compromises Lady Wishfort into releasing Millamant's fortune and approving the marriage.

The play's distinction lies principally in its fashionable setting, witty language, and cross-currents of marital complications. Lady Wishfort, old enough to know better, seeks a new lover and is embarrassingly deceived. Mrs. Fainall and her husband live a marriage based on deceit. Watching these failures, Mirabell and Millamant, in a charming dialogue in Act IV, discuss their marital prospects with clear minds and express their abhorrence of the sentimental and conformist ways of conventional marriages.

Frequently revived in the 18th century and acted by Robert Wilks, Anne Oldfield, Kitty Clive, Peg Woffington, and David Garrick, it was rarely given in the 19th century. It has been successfully staged in London and New York in the 20th century.

EMMETT L. AVERY,
Professor of English, Washington State University.

WAYCROSS, wā'krŏs, city, Georgia, Ware County seat, about 106 miles by road southwest of Savannah and 76 miles northwest of Jacksonville, Fla., at an altitude of 137 feet. It is an important rail and highway hub, as well as a tourist center and convention city, with daily airline service. The Atlantic Coast Line Railroad provides its leading industry. It is a marketing center for naval stores, livestock, forest products, tobacco, honey, and pecans. Manufactures include footwear, cigars, crates and boxes, mobile homes, concrete bricks and blocks, and missile parts.

An Off-Campus Center of the University of Georgia is located at Waycross, and the city's library is headquarters for Okefenokee Regional Library, serving five counties. The Waycross *Journal-Herald* serves 11 nearby counties. Just south of Waycross is the world-famous Okefenokee Swamp. The State Midget Football Tournament is held annually in the athletic stadium, and an annual rodeo and the Regional Fall Fair and Forestry Festival attract many more visitors.

Named for its strategic location in the days of stagecoaches, Waycross was settled in 1872, incorporated in 1874, and chartered in 1909. It is governed by a commission of five members who appoint a full-time city manager. Pop. 19,371.

BUNA TURNER FAIN.

WAYFARING TREE, wā'fâr-ĭng trē, a shrub or small tree, *Viburnum lantana,* in the honeysuckle family, Caprifoliaceae, native of Europe and western Asia, planted and escaped in the eastern United States. It grows commonly in hedges and along roadsides in England—hence its colloquial name. It has opposite, ovate, toothed leaves, small, white, cymose flowers, and fruits which are red, becoming black. The American wayfaring tree, *V. alnifolium,* of eastern North America, is similar but has the outer flowers of the cyme enlarged, and dark purple fruits (see HOBBLEBUSH).

EDWIN B. MATZKE.

WAYLAND, wā'lənd, **Francis,** American clergyman and educator: b. New York, N.Y., March 11, 1796; d. Providence, R.I., Sept. 30, 1865. He was graduated in 1813 from Union College (Schenectady, N.Y.) and after medical and theological studies was a tutor there from 1817 to 1821. He then became pastor of the First Baptist Church in Boston, where, through published sermons such as *The Moral Dignity of the Missionary Enterprise* (1823) and *The Duties of an American Citizen* (1825), he won a leading place in the ranks of American preachers.

In 1827 he was made president of Brown University, in Providence. In the years until his resignation in 1855, he broadened and vitalized the curriculum, expanded the university plant and equipment, and enlarged the faculty and student body. In addition he was himself an inspiring teacher, wrote many widely used textbooks and other works in the fields of moral and intellectual philosophy and political economy, was active in planning the city and state school systems, and became nationally known as a pioneering leader in education. He was first president (1830) of the American Institute of Instruction, earliest national educational association.

His sons Francis (dean of the Yale Law School 1873–1903) and H. L. Wayland wrote A *Memoir of the Life and Labors of Francis Wayland* (1867).

WAYLAND THE SMITH (Ger. WIELAND; Old Norse VÖLUND), the smith hero of the Germanic peoples. He appears to have been originally a local Westphalian saga figure. The oldest extant account of him is the "Völundarkvitha," a song in the *Elder*, or *Poetic, Edda,* probably of the 9th century. The first part, in which Völund and his two brothers marry Valkyries who leave them after seven years, may be a later addition. Völund works in Ulfdal, accumulating many gold rings. Nithoth, king of Sweden, has him captured while sleeping, accuses him of stealing the rings, takes Völund's sword for himself, and gives a ring to his daughter Böthvild. On the advice of his queen, he retains Völund's services by laming him cruelly. In revenge Völund kills the king's sons, sending their skulls to him set in silver, and rapes Böthvild. He then makes himself wings to escape.

In all versions, Wayland is the greatest of armor makers. He forges arms in the epics *Beowulf* and *Waltharius* and made the famous sword Mimung; he appears in the Anglo-Saxon *Complaint of Deor* and the Norwegian *Thidreks saga.* He has many similarities to the classical smith figure Hephaestus, or Vulcan (the lameness and armor making), and to Daedalus (his skill, imprisonment, and escape on wings), but this is more likely to reflect social conditions (the lame skilled artisan) than direct influence. There is a representation of Wayland on a Northumbrian ivory carved casket of the late 7th century.

W. T. H. JACKSON,
Professor of German, Columbia University.

WAYNE, wān, **Anthony,** American Revolutionary officer: b. Waynesborough, Chester County, Pa., Jan. 1, 1745; d. Presque Isle (now Erie), Pa., Dec. 15, 1796. He was the son of Isaac and Elizabeth Iddings Wayne, and grandson of Capt. Anthony Wayne, who had emigrated from Ireland and in 1724 acquired a tannery and some 500 acres of land near Paoli, Pa., naming the estate Waynesborough.

Young Anthony attended his uncle Gilbert Wayne's local school, and in 1759 his father sent him to the Philadelphia Academy (now the University of Pennsylvania).

The Bettmann Archive

"Mad Anthony" Wayne, soldier of the American Revolution.

In 1765 Wayne was sent by a Philadelphia land company to survey a wild tract of about 100,000 acres in Nova Scotia and supervise its settlement. He returned to Philadelphia to marry Mary Penrose, daughter of a wealthy merchant, on March 25, 1766, and the couple immediately sailed for Nova Scotia. Wayne, however, was able to persuade only about 50 European immigrants to take up homes there; the soil would not grow sufficient grain to feed the settlers, and the threat of starvation ended the venture early in 1767. Back at Waynesborough, Anthony helped his father run the farm and tannery, a profitable business to which he succeeded upon the elder Wayne's death in 1774.

As anti-British feeling mounted in the colonies, Wayne became active in politics, was elected to the Pennsylvania Assembly in 1774, and organized a regiment in Chester County in 1775. On Jan. 3, 1776, he was commissioned colonel of the 4th Pennsylvania Battalion ordered to assist Benedict Arnold in his retreat from Quebec.

Wayne reached Albany, N.Y., by sloop and then marched his troops to Lake George, where small boats carried them up Lake Champlain and the Sorel (Richelieu) River in Canada to the St. Lawrence River. On June 10, 1776, there was a sharp battle at Three Rivers, near Quebec, where Wayne unexpectedly met an overwhelming force of British. He withdrew to Fort Ticonderoga, N.Y., and remained there for almost a year as commander, with a force of 2,500 men. He was promoted to the rank of brigadier general on Feb. 21, 1777, but this did little to offset his disgust with the wretched conditions and inactivity at the fort.

On April 12 Wayne joined Washington at Morristown, N.J., and took command of eight regiments known as the "Pennsylvania Line," composed of descendants of Scotch-Irish and German settlers. He instilled magnificent *espirit de corps* into this group, which he was to lead through many trying months. On July 24, 1777, he was sent to Chester, Pa., to train militia recruits, and after a short visit at Waynesborough returned to the Army, then camped north of Philadelphia.

The American cause was now approaching its gravest crisis, as Sir William Howe with a formidable force advanced on the capital at Philadelphia. Wayne took a prominent part in the fighting around the city. On September 11 his division held back 7,000 Hessians at Brandywine Creek (Chadds Ford), Pa., while the rest of Washington's army escaped Howe's flanking movement and retreated. At Paoli, late in the evening of September 20, while obeying orders to harass the enemy, Wayne was driven back by a bayonet charge under Gen. Charles ("No Flint") Grey, who had superior numbers. Accused of negligence in this defeat, Wayne demanded a court-martial, which acquitted him "with the highest Honor." At the Battle of Germantown, October 4, his command pushed the British almost three miles south, but he was later forced to retreat because of confusion in a heavy fog.

Philadelphia had been lost, and the American Army withdrew to Valley Forge. There, during the terrible winter of 1777–1778, Wayne shared the sufferings of his men, although his comfortable estate was only five miles south. After a month's furlough due to ill health he successfully raided New Jersey for cattle desperately needed at the Valley Forge encampment.

In the latter part of June, 1778, Sir Henry Clinton began the evacuation of Philadelphia and headed for New York. On June 28, at Monmouth, N.J., Washington attacked his long baggage train. The crack British guards, flower of the army, retaliated with a bayonet charge against Wayne's forces which had been ordered by Washington to harass the enemy's center. The guards were repulsed with great loss, but the American Army was incapable of resuming the offensive and during the night the British continued their march north.

During an indefinite leave of absence beginning Feb. 1, 1779, Wayne lobbied in the Pennsylvania Assembly for more effective aid for his ragged soldiers. On June 24 he received Washington's letter to join him below West Point, N.Y., and take command of the new light infantry, composed of picked troops from several states. At midnight July 15, 1779, Wayne stormed Stony Point, N.Y., an almost impregnable fort standing out on a high rock near the west bank of the Hudson River, threatening the security of West Point. Three columns waded waist-deep over a flooded marsh to the attack, the center firing noisily while the other two flanked the fort with bayonets on empty muskets. Personally leading one of the columns, Wayne subdued the garrison in the most brilliant action of his career, one of the great exploits of the Revolutionary War. His astonishing victory—followed by clemency for the defeated, so that only 63 British soldiers were killed—sparked the morale of troops and civilians throughout the country. Messages of congratulation and rejoicing flooded Congress. The Marquis de Lafayette warmly congratulated Wayne. The following day Washington rode down to express his thanks, and on July 20 sent a message to Congress declaring that Brigadier General Wayne's "own conduct throughout the whole of this arduous enterprise merits the warmest approbation of Congress. He improved upon the plan recommended by me, and executed it in a manner that does signal honor to his judment and to his bravery. In a critical moment of the assault, he received a flesh-wound in head with a musket-ball, but continued leading on his men with unshaken firmness." Congress presented a medal to Wayne in recognition of his gallant achievement. His victory was a great blow to British prestige.

It was such headlong daring, often bordering on recklessness, which won for Wayne the appellation "Mad Anthony." Always in the heat of every action, he chose the post of greatest danger, exhibiting a boldness that gained him the universal affection of his troops.

The light infantry was dissolved on Jan. 1, 1780, and Wayne returned to Philadelphia to plead once more for the Army, then at Morristown. On the evening of Sept. 26, 1780, while camped at Haverstraw, N.Y., Wayne received word from Washington of Benedict Arnold's treason at West Point. Wayne marched his Pennsylvania regiments 16 miles in four hours to protect the fortress, his prompt movement forestalling a possible British attack.

The Pennsylvania Line, payless for nearly a year, lacking food and clothing, and with many serving beyond their period of enlistment, mutinied at Morristown on the night of Jan. 1, 1781. Wayne, chosen as their intermediary to the State Assembly, won most of their demands. Yet, when ordered to join Gen. Nathanael Green and Lafayette in the South, Wayne could muster only 800 men. Before they were ready to leave York, Pa., a court-martial condemned three mutineers to death when another revolt seemed imminent.

At Green Spring, Va., July 6, 1781, false information lured Wayne into a trap with a swamp behind him and Gen. Charles Cornwallis' entire army of 4,000 men waiting in ambush before him. Wayne called for a daring advance, leading the British to believe American reinforcements had arrived. Before Cornwallis could recover, Wayne's 500 troops had steadily retreated over a narrow causeway. One of Lafayette's sentries accidentally shot Wayne in the thigh on September 2, an injury which limited his activity at the siege of Yorktown, Va., where Cornwallis surrendered on Oct. 19, 1781.

British resistance continued in the South, and in February 1782 Wayne was sent by Washington to serve under Greene in Georgia. He camped at Ebenezer, near Savannah, with 600 men, while Gen. Alured Clarke held the port with 1,800 British regulars. Wayne made a remarkable four-mile march over a causeway and crossed a vast swamp on the night of May 24 to assault 450 redcoats under Col. Thomas Browne, completely unnerving them and forcing them back to Savannah. On June 24 he roused his sleeping men in time to rout 300 Creek Indians—British allies—killing their leader, Chief Guristersijo (Emistisiguo), with a sword thrust. No longer able to hold Savannah, the British evacuated the city on July 11. In September Wayne had a violent attack of fever from which he never completely recovered, and late in July 1783 at last sailed for home. He had liberated Georgia with an incredibly small force, and that state rewarded him with an 847-acre rice plantation located 12 miles northwest of Savannah.

Wayne arrived in Philadelphia in shattered health, but the care of his close friend and physician, Sharp Delany, and the companionship of old friends proved a good tonic. Upon his retirement in October 1783 Congress belatedly appointed him brevet major general, and he became a member of the Pennsylvania Council of Censors, a body which tested the validity of Assembly acts. He spent his evenings lavishly entertaining the most famous people of the day, forgetful that such indulgence aggravated his frequent attacks of gout. As representative of Chester County in the Pennsylvania Assembly in 1784 and 1785 he worked for fair treatment of loyalist refugees and for the licensing of his favorite art, the theater, which was still forbidden in Quaker Philadelphia.

Late in 1785 Wayne went to live on his Georgia plantation, which he eventually lost to creditors after a bitter financial struggle. After he had served for a year (1791–1792) as congressman from Georgia, his seat was declared vacant following evidence of fraud in his election and irregularity in his residence qualification.

Meanwhile, ignoring the peace treaty of 1783, the British had still been holding forts in the Northwest Territory and inciting various Indian tribes to attack American settlers; and in November 1791 Gen. Arthur St. Clair had suffered a crushing defeat by the Indians. To cope with the situation, President Washington recalled Wayne and in April 1792 named him major general in command of the Army in the West. Wayne enlarged the Army and began training his raw recruits. In the midst of this program (April 1793), he learned of his wife's death at Waynesborough.

On April 30 Wayne began a march of over 400 miles into enemy territory. Profiting by St. Clair's mistakes, he maintained constant vigilance, sent out excellent scouts, and built three strong forts on the way. On Aug. 20, 1794, he met about 2,000 Indians at Fallen Timbers (near present Toledo), Ohio, and with only a third of his 3,000 men taking part, drove the Indians in 40 minutes to British-held Fort Miamis, and thoroughly cowed them. Washington appointed Wayne sole commissioner to negotiate peace with the Indians. While awaiting their reply he built Fort Wayne, Indiana, to command the waterways to Lake Erie. On Aug. 3, 1795, the Indians finally signed a treaty at Fort Greenville, Ohio, which brought peace for 15 years.

After a brief and triumphant return to Philadelphia on Feb. 6, 1796, Wayne was sent west again to take possession of the British forts abandoned under Jay's Treaty of 1795. He sailed from Detroit, Mich., to the Presque Isle, Pa., blockhouse on Nov. 17, 1796, and died there December 15. He left two children, Margaretta and Isaac, who subsequently brought their father's remains to the family plot in the graveyard of St. David's Church in Radnor, Pa., July 4, 1809.

GEORGE M. TODD

Bibliography

Johnston, Henry P., *The Storming of Stony Point on the Hudson, Midnight, July 15, 1779* (1900; reprint, Da Capo 1971).

Nelson, Paul D., *Anthony Wayne: Soldier of the Early Republic* (Ind. Univ. Press 1985).

Stille, Charles J., *Major-General Anthony Wayne and the Pennsylvania Line in the Continental Army* (1893; reprint, Kennikat 1968).

Wayne, Anthony, *Anthony Wayne: A Name in Arms,* ed. by Richard C. Knopf (1960; reprint, Greenwood Press 1975).

WAYNE, James Moore, United States Supreme Court justice: b. Savannah, Ga., c. 1790; d. Washington, D. C., July 5, 1867. He was tutored at an early age by an Irish graduate of Dublin's Trinity College (which may account for his lack of Southern parochialism), graduated in 1808 from the College of New Jersey (now Princeton University), and then studied law under a judge in New Haven, Conn. He was an officer in the Georgia Hussars in the War of 1812, interrupting his practice in Savannah. After the war he entered politics, first as a member of the Georgia legislature, then as mayor of Savannah, where he brought about many improvements in municipal government. In 1824 he became a judge of the Georgia circuit court, from which he resigned to take a seat in the federal House of Representatives in 1829. There he was a stalwart supporter of President Andrew Jackson and held many important committee posts, including that of chairman of the foreign relations committee.

In January 1835, President Jackson appointed him to the Supreme Court, where he served without great distinction for over 32 years. His particular forte was in admiralty cases, but even in this area he wrote no distinguished opinions. When the Civil War came—to which he made his contribution by joining in the opinion of Chief Justice Roger B. Taney in the Dred Scott case (q.v.)—he remained loyal to the Union, although his contemporary, John Campbell of Alabama, resigned his post and his own son became an officer in the Confederate Army, rising to the rank of brigadier general. An analysis of his many opinions reveals that he was assigned generally to deal with the comparatively unimportant cases which that court heard in great numbers during his extended tenure.

PHILIP B. KURLAND
Professor of Law, University of Chicago

WAYNE, John, American film actor: b. Winterset, Iowa, May 26, 1907; d. Los Angeles, Calif., June 11, 1979. Marion Michael Morrison (John Wayne) attended the University of Southern California on an athletic scholarship from 1925 to 1927. He then worked in Hollywood as a prop man and bit player and between 1930 and 1939 appeared in innumerable "quickie" Westerns and a few non-Westerns at various studios.

In 1939, Wayne became a star when he played the Ringo Kid in John Ford's *Stagecoach,* and he remained a star and a top moneymaker for more than 35 years. He appeared in such films as *The Long Voyage Home* (1940); *Red River* (1948); *The Quiet Man* (1952); *The High and the Mighty* (1954); *The Green Berets* (1968), which he co-directed; and *True Grit* (1969), for which he won an Academy Award for best actor.

CULVER PICTURES

John Wayne in *True Grit* (1969), for which he won an Academy Award as the year's best actor.

Later pictures include *Chisum* (1970), *The Cowboys* (1972), and *Rooster Cogburn* (1975).

On screen and off, "Duke" Wayne was a vigorous spokesman for conservative American values—anticommunism, law and order, and rugged individualism. In the 1960's and 1970's, he strongly supported the Vietnam War. In June 1979, shortly before his death, the U. S. Congress awarded him a commemorative gold medal.

WAYNE, city, Michigan, in Wayne County, on the South Branch of the River Rouge, about 17 miles by road southwest of Detroit, at an altitude of 660 feet. Wayne is an industrial center, principal manufactures being automobile and aircraft parts; there is truck and poultry farming in the vicinity. Industrial activity grew rapidly after World War II, and the population nearly quadrupled between 1940 and 1960. A single log cabin built in 1824 marked the beginning of the settlement which came to be called Derby's Corners. The village was first called Wayne in a land plat in 1836, presumably in honor of the Revolutionary War hero Gen. "Mad Anthony" Wayne, who secured the Northwest Territory for settlement. Having been incorporated as a village since 1869, Wayne became a city in July 1960, its limits somewhat enlarged and an estimated 3,000 residents added to the population figure of the 1960 census. Government is of the council-manager type. Pop. 21,159.

HELEN F. BIRD

WAYNE, township, New Jersey, in Passaic County, about 15 miles north of Newark and 20 miles west of New York City. Bounded on the south and west by the Pompton, Passaic, and Ramapo rivers, its area of 25.6 square miles varies from woody ridges (subranges of the Watchung Mountains) to flat meadowlands. There are three lakes—Pines, Packanack, and Lionshead. The township shares an airport with Totowa.

Although still mainly residential in character and about 50 percent undeveloped, Wayne is the site of several important installations of the rubber and chemical industries. Just south of Wayne is a major shopping center for the region.

Wayne's early settlers were farmers of Dutch, English, or Huguenot origin. The township was incorporated in 1847 and named in honor of Gen. Anthony Wayne, the Revolutionary War hero, who was stationed here in 1780. The Dey Mansion, now a national historic site, was George Washington's headquarters in the same year. The township has a mayor-council form of government. Population: 46,474.

WAYNE STATE UNIVERSITY, wān, a state-supported institution of higher education located in Detroit, Mich., the seat of Wayne county. The university, which offers bachelor's, master's, and doctor's degrees, includes the College of Liberal Arts, the School of Business Administration, the College of Education, the College of Engineering, Monteith College (for interdisciplinary training through such methods as tutorials and seminars), the College of Nursing, the Law School, the School of Medicine, and the School of Social Work. In addition, in conjunction with the University of Michigan, there are the Graduate Division of Instruction and Research, the Division of Adult Education, and the Institutes of Labor and Industrial Relations and Continuing Legal Education.

Wayne State began in 1868 as the Detroit Medical College. In that year the College of Education also was established under the authority of the Detroit Board of Education. In 1933 the medical college and the College of Education were formally joined as a university. The present institution, under state control, was created in 1956. Enrollment totals about 33,000.

WAYS AND MEANS, Committee on, a standing committee of the U.S. House of Representatives to which all bills relating to taxation and public finance are referred for consideration and report. It consists of 36 members divided between the two major parties generally in the same proportion as the total membership of the House. Because of the great importance to the national economy of the subject matter confided to this committee, it is considered as being second only to the Committee on Rules among the committees of the House. See CONGRESS OF THE UNITED STATES—*The Committee System.*

While the members of this committee are chosen in the same manner as those of other committees—by elections by the House on recommendation of the party caucuses—the Democratic members of the Committee on Ways and Means have the special function of determining for the Democratic caucus the assignments to be given to Democratic members on all other committees of the House.

The Committee on Ways and Means has had a long history. It appeared in the First Congress and became a standing committee in 1795. In 1850 its reports were given precedence over those of other committees (except Rules) on a temporary basis. During the Civil War period this precedence was made permanent by an amendment to the House rules. This committee controls the work of the Committee of the Whole House while it is considering tax measures that have been placed on the Union Calendar.

The committee appoints from among its own members the representatives from the House who serve—with similar representatives chosen by the Committee on Finance of the Senate—on the Joint Committee on Internal Revenue Taxation. The Committee on Ways and Means is the principal one of four, two from the House and two from the Senate, that are charged under the Legislative Reorganization Act of 1946 with the preparation of a legislative budget that must be reported to the two houses by March 15. This provision of the act has suffered from some neglect as budgetary matters have come to be considered solely upon the Executive Budget submitted by the president and approved by the appropriate committees of each house of Congress.

Under the Constitution of the United States all bills for the raising of revenue must originate in the House of Representatives. They are then reviewed by the Senate, through its Committee on Finance. This situation makes the Committee on Ways and Means of the House of Representatives the principal source of revenue legislation. All revenue bills are drafted by or for this committee, or it reviews drafts prepared by the Treasury Department or other interested executive agencies and revises them before sending them to the floor. The area of competence of the committee includes not only internal revenue but also public bonded debt, deposit of moneys, reciprocal trade agreements, customs duties, excise taxes, and even the payroll taxes collected as a basis for social security. Because of the great complexity and high importance of such legislation, the final drafts are nearly always prepared by or under the supervision of the Committee on Ways and Means.

HARVEY WALKER, *Ohio State University*

WAYSIDE INN, historic house in South Sudbury, Mass., 20 miles (32 km) west of Boston. It is the oldest operating inn in the United States. Built by Samuel Howe and opened as Howe Tavern in 1686, it was maintained from father to son for 174 years. In 1746 the third owner, Ezekiel Howe, renamed it the Red Horse, and in 1863, when Henry Wadsworth Longfellow's popular poem *Tales of a Wayside Inn* clearly indicated its identity, it took its present name. Longfellow had visited it, but whether he actually met any of the poem's characters there is uncertain.

The original structure had four ground-floor rooms and a kitchen ell, four bedrooms on the second floor, and an unfinished attic. In 1800 the west wing, including a dining room and a ballroom above, was added. Henry Ford bought the inn in 1923, added a two-story wing, and traced many pieces of the original furnishings, which were restored to the house. After a fire in 1955, the inn was restored and reopened in 1958, and it again served its original function of providing meals and lodging to wayfarers.

WAZIRISTAN, wə-zēr-i-stän′, a mountain region of over 5,000 square miles (14,950 sq km) in Pakistan, on the Afghanistan border. It is in the northern part of the Sulaiman Mountains, with the Gumal River forming its southern border. Waziristan takes its name from the Waziri, a hardy Pushtun (Pathan or Afghan) people comprising the related Darwesh Khel and Mahsud tribes. In this rugged country the people maintained the democratic independence dear to the Afghan-Pathan tribes, and when in 1893 the boundary between Afghanistan and British India was fixed by the Durand Line, Waziristan became an independent territory between the Durand Line and the boundary of effective British rule. Waziri raids into British territory were countered by force, but friendly chiefs were granted subsidies.

When, in 1947, British India was partitioned between Pakistan and India, Waziristan became a part of Pakistan. Afghanistan, however, proposed that a separate Pushtun state be set up to include all the Pushtun peoples in Pakistan, including Waziristan. The Waziri, unfamiliar with state government (they have no paramount chief and give allegiance to regional-kin chiefs only as long as a chief merits respect), maintained their independence by the traditional tribal device of playing off Pakistan against Afghanistan. One member of a chiefly family accepts a subsidy from the Pakistan government, while another member cultivates the Afghan government. With friendly relations established on both sides, the Waziri follow their own way of life, dwelling in mountain villages or black-tent camps, raising sheep, goats, and some horses and cattle, and cultivating crops of wheat, maize, and barley. The export of timber and firewood, hides, and ghee (clarified butter) brings a cash income.

Administratively, insofar as there is outside administration, Waziristan is divided into two political agencies: North Waziristan, with headquarters at Miram Shah; and South Waziristan, with headquarters at Wana. Until 1955 these agencies were attached to the North-West Frontier Province, after that date to the Commissioner's Division of Dera Ismail Khan.

ELIZABETH E. BACON, *Author of "Central Asians Under Russian Rule"*

WEAKFISH, also called sea trout or squeteague, a group of about 15 edible fishes. They are important commercially and as game on both the Atlantic and Pacific coasts, from Cape Cod to Florida and the Gulf of Mexico and from the Gulf of California to Chile. The name of the group derives from their weak mouth tissues, from which fish hooks tear easily.

Weakfish are slender, silvery bluish above and pinkish below, with orange-red or yellow fins. Some species are dotted with black. Most have two large caninelike teeth in the upper jaw. Their weight ranges from 5 to 25 pounds (2.3 to 11.3 kg). They school in shallow open water, feeding on other fish and crustaceans. They are members of the drum family.

WEALTH. To most people a wealthy person, community, or nation is one that is "well off" or "rich" in the sense of possessing those things that contribute to material welfare. These notions convey the essential idea but they must be refined, made more explicit, and placed in appropriate perspective if they are to provide a useful concept for economic analysis, which is often defined as the study of wealth. Adam Smith, the father of English political economy, entitled his famous treatise *An Inquiry into the Nature and Causes of the Wealth of Nations.*

WEALTH AS AN ECONOMIC CONCEPT

The word wealth originally meant state of well-being (weal) but by usage came more and more to refer to those things that generally promote well-being rather than the state of well-being itself. Thus wealth consists of an aggregation of substantive things that contribute to well-being, and these things are called economic goods. The definition may be broadened or narrowed by modifying the meaning of economic goods. In early pastoral economies the principal wealth was sheep or cattle. In agricultural civilizations it was land. In modern industrial societies it is real estate, machinery, and durable consumers' goods. But in modern economies the ownership of wealth has become more indirect and is often represented by stocks, bonds, and other such instruments of ownership. Wealth, therefore, is often thought of as consisting of these instruments, their money value, or even money itself. We shall try to show the sense in which this can be misleading but also the conditions under which it is meaningful.

Wealth and Income. Wealth, as distinguished from income, is the stock of economic goods on hand as of a specific date, while income is the economic goods produced during a specific period, say a year. Thus wealth is a *stock*, while income is a *flow* of economic goods. Wealth as a stock of economic goods aids in increasing the flow of income. But income production also contributes to the growth of wealth. If the portion of income received but not consumed during the income period is larger than the wealth used up in the income-producing process, then wealth will increase. The concepts of wealth and income are so interrelated that even technical writers often use them interchangeably. A man may be called wealthy because he has a large income, even though he may not possess a large stock of economic goods. Thus the term wealth is used broadly to include what has been called income-wealth as well as capital-wealth, and it is this broad concept that makes it reasonably accurate to define economics as the study of wealth. In the present article, however, we shall treat wealth in the narrower sense of capital-wealth or the stock concept, and show that it is, in accounting terms, a balance sheet or stock-of-goods concept, rather than an income or flow-of-goods concept.

Actually, the measurement of wealth is subsidiary to the measurement of income. The national income is a much more direct index of the success and efficiency of an economy and also of the basis upon which its wealth, broadly or narrowly defined, is really evaluated. The value of wealth is nothing more than the reflection of its

NEW YORK ZOOLOGICAL SOCIETY

Weakfish, or sea trout, are important game and commercial fishes on both coasts of North America.

income-contributing power, and no item can be classified under wealth that does not have income-producing potential.

Material Economic Goods. Economic goods defined most broadly include all sources of satisfaction that are scarce and therefore able to command a price. They include not only objects external to individuals but individuals themselves, or, at least, their useful capacities. Generally, however, wealth is restricted to those economic goods that are external to the owner, so that individuals and their capacities are excluded. Furthermore, only material economic goods that can be bought and sold and are external to the owner are ordinarily included. Such things as the reproductive power of seeds, the "goodwill" of a firm or the acumen of its management, the life-supporting qualities of sunshine, or the efficiency of organized institutions are excluded, except insofar as they are reflected in the market value of material objects.

Irving Fisher's definition of wealth as "material objects owned by human beings and external to the owner" is the general connotation given the term in economics. For many interpretations of national productiveness, however, the concept of the resources of a nation (its wealth, broadly speaking) must be extended to include the number and capacities of its population, the efficiencies of its functioning institutions, and the life-promoting and sustaining power of its climate.

Ownership Claims. This view of wealth, in either its narrow or broader aspects, places emphasis on the substantive items that compose it. The ownership rights in such items that govern the use, enjoyment, and disposal of their services often are spoken of as "claims" on wealth. Shares of stock, bonds, bank deposits, or paper money are tangible instruments that give "rights" to wealth. Individuals often speak of them as wealth per se. The right to use a public park or library is also a claim on wealth—the public park is the wealth. Since all wealth must be owned by individuals either as individuals or collectively as members of a social group, the instruments that indicate the ownership make it perfectly sound, for some purposes, to speak of ownership claims as if they were wealth. But, if this is done, then in order not to count the same things twice, the substantive items themselves must be excluded. It has seemed preferable to economists to think of the substantive items as the wealth and the "rights" to the use and disposal of the benefits from these items as claims on wealth. It must be recognized, however, that the arrangements by which wealth is owned and its uses facilitated are in themselves part of the institutional framework within which an economy functions. It also must be recognized that these arrangements have pertinence and usefulness in themselves.

How Wealth Is Measured. The concept of wealth as a stock of a great variety of useful things raises the question of how wealth can be measured other than by listing all such things. Since they are heterogeneous they cannot be added to form a single total. Care has been taken, however, at least in the narrower definition, to restrict the things included in wealth to those that are bought and sold. Thus wealth can be measured as the sum of money values. A money valuation is particularly appropriate for assessing the quantity of wealth in a single total because prices measure the marginal utilities of different goods. The marginal utility of any particular goods is the increase in total satisfaction (or weal) yielded by one additional unit of the good. For expressing in homogeneous terms the heterogeneous satisfactions yielded by different goods, prices provide a basis for assigning a meaningful and useful relative importance to the various categories of wealth.

Money Value of Wealth Stock. To estimate accurately the money values of the wealth stock presents many difficulties. The value of an item of wealth may be viewed in two ways. First it can be thought of as the price that can be received for the use of the item for a restricted period of time, say a year, the item to be returned intact; or, second, as the purchase price that gives the buyer the right to use or otherwise dispose of the services of the item for the entire period of its usefulness. These two values are closely related. The purchase price, which is what is usually meant by the value of an item of wealth, is, excluding sentimental factors, nothing more than a present value assigned to an estimate of the use value of the item for the period of its usefulness. Any present value of future services involves discounting these anticipated services at a current interest rate. Sales values of wealth are thus seen to be reflections of anticipated service values.

Book Value and Current Market Value. If each item of wealth were sold currently, the prices (market values) thus established could be taken as appropriate values. This seldom happens. It becomes necessary, therefore, to assign to the stock not sold the prices secured for the units that were recently transferred. For some items of wealth such as public roads, parks, or even many factory buildings, no representative items are transferred, so that some appraised or book value must be assigned. Book values are usually original purchase price values and these may be quite different from either the current costs of producing a similar item or the price at which the item could be bought or sold. Where marketable instruments such as stocks and bonds exist as ownership claims against the property, the market values of such instruments constitute still another basis for valuing wealth.

Current practice in wealth estimating is to secure, as nearly as possible, current market value. Even if this is obtained the task is only half over if time comparisons are to have any significance. Since the value of money changes, wealth measured in money values would not tell us whether the total of substantive wealth (useful resources) had increased or decreased in quantity. To answer this question we would have to express the totals in dollars of constant purchasing power. For this reason historical estimates of wealth often have only limited usefulness unless they provide the information by which they can be made comparable—namely, constant price valuations.

Reproducible Wealth. Two major categories of substantive wealth, reproducible and nonreproducible wealth, present somewhat different aspects and difficulties for the estimating of money values. Reproducible wealth, which is generally destructible as well, is composed of things man has made and can make again—or he can make closely similar things. The market value of this type of wealth tends, under competition, to equal its cost of reproduction. At any given time the market values of reproducible wealth may deviate from reproduction costs. But competition, by increasing or decreasing the quantity of such items, tends to bring their market values into equality with reproduction costs. To secure a measure of the changing quantity of reproducible wealth over a period of time we can select (1) their reproduction costs, (2) their market values, or (3) their original costs, adjusting each to a given base year of costs for comparability over time.

Nonreproducible Wealth. Thus for reproducible wealth it is clearly permissible to talk of an increasing or decreasing quantity of substantive wealth irrespective of how difficult it may be to measure such changes in the composite of all such items. For nonreproducible wealth it is equally clear that we cannot properly speak of an increase in the quantity of such wealth since by definition it cannot be produced. Land is the major item in such wealth, and if, as is customary, we include under land all natural resources, it encompasses the total of nonreproducibles, with the minor exception of produced works of genius, which are unique and therefore not replaceable.

David Ricardo spoke of land as the "original and indestructible properties of the soil," but our definition of land as all natural resources certainly includes things that are destructible. The various minerals and other ingredients available in nature, while not produced, certainly are destroyed, at least in form, by use. While their quantity may not be increased, it can be decreased. The measurement of such resources for quantification over time presents almost insuperable obstacles. While strictly speaking the quantity of such resources in existence may not be increased, they may be discovered from time to time, or, if known, may be brought into use gradually with the expansion of the economy. These considerations raise the questions whether such discoveries and inclusions in productive uses should be considered additions to the stock of wealth and whether the depletion of known resources should be subtracted.

For many purposes the addition of newly discovered national resources are important considerations, as are the exhaustion of known minerals and the expansion of useful areas. Such resources are in part substitutes for reproducible wealth and certainly increase the output of the economy. Their measurement in terms of money values is so difficult, however, that generally they should be treated separately from the measurement of reproducible wealth.

NATIONAL WEALTH

The wealth of a nation is the sum of the wealth owned by all its people, both in their private capacities as individuals and collectively as citizens of the nation. It should be noted that the wealth of a nation may be larger or smaller than the wealth physically located within its geographic boundaries. Residents of one national state, say the United States, may own property in other nations, and the citizens of other nations may own property in the United States.

A nation's net ownership may be negative or positive and is generally referred to as "net foreign assets" with the proper sign indicated. If positive, as has been true for the most part in the United States, it means that the wealth of the people of the United States is somewhat greater than the wealth located within the nation's boundaries.

National Balance Sheet. If every individual in the United States, every business and other institution, and every government—federal, state, and local—prepared a balance sheet, then the wealth of the United States would be the sum total of such balance sheets, or a consolidated balance sheet for the nation. Such balance sheets would show not only substantive things actually in the possession of each individual or other unit but also the claims each had on the substantive things in the possession of other individuals. Regarding nonsubstantive things, it should be clear that where one balance sheet lists stocks or bonds as assets, some other balance sheets must list the same items as liabilities. Similarly, bank deposits listed as assets by individuals, businesses, and governments will be listed by the banks as liabilities. Money, listed as assets on some balance sheets, will be classed with liabilities to banks and the government, since paper money and even metallic money, other than gold, is really only a promise to pay, used to facilitate exchange.

It is obvious, then, that in consolidated balance sheets, assets to one unit that are liabilities to another will cancel, and the only items that will remain are the substantive things themselves, except for international assets and liabilities. International assets and liabilities would, of course, cancel out if the consolidation was worldwide. The wealth of the United States is then the sum of the substantive economic goods located in the United States, plus the net foreign assets.

Net Worth. Another way to look at a consolidation of balance sheets is to compute for each unit the difference between its assets and the liabilities owed to other units. This difference is called net assets or net worth. The sum of such net worth for all individual units is the national wealth and is equivalent to the value of all substantive economic goods plus net foreign assets. Individuals, proprietorships, and partnerships would have net worths. Corporate business and nonprofit organizations would have no net worths, since the ultimate owners are the stockholders. Governments might have net worths, negative or positive, but in an ultimate sense this net worth also belongs to the people. In summary, then, the wealth of a nation is the net worth of individuals plus the net worth of government.

DISTRIBUTION OF INCOME AND WEALTH

Income Distribution. The most usual meaning of wealth distribution refers to the distribution of wealth ownership among the individuals or households of a nation. There is little valid information that can be summarized meaningfully on wealth distribution in this sense. By contrast, a rather extensive body of information has been built up with respect to the distribution of income. In the United States in the late 1970's, 18.1% of all households had incomes of over $25,000 and received 41.3% of all income, while 16.5% of households were in the low-income bracket (below $5,000) and received only 3% of all income.

Among U.S. families receiving income from wages or salaries in 1977, 25.5% were in the high-income bracket (over $25,000), and they received 78.7% of their total income from these sources. Only 1.7% of families receiving income from wages and salaries were in the lowest-income bracket (under $3,000), receiving 58.4% of their income from these sources.

Among families receiving income from dividends, interest, and rent, 32.6% were in the high-income bracket (6.2% of their total income was from these sources) and only 1.2% were in the low-income group (6% of their income was from these sources).

DISTRIBUTION OF WEALTH

Wealth Distribution. The distribution of wealth may also refer to distribution of control or use, as contrasted with ownership. Modern industrial and market economies, such as that of the United States, concentrate control and use of wealth in the form of productive equipment in large industrial and commercial units. Also banks, insurance companies, and investment trusts concentrate large financial holdings of industrial assets in the form of stocks and bonds by acting largely as intermediaries for individual savers and investors. Thus these types of organizations are called financial intermediaries. It is this type of financial and industrial organization that both facilitates the accumulation of wealth and raises problems of social control and management.

In certain other respects, however, there is a large diffusion of certain kinds of wealth in prosperous economies such as the United States. It has been estimated that approximately one fourth of the wealth of the United States is in the form of residences and durable consumer goods. Early in the 1970's about 63% of all occupied dwelling units were owned by their occupants. Late in the 1970's about 48% of all households owned at least one automobile, while 99.9% of households had at least one television set. The wide distribution of a variety of household appliances is well known. The wealth allocation required by the various industries has become of major interest as efforts are extended for the development of the underindustrialized nations of the world. The investment requirements in capital goods for the different industries are often expressed as capital coefficients indicating the amount of capital (wealth) of different kinds required per unit of industrial output.

Distribution of wealth may also refer to geographic distribution. This may refer to different regions of a nation or to the distribution among nations. In either of these respects also, more is known about income than wealth. It may generally be presumed, however, that income and wealth distributions by geographic areas are significantly correlated. It will suffice for the purposes of this article merely to note that the United States, as compared with the rest of the world, is extremely wealthy. This can be brought out by noting that the world population is approximately 4.4 billion people, of which some 226.5 million or 5% comprise the population of the United States. This 5% of the world's population probably has about one third of the world's income and certainly as much of the world's wealth. But China and India, which together account for more than one third of the world's population, probably have no more than 8 or 9% of the world's income or wealth.

See also INCOME; STANDARD OF LIVING.

RAYMOND T. BOWMAN
Assistant Director of Statistical Standards Bureau of the Budget

Bibliography

Atkinson, Anthony B., and Harrison, J. J., *Wealth* (Pergamon Press 1978).
Cook, Wade, *Real Wealth* (Warner Bks. 1986).
Dodd, M. H., *Theories of Value and Distribution Since Adam Smith* (Cambridge 1975).
Foxley, Alejandro, ed., *Income Distribution in Latin America* (Cambridge 1976).
Giesbrecht, Martin, *Wealth of People* (Kaufmann 1977).
Hamberg, Daniel, *Economic Growth and Instability* (Greenwood Press 1978).
Handlin, Oscar, and Handlin, M. F., *The Wealth of the American People: A History of American Affluence* (McGraw 1979).
Jones, Alice H., *American Colonial Wealth: Documents and Methods*, 3 vols. (Arno Press 1977).
Langmore, John, and Peetz, David, eds., *Wealth, Poverty, and Survival* (Allen & Unwin 1983).
Lebergott, Stanley, *The American Economy: Income, Wealth, and Want* (Princeton Univ. Press 1975).
Mayer, Thomas, *Permanent Income, Wealth, and Consumption* (Univ. of Calif. Press 1972).
Peterson, Wallace C., *Income, Employment, and Economic Growth*, 3d ed. (Norton 1974).
Walras, Leon, *Elements of Pure Economics: Or the Theory of Social Wealth*, tr. by William Jaffe (Porcupine Press 1984).
Weintraub, Sidney, *An Approach to the Theory of Income Distribution* (Greenwood Press 1972).

WEALTH OF NATIONS, The,

WEALTH OF NATIONS, The, the title by which Scottish economist Adam Smith's most famous work, *An Inquiry into the Nature and Causes of the Wealth of Nations*, first published in 1776, is generally known. It is commonly described as being one of the foundations of modern economic literature.

Labor and Value. *The Wealth of Nations* begins with an account of the gains in productivity to be had from extensive division of labor, the application of which necessarily leads to exchange. This, in turn, leads to the use of money. The common use of money implies the reduction of the "exchangeable value" of commodities to terms of money, that is, to terms of price. Thus Smith is led to consider the relative values of things bought and sold in the market. This is the occasion for the statement of what has become known as Smith's labor theory of value, or perhaps more accurately as the labor theory aspect of Smith's theory of value: The value of any commodity is measured by the amount of labor, embodied in goods or services, which the owner of that commodity can command by offering it in exchange. However, the value of labor is itself invariable; that is, labor is not like a commodity in the sense of having a variable value; rather, "Equal quantities of labour, at all times and places, may be said to be of equal value to the labourer." Nevertheless, since it is obvious that different quantities of goods are, from time to time and place to place, given for identical amounts of labor, there is at the very least an appearance of variability in the valuableness of labor. To this extent Smith admitted a similarity between labor and commodities. Nevertheless, he maintained that it was the value of the things given in exchange for labor, not the value of labor, that underwent change. In fact, the foodstuff of laborers would, more nearly than any other thing, have a constant power to command labor, or be constant in value. This means that, by and large, over long periods, a day's labor will tend to bring the seller of it a fairly unvarying compensation in terms of food.

Smith's reason for this line of thinking lay in his assumption that the size of the population responds to the increased or decreased availability of food ("corn"). The number of people increase as food becomes more abundant and decreases as it becomes less so, which keeps the share of each consumer more or less steady. "Equal quantities of labour," Smith observed, "will at distant times be purchased more nearly with equal quantities of corn, the subsistence of the laborer, than with equal quantities of gold and silver, or perhaps of any other commodity." His analysis is thus connected with a form of the subsistence theory of wages and with the population concept that men tend to breed up to the level of subsistence.

Smith discusses the price of commodities as a composite of the rewards going to those who supply the means for producing the thing in question. Thus the price of each good is the sum of the rent, wages, and profit received respectively by the landowners, laborers, and owners of the stock of food and implements used by the laborers during their work. Not only each price but the whole revenue of the people is ultimately reducible to wages, profit, and rent. As to price itself, Smith distinguishes between natural and market price. The natural price is the sum of the natural wages, rent, and profit of those who produce the good, with the understanding that "natural" in this context means what is average or usual to all laborers, landlords, and entrepreneurs in the given neighborhood or society. The market price, which need not at any stated time equal the natural price, is governed by the mutual pressure of supply and demand.

Since the natural price depends upon the natural rates of wages, rent, and profit, Smith must go on to explain the circumstances that control these latter. He traces them to (1) the institutions that prevail in the community and (2) what would now be called the dynamic conditions present in the economy: "the advancing, stationary, or declining state of the society." These in turn are related to the supply of and demand for the primary factors of production—labor, land, and capital. Smith's treatment of that subject led him into broad speculations on wages, population, rent, capital formation, and public policy.

The Nature of Capital. Smith was keenly conscious of the necessity to accumulate capital in order to increase the output of the nation. He classified capital as fixed and circulating, the latter to include money, itself something which is instrumental and neutral to the economic process and hence of a quantity governed by the objective needs of the economy. Partly because he conceived money as simply a passive instrument of circulation, he was bound to argue that the export of monetary metal was not in itself harmful; rather it pointed to a surplus of money within the nation, the export of which is reminiscent of a salutary bloodletting.

Mercantilism. Smith's teaching with respect to the export of money, or gold, was part of his doctrine with respect to restraints on commerce generally. At the time of his writing, the belief was by no means extinct that economic life—indeed the particular economic actions of individuals needed considerable supervision for the sake of the public interest. The view that unguided economic activity might—even must—have consequences harmful to many individuals as well as to the people collectively and to the sovereign is central to the position called "mercantilism." It could be regarded as regulation of economic activity mainly to produce an excess of exports of goods and services over imports, with everything that that implies. Mercantilism was a feature of European policy in the few centuries prior to Smith's writing and was still widespread in his day despite the emergence in France, among the so-called "physiocrats," of the theory that came to be known as laissez faire.

Smith believed that mercantilistic practices were designed by, and for the singular benefit of, particular classes rather than the whole community. It is clear that mercantilism dictated a policy of far-reaching domestic regulation as well as control of foreign trade, but Smith's larger emphasis is on the latter. He is renowned for his massive rejection of mercantilism, or more affirmatively for his advocacy of free commercial relations both internally and among the nations. His argument, however, was not doctrinaire. It conceded the usefulness of control in behalf, for example, of military preparedness. But the main point of his position is that the measure of harmony between private and public interests decisely outweighs the measure of tension between them. From this point the conclusion is reached that the public interest is best served when individuals are left largely free to seek their own gain. The public interest is an unintended by-product of their aggregate acquisitive activity. Smith's aversion to a policy of unusual interventions in favor of merchant activity was accompanied by an equal aversion to such a policy in favor of agriculture. He believed that natural necessity dictated better than government could the order in which economic activities should be undertaken and the amount of emphasis properly belonging to each. The history of Europe illustrated, perhaps embodied, the force generated by men's strivings as they respond to the necessities with which nature confronts them. Government is not by any means left without a role. Rather its duties are proportioned to the degree in which human wisdom and virtue must defer to the surpassing power of men's raw nature.

Influence. *The Wealth of Nations* deserves its reputation as a masterpiece of economics. Many of the issues and problems that have occupied, perhaps will always occupy, social scientists, are raised. Smith's theory of value, of population, and of distribution was of profound influence upon the literature that grew under the hands of David Ricardo, Thomas Malthus, Karl Marx, and their contemporaries. His conception of the wealth of the nation as related to its annual income was by his writing forever impressed on the substance of economics. His speculations on public finance, on the nature of costs, and on a score of other subjects will always be relevant.

The broad teaching of Smith's work has had an immeasurable influence on public practice and private conviction, and the book as a whole represents a most ingenious and successful application of abstract principles to concrete circumstances. Those remote principles had sprung up in widely separated places between Niccolò Machiavelli and David Hume. Their juxtaposition, in *The Wealth of Nations,* with a cogent and well conceived economic doctrine, accounts for the great interest of the book.

JOSEPH CROPSEY
The University of Chicago

WEAPONS. See ARMORED FORCES; ARTILLERY; BOMB; BULLET; EXPLOSIVE; GUIDED MISSILE; GUN; GUNBOAT; GUNNERY; HYDROGEN BOMB; MINE, MILITARY; NUCLEAR WEAPONS; SMALL ARMS; SUBMARINE; TANK; TORPEDO; WEAPONS, PRIMITIVE.

AMERICAN MUSEUM OF NATURAL HISTORY

(Above) Neolithic stone axes with wooden handles, from France. *(Below)* A ballhead club made by the Iroquois of North America.

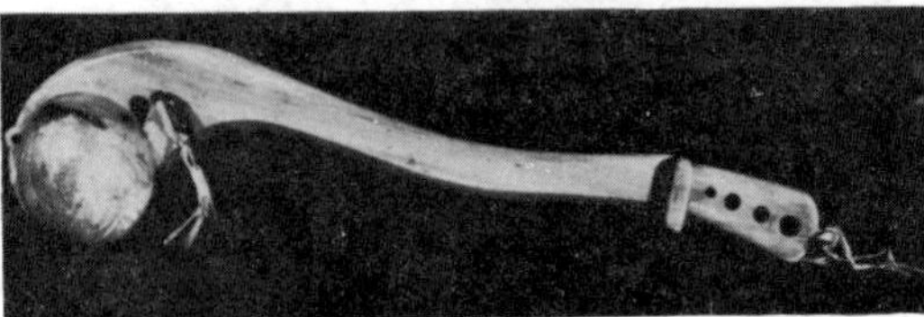

ROYAL ONTARIO MUSEUM, TORONTO

AMERICAN MUSEUM OF NATURAL HISTORY

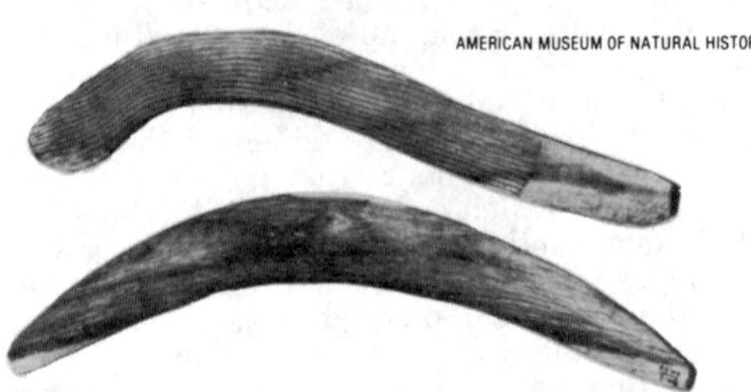

(Above) Two Australian boomerangs: a returning type placed below a nonreturning type.

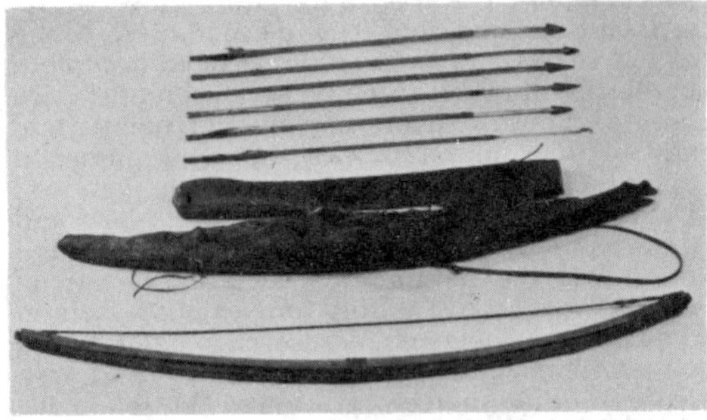

ROYAL ONTARIO MUSEUM, TORONTO

(Above) Bow, arrows, and quiver made by the Inuit of Canada's Northwest Territories. *(Below)* A sword and scabbard from Africa.

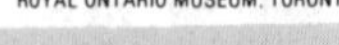

ROYAL ONTARIO MUSEUM, TORONTO

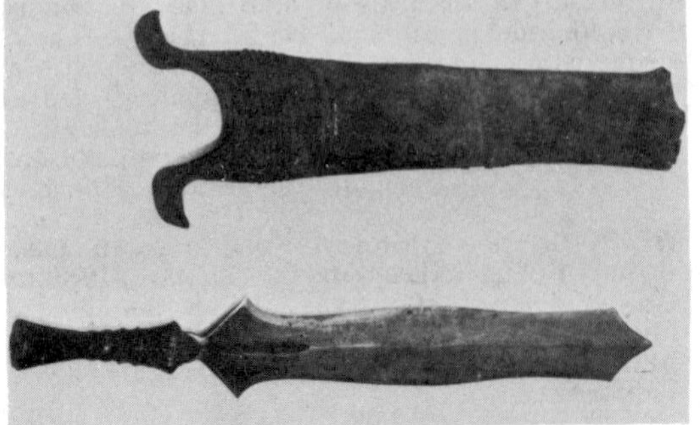

WEAPONS, Primitive. The bodily equipment of humans for combating or preying on other animals is slim; humans have no great strength and possess neither fangs nor claws. Among the tools extending their ability to cope with their environment are weapons for securing food and for defense.

Early humans of the Middle Pleistocene period (Ice Age) first used hand-held stones, to which they gave cutting edges, and also clubs; later the hafting of weapons extended the power of attack, with stone-bladed spears, stone axes, and, still later, arrows. The weapons of historical antiquity, persisting through the Middle Ages, were much like those of primitive peoples. The major change was the substitution of metals for stone, with a shift to the greater use of sword and knife. Improvements of the bow also were made in antiquity, producing the composite (reinforced) bow and crossbow, both with very powerful spring action, which threw a heavier missile to a greater distance and with greater penetration. The huge crossbows and slings developed as siege engines (corresponding to artillery) by the ancients, including the early Chinese, and by medieval Europeans were simply magnified forms of primitive weapons. With the invention of explosives, gun and cannon put an end to the primitive forms, yet as late as the 18th century the bow was considered as effective as the clumsy musket.

Primitive peoples' armament was little differentiated for war and hunt except as the nature of the quarry necessitated specialization. Supplementary weapons for both types of activity were furnished by traps and snares, often complex and ingenious. The commonest weapon was the club, usually given special form and handling, such as the cylindrical upward-thrust club of the Indians of the lower Colorado and the twisted return-boomerang of the Australian aboriginals. Other specialized weapons included the spear and its thrower, the rear end of the shaft engaging a stick held in the throwing hand, increasing the cast by extending the arm's reach. The blowgun (blowpipe) was a bamboo or wooden tube through which a tufted dart was blown by a forceful puff of breath. Each area had specialized equipment involving the acquisition of special skills in its handling.

Old World Specialization. Pacific islanders used mainly slings, javelins, long spears, and clubs. Shields were unknown. Exceptionally, Kiribatians had coconut-fiber armor as protection against spears and clubs edged with shark teeth. Bows were little used in Polynesia and Micronesia except where Melanesian influence was felt. In Melanesia the spear was preferred in eastern New Guinea and the Solomon Islands; the bow, elsewhere. Slings had a secondary use. Sword, spear, bow, blowgun, and shield equipped the Indonesians, with the bow predominating in the east and the blowgun (using clay pellets or poisoned darts) in the west. Many Southeast Asians made use of a crossbow. Central Asian mounted warriors relied on short composite bows (a practice shared with the Chinese and Japanese) and bore sword, mace, lance, and heavy whips, with shield and hide cuirass for protection. In northern Asia, reliance was on bow and spear.

Everywhere in Africa south of the Mediterranean zone, except in the extreme south, primitives used iron-headed spears and knives. Northerly people southward through the Congo Basin and toward the northeast coast used swords and clubs; throwing knives (often multibladed) characterized the northern Congo Basin and javelins the east. Slings were in use in east and west coastal areas. Only in a few regions near the west coast, as well as among Pygmies of Zaire and Bushmen of the southern African deserts, were bows primary weapons. Body armor was worn in the western Sudan, sometimes chain mail, a derivative from the Mediterranean. Skin shields were carried in the eastern parts of the continent, wicker or reed shields in the Congo area.

New World Specialization. In South America, throwing weapons prevailed in the open country and the bow and blowgun in the forests. Peoples of the Andes preferred stone-casting slings, macelike clubs, thrusting lances, darts, and spear throwers. In the warfare of Inca days, auxiliary companies of forest people using their customary bows were organized. In the central and southern plains dependence was on bolas, throwing clubs, and lances, with bows less commonly employed. The horse, introduced from Europe, augmented use of the throwing weapons and lance, discouraging use of the bow.

North American Indians gave first place to the bow, with supplementary use of club, ax, and short spear. On the introduction of the horse, the reinforced bow known in the Northwest and in the Plains was adapted in the latter area for use on horseback. Stone-headed clubs were common east of the Rockies and flat forms east of the Mississippi. Some of the latter had protruding spikes, others a weighted head. Shields afforded protection widely east of the Rockies and in the Southwest, while body armor of hide or linked slats was used in the Northwest. Cotton-quilted armor, sling, spear thrower, and obsidian-studded swords were central Mexican specializations. Warriors there and northward to the lower Colorado tribes were specialized so that those armed with clubs and swords operated tactically in balance with companies of bowmen.

LESLIE SPIER
University of New Mexico

ROBERT J. ERWIN/PHOTO RESEARCHERS

Weasels make themselves useful in rural areas by killing mice and other pests. *(Above)* Long-tailed weasel in winter coat. *(Below)* Least weasel in summer coat.

KARL H. MASLOWSKI/PHOTO RESEARCHERS

WEARING APPAREL. See CLOTHING; CLOTHING INDUSTRY; DRESS; and the Index entry *Dress*.

WEASEL, wē'zəl, in American usage, any small species of the genus *Mustela* of carnivorous mammals, to which the larger mink, ferret, and European polecat also belong. The British restrict the name to the species *M. nivalis,* which in America is called "least weasel." This and a larger weasel, the ermine, occur all across northern North America, Asia, and Europe. The British refer to the ermine *(M. erminea)* as the stoat. The still larger long-tailed weasel *(M. frenata),* the best-known American species, occurs from southern Canada to South America. The male is about 18 inches (45 cm) in length, of which the tail makes up a third. The female, about a fifth shorter, is half as heavy.

Each of the three species molts into a white winter coat in the northern part of its geographic range. In summer the upper parts, tail, and outside of the legs are uniform reddish brown, and the underparts white or yellowish white. The part of the taii nearest the body is black in all seasons except in *M. nivalis.* The slender body, strong flexible neck, flattened head, and short legs (each having five toes with sharp, compressed, curved claws) enable the weasel to pass through any opening that admits its head. The teeth are highly specialized for a diet of flesh. Among mammals the weasel is unsurpassed in speed of killing mice and some animals larger than itself. When given the opportunity, it may kill more food than it needs immediately, storing the excess for future consumption. In temperate latitudes, weasels help to check undue increases of rodents that damage cultivated crops.

The long-tailed weasel, annually about April, bears a single litter of up to nine young in an enlargement of a burrow in the ground after an average gestation period of 279 days. After months of quiescence the fertilized eggs become attached to the uterus and in less than 27 days develop into full-term embryos. Implantation of the eggs is delayed also in the ermine, but not in the least weasel.

Other species that never become white are: in South America, the tropical weasel *(M. africana);* in Asia, the Altai weasel *(M. altaica),* the yellow-bellied weasel *(M. kathiah),* the Siberian weasel *(M. siberica),* and, in India, the back-striped weasel *(M. strigidorsa).* Australia and most oceanic islands lack weasels. In the southern halves of South America and Africa other small mustelid mammals replace weasels.

E. RAYMOND HALL
University of Kansas

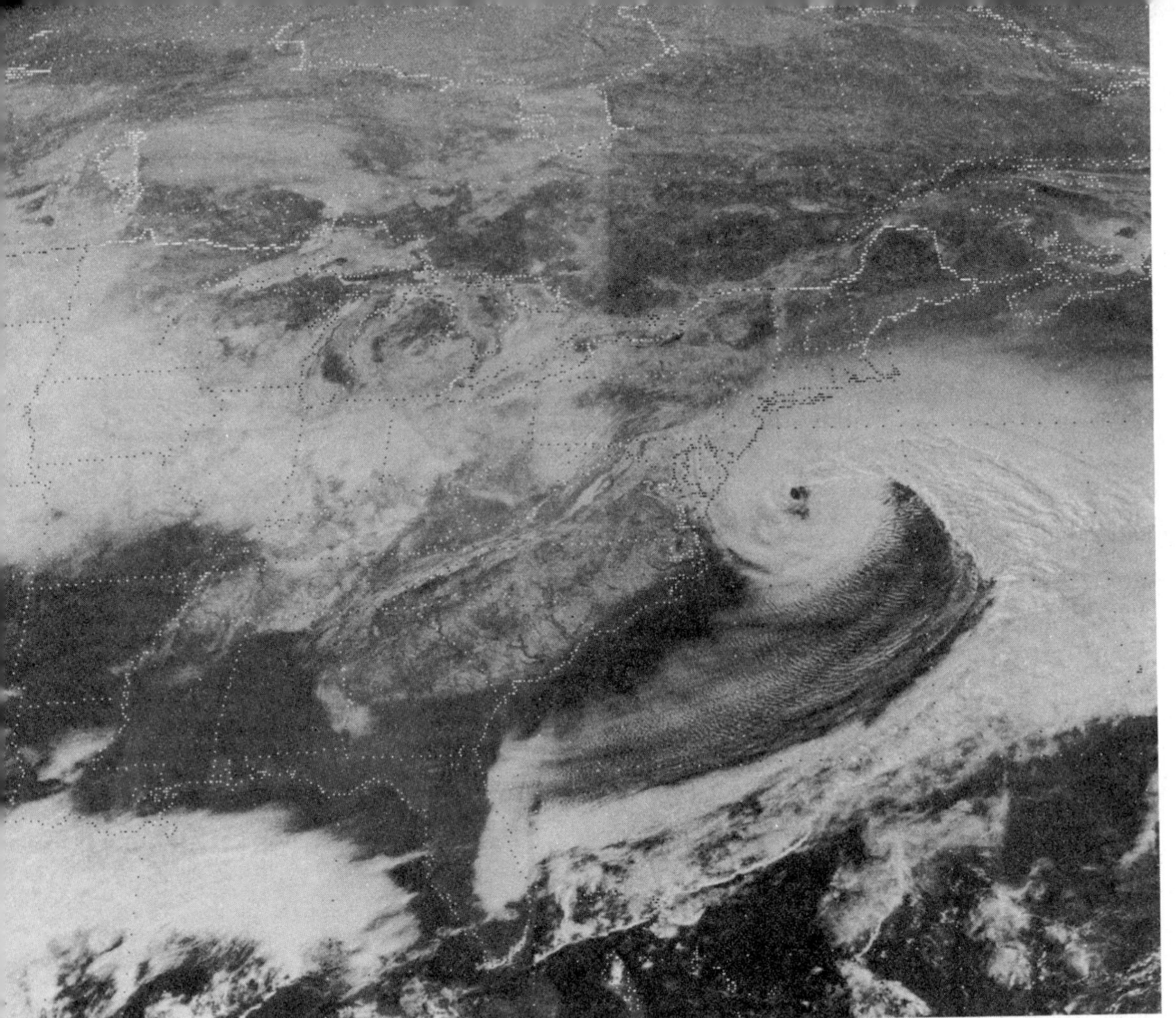

COURTESY NOAA/NATIONAL EARTH SATELLITE SERVICE

Weather satellite photograph of a stage-3 cyclone.

WEATHER. Weather affects all aspects of human endeavor. Thousands of lives are lost each year through weather-related disasters involving flash floods, lightning strikes, tornadoes, and severe snow and ice storms. Direct economic losses amount to hundreds of millions and even billions of dollars a year. Indirect losses are substantially higher. Environmental influences such as sustained high air-pollution levels in major urban areas pose a long-term threat to human health and produce short-term economic losses in the agricultural industry.

Weather, a general term, refers to aspects of the atmosphere near the observer—such as temperature, humidity, and whether conditions are fair or rainy. The weather of a region, considered over a period of many years, is called the climate of that region. (See also CLIMATE.) Weather takes place primarily in the lower 6 miles (10 km) of the atmosphere.

ELEMENTS OF WEATHER

Weather is a complex phenomenon. Basic elements of weather include pressure, temperature, wind, moisture, and precipitation.

Pressure. Imagine a column of air extending from sea level to the top of the atmosphere. This column has weight. In English units, if the area of the bottom of the column is one square inch, the weight of the column would be about 14.7 pounds. Thus, atmospheric pressure at sea level is about 14.7 pounds per square inch. Meteorologists are accustomed to measuring atmospheric pressure in the metric unit millibar, abbreviated mb. A newer metric (SI) unit coming into general use is the kilopascal (kPa). Normal atmospheric pressure at sea level is 1013.2 mb, or 101.3 kPa. (For convenience, mb will be used in this article.)

Atmospheric pressure can differ considerably from what is considered "normal." Two examples of extreme sea-level atmospheric pressure are 870 mb in a Pacific typhoon and 1084 mb in a polar high-pressure center. (Unless specified otherwise, pressure figures indicate pressure at sea level. At higher altitudes pressure decreases.)

Weather maps contain lines called *isobars*. An isobar is a line that connects points of equal pressure. Fig. 1 shows several isobars around a center of high pressure.

Temperature. Most countries measure temperature in degrees Celsius or centigrade, abbreviated °C. (Surface temperature in the United States is still measured in degrees Fahrenheit, or °F.) The global average temperature is about 15°C (59°F). To measure temperature, a thermometer should be placed in the shade in a well-ventilated location about 1.5 meters (5 feet) above the ground.

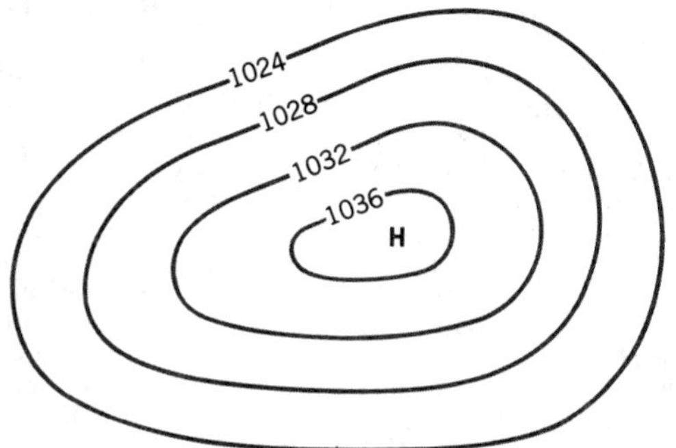

Fig. 1. An isobar is a line that connects points of equal pressure. For example, all points on the outermost isobar shown are at a pressure of 1,024 millibars. The point of highest pressure is marked **H.**

Wind. Winds are identified by the direction from which they blow. They are usually measured in knots (kt) at the surface and in meters per second (m/sec) in the rest of the atmosphere. One knot is one nautical mile per hour (1.15 statute miles per hour, or 0.52 m/sec).

Moisture. Moisture refers to the water vapor that is dissolved in air. The water vapor is in invisible, gaseous form. At a constant pressure, the higher the temperature of the air, the more water it can hold in solution. The capacity of the air to hold water vapor roughly doubles for every 10 Celsius degrees of increase in temperature. Air at 30°C (86°F) can hold twice as much water vapor as air at 20°C (68 °F) and four times as much as air at 10°C (50°F), for example.

Relative Humidity. The ratio of the amount of water vapor in the air to the maximum amount the air can hold at that temperature is called the *relative humidity*. It is expressed as a percentage. Air that holds the maximum amount of water vapor possible is said to be saturated; its relative humidity is 100%. Suppose that a body of air at 10°C and with a relative humidity of 100% is heated to 20°C, with the pressure and the amount of moisture kept constant. Its relative humidity would then be 50%, because at that temperature it can hold twice as much water vapor.

Dew Point Temperature. A useful indicator of atmospheric moisture content is the *dew point temperature*. When a body of unsaturated air is cooled (with no change in pressure) to the temperature at which it becomes saturated, that temperature is called its dew point. The more moisture in the air, the higher the dew point of that body of air.

Clouds. Another indication of atmospheric moisture is the presence of cloud or fog. Clouds can be grouped into three predominant types: high—6 miles (10 km); middle—3 miles (5 km); and low—0.6 mile (1 km). Fog is simply a low cloud that touches the ground. Flat clouds are called stratus; puffy ones are called cumulus. Layered clouds such as cirrostratus (high), altostratus (middle), and nimbostratus (low) are common across the United States in winter; they are often associated with prolonged spells of bad weather. Cumuloform clouds dominate the country during the warm season. The thunderstorm cloud, cumulonimbus, is by far the most spectacular cloud. It is usually a very tall cloud and is associated with the brief, violent thunderstorms of spring and summer.

The cloudiest regions in the United States are the northwest Pacific coast and the Great Lakes; the clearest regions are in the extreme southwest. A clear day is defined as one in which the local cloud cover averages 30% or less.

Precipitation. The average annual precipitation across the United States is about 30 inches (750 mm). Rainfall characteristics vary from place to place, even for places with the same annual rainfall. For example, Buffalo, N.Y., Kansas City, Mo., and Seattle, Wash., all have annual precipitation totals of about 35 inches (900 mm). However, rainfall is evenly distributed throughout the year in Buffalo, with slightly more in winter; Kansas City gets most of its rain in the warm season, particularly in May and June; and Seattle gets most of its rain in winter.

GLOBAL CIRCULATION

The basis of weather is the unequal heating of the combined atmosphere-ocean system of the earth. Because of the earth's rotation around its axis, the tropical regions (regions near the equator) are heated more than the polar regions. Yet we do not observe the tropical regions to be getting steadily hotter and the poles to be getting steadily colder. This is because the excess heat of the tropics is routinely transported to the polar regions. This transport of heat is accomplished primarily by the movement of air in the atmosphere; it is called the general circulation of the atmosphere. The transport of heat to the poles is also carried out by oceanic circulations. For example, the Gulf Stream east of North America and the Kuroshio (Japan) Current east of Japan carry enormous amounts of heat northward toward the pole.

Circulation Models. To understand the nature of the global circulation, it is best to start with very simple—indeed, oversimplified—models. When air is heated, it expands and becomes less dense. It therefore rises. Since air at the equator is heated the most, it rises. Cold air is dense and tends to sink. This takes place in the cold polar regions. Thus in our simple model the global circulation of the atmosphere would assume the pattern shown in Fig. 2. Warm air would rise at the equator and diverge at high altitudes to move toward the poles. Cold air sinks at the poles and moves along the surface toward the equator. Thus in the Northern Hemisphere there would always be a north wind, and in the Southern Hemisphere there would always be a south wind.

Coriolis Effect. The simple circulation pattern described above does not exist. The reason is that we live on a rotating planet. This rotation gives rise to a phenomenon called the Coriolis effect.

The Coriolis effect can be demonstrated by a simple experiment. Put an old record on a record player and turn on the machine. Let us assume that this record player turns in a counterclockwise direction rather than in the usual clockwise direction. Place a straight-edge or a ruler just above the spinning record. With a sharp knife cut into the record from the center of the record out to the rim along the straight edge. Do this quickly. Turn off the record player and examine the newly scratched record. The "straight" line that was scratched with the aid of the ruler is in fact a curved line on the record. It curves to the right as it travels from the center of the record to the rim. The reason is that while

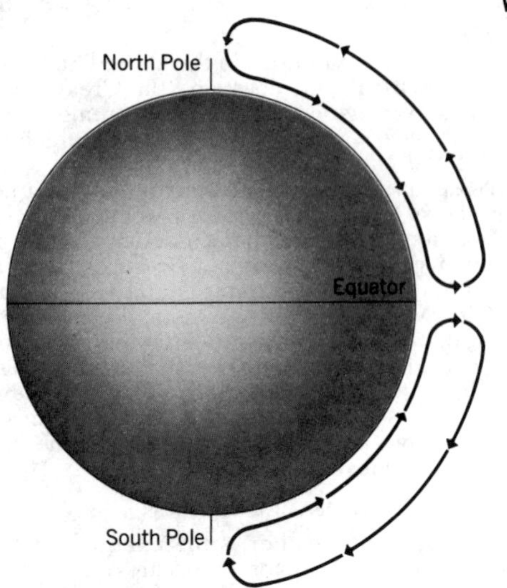

Fig. 2. Cold, sinking air at the poles and warm, rising air at the equator would produce this simple circulation pattern if other factors were not present.

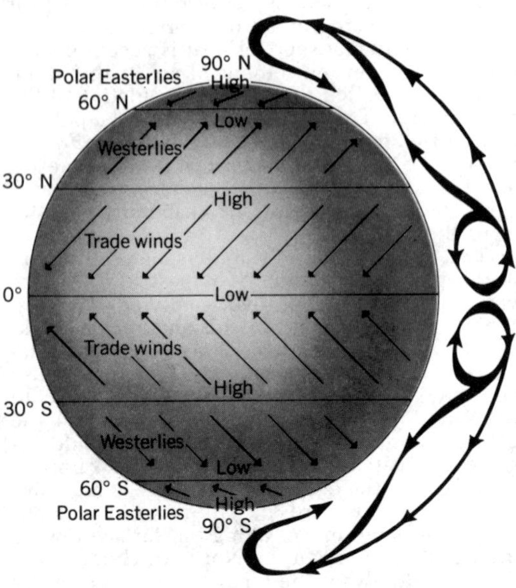

Fig. 3. The actual, very complicated circulation pattern of the atmosphere is shown here in schematic form.

the knife is moving away from the center of the record in a straight line, the surface of the record is moving to the left underneath it. Therefore, relative to the surface of the record, the knife is moving along a path that curves to the right. Now imagine that you are standing at the North Pole. (It is analogous to the center of the record.) You fire a high-speed bullet horizontally. As the bullet travels away from you, the surface of the earth is moving left (from west to east) underneath it. Thus, although the bullet travels in a straight line relative to you, it is curving to the right relative to the surface of the earth.

Further examples would show that this curving to the right is true of all bullets (or any other moving body, such as a body of air) in the Northern Hemisphere, no matter what particular spot you fire from or what direction you fire in. In the Southern Hemisphere the bullet would curve to the left. (Only for motion directly east or west along the equator is there no sideways deflection.) This rightward deflection in the Northern Hemisphere is called the Coriolis effect. We usually do not notice this effect because it is so insignificant over short distances. For example, suppose that in a football stadium located at 40° north latitude, a punter kicks a ball for 50 yards, with the ball in the air for 5 seconds. Would the receiver have to worry about the Coriolis effect? The answer is no because the deflection would be less than half an inch.

Actual Circulation. Because of the Coriolis effect, the actual circulation pattern of the atmosphere is quite complex. It is shown (again in simplified, schematic form) in Fig. 3. There are areas of high pressure at the poles and along latitudes 30°N and 30°S, and there are areas of low pressure along the equator and latitudes 60°N and 60°S. Winds move from areas of high pressure to areas of low pressure. The circulation pattern above the ground is also shown in Fig. 3. There is rising at the equator and sinking at the poles, as in Fig. 2, but more complex patterns exist within this overall pattern.

A more realistic picture of surface pressures and winds is given in Fig. 4, which also shows the variation in the pattern between summer and winter. The easterlies that typically are found in the equatorial and tropical regions are separated by belts of high pressure from the westerlies typical of the middle latitudes. (These belts are not neat straight lines falling exactly along latitudes 30°N and 30°S, as shown schematically in Fig. 3, but are curved and shift with the seasons.) Air sinks along these belts, producing clear skies. Most of the world's major deserts are located in these subtropical high-pressure belts. From these belts, the climate changes significantly toward the equator and toward the poles. The heavy line in the maps in Fig. 4 is the intertropical convergence zone (ITCZ), where northeast winds from the Northern Hemisphere and southeast winds from the Southern Hemisphere meet. On charts of monthly average weather, a distinct east-west cloud can be seen across the Pacific and Atlantic Oceans along the ITCZ. The cloudiness and precipitation along this region are caused by warm, moist air rising and cooling to below its dew point.

Movement Around Highs and Lows. Air moves from centers of high pressure to centers of low pressure. However, it does not move directly from the highs to the lows, as in Fig. 5a. Rather, because of the Coriolis effect, it moves along curved paths. In the Northern Hemisphere, air moving out of a high and turning to the right would produce a clockwise spin around the high; air moving into a low would produce a counterclockwise spin around the low. In the Southern Hemisphere this is reversed: counterclockwise around a high and clockwise around a low.

A typical circulation pattern found on the earth's surface can be seen in Fig. 5b. The winds tend to cross the isobars at an oblique angle, primarily because of friction between the moving air and the surface. A useful rule in the Northern Hemisphere is: if you stand with your back to the wind, the *l*ow will be on your *l*eft.

Higher up in the atmosphere—above the friction layer or lowest kilometer—a balance can be

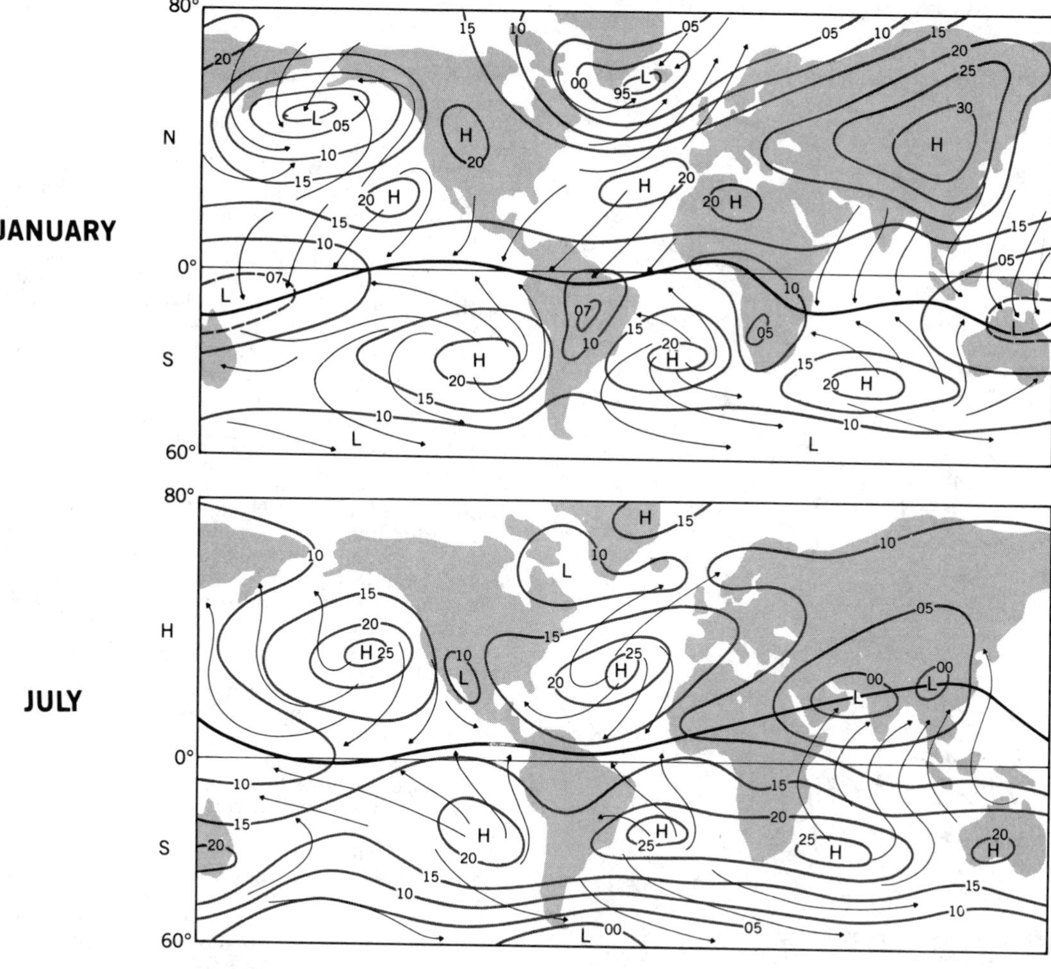

Fig. 4. The pattern of pressure and wind *(shown by arrows)* varies from season to season.

reached between the Coriolis effect, which tends to continuously deflect the wind to the side, and the force arising from differences in pressure, which tends to move the air directly from high to low. This balance is called *geostrophic equilibrium*. Under geostrophic equilibrium, air moves parallel to the isobars, as in Fig. 5c.

Storm Belt. A major storm belt is found in the middle latitudes between 40° and 60° north latitude. Semipermanent low-pressure centers are found near Iceland and south of the Aleutians in January. During July the Icelandic low is weakened and displaced farther northward while the Aleutian low nearly disappears (see Fig. 4). This change is accompanied by a northward displacement and strengthening of the oceanic subtropical highs—a development that exerts a major influence on the climate of the west coast of middle-latitude continents. For example, the clockwise circulation around high-pressure centers in the Northern Hemisphere produces north to northwesterly surface winds along the Pacific coast of the United States. The ocean responds to this persistent wind stress as well as the Coriolis effect in such a way that surface water is forced to move to the right—that is to the west—of the prevailing wind. The net effect is that oceanic surface water is forced to move away from the coast. Water from deeper in the ocean rises to the surface to replace the water that has been forced westward—a process called *upwelling*. This upwelled water tends to be considerably colder than the surface water that it replaces, as swimmers along the coast of central California and Oregon can attest.

Effects of Upwelling. On a global basis the climatic consequences of upwelling are profound. Relatively cold water is found along the west coasts of continents in both hemispheres—for example, California, Peru, northwest Africa, and southwest Australia. During summer the overlying air tends to be warmer than the sea surface. The air also is rather dry owing to the gradual sinking and warming on the eastern margin of the subtropical high. The warm air in contact with the relatively cold sea surface creates a situation in which the air temperature tends to increase upward from just above the surface to about 5,000 feet (1,500 meters) above the ground. (Above this level the temperature again decreases upward.) This upward increase is in direct contrast to the normally observed decrease of temperature with increasing elevation. Vertical mixing of air is not favored under such conditions. Under such conditions satellite photographs often reveal the presence of thin stratocumulus clouds and fog patches over the ocean and adjacent coastal regions, while just inland the weather is characteristically sunny and warm. The lack of vertical mixing means that populated areas will suffer repeated buildups of pollutants from a variety of sources, primarily

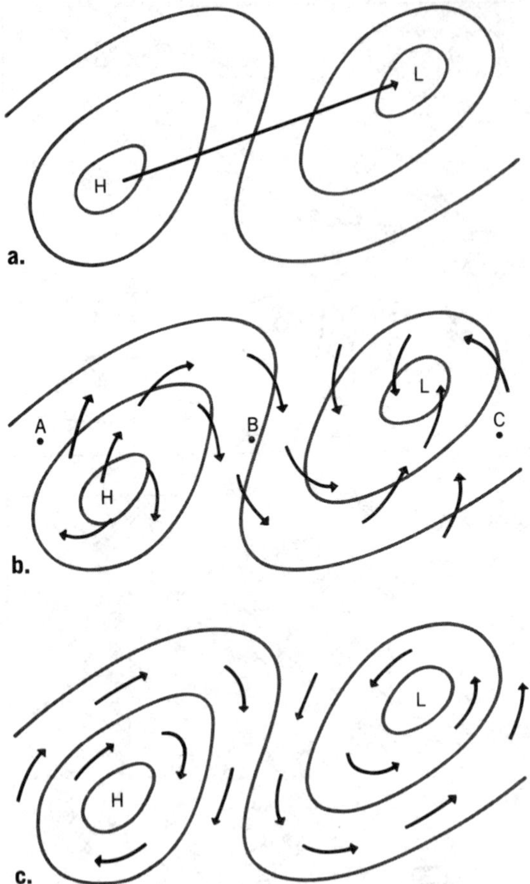

Fig. 5. Air does not move directly from high to low, as shown in **a.** Instead, because of the Coriolis effect, it moves along curved paths. Surface winds in the Northern Hemisphere typically move in the pattern shown in **b.** Part **c** shows the wind pattern higher up.

automobile exhaust. Excessive automobile usage combined with a lower atmosphere that is not well mixed makes Los Angeles the most polluted major metropolitan area in the United States.

A comparison of the weather of San Diego and Charleston is instructive. These two cities are located at approximately the same latitude, but the summer weather is as different as night and day. San Diego's weather is sunny and warm with little, if any, rain for the reasons given above. Charleston is very warm and uncomfortably humid, with frequent afternoon showers and thunderstorms. Upwelling is not a factor in the Charleston climate. The South Atlantic coast is located along the western margin of the subtropical high-pressure belt. The clockwise circulation around the high-pressure region in the Atlantic brings warm, moist air northward along the coast. Such air is generally unstable, and afternoon heating is often sufficient to set off numerous showers and thunderstorms.

500-mb Pressure Surface. In order to understand how the surface wind and pressure patterns evolve, it is necessary to examine the wind and pressure pattern in the middle and upper troposphere. (The troposphere extends from the ground to about 5 to 12 miles, or 8 to 20 km.) Meteorologists find it useful to consider all points in the atmosphere that are at a certain pressure. These points form a surface. Such a surface is depicted in Fig. 6. The surface shown is the 500-mb surface. The lines are analogous to the contour lines (height contours) that connect points of equal elevation on a topographic map. For example, the outer line in the January map in Fig. 6 connects points at an altitude of 5,850 meters (5.85 kilometers, or 3.63 miles) and with a pressure of 500 mb. The next inner line connects points at an altitude of 5,790 meters and with a pressure of 500 mb, and so forth. On a flat map we can think of this 500-mb surface as a shallow pit, with the bottom located over the letter L within the 4,940-meter height contour and the rim located over the tropics. The slope of the pit is steepest where the height contours are close together, and gentlest where the height contours are far apart. Actually, no part of the surface is steep. On the average, the surface slopes about 0.6 mile (1 km) from the subtropics (the outer lines) to the polar regions (the inner lines), a distance of 3,000 miles (5,000 km). So for all practical purposes the 500-mb surface is "horizontal," yet the miniscule slope of 1/5,000 is vital to the wind pattern. The greater the north-south slope of the 500-mb surface, the stronger the winds will be.

If the Coriolis effect did not exist, the winds would move directly from the rim of the pit to the bottom; they would be stronger where the slope is steeper (height contours close together) and weaker where the slope is gentler. However, as soon as the parcels of air start to move, the Coriolis effect comes into play. In the Northern Hemisphere, it causes the air parcels to deviate to the right (eastward) as they move from the tropics northward to the polar regions. Ultimately an equilibrium is reached whereby the individual air parcels are moving just fast enough for the Coriolis effect to balance the tendency of the air parcels to move from south to north. Under this balance, or geostrophic equilibrium, the air parcels (the winds) move parallel to the height contours from west to east. The closer together the height contours the stronger the wind. A belt of strong westerlies is marked in the January map of Fig. 6.

The maps in Fig. 6 are typical of the 500-mb surface in the Northern Hemisphere. Note that the surface in both maps is higher over the tropics (the "rim") than over the polar regions. This is because the air over the tropics is warmer than the air over the polar regions. Warm air occupies more space than cold air. A column of warm air extending from the ground to the 500-mb level would be taller than a column of cold air extending from the ground to the 500-mb level.

Over certain parts of the tropics, the 500-mb surface slopes down toward the equator. As air parcels move down this slope from the tropics toward the equator, the Coriolis effect again makes them turn to the right, and geostrophic equilibrium results in an east wind over some parts of the tropics.

Seasonal Variation. Various seasonal changes can be seen in Fig. 6. In both summer and winter there is a westerly flow of wind above the mid-latitudes, but the general pattern of flow is stronger in winter than in summer. From winter to summer, the band of strongest westerly flow over the Northern Hemisphere is displaced northward by 10 to 15 degrees of latitude, and its speed drops by about a half. The seasonal north-

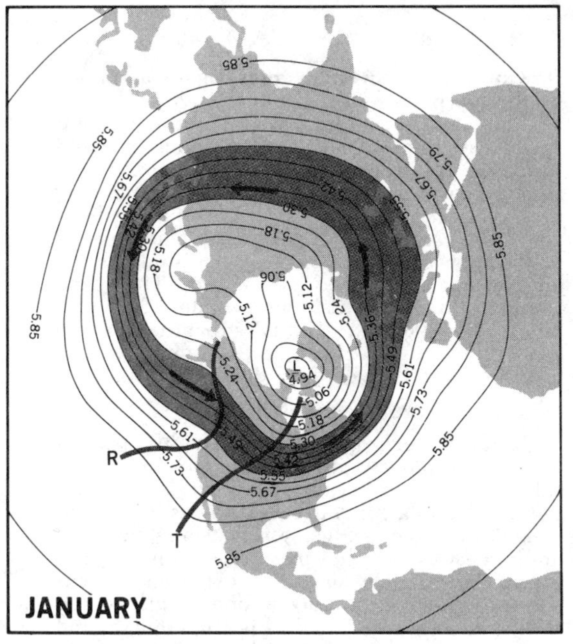

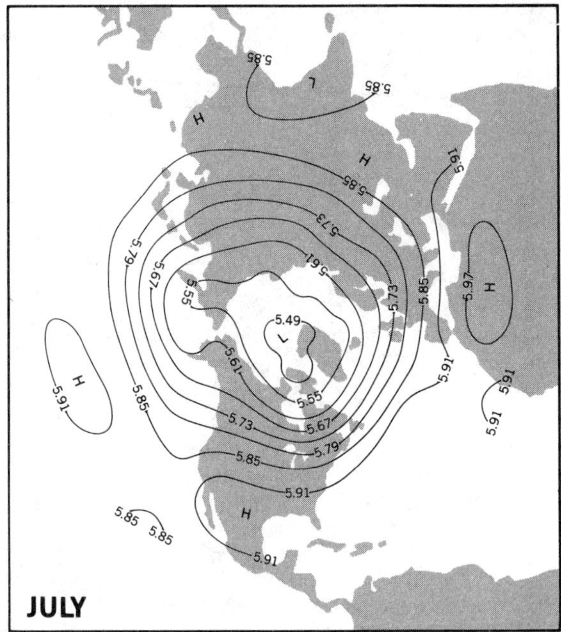

Fig. 6. If all points in the atmosphere that are at a certain pressure are considered together, they form a continuous surface. The surfaces shown are the 500-millibar surface in January and in July. Such a surface can be thought of as a gently rolling prairie with low points at each L and high points at each H. The contour lines show the height above sea level in kilometers. The closer the lines, the steeper the slope and the stronger the wind.

south shift of this band is greater over land than over the ocean. Corresponding changes take place in the Southern Hemisphere, but the variations are not as great.

Troughs and Ridges. Weather is closely associated with what meteorologists call pressure troughs and ridges. These can be visualized with the help of Fig. 7, which shows an imaginary pit in the earth, with the bottom at the letter L. The height contours represent increasing elevations away from the bottom. If we walked from the bottom up to the rim along line A, we would be along the bottom of a valley, or trough. If we walked up along line B, we would be along the crest of a ridge. Line C again represents a trough. A trough is located where height contours curve away from the bottom, and a ridge is located where height contours curve toward the bottom.

Using this analogy of a land surface, let us again look at the pressure surface in the January map of Fig. 6. Along the west coast of the United States, the westerlies from the Pacific travel northward before they turn southward again toward the eastern United States. The height contours along the west coast curve northward (toward the low, the bottom of the pressure surface). They represent a ridge. This ridge is indicated by the line R. Eastward from the ridge is a trough, indicated by the line T. On the average, three to six trough-ridge pairs are found in the Northern Hemisphere.

The region from a trough eastward toward the downstream ridge is characterized by a broad southwesterly flow in the middle and upper troposphere, and by warm, moist air moving in from lower latitudes. Most of the major rain-producing systems in the Northern Hemisphere are found in these regions of westerly flow. In contrast, the northwesterly flow region between the ridge and downstream trough is characterized by cooler, drier air moving in from higher latitudes. Such regions then have typically clear skies.

Direct observation reveals that the atmosphere is characterized by a progression of troughs and ridges in the mid-latitude westerlies. At any given point, trough and ridge conditions alternate. Deteriorating weather and precipitation can be expected in the wake of a ridge as an upstream trough begins to approach a given place. After the passage of the trough, the sky usually clears and pleasant weather returns as the next ridge approaches. At most mid-latitude locations in the Northern Hemisphere, the rate of alternation of troughs and ridges depends on the season. Typical values might be four to five

Fig. 7. To understand the concept of troughs and ridges, imagine walking from the bottom of a pit (L) up to the rim. If our path is along **A** or **C**, we would be walking along the bottom of a trough. If our path is along **B**, we would be walking along the top of a ridge.

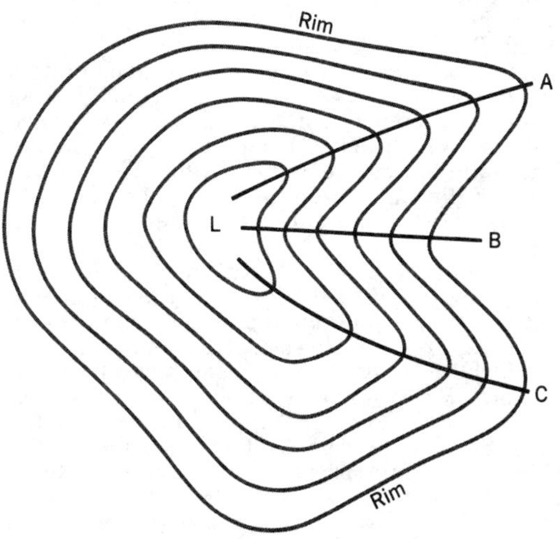

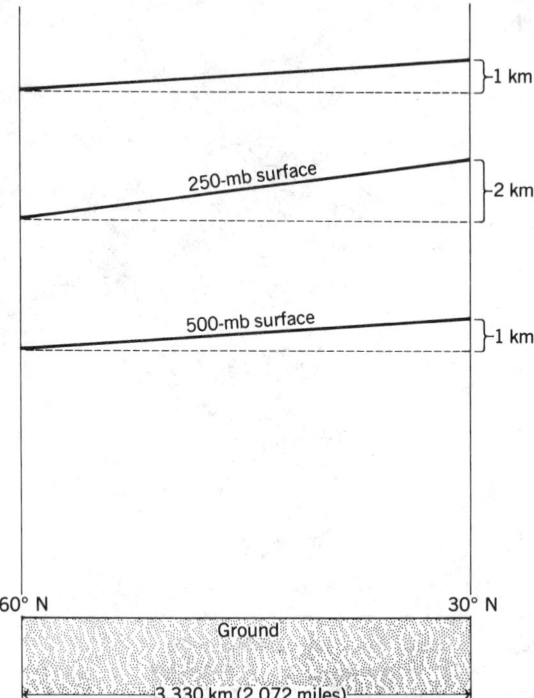

Fig. 8. Different pressure surfaces have different slopes. In this imaginary slice through the atmosphere, it can be seen that the 250-millibar surface is sloped more steeply than the 500-millibar surface below it and another pressure surface above it. The steeper the slope, the stronger the wind. The difference in wind speeds at different altitudes gives rise to the jet stream. (Wind is blowing into the page, away from the reader.)

days in winter and six to seven days in summer. Occasionally the normal west-to-east propagation of trough-ridge systems is interrupted or even reversed. Prolonged periods of extreme heat or cold or extended wet or dry spells can then occur at a given location. In certain regions, also, troughs are particularly apt to be strong and persistent, as along the eastern sides of continents.

Jet Stream. Fig. 8 is a vertical cross-section through the earth and the atmosphere. It cuts the earth's surface along a longitude. For convenience, the surface is shown as a straight line, though it actually is curved. The figure shows only the section between 30°N and 60°N; the North Pole is to the left, the equator to the right. Three pressure surfaces are shown. The bottom one is a 500-mb surface similar to the one in Fig. 7. The difference in the height of this surface between 30° and 60°N is about 0.6 mile (1 km). The middle pressure surface is the 250-mb surface. With this surface the difference in height between those latitudes is greater, about 1.2 miles (2 km).

As indicated previously, the geostrophic wind flows not directly down the pressure slope but sideways, parallel to the height contours—in this case, from west to east. (In Fig. 8, the wind would be flowing into the page, away from the reader.) At the 500-mb level, a west wind of about 80 to 90 knots is required for geostrophic equilibrium to prevail. At the 250-mb level, the slope of the pressure surface is twice as steep, and a wind twice as fast is required for geostrophic equilibrium—about 160 to 180 knots. Above the 250-mb surface, the slope of the pressure surfaces begins to decrease again, as shown by the top pressure surface in Fig. 8.

This wind pattern, with different wind speeds at different altitudes, produces a wind called the *jet stream.* Fig. 9 shows an imaginary slice through the jet stream, which is blowing away from the observer toward the distant horizon. The core of the jet stream can reach speeds of 200 knots or more. The typical altitude for the jet stream is 6 to 8 miles (10–12 km). The north-south width of the jet stream is about 125 to 250 miles (200–400 km). The jet stream is one reason why airliners traveling the same distance take longer to fly westward than eastward.

CYCLONES AND FRONTS

In the upper troposphere, individual parcels of air continuously stream through the trough-ridge pattern, turning alternately north and south but moving in a generally west-to-east direction. (The entire trough-ridge system also moves generally west to east, but more slowly, perhaps at only 20 knots.) The air parcels experience a centrifugal effect, as a person does while going around a curve in a car. In Fig. 10, points A and C are ridges, and points B and D are troughs. At points A and C, the centrifugal effect tends to move the air parcels northward, while at points B and D the centrifugal effect tends to move the air parcels southward.

At all four points, the pressure force tends to move the air parcels northward (down the pressure slope). Thus, at points B and D the centrifugal and Coriolis effects combine to balance the northward pressure force, while at points A and C the Coriolis effect alone must balance the combined pressure force and centrifugal effect. Geostrophic balance can be achieved at all points only if the Coriolis effect is stronger at points A and C than at points B and D. This is tantamount to the requirement that wind blows faster through ridges than through flanking troughs, despite a uniform pressure force.

For the typical mid-latitude trough-ridge systems that are observed on weather maps, this speed variation from ridge to trough to ridge has a subtle but important effect on weather patterns. In the upper tropospheric flow pattern shown in Fig. 11a, the length of the arrows is proportional to the observed wind speed. Thus individual air parcels moving from the ridge toward the downstream trough must slow down. This "piling-up" of air results in what is called *mass convergence* in the upper-tropospheric northwesterly flow in advance of the ridge. As the individual air parcels pass through the trough, they must accelerate toward the downstream ridge. This speeding-up of air results in *mass divergence* in the southwesterly flow ahead of troughs in the upper troposphere.

Cyclones and Anticyclones. A barometer at ground level will sense this mass divergence and convergence in the upper troposphere as the trough-ridge system passes a region. Below the region of upper-tropospheric mass convergence, the surface pressure will rise. Similarly, below the region of mass divergence, the surface pressure will fall. The resulting circulation pattern is shown in Fig. 11b. The high-pressure centers are called *anticyclones;* air diverges from an anticyclone, producing the clockwise spin pattern shown in Fig. 5b (left). The low-pressure centers are called *cyclones;* air converges there, producing a counterclockwise spin, as in Fig. 5b (right).

Sinking air produces clear skies. It tends to be found beneath a northwesterly flow in the upper troposphere, halfway between the ridge and the downstream trough (see Fig. 11b). Similarly, rising air, with its attendant cloudiness and precipitation, tends to be associated with cyclones, which lie beneath a southwesterly flow aloft, halfway between the trough and the downstream ridge. This is why weather forecasters are interested in predicting the motion of migratory troughs and ridges in the upper troposphere. Surface cyclone and anticyclone centers tend to be located below the axis of the upper-tropospheric jet stream. The maximum upper-level convergence and divergence generally lie along the jet-stream axis, where wind-speed variations from trough to ridge to trough are largest. The strongest low-level convergence and divergence, and resulting vigorous ascent and descent, are found directly beneath such regions. Therefore, the professional weather forecaster is also concerned with predicting the location of the jet-stream axis in the upper troposphere.

One may suspect that these migratory-surface cyclones and anticyclones, seen so regularly on the daily weather map, are significantly involved in the process of exchanging tropical and polar air masses so as to even out the earth's temperature differences. This is indeed the case, as can be seen from Fig. 5b. Warm, moist air is transported northward at points A and C in the wake of anticyclones, or in advance of cyclones. Between these points, at point B, cool dry air is transported toward the equator.

Individual cyclones and anticyclones thus play a central role in the general circulation of the atmosphere. As a consequence of unequal solar heating of the poles and tropics, the north-south temperature difference would increase steadily throughout the troposphere were it not for the moderating function of the cyclones and anticyclones.

Fronts and Cyclones. Like the jet stream, fronts often are given the role of scapegoat in the popular media during periods of bad weather. A front is simply a line drawn on a weather map to separate air masses of different origin and hence of different weather characteristics. (An air mass is a large, possibly continent-size, body of air.) The choice of exactly where to place a front is subjective. At many times, frontal contrast may be so weak that it is hard to decide whether to carry the front on the official analysis.

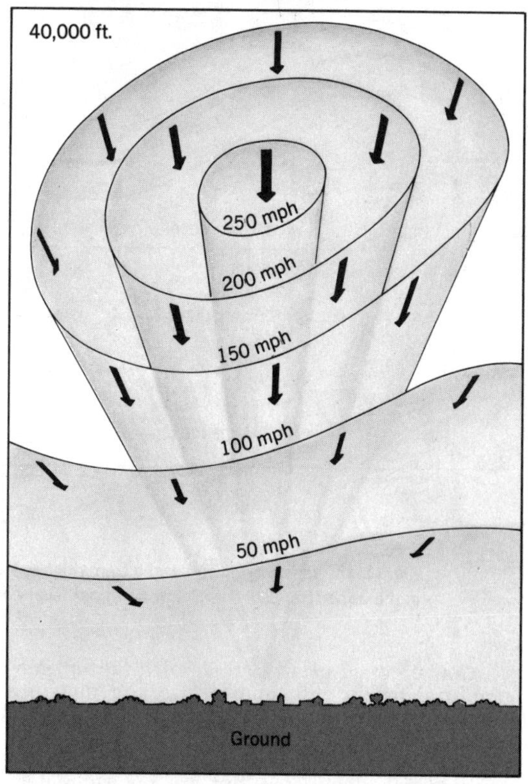

Fig. 9. An imaginary slice through the jet stream.

Fig. 10. The general movement of air is from west to east *(from left to right in this diagram)*. Air moves faster through the ridges (**A** and **C**) than through the troughs (**B** and **D**).

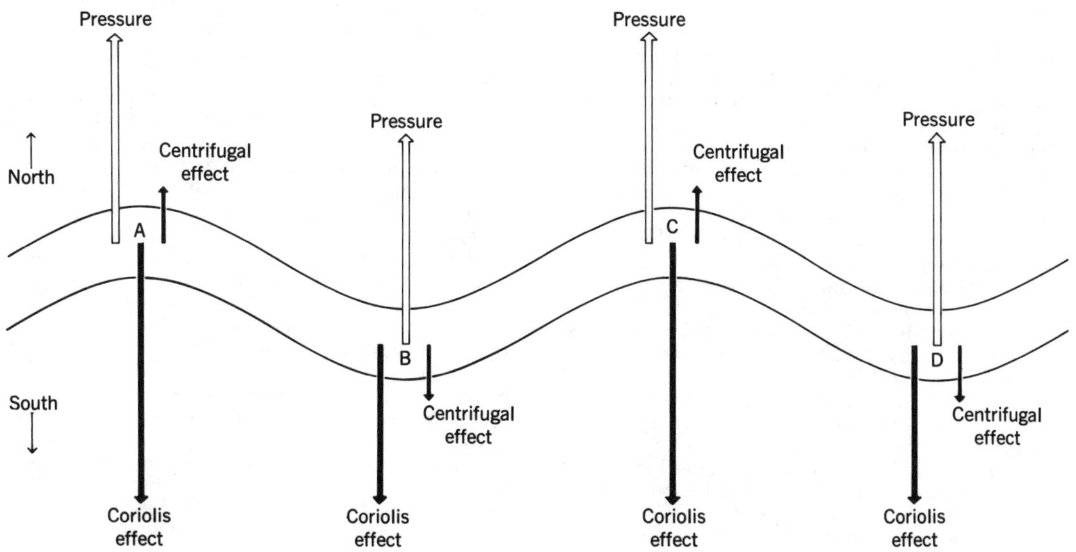

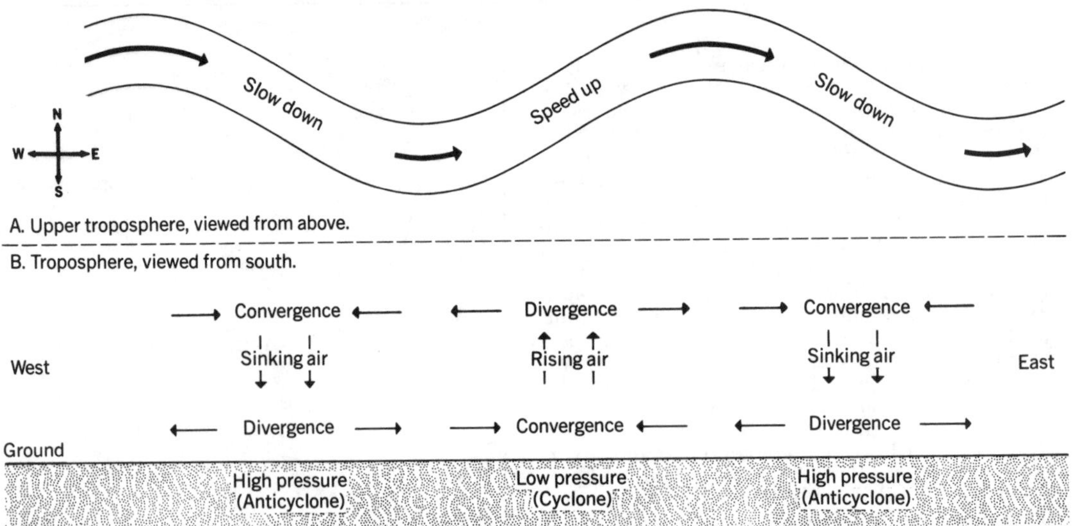

Fig. 11. The variation in wind speed from ridge to trough to ridge causes convergence and divergence of air in the upper troposphere. Below an upper-level convergence there is a high; below a divergence, a low.

Convergence of air parcels of different geographical origin and temperature and moisture characteristics is required to create and maintain a front. For this reason, fronts are found routinely in association with cyclone centers, where convergence dominates, but are not seen near anticyclone centers, where divergence prevails.

A *cold front* is one in which cold air replaces warm air near the ground. It is marked with triangles on weather maps. In a *warm front* warm air replaces cold air near the ground. It is marked with semicircles.

Fig. 12 is a schematic illustration of the evolution of fronts during the development of a typical mid-latitude cyclone. The arrows show the approximate direction of the surface wind, and the scalloped line shows areas of cloudiness. In stage 1, the front is more or less stationary; this is indicated by the alternating semicircles and triangles. A weak cyclone is forming, with its center (marked L) at a pressure of 1010 mb.

By stage 2, approximately 12 to 24 hours later, a cold front is sweeping southeastward and a warm front is moving northward. The pressure at the center of the intensifying cyclone may have dropped to 1000 mb or less, and the typical swirling circulation pattern of a cyclone has developed. The cloud cover has expanded and has begun to wrap around the back (southwest) side of the cyclone center. By stage 3, the pressure has dropped to as low as 970 mb over land or 940 mb over the ocean surface. The frontal structure has become more complicated. The stretch of front originating from the cyclone center and marked with semicircles and triangles on the same side of the line is called an *occluded front*. Conventional wisdom holds that an occluded front forms when rapidly moving cold air overtakes warm air at the surface, forcing it to rise. Evidence suggests however, that an occluded front may be simply a manifestation of a strongly intensifying cyclone that keeps churning deeper into the cold air in response to strong divergence in the upper troposphere.

A remarkable example of a stage 3 cyclone is shown in Fig. 13, a photograph taken at 1:30 P.M., Eastern Standard Time, on Feb. 19, 1979, from a satellite at an altitude of 22,000 miles (35,000 km). An intense cyclone is centered east of the Delmarva (Delaware-Maryland-Virginia) peninsula. The storm center is marked by a circular area devoid of cloud and very much like a hurricane eye. Winds of hurricane force were reported by ship observation a short distance to the west of the storm center, although the evolution of this disturbance was unlike that of a true tropical hurricane.

The giant comma shape of the white cloud mass is created by the entrance of drier air into the storm system from the south and west. Lumpy, convective clouds are present along the leading edge of the cold front and reaching into the cyclone center from the east. Smaller convective clouds aligned with the wind can be seen to the rear of the cold front. The clouds appear to originate about 124 miles (200 km) offshore in a cold air mass that is gradually being heated and moistened from below by a much warmer ocean surface. The extreme western edge of the cloud mass is about to clear the New Jersey and Delaware coast as an all-time-record snowfall of 24 inches (610 mm) ends in the Middle Atlantic states. A swath of snow deposited by this storm in the previous 36 hours can be seen as far south as Georgia, eastern Alabama, and Tennessee. The snow line extends almost to the coast from Savannah to Cape Hatteras. Individual unfrozen rivers can be distinguished in the southeastern U.S. snow cover. In sharp contrast, the Great Lakes are almost totally frozen over, including Lake Superior—a tribute to the especially severe winter of 1978–1979 in that region.

Fronts and Weather. Fig. 14 depicts an idealized vertical cross section through a warm and cold front, or approximately along the dashed line in Fig. 12, stage 2. The approach of the warm front is first evidenced by the arrival of cirrus and cirrostratus clouds at high levels (6 miles, or 10 km). The sun or moon begins to look watery, and optical phenomena such as halos may appear. Next, middle clouds in the form of altostratus and altocumulus begin to shroud the sky, and rain or snow falls from the cloud base, but does not necessarily reach the ground. Precipitation at the ground usually begins with the arrival of low-level nimbostratus clouds. The careful observer will note a variation in the precipitation. Lighter periods of rainfall occasionally are interrupted by heavier periods. The heavier rain is produced when the warm, moist air is forced to rise over the cold air. As it rises, it is cooled below its dew point and rain is formed. In extreme cases thunderstorms may occur just before the arrival of the warm air at the surface.

In the warm sector itself the weather is variable, depending on the time of the year or day and the geographical location. An especially moist air mass, coupled with weak winter solar heating, allows fog, drizzle, and low stratus clouds to persist in the warm sector. During spring and summer, strong solar heating results in partly cloudy skies and high temperatures. Warm-sector air is apt to be turbulent, particularly in the Midwest, so that squalls and other kinds of severe weather are common. More than 95% of all reported tornadoes occur in the warm sector of a mid-latitude cyclone.

The arrival of the cold front may or may not be marked by precipitation. A strong cold front, pushing under the warm air and forcing it to rise sharply, may produce sudden, violent but fortunately brief thunderstorms. Precipitation produced by a cold front typically lasts a few hours, in contrast to the 12 hours or more commonly observed with warm-front precipitation. An exception sometimes occurs when a slow-moving cold front becomes more or less stationary, and a disturbance similar to that in stage 1 of Fig. 12 develops along the front. In this case rainfall may be prolonged and heavy just north of the front, as is commonly seen in winter along the U.S. coast of the Gulf of Mexico.

AIR MASSES

North American Air Masses. Fig. 15 shows the principal air masses that affect North America. An air mass can be thought of as having relatively homogeneous temperature and moisture properties. The source region itself must also be fairly homogeneous in these properties. Over the tropical oceans the subtropical anticyclones provide the source for maritime-tropical air (mT), while the polar oceans act as a source of maritime-polar air (mP). Similarly, a strongly heated continent can act as a source of continental-tropical air (cT), while a snow-covered polar region makes an excellent source for continental-polar air (cP). Further breakdowns into equatorial and arctic sources dependent upon temperature and season of the year are possible.

The principal source of maritime-tropical air for North America is the Gulf of Mexico, the adjacent western Atlantic, and the Pacific west of Mexico. Maritime-polar air is produced in the North Pacific and North Atlantic oceans. Continental-tropical air is produced over Mexico and parts of the southwestern United States, while continental-polar air is produced over northern Canada. An additional source of continental-polar air for North America in winter is the Siberian region of the Soviet Union.

The climate of a particular region of North America is determined by the frequency and persistence of these four basic types of air masses. During summer, Miami is exclusively under the influence of mT air, while Boston alternates between mT, mP, and cP air. Kansas City can feel the influence of mT, cT, and cP air masses. Extremely high temperatures can occur in the Midwest when cT air leaves its desert source region and is warmed by subsidence heating as it descends the east face of the continental divide. Seattle is almost exclusively under the influence of mP air in summer, although occasionally cT air comes in from the east and is warmed by subsidence west of the Cascade Mountains.

In winter the frequency and persistence of these air-mass types change. Then, cT air is essentially absent from the United States while cP air is much more dominant across the northern reaches of the country. The dominant air mass at Miami remains mT air, but mP and cP air masses occasionally penetrate that far south, much to the chagrin of vacationers. The climate of Boston is now dominated by cP and mP air with only occasional incursions of mT air, while Kansas City alternates between mT and cP air masses with abrupt temperature changes at occasional intervals. Seattle experiences predominantly mP air, although occasional intrusions of cP air do occur during brief very cold periods. The difference between a cold and warm January at a location like Kansas City is then a measure of the frequency of the two predominant air-mass types. During a warm January cP air may be present roughly 30% of the time, while during a cold January the same air mass may be present 70% of the time.

Cyclone and Anticyclone Paths. Typical North American cyclone and anticyclone paths are shown in Fig. 16. In winter, cyclones tend to

Fig. 12. Evolution of fronts during a typical middle-latitude cyclone.

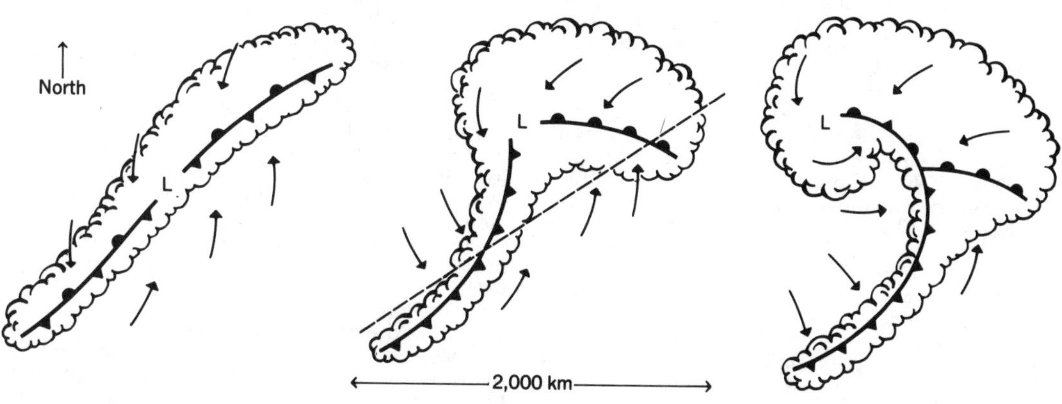

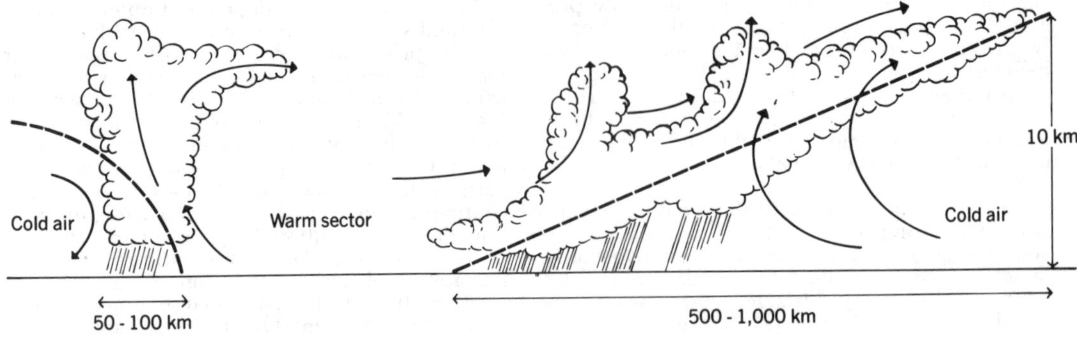

Fig. 13. Vertical cross section through a warm front and a cold front.

congregate in the Gulf of Alaska and Icelandic areas. Cyclones that originate along the downwind slopes of the Rockies in Colorado tend to track toward the Great Lakes, bringing considerable snow to the upper Midwest. Cyclones that track along the U.S.-Canadian border draw warmer air northward ahead of them and are associated with relatively mild and dry conditions across the northern United States. Cyclones originating in the western Gulf of Mexico bring copious rain to the Mississippi and Ohio valley areas accompanied by dramatic changes in temperature as mT and cP air masses alternate in rapid sequence along the track of the storm. Cyclones tracking northeastward along the Atlantic coast are prolific rain and snow producers and are associated with the classic "northeasters" of New England.

Summer cyclones can occur along the Atlantic coast but are much less frequent than in winter. The track along the U.S.-Canadian border is displaced northward. Cyclones originating in northwestern Canada may move southward into the northern plains while the north Pacific area becomes less active. Westward-moving cyclone tracks show up in the Caribbean and off the west coast of Central America. This reflects the passage of occasional tropical storms and hurricanes, as does the track from the southern Gulf of Mexico toward Florida.

The dominant winter anticyclone track is from the northern part of the Soviet Union across the polar region and Canada and into the United States. Repeated cold-air outbreaks accompany the passage of such cyclones into the American Midwest. An alternate anticyclone track runs across southern Canada to the Maritime Provinces. This brings cold air to the northeastern United States. Warm winter weather in the eastern and central United States is associated with the anticyclone track from Texas to New Jersey, while the occasional cold-air outbreak west of the continental divide may be associated with the track from British Columbia to New Mexico.

During the summer, anticyclones exhibit a more eastward movement across the United States, as cold cP air masses tend to remain in Canada. The oceanic tracks change little from summer to winter.

Mountains and Weather. Mountain ranges exert a major influence on weather. When air moves against a mountain range, it is forced to rise. As it rises it cools. Eventually it is cooled past its dew point, and the moisture in it condenses out as precipitation. Then, as it flows down the downwind side of the range, it is compressed because the atmospheric pressure is greater at lower altitudes. This compression heats the descending air. Consequently the relative humidity of the air becomes increasingly lower, and the air is less and less likely to produce rain. For these reasons, the windward side of the mountain range, as well as the crest and the upper part of the downwind slope, tend to have much precipitation. The foothills of the downwind are apt to have little precipitation.

A more or less continuous mountain range runs along the western edge of the North and South American continents (the Cascades, the Sierra Nevada, the Andes). Copious precipitation is produced in these regions when there is a persistent flow of Pacific air inland. Downwind (east) of these mountains the climate is dry.

The north-south orientation of the Rocky Mountains favors the north-south exchange of air masses and hinders east-west exchanges. Cold air can rush across the U.S.-Canadian border in winter and reach the Texas Gulf coast 24 to 36 hours later. Texans remark that there is nothing between them and the North Pole but barbed-wire fences! The Rocky Mountains to the west help to funnel the cold air southward and tend to prevent the cold, dense air from spilling across the continental divide. East-west mountain ranges such as the Himalayas and to a lesser extent the Alps hinder the north-south exchange of air masses by serving as a dam to outbreaks of cold air.

Local Circulation. Mountains also produce local circulation patterns. At night, when the ground cools, the air next to the ground is also cooled. Since cool air is denser, it slides down the slope, producing a breeze from the mountain to the valley. The direction is reversed during the day, when air from the warmed valley blows out of the valley and up the mountainside.

Another local circulation pattern is found at the seashore. During the day, air rises from the heated land, helping to produce a sea breeze from the ocean to the land. At night, air sinks over the cooled land, and the breeze blows from land to sea.

Individual lakes and rivers also have an appreciable influence on regional and local weather. The most obvious examples in the United States are the five Great Lakes. During the fall and early winter, when the water is still unfrozen, much colder air passing over the relatively warmer water picks up appreciable moisture. This results in persistent cloudiness and occasional showers or storms along the lee (downwind) shores of the Great Lakes. Snowfall totals can be phenomenal, as residents of Buffalo can attest. The annual snowfall at Muskegon, Mich., is about twice that of Milwaukee, Wis., on the other side of Lake Michigan.

In the summer the picture is reversed, with the shore areas often sunnier than inland areas. A lake breeze cools the shore areas, reducing the possibility that hot air will rise and produce a storm. The arrival of the autumn frost may be delayed for several weeks compared with inland locations because of the influence of the still relatively warm water. The last frost of spring will come earlier along the lakeshore for similar reasons. To a lesser extent, a similar variation may be noticed in major river valleys; one can often stretch the growing season a bit along the immediate riverbanks. Fog, which has a tendency to accumulate in river valleys, helps further to ward off frost in near-freezing conditions. Satellite pictures routinely disclose the presence of river-valley fog, with the fog being more persistent in the deeper valleys.

Small lakes also have an impact on the local weather, especially in summer. Even a shallow lake, such as Lake Okeechobee in Florida, has a measurable impact on the local weather. The warm lake water is still cooler than the adjacent land areas on a summer afternoon. Showers and thunderstorms tend to avoid the central lake region while concentrating along some shore margins.

HUMAN ACTIVITY AND WEATHER

Human activity can have an effect on weather. Table 1 lists some of these effects. The figures show how urban areas differ from rural areas in various categories. For example, the amount of atmospheric contaminants in urban areas differs from rural areas by +1000% a year. That is, the annual amount of atmospheric contaminants in an urban area is 1000% (or ten times) the annual amount in a rural area. A negative quantity means that an urban area receives less of that category. For example, an urban area receives 22% less solar radiation a year than a rural area. The figures for the bottom four categories are somewhat controversial; some scientists feel that there is not enough evidence to support these figures.

Fig. 14. Principal air masses that affect North America.

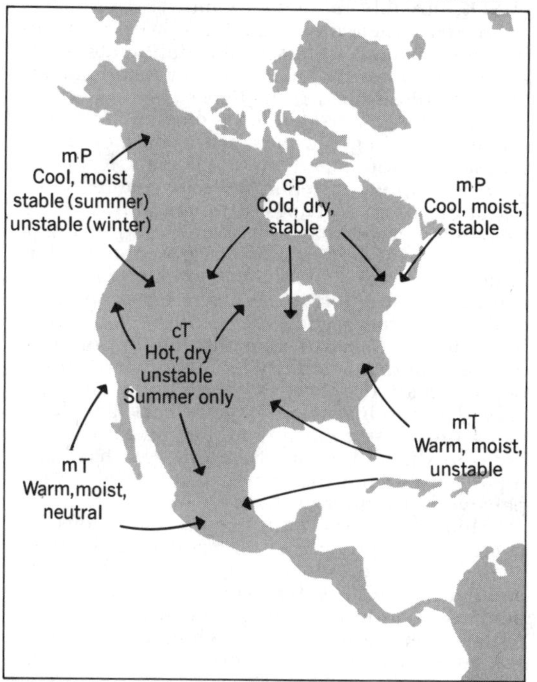

TABLE 1: PERCENTAGE DIFFERENCE IN VARIOUS METEOROLOGICAL FACTORS, URBAN VS. RURAL AREAS

	Annual	Cold Season	Warm Season
Atmospheric contaminants	+1000	+2000	+500
Solar radiation	−22	−34	−20
Temperature	+3	+10	+2
Humidity	−6	−2	−8
Visibility	−26	−34	−17
Fog	+60	+100	+30
Wind speed	−25	−20	−30
Cloudiness	+8	+5	+10
Rainfall	+11	+13	+11
Snowfall	±10	±10	—
Thunderstorms	+8	+5	+17

Source: *Patterns and Perspectives in Environmental Science*, National Science Foundation, 1972.

Temperature. Cities are warmer than the countryside. Urban-rural temperature differences are well documented in both large and small cities all over the globe—persuasive evidence that human activity has altered the weather. During the day, the concrete, brick, and asphalt of the city absorb heat better than the trees and vegetation of the countryside. The excess heat collected during the day is partially radiated back to space at night, but the city does not cool down as much as the countryside. Cities are islands of heat.

Evaporation also contributes to the urban-rural temperature difference. Evaporation is a cooling process. When you step out of a shower or a swimming pool, you feel cool because water is evaporating from your skin. In the countryside, after a summer rain that saturates the soil and leaves the vegetation damp, evaporation may hold down the temperature by one or two Celsius degrees. However, a major portion of the rain that falls on the city is lost down the storm drains. Such water is then unavailable for evaporation.

Atmospheric Contaminants. Atmospheric contaminants strongly affect air quality and visibility in metropolitan areas. Dust and smoke layers often shroud cities, with the automobile acting as a major contributor to air pollution. Automobile exhaust contains unburned hydrocarbons, oxides of nitrogen, and carbon monoxide. In the presence of sunshine the hydrocarbons combine with the oxides of nitrogen to produce ozone and other complicated organic particles. The net result is an eye-stinging photochemical smog that plagues such diverse locations as Los Angeles, Denver, and Washington, D.C. The long-term effect on human health is just beginning to be appreciated. Crops can also be damaged by air pollution. Economic losses in agriculture and business may run to billions of dollars a year across the United States.

Precipitation. There is increasing evidence that human activity can affect the rainfall characteristics of an area. The Metropolitan Meteorological Experiment (METROMEX) was a comprehensive study of urban weather influences

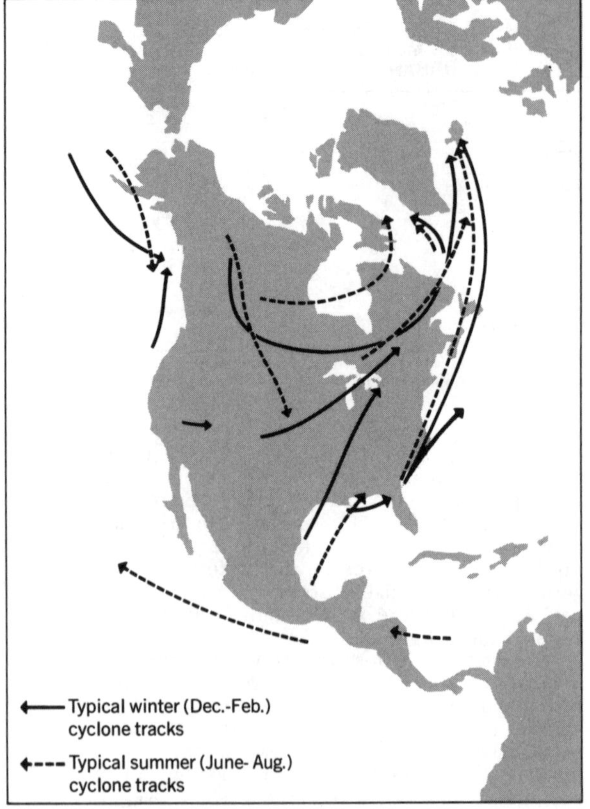

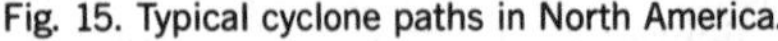
Fig. 15. Typical cyclone paths in North America.

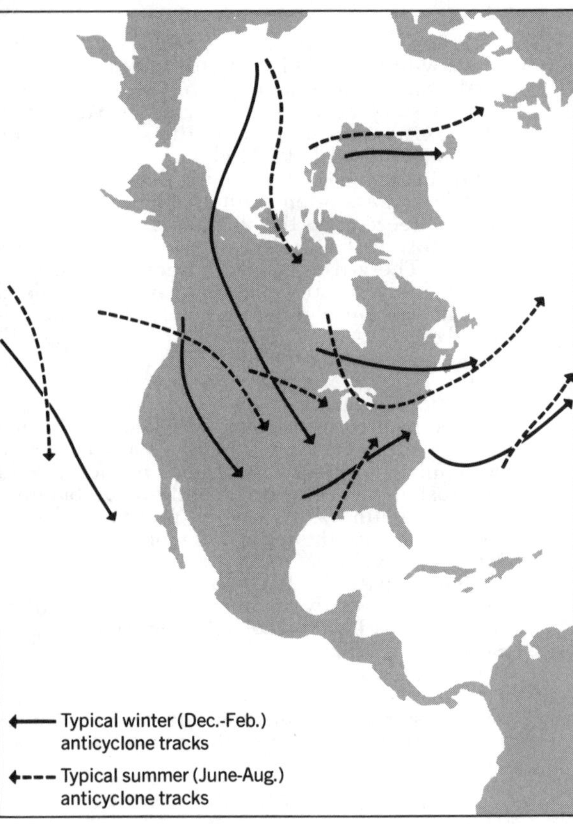

Fig. 16. Typical anticyclone paths in North America.

carried out in the St. Louis area in the early 1970's. Among the more interesting findings was the existence of a summer rainfall maximum in a swath downwind of St. Louis. The rainfall in this swath was 10% to 30% above precipitation levels of the immediate surrounding areas.

Other cases of increased rainfall have been reported downwind from some paper and pulp mills in western Washington, the Chicago-Gary industrial complex, and large power plants in western Pennsylvania. These statistical correlations are debatable: rainfall has a large natural variation, and systematic measurements of rainfall were not made before industrialization. However, even a casual observer can see that large power plants sometimes create their own local weather in the form of growing cumulus clouds over them. This formation of clouds is analagous to the cumulus clouds and even thunderstorms observed above forest fires in some areas.

In certain winter conditions, when the air is very still, the exhaust plume from high smokestacks of a power plant can reach the ground and create a local fog. Accidents due to poor visibility or icing produced by such fog have been reported along some major highways.

Acid rain has become a major global problem. Acid rain contains sulfuric acid, which is formed when the pollutant sulfur dioxide (SO_2) dissolves in rain. The SO_2 is a by-product of the burning of coal and oil. It is produced most heavily in the major industrial regions of the American East and Midwest and in western Europe. Acid rain can be quite strongly acidic, with a pH as low as 3.5. Over many years, acid rain has damaged forests and aquatic life in freshwater lakes of the northeastern United States and Scandinavia. Elimination of acid rain presents a difficult political and technical problem because many nations may be involved, and the worst of the damage often occurs far downwind of the original source of SO_2, possibly in another country.

Weather Modification. The term "weather modification" usually refers to the deliberate alteration of weather by humans rather than inadvertent modification as in the cases described above. The dispersal of fog is one area of experimentation. Fog is a nuisance to both civil and military aviation, and meteorologists for years have attempted to refine methods for reducing fog at airports. For fogs at temperatures above freezing, methods have involved the squirting of fine water droplets or other hygroscopic (water-attracting) particles, such as common salt, over runways in an effort to cause the fog droplets to coalesce on the particles. Visibility would thus be improved because a smaller number of large droplets hinders visibility less than a large number of small droplets. Other efforts have involved the flying of helicopters back and forth along runways or burning fuel along runways in order to stir up the air. Some success has been reported, but the experiments not only are expensive but hinder air traffic.

Modification is easier with cold fogs or clouds. In a mixture of ice crystals and supercooled water droplets (droplets that have remained as liquid water even though their temperature is below freezing), the water tends to coalesce on the ice crystals, which increase to a size at which they are heavy enough to fall as precipitation. Cloud seeding is a method in which crystals of dry ice (frozen carbon dioxide, CO_2) or of silver iodide (Ag I), which has a structure like that of ice, are scattered on the cloud. The crystals serve as centers of coalescence. Results have been mixed, but seeding appears to increase precipitation in mid-tropospheric clouds when the temperature is between −11° and −20°C (12° and −4°F), and to decrease precipitation when the temperature is between −27° and −39°C (17° and −38°F). Dispersal of cold airport fog in Canada and Alaska by seeding has proven successful and reasonably inexpensive. Pioneering experiments in cloud seeding began shortly after World War II.

Long-Term Effects. The gas carbon dioxide is present in the atmosphere only in small amounts, but it exerts an important influence on weather through what is called the "greenhouse effect." Sunlight is absorbed by the ground and subsequently radiated out again, but as energy of wavelengths longer than the wavelengths of the original incoming radiation. The carbon dioxide in the atmosphere lets in the original short-wavelength radiation but blocks the long-wavelength radiation from escaping back into space. Thus the carbon dioxide tends to keep the earth warm. (The glass or translucent plastic in a greenhouse has the same effect.) Since industrialized times, the amount of carbon dioxide in the atmosphere has increased steadily because of the burning of fossil fuels (in factories, power plants, motor vehicles). This may lead to a general warming of the earth. On the other hand, the steadily increasing amounts of pollutants in the atmosphere may block out some solar radiation, possibly leading to a general cooling. Many scientists believe that a global cooling of only a few Celsius degrees would be enough to trigger another massive advance of the polar ice sheets, leading to another ice age, and that a global warming would partly melt the polar ice sheets, causing the sea level to rise and coastal cities to be inundated.

LANCE F. BOSART
State University of New York at Albany

Bibliography

Anthes, Richard A., and others, *The Atmosphere,* 2d ed. (Merrill 1978).
Battan, Louis J., *Fundamentals of Meteorology,* 2d ed. (Prentice-Hall 1984).
Battan, Louis J., *Weather in Your Life* (W. H. Freeman 1985).
Calder, Nigel, *The Weather Machine* (Viking 1974).
Dunn, Gordon E., and Miller, B. I., *Atlantic Hurricanes* (La. State Univ. Press 1964).
Edinger, James G., *Watching for the Wind: The Seen and Unseen Influences on Local Weather* (Doubleday 1967).
Fleagle, Robert G., and others, *Weather Modification in the Public Interest* (Univ. of Wash. Press 1974).
Herman, John R., and Goldberg, Richard A., *Sun, Weather, and Climate* (Dover 1985).
Mather, John R., *Climatology: Fundamentals and Applications* (McGraw 1974).
Miller, Albert, and Thompson, J. C., *Elements of Meteorology,* 3d ed. (Merrill 1979).
Moran, Joseph M., and Morgan, Michael D., *Meteorology: The Atmosphere and the Science of Weather* (Burgess 1986).
Riehl, Herbert, *Introduction to the Atmosphere,* 3d ed. (McGraw 1978).
Scorer, Richard, *Clouds of the World: A Complete Color Encyclopedia* (Stackpole 1972).
Trewartha, Glenn T., *An Introduction to Climate,* 4th ed. (McGraw 1968).
Trowbridge, Leslie W., *Experiments in Meteorology: Investigations for the Amateur Scientist* (Doubleday 1973).
Wallace, John M., and Hobbs, Peter V., *Atmospheric Sciences: An Introductory Survey* (Academic 1977).

WEATHER FORECASTING, the application of scientific principles and procedures to the prediction of future states of the atmosphere. Modern weather forecasting is done with exact, quantitative methods; much of the processing of weather data is done by high-speed digital computers. For a discussion of the causes of weather, see the article WEATHER.

Weather forecasts came to public attention around 1860 as people began to see the possibility of simultaneously collecting weather information from scattered locations and transmitting this information to the appropriate agencies by means of the newly invented telegraph. The U.S. Weather Bureau (now called the National Weather Service) came into being in 1870, and before long the first attempts at day-to-day weather forecasting began. The results were notably unsuccessful. Weather forecasting was done empirically, without theoretical understanding. Many serious scientists washed their hands of the practical side of meteorology—a problem that to some extent remains.

At the close of World War I, Vilhelm Bjerknes, his son Jacob Bjerknes, and Halvor Solberg brought about a meteorological revolution. Working as a team in Bergen, Norway, they set down some ideas on the life cycle and structure of cyclones in three dimensions, based on solid physical understanding. The concept of the occlusion process and of warm and cold fronts was elucidated for the first time. The frontal concepts revolutionized the practice of surface weather analysis. During the next 30 years the availability of upper-air soundings advanced the science of predicting middle-latitude weather systems by quantitative application of fundamental physical ideas. The advent of the high-speed computer around 1950 accelerated the growth of quantitative methods in numerical weather prediction, and since then progress in the field has been startling. Some of these developments will be summarized in the body of this article. The cornerstone of this progress is a union of technological innovation, observational knowledge, and theoretical understanding.

DATA COLLECTION

Instrumentation. Successful weather prediction depends on the availability of observations. Observations of pressure, temperature, moisture, wind, cloud type, visibility, present weather, and other factors must be collected from all over the globe. These observations are required both at the surface and at many different levels in the troposphere and stratosphere. (The troposphere is the lower part of the atmosphere. It extends from the ground up to about 8 km [5 miles] over the poles and 18 km [11 miles] over the equator. The stratosphere is above the troposphere. Most weather is confined to the troposphere.) Most observations are made in the more developed, middle-latitude countries; there are few or no observations collected in less developed countries and across the oceans, which cover most of the globe. Commercial ships and aircraft provide valuable observations from the major shipping lanes and aircraft routes, while upper-air information is routinely obtained from selected continental, island, and a few ship locations. Satellite-based remote sensors offer the exciting possibility of eventually measuring atmospheric structure with sufficient accuracy to obviate the need for an expensive people-based system.

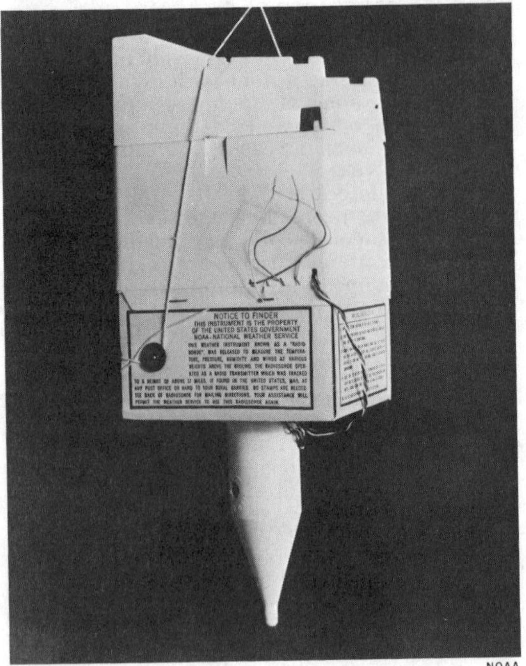

NOAA

A workhorse of meteorological data collection, the radiosonde transmits temperature, pressure, and moisture information. It is attached to the base of a balloon used to sound the atmosphere. Eventually, remote-sensing satellites will replace radiosondes.

Temperature, Pressure, Humidity, Wind. Temperature, pressure, humidity, and wind are measured by means of a thermometer, barometer, hydrometer, and anemometer respectively. (See separate articles on these instruments.) The first three instruments work on the idea of expansion or contraction of an element that is sensitive to heat (alcohol or mercury), pressure (mercury, or pressure differences across a known volume of space), and moisture (human hair, horse hair, or carbon). The anemometer works on the principle that the rate at which the wind spins a fanlike device, or the pressure on a building produced by the wind, is proportional to the speed of the wind.

Temperature is measured in degrees Celsius or centigrade, abbreviated °C. (The freezing point of water is 0°C, and the boiling point of water is 100°C.) Pressure is measured in millibars, or mb. A pressure at sea level of 1013 mb is taken as the standard normal atmospheric pressure. Pressure decreases with increasing altitude. Humidity refers to the amount of water vapor dissolved in the air. The ratio of the actual amount of water dissolved in the air to the maximum amount that could be dissolved in the air at that temperature and pressure is called the relative humidity. It is expressed as a percentage. The lower the temperature, the less the amount of vapor that the air can hold. When a body of air is cooled to the temperature at which it is holding the maximum amount of vapor possible, the relative humidity of that body of air reaches 100%; that temperature is called the dew point. Wind speed is measured in knots or in meters per second. One knot is equal to 0.52 m/sec.

Radiosonde. The radiosonde is the workhorse of meteorological data collection. The radiosonde is a simple electronic device that transmits temperature, pressure, and moisture information. It measures about 50 cm (20 inches) long and is attached to the base of a meteorological balloon used to "sound" the atmosphere. The balloons are launched from a regular surface network at internationally specified times. The balloon ascends at the approximate rate of 300 meters (1,000 feet) per minute. As it rises, it radios back information on temperature, pressure, and moisture at various heights. Wind speed and direction at various heights are obtained by radar tracking of the balloon.

The radiosonde is a good device, but maintenance of the far-flung radiosonde system is expensive. Approximately 100 balloon-borne radiosonde packages are launched by U.S.–controlled stations every day. At $50 per radiosonde package, the cost works out to $5,000 daily and $2 million yearly. This equipment cost is small compared with the manpower cost of launching the radiosondes and collecting and communicating the collected data. Personnel and service costs to the U.S. government amount to many millions of dollars a year. It is hoped that eventually remote-sensing satellites will replace the radiosonde as the workhorse of the global data bank.

Remote Sensing. Since about 1960, many techniques have been developed for collecting data from satellites. Visible-light cameras, infrared detectors, and other remote-sensing instruments on the satellites can detect, measure, and radio back to earth many kinds of information.

The temperature sensor on a satellite deduces temperature by measuring infrared radiation from cloud tops or, where there is no cloud, from the surface. In this manner approximate temperature profiles can be constructed over data-sparse areas. (A profile is a series of readings together with the altitude at which each reading is taken.)

Profiles of temperature, moisture, and other conditions are important in weather forecasting. The technique is not perfect. There are difficulties in matching cloud-top heights with cloud-top temperatures, and in regions of thin clouds the sensor is not sure whether it is picking up surface or cloud-top radiation. New satellites such as the TIROS-N series have advanced sensors that can partially alleviate these problems.

The satellite has proven spectacularly successful in keeping track of global weather patterns. Gone are the days when a devastating tropical cyclone can move undetected onto a land area. Global snow and ice cover, as well as sea surface temperature, is now monitored as never before. Land and agricultural use can now be closely supervised.

Satellites are also useful in tracking clouds. On the assumption that the cloud moves with the mean wind, it is possible to determine the atmospheric wind speed and direction at cloud level. The method works best for reasonably long-lived cloud systems that do not have much vertical structure.

Another technique, satellite microwave sensing, enables a satellite to see through a cloud system and detect the amount of liquid water and water vapor in a column from the surface to the tropopause (the top of the troposphere) over oceanic regions. Research suggests that this tech-

WIDE WORLD PHOTO

(Top) In the Severe Storm Center of the National Weather Service in Kansas City, Mo., weather analysts look for signs of impending storms. The screen shows satellite pictures. Satellite photographs *(below left)*, radar images *(bottom left)*, and surface maps *(below right)* are all essential to modern weather prediction.

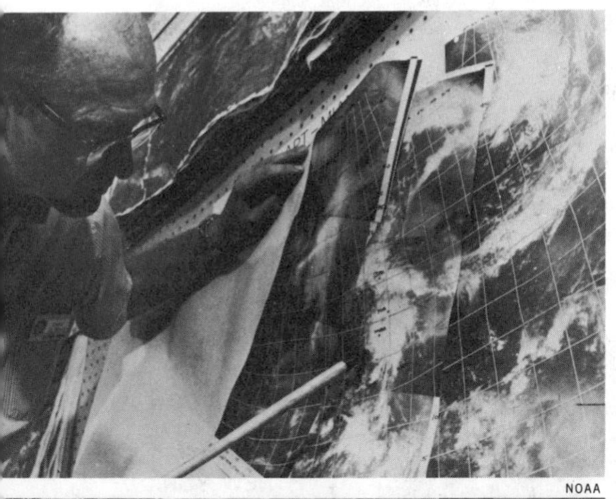

NOAA

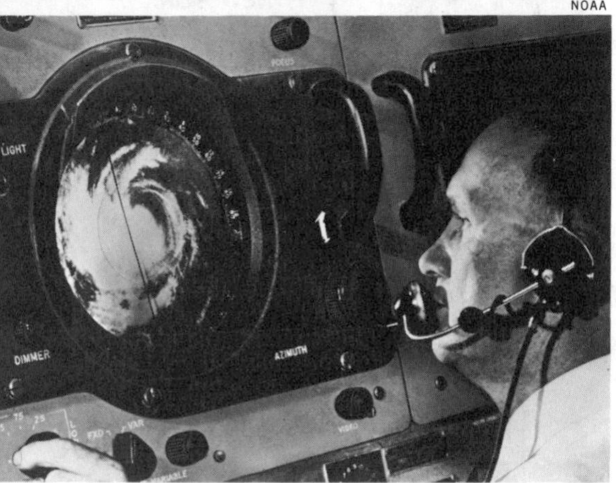

NOAA

NOAA

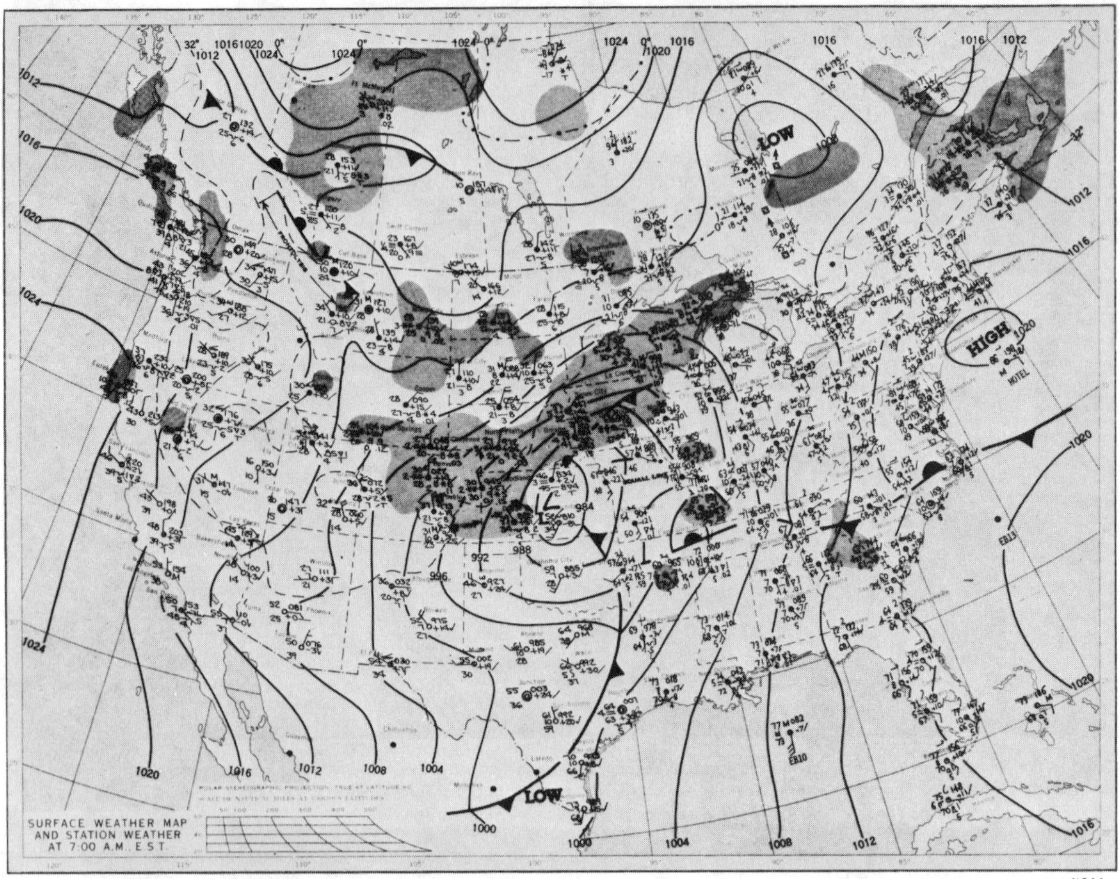

SURFACE WEATHER MAP AND STATION WEATHER AT 7:00 A.M., E.S.T.

NOAA

Detailed weather maps, published by the National Oceanographic and Atmospheric Administration at regular intervals, enable those interested in the weather to follow its development.

Many newspapers publish simplified versions of the daily weather map, such as this one by the United Press International. A cold front is shown sweeping into the Rocky Mountain states from the northwest, producing extensive areas of rain. Its progress may be slowed by the centers of high pressure. Another cold front, pivoting about a low, is advancing toward the Atlantic coast. The numbers at top give barometric pressures.

UPI

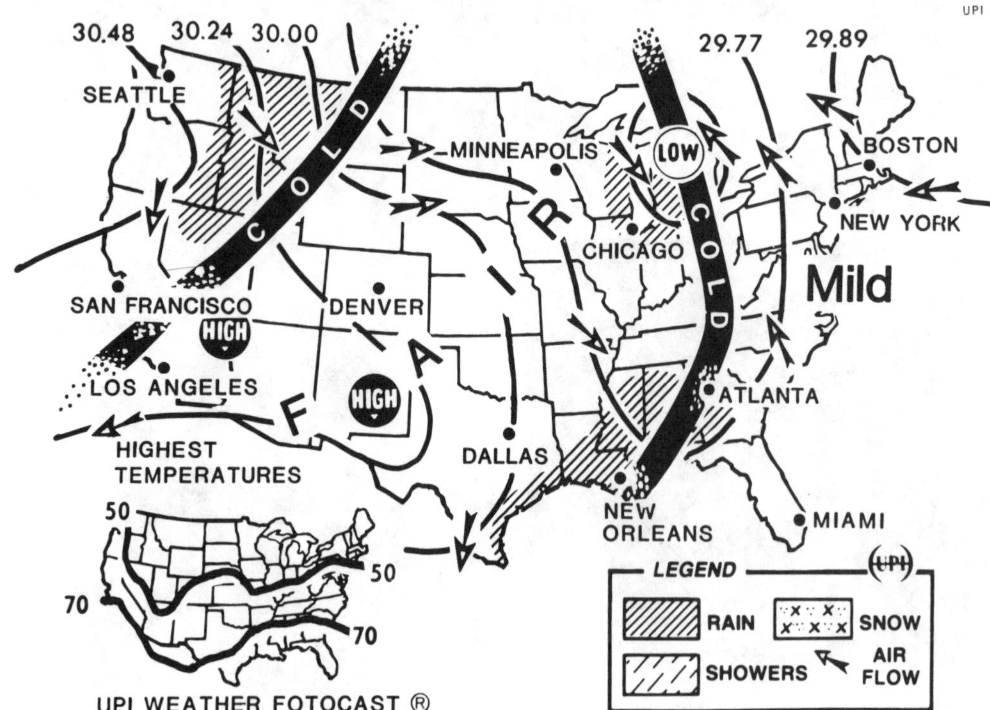

SOME WEATHER CHART SYMBOLS

WIND SPEED (knots)

Pennant = 50 knots
Full barb = 10 knots
Half barb = 5 knots

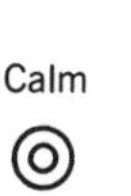
Calm
0

5

10

15

25

50

100

WIND

Feathers always point toward lower pressure

Direction given is direction *from* which the wind blows.

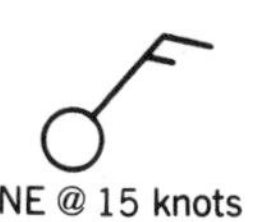
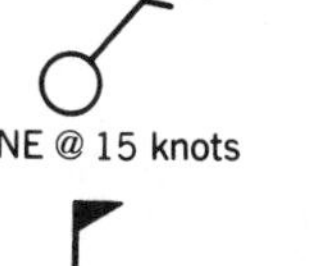
NE @ 15 knots

SE @ 20

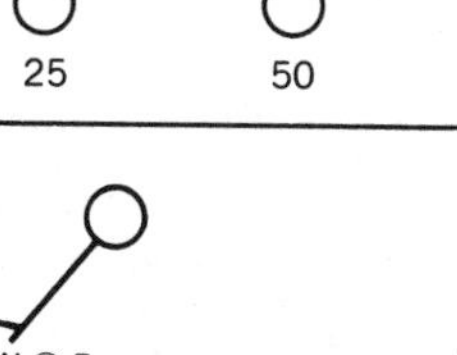
SW @ 5

NW @ 30

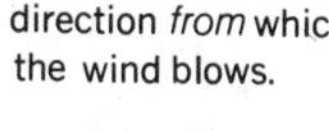

N @ 50

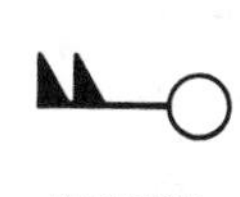
W @ 100

S @ 25

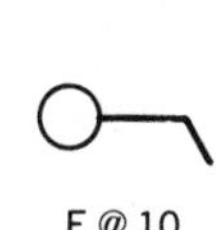
E @ 10

SKY COVER

Clear

Scattered clouds

Partly cloudy

Completely overcast

Obscured

WEATHER

Light rain

Moderate rain

Heavy rain

Dense fog

Ice pellets

Freezing rain

Light drizzle

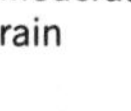
Light snow

Moderate snow

Heavy snow

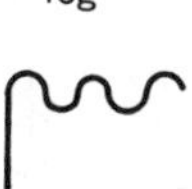
Smoke

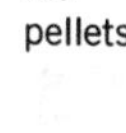
Haze

Dust or sand in air

Lightning

Rain shower

Snow shower

Moderate thunderstorm

Heavy thunderstorm with hail

Squall

Rain and snow mixed

Heavy rain and snow showers

SIMPLIFIED WEATHER CHART PLOTTING CONVENTION

SURFACE

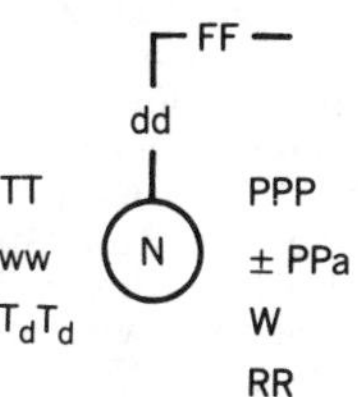

UPPER AIR

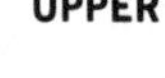
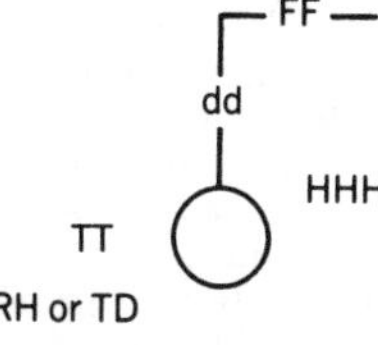

FF Wind speed (knots)
dd Wind direction
TT Temperature (°C)
T_dT_d Dew point (°C)
PPP Pressure (tenths of mb, leading 10 or 9 omitted)
± PPa Pressure tendency last three hours
N Sky cover

ww Present weather symbol
W Past weather symbol
RR 6-hour precipitation (inches)
RH Relative humidity (%)
TD Dew point depression (°C)
HHH Height of constant pressure surface (meters or dekameters)

nique will have a powerful application in the preparation of atmospheric moisture analysis over oceanic regions.

Frequency of Data Sampling. By international agreement all nations use Greenwich Mean Time (GMT) as the official time standard for a 24-hour day. (In the 24-hour system, midnight is 0000, 8:30 A.M. is 0830, noon is 1200, 1 P.M. is 1300, and 9:14 P.M. is 2114, for example.) Greenwich Time is five hours ahead of Eastern Standard Time (EST) and eight hours ahead of Pacific Standard Time (PST). Surface land and marine observations are required every six hours at 0000, 0600, 1200, and 1800 GMT, and thousands of stations routinely make such observations. Many of these land stations and even ships collect weather information hourly or every three hours. Unfortunately, some observations are available only once or twice a day from regions lacking the technology or financial means to support a national meteorological service.

A complete surface observation must include temperature, dew point, pressure, change in pressure over the last three hours, present weather, state of the sky, cloud type, and height and amount of precipitation if it occurred. Numerous other types of information are added as required. In addition weather ships, buoys, and commercial ships report water temperature and information on the state of the sea including the period and height of waves. (Period is the length of time between the passage of one wave crest and the next wave crest.)

Station coverage is heavily biased toward the major industrial nations and principal ship routes. In such regions station separation may be as small as 50 kilometers (30 miles), with 100 kilometers (60 miles) more typical. In the more remote corners of the globe the station separation can easily reach 1,000 kilometers (600 miles).

Radiosonde information is obtained every 12 hours at 0000 and 1200 GMT from the global station network. All stations are required to transmit temperature, moisture, height, and wind measurements at internationally agreed-upon levels. For the troposphere, these are the levels at which the pressures are 1000, 850, 700, 500, 400, 300, 200, and 100 mb.

Data Communication. There is nothing so ancient as yesterday's weather information. All collected surface and upper-air data must be transcribed and sent to one of the three world data centers (Washington, Moscow, and Melbourne) as soon as possible. Computers play a major role in this operation. The data are usually coded into five digit groups, which may look like so much hash to the untrained eye but which can be very efficiently processed by the computer. Time is of the essence because, in the United States, for example, operational weather prediction models are begun from data received within one and a half hours of 0000 and 1200 GMT. Much valid data never gets into the operational forecast cycle. Communication problems are often the culprit. The civilian and military weather services in the United States have introduced new computer systems designed to speed up the process of managing the data flow. Because a forecast center may become overwhelmed with data, computer editing is essential. The system seems to work reasonably well as long as experienced forecasters have the time to oversee and react to the huge flow of data.

DATA ANALYSIS

The final step in the chain before a forecast can be generated is the analysis in time and space of the data. In precomputer times, this used to be done laboriously by experienced analysts working regular shifts.

Analysis was taken very seriously in the early days of the U.S. Weather Bureau, as can be seen from the following memorandum issued in 1894: "Neglect of duty, insubordination, grave-robbing, amending of an original telegraphic report, nonpayment of debts, and omission of isotherm lines on weather maps will be accompanied by penalties ranging from dismissal to sizeable reduction in salary."

Today all routine analyses are prepared by machine. The hub of the operation in the United States is at the National Meteorological Center (NMC) located just outside Washington, D.C. As data are received, the computer checks them for gross errors, and reports that exceed certain specified error limits are thrown away. Manual intervention in various stages of the forecast cycle occasionally is necessary.

Next the computer plots the accepted data for each station at the previously mentioned pressure levels. The computer then prepares an analysis of various meteorological parameters at a discrete array of points called a *grid* on each of these pressure levels. A grid spacing of roughly 100 kilometers (60 miles) is used. From this analysis the computer begins to prepare the forecast.

The actual analysis procedure involves a statistical technique called *optimum interpolation*, the end result of which is a series of lines such as isobars (lines connecting points of equal pressure) or isotherms (lines connecting points of equal temperature) on a weather map, as well as values at the grid points. The maps are transmitted over a national facsimile network from Washington to field offices of the National Weather Service as well as to many other government agencies, private employers, and universities. The national facsimile network is being replaced by a sophisticated computer processing system designed to expedite the flow of weather information.

Preparation of Weather Forecasts. After the data are collected, analyzed, and put into a form that a computer can understand, a forecast can be prepared. Various forecast models are used at the National Meteorological Center, depending upon the complexity desired.

Horizontal and Vertical Movement. To predict the weather, it is necessary to know how fast and in what direction various bodies of air are moving. Air movement takes place both horizontally and vertically. Horizontal movement is much the faster. A typical tropospheric wind speed over the middle latitudes is 10–30 meters (30–100 feet) per second, whereas vertical motions are typically a few centimeters (an inch) per second, or about 1,000 times smaller.

When air is holding all the water vapor that it can hold at that temperature and pressure, it is said to be saturated (relative humidity 100%). Air cools as it rises. If this saturated air rises, precipitation in the form of rain or snow will form, because the cooled air is no longer able to hold so much moisture.

The typical vertical motion of a few centimeters a second, though it is small, is by no means inconsequential. Rise of saturated air at a few

Weather forecasters are a familiar sight on most local television news broadcasts.

SEPP SEITZ/WOODFIN CAMP

centimeters per second is enough to produce 2 to 3 centimeters (1 inch) of rain in less than one day.

Saturated air cools at about 6 Celsius degrees per kilometer (3 Fahrenheit degrees per 1,000 feet) when it is lifted. Sinking air warms and dries out by compression.

In order to make a quantitative precipitation and cloud forecast, a knowledge of vertical motions is essential. Clear skies tend to be associated with downward motion and cloudy or precipitating skies with upward motion (see WEATHER). Unfortunately, the computation of vertical motion presents a complex problem.

Equations of Weather. The basic elements of weather, such as movement of air and the gain or loss of heat, obey the laws of classical physics. For example, one law basic to the calculation of motion is Newton's second law. It states that the force applied to a body (of air or anything else) is equal to the mass of the body times the acceleration imparted to the body by the force, or $F = ma$, where F is force, m is mass, and a is acceleration. This law is also known as the momentum equation, as it can be expressed in the form $F = \frac{mv}{t}$, where v is velocity, t is time, and mv is momentum. In this form it states that the force applied to a body is equal to the rate of change of momentum of that body. This equation must be modified in order to be applicable to the calculation of vertical air motion, because air is subject to two opposing forces—an upward force (buoyancy) due to decreasing pressure with increasing altitude, and a downward force due to gravity. The resulting balance between these dominant forces is called *hydrostatic equilibrium*. There are also two horizontal-momentum equations based on Newton's second law. Additional relations include: the equation of state, the equation of mass continuity, the first law of thermodynamics, and an equation representing the water cycle.

In theory, the complete set of seven equations in seven unknowns governs atmospheric behavior for all time if the proper initial and boundary conditions are known; this, however, is not the case. The equations themselves are highly nonlinear and not amenable to direct analytic solution. Approximations to simulate physical processes must be made. Numerical techniques must be used to evaluate complex terms based upon the input data. This process introduces a certain error into the forecast procedure. The resulting simplified set of equations governing atmospheric behavior is called the *primitive equations* and constitutes the basic model for atmospheric behavior.

In order to generate a forecast, the primitive equations must be integrated in time. This numerical procedure is somewhat analogous to an air-traffic controller tracking an incoming plane on radar. Suppose an aircraft is 600 kilometers (375 miles) from the airport and moving toward the field at 400 kilometers (250 miles) per hour. Assuming that the aircraft will maintain a constant speed, it is then known that the aircraft will travel 400 kilometers in the next hour. Thus it can be "predicted" that the position of the aircraft one hour later will be 600 kilometers minus 400 kilometers or 200 kilometers (125 miles) from the field.

The initial temperature is known from the initial analysis, and the rate of change of temperature is known from the solution of the first law of thermodynamics. The predicted new temperature is equal to the old temperature plus the rate of change of temperature, times a specified time interval over which it is assumed the computed rate of change of temperature is valid. Because of various physical and numerical constraints on our system of equations, the time interval ranges from 5 to 20 minutes. Thus a predicted temperature is computed to be valid, say, ten minutes after the initial time. Similarly the other variables, such as wind speed and direction, are computed to be valid ten minutes later. Next the first law of thermodynamics is solved again to yield still another rate of change of temperature. Then the predicted temperature 20 minutes into the forecast is equal to the previously calculated temperature valid after ten minutes, plus the rate of change of temperature valid at ten minutes times the ten-minute interval. This procedure cycles repeatedly until it is desired to terminate the forecast.

In operational practice the primitive equation models in use at the National Meteorological Center are integrated twice per day beginning one and one half to three and one half hours after the 0000 and 1200 GMT upper-air sampling times. Each model run consumes up to four hours of central processing unit time on a very fast computer. In addition, considerable time must be consumed in translating the model forecast into weather maps and other documents that can be used by the field forecaster—that is, by the local forecasters all over the country.

Dissemination of Public Weather Forecasts. The computer weather forecasts from the National Meteorological Center are routinely printed out at 12-hour intervals as much as 96 hours ahead of time and sent out to the field. Forecasts of precipitation, temperature, wind, and relative humidity at various atmospheric levels, among many other elements, are routinely sent to the field. In addition, a wealth of statistical information including maximum and minimum temperatures, precipitation probability, precipitation type and amount, wind direction and speed, and ceiling and visibility for selected cities is prepared on the basis of model forecast output.

Additional products include a daily three- to five-day temperature and precipitation anomaly forecast accompanied by the expected surface weather map; a six- to ten-day temperature and precipitation outlook that is prepared three times per week; a 30-day temperature and precipitation outlook prepared bimonthly; and a 90-day experimental seasonal forecast prepared four times a year. Charts of daily snow and ice cover, Gulf Stream position, and drought and crop-moisture indexes also are routinely prepared.

To recapitulate, the job of the National Meteorological Center is to prepare a global and regional forecast for North America valid at fixed 12-hour intervals. The forecast guidance "package" also includes the statistical selected-cities forecasts. This forecast guidance package is then sent to the field offices of the National Weather Service as well as to numerous other users, including government agencies such as the Federal Aviation Administration, universities and schools, and private weather-forecasting services.

Local Forecasts. The local National Weather Service forecast offices, totaling about 50 around the country, have the responsibility of preparing a local and regional forecast for the next 48 hours based upon the guidance package. The guidance package can be accepted in its entirety, modified according to local experience and knowledge, or disregarded completely. A forecaster who selects the last option must be prepared to defend his actions. The most common option is to modify the guidance package, based upon current local conditions and the forecaster's meteorological experience. The forecaster has access to the latest radar and satellite data plus the current surface weather.

The public forecast prepared by the local National Weather Service office is necessarily general. The forecast is communicated to the various media outlets for public dissemination. Hazardous weather warnings or watches are communicated to the responsible local officials, police, and civil-defense agencies. Likewise marine and agricultural forecasts, including freeze and frost warnings, are routinely prepared.

Private Forecasters. Many companies and individuals prepare private weather forecasts for specific users. A public utility, for example, needs much more specific information on temperature and wind than can be provided by the local National Weather Service office if it is to provide economical and efficient gas and electric service. The same can be said of suppliers of home heating oil. Private meteorologists provide a valuable service in forecasting snow and ice amounts for ski areas, major shopping areas, and local public-works agencies in charge of snow removal and salting and sanding operations. They are also active in preparing specific forecasts for commercial, recreational, and agricultural interests such as aviation, boating, and crop spraying. Major airlines have meteorological staffs to keep track of special aviation hazards. The commodities market is also sensitive to forecast trends. Speculators want to know about droughts and floods in the major food-producing regions.

The general public is most familiar with private meteorologists through local TV and radio broadcasts. In some markets, such as Oklahoma City, Tampa, Minneapolis, and Boston, competition among the media meteorologists is keen. Some stations have their own radars and satellite receivers. However, both public and private weather forecasters essentially have access to the same weather information from the government. Why then do the forecasts on occasion disagree within the same area? Often there is a difference in interpretation of the forecast guidance. This is a natural by-product of the forecaster's experience and training. Media forecasters have nearly instant access to radio and TV and can update their forecasts almost immediately if conditions warrant. There is no "middleman" in this operation.

National Weather Service forecasters rarely have such a luxury, as several hours often elapse before their forecasts reach the public. The National Weather Service communicates to the public through middlemen represented by local media and newspapers. Broadcasters frequently read obsolete forecasts or edit the forecast for broadcast convenience, which often alters or destroys the content of the forecast. Local newspapers, with rare exceptions such as the New York *Times*, decline to put the time on their printed forecast. The forecast that you read in the morning was probably prepared the previous day and based on information 24 hours old.

Fortunately no such delay exists when it comes to providing watches and warnings to the public on severe local storms such as tornadoes, thunderstorms, and hurricanes. The National Severe Storms Forecast Center in Kansas City and the National Hurricane Center in Miami have the sole responsibilities of monitoring these storms and alerting the public where appropriate. Both of these centers are plugged into the National Meteorological Center in Washington so that up-to-the-minute data and computer forecasts can be exchanged.

Forecast Verification. The assessment of skill involved in the preparation of weather forecasts by public and private sources has not been without controversy. Very often verification methods are chosen so as to cast a particular forecast scheme in the most favorable light. This makes it very difficult to measure objectively the true state of the art. Mindful of the problems, the American Meteorological Society in 1976 adopted an official policy statement on weather forecasting. The portion dealing with skill in weather forecasts is quoted below.

"Accuracy in weather forecasting depends on many factors, for example, the meteorological situation, geographical area, and season; nevertheless it is possible to assess the typical accuracy of different forecasting methods. Forecast skill can be determined objectively by comparing the accuracy of the forecasts with the accuracy of forecasts produced by simple procedures such as predicting that the weather will remain unchanged (persistence) or predicting average weather based upon past weather records (climatology). Skill cannot be said to exist unless forecast accuracy exceeds levels achieved by basic methods such as these. . . .

"The statements of skill herein refer to conditions within the Northern Hemisphere. Skill levels in the Southern Hemisphere are lower, owing to the reduced number of meteorological observations. Weather forecasts prepared by professionally trained personnel presently achieve the following average levels of skill in middle latitudes:

1) *For periods up to 12 hours:* Weather forecasts of considerable skill and utility are attained. The detail that can be included decreases with the time period, ranging from phenomena on the scale of a few kilometers, including severe local storms, for periods out to about 1 hour, to larger features such as fronts, squall lines, and organized precipitation areas for up to 12 hours. . . .
2) *For periods of 12 to 48 hours:* Considerable skill in forecasting 12-hour changes in weather systems having horizontal dimensions of 1000 kilometers or more has been demonstrated, particularly through the use of numerical models. The general area of severe storm activity, and of events such as heavy precipitation or damaging winds, can often be predicted up to 24 hours in advance although the exact location of tornadoes cannot be predicted. General forecasts of cloudiness, air quality, temperature, and precipitation occurrence can be made out to 48 hours.
3) *For periods of 2 to 5 days:* Daily temperature forecasts of moderate skill and usefulness are possible. Precipitation forecasts at an equivalent level of skill can be made to 3 days. The precipitation forecast skill decreases through the fourth and fifth days but maintains a slight margin over climatology.
4) *For periods of 5 days to 1 month:* Average temperature conditions can be predicted with some skill, particularly in the 6–10 day period. There is slight skill in forecasting precipitation amounts for the 6–10 day period but skill for longer periods is marginal. Week-to-week forecasts beyond 10 days have not demonstrated skill.
5) *For periods of more than 1 month:* A minimal skill exists in seasonal outlooks."

Storms, Hurricanes, and Floods. Local storms, hurricanes, and flash floods are major hazards to public safety. Unfortunately, current forecasting models cannot forecast these local weather phenomena accurately. The models at best can only indicate the general region within which these phenomena are likely to occur. For tornadoes and severe thunderstorms, experienced forecasters at the National Severe Storms Forecast Center in Kansas City make the final decision on where such phenomena can be expected. Lightning is another phenomenon about which we can predict only the general area where it is likely to occur, and not the exact spot.

Weather Forecasting of the Future. There will be continued emphasis in the future on the use of numerical models. The models will become increasingly more sophisticated. They will be able to handle both large-scale weather systems and localized, small systems. Improved remote-sensing techniques will furnish the computers with data of increasing accuracy and detail. Theoreticians will concentrate more on phenomena associated with air masses and on the behavior of very long planetary scale waves (troughs and ridges) in an effort that might ultimately result in fairly accurate six- to ten-day forecasts.

Local forecast systems will be devised to take advantage of sophisticated ground-based radar and remote-sensing techniques to give the populace of an urban area up-to-the-minute detailed information on local weather conditions. New radar techniques may make it possible to detect a tornado many minutes before the first visible funnel appears.

Hints for Amateur Weather Forecasters. First and foremost an amateur forecaster must be a keen observer of local conditions. Temperature, relative humidity, pressure, wind speed and direction, and precipitation should be recorded as often as possible. Upper-level winds can often be deduced by following cloud motions. A knowledge of the local climatology is essential. Visit your local forecast office and television station and talk to some of the forecasters. Be an information absorber. Get one of the many radios on the market capable of picking up the NOAA weather radio broadcasts. Listen to long-distance AM radio stations at night and note weather conditions in other cities. Subscribe to the *Daily Weather Map* and the *Weekly Weather and Crop Bulletin.* Join the National Weather Association and the American Meteorological Society.

Forget most of the stated rules about the association of pressure and weather. True, a sharply falling barometer for at least 12 hours usually heralds a period of inclement weather. But even with a high barometer, if it falls rapidly the weather can be just as nasty as if the pressure was much lower. During the Washington snow disaster of Feb. 18–19, 1979, the barometer never went lower than 1020 mb despite a record snow. The opposite case is present at a location like Denver, just to the east of the continental divide. Most precipitation there occurs with an east wind and a *rising* barometer as cold moist air is forced to rise westward toward the divide ahead of a cold Canadian anticyclone moving southeastward into the western plains.

Standard textbooks and forecast rules of thumb never tell you about these conditions, so a knowledge of the local climatology is absolutely essential to the armchair meteorologist. Visit your local library or contact the National Climate Center in Asheville, N.C., for published information on your local and regional climate.

LANCE BOSART
State University of New York at Albany

Further Reading: See bibliography for WEATHER.

RUSS KINNE/PHOTO RESEARCHERS

A weather vane. Because the pivot axis is near the front part of the horse, the horse points into the wind.

WEATHER VANE, a device attached to some elevated object to show by movement which way the wind blows. For a long time, people relied for this purpose on simple observation of the bending of trees, the drifting of smoke, or the like. Eventually devices of various designs were developed for indicating the direction from which the wind came.

Early European history carries many references to "weathercocks," as does the poetry of that era. These were decorative weather vanes, for some reason often made in the image of roosters or cocks. They were designed so that they faced into the wind to indicate the direction from which it came.

In dealing with the weather and with weather forecasting, it is important to know the direction from which the wind blows. The weather producing systems have wind structures by which they can be identified. In the Northern Hemisphere, for instance, counterclockwise winds around a low-pressure center and clockwise winds around a high-pressure center have long been recognized as the laws of storms. The wind belts of the world are established because, through the ages, observers have watched the wind and made records of its direction., Farmers use information about wind direction in planning spraying operations; city planners locate incinerators so that the prevailing winds will carry odors and impurities away from population centers; runways at airports are designed in accordance with the percentage of time the wind blows from the different points of the compass; and sailors set their sails in such fashion as to take advantage of the wind direction.

ERNEST J. CHRISTIE
U.S. Weather Bureau

WEATHERFORD, weth'ər-fərd, **William** (c. 1780–1824), American Indian chief. Weatherford, also known as Red Eagle, is remembered for his role as Indian leader in the Creek Indian war of 1812–1814, in which Gen. Andrew Jackson led the U.S. forces. Weatherford led a large band of Creek Indians in a successful attack on Fort Mims on Aug. 30, 1813, after which he put to death with great cruelty hundreds of the inhabitants of the fort. He was also the leader, or one of the leaders, of the Creek Indians at the battle at Horseshoe Bend on the Tallapoosa River in 1814. The disastrous defeat of the Indians there ended the war. After the battle, Weatherford surrendered himself to Andrew Jackson but was released. The rest of his life was uneventful.

Weatherford's parentage is unclear. According to some, his father was Charles Weatherford, an English or Scotch trader; his mother may have been a Seminole. He lived most of his life on the right bank of the Alabama River, near the site of Montgomery, Ala. He married three times and had many children, who married among the whites. Descriptions of his character vary from the depraved to the noble.

WEATHERING. See EROSION.

WEAVER, wē'vər, **James Baird** (1833–1912), American soldier, congressman, and presidential candidate on the Greenback and Populist tickets. He was born in Dayton, Ohio, on June 12, 1833, and graduated from the Cincinnati Law School in 1856. He entered the Union Army as a lieutenant in 1861 and fought in the battles of Fort Donelson, Shiloh, and Corinth. In 1862, he was promoted to colonel, and in 1856 he was named brigadier general.

After the Civil War, Weaver, then a Republican, was district attorney and federal assessor of internal revenue in Iowa. He found himself increasingly at odds with his own party, however. In the mid-1870's he transferred his allegiance to the Greenback party, a political group that supported an easy money policy of increasing the number of federal greenback paper dollars in circulation to offer relief to debtor groups such as farmers and laborers. Weaver was elected to the U.S. Congress on the Greenback ticket in 1878 and was the Greenback candidate for President in 1880, polling more than 300,000 votes. He was reelected to Congress in 1884 and 1886. He later helped organize the People's, or Populist, party, and was nominated as its candidate for president in 1892, gaining more than one million popular votes and 22 electoral votes. He died in Des Moines, Iowa, on Feb. 6, 1912.

WEAVER, wē'vər, **Robert Clifton** (1907–) American economist, teacher, author, and public official, who was the first black appointed to a U.S. presidential cabinet. Born in Washington, D.C., on Dec. 29, 1907, he attended public schools there and graduated from Harvard with honors in 1929. Harvard granted him an M.A. in 1931 and a Ph.D. in economics in 1934. Weaver then entered federal government service, and throughout Franklin D. Roosevelt's administration advised the government as an expert on manpower, housing, and urban and black affairs. After World War II he taught at Columbia and New York universities and published *Negro Labor, a National Problem* (1946), *The Negro*

Ghetto (1948), *The Urban Complex* (1964), and *Dilemmas of Urban America* (1965).

Weaver was rent commissioner of New York state from 1955 to 1959 and vice chairman of New York City's Housing and Redevelopment Board from 1960 until his appointment in 1961 as administrator of the federal Housing and Home Finance Agency. In 1966, President Lyndon B. Johnson appointed him secretary of the Department of Housing and Urban Development, where he served until 1968. He then was president of Bernard M. Baruch College in 1969–1970, professor of urban affairs at Hunter College in 1970–1978, and director of urban programs for Hunter College's Brookdale Center on Aging after 1978.

WEAVER, wē'vər, any of approximately 275 species of birds that typically weave an enclosed nest composed of grass stems or other fibers. They are best represented in Africa and Australia, and there are a few species in Asia and Europe. With the exception of two or three introduced species, they are entirely lacking in the New World.

Very similar to finches in general appearance, they have a heavy finchlike conical bill, used to crush the seeds of grasses and other plants, which are their principal food. Many weavers are highly sociable, and dozens of pairs often gather in the breeding season to hang their swinging nests from the fronds of a single palm tree. The male weaverbird often builds most of the nest, leaving his mate to line it with fine grass and prepare it for the reception of the eggs. Weaverbirds in general, are poor singers, but they have a variety of whistles and call notes.

Formerly all weavers were placed in the family Ploceidae, but they are not usually divided into two families. One, the weaver finches (family Estrildidae), includes waxbills (*Estrilda*), mannikins (*Lonchura*), fire finches (*Lagonosticta*), the white-cheeked Java sparrow (*Padda*), and sometimes the nest-parasitizing whydahs (*Vidua*).

The other family (Ploceidae) includes the true weavers, the true sparrows (*Passer*), the Buffalo weavers (*Bubalornis* and *Dinemellia*), and sometimes the whydahs. The true weavers include the many species of *Ploceus* as well as the malimbes (*Malimbus*), the queleas (*Quelea*), and the bishops (*Euplectes*).

The males of typical weavers (especially *Ploceus* and *Malimbus*) are yellow, red, or orange, often with black or brown markings on the head or breast, while the females are usually brown or gray and much less colorful than their mates. In some species the males have roosterlike tails.

The sparrows are rather primitive weaverbirds and usually build their untidy nests in the crannies of buildings, though occasionally they weave a crude domed nest in the branches of a tree. Related to them is the social weaver (*Philetairus*) of South Africa, colonies of which build an immense community nest 10 feet (3 meters) or more in height, each pair of birds in the flock having a separate nesting cavity in the side of this structure.

Because of their variety, sprightliness, beauty, and vigor, weaverbirds are highly regarded as cage birds. The names of a few of the species give an indication of the richness of this family: cordon bleu, quail finch, twin-spot, cut-throat finch, seed cracker, zebra waxbill, paradise whydah, Fiji parrotbill, rainbow finch, and Timor fireball. See also QUELEA; SPARROW; WHYDAH.

FAWCETT/ANIMALS ANIMALS

Masked weavers (*Ploceus velatus*) weave their flaskshaped nests from grass and strips from palm fronds.

DEAN AMADON*
The American Museum of Natural History

WEAVERS, The, wē'vərz, a drama written in 1892 by the German playwright Gerhart Hauptmann. The play, about the Industrial Revolution, presents the misery of the Silesian weavers of the second quarter of the 19th century, the development of their minor rebellion, and its failure. *The Weavers* (*Die Weber*, in German) is a series of five one-act dramas rather than a drama in five acts. Different groups of persons appear in five different places, though they belong to the same community. Each of the five acts is a unit, with skillful exposition and a theatrical conclusion. At the same time the five parts constitute a greater whole, in which rebellion is carried to temporary success but is impressive mainly for the presentation of conditions that cry out for a remedy.

There is no hero in *The Weavers*. Every person is an integral, realistic character. To the tragedy of starvation as the only reward for toil is added the pathos of vicarious atonement: an old weaver who refuses to leave his loom instead of joining his fellows in rebellion is shot by a stray bullet.

Hauptmann's method is unqualifiedly naturalistic. The play was first written in the harsh Silesian dialect, and the revised version only approximates the literary language, smacking of the soil. The drama's power lies in its apparent artlessness, in the impressiveness of truth naked and unadorned. There is, however, a high degree in art in the treatment of squalor, which arouses unqualified sympathy, as there is also in its social indictment that is all the more eloquent for being only inferred. The text of the play is the simple precept: "Give them their daily bread."

WILLIAM G. HOWARD
Harvard University

©MANLEY PHOTO/SHOSTAL ASSOCIATES

Navajo woman weaves on an upright loom. American Indians were expert weavers before arrival of Europeans.

WEAVING, the interlacing of two sets of threads at right angles to each other so as to form a web of fabric. The modern weaver uses the same basic principles that the primitive weaver did, but numerous inventions, such as the commercial jacquard loom, have changed the slow laborious handweaving process into a highly productive mechanized industry. However, people continue to use the old methods of weaving, inheriting a tradition that enables them to produce fabrics rich in design and color. Beginning about 1960 interest in handweaving has been revived, and many hobbyists have acquired lap, table, or floor looms, modeled after early craft types, for home weaving.

The two sets of thread used in weaving are called the warp and the weft. The warp threads are the foundation threads that are stretched taut and lengthwise on the loom. The weft threads are those that are laid through the warp threads in various ways to produce different types of cloth. The weft threads are sometimes called woof, filler, or, simply, weaving threads.

Dressing the Loom. Preparing the loom for weaving is known as dressing the loom. Many steps that follow in a logical order must be completed before the actual weaving can begin.

The first steps involve preparing the warp. The weaver must calculate the number of warp threads and their length, as well as the total yardage, needed to complete the project. Both the width and the length of the warp must be considered. The width of the warp corresponds to the width of the finished fabric, plus about 10% for pulling at the selvages (the nonraveling edges created by turning the weft around the outside warp threads). The length of the warp is determined by how long the finished fabric will be, plus 10 inches (25.4 cm) at each end for winding and finishing and an additional 10% for fabric shrinkage. A third factor to be considered when calculating the warp is the openness of the weave. This determines the number of warp ends per inch (epi), also called the warp sett (set).

Once the length of the warp has been determined, a piece of heavy, contrasting cord (the measuring cord or guide string) is cut to a length that measures the distance the warp is to take during warping. When tied into position on a warping board, the cord will guide the weaver in winding the warp threads. There are several methods of winding the warp, determined by the article to be made and the type of loom used. A common method is the cross. This technique keeps the warp threads in sequence and ensures that when they are placed on the loom they do not become tangled or crisscrossed.

After the warp threads are wound, warping the loom may begin. When warping, every thread must be of equal tension and length. Beginning weavers should experiment with various warping methods to decide which is best for them. The method chosen is not important. The importance lies in the ease of the technique, one that will result in an evenly wound warp.

In dressing the loom, one end of the warp is attached to the back apron bar and then rolled onto the warp beam—the most tedious (and often frustrating) step in weaving. When enough warp has been rolled so that it reaches the breast beam, the warp threads are threaded through the heddles. Finally, the warp is attached to the front apron bar, and the tension is adjusted.

Yarns. It is necessary to find suitable yarns, especially for the warp. Among the various catagories of available fibers and threads, all have special uses in weaving fabrics, and the choice

STANDARD TREADLE LOOM

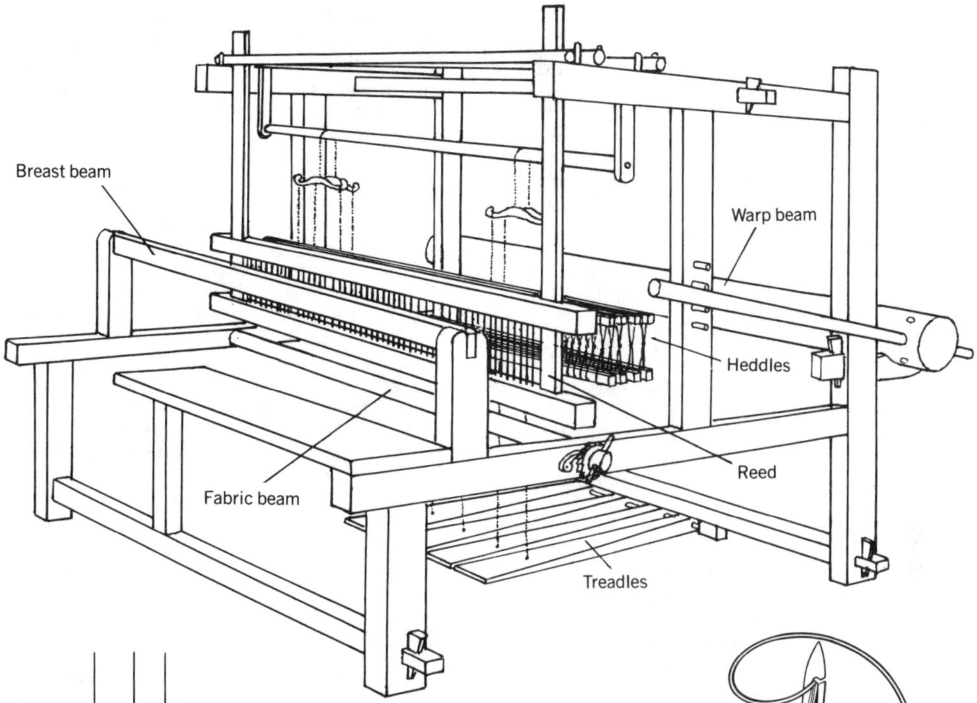

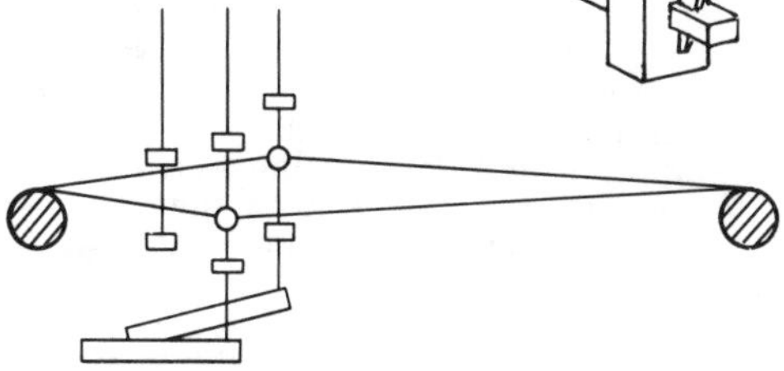

Breast beam

Warp beam

Heddles

Reed

Fabric beam

Treadles

CROSS SECTION OF LOOM, SHOWING WARP THREADS

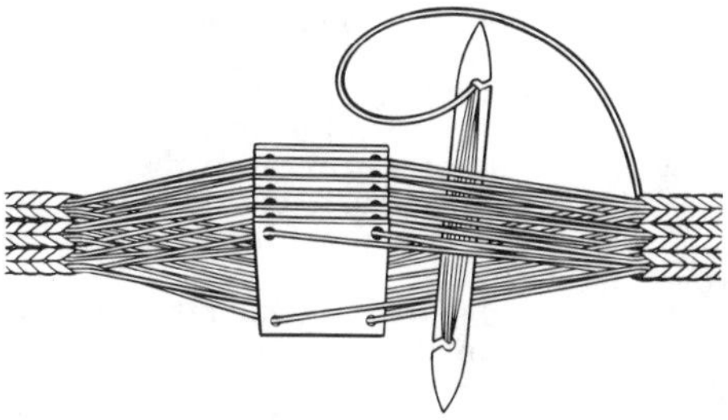

CARD, OR TABLET, LOOM

TYPES OF WEAVES

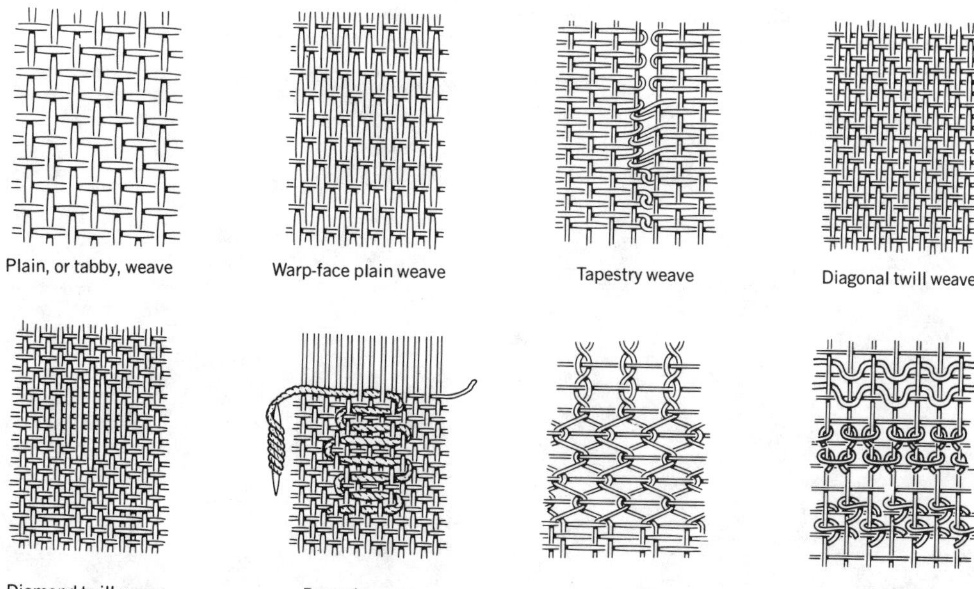

Plain, or tabby, weave

Warp-face plain weave

Tapestry weave

Diagonal twill weave

Diamond twill weave

Brocade weave

Gauze weave

Pile, or rug, weaves

determines the design, pattern, and function of the cloth. Most handweaver hobbyists prefer natural fibers, but there are valid reasons for choosing one of the synthetics.

Among the natural fibers are wool and silk, classified as "animal fibers." Raw wool is a short and kinky fiber, while silk is a smooth, long fiber. The major plant fibers are cotton, produced in the seed pods (balls) of the cotton plant, and linen, made from the stem of the flax plant. Other plant fibers suitable for weaving are derived from yucca, jute, ramie, and kapok.

Fibers have been developed artificially by combining a variety of materials. These fibers are commonly called "man-made fibers." Among the man-made fibers are the cellulose fibers, such as rayon and acetate, and the synthetic noncellulose fibers, such as nylon and polyester. Man-made fibers offer certain advantages over natural fibers. They are quick-drying, flame-resistant, easy to care for, and available in a wide variety of vibrant colors.

The quality of a woven cloth depends on the yarns or threads chosen for both the warp and weft. Because the warp thread is under constant tension and is beaten during the weaving process, it must have considerable strength. If the warp yarn or thread breaks when tested by yanking on it, another selection should be made. Also, warp threads should not shed or fray easily, because shedding and stray fibers make weaving difficult. Linen, cotton, wool, and synthetics are all well suited for warp threads.

Weft threads do not require the strength of warp threads. However, consideration should be given to the color, pattern, and texture of the woven fabric.

A weft-faced fabric, in which the weft threads predominate and the warp threads are hidden, requires a heavier yarn for the weft than for the warp. On the other hand, for a warp-faced fabric, the warp thread is heavier than the weft. For an even, plain weave (50/50) threads of the same weight and thickness should be used for both the weft and the warp.

Looms. In deciding the best loom for a particular weaving project, the size of the woven article and the use to be made of it are the primary considerations. For example, weaving a narrow belt on an inkle loom is quicker and easier than weaving the same article on the larger four-harness loom. In general, weaving large items requires large looms. However, small looms can be used for large items by sewing narrow strips of woven cloth together, but the effect of the finished piece is quite different than that of a continuously woven fabric.

Attention also should be paid to the space in which a loom is to be used. It is difficult to operate a large table or floor loom in a cramped area. In addition, certain looms are easily movable and therefore more suitable for the peripatetic weaver. Other factors affecting the choice of a loom include its complexity and price. The frame loom is the simplest and most primitive type of loom. There are several variations of the frame loom, but they all lack heddles and beaters. The weaving is done by passing the weft threads, usually wound on a shuttle, over one warp thread and under another. Some frame looms have a triangular shed stick with slots that may be turned in various ways to control the warp threads and create a shed, the V-shaped opening between warp threads through which the shuttle passes. Most primitive models simply have a flat stick inserted into the warp. This stick then is turned on end to form the shed. The alternate warp threads then are threaded through string loops that are attached to another stick, which is raised and lowered to form the second shed, not controlled by the flat stick.

The fabric woven on a frame loom, for which the warping is relatively simpler, is limited by the size of the loom, and there usually is no roll-up bar permitting additional length. Patterns may be produced on a simple frame loom, and

The inkle loom, with a fixed heddle, makes narrow strips of fabric, such as belts and straps.

CREATIVE CRAFTS MAGAZINE

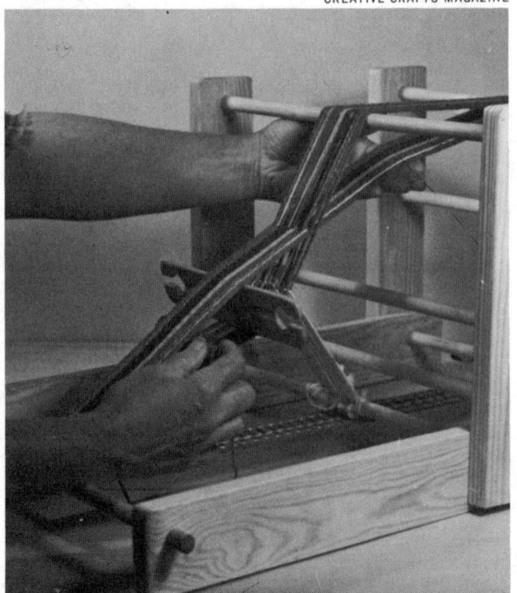

Table looms, like this four-harness model, are especially useful if the space for weaving is limited.

CREATIVE CRAFTS MAGAZINE

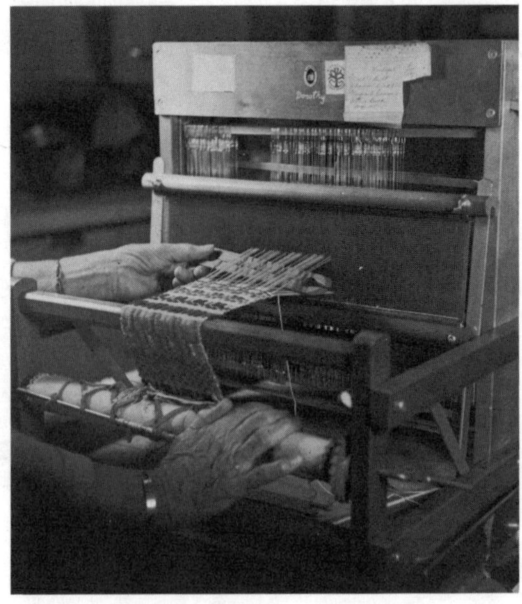

the individual weavings may be sewn together to create larger pieces.

The tapestry loom permits greater flexibility than the frame loom by introducing heddles to create the shed. This flexibility adds to the artistic opportunities for working freely in color and texture and for arranging shapes to visually balance each other.

A tapestry loom, whether large or small, must be sturdy to withstand the necessary tension of the traditional linen warp. Small vertical looms generally are leaned at an angle on a table, while large upright looms sit stationary on the floor in front of the seated weaver. Tapestry-loom heddles usually are made of string, but other models have wire heddles. The heddles are attached after the loom has been warped.

To make string heddles, tie one end of the cord to a heddle rod, setting it into the first slot of the loom support frame. Loop the free end of the cord under the first warp thread and bring it up behind and wrap it around the heddle rod. Continue in this manner across the entire warp, looping under every other warp thread and then over the heddle rod. This forms the first shed. Repeat the technique with the second heddle rod, looping under threads that have not been attached to a heddle. This forms the second shed. After checking the loom for the proper warp tension, the weaving may begin.

As with all looms, as the fabric begins to develop, the sheds become less defined. By relaxing the tension slightly and moving the warp moving bar, the loomed fabric will be pulled around the loom, reestablishing the shed. Before proceeding to weave, readjust the tension.

A rigid heddle loom speeds up the weaving and requires less work by the weaver than the tapestry loom. The difference between the looms is a rigid heddle. In a rigid heddle, holes and slots set a precise spacing of the warp threads and provide the means of creating two sheds. The slots allow the heddle to move along the warp threads while moving the hole and slot threads higher or lower to create the sheds.

Rigid heddles commonly have five slots and five holes per inch, providing for ten ends per inch. The rigid heddle must be strong because it also serves as a beater, pushing against the fell (the woven edge of the cloth) after each pass of the weft. In addition, rigid heddle looms have a rotating warp beam on which the warp is stored, to be let out as more length is needed for the fabric. Fabric that has been woven is rolled on a fabric beam, located at the front of the loom.

The rigid heddle loom, like any frame-type loom, should be strong and squarely built, preferably of hardwood. It should be easy to release and tighten the knobs or nuts that control the rotating warp beam and the fabric beam. Some looms have toothed beams that simplify warping. Others have an additional piece across the back and the breast beam, which helps to adjust the separation of the warp.

Generally, a clean shed formation is an aid to the beginning weaver. The greater the distance between the beam and the heddle, the longer one can weave without unwinding and winding the warp. Warping is relatively simple on a rigid heddle loom, but as with all looms, it is an important preliminary to correct weaving.

To weave on a rigid heddle loom, set the heddles in the "up" position. Throw the shuttle through the shed opening to carry the weft thread across the warp. Beat with the heddle. Push the heddle to the "down" position and pass the weft through in the opposite direction. Beat again. The rigid heddle loom is simple to operate and speedy, and it produces a variety of interesting fabrics.

Many weavers use an inkle loom because it is simple and fast to operate and makes belts and straps that can be combined with other handweavings. The inkle loom, which makes a warp-faced fabric, is a fixed heddle loom, with the heddles made of string. The shed is changed by hand, and the weft is beaten down with a belt shuttle or a table knife. An inkle loom is portable and relatively inexpensive.

Card weaving or tablet weaving is a form of warp twining, producing a warp-faced weave. The technique, somewhat more complicated than that of the loom, provides considerably more versatility. The appearance of a card-woven fabric depends on the selection of warp threads, warp arrangement, and the number of times and the direction that the cards are turned. The weft is beaten with a belt shuttle or a table knife. When weaving, the cards are turned after each pass of the weft in the desired direction. After each turn, the weft is beaten, and the weft shuttle is passed through again.

The card weaver may choose one of two models: a backstrap model or a plank model with pegs to hold the warp. Both types are portable and provide obvious advantages over the inkle loom with regard to the greater variety of color and weave. Backstrap weaving does not represent another type of loom. Instead, it is a different method of controlling warp tension—by the use of the weaver's body. In backstrap weaving, the weaver is actually tied to the loom and becomes a part of it. The opposite end is attached to a tree or other stationary object.

In addition to card weaving, backstrap weaving may use string heddles or change the shed with a rigid heddle. For the beginning weaver, the simplest method is to use the heddle from a rigid-heddle loom. If the weaver desires a 50/50 weave, in which the warp and the weft threads are equally visible in the finished piece, the color pattern can be planned on graph paper, to achieve stripes or plaids.

Among the more sophisticated looms are the harness looms, in which movable frames in the center of the loom contain the heddles. As the frames (harnesses) move up and down, the warp sheds are formed, through which the weft is interlaced.

A two-harness loom produces plain weaves in many variations, depending on the yarn texture and color and the way the warp is handled. A four-harness loom creates a greater variety of patterns and designs. In effect, as the number of harnesses increases, so do the possible weaves, in almost geometric progression.

Looms with four, six, and eight harnesses are available in table models. Table looms solve the problem of limited space. Such looms are operated from the front by pushing levers by hand to change the shed.

A weaver who wishes to move from simple woven patterns to more intricate ones should use a four-harness floor loom. These looms are named after the mechanism that changes the shed—a jack loom or counterbalanced loom. Each has its advantages, although a greater selection of jack looms is available. Jack looms are operated by raising particular harnesses higher than the remaining warp. The harnesses almost always are tied in combination, as determined by the pattern, and lifted by a floor pedal. The counterbalanced loom is operated with sets of harnesses tied so that when the weaver presses certain treadles (levers either hand or foot operated), the attached harnesses are lowered.

Other Weaving Tools. Weaving requires tools in addition to the loom. The tools are needed for handling the warp and weft threads and to facilitate weaving.

Various ways may be used to carry the weft threads through the shed: the butterfly (finger bobbin), stick shuttle, and boat shuttle. These may be used separately or in combination, depending on the loom and the complexity of the woven design. The butterfly is created by winding the weft threads on the hand. The thread is wound around the thumb and then around the second and third fingers, creating crisscrossed threads in between. When the butterfly is approximately 1 inch (2.5 cm) thick, it is slipped off the hand and the thread is tied where the threads cross. The loose end of the wound thread is let out as weft during weaving. Butterflies are used for tapestry, rug and inlay weaving, or when the shed is narrow.

The stick shuttle is wound with weft threads from end to end. The shuttle, usually made of wood or plastic, is 6 to 14 inches (15–36 cm) long. Notches in the ends of the shuttle hold the wound thread securely. When winding the shuttle, care must be taken that the thread is not wound too tightly. This can be avoided by sliding the fingers between the thread and the shuttle during winding. In addition, an excess of thread should not be wound on the shuttle, as it is difficult to pass an overloaded shuttle through the shed.

The boat shuttle is used for inserting the weft through the shed on a four-harness loom. The boat shuttle requires a bobbin winder, which winds the weft threads on a bobbin that fits into a hollowed-out section in the middle of the shuttle. The bobbin winder consists of a wheel that turns a metal rod on which the bobbin is placed, and the bobbin, also called a cop or quill, is a simple small spool that holds the weft threads.

Tools for preparing the warp and dressing the loom are used to control the length and tension of the warp threads. When a long, heavy warp is needed, a warping board is used. In order to withstand the tension of the many tightly wound warp threads, the board is made of heavy oak or maple, with sturdy spaced pegs sunk through the frame. When in use, a warping board may be hung on a wall or laid on a table. During winding, the warp zigzags across the frame until the number of threads required for the warp have been wound.

If a warping board is unavailable, a door frame can be converted into a warping board. Holes are bored into the door frame, and pegs (pieces of a broomstick work well) are placed in the frame. If the pegs are spaced about 36 inches (91 cm) apart, the length of warp being wound can be checked easily.

A table warping reel is designed especially for the home weaver and for those with limited working and storage space. The reel, which requires little storage space, can be assembled and disassembled quickly. The technique is simple and fast. The table model has a maximum capacity of 300 threads each about 8 yards (7.3 meters) long.

A floor warping reel is recommended when many long warp threads are required, as in weaving blankets, rugs, or bedspreads. Because of its size, the floor warping reel is used primarily in craft schools and weaving studios and by home weavers who have an entire room for weaving.

Types of Fabric. There are hundreds of kinds of fabrics—some thick, some thin; some tightly woven, some loose. In almost every piece of fabric, the threads pass over and under each other, one by one, although in some fabrics, threads go over and under more than one thread at a time.

When threads are the same size and weight, and an equal number of threads are used for both the warp and the weft, the woven cloth is a 50/50 plain web, also commonly called a tabby weave or, simply, plain weave. Plain weaves are difficult to make because the beating must be done carefully to avoid streaks, which are clearly visible when the material is held up to the light. When weaving a short length of 50/50 tabby cloth, it is advisable to do so in one sitting because matching the beat after time has elapsed is difficult.

All threads are not beaten in the same manner. Wool threads are pressed, rather than beaten, into place, while cottons and linens are given a swift, firm beat after the shed has been changed. The type of fabric being woven is also a factor that determines the method of beating. For example, a delicate fabric for a scarf is lightly beaten, while the fabric for a coat is firmly beaten.

There are two types of plain weaves: one is controlled by the action of the loom, and the other is manipulated by the fingers. Among loom-controlled weaves are balanced weaves, in which the weft and warp are the same size; and unbalanced weaves, in which the warp and weft differ.

In finger-controlled weaving, decoration and design are the primary considerations. The decoration may be created by weaving in more threads by hand after the basic fabric is complete

Warp threads are being laced through a rigid heddle that has five slots and five holes per inch. The holes and slots provide for exact spacing of the warp.

CREATIVE CRAFTS MAGAZINE

but still on the loom, by knotting in threads as the weaving progresses, or by adding threads by hand at any stage of the weaving and finishing. The beginning weaver should concentrate on fundamental weaving before embarking on skilled decorative techniques. This does not mean, however, that the weaver is restricted to creating a monochromatic cloth. Varied colored threads in either the warp or the weft or in both will produce stripes, plaids, or checks.

The 50/50 balanced weave is found in twill and overshot weaves. (Unbalanced weaves vary from that of rough utilitarian woven rag rugs to artistically textured woven scarves.) The interest created in a balanced weave lies usually in the weft threads, although the warp thread also plays a role. All the possible patterns in balanced weaves may be created in unbalanced weaves.

The twill weave is popular for its pleasing texture and pattern. It is characterized by diagonal lines forming slanted rows of color and design. Twill has an all-over surface design, and twill fabric is both attractive and durable. Woolen twill cloth is known as serge. Twills include many well-known patterns, such as herringbone and goose-eye. These can be woven with two, three, or more different colored threads to achieve striking results, such as bright tartans.

Like the plain weave, twill requires only one shuttle and is the simplest pattern to weave on a four-harness loom. Treadling the harnesses for twill is done in numerical order (1, 2, 3, 4) instead of treadling alternate harnesses (1, 3, 2, 4) as in the tabby weave. The short spaces that the weft travels in twill weaving gives the fabric both its distinctive pattern and strength. All the twill weaves and their variations make attractive fabrics, but the most interesting effects are obtained by using a warp of one color and an equal-size weft of a different color or shade.

A variety of textures are created by twill weaves. The waffle weave results in a textured fabric composed of small pockets of plain weave embedded in raised ridges. These pockets are formed by heavy warp and weft threads coming up and over the regular tabby surface to form small squares.

The raindrop pattern is a reverse twill woven to form small diamond designs. It is well suited for toweling, table cloths, and dress goods.

The basket weave is created by using pairs of warp and weft threads, interlocked to form a basketlike mesh. This type of fabric is commonly used for draperies, pillow covers, and textured mats. When woven in wool, the basket weave makes an excellent blanket.

Different harness treadling is used for the herringbone weave. Whereas the basic twill weave requires treadling in numerical order (1, 2, 3, 4), the herringbone treadling is in numerical order for a number of treadles and then reversed (1, 2, 3, 4, 3, 2, 1).

The overshot weave, derived from the twill weave, consists of repetitive treadling sequences in numerical order (1–2, 2–3, 3–4, 4–1), creating a popular pattern in design and texture. The fabric has a long overshot weave appearing at regular intervals across the surface of the plain-weave web. A complicated weave, such as the overshot, requires a good working knowledge of weaving drafts, which are plans to instruct the weaver how to treadle and manipulate the loom.

The satin weave is by far the most complex, requiring a loom with at least five harnesses.

LAIMUTE E. DRUSKIS/EPA

Weaving instructor demonstrates on a frame tapestry loom. The string heddles are attached to wooden rods.

Because of its complexity, it is done by machine and seldom by handweaving. Damask is a variation of the satin weave that lends itself successfully to handweaving. Damask has long been a favorite for fine table linens and draperies.

History. Primitive people first began to weave when they interlaced twigs and grasses to form mats and baskets. Later, they began to split bark and tree-root fibers into finer fibers that could be woven into clothlike materials. Cloth weaving grew out of basketry, the basic difference being that cloth weaving requires a loom while basket weaving uses stiff fibers. The development of the loom allowed the use of flexible fibers, such as wool, cotton, and linen.

There is evidence of weaving as early as 4400 B.C. A pottery dish found in a prehistoric Egyptian tomb depicts a primitive loom, which has the essential elements of the modern-day loom. Two weaving tools were also found in the tomb—a simple comblike beater and a heddle rod, indicating that significant advances had already been made in manipulating the shed.

Weaving seems to have been common to most cultures. The oldest extant examples of woven cloth were done by Stone Age dwellers about 3000 B.C. These bits of flax fabric were found with the simple tools used to weave them. In Genesis the story of Joseph's coat of many colors indicates that dyeing natural fibers for woven cloth is long-known art. In ancient Egypt it was the custom to enshroud the dead in woven linen, of which many examples exist, since linen is remarkably durable.

In Asia, weaving antedates recorded history. The Chinese made cloth of fine silk, and in Arabia and Persia fabrics were woven of gold and beautifully dyed threads. These fabrics were so highly valued that they were often used for barter. Though few examples of ancient Greek weaving remain, Greek statues indicate a superb knowledge of weaving techniques.

The American Indian, both in North and South America, was already an expert weaver when the first colonists arrived. Indian weaving often has religious symbolism and shows a love of nature. Indians valued their cloth highly, and wasted none of it by cutting.

The horizontal loom with treadle-operated harnesses was developed in Europe in the 13th century. The warping board was also introduced at that time. Little change was made in weaving until the mid-18th century, when the English began to develop improved weaving mechanisms and tools. By the 19th century, handweaving almost had become a lost art in industrialized Europe, although it continued to flourish in Scandinavia, the more remote areas of Europe, and the rural areas of the United States. In the 20th century, however, there was a resurgence of interest in handweaving as a craft that is nearly an art form in its beauty.

WENDIE BLANCHARD
Editor, "Creative Crafts" Magazine

Bibliography

Atwater, Mary M., *Byways in Handweaving* (Macmillan 1954).
Black, Mary E., *New Key to Weaving* (Macmillan 1957).
Bress, Helene, *Inkle Weaving* (Scribner 1975).
Scarlett, James D., *How to Weave Fine Cloth* (Prentice-Hall 1981).
Tod, Osma Gallinger, *The Joy of Handweaving* (Dover 1964).
Gustafson, Paula, *Salish Weaving* (Univ. of Wash. Press 1980).

WEB AND THE ROCK, a novel by the American author Thomas Wolfe, published posthumously in 1939. *The Web and the Rock* was the third large segment—after *Look Homeward, Angel* (1929) and *Of Time and the River* (1935)—of Wolfe's fictional recapitulation of his life and experience. However, the name of the hero, Eugene Gant, in the first two books was changed to George Webber, and the town of Altamont (Ashville, N.C.) became Libya Hill.

Wolfe himself declared that these changes marked a new "objectivity" in his fiction, a development from youthful revolt to a mature and communal sense of life, along with a new stress on the "satiric exaggeration" of human experience. There are still the romantic element and the familiar poetry (and rhetoric) in this third novel—Wolfe could not escape his Southern heritage—but he was becoming a social realist and satirist of note, in the strain of American fiction extending from Herman Melville to Theodore Dreiser and Sinclair Lewis.

The central section of *The Web and the Rock* deals with the arrival of the provincial hero in New York; his love affair with "Mrs. Jack," the symbol of the "enfabled rock"; and his introduction to the highest levels of cosmopolitan culture. The book ends with the tormented dissolution of the love affair; the escape of the hero to Europe; and his first true understanding of Germany under Nazi rule. Although imperfect in structure and detail, the novel contains brilliant descriptions of provincial life, the civilization of cities, and modern man's latent barbarism.

MAXWELL GEISMAR
Author of "Writers in Crisis"

WEB PRESS, a printing press that prints on a continuous roll of paper, called a web, rather than on cut sheets of paper. Web presses are fast and are economical for long printing runs. See also PRINTING.

WEBB, Beatrice (1858–1943), English writer on economics and sociology. Martha Beatrice Potter was born near Gloucester on Jan. 22, 1858, the daughter of a railway and industrial magnate. She was educated privately and, after her mother's death in 1882, became a close business associate of her father. She investigated working-class conditions as part of the survey *Life and Labour of the People in London* (1891–1903), directed by Charles Booth. In 1891 she published *The Co-operative Movement in Great Britain*.

In 1892 she married a kindred spirit, the Socialist leader and Fabian Society member Sidney Webb. The husband-and-wife team served on numerous royal commissions and wrote several masterly studies of economic problems, notably their *History of Trade Unionism* (1894), *Industrial Democracy* (1897), and *English Local Government* (10 vols., 1906–1929). Mrs. Webb also served on the Poor Law Commission (1906–1909) and was joint author of its minority report, thereby awakening public interest in the principles of social insurance. In 1913 they helped to found the *New Statesman*. The Webbs' London house became a socialist salon, and they played an increasingly influential role in guiding the intellectual development of the Labour party. She died in Liphook, Hampshire, on April 30, 1943. See also WEBB, SIDNEY JAMES.

Further Reading Webb, Beatrice, *Our Partnership* (1948; reprint, Cambridge 1975).

WEBB, Sidney James (1859–1947), English social reformer and economic historian. He was born in London on July 13, 1859, and was educated in Switzerland; in Mecklenburg-Schwerin, Germany; and at the Birkbeck Institute and the City of London College. He entered the civil service in 1878 but resigned in 1891 when elected to a seat on the London County Council, which he held until 1910.

Webb, who was an early and active member of the Fabian Society, expounded his gradualist views in *Socialism in England* (1890). In time he emerged as one of the leading intellectuals of the Labour movement. In 1892 he married Beatrice Potter, and together they waged a lifelong crusade for social justice. They helped to found the London School of Economics and Political Science (1895) and the *New Statesman* (1913) and collaborated on a number of authoritative treatises on social and economic history.

As a member of the Coal Industry Commission (1919), Webb drew up a comprehensive scheme for the nationalization of the industry. He was elected member of parliament for Seaham in 1922 and, on the formation of the first MacDonald administration, became president of the Board of Trade in 1924. On the return of the Labour party to office in 1929, Webb was created Baron Passfield and became secretary of state for the colonies (1929–1931) and dominions (1929–1930). On the breakup of the Labour government in 1931, he retired from politics. In 1932 he and his wife visited Russia to study the Soviet way of life. The results of their investigations were published in *Soviet Communism: A New Civilization?* (2 vols., 1935), in which admiration for Russia's economic planning was tempered by dislike for its system of government. He was made a member of the Order of Merit in 1944. Webb died in Liphook, Hampshire, on Oct. 13, 1947. See also WEBB, BEATRICE.

WEBB, William Henry (1816–1899), American shipbuilder. He was born in New York, N.Y., on June 19, 1816, the son of Isaac Webb from Stamford, Conn., who learned shipbuilding at the East River (New York) yard of Henry Eckford and later took it over. On Isaac's death in 1840 the shipyard was passed along to William. Isaac trained the two foremost American shipbuilders of the day: the Nova Scotian Donald McKay, who later built superlative clippers in East Boston, and his own versatile son, whose excellent packets, clippers, steamships, and foreign warships exceeded in total tonnage the production of any other American builder until that time.

In transatlantic sailing packets, the Webb yard built all 16 ships of the crack Black Ball Line to Liverpool between 1836 and 1869, including the Yorkshire, fastest of all packets, as well as all ten ships of the Union Line to Le Havre between 1836 and 1851. Even in the McKay specialty of clippers, Webb produced several excellent ships, including the *Swordfish*, which made the fourth-fastest run between New York and San Francisco.

Webb also built the hulls for numerous crack American steamships, the machinery and boilers coming from the nearby Novelty Iron Works. In particular, he built 16 steamships for the Pacific Mail, in which he had a financial interest. In a dramatic demonstration of his versatility, on a single day (Jan. 21, 1851), Webb launched a Havre packet, a clipper ship, and a Pacific Mail liner.

By the late 1850's the boom had passed, and Webb went after orders for foreign warships. Between 1858 and 1864 he completed the wooden *Japanis* and *General-Admiral* for the Russians and the ironclads *Re d'Italia* and *Re di Portogallo* for the Italians. His only ship for the Union Navy, the huge ironclad ram *Dunderberg*, was completed so late that it was sold to the French. The Black Baller *Charles H. Marshall* in 1869 was Webb's last ship, and also the last square-rigger built in New York. He died in New York City on Oct. 30, 1899.

ROBERT G. ALBION
Harvard University

WEBER, vä′bər, **Carl Maria von** (1786–1826), German composer, whose works helped introduce Romanticism into German music.

Life. Carl Maria Friedrich Ernst von Weber was born in Eutin, Schleswig-Holstein, on Nov. 18, 1786. During his childhood he traveled with his father's theatrical company, acquiring knowledge of the lyric stage and receiving some musical training. His first published music appeared when he was only 12.

In 1800, Weber's opera *The Forest Maiden* was staged in Freiburg. Another opera, *Peter Schmoll*, was first performed in Augsburg in 1803. After additional studies, Weber held various theatrical and court positions. During this period he completed two more operas, *Silvana* (Frankfurt, 1810) and *Abu Hassan* (Munich, 1811) and won acclaim as a pianist. In 1813 he was named conductor of the German Opera at Prague, and soon after he became director of the Dresden German Opera.

In 1817, Weber began writing the opera *Der Freischütz*, his most famous work. Using a libretto by Friedrich Kind, based on a fairy tale by Johann August Apel and Friedrich Laun, Weber set out to compose a specifically German *Singspiel*. Viewed as a challenge to the Italo-French domination of opera in Germany, *Der Freischütz*, produced in Berlin in 1821, proved to be the first triumph of consciously romantic German music. Weber's next opera, *Euryanthe*, was introduced in Vienna in 1823.

Though suffering from tuberculosis, Weber accepted an invitation to compose an English opera for production in London and set to work on *Oberon*. Weary and ailing, he conducted the premier on April 12, 1826, and 11 more performances, and also played at several concerts, the last only one week before he died in London on June 5, 1826. His body, first buried in London, was reinterred in Dresden in 1844. He had become a German national hero, and Richard Wagner delivered the burial oration and conducted special ceremonial music.

Importance. Although Weber's operas have not remained in the active repertoire outside Germany, they nevertheless are important steps in the evolution of romantic music and German opera, and selections from them, notably their fine overtures, often are heard. The considerable body of Weber's nontheatrical music includes choral works; symphonies; concertos, including the familiar *Konzertstück* for piano and orchestra; overtures; chamber music; piano works, among them *Invitation to the Dance*, later orchestrated by Hector Berlioz; and miscellaneous pieces. A master of orchestration, Weber emphasized the literature-based folk elements of German romantic art, its forest lore and supernatural, often grisly elements, as well as its *Gemütlichkeit*.

Weber was also a masterly composer for the voice. He strongly influenced not only such primarily operatic composers as Wagner, but also the entire character of early German romantic music by such composers as Felix Mendelssohn and Robert Schumann.

See also FREISCHÜTZ, DER; OBERON.

HERBERT WEINSTOCK
Author of "Music as an Art"

WEBER, vābər, **Ernst Heinrich** (1795–1878), German anatomist and physiologist, who founded experimental psychology. He was born in Wittenberg, Germany, on June 24, 1795. Educated at Wittenberg, he taught anatomy (1818–1840) and later physiology (1840–1871) at Leipzig. Weber described the chain of small bones between the labyrinth and swim bladder of some freshwater fish. These bones, named "Weberian ossicles," aid sound reception. He was also a pioneer in experimental studies of the nervous impulses controlling heartbeat.

Weber's investigation of the threshold for just noticeable differences in sensation marks the beginning of experimental psychology. He was particularly interested in cutaneous sensations, and his *Der Tastsinn und das Gemeingefühl* (*Sense of Touch and Common Sensibility*), published in Rudolph Wagner's *Handwörterbuch der Physiologie* (1846), is still regarded as a classic in psychology and physiology. Gustav Theodor Fechner summarized Weber's investigations dealing with judgments of least noticeable differences between pairs of stimuli and referred to the inference therefrom as Weber's law (also called the Weber-Fechner law). Weber died in Leipzig on Jan. 26, 1878.

PHILIP L. HARRIMAN
Editor of "Encyclopedia of Psychology"

COLLECTION OF THE WHITNEY MUSEUM OF AMERICAN ART

American artist Max Weber was deeply influenced by the artistic developments that took place in Paris in the early 20th century. *Chinese Restaurant* (1915) is generally regarded as his major painting in the Cubist style.

WEBER, web′ər, **Max** (1881–1961), American painter, who exerted a vital influence on art in the United States in the early 20th century.

Life. He was born in Bialystok, Russia (now in Poland), on April 18, 1881, and went to the United States with his parents in 1891. He studied at the Pratt Institute in Brooklyn N.Y., from 1898 to 1900, where he was introduced by Arthur Wesley Dow, his instructor in composition, to Japanese art and Gauguin's nonnaturalistic use of color.

After teaching for five years, Weber went to Paris. It was a time of intense artistic excitement over Matisse and the Fauvists, and he saw the Salon d'Automne exhibition with Cézanne's paintings that provided the inspiration for the Cubist movement. He also met Henri Rousseau, whose work he later introduced to America by arranging a showing at Alfred Stieglitz' "291" gallery.

Upon Weber's return to the United States, his work was first shown at the Hass Gallery in New York City in 1909. The following year he was included in a group show of American painters at "291," described at the time as an "insult to the American people." His first one-man show, held at "291" in 1911, was called by one critic a "brutal, vulgar and unnecessary display of art license." He was also one of the American exhibitors in the famous Armory Show of 1913. Later one-man shows of his paintings were held at the Newark Museum in 1913 and 1959, the Museum of Modern Art in 1930, and the Whitney Museum of American Art in 1949. Weber wrote on cubism and the significance of primitive art to the modern mind in *Camera Work* (1910), *Cubist Poems* (1914), *Essays on Art* (1916), *Primitives* (1926), and *Woodcuts* (1957). He died in Great Neck, N.Y., on Oct. 4, 1961.

Influence. Weber's work has been criticized for being too eclectic, but his importance probably lies in that very quality, for he was one of the few American artists consistently to perceive and absorb the 20th century developments in Paris. The general effect of his paintings is of rich, jewel-like color, and, despite sorties into abstractionism, the subject matter often has a religious or mystical mood. The violence of the language and the strong reactions of the critics in the early reviews of his paintings eventually gave way in the 1940's to a greater appreciation of his style and a tendency to regard him as the dean of America's modern painters.

JEAN ANNE VINCENT*
Author of "History of Art"

WEBER, vā′bər, **Max** (1864–1920), German social scientist, who had a major influence on modern sociology and, more broadly, on the history of ideas. A wide-ranging scholar and prolific writer as well as a respected professor, he contributed important studies on social organization, the nature of the modern state, jurisprudence and ethics, authority and leadership, and, most notably, the relation between religion and capitalist economics.

Life. Weber was born in Erfurt, Thuringia, on April 21, 1864, and was raised in Charlottenburg, a suburb of Berlin. He studied two years at the University of Heidelberg and completed his education at Berlin, with a degree in law and a doctorate in economics.

Weber's brilliance earned him prestigious appointments in economics at the universities of Freiburg, Heidelberg, and Munich, which he held sporadically owing to periodic emotional breakdowns.

Between travels for his health, he edited the influential *Archive for Social Science and Social Policy*, for which he wrote numerous monographs, and began his multivolume study *Economy and Society*, most of which was published and translated posthumously. He died in Munich on June 14, 1920.

Thought. Weber's early studies were on medieval trading companies, the agrarian societies of Rome and western Europe, and the German stock exchange. His interest in religion as a social institution led him to make in-depth analyses of Buddhism, Confucianism, Hinduism, Taoism, and ancient Judaism. Comparing their values with those of European Christianity, he observed that Protestantism—notably Calvinism—encouraged individual enterprise and the accumulation of capital, enabling one to demonstrate that by achieving economic success he would be favored by God. This formed the basis of his classic work *The Protestant Ethic and the Spirit of Capitalism* (1904–1905).

In Weber's view, Western civilization was marked by a steady trend toward organization, rationalization, and bureaucracy in government, politics, and social institutions. With bureaucracy came social stratification, for which he developed a model consisting of class—concerned with income and economic position; status—with rank, life-style, and prestige; and party—with political affiliation and power.

Formulating a model for politics, Weber delineated three types of authority, each with its base of legitimacy: traditional—confirmed by historical precedent, as in the lord-serf relationship under feudalism; charismatic—reflecting the compelling style of inspired leaders, as in dictatorships; and bureaucratic—resulting from the rational-legal codes of a nation or corporate organization.

Basic to Weber's contributions to sociology were his insistence on rigorous methodology, the elimination of value judgments, and the formulation of models and ideal types for the study of social organization. Almost all social scientists have felt his influence.

Bibliography

Beetham, David, *Max Weber and the Theory of Modern Politics,* 2d ed. (Basil Blackwell 1985).
Brunn, H. H., *Science, Value, and Politics in Max Weber's Methodology* (1972; reprint, Humanities Press 1977).
Giddens, Anthony, *Politics and Sociology in the Thought of Max Weber* (Humanities Press 1972).
Portis, Edward B., *Max Weber and Political Commitment* (Temple Univ. Press 1987).
Weber, Marianne, and others, eds., *Max Weber: A Biography,* ed. and tr. by Harry Zohn (Krieger 1975).

WEBER, (web'ər), symbol Wb, the unit of magnetic flux in the meter-kilogram-second (MKS) system of units and in the International System (SI). If a uniform magnetic field **B** is perpendicular to a surface of area *A*, the magnetic flux is equal to **B***A*.

WEBER AND FIELDS, web'ər, fēldz, American comedy team that starred on Broadway and in vaudeville. Joseph M. Weber was born in New York City on Aug. 11, 1867, and died in Los Angeles, Calif., on May 10, 1942. Lew Fields was born in New York City on Jan. 1, 1867, and died in Los Angeles on July 20, 1941. They formed their partnership when they were nine or ten years old, appearing in variety theaters in New York City in a slapstick act that featured German dialect humor.

In 1885 they formed their own company and toured the vaudeville circuits for ten years. In their sketches, Fields was the tall, thin, trickster and Weber the short, squat innocent. In 1896 they bought the Broadway Music Hall in New York City and renamed it the Weber and Fields Music Hall. They also managed the theater, presenting and acting with such stars as Lillian Russell and DeWolf Hopper in extravagant comedies burlesquing current stage successes—*Cyranose* and *Quo Vass Iss?*, for example.

The team quarreled and dissolved their partnership in 1904, and Weber became the owner and manager of Weber's Theatre. They were reunited in 1912 for a successful Broadway run. After 1914, Fields generally appeared alone until he retired in 1930. Weber retired from acting in 1918 but directed plays until 1928.

WEBERN, vā'bərn, **Anton** (1883–1945), Austrian composer, who was a major force in the development of 20th century atonal and serial music.

Life. Anton Friedrich Wilhelm von Webern was born in Vienna on Dec. 3, 1883. With Alban Berg, he was an early pupil of Arnold Schoenberg, with whom he studied from 1904 to 1910.

Webern spent most of his life in and around Vienna, where he held various conductorships and taught composition. When the Germans occupied Austria in 1938, his music was banned, and he was forbidden to teach. Shortly before the end of World War II, he and his family moved to the town of Mittersill, near Salzburg. On Sept. 15, 1945, he was accidentally shot and killed in Mittersill by an American soldier.

Works. Webern was not a prolific composer. Of the 31 works published during his lifetime—none lasting more than about ten minutes—approximately half are instrumental and half vocal. Apart from the *Passacaglia* (1908), which is tonal, his earlier works are written in the free atonal style invented by Schoenberg in 1908; the later works use Schoenberg's 12-tone (serial) technique.

But Webern was far more radical than Schoenberg, and his music shows a concentration and purity of style that has had an enormous effect on modern music and influenced such composers as Pierre Boulez, Luigi Nono, and Karlheinz Stockhausen. In Webern's music each single tone is of the utmost importance, and the architecture is based on the relations between the individual tones. The sound of his music is usually magical—he had an extraordinarily acute ear—but this is always subordinated to the structural design. He normally avoided large orchestras and wrote for smaller but unusual combinations of instruments. Among his last works are three cantatas for chorus and small orchestra.

HUMPHREY SEARLE, *Author of "Twentieth Century Counterpoint"*

Weber (*left*) always played the butt of the jokes in the vaudeville sketches of the great Weber and Fields.

THE BETTMANN ARCHIVE

WEBSTER, wĕb'stər, **Daniel,** American orator and statesman: b. Salisbury, N.H., Jan. 18, 1782; d. Marshfield, Mass., Oct. 24, 1852. His father, Ebenezer Webster, a Revolutionary veteran, was a man of tenacity and character. The boy's early teachers were mostly semi-itinerant, but he mastered the three R's and was ready in 1796 for the Phillips Exeter Academy, where he spent nine months. He was then prepared by the Rev. Samuel Wood for Dartmouth College, from which he was graduated Aug. 27, 1801, with Phi Beta Kappa rank. He is commemorated at Dartmouth in a professorship of Latin and the Daniel Webster Hall.

Daniel Webster

The seven years following Webster's graduation were a preparatory and probationary period during which he was serving his apprenticeship to the law. He earned some necessary money by teaching at Fryeburg Academy in Maine, and then studied for several months under the eminent attorney, Christopher Gore, in Boston; having been admitted to the bar in March 1805, he opened practice in Boscawen, N.H. In 1807 he was admitted as counselor to the superior court of New Hampshire and moved to Portsmouth, hoping to broaden his practice.

On May 29, 1808, Webster married Grace Fletcher, a schoolteacher in Salisbury, by whom he had five children. Of these, two died in childhood, Edward was a victim of typhoid in the Mexican War, Col. Daniel Fletcher Webster was killed at the head of his troops in the Second Battle of Bull Run (Aug. 30, 1862), and Julia, married to Samuel Appleton in 1839, died in 1848. No descendant bearing the Webster name is now alive.

In the competitive give-and-take of the New Hampshire courts, Webster gained skill and confidence, rising rapidly to leadership at the state bar. Drawn into politics as a Federalist, he denounced Thomas Jefferson's policies and strongly opposed the second war with Great Britain. He drafted and read, Aug. 5, 1812, the "Rockingham Memorial," vigorously attacking the administration. This facilitated his election in November to the 13th Congress, and he served two terms as a member of the opposition. In June 1816, he moved to Boston, and the remainder of his life was spent mostly in Massachusetts and Washington.

Webster's legal reputation was enhanced by his part in the Dartmouth College Case (*Dartmouth College* v. *Woodward*, 4 Wheat., 518), which he argued for the plaintiff before the Supreme Court of the United States in 1818, and which was decided in his client's favor in February 1819. Stripped of technicalities and nonessentials, the immediate issue was the permanence and validity of the charter of an institution of learning; and by implication, the whole subject of the stability of contracts was involved. Chief Justice John Marshall's opinion determined that the Dartmouth College charter was a contract "the obligation of which cannot be impaired without violating the Constitution of the United States." Today Webster's plea is chiefly remembered because of its moving reference to his alma mater: "It is, sir, as I have said, a small college,—and yet there are those who love it!"

In several other crucial cases Webster, as a lawyer, usually supported by Marshall as chief justice, exerted the full power of his reasoning and eloquence to favor a strong national government and a wise freedom in interpreting the provisions of the Constitution. Through *McCulloch* v. *Maryland* (4 Wheat., 316), decided in 1819, and other related cases he became known as "the Expounder of the Constitution," and his function as its elucidator at a critical period was historically of hardly less importance than that of Alexander Hamilton as framer.

Although not often in the criminal courts, Webster in the summer of 1830, at Salem, Mass., aided the prosecution in the trial of the Knapp brothers for the murder of Capt. Joseph White, describing the remorse of the assassin in the words, "There is no refuge from confession but suicide, and suicide is confession."

Webster's activity and ambition in the 1820's seemed boundless. His forensic successes brought him many invitations, and several occasional speeches of that period have placed him as an orator beside Demosthenes, Cicero, and Edmund Burke. First came the Plymouth Oration, delivered Dec. 22, 1820, at the bicentennial of the landing of the Pilgrims. A second address of unusual interest was that on June 17, 1825, at the laying of the cornerstone of the Bunker Hill Monument, at Charlestown near Boston. Its verbal felicity and intensely emotional quality added distinction to its theme. On Aug. 6, 1826, he spoke in commemoration of John Adams and Thomas Jefferson, who by a remarkable coincidence had died within a few hours of one another on the preceding Independence Day.

Inevitably Webster was elected to the national House of Representatives in 1822, and in June 1827, was chosen to succeed Elijah H. Mills in the United States Senate. This was the political arena which, with John C. Calhoun and Henry Clay, he was to dominate for many years. Shortly after taking his seat, he spoke in favor of the protective tariff act of 1828, thus reversing a position which he had taken in 1824, doing this quite frankly in the interests of the industrial area of which he had come to be the spokesman. He was welcomed as a leader of the amorphous anti-Jackson group which became the working nucleus of the ill-fated Whig Party.

Mrs. Webster had died, Jan. 21, 1828, before her husband took his seat in the Senate. On Dec. 12, 1829, he married Caroline Le Roy, of New York City, 17 years younger than he. A few weeks after this second marriage he delivered in January 1830, before the Senate, the speech best known as the Reply to Hayne (q.v.). The basic issue was sectionalism, and Webster hoped to determine the point at which the authority of a sovereign state ceased and that of the federal government began. Senator Robert Young Hayne of South Carolina had defended the doctrine of states' rights, declaring that "there is no evil more to be deprecated than the consolidation of this government." Concurrently he criticized the "disloyalty" of New Englanders during the War of 1812 and Webster's conversion to protectionism. He also explained and defended what came to be known as the South Carolina theory of nullification (q.v.).

Webster's Reply, filling 73 printed pages, first vindicated himself and New England against the slurs of Hayne and then presented his own conception of the nature of the federal Union. He contended that it was established, not by the states severally but by the people as a governmental unit, with certain specified and restricted powers, superior in various respects to the state governments. He closed his peroration with the sonorous words, "Liberty *and* Union, now and forever, one and inseparable!" which have become part of the American heritage. This speech was not merely a refutation of Calhoun's nullification theory. It also rounded out majestically the governmental philosophy which Webster had previously expressed in his arguments before the Supreme Court. He gave brilliant and much-publicized expression to American nationalistic longings and ideals, with which he was popularly identified during his later life.

Webster and Andrew Jackson were together in their insistence that the Union must be preserved. However, in the controversy between President Jackson and the Bank of the United States, Webster supported the bank, whose retainers he had accepted; and in 1836 he was a Whig candidate for the presidency, although he received only the electoral votes of Massachusetts. In 1839 he took a trip to Europe, where he was received as a celebrity and met everyone of any importance.

Webster campaigned vigorously for William Henry Harrison in 1840 and was rewarded with the position of secretary of state. When, after Harrison's death, the strict constructionist, John Tyler, became president, all the cabinet except Webster resigned, under the autocratic pressure of Henry Clay. Webster, however, wished to carry through to a successful conclusion the complicated negotiations with Great Britain over the Maine boundary which resulted in the Webster-Ashburton Treaty (q.v.) of 1842. Rather reluctantly he left the cabinet, May 8, 1843, and was soon reconciled to his former Whig associates. In 1845 he allowed himself to be returned to the Senate, where he opposed the acquisition of Texas and the Mexican War.

The problem of Negro servitude was to trouble Webster to the end of his days. Although he believed the South's "peculiar institution" to be a great moral and political evil, he felt also that it was, within the Southern states, a matter of domestic policy with which the federal government ought not to interfere. Slavery was bad, but not so bad as disunion. During a period of increasing agitation, he had in 1848 renewed presidential aspirations, but the Whig Party again preferred a military hero, Zachary Taylor.

In 1850 the Union seemed seriously in danger from radicals in both North and South. Henry Clay, near the close of his career, sponsored in the Senate a group of measures, including a Fugitive Slave Act, which became known as the Compromise of 1850 (q.v.). Webster, in his "Seventh of March Speech," undertook "to beat down the Northern and Southern follies, now raging in equal extremes." He had resolved not to allow his personal ambitions or desire for popularity to obscure his sense of public duty. The resulting argument, temperate in tone and moderate in language, was deliberately prepared to meet a national crisis and avert disunion. Because of the Fugitive Slave Act, the abolitionists were angered, and John Greenleaf Whittier, in a passionate poem, denounced Webster as "Ichabod." But the best historical judgment has recognized that Webster's effective sponsorship of the compromise probably postponed civil war for a decade.

When Millard Fillmore succeeded Taylor as president in July 1850, Webster again became secretary of state. His most noteworthy act in that capacity was the Hülsemann note, a reply to the Austrian chargé d'affaires in Washington, who had accused the United States of being "impatient for the downfall of the Austrian monarchy." This attracted attention because of its truculent tone, unusual for Webster.

In failing health, Webster spent the early autumn of 1852 at Green Harbor, his homestead in Marshfield, Mass., which he had bought in 1832 and where he found solace in his declining years. There, on Oct. 24, 1852, he died, surrounded by relatives and friends. His last words were, "I still live!" He was buried in the secluded Marshfield cemetery, where his grave is marked by a simple block of granite.

With his Jovian head, cavernous black eyes, swarthy complexion, broad chest, and massive rotundity, Webster stood out in any company through sheer physical dominance. He was compared with stupendous natural phenomena, like Niagara Falls and Mount Washington. When in 1901 the candidates for the American Hall of Fame were chosen, 97 electors cast their votes unanimously for George Washington, but Lincoln and Webster were tied for second place with 96 votes each. Webster was recently named by the United States Senate as one of the five "most useful" members of that body. He was the folk hero of Stephen Vincent Benet's *The Devil and Daniel Webster* (1937), and John F. Kennedy, in his *Profiles in Courage* (1956), included him as one of the conspicuous examples of his thesis.

The "God-like Dan'l" had some very human weaknesses. Humility was not one of his virtues. In his later years, unrestrained by the salutary influence of his first wife, his self-indulgence became notorious. In money matters he was elusive, almost constantly in debt, and allowed himself to be rescued from bankruptcy more than once by admirers. To his critics he seemed too much identified with the wealthy and wellborn, and indifferent to those less fortunate. His instinctive and philosophical conservatism did not please the liberals of his generation.

It was, however, Webster's historic function to strengthen the republic of the Founding Fathers and to use compromise and conciliation to preserve it when it was in danger from sectionalists. It was to emphasize his conception of a united nation that his two ablest Senate speeches were delivered; and when the Civil War did break out, it was his Unionist doctrine, rephrased by Abraham Lincoln, which animated the North and ensured its victory.

CLAUDE MOORE FUESS
Author of "Daniel Webster"

Bibliography

Bartlett, Irving H., *Daniel Webster* (Norton 1981).
Dalzell, Robert F., Jr., *Daniel Webster and the Trial of American Nationalism, 1843–1852* (Norton 1975).
Erickson, Paul D., *The Poetry of Events: Daniel Webster's Rhetoric of the American Dream* (N. Y. Univ. Press 1986).
Fuess, Claude M., *Daniel Webster*, 2d ed., 2 vols. (1930; reprint, Da Capo 1968).
Webster, Daniel, *The Papers of Daniel Webster: Correspondence*, ed. by Charles M. Wiltse and Michael J. Birkner (Univ. Press of New England 1974–1986).
Webster, Daniel, *The Papers of Daniel Webster: Legal Papers*, ed. by Alfred S. Konefsky and others, 2 vols. (Univ. Press of New England 1982–1983).

WEBSTER, H(arold) T(ucker), American cartoonist: b. Parkersburg, W.Va., Sept. 21, 1885; d. Stamford, Conn., Sept. 22, 1952. At the age of 7 he began to draw, and when he was about 12 he sold his first cartoon. After studying art in Chicago for a short time, he began his career as a newspaper cartoonist, working for some of the leading papers in the United States. In 1931 he began to draw for the New York *Herald Tribune*, and eventually his work was syndicated in over 120 North American newspapers.

In thousands of cartoons, Webster commented with acute insight on the American character and social scene. Among his popular cartoon series were "The Timid Soul," which with Caspar Milquetoast added a beloved figure to the national mythology; "Life's Darkest Moment" and "The Thrill That Comes Once in a Lifetime," which nostalgically evoked his boyhood in Wisconsin.

WEBSTER, Jean (in full ALICE JANE CHANDLER WEBSTER), American writer: b. Fredonia, N.Y., July 24, 1876; d. New York, June 11, 1916. After graduating from Vassar College in 1901 she spent a few years in Italy and traveled around the world, then settled in New York City. In 1915 she married Glenn Ford McKinney, a New York lawyer. Her interest in underprivileged children led her to write her most popular novel, *Daddy Long-Legs* (1912), which was successfully dramatized in 1914 and was translated widely. A sequel, *Dear Enemy*, appeared in 1914. She was also the author of *When Patty Went to College* (1903) and other Patty stories.

WEBSTER, John, English dramatist: b. probably 1570/1580; d. probably by 1634. Almost nothing is known of his life: in the dedication to his pageant *Monuments of Honour* (1624), he tells us that he was born free of the Merchant Taylors' Company. He was, however, active as a writer in the years immediately following 1600, collaborating at times with Thomas Dekker and others; Thomas Middleton and John Ford were among those who paid tribute to him in commendatory verse. Apart from the two famous tragedies, *The White Devil* (c. 1612) and *The Duchess of Malfi* (c. 1613), only one extant play, a "dark" comedy called *The Devil's Law Case* (of uncertain date), seems to be wholly his.

The White Devil presents a story of adultery, murder, and revenge, in which the main characters act without scruple and yet deeply engage the reader's and spectator's interest. The "good" characters are shown as powerless to affect the course of events, and are, moreover, presented with some degree of aloofness and dubiety. Outside the dark immediate world of the play there is suggested only a profounder darkness. The dramatist's vision would be a nihilistic one were it not for the keen sense of life in the central figures, the firm recognition of evil, and the insistence on a man's responsibility for even those acts to which he seems compelled.

The Duchess of Malfi, despite its full demonstration of evil and suffering, is basically a gentler, an elegiac, tragedy. Its duchess, who incurs her brothers' enmity through her secret second marriage, combines courage and personal authority with a capacity for warm affection and a scant regard for her duties as a ruler.

Webster's dramatic manner owes much to Shakespeare, whom he frequently echoes, but the two tragedies are securely the work of an individual mind. In his own time he was described as a laborious writer, and his heavy dependence on his reading—for image, phrase, and incidental idea—has been documented at length in Robert W. Dent's *John Webster's Borrowing* (Berkeley 1960). But what he borrowed fitted both the main structural pattern of the drama and the pattern of his grotesque and nerve-stretching imagery. Moreover, he was capable of the direct and moving utterance at a moment of crisis, most of all at a moment of death. In that he followed the example of Shakespeare, but the words and the deeply imagined situations are his own. Webster's is an especially precarious kind of tragedy, for his view of human nature shirked little of its baseness. His satiric strain links him with the fiercer comic writers of Jacobean years, notably John Marston and Ben Jonson, but this element in his work—considered in Travis Bogard's *The Tragic Satire of John Webster* (Berkeley 1955) and Gunnar Boklund's *The Sources of The White Devil* (Uppsala 1957)—did not stand in the way of a deep involvement with and wonderment at the men and women he presented.

After long neglect, the two tragedies have been acted with some frequency on British and American stages during the 20th century. In the range of their language and in the amplitude and humanity of their spectacle, they are major achievements of the English-speaking theater.

CLIFFORD LEECH,
University of Durham, England.

Further Reading: Bradbrook, Muriel, *John Webster* (Columbia Univ. Press 1980); Forker, C. R., *The Skull Beneath the Skin: The Achievement of John Webster* (Southern Ill. Univ. Press 1986); Leech, C., *John Webster* (1951; reprint, Haskell 1969); Moore, Don, *Webster: The Critical Heritage* (Methuen 1982); Webster, John, *The Complete Works of John Webster*, ed. by F. L. Lucas, 4 vols. (1927; reprint, Gordian Press 1966).

WEBSTER, Margaret, Anglo-American actress, director, and producer: b. New York, N.Y., March 15, 1905; d. London, Nov. 13, 1972. Her father, Ben Webster, was a well-known English Shakespearean actor, and her mother was Dame May Whitty, a popular stage and film actress. Miss Webster was born in New York while her father was playing there, but she spent her first 29 years in England. In 1924 she made her first professional appearance in the chorus of Euripides' *Trojan Women* with Sybil Thorndike, and the following year she made her Shakespearean debut with John Barrymore in *Hamlet*. During the next 10 years while appearing in many plays she gradually began directing. When in 1937, Maurice Evans invited her to stage his *Richard II* on Broadway, her distinguished career as a director began. She also continued to act in many productions. In 1944 she emerged as a producer as well as director and in 1948 formed the Margaret Webster Shakespeare Company, which brought exciting, swift-moving drama to most of the states and many Canadian provinces. In 1950 she directed her first opera, *Don Carlos,* at the Metropolitan Opera House, and she appeared in *An Evening with Will Shakespeare* (1952) and *Measure for Measure* (1957). She wrote *Shakespeare Without Tears* (1942) and *The Same Only Different* (1969), the chronicle of five generations of her theatrical family.

WEBSTER, Noah, American lexicographer and writer: b. West Hartford, Conn., Oct. 16, 1758; d. New Haven, May 28, 1843. He attended Yale College from 1774, during a period much unsettled by the American Revolution. The students were dismissed a number of times because of inability to get food, a typhoid fever epidemic, and the fighting of the war. Webster set off to fight at Saratoga, but the battle was finished before he got there. After receiving his bachelor of arts degree in 1778, he studied law and

Noah Webster

was admitted to the bar, but that profession did not offer a living in those troubled times, and he became a schoolteacher. At Goshen, N.Y., in 1782, he began to write a series of elementary textbooks, and this pursuit throughout his long life made him the most important figure in the history of American education. Under the title *A Grammatical Institute of the English Language,* he produced in part 1 a speller (1783). In 1787 the title was changed to *The American Spelling Book* and in 1829 to *The Elementary Spelling Book,* but it was known informally as the "Blue-backed Speller" because of the usual blue binding. In spite of many competitive works, it sold phenomenally, rising to about a million copies a year in the latter part of the 19th century; and it did much to settle and standardize American spelling. Before 1790 Webster experimented with various reforms in spelling, but he became more conservative later in life, and his early radicalism was used by his opponents to plague him. To safeguard the rights of his speller and other writings, he advocated the establishment of copyright laws and was instrumental in getting state laws passed in the 1780's and a federal law in 1790. More than anyone else, he was the "father of American copyright."

Part 2 of the *Grammatical Institute* was a grammar (1784), extensively revised in 1807 and 1831, and part 3 was the first reader compiled in America (1785), revised in 1787 under the title *An American Selection of Lessons.* Other educational works were *Elements of Useful Knowledge* (4 vols., 1802–12), *Biography for the Use of Schools* (1830), *History of the United States* (1832), and *A Manual of Useful Studies* (1839).

In the 1780's Webster traveled extensively, giving lectures on the English language and on education. He wrote much on political matters, often in the newspapers, and his pamphlet *Sketches of American Policy* (1785) helped to shape the developing principles of the Constitution. He was the object of vitriolic abuse, some of it by William Cobbett. In 1787–1788 he edited the *American Magazine,* in New York City, a monthly of general interest. His lectures were published in 1789 as *Dissertations on the English Language,* incorporating new notions from Horne Tooke. They were imbued with linguistic patriotism, welcoming divergence from British English, although later in life he tried to bring the branches of the language into uniformity. He moved to Hartford to practice law and there wrote *The Prompter* (1791), a series of moralistic essays for children, with a quiet humor in the style of Poor Richard. It was widely reprinted and extremely popular, the more so because it was anonymous.

In 1793 Webster was called back to New York by the Federalists to edit a daily newspaper, the *American Minerva* (1793–1798), and a semiweekly, the *Herald* (1794–1797). He moved to New Haven, Conn., in 1798 to write and do research, but the papers continued under his control until 1803, under new titles, the *Commercial Advertiser* (daily) and the *Spectator* (semiweekly). He wrote an important study of epidemics, *A Brief History of Epidemic and Pestilential Diseases* (2 vols., 1799), arguing that the scourges of yellow fever had their source in noxious vapors arising from openings in the earth. In these years and throughout his life he contributed studies to scholarly journals on a remarkably wide range of topics: "Remarks on the Late Meteor" (1788), "On Raising Potatoes" (1798), "On the Affinity Between the Languages of Europe and Asia" (1807), "Experiments Respecting Dew" (1809), "Origin of Mythology" (1810), and many others.

Dictionaries.–In 1800 Webster announced plans for compiling three dictionaries, and his lexicographical activities took the bulk of his time for the rest of his life. In 1806 he brought out *A Compendious Dictionary of the English Language,* based on John Entick's dictionary, and in 1807 *A Dictionary . . . for the Use of Common Schools.* He underwent years of careful preparation for his big dictionary and took subscriptions for it as he traveled about supervising the printing of his spelling book. In 1812 he moved to Amherst, Mass., where he continued his research and engaged in civic activities such as serving in the Massachusetts legislature, acting as trustee and president of Amherst Academy, and helping to found Amherst College. His studies of etymology were especially intensive. He compiled a "Synopsis," comparing the forms of words in 20 languages as found in dictionaries. It was too costly to print, but it formed the basis of his etymologies and put them far ahead of all predecessors. Unfortunately, the new discoveries of Jacob Grimm, Franz Bopp, and others soon superseded a considerable part of his findings, and his genuine advances over 18th century philology have not been fully recognized. In 1822, when he had reached the letter *H,* he moved back to New Haven, where he lived until his death. Yale honored him with a doctor of laws degree in 1823.

Webster sailed for Europe in 1824 to consult books not available in America and to ascertain the state of the English language in England. He spent about five months at Cambridge University and finished the manuscript there in January 1825. Unable to find an English publisher, he brought the manuscript home and arranged for it to be printed at New Haven. Some exotic type had to be imported from Germany. It appeared in 1828 as his crowning lifework, *An American Dictionary of the English Language*, and was immediately recognized as the best work up to its time. It had 70,000 words (12,000 more than the latest edition of Samuel Johnson's) and the definitions and meaning analyses were excellent. A revised edition appeared in 1841. In succeeding decades it ran into competition with the works of Joseph Emerson Worcester (q.v.), creating a "War of the Dictionaries"; but continued re-editions have kept it in the forefront to the present day.

ALLEN WALKER READ,
Associate Professor of English, Columbia University.

Further Reading: Ford, Emily, *Notes on the Life of Noah Webster*, 2 vols. (1912; reprint, B. Franklin 1971); Monaghan, E. Jennifer, *A Common Heritage: Noah Webster and His Blue-Back Speller* (Shoe String 1982); Moss, R. J., *Noah Webster* (G. K. Hall 1984); Shoemaker, Ervin C., *Noah Webster: Pioneer of Learning* (Columbia Univ. Press 1936); Warfel, Harry R., ed., *Letters of Noah Webster* (1953; reprint, Norwood Eds. 1979).

WEBSTER, Pelatiah, American political economist: b. Lebanon, Conn., Nov. 24, 1726; d. Philadelphia, Pa., Sept. 2, 1795. Graduating from Yale College in 1746, he was ordained to the Congregationalist ministry in 1749 and held pastorates in New England until 1755, when he entered business in Philadelphia. During the Revolutionary War he was twice imprisoned by the British, and his property was confiscated. He favored financing the war by taxation rather than by loans, and supported a free-trade policy and the curtailment of paper money issues.

A strong supporter of the Constitution after the war, Webster wrote a pamphlet, *A Dissertation on the Political Union and Constitution of the Thirteen United States of North-America* (1783), which is credited with playing an important role in influencing the public to adopt the federal form of government. In 1787, during Pennsylvania's debates over ratification of the Constitution, he once more published pamphlets urging a strong federal government. Some later writers, notably Hannis Taylor (1851–1922), have tried to establish that Webster was one of the joint authors of the Constitution, or that it was based on his ideas, but that contention has been largely discredited. Webster's contributions to the Union were his cogent arguments for the Constitution and his vigorously stated views on money, credit, taxation, and trade.

WEBSTER, Richard Everard, 1ST VISCOUNT ALVERSTONE, English judge: b. London, England, Dec. 22, 1842; d. Cranleigh, Surrey, Dec. 15, 1915. Educated at Cambridge University, he was called to the bar in 1868. The Conservative government selected him as attorney general in June 1885, and the next month he secured election to Parliament, a necessary prerequisite to occupying the post. He was attorney general until 1892, and again from 1895 until 1900. In the Bering Sea Controversy (1893) and in the Venezuelan Boundary Dispute (1899), he acted as representative of Great Britain. Knighted in 1885, he was raised to the peerage as Baron Alverstone in 1900 on appointment as master of the rolls and later in the year as lord chief justice. During 1903 he served on the commission for settling the Alaska Boundary Dispute. He retired in 1913 and was made viscount.

WEBSTER, town, Maine, in Androscoggin County, now renamed Sabattus. The town was settled in 1775 and soon had important gristmills and sawmills. Woolen mills were opened later. First called Burnt Meadows, the town bore various other names until 1840, when it was incorporated as Webster. It was bordered on the north by a village called Sabattus, and Sabattus was the seat of its post office. By the time of the 1980 census, Webster had been renamed Sabattus. Its chief industries include the manufacture of rubber soles and heels and of plastic products. Pop. 3,081.

WEBSTER, town, Massachusetts, in Worcester County, located on the French River, 16 miles south of Worcester, at an altitude of 458 feet. The major industries are the manufacture of cotton and woolen goods, and shoes. The chief attraction of the town is Webster Lake with the Indian name Chargoggagoggmanchaugagoggchaubunagungamaugg, which translated means "You fish on your side, I fish on my side, nobody fish in the middle." Webster was founded about 1713 and in 1811 Samuel Slater built the town's first cotton mill. Incorporation took place in 1832. Government is conducted by town meeting. Pop. 14,480.

RUTH ELY DICKINSON.

WEBSTER, village, New York, in Monroe County, located 12 miles northeast of Rochester, at an altitude of 410 feet. Formerly in an agricultural area, the community is now suburban, with growing industries including the manufacture of duplicating machines, photographic equipment, and chemicals. Webster was incorporated as a village in 1905. Pop. 5,499.

WEBSTER-ASHBURTON TREATY, an agreement signed in Washington, D.C., Aug. 9, 1842, which settled several outstanding disputes between the United States and Great Britain. The chief point at issue was the location of the boundary between Maine and New Brunswick, Canada, which, because of imperfect geographical knowledge, had been erroneously defined in the Treaty of Paris, 1783. The compromise reached by Daniel Webster and 1st Baron Ashburton (Alexander Baring) awarded 7,015 square miles to the United States and 5,012 to Great Britain. Retention by the British of the northern area assured them of year-round overland military communications with Montreal. Webster used a map, said to have been marked with a red line by Benjamin Franklin at Paris in 1782, in persuading Maine and Massachusetts to accept the agreement. (See RED LINE MAP.) Britain agreed to pay these states $150,000 each, and they were to be reimbursed by the United States for expenses incurred defending the area against encroachment.

The treaty also provided for the free navigation of the Saint John River for all American forest and field products; it defined the source of the Connecticut River; and it retained for the United States the line incorrectly surveyed along the 45th parallel between 1771 and 1774 from the Connecticut River to the St. Lawrence, as a consequence of which Rouses Point remained American territory. The treaty also provided for freedom of navigation in the St. Lawrence, Detroit, and St. Clair rivers and Lake St. Clair. A compromise line was agreed upon between Lake Superior and the Lake of the Woods, which assured that the immensely valuable Mesabi Range iron ore deposits would become the property of the United States.

A compromise agreement was reached on extradition to include surrender of all persons charged with murder, piracy, arson, and forgery. It was found impossible to include desertion, return of runaway slaves, burglary, theft, mutiny, and revolt because of the status of slavery in the United States. An effort to agree upon control of the slave trade resulted in an article by which the United States and Great Britain agreed to maintain separate cruising squadrons off the coast of Africa to suppress the slave trade, but without mutual right of visit and search to determine the character of suspected slavers. Finally, Ashburton expressed regret "that some explanation and apology" had not been immediately made by the British for the destruction on Dec. 29, 1837, of the *Caroline*, an American vessel carrying supplies to Canadian rebels, that had been attacked at Fort Schlosser (Niagara Falls, N.Y.) by a British naval force.

See also Caroline Affair.

Albert B. Corey,
New York State Historian.

WEBSTER CITY, city, Iowa, seat of Hamilton County, on the Boone River, 17 miles east of Fort Dodge and about 75 miles northwest of Des Moines, at an altitude of 1,050 feet. An industrial and commercial center surrounded by rich agricultural land, Webster City produces agricultural machinery and supplies, nonferrous metal castings, electric scoreboards, aluminum boats, washing machines, and frozen foods.

Municipal facilities include an airport and the Kendall Young Library (endowed), and there is a county hospital and a community junior college. The site of Webster City was settled in 1850 and platted in 1857, shortly before a rescue expedition went out from here to aid victims of the Spirit Lake Indian massacre. Webster City was incorporated in 1874, and a council-manager government was instituted in 1915. Pop. 8,572.

Margaret E. Davidson.

WEBSTER COLLEGE, a Roman Catholic institution of higher education, located in suburban St. Louis, Mo. Established in 1915, it is conducted by the Sisters of Loretto at the Foot of the Cross. Essentially aimed at a liberal arts education, the curriculum leads to the degrees of bachelor of arts, music, or science. The program for preparation of specialist teachers for elementary schools is supported by Ford Foundation and National Science Foundation grants. Full-time enrollment in the college numbers more than 650.

Mary O'Connor.

WEBSTER GROVES, city, Missouri, in St. Louis County, located on the southwestern outskirts of St. Louis, of which it is a residential suburb. Eden Seminary for theological students and Webster College, a Roman Catholic school, are located here. The city was incorporated in 1896. Government is under the council-manager system. Pop. 23,097.

Marguerite Norville.

WEBWORMS, wĕb'wûrms, various species of caterpillars (lepidopterous larvae) which form shelters by spinning webs of silk around the ends of branches and leaves upon which they feed. This habit is not so highly developed as it is in the tent caterpillar (q.v.). The latter also always form their webs in the forks of branches and crotches of young trees causing their webs to have a tentlike appearance. Webworms are numerous and belong to a number of genera of several families of moths. Some of them do a great deal of damage in defoliating trees and other plants. One of the commonest species is the fall webworm (*Hyphantria cunea*), which lives in large colonies forming very large webs. They wander far from the web while feeding but always return after eating. Another common species is the garden webworm (*Loxostege similalis*) which also lives in colonies in webs on all kinds of garden plants. The vagabond crambus (*Crambus vulgivagellus*) is a common and sometimes very destructive species that makes its web around the roots of corn and grass and feeds upon these plants.

William D. Field.

WEDDELL, wĕd'əl, **James,** British navigator: b. Ostend, Belgium, Aug. 24, 1787; d. London, England, Sept. 9, 1834. Son of a Scottish upholsterer who had settled in London, Weddell went to sea at an early age, shipping to the West Indies in 1805 on board a British merchant vessel. Despite his lack of formal education and an arrest in 1808 on charges of insubordination and mutiny, he qualified as a midshipman in the navy, where he taught himself navigation. Weddell managed to overcome the inauspicious beginning of his naval career and rose rapidly in rank. In 1810 he was appointed acting master of the *Firefly*, and two years later was promoted to master of the *Hope*.

Weddell's fame rests on his exploration of Antarctic waters from 1819 to 1823, while in command of sealing expeditions to the newly discovered South Shetland grounds. Finding his naval career barred by reductions in fleet strength after the Napoleonic wars, he joined the merchant marine in 1819 and sailed to the Antarctic in command of the 160-ton brig *Jane*. He cruised among the South Orkney and South Shetland Islands, and in 1822 made a second voyage to these waters, this time in command of the *Jane* and the 65-ton cutter *Beaufoy*. Crossing the Antarctic Circle after touching the South Orkneys, he discovered the Weddell Sea (q.v.) and advanced toward the South Pole. On Feb. 20, 1823, he reached the unprecedented latitude of 74° 15′ S. at 34°17′ W., before winds and ice turned him back.

On his return to England, Weddell published *A Voyage towards the South Pole* (1825), in which he advanced the hypothesis that the open sea continued to the Pole. This theory remained in doubt until disproved by the explorations of William S. Bruce in 1904 and Wilhelm Filchner in 1912. Weddell apparently continued to serve as a merchant captain until he died, unmarried, in 1834, but he left no accounts of any further explorations.

FINN RONNE,
Captain, United States Naval Reserve.

WEDDELL SEA, arm of the South Atlantic Ocean (latitude 73° S., longitude 45° W.), forming a large indentation in the coastline of Antarctica between Coats Land and the Palmer Peninsula. To the north its basin is partially blocked by a loop of the submerged Scotia Ridge, a continuation of the Andes Mountains of South America, which emerges in Antarctica as the Palmer Peninsula. The ridge breaks the surface as the South Shetland, South Orkney, and South Sandwich islands.

In the north the Weddell Sea averages 16,000 feet in depth, with a maximum of 27,108 feet in the South Sandwich Trench. The bottom shoals regularly toward the Palmer Peninsula and the continent, the continental shelf being steeper and deeper than is normal. This shelf is transversely breached beneath the Filchner Ice Shelf by the Crary Trough about 3,500 feet deep, which was probably glacially cut during lower stages of sea level.

The southern portion of the sea is covered by the Filchner Ice Shelf (also called Lassiter Ice Shelf), an area of 160,000 square miles and 750 to 1,600 feet thick. It is grounded near its center by ice-covered Berkner Island. The shelf is fed by adjacent continental glaciers and local precipitation. Almost the entire sea contains pack ice. Along the east coast a westerly setting current removes the pack ice in summer and allows ship access to the coast. The current originates in the Indian Ocean where it attains high salinity and temperature. This current is cooled as it flows along the continental shelf. It then flows downslope becoming significant as Antarctic bottom water—the Cold Deep Current of the Weddell Sea.

Precipitation varies from 7.8 inches on the ice shelf to 14 inches at Cape Norvegia. The variation is due to the Filchner area being a preferred breakout position for the inland high pressure system which forces easterly moving moisture-laden cyclones to seaward until they hit Cape Norvegia. The average annual temperature is –26° C. (–14.8° F.).

The Weddell Sea has been a focus of exploration. Early expeditions include those of James Weddell (Great Britain, 1823); Nils Otto Gustaf Nordenskjöld (Sweden, 1901–1903); William S. Bruce (Scotland, 1902–1904); Wilhelm Filchner (Germany, 1911–1912); Ernest Henry Shackleton (United Kingdom, 1914–1916), and whaling expeditions of Carl Anton Larsen (Norway, 1892–1924).

During the International Geophysical Year, 1957–1958, scientific stations were set up in the Coats Land-Filchner Ice Shelf area at Ellsworth (United States), General Belgrano (Argentina), Shackleton (United Kingdom), Halley Bay (United Kingdom), and Norway. Halley Bay and Ellsworth stations (now under Argentine administration) remain in operation.

See also ANTARCTIC REGIONS; POLAR EXPLORATION, SOUTH; and individual biographies of the explorers.

WILLIAM W. VICKERS,
Institute of Polar Studies, The Ohio State University.

WEDDERBURN, wĕd'ər-bûrn, **Alexander, 1st Baron Loughborough** and **1st Earl of Rosslyn,** British judge and statesman: b. Edinburgh, Scotland, Feb. 13, 1733; d. near Windsor, England, Jan. 2, 1805. He was a member of the Scottish bar from 1754 until 1757, and thereafter of the bar of England. Elected to the House of Commons in 1761 as member for Ayr, he subsequently represented various constituencies and was by turn Tory and Whig as expediency suited him. He was appointed solicitor general in 1771, and attorney general in 1778, by Lord North, of whose North American policies he strongly approved. In 1780 he was created baron and made chief justice of the Court of Common Pleas. He served on the bench until 1792, when he became lord chancellor. On retirement in 1801, he was made 1st earl of Rosslyn. As judge he displayed great clarity of judgment; but as politician, despite considerable oratorical powers, he was widely distrusted.

WEDDING. See MARRIAGE, HISTORY OF.

WEDDING ANNIVERSARY, wĕd'ĭng ăn-ə-vûr'-sə-rĭ, the commemorative celebration of a wedding, on the same date each year. Such celebrations are not found in most parts of the world; for one reason, keeping track of the anniversary date requires a literate familiarity with a calendar, a familiarity not possible among nonliterate peoples or in countries where a majority of the people are illiterate. The Shī'ite Muslims of Iran celebrate the anniversary of the marriage of Fatima, daughter of Mohammed, with Ali, his cousin, but this marks a major event in the history of the Shī'ite religion, and is part of the ritual lunar calendar watched over by the priests.

The family practice of observing wedding anniversaries seems to have grown up in western Europe. The earliest references in English literature occur in the 17th century: In the *Diary* of John Evelyn for 1659 there is mention of an invitation to a "forty-first wedding-day feast," and Samuel Pepys, in his *Diary,* wrote of going home "to be merry, it being my sixth wedding night."

Although a church record of 1624 mentions "sylver brydells," the silver wedding anniversary was apparently not widely celebrated (perhaps because few people in those days lived so long), for an author in 1796 felt it necessary to explain that the "silver-feast" was the 25th wedding anniversary, and Mrs. Anna Letitia Barbauld, friend of Dr. Samuel Johnson, writing in 1806, attributed the term "silver feast" to the Germans. The first reference to the golden wedding appears in an 1860 London newspaper, and the first to a diamond wedding in *Punch* in 1872. The symbols for other anniversaries seem to have evolved comparatively recently. But whereas Pepys' and Evelyn's references to the 6th and 41st wedding feasts suggest that in 17th century England every anniversary was the occasion for a party of family and friends, in present-day United States the 2d, 5th, 10th, 15th, 20th, 25th, and 50th are the most frequent occasions for parties, although husband and wife often celebrate annually with an exchange of gifts or a special meal or entertainment.

The symbols for wedding anniversaries are: 1st—paper; 2d—cotton, calico; 3d—leather; 4th—fruit, flowers, books; 5th—wood; 6th—candy, sugar, iron; 7th—wool, copper, brass, bronze; 8th—rubber, electrical appliances; 9th—pottery;

10th–tin, aluminum; 11th–steel; 12th–linen, silk, nylon; 13th–lace; 14th–ivory; 15th–crystal; 20th –china; 25th–silver; 30th–pearl; 35th–coral, jade; 40th–ruby; 45th–sapphire; 50th–golden; 55th–emerald; 60th or 75th (formerly the 60th, now more often the 75th)–diamond.

ELIZABETH E. BACON.

WEDDING CAKE, a large cake, iced and elaborately ornamented, which is served to guests at the repast or reception following a wedding. Small pieces are often sent to absent friends. In modern American usage figures of a bride and groom usually top the confectionery edifice, and the bride, assisted by the groom, makes the first cut into the cake. Until recently, pieces of cake in tiny containers were given to unmarried girls to take home in the belief that if the cake was placed under the girl's pillow she would dream of her future husband.

The wedding cake has its origins far back in time. Among many peoples throughout the world the sharing of food by bride and groom is a significant part of the marriage rite. In ancient Greece the eating of a cake of sesame seed meal mixed with honey was the final act of the ritual, and such cakes were distributed among the guests. In Rome the early marriage rite was called *confarreatio* from the cake of wheat (*farreus panis*) which the couple first offered to the gods, then ate together.

The serving of cakes was also an important part of the marriage celebration in western Europe. The early cake was a small, unleavened biscuit. With the development of baking technology, the small biscuits evolved into a large bride cake, increasingly rich and elaborately ornamented, but always an essential part of the wedding feast.

ELIZABETH E. BACON.

WEDEKIND, vā'də-kĭnt, **Frank,** German dramatist: b. Hannover, Germany, July 24, 1864; d. Munich, March 9, 1918. The son of a physician and reared in Switzerland, he spent his mature years mainly in Munich. He was active as dramatist, poet, short-story writer, cofounder of the satiric periodical *Simplicissimus*, inspirer of the Munich *Überbrettl* or supervaudeville, and actor primarily in his own plays. Abused by some as a pornographic clown and satanic sensualist, he was hailed by others as literary creator of a freer world wherein beauty was not marred by taboos, and natural impulses of body and soul were not stifled by social and moral conventions. His characters are smoldering volcanoes that erupt with elemental power under the impact of inner urges.

In his most famous heroine, Lulu, the central character of *Erdgeist* (1895; Eng. tr., *Earth Spirit,* 1914) and of *Die Büchse der Pandora* (1903; Eng. tr., *Pandora's Box,* 1918), he depicted womanhood per se, sex desire that demanded satiety, instinct that demoniacally rushed on to fulfillment and destruction. He maintained that in Lulu, the wild, untamed, beautiful, sweet, female primitive, he reproduced the eternal feminine, woman's primary configuration, more faithfully than did his contemporaries Henrik Ibsen and Gerhart Hauptmann with their well-groomed, continually jabbering domestic creatures. Wedekind's *Frühlings Erwachen* (1891; Eng. tr., *Spring's Awakening,* 1909) dealt with the devastating effect which the imposition of artificial adult restraints had upon adolescents in whom the stifled cry for life had to find morbid, miserable outlets.

German expressionism was strongly influenced by Wedekind's nervous dramatic dialogue which stressed the mutual unintelligibility of people who could not bridge the chasm between soul and soul; by his substitution of types for individuals, of oversimplified demonic personalities for complex real beings; by his hatred of sham and cant; by his ridicule of monarchy and bourgeoisie; and by his flight to the lower depths of human society, to harlots, criminals, and charlatans.

SOLOMON LIPTZIN,
Professor of German, The City College of New York.

WEDEMEYER, wĕd'ə-mī-ər, **Albert Coady,** American army officer: b. Omaha, Nebr., July 9, 1897. Graduating from West Point in 1918, he rose through the grades to the temporary rank of lieutenant general in 1945. His service included duty in the Philippines and China, study at the Command and General Staff School, and the Kriegsakademie (German General Staff School).

In 1940, he was assigned to Washington, D.C., in connection with the training of the greatly expanded United States Army, and the next year he was transferred to the war planning branch of the General Staff where he continued to serve after the United States entered World War II. In 1943 he was decorated with the Distinguished Service Medal for his outstanding work as chief of the strategy section and later of the strategy and policy group of the operations division.

In the same year he was appointed American deputy chief of staff of the Southeast Asia Command, then operating under Admiral Lord Louis Mountbatten against the Japanese in Burma. He was transferred to Chungking, China, in 1944 to succeed the controversial Gen. Joseph Warren Stilwell in command of United States Army forces in the China area and to serve as chief of staff to Chiang Kai-shek. Promoted to the rank of temporary lieutenant general, he continued to serve in China until war's end, then remained there commanding American troops until the summer of 1946. His report on the conditions in both China and Korea became so controversial in United States Asian policy that it was not published until 1951, when he retired from active service and became an executive in an aircraft-manufacturing company.

WEDGE, wĕdj, a double inclined plane having two or more tapering sides, thick at the head and coming to a sharp edge or point. The most common wedges are of wood or metal. They are usually actuated by percussion, as from a hammer, applied to the head along the direction of the length. Friction is important in the tool's effectiveness, for without it the resistance of the object through or against which the wedge is being driven would force it back out of the crevice it makes. Because of this great friction, it is difficult to determine mechanical advantage accurately, but in general it depends upon the ratio of length to thickness. Ordinary uses include splitting wood and rock, exerting great pressure, and raising heavy bodies. Axes, knives, chisels, nails, carpenter's planes, and other cutting and piercing tools are forms of wedges. The cam is a rotating wedge.

FRANK DORR.

WEDGWOOD, wĕj′wo͝od, **Josiah,** English potter: bap. Burslem, Staffordshire, England, July 12, 1730; d. Etruria, Staffordshire, Jan. 3, 1795. He was the thirteenth child of Thomas and Mary Wedgwood. For generations his family had been engaged in the making of peasant pottery, so it was natural that, when he left school at the age of nine, he should become apprenticed to his brother Thomas to learn the craft of potting.

Wedgwood went into partnership with Thomas Whieldon of Fenton in 1754 and began the research and experimentation which eventually led to his becoming one of the great potters of all time. He started at the Ivy House works in 1759 on very little capital, but such was his success that he was enabled to build his own factory in 1769, which he called Etruria, thus reflecting his love of the neoclassical style of design which he developed to the highest degree. He took Thomas Bentley into partnership in 1769, and they were successful in obtaining many important commissions.

In 1764 he married his third cousin, Sarah Wedgwood; they had eight children of whom the eldest, Susannah, was the mother of Charles Darwin; the youngest son, Thomas, was a pioneer in the invention of photography.

Besides contributing so greatly to "the important work of uniting art with industry" (as quoted from William E. Gladstone), Wedgwood was a leading scientific thinker, a great philanthropist, and a liberal thinker who "thanked his stars and Lord that North America is free from the iron hand of tyranny." He died in 1795, having "converted a rude and inconsiderable Manufactory into an elegant Art and an important part of the National Commerce." The Wedgwood Institute in Burslem honors his memory.

See also WEDGWOOD WARE.

HENSLEIGH C. WEDGWOOD.

WEDGWOOD, Thomas, English scientist and philanthropist: b. Etruria, Staffordshire, England, May 14, 1771; d. Eastbury, Dorsetshire, July 10, 1805. The son of Josiah Wedgwood (q.v.), he is credited as the first to conceive the basic process of photography (q.v.). He described his experiments in a paper, "An Account of a Method of copying Paintings upon Glass, and of making Profiles by the agency of Light upon Nitrate of Silver, invented by T. Wedgwood, esq., with Observations by H. Davy" (Sir Humphry Davy), published in the *Journal of the Royal Institution of Great Britain* (1802), but he found no methods for allowing a moderate exposure time in the camera obscura or for making his pictures permanent. On his father's death in 1795, he inherited a considerable fortune and financially assisted such men as the poet Samuel Taylor Coleridge and the Scottish mathematician Sir John Leslie.

WEDGWOOD WARE. During his partnership with Thomas Whieldon from 1754 to 1759, Josiah Wedgwood (q.v.) began an Experiment Book in which he recorded his efforts toward "the improvement of our manufacture of earthenware, which at that time stood in great need of it." Wedgwood's inveterate and lifelong devotion to invention and improvement enabled him to

Top: **Wedgwood ware of the 18th century or made from 18th century patterns. Some of these were found on the Wedgwood-Whieldon factory site.** ***Bottom:*** **Early queen's ware, made in the late 18th century.**

Josiah Wedgwood & Sons Ltd., London

Top: **Part of a dessert service in the "Nautilus" shape. These products were made at the Wedgwood factory in 1798.** ***Bottom:*** **Wedgwood bone china of the early 19th century, decorated with English landscapes.**

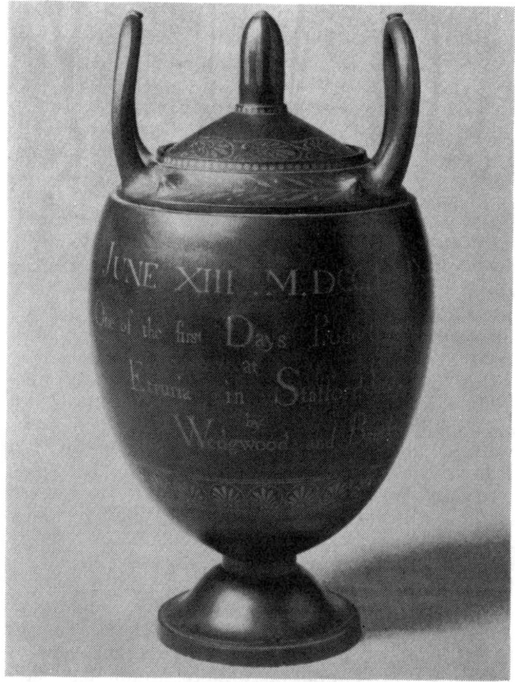

Josiah Wedgwood & Sons Ltd., London

One of six black basalt vases made on June 13, 1769, by Josiah Wedgwood and his partner Thomas Bentley to commemorate the opening on that day of the Etruria factory.

achieve the premier place among the world's great potters.

His first and greatest success was in the perfection of a cream-colored earthenware which was well designed, well potted, and of a quality superior to the contemporary salt-glazed and tin enamelwares, and was, moreover, inexpensive enough for common use as tableware. As a result of the patronage of Queen Charlotte in 1765, this ware became known as queen's ware. It has continued to be the staple product of the Wedgwood potteries up to the present time.

While queen's ware formed the backbone of his business and was the chief reason for the establishment of his fame and fortune, Wedgwood found time to develop and improve numerous other bodies—black basalt, for instance. A dense, hard, vitreous black stoneware, basalt was the ideal medium for the reproduction of the classical red-painted Greek vases known as Etruscan vases, the disinterment of which in Italy gave such a strong impetus to the popularity of the neoclassical style of design during the mid-18th century. Basalt was employed for the making of a bewildering variety of vases, plaques, portrait medallions, intaglios, and teaware.

Most famous of Wedgwood's inventions, however, was the jasper ware which he perfected in 1774. A fine stoneware "of a porcelainous nature," this body was stained with mineral oxides to produce pastel shades of blue, green, lilac, yellow, and black, upon which were applied white classical figures. No type of ware is more instantly recognizable than this jasper ware, even today. Wedgwood also invented numerous other "dry bodies" (so called because they did not require a glaze), such as the bamboo-colored caneware, the red rosso antico, and the composition for the making of mortars.

It was left to Josiah Wedgwood II to introduce bone china on behalf of the Wedgwood company in 1812. Although this type of porcelain was only made by Wedgwood for a period of eight years in the first instance, it has become an increasingly important part of the firm's productions since 1878. Josiah Wedgwood II also introduced colored queen's ware, a pale blue-lavender, a sage green celadon, and a glazed bamboo-colored cane.

During the Victorian era the Wedgwood firm turned out statuesque groups of figures in a body imitative of marble, called Parian, and great quantities of wares with highly colored glazes called majolica.

The firm which Josiah Wedgwood founded in 1759 still flourishes and is carried on by his direct descendants. Queen's ware and bone china dinnerware make up the bulk of the production, but jasper and basalt wares, in reproduction of the original 18th century designs, still remain in popular demand. See also POTTERY—*History* (England).

HENSLEIGH C. WEDGWOOD.

WEDMORE, wĕd′mōr, agricultural village and parish, England, in Somersetshire, seven miles northwest of Wells. It has a 15th century church. In 878 A.D., Alfred the Great, who had overthrown the Danes of East Anglia, signed here with King Guthrum the Peace of Wedmore. By this treaty the king and his chieftains agreed to withdraw into the Danelaw (q.v.), the territory in northeast England north of Watling Street, and to embrace Christianity. Guthrum changed his name to Athelstan with Alfred as his sponsor. Pop. (1951) 2,324.

WEDNESBURY, wĕnz′bər-ĭ, municipal borough, England, in Staffordshire, eight miles northwest of Birmingham, in the Black Country. It is a center for the manufacture of steel products. An ancient market town, it is believed to have been the site of a temple to Woden. A battle between Saxons and Britons took place here in the late 6th century, and early in the 10th century Æthelflæd, daughter of Alfred the Great, built a castle on the site. Pop. (1961) 34,511.

WEDNESDAY, wĕnz′dē, the fourth day of the week. The English name is derived from the old Scandinavian god Odin or Woden. In Anglo-Saxon, it is *Wōdnes dæg;* in Danish and Swedish, *Onsdag;* in Dutch, *Woensdag.* The Romans called it *Dies Mercurii* (Mercury's Day) and the Germans call it *Mittwoch* (midweek). See also ASH WEDNESDAY; WEEK.

WEED, wēd, **Thurlow,** American journalist and political leader: b. Green County, N.Y., Nov. 15, 1797; d. New York City, Nov. 22, 1882. After failing in two newspaper-publishing ventures in Norwich and Manlius, N.Y., he joined the staff of the Rochester *Telegraph* in 1822. Here he wrote editorials proposing John Quincy Adams for president. In 1824 he was sent to Albany as a lobbyist, and worked to align Adams' friends and those of Henry Clay, also a presidential candidate, in a common front against William H. Crawford, backed by Martin Van Buren. This was the first display of Weed's skill in political management that was to mark most of his public life. He was active in the successful campaigns in 1824 of Adams, as a National Republican, for president, and De Witt Clinton for governor of New York, and himself was elected to the state assembly. Prospering in business as in politics, he bought the *Telegraph* in 1825.

During the Anti-Masonic excitement, Weed abandoned the *Telegraph* and published the *Anti-Masonic Enquirer.* (See ANTI-MASONIC PARTY.) In 1830 he established the Albany *Evening Journal,* which he edited until 1863. Weed supported William Wirt, the Anti-Masonic nominee for president in 1832, but he made sure that the candidates for state offices were National Republicans, and his paper attacked the Democrats of the Albany Regency (q.v.). The National Republicans adopted the name of Whigs, and Weed's influence contributed to the victories of William H. Seward, elected governor in 1838, and of William Henry Harrison, elected president in 1840. Regarded by now as the directing genius of the Whig Party, Weed helped to win the presidential nomination for Henry Clay in 1844 and for Zachary Taylor in 1848. The party divided over national issues after Taylor's death in office (July 9, 1850), and Weed joined the newly formed Republican Party in 1854 after Seward, his close friend, was reelected to the United States Senate.

In 1860 he tried to obtain the presidential nomination for Seward, but when this move failed he turned to Abraham Lincoln, who sought his advice during the campaign and after his election. Weed had some voice in federal appointments and in 1861 was sent to Europe with a mission to placate English and French opinion after the Trent affair. (See TRENT AFFAIR, THE.) He supported Lincoln in the 1864 election and his influence with the administration was substantial, but his power waned rapidly after Lincoln's death. After 1863 he resided in New York City and wrote for the press on political topics. He published *Letters From Europe and the West Indies* in 1866. His autobiography appeared posthumously in 1884.

WEED, a plant growing out of place, where it is not wanted, either because of its inherent disagreeable or poisonous character or because it is taking the place reserved for something else. Corn is not a weed in a cornfield, but if some of its seed overwinters in the ground, then it may be a weed in the soybeans which are grown on that plot the following summer. If, as sometimes happens in the corn belt, the soybeans are being used to isolate a breeding plot of corn, then the volunteer corn in these soybeans may be a very annoying kind of weed to the corn breeder.

Propagation.—Weeds have marked capacities to spread and to succeed under a great variety of conditions. A single plant of some species may bear half a million seeds or more, enough to plant several farms. The seeds of weeds are long lived; of those which have been tested, all but a very few kinds still had viable seeds after 5 years. In a test at Michigan State University, seeds of 20 common weeds were buried in soil in glass bottles in 1879, and one lot was dug up and planted every 5 to 10 years. After 25 years over half of the kinds were producing healthy seedlings; three were still producing viable seedlings after 80 years. For the moth mullein (*Verbascum blattaria*) the percentages of germination are going down so slowly, decade by decade, that it bids fair to show viable seeds for more than a century. In the light of these results it is not surprising that tests of an English field where wheat had been continuously grown produced an estimate of 158 million viable weed seeds per acre.

Many weeds have specialized ways of spreading their seeds. The whole plant may be a tumbleweed, as in the semidesert areas of the world; or as with the dandelion, each seed may have a parachute of tiny hairs so that it is carried long distances by the wind and will float if it lands in the water. Transport of weed seeds by water is particularly important in irrigated districts. Many kinds are buoyant and studies of an irrigation ditch have shown that weed seeds were coursing down it at the rate of over a million each 24 hours.

Habitats.—The history of weeds is closely allied with the history of man. Wherever man goes he disturbs the natural vegetation, sometimes a little, more frequently catastrophically. He produces disturbed habitats, paths, dump heaps, and areas of raw open soil, which are unlike the preexisting habitats in that area. In these disturbed habitats the native vegetation for the most part cannot germinate, much less succeed in growing to maturity. Weeds bred elsewhere penetrate into these characteristic habitats produced by man and continue to evolve as they travel about with him, becoming more and more adaptable to his ways. Weeds might even be best defined as plants which succeed in disturbed habitats.

In areas such as the eastern United States, where there were few open soil habitats in prehuman times, a large percentage of the weeds are introduced. Though we usually think of them as European, some of them have an even longer history of association with man, having spread into Europe along with him. It has definitely been shown that the common narrow-leaved plantain (*Plantago lanceolata*), which we ordinarily think of as a European weed, spread into Europe from the East along with primitive agriculturists in prehistoric times. For some European weeds it has even been shown that the strains in European meadows are not precisely like those which are wild in the European mountains, but resemble more closely those from the Altai Mountains in Asia. Presumably they spread into Europe in early times along with flocks and herds from the East.

In naturally wooded areas a larger percentage of the weeds will spread in from elsewhere than in such a place as the Central Valley (Great Valley) of California where there were many open soil habitats in prehistoric times. The Central Valley is therefore a source of New World weeds and the evolution of weedy strains is still going forward there. Some of these have even been studied experimentally. The common weed sunflower (*Helianthus annuus*) has hybridized with *H. bolanderi,* native to the Central Valley. One hybrid population has been followed over an eight-year period and the evolution of the hybrid strain has been plotted in detail.

One of the habitats in which species were preconditioned for roles as weeds is the floodplains of large rivers. Such rivers are continually changing their courses, producing sand bars,

Roche

Some of the more common weeds are: (*left*) English plantain; (*center*) ragweed; (*right*) pokeweed or pokeberry.

gravel bars, mud flats, eroded banks, and other open soil areas. Species which can succeed in these conditions have to be able to germinate and grow in raw soil; furthermore, they have to be adaptable to change. Of the weeds which are apparently native to the eastern United States, a considerable number seem to have been bred along river systems, notably the giant ragweed (*Ambrosia trifida*), pokeweed (*Phytolacca decandra*), and trumpet vine (*Campsis radicans*). In times of flood the larger rivers deposit extensive waste heaps of miscellaneous driftwood and wreckage. These must have accumulated along rivers since time immemorial. Species gradually evolved to do well in such habitats might be expected to flourish in man's artificial dump heaps.

Evolution.—The evolution of weeds is frequently associated with that of closely related cultivated plants. We can point to crop plants (rye, oats) which originated from weeds in grainfields, and which eventually took over as the crop was grown on poorer and poorer soils. We can also demonstrate the reverse—weeds which came from cultivated plants, as for instance the orange day lily (*Hemerocallis fulva*), introduced into the United States from the Orient as an ornamental and now a common roadside weed in nearly every state east of the Great Plains. From the few studies which have been made, it appears that the relationships of weeds to cultivated plants are prevailingly complex. The cultivated wheats have already been proved to have incorporated two weed grasses into their germ plasms, and some experts believe that still others may have played minor roles in their development. For the weed lettuce and cultivated lettuce we have precise information that the weeds have entered into the ancestry of the cultivated ones, and that they in turn have contributed to the continuing evolution of the weeds. Wild lettuce (*Lactuca serriola*) has been used as a source of disease resistance in breeding modern cultivated lettuce (*L. sativa*). On the other hand, much of the variability of *L. serriola* is apparently due to the fact that it crosses with cultivated lettuce. Ordinarily this is not evident because the characteristics of the weed lettuce dominate over those of the cultivated sorts in the hybrids. However, this is not true of the red leaf color of a few cultivated varieties and, when they cross, the red color shows in the resulting hybrids. Under these circumstances it is easy to demonstrate that a good deal of natural crossing goes on between cultivated lettuce and the colonies of *L. serriola* which are growing nearby. The evolutions of cultivated lettuce and of weed lettuce are therefore processes and not events, and we can demonstrate that though these processes began long ago they are still continuing.

WEED CONTROL

Weeds have been controlled for centuries by good farming practice: by using weed-free seed, by cultivation before and after planting, and by so encouraging the crop as to enable it to help crowd out its own weeds. Certain crops, such as soybeans and sorghum, are deliberately planted as smother crops for particular weed infestations. The use of a special mulch paper to cover the soil and kill out weeds was first worked out for pineapples and this method is sometimes practiced in home gardens. Biological control through the use of special insects and diseases requires research on a large scale. It has been successfully applied to the eradication of prickly pear cactus in Australia and of St. John's-wort in the Pacific Northwest.

Chemical Control.—Attempts to control weeds with chemicals began about 1900 and developed very slowly until the introduction of 2,4-D (2,4-dichlorophenoxyacetic acid) shortly after World War II. Since that time development has been most active; more new chemicals have been introduced than in the previous century. A very large number of trade preparations (some of them mixtures of more than one chemical) are now on the market. Some are used as sprays, others in granular form. In addition to 2,4-D and similar growth regulators, these preparations include dinitrophenols, carbamates, arsenicals,

Gering Plastics

A tractor digs a furrow and covers it with polyethylene plastic mulch film in one operation. Weed control of this type was first worked out for pineapples.

borax compounds, urea compounds, and many others.

2,4-D and related compounds are selective herbicides. At low concentrations, they are only slightly toxic to grasses, including corn and other grains, but cause abnormal crippling growth, leading to death, in most broad-leaved plants. At higher concentrations they affect all plants though not to the same extent. They are effective at such low concentrations that they have to be used with great caution, particularly on windy days, and the spray equipment has to be washed and rinsed with extreme care after using so that plants are not unintentionally crippled the next time the equipment is used.

Selective herbicides such at 2,4-D can be used for preemergence treatment. This is practical only for crops with large seeds which are so deeply planted that after seeding, the herbicide can be applied to the surface of the soil. It will not damage the germinating seeds of the crop plant and will deal effectively with germinating weed seedlings near the surface. Nonselective herbicides are used as soil sterilants, and newer ones have been developed which are active for only a few weeks after they have been applied. Postemergence treatment is practically limited to selective herbicides and the concentrations to be used; the period in the life cycle when it can best be applied, varies from one crop to another.

Chemical weed control: lawn patch at left was treated with 2,4-D to rid it of dandelions; adjoining patch was untreated. Both patches started with same weed growth.

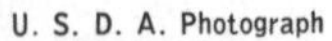

U. S. D. A. Photograph

Flame throwers were developed for use against rank and woody weeds (such as poison ivy). More recently machines have been designed for use with field crops. They focus jets of flame at the base of the weeds and are effective under some conditions.

Chemical weed control is now biologically and economically practical in many cases, but to be effective it needs to be combined with a thorough knowledge of crop management and a detailed understanding of rates of application, precautionary measures, time of application, and the like. It is therefore primarily a matter for the large-scale mechanized operator rather than the small farmer. The homeowner will find it most useful for operations such as crabgrass control for which special herbicides have been developed. Even then the directions need to be read carefully and followed with precision. To be effective, chemical control of lawn weeds needs to be combined with intelligent encouragement of the desired lawn grasses. Dandelions and other weeds have been removed from many lawns by chemical control which was not followed by good lawn care, so that other weeds have spread into the areas vacated by the dandelions.

As an ever-increasing percentage of the world's vegetation is affected (if not destroyed completely) by man's activities, weeds and weedlike plants dominate more and more of the landscapes. In the American Southwest much former grassland is covered with mesquite and similar brush. This is now one of the worst weed problems on Western ranges. Throughout the tropics there are wide areas of thorny scrubland and of grassy savannas dominated by plants which are essentially weeds. The understanding, management, and control of weedy landscapes is one of the world's increasingly urgent biological problems.

Edgar Anderson,
Curator of Useful Plants, Missouri Botanical Garden, St. Louis.

Further Reading: Anderson, Edgar, *Plants, Man and Life* (Little 1952); De Bray, Lys, *The Wild Garden* (Smith Pub. 1978); Holm, Leroy, and others, *A Geographical Atlas of World Weeds* (Wiley 1979); King, Robert D., *Farmers Weed Control Handbook* (Doane Pub. 1985).

WEEHAWKEN, wē-hô′kən, township, New Jersey, in Hudson County, seven miles northeast of Jersey City, at an altitude of 10 feet above the Hudson River, opposite New York City, with which it is connected by the Lincoln Tunnel (vehicular). Industries include the processing of textiles. Weehawken is an Indian name meaning "land of maize." Here, on a small level plot of ground about 20 feet above the river, the famous duel between Alexander Hamilton and Aaron Burr took place on July 11, 1804. The site of the duel was torn away in 1883 to make room for railroad tracks, and the monument which marked the spot where Hamilton fell was moved to the heights above. The town was incorporated in 1859. Government is administered by a commission and mayor. Pop. 13,168.

WEEK, wēk, a period of time in present usage comprising seven days, which stems from a very early origin but has not always been this interval in all civilizations and all times. Periods of eight days were once used in civil practice by the early Romans. The system of subdividing each month into three parts, the *ides, calends,* and *nones,* as employed by both the ancient Greeks and Romans, also persisted for many centuries.

The seven-day week was adopted in pre-Christian times in western Asia, and among Egyptians and Hebrews, and was subsequently carried into Christian civilizations. The Biblical significance of this seven-day period originates in Genesis 2:1–3; in Genesis 29:27, the word "week" is first mentioned.

The astronomical origin of the seven-day week goes back to a very ancient practice of reckoning dates according to a lunar calendar based upon the recurring phases of the moon. Since the period of the moon's synodical revolution (from approximately new moon to new moon), within which the moon undergoes its entire cycle of phases, is roughly 29 to 30 days, it was logical to use this visual indication in setting up the period of the month. To achieve a somewhat shorter period of time reckoning between the month and the day, it was also natural to divide the complete 29.5-day average lunation cycle into four periods of seven days each, each period beginning with one of the principal phases of the moon. (See MOON—*Motions and Appearance.*) However, the length of the year was reckoned by the sun's apparent annual motion among the stars. The incommensurability between the lunar reckoning of the weeks and months of the solar reckoning of the year, when joined in the lunisolar calendar, resulted in discrepancies. These were adjusted in adoption of the solar calendar in the Julian calendar reform of 46 B.C. (See CALENDAR—*Week.*)

The names of the days of the week originate from varied attempts by the ancient peoples to identify the seven subdivisions of the week with the seven heavenly bodies which they saw recurrently in the sky and to each of which they assigned a deity. The Chaldeans were the first to utilize named weekdays in repeating order. Sunday was set as the first day of the week in 321 A.D. by Emperor Constantine, who also established the seven-day week in the Roman calendar and promulgated it to the Christian world. Subsequently, the names given to the days of the week in Latin were adapted through various Germanic languages until they assumed their present designations in English, as follows:

Sunday—the day assigned to the sun.

Monday—the day assigned to the moon.

Tuesday—assigned to Mars, the Roman god of war, who was associated with the Teutonic god called Tiw in Anglo-Saxon. Hence the name "Tiw's day."

Wednesday—assigned to Mercury. This Roman god was associated with the Teutonic god called Woden in Anglo-Saxon, and his day of the week accordingly became "Woden's day."

Thursday—assigned to the Roman god Jupiter, who was identified with the Teutonic god Thor. Thus originated "Thor's day."

Friday—assigned to Venus, the Roman goddess of love and beauty. In Teutonic mythology the corresponding goddess was Freya, who was later confused with Frigg, wife of Odin (Woden). Hence "Frigg's day."

Saturday—assigned to Saturnus, the Roman god of agriculture, which yielded "Saturn's day."

See also separate articles on the days of the week.

FERGUS J. WOOD.

WEEKS, wēks, **John Wingate,** American financier and public official: b. near Lancaster, N.H., April 11, 1860; d. there, July 12, 1926. Reared on his father's farm near Lancaster, he graduated from the United States Naval Academy in 1881 and served in the Navy for two years. In 1888 he entered the brokerage and banking business in Boston as a partner in the firm of Hornblower & Weeks, which became one of the most important houses in the United States. Taking up residence in Newton, Mass., Weeks entered local politics there and in 1903 was elected mayor of the city. The following year he was elected congressman on the Republican ticket and served in the House until 1913, when he entered the Senate for one term. In the 1920 presidential campaign, Weeks managed the New York City headquarters of the Republican Party, and President Warren G. Harding named him to his cabinet as secretary of war. He continued to serve under President Calvin Coolidge until October 1925. At the War Department he did an efficient job in restoring its administration to a peacetime footing following the war.

WEEKS, Sinclair, American industrialist and public official: b. West Newton, Mass., June 15, 1893; d. Concord, Mass., Feb. 7, 1972. Son of John Weeks, he graduated from Harvard in 1914. Weeks began his business career in banking, continuing in that field (except for his service with the artillery in World War I) until 1923, when he became associated with the United-Carr Fastener Corporation of Cambridge, Mass. In 1942 he was named chairman of the board, and in 1945 he assumed the same position in the Reed and Barton Corporation, silversmiths of Taunton, Mass.

A lifelong Republican, he was appointed in 1944 to complete the unexpired term of Henry Cabot Lodge, Jr., in the United States Senate, and in 1949 was chosen national finance committee chairman of the Republican Party. On Jan. 21, 1953, he assumed the post of secretary of commerce, a position to which he was appointed by President Dwight D. Eisenhower, and continued in office until the fall of 1958. Weeks favored United States participation in foreign trade fairs, to raise exports. In addition, he initiated improvements in Patent Office and Weather Bureau operations.

WEEKS, Feast of. See PENTECOST.

WEELKES, wēlks, **Thomas,** English composer: b. possibly about 1575; d. London, England, Nov. 30, 1623. At first in private service to Edward Darcye, groom of the Privy Chamber (1598), he was organist of Winchester College in 1600 and shortly after moved to Chichester. In the meantime he had taken the degree of bachelor of music at New College, Oxford University in 1602. On the title page of his last publication (1608) he calls himself "Gentleman of his Majesty's Chapel" and "Organist of the Cathedral Church of Chichester." In the chapter records of Chichester he is mentioned as organist and choirmaster in 1616. He was replaced as choirmaster in 1617 but continued as organist until his death.

His reputation rests largely on his madrigals. He published *Madrigals to 3, 4, 5, and 6 voyces* (1597); *Balletts and Madrigals to five voyces* (1598); *Madrigals of 5 and 6 parts,* in two sets (1600); and *Ayeres, or Phantasticke Spirites for three voices* (1608). He also contributed a madrigal to Thomas Morley's anthology *The Triumphes of Oriana* (1601). He is one of the most imaginative of the English madrigalists, remarkable both for harmonic subtlety and for spaciousness. A few compositions for instrumental ensemble survive in manuscript, as well as a quantity of church music, which, though less colorful than the madrigals, is marked by taste and dignity.

J. A. WESTRUP
Faculty of Music, Oxford University

WEEMS, wēmz, **Mason Locke** (PARSON WEEMS), American clergyman, book agent, and author: b. Anne Arundel County, Maryland, Oct. 1 or 11, 1759; d. Beaufort, South Carolina, May 23, 1825. Though the place or places of his schooling are not known with certainty, its character was such that John Adams could write of him in 1785 as "a young gentleman of liberal education." One early authority, writing without documentation, affirms that at the early age of 14 years Weems was sent to Edinburgh to study medicine, and there exists some slight corroborative evidence that he practiced that art for a few years in Maryland.

After the American Revolution, he was ordained deacon in the Church of England by the bishop of Chester, on Sept. 5, 1784, and priest by the archbishop of Canterbury a week later. Returning to Maryland he served in different parishes and, in general, played an active part in the life of church and community until in 1792 he took to the road as an itinerant bookseller. That career he followed until he died exhausted, leaving a widow, Frances (Ewell) Weems of Dumfries, Va., whom he had married in 1795, and by whom he had 10 children.

In the course of his career as a preacher and parish priest he was frequently criticized for the informality of his words and actions in the pulpit and out, but John Davis, an English traveler who attended his services at Pohick Church in Mount Vernon parish, Va., nullifies much of this criticism when he writes perceptively that Weems was "cheerful in his mien that he might win men to religion." In 1794 he began the business relationship with Mathew Carey, Philadelphia publisher, which was to make him a familiar figure to those who lived or traveled on the roads from Pennsylvania to Georgia for the next 30 years. His correspondence with Carey, which was published in 1929, is an enrichment of the history of culture in the United States.

Weems' best-known works were his life of George Washington, where first appeared the most famous of American anecdotes, the cherry tree story, and the lives of Francis Marion, Benjamin Franklin, and William Penn. These essays in hero worship, undisguised, were intended honestly and passionately to inculcate patriotic devotion and lofty moral standards in the youth of the country. There can be no doubt of their effectiveness in a country which was still a frontier, not then remarkable for literary sophistication. The Washington biography, for example, was published in 86 editions and issues between 1800 and 1927. Weems' moral pamphlets, directed against the sins of murder, adultery, gambling, and drunkenness, were reprinted throughout his life in many large editions. His 26 known titles have been published in 218 editions and issues.

Weems is a memorable figure in the history of American writing, evangelization, publishing, and bookselling. He was a desperately hard worker in all these fields, a character full of salt and flavor and goodwill to men regardless of race, creed, or color, and he may not be ignored by those who love the land and people he served in his curiously individualistic fashion.

LAWRENCE WROTH
Research Professor of American History, Brown University

WEENIX, vā'nĭks, family of Dutch painters, father and son, who specialized in still life and other popular subjects in the 17th and early 18th centuries.

JAN BAPTIST WEENIX: b. Amsterdam, the Netherlands, 1621; d. Ter May, near Utrecht, 1660. He first studied with Jan Micker, then Abraham Bloemeart, and Claesz Moeyaert. In 1643 he went to Rome where he painted still life and Italianate landscapes showing architectural ruins and tiny figures in modern dress (very much like the work of his pupil Nicolaes Pietersz Berchem, who accompanied him to Italy) and attracted the patronage of Giovanni Battista Cardinal Pampili, who later became Pope Innocent X. In 1647 Weenix returned to Amsterdam, thereafter signing paintings "Giovanni Battista," probably in honor of his patron, for previously his work had been signed simply Jan or Johannes. He changed his style and developed a very popular form of still life painting, specializing in dead game and portraits finished in a very detailed manner (a style his son continued successfully), as well as genre paintings in the manner of Gerard Dou. So rapidly did he paint that he was able to undertake and finish three half-length portraits in a day. His landscape paintings and seaport scenes never lost the brilliant coloration of his Italian period. Although his work is uneven in quality, he has never gone out of fashion. Typical examples of his work are in many museums, including Amsterdam, London (National Gallery, Wallace Collection, and Kenwood), New York (Metropolitan), and Paris (Louvre). His pupils included, besides his son Jan and Nicolaes Berchem, his nephew Melchior d'Hondecoeter.

JAN WEENIX (THE YOUNGER); b. Amsterdam, 1640; d. there, Sept. 20, 1719. A pupil of his father, Jan Baptist Weenix, and his cousin, Melchior d' Hondecoeter, he was listed as a member of the painters' guild in Utrecht in 1664 and 1668. He continued the highly popular refined style of his father and painted landscapes, still life arrangements of fruit, flowers, and dead game, and animals. His paintings were in great demand for the decoration of private houses in Amsterdam and elsewhere. He became successful in his own day, and highly valued centuries later. A most prolific painter, his works are to be found in major museums, among them, New York (Metropolitan), Detroit, and London.

JEAN ANNE VINCENT
Author of "History of Art"

WEEVER, wē′vər, a fish. The name is said to be derived from the Old French *wivre,* meaning "viper," and is applied to the four species of the genus *Trachinus.* The fish is found from the North Sea down the European coast to the Mediterranean and to North Africa. The weevers are usually less than 12 inches long and vary in color from reddish yellow to gray. The eyes are set near the top of the head and the mouth tends to be vertical. The soft dorsal fin is preceded by five or six sharp spines, and there is a similar spine on either side of the gill cover. Through grooves in these spines powerfully irritating poison from glands near their base is injected into the victims. As the fish habitually lies almost covered with sand, it is very dangerous to bathers. CHRISTOPHER W. COATES

WEEVIL, wē′vəl, a general name applied to the adults and larvae of the beetle superfamily Rhynchophora, also frequently called snout beetles because the majority of the species have an elongated and usually downward curved snoutlike head. These beetles have a single median suture (called the gular suture) beneath the head and they have legs with four visible segments on the tarsi. The most characteristic structure is the elongated rostrum or snout, which is better developed in the female than in the male and in the former is used to bore holes into plant tissue for egg laying. There are four families of weevils: Curculionidae, Brentidae, Anthribidae, and Scolytidae (see BARK BEETLES).

Most weevils belong to the Curculionidae, and it has been estimated that there are well over 100,000 species in this family. There are over one dozen subfamilies. These weevils have a pair of elbowed antennae at the sides of their heads. These antennae have a very long first segment with the remaining segments short, the last three of which form a club. The adults of a very large proportion of the species are clothed with scales. Most weevils are of a somber color but a few are brilliantly colored; for example, *Eupholus,* a shining sky-blue species found in New Guinea. Weevil larvae are usually white, stout, distinctly curved and narrowing slightly toward the posterior. They are footless, having at most only small bristly elevations for legs. They have small, dark rounded heads that are equipped with strong mouthparts. Most of them feed inside the plants in which the eggs are laid. Almost all parts of the plant are subject to attack by the many species, including the bark, wood, and roots. Among the many destructive species are: the cotton-boll weevil, *Anthonomus grandis* (see BOLL WEEVIL); the granary weevil, *Sitophilus granarius* (see GRAINS); and the plum curculio, *Conotrachelus nenuphar* (see PLUM).

The weevils or snout beetles of the family Brentidae resemble the Curculionidae in having a strong beak but they differ from them in that the beak does not curve downward. These insects are unusual in that the males are larger than the females, the reverse of the usual condition. Both sexes have rather narrow bodies with straight, not elbowed, antennae. Few species exceed one half inch in length. The male of the species stands guard over the female while she bores a hole to lay each single egg, and he assists her in extracting her beak from the hole or pit. The larvae are borers in dying or dead wood. This family is found chiefly in the tropics and is of little or no economic importance.

Weevil feeding on a leaf. Such so-called snout beetles are noted for damaging crops and stored grain.

The Anthribidae are very small weevils seldom over three tenths of an inch long. They have short and broad beaks or snouts and their mouthparts have a labrum. Their antennae are not elbowed and rarely show a compact club at the end. The larvae of these weevils live in fungus, in dead wood, and in corn and wheat smut. One species, the coffee-bean weevil, *Araecerus fasciculatus* is a pest in stored coffee.

One group of beetles are called weevils although they do not belong to the Rhynchophora. These are the Bruchidae, very small weevils usually less than one eighth of an inch in length. They are oval in shape and have forewings that do not cover all of the abdomen. Their bodies are hairy or scaly. They are brown, gray, or black in color, sometimes mottled with white. The antennae are clubbed and the tarsi are five-segmented, although the fourth segment is small and concealed. They feed mostly in the seeds of leguminous plants and are very destructive, many living in stored seeds. Two of the more important pests in this family are the pea weevil (*Bruchus pisorum*) and the bean weevil (*Acanthoscelides obtectus*).

See also BEETLE—*Classification.*

WILLIAM D. FIELD
Division of Insects, Smithsonian Institution

WEGENER, vä′gĕ-nər, **Alfred Lothar,** German geophysicist and meteorologist: b. Berlin, Germany, Nov. 1, 1880; d. Greenland, November 1930. He was on the staff of the aeronautical observatory at Lindenberg when aviation and its meteorological problems were young. He embarked on four polar expeditions (1906–1908, 1912–1913, 1929, 1930) to test his speculations on meteorology and geophysics, dying in Greenland on his last trip. He was professor of geophysics and meteorology at Hamburg (1919–1924) and at Graz (1924–1930).

Wegener was particularly interested in the thermodynamics of the atmosphere—the conditions in upper and polar air masses that "make" the weather—and published *Thermodynamik der Atmosphäre* in 1911. His most important work, however, was *Die Entstehung der Kontinente und Ozeane* (1915; Eng. tr., *The Origins of Continents and Oceans,* 1924), which went through many editions. It set forth the original theory, known as Wegener's hypothesis of continental drift, that the present continents on the surface of the globe were originally one large landmass that gradually separated and drifted apart. He argued that continents are still in the process of change and that their relative positions have altered greatly even in recent times. He found evidence for this in the shape of the west coast of Africa and the east coast of South America, which appear to fit together. The similarity of rocks and fossils on these two coasts tends to confirm the hypothesis. See CONTINENT—*Continental Drift.* JUSTUS J. SCHIFFERES

WEI HO, wä hō, river, China. It originates at Sinsiang, Honan Province, flows 20 or 30 miles north of the Yellow River, roughly parallel to the course of the latter, and joins the middle section of the Grand Canal at Lintsing in Hopei Province. Its length is about 370 miles. In 1953, with the completion of the 30-mile People's Victory Canal, the Yellow River was linked with the Wei Ho at Sinsiang. The canal helps control the Yellow River, irrigates farmlands alongside, and increases the volume of water in the Wei Ho to facilitate navigation for 100-ton junks from Sinsiang to Tientsin. The freight downstream consists of coking coal, while grain, cotton, and other agricultural products move upstream to Sinsiang from Toakow in northern Honan or downstream from this area to Tientsin over the Grand Canal. RICHARD SORICH

WEI HO, river, China. It originates in Kansu Province about longitude 104°E. and flows eastward through Shensi Province to join the Yellow River at its great eastward bend. The drainage area is approximately 22,400 square miles, and the river is navigable for small craft for 150 miles of its 435-mile length. Near the confluence of the Wei Ho and its left tributary, the Ching Ho, is historic Sian, capital of Shensi Province.

The Wei Ho Valley, extending from Paoki in Shensi Province to the mouth of the Wei Ho, is the center of the population, industry, and agriculture of Shensi Province. As far back as the Chin and Han dynasties, the Chinese have built many irrigation canals in the Wei Ho Valley. As an example of the soil erosion problem that gives the Yellow River its characteristic coloration and its name, the Wei Ho carries away an estimated 150 million tons of earth annually.

RICHARD SORICH

WEIDENREICH, vī′dən-rīKH, **Franz,** German anatomist and anthropologist: b. Edenkoben, Palatinate, Germany, June 7, 1873; d. New York, N.Y., July 11, 1948. After graduating from the Landau Humanist Gymnasium in 1893 he attended the universities of Munich, Kiel, Berlin, and Strasbourg, where he received an M.D. in 1899. He was anatomist at Strasbourg in 1899–1901 and 1902–1918 (with rank of professor from 1904) and at Heidelberg in 1921–1924, professor of anthropology at Frankfurt in 1928–1935, and professor of anatomy at Peiping Union Medical College in 1935–1942. He was associated with the American Museum of Natural History in New York City from 1941 until his death. During World War I, he was president of the Democratic Party of Alsace-Lorraine.

In over 200 publications Weidenreich elaborated the relations between form, growth, and function in blood cells, hemopoietic and lymphatic systems, skin, teeth, bone, and central nervous system, and in human erect posture as related to the evolution of the foot, hand, pelvis, chin, brain, and skull. Weidenreich studied exhaustively the large *Sinanthropus* (Peking Man) population and the later *Homo sapiens* group in the Upper Cave at Chou Kou Tien, North China, and, with Gustav H. R. von Koenigswald, *Pithecanthropus* (Java Man) and the gigantic fossil jaw named *Meganthropus palaeojavanicus* from Java. He also studied Neanderthal skeletons from Ehringsdorf in Europe and, from Russian data, from Teshik Tash in central Asia.

Weidenreich's classic and prophetic work on the evolution of man, defining Archanthropine, Palaeoanthropine, and Neoanthropine stages in a network of differentiating and continuing populations, stresses simple genetic features such as shovel incisor teeth as proof of local racial continuity, and the steady expansion of the brain with growth rate shifts as a cause of change in modern man.

After rejection by three political regimes—French, Nazi, and Japanese—Weidenreich found refuge in the United States. William King Gregory described him as "a brave and tenacious man who never gave in to adversities." Among his many publications may be noted *The Brain and Its Role in the Phylogenetic Transformation of the Human Skull* (1941); *Apes, Giants, and Man* (1946); and *Morphology of Solo Man* (1951). A full bibliography appears in *The Shorter Anthropological Papers of Franz Weidenreich . . . 1939–1948* (1949).

J. LAWRENCE ANGEL
The Daniel Baugh Institute of Anatomy

WEIERSTRASS, vī′ər-shträs, **Karl Wilhelm Theodor,** German mathematician: b. Ostenfelde, Münster, Germany, Oct. 31, 1815; d. Berlin, Feb. 19, 1897. He studied commerce and law at the University of Bonn for four years, at his father's wishes, but left without obtaining a degree. He then prepared for secondary school teaching at Münster Academy, where he studied mathematics under Christof Guderman. Inspired by Guderman's enthusiasm for elliptic functions, as well as by the published work of Neils Henrik Abel and Karl Gustav Jakob Jacobi, Weierstrass constructed a firm foundation for the arithmetization of mathematical analysis, making irrational numbers comprehensible in terms of infinite sequences of rational numbers. He pursued his research at night while teaching successively at the

Münster Gymnasium, the Deutsch-Krone Pro-Gymnasium, and the royal Catholic gymnasium (Collegium Hoseanum) at Braunsberg. Publication of a memoir by Weierstrass on Abelian functions in August Leopold Crelle's *Journal* in 1854 brought him immediate recognition and was followed by teaching posts at the Royal Polytechnic School in Berlin and the University of Berlin, where he was full professor of mathematics from 1864 to 1897. His theory of uniform analytic functions has been the basis of much modern investigation into elliptic functions. He is also known for his work in the calculus of variables.

WEIFANG, wä'fäng', municipality (*shih*), China, eastern Shantung Province, 30 miles northwest of Tsingtao, on the Tsinan railroad. Light industries and other handicrafts include cotton and silk weaving; other manufactures are matches, tobacco products, and flour. It is also a center for the coal mines at nearby Fangtze. Called Weihsien until 1949, it was the site of an infamous concentration camp for Europeans during the Japanese occupation of North China in World War II. Pop. (1953) 148,900.

NORTON GINSBURG

WEIGELA, wī-gē'lə, a genus in the Caprifoliaceae or honeysuckle family represented by about 10 species of woody shrubs. The genus is named in honor of Christian Ehrenfried von Weigel (1748–1831), professor and botanical author of Greifswald, Germany.

Plants of the genus are, by some botanists, included in the genus *Diervilla*. As a result of separating the genus, all the species now commonly known as *Weigela* are native to East Asia, have flowers with quite regular corollas, and produce flowers on wood of the previous season. In comparison, the plants left in the genus *Diervilla* are American species flowering on wood of the current season and having more irregular flowers with a two-lipped corolla.

The plants are deciduous, upright, with opposite leaves often about four inches long, which usually produce an abundance of showy flowers of funnel form about one or one and a half inches long in small clusters. Flower color in weigelas varies from white and yellowish white to intense rose and red, and the flowering period is late spring and early summer. There has been much hybridization within the genus since its introduction into England in 1845, and there are many named varieties which are listed by nurserymen. Some varieties are distinguished by their variegated foliage.

Many of the weigelas are hardy in the northern part of the United States and are very popular for landscaping. They prefer a sunny location and a rich, moist, loamy soil, but often provide a very good show even under conditions which are somewhat unfavorable.

HOWARD W. SWIFT
The New York Botanical Garden

WEIGHING MACHINES, wā'ĭng mə-shēnz', mechanical devices for ascertaining the weights of objects.

Balance Scales. The earliest form, a balance with equal arms, was known to the Egyptians about 5000 B.C. It was, in effect, a lever of the first class, having the fulcrum at the center. When a known weight suspended in a pan (or scale) at one end of the beam exactly balanced a

BLACK STAR

A precision balance. Some are so delicately balanced that they can register the weight of a human hair.

mass suspended in a pan of the same size and weight at the other, the instrument was in equilibrium and the two weights were known to be the same. The name "scale" or "scales," in common use today, is an extension of the entire device of the term used for the two pans. Later refinements, particularly knife-edged pivots invented in the 18th century, gave us the present-day balance.

Precision balances based on the same principle are still the most accurate known. They are used by chemists in quantitative analysis and by assayers for weighing precious metals. Some balances operate on a complex system of levers that have the effect of lengthening their arms to make them more sensitive. They are so delicate that they can register the weight of a human hair or of words written on a paper, and are kept under glass to prevent distortion of the reading by chance drafts. A short-arm balance is quicker to read but not so sensitive.

The ancient Danish and Roman steelyards are examples of unequal-arm balances, and are the basis of beam scales now used by butchers to weigh large pieces of meat. A quarter of beef hung on a hook on the short arm close to the fulcrum can be balanced by moving a small weight or counterpoise along the long beam arm, which is graduated in pounds. Because of the difference in length of the two arms, a known 1-pound weight on the longer lever will balance 10, 100, or 1,000 pounds on the short arm. Some scales used on the counters of grocery and other stores are small versions of the steelyard. See also BALANCE.

Spring Scales. Spring scales are a further development. They operate on the principle that when a helix is subjected to a tension the amount of elongation increases proportionally with the increase in the force of tension. In its simplest form, a spring balance consists of a helical spring of hard steel of high elasticity suspended from a fixed point and carrying the weighing pan at its lower extremity. An automatic-indicating index registers the weight immediately without the necessity for moving a counterpoise manually.

BLACK STAR

A springless scale of the type used for officially weighing a jockey and his tack before a horse race.

Some of these scales employ a system of several springs. Other types, in addition to giving the weight automatically, also compute such data as the price per unit. One form has a fixed line as an indicator, behind which a cylinder, drum, or barrel rotates when a weight is put on the pan.

A fan scale is fitted with a fan-shaped chart over which the indicator describes an arc in moving from zero to the scale's capacity. One form is the familiar computing scale used in post offices and business houses to weigh mail and give the value of stamps required. In addition to weight, the chart carries the cost of mailing letters, books, and packages of various postal classes to different parcel post zones. Instead of using a spring, a fan scale may operate by rotation of a bent rod, or torsion pendulum, its twist being translated through a rack and pinion to move a pointer over a calibrated index.

Platform Scales. A system of multiplying levers, by which a heavy object can be balanced by a relatively small counterpoise on the beam, is used in the platform scale. This scale was patented in 1831 by Thaddeus Fairbanks of St. Johnsbury, Vt., and a number of improvements have been added since then. It is equipped with a load-receiving platform carried on multiplying levers that transmit the weight of the load to a beam which can be balanced by moving a counterpoise. Such a scale has four more lines of support containing bearings that rest directly upon knife-edges in the multiplying levers. Another and newer type of scale for handling heavy weights is the flexure-plate or plate-fulcrum scale, in which the conventional pivots are replaced by steel plates securely fastened to opposing members. This scale operates by bending, or flexing, instead of by friction on the bearings. Still others operate on hydraulic or pneumatic pressure.

Some platform scales accommodate enormous weights, handling heavy artillery at arsenals and even railroad trains moving on suspended lengths of track. One such scale on the New York Central Railroad is 90 feet long and has a capacity of 825 tons. Some are equipped with self-discharging mechanisms that discharge the load when it reaches a given weight; others, using electricity for recording instead of weights, weigh material as it passes by on a conveyor belt.

FRANK DORR
Associate Editor, "Popular Science Monthly"

WEIGHT, wāt, a quantity expressing the relative heaviness of an object or substance, as determined by the measurement of its downward displacement subject to gravity when placed on a beam balance or a spring scale. Physically, the value of any weight W is given by the expression $W = mg$, where m is the mass of the object and g is the local acceleration of gravity. As a physical property resulting from the downward pull exerted on an object by gravity, weight is, therefore, distinct from the *mass* of the object, which term refers simply to the quantity of matter the object contains. The mass of a body is the same anywhere in the universe, but the weight of the body may vary, depending upon the force of local gravity acting upon it, and other influences such as centrifugal force. Any object in free orbit, or coasting without power in outer space, will be in a condition of weightlessness. See also GRAVITATION; GRAVITY; INERTIA; MASS.

WEIGHT, Atomic. See ATOMIC WEIGHT.

WEIGHT CONTROL. See DIET; OBESITY.

WEIGHT LIFTING, a sport in which weights are lifted competitively within prescribed rules. Various versions of the sport were held in Europe, Egypt, Japan, and Turkey before the 20th century, but present-day weight lifting is a development of this century, particularly after 1920, when it was first contested in the Olympic Games.

In the modern sport the athlete lifts a barbell—a one-inch-thick seven-foot-long bar to which disk-shaped weights not over one and one half feet in diameter are attached at either end. Three types of lifts feature the sport. For all specifications for each lift, the official rules should be studied.

Military Press (always performed two-handed). The bar is first lifted from the floor to shoulder height, then rested on the chest or the closely flexed arms and held motionless for two seconds. It must then be lifted vertically until the arms are completely extended and held there two seconds, the arms and legs stiffened.

Snatch (two-handed or with either hand). In simplest terms the weight is lifted overhead in one continuous motion without the pause characteristic of the military press.

Clean and Jerk (two-handed or with either hand). The weight is first lifted to shoulder level ("clean"). The legs are then bent (unlike the military press) and legs and arms are then suddenly stiffened ("jerk") to bring the weight overhead.

In the Olympic Games and in national competition two-handed lifts only are held, and the totals for the three lifts are added to give the competitor's score. There are nine divisions in Olympic competition, classified according to the contestant's weight: flyweight, bantamweight, featherweight, lightweight, middleweight, light heavyweight, middle heavyweight, heavy-

Soviet championship weight lifter Vasili Alekseyev is classed as a super heavyweight, able to lift the heaviest weights.

weight, and super heavyweight. Heavier athletes, naturally, achieve correspondingly heavier lifts. Heaviest lifts are made in the clean and jerk. Next, on the average, comes the military press, with the snatch last, although in a few cases an athlete may score higher in the snatch than in the military press. The world record of 1,184¼ pounds achieved by the Soviet heavyweight Yuri Vlasov in the 1960 Olympic Games for his three lifts serves as a fairly representative example. This was made up of: clean and jerk, 446 pounds; military press, 396¾; and snatch, 341½. In 1972 the press was eliminated from Olympic and international competition.

To qualify for a weight-lifting certificate a candidate must lift the equivalent of his own weight in the two-hands clean and jerk, and come within 20 percent of this in the military press and the two-hands snatch. See also BODY BUILDING.

PARKE CUMMINGS
Author of "The Dictionary of Sports"

WEIGHT THROWING, a term applied to certain of the field events in the sport of track and field. In these events heavy metal weights, made of lead or of brass-covered lead, are thrown for distance. The shot put, the discus throw, the hammer throw and the 35-pound and 56 pound weight throws comprise the common events in this group. Although the javelin is also thrown for distance, it is not regarded as a "weight."

In the *shot put* a heavy metal sphere is propelled from a circle seven feet in diameter; four feet of its circumference—in the forepart of the circle—contains a toeboard four inches high. In this event the shot is not allowed to pass behind or below the shoulder, so that technically it is "put" rather than "thrown." A 16-pound shot is used in major masculine competition, such as in the Olympic Games, national championships, and intercollegiate competition; the 12-pound shot is usually used by males in secondary schools, and the 8-pound shot is used in feminine competition, including the Olympic Games. In the games the shot put is also one of the 10 decathlon events for men. A put of over 72 feet has been made with the 16-pound shot, and a woman has exceeded 73 feet with the 8-pound shot.

The *discus* is a disk, thicker in the center than its circumference. For men this circumference is 8⅝ inches, and the weight is 2 kilograms or 4 pounds 6.4 ounces. The women's discus is about one inch less in circumference and weighs only half as much—1 kilogram. There are other specifications, but these are the essentials. It is thrown from a circle which is 8 feet 2½ inches in diameter, and the athlete rotates several times in the circle before releasing the discus, which must land within a 90-degree sector. The discus is thrown by men and women in the Olympic Games and is a decathlon event for men. The masculine record exceeds 233 feet, and a woman has thrown 232 feet with the 1-kilogram discus.

In the *hammer throw*—for men only—a heavy sphere is attached to a wire which has a grip for the thrower to hold in his hands. The length of the complete implement is 4 feet. The athlete spins the weight around his head several times and then releases it. A 7-foot circle is used, and, like the discus, the weight must land within a 90-degree sector. A 16-pound hammer is thrown in Olympic, national, and intercollegiate competition, while a 12-pound one is used in boys' secondary schools. The 16-pound hammer has been thrown over 263 feet.

The *35-pound* and *56-pound weights* are usually known as the "heavy" weights, and these events are similar in principle to the hammer throw. The handle is bent in triangular fashion, and is much shorter than in the hammer, so that the entire implement is only 16 inches overall. There are no listed world records for these events, and they are not currently held in the Olympic Games, but there is some heavy weight competition in the United States. In the 56-pound weight throw there is a summer contest for the Amateur Athletic Union (AAU) championship; a throw of over 45 feet has been made.

GERHARD GSCHEIDLE/PETER ARNOLD

World record-holder Al Feuerbach competing in the shot put.

The 35-pound weight throw is a winter indoor event, most common in intercollegiate competition in the East. The record exceeds 66 feet.

In all of these events it is a foul to touch the confining circle or step outside of it. The competitor is allowed several attempts, usually three or four.

PARKE CUMMINGS
Author of "The Dictionary of Sports"

WEIGHTLESSNESS. See MASS—*Weightlessness.*

WEIGHTS AND MEASURES. See MEASURES AND MEASURING SYSTEMS.

WEIGL, vī′gəl, **Joseph,** Austrian composer: b. Eisenstadt, Austria, March 28, 1766; d. Vienna, Feb. 3, 1846. The son of a fine cellist, he showed musical gifts at an early age. He was fortunate in his teachers: Florian Leopold Gassman, Johann Georg Albrechtsberger, and Antonio Salieri. Emperor Joseph II favored him after the great Christoph Willibald Gluck had approved the production of his chamber opera, *Die unnützige Vorsicht*, composed at the age of 16. Even more important was Salieri's patronage, to which he owed the assistant conductorship of the Vienna Court Theater (1790); he became composer to the Opera in 1792. In 1823 he resigned this post and in 1827 he was appointed vice Kapellmeister to the court. He was a great favorite of Maria Theresa, daughter of Charles II.

After 1827, Weigl composed only religious works. Of his many operas *Die Schweizerfamilie* (1809), a somewhat mawkish Singspiel with pleasant tunes, remained popular on German stages for years, and may still be revivable. It was rumored that the empress sang the role of Pauline in *Die Uniform* (1805) in a private performance. *Nachtigall und Rabe* (1818) was revived at Hannover, Germany, as recently as 1937. Finally, Beethoven used the air "Pria ch'io impegno," from Weigl's *L'Amor marinaro* (1797) as the theme for the last movement of his trio for pianoforte, clarinet, and cello, Opus 11.

WALLACE BROCKWAY

WEIGLE, wī′gəl, **Luther Allan,** Biblical scholar, translator, and educator: b. Littlestown, Pa., Sept. 11, 1880; d. New Haven, Conn., Sept. 2, 1976. He was ordained a Lutheran minister in 1903 and received a Ph.D. from Yale in 1905. He served as professor of philosophy (1905–1916) and dean (1910–1915) at Carleton College, and professor of religious education (1916–1949) and dean (1928–1949) at the Yale Divinity School. In 1940–1942 he was president of the Federal Council of Churches of Christ, and in 1942–1950 was chairman of the planning committee which organized the National Council of the Churches of Christ in the U.S.A. From 1930 he was chairman of the committee which produced the *Revised Standard Version of the Bible* (New Testament, 1946; Old Testament, 1952; Apocrypha, 1957). Among far-reaching administrative responsibilities he was chairman of the executive committee of the American Association of Theological Schools (1929–1949) and president of Yale-in-China (1946–1956). His early book, *The Pupil and the Teacher* (1916) was a standard text in teacher training for many years and helped create new standards in religious education. His *English New Testament from Tyndale to the Revised Standard Version* (1949) introduced the new version to the English-speaking world.

FREDERICK C. GRANT

WEIHAI, wä'hī' (until 1949 known as WEIHAIWEI), municipality (*shih*), China, in northeast Shantung Province, 140 miles northeast of Tsingtao. A Yellow Sea port situated on Weihai Bay—its harbor is protected by Liukung Island—the city is a commercial center with factories producing rubber products, soap, and matches. Oilseed milling and the weaving of silk and cotton are other important occupations. Eggs, sugar, peanut oil and peanuts are exported.

During the Sino-Japanese War, Weihai (then Weihaiwei) was captured by the Japanese in 1895 and held until 1898, when the city and a surrounding area of 285 square miles was leased by China to Great Britain, which established a naval base called Port Edward. Under the terms of the Shantung settlement agreed to in 1922 at the Washington Conference, Britain offered to return Weihaiwei to China, but unsettled conditions in the country delayed transfer of authority to the Chinese until Oct. 1, 1930. Pop. (1970) less than 50,000.

NORTON GINSBURG

WEIL, vĕy, **Simone,** French philosopher: b. Paris, France, Feb. 3, 1909; d. Ashford, Kent, England, Aug. 24, 1943. Of well-to-do Jewish parents, she studied under Alain (Émile-Auguste Chartier) and was *agrégée de philosophie* from the École Normale Supérieure. She never had the manners of the typical normal school graduate—wit, pride, worldliness—nor did she live the life of the Parisian man of letters of the period. She taught at Le Puy, a provincial *lycée*, but characteristically took off a year to learn as a factory hand at the Renault motor works what labor meant. Depression, politics, and war were problems she faced with others; like André Malraux, André Gide, Ignazio Silone, and Arthur Koestler, she was a militant Leftist. In 1936 she joined the International Brigade against Francisco Franco in the Spanish Civil War. But to these experiences, as to the problems of truth and belief through which she sought to understand them, she brought a questioning radicalism and an astonishing purity all her own.

After the fall of France, when Jews were forbidden to teach by Vichy law, she became a farm servant near Marseilles. Later in 1942, she and her family escaped to the United States, but after a few months she was in London working for the Free French government. Never healthy, she now refused to eat more than the official ration in occupied France. Ravaged by pleurisy, she was admitted to the Middlesex Hospital, from which she was moved to a sanatorium in Ashford, where she died at the age of 34.

Her writings—*La pesanteur et la grâce* (1948; Eng. tr., *Gravity and Grace*, 1952), a collection of religious and philosophical aphorisms; *L'enracinement* (1949; Eng. tr., *The Need for Roots*, 1952), an essay on the obligations of the individual and the state; *L'attente de Dieu* (1950; Eng. tr., *Waiting for God*, 1951), a scriptural autobiography; *La source grecque* (1953), translations and studies; *Oppression et liberté* (1955; Eng. tr., *Oppression and Liberty*, 1958), political and social papers on war, factory work, and language; three volumes of *Cahiers* (1951, 1955, 1956; *Notebooks*, 2 volumes, 1956), a range of topics indicating a mind still finding its direction—all were collected and published after her death. They have made her, while not limited to any orthodoxy, widely known as one of the great spokesmen for religion in our time, one of the subtlest psychologists of spiritual tribulation, and a genuine analyst of force, violence, terror, and death, who found in suffering a source of purity and grace.

EUGENIO C. VILLICANA
Columbia University

WEILL, vīl, Americanized as wīl, **Kurt,** German composer: b. Dessau, Germany, March 2, 1900; d. New York, N.Y., April 3, 1950. After studies in Dessau and Berlin (his teachers included Engelbert Humperdinck and Ferruccio Busoni), he began composing for the stage, the most successful of his early works being *Aufstieg und Fall der Stadt Mahagonny* (1927), *Der Zar lässt sich photographieren* (1928), and—above all—*Die Dreigroschenoper (The Threepenny Opera)*, a satirical, bitter version of *The Beggar's Opera* to a text by Bertolt Brecht. Later, driven from Germany by the Nazi regime, Weill had brief careers in Paris and London before settling (1935) in New York, where he composed both opera—*Street Scene* (1947), *Lost in the Stars* (1949)—and musical comedy—*Knickerbocker Holiday* (1938), *Lady in the Dark* (1941), and *One Touch of Venus* (1943). He composed in many forms, but his fame has been maintained largely by the mordant, deliberately "decadent" pseudo-jazz style of his Berlin works, the spread of which after World War II owed much to his widow, the singing actress Lotte Lenya.

HERBERT WEINSTOCK

WEIL'S DISEASE, vīlz dĭ-zēz', epidemic or spirochetal jaundice, a febrile infection in man, caused by the spirochete *Leptospira icterohaemorrhagiae*. This organism measures about 10 micra in length, and is transmitted to the human by a number of wild and domestic animals, such as mice, dogs, swine, and especially rats. Workers in waterfront areas, slaughterhouses, and fish markets, and cleaners of sewers and canals are particularly likely to be exposed to the disease. The portal of entry may be an abraded skin area or through the respiratory and intestinal tracts.

Six to twelve days after exposure, the victim of Weil's disease develops a high fever, generalized muscular aching, injected conjunctiva, an enlarged tender liver with varying degrees of jaundice, diminished urine output, and, in the severely stricken, hemorrhages in the skin and mucous membranes. Headache and stiff neck are common from meningeal irritation. Laboratory diagnosis may be made by direct dark-field examination of the blood within the first five days. About 90 percent of the cases will show changes in the spinal fluid with 10 to 250 lymphocytes being found per cubic millimeter plus xanthochromia or icteric tinge. Specific agglutination tests become positive in the second week in dilutions above 1:10,000.

Many acute diseases simulate Weil's disease, among them being infectious hepatitis, acute nephritis, typhus fever, influenza, and brucellosis. Treatment of the disease is symptomatic and directed principally toward liver and kidney involvement. Some success in treating the disease with antibiotics has been reported. The disease generally runs a two- or three-week course with a mortality of about 5 percent unless other medical conditions exist.

REAUMUR S. DONNALLY, M.D.
Washington Hospital Center, Washington, D.C.

EASTFOTO

The ancient ducal palace in Weimar, East Germany, with its baroque spire, houses the state art collections.

WEIMAR, vī'mär, city, East Germany, situated at an elevation of 650 feet on the left bank of the Ilm River, 13 miles east of Erfurt. Lying in a picturesque valley, it is primarily a residential center, the small prewar industry of which was not reactivated after 1945.

Cultural Center. Due to the fact that it was simultaneously the residence of Germany's four great literary figures—Johann Wolfgang von Goethe, Johann Christoph Friedrich von Schiller, Johann Gottfried von Herder, and Christoph Martin Wieland—and that at other periods the composers Johann Sebastian Bach and Franz von Liszt, the artist Lucas Cranach the Elder, and the philosopher Friedrich Wilhelm Nietzsche all lived and worked here, Weimar was at one time regarded as the literary and artistic center of the country. Its position as "Germany's Athens" was furthered by the benevolent patronage and encouragement extended by the Grand Duke Charles Augustus (1757–1828), not only to its four great writers but to the cause of art in general, in what was then the capital of Saxe-Weimar (from 1815 Saxe-Weimar-Eisenach).

At every turn in Weimar one is confronted with some facet of the city's magnificent artistic and historical heritage. Central to all is the ducal palace, destroyed by fire in 1774 and rebuilt under Goethe's direction in 1790–1803. Facing it are the so-called Red and Yellow castles, dating respectively to 1576 and 1704 and now housing government offices, while the ducal library of 400,000 volumes is housed in the Green Castle, which dates to 1565 and was rebuilt in rococo style in 1760. Its tower is reached by a spiral staircase of 64 steps, carved in 1671 from a single giant oak.

On a hill across the Ilm River stands the building constructed in 1896 to house the collection of manuscripts and complete editions of the works of Goethe, Schiller, and other notable German writers. The theater at which Goethe directed performances of some of his dramas stands near the house in which Schiller wrote his *William Tell* and in which he died in 1805. Another building associated with Weimar's literary heritage is Goethe's house, dating to 1709 and rebuilt in 1794, which Charles Augustus presented as a gift to the author. Following the death of Goethe's grandson Walter in 1885, it became the state-directed Goethe Museum, with its rooms restored as they appeared at the time of the poet's death in 1832.

Other notable buildings surround the market square. The City House, erected in 1526 (rebuilt 1800), was the scene of many festivities during Weimar's classic period. Opposite it stands the Gothic city hall, dating to 1841, adjacent to which is the home in which Lucas Cranach the Elder worked and died in 1553. The Stadtkirche, or city church, construction of which was initiated in 1498 and which was restored at the beginning of the 18th century, contains work by Cranach. Beneath the church organ stands the tomb of Herder. The Jakobskirche (formerly Hofkirche), or court chapel, erected in 1713, was Schiller's first burial place.

A park, laid out at the beginning of the 19th century and extending from the ducal palace along the riverbank, serves as the setting for Goethe's famous garden house. Many monuments grace the city: the Goethe-Schiller monument in bronze, statues of Herder, Wieland, and the composer Johann Nepomuk Hummel, a fountain of monumental proportions, and a marble bust of Liszt, who lived in the residence on the Marienstrasse that now houses the Liszt museum. Nearby is the house in which Nietzsche died in 1900, now used to house the Nietzsche archives. The patronage of the royal family is recalled by the fact that Goethe and Schiller lie in the ducal vault in the new cemetery.

Modern History. In the 20th century Weimar enjoyed some revival of its former importance when, following World War I, the German National Assembly met here to draft and adopt a constitution for the Weimar Republic on Aug. 11, 1919, and to ratify the provisions of the Treaty of Versailles in the next year. See also GERMANY—27. *The Revolution and the Weimar Republic, 1918–1933*. Beginning in 1919, it recaptured some of its former artistic grandeur as the seat of the Bauhaus, Germany's modern academy of arts and architecture which, however, was removed to Dessau in 1925. In World War II, Weimar was entered by United States forces in April 1945 but later was occupied by Soviet troops. War damage to the central section of the city has been repaired. In 1949, Weimar became part of the German Democratic Republic (East Germany) and now is included in the Erfurt District. Population: (1981 census) 64,000.

WEIMAR REPUBLIC, vī'mär, German republic that came into being after Germany's defeat in World War I. Functioning under the Weimar constitution, it lasted from 1919 until 1933, when it was replaced by Hitler's third Reich. See GERMANY—HISTORY.

WEIMARANER, vī-mə-rä'nər, a sporting dog developed in Germany in the 19th century. The male should stand from 25 to 27 inches (64–69 cm) high at the shoulder; the female, from 23 to 25 inches (58–64 cm). The male's average weight is 70 to 85 pounds (32–39 kg), and the female's is 55 to 70 pounds (25–32 kg). The breed has drop ears, greenish eyes and a distinctive short, sleek gray coat. It is shown with its tail docked to 6 inches (15 cm).

The Weimaraner's special skills are pointing and retrieving and, in some instances, guarding. Like certain other sporting dogs, it is better off in the country than in the city because it ought to be run regularly and does not take at all kindly to being shut up alone in an apartment until its owner gets home from work. Nevertheless many city owners of Weimaraners become so attached to them that they put up with their tendency to be destructive when left alone for long periods.

The breed is stubborn and often too impetuous to be an ideal companion for younger children, but its lively, devoted personality and carefree coat make it a good choice for those who are willing to give it as much exercise as it needs and who have the know-how and persistence to train it to behave properly. The Weimaraner is fairly hardy as big dogs go. It is subject to bloat, but it is less likely to have hip dysplasia than are many other breeds its size.

JOHN HOWE
Author of "Choosing the Right Dog"

WEINBERGER, wīn'bûr-gər, **Caspar Willard** (1917–), American public official, who served in the cabinets of two presidents—as secretary of health, education, and welfare under President Nixon and as secretary of defense under President Reagan. He was born in San Francisco on Aug. 18, 1917, the son of a lawyer. After obtaining a law degree from Harvard in 1941, he practiced law in California and in 1952 was elected to the California Assembly. In 1962–1964 he was chairman of the California Republican Central Committee. During the latter part of the 1960's he held various California state posts, including that of finance director.

His Washington career began in 1970 as chairman of the Federal Trade Commission. He soon moved to the Office of Management and Budget, where, as deputy director (1970–1972) and director (1972–1973), he gained experience with military budgets. In 1973 he became secretary of the Department of Health, Education and Welfare.

In 1975, Weinberger returned to San Francisco as an officer with engineering and construction firms. He was appointed secretary of defense by President-elect Ronald Reagan in December 1980 and was confirmed by the Senate on Jan. 20, 1981. As secretary he secured substantial increases in defense allocations, which by 1985 were larger than during the Vietnam War. Owing to federal budgetary deficits, defense spending was cut back in the next few years over his objections. He resigned on Nov. 5, 1987, citing the illness of his wife.

WEINBERGER, vīn'ber-gər, **Jaromir** (1896–1967), Czech composer. He was born in Prague on Jan. 8, 1896. He was already a noted conductor and teacher when he won world fame with the production, at Prague in 1927, of his first opera, the folk-based *Svanda dudák* (*Schwanda the Bagpiper*). After its 1928 performance at Breslau in German, it was heard throughout Europe. The Metropolitan Opera, New York, staged it on Nov. 7, 1931.

Weinberger moved to London in 1937 and settled in the United States in 1939. Nothing that he composed subsequently approached the success of his first opera. Although he produced a large quantity of music in later years, he has been represented chiefly in the orchestral repertoire—by the popular polka and fugue from *Schwanda* and the variations and fugue on *Under the Spreading Chestnut Tree* (1939). He died in St. Petersburg, Fla., on Aug. 8, 1967.

HERBERT WEINSTOCK
Coauthor of "Men of Music"

WEINGARTNER, vīn-gärt-nər, **Felix** (1863–1942), Austrian composer, conductor, author, and music editor. Paul Felix Weingartner was born in Zara, Dalmatia (now part of Yugoslavia), on June 2, 1863. He began to study piano and composition at an early age, continuing at the Leipzig Conservatory (1881–1883) under Carl Reinecke, Salomon Jadassohn, and Oscar Paul, and later with Franz von Liszt, who was influential in the production of Weingartner's first opera, *Sakuntala* (1884). Beginning his career as a conductor at this time, Weingartner was active in a number of cities, including Berlin, where he led the Royal Opera and the Royal Orchestra. Among the many directorships held by him, the most notable were of the Vienna State Opera (1908–1910) as successor to Gustav Mahler, the Vienna Folk Opera (1919–1924), and the Vienna Philharmonic Orchestra (1919–1927). He made his first appearance in the United States in 1905. Weingartner died in Winterthur, Switzerland, on May 7, 1942.

Weingartner was an excellent pianist and at the turn of the century won high regard as an ensemble performer, touring Europe with his own trio. He was one of the editors of the complete works of Hector Berlioz (from 1899) and of Joseph Haydn (from 1907), among others. As an author he wrote important works, principally in the fields of conducting, aesthetics, and the interpretation of the symphonies of Wolfgang Amadeus Mozart, Ludwig van Beethoven, Franz Schubert, and Robert Schumann. Among those publications translated into English are *Symphony Works Since Beethoven* (1904), *On Conducting* (1906), and *On the Performance of Beethoven's Symphonies* (1908). His activities as a composer continued all his life and included operas (*Orestes*, 1902; *Kain und Abel*, 1914; *Dame Kobald*, 1916; *Der Apostat*, 1938), six symphonies, piano music, and songs. He became a naturalized citizen of Switzerland in 1931.

SAUL NOVACK,
Assistant Professor of Music, Queens College.

WEINHEIM, vīn'hīm (known also as **WEINHEIM AN DER BERGSTRASSE),** city, Germany, in the State of Baden-Württemberg, situated on the Bergstrasse (western slope of the Odenwald hills), 10 miles northeast of Mannheim. The city combines small industries (tires, rubber and leather goods, furniture) with agriculture, serving as a center and railroad junction for the orchards and vineyards in the area. It has several modern trade schools. Founded about 500, Weinheim still possesses ruins of its original fortifications, and above the city stand the remains of Windeck Castle (12th century). Other interesting buildings are the Ulmer Chapel, a Gothic edifice constructed in 1470 (rebuilt 1721); the Catholic church, with notable baroque altars; and the city hall, built in 1725. After World War II, Weinheim was included in the Federal Republic of Germany (West Germany). Pop. (1983 est.) 41,459.

WEINMAN, wīn'mən, **Adolph Alexander,** American sculptor: b. Karlsruhe, Germany, Dec. 11, 1870; d. Queens, N.Y., Aug. 8, 1952. He went to the United States in 1880 and studied at Cooper Union and the Art Students League (at the latter under Augustus Saint-Gaudens). Opening his own studio, Weinman gained his first public recognition at the St. Louis exposition of 1904 with the sculpture *Destiny of the Red Race,* which won a silver medal.

Although Weinman worked in the precise and finished tradition of the medalists of the Italian Renaissance, he achieved success in his large stone and bronze pieces as well, creating an impressive number of symbolic sculptures and war memorials in parks and on public buildings. The work which the artist prized as his best is the pedimental sculpture on the rear of the National Archives Building, Washington, D.C. (1933). Among his other works are the Gen. Alexander Macomb monument in Detroit (1906); the Abraham Lincoln memorials near Hodgenville, Ky. (1909) and at Madison, Wis.; the Lincoln statue in the state capitol at Frankfort, Ky. (1911); and the Lincoln statuette in the Metropolitan Museum of Art, New York City. In Washington, D.C., he executed the monumental frieze for the Supreme Court room in the Supreme Court Building and the sculpture for the façade of the Post Office Department (both 1933). In New York City are found his sculptural decorations on the Municipal Building (1912–1913) and the Pierpont Morgan Library, his portrait bust of Horace Mann in the Hall of Fame (1930), and his figures of Alexander Hamilton and DeWitt Clinton at the Museum of the City of New York (1940).

JEAN ANNE VINCENT

WEIPA, wē'pă, an aboriginal mission station on the western coast of the Cape York Peninsula, Queensland, Australia, which has given its name to the center of a region containing a vast deposit of bauxite. Other known minerals in the general area include gold, tin, wolfram, and mica, but remoteness and inaccessibility of deposits have combined to bar development. The Presbyterian Church established the Weipa mission in 1898. Embracing an area of 2,500 square miles, the reservation is one of the few remaining sites of aboriginal tribal life.

Bauxite was first reported at Weipa in 1902. After 1955, extensive investigation and prospecting showed the deposit of commercial grade ore to exceed 2 billion tons. The ore body is exposed or is at minimum depth, and extends for 150 miles along the coast and some miles inland. Dredging of an access channel for ships began in 1961 as a preliminary to commercial exploitation of the bauxite by a company representing Australian and United States mining interests, and construction of an on-site smelter was planned for refining the bauxite.

R. M. YOUNGER

WEIR, wēr, a family of American artists.

ROBERT WALTER WEIR: b. New York, N.Y., June 18, 1803; d. there, May 1, 1889. After studying with John Wesley Jarvis, he began painting portraits in 1821. In 1824 he went to Italy and studied in Florence under Pietro Benvenuti and also in Rome. He became a member of the National Academy of Design in 1829. In 1834 he was appointed teacher of drawing at the United States Military Academy, where he later became a professor and remained until 1876, teaching such cadets as Ulysses S. Grant, William T. Sherman, and the artist James A. M. Whistler. His best-known but, as architectural decoration, least successful work is the historical composition *Embarkation of the Pilgrims* (completed 1840) in the rotunda of the Capitol, Washington, D.C. Another well-known work is the symbolic *Peace and War* painted for the old chapel at West Point. His best work is a series of sketches made in the Hudson River valley of rock formations and clouds. Other examples of his work include *Red Jacket,* a portrait; *Columbus Before the Council of Salamanca; Our Lord on the Mount of Olives;* and *Virgil and Dante Crossing the Styx.* John Ferguson Weir and Julian Alden Weir were his sons.

JOHN FERGUSON WEIR: b. West Point, N.Y., Aug. 28, 1841; d. Providence, R.I., April 8, 1926. He studied with his father, and in 1866 became a member of the National Academy of Design. From 1869 to 1913 he was the first director of Yale University's School of the Fine Arts. His statues of Yale President Theodore Dwight Woolsey and Professor Benjamin Silliman the elder are on the New Haven campus. Weir painted in the style of the Hudson River school. His book *Human Destiny in the Light of Revelation* (1903) reflected his deep interest in religion.

JULIAN ALDEN WEIR: b. West Point, N.Y., Aug. 30, 1852; d. New York, N.Y., Dec. 8, 1919. He studied first with his father and then with Jean Léon Gérôme in Paris. He was strongly influenced by James A. M. Whistler's lightened color palette and by compositional devices derived from Japanese prints, and he may be called an American impressionist. His painting, *Idle Hours,* now in the Metropolitan Museum, New York City, won the prize of the American Art Association in 1888, and *Breton Interior* won the second-class medal at the Paris Exposition in 1889. Although the refinement and subtlety of his paintings were not widely appreciated in his own day, he is well represented in American museums and in the Luxembourg, Paris. He was one of the first Americans to admire Édouard Manet and to introduce his work into the United States. Weir belonged to the group which formed the Society of American Artists. He was president of the National Academy of Design in 1915–1917.

JEAN ANNE VINCENT.

WEIR, R(obert) Stanley, Canadian jurist and poet: b. Hamilton, Ontario, Canada, Nov. 15, 1856; d. near Lake Memphremagog, Quebec, Aug. 20, 1926. Educated at McGill University, he was called to the bar in Quebec in 1881 and practiced in Montreal. In 1926 he was appointed to the bench of the Exchequer Court of Canada. In addition to his authorship of several legal and historical works, he wrote two volumes of verse, *After Ypres and Other Verses* (1917) and *Poems, Early and Late* (1923). He is best remembered as the author (1908) of the most generally used English lyric to *O Canada!* (French lyrics by Adolphe-Basile Routhlier; music by Calixa Lavallée), which was designated as Canada's national anthem by Parliament in 1980.

WEIRS, wērz, in the broadest sense, dams, embankments, or bulkheads used to keep back a body or stream of water or to divert or measure the flow. A fence of stakes or brushwood known as a weir is sometimes set in a stream or an inlet of the ocean for catching fish. Structures of willows, brush, and the like, weighted with stones or earth, are also called weirs; they are used in the construction of embankments, dikes, or levees (see LEVEE) for directing rivers in their channels, protecting the surrounding land from floods, or diverting water for irrigation or other purposes. Dams constructed of such relatively permanent materials as concrete, rock fill, and earth have largely supplanted the older brush, stake, or timber-crib structures.

In hydraulic engineering, a weir is a bulkhead or dam over which water flows, or a notch in the top of such a structure through which water flows. The flow in large natural channels is usually measured with a current meter, but notches of rectangular, trapezoidal (Cipolletti), triangular, or proportional (Sutro) shapes are used for the measurement of flow in small streams or man-made channels. A Francis formula is widely used for the measurement of flow through a rectangular weir, with variations for such factors as the end shape of the weir, the velocity of approach of the water, and for very low heads of water. All of these factors have an effect on weir discharge rates.

See also DAMS; HYDRAULICS; HYDRODYNAMICS.

WEIRTON, wēr'tən, city, West Virginia, in Hancock and Brooke counties, on the Ohio River, 30 miles west of Pittsburgh and 25 miles north of Wheeling, at an altitude of 640 feet. In the Northern Panhandle of the state, it is a steel manufacturing center with a large tin-plating installation and plants producing zinc-coated steel goods (including automobile parts), chemicals, and cement products. Coal and clay deposits are worked in the vincinity. With Steubenville, Ohio, Weirton forms a metropolitan area with a population (1980) or 163,099. There is an airport. Originally settled by John Holliday and his family during the American Revolution, the area became one of the first iron-manufacturing centers west of the Allegheny Mountains when a blast furnace was built here in the late 1790's by Peter Tarr, who in 1813 supplied cannonballs for Oliver Hazard Perry's fleet on Lake Erie. The furnace is preserved by a local commission. Although the community grew rapidly after 1910, it remained unincorporated until 1947, when Weirton, Weirton Heights, Marland Heights, and Hollidays Cove were organized as a city with a council-manager government. Pop. 25,371.

WEISBACH-DARCY FORMULA, vīs'bäkн-där'sĭ fôr'mū-lə, a basic equation used for determining the loss of head, or friction head, due to friction in pressure conduits or pipes. For circular pipes, whether the flow of the liquid or gas is laminar or turbulent, the equation is

$$h_L = f\ \frac{L}{D}\ \frac{V^2}{2g}$$

where h_L is the head loss or friction head, measured in feet or centimeters of the flowing liquid or gas; L and D are the length and diameter of the pipe, respectively; V is the velocity of flow through the pipe; g is the acceleration of gravity; and f is a friction factor which is a function of both the relative roughness of the pipe and the Reynolds number of the flow. The relative roughness (ε/D) depends on the absolute roughness ε of the interior surface and the pipe diameter D. Empirical curves have been developed for determining the friction factor f and the values of absolute roughness ε, based on extensive tests of commercial pipe. The Reynolds number expresses the viscosity of the fluid.

See also FLUID MECHANICS; HYDRAULICS; HYDRODYNAMICS.

WEISER, wē'sər, city, Idaho, seat of Washington County, at the junction of the Snake (which here forms the border with Oregon) and Weiser rivers, 60 miles northwest of Boise; altitude 2,115 feet. It is a commercial center for a fruitgrowing region, in which irrigation is used extensively. Industries include flour mills, beverage works, and metalworking plants. Dairying is also conducted, and vegetables, especially potatoes and sugar beets, are grown. Copper mines are located here. Laid out in 1877, Weiser was incorporated in 1887; the city was rebuilt (one mile west of the original settlement) after a destructive fire in 1890. The modern city has an airport, and is headquarters for Weiser National Forest. Pop. 4,771.

WEISMANN, vīs'män, **August,** German biologist: b. Frankfurt am Main, Germany, Jan. 17, 1834; d. Freiburg, Nov. 5, 1914. The son of a classical philologist and an artistically gifted mother, Weismann exhibited an active interest in natural history as a child, collecting plants and insects, and raising caterpillars. The Frankfurt environment, with the recently established Senckenberg Natural History Museum, was a favorable one for the nurture and development of such scientific interests as Weismann displayed during the boy's years in the elementary schools.

Weismann's university education led to a degree in medicine at Göttingen (1852–1856), which was followed by an assistantship in the Medical Clinic at Rostock. In the interest of broadening his education in the sciences, he transferred to the Chemical Institute in 1857, and then made a tour of German universities, ending with a more extended stay at the University of Vienna. Toward the end of 1858 he settled down and began a career as a practicing physician in Frankfurt.

The Austrian war in Italy diverted the young

medical graduate into practice at the field hospital at Verona, and gave him a vivid experience with human suffering. Subsequent travels in northern Italy enabled him to see something of the natural beauties and artistic treasures of that country. The year 1860 found him again engaged in his practice in Frankfurt, with time on his hands for reading and thinking about biological problems and for the preparation of a few anatomical papers.

August Weismann

The Bettmann Archive

Seeing clearly that only a career in biological research could satisfy him, Weismann gave up his practice and went first to Paris, where Étienne Geoffroy Saint-Hilaire, Henri Milne-Edwards, and André M. C. Duméril were lecturing. From Paris he went to Giessen in 1861; there he was much stimulated by the lectures and personal influence of Rudolf Leuckart, with whom he maintained a lifelong association, and under whom he began his notable early work on insect embryology. Two years followed at Schloss Schaumburg (in what is now Lower Saxony) as personal physician to the archduke, and this period gave him leisure to complete his first major work, "On the Development of the Diptera in the Egg," and to offer a second paper as the "Habilitation Address" with which he joined the medical faculty of the University of Freiburg im Breisgau in May 1863. In this university he was to remain for the rest of his life.

At first Weismann continued his studies on insect embryology, but failure of his eyesight forced him to give up the use of the microscope and to turn to more general problems of biology. In the decade of the 1860's this meant an interest in evolution. With a lecture on "The Evidences for the Darwinian Theory," with which he became extraordinary professor in 1865, he became one of the more active proponents in Germany of evolution.

The onset of difficulties with his eyes was compensated by the direction of his studies, and still more by his fortunate marriage in 1867 to Marie Gruber, the daughter of a German family in Genoa whom he had met in the course of his Italian travels in 1859. In her he found a congenial and soon indispensable helpmeet, who was not only wife but capable amanuensis and laboratory assistant. Through her constant reading to him during the decade of partial blindness he kept abreast of the developments in biology in one of its most active decades. The Weismann home, in which five children grew up, was filled with literary and artistic interests, and was the center of an active musical circle.

The scientific career of Weismann was that of the natural scientist who begins the accumulation of facts and their classification and then turns to the search for the underlying broad generalizations and principles. His earliest papers were on biochemistry and histology. From these he turned to a series of major studies on insect embryology, on the alternation of generations in the Cladocera of Lake Constance, and on the Mediteranean Hydromedusae. These works involved collecting and field studies, and continued through his first 20 years at Freiburg.

The second series of researches falls into relation with evolution, and gradually came to bear mainly on the problems of heredity. The germ cells of the Hydromedusae had called Weismann's attention to differences in their position in the different types, and to their mode of origin. These observations led directly to the intensive studies of the embryological fate of the germ plasm in other animals. In the development of sexually reproducing animals from the single cell represented by the fertilized egg, the sex cells, or germ plasm, are set apart at an early stage, while the cells that develop into the body (the somatoplasm) grow into the adult animal, enclosing and protecting the germ plasm. The spermatozoan and egg that unite to form a fertilized egg, which will begin the next generation, thus have a continuity with the former one, and are essentially unexposed to the effects of the environment. Samuel Butler's phrase is that "a hen is only an egg's way of producing another egg." The continuity of the germ plasm in question is demonstrated in the development of many animals, notably in the roundworm *Ascaris,* in which the capacity for reproduction is limited to one of the two cells formed by the first division of the fertilized egg, to only one of the four in the next division, to only one of the next division into eight, and so on until the germ cell itself is contained in the completed body of the adult and on further division produces further germ cells like itself.

Building upon the fact that one-celled animals sometimes reproduce by mere division, so that neither of the resulting pair can be regarded as parent or offspring, he developed the concept of potential immortality of these forms. Death becomes a natural phenomenon when more complex multicellular bodies are developed, in which the germ plasm preserves its continuity, while the cells of the body die. In one-celled animals there is continuity of the individual. In the more complex organism this kind of continuity becomes the continuity of the germ plasm.

With attention thus centered on the germ plasm, the problem of the mechanism of heredity, whereby each species of animal and plant reproduces its own kind, was brought sharply into focus; but the theoretical discussions of Weismann and his followers remained sterile until a whole new science of heredity was established by the rediscovery of the facts of the Mendelian process (See HEREDITY; GENETICS). The problem of the continuity of the germ plasm is less clear than Weismann believed, for the segregation of the germ plasm in plants (as undifferentiated tissue) is quite unlike that in animals, though the mechanisms of variation and heredity are essentially similar in the two kingdoms.

The idea of the continuity of the germ plasm comes into sharp conflict with ideas of the hereditary transmission of the effects of use and disuse, or of other environmental influences on the adult body. This brought Weismann into opposition to all Lamarckian ideas (see LAMARCKISM), and thus to their revival during the period when biologists began to doubt the possibility of transformation by the natural selection of chance variations. He went to the extreme of regarding natural selection as the sole effective cause of evolution, and defended his position with vigor, pointing to the adaptive characteristics of the sterile worker and soldier castes of ants as the most positive proof that adaptation cannot result from the transmission of acquired characters.

One of Weismann's most effective contributions to the study of heredity was the conclusion that a reduction division must take place in the germ cells before fertilization, to prevent doubling of the number of chromosomes during each successive generation.

Weismann also propounded the theory of germinal selection, which he built upon the idea of Wilhelm Roux, of the struggle of the parts within the body. Weismann envisaged a struggle for nutriment between the elementary bearers of heredity (which he termed "ids") within the germ cells. This he thought might at last solve the problem of change in hereditary characters in the course of evolution; he thought that it also afforded a clue to directed variation, and hence to directed evolution.

In summary, the name of August Weismann has become associated in biology with the doctrines of immortality of one-celled organisms, continuity of the germ plasm, the noninheritance of acquired characters, germinal selection, and the omnipotence of natural selection.

A complete list of Weismann's publications is available in Ernst Gaupp, *August Weismann, Sein Leben und sein Werk* (1917). His most important works were translated into English. They include: *Studies in the Theory of Descent* (2 vols., 1882); *The Germ-plasm, a Theory of Heredity* (1893); and *The Evolution Theory* (2 vols., 1904).

KARL P. SCHMIDT.

WEISSENFELS, vī'sən-fĕls, city, Germany, situated at an altitude of 300 feet on the Saale River, 20 miles south of Halle and an equal distance west-southwest of Leipzig. An industrial community, it specializes in the production of machinery and shoes, and there are sugar refineries and metalworking plants. Lignite is mined in the surrounding area. The city is a rail junction. Dominating Weissenfels atop the neighboring Schlossberg are the remains of a castle destroyed in 1644 (in the Thirty Years' War) and rebuilt in 1660–1693 as the residence of the dukes of Saxe-Weimar. The oldest structure in the city is the Marienkirche (1157, expanded 1465); notable also is the city hall (erected 1718–1722). Chartered in 1185 after growing around an early Slav settlement, Weissenfels was ceded to Prussia in 1815. After World War II it became part of the German Democratic Republic (East Germany), in Halle District. Pop. (1956 est.) 46,900.

WEISSHORN, vīs'hôrn, mountain peak, Switzerland, in the Pennine Alps, rising to 14,792 feet. Located six miles north of Zermatt, the mountain was first ascended in 1861.

WEIZMANN, vīts'män, **Chaim,** Israeli statesman and scientist: b. Motol, near Pinsk, Russia, Nov. 27, 1874; d. Rehovot, Israel, Nov. 9, 1952. He studied at the universities of Berlin and Freiburg, and in 1901 was appointed lecturer in chemistry at the University of Geneva. In 1904 he went to England, subsequently becoming reader in biochemistry at the University of Manchester, and in 1910 became a naturalized British subject. Soon after his appointment in 1916 as director of the laboratories of the British Admiralty, he discovered a process of synthesizing acetone, employed in the manufacture of high explosives; he remained in his post with the Admiralty until 1919.

An ardent Zionist for many years, Weizmann in 1917 was largely instrumental in obtaining the British government's undertaking (the Balfour Declaration) to establish a national home for Jews in Palestine. He served as president of the World Zionist Organization from 1920 to 1929, and of the Jewish Agency for Palestine during the next two years; in 1931 he was elected president of the Zionist Federation of Great Britain and Ireland. From 1935 to 1946 he was again president of the Jewish Agency, in this capacity taking a prominent part in the events that led to the establishment of the state of Israel. Weizmann was president of the board of governors of the Hebrew University in Jerusalem from 1932 until his death, and was also director of the Daniel Sieff Research Institute, in Rehovot, where he spent much of his time. His scientific work there was largely in the field of agronomics, notably research and experimentation on the castor bean; he also played an important part in the development of synthetic rubber. On May 16, 1948, after proclamation of the new state of Israel, the Council of the Provisional Government elected him its president, a post tantamount to provisional president of the state. He was elected president of Israel in 1949 and re-elected in 1951, serving until his death.

WEIZSÄCKER, vīts'zĕk-ər, **BARON Carl Friedrich von,** German nuclear physicist, cosmogonist, and philosopher of science: b. Kiel, Germany, June 28, 1912. Educated at the University of Leipzig, he taught and did research in institutes of the Kaiser Wilhelm Gesellschaft (Berlin-Dahlem) during the 1930's and early 1940's. It was while he was professor of theoretical physics at the University of Strasbourg (1942–1945) that he propounded his well-known cosmogonic theory. Starting from the Kant-Laplace hypothesis, but avoiding its gaps and contradictions by utilizing new knowledge of the chemical constitution of matter in the universe, he developed an unusually consistent explanation of the origin of the planets by dust aggregation (rather than collision between the earth's sun and another star), the first such explanation to account adequately for the law of planetary distances. The theory revolutionized cosmogonic thinking, which previously, with misgivings, had generally relied on the collision hypothesis. The nuclear process described by Weizsäcker is a carbon cycle in which the carbon nucleus captures four protons in turn, converts two into neutrons, and emits them as alpha particles.

From 1945 to 1957, Weizsäcker taught at the Max Planck Institute for Physics in Göttingen. Long concerned with the relation of modern science to the whole of human life, he has since 1957 been professor of philosophy at Hamburg University. He won the Goethe Prize in 1958.

English translations of his published works include *The History of Nature* (1949), *The World View of Physics* (1952), and *Ethical and Political Problems of the Atomic Age* (1958).

See also SOLAR SYSTEM—*Origin of the Solar System.*

WELCH, wĕlch, **Joseph Nye,** American lawyer: b. Primghar, Iowa, Oct. 22, 1890; d. Hyannis, Mass., Oct. 6, 1960. A 1914 graduate and Phi Beta Kappa from Grinnell College, he received an LL.B. from the law school of Harvard University in 1917. He was in Officers' Training School when World War I ended. Admitted to practice law in Massachusetts in 1919, he joined the firm of Hale and Dorr of Boston, becoming a partner in 1923. He specialized in trial practice before federal and state courts and won wide respect in the legal profession.

In 1954, Welch was appointed counsel for the United States Army in the Army-Senator Joseph R. McCarthy hearings before the permanent subcommittee on investigations of the Senate Committee on Government Operations. During the course of these proceedings, which were televised nationally, he became well known to the American public. His performance at the hearings brought new assignments as television narrator and as actor in the role of a judge in the movie *Anatomy of a Murder* (1959). He was the author of *The Constitution,* published in 1956.

ALAN MATHESON.

WELCH, William Henry, American pathologist and bacteriologist: b. Norwalk, Conn., April 8, 1850; d. Baltimore, Md., April 30, 1934. He received his bachelor's degree at Yale in 1870 and was graduated from the College of Physicians and Surgeons (now part of Columbia University) in 1875. There followed three years of study in Europe, at the universities of Strasbourg, Leipzig, Breslau, and Berlin. At Breslau he became associated with several students who also were to win renown in medicine (including Paul Ehrlich and Carl Weigert), and while there he witnessed a demonstration by Robert Koch. Inspired by the new ideas in pathology, bacteriology, and other branches of medicine which were then unfolding in Europe, Welch returned to the United States in 1878 and established that year at Bellevue Hospital Medical College, New York City, the country's first pathology laboratory.

In 1884, Welch began an association with Johns Hopkins University which continued throughout the remainder of his active career, and which reflected great credit on both man and institution. After accepting the Baxley chair of pathology, he went again to Berlin to study under Koch, and from that time concentrated mainly on the new bacteriology. With Simon Flexner, he demonstrated (1891) the pathology of diphtheria, and in 1892, with George H. F. Nuttall, he discovered the cause of the gas gangrene which affected wounded troops in World War I (*Bacillus aerogenes capsulatus,* known as Welch's bacillus). He also contributed to the knowledge of embolism and thrombosis.

Welch's greatest contribution to medicine, however, lay in the field of medical education. Through his establishment of sound, modern training methods, his part in the founding of the Johns Hopkins Medical School in 1893, and the wise counsel which he lent to various educational institutions and foundations he profoundly influenced the course of American medicine. His advice helped to shape the Rockefeller Institute of Medical Research, whose board of scientific directors he headed from 1900 until his death. He showed exceptional judgment in the selection of colleagues for responsible positions, as well as a talent for administration. In addition to serving as first dean of the medical faculty, he became director of the newly established School of Hygiene and Public Health (1918), and finally occupied the chair of history of medicine (1926), remaining until his retirement in 1931. He was also pathologist to Johns Hopkins Hospital for 27 years, to 1916.

Despite the demands of his manifold interests, Welch delivered hundreds of public lectures on various phases of medicine. A large number of these were collected as *Papers and Addresses by William Henry Welch* (3 vols., 1920); his other publications include *General Pathology of Fever* (1888) and *Bacteriology of Surgical Infections* (1895). Welch's portrait appears in John Singer Sargent's famous painting of the *Four Doctors* of Johns Hopkins (the other subjects being Sir William Osler, Howard A. Kelly, and William S. Halstead).

WELCH, city, West Virginia, 24 miles northwest of Bluefield, at an altitude of 1,300 feet. It is the commercial center for a large semibituminous coalmining region (the "Billion Dollar Pocahontas Coal Fields"), upon which its economy entirely depends. The city, which serves a population of 80,000, has two radio stations, three large hospitals, and a municipal airport. Situated nearby are Premier Cut, reputed to be the deepest highway defile in the world; a state forest and state park; and a "show mine" at Pocahontas, Va. Welch was settled in 1885 and incorporated in 1894. The government is administered by city manager and council. Population: 3,885.

WELD, wĕld, **Theodore Dwight,** American abolitionist: b. Hampton, Conn., Nov. 23, 1803; d. Hyde Park, Mass., Feb. 3, 1895. Reared in Utica, N.Y., he became an evangelist after meeting the revivalist preacher Charles G. Finney in 1825, and, with Charles Stuart, a British advocate of the emanicipation of slaves in the West Indies, joined Finney's "holy band" of evangelists. For two years, Weld preached throughout western New York, laboring for the cause of temperance. In 1830, he espoused antislavery, and was one of the founders of the American Anti-Slavery Society in 1833. As the movement gained momentum, its members traveled throughout Indiana, Ohio, western Pennsylvania, and New York, preaching and lecturing against slavery.

In 1836, Weld trained a band of 70 abolitionists, including his future wife, Angelina Emily Grimké (1805–1879), a writer of antislavery tracts. The group took up the cause of abolition with renewed vigor, preaching and distributing pamphlets, most of them written by Weld, either anonymously or under other authors' names. Antislavery petitions were presented to Congress, and the abolitionist movement was consolidated. Weld went to Washington, where he became a lobbyist in Congress for the antislavery cause, and when several congressmen decided to break with the Whig Party on this issue, he guided their efforts. He also was an adviser to John

Quincy Adams when Adams tried to introduce constitutional amendments against slavery. He retired from activity when a strong antislavery bloc had been formed in the Whig Party in 1843.

Weld's was one of the major voices in the pre-Civil War abolitionist movement. One of his works, *American Slavery As It Is*, published anonymously in 1839, was the basis of Harriet Beecher Stowe's *Uncle Tom's Cabin*.

WELDING, wĕld'ĭng, a modern method of joining materials by the use of one of a number of processes in which heat is supplied either electrically or by means of a torch. The large bulk of materials that are welded are metals, although the term "welding" is sometimes applied to the joining of other materials such as thermoplastics. In order to join two or more pieces of metal together by one of the welding processes, the most essential requirement is heat. Pressure may also be employed, but this is not, in many processes, essential.

The application of welding in today's technology is extensive. The use of welding in joining metals has had a phenomenal rise since about 1930; this growth has been faster than the general industrial growth. Many common everyday items are dependent upon welding for their economical construction. Our modern automobiles are of welded construction; many thousand welds are used in the fabrication of each automobile. Many items in the nuclear and missile field could not be fabricated except by the use of welding for assembly. Electronic equipment in wide use today requires special welding techniques for assembly. Household appliances, kitchen utensils, bridges, ships, aircraft, buildings, farm machinery—all are made more economically in today's technology by using one or more methods for joining by welding.

Modern devices and appliances are complicated, and engineering knowledge is essential in the application of today's tools for welding. Welding is no longer an art in which a craftsman is in complete control. Engineers with training in the fields of electricity, mechanics, materials, and structures ensure the usefulness of welding as a modern means of joining metals into structures with strength and stability. Welding depends upon the application of principles taken from many branches of science. For example, the physicists measure the thermal behavior and electrical characteristics which control the preparation of welded joints. The chemist is helpful in compounding fluxes and special alloys for many applications. The metallurgist provides much of the fundamental information which is required in modern welding. By application of engineering principles, the techniques which are necessary in order to produce sound, serviceable welded joints can be developed. The contributions of many branches of physical science have been important. Although the ease of joining by welding varies among the modern metals, techniques have been developed for producing satisfactory joints in almost all metals and alloys.

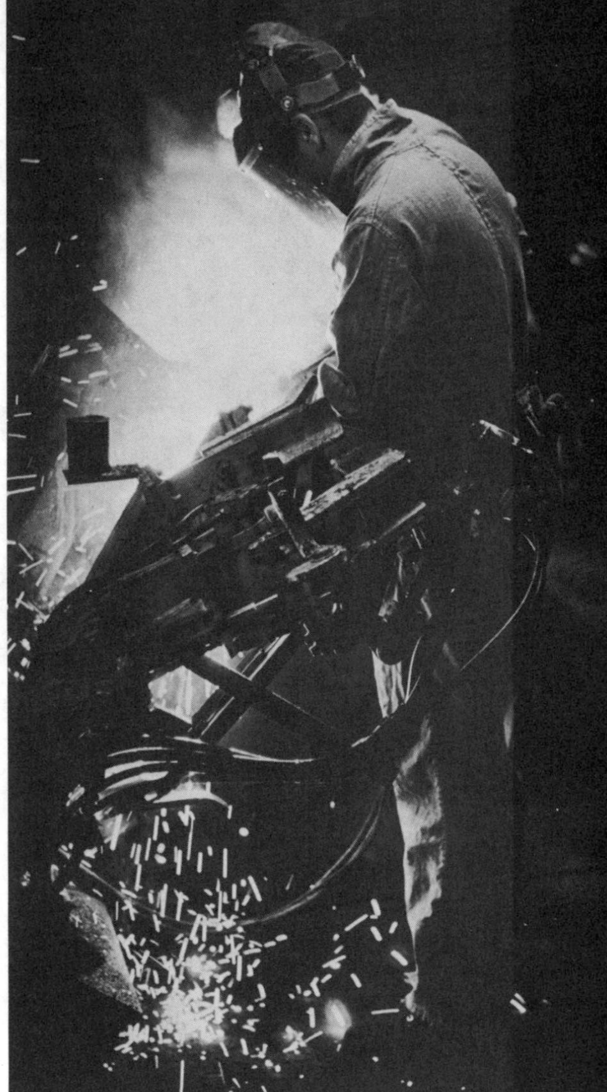
MICHAEL HAYMAN/STOCK, BOSTON

The automobile industry makes extensive use of welding techniques. Here an assembly worker joins body parts.

HISTORY

Arc Welding. Sir Humphry Davy, an Englishman, first described an electric arc in 1809. His experimental work was described soon after the

Historical development of arc welding.

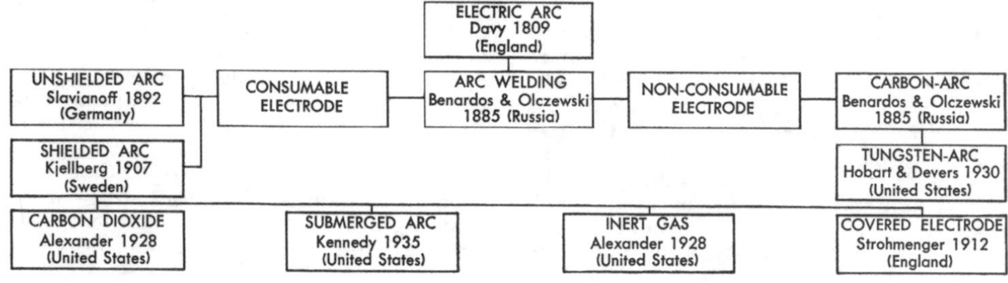

ARNOLD ZANN/BLACK STAR

Completely automated industrial robots weld the joints on an auto body at a Chrysler plant.

voltaic cell was developed for producing electric current; he used a series of 1,000 cells to produce an arc between platinum electrodes. It was in 1885, almost 80 years after this experiment, that Nikolas von Benardos and Stanislav Olczewski, a Russian, patented the first process for arc welding. A single carbon electrode was used in this early development, and fusion was obtained by the heat from an arc drawn between the metal to be joined and the carbon electrode. Metal was added from an auxiliary filler rod fed into the arc or molten puddle. This method of welding is still in use with some modifications.

A little later, in 1889, Dr. H. Zerener, a German, introduced the process which consists of drawing an arc between two carbon electrodes and deflecting the arc outward by means of an electromagnet placed between the electrodes. This method did not find much commercial use. In 1892, Nicholas Slavianoff suggested what may now be recognized as one of the leading methods of welding. He proposed the use of a metallic electrode in wire form in place of the carbon electrode used by Benardos. The bare wire is melted by the arc and is deposited in the joint. This process was the prevailing electric arc welding method until almost 1930 in the United States.

The mechanical properties of the weld metal deposited in air using bare wire are low in ductility since the nitrogen in the arc atmosphere reacts with iron, forming brittle iron nitride. Oscar Kjellberg, a Swedish engineer, applied for a patent in 1907 on the use of a coating on the bare wire. In these early electrodes, which were further developed in the years following 1910, the coating was thin and acted more as an arc stabilizer than as a purifier of the weld metal. The welds produced with this type of electrode showed little improvement in properties over those which were obtained with bare wire electrodes. The common test was to drop the piece on the floor to see whether it would hold together, and welding at this time generally was recommended only as a repair maintenance tool.

The first heavy coated electrode for electric arc welding was developed in England. Arthur P. Strohmenger in 1912 obtained a United States patent for an electrode coated with blue asbestos with a binder of sodium silicate or water glass. From this time on, numerous covered electrodes were developed. Their merit and usefulness depended upon arc protection from the surrounding air; this was obtained by vaporized mineral coatings which melted simultaneously with the core rod and produced a fusible slag covering of the deposit.

Late in the 1920's, cellulose was introduced as a component in the coating; the gaseous products formed by decomposition of the cellulose protected the molten weld metal from the surrounding air. The use of the covered electrode for arc welding has been one of the most important factors in the phenomenal growth of welding. Other methods have been developed more recently. Henry M. Hobart and Philip K. Devers were issued patents in 1930 in which the molten metal in the arc stream was protected by a mantle of inert gas, such as argon or helium. In the early applications of the inert gas arc welding, a nonconsumable tungsten electrode was used for striking the arc. Into this zone was introduced additional filler metal in wire form as necessary to complete the joint. This method is widely used for welding aluminum, stainless steel, magnesium, and many more modern metals which are increasing in use as engineering materials.

As argon and helium became more available, experimental work resulted in a process in which a consumable electrode in wire form carried the electrical current into the arc zone with a stream of inert gas protecting the molten metal. Other gases have been used in blanketing the arc zone, such as carbon dioxide and mixtures of argon and oxygen, and in some cases even nitrogen and hydrogen have been used for protection. In 1935, Harry E. Kennedy, Lloyd T. Jones, and Maynard A. Rodermund applied for a United States patent on a process involving electric arc welding underneath a blanket of granulated welding flux. The welding zone was completely blanketed or submerged under a complex silicate flux. Recently, various modifications of the arc-welding process have been introduced in which consumable electrodes from coils have been used with either magnetic fluxes or fluxes encased in a tubular electrode. The possibilities of applying arc welding to unusual engineering structures has increased many times because of the new developments.

Other Types. The discussion, so far, has had to do with arc welding; there are two other types of welding which have found extensive use in our modern technology. The first of these is called *resistance welding* and is an electrical method in which a high current is passed through the parts being joined; the electrical resistance at the point of contact of these two pieces is such that sufficient heat is generated to melt the metal and form a weld joint. Elihu Thomson, a professor at Franklin Institute in Philadelphia, was the first to demonstrate the possibility of joining metals by resistance welding. His experiments, which were completed in 1886, led to the very extensive, complex welding methods which are useful in the assembly of many of our modern structures. Today, multiple electrode units are employed in high production units for completing hundreds of welds in fast-moving production lines. Electrical controls maintain the uniformity and quality of these welds.

A third process which has had a very extensive use and is still important in welding technology is *oxyacetylene welding*. The oxyacetylene process was an outgrowth of the discovery of Henry Louis Le Chatelier, a French chemist, who in 1895 showed that the combustion of acetylene with oxygen produced a flame having a temperature far higher than that of any gas flame previously known. The commercial success of the oxyacetylene process depended upon the availability of both oxygen and acetylene in sufficient quantities to make the process practical. In 1895, the production of liquid air was initiated, and the evaporation of liquid air provided a means for manufacture of commercial oxygen. In 1892, as a result of an experiment aimed at the production of calcium metal by the reduction of calcium oxide or lime in an electric furnace, the product calcium carbide was formed. Calcium carbide reacts with water to form acetylene gas. With the availability of oxygen and acetylene, many investigators attempted to devise suitable torches which would permit the control of the oxyacetylene flame necessary for its application in welding. In the early 1900's, torches of a practical type were introduced, and by 1903 the process began to be used industrially. This process was used extensively in early applications of welding with improved facilities for handling oxygen gas compressed into steel cylinders and, finally, the production of tanks for storage of acetylene. The oxyacetylene process was used widely for repair and maintenance. As the field of welding expanded in the 1920's and early 1930's, the use of oxyacetylene continued to grow, although at the present time welding practice is roughly divided into about 65 percent arc welding with the balance divided between resistance welding and oxyacetylene welding.

AMERICAN WELDING SOCIETY

In a special application, a plasma arc is used to cut a thick aluminum block at high speed.

WELDING PROCESSES

Arc Welding. In the arc-welding processes, an arc is struck between the electrode and the work. Although there are some arc-welding processes in which a carbon or a bare wire is used as an electrode, these are not extensively used in practice. In order to improve the ductility of the molten metal in the arc, techniques must be devised which will eliminate the air from the weld zone so that the molten iron cannot react with the nitrogen and oxygen in the air. If iron nitride, for example, is formed, the metal in the weld may be brittle and have low ductility. The use of a flux covering on a wire which either produces a gas or a molten slag over the weld deposit has been extensive. With the availability of argon and helium, a tungsten electrode with a filler wire has been extensively employed in a process commonly referred to as the Heliarc process. In this the electrode is a round rod of tungsten and the molten metal is protected by an inert gas such as argon or helium. Additional processes in arc welding include the consumable electrode in which a wire is fed into the weld zone at a rate equal to its melting rate and the molten metal is protected by an inert gas such as argon. The submerged-arc process, in which a bare wire is fed into the weld zone and melted

TYRONE HALL/STOCK, BOSTON

Lightweight arc-welding equipment has many applications at a construction site.

off under a bed of granulated flux, has found extensive use in production applications. Recently, heavy weldments have been made using the electroslag process, in which a molten bath of slag is maintained over the molten weld metal; the joint is made in the vertical position with water-cooled copper shoes quenching the metal in the joint.

Many special tools are available for welding, some of them controlled by an operator who guides the process as it proceeds and feeds wire into the zone as needed. Mechanical means have also been introduced, making the process semiautomatic by controlling the rate of feeding of a wire. Processes have been developed in which a tractor carrying the welding torch proceeds along the joint so as to provide an almost entirely automatic process. Various electronic timing devices are available which control the feed of the wire; for some applications, positioning and sequence have been set up on punched tape. The weld may vary from a continuous joint to spot welds, depending upon the needs of the item being manufactured. Recently a process has been introduced in which the spreading arc is constricted through a narrow orifice, and a process commonly called the plasma arc has characteristics which make it useful for special applications. A process using an electron beam for heating the parts locally in a vacuum chamber has been introduced for joining reactive metals such as zirconium alloys.

Oxyacetylene Welding. In the oxyacetylene welding processes, applications are often of a maintenance type. Many sheet metal applications are also readily handled by oxyacetylene processes. Rather extensive use of the oxygen and acetylene gases is made in the cutting of steel. By preheating a piece of steel and directing a constricted stream of oxygen on the surface, it is possible to cut through heavy thicknesses of steel. If this operation is directed and travels uniformly, the oxygen cutting of steel can provide a shape or straight cut useful for further employment in welded parts.

Resistance Welding. The simplest resistance weld is a single spot weld. The factors important in the control of the resistance-welding process are the amplitude of the current, the time duration of the flow of the current, and the pressure between the parts being welded. By timing the spots and overlapping them, it is possible to make a seam weld. In the automotive field, multiple-spot units have been designed which will make a large number of welds between sheet metal at a fast rate. Flash welding, in which parts are heated by a heavy arc drawn across a gap between them and then pressed while they cool, has been useful in the joining of pipe and bar stock. Resistance welding is applicable to a range of shapes and materials.

Other Processes. Many other processes have been used to a limited extent. The thermit process produces molten metal by reacting aluminum with iron oxide. The molten iron and slag are allowed to flow into the joint and retained there by means of refractories. This process has found use in the repair of heavy machinery and to a certain extent in the joining of rails. Another process which has been introduced during the past few years is that of employing high frequency induced electrical currents to heat the parts to a sufficiently high temperature to enable the joint to be made. Electrical, mechanical, and chemical sources of heat have been employed in order to raise the temperature of the metals so that the parts can be joined with pressure. Ultrasonic energy has been used to join parts at room temperature under pressure. Thin sheets of aluminum can be cold welded by high pressure at room temperature. In recent investigations, friction has been used to generate the temperature necessary to join the parts.

WELDING ENGINEERING

In modern technology welding requires, for its broadest application, a knowledge of many of the associated fields of engineering. After a structure has been designed and a material selected for fabricating a particular unit, it is then possible to select or specify the type of welding process that will be used in the fabrication. A surprising number of methods may be recommended for low carbon mild steel and even medium carbon steel materials. As structures become more complicated and the base metal more highly alloyed, the latitude for process selection becomes more limited.

There are many factors involved in the proper application of welding. These become increasingly important as the specification tolerances become more stringent. Those interested in quality control must recognize many of the elements involved in production fabrication. Before a structure can be designed and built, whether it is welded or not, it is necessary to know the service requirements of the product. An engineering review of the structure must be provided in order to determine the magnitude and distribution of the loads or stresses to be carried. It is important to know whether oil- or watertightness is involved, and corrosion environment to be encountered must be reviewed. Appearance must also be considered in order to determine the successful performance of an engineering structure. After a unit has been properly designed and the initial units built and tested, the control of production of future items must be left to those charged with inspection of the product. First, it is common to use visual inspection. If this is satisfactory, there are many nondestructive tests which can be applied to welded products which require further control. For example, soundness is examined by the use of X-rays or other radiation. A vessel may be tested using water or pressure applied by hydraulic means. Actual dimension tolerance can be measured. These all lead to improved workmanship and the production of a more uniform quality of product.

APPLICATIONS

The applications of welding may be divided generally into three groups: The first is a low-volume type of production in which units are custom built to exacting specifications. In this type, welding is widely applied to manufacture parts for nuclear, missile, and high pressure containers for various chemical processes. The second group of applications which have less stringent requirements is found in the broad field of activity represented by railroad equipment, buildings, bridges, household appliances, garden tools, and farm machinery. The third group of applications occur where a high rate of production is required, as in automobile manufacture. In this type, almost unlimited tests are carried out on the pilot model. Service tests are limited on the initial plant production, and quality of the final product is based on the attempt to manufacture uniform production parts which can be assembled into units for distribution.

CAREW/MONKMEYER PHOTO

A welder uses a stick electrode to join and seal pipe lengths with different diameters.

In a growing economy, welding has taken its place and will continue to assist in the production of articles at a lower cost than by other means or of those items which can be fabricated only by welding. New methods of welding will find their use in our engineering technology. Welding will continue to provide an economical and sound method of joining materials.

CLARENCE E. JACKSON
Union Carbide Corporation

WELFARE, Public. See WELFARE ORGANIZATIONS.

WELFARE ECONOMICS, wel′fâr ē-kə-nŏm′ĭks. Welfare economics is an approach to economic problems that is specifically oriented to the evaluation of the impact of various economic activities and measures on the well-being of individuals. It is a frankly normative and prescriptive approach, in that it attempts to evaluate results and prescribe changes, as distinguished from positive or descriptive economics which merely correlates causes and effects without appealing to any explicit value judgments. The usual scope of welfare economics is further limited in that while business cycles and unemployment obviously have major effects on the welfare of the individual, the waste of idle resources is so patent a failure that the more refined tools of welfare economics are largely unnecessary in dealing with these problems. In practice, welfare economics concerns chiefly the possibilities for improving the way that given aggregates of resources may be allocated to different uses to satisfy better individual wants.

The basic starting point of much of welfare economics is the theorem that the result of a system of perfect competition under ideal conditions is a "Pareto optimum." A Pareto optimum is a state of affairs which cannot be altered to the advantage of one participant without at least some disadvantage to some other person. In general, for any state which is not a Pareto optimum, there will exist another feasible state which would be preferred to the original one by all concerned. A non-Paretian state is thus capable of being changed in a way that will be an improvement by almost any reasonable criterion, whereas if a Paretian state is changed in a way considered to be an improvement, this judgment must necessarily involve the weighing of the gains of those benefited against the losses of those injured. Interpersonal comparisons of this sort are often quite subjective, and they are accordingly avoided as far as it is possible to do so.

The conditions under which this "optimality of competition" theorem holds are very strict: there must be no "neighborhood effects" of one entity upon another outside the operations of the market, such as smoke and noise nuisances, or enjoyment of a neighbor's garden; further, each individual or firm must act as though prices will not be affected by what they do. This latter condition is met by most farmers and consumers, but the condition is met by relatively few if any manufacturers.

Indeed, this last condition is incompatible with the profitable operation of a process involving economies of scale, and one of the major preoccupations of welfare economics has been the problem of how to handle such situations so as to restore the Pareto-optimum conditions. The English economist Alfred Marshall (1842–1924) pointed out very early that where significant economies of scale exist, as in most public utility operations, and also in such undertakings as book publishing, the public welfare can be improved by subsidizing these "decreasing cost" industries at the expense, if need be, of taxes on land, agriculture, and other constant cost or increasing cost industries. The American Abba Lerner later showed how, if all decreasing cost operations are placed in the hands of managers instructed to set their prices at levels covering only "marginal cost"—that is, the additional costs arising because of the production of the last units of output—and if the resulting deficits or intramarginal residues, reflecting the higher costs of producing the initial units of output, can be met from sources which do not themselves disturb the equilibrium, such as taxes on the site value of land, then a Pareto-optimal result can be reached without resort to any extreme centralization.

Unfortunately, the prevalence of economies of scale in modern technology makes it unlikely that these deficits could all be met out of such repercussion-free taxes. Even income taxes introduce distortions of their own, for example in enhancing the attractiveness of do-it-yourself activities yielding a nontaxable return in direct satisfaction, relative to paid work and paid service. This difficulty has given rise to the "general theory of second-best," according to which, since it is impossible to maintain all prices at marginal cost, as would be required for a Pareto optimum to obtain, it is in general better for all prices to deviate somewhat, rather than keep most prices equal to marginal cost and have some prices deviate more drastically from this norm. The complex interrelationships between commodities, such as the complementarity between trucks and gasoline, or the substitutability between coal and oil, make it very difficult to say just what the relative deviations should be: they cannot simply be made proportional to marginal cost.

But welfare economics has more to say about the price structure than merely that decreasing cost industries should be subsidized: even if subsidy is ruled out, welfare can be significantly increased by adopting a proper pattern of prices for the numerous varieties of product and service produced within each industry. Thus welfare economics indicates that much sharper differentials between low off-peak and high peak rates for such services as electricity, telephone calls, and transportation than are ordinarily found can greatly increase the benefits derived from such services, even when no change in the level of profits is involved. In some cases the indicated pricing pattern is quite different from that which might be thought of as "equitable" at first glance, as when it is shown that the rush-hour subway rider should be charged substantially more than the nonrush-hour rider, in spite of the fact that the latter has a more comfortable ride and may be riding for a less praiseworthy purpose.

While welfare economics can show that it would in principle be possible, given omniscience, to accompany such price reforms with income redistributions such that everyone is benefited by the combined change, thus making the combined change unequivocally desirable, in practice it may not be possible to carry out the income redistribution with quite this precision. This has led to considerable discussion of the problem of evaluating reforms which benefit some but hurt others, and to the enunciation of what is termed the "compensation principle," according to which a reform is desirable if it is such that those who gain from the reform could, in principle, fully compensate the losers by appropriate payments and still have some gain left over. The compensation principle thus approves a reform even though the compensation cannot actually be carried out, for example, because even though the aggregate amount to be paid can easily be estimated statistically, identification of the individuals who are to make the payments and those who are to receive them might be prohibitively expensive.

The use of the compensation principle and its corollaries has been attacked, partly for making tacit assumptions concerning the relative value of money to the gainers and to the losers, and partly by showing that in extreme cases its use might show that state *A* is preferable to state *B*, and symmetrically that state *B* is preferable to state *A*, through the application of the criterion from a different base point. Such a paradoxical result is likely to be rare, however, and where it does occur it would be possible to consider the compensation criterion inapplicable.

Actually the adoption of the compensation principle as a broad principle to be applied in a wide array of particular cases rests on a stronger foundation than its application in any one case: while particular individuals might lose in one application of the principle, they have a chance to gain in others, and as long as in each case the gains outweigh the losses, measured in money terms, the chances are good that in the application of the principle over any wide range of cases the net losers for the set of reforms as a whole will be small in number and impossible to pick out in advance. Thus looking at the prospect of the whole series of changes in advance, every individual is likely to have an expectation of gaining, on the average, even though in the event some may lose, so that rational individuals might be expected to vote unanimously in favor of the adoption of the principle. Where this is not the case it can often be made the case through suitable accompanying changes in income tax rate schedules, or the like.

While most of the significant results of welfare economics concern the allocation of resources to different purposes and processes, independently of income distribution considerations, welfare economics does also deal with problems associated with the distribution of income among persons. In this area, however, specific results have been scanty. Various methods have been put forward for the measurement of the relative amounts of "utility" or satisfaction derived by individuals from different levels of expenditure, and for using such a "utility function" in evaluating alternative distributions of income among individuals. These range from deducing a utility function by observing how individuals choose among prospects involving known risks, as in gambling situations, to simply asking representative individuals to compare the amounts of satisfaction they imagine they would obtain from different levels of expenditure. The results have not been encouraging, however, and the question of how income should be distributed among individuals remains one left largely to individual predilections.

Another major area of welfare economics is the analysis of neighborhood effects, also termed "external economies" and "diseconomies." Here the objective is to devise suitable taxes, penalties, bounties, subsidies, or regulations which will have the effect of inducing each individual or firm to adjust his behavior so as to take due account of these direct nonmarket effects which his actions have on others. While in many particular instances these matters are adequately taken care of by regulation under the police powers of the state, it is the special concern of welfare economics to devise economic measures which will avoid as far as possible the need for arbitrary and rigid regulation.

While the achievements of welfare economics have not been as spectacular as those of macroeconomics (national income analysis, in particular Keynesian analysis), the theory is still well ahead of practice, partly because so many of the applications of welfare economics involve disturbing deeply held prejudices as to the proper function of prices and the proper relationships between them. Indeed, many of the prescriptions of welfare economics are difficult to carry out under private ownership, and thus become entangled in the issue of private versus public ownership. Currently, new areas for the application of welfare economics are opening up as the development of electronic devices and data-processing methods render feasible the use of prices to stimulate an efficient use of facilities to a degree hitherto unattainable. It remains to be seen what use will be made of these potentialities.

William Vickrey,
Professor of Economics, Columbia University.

Bibliography

Ashford, Douglas, *Financing Urban Government in the Welfare State* (St. Martin's Press 1980).
Bailey, Elizabeth E., ed., *Selected Economic Writings of William J. Baumol* (N.Y. Univ. Press 1976).
Hicks, John, *Collected Essays on Economic Theory: Wealth and Welfare,* vol. 1 (Harvard Univ. Press 1981).
Higgins, Joan, *States of Welfare: A Comparative Analysis of Social Policy* (St. Martin's Press 1981).
Little, Ian M. D., *A Critique of Welfare Economics* (Oxford 1950).
Mishra, Ramesh, *The Welfare State in Crisis* (St. Martin's Press 1984).
Ng, Yew-Kwang, *Welfare Economics: Introduction and Development of Basic Concepts* (Halsted Press 1980).
Pigou, Arthur C., *Economics of Welfare* (1920; reprint, Macmillan 1960).
Sanger, Mary B., *Welfare of the Poor* (Academic Press 1977).
Vickrey, William, "Utility, Strategy and Social Decision Rules" in *Quarterly Journal of Economics,* vol. 74, pp. 507–535 (Harvard Univ. Press 1960).
Walker, Bruce, *Welfare Economics and Urban Problems* (St. Martin's Press 1981).

WELFARE ISLAND, island, part of New York City's Borough of Manhattan, in the East River between Manhattan and the Borough of Queens. It extends about one and one half miles, from a point opposite 51st Street to a point opposite 86th Street, Manhattan; its area is 139 acres. The island, acquired by the Dutch from the Indians, was granted to Capt. John Manning in 1668; after his death it passed to his stepdaughter, Mrs. Robert Blackwell, and was called Blackwell's Island. The city purchased it from the Blackwell family in 1828, and in 1921 gave it the name Welfare Island. It has been the site of a city workhouse and penitentiary and of city hospitals. In August 1973 its name was changed to Franklin D. Roosevelt Island.

WELFARE ORGANIZATIONS. Welfare organizations exist in large numbers and great variety throughout the United States. Many of them have long histories of humanitarian service while others, including some of the largest, are of more recent origin. Together they constitute a vast network of instrumentalities for conserving and advancing the well-being of the American people.

Governmental agencies make up a large part of this network. Under the provisions of the Social Security Act of 1935, as amended, the federal, state, and local governments share in the provision of numerous forms of social service. The organizations administering these programs are the United States Department of Health, Education, and Welfare and state and local welfare departments located in all political jurisdictions of the nation. Public assistance, child welfare services, and aid to the aged and the handicapped are among the service responsibilities of these organizations. These and other governmental units also administer programs in the fields of recreation, penology, institutional care, health, veterans' benefits, and other welfare areas. All told, governmental welfare organizations number well into the thousands, serve millions of people, and disburse billions of dollars in services and benefits.

Voluntary agencies comprise the other large sector of the welfare network. They may be classified by purpose, auspices and support, and geographical level of operation.

Purpose.—As the United States moved out of the frontier stage and became increasingly industrialized and urbanized, problems of poverty, delinquency, health, family breakdown, and others challenged the conscience of the community. As a result, voluntary associations of citizens such as family service societies and settlement houses were formed to bring relief to the needy and to cope with inadequate living and social conditions through preventive and rehabilitative activities on a broad front. Although many of their functions have been modified by the growth of the public services in recent years, there has been no decrease in the number or importance of the voluntary agencies. Their purposes and programs are varied: to provide casework and counseling services to families, children, the aged, and other individuals; to make leisure-time, informal educational, and recreational opportunities available to groups of all ages; to provide specialized health services to many groups including the handicapped; to engage in social action, as for housing reform, community improvement, and so on; and to bring about better coordination and support of services through joint planning and federated fund raising.

Auspices and Support.—Voluntary welfare organizations may be operated by and receive their support from special groups (church, ethnic, civic, labor), citizens generally (community chests), foundations, or individual members and contributors. More than 2,000 communities federate a large part of their support of agencies through chests and united funds.

Geographical Level.—While most voluntary welfare services are made available to the people through local organizations, national agencies also have an important role to play. Some of these, such as the American Red Cross, have local chapters which undergird the national program. Some, such as the Boy Scouts of America, organize and direct local activities according to a fixed pattern. Some are affiliations of autonomous local agencies having similar programs, as for example the Family Service Association of America. Others, particularly in the health field, raise funds locally in support of nationally conducted research and education. Some agencies operate solely on the national level, as, for example, the National Social Welfare Assembly. The National Association for Social Workers, the Council on Social Work Education, and the National Conference on Social Welfare are important personnel groups. There are state and regional organizations in a few fields.

See also CHILD WELFARE; COMMUNITY CENTER; HULL HOUSE; MENTAL HEALTH; SOCIAL AND UNIVERSITY SETTLEMENTS; SOCIAL SERVICE; SOCIAL WELFARE; TRAVELERS AID.

RUSSELL H. KURTZ,
Editor of "Social Work."

Bibliography

Bell, Winifred, *Contemporary Social Welfare* (Macmillan 1987).
Hasenfeld, Yeheskel, *Human Service Organizations* (Prentice-Hall 1983).
Kruzas, Anthony T., ed., *Social Service Organizations and Agencies Directory* (Gale Res. 1982).
Timms, Noel, and Timms, Rita, *Dictionary of Social Welfare* (Methuen 1982).

WELFARE STATE. The welfare state is a form of government in which the state assumes responsibility for minimum standards of living for every person. Welfare as a purpose of government is not an invention of this century. The Preamble to the Constitution of the United States speaks of "general welfare" as one of the purposes of the Constitution. Yet the term "welfare state" with its specific meaning of social and economic security of a basic minimum came into widespread use only during and after World War II. Such general publicly sponsored programs of social and economic welfare were first called "welfare state" programs in Britain; later the term became accepted in the United States and other nations. Unemployment, sickness, and old age are the three main areas broadly covered by the policies of the welfare state.

The main two reasons of the rise of the welfare state are economic and political. Economically, the welfare state recognizes the fact that most persons in the modern economy are earning their livelihood as wage or salary earners, that is, they are dependent economically upon their employer. This condition of dependence contrasts with the earlier stages of the economy of a century or two ago, when most persons were independent farmers, artisans, and small shopkeepers. Another economic fact is the growing concentration of the population in large urban centers in which the sense of responsibility for one's fellow men has greatly weakened as a result of the anonymous style of living. Finally, the high degree of mobility from job to job throws people constantly into contact with new environments in which they have few or no friends. These economic changes have led to the political recognition that the state must do now what the family and community used to do in the past. Behind this political recognition lies also the fact of the growing political consciousness of the masses and their conception of being rightfully entitled to a minimum standard of living under all circumstances.

Because the welfare state expresses long-term economic changes and their recognition by the government, it is not tied to a particular form of government, such as democratic, authoritarian, or totalitarian. Whenever a society embarks upon a large-scale program of industrialization, some form of welfare state program is put into effect. Where the sense of responsibility for one's fellow men is high, the welfare state will be more advanced than in countries in which such a sense of compassion and responsibility is less strongly developed. Democratic nations generally have a higher sense of such public responsibility for the social and economic welfare of the individual, because the whole democratic philosophy is based on respect for the individual. This difference can be illustrated by the divergent approaches to unemployment relief. Most democratic governments have established systems of unemployment relief, not because an unemployed person would be unable to find any kind of a job in any locality, but because the individual worker is respected as an individual entitled to retain his self-respect by working in his own line; nor should he be forced to leave his home and community, abandon his friends solely in order to avoid starvation. By contrast, totalitarian states (as Communist Russia, for example) do not pay unemployment relief, because they hold that a person can always find a job if he is willing to accept lower pay, work in a less skilled occupation, and leave his community.

The main attack against the welfare state has been on the ground that such policies make the mass of the people too dependent on government, thus undermining the foundations of both economic individualism—free enterprise—and of political individualism—democratic self-government. Since the welfare state in its more advanced form has been in operation for only a relatively short time, it cannot be stated as yet with any degree of certainty to what extent such fears are justified.

WILLIAM EBENSTEIN,
Author of 'Today's Isms'

WELFARE WORK. See SOCIAL WELFARE.

WELHAVEN, vĕl′hä-vən, **Johan Sebastian Cammermeyer,** Norwegian poet: b. Bergen, Norway, Dec. 22, 1807; d. Christiania (Oslo), Oct. 21, 1873. Lecturer (1841) and professor (from 1846) of philosophy and literature at the University of Oslo (then Christiania), Welhaven was one of the two great poets whose names are forever linked as the first poets of modern Norway. The other, Henrik Wergeland (q.v.), was his diametric opposite in temperament and poetic form, an inspired genius whose wildness and formlessness irritated Welhaven and stung him into a vigorous attack. Welhaven also angered his countrymen by a satirical sonnet sequence called *Norges Daemring* (1834; *Dawn of Norway*), in which he accused them of cultural immaturity and provinciality, and by a short verse called *Digtetsand* ("The Spirit of Poetry"). But in most of his poetry he evoked the idyllic charms of nature or the lyric figures of folklore, and he retold some vigorous tales of folk life. His later poems were deeply religious in their tone.

He was a passionate advocate of education, artistic development, and the retainment of culture as a means to achieve national progress. In addition, he adamantly opposed Henrik Wergeland's theory of complete nationalism.

Welhaven valued form above content, and his poems have become classics of the romantic period, following a tradition which reached Norway from Germany by way of Denmark. His unhappy love affairs with Camilla Collett (Wergeland's sister) and Ida Kjerulf are celebrated in literary history. His poems have lent themselves well to the work of later composers. He may be compared with Heinrich Heine in German poetry and Edgar Allan Poe in the American tradition.

EINAR HAUGEN,
Department of Scandinavian Studies, University of Wisconsin.

WELL-TEMPERED CLAVIER, The (*Das wohltemperiertes Clavier*), two series (1722, 1744) of 24 preludes and fugues each for keyboard instrument (harpsichord or clavichord) by Johann Sebastian Bach. Each series contains one prelude and related fugue for each of the 24 major and minor keys, whence the title (which Bach himself gave to only the first series), referring to the then new system of tuning known as equal temperament. The equal temperament system allows performance in all keys, without retuning, on a single instrument of fixed pitch. Earlier composers had produced series approaching this completeness, but Bach's was the first set to encompass all 24 keys. Aside from their historic importance, Bach's preludes and fugues, known familiarly as "The Forty-Eight," belong to the enduring canon of great music. Both were first published in London in 1799.

HERBERT WEINSTOCK.

WELLAND, wĕl′ənd, city, Ontario, Canada, seat of Welland County, 12 miles southwest of Niagara Falls and 20 miles west of Buffalo, N.Y., on the Welland River and the Welland Ship Canal. An early trading center, Welland was chosen as the site of a courthouse in 1856, and was incorporated as a village in 1858, a town in 1878, and a city in 1917. It is an industrial center with 55 factories, employing more than 3,300 workers, producing goods worth about $40 million annually. The principal products are steel and steel tubing, iron castings, brass and brass tubing, cordage, textiles, rubber goods, chemicals, and commercial fertilizers. The city is one of the extension centers served by McMaster University. Population: 45,448.

D. F. PUTNAM.

WELLAND SHIP CANAL. See CANADA—*18. Transportation and Communications* (canals).

WELLER, wĕl′ər, **Sam,** Mr. Pickwick's body servant in Charles Dickens' *Pickwick Papers.* He appears in chapter 10 as Boots at the White Hart, Southwark; enters Pickwick's service in chapter 12; and thereafter does more than any other character to hold the story together. A cheerful Cockney whose knowledge of London and humanity is "extensive and peculiar," he is a supreme humorous creation.

DELANCEY FERGUSON.

WELLER, Thomas H(uckle), American bacteriologist and virologist: b. Ann Arbor, Mich., June 15, 1915. He took his B.A. degree in 1936 and his M.S. in 1937, both at the University of Michigan—where his father, Carl V. Weller, was chairman of the department of pathology in the Medical School—and entered Harvard Medical School. As a senior student there, he worked under Dr. John Franklin Enders (q.v.) on continuous *in vitro* (test tube) virus cultivation. After receiving his M.D. degree in 1940, he was an intern and teaching fellow in pathology (1941) and medicine (1942), then served in the United States Army Medical Corps as chief of the parasitology, bacteriology, and virology sections of the Antilles Department Medical Laboratory, in Puerto Rico, from 1942 to 1946. He returned to Harvard after the war as assistant director of Enders' new infectious disease research laboratory at the Children's Medical Center.

Working with Enders, and Dr. Frederick C. Robbins, Weller succeeded in developing a technique for growing and recognizing poliomyelitis virus *in vitro* in non-nerve tissue, thus making possible subsequent advances against virus diseases, including the breakthrough to a safe antipolio vaccine. For their new tissue culture technique, which they first reported in 1948, Drs. Weller, Enders, and Robbins received the 1954 Nobel Prize in physiology and medicine. Previously an instructor, assistant professor, and associate professor, Weller in 1954 became Richard Pearson Strong professor and chairman of the department of tropical public health in the Harvard School of Public Health. He also isolated from human cell cultures the causative agents of chicken pox and shingles and was able, in collaboration with Franklin Neva, to grow the German measles (rubella) virus in the laboratory. His work with the mumps virus helped to prepare the way for the discovery of the polio vaccine.

WELLERISM, wĕl′ər-ĭzəm, a proverb consisting of a quoted cliché plus an implied story: " 'Everyone to his taste,' said the old woman as she kissed the cow." The form is at least as old as Theocritus (3d century B.C.): " 'All the women we need are inside,' said the bridegroom and closed the door on the bride." Sir Francis Bacon credits Aesop with " 'What a dust I have raised,' quoth the fly upon the coach." But the name "wellerism" is derived from the Cockney Sam Weller and his father in Charles Dickens' *Pickwick Papers:* "Now gen'l'm'n, 'fall on,' as the English said to the French when they fixed bagginets."

Since the 16th century, wellerisms have been common in Germany, Sweden, the British Isles, France, and Italy. Henry David Thoreau was not above " 'Very nice,' as the old lady said when she had got a gravestone for her husband." The English comic weekly *Punch* (1842) has " 'I'll blush for you,' as the rouge-pot said to the old dowager." From American periodicals before, during, and after the vogue of the *Pickwick Papers* come: " 'This suspense will kill me,' as the murderer said upon the gallows"; " 'I've got that down Pat,' said Mrs. Flanigan, as she gave her son a dose of castor oil"; " 'For goodness sake,' sighed the girl, as she wearily trudged home from an auto ride"; and one to end all punning: " 'You have scent for me and I am here,' as the mustard remarked to the Limburger cheese."

FRANCIS LEE UTLEY,
Professor of English, The Ohio State University.

WELLES, wĕlz, **Gideon,** American political leader, writer, editor, and secretary of the navy: b. Glastonbury, Conn., July 1, 1802; d. Hartford, Feb. 11, 1878. After formal schooling at the Episcopal Academy in Cheshire, Conn., and the American Literary, Scientific, and Military Academy in Norwich, Vt., he became part owner and editor (1826–1836) of the Hartford *Times.* A Democrat supporting Andrew Jackson, he was appointed postmaster at Hartford (1836–1841). In the Connecticut legislature (1827–1835) he opposed imprisonment for debt and obtained the passage of Connecticut's corporation law. He was thrice elected comptroller of Connecticut. James Knox Polk appointed him chief of the naval Bureau of Provisions and Clothing (1846–1849), where he obtained invaluable experience during the war with Mexico.

Leaving the Democratic Party on the slavery issue, he helped organize the Republican Party in New England and from 1855 to 1864 was on the Republican National Committee. He headed Connecticut's delegation to the Chicago convention that nominated Abraham Lincoln. Lincoln appointed him secretary of the navy in March 1861.

In the confused first month the new administration, fearing to antagonize Virginia, postponed proper defense measures and lost to the Confederacy the Norfolk Navy Yard, with the steam frigate *Merrimack* and a tremendously important stockpile of naval cannon. Welles disagreed with Lincoln over the proclamation of the blockade, preferring simply to close the ports and regard the rebellion as a domestic matter. Most loyally, however, he supported the president after the blockade had been proclaimed. To improvise a navy to blockade the extensive Southern coast he put through a huge purchasing and building program. Braving the political wrath of Congress, he gave his brother-in-law George D. Morgan power to beat down prices of shipowners.

After the appointment of Gustavus V. Fox as his assistant, Welles could draw on the wide experience of an energetic ex-naval officer and businessman. Together the two made a successful team. Fox, frequently traveling to New York and Hampton Roads, kept in touch with practical affairs of the fleet, while his chief kept a wary eye on his cabinet colleagues in the State and War departments. With a passion for "correct" administration, Welles would not tolerate the interference of William Henry Seward and Edwin McMasters Stanton in affairs of the Navy Department. Welles' single-minded attention to the great blockade, despite Confederate raiders, his early support of John Ericsson in the development of turret ironclads, and his painstaking selection of such commanders as David Glasgow Farragut, David Dixon Porter, and Andrew Hull Foote are his chief wartime accomplishments.

In the administration of Andrew Johnson, Welles brought the navy back to a peacetime status by eliminating several hundred jerry-built ships from the navy list and concentrating on the new class of oceangoing monitors. In the political battles over reconstruction he supported the president. After his retirement in 1869, he published a notable series of wartime reminiscences in the *Galaxy* and the *Atlantic,* and a book *Lincoln and Seward* (1874), drawing much of his material from the manuscript of his wartime diary. The three-volume *Diary of Gideon Welles,* published in 1911, 33 years after his death, is a chief source for the Civil War and reconstruction eras.

RICHARD S. WEST, JR.,
United States Naval Academy.

WELLES, (George) Orson, American actor and radio, motion picture, and theatrical producer: b. Kenosha, Wis., May 6, 1915, d. Oct. 10, 1985. He graduated from high school in Woodstock, Ill., and began his acting career with the Gate Theatre in Dublin, Ireland, in 1931. Two years later he toured the United States with Katherine Cornell, and in 1937 founded the Mercury Theatre, the same year producing a modern-dress version of Shakespeare's *Julius Caesar.* Among his other stage productions were Christopher Marlowe's *Dr. Faustus* (1937), in which he played the title role, and Thomas Dekker's *The Shoemaker's Holiday.* Welles made Mercury text recordings of Shakespeare's plays, at the same time producing radio broadcasts. *The War of the Worlds,* broadcast in 1938, a fictionalized narrative of the invasion of earth by creatures from other planets, caused panic in the New York area because of its realism. Listeners believed it to be a report of an actual Martian invasion.

In 1940 began Welles' motion picture career, as producer, writer, director, and actor. His most notable motion pictures include *Citizen Kane* (1941), *The Magnificent Ambersons* (1942), *Journey Into Fear* (1942), *Macbeth* (1947), *Touch of Evil* (1958), and Kafka's *The Trial* (1963). Films by other directors in which Welles starred include *Jane Eyre* (1944), *The Third Man* (1949), *Moby Dick* (1956), *Compulsion* (1959), *A Man for All Seasons* (1966), *House of Cards* (1969), *The Kremlin Letter* (1970), *Catch 22* (1970), *The Other Side of the Mountain* (1975), and *Voyage of the Damned* (1976). In 1975 he was honored by the American Film Institute, which presented him its Life Achievement Award.

WELLES, Sumner, American diplomat: b. New York, N.Y., Oct. 14, 1892, d. Bernardsville, N.J., Sept. 24, 1961. Graduating from Harvard University in 1914, he began his diplomatic career the following year as secretary of the United States Embassy in Tokyo. From 1917 to 1919 he served in a similar post in Buenos Aires, Argentina. He was assistant chief of the Latin

American affairs division of the Department of State from 1920 to 1921, and chief of the division from 1921 to 1922. After several diplomatic missions to Central America, he was named assistant secretary of state in 1933, a post he held until 1937, with a brief tenure as ambassador to Cuba; from 1937 to 1943 he served as undersecretary of state.

Welles was President Franklin D. Roosevelt's personal envoy on a fact-finding mission to the belligerent nations of Europe in 1940, and accompanied Roosevelt at his meeting at sea with Prime Minister Winston Churchill in 1941, before the entry of the United States into World War II. He is regarded as one of the architects of the "Good Neighbor Policy" of the United States toward the Latin American states. He was the author of *Naboth's Vineyard* (1928); *Four Freedoms* (1942); *The Time for Decision* (1944); *Where We Are Heading* (1946); *We Need Not Fail* (1948); and *Seven Decisions That Shaped History* (1950).

WELLESLEY, Arthur. See WELLINGTON, 1ST DUKE OF.

WELLESLEY, wĕlz'lĭ, **Richard Colley,** 1ST MARQUESS OF WELLESLEY, British statesman: b. Dublin, Ireland, June 20, 1760; d. London, England, Sept. 26, 1842. The elder brother of Arthur Wellesley, 1st duke of Wellington, he was educated at Oxford, and in 1781 entered the Irish House of Peers as Lord Mornington, a title he inherited from his father. In 1784 he became a member of the English House of Commons. Although politically a liberal, his observations of the French Revolution led him to oppose parliamentary reform.

William Pitt the Younger appointed Wellesley to the board of control for Indian affairs in 1793, and four years later he was appointed governor general of India. The British foothold in India was at the time not completely firm, and on his arrival Wellesley was confronted with unrest and enmity in the south. Using diplomacy and military power, he strengthened England's authority. A treaty with the Nizam of Hyderabad in effect subjugated that state to the crown. The rousing victory at Seringapatam on May 4, 1799, broke Mysore's resistance, and a series of battles against the Maratha Confederacy of central India led eventually to the confederacy's defeat. Wellesley also formulated a plan for the establishment of a college to train Indian civil servants, at Fort William in Calcutta.

Wellesley was created 1st marquess of Wellesley in the Irish peerage in 1799. He returned to England in 1805 after a series of disputes with the colonial authorities, and in 1809 was appointed ambassador extraordinary to Seville, Spain, to deal with the Spanish junta in consolidating plans for the Peninsular War. Subsequently he served (1809–1812) as foreign minister under Spencer Perceval.

In 1820, Wellesley was made lord lieutenant of Ireland, and began a benevolent, liberal administration that lasted eight years. When his brother, now the 1st duke of Wellington, became prime minister in 1828, Wellesley was not asked to serve in the administration because of a divergence in the two brothers' views, Wellesley being more liberally inclined toward Roman Catholics. Wellesley served again as lord lieutenant of Ireland from 1832 to 1834. With Warren Hastings and James Andrew Broun Ramsay, he is considered one of the three men who won for Great Britain the empire of India.

WELLESLEY, town, Massachusetts, in Norfolk County on the Charles River, 14 miles southwest of Boston by road; altitude 140 feet. There are some light industries, and in recent years the town has become a major shopping center for many of the surrounding communities, but it is essentially a residential community with a number of educational institutions. Wellesley College (q.v.), Babson Institute, and a branch of the New England Conservatory of Music are located here, as are Pine Manor Junior College, the Dana Hall schools, Tenacre Country Day School, and the Academy of the Assumption. Two modern buildings, the Jewett Arts Center at Wellesley College and the Wellesley Free Library, attract hundreds of visitors each year, and there is an annual art festival. A relief map of the United States and a massive outdoor globe are attractions at Babson Institute.

Originally a part of the Dedham Grants, the town was settled in 1659. The name is derived from Samuel Welles, an early settler. It was incorporated in 1881 and is governed by a town meeting and a board of selectmen elected annually. Included in the town are the villages of Wellesley Farms and Wellesley Hills. Pop. 27,209.

MARGARET J. ARNOLD.

WELLESLEY, Province. See PENANG.

WELLESLEY COLLEGE, a residential liberal arts college for women situated in the town of Wellesley, Mass. The 400-acre campus was once the country estate of Henry Fowle Durant, a wealthy Boston lawyer, who decided after the death of his only son to found a college which would "offer to young women opportunities for education equivalent to that usually provided in colleges for young men." The college was founded in 1870 and opened in 1875.

The physical history of the college falls into three fairly distinct periods. Until March 17, 1914, most of the academic and residential life centered in College Hall, the first and principal building. On that night it was destroyed by fire. Thereafter, freshmen and some upperclassmen lived in small houses in the village and much of the academic work was taught in temporary frame structures until, one by one, they were replaced. The third period began in 1952 when additional large campus residence halls were built and village housing was discontinued. Today all students, who come from every part of the United States and some 30 foreign countries, live in 13 large dormitories, the newest of which, McAfee Hall, was opened in the fall of 1961.

An addition doubling the size of the library building was completed in 1958, and a modern language laboratory constructed. In 1958, too, was opened the Jewett Arts Center, which provides exceptional facilities for art, music, and theater, and is a significant achievement in college architecture. The annual enrollment averages about 1,600 students.

JEAN GLASSROCK.

WELLESLEY ISLANDS, island group, Australia, an uninhabited group at the head of the Gulf of Carpentaria, off the northwest coast of Queensland. Mornington Island, the largest, is 28 miles long and 8 miles wide. Others are Bentinck and Sweers islands and several scattered islets and rocks. The group, first explored in 1802, was named for Richard Colley Wellesley, 1st marquess of Wellesley.

WELLESZ, vĕl′ĕs, **Egon,** Austrian musicologist and composer: b. Vienna, Austria, Oct. 21, 1885; d. Oxford, England, Nov. 9, 1974. After he had studied composition with Arnold Schoenberg, he taught in Vienna at the Neues Conservatorium and at the university. The Nazi regime drove him to England, where he became a lecturer in the history of music at Oxford University (1943), a member of the editorial board of the *New Oxford History of Music* (1946), and the University Reader in Byzantine Music (1948). An authority on the life and music of Schoenberg and on dodecaphony (12-note technique), he also has been recognized as a creative student of Byzantine and other early church music and of early opera. His extremely numerous, dense, complex, "dissonant" compositions were not intended for, and have not won, widespread popular acceptance, but his extensive critico-historical writing has established him as one of the foremost musicologists of his era.

HERBERT WEINSTOCK.

WELLINGBOROUGH, wĕl′ĭng-bə-rə, market town of considerable antiquity, and urban district, England, in Northamptonshire, on the river Nene, 10 miles northeast of Northampton. Industries include the making of boots and shoes, leather tanning and dressing, and the manufacture of ready-to-wear clothes, cardboard boxes and containers, plastics, scientific instruments, and ecclesiastical ornaments. Iron ore has been quarried locally since the 19th century; works for smelting the ore were erected in 1852. Educational facilities include a well-known public school dating from 1595 and a technical college established in 1895. Pop. (1961) 30,579.

H. GORDON STOKES.

WELLINGTON, wĕl′ĭng-tən, **1ST DUKE OF (ARTHUR WESLEY, later WELLESLEY),** Anglo-Irish soldier, administrator, and statesman: b. Dublin, Ireland, on or about May 1, 1769; d. Walmer Castle, Kent, England, Sept. 14, 1852. Fourth son of Garrett Wesley, 2d baron and 1st earl of Mornington, by his wife Anne, daughter of Viscount Dungannon, he was educated at elementary schools at Trim, Ireland, and Chelsea, England; at Eton and Brussels; and in 1786 at the military academy of Angers, France. He was gazetted ensign on March 7, 1787, and on December 25 of the same year was appointed aide-de-camp to the lord lieutenant of Ireland with the rank of lieutenant. From 1790 he sat as member for the family borough of Trim in the Irish Parliament, and acted as land agent to the family estates. He was gazetted captain on June 30, 1791. He became engaged to the Honorable Catherine Pakenham, but her brother, Lord Longford, refused consent to the marriage because Wesley was poor.

By purchase with funds supplied by his eldest brother, Wesley became major in April 1793, and in September, lieutenant colonel of the 33d Foot. His public spirit and devotion to duty made him a conscientious soldier from the beginning, and he first showed his military skill as commander of the rear guard during the duke of York's disastrous retreat in the Netherlands, 1794–1795. Disillusioned by the conduct of the campaign, Wesley tried hard to find official employment as a civilian, but, disappointed in this as in his hope of marriage, he went to India with his regiment, as colonel (May 1796), reaching Calcutta in February 1797.

India.—His eight years' service in India was of the highest value in developing Wesley's great qualities as soldier and administrator. In 1797 he went with the force which occupied Penang in Malaya. Lord Mornington, his brother, arrived in India as governor general in April 1798, at which date the family name was changed to Wellesley. After much devoted and unrecognized work in reorganizing the Indian Army, Colonel Wellesley left Madras with the army sent against Tipu Sultan (Tipu Sahib), as commander of the 16,000 men furnished by the Nizam of Hyderabad. He planned the campaign, and with endless patience and competence dealt with complex problems of transport and supply. On May 4, 1799, Seringapatam was stormed, and Tipu slain.

To the annoyance of senior officers Wellesley was then named military commander of Seringapatam and became virtual ruler of Mysore, though interrupted by the need for punitive expeditions against hostile guerrillas, such as the Maratha Dundia, self-styled "King of the Two Worlds." Disappointed in his hopes of joining the Indian expeditionary force to Egypt against Napoleon Bonaparte, Wellesley returned to Mysore, where he heartily cooperated with the vizier, Purniya, in public works of irrigation and agriculture intended to benefit the peasants.

On April 29, 1802, he was at last gazetted major general, which at that time was the summit of his ambition. Next year he was in command of an expedition against the warlike Marathas under Holkar for the restoration of the peshwa, capturing Poona by surprise after a 40-mile forced night march of the cavalry led by Wellesley in person. Having thus defeated Holkar, Wellesley conducted a brilliant campaign against a Maratha army, led by Mahadaji Sindhia and the raja of Berar, of native troops with French officers. After capturing the supposedly impregnable fortress of Ahmadnagar with its immense stores, Wellesley with his force of 5,000 men and 17 guns unexpectedly came upon the enemy force of 50,000 men and 100 guns at Assaye. He attacked at once, and, though suffering heavy casualties, won a complete victory, capturing 98 guns. For this success he was made Knight of the Bath and received the thanks of Parliament. His officers presented him with a gold sword and an address, and when he left India in March 1805 other congratulatory addresses came from distinguished Indians, both Hindu and Muslim.

Service at Home.—Sir Arthur Wellesley reached England in September 1805, but in spite of his rank and services he was employed at first only as a brigadier, a snub which he endured calmly and with cheerful devotion to duty. William Pitt and Lord Castlereagh saw his merit at once, but the old "Horse Guards" generals suspected him as a "politician." On April 10, 1806, he married Catherine Pakenham, but the Beau, as London society nicknamed him from his austere neatness, was afterward involved in numerous love affairs.

Early in 1806, Wellesley accepted the Whig pocket borough of Rye, to defend in the Commons his brother, Lord Wellesley (formerly Mornington), against charges of malpractices as governor general. A year later he returned to Dublin, not as a humble aide-de-camp, but as chief secretary for Ireland (and its virtual ruler) on a salary of £7,000 a year, privately determined "to obliterate as far as the laws will allow us the distinction between Protestants and Catholics," and taking as his guiding maxim that "government ought to do what is just towards the governed, be the consequences what they may."

He was temporarily recalled for active service as commander of the military force landed by the fleet which attacked Denmark. The jealous Horse Guards sent along one of their own protégés to act as "military wet nurse" to "the politician." Wellesley contemptuously allowed him to give orders until the moment of battle arrived, brushed him aside, gave his own orders, and triumphantly captured Køge on Aug. 29, 1807. It is worth noting that he received grateful acknowledgment from the Danes for his care in protecting the civilian population. After receiving the more formal thanks of Parliament he returned to his Dublin duties, distributing patronage with a "mixture of aristocratic hauteur and cold contempt" for the gentlemanly hunters of money and jobs.

Peninsular War.—He was promoted lieutenant general on April 24, 1808, and in June the government, despite the opposition of the Horse Guards and George III, sent Wellesley to command the expeditionary force intended to aid the Portuguese and Spanish people in their heroic resistance to French invasion. Thus began the Peninsular War, which ended with the invasion of France and the abdication of the emperor.

With an army, mainly infantry, which never exceeded 17,000, Wellesley marched from Figueira da Foz on Aug. 9, 1808, defeated a small force under Gen. Henri François de Laborde at Roliça, and Gen. Andoche Junot himself with the main French army of Portugal at Vimeiro, on August 21. At the very moment of victory Wellesley was superseded by two elderly generals sent by the Horse Guards, who, to his disgust, refused to allow him to pursue the beaten enemy as he wished; and, despite his expressed disapproval of the terms, forced him to sign with them the needlessly timid Convention of Cintra. The convention was most unpopular in England, and Wellesley, while little praised for his victories, was bitterly censured for a document not drawn up by him, of which he had disapproved. Once more he returned to his administrative duties in Dublin.

After Sir John Moore's strategically brilliant but tactically disastrous campaign against Napoleon in Spain, which ended with Moore's death at La Coruña and the evacuation of his army, Wellesley was ordered to Lisbon (which he reached on April 22, 1809) as commander of a larger army (soon to be brigaded with Portuguese troops), and for the next five years never quitted his post. A dispirited and idle army was suddenly thrilled into action by his arrival; and within three weeks he captured Oporto, after a most daring crossing of the Tagus River, and drove Marshal Nicolas Jean de Dieu Soult and the remnants of his army into Spain. The only French troops left in Portugal were one garrison and the prisoners of war.

Wellesley now felt that the situation warranted an attack on the French forces in Spain, in liaison with the Spanish regular army commanded by the very elderly Gen. Gregorio Garcia de la Cuesta, whose incapacity and obstinacy frustrated operations and led to many difficulties and dangers. In spite of a great tactical victory at Talavera de la Reina (July 27–28, 1809), where a numerically stronger army under Marshal Claude Victor was defeated and forced to retire, Wellesley felt Cuesta was so unreliable that he ordered a retreat. Owing to the failure of the Spanish junta to produce the supplies they had promised, the British troops had nothing to eat but flour, and ironically called their position "Dough Boy Hill." The victory of Talavera was popular in England, and Wellesley was created Baron Douro and Viscount Wellington—the name by which he is known to history.

With his inflexible sense of justice Wellington insisted that his troops must be paid for the rations they had not received. He resolved never again to hazard his troops with the Spanish regulars unless he had command, though throughout the war he received and acknowledged the valuable services and intelligence given by the guerrilla leaders. He at once set to work to make himself independent of foreign governments by organizing his own system of supplies and transport (as he had done in India) and, foreseeing a future French attempt to capture Lisbon, he personally surveyed the area and gave orders that resulted in the celebrated Lines of Tôrres Vedras.

The Mansell Collection, London

The Duke of Wellington.

The French invasion was, fortunately for Wellington, slow in starting. It was not until July 20, 1810, that the French "Army of Portugal" crossed the frontier under the command of Marshal Prince André Masséna, with Marshal Michel Ney as second. The accidental explosion of the powder magazine destroyed the Allied fortress of Almeida, and allowed Masséna to advance more quickly than had been expected. Wellington all along had determined to fight the decisive battle at Tôrres Vedras, but on September 26 he fought a very successful delaying action at Buçaco (Bussaco), inflicting heavy losses on the attackers. The planned Tôrres Vedras battle never took place, for when Masséna had surveyed that formidable series of field defenses and the large forces occupying them, he decided not to attack.

By Wellington's orders the Portuguese adopted scorched-earth tactics, and though not all the food stored by the peasants could be destroyed, Masséna's army, accustomed to live by marauding, was soon hungry. After some weeks the French retreated 50 miles to Santarém, where Masséna obstinately remained until March 4, 1811, suffering very heavy losses by sickness, hunger, and desertion. Wellington again pursued the retreating French, fighting a series of brilliant advance-guard actions against Ney's equally brilliant rear-guard defense. The French attack on Lisbon had utterly failed.

In late April 1811, Masséna made another attempt on northwestern Portugal. Gen. William Beresford was left with part of the Allied army to blockade Badajoz, and fought the bloody battle of La Albuera against Soult, while Wellington met and repulsed Masséna at Fuentes de Oñoro, May 3–5, 1811. The rest of the year passed without any major action, but Napoleon began to withdraw troops (including Marshal Soult) from Spain for his invasion of Russia, and Masséna's place was taken by Marshal Auguste Marmont. Fully informed of French movements by the Spanish guerrillas, Wellington made his plans. His first blow was at the fortress of Ciudad Rodrigo, invested and stormed (Jan. 19, 1812) before Marmont was able to move. Badajoz was stormed on April 6, with very heavy British casualties. To conciliate the Spaniards, Wellington handed both fortresses over to their troops. He invaded Spain, and fought a great battle near Salamanca (July 22, 1812), completely defeating Marmont, who was seriously wounded. One of the French generals noted in his diary that Salamanca "raises Lord Wellington almost to the level of Marlborough." Wellington's army entered Madrid, and he pursued the enemy as far as Burgos, where an overwhelming concentration of French forces determined his decision to avoid another general action that year and to retire once more into Portugal.

Napoleon's disasters in Russia encouraged further action in Spain in 1813. Wellington made a triumphal march across Spain, continually outflanking his enemy, and on June 21, 1813, completely defeated Joseph Bonaparte (king of Spain 1808–1813) and Marshal Jean Baptiste Jourdan at Vitoria, compelling them to retire into France. For this campaign Wellington was made field marshal and a marquess. Soult was sent to oppose him, and heavy actions, known as the Battles of the Pyrenees, were fought in the mountains. Wellington invaded France on October 7, and gained another victory on November 10. In 1814 battles were fought at Orthez (February 27) and at Toulouse (April 10), almost immediately followed by the news of Napoleon's abdication.

Wellington was made a duke, and sent to Madrid on a special mission to the restored Ferdinand VII, in the hope of persuading that monarch to adopt less despotic and reactionary measures; but all the envoy obtained was pardons for some of the Spanish liberals. He wrote a farewell order to the Army of the Peninsula—"my old Spanish infantry," as he proudly called them—and, after a brief period in England, acted as British ambassador in France until January 1815, when for a time he took the place of Robert Stewart, Viscount Castlereagh, as England's representative at the Congress of Vienna. Word of Napoleon's escape from Elba reached Vienna on March 7, 1815, and Wellington was dispatched to Brussels (April 5) to command troops from England and other countries, in liaison with Prince Gebhard von Blücher and the Prussians. See also PENINSULAR WAR, THE.

Waterloo.—On June 16, 1815, Napoleon defeated the Prussians at Ligny. Wellington could not come to their help, for his concentration was late, and he had to fight off a series of attacks from Ney at Quatre-Bras. He fell back on a previously selected "Wellingtonian" position in front of the forest of Soignies; and on Blücher's promise of aid decided to fight the battle of Waterloo, June 18, 1815. The Prussians in their turn were late, and for hours Wellington's army met and beat off powerful French attacks, including two hours of repeated cavalry charges. The British Guards held the outpost of Hougoumont throughout, but in the afternoon the French carried the important outpost of La Haye Sainte. The Prussians were now arriving in force, and Napoleon was compelled to send Gen. Georges Lobau and then the Young Guard to meet them. After all previous attacks on Wellington's position had failed, Napoleon sent in a last desperate assault of the Old Guard, met and beaten off by the British Guards, with Wellington himself at their head. The whole French Army now went off in complete confusion, pursued all night by the Prussian cavalry. Blücher and Wellington entered Paris July 7, and on July 14 Napoleon surrendered to the prince regent.

Statesman.—Wellington was now at the height of his fame and power. For a time he was supreme commander of all the Allied troops in France, amounting to over a million—a huge number in those days. Innumerable honors came to him, and in addition to his rank as British field marshal, he was a marshal of the armies of Portugal, Spain, France, the Netherlands, Prussia, Austria, and Russia. This immense influence he used in general with moderation, a sense of justice, and an earnest desire for world peace. He could not, indeed, avert the excesses of the White Terror in the Midi, but he secured the peaceful restoration of Louis XVIII, and steadily refused to support any of the despots' plans for dismembering France. When others failed, he succeeded in settling the difficult problems of war reparations. Although the event caused him financial loss, he urged and succeeded in producing the evacuation of all occupying troops from France in 1818, two years ahead of the date fixed in 1815.

He reentered political life in January 1819, when he joined the cabinet of the 2d earl of Liverpool (Robert Jenkinson) as master general of the ordnance. Many of his admirers regretted this step, wishing that he had remained "the soldier of Europe," but he preferred to think of himself as "the retained servant of the monarchy," ready to serve cheerfully wherever he was needed. George Canning sent him in 1822 to represent England at the Congress of Verona where, in spite of every pressure, Wellington refused to be entrapped into any formula committing England to a policy of support for the reactionary autocracies. He was sent on a special mission to Russia in March 1826, and succeeded in averting for a time the war threatening between Russia and Turkey. For a short time he abandoned active politics to serve as commander in chief of the army, a post he resigned in January 1828 on becoming prime minister. In the face of strong opposition, his government repealed the Corporation Act of 1661 directed against Dissenters, and the Test Act of 1673 directed against Roman Catholics. In 1829 there was even greater religious opposition to his Catholic Relief Bill for Ireland, and he actually had to fight a duel with George William Finch-Hatton, earl of Winchilsea, who impugned the honesty of his motives.

The French revolution of July 1830 had an immediate effect in England, especially in stimulating agitation for the long overdue reform of Parliament. Wellington's government was defeated in the Commons, and he resigned on Nov. 16, 1830. His opposition to the reform bills rapidly changed him from the nation's hero to its most unpopular politician; the windows of Apsley House, his residence in London, were smashed, and his life even was in danger from London mobs. When at last Wellington became convinced that reform was inevitable, he withdrew his opposition, and used his immense personal influence to get the bill passed by the Lords, in June 1832.

He virtually acknowledged that he could not successfully lead a political party by serving under Sir Robert Peel in 1834 and again in 1841. He had not lost his skill as administrator, for during a parliamentary interregnum in 1834 he was for a short time the whole government, daily visiting the ministries, transacting contemporary business, and even clearing up the arrears of his predecessors. In 1846 he helped Peel to carry the repeal of the Corn Laws (q.v.), and in 1848 he was called on by the Whig government to organize the defense of London against a threatened Chartist rebellion. His temporary unpopularity had soon vanished, and more and more he became the symbol of national unity, a venerable elder statesman consulted by the crown and both political parties on all occasions requiring the advice of wisdom and experience. His death in 1852 caused nationwide mourning from the queen to the humblest of her subjects, and Alfred, Lord Tennyson expressed the feelings of his countrymen when he wrote in his ode on the *Death of the Duke of Wellington:* "The last great Englishman is low."

RICHARD ALDINGTON
Author of "The Duke"

Bibliography

The Dispatches of Field Marshal the Duke of Wellington . . . from 1799–1818, comp. by Lt. Col. John Gurwood, 12 vols. (J. Murray 1834–1839)

Dispatches, Correspondence and Memoranda . . . from 1818–1832, ed. by his son, the 2nd Duke of Wellington, 8 vols. (J. Murray 1867–1880).

Supplementary Despatches and Memoranda . . . from 1794–1818, ed. by his son, the 2nd Duke of Wellington 14 vols. (J. Murray 1858–1872).

Aldington, Richard, *The Duke* (Viking 1943).

Croker, John Wilson, *The Croker Papers, 1808–1857*, ed. by Bernard Poole (Barnes & Noble 1967).

Griffith, Paddy, and others, *Wellington Commander: The Iron Duke's Generalship* (Faber 1986).

Guedalla, Philip, *Wellington* (1931; reprint, Arden Library 1979).

Lachouque, Henry, and Carmigniani, Juan C., *Waterloo* (Hippocrene Bks. 1978).

Longford, Elizabeth, *Wellington: Pillar of State* (Academy Chicago 1982).

Stanhope, P. H., *Notes on Conversations with the Duke of Wellington 1831–1851* (1888; reprint, Da Capo 1973).

Strachan, H. W., *Wellington's Legacy: The Reform of the British Army 1830–1854* (Longwood 1984).

WELLINGTON, township and municipality, Australia, in central New South Wales, about 230 miles northwest of Sydney, at the junction of the Macquarie and Bell rivers. Wheat growing, sheep production, flour mills, a butter factory, freezing works, and a sawmill are the principal industries. Burrendong Dam, which will be a source of rural water supply and an aid in flood control, is under construction 19 miles upstream from Wellington on the Macquarie River. There is gold dredging in the Macquarie River.

An explorers' depot was established at the site of Wellington in 1818, followed by a settlement for convicts and a Christian mission. Wellington was gazetted in 1846 and declared a municipal district in 1879. In 1950, it was amalgamated with Macquarie Shire and part of Cobbora Shire to form Wellington Shire. Pop. (1960) town 6,000; municipality 11,021.

R. M. YOUNGER.

WELLINGTON (formerly **JAKATALA**), a hill station and military cantonment, India, in Nilgiri District, Madras State. A suburb of Coonoor, Wellington lies nine miles southeast of Ootacamund at an elevation of 6,100 feet. Known for its healthful climate—temperatures rarely exceed 75° F. and the yearly mean is 62° F.—the town has an important military sanitarium in addition to the military staff college. Chemical works constructed in 1949 manufacture cordite, used in explosives, and other products. The surrounding hill area produces a variety of temperate fruits and vegetables.

JOSEPH E. SCHWARTZBERG.

WELLINGTON, city, Kansas, the seat of Sumner County, about 30 miles south of Wichita by road and 20 miles north of the Kansas-Oklahoma border; altitude 1,223 feet. Wellington is a trade center in the largest wheat-producing county of Kansas. Dairying and beef cattle are also important. Industries include flour milling and the manufacture of aircraft components and furniture, and there are over 100 producing wells in the Wellington Oil Field. Wellington is on the Kansas Turnpike, and has a municipal airport. There are three parks with a total of 1,037 acres.

Wellington was a favorite camping ground for travelers on the old Chisholm Trail. In 1871 a townsite was laid out by a company from Paola, Kans., who named it after the duke of Wellington. The mayor-commission type of government has been in force since 1872 when the town was incorporated. Pop. 8,212.

OLIVE B. MCCOY.

WELLINGTON, provincial district, New Zealand, occupying the southern part of North Island, area 10,870 square miles. (Provincial districts, originally self-governing units, have been merely geographical areas, used primarily for statistical purposes, since the centralization of the New Zealand government in 1875.)

The north-south Tararua and Ruahine mountains divide Wellington into the Wairarapa Plain on the east, predominantly sheep-raising country, and the western coastal area, with sheep and dairy cattle. In the north lies Tongariro National Park, whose 235 square miles include three intermittently active volcanoes: Ruahepu, 9,175 feet high; Ngauruhoe, 7,515 feet; and Tongariro, 6,517 feet, with developed ski grounds. The district is irrigated by several rivers, one of which,

HABGOOD/PHOTO RESEARCHERS

Wellington, the capital of New Zealand, is situated on an excellent harbor, an inlet of Cook Strait.

the Manawatu, cuts a deep gorge through the central range, providing the major road and rail access between east and west. Palmerston North and Wellington are the chief cities. Wool, meat, and dairy products, the principal exports, are shipped through the city of Wellington.

IAN A. GORDON

WELLINGTON, city, New Zealand, the national capital, situated on Wellington Harbor, on Cook Strait. It is the southern terminal of the North Island railway system, and the northern terminal of the ferry services to South Island. The port has a floating dock and wharves for ocean-going and coastal vessels. The level business and port areas include more than 300 acres of land reclaimed from the sea; the residential areas rise steeply from the sea.

Industries and Business Activities. The most important industries in the urban area (which, economically, includes two nearby independent municipalities, the borough of Petone and the city of Lower Hutt) are meat processing, building, woolens manufacture, automobile assembly, food processing, printing, and manufacture of brick, soap, tobacco, and matches. Wellington is the seat of the Reserve Bank, which issues the country's currency, the stock exchange, offices of principal insurance firms, and five trading banks. Many of its citizens are in government service.

Buildings. The majority of residential buildings are made of wood, because of the mild New Zealand winters. In contrast, the government and business area is substantial and imposing. Among the important buildings are the House of Parliament, the old wooden (built in 1876) and the new government buildings, the railway station, town hall and civic buildings (built in 1956), and Victoria University College, which dominates the city from nearby heights. Notable architecturally are the Dominion Museum, Dairy and Wool Board building, and the Hutt city library.

Educational and Cultural Facilities. Victoria University College, founded in 1897, a part of the national university system, has faculties of arts, science, commerce, and law. Its library, with those of the Royal Society, the city, the national library service, the Supreme Court, Parliament (General Assembly), and the Alexander Turnbull Library of rare books and manuscripts (the national repository) make Wellington a notable library center. The National Art Gallery and the Dominion Museum house permanent collections. The New Zealand Players are based here. The city has public parks with commanding views of the city and the sea. There are facilities for sports, and easy access to beaches.

History and Government. The first settlement of 2,000 immigrants from the United Kingdom was established in 1840 at Petone, and shortly afterward was moved seven miles south to the present site. The city was named for Arthur Wellesley, 1st duke of Wellington. The seat of dominion government was transferred from Auckland in 1865. Wellington has its own city government. Pop. (1971) 135,515.

IAN A. GORDON
Victoria University College

WELLINGTON, village, Ohio, in the southern, rural section of Lorain County, 40 miles southwest of Cleveland by road; altitude 856 feet. It is a residential community and shopping center for a farming country famous for its dairy products and thoroughbred horses. In addition to a large foundry there are several small industries. Wellington was settled in 1818, and in 1878, before the introduction of pasteurization, was the cheese center of the United States. The Herrick Memorial Library houses a collection of the pictures of Archibald M. Willard (1836–1918), painter of the *Spirit of '76*. The village has a mayor and council form of government. Pop. 4,146.

MARTHA MORSE

WELLINGTON, Mount, mountain, Australia, in southern Tasmania, rising 4,165 feet, immediately west of Hobart, the state capital, which is built on its foothills. Much of Hobart's water supply comes from small streams on Mount Wellington. First sighted in 1788 by Lt. William Bligh, it was first called Table Hill because of its flat top; the present name has been used since 1834.

WELLMAN, wĕl′mən, **Walter,** American explorer, aeronaut, and journalist: b. Mentor, Ohio, Nov. 3, 1858; d. New York, N.Y., Jan. 31, 1934. At the age of 14, he established himself as a journalist by founding a weekly newspaper in Sutton, Nebr., and seven years later organized the evening Cincinnati *Post.* From 1884 to 1911 he was the Washington correspondent of the Chicago *Herald,* and its successor, the *Record-Herald.* It was, however, as an explorer and pioneer in air travel that he won his fame. In 1891 he journeyed to the Bahama Islands, where, he claimed, he located the exact landing spot of Christopher Columbus on Watling Island, or San Salvador; a permanent marker was erected there.

Turning his attention to the north, Wellman in 1894 led an expedition that reached a latitude of 81° north, northeast of Spitsbergen. In 1898–1899, a similar expedition reached 82° north, near Franz Josef Land. He then tried to reach the North Pole by air. Frank B. Noyes, publisher of the *Record-Herald,* commissioned Wellman in 1906 to fly to the pole in a lighter-than-air ship. The first attempt, in 1907, was abandoned because of violent weather. On the second try, in 1909, Wellman set out again, but the ship traveled only 12 miles before the equilibrator broke and the crew was forced to turn back. By then, Robert E. Peary had reached the pole by foot.

Wellman next began preparing for his most ambitious attempt: a transatlantic crossing by air. The *America,* the airship used in his polar attempts, was rebuilt to a length of 228 feet. Wellman and his five-man crew left Atlantic City, N.J., on Oct. 15, 1910. The voyage was a failure from the start: One of the two motors stalled, and the other almost set the ship afire; cooling and contraction of the ship in the cold night air caused it to lose altitude and drift dangerously close to the water; wind drove it off course. Eventually, after 72 hours, the *America* was forced down 375 miles off Cape Hatteras; the ship drifted away and was lost, and the crew was picked up by a freighter. But the attempt established several records—the length of time in the air, the distance traveled (1,008 miles), and the first regular transmission of wireless messages between shore and an airship. Wellman was given a hero's welcome when he returned to New York.

His published works include *The Aerial Age* (1911), *The German Republic* (1916), and *The Force Supreme* (1918).

WELLS, wĕlz, **Charles Jeremiah** (pseudonym H. L. HOWARD), English poet: b. probably London, England, about 1799; d. Marseille, France, Feb. 17, 1879. In his youth the associate of William Hazlitt and John Keats, Wells began the practice of law about 1820, and in 1822 published a prose collection, *Stories After Nature.* His outstanding work is a verse drama in the Elizabethan style, *Joseph and His Brethren* (1824), which was completely ignored by reviewers until 1837. It did not win fame until 1875, when Algernon Charles Swinburne and Dante Gabriel Rossetti wrote complimentary reviews of the drama and of Wells. Reprinted in 1876, with a preface by Swinburne, *Joseph and His Brethren* brought considerable fame to Wells in his last years. He is said to have destroyed the manuscripts of a novel, two tragedies, poems, and one epic after the death of his wife in 1874.

WELLS, David Ames, American political economist: b. Springfield, Mass., June 17, 1828; d. Norwich, Conn., Nov. 5, 1898. He graduated from Williams College in 1847, and joined the staff of the Springfield *Republican,* where he invented a device for folding newspapers. In 1851 he was graduated from the Lawrence Scientific School in Cambridge, Mass., where he studied under Louis Agassiz. In 1850, he and George Bliss began publishing *The Annual of Scientific Discovery,* which continued until 1866.

Despite his early scientific interests, Wells won fame as an economist. A pamphlet issued in 1864, *Our Burden and Our Strength,* helped to restore the confidence of foreign investors in American bonds and greenbacks, which had fallen to half their face value because of a lack of belief in the North's ability to discharge its debts. The pamphlet, translated into several foreign languages, brought Wells to the attention of President Abraham Lincoln, and the following year Wells was appointed chairman of the National Revenue Commission. In 1866, the post of special commissioner of the revenue was created for him, and shortly thereafter the Bureau of Statistics was established. In *The Reports of the Special Commissioner of the Revenue,* from 1866 to 1869, Wells discussed the subject of indirect taxation and recommended the use of stamps for collecting excise taxes on liquor and tobacco.

A protectionist at first, Wells changed his views after a study of European industries and supported free trade; for 30 years he was a leading advocate of abolition of the tariff. He later became a consultant on tariff matters to Presidents James A. Garfield and Grover Cleveland. When the office of special commissioner was abolished by President Ulysses S. Grant in 1870, Wells was made chairman of the New York State Tax Commission, and in 1871 published *Local Taxation,* one of the early competent surveys of the subject. He became active in railroad affairs, and served as a member of the board of arbitration of the Associated Railways.

Among his other writings are *The Relation of the Government to the Telegraph* (1874), *The Relation of the Federal Government to the Railroads* (1874), *The Silver Question* (1877), *A Primer of Tariff Reform* (1884), and *The Theory and Practice of Taxation* (published posthumously in 1900).

WELLS, Frederic Lyman, American psychologist: b. Boston, Mass., April 22, 1884; d. June 2, 1964. He studied at Columbia University (Ph.D. 1908) and served on the faculties of Columbia and Harvard universities and on the staffs of McLean Hospital in Waverly, Mass., and Boston Psychopathic Hospital. He also worked as consultant in the Office of the Adjutant General of the United States War Department. Wells is noted for his work in clinical psychology and his special research in the mental measurements of superior adults. His works include *Mental Adjustments* (1917), *Pleasure and Behavior* (1924), *Mental Tests in Clinical Practice* (1927), and (with Jurgen Ruesch) *Mental Examiners' Handbook* (1945).

WELLS, H(erbert) G(eorge), English novelist: b. Bromley, Kent, England, Sept. 21, 1866; d. London, Aug. 13, 1946. His father was a shopkeeper in a small way and a professional cricketer; his mother served from time to time as housekeeper at the nearby estate of Uppark ("Bladesover" in *Tono-Bungay*). Though Wells attended Morley's School in Bromley, his real education came from omnivorous reading, a habit formed in 1874 while he was laid up for some months with a broken leg. Between 1880 and 1883 he spent most of his time as a draper's apprentice in Windsor and Southsea, a way of life for which he later recorded his profound detestation in *Kipps*. After a year as a teacher in a private school, he won a scholarship to the Normal School of Science in South Kensington in 1884. There he made a promising start as a student under Thomas Henry Huxley, but his interest faltered in the following year, and he left without a degree in 1887. He then taught in private schools for four years, not taking his B.S. degree until 1890.

H. G. Wells

Bassano Ltd., London

The year 1891 saw Wells established in London, teaching in a correspondence college, married to his cousin Isabel, and the author of a remarkable article on "The Rediscovery of the Unique" in the *Fortnightly Review*. After much writing on educational subjects, he began his sensational literary career with *The Time Machine* in 1895. Meanwhile, he had given up teaching and had left Isabel for one of his brightest students, Amy Catherine ("Jane") Robbins, whom he married in 1895. There followed a series of scientific romances (most notably *The Island of Dr. Moreau,* 1896; *The Invisible Man,* 1897; *The War of the Worlds,* 1898; *The First Men in the Moon,* 1901; and *The War in the Air,* 1908), which form the most familiar part of his work to modern readers. But he grew dissatisfied with the limitations imposed by this kind of writing, and in 1900 he moved into the novel proper with *Love and Mr. Lewisham,* a story of his student days at South Kensington. On this and particularly on *Kipps* (1905), *Tono-Bungay* (1909), and *The History of Mr. Polly* (1910), his serious literary reputation primarily depends.

Though these books are true novels, they are informed by a spirit of profound hostility to the Victorian social order and to the body of orthodox opinion which supported it. Desiring to make explicit his criticism of the past and his hopes for the future, Wells embarked on his career as a prophet with *Anticipations* (1901), *Mankind in the Making* (1903), and *A Modern Utopia* (1905). He thereby came to know George Bernard Shaw, who claimed that he and Wells between them had "changed the mind of Europe," and the other leaders of the Fabian Society. Joining this organization in 1903, he tried in 1906 and 1907 to turn it into a large-scale operation devoted to mass propaganda and political action. He was defeated in this effort by the "Old Gang" under Shaw's leadership, however, and he resigned from the society in 1908. This experience was the starting point for his last novel of literary importance, *The New Machiavelli* (1911), into which he introduced brilliant portraits of Sidney and Beatrice Webb and other noted Fabians.

Beginning in 1898, Henry James, who saw in Wells the most gifted writer of the age, had sought to make him a disciplined artist in fiction. For a time Wells tried to learn the lesson of the master, but after *The New Machiavelli* he turned frankly to the "dialogue novel" in which he could freely and rapidly give expression to his current preoccupations. He sealed his repudiation of James by a devastating parody in *Boon* (1915). During World War I, Wells proved himself to be an expert publicist, particularly in *Mr. Britling Sees It Through* (1916), which made him famous in the United States as well as England.

Having coined the hopeful phrase "the war that will end war" in 1914, Wells was thoroughly disillusioned by the peace settlement at which the Allies actually arrived. In the conviction that the future would be "a race between education and catastrophe," he endeavored to make the essentials of knowledge available to the great public through three massive works: the best-selling *Outline of History* (1920); *The Science of Life* (1931), in which he collaborated with his older son, George Philip Wells, and Sir Julian Huxley; and *The Work, Wealth, and Happiness* (1932). Meanwhile he had emerged as a popular celebrity, living the life of "telegrams and anger" in the great world, with each new shift in his opinions announced through syndicated articles. His key work of this period is *The Open Conspiracy: Blue Prints for a World Revolution* (1928), in which he urged the case for an integrated global civilization.

Wells' last book of enduring value was his *Experiment in Autobiography* (1934). But he continued to average two titles a year: some widely influential like *The Shape of Things to Come* (1933), which did much to awaken a large audience to the dangers threatening the West; and some vastly entertaining like *Apropos of Dolores* (1938), his hilarious tribute to an ex-mistress. He lived through World War II in his house on Regent's Park, abusing the current objects of his disfavor, large and small, from the Roman Catholic Church and Gen. Charles de Gaulle to a neighbor who had erected a large sign to mark the entrance to a servicemen's club some houses down Hanover Terrace. In his last book, a brief essay entitled *Mind at the End of Its Tether* (1945), he expressed the blankest pessimism about mankind's future prospects.

GORDON N. RAY,
Secretary General, John Simon Guggenheim Foundation.

Works

Philmus, Robert M., and Hughes, David, eds., *Early Writings in Science and Science Fiction* (Univ. of Calif. Press 1985).

The Works of H. G. Wells, the Atlantic Edition, 28 vols. (Scribner 1924–1927).

Correspondence

Gettmann, Royal, ed., *George Gissing and H. G. Wells* (Univ. of Ill. Press 1961).

Ray, Gordon N., and Edel, Leon, eds., *Henry James and H. G. Wells* (Univ. of Ill. Press 1958).

Wilson, Harris, ed., *Arnold Bennett and H. G. Wells* (Univ. of Ill. Press 1960).

Bibliography

Hammond, J. R., *Herbert George Wells: An Annotated Bibliography of His Works* (Garland 1977).

Biography

Brome, Vincent, *H. G. Wells: A Biography* (1951; reprint, R. West 1979).

Smith, David, *H. G. Wells: Desperately Mortal: A Biography* (Yale Univ. Press 1986).

Wells, H. G., *Experiment in Autobiography* (1934; reprint, Little 1984).

West, Anthony, *H. G. Wells: Aspects of a Life* (Random House 1984).

Criticism

Bloom, R., *Anatomies of Egotism: A Reading of the Last Novels of H. G. Wells* (Univ. of Neb. Press 1977).

Huntington, John, *The Logic of Fantasy: H. G. Wells and Science Fiction* (Columbia Univ. Press 1982).

Ray, Gordon N., "H. G. Wells Tries To Be a Novelist," *Edwardians and Late Victorians*, ed. by Richard Ellman (Columbia Univ. Press 1960).

WELLS, Horace, American dentist: b. Hartford, Vt., Jan. 21, 1815; d. New York, N.Y., Jan. 24, 1848. With William T. G. Morton, Charles T. Jackson, and Crawford W. Long (qq.v.), he was one of the four principals in the controversy over who deserved credit for the introduction of surgical anesthesia. Wells studied dentistry in Boston and opened his practice in Hartford, Conn. As early as 1840, he became interested in the narcotic effect of the inhalation of nitrous oxide, which had been known since the experiments of Sir Humphry Davy in 1799, and suggested its use as a means of lessening pain in the extraction of teeth. (In 1824, an Englishman, Henry Hill Hickman, had produced unconsciousness in animals by the use of nitrous oxide.) In 1844, Wells attended a demonstration by Gardner Q. Colton on the effects of the gas; he observed that at least one subject was apparently insensitive to pain of sufficient severity to suggest that nitrous oxide could be useful for dental extraction. Wells persuaded Colton to administer the gas to him, while another dentist, John W. Riggs, extracted one of Wells' teeth. Satisfied with the results, and having learned from Colton how to make nitrous oxide, Wells put the method to use in his practice. He was anxious to popularize his discovery, and in 1845, before he had mastered the technique of administering the gas, he went to Boston to see Morton, with whom he had formerly been engaged in an unsuccessful partnership, and who had entered Harvard University as a medical student. Morton took Wells to see Jackson, a chemist, who expressed an unfavorable opinion. However, Wells obtained permission to demonstrate his discovery before the class of John Collins Warren in the Harvard Medical School. The patient was not adequately anesthetized, the demonstration was a failure, and Wells was hissed out of the lecture room. He returned to Hartford, and, after one of his patients almost died of an overdose of nitrous oxide, he abandoned dentistry and turned to a variety of unsuccessful ventures.

In the meantime, Morton learned about ether from Jackson, and in October 1846 he successfully extracted a tooth in a demonstration at the Massachusetts General Hospital. Morton claimed he was using a special preparation of his own invention, called "letheon," and obtained a patent under that name. Long entered into the controversy because he employed ether in 1842, during the removal of a neck tumor; this was not reported until 1848.

In 1846, Wells claimed discovery of the use of nitrous oxide, and in 1847 brought out a pamphlet, *A History of the Discovery of the Application of Nitrous Oxide Gas, Ether, and Other Vapors, to Surgical Operations*. He had previously rejected the use of ether as potentially more harmful than nitrous oxide. After ether had been recognized as an anesthetic agent, he made abortive efforts to prove nitrous oxide superior, and induced a number of physicians to carry out major surgical operations with the gas. Opening an office in New York City, Wells continued his efforts, and also experimented with chloroform, often inhaling it for the exhilarating effect it produced. While under its influence, he created a disturbance and was imprisoned. Dejected, ashamed, and fearful for the loss of his mind, he slashed an artery in his thigh and died in a jail cell. Wells is generally given credit for priority in the use of inhalation anesthesia.

FREDERICK A. METTLER,
Professor of Medicine, College of Physicians and Surgeons, Columbia University.

WELLS, cathedral city, market town, and rural district, England, in Somerset, at the foot of the Mendip Hills, 16 miles southwest of Bath. Stone walls enclose not only the cathedral church, cloisters, chapter house, and burying ground, but the bishop's palace, the deanery, and the subdeanery—the whole a remarkable example of a complete, exclusive, ecclesiastical city. Wells has always been a secular cathedral, never a monastic or parish church.

A church appears to have been built here by King Ine of Wessex in the 8th century. It was later rebuilt and in 909 the bishopric was founded by Edward the Elder, son of Alfred the Great. About the end of the 11th century the see was transferred to Bath, but under Bishop Jocelyn (1206–1242) it returned to Wells and since 1224 successive bishops have always been "of Bath and Wells." The present church was begun about 1186 and building continued for some 200 years. Externally it is famed for its magnificent west front, adorned with more than 300 colored figures in the act of adoration, "a *Te Deum* in stone." Within the church the most striking feature is the inverted arch at the crossing, added in 1337 when the foundations of the tower began to give way in the watery soil. The nave and part of the choir are Transitional in style; the Lady Chapel is Decorated. Transepts and side chapels are of great interest and the Decorated chapter house is outstanding even in this distinguished company. Pop. (1961) 10,545.

H. GORDON STOKES.

WELLS AND WELL SINKING. Any excavation made to obtain water, oil, brine, gas, or information about the interior of the earth may be properly called a well. Since these excavations are made for many purposes and the complete treatment of the subject is very complex, this discussion is confined to wells constructed for the purpose of obtaining water and to a classification based on methods used in their construction. These basic methods are: (1) *digging*, (2) *tunneling*, (3) *drilling* or *boring*, and (4) *driving*. The first three methods are so ancient that their origin is lost in the mists of antiquity. Although new techniques have been introduced and effi-

Ewing Galloway

Above: **Old-fashioned country well with a wooden bucket.** *Below:* **Percussion drilling for water. The bit at the end of the cable first drills a hole, then drives down piping. Earth is removed from piping with a bailer-bucket.**

ciency has been increased many times, especially in the methods of drilling, developing, and pumping water, in many parts of the world the ancient procedures are still used.

Dug Wells.—Almost certainly, the first successful attempts to dig wells were made in North Africa, Asia Minor, and the arid parts of China. The art of well construction was already well known to the Egyptians by 2100 B.C., for Henu, an officer of the 11th dynasty, in describing one of his campaigns, says, "I went forth. . . . I made twelve wells in the bush and two wells in Idehit." Fourteen centuries later the Assyrian ruler Sennacherib made free use of dug wells, and the Old Testament of the Bible makes frequent references to wells. In the 6th century B.C., many houses in Athens were supplied with water from wells, and in Rome many of the houses had dug wells before the first aqueduct was constructed in 312 B.C. In many parts of the world where labor is cheap and machinery is scarce, well digging is still the most practical way to obtain groundwater.

Dug wells are essentially shafts sunk by manual labor from the land surface to a depth some distance below the water table, or groundwater level. If they are dug through hard rock, a wall is commonly built around the mouth of the well in order to limit the entrance of water from the land surface during storms and to prevent soil from sloughing into the well. However, if they are dug through material such as sand and clay, the walls must be shored up as the digging progresses in order to prevent caving in. The materials used for this purpose were originally stone blocks, but in modern times other materials such as wooden staves, brick, concrete tile, and sheet metal have been used. Even with the best of protection, debris accumulates in these wells and they must be cleaned out periodically. Thus, Jacob's well, which is one of the few mentioned in the Bible identified by all authorities, was originally 150 feet deep and more than 7½ feet in diameter, but its present depth is 75 feet and it is no longer usable. Most dug wells are less than 100 feet deep, but depths of 400 to 500 feet are not uncommon.

Generally the water is raised from the wells by a rope attached to a bucket made of skin, or, later, of such materials as wood and steel. However, some wells were so constructed that people and even animals had direct access to the water by means of stairs or ramps built during the construction of the well. Where the water is found within 30 or 40 feet of the surface it is not uncommon to raise the water to the surface by means of small buckets attached to an endless chain that passes over a large wheel at the surface and dumps its water into a trough leading away from the well. This system is in common use throughout the Orient today. Other methods of raising water to the surface, such as Archimedes spirals (see ARCHIMEDES' SCREW), were also devised.

Tunneling.—perhaps the most ingenious device for obtaining groundwater was the kanat, *ghanat* or *qanat* (many other names are also used), an inclined tunnel driven into the detrital materials or outwash fans bordering mountain ranges. These are very common in the region extending from the western end of the Atlas Range in Morocco eastward across North Africa, in Arabia, northern Syria, and in Iran. After an exploratory shaft has been sunk to find the water table, the chief of the diggers' guild selects the site for the portal with appropriate ceremonies, and tunneling begins. The direction and slope are determined by crude surveying instruments consisting of a plumb bob and a notched stick. At distances upslope, rarely exceeding 100 yards, new shafts are sunk as tunneling progresses. The joining of these tunnels from shaft to shaft, even with modern surveying instruments, is difficult, but with the crude instruments used by kanat diggers their construction is nothing less than marvelous. The tunnels are just large enough for a small man, kneeling or lying, and they are not lined, so that fatal accidents due to caving in are common. When the work is completed, water flows freely from the portal by gravity, and a satisfactory water supply is assured. Formerly, when Teheran, capital of Iran, was a city of 275,000, its water supply came from 36 of these kanats, 8 to 16 miles long. Some kanats reach a depth of 500 feet below the land surface, and depths of 200 feet are fairly common. Because they are not supported by lining, the average life of any single kanat is probably not more than a few scores of years. Moreover, if the water level should decline, the yield of the kanat would also decline and it would be necessary to construct a new kanat, possibly at a lower level. However, the kanats of Teheran were said to be more than 200 years old. The earliest kanat on record seems to have been that at Nineveh, which was constructed about 800 B.C.

***Below:* Well, windmill, and tank—standby of the old West.**

Ewing Galloway

Ewing Galloway

***Above:* Water for irrigating an Arizona farm is raised from a well with lift pump driven by a diesel engine.**

Well Drilling.—Long before the Christian era, wells were drilled to depths of hundreds of feet by the Chinese and the Egyptians to obtain flowing water (see ARTESIAN WELLS). The method and the equipment were crude forerunners of modern cable-tool or percussion drills. (See PETROLEUM—5. *Drilling and Production Methods.*) To prevent caving in of the wells, the Chinese used lengths of hollow bamboo stalks. Apparently the Egyptians used logs hollowed out at great effort. Many of the Egyptian wells, some still flowing, have recently been uncovered in the oases of the Western Desert, and fragments of casing have been recovered. Radiocarbon dating (q.v.) may tell us their age; they are believed to date as early as 1500 B.C.

Drilling for water was introduced in Europe about 1126 A.D., when a deep-flowing well was drilled at Artois, France, and about the same time flowing wells were completed in northern Italy. These successes led to more general interest in well drilling, and by the beginning of the 19th century a number of drilled wells had been completed. However, progress was retarded to some extent by lack of adequate pumping equipment in areas where the artesian pressure was insufficient to produce a flow of water, and by the difficulties of supporting the walls of deep wells drilled through soft materials. Although drilling had been adopted in other parts of Europe, the most famous deep wells were drilled in the Paris Basin at Passy, La Chappelle, and Grenelle. These wells penetrated numerous caving formations, and the lining had to be lowered steadily as the drilling proceeded. Because the lining was structurally weak cave-ins were common, the linings collapsed, and drilling tools were lost. Altogether, these wells were costly and time consuming. For example, the well at Grenelle was completed at a depth of 1,741 feet in 1841 after seven and one-half years of unremitting labor. However, the experience gained in repairing linings and retrieving lost tools has since proved of great value to the well-drilling industry.

In the United States the methods of drilling were imported from England and France. Among the earliest drilled wells reported were those drilled for brine in West Virginia and Pennsylvania about 1805. But many other wells were drilled for water, and the practice of drilling grew until it practically replaced digging.

Percussion drilling is best adapted to hard-rock areas, but it is still used in some areas where caving walls are hazardous. However, in many parts of the country it has been almost entirely replaced by rotary or other methods. Since about 1955, a revolutionary system for hard-rock drilling, *down-hole drilling,* has been gaining favor. The working head is essentially similar to a jackhammer, suspended from a hollow drill stem and controlled from a movable truck-mounted mast. The hammer, or bit, pulverizes the rock at the bottom of the hole and the cuttings are literally blown out of the hole by highly compressed air, forced downward through the drill stem. This method proceeds many times faster than cable-tool drilling. However, it is limited to depths of about 125 feet, as compared to about 5,000 feet for the cable-tool drill.

Rotary drilling (see PETROLEUM—5. *Drilling and Production Methods*), first used in the United States about 1901, has gained favor in the oil and gas industry in most areas where unconsolidated sediments are penetrated, and in many areas it is the standard method for drilling water wells, especially where large yields are required. Other standard methods, less widely used, are *augering* with a tool similar to a carpenter's auger, and *jetting* with a high velocity stream of water which erodes soft materials from the bottom of the hole and carries the cuttings to the surface. Various combinations of the above methods are used when the rock conditions require.

Driving.—In areas where the rock formations are soft and the water table is near the surface, small-yield wells are often obtained by driving a small pipe fitted with a screen or perforated pipe into the ground by means of a heavy weight mounted on a derrick or tripod, raised and lowered by hand or by machine. These wells are rarely more than 50 feet deep. They are used for water supply, but more commonly several of them are connected to a single suction pump and used to dewater foundations for piers and other structures.

Casing, Screening, and Development.—Many wells drilled in hard rocks require only enough casing to retain the walls through the soil zone where caving in might occur. The remainder of the well is supported by the strength of the rocks themselves. However, in unconsolidated materials it is generally necessary to support the walls for the entire depth of the hole. The casing usually consists of threaded steel pipe of approximately the same diameter as the hole. The best practice is to string separate joints together in such a way that, when they are in position, specially selected screens will be opposite the water-bearing sands so as to permit water to enter the well. In some cases blank steel casing is set, and a special device is lowered into the well to perforate the casing opposite water-bearing sands. However, other materials, such as concrete pipe, may be used where local conditions warrant. If large yields are desired (100 to 3,000 gallons per minute) the development of the well may be as important as any other part of its construction. In hard rocks this consists of opening or enlarging as many crevices as possible by setting off explosive charges in the water-bearing zone, by introducing carbon dioxide under pressure, or with strong acid solutions or other chemicals. If the water is found in unconsolidated sand, the yield may be increased many times by extremely heavy pumping (overpumping) or by alternate pumping and back-pressuring so as to create a surging action. This pulls the finer materials into the well, where they are carried along with the discharging water, and leaves the coarser, more pervious, materials around the screen. Thus, the water enters the well more readily. The same purpose is served by introducing gravel (usually pea-sized) into the sand around the screen by one of several methods prior to the development by pumping.

The selection of the proper pumping machinery is a most important consideration in the development of water supplies (see PUMPS AND PUMPING MACHINERY). There are many types of pumps and each has certain advantages and serves a special purpose. The type of pump selected for a well depends on a variety of factors such as the depth to water, the diameter of the well, the quantity of water desired or available, and quite often the local preferences. Where the water level during pumping is less than 20 feet below the surface of the land, one of several types of suction pumps is suitable. Where the water level is deeper, one of the lift types of pump must be used. If relatively small quantities of water are required, as for household use or stock wells, the reciprocating or displacement type of pump is efficient and satisfactory, but where quantities ranging from about 100 to several thousand gallons per minute are needed, one of the impeller-type pumps having a diameter small enough to be lowered into the well is generally used.

The power used for pumping also depends on many factors. During the period of the settlement of the West, windmills were in common use for farmsteads and stock watering, but, where a dependable water supply was needed, steam engines were used. These have been replaced to a very large extent by internal combustion engines or by electric motors, especially where large supplies are needed and dependability is essential.

Depth of Wells.—The depth to which wells can be drilled has been increasing steadily for scores of years. Several oil wells have been drilled to depths greater than 25,000 feet, and it seems likely that, as technology advances, much greater depths may be reached, providing economic considerations warrant the cost. For water wells, the limiting factors are not only cost, but the potability of the water. In general, potable water is not likely to be found at depths greater than

5,000 feet, and relatively few wells produce potable water from this depth. Some large-yield wells are as much as 3,000 feet deep, but most are 2,000 feet deep or less. This depends chiefly on the geology and hydrology of the area in which the well is situated. The geology of the United States is widely varied, but on the average the range in depth of wells yielding potable water would be much less than 1,000 feet and probably less than 500 feet.

A. NELSON SAYRE, *U.S. Geological Survey*

Further Reading: Brantly, J. E., *History of Oil Well Drilling* (Gulf Publishing 1971); Chenevert, M., and Williams, F., *Applied Drilling Engineering Manual* (Gulf Publishing 1983); Craft, B. C., and others, *Well Design: Drilling and Production* (Prentice-Hall 1962); Gibson, U. P., and Singer, R. D., *Water Well Manual: A Practical Guide for Locating and Constructing Wells for Individual and Small Community Water Supplies* (Premier Press 1971).

WELLS CATHEDRAL. See under WELLS.

WELLS FARGO, a corporation controlled by the American Express Company, active in the United States in armored-car services and in Mexico in the travel agency and hotel business. The original Wells Fargo & Company was organized in 1852 by Henry Wells, William G. Fargo, and others after the California gold rush. By 1853 it was established as a shipper and banker for miners, and by 1856 was the leading express company in California. The company owned the Pony Express during the last few months before the transcontinental telegraph replaced the service in 1861. With its incorporation in 1866, the company absorbed the Holladay Overland Mail and Express Company, became the owner of the most extensive stagecoach network in the United States, and controlled almost all express service west of the Missouri River. Adjusting to the replacement of stagecoaches by railroads, the company gradually bought rail rights, completing its transcontinental rail route in 1888.

The pioneering mail service of Wells Fargo in California and Oregon ended in 1895. In 1905, the company's banking operation was sold, becoming the Wells Fargo Nevada National Bank (now the Wells Fargo Bank, with headquarters in San Francisco). The inauguration of government parcel post service in 1912 doomed Wells Fargo as an express company. In 1918 it transferred its domestic express operations to American Railway Express Company. Mexican and Cuban subsidiaries continued express operations for three decades. As the Latin-American express business ceased, armored service to banks in the United States grew.

WELS, vels, a city in Austria, the second-largest city in the province of Upper Austria, in the Alpine Foreland on the Traun River, about 25 miles (40 km) southwest of Linz. A trading and industrial center, the city manufactures agricultural implements and machinery, food products, and earthenware. It has natural-gas deposits and hydroelectric power. The Welser Fair is held during September in alternate years.

Wels was founded in 15 B.C. as the Roman Ovilava, and was an important crossroad center and stronghold against the Avars and the Magyars. Holy Roman Emperor Maximilian I died in the castle in Wels in 1519. The city has buildings in the late Gothic and Baroque styles of architecture. Population: (1981) 51,024.

GEORGE W. HOFFMAN, *University of Texas*

WELSBACH, vels′bäKH, **Carl Auer von** (1858–1929), Austrian chemist and inventor, best known for his invention of the gas mantle still used in camping lanterns. Carl Auer was born in Vienna on Sept. 1, 1858. He received his Ph.D. in chemistry at Heidelberg under Robert Bunsen in 1882. Three years later, in 1885, he isolated two new rare-earth metals, neodymium and praseodymium. This work made him the first and only Austrian to discover a new element. Auer continued to publish fundamental studies on the rare earths throughout his career.

In 1885, Auer found that certain earths were intensely luminous when heated, and in 1886 he applied this discovery in a revolutionary lighting device, the gas mantle. After a fabric net (mantle) impregnated with a mixture of thorium and cerium compounds is burned, the remaining oxide ash structure is readily heated to a brilliant incandescence. Gas lamps equipped with Welsbach mantles were far superior to the smoky, noxious gas burners then common and permitted the gas illumination industry to survive another two decades in competition with the newly invented incandescent electric lamp.

Auer's other important inventions included misch metal, the rare-earth alloy used for lighter flints, and an osmium filament for electric lamps that displaced Edison's carbon filament. Although the osmium filament was in turn displaced by the tungsten filament, Auer's method for shaping infusible metals for filaments and some other applications is still preferred.

Auer was raised to a hereditary baronage in 1911, after which his name became Carl Auer von Welsbach. He died at his estate near Treibach in Carinthia on Aug. 4, 1929.

A. J. ROCKE
Case Western Reserve University

WELSH CORGI. See CARDIGAN WELSH CORGI; PEMBROKE WELSH CORGI.

WELSH LANGUAGE AND LITERATURE. See CELTIC LANGUAGES; CELTIC LITERATURES; WALES—*The People and Their Cultural Heritage*.

WELSH PONY, an ancient breed of small Welsh horses and one of the most popular and numerous of the ponies. Related to the Welsh mountain pony and the Welsh cob, it may be traced to

The trim, delicate lines of the Welsh pony result from an infusion of Thoroughbred genes in the 19th century.

early Saxon times. Early in the 19th century, Welsh ponies were interbred to some extent with the Thoroughbreds. As a result modern Welsh ponies tend to have the delicate head and trim limbs characteristic of that breed. In spite of their small size they are outstanding jumpers. For many years a Welsh pony was the U.S. open jumping champion.

Welsh ponies are usually nearly a foot (30 cm) taller than the better-known Shetland ponies. They average about 12.2 hands (49 inches, or 125 cm) in height at the withers.

WELSH SPRINGER SPANIEL, a flushing and retrieving sporting dog from Wales that somewhat resembles both the Brittany and the English springer spaniels. Its average height is 17 inches (43 cm), and its average weight is 40 pounds (18 kg). Its medium-length red-and-white coat is flat, silky, and somewhat feathered. It has drop ears, and its tail is docked.

As a pet the Welsh springer has much more to recommend it than its lack of popularity in the United States would suggest. It is not only easy to groom but also easy to live with, since it is as gentle, obedient, and loving as any of the other spaniel breeds. An additional virtue is that it is less outgoing than the other spaniels. Indeed, for families who want a fairly retiring dog, the Welsh springer might well be the breed of choice, provided that it is socialized very early so that it does not grow up timid. Prospective owners should check the puppy's bloodlines for epilepsy, to which the breed is predisposed. This problem aside, the Welsh springer is likely to be healthier than the overbred cocker spaniel.

JOHN HOWE
Author of "Choosing the Right Dog"

The Welsh springer spaniel is a good dog for people who want a quiet, gentle, obedient, and easy-to-groom pet.

WELSH TERRIER, one of the more popular of the dog breeds that originated in Wales. The male's height at the shoulder should be 15 inches (38 cm), and the female's slightly less. For either sex the standard weight is about 20 pounds (9 kg). The breed's short wiry coat is either black and tan or grizzle and tan and requires regular stripping and trimming. The dog has fold-over ears, and its tail is docked.

Compared with milder-mannered breeds, most terriers are handfuls to manage: high-spirited, feisty, and impulsive. They are also loyal, loving, vigilant, hardy, and fine for older children to roughhouse with. Less excitable than the fox terrier, less scrappy than the Irish, and less rowdy than the young Airedale, the Welsh terrier presents only one real drawback to terrier lovers: the amount of work entailed in keeping its coat looking spruce. Occasional female puppies are hard to housebreak.

The Welsh terrier has a look-alike: the less well-known Lakeland terrier, which is slightly smaller and possibly slightly more headstrong.

JOHN HOWE
Author of "Choosing the Right Dog"

The high-spirited Welsh terrier is a reliable watchdog and a good companion for those who like an active dog.

WELSH v. UNITED STATES, a 1970 decision of the U.S. Supreme Court that held that moral or ethical objections to war could justify draft exemption. The decision interpreted the Universal Military Training and Service Act as allowing a person who was "conscientiously opposed to participation in war in any form" to avoid induction into the armed forces.

Four justices decided that the objector's sincere and meaningful beliefs need not be confined in either source or content to traditional or parochial concepts of religion. Justice John Harlan agreed with the result but thought that the congressional limitation of this draft exemption to those opposed to war because of theistic beliefs was unconstitutional under the 1st Amendment.

RICHARD L. HIRSHBERG, *Attorney at Law*

WELTY, wel'tē, **Eudora** (1909–), American writer, whose short stories and novels, through precisely observed details and graceful prose, convey the nuances of human behavior.

Eudora Welty was born on April 13, 1909, in Jackson, Miss. She attended Mississippi State College for Women and in 1929 received a B.A. degree from the University of Wisconsin. During the Depression she traveled throughout Mississippi as a publicity agent for the Works Progress Administration. (An outgrowth of this work was her series of photographs of the people and places she encountered, a selection of which was published in 1971.) She had trained to be a

© MISSISSIPPI DEPARTMENT OF ARCHIVES AND HISTORY

U.S. author Eudora Welty won a Pulitzer Prize in 1973.

writer since girlhood, when she had listened intently to the anecdotes and gossip of the adults around her. Her short story *Death of a Traveling Salesman* was published in 1936, and her first collection of stories, *A Curtain of Green*, appeared in 1941. For one of these stories, *The Worn Path*, Welty won the first of several O. Henry Memorial Contest awards. Her second collection of stories, *The Wide Net* (1943), also was critically acclaimed, and accolades continued for her first full-length novel, *Delta Wedding* (1946).

Welty lived virtually her entire life in Jackson, and most of her works are set in Mississippi. Despite this, and despite her unfailing ear for Southern dialect, her themes go beyond regional concerns. Recurring motifs are the duality of human nature—the essential isolation of the individual that conflicts with the desire for relationships—and the responsibilities and rewards of family and community bonds. Her novels tend to focus on family complexities, while her stories more often deal with isolated individuals. Her writing is distinguished by extensive use of monologue and dialogue and by an acute awareness of life's ironies and ambiguities.

Eudora Welty won the William Dean Howells Medal of the American Academy in 1955 for her novel *The Ponder Heart* (1954). Both it and *The Robber Bridegroom* (1942) were produced on Broadway. In 1973 she received the Pulitzer Prize for *The Optimist's Daughter* (1972), another novel. Her other works include *The Golden Apples* (1943), a group of interrelated stories; the novel *Losing Battles* (1970); and *Collected Stories* (1981). *One Writer's Beginnings* (1984), is an autobiographical sketch based on a series of Harvard lectures.

WELWITSCHIA, wel-wich′ē-ə, one of the most extraordinary of all plants, found only in a narrow belt of coastal desert, extending from the vicinity of Moçâmedes in Angola to the Namib Desert in South West Africa. In appearance *Welwitschia* resembles a huge wooden carrot with its top barely protruding from the ground. Beneath the ground the trunk tapers into a long taproot often 20 to 40 feet (6–12 meters) deep and sometimes as deep as 60 feet (18 meters). The huge taproot enables *Welwitschia* to survive in regions where rains may be years apart.

The protruding part of the trunk, which may be more than 3 feet (1 meter) in diameter, has a bowl-shaped top. Two leathery strap-shaped leaves, sometimes more than 10 feet (3 meters) long, lie on the ground beside the trunk—one growing from each side of the "bowl." The two leaves—the only ones the plant will ever have—grow continually from the base. Wind action wears away their tips and splits them lengthwise, so a mature plant seems to have several leaves. Some specimens may be 1,500 to 2,000 years old—not so old as bristlecone pines but comparable to redwoods.

Male and female cones are borne on separate plants from January to April. Pollination is by insects. The mature seeds have broad wings and are dispersed by wind.

The only species is *Welwitschia mirabilis*, the sole member of the family Welwitschiidae in the division Pinophyta (gymnosperms).

WEN, a benign, globular, cystic tumor of the skin, which may grow to be the size of a walnut or larger. It occurs mostly on the head, less often on the trunk and scrotum. As a rule, wens appear singly but may be multiple, especially on the scalp. Most of them contain horny material (keratinous cysts); others are filled with sebum (sebaceous cysts). The contents of the latter are frequently putrid and occasionally may become infected.

Generally, wens do not have an opening on the skin surface. The epidermal cells that line their walls produce sebum, horny material, or both. These products distend the walls, resulting in a slow growth over many years. Treatment consists either of complete excision or scraping off of the entire cyst wall. Unless the lining cells are fully removed, the wen will recur. Cancerous degeneration is very rare.

PETER FLESCH, *University of Pennsylvania*

Welwitschia in the Namib Desert. The plant's two long leaves have been torn to thin ribbons by wind.

© CAROL HUGHES/BRUCE COLEMAN, INC.

WENATCHEE, wə-năch'ē, city, Washington, seat of Chelan County, on the Columbia River just below the mouth of the Wenatchee River (Wenatchi is Indian for "river issuing from a canyon"); at an altitude of 636 feet. Situated at the geographical center of the state, it is almost equidistant from Spokane and Seattle. The city claims the title of "Apple Capital of the World" because of the extensive apple orchards in the district, for which it is the shipping and processing center, and it is host to the annual Washington State Apple Blossom Festival. A balmy sun and cool nights also give Wenatchee an ideal climate for producing soft fruits, such as cherries, apricots, and peaches. There is an aluminum plant and a flour mill. Its airport is named after Clyde Pangborn, a native son who landed in Wenatchee after his nonstop transpacific flight in 1931.

As a gateway to central Washington's recreational facilities in the Cascade Range—swimming, boating, fishing, camping, and skiing—Wenatchee receives a large number of tourists. It is the site of Wenatchee Valley College, Washington State University Tree Fruit Experiment Station, the United States Public Health Service Toxicology Laboratory, the North Central Washington Museum, and the North Central Regional Library serving a five-county area of 15,000 square miles. Founded in 1888, the city was incorporated on a new site in 1892. It has a commission form of government. Pop. 17,257.

ANNIE KOINZAN.

WENCESLAS, wĕn'səs-lôs, **SAINT** and **DUKE OF BOHEMIA** (Czech **SVÁTÝ VÁCLAV**; Ger. **WENZEL**): b. about 907; d. Stará Boleslav (Bohemia), Sept. 28, 929. Václav was descended from the Přemyslid dynasty, the origin of which is shrouded in legend. The Přemyslids acquired control over a Slav tribe, the Czechs, who were settled in the area around Prague (now in Czechoslovakia). During the 9th century the Přemyslids gradually united most of Bohemia (western Czechoslovakia). Historical records mention the grandparents of Václav: the duke Bořivoj and his wife Ludmila, already Christians. Václav's father, Vratislav (r. about 915–920), married Drahomíra, daughter of a prince of the still heathen Lutices (a tribe in Lusatia, East Germany). Upon Vratislav's death, when Václav was only about 13, his mother, Drahomíra, ruled. Drahomíra, resenting the influence that Václav's grandmother, Ludmila, exercised on her son's upbringing, had Ludmila murdered. Ludmila had been responsible for the thorough Christian education of Václav. Following Ludmila's reburial in 925 at the St. Vitus Church in Prague there spread legends about her, culminating in her sainthood. Drahomíra's rule caused strife which resulted in the 15-year-old Václav's assuming power about 922. He was killed by his brother, Boleslav, in 929 while visiting the latter's castle.

His seven-year rule was marked by relatively good relations with the German neighbors, in spite of a military defeat administered by the German king Henry I, and by the spread of Christianity among his subjects, as evidenced by the construction of many stone churches. Acceptance among his Christian German neighbors as a Christian Slavic ruler gave Václav sufficient prestige to combat centrifugal forces in his lands, thereby continuing the Přemyslids' efforts at unifying the Slavs in Bohemia. Václav became a symbol of the Czech nation as well as the patron saint of Czechoslovakia. The crown of subsequent Czech rulers was named in his honor. His statue occupies a dominant position in Václavské Náměsti (Wenceslas Square), the main thoroughfare in Prague. His efforts to Christianize his people at a time when Bohemia had only a thin Christian veneer, coupled with his dramatic murder, gave rise to many legends leading to his sainthood. His murderer and brother, Boleslav, who succeeded him as ruler (929–967), had Václav's relics brought to the St. Vitus Church in Prague about 932. The well-known English Christmas carol, *Good King Wenceslaus,* written by John Mason Neale in the 19th century, is based on a somewhat far-fetched legend about the deeds of the martyred king.

CURT F. BECK,
Professor of Political Science, The University of Connecticut.

WENCESLAS or **VÁCLAV** (Ger. **WENZEL**), four kings of Bohemia. Although Wenceslas is the name most familiar to English-speaking readers, Václav is the preferred Czech form and will be employed in the text.

WENCESLAS or VÁCLAV I: b. 1205; d. Sept. 22, 1253. A member of the Přemyslid dynasty, he was the son of Otakar I and the father of Otakar II, both stronger rulers than he. He married Kunigunde of Hohenstaufen in 1224 and was crowned king of Bohemia in 1228 while his father was still ruler, thereby preventing a battle over the succession, a perennial plague of the Přemyslid dynasty.

Václav became sole ruler on his father's death, Dec. 15, 1230. Under his father's reign Bohemia's position within the Holy Roman Empire had been considerably strengthened, the Bohemian kingdom having been given permanent recognition by the German Emperor Frederick II. Under Václav's reign there was substantial economic growth and cultural development, especially in art, poetry, and chivalry. German settlers were attracted to Bohemia and were granted special rights, and towns were founded. All this occurred in spite of frequent warfare. Václav aligned himself at one time with the emperor, at another with the pope, and in 1241 he succeeded in repelling the Mongols who had invaded Moravia. The years 1248–1250 were marred by an insurrection of his nobles in which his son, Otakar, joined forces with the insurgents, but Václav held the throne until his death.

WENCESLAS or VÁCLAV II: b. 1271; d. June 21, 1305. He was only seven when his father, Otakar II, the most powerful of the Přemyslid kings, was decisively defeated at the Battle of Marchfeld, Aug. 26, 1278. Neighboring rulers interfered in Bohemian affairs, and Václav spent five years as a prisoner of Otto of Brandenburg. In 1283, though only 12, Václav nominally assumed the government of Bohemia, but the real ruler was Zaviš, a nobleman who married Václav's mother. In 1287, Václav assumed full control, banishing and then killing Zaviš. Václav married Guta of Habsburg in accordance with a political arrangement made by his father in 1276. After her death in 1298 he married a Polish princess and became king of Poland (1300). In spite of the inauspicious beginning and his premature death, Václav's reign was marked by territorial expansion and economic prosperity. Mining towns prospered, and riches in ore resulted in coinage reform. The mining industry was also organized at this time.

WENCESLAS or VÁCLAV III: b. 1289; d. Olomouc, Moravia (now Czechoslovakia), Aug. 4, 1306. He was the son of Wenceslas (Václav) II. In 1301 he assumed the Hungarian crown, which he kept until 1304. On his father's death in 1305, he took the Bohemian crown and was about to deal with a revolt by the Polish nobility when he was murdered. With him the Přemyslid dynasty ended.

WENCESLAS or VÁCLAV IV, German emperor (1378–1400) and king of Bohemia (1378–1419): b. Feb. 26, 1361; d. Prague (now in Czechoslovakia), Aug. 16, 1419. He was the son of Charles I (Charles IV as German emperor) of the Luxemburg dynasty under which Bohemia had prospered economically and culturally. In 1394 the Bohemian nobility formed a conspiracy against him, holding him a prisoner for three months. Through the influence of the archbishop of Mainz, whose enmity he had aroused, he was deposed as German emperor by the imperial electors in 1400. He continued as king of Bohemia until his death. His reign in Bohemia was marked by a widespread reaction against the excesses of the nobility and clergy and the rivalry between Czechs and Germans which led to the meteoric rise of Jan Hus. Václav lacked the inclination and power to break the Hus heresy, and violent civil war followed in the wake of Václav's death.

CURT F. BECK,
Professor of Political Science, University of Connecticut.

WENCHOW or **WEN-CHOU,** wĕn'chou, Chin. wŭn'jō', municipality (*shih*) and city, China, in southeastern Chekiang Province. The principal commercial center for the province, Wenchow is a port on the south bank of the Wu Kiang estuary, 15 miles inland from the East China Sea, and 160 miles south-southeast of Hangchow. It is an important timber and bamboo shipping port, and also manufactures paper umbrellas, leather goods, and straw mats. Wenchow was opened to foreign trade in 1876, and the city was a major tea-exporting port during the latter part of the 19th century. During the Sino-Japanese War of 1937–1945, Wenchow was occupied briefly by the Japanese (1944–1945), but control of the area subsequently passed to the Chinese Communists in 1949, when it became a municipality. Pop. (1982 census) 325,000.

NORTON GINSBURG.

WENDELL, wĕn'dəl, **Barrett,** American teacher and man of letters: b. Boston, Mass., Aug. 23, 1855; d. there, Feb. 8, 1921. He was graduated from Harvard University in 1877 and prepared himself for a law career, but found that the prospect did not appeal to him. He was asked to help Professor Adams Sherman Hill teach English composition to Harvard undergraduates; he accepted the position, and stayed at Harvard until his retirement in 1917 as professor emeritus of English.

An inspired teacher and critic, Wendell introduced the first course in American literature at Harvard in 1898, publishing *A Literary History of America* in 1900. He also inaugurated the exchange of professors between Harvard and French universities in 1904–1905 and wrote *The France of Today* (1907), considered by many his best work. Other books are *Cotton Mather, the Puritan Priest* (1891) and *The Traditions of European Literature from Homer to Dante* (1920).

WENDS, wĕndz, the name of a group of Slavonic tribes which, by the 5th century A.D., occupied the region in Germany between the Oder River on the east and the Elbe and Saale rivers on the west. They constituted the western rim of the great mass of Slavic peoples who had pressed in behind the Germans south of the Baltic, as the latter moved westward and southward during the period of the *Völkerwanderung*. Even before the time of Christ small bands may have begun to infiltrate among the Germans. Later it became a mass movement as the Germans vacated the land.

The German reaction against the Slavs had its inception in the rise of the Frankish kingdom, which conquered Thuringia in 531. The real offensive began with the founding of the mission posts of Boniface in the 8th century; and the military and religious subjugation of the pagan Wends got into full swing after the completion of Charlemagne's conquest of the Saxons in 804. Halted in the later 9th century, the movement was resumed under Henry I in the 10th century. In 929 a coalition formed by the threatened Wendish tribes was defeated and crushed, and German military control was quickly extended to the Oder and the Erzgebirge. But the success was only temporary. German power east of the Elbe, except in Nordalbingia and Holstein, collapsed during the Wendish rebellion of 983. Not until the accession of Lothar II in 1125 did German eastward expansion resume, this time involving a great movement of colonization by German peasants into the lands wrested from the Wends. Merchants and princes also moved in to found towns that began the commercial development of northern Germany. In 1147 the church authorized a crusade which furthered the work of destruction of the Wends.

Great numbers of the Wends were exterminated in the centuries-long conflict; the rest were Christianized and reduced to serfdom. Some were absorbed by the Germans who surrounded them, but scattered groups held tenaciously to their ancient language and customs. Today the Wends are mostly confined to a small territory in the Upper Spree Valley, in Lusatia. Their dialects (Upper and Lower Lusatian, with subdivisions based on minor shades of pronunciation) belong to the western stem of Slavonic languages, which also includes Polish and Czech. Many German words have entered the present language of the Wends, and German letters are used in their publications. Early writings are generally of a religious nature, but since the revival of national feeling about the middle of the 19th century a number of writers, chiefly poets, have appeared. The recognized literary leader in Lower Lusatian is Mato Kósyk (1853–1940). Outstanding in Upper Lusatian is Handrij Zejleř (1804–1872) and Ćišinski (Jakub Bart, 1856–1909). Their works reflect the peasant milieu as well as the heroic and tragic history of the medieval Wends. Ćišinski, generally considered the finest of the Lusatian poets, exhibits an intense preoccupation with the problem of the national survival of his people. These writers, and others, have also produced some prose works in the Lusatian dialects, but they are of lesser significance.

FRED C. HAMIL
Professor of History, Wayne State University

WENNER-GREN, vĕn'nər-grān, **Axel Leonard,** Swedish industrialist: b. Uddevalla, Göteborg och Bohus County, Sweden, June 5, 1881; d. Stockholm, Nov. 24, 1961. The son of a well-to-do import-export merchant, he became a sales representative of the Lux Company, a Swedish concern making light bulbs, for which he gained the contract to light the Panama Canal when it opened in 1914. In 1920 he formed the Electrolux Company, through which he made a fortune producing vacuum cleaners and later refrigerators. Meanwhile he had married Marguerite Gauntier of Kansas City, Mo., a former opera singer. In 1935, with a group of other Swedish businessmen, Wenner-Gren bought a major interest in the Bofors Munitions Works, the Swedish branch of Krupp, and in the years that followed he was active in behind-the-scenes international political maneuvers that were generally regarded as favoring appeasement of the Nazis. He was blacklisted by the United States State Department in 1942 for supposed business dealings with the Hitler regime after World War II began, but continued to spend considerable time in Latin America, where he acquired extensive, diversified holdings, notably in Mexico. By the end of the war he was believed to be one of the richest men in the world. His postwar fields of activity included heavy investments in Canada and development of the Alweg monorail system. He gave large sums to philanthropic enterprises, including various foundations for scientific and social research and cultural activities in Sweden and the other Scandinavian countries, and the Wenner-Gren Foundation for Anthropological Research, in New York City.

WENTWORTH, wĕnt'wûrth, **Benning,** English provincial governor of New Hampshire: b. Portsmouth, N.H., July 24, 1696; d. there, Oct. 14, 1770. He was graduated from Harvard in 1715 and became a merchant in Portsmouth, which he represented in the provincial assembly for a time. He was appointed a king's councilor in 1734 and was named the first royal governor of the province in 1741. Between 1749 and 1764 he made large grants of unoccupied land west of the Connecticut River in what is now southern Vermont, known as the New Hampshire Grants (q.v.). The first of these (now Bennington, Vt.) was named in his honor. The land affected by the various grants was claimed by the colonial government of New York, but Governor Wentworth maintained his authority and a long wrangle followed (see also VERMONT—*10. History*).

Meanwhile, complaints were being made in England that Wentworth had been guilty of nepotism, had taken exorbitant fees for land grants, had set aside 500 acres for himself in each township, and had been informal and inaccurate in awarding the grants. His conduct as surveyor of the King's Woods also was criticized. Finally permitted to resign, he was succeeded by his nephew, John Wentworth (q.v.). The story of Benning Wentworth's second marriage, to Martha Hilton, a serving maid in his house, is told in Henry Wadsworth Longfellow's poem *Lady Wentworth.*

WENTWORTH, Charles Watson-. See ROCKINGHAM, 2D MARQUIS OF.

WENTWORTH, John, American journalist and political leader: b. Sandwich, N.H., March 5, 1815; d. Chicago, Ill., Oct. 16, 1888. He was graduated from Dartmouth in 1836 and the same year went to Chicago, where friends helped him to buy the *Weekly Democrat*. Establishing it as a daily in 1840, he made it the foremost newspaper of the Northwest. At the same time he studied law and was admitted to the Illinois bar in 1841. He was elected to the United States Congress in 1843 and served six terms (over a 24-year period). Wentworth was active in obtaining issuance of the Chicago city charter and was elected mayor in 1857; he served one year, declined a second term, but was elected again in 1860. He introduced the city's first steam fire engine and first paid fire department, and as an editor he was an earnest promoter of the public schools. The *Democrat* was sold to the Chicago *Daily Tribune* in 1861, but Wentworth remained active in public life for many years thereafter.

WENTWORTH, SIR John, English colonial administrator: b. Portsmouth, N.H., Aug. 20, 1737; d. Halifax, Nova Scotia, April 8, 1820. He was graduated from Harvard in 1755 and became associated with his father, a merchant and landowner. In 1763 he went to England and while there was named an agent for the province of New Hampshire. When complaints were made in England against his uncle, Benning Wentworth (q.v.), governor of New Hampshire, John was appointed in 1766 to succeed him. He also was named captain general of the militia and surveyor general of the King's Woods in America.

Taking the oath as governor at Portsmouth in 1767, John Wentworth applied himself energetically to developing the interior of the province—guiding its division into five counties, granting land, organizing towns, and building roads. He was a leader in the establishment of Dartmouth College (chartered 1769), granting land and contributing money. Wentworth's administration was popular in its early years but his position grew difficult as tension increased between the American colonies and England. He remonstrated against the taxes imposed by the British government but remained loyal to the crown and tried to block cooperation between New Hampshire and the other colonies. Finally, in 1775, he was forced to flee to Boston and later to England. From 1792 to 1808 he was lieutenant governor (in effect, governor) of Nova Scotia, and was created a baronet in 1795.

WENTWORTH, Thomas. See STRAFFORD, THOMAS WENTWORTH, 1ST EARL OF.

WENTWORTH, William Charles, Australian explorer and statesman: b. Norfolk Island, New South Wales, October 1790; d. Wimborne Minster, Dorsetshire, England, March 20, 1872. Taken to Sydney in 1793 from Norfolk Island, where his father was surgeon in the penal colony, Wentworth was sent to England for his education. Returning to Sydney in 1810, he was appointed acting provost marshal, and in 1813 he was a member of the exploring party that broke through the Blue Mountains, then constricting the Sydney settlement. Back in England, he studied law at Peterhouse College, Cambridge, from 1816 and was admitted to the Middle Temple. His influence helped to liberalize provisions of the Bill of 1823 instituting a legislative council for New South Wales, and his *Statistical, Historical, and Political Description of the Colony of New South*

Wales and Van Diemen's Land (1819), advocating parliamentary government, stimulated the flow of free settlers.

Wentworth returned to Sydney in 1824 and, defying local conceptions of government authority over the press, began a newspaper, the *Australian*. He sharply attacked some individual acts of Gov. Sir Ralph Darling, who then sought to license newspapers and impose a stamp duty. Wentworth challenged the duty clauses and won his case, thereby establishing a free press.

The 1842 Constitution Act, providing for 24 legislative council members to be elective, was a triumph for Wentworth's advocacy of representative government. Elected in 1843, he became leader of the council's nonofficial majority. The council quickly gained some control over revenues and redrafted land regulations to suit grazier interests. In 1848–1849, Wentworth helped to formulate a state primary education system for New South Wales and to institute a university (opened 1851). He was mainly responsible for drafting the Act of 1855 which gave the colony a parliament modeled on Westminster, with a lower house elected on manhood suffrage. In London, he sought to create a federal assembly of Australian colonies, but this was not enacted. After a brief visit to Sydney (1861–1862), he returned to England, where he died. He is buried near his former Sydney home, Vaucluse House, which is now preserved as a national monument.

R. M. YOUNGER.

WENZEL. See WENCESLAS.

WEREWOLF, wĭr'wo͝olf, a human being believed capable of transforming himself—or of being transformed—into a wolf. In many parts of the world the belief is prevalent that certain humans have the power of taking the shape and behavior of some animal. This belief is usually associated with the most terrifying animal in the area. In India and southeast Asia it is the tiger; in Africa, the lion, leopard, or hyena. In early Europe, all the way from Russia to the Atlantic and from Scandinavia to the Mediterranean, it was the wolf. (When wolves became scarce a belief arose that witches could transform themselves into cats.)

In Europe the belief in lycanthropy, as the transformation is called, is very old. Herodotus, the Greek historian of the 5th century B.C., recounted a tradition concerning the Neuri, a people who turned into wolves for a few days every year; and Virgil, Roman poet of the 1st century B.C., wrote of a sorcerer who used poisonous herbs to turn himself into a werewolf. In the time of St. Augustine (4th–5th centuries A.D.), magicians sold herbs guaranteed to effect such a transformation. In 16th century France the belief was so prevalent that the parliament of Franche-Comté passed a law expelling werewolves. In the 17th century, English sorcerers were described as taking the shape and nature of wolves by anointing their bodies with a special ointment and putting on an enchanted girdle; while in the last year of the Swedish war with Russia in the early 18th century the wolves which plagued certain districts of Russia were thought to be transformed Swedish prisoners.

The belief in lycanthropy persisted even into the late 19th century, when French peasants in remote regions feared to go out at night lest they be attacked by *loup-garou,* the French name for werewolf. Country people in north Germany thought that speaking the word "wolf" in the month of December laid them open to attack by a werewolf; Danish countryfolk claimed to be able to detect a werewolf by the shape of his eyebrows; while Greeks believed epileptics to be lycanthropes.

A form of insanity in which the victim believes himself a wolf and assumes wolfish behavior is also known as lycanthropy.

ELIZABETH E. BACON.

WERFEL, vĕr'fəl, **Franz,** Austrian poet, novelist, and playwright: b. Prague, Bohemia (now Czechoslovakia), Sept. 10, 1890; d. Hollywood, Calif., Aug. 26, 1945. He published his first verse collection, *Der Weltfreund,* in 1911, and soon became identified with the expressionist movement. This early volume, revealing his innate musical qualities, set a new tone in German poetry, combining some of the tempestuousness of Walt Whitman with the introspection of Fyodor Dostoyevsky. A free adaptation of Euripides' *The Trojan Women* (*Die Troerinnen*) in 1915 established him as a spokesman of pacifism, but he did army service on the Russian front. In 1917 he was transferred to the war press bureau in Vienna, and there he soon met Alma Maria Schindler, the widow of Gustav Mahler, the composer, who was later to become his wife. He continued to live in Austria until Nazi occupation forced him into exile in 1938. After escaping to France, then Spain, he reached the United States in 1940.

By 1920 other verse collections had increased his fame as a lyric poet: *Wir sind* (1913), *Einander* (1915), and *Der Gerichtstag* (1919). He published his verse trilogy *Der Spiegelmensch* in 1921, a colossal mystery play in the style of Johann Wolfgang von Goethe's *Faust* and Henrik Ibsen's *Peer Gynt*. Other important plays include the historical dramas *Juarez und Maximilian* (1924; Eng. tr. 1926) and *Paulus unter den Juden* (1926). The latter, together with his pageant *The Eternal Road* (1936), explores his own border position between Jewish background and a devotion to Catholicism without ever actually entering the church. His play, *The Goat Song* (1926), was adapted from the drama *Bocksgesang* (1921). Another play, *Jacobowsky and the Colonel* (1944), American version in collaboration with S. N. Behrman, translated his bitter experiences as a refugee into a pronouncement of affirmation and ultimate hope.

Werfel's popular international reputation came from his fiction. His *Nicht der Mörder, der Ermordete ist schuldig* (1915) is a mystical variation on the Oedipus theme. With *Verdi: Roman der Oper* (1924; Eng. tr., *Verdi: A Novel of the Opera,* 1925) he contributed to the understanding of the Italian master whom he later described as an *"anima naturaliter Christiana."* Though he continued the lyrical fervor of his youth (he died correcting galley proofs of his last book of verse), he extended his narrative style to novels of impressive proportions. *Barbara oder die Frömmigkeit* (1929; Eng. tr., *The Pure in Heart,* 1931) extolled the simple goodness of a Czech maidservant against the historic panorama of the decline of the Habsburg monarchy. *Die Geschwister von Neapel* (1931; Eng. tr., *The Pascarella Family,* 1932) glorified, in allegorical form, the majesty of music. *Die vierzig Tage des Musa Dagh* (1933; Eng. tr., *The Forty Days of Musa Dagh,* 1934) described the extinction of an Armenian community during World War I as a forewarning of the fate of European Jews after 1933. *Das Lied von Bernadette* (1941; Eng. tr., *The Song of Bernadette,* 1942), a novel based on the life of St. Bernadette of Lourdes, brought him popular acclaim and was made into a successful motion picture. *The Star of the Unborn* was published posthumously in 1946 and, in the guise of a Utopian travelogue, serves as a statement of his final religious creed. His work was diversified in form, theme, and degree of accomplishment, but it was united by his confession of *Weltfreundschaft* or faith in the ultimate brotherhood of all men.

HEINZ POLITZER
Professor of German, University of California

WERGELAND, văr'gə-län, **Henrik Arnold,** Norwegian poet: b. Kristiansand, Norway, June 17, 1808; d. Christiania (now Oslo), July 12, 1845. In his short but intense life he accomplished more for the cultural development of his country than any other one man. His collected works fill many volumes and his name has become the symbol of Norwegian national striving and achievement. His father, Nicolai, was a member of the Constitutional Convention of 1814, when modern Norway was founded, and in 1817 he became a minister at Eidsvoll, where the convention had been held. Henrik was an unusually gifted youth, who received an indelible impression of the national memories that surrounded him here and of his father's teaching and encouragement of his talents.

While a student at the university in Christiania, Wergeland published a huge dramatic poem, *Skabelsen, Mennesket og Messias* (1830; Creation, Man and Messiah), which was intended to rival *Paradise Lost* and similar cosmic poems. He also published collections of poems and several plays, all of them exuberant, chaotic expressions of his rebellious and unruly spirit. His writings were easy targets for the keen but often petty criticism of Johan S. C. Welhaven and others, who picked flaws in the verse and pointed out his lapses from good taste. Wergeland replied in kind, satirizing Welhaven in two farces written under the pseudonym of Siful Sifadda, and became the central figure in Norway's first great literary controversy.

Wergeland was a vigorous advocate of freedom for all oppressed peoples, a sympathizer with the French Revolution, and a worker on behalf of the enlightenment of the common man. He urged the Norwegians to celebrate May 17, the date of the signing of the constitution in 1814, as their national holiday, and carried on an unceasing agitation for the cultural and political liberation of Norway, then united with Sweden. He studied theology, but was regarded as too radical and undisciplined in his personal life to receive a charge. Yet in his later years he became an archivist in the government service and received a pension from the king. Among the causes which he espoused was that of the Jews, who before his time had been excluded from Norway. His best-loved poems were written during his final illness, which lasted for more than a year before he died of tuberculosis. Wergeland combined the ideas of the enlightenment with the lyric form and cosmic perspective of romanticism, and he expressed in his person all the vivid aspirations and hopes of the young Norwegian nation. His position combines that of Percy Bysshe Shelley in England and Walt Whitman in the United States.

EINAR HAUGEN
Professor of Scandinavian Languages, The University of Wisconsin

WERGILD, wûr'gĭld, in Anglo-Saxon law, the money value set on a man and imposed as a fine in atonement for homicide or other injury. Payable to the kindred of the deceased by the kin of the offender, wergild or "wer" at first supplemented, then replaced blood-feud settlement of wrongs. The amount to be paid was determined by a comprehensive tariff graduated according to the rank of the person injured. Rank was based upon birth, number of kindred, possession of land, or official station. For many purposes the amount of a man's own wer was often the measure to be paid for his own offenses. Paternal and maternal kindred paid or shared the wergild in proportions generally of two thirds and one third, respectively. Wergild was part of a larger system of compensation by which various injuries were rectified by specified pecuniary payments to the injured person himself, his relatives, and in some cases also to his lord, the king, or other public authority.

ALAN MATHESON

WERNER, vĕr'nər, **Abraham Gottlob,** German geologist and mineralogist: b. Wehrau, near Görlitz, Saxony, Germany, Sept. 25, 1750; d. Dresden, June 30, 1817. Becoming interested in minerals as a youth, he studied at the college of mines in Freiberg and at the university in Leipzig. In 1775 he returned to the Freiberg college as a teacher of mining and mineralogy, and for the next 40 years he worked in making it a major center of scientific learning. Studying the rocks in the Harz mountains of Saxony, he found that certain fossils (a term which he used for minerals) occurred only at certain levels, and theorized that the rocks had been laid down in orderly chronological succession. This new science, which he called geognosy, represents his most important contribution to geology, and, together with his pioneering in the systematic classification of rocks and minerals, distinguishes him in the view of many as the father of modern geology.

Werner also developed the now discarded neptunian theory (q.v.), a doctrine which held that the rocks were precipitates of a universal primeval sea, and that crystalline rocks, mixed crystals and sediments, layered sediments, and sands and muds were deposited in order. He included even basalt and granite in this category. A highly influential teacher, he and his followers were called neptunists (after Neptune, god of the sea). A heated controversy arose when their ideas were challenged by the plutonists or vulcanists, led by the Scottish geologist James Hutton (1726–1797), who considered the role of subterranean heat the prime factor in rock structure. Hutton's position in this dispute was upheld by later findings. Despite the fact that much of Werner's theoretical work was erroneous, however, he made a tremendous contribution to science in demonstrating the chronological succession of rocks.

See also GEOLOGY—*The History of Geology* (Plutonists versus Neptunists).

WERNER, Alfred, Swiss chemist: b. Mulhouse, France, Dec. 12, 1866; d. Zurich, Switzerland,

Nov. 15, 1919. Educated in German and Swiss technical schools, he earned his doctorate at the Zürich Polytechnic School, where he became an assistant in 1889. After teaching at the Collège de France, Paris, he returned to Switzerland and served as professor of chemistry in the University of Zürich from 1893 until his death. In 1913 he received the Nobel Prize in chemistry "in recognition of his works on the linking up of atoms within the molecule, whereby new light has been thrown upon older fields of research, and new fields have been opened up, especially within the realm of inorganic chemistry."

Werner's chief merit was to supersede the hypothesis of fixed valency—which was supported principally by Friedrich August Kekulé von Stradonitz (1829–1896), the German chemist—by his theory of variable residual valency with a maximal coordination number. This doctrine inaugurated the modern development of inorganic chemistry and induced important discoveries therein. Werner directed more than 200 doctoral dissertations by his students and contributed over 150 articles to scientific periodicals. His works include *Lehrbuch der Stereochemie* (1904); *Neuere Anschauungen auf dem Gebiete der anorganischen Chemie* (1905; 5th ed. 1923); and *Über die Konstitution und Konfiguration von Verbindungen höherer Ordnung* (1914).

WERNIGERODE, vĕr-nē-gə-rō′də, is a town in East Germany at an elevation of 1,000 feet at the end of the Holtemme Valley, at the north foot of the Upper Harz mountain range, 40 miles southwest of Magdeburg. It is a railroad and manufacturing center, producing metal, paper, wood, and glass products, chemicals, and electrical goods. There are several pharmaceutical plants and distilleries. A tourist attraction, Wernigerode has a city hall which was constructed in the 1490's in medieval style from a playhouse (originally built in 1420) of the princes of Stolberg-Wernigerode. The town is dominated by a hillside castle, first mentioned in 1213, and is the site of the Gothic Church of St. Sylvestri, several minor religious edifices, and a meteorological observatory. Wernigerode was founded in the 10th century, was a recognized town in 1100, received its charter in 1229, and joined the Hanseatic League in 1267. In April 1945 it was occupied by United States troops and subsequently invested by Soviet forces. After World War II, it became part of the German Democratic Republic (East Germany), in the Magdeburg District. Population: (1981 census) 35,684.

WERRENRATH, wĕr′ən-răth, **Reinald,** American baritone: b. Brooklyn, N.Y., Aug. 7, 1883; d. Plattsburgh, Sept. 12, 1953. A singing pupil of his father and several other teachers, including David Bispham and Herbert Witherspoon, he made his debut, in oratorio, at the Worcester (Massachusetts) Festival in 1907. He was well known as a concert and oratorio singer before making his operatic debut at the Metropolitan Opera House, New York City, on Feb. 19, 1919, as Silvio in *I Pagliacci* (Enrico Caruso was the Canio). Although successful in that role and as Escamillo in *Carmen* and Valentin in *Faust,* he abandoned opera in 1921 to teach and to tour widely as a recitalist. He became a popular recording artist both as a soloist and as a member (with Lucy Isabelle Marsh, Sophie Braslau, and Lambert Murphy) of the Victor Opera Quartet. He sang in public for the last time at Carnegie Hall, New York City, on Oct. 23, 1952.

HERBERT WEINSTOCK
Coauthor of "Men of Music"

WERTENBAKER, wûr′tən-bā-kər, **Thomas Jefferson,** American historian and educator: b. Charlottesville, Va., Feb. 6, 1879; d. Princeton, N.J., April 22, 1966. He graduated in 1902 from the University of Virginia and in 1910 was appointed instructor in American history at Princeton. He was Edwards professor of American history there from 1925 to 1947 (afterward professor emeritus). The author of numerous distinguished works on the American colonies in the period just before the Revolution. Wertenbaker examined particularly the structure and evolution of their society, largely through a study of education, architecture, literature, and other cultural fields. His writings include *The First Americans* (1927), *The Founding of American Civilization* (1938), *Torchbearer of the Revolution* (1940), *The Old South—The Founding of American Civilization* (1942), *The Golden Age of Colonial Culture* (1942), *The Puritan Oligarchy—The Founding of American Civilization* (1947), and *The Shaping of Colonial Virginia* (1958), a one-volume reprint of three earlier works: *Patrician and Plebeian in Virginia* (1910), *Virginia Under the Stuarts, 1607–1688* (1914), and *The Planters of Colonial Virginia* (1922).

WESBROOK, wĕs′brŏŏk, **Frank Fairchild,** Canadian pathologist and educator: b. Brent County, Ontario, Canada, July 12, 1868; d. Vancouver, British Columbia, Oct. 20, 1918. He received his medical degree at the University of Manitoba and studied at McGill University, Cambridge, England, and Marburg, Germany. In 1896 he was appointed professor of pathology and bacteriology at the University of Minnesota, becoming dean of the medical school in 1906. He returned to Canada in 1913 as first president of the University of British Columbia at Vancouver, a post he held until his death. Named president of the American Public Health Association in 1905, he specialized in the fields of public health and sanitation. In World War I he was chairman of the British Columbia Committee on Food Resources.

WESCOTT, wĕs′kət, **Glenway,** American author: b. Kewaskum, Wis., April 11, 1901; d. Rosement, N.J., Feb. 22, 1987. He is best known for his stories of Wisconsin settlers and especially for his novel *The Grandmothers,* which was awarded the Harper Prize for 1927.

After two years at the University of Chicago (1917–1919), Wescott lived mostly in Europe until the mid-1930's. During the 1920's he published two volumes of poems—*The Bitterns* (1920) and *Natives of Rock* (1925); two novels of frontier life in Wisconsin—*The Apple of the Eye* (1924) and *The Grandmothers* (1927; British title, *A Family Portrait*); and two volumes of short stories—*Like a Lover* (1926) and *Good-Bye, Wisconsin* (1928).

His other works include the novelette *The Pilgrim Hawk* (1940), about Americans in Paris, considered by some his best; *Apartment in Athens* (1945), a novel of Greek underground resistance to the Nazis; and *Images of Truth: Remembrances and Criticism* (1962), about writers he had known.

WESEL, vā'zəl, town, Germany, in the state of North Rhine-Westphalia, located at the confluence of the Lippe and Rhine rivers, 17 miles south of Bocholt and 35 miles north-northwest of Düsseldorf. Situated at the entrance to the Lippe Lateral Canal, it is a rail junction, transshipment port, and industrial center producing mine locomotives, pipes, and machinery; the adjacent countryside engages in dairying and flour milling. Its most notable structure is the Church of St. Willibrordi, built in 1424–1526; and the so-called Berlin Gate still survives as a memento of the massive Prussian fortifications, constructed at the beginning of the 18th century, that guarded the town until 1891.

Wesel was first mentioned in 750 and received its city charter in 1241; it became a member city of the Hanseatic League in 1407. Peter Minuit, governor of the Dutch colony of New Netherland (New York), was born here. In World War II (February 1945) Wesel was almost totally destroyed by bombing, which wrecked a number of historic buildings including the Gothic city hall, built in 1396. In the following month the town was the scene of major air transport activity leading to the Allied crossing of the Rhine. Wesel became part of the Federal Republic of Germany (West Germany) after the war. Pop. (1959 est.) 31,400.

WESER RIVER, vā'zər, river, Germany, formed at Münden in Lower Saxony, Federal German Republic, by the junction of the Fulda and Werra rivers. One of the principal rivers of northwestern Germany, it flows generally north past Hameln (or Hamelin), and turns westward and then north again through the Porta Westfalica, a gap in the Weser Mountains. It continues past Minden, through Bremen and past Bremerhaven, below which it forms a 10-mile-long estuary emptying into the North Sea. The Weser is navigable for all of its 300 miles (with the Werra it totals about 470 miles). Its chief tributaries are the Diemel and Hunte rivers on the left bank and the Aller on the right. The Weser's flow is controlled by large dams on the Diemel, at Helminghausen, and on the Eder, at the Hemfurth. In 1883–1894 the river was deepened below Bremen. It is connected by canals with the Rhine, Ems, and Elbe rivers. According to legend, in 1284 the Pied Piper rid Hameln of a plague of rats by luring them into the Weser, as recounted in Robert Browning's poem, *The Pied Piper of Hamelin.*

WESERMÜNDE, vā-zər-mün'də, former name for the city of Bremerhaven, Germany. Wesermünde was created in 1924 as a Hanoverian city from the union of the port of Geestemünde and the town of Lehe. Bremerhaven itself was absorbed by Wesermünde in 1939, but in 1947 the entire community was renamed Bremerhaven (q.v.).

WESLACO, wĕs'lə-kō, city, Texas, in Hidalgo County, 7 miles north of the Rio Grande, 35 miles west-northwest of Brownsville, at an altitude of 70 feet. It is a processing and distributing center in an irrigated farm area producing citrus fruits, cotton, and truck crops. It serves also as a financial center for the region. The city is on a federal highway, and there is an airport. Agricultural research and training centers are maintained here by the federal government and state colleges. The city's name derives from the initials of the W. E. Stewart Land Company, which promoted the townsite in 1917. It was incorporated in 1921. Civic development plans required all buildings in the business section to be remodeled in Spanish architectural style. A council-manager government was instituted in 1929. Pop. 19,331.

VERNA J. MCKENNA.

WESLEY, wĕs'lē, **Charles,** English evangelist and hymnologist: b. Epworth, Lincolnshire, England, Dec. 18, 1707; d. London, March 29, 1788. He was the 18th child, youngest and third surviving son of Samuel Wesley (q.v.) and Susanna Wesley. At Westminster school, London, he was king's scholar and captain of the school, and then was elected student of Christ Church, Oxford. "My first year in college," he says, "I lost in diversions. The next I set myself to study. Diligence led me into serious thinking. I went to the weekly sacrament and persuaded two or three young scholars to accompany me, and to observe the [monastic] method of study prescribed by the Statutes of the University. This gained us the harmless nicknames of Methodists. In half a year my brother [John Wesley, q.v.] left his curacy at Epworth and came to our assistance. We then proceeded regularly in our studies and in doing what good we could. . . ."

Wesley was ordained in 1735 and went to America as a member of the Georgia Mission of the Holy Club, but he fled the project within five months and landed in England in late 1736. After an evangelical awakening (May 21, 1738, three days before his brother's more famous Aldersgate Street experience), he began a successful preaching ministry in and around London. For 15 years thereafter he was his brother's chief associate in the direction and extension of the Methodist Revival. Although quite as "irregular" as his brother in matters of outdoor and lay preaching, extempore prayer and hymn singing, he was passionately opposed to "separation" from the Church of England, holding, against John, that it was not even "lawful," much less "expedient," to contravene episcopal polity. After 1756 he gradually curtailed his active leadership among the Methodists, discouraged by what he regarded as their drift into Dissent. In 1771 he settled permanently in London, where he continued to minister at the Methodist chapels there. His sons, Charles and Samuel, became prominent musicians and composers. Upon his death, he was buried in St. Marylebone's churchyard at his special request.

Wesley's chief service to the revival and to Christendom was as a Christian poet, one of the greatest hymnologists of all time. He wrote in verse almost as readily as in prose and on nearly as wide a range of topics. He published more than 4,000 hymns—including *Hark, the Herald Angels Sing; Jesus, Lover of My Soul;* and *Love Divine, All Loves Excelling*—and left some 2,800 in manuscript. In them, the Wesleyan message was faithfully expressed and effectively disseminated. He made the Methodists a singing people and provided them with a unique body of hymns. One point of significant doctrinal divergence between the two brothers was Charles' reservations about John's doctrine of *professed* sanctification, which the former set forth in *Short Hymns on Select Passages of the Holy Scripture* (1762).

ALBERT C. OUTLER
Professor, Perkins School of Theology
Southern Methodist University

Bibliography: Charles Wesley

Green, Richard, *The Works of John and Charles Wesley*, 2d rev. ed. (1906; reprint, AMS Press 1974).
Rogal, S. J., *John and Charles Wesley* (G. K. Hall 1983).
Tyson, John R., *Charles Wesley on Sanctification: A Biographical and Theological Study* (Zondervan 1986).
Whaling, Frank, ed., *John and Charles Wesley: Selected Writings and Hymns* (Paulist Press 1981).
Wilder, F., *The Methodist Riots* (Todd & Honeywell 1982).

WESLEY, John, English evangelist and theologian, founder of the Methodist Societies: b. Epworth, Lincolnshire, England, June 17, 1703; d. London, March 2, 1791. He was the 15th child and second surviving son of Samuel Wesley (q.v.) and Susanna Wesley, and was reared in a home atmosphere of Anglican piety and Puritan discipline. His dramatic rescue from the rectory fire of 1709 gave him a sense of special providence which he retained throughout his life. He was educated at the Charterhouse school, London (1714–1720) and at Christ Church, Oxford (B.A., 1724; M.A., 1727). In 1727 he was elected Fellow of Lincoln College, Oxford, and except for a brief period as his father's curate at Epworth, he was there in residence until 1735, serving as tutor, moderator (logic), Greek lecturer (New Testament), and claviger (keeper of the keys).

Under the influence of Jeremy Taylor's *The Rules and Exercises of Holy Living*, he was converted in 1725 ("Instantly I resolved to dedicate all my life to God. . ."). His other spiritual guides at this stage were Thomas à Kempis and William Law. He was ordained deacon in 1725 and priest in 1728. In 1729 he assumed the leadership of the semimonastic group that had been formed in Oxford by his younger brother Charles Wesley (q.v.) and derisively labeled "The Holy Club" or "The Methodists" by the university wits. Wesley did not like the nickname "Methodist" but he adopted it as a badge of honor and proceeded to define it as meaning an authentic Christian *(The Character of a Methodist)*.

In 1735, with three other members of the Holy Club, including Charles, he set out for the new colony of Georgia as missioner to the Indians and pastor of Savannah. This experience, despite its resounding failure, proved decisive as background for Wesley's subsequent career.

Back in England (Feb. 1, 1738) he made several unsuccessful attempts at evangelistic preaching. On May 24, at a meeting of a religious society in Aldersgate Street, London, he underwent a vivid awakening of personal faith and assurance ("I felt my heart *strangely* warmed . . ."). Having learned the doctrine of assurance from the Moravians in Georgia and England (Peter Boehler), he set out on a visit to their centers in Germany. On his return (September 1738) he resumed his preaching mission, still with scant effect. The following spring, however, influenced by Jonathan Edwards' account of the Great Awakening in New England and by George Whitefield's successes at outdoor preaching, Wesley achieved his first significant results as an evangelist, and the Methodist Revival was fully launched. Thereafter, for more than 50 years of incessant activity, he was its head and heart. His prodigious program of preaching, travel, writing, and administration is amply recorded in his *Journal* and letters.

Methodist Societies and The Conference.—In his direction of the revival, Wesley's practical genius flowered in the various procedures he developed to extend and conserve its fruits. The organization of the Methodist Societies into "classes" and "bands," with their own "leaders" and "stewards," provided his converts with a unique pattern of group association and religious nurture. His employment of lay preachers, directly responsible to him, gave him an itinerant militia which he deployed over England, Ireland, and Scotland with great skill and effectiveness. The Conference, an annual gathering of the preachers at Wesley's invitation for consultation, became a parliament where doctrinal and administrative questions were decided. After his death, it served as the agency which perpetuated his authority among the Methodists of Great Britain.

Thus Methodism emerged as an evangelical order within the Church of England, warranted by the parlous state of religion but never approved or appreciated by the hierarchy. Its chief design, as Wesley put it, "was not to form any new sect but to *re*form the nation—particularly the (national) Church—and to spread scriptural holiness over the land."

Despite Wesley's unswerving loyalty to the Church of England, some of his preachers began to agitate as early as 1750 for ministerial standing and "separation" (Nonconformity). They were vehemently opposed in this by Charles Wesley and repeatedly vetoed by John, who held that "separation was lawful but not expedient." However, after the American Revolution (which he heartily deplored) had created an anomalous situation for the Methodists in the United States, Wesley was persuaded to "ordain" Dr. Thomas Coke to join with Francis Asbury in organizing American Methodism and providing the Methodists in the new nation with a necessary ministry. Subsequently he ordained several others of his preachers "to administer the sacraments of baptism and the Lord's Supper, according to the usage of the Church of England . . ." in Scotland and Ireland and finally in England as well. He steadfastly denied, however, that these acts amounted to "separation," and he died a loyal Anglican.

Theology.—The core of Wesley's theological position was formed long before the revival began and from sources chiefly Anglican and patristic. Besides Taylor, Thomas à Kempis, and William Law, he was greatly influenced by the Caroline divines, the Nonjurors, and by the early Eastern fathers of the church. The dynamic center of his message was the quest for holiness, in the sense defined first in his Oxford sermon (Jan. 1, 1733) on *The Circumcision of the Heart*, and maintained thereafter, as he says, "without any material addition or diminution." His Aldersgate Street experience, however, reordered his emphasis on the primacy of faith, so as to stress "saving faith" (justification) as the threshold of the Christian life and "the fullness of faith" (sanctification) as its proper goal.

The subsequent development of Wesley's theology was guided almost exclusively by the needs and occasions of the revival. He is, therefore, best understood as a folk theologian rather than a speculative one. Against Moravian quietism, he stressed good works, "the faith that *works* by love." Against Calvinistic predestinarianism, he insisted on universal redemption and conditional election. Against Anglican formalism, he urged the spontaneity and "witness" of the Holy Spirit. Against the rationalists, he argued for the primacy of revelation in the Scriptures. In every instance, his avowed norm is Biblical. Thus he fused the Protestant traditions of faith and Biblical authority with the ancient catholic traditions of grace and community.

As chief tutor to the Methodists, Wesley undertook to supply them with an abundance of cheap and edifying literature—the printed word in place of his personal presence. He felt quite free to reprint, abridge, or digest the writings of others or to produce his own, according to the circumstances. The bulk of his publication concerns the revival and its progress: the *Journal,* the *Sermons,* the *Hymns,* the *Appeals,* the *Plain Account of Christian Perfection,* the *Explanatory Notes on the New Testament,* and so on. But he also provided his people with textbooks of various sorts, with histories, political commentaries, and a medical handbook called *Primitive Physick,* which went through 23 editions in his lifetime and 9 thereafter.

In line with his concern "to reform the nation," Wesley pioneered in most of the good causes of his day: legal and prison reform, the abolition of slavery ("the execrable sum of all villainies"), civil rights, popular education. He had a special talent for rising to new occasions, for holding a steady course, and for inspiring his associates to their best efforts. No other Christian teacher in 18th century England set his mark in so many lives and places. Even today, the legacy of his heart and mind continues relevant in modern ecumenical Christianity.

ALBERT C. OUTLER,
Professor, Perkins School of Theology, Southern Methodist University.

Bibliography

The Journal of John Wesley, 2 vols. (Zondervan 1986).
Wesley's Standard Sermons, 2 vols., ed. by E. H. Sugden and Joseph Allison (Zondervan 1986).
The Works of John Wesley, ed. by Albert C. Outler (Abingdon 1984–).
Cell, George C., *The Rediscovery of John Wesley* (Univ. Press of Am. 1983).
Moore, Robert L., *John Wesley and Authority: A Psychological Perspective* (Scholars Press 1979).
Slatte, Howard P., *Fire in the Brand: An Introduction to the Creative Work and Theology of John Wesley* (Univ. Press of Am. 1983).
Tuttle, Robert G., Jr., *John Wesley: His Life and Theology* (Zondervan 1982).
Tyerman, Luke, *The Life and Times of the Reverend John Wesley,* 3 vols. (1872; reprint, B. Franklin 1973).

WESLEY, Samuel, English clergyman and poet, father of John and Charles Wesley (qq.v.): b. Winterborne Whitchurch, Dorsetshire, England, Dec. 17, 1662; d. Epworth, Lincolnshire, April 25, 1735. The son and grandson of ejected Nonconformist ministers, he began his education in Dissenting academies near London but in 1683 he transferred to Exeter College, Oxford, where he became a staunch royalist and High Churchman. Ordained priest in 1690, he served two Lincolnshire parishes: South Ormsby (1690–1695) and Epworth (1695–1735).

Wesley was a diligent scholar and a prolific writer. The author of many articles for *The Athenian Gazette,* he also wrote *Elegies on the Queen and the Archbishop* (Mary, and John Tillotson, archbishop of Canterbury); several hymns still in use, a *History of the Old and New Testaments Attempted in Verse,* and a mammoth Latin folio, *Dissertationes in Librum Jobi* (53 miscellaneous essays and a polyglot text of Job). His *Treatise on Baptism* was published, unaltered and unacknowledged, by his son John in the latter's collected *Works.*

Wesley's vivid convictions and fearless zeal made for a stormy and difficult life, both in his Epworth parish and elsewhere. His pamphlet war with the Dissenters resulted in his being jailed in 1705, ostensibly for debt. From prison he wrote: "Thanks be to God, my confinement is comfortable to me since I need not have suffered it if I would have deserted the cause of the universities and the Church. . . . I will never drop the controversy unless I lay my bones here." In 1710 he was active in the defense of Henry Sacheverell and the High-Church party. His chief fame, however, rests in his role, as he said, of being "the grandfather of the Methodists."

Consult Clarke, Adam, *Memoirs of the Wesley Family* (London 1823); Tyerman, Luke, *The Life and Times of the Rev. Samuel Wesley* (London 1866).

ALBERT C. OUTLER,
Professor, Perkins School of Theology, Southern Methodist University.

WESLEYAN COLLEGE, wĕs'lē-ən, an institution of higher learning for women in Macon, Ga. Receiving its charter in 1836, it became the first college chartered to grant degrees to women. It was originally known as Georgia Female College, later (1843) as Wesleyan Female College, and the present name was adopted in 1919. Related to the Methodist Church, it is open to students of all denominations. The present 240-acre campus, located in suburban Macon (Rivoli), was first occupied in 1928.

Wesleyan College emphasizes both liberal arts and fine arts. It confers bachelor's degrees in four areas: arts, science, music, and fine arts. Scholarship help and grants-in-aid, as well as loan funds, are available for students of ability who require financial assistance. The library has special collections of Americana and Georgiana. Full-time students number about 500. School colors are lavender and purple.

W. EARL STRICKLAND.

WESLEYAN METHODISTS. See METHODISM—*Division and Reunion* (In Great Britain).

WESLEYAN UNIVERSITY, an independent college of liberal arts and sciences for men, located in Middletown, Conn., on the Connecticut River about 16 miles south of Hartford. The institution offers courses leading to the degrees of bachelor of arts, master of arts, master of arts in teaching, and master of arts in liberal studies. Although no longer affiliated with the Methodist Episcopal Church, it is the oldest of the institutions of higher education founded in America by that denomination. The curriculum offers more than 300 courses in 21 departments, and in addition there are three experimental colleges (one in language and literature, one in quantitative studies, and one in social studies) where students are given broad freedom in charting their educational programs. In these "college plans" students assume much greater responsibility for their own education, and move rapidly into advanced independent study. In 1959 Wesleyan established a Center for Advanced Studies and to it distinguished persons from the United States and abroad come for from a few weeks to a full year. Wesleyan also has a library; an observatory with a 20-inch telescope; a graduate summer school for teachers; and a university press. The college nickname is the "Cardinals," the colors are cardinal red and black. The average enrollment numbers 2,600 students.

WESSEX, wĕs′ĭks, a kingdom of Anglo-Saxon England, one of the most important of the Heptarchy. It originally covered the country between the valley of the Thames and the south coast, excepting the kingdoms of Kent and Sussex. Wessex, signifying West Saxons, may have been founded by Cerdic, who landed near Southampton in 495 and with the aid of his son, Cynric, established his rule in the southern part of what later became Hampshire. Later kings extended Wessex to the north, and Egbert, who became king in 802, overthrew the kingdom of Mercia and in 829 was recognized as bretwalda. Attacks on England by Danes or Northmen gradually developed, until by 870 they had practically mastered the northern kingdoms and East Anglia. Then began the struggle for Wessex, in which Alfred the Great, who had become king of Wessex in 871, proved victorious. At his death in 899 the king of Wessex was in fact the master of all England west and south of a line drawn roughly from Chester to London, and his sovereignty was also vaguely acknowledged over the rest of the country, known as the Danelaw or Danelagh. It remained for Alfred's son, Edward (Eadward) the Elder, to translate this sovereignty into a definite mastery, the king of Wessex becoming king of England.

The Wessex which is the scene of the novels of Thomas Hardy is the southwestern area of England, principally the county of Dorset.

WESSON, wĕs′ən, **Daniel Baird,** American firearms inventor and manufacturer: b. Worcester, Mass., May 18, 1825; d. Springfield, Aug. 4, 1906. In 1853 he went into partnership with Horace Smith to manufacture a rim-fire metallic cartridge he had improved from another's design. The next year they patented a pistol which fired a cartridge and had a new repeating action. This principle was embodied later in the Winchester repeating rifle. In 1855 the partners sold their rifle patent rights.

Wesson further improved the metallic cartridge and perfected the repeating action for revolvers, and in 1857 he and Smith formed the Smith & Wesson Company to manufacture them. This revolver was unique in having an open cylinder and firing a metallic cartridge, and it was marketed with great success in the United States, Europe, Asia, and South America. The partners continued to refine the weapon with their own inventions and by buying others, such as the shell-extracting device of W. C. Dodge (1869). In 1887, Wesson patented a hammerless safety revolver which could not be fired accidentally.

WEST, wĕst, **Benjamin,** American painter; b. Springfield, Pa., Oct. 10, 1738; d. London, England, March 11, 1820. He began painting at the age of six and acquired the reputation of a prodigy. During his twenties he painted many portraits in Philadelphia and spent 11 months in New York. In 1760 he was sent to Europe through the interest of Philadelphia merchants, and he created a sensation on his arrival in Rome, where he was considered a "noble savage" by the aristocracy. The effect of being lionized, of his sudden exposure to the old masters, and to the different life in Europe caused a nervous collapse. Under the moral influence of the neoclassical critic Johann Winckelmann and his painter-disciple Anton Mengs, West recovered and began his career in historical painting.

In 1763, West arrived in London and showed his Roman paintings with success; he was soon London's most popular painter. He shocked the art world with *Death of General Wolfe* (1771), among the first historical paintings in the grand

NATIONAL GALLERY OF CANADA, OTTAWA, GIFT OF THE DUKE OF WESTMINSTER, 1918.

Benjamin West's *Death of General Wolfe* was at first criticized for showing the figures in contemporary clothing, but it soon became a major influence on the development of English historical painting.

manner to show the figures in contemporary dress rather than in Graeco-Roman costumes. He enjoyed the patronage and friendship of George III and was appointed historical painter to the king in 1772, working on paintings for Windsor Chapel between 1781 and 1801. After 1776, West turned from classical to religious subjects. His *Death on the Pale Horse* (1802) was a precursor of romantic painting. He was a founder of the Royal Academy and its president in 1792–1805 and 1807–1820.

West helped and taught the young Americans who came to London, such as John Singleton Copley, Gilbert Stuart, Thomas Sully, Charles Willson Peale, Matthew Pratt, John Trumbull, Samuel F. B. Morse, and Ralph Earl. The Pennsylvania Academy of Fine Arts, Philadelphia, and Swarthmore College, Swarthmore, Pa., have two of the largest collections of West's work.

HERBERT D. HALE, *"Art News" Magazine*

WEST, Nathanael (1902–1940), American novelist. He was born Nathan Weinstein in New York City on Oct. 17, 1902. After graduating from Brown University in 1924, he worked in New York City as a hotel manager and was an associate of William Carlos Williams in editing the magazine *Contact*. From the mid-1930's he was employed in Hollywood as a motion-picture scriptwriter. On Dec. 22, 1940, West and his wife, the former Eileen McKenney (the inspiration for Ruth McKenney's *My Sister Eileen*) were killed in an auto accident near El Centro, Calif.

West published only four novels, but they all showed great talent and promise, and two became classics of the 1930's: *Miss Lonelyhearts* (1933) and *The Day of the Locust* (1939). The first is a masterpiece of bizarre humor concerning the fatal disintegration of a New York columnist who gives advice to the lovelorn. The second, his most mature work and a striking commentary on his Hollywood experience, exposes the bizarre characters and the boredom surrounding the motion-picture industry. West's first novel, *The Dream Life of Balso Snell* (1931), has the quality of a surrealist fantasy. *A Cool Million* (1934), his third, is ingenious in its debunking of chauvinism and the Horatio Alger myth.

When they first appeared, West's novels received little attention apart from the praise of a few perceptive critics. However, after World War II, they gained recognition for their originality, striking imagery, precision of language, and masterful satire—qualities that place West among the significant American novelists of the early 20th century.

WILLIAM BRACY, *Beaver College*

WEST, Rebecca (1892–1983), English novelist, journalist, and critic. She was born Cicily Isabel Fairfield in County Kerry, Ireland, on Dec. 25, 1892. After attending George Watson's Ladies' College, Edinburgh, she appeared for a short time on the London stage. An ardent feminist, she adopted as her pseudonym the name of Ibsen's heroine in the play *Rosmersholm*—the passionate, strong-willed Rebecca West. She then turned to journalism and continued throughout her life to contribute to important British and American periodicals, beginning with the feminist *Freewoman* in 1911. She joined *The Clarion* the following year as a political writer, reviewed novels for *The New Statesman*, contributed studies of post-World War II treason trials and other crimes to *The New Yorker* (published as *The Meaning of Treason* in 1947 and *A Train of Powder* in 1955), and wrote various political and literary essays and reviews.

Rebecca West's early novels treat psychological problems: amnesia in *The Return of the Soldier* (1918) and the Oedipus complex in *The Judge* (1922). Later fiction includes *Harriet Hume* (1929), *The Harsh Voice* (1935), *The Thinking Reed* (1936), and, after a hiatus of 20 years, *The Fountain Overflows* (1956), about the problems of a London family during the Edwardian era. Nonfictional volumes include *Henry James* (1916), *D. H. Lawrence* (1930), and *St. Augustine* (1933); *The Modern Rake's Progress* (1934) and other works in collaboration with the caricaturist David Low; and a remarkable travel book recounting Balkan history and politics, *Black Lamb and Grey Falcon: A Journey Through Yugoslavia* (2 vols., 1941), generally considered her greatest work.

About 1911, Rebecca West began a 10-year liaison with the novelist H. G. Wells, by whom she had her only child, Anthony West, who also became a prominent writer. From 1930 until his death in 1968 she was married to Henry Maxwell Andrews, a banker. Rebecca West was created a Dame Commander of the British Empire in 1959. She died in London on March 15, 1983.

WILLIAM BRACY, *Beaver College*

WEST, Thomas, 3D BARON DE LA WARR. See DE LA WARR, 3D BARON.

WEST, The, See WESTWARD MOVEMENT.

WEST ALLIS, al'is, a city in Wisconsin, in Milwaukee County, 7 miles west of downtown Milwaukee, at an altitude of 700 feet. It is a manufacturing and banking city, site of the home plant of the Allis-Chalmers Manufacturing Company, makers of industrial and farming machinery. About 120 other plants in the city produce trucks, motors, iron and steel products, wood products, and industrial gases. The city is served by the Chicago and North Western, the Chicago, Milwaukee, St. Paul and Pacific, and the Minneapolis, St. Paul and Sault Ste. Marie railroads. The Wisconsin State Fair Grounds, established in 1892, are situated here.

The first settler in what is now the city of West Allis was Francis Weld, who claimed a homestead in 1827. The community that grew around his home was known as Honey Creek until 1881, when the name was changed to North Greenfield. In 1902, North Greenfield was incorporated as a village and its name changed to West Allis, in recognition of the new Allis-Chalmers plant. In 1906 the village was incorporated as a fourth-class city. In 1954 annexations increased the area of the city and its population. Government is by mayor and council. Population: 63,982.

WEST BEND, city, Wisconsin, seat of Washington County, on the Milwaukee River, 30 miles north-northwest of Milwaukee and 20 miles west of Lake Michigan, at an altitude of 943 feet. West Bend is a manufacturing city whose chief products (and those of the surrounding area) are aluminum utensils, household appliances, outboard motors, farm machinery, automobile accessories, material-handling equipment, and beverages. There are a municipal airport and a 75-acre city park. West Bend was founded in 1845 by Byron Kilbourn, who chose the site because of its excellent water power for a sawmill and gristmill. The first city charter was granted in 1885. Rapid industrial growth began with the founding of the West Bend Aluminum Company in 1911. Government is by mayor and council. Population: 21,484.

LOMA BARRINGTON

WEST BENGAL. See BENGAL—*West Bengal.*

WEST BROMWICH, wĕst brŭm′ĭch, a locality in the West Midlands (formerly Staffordshire) metropolitan county of west central England, on the outskirts of Birmingham. Formerly a county borough, West Bromwich was integrated into West Midlands in 1974. It is a coal-mining region and has important steel-casting and metalworking plants, as well as oil, chemical, and electrical-engineering industries.

Historic buildings include the 16th century Oak House (restored), now a museum; the 13th century manor house; and the Asbury Cottage, where Francis Asbury, one of the first missionaries of Methodism to the United States, spent his early life. Population: (1981) 154,930.

H. GORDON STOKES

WEST CARROLLTON, wĕst kăr′əl-tən, town, Ohio, in Montgomery County, on the Miami River, eight miles by road south-southwest of Dayton, at an altitude of 715 feet. It is an industrial center, with excellent water power. The paper mills, the first of which was converted from a distillery in 1872, are the town's chief industry and rank among the largest in Ohio. Incorporated in 1887, it is governed by a mayor and council. Population: 13,148.

ELIZABETH FARIES

WEST CHESTER, wĕst chĕs′tər, borough, Pennsylvania, seat of Chester County, 25 miles west of Philadelphia by road, at an altitude of 459 feet. A residential community, it has been called "the Athens of Pennsylvania" because of its many buildings of Greek Revival architecture. It is a banking town and trade center of a dairy and agricultural region; industries include the manufacture of air compressors, tags, penicillin, Foamite, dairy equipment, wheels, springs, wind turbines, and paper boxes, and the canning of mushrooms. There is an airport. The West Chester State Teachers College and the Chester County Historical Society are situated here. Brandywine Battlefield State Historical Park is two miles to the south. West Chester grew from a crossroads village called Turks Head (after a tavern which was licensed in 1762). The county seat was moved from Chester in 1786. The community was named West Chester in 1799, when it was incorporated into a borough. It has a mayor-council government. Population: 17,435.

DOROTHY B. LAPP

WEST CHICAGO, wĕst shə-kä′gō, city, Illinois, in Du Page County, 30 miles west of Chicago, at an altitude of 765 feet. In an agricultural area, the city has railroad shops and manufactures of movable buildings, building materials, rare-earth chemicals, gas mantles, and lighting implements. There is an airport. The city was incorporated in 1906. Population: 12,550.

WEST COVINA, wĕst kō-vē′nə, city, California, in Los Angeles County, in the east San Gabriel Valley, 18 miles (by highway) east of the Los Angeles civic center, at an altitude of 425 feet. It is a residential city, part of the Los Angeles metropolitan complex, and a center of trade and service in the San Gabriel Valley—an agricultural area, where citrus fruit farming is important. One third of the city's residents are employed in Los Angeles and only 10 percent in West Covina, principally in retail trade. The West Covina Unified School District, embracing 13 elementary schools and two high schools, was established in 1960. Mount San Antonio Junior College is in Walnut, six miles southeast. The city has a council-manager form of government, adopted in 1955. West Covina was incorporated as a city in 1923.

In the 1870's vineyards were planted in the area. The experiment failed, but left a legacy in the name Covina, derived from "vineyard in a cove." With the expansion of the Los Angeles area, the city's population growth has been spectacular. In 1950 the population was 4,499, and a special census in 1957 counted 40,915. Population: (1980) 80,291.

VERA E. FITCH

WEST DES MOINES, wĕst də moin′, city, Iowa, Polk County, five miles west of Des Moines, at an altitude of 813 feet. It has manufactures of cement and foundry products. Incorporated as Valley Junction in 1893 and renamed in 1938, it has a mayor-council government. Population: 21,894.

WEST ELMIRA, village, New York, in Chemung County, just west of Elmira, the county seat. Population: 5,485.

WEST FLANDERS. See FLANDERS, WEST.

WEST FRANKFORT, wĕst frăngk′fərt, city, Illinois, in Franklin County, 45 miles south-southeast of Centralia, at an altitude of 405 feet. It is an industrial and trade center in a bituminous coal, oil, and agricultural area, which produces livestock, garden truck produce, poultry, and fruit. The name derives from Francis Jordan's Fort, built against the Indians early in the 19th century. This was shortened to Frank's Fort and then to Frankfort. When the railroads were built, the town was moved to the west and renamed. It was incorporated in 1905, and a commission form of government was adopted in 1932. Population: 9,437.

HELEN L. CLEM
West Frankfort Public Library

WEST FRISIAN ISLANDS. See FRISIAN ISLANDS.

WEST GERMAN FEDERAL REPUBLIC. See GERMANY.

WEST HARTFORD, wĕst härt′fərd, town, Connecticut, in Hartford County, 4 miles west of Hartford and 28 miles south of Springfield, Mass., at an altitude of 150 feet. It is a residential suburb within the Greater Hartford metropolitan area, but possesses important industries, including the manufacture of turbines, automobile parts, coil springs, electrical supplies, small tools, precision machine tools, dies, chemical products, plastics, and accessories for aircraft engines. The Amtrak

Railroad provides passenger service at Hartford and maintains two sidings in the town for freight shipments. Truck operators and bus lines serve the town on federal and state highways. Air passenger service is available at Bradley Field, Windsor Locks, 18 miles away. The town has one weekly newspaper, one television outlet, and one radio (AM) station. St. Joseph College for women is situated here, as are three private secondary and preparatory schools—Kingswood School, Mount St. Joseph Academy, and the American School for the Deaf, founded in 1817. There are a public library and a children's museum. The rose gardens in Elizabeth Park attract thousands of visitors annually.

The town's council-manager government, the first in Connecticut, was adopted in July 1919. Settled in 1679, West Hartford was originally an agricultural area. It was incorporated in May 1854, as a separate town from Hartford. Noah Webster, the lexicographer, was born here. Population: 61,301.

ROBERT C. SALE,
Former State Librarian, Connecticut State Library.

WEST HAVEN, wĕst hā'vən, town, Connecticut, in New Haven County, on New Haven Harbor, adjoining the city of New Haven on the southwest, 14 miles east of Bridgeport. Suburban in character, West Haven has many small industries with diversified products, of which automobile tires, buckles, textiles, and die castings are representative. Commercial air service is available at the New Haven municipal airport, four miles from the center of West Haven. The town includes the amusement resort of Savin Rock. The first permanent settlement in the town was made in 1646, but it did not separate from New Haven until 1712, when the town of Orange was established. In 1873 the borough of West Haven was created as a part of Orange. In 1921 it became a town and is still the youngest in the state. Its form of government is the representative town meeting and board of selectmen. Population: 53,184.

ROBERT C. SALE.

WEST HAVERSTRAW, wĕst hăv'ər-strô, village, New York, in Rockland County, directly northwest of Haverstraw, near the west bank of the Hudson River. Chemicals, textiles, and clothing are manufactured. In the village is a state home for crippled children. The area was incorporated in 1883. Population: 9,181.

WEST HAZLETON, wĕst hā'zəl-tən, borough, Pennsylvania, Luzerne County, adjoining Hazleton, in the east central part of the state. A residential borough, situated in the middle coalfield of the anthracite area, it formerly was the site of some mining, but now has diversified, mostly small industries. It is served by the Hazleton municipal airport. A branch center of Pennslyvania State University is at Hazleton. The borough was incorporated in 1889 and has a mayor-council form of government. Population: 4,871.

ROBERT N. COHEE.

WEST HELENA, wĕst hĕl'ə-nə, city, Arkansas, Phillips County, 3 miles west-northwest of Helena and the Mississippi River, and 92 miles east-southeast of Little Rock. Lumber is milled and wood products are manufactured. Founded in 1909, it was incorporated in 1917 and has a mayor-council government. Population: 11,367.

WEST HIGHLAND WHITE TERRIER, a Scottish breed, hardy in appearance, possessed of a distinctive white coat, and exhibiting strength and activity. It originated on the estate of the Malcolms of Poltalloch in Argyllshire and the breed name was taken from the western Highlands where it was developed. Its white coat distinguishes it from the Cairn terrier, with which it shares a common ancestry. Some say the breed was derived from white puppies produced in Cairn litters. The West Highland white is not unlike the Scottish terrier, although fanciers do not want the "Westie" confused with the "Scottie." The West Highland white's coat is serviceable as well as attractive, the longer outer hair harsh and straight, the underlayer soft and plentiful. The breed, which came to the United States in the early 1900's, stands 11 inches high at the shoulder and weighs 14 to 16 pounds.

WILLIAM F. BROWN.

WEST INDIES, west in'dēz, the islands scattered in the tropic basin between continental North America and South America, east of Central America and Mexico. Discovered and named the Indies by Christopher Columbus, these islands eventually came to be known as the West Indies to distinguish them from the East Indies archipelago of southeast Asia.

The two main groups of the West Indies form the northern and eastern limits of the Caribbean Sea, which is bounded on the south by Colombia and Venezuela and on the west by Central America. The larger group is the *Greater Antilles,* or northern chain formed by Cuba, Jamaica, Hispaniola, and Puerto Rico; the smaller is the *Lesser Antilles,* which curve southward from Puerto Rico to Trinidad and then westward along the coast of South America to Aruba. A third group, the 2,700 keys and islands of the Bahamas, lies outside the Caribbean, just east of Florida.

The People. The pre-Columbian population of the West Indies disappeared long ago. The American Indians who inhabited the islands were replaced rapidly as Europeans settled island after island. The Europeans introduced African slaves, whose descendants have remained to claim most of the West Indies.

The Europeans were rarely in the majority even on those islands like Cuba and Puerto Rico where the introduction of slaves was severely restricted. The Spaniards mixed with the Africans with relative ease in comparison with the exclusive English. Thus today in these two islands the pure African descendants are a decided minority, as are also the pure descendants of the Spanish colonizers. On other islands, like Aruba and Curaçao, where agriculture never prospered, the descendants of the Dutch are more noticeable though again the population is heterogeneous.

The island of Hispaniola (Santo Domingo) presents a special case. It was colonized first by Spaniards, who later were forced to recognize the sovereignty of the French over Haiti, the western section of the island. The whole island was caught up in a slave rebellion which produced the first black republic in the New World. Haiti remains a black republic, but the people of the eastern part of the island—the Dominican Republic, independent since 1844—are of mixed extraction. The blending continues, since European immigrants are encouraged to settle in the republic, and the black Haitian laborer has often been brought in to cut sugar cane.

Besides the European and his descendants, other racial minorities can be found in the West Indies. The Chinese were imported in the 19th century to Cuba and Jamaica. Originally used to build roads and later to cut sugarcane, the Chinese rapidly left the rural areas to develop small businesses in the urban centers. They number about 1% of Jamaica's population.

After the abolition of slavery in the West Indies, laborers were imported under contracts of five to ten years from many other sections of the world. Along with the Chinese came Portuguese from the Madeira Islands and Spaniards from the Canary Islands, but the hardest working and most adaptable to the climate of the Caribbean were the East Indians. Thousands were imported from what are now India and Pakistan, mostly into the Lesser Antilles, right up into the first decades of the 20th century. Their descendants can be found in Jamaica, Martinique, and Guadeloupe, but above all in Trinidad, where, out of an estimated population of about a million, more than one third is East Indian.

The Land and Natural Resources. The islands of the West Indies are formed by two principal chains of mountains, one running east and west and the other north and south. The Atlantic and the Caribbean have left only the most prominent peaks of these mountain chains visible above the water. On some of the islands, like Cuba and Hispaniola, the mountain peaks are joined together by extensive and fertile island valleys, while on others, like Puerto Rico and Nevis, the fertile land is limited for the most part to a coastal fringe around the principal elevations.

The mountains reach their highest point in Hispaniola—10,417 feet (3,175 meters) on Pico Duarte—and, in contrast, the sea drops to a depth of about 27,000 feet (about 8,200 meters) just north of Puerto Rico. Some of the more recently formed mountains in the Lesser Antilles are still active volcanos. Other islands in the Lesser Antilles, including Barbados and Antigua, were formed by geologically older mountains which have been worn away.

The climate of the West Indies is temperate all year. In January and February the temperature drops at night to the lower 70's F (lower 20's C) in the coastal areas and to the mid-60's F (17°–19° C) in the high mountains of Haiti and Cuba, but during the day it rises to 80° F (27°C) and above. The months of August and July are the hottest in the West Indies, but the gentle breezes of the Trade Winds keep the high temperature below 90° F (32° C). Torrential rains also help to keep the temperature down during June, July, and August. These are the months during which hurricanes may occur.

With fertile alluvial plains, abundant rain (except perhaps in the dry months of March and April), thick tropical foliage, and an ideal climate, the West Indies seem to combine all the elements necessary for a rich tropical garden. The islands are not blessed, however, with rich mineral resources. The few exceptions of Trinidad, Jamaica, and possibly Cuba only serve to emphasize the plight of the other smaller islands. Petroleum is found in Trinidad, and, since World War II, Jamaica has become one of the largest producers of bauxite, from which aluminum is extracted. In Puerto Rico, copper has been found. Cuba has workable deposits of copper, nickel, manganese, chromium, and iron. Some bauxite is mined in the Dominican Republic.

THE WEST INDIES

Political component	Population (1979 est.)	Capital
Independent nations:		
Antigua and Barbuda	75,000	St. John's
Bahamas	224,000	Nassau
Barbados	251,000	Bridgetown
Cuba	9,775,000	Havana
Dominica	79,000	Roseau
Dominican Republic	5,275,000	Santo Domingo
Grenada	109,000	St. George's
Haiti	4,919,000	Port-au-Prince
Jamaica	2,162,000	Kingston
St. Christopher and Nevis	44,400[2]	Basseterre
St. Lucia	118,000	Castries
St. Vincent and the Grenadines	97,000	Kingstown
Trinidad and Tobago	1,127,000	Port of Spain
British dependencies:		
Anguilla	6,500[2]	The Valley
British Virgin Islands	13,000	Road Town
Cayman Islands	17,000	Georgetown
Montserrat	11,000	Plymouth
Turks and Caicos Is.	6,000	Grand Turk
French departments:		
Guadeloupe	319,000	Basse-Terre
Martinique	315,000	Fort-de-France
Netherlands Antilles[1]	260,000	Willemstad
Associated with U.S.:		
Puerto Rico	3,188,000[2]	San Juan
U.S. Virgin Islands	95,600[2]	Charlotte Amalie
Navassa Island	. . .	. . .
Total West Indies	*28,485,500*	

[1]Includes Aruba, Bonaire, Curaçao, Saba, St. Eustatius, and part of St. Martin. [2]1980 census (rounded).

The Economy. For centuries the West Indies have been known for the production of sugar, coffee, tropical fruits, and spices. While this continues to be true for most of the islands, industry and commerce are beginning to dominate. Industry first touched the almost deserted and barren islands of Curaçao and Aruba, where oil refineries were built by the Dutch and Americans to refine Venezuelan oil. Trinidad soon followed with its own refineries, but the depression of the 1930's prevented any further development of industry or commerce in the West Indies.

After World War II, Puerto Rico led the way with an impressively successful industrial development program, which facilitated the establishment of over a thousand new industrial plants. Other islands, like Jamaica, Trinidad, Martinique, and Antigua, hoping to imitate Puerto Rico's success, initiated their own industrial development programs with varying degrees of failure or success. Ready and direct access to the vast North American market, which producers in Puerto Rico have, was not available to other islands of the West Indies since they do not lie within the U.S. tariff walls. Nevertheless, industry can be found on the sugar island of Antigua in the form of a modern oil refining plant. St. Croix, one of the American Virgin Islands, has harvested its last sugar crop; its people, who cut cane for 300 years, are now working in chemical plants and in oil and bauxite refineries.

The West Indies received some of the benefit of North American and European prosperity after World War II through the increased tourist trade, which previously had been almost monopolized by Havana. Small islands like St. Barthélemy (French), St. Martin (French and Dutch), and St. John (U.S.) joined the list of ports-of-call for tourist ships which usually put in at the standard colorful West Indian communities of Charlotte Amalie (U.S. Virgin Islands), Port-au-Prince (Haiti) and Willemstad (Curaçao).

Either through industry or through commerce stimulated by tourism, the West Indies have enjoyed a certain degree of prosperity since the late 1960's. The average per capita annual income has risen, especially in Puerto Rico, the U. S. Virgin Islands, and Curaçao. But pockets of poverty continue to exist, as in Haiti, where political instability and uncertainty, combined with a high density of population, tend to keep down the standard of living.

Educational and Cultural Life. The first university in the New World was founded in 1538 (nearly a century before Harvard) in Santo Domingo, the present capital of the Dominican Republic. Now the West Indies have at least a dozen universities and colleges, a clear indication of the attention paid to education in the Caribbean. With the notable exception of the island of Hispaniola, illiteracy has been all but eliminated from the West Indies. Popular libraries on all the islands, scientific centers of research (like the nuclear center in Mayagüez, Puerto Rico), educational television (found in Puerto Rico and Antigua), and graduate schools of medicine (in Cuba, Puerto Rico, Jamaica, and the Dominican Republic) are some of the institutions which attest to the intellectual progress of the West Indies.

The West Indies are famous for their popular forms of music such as the calypso and the rumba. Less known are their poets, like Aimé Césaire (Martinique), founder of the school of negritude; their anthropologists, like Fernando Ortíz (Cuba) and Jean Price Mars (Haiti), pioneers in the study of West Indian culture; and their novelists, like Alejo Carpentier (Cuba), V.S. Naipaul (Trinidad), and George Lamming (Barbados), or short story writers, like Juan Bosch (Dominican Republic) and John Hearne (Jamaica). The list could be extended to include many others.

Creole culture is typical of the West Indies, where ancient folkways of expression in speech and art have not been wiped out by modernization. The people of Haiti prefer to speak a French Creole rather than pure French; the multilingual people of Curaçao, fluent in Dutch, English, and Spanish, prefer to use Papiamento (a Spanish-based Creole language) to converse among themselves.

The West Indies present the contrasting cultural patterns which reflect the varied European heritage of the colonial period. However, beneath this heterogeneous pattern lies a common cultural base which serves to identify and in a way bind together all the island communities.

History. Columbus' first landfall was in the West Indies on what is believed to be the island of San Salvador in the Bahamas. The Spaniards explored the whole Caribbean Sea and eventually settled the Greater Antilles. The indigenous Arawaks of the larger islands were either eliminated or absorbed by the Spanish in the first years of the 16th century. The Caribs, who gave their name to the Caribbean Sea, were confined to the Lesser Antilles, which the Spanish felt were not valuable enough to colonize. Thus, in the 17th century, when the French, Dutch, Danish, and English invaded the Spanish domain, they were at first limited to the islands of Barbados and St. Christopher (St. Kitts) and later St. Eustatius, Antigua, and Martinique. In 1655, under Oliver Cromwell's directives, the English made a major attempt to conquer Hispaniola but, when repelled by the Spanish, were forced to settle for Jamaica. The French, by the end of the 17th century, had succeeded in securing Spanish recognition of their occupation of Haiti.

Spices and productive sugar plantations converted the West Indies into precious jewels in the crowns of European monarchs, and throughout the 18th century, possession of the islands was hotly contested. By the end of the Napoleonic era, however, the lines of control were established. Spain had lost Trinidad and Jamaica to the British; and France had taken Haiti, only to lose it in 1794 to Toussaint L'Ouverture, who led his slave companions to a successful revolt.

At the close of the 19th century the United States wrested from Spain its remaining two colonies in the New World: Cuba achieved nominal independence, but Puerto Rico remained a colony of the United States at the end of the Spanish-American War. In 1917 the Danes sold their Virgin Islands to the United States, thus completing American territorial expansion in the Caribbean.

Cuba, Haiti, and the Dominican Republic, the only independent countries in the West Indies until 1962, have fluctuated between revolutionary anarchy and bloody dictatorships. On various occasions the United States intervened in Cuba under the Platt Amendment (see PLATT, ORVILLE HITCHCOCK), and in 1965 in the Dominican Republic—on each occasion to prevent bloody civil strife. Some material progress was realized under ruthless dictators like Rafael Trujillo in the Dominican Republic and Fulgencio Batista in Cuba.

Since World War II, the United States and Britain have moved to liquidate their colonial empires in the Caribbean. Puerto Rico enjoys a high degree of prosperity and stability in a voluntary association with the United States which allows complete local autonomy. Jamaica and Trinidad, with its satellite island of Tobago, achieved independence in 1962, and Barbados in 1966—all within the Commonwealth of Nations. Antigua, Dominica, Grenada, St. Kitts-Nevis-Anguilla, and St. Lucia in 1967 and St. Vincent in 1969 became associated states with Britain. The Bahamas became independent in 1973, Grenada in 1974, Dominica in 1978, St. Lucia and St. Vincent and the Grenadines in 1979, Antigua and Barbuda in 1981, and St. Christopher and Nevis in 1983. All remained within the Commonwealth.

In one respect, the West Indies have experienced disappointing failures. Attempts were made after World War II to bind the West Indies closer together in a regional federation or association. These attempts, such as the Caribbean Organization and the West Indies Federation, were made both at the national and international levels, but after a few years were disbanded. However, steps are taken periodically to seek closer cooperation, particularly in the economic field, with the hope that political cooperation will follow.

THOMAS MATHEWS*
University of Puerto Rico

Bibliography

Burn, William L., *The British West Indies* (Greenwood Press 1975).
Evans, F. C., *The West Indies* (Cambridge 1973).
Kiple, K. F., *The Caribbean Slave* (Cambridge 1985).
Lowenthal, David, *West Indian Societies* (Oxford 1972).
Phillips, Sir Fred, *West Indian Constitutions: Post-Independence Reforms* (Oceana Pub. 1985).
Sherlock, Sir Philip, *West Indian Nations* (St. Martin's Press 1973).

WEST LAFAYETTE, wĕst lä-fĭ-ĕt', city, Indiana, in Tippecanoe County, 60 miles northwest of Indianapolis and across the Wabash River from Lafayette, the county seat, with which it is connected by four bridges. Purdue University, a land-grant institution, is within the city limits. Six miles to the north is the Tippecanoe Battlefield, where William Henry Harrison and Tecumseh fought in 1811. Fort Ouiatenon, four miles to the south, is on a site used by many Indian tribes as camping grounds until the French built a trading post there in 1719–1720. West Lafayette was called Kingston from 1845 until 1888, when the adjoining town of Chauncey was annexed and the present name was adopted.

Incorporated in 1924, the city is governed by a mayor and council. West Lafayette has an airport and is served by the Lake Central Airlines and by state and federal highways. The surrounding region is agricultural. The humorist and playwright George Ade, a one-time resident of the town, was part donor of the Ross Ade Stadium, where Purdue's football games are played. Pop. 21,247.

Blanche G. Lloyd.

WEST LIBERTY STATE COLLEGE, wĕst lĭb'ər-tē, a state-controlled, coeducational college, with its main campus at West Liberty, W.Va., and a downtown branch in Wheeling. Founded in 1837 as West Liberty Academy, the school was known as West Liberty State Normal School from 1870, and West Liberty State Teachers College, from 1931, before acquiring its present name in 1943. Curriculums offered include liberal arts and preprofessional courses, teacher education, business administration, and dental hygiene. The average enrollment is 1,600.

WEST LINN, wĕst lĭn, city, Oregon, in Clackamas County, on the Willamette River, opposite Oregon City and about 11 miles south of Portland. It is a paper-milling center, incorporated in 1913. Pop. 12,956.

WEST LONG BRANCH, wĕst lŏng brȧnch, borough, New Jersey, in Monmouth County, located about 55 highway miles south of New York City, 2 miles from the Fort Monmouth military installation, and 1 mile from the Atlantic Ocean. It is primarily a residential area. The borough is the home of Monmouth College, with its beautiful buildings and campus, and was the site of President Woodrow Wilson's summer White House, called "Shadow Lawn." West Long Branch has a council form of government, established in 1908, with a mayor and six councilmen. Pop. 7,380.

Nina J. Klein.

WEST LOTHIAN, wĕst lō'thē-ən (formerly **LINLITHGOWSHIRE**), county, Scotland, covering 120 square miles in south-central Scotland. From its northern border on the Firth of Forth, it extends southward into hilly country drained by the Avon and Almond rivers. The county town is Linlithgow (1961 pop., 4,327). West Lothian is a farming and dairying region, and has important coal, oil-shale, iron-mining, and quarrying industries. There are prehistoric and Roman remains. Pop. (1961) 92,764.

WEST MEMPHIS, wĕst mĕm'phĭs, city, Arkansas, in Crittenden County, in the so-called Tri-State District of Arkansas, Tennessee, and Mississippi, on the west bank of the Mississippi River, less than 10 miles west of Memphis, Tenn. It is served by the Missouri Pacific, Cotton Belt, and St. Louis-San Francisco railways, and is on a federal highway. A privately owned airport offers chartered service. The city is an agricultural trading center in a region whose rich alluvial soil supports such crops as corn, small grain, soybeans, alfalfa, rice, and cotton, the latter being the primary crop. Originally a logging camp, West Memphis became a lumber-milling center and now boasts several light industries. Facilities for processing and marketing food and othewise serving the farmer include canning factories, fertilizer-mixing plants, cotton oil mills, compresses, and meat-packing plants. The city has a modern hospital, a daily newspaper, and a radio station. West Memphis was incorporated in 1920. Government is by mayor and council. Pop. 28,138.

M. W. Hightshoe.

WEST MIFFLIN, wĕst mĭf'lĭn, borough, Pennsylvania, the largest in Allegheny County, lying along the south bank of the Monongahela River, about 10 miles southeast of Pittsburgh. An industrial center, it is the site of many important industries which manufacture steel and coal products, automobile bodies, and cans, and there is an atomic energy plant. Freight service is provided by five railroads, including the Pennsylvania Railroad, which also serves passengers. The Allegheny County Municipal Airport is located in the borough. The comunity was formerly Mifflin Township, created in 1788 and named for Thomas Mifflin, the first governor of the state. It became a borough in 1944 and is governed by a mayor and seven councilmen. Kennywood Amusement Park, one of the nation's largest, is in West Mifflin. Pop. 26,552.

Dorothy English.

WEST MILWAUKEE, wĕst mĭl-wô'kē, village, Wisconsin, in Milwaukee County, on the southwest border of the City of Milwaukee. This two-square-mile village has the heaviest concentration of industry in the Milwaukee area. Eighty percent of its land is zoned for industrial and mercantile establishments, which employ more than twice the number of people who reside in the village. Industries manufacture power shovels, diesel engines, industrial cranes, preassembled homes, conveyor belts, malt, candy and cookies, dishwashers, X-ray units, and water heaters.

West Milwaukee was incorporated in 1906 and operates under a village president and six trustees who are popularly elected. The village is chiefly noted for its great industrial complex, which gives it the appearance of an industrial park. Pop. 3,535.

Richard E. Krug.

WEST MONROE, wĕst mən-rō', city, Louisiana, in Ouachita Parish, on the west bank of the Ouachita River, opposite Monroe, in the north-central part of the state, at an elevation of 75 feet. It is an attractive residential community, with many homes built in the rolling pine hills. The surrounding country is agricultural. Cotton, cottonseed oil, and soybeans are processed and a chemical plant is located here. The city is on state and federal highways and is served by the same carriers which accommodate its larger neighbor, Monroe (q.v.), whose cultural and educational facilities are also available to West Monroe's citizens. Known for some years as Cottonport, the community was founded in the 1860's, two miles south of the bustling river port of Trenton. After the Illinois Central Railroad had bridged the Ouachita at West Monroe in 1880, Trenton was gradually eclipsed and eventually absorbed by the younger town. West Monroe was incorporated in 1926 and is governed by a mayor and council. Population: 14,993.

FRANCES FLANDERS.

WEST NEW YORK, wĕst nōō yôrk′, town, New Jersey, in Hudson County, situated atop the Palisades, several miles north of Jersey City and directly west across the Hudson River from midtown New York City. One of the country's largest "towns," it exceeds many "cities" in population. West New York is a combined residential and light industrial community and an embroidery-manufacturing center. It has been estimated that as much as 90 percent of the country's embroidery industry can be found in the town or within five miles of it, the products being exported throughout the country and the world. Textiles, clothing, radio parts, leather goods, and toys are also manufactured, and the town is a leading commercial shopping area. The Hudson River frontage is a mile-long saltwater port which accommodates ocean-going vessels. Beyond it at the riverside are extensive New York Central Railroad facilities. West New York's parks, along the top of the Palisades, command unsurpassed views of the Hudson and the New York skyline. The Statue of Liberty and the Weehawken site of the duel between Alexander Hamilton and Aaron Burr are also visible.

Settlement was begun by the Dutch in 1661, and Gov. Peter Stuyvesant's patents were later recognized by the English governor, Philip Carteret. During the Revolutionary War, a spirited skirmish was fought in the vicinity when Gen. Anthony Wayne led an unsuccessful attack by colonists on a Tory blockhouse. After the Revolution, New Jersey's status as a link between New York and Philadelphia led to the quick settlement of the area, which has been densely populated and economically active ever since. West New York was organized as an independent town in 1898, when it had a population of about 5,000. It is governed under the commission form, with five popularly elected commissioners selecting the mayor. Population: 39,194.

HELEN OSIENSKI.

WEST NEWTON, wĕst nū′tən, borough, Pennsylvania, in Westmoreland County, on the Youghiogheny River, about 20 miles southeast of Pittsburgh, and 15 miles by state highway southwest of Greensburg, the county seat, at an elevation of 770 feet. It is a residential district with a few small industries, truck and dairy farming, some cattle raising, and coal mining in the vicinity. It is served by the Baltimore & Ohio Railroad and is governed by a burgess and council. Settled in the 18th century, it was the site of an Indian massacre in 1763. First named Simerals Ferry, the name was changed to Robbstown and then to West Newton. Population: 3,387.

NELL PENNEY.

WEST ORANGE, wĕst ŏr′ĭnj, town, New Jersey, in Essex County, four miles by road northwest of Newark. The town covers 12 square miles and part of it lies in the Watchung Mountains, also called the Orange Mountains, which are two ridges of volcanic origin. Primarily a residential community, West Orange has some manufacturing, including pharmaceuticals, clothing, batteries, office equipment, and chemical and electronic research. Traprock is quarried within the town limits. Although the town has no hospital of its own, the Kessler Institute for Rehabilitation, which treats paraplegics, amputees, and other physically disabled persons, is located here. A year-around ice-skating rink is maintained in the South Mountain Arena by the County Park Commission.

Thomas A. Edison, the inventor, was a resident of West Orange from 1887 until his death in 1931. His 10,000-volume library and his laboratory, with its original working equipment, is a national monument. His home, a 23-room Victorian mansion in the Llewellyn Park section of the town, is now a national museum.

West Orange was incorporated as a town in 1900. The area it occupies had been formed from portions of various communities into the Township of Fairmount in 1862, the name being changed to West Orange the following year. A commission form of government has been in effect since 1922. Population: 39,510.

ROBERT JONAS.

WEST ORANGE, village, Texas, in Orange County, near the Louisiana border, about 20 miles east of Beaumont, at an altitude of 10 feet. The village is a residential suburb just southwest of the city of Orange, a manufacturing center and deep-water port on the Sabine-Neches Waterway. Population: 4,610.

WEST PALM BEACH, wĕst päm bēch, city Florida, seat of Palm Beach County, located on the east coast of Florida, on Lake Worth, across from the resort town of Palm Beach and 68 miles north of Miami on a federal highway and the Intercoastal Waterway, at an elevation of 15 feet. It is served by the Florida East Coast and Seaboard Airline railroads, the Palm Beach International Airport, and the Port of Palm Beach. It is a commercial center for Everglades farm products, cattle, and citrus. Industries include the manufacture of tents and awnings, furniture, building materials (especially concrete blocks), and food and beverages. Since 1950, electronics and jet-engine manufacturing plants have opened in the county.

A tourist center as well as a trade center, West Palm Beach has a municipal golf course and swimming pools, and maintains supervised parks with tennis courts, lawn bowling, and shuffleboard courts. Swimming, fishing (both fresh- and saltwater), and boating are possible during the entire year. For cultural and intellectual activities, there is a public library, a junior museum, and the Norton Gallery and School of Art, noted for its collection of Chinese jade. The city also has a Little Theatre and a number of music, art, and garden clubs. The Atlanta Braves baseball team has its winter training quarters in West Palm Beach, and the city is a center for boat derbies and regattas.

The city was founded in 1893 by Henry M. Flagler as a trade and industrial center for Palm Beach, and was incorporated the following year. It has had a commission-city manager form of government since 1919. Population: 63,305.

ZELLA D. ADAMS.

WEST PATERSON, wĕst păt'ər-sən, borough, New Jersey, a southwest suburb of Paterson, in Passaic County, about 30 miles by road northeast of New York City, at an elevation of 190 feet. It is primarily a residential area, stretching from Garret Mountain to the Passaic River. Formerly a part of Little Falls, it was incorporated in 1917 and is governed by a mayor and council. The major portion of the Garret Mountain Reservation (570 acres), the largest of the Passaic County parks, is located here. Population: 11,293.

WEST PITTSTON, wĕst pĭts'tən, borough, Pennsylvania, in Luzerne County, 10 miles southwest of Scranton, in the heart of northeastern Pennsylvania's anthracite region, on the west bank of the Susquehanna. It is across the river from Pittston, with which it is connected by two bridges. The borough is largely residential but has a trailer assembly plant and factories manufacturing clothing, buckets, chains and cables, plastics, and cigars. Sometimes known as "The Garden Village," West Pittston is noted for its spacious homes and lawns. It was originally called Jenkins' Ferry, the ferry having once been its only link with Pittston. The borough was chartered in 1857 and is governed by a burgess and council. A marker identifies the former site of Fort Jenkins, one of the main defenses of the Wyoming Valley in colonial times. Population: 5,980.

MYRA SIMONS.

WEST PLAINS, wĕst plānz, city, Missouri, seat of Howell County in the Ozark Mountains region of southern Missouri, about 90 miles east-southeast of Springfield and 20 miles north of the Arkansas boundary, at an altitude of 955 feet. It is served by federal and state highways and by the St. Louis-San Francisco Railroad. West Plains is a shipping center for local livestock, dairy products, lumber, and grain, and it has some light industry, including food processing, woodworking, and shoe manufacturing. It was laid out in 1858 and is governed by a commission. Population: 7,741.

WEST POINT, wĕst point, city, Georgia, in Troup County, on the Chattahoochee River, at the point where the river becomes the Georgia-Alabama boundary, at an altitude of 580 feet. It was once thought to be the westernmost spot in Georgia. It is on state and federal highways. West Point has a textile manufacturing industry in operation since 1866, and is a trading center for five textile communities on the Alabama side of the border. Textile machinery is manufactured in a foundry and machine works. The city was incorporated in 1831 and is governed by a mayor and council. Here Fort Tyler, the last fort of the Confederacy, fell on April 16, 1865, to 3,000 of James Harrison Wilson's troops ("Wilson's Raiders"), after a defense by less than 300 Confederates, including boys, militia, and convalescents of Reid Hospital. Population: 4,294.

WEST POINT, city, Mississippi, seat of Clay County in the northern part of the state, at an altitude of 243 feet. It is about 140 road miles northeast of Jackson, is on a federal highway, and is served by the Illinois Central and other railroads. Situated in the so-called "Prairie Belt," well adapted to livestock and dairying, the community is nearly balanced between agriculture and industry. Manufactures include boilers, pajamas, boats, fishing equipment, and fertilizer, and there are meat-packing, dairy products, and feed-processing plants. The city has a radio station, a daily newspaper, and a small junior college for Negroes. Within 22 miles of the town are Mississippi State University and the Mississippi State College for Women. The Columbus Air Force Base is 11 miles to the east. Incorporated in 1858, West Point is governed by a mayor and a board of aldermen. Population: 8,811.

D. H. COLEMAN.

WEST POINT, town, Virginia, in King William County, situated at the point where the Pamunkey and Mattaponi rivers converge to form the York River, at an altitude of 16 feet.

The town was founded in the early 17th century and was named for the four West brothers: Thomas, Francis, John, and Nathaniel, the first three of whom were governors of Virginia. In 1691 the state General Assembly designated West Point as a port of entry and in 1705 as a free borough. George Washington often stopped at the town on his way to Williamsburg from Mount Vernon, and Martha Washington was born nearby.

During the Civil War the town was of strategic importance because it lay at the head of navigation on the York River and was the terminus of the Richmond and York River Railroad. On May 7, 1862, the immediate area was the scene of an engagement between Union and Confederate troops (see PENINSULAR CAMPAIGN OF 1862). The town was incorporated in 1870 and continues to function as a port. In addition to fisheries, there are pulp mills, pickle factories, and manufactures of wood products.

West Point has a mayor-council form of government. Population: 2,726.

WEST POINT, United States military reservation, New York, located in Orange County, on the west bank of the Hudson River, about 50 miles north of New York City. The West Point Military Reservation is the site of the United States Military Academy (q.v.), established by Congress on March 16, 1802.

West Point is the oldest military post in the United States in continuous occupation by American troops. The area, in the Hudson Highlands, was first occupied on Jan. 20, 1778, because of its strategic importance in controlling the Hudson River. Large fortifications were built, the restored remains of which are still visible, and a heavy iron chain was stretched across the river to Constitution Island to prevent British vessels from ascending. In 1780 the area was under the command of Benedict Arnold, whose conspiracy to betray this key military post to the enemy was frustrated by the capture of Major John André. After the Revolutionary War, West Point was retained as a military post.

The scenic beauty of the site is enhanced by the West Point Plain, a broad terrace about 150 feet above the level of the river, by the view of the river north to Newburgh, and by the nearby hills, including such peaks as Crow's Nest and Storm King. To the south is the village of Highland Falls. The reservation, including Constitution Island contains about 16,000 acres.

SIDNEY FORMAN.

WEST POINT MILITARY ACADEMY. See UNITED STATES MILITARY ACADEMY.

WEST PRUSSIA, wĕst prŭsh'ə (Ger. **WESTPREUSSEN**), a province of the former Kingdom of Prussia, in Germany, between Pomerania (west) and East Prussia. The capital was Danzig (Pol. Gdansk). Most of the area was ceded to Poland after World War I, recovered by Germany in 1939, and returned to Poland after World War II.

WEST READING, wĕst rĕd'ĭng, borough, Pennsylvania, in Berks County, in the eastern part of the state, on the western side of the Schuylkill River, across from Reading. Settled as early as 1748, West Reading was divided into lots in 1873 and incorporated in 1907. It has a council-manager government. There are 20 acres of parks. Hosiery manufacture is the principal industry. Population: 4,507.

RICHARD L. BROWN.

WEST RIVER. See SI KIANG.

WEST SAINT PAUL, wĕst sānt pôl', city, Minnesota, in Dakota County. It is in the "Twin City" area, on the south bank of the Mississippi River. At its original incorporation in 1858, it included the present city of South St. Paul. Reincorporated in 1889, West St. Paul now covers an area of about five square miles. It has been governed by a mayor and council since 1907. The city has no large industries and is primarily a residential suburb for the neighboring cities of St. Paul, Minneapolis, and South St. Paul. Population: 18,527.

ROBERT E. HOAG.

WEST SPRINGFIELD, wĕst sprĭng'fēld, town, Massachusetts, in Hampden County, in the southwestern part of the state, on the west bank of the Connecticut River, across from Springfield. The town is both residential and industrial, the principal manufactures being paper, fiber boxes, machine gears and tools, magnetos, chemicals, and gasoline pumps. There are also bookbinderies, a farm supply cooperative, and an electric generating plant. The first permanent house was built in 1654. The town became a separate parish in 1696 and was incorporated as an independent township in 1756. The Day House, built in 1754, is now a historical museum. From the nearby farm of Justin Morgan, born in West Springfield in 1747, came the stallion Justin Morgan, progenitor of the breed of Morgan horses.

The Eastern States Exposition is held annually in West Springfield. The exposition grounds are also the site of Storrowton Village, a reconstructed colonial community. The town has a public library, a radio station, and three theaters (plus a music tent during the summer months). The form of government is the elective town meeting system. Population: 27,042.

HILDA M. HOLMAN.

WEST SUMMERLAND, wĕst sŭm'ər-lənd, village, Province of British Columbia, Canada, a part of the Summerland District Municipality. It adjoins the town of Summerland on the west side of Okanagan Lake, about 10 miles northwest of Penticton and 45 miles north of the United States border. It is served by the Canadian Pacific Railway. Since there is a long frost-free period, tree-fruit is produced on the benchlands by irrigation. Within the municipality are to be found a hospital, a library, and a weekly newspaper, and there is a government experimental farm and entomological laboratory.

WEST TERRE HAUTE, wĕst tĕr'ə hōt, city, Indiana, in Vigo County, on the western bank of the Wabash River, opposite Terre Haute, at an altitude of 476 feet. It is served by the Pennsylvania Railroad. Once a thriving coal-mining town, it is now principally a residential suburb. It became a city in 1933. Population: 2,806.

WEST TEXAS STATE COLLEGE, wĕst tĕk'səs, a coeducational, state-controlled liberal arts and teachers college at Canyon, Texas. It was established as the West Texas Normal College in 1910, but degrees were not granted until 1919. In 1923, the name was changed to West Texas State Teachers College. A fifth year of college work and the granting of the master's degree was authorized in 1930. In recognition of the wider scope of the college in general education, the Texas legislature in 1949 changed the name to West Texas State College. The seven degrees now granted include the bachelor of arts, bachelor of science, bachelor of business administration, bachelor of music education, master of arts, master of education, and master of business administration. The library has a collection of over 50,000 volumes and nearly 400,000 government documents, including a collection of newspapers, letters, and other materials relating to the early history of the Texas Panhandle. In addition to regular day-time classes, a full week's schedule of evening classes is offered. The school colors are maroon and white, and the athletic teams are nicknamed the "Buffaloes." The average enrollment is about 8,000.

BILL R. LEE.

WEST UNIVERSITY PLACE, wĕst yo͞o-nə-vûr'sə-tē plās, city, Texas, in Harris County. It is a residential suburb of Houston, and was developed after 1917 as a planned community of country homes southwest of the larger city, and now maintains independent life within the Houston city limits. There are a few industries, but the community has remained primarily residential, boasting homes of above-average valuation. Extensive building was completed by 1950, development having since been generally limited to improvement of city services and community recreational facilities. West University Place was incorporated in 1925, adopted a home-rule charter in 1940, and is governed by a policy-setting commission and mayor, with a city manager acting as executive. Population: 12,010.

WEST VANCOUVER, wĕst văn-ko͞o'vər, municipal district, Province of British Columbia, Canada. It is situated on the Pacific Great Eastern Railway and on a highway, north of Burrard Inlet, across from the city of Vancouver, with which it is linked by the Lions Gate Bridge. Its mild, maritime climate and its beautiful scenic views of the mountains and the sea make it an attractive residential community. There is easy access to beaches and to the skiing chair lifts on Grouse Mountain and Hollyburn Ridge. Incorporated as a municipality in 1912, West Vancouver has a weekly newspaper. Population: 35,728.

WEST VIEW, wĕst vyo͞o, borough, Pennsylvania, in Allegheny County, on a federal highway, directly northwest of Pittsburgh. Incorporated in 1905, it is one of Pittsburgh's most attractive residential suburbs, distinctive for its many brick houses and its tree-studded lawns. Population: 7,648.

STATE OF WEST VIRGINIA

Harpers Ferry, where the Potomac and Shenandoah rivers meet, is famed as the site of John Brown's 1859 raid.

WEST VIRGINIA

TABLE OF CONTENTS

State Seal of West Virginia

WEST VIRGINIA, vər-jin′yə, one of the South Atlantic states of the United States, known as the Trans-Allegheny Region of Virginia before its separation from the mother state during the Civil War. West Virginia is bounded on the north by Ohio, Pennsylvania, and Maryland; on the south by Virginia and Kentucky; on the west by Ohio and Kentucky; and on the east by Virginia. The narrow strip of land at the north, between Ohio and Pennsylvania, is called the Northern Panhandle, and that at the east is called the Eastern Panhandle. The latter is almost entirely surrounded by Maryland and Virginia, the three easternmost counties being joined to the rest of West Virginia by a neck of land less than 10 miles (16 km) wide.

Because of the state's rugged terrain, it is nicknamed the Mountain State and sometimes referred to as "the Switzerland of America." It is the second-largest coal producing state in the United States, but the economic depression characteristic of the Appalachian states resulted in a declining population in West Virginia. The state is trying to counteract this trend by adding new industries to such old ones as the manufacture of fine glass, for which it has long been famous.

1. The Land

Because of its natural character the state boundary is perhaps the most irregular in the Union. The West Virginia–Ohio line is the low water mark on the western bank of the Ohio River, thus throwing the islands within West Virginia. The center of the Big Sandy and of Tug Fork of that stream is the boundary between West Virginia and Kentucky. The Virginia–West Virginia line is made up of portions of the boundaries of border counties and generally follows the crest of meandering mountain ridges. The West Virginia–Maryland line is the south bank at the low water mark of the Potomac and its North Branch to the source of the latter at Fairfax Stone, thence by a line due north about 35 miles

EWING GALLOWAY

Hawk's Nest State Park, southeast of Charleston, offers visitors breathtaking views of the New River Gorge.

(56 km) to the Mason and Dixon line, which forms the boundary between West Virginia and Pennsylvania to its western terminus at a point about 20 miles (32 km) east of the Ohio River. Thence the Pennsylvania boundary extends due north 61 miles (98 km) to the northern bank of the Ohio.

Major Physical Divisions. West Virginia has two major land divisions, the Appalachian Plateau and the Appalachian Ridge and Valley Region. The Appalachian Plateau, where the state's minerals, including coal, and larger cities are located, lies to the west of the Allegheny Front on the western border of the Appalachian Ridge and Valley Region. The rugged, irregular border between the two regions is formed where the sharply folded layers of rock of the Ridge and Valley Region meet the more gently folded layers of the plateau.

The Ridge and Valley Region is in the eastern part of the state and takes in the Eastern Panhandle. Here heavily forested mountain ridges are separated by narrow valleys. The soil is rich, supporting the state's agriculture and livestock.

The average elevation of the surface of West Virginia is about 1,500 feet (458 meters) above sea level. The range in altitude is 4,613 feet (1,400 meters), the lowest point being Harpers Ferry at 240 feet (73 meters) and the highest the summit of Spruce Knob, Pendleton county, at 4,863 feet (1,483 meters). The lowest point in the Mississippi Valley drainage is at Kenova (500 feet, or 152 meters). Of the total area, over 20,635 square miles (53,435 sq km) drain into the Ohio either directly or indirectly; nearly 3,500 square miles (9,065 sq km) drain into the Potomac; and about 80 square miles (207 sq km) in Monroe county drain into the James. The predominant feature of West Virginia topography is ruggedness. There are no natural lakes or pools of considerable size, and the areas of poorly drained land are few and small.

Rivers and Lakes. The Allegheny Front divides the state of West Virginia into two separate drainage systems. The rivers and streams to the west of the front drain into the Ohio River. To the east the waters flow across the eastern seaboard into Chesapeake Bay. The Ohio River, which flows for over 275 miles (443 km) along the western border of the state, is navigable and connects with the Mississippi River. The principal tributaries of the Ohio River are the Monongahela, Little Kanawha, Kanawha, Guyandotte, and Big Sandy rivers. The Elk, Gauley, and New rivers are branches of the Kanawha River, the largest Ohio tributary in the state. The Cheat, Tygart, and West Ford rivers are branches of the Monongahela. The Shenandoah and other rivers in the Eastern Panhandle flow north and east into the Potomac. The principal tributaries of the Potomac are the North Branch and the South Branch.

West Virginia has no large natural lakes, but locks and dams for flood control have created large reservoirs that serve as lakes for fishing and recreational purposes. The largest of these is Summersville Lake on the Gauley River. Others include Bluestone Lake on New River, Sutton Lake on Elk River, Tygart Lake on the Tygart Valley River, and East Lynn Lake on Twelvepole Creek. Lake Lynn, also known as Cheat Lake, on Cheat River, is used primarily for power.

INFORMATION HIGHLIGHTS

Location: West Virginia is a South Atlantic state bounded on the north by Ohio, Pennsylvania, and Maryland, on the south by Virginia and Kentucky, on the west by Ohio and Kentucky, and on the east by Virginia.
Elevation: *Highest point*—Spruce Knob, 4,863 feet (1,483 meters); *lowest point*—Potomac River, 240 feet (73 meters); *approximate mean elevation*—1,500 feet (458 meters).
Area: 24,231 square miles (62,758 sq km); rank, 41st.
Population: 1980 census, 1,950,279; rank, 34th. Increase (1970–1980), 11.8%.
Climate: Warm, humid summers and cold, humid winters, with sudden changes possible in all seasons; abundant rainfall.
Statehood: June 20, 1863; order of admission, 35th.
Origin of Name: Was the western part of Virginia until the Civil War, when it broke away to remain part of the Union.
Capital: Charleston.
Largest City: Huntington.
Number of Counties: 55.
Principal Products: *Manufactures*—chemicals; primary metals; stone, clay, and glass products; metal products; nonelectric machinery; *farm products*—milk, beef, cattle, apples, poultry, eggs; *minerals*—coal, petroleum, natural gas and natural gas liquids, sand and gravel.
State Motto: *Montani semper liberi* ("Mountaineers are always free").
State Songs: *West Virginia, My Home Sweet Home; West Virginia Hills; This is My West Virginia.*
State Nicknames: Mountain State; Panhandle State; Switzerland of America.
State Bird: Cardinal.
State Flower: Great rhododendron.
State Tree: Sugar maple.
State Flag: State coat of arms in a field of white bordered by a strip of blue; above the coat of arms a ribbon with the words "State of West Virginia," and below, a wreath of Great rhododendron. See also FLAG—*Flags of the States.*

Climate. Because the range in altitude is equivalent to about 10 to 15 degrees of latitude, West Virginia has a great diversity of climate. Only the Eastern Panhandle is affected perceptibly by the Atlantic Ocean, and the climate of the major part of the state is decidedly continental and thus subject to great and frequent changes in temperature. The mean annual temperature ranges from 56° F (13° C) in the southwestern counties to 48° F (9° C) in the mountain counties. For the greater part of the state the mean annual temperature is between 52° and 53° F (11°–12° C), and the range is from −15° to 100° F (−26°–38° C), but temperatures as low as −35° F (−37° C) and as high as 107° F (42° C) have been recorded. In the low-lying counties the growing season is about six months and in the highest about five months. The prevailing winds are from the southwest.

The annual precipitation varies from well over 50 inches (1,270 mm) in a few of the highest counties to 35 to 40 inches (889–1,016 mm) in counties of the panhandles. The mean for the greater part of the state is between 45 and 50 inches (1,143–1,270 mm) and is usually fairly evenly distributed, but some seasons are very dry.

Plant and Animal Life. Before the first white settlers came, present-day West Virginia was almost completely covered by a mixed hardwood growth known as the Appalachian Hardwood Forest. Among the trees were tulip (or poplar), locust, hickory, ash, oak, maple, walnut, beech, chestnut, cherry, sycamore, elm, birch, and mulberry. Some idea of the primeval forest of West Virginia may be had from the Mingo Oak, located near the Mingo-Logan county line. At the time of its death in 1938 this tree was said to be the largest and the oldest living thing in the state. It was about 600 years old and had attained a height of 145 feet (44 meters) and a circumference of 30 feet 9 inches (9.4 meters).

Very little of the virgin forest is now standing. Blights, rusts, and insects took their toll. Consequently the chestnut and certain kinds of pines are all but gone.

Because of its abundant plant life, West Virginia is a botanist's paradise. Among rare plants are coltsfoot, sundew, and bog rosemary. Because of the varied climate and wide drainage system, the more common plants include many of those found in Canada and in the subtropical areas of the Appalachian Highlands. Among favorite shrubs are azalea (wild honeysuckle), rhododendron (big laurel), kalmia (laurel), and the American wisteria. Box huckleberry may be older than the Mingo Oak, and a lone hawthorn tree in the Cranberry Glades of Pocahontas county has attained a height of 40 feet (12 meters).

Animal remains found here and there indicate that West Virginia once was inhabited by many kinds of huge, clumsy slothlike animals. They indicate also that the climate has at times been much colder and at other times much hotter than at present.

The first white settlers found deer, wolves, bears, pumas, beavers, and elk in large numbers, and there were a few buffaloes in the Kanawha Valley. Except for protected deer, many of these animals are now almost extinct, but smaller animals such as foxes, skunks, and raccoons, along with beavers, are tending to increase in numbers.

Waste from mines and sawmills has destroyed many of the game fish, but numerous streams have been restocked with bass, trout, and pike of several varieties. There are several kinds of frogs, toads, water dogs, turtles, and snakes. Only two species of snakes, rattlers and copperheads, are poisonous. There are about 300 species and subspecies of birds. Among favorites are the robin, wren, tanager, and cardinal, which became the state bird in 1949.

STATE OF WEST VIRGINIA

Barges transport coal from mines to consumers along the Ohio River near Point Pleasant, W. Va.

Mineral Resources. Bituminous coal is the state's most valuable mineral resource. Deposits lie beneath about half of the state, including all the central counties and almost all of the western counties.

West Virginia also ranks high in the production of oil and gas and their by-products. Salt

Blackwater Falls near Davis in the Eastern Panhandle is one of the state's outstanding recreational areas.

STATE OF WEST VIRGINIA

GRUBER STUDIO, WHEELING, WEST VIRGINIA

Wheeling, in the highly industrialized Northern Panhandle, is renowned for its iron and steel production.

brine and rock salt are widely distributed west of the Alleghenies. Among other minerals found are barite, bromine, and fluorspar. The state is famous for its mineral springs, such as those at White Sulphur and Berkeley Springs.

Conservation. West Virginia's main conservation concerns are with the regulation of strip mining and soil and forest conservation. Strip mining has been banned in many counties because of the failure of the coal companies to restore the land after stripping. Conservationists urge the use of terracing, contour plowing, and strip cropping to prevent soil erosion. Conservation programs also protect the quality of the state's water resources, preserve oil and natural gas, and control air pollution.

Much is being done to conserve fish and game through the use of hatcheries and refuges. The state department of natural resources maintains the 127-acre (51-hectare) Palestine Bass Hatchery in Wirt county and several smaller hatcheries, including the Ridge Bass Hatchery in Morgan county, the Marlinton Trout Hatchery in Pocahontas county, and the Spring Run and the Petersburg Trout hatcheries in Grant county. In addition, there are federal hatcheries at White Sulphur Springs and Leetown. Game refuges include the Nathaniel Mountain and Short Mountain reservations (in Hampshire county) and the Elk River refuge (Braxton county), covering nearly 9,000, 8,000, and 7,000 acres (3,645, 3,240, and 2,835 hectares), respectively. There are also a much smaller State Game Farm in Upshur county, the Hornor Game Refuge in Lewis county, and the Plum Orchard Public Hunting Area in Fayette county.

2. The People

Backed by a rich heritage of folk art and fine handicrafting, the people of West Virginia have preserved the best of their past as a security against an uncertain future. A turbulent history has kept the pioneer spirit alive among the people who are descended from the original Scotch-Irish and German settlers.

Characteristics of the Population. Almost two thirds of West Virginia's population live in rural areas, including small mining towns and trading centers. At the close of the Civil War an influx of freed slaves swelled the population when they arrived to find work in the coal mines. In the late 1800's and early 1900's many immigrants arrived from Hungary, Ireland, Italy, and Poland to work in the mines.

The largest religious groups in West Virginia are Methodists and Baptists, followed by Episcopalians, Presbyterians, and Roman Catholics. The Disciples of Christ Church originated in West Virginia, and the first settlement of Seventh Day Adventists west of the Allegheny Mountains was at Salem.

Since 1864, West Virginia has divided its vote almost equally between Republican and Democratic candidates, but since the early 1930's, the voters have favored the Democratic presidential candidates.

In the 1960's, West Virginia lost about 6.2% of its population. The greatest population declines were in rural countries when many unemployed persons went north and west in search of jobs. In the 1970's, however, the population increased by 11.8%, according to the 1980 census.

Way of Life. The earliest settlers of West Virginia were cabin-dwelling farmers of English, Scotch-Irish, and, in fewer cases, German descent. These were a hardy, gregarious, but often fiercely individualistic people, with more than a little pride in the democratic equality of frontier life. The Trans-Allegheny Region remained virtually a frontier territory until the time of the Civil War. Because the plantation system and slaveholding were economically impractical in this mountain region, there was neither a large black population nor any real equivalent of eastern Virginia's landed aristocracy. After the Civil War and separation from the parent state, however, West Virginia's mode of living patterned itself more closely on Southern than on Northern models. This tendency still can be observed in the relatively leisurely pace of life in West

WEST VIRGINIA

COUNTIES

Barbour 16,639 F2
Berkeley 46,775 K2
Boone 30,447 C4
Braxton 13,894 E3
Brooke 31,117 K5
Cabell 106,835 B4
Calhoun 8,250 D3
Clay 11,265 D4
Doddridge 7,433 E2
Fayette 57,863 D4
Gilmer 8,334 E3
Grant 10,210 H2
Greenbrier 37,665 F5
Hampshire 14,867 J2
Hancock 41,053 K4
Hardy 10,030 J2
Harrison 77,710 F2
Jackson 25,794 C3
Jefferson 30,302 L2
Kanawha 231,414 C4
Lewis 18,813 E2
Lincoln 23,675 B4
Logan 50,679 C5
Marion 65,789 F2
Marshall 41,608 K6
Mason 27,045 B3
McDowell 49,899 C6
Mercer 73,942 D6
Mineral 27,234 J2
Mingo 37,336 B5
Monongalia 75,024 F1
Monroe 12,873 E5
Morgan 10,711 K1
Nicholas 28,126 E4
Ohio 61,389 K5
Pendleton 7,910 H3
Pleasants 8,236 D2
Pocahontas 9,919 F4
Preston 30,460 G2
Putnam 38,181 C4
Raleigh 86,821 D5
Randolph 28,734 G3
Ritchie 11,442 D2
Roane 15,952 D3
Summers 15,875 E5
Taylor 16,584 F2
Tucker 8,675 G2
Tyler 11,320 E2
Upshur 23,427 F3
Wayne 46,021 B4
Webster 12,245 F4
Wetzel 21,874 E1
Wirt 4,922 D4
Wood 93,648 D2
Wyoming 35,993 C5

CITIES and TOWNS

Accoville 975 C5
Acme 165 D4
Ada 250 D6
Addison (Webster Springs)⊙ 939 F4
Adolph 80 F3
Adrian 510 F3
Advent 120 C3
Albright 357 G1
Alderson 1,375 E5
Alexander 50 F3
Algoma 200 D6
Alkol 500 C4
Alma 197 E2
Alpena 110 G3
Alpoca 200 D5
Alton 139 F3
Alum Bridge 150 E2
Alum Creek 900 C4
Alvon 75 F5
Alvy 150 E2
Ameagle 230 D5
Amherstdale-Robinette 1,075 C5
Amma 200 D3
Anawalt 652 D6
Anmoore 865 F2
Ansted 1,952 D4
Apple Grove 900 B3
Arbovale 610 G4
Arbuckle 70 C3
Arden 130 G2
Arnett 300 D5
Arnoldsburg 175 D3
Arthur 350 H2
Arthurdale 1,063 G1
Asbury 280 E5
Asco 175 C6
Ashford 400 C4
Ashley 75 E2
Ashton 259 B3
Athens 1,147 E6
Auburn 116 E2
Augusta 750 J2
Aurora 250 G2
Avondale 250 C6
Baisden 500 C5
Baker 200 J2
Bakerton 125 L2
Bald Knob 356 C5
Baldwin 92 E3
Ballard 220 E6
Ballengee 170 E5
Bancroft 528 C3
Barboursville 2,871 B4
Barnabus 750 C5
Barrackville 1,815 F1
Barrett 950 C5
Bartley 900 C6
Bartow 500 G3
Bath (Berkeley Springs) 789 K1
Bayard 540 H2
Beards Fork 400 D4
Beartown 500 C6
Beaver 1,122 D5
Bebee 125 E1
Beckley⊙ 20,492 D5
Bedington 150 L1
Beech Bottom 507 K5
Beeson 300 D6
Belington 2,038 F2
Belle 1,621 C4
Belleville 105 C2
Belmont 887 D2
Belo 90 B5
Belva 275 D4
Bens Run 85 D2
Benwood 1,994 K5
Bergoo 220 F4
Berkeley 600 L2
Berkeley Springs (Bath)⊙ 789 K1
Berlin 100 F2
Berwind 615 C6
Beryl 80 H2
Bethany 1,336 L5
Bethlehem 3,045 K5
Beverly 475 G3
Bickmore 300 D4
Bigbend 120 D3
Big Chimney 450 C4
Big Creek 500 B5
Big Four 150 C6
Big Isaac 83 E2
Big Otter 150 D3
Big Springs 485 D3
Bim 500 C5
Birch River 650 E4
Bismarck 100 H2
Blacksville 248 F1
Blair 800 C5
Blakeley 76 D4
Bloomery 200 K2
Blue Creek 650 D4
Bluefield 16,060 D6
Boggs 131 E4
Bolair 950 F4
Bolivar 672 L2
Bomont 170 D4
Boomer 1,051 D4
Borderland 250 B5
Bowden 135 G3
Boyer 95 G3
Bradshaw 1,002 C6
Bramwell 989 D6
Brandonville 92 G1
Brandywine 300 H3
Breeden 600 B5
Bridgeport 6,604 F2
Bristol 60 F2
Brohard 80 D2
Brooks 196 E5
Brounland 900 C4
Brown 100 F2
Brownton 400 F2
Bruceton Mills 296 G1
Buck 150 E5
Buckeye 125 F4
Buckhannon⊙ 6,820 F3
Bud 400 D5
Buffalo 1,034 C3
Bunker Hill 600 K2
Burlington 300 J2
Burning Springs 137 D3
Burnsville 531 E3
Burnt House 175 D2
Burnwell 140 D4
Burton 200 F1
Cabin Creek 900 C4
Cabins 300 H2
Cairo 428 D2
Caldwell 795 F5
Calvin 400 E4
Camden on Gauley 236 E4
Cameron 1,474 L6
Camp Creek 200 D5
Canebrake 300 C6
Canvas 300 E4
Capon Bridge 191 K2
Capon Springs 580 K2
Carbon 300 D4
Caretta 650 C6
Cascade 103 G1
Cashmere 120 E6
Cass 148 G4
Cassity 150 F3
Cassville 800 F1
Catawba 186 F1
Cedar Grove 1,479 D4
Cedarville 90 E3
Center Point 250 E2
Centralia 100 E3
Central Station 200 E2
Century 250 F2
Ceredo 2,255 B4
Chapmanville 1,164 B5
Charleston (cap.)⊙ 63,968 D4
Charleston‡ 269,595 D4
Charles Town⊙ 2,857 L2
Charmco 800 E4
Chattaroy 1,383 B5
Cherry Run 120 K1
Chesapeake 2,364 C4
Chester 3,297 L4
Christian 200 C5
Cinco 200 D4
Cinderella 100 B5
Circleville 180 H3
Clarksburg⊙ 22,371 F2
Clay⊙ 940 D4
Clayton 100 E5
Clear Creek 300 D5
Clearview 740 K5
Clendenin 1,373 D3
Cleveland 74 F3
Clifftop 100 E4
Clifton 325 B3
Clifton Mills 136 G1
Clifty 250 E4
Clinton 350 K5
Clintonville 258 E5
Clio 300 D3
Clothier 900 C5
Clover 350 D3
Clover Lick 250 F4
Coal City 2,324 D5
Coal Fork 2,775 D4
Coalton 306 G3
Coalwood 650 C6
Coburn 230 F1
Coco 100 D4
Coketon 61 G2
Colcord 600 D5
Colliers 864 L5
Copen 50 E3
Core 250 F1
Corinth 195 H2
Costa 250 C4
Cottageville 300 C3
Cove Gap 650 B4
Cowen 723 E4
Coxs Mills 275 E2
Craigsville 1,562 E4
Cranberry 315 D5
Cranesville 106 G1
Crawley 395 E5
Creston 108 D3
Crum 500 B5
Crystal 150 D6
Cucumber 274 C6
Culloden 2,931 B4
Cyclone 500 C5
Czar 120 F3
Dallas 450 K5
Daniels 1,959 D5
Danville 727 C4
Darkesville 150 L2
Davis 979 H2
Davisville 200 C2
Davy 882 C6
Dawes 800 D4
Dawson 300 E5
Decota 800 D4
Deerwalk 150 D2
Delbarton 981 B5
Dellslow 300 G1
Diana 300 F3
Dickson 200 B4
Dille 300 E4
Dingess 600 B5
Dixie 985 D4
Dola 200 F2
Dorcas 49 H3
Dorothy 400 D5
Dry Creek 441 D5
Dryfork 425 H3
Duck 500 E3
Dunbar 9,285 C4
Duncan 40 C3
Dundon 85 D4
Dunlow 169 B4
Dunmore 286 G4
Durbin 379 G3
East Bank 1,155 D4
Eastgulf 300 D5
East Lynn 150 B4
East View 1,222 F2
Eccles 1,162 D5
Eckman 750 C6
Edgarton 415 B5
Edray 175 F4
Edwight 31 C5
Egeria 150 D5
Eglon 70 G2
Elbert 400 C6
Eleanor 1,282 C3
Elgood 125 E6
Elizabeth⊙ 856 D2
Elk Garden 291 H2
Elkhorn 150 D6
Elkhurst 120 D4
Elkins⊙ 8,536 G3
Elkridge 500 D4
Elkview 1,161 C4
Ellamore 250 F3
Ellenboro 357 D2
Elton 200 E5
English 500 C6
Enoch 125 E4
Enterprise 1,110 F2
Erbacon 350 E3
Eskdale 400 D4
Ethel 450 C5
Eureka 125 D2
Evans 400 C3
Everettville 175 F1
Fairmont⊙ 23,863 F2
Fairplain 200 C3
Fairview 759 F1
Falling Spring (Renick) 240 F4
Falling Waters 130 L1
Farmington 583 F1
Fayetteville⊙ 2,366 D4
Fellowsville 100 G2
Fenwick 500 E4
Ferguson 150 B4
Ferrellsburg 300 B4
Filbert 130 D6
Fireco 200 D5
Fisher 500 H2
Flat Top 550 D5
Flatwoods 405 E3
Flemington 452 F2
Follansbee 3,994 K5
Folsom 360 E2
Forest Hill 314 E5
Fort Ashby 1,205 J2
Fort Gay 886 A4
Fort Seybert 200 H3
Fort Spring 250 E5
Foster 500 C4
Four States 500 F2
Frame 76 C3
Frametown 150 E3
Frankford 200 F5
Franklin⊙ 780 H3
Fraziers Bottom 250 B3
French Creek 200 F3
Frenchton 102 F3
Friendly 242 D1
Frost 125 G4
Gallipolis Ferry 325 B3
Galloway 500 F2
Gandeeville 150 D3
Gap Mills 300 F5
Gary 2,233 C6
Gassaway 1,225 E3
Gauley Bridge 1,177 D4
Gauley Mills 165 E4
Gay 300 C3
Gerrardstown 240 K2
Ghent 500 D5
Giatto 400 D6
Gilbert 757 C5
Gilboa 500 E4
Gilmer 110 E3
Glady 175 G3
Glasgow 1,031 D4
Glen 175 D4
Glen Dale 1,875 K5
Glen Daniel 300 D5
Glen Easton 105 K6
Glen Ferris 200 D4
Glengary 250 K2
Glenhayes 175 A4
Glen Rogers 500 D5
Glenville⊙ 2,155 E3
Glen White 300 D5
Glenwood 400 B3
Glovergap 100 F1
Gordon 300 C5
Gormania 100 H2
Grafton⊙ 6,845 G2
Grantsville⊙ 788 D3
Grant Town 987 F1
Granville 992 F1
Grassy Meadows 100 E5
Great Cacapon 750 K1
Green Bank 115 G4
Green Sulphur Springs 225 E5
Greenview 250 C4
Greenville 125 E5
Greenwood 750 E2
Griffithsville 300 B4
Grimms Landing 350 B3
Guardian 175 F3
Hacker Valley 440 F3
Halltown 375 L2
Hambleton 403 G2
Hamlin⊙ 1,219 B4
Hampden 300 C5
Hancock 175 K1
Handley 633 D4
Hanover 300 C5
Harding 100 G3
Harman 181 G3
Harmony 600 D3
Harper 400 D5
Harpers Ferry 361 L2
Harrisville⊙ 1,673 E2
Hartford 556 C2
Hartland 90 D4
Harts 400 B4
Harvey 300 D5
Havaco 350 C6
Heaters 440 E3
Hedgesville 217 K1
Helvetia 130 F3
Hemphill 700 C6
Henderson 604 B3
Hendricks 390 G2
Henlawson 900 B5
Hepzibah 600 F2
Herndon 500 D5
Hico 750 D4
Hillsboro 276 F4
Hinton⊙ 4,622 E5
Hodgesville 200 F2
Holcomb 200 E4
Holden 2,036 B5
Hollywood 150 F5
Hominy Falls 175 E4
Hookersville 250 E4
Horner 125 F3
Horse Shoe Run 500 G2
Howesville 600 G2
Hubball 145 B4
Hundred 485 E1
Huntersville 125 F4
Huntington⊙ 63,684 A4
Huntington-Ashland‡ 311,350 A4
Hurricane 3,751 C4
Hutchinson 285 F2
Huttonsville 242 G3
Iaeger 833 C6
Independence 200 G2
Indian Mills 150 E5
Indore 300 D4
Institute C4
Inwood 1,159 K2
Itmann 600 D5
Ivanhoe 200 F3
Ivydale 800 D3
Jacksonburg 400 E1
Jane Lew 406 F2
Jarvisville 250 F2
Jeffrey 900 C5
Jenkinjones 750 D6
Jesse 400 C5
Jodie 440 D4
Jumping Branch 700 E5
Junction 75 J2
Junior 591 G3
Justice 600 C5
Kanawha Falls 105 D4
Kearneysville 250 L2
Keenan 95 F5
Kegley 900 D6
Keith 175 C4

⊙County seat. ‡Population of metropolitan area.

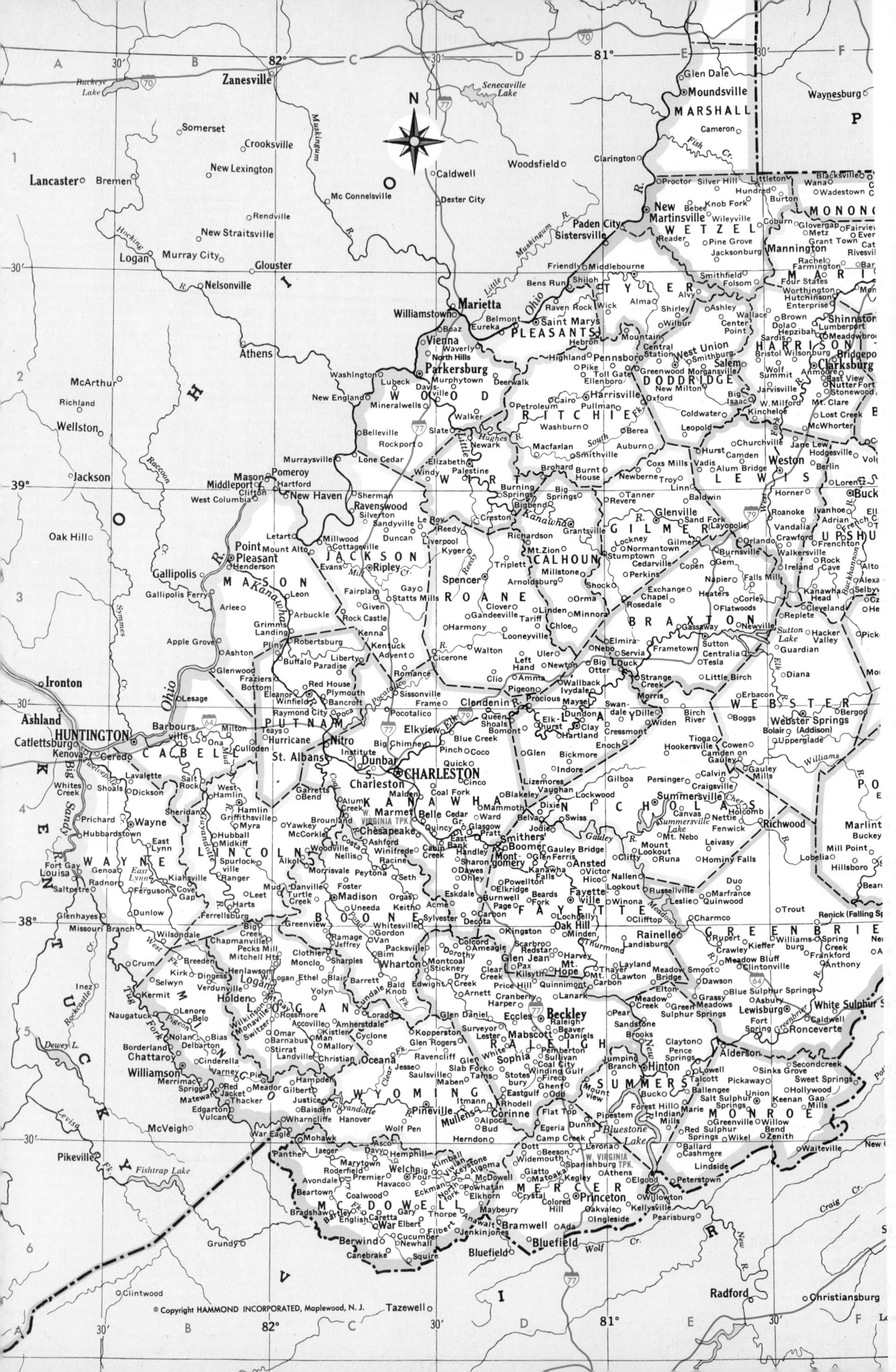

A
B
C
D
E
F
30′
82°
81°
Buckeye Lake
Zanesville
Senecaville Lake
Glen Dale
Moundsville
MARSHALL
Waynesburg
N
P
Somerset
Crooksville
Muskingum
Cameron
Fish Cr.
Clarington
Woodsfield
New Lexington
Caldwell
Lancaster
Bremen
O
Mc Connelsville
Dexter City
Proctor
Silver Hill
Littleton
Blacksville
Wana
Wadestown
Hundred
Burton
New Martinsville
Bebee
Knob Fork
Wileyville
Coburn
MONONG
Rendville
New Straitsville
Hocking
Paden City
Sistersville
WETZEL
Reader
Pine Grove
Jacksonburg
Mannington
Glovergap
Metz
Grant Town
Fairview
Rivesville
Logan
Murray City
Glouster
Friendly
Middlebourne
Smithfield
Folsom
Rachel
Farmington
Nelsonville
Bens Run
Shiloh
TYLER
Alvy
Four States
Worthington
Hutchinson
Enterprise
Marietta
Raven Rock
Wick
Alma
Ashley
Shirley
Wilbur
Wallace
Center Point
Brown
Dola
Hepzibah
Shinnston
Lumberport
Meadowbrook
Williamstown
Belmont
Eureka
Saint Marys
PLEASANTS
Mountain
Sardis
HARRISON
Bristol
Wilsonburg
Bridgeport
Clarksburg
Boaz
Vienna
Waverly
North Hills
Hebron
Central Station
West Union
Smithburg
Salem
Athens
Highland
Pennsboro
Pike
Toll Gate
Ellenboro
Greenwood
Morgansville
DODDRIDGE
New Milton
Wolf Summit
Anmoore
Nutter Fort
Stonewood
Parkersburg
Washington
Lubeck
Murphytown
Deerwalk
Davisville
WOOD
McArthur
2
New England
Mineralwells
Petroleum
Cairo
Harrisville
Pullman
Oxford
Big Isaac
Jarvisville
W. Milford
Mt. Clare
Richland
Walker
RITCHIE
Coldwater
Kincheloe
Lost Creek
Wellston
Belleville
Slate
Hughes R.
Washburn
Berea
Leopold
McWhorter
Rockport
Little
Newark
Macfarlan
South Fk.
Auburn
Hurst
Churchville
Camden
Jane Lew
Hodgesville
Raccoon
Murraysville
Lone Cedar
Elizabeth
Palestine
Smithville
Coxs Mills
Vadis
Alum Bridge
Weston
Berlin
Jackson
Mason
Pomeroy
Middleport
Hartford
Clifton
New Haven
Sherman
Windy
WIRT
Brohard
Burnt House
Newberne
Troy
Linn
LEWIS
Lorentz
39°
West Columbia
Burning Springs
Big Springs
Tanner
Revere
Horner
Buckhannon
Ravenswood
Silverton
Bigbend
Glenville
Sand Fork
(Layopolis)
Roanoke
Ivanhoe
Adrian
O
Sandyville
Le Roy
Creston
Kanawha
Grantsville
GILMER
Vandalia
Oak Hill
Letart
Millwood
Cottageville
Reedy
Liverpool
Duncan
Kyger
Richardson
Mt.Zion
Lockney
Normantown
Gilmer
Orlando
Crawford
UPSHUR
Frenchton
Point Pleasant
Mount Alto
JACKSON
Triplett
CALHOUN
Stumptown
Burnsville
Walkersville
Henderson
Evans
Ripley
Mill Cr.
Spencer
Reedy
Millstone
Cedarville
Perkins
Copen
Gem
Rock Cave
Gallipolis
MASON
Leon
Gay
Statts Mills
ROANE
Arnoldsburg
Shock
Napier
Falls Mill
Ireland
3
Gallipolis Ferry
Fairplain
Given
Orma
Exchange
Chapel
Heaters
Corley
Kanawha Head
Arlee
Arbuckle
Clover
Gandeeville
Linden
Minnora
Rosedale
Flatwoods
Cleveland
Symmes
Grimms Landing
Rock Castle
Harmony
Tariff
Chloe
BRAXTON
Gassaway
Newville
Replete
Kenna
Looneyville
Sutton Lake
Hacker Valley
Apple Grove
Pliny
Robertsburg
Kentuck
Walton
Elmira
Sutton
Ashton
Buffalo
Liberty
Paradise
Advent
Cicerone
Left Hand
Uler
Nebo
Servia
Frametown
Centralia
Tesla
Guardian
Glenwood
Romance
Newton
Big Otter
Duck
Strange Creek
Little Birch
Diana
Ironton
Fraziers Bottom
Red House
Plymouth
Clio
Amma
Wallback
Ivydale
Ohio
Lesage
Eleanor
Winfield
Bancroft
Sissonville
Frame
Pocatalico
Pigeon
Procious
Maysel
Morris
Erbacon
Clendenin
Swandale
Dille
Birch River
WEBSTER
Bergoo
Ashland
Barboursville
Milton
Teays
PUTNAM
Elkview
Queen Shoals
Bomont
CLAY
Elk-hurst
Dundon
Clay
Hartland
Widen
Boggs
Webster Springs (Addison)
Bolair
Upperglade
Catlettsburg
HUNTINGTON
Ona
Hurricane
Raymond City
Nitro
Big Chimney
Blue Creek
Cressmont
Tioga
Hookersville
Kenova
Ceredo
CABELL
Mud
Culloden
St. Albans
Institute
Pinch
Coco
Enoch
Cowen
Camden on Gauley
Twelvepole
Lavalette
Salt Rock
Dunbar
Quick
Glen
Bickmore
Williams
Whites Creek
Shoals
Dickson
West Hamlin
CHARLESTON
Cinco
Indore
Calvin
Gauley Mills
Big Sandy
Hamlin
Garretts Bend
Coal
S. Charleston
Malden
Coal Fork
Lizemores
Vaughan
Gilboa
Persinger
Craigsville
4
Sheridan
Griffithsville
Alum Creek
KANAWHA
Blakeley
Mammoth
Lockwood
Summersville
Cherry R.
Prichard
Wayne
Guyandotte
Myra
Hubball
Brounland
W. Marmet
VIRGINIA TPK.
Belle
Cedar Gr.
Ward
Dixie
Belva
Swiss
Canvas
Summersville Lake
Nettie
Holcomb
Fenwick
Richwood
Marlinton
Hubbardstown
Yawkey
McCorkle
Chesapeake
Quincy
Glasgow
Pratt
Smithers
Jodie
Mt. Nebo
Buckeye
East Lynn
Midkiff
LINCOLN
Ashford
Winifrede
Cabin Creek
East Bank
Handley
Boomer
Glen Ferris
Gauley Bridge
Gauley R.
Mount Lookout
Leivasy
Mill Point
Fort Gay
Louisa
WAYNE
Genoa
East Lynn L.
Spurlockville
Woodville
Alkol
Racine
Sharon
Montgomery
Kanawha Falls
Ansted
Clifty
Runa
Hominy Falls
Lobelia
Hillsboro
Radnor
Kiahsville
Ranger
Morrisvale
Peytona
Seth
Dawes
Ohley
Victor
Hico
Nallen
Saltpetre
Ferguson
Cove Gap
Leet
Mud
Danville
Turtle Creek
Foster
Powellton
Elkridge
Fayetteville
Lookout
Russellville
Duo
Harts
Madison
Orgas
Eskdale
Burnwell
Beards Fork
Winona
Leslie
Marfrance
Quinwood
Glenhayes
Dunlow
Ferrellsburg
Uneeda
Keith
Acme
Page
Meadow
Missouri Branch
BOONE
Pond
Sylvester
Carbon
Decota
FAYETTE
Lochgelly
Clifftop
Charmco
Trout
Renick (Falling Spring)
38°
Wilsondale
Big Creek
Greenview
Whitesville
Kingston
Oak Hill
Minden
Rainelle
Landisburg
GREENBRIER
Chapmanville
Ramage
Jeffrey
Gordon
Van
Packsville
Colcord
Ameagle
Scarbro
Redstar
Harvey
Thurmond
Rupert
Crawley
Kieffer
Williamsburg
Spring Creek
Frankford
Pecks Mill
Mitchell Hts
Clothier
Dorothy
Glen Jean
Pax
Mt. Hope
Thayer
Layland
Meadow Bluff
Clintonville
Anthony
West Fk.
Crum
Breeden
Henlawson
Monclo
Bim
Sharples
Wharton
Montcoal
Stickney
Clear Creek
Dry Creek
Kilsyth
Mt. Carbon
Lawton
Meadow Bridge
Smoot
Kirk
Dingess
Logan
Ethel
Blair
Barrett
Bald Knob
Edwight
Price Hill
Quinnimont
Dawson
Selwyn
Verdunville
Yolyn
Lundale
Arnett
Elton
Grassy Meadows
Blue Sulphur Springs
Asbury
Inez
Kermit
Holden
LOGAN
Cranberry
Lanark
Green Sulphur Springs
Meadow Creek
White Sulphur Springs
Tug Fork
MINGO
Rockcastle
Wilkinson
Monaville
Switzer
Rossmore
Lorado
Glen Daniel
Harper
Beckley
Eccles
Pear
Lewisburg
Caldwell
Naugatuck
Lenore
Belo
Amherstdale
Accoville
Kistler
Kopperston
Surveyor
Mabscott
Raleigh
Beaver
Daniels
Sandstone
Fort Spring
Ronceverte
Pigeon
5
Dewey L.
Borderland
Nolan
Bias
Delbarton
Omar
Barnabus
Man
Cyclone
Glen Rogers
Lester
RALEIGH
Brooks
Greenbrier
Chattaroy
Stirrat
Mallory
Landville
Christian
Oceana
Ravencliff
Glen White
Sophia
Sullivan
Pemberton
Clayton
Pence Springs
Alderson
Cinderella
Williamson
Varney
Merrimac
Sprigg
Red Jacket
Matewan
Thacker
Pie
Meador
Hampden
Gilbert
Jesse
Saulsville
Maben
Slab Fork
Tams
Stotesbury
Coal City
Winding Gulf
Fireco
Ghent
Jumping Branch
Hinton
SUMMERS
Lowell
Talcott
Sinks Grove
Secondcreek
Pickaway
Sweet Springs
Edgarton
Vulcan
Justice
Baisden
WYOMING
Itmann
Eastgulf
Odd
Rhodell
Mount View
Bucko
Ballengee
Salt Sulphur
Union
Keenan
Gap Mills
Hollywood
McVeigh
Wharncliffe
Hanover
Guyandotte
Pineville
Mullens
Corinne
Flat Top
Pipestem
Forest Hill
Indian Mills
Marie
MONROE
Levisa
Wolf Pen
Alpoca
Bud
Egeria
Dunns
Bluestone Lake
Greenville
Willow Bend
War Eagle
Mohawk
Herndon
Camp Creek
Red Sulphur Springs
Wikel
Zenith
Waiteville
New Castle
Pikeville
Fk.
Fishtrap Lake
Panther
Iaeger
Asco
Davy
Hemphill
Kimball
Vivian
Keystone
Dott
Beeson
Widemouth
Lerona
Spanishburg
Ballard
Cashmere
Lindside
Marytown
Roderfield
Premier
Avondale
Havaco
Welch
Big Four
Eckman
North Fork
Algoma
McDowell
Powhatan
Elkhorn
Giatto
Matoaka
Kegley
W. VIRGINIA TPK.
Athens
Elgood
Peterstown
Beartown
Coalwood
MERCER
Crystal
Princeton
Willowton
Bradshaw
MCDOWELL
Gary
Thorpe
Caretta
Bartley
English
War
Elbert
Maybeury
Colored Hill
Oakvale
Ingleside
Kellysville
Pearisburg
Anawalt
Craig Cr.
Filbert
Cucumber
Newhall
Jenkinjones
Bramwell
Ada
Bluefield
6
Grundy
Berwind
Canebrake
Squire
Bluefield
Wolf Cr.
New R.
R
V
I
Clintwood
Radford
Christiansburg
© Copyright HAMMOND INCORPORATED, Maplewood, N. J.
Tazewell

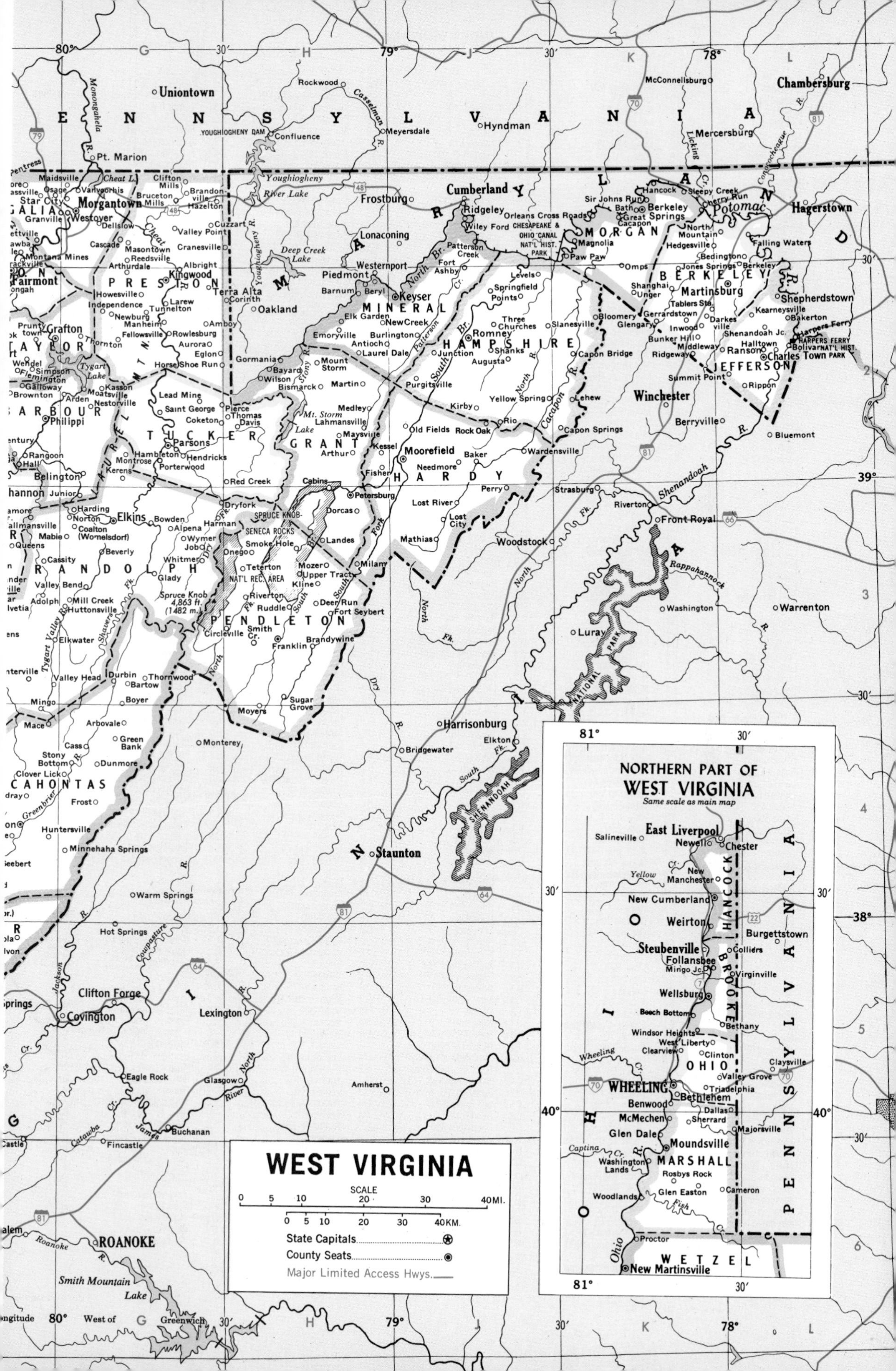
WEST VIRGINIA
SCALE
0 5 10 20 30 40MI.
0 5 10 20 30 40KM.
State Capitals
County Seats
Major Limited Access Hwys.
NORTHERN PART OF
WEST VIRGINIA
Same scale as main map
PENNSYLVANIA
MARYLAND
VIRGINIA
OHIO
PRESTON
TAYLOR
BARBOUR
TUCKER
RANDOLPH
PENDLETON
GRANT
MINERAL
HAMPSHIRE
HARDY
MORGAN
BERKELEY
JEFFERSON
HANCOCK
BROOKE
OHIO
MARSHALL
WETZEL
Uniontown
Morgantown
Cumberland
Hagerstown
Chambersburg
Winchester
Harrisonburg
Staunton
Lexington
ROANOKE
Clifton Forge
Covington
Front Royal
Warrenton
Martinsburg
Charles Town
Keyser
Romney
Moorefield
Petersburg
Franklin
Elkins
Parsons
Kingwood
Grafton
Philippi
Fairmont
Berkeley Springs
East Liverpool
Steubenville
Weirton
Wellsburg
WHEELING
Moundsville
New Martinsville
Spruce Knob
4,863 ft.
(1,482 m.)
SPRUCE KNOB-SENECA ROCKS NAT'L REC. AREA
SHENANDOAH NATIONAL PARK
HARPERS FERRY NAT'L HIST. PARK
CHESAPEAKE & OHIO CANAL NAT'L HIST. PARK
Smith Mountain Lake
Potomac
Shenandoah
80°
79°
78°
39°
38°
81°
40°
Longitude West of Greenwich

WEST VIRGINIA

Kellysville 165 .... E6
Kenna 150 .... C3
Kenova 4,454 .... A4
Kentuck 200 .... C3
Kermit 705 .... B5
Keyser⊙ 6,569 .... J2
Keystone 902 .... D6
Kiahsville 102 .... B4
Kieffer 135 .... E5
Kilsyth 200 .... D5
Kimball 871 .... C6
Kingston 189 .... D5
Kingwood⊙ 2,877 .... G2
Kirby 110 .... J2
Kirk 400 .... B5
Kistler 200 .... C5
Knob Fork 106 .... E1
Kopperston 700 .... C5
Lahmansville 200 .... H2
Lanark 559 .... D5
Landes 88 .... H3
Landisburg 250 .... E5
Landville 400 .... C5
Larew 125 .... G2
Lavalette 600 .... B4
Lawton 100 .... E5
Layland 500 .... E5
Layopolis (Sand Fork) 280 .... E3
Leet 175 .... B4
Left Hand 700 .... D3
Leivasy 200 .... E4
Lenore 800 .... B5
Leon 228 .... C3
Lerona 550 .... D6
Lesage 600 .... B3
Leslie 350 .... E4
Lester 626 .... D5
Letart 350 .... C3
Levels 180 .... J2
Lewisburg⊙ 3,065 .... E5
Liberty 150 .... C3
Lindside 225 .... E6
Linn 165 .... E2
Little Birch 400 .... E3
Littleton 335 .... F1
Liverpool 34 .... C3
Lizemores 400 .... D4
Lochgelly 250 .... D4
Lockney 190 .... E3
Lockwood 300 .... D4
Logan⊙ 3,029 .... B5
Lookout 200 .... E4
Lorado 400 .... C5
Lorentz 200 .... F2
Lost City 130 .... J3
Lost Creek 604 .... F2
Lost River 500 .... J3
Lowell 140 .... E5
Lubeck 1,356 .... C2
Lumberport 939 .... F2
Lundale 525 .... C5
Maben 450 .... D5
Mabie 550 .... F3
Mabscott 1,668 .... D5
Macfarlan 436 .... D2
Madison⊙ 3,228 .... C4
Maidsville 500 .... F1
Malden 900 .... C4
Mallory 1,330 .... C5
Mammoth 563 .... D4
Man 1,333 .... C5
Manheim 45 .... G2
Mannington 3,036 .... F1
Marfrance 225 .... E4
Marie 125 .... E5
Marlinton⊙ 1,352 .... F4
Marmet 2,196 .... C4
Martin 80 .... H2
Martinsburg⊙ 13,063 .... K2
Marytown 118 .... C6
Mason 1,432 .... B2
Masontown 1,052 .... G1
Matewan 822 .... B5
Mathias 110 .... J3
Matoaka 613 .... D6
Maybeury 300 .... D6
Maysel 350 .... D3
Maysville 150 .... H2
McCorkle 300 .... C4
McDowell 500 .... D6
McMechen 2,402 .... K5
McWhorter 150 .... F2
Meador 225 .... B5
Meadow Bluff 250 .... E5
Meadow Bridge 530 .... E5
Meadowbrook 500 .... F2
Meadow Creek 300 .... E5
Merrimac 140 .... B5
Metz 150 .... F1
Middlebourne⊙ 941 .... E1
Middleway 350 .... K2
Midkiff 650 .... B4
Mill Creek 801 .... G3
Mill Point 148 .... F4
Millstone 850 .... D3
Millwood 800 .... C3
Milton 2,178 .... B4
Minden 800 .... D5
Mineralwells 325 .... C2
Mingo 350 .... F3
Minnora 500 .... D3
Missouri Branch 250 .... A5
Mitchell Heights 342 .... B5
Moatsville 150 .... G2
Monaville 950 .... B5
Monclo 242 .... C5
Monongah 1,132 .... F2
Montana Mines 200 .... F1
Montcoal 150 .... D5
Monterville 250 .... F3
Montgomery 3,104 .... D4
Montrose 129 .... G2
Moorefield⊙ 2,257 .... J2
Morgansville 164 .... E2
Morgantown⊙ 27,605 .... G1
Morrisvale 450 .... C4
Moundsville⊙ 12,419 .... K6
Mountain 200 .... E2
Mount Alto 200 .... C3
Mount Carbon 450 .... D5
Mount Clare 950 .... F2
Mount Gay-Shamrock 4,366 .... C5
Mount Hope 1,849 .... D5
Mount Lookout 500 .... E4
Mount Nebo 535 .... E4
Mount Storm 500 .... H2
Mountview 108 .... D5
Mud 143 .... C4
Mullens 2,919 .... D5
Murphytown 600 .... D2
Murraysville 20 .... C2
Myra 90 .... B4
Nallen 250 .... E4
Napier 158 .... E3
Naugatuck 500 .... B5
Nebo 200 .... D3
Nellis 600 .... C4
Neola 300 .... F5
Nestorville 100 .... G2
Nettie 500 .... E4
Newark 100 .... D2
Newburg 418 .... G2
New Creek 95 .... J2
New Cumberland⊙ 1,752 .... K4
Newell 2,032 .... K4
New England 335 .... C2
Newhall 400 .... C6
New Haven 1,723 .... C3
New Manchester 800 .... K4
New Martinsville⊙ 7,109 .... E1
New Milton 44 .... E2
Newtown 390 .... D3
Newville 160 .... E3
Nitro 8,074 .... C4
Nolan 250 .... B5
Normantown 112 .... E3
Northfork 1,105 .... D6
North Hills 940 .... D2
North Mountain 100 .... K1
Norton 400 .... G3
Nutter Fort 2,078 .... F2
Oak Hill 7,120 .... D4
Oakvale 208 .... D6
Oceana 2,143 .... C5
Odd 500 .... D5
Ohley 450 .... D4
Omar 900 .... C5
Ona 200 .... B4
Onego 400 .... H3
Orgas 500 .... C4
Orlando 700 .... E3
Orleans Cross Roads 150 .... J1
Orma 370 .... D3
Osage 285 .... F1
Packsville 225 .... C5
Paden City 3,671 .... D1
Page 600 .... D4
Palestine 110 .... D2
Panther 450 .... C6
Paradise 50 .... C3
Parkersburg⊙ 39,967 .... D2
Parkersburg-Marietta‡ 162,836 .... D2
Parsons⊙ 1,937 .... G2
Patterson Creek 157 .... J1
Paw Paw 644 .... K1
Pax 274 .... D5
Pear 100 .... E5
Pecks Mill 350 .... B5
Pemberton 300 .... D5
Pence Springs 300 .... E5
Pennsboro 1,652 .... E2
Pentress 250 .... F1
Persinger 100 .... E4
Petersburg⊙ 2,084 .... H3
Peterstown 648 .... E6
Peytona 175 .... C4
Philippi⊙ 3,194 .... G2
Pickaway 225 .... E5
Pickens 240 .... F3
Pie 250 .... B5
Piedmont 1,491 .... H2
Pike 120 .... D2
Pinch 800 .... D4
Pine Grove 767 .... E1
Pineville⊙ 1,140 .... C5
Pipestem 100 .... E5
Pliny 900 .... B3
Plymouth 125 .... C3
Poca 1,142 .... C4
Pocotalico 2,420 .... C4
Point Pleasant⊙ 5,682 .... B3
Points 250 .... J2
Powellton 1,339 .... D4
Powhatan 400 .... D6
Pratt 821 .... D4
Premier 400 .... C6
Price Hill 175 .... D5
Prichard 500 .... A4
Princeton⊙ 7,493 .... D6
Procious 600 .... D3
Proctor 350 .... E1
Pruntytown 145 .... F2
Pullman 196 .... D2
Purgitsville 450 .... J2
Queens 100 .... F3
Queen Shoals 120 .... D4
Quick 400 .... D4
Quincy 150 .... C4
Quinwood 460 .... E4
Rachel 550 .... F1
Racine 725 .... C4
Radnor 300 .... A4
Rainelle 1,983 .... E5
Raleigh 900 .... D5
Ramage 350 .... C5
Ranger 300 .... B4
Ranson 2,471 .... L2
Ravencliff 350 .... C5
Ravenswood 4,126 .... C3
Raymond City 400 .... C4
Reader 950 .... E1
Red Creek 125 .... H2
Red House 650 .... C3
Red Jacket 850 .... B5
Redstar 200 .... D5
Reedsville 564 .... G1
Reedy 338 .... D3
Renick 240 .... F4
Replete 200 .... F3
Rhodell 472 .... D5
Richwood 3,568 .... F4
Ridgeley 994 .... J1
Ridgeway 200 .... K2
Rio 140 .... J2
Ripley⊙ 3,464 .... C3
Rippon 500 .... L2
Rivesville 1,327 .... F1
Robertsburg 140 .... C3
Rock Castle 100 .... C3
Rock Cave 400 .... E3
Rock Oak 100 .... J2
Rockport 100 .... C2
Roderfield C6
Romance 55 .... C3
Romney⊙ 2,094 .... J2
Ronceverte 2,312 .... F5
Rosbys Rock 100 .... K6
Rosedale 400 .... E3
Rossmore 200 .... C5
Rowlesburg 966 .... G2
Ruddle 36 .... H3
Runa 150 .... E4
Rupert 1,276 .... E5
Russellville 280 .... E4
Saint Albans 12,402 .... C4
Saint George 150 .... G2
Saint Marys⊙ 2,219 .... D2
Salem 2,706 .... E2
Salt Rock 350 .... B4
Sand Fork 280 .... E3
Sandstone 300 .... E5
Sandyville 500 .... C3
Sardis 100 .... F2
Saulsville 250 .... C5
Scarbro 800 .... D5
Seebert 100 .... F4
Selwyn 500 .... B5
Seth 950 .... C4
Shanghai 200 .... K2
Shanks 500 .... J2
Sharon 750 .... D4
Sharples 250 .... C5
Shepherdstown 1,791 .... L2
Sherman 104 .... C3
Sherrard 400 .... K5
Shinnston 3,059 .... F2
Shirley 275 .... E2
Shoals 150 .... B4
Shock 200 .... D3
Silver Hill 125 .... E1
Silverton 250 .... C3
Simpson 250 .... F2
Sinks Grove 156 .... F5
Sissonville 450 .... C3
Sistersville 2,367 .... D1
Slab Fork 210 .... D5
Slanesville 250 .... K2
Slate 50 .... D2
Smithburg 130 .... E2
Smithers 1,482 .... D4
Smithfield 278 .... E2
Smithville 200 .... D2
Smoot 300 .... E5
Sophia 1,216 .... D5
South Charleston 15,968 .... C4
Spanishburg 550 .... D6
Spencer⊙ 2,799 .... D3
Sprigg 225 .... B5
Springfield 250 .... J2
Spurlockville 250 .... B4
Squire 900 .... C6
Star City 1,464 .... F1
Statts Mills 400 .... C3
Stickney 150 .... D5
Stirrat 250 .... C5
Stonewood 2,058 .... F2
Stotesbury 199 .... D5
Strange Creek 175 .... E3
Stumptown 125 .... E3
Sullivan 700 .... D5
Summersville⊙ 2,972 .... E4
Summit Point 455 .... K2
Surveyor 300 .... D5
Sutton⊙ 1,192 .... E3
Sweet Springs 46 .... F5
Swiss 500 .... D4
Switzer 1,034 .... B5
Sylvester 256 .... C4
Tablers Station 75 .... K2
Talcott 800 .... E5
Tallmansville 140 .... F3
Tams 30 .... D5
Tanner 375 .... E3
Tariff 85 .... D3
Teays 200 .... B4
Terra Alta 1,946 .... H2
Tesla 300 .... E3
Thacker 525 .... B5
Thomas 747 .... H2
Thornton 200 .... G2
Thorpe 600 .... D6
Three Churches 350 .... J2
Thurmond 67 .... D5
Tioga 825 .... E4
Triadelphia 1,461 .... L5
Troy 110 .... E2
Tunnelton 510 .... G2
Turtle Creek 743 .... C4
Uneeda 700 .... C4
Unger 300 .... K2
Union⊙ 743 .... E5
Upperglade 750 .... F4
Upper Tract 155 .... H3
Vadis 130 .... E2
Valley Bend 950 .... F3
Valley Grove 597 .... L5
Valley Head 900 .... G3
Van 800 .... C5
Varney 750 .... B5
Vaughan 375 .... D4
Verdunville 950 .... B5
Victor 500 .... D4
Vienna 11,618 .... D2
Vivian 500 .... D6
Volga 125 .... F2
Vulcan 130 .... B5
Wadestown 300 .... F1
Waiteville 230 .... F6
Walker 100 .... D2
Walkersville 135 .... F3
Wallace 325 .... E2
Wallback 150 .... D3
Walton 500 .... D3
Wana 150 .... F1
War 2,158 .... C6
Ward 850 .... D4
Wardensville 241 .... J2
Washington 450 .... C2
Washington Lands 400 .... K6
Waverly 500 .... D2
Wayne⊙ 1,495 .... B4
Webster Springs⊙ 939 .... F4
Weirton 25,371 .... K5
Weirton-Steubenville‡ 163,099 .... K5
Welch⊙ 3,885 .... C6
Wellsburg⊙ 3,963 .... K5
West Columbia 245 .... B3
West Hamlin 643 .... B4
West Liberty 744 .... K5
West Logan 630 .... C5
West Milford 510 .... F2
Weston⊙ 6,250 .... F2
Westover 4,884 .... G1
West Union⊙ 1,090 .... E2
Wharncliffe 900 .... C5
Wharton 450 .... C5
Wheeling⊙ 43,070 .... K5
Wheeling‡ 185,566 .... K5
Whites Creek 500 .... A4
White Sulphur Springs 3,371 .... F5
Whitesville 689 .... C4
Whitmer G3
Widemouth 100 .... D6
Widen 230 .... E4
Wiley Ford 1,224 .... J1
Wileyville 175 .... E1
Wilkinson 975 .... B5
Williamsburg 350 .... F5
Williamson⊙ 5,219 .... B5
Williamstown 3,095 .... C2
Willowton 110 .... E6
Wilsonburg 350 .... F2
Wilsondale 250 .... B5
Windsor Heights 800 .... K5
Winfield⊙ 329 .... C3
Winifrede 750 .... C4
Winona 250 .... E4
Wolf Summit 750 .... F2
Womelsdorf (Coalton) 306 .... G3
Woodlands 200 .... K6
Woodville 300 .... C4
Worthington 329 .... F2
Yawkey 985 .... C4
Yellow Spring 280 .... J2
Yolyn 400 .... C5

OTHER FEATURES

Big Sandy (riv.) A4
Bluestone (lake) E5
Buckhannon (riv.) F3
Cacapon (riv.) J2
Cheat (lake) G1
Cheat (riv.) G1
Cherry (riv.) E4
Chesapeake and Ohio Canal Nat'l Hist. Park J1
Clear Fork, Guyandotte (riv.) C5
Coal (riv.) C4
Dry Fork (riv.) C6
Dry Fork (riv.) G3
Elk (riv.) D4
Fish (creek) E1
Gauley (riv.) D4
Greenbrier (riv.) F4
Guyandotte (riv.) B4
Harpers Ferry Nat'l Hist. Park L2
Hughes (riv.) D2
Kanawha (riv.) C3
Little Kanawha (riv.) D3
Meadow (riv.) E4
Mill (creek) C3
Monongahela (riv.) G1
Mount Storm (lake) H2
Mud (riv.) B4
New (riv.) E5
North (riv.) J2
Ohio (riv.) B3
Patterson (creek) J2
Pigeon (creek) B5
Pocatalico (riv.) C3
Pond Fork (riv.) C4
Potomac (riv.) L1
Potts (creek) F5
Reedy (creek) D3
Shavers Fork (riv.) G3
Shenandoah (riv.) K2
Spruce Knob (mt.) G3
Spruce Knob-Seneca Rocks Nat'l Rec. Area H3
Stony (riv.) H2
Summersville (lake) E4
Sutton (lake) F3
Tug Fork (riv.) B5
Twelvepole (creek) A4
Tygart (lake) G2
Tygart Valley (riv.) F3
West Fork (riv.) E3
Williams (riv.) F4

⊙County seat. ‡Population of metropolitan area.

PHOTO RESEARCHERS

West Virginia's rich tradition of handicrafts and folk art are celebrated each summer at fairs in Ripley (*left*) and Glenville (*right*).

RON SNOW/STATE OF WEST VIRGINIA

LARGEST CENTERS OF POPULATION

(Incorporated places and metropolitan areas[1])

City or metropolitan area	1980	1970	1960
Charleston	63,968	71,505	85,796
Metropolitan area	269,595	257,140	252,925
Huntington	63,684	74,315	83,627
Metropolitan area[2]	311,350	286,935	254,780
Wheeling	43,070	48,188	53,400
Metropolitan area	185,566	181,954	190,342
Parkersburg	39,967	44,208	44,797
Morgantown	27,605	29,431	22,487
Weirton	24,736	27,131	28,201
Fairmont	23,863	26,093	27,477
Clarksburg	22,371	24,864	28,112
Beckley	20,492	19,884	18,642
Bluefield	16,060	15,921	19,256
South Charleston	15,968	16,333	19,180

[1]Standard metropolitan statistical areas.[2] Huntington-Ashland.

URBAN-RURAL DISTRIBUTION

Year	Percent urban	Percent rural
1920	25.2 (U.S., 51.2)	74.8
1930	28.4 (U.S., 56.2)	71.6
1940	28.1 (U.S., 56.6)	71.9
1950	34.6 (U.S., 64.0)	65.4
1960	38.2 (U.S., 69.9)	61.8
1970	39.0 (U.S., 73.5)	61.0
1980	36.2 (U.S., 73.7)	63.8

GROWTH OF POPULATION SINCE 1790

Year	Population	Year	Population
1790	55,873	1920	1,463,701
1820	136,808	1940	1,901,974
1840	224,537	1950	2,005,552
1860	376,688	1960	1,860,421
1880	618,457	1970	1,744,237
1900	958,800	1980	1,950,279

Gain, 1970–1980: 11.8% (U.S. gain, 11.4%). **Density,** 1980: 80.8 persons per sq mi (U.S. density, 62.6).

Virginian cities, the exceptions being Wheeling and Weirton, communities that have more in common with the industrial cities of neighboring Ohio and Pennsylvania.

The 20th century brought certain discernible changes in the character of West Virginia and its citizens. After many decades of gradual shift from rural to urban and suburban living, the extreme individualism that marked the personality of the typical West Virginian in the early years of the republic seemed to have given way to an interest in collective activities. West Virginians in large numbers joined secret orders such as the Masons and Odd Fellows, as well as civic organizations such as the Kiwanis and Lions, local chambers of commerce, women's clubs, and veterans' organizations. The state's Puritan tradition, which had long inhibited such activities as dancing, card playing, and even attendance at theatrical shows, has lost much of its force.

In the early 1800's, social gatherings took place on such occasions as weddings and cornhuskings. The large family reunion was a later phenomenon, a product of the traditional clan-consciousness of West Virginians. It reached a peak of popularity in the period between the two world wars, when many thousands of visitors could be attracted to a single event of this kind. For example, in the 1930's and 1940's the Lilly family reunion sometimes drew as many as 75,000 people, most of whom could claim some sort of kinship with the 17th century colonist Robert Lilly.

Hunting and fishing have always been popular among West Virginians, and skiing is a recent addition to the list of standard recreational pursuits. Among the spectator sports, football and

CLARENCE DELAND/PHOTO RESEARCHERS

Strip-mining methods uncover a seam of bituminous coal, the state's most valuable natural resource.

basketball have large followings. Facilities for all kinds of sports have been much expanded since World War II.

White Sulphur Springs, which is in the southeastern part of the state, is especially famous for such facilities, including one of the nations's outstanding golf clubs.

Main Centers of Population. The state's four largest cities contain about 11% of the state's population. The largest city is Charleston, the capital. Charleston has not always been the seat of government. From June 20, 1863, to April 1, 1870, and again from May 23, 1875, to May 1, 1885, the capital was Wheeling. Because of the frequent removals, the seat of government was often called the "Capital on Wheels." The second-largest city, only slightly smaller than Charleston, is Huntington, an industrial city on the Ohio River in the western part of the state. Huntington is a transportation hub, a trade center, and the state's only tobacco market. Wheeling, the third-largest city, is in the northern part of the state on the Ohio River. Other leading cities are Parkersburg, Morgantown, Weirton, and Fairmont.

The percentage of the state's urban population has followed a consistent trend upward from 1870, with the exception of the period 1930–1940, when movement to suburban areas helped produce a decline.

PERSONAL INCOME IN WEST VIRGINIA

Source	1960	1970	1980
	(Millions of dollars)		
Farms	57	33	45
Mining	361	568	1,889
Construction	112	312	737
Manufacturing	741	1,125	2,615
Transportation, communications, and public utilities	254	395	993
Wholesale and retail trade	360	611	1,538
Finance, insurance, and real estate	72	126	357
Services	255	500	1,397
Other industries	3	7	19
Government	273	575	1,629
		(Dollars)	
Per capita personal income	1,597	3,043	7,800
Per capita income, U.S.	2,216	3,945	9,521

Source: U.S. Department of Commerce, *Survey of Current Business.*

3. The Economy

Although the economy of the state once was based almost exclusively on coal mining, forestry, and petroleum, the trend has been toward economic diversification. In keeping with this trend some portions of the state, particularly the Ohio and Kanawha valleys, have experienced extensive industrial development and are today the seats of important chemical and metal industries.

The state possesses many advantages in its natural resources, transportation facilities, and location in proximity to large market areas that should favor the continuation of the process of industrialization. Despite such factors, however, per-capita income has continued to lag below the national average.

The economic activities of the people of West Virginia are widely diversified, but manufacturing, commerce, and mining furnish the major portion of the state income. General manufacturing activities, with chemical production and the fabrication of metal products heading the list, normally supply more than a fifth of the state's income. Trade, commerce, and service activities supply a similarly large portion of the total, while mining accounts for another 15% to 20%.

Manufacturing. The leading manufacturing industries in the state are chemicals and allied products, including dyes, detergents, paints, plastics, synthetic rubber, and salt cake. The chemical industry is concentrated in the Kanawha and Ohio valleys. The manufacture of iron and steel products is centered in the Northern Panhandle. Stone, clay, and glass products are also important industries in West Virginia. The state is well known for its pottery and glassware, which includes blown glass, bottles, crystalware, plate glass, and stained glass.

Other leading industries produce food products, petroleum and coal products, fabricated metals, electrical machinery, lumber and timber products, paper and pulp, hand tools, and transportation equipment.

Agriculture and Forestry. Farming, although widely practiced, is no longer an important source of income. Livestock, poultry, dairy products, hogs, and sheep are raised on West Virginia farms. Corn is the largest field crop, but barley, potatoes, oats, and wheat also are grown. The orchards produce apples, peaches, cherries, grapes, pears, and plums. The Shenandoah Valley is one of the finest apple-growing regions in the country.

Forest industries are still important. Nearly 12 million acres (4.8 million hectares) of commercial forestlands are located within the state. The most important trees for commercial timber are cherry, oak, and tulip. Hemlock, white pine, and red spruce are also in abundance in the mountains.

Mining. The most important mined product in West Virginia is bituminous coal. The state has been one of the leading producers in the country since 1931. West Virginia produces large quantities of natural gas from gas fields that lie beneath the Appalachian Plateau. The state is also a large producer of salt from underground beds, and of stone, sand, gravel, and clay.

Transportation. Water transportation has always been important in West Virginia because of the difficulties of traveling over the rugged terrain. Great amounts of freight still are carried on the Ohio, Monongahela, Kanawha, and Big Sandy rivers.

The first railroad, the Baltimore & Ohio, reached Wheeling in 1853. The state is covered by about 4,000 miles (6,430 km) of track. The major rail arteries generally run east and west. In order to reach Wheeling from Cumberland, Md., in 1852, railroad crews had to build 11 tunnels and 113 bridges.

© RAY ELLIS/PHOTO RESEARCHERS

A worker in Morgantown marks a crystal goblet for etching. The state has long been a producer of glassware.

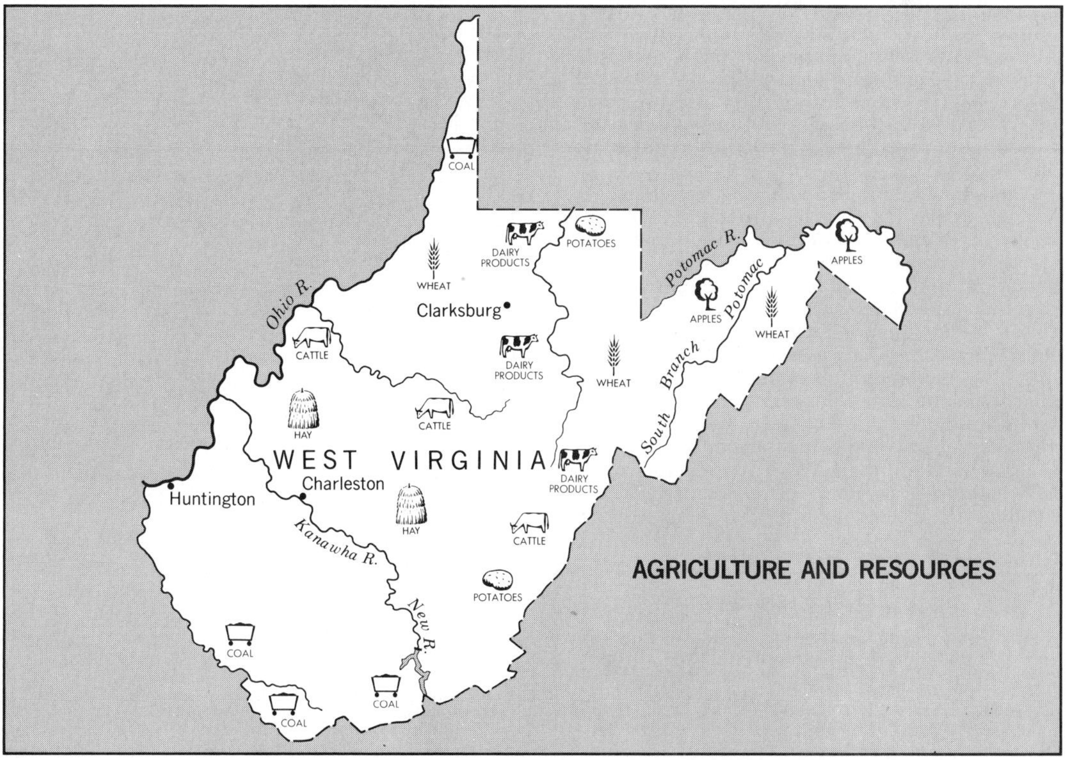

West Virginia has about 36,000 miles (57,900 km) of roads and highways, including the West Virginia Turnpike between Charleston and Princeton. Road building was complicated by the rocky terrain and rugged mountains.

AGRICULTURE AND RESOURCES

WEST VIRGINIA
Clarksburg
Charleston
Huntington
Ohio R.
Potomac R.
South Branch Potomac
Kanawha R.
New R.
COAL
DAIRY PRODUCTS
POTATOES
APPLES
WHEAT
CATTLE
HAY

FPG

The chemical industry, a leading economic activity in the state, is part of a trend toward diversification.

Aviation developed more slowly in the state because of the difficulty in building runways. The aviation hub of the state is Charleston, which is served by four domestic airlines.

4. Government

The present state constitution went into effect in 1872. The state's first constitution was adopted in 1863, when West Virginia was admitted to the Union, and was replaced in 1872. Amendments must be passed by a two-thirds vote of the legislature and ratified by a majority of voters. The constitution may also be amended by a constitutional convention, which can be called if approved by a majority of the legislators and voters.

Structure of Government. The governor of West Virginia is elected to a four-year term. He may serve any number of terms, but no more than two terms consecutively. There is no lieutenant governor, and in the event a vacancy in the governorship occurs because of death, disqualification, resignation, or removal from office, the president of the Senate serves as governor until the next gubernatorial election. Other elected officials in the state who are elected to four-year terms are the secretary of state, auditor, treasurer, attorney general, and commissioner of agriculture.

The legislature in West Virginia consists of a Senate and a House of Delegates. The 34 senators are elected to four-year terms, and the 100 delegates are elected to two-year terms. The state legislature convenes annually on the second

GOVERNMENT HIGHLIGHTS

Electoral Vote—6. **Representation in Congress**—U. S. senators, 2; U. S. representatives, 4. **State Legislature**—Senate, 34 members, 4-year terms; House of Delegates, 100 members, 2-year terms. **Governor**—4-year term; may succeed himself only once but may serve any number of terms.

GOVERNORS

Arthur I. Boreman	Republican	1863–1869
Daniel D. T. Farnsworth[1]	"	1869
William E. Stevenson	"	1869–1871
John J. Jacob	Democrat	1871–1877
Henry M. Mathews	"	1877–1881
Jacob B. Jackson	"	1881–1885
E. Willis Wilson[2]	"	1885–1890
A. Brooks Fleming	"	1890–1893
William A. MacCorkle	"	1893–1897
George W. Atkinson	Republican	1897–1901
Albert B. White	"	1901–1905
William M. O. Dawson	"	1905–1909
William E. Glasscock	"	1909–1913
Henry D. Hatfield	"	1913–1917
John J. Cornwell	Democrat	1917–1921
Ephraim F. Morgan	Republican	1921–1925
Howard M. Gore	"	1925–1929
William G. Conley	"	1929–1933
H. Guy Kump	Democrat	1933–1937
Homer A. Holt	"	1937–1941
M. Mansfield Neely	"	1941–1945
Clarence W. Meadows	"	1945–1949
Okey L. Patteson	"	1949–1953
William C. Marland	"	1953–1957
Cecil H. Underwood	Republican	1957–1961
William W. Barron	Democrat	1961–1965
Hulett C. Smith	"	1965–1969
Arch A. Moore	Republican	1969–1977
John D. Rockefeller 4th	Democrat	1977–1985
Arch A. Moore	Republican	1985–1989
Gaston Caperton	Democrat	1989–

[1]As president of the Senate, Farnsworth, succeeded as governor and filled the unexpired term of Boreman, who resigned to become a U.S. senator.

[2]The election of Fleming over Nathan Goff in 1888 was contested, and Wilson served until the contest was determined by the legislature.

Wednesday of January except in the year after a gubernatorial election, when the regular session is opened on the second Wednesday in February.

The highest court in West Virginia is the supreme court of appeals, made up of five judges elected to 12-year terms. The state has 29 judicial districts, each with a judge elected to an eight-year term. State courts with limited jurisdiction include county, common pleas, domestic relations, criminal, police, intermediate, juvenile, municipal, and justice-of-the-peace courts. Judges of all these courts are elected.

Public Finance. The bulk of the state's income from taxes is derived from business, occupation, and sales taxes. Other sources of revenue come from horse-racing fees, profits from the state-controlled sale of liquor, corporate and personal income taxes, taxes on cigarettes, gasoline, and insurance, and licensing.

Social Agencies. State social agencies cooperating with the general program of the U. S. Department of Health and Human Services include a department of welfare, a department of employment security, and a division of vocational rehabilitation. A department of labor is the enforcement agency for all labor legislation except that pertaining to mines and mining. The latter is the province of a separate department of mines, which also directs training in mine-rescue work.

Matters pertaining to sanitation, immunization, sewage disposal, and water supply are controlled by a department of health. The department of mental health supervises the state's five mental hospitals and conducts research and training programs in the field of mental health.

A state department of natural resources directs the maintenance and development of state forests, the protection of wildlife, and the general beautification of the state. There is also a state water commission that concerns itself with the causes and control of stream pollution.

Other social agencies include a commission on aging, which collects information about the problems of the aged and makes recommendations to the governor and legislature; a human rights commission; and a department of veterans affairs, which furnishes aid and counsel to veterans and to widows and orphans of deceased veterans.

5. Education and Culture

Elementary and Secondary Education. The pioneer schools in West Virginia were supported by subscription. The teachers were paid by the parents in cash, farm produce, or bed and board. In 1796 legislation was enacted providing for free schools in counties that wished to establish them, but the program's success was limited because county officials felt that the parents of the children should pay for their education. In 1810 a literary fund for the education of poor children was established. The free-school system came into being in 1863, and in 1872 the constitution provided for tax funds to support the schools. The ungraded rural school classes were improved in 1890 by the Wade Plan, a method for teaching subjects at various grade levels to children of different ages, developed by Alexander L. Wade in West Virginia. Once adopted by the legislature, the plan gained wide acceptance in rural schools throughout the country.

Public secondary education did not become available in West Virginia until 1908. Before that time, high-school subjects were taught only at private academies.

WEST VIRGINIA INDUSTRIAL AND PUBLICITY COMMISSION

The State Capitol in Charleston, completed in 1932, is a masterpiece by architect Cass Gilbert.

The public-school system is supervised by a state superintendent appointed by the board of education. The magisterial and independent school districts were abolished in 1933 and merged into 55 county units for the administration of both the elementary and the secondary schools. The state provides tax funds to the counties to maintain the schools and pay for textbooks for those who cannot afford to buy them. Each county's schools are controlled by a single board that functions through a county superintendent and his assistants. There are no independent city school systems.

Higher Education. Bethany College, founded in 1840 in Bethany, is the oldest in the state. West Virginia University, established on a land grant in 1867, is the oldest state-supported institution. Other state schools are Concord College in Athens, Marshall University in Huntington, Shepherd College in Shepherdstown, and West Virginia Institute of Technology in Montgomery. State colleges are located in Bluefield, Fairmont, Glenville, Institute, and West Liberty; the last-named is the oldest state college in West Virginia. Included among the private institutions of higher learning are Bethany, Alderson-Broaddus in Philippi, Davis and Elkins in Elkins, West Virginia Wesleyan in Buckhannon, the University of Charleston, Salem College in Salem, and Wheeling College. There are also a number of accredited nursing schools in the state.

Libraries and Museums. As early as 1809, West Virginia had a subscription library whose paying members could read its books without additional charge. Public libraries, which were first established about 1900, operate in most of the 55 counties.

The largest library in the state is the West Virginia University Library. In the state capitol in Charleston the department of archives and history maintains an extensive library collection

STATE OF WEST VIRGINIA

The University of Charleston occupies a spacious city campus on the banks of the broad Kanawha River.

that features files of public records, official reports of state departments and officials, newspapers, and other materials bearing on the history and development of the state. In some of the libraries, both public and college, small museums are maintained.

Fine arts museums include the Huntington Galleries in Huntington. Among the historical museums are the Jackson's Mill Museum in Jackson's Mill on the original 5-acre (2-hectare) site of the boyhood home of "Stonewall" Jackson; the Science and Culture Center in the Capitol Complex in Charleston, containing a library, archives, and exhibits that include a settler's cabin, a country store, and a Civil War display; Master Armorer's House in Harpers Ferry, where the story of gunmaking is told; and the Pocahontas County Historical Museum in Marlinton, containing documents, implements, clothes, and toys.

Other Cultural Activities. Backed by a rich heritage of folk art and fine handicrafting, the state has had no lack of accomplished practitioners in the fields of literature, music, and the other arts. Painters and sculptors banded together to form the West Virginia Artists Association in 1928. The state's Federation of Music Clubs was organized in 1917. A popular event of the musical calendar is Huntington's annual State Band Festival. The University School of Music (1897) is one of the nation's oldest. The Children's Theater, established in Charleston in 1932, has had notable success, and Wheeling's Little Theater group has staged open-air performances in that city.

The systematic study and preservation of West Virginia's wealth of folk literature and folk music has been a fairly recent development, gathering momentum only in the 1950's, although several useful collections of local folklore became available in print in the 1930's. Many ballads heard in the West Virginia hills have been traced to early English origins. Both Wheeling and Charleston have symphony orchestras.

Communication. The first newspaper published in the region was the *Potomak Guardian and Berkeley Advertiser* in Shepherdstown in 1790. The oldest paper still in existence is the *Roane County Reporter,* which has been publishing weekly in Spencer since 1800. The leading West Virginia daily newspapers include the Charleston *Gazette* and *Daily Mail,* the *Herald-Dispatch* in Huntington, and the *News-Register* in Wheeling.

The state's first radio station, WSAZ, began broadcasting in 1923 from Huntington. The first television station, WSAZ-TV, began operating in Huntington in 1949.

6. Recreation and Places of Interest

The recreational opportunities in West Virginia are varied, ranging from magnificent national forests to health spas. Favorite sports include fishing, hunting, skiing, tobogganing, and skating. The beautiful scenery attracts tourists and campers, as do the historical landmarks, parks, and recreation areas.

Parks, Forests, and Recreation Areas. The National Forest at Monongahela covers 840,000 acres (340,000 hectares) in the Allegheny Mountains. Its outstanding scenery includes the 57-foot (17-meter) falls in Blackwater Canyon, unexplored limestone caverns, and the Cranberry Glades. The Spruce Knob–Seneca Rocks National Recreation Area is another major tourist attraction. State forests of over 10,000 acres (4,000 hectares) include Cooper's Rock, Seneca, and Calvin Price. State forests with at least 5,000 acres (2,000 hectares) include the Cabwaylingo, Kumbrabow, Greenbrier, Kanawha, Camp Creek, and Panther Creek.

Watoga in Pocahontas county, with more than 10,000 acres, is the largest state park. It is followed in size by Holly River at Hacker Valley, Cacapon near Berkeley, Lost River at Mathias, and Babcock near Clifftop. The many other parks include Blackwater Falls near Davis, Bluestone at Hinton, Caywaylingo near Dunlow, Canaan Valley near David, Cedar Creek at Glenville, Chief Logan at Logan, Hawk's Nest near Gauley Bridge, Kumbrabow near Elkwater, Lost

FAMOUS WEST VIRGINIANS

Baker, Newton Diehl (1871–1937), political leader and secretary of war under President Woodrow Wilson, 1916–1921.
Boyd, Belle (1843–1900), Confederate spy, actress, and author who was tried twice but not convicted. Later married former Union officer. Wrote *Belle Boyd in Camp and Prison* (1865).
Buck, Pearl (1892–1973), author whose best known work was her novel *The Good Earth* (1931).
Cooke, Philip Pendleton (1816–1850), poet and storywriter.
Davis, Henry Gassaway (1823–1916), political and business leader; member of state legislature, 1865–1871; U. S. senator, 1871–1883; U. S. vice presidential candidate, 1904.
Davis, John W. (1873–1955), politician; U. S. solicitor general, 1913–1918; ambassador to Great Britain, 1918–1921; Democratic presidential candidate, 1924.
Delany, Martin Robinson (1812–1885), abolitionist, physician, and first black major in the U. S. Army.
Gates, Horatio (1727–1806), Revolutionary War general.
Jackson, Thomas "Stonewall" (1824–1863), Confederate general.
Lorentz, Pare (1905–), motion picture director of film documentaries.
Lucas, Daniel Bedinger (1836–1909), author known as "poet of the Shenandoah Valley."
Montague, Margaret Prescott (1873–1955), author and short story writer who won O. Henry Prize 1920 for *England to America*.
Morrow, Dwight Whitney (1873–1931), lawyer, banker, and diplomat.
Owens, Michael Joseph (1859–1923), inventor and glass manufacturer.
Payne, Christopher Harrison (1848–1925), black clergyman, lawyer, federal official.
Reno, Jesse Lee (1823–1862), military leader in Mexican War and Civil War for whom Reno, Nev., was named.
Reuther, Walter Philip (1907–1970), union leader.
Skidmore, Hubert (1909–1946), novelist.
Steber, Eleanor (1916–), opera singer.
Strauss, Lewis L. (1896–1974), financier, naval officer, and chairman of the Atomic Energy Commission.
Vance, Cyrus R. (1917–), lawyer, government official, diplomat, and secretary of state in the Carter administration, 1977–1980.
Webster, Harold Tucker (1885–1952), cartoonist, creator of Casper Milquetoast.
White, Israel Charles (1848–1927), geologist who developed new techniques for exploitation of gas and oil resources.

River at Mathias, North Bend at Cairo, Pipestem Resort near Hinton, Tomlinson Run at New Manchester, Twin Falls at Pineville, Tygart Lake at Grafton, and Watoga at Huntersville. There are also a number of city parks and zoos.

Historical Sites and Monuments. Among the historical sights in West Virginia are the Morgan Morgan monument, marking the site of the state's first settlement; Rumsey Memorial Monument in Shepherdstown, commemorating a steam-propelled boat invented by James Rumsey in 1787; a monument in Point Pleasant, commemorating the battle between the settlers and the Indians in 1774; and the Andrews Methodist Church in Grafton, where the first Mother's Day was observed on May 10, 1908. Others include the John Brown Monument at Harpers Ferry; the Old Stone Church in Lewisburg, built of native stone by Scotch-Irish settlers in 1796; Mammoth Mound in Moundsville, the tallest prehistoric Indian burial mound in the world, built between 1,000 and 2,000 years ago; and the Centennial Cabin and Museum at Parkersburg.

Restorations. The Campbell Mansion, formerly the home of Alexander Campbell, the founder of Bethany College, is a 27-room restoration of a structure originally built between 1793 and 1840. Also on the grounds are a schoolhouse and cemetery. Other restorations include Contentment, an antebellum home and museum in Ansted; Sunrise in Charleston, which houses a planetarium, animal fair, and garden center; Harper House at Harpers Ferry, a home dating back to 1782; and Willow Glen in Wheeling, a 40-room mansion built by a local coal baron.

Other Points of Interest. Blennerhassett Island, in the Ohio River just south of Parkersburg, is interesting historically. Here was the home of Harman Blennerhassett, a wealthy Englishman who had come to America to pursue his interests in the natural sciences without family interference. In 1805, Aaron Burr persuaded him to join in schemes the nature of which he seems not to have understood but which were later interpreted as treasonous. As a consequence, Blennerhassett lost his home and fortune.

Two West Virginia towns became renowned through John Brown, the antislavery leader from Kansas. His raid on Harpers Ferry in 1859 resulted in the death of several men and his capture. He was tried, sentenced, and hanged in Charles Town (then Charlestown, Va.). The Harpers Ferry National Monument, established in 1957, is visited annually by more than a million people.

Also of unusual interest are the Beckley Exhibition Coal Mine in New River City Park in Beckley; Berkeley Springs, a health resort once visited by Martha and George Washington; the Cass Scenic Railroad; the State Capitol in Charleston, a masterpiece of architect Cass Gilbert; the Gauley Bridge; the National Radio Astronomy Observatory in Deer Creek Valley; the Leetown National Fish Hatchery; Smoke Hole

West Virginia's topography is typified by Seneca Rocks near Petersburg, part of a national recreational area.

EARL PALMER/MONKMEYER

Cavern at Petersburg and Seneca Caverns at Riverton; and Reymann Memorial Farms (the West Virginia University experimental farm) and the Lost River, both in Wardenville.

Annual Events. In West Virginia the most spectacular season is spring, when the dogwood and redbud are in bloom. But festivals and special events occur throughout the year. These include the Alpine Festival in Davis in March; White Water Weekend in Petersburg in March; Wildflower Pilgrimage at Blackwater Falls State Park; a Strawberry Festival in Buckhannon in May; the Folk Festival in Glenville in June; *Hatfields and McCoys*, a play about West Virginia history presented at Grandview State Park throughout the summer; the Mountain State Art and Craft Fair held on July 4th weekend at Cedar Lakes; the West Virginia State Fair at Lewisburg; the Poultry Festival in Moorefield; the Cherry River Festival in Richwood in August; and the five-day Appalachian Arts and Crafts Festival at Beckley. Later events are the New Martinsville's Saddle Club Show, Town & Country Days, and Inboard Regatta in September; the Preston County Buckwheat Festival in Kingwood in September; and in October the Annual Black Walnut Festival in Spencer and the Mountain State Forest Festival at Elkins featuring a parade, forest tours, and woodsmen's contests. Music festivals are held in Wheeling in April and in Charleston in May.

7. History

The early history of the state is closely tied to that of Virginia, of which West Virginia was once a part. When Virginia joined the Confederacy in 1861, the people of the western counties were sympathetic with the Union cause. They formed their own government and became a separate state in 1863.

Exploration. The earliest Indians in the area that is now West Virginia were the moundbuilders who occupied the land about 1000 B. C.–1000 A. D. Ancient mounds and relics of this civilizations have been found in the Ohio Valley. The uncharted and unexplored region was granted to the London Company by King James I in 1606. In 1609 the royal charter for the Virginia colony extended its boundaries from South Carolina, north to Pennsylvania, and westward and northwestward indefinitely, but the western reaches of this grant were left relatively undisturbed because of the mountains that separated them from the coastal sections of Virginia.

In the 1640's the Iroquois Indians drove the weaker tribes out of the area. When the first white man, John Lederer, arrived in the western Virginia region in 1669, the unpopulated country was being used as a hunting ground and source of salt for the remnants of the tribes that remained nearby. These included the Cherokee, Tuscarora, Mingo, Delaware, and Susquehanna. In 1671, Thomas Batts and Robert Fallam went beyond the Blue Ridge reached by the Lederer expedition. Batts and Fallam crossed the Appalachian Mountains in their search for a water route to the Pacific Ocean, and claimed the Ohio Valley for England.

Settlement. The state's first white settler arrived in 1726 when Morgan Morgan came from Delaware and built a log cabin at Bunker Hill. Other settlers followed, many of them German or Scotch-Irish. In 1727, Germans from Pennsylvania, seeking religious freedom, settled at New Mecklenburg (now Shepherdstown), but these early pioneers were frequently under Indian attack. They built forts and blockhouses, many of which were the nuclei of today's cities. In 1742, John P. Salley discovered coal on the Coal River near Racine, but it was not immediately developed. The French and Indian War raged from 1754–1763. In 1755, George Washington led an unsuccessful raid against the French and Indians, who were closely allied, and British Gen. Edward

John Brown's Fort in Harpers Ferry, now a museum, commemorates the site of his last stand against federal troops.

STATE OF WEST VIRGINIA

Braddock's forces were almost annihilated by the Indians in this battle. The turning point came in 1758 when the British captured the French Fort Duquesne (now Pittsburgh), breaking the French power in the Ohio Valley and weakening their alliance with the Indians.

To avoid further bloodshed, King George III decreed that the colonists should not take any more land west of the Alleghenies unless a peaceful treaty was reached with the Indians. The Scotch-Irish ignored the royal proclamation, and the German and Dutch could not read it. The skirmishes continued.

In 1769 a treaty was signed with the Cherokee and Iroquois Indians in which they gave up all land between the Allegheny Mountains and Ohio River, and the settlers streamed across, but many of them still fell victim to the Shawnee. In 1774, Governor Dunmore took retaliatory measures against the Shawnee. The day-long battle at Point Pleasant on Oct. 10, 1774, resulted in a meeting at Pittsburgh in 1775 that led to the promised neutrality of seven important Indian tribes in the Revolutionary War, which had just begun. The Indians kept their neutrality for two years, but ultimately the British turned them against the colonists.

During the "Bloody Year of the Three Sevens" (1777) western Virginians suffered major Indian invasions. It was not until 1794, more than a decade after the end of the Revolutionary War, that the Indians retreated from the Ohio River and released their prisoners, making western Virginia a safe place in which to live. The last battle of the American Revolution took place on Sept. 11, 1782, when a British and Indian attack on Fort Henry near Wheeling ended in their defeat.

Separation and Statehood. As early as 1776 the settlers in western Virginia petitioned the Continental Congress for their own government. The social and economic differences between the two contrasting sections of the Virginia colony were vast. To the east were prosperous tobacco plantations and an aristocratic lifestyle. West of the mountains were hardworking frontiersmen, farming and raising livestock as they carved their rough-hewn lives out of the wilderness. Because the heaviest concentration of population was in the east, it was they who controlled state affairs, and it was they who benefited from legislation covering slavery, taxes, public funds, and education. The breach continued to widen.

During the evolution of the Jacksonian program of democracy and expansion, the interests of present West Virginia were largely political and economic. Located at the crossroads of the United States and favored by boundless resources, the area was chiefly concerned, after the War of 1812, with banks, internal improvements, and industry. When these, particularly the banks and the internal improvements, were not provided by the federal government, the local inhabitants generally sought to increase their influence in state government as a means of providing them. To this end they demanded white manhood suffrage, equal representation in the General Assembly for equal numbers of white residents, and reforms in the local government. Most of these demands were conceded in the reform convention in 1851.

Following 1851 the chief differences between eastern and western Virginia were economic. Although representation in the General Assembly was still arbitrarily apportioned, the question of reapportionment on the basis of white population was, under a constitutional requirement, to be submitted to the voters in 1865, and the westerners felt confident of its approval. But they had paid a high price for the concessions the east made in 1851. Among other things, that section demanded and secured a property classification under which black slaves under 12 years of age were exempt from taxation and those over that age, however valuable, could not be assessed in excess of $300. Moreover, through their control of the General Assembly, the easterners had appropriated to themselves all the state institutions and a fairly adequate system of railroads, financed in part by the state, whereas the westerners were given only macadam and dirt roads and an asylum for the insane. Worse still, the eastern-controlled assembly had refused the Baltimore & Ohio Company a franchise for a track to extend from Harpers Ferry to the Ohio River by way of the Shenandoah, New, and Kanawha valleys. The question of slavery was not, in itself, an issue between east and west. The middle-class white residents of the west tended to abhor abolitionists and, without notable exception, deplored John Brown's attempt to incite slaves to revolt against their masters.

EARL PALMER/MONKMEYER

A coal museum in Stotesbury features a replica of a mine and artifacts of the 19th century coal industry.

Nevertheless, when the Virginia state convention voted (April 17, 1861) to secede from the Union, the westerners, in the First Wheeling Convention (May 13–15), repudiated the action, naming a central committee that proceeded at once to put the northwest in a state of defense. The state authorities in Richmond meanwhile proceeded to make a formal alliance with the Confederate States of America, which thereupon moved its capital from Montgomery, Ala., to Richmond, Va.

DAVE CRUISE/PHOTO RESEARCHERS

Harewood, built in 1770 near Charles Town, was the home of Col. Samuel Washington, brother of George Washington.

Under the circumstances, loyal leaders in the northwest abandoned their long-cherished desire for separate statehood and joined President Lincoln in his efforts to preserve the Union. To that end it was considered necessary to reorganize the government of Virginia on a loyal basis. The initial steps were taken in the first session of the Second Wheeling Convention (June 11–25). Acting as a constituent assembly, that body elected Francis H. Pierpont governor of the restored government of Virginia and authorized such changes in the wording of the existing constitution as were considered necessary to permit him and the other state agencies, particularly the General Assembly, to function. The work of reorganization was then completed by the General Assembly, which elected John S. Carlile and Waitman T. Willey to the U. S. Senate to fill vacancies caused by the withdrawals of R. M. T. Hunter and James M. Mason to cast their lots with the Confederacy. As expected, the new senators were seated, and the reorganized government was accepted as sufficient for any contingency, even the approval of the dismemberment of Virginia and the formation of a new state.

The Confederate defeat at Rich Mountain (July 11, 1861) and Gen. Henry A. Wise's retreat from the Kanawha Valley had meanwhile given impetus to a new state movement. Fortunately for those who wished it, the Second Wheeling Convention had only recessed. For the purpose of dealing with the altered situation it was reconvened on Aug. 6, 1861, and on August 20 it adopted a dismemberment ordinance that also provided for the formation of a new state to be called Kanawha. With only "Black Republicans" and abolitionists voting against the proposed new state, the ordinance authorizing it was approved by the participating voters on October 24. An attempt directed by Gen. Robert E. Lee to recover northwestern Virginia for the Confederates having failed meanwhile, the makers resolved to widen the bounds of the proposed new state. In fact, some of them wished to include all western Virginia. As a consequence, a constitutional convention, meeting on Nov. 26, 1861, extended the boundary to the south so as to make a "well-rounded-out state" and to the east so as to include all of Virginia traversed by the Baltimore & Ohio Railroad. At the same time the name was changed from Kanawha to West Virginia.

With the sole provision that the proposed state change its constitution to provide for the gradual abolition of black slavery, the constitution, ratified on April 3, 1862, was accepted by the Congress as drafted. As this was a political matter wholly within the province of Congress, its legality has never been questioned by the courts. Governor Pierpont having agreed to transfer the capital of the reorganized government from Wheeling to some available point in Virginia, Lincoln approved the separate statehood bill as a war measure, and West Virginia was admitted as the 35th state on June 20, 1863.

Since Statehood. Since statehood, West Virginia has had major disputes with neighboring states. A suit brought by Virginia to recover Berkeley and Jefferson counties was settled in favor of West Virginia (1871). The action growing out of the abduction by Kentucky authorities of West Virginia citizens during the Hatfield-McCoy feud was resolved in favor of Kentucky (1888). Litigation initiated by Maryland for the adjustment of common boundaries was settled in 1910 in favor of West Virginia. The Virginia debt issue was finally settled in favor of Virginia (1911–1919). Ohio and Pennsylvania succeeded in enjoining the state from restricting the exportation of natural gas (1923).

Following the Civil War, West Virginia experienced a reconstruction not unlike that to which the former Confederate states were subjected. In 1872 this was ended in part through a new constitution (ratified August 22) drafted by ex-Confederates and liberal Democrats.

Thereafter the best efforts of its leaders were directed largely at solving transportation problems and developing the state's natural resources. For a time the new state led the entire country in developing a progressive free public school system. Later the leadership became preoccupied with material things, and the state fell behind in educational development on both the lower and the higher levels.

From 1871 to 1897, West Virginia was controlled by the Democratic party. Of the six Democratic governors, E. Willis Wilson alone was a reform liberal. Throughout this period the state rarely exercised its regulatory powers, and reform was at a standstill. In 1882 certain exemptions from taxation accorded to the railroads and the farmers were nullified by court decision.

The Republicans controlled the state administration from 1897 to 1933, with the exception of the administration of Democrat John J. Cornwell (1917–1921). Like their predecessors, the Republicans were economy minded and eager to attract nonresidential capital. They were more interested in business promotion than social reform. But the impact of the progressive movement with its demand for better schools, conservation of natural resources, improved highways, public health programs, and fair labor practices did not go unnoticed.

From the great railway strike of 1877, which had its inception at Martinsburg, to the enactment of the National Labor Relations Act in 1935, West Virginia was the scene of industrial strife that on occasion erupted into open warfare. On the one hand there were the West Virginia coal operators resisting unionization of their mines; on the other, the United Mine Workers of America (aided and abetted by the operators of Pennsylvania, Ohio, Indiana, and Illinois) asserting their right to bargain collectively. The last citadel of resistance was the southern West Virginia "smokeless" field, where the operators were a law unto themselves during the "Golden Twenties."

Labor problems in the 1920's came to a climax at the Battle of Blair Mountain in 1921, when a four-day battle between unionizing coal miners and 2,100 federal troops, backed by a squadron of U. S. bombers, resulted in the miners' defeat. The labor movement in the state was crippled for the next decade by court injunctions, but with the paralysis of the coal industry in the 1930's, operators and miners alike welcomed the labor legislation of the New Deal, and unionization was effected by default.

Help for the 11 Appalachian Mountain states came from Presidents John F. Kennedy and Lyndon B. Johnson when federal-aid programs for building roads, developing water resources, restoring forests, and retraining workers were instituted. More than $100 million were poured into the state, $45 million of which was for the relief of hungry people. In 1965, West Virginia abolished capital punishment, and in 1965 state laws were passed to control water and air pollution and strip mining. These advances in the 1960's were countered, however, by floods and mining disasters that took many lives. Following the explosion and fire at Farmington in 1968 that killed 78 miners, Congress passed stronger regulatory laws for mine safety, better working conditions, and increased benefits for the miners.

During the early 1960's, West Virginia was one of the poorest states in the country, but noticeable economic gains in the 1970's resulted in an increase in per-capita income and a decrease in unemployment. New demands for coal and a growth in industry are the basis for a steady economic growth in the state.

The Modern Era. From 1933 to 1957 the political history of the state belonged to the Democrats, whose problems stemmed chiefly from depression, war, transition from wartime to peacetime economy, the coal depression, and the need for constitutional reform. The Republicans, assuming control of the executive branch of the state government in 1957, continued the effort to keep West Virginia abreast of neighboring states in conservation, education, highway improvements, promotion of tourism, and industrial expansion, but failed to solve its most persistent problem, that of extensive unemployment. The high level of joblessness, deriving in large measure from chronic weakness in the coal industry, was aggravated by advances in automation.

CHARLES H. AMBLER* AND FESTUS P. SUMMERS*
West Virginia University

HISTORICAL HIGHLIGHTS

1669 John Lederer and his companions became the first white men in the West Virginia region.
1671 Thomas Batts and Robert Fallam gave England claim to the Ohio Valley.
1726 Morgan Morgan established the state's first white settlement at Bunker Hill in Berkeley county.
1727 Germans from Pennsylvania settled at New Mecklenburg (now Shepherdstown).
1742 Coal was discovered on the Coal River.
1755 French and Indians defeated troops led by George Washington and Gen. Edward Braddock.
1774 Lord Dunmore's War was fought against the Indians.
1776 People of West Virginia petitioned Continental Congress for separate government.
1815 Gas was discovered near Charleston.
1859 John Brown and his followers raided the arsenal at Harpers Ferry.
1861 The counties of western Virginia supported the Union and refused to comply with the Virginia legislature's decision to secede.
1863 West Virginia became the 35th state of the Union on June 20.
1872 The present state constitution was adopted.
1885 Charleston became the permanent capital of West Virginia.
1915 The U. S. Supreme Court settled the debt issue, ruling that West Virginia owed Virginia $12,393,929.50 at the time of separation.
1921 A union dispute involving the coal miners erupted into the Battle of Blair Mountain.
1929 West Virginia ranked first in the country in the production of coal.
1939 West Virginia made the final payment on its debt to Virginia.
1943 Vast salt deposits were discovered in the northwestern part of the state.
1965 West Virginia abolished capital punishment.
1968 A mine disaster at Farmington took 78 lives, leading to new mine safety laws.
1972 Floods near Man killed more than 100 persons.

Bibliography

Bice, David A., and Jones, Helen, *West Virginia and the Appalachians* (Jalamap Pub. 1983).
Clagg, S. *West Virginia Historical Almanac* (McClain 1975).
Cohen, Stan B., and Pauley, Michael J., *Historic Sites of West Virginia,* 2d ed. (Pictorial Hists. 1985).
Lambert, Oscar D., *West Virginia and Its Government* (Greenwood 1972).
Summers, Festus P., and Ambler, C. H., *West Virginia: The Mountain State,* 2d ed. (Prentice-Hall 1958).
Williams, John A., *West Virginia* (Norton 1984).
Williams, John A., *West Virginia and the Captains of Industry* (West Va. Univ. Lib. 1976).

WEST VIRGINIA INSTITUTE OF TECHNOLOGY, a coeducational, state-controlled college of liberal arts and technical school, at Montgomery, West Virginia, some 25 miles southeast of Charleston. Originally chartered in 1895 as a branch of West Virginia University, it became a junior college in 1921 and was named the New River State School. Ten years later it was authorized to grant four-year degrees and its name was changed to New River State College. The present name was adopted in 1941. Accredited by the North Central Association of Colleges and Secondary Schools, the West Virginia Institute of Technology grants the standard baccalaureate degrees. Departments include: biology; business administration and economics; chemistry; education and psychology; English; history, government, and social studies; home economics; industrial arts; mathematics; music; physics; physical education; and printing management. There is also an engineering division. The library contains over 84,000 volumes, including a West Virginia collection. The average enrollment is about 3,300.

WEST VIRGINIA STATE COLLEGE, a coeducational college at Institute, West Virginia. By an act of the state legislature, it was established in 1891 as the West Virginia Colored Institute, in the valley where Booker T. Washington, the renowned Negro educator, spent his boyhood and later began his teaching career. It was opened to students in 1892. In 1915 the name was changed to West Virginia Collegiate Institute; it became West Virginia State College in 1929, by another legislative act. In 1954, the United States Supreme Court's desegregation decision unlocked the doors of the college to white students, previously barred by the state constitution from attending classes with Negroes. Within the first semester after the court's decision, quiet integration was transforming the school into what one educator since has called "the South's and the nation's most thoroughly integrated college."

A tax-supported institution, accredited by the North Central Association of Colleges, State offers a comprehensive undergraduate program leading to baccalaureate degrees in the arts, science, and music. The college has departments of arts survey, biology, business, chemistry, economics, education, English, foreign languages, geography, history, home economics, industrial technology, law enforcement, mathematics, music, philosophy, physical education, physics, political science, psychology, sociology, and speech-drama.

Candidates for the degree of bachelor of arts may qualify for the specialized degree in elementary education, and candidates for the bachelor of science degree may qualify for the specialized degrees in business administration, technical science, home economics, mechanic arts, or secondary education.

The college is in a small community 10 miles (16 km) west of Charleston. The library has some 110,000 volumes and 750 current periodicals. Old gold and black are the school's colors, and the athletic teams are nicknamed the "Yellow Jackets." Enrollment is about 4,000.

A. H. CALLOWAY, *West Virginia State College*

WEST VIRGINIA UNIVERSITY, a coeducational, state-controlled institution of higher learning, located at Morgantown, W. Va., about 60 miles south of Pittsburgh, Pa. Its three campuses occupy 475 acres in Morgantown, and its experimental farms, forests, and camps cover another 11,000 acres in six West Virginia counties. Chartered in 1867 as the Agricultural College of West Virginia under the national land-grant act, it was established on the site of the 50-year-old Monongalia Academy, overlooking the Monongahela River. The name was changed to West Virginia University the following year.

In addition to the original college of arts and sciences, the university maintains colleges of agriculture and forestry, engineering, human resources and education, journalism, mines, nursing, pharmacy, physical education, social work, dentistry, law, and medicine. There are also a creative arts center and a graduate school.

Affiliated with the university are Potomac State College at Keyser, the Parkersburg Branch of West Virginia University at Parkersburg, and agricultural and engineering experiment stations, a bureau of government research, a bureau of business research, an institute of industrial relations, four extension divisions (agriculture, mining and industrial, general, and labor education), and divisions of military and air science. There is an extension center at Greenbrier Valley, in Lewisburg. The Kanawha Valley Graduate Center, once an extension facility of the university, is now independent.

All educational, administrative, financial, and business affairs of the university are vested in a bipartisan Board of Governors, made up of nine members appointed by the governor of the state for staggered nine-year terms. At least one and not more than two members must be appointed from each Congressional district. The board selects the president. There is a library containing over 720,000 volumes, 7,100 current periodicals, and special collections of newspapers on microfilm, court records, and other materials relating to the history of the state. The school colors are gold and blue, and athletic teams are known as the "Mountaineers." The average enrollment is about 21,500.

HAROLD J. SHAMBERGER
Assistant to the President
West Virginia University

WEST VIRGINIA WESLEYAN COLLEGE, a privately controlled, coeducational college of liberal arts, located in Buckhannon, a city of more than 6,000 inhabitants near the geographical center of West Virginia. The school was founded in 1890 as the West Virginia Conference Seminary by the West Virginia Conference of the Methodist Episcopal Church. For 14 years it operated as an academy, or preparatory school. In 1904, however, it became an institution of collegiate rank and it has since been known as West Virginia Wesleyan College. It is fully accredited and offers baccalaureate degrees in the arts, science, and music education.

The 50-acre campus at Buckhannon is shaded by a grove of native oaks and by hundreds of other trees and shrubs planted by the founders and friends of the institution. Its beauty is further enhanced by its larger setting, the scenic foothills of the Alleghenies. The school colors are orange and black, the athletic teams being known as the "Bobcats." There is a library with approximately 100,000 volumes, including special Abraham Lincoln and Civil War collections. The average enrollment is about 1,800.

JAMES STANSBURY
West Virginia Wesleyan College

WEST WARWICK, wĕst wŏr′ĭk, town, Rhode Island, in Kent County, on the Pawtuxet River, 11 miles southwest of Providence, at an altitude of 135 feet. Manufactures include cottons, woolens, worsteds, velvet, lace, and bookbinding cloth. There are dairy, poultry, and truck farms in the area. The town was set off from Warwick and incorporated in 1913. Population: 27,026.

WEST YORKSHIRE, a metropolitan county of northern England, created in 1974 out of a portion of the former West Riding section of Yorkshire. It occupies an area of 787 square miles (2,039 sq km), extending eastward from the Pennine highlands, which rise to about 1,500 feet (460 meters) on the western border. Its largest city and financial center is Leeds. Huddersfield and Bradford are important textile centers.

Early settlement of the area by Scandinavians and Anglo-Saxons was followed by establishment of several medieval feudal towns and the gradual development of the West Riding woolen mills.

Today West Yorkshire is the heart of Britain's woolen industry. Specialized factories in an area extending roughly from Keighley on the west to Leeds and Wakefield on the east perform all the combing, spinning, and weaving operations involved in producing woolen textiles. The county is also a coal-mining region, although exhaustion of mines in the western highlands has necessitated opening deeper reserves in the east. Agriculture is diversified, ranging from sheep raising in the Pennine highlands to dairying and food-crop farming in the eastern lowlands. Population: (1979) 2,064,000.

WESTBOROUGH, wĕst′bûr-ō, town, Massachusetts, in Worcester County, 29 miles west of Boston, at an altitude of 300 feet. The Assabet River flows through the town. Settled about 1675, the town was incorporated in 1717. Predominantly residential, it has a considerable number of small industries including abrasives, leather, machinery, and paper manufacture. Eli Whitney was born here and it was the home of Jack Straw, believed to be the first Indian in Massachusetts converted to Christianity. Ebeneza Parkman, a Protestant minister who came to Westborough in 1724, kept a day-by-day diary for 58 years, and this valuable record of colonial living is now in the Worcester Antiquarian Society. Lyman School for Boys, a state correctional school, and Westborough State Hospital are located here. Westborough has a town meeting system of government. Population: 13,619.

GLADYS E. AINSWORTH.

WESTBROOK, wĕst′brŏŏk, city, Maine, in Cumberland County, six miles morthwest of Portland, on the Presumpscot River, at an altitude of 85 feet. Settled in 1628, it was called Saccarappa and until 1814 was part of the town of Falmouth, from which it was separated and incorporated as Stroudwater. Later that year the name was changed in honor of Thomas Westbrook, a man prominent in local civil and military affairs. In 1871 a section of Westbrook was separated and set up as a new town, Deering, now a part of Portland. Westbrook was incorporated as a city in 1891 and is governed by a mayor and council. The city manufactures paper, wood products, machinery, shoes, textiles, crushed-stone products, and jewelry. Population: 14,976.

CHRISTINE LOWELL

WESTBURY, wĕst′bĕr-ē, village, New York, in Nassau County, 23 miles east of New York City, at an altitude of 105 feet (32 meters).

The village was named after the town of Westbury, England, from which the original settlers arrived about 1665. These people were Quakers and established one of the first Friends' meetings here, and services have been regularly held since 1700. The village is primarily a residential suburb of New York City. Located in Westbury are the Robert Bacon Memorial Children's Library, the only independent children's library in the United States; the Country Art Gallery and School; Old Westbury Gardens (John S. Phipps Foundation); and the Westbury Music Fair. Of interest nearby are the Nassau County Historical Museum in Salisbury Park, the site of Charles A. Lindbergh's takeoff on the first Atlantic solo flight, and Roosevelt Raceway.

The village was incorporated in 1932, and is governed by a mayor and council. Population: 13,871.

ESTHER HICKS EMORY.

WESTCHESTER, wĕst′chĕster, village, Illinois, in Cook County, 14 miles west of Chicago, on state and federal highways. The village is primarily a residential suburb of Chicago. The streets of the village, lined with 15,000 American elms, bear English names—Kent, Canterbury, Chaucer, Robin Hood Lane, and so on. The village was founded by Samuel Insull, public utility magnate, and was incorporated as a village in 1925. It is bounded by three forest preserve areas operated by the Cook County Forest Preserve District. Village government is administered by a council and manager. Population: 17,730.

LILLIAN R. O'BOYLE.

WESTCOTT, wĕs′kət, **Brooke Foss,** English prelate and theologian: b. Birmingham, England, Jan. 12, 1825; d. Bishop Auckland, Durham, July 27, 1901. Graduated from Trinity College, Cambridge, in 1848, he was a fellow there for two years and in 1851 was ordained in the Church of England.

Entering Harrow in 1852 as an assistant master, Westcott remained at the school until 1869, when he became residentiary canon of Peterborough. While at Harrow, he began to make a name for himself as a biblical exegete and historian. The views expounded in his *General Survey of the History of the Canon of the New Testament during the First Four Centuries* (1855) have come to be generally accepted. In 1860 he published *Introduction to the Study of the Gospels*, dealing with the authorship of the Synoptic Gospels. In the *Gospel and the Resurrection* (1866) he dealt with the final problems of existence. He also contributed many articles to William Smith's *Dictionary of the Bible* (1863). The appearance of two-volume *The New Testament in the Original Greek* (1881), written with Fenton J. A. Hort after 28 years of work, was hailed as a major achievement.

The turning point of Westcott's life came with his appointment as regius professor of divinity at Cambridge in 1870. Together with Fenton J. A. Hort and Joseph Barber Lightfoot, he led the Cambridge tradition of biblical scholarship and hermeneutics. While at Cambridge he played a leading role in the reorganization of the Divinity School, the establishment of the Cambridge Mission to Delhi, and the Cambridge Clergy Training

School. From 1870 to 1881 he was a member of the company that brought out a revised edition of the New Testament. He was a strong supporter of the cooperative movement and was president of the Christian Social Union from 1889 until his death. In 1883 he became canon at Westminster and in 1890 was appointed bishop of Durham. While at Durham he took a lead in trying to bring the church and the miners closer together and he was influential in settling the strike by the coal miners of 1892. Some of his sermons are collected in *Christian Aspects of Life* (1897) and *Lessons of Work* (1901).

WESTCOTT, Edward Noyes, American novelist and banker: b. Syracuse, N.Y., Sept. 26, 1846; d. there, March 31, 1898. Educated in the local schools, he became a clerk at the age of 16. After working in the insurance and banking fields for a number of years, he organized his own banking and brokerage firm.

Tuberculosis forced his retirement and during the summer of 1895, at Lake Meacham, N.Y., he started to write the novel *David Harum: a Story of American Life* (q.v.). Completed in Naples, Italy, the following year, it was refused publication by several publishing houses. Finally shortly after Westcott's death, it appeared in print. The book proved to be a great success, more than one million copies having been sold in the next forty years. It has also been made into a play and a motion picture.

WESTERLIES, The. See WINDS—*Glossary of Winds*.

WESTERLY, wĕs'tər-lē, town, Rhode Island, in Washington County, 37 miles southwest of Providence, between the Pawcatuck River and Block Island Sound, at an altitude of 15 feet. It was noted in former years for its shipbuilding, granite quarrying, and textile industries. Today it manufactures bleach and dye, printing presses, elastic webbing, furniture, food products, and electronic equipment, and is famous for Westerly granite used in fine monumental work.

The town was first settled in 1648 on the site occupied by the Niantic Indians under the sachem Ninigret. In 1661 a substantial settlement called Misquamicut was founded and in 1669 the town was incorporated as Westerly because of its geographical location. It was called Haversham from 1686 to 1689. The town includes nine villages, the most important to its economy being the summer resorts of Watch Hill, Misquamicut, Weekapaug, and Shelter Harbor. The largest industrial enterprise, bleaching and dyeing, is located in Bradford. Wilcox Park is in the center of the town, and a state beach is maintained at Misquamicut. Government is by a council. Pop. 18,580.

SALLIE E. COY.

WESTERMARCK, vĕs'tĕr-märk, Eng. wĕs'tər-märk, **Edward Alexander,** Finnish anthropologist, sociologist, and philosopher: b. Helsingfors (now Helsinki), Finland, Nov. 20, 1862; d. Lapinlahti, Sept. 3, 1939. Westermarck was educated at the University of Helsingfors, where he later became a professor of moral philosophy. He served as professor of sociology at the University of London, 1907–1930; and from 1930 to his retirement in 1935, as professor of philosophy at Turku University in Finland. Westermarck is chiefly noted for his studies of marriage. In his *History of Human Marriage* (1891; 5th ed., 3 vols., 1929) and other writings, he refuted the theory of Lewis Henry Morgan (q.v.) that monogamy arose out of earlier stages of promiscuity and polygamy. Marriage, Westermarck held, is the foundation of human society; monogamy appears among the most primitive peoples and in certain forms even among the anthropoids.

In *The Origin and Development of the Moral Ideas* (2 vols., 1906–1908), he investigated the emotional basis of moral judgments and the relation of moral feelings to ethical concepts and attitudes in different societies. In *Ethical Relativity* (1932), Westermarck maintained that moral judgments reflect attitudes of approval and disapproval inculcated in the individual by society. Based on his ethnological researches in Morocco were his *Ritual and Belief in Morocco* (2 vols., 1926), and *Wit and Wisdom in Morocco* (1931). Other writings include *Memories of My Life* (1929); *Early Beliefs and Their Social Influence* (1932); *Three Essays on Sex and Marriage* (1934); *The Future of Marriage in Western Civilization* (1936); and *Christianity and Morals* (1939).

MURRAY GREENE.

WESTERN AUSTRALIA, wĕst'ûrn ôs-trāl'yə, state, Australia, occupying the western sector of the continent, bounded on the north by the Timor Sea, on the northwest, west, and south by the Indian Ocean, on the southeast by the Great Australian Bight, on the east by South Australia and the Northern Territory, with an area of 975,920 square miles. It is the largest state of the Commonwealth, having 32.81 percent of the land area. Over one-third of the state lies north of the Tropic of Capricorn. The capital city is Perth. Other major towns are the twin gold-mining centers of Kalgoorlie and Boulder, and Bunbury.

Physical Features.—The terrain is generally low and flat. The plains are vast, relieved in some

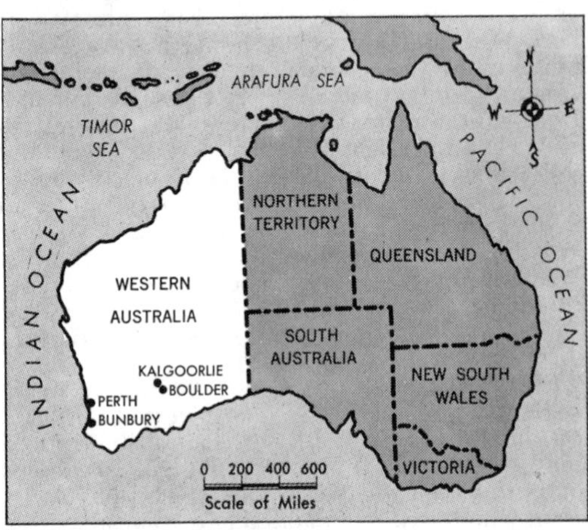

Location map of Western Australia.

parts by residuals of the hardest rocks. A great part of the state is devoid of rivers, and there are no significant freshwater lakes. Artesian water augments surface supplies in some areas. Rivers in the north are spasmodic, depending upon seasonal rains, while those in southern areas flow fairly regularly. Principal rivers are the Ord and Fitzroy, in the north, and the De Grey, Fortescue, Ash-

The low, gently undulating terrain in this view of east central Western Australia is typical of the state's dry "outback."

AUSTRALIAN NEWS AND INFORMATION BUREAU

burton, Gascoyne, Murchison, and Swan. A remnant of very ancient landmasses, the gently undulating Great Plateau covers more than nine tenths of the state; fringing it is a coastal plain which is generally narrow. To the east of Perth and leading up from the coastal plain, the Darling Range is an escarpment extending some 300 miles north and south and averaging about 1,000 feet above sea level; it forms the western margin of the ancient landmass. To the north and east, the plateau becomes more arid, merging into the Great Sandy Desert where scattered aboriginal tribes gain a living from country that will not support white settlement; they number about 2,000 persons. A few elevations bear the names of mountains but these are generally only a few hundred feet above the general level. The King Leopold and Hamersley ranges in the north and the Stirlings in the south are no more than high plateaus, each an eroded residual; the Porongorups (in the south) are mere granite outcrops. The highest point is Mount Bruce, 4,024 feet, near the Hamersley Range.

More than half of the state receives an average rainfall of less than 10 inches. In the tropical highlands of the far north, there is a considerable area with good summer rainfall (the Kimberleys), while in the southwest corner and along the southern coast some 100,000 square miles have a mild Mediterranean climate with reliable winter rains. Between these zones lies the dry "outback," a highly mineralized area receiving sporadic rainfall and covered for the most part with small eucalyptus, saltbush, spinifex, mulga, and other drought-resistant plants. The flora of the southwest sector of the state is particularly rich. It is characterized by an extraordinary variety of flowering plants (over 7,000 species). Hardwood forests (located in the southwest) cover more than 10,000 square miles.

Population. The population of the state is 1,222,300 (1978 est.), with more than half of the people living in the Perth metropolitan area. The populations for the major cities (1966) were: Perth metropolitan area 499,969; Kalgoorlie urban area 19,908; Bunbury 15,459; Geraldton 12,125; Albany 11,419; Northam 7,400. The latest census (1954) showed that there were 20,786 full-blooded aborigines in the state.

The Economy. Sheep are grazed throughout the agricultural regions and extend well into the low-rainfall areas, where large flocks forage on rough but nutritious natural pasture. In the north, an ambitious project to dam the Ord River began in 1960; it visualized eventual agricultural as well as some pastoral development. Beef cattle predominate in the summer-rain areas in the north and, in conjunction with dairy herds, form an important industry in the southwest sector. About 25,000,000 acres, mainly in the south, have been cleared and developed for agriculture, with nearly 10,000,000 acres brought into production between 1946 and 1960. Increased productivity has come with mechanized farming and improved pastures (arising from the introduction of new pasture species, increased use of superphosphate as top-dressing, and correction of soil deficiencies by use of trace elements). Wool provides about one third of the state's rural wealth, and grains (wheat, oats, and barley) account for 40 percent. Other products include milk, meat, fruit, vegetables, poultry, and honey.

With 80 percent of national output, Western Australia is the principal gold-producing state. Steam-raising coal is mined in the southwest. Extensive and rich iron ore deposits at Yampi Sound and at Koolyanobbing (near Southern Cross) are now being worked. Other industrial minerals include blue asbestos (crocidolite), manganese, ilmenite, tin, and lead, while large-scale deposits of bauxite are known to exist. Oilfields of commercial size exist at Barrow Island. Income from fisheries derives largely from the crayfish catch and whaling. Frozen crayfish (rock lobster) tails are sent to the United States.

Imports are mainly from the eastern states. They include metals and manufactures, machines and machinery, apparel, electric appliances, chemicals, and textiles. Oil is imported from the Middle East, and refined. Most exports are shipped overseas. Refined petroleum products are sent to other states.

A power grid has been developed across the southwest by the state-owned electricity commission, the main producer of electricity. Water conservation has been developed considerably; linked with the storages are pipelines carrying water to the dry inland. The 346-mile pipeline to Kalgoorlie (opened 1903) has been extended to serve towns and farms over an area of 4,000,000 acres.

AUSTRALIAN TOURIST COMMISSION

Perth, on the Indian Ocean, is the capital and chief commercial and cultural center of Western Australia.

Transportation. Railroads have been substantially modernized. There are 4,851 miles of track open to traffic. The single link with the eastern states is by the Commonwealth railways' transcontinental line. The arterial and secondary road network covers 11,000 miles. Air services operate between Perth and eastern states, and international routes link with South Africa and Singapore. Intrastate air services operate over more than 16,000 route miles. The Royal Flying Doctor Service operates from six bases to cover all inland areas. Regular shipping services link with the eastern states and with Asia, Africa, Europe, and the United States, operating from Fremantle, Australia's main bunkering port.

A flock of stud Suffolk sheep in a pasture outside Bunbury, in the far southwestern part of the state.

AUSTRALIAN NEWS AND INFORMATION BUREAU

Cultural Activities. The state has two daily newspapers, the *Daily News* and *The Western Australian*, both published in Perth. The State Library is the chief library. The principal scientific institutions are the Royal Society of Western Australia, the Australian Institute of Agricultural Science, and the Astronomical Observatory. The chief museum is the Museum of Western Australia, with a fine natural history collection. The University of Western Australia is the only university in the state, and provides free tuition to all students with residential qualifications. All these institutions are located in Perth. Education is compulsory to the age of 14. There are both state and church schools. Professional, commercial, and technical training is provided at all levels.

Government. The state has a bicameral legislature consisting of a 30-member Legislative Council and a 51-member Legislative Assembly. The first is elected by a more restrictive franchise and consists of three persons elected from each of 10 districts for a period of six years, one of whom retires biennially. The second chamber is elected by a universal franchise for a period of three years. Executive power is exercised by a cabinet headed by a premier and responsible to both houses. The government is headed by a governor appointed by the sovereign of Australia.

History. Dutch navigators first touched the northwest coast early in the 17th century and the English buccaneer William Dampier spent some months there in 1699, but all found the land unprepossessing. Known as New Holland, the territory west of 135° east longitude was not claimed by Britain until 1829, three years after settlements had been made at Albany on King George Sound under Major Edmund Lockyer, and in the far north, both largely to forestall the French. The Swan River Colony was set up direct from London in 1829 under a privately-sponsored plan, with Sir James Stirling as governor. Settlement proceeded slowly, however. The economic development of the country received an impetus with the transportation of convicts from England starting in 1850. In the following 18 years, 9,700 men were brought to the colony. They helped not only to build roads and bridges but were a source of cheap labor for the settlers. The discovery of gold in the 1880's brought about a spurt in the development of the interior. In 1890 the colony received responsible government and the first Parliament was opened on Dec. 30, 1890. In 1900 Western Australia joined the Commonwealth as the sixth state. The early 1900's saw the establishment of the wheat belt and in the 1920's rural industries developed in the southwest. During the 1930's a strong movement arose to secede from the Commonwealth but with the end of the economic depression and start of World War II the movement died. Fremantle was developed as a United States submarine base during World War II. Monte Bello Island was the site of the first atomic bomb explosion by Great Britain in September 1952.

See also AUSTRALIA.

R. M. YOUNGER.

Further Reading: Aveling, Marion, ed., *Westralian Voices: Documents in Western Australian Social History* (Intl. Spec. Bk. 1980); Cameron, J. M. R., *Ambition's Fire: The Agricultural Colonization of Pre-Convict Western Australia* (Intl. Spec. Bk. 1982); Firkens, Peter, ed., *A History of Commerce and Industry in Western Australia* (Intl. Spec. Bk. 1980); Russell, E., *A History of the Law in Western Australia* (Intl. Spec. Bk. 1980); Stokes, John P., *The Western State: Some of Its People and Ports*, 3d ed. (Intl. Spec. Bk. 1976).

WESTERN AUSTRALIA, University of, a state-supported, coeducational institution of higher learning in Crawley, Western Australia, on a bay of the Swan River, about three miles from Perth. The university was founded in 1911. Nine faculties award bachelor degrees: arts, law, education, economics, science, engineering, agriculture, dental science, and medicine. There are three residential colleges: St. George's (Anglican), St. Thomas More (Roman Catholic), and St. Catherine's (nondenominational), plus a Hall of Residence; all provide residence for men students with the exception of St. Catherine's which is a college for women. Among the outstanding buildings are Hackett Memorial Hall, named for Sir J. Winthrop Hackett, a benefactor of the university, and Winthrop Hall with its aboriginal paintings by George Benson. Adult education activities, conducted by the Adult Education Board, are statewide and include extension lectures, orchestral concerts, drama, opera, and ballet. In association with other interested bodies the Adult Education Board also conducts an annual Festival of Perth. The annual enrollment averages 3,500 students.

ARTHUR J. WILLIAMS.

WESTERN CAROLINA COLLEGE, a coeducational college and liberal arts teacher-training institution located in Cullowhee, N.C. Founded in 1889 as the private Cullowhee High School, the state took over its support in 1893, and in 1905 it became Cullowhee Normal and Industrial School. The first instruction on a college level began in 1912. In 1925 it became Cullowhee State Normal School and in 1929 Western Carolina Teachers College. It took its present name in 1953. The school grants bachelor degrees in arts, science, and education, and a degree of master of arts in education. Western Carolina College has achieved a national reputation through its experimental program for gifted children, and for training teachers for both gifted and handicapped children. The school colors are purple and gold and the athletic teams are known as the "Catamounts." The annual enrollment averages 1,600 students.

LILLIAN HIRT.

WESTERN CHURCH, the Catholic Church in the West, under the headship of the pope as Roman pontiff and patriarch. The term is also used to include Eastern groups under the rule of the Roman Catholic Church such as the Uniats, and even separated churches in the West like the Anglican (Church of England) or Episcopal Church. In the widest sense of all it includes Protestantism and is virtually equivalent to "Western Christendom."

Historically the term Western Church arose in contradistinction to the Eastern Church, that is, the Holy Orthodox Church (or Churches) of the East (see ORTHODOX CHURCHES), and the distinction rests upon tendencies and events far older than the date of 1054 A.D. given for the final division between Eastern and Western Christianity called the Great Schism. Tensions between East and West are as old as the beginnings of history, according to Herodotus and others; and such events as the attempt to divide the Roman world by Antony and Cleopatra, or the reorganization of the Roman Empire by Diocletian and Constantine, are examples of factors which influenced and led to the eventual separation. Language differences (Western Latin versus Eastern Greek) also had much to do with it. Efforts are being made in the mid-20th century to heal the breach (see ECUMENICAL MOVEMENT).

FREDERICK C. GRANT.

WESTERN DESERT, one of the five Egyptian frontier districts of the United Arab Republic, bordered on the east by the Nile Valley, on the north by the Mediterranean Sea, on the west by Cyrenaica, and on the south by the Southern Desert. Although the Mediterranean shore has a number of settlements, its main features are the five oases of Bahariya, Dakhla, Farafra, Kharga, and Siwa, all lying in extensive depressed basins ranging from 50 to 200 miles in length and from 10 to 30 miles in width. They embody small cultivated areas of from 1 to 40 square miles, the population of which gains a precarious living by cultivating dates, olives, apricots, and rice. In the Libyan Desert, one of the most forbidding areas of the Sahara, it lies in a region of scant rainfall, extreme temperatures, and violent winds. Except for small airfields near Bahariya and Mersa Matruh, and a rail connection between Mersa Matruh-Alexandria, and Kharga-Nag Hammadi, its only contact with the outside world is by caravan routes, which connect the various oases and extend to the Nile Valley and the Mediterranean coast. The people are predominantly Muslim; the area is administered, as are all frontier districts, by the minister of war. The population, largely nomadic, is believed to number 100,000 (1961).

The region is rich in historical associations. Southwest of El Qasr is a large ruined temple of the Roman era; in the Kharga district lie the ruins of the temples of Hibis (c. 500 B.C.) and of Nadura (c. 150 A.D.), a Christian convent, and a Christian cemetery, and here axes of the Stone Age have been found. In the Siwa Oasis lie the ruins of temples and rock tombs of the Ptolemaic and Roman periods, and it once harbored the oracle of Jupiter Ammon, to which Alexander the Great is believed to have made a pilgrimage. To the north lies the Qattara Depression in which, in October 1942, was fought the Battle of El Alamein, which ended the danger of Nazi engulfment of Egypt in World War II.

See also EGYPT—3. *The Land and Its Resources.*

WESTERN ELECTRIC COMPANY, an industrial manufacturer of telephone apparatus, cable, electronic military devices, and special communications equipment, with its head office in New York City. Incorporated in 1915, it was the successor to the Western Electric Company of Illinois, which was purchased by the American Bell Telephone Company in 1881. This acquisition enabled the Bell System to take advantage of Western Electric's strong patent position and assured the system of the large and steady supply of telephone equipment. In its early years the company developed a large business in industrial power apparatus—arc lamps, switchboard equipment, motors, and generators. In 1910 it disposed of its power equipment business to the Westinghouse Electric and General Electric companies.

After 1900, when the American Telephone and Telegraph Company became the parent company of the Bell System, Western Electric became its chief operating company for the manufacture and supply of telephone equipment. Western Electric pioneered in the development of radio equipment, including the three-element tube and the cone speaker. By 1960 it employed an average of 134,000 employees and was one of the largest suppliers of radar and electronic military equipment in the United States. The principal subsidiaries of Western Electric are the Sandia Corporation, which is engaged in atomic energy development; the Nassau Smelting and Refining Company; and the Teletype Corporation. Western Electric maintains offices in Canada and Great Britain to care for its foreign patent holdings. Bell Telephone Laboratories carries on research and development for both the American Telephone and Telegraph Company and Western Electric.

COURTNEY R. HALL
Professor of History, Queens College, New York

WESTERN EMPIRE, the western portion of the Roman Empire that was permanently detached from the Eastern Empire after the death of Theodosius the Great in 395 A. D. The Roman Empire had been split, then reunited, several times before the permanent separation. After 395 the Western Empire was ruled first from Milan, then Ravenna. It included Italy, Illyria, Pannonia, Noricum, Gaul, Britain, Spain, Mauretania, Numidia, as well as Libya as far as the Gulf of Syrte. The Western Empire ended in 476, when Odoacer, king of the Heruli, forced the emperor Romulus Augustulus to abdicate. See also ROME.

WESTERN EUROPEAN UNION (WEU). Following the collapse of the European Defense Community (q.v.) plan in August 1954, the six nations involved in that enterprise conferred in London with Great Britain, Canada, and the United States with a view to finding another formula for the rearming of West Germany. On the initiative of the British foreign secretary, Anthony Eden, it was decided to rearm Germany within the framework of a revised version of the European defense organization set up by the Brussels Treaty of 1948 (signed by Britain, France, and the Benelux countries) and later absorbed (1949) into the North Atlantic Treaty Organization (NATO).

This proposal was embodied in a series of protocols signed at Paris on Oct. 23, 1954, providing for termination of the occupation regime in Germany, inclusion of Germany and Italy in the Brussels organization (now to be known as the Western European Union), and admission of Germany to NATO. To allay fears of German aggression, limits were set on the size of national forces, subject to review by unanimous consent of the members of WEU. Germany accepted the restrictions on her forces and also a prohibition against the manufacture of nuclear, chemical, and bacteriological weapons and of certain types of conventional weapons. An agency was established to supervise these limits and to collate information on the annual strength of all members. At the same time the Western powers made certain pledges to Germany concerning reunification and the illegitimacy of the East German regime. As part of the price of agreement, Britain made an unprecedented promise not to reduce her forces on the Continent without the consent of WEU.

The Western European Union comprises a council and secretariat, with headquarters in London, and an assembly identical in membership with the delegations of these nations to the Council of Europe (see EUROPE, COUNCIL OF). Militarily, WEU has had little importance, being overshadowed by NATO, but it gained new potential interest as a framework within which the nuclear armament of Germany might be achieved through the establishment of a European nuclear force.

See also NORTH ATLANTIC TREATY AND WESTERN EUROPEAN UNION.

LAURENCE W. MARTIN, *Author of "Diplomacy in Modern European History"*

WESTERN ILLINOIS UNIVERSITY is a state-supported, coeducational institution of higher learning in Macomb, Ill. Founded in 1899 as Western Illinois Normal School, it became Western Illinois State Teachers College in 1921 and received its present name in 1957. The university consists of schools of arts and sciences; education; applied sciences; business; fine arts; health, physical education, and recreation; and graduate studies. The bachelor's and master's degrees are given. Enrollment in the 1970's exceeded 14,000.

WESTERN KENTUCKY UNIVERSITY is a state-supported, coeducational institution of higher learning in Bowling Green, Ky. Founded in 1906 as Western Kentucky State Normal School, it merged with Southern Normal School in 1907 and first granted degrees in 1922. Called Western Kentucky State Teachers College in 1930, it received its present name in 1966. It includes colleges of arts and humanities, science and technology, business and public affairs, education, and applied arts and health; a graduate school; and a community college. It offers bachelor's and master's degrees. The library has a collection of Kentuckiana and American folklore. Enrollment in the 1970's exceeded 11,000.

WESTERN MICHIGAN UNIVERSITY is a state-supported institution of higher education in Kalamazoo, Mich. Since its founding in 1903 as Western State Normal School, the institution has continued to meet its initial obligation—the preparation of teachers. But the growing educational needs of the state have changed its role to that of a multipurpose university. Its changing status and role are reflected in successive changes of name—to Western State Teachers College in 1927, Western Michigan College of Education in 1941, and Western Michigan College in 1955. The present name was adopted in 1957.

Both undergraduate and graduate programs are offered in colleges of applied science, arts and sciences, business, education, and fine arts and in schools of librarianship and social work. Master's degree programs number about 60. Doctoral programs include those in education, chemistry, mathematics, and sociology. Enrollment in the 1970's exceeded 20,000.

WESTERN ONTARIO, University of, a coeducational institution of higher education, situated to the northwest of London, Ontario, Canada. It was chartered in 1878 as the Western University of London, Ontario, under the auspices of the Church of England. In 1908 it became a nondenominational municipal university. Under a provincial act of 1923 it received its present name and was given particular responsibility for serving 14 counties in the western part of the province. The first buildings on the present campus were completed in 1924.

The divisions of the university include faculties of arts, music, science, social science, engineering science, dentistry, medicine, law, nursing, and graduate studies; schools of business administration and library and information science; and the Althouse College of Education. Programs in most of these divisions lead to the usual range of undergraduate and graduate degrees. Institutions affiliated with the university include Huron College, a theological school and general arts college; King's College, a seminary and college of arts; and Brescia College, which specializes in art subjects. All these affiliated colleges are situated in London. Among notable facilities of the university are the libraries, with special collections in regional history; the Talbot Theatre; and the Museum of Indian Archaeology and Pioneer Life.

WESTERN RESERVE, that part of Connecticut's land claims in the Northwest Territory that Connecticut had refused in 1786 to yield to the United States and had "reserved" for settlement by its own citizens. The Western Reserve occupied a tract of what is now northeastern Ohio. The boundary extended west from the Pennsylvania border along the 41st parallel to the vicinity of Willard and then north to Port Clinton. The shore of Lake Erie, from Port Clinton to the Pennsylvania state line, constituted the northern boundary of the reserve. Within the 6,000-square-mile (10,000-sq-km) area are some of Ohio's principal cities, including Cleveland, Sandusky, Akron, and Youngstown.

Connecticut's claims to a much larger region of the Northwest Territory were based on its charter of 1662, granted by Charles II of England, which gave the colony dominion over all lands west of it "from sea to sea." The grant conflicted with subsequent grants by the same king to the proprietors of New York and Pennsylvania.

Congress sought to untangle this and other territorial conflicts by persuading the states to cede their western claims. But Connecticut retained the Western Reserve and in 1792 opened 500,000 acres (200,000 hectares) to Connecticut townsfolk who had suffered losses from British raids during the Revolution. This section was called "The Sufferers' Lands" or "The Firelands." In 1795 the remaining 3 million acres (1,200,000 hectares) of the reserve were sold to the Connecticut Land Company, a consortium made up of 35 landowners. In 1800, Connecticut agreed to yield its longtime claim to the entire Western Reserve to the newly organized Ohio territory.

WESTERN RESERVE UNIVERSITY. See CASE WESTERN RESERVE UNIVERSITY.

WESTERN SAHARA. See SPANISH SAHARA.

WESTERN SAMOA. See SAMOA.

WESTERN SPRINGS is a village in Illinois, in Cook county, 15 miles (24 km) west of Chicago. Originally named East Hinsdale in 1871, it was incorporated under its present name in 1886. The Potawatami Indians and trappers once frequented the area. The village was named for the mineral springs situated in what is now Spring Rock Park. The village, a residential suburb of Chicago, is governed by a manager and board of trustees. Population: 12,876.

ANN VANCE, *Western Springs Public Library*

WESTERN UNION TELEGRAPH COMPANY, a communications company with its head office in Mahwah, N. J. It was established in April 1851 as the New York & Mississippi Valley Printing Telegraph Company to build a telegraph line from Buffalo, N. Y., to St. Louis, Mo. In 1856 it adopted its present name. By 1861 the company had completed the first transcontinental telegraph line and was supplying service over a wide area in the East.

In 1876, Alexander Graham Bell offered to sell the company his telephone patents for $100,000. Western Union refused the offer but decided later to enter the telephone field, having acquired equipment patents from Edison and Elisha Gray. In 1879, however, the company lost infringement cases brought against it by the Bell interests. Forced out of the telephone field, Western Union devoted itself exclusively to the development of its telegraphic lines. By 1900 the system had grown to a million miles of telegraph lines plus two international cables.

The company continued to grow, reaching a dominant position in the United States telegraph field by absorbing more than 500 smaller companies. In October 1943 it acquired Postal Telegraph, Inc., its most serious competitor, which had been under control of the International Telephone and Telegraph Company. American Telephone and Telegraph challenged Western Union in 1931 by instituting its TWX direct telegraph exchange system, but Western Union met this move by developing its own TELEX system. In addition to telegram service, Western Union provides facsimile and private wire services, reservation and money order services, as well as nontelegraphic messenger and distribution services.

As late as 1914, some 80 percent of all telegraphic messages were transmitted over manually operated circuits but since that time the system has been largely mechanized, especially since World War II. By 1950 a huge network of 15 high speed switching centers was completed, which provided nationwide distribution of messages automatically with but one manual operation: the typing of the message at the point of origin. In the direction of increased automation, facsimile telegraphy and transmission over radio beam have been expanded. Thousands of business firms utilize the automatic Desk-Fax system which transmits both statistical data and messages directly from their message centers. In 1960 the company began the construction of a transcontinental microwave beam system capable of handling every form of electronic communication to link directly or by extension most of the large cities of the United States. In 1974, Westar I, a communications satellite, was launched by NASA for Western Union.

COURTNEY HALL*, *Queens College, New York*

WESTERNS is the term applied to novels, short stories, motion pictures, and radio and television dramas that purport to represent life in the American West, especially during the period between the Civil War and the late 1890's. The open rangelands, rugged mountains, and deserts between the Missouri River and the Pacific Ocean—known popularly in this context as the "Wild West"—furnished a seemingly endless supply of raw materials for adventure stories, as well as the inspiration for works of art, music, ballet, and musical theater.

The dominant figure of the Western, the cowboy, emerged in Texas after the Civil War, when large numbers of men were needed by ranchers to tend the growing herds of longhorn cattle on the open range. The cowboys' experiences while driving cattle across hundreds of miles from the range to market became standard subjects for Western stories. As towns sprang up around cattle markets and mining camps, another archetypal Western figure developed—the territorial marshal, whose shoot-outs with notorious badmen became legendary. Cultural historians have come to regard the cowboy and the lawman as authentic American folk heroes. See also COWBOY.

Background Figures and Locales. Certain actual persons and places, because of their frequent appearance in Westerns, achieved legendary status. Prominent among the frontiersmen were Kit Carson, Davy Crockett, and Buffalo Bill. Women were represented by the frontierswoman Calamity Jane and sharpshooter Annie Oakley. Wyatt Earp, Bat Masterson, Wild Bill Hickok, and Pat Garrett upheld law and order, against such notorious outlaws as Billy the Kid, Cole Younger, Jesse James, Sam Bass, Cherokee Bill, and Belle Starr. Justice was meted out by "Hanging Judge" Isaac C. Parker of the Arkansas-Oklahoma border and "Fining Judge" Roy Bean of Texas. Indians, the traditional enemies of incoming settlers, were led by chiefs Sitting Bull, Crazy Horse, Geronimo, and Red Cloud.

Recent studies have disclosed the existence of a number of black cowboys. Many of them, such as Joe McCloud, Broncho Sam, Bill Nunn, Bob Lemmons, and Will Peoples, were noted for their ability to capture and tame wild mustangs, the horses used for herding and driving cattle.

Place-names that recur throughout Westerns include the Chisholm, Shawnee, Bozeman, and Western trails, along which cattle were driven to market. Cattle towns, such as Abilene and Dodge City, and mining towns, such as Tombstone, Deadwood, and Cripple Creek, were famous for their saloons, dance halls, and gambling parlors. Texas cattle ranches—the King, XIT, Three D, JA, and Matador—with thousands of acres of range, figured prominently in Western lore.

Fiction. From the earliest dime novels published in the mid-19th century, Western fiction has been dominated by the exploits of cowboys and lawmen. In a typical story, a lone figure on horseback—equally adept with fists and gun—triumphs over hostile Indians or over cattle rustlers, marauders, gunmen, and other assorted villains. This plot, repeated over and over, dominates the "Buffalo Bill" stories of Ned Buntline, the "Deadwood Dick" adventures of Edward L. Wheeler, the "Hopalong Cassidy" yarns of Clarence E. Mulford, and scores of novels and stories by such writers as Zane Grey, Luke Short, and Max Brand.

A more serious approach to Western fiction was introduced with Owen Wister's *The Virginian* (1902) and Andy Adams' *The Log of a Cowboy* (1903), which treat range life more realistically or pay greater attention to actual historical conditions in the period represented. Other acknowledged early leaders in this vein include B. M. Bower (*The Lonesome Trail*, 1909), Eugene Manlove Rhodes (*Good Men and True*, 1910), Hamlin Garland (*They of the High Trail*, 1914), Rex Beach (*Heart of the Sunset*, 1915), Emerson Hough (*The Covered Wagon*, 1922), and Will James (*The Drifting Cowboy*, 1925). Among later writers of serious fiction were Ernest Haycox (*Starlight Rider*, 1933), Conrad Richter (*The Sea of Grass*, 1937), Walter Van Tilburg Clark (*The Ox-Bow Incident*, 1940), A. B. Guthrie (*The Big Sky*, 1947), and John Houghton Allen (*Southwest*, 1952).

Motion Pictures. In addition to fiction, the Western experience has furnished materials for the entertainment media and the arts. From the beginning of the motion-picture industry, Western fiction provided a virtually inexhaustible source for both silent films and "talkies." Hundreds of novels and stories were adapted for full-length movies and serials, which were viewed enthusiastically throughout the United States and in other parts of the world. In the early decades of the 20th century, the Western movie, or "horse opera" as it came to be called, reinforced more than any other medium the status of the cowboy and the marshal as folk heroes.

A vast number of Western films were produced, most of which had standard plot formulas. Some, however, became motion-picture classics: *The Great Train Robbery* (1903), *The Covered Wagon* (1923), *Cimarron* (1931), *Stagecoach* (1939), *Red River* (1948), *The Gunfighter* (1950), *High Noon* (1952), and *Shane* (1953). Success inevitably led to parody, as in *Destry Rides Again* (1939), *Cat Ballou* (1965), *Butch Cassidy and the Sundance Kid* (1969), and *Blazing Saddles* (1974), and occasionally to "message" films, such as *The Ox-Bow Incident* (1943) and *Tell Them Willie Boy Is Here* (1969).

For their roles in Western films, many actors achieved legendary status in their own right. Notable among them are William S. Hart, William Boyd, Hoot Gibson, Buck Jones, Tim McCoy, Tom Mix, Ken Maynard, Gary Cooper, Randolph Scott, Joel McCrea, and John Wayne.

Radio and Television. In the 1930's and 1940's serialized Westerns were offered as standard radio fare. The most famous were *The Lone Ranger*, in which a masked rider, accompanied by his Indian companion Tonto, performs good deeds throughout the Western plains, and *Death Valley Days*, a series of semihistorical dramas about mining camps in California and Nevada.

Among televised Westerns, two are especially noteworthy for sustaining viewer interest: *Gunsmoke*, which was first produced for radio in 1950, featuring the heroics of Matt Dillon, a frontier marshal in Dodge City, and *Bonanza*, recounting the exploits of the Cartwright family of cattle ranchers. Other series that achieved steady followings include *Have Gun, Will Travel*, about a Western knightly adventurer aptly named Palladin, and *Wyatt Earp* and *Bat Masterson*, relating episodes from the legendary careers of two historical Western marshals.

Art. The vast and colorful Western terrain, with its Indians, cowboys, hunters, mountain men, and miners, its prairies, mountains, and des-

MUSEUM OF MODERN ART, FILM STILLS ARCHIVE

The Covered Wagon (1923), a silent-film classic, gave an epic grandeur to motion pictures about the Old West.

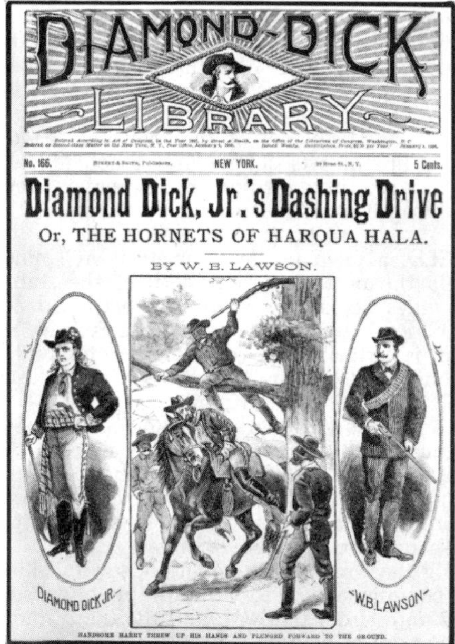

BETTMANN ARCHIVE

Western adventure dime novels—which often sold for 5 cents—were a popular form of fiction in the United States in the 19th century.

CULVER PICTURES

The film *Destry Rides Again* (1939), with James Stewart (*center*) as a lawman who would not tote a gun and Marlene Dietrich as a barroom singer of easy virtue, satirized traditional Westerns.

CULVER PICTURES

Popular TV Western series *Gunsmoke,* first produced in 1955, starred James Arness (*left*) as heroic Dodge City Marshal Matt Dillon. Dennis Weaver (*center*) was his deputy Chester, and Milburn Stone played Doc Adams.

erts, and its horses, cattle, buffalo, and other animal life provided American painters with abundant materials. Among the leading artists who interpreted the Old West are George Catlin, who specialized in Indians of the Great Plains and the Northwest, Frederic Remington, whose works comprise a virtual history of Western life through paintings and book illustrations, and Charles M. Russell, who devoted his talent to recording Montana cowboys, Indians, and wildlife. Writers of Westerns who illustrated their own books include Will James, Ross Santee, and Tom Lea.

Music. Western music traditionally consists of sentimental ballads with simple melodies and lyrics that express the emotions and experiences of range life. The guitar, banjo, and occasionally the ukulele are the principal accompaniment for singing, and these, together with the fiddle and the accordion, comprise the fundamental instruments for the Western-style square dance. Among the all-time favorite songs are *Home on the Range, Red River Valley, The Cowboy's Lament* (*Streets of Laredo*), *I Ride an Old Paint, The Old Chisholm Trail, Rye Whisky, The Buffalo Skinners,* and *Little Joe the Wrangler.*

Some cowboy actors, such as Gene Autry, Tex Ritter, and Roy Rogers, were also singers. Other popular singers of Western ballads, which form part of the country-music scene, include Eddy Arnold, Elton Britt, Johnny Cash, Red Foley, Montana Slim, Hank Snow, Merle Travis, Hank Williams, and Bob Wills. Ballads of social commentary by Woody Guthrie and Cisco Houston added an important dimension to Western music. See also COUNTRY MUSIC.

However, Western themes in music extended beyond the purely popular idiom. *Oklahoma!* (1943), in which Richard Rodgers and Oscar Hammerstein II utilized traditional Western material to dramatize the conflict between ranchers and farmers, marked a milestone in the American musical theater. Ferde Grofé composed the orchestral *Grand Canyon Suite* (1931), which programatically recalls the Western landscape. In ballet, *Billy the Kid* (1938; choreography by Eugene Loring, score by Aaron Copland); *Rodeo* (1942; Agnes de Mille, Copland), and *Western Symphony* (1954; George Balanchine, Hershy Kay) exploit Western material. Even opera has found its source in the American West, as in Puccini's *The Girl of the Golden West* (1910), based on a play by David Belasco, and Douglas Moore's *Ballad of Baby Doe* (1955), a romantic drama set in a Colorado mining town.

Bibliography

Botkin, B. A., *A Treasury of Western Folklore* (Crown 1951).

Branch, Douglas, *The Cowboy and His Interpreters* (1926; reprint, Cooper Square 1961).

Curry, Larry, *The American West: From Catlin to Russell* (Los Angeles County Mus. of Art 1972).

Dobie, J. Frank, *Guide to Life and Literature of the Southwest* (Southern Methodist Univ. Press 1952).

Durham, Philip, and Jones, Everett L., eds., *The Frontier in American Literature* (Macmillan 1969).

Durham, Philip, and Jones, Everett L., *The Negro Cowboys* (1965; reprint, Univ. of Neb. Press 1983).

Erickson, John B., *Cowboys are a Separate Species* (Maverick Bks. 1986).

Folsom, James K., *The American Western Novel* (College & Univ. Press 1966).

Frantz, Joe B., *Aspects of the American West* (Texas A & M Univ. Press 1976).

Frantz, Joe B., and Choate, Julian Ernest, Jr., *The American Cowboy: The Myth and the Reality* (Univ. of Okla. Press 1955).

Lomax, John A., *Cowboy Songs and Other Frontier Ballads* (1916; reprint, Macmillan 1986).

Steckmesser, Kent L., *The Western Hero in History and Legend* (Univ. of Okla. Press 1967).

WESTERVILLE, a city in Ohio, is a residential community about 10 miles (16 km) northeast of Columbus, in the central part of the state. It is the home of Otterbein College, a United Methodist school founded in 1847 by the United Brethren Church. Hanby House, the residence of Benjamin R. Hanby, who wrote the song *Darling Nellie Grey,* is maintained as a state historical site.

Founded in 1839, Westerville was known as the "dry capital of America" from 1909 to 1948, when it was the national headquarters of the Anti-Saloon League. Government is by a city manager and city council. Population: 23,414.

JOHN BECKER, *Otterbein College*

WESTFIELD, a city in Massachusetts, is in the western portion of the state, in Hampden county, about 9 miles (15 km) west of Springfield. It is on the Westfield River, a tributary of the Connecticut River, and is a mixed manufacturing and residential community. The city was once the source of nearly all the whips manufactured in the United States but is now industrially diversified, producing bicycles, school furniture, firearms, cast-iron boilers, leather goods, paper, brushes, cigars, tools, dies, and various precision instruments.

In 1669 the General Court of Massachusetts authorized the town of Westfield–so called because it was then the westernmost settlement in the colony. Westfield was incorporated as a city in 1921. It is the home of the Westfield State College, a liberal arts school and teachers college. The city is governed by a mayor and council. Population: 36,465.

WESTFIELD, a town in New Jersey, is in Union county, in the northeastern portion of the state, about 5 miles (8 km) west of Elizabeth and 20 miles (32 km) southwest of Manhattan, N.Y. Westfield is primarily a residential community for persons employed in New York City, Elizabeth, and nearby industrial plants.

The area was first settled about 1700, when it was considered a part (the "west fields") of the town of Elizabeth. It became an independent township in 1794 and, in 1903, was reorganized and incorporated as the Town of Westfield, with a mayor-council form of government.

During the American Revolution, several skirmishes took place in and around the town. A cemetery dates from that era, and there are some pre-Revolutionary homes. One of these is now a "living museum" in which colonial crafts are demonstrated. Population: 30,447.

WESTFORD, a largely residential town in northeastern Massachusetts, in Middlesex county, is 17 miles (27 km) northwest of Boston. Industries include offset printing and granite quarrying. Two old homes have witches' stairs opposite regular staircases. Once part of Chelmsford, Westford was incorporated in 1729. Government is by town meeting. Population: 13,434.

WESTINGHOUSE, wes'ting-hous, **George** (1846–1914), American inventor of the air brake that made high-speed railroad travel safe and the founder of the Westinghouse Electric Corporation. He was born in Central Bridge, N.Y., on Oct. 6, 1846, and died in New York City on March 12, 1914. Leaving his father's shop, he joined the Union Army at the age of 15 and served throughout the Civil War, terminating his service as an assistant engineer in the navy. After he briefly attended Union College, machinery and invention lured him back to his father's shop. There he developed and patented a rotary steam engine, a device for replacing derailed freight cars on the track, and a railroad frog.

Westinghouse's first major achievement, the one that first brought him great wealth, was his development of a fail-safe braking system for trains that was under the direct control of the locomotive engineer. Formerly, train accidents had occurred frequently because the brakes on each car of a train had to be applied manually by brakemen following a signal from the engineer.

When his first brake, operated by steam, proved impracticable, he turned to compressed air and on April 13, 1869, was awarded the first of many air-brake patents. In September he organized the Westinghouse Air Brake Company to develop on a standardized basis the apparatus that, continuously improved, was to be adopted on the vast majority of the world's railroads.

To control the increased speed and flexibility made possible by the air brake, Westinghouse now undertook to develop railroad signals and interlocking switches. In 1882, having purchased the patents of others and combined them with his own inventions, he organized the Union Switch and Signal Company. He also developed apparatus for the safe transmission of natural gas, hitherto a dangerous procedure.

Westinghouse's other major achievement was his central role in the development and commercial exploitation of alternating-current electric power. In 1884, attracted to the potential of electricity, he founded the Westinghouse Electric Company. Foreseeing the possibilities of alternating current, which could be distributed over great distances, whereas direct current was limited to a radius of two or three miles, Westinghouse bought the patents of foreign and domestic inventors of transformers, which were the key to high-voltage distribution. He thus came into conflict with Thomas Alva Edison, the proponent of direct current, in the famous "War of the Currents." Despite the fact that, at equal voltages, direct current is more deadly, Edison's warning that alternating current was a potential threat to life was accorded a strange but spurious confirmation in the public mind when the state of New York decided to employ alternating current in electrocution of condemned criminals for capital crimes.

Westinghouse persevered, however, enlisting the services of Nikola Tesla and other inventors in the development of alternating-current motors and apparatus for the transmission of high-tension current. They pioneered in large-scale municipal lighting and engaged in the utilization of the extensive hydroelectric power resources of Niagara Falls.

Westinghouse was an extraordinarily prolific inventor and a brilliant industrial manager. He took out about 400 patents in his lifetime and was experimenting with steam turbines and air springs for automobiles up to the time of his death. As a manager, by encouraging the ideas and exploiting the patents of the many engineers he employed, Westinghouse made his company one of the greatest electric manufacturing organizations in the United States and the outstanding competitor of the General Electric Company, which in 1896 arranged to use his patents by a cross-licensing agreement. By the turn of the century, the various Westinghouse enterprises were capitalized at $120 million and had grown to employ perhaps 50,000 workers, but in the financial panic of 1907 their founder lost control of his companies. In 1911 he severed his connections with them completely.

Westinghouse spent his last years mostly in public service, particularly in the reorganization of the Equitable Life Assurance Society from a bankrupt stock company to a viable mutual company.

See also AIR BRAKE.

WESTLAKE, a city in northern Ohio, in Cuyahoga county, 12 miles (19 km) west-southwest of downtown Cleveland. Predominantly a residential suburb, the community has some light manufacturing of such products as construction components, small metals, cosmetics, and plastic tubing. The surrounding area produces potatoes, corn, wheat, and grapes.

Once part of the Western Reserve, the original settlement was occupied in 1810 by New Englanders. The area was called Dover or Dover Center. In 1940 a small segment of that area was changed to Westlake, and the city was incorporated in 1957. Westlake has a mayor-council form of government. Population: 19,483.

WESTMEATH, west'mēth, a county in the north central part of the Republic of Ireland, in Leinster province. Bounded by the counties of Longford, Cavan, Meath, Offaly, and Roscommon, it has an area of 681 square miles (1,763 sq km). The county of Westmeath is level with many bogs, especially in the south, and lakes, which are noted for their fine trout. The rivers Shannon and Brosna flow through it, and it is crossed by the Royal Canal. The principal occupations are dairy farming, cattle raising, and the growing of oats, wheat, and potatoes. Other industries include alcohol distilling, tweed and cotton milling, limestone quarrying, and the manufacture of furniture.

Originally part of Teffia, in the ancient kingdom of Meath, Westmeath was made an independent county in 1541. The county's chief towns are Mullingar, the county town, and Athlone. Population: (1981) 61,523.

WESTMINSTER, west'min-stər, a city in southern California, in Orange county, 12 miles (19 km) east of Long Beach. Situated in a truck-farming and citrus-fruit region, it is a residential suburb of both Long Beach and Los Angeles, which is approximately 25 miles (40 km) to the northwest. Westminster has several industrial parks. A U.S. naval weapons station and Los Alamitos Naval Air Base are nearby.

Westminster was founded in 1870 by the Rev. L. P. Weber as a colony for Presbyterians. Incorporated in 1957, it is governed by a council and manager. Population: 71,133.

WESTMINSTER, west'min-stər, a city in north central Colorado, in Adams county. It is primarily a residential suburb of Denver, which is situated 9 miles (14 km) to the southeast. Westminster's manufactures include telephone switching equipment and electromechanical products. Stapleton International Airport is nearby.

At the turn of the century the Presbyterian Church started a college and erected a building designed by Stanford White. However, the school survived only briefly, except for Westminster Law School, which moved to Denver. In 1920 the Pillar of Fire, an independent fundamentalist church group, bought the property and has maintained Belleview College there. Incorporated in 1911, Westminster has a council-manager government. Population: 50,211.

WESTMINSTER, west′min-stər, a city and inner borough of Greater London, England. It was established in 1965 by the consolidation of the former boroughs of Westminster, Paddington, and St. Marylebone. Situated on the River Thames, immediately west of the City of London, Westminster contains some of the finest buildings in England and teems with historical associations. Buckingham and St. James's palaces and the houses of Parliament are here, as well as Westminster Abbey, Westminster School, Westminster Cathedral, and St. Martin's-in-the-Fields and St. Margaret's churches. Royal Albert Hall, Whitehall and the principal government buildings, No. 10 Downing Street, and New Scotland Yard also are in Westminster, as are the National, Tate, and National Portrait galleries and the principal theaters. Victoria and Charing Cross railroad stations are located in the city, as is Trafalgar Square. Because of their strategic locations, a number of these historic buildings suffered damage from World War II bombing raids.

The history of Westminster dates from a very early period. It became a city when, in 1540, Henry VIII made it the see of a bishop. Even though the see was merged with that of London 10 years later, Westminster retained the right to the title of a city. Population: (1981) 190,661.

GORDON STOKES
Author of "English Place-Names"

WESTMINSTER, Statute of, west′min-stər, an act of the British Parliament passed on Dec. 11, 1931. The most significant effect of World War I upon the constitutional organization of the British Empire was the creation of the Commonwealth of Nations. Strongly aware of their contribution to British victory and of their national strength, the dominions asked for political autonomy and for increased participation in discussions affecting them and the British Isles. In 1931, therefore, the English Parliament enacted the Statute of Westminster, which gave legal sanction to the British Commonwealth and to the recommendations made by imperial conferences since 1918.

The ultimate result of the statute was to make the dominions independent and to give them the legal right, if they so desired, of withdrawing from the Commonwealth. Specifically, the statute abolished the authority of the English Parliament over legislation of dominion parliaments, ruled that no statute passed by the English Parliament had authority in a dominion unless expressly requested, defined the legislative powers of the dominion parliaments, and required the consent of dominion parliaments to any legislation dealing with the royal succession. Since 1931 the members of the British Commonwealth have been politically independent and self-governing, but united in an allegiance to the English crown.

BRYCE LYON
University of California at Berkeley

WESTMINSTER, Statutes of, west′min-stər, three legal codifications enacted by Edward I of England between 1275 and 1290. Called the "English Justinian," Edward I was one of the great lawgivers of the Middle Ages. During his reign more legislation was enacted than in any succeeding time. In the Statutes of Westminster, Edward promulgated principles that have become important parts of Anglo-American law.

The Statute of Westminster I (1275). This statute dealt with many aspects of English law—civil, criminal, constitutional, and procedural. Its 51 clauses regulated and defined such matters as wardship, limitations of legal actions, and essoins (legal delays). Undoubtedly the most important clause was that regulating trial procedure, which held that notorious felons who would not submit to trial by jury should be kept in strong and hard imprisonment (*en le prison forte et dure*). Until 1772, when this clause was abolished, prisoners were loaded with heavy chains and fed only bread and water until they consented to jury trial. Some died under such pressure of the chains rather than submit to the verdict of a jury. Despite its severity, this clause hastened the development of trial by jury and contributed to making the Statute of Westminster I one of the most influential enactments to have been promulgated in English legal history.

The Statute of Westminster II (1285). Often called *De Donis Conditionalibus* (concerning conditional gifts), the statute probably ranks as one of the most important laws in the development of England land law. Its 50 clauses embraced many phases of land law and initiated new legal procedures. The clause regulating conditional gifts created the modern fee tail (estates tail), so named because it was restricted (*taille* in French meaning "cut down") to the line of descent specified in the legal instrument. This meant that if land was passed on to an heir under the condition that it should not be sold or in any other way alienated outside the family, the condition had to be upheld and free alienation was thereby thwarted.

In the area of criminal law this statute started a trespass on the way to being a tort; power was granted to the royal courts to liberalize their interpretation of trespass so that almost any type of trespass could be viewed as a kind of wrong (tort). Procedurally this statute expedited justice by providing that, whenever possible, cases should be tried locally in the counties by royal justices of assize rather than in the central courts at Westminster. This innovation alleviated the crowded courts of Westminster and relieved the litigants and jurors from traveling long distances to court. Incorporated in the Statute of Westminster II was a clause that could be interpreted to give the chancery general authority for the expansion of legal remedies by the issuance of new writs.

The Statute of Westminster III (1290). Sometimes called *Quia Emptores* (since purchasers), this statute terminated the feudal practice of subinfeudation. Henceforth when a man (M), holding land in fief of another (A), sold the land to a purchaser (P), the purchaser became the tenant of A rather than of M. The result of this statute was eventually to bring all English landholders into immediate tenurial relations with the king and thereby to hasten the end of the feudal system.

BRYCE LYON
University of California at Berkeley

WESTMINSTER ABBEY, west′min-stər (officially, the Collegiate Church of St. Peter in Westminster), the most famous church in the Commonwealth, located in London, England. Legend relates that the first church was erected about 605 by Sebert, king of the East Saxons. The recorded history of the Benedictine abbey begins with Edward the Confessor, who started construction of a new church about 1050. Built in the Norman style, it was consecrated in 1065 and was the scene of the coronation of William the Conqueror (1066). The entire east end was torn down by Henry III, who in 1245 began to build the present church.

A cruciform structure in the Gothic style, the abbey is 531 feet (162 meters) long and almost 102 feet (31 meters) high; the nave itself is nearly 39 feet (12 meters) wide. The church's principal architectural features are the transepts with aisles; the nave with aisles finished in the late 15th century; the choir with six chapels opening north and south of it; the majestic west towers, designed by Christopher Wren but not completed until 1740; and the Henry VII Chapel, built about 1503–1519. This chapel is famous both for its exquisite fan-vaulted roof and for its carved oaken stalls, above which hang the banners of the Knights of the Bath.

Steeped in history, Westminster Abbey is a veritable national shrine. In the center nave, near the west entrance, is the grave of the Unknown Warrior of World War I. At the east end of Henry VII Chapel is the Royal Air Force Memorial Chapel. It contains a superb stained-glass window commemorating the 63 squadrons that fought in the Battle of Britain in 1940 and embodying all their badges. Many distinguished Britons are buried in the abbey, including Geoffrey Chaucer, Edmund Spenser, Alfred Tennyson, Robert Browning, Ben Jonson, Isaac Newton, Charles Robert Darwin, and David Livingstone. Outstanding statesmen such as William Pitt, Robert Peel, Benjamin Disraeli, and William Gladstone are honored with monuments. Many of England's monarchs from Edward the Confessor to George II are also buried here. Their tombs are in the chapels of Edward the Confessor and Henry VII. In the chapel of Edward the Confessor is the coronation throne, enclosing the Stone of Scone upon which the Celtic kings were crowned. On this throne, in front of the High Altar, every monarch of England from William I has been crowned, with the exception of Edward V and Edward VIII.

WESTMINSTER CHOIR COLLEGE, west′min-stər, a private institution of higher learning for training in music, particularly church-related choral music and organ. The school was founded in Dayton, Ohio, in 1926 and moved to Ithaca, N.Y., in 1929 and to its present location in Princeton, N.J., in 1932. It offers bachelor's through doctor's degrees.

WESTMINSTER COLLEGE, west′min-stər, a small liberal-arts college located in Fulton, Mo. Its campus occupies about 197 acres (80 hectares) on a slope bordering Stinson Creek.

Founded by the Presbyterian Church in 1851 as Fulton College, it was renamed Westminster College in 1853. Originally a men's college, it began to admit full-time women students in 1979. The college grants a bachelor of arts degree, with major study available in 15 areas.

The library features a special collection on Sir Winston Churchill, who delivered his famous "iron curtain" speech at the college in March 1946.

WESTMINSTER CONFESSION OF FAITH. See CONFESSION OF FAITH, WESTMINSTER.

WESTMINSTER KENNEL CLUB, a New York City kennel club whose annual bench show is the outstanding dog show in the United States. The show attracts dogdom's elite, with entries limited to about 2,500 dogs. To be eligible for entry, a dog must have won at least one championship point in a show sponsored by the American Kennel Club or be a champion of record. Typically, more than half of the dogs entered at the Westminster show are champions of record.

The Westminster Kennel Club was established in 1877 by a group of sportsmen primarily interested in field dogs. During the club's early days, field dogs dominated the show to such an extent that pointers and setters accounted for more than half of the number of entries. A silhouette of a celebrated early pointer, Sensation, remains the club's symbol.

WILLIAM F. BROWN*, *"The American Field"*

Westminster Abbey, in London. Its majestic towers were designed by Christopher Wren and completed in 1740.

BRITISH TOURIST AUTHORITY

BRITISH TOURIST AUTHORITY

Westminster Palace, the largest Gothic building in England, is the seat of the British Houses of Parliament.

WESTMINSTER PALACE, west′min-stər, the seat of the Houses of Parliament, the largest Gothic edifice in England. The structure covers 8 acres (3 hectares) in the heart of London. Originally a royal residence, it was built by Canute in 1035. After it was destroyed by fire the following year it was replaced by Edward the Confessor's palace in 1054. It continued to be an abode of the kings of England until 1512, when a large part of it was burned. From then on it was the meeting place of Parliament until the great fire of Oct. 16, 1834, when most of its buildings were gutted.

The present Perpendicular Gothic structure was erected in 1840–1867 under the direction of Sir Charles Barry, at a cost of £3 million. On May 10, 1941, the House of Commons was destroyed by German airplanes in bombing raids. The clock tower, containing the famous Big Ben, named after Sir Benjamin Hall, was also damaged in the bombardment. The new chamber, which was designed by Sir Giles Gilbert Scott, was opened on Oct. 26, 1950.

Westminster Hall, an original and integral part of the palace, was built in 1097–1099 by King William Rufus and enlarged by several of his successors, notably Richard II, who added the magnificent hammer-beam roof. From 1305 to 1806, the hall was the seat of the highest court in the realm and many state trials were held there over the centuries. In more recent times it witnessed the lying-in-state of George V and George VI after their deaths.

WESTMINSTER SCHOOL, west′min-stər, an ancient English public school, originally attached to the Benedictine Monastery at Westminster Abbey, London. The date of its original establishment by Henry VIII is not known. It was refounded by Elizabeth I in 1560 as St. Peter's College. The school's buildings closely adjoin the abbey; several of them once were part of the domestic buildings of the abbey. The great schoolroom was once the monks' dormitory. Other buildings such as Ashburnham House belong to the post-Reformation period. Many of the buildings were remodeled after World War II.

The school is one of the seven principal public schools of England. It was long noted for its annual play in Latin, a practice that was discontinued at the end of World War II. Among the famous school customs is the struggle for a tossed pancake on Shrove Tuesday, the ceremony of the Pancake Greaze. Many eminent Englishmen were educated at Westminster.

WESTMORELAND, west-môr′lənd, **William Childs** (1914–), American general, who commanded U.S. forces in South Vietnam during the Vietnam War. He was born in Spartanburg county, S.C., on March 26, 1914. After attending The Citadel, in Charleston, S.C., he won an appointment to the U.S. Military Academy at West Point, N.Y. He graduated in 1936.

During World War II, Westmoreland led battalions in North Africa and Europe. After the war he took glider and paratroop training and taught at the Command and General Staff College, Fort Leavenworth, Kans., and at the Army War College. He saw further combat in the Korean War, leading the 187th Airborne Regimental Combat Team in two combat missions. In 1956 he was promoted to major general, becoming the youngest officer of that rank in the Army. In 1958 he was made commanding general of the 101st Airborne, the elite "Screaming Eagle" division.

Westmoreland served as superintendent of West Point from 1960 until 1963, when he was

The American photographer Edward Weston was noted for his studies of natural forms and landscapes, such as the sand dunes of *Oceano* (1936).

placed in command of the 18th Airborne Division, Fort Bragg, N.C. In 1964, President Lyndon B. Johnson appointed him senior military commander in Vietnam. Westmoreland favored a strategy of U.S. troop escalation in Vietnam. During his tenure there, the U.S. presence grew from a few thousand advisers to more than 500,000 ground forces. Replaced in 1968, Westmoreland returned to the United States and became Army Chief of Staff. He retired in 1972.

WESTMOUNT, west′mount, a city in southern Quebec, Canada, on Montreal Island. Situated within the city limits of Montreal, with an area of 1.53 square miles (3.96 sq km), it is mainly an English-speaking residential suburb. It is noted for its fine public parks.

Formerly Notre-Dame-de-Grâce, the village was renamed Westmount in 1895 for its location just southwest of Mount Royal. Incorporated as a city in 1908, Westmount has a council-manager government. Population: 20,480.

FERNAND GRENIER, *President*
Télé-université, University of Quebec

WESTON, Edward (1850–1936), American inventor and manufacturer noted for his electrical instruments. Weston was born and raised in England's industrial Midlands. Although he was trained in medicine, his interests turned to physics and chemistry. After immigrating to the United States about 1870, he entered the nickel-plating industry and conceived the idea of using generators instead of batteries to supply the power needed for plating.

He soon organized his own company, which became a leading manufacturer of electroplating generators. Weston next entered the field of electric lighting, but his ventures in arc lighting and incandescent electric lighting both failed. About 1886 he turned to electrical measurement and instrumentation, in which he was an unqualified success, and the Weston Electric Instrument Company became world famous for the quality of its products. Weston's cadmium amalgam cell was for many decades the official standard of electromotive force.

WESTON, Edward (1886–1958), American photographer, whose work was noted for its composition and clarity of detail. He was born in Highland Park, Ill., on March 24, 1886. When he was 18, he opened a photographic portrait studio in Glendale, Calif., but in 1923 he abandoned commercial photography and went to Mexico for three years. After returning to the United States, he began his famous nature studies, limited at first to California. However, in 1937, after receiving a John Simon Guggenheim Memorial Foundation fellowship, he was able to photograph extensively during travels throughout the American West.

A master craftsman, Weston never relied on artificial light, and seldom cropped, enlarged, or retouched the negatives. His work demonstrated the artistic potential of the photographic medium. It was frequently seen in exhibitions, including a major one-man show at New York City's Museum of Modern Art in 1947. Although he did not use color photography until late in life, those color pictures that he did take show the same precision that characterizes his black-and-white studies.

His art has been collected in a number of volumes, including *Seeing California with Edward Weston* (1939), *Photographs* (1936), *Fifty Photographs* (1947), and *My Camera on Point Lobos* (1950). *California and the West* (1940) and *The Cats of Wildcat Hill* (1947) have texts by his second wife, Charis Wilson Weston. He died in Carmel, Calif., on Jan. 1, 1958. Two volumes entitled *The Daybooks of Edward Weston* were published posthumously in 1973.

WESTON, Edward Payson (1839–1929), American long-distance walker. He was born in Providence, R.I., on March 15, 1839, and was raised in Boston, where he overcame a sickly childhood by extensive walking. As a young reporter on the *New York Herald*, he could turn in his night copy more quickly on foot than others could by horsecar. In 1861 he attracted attention by walking 443 miles (713 km) from Boston to Washington in 208 hours to attend the inauguration of Abraham Lincoln.

Weston began his professional career in 1867, walking 1,326 miles (2,133 km) from Portland, Me., to Chicago in 26 days. He repeated the trip 40 years later, in 1907, bettering the time by 29 hours. He also took part in six-day races, in which he walked and ran a total of 500 miles (805 km) in a week. In 1909 he walked 3,895 miles (6,270 km) from New York to San Francisco in 104 days and 7 hours. In 1910 he walked 3,500 miles (5,635 km) from San Francisco to New York in 76 days and 23 hours. Weston died in Brooklyn, N.Y., on May 13, 1929.

WESTPHALIA, west-fāl′yə, a historic region of northwestern Germany, part of which is now included in the West German state (Land) of North Rhine–Westphalia.

In the early Middle Ages, from about the 9th century, Westphalia was the name of the western third of the tribal duchy of Saxony, between the Weser and the Rhine rivers. In 1180 the duchy was awarded to the archbishops of Cologne. But the archbishops' control was ultimately limited to part of the Sauerland, to which the term duchy was later restricted. Ecclesiastical and secular princes ruled over other parts of the region.

In 1807, Napoleon combined several German regions into the kingdom of Westphalia, which he gave to his brother Jérôme to rule. The kingdom ended with the Congress of Vienna (1815) settlement.

WESTPHALIA, Peace of, west-fāl′yə, the treaties ending the Thirty Years' War that were negotiated in two towns in Westphalia and signed in 1648. The peace negotiations were long drawn out, beginning in 1641 and actively pursued from 1643, after the French victory over Spain at the Battle of Rocroi. A new ruler in Sweden (Christina), a new pope (Innocent X), and a new cardinal-minister of France (Jules Mazarin) seconded the desires for peace expressed by the Dutch, who no longer felt threatened by Spain after Rocroi, and by Emperor Ferdinand III, for whom the war had been going badly since 1640.

The peace congress opened in 1644. Two separate sets of negotiations were necessary. One, between the Bourbons and the Habsburgs, took place at the Westphalian town of Münster. The other, between Sweden and the Holy Roman Empire, took place at the nearby town of Osnabrück. Even then France refused to negotiate with Spain, and a state of war between them existed until the separate Treaty of the Pyrenees was concluded in 1659.

There was much hair-splitting and fantasy about these typically 17th century peace parleys. Both France and Sweden maintained the fiction that they were protecting the Holy Roman Empire against the Habsburgs, a dynasty that had been ruling the empire uninterruptedly since 1438. The different estates of the empire, some of which fought on one side and some on the other, and not a few of which changed sides during the course of the war, all insisted on being represented at the peace negotiations. Meanwhile the war went on, and the French armies took fire and sword through the Bavarian Palatinate right up to the moment of the final signing of the peace on Oct. 24, 1648. (Earlier, on Jan. 30, 1648, Spain and the Dutch had ended their hostilities with the Peace of Münster.)

The Political Settlements. The peace, when it came, settled many things, though it left many others undone. While Spain and France remained at war, Spain and the United Provinces did not. The complete independence of the United Provinces was recognized at last, after a century of struggle between the Dutch and their former overlords, the Spanish Habsburgs. Likewise, the Swiss, whose independence had been first asserted in the three small forest cantons as early as the middle of the 13th century, now saw their 400-year-long fight for liberation from the Habsburgs crowned with success. Both Switzerland and the United Provinces had, of course, been independent in all but name for many years before this final recognition came in 1648.

France, who had intervened in and prolonged the war for territorial gain and whose cardinal ministers Richelieu and Mazarin had allied themselves with Protestants against the Roman Catholic leaders of the Counter Reformation for this purpose, gained the rights (deliberately undefined) of the emperor in Alsace and the disarmament of the right bank of the Rhine from Basel to Philippsburg. The way thus lay open for the ultimate annexation of Alsace by France. France also kept the three bishoprics of Metz, Toul, and Verdun, which it had seized.

The Baltic Sea was turned into a virtually Swedish lake by Sweden's acquisition of western Pomerania (Hither Pomerania; German, Vorpommern), Rügen, the city of Stettin, and the bishoprics of Bremen and Verden. The bishoprics gave Sweden control of the North Sea coast of Germany. Eastern Pomerania (Farther Pomerania; German, Hinterpommern) was awarded to the elector of Brandenburg, as were the former bishoprics of Kammin, Halberstadt, and Minden, and the right to future possession of the archbishopric of Magdeburg. By this settlement Brandenburg may have been the chief beneficiary of Westphalia in the long run since it was now firmly established on the Elbe River and had emerged as a power of importance and potential greatness in Europe.

Saxony retained Lusatia, which had been awarded to it by the Treaty of Prague (1635). The war-devastated Palatinate was divided between Bavaria, which retained the Upper Palatinate, and Charles Louis, son of Frederick V, to whom the Rhenish Palatinate was restored and for whom a new electoral dignity was created.

The political settlement in the treaties gave the death blow to the Holy Roman Empire, though it lingered on until 1806. By recognizing the full sovereignty of each German principality within the empire, it left little power to the emperor. Both Sweden and France were enabled by the treaties to intervene and "protect" the constitution of the empire, even against the emperor himself.

The Religious Settlement. The religious settlement can be said to have completed the Reformation begun in the 16th century, for the peace now extended toleration to the Calvinists to the same extent (and indeed in some respects beyond that) which Lutherans had enjoyed since the Peace of Augsburg (1555). Each prince retained the right to determine the religion of his subjects. Church properties were to be returned to those who had held them on Jan. 1, 1624. Pope Innocent X refused to accept the treaties, and in the bull *Zelo domus dei* he attacked them furiously.

Religious peace was almost as great a boon to

Germany and the Holy Roman Empire as the cessation of the terrible material devastation and rapine itself. But the political settlement in Central Europe may be said to have set back German unification for at least 200 years and to have left wounds on the body politic that has lasted for more than 300 years. Nevertheless, the Peace of Westphalia was a major landmark and turning point in European history. See also THIRTY YEARS' WAR.

JOHN A. HAWGOOD*
Author of "The Evolution of Germany"

WESTPORT, a town in southwestern Connecticut, in Fairfield county. Situated on Long Island Sound at the mouth of the Saugatuck River, it adjoins the city of Norwalk on the west. Although chiefly a residential community, which has attracted writers and artists, Westport has some light industry. Hardware, plastics, chemicals, embalming fluid, liquid soaps, tacks, twine, and toys are produced. The Westport Country Playhouse, which offers summer theater, and the Sherwood Island State Park are located within the town.

An early event of importance to the future security of the colonists occurred in the area in July 1637, when the Great Swamp Fight ended the Pequot Indian War. With sections from the towns of Fairfield, Norwalk, and Weston, the new town of Westport was incorporated in 1835. Westport is governed by a representative town meeting. Population: 25,290.

WESTWARD HO!, a historical romance by the English writer Charles Kingsley, published in 1855. Its action spans the years 1574–1588. The English episodes center on Bideford in north Devonshire; the overseas adventures, on the Spanish Main.

Amyas Leigh and his brother Frank are among the suitors of Rose Salterne. While Amyas is cruising with Francis Drake in the *Golden Hind*, Rose elopes with Don Guzman, a Spanish officer captured at Smerwick and now on parole. The don is abetted by Lucy Passmore, a "white witch," and by Eustace Leigh, Amyas' cousin, a Jesuit priest. Guzman takes Rose to La Guayra (La Guaira, Venezuela). The Leighs fail in an attempt to rescue her, and Frank falls into the hands of the Inquisition. Both he and Rose are put to death. Amyas vows revenge on Guzman, and finds opportunity when the Spaniard returns to British waters as commander of a galleon in the Armada. When the Spanish Fleet is dispersed, Amyas follows the don, only to be balked of his vengeance when the galleon perishes, with all hands, on the rocks of Lundy Island. As if to rebuke his vengefulness, a bolt of lightning strikes Amyas blind in the same storm that destroys Guzman and his crew. Amyas returns to his home, where he ultimately finds peace of mind.

The novel is packed with action, polemic, and didacticism. Kingsley views history as an intensely Protestant Victorian. Encomiums on the English character alternate with denunciations of the Church of Rome. When read by the young, the book has enough narrative movement to carry the reader past the tendentious passages. Older readers are likely to be repelled by them.

DELANCEY FERGUSON
Brooklyn College

WESTWARD MOVEMENT, the historical process through which the United States was gradually populated. Between 1607, when the first assault on the wilderness was made by Anglo-American pioneers at Jamestown in Virginia, and 1890, when the director of the census announced that an unbroken line no longer separated the settled from the unsettled portions of the continent, population surged westward in a series of migrating zones, each representing a more advanced stage in the evolution of society from primitive to more complex forms. During the three centuries of frontiering required to settle the continent, it may be argued that the American people were endowed with many of the traits and institutions that distinguish them today.

Patterns of Movement. What force impelled these pioneers, luring them into the unknown? Opportunity was the magnet that drew men and women from Europe or the eastern United States into the sparsely settled West, for there nature's bounties were so abundant that individuals needed only their own brawn, brains, and courage to improve themselves economically and socially. Opportunity was present in a variety of forms, and these in turn accounted for the nature of the zones that were discernible within the frontier area. Far to the west, along the cutting edge of civilization, roamed trappers and fur traders seeking wealth in the form of deer or buffalo hides, and shiny packs of beaver pelts. Behind them, wherever conditions warranted, came the miners, searching streams and mountain slopes for the telltale glint of dull metal that might spell a fortune in gold or silver or lead. Not far to the rear of the prospectors were the cattlemen in quest of lush fields where they could fatten their roaming herds without the restraint of farmers' fences. These shock troops of civilization made little impression on the wilderness; instead they succumbed so completely to the forces of nature that they reverted to a primitive way of life resembling that of the Indians.

This was not the case with the next wave of settlers: the pioneer farmers. Restless nomads impelled westward by a desire for self-improvement or the search for adventure, they viewed the wilderness as an enemy of progress; to them every tree was a barrier between themselves and as ever-expanding civilization. So they cut away the forests or broke the prairie sod, built their cabins, raised their crops, and then succumbed to restlessness again as neighbors pressed in on them. When they moved on to begin the process anew, they sold their "improvements" to a new wave of "equipped farmers" who were blessed with both stability and capital. These permanent settlers completed the forest clearings, fenced their fields, built homes, and financed roads that would connect their communities with Eastern markets. As commercial activity quickened, a final group of frontiersmen appeared as though by magic—merchants and millers and distillers and lawyers—to scatter villages through the backcountry. With their coming the region automatically became part of the East; to the westward their predecessors were already wresting a new West from nature.

Atlantic Coast. When this process began in the early 17th century the "East" was Europe and the "West" the strip of coastal lowlands hugging the Atlantic. From beachheads at Jamestown in Virginia, St. Marys in Maryland, Plymouth and Boston in Massachusetts, and at

THE BETTMANN ARCHIVE

Pioneers moved westward in caravans of covered wagons, their goal the Rocky Mountain or California goldfields or the fertile lands of the Oregon territory.

other isolated points, Anglo-American pioneers began their assault on the vast forests that extended limitlessly westward. For a time they seemed destined to lose their battle with nature; Englishmen died like flies at Jamestown as they went through the "seasoning" process that gave them immunity to America's diseases and knowledge of the techniques needed to combat its wilderness. Yet within half a century the battle was won and the first West conquered, for by the 1670's the coastal plain and river bottoms were occupied by sturdy farmers busily producing tobacco in the South and cereals and livestock in the North.

So persuasive was the environmental influence that even within this short span a frontier pattern had evolved. That of Virginia was typical. Far to the west, beyond the "fall line" where waterfalls checked direct navigation from the sea, lay an unoccupied wilderness where fur traders roamed in their perpetual quest for deer hides and beaver pelts. Along the fall line herdsmen pastured their cattle in pea-vine marshes or fields cleared by the Indians, moving, as one traveler put it "(like unto the ancient patriarchs or the modern Bedouins in Arabia), from forest to forest in a measure as the grass wears out or the planters approach them." East of cattle frontiers lay a band of small farms where half-cleared fields produced corn and other grains. Still farther eastward was a land of larger farms, owned by prosperous planters who lived in elaborate manor houses, grew tobacco with hired labor, and invested their profits in imported luxuries that would allow them to ape the English country gentry. Hugging the coastline were bustling towns where merchants fattened on the growing trade between the interior and Europe.

Appalachians and Beyond. By the time this first West was won, pioneers were beginning the conquest of a new West that lay beyond. The occupation of the hilly upland that comprised the Appalachian Mountain system and its foothills began in the 1670's when a growing population caused prices for lowland acreages to rise to the point that younger sons, freed servants, and new arrivals from Europe could no longer afford land there. As they moved, they found themselves in a new environment, so distant from the coast that the influence of their European heritage rapidly waned. Thus freed from tradition, they adopted practices adjusted to the strange new world in which they found themselves. They abandoned frame houses for log cabins, clothed themselves in deerskins rather than imported fabrics, developed the "long rifle" and the ax as essential tools, and became so familiar with the forest that they seemed more at home there than in the lanes of Boston or New York. Their divorce from the past was hastened with the arrival in the backcountry of two alien groups—the Scotch-Irish from Ulster and the Palatines from Germany—who migrated in large numbers during the early 18th century and moved directly to the interior in quest of cheap lands. As in all frontier communities, this mingling of racial strains strengthened the social order by allowing each to contribute something to the resulting civilization. The great "Palatine barns" of the Germans and the roving "circuit riders" of the Scotch-Irish typified the contributions of these groups to the American way of life.

Frontiersmen from the outer fringes of this West were ready to push beyond the Appalachians by the mid-18th century, but for a time they were held back as England won the region from France (1763) and English statesmen struggled to devise a settlement policy that would not provoke Indian retaliation. In the end this system broke down, as would all designed to hold frontiersmen back when good lands lay ahead. By 1775, pioneers were pouring through the mountain gaps to build their communities about the Forks of the Ohio, in modern West Virginia, in the Bluegrass country of Kentucky, and in eastern Tennessee. For a time they were driven back by Indian fighting during the Revolutionary War, but so compulsive was their eagerness to move westward that migration began with a lull in the warfare after 1778. By the close of the Revolution some 25,000 persons lived in Kentucky, while settlements straggled westward from Pittsburgh and engulfed both eastern Tennessee and lands about Nashville.

A sympathetic government paved the way for the next major migrations by drafting the Ordinance of 1785, allowing settlers to buy surveyed lands, and the Ordinance of 1787, providing for the eventual division of the West into states. Thus assured of clear land titles and political equality, pioneers swept westward in a mighty flood between the 1790's and 1810. They filled western New York, peopled Ohio, Kentucky, and Tennessee with enough newcomers to justify statehood, and formed a thin line of settlements in southern Indiana and Illinois. Only another war—the War of 1812—checked the flood as Indians seized the opportunity to fight back against usurpation of their hunting grounds. In the end the Indians lost more than they gained, for their decisive defeat during the war so broke their spirit that they retreated once more, opening most of the Mississippi Valley to settlement.

Lake Plains and Gulf States. The "Great Migration" that resulted after 1815 flowed in two directions. One was toward the fertile "Lake Plains" country where pioneers from the upper South, the Northeast, and Germany met and mingled to create a new society that showed the stamp of all of the civilizations that contributed to its strength. By the end of the 1840's the whole area north of the Ohio had been carved into states while Missouri and Iowa were also sufficiently peopled to earn a place in the Union. In all these states, self-sufficient, small-scale agriculture emphasizing cereals and livestock was the rule, and all reflected the democratizing influence of these economic units by constitutions barring slavery (save in Missouri), providing for manhood suffrage, and assuring popular control of the legislative, executive, and even judicial branches of government.

The civilization evolving from the second post-1815 migration—that into the plains that bordered the Gulf of Mexico between western Georgia and Louisiana—differed markedly. There newcomers were drawn almost solely from the Southeast, as the existence of slavery deterred the coming of Northerners or Europeans. There the objective of each pioneer was not self-sufficiency but the production of salable surpluses in the form of cotton. As this profitable crop could be most economically grown on large-scale agricultural units, there was a tendency in all good-soil areas to consolidate holdings into plantations of about 1,000 acres, even along the fringes of settlement. This process meant a constant displacement of small farmers who were driven westward to virgin lands. The Gulf Plains were settled rapidly as a result—Alabama, Mississippi, and Louisiana were all states before the end of the 1820's and Arkansas followed in 1836—but the social system that evolved denied the pioneer his birthright by barring him from the best lands and foisting on him an aristocratic political philosophy geared to the defense of slavery.

Great Plains to Pacific. The westward movement in both the Gulf states and Lake Plains came to a halt when settlers reached the western edge of the first tier of states lying beyond the Mississippi, for there they encountered a physical environment that their forest-adjusted frontier skills could not conquer. The Great Plains province, stretching limitlessly away to the Rockies, was a giant grassland where wood for housing, fencing, and fuel was nonexistent, and where a semiarid climate defied farmers whose techniques had been developed in the humid East. The orderly march westward halted before this barrier, while a few of the more venturesome pioneers explored the possibilities of the unknown lands that lay beyond. These were the men who formed caravans of covered wagons and during the early 1840's defied nature by moving westward over the Oregon and California trails to the fertile farm lands that awaited them in the Willamette and Sacramento valleys. Although few in numbers, they played yeomen's roles in paving the way for later comers. Oregon pioneers helped force the settlement that added that disputed land to the United States, while their counterparts in California precipitated the crisis which led Mexico to surrender its hold on all the Southwest.

The occupation of this distant land would still have proceeded at a snail's pace had not the discovery of gold in a stream cascading westward from California's Sierra Nevada Mountains launched the fabulous rush of the Forty-niners (q.v.). Most of the 100,000 gold seekers who reached the West failed to "strike it rich" and turned to farming or shopkeeping instead, forming a stable population that allowed California to win statehood in 1850. Others, hopelessly infected with the prospecting fever, streamed out of the state in their search for wealth. Wherever they went—in Nevada and Arizona, across Idaho and Montana and Wyoming, into Colorado and the Black Hills of South Dakota—strike after strike was made, and each attracted an influx of starry-eyed miners. During the two decades after 1849 their isolated mining camps blossomed into permanent settlements as farmers flocked in to produce food and politicians courted their favor by dividing all the trans-Rocky Mountain West into states or territories.

With the eastward thrust of the mining frontier, only the Great Plains province remained largely unsettled at the close of the Civil War. This last great West could be subdued in one of two ways: either by adapting economic practices to its unique environment or by conquering that environment with man-made devices. Both methods were tried, the first by cattlemen who transformed the Great Plains into a giant pastureland between 1865 and 1887, the second by small farmers whose fenced fields, relentlessly intruding from the East, gradually drove the ranchers westward as the open range diminished. Their advance was made possible by technological developments stemming from the wave of postwar industrialism; barbed-wire fences, windmills, railroads, and efficient farm machinery were the tools used in the conquest of America's last West. So effectively did they allow the westward-sweeping farmers to transform barren grasslands into fertile fields that by 1890 the director of the census could announce that "there can hardly be said to be a frontier line" remaining in the United States. One era in history had drawn to a close.

Effect on National Character and Institutions. Reactions varied greatly as Americans during the next decades adjusted themselves to a closed-space existence. Some feared that dwindling resources and a mounting population would usher in an era of starvation; the president of one Western railroad prophesied that "in twenty-five years we shall have a nation-wide famine." Others, such as President Theodore Roosevelt, sought to awaken the nation to the need of conserving what was left of its natural heritage. Still others, with Presidents Woodrow Wilson and Franklin Delano Roosevelt in the van, advocated a positive role on the part of the federal government as a means of providing individuals with the security and opportunity formerly offered by the open frontier. "Today," wrote Franklin D. Roosevelt in 1935, "we can no longer escape into virgin territory: we must master our environment."

Less spectacular, but nonetheless important, was the impact of the passing of the West on the nation's historians and social scientists. Inspired by the writings of the pioneer historian of the frontier, Frederick Jackson Turner of Wis-

THE BETTMANN ARCHIVE

Some American Indian tribes saw the westward movement as a threat to their lands and traditional way of life and fought against the encroachments of settlers. The lithograph shown is based on a painting by Carl Wimar.

consin, they began an appraisal of both past and future as viewed in the light of this unique national experience. Their findings indicated that much which was typically American in both the characteristics of the people of the United States and their institutions was traceable to the three centuries of expansion which had marked their history.

This expansion, historians concluded, had led to a constant rebirth of civilization in the West. As pioneers moved into a wilderness environment, they found that habits as well as artifacts acquired in regions of compact settlement were no longer essential. Complex political institutions proved only burdensome in sparsely settled Western communities; economic specialization was valueless in a region where each man provided for his own needs; social status based on inherited prestige vanished in a land where the individual's contribution was judged by his skill with rifle or ax; cultural pursuits seemed outmoded in a primitive social organism where so many material tasks demanded completion. Hence practices and institutions common in the East were discarded as life reverted toward simpler forms. Thus did man in the virgin West forsake much of his heritage, and prepare himself to develop new traits and devices suited to the environment in which he found himself.

These slowly evolved as new settlers flocked in to thicken the population of each frontier community. With social controls increasingly necessary, governmental activities were expanded, economic specialization set in, society developed along familiar hierarchal lines, and cultural activities quickened. Eventually a full-blown civilization emerged, but this differed significantly from the civilizations of the East on which it was based. The impact of the environment, the accidental divergencies natural in areas of separate evolution, and the contributions of representatives from many cultures present among the founders, all helped mold each Western community into a social organism that was similar to, but differed from, the many that had contributed to its growth. As this process went on, over and over again for three centuries, an "Americanization" of men and their institutions took place. This transformation, obviously, was not alone responsible for the distinctive nature of civilization in the United States. That stemmed from the European heritage, the mingling of peoples from many lands, the continuing impact of ideas from abroad, the Industrial Revolution, and other forces. But those features of life and thought that are usually considered to be most typically American can be traced in some degree to the influence of the West during the nation's formative period.

This is the case with certain individual traits or characteristics. The Americans are a mobile people, loosely bound to any one place and ready to move when opportunity beckons; the typical frontiersman drifted westward so often that his allegiance to any locality could not be deeply rooted. They are an inventive people who accept innovation unquestioningly and prefer change to adaptation; their pioneer ancestors acquired this frame of mind by constantly facing new situations where past precedents did not apply. They are a materialistic people, with less time for culture than most peoples of the Western World; Westerners could pay little attention to the arts in a primitive land where the battle against nature absorbed all of their energies. They are an individualistic people, resenting any attempt by the government to interfere with their economic activities; frontiersmen lived amidst such abundance that each man could care for his own needs without the aid or intrusion of society. With the passing of the West, American individualism, materialism, and mobility began to diminish, but they remain as noticeable characteristics among many people.

Equally notable was the frontier's effect on many institutions. Economic practices in the United States are geared to the need of constantly replacing artifacts and machines that would be carefully preserved in other countries of the world, for Americans have a tendency to discard the old as soon as a new model appears. This habit they acquired from their pioneer forebears who lived amidst such an abundance of natural resources that waste became second nature to them. Political institutions also bear the stamp of the nation's formative years in their emphasis on democratic practices. Democracy did not originate in the forests of the New World, of course; it was well developed in European theory and practice when the Anglo-American frontier was in its infancy. Yet conditions in the West tended to deepen faith in democratic practices. There poverty served as a great leveler; there nature emphasized the equality of men by diminishing the importance of wealth and hereditary privilege; there the urge to self-rule was strong among men who realized that Eastern legislators did not understand their unique problems. On the frontier, as nowhere else in the new land, was born a deep-seated faith in democracy that has remained a part of the national heritage.

See also FRONTIER LIFE; HOMESTEAD MOVEMENT; MOUNTAIN MEN.

RAY ALLEN BILLINGTON
Author of "Westward Expansion"

Bibliography

Billington, Ray Allen, *Westward Expansion: A History of the American Frontier,* 5th ed. (Macmillan 1982).
Buley, Roscoe C., *The Old Northwest: Pioneer Period, 1815–1850,* 2 vols. (1950; reprint, Ind. U. Press 1983).
Clark, Thomas D., *Frontier America,* 2d ed. (Scribner 1969).
De Voto, Bernard, *The Course of Empire* (1952; reprint, Univ. of Nebr. Press 1983).
Horsman, Reginald, *The Frontier in the Formative Years, 1783–1815* (Univ. of N. Mex. Press 1979).
La Feber, Walter, *The New Empire: An Interpretation of American Expansion, 1860–1898* (Cornell 1967).
Merk, Frederick and Lois B., *Manifest Destiny and Mission in American History* (1963; reprint, Greenwood 1983).
Paxson, Frederic L., *History of the American Frontier, 1763–1893* (1924; reprint, Berg 1964).
Riegel, Robert E., *America Moves West,* 5th ed. (Holt 1971).
Smith, Henry Nash, *Virgin Land: The American West as Symbol and Myth* (Harvard Univ. Press 1970).
Turner, Frederick Jackson, *The Frontier in American History* (1920; reprint, Krieger 1976).
Webb, Walter Prescott, *The Great Plains* (1931; reprint, Univ. of Nebr. Press 1981).

WET, Christiaan Rudolph de. See DE WET, CHRISTIAAN RUDOLPH.

WETHERSFIELD, weth′ər-fēld, a town in central Connecticut, in Hartford county, situated on the Connecticut River immediately south of Hartford. Though primarily residential, the town has some light industry. The chief products are seeds, tools and dies, hydraulic valves, and electrical components.

Originally known as Pyquag, the area was the site of the first permanent English settlement in Connecticut, dating from 1634, when settlers from Watertown, Mass., arrived. The name Wethersfield was adopted in February 1637. Several houses predate the American Revolution; more than 100 were built before 1800. The foremost is the Webb House (1752), where Gen. George Washington and the Count de Rochambeau met in 1781 to coordinate the efforts of the French and American forces. Another notable structure is the Buttolph-Williams House (1692), which features a 17th century kitchen.

Wethersfield is governed under the town council-manager system, adopted in 1954. Population: 26,013.

WETLAND. See MARSH; SWAMP; TIDAL MARSH.

WETMORE, wet′môr, **Alexander** (1886–1978), American ornithologist. He was born in North Freedom, Wis., on June 18, 1886. He was educated at the University of Kansas and George Washington University, from which he received a doctorate in zoology in 1920. He served as a staff biologist for the U.S. Department of Agriculture from 1910 until 1924, when he was named superintendent of the National Zoological Park in Washington, D.C. From 1925 to 1944 he was assistant secretary of the Smithsonian Institution and had charge of the United States National Museum. He then served as secretary (the principal executive officer) of the Smithsonian until his retirement in 1952, when he became a research associate at the institution. He died in Washington on Dec. 7, 1978.

Wetmore studied both living and fossil birds. In addition to scores of technical papers, he published *The Migration of Birds* (1926), several books on the birds of South America and the Caribbean, *Checklist of the Fossil and Prehistoric Birds of North America and the West Indies* (1956), and was general editor of the fifth edition of *Checklist of North American Birds* (1947).

WETTING AGENTS, compounds that concentrate in the surface film of the substance in which they dissolve and thereby lower the surface tension of that substance. They are also, for this reason, called "surface-active agents." Since only small amounts of a wetting agent are required to fill the surface of a system, they exert their full influence in small concentrations. By lowering the surface tension, wetting agents make it possible to extend the surface of the system with little input of energy. Thus, whereas pure water will foam only with continuous, vigorous shaking, water with surface-active agents added will foam easily and, moreover, will form bubbles that are stable and break down slowly.

A liquid with a lowered surface tension will spread more easily over solids, into fine cracks, and around insoluble particles. Such liquids will wet larger areas more efficiently (hence the term "wetting agents"). For this reason, wetting agents are useful additives in paints, inks, lubricants, and other compounds that are applied to surfaces.

Generally the molecules of a wetting agent contain two parts with significantly different properties. For example, one part may be soluble in water, while the other part is not. Such molecules tend to concentrate at the surface, since only there can one part of a molecule be in the water and another part out of the water.

In a typical wetting-agent molecule, the water insoluble part is soluble in oils or fats. Thus, in a mixture of oil and water the agent concentrates in the oil-water interface, so that part of the molecule can be in water and part in oil. If the mixture is stirred vigorously, small bubbles of water in oil or oil in water are produced, resulting in more interface for the wetting agent to occupy. The small bubbles cannot coalesce without ejecting the wetting agent molecules, which would require a considerable energy input. A wetting agent therefore promotes the formation of emulsions. The natural soaps and synthetic detergents are wetting agents that greatly increase the washing efficiency of water through this encouragement of emulsification.

Many of the molecules produced by living organisms serve as wetting agents. The bile salts bring about the emulsification of fat in the intestine and aid digestion in this way. Proteins and phospholipids are wetting agents, and the fact that milk can be homogenized is the result of the stabilization of the fine droplets of cream by the protein molecules concentrated in the surfaces of those droplets.

See also DETERGENT; SOAP.

ISAAC ASIMOV, *Author of "The Intelligent Man's Guide to Science"*

WEXFORD, weks′fərd, a county in southeastern Ireland, in the province of Leinster, about 908 square miles (2,350 sq km) in area. It is bounded on the south by the Atlantic Ocean, on the west and north by the counties of Waterford, Kilkenny, Carlow, and Wicklow, and on the east by St. George's Channel. The county seat is Wexford.

Fishing, iron founding, tanning, woolen milling, bacon and ham curing, and brewing are the chief industries. Marble, slate, and granite are quarried. The farm regions produce poultry, cattle, wheat, barley, potatoes, and dairy products.

Wexford was the first county in Ireland to be occupied by the English. Ancient castles and church ruins are near the town of Enniscorthy and Ferns. Population: (1981) 99,016.

WEXFORD, weks'fərd, a town in southeastern Ireland, the seat of county Wexford. It is situated at the mouth of the river Slaney, 70 miles (110 km) south of Dublin. Industries include brewing, meat curing, and the manufacture of textiles, agricultural implements, and furniture. Tourism is important to the economy. The town takes its name from the 9th century Danish settlement of Waesfjord. Wexford was the headquarters of the rebellion of 1798. Population: (1981) 11,396.

WEYDEN, Rogier van der. See VAN DER WEYDEN, ROGIER.

WEYL, vīl, **Hermann** (1885–1955), German mathematician and mathematical physicist. Weyl was born in Elmsborn, Germany, on Nov. 9, 1885, and graduated in 1908 from the University of Göttingen, where he was David Hilbert's most gifted student. His early work was deeply influenced by Hilbert's analytic approach, although he later diverged from his teacher. In 1913 he was appointed a professor at the University of Zürich, where he worked with Albert Einstein.

Fascinated with Einstein's theory of relativity, Weyl developed a unified field theory, in which electromagnetic and gravitational fields could be treated as geometrical properties of space-time. In the 1920's he showed how quantum-mechanical phenomena could be most easily expressed in terms of group theory. His application of function theory to geometry and his work in analytic theory of numbers and topology distinguished him as one of the most universal mathematicians of the 20th century.

In 1930, Weyl returned to Göttingen, only to leave three years later in protest over Nazi treatment of his Jewish colleagues. He then accepted an appointment at the Institute for Advanced Study, in Princeton, N.J., where he remained until his death on Dec. 8, 1955.

STEVE HARRIS, *University of Wisconsin*

WEYMOUTH, wā'məth, a town in eastern Massachusetts, in Norfolk county, about 12 miles (19 km) southeast of Boston, on Boston Bay. Although mainly a residential suburb, Weymouth manufactures shoes, shoe counters, belting, electronics components, paper boxes, industrial resins, and chemicals. The town is made up of four major villages—Weymouth Landing and North, East, and South Weymouth. A United States naval air station is in South Weymouth.

Thomas Weston, an English merchant adventurer, sent a party to establish a trading station at Wessagusset, the Indian name for the present town, in 1622. In 1634, 21 families from Weymouth, England, arrived, and the town was incorporated in September 1635.

Abigail Adams, wife of the second president of the United States, was born in Weymouth in 1744. Her birthplace has been restored and opened to the public. Government is by representative town meeting. Population: 55,601.

WHALE, any of a group of exclusively aquatic mammals that includes the largest animals that ever lived. Whales (order Cetacea) are found in all oceans and contiguous seas, and in certain rivers and lakes of southeastern Asia, tropical South America, northern North America, and northern Eurasia.

This article deals mainly with larger members of the whale order. For further information on some smaller whales, see BELUGA; DOLPHIN; KILLER WHALE; NARWHAL; and PORPOISE.

Whales are typically characterized by torpedo-shaped bodies with forelimbs shaped as flippers and no external hind limbs. Most whales have a dorsal fin, and the tail is horizontal in contrast to the vertical tail of most fishes. A layer of blubber underlies the almost hairless skin, which has no sebaceous or sweat glands. The eyes are small in comparison to body size, and there are no external ears. Adult whales are 4 to 100 feet (1.2–30 meters) long and weigh from 45 pounds to 220 tons (20–200,000 kg).

Whales swim by means of up and down movements of the tail. The flippers function as balancing and steering organs. The large baleen whales can attain a maximum speed of 16 mph (26 km/h), and some dolphins have been clocked at speeds of up to 20.5 mph (33 km/h).

The two groups of living whales are the baleen whales (Mysticeti), characterized by a filter-feeding mechanism known as baleen, and the toothed whales (Odontoceti), known for their complex echolocation systems. A third group, the Archaeoceti or zeugeodonts, became extinct about 25 million years ago. These primitive toothed whales are neither filter feeders nor echolocators. All three groups of whales probably had a common origin from terrestrial mammals. Studies suggest that the most likely ancestors of whales were derived from terrestrial mesonychids. The mesonychids were a group of large-bodied mammals (condylarths) that lived during the Paleocene and Eocene epochs more than 50 million years ago.

The main ecological difference between the baleen and toothed whales is in their place in the food chain. The toothed whales feed mainly on carnivores, including fish, squid, and octopus. Their conical teeth are for seizing and holding prey, which they swallow whole. Baleen whales, on the other hand, feed mainly on various species of zooplankton—small, largely herbivorous invertebrates such as euphausiids (krill), copepods, and certain types of amphipods. Small fish are also eaten, especially in coastal waters. These food items are strained from the seawater by means of a mat formed by intertwined bristles attached inside the baleen.

The estimated life expectancies of whales range from less than 20 years for some of the smaller species to 70 years for Baird's beaked whales. Except for humans, the only predators of large whales are killer whales *(Orcinus orca)*. Any of the whales that live in polar waters are vulnerable to ice entrapment and consequent starvation or suffocation.

Whales have long been hunted by humans, and some populations were brought to the verge of extinction. Most large species are now protected by regulations of the International Whaling Commission (IWC). All large whales are completely protected by the international Convention for the Regulation of Whaling, effective in 1986.

Historically the most valuable whale products were the baleen (also called whalebone) and the oil derived from blubber. Until kerosine became available in the late 19th century, whale oil was used chiefly for lighting. During the 20th century, whale oil was used in the production of margarine, soaps, lubricants, waxes, explosives, and numerous other products. Sperm-whale oil was especially valued as a high-quality lubricant. By the 1980's artificial substitutes had been found for all whale products. The most important of these is a desert plant native to the southwestern United States, the jojoba *(Simmondsia chinesis)*, which can provide an economic substitute for sperm oil. Whale meat is still eaten by the people of a few countries, but it is no longer an important part of their diet.

See also WHALING.

GENERAL CHARACTERISTICS

Anatomy and Physiology. Whales have several characteristic anatomical features. Their lungs and livers are not lobed, but the kidney is divided into many lobes—each acting as an individual filtering unit. Whales have three or more chambers in the stomach, and there is no gallbladder. The diaphragm crosses the body on an oblique angle. Highly developed retia mirabilia are present in both the lower part of the head and the thorax. These retial masses help moderate pressure changes that occur during diving. They may prevent overstressing sensitive regions such as the brain and spinal cord.

Sperm whales and some beaked whales can dive to depths of more than 3,280 feet (1,000 meters), where they are subject to pressures in excess of 100 atmospheres. These dives can last over an hour. Three important factors make it possible for whales to go without breathing for such a long period. The first is the high oxygen-storing capacity of their muscles and blood. The proportion of oxygen-storing myoglobin in a whale's muscles is about two to nine times that found in terrestrial mammals. The high oxygen-storage capacity of whale blood is due to the fact that the proportion of red blood cells is as much as twice as high as it is in most land mammals. Second, whales are less sensitive than land mammals to the effects of the lactic acid and carbon dioxide that accumulate in the blood and tissues when breathing stops. Third, the oxygenated blood in the arteries is redistributed during a dive by constriction of arteries that supply noncritical parts of the body. This allows most of the blood to flow to the central nervous system, including the brain. This redistribution is accompanied by a drastic reduction in heart rate. In dolphins, for example, the heart rate at the surface of the water is 90 to 100 beats per minute, but it is only 12 to 20 beats per minute while the dolphin is underwater. Baleen whales are not deep divers.

Whales have five mechanisms to maintain or regulate their body temperature: (1) The large size typical of whales means that, relative to body mass, the proportion of heat-losing surface area is less than in small animals. (2) A layer of insulating blubber with a minimal supply of blood reduces heat loss to the water. (3) The flippers, dorsal fin, and flukes have countercurrent heat-exchange systems, in which the arteries carrying warm blood from the heart are surrounded by veins. This ensures that the heat contained in the outflowing arterial blood is at least partly recovered by inflowing venous blood instead of being lost to the cold seawater. (4) A relatively high metabolic rate enables whales to generate more heat per unit of body weight than do land mammals. (5) Finally, the relatively low respiration rates of whales result in low heat loss to the atmosphere.

A humpback whale leaps out of the water. This and many other characteristic behaviors are not well understood.

Most scientists believe that the whale's spout is vapor caused by condensation of air escaping the lungs. However, further research has shown that the gray whale's spout consists mainly of seawater blown up during expiration, at least on the breeding grounds.

The brain weight of whales ranges from 20 pounds (9.2 kg) in the sperm whale to only 4.5 pounds (0.2 kg) in the smaller river dolphins *(Pontoporia blainvillei)*. The large whales and the elephants are the only animals with brains larger than human brains. However, their brains are much smaller in relation to their body size than those of humans and bottlenose dolphins *(Tursiops truncatus)*. This suggests that the baleen whales may be less intelligent than both humans and these dolphins. The level of intelligence in captive dolphins seems comparable to that of chimpanzees.

Behavior. The social organization of baleen whales is still poorly understood. It is known that groups generally include only two to five individuals, although larger temporary aggregations often form on rich feeding grounds or during the breeding season. However, studies of humpback and right whales are yielding much new information. These studies track the behavior of individual whales, recognized by their markings, and show that these whales are not monogamous, as some scientists formerly thought.

In humpback whales, solitary adult males often "sing" for long periods, emitting a complex series of low-frequency moans. The singers are sometimes approached by other males, and the encounters often lead to fights. Groups of three individuals usually include a male, a female, and her calf. Larger groups usually consist of a female in heat and many males. Males in such groups attempt to block other males from access

BLUE WHALE
A baleen whale. The streamlined blue whale is the largest of all animals.

Whales include the largest animals alive today and the largest animals that ever lived. Even *Brachiosaurus,* the largest of the dinosaurs, weighed less than half as much as a female blue whale. Whales fall into two main groups: the baleen, or whalebone, whales and the toothed whales.

The baleen whales have a distinctive sieve-like structure for straining small food animals from the water. The group includes the largest whale (the blue whale) and one of the smallest (the minke whale). Other baleen whales shown here are the humpback, right (or bowhead), and gray whales.

The toothed whales are more closely related to the dolphins and porpoises than to the baleen whales. They prey on squid, fish, and other large marine animals. The largest of this group is the sperm whale, which is by far the most numerous of the large whales. The only other toothed whales are the beaked whales, including Baird's beaked whale and the northern bottlenose whale.

MINKE WHALE
A baleen whale. It is both the smallest and the most widespread of the rorquals.

HUMPBACK WHALE
Adult female and young. A baleen whale, the humpback is noted for its leaps from the water and for the songs of adult males (available on commercial recordings).

PAINTINGS BY LARRY FOSTER

RIGHT (BOWHEAD) WHALE
A temporary mating group consisting of a female (background) and two males. A baleen whale with a high yield of oil, the right whale was the first to be hunted commercially.

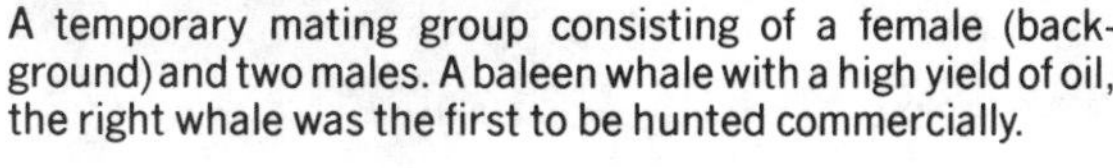

GRAY WHALE
A medium-size baleen whale. Now extinct in the North Atlantic and rare in the western Pacific, it is numerous in the eastern Pacific off California.

SPERM WHALE
A toothed whale made famous by Herman Melville's *Moby-Dick*. It is the most numerous of all large whales.

BAIRD'S BEAKED WHALE
A toothed whale. Little is known about the beaked whales. Only two kinds, Baird's beaked whale and the northern bottlenose, have been hunted commercially.

NUMBERS OF WHALES

Species	Before commercial whaling	1985	Percent
BLUE	210,000	11,000	5
FIN	450,000	100,000	22
SEI	200,000	80,000	40
BRYDE'S	100,000	40,000	40
MINKE	360,000	250,000	70
RIGHT	100,000	4,000	4
BOWHEAD	100,000	4,000	4
GRAY	15,000	15,000	100
SPERM	1,500,000	1,250,000	83

to the female, and the ensuing fights may be violent—at times resulting in bloody wounds.

Right whales form similar temporary groups consisting of a female in heat and several competing males. Females are larger than males in all baleen whales. This is thought to be related to the biological requirements of reproduction rather than to social structure.

Sperm whales are polygynous. The basic social unit appears to be a mixed school of 20 to 40 animals, consisting of adult females and their calves. During the breeding season each of these groups is joined by a few adult males. The young of both sexes form separate juvenile schools after they are weaned. Young females rejoin the mixed schools before maturity, but males remain in bachelor groups for many years until they reach breeding age. Like most highly polygynous terrestrial mammals, males far exceed females in size.

Beaked whales mostly form smaller schools of three to six individuals, and there is relatively little difference in size between the sexes. Little more is known about the social structure of these whales.

Mass strandings usually involve gregarious offshore species such as sperm whales, pilot whales, and several species of dolphins. Many of these strandings may be simply the result of navigational errors. Because of the social ties among members of a group, individual animals put back in the water usually return to the beach to rejoin their companions. Trematode infestations in the ears of some whales also have been suggested as a factor in some strandings. Whales or dolphins that strand singly are almost always sick.

Communication. Baleen whales produce four types of sounds: (1) the typical low-frequency moans, including the "songs" of humpback whales, which have a pitch usually between 20 and 200 Hz (Herz, cycles per second) and last between 0.4 and 36 seconds; (2) gruntlike thumps and knocks of short duration, mainly between 40 and 200 Hz and lasting from 50 to 500 milliseconds; (3) chirps, cries, and whistles with frequencies above 1000 Hz; and (4) clicks or pulses with upper ranges of 20 to 30 kHz (kiloherz). The origin of these sounds is suspected to be the larynx, although the whales have no vocal cords.

Sounds produced by toothed whales include two main types: clicks and whistles. Clicks may be emitted singly, in individual bursts, or in long trains. These sounds usually span a very broad bank of pitches (0.1 to 120 kHz). Long trains of clicks may be heard as a single sound and have been given a variety of names such as barks, chirps, and squawks. Clicks are used for echolocation of prey. Whistles are pure-tone, frequency-modulated signals with a pitch from 4 to 20 kHz and last about half a second.

Clicks appear to be emitted from the right nasal plug and its associated diverticula, and whistles are associated with movements of the last nasal plug. A few investigators believe that both sounds are produced by the larynx.

Life Cycle and Reproduction. Most baleen whales migrate twice a year between rich feeding areas in the Antarctic and Arctic regions and temperate or subtropical breeding and calving grounds. The entire reproductive cycle is correlated with these migrations. In sperm whales, only the adult males migrate to colder waters in the nonbreeding season; the females and juveniles remain in warmer waters all year.

All whales mate in the water. Mating usually occurs with the pair swimming on their sides belly to belly. The male's testes are retained permanently inside the abdominal cavity. In the adult gray whale the testes weigh over 84 pounds (38 kg) and the penis is about 43 inches (110 cm) long.

The gestation periods of whales range from about 10 to 13.5 months in baleen whales and from 10 to 17 months in toothed whales. The larger toothed whales have the longest gestation periods. Only a single young is born, and it is usually one fourth to one third the length of the mother. The teats of the mammary glands are found within paired slits on either side of the female reproductive opening. Contact with the teats during suckling causes the milk to spurt freely into the mouth of the calf. The milk of baleen whales is unusually high in fat content—30%–53%. It also contains 10%–14% protein, and only about 2% sugar (lactose). The high fat content probably accounts for the rapid growth of the calf during the suckling period. During this period the calf may increase its body weight five to eight times. Sperm-whale milk contains only 17% to 34% fat, 8% to 12% protein, and a very small amount of sugar.

The smaller toothed whales (dolphins and porpoises) are weaned in four or five months, but the young of larger species continue to suckle for two years or longer. Whales become sexually mature at two or three years in some of the smallest dolphins and porpoises but not until 10 years or more in the larger toothed whales and baleen whales. The maximum life span is estimated at up to 40 years for baleen whales and up to 70 years for toothed whales.

BALEEN WHALES

This group of whales (suborder Mysticeti) is distinguished by the presence of baleen and by external paired blowholes. Baleen whales feed mainly by straining krill and other crustaceans from the water as they swim along the surface with their mouths open. They are found in all oceans and contiguous seas except the Black Sea. There are three living families: The Balaenopteridae includes the rorquals—the blue whale, the fin whale, the sei whale, Bryde's whale, the minke whale, and the humpback whale. The Balaenidae includes the right whales, the Greenland or bowhead whale, and the pygmy right whale. The Eschrichtidae contains only the gray whale.

Rorquals. The rorquals, including the blue whale and the humpback, have similar shapes and differ mainly in size. All have deep lengthwise furrows in the skin of the throat.

Blue Whale. The blue whale (*Balaenoptera musculus*) is the largest of all whales and the biggest animal that ever lived. One female caught in the Antarctic measured 100 feet (30.5 meters), with an estimated weight of more than 160 tons. This species is long and streamlined, as are other rorquals, in contrast to the more heavyset right whales and the humpback whale. The color is a mottled blue-gray. Other distinctive characteristics are a strikingly small dorsal fin located on the posterior third of the body; a flat rostrum (upper jaw or snout) that appears U-shaped when viewed from above; and a tall, dense spout. In the Antarctic a yellowish film of diatoms is often present on the ventral and lateral surfaces of these whales, which prompted the whaler's term "sulfur-bottom." The diatoms accumulate on the whales during long stays in cooler waters.

The baleen of blue whales is black and relatively short and coarse. Blues feed almost exclusively on swarms of small crustaceans known as krill (euphausiids). However, off Baja California, Mexico, they also may eat seagoing crabs (*Pleuroncodes planipes*) during the winter. In the Antarctic region, daily food consumption for a single whale is up to 8 tons of krill.

The age of sexual maturity for both sexes is about 10 years. Individual females give birth only at two- or three-year intervals. Gestation is about one year. Calves are conceived and born at low latitudes during the winter. At birth the calves are about 23 feet (7 meters) long and usually weigh more than 2.5 tons. Calves are weaned about eight months after birth, at a mean length of approximately 53 feet (16 meters), after a weight gain of up to 200 pounds (90 kg) per day.

Blue whales have been protected worldwide by the IWC since 1966. However, it is uncertain whether blue whale populations will ever recover from their low levels, if they survive at all. The current estimate of 5,000 whales in the Southern Hemisphere is only 2.5% of the estimated 200,000 present in the early 1900's.

Other Rorquals, Including Humpbacks. The approximate maximum lengths of the smaller rorquals are 88 feet (26.8 meters) for the fin whale (B. *physalus*), 69 feet (21 meters) for the sei whale (B. *borealis*), 46 feet (14 meters) for Bryde's whale (B. *edeni*), 35 feet (10.7 meters) for the minke whale (B. *acutorostrata*), and 53 feet (16 meters) for the humpback whale (*Megaptera novaeangliae*).

The other major distinctive features of the rorquals are a white right lower lip and a white edge on the upper jaw in fin whales; a single rostral ridge extending forward from the base of the blowhole in sei whales; three prominent ridges on the rostrum in Bryde's whale; and a triangular-shaped rostrum with a single prominent ridge in the minke whale.

Fin and sei whales are widely distributed in temperate and polar waters of both hemispheres. Bryde's whales are found in tropical and temperate waters around the world. They are especially abundant in areas of high food productivity. Minke whales, the most widespread of the rorquals, are found in tropical, temperate, and polar waters of both hemispheres.

The main food of rorquals is various species of krill (euphausiids). Sei whales prefer copepods if available. Animals such as small squid, lantern fish (Myctophidae), and certain amphipods are occasionally taken by rorquals. Bryde's whales feed on krill in pelagic waters and fish in coastal areas. In certain feeding areas, one or two humpbacks swim in an upward spiral around swarms of krill found on or below the surface. As they circle the krill they expel air in a chain of bubbles from the blowhole. The rising bubbles form a "bubble net" that causes the krill to mass in the center of the ring of bubbles. The whales then feed on the concentrated krill.

The gestation period is a year or slightly longer in all rorquals except the minke, in which it is approximately 10 months. The mean length at birth ranges from 9 feet (2.8 meters) in the minke whale to about 20 feet (6 meters) in the fin whale. The larger mature rorquals breed every two or three years; in the smaller minke whales the females calve almost every year. Sexual maturity is attained in both sexes between the ages of 5 and 15 years. Whales in depleted populations attain sexual maturity at an earlier age than those in populations that have reached the environment's carrying capacity.

Whaling during the 20th century has greatly reduced almost all populations of all the rorquals and the humpback. Commercial exploitation of humpback whales has been prohibited by the IWC since 1966.

Right Whales. The family Balaenidae includes three types of whales: the right whales (*Eubalaena glacialis* and *E. australis*), the Greenland right or bowhead whale (*Balaena mysticetus*), and the pygmy right whale (*Caperea marginata*). Historically, right whales occurred mainly in cold and warm-temperate coastal waters around the world. Bowheads are found only in the Arctic, and pygmy right whales are found only in the Southern Hemisphere.

Right and bowhead whales grow to about 60 feet (18 meters), of which the head is about a third of the total length. Other distinguishing features of right and bowhead whales are the absence of a dorsal fin, large broad flippers, and a large girth (equal to total length). These whales are all black except for a white blotch on the ventral surface in right whales and a white chin in bowhead whales. The most distinctive external feature of the right whale is several patches of grayish, roughened skin called callosities located on the head. The pattern formed by callosities enables observers to recognize individual whales.

Right whales feed almost exclusively on copepods and krill. The age of sexual maturity is unknown. The gestation period is probably about 11–12 months. The length at birth is between 16 and 20 feet (5–6 meters). The lactation period has been estimated at 6 to 12 months. The average interval between births in southern right whales is three years. Bowheads are similar to right whales in feeding habits and reproductive behavior.

The pygmy right whale grows to 21 feet (6.4 meters) in length. It is more slender than the right whale, and its head is a quarter of its total length. It has a sickle-shaped dorsal fin and narrow flippers. Its body is countershaded dark gray above and white below. Pygmy right whales are known to feed only on copepods. Little is known about their reproductive biology.

All populations of right whales were severely reduced by whalers during the 19th century, and only a few of the Southern Hemisphere populations have showed any signs of increase. Bowhead whales are still hunted by Alaskan natives. This hunt has been the focus of controversy because the bowhead is considered the most critically endangered species of baleen whale. The world population of bowhead whales is probably less than 5,000, with the majority occurring in the western Arctic of North America.

Gray Whales. The gray whale (*Eschrichtius robustus*) is now extinct in the North Atlantic, but two populations occur in the North Pacific Ocean: the western Pacific or Korean stock and the eastern Pacific or California stock. The California population is well known for its annual migration along the west coast of North America during November through May.

Gray whales are of medium size. Adult females range between 38 and 49 feet (11.7–15.0 meters) in total body length and adult males between 36 and 47 feet (11.1–14.3 meters). No dorsal fin is present, but a series of bumps or ridges occur on the back behind a larger bump. The color is a mottled gray, and numerous flat barnacles and "whale lice" (small parasitic amphipods) usually are attached to the skin. Gray whales are bottom feeders. They feed mainly by sucking up minute shrimplike crustaceans (gammaridean amphipods).

The two Pacific gray whale populations were greatly reduced by overexploitation in the late 1800's and early 1900's. The western Pacific population is still at a very low level (perhaps only a few hundred whales), but the eastern Pacific population has increased to about 16,000 individuals (1980). This is about 80% of the estimated unexploited population of 20,000 animals. Although protected from commercial whaling, approximately 180 gray whales are taken each year by Soviet catcher boats for use by Siberian natives.

TOOTHED WHALES

The toothed whales (suborder Odontoceti) are distinguished by the presence of teeth, a single blowhole, and the fatty "melon," an acoustic lens that focuses incoming echolocation signals. Toothed whales are found in all oceans and contiguous seas. In addition, some dolphins are found in a few rivers and lakes. Toothed whales feed mainly on fish, squid, and shrimp.

The three living superfamilies of toothed whales are the Platanistoidea, including all the river dolphins; the Delphinoidea, including the various types of mainly marine dolphins and porpoises, narwhals, and belugas; and the Physeteroidea, which includes the sperm and beaked whales. Adults range in size from 4 feet (1.2 meters) in the smallest dolphins to about 65 feet (20 meters) in sperm whales. Only the last superfamily is discussed here. Dolphins, porpoises, belugas, and narwhals are described in separate articles.

Sperm Whales. The sperm whale family (Physeteridae) contains the sperm whale (*Physeter catodon*), the largest of the toothed whales; the pygmy sperm whale (*Kogia breviceps*); and the dwarf sperm whale (*K. simus*). All three are characterized by the spermaceti organ and associated structures inside their heads, asymmetric skull, underslung lower jaw, and functional teeth mainly in the lower jaw. A few upper teeth are commonly found in *K. simus*.

The spermaceti organ contains a white waxy substance called spermaceti, once valued for making cosmetics and candles. The most likely function of the organ is that it serves as an acoustic lens to focus echolocation signals used for finding prey, but some investigators have argued that it is a buoyancy regulator.

In adult male sperm whales the head makes up about 35% of the total length. The blowhole is located far forward on the left side of the head, with a spout that comes out at a sharp angle from the head and toward the left; and a rounded or triangular dorsal hump replaces the dorsal fin. The skin has a shriveled appearance.

The Sperm Whale. The length of adult female sperm whales is 28 to 41 feet (8.5–12.5 meters) and that of adult males is 36 to 65 feet (11–20 meters). The mean age of sexual maturity of female sperm whales is nine years, when they have an average length of about 30 feet (9 meters). Males do not join the mixed schools of females and young and also do not participate in breeding until they are about 30 years old (long after reaching sexual maturity) and about 43 feet (13 meters) in length. Females produce a calf every three to five years. Newborn sperm whales average about 13 feet (4 meters) in length. The gestation period is approximately 15 months, and the lactation period lasts between one and two years.

Sperm whales feed mostly on larger squid, including the giant squids (*Architeuthis* and *Moroteuthis*), and a wide variety of large sea-bottom and midwater sharks, skates, and fishes. Items recovered from sperm whale stomachs include rocks, glass fishing floats, deep-sea sponges, crab meat, cut meat of baleen whales,

CLASSIFICATION

The classification or taxonomy of all living whales, including dolphins and porpoises, follows. The number of species is given in parentheses after each genus.

ORDER CETACEA

Whales, dolphins, porpoises, belugas, and narwhals.

Suborder Mysticeti

Whalebone or baleen whales.

FAMILY ESCHRICHTIIDAE.
Eschrichtius (1): Gray whale.

FAMILY BALAENOPTERIDAE: Rorquals
Balaenoptera (5): Blue, fin, sei, Bryde's, and minke whales.
Megaptera (1): Humpback whale.

FAMILY BALAENIDAE: Bowhead and right whales.
SUBFAMILY NEOBALAENINAE
Caperea (1): Pygmy right whale.
SUBFAMILY BALAENINAE
Balaena (1): Bowhead whale.
Eubalaena (2): Right whales.

Suborder Odontoceti.

Toothed whales, dolphins, and porpoises.

SUPERFAMILY PLATANISTOIDEA: River dolphins.

FAMILY INIIDAE
Inia (1): Boutu.

FAMILY LIPOTIDAE
Lipotes (1): Beiji.

FAMILY PLATANISTIDAE
Platanista (2): Indian River dolphins.

FAMILY PONTOPORIIDAE
Pontoporia (1): Franciscana.

SUPERFAMILY DELPHINOIDEA: Marine dolphins and porpoises.

FAMILY MONODONTIDAE: Narwhals and belugas.
SUBFAMILY DELPHINAPTERINAE
Delphinapterus (1): Beluga.
SUBFAMILY MONODONTINAE
Monodon (1): Narwhal.
SUBFAMILY ORCAELLINAE
Orcaella (1): Irrawaddy dolphin.

FAMILY DELPHINIDAE: Dolphins and grampuses.
SUBFAMILY STENONINAE
Sotalia (1): Tucuxi.
Sousa (2): Humpback dolphins.
Steno (1): Rough-toothed dolphin.

SUBFAMILY DELPHININAE
Delphinus (1): Common dolphin.
Grampus (1): Risso's dolphin.
Lagenodelphis (1): Fraser's dolphin.
Lagenorphynchus (6)
Stenella (5)
Tursiops (1): Bottlenose dolphin.

SUBFAMILY GLOBICEPHALINAE: Killer whales.
Feresa (1): Pygmy killer whale.
Globicephala (2): Pilot whales
Orcinus (1): Killer whale.
Peponocephala (1): Melon-headed whale.
Pseudorca (1): False killer whale.

SUBFAMILY LISSODELPHININAE
Lissodelphis (2): Right-whale dolphins

SUBFAMILY CEPHALORHYNCHINAE
Cephalorhynchus (4)

FAMILY PHOCOENIDAE: Porpoises.
Neophocaena (1): Finless porpoise.
Phocoena (4): Common porpoise and others.
Phocoenoides (1): Dall's porpoise.

SUPERFAMILY PHYSETEROIDEA: Beaked and sperm whales.

FAMILY ZIPHIIDAE: Beaked whales.
Berardius (2): Beaked whales.
Hyperoodon (2): Bottlenose whales.
Mesoplodon (12): Mesoplodonts.
Tasmacetus (1): Tasman beaked whale.
Ziphius (1): Cuvier's beaked whale.

FAMILY PHYSETERIDAE: Sperm whales.
Kogia (2): Dwarf and pygmy sperm whales.
Physeter (1): Sperm whale.

clams, and a human boot. Some of the objects are evidence that sperm whales sometimes feed along the seafloor. Adult males can remain submerged for periods of an hour or more. Sonar operators have actively tracked sperm whales to depths of 9,200 feet (2,800 meters).

The IWC prohibited factory-ship whaling for sperm whales in 1979. Beginning about 1982 the remaining catch, from North Pacific shore stations, was reduced to 400 sperm whales a year, compared with a peak total North Pacific catch of 29,000 in the mid-1960's. Although female sperm whales are still numerous, the number of adult males is greatly reduced.

Sperm whales are the source of ambergris, a waxy substance once highly prized as a base for perfumes and cosmetics. Masses of ambergris up to 220 pounds (100 kg) accumulate in the whale's lower intestine. Ambergris is sometimes found on beaches or floating in the sea.

Dwarf and Pygmy Sperm Whales. The range of sizes in sexually mature *Kogia* is 7 to 11 feet (2.1–3.4 meters). The diet of both whales consists mainly of various species of smaller squid but also includes fishes and crustaceans. Stomach contents from dwarf sperm whales indicate that they dive to depths of at least 985 feet (300 meters). Age of sexual maturity is unknown, as are most other details of the reproductive cycle.

Little is known about either species of *Kogia*. Most historical records are not accurate as to species, since the dwarf sperm whale was only recently accepted as a distinct species. They are rarely sighted at sea but appear to be solitary or to form small schools of about six or seven animals. Nothing is known about the overall abundance of these whales, but because they are commonly stranded in some areas they must be locally abundant.

Beaked Whales. These are a diverse family of 18 species in five genera. They are exclusively oceanic in distribution. Beaked whales are of medium size, with adults ranging in length from about 13 feet (4 meters) in *Mesoplodon* to slightly more than 39 feet (4 meters) in *Berardius*. In all species except the Tasman beaked whale the upper teeth are absent or vestigial and no more than four teeth are present in the lower jaws. Other characteristics of the family include a pair of deep throat grooves and flukes with no median notch. The two best-known species are the northern bottlenose whale *(Hyperoodon ampullatus)* and the Baird's beaked whale *(Berardius bairdii)*.

Very little is known about this group, since they are infrequently observed and difficult to identify at sea. They feed mainly on various squid and some fishes and appear to be deep divers. The northern bottlenose has been re-

ROBERT COMMER/EARTH VIEWS

Unlike most other sharks, the docile whale shark feeds on small crustaceans and other plankton.

ported to dive for up to two hours. They are usually seen in groups of up to six whales.

The only information on reproductive cycles is for the two species taken commercially. The estimated age of sexual maturity in Baird's whale is 8 to 10 years. The mating season is October and November. The gestation may be as long as 17 months, and most births occur from November to July, with the majority in March and April. The interval between calves is probably three years. The mean age of sexual maturity for the northern bottlenose whale is 11 years for females and 7 to 11 for males. The peak of breeding is in April, and gestation is estimated at one year. The calving interval is about two or three years.

The status of all the beaked whale populations except the northern bottlenose is generally good, but a few species may be naturally rare. Longman's beaked whale *(M. pacificus)* is known from only two individuals. The IWC prohibited commercial catches of the northern bottlenose in 1978.

ROBERT L. BROWNELL, JR.
U. S. Fish and Wildlife Service

Bibliography

Ellis, Richard, *The Book of Whales* (Knopf 1980).
Ellis, Richard, *Dolphins and Porpoises* (Knopf 1982).
Gaskin, D. E., *The Ecology of Whales and Dolphins* (Heinemann 1982).
Haley, D. D., ed., *Marine Mammals of Eastern North Pacific and Arctic Waters* (Pacific Search Press 1978).
Howell, A. Brazier, *Aquatic Mammals* (reprint, Dover 1970).
Leatherwood, S., and Reeves, R. R., *The Sierra Club Handbook of Whales and Dolphins* (Sierra Club 1983).
Norris, Kenneth S., ed., *Whales, Dolphins, and Porpoises* (Univ. of Calif. Press 1966).
Payne, Roger, ed., *Communication and Behavior of Whales* (Western Press 1983).
Ridgway, Sam H., ed., *Mammals of the Sea: Biology and Medicine* (C. C. Thomas 1972).
Schevill, W. E. ed., *The Whale Problem: A Status Report* (Harvard Univ. Press 1974).
Slijper, E. J., *Whales* (Cornell Univ. Press 1979).

WHALE OIL. See under WHALING.

WHALE SHARK, the largest of all sharks and the largest of all fishes. The biggest specimen measured was nearly 45 feet (15.2 meters) in length. The whale shark is the only large shark covered with white spots and the only shark with the mouth at the end of the snout rather than below it. Unlike the vast majority of sharks, the whale shark does not prey on large fish or other large vertebrates. Instead, it strains small animals from the water like the baleen whale and like the basking shark, which is the next-largest fish.

Whale sharks are open-sea fishes found in tropical waters around the world. They sometimes range as far north as New York and as far south as southern Brazil and Australia. They are especially abundant in the Philippines, the Red Sea, the Caribbean region, and the Gulf of California. In the Caribbean, whale sharks have been observed commingled with tunas, apparently feeding on the same schools of small fish.

The huge mouth measures 5 feet (1.5 meters) across in medium-size individuals. The numerous tiny teeth are not used to catch food. Instead, the whale shark uses its gill rakers to strain plankton, small fishes, and squid from the water. The rakers are attached to the bottom of the gill bars and extend forward into the throat, where they form an interlocking net somewhat like the baleen (whalebone) plankton strainer in whales. When water is strained through the rakers, food animals are trapped and swallowed.

Sometimes whale sharks feed while cruising slowly along the surface. At other times they take up a vertical, tail-down position and bob up and down in the water, gulping their prey on each upward bob.

Whale sharks are egg layers. An egg case found in the Gulf of Mexico contained a young whale shark 14 inches (36 cm) long.

Whale sharks are of no economic importance. Their livers lack the concentration of vitamin A that makes the basking shark and some other sharks valuable catches.

The whale shark, *Rhiniodon typus,* is the sole member of the family Rhiniodontidae in the order Orectolobiformes, which also includes carpet sharks and nurse sharks.

E. O. WILEY
Museum of Natural History
University of Kansas

WHALEBONE. See under WHALE.

A harpooner prepares to lance a dying, upside-down sperm whale. In the background a whaleboat is overturned by another whale. The four whaleboats visible were launched from a mother ship in the background. (1862 lithograph)

WHALING. The origins of whaling are unknown. When, where, and how men first began to catch the world's largest animals remain matters of speculation. However, the earliest evidences of whaling have been found where whales migrate close to shore: the coasts of Alaska and Siberia (about 2000 B.C.), northern Norway (about 900 A.D.), and the Bay of Biscay (about 1000 A.D.).

Subsistence Whaling. The first whale hunters killed whales for subsistence. They used the meat and blubber for food and the oil for light and heat. In addition, in the Arctic, whale bones, baleen, and sinews were used for building materials. All of these early hunters were shore whalers. Their open boats—whether umiaks, dugout canoes, or sampans—were too fragile to venture far from land. Besides, the dead whales had to be towed to shore, an arduous task that usually required many boats. Once ashore, the whale was butchered to obtain the meat, blubber, bone, and baleen.

The most effective subsistence whalers were the Eskimos, whose survival on the Arctic coast depended on their ability to take sea mammals, including large whales. Other subsistence whalers of the North Pacific were the Nootka and related Indian tribes of the Northwest Coast, the Aleuts, the Japanese, and the Chukchis of the Siberian coast.

Beginnings of Commercial Whaling. Commercial whaling emerged in Europe in the Middle Ages. Along the Bay of Biscay, French and Spanish Basques had long taken whales that migrated close to shore. The reduction of these stocks or the increasing wariness of the whales led by 1300 A.D. to voyages farther out to sea, using sailing vessels capable of carrying and launching open whaleboats.

Whales taken in the open ocean were towed to the ship rather than to the shore. As the whale lay alongside, the baleen was removed from its mouth and the blubber was flensed (stripped from the carcass) and packed in casks for rendering later. Ashore the oil was tried out (extracted) from the blubber by cooking it in large cauldrons set in brick furnaces known as tryworks. Whale oil found a ready market as a high-quality lubricant, fuel for lamps, and dressing for leather and textiles.

Baleen was also a valuable commodity. It consists of the strong flexible strips that make up the filter-feeding mechanism characteristic of most species of large whales. Known erroneously as whalebone or whale fins, it was used to make a wide variety of products, ranging from corset stays and umbrella ribs to combs and brushes.

Well established by 1300 A.D., commercial whaling remained largely in the hands of the Basques for about 300 years. The only species that they hunted was the right whale. It was called "right" because it was rich in oil and baleen; slow enough to be chased and killed with rowed boats; and recoverable, since it floated when dead—unlike many other species. As the nearby stocks of right whales were depleted—first in the Bay of Biscay, then elsewhere along the European coast—the Basques began in the 1550's to make long-distance whaling voyages across the Atlantic to the coast of Labrador. There, from Red Bay and other bases, they intercepted right whales as they migrated along the coast of the western Atlantic.

Spread of Commercial Whaling. The high profits of the Basque whalers attracted people elsewhere in Europe to undertake commercial whaling under Basque tutelage. After English explorers reported seeing many whales in Arctic waters around Spitsbergen (now Svalbard), the first English whaling expeditions—using Basque whaling specialists—were launched. An oil rush followed, as the Dutch, Germans, and French sought to share in the harvest. The whale they hunted was a newly discovered species known as the Greenland right whale, a species closely related to the right whale but yielding even more oil and baleen.

The intense rivalry for so rich a prize verged on open warfare. When England tried to claim a monopoly over the whale resources of Spitsbergen, the Dutch responded vigorously. First they forced a division of the island into zones of national influence, then they gained ascendancy. They established the town of Smeerenburg (Blubbertown) for trying out whale oil, and maintaining the whaling fleet. Dutch whaling at Spitsbergen peaked in 1684, when 246 ships hunted the bowhead whale.

By the end of the 17th century so few whales were left near Spitsbergen that Dutch and En-

© ANTHONY P. STATILE/D.P.I.

A 1960's whaling fleet in the Ross Sea near Antarctica. Whales killed by the small catcher boats were butchered and processed into oil, meat, and other products on the large factory ship (*right center*).

glish whalers were forced west to Greenland. In the early 1700's they sailed beyond Greenland to Davis Strait and Baffin Bay. Aided by government subsidies and bounties, English whalers regained the lead in whaling, and soon the Dutch withdrew from whaling west of Greenland. In their place in the 1740's came the colonial whalers of Nantucket and Cape Cod.

Whaling in America. Whaling had emerged as a recognized enterprise in New England by 1650. It began with shore whaling where migratory routes brought right whales close to the coast at Cape Cod, Nantucket, and the south shore of Long Island. The reduction of inshore stocks of whales led to ventures farther from shore. These early voyages were made in small sloops or schooners carrying one or two whaleboats and lasted three to six weeks. Because the voyages were short and the climate cool, the blubber was stored on board in casks and rendered ashore. At first the only prey was right whales, which were followed on their migrations north to the Gulf of St. Lawrence and Davis Strait.

A rapid expansion of American whaling began about 1712 with the exploitation of a previously ignored species—the sperm whale. Unlike the right and bowhead whales, sperm whales inhabit deep waters beyond the continental shelves. Catching them meant sailing far from shore, usually in temperate climates, where blubber would not keep for long. This problem was solved by one of the major technological innovations in the history of whaling: the onboard tryworks. Equipped with this means of rendering oil from blubber, the whaleship was a primitive factory ship, capable of processing its catch at sea and limited in range only by the endurance of vessel and crew. In the 1750's, American whaleships with tryworks aboard began a century of exploration that opened up all of the world's whaling grounds except those of the Antarctic. Their success made America the dominant whaling nation in the 19th century.

Whaling in the Pacific. American and British whaleships penetrated the Pacific in the 1790's. Within 50 years all of the sperm and right whale grounds of the Pacific had been discovered, as had those of the Indian Ocean. In 1848, whalers passed through the Bering Strait and found bowhead whales, the western Arctic counterpart of the Greenland right whales. In the 1850's whalers invaded the bays and lagoons of Baja California, where gray whales gathered to mate and calve. After a decade of hectic hunting, the gray whale was on the verge of extinction. By midcentury more than 700 whaleships, most of them American, hunted whales worldwide. Almost half of this fleet sailed from New Bedford, Mass., the greatest whaling port. To observers, if not to participants, there was romance and adventure in this era of whaling, reflected enduringly in Melville's novel *Moby-Dick* (1851).

The End of Sailing-Ship Whaling. Three factors led to a decline in whaling after the American Civil War. First, the loss of ships to Confederate raiders was followed by a series of disasters in the Arctic, beginning in 1871, when 32 vessels were abandoned in the ice. Second, the stocks of whales had declined so drastically that the cost of catching them was becoming prohibitive. Third, and even more serious, the discovery of commercial quantities of petroleum in Pennsylvania in 1859 provided cheap substitutes for whale oil as a fuel for lamps and as a lubricant.

The remaining market for baleen led to a concentration of whaling in the western Arctic, where auxiliary steam power enabled sailing whaleships to penetrate into the last refuge of the bowhead whale. Only the introduction of a less costly replacement for baleen—spring steel—saved the species from extinction.

The Modern Era. In the last quarter of the 19th century the whaling industry was in a severe decline with no apparent prospect of recovery. But at this point two revolutionary technologies ushered in the modern age of whaling.

The first new technology was developed in Norway about 1870 by a whaling merchant, Svend Foyn. Foyn devised a cannon-fired explosive harpoon that could both fasten to and kill a whale. The gun required a stable platform, which Foyn provided in the form of an engine-powered catcher boat fast enough to catch the fastest whales and sturdy enough to recover them after the kill. Together, the gun and boat made it possible to hunt for the first time the rorquals, including the blue and fin whales—the two largest animals ever to inhabit the earth. Rorquals were too fast and too strong to be caught with open boats and hand harpoons. Even if caught,

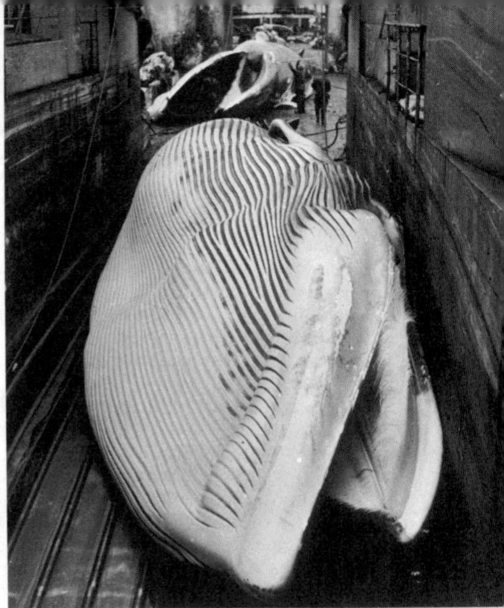

(*Left*) A catcher boat tows a dead whale to the factory ship. (*Right*) The whale is dragged up the slipway to the flensing deck, where blubber, meat, and useful organs are cut from the carcass.

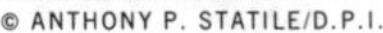

they usually sank when they were killed and could not be recovered and towed back to the mother ship by an open boat.

The commercial incentive for renewed whaling was provided by the second technology—hydrogenation—developed by the German inventor K. P. W. T. Normann in 1902. Hydrogenation removed the fishy flavor from whale oil and transformed it into a solid fat suitable for margarine, thus opening up an entirely new market for the oil.

Whaling in the Antarctic. With new tools and incentives, whalers moved on to previously unexploited fishing grounds. In 1904 a shore fishery established on South Georgia Island in the South Atlantic provided the base for invading Antarctic waters—inaugurating the most destructive period in the history of whaling.

For the first two decades of Antarctic whaling the whales caught by catcher boats were flensed at shore stations (mostly on South Georgia Island), as at Spitsbergen three centuries earlier, or alongside specially equipped whaleships. But in 1925 another Norwegian invention, the floating factory ship, led to the greatest expansion in the history of whaling. The floating factory had a stern slipway through which an entire whale could be dragged on deck for quick and efficient processing. Virtually all parts of the whale were used: meat for human consumption; oil for margarine, soap, and specialized lubricants; bone meal for livestock fodder and fertilizers; organs for vitamins; and waxes for cosmetics.

The intense whaling in Antarctic waters—by Norway and Great Britain up to World War II and by Japan and the Soviet Union afterward—led to the successive depletion of the blue, the fin, and the sei whales. Despite a growing realization that the survival of these species was in doubt, restraints proved ineffective. The International Whaling Commission (IWC) had been established in 1946 to protect endangered species, but it was hindered by uncertainty among scientists as to the status of various whale populations, and it lacked authority to enforce its decisions. As late as 1964, 357 catcher boats and 23 factory ships were in operation, mostly in the Antarctic, and there were 39 shore stations worldwide. The total catch in that year was 63,001 whales.

The End of Commercial Whaling. The failure of the IWC's regulations led to a growing number of people in favor of halting all commercial whaling. In Stockholm in 1972, the United Nations Conference on the Human Environment called for a 10-year moratorium on all commercial whaling. Ten years later, in 1982, the IWC voted overwhelmingly to ban all commercial whaling after 1986. However, the IWC still lacked power to compel compliance, and the three nations with major whaling industries—Japan, the Soviet Union, and Norway—filed objections to the decision. Nonetheless, the long history of commercial whaling will come to an end—if not in 1986 then soon after—not because no whales are left but because the threats to their survival have come to symbolize the need for more careful management of the world's resources.

RICHARD C. KUGLER, *Old Dartmouth Historical Society Whaling Museum*

YIELDS OF WHALE OIL

Species	Average approximate yield	
	Barrels	Metric tons
Rorquals		
Blue	120	20
Right	120	20
Bowhead	120	20
Fin	60	10
Humpback	50	8
Sperm	50	8
Gray	35	6
Sei	20	3.4
Bryde's	20	3.4
Minke	3.5	0.6

Further Reading: Ellis, Richard, *The Book of Whales* (Knopf 1980); Jackson, G., *The British Whaling Trade* (Shoe String Press 1978); Matthews, L. H., ed., *The Whale* (Simon & Schuster 1968); Starbuck, A., *History of the American Whale Fishery* (1878; reprint, Argosy-Antiquarian 1964); Tønnessen, J. N., and Johnsen, A. O., *The History of Modern Whaling* (Univ. of Calif. Press 1982).

WHARTON, hwôr'tən, **Edith (Newbold Jones),** American novelist: b. New York, N.Y., Jan. 24, 1862; d. St.-Brice-sous-Forêt, France, Aug. 11, 1937. She was descended from wealthy and socially prominent New York families and was privately educated. In 1885, after her formal debut, she married Edward Wharton, a Boston banker. They spent much time in Europe, moved to France in 1907, and were divorced in 1913. Wharton never remarried. She maintained a residence in the United States but continued to live in France.

During her rather lonely and isolated childhood she had learned to make up stories for her own amusement, and later she had published some of her verse, but apparently it was her husband's mental illness which caused her, as a therapeutic measure, to take up the profession of writing. In the 1890's she began to contribute short stories and poems to *Scribner's Magazine*, and by the turn of the century she was publishing short story collections and novels. Her first popular success came with *The House of Mirth* (1905), a symbolic depiction of the manners of New York society. The novel deals with the plight of a young woman who lacks the financial means to maintain her high social position. It was followed by several other novels about the New York scene, the most successful of which is *The Age of Innocence* (1920), awarded a Pulitzer Prize. This story explores the moral hypocrisy which is the foundation of the apparently "innocent" New York social world. The plight of two lovers, trapped in a situation which makes their own happiness impossible because they have prior obligations to others, is the basic situation. The same dilemma is used in her novelette *Ethan Frome* (1911), a stark and tragic story set in an imaginary New England town reminiscent of the region around Lenox, Mass., where Wharton had often spent her summers. *Ethan Frome* achieved enormous popularity.

Her other novels present a wide range of interest. The first, *The Valley of Decision* (1902), had an 18th century European setting. *The Fruit of the Tree* (1907) treats an American executive's conflicts of love and business, and *Summer* (1917) returns to the New England realism of *Ethan Frome*. She then depicts Americans in France in *The Reef* (1912) and *The Custom of the Country* (1913); war themes in *The Marne* (1918) and *A Son at the Front* (1923); international manners in *The Glimpses of the Moon* (1922); parent and children relationships in *The Mother's Recompense* (1925), *Twilight Sleep* (1927), and *The Children* (1928); and Midwestern versus New York society in *Hudson River Bracketed* (1929) and its sequel *The Gods Arrive* (1932). Her final novel, *The Buccaneers* (1938), was left unfinished.

Wharton was also a master of the novelette and short story. Besides *Ethan Frome* her novelettes are *The Touchstone* (1900), an ethical dilemma about love letters; *Sanctuary* (1903); *Madame de Treymes* (1907), contrasting French and American ideals; and her Old New York tetralogy (1924): *False Dawn, The Old Maid, The Spark,* and *New Year's Day*. Her short story collections are *The Greater Inclination* (1899), *Crucial Instances* (1901), *The Descent of Man and Other Stories* (1904), *The Hermit and the Wild Woman* (1908), *Tales of Men and Ghosts* (1910), *Xingu and Other Stories* (1916), *Here and Beyond* (1926), *Certain People* (1930), *Human Nature* (1933), *The World Over* (1936), and *Ghosts* (1937).

Wharton is often compared to Henry James, with whose work her own has much in common. Both depict an orderly, mannered world of delicate scruples and quiet heroism, where commonplace tragedy, usually of their own devising, frustrates the hopes or destroys the happiness of worthwhile people. She was a close friend of James during the last 12 years of his life, a significant period in her own creative development. She even read her work aloud to him for criticism, but she was no slavish imitator of his and viewed with suspicion his preoccupation with pure artistic technique. At one point, hearing that he was in financial difficulties she arranged for some of her own royalties to be transferred to his account, handling the transaction so that James never knew, a gesture befitting some of her fictional heroes.

James K. Folsom
Yale University

WHARTON, Thomas, 1st Marquess of Wharton, English political leader: b. England, August 1648; d. London, April 12, 1715. The third but eldest surviving son of Philip, 4th Baron Wharton, he entered Parliament in 1673 and was an active supporter (1679–1680) of the unsuccessful bill to exclude James, duke of York (later James II); from the succession to the throne. During James' reign, Wharton corresponded secretly with William of Orange and composed the popular Whig ballad *Lilliburlero (Lilli Burlero)*, later boasting that he "sang James II out of three kingdoms." William III rewarded Wharton's services to the Glorious Revolution of 1688 by appointing him a privy councilor and comptroller of the household. On the accession (1702) of Queen Anne, who disapproved of his licentious private life and his views on religion, he was deprived of all his offices. In retaliation, he resisted the policies of the court party, especially in their attempts to pass in Parliament the Occasional Conformity Bill, aimed against the Nonconformists.

When his Whig friends entered the administration of the 1st earl of Godolphin, Wharton was created an earl (1706) and appointed lord lieutenant of Ireland (1708–1710). In 1710, after the Tory victory, he once more opposed the administration's policies, especially the Treaty of Utrecht (1713) and the Schism Act (1714). After the death of Queen Anne in 1714, he was one of the Whig lords who contrived the peaceable accession of George I, with whom, as elector of Hannover, Wharton had been in correspondence as early as 1706. In 1715, two months before his death, George made him a marquess and lord privy seal.

WHARTON, city, Texas, seat of Wharton County, on the Colorado River, 55 miles southwest of Houston, at an altitude of 110 feet. A trading center for the oil and sulfur industries of the area and its rice and cotton plantations, the city also has plants for hide processing, alfalfa dehydrating, meat packing, poultry processing, and fertilizer manufacturing.

Founded in 1847, it was incorporated in 1902. It is governed by a mayor and council. Population: 9,033.

WHARVES. See Harbor.

WHAT EVERY WOMAN KNOWS, a play by James M. Barrie, Scottish novelist and dramatist, produced in 1908 and published in 1918. Maggie Wylie is a plain, small, modest but resolute spinster of 27, with no prospects of marriage. John Shand, an ambitious but impecunious student five years younger than Maggie, breaks into the Wylie library in an effort to advance his learning. Maggie's father and two brothers seize the incident as an opportunity: they will finance John's education if he will promise to marry Maggie at the completion of his studies. Barrie portrays all the characters as typically Scottish.

John lacks a sense of humor, but in other ways does amazingly well. After six years he wins election to Parliament, and marries Maggie, although he frankly admits that he does not love her. Her single desire, which she carries out with passionate devotion and self-effacement, is to help him realize his political ambitions. She types his speeches, which win a reputation for their wit and novel ideas.

But John falls in love with Lady Sybil Tenterden, who is all that Maggie is not—worldly, charming, beautiful. Maggie faces this problem with determination, and offers to give up John if he can find greater help and inspiration in her rival. After a brief period in the company of Sybil, it becomes apparent that John's speeches lack the qualities that propelled him to the top. He is unable to understand why; for, as is the way with men, he has believed in his strength, and gloried in the conviction that he has risen by himself. Finally he realizes that his success is due primarily to Maggie. She explains to him that the wife of every successful man knows how her husband's success has been achieved: this is every wife's private joke.

WHAT MAISIE KNEW, a novel by Henry James published in 1897. It has an important place in the author's development as a novelist and gives an incisive preview of a peculiarly modern problem—the relations of children and parents. The parents of Maisie, a child of six, get a divorce, and each lovelessly agrees to care for her six months of the year. Thus the child is subjected to their bitter notions of each other as well as to a sequence of affairs and entanglements which only deepen Maisie's uncertainty about her life and compel an early maturity. Only in Mrs. Wix, her second governess, does Maisie find some security and a growing ability to manage "what she knows." She belongs to that gallery of children—like Charles Dickens' Oliver Twist or Mark Twain's Huckleberry Finn—conceived by the novelist out of a need to assess the complexities of the moral life in the individual and society in the context of the unequivocally sharp and innocent vision of the child.

The theme of the novel—the growth of conscience and heart—relates to James' middle period; in form and style it is the first work to indicate the later style of the novelist. The plot begins to center, not on external setting and event, but on internal thought and feeling; the prose begins to be denser, tauter in construction, richly metaphorical and suddenly colloquial, leisurely paced and unexpectedly abrupt. This lasting and remorseless light on the fate of the child in our time is difficult reading, and it is perhaps best read after *Roderick Hudson* (1876) or *The Portrait of a Lady* (1881).

EUGENIO VILLICAÑA.

WHAT PRICE GLORY?, a play about World War I by Maxwell Anderson and Laurence Stallings, produced in New York in 1924 under the direction of Arthur Hopkins, and published in 1926. It is usually ranked with Robert C. Sheriff's *Journey's End* as the best dramatization of the ordeal of trench fighting in the war.

The play owed its success to vivid creation of character and atmosphere rather than to plot. The characters are United States Marines—old-time professional soldiers mingled with green recruits. The thread of formal plot is the long-standing rivalry between two of the old-timers, Captain Flagg and Sergeant Quirt, who have come up together in the service. As the play opens, Quirt has just been reassigned to Flagg's company as top sergeant; the company is in rest camp in a French village, and Flagg is going off on leave. In his absence, Quirt supplants him as lover of Charmaine, the daughter of the local innkeeper. On Flagg's return, the girl's father complains that she has been seduced. Flagg orders Quirt to marry her, but before the ceremony can be performed the company is ordered to the front.

Act II is staged in a frontline dugout. On accomplishing its mission, the remnant of the company is relieved, but in Act III, before the weary men have had a chance to rest, all leaves are canceled and the company is ordered back to the trenches. The curtain falls as the wounded Quirt hobbles after the others, calling, "What a lot of . . . fools it takes to make a war!"

When originally produced, the play created a sensation because of the relatively uncensored profanity put in the mouths of the soldiers. Flagg and Quirt are tough, hard drinking, unromantic, but they know how to take care of their men, and to lead them. For such professionals, war is neither a noble crusade for an ideal nor a dashing quest of glory. It is a messy job which they are paid and trained to carry through as best they can.

WHATELY, hwāt'lē, **Richard,** English prelate, archbishop of Dublin: b. London, England, Feb. 1, 1787; d. Dublin, Ireland, Oct. 1, 1863. Educated at Oriel College, Oxford, he returned there as a fellow, and in 1819 published his famous *Historic Doubts Relative to Napoleon Buonaparte*. Among the most popular of Whately's writings, the pamphlet aims a barbed shaft at the skeptical philosophy of David Hume, by reducing to absurdity the application of logic to the Scriptures. Nonetheless, Whately was famed as a logician. His scholarly reputation rests on his *Elements of Logic*, published in 1826, and the *Elements of Rhetoric*, in 1828, for the main part, although he is also remembered for his views on economics, summarized in the *Introductory Lectures on Political Economy*, published in 1855. In 1822 he was appointed parish priest in Halesworth, Suffolk, but in 1825 returned once more to Oxford, as principal of St. Alban Hall. In 1829 he was appointed to the chair of political economy. Always a liberal in religion and politics, Whately minimized theology and metaphysics, was against Tractarianism (q.v.), supported Roman Catholic emancipation and the state endowment of Roman Catholic clergy, and was a founder of the broad-church movement. He was also opposed to the transportation of convicts to Australia. In 1831 he was appointed archbishop of Dublin, and warmly embraced the cause of common religious education for Protestants and Roman Catholics, but did not see his ideas adopted.

DAVID REPP/PHOTO RESEARCHERS, INC.

Wheat is the major food crop throughout the world except in Asia, where rice is more widely grown.

WHEAT, hwēt, a grass of the Gramineae family, of the tribe Hordeae, and of the genus *Triticum,* is the most widely grown of all the cereal grains. Except in the rice-eating regions of Asia, wheat products are the principal cereal foods of an overwhelming majority of the world's inhabitants. In the United States, food products from wheat contribute about one fourth of the total food energy requirement of man, and in European countries, particularly France and Italy, they make up a considerably greater proportion of the diet.

The preeminence of wheat as a food is due to several factors. It is adapted to a wide variety of soil and climatic conditions, and can be grown extensively throughout the world. It is economical to produce, and gives good yields of grain with excellent storage properties. Its great popularity as a human food is due to its mild, acceptable flavor, and the unique ability of its principal proteins to form gluten when mixed with water to make a dough. The gluten gives a soft, springy quality to bread doughs, and enables them to retain the carbon dioxide which is produced by yeast fermentation; this permits the production of light, finely textured loaves of bread. Flour from other cereals such as barley, corn, rice, and rye, which do not have gluten-forming properties, yield rather heavy loaves.

Wheat played an important part in the development of civilization, and was grown before the beginnings of recorded history, so that its origin is obscure. The most ancient languages mention wheat, or corn, and archaeologists have found carbonized grains of wheat in the prehistoric lake dwellings in Switzerland, in remains from the Stone Age in England, in the tombs of the pharaohs in Egypt, and in the excavations of ruins in Turkey, some of which date back to 4000 B.C. There is evidence that wheat was cultivated in China in 3000 B.C. Some scientists believe that wheat originated in Mesopotamia (Iraq), although many others hold the view that the plant once grew wild in the valleys of the Euphrates and Tigris rivers, and spread from these regions to the rest of the world.

It is not believed that wheat existed in America before Christopher Columbus discovered the continent. Columbus brought wheat to the West Indies in 1493; the grain was taken to Mexico by Hernán Cortés in 1519, and Jesuit and Franciscan missionaries carried it into what is now Arizona and California. Colonists in Massachusetts and Virginia began production of the grain early in the 17th century. Wheat was not as well adapted to the coastal area as corn, but as settlers moved into the Ohio Valley and the West, wheat became one of their main crops.

1. Chemical Composition and Structure

Chemical Composition. Wheat consists principally of proteins and starch with smaller quantities of other carbohydrates, fats, pigments, certain vitamins, and minerals. It contains the important B vitamins—thiamine, riboflavin, and niacin—but no vitamin C unless the grain is sprouted. The yellow pigments present in wheat consist chiefly of xantophyll, which does not give rise to vitamin A when ingested. The embryo (germ) of wheat is a rich source of vitamin E.

The protein content of wheat is influenced chiefly by the soil and climatic conditions under which it is grown. Considering the United States as a whole, the protein content varies from 7 to 19 percent. In general, regions with a mild, humid climate, which is typical of land areas near large bodies of water, result in a long growing and ripening period and produce starchy kernels of low protein content. In contrast, the Great Plains area is characterized by relatively hot, dry weather during the ripening of the grain, and yields wheat with a high protein content. Within a climatic zone, seasons of high rainfall or the use of irrigation, especially during the ripening period, result in a decrease in protein content with an increase in yield.

The moisture-retaining properties of soil have more influence on the protein content of wheat than on the level of fertility; nitrogenous fertilizers frequently enhance the yield quite markedly without greatly affecting protein content. In general, however, the protein content of wheat is raised by increasing the available nitrogen in the soil; thus, wheat grown on summer fallow or after legumes is usually of higher protein content than when grown after cereal grains or grasses. Although soil and climatic conditions have the greatest influence on protein content, genetic factors are involved, since some varieties produce wheat of higher protein content than others, when grown in the same environment.

Structure. The parts of a typical wheat kernel and their relation to one another are shown in the accompanying figures. Flour is produced from the starchy endosperm. Bran is composed of the pericarp and aleurone layer, together with the brush, the vascular bundle (in crease), pigment strand, and nucellar projection (and associated structures not distinguishable in the figures). The seed, properly so called, comprises the germ, endosperm (aleurone layer plus starchy endosperm), nucellar tissues, and a very thin seed coat. The structure at the lower right in the longitudinal section is the germ (see WHEAT GERM). The entire kernel, composed of the seed and its protective layers of cells, is a special kind of fruit, called a caryopsis.

2. Production

World Production. Wheat has a range of cultivation which is probably greater than that of any other crop, and is being seeded and harvested somewhere in the world each month of the year.

Wheat is grown at elevations of 8,000 to 10,000 feet in the tropics of Mexico, northwestern South America, and Abyssinia, and below sea level in the Imperial Valley of California. It grows within the Arctic Circle in Europe, Asia, and North America, and in such warm countries as Brazil and the tropics of the Philippines. In the world as a whole, several thousand varieties are grown. The cultivation of wheat on a large scale is confined pricipally to temperate regions where the annual rainfall is from 15 to 35 inches; it does not do well on sandy and peat soils, and is best adapted to loam and clay soils which are well supplied with organic matter (humus).

In Europe there are three principal wheat-growing regions: (1) the plains of southern Russia and the Danube Basin (including Romania and Hungary); (2) the countries bordering the Mediterranean Sea, especially Italy; and (3) northwestern Europe (Germany, France, Holland, Belgium, and Great Britain). In North America, wheat is grown principally in the Great Plains area of the United States and Canada and in the Columbia River basin (eastern Washington and Oregon). Other leading wheat-producing areas are located in the central part of Argentina,

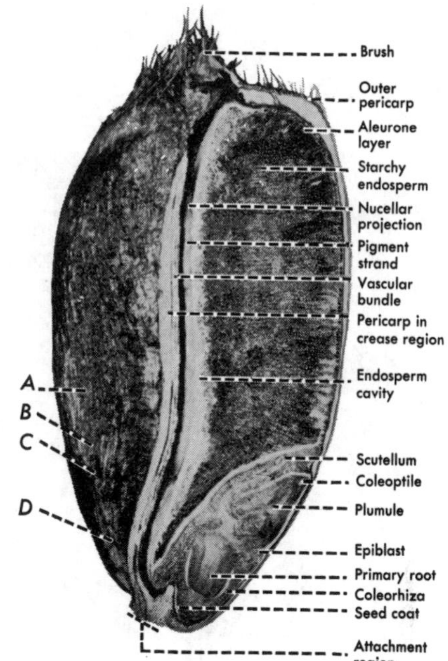

Diagram of a longitudinal section (through crease) of a typical wheat kernel.

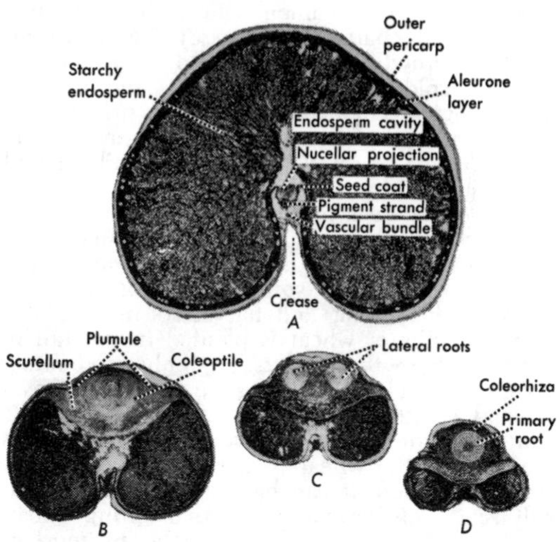

NORTHERN UTILIZATION RESEARCH AND DEVELOPMENT DIVISION, U. S. DEPARTMENT OF AGRICULTURE

Cross section of a typical wheat kernel, cut at the levels and angles marked *A, B, C,* and *D* in the longitudinal section shown in the upper diagram.

southern Australia, and Pakistan. The inequality in wheat production and consumption results in a large international trade in wheat. Under normal world conditions, vast streams of wheat pass from the surplus-producing countries of North America, Argentina, and Australia to the countries of deficit production, principally in western Europe.

United States Production. Three botanical species of wheat, *Triticum vulgare* (common wheat), *T. durum* (amber and red durum wheats), and *T. compactum* (white and red club wheats), each representing several varieties, are grown in

Combines work in tandem to harvest a prairie of wheat. In one operation a combine cuts and threshes the grain.

the United States, but members of the *T. vulgare* group represent nearly 95 percent of the total production. The common wheats differ in such physiological characteristics as spring or winter habit of growth, earliness, yield, resistance to drought, cold, and plant diseases, and in such morphological characteristics as the presence or absence of awns; color (red or white); and kernel texture (hard or soft), as well as in milling and baking behavior.

For commercial purposes, the common wheats are classified in four major groups: hard red spring, hard red winter, soft red winter, and white wheats (winter and spring). Spring wheat is sown in the spring and harvested in the later summer. Winter wheat is planted in the fall in regions where the winters are only moderately severe; it develops a root system before the onset of cold weather, and becomes dormant during winter. In the spring, the plants make a vigorous growth and the wheat is harvested in the early summer. Where it can be grown, winter wheat will usually give greater yields than spring wheat.

As wheat is essentially a food grain, most of each year's crop goes into food uses, chiefly as flour. Some grain is required for seed, and the rest is used for feed.

Hard red winter wheat is grown principally in the southern and central portions of the Great Plains, with the greatest acreages in Kansas, Nebraska, Oklahoma, Montana, Texas, and Colorado. Hard red spring wheat is grown in the northern portion of the Great Plains area, in the states of Minnesota, North Dakota, South Dakota, and Montana, where the winters are severe, and semiarid conditions prevail. Soft red winter wheat is grown east of the Great Plains area and south of Wisconsin, in regions which are usually characterized by ample rainfall and moderately cold winters. It is the leading class of wheat in Ohio, Indiana, Illinois, Missouri, Pennsylvania, Maryland, Virginia, West Virginia, New Jersey, Delaware, North Carolina, South Carolina, Georgia, Kentucky, Tennessee, and Alabama. White wheats are grown chiefly in the Pacific coast states and in New York and Michigan; the leading producing states are Washington, California, Idaho, and Michigan.

Durum wheat was introduced into the United States from Russia by Mark A. Carleton, cerealist of the United States Department of Agriculture, in the late 19th century for cultivation in the north-central regions of North Dakota. Existing spring wheat varieties gave relatively poor yields there because of arid conditions and their relatively greater susceptibility to the prevailing physiologic strains of wheat stem rust.

Wheat is grown on about one third of the farms in the United States; in some areas it is almost the sole source of farm income. In the major producing regions of the Great Plains and the Pacific Northwest where there is limited rainfall, wheat is often grown on the same land year after year, or the land is allowed to remain idle, with occasional cultivation every second or third year to conserve moisture and nitrates for the following crop. In the Eastern United States

WHEAT PRODUCTION

Country	U. S. Tons (millions)	Metric Tons (millions)
Soviet Union	106,800	96,900
United States	64,300	58,300
China	47,400	43,000
India	31,700	28,800
Canada	26,000	23,600
Turkey	18,300	16,600
France	17,700	16,100
Australia	12,900	11,700
Argentina	12,300	11,200
Italy	10,500	9,500
Pakistan	9,600	8,700
Romania	7,400	6,700
West Germany	7,400	6,700
Iran	6,600	6,000
Yugoslavia	6,600	6,000

Source: Food and Agriculture Organization, 1976.

wheat is almost always grown in rotation with other crops; when it follows corn or soybeans, the land is usually prepared by disking. The application of fertilizers is seldom profitable in the major wheat-growing areas of the West, but in the Central and Eastern states mixtures containing phosphorus and potassium compounds are commonly applied at seeding time. Nitrogen is usually supplied through the use of legume crops in rotation, although a late winter or early spring application of nitrogenous fertilizers is beneficial in the South, and in wet seasons in the East.

In states where wheat is extensively grown, it is usually harvested and threshed in one operation by a machine called a combine. It is necessary to delay harvesting from 7 to 14 days after the normal time for cutting with a binder in order that the moisture content will be reduced to 14 percent or less, so that the grain can be stored safely. The culture of wheat in the United States has been so completely mechanized that only about three man-hours of labor are now required per acre (20-bushel yield), compared with 58 man-hours in the mid-19th century.

Commercial Classification. The United States Grain Standards Act, passed in 1916, provided for the establishment of official standards for the common grains, and the federal licensing and supervising of grain inspectors. These standards have been revised from time to time, and are designed to sort each grain into a number of categories according to quality. Wheat is divided into seven classes on the basis of botanical species, habit of growth, and color: hard red spring, durum, red durum, hard red winter, soft red winter, white wheat, and mixed wheat. Five of these are divided into subclasses on the basis of such factors as kernel density, geographical origin, or the presence of certain varieties. Each subclass is separated into a number of grades on the basis of plumpness, soundness, cleanliness, extent of weathering, and the presence of insects, smut, garlic, and the like. The standards also specify maximum moisture limits for all the regular grades (14.5 percent for hard red spring, durum, and mixed wheat, and 14 percent for the other classes). The hard wheats, which include hard red spring, hard red winter, and hard white, are valued for the production of flours used in making yeast-leavened bread. Soft red winter, soft white, and white club wheats are best suited for making chemically leavened baked products such as biscuits, cakes, and pastries. Amber durum is prized for the manufacture of such alimentary pastes as macaroni, spaghetti, and noodles. Red durum is less satisfactory for alimentary paste than is amber durum.

The suitability of wheat for these various purposes depends primarily on its protein content, which is reflected in a general way by the hardness and translucency of the kernels. Usually the hard, translucent types are considerably higher in protein content than soft wheats with a starchy, opaque appearance.

W. F. GEDDES
Professor of Agricultural Biochemistry
University of Minnesota
Revised by J. A. SHELLENBERGER
Head, Department of Flour and Feed Milling Industries, Kansas State University

3. Wheat Pests

Several species of insects and mites are injurious to growing wheat plants and to the wheat kernels in storage. In the principal wheat-growing regions of the United States, the hessian fly (*Phytophaga destructor*) has for many years been a very injurious enemy of the wheat crop. Damage estimated at $100 million in a single year has been caused by this pest. The insect received its common name at the time of its depredations on Long Island in 1779 on the supposition that it had been brought into this country from Europe in straw used for the bedding of Hessian soldiers. The fly also occurs in Canada, northern Africa, western Asia, Great Britain, and New Zealand. It looks much like a gnat or mosquito. The female lays pale red eggs in the grooves of the upper surface

Before shipment, wheat is stored in grain elevators. This elevator at Hutchinson, Kans., is a quarter-mile long.

GEORG GERSTER/PHOTO RESEARCHERS, INC.

of the wheat leaves in the spring and again in the fall. Larvae or maggots hatch in about a week and make their way down behind the sheaths where they feed on the plant juices, causing the plants to wilt and die. When full grown, in about 10 days, the maggots change to pupae, commonly termed "flaxseeds," and remain in this stage for part of the summer and throughout the winter. The adults emerge from these pupae.

Other flies attack wheat. The wheat stem maggot (*Meromyza americana*) occurs in the United States, Mexico, and Canada, and at times may injure 2 percent of the crop. The larvae tunnel into the wheat stems, sometimes severing them and causing the heads to turn white and die. The wheat bulb fly (*Leptohylemyia coarctata*) is one of the most serious pests of wheat in Great Britain and in certain years causes heavy losses. The maggots which hatch from eggs laid in the soil by this fly burrow into the new shoots of wheat and destroy them. Another insect injuring wheat in that country is the frit fly (*Oscinella frit*). It affects the plant in much the same way as the bulb fly.

The chinch bug (*Blissus leucopterus*) is another destructive insect of wheat in central United States, especially in outbreak years. The adult is black with white markings and about one-sixth inch long. After spending the winter in clumps of wild grasses, the adults move in large numbers to young growing wheat where they suck the juices of the plants, thus killing them. The females lay their eggs on the lower parts of the plants. The young reddish nymphs feed on the plants but fortunately the wheat usually ripens before they become full grown and migrate to more succulent crops such as corn or sorghum. Wet open winters and warm damp weather in the spring are unfavorable to chinch bugs. Such conditions and a white fungous disease often reduce their numbers so that they cause little damage.

Aphids or plant lice attack the wheat plant and in certain years, the worst of these pests, commonly known as the greenbug (*Toxoptera graminum*), appears in outbreak numbers in the Great Plains states. Since 1882, when the greenbug was first reported in the United States (from Virginia), there have been 14 outbreaks. In the most serious one, which occurred in 1942, more than 61 million bushels of grain were lost in Texas and Oklahoma. In the spring of 1950 over 1,500,000 acres of wheat in northern Texas and western Oklahoma were abandoned because of damage by the greenbug and more than 600,000 other acres were treated with insecticides to control the insect. The greenbugs suck the sap from the young overwintering wheat plants, causing the leaves to turn yellow. Both wingless and winged forms occur. All the wingless forms are female and during the spring and summer they give birth to living young. On the approach of cold weather, winged males and females are produced and the mated females lay shiny black eggs which overwinter on the leaves of the plants. There may be 20 generations a year in Indiana and even more in Texas and Oklahoma. Several other aphids attack wheat in the United States. Among them the most injurious are the apple grain aphid (*Rhopalosiphum fitchii*) and the English grain aphid (*Macrosiphum granarium*). These aphids feed in the heads of the wheat, causing the growing kernels to shrivel. Several of the aphids transmit a serious disease of wheat known as barley yellow dwarf virus.

The wheat stem sawfly (*Cephus cinctus*) caused an estimated $17 million loss of wheat in Montana and North Dakota in 1952, and is considered the most important insect pest attacking wheat in the Prairie Provinces of Canada, where in some years it has destroyed up to one third of the crop over large areas. The wheat stem sawfly is apparently a native grass-feeding insect which has acquired an appetite for wheat in the more northern part of the wheat belt. The female sawflies insert their eggs into the plant stems. The hatched larvae bore down through the joints until late summer when they girdle the stems and plug themselves in with frass near the base of the plant. The weakening of the plant stems by the larvae feeding inside and the breaking off due to the girdling reduce the yield and quality of the grain. Two other sawflies, the black grain stem sawfly (*C. tabidus*) and the European wheat stem sawfly (*C. pygmaeus*), frequently damage wheat in the eastern United States. Both are widely distributed in Europe, and the former also occurs in southeastern Asia and northern Africa.

Grasshoppers are a constant threat to wheat in the western wheat-producing areas of the United States and Canada, and in some years they destroy wheat worth millions of dollars. When abundant the grasshoppers strip off all the leaves of the wheat plants and cut off the heads. Although many kinds of grasshoppers attack wheat, five species are responsible for most of the loss. These are the migratory grasshopper (*Melanoplus bilituratus*), the differential grasshopper (*M. differentialis*), the two-striped grasshopper (*M. bivittatus*), the red-legged grasshopper (*M. femur rubrum*), and the clear-winged grasshopper (*Camnula pellucida*). Several species of migratory grasshoppers, widely referred to as locusts, cause extensive damage to wheat in South America, Africa, south Asia, and the Near East. If not controlled in some areas they may practically wipe out the food crop of an entire population. Mormon crickets (*Anabrus simplex*), which are really wingless grasshoppers, sometimes migrate into wheat fields in large bands in a number of Western states and Canadian provinces, where they damage the crop in any stage of growth, especially by feeding on the ripening kernels.

Tiny mites, which are not insects, since the adults have four instead of three pairs of legs, are also pests of wheat, especially in the western parts of Kansas, Oklahoma, and Texas. The brown wheat mite (*Petrobia latens*) at times infests the plants in enormous numbers and sucks the plant juices. The winter grain mite (*Penthaleus major*) damages wheat as well as other small grains. The wheat curl mite (*Aceria tulipae*), especially in Kansas and Nebraska, feeds on the wheat and transmits the serious wheat streak virus disease.

In the wheat-growing areas east of the Mississippi, the wheat jointworm (*Harmolita tritici*) ranks next to the hessian fly as a most important enemy of wheat. It has been in the United States since 1821 when it was first observed in eastern Pennsylvania. The adult of this insect resembles a small black ant with wings. The female lays her eggs in the wheat stem near the joints and they hatch into small grubs which feed on the juices of the plant. Their presence in the stems causes hard woody galls to form and the plants bend or break over. A closely related insect, the wheat strawworm (*H. grandis*), attacks the wheat plants in the spring so that they become stunted and sometimes die.

Several members of the Pentatomidae or stinkbugs attack wheat. In Europe, Asia, and Africa, and especially in Iran and Iraq and other countries in the Near East, some of these bugs of the genus *Eurygaster* are very destructive pests. *E. integriceps*, sometimes known as the "sen" pest, is probably the worst. These bugs pierce the soft wheat kernels and suck the juices. As a result the yield of ripened grain is low, the quality is poor, and flour made from it is not palatable. The Say stinkbug (*Chlorochroa sayi*) is an important pest of wheat in some years in Montana, North Dakota, and Canada's Prairie Provinces. The bugs suck the juices from the developing kernels and the grain when harvested is shriveled.

The pale western cutworm (*Agrotis orthogonia*), and the army cutworm (*Chorizagrotis auxiliaris*) are major wheat pests in the Great Plains area of the United States and Canada. The former species kills the plants by feeding on them beneath the soil surface, while the latter crawls up on the plants late in the day and at night and devours the leaves, stem, and head. The armyworm (*Pseudaletia unipuncta*) is also sometimes destructive to wheat. The larvae of several species of wireworms (Elateridae) eat the germinating wheat seeds in the soil, causing poor plant stands. The adults are common click beetles. These insects are long lived, some of them living for several years. Wheat sown early on ground heavily infested with white grubs (*Phyllophaga*) may have its roots eaten off by these insects and the young plants become seriously damaged. Billbugs (*Calendra* spp) sometimes feed in the lower part of the stem and crown of the wheat plant, causing the stems to die.

Only the most important known pests of wheat have been mentioned. Many other insects feed on the plant and at times some of them may be numerous enough to cause economic injury.

Great progress has been made in recent years by entomologists, in cooperation with chemists, plant breeders, and agricultural engineers, in the control of pests of wheat. New powerful insecticides have become available and modern means for their application, such as aircraft and improved ground equipment, have made it economically practical to treat large acreages of wheat infested by injurious insects. For example, nearly 2 million acres of wheat and other small grains in Oklahoma were treated with insecticides to control the greenbug in 1951. Grasshoppers, cutworms, aphids, and other insects feeding on the wheat plants can be readily controlled with insecticides. It is important now to discover the insect infestations early enough so that they can be treated with the proper insecticide before the crop is damaged.

On the other hand, some pests of wheat, such as sawflies, the wheat jointworm, and the wheat strawworm, all of which tunnel within the stems, cannot be controlled effectively with insecticides. Certain cropping practices or cultural control, and the use of resistant varieties of wheat when possible, must be depended upon to reduce infestations of such insects. The threat of serious damage by the hessian fly in the United States has largely disappeared as a result of the widespread adoption by growers of safe planting dates and, more recently, by the use of resistant varieties of wheat. Years ago it was discovered that wheat planted moderately late in the fall, after most of the hessian flies had disappeared, suffered little if any damage. Entomologists determine the safe dates for planting in each state and advise the growers. Fifteen varieties of wheat, some of the most important of which are Pawnee, Ponca, Dual, Monon, and Redcoat, are resistant to the hessian fly.

Most pests of wheat are controlled to some extent by their natural enemies, such as birds, rodents, insect parasites and predators, and disease. Usually, however, the amount of control by these agents is not sufficient to prevent serious crop damage by the injurious species.

Many species of insects attack stored wheat. In the United States, they are most abundant in the southern part of the country, where the winters are mild, and least abundant in the Canadian border states, where low winter temperatures usually kill them out annually. Infestations by these insects rarely start in the field, but rather develop after the grain is placed in storage, from small numbers living around the storage sites, often in waste grain, feed, or trash, or in hiding places in the storage bins themselves.

The most damage is done by those species that attack the sound kernels of wheat, such as the granary weevil (*Sitophilus granarius*), the rice weevil (*S. oryzae*), the lesser grain borer (*Rhyzopertha dominica*), and the Angoumois grain moth (*Sitotroga cerealella*). The larvae of all these species live within the wheat kernels and ruin them.

Many other insects are secondary pests of stored wheat, feeding on grain dust, broken or moldy kernels, or dockage, in both adult and larval stages. Their feeding activity may cause spoilage due to heating and an increase in moisture content of the grain. These insects are generally considered in groups, such as the flour moths, including the Indian-meal moth, Mediterranean flour moth, and meal moth; the grain and flour beetles, including the cadelle, the saw-toothed grain beetle, the confused flour beetle, and the flat grain beetle; the mealworms, including several species of beetles belonging to the Tenebrionidae; the fungus beetles; the dermestid beetles; and the spider beetles.

Damage to stored wheat from insects may be prevented by destroying the sources of infestation around the storage site, by thorough cleanup of waste grain or other material, by the application of insecticidal sprays to the interior walls of the empty bins, and by applying a protective spray to the wheat. Stored wheat should be inspected frequently and fumigated promptly when infestation is found.

Arlo M. Vance
Randall Latta
Entomologists, United States Department of Agriculture

4. Diseases of Wheat

Diseases of wheat are caused chiefly by fungi, bacteria, nematodes, and viruses. They cause enormous losses and are among the greatest of obstacles to efficient and stable production of wheat. Many of them are insidious and widely prevalent every year, others are destructive locally, while still others are widespread and become epidemic only in certain years. The amount of damage they cause varies greatly from season to season, and, for most diseases also from one field to another. In some areas, epidemics of diseases such as leaf and stem rusts, smuts, scabs, and root rot cause losses of 25 to 50 percent or more of the potential crop; sometimes there may be enormous losses over wide areas.

In 1916 one of the most disastrous epidemics of stem rust on record swept over the spring wheat-growing areas in the United States and Canada and destroyed approximately 280 million bushels of wheat. In 1935 and 1937 there were destructive epidemics of stem rust which virtually ruined the wheat crop in the upper Mississippi Valley. Again in 1953 a widespread and extremely destructive stem rust epidemic almost annihilated durum wheats in Minnesota and the Dakotas; the estimated loss for all durum wheats was 65 percent of the potential crop. In most countries rusts are definitely a limiting factor in wheat improvement and production. Because of frequent epidemics of certain diseases and the vast areas involved, it is difficult to estimate accurately the average annual percentage of loss caused by diseases of wheat. In many parts of the world it usually amounts to 10 to 15 percent or more of the potential crop.

The more important diseases of wheat are: stem rust caused by *Puccinia graminis* var. *tritici;* leaf rust caused by *P. recondita;* stripe rust caused by *P. striiformis;* bunt caused by *Tilletia foetida* and *T. caries;* scab or fusarium head blight caused by many species of *Fusarium,* particularly *F. graminearum;* and seedling blight and root rot also caused by many species of fungi, especially of the genera *Fusarium, Helminthosporium, Pythium,* and by *Ophiobolus graminis.* In addition there are many other diseases of less importance. These may be of considerable economic consequence in some areas every year and in some years they may cause severe damage, particularly when susceptible varieties are grown.

Bunt or stinking smut since historical times has been one of the major diseases of wheat. Bunt decreases yield, creates difficulties in threshing and processing, and lowers the quality of the grain. It is worldwide in distribution, although it is usually more prevalent in the drier regions of the world. In the United States, bunt is particularly destructive in the Pacific Northwest. In contrast, loose smut, *Ustilago tritici,* is prevalent only in regions where there is high relative humidity during the blooming period in wheat—a situation which is usually encountered in the soft winter wheat regions of the United States.

Stinking smut usually modifies the spike so that each kernel or seed is replaced by a smut ball that contains 5 to 10 million blackish spores (called chlamydospores). A fishlike odor, caused by trimethylamine, is characteristic, hence the name stinking smut. Smutty wheat commands a lower price on the market because spores adhere to threshed grain and must be washed off before milling.

Fusarium head blight (scab) damages wheat severely, especially in the corn belt where temperature and relative humidity are high during the blossoming period. The growth of the fungus (species *Fusarium*) in the developing kernel results in the production of substances toxic to man and certain animals. Violent nausea and stomach soreness result from eating scabbed grain. In Russia where infected grain was once used extensively for making bread, the product was known as intoxicating bread. At present scabby kernels are removed effectively from seed lots by cleaning equipment; hence scabby kernels do not occur in large quantities in milled-wheat products. Certain animals, especially pigs, strongly dislike scabby grain and fail to make normal gains in body weight when fed scabby wheat and barley.

Root rots of wheat are caused by many microorganisms and are among the more important diseases of wheat. They are debilitating, insidious, and usually inconspicuous. The destructiveness varies greatly with the season, the locality, and the variety of wheat grown. The pathogens live on or in the seed, soil, and dead plants. They invade all underground parts of the plant and induce seedling blight, root decay, and premature death of older plants. They tend to multiply in the soil when wheat or other susceptible crops are grown year after year.

Since the soil is actually teeming with microscopic life—protozoa, bacteria, fungi, and nematodes—there is actually a biological warfare among them. Because of such intense competition among soil organisms many of the pathogens are destroyed, including those that cause bunt, scab, foliage blight, and root rot; hence many diseases fail to develop. In fact, if it were not for this constant natural biological warfare in the soil, it would be virtually impossible to grow wheat continuously on our vast prairies and plains.

Sources of Infection. Wheat kernels frequently are invaded and discolored by fungi and bacteria. Such seeds often are the source of primary infection for root-rotting pathogens, especially species of *Fusarium* and *Helminthosporium.* Moreover, badly discolored seeds—a condition known as black point—are undesirable in making semolina. In addition, storage molds, usually *Aspergillus* and *Penicillium* species, often invade the kernels after harvest and cause "sick wheat," making such wheat undesirable for milling and baking. If the wheat is stored at moisture contents above 13 percent, molds grow into the germ of the grain and gradually weaken and finally kill it. In most seed lots the infection by storage molds is invisible and can be detected only by special techniques.

The microorganisms that cause rusts, smuts, mildew, root rot, foliage blight, and other diseases of wheat are living, moldlike parasitic plants. They grow, hybridize, and produce spores ("seeds") by which they multiply and spread. Under environmental conditions favorable to their growth, the spores germinate and penetrate the wheat plant where they establish parasitic relationships. Bacteria, viruses, and nematodes also cause destructive diseases of wheat.

Pathogens such as fungi and bacteria are readily carried on or in the seed, by insects, and by wind. The wind is the most effective agent of dissemination of many fungi. Spores of rust and other pathogens have been caught more than three miles above the ground and there is good circumstantial evidence that they are carried hundreds of miles by strong winds. As insects and wind have no respect for national boundaries, many diseases are of international importance.

Sometimes stem and leaf rust spores settle down at the rate of 1 million or more per square foot in a 24-hour period. An acre of wheat with 10 percent rust infection would produce 20 pounds of rust spores and there are about 180 billion spores (uredospores) in a pound. In epidemic years there are vast areas of wheat with 65 to 95 percent of rust infection, and the enormous number of spores produced on 20 to 30 million acres of wheat is almost incredible. In the fall the rust spores are usually blown from Canada and northern United States southward where they initiate new infection on winter wheat. Obviously, the control of rust is an international problem.

Parasitic Races of Fungi. Not only are diseases of wheat caused by many distinct species of fungi but most of the species comprise many parasitic races. Thus, within the species of *Helminthosporium sativum* there are hundreds of distinct cultural races that can be identified as such when grown on artificial media. Many of these races differ greatly in their parasitic capabilities on wheat and other cereals. Perhaps *Puccinia graminis* var. *tritici* (stem rust) is a better example of physiologic specialization. In the variety *tritici* of stem rust, more than 300 distinct parasitic races are delimited and there are perhaps many more. Further, each race consists of many biotypes with minor differences.

Rusts are obligate parasites, and spores from races of the same species are similar under the microscope. Hence, races of a rust can only be distinguished and identified by their parasitic effect on certain varieties of wheat, called rust differentials. Each such wheat variety may be resistant to some races, moderately resistant to others, and completely susceptible to still others. Extensive rust surveys over much of the world indicate that the prevalence of races may vary from one place to another and from one year to another. Thus, a variety of wheat may be resistant in one area or country but completely susceptible in another, and vice versa, because of the existence of different races of the pathogen and the precedence or predominance of different races in different countries at a specified time.

Changing Disease Problems. Disease problems in wheat are continually changing, chiefly because new pathogens evolve, or are introduced from other regions. Sometimes problems change because minor diseases become major diseases. The probability of establishing a foreign pathogen or new virulent race of a native pathogen is even greater now than it was in the past because of the mass movement of many materials and men throughout the world.

The introduction of a new variety of wheat frequently brings about tremendous shifts in the prevalence of diseases hitherto considered unimportant in a particular region. When Marquis wheat replaced Preston, Haynes bluestem, and Glyndon fife in spring wheat regions from 1910 on, scab, hitherto a minor disease, became a major one, whereas the bunt problem decreased greatly. Then, with the introduction of the two stem rust resistant varieties, Kota and Ceres, about 1925, leaf rust, bunt, and loose smut became major diseases simply because these varieties were especially susceptible to certain races of the fungi that cause these diseases and that were present when the new varieties were grown. The release of many other varieties has repeatedly shifted the relative importance of diseases. Population shifts in the prevalence of parasitic races frequently are responsible for severe rust attacks on varieties that are resistant to the previously prevalent rust races.

Extensive surveys have shown that the prevalence and distribution of physiologic races of rust may change gradually over a period of many years or they may change rapidly in a single year. Stem rust race 56 was first found near rusted barberries in the North Central United States in 1928, but it did not become widely prevalent until 1935 when it virtually eliminated the growing of the wheat variety Ceres. Race 15 B, found occasionally near barberry bushes in the Eastern United States prior to 1950, became the dominant race in the United States and Canada in that year, and in the following year it became prevalent also in Mexico. This race attacks all of the commercial, hitherto resistant varieties of wheat, and it was responsible for the destructive epidemic in the hard red spring and durum wheat areas in the United States and Canada in 1950 and 1953.

Past history has shown that new races of the bunt fungus developed following the release of a new bunt-resistant variety of wheat in the Pacific Northwest. The population of the new races of bunt is greatest in regions where the new smut-resistant varieties are grown. If a new race of a pathogen can attack a so-called resistant variety, then the chances are good that the more extensively this variety is grown, the more rapidly will the new race multiply. Thus, a new variety may appear to lose its resistance, but in most cases it can be demonstrated that this is due to the increase of new parasitic races of the pathogen.

Hybridization of Plant Pathogens. Plant pathogens are not static; they hybridize and mutate just as higher plants do. Many new and virulent races of smuts and rusts have been produced by hybridization between existing races or biotypes. Fertile interspecific hybrids have been obtained by hybridization between two species of smut, *Tilletia caries* and *T. foetida.*

Hybridization frequently results in marked changes in pathogenicity, and new races often are produced that are more virulent than the parents. New races may attack hitherto resistant varieties of wheat that have recently been released to growers. The practical importance of hybridization in nature is most clearly apparent in stem rust.

Races of stem rust can hybridize readily on common barberry, and apparently this occurs frequently in nature. As many as 18 races have been derived from a single cross between biotypes of a single race. Extensive studies made cooperatively by the United States Department of Agriculture and the University of Minnesota have shown that different kinds of races and biotypes are 10 to 20 times more numerous near barberries than away from them.

The sexual stage of stem rust occurs only on barberry and this has been one of the major reasons for the eradication of rust-susceptible barberries in at least 18 states. The role of barberries, however, in the production of initial inoculum resulting in primary infection centers was of tremendous importance before these bushes were eradicated from spring wheat areas. Although more than 448 million barberry bushes have been destroyed, some still remain and the campaign to eliminate them continues.

Treatment and Control. Although many diseases of wheat such as root rots, scab, and bunt cannot be completely prevented, particularly where wheat is grown extensively and intensively, they can be materially reduced by good agricultural practices. Sound seed of recommended varieties should be treated with a fungicide to eliminate the pathogens from the seed and to protect the seed and seedlings against soil- and seed-borne organisms, such as species of *Fusarium, Helminthosporium, Pythium,* and *Tilletia.* The seed should be sown only deep enough to provide adequate moisture for germination. Also, a good cropping sequence should be followed. The seedbeds should be well prepared, and fertilizers should be applied if there is a deficiency of essential elements. As varieties differ greatly in susceptibility, only the varieties recommended for particular regions should be grown in those localities.

Despite many difficulties in controlling plant diseases, much progress has been made in the development of disease-resistant varieties of wheat. Although varieties may be only temporarily resistant, they have greatly reduced the danger of destructive epidemics and lowered the cost of production. Since most pathogens consist not only of parasitic races but also of biotypes, collections of them from diverse sources must be used in testing for disease resistance. Because of the frequent shifts in diseases and in parasitic races, the breeding program for the development of resistant varieties of wheat must be carried on continuously.

J. J. Christensen
Department of Plant Pathology and Botany
University of Minnesota

Bibliography

Ackroyd, W. R., and Doughty, Joyce, *Wheat in Human Nutrition* (Univ. of Toronto Press 1970).
Britnell, G. E., *Wheat Economy* (Univ. of Toronto Press 1974).
Brumfield, Kirby, *This Was Wheat Farming* (Superior Pub. 1968).
Evans, L. T., and Peacock, W. J., eds., *Wheat Science—Today and Tomorrow* (Cambridge 1981).
Ferns, G. K., and others, *Australian Wheat Varieties: Identification According to Growth, Head and Grain Characteristics* (Intl. Specialized Bk. Ser. 1977).
Hadwiger, Don F., *Federal Wheat Commodity Programs* (Iowa State Univ. Press 1970).
Inglett, George E., *Wheat: Production and Utilization* (Avi 1974).
International Maize and Wheat Improvement Center, *Bibliography of Wheat* (Scarecrow 1971).
Kihara, H., *Wheat Studies: Retrospects and Prospects, The Birthplace of Genetical Research on Wheat* (Elsevier Pub. Co. 1982).
Quisenberry, K. S., and Reitz, L. P., eds., *Wheat and Wheat Improvement* (Am. Soc. of Agronomics 1967).
Villareal, Reynaldo L., and Klatt, Arthur P., eds., *Wheats for More Tropical Environments* (Agribookstore/Winrock 1985).

WHEAT GERM, the embryo of the wheat seed, comprising about 2 to 3 percent, by weight, of the entire kernel. There is special interest in wheat germ from the nutritional standpoint, because it is a rich source of certain vitamins, especially vitamin E, and also because the oil it contains has a considerably higher proportion of unsaturated fatty acids than is found in animal fats.

Structure. The germ lies near the base of the wheat kernel on the side opposite the crease (see figures under Wheat). The germ is made up of an embryonic plant partly surrounded by a shield-shaped structure, the scutellum, to which it is connected by conducting tissues. The embryonic plant, or embryonic axis, is composed of a rudimentary stem and leaves protected by the enclosing coleoptile, and the primary root, which is covered by the coleorhiza. Two pairs of secondary lateral roots are also present. All tissues of the embryonic axis are, as the name implies, in a rudimentary state. At the time of germination, they develop to form the seedling plant.

The scutellum contains food, chiefly oil and protein, for development of the embryonic axis during germination. On the side that is embedded in the endosperm, the surface cells of the scutellum (scutellar epithelium) are modified to carry out digestion and absorption of food from the endosperm at the time of germination. The entire germ forms a separate structure within the kernel, so that there is no need to break cell walls to separate the germ from the endosperm (the part from which flour is made) and the bran. However, there is a very thin layer of amorphous material between the endosperm and the scutellar epithelium that tends to cement the two structures together. For good separation, the amorphous cementing layer must be softened to weaken its adhesive power.

Separation. Wheat germ is produced in the United States as a byproduct of milling for flour production. The germ is flattened by sizing rolls following the first reduction grinding. This is possible because the larger content of both oil and water in germ than in the endosperm, which, in being reduced to flour particles, allows the former to be more easily flattened without breaking. The friable pieces of endosperm pass through a sieve on which the flattened germs are retained. The latter constitutes "mill germ." In some countries, special milling systems are used for germ separation.

Composition. A number of analyses have been made of germ hand-dissected from the kernel. More commonly, however, data have been obtained for mill germ, which not only contains small amounts of bran and endosperm, but also usually lacks a portion of the scutellum. The composition of mill germ is variable, depending on how much the fraction differs from pure germ. In general, however, it more or less closely reflects the composition of the pure germ. The accompanying table shows the approximate amount of most of the important constituents in pure germ.

COMPOSITION OF WHEAT GERM
HAND-DISSECTED FROM THE KERNEL
(on basis of 14% moisture content)

Constituent	Part of germ	Amount
Protein	Total	26–28 percent
Sugars	Total	17–18 percent of defatted germ
Lipids	Total	20 percent
Phosphorus	Total	1.5–1.75 percent
Thiamine	Embryonic axis	5–25 parts per million
	Scutellum	130–240 parts per million
Niacin	Embryonic axis	30–55 parts per million
	Scutellum	40 parts per million
Pyridoxin as the hydrochloride	Total	23 parts per million
Pantothenic acid as the calcium salt	Embryonic axis	18 parts per million
	Scutellum	15 parts per million
Riboflavin	Embryonic axis	15 parts per million
	Scutellum	14 parts per million

Wheat germ also contains numerous enzymes, including phytase, lipase, lipoxidase, amylase, proteinase, dipetidase, phosphomonoesterase, and others. Phosphatases and catalases of wheat, for example, are largely concentrated in the germ. Mineral constituents that have been reported to occur in wheat germ include potassium, phosphorus, magnesium, calcium, iron, manganese, zinc, sulfur, copper, aluminum, sodium, lead, tin, silver, silicon, nickel, and traces of cobalt and boron. The lipids of the germ contain sterols, tocopherols, and pigments, as well as wheat oil. The vitamin E activity of mill germ is reported to be about 165 to 320 parts per million, the exact amount probably depending largely upon the purity of the mill fraction. Wheat oil is of the linoleic acid type, in contrast to corn and rice oils, which are of the oleic-linoleic acid type. Unlike the other commercial cereal oils, wheat oil contains an appreciable amount of linolenic acid (reported amounts range from 3.5 to 29.2 percent).

The germ pigments are considered to be chiefly xanthophylls.

Uses.—Wheat germ is used chiefly as a valuable nutritional component of animal feeds. A relatively small percentage of the wheat germ produced in the United States is used as a specialty food adjunct. Another small percentage is processed for separation of wheat oil, by either hydraulic expression or solvent extraction. The oil is used principally, in the United States, as a specialty product supplying natural vitamin E and unsaturated fatty acids for nutritional supplement. The oil cake remaining after removal of the oil from mill germ is used in animal feeds.

The high degree of unsaturation of the fatty acids in wheat oil raises the problem of rancidity that may occur in both the oil and the undefatted germ. This is why germ is removed from flour and the flour enriched with pure vitamins to compensate.

MAJEL M. MACMASTERS,
Professor of Flour and Feed Milling Industries. Kansas State University.

WHEATEAR, hwēt'ĭr, the name applied to thrushes of the chat group, comprising the genus *Oenanthe,* about 12 in all. They inhabit open rocky or desert country. The common wheatear, *O. oenanthe,* inhabits northern Asia and Europe, including the British Isles. In summer it reaches Alaska and Greenland in small numbers, and is called the Greenland wheatear in American usage. About six inches long, the bird has a gray back, black tail and wings, and a conspicuously white rump, from which it derives its name—an adaptation of "white rear." Its blue eggs, up to six in number, are laid in a nest of wool, fur, and grass, hidden in a crevice in a rock or in a rodent burrow. All the other species of wheatears are seen exclusively in the Old World, chiefly in the stony deserts of Asia and Africa; they are conspicuously black and white in color.

DEAN AMADON.

WHEATLEY, hwēt'lĭ, **Phillis,** Afro-American poet: b. Africa, 1753?; d. Boston, Mass., Dec. 5, 1784. Brought to Boston as a slave while still a child, she was purchased by John Wheatley, a tailor, as a servant for his wife. In the Wheatley household she learned to read English and the rudiments of Latin, and became versed in mythology, ancient history, and the contemporary English poets. She wrote her first verses when she was 13 years old, and published her first in 1770. When she was about 20 years old she was taken to England, where she was cordially received and became greatly popular because of her personality and her easy conversation.

The first bound volume of her verse, published in 1773 and dedicated to Selina Hastings, Countess of Huntington, was *Poems on Various Subjects, Religious and Moral, by Phillis Wheatley, Negro Servant to Mr. John Wheatley of Boston, in New England.* After her return to America, she published several poems, including an address to George Washington. In 1778, the Wheatley family having been broken up by death and Phillis Wheatley having been granted her freedom, she married John Peters, a free black. She died in extreme want.

In 1834 Margaretta M. Odell published the *Memoir and Poems of Phillis Wheatley,* and in 1864 appeared *The Letters of Phillis Wheatley, the Negro Slave-Poet of Boston.* The work of Wheatley was imitative but well fashioned, and it won much praise from critics.

WHEATON, hwē'tən, **Henry,** American jurist and diplomat: b. Providence, R.I., Nov. 27, 1785; d. Dorchester, Mass., March 11, 1848. After he was graduated from Rhode Island College (now Brown University) in 1802, he studied law in France, and began his practice as an attorney in Providence.

He later became editor of a political journal, and subsequently a justice in New York. In 1816 he became reporter for the Supreme Court of the United States; his reports, published in 12 volumes, are exceptionally complete, with valuable annotations.

Wheaton began his diplomatic career in 1827 as chargé d'affaires to Denmark, the first regular diplomatic agent from the United States to that nation. During his tenure in Copenhagen, he negotiated a treaty, which later became the prototype of similar agreements with France and Naples, settling the question of indemnity for seizure of American ships. In 1835 he was appointed chargé d'affaires to the court of Prussia, and two years later was created minister plenipotentiary, an office he retained until 1846. He negotiated a treaty in 1844 for the reduction of import duties between the United States and Germany; the treaty, although rejected by the United States Senate, served as a basis for subsequent agreements.

Wheaton is also remembered as a scholar. His most widely known work is *Elements of International Law,* published in 1836, and later translated into French, Italian, Spanish, Chinese, and Japanese. Elected to membership in the Scandinavian and Icelandic literary societies in 1830, Wheaton the following year published *History of the Northmen,* a book that supported the theory of the exploration of North America by Scandinavian sailors centuries before Christopher Columbus. He was elected to the French Institute in 1842, and the Prussian Academy of Science in 1843.

His writings include *Some Accounts of the Life, Writings, and Speeches of William Pinkney* (1826); *Histoire du progrès du droit des gens en Europe . . .* (1841; English tr., *History of the Law of Nations in Europe, and America . . .* 1845); and *An Inquiry into the Validity of the British Claim of a Right to Visitation and Search of American Vessels* (1842).

WHEATON, city, Illinois, seat of Du Page County, 26 miles west of Chicago, at an altitude of 760 feet. Primarily a residential community, Wheaton is in an agricultural region (corn, oats, and barley), and has light manufacturing and nurseries. It is the seat of Wheaton College (q.v.), and the headquarters of the Theosophical Society of America. Elbert H. Gary, a steel industry pioneer, was born here.

Settled in 1837 by Jesse and Warren Wheaton of Pomfret, Conn., Wheaton was incorporated as a village in 1859, and in 1890 was chartered as a city. The former estate of the late Robert R. McCormick, owner of the Chicago *Tribune,* located near Wheaton, has been converted into the Robert R. McCormick Museum and the Cantigny War Memorial Museum of the First Division. Government of the city is by commission. Population: 43,043.

WHEATON COLLEGE, an independent Christian coeducational institution of liberal arts and science in Wheaton, Ill. Founded in 1853 as Illinois Institute, it was chartered as Wheaton College in 1860. A graduate school of theology was added in 1936, and a school of nursing in 1947. The college offers work leading to the bachelor of arts and bachelor of science degrees in various arts and sciences, including preprofessional courses in medicine, law, theology, dentistry, and engineering, a course in professional chemistry, and professional music courses leading to the bachelor of music and the bachelor of music in education degrees. There is a teacher-training program for elementary and high school teachers which is approved by the National Council for Accreditation of Teacher Education. The graduate school and seminary awards the master of arts degree in Christian education, Old Testament, New Testament, church history, and theology, and the bachelor of divinity degree.

The original campus was donated by Warren Wheaton, one of the founders of the city of Wheaton. About 75 percent of the student body comes from outside Illinois, including 30 foreign countries. More than 1,700 full-time students are registered in the college. The library has approximately 115,000 volumes. School colors are orange and blue; athletic teams are nicknamed the "Crusaders."

ENOCK C. DYRNESS.

WHEATON COLLEGE, a nondenominational college of arts and sciences for women, located in Norton, Mass., 30 miles from Boston. It was one of the pioneer institutions in education for women. Founded in 1834 by Judge Laban Wheaton in memory of his daughter, Eliza Wheaton Strong, who died in that year, the institution was first named Wheaton Female Seminary. It received its first students in 1835, and was incorporated in 1837. Under Dr. Samuel Valentine Cole, one of its outstanding presidents, it was chartered by an act of the Massachusetts legislature in 1912 as Wheaton College, thus becoming the first educational institution in the Old Colony, the land settled by the Pilgrims.

Wheaton College draws the majority of its students from New England and the Middle Atlantic states, but also numbers in its enrollment women from the rest of the United States and from other nations. It has almost 700 students, and a faculty of 65. The campus contains 33 buildings. The college provides honors work, independent work, tutorial or seminar work for senior majors, and interdepartmental courses and majors. Its library contains about 73,000 volumes.

WHEATSTONE, hwēt'stōn, **SIR Charles,** English scientist and inventor: b. Gloucester, England, February 1802; d. Paris, France, Oct. 19, 1875. He entered business in London as a maker of musical instruments, and early attracted the attention of scientists with his experiments in the field of sound. In 1834 he was appointed professor of experimental philosophy in King's College, London, and in the same year exhibited experiments for measuring the speed of light, using a half mile of copper wire. He then conceived the idea of applying this apparatus to telegraphic equipment, and, in 1837, he and William F. Cooke obtained the first patent for a magnetic telegraph; however, no practical application of the principle was made until after the telegraph devised by Samuel F. B. Morse (q.v.) had been put into operation. Wheatstone was also active in the fields of submarine telegraphy, vision, magnetoelectric machines, and cryptography. He is credited with the invention of the rheostat and the stereoscope. He became a fellow of the Royal Society in 1836, and was also a corresponding member of the Academie des Sciences, of Paris, and of the principal scientific societies of Europe. He was knighted in 1868. Although he left no major writings, he was the author of numerous papers on scientific subjects, published in professional journals. A volume of his collected writings was brought out after his death, in 1879.

WHEATSTONE BRIDGE, a commonly used instrument for measuring electrical resistance. Invented in 1833 by Samuel Hunter Christie, it was publicized in 1843 by Sir Charles Wheatstone

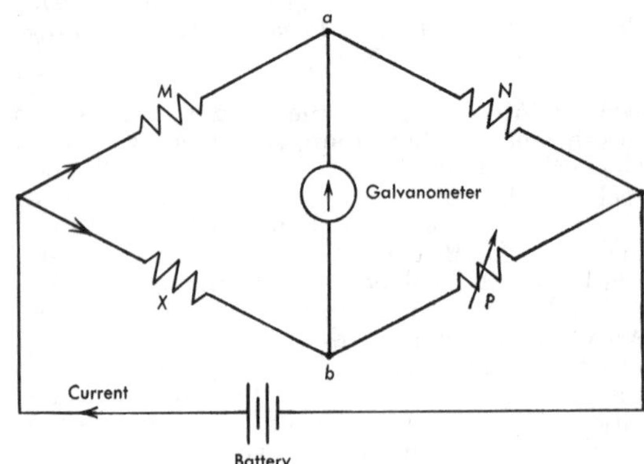

(q.v.), who showed its application to electrical measurement. The circuit is shown in the accompanying figure, in which *M* and *N* are known resistances, *P* is a variable known resistance, and *X* is the unknown resistance to be measured. To make the measurement, *P* is adjusted until the galvanometer shows no current flowing from *a* to *b*. It is then true that

$$X = \frac{M}{N}P.$$

The usefulness of the circuit is due to the fact that the accuracy of the results depends only on the accuracy with which the resistances *M*, *N*, and *P* are known, and on the sensitivity of the galvanometer to small currents. Measurements accurate to 0.1 percent are readily made of resistances from small fractions of 1 ohm to several hundred thousand ohms. Below 0.1 ohm, the resistances of the connections begin to affect the results, and above 1,000,000 ohms, the circuit currents are often too low for an ordinary galvanometer.

J. E. NANKIVELL,
Research Assistant Professor of Physics, Stevens Institute of Technology.

WHEEL, hwēl, a mechanical device providing rotary motion by means of a disk or circular frame revolving on an axis. The rotary motion provided by the wheel is so basic to machinery that it is doubtful that mechanized civilization could have developed without it. Since the invention of the wheel in protohistoric times, its exploitation has gradually brought innumerable derivatives. It led first to a revolution in land transport; subsequently, by a series of mutations, machines were devised to lessen labor, increase its efficiency, and substitute power sources for the limited muscular capacities of man and beast. Enumeration of even a few of the derived forms suggests the magnitude of developments from the wheel: revolving shafts, pulleys, gears, and flywheels are involved in complex devices such as turbines, internal combustion engines, and electric motors. Some permit application of power directly at a working point, as in the winch and the circular saw; others transform natural sources of power into forms that can be transmitted, as in the windmill and the dynamo.

A wheel operates as an infinite series of levers. In a cartwheel, for example, each spoke is a lever, with the rim on the ground as its fulcrum. A connecting rod at an intermediate point on the radius of the wheel, as in a locomotive drive wheel, delivers power to the rim, the axle serving as the fulcrum. Reversing this, with a fixed axle, power applied to the rim provides reciprocating motion to a connecting rod. A set of gears of different sizes modifies power or speed in proportion to the lengths of their radii. Not only does a wheel, in effect, lever its load forward, but in contrast to a dragged object, it also minimizes friction. A man or horse is thus able to pull a load many times as great as he could carry on his back.

Early History. Knowledge of the wheel's origin can be projected from its earliest known form, the two-wheeled cart of the Bronze Age in Sumer (3500 B.C.). Like all inventions it involved a combination of previously known devices. For 2,000 years rollers had been used to move heavy weights; loads had been transported on dry-land sledges or shafts dragged by animals; and plows were drawn by pairs of oxen. With rollers under such sledges, held in place by guides, traction was greatly improved. The sequence may have been, first, to trim the excess at the middle of the roller to overcome difficulties with the guides, leaving the ends as rudimentary wheels; and then to mount free-turning wheels on fixed axles. The difficulty of cutting cross sections of sufficiently large logs with inadequate tools was surmounted by forming solid disks of three sections of plank crossed by two battens. The earliest vehicles had a single pole, indicating that pairs of plow oxen were put to the new task. The point of origin is uncertain: it may have been inner Asia, for all that the archaeological record points to the Near East.

Wheeled vehicles were known in Sumer in 3500 B.C.; Assyria, 3000 B.C.; Indus Valley, 2500 B.C.; central and northern Europe, soon after 1000 B.C.; and Britain, about 500 B.C. This sequence indicates a single origin of the wheel, and its subsequent slow adoption over the Old World. The only other independent invention approximating the wheel is from ancient Mexico, where toy clay animals resting on clay tubes acting as rollers have been found, but there is no indication that practical application followed.

Evolution and Applications. The earliest wheeled vehicles had limited use until inherent problems were solved. The four-wheeled wagon, almost as old as the cart, could be steered only by lifting it bodily until a swiveling front axle was devised. Draft by pairs of oxen or asses was slow. With the introduction of the swifter horse from the Asiatic steppes into Mesopotamia just after 2000 B.C., the cart was transformed into a lighter military chariot. The spoked wheel then widely adopted was first given a tire or binding of leather, later of copper. To withstand wear wheels were provided with studs, or the spokes were extended through the rims.

CHRISTOPHER S. JOHNSON/STOCK, BOSTON

Belted wheels, such as these used to transfer power from waterwheels, appeared in Europe in the Middle Ages.

The first adaptation of the wheel for a machine was the waterwheel. A horizontal wheel set in a flowing stream, with its vertical shaft turning a millstone above, spread from the Near East in the 1st century B.C. Not long after, Roman engineers devised the more efficient vertical wheel to raise water for irrigation and, with simple gears, to operate flour mills. Extended use followed the development of the even more effective overshot wheel in the 3d century A.D. Greatly expanded employment came in the early Middle Ages when the waterwheel operated mechanical hammers, ore stamp mills, and bellows by means of cams. Windmills (see WINDMILL) harnessed another natural source of energy. The Eastern type, turning on a vertical axle, originated in Persia in the 5th to 7th centuries A.D.; probably independently, in western Europe, windmills with horizontal shafts first appeared in the 12th century. Pulleys were in use before 1500 B.C.; in the 1st century A.D. they were used in cranes where the windlass was powered by men inside a huge wheel built as a treadmill.

The adaptation of wheels as gears was a conceptual leap. Engaging wheel rims to transmit or modify motion is not obvious, and the invention may have been due in part to accidental juxtaposition of studded wheels. The first gear set was a pair of toothed wheels, axles at right angles, in vertical waterwheels. Cyclometers to be attached to vehicles, involving multiple gears, were invented about the 1st century B.C. and ultimately became the source of clock mechanisms. Far more sophisticated reduction gears and belted wheels did not make their appearance until the Middle Ages.

Other mechanisms providing rotary motion, as old or older than the wheel, entered into machine combinations with it. The weighted spindle was employed from Neolithic times for spinning thread; the spinning wheel, coupling this with a wheel, was an ancient Asiatic invention which reached Europe in the Middle Ages. The so-called potter's wheel (q.v.), a flywheel (q.v.), probably antedating the cart, was developed by pivoting the plate on which clay was hand molded. Equally ancient is the rotary hand mill (two superimposed stones for grinding flour), to which waterwheel power was added shortly before the Christian era. Grinding disks rotated by crank were known in China about 1500 B.C.; the independently invented grindstone reached Europe after 500 A.D. Two devices, essentially rotating shafts, may have appeared independently of the wheel, but became elaborated under its stimulus: the lathe, dating from the 2d millennium B.C. in Egypt and put to widespread use by the Greeks after the 7th century B.C.; and the windlass, which came into use about 1000 B.C.

See also WHEEL AND AXLE.

LESLIE SPIER,
Late Professor of Anthropology, University of New Mexico.

Further Reading: Hall, A. Rupert, and Smith, Norman, *A History of Technology*, 8th ed. (Mansell 1984); Piggott, Stuart, *The Earliest Wheeled Transport: From the Atlantic Coast to the Caspian Sea* (Cornell Univ. Press 1983); Turner, Susan, *Wheels and Grindstones* (Strode Pub. 1980).

WHEEL AND AXLE, one of the so-called six simple machines, incorporating the basic principles of most hoisting machines. In its fundamental form, it consists of a large wheel, often grooved, rigidly mounted on an axle. A rope or chain is attached to the grooved rim and another to the axle. A small force applied to the wheel is sufficient to lift a heavy load at the end of the rope on the axle, but through a shorter distance; the ratio is in proportion to the circumference of the axle to that of the wheel. The mechanical advantage thus equals the circumference, or radius, of the wheel, divided by the circumference, or radius, of the axle. The wheel may be replaced by a crank and the axle by a drum or cylinder, as in the windlass, winch, and capstan, or both may be replaced by gears of different sizes, as in bicycle sprockets and the mechanism of ice-cream freezers.

FRANK DORR.

WHEEL ANIMALCULES. See ROTIFERA.

WHEEL CRANK. See CRANK.

WHEEL LOCK. See SMALL ARMS.

WHEELBARROW, hwēl'băr-ō, a hand-pushed vehicle, consisting of a boxlike or dish-shaped body supported on two shafts, arranged in a V with handles at the spread end and a wheel and axle at the point. The wheelbarrow is a lever of the second class (see LEVER), with the fulcrum at the axle, the force applied at the handles, and the load or resistance between the two, in the body. It is used by laborers, farmers, gardeners, and others for transporting loads too heavy or bulky to be carried by hand, and is similar to hand trucks used by warehousemen and industrial workers, except that the latter have two wheels. Modern wheelbarrows are made of wood or of a light metal, such as aluminum, and have a rubber tire on the wheel. A two-wheeled vehicle for carrying garden material is more properly called a garden cart.

FRANK DORR.

WHEELER, hwē'lər, **Benjamin Ide,** American scholar and educator: b. Randolph, Mass., July 15, 1854; d. Vienna, Austria, May 2, 1927. After receiving his bachelor of arts degree in 1875 and his master of arts in 1878, both from Brown University, he taught in high school and at Brown, traveled and studied in Germany, and in 1885 won his doctorate at the University of Heidelberg in Germany. He returned to the United States as instructor of Latin at Harvard University, and then went to Cornell University in 1886 as professor of Greek and comparative philology. He remained at Cornell until 1899, and during this period wrote most of his scholarly works. In 1899 he became president of the University of California in Berkeley, and during the following 20 years guided that institution's growth into one of the largest and foremost universities in the United States. In 1909–1910 he returned to Germany as Theodore Roosevelt professor at the University of Berlin; a course of his lectures there was later published under the title *Unterricht und Demokratie in Amerika* (1910). Wheeler retired from the University of California in 1919 as professor of comparative philology and president emeritus.

His writings include: *Analogy and the Scope of Its Application to Language* (1887); *Introduction to the Study of the History of Language* (1891); *Organization of Higher Education in the United States* (1896); and *Alexander the Great: The Merging of East and West in Universal History* (1900).

WHEELER, Burton Kendall, American senator and lawyer: b. Hudson, Mass., Feb. 27, 1882; d. Washington, D. C., Jan. 7, 1975. He attended the University of Michigan (LL. B., 1905), was admitted to the Montana bar in 1906, and practiced law in Butte until 1911, when he was elected to the Montana state legislature. From 1913 to 1918 he served as federal district attorney for Montana, and in 1922 was elected to the United States Senate for the first time, campaigning as a Democrat. He was presidential candidate Robert M. La Follette's running mate on the Progressive Party ticket in 1924, but after the party was defeated Wheeler reentered the Democratic Party. After the election of President Franklin D. Roosevelt in 1932, Wheeler generally supported Roosevelt's New Deal, but opposed the proposed Judiciary Reorganization Bill in 1937, and was one of the leaders of the isolationist movement in the years immediately preceding the entry of the United States into World War II. He vigorously opposed the preparedness bill and the lend-lease bill of 1941, and also spoke out against repealing three sections of the Neutrality Act of 1939. After serving four terms in the Senate, Wheeler was defeated in the 1946 primaries, and returned to the practice of law in Montana.

WHEELER, John Neville, American newspaper executive: b. Yonkers, N.Y., April 11, 1886; d. Ridgefield, Conn., Oct. 13, 1973. A sportswriter for the New York *Herald*, he formed the Wheeler Syndicate in 1913 to specialize in sports features, and arranged with Harry Conway (Bud) Fisher, one of the first comic strip artists, and Fontaine Talbot Fox, Jr., well-known cartoonist, for the release of their work; Fisher received a guarantee of $52,000 a year, the highest payment ever made to a newspaper artist up to that time. In World War I the syndicate sent Richard Harding Davis, noted writer and war correspondent, to Belgium, where he produced notable reports on early actions. Lacking full stock control in the syndicate, Wheeler sold out to the McClure Syndicate (oldest American newspaper syndicate, founded in 1884) in 1916 but immediately formed the Bell Syndicate. After World War I (in which he served at home and in France as a field artillery lieutenant), he persuaded Ring Lardner, writer, to contribute to the Bell Syndicate, while Fisher and Fox also joined the group. From 1924 to 1926 Wheeler served as both the executive editor of *Liberty* as well as Bell Syndicate director.

In 1930, he became general manager of the North American Newspaper Alliance, Inc. (NANA), which had been formed in 1922 by 50 major United States and Canadian newspapers. At the same time, NANA absorbed the Bell Syndicate, the Associated Newspapers, Inc. (a service formed in 1912 by other major American newspapers), and Consolidated News Features, Inc., founded in 1920. In 1952, the McClure Syndicate was brought into the Bell-NANA combination, and in 1958 the Bell Syndicate bought effective stock control in NANA. Although comprising a single administrative unit, the various components in the Bell-NANA group have retained their separate corporate entities, with Wheeler, in 1961, serving as president and/or chairman of the board of each syndicate.

He is the author of *I've Got News for You* (1961).

ROBERT W. DESMOND,
Professor of Journalism, University of California.

WHEELER, Joseph, American soldier and legislator: b. near Augusta, Ga., Sept. 10, 1836; d. Brooklyn, N.Y., Jan. 25, 1906. A graduate of the United States Military Academy (1859), he resigned from the Army in April 1861 to join the Confederate forces. He became colonel of the 19th Alabama Infantry, fought with distinction at Shiloh (April 6–7, 1862), and in July 1862 was promoted to commander of cavalry of the Army of the Mississippi; subsequently he led the Confederate cavalry in the Western theater throughout the war, during which he rose to lieutenant general (February 1865) and earned the nickname "Fighting Joe."

During the Civil War, Wheeler participated with skill and energy in many significant engagements. He led General Braxton Bragg's advance into Kentucky in August and September of 1862, fought gallantly at Perryville (Oct. 8, 1862), and covered the retreat into Tennessee. He was prominent at Stone River (Dec. 31, 1862–Jan. 2, 1863), and Chickamauga (Sept. 19–20, 1863), and after the latter engagement made a brilliant raid into Union territory, destroying over 1,200 wagons with their valuable supplies. He also took part in the siege of Knoxville (Nov. 17–Dec. 4, 1863). During 1864–1865 he continuously harassed Gen. William T. Sherman's forces in their progress from Dalton to Atlanta, and on their match to the sea and through the Carolinas. Still only 28 when the war ended, he was classed by Gen. Robert E. Lee as one of the two outstanding Confederate cavalry leaders, the other being Gen. James Ewell Brown ("Jeb") Stuart.

After the war and a short residence in New Orleans, Wheeler became a planter and lawyer in Wheeler, Ala. (named in his honor). Elected to the United States House of Representatives, Wheeler served in Congress in 1881–1882, 1883, and 1885–1900, and was an outspoken advocate of reconciliation between the North and South. In the Spanish-American War of 1898 he returned to service as a major general of volunteers, defeated the Spanish at Las Guasimas (June 24), was present at the Battle of San Juan Hill (July 1), and participated in the siege of Santiago de Cuba. In 1899–1900 he briefly commanded a brigade in the insurrection in the Philippine Islands, and in September 1900 he retired, having been commissioned a brigadier general in the Regular Army. He was buried in Arlington National Cemetery. He wrote *Cavalry Tactics* (1863), "Bragg's Invasion of Kentucky," vol. 3, *Battles and Leaders of the Civil War* (1887–1888; new ed. 1956), and *The Santiago Campaign* (1898).

WHEELER, Wayne Bidwell, American prohibitionist and lawyer: b. near Brookfield, Ohio, Nov. 10, 1869; d. Battle Creek, Mich., Sept. 5, 1927. Graduating from Oberlin College in 1894, he became active in the Anti-Saloon League of Ohio and, upon realizing that it needed legal guidance, he went to law school at Western Reserve University, graduating in 1898. He immediately became attorney for the Ohio unit and later served as its superintendent (1904–1915) and as general counsel in Washington of the Anti-Saloon League of America (1915–1927). In the latter post, he worked militantly for prohibition on many fronts, at both the state and national levels, and played a leading role in obtaining the passage by Congress in 1919 of the Prohibition Amendment to the Constitution. The Amendment was subsequently ratified by the states.

WHEELER, William Almon, American legislator and businessman, and vice president of the United States: b. Malone, N.Y., June 30, 1819; d. there, June 4, 1887. He attended the University of Vermont for two years, was admitted to the bar in 1845, and in the earlier part of his career served as United States district attorney for Franklin County (1846–1849), Whig member of the New York Assembly (1850–1851), Republican state senator and president pro tem of the Senate (1858–1859), and member of the United States House of Representatives (1861–1863); during part of this time he was associated with a bank in Malone and was president of the New York Northern railroad. He presided over the New York constitutional convention of 1867–1868 and served again in Congress for four consecutive terms (1869–1877), during which he built a reputation for scrupulous integrity (having opposed the "salary grab" act of 1873, he used the excess salary granted him to purchase government bonds which he then extinguished by having them canceled). He was also the author of the "Wheeler Compromise" of 1874 which resolved a disputed election in Louisiana to the satisfaction of all parties. He was vice president in 1877–1881, having been elected in 1876 as running mate of the Republican nominee, Rutherford B. Hayes.

WHEELER, William Morton, American educator and zoologist: b. Milwaukee, Wis., March 19, 1865; d. Cambridge, Mass., April 19, 1937. Educated at German-American Normal College, Milwaukee, from which he graduated in 1884, and at Clark University (Ph.D., 1892), he specialized in entomology, more particularly insect embryology, and held posts as instructor at the University of Chicago (1893–1899), professor at the University of Texas (1899–1903), and curator of invertebrate zoology at the American Museum of Natural History, New York City (1903–1908). He then became professor of entomology at the Bussey Institution, Harvard University, and remained there for 26 years (until his retirement in 1934), serving as its dean of faculty from 1915 to 1929. He wrote: *Ants, Their Structure, Development and Behavior* (1910), *Social Life Among the Insects* (1923), *The Social Insects, Their Origin and Evolution* (1928), *Foibles of Insects and Men* (1928), *Demons of the Dust, a Study in Insect Behavior* (1930), and, published posthumously, *Essays in Philosophical Biology* (1939).

WHEELING, hwē'lĭng, city, West Virginia, seat of Ohio County. An industrial and commercial center, it is situated in the Northern Panhandle on the east bank of the Ohio River and includes Wheeling Island, a residential island in midstream. Bridges cross the Ohio via Wheeling Island to Bridgeport and Martins Ferry, Ohio, while south of the city a bridge spans the river to Bellaire, Ohio. The city lies 56 miles southwest of Pittsburgh by road. Its altitude is 687 feet. Wheeling Creek winds through the city and empties into the Ohio.

Known for a century as "the Nail City" but more recently as "the Friendly City," Wheeling is surrounded by vast coal and natural gas fields which, together with steam-generated electric power, have contributed largely to its economy Its chief industry is iron and steel but there are also railroad shops and diversified manufactures including tinplate, sheet metal products, nails, china, tiles, glass, paper, textiles, clothing, tobacco and food products, medicines, furniture, and plastics. The discovery of rock crystal deposits nearby has led to a chemical industry. The city is served by two federal highways, three railroads (Baltimore & Ohio, Nickel Plate, and Pennsylvania), and an airport. It is a port of entry and has a busy river barge traffic. There are three radio and one television broadcasting stations.

Besides public and parochial schools, the city is the site of Linsley Military Institute, founded in 1814, Mount de Chantal Academy for girls (1848), and Wheeling College (Jesuit; 1954), while nearby are West Liberty State College (1837) and Bethany College (1840). The Ohio County Public Library at Wheeling dates back to 1859. Of the two large municipal parks, Oglebay Park, 5 miles to the northeast, covers 1,083 acres, while Wheeling Park, in the southeast, comprises 170 acres. The city has 35 playgrounds and 6 municipal swimming pools. There is a half-mile horse-racing track on Wheeling Island.

History.—Captain Celeron de Bienville and his party of French explorers visited the site in 1749. Settlement began in 1769 with the arrival of the three Zane brothers, Ebenezer, Jonathan, and Silas. In 1774, the British built Fort Fincastle on the site; in 1776 its name was changed to Fort Henry in honor of Patrick Henry, first governor of Virginia, and at Fort Henry the last engagement of the American Revolution was fought on Sept. 11–13, 1782 (a stone marker in the city marks the site of the fort). After growing up as Zanesburg, the city was chartered in 1806 as Wheeling (the name is believed to come from the Indian *Weeling*, "place of the skull," a designation supposedly used by the Indians because it was here that the heads of a group of massacred whites were once displayed on poles as a warning to others). The National Road reached Wheeling in 1818 and the Baltimore and Ohio Railroad in 1853. A suspension bridge to Wheeling Island was built in 1849 (and replaced in 1856 after being blown down) despite legal opposition by Pittsburgh, 90 miles upstream; the bridge was designated a national monument in 1956. A new span to Wheeling Island named Fort Henry Bridge was opened in 1955. During the Civil War the Wheeling conventions of Virginians loyal to the Union were held in the city in 1861–1862, leading to the formation of West Virginia from Virginia's western counties, and Wheeling was the capital of West Virginia in 1863–1870 and 1875–1885. The old capitol erected in 1876 was razed in the late 1950's and replaced in 1959 by a new city-county building. The city was incorporated in 1836, and today has a manager-council form of government. Population: 43,070.

VIRGINIA EBELING,
Librarian, Ohio County Public Library.

WHEELOCK, hwē'lŏk, **Eleazar,** American clergyman and educator: b. Windham, Conn., Apr. 22, 1711; d. Hanover, N.H., Apr. 24, 1779. He graduated from Yale College in 1733, was licensed to preach in the following year, and in 1735 became pastor of a Congregational church at Lebanon, Conn., which he served for the next 35 years despite his supposed involvement in the Separatist movement. Emulating many preachers, on whom the educational system of the time depended, Wheelock tutored pupils for admission to college. In 1743, however, his educational efforts took a new turn when he determined to instruct young Indians, convert them to Christianity, and return them to their tribes as teachers and missionaries. To this end, he established Moor's Indian Charity School, but his efforts met with only minor success.

Disappointed in his pupils, in conflict over policy with the royal superintendent of Indian affairs, dissatisfied with his salary arrangements with his parishioners, and wishing to expand his educational program, in 1769 Wheelock obtained from New Hampshire a royal charter and 44,000 acres of land for a college to be located in that state, and chose Hanover as its site. Arbitrarily naming the new college after the earl of Dartmouth, president of a board of trustees administering a fund of £12,000 raised in England for the education of Indians, Wheelock devoted the last nine years of his life to establishing the new college, serving as its president and teaching and preaching. He adhered to his original objectives in recruiting young Indians from Canada as students and showed marked administrative ability in raising money for the new institution, which was often debt ridden, and in sustaining the college through the tumult and conflicts of the American Revolution. He was succeeded as president of Dartmouth College by his eldest son, John Wheelock (q.v.)

See also DARTMOUTH COLLEGE.

WHEELOCK, John, American educator: b. Lebanon, Conn., Jan. 28, 1754; d. Hanover, N.H., Apr. 4, 1817. The son of Eleazar Wheelock (q.v.), he transferred from Yale to the new Dartmouth College, graduating in its first class in 1771. He served with distinction as an officer during the American Revolution and, upon the death of his father in 1779, succeeded to the presidency of Dartmouth under the provisions of his father's will. As president, he faced the formidable task of providing buildings for the college, hitherto housed in log cabins, and raising funds to continue the elder Wheelock's program of educating, not only whites, but Indians. Soliciting individual contributions in England and the United States, conducting lotteries, obtaining grants from the New Hampshire legislature, and selling the college's extensive landholdings, Wheelock obtained funds sufficient to construct a chapel and the first college building and to establish professorships on a salaried basis. He was also instrumental in founding the medical school in 1798.

Although his tenure during this period of growth and construction had been relatively calm, increasing friction over religious matters between Wheelock and his board of trustees came to a head in the appointment of a theological professor contrary to the president's wishes. The controversy simmered until 1815, when an enlarged board of trustees dismissed the president, who appealed to the public, while the issue became political. In 1816 the New Hampshire legislature amended the college charter, changing Dartmouth to a university with an enlarged board of trustees, which elected Wheelock president. The college sued for the restoration of its property and in 1818 was vindicated by the United States Supreme Court under Chief Justice John Marshall in a landmark decision with implications far beyond the terms of the original dispute. Before the case went to court, Wheelock became so ill that he was unable to fill his new post, and he died before the final decision on the dispute was handed down.

See also DARTMOUTH COLLEGE CASE, THE.

WHEELWRIGHT, hwēl'rīt, **William,** American shipping and railroad pioneer in South America: b. Newburyport, Mass., March 16, 1798; d. England, Sept. 26, 1873. He attended Phillips Academy, Andover, and at 16 shipped as a cabin boy to the West Indies, later becoming a ship's master in South American waters. In 1823, Wheelwright survived a shipwreck in the ocean near Buenos Aires. In 1824–1829, he was United States consul at Guayaquil, Ecuador, and then moved to Valparaiso, Chile, where he built gas- and waterworks, a lighthouse, and other port facilities. By 1838 he had obtained concessions from South American west coast countries for a steamship line, and in 1840 he secured British financial backing and a charter for the Pacific Steam Navigation Company, which inaugurated service between Valparaiso and Callao, Peru, which was later extended to Panama.

Between 1849 and 1852 he built the first railroad in South America, connecting the Chilean port of Caldera with the rich copper and silver mines of Copiapó, and in 1850, also in Chile, the first telegraph line. His greatest ambition was to build a transcontinental railroad across the Andes between Argentina and Chile, and in May 1870, with British financial support, he completed a line from Rosario, on the Paraná River 170 miles above Buenos Aires, to Córdoba, 246 miles northwest; however, political and financial complications delayed further work and the trans-Andean part of the line was not completed until 1910. In 1872, Wheelwright completed a railroad from Buenos Aires to Ensenada, on the Río de la Plata gulf, thereby permitting development of the port of La Plata. Although he rarely visited the United States, he maintained ties with his hometown and left part of his fortune for the technical education of Newburyport youths. In 1877, the people of Chile erected a statue of him in Valparaiso as a gesture of appreciation.

WHELK, hwĕlk, a term applied to many diverse genera of marine snails in various English-speaking countries. Originally, this was the common name for *Buccinum undatum*, Linné, a marine snail occurring in the North Atlantic on the coasts of both Europe and North America. Since early colonial times, both in North America and in Australia, the name has also been used for *Busycon* and *Fasciolaria* in the Western Atlantic, and for *Charonia, Monoplex,* and other genera in Australia. *Thais lapillus* Linné of Europe and eastern North America is referred to as the dog or rock whelk, and *Nassarius obsoletus* Say of eastern North America as the mud whelk. The former lives on exposed rocky shores and the latter on mud flats in bays and inlets where there is some admixture of freshwater. Since the word "whelk" has been so loosely used for so many and completely unrelated mollusks it has no identification value. Many of these so-called whelks, along with other marine snails, are occasionally used for food by man, but more frequently they are used for fish bait as the muscular foot is tough and clings firmly to the hook.

See also SNAIL AND SLUG.

WILLIAM J. CLENCH.

WHEN LILACS LAST IN THE DOORYARD BLOOM'D an elegy by Walt Whitman on President Abraham Lincoln, written shortly after his assassination and first printed in 1865. Like all of Whitman's other major poems, it is included in *Leaves of Grass* as finally edited by the poet. The elegy reflects feelings in the author, that had grown during the Civil War, "for the sweetest, wisest soul of all my days and lands." More importantly perhaps, it is also a product of the mature artist's ability to give universality to emotion.

Whitman never knew Lincoln personally, although he once recorded exchanging cordial bows. Also, Whitman did not like hero worship. So this elegy is completely without tributes to power and leadership, and Lincoln is not even mentioned by name. The poem is constructed on the use of three primary symbols: "powerful western fallen star"—Lincoln; the lilac—youth, nature recreating itself, life; and the song of the hermit thrush—the gift of feeling and expression, "Death's outlet song of life." The form of the poem is a simple series of associations: the passage of the president's coffin across the United States; the poet's presentation of a sprig of lilac, and bestowal on the burial house of the sounds, sights, and smells of America; the bird's carol of death, a "victorious" song of "fullest welcome"; and the poet's "long panorama of visions"—armies with splintered battle staffs and myriads of corpses. After these associations, Whitman comes to mourn not Lincoln alone, but all the Civil War dead, and to feel with the living the real anguish—" . . . the mother suffer'd, And the wife and the child and the musing comrade suffer'd, And the armies that remain'd suffer'd." Finally, a coda-like reprise of star, lilac, and song of the thrush affirms keeping the memory of "the dead I loved so well."

JOHN ASHWORTH.

WHETSTONE, hwĕt'stōn, any stone used for sharpening tools. Sandstones and fine mica schists form the coarser kinds. Siliceous clay rocks and particularly the fine compact rocks made of quartz grains, such as Arkansas stone or novaculite, form the more desirable varieties for oilstones and delicate hones.

WHEY. See CHEESE AND CHEESE MAKING.

WHIG PARTY, hwĭg pär'tē, a political party in the United States during the second quarter of the 19th century, formed to oppose President Andrew Jackson and the Democratic Party. The term Whig came into common use in 1834, and persisted until the disintegration of the party after the presidential election of 1856. The anti-Jackson groups drew upon the political history of two revolutions, the American and 17th century English, for their name. In both cases the opposition to the king had called themselves Whigs (q.v.). Now it was "King Andrew" Jackson who was the alleged tyrant.

The Whigs' direct political antecedents were the National Republicans, the administration party during John Quincy Adams' presidency (1825–1829). They advocated a nationalistic economic policy (the "American System"), but were stymied by the rising power of the Jacksonians, who were thereafter called Democrats. Jackson's inauguration in 1829 began the period of National Republican opposition and prepared the ground for the coalition of political forces which formed the Whig Party. Henry Clay of Kentucky, and Daniel Webster of Massachusetts became the party's leading figures. Webster was more of a nationalist than Clay, as he demonstrated in his famed Reply to Hayne of South Carolina (Jan. 26–27, 1830). But both men urged a program of tariff protection, federally sponsored communication projects (internal improvements), continuation of the national bank, and a conservative public land sales policy—the "American System," much of which could be traced back to Alexander Hamilton's Federalist economic policy of 1791. This was a program with especially strong appeal to merchants and manufacturers whose business operations went beyond state lines. Clay made the president's veto of a bill to recharter the second Bank of the United States the key issue of the election of 1832, but Jackson easily won reelection.

State sovereignty, not economic nationalism, was the idea which brought a significant addition to the ranks of those opposing Jackson. John C. Calhoun of South Carolina broke his alliance with Jackson when he realized that he would not be the next Democratic president, and the split widened during South Carolina's attempt of nullification of federal tariff laws. Jackson reacted sternly to this defiance, giving Clay an opportunity to introduce a compromise tariff bill in February 1833. Calhoun approved the compromise and for several years acted in uneasy association with other anti-Jacksonians. Another source of recruits was the Anti-Masonic Party, particularly strong in New York and Pennsylvania. The stated purpose of this strange phenomenon in American history was to combat the supposed threat of Masonic power over judicial and political institutions. It also provided younger politicians with a convenient means for advancement. Among those Anti-Masons who became important Whig leaders were William H. Seward and Thurlow Weed of New York, and Thaddeus Stevens of Pennsylvania. With the addition of two more groups, antinullification states' rights Southerners and the so-called Democratic Conservatives, who opposed their party's financial policies after 1836, the Whig coalition was complete, but hardly united.

Hard times following the panic of 1837 and the popularity of their candidate, Gen. William Henry Harrison, brought the Whigs victory in 1840 over Jackson's successor, Martin Van Buren. The new Whig managers stole a turn from the Democrats by outdoing them in raucous electioneering during the "Log Cabin" campaign—the most tumultous presidential campaign the nation had yet seen. (This was the formula for the only other Whig victory, that of Gen. Zachary Taylor in 1848). Harrison's death on April 4, 1841 (one month after assuming office), was especially disastrous for the party. John Tyler, a Virginia states' rights former Democrat, replaced him and vetoed a succession of key Whig tariff and banking bills. The frustrated Whigs read their president out of the party, but the last pre-Civil War opportunity for passage of a modified "American System" had slipped by.

When the Whigs next won the presidency in 1848 the nation was deeply involved in the problems of slavery and national expansion. With disunion threatening, the aged Whig leaders Clay and Webster tried, in January and March 1850, to compromise the main points of sectional friction. President Taylor blocked their moves, but his death on July 9, made Millard Fillmore, a party man from New York, president. While the Compromise of 1850 was not solely a Whig accomplishment, the Whig leadership had been prominent in its passage. Webster, now Fillmore's secretary of state, dreamed of capturing the presidency at the head of a Union movement in 1852. But both major parties accepted the Compromise, and on June 16, 1852, the Whigs reverted to form in nominating another general, Winfield Scott. Two weeks later Clay was dead and Webster died in October. The passing of these two great figures heralded the Whig disaster of 1852. The party never recovered from this defeat. Its call for moderation and Union, by now far more prominent than the national economic policy, became increasingly ineffective as the Civil War approached. Southern Whigs, fearful of Northern encroachment on slaveholding rights, thought the Democratic Party more receptive to their interests; and a significant number of Northern Whigs had already moved into the antislavery Free Soil Party, which had been formed on the eve of the election of 1848.

The Bettmann Archive

An 1848 cartoon attacks the Whigs for refusing the presidential nomination to their ranking statesman, Henry Clay.

The rise of the Republican and the anti-immigrant Know-Nothing parties completed the Whig downfall. Defections to Republicanism were numerous, while the former Whig president, Fillmore, accepted the Know-Nothing nomination. A Whig national convention met in 1856, but simply endorsed the Fillmore ticket. Thus the party of Unionism came to an end, a victim of sectional controversy. In 1860 a feeble remnant of Whiggery organized a Constitutional Union Party, a last-ditch attempt to prevent disruption of the Union. They fared badly in the election; their constitutional conservatism was politically dead, and with it had perished the Whig Party.

It is difficult to speak of Whig doctrine in a party of such diverse elements. Politically, the opposition to Jackson dictated an attack on excessive presidential energy. Whigs believed Congress should initiate policy, not the president. Whig views of the Constitution ranged from Webster's nationalism to Tyler's states' rights views, with the nationalistic view predominating. But its national economic policy best characterized the Whigs, although not all those calling themselves Whigs accepted it. Politically, this was a premature nationalism, at a time when the effective power of government remained to a large extent with the states. The Democrats, through their generally superior state political organizations and greater identification with popular interests, were usually able to maintain their ascendancy. The absence of true nationalism before the Civil War, meant that the party with a national economic policy had to depend on nonsense and war heroes for its two national victories. With no Southerners in Congress during the Civil War, and with a former Illinois Whig, Abraham Lincoln, in the White House, the Republican Party finally passed much of the economic legislation on tariff and banking which the Whigs had long advocated.

FRANK OTTO GATELL.
Department of History, University of Maryland.

Bibliography

Brown, Thomas, *Politics and Statesmanship: Essays on the American Whig Party* (Columbia Univ. Press 1985).
Carroll, E. Malcolm, *Origins of the Whig Party* (1925; reprint, Da Capo 1970).
Cole, Arthur C., *The Whig Party in the South* (1913; reprint, P. Smith 1959).
Ershkowitz, Herbert, *The Origin of the Whig and Democratic Parties* (Univ. Press of Am. 1983).
Howe, Daniel W., *The Political Culture of the American Whigs* (1980; Univ. of Chicago Press 1984).
Poage, George R., *Henry Clay and the Whig Party* (1936; reprint, P. Smith 1965).

WHIGS, hwĭgs, a word of Scottish origins, significant in the political histories of both Great Britain and the United States (for the latter, see WHIG PARTY). Its origins are disputed, but the place of origin, western Scotland, is not. The most widely accepted derivation is from *whey;* an alternate form is *whiggamore.* The poorer rural folk who drank such inferior dairy products as whey, buttermilk, or soured milk were themselves called whigs or whiggamores, and the term was not a complimentary one. Other suggested derivations are: (1) from *whiggam,* supposedly used by peasants of that area in driving horses; from the verb *whig,* meaning "to spur on"; or (2) *whig,* a Scots Gaelic term for horse thieves.

Historically, the word was first important during the English Civil War, when it was applied to the Presbyterian Covenanters of west Scotland who marched on Edinburgh in 1648 to seize control of the government from the Royalist Party. There are also suggestions, but little evidence, to the effect that in the Covenanter's motto "We Hope In God" lies the origin of the word whig. After the Stuart Restoration it was again in use to denominate the exclusioners who after 1679 opposed the right of succession of the duke of York (later James II) to the throne (see EXCLUSION, BILL OF). The accession of the Catholic James in 1685 provoked the Glorious Revolution of 1689. This overthrow was decidedly a Whig triumph and settled permanently the question of constitutional sovereignty in England, that is, that Parliament—not the king—was to have the effective voice in governing the realm. Although they chiefly accomplished the revolution, the king the Whigs put in power, William of Orange, was indifferent to party sources of support, and his successor, Queen Anne, preferred Tory ministers.

Not until Anne's death and the accession of the Hanoverian line did the period of the Whig oligarchy begin (1714–1760). For nearly half a century the Whigs ruled Britain, but did so moderately. Robert Walpole's long ministry (1721–1742) best exemplified Whig moderation, a policy as much the product of prudence as philosophical commitment. A minority among the great landowners, the Whig oligarchs left local government in the hands of Tory justices of the peace, while they cultivated central power at London in cooperation with the town merchants and through the use of rotten boroughs to ensure parliamentary control. Their principal party dogma was opposition to unconstitutional royal power. The first two Hanoverians gave no trouble on that score. Walpole's motto was "Let Sleeping Dogs Lie." When George III came to the throne in 1760 he sought to build up a Royal Party in Parliament. The Whigs were intellectually played out by then, and politically shattered by their mismanagement of the early phases of the Seven Years' War, the struggle which led to the rise of William Pitt the Elder as a national statesman. When the Whigs under the 2d marquis of Rockingham briefly regained office in 1780 the ways of the oligarchy were past. Now they appealed to public opinion. But the result, after several inconclusive years, was a new oligarchy, Tory this time, which ruled until 1830.

The last decade of power of English Whiggery saw the passage of the great Reform Bill of 1832. Lord Grey utilized the widespread discontent over the long-standing abuses in parliamentary representation. The Reform Bill widened voting privileges and abolished many of the so-called pocket and rotten boroughs. The Whigs, in power since 1830, followed up this measure with a municipal elections reform bill in 1835. Both bills were conservative, but the changes they wrought were considerable considering the previous atrophy of representative machinery in Britain. (In addition, the Whig ministry had obtained, in 1833, the abolition of slavery in the British colonies.) But the Whigs could not cope with the problems of 19th century industrial Britain. Robert Peel organized the Conservative Party from the Tory wreckage and took office in 1841. Gradually the Whigs began to merge into the new Liberal Party. With the beginning of William E. Gladstone's Liberal ministry in 1868, the Whig Party as a distinguishable political entity ceased to exist. For a decade or two the word Whig was used to denote a person of extremely old-fashioned ideas.

See also GREAT BRITAIN—*21. History*.

FRANK OTTO GATELL,
Department of History, University of Maryland.

WHIMBREL. See CURLEW.

WHIN. See FURZE.

WHINCHAT, hwĭn'chăt, a small thrush, *Saxicola rubetra,* nesting throughout much of Europe and northern Asia and wintering in Africa. In the British Isles it is common in upland moors and open areas where there are scattered bushes; it received its name from its habit of perching on whin bushes, that is, gorse and other thorny gowth. Six inches in length, the male is attractively but modestly marked with ruddy breast, black cheeks, and white wing patches.

The hair-lined nest is hidden in the grass, often at the base of a bush; the eggs are spotted.

DEAN AMADON.

WHIP, hwĭp, in politics, a person designated by a political party to seek party discipline in a legislative chamber, especially in voting, and to see that party members are present for important debates. An outgrowth of the whip system long in use in the British Parliament, the use of whips in the United States Congress dates back to 1899, when the Republican caucus in the House of Representatives designated Representative James E. Watson of Indiana as whip; in the Senate it goes back to 1913, when Senator James H. Lewis of Illinois was named whip by the Democrats. In modern practice, in the House of Representatives, the Republican and Democratic parties each employ a chief whip aided by a number of assistant whips. However, the well-known independence of American congressmen indicates that the efforts of the party whips are not uniformly or universally successful. One principal reason for this is the lack of sanctions that can be applied by the party to secure support for its policies. The chief one available relates to committee assignments, controlled by the party caucuses.

In the British House of Commons, the government and opposition whips have duties similar to but somewhat more extensive than Congressional whips, their work extending even to the arrangement of the daily agenda and the fixing of time limits for debate.

HARVEY WALKER.

WHIP SCORPION. See SCORPIONS.

WHIP SNAKE, hwĭp'snāk, or **COACHWHIP,** kōch'-hwĭp' (*Coluber flagellum* or *Masticophis flagellum*), a common, slender, agile, speedy snake, often aggressive, related to the black snake and blue racer. It occupies the southern half of the United States and northern Mexico. The upper surface is variously yellow, gray, reddish, or black. Whip snakes climb bushes or trees and feed on rodents, birds and eggs, lizards, other snakes, and insects. Some very slender leaf-green poisonous tree snakes (Dipsadinae) of Africa and Asia also are called whip snakes.

TRACY I. STORER.

WHIPPET, hwĭp'ĭt, a breed of dog, youngest of the coursing hounds, that was developed from a greyhound-terrier cross made by breeders in the north of England in the mid-1800's. Their object was to produce a "snap dog"—a term referring to dogs used in coursing rabbits in an enclosure, the winner being the dog which "snapped up" the largest number of rabbits. Later, crosses with the Italian greyhound were made. This alert sporting hound is quiet, dignified, elegant, regarded by some as a miniature greyhound, standing 18 to 22 inches in height and weighing from 10 to 28 pounds. The whippet is sensationally swift for approximately one eighth of a mile, establishing marks of 35 miles per hour, and is, of course, best known for racing (it is often referred to as "the poor man's race horse"). The breed was given official recognition by the Kennel Club of England in 1891. It is noted for its rabbit-coursing ability and as a proficient rat killer.

WILLIAM F. BROWN.

WHIPPING POST, hwĭp'ĭng pōst, a post at which criminals were formerly whipped in England and some states of the United States. Whipping was gradually eliminated in England and was finally abolished by the Criminal Justice Act of 1948. In the United States, only Delaware and Maryland have used the whipping post in modern times. While it was abolished in Maryland in 1953 (by repeal of the law prescribing whipping for wife beaters), it still exists in Delaware. There, although whipping of women was abolished in 1889, public whippings may still be administered to males for 25 different crimes. However, the whipping post in Delaware has not been used since 1952. In early Delaware the whipping post and the pillory were structurally combined, but since 1905, when the pillory was abolished, the post has stood alone in each of the state's three counties.

WHIPPLE, hwĭp'əl, **Abraham,** American naval officer: b. Providence, R.I., Sept. 26, 1733; d. near Marietta, Ohio, May 27, 1819. In the French and Indian War he commanded the privateer *Game Cock,* and on one cruise captured 23 prizes. He led the prerevolutionary raid on June 9–10, 1772, which resulted in the burning of the British revenue cutter *Gaspée,* aground in Narragansett Bay. In the American Revolution, after being commodore of Rhode Island's small fleet, he became an officer of the Continental Navy, and in 1778 sailed the frigate *Providence* to France on a munitions-procuring and courier mission. On his return he was engaged in cruises off the American shore. One morning in the summer of 1779, during a dense fog, Commodore Whipple's squadron of the *Providence* and two other ships fell in with a large British merchant fleet under convoy; when the fog lifted (according to one account), his squadron stayed with the enemy fleet under pretense of being British vessels and sent men aboard 11 of the merchantmen, detaching them from the convoy and bringing 8 of them safely to port. The captured ships constituted one of the richest prizes of the war. Subsequently he was charged with the naval defense of Charleston, S.C., but most of his guns were taken ashore to reinforce land batteries and upon the fall of the city in 1780 he was captured and remained in prison until the end of the war.

WHIPPLE, Fred Lawrence, American astronomer: b. Red Oak, Iowa, Nov. 5, 1906. Educated at the University of California (A.B., Los Angeles, 1927; Ph.D., Berkeley, 1931), he became a staff member of the Harvard College Observatory in 1931 and the following year joined the Harvard University faculty, advancing to professor of astronomy in 1950 and serving as chairman of the department in 1949–1956. In 1955, he became director of the Smithsonian Astrophysical Observatory in Cambridge, Mass., and in 1959 he was appointed director of the Harvard Radio Meteor Project.

Known especially for his research on comets, meteors, and the upper atmosphere, he was awarded the Donohue medals for the independent discovery of six new comets (the last reported in 1942). During World War II, as radio laboratory research associate (1943–1945) of the Office for Scientific Research and Development, he was in charge of developing confusion reflectors, or "windows," used extensively as radar countermeasures. Since World War II he has held many government appointments connected with missile, upper-atmosphere, and space research. At the Smithsonian observatory he developed, under the International Geophysical Year (IGY), the optical system for tracking artificial satellites, and continued to direct it under the National Aeronautics and Space Administration; the program in 1961 included a worldwide network of 12 Baker-Nunn tracking camera stations and 100 Moonwatch volunteer observation teams. In 1946, he became a member of the Rocket Scientific Panel, United States, and in 1955 a member of the United States National Committee Technical Panel on the earth satellite program. He is a member of many scientific bodies, is chairman of Commission 22 (Shooting Stars) of the International Astronomical Union, and is an editor of the *Astronomical Journal* and *Planetary and Space Science,* editor of *Smithsonian Contributions to Astrophysics,* and author of *Earth, Moon and Planets* (1958) and *Orbiting the Sun* (1981).

WHIPPLE, George Hoyt, American pathologist, educator, and Nobel Prize winner: b. Ashland, N.H., Aug. 28, 1878; d. Rochester, N.Y., Feb. 1, 1976. He obtained his M.D. degree from Johns Hopkins University in 1905 and taught pathology there from 1909 to 1914. From 1914 to 1921 he taught research medicine and was director of the Hooper Foundation for Medical Research at the University of California, where he was dean of the medical school in 1920–1921. Then, from 1921 to 1952, at the University of Rochester, he was dean of the School of Medicine and Dentistry (1921–1953) and professor of pathology (1921–1955). He is chiefly known for his work on the treatment of pernicious anemia with liver, and in 1934 was one of three American physicians (the others were George R. Minot and William P. Murphy) to receive jointly the Nobel Prize in physiology and medicine for their separate efforts in this field. As an extension of his research, he was the author of more than 200 publications on anemia, pigment metabolism, blood plasma proteins, bile salt metabolism, liver injury and repair, and related subjects.

WHIPPLE, William, American soldier, legislator, and signer of the Declaration of Independence: b. Kittery, Me., Jan. 14, 1730; d. Portsmouth, N.H., Nov. 10, 1785. Formerly a sea captain, he became a merchant in Portsmouth about 1760, was prominent in prerevolutionary currents against British rule, and in 1775 quit business to devote himself to public life. He was a member of the Continental Congress in 1776–1779, and was one of three New Hampshire signers (the others being Josiah Bartlett and Mathew Thornton) of the Declaration of Independence. Whipple took part in the brief Saratoga and Rhode Island campaigns as a militia leader, and helped in negotiations for the surrender of the British general John Burgoyne in 1777. In 1782–1785 he was associate justice of the state Superior Court.

WHIPPOORWILL, hwĭp-ər-wĭl', a species of bird, *Caprimulgus vociferus,* of the nightjar or goatsucker family, found in North America. About 10 inches long, it nests in brushy or forested areas in central Canada and in the eastern and central United States, and in winter migrates to the

Its mottled plumage blends with the natural background and protects a whippoorwill from predators.

Allan D. Cruickshank from National Audubon Society

Gulf of Mexico coast and Mexico, arriving back in its nesting haunts about April 1st. Other races of the species nest locally in the mountains of the southwestern United States and in Mexico and Central America. The plumage of the whip-poorwill is beautifully mottled with shades of brown, gray, and white, and blends perfectly with the leaves on the ground. Far this reason, and because it is entirely nocturnal in habits, it is seldom seen except by those who enter its haunts and flush it from the ground or from a low limb, on which, because its feet are very tiny, it perches lengthwise. Its voice on the other hand is loud, arresting, and unmistakable, consisting of three rapidly uttered syllables, suggesting its name. This call it utters over and over with breathless rapidity. It calls just as darkness is descending, and again shortly before dawn, but also at intervals during the night, especially if the moon is out.

The food is entirely moths and other insects, engulfed in its capacious mouth as it sallies out from a low perch or flutters through the dusk on its long wings. The whippoorwill lays its two eggs on the leaves of the forest floor, without making a nest. The eggs and also the young are protectively colored and very difficult to detect.

DEAN AMADON.

WHIPSNAKE. See WHIP SNAKE.

WHIRLIGIG BEETLE, hwûr'lə-gĭg bē'təl, an aquatic beetle of the family Gyrinidae, so called because of its habit of swimming about in a circular fashion, sometimes in large groups, on the surface of water. The adults are easily distinguished from other beetles by having each compound eye divided into a dorsal portion and a ventral portion that is submerged. They feed chiefly on the bodies of insects that fall into the water. The larvae are more predaceous than the adults and roughly resemble small centipedes. They make a squeaking noise when disturbed by rubbing the tip of the abdomen against the elytra.

WILLIAM D. FIELD.

WHIRLPOOL, hwûrl'pōōl, a circling inrush of water to fill the central maw of a spiraling vortex, often with complete disappearance to a lower level through a subsurface channel, pothole, or sink. The vortex motion results from a combination of opposing current flow, hydrodynamic gradient (inward or centripetal force), outward or centrifugal force, and the downward pull of gravity. Whirlpools may be found wherever conflicting currents and subsurface drainage channels or flow patterns exist, as in the Whirlpool Rapids below Niagara Falls on the Canadian-United States border, the Maelstrom of the Norwegian Sea, and the wind-driven Garofalo (or Galofalo) whirlpool (known as Charybdis to the ancients) in the Strait of Messina between Italy and Sicily.

FERGUS J. WOOD.

WHIRLWIND. See CYCLONE; TORNADO; WATERSPOUT; WINDS—*Glossary of Winds* (Storms and Squalls Producing High Winds).

WHISKEY or **WHISKY,** hwĭs'kē, an alcoholic liquor made differently in different countries, but always from a fermented mash of grain. To be fermentable the mash must contain malt, generally barley malt, the malting consisting of steeping the bearded kernels in warm water, heaping and turning them on a malting floor until they sprout, and then drying them in a kiln. This germination generates a chemical agent, called diastase, that converts starches into sugar. Letting the malt convert his entire mash, the distiller brews with the aid of yeast his "distiller's beer," wherein alcohol is born weak to become (via the still) something stronger, roughly recognizable as whiskey even though it flows out colorless.

In America the indigenous flavors were—and are—rye and corn. Scotch-Irish settlers in western Pennsylvania who grew rye found it easier and more profitable to transport their crop over the mountains to seaboard markets as potation goods rather than as farm produce. In addition, the limestone water of their New World area was exactly right for whiskey making, the knowledge of which they had brought from Northern Ireland. When in 1791, Alexander Hamilton, with a depleted Treasury, imposed an excise tax on liquor, the farmer-distillers rose in armed defiance. President Washington, himself a rye distiller on a small scale, took stern action, dispatching 15,000 Virginia militiamen to quell this one and only Whiskey Rebellion (q.v.) in United States history. Certain irreconcilables departed downstream to Kentucky and its unsurpassed limestone water. In a county called Bourbon stills were set up, served by a mash consisting primarily of corn and secondarily of rye, with a barley malt supplement.

One thing the consumer waited for overlong was dependable aging. Whiskeys acquire their ages in sturdy oak barrels, traditionally white oak. Under favorable conditions, the oak extracts some of the factors that make young whiskey harsh; in exchange it contributes flavors from the wood, rounding out the flavors that came from the grain. A shortage of barrels in the mid-19th century is credited with the discovery that wrought a revolution in whiskey making. It seems that the only barrels that had not been procured were some in which salt fish had been shipped. Undeterred by their apparent unsuitability, one purchaser took drastic measures to eliminate the fishy odor: he burned the interiors of the staves and heads to a considerable depth. The whiskey that resulted mellowed so early as to be almost startling; it was evident that the charred wood had accelerated the aging process. News spread in varied versions of origin, resulting in general adoption of the innovation. Eventually the federal alcohol authorities made charring compulsory, and added the stipulation that barrels for storing whiskey in warehouses be new and made of unused oak. Aging, given this double stimulus, still was plagued with halts and gaps caused by weather. However, the modern distiller has overcome intermittance by installing air conditioning and humidity control which are kept in constant operation. Representative types of whiskeys, beginning with the American varieties, are as follows:

Bourbon Whiskey.—This type is prepared from a mash of not less than 51 percent corn, or from a combination of such whiskeys. Age or ages are unstipulated. *Sour mash bourbon* is a special Southern traditional type of bourbon, owing its individuality to the yeasting-back process of fermentation whereby each batch in the fermenter is activated chiefly by working-yeast brought over from a previous batch. This is a more leisurely procedure than that used with *sweet mash*, which is fresh. Neither type tastes sour.

Rye Whiskey.—This is made from a mash of not less than 51 percent rye, or a combination of such whiskeys. Age or ages are unstipulated. Rye tends to taste younger than bourbon of the same age.

Corn Whiskey.—A specialty of the South, its mash is not less than 80 percent true to its name grain. Corn whiskey is exempted from char influence lest its accent be impaired.

Straight Bourbon Whiskey, Straight Rye Whiskey, Straight Corn Whiskey.—Twenty-four months is the aging requirement for this class, which bourbon greatly leads in popularity.

Whiskey—A Blend.—Straight whiskey of 100 proof (50 percent alcohol by volume) participates to the extent of not less than 20 percent of the mixture's volume. The balance is made up of other whiskey and/or grain neutral spirits. It is bottled at not less than 80 proof. Note that the fomula is flexible. Top-grade versions increase the age of the straight whiskey employed, and raise its participation well above the 20 percent minimum.

Bourbon Whiskey—A Blend; Rye Whiskey—A Blend; Corn Whiskey—A Blend.—These contain not less than than 51 percent straight whiskey, lightened with grain neutral spirits.

Blended Straight Whiskeys, Blended Straight Bourbon Whiskeys, Blended Straight Rye Whiskeys, and So On.—These are balanced stock selections with no stipulations as to quantities and qualities except that the youngest component must be at least two years old; grain neutral spirits automatically excluded.

Bottled in Bond.—Straight whiskey not less than four years old is permitted to be bottled, at 100 proof, while held under federal government lock and key as security for the excise tax to be paid thereon just before withdrawal. The government supervises the bottling, grants the designation "Bottled in Bond," and authorizes the affixing of the distinctive green revenue stamp over the cork; but it does not in any manner guarantee the quality nor the purity of the whiskey.

Scotch Whisky (never spelled with an *e*).—Pot-still malt whisky, hearty and smoky, long has been the peculiar treasure of the Scots. Some was smuggled across the border sporadically during the 17th and 18th centuries, but not until blending was introduced late in the 19th century did Scotch become an article of legitimate export. Oddly light for whisky, Scotch is lightened by "grain whiskies"—patent-still products from mixed mash of cereals in which maize is prominent—turned out at about 180 proof, just short of being grain neutral spirits. They qualify as whiskies by possessing characters which the blender can distinguish and utilize in working out his combinations. Grain whiskies are aged individually and further aged as components of blends. The container is of uncharred oak, preferrably one that has held sherry. By law, the minimum age for Scotch is three years; export trade agreements raise that minimum to four years. Choice Scotches have the benefit of much greater age. As compared with the foundation dates of the more than 100 small distilleries that make the malts—classed as Highland, Lowland, Campbelltown, and Islay—even the most patriarchal "liqueur" Scotch is but a youth.

Irish Whiskey.—The other Gaelic classic is nonsmoky in flavor because the kiln floor on which this whiskey's malt is roasted has no perforations to admit peat fumes. In Northern Ireland the mash is malted barley only; in Eire it may comprise a dozen grains. In both, distillation is by pot stills—large, impressive, and not to be confused even remotely with the "little pot" in which illicit poteen, from potatoes, is cooked. Straight or blended, Irish whiskeys are exported at not less than seven years of age. Very old straight Irish is a virtual elixir.

Canadian Whiskey.—These whiskeys, distilled at somewhat higher proof than those of the United States, are consequently lighter in body, their bourbon and rye flavors more delicate. Less aging is required, and loss by evaporation during that aging is made up, by Canadian custom, through replenishing with new whiskey or grain neutral spirits. For this reason all Canadian whiskey exported to the United States is classified as blended whiskey. At two years Canadian whiskey may be bottled in bond at 90 proof.

See also DISTILLATION; DISTILLED LIQUORS; DISTILLING INDUSTRY.

LAWTON MACKALL.

Further Reading: Carson, Gerlad, *The Social History of Bourbon* (Univ. Press of Ky. 1984); Cooper, Derek, *Guide to the Whiskies of Scotland* (Cornerstone 1979).

WHISKEY INSURRECTION. See WHISKEY REBELLION.

WHISKEY REBELLION, an insurrection in western Pennsylvania which reached its climax in 1794. It was a consequence of the excise law of 1791 which imposed a tax on distilled liquors. In western Pennsylvania, where distillation was the most economical way of consuming surplus corn—to the extent that jugs of corn liquor were utilized as currency—the farmers considered the tax to be burdensome and a violation of their rights. Despite modifications in the original legislation, the grievance continued to rankle.

The mountain people, not far removed from the tactics of the American Revolution, and with the Stamp Act in mind, refused to pay the duty and gave the excise agents rough handling. There was something like a revival of the spirit of 1776 as the framework of a revolutionary situation came into existence, with demagogues haranguing mass meetings and committees of public safety organized in defense of rights presumed to be outraged. Among the hotheaded farmers, there was secession talk and even independence talk, moderated by the good sense of the youthful Albert Gallatin (q.v.).

The tax delinquency of the distillers provided a test of the powers of the fledgling federal government. Alexander Hamilton, particularly, was eager for the power of the new government to be demonstrated and thought that the situation in Pennsylvania justified exemplary action. Besides, it offered Hamilton the opportunity, his last chance as matters turned out, to show himself a soldier. It was at Hamilton's insistence that President George Washington acted to call out the militia.

In the fall of 1794, the militia of four states including Pennsylvania, was on its way across the Alleghenies. In face of this opposition, the leaders of the farmers fled, and the rebellion collapsed.

EDWARD N. SAVETH

WHISKEY RING, The, in American history, a national internal revenue scandal, which was exposed in 1875 through the efforts of Secretary of the Treasury Benjamin H. Bristow. Statistics showed that for some years prior to 1875 the United States had, in St. Louis, Mo., alone, lost at least $1,200,000 of tax revenue which it should have received from whiskey, yet special agents of the Treasury set to work from time to time had failed to do more than cause an occasional flurry among the thieves. The Whiskey Ring was organized in St. Louis when the Liberal Republicans there achieved their first success. It occurred to certain politicans to have revenue officers raise a campaign fund among the distillers. This idea the officers modified later, raising money in the same way for themselves, and in return conniving at the grossest thievery. As it became necessary to hide the frauds, newspapers and higher officials were hushed, till the ring assumed national dimensions. Its headquarters were at St. Louis, but it had branches at Milwaukee, Chicago, Peoria, Cincinnati, and New Orleans, and an agent at Washington, D.C. A huge corruption fund was distributed among gagers, storekeepers, collectors, and other officials, according to a fixed schedule of prices. As a result of the investigation by Secretary Bristow arrests were made in nearly every leading city. Indictments were found against 152 liquor men and other private parties, and against 86 government officials, notably the chief clerk in the Treasury Department, and President Ulysses S. Grant's private secretary, Gen. Orville E. Babcock.

WHISPERING GALLERY, a gallery or dome of an elliptical or circular form in which faint sounds, such as a whisper, produced at certain points on the circumference are heard with startling clarity at certain other distant points along the circumference; or such a sound may be conveyed with similar distinctness all around the gallery's circumference. The phenomenon is attributed to peculiar acoustic qualities resulting in concentration of the sounds by reflection from the walls. One of the most famous whispering galleries is at St. Paul's Cathedral, London, England. Others are in the Capitol at Washington, D.C., the Mormon Tabernacle in Salt Lake City, Utah, and in Gloucester Cathedral, England.

WHIST, hwĭst, a card game for four people, those sitting opposite each other being partners. It was first clearly described by Edmond Hoyle in his *Short Treatise on the Game of Whist* (1742). Whist was the forerunner of, and has largely been superseded by, bridge.

WHISTLE, hwĭs'əl, in music, a small, high-pitched pipe of metal, wood, cane, or plastic, with six holes. Classified as fipple flutes (the upper end is stopped by a fipple or plug in which a narrow slit is cut), whistles are blown through a flue, the air current striking a sharp edge cut into the wall of the instrument. The families of flageolets and recorders are classified as (or as closely related to) the whistles. Pipe organs often include whistle stops; various powered whistles have been experimented with for musical purposes. In primitive forms, whistles may be nose blown or mouth blown. Such contemporary examples as the common tin whistle have little place in serious composed music, but are widely used as toys and for signaling.

HERBERT WEINSTOCK

WHISTLER, hwĭs'lər, **James Abbott McNeill,** American painter and etcher: b. Lowell, Mass., July 10, 1834; d. London, England, July 17, 1903. He took his first drawing lessons in the Academy of Fine Arts, St. Petersburg (now Leningrad) for his father had taken the family to Russia while he built a railroad from St. Petersburg to Moscow. His sister married Seymour Haden, who later became an important etcher, and moved to England where James soon joined her. In 1849 his father died, and the Whistlers returned to the United States. He went to school in Pomfret, Conn., received an appointment to the United States Military Academy at West Point in 1851, but failed chemistry in his third year and was discharged. He worked for a time as draftsman for the United States Geodetic and Coastal Survey. In 1855 he went to Paris and never returned to America. He became a pupil of Charles Gabriel Gleyre, an artist of the school of Jean Auguste Dominique Ingres, and became associated with Édouard Manet, Henri Fantin-Latour, and Claude Monet. He maintained studios in Paris and London. He exhibited paintings in the Royal Academy, and *The White Girl* (National Gallery of Art, Washington, D.C.), which was refused at the Salon, was finally exhibited at the Salon des Refusés (Paris) in 1863 and caused a sensation.

Whistler was not widely appreciated in the early years and was never invited to become a member of the Royal Academy although he exhibited there for a number of years. His *Portrait of My Mother*, first entitled *An Arrangement in Grey and Black*, was received reluctantly by the academy, although it now is in the Louvre, Paris. Some of his best work was shown at the Grosvenor Gallery, opened by Sir Coutts Lindsay in 1877, and included the very original series called *Arrangements, Harmonies, Nocturnes,* and *Etudes,* which took their names from the most abstract of the arts—music—for Whistler wished to avoid the emphasis on storytelling which characterized the painting of his time. He liked to frame his paintings in colors which best set them off and in one instance, in 1874, gave a special exhibition in which even the gallery walls and the livery of the attendants harmonized with the compositions on view. It was in this period that Whistler began to paint portraits in the rather attenuated, almost ghostly, style of his protrait of Sir Henry Irving.

When Whistler moved to Chelsea in London, he met the Pre-Raphaelites, and Algernon Swinburne and Oscar Wilde. He became noted for his elegant, if eccentric, dress, and for his pointed witticisms, and was better known as a personality rather than as an artist, for his sharp tongue rather detracted attention from his serious achievements as an artist. However, his etchings were admired from the beginning of his career. His earliest etchings were made in France and published in 1858, consisting of 12 plates of figures, street scenes, and interiors. The second set, the *Thames Series* (1860), was a collection of 16 scenes along the river while he lived in Chelsea. These were first published in 1871. Whistler's etchings have been ranked with

Rembrandt's. No complete listing of his prints has ever been made, and Whistler was not systematic about keeping proofs of "stages" or memoranda, but it is estimated that there were more than 400 etchings. In them is perhaps the best evidence of his study of Japanese art, for the increasing economy of means, the precision, the flexibility of line, indicate that he fully understood the manner by which the Japanese could suggest a whole scene by a mere horizon line and a fragment of a pier. The Fine Arts Society commissioned him to make a series of etchings of Venice in 1880; the *First Venice Series* consisted of 12 plates, the *Second* of 53. In his etchings as well as in his paintings, Whistler was able to capture the atmospheric conditions, and in this he demonstrated a very English quality, despite his American background. He was even more successful than Monet in his rendering of atmosphere. Besides series of etchings, Whistler made a good many significant single plates. Examples of his etchings are found in the British Museum, London, the New York Public Library, the Metropolitan Museum of Art, New York City, the Bibliothéque Nationale, Paris, and the Academy of Fine Arts, Venice, Italy.

Whistler also was noted for his lithographs and dry points. He also produced some remarkable watercolors and pastel paintings. He did some work in interior decoration, such as the Sarasate music room in Paris and the Peacock Room in Prince's Gate, London, of which the latter is now in the Freer Gallery of Art, Washington, D.C. The owner of the Peacock Room, F. R. Leyland, objected to the aesthetic theories of the artist, for the Spanish leather walls of this dining room were painted over to harmonize with the painting, *Princess of the Land of the Porcelain,* and the collection of porcelains in the room.

Whistler's paintings cover a broad range of subjects. There are numerous portraits (*Cicely Alexander—Harmony in Grey and Green, Rosa Corder,* and *Thomas Carlyle,* the latter a very strong characterization, later sold to the city of Glasgow), marine scenes, and landscapes, especially night scenes. He was a technician in his paintings as well as in his print making. His method was to apply successive thin layers of color, thereby gaining great permanency for his canvases.

Whistler imposed himself on his age, not only because of the distinctness of his personality and his articulateness, but because of his dissatisfaction with the detail and clutter of conventional painting in his time. He restored simplicity and light, fresh color to painting. Many young American artists abandoned the muddy palettes they had been taught to use when they saw the work of their expatriate brother. He was the defender of artistic individuality and very critical of poseurs, although accused of being one himself. He promulgated the doctrine of "art for art's sake." He stated his creed as a painter in two series of *Propositions* and the lecture *Ten O'Clock* (published in 1888). One of the propositions was that a painting had "no mission to fulfill" but was a "joy to the artist, a delusion to the philanthropist, a puzzle to the botanist." He considered critics ignoramuses but useful—"they keep one always busy, always up to the mark, either fighting or proving them idiots." The severity with which he attacked those whom he disliked was legendary and qualified him to write the book, published in 1890, entitled *The Gentle Art of Making Enemies.*

HARRIS WHITTEMORE COLLECTION, THE NATIONAL GALLERY OF ART

James Whistler's *The White Girl* created a sensation at its showing at the Paris Salon des Refusés in 1863.

A famous incident in the history of modern art is the lawsuit between the critic John Ruskin and Whistler. In 1877 Ruskin wrote in *Fors Clavigera* about a Whistler painting then showing at the Grosvenor Gallery, *Nocturne, Black and Gold—The Falling Rocket:* "I have seen, and heard, much of Cockney impudence before now; but never expected to hear a coxcomb ask two hundred guineas for flinging a pot of paint in the public's face." Whistler brought suit for slander and was awarded damages of one farthing, which he thereafter wore on his watch chain. The costs against Ruskin were met by a public subscription. Whistler later wrote the satiric pamphlet *Whistler v. Ruskin: Art v. Art Critics.*

Whistler became a member of the Royal Society of British Artists in 1884 and its president in 1886. During his administration the quality of the exhibitions improved but they were a commercial failure. When Whistler failed to be reelected, many of his followers resigned. His explanation was characteristic: "It is all very simple. The Royal Society of British Artists has disintegrated—the 'artists' have come out, the 'British' remain." Whistler became an officer of the Legion of Honor and a member of academies in foreign countries and in 1900 received gold medals at the Paris Exposition. His works are highly valued.

JEAN ANNE VINCENT
Author of "History of Art"

Bibliography

Arts Council of Great Britain, *James McNeill Whistler: An Exhibition* (1960).
Curry, David P., *James McNeill Whistler* (Norton 1984).
Fine, Ruth E., *Drawing Near* (Univ. of Wash. Press 1984).
Gregory, Horace, *The World of James McNeill Whistler* (Nelson 1959).
Sutton, Denys, *Nocturne: The Art of James McNeill Whistler* (Lippincott 1963).
Young, Andrew M., and others, *The Paintings of James McNeill Whistler,* 2 vols. (Yale Univ. Press 1980).

WHISTLING SWAN, a North American swan that produces a variety of hornlike calls having little resemblance to a whistle. The whistling swan (*Olor columbianus*), also called the common American swan or wild swan, is of the same species as the European Bewick's swan (*O. c. bewickii*). The whistling swan breeds and raises its young in the American Arctic in the spring and summer and usually winters along certain stretches of the Atlantic and Pacific coasts.

LEONARD LEE RUE III, FROM NATIONAL AUDUBON SOCIETY

Whistling swans have a high, musical call.

It is about 4.5 feet (1.4 meters) long and pure white except for the black beak marked with yellow next to the eyes. Its nest in the Arctic is usually a large mound of moss, grass, or other plants, sometimes 6 feet (1.8 meters) in diameter.

WHITBY, hwit'bē, a town in North Yorkshire, England, is on the North Sea, 16 miles (26 km) north-northwest of Scarborough. It is a seaport, market town, and resort. The older part lies in the steep valley cut through the limestone cliffs by the Esk River, which here runs into the sea and provides a harbor for fishing boats. Modern Whitby occupies higher ground on the west side. There are good sands and bathing. Adjacent to the town are the far-spreading Yorkshire moors. Its economy is based on fishing, shipbuilding, metalworking, the export of coal, and tourism.

High on the harbor's east side are the ruins of St. Hilda's Abbey, founded in 657, though the present remains date only from the 12th century. The Synod of Whitby, held here in 664, turned England toward the observances of the Roman Church and away from the usages of the Celtic Church. The poet Caedmon (died about 680) was a monk at the abbey. It was destroyed by the Danes in 867 but reestablished by the Benedictines in 1078. Adjoining the ruins is the much-restored St. Mary's Church, which was originally Norman. Population: (1971) 12,717.

WHITBY, hwit'bē, is a town in Ontario, Canada, and the seat of Ontario county. It lies on Lake Ontario, 28 miles (45 km) northeast of Toronto. Providing services for an agricultural hinterland, Whitby also has factories producing canned goods and other food products, hardware and metalwork, automobile tires, and rubber goods. It is the site of Ontario Ladies' College and a large provincial hospital.

The community was founded in 1836 and named Perry's Corners after its founder, Peter Perry, a politician. Incorporated in 1855, it was renamed for the Whitby in Yorkshire, England. Whitby, Ontario, was once an important port, shipping lumber and wheat to the United States. Population: 36,698.

D. F. PUTNAM, *University of Toronto*

WHITCHURCH-STOUFFVILLE, hwit'chûrch stō'-vil, is a town in Ontario, Canada, 24 miles (38 km) northeast of Toronto. It is situated in a rich farming region of York regional municipality (formerly York county). The community's center is Stouffville, named for Abraham Stouffer, who settled there after leaving Pennsylvania in 1804. The village of Stouffville and the township of Whitchurch were merged to form the present town. Population: 13,557.

WHITE, Andrew Dickson (1832–1918), American educator, diplomat, and historian, who helped found Cornell University. He was born in Homer, N. Y., on Nov. 7, 1832. A student of history, White graduated from Yale College in 1853, studied in Europe, served as an attaché in the U. S. legation in St. Petersburg, Russia (1854–1855), and received his M. A. from Yale in 1856. After a period as a professor at the University of Michigan, White served in the New York state Senate in the mid-1860's.

As chairman of the Senate's committee on education, he became especially interested in the establishment of a new university for the state. With Ezra Cornell as a benefactor, White wrote the charter for a model university to be located at Ithaca. White's plans called for the admission of women and for the treatment of students as adults. Blessed by private money and a large federal land grant, Cornell University opened in 1868. White was its president until 1885.

He was also the first president of the American Historical Association, minister to Germany (1879–1881, 1897–1902), minister to Russia (1892–1894), and chairman of the U. S. delegation to the first Hague Conference (1899).

A prolific author, White wrote *History of the Warfare of Science with Theology in Christendom* (1896) and a two-volume autobiography (1905). He died in Ithaca on Nov. 4, 1918.

WHITE, Byron (1917–), American lawyer and justice of the U. S. Supreme Court. White was born in Fort Collins, Colo., on June 8, 1917. At the University of Colorado (B. A., 1938), he was elected to Phi Beta Kappa. "Whizzer" White played basketball and baseball and was an All-American halfback in football. He later studied at Oxford as a Rhodes Scholar; played professional football in Pittsburgh and Detroit; served in the Navy in World War II; and received an LL.B. from Yale (1946). In 1954 he was elected to the National Football Hall of Fame.

White practiced law in Denver from 1947 to 1961. He worked for the election of John F. Kennedy as president in 1960 and served as deputy U. S. attorney general in 1961 and 1962. President Kennedy named him to the Supreme Court in 1962.

Somewhat unexpectedly, White did not join the court's liberal majority bloc. Rather, he often wrote dissenting opinions in the areas of the rights of criminal defendants and the protection of 1st Amendment guarantees. In criticizing the majority in *Miranda* v. *Arizona* (1966), which imposed strict rules for police when questioning criminal suspects, White warned that the court's ruling "will return a killer, a rapist or other criminal to the streets . . . to repeat his crime. . . ." When the court moved to the right with the addition of four Nixon appointees, White often sided with them to create a new majority.

WHITE, E. B. (1899–1985), American writer, whose crisp, graceful, and highly individual style, as well as his independence of thought, made him one of America's leading essayists.

Elwyn Brooks White was born in Mount Vernon, N. Y., on July 11, 1899. After service as an Army private in 1918, he graduated from Cornell University in 1921. He worked as a reporter on the Seattle *Times* and as an advertising copywriter before joining *The New Yorker* magazine in 1926, a year after its founding. For 12 years he wrote the editorial essays in the magazine's "Notes and Comments" and contributed verse and other pieces. In 1937 he moved to a farm in North Brooklin, Me., and from this retreat continued writing, including a column, "One Man's Meat," in *Harper's* (1938–1943) and free-lance pieces for *The New Yorker*.

White's publications include two books of verse, *The Lady Is Cold* (1929) and *The Fox of Peapack* (1938); *Is Sex Necessary?* (1929), satirical essays with James Thurber; collected pieces, including *Every Day Is Saturday* (1934), *Quo Vadimus?* (1939), *One Man's Meat* (1942; enlarged ed. 1944), *The Second Tree from the Corner* (1953), and *The Points of My Compass* (1962); children's books, *Stuart Little* (1945), *Charlotte's Web* (1952), and *The Trumpet of the Swan* (1970); *Here Is New York* (1949), a personal characterization; and *The Wild Flag* (1946), a plea for world law.

With his wife, the former Katharine Sergeant Angell, a *New Yorker* editor, he edited *A Subtreasury of American Humor* (1941). His revised edition of William Strunk, Jr.'s *The Elements of Style* was issued in 1959.

He was awarded the gold medal for essays and criticism of the National Institute of Arts and Letters (1960) and the American Academy of Arts and Letters (1973), the Presidential Medal of Freedom (1963), and a special Pulitzer Prize (1978). He died in Brooklin, Me., Oct. 1, 1985.

WHITE, Edward Douglass (1845–1921), 9th chief justice of the United States. He was born in Lafourche parish, La., on Nov. 3, 1845. His father, Edward Douglass White (1795–1847), was a lawyer who served both as congressman from Louisiana (1829–1834, 1839–1843) and governor (1835–1839). The younger White was educated at Mount St. Mary's College in Maryland, the Jesuit College in New Orleans, and Georgetown College (now Georgetown University) in Washington, D. C. His education was interrupted by a short term of service in the Confederate Army.

In 1868, White was admitted to the Louisiana bar and immediately entered politics. He was elected to the state Senate in 1874 and served on the Louisiana supreme court in 1879–1880. A leader of the antilottery forces in the state, he was named to the U. S. Senate in 1890. When President Grover Cleveland was twice thwarted by his political foe, Sen. David B. Hill of New York, in his efforts to appoint two New York lawyers, William Hornblower and Wheeler Peckham, to a vacant seat on the Supreme Court, he nominated White, whom the Senate could not reject because he was a member of "the club."

White was associate justice from 1894 to 1910, when he was promoted to chief justice, succeeding Melville Fuller, by President William H. Taft, who, in turn, was to succeed him in that post. White was the first justice to be appointed to the center chair from a position on the court. He held his post until his death in Washington on May 19, 1921.

His work on the court during 27 years of service does not permit of neat categorization. Taft said in his eulogy of White that his primary commitment was to nationalism. Certainly this was evident in his recognition of Congress' extensive power over interstate commerce, as revealed in *Clark Distilling Co.* v. *Western Md. Ry.* (1917), and *Wilson* v. *New* (1917).

White's position on state economic regulation, however, was entirely unpredictable. For example, he dissented in *Lochner* v. *New York* (1905), when the court struck down the New York maximum hours law. But he also dissented in *Bunting* v. *Oregon* (1917), which sustained an Oregon maximum hours statute and overruled the *Lochner* decision. Probably his most important judicial accomplishment was reading the "rule of reason" as a criterion for illegality into the antitrust laws, in the case of *Standard Oil Co.* v. *United States* (1911).

His judicial writing style was incredibly bad. Felix Frankfurter once described his opinions as "models of what judicial opinions ought not to be." A more recent commentator, James Watts, suggested that "He moved portentously across the thinnest ice, confident that a lifeline of adverbs—'inevitably,' 'irresistibly,' 'clearly,' and 'necessarily'—was supporting him in his progress." But he had a remarkable memory, and he presided over the court with energy, dignity, and charm. He was almost universally liked by his brethren on the court and the bar, even by those who, like Justice Oliver Wendell Holmes, had more respect for him as an individual than they had for him as a judge.

PHILIP B. KURLAND, *University of Chicago*
Author of "Politics, the Constitution and the Warren Court"

WHITE, Edward H. See ASTRONAUTS.

WHITE, Henry (1850–1927), American diplomat. He was born in Baltimore, Md., on March 29, 1850, and educated privately in the United States and Europe. His early diplomatic service was in the U. S. legation in Vienna (1883) and the embassy in London (1883–1893), where he became first secretary before being replaced by President Grover Cleveland.

White was reappointed to the London post by President William McKinley in 1897. For the next eight years he played an important behind-the-scenes role in diplomatic affairs, winning the high regard of British and American leaders. He was ambassador to Italy from 1905 to 1907 and to France from 1907 to 1909. As U. S. representative at the Algeciras Conference (1906), he helped settle the dispute between Germany and France over Morocco.

During World War I, White served as regional director of the Red Cross and president of the War Camp Community Service. He was appointed to the U. S. Peace Commission by President Woodrow Wilson in 1918. Although at first opposed to the League of Nations, he soon became a strong advocate of U. S. membership. He died in Pittsfield, Mass., on July 15, 1927.

WHITE, Hugh Lawson (1773–1840), American judge and political leader. He was born in Iredell county, N. C., on Oct. 30, 1773. After reading law, he began his practice in Knoxville, Tenn., in 1796. Entering public affairs, he held several positions, including judge of the state supreme court, member of the state senate, and president of the state bank.

White served in the U. S. Senate from 1825 to 1840. A Jeffersonian and Jacksonian Democrat, he supported President Andrew Jackson at first. But he broke with the president by not supporting as his successor Martin Van Buren, who was not popular in Tennessee. White's speech in 1835 favoring a limitation on executive patronage was regarded as an attack on the administration. White ran for president in 1836 as an independent and carried two states, but he failed to prevent Van Buren's election. A man of high principles, White resigned from the Senate in 1840 when the Tennessee legislature sent him instructions he felt unable to obey. White died in Knoxville on April 10, 1840.

WHITE, Josh (1908–1969), American spiritual and blues singer, who became a popular folksinger in urban cabarets during the 1940's.

Joshua Daniel White was born in Greenville, S. C., on Feb. 11, 1908. As a young boy, traveling with a group of blind musicians, he taught himself to play the guitar and also learned the spirituals and blues that later became his repertoire. During the 1930's he recorded for Columbia and made several radio broadcasts.

Josh White also appeared on the Broadway stage, performed at the White House, toured Europe successfully, and ended his career as a popular attraction on the college concert circuit. He usually performed seated on a stool.

His hit songs included *One Meatball, Outskirts of Town, Hard-Time Blues,* and *John Henry.* An album of Southern prison songs, *Chain Gang,* was nationally famous. He died in Manhasset, N. Y., on Sept. 5, 1969.

WHITE, Margaret Bourke. See BOURKE-WHITE, MARGARET.

WHITE, Patrick (1912–), Australian author, who was awarded the Nobel Prize for literature in 1973. In the Nobel citation, White was commended for his "epic and psychological narrative art," his "onslaught against vital problems," and his ability to extract from language "all its power and all its nuances, to the verge of the unattainable."

Patrick Victor Martindale White was born in London, England, on May 28, 1912, while his parents were on vacation. His early years were spent in Sydney, after which he returned to England for his secondary and college education (B. A., Cambridge University, 1935). In 1939–1940 he visited the United States, and during World War II he served in the Royal Air Force as an intelligence officer in the Middle East and Greece. Following the war he settled on a small farm near Sydney.

White's early novels—*Happy Valley* (1939), *The Living and the Dead* (1941), and *The Aunt's Story* (1948)—were published in London and New York, and, while they were admired in Britain and the United States, they went generally unrecognized in Australia. Not until *The Tree of Man* (1955), set in the near-suburban countryside of 20th century Australia, was White acclaimed in his homeland. Now an international literary figure, White published *Voss* (1957), *Riders in the Chariot* (1961), *The Solid Mandala* (1966), and *The Vivisector* (1970). In 1973, *The Eye of the Storm* appeared. This novel of character, set in Sydney and the Australian outback, was regarded as White's most important book—a lacerating view of family relationships, painted on a sweeping canvas. White's shorter fiction is collected in *The Cockatoos* (1974).

WHITE, Paul Dudley (1886–1973), American physician, who was one of the world's leading authorities on heart disease. He was born in Roxbury, Mass., on June 6, 1886. After receiving his M. D. degree from Harvard Medical School in 1911, he began a lifelong association with Massachusetts General Hospital in Boston. He headed the hospital's cardiac clinics and laboratory, and in 1949 became a consultant in medicine. From 1914 to 1956 he taught at Harvard Medical School.

White was a pioneer in the diagnosis, treatment, and prevention of diseases of the heart and circulatory system. He was among the first to use the electrocardiograph to detect cardiac disorders, and was a staunch advocate of weight control, proper diet, and daily exercise. When President Dwight Eisenhower was stricken with a coronary thrombosis in 1955, White became his chief medical consultant. In 1971 he visited the People's Republic of China to study its medical practices.

White was a founder of the American Heart Association and served as its president from 1942 to 1944. His book *Heart Disease* (1931), a standard reference work in its field, went through many editions. He died in Boston, Mass., on Oct. 31, 1973.

WHITE, Peregrine (1620–1704), the first person born in New England of English parents. His given name means "pilgrim." The son of William and Susanna White, he was born on the *Mayflower* as it lay at anchor off Cape Cod on Nov. 20 (Nov. 30, New Style), 1620. Another child, Oceanus Hopkins, had been born at sea.

After the death of William White during the Plymouth settlement's first winter, Susanna White in 1621 married Edward Winslow, later the colony's governor. As an adult, Peregrine White settled in Marshfield, Mass., where he was given land and held minor civil and military posts. He died in Marshfield on July 22, 1704.

WHITE, Stanford (1853–1906), American architect, who created handsome buildings in the neoclassical style. White was born in New York, N. Y., on Nov. 9, 1853, the son of literary critic R. G. White. He was trained by H. H. Richardson, with whom he worked on the great Romanesque Trinity Church in Boston. After traveling in Europe with C. F. McKim and the sculptor Augustus Saint-Gaudens, White in 1880 became the third partner in the influential New York firm of McKim, Mead, and White.

Exuberant, inspired, and devoted to beauty, White designed opulent town and country mansions and other buildings that reflected the increasing wealth and cultural awareness of the age. He worked first in the firm's romantic shingle style, as in the Casino at Newport, R. I. (1881). Then he shifted to the Italian Renaissance style for which the firm became famous. He specialized in classical detail and in interiors and furnishings, which he brought from Europe. His extant New York buildings include the Villard houses (begun 1882), Century Club, and Washington Square Arch. The Herald Building, old Madison Square Garden (1889), Madison Square Presbyterian Church, Metropolitan Club, and Gorham and old Tiffany buildings have all been destroyed. White was shot and killed in New York on June 25, 1906, by Harry Thaw, apparently out of jealousy over Thaw's wife, former chorus girl Evelyn Nesbit.

WHITE, T. H. (1906–1964), English author, whose best-known work is the multivolume fictional chronicle of King Arthur and his court, published under the omnibus title *The Once and Future King* (1938–1958). Terence Hanbury White was born in Bombay, India, on May 29, 1906, and educated at the University of Cambridge, from which he received his bachelor's degree in 1928. He had already published a book of poetry, *Loved Helen,* in 1927. He taught until he was 30, when he retired to devote his full time to writing. His early books include *Dead Mr. Nixon* (1930), *Darkness at Pemberley* (1932), *Earth Stopped* (1935), and *Gone to Ground* (1937). *England Have My Bones,* published in 1937, praises the English character.

Long a student of medieval lore and Arthurian romance, White brought out *The Sword in the Stone,* the first volume of his Arthurian pentalogy, in 1938. The final volume, *The Once and Future King,* was published 20 years later. White's other books include *Burke's Steerage* (1939), *Mistress Masham's Repose* (1946), *The Elephant and the Kangaroo* (1947), *The Goshawk* (1952), and *The Scandalmonger* (1952). White died in Piraeus, Greece, on Jan. 17, 1964. See also ONCE AND FUTURE KING.

WHITE, Theodore Harold (1915–1986), American author and journalist, best known for his series of books detailing presidential campaigns. He was born in Boston, Mass., on May 6, 1915, and graduated from Harvard University in 1938.

After serving as a correspondent in China for *Time* magazine in 1939–1945, White coauthored *Thunder Out of China* (1946), which was critical of the Nationalist government, and edited *The Stillwell Papers* (1948). His work as a correspondent in Europe for the Overseas News Agency and *The Reporter* magazine led to his book *Fire in the Ashes: Europe in Mid-Century* (1953).

White's *Making of the President, 1960,* on the campaigns of John F. Kennedy and Richard M. Nixon, won the Pulitzer Prize. Additional volumes followed on the presidential campaigns of 1964, 1968, and 1972. The Watergate episode and its aftermath formed the basis of *Breach of Faith: The Fall of Richard Nixon* (1975).

In a memoir, *In Search of History: A Personal Adventure* (1978), White reviewed his career as a journalist-historian. He also wrote two novels: *The Mountain Road* (1958), about China; and *The View from the Fortieth Floor* (1960), about the corporate world of a magazine. White died in New York City on May 15, 1986.

WHITE, Walter Francis (1893–1955), American author and a leading black spokesman, who was executive secretary of the National Association for the Advancement of Colored People (NAACP) for over 20 years. He was born in Atlanta, Ga., on July 1, 1893. Although light-skinned, he chose to live as a black man after witnessing racial discrimination and persecution while growing up in Atlanta. He graduated from Atlanta University in 1916, and in 1918 joined the NAACP, becoming executive secretary in 1931.

As investigator, spokesman, lobbyist, and author, White fought ceaselessly against racial discrimination, and was especially prominent in the campaign against lynching. Although unsuccessful in obtaining a federal antilynching law, his efforts helped achieve the almost complete elimination of that crime. He wrote accounts of lynchings in his novel *Fire in the Flint* (1924) and in his report *Rope and Faggot: A Biography of Judge Lynch* (1929).

White received several notable awards, including the Spingarn Medal in 1937. His other books include his autobiography, *A Man Called White* (1948), and the posthumous *How Far the Promised Land?* (1955), a report on the progress made by black Americans. He died in New York City on March 21, 1955.

WHITE, William (1748–1836), American clergyman, who was one of the founders and earliest leaders of the Protestant Episcopal Church in the United States. White was born in Philadelphia, Pa., on April 4, 1748. After graduating from the College of Philadelphia (now the University of Pennsylvania), he went to England to be ordained a priest in 1772. Returning to America, he became assistant rector and then rector of Christ Church, Philadelphia, a position he held for 60 years until his death.

After the Revolution, White led in organizing the Church of England parishes into the independent Protestant Episcopal (now the Episcopal) Church. He drafted and worked for the adoption of its first constitution (1785), which introduced the principle, new to Anglicans, of lay participation in church government. He helped prepare the American revision of the Book of Common Prayer and proposed the ordination of bishops in America rather than in England. Elected bishop of Pennsylvania in 1786, he was consecrated in England the following year under an act of Parliament that dispensed with the usual oath of allegiance to the crown. He was presiding bishop of the church in America in 1789 and from 1796 to 1836.

As leader of a denomination retaining ties with England, White tactfully guided the church through the post-Revolutionary period. Preventing incipient dissension over episcopal ordination, he arranged the first consecration of a bishop on American soil in 1792, thus ensuring the continuity of episcopal orders from the mother church to the daughter church. He also promoted Sunday schools, then considered radical, and encouraged cooperation with Quakers and other denominations. White also trained clergy, served as chaplain to Congress, and wrote articles for church periodicals as well as such works as *Memoirs of the Protestant Episcopal Church in the United States of America* (1820). He died in Philadelphia on July 17, 1836.

WHITE, William Allen (1868–1944), American newspaper editor and author, who as a small-town editor for nearly 50 years was an influential voice for the ideas of Main Street America. Born in Emporia, Kans., on Feb. 10, 1868, he moved with his family when he was ten to El Dorado, Kans. He studied at the College of Emporia and the University of Kansas (1886–1890), which he left before graduation in order to become business manager of the El Dorado *Republican*. In 1891 he went to Kansas City, and in 1892 he became editorial writer for the Kansas City *Star*.

In 1895 he borrowed $3,000 and bought the Emporia *Gazette*, which he edited and published for the rest of his life. Through the columns of the *Gazette*, an obscure country paper when White acquired it, he became known throughout the United States as the "Sage of Emporia," a genial and warmly human person who epitomized the middle-class Midwest. At first a straight-line Republican, he later espoused the liberal politics of Theodore Roosevelt, whose Progressive party bid for the presidency he supported in 1912. Thereafter White fought to liberalize Republican party policies, usually without success.

White's editorial "What's the Matter with Kansas?" (1896), an attack on the People's party (Populists), first attracted national attention to the country editor. His essay "Mary White," on the death of his daughter in a riding accident in 1921, is considered a classic. His 1922 editorial "To an Anxious Friend" won him the first of two Pulitzer prizes; the second came posthumously for his *Autobiography* (1946).

White was a prolific contributor to magazines and published much widely read fiction, including a novel, *A Certain Rich Man* (1909), and a collection of short stories, *In Our Town* (1906). He also wrote biographies of Woodrow Wilson (1924) and two of Calvin Coolidge (1925, 1938). His newspaper writings were collected in *The Editor and His People* (1924) and *Forty Years on Main Street* (1937). White died in Emporia on Jan. 29, 1944.

WHITE is a color at one extreme end of a scale of grays, with black at the other extreme end of the scale. White, grays, and black have no hue and therefore are called achromatic, or neutral, colors. They differ in that white objects reflect most of the light shining on them, gray objects reflect intermediate amounts of light, and black objects reflect very little light.

Many persons analyze the colors they experience as red, yellow, green, blue, black, and white. For this reason these six colors are called the psychologically primary colors. However, most so-called whites are very light grays. For example, fresh snow reflects about 80% of the light falling on it, but snow would have to reflect 100% of the incident light to be truly white.

White light is light that has approximately the same spectral energy distribution as noon sunlight. White light also is approximately the same as the light radiated by a black body at a temperature of about 6000° C (10,800° F).

White paints are made with such pigments as white lead, titanium white (titanium dioxide), and zinc white (zinc oxide). See also COLOR; LIGHT—*Behavior of Light* (Refraction); PAINT—*Ingredients Used in Paints and Coatings*.

WHITE ANT. See TERMITE.

WHITE BEAR LAKE is a city in eastern Minnesota, in Ramsey county, about 10 miles (16 km) northeast of St. Paul. Situated on the western shore of 3-mile (5-km)-long White Bear Lake, one of many scenic lakes in the area, the city is a popular resort and residential suburb of St. Paul. Sailboat building and truck farming are among the main commercial activities in the area. Ice-fishing contests are held as part of the St. Paul Winter Carnival. First settled in 1851 and incorporated in 1921, it has a city manager government. Population: 22,538.

WHITE BIRCH. See BIRCH.

WHITE BLOOD CELL. See BLOOD—*Composition of Human Blood*.

WHITE CAMELIA, Knights of the. See KNIGHTS OF THE WHITE CAMELIA.

WHITE CEDAR. See CEDAR.

WHITE CLOVER. See CLOVER.

WHITE FIR. See FIR.

WHITE-FOOTED MOUSE. See MOUSE.

WHITE-FRONTED GOOSE, a large dark-bodied goose that breeds in far northern regions of Europe, Asia, and North America and migrates southward before the onset of winter. The goose, *Anser albifrons*, has a white forehead, tan or pink bill, gray or brown front, black or brown back, white rear bottom, and yellow or orange legs. It is an excellent swimmer, walks well, and flies in slanted or V formations.

The European white-fronted goose (*A. albifrons albifrons*) winters in southern Scandinavia, England, central Europe, Italy, and Greece. The larger tule goose (*A. albifrons gambelli*) winters in California in the Sacramento Valley.

The white-fronted goose is a member of the family Anatidae. See also GOOSE.

WHITE GRUB, the larva of any of several members of the scarab family (Scarabaeidae), especially the larva of the May beetle (*Phyllophaga*). The grubs have a brown head and a white C-shaped body with six legs. They feed on roots, chiefly those of grasses, but injure many other kinds of crops planted in newly cultivated sod.

UPI

The north facade of the White House, the official residence of the president of the United States.

WHITE HOUSE, the mansion at 1600 Pennsylvania Avenue, N. W., in Washington, D. C., that has served as the home of every American president since John Adams. Although the building is not so imposing as the palaces of many heads of state, it has become a symbol of the grandeur and burden of the presidency, as well as of the greatness of the United States.

Description. The main section of the White House measures 170 feet (51 meters) long and 85 feet (25.5 meters) deep. The building's 2½ stories are mounted on a basement, which because of the slope of the land is actually a ground floor on the south side. The West Wing, completed in 1902 and containing the presidential office and the Cabinet Room, and the East Wing, built in 1942 for offices, flank the mansion. The White House is situated on some 18 acres (7.2 hectares) of land. The beautifully landscaped grounds include the famous Rose Garden and the Jacqueline Kennedy Garden.

James Hoban, the Irish-born architect who designed the White House in 1792, drew heavily on the Palladian style popular at the time. Chosen after an open competition, his plan for a boxlike stone structure with a hipped roof, balustrade, and columned entrance was not original, but it was attractive, dignified, and flexible.

The rooms on the state (first) floor have not been altered significantly since Hoban's time. The East Room serves as the great reception room. It is dominated by huge chandeliers, a mahogany piano supported by gilt eagles, and a Gilbert Stuart portrait of George Washington. The bodies of eight presidents have lain in state in the East Room, and during the Civil War, Union troops were quartered there. The adjacent Green Room, used by Thomas Jefferson as a dining room, is furnished as a parlor in early 19th century style. The elegant, oval Blue Room, overlooking the south grounds, contains the exquisite French Empire furniture installed by the James Monroes in 1817. The Red Room, used as a parlor or sitting room, is decorated in the American Empire style. In the large white and gold State Dining Room at the west end of the house is a multisectioned bronze-doré (gilt-bronze) centerpiece purchased by Monroe.

On the second floor are the Lincoln Bedroom, where the Emancipation Proclamation was signed; the rose and white Queen's Bedroom, which is occupied by visiting royalty; and the Treaty Room, which is furnished as a conference room of the Grant era.

Among the noteworthy rooms on the ground floor are the China Room, a library, and the Diplomatic Reception Room, which was a boiler room until it was renovated in 1902. Franklin Roosevelt made his fireside chats from that room, which now features American Sheraton furniture and a rare scenic wallpaper from 1834.

History. When President Adams arrived in the new Federal City in November 1800, he was dismayed to discover that the executive mansion was far from finished. Rooms were unplastered and the main staircase was incomplete. Since no laundry yard was available, Abigail Adams hung her wash in the unfinished East Room. Soon, however, the Adamses were entertaining at formal receptions at which the President, dressed in black velvet breeches, stood on a dais and bowed stiffly to his guests.

Such formality seemed undemocratic to the next president, Thomas Jefferson. He displeased traditionalists by shaking hands with visitors and by entertaining at small dinner parties where good food and conversation took precedence over ritual. During Jefferson's tenure (1801–

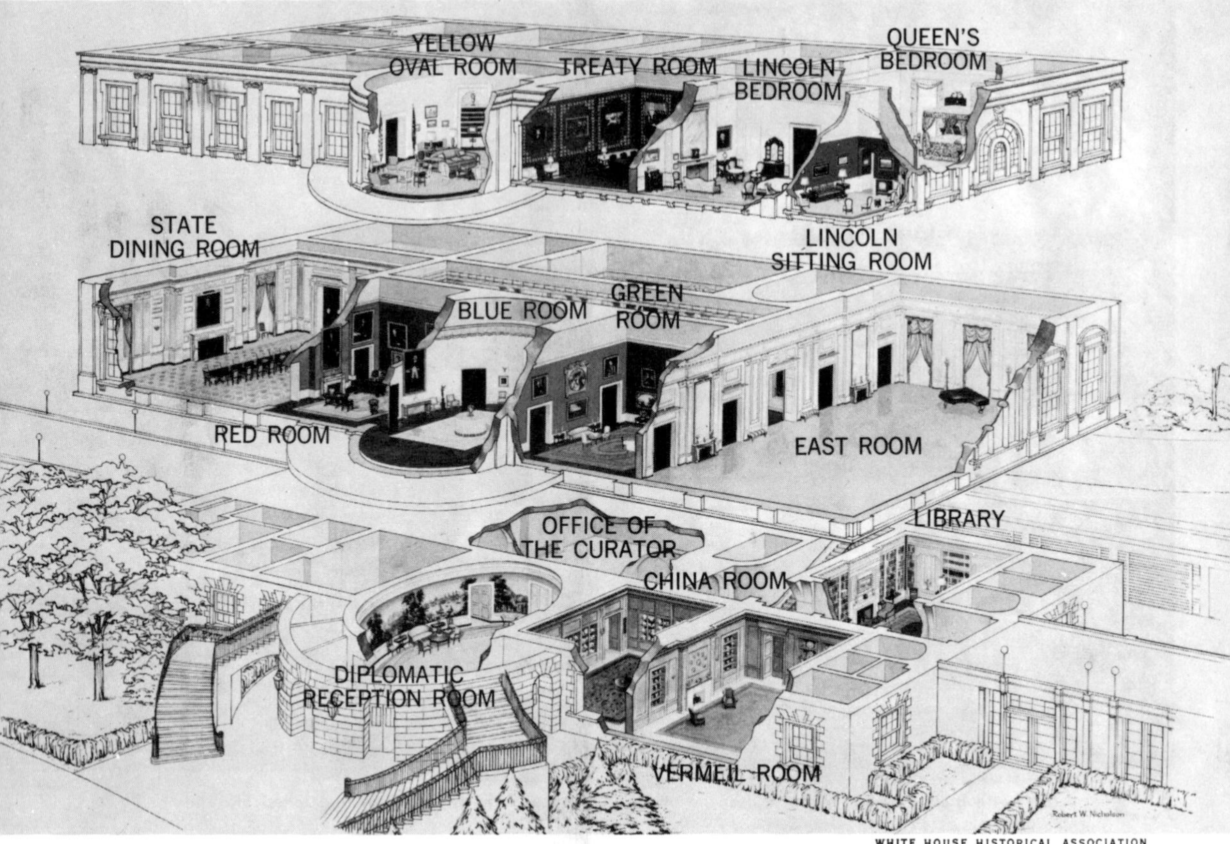

WHITE HOUSE HISTORICAL ASSOCIATION

This cutaway view shows the principal rooms of the White House.

1809), work on the White House was completed by the architect Benjamin Latrobe. A terrace and pavilions were added on each side.

A Jefferson grandchild was the first baby born in the White House. The first wedding occurred during the administration of James Madison (1809–1817). The bride was a sister of Dolley Madison, who later saved the Stuart portrait of Washington, which she removed before British troops burned the mansion in 1814. Only the charred exterior walls survived, but the White House was rebuilt and was reoccupied in 1817.

In the ensuing years, the mansion has undergone frequent redecoration and renovation. The North and South porticos were erected in the 1820's. New heating and plumbing systems were installed in the 1850's, as was a stove—previously, cooking was done in open fireplaces. A glass conservatory was built during the Buchanan administration. In 1873, during the Grant administration, rotting timbers and failing ceilings led to a major, ornate renovation.

The first telephone was installed during the tenure of Rutherford B. Hayes (1877–1881). His wife—called Lemonade Lucy because she did not permit liquor to be served—instituted the annual Easter egg-rolling on the White House lawn. Chester Arthur was president when the first elevator was put in. Electricity came during the Benjamin Harrison administration (1889–1893). Mrs. Harrison, who was afraid to turn off the lights for fear of shocks, began the now-famous White House china collection.

With the arrival of Theodore Roosevelt and his six exuberant children in 1901, it became clear that the first family required more room and more privacy. Consequently, the presidential offices on the second floor were converted into additional family space, and the new West Wing offices were constructed. More family rooms were added on the third floor in the late 1920's.

During the Truman administration, the entire mansion was discovered to be perilously close to collapse. Instead of razing the house altogether, it was decided to shore up the historic exterior walls while gutting the interior, which was rebuilt over the next four years (1948–1952) with as much of the original materials as possible. President Truman was criticized for having a balcony built on the second-floor level of the South portico, but it has been a favorite spot for presidential families ever since.

The concept of the White House as a repository for authentic antiques and fine paintings is relatively recent. Mrs. Kennedy sought contributions from private individuals when she redecorated the mansion. Subsequent first ladies have followed her lead. President Johnson in 1964 established the Committee for the Preservation of the White House and established the permanent office of curator.

Today some 1.5 million visitors tour the White House annually and see rooms furnished with items of both artistic and historical significance.

KENNETH W. LEISH
Author of "The White House"

Further Reading: Jensen, Amy L., and Jensen, H., *The White House and Its 35 Families* (McGraw 1970); Leish, Kenneth W., *The White House* (Newsweek 1972); Pearce, Mrs. John N., and others, *The White House: An Historic Guide* (The White House Historical Assn. 1971); Seale, William, *The President's House: A History* (The White House Historical Assn. 1986); Singleton, Esther, *The Story of the White House* (1907; reprint, Ayer 1972).

The Oval Room office in the West Wing of the White House was redecorated during the Nixon administration. Mrs. Richard Nixon designed the rug, which is flag blue with gold stars and a gold presidential seal.

UPI

The Red Room is in French Empire style. Furniture with historical associations includes sofas that had belonged to Nellie Custis and Dolley Madison.

WHITE HOUSE HISTORICAL ASSOCIATION

WHITE HOUSE HISTORICAL ASSOCIATION

The Green Room is in the Federal style. The furniture, which is chiefly Sheraton and Hepplewhite, includes a sofa that was once the property of Daniel Webster.

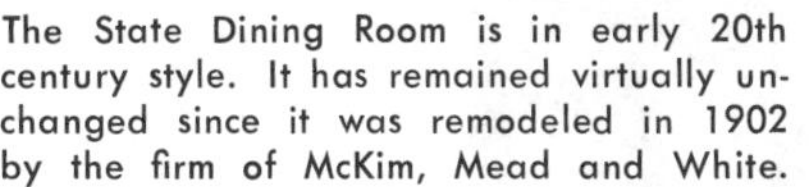

The State Dining Room is in early 20th century style. It has remained virtually unchanged since it was remodeled in 1902 by the firm of McKim, Mead and White.

WHITE HOUSE HISTORICAL ASSOCIATION

WHITE-JACKET is a novel by the American author Herman Melville, first published in 1850. It is a semiautobiographical work, based on the author's experiences on the U. S. Navy frigate *United States* in 1843–1844. The book, subtitled *The World in a Man-of-War*, recounts the voyage of the naval vessel *Neversink* from Hawaii to Virginia. The title derives from the white pea jacket that the narrator, a young seaman, purchases in Peru—a symbol of youthful innocence. The novel is a realistic account of life at sea, both its pleasures and its brutalities.

WHITE LEAD is any of several poisonous lead compounds used chiefly as white pigments in exterior paints. These pigments include basic carbonate white lead, basic sulfate white lead, and basic silicate white lead. Basic carbonate white lead, $2PbCO_3 \cdot PbO(OH)_2$, the oldest white pigment, is a powder marketed as a dry pigment or a paste. Basic sulfate white lead, $2PbSO_4 \cdot PbO$, introduced commercially in 1876, is now of secondary importance. Basic silicate white lead consisting mainly of lead monoxide and silicon oxide is used in exterior house paints. Another type consisting of silicates of lead is used in paints to protect metal surfaces from corrosion. See also Lead Poisoning.

WHITE MOUNTAINS, a continuation of the Appalachian system, stretching across north central New Hampshire into west central Maine. Except for the Great Smokies, the White Mountains have the highest peaks in the United States east of the Rockies. They derive their name from the grayish white appearance of the taller peaks, whose rocky summits extend far above the green timberline. As high as they are, the White Mountains are but the core of a much higher range that was formed at the close of the Paleozoic era, when sedimentary material washed from adjacent land areas was compacted into rock and elevated, and granite, syenite, and related rock types were thrust into place by igneous activity. The heat and pressure accompanying these forces account for the intense folding and crumbling characteristic of the rocks in the region and their highly metamorphic character.

The larger peaks—some 86 in number—are confined to an area of about 1,300 square miles (3,370 sq km). Eleven of these (counting the three summits of Mt. Adams as separate peaks) rise over 5,000 feet (1,500 meters), 25 others more than 4,000 feet (1,200 meters), and 26 others more than 3,000 feet (900 meters). Although not nearly so high above sea level as the Rockies, the White Mountains have the lofty grandeur of much higher peaks because they rise so abruptly from a central plateau. They are grouped into a number of ranges by the "notches" and valleys worn by the headwaters and tributaries of the four river systems that flow out of the region—the Androscoggin, the Ammonoosuc, the Pemigewasset, and the Saco.

The Presidential Range in north central New Hampshire contains the loftiest peaks: Mt. Washington, the highest, reaches 6,288 feet (1,917 meters); Adams, Jefferson, Clay, Monroe, Madison, and Franklin are over 5,000 feet. The peak of Mt. Washington, accessible by road and cog railway, can be seen occasionally from the Atlantic Ocean, 75 miles (120 km) away. Some 20 to 30 miles (30–50 km) to the southwest lie the equally spectacular Kinsman Mountain and the Franconia Mountains and their notches. From the valley of the Pemigewasset one can see, looking east, Mt. Lafayette, Mt. Lincoln, and the spectacular gorge and waterfall known as the Flume. To the west lie Profile (Cannon) Mountain, with its aerial tramway and celebrated Old Man of the Mountain—the "Great Stone Face" of Nathaniel Hawthorne's tale; and the glacial caverns of the Lost River near Kinsman Notch.

In 1925 most of the region, including a relatively small tract in Maine, was made into a national forest. For the convenience of campers and tourists, the state of New Hampshire has provided a number of state parks and reservations; the United States Forest Service maintains roadside company sites; and the Appalachian Mountain Club has established a network of mountain trails and shelters. The area is a popular summer resort, and it attracts winter sports enthusiasts, especially skiers.

Robert B. Dishman
University of New Hampshire

GRANT HEILMAN

Mount Washington, New Hampshire, in the Presidential Range of the White Mountains, is the highest peak in the northeastern states.

JEANNE WHITE, FROM NATIONAL AUDUBON SOCIETY

JOHN R. TERRES, FROM NATIONAL AUDUBON SOCIETY

Two monarchs of the eastern forests: the white oak (*above*), which ranges throughout eastern United States, and the white pine (*left*), common in northeastern United States and eastern Canada.

WHITE NOISE is an electronic or acoustic noise having the same intensity at every frequency within a given range of frequencies. The term was coined by analogy to white light, which contains every frequency within the visible-light spectrum.

Electronic white noise arises mainly from the random motion of electrons in conductors and such devices as resistors, vacuum tubes, and semiconductors. White noise generally is unwanted in electronic systems because it interferes with the reception of information-bearing signals. Acoustic white noise is a complex sound whose frequency components are so numerous and so closely spaced that the sound has no pitch. It sounds like a prolonged hiss similar to that of an amplifier-loudspeaker system turned to maximum volume. See also ELECTRONIC MUSIC—*Sound Sources;* HEARING.

WHITE OAK, a large, majestic, long-lived tree found in the United States from Maine to Minnesota and southward to the Gulf of Mexico. Its close-grained light-brown wood is handsome, strong, heavy, hard, and durable, making it especially valued for furniture, home interior paneling, floors, barrels, and boats.

The white oak, *Quercus alba,* generally grows 80 to 100 feet (24–30 meters) high, has stout wide-spreading branches, and a trunk 3 to 4 feet (0.9–1.2 meters) in diameter. Some reach a height of 150 feet (45 meters) and a trunk diameter of 8 feet (2.4 meters). The tree has a lifetime of 200 to 300 years, or even longer.

The white oak has round-lobed bright-green leaves, 4 to 9 inches (10–23 cm) long, that turn deep red and golden brown in the fall. After 20 years or more, the tree begins to bear smooth-shelled nuts (acorns). See also OAK.

WHITE OWL. See BARN OWL.

WHITE PERCH, a small perchlike food fish found in brackish waters from Nova Scotia to South Carolina and sometimes found landlocked in freshwater lakes. It grows to a length of about 10 inches (25 cm) and is dark green on top and silvery white on its sides and belly. Those living in salt water ascend rivers in the spring to breed.

The white perch, *Roccus americanus* or *Morone americana,* was once classified in the sea bass family, Serranidae. In 1966 it was reclassified in the temperate bass family, Percichthyidae.

WHITE PINE, any of several large coniferous evergreen trees having needles in clusters of five and a close-grained, light-colored soft wood widely used in buildings. The eastern white pine (*Pinus strobus*), the largest in northeastern North America, generally grows about 100 feet (30 meters) high with a trunk 3 to 4 feet (0.9–1.2 meters) in diameter. It has tiers of plumelike branches, clusters of blue-green needles, and slender cones 4 to 8 inches (10–20 cm) long that discharge small winged seeds in the fall.

The western white pine (*Pinus monticola*) is found from British Columbia to California and in Idaho and Montana. It generally grows about 100 feet (30 meters) high with a trunk diameter of 4 feet (1.2 meters). It has blue-green needles and cones 5 to 11 inches (13–28 cm) long.

The sugar pine (*Pinus lambertiana*), the largest American pine, is found in mountain regions in Oregon and California. It generally grows to a height of about 210 feet (64 meters) with a trunk diameter of about 7 feet (2 meters). It has blue-green needles and very large cones more than 12 inches (30 cm) long. See also PINE.

WHITE PLAINS is a city in southern New York state, the seat of Westchester county, midway between the Hudson River and Long Island Sound. It is situated in the New York metropolitan area, about 25 miles (40 km) northeast of downtown Manhattan.

A residential community with a large commuting population, White Plains is the financial, commercial, and shopping center for the county. It has also become the national and regional headquarters of many large corporations and is the site of a variety of light industrial and research firms. The Westchester County Airport is a few miles northeast of the city.

White Plains is the home of the College of White Plains (formerly Good Counsel College), and many other colleges are located nearby. It is also the site of the Westchester County Center, which presents cultural and athletic programs throughout the year.

White Plains was settled in 1683 by families who purchased the land from the Indians. In the 18th century it was an important post station for stagecoaches. White Plains was the site of the first official reading of the Declaration of Independence in New York state. The Battle of White Plains (1776) was fought just north of the settlement. George Washington's headquarters has been preserved and is open to the public. White Plains was chartered as a village in 1866 and as a city in 1915. Government is by a mayor and common council. Population: 46,999.

WHITE PLAINS, Battle of, an engagement in the American Revolution, fought on Oct. 28, 1776. Following the indecisive battle of Harlem Heights on September 16, George Washington decided to evacuate Manhattan and move north into Westchester. The British general, Sir William Howe, sent forces up the Hudson and East rivers in the hope of encircling the Americans and cutting off communication with New England. Both armies moved slowly and inefficiently. By the time Howe landed near New Rochelle, Washington had taken up a good position on the heights near the village of White Plains.

Howe, who had advanced on White Plains with about 13,000 men, finally attacked on October 28. The American line was anchored on Chatterton Hill, west of the Bronx River, and defended only by 1,600 inexperienced militia under Gen. Alexander McDougall, but the crack Delaware Continentals and Marylanders stood in reserve. The British and Hessians stormed the hill with determination, but the militia acquitted themselves surprisingly well, and for a long time the fighting in the thick foliage was pressed with vigor on both sides. At length, Howe ordered the 17th Dragoons into action (in the first formal cavalry charge of the war), and their onslaught proved too much for the weary militia, who retreated in confusion into the nearby woods. But the Delaware and Maryland regiments, fighting with their usual cool doggedness, formed a knot of resistance that permitted an orderly retreat and saved the rest of the army. The next day a skirmish took place, but Howe waited for reinforcements before resuming the offensive. Meanwhile, the Americans retired a few miles to a stronger position at North Castle, and Howe returned to the south. The American and British armies each lost about 300 men in killed, wounded, and prisoners in the engagement. The battleground is a National Battlefield Site.

WHITE RIVER, a tributary of the Arkansas River, flowing 720 miles (1,150 km) in Arkansas and Missouri. The river rises in the Boston Mountains of the Ozarks in northwestern Arkansas. It flows northeast into Missouri, then southeast back into Arkansas, turning south at Newport. Eventually it joins the north channel of the outlet of the Arkansas River to the Mississippi.

More than half of the White River's course is through uplands, where it has cut a deep valley and in some places is confined by narrow gorges. From Newport it meanders across the Mississippi plain through forested swampland.

Flood-control and power dams on the upper course have created lakes (Beaver, Ark.; Table Rock, Mo.; Bull Shoals, Mo.-Ark.), which are also used for recreational purposes. The White River can be navigated by vessels of shallow draft for its last 300 miles (480 km) from Batesville, Ark., just above Newport.

WHITE RIVER, in Indiana, the chief tributary of the Wabash River. From near Petersburg in southwestern Indiana, it flows southwestward over a 52-mile (84-km) course and enters the Wabash near Mt. Carmel, Ill. The White River is formed by the junction of its West Fork and East Fork near Petersburg. Its West Fork rises in Randolph county in eastern Indiana and flows southwestward past Muncie, Indianapolis, and Bicknell, Ind., before joining the East Fork. Its East Fork rises in Henry county in eastern Indiana, flows southwestward past Columbus and Shoals, Ind., and joins the West Fork.

WHITE RIVER, a tributary of the Missouri River, flowing 507 miles (811 km) in Nebraska and South Dakota. The river rises in the hilly Pine Ridge of northwestern Nebraska and runs northeast through irrigated farmland into South Dakota. There it traverses the grassy hills of the Pine Ridge (Sioux) Indian Reservation and turns eastward, marking the southern edge of the intricately eroded Badlands. Continuing eastward, it winds through a long stretch of cattle country before emptying into Lake Francis Case, a widening of the Missouri River, near Chamberlain, S. Dak.

WHITE ROCK is a city in British Columbia, Canada, on Semiahmoo Bay of the Strait of Georgia, 25 miles (40 km) southeast of Vancouver. Situated just north of the U. S. (Washington state) border, it is a customs port on the main route between Seattle and Vancouver. The Peace Portal, an arch erected in 1921, marks the western end of the undefended international boundary.

The site of White Rock was cleared for settlement in 1905, and the community was incorporated as a city in 1957. Its mild climate and extensive beaches have made it a popular vacation resort and retirement center. Population: 13,550.

WHITE RUSSIA, or Belorussia, was the name given to the Russian lands that paid no tribute to the Tatars or Lithuanians. See BELORUSSIAN SOVIET SOCIALIST REPUBLIC.

WHITE SANDS MISSILE RANGE is the largest overland rocket- and missile-testing range in the United States. It lies west of Alamogordo, N. Mex. See also MISSILE RANGES; NEW MEXICO (map).

JOSEF MUENCH

Huge dunes of white gypsum sand rise above the valley floor at White Sands National Monument in New Mexico.

WHITE SANDS NATIONAL MONUMENT, a federal nature preserve containing a large and beautiful gypsum desert. The monument, which was established in 1933, is 15 miles (24 km) southwest of Alamogordo, N. Mex. Snow-white gypsum dunes, constantly shifting, rise from 10 to 40 feet (3–12 meters) above the floor of the Tularosa basin. The monument contains almost 147,000 acres (59,500 hectares).

Mountain ranges flanking the valley contain tons of gypsum, which is carried with rainwater and melted snow into Lake Lucero at the southwest corner of the monument. When the lake evaporates, the fine crystals are picked up by the wind and deposited on the dunes.

Most of the monument is bare of vegetation, but a few hardy plants, including species of sumac, yucca, rabbit brush, and saltbush, have resisted burial. In some instances, plants have grown stems 40 feet (12 meters) long. Small animals have also adjusted to the harsh environment. Pocket mice and lizards have white coats that help them evade foxes, coyotes, and hawks.

The geology, flora, and fauna within the monument are explained in exhibits at the visitor center. In a legendary but more romantic version, the snowy wraiths that swirl across the dunes are Spanish maidens searching for lost lovers.

The White Sands Missile Range lies to the north of the monument.

WHITE SEA, a sea extending 365 miles (587 km) southwest from the Barents Sea, in the northwestern USSR, between Kola Peninsula on the west and Kanin Peninsula on the east. The White Sea (Russian, Beloye More) is joined to the Barents Sea by the Gorlo Strait. Near its mouth on the eastern side is Mezen Bay, which receives the waters of the Mezen River.

The inner part of the White Sea contains three large bays: Kandalaksha Bay to the northwest; Onega Bay, to the southeast, into which the Onega River flows; and Dvina Bay, which receives the Northern Dvina River. Solovets Island is the largest island in the sea.

The White Sea has an area of about 35,000 square miles (90,650 sq km) and is comparatively shallow, with an average depth of 325 feet (100 meters). It freezes over from November to May, although icebreakers keep the main port of Archangel open. Fishing (herring and cod) and shipping are the main economic activities. Other ports on the White Sea are Belomorsk (the terminal of the White Sea–Baltic Canal), Kandalaksha, Kem, Severodvinsk, and Onega.

WHITE SEA–BALTIC CANAL, an inland waterway in the northwestern USSR, extending from the port of Belomorsk on the White Sea to Povenets Harbor on Lake Onega. The canal is 140 miles (230 km) long and runs in a generally north-south direction, crossing the hills dividing the Baltic and White Sea watersheds by a series of 19 locks. The central part of the waterway crosses Lake Vygozero, from which the canal makes an abrupt and spectacular descent through locks into Lake Onega.

The White Sea–Baltic Canal (Russian, Belomorsko-Baltiski Kanal) derives its name from the fact that ships can sail from the White Sea via the canal to Lake Onega, and then to the Baltic Sea via the Svir River, Lake Ladoga, the Neva River, and the Finnish Gulf. By using it, Soviet ships can sail quickly between the Baltic and White seas, avoiding the long route circling the Scandinavian peninsula.

Czarist Russia planned to build such a canal, but the actual construction took place under the Soviets from 1931 to 1933. It was the first large inland waterway constructed by the USSR, first named the Stalin Canal, and built by prison labor. Maksim Gorki, the famous Russian writer, wrote a pamphlet justifying the use of prison labor for such an important project. During World War II, invading Finnish troops captured and damaged the canal's southern locks. These were reconstructed, and the canal was back in operation by 1946.

The canal is sufficiently deep to accommodate submarines, destroyers, and merchant ships of up to 1,250 tons. It has aided the development of Soviet Karelia; a number of new industrial towns have arisen along its route. The main canal cargoes are timber, apatite for fertilizer, and building stone moving south to Leningrad. Timber, coal, and oil move north to the White Sea for shipment to Western Europe.

ELLSWORTH RAYMOND,
Associate Professor of Soviet Government and Economics, New York University.

WHITE SETTLEMENT, town, Texas, in Tarrant County, nine miles west of Fort Worth and just south of Lake Worth. A residential and commercial suburb of Fort Worth, formerly called Liberator Village or Liberator, the town was incorporated after 1940 and in 1954 adopted a home-rule charter with a mayor-council form of government. Pop. 13,508.

WHITE SULPHUR SPRINGS, town, West Virginia, in Greenbrier County, 115 miles by road from Charleston and 8 miles east of Lewisburg, near the Virginia border, at an altitude of 1,917 feet. It is a residential community and health resort in the Allegheny Mountains, famed for its mineral springs. There is a municipal airport. The town was founded in 1750 and incorporated in 1909; its mineral springs have been popular since the early 1800's. Buildings of interest are the President's Cottage (1816), which served as a summer White House for Presidents Van Buren, Tyler, and Fillmore, and the White Sulphur Springs Hotel (1854, now Greenbrier). German, Italian, and Japanese diplomats were interned here during World War II. Of national interest is the Sam Snead (golf) Festival each May. The government, adopted in 1910, is by mayor and five councilmen. Pop. 3,371.

CARSON W. TURNER.

WHITE-THROATED SPARROW. See SPARROW.

WHITE WHALE or **BELUGA,** bə-lo͞o′gə, a species (*Delphinapterus leucas*) of cetacean, the only cetacean that is white as an adult. White whales are medium sized, reaching 16 feet for the adult bulls and perhaps a foot or two smaller for adult cows. At 16 feet, the weight would be in the neighborhood of 1½ tons. Calves are born in the spring or early summer and are from 5 to 6 feet long and dark gray. As they grow, they turn progressively lighter until the white color is attained at 10 to 12 feet. The range of the white whale is throughout ice-free Arctic and sub-Arctic seas, mostly near coasts. The most southerly places in which they are found are the St. Lawrence River and the southern Bering Sea. The name "beluga," by which they are most often called, is from a Russian word meaning "whitish." This name is also applied to the white river sturgeon, source of caviar. The beluga is primarily a fish eater, but it also eats a great variety of worms, squids, crustaceans, and other invertebrates, which it finds mainly on the bottom in rather shallow water. Commonly, in summer, it travels up rivers with the tide, following the schools of migratory fishes, such as smelt and salmon, to feed on them. It is a timid creature, very sensitive to its surroundings, and possesses excellent echolocation (sonar) ability, which it uses to find food and to navigate in the murky, shallow river waters where it feeds.

CARLETON RAY.

WHITEAVES, hwīt′ēvz, **Joseph Frederick,** Canadian paleontologist and zoologist: b. Oxford, England, Dec. 26, 1835; d. Aug. 8, 1907. He studied at the University of Oxford (1858–1861) and made investigations of the land and freshwater mollusca and fossils of the oolitic rocks in the vicinity of Oxford, adding considerably to the information possessed. He visited the United States and Canada and became engaged in geological investigations in Montreal and Quebec in 1861 to 1862. From 1863 to 1875 he was scientific curator of the museum and secretary of the Natural History Society of Montreal. He made a special study of the land and freshwater mollusca of lower Canada between 1867 and 1873. He was appointed to the Canada Geological Survey in 1875, became its paleontologist in 1876, one of the assistant directors in 1877, and zoologist in 1883. He was one of the original fellows of the Royal Society of Canada, founded in 1882.

WHITEBAIT, hwīt′bāt, a small fish, which is regarded by naturalists as merely the fry of the herring or of similar fish. In America, the term is applied to small (two- to three-inch) North Atlantic herring, as well as to some small smelts on the northern Pacific coast of California. The whitebait fishery is actively prosecuted on some parts of the British coast, particularly in the estuary of the Thames, where the whitebait is very abundant in spring and summer, beginning to appear at the end of March or early in April. Adult whitebait are caught on the coasts of Kent and Essex during winter, and in this condition are about six inches in length. Whitebait is found also in the Firth of Forth. It is much in demand as a delicacy for the table. When ordinarily captured, whitebait are only from one and one-half to four inches in length. They are caught by means of bag nets sunk four or five feet below the surface of the water. For several months they continue to ascend the river in shoals with the flood tide and descend with the ebb tide, not being able to live in freshwater.

WHITEBEAM, hwīt′bēm, **WHITEBEAM TREE,** or **BEAM TREE,** a small tree or shrub, *Sorbus Aria,* in the rose family, related to the mountain ash, apple, and pear. Its simple, toothed leaves are dark green above, white-wooly below; the young twigs are also white. The strongly scented, clustered, white flowers are about one-half inch across. Whitebeam is native to Europe, widely cultivated there, and grown in avenues and parks, and in sunny, exposed locations. The small, mealy, scarlet to orange, applelike fruits have been used in making a brandy, jam, and bread. The wood is hard and tough.

EDWIN B. MATZKE.

WHITECAP or **WHITE HORSE,** the plume of froth whipped up at the surface of a deep-sea swell or a partially breaking deep-sea wave under the force of a strong wind blowing over the water. The surface water is churned up by friction with the moving air stream and becomes flecked with foam at the crests of the waves. Thus whitecaps seen in open water are always a sign of high wind, from which a *spindrift* of spray may also result, streaming from the whitecap in the direction of wind flow. Near shore, white water may also indicate a line of spilling or plunging breakers, or the presence of rocks, and is produced by turbulent mechanical action of the water.

FERGUS J. WOOD.

WHITECHAPEL, hwīt'chăp-əl, a district in the Borough of Stepney in the east end of London, England. It is a center of clothing manufacturing. Within its boundaries are a bell foundry dating from 1570 and the London Hospital built in 1757. Whitechapel Art Gallery was founded in 1901 by Canon Samuel Augustus Barnett (1844–1913), who was also one of the founders of Toynbee Hall (1884), a model educational and social center named after Arnold Toynbee (1852–1883), the sociologist and economist. With other East London districts, Whitechapel suffered heavy bomb damage during World War II.

H. GORDON STOKES.
Author of "English Place Names"

WHITEFIELD, hwīt'fēld, **George,** English evangelist, founder of the Calvinist Methodists: b. Gloucester, England, Dec. 16, 1714; d. Newburyport, Mass., Sept. 30, 1770. An innkeeper's son, Whitefield attended the grammar school of St. Mary de Crypt at Gloucester. According to his self-accusing *A Short Account* (1740), he was given to truancy and "very fond of reading Plays" and acting. But at Pembroke College, Oxford, where he entered as a servitor and matriculated in 1732, Whitefield met the Wesleys and joined the "methodist society" in 1735, in which year he dated his conversion. He was ordained a deacon in the Church of England in 1736; within a year the power and novelty of Whitefield's preaching had already made him a controversial figure.

Having proposed himself to the Wesleys as a missionary, Whitefield began the first of seven voyages to America on Feb. 2, 1738 for Georgia, where he preached, organized schools, and planned the Bethesda orphanage. Late in 1738 he returned to England to solicit funds for it. His mingling with dissenters was disapproved by the church, and his extempore, dramatic preaching caused him to be excluded from several pulpits. He then began to speak in the "fields," often to audiences of 20,000 and more, and on Aug. 1, 1739 was denounced by the bishop of London. Two weeks later Whitefield embarked for America. Whitefield's journals describe these events in detail.

Whitefield's arrival in the colonies acted as the catalyst of the "Great Awakening." In Philadelphia (where he impressed Benjamin Franklin) Whitefield preached to throngs; traveling southward, he attracted immense audiences from Maryland to Georgia. When he returned to the north he preached to tens of thousands in Pennsylvania and moved into New England, where he drew some 50,000 hearers to Boston Common. To Jonathan Edwards (1703–1758), whom Whitefield met and impressed, these prodigious feats were among the evidences of an impending millennium. But Whitefield was censured by the Anglican Commissary of Charleston, derided by conservative Philadelphians, and denounced in the Harvard faculty *Testimony* (1744) as "an Enthusiast, a censorious, uncharitable Person, and a Deluder of the People." He retained his popularity, however, through five subsequent visits to America and during each contributed profoundly to intercolonial unity. By attacking the parish system and by scorning religious "names and parties," he helped forge an alliance of dissenters from New England to the South.

In the spring of 1740 Whitefield publicly condemned John Wesley's doctrine of "free grace." Thereafter Whitefield was the acknowledged leader of "Calvinist Methodism" and, indirectly, through his chaplaincy to the countess of Huntingdon, the founder of the "Connexion" that bore her name. He spent the rest of his life touring Great Britain, Ireland, and America to advance the cause of the evangelical revival. Yet he was not a theologian. Rather he was, as an American admirer observed in 1740, "a great master of pulpit oratory," for whom the test of any doctrine was its efficacy in converting souls. Of more than 18,000 sermons Whitefield preached, less than 90 survive in any form, and these contain only hints of the emotional power that moved millions in America, England, Scotland, and Wales. Nor was Whitefield's presence in itself imposing; childhood measles had left him squint eyed. But his gestures, though novel and dramatic, were never forced, his voice was graceful, and through all shone the zeal that made him the prototype of evangelical Protestantism in his century and the next.

ALAN HEIMERT,
Assistant Professor of English, Harvard University.

WHITEFISH BAY, hwīt'fĭsh, village, Wisconsin, in Milwaukee County, on wooded bluffs overlooking Lake Michigan, about six miles north of downtown Milwaukee, at an altitude of 653 feet. An entirely residential suburb of Milwaukee, it is the largest village in the state in population. Settled in 1842 and incorporated in 1892, Whitefish Bay has a council-manager form of government, which was adopted in 1938. Population: 14,930.

JANET M. EGGUM.

WHITEFISHES, hwīt'fĭsh-əz, a group name for the numerous species of the genus *Coregonus* which belong to and look like the Salmonidae family. They occur in northern freshwaters throughout Eurasia and North America and are important commercially in the Great Lakes. These fishes are silvery, with dark backs. The short dorsal, set in the middle of the length, is followed by a small adipose fin, typical also of the trouts and salmons from which these fishes are chiefly distinguished by their conspicuous scales and small teeth. There are numerous species, some of which hybridize. They generally live in the deeper part of lakes or streams, but return to spawn nearer shore. Whitefish feed on tiny crustaceans.

Due to the opening of the Welland Canal, which gave saltwater fishes access to the Great Lakes, sea lampreys arrived and began serious depredations on the whitefish population. Two methods are being used to hold the lamprey population in check—poison, and electric barring from the streams which it ascends for spawning. Whitefish are marketed fresh or smoked and the roe is sometimes used for making caviar.

CHRISTOPHER W. COATES.

WHITEHALL, hwīt'hôl, a street in London, England, leading north from the Houses of Parliament to Trafalgar Square. It contains many important government offices, including the Admiralty and the War Office. In Whitehall stands the Cenotaph, designed by Sir Edwin Landseer Lutyens (1869–1944), a memorial to those who fell in the two world wars. Whitehall is named after a palace purchased in 1298 by the Archbishop of York, which, altered and embellished and known as York House or York Place, was

Radio Times Hulton Picture Library

A memorial service is held at the Cenotaph in Whitehall.

the London abode of his successors. Henry VIII seized the property and changed its name to Whitehall on the fall of Thomas Cardinal Wolsey (1529). All that now remains of it is the banquet hall which was designed by Inigo Jones (1573–1652) in the reign of James I. Long used as a chapel, it is now the United Services Museum. Charles I was beheaded in front of Whitehall in 1649, walking to the scaffold through one of the windows.

ALLAN M. FRASER.

WHITEHALL, village, New York, in Washington County, at the southern end of Lake Champlain and the northern terminus of the Champlain Division of the New York State Barge Canal; 77 miles north of Albany and 21 miles northeast of Glens Falls, at an altitude of 125 feet. It is a summer resort and industrial center, with railroad and machine shops, boatbuilding yards, and factories for metal products and ladies' coats. It was settled in 1759 by Major Philip Skene, a British army officer, with some 30 families, and called Skenesborough; in 1806 it was incorporated as Whitehall. It is popularly known as the birthplace of the United States Navy, because ships were constructed there by Benedict Arnold in 1776 to stop the British invasion down Lake Champlain; the American ships were destroyed in the Battle of Valcour Island on the lake, the first naval action after the Declaration of Independence, but the invasion was delayed for a year. After the Battle of Plattsburgh in the War of 1812, the American and British fleets were brought to Whitehall and later sunk. Pop. 3,241.

LORRAINE DANNEHY.

WHITEHALL, city, Ohio, in Franklin County, seven miles east of Columbus, of which it is a suburb. Incorporated as a city in 1956, it has mayor-council government. Pop. 21,299.

WHITEHALL, borough, Pennsylvania, in Allegheny County, five miles directly south of downtown Pittsburgh. Formed from parts of Baldwin and Bethel townships in 1947, it is a suburb of Pittsburgh with a mayor-commission form of government. Pop. 15,143.

WHITEHEAD, hwīt′hĕd, **Alfred North,** English philosopher and mathematician: b. Ramsgate, Isle of Thanet, Kent, England, Feb. 15, 1861; d. Cambridge, Mass., Dec. 30, 1947. His grandfather, father, uncles, and brothers engaged in activities concerned with education, religion, and local administration in Kent. His father was an ordained clergyman of the Anglican Church and in his later years was vicar of St. Peter's Parish. The history of the region and the religious family background made lasting impressions upon the boy, whose early education conformed to the traditions of the time. He began studying Latin at the age of 10, and Greek at 12. In 1875 he was sent to school at Sherborne, in Dorsetshire, where "the relics of the past were even more obvious" than in Kent. In his spare time he read Wordsworth and Shelley, and poetry and history became his major interests.

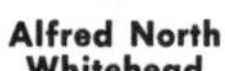

Alfred North Whitehead

Walter Stoneman

In the fall of 1880 he entered Trinity College, Cambridge. There he resided without interruption until the summer of 1910, first as a "scholar," then as a "fellow," and finally as senior lecturer. His undergraduate studies were devoted almost exclusively to mathematics, pure and applied. His course work, however, was augmented by regular and long discussions with fellow students and friends on religion, philosophy, and especially literature. His friends included Henry Head, D'Arcy Thompson, G. Lowes Dickinson, Henry Sidgwick, William R. Sorley, Frederic W. Maitland, and other persons prominent or to become prominent in English philosophy and letters. Whitehead obtained his fellowship at Trinity and also a lectureship in mathematics in 1885. In 1890 he married Evelyn Willoughby Wade and they had two sons and a daughter. The younger son was killed in action in 1918.

Whitehead moved to London in 1910, and from 1911 to 1914 he held various positions in mathematics at University College, University of London. From 1914 until the summer of 1924 he held a professorship in mathematics at the Imperial College of Science and Technology at Kensington. Here he became dean of the faculty of science in the university, and chairman of the council which managed Goldsmith's College. In 1924, at the age of 63, Whitehead joined the faculty of Harvard University as professor of philosophy, where he remained until his retirement in 1937. In recognition of his contributions in his field he had been made a fellow of the British Academy in 1931 and was awarded the British Order of Merit in 1945.

Whitehead's first book, *A Treatise on Universal Algebra,* appeared in 1898. Hermann Grassmann's theory of extensions, Sir William R. Hamilton's work on quaternions, and George Boole's symbolic logic had influenced him strongly and largely determined his own work in mathematical logic. In 1903, the year Whitehead was elected to the Royal Society, Bertrand Russell published his *Principles of Mathematics.* Both men discovered that they had projected further works along almost identical lines and therefore began to collaborate on the monumental *Principia Mathematica* (3 vols., 1910–13). Whitehead's philosophical writings did not begin until the end of World War I. Beginning at this time, however, his thinking underwent a transition that resulted in some profound changes.

The beginnings of these changes can be observed in *An Enquiry Concerning the Principles of Natural Knowledge* (1919), the less technical *The Concept of Nature* (1920), and *The Principle of Relativity With Applications to Physical Science* (1922). The transition was accelerated in *Science and the Modern World* (1925), *Religion in the Making* (1926), and *Symbolism; Its Meaning and Effect* (1927). It culminated in the key work of his mature philosophy, *Process and Reality* (1929), the Gifford Lectures at Edinburgh University (1927–1928). This difficult work has been compared to that of Plato and Leibniz as being a combination of formal thought with speculative metaphysics. Nature was no longer conceived as the terminus of sense perception but as a great expanding nexus of occurrences. The basic conceptions developed in *Process and Reality* were intended to be all-inclusive and interlocking. They aimed at the elimination of all dualisms: mind-matter, God-world, permanence-transience, causality teleology, atomism-continuity, sensation-emotion, and subject-object. The work achieved a reconciliation of the realistic and the conceptualistic strands in Whitehead's own earlier philosophy. (See also Process and Reality.)

After *Process and Reality,* no essential changes occurred in Whitehead's system, although in *Adventures of Ideas* (1933) he discussed his basic concepts further and in *Modes of Thought* (1938) an illuminating comparison was made of logical and aesthetic consistency. His *Aims of Education and Other Essays* (1929) gained a wide readership after World War II.

W. H. Werkmeister
Author of "Philosophy of Science"

WHITEHEAD, William, English poet: b. Cambridge, England, February 1715; d. London, April 14, 1785. He was educated at Winchester College and Clare Hall, Cambridge, was appointed secretary and registrar of the Order of the Bath in 1755, and in 1757, through the influence of the earl of Jersey, whose son he tutored, he was appointed poet laureate of England in succession to the poet and dramatist Colley Cibber (1671–1757). He was the author of the tragedies: *The Roman Father* (1750); and *Creusa, Queen of Athens* (1754); the comedy, *The School for Lovers* (1762), his most successful play; a farce, *The Trip to Scotland* (1770); and numerous minor poems. His identity is sometimes confused with that of the English satirist, Paul Whitehead (1710–1774). His collected poems were published (1788) with a memoir by William Mason.

WHITEHILL, hwĭt'hĭl, **Clarence Eugene,** American opera singer: b. Marengo, Iowa, Nov. 5, 1871; d. New York, N.Y., Dec. 19, 1932. After studies in Chicago he went to Paris for instruction under Giraudet and Sbriglia. Following his operatic debut in the bass role of Friar Lawrence in Gounod's *Roméo et Juliette,* at Brussels in 1899, he became (1900) the first American male singer to be engaged by the Opéra-Comique, Paris (debut as Nilakantha in Délibes' *Lakmé*). He then toured the United States with the Savage English Grand Opera Company before further study and operatic performances in Germany. On Nov. 25, 1909, Whitehill made his debut with the Metropolitan Opera Company in New York City, excelling in Wagnerian roles, but also succeeding in French and Italian operas, winning high critical esteem for his Golaud in the Metropolitan's first production of Debussy's *Pelléas et Mélisande* in 1924.

Herbert Weinstock.

WHITEHORSE, hwĭt'hôrs, city, Yukon Territory, Canada, in the south, at an altitude of 2,079 feet, at the head of navigation on Lewes River, a name for the upper part of the Yukon River, 65 miles directly north of the Alaska border and 95 miles north of the seaport of Skagway, Alaska. Northern terminal of the White Pass and Yukon Railway and on the Alaska Highway, it serves as a distributing center for the surrounding mining, hunting, and trapping region. It has been the capital of the Territory since 1951. It is the base for highway maintenance in Canada, and also for the Royal Canadian Air Force and various government departments. Whitehorse has a modern airport with scheduled airline services, and radio and meteorological stations. A staging area for the Klondike gold rush, it was founded in 1900 and incorporated as a city in 1950. Of interest are Miles Canyon and Whitehorse Rapids, an old log church (Anglican), an Indian graveyard, the MacBride Historical Museum, which contains Indian artifacts and crafts and material on the history of the Yukon Territory, and the original cabin of Sam McGee, made famous by Robert W. Service in his poem, *The Cremation of Sam McGee.* Population: 14,814.

W. D. MacBride.

WHITELOCKE, hwĭt'lŏk, **Bulstrode,** English lawyer and statesman: b. London, England, Aug. 6, 1605; d. Chilton, Wiltshire, July 28, 1675. He was educated at Oxford University and studied law at the Middle Temple. In 1626, he was called to the bar and entered Parliament in the same year. Whitelocke was chairman of the committee of the Long Parliament of 1640 which drew up charges of impeachment against Sir Thomas Wentworth, 1st earl of Strafford, but he refused membership on the tribunal which tried Charles I in 1649. As ambassador to Sweden

(1653–1654), he showed diplomatic skill in negotiating a treaty of friendship with that country. A commissioner of the Great Seal (1649; 1654–1655), he was dismissed because he opposed Oliver Cromwell's changes in chancery court procedure, but he was made a member of the upper house in 1657. He regained his commission under Richard Cromwell and, on the latter's resignation, became president of the council of state and a member of the committee of safety which superseded it. Pardoned at the Restoration, Whitelocke lived out his days in quiet retirement.

ALLAN M. FRASER.

WHITEMAN, hwīt'mən, **Paul,** American conductor: b. Denver, Colo., March 28, 1891; d. Doylestown, Pa., Dec. 29, 1967. He played the viola in symphony orchestras in Denver and San Francisco and later conducted a U. S. Navy band. Then, with his own dance band in Santa Barbara, Calif., he evolved the mixed style of orchestration and performance called "symphonic jazz." At his historic concert, called an "experiment in modern music," at Aeolian Hall, New York, on Feb. 12, 1924, he conducted the first performances of two pieces of "symphonic jazz" which he had commissioned: Victor Herbert's *Suite of Serenades* and George Gershwin's *A Rhapsody in Blue* (orchestrated by Ferde Grofé, who later composed his *Grand Canyon Suite* for Whiteman). Very popular as a recording artist, Whiteman also toured widely in the United States and Europe. He established the annual Whiteman Awards for "symphonic jazz" compositions by Americans and wrote or was coauthor of several books: *Jazz* (with M. M. McBride, 1926), *How to Be a Bandleader* (with L. Lieber, 1941), and *Records for the Millions* (1948).

HERBERT WEINSTOCK.

WHITESBORO, hwīts'bûr-ō, village, New York, in Oneida County, four miles northwest of Utica on the Mohawk River and the New York State Barge Canal, at an altitude of 415 feet. It is a residential and commercial community, manufacturing baskets, furniture, wood products, and heaters. It was first settled in 1784 by Judge Hugh White, who left his Middletown, Conn. home, shipped by water to Albany, traveled overland to Schenectady, and then up the Mohawk by bateau. The village was incorporated in 1813. Population: 4,460.

WHITESTONE, hwīt'stōn, community, New York, in the Borough of Queens, New York City, on the East River (north shore of Long Island). It is connected with the Borough of The Bronx by the Bronx-Whitestone Bridge, opened in 1939 and owned and operated by the Triborough Bridge Authority.

WHITETHROAT, hwīt'thrōt, a name applied to various birds, notably two species of Old World warblers, the common whitethroat, *Sylvia communis,* and the lesser whitethroat, *S. curruca.* Both occur in England where the former, though a small, modestly colored bird, makes itself conspicuous, especially when singing, and was known to farm boys and milkmaids as Peggy Whitethroat. Both species winter in Africa. Their song is not very musical. In America the white-throated sparrow, *Zonotrichia albicollis,* is often called by the name of whitethroat.

DEAN AMADON.

WHITEWASH, hwīt'wŏsh, a milky fluid produced by mixing slaked or hydrated lime with water, used as an inexpensive, impermanent coating for such surfaces as walls, ceilings, and fences. When mixed with size and sometimes colored, it is used on interior surfaces under the name of calcimine.

WHITEWATER, hwīt'wô-tər, city, Wisconsin, in Walworth County, on Whitewater Creek, about 43 miles southeast of Milwaukee, at an altitude of 822 feet. The name derived from the Algonquian Wau-be-gan-naw-po-cat meaning whitish or muddy water. The city is the center of a dairy, poultry, truck- and grain-farming region; its industries include manufacturing and food-processing plants. The coeducational Wisconsin State College (for teachers) was established in the city in 1868. The first settlement on the present site was in 1837; the Old Mill was built in 1839; the village plat was surveyed in 1840 and was incorporated in 1858. Whitewater became a fourth-class city in 1909. A city-manager form of government with eight councilmen was adopted in 1955. Population: 11,520.

WHITEWOOD, hwīt'wŏŏd, the name applied to numerous trees having light-colored wood, and to their lumber. In North America, the tulip tree, *Liriodendron tulipifera,* which has greenish yellow heartwood and white sapwood, is often called whitewood; other American plants sometimes designated whitewood are basswood (also called linden), *Tilia americana;* sycamore, *Platanus occidentalis;* cottonwood, *Populus deltoides;* maleberry or male blueberry (a shrub), *Lyonia ligustrina;* and in Florida *Drypetes diversifolia* and *Schoepfia chrysophylloides.* In Great Britain, European lindens and Norway spruces are sometimes called whitewood, and in other regions the name is used for various trees.

EDWIN B. MATZKE.

WHITFIELD, hwĭt'fēld, or **WHITFELD,** hwĭt'fĕld, **Henry,** English clergyman: b. near London, England, ?1597; d. Winchester, ?1657. Nothing is definitely known of his early life. He appears to have been appointed to the living of Ockley, Surrey, in 1616, but incurred the displeasure of Archbishop William Laud by protecting several Puritan clergymen. He therefore emigrated to New England with a number of followers from Kent, Surrey, and Sussex and was one of the founders of Guilford, Conn. His stone house there, built in 1639 and used as a place of worship until a meetinghouse could be erected, now serves as a museum. In 1650 he returned to England and settled at Winchester. His writings include *Some Helpes to stirre up to Christian Duties* (3d ed., 1636); *The Light appearing more and more towards the Perfect Day* (1651); and *Strength out of Weakness* (1652).

WHITGIFT, hwĭt'gĭft, **John,** English prelate: b. Great Grimsby, Lincolnshire, England, ?1530; d. Lambeth, London, Feb. 29, 1604. Educated at Cambridge University, he was elected a fellow of Peterhouse (1555) and took holy orders in 1560. He gained many academic preferments at Cambridge and was vice chancellor of the university (1570, 1573). He was made dean of Lincoln in 1571 and, in 1577, bishop of Worcester. In 1583, he was appointed archbishop of Canterbury and became a member of the Privy Council in 1586. In theology he had strong Calvinist convictions, which later found formal expression in the Lambeth Articles (q.v.) which he helped to draft (1595). He was, however, a firm believer in the episcopalian system of church government and a vigorous opponent of the Presbyterian polity advocated by Thomas Cartwright, whom he caused to be deprived of his professorship at Cambridge (1570) and his fellowship at Trinity (1571). A stern disciplinarian, he strove to establish rigid religious uniformity, a policy in which he enjoyed the full support and confidence of Elizabeth I, who referred to him as "her little black husband." In 1583, he drew up stringent articles compelling all clergymen to subscribe to the royal supremacy, the Book of Common Prayer, and the Thirty-nine Articles. In 1586, at his instigation, the press was muzzled by means of a star-chamber decree which forbade the printing of any publication without the license of the archbishop of Canterbury or the bishop of London. Because of his anti-Puritan measures he was libeled, with other bishops, in the Marprelate tracts. In retaliation, he obtained increased powers for the court of high commissions to punish ecclesiastical offenses, and, in 1593, he had a law passed making Puritanism a statutory offense. He attended Elizabeth on her deathbed, crowned James I, and was present at the opening of the Hampton Court Conference (1604).

ALLAN M. FRASER,
Provincial Archivist, Newfoundland, Canada.

WHITHORNE, hwĭt'hôrn, or **WHITTERN,** hwĭt'ûrn, **Emerson.** American composer: b. Cleveland, Ohio, Sept. 6, 1884; d. New York, N.Y., March 22, 1958. After boyhood musical studies and tours as a young pianist, he spent 11 years in Europe as a student (his teachers having included Theodor Leschetizky, Robert Fuchs, and Artur Schnabel), critic, and concert manager for his wife, the pianist Ethel Leginska. Returning to America in 1915, he composed in then novel idioms, including so-called "machine music," and became a leading figure in the League of Composers (New York). His music never attracted more than a small audience; it now is seldom performed.

HERBERT WEINSTOCK.

WHITIN, hwīt'ĭn, **Paul,** American businessman and civic leader: b. Roxbury, Mass., Dec. 3, 1767; d. Feb. 8, 1831. Born Paul Whiting, he was 18 months old when his father died; within a year his mother married James Prentice of Sutton, Mass. He was essentially self-educated, having attended school no more than six months. At 14 he was apprenticed to Jesse White of South Northbridge to learn the trade of blacksmith. In 1793 he married Betsy Fletcher of Northbridge; he signed the marriage certificate "Paul Whitin," dropping the "g," and thereby became the progenitor of the Whitin families. In 1794 he entered business with his father-in-law, James Fletcher, under the name of Fletcher and Whitin, making bar iron from scrap iron and later manufacturing hoes and scythes. In 1809 he financed the erection of the first cotton mill in the Northbridge area, the Northbridge Cotton Company. He bought out his partner in Fletcher and Whitin in 1826 and founded P. Whitin and Sons; in time half a dozen mills came under its ownership. The company was dissolved in 1864, the eldest son, John C. Whitin, taking the shop which made the mill machinery, which became the well-known Whitin Machine Works. In 1795 Whitin was elected town clerk of Northbridge, holding this office for 13 years; he was justice of the peace from 1805 to 1819. He was active in the state militia, rising through the ranks to lieutenant colonel (1807), after which he was known as "Colonel." Four years after he died the anomalous name of the village of South Northbridge was changed to Whitinsville in his honor.

PETER HACKETT.

WHITING, hwīt'ĭng, city, Indiana, in Lake County, near the southern end of Lake Michigan between Gary and southeast Chicago, at an altitude of 585 feet. In the Calumet industrial complex, it has large oil refineries and chemical plants. It is the birthplace of the Standard Oil Company (Indiana), which operates its refinery in Whiting as a subdivision (since Jan. 1, 1961) of the American Oil Company, wholly owned by Standard. The cultural life of the community is particularly concerned with music; the Memorial Community House, built by Standard Oil in 1923 in memory of soldiers of World War I, contains a concert hall as well as other recreational facilities; Lake Front Park has a fine beach. The city was settled on the site of Whiting's Crossing (station 1874) and incorporated as a town in 1895 and as a city in 1903. Government is by a mayor and six councilmen. Population: 5,630.

DANA BROWN.

WHITING, the several species of fishes of the genus *Menticirrhus*, one of the croaker group, and also known as corbina and kingfish, the latter popular name more widely used for the unrelated *Scomberomorus* species of which the cero is one. *Menticirrhus* is found only in North and South America. These fishes are usually less than two feet long. Their body is elongated, the snout projects, and the teeth are very fine. There is a single barbel on the chin. The outer margin of the caudal fin is concave above and convex below. The whitings have no air bladder. They are metallic greenish fishes found coastally in surf and over sand and are bottom feeders on small fishes and crustaceans. They are popular with anglers and are marketed where not legally protected.

CHRISTOPHER W. COATES.

WHITING. See CHALK.

WHITLAM, hwit'ləm, **Gough** (1916–), prime minister of Australia. He was born in Kew, Victoria, Australia, on July 11, 1916. After World War II he practiced law. In 1952 he was elected as a Labour member to the national House of Representatives. Becoming parliamentary leader of the party in 1967, he steered the party away from doctrinaire socialism and toward a more pragmatic approach to reform.

On Dec. 2, 1972, in a general election, the Labour party defeated the Liberal-Country party coalition that had governed Australia for 23 years. Whitlam, who succeeded William McMahon as prime minister on Dec. 5, 1972, had campaigned on the need for increasing social and economic benefits. Retaining the foreign affairs portfolio, Whitlam suspended military conscription, freed imprisoned draft resisters, established diplomatic relations with Communist China, and announced withdrawal of Australian forces from Vietnam. Eventually inflation, business bankruptcies, and unemployment eroded public confidence in his government, and in November 1975 he was dismissed by Governor General Sir John Kerr, to be succeeded by Malcolm Fraser.

WHITLOCK, hwĭt'lŏk, **Brand,** American writer, politician, and diplomat: b. Urbana, Ohio, March 4, 1869; d. Cannes, France, May 24, 1934. He worked as a journalist in Toledo and Chicago from 1887 to 1893, and then served as clerk in the office of the Illinois secretary of state. In this capacity he became friendly with John Peter Altgeld, Illinois reformer, who was governor at the time, making out for Altgeld in secret the pardons for the last three prisoners of the 1886 Haymarket Square riot and becoming involved in the resulting controversy. Whitlock studied law, was admitted to the Illinois bar in 1894 and to that of Ohio in 1897, and established his practice in Toledo. There he crusaded for improved legal procedures, for prison reforms, and against capital punishment, working with Mayor Samuel M. "Golden Rule" Jones in the local reform movement of the time. After Jones died in 1904, Whitlock was elected mayor of Toledo in 1905 on a home-rule, nonpartisan, antimonopoly platform. He succeeded in securing a new city charter providing for the initiative, referendum, recall, and direct nominations. He was by this time a well-established magazine writer, producing both verse and prose, the latter dealing in the main with politics and economics in an uncompromising fashion.

President Wilson appointed Whitlock minister to Belgium in 1913, and he was in office at the outbreak of World War I. He was entrusted with the representation of seven of the warring nations and remained at his post after the German invasion. His skill in dealing with the difficulties under the German occupation earned him a worldwide reputation, and he won scarcely less praise for his handling of Belgian relief work.

After the signing of the armistice in November 1918, Whitlock resumed his duties in Brussels and served with the rank of ambassador from 1919 to 1922. He was showered with honors by the Belgian and other Allied governments, and a boulevard in Brussels was named for him. He retired because of ill health and spent his last years in Europe. He was buried at Cannes.

His books include *The Thirteenth District* (1902); *Her Infinite Variety* (1904); *The Turn of the Balance* (1907); *Abraham Lincoln* (1908); *The Gold Brick* (1910); *On the Enforcement of Law in Cities* (1913); *Forty Years of It; an Autobiography* (1914); *Memoirs of Belgium Under the German Occupation* (1918); *Belgium: a Personal Record* (2 vols., 1919); *J. Hardin and Son* (1923); *La Fayette* (2 vols., 1929); *The Strangers on the Island* (1933).

WHITLOCK, Elizabeth Kemble, English actress: b. Warrington, Lancashire, England, April 2, 1761; d. Feb. 27, 1836. The fifth child of Roger Kemble, she went to London with her two elder sisters, Sarah (Mrs. Siddons) and Frances (Mrs. Twiss), after some stage experience in the country. She first appeared at Drury Lane Theatre in 1783 as Portia in *The Merchant of Venice*. In 1785 she was married to Charles Edward Whitlock, a provincial manager and actor, and seven years later accompanied her husband to the United States, where they performed for many years in the principal cities. Mrs. Whitlock became the most popular actress of the day in America and frequently performed before President Washington and other distinguished persons in Philadelphia. She returned to England in 1807 with a competence and retired from the stage.

WHITMAN, hwĭt'mən, **Charles Otis,** American zoologist: b. Woodstock, Me., Dec. 14, 1842; d. Chicago, Ill., Dec. 6, 1910. He graduated from Bowdoin College in 1868, taught for some years, then studied (1873) under Louis Agassiz on Penikese Island and under Rudolf Leuckart at Leipzig, where he received his Ph.D. in 1878. He was professor and chairman of zoology at the Imperial University in Tokyo, Japan, from 1879 to 1881, worked at the Naples Zoological Station (1881–1882), and assisted in zoology at the Harvard Museum of Comparative Zoology (1882–1886). He became director of the Allis Lake Laboratory, Milwaukee (1886–1889), founded by E. P. Allis, Jr., and established the *Journal of Morphology* (1887) with Allis. He taught zoology at Clark University (1889–1892) and was professor and head of the department of zoology at the University of Chicago from 1892 until his death. He was the first director (1888–1908) of the Marine Biological Laboratory at Woods Hole, Mass., and the leader in establishing (1890) the American Morphological Society, which became the American Society of Zoologists.

Whitman published 67 papers, principally on eggs, development and anatomy of vertebrates and annelids, microscopic methods, marine laboratories, the cell theory, animal behavior, origin of species, and genetics and evolution. His first publication, *The Embryology of Clepsine* (1878), established the concept of cell lineage (tracing the history of cleavage cells through to their ultimate fates in development) and stimulated a brilliant group of young Americans to emulate him. He stressed egg organization as preceding and regulating cell formation during development. Probably no teacher except Louis Agassiz (1807–1873) or William Keith Brooks (1848–1908) exerted so great an influence on the course of American zoology.

DONALD P. COSTELLO,
Kenan Professor of Zoology, The University of North Carolina.

WHITMAN, Charles Seymour, American lawyer and politician: b. Hanover, Conn., Aug. 28, 1868; d. New York, N.Y., March 29, 1947. He went to Amherst College, did postgraduate work at Williams College, then studied law at New York University, and was admitted to the bar in 1894. In 1901 he was appointed assistant corporation counsel of New York City, where his work won him the post of city magistrate. In this capacity he helped to establish the night court in the city for the immediate trial of offenders arrested at night. In 1907 Gov. Charles Evans Hughes appointed Whitman a judge of the Court of General Sessions, and in the following year deputy attorney general. He was elected district attorney of New York County on a fusion ticket in 1909, reelected in 1913, and in 1914 was elected governor of New York State on the Republican ticket. Whitman was chairman of the Republican National Convention in 1916, where he urged the nomination of Charles Evans Hughes for president. In September of the same year he was reelected to the governorship of New York and served until the end of 1918 when he was defeated for reelection by Alfred E. Smith, the Democratic candidate. He resumed the practice of law in New York in 1919, was appointed a commissioner of the Port of New York Authority in 1935, and became chairman of the Committee on Port Planning in 1945.

WHITMAN, Marcus, American missionary and pioneer: b. Rushville, N.Y., Sept. 4, 1802; d. Waiilatpu, Walla Walla Valley, Nov. 29, 1847. He studied medicine with a local physician and earned a degree from Berkshire Medical College, Pittsfield, Mass. and practiced this profession for eight years. In January 1835, he was accepted for missionary service among the Indians by the American Board of Commissioners for Foreign Missions, and in that year he accompanied Samuel Parker on an exploratory tour beyond the Rockies. After interviewing Indians from Oregon at the fur-trading rendezvous on Green River, he returned to the East to make preparations for a mission among the Nez Percé Indians. He married Narcissa Prentiss, also a missionary under the American board, at Angelica, N.Y., on Feb. 18, 1836; accompanied by the Reverend and Mrs. Henry Harmon Spalding and W. H. Gray, they journeyed west, reaching Fort Walla Walla in September. Mrs. Whitman and Mrs. Spalding were the first American women to cross the Rockies and reach Oregon by the overland route. Late in 1836 this party established a station at Waiilatpu, on the Walla Walla River near the present city of Walla Walla, Wash., and another station at Lapwai, near present-day Lewiston, Idaho. Progress at both missions was slow and disappointing. Whitman and Spalding helped the Indians build houses, showed them farming techniques, and taught them how to erect mills. In 1838, after the arrival of a reinforcement, two other stations were established—one at Tshimakain, 25 miles northwest of Spokane, and another at Kamiah, 40 miles southeast of Lapwai, in present-day Idaho. Because of dissension in the mission, early in 1842 the American Board ordered the recall of some of the missionaries and the abandonment of Waiilatpu and Lapwai. To persuade the board to rescind this order, Whitman made his famous 3,000-mile ride to the East in the fall and winter of 1842–1843, a ride which gave rise to the myth that he undertook this journey to save Oregon from the British. Historical research has proved, however, that Whitman rode primarily to save the Oregon mission. His effort was successful, and he returned to Oregon with the overland migration of 1843. The mission continued its work until the murder of the Whitmans and 11 of their associates by Cayuse Indians in November 1847 induced the American Board to abandon its effort in the Oregon Territory.

See also WHITMAN NATIONAL MONUMENT.

J. ORIN OLIPHANT
Professor of History, Bucknell University

WHITMAN, Sarah Helen Power, American poet: b. Providence, R.I., Jan. 19, 1803; d. there, June 27, 1878. She was married to John W. Whitman, a Boston lawyer who died in 1833, and was engaged briefly in 1848 to Edgar Allan Poe (1809–1849), afterward writing a defense of him entitled *Edgar Poe and His Critics* (1860); some of her verse was considerably influenced by his. She contributed numerous critical articles and poems to periodicals and was noted for her conversational powers. Her verse was in part collected in the volume *Hours of Life, and Other Poems* (1853), and fully in the posthumous *Poems* (1879). *Fairy Ballads* and some other works were written with her sister, Anna M. Power. Her finest poem, *A Still Day in Autumn,* has much melody and beauty of expression and retains an honored place in anthologies. In 1909, *The Last Letters of Edgar Allan Poe to Sarah Helen Whitman* was published.

WHITMAN, Walt (in full WALTER), American poet: b. West Hills, Long Island, N.Y., May 31, 1819; d. Camden, N.J., March 26, 1892. The son of a Quaker carpenter and a mother descended from New York Dutch farmers, he grew up and attended public elementary schools

The Bettmann Archive

Walt Whitman, immortal of 19th century American poetry.

in Brooklyn, spending summers in central Long Island, the Paumanok of his poems. He began his working life with teaching in rural schools, and with setting type and writing for several newspapers and magazines.

From 1846 to 1848 he was editor of *The Brooklyn Eagle,* the leading newspaper in the city at that time. In his editorials he showed himself an abolitionist; a democrat in the libertarian tradition of Thomas Jefferson; an expansionist regarding the issues of the Mexican War, like most of the intellectuals of that period; a Jacksonian in opposition to the bankers; an opponent of capital punishment; and "a free trader by instinct," as he called himself. He was discharged from *The Eagle,* apparently because of the strength of his convictions for abolishing slavery and for free soil.

Three months on a New Orleans paper gave him a chance to see much of the country he later described so richly in his poems. Back in New York, he worked with his father and free-lanced. He edited *The Brooklyn Times* from 1857 to 1859, when he was let go because of church opposition to his frankly expressed ideas on the sexual problems of the unmarried, abortion, prostitution, and slavery. He continued to earn his living mainly from undistinguished hack work, and whatever craftmanship he learned had little relation to his poetry. But the opportunity to observe the growing metropolis—with its theaters, many occupations, and diverse national cultures—had a profound effect. Later in life, he said that his great work, *Leaves of Grass,* arose out of his "life in Brooklyn and New York from 1838 to 1853, absorbing a million people, for fifteen years, with an intimacy, an eagerness, an abandon, probably never equalled."

The slim first edition of *Leaves of Grass,* his main work and probably the most influential single volume of verse in American literature, appeared in 1855. It was not a popular success; but part of literary America, led by Ralph Waldo Emerson, greeted it with warm appreciation. In a letter to Whitman, Emerson wrote: "I find it the most extraordinary piece of wit and wisdom that America has yet contributed. . . . I greet you at the beginning of a great career. . . ." Whitman's poems about the Civil War were published in a separate volume called *Drum Taps* in 1865. With other later work, this volume was subsequently included in expanded editions of *Leaves of Grass.*

A sensitive and passionate humanitarian, he worked as a volunteer nurse in Army hospitals in Washington, D.C., during the Civil War. After acquiring some small fame for this service, he was given a clerkship in the Indian Department. But he was dismissed when his chief, Secretary of the Interior James Harlan, discovered his authorship of *Leaves of Grass* and labeled it "an indecent book." Many friends then rallied to his defense and effected his transfer to the attorney general's office. One of these friends, William Douglas O'Connor, wrote a pamphlet, *The Good Gray Poet* (1866)—a title that became a common public image of Whitman and thenceforth provided some antidote to slander and misunderstanding. Whitman collected and published his most significant prose in *Democratic Vistas* (1871).

A paralytic attack in 1873 forced the poet to give up his work in Washington. He spent almost all the rest of his life in Camden, N.J., living mainly by lecturing, sale of his books in England, and the help of friends. After living with his brother, in 1884 Whitman bought a house on Mickle Street that was turned into a memorial after his death. The details of his life before 1873 have remained obscure, so that biographers have indulged in much conjecture and debate. But the period after 1873 was chronicled by a frequent companion, Horace Traubel. The "good gray poet" was fond of sociability, and a little intellectual circle formed around him. This included John Burroughs, the naturalist; Peter Doyle, a horse-car conductor; and Mrs. Anne Gilchrist, an English author. Like Whitman himself, this circle was libertarian and nonconformist in sentiment.

Whitman conceived of literature as "a means whereby men may be revealed to each other as brothers"; and most simply, *Leaves of Grass* may be described as a long paean to brotherhood. Yet both content and artistic method reflect a rich fusion of social, political, and aesthetic conflicts of the time.

The poet's equalitarianism was a fierce affirmation accompanying awareness of an opposing spirit in America, which he saw as "pride, competition, segregation, vicious wilfulness, and license beyond example. . . ." In this ardent equalitarianism he found (paradoxically, to some readers) his central subject—himself: "I celebrate myself, and sing myself, And what I assume you shall assume, For every atom belonging to me as good belongs to you. I loafe and invite my soul, I lean and loafe at my ease observing a spear of summer grass. . . . I guess it must be the flag of my disposition, out of hopeful green stuff woven. . . And now it seems to me the beautiful uncut hair of graves. . . The smallest sprout shows there is really no death. . . ."

Thus, the central theme in *Leaves* is a symbolic identification of regeneration in nature with the deathless self. In developing this theme Whitman seems completely unaffected by that unresolved philosophical conflict between the individual and the collective that has troubled so many 19th and 20th century thinkers; "One's-Self I sing," he wrote, "a simple separate person, Yet utter the word Democratic, the word En-Masse." As "mate and companion of people" he hails all races and continents, all cities and countries, and the workmen of all occupations.

Time and again the poet refused to expurgate from new editions of *Leaves of Grass* lines with sexual content. To him a sexless individuality was inconceivable. "I am the poet of the Body and I am the poet of the Soul," he wrote; ". . . Of physiology from top to toe I sing." In 1881 an edition of *Leaves* was in effect banned in Boston because the New England Society for the Suppression of Vice threatened the publisher with suit. But most modern scholars, regardless of how they estimate other aspects of Whitman's work, find such old scandals more an indication of the surviving Puritanism of the times than a significant commentary on the poet.

As a technician, Whitman may be regarded as the father of free verse in American literature. He used rhyme rarely, as in the popular but uncharacteristic "O Captain! My Captain!" Seeking a new poetic form to fit his new poetic content, he found models in operatic recitative, the English Bible, Shakespeare, and translations of Greek and Latin oratory. Also, he searched endlessly for fresh idiom and vocabulary, adopting words freely from other languages, especially French. His poems were written to be spoken, and in rhythm and tonal volume there is great dynamic range—from fierce declamation to the aria from "the mocking bird's throat, the musical shuttle."

A complex man and artist, Whitman exhibits many seeming contradictions. He voiced a personal religion at the same time as he hailed science and materialism. While denying death, he heard on Paumanok "the sweet and delicious word death," and wrote what has often been regarded as the great elegy of American literature (*When Lilacs Last in the Dooryard Bloom'd*). He celebrated peace but at the same time regarded his book as an instrument of humanity's struggles. Like the transcendentalists and in particular Emerson, who he said brought him "to a boil" as a creative artist, he abjured a foolish consistency.

JOHN ASHWORTH, *Columbia University*

Bibliography

Allen, Gay W., *The New Walt Whitman Handbook* (1975; reprint, N.Y. Univ. Press 1986).
Arvin, Newton, *Whitman* (1938; reprint, Russell & Russell 1969).
Bloom, Harold, ed., *Walt Whitman* (Chelsea House 1985).
Boswell, Jeanetta, *Walt Whitman and the Critics: A Checklist of Criticism 1900–1978* (Scarecrow 1980).
DelloBuono, Carmen J., *Rare Early Essays on Walt Whitman* (Norwood Eds. 1980).
Fausset, Hugh I., *Walt Whitman: Poet of Democracy* (1943; reprint, Russell & Russell 1969).
Giantvalley, Scott, *Walt Whitman, 1838–1939: A Reference Guide* (G. K. Hall 1981).
Hutchinson, George, *The Ecstatic Whitman: Literary Shamanism and Crisis of the Union* (Ohio State Univ. Press 1986).
Kaplan, Justin D., *Walt Whitman: A Life* (Simon & Schuster 1980).

WHITMAN, town, Massachusetts, in Plymouth County, about four miles directly east of Brockton, at an altitude of 80 feet. It is chiefly a manufacturing town, largely of shoes, but also of leather findings, shoe machinery, and tacks. More recently many small plastics concerns have replaced some of the larger factories. Originally a part of Abington, Whitman was settled about 1670 and was known as Little Comfort or South Abington. Under the latter name it was set off and incorporated in 1875, but in 1886 the present name was adopted to honor Augustus Whitman, who willed a large tract of land for a public park. Paul Revere learned cannon making in a foundry in the town, and Francis Cardinal Spellman was born here. Government is by annual town meeting and five selectmen. Population: 13,534.

WHITMAN COLLEGE, a coeducational, privately endowed, nonsectarian liberal arts residence college, in Walla Walla, Washington, founded by the Reverend Cushing Eells as a memorial to his friend and fellow missionary, Dr. Marcus Whitman. It was chartered by the Territorial Legislature of Washington in 1859. The college offers the bachelor of arts degree with majors in 18 subject matter areas, and a professional bachelor of music degree with majors in piano, voice, violin, and organ. Enrollment averages 1,000.

WHITMAN NATIONAL MONUMENT, located six miles west of Walla Walla, Washington, at a site called Waiilatpu (place of the rye grass) by the Cayuse Indians. It contains the mission founded in 1836 among these Indians by Dr. Marcus Whitman and his wife, Narcissa Prentiss Whitman (see WHITMAN, MARCUS). Until the mission was destroyed and the Whitmans and 11 of their associates killed by the Cayuse in 1847, Whitman treated the Indians' diseases and taught them agriculture, letters, and religion. The mission was a landmark on the Oregon Trail, and the Whitmans gave much aid to passing emigrants. The national monument, established in 1940, commemorates the courage and dedication of the Whitmans. It contains 93 acres and has a visitor center which tells the story of missionaries in the Pacific Northwest.

WHITMER, hwĭt'mər, **David,** American Mormon leader: b. near Harrisburg, Pa., Jan. 7, 1805; d. Richmond, Mo., Jan. 25, 1888. He brought Joseph Smith (1805–1844) to his father's farmhouse near Palmyra, N.Y., where the golden plates were translated in 1829 and published as the *Book of Mormon* in 1830. After baptism by Smith, he was one of three men privileged to examine the gold plates to testify to their supernatural source, yet material character. In 1834 Smith made him president of the High Council of Zion, managing Mormon interests in Missouri. Differences developed, however, and Smith excommunicated him in 1838. Whitmer lived thereafter in Richmond, Mo., where he became a member of the city council and was once elected mayor. In 1867 he and his family revived the Church of Christ, which had split from Smith's organization, but had made only 150 proselytes at his death.

WHITNEY, hwĭt'nē, **Anne,** American sculptor: b. Watertown, Mass., Sept. 2, 1821; d. Boston, Jan. 23, 1915. Self-taught, she began sculpturing in her 30's and in 1872 opened a studio in Boston. Very shortly, she was commissioned by Massachusetts to do the marble statue of Samuel Adams for the Capitol in Washington. The work, which she executed in Italy, has been praised for its "feminine power." Her statues of Charles Sumner in Harvard Square, Cambridge, and of Leif Ericsson on Commonwealth Avenue, Boston, are other major works.

WHITNEY, Asa, American inventor and manufacturer: b. Townsend, Mass., Dec. 1, 1791; d. Philadelphia, Pa., June 4, 1874. As a boy he worked in his father's blacksmith shop, and then became a machinist in shops in New Hampshire and New York and began his own manufacture of axles in Brownsville, N.Y. In 1830 he was made master machinist of the Mohawk and Hudson Railroad shops, and three years later became superintendent of the road. From 1839 to 1842 he was New York State canal commissioner. He settled in Philadelphia in 1842 after forming a partnership with Matthias W. Baldwin for the building of locomotives. In May 1847 he obtained a patent for a cast-iron car wheel with a corrugated center web, and a patent for his method of manufacturing it; and in April 1848 he obtained a patent for an improved process of annealing and cooling cast-iron wheels. With these three patents he developed his own firm into the largest car-wheel works in the country. He left money to the University of Pennsylvania to establish a chair of dynamic engineering.

WHITNEY, Asa, American merchant and railroad promoter: b. North Groton, Conn., March 14, 1797; d. Washington, D.C., Sept. 17, 1872. He began his business career about 1817 as buyer for a New York dry-goods merchant and traveled abroad extensively. In 1836 he formed his own firm, but failed in the panic of 1837. He went to China where he made another fortune in a little over a year. Upon his return to the United States he worked tirelessly to get Congress to authorize the building of a transcontinental railroad in order to expand trade with the Orient. Before his death one railroad to the Pacific coast had been completed and three others were begun.

WHITNEY, Eli, American inventor and manufacturer: b. Westborough, Mass., Dec. 8, 1765; d. New Haven, Conn., Jan. 8, 1825. Possessed of an inquiring mind and exceptional manual dexterity, with only an elementary schooling, at the age of 16 he built up a workshop on his father's farm and launched a successful business producing nails and small wares difficult to buy during the Revolution. When he was 19 he decided to seek a college education, an ambition achieved when he graduated from Yale in 1792. Prospect of work as a tutor then took him to Savannah, Ga., where a new acquaintance, Gen. Nathanael Greene's widow, inspired him to turn his inventive talents to the design of a machine to clean the tight-clinging green seeds from short-staple cotton, work previously done tediously by hand. By April 1793, he demonstrated the resulting "gin," a device easy to build, simple to operate by hand, horsepower, or water power, and extraordinarily effective. He returned to New Haven and obtained a patent on March 14, 1794. In partnership with Phineas Miller, a friend in Georgia, he undertook to build gins to install throughout the cotton country. Financial disasters quickly overtook the enterprise, as pirating of the invention became widespread and expensive lawsuits failed to stop the multiplication of the "surreptitious" gins. Not until 1807 did a successful suit bring Whitney a modest return. In the preceding 13 years, use of his gin had given the Deep South a salable commodity, the demand for which was destined to grow steadily.

Eli Whitney

Yale University Art Gallery, from Bettmann

Meanwhile, when war with France threatened, Whitney, burdened with crushing debts, had obtained a contract in 1798 to make 10,000 muskets for the United States government. While building gins, he had devised several machines which led him to believe he could apply to musket manufacture what he called later "the uniformity system," whereby power-driven tools would reproduce each component with sufficiently close tolerances to make it interchangeable with any like part without hand filing and fitting. Although failing to meet the specified time schedule, in his new shop in what is now Whitneyville near New Haven, he carried out his general plan of fabrication by machine tools, some of which were of his own invention. Government officials were extremely patient since they were anxious to promote American manufactures, particularly of munitions, in order to make the United States independent of Europe in wartime. They received the last of the 10,000 muskets in 1809 instead of 1800, the promised delivery date. But in that interval the "Mill Rock" shop had proved the feasibility of the uniformity system. Within 15 years the newly formed Army Ordnance Department required use of that mode of manufacture in all contracts for small arms.

French arms makers had developed the system before Whitney tried it in America, and recent investigation indicates that he may have studied reports of French methods in the 1790's. Furthermore, as the trip hammer was in use in several American establishments by the turn of the century, and Simeon North (1765–1852), pistol maker of Middletown, Conn., certainly was employing some simple machine tools before 1810, doubts multiply about the extent to which Whitney was truly an innovator. Whether he invented the first milling machine in 1818 is also uncertain. Nevertheless, whether originating genius or merely one of several men pursuing similar ideas, Whitney early acquired a prestige that promoted acceptance of his techniques. As the source of the modern assembly line, they have made the United States a leading industrial nation.

CONSTANCE MCLAUGHLIN GREEN,
Washington History Project,
American University.

WHITNEY, Gertrude Vanderbilt, American sculptor: b. New York, N.Y., April 19, 1877; d. there, April 18, 1942. The daughter of Cornelius Vanderbilt (1843–1899), in 1896 she married Harry Payne Whitney, son of William Collins Whitney. She studied sculpture in New York and Paris, where she was inspired by the renowned French sculptor Auguste Rodin to express her artistic aspirations and tragic sense through plastic, dynamic figures.

Her works include the Titanic Memorial and the Aztec Fountain (in the Pan American Building), both at Washington, D.C.; the El Dorado Fountain at San Francisco; the St. Nazaire War Memorial in France; and many equestrian statues. She was known equally well as a distinguished sculptor and a sponsor of aspiring artists, and much of her effort and wealth was directed toward developing and encouraging a national artistic taste. Outstanding among her many benefactions is the Whitney Museum of American Art in New York City, which she conceived and financed.

WHITNEY, John Hay (nickname "Jock"), American financier, ambassador, and publisher: b. Ellsworth, Me., Aug. 17, 1904. Both of his grandfathers, John Hay and William Collins Whitney, had been cabinet officers. He was educated at the Groton School and at Yale and Oxford universities, returning in 1927 to administer the estate of his late father, Payne Whitney. In time, he became active in industry, civic affairs, government, the arts, philanthropy, publishing, and, in the world of sports, as a leading polo player and breeder of racehorses. In the 1930's, his film-producing firm, Pioneer Pictures, was the first to exploit the Technicolor process, and he served as board chairman of Selznick-International. He also financed many Broadway plays. In 1940, he helped to organize the Office of the Coordinator of Inter-American Affairs, heading its motion-picture division until 1942. While with the Army Air Force (1942–1945), he rose to the rank of colonel and, on one occasion, was captured by the Nazis but escaped, and in 1945 he was awarded the Legion of Merit. He founded the philanthropic John Hay Whitney Foundation in 1946, and from 1957 to 1961 was ambassador to Britain. He acquired control of the *New York Herald Tribune* in 1958 but closed the paper in 1966 and later became chairman of *The International Herald Tribune*. Many of his financial interests, particularly publishing, were handled through the Whitney Communications Corporation. He died in Manhasset, N.Y., on Feb. 8, 1982.

WHITNEY, Josiah Dwight, American geologist: b. Northampton, Mass., Nov. 23, 1819; d. Sunapee, N.H., Aug. 19, 1896. He was the brother of William Dwight Whitney (q.v.). After graduating from Yale in 1839, he spent the years 1842–1847 studying in Europe, and subsequently took part in a geological exploration of the Lake Superior region. In 1854 he published *The Metallic Wealth of the United States,* a pioneering work in mining geology, and from 1855 was engaged in surveys of Iowa and parts of Wisconsin. In 1860 he was made state geologist of California, where he worked for more than a decade, producing several volumes of a *Geological Survey of California* between 1864 and 1870. Mount Whitney, the highest peak in the United States outside of Alaska, was named in his honor as the head of the expedition which first measured its height in 1864. Connected with Harvard University after 1865, he became professor of geology in 1875. His *Climatic Changes of Later Geological Times* (1882) aroused considerable controversy in scientific circles, as did the Calaveras skull, which he discovered in 1866.

WHITNEY, Robert Sutton, American conductor: b. Newcastle-upon-Tyne, England, July 9, 1904. He studied music in Chicago with Leo Sowerby and Rudolph Reuter, conducting with Eric De Lamarter and Frederick Stock. He made his debut as a conductor with the Chicago Civic Orchestra in 1932 and became conductor of the Louisville (Kentucky) Philharmonic (later Louisville Orchestra) in 1937. In 1948 he began to specialize in contemporary music, including at least one recent composition in each concert. From 1953 on, the Louisville Orchestra received large grants from the Rockefeller Foundation for commissioning symphonic and operatic scores. Whitney thus led very numerous world premières (some 150 by 1959) of works of living composers, both American and foreign, and recordings gave wide circulation to their works. Whitney also was dean of the school of music at the University of Louisville, 1956–1972.

WHITNEY, William Collins, American politician and financier: b. Conway, Mass., July 5, 1841; d. New York, N.Y., Feb. 2, 1904. Graduating from Yale in 1863, he entered the Harvard Law School and was admitted to the New York bar two years later. He took part in the proceedings against the Tweed ring and, as corporation counsel of the city (1875–1882), thoroughly reorganized the legal department. He was an organizer of the Metropolitan Street Railway System which consolidated the rail transit lines in the city. He promoted the election of Grover Cleveland as governor of New York in 1882 and as president in 1884. Serving as secretary of the navy during Cleveland's first national administration (1885–1889), Whitney initiated a program for the improvement of naval ships, including armor plating. He was Democratic campaign manager during Cleveland's second successful race for the presidency in 1892. Subsequently he devoted his main energies to business, was a director of many corporations, and became one of the largest landholders in the East. He also developed one of the nation's finest racing stables.

HARRY PAYNE WHITNEY (1872–1930), a son, took over the direction of his father's financial interests, developed mining properties in the United States and Mexico with Daniel Guggenheim, and became an influential financier. He was a noted polo player, captain of the United States polo team, and extended his father's success in horse breeding and racing.

WHITNEY, William Dwight, American philologist: b. Northampton, Mass., Feb. 9, 1827; d. New Haven, Conn., June 9, 1894. He was the brother of Josiah Dwight Whitney (q.v.). After graduating from Williams College in 1845, he studied at Yale (1849–1850) and then went to Germany, where he continued his philological and Sanskrit studies under Franz Bopp at Berlin and Rudolf von Roth at Tübingen. He was appointed professor of Sanskrit at Yale in 1854, and in 1870 professor of Sanskrit and comparative philology, retaining this post until his death. In 1856 he published, with Roth, an edition of the *Atharva-Veda Sanhita,* and in 1862 issued at New Haven an edition, with translation and notes, of the *Atharva-Veda Prâtiçâkhya*. His *Language and the Study of Language* (1867) was an admirable exposition of the main principles of comparative philology. Among his many other published works, his *Sanskrit Grammar* (1879) was outstanding. He was also editor in chief of the *Century Dictionary: an Encyclopedic Lexicon of the English Language* (6 vols., 1889–91) and first president of the American Philological Association (1869).

WHITNEY, Willis Rodney, American scientist: b. Jamestown, N.Y., Aug. 22, 1868; d. Schenectady, Jan. 9, 1958. He graduated from Massachusetts Institute of Technology in 1890, received his doctorate in chemistry from the University of Leipzig (1896), and returned to teach at M.I.T. (1896–1904). While there, he proposed the now universally accepted electrochemical theory of corrosion (see CORROSION). In 1900 he helped to establish the General Electric Research Laboratory at Schenectady. He moved permanently to that city in 1904, was director of the laboratory until 1928, and from 1928 to 1941 was vice president of the General Electric Company in charge of research. Under his guidance, the laboratory made many important contributions to the electrical industry, including fundamental developments in the radio tube, applications of the cathode-ray tube in radar and television, improvements in incandescent lighting, and development of high-voltage X-ray equipment. Whitney's personal researches were devoted to the metalized lamp filament; the inductotherm machine for applying energy to local parts of the body or to produce general artificial fever; heating units for electric ranges; and the hydrogen cooling system for turbine generators.

WHITNEY, Mount, a peak of the Sierra Nevada, California, on the line between Tulare and Inyo counties, in the southeastern part of the state; altitude 14,494 feet (4,418 meters), the highest elevation in the United States outside of Alaska. The slope is precipitous on the east, rising abruptly for about 11,000 feet (3,350 meters) from Owens Valley. The peak was named for Josiah Dwight Whitney, chief of the survey party that first measured its height in 1864. It was first climbed in 1873.

WHITSUNDAY, hwĭt'sən-dē, or **WHITSUNTIDE,** hwĭt'sən-tīd, the English name for the feast of Pentecost, probably from the white robes worn by the newly baptized on that day (or its eve), or perhaps from such flowering trees as the whitethorn (English) or hawthorn, which was said to be often in bloom at that season. It is the seventh Sunday or 50th day (Greek *pentēcostē hemera*) after Easter, commemorating the descent of the Holy Spirit upon the Apostles on that day (Acts 2:1–4). Among the Jews it commemorates the giving of the law, occurring on the 50th day after Passover, the departure of Israel from Egypt. With Christmas and Easter, it is one of the three greater festivals of the Christian year. The observance of a period of Pentecost between Easter and Whitsunday began early in church history, as Tertullian (*On Baptism, The Military Crown*), Origen (*Against Celsus*), the *Apostolic Canons,* and other ancient sources attest. About 385 A.D. the Christian lady Etheria (or Silvia), in her *Peregrinatio,* described the elaborate observance of the feast day at Jerusalem. In the Church of England and the Episcopal Church the Sunday and the two following days have special collects, epistles, and gospels. The most general designation of the Sundays from Pentecost to Advent is the traditional one, the "Sundays after Pentecost"; but the Anglican Church names them "after Trinity," which is the first Sunday after Pentecost. This Sunday was so named in honor of the Blessed Trinity and the usage was universally enjoined by Pope John XXII in 1334 A.D. But the result is a confusion in numbering, and the tendency to return to the original designation is growing.

FREDERICK C. GRANT,
Professor of Biblical Theology, Union Theological Seminary, New York City.

WHITSUNDAY GROUP, the name now commonly applied to the 20 or so continental islands lying off the coast of Queensland, Australia, about latitude 20° S., the largest being Whitsunday Island, 42 square miles in area and rising to 1,430 feet. Through the group runs the 20-mile-long Whitsunday Passage leading to the shipping channel inside the Great Barrier Reef. The group forms part of the Cumberland Islands chain named by Capt. James Cook in 1770. Fragments of a former coastal range, the islands are varied in topography. Most have a fringing reef of coral and a rich marine fauna similar to that of the outer reef (about 30 miles to the east). Five of the islands, including Lindeman, Hayman, and South Molle, have been developed as vacation resorts. Whitsunday Island, a national park, is uninhabited, as is adjacent Hook Island, which has ceremonial relics of the now extinct Whitsunday tribe of aborigines.

R. M. YOUNGER
Author of "Australia and the Australians"

WHITTAKER, hwĭt'ə-kər, **Charles Evans,** American lawyer and judge: b. Troy, Kans., Feb. 22, 1901; d. Kansas City, Mo., Nov. 27, 1973. After a ninth-grade education he worked on a farm for a period of three years. He then moved to Kansas City, Mo., where he entered the school of law of the University of Kansas City, attending law classes, making up his high school deficiencies, and working part time as an office boy in a law firm. He received his law degree in 1924, having been admitted to practice in Kansas during the previous year. The practice of law was his sole dedication; he concentrated on corporation cases and rose, over a period of 30 years, to be one of the senior partners in Kansas City's most prominent law firm. He was active in bar association activities and was president of the Missouri bar immediately prior to his appointment to the United States District Court for the Western District of Missouri in 1954. He was elevated to the Court of Appeals for the Eighth Circuit in 1956 and was appointed to the United States Supreme Court by President Dwight D. Eisenhower in 1957. He thus became the first justice to be appointed to the court from Missouri and the first justice who was born in Kansas. On all three courts in the federal judicial system, his work has been that of the legal technician, dispassionate in his judicial decisions.

PHILIP B. KURLAND,
Professor of Law, University of Chicago.

WHITTIER, hwĭt'ē-ər, **John Greenleaf,** American poet and abolitionist: b. Haverhill, Mass., Dec. 17, 1807; d. Hampton Falls, N.H., Sept. 7, 1892. Unlike most of the other New England writers of his time, Whittier was not heir to the respectable Calvinist-Unitarian-Transcendentalist orthodoxy. The son of a Quaker farmer, he was himself a Quaker. As a boy he worked on his father's farm, which he celebrated later in his most famous poem, *Snow-Bound.* Early life was not easy for Whittier, who worked so hard at farming and later at shoemaking that it may have affected his health. He managed to save enough money from his cobbling to pay for two terms at Haverhill Academy in 1827–1828, but other than this had little formal schooling, though he read widely and was interested all his life in politics.

Whittier drifted into writing more or less by chance. A schoolmaster at Haverhill introduced him to the poetry of Robert Burns, and his first poem happened to be published in the Newburyport *Free Press* in 1826. The *Free Press* at this time was edited by William Lloyd Garrison, the influential abolitionist, who took an immediate interest in the young Whittier and became his lifelong friend. In 1829, Garrison's influence obtained for Whittier the editorship of *The American Manufacturer,* a Boston weekly magazine ostensibly concerned with industry and agriculture, but actually a pro-Henry Clay political paper. This appointment brought Whittier into active participation in the abolitionist movement. He became a writer of antislavery material, contributing to and editing the *New England Weekly Review* (1830–1832), the *Pennsylvania Freeman* (Philadelphia 1838–1840), and the *Middlesex Standard* (Lowell, Mass., 1844–1845), and finally becoming corresponding editor of the Washington *National Era* from 1847 to 1860. In addition, his abolitionist pamphlet *Justice and Expediency* (1833) quickly became one of the most widely known pieces of abolitionist propaganda, and he published an entire volume, *Poems Written During the Progress of the Abolition Cause in the United States* (1837), dedicated to furthering the antislavery movement. His devotion to the cause of freeing the slaves was not, however, only literary. In 1833 he acted as a secretary of the Anti-Slavery Convention at Philadelphia, as well as being one of the committee which drafted the declaration of principles. Largely on the basis of his abolitionist sympathies, he was elected to the Massachusetts legislature from Haverhill in 1835, and in 1836, he became secretary of the Anti-Slavery Society.

John Greenleaf Whittier

The Bettmann Archive

Whittier was abolitionist in principle, but he was also a staunch Quaker, and as such committed to a belief in nonviolence. He himself twice suffered the effects of mob frenzy, once in 1835 when he and the English lecturer George Thompson were mobbed in Concord, N.H., and again in 1838 when the offices of the *Pennsylvania Freeman* were burned by a rioting crowd. As the American Civil War approached, Whittier's pacifist views seemed indecisive in the eyes of other more extreme abolitionist leaders. His poem *A Word for the Hour* (1861) explicitly states that he would be willing to let the South secede rather than risk war, and while other abolitionist leaders made John Brown into a national martyr-hero, Whittier wrote privately that "the distinction should be made clear between the natural sympathy with the man and approval of his mad, and, as I think, most dangerous and unjustifiable act."

Because of his moderate stand on the issue of secession and his hopes for compromise, Whittier appeared almost traitorous to radicals on both sides, since political passions in 1861 were too violent for conciliation to seem other than cowardice. True to his principles, at the end of the Civil War Whittier welcomed the South back with delight, approving Lincoln's idea of a generous peace, and deploring the vindictive and revengeful reconstruction government which Congress actually imposed on the beaten Confederacy. Having sold the family farm in 1836, Whittier moved to a new home in Amesbury, Mass. After 1876, he spent much of his time at the home of his three cousins, daughters of Edmund Johnson, in Danvers, Mass.

It is perhaps ironic that the Whittier who is known today is not remembered as a fiery political radical, but rather as a nostalgic poet of peaceful rural New England. His reputation rests on a few bucolic poems known to everyone, notably *The Barefoot Boy* (1855) and *Snow-Bound* (1866), while his political writings are ignored, except by scholars. Once considered one of the greatest of American poets, his fame has steadily declined since his death, partly as a result of 20th century changes in taste and partly due to his own imperfections. A prolific writer—his works run to seven volumes—his poetry is often facile and bland. He is overly fascinated by involved stanzaic forms, most of which are not necessary to the rather commonplace content of his verse. He succeeds best in the ballad, where his simplicity is untainted by pretentiousness or by the consciously "literary" poetic diction which caused him to write in imitation of Tom Moore or the Scottish dialect of Robert Burns. Whittier himself realized the limitations of his genius. The *Proem* to his first collected *Poems* (1849) states wistfully his love for "the old melodious lays" of Edmund Spenser and Sir Philip Sidney, yet continues honestly that he only "vainly" tries "to breathe their marvelous notes," and concludes sadly that he has "Nor mighty Milton's gift divine, / Nor Marvel's wit and graceful song."

Yet disesteem for Whittier is as misguided as the adulation of his contemporaries. His poem *Ichabod* (1850), telling of his grief at the defection of Daniel Webster from abolitionist principles, still stirs our hearts and his *The Kansas Emigrants* (1854) is as fresh today as it was when it was sung on the long trail west. If much of his verse is conventional and uninteresting, so is much sincere and honest, and worthy to survive.

Most important of Whittier's works are the following: *Legends of New England in Prose and Verse* (1831); *Justice and Expediency* (1833); *Mogg Megone* (1836); *Poems* (1838); *Lays of My Home and Other Poems* (1843); *Voices of Freedom* (1846); *Supernaturalism in New England* (1847); *Old Portraits and Modern Sketches* (1850); *Songs of Labor, and Other Poems* (1850); *Snow-Bound: a Winter Idyl* (1866); *The Tent on the Beach, and Other Poems* (1867); *Among the Hills, and Other Poems* (1869); *Miriam, and Other Poems* (1871); *The Pennsylvania Pilgrim, and Other Poems* (1872). His complete writings appeared in seven volumes in Boston (1888–1889) and a one-volume edition of his poems in Cambridge (1895). A complete bibliographical listing may be found in Currier, Thomas F., *A Bibliography of John Greenleaf Whittier* (Cambridge, Mass., 1937).

See also AMERICAN LITERATURE—3. *19th Century* (The New England Renaissance); BARBARA FRIETCHIE; MAUD MULLER; SNOW-BOUND.

JAMES K. FOLSOM,
English and American Studies Departments, Yale University.

Bibliography

Fields, A. A., *Whittier* (1893; reprint, R. West 1978).
Kribbs, Jayne K., *Critical Essays on John Greenleaf Whittier* (G. K. Hall 1980).
Linton, W. J., *Life of John Greenleaf Whittier* (1893; reprint, Century Bookbindery 1982).
Rowntree, A., *Whittier* (1946; reprint, Folcroft 1973).
Von Frank, Albert J., *Whittier: A Comprehensive Annotated Bibliography* (Garland 1976).

WHITTIER, city, California, in Los Angeles County, 13 miles southeast from the center of Los Angeles, at an altitude of 245 feet. While it is primarily a residential suburb of Los Angeles, there is some light industry, such as oil tools, automobile radiators, cameras, and clay and electronic products. The city is the seat of Whittier College, a liberal arts college founded by the Society of Friends and chartered in 1901, and the largest Friends' meetinghouse in the world is situated there. In nearby Pico-Rivera is the two-story adobe mansion of Don Pio Pico, last Mexican governor of California, now preserved as a state historical monument. The city was founded in 1887 by a colony of the Society of Friends, who named it after John Greenleaf Whittier, the Quaker poet; it was incorporated in 1898. Many of its original settlers were Quakers from Indiana, Illinois, and Iowa. Richard Milhous Nixon was born in nearby Yorba Linda, attended Whittier College, and practiced law in the city until 1942. A council-manager form of government with 10 council seats was adopted in 1949. Population: 68,872.

BENJAMIN WHITTEN.

WHITTIER COLLEGE, a four-year coeducational nonsectarian liberal arts college in Whittier, Calif. It originated as an academy in 1888, a year after the founding of the town of Whittier by pioneer Quakers, who named both the town and the college for John Greenleaf Whittier, the American Quaker poet. The college, as such, was chartered by the State of California in 1901. Its 115-acre campus is situated about 15 miles from Los Angeles.

Whittier offers the bachelor of arts, master of arts, and master of science and education degrees. It is noted for its general studies program; it also administers an overseas program in Copenhagen, Denmark. School colors are purple and gold, and teams are known as the "Poets." Average enrollment in the regular session is 1,500.

WHITTINGHAM, hwĭt′ĭng-əm, **Charles,** English printer: b. Caludon, Warwickshire, England, June 16, 1767; d. Chiswick, near London, Jan. 15, 1840. He served his printing apprenticeship at Coventry, and in 1789 he established his own press in London. In 1809 he removed to Chiswick, at that period still outside London, and there, in 1811, he founded the Chiswick Press, which became distinguished for excellence and beauty of workmanship. He was one of the first to issue inexpensive reprints of the classics, and he pioneered in bringing out India-paper editions.

Soon after Whittingham took his nephew, Charles Whittingham (1795–1876), into partnership in 1824, the Chiswick Press issued Washington Irving's *Knickerbocker's History of New York* (1824) and Pierce Egan's *Life of an Actor* (1825). The younger Whittingham began block-color printing in 1840, and in 1844 reintroduced William Caslon's old-style type. In 1852 the Chiswick Press was moved back to London, where it continued to print many fine books for the publisher William Pickering (1796–1854), including the "Aldine" edition of the English poets.

WHITTINGTON, hwĭt′ĭng-tən, **Richard,** English merchant and mayor of London: b. near Newent, Gloucestershire, England, 1358?; d. London, March 1423. The son of Sir William Whittington of Pauntley Manor, Newent, he became a mercer in London, supplying velvet and damasks to the household of the earl of Derby, later Henry IV. On the death of London's mayor in June 1397, the king appointed Whittington to serve out the remainder of the term; in October he was elected mayor for the ensuing 12 months. He often made substantial loans to Richard II and his successors Henry IV and Henry V. He was again mayor in 1406–1407 and 1419–1420. A childless widower, Whittington used his wealth in public benefactions, including a college and hospital connected with his church of St. Michael Royal. Upon his death, he bequeathed his considerable fortune to charitable and public causes. There is no evidence that he was ever knighted.

The Dick Whittington legend and nursery rhymes picture a poor country orphan who makes his way to London where a rich merchant, Hugh FitzWarren, taking pity on him gives him work as a scullion. Dick, having bought a cat for a penny to protect him from the rodents in his garret, contributes this sole possession as his personal venture in his master's trading ship the *Unicorn*. The cat is sold to a Barbary prince for 10 times the value of all the other freight. Meanwhile, disappointed at not finding that London's streets were paved with gold and made desperate by the cook's abuse, Dick steals from the house early on All Hallows morning and trudges sadly out of the city. Resting at Holloway he hears the distant chimes of Bow bells and they seem to say:

Turn again, Whittington,
Lord Mayor of London.

He hastens back to his pots and spits, soon learns of his fortune on the arrival of the *Unicorn*, marries his master's daughter, Alice, and thrice becomes lord mayor of London. There is no record of the legend's existence prior to the publication in 1605 of a play and a ballad on the theme. The license for the ballad gives its title as *The vertuous Lyfe and memorable Death of Sir Richard Whittington, mercer, some-time Lord Maiour*. Neither the play nor the ballad has survived.

WHITTLE, hwĭt′əl, SIR **Frank,** British aeronautical engineer and inventor: b. Coventry, England, June 1, 1907. After graduation from Leamington College, in 1923 he became an apprentice at the Royal Air Force College, then cadet, pilot officer, and flying instructor (1930). He was the first engineer to produce a British gas turbine engine for the jet propulsion of aircraft. He applied for his first patent on his gas turbine in 1930. After further study in the mechanical sciences at Cambridge University and serving as test pilot for the Marine Aircraft Experimental Establishment at Felixstowe, Whittle joined Power Jets, Ltd. to continue his experiments and a jet propulsion turbine was built to his design. In May 1941, the first flight using the Whittle jet engine was successfully made. While an officer of the Royal Air Force, he refused to claim any remuneration for his work or inventions; however, in 1948, the government awarded him £100,000 in recognition of his achievements. Air Commodore Whittle has been awarded many honors, among them the Gold Medal of the Royal Aeronautical Society, the Daniel Guggenheim Medal, and the Franklin Medal of the Franklin Institute. He was knighted in 1948.

See also JET ENGINE.

ELIZABETH B. BROWN.

WHITTREDGE, hwĭt′rĭj, **(Thomas) Worthington,** American painter: b. Springfield, Ohio, May 22, 1820; d. Summit, N.J., Feb. 25, 1910. He studied painting in Cincinnati from 1840 to 1849 and showed such promise that he went to Düsseldorf in 1849. He spent three years there as a pupil of Andreas Achenbach, posed as Washington for Emanuel Leutze's (1816–1868) *Washington Crossing the Delaware*, and met Albert Bierstadt (1830–1902). From 1854 to 1859 he lived in Rome where he met Frederick Edwin Church (1826–1900) and others, and traveled around Europe. On his return to America in 1859 he submitted a Roman Landscape to the National Academy, to which he was elected in 1861 and of which he became president (1865; 1874–1877). Settling in New York, he became a popular painter of the Hudson River school (q.v.). While he made several trips to the West and to Mexico, he preferred to paint the gentler aspects of Catskill woods and streams to the grand or exotic landscapes of his travels. His notable works include *Evening in the Woods, The Trout Pool, Trout Brook in the Catskills,* and *The Poachers.*

HERBERT D. HALE.

WHITWORTH, hwĭt′wûrth, SIR **Joseph,** English mechanical engineer: b. Stockport, Cheshire, England, Dec. 21, 1803; d. Monte Carlo, Monaco, Jan. 22, 1887. He started as a mechanic in Manchester and London, discovered the method of making a truly plane surface by scraping, and in 1833 established himself as a toolmaker at Manchester, making many improvements in machine tools over the next 20 years. Between 1840 and 1850 he developed his standard system of uniform measures and gages of great utility in engineering and designed measuring machines accurate up to one millionth of an inch. He established a uniform system of screw threads, known as the Whitworth thread. After experimentation with rifles, by 1857 he perfected a hexagonal-barreled rifle (Whitworth gun) of great range, accuracy, and penetrative power, greatly excelling the Enfield then in use. The War Office did not accept it, as being of too small a caliber for a military weapon; but in 1869 the War Office declared that a weapon of such caliber would appear to be the most suitable. Whitworth was equally successful in designing a cannon, but his rifled model with a 250-pound shell and a six-mile range was rejected by the ordnance board in 1865, much to the detriment of British ordnance. His method of compression of ductile cast steel for ordnance was a great advance and came into general use. His works at Manchester were converted into a limited-liability company in 1874, and in 1897 merged with the Elswick works, established by Sir William Armstrong (1810–1900). His fortune was devoted to the endowment of 30 Whitworth scholarships in mechanics and to the furthering of charitable and educational work. He was made a baronet in 1869.

WHITWORTH COLLEGE, a coeducational Presbyterian liberal arts college at Spokane, Wash. Originating as Sumner Academy in Sumner, near Tacoma, in 1883, it became a college in 1890 and was renamed to honor its founder, George Frederic Whitworth (1816–1907), pioneer Presbyterian missionary and educator. In 1914 the school was moved from the Puget Sound area to its present site, a 150-acre campus, 7 miles north of Spokane. A major expansion program was launched in the 1950's. Whitworth offers majors in 25 academic departments. Crimson and black are the school colors, and the teams are known as the "Pirates." Average annual full-time undergraduate enrollment is about 875.

WHITWORTH GUN. See PROJECTILES; WHITWORTH, SIR JOSEPH.

WHOLE-TONE SCALE, in music, a scale bridging an octave in six equal steps, either c-d-e-f♯-g♯-a♯-c or c♯-d♯-f-g-a-b-c♯ or a transposition thereof. Although found in some Oriental music and dipped into passingly by earlier Western composers (Gioacchino Antonio Rossini, Mikhail Ivanovich Glinka, Hector Berlioz), it was employed first for its inherent indecisiveness, its "impressionistic" effect, by Claude Debussy. Because it lacks important structural integers of the traditional Western major and minor scales (leading tone, perfect fifth, perfect fourth), it cannot be used in pure state for developing a harmonic structure. Debussy, having experimented with it fitfully (notably in his piano prélude *Voiles*), tacitly admitted its limitations; his contemporaries and successors have regarded it as a minor means to be called upon only for modulatory passages and coloristic touches.

HERBERT WEINSTOCK.

WHOLESALING, hōl′sāl-ĭng, the functions performed in the process of moving goods from producers to retailers or to industrial and institutional users. Generally speaking, these functions are performed by individuals or organizations known as wholesalers or wholesale middlemen. The American Marketing Association defines the wholesaler as a "merchant middleman who sells to retailers and other merchants and/or to industrial, institutional, and commercial users, but who does not sell in significant amounts to ultimate consumers." Since a major part of consumer goods pass through wholesale organizations, their effectiveness and efficiency have a direct bearing on the standard of living of every American. In recent decades, with the growth of large retail organizations, many of which operate on a national scale, there has been some tendency among retailers and large manufacturing organizations of consumer goods to deal directly with each other and thereby perform the wholesale functions between them.

The wholesaling job consists of several important functions. Assembling involves the task of gathering into one place many kinds of goods made in many places. With this function goes storage of goods for various periods of time. Then, in order to distribute merchandise, wholesalers have to perform the double function of buying and selling; involved with these functions is merchandising. Merchandise cannot be produced and distributed without risk bearing, and sharing in risk taking is one of the contributions of wholesaling. In addition, merchandise must be financed from raw material to ultimate consumer, and wholesalers contribute to financing of merchandise through certain parts of the distributive process. Stockkeeping of the multitude of finished goods is also an important task along with delivery of the merchandise to retail sellers.

In 1929 there were 162,936 wholesale establishments in the United States doing over $65 billion worth of business. By 1972 the number had increased to 348,200 and the sales to $684 billion.

Of the several major kinds of wholesalers, *merchant wholesalers* make up by far the largest group, both in numbers and in volume of business. This type of wholesaler takes title to the merchandise handled, usually offers credit, makes deliveries of merchandise, issues catalogues, maintains a force of salesmen to call on customers, and provides other services to retailers. The next most important group in volume of merchandise handled are the *manufacturers' sales branches*. They are owned and operated by manufacturers in market areas important to the manufacturer.

Other wholesalers are the *petroleum bulk stations and terminals*, which are limited to petroleum and gas products. As a group they are growing in importance.

Merchandise agents and brokers represent manufacturers, usually in a particular region. Agents and brokers do not take title to merchandise but usually negotiate sales between the buyer and seller. They are useful in introducing new products and do not handle competing lines of merchandise. *Rack jobbers* provide merchandise displays such as records in retail stores. They do the complete job of merchandising, choosing items, providing inventory, and maintaining adequate displays and stock. This group of wholesalers is growing in importance, particularly in food supermarkets.

The two general classifications of wholesalers are the *full-service* and the *limited-function* establishments. The first offers full service to its customers, and the second only a limited number of the wholesale functions. Among the limited-function wholesalers are the cash-and-carry, mail-order, truck-jobber, and drop-shipper types. They generally are not large operations in volume and size, and, with the exception of mail-order organizations, usually operate in a restricted area.

Wholesalers render many important services to retailers and through them to customers. They anticipate customers' merchandise requirements and assemble different lines of goods. They buy in economical quantities and maintain a reservoir of merchandise that may be drawn on by retail stores. Often they maintain prompt deliveries, grant credit, and provide advisory services in connection with merchandising, advertising, and selling.

PAUL J. SOUTHARD
Formerly, Columbia University

Bibliography

Beckman, Theodore N., and others, *Marketing,* 9th ed. (Ronald 1973).
Brown, Milton P., and others, *Strategy Problems of Mass Retailers and Wholesalers* (Irwin 1970).
Bucklin, Louis P., *Competition and Evolution in the Distributive Trades* (Prentice-Hall 1972).
Buell, V. P., *Handbook of Modern Marketing,* 2d ed. (McGraw 1986).
Dannenberg, William P., and others, *Introduction to Wholesale Distribution* (Prentice-Hall 1978).
Ertel, Kenneth, and Walsh, Lawrence, *Wholesaling and Physical Distribution,* ed. by E. Dorr (McGraw 1978).
Schewe, Charles, and Smith, Reuben, *Marketing Concepts and Applications,* 2d ed. (McGraw 1983).
Revzan, David A., *Wholesaling in Marketing Organization,* ed. by Henry Assael (1961; reprint, Ayer 1978).
Vance, James E., *Merchant's World: The Geography of Wholesaling* (Prentice-Hall 1970).

WHOOPER. See WHOOPING CRANE.

WHOOPING COUGH, or pertussis, an infectious disease that most commonly attacks children, generally but once in their lives. It is a contagious, bacterial infection caused by *Bordetella pertussis* (called *Hemophilus pertussis* until 1957). Typically, severe spasmodic coughing is followed by prolonged inhalation, during which a shrill whistling sound—the whoop—is produced.

The first symptoms are those of the common cold, appearing usually within ten days after exposure, and include runny nose, sneezing, cough, and low-grade fever. During the next seven to ten days the cough gradually becomes more severe, is likely to be troublesome especially at night, and begins to occur in explosive bursts. The characteristic high-pitched crowing whoop now appears as the patient gasps for air following the explosive cough. Several fits of coughing commonly succeed one another until some mucus is expelled. Vomiting frequently follows a coughing attack. The number of coughing fits varies from four or five daily, in mild cases, to as many as 40 or more in severe cases.

Between these attacks the patient is usually comfortable and does not seem sick. In some instances the typical whoop is not heard in spite of the severity and frequency of coughing fits. This is particularly true of young infants, adults, or those partially protected by vaccine. During the first week or two of the spasmodic coughing stage the attacks increase in severity and frequency. They then remain at about the same level for a variable period, usually one to three weeks, and then gradually decline until the whooping and vomiting stop altogether. Some coughing usually lingers awhile, but its character is that of ordinary bronchitis. It usually fades away in another two or three weeks.

With subsequent respiratory infections, some patients will develop recurrent spasmodic coughing attacks complete with whoops and vomiting. These may occur repeatedly for months or even for a year or two. The commonest and usually most severe complication of this disease is pneumonia. Whooping cough is seldom fatal in older children or adults but is often fatal in the first year of life. For this reason the routine immunization program of all infants should include injections of pertussis vaccine, by itself or in combination with vaccines for diphtheria, polio, and tetanus. This is known to be 75% to 80% effective in preventing the disease. Furthermore, immunized children who subsequently contract whooping cough usually will acquire a mild case. Exposed unvaccinated persons may obtain temporary passive protection against the disease by injections of hyperimmune rabbit or human antipertussis serum. Such protection lasts four to six weeks.

An acute attack of whooping cough is usually treated with one of the broad-spectrum antibiotics, but such treatment must be started early in order to be effective in reducing the severity of the infection. Little is to be gained by antibiotic therapy if even slight symptoms have been present for more than a week. Supportive therapy is an important factor in the management of the disease, particularly in small infants. Sedative cough mixtures are not recommended. An atmosphere of increased humidity with the addition of oxygen as needed is often helpful.

GLADYS J. FASHENA, M. D.
Southwestern Medical School
The University of Texas

BUREAU OF SPORT FISHERIES AND WILDLIFE

An adult whooping crane, in white plumage, and its rust-colored young, at Aransas National Wildlife Refuge.

WHOOPING CRANE, a large crane with a loud "whooping" cry that is one of the world's rarest birds. Long on the verge of extinction, the whooping crane has slowly increased its numbers since about 1954, when only 21 birds remained. To promote a more rapid increase in the whooper population, eggs have been taken from crane nests to establish a captive flock at the Patuxent Wildlife Research Center in Maryland and placed in the nests of the much more numerous sandhill cranes, which serve as foster parents for the young whoopers.

Whooping cranes usually are slightly more than 4 feet (1.2 meters) in height, with a wingspan of about 7.5 feet (2.25 meters). The adult plumage is mostly white, with black wing tips and bare red skin on the crown and cheeks. The bill is gray, and the legs are black. Whoopers feed on a wide variety of aquatic animals such as snails and frogs and also eat seeds and other plant materials.

Whooping cranes breed at their isolated summer grounds in Wood Buffalo Park in northern Canada. They winter 2,600 miles (4,200 km) away at Aransas National Wildlife Refuge, a 47,000-acre (19,000-hectare) preserve on the Texas coast. Because of the whooper's large territorial requirement—about 400 acres (160 hectares) per pair—the capacity of the Aransas Refuge, only part of which is suitable habitat, is probably not more than a few dozen adult birds.

Whooping cranes are believed to pair for life. Their elaborate courtship dances include bowing, jumping, and wing-flapping. Nests consist of piles of vegetation above water level on wet ground. Usually two eggs are laid, but only one chick normally survives to fly south for the winter.

The whooping crane, *Grus americana,* belongs to the family Gruidae, order Gruiformes.

WHORTLEBERRY, hwûr′təl-ber-ē, also called bilberry or whinberry, a small shrub (*Vaccinium myrtillus*) of Europe and northern Asia related to the blueberry. It grows as tall as 2 feet (60 cm). Its edible fruits, the size of small blueberries, are black with a powdery coating.

WHO'S AFRAID OF VIRGINIA WOOLF?, a drama by the American playwright Edward Albee. First produced in 1962, *Who's Afraid of Virginia Woolf?* won the New York Drama Critics Circle Award. The play was made into a film in 1966, with Elizabeth Taylor and Richard Burton.

Who's Afraid of Virginia Woolf? centers on the relationship between George, a college professor, and Martha, his wife. Their marriage is marked by mutual hatred, which is expressed through cruel accusations and vituperative arguments. A second couple, Honey and Nick, is introduced into their lives, and George and Martha set about to draw them into their own marital quagmire. In three acts, entitled *Fun and Games, Walpurgisnacht,* and *Exorcism,* the deepest psychological problems of the characters are revealed. In the end, George and Martha seem about to start anew, with a possibility for happiness or, at least, mutual respect, while Honey and Nick appear to be taking their place in regard to mutual revilement.

WHYDAH, hwid′ə, or widowbird, any of about ten species of small African birds that parasitize the nests of weaver finches. Whydahs are chiefly seed-eating birds that live in open plains and savannas but lay their eggs in the nests of weaver finches in nearby forests. Each kind of whydah parasitizes the nests of a particular kind of weaver finch. The eggs of the whydah resemble those of its particular host finch, and the begging calls and mouth markings of young whydahs mimic those of the host young.

Female whydahs are plain and somewhat sparrowlike. Males take on a special plumage, mostly glossy black, for the breeding season, and some species have very long tails. The male pin-tailed whydah (*Vidua macroura*), for example, develops a black and white breeding plumage with a pink bill, and its roughly 10-inch (25-cm) tail is twice as long as the rest of its body. Most whydahs belong to the genus *Vidua,* family Ploceidae, order Passeriformes.

A male shaft-tailed whydah (*Vidua regia*) in breeding plumage, with four greatly lengthened tail feathers.

SAN DIEGO ZOO

WHYMPER, hwim'pər, **Edward** (1840–1911), English mountaineer and author, who was the first person to climb the Matterhorn in the Alps. Whymper was born in London, England, on April 27, 1840. After traveling to make sketches of Alpine peaks, he climbed Mount Pelvoux in the French Alps in 1861 and the Pointe des Écrins in 1864. In 1865, after many attempts, he reached the summit of the Matterhorn, at an altitude of 14,690 feet (4,478 meters). This was the first time the rugged mountain had been scaled. The expedition ended in disaster when four of Whymper's party of seven lost their lives during the descent.

On visits to Greenland in 1867 and 1872, Whymper collected rare fossils and shrubs that later were acquired by the British Museum. In 1880 he explored the Andes in Ecuador, where he discovered Andean glaciers and collected specimens of fossils, plants, and animals. In 1880 he was the first to reach the summit of Chimborazo (20,577 feet, or 6,272 meters) in Ecuador. He also ascended Cotopaxi (19,700 feet, or 6,003 meters), the highest active volcano in the world. In 1901–1905 he made exploring tours in Canada and ascended mountains and made investigations in the Great Divide region of the Rockies.

Whymper's writings include *Scrambles Amongst the Alps* (1871) and *Travels Amongst the Great Andes of the Equator* (1892). He died in Chamonix, France, on Sept. 16, 1911.

WICHITA, wich'i-tô, in south central Kansas, the state's most populous city and the seat of Sedgwick county. Situated at the junction of the Arkansas and Little Arkansas rivers, it is 190 miles (305 km) southwest of Kansas City, Kans. Wichita is the commercial and industrial center of a rich agricultural and oil- and gas-producing region. The city is the petroleum capital of Kansas, with many oil companies represented. More wheat is milled in Wichita than anywhere else in the state, and the city serves as the meat and soybean oil processing center of Kansas.

Wichita ranks as the largest manufacturing center in Kansas. Aircraft manufacture is the biggest industry, represented by the Beech Aircraft Corporation. Cessna Aircraft Company, Gates Learjet Corporation, and the Boeing Military Airplane Company. Household appliances, oil-field equipment, camping equipment, farm equipment, metal and wood products, home and office equipment, and computers also are manufactured.

Wichita is on the Kansas Turnpike and several interstate highways. The Wichita Mid-Continent Airport, 6 miles (10 km) from downtown, is served by several airlines. The McConnell Air Force Base is southeast of the city.

Wichita State University was founded in 1892. Friends University (1898) is affiliated with the Society of Friends, and Kansas Newman College (1933) is a Roman Catholic institution.

A new 14-story city hall was completed in 1975. The old city hall, built in 1892, now serves as home for the Historical Museum. Century II, a circular structure completed in 1969, is a cultural and convention center that includes a concert hall, where performances by the Wichita Symphony Orchestra are given, exhibition halls, and a theater. The Kansas Coliseum, seating 12,000, provides an arena for sports events, concerts, exhibitions, and other shows.

Among the city's art museums are the Wichita Art Museum, which has the Murdock collection, one of the largest collections of American art in the United States; the museum of the Wichita Art Association; and the Ulrich Museum of Wichita State University. Other museums include the Fellow-Reeve Museum of Friends University, concentrating on historical relics, paleontology, and zoology; the Wichita Historical Museum; Historic Wichita Cow Town, a replica of early Wichita; and the Mid-America All Indian Center Museum, displaying Plains Indian artifacts. The city also is the site of a fine natural habitat zoological garden.

History and Government. In 1864, James R. Mead and Jesse Chisholm established a trading post at the junction of the Arkansas and Little Arkansas rivers. Soon after the removal of the Wichita Indians to Oklahoma Territory in 1867, a white settlement grew up at the trading post. The trail followed by Chisholm on a trading expedition in 1865, later called the Chisholm

KANSAS DEPT. OF ECONOMIC DEVELOPMENT

Century II, a cultural and convention center in Wichita, Kansas, includes exhibition halls, a concert hall, and a theater.

Trail, quickly became an important overland cattle route, and the settlement of Wichita, whose name is derived from the Indian tribe, became a stopping point for cattle drivers.

The first settlers arrived in 1868. Wichita was laid out in 1869 and incorporated as a town in 1870. In 1872 the Santa Fe Railway reached Wichita, a U.S. land office was opened, and the Wichita *Eagle* and *Beacon* newspapers were founded. Development of the rich lands, the oil, and commerce and industry brought a rapid increase in population. Wichita was chartered as a city in 1886. It adopted a city manager-commission form of government in 1917. Population: 279,835.

DOWNING P. O'HARRA*, *University of Wichita*

WICHITA FALLS, wich'i-tô, a city in Texas and the seat of Wichita county. It is situated on the Wichita River, 114 miles (183 km) northwest of Fort Worth and 12 miles (19 km) south of the Oklahoma border. Wichita Falls is a commercial, oil, and industrial center for a wide area in north central Texas and south central Oklahoma.

In the midst of oil fields, the city serves as headquarters for independent operators and producing companies. Oil is refined, and oil-field equipment and machinery are manufactured. Other industries include flour milling and the manufacture of clothing, leather goods, foundry products, feedstuffs, house trailers, bedding, seat covers, and air conditioning equipment. There is a large wholesaling business in oil-field supplies, building materials, and farm machinery.

Agricultural production from the surrounding area, which is rich farming and stock-raising country intensively developed by irrigation, is devoted largely to cattle, grain, dairy products, and fruits such as peaches and plums.

Two railways provide service to the city. There is a municipal airport served by scheduled airlines. Sheppard Air Force Base, opened as Sheppard Field in 1941, was declared a permanent installation in 1950.

Midwestern University, a state institution, grew out of Wichita Falls Junior College, established by the city in 1922. The Kemp Public Library was given to the city in 1918 by the J. S. Kemps, a pioneer family. The Wichita Falls Symphony Orchestra gives concerts in the city's Memorial Auditorium.

A favorite camping site in the 1850's, the land near the falls of the Wichita River was laid out as a townsite in 1876. Reached by the Fort Worth and Denver City Railroad in 1882, Wichita Falls became the county seat in 1883 and was incorporated as a city in 1889. In 1886 the five-foot falls in the river were destroyed by heavy floods. Irrigation began in 1900. The first oil well came in in 1901, the Burkburnett boom began in 1919, and a second boom in oil came in 1937. The city operates under a city manager-commission form of government, adopted in 1928. Population: 94,201.

BARBARA C. JAMISON

WICHITA INDIANS, one of the principal tribes of the Caddoan linguistic family of North American Indians. Their name was derived from the Choctaw *wia chitoh*, "big arbor," referring to the large grass-thatched structures for which they were noted. Their traditional home was the Wichita Mountains of Oklahoma, but they have ranged far; Francisco Coronado encountered them in central Kansas in 1541 and recorded their homeland as the Province of Quivira. The Wichita custom of tattooing the body earned them the French name of *Pani Piqués;* they called themselves *Kitikitish*, meaning "raccoon-eyed people," a reference to their manner of face painting. They have enjoyed a high reputation for honesty and hospitality, but were quick to take offense; they were able warriors in battle. Theirs was a highly developed agricultural way of life, raising great crops of corn, pumpkins, beans, and other crops; they depended upon the buffalo for meat. At the time of the Treaty of Camp Holmes with the Plains tribes in Oklahoma in 1835, the sight of more than 200 huge grass-thatched dwellings arrayed on the plains tremendously impressed the military negotiators from the United States. Among some of the most interesting types of Indian homes, these testify to the ingenuity of the aboriginal architect in solving environmental problems.

Following the signing of the treaty, the Wichita continued to live in Oklahoma until the outbreak of the Civil War, whereupon they fled to Kansas as refugees. The founding of Wichita, Kans., on this site is a reminder of that period in their history. Many Wichita warriors served in the Union forces. In 1867 the tribe returned to Oklahoma, where they were placed on a reservation north of Anadarko in the vicinity of Gracemont, in Caddo County. Their closest kinsmen, the Tawakoni and the Waco, have affiliated with the Wichita so much that for most purposes the three are regarded as one. The Tawakoni, whose name means "river bend at the red sand hills," were noted middlemen in the Southern Plains Indian trade, and their villages were favorite marketplaces for neighboring tribes. The Waco, whose name apparently comes from *Wéhiko*, a corruption of Mexico (a reference to their constant warfare with the Mexicans), have always been a small tribe. Like the Tawakoni, their culture reflects the agricultural pattern of the parent body. Approximately 250 Wichita descendants live on reservation lands, with some 190 Tawakoni and 60 Waco.

FREDERICK J. DOCKSTADER
Director, Museum of American Indian, Heye Foundation

WICKERSHAM, wĭk'ər-shəm, **George Woodward,** American cabinet officer and lawyer: b. Pittsburgh, Pa., Sept. 19, 1858; d. New York, N.Y., Jan. 25, 1936. He studied at Lehigh University, then took his degree in law at the University of Pennsylvania in 1880. He first engaged in practice in Philadelphia, but practiced in New York after 1882. He was for many years a member of the law firm of Strong and Cadwalader, which later became Cadwalader, Wickersham and Taft. He specialized in business problems, became one of the leading corporation counsels of New York State, and had wide experience in railway litigation in the United States. During the Taft administration he was attorney general of the United States (1909–1913) and handled successfully much antitrust litigation under the Sherman antitrust law. He was American member of the Committee on Progressive Codification of International Law under the League of Nations from 1924 to 1929.

In 1929 President Herbert Hoover appointed Wickersham chairman of the National Commission on Law Observance and Enforcement, popularly known as the Wickersham Commission. During a two-year period the commission delved into the twin problems of observance and enforcement. One of its major conclusions was that the machinery for criminal law enforcement in the United States was entirely inadequate and that the annual cost of crime amounted to a staggering total of a billion dollars. It was, however, the report on prohibition, released Jan. 13, 1930, that attracted widest attention. A majority of the commission disapproved the "noble experiment"; but the chairman and three colleagues favored further trial. Less than two years later Wickersham conceded that prohibition had been a failure and urged that it be replaced by regulation of the sale of alcoholic beverages.

WICKFORD, wĭk'fərd, village, Rhode Island, in the Township of North Kingstown (incorporated 1674), in Washington County, on Narragansett Bay, 20 miles by road south of Providence, at sea level. It was named for Wickford, England. The village is primarily a residential community for persons employed in Providence and also serves the Quonset Point Naval Air Station 3½ miles to the north, where the famous Quonset huts were first used.

Wickford has one of the finest small-boat harbors on the Atlantic seaboard, with a large marina, and does considerable tourist trade. Wickford is rich in colonial history and architecture, possessing more well-preserved 18th century houses than any other village its size in New England. The Old Narragansett Church (1707) is the oldest Episcopal church building in the North. The Gilbert Stuart Birthplace (1750) nearby, where the famous portrait painter was born, is a museum, as is "Smith's Castle" (1677), where Roger Williams traded with the Indians. Settlement began about 1637, and the village was founded in 1709. The town manager form of government was adopted in 1954.

GLADYS S. HELLEWELL

WICKHAM, William of. See WILLIAM OF WYKEHAM.

WICKLIFFE, wĭk'lĭf, city, Ohio, in Lake County, 2 miles south of Lake Erie, and 13 miles northeast of downtown Cleveland, at an altitude of 655 feet. This is chiefly a residential area, but small manufactures include pipe machinery, patterns, lubricants, tools, and cranes. Wickliffe is the seat of the Telshe Yeshiva College (Rabbinical) and the Borromeo Seminary (Roman Catholic). The earliest white settler was William Jones in 1817, although Indians inhabited the area until 1840. The post office was established in 1842 and the town named after the then Postmaster General Charles A. Wickliffe. The area was incorporated as a village in 1916 and became a city in 1951; government is by mayor and six councilmen. Population: 16,790.

DORIS H. SHACKSON

WICKLOW, wĭk'lō, county, Ireland, in Leinster Province, on the east coast (Irish Sea), between Dublin (north) and Wexford (south). The county town is Wicklow, 26 miles southeast of Dublin. Inland, the county is hilly, with picturesque valleys where sheep and cattle are raised; there is also mining of iron, copper, and lead. Bray and Arklow are fishing ports and shore resorts. Pop. (1956) 59,906.

WICKSELL, wĭk'səl, **(John Gustav) Knut,** Swedish economist: b. Stockholm, Sweden, Dec. 20, 1851; d. Stocksund, May 3, 1926. Educated at the University of Uppsala and several European universities, he completed his doctorate at Uppsala in 1895, but had to obtain a law degree before receiving a professorship in political economy and fiscal law at Lund University in 1904, a post which he held until 1916. He was the initiator of the modern Swedish school of economists, which includes Gunnar Myrdal, Bertil Ohlin, and Erik Lindahl. He was particularly associated with the application of marginal productivity analysis in both price and monetary theory. He restated Eugen Böhm-Bawerk's interest theory in terms compatible with the equilibrium system of Léon Walras. His was one of the earliest treatments of a real investment analysis of the business cycle. His work also served as one foundation of Keynesian macroeconomics, and the beginning of truly dynamic economic analysis.

Wicksell was deeply concerned with political and social issues. His policy recommendations developed from his economic analysis. Regarded as shockingly radical when first advocated, many of his ideas were adopted as part of the national policy in Sweden during his lifetime. He was a prolific writer. Major works translated into English are: *Lectures on Political Economy* (1934); *Interest and Prices; a study of the Causes Regulating the Value of Money* (1936); *Value, Capital and Rent,* containing a bibliography of his published works (1954).

WILLIAM N. KINNARD, JR.

WICLIF, John. See WYCLIFFE, JOHN.

WIDDIN. See VIDIN.

WIDDRINGTONIA wĭd-drĭng-tōn'yə, a genus including about six species of drought-resistant trees and shrubs of South Africa, belonging to the Cupressaceae family. The leaves are evergreen and scalelike and the individual plants have both staminate and pistillate flowers. The carpellate cones usually have four scales. Although mostly quite limited in range and occurring only in patches, they have some economic value for their timber and for the fragrant resin. They are found in mountainous districts of Cape Province, ranging to Natal, Mozambique, Zimbabwe, and Madagascar. The present ranges are somewhat of the nature of relict colonies, but fossil remains of apparently related trees indicate ancestors of present-day species may have been widespread in Europe and North America in the Mesozoic. *Widdringtonia juniperoides,* a tree about 65 feet tall, popularly known as cedar, gives its name to Cedar Berg (mountain) in Cape Province, where it grows in relatively inaccessible positions. *W. schwarzii,* on Konka Berg (mountain) in southwestern Cape Province, resembles the preceding but has smaller cones. *W. whytei,* of Zimbabwe and northern Transvaal, is a tree up to 150 feet high. Known as Mlanje cypress (from Mount Mlanje), it is a valuable tree, since its wood is immune to attacks of termites, and its growth is being encouraged. *W. cupressoides,* ranging from Cape Town to Grahamstown, Cape Province, is a shrub only 10 to 15 feet high.

EARL L. CORE
Chairman, Department of Biology, West Virginia University

WIDE, WIDE WORLD, The, domestic novel by Susan Warner (q.v.) published in three volumes in 1851 under the pseudonym Elizabeth Wetherell. For several generations it was one of the most widely read works ever written in the United States. Said to have been accepted for publication only on the insistence of the first publisher's mother, it describes the adventures of a model child who grows perfect in all the religious, moral, and social virtues as family difficulties send her to live successively with a harsh aunt, a kindly minister, and her stern Scottish grandparents. Though persistently ridiculed for its sentimental and preachy tone, it is not without shrewdness and is still readable by those who can accept what was regarded even in its own day as overinsistent moralizing and priggish propriety. Perhaps it is best regarded not as literature but as a document illustrating changes in popular taste.

JOSEPH WOOD KRUTCH.

WIDENER, wĭd'nər, **Peter Arrell Brown,** American financier and philanthropist: b. Philadelphia, Pa., Nov. 13, 1834; d. Elkins Park, Nov. 6, 1915. Owner of a meat business in Philadelphia, he made a large profit from government contracts during the Civil War. This sum, combined with wise investments and municipal political activity, enabled him to amass a moderate fortune. He then joined with his friend William L. Elkins in gaining control of all street railway lines in the city, and Widener later extended his holdings to rapid transit systems in Chicago, Pittsburgh, and Baltimore. By now his investments had become diverse and widespread; among the companies he helped to establish were the United States Steel Corporation and the American Tobacco Company. An avid art collector, he acquired many treasured works of painting and sculpture, and as a philanthropist he gave away an estimated 11 million dollars to charitable enterprises, as well as his entire art collection to the city. Two of his major contributions were his Philadelphia residence, which he donated for use as a public library, and the Widener Memorial Industrial Training School for Crippled Children, which he built and endowed.

HARRY ELKINS WIDENER (1885–1912), his grandson, became an eminent collector of rare books. After young Widener's death in the *Titanic* ship disaster, his valuable library went to Harvard College and was housed in the Harry Elkins Widener Memorial Library, a gift of his mother.

WIDGEON, wĭj'ŭn, or **WIGEON,** the name of three species of freshwater ducks of the genus *Anas*, placed by some authorities in a special genus called *Mareca*. Two species are found in the Northern Hemisphere, the European widgeon (*A. penelope*) in northern Eurasia, and the American widgeon (*A. americana*) in northwestern North America; the third, the Chiloë widgeon (*A. sibilatrix*), inhabits southern South America. They are about 19 inches in size with a heavy rounded body, although they walk, swim, and fly easily. The males are more colorful than the females, except for the Chiloë widgeon in which both sexes are colorful and alike. In the American widgeon the male has a gray head with a broad streak of metallic green behind the eye, and a white forehead and crown, hence the name "baldpate" by which it is commonly called in America. The male European widgeon has a rusty red head and a golden buff forehead and crown. The Chiloë widgeon has a white face and a black crown and neck, with a band of metallic green behind the eye. It is chiefly sedentary but the other two species are migratory. The American widgeon winters south to the West Indies and Panama, and the European widgeon in Africa and southern Eurasia, though it is also a rare but regular winter visitor in North America. The widgeons breed on lakes, rivers, and ponds, and also on marshes, moors, and tundras, and their food consists almost entirely of vegetable matter. On migration and in their winter quarters they frequent chiefly the seacoast and muddy estuaries.

CHARLES VAURIE.

WIDNES, wĭd'nĕs, municipal borough, Lancashire, England. Incorporated in 1892, this manufacturing town lies on the river Mersey, 12 miles southeast of Liverpool, on the Liverpool-to-London railroad. A hamlet until the early 19th century, it was swiftly developed after the opening, in the 1830's, of John Hutchinson's limekiln. The growth was due to its riverside location between Manchester and Liverpool and to its easy access to the Lancashire coalfields and the Cheshire salt mines. Docks were built and extended in 1866 and 1884. Industries include chemical, metallurgical, and engineering works, soap, paint, glass, and textiles; a technical college provides related training. The railroad line and a transporter bridge connect Widnes with Runcorn across the river. The Queen's Hall was opened as a civic hall in 1957. Pop. (1961) 52,168.

RICHARD WEBB.

WIDOR, vē-dôr', **Charles Marie (Jean Albert),** French organist and composer: b. Lyon, France, Feb. 21, 1844; d. Paris, March 12, 1937. Son of the organist at St. François in Lyon, he learned the instrument as a boy and, after studying organ and composition in Brussels, succeeded to his father's post in 1860. Appointed organist at St.-Sulpice in Paris in 1869, he remained in that distinguished church office for 65 years until his retirement in 1934. He succeeded César Franck as professor of organ at the Paris Conservatoire in 1890, and in 1896 became also professor of composition there. Until his retirement, he was also director of the American Conservatory of Music in Fontainebleau. Widor's copious and diversified compositions included 10 symphonies for organ, a ballet, operatic works, pianoforte concertos, and other pieces, orchestral suites, 2 symphonies for orchestra, and sacred music. Several movements from his organ symphonies (or suites) have attained wide popularity and have become part of the standard organ repertory. His many noted pupils include Albert Schweitzer, with whom he collaborated in compiling a major edition of the organ works of Johann Sebastian Bach.

WIDOW, wĭd'ō, a woman who has lost her husband and has not married again. A "grass widow" is a divorcée. In most countries of the world the number of widows far exceeds the number of widowers (men who have lost their wives and not remarried). This is due primarily to two factors:

(1) the greater longevity of females and (2) the reluctance of males to take previously married wives.

The United States is typical of modern cultures; three out of four wives survive their husbands. Although widowed men and women are more likely to remarry at any given age than are single persons to marry for the first time, the ratio of female to male widows is high. There were (1960) approximately 1,500,000 widowed males in the United States, but 4,259,000 widowed females.

In Asiatic cultures, customs tend to taboo marriage of widows. Hindu culture has long forbidden it, even though sanctioning a type of child betrothal which has the sanctity of marriage. As a result of this custom, many girls are widowed before consummating the marriage and by age 40 more than half of all women are widowed. Muslims in India and Pakistan, because of their long association with Hindus, have adopted almost as rigid customs. In both cultures, widowed males are expected to remarry, taking virgins.

Only very slowly are these customs breaking down. The taboos on marriage of widows are passing with westernization, as has *suttee,* the burning of the widow on the funeral pyre of her husband, once practiced among upper classes in India and in certain other cultures of the world. In fact, the Indian Parliament has passed a law permitting remarriage of widows, but this ancient custom is likely to persist for many decades to come.

PAUL H. LANDIS,
Washington State University

WIDOW BIRD. See WEAVER.

WIDOW IN THE BYE STREET, The, a narrative poem by John Masefield (q.v.), first published in 1912. Together with *The Everlasting Mercy* (1911), *Dauber* (1913), and *The Daffodil Fields* (1913), it established the author's place as one of the leading English poets of the 20th century.

Beginning with a deliberate imitation of the opening of Geoffrey Chaucer's *Nun's Priest's Tale,* Masefield tells the story of a poor widow in a little Shropshire town, and her son, Jim Gurney. The mother, widowed while Jim was still a baby, supported herself as a seamstress while the child was growing, and broke her health in so doing. When the lad reached his teens, and went to work as a laborer, there followed a brief period of happiness, shadowed always by the mother's dread of the day when another woman would take her son from her. The woman came, in the person of Anna, a clandestine prostitute much older than Jim, whom he met at the fair. Having a tiff with her current lover, Sheperd Ern, Anna led on and ensnared the boy in order to make Ern jealous; she succeeded in both endeavors. When Ern returned to her, she callously dismissed Jim, and he, crazed with anger and humiliation, murdered Ern. He was condemned and hanged. His mother lived on to mourn her son, her mind broken with grief.

When the poem was first published, it, like *The Everlasting Mercy,* created a sensation. Long narrative poems had almost gone out of fashion; Masefield's colloquial vigor fascinated a public whose idea of narrative verse still was influenced by memories of Alfred, Lord Tennyson and William Morris. The sweep of the story, the skill with which Masefield fitted fast-moving dialogue into the metrical framework of Chaucer's rime royal stanza, obscured the poem's defects, chief of which is an excess of emotionalism. Nevertheless, the emotion, though overwrought, is genuine; the situation of a guileless youngster enslaved by a worthless woman is convincingly handled, and the poem contains passages of great lyric poetry.

DELANCEY FERGUSON
Formerly, *Brooklyn College*

WIDUKIND. See WITTEKIND.

WIECHERT, vē′kərt, **Ernst Emil,** German author: b. Kleinort (a forester's lodge), Sensburg, East Prussia, Germany, May 18, 1887; d. Uerikon, Switzerland, Aug. 24, 1950. The son of a forester, he went to school in Königsberg, studied science, philosophy, and foreign literatures, and taught school in Berlin until 1933. Wiechert served and was wounded in World War I. Later he settled in Bavaria and, because of his critical attitude toward the National Socialist regime, was interned for four months in the Buchenwald concentration camp in 1938—an experience which he recounts in *Der Totenwald* (1945; Eng. tr., *The Forest of the Dead,* 1947). He visited the United States briefly in 1949 as a guest lecturer at Stanford University.

In spite of the persistent despair and melancholy that characterize most of his novels, and his often excessive romantic individualism, Wiechert was one of the most popular modern German novelists. In his autobiographical works *Waelder und Menschen* (1936; Forests and Men) and *Jahre und Zeiten* (1949; Years and Ages) he points to his East Prussian heritage of somber mysticism and to the disillusioning experience of World War I as the central impulses in his writings.

Weichert is always intensely introspective and preoccupied with the inescapable reality of evil. His early novels *Der Wald* (1922; The Forest) and *Der Totenwolf* (1924; The Death Wolf) show his pessimism rendered in a highly lyrical manner; only a withdrawal into the hearing realm of nature makes it possible to bear a life emptied of meaning. In the short stories *Die Magd des Juergen Doskovil* (1932) and *Hirtennovelle* (1935; The Shepherd's Tale) he achieves perhaps his best fiction; simple human beings seek in these works to break through solitude and bitterness to a communion with God. *Die Majorin* (1934; Eng. tr., *The Baroness,* 1936) deals with the returning soldier whose shattered faith in life is restored by the love and devotion of a proud woman. All of Wiechert's themes are represented in *Die Jerominskinder* (2 vols., 1945–47), a chronicle of an East Prussian family, and in the post-humous *Missa sine nomine* (1950; Eng. tr. with same title, 1953; Eng. tr. as *Tidings,* 1959).

His lyrical poem *Totenmesse* (1945), his highly symbolic plays *Das Spiel vom Deutschen Bettelmann* (1933; The German Beggar) and *Der Verlorene Sohn* (1935; The Prodigal Son), as well as his many addresses (*Reden an die Deutsche Jugend,* 1951), made Wiechert, during the National Socialist regime, a conspicuous representative of the "resistance from within." In all his works, the recurring motif of the "simple life" is sometimes movingly conveyed; but especially his later publications lack not only an articulate philosophy but a convincing attachment to reality, and therefore tend to produce an uncomfortable feeling of excessive sentimentality and effusiveness. The publication of Wiechert's collected works in 10 volumes began in 1956.

VICTOR LANGE,
Chairman, Germanic Department, Princeton University.

WIELAND, vē'länt, **Christoph Martin,** German author: b. Oberholzheim, near Biberach, Württemberg, Germany, Sept. 5, 1733; d. Weimar, Jan. 20, 1813. The son of a country clergyman, he was educated in a severely Protestant fashion and, from 1750 to 1752, studied law and literature at the University of Tübingen. Subsequently he lived for eight years in Switzerland, first in Zurich in the house of the critic Johann Jakob Bodmer, and later in Bern where he became for a time engaged to Jean Jacques Rousseau's friend Julie de Bondeli.

Wieland's early philosophical essays, *Zwölf moralische Briefe* (1751; Twelve Letters on Morality), his stories, *Erzaehlungen* (1752), his epic poems, *Hermann* (1751) and *Cyrus* (1759), and his tragedy, *Lady Johanna Gray* (1758), all reflect the several stages of his literary development from Christian idealism to the sensuous aestheticism that was characteristic of the 18th century French enlightenment.

In 1760 Wieland was appointed a city official at Biberach and joined the elegant circle of Count Friedrich von Stadion at Warthausen. During the following years he wrote, partly for this worldly and cultivated society, his celebrated prose translations of William Shakespeare (published in 8 vols., 1762–1766). His first great success was a novel in the manner of Miguel de Cervantes Saavedra, *Die Abenteuer des Don Sylvio de Rosalva* (1764; The Adventures of Don Sylvio de Rosalva). Perhaps his best-known work, *Agathon* (2 vols., 1766–67), is an account of the development of a young man from emotional "enthusiasm" to philosophical scepticism. *Musarion oder die Philosophie der Grazien* (1768; Musarion or the Philosophy of the Graces) sets forth in the form of a graceful poem Wieland's indebtedness to the ideas of sensual and intellectual beauty expressed by the 3d earl of Shaftesbury (Anthony Ashley Cooper).

In 1765 Wieland married Dorothea von Hillenbrand, who bore him 14 children. After three years as professor at the University of Erfurt he accepted in 1772 an appointment as tutor to the young children of the Duchess Anna Amalia of Saxe-Weimar, who was impressed by Wieland's work *Der goldene Spiegel oder die Könige von Scheschian.* There and in nearby Ossmannstedt he lived a busy and widely respected life as poet, novelist, and editor. Johann Wolfgang von Goethe, who had earlier attacked Wieland for his conventional French classicism (*Götter, Helden und Wieland,* 1774; Gods, Heroes, and Wieland), composed in 1813 a moving necrologue for his distinguished fellow citizen. Wieland's effectiveness as a preceptor of cultural cosmopolitanism and literary taste was due in large measure to his conscientious editorship from 1773 to 1810 of the monthly review, *Der teutsche Merkur* (later *Der neue teutsche Merkur*). Here, in the manner of the *Mercure de France,* he introduced his German readers to the most important aspects of contemporary literature and thought. At the same time he translated the works of many of the major figures of the European tradition, especially the Roman poet Horace, the orator Cicero, and the Greek poet Lucian.

Wieland's chief writings during the early years in Weimar were the 14 cantos of the romantic poem *Oberon* (q.v.; 1780), perhaps the finest of all modern epic poems written in German, and the satirical novel *Die Abderiten. Eine sehr wahrscheinliche Geschichte* (1774; The Abderites. A Most Probable Tale), in which he caricatured life in the provincial German towns such as Erfurt.

In a prolific series of urbanely ironical works he continued during the next 20 years to criticize the intellectual pretensions of his contemporaries: *Geheime Geschichte des Philosophen Peregrinus Proteus* (1791; Secret History of the Philosopher Peregrinus Proteus) ridicules the religious fanatic Johann Kaspar Lavater and certain German preromantic writers; *Aristipp* (4 vols., 1800–01), Wieland's last novel, shows the hero at the time of Socrates and Plato, maintaining himself as a critical individual against the fashionable temptations of either intellectualism or sentimentality. Besides these major works Wieland produced an astonishing variety of verse, operatic libretti (*Alceste,* 1773; *Rosamund,* 1778), comedies, modern fairy tales, and critical commentaries on the literature and culture of his day.

The importance of Wieland's work is only now being appreciated. Sober judgment and civilized good taste, a superb ease of style and versification, and a thorough familiarity with all aspects of European civilization made him one of the most important representatives of 18th century literature. He was the first German writer to devote himself seriously to the craft of fiction, and his intense, serious interest in Henry Fielding and Laurence Sterne made these distinguished English novelists accessible in translation to the German public.

Wieland's part in the shaping of German as a poetic and critical language cannot be overrated. With Goethe, Johann C. F. von Schiller, Johann Gottfried von Herder, and Baron Wilhelm von Humboldt, he developed the canons of German classicism; his wit and independent intelligence gave him a standing almost comparable to Voltaire.

VICTOR LANGE,
Chairman, Germanic Department, Princeton University.

WIELAND, Heinrich Otto, German chemist: b. Pforzheim, Germany, June 4, 1877; d. Munich, Aug. 5, 1957. Educated at the University of Munich (Ph.D., 1901) and at other German universities, and holder of doctorates also in engineering and medicine, he taught at Munich from 1904 to 1917 and from 1925 to 1952, in the latter period as professor and director of the chemical laboratories. His research on cholic (bile) acids and related substances won for him the 1927 Nobel Prize in chemistry. Wieland and Adolf Windaus (q.v.), the 1928 Nobel laureate, were honored for their discovery of the complex structure of cholesterin (see CHOLESTEROL), a substance found in bile. Their formula later was found to be incorrect, however, and the problem was not solved until 1932 when British scientists found the key. Wieland also engaged in research in the alkaloids, anesthetics, biological oxidation, and organic nitrogen compounds. He was the author of works on organic chemistry and biochemistry, notably *Über den Verlauf der Oxydationsvorgänge* (1933), and he was the editor of *Liebig's Annals of Chemistry*.

WIEN, vēn, **Wilhelm,** German physicist: b. Gaffken, East Prussia, Germany, Jan. 13, 1864; d. Munich, Aug. 30, 1928. He became an assistant to the German physicist Hermann L. F. von Helmholtz in 1890, following studies at the universities of Göttingen, Heidelberg, and Berlin. From 1899 until his death he held professorships at Giessen, Würzberg (1900–1920), and Munich (from 1920). His scientific research centered especially on radiation, a field in which he and his colleagues pioneered.

Wien's Laws. In 1896, employing the principles of thermodynamics, he proposed three laws concerning the relationships between the wavelength distribution of radiant energy emitted by and entirely dependent upon the absolute temperatures of a black body (a theoretical completely perfect radiator which absorbs all of the radiation incident upon it, reflecting none and transmitting none). Wien's displacement law states, in effect, that while the energy emitted from a black body increases at all wavelengths as its temperature increases, such energy increases do not appear in equal proportions at all wavelengths, and that there is a shift or displacement in the distribution of energy toward shorter wavelengths. His radiation law and a third law, known as Wien's distribution law, relate to radiant energy emission and distribution from a black body at different absolute temperatures and are in essential agreement with the work of Max Planck, but the third law is applied accurately only at short wavelengths.

Wien's work in this area, which paralleled the studies of Planck and contributed to the latter's historic findings, resulted in his selection as the 1911 Nobel Prize winner in physics. His investigations also carried over into optics, cathode rays, X rays, and hydrodynamics.

WIENER, wē'nər, **Norbert,** American mathematician: b. Columbia, Mo., Nov. 26, 1894; d. Stockholm, Sweden, March 18, 1964. A son of the philologist Leo Wiener, he graduated from Tufts College in 1909. He later studied at Harvard (Ph.D., 1913), Cornell, and Columbia, and abroad at Cambridge and Göttingen universities. From 1919 until his retirement in 1960, he taught in the department of mathematics at the Massachusetts Institute of Technology, where he became a full professor in 1932.

While working for the government during World War II, Wiener became interested in the nature of information processes as pertaining to automatic electronic computers and similar mechanisms. From further research, working particularly with automatic predictors used in antiaircraft systems, he developed the branch of science (or combination of sciences) known as cybernetics, a term which he coined from the Greek word for governor or steersman, and which concerns the relationship between communication and control in the human (or animal) brain and nervous system and that which functions in machines. Wiener set forth his findings in *Cybernetics, or Control and Communication in the Man and the Machine* (1948), a work which won high acclaim and aroused interest among members of several scientific disciplines. He also wrote *The Human Use of Human Beings* (1950), *God and Golem, Inc.: A Comment on Certain Points Where Cybernetics Impinges on Religion* (1964), and *Cybernetics of the Nervous System* (1965). Two volumes of memoirs, *Ex-Prodigy* (1953) and *I Am a Mathematician* (1956), trace his early years. A novel, *The Tempter*, appeared in 1959.

WIENER NEUSTADT, vē'nər noi'shtät, a city in Austria, in Lower Austria Province, 25 miles (40 km) south of Vienna. An industrial center and a regional transportation hub, the city has metalworking and textile industries. It was founded in 1194 as a fortress town to guard against the Magyars. Largely rebuilt after a disastrous fire in 1834, it was almost leveled by Allied air attacks during World War II because of its armaments production, and was again rebuilt after 1945. Remaining from its early history is a 13th century castle built by the ducal family of Babenberg and converted into a military academy in 1752. Among the old churches is St. George's of the Castle (13th century), containing the remains of Emperor Maximilian I, and a Cistercian abbey church with the fine tomb (1467) of Eleanor of Portugal, wife of Emperor Frederick III. Population (1981 census) 35,050.

WIENIAWSKI, vye-nyäf'skē, **Henryk,** Polish violinist and composer: b. Lublin, Poland, July 10, 1835; d. Moscow, Russia, March 31, 1880. A violin student as a young child, he showed such precocity that his mother took him to Paris where he entered the conservatory at the age of 8. His progress was so rapid that in one year he was placed in the advanced class under Lambert Joseph Massart, and at 11 was graduated with the first prize in violin, an unprecedented feat. Becoming a concert violinist at 13, he delighted audiences in St. Petersburg and Warsaw before resuming his studies at the Paris Conservatoire, again graduating with first prize in 1850. After serving as court violinist to the czar and teaching for several years at the St. Petersburg Conservatory, he joined Anton Rubenstein on a concert tour of the United States in 1872, remaining until 1874 when he was named professor of violin at the Brussels Conservatory. One of the great violin masters of the century, Wieniawski developed a technique that was said to be flawless, and he executed the most difficult pieces with remarkable ease and assurance. His compositions were intended mainly to exhibit his virtuosity, but some of them remain popular, notably his violin concerto in D minor. Among his other works are two collections of violin etudes, the violin concerto in F♯ minor, and Légende for violin and orchestra.

WIESBADEN, vēs'bä-dən, a city in West Germany, attractively situated between the Rhine River and the foot of the wooded Taunus mountain range, 20 miles (32 km) west of Frankfort. It is the capital of the state of Hesse.

Noted for its 27 thermal springs and its mild climate, Wiesbaden is one of Europe's leading spas. It is also a manufacturing, publishing, film making, and convention center, and has an important trade in locally produced sparkling wine (*Sekt*). The castle (1841) houses the Hesse state legislature and government offices. Music, ballet, and drama are performed in the state theater (1894), and the municipal museum contains an excellent art gallery. In the spa district is a noted casino.

During the 1st century A.D. the site became a Roman spa called Aquae Mattiacorum. The city was first recorded in 829 as Wisibada and chartered in the 13th century. Wiesbaden was the capital of Nassau from 1806 to 1866, when that duchy was incorporated into Prussia.

After World War I the city was the headquarters of the interallied commission for the demilitarized Rhineland from 1918 to 1929. Following World War II it was chosen as the capital of the new West German state of Hesse. Meanwhile the U.S. Air Force established a large military base and hospital at Wiesbaden. Despite some industrialization the city preserved its essentially residential character, with handsome buildings of the Victorian era and open green spaces. Population: (1982) 273,703.

WIESEL, vē-sel′, **Elie** (1928–), American writer and educator, widely regarded as the spokesman for the victims and survivors of the Nazi Holocaust during World War II. Most of his fiction, essays, and commentaries are informed by his mission to bear witness to the starkest event in human history. In recognition of his efforts as "a messenger to mankind," he was awarded the Nobel Peace Prize in 1986.

Eliezer Wiesel was born in Sighet, Romania, on Sept. 30, 1928. He received a thorough grounding in Jewish religious studies seasoned with Hasidic lore. In 1944 the Jews of the town were deported by the Nazis to concentration camps. Wiesel managed to survive and was liberated in 1945. Settling in Paris, he studied at the Sorbonne and worked as a reporter for French and Israeli newspapers. He went to the United States in 1956 and was naturalized in 1963. He taught at the City College of New York and in 1976 was appointed professor of humanities at Boston University.

Wiesel's first novel, *Night* (1960), originally published in Yiddish (1956) and then in French (1958), concerns a boy's experiences in a death camp. In *Dawn* (1961) a young Jewish terrorist in Palestine is assigned the retaliatory execution of a British officer. In *The Accident* (1962) a journalist in New York is struck by a car and, while recovering, meditates on guilt for having survived the Holocaust. In *The Town Beyond the Wall* (1967) the central theme is apathy in the face of evil. *The Gates of the Forest* (1967) examines man's relationship with God during the Holocaust. The plight of Jews in the Soviet Union is the subject of *Jews of Silence* (1967) and of the play *Zalmen, or The Madness of God* (1968). A collection of stories and essays makes up *Legends of Our Times* (1968). In *Beggar in Jerusalem* (1970) the protagonist muses on the Israeli victory in the six-day war of 1967. Other works include *Souls on Fire* (1972), Hasidic tales; and *The Fifth Son* (1985).

WIESENTHAL, vē′zən-täl, **Simon** (1908–), Austrian investigator, who was instrumental in bringing to justice more than 1,100 Nazi war criminals. Among his most celebrated feats were the discoveries of Adolf Eichmann in Argentina and of Franz Stengl, commandant of Treblinka, in Brazil. Asserting that the search for Nazi criminals was in the spirit of justice and not vengeance, Wiesenthal and his associates prepared meticulous dossiers on their suspects and urged that they be captured and tried in the countries of their crimes.

Wiesenthal was born in Buczacz, Austria-Hungary (now Soviet Union), on Dec. 31, 1908. He practiced architecture in Lvov, Poland, until World War II. He and his wife were interned in separate concentration camps but survived and were reunited after five years. More than 80 members of their families were killed. Wiesenthal then headed the Jewish Documentation Center in Linz, Austria (1947–1954), for the aid of Jewish victims of Nazi persecution. In 1961 he became director of the Jewish Documentation Center in Vienna.

The Simon Wiesenthal Center for Holocaust Studies, with headquarters in Los Angeles, is a document and film archive and maintains a Nazi Watch Program to monitor the activities of former Nazis and neo-Nazis.

Wiesenthal wrote several books based on his concentration camp experiences and his work as an investigator. Notable among them are *KZ Mathausen* (1947); *The Head Mufti: Agent of the Axis* (1947); *I Hunted Eichmann* (1961); *Limitation* (1964); *The Murderers Among Us: The Simon Wiesenthal Memoirs* (1967); *Sunflower* (1969); *Sails of Hope* (1973); *The Case of Krystyna Jaworska* (1975); and *Max and Helen* (1982).

WIG, (shortened form of *periwig*), an artificial hair covering for the head, worn to conceal baldness, to effect a disguise, or for ceremonial or theatrical purposes. The use of wigs as adornment originated in early times. They were worn by both men and women in Egypt for reasons of cleanliness and comfort as well as decoration, often in unnatural colors or interwoven with gold jewelry. An elaborate wig was found in the Danish Bronze Age burials (about 1500–800 B.C.), indicating the widespread usage. In Greece, which probably imported the wig from the Persians, it was worn by both sexes and also used as part of theatrical costume. Wigs came into fashion in late Republican or early Imperial Rome; Caesar used a wig as well as the laurel to hide his baldness, and it was worn by emperors also. Upper-class Roman women favored wigs made of blonde or red hair taken from the heads of captured women from the north.

The great vogue of wig wearing in France and England in the 17th and 18th centuries began at the court of Louis XIII, who was bald. From there it spread to England, although women had worn wigs earlier in Elizabethan times. (Elizabeth herself had a large and varied wardrobe of wigs, and Mary, Queen of Scots wore a wig to her beheading.) The peruke was a familiar part of the gay costume of the Cavaliers, and it came into general use in the reign of Charles II, especially among fashionable gentlemen of the day.

The full-bottomed periwig of the Restoration was a large, elaborate construction usually made in natural colors (the white-powdered type did not come into prominence until the 18th century), and necessitated the shaving or close cropping of the head. This form continued through the reign of Anne (1702–1714), but by 1730 a neater, soldier's style (tie wig), confined in back with a black ribbon, was favored by young men. One version was known as the Ramillies wig, consisting of long braided queues tied at top and bottom with a small ribbon bow, which was supposedly worn by soldiers at the Battle of Ramillies in 1706.

The pigtail was popular in the early Georgian period, and remained in use by British sailors until the mid-19th century. Another popular style was the *bag wig,* in which the hair was gathered in back and enclosed in a black silk bag drawn up with a string. Further modifications in the 18th century resulted in simpler styles, evolving into stiff corkscrew curls around the head. By 1790 the wig had disappeared from general use in England, although it is worn there today as a symbol of office by the lord chancellor, judges, barristers, and bishops. A widely used modern form, the toupee, is designed to simulate natural hair.

WIGAN, wig′ən, a district of Greater Manchester metropolitan county in northwestern England. Coal has long been mined in the vicinity, and the availability of cheap coal during the Industrial Revolution made Wigan a center of cotton-textile milling, clothing manufacture, and heavy engineering. In the 1930's the local economy was hard hit by the Great Depression. After World War II, Wigan's traditional economic activities were supplemented by the establishment of new industries that broadened its production base. Among these were food processing, electrical and electronics engineering, and the manufacture of plastics and paper.

The site of Wigan was probably the Roman outpost of Coccium. Wigan was made a borough in 1100. The working conditions and daily lives of the coal miners before World War II were vividly described by George Orwell in *The Road to Wigan Pier* (1937). Population: (1981 census) 79,535.

WIGGIN, wig′in, **Kate Douglas** (maiden name **SMITH**), American children's author and educator: b. Philadelphia, Pa., Sept. 28, 1856; d. Harrow, England, Aug. 24, 1923. Educated at Abbott Academy, Andover, Mass., she became interested in the new art of kindergarten teaching, as did her sister, Nora Archibald Smith (1859?–1934). In 1877, Kate Smith studied under Emma J. C. Marwedel, a pioneer kindergarten worker who had gone to the United States at the urging of Elizabeth Peabody. In 1878, Kate joined with others in founding the Silver Street Kindergarten in San Francisco, the first free kindergarten in the Far West; two years later she and her sister established the California Kindergarten Training School for teachers.

Mrs. Wiggin began her literary career as a writer of stories for children; the early ones, including the enormously popular *The Birds' Christmas Carol* (1887), were intended to raise funds for kindergarten work. Among the later ones were *Rebecca of Sunnybrook Farm* (1903) and *Mother Carey's Chickens* (1911).

Mrs. Wiggin frequently visited England, and several of her books for adult readers grew out of these visits—among them the "Penelope" volumes, half novel, half travelogue, which dealt lightly with the Henry Jamesian theme of the interaction of British and American cultures.

Mrs. Wiggin's earlier stories for children tended to sentimentalism, and have gone out of fashion. *Rebecca,* however, is one of the few girls' stories to rival Louisa May Alcott's in popularity. The adult novels are neat, often witty, but thin. Mrs. Wiggins kept up her interest in education, and collaborated with her sister in preparing textbooks.

DELANCEY FERGUSON, *Author of "Mark Twain: Man and Legend"*

WIGGLESWORTH, wig′əlz-wûrth, **Michael,** American clergyman and author: b. probably Yorkshire, England, Oct. 18, 1631; d. Malden, Mass., May 27, 1705. His Puritan parents brought him to America as a child in 1638, staying briefly at Charlestown and then settling in New Haven. He graduated from Harvard in 1651 and remained as a fellow and tutor until 1654. During this period he began preaching and about 1656 was ordained as minister of the Congregational church at Malden. In spite of extended poor health, he remained in the post for the rest of his long life, at the same time studying and practicing medicine and writing theological verse.

The most famous of these works was *The Day of Doom,* believed to have been first published in 1662. Reflecting Wigglesworth's stern Calvinist beliefs, the long poem, composed in ballad meter, presents a terrifying account of the Last Judgment, although its lurid and inhuman descriptions were not uncommon in the theological climate of early New England. Five editions appeared in Massachusetts by 1701, and at least two editions in England, and it was reprinted frequently thereafter. Although this and other verse showed evidence of some latent artistic talent, his writing was intended only for spiritual edification and to inspire a fear and reverence of God. This theme was repeated in *Meat Out of the Eater or Meditations Concerning the Necessity, End, and Usefulness of Afflictions Unto Gods Children* (1669) and in "God's Controversy with New-England" (*Proceedings of the Massachusetts Historical Society,* 1873).

EDWARD WIGGLESWORTH (c. 1693–1765), a child by his third marriage, was the first occupant of the Hollis chair of divinity at Harvard (from 1722), and published a number of pamphlets and sermons defending orthodoxy against criticism, especially that of evangelist George Whitefield.

WIGHT, Isle of, wīt, an island and county in southern England off the coast of Hampshire. It is separated from the mainland by a deep seawater channel—the Solent on the west and Spithead on the east—up to 5 miles (8 km) wide. Known locally as the Wight, the island measures 22.5 miles (36 km) from east to west and 13.5 miles (22 km) from north to south. Its area is 147 square miles (381 sq km). The highest point is St. Boniface Down (787 feet, or 240 meters), overlooking Ventnor, one of the popular resorts on the sheltered southeast shore of the island. Newport, near the center, is the county seat; Cowes, to the north, is the principal commercial port and a noted yachting center.

The name Wight is probably the *Vectis* known to the Romans at the time of the island's conquest by the emperor Vespasian in 43 A.D. The island, which has more sunshine than any other part of the British Isles, is known as the "Garden Isle" for its mild climate and profusion of wild flowers. It is also referred to fondly as "Little England," and embodies, in microcosm,

British insular pride, veneration of tradition, and the love of well-kept gardens, athletics, boating, and the sea. Yacht building and tourists are the main sources of revenue, but sheep are raised on the chalk downs, and fruit and vegetables are grown. Population: (1971) 109,284.

WIGHTMAN, wīt'mən, **Hazel (Hotchkiss),** American tennis player: b. near Healdsburg, Calif., 1886; d. Chestnut Hill, Mass., Dec. 5, 1974. Entering her first major competition in 1909, she won the national singles title and played on the victorious doubles and mixed doubles teams. She gained nationwide fame when she repeated this performance in 1910 and 1911. In 1919 (the year she won her fourth national singles title), she donated a trophy for international women's team competition; the United States and Great Britain began competing for the Wightman Cup in 1923 and have continued ever since. In 1954, at the age of 68, Mrs. Wightman captured the last of some 45 national titles to her credit.

WIGMORE, wĭg'mōr, **John Henry,** American lawyer and educator: b. San Francisco, Calif., March 4, 1863; d. Chicago, Ill., April 20, 1943. Educated at Harvard (B.A., 1883; LL.B., 1887), he practiced law in Boston for two years, then became professor of Anglo-American law at Keio University, Tokyo (1889–1892). From 1893 to 1929 he was professor of law at Northwestern University, and from 1901 to 1929 dean of the Law School. A voluminous writer and editor on legal subjects, he was best known as an authority on evidence. His major work in this field, and his outstanding contribution to legal literature, is his 10-volume *Treatise on the Anglo-American System of Evidence in Trials at Common Law* (3d ed., 1940), a penetrative and comprehensive treatment of the subject. Shorter works include *Students' Textbook of the Law of Evidence* (1935), *Panorama of the World's Legal Systems* (1936), *Science of Judicial Proof* (3d ed., 1937), *Code of the Rules of Evidence in Trials at Law* (3d ed., 1942), and *Guide to American International Law and Practice* (1943). Wigmore was president of the American Institute of Criminal Law and Criminology (1909–1910), served on the staff of the judge advocate general of the United States (1916–1919), and was a member of the United States Section of the Inter-American High Commission (1915–1919).

WIGNER, wĭg'nər, **Eugene Paul,** Hungarian-American mathematical physicist: b. Budapest, Hungary, Nov. 17, 1902. Educated as a chemical engineer at the Technische Hochschule in Berlin, he taught there and in Göttingen until 1930, when he went to the United States; he became a naturalized American citizen in 1937. He taught mathematical physics at Princeton University from 1930 until 1937, was professor of physics at the University of Wisconsin for one year, and returned to Princeton in 1938 as professor of theoretical physics. Associated with the preliminary organization of nuclear research in the United States, he was one of a group of foreign-born scientists who helped to obtain government sponsorship for atomic research. He engaged in research at the University of Chicago Metallurgical Laboratory and other installations during the period of the Manhattan Project. After World War II, while on leave of absence from Princeton, he became director of research at the Clinton Laboratories in Oak Ridge, Tenn., devoted to the production of radioactive isotopes for civilian uses, and to peaceful uses of atomic energy. He returned to Princeton in 1947, and in 1963 shared the Nobel Prize in physics.

In addition to writing numerous papers on nuclear theory, he has applied the mathematical methods of group theory to quantum mechanics and molecular structure, and has done research in theories of chemical reaction rates and the solid state. His book, *Gruppentheorie und ihre Anwendungen auf die Quantenmechanik der Atomspektren* (1931), is widely used as an advanced text in quantum mechanics. Wigner is also the coauthor of *Nuclear Structure* (1958) and *Physical Theory of Neutron Chemical Reactors* (1958).

WIGTOWN, or **WIGTON,** wĭg'tən, county, Scotland, bounded on the west by the North Channel, on the north by Ayrshire, on the east by Kirkcudbright and the Solway Firth, and on the south by the Irish Sea. The county is about 33 miles from east to west and 26 miles from north to south. Its area is 487 square miles, of which about 46 percent is arable.

Wigtown is irregular in form, being deeply intersected by two arms of the sea, Luce Bay on the south and Loch Ryan on the north. The western part, known as the "Rhinns of Galloway," forms a peninsula; its northern extremity is Corsewall Point, and its southern the Mull of Galloway. The southeastern half of the county extends south in the form of a blunt triangle, terminating in Burrow Head. The soil is varied and mostly inferior, except for a portion along the seashore, especially in the southeastern part, which consists of rich loam. The climate is mild but moist, with comparatively heavy rainfall. There are many dairy establishments. Wigtown has two rivers, the Cree and the Bladnoch, which are navigable for a few miles, and has numerous smaller rivers and creeks, and freshwater lakes.

The county was formed about 1341. A church near the present village of Whithorn, founded by St. Ninian in the 4th century, is believed to be the oldest in Scotland. There are hill forts and standing stones dating from the times of the Picts, and numerous ancient Christian crosses. The capital is Wigtown; other municipalities are Newton-Stewart and Stranraer. Population: (1974) 27,410.

WIGWAGGING, wĭg'wăg-ĭng, a system of signaling by waving to and fro a flag or a light, in accordance with an established code, usually the Morse code. See also TELEGRAPHY.

WIGWAM, wĭg'wŏm, an Algonquian Indian term applied to any of several arborlike dwelling structures. The word first appeared in English in 1628, as used by Massachusetts colonists to refer to Indian habitations. It was borrowed from the Abnaki *wigwâm*, meaning "dwelling." The term has been erroneously applied to many kinds of Indian structures, including the *tepee* of the Plains tribes and the *wickiup* of the Southwestern area, but correctly it refers to the type of dwelling found among the Eastern Woodlands Algonquian-speaking folk from Massachusetts to Michigan, and Virginia to Maine, most of whom use some variant form of the word in their own dialect.

Bark-covered wigwams: at left is a dome-shaped dwelling of the Winnebago Indians; below, a Seneca Indian wigwam, resembling the conical tepees of the Western Plains.

MUSEUM OF THE AMERICAN INDIAN, HEYE FOUNDATION

Most wigwams are made of saplings or poles inserted in the ground and lashed together to form a loaf-shaped or conical framework, converging at the top. The frame is covered with bark or rush matting, with a hole for the smoke to escape. The wigwam may be permanent, as is usually the case, or portable, and is occasionally covered with hides instead of bark. Some tribes use rectangular structures.

The term was also applied to the headquarters of the Tammany Society (see TAMMANY HALL), and, by extension, to any temporary structure used for a nominating convention or any other political meeting.

FREDERICK J. DOCKSTADER

WILBERFORCE, wĭl'bər-fōrs, **Samuel,** English Anglican bishop: b. London, England, Sept. 7, 1805; d. near Dorking, Surrey, July 19, 1873. The third son of the abolitionist William Wilberforce, he was educated at Oxford University and became bishop of Oxford in 1845. A High churchman, he opposed the appointment in 1847 of Renn Dickson Hampden as bishop of Hereford. Hampden was an evangelist who held the authority of the Scriptures to be superior to that of the church. In 1863, Wilberforce drew up the address of the bishops demanding, in vain, the resignation of John William Colenso as bishop of Natal, Union of South Africa, because of what the bishops called heretical views. Though several of his family and friends had joined the Roman Catholic Church, Wilberforce had no sympathy for the Oxford Movement, which leaned toward Romanism. In 1869 he was created bishop of Winchester. Although nicknamed "Soapy Sam" by his opponents because of his alleged expediency, he nonetheless improved the efficiency of the Church of England administration and strengthened the authority of its convocation. His publications include *Agathos and Other Sunday Stories* (1840), *A History of the Protestant Episcopal Church in America* (1844), and, with his brother, Robert Isaac Wilberforce, a five-volume *Life* of William Wilberforce (1838).

ALLAN M. FRASER
Provincial Archivist, Newfoundland, Canada

WILBERFORCE, William, English philanthropist and abolitionist: b. Hull, Yorkshire, England, Aug. 24, 1759; d. London, July 29, 1833. He was educated at St. John's College, Cambridge University. He was left independently wealthy, and entered politics at 21 as a member of the House of Commons for Hull (1780–1784), Yorkshire (1784–1812), and Bramber, Sussex (1812–1825). He became a close friend and stanch supporter of William Pitt the Younger. The turning point in his life occurred in 1784, when he was converted to evangelicalism. Within two years he became the tireless champion and impassioned spokesman in the House of Commons for the abolition of slavery, helping also to finance publicity for the cause. He was one of the leaders of the "Clapham Sect," a group of evangelical social reformers in London, and it was chiefly as a result of his efforts that Parliament, in 1807, abolished the slave trade in the British colonies. He then pressed for liberation of Africans still enslaved because they had been purchased before the act of 1807. He sponsored the establishment of the Anti-Slavery Society in 1823, but failing health forced him, two years later, to relinquish leadership of the emancipation crusade to Sir Thomas Fowell Buxton. Wilberforce died just one month before final passage of the act of Parliament that abolished slavery throughout the British Empire, and he was buried in Westminster Abbey. His life exemplified practical Christianity, the principles of which he expressed in *A Practical View of the Prevailing Religious System of Professed Christians* (1797). His *Appeal to the Religion, Justice and Humanity of the Inhabitants of the British Empire on behalf of the Negro Slaves in the West Indies* appeared in 1823.

ALLAN M. FRASER
Provincial Archivist, Newfoundland, Canada

WILBUR, wĭl′bər, **Curtis Dwight,** American public official and jurist: b. Boonesboro (now Boone), Iowa, May 10, 1867; d. Palo Alto, Calif., Sept. 18, 1954. The brother of Ray Lyman Wilbur, he was graduated from the United States Naval Academy in 1888, but that same year resigned his commission in the navy to study law. He entered practice in Los Angeles, was elected judge of the county's superior court (1903–1918), and then associate justice of the state Supreme Court, serving as chief justice from 1922 to 1927. During his years on the bench he helped formulate California's juvenile laws. Wilbur was secretary of the navy from 1924 to 1929. In that capacity he utilized his naval and judicial background to improve the status of his department. He advocated a larger navy, and urged greater use of heavier-than-air craft. To lead the way, he introduced a course in aviation at the Naval Academy. He served as judge of the 9th United States Circuit Court of Appeals from 1929 to his retirement in 1945, acting as presiding judge from 1931.

WILBUR, wĭl′bər, **Richard Purdy,** American poet: b. New York, N.Y., March 21, 1921. He studied at Amherst College (B.A. 1942) and Harvard University (M.A. 1947) and taught at Harvard, Wellesley College, Wesleyan University, and Smith College. His poetry combined a genuine lyric gift with traditional devices, marked by wit and a sense of paradox.

Wilbur's works include *The Beautiful Changes and Other Poems* (1947); *Ceremony and Other Poems* (1950); *Things of This World* (1956), which won a Pulitzer Prize and National Book Award; and *Poems* (1957). Wilbur wrote the lyrics for the acclaimed musical comedy *Candide* by Leonard Bernstein and Lillian Hellman, produced in 1956. He also edited the *Complete Poems of Poe* (1959), and his translations of Molière's plays *Tartuffe, The Misanthrope*, and *The School for Wives* were highly regarded.

In 1987, Wilbur became poet laureate of the United States, succeeding Robert Penn Warren.

WILLIAM BRACY, *Beaver College*

WILD CAT or **WILDCAT,** wīld′kăt, the common name given to five or six intimately related Old World species of small cats, hardly distinguishable in size, color, and bodily proportions from the aggregate of domestic cats. Animals in North America called wild cats are lynx and bobcat.

The Old World wild cats—with the possible exception of the so-called jungle cat (see below)—can interbreed with, and are the immediate progenitors of, the house cat. They are widely distributed over Europe, except in the Scandinavian countries, and are found in most parts of continental Asia from Mongolia southward, and in all Africa except the heavily forested parts. Collectively, wild cats average larger in size of body and teeth than domestic cats, a difference that reflects physical degeneration on the part of the domestic form. The head of wild cats is short and broad; the ears are comparatively large and pointed, never with a white spot behind; the feet are small compared with those of other wild species. There are normally two premolars in each upper jaw, the anterior one being minute.

The so-called European wild cat (*Felis sylvestris*) is found in the three continental areas defined above, with the exception of extreme southern Asia, where the jungle cat alone occurs. The color and pattern of its stripes and spots run the gamut of variation common to the striped or "tiger" varieties of house cat. The ground color of the European wild cat normally varies from brownish to gray, with two cheek stripes and five crown stripes, the middle one of which can be traced back over nape, shoulders, and along the spine, where it becomes quite conspicuous. The pattern on flanks, shoulders, and thighs consists of transverse stripes, blotches, or chains of spots. There is usually an irregular pattern of spots on the underside, often with one or two bands on neck and throat. The tail may be bushy or thinly haired, the tip always black, the length from a half to two thirds of the combined head and body dimensions. As among all cats, there are black and reddish varieties among the various species of wild cats.

Many races of the European wild cat have been described by naturalists, and some of these were believed to be distinct species. However, the African wild cat (*F. sylvestris libyca*), long regarded as a separate species, is merely the pale race of the common European wild cat, living in the semidesert districts of north Africa. Animals of arid regions are, as a rule, paler than others of the same species living in humid lands. In the African race, the stripes of head and body are less defined than in the European representatives of the species, the ears are usually tufted, and the hairs along the spine are generally raised to form a crest. The Indian desert wild cat (*F. sylvestris ornata*), of the deserts of central and western India, is another very pale race of the common wild cat. Its combined head and body is about two feet long, and its tail is half that length.

The Chinese desert cat (*F. bieti*), of southern Mongolia, Kansu, and Szechwan, is almost uniformly yellowish gray because of the great reduction or complete suppression of the stripe and spot pattern of the body. This cat is known from very few specimens and its exact relationship to the common wild cat is not fully established.

The wild cat is so closely related genetically to the domestic cat that the two can interbreed.

The sand wild cat (*F. margarita*), of the deserts of Sahara, Arabia, and Turkestan, is most adapted for desert life. It is extremely pale, with the stripe pattern obsolete (indistinct or absent), the ear tufts absent, and a mat of hairs present on the soles of the feet. This last feature permits the cat to travel easily over sandy or rocky terrain. Some authorities regard the sand cat of Turkestan specifically distinct from the one of the Sahara and list it as *F. thinobius.*

The jungle cat or chaus (*F. chaus*) is the largest and most distinctive of the wild cat group. It ranges from the Caucasus and Caspian districts southward into India, Ceylon, Burma, and Indochina, and westward into Egypt. It is an inhabitant of more humid regions than its Asiatic and African relatives and is correspondingly more richly pigmented, with the pattern of dark stripes and spots more fully developed. In the jungle cat there is a distinct crest of hair on the back, and small tufts on the tips of the ears. The tail is comparatively short: always less than half its total length. A male may attain a head and body length of 31 inches and weigh up to 20 pounds. The female is 4 to 5 inches shorter and weighs 5 to 6 pounds less.

The last and smallest member of this group is the black-footed cat (*F. nigripes*), of the arid parts of southwest Africa. Very little is known of this species.

In spite of the tricontinental scope of their range and the great diversity of their habitats, wild cats behave very much alike everywhere. The forest-dwelling species is just as much at home on the ground as is the desert-dwelling wild cat. All eat whatever animal they can seize and kill, whether it be frog, rabbit, poultry, lamb, beetle, or fish. All make dens in holes under tree roots or among rocks and boulders, or make nests in brush heaps or thick clumps of grass. They breed once or twice a year. The period of gestation lasts from 53 to 68 days, depending on the species and locality, and four or five young are produced in one litter.

See also CAT; JAGUARUNDI; JUNGLE CAT.

PHILIP HERSHKOVITZ
Chicago Natural History Museum

WILD DUCK, The. In his social plays Henrik Ibsen presented his demands for the improvement of society, such as sacrifice, marriage founded "upon entire candor on both sides," and the cure of society's ills by telling the truth about them. But he came to disbelieve in universal standards; hence this tragicomedy, published in 1884, in which a would-be idealist, Gregers Werle, brings about untold misery by his very "idealism."

Gregers' father, a wealthy businessman, had engaged in a dishonest project with his partner, Ekdal, and had managed to have himself absolved, while the latter was found guilty and sent to jail. Furthermore, the elder Werle had seduced his housemaid, Gina, and avoided scandal by marrying her off to Ekdal's son, Hjalmar, at the same time setting the couple up in a photography business. Here Gina does the work while Hjalmar eats and sleeps in comfort, continually prating of what he will do for his family when he succeeds with his "invention." Gregers Werle feels that he has the mission to snatch Hjalmar out of the "swamp atmosphere of lies" in which he is living, by revealing to him the truth about his marriage. Gregers' meddling causes Hjalmar to assume a ludicrous melodramatic pose by rejecting his 13-year-old daughter, Hedwig. Gregers talks to her about winning her father back by sacrificing her dearest possession, a pet wild duck. But instead of sacrificing the duck, the sensitive girl shoots herself. Dr. Relling, a kindly cynic, says to Gregers that he should not dun simple people with "ideals," and adds: "Rob the average man of his life-illusion and you rob him of his happiness." The crowning irony is that the old roué Werle marries a woman with a past after each has told all—and Gregers asks: "Is this not the ideal marriage?"

To see this play—perhaps the most gripping of Ibsen's dramas—is, in the words of Bernard Shaw, "to look on with horror and pity at a profound tragedy, shaking with laughter all the time at an irresistible comedy; to go out, not from a diversion, but from an experience deeper than real life ever brings to most men. . . ."

ADOLF E. ZUCKER
Chairman, Division of Humanities
University of Maryland

WILDE, Oscar (Fingal O'Flahertie Wills), Irish poet and dramatist: b. Dublin, Ireland, Oct. 16, 1854; d. Paris, France, Nov. 30, 1900. His father, Sir William, was a famous surgeon; his mother, Jane Francesca Elgee, wrote, under the name of "Speranza," inflammatory prose and imitative verse for the "Young Ireland" party.

At Trinity College, Dublin, John Pentland Mahaffy instilled in Wilde a deep interest in Greek life and literature. In 1874 Wilde won a scholarship to Magdalen College, Oxford, where he spent four years and was influenced by John Ruskin's views on art and Walter Pater's aesthetic hedonism. In 1878 he won the Newdigate poetry prize with *Ravenna;* later in the same year he toured Greece with Mahaffy. Settling in London, he quickly became famous, or notorious, for wit and for oddities of dress and behavior. His *Poems* (1881), though mainly derivative, sold widely. Du Maurier caricatured him in *Punch* as Jellaby Postlethwaite; Gilbert and Sullivan did the same as Bunthorne in the opera *Patience* (1881). In 1882 he made a successful lecture tour of the United States. On May 29, 1884, he married Constance Lloyd, by whom he had two sons, Cyril and Vyvyan.

Until the late 1880's Wilde's literary output was minor. He lectured occasionally; edited a magazine, *The Woman's World;* wrote a few essays; and published *The Happy Prince and Other Tales* (1888), a collection of witty fairy tales marking the beginning of his most productive period of writing. In 1891 he published among other works his *Intentions*, dialogues and essays in aesthetic criticism, and *The Picture of Dorian Gray*, a decadent novel partly imitative of Joris K. Huysmans' *À rebours* (1884).

On Feb. 20, 1892, George Alexander produced *Lady Windermere's Fan* at the St. James's Theatre, and a new age of English comedy began. Next came *A Woman of No Importance* (April 19, 1893), *An Ideal Husband* (Jan. 3, 1895), and *The Importance of Being Earnest* (Feb. 14, 1895). In the first three plays Wilde used conventional plots, but hid them behind veils of some of the wittiest dialogue ever written in English. In the last, contriving a plot as delightfully absurd as the speeches, he produced a unique work.

THE BETTMANN ARCHIVE

Oscar Wilde was photographed in a pensive mood during his successful lecture tour of America in 1882.

At the peak of success came disaster. Wilde had become intimate with Lord Alfred Douglas, son of the marquis of Queensberry. The marquis publicly accused Wilde of homosexual practices, and Wilde rashly brought suit for libel. He lost the suit, was arrested and convicted on the morals charge, and served two years in Reading Gaol (1895–1897) for the offenses under the Criminal Law Amendment Act. There he wrote *De Profundis*, a long letter to Douglas, which appears in its most complete version in Rupert Hart-Davis' edition of Wilde's letters, published in 1962. After his release, Wilde composed his best poem, *The Ballad of Reading Gaol* (1898). Shortly afterwards, Wilde went bankrupt. But he was then a broken man and spent his last years on the Continent, where he subsisted on "loans" from friends.

Most of Wilde's poetry is derivative and insincere; his attempts at tragedy, as in *Salomé* (1893), come perilously near to rant. A few stories and essays such as *Lord Arthur Savile's Crime, The Portrait of Mr. W. H.,* and *The Soul of Man Under Socialism* (all published originally in periodicals in 1887, 1889, and 1891, respectively) are still read. But he is permanently important in the history of English comedy. He took the realistic problem plays of Henrik Ibsen and Victorien Sardou, as these had been anglicized and diluted by Arthur Wing Pinero and Henry Arthur Jones, and by setting new standards of wit prepared the way for George Bernard Shaw.

See also BALLAD OF READING GAOL; IMPORTANCE OF BEING EARNEST; LADY WINDERMERE'S FAN; PICTURE OF DORIAN GRAY.

DELANCEY FERGUSON
Formerly, Brooklyn College

WILDEBEEST, wil'də-bēst, either of two species of African antelope. It is also called a *gnu* (pronounced nōō).

The blue wildebeest (*Connochaetes taurinus*), also called the brindled gnu, varies in color from brown to bluish gray, with dark brown bands (the brindling) on the forequarters. The face, beard, mane, and tail are black, except in *C. t. albojubatus,* a subspecies having a white beard. The black wildebeest (*C. gnou*), also called the white-tailed gnu, is dark brown and has a stiff upright mane and white tail. The horns, borne by both sexes, project sideways and back in the blue wildebeest and forward and back in the black wildebeest. The blue wildebeest reaches about 52 inches (1.3 meters) in height at the shoulders and about 500 pounds (225 kg) in weight; the black wildebeest, 44 inches (1.1 meters) and 350 pounds (160 kg).

The blue wildebeest, found from Kenya south, is one of the most common antelopes of eastern Africa. The largest population, numbering about 400,000, inhabit Tanzania's Serengeti Plains. The black wildebeest once existed in enormous numbers in South Africa, but was decimated by hide hunters in the late 19th century. From the few hundred survivors the species has increased to about 2,000, but all are confined to fenced farms and reserves, mainly in the Orange Free State.

Wildebeests are highly gregarious. Though they usually live in small herds, they may congregate by the tens of thousands on a new flush of grass or during migration. Bulls become territorial, defending a piece of land as their own, and remain alone except when herds enter their grounds. Black wildebeest bulls, though smaller than blue wildebeest bulls, defend larger territories, are seemingly more aggressive, and have perhaps the most lethal horns of any antelope.

Both rutting and calving are highly seasonal. The female bears a single calf weighing about 40 pounds (18 kg) after an 8-month gestation. Wildebeest calves can run beside their mothers within 5 minutes after birth. Hyenas take a heavy toll of calves, and adults are the lion's favorite prey.

RICHARD D. ESTES, *Museum of Comparative Zoology, Harvard University*

The blue wildebeest, one of two species of wildebeest, is a common African antelope found from Kenya south.

© LEONARD LEE RUE/PHOTO RESEARCHERS

WILDER, wīl′dər, **Laura Ingalls,** American writer: b. Pepin, Wis., Feb. 7, 1867; d. near Mansfield, Mo., Feb. 10, 1957. A few years after her marriage (1885), Laura moved to Florida with her husband and daughter (also a writer, Rose Wilder Lane). In 1894 the family settled in the Ozark country. At the age of 65 she began a series of novels for young people based mainly upon her own pioneering experiences from age 5 to 18. The first of her Laura novels, *Little House in the Big Woods* (1932), is about frontier life in Wisconsin. It was followed by *Farmer Boy* (1933), early childhood experiences of her husband Almanzo. *Little House on the Prairie* (1935) continues her story into Kansas and is followed by five other Laura novels in chronological sequence: *On the Banks of Plum Creek* (1937), in the Minnesota wheat country; *By the Shores of Silver Lake* (1939), age 13 in Dakota territory; *Long Winter* (1940), reintroducing the Wilder brothers of *Farmer Boy; Little Town on the Prairie* (1941), further Dakota experiences; *These Happy Golden Years* (1943), pioneer schoolteaching begun at the age of 15 and marriage; and finally, the posthumously published *The First Four Years* (1971), the early years of Laura's marriage.

The American Library Association established in 1954 the Laura Ingalls Wilder Award for lasting contributions to children's literature.

WILDER, Thornton Niven, American playwright and novelist: b. Madison, Wis., April 17, 1897; d. Hamden, Conn., Dec. 7, 1975. He attended school in Hong Kong and Chefoo, China, where his father was in the consular service, and subsequently in California. He studied at Oberlin College for two years, graduated from Yale in 1920, and in the next year studied archaeology at the American Academy in Rome. He then taught at the Lawrenceville School, New Jersey, 1921–1928, taking out time for an M. A. degree at Princeton in 1925. At the University of Chicago, 1930–1936, he taught literature and writing; and in 1950–1951 he was Charles E. Norton professor of poetry at Harvard. He served in the coast artillery in 1918; during World War II he became an air intelligence officer.

Wilder's first published book was *The Cabala* (1926), a novel about fallen pagan gods in 20th century Rome. His second novel, *The Bridge of San Luis Rey* (1927), brought him fame and a Pulitzer Prize. It analyzes the life and fate of the victims of an early 18th century bridge disaster in Peru. Other novels are *The Woman of Andros* (1930), a story of ancient Greece based partly on a comedy by Terence; *Heaven's My Destination* (1935), a satirical study of a Midwestern book salesman with a religious complex; and *The Ides of March* (1948), which the author calls "a fantasia on certain events and persons of the last days of the Roman republic." Both in his novels and in his plays, he is a skillful and imaginative craftsman. Among his literary precursors James Joyce and Gertrude Stein have special importance.

Wilder began writing one-act plays during his student years at Yale, and *The Trumpet Shall Sound* was produced in 1926 by the American Laboratory Theatre. *The Angel that Troubled the Waters and Other Plays* (1928) and *The Long Christmas Dinner and Other Plays* (1931) are collections of his early dramatic work. In 1938 *Our Town* was produced in New York and awarded a Pulitzer Prize as the best play of the year. As a classic of the American theater, it is representative of Wilder's technique and philosophy as a dramatist, illustrating his acceptance of obvious theater conventions and make-believe. He uses a narrator and improvised staging in portraying the simple everyday life of Grover's Corners, N.H., a typical American small town.

The Skin of Our Teeth (1942), his second Broadway success, was also awarded a Pulitzer Prize. It combines farce and allegory, partly based upon James Joyce's *Finnegans Wake*, and projects a sort of history of mankind through the struggles of a contemporary New Jersey family. *The Merchant of Yonkers* (1938) was revised later as *The Matchmaker* (1954) and performed with great success at the Edinburgh festival and in New York. The musical comedy *Hello, Dolly!* was adapted from it.

His minor dramatic works include adaptations, translations, and an Alcestis trilogy, *A Life in the Sun*. Three one-act plays from his "Seven Ages of Man" and "Seven Deadly Sins" cycles were performed in 1962 as *Plays for Bleecker Street*. Wilder's last major works, written in semiretirement, were *The Eighth Day* (1967), the theme of which is that man is not an end but a beginning, and *Theophilus North* (1973), which is a partly autobiographical story of a retired schoolteacher.

See also BRIDGE OF SAN LUIS REY; OUR TOWN.

WILLIAM BRACY
Beaver College

WILDERNESS, Battle of the, wĭl′dər-nĕs, on May 5–6, 1864, during the American Civil War, a battle fought in the tangled forest fringing the south bank of the Rapidan River in Virginia. It was the first encounter between Gen. Robert E. Lee, foremost soldier of the Confederacy, and Lt. Gen. Ulysses S. Grant, supreme commander of all the United States armies.

At midnight May 4, Gen. George G. Meade's Army of the Potomac and Gen. Ambrose E. Burnside's independent 9th Corps, aggregating 101,895 effectives and operating under Grant's personal direction, quit their encampments around Culpeper, Va., and initiated the final grand campaign of 1864–1865, a concerted movement of four Federal armies designed to crush the Confederacy.

General Lee's Army of Northern Virginia, 61,025 strong, held the south bank of the Rapidan River. With the intention of passing Lee's right by a circuitous march through the wilderness, Grant advanced his four armies in two parallel columns. The right, composed of Gen. Gouverneur K. Warren's 5th Corps and Gen. John Sedgwick's 6th Corps, crossed the river at dawn and halted near Wilderness Tavern. Holding the left, Gen. Winfield S. Hancock's 2d Corps went to Chancellorsville, Va. General Burnside closed on Sedgwick's rear; the artillery reserve and the supply trains followed Hancock. From dawn until midafternoon of the next day these two columns thumped and rumbled over the pontoon bridges that had been hurriedly thrown across the river.

Apprised of General Grant's movement, General Lee sent Gen. Richard S. Ewell's 2d Corps eastward on the Orange turnpike toward the wilderness. Gen. Ambrose P. Hill's 3d Corps took the parallel Orange plank road, his advance marching on the right rear of Ewell's column. Gen. James Longstreet's 1st Corps broke camp at Mechanicsville, Va., to come up on Hill's right. General Grant, being surprised by Ewell's appearance in the wilderness, ordered Warren to suspend his march to Parker's Store, on the Orange plank road, and, supported by Sedgwick, to attack along the turnpike. Striking before Sedgwick connected on his right, Warren was stopped. The battle shifted to General Sedgwick's front and raged until nightfall.

Meanwhile, with the report that Hill's corps was near Parker's Store, Grant decided to abandon his plan of deployment on the line running from Shady Grove Church to Parker's Store to Wilderness Tavern. He instructed Hancock, who was marching toward the Shady Grove Church, to proceed northward on the Brock road to its intersection with the plank road and attack toward the store. The mounting violence of Hancock's assault compelled General Lee to forego his attempt to extend Hill's left to Ewell's right. The protective cover of darkness saved Hill from destruction. General Lee then ordered Longstreet to hasten forward and take over Hill's front. Although failing to establish a connected line favorable to a counteroffensive action, Lee drew Grant into the battle he sought to avoid.

At dawn on May 6 Hancock renewed his assault. General Burnside proceeded to move toward the gap in Lee's line. Warren and Sedgwick struck Ewell in unison, endeavoring to pin him to his front. While Hancock's power drive staggered Hill's battered brigades, Ewell, holding firmly, extended his right across the gap. Burnside faltered. At this juncture Longstreet arrived, met the Federal attack head on, sent four brigades by the right, and struck Hancock's left rear and drove him back to his reserve trenches along the Brock road. General Lee was now unable to exploit the initiative conferred by General Longstreet's masterful stroke. At 4 P.M. Hancock repelled a frontal assault on his reserve position. At twilight an ill-timed attack on the Federal right flank failed, in the confusion of darkness, to fulfill the promise of initial success.

General Grant sustained a loss of 17,636 men—killed, wounded, and missing. General Lee's loss was probably in the same proportion to his strength though the exact figures are unknown. The battle of annihilation which Grant hoped to fight on open ground beyond the wilderness ended in a tactical draw in the thick woodland. At the same time, General Lee failed to repeat his performance at Chancellorsville, Va. In reality, the clash in the wilderness became the initial engagement of a 44-day battle of attrition, the storm center sweeping around Richmond and over the James River to the south side of Petersburg.

EDWARD STEERE

WILDERNESS ROAD or **WILDERNESS ROUTE,** in American history, an important passageway through the Appalachian Mountains for the westward spread of English colonization. It was one of a vast and ancient network of Indian trails in eastern America which the frontiersmen discovered and used on long hunts to reach the game-filled savannas of the Dark and Bloody Ground (Kentucky). In 1775 Col. Richard Henderson, head of the Transylvania Company,

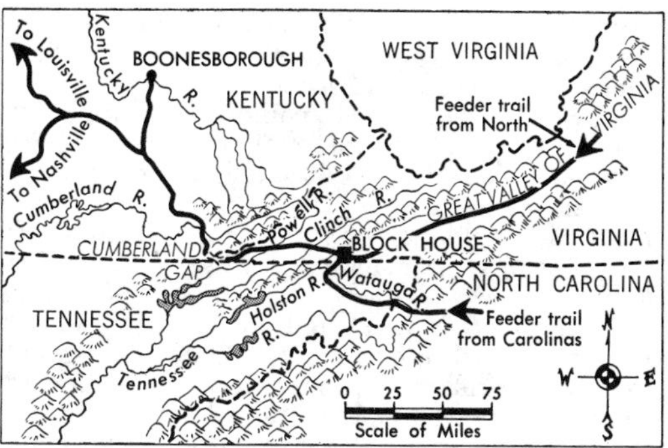

Map of the Wilderness Road and its feeder trails.

purchased from the Cherokee Indians a huge tract of land between the Kentucky River and the southern edge of the Cumberland River watershed. To help settlers reach this area Daniel Boone was hired to mark out and improve the existing Indian trail, and it then became the Wilderness Road.

It began in southwestern Virginia at the Block House, where two feeder trails converged, one coming from the north down the Great Valley of Virginia, the other from the Carolinas. Here travelers waited to form companies as protection against Indians, then set out for the wilderness. Once past the mountainous terrain the route continued through central Kentucky to Louisville, on the Ohio River. One branch trail led to Nashville, Tenn., and another, a new one made by Boone, to the company's first settlement at Boonesborough. The Wilderness Road was the most important land route connecting the settled East with the virgin western regions until the early 1800's when the newly created National Road north of the Ohio River drew the westward traffic.

WILLIAM O. STEELE

WILHELM II, German emperor. See WILLIAM II (Friedrich Wilhelm Viktor Albert).

WILHELM II COAST (also known as KAISER WILHELM II LAND), that part of the Antarctic coast between Cape Penck, about 66° 40′ S, 87° 35′ E, and Cape Filchner, about 66° 28′ S, 92° 18′ E. The coast was named for Kaiser Wilhelm II by the German Antarctic expedition of 1901–1903, which landed at Gaussberg (89° 19′ E), an extinct volcano which is the only rock outcrop on the coast. The subsequent exploration of Wilhelm II Coast has been conducted by the Australian expedition of 1911–1914, the United States expedition of 1946–1948, and the Soviet expedition begun in 1956.

Wilhelm II Coast is claimed by Australia as part of its Antarctic Territory.

JOHN T. HOLLIN

WILHELM MEISTER, vĭl′hĕlm mīs′tər, the general title and main character of a novel in two parts by Johann Wolfgang von Goethe. The work was begun in 1777 as an autobiographical novel of the theater, which breaks off abruptly with the preparations for a performance of Shakespeare's *Hamlet* conformable to the ideas of the master-actor, producer, and hero. This torso of an early version was discovered in

Switzerland in 1909 and called *Wilhelm Meisters theatralische Sendung* (1911; Wilhelm Meister's Theatrical Mission).

In 1795–1796, not without Friedrich von Schiller's influence, the fragment was revised and expanded into a full-length novel of development according to Goethe's new renaissance ideal of unfolding one's gifts to the utmost for better service to mankind. It appeared as *Wilhelm Meisters Lehrjahre* (1796; *Wilhelm Meister's Apprenticeship*), and in its new form it became one of the world's famous novels, with tremendous influence upon literature in general. The hero's new aim is to be a "master" of life, striving for ever greater humanistic virtues and, though a commoner, communing with aristocratic circles as the best representatives of 18th century culture. The theater still serves as a means to higher goals but is secondary to the new ideals. There are scenes and love affairs with autobiographical overtones involving actors, commoners, and noblemen. There is romanticism, largely supplied by the mysterious Harper and the sad little hermaphrodite Mignon, who yearns for Italy, is infatuated with Wilhelm, and turns out to be of noble stock. The interspersed songs they sing, among the most famous of Goethe's lyrics and often set to music, helped to inspire the opera *Mignon* (1866) by Ambroise Thomas. Another feature of the *Apprenticeship* is the profound discussion of European drama, particularly the plays of Shakespeare, who had become one of Goethe's "universal geniuses." Such passages, already conspicuous in the early version or *Theatralische Sendung*, make clear why the theater today is an integral part of German culture and why Shakespeare is viewed almost as a native German.

But in the *Apprenticeship* the story of Wilhelm was not concluded. In 1821 the septuagenarian author took up the theme again, and three years before his death he published a continuation entitled *Wilhelm Meisters Wanderjahre* (1829; *Wilhelm Meister's Wanderings*). Although in a sense it carries the story forward, it reveals a new philosophy and style, in keeping with the changed times. The perfectibility of the individual, in the humanistic sense, makes way for the preparation of a specialist, who is able to cope with the new industrial era as a technically trained practitioner. As a novel and a work of art it falls short, compensating only to a degree by offering fruits of wisdom in the fields of morality, education, and social philosophy. Separate short stories and disquisitions—a notable one on education—overshadow the plot. In the end Wilhelm and his group decide to emigrate to America to work together in an environment of free democratic enterprise.

EDWIN H. ZEYDEL
Professor of German, University of Cincinnati

WILHELM TELL. See WILLIAM TELL.

WILHELMINA, wĭl-hĕl-mē′nə, Du. vĭl-hĕl-mē′nə (in full, WILHELMINA HELENA PAULINE MARIA), queen of the Netherlands: b. The Hague, Aug. 31, 1880; d. Apeldoorn, Nov. 28, 1962. She was the daughter of William III by his second wife, Emma of Waldeck. Upon her father's death in 1890, Wilhelmina became queen under the regency of her mother during the remaining years of her minority. Soon after her 18th birthday, on Sept. 6, 1898, she was crowned at Amsterdam.

THE BETTMANN ARCHIVE
Queen Wilhelmina ruled the Netherlands from 1898 until she abdicated in favor of her daughter in 1948.

On Feb. 7, 1901, she married Henry Wladimir Albert Ernst, duke of Mecklenburg-Schwerin (1876–1934).

Queen Wilhelmina led a stern and exemplary life, took pride in being a good housewife, and received popular support in her public activities. She respected the powers of Parliament under the constitutional monarchy and maintained the traditional peace and neutrality of her country until the outbreak of World War II. An economic crisis brought on by World War I was faced with great courage and initiated a program of extensive social reform. The development of industry and foreign trade under Queen Wilhelmina's rulership brought prosperity to an expanding population.

After Germany's invasion of the Netherlands on May 10, 1940, Queen Wilhelmina escaped to England with her family and leading government officials. In 1942 she visited Canada and the United States, addressed a joint meeting of Congress, and the following summer visited President Franklin D. Roosevelt at Hyde Park. After the invasion of France by Allied armies in 1944, the queen remained in London until March 1945, when she visited liberated areas of her kingdom and began to apply herself to the problems of reconstruction. Crown Princess Juliana, her daughter and only child, had rejoined her in London after spending a few years in Canada. After the celebration of the queen's 50th anniversary of rulership in 1948, Wilhelmina abdicated and was succeeded by Juliana.

WILHELMJ, vĭl-hĕl′mē, **August,** German violinist: b. Usingen, Germany, Sept. 21, 1845; d. London, England, Jan. 22, 1908. As a child prodigy he attracted the attention of Franz Liszt, who successfully recommended advanced studies in both theory and interpretation. He won international renown as a virtuoso, touring throughout Europe, North and South America, Asia, and Australia. Richard Wagner appointed him concertmaster of the orchestra for the first cyclic performances of *Der Ring des Nibelungen* at Bayreuth in 1876. He also composed, prepared cadenzas for violin concertos, and arranged pieces for violin.

HERBERT WEINSTOCK

WILHELMSHAVEN, vĭl-hĕlms-hä′fən, city, Germany, in the State of Lower Saxony, situated on the North Sea at the mouth of Jade Bay, 40 miles northwest of Bremen. Its artificial harbor, walled with granite, is connected with the bay by way of a canal. It is a rail terminus and industrial center, manufacturing cranes, electric motors, refrigerators, vacuum cleaners, furniture, leather goods, and a great variety of industrial products; and it serves as the harbor for a deep-sea fishing fleet. It is also the starting point for a pipeline extending to the Ruhr industrial district, thus important as a port for oil tankers. Among important institutions here are three colleges for teachers—vocational, agricultural, and social science—and both an ornithological station and the Max Planck Institute of Oceanography.

The area was part of the state of Oldenburg when it was purchased by Prussia in 1853 for the construction of a naval base. The city was planned in 1856 and named in 1869. The famous sailors' mutiny of Oct. 30, 1918, contributing to Germany's capitulation in World War I, occurred here. In 1937 Wilhelmshaven was enlarged through its incorporation with the neighboring town of Rüstringen and returned to the state of Oldenburg, under which it remained until 1945. Many of its naval installations were damaged by Allied aerial bombing during World War II. After 1945 the remaining naval facilities were destroyed, and its industry was completely oriented toward peacetime production. The city is located in the Federal Republic of Germany (West Germany). Pop. (1950) 101,210; (1959 official est.) 99,600.

WILKES, wĭlks, **Charles,** American naval officer and explorer: b. New York, N. Y., April 3, 1798; d. Washington, D. C., Feb. 8, 1877. He entered the Navy as a midshipman in 1818, did service during the next few years in Mediterranean and Pacific areas, and in 1832–1833 did survey work in Narragansett Bay which led to his appointment in Washington, D. C., to head a depot of charts and instruments which eventually became the United States Naval Observatory.

In 1838 he was put in command of an important expedition for scientific exploration which took him to several island groups of the South Pacific, Australia, the Antarctic coastal areas now known as Wilkes Land, the Hawaiian Islands, the Northwest coast of the United States, and islands of Oceania, completing a voyage around the world before his return to New York in the summer of 1842. During the next 20 years his main occupation was the preparation of records of this expedition. He wrote a five-volume *Narrative of the United States Exploring Expedition* (1844), and in addition to editing the 20-volume report of the expedition he prepared two of the special volumes himself—the meteorology (1851) and the hydrography (1861). He also prepared atlases for these projects and published *Western America* (1849) and other books, articles, and reports. He was the first to make a defensible claim of having discovered an Antarctic continent.

At the beginning of the Civil War in 1861, Wilkes was placed in command of the U. S. S. *San Jacinto* and ordered to search for a Confederate vessel in the Caribbean area. On November 8, 1861, he stopped the British steamer *Trent* and unlawfully removed the Confederate commissioners James M. Mason and John Slidell, who were en route to England (see TRENT AFFAIR, THE). He received promotions and further war assignments, but later he incurred disfavor which resulted in his being placed on the retired list. When he incurred further conflict with the Navy Department, he was subjected to court-martial, reprimanded, and suspended from duty. But in 1866 he was commissioned a rear admiral and retained on the retired list.

WILKES, John, English politician and rake: b. London, England, Oct. 17, 1727; d. there, Dec. 26, 1797. The precocious son of a wealthy brewer, Wilkes was first educated by a Presbyterian minister named Leeson, allegedly infected with Arianism, who provided him with sound classical training and may have stimulated his taste for freethinking. In 1744 he entered the University of Leiden, remaining abroad for two years and traveling extensively.

Soon after his return to England, Wilkes married Mary Mead, daughter of a wealthy dissenting grocer, but his licentious habits quickly brought about their separation. Sir Francis Dashwood, one of his close friends among the rakes, had enrolled him in a secret club of profligates known as "Mad Monks of Medmenham," to which the poet Charles Churchill as well as many prominent politicians and nobles also belonged. Wilkes is said to have terrified the members upon the occasion of a Black Mass by releasing into their midst a baboon disguised as Satan.

In 1757, elected to Parliament as member from Aylesbury, he became one of William Pitt's supporters and a critic of John Stuart, 3d earl of Bute, and the incumbent government. His campaign against Bute culminated in an attack on George III in the *North Briton,* No. 45 (1763), which led to his arrest and prosecution for libel. A second charge was brought against him for printing *An Essay on Woman,* an obscene and blasphemous poem. Though he was found guilty of both blasphemy and libel, he was released from prison on the ground that his arrest had been a breach of parliamentary privilege. He then fled to France. When he failed to appear for sentencing, he was expelled from the House of Commons in 1764 and outlawed. While in France, however, he was lionized in the radical salons.

Returning to England in 1768, he was elected to Parliament for Middlesex but soon arrested, fined, and imprisoned. In 1769 Commons expelled him, but Middlesex reelected him. Once again he was expelled, and for a third time he was elected. Commons responded by seating the defeated candidate. In this controversy Junius championed Wilkes in the famous *Letters,* and Dr. Samuel Johnson defended the government in *The False Alarm.* Meanwhile, in 1769, Wilkes had sued the secretary of state for illegal arrest and had been awarded damages, thus establishing the important legal principle that general warrants are unconstitutional.

When he was released from prison in 1770, he found himself the hero of the London mobs, who delighted in the cry "Wilkes and Liberty," and he received as well the more substantial backing of the London merchants, whose program he urged in Parliament. Admirers in America as well as in England cooperated in paying his extensive debts. As an opposition member, he worked for parliamentary reform and religious toleration, and he championed the cause of the American colonists. He also held the offices of alderman of the city of London, sheriff for Middlesex, and lord mayor of London.

Wilkes' features were irregular and unattractive, as suggested by William Hogarth's famous caricature, but his wit could charm even men like Johnson and Edward Gibbon, who detested his political opinions. As a writer, however, he was undistinguished. Recent estimates of Wilkes are likely to be much less favorable than those current during the 19th century. He was by no means, it is generally considered, a principled reformer, but a colorful and witty opportunist, a scoundrel who happened to serve the cause of reform.

Jeffrey Hart
Professor of English, Columbia University

WILKES-BARRE, wĭlks'băr-ē, city, Pennsylvania, seat of Luzerne County, on the east bank of the Susquehanna River, at an altitude of about 575 feet. It is in the scenic and historic Wyoming Valley between outlying ranges of the Blue Ridge Mountains, about 18 miles southwest of Scranton. At nearby Avoca is the Scranton–Wilkes-Barre Airport, which serves the area. The city was named in honor of John Wilkes and Isaac Barré, champions of the colonial cause in the British Parliament during the Revolutionary War.

Wilkes-Barre is principally an industrial center, producing a wide diversity of goods such as cigars, steel wire, blasting powders, slippers, lace curtains, furniture, television and radio parts, pencils, locomotives, heavy machinery, and electronic transistors. Local institutions include Wilkes College, a four-year coeducational institution; King's College for men; the Wyoming Historical and Geological Society; and the Osterhout Free Library. Fell Tavern, erected in 1897, stands on the site of an old tavern built in 1787, where, in 1808, anthracite coal was first burned in an open grate. Monuments in the river common mark the site of old Fort Durkee and Wyoming Fort. The public square has a monument to John Wilkes and Isaac Barré. The Frances Slocum playground commemorates the house from which Frances Slocum, at the age of five, was seized and carried away in 1778 by the Delaware Indians. An outdoor fine arts fiesta, held every May for three days, displays arts and crafts and provides free musical and theater entertainment. The Battle of Wyoming is commemorated annually on July 3 at the Wyoming Monument.

Wilkes-Barre was originally settled in 1769 by the Susquehanna Company. In the spring of that year John Durkee led a group of emigrants from Norwich, Conn., to the spot, laid out a settlement, and built a stockade called Fort Durkee. Their right to the land was challenged by the Penns, who held conflicting claims, and the Yankee-Pennamite wars (see Pennamite Wars) soon began. Indian hostility, encouraged by Tories during the Revolutionary War, led to the Wyoming Massecre of July 3, 1778. The following day Wilkes-Barre was burned, and it was burned again in 1784. It became a county seat in 1786, was incorporated as a borough in 1806, and became a city in 1871. It has a mayor-council form of government. Population: 51,551.

Josephine Pedigo

WILKES LAND, a large area of the Antarctic continent, roughly south of western Australia. Its limits are not yet strictly defined: the northern coast fronts on the Indian Ocean and lies roughly on the Antarctic Circle (66–67° S); longitudinally it extends from about 100° 26′ E to about 142° 05′ E. The interior of Wilkes Land is not well explored, and its poleward limit is completely undefined. It is named after Charles Wilkes, commander of the United States expedition of 1838–1842, whose numerous sightings of the ice sheet in this area provided the first strong evidence that Antarctica is a continent. Subsequent exploration and investigation were conducted by expeditions from Australia, France, Russia, and the United States, all of which have maintained bases there for various periods. Only Dumont d'Urville Station (France) and Wilkes Station (Australia and United States) are currently in full operation. Except for a few rock islets and peninsulas in the vicinity of the bases, Wilkes Land is completely covered by the Antarctic ice sheet, which rises from the coastal cliffs, steeply at first and more gently later to a probable height of 8,000 or 9,000 feet, approximately 400 miles inland.

John T. Hollin
Institute of Polar Studies, Ohio State University

WILKIE, wĭl'kĭ, Sir **David,** Scottish genre and portrait painter: b. Cults, Fifeshire, Scotland, Nov. 18, 1785; d. at sea, off Gibraltar, June 1, 1841. After studying painting at the Trustees' Academy, Edinburgh, he returned to Cults and soon began a series of works which brought him fame. Among his important paintings are *Pitlessie Fair* (1805), in the National Gallery of Scotland, Edinburgh; *The Village Politicians* (1806), in the Earl of Mansfield collection; *Blindman's Buff* (1813), in the royal collection at Buckingham Palace, London; and *The Blind Fiddler* (1806), *The Village Festival* (1811), *The Rabbit on the Wall* (1816), *The Reading of the Will* (1920), and *The Parish Beadle* (1823), all in the Tate Gallery, London. These scenes of humble life reflect the manner of the Dutch school, but after travel in southern Europe he came under the influence of Italian and Spanish masters in both style and subject matter. *The Preaching of Knox Before the Lords of the Congregation, June 10, 1559* (1832) is the best example of his late and less distinguished work. It is also in the Tate Gallery. In 1830 Wilkie was made painter in ordinary to the king, and in 1836 he was knighted.

WILKINS, wĭl'kĭnz, Sir **(George) Hubert,** Australian polar explorer and aviator: b. Mount Bryan East, Australia, Oct. 31, 1888; d. Framingham, Mass., Dec. 1, 1958. He was educated in electrical engineering at the School of Mines and Industries in Adelaide, after which he took up photography and learned the fundamentals of flying. From 1912 to 1913 he was a newsreel photographer in the Balkans, covering the Balkan

War for British newspaper and motion-picture concerns. Vilhjalmur Stefansson selected him as official photographer for the Canadian Arctic Expedition of 1913–1917, and his loyalty and devotion to the aims of the expedition resulted in his promotion to second in command. In September 1917 he joined the Australian Flying Corps on the French front as a photographer. In 1919 he competed unsuccessfully for the London *Daily Mail* prize of $50,000 for a flight from England to Australia. He was second in command of the British Imperial Antarctic Expedition (1920–1921) and returned to the Antarctic in 1921 as naturalist on Sir Ernest Shackleton's Quest Expedition. From 1923 to 1925 he headed an expedition to tropical Australia and neighboring islands for the British Museum.

On April 15, 1928, with Carl Ben Eielson as pilot, Wilkins flew from Point Barrow, Alaska, to Spitsbergen, Norway, a distance of 2,100 miles in 20½ hours, on the first west-to-east Arctic crossing, hailed as the greatest of all Arctic flights. On June 14, 1928, he was knighted by King George V. He led the Wilkins-Hearst Antarctic Expedition in the fall of 1928, becoming the first to use an airplane in the Antarctic and the first to have flown over both polar regions. With Ben Eielson as pilot, his outstanding 1,200-mile round trip flight down the coast of Palmer Peninsula revealed many new geographical features. In 1931 Wilkins went around the world in the *Graf Zeppelin*, and during the same year he made the first under-ice explorations in the Arctic. However, after several short-distance penetrations in an antiquated Navy submarine renamed the *Nautilus*, repeated breakdowns forced him to abandon his attempt to cross the pole. From 1933 to 1939 he managed four of Lincoln Ellsworth's Antarctic expeditions. He was associated from 1942 until his death as a consultant with various branches of the United States government, including the Navy, Weather Bureau, and Army Quartermaster Corps. His ninth visit to the Antarctic was made during the International Geophysical Year's 1957–1958 season.

Wilkins contributed to numerous scientific journals, magazines, and newspapers, and he was the author of four books: *Flying the Arctic* (1928); *Undiscovered Australia* (1929); *Under the North Pole, the Wilkins-Ellsworth Submarine Expedition* (1931); and, with Harold H. Sherman, *Thoughts Through Space, a Remarkable Adventure in the Realm of the Mind* (1942).

EDITH M. RONNE,
Specialist on Antarctic Affairs.

WILKINS, Mary Eleanor. See FREEMAN, MARY E. WILKINS.

WILKINS, Maurice Hugh Frederick (1916–), British biophysicist whose X-ray diffraction studies contributed much to the determination of the structure of DNA. For this work, he was awarded the 1962 Nobel Prize in physiology or medicine, with Francis H. Crick and James D. Watson, who discovered the structure of DNA.

Shortly after World War II, Wilkins became interested in DNA and observed that the thin fibers of DNA are uniform, suggesting a regular arrangement of molecules. To learn more about DNA, he subjected it to X-ray diffraction analysis, a technique in which crystalline materials are exposed to X-rays and the subsequent diffraction patterns are studied. This technique revealed that the molecular arrangement of DNA is regular and indicated that the structure might be a helix. Further analysis of diffraction photographs, much of which was done by Wilkins' colleague Rosalind Franklin, showed that the structure repeats itself regularly at a certain constant distance and suggested that the phosphate groups known to be present in DNA might be on the outside of a helical structure.

Biochemical analysis had previously revealed that DNA is composed of alternating phosphate and sugar groups along with nitrogenous bases joined to the sugars. Armed with this data and the diffraction studies of Franklin and Wilkins, Watson and Crick were able to construct a molecular model of DNA. Their model showed DNA as a double helix resembling a spiral staircase whose sides consist of chains of sugars and phosphates, with steps formed by pairs of bases. After Wilkins, Crick, and Watson published their findings in 1953, Wilkins went on to verify that the Watson-Crick model of DNA is the only model that would account for the diffraction patterns observed.

Wilkins was born in Pongaroa, New Zealand on Dec. 15, 1916. He studied at Cambridge University and received his Ph. D. in physics at Birmingham University in 1940. In 1946 he became associated with King's College in London, where he did his award-winning research on DNA.

WILKINS, wĭl'kĭnz, **Roy** (1901–1981), American civil rights leader. He was born in St. Louis, Mo., on Aug. 30, 1901, but grew up in St. Paul, Minn., where he attended public schools. He graduated from the University of Minnesota in 1923. Young Wilkins began his professional career as a journalist with the Kansas City (Mo.) *Call*, a black weekly. He joined the National Association for the Advancement of Colored People in 1931 as assistant executive secretary. He edited the *Crisis*, the official organ of the association, from 1934 to 1949.

Wilkins was named administrator of internal affairs of the NAACP in 1950. He became its executive secretary in 1955 and its executive director in 1964. Under his leadership the NAACP reached a strength of about 500,000 members in 2,000 branches. He resigned as of July 28, 1977, and was succeeded by Benjamin Hooks. Wilkins died in New York City on Sept. 8, 1981.

A shrewd political strategist, Wilkins consistently pursued a policy designed to produce economic and civil rights gains for blacks without alienating significant segments of the white power structure. Considered one of the most powerful and respected civil rights leaders in America, he served on the boards of many national organizations concerned with labor, civil rights, and education.

C. ERIC LINCOLN
Union Theological Seminary, New York

WILKINSBURG, wĭl'kĭnz-bûrg, borough, Pennsylvania, in Allegheny County, 7 miles east of Pittsburgh at an altitude of about 920 feet. It is the second largest borough in Pennsylvania. Originally settled in 1780, it was known successively as McNairsville and Rippeysville, and incorporated in 1887 as Wilkinsburg in honor of Judge William Wilkins, a minister to Russia and secretary of war under President John Tyler.

Wilkinsburg is principally a residential community for persons working in Pittsburgh proper; it has an urban renewal program, serves as a retail commercial center for the rapidly developing suburban area, but has no major industrial firms. This "City of Churches" has 30 churches of various affiliations. It also has civic and junior civic symphony orchestras. This was the original home of radio station KDKA, which initiated commercial broadcasting in 1920. A borough manager governs with the assistance of a mayor and council. Population: 23,669.

AGNES M. MURDOCK.

WILKINSON, wĭl'kĭn-sən, **Ellen (Cicely),** British political leader: b. Manchester, England, Oct. 8, 1891; d. London, Feb. 6, 1947. Daughter of a millworker, Ellen Wilkinson was educated through the aid of secondary school scholarships, and she completed the M.A. degree at Manchester University. In 1912 she joined the Independent Labour Party; she became an organizer of the National Union of Women's Suffrage Societies (1913) and the National Union of Distributive and Allied Workers (1915). She was also a founder of the Communist Party of Great Britain in 1920. Failing to win a parliamentary seat in 1923, she was elected as a Communist to the Manchester City Council in the same year. Having severed her Communist connection, she was elected to Parliament in 1924 as a Labour member for Middlesbrough East, a seat she held until 1931. Elected in 1935 for Jarrow, she led the march of the Jarrow workers on London in 1936 and published *The Town that Was Murdered* (1939), describing conditions in Jarrow. She criticized the Conservative government's policies on appeasement and unemployment, and in 1938 she sponsored a bill protecting installment buyers. Mrs. Wilkinson joined the Churchill coalition government in 1940, first as parliamentary secretary to the Ministry of Pensions, then as parliamentary secretary to the Ministry of Home Security. Appointed minister of education in 1945, her function was to translate the 1944 education act into reality (see GREAT BRITAIN—*12. Education*). She was a member of the British delegation to the 1945 United Nations Conference at San Francisco. Other writings include *Why War?* (1934) and, with Edward Conze, *Why Fascism?* (1934).

RICHARD WEBB,
British Information Services.

WILKINSON, James, American army officer and adventurer: b. Calvert County, Md., 1757; d. Mexico City, Mexico, Dec. 28, 1825. Educated on his father's plantation by private tutors, Wilkinson briefly studied medicine before being commissioned a captain in the Continental Army in 1776. He served with Benedict Arnold's expedition against Montreal and, in December, became aide-de-camp to Horatio Gates. He was made the official messenger to carry the news of the American victory at Saratoga to Congress, a mission which took him 18 days because, as Samuel Adams charged, he "dawdled with a tavern keeper's daughter." To commemorate the event, Congress presented him with a sword, rejecting Adams' suggestion that he be given spurs. Through Gates' influence, he was brevetted a brigadier general, but he lost this rank because he openly participated in the Conway cabal. He next became Continental clothier general, an office he was forced to resign in 1781 after irregularities in his accounts were discovered.

Following the American victory at Yorktown in 1781, Wilkinson lived briefly in Pennsylvania, then moved to Kentucky in 1784, where he became immediately involved in a Spanish conspiracy to gain control of the region. He made several trips down the Mississippi to New Orleans, where he conferred extensively with the Spanish governor and ultimately took an oath of allegiance to the Spanish crown, promising to encourage western territories to separate from the Union. For this service he was rewarded with a trade monopoly on goods entering the port from the north. He was later granted an annual pension of $2,000 to work for the interests of Spain in the United States.

Wilkinson returned to active service in 1791 when Indian warfare broke out in Ohio. In 1792 he was commissioned a brigadier general and served under Anthony Wayne. He immediately launched a sustained campaign to discredit his superior and to gain the command for himself. Upon Wayne's death in 1796, Wilkinson, technically a Spanish subject and still a pensioner of the Spanish king, became the ranking officer in the American Army.

In 1803 Wilkinson took formal possession of Louisiana for the United States. Shortly thereafter, as commanding general, he began a close association with Aaron Burr, who had been discredited within his own party for congressional maneuverings against Jefferson in 1801, more generally discredited throughout the country for his duel with Alexander Hamilton in 1804. Recent scholarship tends to support rumors widespread at the time: that Burr hoped to detach a large segment of the American West from the Union to form his own republic. James Wilkinson, then governor of Louisiana Territory, was to be his second in command. By 1806 the Burr conspiracy was an open secret in the West and a major target for John Randolph's attacks on the Jefferson administration in Congress. When Burr's indiscretions seemed to destroy all hope of success, Wilkinson denounced his colleague, arrested his collaborators in Louisiana, and declared martial law to protect the territory.

At Burr's trial in Richmond, Va., in 1807, the general was the chief witness for the prosecution. His own position was so equivocal, however, that he himself narrowly missed indictment for treason. He challenged Randolph, the foreman of the grand jury, to a duel, but was rebuffed as a "finished scoundrel" who was "unworthy" of a gentleman's attention. For the next four years, most of Wilkinson's time was spent defending what was left of his reputation. He faced a series of inquiries and courts-martial, the last of which, in 1811, unearthed such damaging evidence that President Madison restored him to his command "with regret."

In 1813 Wilkinson occupied Mobile, thus acquiring the only territory obtained by the United States in the War of 1812. Later that year he was responsible for an abortive attempt to take Montreal. Relieved of command in 1814, he was again brought before a court of inquiry and again acquitted. He was honorably discharged in 1815, went to Mexico in 1821 to negotiate a Texas land grant, and served briefly as adviser to Emperor Iturbide.

WILLIAM E. STOKES, JR., *Coauthor*
"The Papers of Randolph of Roanoke"

WILKINSON, Jemima, American religious leader: b. Cumberland, R.I., Nov. 29, 1752; d. Jerusalem, Yates County, N.Y., July 1, 1819. Her mother, although she died when Jemima was only 10 years old, educated her in the Quaker faith. During her early twenties, after a severe attack of fever, she professed that she had been raised from the dead, that her carnal life was ended, and that henceforth her body was reanimated by the spirit and power of Christ. She called herself the "Universal Public Friend" and pretended to work miracles. Although she was illiterate, she induced many intelligent people to become her followers. Churches were established by her adherents in Rhode Island and Connecticut, and in 1788 it was decided to found a colony of Universal Friends in Jerusalem Township in Yates County, N.Y., near Seneca Lake. She joined the colony in 1790, accompanied by two "witnesses," Sarah Richards and Rachel Miller, and she exacted from the group the most complete submission and the most menial services, her influence over them being practically supreme. She insisted on the Shaker doctrine of celibacy, and the exercises at her religious meetings resembled those of that controversial sect. Wilkinson also taught mystical dream interpretation and professed that she was a divine messenger from God, even perhaps, that she was Christ reincarnated.

Although she never relinquished her pretensions, after some years her influence began to wane, she lost her physical beauty, and the latter part of her life was embittered by illness, jealousies, annoyances, and controversies between herself and her followers, which she bore with no great fortitude. The sect was broken up after her death.

WILKINSON, John, American Confederate naval officer: b. Norfolk, Va., Nov. 6, 1821; d. Annapolis, Md., Dec. 29, 1891. He became a midshipman in 1837 and served several years in the United States Navy before resigning in 1861 to join the Confederacy.

During the Civil War he achieved great fame as commander of the Confederate blockade runner *Robert E. Lee* and other ships. He also led a daring but unsuccessful party of adventurers who attempted to capture Johnson's Island in Lake Erie in order to free the thousands of Confederate prisoners that were being held there. His *Narrative of a Blockade-Runner* was published in 1877.

WILKINSON, Marguerite Ogden (nee **BIGELOW**), Canadian-American poet and anthologist: b. Halifax, Nova Scotia, Canada, Nov. 15, 1883; d. New York, N.Y., Jan. 12, 1928. She completed her education at Northwestern University and in 1909 married James G. Wilkinson, principal of the Roosevelt School, New Rochelle, N.Y. She wrote verse, reviewed poetry for the New York *Times Book Review*, and became a popular lecturer on poetry for school and club groups. She published *In Vivid Gardens* (1911) and *By a Western Wayside* (1912), her first collections of verse; *The Great Dream* (1923), a long visionary poem; and *Citadels* (1928), religious poems. Her popularity during the 1920's is attributed mainly, however, to her anthologies of poetry, which include *Golden Songs of the Golden State* (1917), *New Voices* (1919), *Contemporary Poetry* (1923), and *Yule Fire* (1925). She drowned while swimming at Coney Island.

WILL, wĭl, in law, an effective declaration of intention of what shall be done at the death of the maker or testator, usually relating to a disposition of property. Formerly, the term "will" was employed only with reference to real property, and the term "testament" applied to personalty; will is now used to designate a disposition of either or both. A will takes effect at the death of the testator and passes interests held at that time. Failure to make a will or to provide proper execution subjects the decedent's property to distribution under the intestate succession statutes.

Capacity to make a will is defined by the laws of each state. Generally, any person of sound mind and memory and of legal age at the time of executing a will may make a testamentary disposition. Legal age is usually 21, although distinctions vary in some states according to the maker's sex or the nature of the property disposed. Former restrictions upon married women and aliens have largely disappeared, and illiterate, incapacitated, and aged persons can, with some qualifications, dispose of property by will. Absolute soundness of mind is not essential; the testator must, however, understand the nature of his action, the nature and extent of his property, must be able to recollect the persons who are the natural objects of his bounty, and be able to formulate a plan of disposition. To cause incapacity, any mental derangement must affect the disposition itself. An adult may be presumed to have had testamentary capacity at the time of the will's execution, although some states require the proponent of a will to show capacity by positive evidence.

Rights of Testator.—A testator in the United States has relative freedom to bequeath or devise his property as he chooses. As a rule, property which is descendible is distributable by will; yet, some interests are reserved to family members by law. Legislative techniques for protecting a surviving spouse against the will of a decedent are statutory dower, forced heir, or distributive share statutes and community property. Where testamentary provision is made and a statutory or common law right is given the same person, the spouse may be required to elect between the two. Further family protection is provided in many jurisdictions by means of securing a homestead, specific personal property, a family allowance, or by limiting charitable donations. Statutes granting an interest to afterborn or omitted children are designed to prevent inadvertent disinheritance.

Subject to qualifications of this nature and to the demands of tax, perpetuities limitations, and creditors' claims, a testator is at liberty to dispose of his interests in any legal manner. He may disinherit one who would otherwise have an intestate claim, impose conditions upon his gifts, create trust estates, and pass property to most persons and institutions. More severe limitations on disposition are imposed in France and other civil law countries where certain relatives of the testator are absolutely entitled to a specified portion of the estate. In the United States, a devise in unlimited terms is generally held to pass all interest held by the decedent, including real property acquired after the execution of the will. A property owner may, of course, distribute his interests by means other than a will. Nontestamentary arrangements such as contracts, deeds, living trusts, or gifts—if properly executed—may effect lifetime transfers of interests even though enjoyment of the property is deferred until the transferor's death. Some property rights—for example, an interest in joint tenancy with survivorship—pass at death but outside the will.

Preparation and Execution of Will.—Although no set wording is essential to constitute a will, the instrument must evidence the maker's testamentary intent. A will may be written on any writing material and on several sheets as long as their coherence is apparent. A general rule is that a separate document may be incorporated into a will if the document exists when the will is executed and is described in the will with sufficient accuracy to permit identification.

To be valid, wills must be executed strictly in accordance with statutory formalities. All wills in the United States, with the exception of nuncupative or oral wills, must be in writing and signed by or for the testator. The signature, or any visible impression intended as such, must come at the end of the will in some states; others permit the testator to sign elsewhere.

Attestation—the bearing witness to the will, to the testator's act, or to the signature—and subscription by two or sometimes three witnesses are required. The will must either be signed in the presence of the witnesses, or the signature or the will must be shown to them and acknowledged by the testator as his own. Where expressly required by statute, there must also be publication, the testator's making known that the instrument is his last will, with a request that the witnesses act. Witnesses to a will sign in the presence of the testator and preferably of each other. Persons selected to witness must be competent to testify concerning the material facts of execution and should be chosen from those most likely available at the time the will is probated. They should not be beneficiaries under the will. An attestation clause preceding the signatures of the witnesses and reciting that all formalities have been complied with is desirable evidence of due execution but not mandatory.

Holographic wills are entirely in the handwriting of the testator and are valid without attestation in a few states. The testator must sign personally; a dated holograph may be required. An oral will disposing of personal property of a limited value is permitted in most jurisdictions where the testator is in his last illness, the declaration is witnessed at his request, and the testimony of witnesses is reduced to writing or the will probated within a designated period. A similar oral testamentary disposition is recognized for military personnel in active service.

By a wills act in Great Britain, a valid will must be in writing, signed by the testator or his proxy, signed or acknowledged in the presence of two or more witnesses, and attested and subscribed by the witnesses in the presence of the testator. The testator's knowledge of the contents of the will is essential. Three kinds of wills are permitted in France: a holographic will; a notarial will executed in the presence of notaries and witnesses and dictated to a notary; and a "mystic" will, signed by the testator, sealed, and presented to a notary for endorsement before witnesses. Somewhat similar wills are recognized in other civil law jurisdictions and in the State of Louisiana.

Alteration and Revocation.—Alterations and amendments to a will may be made at any time before the death of the testator. An amendment, known as a codicil, must be signed by the testator and witnessed in the same manner as the original will. Revocation of a will may be accomplished by the testator's act or by operation of law. A will is revoked by a subsequent testamentary instrument containing an express clause of revocation or provisions inconsistent with those of the former will and by physical acts such as tearing, burning, or canceling carried out with the intention to revoke. However, mutilation alone may result in only partial revocation. In some states, subsequent marriage of the testator, divorce with property settlement, or birth of issue invalidates a will. While some jurisdictions provide for revival of an earlier will at the destruction or revocation of a later one, others recognize revival only by republication, unless the intent appears otherwise.

Probate of Will.—At the death of the testator, the will, unless a settlement is contracted, is placed on file for probate, the process by which a court of competent jurisdiction, usually called the probate court, establishes that an instrument is the valid last will of a decedent and that the will was executed by a competent testator in the manner required. In most states, a will has no effect as an instrument of title until probated, except perhaps for land. Probate is therefore to establish the rights of the beneficiaries. The primary place of probate is in the state and county where the deceased was domiciled at his death. If the will passes real estate at a different location, it must thereafter be submitted for probate at the situs of the land. Notice of petition for probate usually must be given to heirs at law and other interested persons, though some jurisdictions permit ex parte proceedings without notice. A will may be contested by one whose legal or equitable interest would be affected adversely. In part or in whole, a will may be set aside by a successful contest on the grounds of improper execution, an absence of testamentary capacity or intent, or a disposition induced by fraud, mistake, or undue influence upon the mind of the testator. A person or corporation nominated in a will to administer the testator's estate is known as an executor. If none is named or available, the court appoints an administrator.

Judicial construction of a will may become necessary. The primary object in construing a will is to learn the testator's intention and to give it effect as far as possible. Intent is determined by an examination of the entire instrument, with every provision considered. Wills are liberally construed, and technical rules of construction are utilized only if the testator's intent is obscure and the language of the will ambiguous.

ALAN A. MATHESON,
School of Law, Columbia University.

WILL, in philosophy and psychology, the faculty or function which is directed to conscious and intentional action. The will, considered either as an activity or a faculty specifically devoted to an activity, has had a long history in philosophic and psychological literature. Human actions, more than those of any other animal, are goal directed and most often explainable primarily in terms of ends to be achieved.

Ancient Concept.—Both Plato and Aristotle considered explanations in terms of purposes applicable to all of nature, finding nature always acting toward some end in the most economical way possible. For both of these thinkers, however, man's possession of reason was his uniquely distinguishing characteristic. The rational faculty, they believed, enables man to choose from among a diversity of possible means in the pursuit of his endeavors. Nevertheless, Greek philosophy in its classical period is generally considered not to have developed a very clear-cut notion of the will. Plato taught that no man deliberately desires evil. Aristotle believed that all deliberation is about means and never about ends, since the end—happiness—is ever the same. The Platonic position resulted in the doctrine that virtue is knowledge, a view which has the effect of defining wrongdoing as ignorance, thereby eliminating the possibility of an inherently bad intention.

The absence of a clearly developed doctrine of the will in Greek philosophy is therefore to be traced to the primacy of reason over will in the classical tradition. It is reason that presents to the will its possible choices, and the choice which results is primarily the consequence of the light in which the respective choices are perceived by the rational faculty. In this view the will is not a faculty that chooses from among equally desirable alternatives, but rather its choice is conditioned by reason, which presents this or that alternative as the desirable one. A bad choice therefore is the result of defective reason. Aristotle's discussion of the problem of choice is restricted largely to distinguishing voluntary from involuntary actions. He sees the distinction essentially in the agent's awareness of prevailing circumstances. He terms as voluntary that action having its origin in the agent who is aware of the circumstances in which he is acting; whereas the involuntary consists of an incomplete awareness of the facts rather than of the ethical issues involved.

Will and Sin.—It is with the development of the doctrine of sin in Christian thought that the will begins to assume more significant proportions in philosophic thought. For sin to be real, the sinner must be fully aware of the good and yet choose its opposite. This choice cannot be the result of a defect in reason because, if that were the case, the act of sinning would not then be the conscious rejection of the good that it is. The existence of a free and independent will, which is in effective control of human action and which has in its power the rejection of the good, is thus seen to be a precondition of the possibility of sin. At the same time, St. Augustine is careful not to make of human will a power independent of God —a power whose actions God cannot foresee—thereby limiting His omniscience. While God foresees the choices of the will, He does not compel them but acts only as an observer who witnesses future rather than contemporary events (though this very distinction between the future and the present is not ultimately applicable to God, who is beyond all time).

The prominence of the notion of grace in Augustine, while sometimes taken as indicating a denial of the efficacy and independence of the human will, is in fact made necessary by the importance his doctrine of will assumes in his thought. (See AUGUSTINIANISM.) The doctrine of grace is directed against the Pelagian heresy, according to which the will is equally posed between the good and the bad without being determined in the one or the other direction. (See PELAGIANISM.) The effect of the Augustinian doctrine of grace is to deny this theory of equal balance and to substitute for it a will whose natural inclination is evil, unless otherwise directed by saving grace. If anything, it is the doctrine of the absolutely free will that suffers, not the efficacy of the will as such; for the will, whether directed toward the good by saving grace or toward evil by its natural tendency, remains in control of human action. In later medieval philosophy the Augustinian tradition is represented by Duns Scotus, who argues for the primacy of will over reason, whereas Thomas Aquinas teaches the primacy of reason over will. See also SCHOLASTICISM.

Modern Views.—In pre-Kantian modern philosophy the surprising unanimity of opinion in the direction of determinism, a unanimity that embraces empiricists as well as rationalists, prevents the development of any great emphasis on the will as a philosophically ultimate category. Thus, for René Descartes, the will is free only as long as it does not go beyond what is clear and distinct to reason. Its virtue therefore consists of permitting itself to be guided by reason, and it is the cause of error when it rejects this guidance and decides upon judgments for which reason provides no sanction. In the empiricist camp, David Hume finds the will subject to the universal principle of causality. He distinguishes free acts from those performed under compulsion by claiming that in the case of the former the causes operate through the will, but that in the latter they bypass the will, producing the familiar feeling of compulsion.

It is in fact not until Immanuel Kant that the will comes into its own as a decisive element in the philosophy of western Europe. In Kant's *Critique of Pure Reason* the will does not play a very important role. It is only when Kant turns his attention to the demands of the moral life that his thinking leaves the domain of the phenomenal world and penetrates to the deepest layers of the self which—as author of categories of understanding operative in the phenomenal world—extends beyond it into the world of the noumenon where freedom and autonomy, instead of causality and determinism, are supreme. Kant's notion of the free will is therefore not to be identified with the empirical will which is the object of cognition and which is subject to psychological research. Instead, as the noumenal root of the self, it escapes all objectification, its very existence being postulated from the fact of moral responsibility. The relation established by Kant between the will and reason is a complex one, a thorough discussion of which requires more space than this article permits. Suffice it to say that while Kant insists that only a rational being can possess will, he also strongly implies, even if he never states explicitly, that the will, as the expression of the noumenal self, is metaphysically the more original or dominant faculty.

This implication is taken up and developed assiduously by German Romantic philosophy, for which the will moves into the forefront of metaphysical discussion. For Arthur Schopenhauer the will is identified with the very nature of being. Everything that is, he argues, offers resistance to its dissolution, thus justifying the philosopher in finding will the fundamental principle of all being. Influenced by oriental thought, he finds in the endless and insatiable willing that is reality the root of all suffering in the world, especially that of man. The will cannot be defeated by being exercised since the more it is satisfied, the more avaricious it becomes. The solution advocated by Schopenhauer is the cessation of the activity of willing. Such a cessation produces the final liberation from the endless cycle of will and frustration that is the tragic fate of mankind. Schopenhauer finds in art that will-less contemplation of reality which he advocates, and in this view he returns to Kant, for whom the essence of the aesthetic attitude is a nonutilitarian perception of objects.

Friedrich Nietzsche, who shares many of Schopenhauer's metaphysical views, differs with Schopenhauer's negative attitude toward the will. For him all philosophies which attempt to undermine the exercise of the will to power are more or less thinly disguised versions of Christian slave morality whose purpose it is to protect the weakest and least valuable portions of humanity against the legitimate rule of the powerful, a rule that is ordained by nature itself.

Twentieth century psychology has not emphasized the will as a significant factor in personality. The psychology of conditioning as developed by Ivan Petrovich Pavlov is too deeply committed to a physiological model of explanation to recognize the will as an independent force in guiding human conduct. Similarly, Freudian psychology, with its emphasis on unconscious motivations, cannot avoid considering the conscious will as a relatively surface phenomenon controlled by deeper, unconscious forces over which it has no effective control.

It is in existential philosophy, as originated by Søren Aabye Kierkegaard and developed by Martin Heidegger, Karl Jaspers, and Jean-Paul Sartre, that the will once more plays a dominant role. Thus Kierkegaard says in *Either—Or* (1843) that only he who "chooses himself" can truly be himself, "and this everyone can be if he wills it." Sartre's notion of "project," as the basic characteristic of human existence, places free choice and, indirectly, the will into the center of his thought. The existential notion of authenticity is also inconceivable without the primacy of the will which accepts its responsibilities and shapes its existence in accordance with them. The development of existential psychoanalysis by Otto Ludwig Binswanger and others in Europe and the gradual introduction of these ideas in America is beginning to show its influence in American psychology, where it represents an alternative to the more deterministic views that have been dominant.

See also FREE WILL AND DETERMINISM and biographies of philosophers mentioned.

Bibliography

Aveling, F., *Personality and Will* (1931; reprint, R. West 1978).
James, William, *The Will to Believe* (1897; Harvard Univ. Press 1979).
Kant, Immanuel, *Fundamental Principles of the Metaphysics of Morals,* tr. by Otto Manthey-Zorn (1797; Irvington 1966).
Kenny, A. S., *Aristotle's Theory of the Will* (Yale Univ. Press 1979).
Mahan, Asa, *Doctrine of the Will* (AMS Press 1975).
O'Shaughnessy, B., *The Will,* 2 vols. (Cambridge 1980).
Schopenhauer, Arthur, *The World as Will and Idea,* tr. by R. B. Haldane and J. Kemp, 3 vols. (1896; reprint, AMS Press 1975).
Southerland, Paul G., *Friedrich Nietzsche and the Theory of the Will to Power* (Am. Classical College Press 1982).

MICHAEL WYSCHOGROD,
Assistant Professor of Philosophy, Hunter College of the City University of New York.

WILL-O'-THE-WISP. See IGNIS FATUUS.

WILLAERT, vĭl'ärt, **Adrian,** Flemish composer: b. Bruges, Flanders, 1490?; d. Venice, Italy, Dec. 8, 1562. After studies in Paris, he became a household musician to the Este family at Ferrara and elsewhere. Appointed *maestro di cappella* at St. Mark's Cathedral in 1527, he settled permanently in Venice, in effect becoming an Italian. His pupils at the singing academy that he founded included such famous composers as Andrea Gabrieli and Cipriano de Rore. As a master of both vocal and instrumental polyphony, he initiated the great school of Venetian music. Taking musical advantage of the architecture of St. Mark's, he evolved a magnificent manner of antiphonal scoring for two choirs and two organs. His surviving compositions, many available in scholarly modern editions, include masses, motets, madrigals, *ricercari, canzone,* and vesper psalms.

HERBERT WEINSTOCK.

WILLAMETTE RIVER, wĭ-lăm'it, a river in western Oregon, formed by the junction near Eugene, in Lane County, of Coast Fork and Middle Fork, streams which flow from the Cascade Range. The river flows northward through a fertile valley of farmland, forests, and populous cities, including Eugene, Corvallis, Albany, Salem, Oregon City, and Portland. It enters the Columbia River just north of Portland. The river is navigable all the way to Eugene, but rail and motor traffic make water transportation south of Portland of minor commercial importance. The river is a source of fish and hydroelectric power, and dams have been constructed along a few of its tributaries. Its total distance from the forks which mark its beginning to the Columbia River is about 190 miles.

WILLAMETTE UNIVERSITY, a coeducational, privately controlled university at Salem, Oregon, the oldest institution of higher learning west of Missouri. It is associated with Methodist Church. In 1834 a school for Indian children was established in Salem by missionaries, and in 1842 a constitution and bylaws were adopted for Oregon Institute, renamed Willamette University in 1853. Advanced instruction began in 1844. Today there are three colleges: liberal arts, music, and law, all granting bachelor degrees. Graduate study leads to a master of arts in education for secondary school teachers; the college of law grants a doctor of jurisprudence. Though located near the capitol buildings in the heart of the city it is largely a residential school. An honor's program is offered for superior students. Athletic teams are known as the "Bearcats"; college colors are cardinal red and gold. The annual enrollment averages 1,200 students.

G. HERBERT SMITH.

WILLARD, wil'ərd, **Archibald M.,** American painter and illustrator: b. Bedford, Ohio, Aug. 26, 1836; d. Cleveland, Oct. 11, 1918. He served in the Civil War as a color bearer and afterward earned a living as a carriage painter. In 1873 he went to New York City to study art, concentrating on battle scenes and other dramatic events. One of Willard's paintings, *The Spirit of '76,* became familiar to generations of American schoolchildren and stands as one of the nation's best-loved patriotic symbols. Originally entitled *Yankee Doodle,* the scene was sketched while Willard was watching a Fourth of July

The Bettmann Archive

***The Spirit of '76*, painting by Archibald M. Willard.**

parade in Wellington, Ohio, in 1875. It was subsequently made into a painting for the 1876 Centennial Exhibition in Philadelphia. The painting was finished shortly after the death of his father, who had posed for the central figure, in 1876. *The Spirit of '76* captures the fighting qualities of the colonial troops in the three main figures (two drummers and a fife player) who march indomitably onward through the smoke and din of battle. John H. Devereux, the railroad pioneer whose son was the model for the drummer boy, acquired the painting in 1880 and presented it to the town of Marblehead, Mass., where it now hangs in Abbott Hall.

WILLARD, Emma (nee HART), American educator: b. Berlin, Conn., Feb. 23, 1787; d. Troy, N. Y., April 15, 1870. In 1807 she took charge of the Middlebury, Vt., Female Academy, which she left in 1809 to marry Dr. John Willard (1759–1825) of Middlebury. In 1814 she opened a school for young ladies in her own home, introducing mathematics and philosophy, subjects unheard of for women, and proved that they could master them and retain their health and charm. Ambitious for the progress of women's education, she sent the New York governor, DeWitt Clinton, in 1818, her *Plan for Improving Female Education*, published in 1819, and pleaded for it herself before the state legislature. She asked that state aid be provided for female seminaries and that women be given the same educational advantages as men. In 1819 she moved her school to Waterford, N.Y., and in 1821 (aided by local citizens but without state aid) she established the Troy Female Seminary, continuing her policy of teaching higher subjects including science. She evolved new methods of teaching geography and history, published textbooks which won immediate recognition, and trained hundreds of teachers whom she sent into the South and West, making her seminary a model in America and Europe.

After a trip to Europe in 1830, she published a volume of poems (1831), including *Rocked in the Cradle of the Deep*, and *Journal and Letters from France and Great Britain* (1833). She also helped found a training school for teachers in liberated Greece in 1833. In 1838 she turned her seminary over to her son and his wife and devoted herself to improving public schools, traveling widely to hold teachers' institutes and asking that women serve as teachers. She continued to publish textbooks, among them *Last Leaves of American History* (1849). The first woman to prove the value of higher education for women, she opened the way for high schools for girls and women's colleges. The seminary that she founded became the Emma Willard School in 1895.

Her published works include *Nineteen Beautiful Years* (1864), a life of her sister; *How to Win: A Book for Girls* (1886); and *Glimpses of Fifty Years* (1889).

See also COEDUCATION.

ALMA LUTZ

WILLARD, Frances Elizabeth Caroline, American educator, reformer, and lecturer: b. Churchville, N. Y., Sept. 28, 1839; d. New York, Feb. 18, 1898. She grew up on a farm at Janesville, Wis., and graduated from Northwestern Female College, Evanston, Ill., in 1859. She began teaching and eventually became president of the Evanston College for Ladies (1871) and, when this institution became part of Northwestern University, dean of women.

In 1874 she became secretary of the Woman's Christian Temperance Union (WCTU), and she was president of the organization from 1879 until her death. Under her leadership it grew to 10,000 local units with a paying membership of 250,000 women, the great woman movement of the century. In addition to working boldly for the controversial franchise, she established 39 departments of activities related to home protection, including temperance, better schools, politics, lobbying, labor reform, prison reform, police matrons, peace, nutrition, and kindergarten. The power and prestige of the union was amplified by its warm endorsement by other important and kindred organizations, such as the Young Men's Christian Association, the Ministerial Alliance, the Sunday School Association, the Knights of Labor, and the Grange.

She also became president of the National Council of Women in 1890. Acclaimed as a brilliant and charming speaker, she traveled widely to present her views and win recruits. By the end of the century she had established a temperance hospital, a publishing association, lecture bureau, an office building in Chicago, and a world WCTU organization with membership of two million women; and 20 states had enacted woman suffrage in whole or in part. After her death, Congress voted to place her statue in the rotunda of the Capitol in Washington, D. C., extolling Frances Willard as "the first woman of the 19th century, the most beloved character of her times."

MARY EARHART DILLON
Professor of Political Science, Queens College, City University of New York

WILLARD, city, Ohio, in Huron County, about 75 miles by road southwest of Cleveland. It has an airport for private planes. Willard is located in a truck-gardening area and has rubber, metal toy, and printing industries. It was incorporated in 1882 as Chicago Junction and renamed in 1917 in honor of Daniel Willard, president of the Baltimore & Ohio Railroad. The city manager form of government was adopted in 1959. Population: 5,674.

WILLCOCKS, wĭl′kŏks, **Sir William,** British engineer and irrigationist: b. India, 1852; d. Cairo, Egypt, July 28, 1932. Educated at Roorkee College in India, he was employed on public works in that country from 1872 to 1883, and on Egyptian works and reservoirs from 1883 to 1897. Willcocks designed and supervised the building of the Aswan Dam from 1898 to 1902, and was knighted in the latter year for this achievement. His irrigation projects in Mesopotamia in 1911 were equally important. He wrote *Egyptian Irrigation* (1889); *The Irrigation of Mesopotamia* (1905); *From the Garden of Eden to the Crossing of the Jordan* (1918); and an autobiography, *Sixty Years in the East* (1935), published posthumously.

WILLEBRANDT, wĭl′ə-brănt, **Mabel** (née Walker), American lawyer and public official: b. Woodsdale, Kans., May 23, 1889; d. Riverside, Calif., April 6, 1963. She graduated from Tempe (Ariz.) Normal School in 1911, and was principal of a South Pasadena, Calif. school while she studied law at the University of Southern California. Admitted to the California bar in 1915, she went into private practice and was appointed public defender for Los Angeles city and county, handling over 2,000 cases. In 1921 she became assistant attorney general of the United States in charge of cases arising from violation of the Prohibition Amendment. She also supervised the federal Bureau of Prisons. During the 1920's she was famous for her relentless enforcement of prohibition. Resigning from her federal posts in 1929, she returned to private practice in California. In 1938 she became the first woman to serve as chairman of an important committee of the American Bar Association (the committee on aeronautical law).

WILLEMITE, wĭl′əm-īt, a mineral, orthosilicate of zinc, Zn_2SiO_4, named for King William (Willem) I of the Netherlands. It is found in Belgium, Africa, and several parts of the United States; the mine at Franklin Furnace, N.J., which had been the chief United States source, was exhausted in 1954. In its pure form, willemite is an opaque or transparent white; when mixed with iron or manganese, it may be green, yellow, red, or brown. The crystals are commonly hexagonal prisms ending in obtuse rhombohedra, but a granular form is also found mixed with franklinite. Crystals from Belgium differ from the New Jersey type in having an easy basal cleavage. The mineral has a hardness of 5.5 and a specific gravity of 3.9 to 4.2. It sometimes appears phosphorescent, and under ultraviolet rays shows a bright yellow-green fluorescence. A variety in which manganese partially replaces the zinc is known as troostite.

WILLEMS, vĭl′əms, **Florent (Joseph Marie),** Belgian genre painter: b. Liège, Belgium, Jan. 8, 1823; d. Neuilly-sur-Seine, France, Oct. 23, 1905. He studied at the Academy of Mechlin, where his style was influenced by the Dutch masters of the 17th century. About 1840 he moved to Paris and won success both as an artist and as a teacher. Scenes of everyday life and historical subjects were his specialties. His paintings may be seen in the museums of Antwerp, Liège, and Brussels.

WILLEMSTAD. See Curaçao.

WILLESDEN, wĭlz′dən, municipal borough, England, in Middlesex County, six miles northwest of St. Paul's, London. At the beginning of the 19th century it was a rural community with a population of 751. The flood of London's growth reached it about 1875, when its population was 15,500. By 1905 it had become established as a "dormitory" town with a population of nearly 149,000. During World War I, Willesden became a center of light industry, and since then it has developed as a densely built-up residential and industrial suburb. Its growth has been helped by the fact that it is an important railroad center. It is also on the Grand Union Canal, which connects the Thames with the Midlands. Watling Street, which forms the eastern boundary of the borough for some distance, also leads to the Midlands. The only early building is St. Mary's Church, which retains a few Norman features. Pop. (1961) 170,835.

H. Gordon Stokes.

WILLET, wĭl′ĭt, a large North American sandpiper, *Catoptrophorus semipalmatus,* so named because of its call, *pilly-will-willet.* It nests on the Atlantic and Gulf coasts from New Jersey south, with an isolated colony in Nova Scotia, and on lakeshores in the interior from Saskatchewan to Nevada. In winter it migrates to the Gulf states, the coasts of Mexico, and southern California. About a foot in length, the willet is mottled with ashy gray and black above and white below. The winter plumage is a uniform grayish brown above. The name *Catoptrophorus,* meaning "mirror bearer," refers to white areas in the wing, which are conspicuous in flight. The spotted eggs, four in number, were formerly prized as food; the flesh, less so.

Dean Amadon.

WILLETT, wĭl′ĭt, **Marinus,** American Revolutionary officer: b. Jamaica, Long Island, N.Y., July 31, 1740; d. New York, N.Y., Aug. 22, 1830. After serving in the French and Indian Wars, he became a leader of the Sons of Liberty, who in 1775 seized arms from the English in New York to prevent their being sent to Boston. In 1777, with the rank of lieutenant colonel, he was second in command at Fort Stanwix, N.Y., holding it against Col. Barry St. Leger until relieved by Benedict Arnold. Two years later he was with the expedition of Gen. John Sullivan against the Iroquois, and later commanded the American forces in the Mohawk Valley, where in 1781 he checked the English at the Battle of Johnstown. Early in 1783 he led the last attack of the Revolutionary War, against the British garrison at Oswego, N.Y.

Willett was sheriff of New York County from 1784 to 1788, and in 1790 he was sent by President George Washington on a mission to the

Creek Indians, whose leaders he induced to go to New York City, where they signed a treaty of peace. From 1807 to 1808 he served as mayor of New York. He was buried in a coffin made of wood that he had collected on various battlefields. From his manuscript journals, his son published *A Narrative of the Military Actions of Colonel Marinus Willett* (1831).

WILLETT or **WILLET, Thomas,** American colonial leader: b. Barley, Hertfordshire, England, August 1605; d. Swansea, Mass., Aug. 4, 1674. He went to Holland with a group of Puritans in the 1620's and emigrated to Plymouth Colony about 1630. Willett became a prominent trader and shipowner, acquiring considerable property in New Amsterdam; his knowledge of English made him the choice of Gov. Peter Stuyvesant there to serve on a committee to settle boundaries with the English colonies in 1650. Willett subsequently became a magistrate of Plymouth Colony, accompanied the English expedition against New Amsterdam in 1664, and helped to negotiate the surrender of the city. In 1665 the English governor, Richard Nicolls, appointed him mayor of the renamed city of New York, and he was mayor again in 1667. His property was confiscated when the Dutch briefly recaptured New York in 1673, and he retired to his home in Swansea.

WILLETTE, vē-lĕt′, **Adolphe (Léon),** French painter and illustrator: b. Châlons-sur-Marne, France, July 31, 1857; d. Paris, Feb. 4, 1926. A pupil of Alexandre Cabanel, he made his debut in the Paris Salon of 1881 with *The Temptation of St. Anthony* and other paintings, but soon turned to illustration, for which he is best known. As a political and moral satirist, he contributed to *Chat noir, Courrier français, Rire, Triboulet, Boulevard,* and 20 other illustrated publications, later founding *Pierrot* and *Pied-de-nez.* He worked in lithograph and pastel as well as black and white. His most famous illustrations are the Pierrot and Colombine cartoons. Influenced by the tradition of the 18th century, they are witty, good-natured, and tender depictions of life on Montmartre.

WILLEY, wĭl′ē, **Gordon Randolph,** American archaeologist and anthropologist: b. Chariton, Iowa, March 7, 1913. Because of an early interest in archaeology, he chose the University of Arizona for his undergraduate studies (A.B., 1935), completing his Ph.D. at Columbia University in 1942 after doing field work in Peru. Between 1943 and 1950 he was on the staff of the Bureau of American Ethnology, Smithsonian Institution, where he worked on the *Handbook of South American Indians.* In 1950 he was appointed Bowditch professor of Central American and Mexican archaeology and ethnology at Harvard University. Field work in the years that followed took him to Panama, British Honduras, Nicaragua, and Guatemala. Willey's major contributions are in synthesis and theory. His significant publications include *An Interpretation of the Prehistory of the Eastern United States* (1951), with James A. Ford; *Archeology of the Florida Gulf Coast* (1949); *Prehistoric Settlement Patterns in the Virú Valley, Peru* (1953); and *Method and Theory in American Archaeology* (1958), with Philip Phillips.

STEPHEN WILLIAMS.

WILLIAM, wĭl′yəm, (WILHELM FRIEDRICH HEINRICH; known as WILLIAM OF WIED), king of Albania: b. Neuwied, Prussia, March 26, 1876; d. Predeal, Rumania, April 18, 1945. Member of a German princely family (Wied), he was the cousin of Emperor William II of Germany and of Czar Nicholas II of Russia. In 1913 he was offered the throne of Albania by the Great Powers, which had sponsored the creation of the new kingdom. Crowned at Durrës (Durazzo) in March 1914, he was soon faced by an uprising and fled the country in September, but never formally abdicated. See also ALBANIA—*History.*

WILLIAM, the name of four kings of England:

WILLIAM I (called THE CONQUEROR): b. Falaise, Normandy, 1027 or 1028; d. Rouen, Sept. 9, 1087. He was the son of Robert the Devil, duke of Normandy, and Arlette, daughter of Fulbert, a tanner of Falaise. Though an illegitimate son, William succeeded his father as duke of Normandy in 1035, at the age of eight. He lived in obscurity for 12 years in the care of guardians until the Battle of Val-ès-Dunes (1047), won for him against rebellious vassals by his overlord King Henry I of France, allowed him to consolidate his position and power. In 1053 he married Matilda, daughter of Baldwin V, count of Flanders, by whom he had four sons and five daughters. He acquired Maine by force in 1063 and was even able to act independently of his lawful sovereign.

Mansell Collection, London

William I (called the Conqueror).

The lack of heirs to the English throne and Edward the Confessor's predilection for Normans (among whom he had been brought up) made it possible for William to put forward his candidature, though he was only Edward's cousin by marriage. Despite a promise made by Edward to William on his only visit to England in 1051, Harold Godwin became king in 1066; his title seemed indisputable, and no Englishman supported William. William therefore submitted his claims to trial by battle, invading England in 1066, and, favored by good fortune, won the Battle of Hastings (see HASTINGS, BATTLE OF).

This victory saw the death of Harold and every adult member of the Godwin family, leaving William as the only competent candidate for the throne. As such, the country accepted him, and he was crowned in London on December 25.

Since there was little native resistance, William left England for a nine months' visit to Normandy in March 1067; he was, indeed, to spend far more than a third of his reign out of England. By 1068 the English fyrd (army) was fighting on his behalf. English resistance was incoherent and fitful: Edric the Wild on the borders of Wales; the earls Edwin of Mercia and Morcar of Northumbria in 1068 and 1069; Hereward the Wake, legendary hero of the common people, in 1070. The policy of terrorization, already used in the conquest of Maine, was applied to England, particularly in the frightful devastation of the northern parts between the North Sea and the Irish Sea in 1069. Furthermore, since there had to be close cooperation between William and his barons in defense of their common security and interest, William had no difficulty in suppressing occasional insurrections such as those of Eustace of Boulogne (1067), Ralph, earl of East Anglia, and Roger, earl of Hereford (1075), and Bishop Odo of Bayeux, earl of Kent (1082). William was content to protect his new realm on the west by establishing marcher earldoms on the borders of Wales; and after extracting a vague promise of allegiance from Malcolm Canmore, king of Scots, in 1072, he constructed Newcastle as a permanent defense for the northern frontier. The new factor was that England was now directly involved in the politics of Europe, and most of William's later years and resources were spent in defeating the machinations of Count Robert of Flanders, Count Fulk of Anjou, and Philip I of France against his Norman duchy.

Mansell Collection, London

Seals of William the Conqueror.

No single fact in the history of England in the 40 years after 1066 is more notable than the continuance of the old English state, its institutions, and language. William regarded himself not as a conqueror, but as a legitimate heir. He was crowned with the ceremonial of old English kings and swore their oath at his coronation. He inherited a paramount right to the allegiance of all his subjects; the Salisbury Oath of 1086, which asserted the precedence of fealty to the king over obligations to inferior lords, merely exhibited the king's right. The witan continued, though with an altered complexion, as the king's council. The revenues of the English kings became those of their Norman successors. The shire courts and hundred courts remained as the indispensable agents of local government, and manorial courts simply continued pre-Conquest tribunals. Thus the structure of the state was substantially the same as it had been before 1066, and the English way of life was not radically altered; for, in contrast with Normandy, England was an ordered polity, and neither in political concepts nor in administrative agencies did William know anything more advanced than what he found.

William's addition to the stock of native institutions was not large: mainly a clumsy, ineffective, and short-lived organization of the military resources of the crown which brought in new elements of feudal law and a modest source of revenue through feudal incidents. Norman, that is, French, feudalism differed little from the English variety: the mounted soldier was called by the English word "knight" because he resembled the knight the English already knew, and the service owed by thegns (thanes) was easily transmuted into service owed by knights. The old English nobility disappeared and was replaced by foreigners, but William made no redivision of land, merely confiscating the estates of his enemies and conferring them on his followers. In landholding, as in government, there was continuity.

Similarly, in the church, the higher clergy saw a growing infusion of foreign elements, and the monasteries were Gallicized, but the parochial clergy was necessarily left undisturbed. With the wholehearted cooperation of Lanfranc, who was made archbishop of Canterbury in 1170, William gave the church courts of its own in which to try ecclesiastical causes; but even this development must have come sooner or later, for it is inconceivable that England would have stood outside the organization of Latin Christianity. Neither William nor Lanfranc was an ardent reformer or papalist, and relations with Rome, regulated in accordance with previous custom, evoked no serious problems.

William was ruthless and unscrupulous, masterful and indomitable; with no originality of mind, he was nevertheless a highly efficient ruler. The Domesday Book (q.v.), though a costly mistake, never finished and rarely used, survives as a memorial to the drive that he gave to administration in thus setting on foot a nationwide inquiry into the wealth of his kingdom.

On William's death, due to an injury on horseback during fighting in France, his inheritance, the duchy of Normandy, went by rules of tenure to his eldest son, Robert; but he left his prize of war, England, to his second surviving son, William (see *William II* in this article). Had the terms of his will been maintained, England and Normandy would have gone their different ways, and the Norman Conquest would have been no more than a footnote in English history. See also GREAT BRITAIN AND NORTHERN IRELAND—*21. History* (Norman Conquest).

Bibliography

Belloc, Hilaire, *William the Conqueror* (1938; reprint, Darby Bks. 1983).
Chambers, James, *The Norman Kings* (Biblio. Dist. 1981).
Douglas, David C., *William the Conqueror: The Norman Impact Upon England* (Univ. of Calif. Press 1964).
Freeman, E. A., *William the Conqueror* (Gordon Press 1984).
Loyn, H. R., *The Norman Conquest,* 3rd ed. (Longwood 1984).

WILLIAM II (called RUFUS, because of his ruddy complexion): b. 1056/1060; d. Hampshire, England, Aug. 2, 1100. Third son of William I the Conqueror and Matilda of Flanders, he was nominated king of England by his father and, with the support of Lanfranc, archbishop of Canterbury, acceded to the throne on Sept. 26, 1087. He died unmarried and was succeeded by his younger brother, Henry I.

The Norman nobles, having property on both sides of the Channel, opposed the division of England and Normandy willed by the Conqueror. Led by Bishop Odo of Bayeux, earl of Kent, they revolted against William in 1088, with the object of placing his elder brother Robert, duke of Normandy, on the throne. Eager to avoid anarchy, the native English rallied to the support of William, and the rebellion was suppressed. A second and last baronial revolt under Robert de Mowbray, earl of Northumberland, in 1095 was also unsuccessful and was put down with the utmost severity.

Scotland presented no difficulty. The homage done by her king, Malcolm Canmore, in 1091 did not prevent William from forcibly incorporating Cumberland and Westmorland into his English kingdom and turning Carlisle into a garrison town. After the ambush and death of Malcolm at Alnwick (1093), Scotland remained quiescent under English control.

At home, William's insatiable greed led him to exploit to the full every fiscal right that he had. The able and ambitious Rannulf Flambard, rewarded with the bishopric of Durham in 1099, became the king's chief agent in devising ostensibly legal means of financial extortion. The worst effects of the royal avarice were seen in the church, where William prolonged vacancies in high ecclesiastical offices so that he could keep the profits for himself. Thus, though Lanfranc died in 1089, William did not appoint a successor at Canterbury until 1093, when the saint and scholar Anselm of Aosta was named archbishop. Anselm became a more uncompromising reformer with every year, and the first open rupture between church and state became visible at the Council of Rockingham in 1095. Two years later, Anselm went into exile, leaving the church leaderless and the revenues of his see in the king's hand.

Meanwhile, Normandy had fallen to pieces under the feckless Duke Robert. Maine was appropriated by Anjou; and Henry, younger brother of Robert and William, had purchased the Cotentin district, which William subsequently recovered for Robert and himself. From the beginning of his reign, William had been buying up parts of the duchy, and from 1096 he held what was left of it in pledge for 10,000 marks, though he never was duke.

William was given to unnatural vices, blasphemy, and uncurbed violence. His death came while hunting in the New Forest, from an arrow presumably shot by Walter Tirel, lord of Poix in Ponthieu, and may have been the result of a planned assassination. The most that can be said in his favor is that English monarchy had retained its strength.

See also GREAT BRITAIN—*31. History* (William Rufus).

G. O. SAYLES,
Burnett-Fletcher Professor of History, University of Aberdeen.

Further Reading: Chambers, James, *The Norman Kings* (Biblio. Dist. 1981); Freeman, Edward A., *Reign of William Rufus* (1882; reprint, AMS Press 1980); Poole, Austin L., *From Domesday Book to Magna Carta* (Oxford 1951); Rowley, Trevor, *The Norman Heritage 1066 to 1200* (Methuen 1983).

WILLIAM III: b. The Hague, the Netherlands, Nov. 4, 1650; d. London, England, March 8, 1702. He was the only child of William II, prince of Orange, and Mary, eldest daughter of Charles I, king of England. The father died eight days before the son's birth, leaving the house of Orange leaderless against the powerful republicans of Holland, although it retained its popularity with the masses. William's youth was dominated by the struggle between these groups. He was delicate and undersized, with a tendency to asthma. Carefully educated, he grew up with a stern self-control, frugal and temperate, with a mastery of languages and an impenetrable reserve. He was a dedicated political and soldierly type.

In 1667 the republicans, headed by the brothers Jan and Cornelis De Witt, succeeded in abolishing the stadholdership of the Netherlands; but the young prince came into his own in the grave crisis of 1672, when the French invaded the country with immensely superior forces. William was appointed captain general and stadholder for life, and an angry mob at The Hague murdered the De Witts, who had stood for an appeasement policy with France. William had the dikes opened and the country flooded, and thus won Holland a breathing space. The next year he concluded a defensive alliance with Spain and the Austrian Empire, and henceforth his life was dedicated to the single-minded aim of resisting Louis XIV's threatened domination of Europe.

In pursuit of this objective, in 1677 William married his cousin Mary, daughter of the future James II of England and heiress presumptive to the throne on her father's succession. Meanwhile, he had displayed much doggedness, perseverance, and personal bravery in the field, but did not have much luck as a commander. As a soldier he was competent but unimaginative; his great gifts were for politics and diplomacy. His diplomatic efforts were rewarded by the Peace of Nijmegen in 1678, which secured the integrity of the Netherlands, temporarily halted Louis XIV's career of aggression, and marked out William as the leader of European resistance to it.

The key to the situation and all hope of a grand alliance to restrain Louis XIV lay with England, temporarily misled by the ambivalent pro-Catholic policies of Charles II and James II. In consequence, by 1685, when James II succeeded his brother, France was more powerful than ever. William's own principality of Orange had been occupied in 1682, and the Huguenots expelled. William welcomed refugees in the Netherlands from Louis XIV's persecution, while preventing any countermeasures against Dutch Catholics; though a Calvinist himself, he stood constantly by the principle of toleration.

As James II's plans to bring England over to the Catholic side unfolded, William inevitably became the leader to whom the opposition looked for redress. On July 1, 1688, an invitation was sent by a number of English political leaders to William to head an armed expedition to intervene by force, since James had built up a standing army to enforce his policy. The birth of a son to James and his second wife, Mary of Modena, had made it essential for William to take over the government from the threatened Catholic dynasty.

Infatuated, James refused Louis XIV's offers of help and of an alliance against the Netherlands. Louis therefore declared war against the Austrian Empire and sent his armies to the Rhine. This freed William for his expedition down the Channel, and he landed with his Dutch army at Torbay on Nov. 5, 1688. He moved slowly up through the country, gradually gaining adherents, while supporters fell away from the king, among them his second daughter Anne and her intimate friends, the Churchills. The king's nerve gave way, while his projects fell about his ears; the commissioners to whom he entrusted the government came to terms with William, while James planned to flee from the country. William did nothing to impede this; indeed it simplified his problem when James ultimately escaped to France. The vacant throne was offered to William and Mary as joint sovereigns, and they were crowned on April 11, 1689. England was at once brought into the coalition against Louis XIV, which became the Grand Alliance later that year.

James invaded Ireland with French aid, but William's victory at the Boyne (July 1, 1690) destroyed James' hopes of regaining his kingdom. William was free to conduct the war in the Netherlands, where he displayed much valor at the sanguinary Battle of Landen in 1692. The political situation in England, where he was never popular, gave him constant anxiety; and in 1694 his wife Mary who had displayed the utmost loyalty, died. After her death, however, he was reconciled with her sister Anne and even with the earl (later 1st duke) of Marlborough, who had resented Dutch leadership of the English armies. William achieved a favorable peace at Ryswick in 1697, recognizing his position in England, and during the next few years attempted to regulate the succession to the Spanish possessions by diplomatic agreements with Louis XIV.

William's hand was weakened by English insistence upon disarming and unwillingness to support his policies. Only Louis' open breach of his engagements, by accepting the entire Spanish inheritance for his grandson and recognizing the son of James II as king of England, aroused the country to its danger and gave William support for the renewal of the Grand Alliance. He spent his last strength making diplomatic and military preparations for war (War of the Spanish Succession), begun in 1701, the conduct of which he left to Marlborough. Although Marlborough was a genius as a soldier and William's equal in diplomacy, he did not have the king's political courage or moral grandeur. William was indeed a heroic figure: although he did not live to accomplish it, his life's work was ultimately fulfilled in the defeat of Louis XIV and the reduction of France's ascendency in Europe.

For the important domestic events of William III's reign, and other details, see GREAT BRITAIN AND NORTHERN IRELAND—*21. History*.

Further Reading: Barany, George, *The Anglo-Russian Entente Cordiale of 1697–1698* (East European Quarterly 1986); Baxter, Stephen B., *William III and the Defense of European Liberty from 1650 to 1702* (1966; reprint, Greenwood Press 1976); Haley, K. H., *William of Orange and the English Opposition, 1672–1674* (1953; reprint, Greenwood Press 1975); Robb, N. A., *William of Orange: Personal Portrait*, 2 vols. (St. Martin's Press 1966–1969).

WILLIAM IV: b. London, England, Aug. 21, 1765; d. Windsor, June 20, 1837. The third son of George III, he served as a young man in the Navy, where he became a friend and admirer of Horatio Nelson. In 1782 he narrowly escaped being kidnaped by an agent of George Washington in New York. As duke of Clarence, he lived for 20 years with the actress Dorothea Jordan, by whom he had 10 children. In 1811 he severed relations with Mrs. Jordan, and seven years later married Adelaide of Saxe-Meiningen. On the death of his brother George IV in 1830, he succeeded to the throne, an elderly, kindhearted, simple gentleman of popular sympathies, interested in the welfare of the poor. This aided him in the prolonged crisis over the reform of Parliament; attached to constitutional principle, with common sense in spite of his garrulity, he gave his support to the Reform ministry, enabling it to carry the Reform Bill in 1832. (See also GREAT BRITAIN—*21. History*.) He was known affectionately as the "sailor-king."

William's two daughters by Queen Adelaide died in their infancy, and he was succeeded on the throne by his niece Victoria.

Further Reading: Allen, W. Gore, *King William IV* (Cresset Pub. 1960); Somerset, Anne, *The Life and Times of William IV* (Weidenfeld & Nicholson 1980); Ziegler, Phillip, *King William IV* (Harper 1973).

A. L. ROWSE,
All Souls College, Oxford University.

WILLIAM (Ger. WILHELM), the name of two emperors of Germany and kings of Prussia:

WILLIAM I (WILHELM FRIEDRICH LUDWIG): b. Berlin, Germany, March 22, 1797; d. there, March 9, 1888. He was the second son of King Frederick William III of Prussia and Queen Louisa, a princess of Mecklenburg-Strelitz. His youth was clouded by Napoleon I's defeat of Prussia in 1806–1807 and the early death of his mother in 1810. Since he was not expected ever to become the ruler of Prussia, he received an exclusively military training and chose a military career. He took part, as a captain, in the campaigns in France in 1814–1815 and proved his bravery in battle. By 1825 he had become a lieutenant general and commander of the guard corps. In 1829 he married Princess Augusta of Saxe-Weimar. In 1840, when his brother Frederick William IV, who was without offspring, ascended the throne, he was declared prince of Prussia (heir presumptive).

William, who throughout his life was to hold to the doctrine of the divine right of kings, disapproved of his brother's attempts to introduce some representative forms of government in 1847, and proposed in March 1848 to put down the revolutionary movements by force of arms. His activities in the disturbances in Berlin brought him the nickname of "prince of cartridges." After the king accepted a conciliatory policy, William found temporary security in England, but returned to Berlin in June 1848. In the summer of 1849 he commanded the army that defeated the revolutionary uprisings in Baden and the Palatinate. William was willing to accept the Prussian constitution of 1850, which, in spite of liberal elements, left the essential governmental power in the hands of the monarch. In the following years, therefore, he opposed the attempts of the reactionary groups to undermine the constitution.

When, in 1857, William was made deputy of his mentally incapacitated elder brother and in 1858 prince regent of Prussia, he opened what was considered a new era by selecting a cabinet containing some moderate liberals. When he became king upon the death of his brother in 1861, however, he entered upon his reign with the intention of strengthening the army by rejuvenating it and giving the professional element more complete control at the expense of the national guard. An army reform bill was drafted with the help of his minister of war, Count Albrecht von Roon, and met with the stern opposition of the liberal majority of the Prussian Parliament. The ensuing constitutional conflict made William ready to resign in 1862. As a last resort, on the suggestion of Roon, he appointed Otto von Bismarck as minister president in September 1862. For almost four years Bismarck ruled the state by unconstitutional means, but attempted at the same time to satisfy the national aspirations of the German liberals through an active foreign policy. The war against Denmark over Schleswig-Holstein and the war against Austria in 1866, both of which William originally opposed, made Prussia master of North Germany. Schleswig-Holstein, Hannover, Hesse, Nassau, and Frankfurt were annexed, and the remaining states united with Prussia in the North German Confederation, of which William became president.

Bismarck, who wished to bring Bavaria into the confederation at a future date and also saw in Austria a future ally of Germany, dissuaded William only with great difficulty from imposing humiliating peace on the two states in 1866. He also encountered great initial resistance on the part of the monarch when he advocated concessions to the liberal Parliament in order to end the constitutional conflict. Bismarck's policy actually achieved the exclusion of all parliamentary controls over the army, which remained an exclusive instrument of monarchical authority. The war with France in 1870–1871 brought the accession of the South German states to the North German Confederation, and the German Empire came into being. On January 18, 1871, during the siege of Paris, William I was proclaimed German emperor by the German princes in the Hall of Mirrors in the palace at Versailles.

Both in the war of 1866 and that of 1870–1871, William had assumed supreme command. But though he understood well the problems of internal military service, he had no ability in strategy. It was the military genius of his chief of staff, Count Helmuth von Moltke, that won the German victories of that period. William, however, made a great contribution to winning the war of 1870–1871 by settling the bitter conflict which arose between Bismarck and Moltke over the direction of the war.

After 1871, William accepted the political advice of Bismarck, though he always insisted on being fully convinced of the wisdom of all political actions. This demand led to many letters of resignation from Bismarck until William wrote his "Never" on one in 1877. Empress Augusta, too, opposed some of Bismarck's policies, as in the case of the anti-Catholic May laws of 1873 which Bismarck favored (see KULTURKAMPF) and which created so much bitterness that they ultimately had to be repealed. The last serious struggle between emperor and chancellor took place in 1879, when Bismarck's negotiations of an alliance with Austria-Hungary appeared to William as a betrayal of the old friendship between Prussia and Russia. Though William's influence on Bismarck's policy between 1862 and 1888 was not very great, the nature of the king imposed certain restraints on the chancellor, compelling him to follow less subjective tactics than Bismarck might have liked. William's modesty and tactfulness were of great service in winning the cooperation of princes and people for the new empire, and also in its international relations. In 1878 two attempts on his life were made, which Bismarck used as justification for an antisocialist law, though neither would-be assassin was a member of the Socialist Party.

See also BISMARCK, PRINCE OTTO (EDUARD LEOPOLD) VON; GERMANY—26. *The North German Confederation and the German Empire, 1866–1918.*

Further Reading: Stern, Fritz P., *Gold and Iron: Bismarck, Bleishroder, and the Building of the German Empire* (Random 1979).

WILLIAM II (FRIEDRICH WILHELM VIKTOR ALBERT): b. Potsdam, Germany, Jan. 27, 1859; d. Doorn, the Netherlands, June 4, 1941. He was the son of the crown prince, Frederick William (later Emperor Frederick III), and his

William II

Culver Service

wife Victoria, a daughter of Queen Victoria of Great Britain. At his birth he suffered an injury that slightly crippled his left arm. He received his education under the tutorship of a narrowly sectarian religious teacher, but also attended the gymnasium in Kassel and Bonn University. His character and manners, however, were more permanently shaped by the Guards officers after he entered the army in 1880 and became colonel of the Guard Hussars in 1885. His parents, both of whom held liberal convictions and were critical of Prince Otto von Bismarck (q.v.) as chancellor, failed to instill their political views in the prince who, from his youth, embraced the divine right concept of kingship. In 1881 he married Augusta Victoria of Schleswig-Holstein-Sonderburg-Augustenburg, who bore him six sons and one daughter.

William II came to the throne on June 15, 1888, practically the successor of his grandfather, William I, since his father, already deathly ill when he became emperor, ruled for only 99 days. The young emperor was of about the same age as his illustrious ancestor Frederick the Great when the latter became king in 1740. The Prussian kings of the 19th century had contented themselves with ruling through their ministers. However, William II felt that the personal regime of a former century could be restored. His autocratic ambitions lay behind his dismissal of Bismarck in March 1890, though ostensibly the conflict concerned the wish of the emperor to end the repressive policy that Bismarck had conducted against the working class.

William II attempted to persuade the world as well as himself that he ruled Germany. In fact, he was quite unequal to the task. Ministers like Bernhard von Bülow (q.v.) and Friedrich von Holstein did the actual governing, while even in the matter of choosing his ministers and advisers the emperor proved to be a poor judge of men. As a divine rightist, he did not tolerate criticism, though his impulsive actions and aggressive speeches endangered Germany both at home and abroad. However, after one particularly unfortunate press interview held by the emperor on German and British naval armament, the Reichstag in 1908 insisted he seek his chancellor's advice on all important political matters.

In the field of foreign affairs, the dismissal of Bismarck led to the weakening of Russo-German friendship. William allowed the Russo-German Reinsurance Treaty, central to Bismarck's policy, to lapse in 1890. When Germany in the same year concluded a treaty with Britain by which Helgoland was ceded to Germany in exchange for the island of Zanzibar in East Africa, Russia countered by concluding a defensive military alliance with the French Republic in 1893. The emperor's attempts to restore friendly relations with Russia by personal diplomacy, as in the case of the so-called Treaty of Björkö (1905), could not succeed while he was at the same time following an expansionist policy in the Middle East, an area of particular concern to Russia. Similarly, his efforts to win English friendship by the occasional display of personal amiability toward England were equally unavailing since he permitted Admiral Alfred von Tirpitz to build up a navy large enough to threaten Britain's control of the seas. To maintain the balance of power in Europe, England was forced to conclude the Anglo-French Entente of 1904 and an entente with Russia in 1907.

In the diplomatic crisis of July 1914, following the assassination of Archduke Francis Ferdinand, William II first encouraged Austria to take stern action against Serbia, then wavered as he realized there was danger of a European war; nevertheless, he failed to accept methods of diplomatic negotiation which might have prevented the outbreak of World War I. During the war the emperor moved from the center of the stage, though he did not support those civilian advisers who, like the chancellor, Theobald von Bethmann-Hollweg, attempted to moderate German war policies. He approved the policy of unlimited submarine warfare in March 1917, which brought the United States into the war, and on the insistence of generals Paul von Hindenburg and Erich Ludendorff he replaced Bethmann-Hollweg in July 1917. For the next 14 months the two generals were the virtual dictators of Germany. William II followed their advice again when he appointed, in early October, Prince Max of Baden as chancellor. The latter proposed to introduce parliamentary government and to negotiate an armistice and a peace with the Allied powers on the basis of President Woodrow Wilson's Fourteen Points. The sudden admission that the war could not be won by military means, which was implied in the German demand for an armistice on October 5, 1918, made the exhausted people wish for immediate termination of hostilities. When it appeared from President Wilson's notes that the Allied powers would not accept William II as a partner in peace negotiations, his abdication was demanded. The whole monarchical system was now in jeopardy. Prince Max took it upon himself to announce the emperor's abdication on November 9, but could not stop the revolution. On the same day Field Marshal von Hindenburg informed William II that the army would not fight for his throne and advised him to take refuge in the Netherlands. He arrived there on November 10, living at first at Amerongen, then on his own estate at Doorn. The plan of the Allied powers to place William II on trial as author of World War I, embodied in Article 232 of the Versailles Treaty, was frustrated by the refusal of the Dutch government in 1920 to extradite him. A year after the death of his wife in 1921, he married the widowed Princess Hermine of Schönaich-Carolath.

See also GERMANY—26. *The North German Confederation and the German Empire, 1866–1918.*

HAJO HOLBORN,
Yale University.

Bibliography

Balfour, Michael, *The Kaiser and His Times* (Norton 1972).
Cowles, Virginia, *The Kaiser* (Harper 1964).
Durr, Volker, and others, eds., *Imperial Germany*, vol. 3 (Univ. of Wis. Press 1986).
Fischer, Fritz, *From Kaiserreich to Third Reich: Elements of Continuity in German History, 1871–1945*, tr. by Roger Fletcher (Allen & Unwin 1986).
Hull, Isabel V., *The Entourage of Kaiser Wilhelm II, 1888–1918* (Cambridge 1982).
Ludwig, Emil, *Wilhelm Hohenzollern: The Last of the Kaisers* (1927; reprint, AMS Press 1970).
Rohl, John, and Sombart, Nicolaus, eds., *Kaiser Wilhelm II—New Interpretations: The Corfu Papers* (Cambridge 1982).
Viktoria Luise, *The Kaiser's Daughter: Memoirs of H. R. H. Viktoria Luise, Princess of Prussia* (Prentice-Hall 1977).
Wilhelm II, *The Kaiser's Memoirs, 1888–1918* (1922; reprint, Fertig 1977).
Whittle, Tyler, *The Last Kaiser: A Biography of Wilhelm II, German Emperor and King of Prussia* (Quadrangle Bks. 1977).

WILLIAM (Du. **WILLEM**), the name of five stadholders and three kings of the Netherlands. The stadholders also had the titles of counts of Nassau and princes of Orange. For general background on the periods covered, see also NETHERLANDS, KINGDOM OF THE—*History*.

STADHOLDERS

WILLIAM I (called **THE SILENT**): b. Dillenburg, Germany, April 24, 1533; d. Delft, the Netherlands, July 10, 1584. Founder of the independent Dutch Republic, William was one of the supreme figures in the history both of the Low Countries and of Europe in the 16th century. He embodied the strengths and virtues of the great nobility, yet became a revered leader of the common people. Born a German, he was French by language and culture, made the Netherlands his residence and spiritual home, but remained always a European in interest and feeling. Though mediocre as a general, he was a master of statecraft. To his devotion and judgment, the modern Dutch state ultimately owes its existence.

The eldest son of Count William of Nassau and Countess Juliana of Stolberg-Wernigerode, he was raised as a Protestant until 1544, when Emperor Charles V required that he become a Catholic and reside in the Low Countries in order to inherit the possessions of his cousin René de Chalon; William also inherited René's principality of Orange, a sovereign enclave in southern France, so that he and his descendants were thereafter known as princes of Orange.

At the court of the regent of the Netherlands, Mary of Hungary, William emerged as a Catholic of the Erasmian type, committed to piety rather than doctrine and reluctant to command faith by the sword. At this time he was wholly the great nobleman, the wealthiest in the Low Countries and the favorite of Charles V, who entrusted him with supreme military command in operations against France in 1555. Charles' son and successor, Philip II, at first continued William in the same honor, naming him to the Order of the Golden Fleece and a member of the Council of State in 1555, a deputy to the peace negotiations concluded at Cateau-Cambrésis in 1559, and stadholder (lieutenant) in Holland, Zeeland, Utrecht, and Franche-Comté the same year.

Soon, however, Philip's attempt to rule in the Low Countries as he did in Spain led to William's estrangement and then finally to rebellion. The prince of Orange envisioned the government of the Netherlands as one based on collaboration between the sovereign, the great nobles, and the provincial "States" (representative assemblies); hence he opposed more and more openly and energetically Philip's policy of absolutism and centralization, as his hopes for a compromise were wrecked by the king's intransigence. His careful secrecy in this period won him the sobriquet of "Silent," although he was usually anything but taciturn.

In 1566 William, though not a direct participant, was closely linked with his brother Louis of Nassau to the quasi rebellion of the lesser nobility known as the Gueux (Beggars). The next year, when the duke of Alva brought a Spanish army to the Low Countries and began to rule by virtual military dictatorship, William withdrew to his castle at Dillenburg and began to organize armed resistance to what he saw as Spanish tyranny. In the spring of 1568, having been branded as an outlaw by Alva, he crossed the borders of the Netherlands with an army largely paid for by German Protestant princes, but was defeated. Thereafter, he placed his main reliance on indigenous forces of resistance, notably the Calvinists, the "Sea Beggars" (Dutch seamen who fought the Spaniards as privateers), and the bulk of the business community.

In 1572 William tried to back the Sea Beggars' capture of the port of Brielle by attacking the Spaniards who were besieging Mons. When he failed, he withdrew to Holland, where the Sea Beggars and Calvinists seized the governments of many towns. The States of Holland, Zeeland, and Utrecht acknowledged William as their stadholder, and thereafter it was by virtue of their authority that he commanded the forces of rebellion against Spain and governed within the emerging independent state. In 1573 he became a member of the Reformed (Calvinist) Church, but remained an Erasmian in spirit.

William's basic aim continued to be the independence of all 17 provinces of the Low Countries, and for a period (1576–1578) his policy of political unity and religious compromise, embodied in the Pacification of Ghent (1576), seemed hopeful of success. The arrival of Alessandro Farnese, duke of Parma, as Philip's new commander, confronted William at last with an opponent of equal political mastery and far greater generalship. William reluctantly accepted the Union of Utrecht (Jan. 23, 1579), an alliance of the five (later seven) northern provinces where the rebels continued to hold out, though it represented the collapse of his hopes for an all-inclusive "Greater Netherlands" because three of the southern provinces in allegiance to Philip had formed the nearly simultaneous Union of Arras.

In 1580 Philip again outlawed William, promising wealth and noble rank to a successful assassin. William survived a first attack in 1582, but two years later he was ambushed and shot in his home in Delft by Balthasar Gérard. His death halted plans to make him hereditary count of Holland and Zeeland.

Bibliography

Burnchurch, R., *An Outline of Dutch History* (Heinman 1982).

Geyle, Pieter, *The Revolt of the Netherlands, 1555–1609*, 2d ed. (B&N Imports 1980).

Harrison, Frederick, *William the Silent* (1897; reprint, Associated Faculty Press 1970).

Hibben, C. C., *Gouda in Revolt: Particularism and Pacifism in the Revolt of the Netherlands, 1572–1588* (Benjamins N. Am. 1983).

Parker, Geoffrey, *Spain and the Netherlands, 1559–1659* (Enslow Pub. 1979).

Wedgwood, Cicely V., *William the Silent: William of Nassau, Prince of Orange, 1533–1584* (Norton 1968).

WILLIAM II: b. The Hague, the Netherlands, May 27, 1626; d. there, Nov. 6, 1650. The son of Frederick Henry (a younger son of William the Silent), who became stadholder in 1625, and of Amalia van Solms, a German-born noblewoman, he was raised from boyhood as the future leader of the Dutch Republic. His marriage (1641) to Mary, daughter of Charles I of England, established the fateful alliance of the Orange and Stuart dynasties. During his father's lifetime, William was elected to follow him in his offices. Becoming stadholder and captain general on Frederick Henry's death in 1647, he endeavored vainly to prevent the conclusion of peace with Spain. Although the Treaty of Münster (Peace of Westphalia, 1648) recognized the independence of the Dutch Republic, William hoped to gain all of the Low Countries and hence sought renewal of the war in alliance with France. The Province of Holland opposed this policy, however, wishing to reduce its immense burden of debt inherited from the war of independence. Amsterdam in particular was hostile to territorial aggrandizement in the southern Netherlands, fearing that if Antwerp, its arch rival, came under Dutch sovereignty, it would no longer be possible to maintain Antwerp's exclusion from seaborne trade. The effort of the Province of Holland to reduce the military forces in its pay, despite a contrary ruling by the stadholder and the States-General, led to a near civil war in 1650. William arrested leaders of the hostile faction in Holland and briefly besieged Amsterdam. A compromise settlement gave him most of the advantage. Shortly thereafter, before he could consolidate his expanded powers, he died of smallpox.

WILLIAM III. See WILLIAM (kings of England)—*William III*.

WILLIAM IV (CHARLES HENRY FRISO): b. Leeuwarden, the Netherlands, Sept. 1, 1711; d. The Hague, Oct. 22, 1751. An offspring of the cadet (Nassau-Dietz) line of the house of Orange, he was born posthumously and was named immediately to the stadholderate of Friesland, which his father, John William

Friso, had held. Over a period of years he was elected to the stadholderate of the other provinces, which had been vacant since the death of William III in 1702. Groningen, Gelderland, and Drenthe chose him while he was still a child, but Holland, Zeeland, and Utrecht did so only under the pressure of popular rioting after the disaster of the French invasion of 1747. His stadholderate and captain generalcy were declared hereditary in his family in both the male and female lines. These successes were due not to his personal gift (he lacked both intelligence and drive), but to the prestige of the house of Orange, to which the people continued to be devoted.

William V: b. The Hague, the Netherlands, March 8, 1748; d. Brunswick, Germany, April 9, 1806. The son of William IV, he followed his father in his offices in 1751 but assumed the duties of government only in 1766, on reaching his majority. He was jealous of the honor and prerogatives of his house but was ineffectual in their defense and in the government of the republic. He broke with the century-old English orientation of the house of Orange, preferring the friendship of Prussia, to which he was allied by marriage.

Dutch defeats during the war against Great Britain as an ally of the Americans in the Revolution produced mounting dissatisfaction, led by the pro-French party of the "Patriots," which demanded constitutional reform. In 1784 William left The Hague to live outside the turbulent Province of Holland but was re-established in his full powers three years later by Prussian armed intervention. The invasion of the French revolutionary armies in 1794–1795 led to his flight (Jan. 18, 1795) to England, where he asserted that he retained his authority as stadholder and approved English occupation of the Dutch colonies. He supported the unsuccessful Anglo-Russian invasion of Holland in 1799, but thereafter lost hope, and in 1801 permitted his followers to accept offices in the French-sponsored Batavian Republic.

KINGS

William I (Willem Frederik): b. The Hague, the Netherlands, Aug. 24, 1772; d. Berlin, Germany, Dec. 12, 1843. Eldest son of the stadholder William V, he commanded the Dutch armies in the war against revolutionary France from 1793 to 1795, when he fled to England with his father. More vigorous and purposeful than William V, he endeavored to achieve a restoration, first with Prussian and then with Anglo-Russian help; during the Anglo-Russian landings of 1799, he sought conciliation with the anti-Orange "Patriots." William changed his place of residence to Berlin and came briefly to terms with Napoleon, receiving Fulda as a principality; but he would not join the Confederation of the Rhine and was thenceforth treated by Napoleon as an enemy. Captured at Jena in 1806 while serving as a Prussian general, he was paroled and joined the Austrian service in 1809.

With the debacle of French power after 1812, William received an invitation (Nov. 21, 1813) from Dutch rebels against Napoleon to take the lead in the national war, and he landed at Scheveningen, near The Hague, on November 30. Sentiment ran strongly in favor of a constitutional monarchy, and he took the title of sovereign prince on December 2, promising a constitution. By the first Treaty of Paris (1814) he obtained the unification, in a single state, of the northern Netherlands (former Dutch Republic) and the southern Netherlands (former Austrian Netherlands). On March 16, 1815, he took the title of king of the Netherlands in order to consolidate the re-established unity of the Low Countries.

William's government was marked by the spirit of "enlightened despotism" rather than constitutional monarchy. He encouraged the commercial and industrial reorganization of the country, notably by the formation of the Netherlands Trading Company (Nederlandsche Handel-maatschappij), to which he contributed both funds and leadership. He also retained and made effective use of the centralized administration of government introduced by Napoleon. The domination of the northern provinces and William's attempt to make all the churches arms of the state led to the revolt of 1830 in the southern provinces. He balked at accepting the independence of Belgium until 1839 and retained eastern Luxembourg as a grand duchy in his own name.

Despite the proclamation of a new, more liberal constitution in 1840, he continued his autocratic habit of government. Increasing popular discontent caused him to abdicate on Oct. 7, 1840, in favor of his son, William II. He took up residence in Silesia but retained his ties with his homeland. In 1843 he sent a gift of 10,000,000 guilders to the Dutch treasury to tide it over fiscal difficulties.

William II (Willem Frederik George Lodewijk): b. The Hague, the Netherlands, Dec. 6, 1792; d. Tilburg, March 17, 1849. The son of William I, he was trained in Prussia for military command and served the 1st duke of Wellington as an adjutant (1811–1813) during the Peninsular Campaign. He then commanded the Dutch Army in the war of liberation against Napoleon and at the battles of Quatre-Bras and Waterloo (1815). As crown prince, he supported the liberal opposition to his father's autocratic policy, even resigning his army command in 1817. He led the Dutch troops opposing the Belgian revolution of 1830 but used force reluctantly and sought a compromise, to his father's indignation. Becoming king after the abdication of William I in 1840, he was not content to reign without ruling, and consequently broke with the liberals; but he accepted reform of the constitution in March 1848 under the impact of revolutionary events abroad.

William III (Willem Alexander Paul Frederik Lodewijk): b. Brussels (present Belgium), Feb. 19, 1817; d. Het Loo, near Apeldoorn, the Netherlands, Nov. 23, 1890. The son of William II, he ascended the throne on March 17, 1849. Primarily a soldier in his interests, he found it difficult to adapt himself to the system of full-fledged parliamentary government introduced by the Constitution of 1848. In foreign affairs, he supported Napoleon III of France against the rising power of Prussia. His proposal in 1867 to cede the grand duchy of Luxembourg to France aroused furious German resistance and had to be dropped. During his final illness (1889–1890) the regency was held by Queen Emma, his second wife, mother of his daughter and successor Wilhelmina.

Herbert H. Rowen,
Associate Professor of History, The University of Wisconsin-Milwaukee.

WILLIAM I (called THE LION), king of Scotland: b. 1143; d. Stirling, Scotland, Dec. 4, 1214. He was the second son of Henry, earl of Northumberland and Carlisle, heir of David I. He succeeded his older brother, Malcolm IV, to the throne of Scotland in December 1165. His reign is important in the history of Scottish-English relations, the Scottish Church, and the growth of towns.

After an unsuccessful attempt to persuade Henry II of England to cede Northumberland and Cumberland, which Malcolm IV had lost in 1157, William made a treaty with Louis VII of France. This agreement was the forerunner of the Auld Alliance between Scotland and France. In 1173 Henry's sons rebelled and offered William the earldom of Northumberland in exchange for his support. Invading England the next year, he was captured at Alnwick, taken to Normandy, and forced to accept the Treaty of Falaise in exchange for his release. He thereby recognized Henry II as suzerain over Scotland and his own vassals, and also the superiority of the English archbishops over the Church of Scotland.

During the next 15 years, William or his advisers showed considerable skill in working for the restoration of Scottish independence in church and state. He founded (1178) a great abbey at Arbroath dedicated to St. Thomas à Becket, for whose martyrdom Henry II had been responsible. His bishops refused to recognize the control of the English archbishops and, in spite of a quarrel between William and the papacy over the appointment of a bishop of St. Andrews, they obtained from Clement III in 1192 a bull declaring the Scottish Church to have no superior but the pope. The next year, Henry's successor, Richard I, cancelled the Treaty of Falaise in return for 10,000 marks to finance his Crusade, and restored Scottish political independence by the Treaty of Canterbury. William had a number of disagreements with John of England, Richard's successor, but avoided war. His reign of 49 years was the longest in Scottish medieval history and was marked by the grant of charters founding many of the most important burghs.

William married in 1186 Ermengarde de Beaumont, a cousin of the English king; his son, the future Alexander II, who succeeded him, was born in 1198. He also had two daughters, Margaret and Isabella, both of whom married English noblemen. There are indications that William's epithet "the Lion" was due to his appearance and character in youth. It was not until his son's reign that the lion became the heraldic symbol of Scottish kingship.

J. M. REID,
Author of "Scotland, Past and Present."

WILLIAM, kings of Sicily:

WILLIAM I (called THE BAD): b. about 1120; d. May 7, 1166. Son of Roger II of Sicily, he succeeded to power in 1154 and continued his father's policy of excluding the barons from the government and curbing the independence of the towns. For this reason he was called "the Bad," although he was a ruler of great merit.

The existence of a strong Sicilian kingdom that included southern Italy inspired the hostility of the Holy Roman emperor, Frederick I (Barbarossa); the Byzantine emperor, Manuel I Comnenus; and the pope, Adrian IV. With the aid of his able minister, Maione, William won a series of victories over his internal and external enemies. Repulsing a Byzantine invasion and suppressing a rebellion of the Sicilian nobles in 1156, he forced Adrian to recognize him as king. He then united with the papacy in opposing the extension of Frederick's power in Italy and was instrumental in obtaining the election of Pope Alexander III (1159). A second victory over the Greeks had induced Manuel to make peace, but loss of Sicily's African possessions and the murder of Maione (1160) by a conspiracy of the nobles were serious setbacks. For a time, the king himself was imprisoned by the barons, but with popular support he quelled the revolt and was thereafter free to pursue his Italian policy to a successful conclusion with the installation of Alexander III in the Lateran (1165).

WILLIAM II (called THE GOOD): b. 1153 or 1154; d. 1189. He succeeded his father, William I, in 1166 at the age of 13. On reaching his majority, he at first followed his predecessor's policy of containing the ambitions of the Holy Roman emperor, and formed an alliance with the pope and the Lombard League against Frederick I (Barbarossa). In 1177 he married Joan, daughter of Henry II of England.

William's attempt to establish Sicilian hegemony in the eastern Mediterranean had serious consequences for the Norman kingdom. To free himself for a war against the Byzantine Empire, he made peace with Frederick I in 1186 by agreeing to the marriage of his aunt and heiress, Constance, with the Roman emperor's son, the future Henry VI. Thus he established the claim of the Hohenstaufen dynasty to the throne of Sicily. The campaign against Constantinople was unsuccessful. William's death prevented him from taking part in the Third Crusade, for which he had cleared the eastern Mediterranean in 1188 by repulsing the fleet of the sultan Saladin off Tripoli.

WILLIAM (Ger. WILHELM), name of two kings of Württemberg:

WILLIAM I: b. Lüben, Silesia, Sept. 27, 1781; d. Stuttgart, Württemberg, June 25, 1864. Son of Frederick I of Württemberg, he succeeded his father in 1816, having participated in the Napoleonic Wars, first on the side of the emperor (1812), then in support of the Allies (1814–1815). He began his reign by instituting a liberal constitution in 1819, which won him great popularity in Germany, and worked for the unification of Germany, defending the rights of the smaller states against Prussia. In 1828–1830 he helped establish the Zollverein (q.v.), but the increasing threat of Prussian domination led him to oppose the unification plans set forth by the Frankfurt Assembly in 1848–1849. Dismissing the liberal ministry that disagreed with his German policy, he had the constitutional reforms of 1848–1849 revoked and the code of 1819 re-established.

WILLIAM II: b. Stuttgart, Württemberg, Feb. 25, 1848; d. Schloss Bebenhausen, Germany, Oct. 2, 1921. Son of Prince Frederick of Württemberg, he succeeded his uncle Charles I to the throne in 1891, the kingdom having become part of the German Empire in 1871. He fought on the side of Austria against Prussia in 1866 and on the side of Germany against France in 1870–1871. Obliged to abdicate in 1918, he took the title of duke of Württemberg.

COLONIAL WILLIAMSBURG

The Wren Building, College of William and Mary, built in 1697 and restored as part of Colonial Williamsburg.

WILLIAM (full name FRIEDRICH WILHELM VIKTOR AUGUST ERNST), crown prince of Germany and eldest son of William II, emperor of Germany; b. Potsdam, Germany, May 6, 1882; d. Hechingen, July 20, 1951. He had the customary military training of a German prince and attended the University of Bonn. Before his marriage in 1905 his escapades were notorious, but after his alliance with Cecilie Auguste Marie of Mecklenburg-Schwerin, he and his wife became popular social leaders and influential in public affairs. William was often opposed to the kaiser. However, when World War I broke out he supported his father and was given a position on the general staff with the rank of lieutenant general. In a purely nominal command of the Fifth Army on the western front, he failed to capture Verdun in 1916. After his father's abdication (1918), he renounced the succession and followed him into exile in Holland.

Allowed to return to his native land in 1923, he took up the cause of Adolf Hitler and joined the Nazi motor corps. Although he was not allowed to enlist in the army in 1939, three of his sons did so. At the end of World War II he was captured by the French but allowed to return to a villa in Hechingen. His second son, Louis Ferdinand, became head of the Hohenzollern family, the eldest son, Wilhelm, having been killed in World War II.

WILLIAM IX (Fr. GUILLAUME), DUKE OF AQUITAINE and COUNT OF POITIERS: b. 1071; d. 1127. He was the earliest of the troubadours. At the age of 15 he became head of one of the most powerful states of feudal France. In 1101 he was one of the leaders of a minor Crusade which ended in disaster. He was equally unsuccessful in his protracted attempt to take over the county of Toulouse. Nor did he distinguish himself as a husband: his first marriage lasted only two years, and his second wife became a nun.

William was of a gay, boisterous nature and prone to entertain his friends with tales of his amorous escapades. Some of these tales he turned into songs. They are written with a great deal of verve and zest, but the humor is at times coarse. His principal title to fame is a group of four songs which contain several of the conceits and expressions later associated with what was to be called courtly love. Especially significant is William's use of the masculine *mi dons* (my lord) in addressing his beloved, since this established her as his liege, whom he was obligated to serve and obey. *Mi dons* constitutes the first linguistic appearance of what is now expressed by "putting Woman on a pedestal." William wrote in the literary language of southern France, usually termed Provençal. The following lines will give some idea of William's poetry (*Song* X, 13–19):

La nostr' amor vai enaissi
Com la branca de l'albespi
Qu'esta sobre l'arbre en treman,
La nuoit, a la ploja ez al gel,
Tro l'endeman, que·l sols s'espan
Pel las fueillas verz el ramel.

(Our love is like
The hawthorn branch
Which shivers at night
In the rain and the cold,
Till the morning sun
Shines on its green foliage.)

The famous Eleanor of Aquitaine was William's granddaughter.

See also PROVENÇAL LITERATURE.

ALFRED FOULET
Princeton University

WILLIAM AND MARY, College of, an accredited, state-supported, coeducational institution located in Williamsburg, Va. The second oldest college in the United States, it was established by royal charter in 1693 after two attempts by Virginia to found a college had failed (1618 and 1661). The Reverend James Blair, who had been commissioned to obtain the charter, became its first president. Lands, tax funds, and other income were assigned for its use, and in 1694 the College of Heralds in London granted it a coat of arms. The main building, named for Sir Christopher Wren, was completed in 1697 and rebuilt with much of the original walls after fires in 1705 and 1859. Brafferton Building, built as an Indian school from funds bequeathed by the scientist Robert Boyle, was finished in 1723, and the foundation of the President's House was laid in 1732. These three colonial structures were restored between 1928 and 1932 through donations by John D. Rockefeller, Jr.

The honor system in American colleges and Phi Beta Kappa began at William and Mary in 1776. Under Thomas Jefferson's guidance in 1779, the college became a university, discontinuing its grammar and divinity schools and establishing schools of law, medicine, and modern languages, the first such departments in the United States. The elective system of study was introduced at this time.

During the Revolutionary War, British, French, and American troops occupied the college and it lost a large part of its endowment and lands. Under the presidency of Thomas Roderick Drew it grew in stature, but suffered damage in the Civil War and was forced to close in 1881 because of financial difficulties. In 1888, however, it resumed operation with an annual appropriation from the legislature of Virginia, and in 1906 it became part of the state educational system. Coeducation was introduced in 1918.

The General Assembly of Virginia, at the 1960 session, established "The Colleges of William and Mary," providing for an expanded board of visitors and the appointment of a chancellor. This system, in addition to the original College of William and Mary in Virginia, comprises the Richmond Professional Institute, the Norfolk College of William and Mary, the Christopher Newport College (Newport News), and the Richard Bland College (Petersburg), the last two being junior colleges.

William and Mary alumni include three presidents of the United States (Thomas Jefferson, James Monroe, and John Tyler), besides many other persons distinguished in civil and military life, in letters, science, and the church. George Washington, while not an alumnus, held his first and last public offices under the auspices of the college: his license as surveyor of Culpeper County was awarded by the faculty in 1749, and from 1788 until his death in 1799 he was William and Mary's first American chancellor. The annual enrollment averages 3,000 students.

Davis Y. Paschall,
President, The College of William and Mary in Virginia.

WILLIAM AUGUSTUS, wĭl'yəm ô-gŭs'təs, **Duke of Cumberland,** English military commander: b. London, England, April 15, 1721; d. there, Oct. 31, 1765. Third son of George II (then prince of Wales) and Caroline of Brandenburg-Ansbach, he was trained for a naval career but chose the army instead. In the War of the Austrian Succession (1740–1748), the Jacobite Rebellion (1745–1746), and the Seven Years' War (1756–1763), he distinguished himself by his courage but was not a great commander, and his ruthless suppression of the Scottish clans in 1746 won him the epithet of "butcher."

Wounded in the Battle of Dettingen (1743), he was given command of allied forces in the Netherlands the next year as captain general, but lost the Battle of Fontenoy in 1745 to Marshal Maurice de Saxe. After defeating the Jacobite rebels of Prince Charles Edward at Culloden Moor (1746), he returned to the Netherlands, where Saxe again overcame him, at Lauffeld (Val) in 1747. On the outbreak of the Seven Years' War, he was sent to defend Hannover, but after his defeat at Hastenbeck (1757) the king empowered him to make a separate peace. Under pressure from his ministers and allies, however, George II changed his mind and repudiated the convention by which Cumberland had agreed to withdraw from Hannover and disband his army. The duke returned to England in disgrace, resigned from the army, and retired to Windsor. In his last years, he played an important role in English politics, supporting his former enemy, William Pitt, because of their mutual opposition to concluding the war. He also regained much of the popularity that he had lost by oppressing the Scots, and in 1765 was reinstated as captain general by George III.

WILLIAM JEWELL COLLEGE, wĭl'yəm jo͞o'əl, an accredited coeducational, private institution of liberal arts, located in Liberty, Mo., a suburb of Kansas City. Founded in 1849 by the Baptists of Missouri, it was named for a leader in its establishment, donor of $10,000 in lands toward its initial endowment.

The college offers a four-year course leading to the bachelor of arts degree only. Some work is given in teacher training and the preparation of physical education personnel. The college grants scholarships with special aid to students dedicated to full-time Christian service.

The campus, covering 106 acres, includes two dormitories for men and three for women; Jewell Hall, the principal classroom building; Marston Hall, the science building; Gano Chapel; Brown Gymnasium; the Carnegie Library (containing the Charles Haddon Spurgeon Collection); Yates College Union; and a floodlighted concrete sports stadium. The student body numbers about 1,000; the faculty about 60.

Joseph C. Clapp.

WILLIAM OF MALMESBURY, wĭl'yəm, mämz'-bər-e, English historian: b. probably in Somerset, England, 1090/1096; d. Malmesbury Abbey, ?1143. He was educated at the abbey for which he was named and served as its librarian. His chief works are *De gestis regum Anglorum,* a history of the kings of England from 449 to 1127, and its sequel, *Historia novella,* continuing the narration to 1142. In them he emulated the Venerable Bede, attempting to give his material a systematic connection showing causes and effects. *De gestis regum Anglorum* has great literary value as well as historical importance, since William made use of early ballads and interrupted his narrative with tales designed to entertain the reader. He also wrote an ecclesiastical history of England, *De gestis pontificum Anglorum,* and lives of saints.

WILLIAM OF NEWBURGH, wĭl'yəm, nū'bə-rə, English historian: b. Bridlington, Yorkshire, England, 1136; d. 1198/1201. He was educated at the Abbey of Newburgh and is generally believed to have spent his entire life there. His *Historia rerum Anglicarum* (History of English Affairs), covering the period from 1066 to 1198, is highly valuable as a broad-minded, just, and clear picture of the happenings of the times, though his statements are not always accurate. It is one of the chief authorities for the reign of Henry II. Because of his ability to sift the facts and make unbiased judgments without lengthy moralizing or digression, William has been called "the father of historical criticism."

WILLIAM OF OCKHAM. See Ockham, William of.

WILLIAM OF SAINT CARILEF, wĭl'yəm, săɴ' kȧ-rē-lĕf', or **SAINT CALAIS,** săɴ' kä-lĕ', Norman bishop of Durham: d. Windsor, England, Jan. 2, 1096. He entered the monastery for which he was named, rose rapidly in position, and came to the attention of William the Conqueror, who made him bishop of Durham (1081). In this office he was a wise administrator, reformer, and builder, but as chief minister of William II he was an unscrupulous opportunist. He supported the revolt of Bishop Odo of Bayeux against the king, but at his trial for treason he conducted his defense so skillfully that he was allowed to go to Normandy. Pardoned, he returned to his see in 1091 and sided with the king against Anselm, archbishop of Canterbury;

Scene from an open-air performance of *William Tell* at Interlaken, Switzerland. Schiller's poetic drama of Swiss revolt against Austrian rule in the 14th century inspired Rossini's opera *Guillaume Tell*.

Swiss National Tourist Office

at the Council of Rockingham he argued in favor of the king's authority over the bishops, a position that was in complete opposition to that which he had previously taken in his own defense. The cathedral of Durham is his finest achievement: he began its reconstruction in 1093, advancing the work far enough to determine its lasting form.

WILLIAM OF TYRE, wĭl'yəm, tĭr, historian and prelate: b. about 1130; d. 1184/1190. His early life is obscure, but he was probably born in the Latin kingdom of Jerusalem, possibly of French parents, and studied in Europe. He was attached to the chancellory of Amalric I of Jerusalem, whom he served as ambassador. After Amalric's death, he became chancellor of the kingdom of Jerusalem, was made archbishop of Tyre in 1175, and attended the Lateran Council in 1179. His *Historia rerum in partibus transmarinis gestarum*, in 23 books, is the chief source of the history of the Latin kingdom from 1127 to 1184 and one of the principal accounts of the French crusaders from 1095 to 1184. It extends from the preaching of the first crusade by Peter the Hermit and Pope Urban II to the end of 1183 or the beginning of 1184.

WILLIAM OF WIED. See WILLIAM, king of Albania.

WILLIAM OF WYKEHAM or **WICKHAM,** wĭl'yəm, wĭk'əm, English prelate and statesman: b. Wickham, Hampshire, England, 1324; d. Waltham, Hampshire, Sept. 27, 1404. Educated at Winchester, he entered the service of the royal court about 1347 and superintended Edward III's additions to Windsor Castle. Ordained as a priest in 1362, he was consecrated bishop of Winchester in 1367. His advancement in the king's service was equally rapid. Appointed lord privy seal in 1364, he became, in 1367, lord chancellor, an office in which, owing to the senility of Edward III, he was the virtual head of government. Blamed for the military reverses in France and attacked by the anticlerical party led by John of Gaunt, he was driven from office in 1371. In 1376 he was one of the leaders of the Good Parliament in opposition to John of Gaunt's misrule, but the death of the Black Prince, his political ally, exposed him to the vengeance of his powerful adversary, who had him impeached and severely punished. He was pardoned on the ascension of Richard II and, an enlightened patron of learning, he founded New College, Oxford (built 1380–1386) and Winchester College (built 1387–1394), the first of England's public schools. In 1389 he again assumed the duties of the lord chancellorship, in order to guide the young king, who had recently thrown off the tutelage of the lords appellant. Dismayed by Richard's absolutist tendencies, he resigned in 1391. He devoted the remainder of his life to clerical reform and to the complete rebuilding of the nave of Winchester Cathedral in the perpendicular style.

ALLAN M. FRASER.

WILLIAM TELL, wĭl'yəm tĕl', (**WILHELM TELL**), a poetic drama by Johann Christoph Friedrich von Schiller (q.v.), completed and produced in 1804. It immediately became one of the most popular of all German plays and has been frequently revived in the original and in translated versions. Through the colorful legend of William Tell (q.v.) it presents scenes of political oppression, rebellion, and heroic defiance of tyranny.

The play opens with a description of the idyllic Swiss countryside where the action takes place. The peaceful life of the people is shown in dramatic contrast to the cruelty and abuse of their Austrian overlords, and the local patriots of three cantons are eventually roused to open rebellion.

But it is the personal drama of Tell which forces him to participate actively in the uprising to lift the yoke of Austrian oppression. He is a modest huntsman, excelling all others as an oarsman and archer. In the first scene it is he who has the courage and skill to row a peasant safely across the lake during a storm in order to save him from capture by the troopers of Gessler, the viceroy of the Austrian emperor. In Act III, Tell is arrested for failing to salute the viceroy's cap and then ordered by Gessler to shoot an apple from the head of his son Walter. After doing so successfully, he admits that a second arrow, held in readiness, was meant for Gessler himself had he failed. He is taken into custody and ferried across the lake, but a storm rises, the boat is in danger, and Tell is called upon to steer it to safety. He escapes, and later in a mountain pass puts an arrow through Gessler's heart, thus freeing his countrymen from a tyrant and setting off a revolt which brings Swiss independence.

William Tell is an epic drama, somewhat comparable in structure to a Shakespeare chronicle play. It tells the story of one of the earliest European struggles to establish a democratic government. In this panorama of 14th century history, Schiller has made the people as well as their legendary hero important protagonists in the struggle for basic human rights. The patriotic fervor and abhorrence of foreign oppression which Schiller has expressed in this last great drama of his career has had special appeal to German nationalists. There is a timeliness in *William Tell,* moreover, for any people subjected to political and social injustice. It sounds a stirring call to freedom and human dignity.

WILLIAM BRACY.

WILLIAM TELL (GUILLAUME TELL), French opera in four acts by Gioacchino Rossini; libretto, after Johann Christoph Friedrich von Schiller's famous drama *William Tell* (q.v.), by Victor Joseph Étienne de Jouy and Hippolyte Louis Florent Bis. The opera was first performed in Paris on Aug. 3, 1829. Cast: Mathilde (soprano); Hedwig (soprano); Jemmy (soprano); Rudolf (tenor); Arnold (tenor); Ruodi (tenor); William Tell (baritone); Leuthold (bass); Gessler (bass); Walter Fürst (bass); Melchthal (bass). Locale: Switzerland, early 14th century.

Act I.—During a shepherds' festival, William Tell learns that the elderly Melchthal's son Arnold is in love with the Austrian tyrant Gessler's daughter Mathilde, whom Arnold has saved from drowning. Tell convinces Arnold that he must fight for Swiss freedom against Mathilde's father. Leuthold, who has killed an Austrian soldier in defense of his daughter, appears in flight before Gessler's men. Tell saves him by taking him across the stormy Lake of Lucerne by boat. Rudolf, leading the pursuers, sets fire to the fishermen's huts and seizes Melchthal as a hostage.

Act II.—*Scene 1.*—Arnold and Mathilde declare their love and he prepares to abandon the struggle for Swiss freedom. But when Tell and Walter Fürst reveal that Gessler has had Arnold's old father murdered, he joins them in swearing revenge.

Scene 2.—Citizens of the Swiss cantons convene to vow war against the century of Austrian tyranny represented by Gessler.

Act III.—*Scene 1.*—Arnold ceremoniously accepts leadership of the Swiss rebels.

Scene 2.—In honor of a century of Austrian rule, the Swiss are made to bow before the Austrian coat of arms topped by Gessler's hat. When Tell (whom Gessler remembers to be the man who balked the capture of Leuthold) refuses to bow, the tyrant orders him to shoot an apple from his son Jemmy's head. Tell splits the apple with one arrow. When he accidentally drops a second arrow, Gessler demands to know its purpose. Tell replies that it was intended for Gessler if the first arrow struck Jemmy. Despite Mathilde's pleas, Gessler arrests Tell, who quietly sends word to his wife Hedwig to light beacons signaling open revolt.

Act IV.—*Scene 1.*—The grieving Arnold learns of Tell's arrest and exhorts his followers to action.

Scene 2.—Mathilde brings Jemmy to the sorrowing Hedwig, who sets fire to the house as the agreed-upon signal. The escaping Tell arrives, pursued by Gessler—against whom he successfully turns the extra arrow that Jemmy has saved. Arnold appears at the head of the victorious Swiss forces; all join in prayer and in praise of liberty.

Wholly different in musical style from Rossini's comic operas, *William Tell* is magnificent but overlong. It helped set the extravagant, pageantlike manner of French grand opera later developed by Giacomo Meyerbeer. Now seldom produced intact, it is best known by its ever-familiar programmatic overture, Mathilde's aria *Sombre forêt,* and Arnold's aria *Asile héreditaire,* as well as its stirring choruses.

HERBERT WEINSTOCK,
Author of "Music as an Art."

WILLIAM THE CONQUEROR. See WILLIAM (kings of England)—*William I.*

WILLIAM THE LION. See WILLIAM I, king of Scotland.

WILLIAM THE SILENT. See WILLIAM (stadholders and kings of the Netherlands)—*Stadholders* (William I).

WILLIAMS, wĭl'yəmz, **Ben Ames,** American writer: b. Macon, Miss., March 7, 1889; d. Brookline, Mass., Feb. 4, 1953. A highly productive and fluent writer, he produced more than 35 novels and 400 short stories, gaining popular distinction in the fields of historical and detective fiction and for his novels of character set in New England.

Williams spent his early boyhood in Ohio. After a year in Cardiff, Wales, where his father was the United States consul, he entered Dartmouth College, graduating in 1910. He then became a reporter for the Boston *American* and for the next six years combined newspaper work with short story writing. He married in 1912, eventually settling in Maine.

After publishing his first book, *All the Brothers Were Valiant,* in 1919, he turned to novel writing. Touching on a variety of themes, his fiction displays a mastery of storytelling techniques and reveals a careful concern for accuracy in transcribing past and contemporary events and scenes. *Splendor* (1927) is an authentic study of American life between the early post-Civil War years and World War I. *Evered* (1921) and *Immortal Longings* (1927) reflect Williams' recurring interest in New England life. His bent for detective fiction is evidenced in *Death on Scurvy Street* (1929) and *An End to Mirth* (1931), while *Black Pawl* (1922) and *Honeyflow* (1932) are primarily character studies. Broadening his interests to include the full canvas of American history, he wrote *Thread of Scarlet* (1939) and *Come Spring* (1940). His best and most popular work is *House Divided* (1947), which interpreted the effect of the Civil War on the lives of five major characters representing traditional southern attitudes. Its sequel, *The Unconquered,* was published posthumously in 1953.

WILLIAMS, Edward (bardic name IOLO MORGANWG), Welsh poet and Celtic scholar: b. Llancarfan, Glamorganshire, Wales, March 10, 1747; d. Flemingston, Dec. 18, 1826. Though he earned his living by turns as a mason, a bookseller, and a land surveyor, his chief interest lay in collecting ancient Welsh manuscripts. With Owen Jones and William Owen Pughe, he edited the *Myvyrian Archaiology* (1801–1807). Some of the best of his own poetry was published until the title *Poems, Lyric and Pastoral* (2 vols., 1794). He was a friend of the English poet, Robert Southey (1774–1843). Williams played an important part in the controversy over the bardic traditions of Glamorgan, a system which he believed to stem from the prehistoric age of the Druids, but which scholars have since determined to be a more recent development. The *Iolo Manuscripts,* a major collection of the old Celtic manuscripts found by him, was published in 1848, long after his own death and a year after the death of his son, Taliesin Williams (1787–1847), who edited much of the material.

WILLIAMS, Eleazar, American missionary to the Indians: b. probably Caughnawaga, Canada, about 1789; d. Hogansburg, N.Y., Aug. 28, 1858. The half-breed son of Thomas Williams, a St. Regis Indian chief, he received an education while living with relatives in Longmeadow, Mass., and served in the War of 1812 as a United States scout in northern New York and Canada. After the war he became a Protestant Episcopal lay reader, labored among the Oneida Indians of New York, translated the Book of Common Prayer into the Iroquois language, and in 1821 led a group of Oneida chiefs to the Green Bay region of Wisconsin, with some idea of establishing an Indian empire in that region. With the endorsement of the church, he began a school there, but eventually lost the favor of the Indians, apparently because of his vanity, instability, and other failings of character. He is chiefly remembered for representing himself to be the "lost dauphin," heir to the throne of France, a claim which he is not known to have made until he was over 50 years of age. According to his story, he was the son of Louis XVI and Marie Antoinette, kidnapped and brought to the United States as a baby. This account, which has never had any substantiation, became a subject of serious controversy after the publication by an Episcopal minister of a favorably disposed article in *Putnam's Magazine* in 1853. He is credited with simplifying the writing of the Mohawk language.

WILLIAMS, Emlyn, British actor, director, and playwright: b. Mostyn, Flintshire, Wales, Nov. 26, 1905; d. London, Sept. 25, 1987. Of working-class parents, he spoke only Welsh until age eight but eventually became fluent in five languages. He attended the Holywell County School and later, on scholarships, studied at St. Julien in Switzerland and at Christ Church College, Oxford. He first played on the London stage in 1927, but fame eluded him until 1931, when he appeared as Lord Lebanon in Edgar Wallace's *The Case of the Frightened Lady.* He had already written and acted in several of his own plays when the first of his two most famous theater pieces, *Night Must Fall,* was produced in 1935. In it he created the central role of a psychopathic murderer, repeating it the following year in New York. This success was eclipsed by that of *The Corn Is Green,* which ran for nearly two years in London from the fall of 1938. It drew on the author's experiences as a Welsh miner's son, unusually gifted but hardly aware of the world beyond Wales, given an opportunity for self-development through the dedication and harsh discipline of a schoolteacher. Williams played the autobiographical role in the London production. In New York, *The Corn Is Green* won the New York Drama Critics Circle Award as the best foreign play of the 1940–1941 season and drew from Ethel Barrymore one of her most memorable performances in the role of the teacher.

Between his two triumphs in London, Williams played in several Ibsen and Shakespeare productions of the Old Vic Company. He toured extensively with his own plays during World War II, scored again in the leading role of Lillian Hellman's *Montserrat* in New York in 1949, and during the 1950's devoted much of his time to unusual one-man theatrical ventures in which he impersonated Charles Dickens reading from his own works and Dylan Thomas as a youth. Williams also directed numerous plays and acted in motion pictures, winning much praise for his performances in *The Stars Look Down* and *Major Barbara* in 1941. In 1949 he wrote, co-directed, and acted in *The Last Days of Dolwyn,* a film dealing with the slow death of a Welsh mining community.

WILLIAMS, Ephraim, American colonial soldier: b. Newton, Mass., March 7, 1714; d. near Lake George, N.Y., Sept. 8, 1755. In early life he was a sailor, but in King George's War between Britain and France (1744–1748), he served as captain of a company of New England soldiers in Canada. He received from Massachusetts, in return for his services, a grant of 200 acres of land in what was later the township of Adams and Williamstown in Berkshire County, and was made commander of all the frontier posts west of the Connecticut River.

When hostilities broke out afresh (the French and Indian War, 1754–1763), Williams, then a colonel, was ordered to join the New York forces under Sir William Johnson, who, in late summer of 1755, marched northward from Albany with a large body of men to engage the French advance force under Gen. Ludwig August Dieskau. In the vicinity of Lake George, the whole party was entrapped in an ambuscade of French and Indians. Though the battle eventually went to the British, Williams was mortally wounded early in the action. While in camp at Albany, he had made his will, bequeathing his property for the establishment of a free school in Massachusetts. This school was to become Williams College (q.v.). In 1854, the alumni of Williams erected a monument to his memory on the spot where he was supposed to have fallen.

WILLIAMS, G(erhard) Mennen, American public official and six-term governor of Michigan: b. Detroit, Mich., Feb. 23, 1911; d. Detroit, Feb. 2, 1988. He was the grandson, on his mother's side, of the soap manufacturer Gerhard Mennen, to whom he owed his given names and his nickname "Soapy." He earned a bachelor of arts degree (1933) at the School of Public and International Affairs of Princeton University, and a law degree (1936) at the University of Michigan, both with high honors. He was an attorney for the Social Security Board in Washington in 1936–1937 and assistant attorney general of Michigan from 1937 to 1939, under Gov. Frank Murphy. After Murphy had become United States attorney general, Williams served as his executive assistant. During World War II, he was an air combat intelligence officer on various naval aircraft carriers, winning several citations, and after the war he returned to government service in the Office of Price Administration. Early in 1948, with the help of liberal-reform elements in his home state, Williams, an avowed New Deal Democrat, won an uphill battle for his party's gubernatorial nomination, and in November, against even greater odds, he won election as governor of Michigan.

Williams was subsequently reelected five times, serving six consecutive two-year terms, but his program, which called for expanding services in many areas of governmental activity, met much opposition in the legislature, which remained predominantly Republican. Though he accomplished some of his stated goals in such fields as education, housing, and civil rights, the constant struggle between the executive and the legislative branch over tax measures brought Michigan to a financial crisis in the late 1950's. He did not seek reelection in 1960. In President John F. Kennedy's administration, Williams was assistant secretary of state for African affairs (1961–1966). Elected to the Michigan Supreme Court in 1970, he served as chief justice from 1983 until his retirement in December 1986.

WILLIAMS, Sir George, British philanthropist and founder of the Young Men's Christian Association: b. near Dulverton, Somerset, England, Oct. 11, 1821; d. Torquay, Devonshire, Nov. 6, 1905. A farmer's son, he became a zealous church member at about the age of 16, and thereafter was vigorous in his advocacy of the temperate life and in his concern for the religious welfare of others. In 1841 he went to London, where he found work in a dry-goods establishment. In June 1844, in concert with a group of like-minded employees and with the support of many others, he organized the Young Men's Christian Association, which was designed to be "a society for improving the spiritual condition of young men engaged in the drapery and other trades." Largely due to his leadership, the association underwent a rapid development and spread to other countries.

Williams later became a partner in the draper's concern where he had begun employment as a clerk, and was able to give much financial support to the YMCA and to various other societies. He was treasurer of the YMCA for over 20 years from 1863, and he succeeded Lord Shaftesbury (Anthony Ashley Cooper) as its president in 1886. He was knighted in 1894, by which time the organization had more than 5,000 branches throughout the world, including some 2,000 in the United States. See also Young Men's Christian Association.

WILLIAMS, George Henry, American lawyer and politician: b. New Lebanon, N.Y., March 26, 1820; d. Portland, Oreg., April 4, 1910. Admitted to the bar in New York in 1844, he moved to Iowa where he engaged in practice. He was judge of the First Judicial Court of Iowa (1847–1852) and chief justice of the Oregon Territory (1853–1857). One of the framers of the constitution of the state of Oregon, he served as United States senator from that state in 1865–1871. In the Senate he was one of the most virulent of the "Radical Republicans" who blocked President Andrew Johnson's liberal Reconstruction policies, and he voted for Johnson's impeachment. Under President Ulysses S. Grant he was attorney general from 1871 to 1875. Grant nominated him for the post of chief justice of the United States Supreme Court in 1873, but his apparent involvement in a vote fraud in Oregon caused the Senate to reject the nomination. After his retirement as attorney general, he practiced law in Portland, Oreg., and was mayor of that city in 1902–1905.

WILLIAMS, George Washington, a prominent black historian, journalist, and clergyman: b. Bedford Springs, Pa., Oct. 16, 1849; d. Blackpool, England, Aug. 4, 1891. He enlisted at 14 in the Union Army and served with distinction in the Civil War. Later he fought in Mexico against Emperor Maximilian's forces. Reenlisting in the U.S. Army, he saw service in the Indian campaigns on the western frontier, receiving a medical discharge in 1868. He studied at the Newton (Mass.) Theological Institution and was ordained a Baptist minister in 1874.

In 1875, Williams helped to found *The Commoner*, an Afro-American newspaper in Washington, D.C. The next year, he accepted a pastorate in Cincinnati, where he also wrote columns for a newspaper and studied law. He was admitted to the Ohio bar and in 1879 was elected to the state legislature, serving a single term.

A student of the black experience in America, Williams wrote *A History of the Negro Race in America from 1619 to 1880* (1883) and *A History of the Negro Troops in the War of the Rebellion* (1888).

He sought and won the backing of the railroad magnate Collis P. Huntington for a trip to the Congo in 1890. Initially an admirer of the Congo's ruler, Leopold II, king of the Belgians, he soon began to publish denunciations of him for the crimes he saw being perpetrated against Leopold's Congolese subjects. Disillusioned and impoverished, having lost Huntington's financial support, Williams died on his way home.

WILLIAMS, Hank, American singer and composer of country and western songs, who was perhaps best known for his interpretation of his own song *Cold, Cold Heart.* Williams was born near Georgiana, Ala., on Sept. 17, 1923. He taught himself to play the guitar, and when he was 14 he organized his own band, Hank Williams and his Drifting Cowboys, which played for local affairs. From 1937 to 1947 his group had its own program on a Montgomery, Ala., radio station. Nationwide stardom came when he and his band began making recordings in 1947. After they joined the Grand Ole Opry in 1949, Williams dominated country music until his death.

As a singer Williams scored with songs written by others, such as *Love Sick Blues*, and those he wrote himself, such as *Cold, Cold Heart, Hey, Good Lookin', Jambalaya,* and *Your Cheatin' Heart.*

Williams died in Oak Hill, W.Va., on Jan. 1, 1953. He was elected to the Country Music Hall of Fame in 1961, one of the first three to be so honored.

WILLIAMS, John (1664–1729), American clergyman known as the "Redeemed Captive." He was born in Roxbury, Mass., on Dec. 10, 1664. After graduating from Harvard College in 1683, he settled in Deerfield, Mass., and was ordained in 1688. In late February 1704 the town was raided by a band of French and Indians who killed two of his children and his black servant. Williams, his wife, and six surviving children were forced to set out with other prisoners for Canada. His wife was killed on the way.

On his arrival in Canada, Williams was treated with considerable respect by the French. At length he was permitted to return to Massachusetts, arriving in Boston in November 1706 with 57 other captives, including two of his children. He soon resumed his pastoral duties in Deerfield and published a narrative of his captivity entitled *The Redeemed Captive Returning to Zion* (1707), which was widely circulated and has provided later readers with a vivid picture of the dangers of the American frontier in the early 18th century. Williams died in Deerfield on June 12, 1729.

WILLIAMS, Jonathan (1750–1815), American soldier and engineer, who was the first American to apply the principles of scientific engineering to military affairs. He was born in Boston, Mass., on May 26, 1750. At the age of 20 he went to London to engage in business, but in 1776 he moved to Paris to work with his granduncle, Benjamin Franklin, who was ambassador to France. While there he studied European military science and read widely about fortifications. He returned to America with Franklin in 1785.

In 1801, Thomas Jefferson appointed him inspector of fortifications at West Point with the army rank of major. He soon became the first superintendent of the newly established U.S. Military Academy, and in 1805 he was made lieutenant colonel of engineers. Eventually he became known as "the father of the Corps of Engineers." While in charge of New York City's fortifications, he had Castle William built on Governor's Island and became senior officer at that fort. He resigned his commission in 1812. He was elected to Congress in 1814 but died in Philadelphia on May 16, 1815, before he could take his seat.

WILLIAMS, "Old Bill." See WILLIAMS, WILLIAM SHERLEY.

WILLIAMS, Ralph Vaughan. See VAUGHAN WILLIAMS, RALPH.

WILLIAMS, Robert R. (1886–1965), American chemist, known for his work with thiamine (vitamin B_1). He was born in Nellore, India, on Feb. 16, 1886. After graduating from the University of Chicago in 1908, he went to the Philippines to teach. While there he became aware of the incidence of beriberi and spent the next nine years working on the problem with the Philippine Board of Science in Manila and the Bureau of Chemistry in Washington. He was chemical director of the Bell Telephone Laboratories from 1925 to 1945 and also served as chairman of the Committee on Cereals of the Food and Nutrition Board, National Research Council, until his retirement in 1959.

In the 1930's, Williams isolated thiamin, determined its structure and synthesis, and discovered that it is an antiberiberi factor. His patent rights were turned over to the Research Corporation, a foundation in New York City, to ensure that the proceeds from the synthetic processing of vitamin B_1 would be used to support research in combating malnutrition in many parts of the world. See also VITAMIN.

Williams helped establish the "enrichment" process of adding vitamins to bread, flour, and cornmeal—one of the most important factors in the control of beriberi, pellagra, and riboflavin deficiency. He died in Summit, N.J., on Oct. 2, 1965.

WILLIAM H. SEBRELL,* *Columbia University*

WILLIAMS, Roger (1603?–1683), American Puritan intellectual and founder of Rhode Island. He was born in London, England, probably in 1603, the son of James Williams, "citizen and merchant taylor of London," and of Alice Pemberton, the daughter of Robert Pemberton and Catherine Stokes, both of trading families.

While very young, Williams was employed by the jurist Sir Edward Coke, who later arranged for his entrance in 1621 to the Charterhouse. He entered Pembroke College, Cambridge, in 1623 and took his bachelor of arts degree in July 1627. In late 1628 he became chaplain to Sir William Masham, in Otes, Essex County, where on Dec. 15, 1629, he married Mary Barnard (Bernard), the daughter, probably, of the Rev. Richard Bernard, "conformable Puritan" and author of *The Isle of Man.*

In the summer of 1629, Williams attended the conference at Sempringham called by the Puritans, among them John Cotton and Thomas Hooker, to consider the possibility of emigration to America. On Dec. 10, 1630, he sailed from Bristol on the ship *Lyon* and landed at Nantasket on Feb. 5, 1631. Chosen teacher of the Salem church, he declined the appointment, charging that the congregation had not "separated" from the Church of England. He moved to Plymouth, where he preached for a year, but even in that Separatist colony his "strange opinions" caused "some controversie betweene the church & him."

In 1633, Williams accepted a call to the Salem pulpit and immediately demanded that all the New England churches "separate." He also challenged the Massachusetts government, claiming its charter was invalid because the king had no power to grant land, which could be rightly acquired only as the colonists "compounded with the natives." When Williams added that Charles I was an ally of anti-Christ and then conveyed these sentiments in a letter to the king, he was called before the Massachusetts General Court. He apologized, but on April 30, 1635, he was again summoned, charged this time with holding that the government had no right to punish violations of the first four commandments and that "a magistrate ought not to tender an oath to an unregenerate man." The Massachusetts leaders wondered why Williams, whom Gov. John Winthrop considered a "godly minister," should deny them powers that seemed so clearly warranted by Scripture. Cotton privately, then Hooker before the court, examined Williams, but they "could not reduce him from any of his errors." On Oct. 9, 1635, Williams was convicted of venting "newe & dangerous opinions against the aucthoritie of magistrates" and was sentenced to banishment from the colony.

In April 1636, Williams and his few companions reached the spot he was to call Providence—out of his "Sence of Gods mercefull providence unto me in my destresse." He purchased land from the Narragansett Indians and parceled it out for use. He befriended the Indians and learned their language, and during the Pequot War (1637) he served all New England as a negotiator. Yet orthodox Massachusetts remained hostile to Rhode Island, where it was ordered "that no man should be molested for his conscience."

In 1642, Williams sailed for England to procure a charter. While at sea he composed *A Key into the Language of America* (London 1643), a work testifying to his thoughtful appreciation of Indian culture. Williams received his charter on March 14, 1644, and returned to Rhode Island to become the first "chiefe officer" of its "democraticall" government.

The stay in London provided Williams an opportunity to publish his matured views on church-state relationships. On Feb. 5, 1644, appeared his *Mr. Cottons Letter Lately Printed, Examined, and Answered.* In the letter, sent to Williams in 1636, but "providentially" first printed while Williams was in London, Cotton had contended that separatism unnecessarily weakened the church. Williams ignored this argument and asked instead if any government had the right to "persecute" him for his religious opinions. The question he pursued in the *Queries of Highest Consideration* (Feb. 9, 1644), a rejoinder to *The Apologeticall Narration* issued by the five Independent ministers attending the Westminster Assembly. The assembly had been convoked by Parliament to decide what ecclesiastical policy should replace the church deposed by the Puritan Revolution. Williams denied Parliament's right to call the assembly and questioned the very idea of a uniform "national church."

Meanwhile, Williams prepared the volume which would stand as his most imposing monument—*The Bloudy Tenent of Persecution.* In this work (July 15, 1644) Williams disclosed the premises that underlay his lifelong advocacy of religious freedom. Far from anticipating Thomas Jefferson, Williams arrived at his belief in separation of church and state through "typology"—that is, he read the Old Testament not literally, but as a poetic "shadow" of the New Testament. More orthodox divines found in Scripture a "pattern" of civil patronage of religion, but Williams insisted that in the Christian era, "all nations are merely civil, without any such typical, holy respect upon them as was upon Israel." When Williams returned to the issue in 1652 with *The Bloudy Tenet Yet More Bloudy* (a final critique of Cotton's argument that government must sustain the church) and *The Hireling Ministry None of Christs* (an attack on civil maintenance of the clergy), his postulates were still those of a mystic "typologist."

In his last years Williams was plagued by land and boundary disputes, one of which took him to England in 1651 to seek confirmation of the charter. He was reduced to poverty when his trade was disrupted by King Philip's War (1675–1676), during which Williams, though well over 70, bore arms in New England's defense. As an old man he looked on Quaker zeal hopefully as a revival of Puritan piety. He defended the Quaker right to religious freedom,

THE BETTMANN ARCHIVE

Roger Williams, the founder of Rhode Island.

but he nonetheless sought to expose their "errors." Though Williams had briefly joined the Baptists in 1639 and considered himself thereafter a "seeker," his theology had remained soundly orthodox. His *Experiments of Spiritual Life and Health* (London 1652), written originally for his wife, carried an enduring Puritan message: "If riches, if children, if friends, if whatsoever increase, let us watch that the heart fly not loose upon them."

Williams died in Providence, R.I., between Jan. 16 and March 15, 1683. Trader and statesman, friend of New England governors and of Oliver Cromwell, Sir Henry Vane, and John Milton, Roger Williams, who even as a shaker of nations had never been wholly of this world, was perhaps the purest of American Puritans.

See also RHODE ISLAND—*History*

ALAN HEIMERT
Author of "Religion and the American Mind"

Bibliography

Williams' publications and letters are collected in *Writings* (1866–1874). Reprinted separately are *A Key into the Language of America*, ed. by Howard M. Chapin (1936), and *Experiments of Spiritual Life and Health*, ed. by Winthrop H. Hudson (1951).

Brocknuier, Samuel H., *Irrepressible Democrat: Roger Williams* (Ronald 1940).

Carpenter, Edmund J., *Roger Williams* (1909; reprint, Arno 1972).

Easton, Emily, *Roger Williams: Prophet and Pioneer* (1930; reprint AMS Press 1976).

Eaton, Jeanette, *Lone Journey: The Life of Roger Williams* (Harcourt 1966).

Ernst, James E., *Roger Williams: New England Firebrand* (1932; reprint, AMS Press 1976).

Garrett, John, *Roger Williams: Witness Beyond Christendom* (Macmillan, N. Y., 1970).

Gilpin, W. Clark, *The Millenarian Piety of Roger Williams* (Univ. of Chicago Press 1979).

Miller, Perry, *Roger Williams: His Contribution to the American Tradition* (1953; reprint, Atheneum 1962).

Morgan, Edmund S., *Roger Williams: The Church and the State* (Harcourt 1967).

Polishook, Irwin H., *Roger Williams, John Cotton and Religious Freedom: A Controversy in New and Old England* (Prentice-Hall 1967).

Winslow, Ola Elizabeth, *Master Roger Williams* (1957; reprint, Octagon 1973).

UPI

Ted Williams was the last player to bat over .400.

WILLIAMS, Ted (1918–), American baseball player, who ranks as one of the game's foremost hitters. Theodore Samuel Williams was born in San Diego, Calif., on Aug. 30, 1918. He played professional baseball for the Pacific Coast League team in that city for two years (1936–1937) without great distinction, but after a banner season with the Minnesota Millers of the American Association he was called up to the Boston Red Sox in 1939.

A left-handed hitting outfielder with a classic stance and swing, Williams was to be hailed as one of baseball's greatest hitters within a few years of his entry into the major leagues, batting .327 and .344 in his first two seasons and .406 in his third (1941).

Williams, long known as "the Kid," was a colorful, quick-tempered perfectionist. A keen student of hitting, he was intensely preoccupied with his specialty and, in the early years at least, made little attempt to conceal his scorn for baseball fans, sportswriters, and the art of fielding. Nevertheless, he delighted followers of the game with his batting feats. And fellow players seeking advice on hitting problems found him to be a readily available analyst.

Though his career with the Red Sox was twice interrupted by service in the armed forces (1943–1945 and 1952–1953), he recorded six American League batting championships (second only to Ty Cobb's 12), 521 home runs (among the few to pass 500 in major league history), and a lifetime batting average of .344 (exceeded by only four hitters of the modern era). He was named the American League's most valuable player in 1946 and again in 1949.

Williams retired as a player in September 1960 and was elected to the National Baseball Hall of Fame in 1966. In 1969 he became manager of the Washington Senators (later, the Texas Rangers), retiring in 1972.

WILLIAMS, Tennessee (1911–1983), American writer, considered by many to be the nation's finest dramatist of the post-World War II era. His emotionally charged works deal compassionately with sensitive but psychically wounded protagonists seeking to survive in a hostile world.

Life. Thomas Lanier Williams was born in Columbus, Miss., on March 26, 1911. He spent much of his childhood in the home of his maternal grandfather, an Episcopal minister, with whom his parents lived. In 1918, Williams' father moved his family to St. Louis, and thereafter family harmony disintegrated. Williams began writing as early as 1922 and published his first story in 1928. He entered the University of Missouri in 1929 but had to withdraw in 1931 for lack of funds. He then spent what he described as "a season in hell" working for a shoe company until he had a physical breakdown in 1934. He later returned to college and graduated from the University of Iowa in 1938. During the 1930's, Williams wrote a number of plays, several of which were performed by amateur groups.

Williams changed his name to Tennessee, his father's home state, in 1939, the year in which he won a playwriting contest sponsored by New York's Group Theatre. In 1940 his *Battle of Angels* was produced professionally but closed during its pre-Broadway tryout, probably because its mixture of sex and religion offended playgoers of that conservative era. (It was subsequently revised and produced as *Orpheus Descending* in 1957 and filmed as *The Fugitive Kind* in 1960.) After 1940, Williams worked at numerous temporary jobs, including scriptwriter for MGM, before achieving his first success with *The Glass Menagerie* in 1945.

During the late 1950's, Williams became addicted to alcohol and drugs, and in 1969 he suffered a mental and physical breakdown. Although his last major success came with *The Night of the Iguana* (1961), he continued to write regularly until his death in New York City on Feb. 25, 1983. Many of his plays reflect his own experiences, about which he wrote candidly in his *Memoirs* (1975).

Writings. Williams wrote about 30 full-length plays, some 35 short plays, an equal number of short stories, two volumes of poetry, and a volume of essays. He also wrote two novels—*The Roman Spring of Mrs. Stone* (1950) and *Moise and the World of Reason* (1975). Some 15 of his works were made into films, and two of his plays have served as librettos for operas. His output, though prolific, was uneven, but the overall quality of Williams' work assures him a lasting place in American drama.

In *The Glass Menagerie,* Williams drew on his life in St. Louis to create a seriocomic picture of a mother who lives on memories of her romanticized Southern past and on hopes for the future of her children, especially for the painfully shy Laura, who seeks refuge from reality in her menagerie of glass animals.

Williams' best-known play and the one that most fully realizes his major themes is *A Streetcar Named Desire* (1947), in which a once-genteel Southern belle, Blanche DuBois, struggles with psychological and moral decay but finds herself no match for the harsh reality represented by her brother-in-law, Stanley Kowalski. Here, as in others of his plays, Williams depicts a vulnerable and sensitive soul struggling to retain a modicum of dignity and to achieve a degree of salvation in a callous and cruel world.

Although comedy plays a part in almost all of Williams' plays, *The Rose Tattoo* (1951) is one of his few predominantly comic works. Set on the Gulf Coast among Italian Americans, it concerns a widow who is convinced that happiness ended when her husband died but who comes to accept a new love.

In his symbolic fantasy *Camino Real* (1953), fictional, real, and mythic characters—including Don Quixote, Camille, Lord Byron, Casanova, and Kilroy—are caught in a struggle between romantic idealism and deadening reality. Little understood and unsuccessful at that time, it was viewed as a classic when revived in New York in 1970.

Cat on a Hot Tin Roof (1955), one of Williams' greatest successes, develops the theme of mendacity—symbolized by alcoholism, homosexuality, and cancer—as a corrupter of the relationships within the family of a wealthy Southern planter. Following this play, Williams found it increasingly difficult to write, and thereafter he was often accused of turning out pale reflections of his earlier work. Many critics consider *Suddenly Last Summer* (1958) a near parody of his characteristic themes, while others have pronounced it one of his major works. In it a young woman, Catherine, suffers a breakdown when her cousin, Sebastian, whom she has accompanied on a foreign tour, is killed and eaten by a band of homeless boys whose sexual favors he has bought. Like several others of Williams' plays, this one suggests an integral connection between religion and sex. However, despite its sensational nature, Sebastian's sacrifice is no more cruel than his mother's attempt to have Catherine lobotomized to keep her from revealing the truth about Sebastian. Williams recaptured much of his earlier popularity with *The Night of the Iguana*. Set in a seedy Mexican hotel, it focuses on a defrocked minister, now a tour guide, whose breakdown brings him a new vision and acceptance of life.

Williams' subsequent plays show a decreased interest in story and greater concern for symbolism and nonrealistic techniques. In *The Milk Train Doesn't Stop Here Anymore* (1963), a young man, dubbed "the angel of death," arrives at a mountaintop villa where he helps an aging, dying woman accept the inescapable. Throughout, two Japanese-style stage assistants, dressed in black, serve as scene shifters. *Out Cry* (also called *The Two Character Play*, 1967, 1973) has been compared to the dramas of Samuel Beckett and Harold Pinter in its allusive, nonspecific dialogue. On a bare stage, a brother and sister, probably based on Williams and his sister Rose, rehearse a play in which they are trapped by their childhood. Critics have seen *Out Cry* as a personal statement by Williams about himself, his art, and his audience. *Small Craft Warnings* (1972), the most successful of Williams' late plays, is set in a bar peopled with losers and eccentrics. The primary interest resides in the soliloquies, which lay bare the characters' innermost secrets.

In the late 1970's, Williams returned to his earlier style of writing. *Vieux Carré* (1977), like *The Glass Menagerie*, reflects Williams' own life in the 1930's. *Tiger Tail* (1978) is a reworking of his film script for *Baby Doll* (1956). *A Lovely Sunday for Crève Coeur* (1979) depicts the visit of four lonely women to a St. Louis amusement park in the 1930's. Williams' final play, *A House Not Meant to Stand* (1982), concerns the physical and emotional disintegration of an aging married couple.

WIDE WORLD

Tennessee Williams, American playwright

Williams won Pulitzer Prizes for *A Streetcar Named Desire* and for *Cat on a Hot Tin Roof*. The same two plays won New York Drama Critics' Circle Awards, as did *The Glass Menagerie* and *The Night of the Iguana*.

OSCAR G. BROCKETT
Author of "The Theatre, an Introduction"

Further Reading: Hirsch, Foster, *A Portrait of the Artist: The Plays of Tennessee Williams* (Kennikat Press 1979); Jackson, Esther M., *The Broken World of Tennessee Williams* (Univ. of Wis. Press 1965); Londré, Felicia H., *Tennessee Williams* (Ungar 1980); Phillips, Gene D., *The Films of Tennessee Williams* (Art Alliance Press 1980).

WILLIAMS, William (1731–1811), American patriot and public official. He was born in Lebanon, Conn., on April 8, 1731, and graduated from Harvard College in 1751. In 1755 he served on the staff of Col. Ephraim Williams, a cousin, in the Lake George expedition against the French. He subsequently engaged in business in Lebanon.

In 1775 he was elected a representative in the Continental Congress, and in the following year signed the Declaration of Independence. His property was nearly all expended in the Revolutionary War, during which he was tireless in obtaining private donations to supply the Continental Army, going from house to house to collect articles that could relieve the destitution of the soldiers. He held many public offices in Connecticut, his period of service spanning more than 50 years. He helped to frame the Articles of Confederation and was a member of the convention of his state that adopted the federal Constitution. Williams died in Lebanon, Conn., on Aug. 2, 1811.

WILLIAMS, William Carlos (1883–1963), American poet, who was one of the leading 20th century literary figures in the United States. He was born in Rutherford, N. J., on Sept. 17, 1883, to a British businessman and a mother of French-Spanish extraction from Puerto Rico. He was educated at the Horace Mann School in New York City and in Switzerland before attending the University of Pennsylvania, from which he received a medical degree in 1906. From 1910 until his retirement from practice in 1951, he was a successful pediatrician in Rutherford, where he died on March 4, 1963.

While still a practicing physician, Williams achieved international fame as a prolific writer of poetry, fiction, and critical essays that earned him a leading and influential position in contemporary American literature. During his student days at the University of Pennsylvania, he had become a close friend of Ezra Pound, who influenced him greatly in the development of his literary art.

Unlike the imagists, in whose publications his poems first came to public notice, Williams leaned strongly from the beginning on American material and on a diction and free metrical rhythm modeled on American speech, derived from the landscape and the people of his New Jersey surroundings. While the imagists, including Pound, went abroad, Williams stayed at home, to become one of the strongest advocates and exemplars of the nativist movement in American letters. For example, his *In the American Grain* (1925) is a vivid prose depiction of the American emotional heritage.

"By listening to the language of his locality," Williams said, "the poet begins to learn his craft. . . . The commonplace, the tawdry, the sordid all have their poetic uses if the imagination can lighten them." Thus, a piece of broken glass in an alleyway, an old woman munching plums, and the commonest field flowers became the subjects of his poems. In *Paterson* (5 books; 1946–1958), a portrayal of modern man in the microcosm of a New Jersey city, he produced one of the major American philosophical poems of the century. Similarly, in such fiction as his novel *First Act* (1937) and the short stories collected in *Make Light of It* (1950), he accomplished a remarkable rendering and transformation of everyday Americana. Williams' other works include *Poems* (1909), *The Collected Later Poems* (1950), *The Collected Earlier Poems* (1951), *Desert Music* (1954), *Selected Essays* (1954), *Journey to Love* (1955), and *Selected Letters* (1957). Williams was awarded the Pulitzer Prize in 1962 for *Pictures from Brueghel*, a collection of his last three books of poems.

NORMAN HOLMES PEARSON
Yale University

WILLIAMS, William Sherley (died 1849), American trapper and guide. He was known as *Old Bill Williams*. He received some education and was probably, for a time, an itinerant Methodist preacher in Missouri.

Williams accompanied the surveying expedition along the Santa Fe Trail in 1825 and 1826 led by Joseph C. Brown. In the late 1820's he trapped in New Mexico and lived for a while with the Moqui, or Hopi, Indians, whom he apparently tried to convert to Christianity. In 1833 and 1834 he explored California with the trapper Joseph R. Walker, and he later lived among the Ute Indians and trapped in Colorado and Utah. In 1843 he set out from Bent's Fort in southeastern Colorado on a two-year expedition that carried him to the Oregon Territory and back to Santa Fe.

In 1848, the explorer John C. Frémont, eager to redeem himself after a court-martial, left Missouri to seek a new pass through the Rocky Mountains to California. In Colorado he took on Williams as a guide. They entered the upper Rio Grande Valley, an area Williams knew well. As the weather worsened, Williams wanted to swing south to the mountains, but Frémont was determined to reach California more directly.

Williams lost his way in the heavy snow. Trapped in a blizzard, Frémont decided to turn back, and he sent Williams and three other men to Taos, N. Mex., for supplies. Williams ran out of food and nearly starved. Frémont also set out for Taos. In all, 11 men died in one of the worst disasters in American exploration.

In March 1849, Williams and another man retraced the route to recover lost equipment. But both men were killed probably by Indians. Williams, Ariz., is named for the trapper, as are nearby Bill Williams Mountain and the Bill Williams Fork of the Colorado River.

WILLIAMS COLLEGE is a private, coeducational liberal arts college, located in Williamstown, Mass. It is primarily an undergraduate institution, although master's degrees are granted in development economics, history of art, biology, and physics. Until 1970, enrollment was limited to men.

The curriculum at Williams leading to the baccalaureate degree is divided into three divisions: language and the arts, social studies, and science and mathematics. In the freshman year, students follow a course of general study. In the sophomore year they may begin study in a major field of concentration, required of all students in the junior and senior years. The purpose of the program is to provide both a well-rounded education and training in a specific skill, often in anticipation of graduate study. The college has exchange and cross-enrollment agreements with a number of other American colleges, mostly in the Northeastern states. It also provides for study abroad, in Madrid and Hong Kong.

The college owes its origin to Col. Ephraim Williams, whose will provided for the establishment of a "free school" in northwestern Massachusetts. In 1791, after a delay of some 35 years, the school was opened, and in 1793 it was incorporated as Williams College by the Commonwealth of Massachusetts. The college's early years were plagued by financial difficulty and dissension. However, beginning in 1821, under the leadership of President Edward Dorr Griffin, it achieved stability and a reputation for excellence, to become one of the most highly respected small colleges in the United States.

WILLIAMSBURG, a city in Tidewater Virginia, the seat of James City county, is 46 miles (74 km) southeast of Richmond. Established in 1633, the city was the capital of Virginia in the 18th century. One of the great restorations of American colonial life is situated here (see WILLIAMSBURG, COLONIAL). The College of William and Mary is here. The Abby Aldrich Rockefeller Folk Art Collection is one of the finest collections of its kind. Population: 9,870.

COLONIAL WILLIAMSBURG

Raleigh Tavern, Williamsburg, was rebuilt on its original site after having burned to the ground in 1859.

WILLIAMSBURG, Colonial, a historic town in Virginia that has been restored to its appearance in the 18th century. As an experiment in preserving the past, Colonial Williamsburg is without equal, and as a tourist attraction it has few rivals in the United States. The town, once the capital of Virginia, conveys an ambience that may linger always with the visitor. The streets may be crowded with people and horse-drawn carriages, but the prevailing mood is one of serenity. Grace and proportion are present in the Georgian buildings and the formal gardens. Washington, Jefferson, and other statesmen came here often to help shape the course of Virginia on the eve of Revolution, and a little imagination can invoke their presence today.

History of the Town. English settlers founded a town on the site of Williamsburg in 1633 and named it Middle Plantation. In 1693 the College of William and Mary was established here instead of at nearby Jamestown. Six years later, after Jamestown burned for the second time, the Virginia legislature decided to move the capital to Middle Plantation. They renamed the community Williamsburg in honor of William III, the king of England at that time. The royal governor, Francis Nicholson, laid out the new city and produced one of the first major town plans attempted in colonial America. The final design featured a series of three streets running east and west. The middle one, named Duke of Gloucester Street in honor of the son of Queen Anne, was intended to serve as the principal thoroughfare connecting the Capitol with the campus of William and Mary. The Palace Green served as the north-south axis and as the main approach to the new governor's residence.

From 1699 until 1780, Williamsburg led Virginia in culture and political influence. The city witnessed the main events that culminated in Virginia's decision to join with the other colonies in separating from Britain in 1776. Most of the

The Governor's Palace, completed in 1720, was the home of the royal governors during the 18th century. Wrought iron gates frame the walk leading to the ballroom wing.

COLONIAL WILLIAMSBURG

COLONIAL WILLIAMSBURG

(*Above*) The restored Capitol in Williamsburg, where the Virginia House of Burgesses met from 1704 to 1780. (*Below*) Craftsmen in 18th century costume, including a printer (*left*) and a candlemaker, demonstrate their trades for the tourists.

COLONIAL WILLIAMSBURG

COLONIAL WILLIAMSBURG

leaders that Virginia contributed to the new republic were educated at the College of William and Mary or served in the Virginia House of Burgesses. During the early 1770's, George Washington, Patrick Henry, Thomas Jefferson, Richard Henry Lee, and George Mason debated the great questions of the day in Williamsburg. Jefferson studied at the college during the early 1760's, and he worked closely with George Wythe and other prominent lawyers who lived in the colonial capital.

In 1790 the new state of Virginia moved its government to Richmond, and Williamsburg settled into the life of a quiet town with only two principal institutions: the Eastern State Hospital, founded in 1770, and the College of William and Mary. During the next century and a half, Williamsburg's peaceful atmosphere was disturbed but once—during the Peninsular Campaign of Union Gen. George McClellan in the Civil War. Duke of Gloucester Street gradually took on the aspect of a commercial thoroughfare that could be found in any American town. By the 1920's telephone wires, garages, and lines of automobiles tended to screen out most of the buildings that had survived from the colonial period.

THE RESTORATION

In the fall of 1926, Dr. William A. R. Goodwin, former rector of Bruton Parish Church, persuaded John D. Rockefeller, Jr., to restore the colonial city as an educational project. Rockefeller invested millions of dollars in the restoration. After Dr. Goodwin had purchased a considerable amount of real estate in the older portions of the town, a staff of architects, assisted by historical researchers and an archaeologist, began the massive job of returning Williamsburg to its 18th century appearance. This task involved the removal of many modern buildings from the center of town and the reconstruction of hundreds of lost houses, stores, and outbuildings.

Three major monuments of the colonial period had disappeared and had to be reconstructed on their original sites: the Capitol, the Raleigh Tavern, and the Governor's Palace. Nearly 90 buildings from the pre-Revolutionary era stood as reminders of the city's antiquity. These structures were studied thoroughly in preparation for physical restoration.

Some members of the architectural staff of the restoration, under the direction of an archaeologist, excavated nearly all of the building sites known to have existed in the 18th century in order to locate foundations and artifacts that might indicate each building's use. During the early years of research at Williamsburg, the draftsmen took field trips into many parts of southern Virginia so that they could photograph, measure, and study surviving 18th century buildings.

Colonial Williamsburg, Incorporated, operating as a private philanthropy, opened its first exhibition building to the public in 1930 when the Travis House began to serve as a restaurant. Two years later the reconstructed Raleigh Tavern opened as a historical museum, complete with hostesses who told visitors how Virginia legislators met informally after the royal governor dissolved the House of Burgesses to prevent resolutions of protest over the tea tax.

The Williamsburg restoration was officially inaugurated in 1934 when the reconstructed Governor's Palace and Capitol were completed. Subsequent restoration and reconstruction projects have permitted the Colonial Williamsburg Foundation to bring all parts of the old city into the restored area. Architectural, documentary, and archaeological research has been used effectively to help create a picture of 18th century buildings and gardens in an urban setting.

Colonial Williamsburg Today. The visitor to Colonial Williamsburg is now directed to an information center outside of the exhibition area where an orientation motion picture, *The Story of a Patriot,* is presented. Then he may enter the city on a bus provided for ticket holders. Activities and tours within the restored town may occupy the newcomer for several days.

The regular ticket of admission permits the tourist to see a number of buildings that illustrate the different social classes and occupational groups that would have been present in Virginia's colonial capital just before the Revolution. Usually, those who come for a short visit restrict themselves to the Capitol, the Governor's Palace, and a few of the craft shops and houses. Even a brief stay can include several tours to the places where Virginia's leaders faced the crises that eventually led to the decision to break with Britain.

Visitors who remain longer than one day can see something of the life of the middle-class residents who were the craftsmen and professionals. The Brush-Everard and James Geddy houses, with their gardens and outbuildings, serve this purpose adequately. The homes of two prominent lawyers, George Wythe and Peyton Randolph, offer some evidence of the life-style of the older and more established families of 18th century Virginia. Several public buildings, such as the Gaol, the Courthouse, and the Magazine, show the challenges that the colonists encountered in maintaining law and order.

The cultural life of Williamsburg can be illustrated by visits to the Wren Building at the college—the oldest academic structure remaining in America—and to Bruton Parish Church. The discomforts of crowded 18th century lodgings come to life in the common rooms of the Raleigh Tavern and Wetherburn's Tavern. The reconstructed James Anderson House on Duke of Gloucester Street contains an innovative archaeological museum that shows how artifacts excavated in the yards of Williamsburg have contributed to the scholarship of the restoration.

Crafts and Entertainment. The Colonial Williamsburg Foundation offers craft demonstrations for the tourist who wants to observe some aspects of business life 200 years ago. Many shops along the old commercial section of Duke of Gloucester Street display merchandise that the Virginia aristocracy either imported or ordered from local artisans. Silversmiths, cabinetmakers, bookbinders, wigmakers, blacksmiths, coopers, and many other skilled workmen handle the same tools used in the preindustrial era.

A broad program of education and entertainment is offered in the restored area and at the information center. Reconstructed taverns such as the King's Arms and Christiana Campbell's feature luncheon and dinner menus that were common in the city before the Revolution. The theaters in the information center have evening programs that include films and specialized slide shows covering a wide variety of subjects relating to colonial life or to the development of the restoration in the 20th century.

After the exhibition buildings have closed for the day, the visitor may watch a militia muster on the Market Square, with demonstra-

Bruton Parish Church, completed in 1715, was the colony's court church. It has its original walls and windows.

COLONIAL WILLIAMSBURG

COLONIAL WILLIAMSBURG

Archaeologists at Williamsburg study foundations and land adjacent to existing buildings, as in the partly excavated backyard of Wetherburn's Tavern, for information about the use of the buildings or lives of the colonial residents.

tions of colonial firearms, or attend a candlelight concert in the ballroom of the Governor's Palace, or follow a lanthorn (lantern) tour through the craft shops in the evening. The tricorn hat tour enables school-age children to engage in a number of activities in which young people might have taken part 200 years ago in Williamsburg. The Colonial Williamsburg Foundation also sponsors a number of special conferences during the year, including the Antiques Forum and the Garden Symposium.

Evaluating the Restoration. Since the middle 1930's millions of Americans have visited Colonial Williamsburg, so it is no surprise that the restoration has exercised an enormous influence on the study of history and on the design of residential and commercial buildings all over the United States.

The creators of the Williamsburg project used every means available to re-create a functioning community, but they had no intention of inspiring people in other parts of the country to imitate Tidewater Virginia designs. Their work, however, has proven to be one of the largest collaborative enterprises in historical scholarship attempted in the United States. The restoration has had an effect on preservation-restoration techniques throughout the nation, particularly when architects who worked at Williamsburg have been commissioned to supervise similar operations elsewhere.

But there continues to be debate concerning whether the extraordinary beauty of the buildings and gardens in the restored area present a correct picture of a colonial city. In making the past come to life, the interpreters of Colonial Williamsburg have been accused of avoiding unattractive aspects of Virginia's society, such as disease, poor sanitation, slavery, infant mortality, and class distinctions. Both the official guidebook and the tour guides in the restoration area make no attempt to gloss over these controversial topics. The staff freely comments on the less appealing aspects of colonial life, but these troublesome subjects are not stressed. Visitors to the restored area may not care to see domestic animals scavenging for refuse thrown into the streets. Few persons seriously expect to see a working demonstration of the harsh system of discipline imposed upon African slaves. Above all, the central message of the Williamsburg project has been the fundamental importance of the development of self-government in the colony of Virginia during the years that preceded the American Revolution.

Related Activities. The decision in the middle 1920's to carry out the restoration of Williamsburg has influenced the economic development of the modern city. There are no large industries, other than the host of activities normally associated with tourism. The Busch Gardens, known as the Old Country, is a well-planned amusement park with a variety of activities ranging from segments of Shakespeare plays to animal shows. The presence of the Old Country and a large brewery has contributed greatly to the prosperity of James City county, but these facilities also increase the pressures on the tourist accommodations that are available in the Williamsburg area.

The Colonial Williamsburg Foundation sponsors research into every aspect of the life of colonial Virginia through the allied fields of history, architecture, and archaeology. One long-term project is the development of Carter's Grove Plantation, 6 miles (10 km) southeast of Williamsburg, as a working 18th century farm complex. The foundation, together with the Institute of Early American History and Culture at the College of William and Mary, publishes the results of its research, and makes available to educational institutions books and films that help to illustrate Virginia's unique contribution to the development of the United States.

CHARLES B. HOSMER, *Principia College*
Author of "Presence of the Past: A History of the Preservation Movement in the United States Before Williamsburg"

Bibliography

Bruno, Susan, and Quaresima, Donna, *Insider's Guide to Williamsburg, Virginia* (Storie/McOwen 1986).
Goodwin, Rutherford, *Williamsburg in Virginia,* rev. ed. (Williamsburg 1968).
Kocher, A. Lawrence, and Dearstyne, Howard, *Colonial Williamsburg: Its Buildings and Gardens,* rev. ed. (Williamsburg 1971).
Kopper, Phillip, *Colonial Williamsburg* (Abrams 1986).
Noel Hume, Ivor, *Archaeology and Wetherburn's Tavern* (Williamsburg 1969).
Noel Hume, Ivor, *Digging for Carter's Grove* (Williamsburg 1974).
Olmert, Michael, *Official Guide to Colonial Williamsburg* (Williamsburg 1985).
Wamsley, James S., *The Crafts of Williamsburg* (Holt 1984).

WILLIAMSON, Hugh (1735–1819), American scientist and public official. He was born in West Nottingham, Pa., on Dec. 5, 1735. He received bachelor's and master's degrees from the College of Philadelphia (now the University of Pennsylvania) and taught mathematics there. He then studied medicine at Edinburgh, London, and the University of Utrecht, where he received a medical degree. He studied the transits of Venus and Mercury and in 1771 published *An Essay on Comets.*

In England after witnessing the Boston Tea Party in 1773, he warned the Privy Council of rebellion in America unless parliamentary measures were modified. He obtained and revealed startling letters from colonial officials urging "abridgement of . . . English liberties" in the colonies. He aided Benjamin Franklin in his electrical experiments.

In North Carolina in 1776 he began a profitable West Indian trade. As surgeon general of the state's troops, he saved many lives through inoculations and sanitation measures. He served in the state legislature, the Continental Congress, the constitutional convention, and in the U. S. House of Representatives (1789–1793). Thereafter he wrote on scientific subjects, among which his study on climate brought him his greatest recognition. He died in New York City on May 22, 1819.

WILLIAMSON, William Crawford (1816–1895), English naturalist, who was one of the founders of paleobotany. He was born in Scarborough, England, on Nov. 24, 1816. After working as a surgeon at a dispensary, he became a professor of natural history, anatomy, and physiology at Owens College in Manchester in 1851. He taught there for more than 40 years, retiring as a professor of botany in 1892. He died in London on June 23, 1895.

During the 1840's, Williamson wrote monographs dealing with the structure of fish scales, teeth, and bone. In 1858 he published *On Recent Foraminifera,* in which he described a new thin-section technique for studying these marine protozoa.

After extensive paleobotanical research he wrote numerous papers (1872–1894) on fossil plants found in coal beds. Williamson was the first to point out that certain primitive plants related to modern horsetails, ferns, and club mosses had a woody cylinder that grew by the external deposit of new layers.

WILLIAMSPORT, a city in north central Pennsylvania, the seat of Lycoming county, is 86 miles (138 km) north of Harrisburg, the state capital. Located in the foothills of the Allegheny Mountains, it lies on the West Branch of the Susquehanna River at an elevation of 528 feet (161 meters).

Williamsport's economy is primarily industrial, with both light and heavy manufacturing. Its principal products include textiles, wire rope, boilers, furniture, aircraft parts, and electronic equipment. A large industrial park was established in the western part of the city in 1956. The Williamsport-Lycoming County Airport is nearby. The city is also served by major highways and railroads.

Williamsport is the site of Lycoming College and the Williamsport Area Community College. It is the home of *Grit,* the country's largest circulation family weekly newspaper. Also in the city is the Lycoming County Historical Museum, which features exhibits on regional history and has weekly crafts demonstrations. Williamsport is the birthplace of Little League baseball and the site of the league's national headquarters. Every year the city is host to the Little League World Series. The Community Arts Festival is held for one week each spring.

Williamsport was settled in the 1790's. It was incorporated as a borough in 1806 and as a city in 1866. In the second half of the 19th century it was an important lumbering center. But the exhaustion of local forest reserves by the early 20th century meant the end of the lumbering industry, and the city began to diversify its economy. Williamsport has a mayor-council form of government. Population: 33,401.

WILLIAMSTON, a town in northeastern North Carolina, the seat of Martin county, is on the Roanoke River, 95 miles (152 km) east of Raleigh. Although the area is a rich agricultural region, industry is being introduced at an increasing rate. During the mid-1970's, the downtown business district was being rebuilt.

The town was incorporated in 1779 and later named in honor of Col. William Williams of the Martin county militia. It is governed by a mayor-council. Population: 6,159.

WILLIAMSTOWN, a city in Australia, is a port and industrial center of Greater Melbourne, in the state of Victoria. The harbor, at the head of Port Phillip Bay, has ample facilities for docking, cargo handling, and ship construction and repairs. Industries include oil refining, food processing, and the manufacture of textile, chemical, and glass products. There are also railroad yards and workshops.

Williamstown, named for King William IV, was settled in 1835 and became a city in 1919. Population: (1971) 29,983.

WILLIAMSTOWN is a town in the northwestern corner of Massachusetts, in Berkshire county, at the confluence of the Green and Hoosic rivers, 19 miles (31 km) north of Pittsfield. Although principally a picturesque colonial college town, Williamstown manufactures wire and photographic products.

Williams College, originally founded in Williamstown as a free school, was granted a charter by the Commonwealth of Massachusetts in 1793. Many of its beautiful buildings are open to the public, including the art museum and the Chapin Library. The town is also the site of the Sterling and Francine Clark Art Institute, world famous for its collection of 19th century paintings and old silver pieces. The Williamstown Summer Theatre offers an eight-week season.

Established as a plantation called West Hoosuck in 1753, the town was incorporated in 1765. It was renamed in accordance with the will of Col. Ephraim Williams, Jr., who bequeathed his estate for the founding of a free school provided the town was named Williamstown. Government is by a manager and selectmen. Population: 8,741.

WILLIAMSVILLE a village in western New York, in Erie county, is situated about 8 miles (13 km) northeast of Buffalo. It is primarily a suburban community, and has virtually no industrial activity. The campus of Erie County Technical Institute lies east of the village. Here also is the Eagle Hotel, operated as a tavern for over a century. A mill built by Jonas Williams in 1811 has been restored and is now in operation, producing water-ground flour. Dream Island, the village park, and Glen Park, a smaller version of Coney Island, are popular local attractions.

Once a part of the Holland Land Company tract, the site was settled in 1800. It was originally known as Williams' Mills, after Jonas Williams, a local miller. During the War of 1812, soldiers were garrisoned in the town, and when the city of Buffalo was burned by the British in 1813 many of its inhabitants sought refuge here. The village was incorporated in 1869. Classified as a first-class village under New York State law, it has a mayor-trustee type of government. Pop. 6,017.

SUZETTE I. BEREZOWSKA.

WILLIBALD, wĭl'ĭ-bôld, SAINT, Anglo-Saxon missionary and traveler: b. England, ?700; d. Eichstätt, Bavaria, 786. Educated at the monastery of Waltham, he embarked (c. 720–721) on a pilgrimage to Rome, and, having wintered there, set out in 722 for Jerusalem, which he reached after many adventures, including imprisonment as a spy by the Muslims at Emesa (Homs, Syria). After extensive journeys through Palestine and Syria, he ventured back to Italy, spending two years (726–728) at Constantinople on the way. He then entered the famous Benedictine monastery of Monte Cassino, where he remained for 10 years until, at the request of St. Boniface, Pope Gregory III sent him as a missionary to Germany.

Consecrated bishop of Eichstätt in 741, he built a monastery there and, after the death of St. Boniface, became the leader of the missionary monks in Germany. He wrote a narrative of his life and travels which shed some light on the manners and customs of the Near East in his day.

ALLAN M. FRASER.

WILLIBRORD, wĭl'ĭ-brôrd, SAINT, Anglo-Saxon missionary, known as the "Apostle of Frisia": b. Northumbria, 658; d. Echternach, Luxembourg, Nov. 7, 739. Educated in the Benedictine monastery of Ripon, near York, he became a monk and probably sat at the feet of St. Wilfrid himself. In 678 he went to Ireland, where he pursued his studies under Bishop Egbert who, in 690, sent him as a missionary to Frisia (Friesland), where St. Wilfrid, his former teacher, had begun the conversion of the Frisians to Christianity. (See WILFRID, SAINT.) Before embarking upon his missionary labors, he journeyed to Rome to secure the approval and blessing of the pope. His work among the Frisians was carried on under the powerful protection of the Frankish mayor of the palace, Pepin of Herstal, and his son, Charles Martel. Willibrord succeeded not only in Christianizing the pagan but in civilizing the barbarian and in extending the sway of the Franks over the mouth of the Rhine into what is now the northern Netherlands.

In 695, on another visit to Rome, he was consecrated archbishop of Utrecht by Pope Sergius III. His see became a center of Anglo-Saxon culture which attracted renowned scholars. He died in the monastery of Echternach which he himself had founded. His missionary work was continued by St. Boniface, who had been his assistant for several years.

ALLAN M. FRASER.

WILLIMANTIC, wĭl-ə-măn'tĭk, city, Connecticut, seat of Windham County, situated at the junction of the Willimantic and Natchaug rivers; 28 miles east of Hartford, at an elevation of 250 feet. It is within the town limits of Windham. Long known as the Thread City, it has been famed for cotton spinning since 1822. Its chief manufactures have been thread, textiles, yarns, metal products, tools, machinery, hardware, rayon, airplane parts, and optical goods. Educational facilities include the Willimantic State College. Incorporated as a borough in 1833, and as a city in 1893, Willimantic is governed by a mayor and a board of aldermen. Pop. 14,652.

WILLIMANTIC STATE COLLEGE, a liberal arts and teachers college in Willimantic, Conn., 28 miles from both Hartford and New London. It is one of four state colleges in Connecticut. Established in 1889 as a two-year normal school for the training of teachers for the elementary schools, it became Willimantic State Teachers College in 1937, offering a four-year course leading to a bachelor of science degree. For the successful completion of the first two years, the associate in science degree was awarded. Graduates of the four-year program were certified to teach in public elementary and junior high schools in Connecticut. Effective July 1, 1959, the name of the college was changed to Willimantic State College. Beginning in September 1961, two programs became available: a teacher education program culminating in the bachelor of science degree; and a liberal arts program leading to either a science or an arts degree. The school colors are blue and white. There is a library of 25,000 volumes. The annual enrollment averages 1,200 students.

J. E. SMITH.

WILLING, wĭl'ĭng **Thomas,** American merchant, financier, and public official: b. Philadelphia, Pa., Dec. 19, 1731; d. there, Jan. 19, 1821. In 1740 he was sent to England to be educated at schools in Bath and Wells. He entered the Inner Temple, London, in 1748, to read law. Returning to Philadelphia in May 1749, he became a partner in his father's mercantile business, and later entered into partnership with Robert Morris (who was to be a signer of the Declaration of Independence) as Willing, Morris & Company, a firm which became the leading mercantile house in Philadelphia. Willing also engaged in many public activities. In 1763 he was elected mayor of Philadelphia, and in 1764 a member of the Pennsylvania Assembly. Three years later he was appointed a justice of the provincial Supreme Court, in which he served until 1777. He became an active champion of colonial rights but was reluctant to break with Britain. In 1775 he was elected to the Second Continental Congress and voted against the Declaration of Independence, explaining later that he had considered America unequal to an armed conflict with the mother country.

During the Revolutionary War, he remained in Philadelphia, refused to take the oath of allegiance to the crown, and worked assiduously at his business, his successful conduct of which was greatly to assist Robert Morris in the latter's financial support of the war. In 1781, Willing became president of the newly created Bank of North America. Later he was among the commissioners appointed by President George Washington to receive subscriptions to the first Bank of the United States and served as its president from 1791 to 1797, subsequently returning to private business. His health broke suddenly in 1807 and he retired, having amassed a fortune which was estimated to exceed 1 million dollars.

WILLINGBORO, wil'ing-bur-ō, is a township in western New Jersey, in Burlington county, on Rancocas Creek, about 15 miles (25 km) southwest of Trenton.

It is a completely planned residential community of one-family homes and townhouses, which was developed by the real estate firm of Levitt and Sons, beginning in 1958. It was called Levittown from 1959 until 1963, when the residents voted to restore the area's former name of Willingboro. On a tract zoned for light industry, factories make printing rollers, plumbers' wire snakes, and electronic components.

The region was settled by English Quakers late in the 17th century on land formerly occupied by the Lenni Lenape or Delaware Indians. Government is by council and manager. Population: 39,912.

WILLINGDON, wĭl'ĭng-dən, **1st Marquess of (Freeman Freeman-Thomas),** British statesman: b. Ratton, Sussex, England, Sept. 12, 1866; d. London, Aug. 12, 1941. Educated at Eton and Trinity College, Cambridge, he was a Liberal member of Parliament from 1900 until 1910, when he was raised to the peerage as Baron Willingdon of Ratton. His distinguished career as a pro-consul began in 1913 with his appointment as governor of Bombay presidency in India. His transfer to the governorship of Madras presidency in 1919 coincided with the introduction of the system of provincial dyarchy under the Government of India Act of that year. This system he administered with notable success, achieving an unusual degree of cooperation between his two groups of ministers in Madras, responsible respectively for the "transferred" and "reserved" departments of government. Created a viscount in 1924, he led the Indian delegation to the League of Nations Assembly in Geneva in 1925.

Willingdon was appointed governor general of Canada in 1926 and provided constructive leadership during the period of constitutional transition between the Balfour Report of 1926 and the Statute of Westminster (1931). Created an earl and made a member of the privy council in 1931, he returned to India as viceroy and presided over the implementation of the Government of India Act of 1935, handling the passive resistance of the National Congress Party with firmness and skill. On his return to Great Britain in 1936, he was made a marquess and was appointed constable of Dover Castle and lord warden of the Cinque Ports.

Allan M. Fraser.

WILLIS, wĭl'ĭs **Nathaniel Parker,** American writer of journalistic essays, verse, and short stories: b. Portland, Me., Jan. 20, 1806; d. at his Idlewild estate near Tarrytown, N.Y., Jan. 20, 1867. Before graduating from Yale in 1827, he had already won fame with his facile gift for writing sentimental verse, mostly paraphrased from the Bible. In 1829 he founded the *American Monthly Magazine* in Boston, and when it failed two and a half years later he went to New York City and began a lifelong association with George Pope Morris, editor of the New York *Mirror*. The next five years he spent mostly in sophisticated circles in Europe and the Near East as a popular literary journalist, publishing letters in the *Mirror* and other periodicals. Most of his prose works are gatherings from these travel letters; *Pencillings by the Way* (1835; 3 vols., 1844) and *Loiterings of Travel* (3 vols., 1840) are typical.

He continued to write verse, but in the same sentimental and paraphrastic vein. He befriended Edgar Allan Poe, who praised his poem *Unseen Spirits*. He tried his hand at drama: *Bianca Visconti* (1839) was produced in New York in 1837 and followed by *Tortesa, or The Usurer Matched* (1839). His one full-length work of fiction, *Paul Fane: A Novel* (1857), was a failure. Selected short stories were reprinted in *People I Have Met* (1850), *Life Here and There* (1850), and *Fun-Jottings* (1853). According to a couplet by James Russell Lowell, "Willis's shallowness makes half his beauty." Though his affectations might suggest the later Oscar Wilde, he suffered neither the latter's genius nor his tragic reverses of fortune.

William Bracy.

WILLIS, Thomas, English physician and anatomist: b. Great Bedwin, Wiltshire, England, Jan. 27, 1621; d. London, Nov. 11, 1675. He studied at Christ Church College, Oxford, and later practiced medicine at the university and taught there. After 1666, he established a successful medical practice in London. An authority on the brain and nervous system, he discovered a circle of arteries at the base of the brain, since known as the circle of Willis, and described several varieties of nervous affliction and hysteria. He has been credited as the discoverer of diabetes mellitus, since he was the first to distinguish it from other forms of the disease by noting that it increased the sugar content of the urine. His *Cerebri anatome nervorumque descriptio et usus* (1664), the most important treatise on the nervous system produced to that time, contained a wealth of accurate, detailed drawings, many of them attributed to the architect, Sir Christopher Wren.

WILLISTON, wĭl'ĭs-tən, city, North Dakota, seat of Williams County, on the Missouri River, at an altitude of 1,877 feet, 128 miles west of Minot by road and 18 miles from the Montana state line. It has a municipal airport. Williston is a residential city in the heart of a farming, ranching, and distributing center. Oil was discovered in the Williston Basin in 1951, and 10 years later the city had over 1,100 wells within its trade territory. There are also salt and lignite coal mines. The University of North Dakota, Williston is located here, and the Band Festival, held each spring since 1930, attracts thousands of visitors annually.

About 1864, the discovery of gold in Western Montana made the Missouri an artery of commerce, and wood-burning steamboats began to ply the river, stopping at "wood landings" to refuel. One of these landings was the original site of the settlement, founded in 1880. The city was named for Daniel Willis James, a director of the St. Paul, Minneapolis and Manitoba Railway, forerunner of the Great Northern. The Great Northern Railroad came to Williston in 1887 and was largely responsible for making it a permanent community.

Incorporated as a town in 1894, the city adopted the commission form of government in 1913. Population: 13,336.

FLORENCE M. KEARNS.

WILLITS, wĭl'ĭts, city, California, in Mendocino County, situated at an elevation of 1,360 feet, in Little Lake Valley, 132 miles north of San Francisco on the Redwood Highway. There is a municipal airport. The town was named for Hiram Willits, an early local storekeeper from Indiana. Originally a lumbering community, Willits is now also the center for a sheep- and cattle-ranching and poultry-raising area. There is a cylinder-manufacturing plant. Hunting and fishing are popular sports, and the Fourth of July Frontier Days Parade and Rodeo is a tourist attraction. The city has a museum and a public library. Willits was the home of Seabiscuit, the great racehorse. Settled in 1854 and incorporated in 1888, the city is governed by an elected council. Pop. 4,008.

LUCILLE L. ELLIOTT.

WILLIWAW. See WINDS—*Glossary of Winds.*

WILLKIE, wĭl'kē, **Wendell (Lewis),** American lawyer, utility executive, and political leader: b. Elwood, Ind., Feb. 18, 1892; d. New York, N.Y., Oct. 8, 1944. He received bachelor's and law degrees from Indiana University and practiced law with his father for a short time after his graduation. With the outbreak of World War I, he enlisted in the Army as a private, served

Wendell Willkie

Wide World Photos

overseas, and returned home a captain. After the war, he resumed the practice of law for an industrial corporation in Akron, Ohio, and two years later, accepted a position with a firm of utility lawyers. During this period, Willkie made scores of speeches in favor of international cooperation, for the improvement of state governmental administration, and in opposition to the Ku-Klux Klan. He was active in the Democratic Party and was a delegate to its 1924 national convention.

While in Akron, Willkie attracted the attention of Bernard C. Cobb who, in 1929, formed the Commonwealth and Southern Corporation, a utility holding company operating in 11 states. That same year, Willkie was invited to join the New York legal firm which represented Commonwealth and Southern, and in 1933, when Cobb retired, he selected Willkie to be the new president of the corporation. Willkie's principal activities promptly became the rejuvenation of the ailing electrical industry and the assumption of leadership of the utilities' struggle against governmental competition in the Tennessee Valley. Although a Democrat, Willkie fought the administration in the courts and in the mass media, and soon became recognized as one of the most articulate critics of President Franklin D. Roosevelt's economic policies. By 1939, he was the acknowledged spokesman of business opposition to the New Deal.

Willkie's economic associations, frequent speeches, and appealing personality subsequently made him attractive to business leaders within the Republican Party, and ultimately led to his serious consideration by that party as a possible presidential nominee. Across the country, his amateur supporters began conducting an enthusiastic grass roots campaign; in June 1940, at the Republican Convention in Philadelphia, a small band of party leaders, aided by an astute, professionally directed public relations campaign and wildly shouting galleries, swept Willkie into the GOP nomination.

Throughout the autumn of 1940, Willkie waged a vigorous, though uncoordinated, campaign against Roosevelt's economic policies. Aiming his appeal at Democrats and independent voters, he pledged a more unified and prosperous America and an end to unemployment. But because Willkie agreed with many of the New Deal social reforms and the president's attitudes on foreign policies, he did not present a clear alternative to the people. By November, Democratic leaders agreed that Willkie had been the strongest candidate the Republicans could have nominated. But at the polls the votes remained divided along economic lines, and many voters, obviously concerned with the frightening international situation, cast their ballots for the more experienced leader. Consequently, Willkie lost the election by nearly 5 million votes, although he polled more popular votes than any Republican prior to that time.

After the election, Willkie advocated a policy of "loyal opposition"—support for the president in program areas crucial to national defense, with partisan criticism of him in other fields. He attempted to maintain his Republican Party leadership while supporting the administration's program of assistance to the Allies. As a result of his vociferous opposition to all isolationists, however, he lost the support of the conservative forces within the Republican Party. After America's entrance into World War II, Willkie became the Republicans' leading advocate of postwar international cooperation. As the president's personal envoy, he made a trip around the world and later wrote a best-selling book, *One World* (1943), a ringing declaration of the need for understanding and cooperation among the people and leaders of all nations. Eventually, Willkie led the Republican Party to take a public stand supporting membership in a postwar organization. As a result of his activities, however, so many party leaders were alienated that Willkie found he no longer had control of the GOP organization. When he again ran for the presidential nomination in 1944, he was defeated in the Wisconsin primary election, and promptly withdrew from the race. Thereafter, his influence within the Republican party declined rapidly. He suffered a heart attack in August of 1944, and died in New York City in October.

Wendell Willkie, as a corporation president and a recent Democrat who became the Republican presidential candidate, is unique in American political history. Although he never held public office, he made the Republican Party more receptive to international cooperation and was a valuable force for national unity in the realm of foreign policy during World War II.

DONALD BRUCE JOHNSON,
Department of Political Science, State University of Iowa.

WILLMAR, wĭl'mär, city, Minnesota, seat of Kandiyohi County, situated on the southern shore of Foot Lake, about 95 miles west of Minneapolis, at an altitude of 1,123 feet. There is a municipal airport. It is a resort and trade center which processes poultry, livestock, dairy products, and grains; industries include children's furniture, foundries, machine shops, and printing. Important local institutions are the Kandiyohi County-Willmar Library, the Willmar Memorial Auditorium, the Rice Memorial Hospital, and a state mental hospital. A two-day "Kaffee Fest" takes place here annually in June. The site was settled in 1856, but was deserted because of the Sioux Indian uprising in 1862. The trading center established here in 1869 was named for Léon Willmar, a Belgian agent for European bondholders of the St. Paul and Pacific Railroad, which originally owned the site.

Willmar was incorporated as a village in 1874 and adopted a city charter in 1901. Government is by a mayor and a group of eight councilmen. Pop. 15,895.

BURTON L. SUNDBERG.

WILLOUGHBY, wĭl'ō-bē, **Westel Woodbury,** American political scientist: b. Alexandria, Va., July 20, 1867; d. Washington, D.C., March 26, 1945. After graduating from Johns Hopkins University in 1888, he practiced law for several years.

In 1894–1895 he was assistant in political science at Leland Standord Jr. University (Stanford University), and from 1897 to 1933 was professor of political science at Johns Hopkins University. He was adviser to the Chinese delegations at the Washington Conference, 1921–1922, at the International Opium Conference, 1924–1925, and at the Assembly of the League of Nations, held in 1931. Willoughby was the author of numerous books on constitutional law and other subjects, including *The Supreme Court of the U.S.—Its History and Administrative Importance* (1890); *The American Constitutional System* (1904); *Fundamental Concepts of Public Law* (1924); and *The Ethical Basis of Political Authority* (1930).

He was the twin brother of the economist WILLIAM FRANKLIN WILLOUGHBY (1867–1960), professor of government at Princeton (1912–1917) and director of the Institute for Government Research (1916–1932).

WILLOUGHBY, village, Ohio, in Lake County, situated on the Chagrin River near Lake Erie, 17 miles northeast of Cleveland. Manufactures have included auto parts, rubber products, furniture, machinery, metal products, chemicals, and heating apparatus. In the 1950's, Willoughby experienced rapid development as a residential community. The village has a public library and a medical college. The first settlement centered around a grist- and sawmill erected in 1797; the first town meeting was held in 1815. Government is administered by a mayor and council. Population: 19,329.

WILLOUGHBY HILLS, village, Ohio, in Lake County, adjacent to Willoughby, situated near Lake Erie, about 17 miles northeast of Cleveland, at an altitude of about 625 feet. It was incorporated separately as a village in 1954. Pop. 8,612.

WILLOW, wĭl'ō, a genus, *Salix,* of some 300 species of trees and shrubs in the family Salicaceae; over 100 are in North America. Mostly north temperate, they extend from the Arctic to the Gulf of Mexico, Central America, the West Indies, into the Andes in Chile; they also grow in Eurasia, South Africa, Madagascar, Java, and Sumatra. Willows vary from less than 1 inch in height under Arctic and alpine conditions (*S. herbacea,* dwarf willow) to trees of 100 feet or more. The alternate, simple leaves may be narrow as in weeping willow, or rather broad as in the pussy and shining willows. The leaf stalks are short, and stipules are often present. One large scale covers each bud. The flowers are in elongated clusters, aments or catkins, of two types, staminate and pistillate; these are normally on different trees. However, exceptions occur, and both types may be on the same tree, or staminate and pistillate flowers may develop in the same catkin, or in rare instances, the flowers are bisexual. A staminate catkin has an axis bearing numerous bracts which are more or less hairy on the outer surface, each subtending 2 or several stamens and a yellow nectar gland. In the pisillate ament each bract encloses a gland and a single pistil with a divided stigma and an ovary containing 8 or more ovules. The seeds are minute and have a tuft of soft hairs which serve for wind dissemination. Pussy willow catkins appear well before the leaves, and as the staminate ament elongates the backs of the bracts become visible, exposing their silky grayish hairs and giving rise to the "pussy" stage. Later the stamens with their golden pollen are seen. Willow catkins are visited by insects which gather nectar and pollen and effect pollination. In certain northern and Arctic species the pollen is less sticky, and wind pollination apparently occurs, as in catkin-bearing plants generally. Since the sexes are normally on separate plants, cross pollination is the rule; hybridization is thus facilitated and many intermediate forms exist. In various species diploid chromosome numbers of 38, 76, 114, and 152 are found, so that they constitute a polyploid series, as is often the case in hybridization. The perpetuation of these forms is facilitated by natural and artificial propagation by cuttings. In the temperate zone willows thrive along stream banks, and twigs naturally root in the muddy shores. They also reproduce by seeds. Among flowering plants willow is ancient, fossils

Roche

Pussy willow *(Salix discolor)* staminate catkins.

extending back to the Cretaceous.

Largest of the willows of eastern North America is the black willow, *S. nigra.* With its dark brown, ridged bark, reddish to orange twigs, and long, narrow leaves, it is a striking stream bank tree, ranging from the east westward across Texas to California. Although its light, reddish brown wood is soft and not strong, this is the common willow wood of North America. It is used for artificial limbs, boxes, crates, barrels for produce, cores for veneers, furniture, and somewhat for paper pulp. By destructive distillation it yields charcoal and black powder, a constituent of black gunpowder. The peach-leaved willow, *S. amygdaloides,* extends from Washington across Canada to western New York, and south to Oklahoma and Texas; it flourishes along the streams flowing eastward from the Rockies. This shrub or fairly tall tree with leaves suggestive of those of the peach finds limited use for lumber and charcoal. Other conspicuous American species are the shining willow, *S. lucida,* a shrub or tree of the northeast, identified by its leaves which are a deep, rich, shiny green above, paler beneath, and the pussy willow, *S. discolor,* a shrub or small tree, distributed along waterways from Nova Scotia to Manitoba, and southward to Missouri and Delaware. Its "precocious" staminate catkins are ornamental. Similar are the florists' willows, *S. caprea* and *S. cinerea,* introduced from Europe, and sold as pussy willows at Eastertime. In central Europe they are used in churches on Palm Sunday. Numerous other cultivated willows have frequently "escaped." Although native of Europe, Asia, and Africa, the white willow, *S. alba,* is planted and grows wild in North America. It is a tall riparian tree with spreading branches often drooping, and small, narrow, silky leaves. There are forms with bright yellow and others with bright red branches. White willow and crack willow, *S. fragilis,* a similar tall tree but with somewhat larger leaves, and greenish to reddish twigs that snap off in the wind, furnish important European wood. The weeping willow, *S. babylonica,* with pendulous branches and narrow falcate leaves, is native of China; the trees by the rivers of Babylon, upon which the Jews hung their harps as they wept, according to the Psalms, were probably aspens, not weeping willows as often supposed. Willow "rods" or twigs are cut in winter or spring, and the bark is removed. They are then dried and woven into baskets and wicker furniture; osier willow (*S. viminalis*), almond-leaved willow (*S. amygdalina*), and purple osier (*S. purpurea*) are preferred. Pollarded willows are trees which have been cut back to produce a dense head of shoots, such as are employed in basketry. Willow is also a source of tannin, of salicin, and of honey, and the trees are used as windbreaks, shelterbelts, to prevent erosion, and in riverbank revetments.

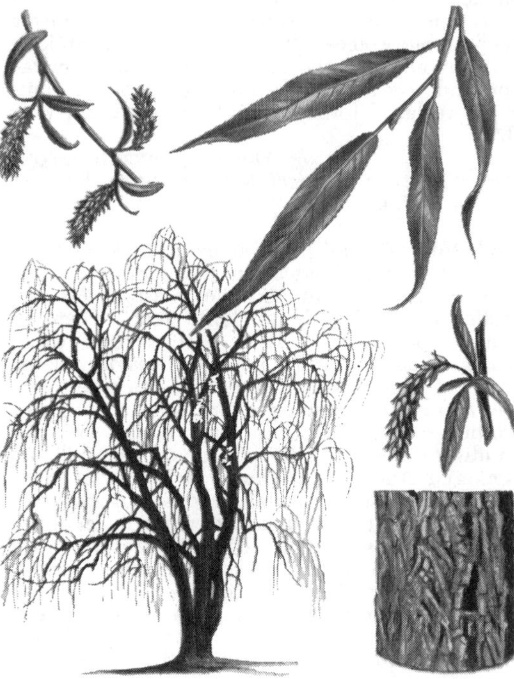

Weeping willow *(Salix babylonica)*: details (clockwise) of leaves, fruit, bark, winter silhouette, and pistillate flowers.

EDWIN B. MATZKE,
Department of Botany, Columbia University.

Further Reading: Brendell, Theresa, *Willows of the British Isles* (Seven Hills Bks. 1985); Hora, Bayard, ed., *Oxford Encyclopedia of Trees of the World* (Oxford 1981); Phillips, Roger, *Trees of North America and Europe* (Random House 1978); Preston, Richard J., Jr., *North American Trees,* 3d ed. (MIT Press 1977); Rehder, Alfred, and Rehder, Harald A., *Manual of Cultivated Trees and Shrubs Hardy in North America* (1940; reprint, Dioscorides Press 1986).

MUSEUM OF THE AMERICAN CHINA TRADE

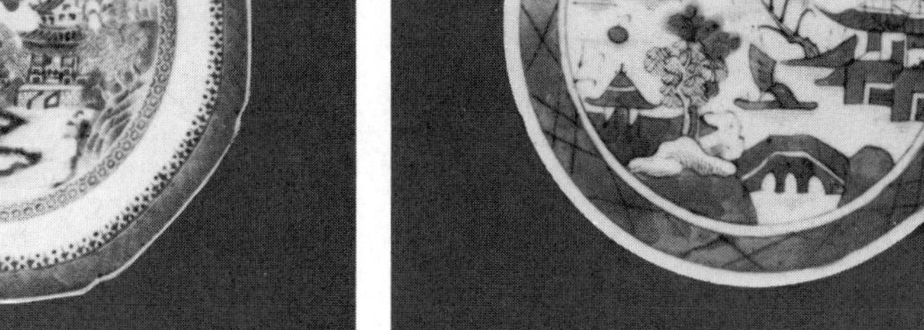

MUSEUM OF THE AMERICAN CHINA TRADE

Chinese willowware. The "Two Birds" pattern (*left*) dates from about 1795, "Canton" (*right*) from about 1895.

WILLOW WARBLER, one of several Old World warblers of the genus *Phylloscopus,* usually *P. trochilus,* a typical species of this genus. It is a small, dull-green bird, measuring only about 4.5 inches (11.5 cm), but it has a most pleasing melodious song, which rises in measured phrases, then becomes faint, and sinks away. It is characteristic of the open woodlands and breeds in northern Eurasia from the British Isles to the Pacific Ocean.

CHARLES VAURIE
The American Museum of Natural History

WILLOWICK, wil'ə-wik, a city in Ohio, in Lake county, on the shore of Lake Erie, 15 miles (24 km) northeast of downtown Cleveland. A residential area, Willowick was incorporated as a village in 1922 and proclaimed a city in December 1956. It is governed by a mayor and a nonpartisan council. Population: 17,834.

WILLOWWARE, wil'ō-wâr. All porcelain and earthenware dishes decorated with this transfer-printed scenic pattern are known collectively as willowware. Adapted from the Chinese decoration on much of the blue and white china imported to England in the 17th and 18th centuries, this design originated in 1780 at the Caughley pottery. The copper plate for it was first engraved by Thomas Minton, who later founded his own famous pottery. This pattern was so popular that soon other potteries like Wedgwood, Spode, and Davenport were using it, and by about 1800 it had become a stock pattern with most English potteries for both porcelain and earthenware dishes. From this it became the most widely used decoration for inexpensive earthenware dishes, which were quantity-produced by the English potteries for home use and export. It was also copied by some of the continental potteries, especially those of the Netherlands.

The willow pattern never went out of style and is still a standard one with pottery manufacturers in England, Holland, the United States, and even Japan for export to Occidental markets. At first, it was printed in cobalt blue and later in a medium green and the reddish shade known as mulberry. The design of this pattern perpetuates the legendary Chinese love story of the scribe, Chang, and Li-chi, daughter of a mandarin. They eloped to an island teahouse surrounded by willow trees on a small lake. Pursued by her father, the lovers were changed by approving gods into a pair of turtledoves. These are shown flying away to safety above the willow trees.

WILLS, wilz, **Helen Newington** (1906–), American tennis player, who was also known as Helen Wills Moody. She was born in Centerville, Calif., on Oct. 6, 1906. Educated at the Anna Head School and the University of California, she later studied art and exhibited in New York City. She won the United States women's singles championship in 1923, 1924, 1925, 1927, 1928, 1929, and 1931; the Wimbledon singles eight times; the French singles four times; and the Wightman Cup singles 18 times, retiring from major tournament play in 1938. She wrote and illustrated

Helen Wills dominated women's tennis in the 1920's, when she won the U. S women's singles six times.

UPI

Tennis (1928) and *Fifteen-Thirty* (1937). Called the "Queen of the Nets" and the greatest woman tennis player of her time, she was known as Helen Wills Moody during the years of her marriage to Frederick S. Moody, Jr. (1929–1937). She later (1939) became Mrs. Aidan Roark.

WILLSTÄTTER, vil′shtet-ər, **Richard** (1872–1942), German chemist, who won the 1915 Nobel Prize in chemistry. He was born in Karlsruhe, Germany, on Aug. 13, 1872, studied at the University of Munich (Ph. D., 1894) under the famous chemist Adolf von Baeyer, and taught there until 1905. He was professor of chemistry at the Federal Polytechnic Institute in Zurich from 1905 to 1912 and then at the Kaiser Wilhelm Institute for Chemistry in Berlin. In 1916 he returned to Munich as professor of organic chemistry and director of the chemistry laboratory, succeeding Baeyer. He resigned in 1925 in protest against the university's anti-Semitic policy, and in 1939 retired to Locarno, where he died on Aug. 3, 1942.

In intensive studies of the alkaloids, Willstätter determined the chemical structure of many compounds, including cocaine, one of those that he successfully synthesized (1902). At Zurich he undertook his most famous researches on plant pigments, especially chlorophyll, the carotenoids, and anthocyanins. In separating and purifying these he perfected a technique called partition chromatography, which revolutionized research in this field. For this work he was awarded the 1915 Nobel Prize in chemistry. He also studied enzymes, but his theory of photosynthesis was disproved by later discoveries.

WILM, vilm, **Alfred** (1869–1937), German metallurgist. He was born in Niederschellendorf, Germany, on June 25, 1869. He studied chemistry at the University of Breslau and the Charlottenburg Technical School, and later was assistant at the University of Göttingen to Friedrich Wöhler, the first to isolate aluminum.

In 1901, Wilm began work at a government research institute near Berlin, and in the following decade discovered and perfected a process for strengthening aluminum alloys through heat treatment and aging. One of these light, high-strength alloys, called duralumin and patented by Wilm, made possible important advances in aircraft construction. He died in Saalberg, Germany, on Aug. 6, 1937.

WILMETTE, wil-met′, a village in Illinois, in Cook county, on Lake Michigan, about 15 miles (24 km) north of downtown Chicago and just north of Evanston. It derives its name from Antoine Ouilmette, a French-Canadian fur trader whose Indian wife received a land grant from the government in 1829; it was subsequently settled as Ouilmette Fields.

Wilmette has retained its character as a village of homes through the use of selective zoning ordinances. Among its churches is the domed, nine-sided temple built by followers of the Bahá'í faith. The temple is partially walled with glass and its facade ornamented with fine grillwork and religious symbols. Wilmette is the site of Mallinckrodt College, a Roman Catholic college for women. Incorporated in 1872, the village has been governed since 1930 by a manager and council. Population: 28,229.

WILMINGTON, the largest city in Delaware, the state's major industrial center, and the seat of New Castle county. Situated 26 miles (42 km) southwest of Philadelphia, Pa., at the junction of the Delaware and Christina rivers and Brandywine Creek, it is a major port with deepwater docks.

Places of Interest. The foremost attraction in the area is the Winterthur Museum and Gardens, 5 miles (8 km) northwest of the city. The museum is housed in a great country mansion of the French château style surrounded by a private park. It features period rooms from historical houses, providing a panoramic view of American interior architecture, furnishings, arts, and crafts, dating from the 17th to the early 19th century. Nearly 200 rooms and displays contain thousands of collectors' items. They include outstanding examples of domestic textiles, pewter, furniture, silver, ceramics, paintings, and prints. Outside the museum is a court surrounded by reconstructed sections of housefronts giving the effect of a small village square, and Shop Lane, a simulated street lined with storefronts. The garden consists of 60 acres (24 hectares) of plantings of trees, flowers, and shrubs. The museum and gardens were opened to the public in 1951.

Of historical interest are the Holy Trinity (Old Swedes) Church and Hendrickson House. The stone church, built in 1698, is believed to be the oldest Protestant church in North America still serving as a place of worship. When the church was consecrated in 1699, it was Swedish Lutheran and severely plain. Now Episcopalian, it is somewhat more ornate. Hendrickson House is a Swedish farmhouse originally erected in Pennsylvania and then dismantled and rebuilt on the church site to hold its library, museum, and office.

Also of historical interest are Rodney Square, with the statue of Caesar Rodney, a signer of the Declaration of Independence; Fort Christina Monument, marking the landing place of the first Swedish expedition in 1638; the Old Town Hall, built in 1798 and now a museum containing colonial and Revolutionary War relics together with displays of decorative arts and silver; and the Hagley Museum, which stands on the site of the original du Pont powder mill on the banks of Brandywine Creek. Outdoor exhibits and demonstrations show an operating hydroelectric plant, a wooden waterwheel, and a steam engine of the 1870's. The main museum has dioramas and displays tracing the industrial and archaeological development of the area from the 17th to the 20th century. Eleutherian Mills, a home built by E. I. du Pont de Nemours in 1802, also is on the museum grounds. Its barn contains a collection of 19th century farm tools, weathervanes, a Conestoga wagon, and a cooper shop.

Another outstanding attraction is the Nemours Mansion, a modified Louis XVI château on a 300-acre (120-hectare) estate with 77 rooms of antique furniture, tapestries, and works of art.

The city also has three parks with recreational facilities—Brandywine Park and zoo, Banning Park, and Brandywine Springs Park. In what is now Brandywine Springs Park, Washington met Lafayette before the Battle of Brandywine (1777). From 1827 to 1845 a famous resort hotel, popular with Southern planters and politicians, was located on the site.

BOB GLANDER/SHOSTAL ASSOCIATES

The modern business district of Wilmington, Del., where large chemical firms have international headquarters.

Cultural Activities. Cultural life in Wilmington is enhanced by an opera house and two museums. Dance, theater, music, and film programs are held on the stage of the Grand Opera House, a restored Neoclassic Revival building of cast iron.

The Delaware Art Museum features the Howard Pyle and John Sloan collections, the Bancroft Collection of Pre-Raphaelites, and the Phelps Collection of Andrew Wyeth's works.

In the Delaware Museum of Natural History the visitor will find the Hall of Birds, the World of Sea Shells, and the Hall of Mammals. Also on view are the largest-known bird's egg and collections of extinct birds from New Zealand.

Industry. Wilmington, the "Chemical Capital of the World," is the headquarters of multidivisional E. I. du Pont de Nemours & Company. Established in 1802, du Pont manufactures synthetic fibers and plastics and other chemical products. It is one of the giant industrial enterprises in the United States.

The city's other manufactured products are vulcanized fiber, glazed leathers, dyed cotton, rubber hose, tanning extract, cork and floor products, ships, malleable iron, automobile wheels, and castings. Other industries are automobile assembly; oil refining; yacht, barge, and ship building; railway car building and repairing; copper smelting; and meat-packing. Wilmington also is an important East Coast shipping center.

History and Government. Swedish colonists led by Peter Minuit landed on the site in 1638 and started a colony they called Christinahamn ("Christian Harbor"). The little village included Fort Christina, Old Swedes Church, and several dwellings.

In 1655, Dutch soldiers under the command of Peter Stuyvesant, the peg-legged governor of New Netherland (now New York), annexed the settlement and ended Swedish rule. Gradually it developed into an important trading center and was taken by the British in 1664.

After a period of decline, the area attracted a group of enterprising Quakers who revitalized the economic life of the community. Renamed Willington in 1731 after Thomas Willing, a prominent settler in the area, the town changed its name in 1739 to Wilmington. The new name honored Spencer Compton, earl of Wilmington and friend of an influential local landowner. During the American Revolution, Washington established military headquarters in Wilmington and reconnoitered the area with Lafayette.

The abundant waterpower from creeks in the Brandywine Valley stimulated the industrial growth of the city, and by the time du Pont built his first powder mill on Brandywine Creek in 1802, the area had been industrialized for 100 years.

Wilmington was incorporated as a borough in 1739 and as a city in 1832. It is governed by a mayor and council. Population: 70,195.

Further Reading: Hoffecker, Carol E., *Corporate Capital: Wilmington in the Twentieth Century* (Temple Univ. Press 1983); Montgomery, Elizabeth, *Reminiscences of Wilmington in Familiar Village Tales, Ancient and New* (1851; reprint, Kennikat 1972).

WILMINGTON, a city in North Carolina, the seat of New Hanover county. It is on the east bank of the Cape Fear River, 30 miles (48 km) from its mouth at the Atlantic Ocean and about 115 miles (185 km) southeast of Raleigh. Bluethenthal Field is the local airport.

Industries and Manufactures. A port of entry situated on a peninsula between the Cape Fear River and the Atlantic, Wilmington is North Carolina's chief deepwater port as well as a tourist, trade, and industrial center. The principal agricultural crops are bulbs, flowers, farm truck, peanuts, corn, and tobacco. Manufacturing enterprises produce clothing, fertilizer, textiles, paper and lumber, petroleum, asphalt, steel tanks and boilers, chemicals, cement, electric power, and gas. A pilot saline conversion plant was authorized by the United States government for this region. The site of the North Carolina state docks, Wilmington is first among the southern Atlantic coast ports in the handling of creosoted products, molasses, bromine, and seed potatoes.

Educational, Cultural, and Recreational Facilities. Until 1910 the largest city in North Carolina and its leading cultural and social community, Wilmington contains a fine old live oak-shaded residential section of many beautiful homes. Its public library, founded in 1760 as the Cape Fear Library, is one of the oldest municipal libraries in the country. The city has concert, choral, and chamber arts groups, and its Thalian Association is one of the state's earliest theatrical organizations. An annual Azalea Festival takes place in early spring, attracting visitors from a wide area, and the Wilmington open golf tournament is held later in the season. Near Wilmington are two popular ocean beach resorts—Wrightsville Beach, 10 miles (16 km) east, and Carolina Beach, 16 miles (26 km) south.

Places of Interest. Wilmington's historic buildings include Cornwallis House, built in 1771, Revolutionary War headquarters of Lord Cornwallis; the City Hall, built in the mid-1850's, of classic design and noted for the theater which it contains; Bellamy mansion, built between 1857 and 1859, a splendid example of Greek Revival architecture, used during the Civil War by occupying Union troops; and Greenfield Park, whose gardens are known for their display of camellias, azaleas, and roses. Fourteen miles (22.5 km) south, in a lovely setting of moss-hung trees, stands Orton Plantation, established in 1725 and famous for its colonial mansion, camellias, and azaleas.

History and Government. The first settlement at Wilmington was made in the early 1730's by English yeomen who called it New Liverpool. Later it was known as New Town. In 1734 its name was changed to honor Spencer Compton, English earl of Wilmington and patron of Gabriel Johnston, an early local governor, and it was incorporated in 1739. Wilmington was the scene of Stamp Act resistance in 1765, and in 1781 the city was occupied by Lord Cornwallis before his march to Yorktown. During the Civil War it was a principal port of entry for Confederate blockade runners. After the bombardment of Fort Fisher, 18 miles (29 km) south of the city, Wilmington surrendered to the Union forces. (See WILMINGTON, CAPTURE OF.) It was rechartered as a city in 1866.

The city manager form of government, with a five-member council, was adopted in 1941. Population: 44,000.

KATHERINE HOWELL
Librarian, Wilmington Public library

WILMINGTON, Capture of, a battle of the American Civil War. The capture by Union forces of Fort Fisher, near the point of the peninsula between the Cape Fear River estuary and the Atlantic Ocean in southeastern North Carolina, was part of a military-naval operation of major strategic importance. Gen. Ulysses S. Grant's objective was twofold. His primary aim, achieved by the fort's capture on Jan. 15, 1865, was to destroy the usefulness of Wilmington, N.C., 30 miles upriver, as the last maritime depot for Confederate army supplies shipped from Europe and the West Indies by blockade runners. His second aim was the seizure of Wilmington itself, to be used as a base for development of a new invasion route into the Southern heartland. Union troops debarking there were to advance due north to Goldsboro, join units of William Tecumseh Sherman's victorious army, and combine in an advance on Richmond from the south.

Gen. Alfred H. Terry, Fort Fisher's conqueror, delayed his attack on an entrenched line two miles north, waiting for reinforcements. On February 9, a 4,400-man division under Gen. Jacob D. Cox, first of Gen. John McA. Schofield's XXIII Corps troops to arrive from Washington, joined him, Schofield himself taking command, and on February 11 the advance began up the peninsula. Five days later an advance was begun up the right bank as well. Confederate Maj. Gen. Robert F. Hoke and Brig. Gen. Johnson Hagood were obliged to fight delaying actions. The Union troops were importantly aided by gunboats and the monitor *Montauk* which bombarded and forced evacuation of Fort Anderson on the right bank, halfway between Fort Fisher and Wilmington. On the night of February 21, Hoke burned steamers, boats, cotton, and naval stores at Wilmington, then abandoned the town, retreating north toward Goldsboro; the next morning Terry's troops entered Wilmington unopposed.

Union losses in the brief campaign were estimated at about 200 killed and wounded. General Schofield's estimate of Confederate casualties was 1,000 killed, wounded, or taken prisoner.

WILMINGTON COLLEGE. See NORTH CAROLINA, UNIVERSITY OF.

WILMOT, wil'mot, **David** (1814–1868), American judge and politician. He was born in Bethany, Pa., on Jan. 20, 1814. Admitted to the bar in 1834, he practiced law in Towanda, and served as a Democratic member of Congress from 1845 to 1851. He favored the Mexican War and other party measures, but opposed the extension of slavery in any territory acquired by the United States. On Aug. 8, 1846, when a bill was introduced appropriating funds to be used in the negotiation of peace with Mexico, Wilmot introduced an amendment providing that "neither slavery nor involuntary servitude" shall be allowed in territory so acquired. This amendment, known as the Wilmot Proviso, became famous in American history.

Wilmot supported Martin Van Buren in 1848 against Gen. Lewis Cass, the Democratic candidate for the presidency. Later he was one of the founders of the Republican party and served as a delegate to the national conventions of 1856 and 1860.

From 1851 to 1861 he served as president judge of the 13th judicial district of Pennsylvania. In 1857 he was the unsuccessful Republican candidate for governor of the state. From 1861 to 1863 he was a U.S. senator and a loyal supporter of President Lincoln. He served as judge of the U.S. Court of Claims from the time of his appointment in 1863 until his death in Towanda, Pa., on March 16, 1868.

WILMOT, John. See ENGLISH LITERATURE—*Restoration* (Poetry).